DATE			
REF.			
		REF.	
			REF.
	REF.		
REF.			
		REF.	REF.
	REF.		

DICTIONARY

OF

NATIONAL BIOGRAPHY

1922—1930

THE DICTIONARY of NATIONAL BIOGRAPHY

Founded in 1882

by

GEORGE SMITH

1922–1930

Edited by J. R. H. Weaver

With an Index covering the years 1901–1930
in one alphabetical series

OXFORD UNIVERSITY PRESS

Oxford University Press, Ely House, London W. 1

OXFORD LONDON GLASGOW NEW YORK
TORONTO MELBOURNE WELLINGTON CAPE TOWN
IBADAN NAIROBI DAR ES SALAAM LUSAKA ADDIS ABABA
KUALA LUMPUR SINGAPORE JAKARTA HONG KONG TOKYO
DELHI BOMBAY CALCUTTA MADRAS KARACHI

ISBN 0 19 865203 8

First Edition 1937
Reprinted 1953, 1961, 1967, 1976

Printed in Great Britain
at the University Press, Oxford
by Vivian Ridler
Printer to the University

PREFATORY NOTE

THIS volume contains the biographies of notable persons who died in the nine years 1922–1930. The number of biographies included is greater than in the preceding volume, which covered ten years, and a somewhat ampler treatment of individual lives has been afforded. If the present rate of selection is continued throughout the rest of the century, the result will be to add approximately 7,000 lives to the Main Work and its Supplement as completed in 1901. To add an appreciably larger number would be out of keeping with the scale and historical perspective of the main Dictionary, the aim of which has been to include the biographies of those persons, and those only, whose activities, ideas, writings, or discoveries are deemed to have made a definite contribution to the annals of their generation, and whose careers are therefore likely to be of consequence to present and future historical inquirers.

The fact that the Dictionary now deals with the lives of contemporaries is not without effect upon the character of the biographical notices. In the first place, ample material both published and private is usually available; contributors have less difficulty, therefore, in procuring information than in selecting what appears to be significant. Secondly, almost all the contributors have been in a position to furnish, where thought desirable, personal appreciations of the subjects of the memoirs. Although the most dispassionate judgement seldom turns out to be entirely flawless, yet it is hoped that such estimates as are here supplied may prove useful to future biographers and historians, in helping them to dispel theory or conjecture which is not founded upon the evidence of contemporaries.

The biographies recorded in this volume cover a period of more than a hundred years. Three of them begin as far back as the reign of George IV: the late Professor G. D. Liveing (who died as the result of a street accident at the age of ninety-seven) was born in 1827; Sir Harry Poland in 1829, and Admiral John Moresby, who charted the coasts of New Guinea, in March 1830. Twenty-nine other lives begin before the accession of Queen Victoria: these include the names of S. Baring-Gould, Bishop G. F. Browne, Dr. John Clifford, Admiral Sir Edmund Fremantle, Sir Archibald Geikie, Frederic Harrison, Sir T. G. Jackson, the architect, Joseph Rowntree (the second of the name), Sir Charles Santley, Lord Eversley (better remembered as Mr. Shaw-Lefevre), and Dean Wace. Lord Eversley, it will be noted, claimed acquaintance with thirteen prime ministers, seventeen lord chancellors, and seven archbishops of Canterbury; he also took photographs at the front in the Crimean War.

The serene figure of the late Queen Alexandra forms a link in the court annals of three reigns, the chief political events of which, from the days of Disraeli, are recalled by the careers of four prime ministers, Lord Rosebery, Lord Balfour, Lord Oxford and Asquith, and Mr. Bonar Law, and four leading statesmen, Lord Morley, Lord Lansdowne, Lord Milner, and Lord Curzon. The political chronicle of fifty years can be amplified from the biographies of five lord chancellors, Lords Birkenhead, Cave, Finlay, Haldane, and Loreburn, of Archbishop Lord Davidson, and of such representative figures (many of them better recalled without their titles) as Henry Chaplin, Herbert Gladstone, Lewis Harcourt, Lord George Hamilton, Walter Long, Edwin Montagu, Lord Northcliffe, and Lord Stanley of Alderley. The various phases of the changing political fortunes of Ireland are reflected in the lives of John Dillon, William O'Brien, Lord Dunraven, Antony MacDonnell, T. P. O'Connor, Arthur Griffith, and Michael Collins.

The obituary roll of these years includes a long list of Dominion statesmen and Colonial administrators. Typical of the hey-day of the Indian Civil Service are the careers of Sir William Duke, Sir Mortimer Durand, Sir Thomas Holderness, Sir William Meyer, and Sir Charles Rivaz. If to these are added the names of Sir Robert Bond (Newfoundland), Sir Clifford Sifton (Canada), J. X. Merriman and Sir Thomas Smartt (South Africa), Andrew Fisher (Australia), W. F. Massey, Sir Robert Stout, and Sir Joseph Ward (New Zealand), Sir Charles Coghlan and Sir Robert Coryndon (Rhodesia), Sir Frederick Jackson (Uganda), Sir John Kirk (Zanzibar), Sir Harry Johnston (East and West Africa), Sir Gordon Guggisberg (the Gold Coast), Sir George Goldie, the founder of Nigeria, Sir Gilbert Clayton and Coles 'Pasha' (Egypt), and Sir West Ridgeway (Ceylon and North Borneo), it will be evident that most aspects of the constitutional and economic development of the British Empire since the late Victorian period are touched upon in these pages.

The years of the European War are now beginning to recede, although its tremendous episodes on land and sea are still unclouded by the mists of Time. Most of those who held the highest commands have now passed, and among them will be found here the names of Lord Ypres, Lord Haig, Lord Horne, Lord Rawlinson, Sir Horace Smith-Dorrien, and Sir Henry Wilson; the naval names include those of Sir John De Robeck, Sir Hugh Evan-Thomas, Sir Henry Jackson, Sir Percy Scott, and Sir Doveton Sturdee, the victor of the Falkland Islands; to an earlier naval generation belong Sir Cyprian Bridge, Sir Edmund Fremantle, Sir William May, and Sir Edward Seymour.

In the field of Letters and Scholarship, especially historical scholarship, many distinguished names are contained in this volume. Among authors and men of letters are Robert Bridges, Joseph Conrad, Edmund Gosse, Thomas Hardy, W. H. Hudson, and D. H. Lawrence; among philosophers and classical scholars, Bernard Bosanquet,

F. H. Bradley, J. P. Postgate, Sir William Ridgeway, and James Ward. The economists include Alfred Marshall; the historians, Edward Armstrong, Lord Bryce, J. B. Bury, Sir Julian Corbett, Sir George W. Prothero, Sir James H. Ramsay, Horace Round, T. F. Tout, Sir George Otto Trevelyan, Sir Paul Vinogradoff, and Sir Adolphus William Ward. To these must be added the names of Sir Sidney Lee and Henry William Carless Davis, editors of the *Dictionary of National Biography*, the former from 1891 to 1916, the latter from 1919 until his sudden death in 1928. Of Sir Sidney Lee's services to the Dictionary a full account is contained in the memoir of him by the late Sir Charles Firth which was specially prefixed to the volume for 1912–1921, published in the year following his death. This is supplemented by the biography which is included here. The loss of Professor Davis's guidance at the time when the present volume was being planned was a severe and wholly unexpected blow.

It is not, of course, upon the biographies of the eminent that the value of the Dictionary mainly depends; but since the work is now arranged in decennial volumes, the yield of the obituary roll of each decade gives some clue to the fertility of the generation which belongs to it. The selection of representative names from the roll of these years could be extended much farther. It must suffice to mention among the men of science and engineers the names of William Bateson, the biologist, Sir James Dewar, De Ferranti, the electrical engineer, Oliver Heaviside, the physicist, Sir Edwin Ray Lankester, Sir J. N. Langley, the physiologist, W. H. Perkin, the chemist, Sir Frederick Treves, the surgeon, and Sir Philip Watts, the naval designer. The stage lost Dame Ellen Terry in this period, and painting, J. S. Sargent. Finally, it is fitting to close this summary with the names of some of the great adventurers—Gertrude Bell, Charles Doughty, Henry Godwin-Austen, surveyor of the Himalaya, Brigadier-General Pereira, who covered 45,000 miles on foot in China, Sir Ernest Shackleton, and Sir Ross Smith, the airman.

The acknowledgements of the Editor are due in particular to the following for much valuable advice and information: Sir Hugh P. Allen, Mr. C. T. Atkinson, Dr. Cyril Bailey, Mr. C. F. Bell, Mr. E. I. Carlyle, Professor J. H. Clapham, Dr. C. R. M. F. Cruttwell, Dr. Geoffrey Dawson, the Rt. Hon. H. A. L. Fisher, Dr. G. S. Gordon, Sir Ian MacAlister, Lord Justice MacKinnon, the late Mrs. Lane Poole, Admiral Sir Herbert W. Richmond, Sir Charles S. Sherrington, Professor N. V. Sidgwick, Major-General Sir Ernest D. Swinton, and Colonel G. H. de Watteville.

In preparing the volume the Editor has again received invaluable assistance from Miss Margaret Toynbee, Ph.D., lecturer of St. Hilda's College, who has, in addition, compiled the Epitomes of this and the previous volume. Mrs. Weaver has given him much secretarial help. He is also specially indebted to the Editor of *The Times* and

Mr. F. S. A. Lowndes for kindly placing at his disposal a file of the obituary notices published in *The Times* during the period; and to the Rev. H. E. D. Blakiston, D.D., President of Trinity College, Oxford, who has read the whole of the proof-sheets and furnished many valuable suggestions.

With the appearance of this volume the present Editor retires from the editorship, and takes leave, with regret, of the large body of contributors, who have shown him so much courtesy and consideration. To the officials of the Oxford University Press he is under great obligations for their advice and unfailing support, which have been the mainstay of his labours.

J. R. H. W.

LIST OF CONTRIBUTORS

1922–1930

The names of deceased contributors are marked thus: †.

ABERCROMBIE, Lascelles:
Hardy.
ADCOCK, Frank Ezra:
Reid (J. S.).
ADY, Cecilia Mary:
Armstrong.
AKERMAN, Richard Frank Martin:
Parratt.
ALCOCK, Sir Walter Galpin:
Bridge (J. F.).
ALDINGTON, Richard:
Lawrence.
ALLEN, Carleton Kemp:
Vinogradoff.
ALLEN, Thomas William:
Brown.
AMOS, Sir Maurice Sheldon:
Coles (C. E.).
APPLEYARD, Rollo:
Heaviside.
ARTHUR, Sir George Compton Archibald, Bart.:
Alexandra.
ASHLEY, Maurice Percy:
Archer; Clutton-Brock.

BADDELEY, Sir Vincent Wilberforce:
Bridgeman; Burney; Evan-Thomas; Kerr; MacGregor; Meux; Scott (P. M.); Sturdee.
BAILEY, Cyril:
Warren (T. H.).
BAIRD-SMITH, David:
Neilson.
BALFOUR, Frederick Robert Stephen:
Elwes.
BALFOUR, Henry:
Hose.
BALLARD, Colin Robert:
Smith-Dorrien.
BARCROFT, Sir Joseph:
Bayliss; Starling.
BARNES, William Emery:
Chase.
BARRINGTON-WARD, Robert M'Gowan:
Sargeaunt.
BATE, Herbert Newell:
Turner (C. H.).
BAYNES, Norman Hepburn:
Bury.
BELL, Charles Francis:
Tuke.
BELL, Eva Mary:
Steel.
BELL, George Kennedy Allen, Bishop of Chichester:
Davidson.
BELL, Harold Idris:
Grenfell (B. P.).
BELL, Kenneth Norman:
Smith (A. L.).
BENECKE, Paul Victor Mendelssohn:
Coolidge.
BETHUNE-BAKER, James Franklin:
Mason.
BINYON, Laurence:
Cust; Image.
BIRON, Sir Chartres:
Hall (E. M.).
BLACK, Arthur:
Kirk (J.).
†BLAIR, Sir Robert:
Jackson (C.).
BLAKISTON, Herbert Edward Douglas:
Verney.
BONHAM CARTER, Sir Edgar:
Howard.
BORENIUS, Tancred:
Brock; Dicksee; Fildes; Frampton; Gleichen; Holiday; Leader; Sargent; Shannon; Thornycroft (W. H.); Wood (F. D.).
BOWER, Frederick Orpen:
Balfour (I. B.).
BOYCOTT, Arthur Edwin:
Shattock.
BOYD, James:
Wright.
BRADDELL, Thomas Arthur Darcy:
George.
BRIERLY, James Leslie:
Holland.
BRISCOE, John Fetherstonhaugh:
Newbolt.
BROAD, Charlie Dunbar:
M'Taggart.
†BUCKLE, George Earle:
Chirol.
BULLOCK, Fred:
Smith (F.).
BURGIN, George Brown:
Jerome.
†BURKITT, Francis Crawford:
Lewis.
BURN, Sir Richard:
Meyer (W. S.).
†BUTLER, Edward Cuthbert:
Gasquet.

CALLENDER, Geoffrey Arthur Romaine:
Corbett; Thursfield.
CAMERON, John Forbes:
Anderson (H. K.).
†CANA, Frank Richardson:
Chisholm.
CARLYLE, Edward Irving:
Acland; Benton; Bryce; Chaplin; Ferranti; Fitzmaurice; Fox; Galloway; Garstin; Kennedy; Lee; Leslie; Matthews; Metcalfe; Norton-Griffiths; Ridgeway (J. W.); Seccombe; Stokes (F. W. S.); Thornycroft (J. I.); Watts.
CATHCART, Edward Provan:
Paton.
CAW, Sir James Lewis:
Guthrie.

List of Contributors

CECIL, Algernon:
Balfour (A. J.); Prothero.
CHALMERS, Robert Chalmers, Baron:
Davids.
CHAMBERS, Raymond Wilson:
Ker.
†CHAPLIN, Sir Francis Drummond Percy:
Coghlan; Michell.
CHAPMAN, Robert William:
Hudson (R. A.).
CHAPPLE, Charles Roberts:
Watson.
CHARTERIS, Hon. Sir Evan:
Gosse; Primrose (Rosebery).
CHEATLE, Sir George Lenthal:
Cheatle.
CHILD, Harold Hannyngton:
Bancroft; Bourchier; Carton; Esmond; Hawtrey; Terry; Walkley; Wood (Lloyd).
CLOSE, Janet Marjorie:
Palmer.
COATE, Mary:
Baring-Gould.
COCHRANE, Alfred:
Bowles; Boyd; Brabazon (Meath); Burge; Caillard; Douglas-Scott-Montagu (Montagu of Beaulieu); Doyle; Furneaux; Guinness (Iveagh); Harrison (F.); Hills; Hulton; Ilbert; Lever (Leverhulme); Mallock; Pearson (Cowdray); Pirrie; Primrose (H. W.); Reid (Loreburn); Salvidge; Samuel (Bearsted); Smith (Hambleden); Spofforth; Stevenson (J.); Sutherland; Wace; Wynn-Carrington (Lincolnshire).
†CONWAY, Robert Seymour:
Postgate; Ridgeway (W.).
COOPER, Wilbraham Villiers:
Gladstone; Strachey.
CORNFORD, Francis Macdonald:
Harrison (J. E.).
COSGRAVE, William Thomas:
Collins; Griffith.
COTTESLOE, Thomas Francis Fremantle, Baron:
Eaton (Cheylesmore).
COUPLAND, Reginald:
Egerton.
CRAIGIE, Sir William Alexander:
Bradley (H.).
CULLIS, Winifred Clara:
Scharlieb.
CUMMING, Sir John Ghest:
Carmichael.

DAFOE, John Wesley:
Sifton.
DAMPIER, Sir William Cecil Dampier:
Darwin (F.); Liveing.
†DARTON, Frederick Joseph Harvey:
Bland (Nesbit).
DAVIES, David:
Channell; Poland.
DAWSON, Geoffrey:
Harmsworth (Northcliffe).
DAWSON, William Harbutt:
Chamberlain.
DESCH, Cecil Henry:
Beilby.
†DICKINSON, Goldsworthy Lowes:
Browning.
DODD, Charles Harold:
Peake.
DODGSON, Campbell:
Colvin; Rawlinson (W. G.).
DRIVER, Godfrey Rolles:
Gray (G. B.).
DUNHILL, Thomas Frederick:
Stanford.
DYSON, Sir Frank Watson:
Christie; Dreyer.

EDE, Harold Stanley:
Harris.
EDMONDS, Sir James Edward:
Repington.
EGERTON, Alfred Charles Glyn:
Callendar.
ELGOOD, Percival George:
Blunt; Clayton; Stack.
ELLIOT, Walter Elliot:
Pringle.
ELTON, Oliver:
Montague.
ENTWISTLE, William James:
Fitzmaurice-Kelly.
ESDAILE, Arundell James Kennedy:
Gilson.

FAIRBAIRN, John Shields:
Champneys.
FALLS, Cyril Bentham:
Lukin.
†FARNELL, Lewis Richard:
Abbott.
FIELD, Sir Arthur Mostyn:
Tizard.
FIRTH, John Benjamin:
Le Sage.
FITZGERALD, Maurice Henry:
Ryle.
FLOWER, Robin Ernest William:
Freeman.
FORSYTH, Andrew Russell:
Burnside; Glaisher.
FREEMAN, George Sydney:
Gray (H.B.).
FULTON, William:
Cooper.

GALBRAITH, Vivian Hunter:
Tout.
†GARROD, Sir Archibald Edward:
Church; Duckworth.
GASELEE, Sir Stephen:
Benson; Headlam-Morley; Jenkinson.
GAUVAIN, Sir Henry:
Treloar.
GIBB, Hamilton Alexander Rosskeen:
Arnold.
†GLAZEBROOK, Sir Richard Tetley:
Darwin (H.).
GODLEY, Hon. Eveline Charlotte:
Godley.
GOOCH, George Peabody:
Ward (A. W.).

List of Contributors

GOODHART, Arthur Lehman:
Kenny.
GOODHART-RENDEL, Harry Stuart:
Jackson (T. G.); Webb (A.).
GOODRICH, Edwin Stephen:
Lankester.
GORELL, Ronald Gorell Barnes, Baron:
Murray.
†GRANT, Sir Alfred Hamilton:
Holdich.
†GRANT, William Lawson:
Bond; McGrath; Mackenzie (W.); Meredith; Parkin.
GRANVILLE-BARKER, Harley Granville:
Trench.
GRIMSDITCH, Herbert Borthwick:
Adami; Cobden-Sanderson; Furniss; Gould; Holme; Jones (H. A.); Lucy; Pain; Sims; Solomon; Ward (L.).
GUNN, James Andrew:
Cushny.
GWYNN, Denis Rolleston:
O'Donnell; Vaughan.
GWYNN, Edward John:
Bernard.
GWYNN, Stephen Lucius:
Dillon; MacNeill; Quin (Dunraven).

†HADOW, Sir William Henry:
Balfour (T. G.).
HALDANE, Elizabeth Sanderson:
Haldane.
HANBURY, Harold Greville:
Joyce; Salter.
HARDIE, Martin:
Greaves; McEvoy.
HARRIS, Sir Charles:
Brett (Esher); Ward (E. W. D.).
HATTERSLEY, Alan Frederick:
Moor.
HAYNES, Edmund Sidney Pollock:
Clodd.
HEADLAM, Sir Cuthbert Morley, Bart.:
Percy (Northumberland).
HEADLAM, Maurice Francis:
Elliot; Sinclair (Pentland); Smith (H. B.); Struthers; Wood (T. M.); Younger.
HEATH, Sir Henry Frank:
McCormick.
HETHERINGTON, Sir Hector James Wright:
Jones (H.).
HILL, Sir Arthur William:
Veitch.
HIRST, Francis Wrigley:
Masterman; Morley; Shaw-Lefevre (Eversley).
HOBLEY, Charles William:
Jackson (F. J.).
HOGAN, James:
O'Higgins.
HOGARTH, William David:
Bell (G. M. L.); Doughty.
HOSIE, Dorothea, Lady:
Jordan.
HOWELLS, Herbert Norman:
Brewer.
HURD, Sir Archibald:
Carden; De Robeck; Troubridge.

HURST, Arthur Frederick:
Stokes (A.).
HUSSEY, Christopher:
Lorimer; Weaver.
HYAMSON, Albert Montefiore:
Gollancz (I.).

JACKS, Maurice Leonard:
McClure.
†JAMES, Montague Rhodes:
Durnford.
JOHNSTON, Thomas:
Wheatley.
JONES, Henry Albert:
Brancker; Butler (F. H.); Scott (G. H.); Smith (R. M.); Thomas (G. H.).
JONES, Thomas:
Law.
JONES, William Henry Samuel:
Browne (G. F.).
†JOSE, Arthur Wilberforce:
Fisher.

KEITH, Sir Arthur:
Macewen; Treves.
KENNEDY, William Paul McClure:
Walker.
KENYON, Sir Frederic George:
Hogarth; Thompson (E. M.).
KEYNES, John Maynard:
Edgeworth; Marshall.
KING, Henry Medwin:
Sanderson (F. W.).

LAMB, David Crichton:
Booth.
†LAMB, Horace:
Taylor.
LANCELOT, John Bennett:
Chavasse.
LANDALE, Stenard Ernest Andrew:
Swinton.
LANDON, Philip Aislabie:
Bray; Coleridge.
†LANSDOWNE, Henry William Edmund Petty-Fitzmaurice, Marquess of:
Petty-Fitzmaurice (Lansdowne).
LAST, Hugh Macilwain:
Bury.
LESLIE, John Randolph Shane:
Logue.
LEVIEN, John Mewburn:
Albani; Santley.
LEWIS, Sir Thomas:
Mackenzie (J.).
LINDSAY, Alexander Dunlop:
Bosanquet (B.).
LIVINGSTONE, Sir Richard Winn:
Dill.
LLOYD, Alan Charles Gore:
Merriman.
†LODGE, Sir Richard:
Ramsay.
LOEWE, Herbert Martin James:
Gollancz (H.).
LONG, Basil Kellet:
Smartt.

LONGSTAFF, Tom George:
Wollaston.
LOVETT, Sir Harrington Verney:
Durand; MacDonnell.
LUCAS, Edward Verrall:
Methuen.
LYNAM, Edward:
Fordham.
LYON, Percy Comyn:
Bayley.

MACCOLL, Dugald Sutherland:
Phillips.
MACDONAGH, Michael:
O'Brien (W.); O'Connor.
MACDONALD, Sir George:
Craik.
MACKINNON, Frank Douglas, Lord Justice Mackinnon:
Chalmers; Pickford (Sterndale).
MACLAGAN, Sir Edward Douglas:
Rivaz; Young (W. M.).
MACMILLAN, Hugh Pattison Macmillan, Baron:
Cave; Ure (Strathclyde).
MACNICOL, Nicol:
Farquhar.
MCWATTERS, Sir Arthur Cecil:
Barbour; Monteath.
MALCOLM, Dougal Orme:
Beit; Maguire; Whibley.
MALCOLM, Sir Ian Zachary:
Long.
MARETT, Robert Ranulph:
Spencer.
MARGOLIOUTH, David Samuel:
Conybeare.
MASON, Kenneth:
Godwin-Austen.
MATHESON, Percy Ewing:
Courtney; Spooner.
MATHEW, David James:
Bégin.
MATHEW, Theobald:
Bailhache; Bigham (Mersey); Bosanquet (F. A.); Lush; Russell; Shearman.
MAURICE, Sir Frederick Barton:
Haig; Horne; Rawlinson (H. S.); Stopford.
MAY, James Lewis:
Lane.
MEDLEY, Dudley Julius:
McKechnie.
MICKLEM, Edward Romilly:
Hastings.
MILFORD, Sir Humphrey Sumner:
Frowde.
MILLAR, Eric George:
Thompson (H. Y.).
MILLER, Sir John Ontario:
Holderness.
MILLER, Steuart Napier:
Phillimore (J. S.).
MONRO, Alida:
Mew.
MOORE, Theodore Conyngham Kingsmill:
O'Brien (Shandon); Ronan.

MOWAT, Robert Balmain:
Loch; Wills.
†MOYNIHAN, Berkeley George Andrew Moynihan, Baron:
Teale.
MURRAY, George Gilbert Aimé:
Leaf.

†NAYLOR, Edward Woodall:
Mann.
NEVINSON, Henry Woodd:
Massingham.
NEWTON, William Godfrey:
Newton.
NICOLSON, Hon. Harold George:
Curzon.
NIGHTINGALE, Albert Darby:
Sanderson (F. W.).

O'BRIEN, Edward:
Carman; Felkin (Fowler); Heseltine (Warlock); Locke; Murry (Mansfield).
OLIVIER, Sydney Olivier, Baron:
Guggisberg; Johnston.
OLLARD, Sidney Leslie:
Coles (V. S. S.).
OMAN, Sir Charles William Chadwick:
Hutton.
ONSLOW, Richard William Alan Onslow, Earl of:
Buchanan; Emmott; Hamilton; Harcourt; Lockwood (Lambourne); Nicolson (Carnock); Thomson (C. B.); Warren (C.).
OWEN, Charles Venn:
Alderson; Anderson (W. H.); Bols; Chermside; Creagh; Ewart; Macdonald; Mackinnon; Mahon.

PAGE, Frederick:
Meynell; Shorter; Whiteing.
PARKER, John:
Barrington; Boucicault; Chevalier.
†PEARCE, Edmund Courtenay, Bishop of Derby:
Pearce.
†PEET, Thomas Eric:
Hall (H. R. H.).
PEREIRA, Sir Cecil Edward:
Pereira.
PETERS, Edwin Arthur:
Milligan.
PHILIP, James Charles:
Thorpe.
PHIPPS, Sir Edmund Bampfylde:
Yoxall.
PICKARD CAMBRIDGE, Arthur Wallace:
Newman.
†POLLOCK, David Stuart Hope:
Robinson.
†PONSONBY, Sir Frederick Edward Grey:
Knollys.
POOLE, Austin Lane:
Stevenson (W. H.).
POWER, Sir D'Arcy:
Bowlby.
PUNNETT, Reginald Crundall:
Bateson.
PYE, David Randall:
Mallory.

†RAIT, Sir Robert Sangster:
Dicey; Forrest.
RASTALL, Robert Heron:
Bonney.
RAYLEIGH, Robert John Strutt, Baron:
Strutt.
REES, James Frederick:
Ashley.
REITZ, Deneys:
De Wet.
RHYS, Ernest:
Dent.
RICHMOND, Sir Herbert William:
Bridge (C. A. G.); Fremantle; May; Seymour.
ROBERTS, Charles Henry:
Montagu.
ROBINSON, Robert:
Perkin.
ROLLESTON, Sir Humphry Davy, Bart.:
Allbutt; Godlee; Leishman; Powell.
ROSS, Sir Edward Denison:
Browne (E. G.).
ROSS, Hugh Munro:
Dewar.
ROSS, William David:
Hicks.
ROWLATT, Sir Sidney Arthur Taylor:
Finlay.
RUDMOSE BROWN, Robert Neal:
Herdman; Keltie; Kirk (J.); Lindsay; Moresby; Shackleton.
RUSHBROOKE, James Henry:
Clifford; Meyer (F. B.).

SADLEIR, Michael:
Conrad; Mackay (Corelli).
SAMPSON, Ralph Allen:
Turner (H. H.).
†SANDARS, John Satterfield:
Akers-Douglas (Chilston).
SANDERS, William Stephen:
Gosling.
SANKEY, John Sankey, Baron:
Phillimore (W. G. F.).
SAUNDERS, John Tennant:
Shipley.
SAWYER, Harold Athelstane Parry:
Magrath.
SCARBROUGH, Alfred Frederick George Beresford Lumley, Earl of:
Goldie.
SCHUSTER, Sir Claud:
Smith (Birkenhead).
†SCOTT, George Forrester:
Sturt.
SCOTT, William Robert:
Nicholson.
SEDGWICK, Walter Bradbury:
Sonnenschein.
SELBY BIGGE, Sir Lewis Amherst, Bart.:
Stanley (Sheffield).
SETON, Sir Malcolm Cotter Caviston:
Duke.
†SHADWELL, Arthur:
Hobhouse.
SHAND, Philip Morton:
Mackintosh.

†SHARPEY-SCHAFER, Sir Edward Albert:
Mott.
SHAW, Sir William Napier:
Dines.
SHERRINGTON, Charles Ely Rose:
Acworth.
SHERRINGTON, Sir Charles Scott:
Ferrier; Langley; Paget.
SIKES, Edward Ernest:
Sandys.
SMITH, David Nichol:
Raleigh.
SMITH, Sir Frank Edward:
Jackson (H. B.).
SMITH, George Charles Moore:
Carpenter (E.).
SMITH, Herbert Maynard:
Weston.
SMITH, John Alexander:
Burnet.
SMITH, Nowell Charles:
Bridges.
SMITH, Reginald Allender:
Read.
†SOOTHILL, William Edward:
Hosie.
†SORLEY, William Ritchie:
Ward (J.).
†SPANTON, Ernest Frederick:
Johnson.
SPENDER, John Alfred:
Asquith (Oxford).
SPENS, Will:
Butler (G).
SRAWLEY, James Herbert:
Fry.
STEBBING, Edward Percy:
Wilmot.
STENTON, Frank Merry:
Round.
STEPHENS, John William Watson:
Manson.
STILL, George Frederic:
Thomson (J.).
STODDART, Jane Thompson
Nicoll.
STRACHEY, Ray:
Aldrich-Blake; Fawcett; Jebb; Pankhurst.
STRAKER, William:
Burt.
†SUTRO, Alfred:
Zangwill.

TAIT, James:
Farrer; Kingsford.
TAYLOR, Alfred Edward:
Bradley (F. H.).
TEMPERLEY, Harold William Vazeille:
Satow.
THOMAS, Frederick William:
Macdonell.
†THOMAS, Herbert Henry:
Geikie; Teall.
THOMPSON, Sir D'Arcy Wentworth:
Thiselton-Dyer.
THOMPSON, Edward John:
Canton.

THOMPSON, Herbert:
Squire.

TILLEY, Sir John Anthony Cecil:
Sanderson (T. H.).

†TINSLEY, Edward Samuel:
Blackburne.

TOYNBEE, Margaret Ruth:
Bell (A. G.).

TRACEY, Herbert Trevor:
Abraham; Roberts.

TREVELYAN, George Macaulay:
Trevelyan.

TREVELYAN, Janet Penrose:
Green.

TROUP, Robert Scott:
Schlich.

TURNBULL, Herbert Westren:
MacMahon.

TURNER, George James:
Rigg.

TWEEDSMUIR, Susan Charlotte Buchan, Baroness:
Webb (M. G.).

VAUGHAN WILLIAMS, Ralph:
Sharp.

VENN, John Archibald:
Venn.

VESEY FITZGERALD, Seymour Gonne:
Ameer Ali; Dyer (R. E. H.); Edge; Jenkins; Knox; Muddiman; Sinha.

WADDINGTON, Sydney Peirce:
Wood (C.).

WALKER, Edward Mewburn:
Ball.

WALPOLE, Sir Hugh Seymour:
Haggard; Hewlett.

†WARREN, Sir Thomas Herbert:
Case.

WATKIN, Alfred Edward:
Baron; Dalziel; Pease; Rowntree; Walsh; Wilson (J. H.).

WATTEVILLE, Herman Gaston de:
Callwell; Clery; Congreve; French (Ypres); Grenfell (F. W.); Harper; Maxwell; Monro; Morland; Townshend; Wilson (H. H.).

†WAUGH, William Templeton:
Shaughnessy.

WEATHERALL, John Henry:
Carpenter (J. E.).

WEAVER, John Reginald Homer:
Davis.

WEBB, Clement Charles Julian:
Rashdall; von Hügel.

WEBB, Maurice Everett:
Knott.

†WELBY, Thomas Earle:
Weyman.

WHATLEY, Norman:
Glazebrook.

WHEARE, Kenneth Clinton:
Bond.

WHITTON, Frederick Ernest:
Willcocks.

WILFORD, Sir Thomas Mason:
Massey; Stout; Ward (J. G.).

†WILKINSON, Henry Spenser:
Crowe.

WILLIAMS, Arthur Frederic Basil:
Childers; Milner; Young (G.).

WILLIAMS, Ifor:
Evans; Morris-Jones.

WILLIAMS, Iolo Aneurin:
Cadbury.

WILLIAMS, Robert:
Owen.

WITHERS, Hartley:
Macara; Mond (Melchett).

WOODWARD, Sir Arthur Smith:
Dawkins.

WOODWARD, Ernest Llewellyn:
Hudson (W. H.).

WORTHINGTON, Frank Vigors:
Coryndon.

WORTHINGTON, Sir Percy Scott:
Waterhouse.

WYLIE, Sir Francis James:
Fairbridge.

ZULUETA, Francis de:
Merry del Val.

DICTIONARY
OF
NATIONAL BIOGRAPHY
(TWENTIETH CENTURY)
PERSONS WHO DIED 1922–1930

ABBOTT, EDWIN ABBOTT (1838–1926), teacher and scholar, was born in London 20 December 1838, the eldest son of Edwin Abbott, headmaster of the Philological School, Marylebone, by his wife, Jane Abbott (a first cousin). Educated at the City of London School under Dr. G. F. W. Mortimer [q.v.], he entered St. John's College, Cambridge, as a scholar in 1857, was senior classic and senior chancellor's medallist in 1861, and was elected to a fellowship at his college in 1862. He resigned this position in 1863 on account of his marriage with Mary Elizabeth (died 1919), daughter of Henry Rangeley, landed proprietor and coal-owner, of Unstone, Derbyshire. He was ordained deacon in 1862 and priest in 1863.

Abbott entered the scholastic profession, which was to be his main life work and in which he was to rise to the highest rank, in 1862, when he was appointed an assistant master at King Edward's School, Birmingham. In 1864 he went to Clifton College, where he worked for a short time under the inspiring influence of John Percival [q.v.]. In 1865, at the early age of twenty-six, he was elected to the headmastership of the City of London School, which he held until his retirement in 1889. During the whole of this period he not only worked with untiring energy at his administrative and teaching duties as head of a great London day-school, but he found leisure for varied literary work, mainly in biblical and English studies. Valuable and even original as much of this was, his claim to be remembered must chiefly rest upon what can only be called his genius for teaching.

The City of London School had already risen greatly in reputation under Abbott's predecessor and teacher Dr. Mortimer; but it was owing to Abbott's inspiration that it won the distinction of providing an intellectual training unsurpassed, if equalled, in any other English school. His greatness as an educator was partly that of an organizer of new methods of teaching, and partly that of an originator of many innovations in the school curriculum. Having a reverence for physical science not often found among the classical scholars of his day, he made an elementary knowledge of chemistry compulsory throughout the upper school. As regards classical instruction, he had the greatest respect—which he instilled into his pupils—for the severe standards of formal scholarship; but he breathed new life into it. He was one of the first to adopt the reformed pronunciation of Latin, thus giving back to that language the old music which it had lost in barbaric English vocalism.

Having caught the enthusiasm then prevalent at Cambridge for the study of comparative philology, at that time in its interesting and hopeful youth, Abbott provided better teaching in the subject for the members of his sixth form than they could find for many years afterwards in the lecture-rooms of Oxford: in order to fortify the subject he introduced his keenest pupils to the study of Sanskrit, and more than one of them—notably Professor Cecil Bendall [q.v.]—rose to eminence as Sanskrit scholars.

Abbott's most fruitful innovation in the traditional curriculum was the introduction of English literature as an integral part of form-teaching throughout the school: every term his sixth form studied a play of Shakespeare as they studied a Greek play; and thus the language and soul of one great world helped to interpret the other. It was his own enthusiasm for great literature, and his masterful exposition of the secrets and principles of style, which opened to many boys a treasure-house that permanently enriched their lives and inspired the careers of such pupils as Arthur Henry Bullen [q.v.], Sir Sidney Lee [q.v.], and others who won fame as English scholars and men of letters.

Of no less importance were the changes which Abbott succeeded in carrying through in the organization of classes and in the personnel of his staff. When he first took up the reins, the school was suffering, as many others suffered at that time, from the great size of some of the classes; as many as seventy boys might be under one form-master. Abbott was able to effect important reforms in this vital matter, though probably not as trenchant as he desired. He was also able markedly to improve the quality of his teachers, and to attract able men from his own and the sister university to work under him. In spite of his loyal devotion to Cambridge, he had a high appreciation of the Oxford course and of the type of men that it tended to produce. Of all the capacities that he strove to evoke in his pupils, he valued most highly that of the clear expression of serious thought, which he conceived to be the chief result of the Oxford 'Greats' training; and of all his pupils he was perhaps proudest of H. H. Asquith, whom he regarded as its best representative.

Apart from any of his special interests and reforming ideas, it was Abbott's whole personality which inspired and controlled those who came most closely under his influence, and which permeated the whole school. He had the mark of the spiritual leader in that he could impart to others something of the 'virtue' that was in him. He was aflame with intellectual energy: without driving or over-taxing his pupils, he made intellectual effort a kind of religion for them; his deep reprobation of intellectual slackness and unveracity was such a spur to them that his sixth form became a most stimulating *palaestra* for eager and receptive spirits. At the same time he was by no means what is called 'an intellectualist', but a great moral and religious teacher.

In spite of a frail and delicate physique, Abbott could keep discipline without effort, for he had the eyes and the voice of the commander, and possessing the enthusiasm of genius, he had none of the official mannerisms of the headmaster. He was an impressive preacher, having an attractive delivery and a pure and distinguished style: in the pulpit he was a bold and original exponent of advanced broad church doctrines; while his religious instruction to his classes was unconventionally spiritual and winning. His own university elected him Hulsean lecturer in 1876, and Oxford invited him to be select preacher in 1877. But, next to teaching, Abbott's vocation lay in writing; and it was probably the attraction of complete leisure for literary work, as well as his weariness of administration, which prompted his retirement at the zenith of his reputation and at the comparatively early age of fifty (1889).

During the active period of his life Abbott had already produced much, for he began to publish in 1870. His writings fall into three categories: school-books, works of literary scholarship, and works of theological scholarship and construction. Some of his publications in the first class rise markedly above the average level of the school primer: his treatise *How to write clearly* (1872) is an original and successful attempt to formulate some of the fundamental rules of style. His *Shakespearean Grammar* (1870) is a work of scholarly research and an original contribution to the linguistic study of Shakespeare. His *English Lessons, for English People* (1871)—written in collaboration with his friend Professor (Sir) J. R. Seeley [q.v.]—contains a luminous exposition of the varied styles and modes of expression to be found in the great English masters of poetry and prose, together with a stimulating selection of illustrative passages; and it deals helpfully with many of the higher problems of literary criticism.

The English classical author on whom Abbott laboured most was Francis Bacon. In 1877 he published a monograph *Bacon and Essex*, a work of critical value, serving to correct the partial judgement of James Spedding [q.v.] of Bacon's action on the occasion of the trial of the Earl of Essex. Of more importance for a general estimate is the introduction which accompanied his seventh edition of Bacon's *Essays* (1886); this contains an original and masterly study of Bacon's varied activities and complex character, based mainly on the self-revelations given in the *Essays*.

More numerous and perhaps more weighty than Abbott's works of secular scholarship are his theological writings. All these have the distinction of his style and bear the stamp of his personality. Their range is wide, for they include treatises of textual criticism, showing the most minute and laborious attention to statistical details and to linguistic interpretation (*Johannine Vocabulary*, 1905;

Johannine Grammar, 1906), as well as works of high religious imagination and bold constructive power, such as *Philochristus* (1878), *Onesimus: Memoirs of a disciple of Paul* (1882), and *Silanus the Christian* (1906). These are striking expositions of the broad church point of view; the first is dedicated to Seeley, the author of *Ecce Homo*, with whom Abbott proclaims his spiritual brotherhood. Not only for the purity of their style but for their religious insight they stand out among the theological writings of Abbott's generation. *Philochristus*, a dramatic account of the life of Jesus as it may have appeared to a contemporary disciple, must be ranked high among modern attempts to reshape the gospel narrative. The later work, *Silanus*, shows a further departure from orthodoxy, in that the miraculous is wholly discarded while the supernatural is retained: it gives a penetrating estimate of the ethical doctrines of Epictetus. Abbott also wrote *Philomythus* (1891), a discussion of J. H. Newman's 'Essay on Miracles', and *The Anglican Career of Cardinal Newman*, 2 vols. (1892).

Abbott died at his home at Hampstead 12 October 1926. He had one son and one daughter. There is a portrait of him by Sir Hubert von Herkomer in the possession of the City of London School.

[Private information; personal knowledge.]
L. R. Farnell.

ABRAHAM, WILLIAM (1842–1922), labour politician and trade union leader, was born at Cwmavon, in the Afon Valley, South Wales, 14 June 1842. He was the fourth son of Thomas Abraham, a working miner, and was himself employed underground for fully twenty years, beginning as a pit boy at the age of nine. His mother's name was Mary Williams. With no more than a scanty education at Cwmavon national school, Abraham became, through his association with the miners' trade union and political organization, a conspicuous and influential figure—popularly known by his eisteddfod pen-name 'Mabon'—in the public life of Wales. He was a pioneer of trade unionism among the Welsh miners, a leader of Welsh Nonconformity, and the first of the miners' representatives to enter parliament from the Welsh coal-field. Politically, he belonged to the radical wing of the liberal party, but as a trade unionist he naturally attached himself to the small group of labour members who emerged from the general election of 1885 and maintained an independent position in the House of Commons until the labour party assumed its present form and title after the general election of 1906. It was not, in fact, until 1909 that the miners' national organization became affiliated to the labour party; so that it was only in the last decade of his parliamentary career, which lasted from 1885 to 1920, that 'Mabon' was formally a member of the labour party; and it cannot be said that he was at any time an ardent advocate of that party's socialistic policy. As a trade unionist he was the leader and spokesman of the most moderate section of the miners' movement in South Wales, and a restraining influence in both the South Wales Miners' Federation and the Miners' Federation of Great Britain.

Abraham began his career as an agent of the miners in 1871, when only a loose form of district organization existed in South Wales; and the part which he played in the industrial conflicts of 1871 to 1873, preceding the establishment of the sliding-scale system of regulating wages in relation to prices and profits in the mining industry, made him the miners' inevitable choice for the chairmanship of their side of the joint Sliding-Scale Association which governed their relations with the coal-owners from 1875 to 1902. During the existence of the Association, Abraham exercised a very high degree of personal authority in the miners' counsels; although disputes were frequent, general stoppages of work in the coal-field occurred but rarely; and 'Mabon' defended the sliding-scale system tenaciously against the younger generation of miners' leaders, who strove to unite the various district organizations and local unions into a single union for the whole coal-field with the minimum wage as its main objective in policy. He assisted willingly to form the South Wales Miners' Federation by the union of seven or eight independent local bodies, including his own Cambrian Miners' Association, and became the Federation's first president in 1898; but he was not in sympathy with the militant policy which it pursued, separately and in conjunction with the Miners' Federation of Great Britain after 1899, culminating in the very serious upheaval in South Wales in 1910–11, and in the first general strike of miners in all the coal-fields in 1912. His control of the miners' policy declined with the passing of the sliding-scale system, but he retained considerable personal influence until the onset of syndicalist doctrines marked the advent of new men and new methods in the coal-field.

Abraham owed much of his popularity in Wales to his skill in arousing the emotions of the miners by fervent oratory and by his readiness to sing to them when he, or they, grew tired of speech-making. Frequently he concluded a speech with a peroration in the vernacular, followed by a spirited rendering of 'Hen Wlad fy Nhadau' ('Land of My Fathers'); and on many occasions he used the song like a charm on unruly or hostile assemblies of miners. At the height of his career he was a striking figure; black-bearded, square-built, though only of medium stature, he left the impression of a dominating personality. In later years he grew stout and moved somewhat heavily, but he kept to the end the imperious carriage of a man who had held the responsibilities of leadership and knew the sense of power in having maintained for so long his place at the head of the miners' organization. As a member of parliament he did not often intervene in House of Commons debates, except where mining matters were raised, but on these he was for many years the miners' chief spokesman in the House.

No serious challenge was ever made to Abraham's tenure of a seat in the House of Commons, even when his liberal-labour politics assumed an old-fashioned appearance. He sat as member for the Rhondda division from 1885 to 1918, and for two years thereafter as member for Rhondda West. He was sworn a member of the Privy Council in 1911. He died at Pentre, in the Rhondda Valley, 14 May 1922.

Abraham married in 1860 Sarah (died 1900), daughter of Thomas Williams, and had three sons and three daughters.

[*The Times*, 15 May 1922; Ness Edwards, *History of the South Wales Miners*, 1926; H. Stanley Jevons, *The British Coal Trade*, 1915; Labour Party and Trades Union Congress *Annual Reports*; private information; personal knowledge.] H. T. Tracey.

ACLAND, Sir ARTHUR HERBERT DYKE, thirteenth baronet, of Columb John, Devon (1847–1926), politician and educational reformer, born at Holnicote, near Porlock, 13 October 1847, was the third son of Sir Thomas Dyke Acland, eleventh baronet [q.v.], by his first wife, Mary, daughter of Sir Charles Mordaunt, eighth baronet, of Massingham, Norfolk. Sir Henry Wentworth Acland [q.v.] was his uncle. He entered Rugby School in 1861, and matriculated from Christ Church, Oxford, in 1866. He obtained a second class in classical moderations (1868) and also in the final school of law and modern history (1870), graduating B.A. in 1870 and M.A. in 1873. At Oxford Acland showed a keen interest in economic and social questions, and gathered round him a group of young Fellows and undergraduates who were known as the 'Inner Circle'.

In 1871 Acland was appointed lecturer, and in 1872 tutor, at Keble College, then newly founded. He was ordained deacon in 1872, but in 1879 resigned his orders under the Clerical Disabilities Act of 1870. In 1875 he gave up his tutorship at Keble, and from 1875 to 1877 held the post of principal of the newly founded Oxford Military School at Cowley. He was also the first treasurer of Somerville College, Oxford. In 1880 he was appointed steward of Christ Church, and from 1884 to 1885 he was a senior student at Christ Church. In 1884 he was appointed senior bursar of Balliol College, and was made an honorary fellow in 1888.

In December 1885 Acland was returned to parliament in the liberal interest as member for the newly formed Rotheram division of the West Riding of Yorkshire. He at once became an authority on educational questions, and between 1885 and 1889 took a considerable part in promoting the Welsh Intermediate Education Act, a private members' bill, which was passed in 1889 and anticipated the Education Act of 1902 in making the Welsh county councils an educational authority. He afterwards contributed a paper on the working of the Act to *Studies in Secondary Education* (1902), edited by himself and (Sir) Hubert Llewellyn Smith. His experience as a member of the West Riding county council had impressed him with the advisability of entrusting the control of educational matters to the county councils, and he took a further step in this direction by persuading the House of Commons in 1890 to make a grant to the county councils for technical education.

In August 1892, when Mr. Gladstone formed his fourth ministry, Acland entered the Cabinet as vice-president of the Committee of Council of Education. To Gladstone the admission of Acland, 'the son of the oldest of all the surviving friends of his youth, Sir Thomas Acland', gave personal gratification [Morley, *Life of Gladstone*, iii, 494–5]. For the first time the vice-president had a seat in the Cabinet, and in consequence Acland had entire control of the department, although Lord Kimberley and Lord Rosebery represented it in the House of Lords. Acland's direction to inspectors to concern themselves with the structural improvement of school buildings was criticized as an attempt to discourage, by putting financial pressure on them, voluntary schools and religious education. He succeeded, however, in 1893 in passing an Act by which the age for compulsory attendance at school was raised from ten to eleven. He also, towards the close of his tenure of office, reorganized the science and art department at South Kensington and abolished payments by examination results, subjecting all subjects taught to inspection, and making a portion of the government grant dependent on the reports of qualified certificated teachers acting as inspectors.

With regard to his general position in the Cabinet, Acland had the reputation among his colleagues of 'keeping in touch with the labour people and their mind' [Morley, *Recollections*, i, 324], and Lord Morley states that, on Gladstone's retirement in 1894, Earl Spencer, Mr. Asquith, Acland, and himself were 'the leading junto inside the Cabinet' who preferred Lord Rosebery to Sir William Harcourt as Gladstone's successor [*ibid.* ii, 15].

When the liberal ministry went out of office in 1895 Acland retired from active politics for reasons of health. He resigned his seat in 1899, but kept in close touch with his party and with the Board of Education. In 1902 he returned to the councils of the party for the purpose of opposing the conservative Education Bill which proposed to make state grants to voluntary schools while leaving the religious teaching under the control of the managers. In December 1905, when Sir Henry Campbell-Bannerman was forming his ministry, Acland was largely instrumental in overcoming Sir Edward Grey's reluctance to take office in a ministry from which Lord Rosebery was excluded, urging on him that he ought not to imperil the whole liberal cause and with it the cause of free trade, by reviving old differences on the eve of a general election [Spender, *Life of Campbell-Bannerman*, ii, 196–7].

Acland was president of the general committee of the National Liberal Federation in 1906. He declined the offer of a peerage in 1908. For some years he was president of the consultative committee of the Board of Education, and in 1912 he was chairman of the Liberal Land Committee. He received the honorary degree of LL.D from the universities of Leeds (1904) and Bristol (1912). Acland published in 1882, in conjunction with Professor Cyril Ransome, *A Handbook of the Political History of England*, which had considerable popularity as a book of reference and reached a new edition in 1913. Another successful manual, published by Acland and Benjamin Jones, was *Working Men Co-operators* (1884), an account of the artisans' Co-operative movement in Great Britain. Acland also published *The Patriotic Poetry of William Wordsworth. A Selection* (1915), and at an earlier date printed for private circulation a life of his father, Sir Thomas Dyke Acland.

Acland succeeded his brother, Sir Charles Thomas Dyke Acland, as thirteenth baronet in 1919. He died in London 9 October 1926 and was buried at Golders Green. He married in 1873 Alice Sophia, daughter of the Rev. Francis Macaulay Cunningham, rector of Witney, Oxfordshire, and afterwards rector of Brightwell, Berkshire. They had two sons and one daughter. Acland was succeeded as fourteenth baronet by his elder and only surviving son, Francis Dyke (born 1874).

[*The Times*, 11 October 1926; Lord Morley, *Recollections*, 2 vols., 1917; J. A. Spender, *Life of Sir Henry Campbell-Bannerman*, 2 vols., 1923; *Rugby School Register, vol. ii, 1850–1874*, 1881; R. L. Archer, *Secondary Education in the Nineteenth Century*, 1921.]

E. I. Carlyle.

ACWORTH, Sir WILLIAM MITCHELL (1850–1925), expert on railway economics, was born at Rothley, Leicestershire, 22 November 1850, the third son of the Rev. William Acworth, vicar of Rothley, by his wife, Margaret Dundas, daughter of Andrew Mitchell, of Maulside, Beath, and Blythswood Place, Glasgow. He was educated at Uppingham and at Christ Church, Oxford, where he obtained a second class in the honour school of modern history in 1872. After taking his degree, he acted for eighteen months as tutor to the two sons of the Crown Prince Frederick of Germany, William (afterwards the Emperor William II) and Henry. On returning to England he was appointed in May 1875 an assistant master at Dulwich College, where he remained until 1885.

The problems of law and government attracted Acworth, and in 1886 he was elected a member, later chairman, of the Metropolitan Asylums Board. Serving on the London County Council from 1889 to 1892, he had meanwhile specialized in railway transport economics, and his first book, *The Railways of England*, was published in 1889, followed by *The Railways of Scotland* in 1890. In the latter year he was called to the bar by the Inner Temple. He served on the royal commission on accidents to railway servants in 1899, on the viceregal commission on Irish railways in 1906, and on the Board of Trade committee on railway accounts and statistics in 1906. He became a director of the Underground Electric Railways of London Limited and of the Midland and South-Western Junction Railway, and was a frequent contributor of articles on railway economics to technical and other periodicals both in Great Britain and in the United States of America, where he was held in high esteem.

Familiar with American railway statistical methods, Acworth criticized the railway accounts of Great Britain in *The Railways and the Traders* (1891). The new form of railway accounts introduced in 1911 was a great improvement, the credit being due largely to Acworth, but only in 1920 did the ton-mile and the passenger-mile statistical units, as advocated by him in 1906, become a requirement of railway accounting. Soon after its foundation in October 1895, Acworth inaugurated lectures for railway students at the London School of Economics, to which institution he gave his unique collection of transport literature. These lectures led to the publication in 1905 of his classic work, *The Elements of Railway Economics*, an admirable text-book which has been widely translated.

As unsuccessful unionist candidate for the Keighley division of the West Riding in 1906, 1910, and 1911, Acworth gained some experience of political activities. From 1914 onwards his interest in transport matters was mainly directed abroad, his advice being sought in many countries. In 1916 he was appointed a member of the royal commission of inquiry into the Canadian railways. He gave evidence before the joint committee on inter-state and foreign commerce of the United States Congress in 1917. In a revised form this evidence was published in 1920 as *A Historical Sketch of State Railway Ownership*, wherein may be found his reasons for preferring private enterprise. Southern Rhodesian railways claimed his attention in 1918, and in 1921 he was appointed chairman of the committee on Indian railway policy and administration. Acworth had, indeed, become the greatest expert in the world on the relationship between railways and governments; consequently, he was asked by the council of the League of Nations in 1923 to undertake an investigation of the Austrian railways. He accepted a similar request with regard to Germany from the Reparations Commission in 1924, being subsequently appointed *zweiter Vizepräsident des Verwaltungsrates* on the Deutsche Reichsbahn Gesellschaft constituted in that year. At the time of his death, which occurred in London 2 April 1925, he was about to embark upon a similar investigation in Rumania.

A supporter of private enterprise, Acworth was, in some instances, led to recommend measures of state control owing to chaotic post-war conditions; but he always strongly emphasized the necessity of separate railway budgets and of adequate safeguards against political interference. It is of interest that where state control has not succeeded, his recommendations against such interference have not been carried out in their entirety.

Acworth was knighted in 1921 and created K.C.S.I. in 1922. He was twice married: first, in 1878 to Elizabeth Louisa Oswald (died 1904), eldest daughter of James Brown, of Orangefield, Ayrshire; secondly, in 1923 to Elizabeth Learmonth, daughter of Thomas Wotherspoon, of Hundleshope, Peeblesshire. There were no children of either marriage.

[*Economic Journal*, June 1925; private information.] C. E. R. SHERRINGTON.

ADAMI, JOHN GEORGE (1862–1926), pathologist, was born 12 January 1862 at Ashton-on-Mersey, Lancashire, the second son of John George Adami, hotel proprietor in Manchester, by his wife, Sarah Ann Ellis, daughter of Thomas Leech, of Urmston, Lancashire. Both families numbered many medical men in their ancestry. He was sent to Old Trafford School and Owens College, Manchester, and in 1880, having passed the first part of the London B.Sc. examination, entered Christ's College, Cambridge. At Cambridge he was greatly influenced by the teaching of (Sir) Michael Foster [q.v.]. He gained a first class in both parts of the natural science tripos (1882, 1884), and after going down worked for eight months at Breslau under

Rudolf Heidenhain. From 1885 to 1887 he was house physician at the Royal Infirmary, Manchester; in 1888 he returned to Cambridge as university demonstrator in pathology; and in 1890 was working at the Pasteur Institute in Paris under Roux, Metchnikoff, and Pasteur. In March 1891 he was elected to a fellowship at Jesus College, Cambridge.

In 1892 Adami was appointed to the chair of pathology and bacteriology at McGill University, Montreal. He found a young university and a department badly hampered by lack of funds, buildings, and equipment. These material needs were met by the generosity of Lord Strathcona; while Adami, by his able teaching and originality in research built up a wide reputation. His contribution on 'Inflammation' to Sir Clifford Allbutt's *System of Medicine* (1896) attracted particular attention. In 1899 he was invited to apply for the chair of pathology at Cambridge, but felt it his duty to refuse. In 1905 he was elected F.R.S., and in 1908 the first volume of his *Principles of Pathology* proved an important book in the teaching of the subject, insisting, as it did, on a closer union between pathology and physiology. The second volume (written in collaboration with A. G. Nicholls) appeared in the following year; and in 1912 Adami produced, in collaboration with John Macrae, a *Text-Book of Pathology* for the general student. In 1911 he was elected president of the Canadian Association for the prevention of Tuberculosis and in 1912 president of the Association of American Physicians. During the European War he served as assistant director of medical services to the Canadian expeditionary force. In 1918 he published *The War Story of the Canadian Army Medical Corps*.

In the autumn of 1919 Adami was appointed vice-chancellor of the university of Liverpool. The university was then in the full throes of post-war expansion, its numbers having grown from under 900 in August 1914 to 2,600 in the session of 1919–20. As vice-chancellor one of Adami's chief services to the university was the raising, by appeal, of a sum of £360,000 for the provision of new buildings and equipment, the endowment of new chairs, and the inauguration of additional lectureships. He had a high conception of the importance of the university in the life of a great commercial community like Liverpool, and he made it his business to strengthen the links between business and academic life and to maintain the interest of the surrounding districts outside the city itself. An untiring and witty public speaker, he was accessible, genial, and energetic, and won both esteem and affection in university and city alike. His last two and a half years were passed under the shadow of a malady he knew to be fatal, but his activity never slackened. He died at Ruthin 29 August 1926.

Adami's chief service to pathology was to link it more closely with clinical medicine, stressing always the importance of preventive medicine. For ten years before the European War he fought a campaign in Canada for public health—insisting especially on child welfare and measures against tuberculosis. He was largely responsible for the standardization of the Wassermann technique in British laboratories, and in 1919 spoke out fearlessly on the subject of venereal disease.

Adami married twice: first, in 1894 Mary Stuart (died 1916), daughter of James Alexander Cantlie, of Montreal, by whom he had one son and one daughter; secondly, in 1922 Marie, elder daughter of the Rev. Thomas Wilkinson, of Litherland, near Liverpool, by whom he had no children.

[Marie Adami, *J. George Adami: a memoir; together with contributions from others, his friends, and an introduction by Sir Humphry Rolleston*, 1930; *British Medical Journal*, 1926, vol. ii, pp. 507–510; *Nature*, 25 September 1926.] H. B. Grimsditch.

AKERS-DOUGLAS, ARETAS, first Viscount Chilston (1851–1926), statesman, born at St. Leonards-on-Sea 21 October 1851, was the only son of the Rev. Aretas Akers, of Malling Abbey, Kent, by his wife, Frances Maria, daughter of Francis Holles Brandram, of Underriver House, Kent. He was educated at Eton and at University College, Oxford, and was called to the bar by the Inner Temple in 1875. The same year he assumed the additional name of Douglas, on succeeding to the estates in Kent and Scotland of his kinsman, James Douglas Stoddart Douglas, of Chilston Park, Kent, and Baads, Midlothian.

In Akers-Douglas's youth the county of Kent was not only a conservative stronghold, but also the nursery of that party's organization. Sir William Hart Dyke, Disraeli's political adjutant, was member for the mid-division, and Lord Abergavenny, who was lieutenant of the county, was chief controller of the party's interests, and from Eridge Castle issued the appointments of the principal staff officers of the conservative head-quarters in London. After his marriage in 1875 Akers-Douglas was encouraged by Lord Abergavenny to take an active part in county politics, and in 1880, after a contest, he was elected member of parliament for East Kent. He represented this constituency until its redistribution in 1885 under the name of the St. Augustine's division, thereafter being returned—on several occasions without a contest—until his retirement in 1911. In 1883, three years after his election, he was appointed an opposition whip—Hart Dyke and Rowland Winn (afterwards Lord St. Oswald) having retired from that position. After Mr. Gladstone's resignation of office in June 1885, Akers-Douglas was appointed patronage secretary in the new government; he held this post until the defeat of Lord Salisbury's administration in the following January. In July 1886, after the rejection of the first Home Rule Bill, Lord Salisbury resumed office, and Akers-Douglas returned to the Treasury, where he remained until the dissolution of parliament in 1892. He was admitted a member of the privy council in 1891.

These six years were the supreme test of Akers-Douglas's exceptional abilities. 'Parties', as Pulteney once said, 'like snakes are moved by their tails'; and, although the conservative government had a majority, its life depended on the dissentient liberals, whose adherence to the government was swayed by the dual and occasionally alternating counsels of Lord Hartington and Mr. Chamberlain. The control of these composite forces required firmness, tempered with delicate handling, and to this task Akers-Douglas brought an industry and supervision which never tired. He acquired an ample and accurate knowledge of parliamentary procedure which he combined with the closest study of party interests. No one knew better the changing mood of the lobby, the exact value of the *frondeur*, or the extent of an intrigue. He possessed a preternatural dexterity in judging the qualifications of men for office or party service, as well as their claims for honorific recognition. In dealing with the importunate suitor he could 'smile without art and win without a bribe'. His will was tenacious; his character strong. He compelled the attendance of ministers at the House with the insistence which he applied to private members. In all the affairs of government or party Lord Salisbury trusted him implicitly.

Akers-Douglas served as chief whip in the brief opposition period from 1892 to 1895: upon the return of the unionist connexion to power in the latter year, he was preferred by Lord Salisbury to the post of first commissioner of works. In this office he shared responsibility for the ceremonial of King Edward VII's coronation in Westminster Abbey in 1902, and for the Mall Memorial to Queen Victoria. In 1902, on the transfer of Mr. (afterwards Lord) Ritchie to the Exchequer, he was appointed secretary of state for the home department, a position which he filled unostentatiously and efficiently until the resignation of Mr. Balfour's government in the winter of 1905. He survived the convulsion of the general election in the following January, but with rare modesty allowed it to be understood that his official career was ended. At the coronation of King George V in 1911 he accepted the conventional viscounty—a promotion which was widely approved—and was created Baron Douglas, of Baads, and Viscount Chilston, of Boughton Malherbe, Kent.

In the last years of Chilston's life his health failed, and he died in London 15 January 1926. He was created G.B.E. (1920) and a knight of grace of St. John of Jerusalem (1916). His portrait by Sir A. S. Cope is at Chilston Park. He married in 1875 Adeline Mary, daughter of Horatio Austen Smith, of Hayes Court, Kent, by whom he had two sons and five daughters. He was succeeded as second viscount by his elder son, Aretas (born 1876).

[*The Times*, 16 January 1926; *Studies of Yesterday, by a privy councillor*, 1928.]

J. S. Sandars.

ALBANI, Dame MARIE LOUISE CÉCILIE EMMA (1852–1930), singer, born at Chambly, near Montreal, 1 November 1852, was the elder daughter of Joseph Lajeunesse, the descendant of an old Breton family, professor of piano, violin, harp, and organ, by his wife, Melina Miguaud, on her mother's side of Scottish descent. Emma began her musical education under her mother at the age of four. At five her father undertook her training, and her strong constitution enabled her so to profit by his lessons that, on going to the Sacré Cœur convent at Montreal at eight, her power of reading vocal and pianoforte classical works at sight evoked some wonder. The mother superior, an Italian, appreciated the child's musical ability and histrionic gifts. She soon made semi-public appearances in Montreal, playing the harp and piano, and improvising. Four years later she made her début as a singer, on that occasion singing 'Robert, toi que j'aime'.

In 1864 the Lajeunesse family removed to Albany, New York, where Emma became first soprano in the choir of the Roman Catholic church of St. Joseph, subsequently undertaking the duties of organist; she also became teacher of piano and singing at the Sacré Cœur convent, Kinwood. By the advice of the bishop, Lajeunesse brought his daughter to Europe in about 1867 or 1868 (his wife had died when Emma was seven) with a view to her adopting singing as a profession. Her first professor was Gilbert Duprez, at Paris, formerly a distinguished singer, celebrated for his excellent declamation and strong dramatic sense. The impresario Maurice Strakosch was brought to hear her by Prince Poniatowsky, a pupil of Rossini. By Poniatowsky's advice she was sent to Milan, to study with Francesco Lamperti, to whose instruction she always expressed herself deeply indebted. Operatic managers who came to hear the students made Emma several offers for public appearances. It was finally decided in 1870 that she should make her début at Messina, as that public was very difficult to satisfy and success there would mean success anywhere. The opera selected was Bellini's *La Sonnambula*. On the advice of her Italian elocution master, Delorenzi, she adopted the name of 'Albani', the patronymic of an old Italian noble family, practically extinct. She sang the whole season in Sicily, and was invited to open the new Bellini theatre at Aci Reale. On this festive occasion crowds came from all parts of Italy to hear her, and she was overwhelmed with gifts. From Sicily she returned to Milan for further study with Lamperti. She next sang at Cento, and afterwards was engaged at the Politeana Theatre at Florence, success attending her constantly. At Florence Albani made the acquaintance of Jenny Lind, finding the ideas of the retired great singer noble and elevating, and a great help to her own art.

From Florence, Albani went to Malta, where she sang for the whole season of 1870–1871. The part of Inez in Meyerbeer's *L'Africaine* she sang after two days' study, having to undertake it at a moment's notice. On leaving Malta, British men-of-war's boats formed a double line through which passed the steamer bearing Albani away.

Albani arrived in London in June 1871, and was engaged by Frederick Gye the younger [q.v.], impresario of the Royal Italian opera, Covent Garden, for five summer seasons. But her début there did not take place till 2 April 1872, when she made an immediate success as Amina in *La Sonnambula*. From now on she sang almost every season there until 1896, displaying great versatility in many parts.

Between the London seasons Albani visited Paris—the first occasion was 1872–1873—to sing Italian opera; she sang also in opera and at concerts at Brussels and in Germany, and toured the United States of America in 1874 and 1889 and Canada in 1883 and 1889. In 1873 and 1874 at Moscow and St. Petersburg her singing was much admired by the court: the Tsar Alexander II sent her a diamond ornament after her performance at a state concert. Her portrayal of Wagner's heroines, Elsa in *Lohengrin* (at Covent Garden in 1875, and in Berlin in 1882), Elizabeth in *Tannhäuser* (1876), culminating in an appearance as Isolde to Jean De Reszke's Tristan in 1896, forms a striking piece of operatic history, for she employed Italian vocal methods, in accordance with the known ideas of that great opera reformer.

While Albani's successes on the operatic stage were of such high order, those in oratorio were equally so. At the Handel festival in 1877 she was principal soprano, and after Thérèse Tietjens's retirement in 1877, she occupied that place at all the festivals. A noteworthy appearance was in Gounod's *Redemption* at the Birmingham festival in 1882. Other composers in whose new works she appeared were Sullivan, Dvorák, Mackenzie, and Cowen. In 1886 Albani sang in the performance of *St. Elizabeth* at which Liszt was present, this being the composer-pianist's last visit to London. Her voice could ring out in telling tones in the largest building, while her mezza-voce was delightful.

The range of Albani's abilities and her personal charm made her not only a great popular singer but a favourite with many royal personages. Queen Victoria keenly appreciated her talents and treated her with much friendship. She received decorations accompanied by valuable gifts from the Empress Eugénie, Kaiser Wilhelm I, and others, but she recorded that she was as proud of receiving the Beethoven gold medal of the Royal Philharmonic Society (1897) as of any of her court honours.

Albani consulted pictures and statuary

in order to obtain correctness in costume when essaying new characters. She believed, too, in going to the fountain-head for instruction and in the influence of environment: for example, she studied *Mignon* with Ambroise Thomas, *The Redemption* with Gounod (who wrote *Mors et Vita* with her in view), and Wagnerian roles with Franz Wüllner, Wagner's friend, at Munich. She also visited Brahms at Vienna, singing part of his *Requiem* to him, in the principal solo affecting him to tears.

Albani retired in 1911, after a farewell concert (14 October) in the Albert Hall, assisted by Madame Patti and Sir Charles Santley [q.v.]. Thereafter she devoted herself to teaching. She was created D.B.E. in 1925. She died in London 3 April 1930.

Albani married in 1878 Ernest Gye, son of Frederick Gye the younger, and had one son. Her husband became lessee of Covent Garden Theatre on his father's death in the same year.

[*The Times*, 4 April 1930; *Grove's Dictionary of Music and Musicians*, 3rd edition, vol. i, edited by H. C. Colles; Herman Klein, *Great Women Singers of My Time*, 1931; Emma Albani, *Forty Years of Song*, 1911; H. Saxe Wyndham and Geoffrey L'Epine, *Who's Who in Music*, 1913; personal knowledge.]

J. M. Levien.

ALDERSON, Sir EDWIN ALFRED HERVEY (1859–1927), lieutenant-general, was born at Capel St. Mary, Suffolk, 8 April 1859, the eldest son of Lieutenant-Colonel Edward Mott Alderson, of Poyle House, Ipswich, by his wife, Catherine Harriett Swainson. At the age of seventeen he joined the Prince of Wales's Own Norfolk Artillery Militia, and two years later (1878) was gazetted to the 97th Foot, now the Queen's Own Royal West Kent Regiment, joining his unit in Halifax, Nova Scotia. After a short term there he went with his regiment to Gibraltar, and thence in 1881 to Natal. Here he was detached for service with the Mounted Infantry at Laing's Nek, and with this arm he was destined to be closely identified for a large part of his military career. In 1882 the Mounted Infantry took part in the Egyptian campaign, being engaged in both actions at Kassassin (26 August and 9 September) and at the capture of Tel-el-Kebir (13 September). For his part in this campaign Alderson received the medal with clasp and the Khedive's star. In the Nile expedition of 1884–1885 he took part with the Mounted (Camel) Regiment in the unsuccessful attempt to relieve General Gordon at Khartoum. For saving a private soldier from drowning in the Nile in 1885 he was awarded the medal of the Royal Humane Society.

In 1887 Alderson was appointed adjutant to the Mounted Infantry at Aldershot, having been promoted to the rank of captain in the previous year; he was given the same office in the Royal West Kent Regiment in 1890, and retained it for four years. He passed out of the Staff College in 1895, and in the following year, with the substantive rank of major, went in command of the Mounted Infantry to South Africa, where he played a prominent part in the quelling of the Matabele revolt (1896). He was then given command of all troops in Mashonaland, and received the brevet of lieutenant-colonel. This active year was followed by a period of duty at Aldershot as deputy assistant adjutant-general and in command of the Mounted Infantry. In 1900 he was made brevet-colonel and appointed inspector-general of Mounted Infantry with the rank of brigadier-general. In the South African War (1899–1902) Alderson commanded the Mounted Infantry in 1901–1902, his force including Canadian, Australian, New Zealand, and other colonial troops. He was three times mentioned in dispatches, subsequently receiving the two medals with seven clasps and the C.B. (1900); he was also appointed successively aide-de-camp to Queen Victoria and to King Edward VII. In 1903 he was promoted to the substantive rank of colonel and for four years commanded the second infantry brigade at Aldershot with the rank of brigadier-general. He was made major-general in 1907. For four years (1908–1912) he commanded the 6th (Poona) division, Southern army, India.

On the outbreak of the European War in 1914, Alderson was appointed (4 August) to command the first mounted division, all troops in the counties of Norfolk and Suffolk, and he was also placed in charge of the defence of that area. In the following October, with the rank of lieutenant-general, he was given the command of the first Canadian division, which embarked for France in February 1915. The division fought at Neuve Chapelle (10–13 March), in the second battle of Ypres (22 April–25 May), at Festubert (15–25 May), and in the second battle of Givenchy (15–16 June). In August the second Canadian division arrived in France, and the two divisions then became the Canadian Army Corps with Alderson in command. A third division was added to the corps in January 1916, and in the following May, when Sir Julian Byng (afterwards Lord Byng of Vimy) took over the command, Alderson became inspector-general, Canadian forces, and held that appointment until the end of hostilities. He was promoted K.C.B. in 1916. In 1921 he was made colonel commandant of the Royal West Kent Regiment.

Retiring from the army in 1920, Alderson devoted himself to the two main recreations of his private life, hunting and yachting. He was a noted horseman and lover of horses, and a great believer in hunting as a school for officers; wherever he was stationed he hunted—at home, in Africa, and in India. He was master of the South Shropshire hunt in 1914, and resumed the mastership in 1920. He was also a member of the Royal Norfolk and Suffolk Yacht Club, owning a considerable number of racing and other craft, and commodore of the Broads Cruising Association. In 1896 he published *With the Mounted Infantry and Mashonaland Field Force*, in 1900 *Pink and Scarlet, or Hunting as a School for Soldiering*, and *Lessons from 100 Notes made in Peace and War*.

Alderson married in 1886 Alice Mary, second daughter of the Rev. Oswald Sergeant, vicar of Chesterton, Oxfordshire. There was one son of the marriage.

Alderson died at Lowestoft 14 December 1927, and on that day the department of national defence at Ottawa paid a notable tribute to the memory of the first commander of the Canadian Corps in France.

[*The Times*, 15 December 1927; Sir J. F. Maurice and M. H. Grant, (Official) *History of the War in South Africa 1899–1902*, 1906–1910; Sir J. E. Edmonds, (Official) *History of the Great War. Military Operations. France and Belgium, 1915*, 1928; *The Queen's Own Gazette* (journal of the Queen's Own Royal West Kent Regiment), January 1928.] C. V. OWEN.

ALDRICH-BLAKE, DAME **LOUISA BRANDRETH** (1865–1925), surgeon, was born 15 August 1865 at Chingford, Essex, the eldest daughter and second child in the family of six of the Rev. Frederick Aldrich, rector of Chingford, by his wife, Louisa Blake Morrison. The surname of Blake was assumed by her father at the time of his marriage. Soon after Louisa's birth her father became rector of Welsh Bicknor, Herefordshire, where her childhood was passed and where she and her brothers and sisters were devoted to open-air sports and to animals. At the age of sixteen (1881) Louisa was sent to a school at Great Malvern, and thence in 1884 to Neuchâtel for two years. From 1886 to 1887 she was a student at St. Hilda's College, Cheltenham, where she proved slow, but very sure, and possessed of a remarkable memory. She was silent, but not unsociable, and distinguished for her skill in boxing and cricket, at that date unusual in a girl.

In 1887 Miss Aldrich-Blake decided to study medicine, and entered the London School of Medicine for Women in Hunter Street, where she became absorbed in her work, and won every available prize. In 1892 she obtained the M.B. of London University with first-class honours, in the following year the B.S. (also with first-class honours) and the gold medal for surgery, and she took her M.D. (London) in 1894 at the age of twenty-nine. A year later (1895) she became master in surgery (the first woman to be so qualified) and decided to specialize in this branch. Thereafter Miss Aldrich-Blake devoted her whole energies to surgery, being successively assistant, senior, and consulting surgeon to the Elizabeth Garrett Anderson Hospital, Euston Road, and to the Royal Free Hospital, Gray's Inn Road. In 1914 she became dean of the London (Royal Free Hospital) School of Medicine for Women, and was largely responsible for the expansion of its work in the following years.

As a surgeon and, indeed, in everything she did, Miss Aldrich-Blake showed not only skill but patient attention to detail, deliberate judgement, and unvarying steadiness; in consequence she had remarkable success in preventing shock after her operations. She was slow to speak, but her very presence inspired security and confidence. She did not seek relaxation or amusement outside her work, but took pleasure in administrative business and even in committee work, the details of which she mastered as thoroughly as those of her profession.

Miss Aldrich-Blake was elected a fellow of the Royal Society of Medicine in 1910, and was created D.B.E. in January 1925. She died at her home in London 28 December of that year.

A portrait of Miss Aldrich-Blake by Sir William Orpen (1923) is at the London School of Medicine for Women.

[Lord Riddell, *Dame Louisa Aldrich-Blake*, 1926.] R. STRACHEY.

ALEXANDRA CAROLINE MARY CHARLOTTE LOUISE JULIA (1844–1925), of Denmark, queen-consort of King Edward VII, was born at the Gule Palace, Copenhagen, 1 December 1844, the eldest daughter and second of the six children of Prince Christian of Schleswig-Holstein-Sonderburg-Glücksburg, by his wife, Louise, daughter of the Landgrave William of Hesse-Cassel. Her parents lived in modest circumstances at Copenhagen, but her mother, as niece to King Christian VIII (1839–1848), was the natural heiress, after her childless cousin King Frederick VII (1848–1863), and subject to the renunciations of her mother and brother, to the throne of Denmark. In the duchies of Schleswig-Holstein, however, the Salic law had not been repealed, and, with the Duke of Sonderburg-Augustenberg ready to reassert his claim, trouble was already brewing over them. At the instigation of the Tsar Nicholas I of Russia, a correspondence was circulated through the courts of Europe, as the result of which a protocol was signed in London in 1852 which set out that, failing male issue to the reigning king, the crown of Denmark, together with the duchies—under a nominal German supervision—should revert to Prince and Princess Christian.

Princess Alexandra was brought up very simply with her brothers and sisters at Copenhagen and at the château of Bernstorff, ten miles from the capital. She was taught foreign languages, including English, and showed a marked aptitude for music. Hans Andersen was a friend of her parents and on intimate terms with the children. She was only thirteen years old when negotiations were set on foot which ultimately issued in her coming to England. In 1858 the question of a bride for Albert Edward, Prince of Wales, was under discussion, and Leopold, King of the Belgians, on whose advice Queen Victoria and Prince Albert largely relied, sent to Windsor a list of seven eligible young princesses with the name of Prince Christian's daughter heavily underlined [see Edward VII]. The project was, however, allowed to simmer until, on 24 September 1861, a meeting between the two young people in the cathedral town of Speier was ingeniously arranged by the crown princess of Prussia, the eldest sister of the Prince of Wales. 'We hear nothing but good of Princess Alexandra; the young people seem to have taken a warm liking to one another', Prince Albert wrote to the crown princess on 4 October. The untimely death of her husband on 14 December only sharpened Queen Victoria's determination to carry out what he had clearly wished. The formal betrothal took place on 9 September 1862 at the palace of Laeken, near Brussels. The princess landed at Gravesend on 7 March 1863, and on 10 March the marriage was solemnized in St. George's chapel, Windsor. Queen Victoria, clad in deepest mourning, witnessed the ceremony from the royal closet above the chancel.

The self-enforced seclusion of the queen quickly gave to her son and daughter-in-law a virtual sovereignty over the social world, and under their kindly sway English society soon assumed a gayer complexion, while the English aristocracy, on which the Prince Consort had looked with scant favour, resumed its former importance in royal circles. The princess was no less desirous than her husband that Marlborough House, their London home, and Sandringham—the Norfolk estate bought in 1861 with the savings from the duchy of Cornwall revenues which had accumulated during the prince's minority—should be open to any one who could claim real and honourable distinction; they both delighted in entertaining and were quite willing, in certain well-recognized circumstances, to be entertained themselves. Their hospitality was large, and at one time a malicious rumour spread that the Prince and Princess of Wales had outrun their income and that the prince was rather heavily in debt. *The Times* was inspired to give an explicit contradiction to a report which was without foundation, but the public was reminded that the prince and princess were carrying out official and social duties which had scarcely been contemplated when their marriage settlement was drawn up.

Meanwhile the Princess of Wales had secured, seemingly without an effort, the affections, not only of those with whom she came in contact, but of the British people at large. Her perfect simplicity played no small part in her perfect correctness. Her presence at any gathering involved no 'stiffness', but she carried to it a peculiar dignity, not easy to define but impossible to deny. Unlike some of her predecessors in the same position, she never allowed herself to be caught in the labyrinth of politics—though she numbered Mr. Gladstone among her closest friends—but certainly no foreign princess ever did half so much to mould the social life of the country of her adoption or strove more eagerly to better and brighten the lot of the poorer classes.

In the first year of her marriage two events occurred to dignify further Alexandra's position. The death in November of King Frederick VII placed the princess's father on the throne of Denmark as Christian IX, and her second brother, William, was chosen by the European powers to be king of the Hellenes, and crowned under the name of George, the patron saint of Greece. The crown proved no easy one to wear; from his accession to his assassination fifty years later, King George's chequered fortunes were a source of constant anxiety to his sister, whose sober advice and substantial help were frequently invoked.

The close of the year 1863 was to be embittered for the princess by the outbreak of the struggle in which three parties were engaged and which issued in the triumph of Prussian might over Danish claims. By signing the new Danish constitution which his predecessor had proclaimed shortly before his death, King Christian had asserted his claim to the duchies of Schleswig-Holstein, which was promptly disputed both by Frederick, Duke of Augustenberg, who repudiated the renunciation made by his father in 1852, and by King William I of Prussia, who induced the Emperor Francis Joseph of Austria to join him in expelling the Danes from the coveted territories, with the understanding that after the struggle they should be the joint possessors. Queen Victoria, though bent on peace, remembered the Prince Consort's desire for a powerful Prussia; her eldest daughter, the crown princess of Prussia, favoured the pretensions of Duke Frederick; while the Princess of Wales, whose anxiety for her country was painful to witness, imposed silence on herself, except when at Windsor she reminded her English relations that the duchies belonged to her father by right and could only be wrested from him by force, a remark which caused the queen to forbid the subject to be mentioned again in her presence.

The reticence of the princess was the more laudable—and cost her no less effort—because she was aware that the Cabinet seriously contemplated armed interference on behalf of Denmark, and that a word spoken by her would have roused the sympathy of many. Her hold over the affections of the English people was further strengthened when on 8 January 1864 she gave birth to a son, Albert Victor, afterwards Duke of Clarence, who stood as successor to the throne in the second generation.

The humiliations which her parents and her country were to suffer at the hands of Prussia were bitterly resented by the princess, but she found much solace in the whole-hearted support of her husband, who shedding for the moment political restraints, openly proclaimed his sympathy with his wife. The war over (August 1864), Alexandra was anxious to go to Denmark to see her parents, but Queen Victoria, who had forbidden her son to visit Copenhagen at the time of his betrothal, again imposed the same veto on him, and it required the intervention of Lord Palmerston—the princess's constant champion—for the queen to withdraw it. The prince and princess left England in September, but the prince had to give his written undertaking that he would say nothing and do nothing which would savour of Danish leanings; and it was further stipulated that the visits to Copenhagen and to Stockholm—to which the tour was to be extended—should be regarded as strictly private. This proviso King Charles XV of Sweden, to Queen Victoria's annoyance, brushed aside when he organized a public reception for the royal travellers and insisted on their being state guests at his palace.

For Bismarck the seizure by Prussia of the duchies of Schleswig-Holstein was but a stepping-stone, and in 1866, after the battle of Sadowa (3 July) had closed the contest between Austria and Prussia, the princess was to see her family further despoiled. By the terms of the Treaty of Prague (23 August), not only did Hesse-Darmstadt, of which her favourite sister-in-law, Princess Alice, was grand duchess, and Hanover pass into Prussian hands, but Hesse-Cassel, where she had found a second home, ceased to be the domain of her uncle and became an incorporated Prussian province. Once more the princess suffered in silence, but through the ensuing decades indignation smouldered in her breast and the very word Prussia would cause her to tighten her lips lest some injudicious expression should escape them. She clung tenaciously to the clause in the Treaty of Prague which gave Denmark the hope of recovering some portion of her lost provinces—viz. the northern district of Schleswig. In vain the people of this area pleaded for a referendum, and for forty years their grievance rankled in Alexandra's mind. Her joy was manifest when she learned that the Treaty of Versailles (1919) provided for an immediate transference of territory to Denmark, while a year later, under the plebiscite for which she had constantly pleaded, Northern Schleswig was handed over to the country of her birth.

'*Le Prussianisme, voilà l'ennemi*', was Gambetta's dictum, and while the Princess of Wales would entirely have endorsed it, she would not allow her subsequent mistrust of Germany or her dislike of Kaiser Wilhelm II to deter her from taking a cheerful part in any occasion which, by improving Anglo-German relations, might promote the peace of Europe. She visited Berlin whenever circumstances demanded it of her, and in later life formed a close friendship with her sister-in-law, the Empress Frederick. At Windsor, Sandringham, and Cowes she would play to perfection the part of hostess, and offer to her imperial nephew a welcome with which he could find no fault.

On 3 June 1865 Alexandra gave birth to her second son who, forty-five years later, was to succeed his father on the throne of England as King George V. Four other children were born to the Prince and Princess of Wales: Louise (20 February 1867) afterwards Duchess of Fife and princess royal; Victoria (6 July 1868); Maud (26 November 1869) afterwards Queen of Norway; and John (born 6, died 7, April 1871). In 1867, immediately after the birth of Princess Louise, Alexandra was severely attacked by an acute form of rheumatism which lodged in the knee-joint, causing her intense pain and for some time baffling the skill of her doctors. So long as there existed any public anxiety Marlborough House was besieged by anxious inquirers. Recovery was slow, and the illness, of which the patient herself was disposed to make light, left a permanent, though almost imperceptible, mark. The princess was a bold and skilful horsewoman, and for more than a quarter of a century afterwards was still a forward figure in the hunting field, but she had to ride on the 'reverse' side.

Mr. Disraeli, on assuming office in February 1868, pressed the queen to allow the Prince and Princess of Wales to be the guests of the newly appointed viceroy of Ireland, the Marquess of Abercorn, who was about to be advanced to a dukedom. The queen showed some hesitation, partly because the prince and princess had been indirectly approached on the subject before her own wishes had been consulted, and partly because she feared lest the presence of the heir to the throne across the Irish channel might be used for political purposes. There was also the element of risk to be considered, since Fenianism was rife, nor was the queen sure whether her daughter-in-law had sufficiently recovered from her illness to undergo the fatigue of the visit. But the princess discounted both the fatigue and the risk in her desire to see Ireland and to let the Irish see her. Accordingly, on 15 April the prince and princess landed at Kingstown and carried out, with evident enjoyment, a nine-days' programme, which included the installation of the prince as a knight of St. Patrick, the unveiling of Edmund Burke's statue in College Green, a review in Phoenix Park, and races at Punchestown; the princess struck a happy note by insisting that her husband should wear a green tie whenever possible, and by herself appearing on every appropriate occasion in Irish poplin with a mantilla of Irish lace. The whole visit, unpunctuated by any manifestation of ill will, proved such a success that before leaving Dublin a message was sent to the queen urging her to come over to Ireland and 'satisfy yourself on the force of affectionate feeling'. The princess was to cross again to Ireland in 1885, and to pay three visits there as queen consort; on each occasion she received the same enthusiastic welcome, which was no less emphatic because of a rumour that she had not been altogether averse from Mr. Gladstone's more moderate schemes of Home Rule.

At Balmoral in the autumn of 1868 the prince and princess informed the queen of their wish to spend the winter abroad and travel to the Near East. The princess had not altogether shaken off the effects of her illness, and change of scene and climate was strongly recommended; they were both anxious to see the Suez Canal, then approaching completion, and thought that it would be polite, and politic, to return the recent visit to London of the Sultan of Turkey. The princess, too, had been annoyed by foolish stories about the high play in which the prince was, quite erroneously, supposed to have indulged, and by ill-founded rumours as to the 'fastness' of some of those who composed the, so-called, Marlborough House set; for these and other reasons both Edward and Alexandra were anxious to leave England for a time, and they cheerfully accepted the terms with which the queen qualified her consent. They set out in November and were absent from England until the following May [see Edward VII]. The tour of Egypt (February–March 1869)—the only occasion on which the princess quitted Europe—was extended to Wadi Halfa, and as, in the meanwhile, threatened hostilities between Turkey and Greece had been averted, Queen Victoria, rather grudgingly, permitted the travellers on their way back in April to accept a very cordial invitation from the sultan and to pay a visit—the first of many—to the newly married king and queen of the Hellenes.

The princess was on a visit to Denmark when, in July 1870, war between France and Germany was declared. Queen Victoria, knowing that France looked to Denmark as a possible ally, and deprecating as usual her daughter-in-law's 'Danish partisanship', insisted on Alexandra returning to England at once. The misfortunes of France provoked the liveliest sympathy in the Princess of Wales, the more so, perhaps, because, with the victories of the German army, the letters of the crown princess of Prussia to her mother assumed an increasingly provocative tone. As often happened, the princess's outlook differed sharply from that of the queen whose expressed view that 'a powerful Germany can never be dangerous to England' she found it difficult to comprehend; the proclamation of the King of Prussia as German Emperor filled her with forebodings.

Except where the country of her birth, or Greece, were concerned, the Princess of Wales made no intrusion into foreign politics, although in 1877, when Russia declared war on Turkey, the report ran that the royal family was as sharply divided in its sympathies as the Cabinet. The queen, leaning wholly on Lord Beaconsfield, and the Prince of Wales, irritated by the trend of events in Russia, were admittedly Turcophil, while the princess was said to take her cue from Lord Salisbury and Lord Derby and to affirm Russia's right to save Christian states from the clutches of the infidel. While the suggestion of any attempt to exercise political influence was wholly unfounded, the princess certainly regarded herself as bound to Russia by family ties; her visits to Russia were frequent and often protracted, and with characteristic disregard of danger, she insisted in March 1881 on travelling to St. Petersburg to be beside her sister, the Empress Marie, after the assassination of the Emperor Alexander II, although at that moment even the police force was known to have Nihilist conspirators in its ranks. Throughout the Empress Marie's troubled life Alexandra was wholeheartedly in sympathy with her, and after the revolution of 1917 her Russian relations became her constant care and proved to be no small strain on her resources.

In 1889 the princess's eldest daughter, Louise, was married to Alexander, Earl of Fife, whom the queen promptly advanced to a dukedom. Five years elapsed before her surviving son, George, was united to Princess Victoria Mary of Teck, the daughter of Francis, Duke of Teck and her favourite cousin, Princess Mary Adelaide, of Cambridge. Meanwhile she had suffered a blow from which she never wholly recovered. On 14 January 1892 her elder son, who had been created Duke of Clarence two years previously and was betrothed to the princess who was yet to become her daughter-in-law, died at Sandringham of an especially vicious form of influenza then prevalent. While the second daughter, Princess Victoria, remained her mother's constant companion, the youngest, Princess Maud, was in 1896 married to her cousin, Prince Charles, the second son of the crown prince of Denmark, an alliance which later proved to have some political significance. When, in 1905, the kingdoms of Norway and Sweden were separated, the Norwegian vote for a new king was accorded by general count to Prince Charles of Denmark, who, largely under Queen Alexandra's advice, declined to leave Copenhagen until summoned to Christiania in virtue of a referendum.

On 19 January 1901 the Princess of Wales, with other members of the royal family, was hurriedly summoned to Osborne, and, three days later, she was close to Queen Victoria's bedside when she died. Through forty years comment had not been infrequent as to the points of contact between a sovereign whose authority brooked neither criticism nor contradiction and a princess whose gentleness of manner concealed much strength of character. The contrast between them, both in outlook and method, was acute. Their divergence of views suffered little change in the passage of time, but in both of them loyalty of purpose was so deeply ingrained that mutual trust and wholehearted affection for one another grew stronger every year; the death of Queen Victoria was felt by the princess, on her own admission, as the loss of a second mother.

The accession to the position of queen consort could not do much to enhance the status of a princess whose popularity with society—in the widest sense of the word—had been supreme for forty years. But King Edward VII was determined to give his queen the most exalted rank it was in his power to bestow, and one of his first acts was tc convene a special chapter of the Order of the Garter and to revive in favour of Queen Alexandra a custom instituted by Richard II but which had fallen into disuse since Henry VII 'Gartered' his mother. Both before and after her accession, Queen Alexandra's energies and a substantial slice of her income were spent in the relief of suffering and poverty. Her charities were perhaps dictated by her heart rather than by her head, and so far as she herself was concerned were wholly unostentatious, but her example unquestionably gave a great stimulus to beneficent work on the part of wealthy and influential people and went some way to solve certain social problems. The dinners which she gave to celebrate Queen Victoria's diamond jubilee in 1897, when 400,000 poor people were her guests; the hospital ship which she equipped for the sick and wounded soldiers in the South African War; the tea given at her coronation to 10,000 maids-of-all-work; the fund—amounting to over a quarter of a million sterling—raised, on her initiative, in 1906 in aid of unemployed workmen; the institution of the Queen Alexandra Imperial Military Nursing Service in 1902; the introduction of the Finsen lamp into the London Hospital in 1899—all these go to testify no less to her fertility in suggestion than to her insistence on the execution of her sometimes rather daring plans.

The death of King Edward occurred 6 May 1910; Queen Alexandra was in Italy and no news calculated to give her special anxiety had reached her, but she had a sudden premonition that the king's hours were numbered, and travelling rapidly from Venice, reached his bedside some thirty hours before he died. After his death the queen withdrew into comparative retirement. There remained plenty to occupy her, and her interest in the London Hospital and in many schemes to alleviate suffering only seemed to grow with her declining years; but she preferred now to help rather than to head any movement. In 1913, in order to mark what she described as 'the fiftieth anniversary of my coming to this beloved country', 'Alexandra Day' (in June) was instituted, with roses for its outward and visible sign; and ever since on every 'rose day' myriads of flowers have been sold, and British hospitals have benefited thereby to the extent of hundreds of thousands of pounds.

The European War fired again Queen Alexandra's desire to help, and now especially to help the wounded; her time and her purse were constantly available for any calls made upon them. Her influence was incessantly invoked for this or that concession, but she declined to interfere at any point except to put in a plea for the mothers who had been doubly bereaved; and to her pleading was largely due a ruling that when two sons in a family had been killed, the others should, if possible, be kept behind the firing-line. Her friendship with Lord Kitchener was of long standing, and she greatly appreciated, and never divulged to any one, the daily bulletin of war news which he caused to be sent to her. Careless of danger for herself, her sense of danger for others was acute, and on learning of the proposed mission of the secretary of state for war to Russia in 1916, she was persuaded that disaster would attend it and begged, but of course in vain, that it might be cancelled. When, after the tragedy of the *Hampshire*, a memorial to Lord Kitchener was inaugurated, the queen mother at once placed herself at the head of the appeal, which quickly produced a sum never before approached by any memorial fund.

The last two years of Queen Alexandra's life were spent quietly at Sandringham, the home which she loved and which King Edward had bequeathed to her. There, without struggle or suffering, she died 20 November 1925. Prior to the burial at Windsor, the queen lay in state for twelve hours in Westminster Abbey, and a long line of 50,000 men, women, and children filed past the bier, headed by a band of 'Queen Alexandra' nurses.

The key to Queen Alexandra's life was her essential goodness, which showed itself not merely in her family relations and private life, but in the use which she made of her public position, alike as princess and as queen consort. All who gave their services to the sick or the sorrowful, who tried to help children, who cared for birds or animals, could rely on her practical sympathy and eager—sometimes perhaps too eager—readiness to help. Simplicity, charm of manner, and a keen sense of humour combined with her attractive character to make Queen Alexandra one of the best loved of British royal personages. Alone of all the royal consorts who have come to Great Britain from abroad she was never regarded as a foreigner.

Queen Alexandra's beauty often provoked the despair of the painter, the sculptor, and the photographer; the deep blue eyes, the swift play of expression, the smile, irresistible because it was absolutely genuine, seemed incapable of reproduction on canvas or in clay. 'Alix looked lovely in grey and white and more like a bride just married than a silver one of twenty-five years' is an entry in Queen Victoria's diary for 10 March 1888, and certainly for a quarter of a century successive years had only seemed to enhance her daughter-in-law's physical attractions. Perhaps the happiest picture of her is by Richard Lauchert, who painted the Princess of Wales at the age of eighteen; Luke Fildes executed the state portrait (1901) and another, painted some eight years earlier; while other, more or less successful, portraits were painted by F. Winterhalter, Sir W. B. Richmond, H. von Angeli, Benjamin Constant, and Edward Hughes. A drawing appeared in *Vanity Fair* 7 June 1911.

[*The Letters of Queen Victoria*, first series edited by A. C. Benson, 3 vols., 1908, second and third series edited by G. E. Buckle, 6 vols., 1926–1928 and 1930–1932; Sir Sidney Lee, *King Edward VII, a biography*, 2 vols., 1925; Sir George Arthur, *Queen Alexandra*, 1934; private information.] G. Arthur.

ALLBUTT, Sir THOMAS CLIFFORD (1836–1925), physician, born at Dewsbury 20 July 1836, was the only son of the Rev. Thomas Allbutt, vicar of Dewsbury, by his wife, Marianne, daughter of Robert Wooler, of Dewsbury. Allbutt was sent to St. Peter's School, York, whence he entered Gonville and Caius College, Cambridge, in 1855, gaining a classical scholarship there a year later. In 1860 he obtained a first class (the only one of the year) in the natural sciences tripos with distinction in chemistry and geology. After studying medicine at St. George's Hospital, London, and taking the degree of M.B. (1861), he went to Paris and attended the clinics of Armand Trousseau, G. B. A. Duchenne, A. P. E. Bazin, and A. Hardy.

Allbutt's active professional life falls into three periods: from 1861 to 1889 he was a consulting physician in Leeds, from 1889 to 1892 a commissioner in lunacy in London, and for the remainder of his life regius professor of physic at Cambridge. Confining himself to consulting practice at Leeds, he utilized the early lean years in wide reading, writing medical essays, and clinical work at the fever hospital, the general infirmary, where he was physician from 1864 to 1884, and the West Riding asylum. During 1865 and 1866 he treated a typhus fever outbreak by open-air methods, a plan which he later advocated for consumption. His invention in 1866 of the present short clinical thermometer facilitated the routine taking of temperatures. His monograph on the use of the ophthalmoscope in nervous and other diseases appeared in 1871, and his pioneer papers on syphilitic disease of the cerebral arteries (1868), the effect of strain on the heart (1870, 1873), and anxiety as a cause of kidney disease (1876) belong to this period. In 1880 he was elected a fellow of the Royal Society; at this time, also, he initiated the practice of consultation between the medical witnesses before the hearing of legal cases. He delivered the Goulstonian lectures on *Visceral Neuroses* at the Royal College of Physicians in 1884, and in 1885 introduced the surgical treatment of tuberculous glands in the neck [see also Teale, T. P.]. In an address at Glasgow in 1888 he began pleading for the study of comparative medicine, and had the gratification of seeing a professorship of comparative medicine established at Cambridge in 1923.

The fatigue of consulting practice necessitated Allbutt's acceptance of a commissionership in lunacy in 1889. In 1892, however, he was appointed regius professor of physic at Cambridge, but, being the first regius professor not a previous resident in Cambridge, did not obtain a footing in Addenbrooke's Hospital until 1900.

Probably Allbutt's greatest service to contemporary medicine was his *System of Medicine* in eight volumes (1896–1899) which went into a second edition in eleven volumes (1905–1911). Two outstanding contributions to medicine were his descriptions of hyperpiesia or high blood pressure apart from kidney disease (1895), and of the aortic origin of angina pectoris (1894). He gave numerous addresses; in his eightieth year he published *Diseases of the Arteries and Angina Pectoris* (1915) and six years later (1921) *Greco-Roman Medicine and other historical essays*. His scholarly care in the use of words was shown in his *Notes on the Composition of Scientific Papers* (1904; third edition 1923).

Allbutt married in 1869 Susan, daughter

of Thomas England, merchant, of Headingley, Leeds. They had no children. He was created K.C.B. in 1907. His portrait by Sir William Orpen was presented by the medical profession to him when president of the British Medical Association in 1920, and is now in the Fitzwilliam Museum at Cambridge. The same year he was admitted a member of the Privy Council. There is good evidence that George Eliot drew the character of Lydgate in *Middlemarch* (1872) in part at least from Allbutt. He died suddenly 22 February 1925 at his house in Cambridge.

[*British Medical Journal*, 1925, vol. i, pp. 428–433; personal knowledge.]

H. D. Rolleston.

AMEER ALI, SYED (1849–1928), Indian jurist and Islamic leader, was born 6 April 1849 at Cuttack, in Orissa, the fourth son of Syed Saadat Ali, by his wife, the daughter of Shamsuddin Khan, landowner, of Sambalpur. He traced his descent from the Prophet Mohammed through the eighth Imam, Ali Raza; and the family, which belonged to the Shia sect and had come to India with Nadir Shah in 1739, was settled at Mohan in the Unas district of Oudh. Ameer Ali's parents were poor, his father being a man of roving disposition and studious tastes. Nevertheless, he was educated at the Hooghly College, Chinsurah, and by the aid of scholarships was able to graduate in arts and law at the university of Calcutta, being the first Moslem to take the M.A. degree. He then came for three years to England, at the end of which he was called to the bar by the Inner Temple in 1873 and returned to practise the law in Calcutta. He was lecturer on Mohammedan law at the Presidency College for several years and held the Tagore law professorship at the university of Calcutta in 1884 and 1885. The Moslems of India were, at this period, a backward community. In spite of the teachings of Sir Syed Ahmad they had not accommodated themselves to the changes whereby, a generation earlier, their traditional culture had ceased to be the passport to office. Combining, as he did, that culture with a Western education, Ameer Ali's position as a political leader was marked out for him almost immediately. Thus in 1877 he founded the first Moslem political organization in India; in 1878 he became a member of the Bengal legislative council, and in 1883 one of the three Indian additional (i.e. legislative) members of the governor-general's council. The outstanding event of his term of office as a legislator was the introduction of a Bill by Sir Courtenay Peregrine Ilbert [q.v.] giving Indian magistrates in the *mufassal* power to try charges against Europeans. Passions ran high: but on a personal appeal from the viceroy, the Marquess of Ripon, Ameer Ali succeeded in negotiating a compromise, and the storm died down. He was much abused by critics of the type to whom all compromise is distasteful; nevertheless, in avoiding a continuance of acrimony, his statesmanship was probably correct. The Koran itself declares that the friendly settlement of disputes is of great merit, a text which found a ready chord in Ameer Ali's nature.

Meanwhile, Ameer Ali had been prospering in his profession: after acting as Presidency magistrate, he had been appointed in 1879 chief Presidency magistrate, a very unusual appointment for an Indian at that period; in 1890 he was created a judge of the high court of Calcutta, and held office for over fourteen years. Throughout his judgeship he made a practice of spending his vacations in England, and on retirement in 1904 he made it his permanent home. In 1909 Lord Morley determined to appoint an Indian judge to the Privy Council: and Ameer Ali, already domiciled in England, was the obvious man for this unsalaried and onerous post. He threw himself with zest into the work of the Judicial Committee and was unfailing in his attendance at the hearing of Indian appeals almost till his death, which occurred at Pollingfold Manor, his house in Sussex, 3 August 1928.

As a judge, Ameer Ali's real merits were obscured by a conversational manner in court and a tendency to prolixity in judgment—superficial failings which grew on him with advancing years. Nevertheless, few, if any, judges in Indian legal history have given more judgments of far-reaching importance: for instance, *Imambandi* v. *Mutsaddi* in Mohammedan law, *Ramachandra* v. *Vinayak*, *Buddha Singh* v. *Laltu Singh*, and *Girjabai* v. *Sadashiv* in Hindu law. He was the author of a treatise on *Mohammedan Law* (2 vols., 1880 and 1884) which has passed through several editions, and he collaborated in many other legal works.

Ameer Ali's international position as a protagonist of Islam came, however, to be of even greater importance than his work as a judge. Moslems all over the world, distressed by the apparent contradiction between Islam and modern civilization, could draw comfort from the example of one who, while a devout and in some ways very conservative upholder of his faith, was yet open to the best of modern thought. He wrote extensively not only on law but on Moslem history and institutions; and if his conviction that the reforms which he favoured (e.g. the legal prohibition of polygamy) had always been the genuine orthodoxy provoked an occasional smile, it is well to remember that other reformers also have found it necessary to deck reform in the garments of the past. As a pamphleteer, a speaker, and an organizer, Ameer Ali was continually before the public in defence of his co-religionists: for instance, in presenting to a public prejudiced by reports of Turkish atrocities, the other side of the case; in the same connexion he took the lead in founding on the occasion of the Italo-Turkish War in Tripoli (1911–1912) the British Red Crescent as a Moslem counterpart to the Red Cross. For modern developments of nationalism, whether in Turkey or India, he had little sympathy: Islam and the British Empire, both transcending merely racial or geographical barriers, were the objects of his loyalty; and that he saw no contradiction between these loyalties was an object-lesson of value to other Moslems during the War of 1914–1919. Though a Shia by origin, he believed in the necessity of the Caliphate as a symbol of Islamic unity: and in 1923 he collaborated with the Aga Khan, also a Shia, in an open letter to the Turkish national assembly protesting against its suppression. Indian nationalism he regarded as a mere cloak for Hindu domination; and, from the time of the first proposals of Lord Morley to the day of his death, he was a strong advocate of community representation and the separate treatment of Indian Moslems.

Ameer Ali was for some years chairman of the Woking mosque committee, and was active in furthering the project, not yet brought to fruition, of establishing in central London a mosque which should be worthy of the capital city of the greatest Islamic power. From the first he felt at home in England, where his simplicity of character attracted an ever widening circle of friends. He was proud of having as a young man attracted the notice of John Bright, who proposed him for the Reform Club, of which he remained a member for nearly half a century. He received curiously little in the way of official recognition, although it is understood that at the close of his life he refused a knighthood.

Ameer Ali married in 1884, at the Unitarian church in Little Portland Street, London, Isabelle Ida, daughter of Heyman Konstam, of London. He was survived by his wife and two sons, the elder of whom was a member of the Indian civil service and the younger became a judge of the Calcutta High Court.

A portrait of Ameer Ali by Oswald Birley is in the Privy Council Office, Downing Street, London.

[*The Times*, 4 August 1928; *Calcutta Weekly Notes*, 13 August 1928; Ameer Ali's own memoirs in *Islamic Culture*, vols. iv and v, 1931 and 1932; personal knowledge.]

S. V. FitzGerald.

ANDERSON, Sir HUGH KERR (1865–1928), physiologist and administrator, was born at Frognal Park, Hampstead, 6 July 1865. His great-grandfather, Alexander Anderson, was a surgeon in the royal navy, his grandfather, John Ford Anderson, a doctor at Peterhead, who died young, leaving a family with their way to make in the world. So it was that the second son, James Anderson, Hugh Anderson's father, set out in 1828 for London, where he joined and ultimately became senior partner of a shipping firm which was later incorporated in the Orient Steam Navigation Company. James Anderson married Eliza, daughter of Surgeon-General John Murray, and Hugh was the third son of their family of four sons and seven daughters.

After four years (1880–1884) at Harrow, Anderson went in 1884 to Gonville and Caius College, Cambridge, with the Sayer scholarship in classics, but then turned to the study of natural science for which he had an inherent aptitude. He became a scholar of his college in 1886, and gained a first class in both parts of the natural sciences tripos. On taking his degree (1887) he might have entered his father's business, but he preferred to devote himself to science, and proceeded to St. Bartholomew's Hospital in 1889 in order to complete his medical qualification.

After taking the degree of M.B. in 1891, Anderson returned to Cambridge, and then began the period of his active scientific work. He was appointed university lecturer in physiology, and elected a fellow of Gonville and Caius College in 1897. In collaboration with Professor John Newport Langley [q.v.] he was the author of some fifteen papers of major importance, and by himself of about six more. The joint papers dealt with the opening of the pupil of the eye under sympathetic stimulation, with a new and unexpected type of neural reaction, with the nerve supply of the lower viscera, with peripheral nerve-degeneration, and with other nerve-fibre problems. While both authors were patient and accurate observers, their critical outlook was fortunately different. Langley was zealous that each fact and each conclusion drawn from it should be rigidly established, while Anderson brought to the partnership a philosophic outlook and considered each new fact in its relation to general biological principles. Though the technique of the authors may now be superseded, it yielded in their hands a succession of results which form an established part of neurology. The principal paper of which Anderson was sole author dealt with the development in their later phases of nerve-cells and their fibres, and he showed that trophic nutrition and functional reaction were separable and largely independent. He meant to return to this problem, but other work began to press upon him and, although he continued to follow and to encourage biological research, from about the year 1907, when he became a fellow of the Royal Society, he ceased to be an active contributor to scientific literature.

The reason for this diversion from active research was that his college and university had discovered Anderson's business ability, and he had become more and more immersed in administration. He became a member of the Medical Board of the university and of the Press Syndicate in 1907, of the Financial Board in 1908, and of the council of the Senate in 1910, and so continued until his death, becoming chairman of the Press in 1918.

In addition to his scientific and administrative work Anderson was engaged in teaching and lecturing in a way that was very stimulating to the better students, until he was elected master of Gonville and Caius College in 1912. During the European War he resumed lecturing in medicine, while doing much in his college for the comfort of the successive schools of staff officers who then filled its buildings.

In 1919 Anderson was appointed a member of the royal commission on the universities of Oxford and Cambridge. That body reported in 1922, and when in 1923 two commissions, one for Oxford and one for Cambridge, were appointed to give statutory effect to the recommendations of the earlier body, Anderson was called upon to continue his labours as a commissioner for Cambridge. His knowledge of university administration and the unremitting care which he gave to details made him a valued member of the commissions, and the messages which were received from Oxford at the time of his death showed that his services were appreciated there as they were in Cambridge.

Anderson became a governor of Harrow School in 1922 and he was an original member of the committee of selection for the Commonwealth Fund fellowships (1925). Of his other activities one requires special mention. When, in 1927 and 1928, the munificent offer of the International Education Board of the Rockefeller Foundation to Cambridge University for buildings and endowment for the biological sciences and for a new university library was being negotiated, the university gave Anderson full powers. He was in constant touch with all the interests concerned, but he acted as a plenipotentiary. The 'Anderson Room' in the new Library commemorates this work.

Anderson married in 1894 Jessie, daughter of Surgeon-General Francis William Innes, and had one son and one daughter. In 1922 he was knighted.

Anderson died in London 2 November 1928 at the summit of his powers. No one who knew him as an undergraduate could have foreseen the influence he would come to wield. As he was of a sensitive nature and often distrustful of his own powers, he avoided the public platform and anything of the nature of self-seeking was entirely absent from him. His work lay in the laboratory, in his study, and in the committee room; his influence came from the width of his outlook, from his capacity for amassing and assembling detailed information, and not least from his great gift of sympathy. In addition to his scientific qualities he had a strong artistic sense and a love of music and of all that was beautiful. There is a mural monument to him designed and executed by Harold C. W. Soper in the college chapel and a portrait (1922) by Sir William Orpen in the Master's Lodge.

[*The Caian*, special obituary number, vol. xxxvii, No. 3 (privately printed); *Proceedings* of the Royal Society, B, vol. civ, 1928–1929; personal knowledge.] J. F. Cameron.

ANDERSON, Sir WARREN HASTINGS (1872–1930), lieutenant-general, born at Aldershot 9 January 1872, was the elder son of General David Anderson, by his wife, Charlotte Christina, daughter of David Anderson, of St. Germains, Haddingtonshire. His father was governor of the Royal Military College, Sandhurst, and, during the absence of General Sir Archibald Alison, commanded for a time at Aldershot. Hastings Anderson was educated at Marlborough, and ended his career there at the head of the modern school. From school he went straight to Sandhurst, and was gazetted to his father's regiment, the Cheshire, in 1890. Both he and his father became colonels of the regiment, the son attaining that honour in 1928. Anderson served with the second battalion as adjutant throughout the South African War, except for a short period in 1900 when he filled the office of deputy assistant-adjutant-general under the military governor of Johannesburg. He passed out of the Staff College in 1905, and spent four years from January 1906 at the War Office in the mobilization and training and staff duties directorates. Thereafter he was specially employed until April 1911, when he was appointed to the general staff of the Southern command at Salisbury.

In February 1914 Anderson joined the instructional staff of the Staff College with the temporary rank of lieutenant-colonel. In the following August, on the outbreak of the European War, he went with a number of the students to France in order to make arrangements for the arrival and railway transport of the British Expeditionary Force. Returning to England, he finally went to the Western front in the following November as chief staff officer with the 8th division formed of regular troops from abroad under General (Sir) Francis Davies, and was on active service throughout the War. With the 8th division he was present at the battles of Neuve Chapelle (10–13 March 1915) and Loos (25 September–8 October 1915), and was promoted shortly after the latter battle to be brigadier-general in the XI Corps commanded by Sir Richard Haking. He remained with the XI Corps until September 1916, when he moved to Lord Horne's XV Corps, which was still engaged in the later stages of the battle of the Somme. A week after Anderson's arrival Lord Horne left the Corps in order to take up the command of the Third Army. After only five months with the XV Corps, Anderson was transferred to the First Army as major-general, general staff, in which appointment it fell to him to make the final preparations for the Vimy offensive in April 1917, and to take general staff control of the operations on the First Army front. These were designed to deceive the enemy into the belief that a great effort was being made to capture Lens. A skilful combination of feint attacks and real ones with but small effectives kept the First Army, and the enemy, busy over a long period, and to Anderson's clever planning must be attributed much of the measure of success attained.

During the great German offensive in the spring of 1918 the First Army front was held by tired divisions from the Third and Fifth Armies and some Portuguese troops. Head-quarters at Ranchicourt passed through a most anxious time, but the front maintained a stubborn defence although the Portuguese were forced to yield ground. Some shells actually fell on Ranchicourt at this time, but the head-quarters did not move back. After the turn of the tide, when the initiative was taken up by the Allies, the advance of the First Army was steady and continuous. The Drocourt-Quéant line was forced on 2 September; then followed the forcing of the Canal du Nord (27 September), the advance on Cambrai (8 October), the battle of the Selle (17 October), the capture of Valenciennes (1–3 November), the final advance and the capture of Mons on the morning of the day on which the armistice was signed (11 November). Anderson was awarded the C.B. in 1918.

It was natural that a soldier of such extensive war experience should be chosen as commandant of the Staff College on its re-opening in March 1919. Anderson held this important post for three years, and in 1922 was created K.C.B. In that year he was appointed chief general staff officer to General Sir Charles Harington, general officer commanding-in-chief the Allied army of the Black Sea; Anderson's great experience was of the highest value to the commander-in-chief in the difficult situation in Asia Minor arising from the rivalry between the Greeks and the Turks while the Allies were in occupation. The British forces held the neutral point at Chanak where, but for patience, tact, and diplomatic skill in the direction of affairs, a major conflagration might easily have broken out. In the following year (1923) he went to India as deputy quartermaster-general at army head-quarters, and in 1924 was transferred to the command of the Baluchistan district, Quetta.

Anderson returned to England in 1927 and was appointed to the high office of quartermaster-general of the forces, with the rank of lieutenant-general, and a seat on the Army Council. He thus became involved in effecting many changes in the army and in important questions such as its mechanization and the employment of aeroplanes as troop carriers. Here again his wide knowledge gave added value to the War Office deliberations, and his ultimate nomination, a few weeks before his death, to the command at Aldershot, where his father had commanded before him, was looked upon as merely another step to the still more important appointment of chief of the Imperial General Staff.

Hastings Anderson was a born soldier, reared amongst soldiers, yet he had none of the insular outlook which sometimes accompanies the innate loyalty of the British officer. He had high ideals and a definite conception of the dignity of a British general and the duties required of that dignity, yet he never lost the grace which led him always to observe a gentle and chivalrous attitude towards others. He was very fair minded, and although he held strong opinions and expressed them with force and complete clarity, no one could be more whole-hearted and loyal in carrying out decisions of a higher authority which were contrary to his views. He possessed a charming gift of illustrating, but not exaggerating, his views with a leaven of wit, and enlivened many a grave situation with a timely story. He was extremely proud of his own regiment, and the studies of his earlier years gave him an armoury of knowledge of military history in general and of British regimental history and customs in particular which was second to none. He was the author of an *Outline of the Development of the British Army* (1930, 3rd ed. 1931) and was a vice-president of the Society for Army Historical Research.

Anderson married in 1910 Eileen Hamilton, only daughter of Hamilton Osborne, of London; there were no children of the marriage. He died in London 10 December 1930.

[*The Times*, 12 December 1930; Sir J. E. Edmonds, (Official) *History of the Great War. Military Operations. France and Belgium, 1915*, 1928; *The Oak Tree* (journal of the second (Cheshire) regiment), January 1931; private information.] C. V. Owen.

ARCHER, WILLIAM (1856–1924), critic and journalist, was born at Perth 23 September 1856, the eldest son of Thomas Archer, formerly of Gracemere, Queensland, by his wife, Grace Lindsay, daughter of James Morison, of Muirton, Perth. Thomas Archer and his wife led a wandering life, but when in Scotland regularly attended the meetings of two small separatist religious sects, the Walkerites and the Glassites. Members of the Archer family were to be found in Norway and in Australia. To these family connexions may be traced William Archer's later love of Norwegian literature and of travel, the strength of his moral principles, his anticlericalism, and, through mental reaction, his vehement rationalism. He was educated at Perth Academy, George Watson's College, Edinburgh, and Edinburgh University. He was trained as a lawyer and called to the bar by the Middle Temple in 1883, but never practised. In 1875 Archer sent an article to the *Edinburgh Evening News* and, while still at college, became a leader-writer for that paper at a salary of £80 a year. After leaving the university he made a tour of the world in visiting his parents in Australia (1876–1877)—he had already travelled in Scandinavia—and after another short spell on the staff of the *Edinburgh Evening News*, he settled in London in 1878.

Archer began his career in London as dramatic critic on the *London Figaro* (1879–1881): he also contributed articles to the rationalist press under a pseudonym. Despite the protests of some of his friends, he devoted himself mainly to a study of the theatre, and subsequently became a critic for the *World*, the *Nation*, the *Tribune*, the *Morning Leader*, and the *Manchester Guardian*.

When Archer first began this work in London, the English stage, occupied for the most part with mechanical French farce and puerile melodrama, was passing through a poor period. But by the 'nineties, when Archer's reputation and influence as a critic had become established, especially through his *Study and Stage* articles in the *World* (reprinted as *The Theatrical World*, 5 volumes, 1893–1897), a definite change was taking place: mingled with plays like *Trilby* and *Diplomacy* the dramas of Pinero, Wilde, Barrie, and Ibsen were beginning to be played and a higher standard of theatrical performances created. This change was largely due to Archer. Although he was not the first translator of Ibsen, his translation of *The Pillars of Society* was the first of Ibsen's plays to be produced in London (at the Gaiety Theatre in 1880); and although his translations were open to certain criticisms they became the most popular, and materially helped the growth of the appreciation of Ibsen by the English public. Archer also edited the prose dramas of Ibsen

(5 volumes, 1890–1891) and the collected works of Ibsen (11 volumes, 1906–1907).

Archer wrote several books about the theatre, the best of which are *Masks or Faces?* (1888) and *Play-making* (1912). He also published *Poets of the Younger Generation* (1901) besides much miscellaneous journalistic work. In 1908 he paid a visit to the United States in order to study the race problem; in 1910 he went to Spain to investigate the case of Francisco Ferrer, who had been executed for what Archer considered unjust and obscurantist reasons; and in 1912 he travelled through India and the East. As results of these visits he published *Through Afro-America* (1910), *The Life, Trial, and Death of Francisco Ferrer* (1911), and *India and the Future* (1917). He also edited the works of Congreve (1912) and a selection of the plays of Farquhar (1906).

On the outbreak of war in 1914 Archer devoted himself energetically to propaganda work for the British government. Long before the War he had joined the Inns of Court Volunteers—and in this corps his only son now received a commission. In 1918 his son was killed, and the shock induced him to make some experiments with spiritualism—not, indeed, for the first time. But his enthusiastic rationalism did not desert him, and for the last seven years of his life he used his pen powerfully, if a little crudely, in regular religious controversy. Archer's last book on the drama, *The Old Drama and the New*, was published in 1923; and in the same year his one successful play, *The Green Goddess*, into which he put his great knowledge of stagecraft and the plot of which he obtained in a dream, was produced at the St. James's Theatre, London: it had been performed in New York two years previously. His other plays are *War is War* (1919), *Martha Washington, Beatriz Juana*, and *Lidia* (all published posthumously, 1927): the last two are in blank verse. He died in London 27 December 1924 after an unsuccessful operation.

Archer is described as 'physically a tall upstanding well-built Scot' [G. B. Shaw, introduction to Archer's *Three Plays*, 1927]. He was a man of wide culture and varied interests, who spoke many languages, and had travelled widely. He was lamented in Norway as her 'unselfish and self-sacrificing friend'. He worked for the abolition of the theatrical censorship, for the formation of a national theatre [see *A National Theatre Scheme and Estimates* by William Archer and H. Granville Barker, 1907], and for a time he was actively connected with the League of Nations Union. As a critic he may have been somewhat harsh in his principles, too rigid in his logic, and lacking in the elasticity of mind of his contemporary, Arthur Bingham Walkley [q.v.]; but his emphasis on good dramatic structure and his hatred of slovenliness in any form were a necessary and vital help to all young dramatists. It is perhaps significant that when Bernard Shaw, a close friend of his, read him his first play, Archer went to sleep. That he was a man of deep and genuine humour is proved both by the testimony of his friends and by a study of his writings. His incorruptible honesty made a real impression on the English stage, and his translations and teaching contributed to the knitting together of European culture.

Archer married in 1884 Frances Elizabeth, daughter of John Trickett, a retired civil engineer, and had one son.

[*The Times*, 29 December 1924; *Manchester Guardian*, 29 December 1924; *Observer*, 4 January 1925; L. Aas, *William Archer*, 1920; Charles Archer, *William Archer—Life, Work, and Friendships* (in MS.); J. M. Robertson, biographical Introduction to *William Archer as Rationalist*, 1925; 'Personal Note' by G. Bernard Shaw prefixed to Archer's *Three Plays*, 1927.] M. P. Ashley.

ARMSTRONG, EDWARD (1846–1928), historian and teacher, was born at Tidenham vicarage, Gloucestershire, 3 March 1846. He was the second son of the Rev. John Armstrong, D.D. [q.v.], by his wife, Frances Whitmore, a clever and accomplished woman to whom her son owed his early instruction in languages. In 1853, his father was made first bishop of Grahamstown, and the family migrated to South Africa. Episcopal journeys among the Kaffirs, still unsettled after their recent rising, made a deep impression upon the boy. His first school was St. Andrew's College, Grahamstown; when, on the bishop's death in 1856, he returned to England, he won a scholarship at Bradfield College. In 1865 he went up to Exeter College, Oxford, as a scholar, and obtained first classes in classical honour moderations (1866) and in *literae humaniores* (1869). On taking his degree in 1869, he was elected to a fellowship at Queen's College.

Except for a brief interval (1871–1873) at Rugby as a classical master, Oxford and Queen's College were the centre of Armstrong's work and interests from that time until his death. A serious illness, in 1872, brought an interlude in his work and an opportunity for long visits to the continent. Throughout his life travelling was his chief recreation. His wanderings took him to remote corners of Europe, where he became intimate, not only with cities and archives, but with the countryside and its flowers, the peasants and their crops. He also acquired considerable proficiency in modern languages. 'I can speak five fluently and mangle two', is his own description of his attainments.

In 1878 Armstrong became senior bursar of Queen's College, and in 1883, on the appointment of Dr. G. W. Kitchin to the deanery of Winchester, he undertook the teaching of modern history for the college, in addition to his bursarial work. This proved to be a turning-point in his career. Hitherto he had won distinction in classical studies; now he entered upon his life-work as an historian. From the first he specialized in foreign history. He became the leading English authority on the Italian Renaissance; thence his studies went back to Italy in the time of Dante, and forward to Italy of the eighteenth century. The great days of the Spanish Empire, France of the Hundred Years' War and the wars of religion, the Netherlands under Charles V and William the Silent, and Germany in and before the era of the Reformation, were among the subjects upon which he wrote and lectured. At a time when few good books on the period were accessible to students, his teaching became the mainstay of all who studied the history of the Renaissance. It was no child's play to follow his lectures. Yet the stream of learning which his pupils struggled to divert to their note-books was interrupted, from time to time, by descriptions of historic sites which he had visited, or by anecdotes illustrating the idiosyncrasies of historic characters; and at such moments history became alive at his word.

Armstrong's books were the offspring of his teaching. *Elizabeth Farnese* (1892), *The French Wars of Religion* (1892), *Lorenzo de' Medici* (1896), and his *magnum opus, The Emperor Charles V* (2 vols., 1902), embodied his mature judgement on matters which had long occupied his mind. Each became a standard work on the subject, wise, witty, scholarly, and marked by characteristic breadth of view. His exhaustive knowledge, and his reluctance to depart from the firm basis of fact, gave to his larger works a certain heaviness. His literary gifts are seen to better advantage in the papers which he contributed to the Oxford Dante Society, the British Academy, and the learned periodicals. Among these, three are noteworthy, as typical of different aspects of his writing. In 'Dante's Political Ideal', published in the *Church Quarterly Review* (1890) and translated into Italian for the *Biblioteca storico-critica della letteratura dantesca*, he is seen as the political philosopher with a grasp upon historical realities. The memoir of his fellow Dantist, Edward Moore [q.v.] (*Proceedings* of the British Academy, vol. vii, 1915–1916), exhibits the sympathy and insight of the model biographer. In lighter vein, his essay on 'An Italian Adventurer' (*Macmillan's Magazine*, 1896) tells with inimitable charm and humour the story of an episode in the war of the League of Cambrai, and rises to the height of poetry in its description of Vicenza, in her setting of river, mountain, and plain.

If Armstrong's place of honour is among the historians, he was quite as much a man of affairs. For forty-four years, first as bursar (1878–1911) and then as pro-provost (1911–1922), he was engaged in the administration of Queen's College, handling with success men of every age and type. It was easy for him to establish contact with college servants and tenants, with dons and undergraduates, with scholars, soldiers, athletes, because their work and ways were alike interesting to him. As a member of the council of Bradfield College (1882–1902), and again as warden (1910–1925), he took an active share in the government of that school, especially in the difficult task of reconstruction which followed the resignation of Dr. Herbert Branston Gray [q.v.] from the headmastership. In Oxford, he served as a curator of the Taylor Institution and of the Botanic Garden, and was among the early friends of women's education. For some years he was chairman of the council of St. Hilda's College, and he regularly devoted two or three hours a week to women pupils. For him there was no gulf between his public life and his work as an historian; both bore the mark of his common sense and knowledge of the world. His interest in the men and women of the Renaissance was akin to that which he showed in the men and women of his own day. It was as natural for him to speak of Duke Cosimo de' Medici as the 'best-looking young man in Florence', as it was to say of a friend of his undergraduate days, 'He was a wonderfully good-looking fellow, and the best-dressed man in Oxford.' His power as a teacher was shown most fully in 'private hours', when one or two pupils at a time listened to his stories and laughed at his quips, conscious all the while that they were receiving, from these friendly conversations, sound training in the subject matter and methods of historical study.

Armstrong married twice: first, in 1879 Mabel (died 1920), the beautiful but delicate daughter of Dr. Joseph William Watson, chevalier of the order of Charles III of Spain, scientific inventor, sometime vice-consul for Spain at Brighton; secondly, in 1921 Geraldine Prynne, daughter of the Rev. James Adolphus Harriss, vicar of St. Andrew's, Oxford; she brought him a 'St. Luke's summer' of happiness. He had no children. In 1905, he was elected a fellow of the British Academy and in 1926 was awarded the Serena medal for distinguished work in Italian history. His election to the Athenaeum Club under rule 2, in 1905, was an honour appropriate to his social gifts. He was a convinced churchman, and until late in life, he walked daily to Queen's College for morning chapel. Until within a few weeks of his death he was at work on articles for the *Cambridge Medieval History*, which were published posthumously. He died 14 April 1928 at the Red House, Oxford, and is buried in Holywell cemetery. In the Creweian oration for that year the public orator spoke of him as *Vir exquisitae doctrinae atque humanitatis*. It was a fitting tribute to a distinguished historian and a most lovable man.

From his school days it was Armstrong's habit to express himself in verse, and a selection of his *Poems*, written between 1861 and 1924, with a memoir by Professor H. J. Paton, was privately printed by the Oxford University Press in 1929.

There is a portrait at Bradfield College, painted by C. Goldsborough Anderson in 1922, of which replicas are at Queen's College and St. Hilda's College.

[*The Times*, 16 April 1928; *Oxford Magazine*, 17 May 1928; *Proceedings* of the British Academy, vol. xiv, 1928; E. Armstrong, *Italian Studies* (ed. C. M. Ady), 1934; personal knowledge.]

C. M. Ady.

ARNOLD, Sir THOMAS WALKER (1864–1930), Orientalist, was born at Devonport 19 April 1864, the third son of Frederick Arnold, who was then in business at Devonport, by his wife, Matilda Sweet. He was educated first at Plymouth High School, and then, from 1880, at the City of London School, whence he proceeded in 1883 with a scholarship to Magdalene College, Cambridge. Although entered for the classical tripos, he was attracted to a variety of other subjects, and more especially to Oriental studies, under the stimulating guidance of Edward Byles Cowell [q.v.] and William Robertson Smith [q.v.]. After his tripos, in which he was placed in the third class, Arnold spent a fourth year at Cambridge, devoting special attention to the history of Islam. His interest in Oriental subjects led to his selection for the post of teacher in philosophy at the Mohammedan Anglo-Oriental College at Aligarh, in the United Provinces.

The ten years (1888–1898) spent at Aligarh left an enduring impress on Arnold's character and outlook. There he formed one of a small band of Englishmen, led by the principal, Theodore Beck, and (Sir) Theodore Morison, who devoted themselves to the service of the ideal laid down by the liberal-minded founder of the college, Sir Syed Ahmad Khan—to reform Islam by a harmonious synthesis of Moslem culture with Western scientific thought and method. Arnold set out with genuine religious fervour to make the ideal a reality in the lives of himself and his students. He dressed like a Moslem, and founded in the college the *Anjuman al-Farz*, or 'Duty Society', the members of which undertook to work individually for the regeneration of their nation. The sympathy, amounting to affection, which he then learned for Indian Moslems, and the insight which he gained into their life, remained with him to the end of his days, and called out in return the affection of a like-minded group of his Indian colleagues and pupils. It inspired his studies and permeated his first important work, *The Preaching of Islam* (1896), which placed him at once in the front rank of Islamic scholars and historians. In 1898 Arnold joined the Indian educational service as professor of philosophy at the government college (now university) of Lahore. There his teaching, although less intimate, exercised a profound influence on his best pupils, among whom was (Sir) Muhammad Iqbal, later one of the leaders of the Indian Moslem community.

Although other posts had been offered to him, Arnold resigned from the service in 1904 and returned to London as assistant-librarian at the India Office, holding simultaneously the part-time professorship of Arabic at University College. In 1909 he was chosen to fill the newly created post of educational adviser for Indian students in England, the duties of which he discharged with conspicuous success for eleven years. His services to Indian education were duly recognized by the conferment of the C.I.E. in 1912 and a knighthood in 1921 after his retirement at the end of 1920.

On the establishment of a School of Oriental Studies in the university of London in 1917, Arnold had been invited to give instruction in his spare time, and after his retirement from the India Office he was appointed as first holder of the chair of Arabic and Islamic studies. The return to academic work was very welcome to him, and the remaining years of his life were devoted to building up the new department, to teaching, and to writing. In spite of medical warnings he continued to work at high pressure. Early in 1930 he went to Cairo as visiting professor at the Egyptian University, and a fortnight after his return to England, he succumbed, on 9 June 1930 at his home in Kensington, to an attack of heart failure. During his later years he received many honours; Magdalene College made him an honorary fellow in 1917, the university of Prague conferred on him an honorary doctorate, and in 1926 he was elected a fellow of the British Academy.

Arnold's output of published work was greatly hindered by his administrative duties, and down to 1920 the *Preaching of Islam* remained his only important publication. This book, however, played a noteworthy part in disseminating the more understanding view of Islam which began to prevail towards the close of the nineteenth century, and a second edition, much revised and enlarged, was issued in 1913. It was translated into Urdu and later into Turkish. An edition of a small but important text on the *Mu'tazilah* (1902) was Arnold's only other Orientalist publication from India. His later work shows in maturer form the same qualities of sympathy and insight that marked his first. In *The Caliphate* (1924) he surveyed the history of that office from its origins to its final abolition; and he compressed the work of many years into a sixpenny booklet on *The Islamic Faith* (1928) for a wider public. Articles contributed to Hastings's *Encyclopædia of Religion and Ethics* on 'Persecution' and 'Toleration' suggested the idea of a book on toleration in Islam, but it was destined to remain unfinished. Since 1910 he had acted also as English editor of the international *Encyclopædia of Islam*, himself contributing several articles relating mainly to India.

In his later years, however, it was on Mohammedan pictorial art that Arnold's chief work was done. A volume on *Court Painters of the Grand Moguls* (1921), in collaboration with Mr. Laurence Binyon, and some minor essays, preceded the publication of his elaborate study of *Painting in Islam* (1928), a work which laid the foundations for the solid study of the history and technique of Islamic art. His conclusions were summarized in *The Islamic Book* (1929; also in German with the title of *Denkmäler Islamischer Buchkunst*), written in collaboration with Adolf Grohmann. A study on *Bihzād and his Paintings in the Ẓafarnāmah MS.* (1930) and the Schweich lectures delivered in 1928 on *The Old and New Testaments in Muslim Religious Art* (posthumously published in 1932) were his last contributions to this subject.

Arnold delighted in teaching, and his humanity made him an ideal teacher. His enthusiasm communicated itself to his students, even in the elementary stages of grammatical study; to the more advanced, both Indian and English, he was unfailing in encouragement, and there were few who did not learn something of his high ideals and wide tolerance. In private life he had a remarkable talent for friendship, nourished by a quiet gaiety and a modesty of manner carried almost to the point of humility, which concealed, none the less, a strong sense of duty and a high intellectual standard which in his administrative career sometimes brought him into collision with his official superiors. For dogmatic judgements he always had a word of humorous but devastating criticism, and nothing repelled him more than dry scholasticism. Yet he was himself something of a scholastic, keenly interested in medieval thought and religious institutions, and a lover of colour and ritual. To this side of his character he left a memorial in a version of *The Little Flowers of St. Francis* (1898, and many subsequent editions), in which his literary gifts were shown at their best.

Arnold married in 1892 Celia Mary, daughter of George Hickson, of Highbury, manufacturer in the city of London, and niece of Theodore Beck, by whom he had one daughter.

[*The Times*, 11–14 June 1930; *Journal* of the Central Asian Society, October 1930; Sir M. Aurel Stein, *Sir Thomas Walker Arnold, 1864–1930*, in *Proceedings* of the British Academy, vol. xvi, 1932; *al-Andalus* (Madrid), vol. i, 1933; personal knowledge; private information.]

H. A. R. Gibb.

ASHLEY, Sir WILLIAM JAMES (1860–1927), economic historian, was born in Bermondsey 25 February 1860, the eldest son of James Ashley, a journeyman hatter, who came from Wrexham, Denbighshire, by his wife, Jane Short. He was educated at St. Olave's grammar school, Southwark, whence he proceeded to Balliol College, Oxford, in 1878 with a Brackenbury history scholarship. In 1881 he was placed in the first class of the honour school of modern history. For the following five years Ashley remained at Oxford, pursuing his studies and doing a certain amount of private coaching. In 1882 he was awarded the Lothian essay prize. His interest in economic history was greatly stimulated by attendance at the course of lectures given in the winter of 1881–1882 by Arnold Toynbee [q.v.] on the Industrial Revolution. It was, indeed, partly from the notes which Ashley took that it was possible to prepare the lectures for publication after Toynbee's death. Toynbee's pioneer work owed little or nothing to continental influences. Ashley, however, during these years made three short visits to Germany which had the most important bearing on his thought and work. Henceforth, the enthusiasm for social reform which he admired in Toynbee was blended with that devotion to scholarship which characterized the German school of economic historians. Ashley mastered the German literature of the subject, although he did not come under the personal influence of its exponents. It was not until 1902 that he met Gustav Schmoller, the leading exponent of the historical approach to economics, whose work had particularly impressed him. In 1885 Ashley was elected fellow of Lincoln College, Oxford, and he was later appointed lecturer at Corpus Christi College. The Oxford tutorial system, however, had no great attraction for him, and it can be gathered from his subsequent references that he was not sorry to escape from it.

The year 1888 proved a decisive one in Ashley's career. In the spring he was appointed professor of political economy and constitutional history in the university of Toronto. Before his departure for Canada he married Annie Margaret (died 1922), daughter of George Birkbeck Hill [q.v.], the Johnsonian scholar. After his arrival in Canada appeared the first part of *An Introduction to English Economic History and Theory* (1888). Dedicated to the memory of Arnold Toynbee and containing a chapter which drew attention to German research on medieval economic thought, the book is an important landmark in the development of the subject. It reveals remarkable skill in planning and exposition together with a freshness and lucidity of style. Although the preface states the case for the study of economic history cautiously and persuasively, it was obviously meant to be a direct challenge to the accepted British method of approach to the subject of economics. Ashley speaks of the neglect of the teaching of Wilhelm Roscher, Bruno Hildebrand, and Karl Knies—the pioneers of the historical method in Germany—and proceeds to enunciate principles that completely undermine the assumptions of the classical school.

Ashley remained four years at Toronto engaged in the organization of a new department. He then removed in 1892 to Harvard, where a chair of economic history, the first in the English-speaking world, had been created for him. The second part of his *Introduction* appeared in 1893. It covered the later Middle Ages with some excursions into the Tudor period. The original plan of dealing with fact and contemporary speculation side by side was retained, but the subjects were treated in greater detail. In the preface Ashley pleads for a truce in the controversy about method, a subject which he had dwelt upon in his inaugural address at Harvard (reprinted in *Surveys, Historic and Economic*, 1900). But he remained thoroughly convinced of the value of the historical approach as a means of interpreting economic phenomena. To the present generation his constant assertion of his point of view and his references, mostly in conversation, to the opposition which it encountered, vehement though it was, suggest that he exaggerated the importance of the conflict. The fact is that the issue has now lost most of its significance. The subjects which mainly occupied Ashley's attention during the years which he spent at Harvard may be gathered from the essays and reviews collected in his *Surveys, Historic and Economic*. He followed with eager interest the work on medieval agrarian and burghal history which was then appearing in England and on the Continent; but his mind was turning to problems of eighteenth-century commercial history, and his essays on *The Tory Origin of Free Trade Policy* and *The Commercial Legislation of England and the American Colonies* are notable contributions to the elucidation of mercantilism in theory and practice.

In 1900 Mason College, Birmingham,

was converted into the university of Birmingham, and in the following year Ashley was appointed its first professor of commerce. The task which he had to face was a formidable one, for he had to work out a scheme of study for which there were no English precedents. Academic opinion was sceptical, if not definitely hostile, and business men had to be converted to the idea. Ashley decided to base the degree in commerce broadly on economics and economic history, with special reference to the structure, organization, and administration of industry. He also made provision in the course for accounting, industrial law, and one or more modern languages. It is a tribute to his wisdom that the courses for degrees in commerce subsequently adopted by other British universities follow the main lines of his original scheme. Ashley held the chair of commerce at Birmingham until his retirement in 1925 when he was made professor emeritus; for the greater part of the period he was dean of the faculty of commerce, and from 1918 to 1925 he was also vice-principal of the university.

Ashley's settlement in Birmingham coincided with the beginnings of the tariff controversy launched by Joseph Chamberlain. His repudiation of *laisser-faire* economics and his experience in Canada and the United States had led him to question the free trade position. He was particularly impressed by the growing economic influence of the United States in Canada, and felt that some kind of imperial commercial understanding was desirable. There was, indeed, a general impression that he was the academic adviser of the new protectionist movement, an impression which tended to obscure his real position. It was a disappointment to him that the tariff question became the subject of acute political dissension. His sympathies with social reform were genuine and abiding: he wished to see the revision of the fiscal system associated with a radical programme of social improvement. Thus to regard Ashley's position from the strictly party point of view would be to discover in him many inconsistencies; but these are due to the manner in which the parties chose to differentiate themselves rather than to any essential contradiction in the principles which he upheld. His own position as defined in *The Tariff Problem* (1903) revealed singular detachment from mere party issues.

From the time of the tariff controversy to his death Ashley was to some degree involved in public affairs. The War and post-War period naturally made great claims on him. Among the numerous committees on which he served were the departmental committee on food prices (1916) and the Sumner committee on the cost of living (1918). He was appointed a member of the royal commission on agriculture (1919) and subsequently of the agricultural tribunal of investigation (December 1922–May 1924). After his retirement he took a great interest in the work of the committee on industry and trade, on which he was appointed in December 1924, and his influence can be detected in some of its reports.

Such claims on his time and the many administrative duties incidental to a growing university, as well as the demands of a busy industrial community, made it impossible for Ashley to devote continuous attention to economic history, but on the two occasions when he was invited to give special courses of lectures he turned to the subject in which he had done such brilliant pioneer work and for which he always retained a peculiar affection. At Hamburg in 1912 he delivered eight lectures in which the whole ground of English economic history was reviewed. They were subsequently published under the title of *The Economic Organisation of England* (1914) and have earned a well-merited popularity. In 1923 he was appointed Ford's lecturer at Oxford, and took as his subject the place of rye in the dietary of the English people. His work on the agricultural tribunal made it impossible for him to deliver the lectures, but on his retirement in 1925 he returned to the subject with great enthusiasm, and explored agrarian history in order to substantiate his thesis. Although soon stricken with disease, he struggled on with great courage, and the manuscript of his book was completed a few weeks before his death, which took place 23 July 1927 at Canterbury, to which place he had retired. It appeared posthumously as *The Bread of our Forefathers; an Enquiry in Economic History* (1928).

Of nonconformist origin, Ashley became in later life a devout churchman. On several occasions he preached in Birmingham cathedral and elsewhere; a selection of his discourses under the title of *The Christian Outlook* (1925) reveals his real concern about the social implications of religion. In public speech his matter was always excellent although his delivery was slow. As an administrator he was cautious. When at his ease he could be delightfully friendly and even playful, but in chance encounters and in conference he was apt to give some offence where a man of greater intuition and perhaps less sincerity would avoid arousing opposition. He was knighted in 1917, and elected an honorary fellow of Lincoln College in 1920. He was survived by one son and two daughters.

[*The Times*, 25 July 1927; Anne Ashley, *William James Ashley*, 1932; *Economic Journal*, vol. xxxvii, 1927; *Economic History Review*, vol. i, 1928; private information; personal knowledge.]

J. F. Rees.

ASQUITH, HERBERT HENRY, first Earl of Oxford and Asquith (1852–1928), statesman, was born at Croft House, Morley, Yorkshire, 12 September 1852, the second son of Joseph Dixon Asquith, a nonconformist wool-spinner and weaver of that place, by his wife, Emily, daughter of William Willans, a wool-stapler of Huddersfield. His father died when he was eight years old, and his mother then went with her four children to live near her father at Huddersfield; there, and for a short time at a Moravian boarding-school at Fulneck, near Leeds, Asquith received his early education. In 1863 he was sent with his elder brother to live with relatives in London, and entered the City of London School, then situated in Milk Street, off Cheapside. He remained at this school for seven years and came strongly under the influence of Dr. Edwin Abbott [q.v.], its most famous headmaster. Abbott early marked him out as a boy of brilliant promise with an especially precocious talent for speech-making, which was shown to great advantage at the school debating society. In 1870 Asquith proceeded to Balliol College, Oxford, having gained a classical scholarship at the age of seventeen. He more than fulfilled his school promise at Oxford where he obtained first classes both in classical moderations (1872) and *literae humaniores* (1874) and was awarded the Craven scholarship (1874), after being *proxime accessit* for the Hertford and the Ireland scholarships. Asquith was also in his last term president of the Oxford Union, where the fame of his exploits was handed on to many generations of undergraduates. Jowett, like Abbott, predicted a great career for him, and all his Oxford contemporaries were of the same opinion.

In 1874 Asquith was elected fellow of Balliol, the other fellowship of the same year being awarded to A. C. Bradley, professor of poetry at Oxford, 1901–1906. About the same time he entered as a student at Lincoln's Inn, and after a short residence at Balliol came to London, and for the next year was a pupil in chambers of the future Lord Justice Bowen, who confirmed what was now the usual opinion of his abilities. He was called to the bar in 1876. In 1877, in his twenty-sixth year, he married Helen, daughter of Frederick Melland, a well-known Manchester physician, and took up his residence at Eton House, in what used to be John Street, Hampstead. Asquith had early decided that his real career was to be in politics, and that the bar was to be only a means to that end. But in making his way at the bar he had six years of struggle and discouragement, in which he added to a slender income by lecturing and writing articles for the *Spectator* and *Economist*. The rare briefs which came his way were well argued, but he lacked some of the superficial qualities which tell with juries and ensure quick success. It was not until 1883 that he began to make his mark at the bar, and then he caught the attention of (Sir) Robert Samuel Wright, afterwards a judge, at that time attorney-general's 'devil', and of Sir Henry James (afterwards Lord James of Hereford), for both of whom he 'devilled', and to whom he always acknowledged a great debt for help in these early years.

During this period Asquith devoted most of his leisure to politics, speaking for the Eighty Club at public meetings and engaging in debate at local parliaments as an ardent Gladstonian liberal. In 1886, being now fairly established at the bar, he decided to stand for parliament, and after a week's campaign was returned for East Fife, a constituency which remained faithful to him for thirty-two years. He at once made his mark in the House of Commons. His speeches were brief, pointed, trenchant, and admirably timed; it was said from the beginning that he spoke with the authority of a leader and not as a back-bencher. During this parliament he concentrated on the Irish question, and distinguished himself as a vehement opponent of the coercive policy of Mr. Balfour, then chief secretary for Ireland. But his chief opportunity came in 1888 when he was appointed junior counsel for Charles Stewart Parnell [q.v.] before the Parnell commission—Sir Charles Russell being leader—and a brilliant cross-examination of one of the principal witnesses for *The Times* not only 'made' him at the bar but greatly enhanced his reputation in the House of Commons, where he made formidable use of the knowledge gained on the commission. From this time forward his legal practice increased by leaps and bounds, and his name became widely known in the country. He took silk in 1890.

As a tragic set-off to these successes came the loss of his wife, who died of typhoid fever in September 1891, when they were on holiday together at Lamlash in the Isle of Arran. 'To me', Asquith wrote to a friend some time afterwards, 'she was the gentlest and best of companions, a restricting rather than a stimulating influence, and knowing myself as I do, I have often wondered that we walked so evenly together. I was only eighteen when I fell in love with her, and we married when we were little more than boy and girl. In the cant phrase our marriage was a "great success"; from first to last it was never troubled by any kind of sorrow and dissension; and when the sun went down, it was in an unclouded sky.' Asquith was now left a widower with five young children (four sons and one daughter), and he had in front of him some of the hardest years of his life.

Up to the autumn of 1890, it was generally believed that the liberal party would come back to power with a large majority at the next election, but the Parnell divorce case in November of that year, and the complications which followed from it, blighted that prospect. Thus, when the election came in 1892, the party had a majority of only 40, with which to undertake the formidable task to which it was pledged of carrying a Home Rule Bill through parliament. That task was doomed to failure from the beginning, but, indomitable as ever, Mr. Gladstone was determined to try, and formed an exceptionally able Cabinet with a strong infusion of younger men. Abandoning his former objection to putting into a Cabinet men who had not served an apprenticeship as under-secretaries, he made Asquith home secretary, and no appointment received more general approval. Asquith thus became a Cabinet minister and the holder of the principal secretaryship of state at the age of thirty-nine.

In lasting three years the liberal government outlived the most sanguine expectations of its friends, and at the end of that time Asquith was held to have justified and increased his reputation. He had shown firmness and good sense on such questions as the demand for the release of Irish dynamiters, the holding of public meetings in Trafalgar Square, and the Featherstone riots (August 1893); any one of these, if mishandled, might have put the government in jeopardy. He also left behind him an excellent administrative record, and steered an important Factory Bill through the House of Commons in 1894 and 1895. His reputation was now firmly established as a debater in the house, and as an admirable speaker on platforms in the country. When parliament was dissolved in 1895, he was generally regarded as a future prime minister.

In May 1894, while he was home secretary, Asquith married as his second wife Margaret (Margot), youngest daughter of Sir Charles Tennant, first baronet [q.v.], a young woman well known in London society for her brilliant gifts and originality of mind and character. A selection (published in his biography) of the letters that he wrote to her before their marriage, reveals a deep and imaginative side of his character which he kept veiled from the public until the end of his life. The world said that they were unequally matched; but he remained as devoted to her to the end as she was to him, and was unqualified in his admiration of her gifts and in acknowledging the stimulus which she gave to his own less lively disposition. There were five children of this marriage, of whom only two, a son and a daughter, survived infancy.

Asquith remained out of office for nearly eleven years—years of trouble and schism for the liberal party, from which at times it seemed doubtful if it could ever recover. The resignation of Lord Rosebery as leader of the party in 1896 was followed by the resignation of Sir William Harcourt from the same position in 1898. In the latter year Asquith was much talked of for the succession to the leadership, but he was resolved not to put himself into competition with Sir Henry Campbell-Bannerman, who had the claim of seniority, if willing to accept this 'bed of thorns', as Lord Rosebery called it. Asquith, moreover, was now busily engaged earning a large income at the bar, to which he had returned in defiance of the convention which was supposed to prevent an ex-Cabinet minister or, indeed, any privy councillor, from engaging in this profession, and he was not yet prepared to give his whole time to public affairs. He was, in fact, very often absent from the House of Commons in these days, and some said that he was tiring of politics.

That was never so, but politics were difficult and thorny enough for a liberal leader between the years 1899 and 1902. The Boer War which broke out in the autumn of 1899 deeply divided the party and its leaders. There were Little-Englanders, so called, who thought the War an iniquity and denounced it in unmeasured terms; there were 'Liberal-Imperialists' who thought it just and inevitable, at all events after President Kruger's ultimatum. Asquith, although he had vigorously criticized the Chamberlain-Milner diplomacy which led up to the War, was of the latter opinion. This brought him into collision with Campbell-Bannerman who, although he admitted the inevitability of the War after the ultimatum, could never be brought to pronounce it just or, taking into consideration the whole course of events, unavoidable. Little-Englanders and Liberal-Imperialists composed their differences temporarily for the 'khaki' election of October 1900, in which both suffered equally, but the trouble broke out anew afterwards, and in June 1901 Asquith publicly protested against Campbell-Bannerman's use of the phrase 'methods of barbarism' as applied to the farm-burning practised by British troops in South Africa under the provocation of guerrilla warfare. Much recrimination followed, and the formation of the Liberal League by the Imperialist group in February 1902 seemed to indicate that the whole group was about to follow Lord Rosebery in the 'definite separation' which he had already announced on his own behalf. But by this time Asquith had come to the conclusion that the quarrel had gone too far, and in the next few weeks he used his influence successfully to make peace.

The situation was eased by the ending of the War in May 1902, and before another year was out the conservative party, by its education policy and still more by raising the fiscal question, had done what liberals had failed to do for themselves—reunited the liberal party. From now to the end of the parliament, Asquith was foremost both in attacking the government and in defending free trade; and the speeches which he made in the country were models of trenchant and lucid exposition of all aspects of the fiscal question.

Mr. Balfour's government resigned early in December 1905, and after ten and a half years of exclusion from office the liberal party again had an opportunity of forming a ministry. The circumstances at the moment were by no means auspicious. Lord Rosebery had just made a speech dissenting emphatically from the line taken by Sir Henry Campbell-Bannerman, with Asquith's consent, on the Irish question; and while the government was being formed a serious hitch occurred owing to the condition which Mr. Haldane and Sir Edward Grey sought to make that Asquith should be leader of the House of Commons while the new prime minister, Sir Henry Campbell-Bannerman, should accept a peerage and go to the Lords. Asquith, who had, in the meantime, accepted the office of chancellor of the Exchequer, was strongly opposed to any step which would lead to a crisis at that moment on an issue personal to himself; and when Campbell-Bannerman declined their condition, Haldane and Grey were persuaded to waive it, and to enter the government as secretary for war and foreign secretary respectively—appointments which were to be momentous in later years. At the election which followed in January 1906 the liberal party obtained an enormous majority mainly on the free trade issue, and for the next two years Campbell-Bannerman remained leader of the House of Commons, a position in which he greatly distinguished himself and—as no one acknowledged more generously than Asquith—belied all the fears that had been expressed about his capacity for leadership.

In these two years the struggle between Lords and Commons, which was to last continuously for the next five years, entered upon its first stage. The House of Lords either rejected or amended out of recognition the bills to which the liberal government attached most importance—education bills, land bills, franchise bills—and feeling ran high on this treatment of liberal legislation just after a great liberal triumph in the country. Asquith, as had been expected, proved the most formidable debater on the government side in these controversies; but his principal work was as chancellor of the Exchequer, and he was responsible for three budgets (1906, 1907, and 1908), the last of which he introduced after he had become prime minister. As a financier, he was orthodox, thrifty, and progressive. In his first budget he took off the 1*s.* per ton coal export tax, and reduced the tea tax from 6*d.* to 5*d.* In his second he established the difference between earned and unearned income for income-tax, and revised the whole system of grants in aid of local authorities, substituting equivalent grants for ear-marked taxes. In his third he made the first provision for old age pensions, at the same time reducing the sugar tax from 4*d.* to 2*d.* He took especial pride in having instituted old age pensions, and was able to claim that, in spite of this new demand on the Exchequer, he had reduced debt at the rate of from 14 to 15 millions a year out of taxation.

In February 1908 Campbell-Bannerman fell dangerously ill, and it soon became known that he was dying. His relations with Asquith had been intimate and affectionate, and Asquith on his side was reluctant to take any step which might be painful to him or retard the hope of his recovery, while it was yet possible to hope. The government was carried on with great difficulty in his absence during the next six weeks, and at the end of that time Campbell-Bannerman's doctors declared his resignation to be imperative. King Edward VII was then at Biarritz, and instead of returning to London, summoned Asquith to 'kiss hands' as prime minister at that French watering-place—a method of procedure which exposed him to no little criticism. Asquith departed for Biarritz on 5 April, 'kissed hands' on 6 April, and came back as prime minister the following day, with the list of his ministers approved. The most important changes which he made in the previous administration were the appointments of Mr. Lloyd George to be chancellor of the Exchequer, of Mr. Reginald McKenna to be first lord of the Admiralty, and of Mr. Winston Churchill to be president of the Board of Trade.

Never was a political succession less disputed than that of Asquith to the prime ministership in April 1908. There were no rivals in the field, and he came to the highest place by common consent. But no one at that moment thought it likely or, indeed, possible that he would hold this place for nearly nine years—the longest continuous period for which it had been held by one man since Lord Liverpool's resignation in 1827. In April 1908 the liberal tide was visibly ebbing from its high-water mark of 1906; almost all the legislation on which the party had set its heart had been brought to a standstill owing to the resistance of the House of Lords; and failing the means of overcoming this obstruction, the government was losing prestige in the country and seemed doomed, if it survived, to a sterile 'ploughing of the sands'. No one then foresaw that the House of Lords itself would provide the issue which would prolong the life of the government and keep the liberal tide flowing until the outbreak of the European War in 1914.

The issue arose out of finance. By the end of 1908, it had become clear that the large and unexpected increase in the German navy would require a corresponding effort on the part of the British government. The necessity was challenged by certain members of the Cabinet, who saw with dismay the prospect of the surplus which they had ear-marked for social reform being absorbed by the demands of the Admiralty. A sharp struggle followed, in which the Admiralty secured an even bigger programme than it had at first demanded; but the Cabinet decided that money should be found both for the construction of new ships and for the social programme which it had previously contemplated. The budget of 1909 which Mr. Lloyd George introduced for this purpose, with its fourteen millions of extra taxation, may seem a modest effort to a later generation, but it led to a violent agitation, in which the proposed new land taxes were specially singled out for denunciation, and on the last day of November it was rejected by the House of Lords. This raised a constitutional question of the first magnitude. For at least 250 years it had been assumed by all parties that the power of the purse belonged to the House of Commons, and to that House alone; and it was clear that, if the House of Lords could establish its right to hold up supply, it would have acquired the power of dissolving parliament and bringing any government to which it objected to a standstill. In fact, the hereditary assembly would have the whip-hand of the elective.

Asquith immediately took up the challenge and appealed to the country. At the election which followed, in January 1910, the government secured a majority of 124—a majority large enough for ordinary purposes, but not large enough to overcome the opposition of the Irish if they carried their objection to certain taxes to the length of voting against the budget, when it was again presented to the House of Commons. For some weeks the fate of both the budget and the government was in doubt, but Asquith stood firm against any change to conciliate the Irish, and in the end the latter gave way and the budget was passed by a majority of 93 in the House of Commons on 27 April 1910, and accepted without a division by the House of Lords on the following day. But the liberal party was now unanimously of opinion that the government could not content itself with procuring the submission of the House of Lords on the one issue of the budget and continue to accept its unqualified supremacy over all other legislation. Simultaneously with the passing of the budget, Asquith had prepared and presented to the House of Commons a scheme for limiting the powers of the House of Lords by providing that a Bill which had been passed by the House of Commons in three successive sessions should, after a minimum period of two years from its first introduction, automatically become law in spite of its rejection in each of those sessions by the House of Lords. This was the plan which the liberal party had adopted in 1907, and it was now the party's unanimous demand that it should occupy the first place in the government programme.

It was evident from the beginning, however, that such a plan would not be accepted by the House of Lords except under pressure of a creation of peers, or the threat of such a creation, to overcome its resistance. No one saw this more clearly than King Edward, who had warned Asquith before the election of January 1910 that if the question of the House of Lords veto was raised in addition to that of the budget in the new house, he would not 'feel justified in creating new peers until after a second general election', at which the veto would be the sole and acknowledged issue. The natural sequence of events was broken by the death of King Edward in May 1910, and for the next few months Asquith endeavoured to reach a settlement of the House of Lords and other constitutional questions through a conference of the leaders of both parties. When this attempt broke down, he decided to dissolve parliament at once and to hold the second election on the House of Lords question for which King Edward had stipulated as the condition of using the royal prerogative to create peers. But before doing so he felt it necessary to satisfy himself that King George V would accept this second election as the final and sufficient test of the popular will, as presumably his father would have done. Accordingly, on 16 November, Asquith put the question to the king in an interview at Buckingham Palace, and obtained from him a 'hypothetical understanding', as he afterwards described it, that, if the government obtained 'a sufficient majority' at the coming election, he (the king) would create peers in sufficient numbers to overcome the resistance of the House of Lords, should it resist in the teeth of the popular verdict. It was agreed that this understanding should be divulged to no one except members of the Cabinet, unless it proved necessary to give effect to it in the new parliament.

Asquith always hoped that this necessity would not arise, and that, if the popular verdict was decisive, the House of Lords would bow to it without waiting for a creation of peers. In this way he hoped that the king would be kept out of the controversy which was bound to follow, if the understanding were made public either before the election or while the measure was being debated in the new parliament. To a considerable extent this hope was realized, but although the election of December 1910 gave the government a majority of 126, the House of Lords continued its resistance up to the last stages of the Parliament Bill which it amended in such a way as to defeat its principal objects. On 24 July, when the House of Commons met to consider the Lords' amendments, Asquith stood at the box for half an hour unable to make himself heard against the organized clamour of his opponents, and the house had to be content with learning the intentions of the government from the report of his undelivered speech in the next day's papers. It now became necessary to reveal that the king was prepared to use his prerogative if the peers persisted in their opposition, but even under this pressure the Bill was only passed by a majority of 17 after agitated debates in which Asquith was hotly assailed for having 'coerced the king'.

To the end of his life Asquith warmly repudiated this charge. The position was one, in his opinion, in which neither king nor minister had any option. The minister could not have undertaken another election without satisfying himself that, if a sufficient majority was obtained, the result would be decisive; the king could not, as the event proved, have obtained another minister who could have survived either in the existing parliament or in the new parliament. Opinions may differ as to the policy of the Parliament Act, but it is now scarcely disputed that the king's action was in strict accord with his constitutional duties and that Asquith, in peculiarly difficult circumstances, chose the method best calculated to keep the crown out of political controversy.

At the election of December 1910, Asquith made it clear that the removal of the absolute veto of the House of Lords was intended by the government to clear the way to other liberal legislation which, till then, had been obstructed by the peers; and in April 1912 he introduced a Home Rule Bill, proposing, for the third time since Mr. Gladstone's effort in 1886, to set up a subordinate parliament in Ireland. The accumulated bitterness of the party struggles of previous years now found vent in the opposition to this Bill. Before the year was out the protestant counties of Ulster, under the leadership of Sir Edward Carson and with the support of unionist leaders, began to drill and arm with a view to resisting the Bill if it became law, declaring this to be the only alternative remaining to them, now that the veto of the House of Lords was removed. This placed the government in extreme difficulty. It was warned that any legal proceedings which it might take would almost certainly be abortive, since in the heated state of opinion it was improbable that juries would convict; and Irish supporters of the government were strongly opposed to 'British coercion' being applied to any party in Ireland. Asquith held his hand, and during the next eighteen months endeavoured by all possible means to narrow down the field of controversy and bring the opposing parties to reason. The agitation continued unabated in the meantime, and among its more serious incidents was the intimation in March 1914 of a group of officers at the Curragh camp in Ireland, in answer to a question put to them by their commanding officer, that they would accept dismissal from the service rather than take part in the coercion of Ulster. Asquith was of opinion that such a question ought never to have been put to them, and that the whole matter had been seriously mishandled by the military authorities. The country and the House of Commons were greatly disturbed by this event, and in order to restore discipline and reassure the public, Asquith himself assumed the secretaryship for war and was actually serving in that capacity when the European War broke out (28 July).

After much patient negotiation, in which the king played a useful part, the Irish controversy was reduced to the question of the precise area to be excluded, and the conditions on which that area should vote itself out or vote itself in. This was submitted to a conference of party leaders at Buckingham Palace on 14 July 1914, but even then the leaders failed to agree, and the future was still in doubt when the War came to suspend the controversy. The Home Rule Bill was passed into law in September 1914 after the War had broken out, but was accompanied by a suspensory Bill postponing its operations until the War was over. A parallel controversy went on during the same years about the Welsh Disestablishment Bill which was dealt with in the same way while the War continued, but was accepted afterwards by general consent.

During these years of agitating controversy between the male parties in the electorate, Asquith became a special target of the militant suffragists who were demanding votes for women and pursuing their campaign with acts of obstruction and violence. For the greater part of his life he was an opponent of women's suffrage, and he both spoke and voted against the resolutions and bills introduced into the House of Commons for the enfranchisement of women. His reasons were frankly sentimental. As his correspondence shows, he rated the capacity and intelligence of women very high, and had no more intimate confidants on serious matters than his wife and a few chosen women friends. But he considered that women in general would lose rather than gain by engaging in the rough and tumble of politics, and he saw no middle course between enfranchising them and admitting them to parliament, and for this final step he was not prepared. His opposition, however, as he explained to the house in one of the debates on the subject (6 May 1913) was 'not dogmatic or final'. He would withdraw it if, first, clear proof were given that an overwhelming majority of women desired to be enfranchised, and secondly, if it were shown that the absence of direct representation in the House of Commons caused the neglect by parliament of the special needs and interests of women. He considered that these conditions had been reasonably fulfilled by the experience of women's work in the War and the new position which they were evidently going to occupy in industry. The demand persisted, and there could no longer be any question of their special interest in legislation. Accordingly he supported their enfranchisement in the Act of 1918, and in the following year the removal of the bar to their sitting in parliament.

Grave and difficult as were the domestic controversies of these years, foreign affairs in the end overshadowed them all. Few British ministers can have had to face more, and more dangerous, crises in the same period of time as Asquith in the six years from the date on which he became prime minister to the outbreak of the European War. His complete accord during these years with Sir Edward Grey, the foreign secretary, he reckoned one of the most fortunate circumstances of his life, and the perfect partnership of the two men saved him from the friction so usual in the relations between prime minister and foreign secretary, and kept the government steadfast to a continuous line of policy. Asquith was anxious to find any means of conciliating Germany, but loyalty to the French *entente* and security against the challenge of the increasing German fleet he considered to be the two essentials of British policy. In the many struggles within his Cabinet about the increases in the British navy deemed necessary to meet the German competition, he was invariably a strong supporter of what the Admiralty thought necessary for safety, and he brought all the arts of persuasion to bear upon his colleagues who were unconvinced or reluctant. On the other hand, he was strongly opposed to scattering the resources of the country between army and navy in time of peace, and in a lively passage in his *Genesis of the War* (1923) has replied to the charge that he did not 'raise an army' on the continental model in the years before the War. He believed, as did most responsible men in both parties, that no government could have persuaded the British people to accept compulsory military service except under the pressure of extreme necessity, and he claimed for his government that in keeping the navy beyond challenge and maintaining the expeditionary force and territorial army, it had made a larger effort in naval and military preparation than any other government in the same space of time.

The successive crises arising out of the annexation of Bosnia-Herzegovina in 1908, the dispatch of the German warship *Panther* to Agadir in 1911, and the Balkan Wars of 1912–1913 tested the nerve of his government to the utmost, and not less because some of them coincided with the tensest moments in domestic affairs. The Agadir crisis, for example, ran side by side with the Parliament Bill in 1911, and while the Peers and Commons were at grips Asquith and his Cabinet had seriously to consider the possibility that in another week Great Britain would be plunged into war with Germany. In all these emergencies Asquith's steadiness and composure were of the highest value.

Asquith has left it on record in his *Memories and Reflections* (1928) that in the final crisis of July to August 1914 he started with five leading ideas on policy: (1) Great Britain has no obligations of any kind either to France or Russia to give them military or naval help; (2) Great Britain must not forget the ties created by her long-standing and intimate friendship with France; (3) it is against British interests that France should be wiped out as a great power; (4) Great Britain cannot allow Germany to use the Channel as a hostile base; (5) Great Britain has obligations to Belgium to prevent her from being utilized and absorbed by Germany. All five of these ideas had been embodied in the policy of Asquith's government in the previous years. In the Grey-Cambon correspondence of 1912 it was laid down for the information of the French that all final decisions rested with the British parliament. In the naval negotiations with Germany following the mission of Viscount Haldane [q.v.] to Berlin in the same year, a German formula which would have detached Great Britain from France and compelled her to remain neutral in the event of a German attack upon France was definitely declined, and in reporting the government's decision Asquith told the king that British interests alone, apart from consideration for France, required its refusal. The British documents in regard to the neutrality of Belgium further show that the British government made it quite clear that it would not be a party to the violation of Belgian territory by any power, and Marshal Joffre has revealed in his *Mémoires* that a French plan, which might have anticipated the German incursion by entering Belgian territory in advance of the Germans, had to be abandoned in November 1912 on that account. When the crisis came, all these ideas and motives worked together to the conclusion that honour and policy alike required British intervention; and Asquith himself never wavered in the view that a victory of Germany over France, leading, as it almost certainly would have done, to German control of Belgium and the Channel ports, and to a combination of hostile fleets in German hands, would leave Great Britain and the British Empire in a position of the gravest peril. His colleagues have left their testimony that when the final crisis came, his handling of the Cabinet was masterly. He knew where he would stand; but he knew also the importance of keeping the government united, and the unwisdom of forcing the hands of colleagues who shared his responsibility. By his patience and suasion he accomplished the feat, which at the beginning had seemed impossible, of bringing Cabinet and country to the all but unanimous conclusion that British participation in the War was a stern necessity.

Asquith's government, by common consent, handled the first stages of the European War with remarkable skill and success. The navy was at its stations at the critical moment; the six divisions of the Expeditionary Force were conveyed to France swiftly, secretly, and without a hitch. The plans devised in previous years to prevent panic and to enable business to continue worked with admirable efficiency. The appointment of Lord Kitchener as secretary for war was hailed as a masterstroke. But in Great Britain, as in other countries, both government and public were utterly unprepared for the prolonged and devastating struggle which followed. When the retreat from Mons had been retrieved by the victory of the Marne (September 1914), hopes ran high that the War would be 'over before Christmas', and the grim war of attrition which now set in presented all the governments concerned with unheard-of problems as to men, munitions, and supply. Within Asquith's government were influential men, especially Mr. Lloyd George and Mr. Winston Churchill, who believed that the war of attrition could be avoided by a 'more imaginative strategy' which would discover alternatives to an incessant hammering at trench barriers on the Western front; and Asquith himself made one exception—in favour of the Dardanelles expedition (February 1915)—to the belief which he otherwise strongly held that victory could only be attained by conquering the main German army in France. The Dardanelles expedition miscarried partly because an initial confusion between a purely naval and joint naval and military attack robbed it of the element of surprise, and partly because, when it had failed as a surprise, sufficient men and munitions could not be spared from the Western front to ensure its success.

The failure of the Dardanelles expedition in its initial stage coincided with an agitation on the subject of munitions on which Asquith had borne uncomplainingly much unfair criticism, and the two things together brought the purely liberal government, which had been in office since 1906 and had survived two general elections, to an end (May 1915). Asquith now formed a coalition Cabinet in which the principal unionist leaders and one member of the labour party (Arthur Henderson) were included.

For the purpose of the War the Coalition government was no improvement on its predecessor. The new men needed to be informed about everything from the beginning; all the parties expected to be represented on any body to which the conduct of the War was deputed; party feeling persisted and caused acute divisions on subjects like compulsory service and the treatment of the Irish question after the rebellion of Easter 1916. Asquith's official biography tells a story of incessant struggles on these and other questions within the Cabinet; and throughout its existence Mr. Lloyd George maintained a running fight with Lord Kitchener and the principal military authorities, demanding a complete change in the direction of the War, by which he meant the transfer of the chief part of the army from the Western to the Eastern front. Then, as later under his own government, this proposal encountered the all but unanimous opposition of the commanding officers, British and French. Both protested that the enemy would have the enormous advantage of interior lines against the long and uncertain communications of the Allies, to say nothing of the inadequacy of the ports and bases of supply and other geographical obstacles to campaigns in the East. The French especially were determined that none other than their own country should be the main theatre of war, while it was in the occupation of the enemy.

The French, nevertheless, made an exception to their own rule in favour of the Salonika expedition (October 1915), which proved a grave embarrassment to the British government. Asquith opposed it to the utmost of his power, but the French forced his hands, and by so doing compelled the evacuation of the Dardanelles, since troops could not be found simultaneously for both expeditions. The evacuation of the Dardanelles (December 1915) without the loss of a man was a great military feat, but in the public mind it set the seal of failure on the greatest military operation of the year 1915, and, combined with the ill success of the great offensives in France in the autumn of the same year, did much to sap the credit of the Coalition government.

Asquith met these troubles with his

usual fortitude, and the next few months were occupied in preparing the Somme offensive and in instituting compulsory service which, after the failure of the Derby scheme of recruiting in the autumn of 1915, he thought inevitable. This, however, encountered fierce opposition from many different quarters, and once more it needed all Asquith's skill and patience to carry it through without breaking up his Cabinet. In the spring of 1916 came the Irish rebellion, which Asquith met characteristically by going to Ireland and informing himself about all aspects of the situation. He came back convinced that the only way to stem the tide of anti-British feeling was at once and without waiting for the end of the War to set up parliamentary Home Rule for the South of Ireland. In this he had the support of Mr. Balfour and Mr. Bonar Law, and even of Sir Edward Carson, but the opposition of other conservative members of the Cabinet, and especially of Lord Lansdowne, proved too strong and, to his great disappointment, he was compelled to drop the project.

In after years German soldiers confessed that the Somme offensive had played the principal part in exhausting the military power of Germany, but this result was not apparent at the time, and when, after heroic struggles and immense losses, the fighting died down in the autumn of 1916, the enemy seemed to be as firmly entrenched as ever on French soil. All the anxieties and disappointments of these times were now concentrated on Asquith, and he became the subject of violent and unscrupulous newspaper attacks which had the avowed object of driving him from office. He had from the beginning accepted the fullest responsibility for everything that went wrong, stood between the soldiers and impatient criticism at all critical moments, and scrupulously refrained from advertising his own activities or claiming credit for himself. These were conspicuous merits which won him the respect and confidence both of the soldiers in the field and of his intimate colleagues. But they left him exposed to critics who knew how to work on popular feeling against a man who never defended himself, and the legend that he was lethargic, that he was 'waiting and seeing' [see *Life*, i, 275, for the origin (1910) of the phrase], and even that he was 'sparing the Germans' obtained a wide vogue in the autumn and winter of 1916.

The cry now went up from these hostile quarters that Asquith should be displaced in favour of Mr. Lloyd George, who had long been pressing for a 'change in the direction of the War'. In the last days of November and the beginning of December 1916 a series of skilful manœuvres in which Sir Edward Carson, Lord Beaverbrook, and finally, though with some reluctance, Mr. Bonar Law, played the principal parts, led the unionist members of the Cabinet to transfer their support from Asquith to Mr. Lloyd George, and Asquith with all his principal liberal colleagues thereupon resigned (5 December 1916). Mr. Lloyd George proposed that the direction of the War should be taken out of the hands of the Cabinet and intrusted to a war council of four with himself as chairman and Asquith exercising only a shadowy and titular control as prime minister. Asquith was not unwilling to delegate some of his executive functions, provided that his final control was unimpaired, but conversations between the two men left it in extreme doubt whether this was Mr. Lloyd George's intention, and the group of newspapers which supported him made it quite clear that nothing less than Asquith's complete supersession was the object aimed at. Throughout this controversy Asquith had the support of all his liberal colleagues, and up to the beginning of December unionist ministers, with the exception of Mr. Bonar Law, had expressed a strong preference for his leadership. But at the critical moment a mistaken belief on his part that they had suddenly deserted him led to obscure cross-purposes between him and them, in the course of which they forced his hands by resigning. Whether the result would have been different if Mr. Bonar Law had acquainted Asquith with the resolution passed by unionist ministers at their meeting (Sunday, 3 December), and thus allowed him to explore the position for himself, has been much debated; but Mr. Bonar Law, for reasons which he thought good, withheld this resolution from Asquith, and the first war Coalition came to a close in a scene of confusion and misunderstanding. Mr. Lloyd George now succeeded Asquith as prime minister.

The change in the direction of the War which Mr. Lloyd George desired, namely, the transfer of the chief part of the British army from the Western to the Eastern front, proved as impossible under the new régime as under the old, and the next year (1917) was one of the blackest of the War for the Allies. As leader of the opposition, Asquith gave a general support to the government and refrained from any but the most moderate criticism; but in the following year an incident occurred which gravely affected his fortunes and those of the liberal party. This was the debate on the letter which General (Sir) Frederick Maurice, the director of military operations, Imperial General Staff, had addressed to the newspapers after the spring disasters of 1918, challenging the statements made by Mr. Lloyd George and other members of the government respecting the strength of the army in France at the time of the great German offensive in March 1918. On the appearance of this letter (7 May), Mr. Bonar Law, speaking on behalf of the government, had said that an impartial inquiry was necessary, and proposed that it should be undertaken by three judges. Asquith, who greatly objected to judges being invoked to decide questions which raised political issues, submitted an amendment in favour of a select committee of the House of Commons as the proper tribunal. Upon that Mr. Lloyd George announced that the government would regard a vote for this amendment as a vote of censure upon itself, and, withdrawing the proposal for inquiry, demanded a vote of confidence from the House of Commons there and then. Asquith persisted in his amendment, and in the division which followed he and 106 other liberals voted for it. No more was heard of this incident at the time, but in the following November, after the conclusion of the armistice, when the liberal and conservative leaders of the Coalition, Mr. Lloyd George and Mr. Bonar Law, decided to hold an immediate election, Asquith and the other liberals who had voted for his amendment found themselves branded as having conspired against the government at the most critical moment of the country's fortunes, and therefore as unworthy to be returned to parliament. Popular feeling ran so strongly at the time, and the joint appeal of the Coalition leaders had so destructive an effect on ordinary party loyalties, that the non-Coalition liberals were to all intents and purposes wiped out, and Asquith himself was defeated in East Fife—the constituency which up till then had returned him continuously for thirty-two years.

This method of electioneering, and the extravagant and embarrassing promises of indemnities and other punitive measures against the late enemy which accompanied it, found few defenders in subsequent years, but the result was decisive at the time. The independent liberals were reduced to 26 in number, and Asquith himself was out of parliament for the whole of the following year (1919). Although his services were available for the Peace Conference at Versailles, the prime minister refrained from including him among the British delegates. He bore these rebuffs with unfailing dignity and fortitude, and at the beginning of the following year (1920) a by-election at Paisley offered him the opportunity of returning to parliament. His campaign on that occasion is generally acknowledged to have been one of his finest oratorical efforts, and he used it to develop an all-round liberal programme and to state his views firmly about what he considered to be excessive and unworkable provisions in the peace treaties. He had by this time come to the conclusion that there was no solution of the Irish question short of Dominion Home Rule, and on that subject he declared himself uncompromisingly.

Returning to parliament, Asquith devoted himself mainly to the Irish question, and hotly denounced the method of reprisals adopted by the special force popularly called the 'Black and Tans', while again constantly urging the solution of Dominion Home Rule. The prime minister spoke of this as madness, and others called it 'treason', but Asquith was undismayed. The policy which he advocated was in fact adopted before the close of the year 1921. From that time onwards the Coalition rapidly disintegrated, and in the election which followed (November 1922), the conservative party, having thrown off Mr. Lloyd George, came back to power with Mr. Bonar Law as prime minister. There were 117 liberals of all sections (64 independents, and 53 followers of Mr. Lloyd George) in the new house, and a reunion between them was effected in the autumn of 1923, when Mr. Baldwin, who had become prime minister on Mr. Bonar Law's retirement in the previous May, suddenly dissolved parliament on the issue of free trade and protection. This reunion undoubtedly saved free trade for the time being, but it presented liberals with a very perplexing problem in the new parliament which met after the general election of December 1923. For although the conservatives were in a minority of nearly a hundred, labour, which was the next strongest party, with 191 seats, could only form a government with the support of liberals, who were 158 strong. Liberals, therefore, had to decide whether they should support labour in taking office, or support Mr. Baldwin in continuing in office, or take office themselves with the support of the conservatives.

There were not a few who urged Asquith to adopt the third course, and he received strong assurances of conservative support, if he would take it. But he was unhesitatingly for enabling labour to take office. He thought that it would be seriously harmful to the public interest and an incitement to class antagonism for the two 'middle-class' parties to combine together to deprive labour of an opportunity which either of them would have claimed as its right in like circumstances; he held it to be impossible for Mr. Baldwin, after he had told the country that he could not carry on without protection, to continue in office as if nothing had happened, when he had been refused permission to try that remedy; and he was not prepared either to enter into a coalition with conservatives or to take office depending on their support. His decision has generally been regarded as constitutionally correct, and in keeping with the instinctive sense of fair play characteristic of great parliamentary leaders; but the sequel was not a happy one for the liberal party. Fruitful co-operation between labour and liberal proved impossible; and after eight months the labour government came to an untimely end (October 1924) in what Asquith called 'two squalid crises, each of which could have been avoided, or at least circumvented, if they had played their cards with a modicum of either luck or skill'. In the election that followed, the strange incident of the 'Zinovieff' letter let loose a storm in the country which overwhelmed both liberal and labour, and Asquith himself was defeated when he presented himself for re-election at Paisley. Thus after thirty-eight years ended his career in the House of Commons.

The king immediately offered Asquith a peerage, and after a short period for reflection he accepted it and entered the House of Lords as Earl of Oxford and Asquith in 1925. He was created K.G. the same year. He remained leader of the liberal party for another eighteen months, but his last days in that capacity were clouded by differences with Mr. Lloyd George, arising first out of the Lloyd George fund and coming to a climax at the time of the General Strike (May 1926), when Mr. Lloyd George took action which, in Asquith's view, made an irreparable breach between them. In this view he was supported by nearly all his liberal colleagues, but the attitude of the rank and file of the party seemed to him ambiguous, and rather than face further dissensions he resigned his leadership in October 1926.

Asquith's health had already begun to fail, but in the next year he had a partial recovery and lived quietly, seeing his friends and working at his book, *Memories and Reflections*. His years of office had left him much impoverished, and for some time past he had turned to writing in order to supplement his income; in addition to many essays and addresses he produced two books, the *Genesis of the War* (1923) and *Fifty Years of Parliament* (1926), which are contributions of high value to history and autobiography. To the end he preserved the dignity, fortitude, and charity which had characterized him throughout his life. He died at his country home, The Wharf, Sutton Courtney, Berkshire, 15 February 1928, and having expressed a strong wish that there should be no public funeral, he was buried in the churchyard of that village.

It was said after his death that Asquith was the 'last of the Romans', and there is much in his character and career to justify that description. In his respect for institutions, his sense of decorum in public affairs, his dislike of mob-oratory and self-advertisement, his high sense of honour, he was in the line of classical English statesmanship. If circumstances made him leader in a great democratic struggle, he was, in his own view, defending the historic House of Commons against an innovation which, if not resisted, would have destroyed its prerogative, and he conducted the controversy on a high plane of serious argument. Like Mr. Gladstone he was defeated in his attempt to give Ireland parliamentary Home Rule, but his effort for a timely settlement on the lines then proposed may well seem conservative in contrast with the solution afterwards adopted. He had certain outward characteristics which lent themselves to the reproach of 'wait and see' which his enemies threw back at him, and his temperamental dislike of showy action undoubtedly was a drawback in war, when the public looks for dramatic qualities in its leaders. But the curtain is seldom lifted on the part which he played behind the scenes without showing him to have been prompt and decisive. He took the War Office into his own hands during the Ulster troubles, and returned to it again at a very critical moment in the War; he played a principal part in bringing Italy into the War; he went to Ireland himself after the rebellion. He was immovable in defence of soldiers in the field, or members of his Cabinet whom he thought unjustly blamed; he did unflinchingly many necessary but unpopular things, and bore the odium without complaint or explanation. In all these ways he earned the respect and trust of his colleagues, and conformed to the highest traditions of public life. In the end he showed certain signs of weariness after his long term of office and the incessant struggles and crises in which he had played the leading part, and he lacked the resilience to defend himself against the attacks which bore him down. But in the long period of his prime ministership he had played a continuous part in great and historic events such as had seldom fallen to any British statesman, and it may be said that only a man of commanding abilities, iron nerve, and high integrity of character could have sustained it.

Asquith's eldest son, Raymond, a man of exceptional brilliance, was killed in action in 1916, and he was succeeded as second earl by his grandson, Julian Edward George (born 1916).

Asquith was of middle height; his frame unathletic, but erect and firmly compacted. Spare till he was in the 'forties, in later life he filled out, and acquired in old age an ample habit of body. His face in early life was pale and ascetic, the eyes wide apart and if anything prominent rather than sunken, the nose substantial, the mouth full but firm; the whole dominated by a massive brow from which a wave of hair swept back. In middle age his complexion acquired a healthy red, the severe cast of feature yielded to a prevailing expression of serenity, the abundant hair silvered, yet his countenance still had austere phases. The mouth had contracted to the firm thin line which it tends to assume in lawyers; the forehead remained salient and formidable; and when he was speaking or under a high light which set off the modelling of the bones, his face could assume a sternness, an expression of command and of authority, which was at least as true a reflection of his character as the geniality which normally overlay them.

There are portraits of Asquith by Sir William Orpen in the Council Room, Lincoln's Inn; by Sir John Lavery at the Reform Club; by Solomon J. Solomon at the National Liberal Club, and by Fiddes Watt in Balliol College hall. The last was thought by his friends to be the best likeness. There are also various busts; one by Mrs. Clare Sheridan at the Oxford Union; others at the City of London School, and in the Town Hall at Morley. Cartoons appeared in *Vanity Fair* 14 July 1904 and 17 March 1910.

[*The Times*, 16 February 1928; J. A. Spender and Cyril Asquith, *Life of Lord Oxford and Asquith*, 2 vols., 1932; H. H. Asquith, *The Genesis of the War*, 1923, *Fifty Years of Parliament*, 2 vols., 1926, *Memories and Reflections, 1852–1927*, 2 vols., 1928, *Occasional Addresses, 1893–1916*, 1918; *Speeches by the Earl of Oxford and Asquith*, edited by J. B. Herbert, 1928; *The Autobiography of Margot Asquith*, 2 vols., 1922; J. A. Spender, *Life of Sir Henry Campbell-Bannerman*, 2 vols., 1923; A. G. Gardiner, *Life of Sir William Harcourt*, 2 vols., 1923; Lord Morley, *Recollections*, 2 vols., 1917.]

J. A. Spender.

AUSTEN, HENRY HAVERSHAM GODWIN- (1834–1923), explorer and geologist. [See Godwin-Austen.]

BABINGTON SMITH, Sir HENRY (1863–1923), civil servant. [See Smith, Sir Henry Babington.]

BAILHACHE, Sir CLEMENT MEACHER (1856–1924), judge, the eldest son of the Rev. Clement Bailhache, a baptist minister and secretary to the Baptist Missionary Society, by his wife, Emma, daughter of Edward Augustus Meacher, of Ivinghoe, Buckinghamshire, was born at Leeds 2 November 1856. His father belonged to a Huguenot family which had settled in Jersey. Bailhache was educated at the City of London School and at London University, where he took the degree of LL.B. in 1877. After admission as a solicitor, he practised successfully for some years at Newport, Monmouthshire. Then, realizing his powers as an advocate, he entered as a student at the Middle Temple and was called to the bar in 1889. He was made a bencher in 1912.

Joining the South Wales circuit, where he was already well known as a solicitor, Bailhache at once became one of its busiest members, and ten years later he was receiving briefs in cases of importance in London. He had made a close study of commercial law, and City firms who had business in the newly established Commercial Court were not slow to recognize his merits. In 1908 he took silk with a group of distinguished juniors, which included the Hon. Frank Russell (afterwards Lord Russell of Killowen), (Sir) John Simon, and F. E. Smith (afterwards Earl of Birkenhead). At the moment (Sir) T. E. Scrutton (afterwards Lord Justice) and

J. A. Hamilton (afterwards Viscount Sumner) were the favourite leaders in the Commercial Court, but their speedy elevation to the bench gave Bailhache an opening of which he took full advantage. His services were so often required in the Commercial Court that he was seldom engaged in cases which attracted public attention; nor had he the showy style which is expected of a jury advocate. But in explaining to a judge a complicated set of facts and applying to them the correct legal principles he had no superior, and his arguments were heard with interest and respect by all tribunals. His addresses lost nothing in lucidity for being brief, and he was a good-tempered and courteous opponent.

In 1912 the congestion in the common-law courts was considerable, and the appointment of a judge under the recently passed Additional Judges Act of 1910 was decided upon. Lord Haldane, who had just succeeded Lord Loreburn as lord chancellor, promoted Bailhache to the bench with the entire approval of the bar. The customary knighthood followed in the same year. As a judge Bailhache was industrious and self-reliant. He often presided in the Commercial Court. Quick to a fault, he disposed of a great quantity of work. Occasional complaints were made that he did not pay sufficient attention to the arguments of counsel, and his summary treatment of a case sometimes led to a successful appeal. His judgments were easily delivered and well expressed, and, however difficult the topics under discussion, he preferred to deliver judgment without delay.

The outbreak of war in 1914 brought a variety of problems to the Commercial Court, and with many of them Bailhache had to deal. *Sanday* v. *British and Foreign Marine Insurance Company* (1915, constructive total loss by declaration of war), *Becker Gray & Co.* v. *London Assurance Corporation* (1915, whether putting into port to avoid capture was a loss covered by insurance), and *China Mutual Steam Navigation Company* v. *Maclay* (1918, the requisitioning of ships by the government) are examples of his war decisions appearing in the *Law Reports*. The first and second of the above-mentioned judgments were affirmed both in the Court of Appeal and in the House of Lords.

Apart from presiding in 1916 over a committee to inquire into allegations as to the inefficiency of the aeroplanes supplied to the Royal Flying Corps and into reports on the administration and command of that body, Bailhache did no public work of the extra-judicial kind. As a criminal judge he was less successful than when he was dealing with civil causes. He saw no reason why swift and businesslike methods should be confined to the Commercial Court. He sometimes tried a prisoner as if he were hearing a commercial summons: and he was known to ask counsel for the defence whether there was really any answer to the charge against his client. His direction to the jury in a murder case, *Director of Public Prosecutions* v. *Beard* (1920), as to the effect of drunkenness upon criminal responsibility, led to the grant of the attorney-general's *fiat* for an appeal to the House of Lords. Bailhache had told the jury that if the accused man was so drunk that he did not know what he was doing, or did not know that he was doing wrong, the defence of drunkenness succeeded to the extent of reducing the crime to manslaughter. It was held that although the judge had been wrong in applying the test of insanity to a case of drunkenness, there had been no misdirection of the jury. The conviction for murder was accordingly upheld, with an intimation that the death sentence would not be carried out.

Greatly disliking pomp of any kind, Bailhache was unconventional in his ways. A pipe was his constant companion, and he smoked it even on occasions of ceremony, not excepting the assize dinner at Bishopthorpe and the Mansion House banquet to the judges. He was a strict teetotaller. His sudden death, which took place at Aldeburgh 8 September 1924, was due to cerebral haemorrhage. Bailhache married in 1881 Fanny Elizabeth, daughter of Herman Liebstein, a member of the Chancery bar, and had a son and two daughters.

[*The Times*, 9 September 1924; *Law Journal*, 13 September 1924; personal knowledge.]

T. Mathew.

BALFOUR, ARTHUR JAMES, first Earl of Balfour (1848–1930), philosopher and statesman, was born at Whittinghame (now Whittingehame), East Lothian, 25 July 1848, the eldest son and fourth child of James Maitland Balfour, of Whittinghame, by his wife, Lady Blanche Mary Harriet, second daughter of James Brownlow William Gascoyne-Cecil, second Marquess of Salisbury. His paternal grandfather, James Balfour, younger son of John Balfour, of Balbirnie, after making a fortune as a contractor in India, had purchased the Whittinghame estate; and this passed in due course to his father, James Maitland Balfour, a country gentleman, sometime chairman of the North British Railway, and a member of parliament for Haddington district 1841–1847, but a man of no great mark. Through his paternal grandmother, Lady Eleanor, daughter of James Maitland, eighth Earl of Lauderdale [q.v.], he was descended from William Maitland, of Lethington [q.v.]; from his mother he inherited the blood of William Cecil, Lord Burghley [q.v.]; but, while these sixteenth-century sources of political ability deserve mention, it might be as difficult to trace any resemblance between his character and that of either of those statesmen as between his career and one or other of theirs.

By common consent his mother's influence, accentuated as it may have been by his father's premature death in 1856, was supreme in Balfour's early education, for the boy was beyond doubt deeply impressed by a personality at once profoundly religious and brilliantly amusing. Handicapped by short sight and delicate health, he owed less perhaps to Eton, where nevertheless he came under the influence of William Johnson (Cory) [q.v.], or even to Cambridge, where from 1866 to 1869 he was a fellow-commoner of Trinity College, than to a home circle of which the indigenous distinction, so to speak, of his brothers and sister, Gerald, the scholar and statesman, Frank, the biologist [see Balfour, Francis Maitland], and Eleanor (Mrs. Sidgwick), subsequently principal of Newnham College, was presently increased by that of his brothers-in-law, Henry Sidgwick [q.v.], the moral philosopher, and John, third Lord Rayleigh [q.v.], the physicist. In such company Balfour, who secured no more at the university than a second in the moral sciences tripos, shone indeed, but as no bright particular star; and many who saw the modesty of his first beginnings failed wholly to foresee the brilliancy of his final ends. His mind was perhaps too independent for a curriculum; and he was in any case always more interested in finding truth for himself than in learning what others had supposed it to be. 'For the history of speculation', he declares, 'I cared not a jot. Dead systems seemed to me of no more interest than abandoned fashions. My business was with the groundwork of living beliefs; in particular with the goodness of that scientific knowledge whose recent developments had so profoundly moved mankind' [*Theism and Humanism*, p. 138]. It followed that his writings showed something less of contact with the old masters and something more of conflict with current theories than was consistent perhaps with the most enduring work. If he thought in any man's tradition, it was in that of Berkeley, of whom he published a study (published originally in the *National Review*, March–April 1883, reprinted in *Essays and Addresses*), and whose lucid style and exquisite dialectic seems to anticipate his own. In the harmonies of his thought and language may be caught, indeed, an echo of the eighteenth century, as was proper enough in one whose considered preference [see his essay 'The Nineteenth Century' in *Essays and Addresses*, 1905, pp. 315 ff.] was for that epoch and whose love of music was stimulated to the uttermost by the oratorios of Handel, a composer possessed, so he maintains in one of his most graceful essays, of 'a more copious, fluent and delightful gift of melody' than any other [*ibid.* p. 169]. His natural taste was, in truth, for a time characterized by 'unity and finish'; and he clung to its legacy, finding Scott and Jane Austen, Coleridge and Wordsworth, Keats and Shelley to be better companions than authors of more recent repute—than Dickens and Thackeray, than Carlyle with his 'windy prophesyings' or Mill with his 'thin lucidity'. What, intellectually, he was not, was a mid-Victorian. No child of the late 'forties more instinctively reverted to the serene mentality of an earlier period; no man of the early 'seventies prepared himself with less effort to assimilate the scientific knowledge of a later one. He was all his life intermittently concerned to formulate the rational grounds of faith in such a manner as to bring metaphysics back into the scales of common thought and so to recover for physics its proper weight, and no more, in the balances. Two things helped him in this endeavour—a mind untiringly interested in scientific development, of which he kept abreast not by experiment but by reading, discussion, and inquiry, and a style, never trite or precious, but illustrating with no little charm and liveliness the virtue of putting the right word in the right place, and rising in such a passage as that upon the prospect of man in a purely physical universe to an impressive and moving eloquence. The passage mentioned shows, indeed, in the opinion of competent judges, his literary power at its highest, and as such merits quotation here:

'We survey the past,' he wrote, 'and see that its history is of blood and tears, of helpless blundering, of wild revolt, of stupid acquiescence, of empty aspirations. We sound the future, and learn that after a period, long compared with the individual life, but short indeed compared with the divisions of time open to our investigation, the energies of our system will decay, the glory of the sun will be dimmed and the earth, tideless and inert, will no longer tolerate the race which has for a moment disturbed its solitude. Man will go down into the pit, and all his thoughts will perish. . . . Matter will know itself no longer. Imperishable monuments and immortal deeds, death itself, and love stronger than death, will be as though they had never been. Nor will anything that *is* be better or be worse for all that the labour, genius, devotion and suffering of man have striven through countless generations to effect.' [*Foundations of Belief*, pt. I, c. 1.]

For all the patent grace and power of such digressions Balfour's real achievement as a metaphysician is not easy to determine, and none the more that his fame as a statesman tended to advertise his work with the vulgar and to depreciate it with the elect. The former took him at his word and proclaimed him without further ado a philosopher; the latter dismissed him without too much consideration as an amateur. His strong conflict was with naturalism; his contention, that the foundations of natural science are no firmer than those of theology, and even perhaps not so firm; his thesis, that Theism clears, instead of confusing counsel. He pushed home these opinions with much ingenuity and without any undue apparatus of technical phraseology; yet the public was long in understanding him. The title of his earliest book—*A Defence of Philosophic Doubt* (1879)—suggested to those who had not assimilated its contents that he was a philosophic doubter; and, though this was far from being the fact, it was nevertheless true that the position there taken up as regards theology fell something short of that adopted later in his *Foundations of Belief* (1895) and his Gifford lectures on Theism (1915 and 1922–3).

Very briefly Balfour's argument was this. The theory of knowledge underlying the scepticism of science in regard to religion should in any dispassionate mind produce a similar scepticism as regards science itself. By its attacks upon religion the scientific mind has in fact manufactured a boomerang; and this point was brought out with all Balfour's dialectical ability. It was, however, as he maintained in a reply to his critics delivered near the end of his life before the British Academy [see *Proceedings* of the British Academy, 9 December 1925], a complete misconception of his meaning to suppose that he had tried to destroy rational values by insinuating philosophic doubts. The aim of his criticism was quite other. 'The sceptic says', he urged, 'that, as we can prove nothing, we may believe anything. I say that, as we believe a great deal and intend to go on believing it, we should be well advised to discover on what assumption we may believe it most reasonably.'

'All men, including all philosophers, are', Balfour maintained, 'believers'; and his aim was fearlessly to recognize that all constructive thought rests upon a foundation of faith and is not on that account insecure. A body of beliefs, he pointed out, that can neither be proved nor ignored nor rejected forms the pre-supposition of what is termed scientific knowledge—the belief, for example, in the existence of others as distinct from ourselves, in our power to communicate with them, in our mental resemblance to them, in our occupation of the same physical universe with them, and so forth. Our awareness of other minds, he argued by way of illustration, is not direct but dependent upon observation of or conjecture about their associated bodies. Though 'inevitable' it is not 'self-evident', is entangled with admissions of faith and theories of knowledge, and lies beyond the sphere of intuitive assurance. Such perceptions, for the rest, are 'no trustworthy purveyors of information about the character of physical reality'. They cannot be treated as a product of evolution, and, if we are to suppose our beliefs upon the way to truth, we are obliged to assume 'a Power transcending the physical universe'. Carrying the attack upon philosophic naturalism into its citadel, Balfour drove home the point that, if naturalism were true, then 'all the convictions we entertain and all the reasoning by which they are supported must be completely dependent on the preterrestrial distribution of electric charges—entities which are guided by nothing more intelligent than the blind forces of attraction or repulsion and do nothing more purposeful than radiate energy at random through the depths of space'. 'Theories', he submitted, 'which give this account of their origin are well on the way to suicide.' Only let the same rights be conceded by science to the values of goodness and beauty that it is accustomed and compelled to claim for truth, and, not only is the case for naturalism gone, but the whole sphere of human experience is welded into a more coherent whole.

Such then was the line of argument, such the pathway of thought that Balfour, had he been left to make a life for himself, would, according to his own belief, have pursued and elaborated. Even as things turned out, his metaphysic possesses for the intellectual development of his age something of the value of a bee-line. Physical science was in fact moving towards a position scarcely distinguishable from philosophic doubt in respect of its theory of knowledge, though neither with his speed nor by his methods. And psychology was presently to sharpen the point of his criticism by raising doubts whether reason can by any rational process clear itself from the suspicion of springing in the last resort from unreasoning impulse. It deserves perhaps to be added that the value of Balfour's apologetic did not go without recognition in the English Church. 'As Lord Balfour argues in his Gifford Lectures,' observes Dr. Inge, 'what makes Naturalism untenable is that the higher values cannot be maintained in a naturalistic setting. . . . This is the chief argument in his book, and I think it is valid' [W. R. Inge, *God and the Astronomers*, p. 230].

The influence that diverted Balfour's energies from philosophy to politics was that of his uncle. At the suggestion of Lord Salisbury [the third Marquess, q.v.] he stood for the borough of Hertford and in 1874 entered parliament as a supporter of Disraeli's last administration. So far as the subtlety and versatility of his mind allowed of a party label, he was a conservative, as well by choice as by tradition. 'Conservative prejudices', he is reported to have said to Alfred Lyttelton, the best-loved of his men friends, 'are rooted in a great past and Liberal ones planted in an imaginary future.' His political talent, however, was of slow growth. His first election-address was without facility and his first parliamentary speech long in coming. He felt diffident and unambitious. But also a far-reaching shadow fell at this time across his path.

In the opening of the year 1875 occurred the death of Miss May Lyttelton, the sister of the remarkable band of brothers who made in their time the fame of their family. Only a month or so earlier Balfour after no little delay had, if not formally, at least in effect, become engaged to her; and this tragic sequel to a reciprocated affection, though it did not absolutely close the door on thoughts of marriage, left him half-hearted or hesitating; and in the event he remained a bachelor.

It was so often discussed, even by some who were well acquainted with him, whether, behind Balfour's easy charm of manner and perfect appearance of interest, there lay any great strength of human feeling, that a word on this point seems to be required. Those who knew him best knew best how deeply he could be moved and how inexhaustible could be his solicitude and his sympathy. A dread, rather than a defect of emotion, explains some part of what was said to the contrary; natural reserve, coupled with a profound dislike of any sort of insincerity in matters of the deepest moment, much of the rest. Yet it may be true to add that in his general attitude towards human life and its conditions there was something less both of passion and compassion than might have been looked for in a man of such fine perception and delicate discernment. 'Philosophy can clip an angel's wings', and seldom if ever in his essays or his speeches does he indicate sensibility to the tears of things or lend words to the stammering tongue of humanity. This limitation, whatever its cause, goes some way to explain why, for all his long lifetime of service, his personality never quite captured the public imagination. His appeal was essentially to the few and not the many, to the salon and to the senate rather than to the street: and on more than one critical occasion he showed a lack of what goes by the name of the 'common touch'.

Though his abilities were such as to have made his reputation in any but a jacobinical society, it must be reckoned a circumstance very favourable to Balfour's career that the public life of the country at the time of his entry into politics was still strongly coloured by aristocratic influences. The landed aristocracy among whom his inheritance placed him had not yet lost its consequence, and the intellectual aristocracy towards which his talents drew him was still gaining in power. But if he found a congenial society, he as certainly founded, though without conscious effort, a congenial clique. The memory of the 'Souls' is intimately associated with his name. They formed a coterie for which it might be difficult to find a parallel in English history. Free from any disastrous exclusiveness either social or conversational, interested in really interesting things, alive to the claims of art and not dead to those of morals, blending politics with fashion and fashion with philanthropy, they contrived, without incurring too much ridicule, to sacrifice to Beauty, Truth, and Goodness against a background of west-end dinner-parties and great English country-houses. Of this circle of clever men and often brilliant and beautiful women Balfour seemed made to be the *arbiter elegantiarum*. The intellectual grace of his appearance, the charm of his manner, the play of his mind, the liberality of his views, the lightness of his touch, all contributed to make him the cynosure of a set whose day-dreams of chivalry and fair women found some sort of expression in the collection of Burne-Jones's paintings that he hung in his London house; whilst his own shattered romance, impoverishing though some felt it to have been to the full development of his character, left him the freer to form and cultivate those great friendships with women which claim some mention in any sketch of his life. Lady Oxford, herself an early friend, has picked out three of these for special notice—those with (Mary) Lady Wemyss, Lady Desborough, and (Alice) Lady Salisbury—and the justice of this choice will be generally agreed to.

An incomparable guest in many well-known houses, an engaging host in his own, a much-prized member of many eminent institutions and learned societies; president of the British Association (1904), of the British Academy (from 1921), of the Psychical Research Society, of the Synthetic Society, and, it might even be claimed, potentially of the Royal Society, since in 1920 he was approached, though without success, on the subject; honorary fellow of his college; chancellor of Cambridge (1919) and Edinburgh (1891) universities; foreign member of the French Academy; Romanes lecturer at Oxford; Gifford lecturer; member of the Order of Merit, and wherever he was, an outstanding figure, exceptionally gifted both as talker and listener, in the conversation piece, Balfour enjoyed a social prestige perhaps unequalled by any statesman since the days of Fox. Of all the eminent men of his day he was possibly the one whom the majority of cultivated people would have preferred to meet and whose opinion in difficult issues they would have been inclined to follow. His indirect influence, imponderable though it is, upon the 'social tissue' of his time was thus certainly large; and the depth of his interests was shown in the breadth of his hospitalities. The doors of Whittingehame, where autumn after autumn he was accustomed to entertain a large family circle with the aid of his devoted sister, Miss Alice Balfour, were thrown open to an assortment of visitors as varied as Bergson, the philosopher, Wilfrid Ward, the Catholic apologist, and Mr. and Mrs. Sidney Webb, the Fabian socialists; whilst with some of his direct opponents in parliament—with Asquith, with Haldane, and with Morley—his relations approximated to friendship.

A lively interest in games and music added pleasing traits to a figure in every aspect possessing the charm of the amateur and eluding the provincialism of the expert; and the great worlds of learning and of leisure marked with equal satisfaction the versatile politician listening rapt to an oratorio of Handel, or celebrating victory, not undemonstratively, at the close of an Eton-and-Harrow cricket match. For the rest, golf and lawn-tennis, which he continued to play almost to the close of his life, rounded off the tale of Balfour's recreations.

There can be little doubt that the exceptional position which he occupied in the intellectual and social life of his time tended on the whole to fortify Balfour's influence in politics; and the growth of the one needs to be remembered in considering the advance of the other, with which this account will now be exclusively concerned. In the course of a six-months' tour round the world with her brother, Spencer, after Miss Lyttelton's death, Balfour visited the United States, Australia, and New Zealand. His parliamentary career opened with his return. In 1876—on 10 August—picking his occasion so as to test his powers before the smallest possible audience, he made his maiden speech on the subject of Indian currency with the House in committee. In 1877 he recommended the grant of university degrees to women. In 1878 he produced his first attempt at legislation by the introduction of a Burials Bill which, however, was 'talked out'. It is, perhaps, of more consequence that in this year he became Salisbury's parliamentary private secretary and in that capacity attended the Congress of Berlin (June–July 1878). It was, however, the conservative disaster at the general election of March 1880 that first brought him into notice. He had retained his seat at Hertford, though only by a small majority, and in the new parliament became associated with the meteoric 'Fourth Party', sometimes described, but not altogether correctly, as 'a party of four', since Balfour's real allegiance remained with his uncle, who presently succeeded Beaconsfield in the conservative leadership.

The Irish question was at this time fast becoming the central issue in politics; and on 16 May 1882 Balfour spoke with telling effect on the so-called Kilmainham Treaty, stigmatizing it, to Gladstone's indignation, as 'an infamy'. Though his speaking lacked fluency, his power of argument made from that date a growing impression. His speech in favour of a conservative amendment requiring a two-thirds majority before the new expedient of the closure could be employed was particularly remarked, and the more that it brought him into conflict with Lord Randolph Churchill, the Fourth Party leader. A deeper rift, however, between these associates presently appeared. The interregnum as regards leadership had plainly to be terminated if the conservatives were to regain power. Churchill saw this, as he also saw that power itself was destined to pass from parliament to the constituencies; and, in the guise of the champion of 'Tory-Democracy', he attempted to transfer the seat of party sovereignty from the Central Committee, of which Salisbury defended the traditional rights, to the National Union of Conservative Associations. During the struggle Balfour, as the friend of one protagonist and the nephew of the other, occupied a mediatorial position, not without adding to his own consequence in conservative counsels; and this consequence was further augmented by the fact that the motion which brought about the downfall of Gladstone's administration was planned in his house, no. 4 Carlton Gardens (June 1885). In the formation of the so-called 'ministry of Caretakers' which followed, he seems to have given further assistance in dealing with Churchill, who went to the India Office, whilst he himself became president of the Local Government Board, an appointment that he filled for six months without any particular distinction.

At the ensuing general election (December 1885) Balfour was returned in East Manchester, for which constituency he sat continuously until 1906. The liberals, however, were in general victorious. Gladstone, for reasons tactically prudent, if morally questionable, had made no clear declaration of policy about Ireland before the polling, and a short period of confusion, during which Balfour as his uncle's nephew became the recipient of confidences both from Gladstone and Joseph Chamberlain [q.v.], resulted. The first Home Rule Bill was, however, eventually introduced in April 1886 only to be rejected by the House of Commons in June. A general election followed; and a clear majority against Home Rule was returned, though no majority was secured by any single party. In the ensuing conservative administration, which depended upon liberal-unionist support, Balfour filled the recently created post of secretary for Scotland. The crofters' agitation against rent was at that time at its height. He dealt firmly and effectively with the Scottish Land League which was active in Skye and elsewhere; the secret of his success, if there was one, lying in his resolve to recover for the law its lost prestige. In November 1886 he was given Cabinet rank, and in March 1887 he was offered the Irish chief-secretaryship. He hesitated, consulted Sir William Jenner about his health, which was passed as sufficient, and finally accepted. The country saw with something like stupefaction the appointment of the young dilettante to what was at the moment perhaps the most important, certainly the most anxious office in the administration. Salisbury knew, however, very well what he was about.

The celebrated Irish 'plan of campaign' for the reduction of rents by the intimidation of landlords had at this juncture already been launched, and an Irish Crimes Bill, to run for a term of unlimited duration, had been drafted in reply (March 1887). Balfour, whilst yielding to liberal sentiment by abandoning the proposed removal to England of the venue of trials by jury, took power to 'proclaim', or in other words to suppress, the National League in any district where he thought this desirable, and made use of these powers in August 1887. But the real tug-of-war came in September with the prosecution, under the Crimes Act, of William O'Brien [q.v.]. Violence was met with force; and the sanguinary result, though only two rioters appear to have been killed, won for the Irish chief secretary the title of 'Bloody Balfour'.

The 'resolute government' which was the foundation of Lord Salisbury's Irish policy achieved its purpose; and the Crimes Act was eventually suspended in every district of Ireland. Constructive measures were not, however, wanting. A Light Railways Act was passed with especial reference to the west of Ireland (1889). A Congested Districts Board was set up to deal with the difficulties of the poorer parts of the country (1890). A Land Purchase Act (1891) attempted to encourage peasant proprietorship and to reduce the scandal, by no one resented more deeply than by Balfour, of the unjust or absentee landlord. And a Catholic college, endowed by the state except only in respect of the teaching of dogmatic theology, would, but for the opposition that it aroused in different quarters, have formed another feature of Balfour's administration. His personal triumph was indubitable. He had put his views into effect in spite of the resistance of what at the end of his life he declared to have been 'in some respects the most brilliant parliamentary party which the British system of representative government has ever produced' [*Chapters of Autobiography*, p. 191]. But if the tactics and eloquence of the Irish were well calculated to bring out Balfour's political ability, their 'miscellaneous scattering of violent adjectives', as Lady Oxford has called it [*More Memories*, p. 99], was not less well calculated to make his political fortune. The House admired the fine courage, the imperturbable temper, the exquisite irony which he opposed to the terrorism and invective of his opponents; and upon the death of Mr. W. H. Smith in October 1891 the leadership in the Commons, with the office of first lord of the Treasury, fell to him almost as a matter of course. Mr. Goschen was the only possible alternative, but for various reasons not an acceptable one. An interesting situation had now arisen with uncle and nephew respectively in command of the conservative forces in their different Houses; and it was none the less interesting that nothing like it had occurred, unless in the case of Pelham and Newcastle, since, under another queen, Burghley and Cecil had held the chief offices of state. The combination worked well and was not without its bearing upon the fact that the opening of the twentieth century saw the prime minister still a member of the House of Lords.

Balfour, however, was not at his best in the early days of his leadership. He gave the impression of being a less hard worker than his immediate predecessor; and he certainly did not think more about politics outside working hours than he must. But, if sometimes a hesitating speaker, he showed himself no less a master of debate—as distinct, that is, from eloquence,—in a House which still contained Gladstone, than a master of the subject which now had Gladstone's and indeed all men's attention. It is, of course, impossible to trace in detail his tactical moves in the great parliamentary game. It must suffice to say that at the general election of July 1892, when the Gladstonians were returned to power, Balfour kept his seat by a reduced majority; that, after a period of opposition, during which Gladstone's second Home Rule Bill was defeated in the Lords, the unionists came back in July 1895 with a majority of over 150; and that in the coalition government which followed, Balfour again became first lord of the Treasury with the leadership in the Commons. His work in this capacity was heavy, various, and of varying merit. In 1896 he piloted into port an Irish Land Bill and an Agricultural Derating Bill, but the Education Bill of that year suffered shipwreck, not without reflecting upon his political management nor, it might be added, without causing him to reflect upon the educational complexities that had led to his failure. In 1897 a Workmen's Compensation Act and in 1898 an Irish County Councils Act were the principal features of unionist policy. Then in October 1899 came the Boer War.

In regard to South African affairs Balfour showed in private some disposition to sympathize with the Jameson Raid (December 1895), to criticize the handling by Mr. Chamberlain of the diplomatic negotiations which preceded the outbreak of war, and to condemn Sir Redvers Buller's conduct of the military operations. These views naturally found no public utterance; and indeed his loyalty to Chamberlain at this time was the making of their subsequent good relations. His individual contribution to the prosecution of hostilities must be sought in his serenity and decision in council—a serenity and decision of particular value during the crisis, which eventuated in the dispatch of Lord Roberts to take over the supreme command (December 1899). On the platform, however, Balfour, failing not for the last time to catch the public mood, did himself less than justice; and to the anxious eyes of the crowd his nonchalance looked too much like flippancy. Yet upon no man's mind was the great lesson of that war more deeply impressed; and a searching and continuous attention to the problem of military efficiency forms thenceforward a marked feature of his political activity.

At the so-called 'khaki' election of October 1900, which resulted in the return of the unionists with a slightly reduced but still very powerful majority, Balfour nearly trebled his own figures at East Manchester. He was nearing the apex of his fortunes, and when, in July 1902, after the conclusion of peace, Salisbury resigned the premiership, the succession fell to him with the full assent of the Duke of Devonshire and of Chamberlain. The recognition of his qualities was ample; yet his position from the first was as much weaker than his uncle's as a majority inherited is a worse title to power than a majority newly won at the polls. Moreover, even as Balfour came into office, the seeds of his difficulties were being sown. The Imperial Conference, that year assembled, passed a resolution in favour of granting preferential duties to the Colonies; and Chamberlain, before he left for a visit to South Africa at the close of the year, sought a Cabinet decision on the issue. The policy agreed upon was to maintain the existing shilling duty upon corn but to remit it in respect of the Empire. Mr. C. T. (afterwards Lord) Ritchie [q.v.], however, whom Balfour had made his chancellor of the Exchequer, was temperamentally antipathetic to his chief and dogmatically attached to free trade. His budget speech (23 April 1903) revealed his sentiments; and his budget proposals repealed the corn-duty. Feeling rose quickly. Balfour tried to allay it by suggesting that the duty might be reimposed as part of some larger policy. But Chamberlain, though not apparently with deliberate purpose, brought the issue to a head by a speech at Birmingham on 15 May; and the battle was joined between the tariff reform and free trade sections of the unionist party. In these circumstances Balfour's attitude was governed by two considerations, the one, to keep the party together, and the other, to secure what he defined as 'liberty of fiscal negotiation'. As his memorandum on the subject shows, he believed that retaliatory duties against the foreigner would promote freedom of trade; and for the imposition of these he held the country to be already prepared. Before, however, the grant of preferential treatment to the Colonies, involving as it must some taxation of food, was made, he considered that a period of propaganda was required; and he attempted, therefore, to treat 'preference' as for the time outside the sphere of practical politics.

These views were not deficient in lucidity; nor was Balfour lacking in firmness in his handling of the situation. Reluctantly convinced, however, by the pressure put upon him that tariff reform must be withdrawn from the category of open questions, he insisted still that his own policy as regards 'preference' must prevail amongst the members of his administration. Chamberlain made no complaint of this procedure but was not himself more willing to forgo the advocacy of preferential tariffs than were Ritchie, Lord George Hamilton, and Lord Balfour of Burleigh to abandon their opposition to retaliatory duties. The disruption of the Cabinet became, therefore, inevitable; and Balfour determined that neither body of dissentients from his own views should gain any advantage from it. But, whilst parting with the extremists, he continued to do his utmost to minimize the party cleavage. He attempted, and for a short time successfully, to retain the Duke of Devonshire, a free-trader; and on the other hand, whilst accepting Joseph Chamberlain's resignation, he made it clear to him that he intended Austen Chamberlain to be Ritchie's successor at the Exchequer. Then, on 14 September, at a meeting of the Cabinet, at which his memorandum *Economic Notes on Insular Free-Trade* (subsequently published) formed the chief item on the agenda, he—in Devonshire's phrase—'summarily dismissed' Ritchie and Balfour of Burleigh. To his regret a speech of his at Sheffield (1 October) caused Devonshire's resignation to follow.

Balfour's administration now entered upon its most difficult phase. The party friction, adversely affected by his own unfortunate, though unavoidable, absence from the debate on the royal address in February 1904, developed rapidly; and the division-lists discovered a wide rift in the unionist ranks. He attempted to mark time, going only so far in the October of that year as to say that, if returned to power, he would summon a colonial conference of which the recommendations were only to be adopted if approved at another election. But, if Balfour had the caution of Fabius Cunctator, Chamberlain had all the energy of an old man in a hurry; and the nation watched with growing impatience the two years' delay in giving battle.

Balfour's procrastination was doubtless due in part to his perception that there were other things besides tariffs to be considered. His administration was, in fact, making its mark both in domestic and foreign policy to a degree but little observed; and he was anxious, so far as possible, to consolidate its achievements. In the military reconstruction which the lessons of the South African War had rendered necessary, he had interested himself, as well in regard to general matters, as more particularly in regard to the rearming of the field artillery with the eighteen-pounder gun (December 1904) and the formation of the Committee of Imperial Defence (December 1902–March 1903), of which he gave some account in speeches at Liverpool (13 February) and in the House of Commons (5 March). Both these preoccupations found full justification a decade later; and the Committee, providing as it does for a consultative, non-party council of experts and statesmen assisted by a secretarial staff, has long taken its place amongst British political institutions. Its fortunes, however, like those of the gun, were none too well assured even so late as the date of Balfour's resignation in 1905. Evolved from the old Defence Committee of the Cabinet and entrusted with the continuous survey of defensive problems of a mixed political, military, and naval nature, it must always be reckoned a remarkable proof of his patriotic foresight. For the first time in history the leaders of rival political parties were enabled to associate in the work of public defence without the difficulties of public debate or the obscurities of private conference.

The liquidation of the South African War formed another of Balfour's anxieties. Whilst the situation there, as the liberals saw, eventually demanded the bold generosity of a grant of self-government—a grant which, when the time for it came, he made the mistake of opposing with vigour—the introduction of Chinese labour on the Rand, unavoidable though it seems to have been in the actual circumstances, stood in some need of defence against doctrinaire denunciation. Again, in the matter of education the Bill, which Balfour had introduced in March 1902 and carried largely by his own efforts to the statute book against a great clamour of opposition, led by Mr. Lloyd George within and by Dr. John Clifford [q.v.] without the House, required the undenominational criticism of time to establish its merits. With the possible exception of the Licensing Act of 1904, into which also he put much personal work with a view to securing both the reduction of licences and the equitable compensation of publicans, it was perhaps the most important piece of legislation that Balfour was ever directly concerned with; and its provisions, controversial as they appeared to be at the date of their enactment, have survived, broadly speaking, a quarter of a century of widespread change. Conceived in conjunction with Sir Robert Morant [q.v.] and designed to secure to every parent, so far as possible, the kind of religious teaching he desired for his child, the new settlement provided rate-aid for voluntary schools, whilst substituting a committee of the county council for the former school board as the local education authority. Though the actual issue has largely lost interest, Balfour's defence of his action, published among his *Essays and Addresses* under the title of 'Dr. Clifford on Religious Education', may still be read with pleasure. It is a small masterpiece of very delicate and finished irony, and shows, perhaps better than anything else that he wrote, what he was capable of in this vein.

It was, however, in regard to foreign policy that Balfour most feared a change of government. His experience of foreign affairs dated back to the days when his uncle during illness or absence would entrust him with their temporary conduct. The inception of the Franco-British *entente*, which followed quickly upon Salisbury's retirement, represented, however, a striking departure in policy from nineteenth-century tradition. Balfour and the foreign secretary, Lord Lansdowne [q.v.], appear, it is true, to have envisaged the diplomatic understanding with France rather as a method of settling old disputes than of providing new defences; and it was only after they had left office that military conversations between the Powers concerned were formally initiated. The fact remains that it was Balfour's administration which for better or worse abandoned the time-honoured plan of an England holding the diplomatic balances in Europe by virtue of sea power for that of an England with its weight, both naval and military, thrown into one of the scales.

A memorandum of Balfour's, furnished at Mr. Winston Churchill's request to Sir Edward Grey in 1913, shows, however, that he fully realized the dangers involved in the policy of an *entente*, and would have preferred a defensive alliance governed by the principle that the fulfilment of its pledges could not be claimed unless the party claiming were ready to submit a case for arbitration. This preference for clear rather than obscure commitments was exemplified in Balfour's treatment of the Far-Eastern alliance with Japan which he had inherited and was resolved, if possible, to renew before quitting office. The outbreak of war between Russia and Japan in 1904 merely intensified his purpose, since he wished to demonstrate Great Britain's fidelity as an ally whilst the outcome was still uncertain. Negotiations for the renewal of the Anglo-Japanese Agreement of 1902 were therefore initiated in the beginning of 1905 and carried to a successful conclusion in the following summer. Any project for a better understanding between Britain and Russia became dormant in these circumstances. The countries were, in fact, in consequence of the Dogger Bank incident, within an ace of war in October 1904. Balfour's private correspondence with Lansdowne indicates, moreover, a grave suspicion of Russian designs in India and an almost uncanny intuition of such a deal between Russia and Austria in the Near East as was later concluded at Buchlau (1908). His personal orientation, in the strict sense of that word, was therefore only towards Japan, whilst his occidentation, if the word may be allowed, was as certainly towards the United States. He was able before the end of his life to give effect to both these feelings in the Washington Naval Agreement of 1921, though the resulting collapse of the Anglo-Japanese alliance showed clearly enough that it was not possible for England, at any rate at that time, to look both to the East and to the West.

As the year 1905 drew to a close, it became increasingly obvious that the tale of Balfour's administration was told and that the nation had tired of the telling. By November, in default of a fiscal truce within the party, he was ready to make an end, and, after considering the respective merits of dissolution and resignation, elected for the latter. On 4 December he resigned the premiership—an office for which he had provided a constitutional recognition and official precedence previously unknown. For three years and a half he had served as the prime minister of a sovereign whose great qualities were too different from his own to make close sympathy or understanding easy.

The storm now fell in full strength upon a minister whose record in regard to national defence was little known, in regard to education widely resented, and in regard to foreign policy imperfectly understood. Even amongst his supporters Balfour's governing resolve to avoid the mistake of Peel and to maintain at all costs the unity of his party was taken for evidence of vacillation. Two incidents had further accentuated the general discontent with his administration. His imprudent extension of the term of office in India of Lord Curzon [q.v.] eventuated in an unseemly dispute between the viceroy and Lord Kitchener [q.v.]; and his reluctant assent to George Wyndham's wish to have Sir Antony (afterwards Lord) Macdonnell [q.v.] appointed as under-secretary in Ireland resulted, unfairly enough, in his being himself charged with deserting a friend.

In the general election of January 1906 the conservative disaster at the polls was complete. Balfour himself was defeated at East Manchester by nearly 2,000 votes; and his following in the House was reduced to a very small remnant. A safe seat, however, was offered him as member for the City of London, and on 12 March he returned to the House, where in spite of the historic attempt of the new prime minister (Sir H. Campbell-Bannerman) to discredit him ('enough of this foolery') his ascendancy in debate was quickly regained. An exchange of letters with Chamberlain reaffirmed fiscal change as the first plank in the unionist platform, but into a detailed programme of economic policy Balfour wisely refused to be drawn. He recognized in the increased representation of labour in parliament the advent of a new era; and he saw the supreme business of his party as that of enabling the ship of state to ride the coming storm. Whilst conservative dissatisfaction with his leadership culminated in the cry that 'Balfour must go', that leadership was directed towards the preservation of a common front in both Houses against legislation calculated, as he saw, to force the question of the House of Lords into the forefront of the battle. He is thus to be found putting up a good fight in the Commons against the Education Bill of 1906, the Licensing Bill of 1908, and the budget of 1909, holding as he did that the rights of parents in regard to religion were attacked by the first, the rights of property by the second, and the rights of the constitution, through the insertion of land valuation clauses in a Finance Bill, by the third. In due course he approved the rejection of the budget by the peers (November 1909) and defended their action as 'abundantly justified'.

The general election of January 1910 which followed, made the Irish nationalists masters of the situation. Resolutions, however, restricting the veto of the House of Lords so as to allow of the passage of a Home Rule Bill were only just carried and the delayed Finance Bill passed, when the death of King Edward VII in May 1910 changed the mood of the nation. The inception of a new reign invited a party truce; and a conference of party leaders met on 17 June and sat until 10 November. Of this conference Balfour was a leading member; and his ability made a deep impression even upon his opponents. The apparent issue upon which the negotiation broke down lay between the liberal plan of resorting to a general election in the event of an irreconcilable difference between the two Houses over constitutional questions and the conservative preference for a referendum. Balfour, however, would, it appears, have yielded the point, if all possible Home Rule bills, and not only the forthcoming one, had been placed within the scheduled category of constitutional measures compelling an appeal to the constituencies.

Towards the close of the conference and on Mr. Lloyd George's initiative, Balfour entered upon an informal, secret negotiation for a settlement of the outstanding political issues in the national interest by the formation of a coalition government. Whilst not altogether unsympathetic, Balfour, haunted as he was by the spectre of Peel, eventually refused to entertain a scheme involving so large a sacrifice of party principles and so great a breach of party ties. To the charge, subsequently brought against him by Mr. Lloyd George, of having made a great refusal he might, perhaps, have replied that he had avoided a great betrayal. A reference to the experienced judgement of Mr. Akers-Douglas had in fact confirmed his opinion that the project was not only impracticable but rendered impossible by the initial difficulty of forming a coalition ministry to put it into effect.

The constitutional battle was therefore resumed. In November 1910 the prime minister, Mr. Asquith, obtained from King George V a pledge to create a sufficiency of peers to carry the Parliament Bill in the event of a favourable response at the polls and, with this pledge in his pocket, appealed to the country. In Balfour's view no guarantee of the sort was constitutionally required until a constitutional crisis had actually arisen and unless the sovereign had no alternative ministry, and, when in July 1911 he learnt that the king's pledge had already been obtained, he summoned a 'shadow' cabinet to consider the situation. Some of his colleagues were for resistance to the Bill; others for surrender. The split spread to the party; and a 'die-hard' revolt was added to a tariff reform division.

Concerned with practical consequences and anxious always to save the Crown from criticism, Balfour had little sympathy with those who regarded the issue as one of high principle and were resolved to die fighting. As he saw things, their action was merely theatrical since they were powerless to stop the impending change in the status of the Upper House and could only aggravate its incidents. The 'die-hards' were, however, unconvinced and carried their opposition to the Bill to a division (10 August). Balfour suffered so keenly from this rejection of his advice as to feel that it put a term to his leadership. At Bad Gastein, which he visited in August, he reviewed the position; in September, upon his return to England, he discussed it with the party organizers; in October he took his decision; and in November he resigned.

The effect of this step was striking. Freed from the trammels of circumstance, his high character, his vast ability, his rare distinction quickly stood out; and as a statesman he now began to receive the recognition which had been refused him as a leader. It happened that the Irish question was once again in the centre of the political stage. There were none on either side of the House who could rival him in knowledge and experience of it, and there were few anywhere who understood so well as he how far beyond any liberal solution of the problem the passions, now fiercely clashing, had carried the issue. He did what he could in a crisis not of his making, recommending the division of Northern and Southern Ireland; emphasizing the view in his *Nationality and Home Rule* (1913) that the Irish national spirit would rest content with no half-measures of separation; advising the opposition not to incur responsibility, by any amendment of the government's amending Bill, for the delimitation at the eleventh hour of a boundary between North-East Ulster and the rest of Ireland; and even holding himself in readiness, should the king desire to take a last opportunity of testing English opinion, to resume office, with or without Lord Rosebery as his colleague, in a 'ministry of Caretakers'.

It was just at this juncture that the outbreak of the European War (28 July 1914) suppressed all smaller quarrels. Balfour turned his mind at once to the new issues. He gave his assurance of support to the bolder section of the Cabinet in the hour of decision, accepted, at the king's wish, when England became involved in the conflict, a seat on the committee of the Prince of Wales's Fund for the relief of distress; resumed, at the prime minister's request, membership of the Committee of Imperial Defence; and assisted in the preparation of plans for dealing with the civil population in the event of coastal raids. From November 1914 he attended the meetings of a 'war-council' or 'inner cabinet' convened by the prime minister at 10 Downing Street, thus involving himself in responsibilities scarcely compatible with the position of an ex-minister in opposition. This state of things was, however, of no long duration. Shortage of munitions and dissensions at the Admiralty led in May 1915 to the formation of a Coalition government, in which Balfour became first lord of the Admiralty, the only 'heavy administrative office', so he told the prime minister, for which he could usefully be responsible.

Mr. Lloyd George in his *War Memoirs* [vol. ii, p. 1017] has conveyed the impression that the minister whom he afterwards placed at the head of the Foreign Office was incompetent for the work of the Admiralty. This was not the opinion of those who saw Balfour there at close quarters. Behind characteristically indolent postures he brought to bear upon the issues submitted to him so penetrating a judgement that it was possible for the secretary at that time to the department to assert that 'at the Admiralty it was felt that, if Balfour personally did not favour any particular action or policy, there was no need for further inquiry'. His speech introducing the navy estimates (7 and 8 March 1916) showed according to the same authority 'as much knowledge of the important questions of naval administration as the speeches of any of his predecessors with more advantages on their side of time and political conditions'. It showed, too, incidentally and in reference to Mr. Churchill a mastery of debate and delicacy of sarcasm equal to anything he had displayed in his prime.

Balfour, in fact, though he attempted no departmental reorganization, believing as he did that the existing system worked well if wisely handled, dealt effectively in a series of board meetings with various matters of naval policy requiring regulation and decision, and quickly restored serenity to a department distracted by the differences between his predecessor, Mr. Churchill, and Lord Fisher [q.v.]. Two considerable events fell within his term of office—the withdrawal from Gallipoli, the wisdom of which he had doubted, and the battle of Jutland (31 May 1916). The former was faultlessly executed. The *communiqué* in which he announced the news of the latter drew, however, much criticism upon his department. Drawn up in his hand and but slightly modified after consultation with his naval advisers, it was dispatched, notwithstanding statements to the contrary, without reference to the secretary to the Admiralty or to Mr. Churchill, and gave the public, as he always maintained it should have done, the unvarnished truth, yet at the same time certainly disseminated a false impression of disaster that was only by degrees removed as the sufficiency of the naval success became plain. A lull followed the engagement, but the German submarine menace was none the less growing; and in November 1916 Balfour created a special department to deal with it. Both Mr. Asquith and Sir Edward Grey, however, were anxious for some change of personnel in the naval membership of the Admiralty Board, and before the fall of the first Coalition, Admiral Jellicoe had been appointed to succeed Sir Henry Jackson [q.v.] as first sea lord. Whether this new combination of talent would have resulted, as one well-qualified observer believed, in a more rapid suppression of the submarine attack cannot be determined, for the downfall of the Asquith administration was coincident with it.

Balfour had nothing to do with organizing the cabal which ousted Asquith from power, but he seems to have taken no exception to it, and his decision to give it countenance was momentous for England and, still more, for Europe. A certain modesty and moral simplicity characteristic of him were apparent in his conduct. In his view the sole question to be considered was how the War might be most efficiently carried on and, once he had satisfied himself that Mr. Lloyd George was of all men available the best qualified for the task, he was characteristically indifferent to all personal considerations, such as that minister's recent but unsuccessful attempt to remove him from the Admiralty. His assistance was undoubtedly essential to the formation of the new Coalition, for without it the administration must have lacked sufficient support in influential conservative quarters. In the new distribution of departments he was given the Foreign Office. His presence there had the greater consequence that, with the break-up of the Asquith government, British counsels had lost the diplomatic experience and moderation both of Lansdowne and of Grey.

The association between the new prime minister, Mr. Lloyd George, and the foreign secretary, which during the late crisis had issued in a marked personal sympathy, was as the meeting of two currents, one turgid and strong, the other refined to a crystal clarity. It was easy to see from the first that the prime minister had planned such a dyarchy in foreign affairs as had not previously been known to the constitution. An amateur foreign office, irreverently termed the 'garden-suburb', arose in the precincts of 10 Downing Street; and by this means Mr. Lloyd George exercised a direct as well as indirect and constitutional influence upon foreign affairs. Balfour's importance to the prime minister and ready access to his presence modified the immediate effect of such a system, but its ultimate consequences were apparent at the Peace Conference, where Balfour's position contrasted unfavourably with that of Castlereagh at Vienna or Salisbury at Berlin.

The change of government meanwhile afforded no spectacular successes. During 1917 the submarine trouble grew at sea, differences between the prime minister and the generals accentuated the difficulties of carrying on hostilities, and the land operations were overshadowed by the slaughter at Passchendaele (August). The entry of the United States into the War, which came early in the year, needed, however, only to be developed to make victory sure. Balfour, to his lasting distinction, seized a diplomatic opportunity which he of all men living was best qualified to use. On 14 April 1917, after ascertaining that his visit would be welcome to President Woodrow Wilson, he sailed for the United States at the head of a diplomatic mission. His enthusiasm for an understanding between the two Anglo-Saxon peoples put a spur to his tact and ability. He made good friends with Wilson, charmed the Americans generally by the grace of his manners, and delivered memorable speeches both before Congress and at Washington's grave. His diplomatic achievement was consummated by the intimation, unofficially conveyed to the president, of the existence of those secret treaties with Russia and Italy which ran counter to the principle of nationality and so to American policy. In brief his mission had secured a success which stood the Allies in good stead as American credit, shipping, and soldiers became increasingly needful, whilst on a longer view it seemed to have laid the foundation of just such a fusion of Anglo-Saxon sentiment as Balfour had long had at heart.

In foreign policy in general Balfour's achievement is less assured. Both the progress of the War and the versatile energy of the prime minister drove him continuously towards those very things which his memorandum for the Cabinet of 4 October 1916 (published in Lloyd George's *War Memoirs*, vol. ii, pp. 884–886) shows that he had wished to avoid, namely, the humiliation of Germany, the dissolution of the Dual Monarchy, and the peril of a pan-German state incorporating or seeking to incorporate a purely German Austria. A stronger diplomacy might perhaps have made more of the Austrian peace move (1917), a subtler one might perhaps have gauged the Bolshevist mentality better; and some uncertainty of aim may be inferred from the countenance, long unsuspected, which he gave to the publication, if not the contents, of the famous 'peace letter' of Lord Lansdowne [q.v.] of November 1917 by referring its writer to Lord Hardinge, at that time permanent under-secretary for foreign affairs. It might indeed be difficult to say whether his foreign policy was in the tradition of the old Europe or of a new order founded, at least in theory, upon nationality, democracy, a league of nations, and an open diplomacy. Salisbury's large wisdom and Mr. Lloyd George's vivacious versatility seemed to dispute possession of a mind constitutionally cool and unfailingly receptive.

One decisive move which he himself rated as his great achievement, did, however. characterize Balfour's tenure of the

Foreign Office. Ever since a conversation with Dr. Weizmann at Manchester during the throes of the general election of 1906, he had been keenly interested in Zionism; and intercourse with Mr. Justice Brandeis in America had strengthened his faith in its political value. In November 1917 he triumphed over opposition both within and without the Cabinet and issued the so-called Balfour Declaration in favour of a Jewish national home in Palestine. The project finally took shape at the Peace of Versailles. Under a British mandate from the League of Nations the Jews were established in the Holy Land on equal terms with the existing inhabitants, and, though Arab feeling was aroused to such a degree as to endanger Balfour's personal safety when he visited Damascus in 1925, the experiment proved so popular among the Jews that at the hour of his death Jewry mourned him with honours perhaps never before accorded to a Gentile.

'It was not so much the war as the peace that I have always dreaded,' Balfour told Lady Wemyss on the evening before he left for the Peace Conference at Paris in January 1919. The two English ministers were lodged in the Rue Nitot, the prime minister on the first, the foreign secretary on the second floor. During the inaugural period of the Conference the two ministers sat alike in the so-called 'council of ten', which contained both the heads and the foreign ministers of the five great, victorious delegations. This period, which lasted for a month from the middle of January 1919, closed with the temporary absence of President Wilson in America, Lloyd George in England, and Clemenceau in bed, and was followed by an interval of three weeks (16 February–8 March) during which Balfour dominated the situation. He altered it vastly for the better, so much so indeed that Clemenceau on recovery named him the Richelieu of the Congress. 'Whereas in the middle of February', remarks Mr. Churchill, 'the work of the Conference was drifting off almost uncontrollably into futility, all was now brought back in orderly fashion to the real' [W. S. Churchill, *The Aftermath*, vol. v, p. 190]. Its commissions, spurred on by this new pressure, had, in other words, got through their work and reported. On the return of Mr. Lloyd George, however, and in consequence of a leakage of information, a 'council of four' was superimposed, with the foreign secretary's full approval, upon the original council of ten. From that time Balfour, whilst as foreign minister he retained his seat on the latter (known thenceforward as the 'council of five') and both by reason of the proximity of his lodgings to those of the prime minister and his prominence on the British Empire Committee remained acquainted with the general course and conduct of the negotiations, no longer participated in the principal discussions and was not in every case made aware of impending decisions, even when of grave moment. The extent to which he thus abrogated his office may be inferred from a statement which he made towards the close of the Conference to his colleague, Lord Robert Cecil, to the effect that, not having been consulted on some point or another, he should not defend the Peace Treaty, which, he added, was not of his making. But even if this *obiter dictum* ought not to be pressed, though in fact it does not lack corroboration, as evidence of his secondary position, the extraordinary circumstance that the Foreign Office apparently worked on the assumption that a peace was to be negotiated, whereas in the event the terms intended for negotiation were dictated without serious discussion or amendment, would still indicate, conclusively enough, the limitations of his influence. To such a degree, then, but at such a price may Balfour's direct responsibility be reduced for a treaty which cannot readily be reconciled with the British tradition of 1814, the British purpose in 1914, the conditions of the Armistice, the aspirations of a League of Nations, or his own, in general, conciliatory dispositions. Had he, however, been in a position to insist upon the conclusion which he desired, of a preliminary agreement imposing a naval and military, and perhaps outlining a territorial, settlement, and had he also concerned himself more with the economic and financial aspects of the peace to be negotiated, the outcome might, perhaps, have been happier.

The signing of the treaty with Germany on 28 June 1919 left Balfour again at the head of the British delegation; and the Treaty of St. Germain with Austria, which followed on 10 September, was his particular contribution to the settlement. Prejudiced by certain previous decisions of the council of four, it cannot be said to have avoided the danger that he had early signalled of a small Austria exciting sentiments both of affinity and cupidity in a great German neighbour. In the retrospect, indeed, Balfour was accustomed to defend the geographical aspect of the peace terms in general by arguing that the frontiers approved could not in practice have been bettered. His apologists may, however, prefer to dwell upon the terrific strain that his office had imposed upon a man now over seventy. There can in fact be little doubt that he felt the conduct of foreign affairs, involving as it did at Paris a social side which he was not the man to wish to avoid, to be getting beyond his strength; and this notwithstanding that, when he left for Paris, Lord Curzon had been inducted as acting foreign secretary at Whitehall. With the conclusion of the Austrian treaty he resigned (24 October 1919), retaining a place in the Cabinet as lord president of the council.

Balfour's association with foreign affairs was, however, by no means finished. In November 1921 he figured as leading British delegate at the Washington Conference which resulted in a Five-Power treaty for a measure of naval disarmament and a Four-Power compact of good understanding in the Pacific, but which also eventuated in the termination of the Anglo-Japanese Alliance of 1905. Then, in August 1922, he gave his name to the British note which he had drafted recommending a general cancellation of war debts as part of a general settlement. And finally, in the October following, as British representative at Geneva, he carried, largely by his own efforts, a scheme, which was successfully put into effect, for the financial rehabilitation of Austria under the auspices of the League of Nations. It might be added that a few weeks earlier he had taken together with Mr. Lloyd George and Mr. Churchill the grave responsibility of issuing a *communiqué* committing Great Britain to resist the crossing of the Straits at Chanak by the Turkish forces.

The same year 1922 brought him, in March, the K.G. and, in May, an earldom. He elected to call himself Earl of Balfour and, as a second title, Viscount Traprain. Thenceforward he figures as an elder statesman, yet—although the fall of Mr. Lloyd George, by whom he stood, a little rushed perhaps by circumstance, in the political crisis of 1922, threw him for a time out of office—not as one on the retired list. As lord president of the Council he was included in Mr. Baldwin's second administration from 1925 to 1929 and in that capacity took occasion to show his abiding sense of the overshadowing importance of physics in relation to politics by the foundation of the Committee of Civil Research, a body conceived on the same lines as the Committee of Imperial Defence but designed to give to men of science direct access to ministers as well as to coordinate scientific investigations throughout the Empire. But of his imperialist outlook those years contained another proof. The so-called Balfour Definition (1926)—embodied in the report of the Inter-Imperial Relations Committee of which he acted as chairman—gave expression to the view that positive ideals and free institutions formed the basic principle of the British Empire and so paved the way for the Statute of Westminster (1931) which recognized the equal status, both in domestic and foreign affairs, of the Colonies with the mother-country. Here was evidence enough that the eye of his mind was not dimmed, even if his bodily strength had abated. Yet there were some who thought that his career should have been earlier closed, some, not without influence in the matter, who would have liked to see him end his life, as but for the War he had himself dreamed that he might do, as head of his old Cambridge college. So graceful a tribute to his life-long interest in all that made for education might, had circumstances allowed it to take effect, have saved him from any ministerial association with the grant of Home Rule to Ireland; an association plainly inconvenient, to say no more, and imperfectly explained away by the fact of his absence in America at the date of its occurrence.

Balfour died at Fisher's Hill, his brother's house near Woking, 19 March 1930, and was buried at Whittingehame with the rites of the Church of Scotland, to which, though without any exclusive attachment—for he was a communicant also in the Church of England—he belonged. His metaphysical studies had satisfied him that personal immortality was implicit in the very structure of man's being. Not less did his patriotic achievement satisfy his contemporaries that political immortality was assured to the spacious record of his life. Yet his place amongst his compeers is no easy one to determine. He was a first minister in King Edward VII's piping times of peace, first lord of the Admiralty when the drums of war were beating at their loudest, foreign secretary at the greatest peace congress, or more strictly conference, the world has ever seen; yet it would be too much to say that he shone with Pitt's beacon-light, burned with Chatham's incandescent fire, or got Europe back to work with Castlereagh's laborious patience. Accomplished parliamentarian as he was, he had neither Canning's gift of speech nor Peel's grand manner. A conservative leader, and very loyal to his trust, he made no such impression, as Salisbury's, of sagacious strength or, as Disraeli's, of romantic vision. His political genius was in fact essentially transitional, evolutionary, and in that sense creative; nor, if it had been other, could he have worked so well in turn with Salisbury, with Chamberlain, and with Lloyd George. It was of a piece with this that he rose by opposing in Ireland the very principle of nationality which he ended by advocating in Palestine and saw in these apparently contrary purposes his own two chief achievements. Yet this seeming inconsequence was not in his case incompatible with a deeper intellectual integrity. For the rapier with which he had first opened the world's oyster seemed, when laid aslant the imperial and constitutional problems of his time in later life, to turn to a fine edge of light cutting their knots and tangles. The native propensity towards mediation which set a limit to his powers of leadership, increased the range and finish of his thoughts; and in a period of unexampled change and far-reaching confusion his serene and luminous cast of politics frequently exemplified the instinctive courtesy of an even mind observing the golden mean. In no derogatory sense, then, he possessed, as John Morley noticed, something in common with Halifax, the 'trimmer'—the Halifax, that is, of Macaulay's portrait with 'his keen, sceptical understanding, inexhaustibly fertile in distinctions and objections; his refined taste; his exquisite sense of the ludicrous; his placid and forgiving, but fastidious temper, by no means prone either to malevolence or to enthusiastic admiration', the Halifax of whom Walter Raleigh, the critic, observed that 'his importance may well be measured by this, that it never depended on the office that he held'. Yet when all the claims of contrast and comparison have been satisfied, Balfour remains, in the eyes at least of many who knew him, a unique figure—one of those rare men, indeed, about whom it may be said without rhetorical exaggeration that neither his own generation nor another will look upon his like again.

There are several portraits of Balfour at Whittingehame—by George Richmond in the 'seventies, by Ellis Roberts in 1890, by P. A. László in 1908, by Sir William Rothenstein in 1923, by Sir James Guthrie in 1927. The Carlton Club contains a full-length portrait painted in 1908 by J. S. Sargent; Trinity College, Cambridge, a portrait in his D.C.L. robes by László, and Eton College one by Fiddes Watt. A bust by Onslow Ford is also at Whittingehame. A cartoon appeared in *Vanity Fair* 27 January 1910.

[Balfour was succeeded as second earl by his only surviving brother, Gerald William (born 1853). Blanche E. C. Dugdale, *Arthur James Balfour, First Earl of Balfour*, 2 vols., 1936, written with intimate knowledge based upon the author's contemporary memoranda. Balfour's own *Chapters of Autobiography* (edited by Mrs. Dugdale), 1930, though only a fragment put together in his last illness, has also great importance for the student of his life and character. His *Essays and Addresses*, 1893 (3rd edition 1905) and his *Essays Speculative and Political*, 1920, contain autobiographical matter and illustrate the development of his views. The student of his philosophy will need to consult his *Defence of Philosophic Doubt*, 1879 (new edition 1920), his *Foundations of Belief*, 1895 (8th edition 1901), and his *Theism and Humanism* and *Theism and Thought*—the Gifford lectures which he delivered in 1915 and 1922–1923 respectively.

Estimates of and allusions to Balfour can be found in such contemporary biographies and recollections as Lady Gwendolen Cecil's *Life of Robert, Marquis of Salisbury*, vols. iii and iv, 1931 and 1932; J. L. Garvin's *Life of Joseph Chamberlain* vol. iii, 1934; *War Memoirs of David Lloyd George*, vols. i–iv (to 1917), 1933–1934; Sir Austen Chamberlain's (forthcoming) *Memoirs*; (Margot) Countess of Oxford and Asquith's *Autobiography*, 1922, and *More Memories*, 1933; Viscount Esher's *Journals and Letters*, ed. M. V. Brett, vols. i and ii, 1934. Sir Ian Malcolm, who was one of Balfour's political secretaries, published in 1930, *Lord Balfour: A Memory*, which deserves notice, as does an article in *Ten Personal Studies*, 1908, by Wilfrid Ward. The present Lord Rayleigh has dealt with the scientific aspect of Balfour's activities in a short obituary notice prepared for the Royal Society, and reprinted under the title *Lord Balfour in his relation to Science*, and Mr. John Buchan (Lord Tweedsmuir) with his literary style in an article in *Homilies and Recreations*, 1926. For the episode of the Lansdowne 'peace letter' of 1917 see *The Nineteenth Century and After*, March 1934 (article by Lord Lansdowne); and in regard to Balfour and the Peace Conference Mr. Harold Nicolson's *Peacemaking 1919*, 1933, will be found useful.] A. Cecil.

BALFOUR, Sir ISAAC BAYLEY (1853–1922), botanist, was born at Edinburgh 31 March 1853, the third child (second son) of John Hutton Balfour [q.v.], professor of botany in the university of

Edinburgh, by his wife, Marion, daughter of Isaac Bayley, of Edinburgh, writer to the signet. He counted among his forebears George Husband Baird [q.v.], principal of Edinburgh University 1793–1840, and James Hutton [q.v.], the geologist.

Balfour was educated at Edinburgh Academy and Edinburgh University, where he graduated B.Sc. in 1873. He studied also under Julius von Sachs at Wurzburg University and with A. de Bary at Strassburg. From 1875 to 1878 he acted as assistant to Sir C. Wyville Thomson, professor of natural history at Edinburgh University, and to T. H. Huxley, Thomson's substitute during his absence on the *Challenger* expedition. He was one of (Lord) Lister's dressers in Edinburgh (1875–1876). He took his M.D. degree in 1877. He had already accompanied, as botanist, the transit of Venus expedition to Rodriguez Island in 1874; in 1879 he explored the island of Socotra in order to collect plants. In that year he was appointed to the chair of botany in Glasgow University and he remained there until 1884, when he was elected Sherardian professor of botany at Oxford, and fellow of Magdalen College. In 1888 he removed to Edinburgh on his appointment as professor of botany in the university, King's botanist in Scotland, and keeper of the royal botanic garden. These positions he held until shortly before his death in 1922.

Balfour's most substantial published work was *Botany of Socotra* (1888), describing about 300 new species from the endemic flora of this oceanic island. He was engaged in systematic botanical work throughout his life, his main interest being in rhododendrons and primulas; he also did valuable work on the propagation of plants and the germination of seeds. But his influence was chiefly administrative. In each of the universities which he served he found a department needing reorganization: in Glasgow he saved the herbarium, and secured rebuilding of the plant-houses; in his few years at Oxford he did the same; and in each he reorganized the teaching on modern lines. But in his own university of Edinburgh the scope was greater: here he reconstituted the botanic garden; rebuilt the plant-houses; enlarged the laboratories, and created the rock-garden. Under his hands Edinburgh became a centre of the finest horticulture. Meanwhile he was conducting one of the largest botanical schools in the country and, as King's botanist in Scotland, directing correspondence with leading botanists both imperial and foreign. For a quarter of a century Balfour was the most efficient all-round botanist in Great Britain.

During his short tenure of the chair of botany at Oxford Balfour established relations with the Clarendon Press, inducing it to found in 1887 the *Annals of Botany*, a quarterly journal which, after nearly half a century, is now of world-wide repute. The Clarendon Press also, on his advice and under his editorship, produced a series of translations of foreign treatises, necessary for the completion of that revival of the study of botany in Great Britain in which he had taken a leading part.

Balfour married in 1884 Agnes Boyd, daughter of Robert Balloch, merchant, of Glasgow, and had one son and one daughter.

Balfour was elected F.R.S. in 1884, and created K.B.E. in 1920. He died at Court Hill, Haslemere, 30 November 1922.

[*Proceedings* of the Royal Society, vol. xcvi, B, 1924; *Proceedings* of the Royal Society of Edinburgh, vol. xliii, 1923; *Kew Bulletin*, No. 1, 1923.] F. O. Bower.

BALFOUR, Sir THOMAS GRAHAM (1858–1929), author and educationist, born in Chelsea 2 December 1858, was the only child of Surgeon-General Thomas Graham Balfour [q.v.], by his wife, Georgina, daughter of George Prentice, of Armagh. On his father's side he was closely connected, through the Balfours of Pilrig, with Robert Louis Stevenson. He was educated at Marlborough and at Worcester College, Oxford. His school life was partly impaired by ill health: at the university he obtained a first class in classical moderations (1880) and a second class in *literae humaniores* (1882), won distinction as a rifle-shot, and captained the shooting eight during his last two years.

In 1885 Balfour was called to the bar by the Inner Temple, but he found the practice of advocacy uncongenial, and his chief piece of work during these years was his contribution (the chapter on 'Battersea') to Charles Booth's *Life and Labour of the People in London* (1891–1903). For a time he travelled extensively, and in 1891, after the death of his parents, he accepted R. L. Stevenson's invitation to make his home at Vailima. On Stevenson's death in 1894 Balfour returned to England: in 1896 he married Rhoda, daughter of Leonard Dobbin Brooke, of Birkenhead, and settled at Oxford, where he wrote his two principal works. His *Educational Systems of Great Britain and Ireland* appeared in

1898 and rapidly became a standard authority: his *Life of Robert Louis Stevenson*, written at the request of Stevenson's family for the Edinburgh edition of his works, followed in 1901, and established Balfour's reputation as a biographer.

During Balfour's residence in Oxford he served the delegacy of local examinations first as examiner, then as assistant-secretary. This experience and the success of his volume on educational systems bore fruit when in 1902 he was appointed director of technical education, and in 1903 general director of education, to the county of Staffordshire. Balfour's appointment came at a critical time. The Act of 1902 had remodelled the educational administration of England and had vitally affected that of every district. The problems of Staffordshire were especially varied and insistent—a population of 600,000, a county mainly agricultural yet including two densely populated industrial areas, five county boroughs, nine boroughs and urban districts with powers over elementary education, twenty-nine school boards to be co-ordinated, a serious lack both of school buildings and of technical classes and colleges, and, above all, the urgent need of conciliating and bringing into line a large number of competing interests on whose co-operation the accomplishment of the task largely depended. To these problems Balfour addressed himself with whole-hearted devotion. He gained the entire confidence of his chairman, F. E. Kitchener, and of his committee, of the Board of Education, and of the neighbouring local authorities; he won the cordial affection of his subordinates, he met every difficulty with admirable temper and judgement, and he administered his office with a steady, far-seeing wisdom which made it an example to the country at large. In his first ten years he built forty-eight new schools, and the number was considerably increased afterwards; he extended the pottery school at Stoke, and established the technical colleges at Wednesbury and Wolverhampton and the mining college on Cannock Chase; he was a pioneer both of school-gardens and of school-libraries. The addresses on educational administration which he gave to the university of Birmingham in 1921 are models of their kind: they are the direct outcome of his own practice and experience.

In 1907 Balfour received the honorary degree of M.A. from Cambridge University and in 1924 that of LL.D. from the university of Birmingham. He was knighted in 1917. Among his many public appointments it may be mentioned that he served as chairman of the association of directors and secretaries of education (1908), as a member of the reconstruction committee on adult education (1917–1919), of the committee on the position of science in education (1916–1918), and of the consultative committee of the Board of Education (1926–1929). During the last year of the European War (1918–1919) he served as director of education in France (lines of communication) for the Young Men's Christian Association, and held that office with conspicuous success until the demobilization in 1919.

Balfour retired in 1926 after more than twenty-three years' service, and returned to Oxford, where he became a member of the city education committee, of the delegacy for extra-mural studies, and of the council of Barnett House. He died at Oxford 26 October 1929, leaving a widow and two sons.

Balfour possessed a true literary gift, and, if the balance had so inclined, might well have maintained his honourable place among English writers. But the claims of administrative work were too strong to be resisted, and in acknowledging them he found his most suitable and most fruitful field of activity. He was a master of his subject; swift in judgement, tenacious in policy, untiring in operation, fearless in pressing his point, yet able to disarm opposition by his tact, his humour, and his complete unselfishness. He lived through a difficult period in the history of English education: that he helped to bring it to a successful issue was alike due to his power of initiative, his wide sympathy, and his unswerving integrity of character.

[*The Times*, 28 October 1929; *Times Educational Supplement*, 2 November 1929; private information.] W. H. Hadow.

BALL, FRANCIS ELRINGTON (1863–1928), historian and antiquary, born 18 July 1863 at Portmarnock, co. Dublin, was the third son of John Thomas Ball [q.v.], of Taney House, Dundrum, co. Dublin, lord chancellor of Ireland from 1875 to 1880, by his wife, Catherine daughter of the Rev. Charles Richard Elrington [q.v.], regius professor of divinity in the university of Dublin. As his health in early life gave cause for anxiety, he was educated by a private tutor, and was not even sent to Trinity College, Dublin, although his father was vice-chancellor of the university.

Ball first came into notice through his work for the unionist cause in Ireland. His modest nature and his distaste for speaking on the platform kept him in the background; but among those who were behind the scenes it was generally recognized that the organization of the unionist party in Ireland and not a few of its successes at the polls were largely due to his untiring and unselfish efforts. At the general election of 1900 he was induced to stand for South County Dublin as an independent unionist, in opposition to Sir Horace Plunkett, the official candidate of the party. Ball polled a respectable number of votes, but the result of the split was that the seat was gained by the nationalists.

Ball thenceforward resolved to abandon politics for letters, and it is as a writer, rather than as a political organizer, that he will be remembered. The first work of any importance from his pen was *A History of the County Dublin* (6 parts, 1902–1920). In 1910 he published volume i of *The Correspondence of Jonathan Swift, D.D.*, the sixth and last volume of which appeared in 1914. In 1911 the honorary degree of Litt.D. was conferred on him by the university of Dublin in recognition of his work as editor. After the completion of his edition of Swift's correspondence, Ball turned to an entirely different subject, *The Judges in Ireland, 1221–1921* (2 vols., 1926). He then returned to the Dean of St. Patrick's, and was engaged at the time of his death on a volume dealing with the poems attributed to Swift. Fortunately, the work was ready for the press, except for the index and the revision of the proofs of the later sheets. It was published in 1929 under the title of *Swift's Verse; an Essay*.

To those who knew him best, Ball's character was summed up in the term *pietas*—loyalty towards his father, his friends, the class to which he belonged, and the order for which it stood. It was his *pietas* to his friend, Caesar Litton Falkiner [q.v.], which first directed his attention to Swift, and led him to carry out the new edition of the letters which Falkiner had planned. It was his *pietas* to his father's memory and to the class from which he sprang that inspired *The Judges in Ireland*. Irish history was to him the history of the English in Ireland, and of the civilization which they had brought into that country. As he explains in his preface, his history of the Irish judges deals solely with 'the seven centuries during which the authority of England was absolute in their appointment'.

The work by which Ball is most widely known is his edition of Swift's correspondence. It was the first annotated edition, and for the work of annotation Ball was admirably qualified by his unrivalled knowledge of the topography and history of Ireland within the Pale. *Swift's Verse* is intended for the student rather than for the general reader; but for the student it settles once and for all a great number of controversial points. Few would question that Ball was the greatest authority of the time on Swift. His work on the Irish judges is a remarkable achievement for one who had not been trained as a lawyer. At every turn it reveals the sure hand of the born researcher. As much of Ball's information was derived from documents which perished in the burning of the Irish Record Office in 1922, his work has become, in many instances, the primary authority.

Ball inherited his father's judicial temper. He never allowed his political sympathies to warp his judgement of individuals, or to lead him to misrepresent facts. He did not, however, inherit his father's grace of style, although his *Judges in Ireland* attests his gift of historical imagination. His industry was immense, and he set himself a severe standard of accuracy. He was shy and retiring by nature, but after his marriage his house in Dublin became one of the centres of social life in the Irish capital. Early in 1918 he left Ireland and settled in London, where his time was divided between the British Museum and the Carlton Club. He was a man of a warm heart and an affectionate nature, and his friendships were deep and lasting.

Ball died at a nursing-home in Dublin 7 January 1928. He married in 1897 Florence Eglantine (died 1913), daughter of the Rev. William Alfred Hamilton, D.D., rector of Taney, Dundrum, and canon of Christ Church, Dublin. There were no children of the marriage.

[*The Irish Times*, 9 January 1928; *Notes and Queries*, 16 February 1929; author's preface to *The Correspondence of Jonathan Swift* and introduction to *The Judges in Ireland*; personal knowledge.] E. M. Walker.

BANCROFT, Sir SQUIRE BANCROFT (1841–1926), actor and theatrical manager, the elder son of Secundus Bancroft White Butterfield, oil merchant, of Rotherhithe, by his wife, Julia, daughter of Thomas Anthony Wright, was born at Cristall's Cottage, Rotherhithe, 14 May 1841. In December 1867 he took the surname of Bancroft, and as Squire Bancroft married in that month Marie Effie Wilton [see below]. One son was born of the marriage.

Fatherless before he was seven, Bancroft was educated at private schools in England and in France, and in January 1861 went on the stage under the name of Bancroft at the Theatre Royal, Birmingham. Till the spring of 1865 he played in provincial stock companies; and at Liverpool early in 1865 he first acted with his future wife, Marie Wilton, who then engaged him for the Prince of Wales's Theatre, London. There, on 15 April 1865, he appeared for the first time in London in the comedietta *A Winning Hazard*, by J. P. Wooler. In 1867 he succeeded Henry James Byron [q.v.] as joint manager with his wife of the Prince of Wales's. In that partnership Bancroft, who was prudent, pertinacious, and laborious, soon came to be predominant, always keenly criticized but loyally supported by his brilliant wife.

Their mainstay at first were the comedies of Thomas William Robertson [q.v.]. *Society* and *Ours* were followed by *Caste*, *Play*, *School* (the most remunerative of all), and *M.P.* Carefully nursed and opportunely revived, they won nearly half the profits made at that theatre. Other successful plays produced there were: *Man and Wife* by Wilkie Collins, *Sweethearts* by (Sir) W. S. Gilbert, and two adaptations from Sardou, *Peril* (*Nos Intimes*) and *Diplomacy* (*Dora*). In April 1875 an elaborate production of *The Merchant of Venice* was quickly withdrawn, owing to Charles Coghlan's failure as Shylock. Revivals of *The School for Scandal*, Bulwer Lytton's *Money*, Dion Boucicault's *London Assurance*, J. B. Buckstone's *Good for Nothing*, and *Masks and Faces* by Charles Reade and Tom Taylor, were all successful. The theatre became too small for the Bancrofts' public; and in 1879 they took the Haymarket Theatre, rebuilt it, and opened it on 31 January 1880. On that night a disturbance was created by spectators who resented the abolition of the pit in order to make room for more stalls. The financial success of the management continued almost unbroken with revivals of *School*, *Ours*, and *Caste*, two new adaptations from Sardou, *Odette* and *Fedora*, new presentations of *The Rivals*, and of Tom Taylor's *Plot and Passion* (1881) and *The Overland Route* (1882) and a new comedy, *Lords and Commons* (1883), by (Sir) A. W. Pinero. On 20 July 1885 Mr. and Mrs. Bancroft retired from management, with a profit on the twenty years of £180,000.

The Bancrofts effected great reforms both in theatrical art and in theatrical business, and their management at the Prince of Wales's Theatre inaugurated a new era in the development of modern dramatic art. In casting plays they thought first of the general effect, and so often themselves took small parts that public and critics complained of their self-suppression. In rehearsing they introduced (with the help of T. W. Robertson), the subtle interaction of characters and situation which is the basis of subsequent dramatic art. In staging they sought for naturalism, reflecting the choicer taste of their own time. They greatly increased the pay and improved the conditions of their players, a reform in which they were soon to be followed by (Sir) Henry Irving. Their heavy expenses were met by raising the price of seats; they were the first to charge (in 1874) half-a-guinea for a stall. This general refinement, before and behind the curtain, together with the social success of Mr. and Mrs. Bancroft themselves, brought 'Society' back to the theatre and attracted to the stage young people of gentle birth.

Bancroft was a good actor. His special part was the 'swell' (such as Captain Hawtree in *Caste*), a type which he rescued from convention and turned into a reflection of real life. But his Triplet (his favourite part) in *Masks and Faces*, his Faulkland in *The Rivals*, and his Orloff in *Diplomacy* showed his power in pathos, high comedy, and tense drama. It was Henry Irving's opinion that Bancroft had 'left his best work as an actor undone' through paying too much attention to management. His choice of plays and players was sagacious; and as producer he knew his limitations well enough to seek help from Robertson, Coghlan, and Pinero.

During his forty-one years of life after retirement, Bancroft returned to the stage twice; to play the Abbé to Henry Irving's Landry in *The Dead Heart* at the Lyceum in 1889, and in 1893 to play Orloff for (Sir) John Hare at the Garrick. For the rest, he was content to watch, and generously to relieve with money or advice, the struggles of his successors in the theatre, and to enjoy, at his house, 18 Berkeley Square, or later at his flat, A1, The Albany, his social success and his many friendships.

Tall, erect, and handsome to the last, he was a well-known figure in the West End of London. About the early 'nineties he began a series of public readings of Dickens's *A Christmas Carol*, by which, in the United Kingdom and in Canada, he raised more than £20,000 for the hospitals. He was president of the Royal Academy of Dramatic Art, and a member of the lord chamberlain's advisory board for licensing of plays. He was knighted in the jubilee honours of 1897, and died at his flat in London 19 April 1926.

Portraits and caricatures of Bancroft are many. The chief is a three-quarter length in oils by H. G. Riviere in the National Portrait Gallery; a replica of this is in the Garrick Club, which also possesses a bust by Count Gleichen and the original cartoon by 'Spy' which appeared in *Vanity Fair* 13 June 1891.

Marie Effie Wilton, Lady Bancroft (1839–1921), actress and theatrical manager, the eldest of the six daughters of Robert Pleydell Wilton, provincial actor, by his wife, Georgiana Jane Faulkner, was born 12 January 1839 at (as she believed) Doncaster. She went on the stage in childhood, and won praise from Charles Macready, with whom she acted Fleance; from Charles Kemble, who saw her play Arthur in *King John*; and from Charles Dillon, manager of the Lyceum Theatre, London, who in September 1856 brought her to London to act Henri in *Belphegor* by Charles Webb, at the Lyceum. In that programme she also appeared as Perdita in William Brough's extravaganza of that name. Thus began her brilliant career in burlesque: at the Haymarket Theatre under John Baldwin Buckstone [q.v.], at the Adelphi Theatre under Benjamin Nottingham Webster [q.v.], and at the old Strand Theatre under Mrs. Ada Swanborough. As Pippo (one of her many boy-parts) in H. J. Byron's *The Maid and the Magpie* she won high praise from Charles Dickens; and there is much contemporary evidence of her great ability and charm.

Marie Wilton's ambition, however, was to play comedy; and in order to be free to do so she borrowed in January 1865 £1,000 from her sister Emma's husband, Francis Drake, took the rather disreputable little Queen's Theatre in Tottenham Street, did it up very prettily, obtained permission to name it the Prince of Wales's Theatre, and on 15 April 1865 opened it in partnership with H. J. Byron. The first programme consisted chiefly of burlesque. In June they produced a new comedy by Byron, *War to the Knife*, and in November Marie Wilton took a bold step in staging *Society* by T. W. Robertson. The acceptance of this comedy and the realism and daintiness of its mounting began a new era in English theatrical art, the chief credit for which belongs to Marie Wilton. *Ours* was produced on 15 September 1866; and after the Christmas programme of that year burlesque was seen no more at the Prince of Wales's.

To the Robertson comedies Marie Wilton's roguish humour and fine technique were invaluable; she was equally good as a well-bred girl, like her favourite Naomi Tighe in *School*, and as a girl of the people, such as Polly Eccles in *Caste* or Nan in Buckstone's *Good for Nothing*; while as Lady Teazle, as Jenny Northcott, first young and then middle-aged, in *Sweethearts*, and as Peg Woffington in *Masks and Faces*, she proved herself an actress of genius in more than one type of comedy. The descriptions of her acting contributed by Sir A. W. Pinero and Sir J. Forbes-Robertson to Sir Squire Bancroft's book, *Empty Chairs*, show wherein her talent consisted. But, as the theatre prospered her acting was more and more sacrificed to its success and to the claims of social life. Her appearances became fewer, and her parts such as she was obliged to 'write up' in order to make them effective.

In private life Lady Bancroft was scarcely less amusing than on the stage, and her warm heart and merry nature won her a host of friends in all classes of society. Soon after her retirement in 1885 she was received into the Roman Catholic Church; and she occupied some of her long leisure in writing three plays and a novel. She died at Folkestone 22 May 1921.

A portrait of Lady Bancroft by T. Jones Barker is in the National Portrait Gallery. A bust by Count Gleichen is in the Garrick Club.

[*The Times*, 14 December 1867, 23 May 1921, and 20 April 1926; *Mr. and Mrs. Bancroft on and off the Stage: Written by themselves*, 1888; revised and brought down to 1909 as *The Bancrofts: Recollections of Sixty Years*, 1909; Squire Bancroft, *Empty Chairs*, 1925; W. D. Adams, *Dictionary of the Drama*, 1904; *Who's Who in the Theatre*, 1912; personal knowledge.] H. H. Child.

BARBOUR, Sir DAVID MILLER (1841–1928), Indian civil servant and economist, was born at Omagh, co. Tyrone, Ireland, 29 December 1841. He was the third son and fifth child of Miller Barbour by his wife, Margaret Denny, and came of stock that had been settled for some three centuries as farmers and small landowners at Calkill, near Omagh. From Omagh Academy Barbour entered Queen's College, Belfast, in October 1858, with a science scholarship, holding also, subsequently, the senior scholarship in natural philosophy. In 1862 he graduated B.A. in the Queen's University of Ireland, and twenty years later received the honorary degree of LL.D. when the Queen's University was dissolved and superseded by the Royal University of Ireland.

Barbour passed into the Indian civil service in 1862 in the early days of the open competition, being sixth in order of merit and first in mathematics in the examination. He arrived in India in December 1863, and was posted to Bengal. His first experience in finance was in 1872 as under-secretary to the government of India in the finance department. Subsequently he held in succession the post of accountant-general in the Punjab, in Madras, and in Bengal, and acted as secretary to the government of Bengal in the finance department and later in the revenue and general department. In 1880 he published a pamphlet over the initials 'D.B.' entitled *Our Afghan Policy and the Occupation of Candahar*. In this pamphlet, writing after the second Afghan War and the British occupation of Kabul and Kandahar, he pressed for prompt withdrawal from Afghanistan at the earliest opportunity and for a return to the policy of Lord Lawrence [q.v.]

In April 1882 Barbour returned to the government of India as secretary in the department of finance and commerce. The decade which followed, when the problems of Indian finance and currency were brought into the forefront of international discussions, was a critical period in the economic history of India. At that time the basis of the Indian currency system was silver freely minted, the gold value of the rupee fluctuating with the gold value of silver bullion. When Germany, after the war of 1870, changed to a gold standard, forces had been set in motion which put an end to bimetallism; there was a continuous decline in the value of silver; trade became disorganized; and the Indian government, with large foreign payments to make, was seriously embarrassed. In his book, *The Theory of Bimetallism*, published in 1885, Barbour argued in favour of the reintroduction of bimetallism by international action. He represented India on the royal commission on gold and silver of 1886 and was one of the minority (5 out of 12) which pronounced in favour of a return to bimetallism. He himself, however, recognized that the re-establishment of bimetallism was impossible except by universal, or almost universal, agreement, and that such agreement could not be obtained. The commission reported in 1888 and on 22 November of that year Barbour became finance member of the governor-general's council. He was made K.C.S.I. on 1 January 1889.

A currency crisis was by this time imminent. When introducing the Indian budget for the year 1891–1892, Barbour made a statement of his personal views which has been often quoted; it indicated clearly that the alternative to which the government of India was being forced was the adoption of the gold standard. In the absence of international action the situation became more and more critical; but although the government of India supported Barbour, it was not until after consideration by a special committee under Lord Herschell [q.v.] that the policy which Barbour advocated was finally accepted. Legislation was passed closing the Indian mints to the free coinage of silver on 26 June 1893.

Barbour left India in November 1893. In 1898 he became a member of Sir Henry Fowler's committee on Indian currency, which marked the next stage in the reform initiated in 1893. In 1899, on the recommendation of this committee, the permanent rate of exchange for the rupee was fixed at 1*s.* 4*d.*, gold was made legal tender at the rate of R.15 to the £, and the profit on coinage was used to form a gold fund to secure the convertibility of rupees into sovereigns at the fixed rate. Thus came into being the gold exchange standard in India, a system which in essentials provides a cheap local currency for internal use, maintained at par with international currency by administrative measures and by the aid of a gold reserve. The final result was admittedly not envisaged from the first, but its success was such that during the next decade it was widely imitated. In *The Standard of Value*, published in 1912, Barbour set out with great clarity and candour the dramatic story of his struggle for bimetallism, and the circumstances in which he, the champion of bimetallism, was forced to deal that system its most fatal blow by the closure of the

Indian mints. In the following year he published an economic study entitled *The Influence of the Gold Supply on Prices and Profits*.

After his return from India Barbour undertook almost continuous service on commissions and committees of imperial importance. A keen Ulsterman, he had always taken a deep interest in Irish affairs. In May 1894 he was appointed a member of the royal commission on the financial relations between Great Britain and Ireland. Dissenting from the majority, which contained a preponderance of home rulers, Barbour maintained that the question referred to them should be considered in all its aspects and on the broadest grounds of equity. His 'Minute of Dissent' is a masterly analysis of the financial relations of the two countries from the time of the Union. In December 1896 he was appointed a member of the royal commission which visited the West Indian Islands in order to report upon their condition and prospects, which were suffering severely from the depression in the sugar industry. In January 1899 he visited Jamaica again, this time alone, to report upon the financial condition of the Colony; and his report made no secret of his view that Jamaica would have been able to pay its way if its affairs had been managed with greater prudence. He suggested the necessary measures to restore financial equilibrium. The same report contains a critical review of the constitution of the Colony, which is of more than ephemeral interest, showing how a compromise between crown and representative government had led to a division of responsibility and weakness in administration. Barbour became K.C.M.G. in June 1899 in recognition of these services.

In October 1899 and November 1902 committees were appointed to report on the currencies of the West African colonies and protectorates and of the Straits Settlements. Of both these committees Barbour was chairman, and in both instances, using the experience gained in India, he was able to recommend arrangements akin in essentials to the system by then successfully working in that country. In the interval between these two committees, in October 1900, he was invited to report on the finances of the Transvaal and the Orange River Colony. In February 1903 he entered upon work of a somewhat different character as chairman of the royal commission on London traffic, which after prolonged deliberations reported in June 1905 and made the first recommendation for a central Traffic Board with jurisdiction over Greater London. The last royal commission on which Barbour served was the commission on shipping rings, which was appointed in November 1906 and reported in May 1909. On this occasion again he found it necessary to dissent from the other members of the commission. He alone was prepared to recommend an effective check on the shipping rings, to be imposed if necessary by legislation.

On two further occasions Barbour took part in discussions affecting India. During 1907–1908 he was a member of the Indian railway finance and administration committee under the chairmanship of Lord Inchcape. Again, in 1919, he gave evidence before the committee on Indian exchange and currency. Recognizing that the prevailing conditions were altogether exceptional, he was totally opposed to any attempt being made at that time to fix a permanent rate of exchange. Had his advice been accepted, the ill-fated attempt made in 1920, with great loss to India, to stabilize the rupee at 2*s.* would have been avoided.

Barbour died 12 February 1928 at Tiltwood, Crawley Down, Sussex. In 1883 he had married Katherine Constance, daughter of Thomas Gribble, who had been connected with the wine trade in Portugal. He left three sons and one daughter.

After his retirement from India Barbour was a well-known figure in London, both at the Athenaeum and in the City. He joined the board of the East Indian Railway Company in 1895, became deputy chairman in 1917, and chairman in 1919, holding that office until 1924. He was also a director of the Standard Bank of South Africa from 1901 until 1927. He was a man of active habits, a keen fisherman and a fine shot, and when in India well known as a shikari in the Simla Hills. On his death in 1928, his old friend Lord Inchcape, who had been a close collaborator in the earlier days of Indian currency reform, paid this tribute to his memory: 'There are few men alive now who worked with Sir David Barbour, but all who remain will, I am sure, venerate his memory, as I do, for his high-minded character, his great ability, his honesty of purpose, his keen sense of humour, and his kindly and affectionate disposition.' But it is for his contribution to currency history that Barbour will be best remembered. He was, both from his position as finance member of the government of India and from his own personal qualifications, the most striking figure of the dramatic conflict over bimetallism, and his action in closing the Indian mints in 1893 opened a new page in currency history of which the final chapter has not yet been written.

[*The Times*, 14 February 1928; *The Theory of Bimetallism*, 1885; *The Standard of Value*, 1912; Indian Financial Statement for the year 1891–1892; *Reports* of royal commissions and committees cited in text; personal knowledge.]

A. C. McWatters.

BARING-GOULD, SABINE (1834–1924), divine and author, born at Dix's Fields, Exeter, 28 January 1834, was the eldest son of Edward Baring-Gould, of Lew Trenchard, Devonshire, by his wife, Sophia Charlotte, daughter of Admiral Francis Godolphin Bond, R.N. He was educated privately, mainly abroad, owing to ill health. In 1853 he entered Clare College, Cambridge, and graduated B.A. in 1856. He was assistant master first at the choir school of St. Barnabas's church, Pimlico (for a few months in 1857), and then for seven years (1857–64) at Hurstpierpoint College. In 1864 he was ordained deacon at Ripon and became curate of Horbury, Yorkshire. In 1865 he was ordained priest. In 1866 he became vicar of Dalton, Yorkshire, and in 1871 rector of East Mersea, Essex. On the death of his father in 1872, he succeeded to the family estate of Lew Trenchard, and in 1881 presented himself to the family living of Lew Trenchard. In 1918 he was elected an honorary fellow of Clare College, Cambridge. He died at Lew Trenchard 2 January 1924. He married in 1868 Grace (died 1916), daughter of Joseph Taylor, of Horbury, by whom he had five sons and nine daughters.

Baring-Gould wrote voluminously on many subjects; his published works from 1857 to 1920 number 159. His most serious writings, based on considerable research, although lacking in the finer details of critical scholarship, are *The Origin and Development of Religious Belief* (2 vols., 1869–1870), *The Lives of the Saints* (15 vols., 1872–1877, new edition in 16 vols., 1897–1898), and *The Lives of the British Saints* (1907). A high churchman, he believed in the catholicity of the Church of England, and had little sympathy with either Calvinism or papalism. His history of *The Evangelical Revival* (1920) is diffuse in style and hardly does justice to the subject. He published numerous collections of sermons and wrote several hymns, the best-known being 'Onward Christian Soldiers'.

Baring-Gould's interest in legend and folk-lore marks his secular writings and is apparent in his *Book of Were-Wolves* (1865) and *Curious Myths of the Middle Ages* (1866, 1868). He travelled extensively in Europe and his descriptive volumes, although lacking in exact historical data, won popularity through a lively style and a gift for fresh observation. The most important are *In Troubadour Land* (1891), *The Deserts of Southern France* (1894), *A Book of the Cevennes* (1907), and *A Book of the Pyrenees* (1907).

Baring-Gould's numerous works on the West of England emphasized the natural beauty of the region and popularized its folk-lore and history. His most important books on this subject are *A Book of the West* (1899), *A Book of Dartmoor* (1900), *Devonshire Characters and Strange Events* (1908), and *Cornish Characters and Strange Events* (1909). He performed a valuable service in collecting from published sources and oral tradition the folk-songs of Devon and Cornwall. His *Songs and Ballads of Devon and Cornwall* (1890) and his *Songs of the West* (1905) are the fruit of much research. He acted as secretary of the Dartmoor exploration committee of the Devonshire Association, was elected president of the Association in 1896, and contributed to its transactions from 1888 to 1920. In 1876 Baring-Gould published *The Vicar of Morwenstowe: a Life of Robert Stephen Hawker*. The book had a wide circulation owing to its lively style and local colour, but it was severely criticized for its serious inaccuracies in the *Athenaeum* of 26 March 1876. Later editions only slightly remedied these defects.

In fiction Baring-Gould's versatility and dramatic power found free scope, and his numerous novels were popular. The best known are *Mehalah* (1880, which Swinburne likened to *Wuthering Heights*), *John Herring* (1883), *Court Royal* (1886), *Arminell* (1890), *Cheap Jack Zita* (1893), and *The Broom Squire* (1896).

A portrait of Baring-Gould by Sydney Carter is in the City Library, Exeter, and a reproduction of a photograph taken of him at Lew Trenchard on 10 October 1923 was published in volume xiii of *Devon and Cornwall Notes and Queries*, April 1924.

[*The Times*, 3 January 1924; Baring-Gould's writings, particularly his *Early Reminiscences (1834–1864)*, 1923, and *Further Reminiscences (1864–1894)*, 1925; *Transactions* of the Devonshire Association for the Advancement of Science, Literature, and Art, vols. xx, xxvi–xxxv, xxxvii, lii, and lvi; *Notes and Queries*, 6th series, vol. ix, 1884; *Notes and Gleanings*, vol. i, 1888; *The Western Antiquary*, vol. v, 1885; *Devon Notes and Queries*, vol. i, 1900–1901, iv, 1906–1907; *Devon and Cornwall Notes and Queries*, vol. vii, 1912–1913, xiii, 1924–1925.] M. COATE.

BARON, BERNHARD (1850–1929), tobacco manufacturer and philanthropist, was born in South Russia of Jewish parents 5 December 1850. Further details of his parentage and birthplace are not available. As a boy he migrated to the United States and found employment at a tobacco factory in New York. He was there befriended by a foreman named Falk, who gave him tobacco leaf for making cigarettes which at that time were providing a new method of consuming tobacco. In search of customers for his cigarettes Baron went to New Haven, Connecticut, where the students of Yale University brought him a profitable trade. He began to save money, which he deposited with a bank in the Bowery, New York: in 1874 the bank failed and Baron's savings were lost. This misfortune led him to obtain employment at the tobacco factory of Kinney Brothers of New York; but as soon as he had again accumulated savings he started a cigar-manufacturing business of his own at Baltimore. This business prospered, and in after years Baron used to recall that it was the largest undertaking of its kind south of Philadelphia. In 1890 Baron was approached by a group of financiers who persuaded him to join in a venture directed against the tobacco trusts, and during the years 1890–1895 he was managing director of the National Cigarette Tobacco Company of New York.

It was during this period that machines for making cigarettes were first projected, and Baron, having himself invented such a machine, came to settle in England in 1895. He immediately formed a limited company in London to which he sold the patent rights in his machine, and in 1895, with a capital of £120,000, the Baron Cigarette Machine Company started operations. This undertaking was successful, until in 1903 its business was brought almost to a standstill by the competition of the newly established Imperial Tobacco Company. Baron now determined to obtain an outlet under his own control for the sale of the cigarettes produced by the Baron company, and accordingly in 1903 he purchased a small London tobacco business which bore the name of its first owner, J. J. Carreras. From that year onwards this business, under Baron's control, was developed until it became one of the most notable commercial undertakings in the country. Baron continued to act as chairman of Carreras Limited until his death, which took place at his home, The Drive, Brighton, 1 August 1929. His estate was proved at £4,944,820 (net personalty £4,937,320).

Baron is chiefly remembered for the romance of his career and for the extent of his benefactions. The experiences of his early life made him intensely sympathetic to appeals on behalf of the poor, and during his lifetime he contributed approximately £2,000,000 to charitable objects. It is estimated that he devoted more than £750,000 to hospitals alone. His donations in 1927 amounted to £180,000, and in September 1928 he created a trust which set aside £575,000 for the benefit of hospitals and homes for crippled children. Baron was a broad-minded philanthropist, and Christian, Jewish, and undenominational charities alike benefited by his generosity. Towards the end of his life he used to celebrate his birthdays by making large gifts to hospitals, orphanages, and other charitable organizations, and to mark his seventy-seventh birthday he distributed £32,000 among two hundred hospitals and philanthropic institutions.

Baron's wife, whose maiden name was Rachael Schwartz, predeceased him in 1920. Their only son, Louis Bernhard (born 1876), succeeded his father as chairman of Carreras Limited, and was created a baronet in 1930. A portrait of Baron, painted by Sir William Orpen, is in the possession of the family, and at Arcadia Works, Hampstead Road, London, there is a bust, the gift of his employees, which was executed by William Reid Dick.

[*The Times*, 3 August 1929; private information.] A. E. WATKIN.

BARRINGTON, RUTLAND (1853–1922), actor and vocalist, whose real name was GEORGE RUTLAND BARRINGTON FLEET, the fourth son of John George Fleet, wholesale sugar dealer in Fenchurch Street, London, by his wife, Esther, daughter of the Rev. Ferdinand Faithfull, rector of Headley, near Epsom, was born at Penge, Surrey (now in Kent), 15 January 1853. He was educated at first by a private tutor, then at Headley rectory, and subsequently at Merchant Taylors School, and on leaving entered business in the City, where he remained until he was twenty-one. His aunt, Emily Faithfull, was a well-known entertainer, and she was instrumental in obtaining his first engagement with the actor, Henry Neville [q.v.]. He made his first appearance on the stage at the old Olympic Theatre on 1 September 1874 as Sir George Barclay in *Clancarty* by Tom Taylor. In the following year he went on tour with Mrs. Howard Paul [q.v.], and he remained with her when she obtained an engagement with Richard D'Oyly Carte [q.v.], and insisted that Barrington should be engaged also.

Barrington made his first appearance under D'Oyly Carte's management at the Opera Comique 17 November 1877, when he took the part of Dr. Daly in *The Sorcerer* by (Sir) W. S. Gilbert and (Sir) Arthur Sullivan, and made an immediate success. This first engagement with D'Oyly Carte lasted for eleven years, first at the Opera Comique and later at the Savoy, during which period he played the following original parts in Gilbert and Sullivan operas: Captain Corcoran in *H.M.S. Pinafore* (May 1878), the sergeant of police in *The Pirates of Penzance* (April 1880), Archibald Grosvenor in *Patience* (April 1881), the Earl of Mountararat in *Iolanthe* (November 1882), King Hildebrand in *Princess Ida* (January 1884), Pooh-Bah in *The Mikado* (March 1885), and Sir Despard Murgatroyd in *Ruddigore* (January 1887); he also appeared at different times as the Counsel for the Plaintiff and the Judge in *Trial by Jury*.

Quitting the Savoy, Barrington entered upon the management of the St. James's Theatre, opening on 13 October 1888 with *The Dean's Daughter* by Sydney Grundy and F. C. Phillips, followed by *Brantinghame Hall* by (Sir) W. S. Gilbert; but both plays proved unsuccessful, and Barrington was forced into bankruptcy.

For a short period Barrington played at the Comedy Theatre under (Sir) Charles Hawtrey [q.v.], but he returned to the Savoy Theatre, under D'Oyly Carte, in December 1889 in order to play the part of Giuseppe in *The Gondoliers* by Gilbert and Sullivan. This second engagement at the Savoy covered a period of four and a half years (1889–1894), in the course of which he appeared in *The Nautch Girl* (1891), *The Vicar of Bray* (1892), *Haddon Hall* (1892), *Jane Annie* (1893), and *Utopia Limited* (1893). None of these operas had the attraction of the previous productions, and in 1894 Barrington joined the late George Edwardes's company in order to play Dr. Brierley in *A Gaiety Girl* on tour and at Daly's Theatre. He was next seen at the Lyric Theatre, October 1894, in *His Excellency* by Gilbert. In 1896 he was back again at the Savoy in *The Mikado*, and as Ludwig in *The Grand Duke*, after which he returned to Daly's Theatre, under Edwardes, and remained there from 1896 to 1904, playing in *The Geisha*, *A Greek Slave*, *San Toy*, *A Country Girl*, and *The Cingalee*.

Thereafter, beyond appearing in *Amăsis* (1906), *The Girl in the Train* (1910), and in occasional revivals at Daly's and the Savoy theatres, Barrington received only minor engagements at various theatres and music halls. From 1916 to 1918 he was engaged with (Sir) John Martin-Harvey. With that manager he played his last part, that of Claus in *The Burgomaster of Stilemonde* at the Lyceum Theatre, Edinburgh, in October 1918. In the following January he had a paralytic seizure; but he lingered on, in very straitened circumstances, for a few years. For his benefit a complimentary performance was given at the Savoy Theatre in February 1921, and in April 1922 he was elected an annuitant of King George's pension fund for actors. He died 31 May 1922 at St. James's Infirmary, Wandsworth Common.

Barrington was the author of a play, *Bartonmere Towers* (1893), a version of Kingsley's *Water Babies*, and of an autobiographical record of his stage career, *Rutland Barrington* (1908) and *More Rutland Barrington* (1911). He also contributed to *Punch* for several years over the signature of 'Lady Gay'. He was an artist of some taste, and his water-colours of river scenes and sea-scapes showed skill and feeling. He was interested in sport and athletics, and was a keen connoisseur of bric-à-brac. In his time Barrington was a man of considerable importance in the theatre. Possessed of a fine figure, an abundant sense of humour, and a soft though penetrating voice, he left a tradition in the parts which he created at the Savoy and Daly's theatres, which long survived him.

[*The Times*, 2 June 1922; *Who's Who in the Theatre*; personal knowledge.]

J. Parker.

BATESON, WILLIAM (1861–1926), biologist, born at Whitby, 8 August 1861, was the elder son of William Henry Bateson [q.v.], master of St. John's College, Cambridge. Through his mother, Anna, daughter of James Aikin, a remarkable woman, he traced Scottish descent. His younger sister was Mary Bateson [q.v.], the historian. Educated at Rugby, William Bateson looked back on his schooldays as neither enjoyable nor profitable. It was not until he went up to St. John's College, Cambridge, in 1879 that he began to find himself. The study of natural science proved most congenial to his temperament, and the first class which he obtained in the first part of the tripos examinations of 1882 led to the award of a college scholarship. The following year he obtained a first class in the second part of the tripos.

At this time, under the influence of Francis Maitland Balfour [q.v.], the study of embryology was the vogue, and Bateson decided to devote himself to working out the development of *Balanoglossus*, a peculiar worm-like creature of which nothing in this respect was known. He spent two years in the United States of America, and the results of his successful solution of the problem, with its revolutionary implications on the origin of the great vertebrate group, are now to be found in any zoological text-book. On the result of this work Bateson was elected in 1885 a fellow of his college, a position which he held for twenty-five years, after which he was elected to an honorary fellowship. But the visit to America held greater consequences for Bateson's career, for here he met W. K. Brooks, of Johns Hopkins University, whose influence had much to do with stimulating an interest in the problems of evolution. This led Bateson in 1886 to set out for Western Central Asia in order to explore the fauna of the salt lakes. On his return in 1887 he turned aside to investigate the brackish waters of Northern Egypt. The biological results were on the whole disappointing, but the experience undoubtedly helped to develop his naturally keen powers of observation [see *Letters from the Steppe*, posthumously published in 1928].

Back again in Cambridge, Bateson at once turned from the current modes of research, which had earlier brought him success, to strike out a line of his own. Convinced that the solution of the problem of species lay in the nature of variation, he embarked on the critical collection of relevant facts wherever he could find them. These eventually took shape in his *Materials for the Study of Variation* (1894), a book which appeared in the same year as his election to the fellowship of the Royal Society. This book, by its insistence upon the phenomenon of discontinuity in variation, gave a fresh orientation to the study of evolutionary problems. Perceiving clearly that the next step was to determine the behaviour of discontinuous variations in the process of heredity, he set to work on the experimental breeding of animals and plants. Then in 1900 the unforeseen happened. With the unearthing of Gregor Mendel's long forgotten and now famous *Versuche über Pflanzen-Hybriden* there suddenly appeared the clue for which Bateson had been seeking—the clue which he was on the verge of discovering for himself. He at once recognized its paramount significance, and in a world where biologists were for the most part indifferent or hostile he constituted himself Mendel's apostle. The new doctrine of heredity was bitterly challenged in circles considered to be authoritative, and the keenness of the ensuing controversy is reflected in Bateson's little book entitled *Mendel's Principles of Heredity—a Defence* (1902). Meanwhile Bateson's experimental work had proceeded vigorously, with the help of a band of younger biologists who gathered round him, fired with his enthusiasm and the inspiration of the new knowledge. The year 1904 proved to be a turning-point. In that year Bateson was president of the Zoological Section of the British Association. The controversy between himself and his critics came to a head, and Mendel was vindicated once for all.

The quieter years which followed were filled with discoveries of interest, many of which were chronicled by Bateson in *Mendel's Principles of Heredity* (1909). The garden of his house at Grantchester, near Cambridge, became a Mecca for biologists from all over the world. The importance of his work was gradually recognized. In 1907 he was invited by the university of Yale to deliver the Silliman lectures, which later appeared in book form as *Problems of Genetics* (1913). In 1908 the university of Cambridge created for him the chair of biology. He held this only until the end of 1909; for in 1910 he moved to Merton, Surrey, in order to take up the directorship, which he retained until his death, of the newly founded John Innes Horticultural Institution.

Here at last, with ample means, Bateson had opportunity to extend the scale of his experiments, and his faculty for organization found full scope. Buildings were planned, gardens laid out, and, most important of all, an enthusiastic and competent band of colleagues gathered round him. The Institution rapidly took its place among the most notable centres of biological research, and workers flocked to it from all parts. They found there something which was not to be found elsewhere; something of that burning passion for truth, and of that high conception of the calling of the naturalist which was of the essence of Bateson's personality.

More than any other man Bateson was the founder of the experimental study of heredity and variation which was now providing a fresh orientation to the biological sciences—a study for which he invented the term 'genetics'. Nor was he neglectful of the utilitarian aspect of biology. The rapid progress of the breeder during the earlier decades of the twentieth century was largely due to Bateson's clear exposition of the nature of the problems involved. There is hardly a marked advance which cannot be traced to his example or precept. But remarkable as were his own achievements, it was his prophetic vision which impressed his younger contemporaries. He realized even at the outset whither these simple experiments with garden plants and mice and poultry were tending. For him they were not merely a new and potent tool at the service of the breeder, but a means whereby man could ultimately clarify his conceptions of himself and of his position in the scheme of things. His views on these matters appeared sporadically before varied audiences—in a Herbert Spencer lecture at Oxford in 1912, a presidential address to the British Association in 1914, an address to the Salt Schools in 1915. That they exerted so little influence in his lifetime is doubtless in some part due to the intermittent manner of their appearance. It was not until 1928 that Bateson's *Essays and Addresses* were collected together in book form. Apart from the importance of their content they show that a man of science can also be a master of fine and forceful prose. The same keen sense of form which infused Bateson's science and writing found another outlet in his appreciation of art. An ardent collector of drawings of old masters, of Japanese colour prints, and of other things Oriental, his connoisseurship was recognized by his election in 1922 as a trustee of the British Museum.

Bateson died at Merton 8 February 1926. He married in 1896 Beatrice, daughter of Arthur Durham, senior surgeon to Guy's Hospital, by whom he had three sons, only one of whom survived his father.

There is a drawing of Bateson by W. Arnold Forster in the National Portrait Gallery.

[*William Bateson, His Essays and Addresses*, with a memoir by Beatrice Bateson, 1928; *Nature*, 27 February 1926; *Edinburgh Review*, July 1926; *Scientific Papers of William Bateson*, 1928; personal knowledge.]

R. C. Punnett.

BAYLEY, Sir STEUART COLVIN (1836–1925), Indian civil servant, was born 26 November 1836, the youngest son of William Butterworth Bayley [q.v.], of the Bengal civil service, by his wife, Anna Augusta, daughter of William Jackson, registrar of the supreme court, Calcutta. The father and the son between them gave 106 years continuous service to India. Educated at Eton and at the East India Company's College at Haileybury, Bayley was posted to Lower Bengal in 1856. From 1862 to 1867 he was junior secretary to the government of Bengal, and was noted at that time by Sir George Otto Trevelyan as 'a dead hand at a minute, and the best amateur literary critic I ever came across'. After service as district officer, judge, and commissioner, Bayley became commissioner of Patna in 1873, and his success in coping with a disastrous famine in this division in 1874 was rewarded with the C.S.I. In 1877 he accompanied the viceroy, the second Lord Lytton, on his visit to Southern India, as private secretary for famine affairs. Promoted K.C.S.I. in 1878, he was appointed in the same year chief commissioner of Assam, and in 1879 he acted for six months as lieutenant-governor of Bengal, in addition to his duties in Assam. In 1881 he was awarded the C.I.E. and transferred to Hyderabad as resident, and in 1882 he was made home member of the viceroy's executive council.

Lord Dufferin found in Bayley a valuable counsellor in connexion with the Bengal Tenancy Act and in composing the racial antagonism roused by the Ilbert Bill, in the final shaping of which Bayley had taken a leading part. He became lieutenant-governor of Bengal in April 1887, and administered its internal affairs with sagacity and firmness, while on its frontiers an aggressive movement of the Tibetans was repelled, and raids by Chin-Lushai tribes in the south were checked and punished. His resignation in December 1890, on his appointment as political secretary at the India Office, was regretted by all classes, and his memory is perpetuated in Calcutta by a statue, the work of Sir Hamo Thornycroft, erected by public subscription. In 1895 Bayley became a member of the India Council, retiring finally from service in 1905. In 1911 he received the signal honour of promotion to the G.C.S.I. Elected to the Athenaeum Club in 1891, as a person 'of distinguished eminence in the public service', he was on the committee of the club from 1900 to 1920 and its chairman for five years. He was also chairman of the council of the Royal Society of Arts from 1906 to 1908. He died in London 3 June 1925 in his eighty-ninth year, and was buried in Brompton cemetery.

Bayley combined with a dignified presence and an old-fashioned courtesy of manner a ready sympathy and wide interests. His conservative outlook in public affairs was tempered by his appreciation of the growth of national feeling in India, while his practical knowledge rendered him a clear-headed administrator and a sound adviser. He was a great and varied reader and wrote with much literary ability and a refreshing humour. He made many friends and no enemies, and his character and his career lent honour to the Service to which he gave nearly fifty years of his life. He married in 1860 Anna, daughter of Robert Nesham Farquharson, I.C.S., and their singularly happy union remained unbroken for sixty-four years. They had thirteen children, of whom five sons and three daughters survived them.

[*The Times*, 4 June 1925; *The Journal of the Royal Society of Arts*, 26 June 1925; Sir G. O. Trevelyan, *Interludes in Verse and Prose*, 1905; E. Axon, *Bayley Family*, 1890; C. E. Buckland, *Bengal under the Lieutenant-Governors, 1854–1898*, 1901; private information; personal knowledge.] P. C. Lyon.

BAYLISS, Sir **WILLIAM MADDOCK** (1860–1924), physiologist, was born at Wolverhampton 2 May 1860, the only son of Moses Bayliss, manufacturer of iron ware, of that town, by his wife, Jane Maddock. He was educated at Mowbray House School, Wolverhampton. He might naturally have entered his father's business, but his tastes lay in the direction of science and medicine. Nevertheless, he maintained a connexion to the end of his life with the family business, of which he was a director: in particular he was interested in the conditions of the employees.

With the object of pursuing medicine, Bayliss was apprenticed at the Wolverhampton Hospital, but he never finished his medical training. In 1881 he entered University College, London, and shortly afterwards came under the influence of (Sir) Edwin Ray Lankester [q.v.] and (Sir) John Scott Burdon-Sanderson [q.v.], particularly the latter. In 1883 Burdon-Sanderson went to Oxford, as the first Waynflete professor of physiology; thither Bayliss followed him, entering Wadham College in 1885. He obtained a first class in the school of natural science (physiology) in 1888.

After taking his degree, Bayliss participated for a time in the teaching of physiology at Oxford, but in 1888 returned to University College, never to leave it. In 1912 a professorship of general physiology was created specially for him. Here may be mentioned Bayliss's association with and attachment to the Physiological Society, which played a great part in his life. His name first appears in its annals in 1885 (21 March), when the society was very small and largely social. At a meeting of eight members at University College, London, Bayliss was a guest; other guests recorded as present were C. D. F. Phillips, Dudley Buxton, Sidney Martin, W. D. Halliburton, (Sir) John Rose Bradford, and Raphael Meldola. Bayliss was secretary from 1900 till 1922 and treasurer from that date until his death. The regularity of his attendance at the meetings was quite exceptional.

Bayliss's scientific researches had begun before going to Oxford with a study of the electric currents developed in the salivary glands and, like much of his other work, was done in collaboration, this time with Rose Bradford. In 1891 Bayliss and Ernest Henry Starling [q.v.] began that collaboration which lasted in one form or another until Bayliss's death and which was productive of a great advance in the knowledge of physiology. Its first-fruit was a paper on the electric currents of the mammalian heart. In 1894 was published their classical paper on venous and capillary pressures, and in 1898–9 appeared papers on the innervation of the intestine, which held the field until X-ray methods shed new light on the subject. The richest fruit of this collaboration, however, came in 1902 with the discovery of secretin. Throughout these years Bayliss was bearing a much lighter burden of administrative work and of teaching than Starling, and consequently, in addition to taking his share in these researches, had time to pursue other investigations. These were mostly concerned with the vascular system—the circulation through the brain, vaso-motor reflexes, antidromic nerve fibres, and the like.

At about this time also (1900) Bayliss evinced a growing interest in the chemical and physical sides of physiology, which were then opening up. He did some work on enzyme action, but the principal form which the interest took was the publication of his book *Principles of General Physiology* (1915), which quickly became a standard authority. It was a monument of erudition, clear statement, and cautious rejection of anything but what was completely established. The book went through four editions, and was so much the creature of Bayliss's own personality that after his death it could not have been perpetuated by others without losing its distinctive character. Bayliss was the author of two shorter books, *The Nature of Enzyme Action* (1908) and *The Vaso-motor System* (1923). His principal contributions to physiology dealt with the use of saline injections for the amelioration of surgical shock, a treatment which met with a considerable measure of success. In the summer of 1918 over 50,000 litres of 'gum-saline' were sent out to the British forces in France.

Bayliss was elected F.R.S. in 1903 and knighted in 1922, and he held many degrees from universities and academies at home and abroad. He was a member of the council of the Royal Society (1913–1915), Croonian lecturer (1904), royal medallist (1911), and Copley medallist (1919). He received the Baly medal of the Royal College of Physicians (1917), and delivered the Oliver-Sharpey lectures (1918), the Sylvanus Thompson lectures (1919), and the Herter lectures (1922). Wadham College made him an honorary fellow in 1922.

Bayliss married in 1893 Gertrude Ellen, daughter of Matthew Henry Starling, clerk of the crown, Bombay, and sister of E. H. Starling: they had three sons and one daughter. They lived at Hampstead, and to physiologists their generous hospitality was a signal feature of the social side of academic life. Indeed, Bayliss delighted in the society of other scientific men: not least that of young physiologists, many of whom gravitated to the Institute at University College in order to work with Starling and himself. Bayliss's honesty and generosity of outlook, the simplicity and nobility of his mind, his faculty of getting to the bottom of problems, coupled with his great erudition, made intercourse with him at once a pleasure and an education. He died at Hampstead 27 August 1924.

[*The Times*, 28 August 1924; *Proceedings* of the Royal Society, vol. xcix, B., 1926 (with portrait); private information.]

J. Barcroft.

BEARSTED, first Viscount (1853–1927), joint-founder of the Shell Transport and Trading Company. [See Samuel, Marcus.]

BÉGIN, LOUIS NAZAIRE (1840–1925), cardinal and archbishop of Quebec, born at La Pointe-Lévis in French Canada 10 January 1840, was the son of Charles Bégin, farmer, by his wife, Luce Paradis. His parents came of farming stock of French descent. He began his education at the Lévis model school, whence he proceeded to the commercial college, St. Michel, and entered the archdiocesan seminary at Quebec in 1857. After graduating B.A. from Laval University, Quebec, he was sent to Rome in 1863 in order to complete his theological studies at the French College and Gregorian University. He was ordained priest at Rome in 1865, and received the degree of D.D. from the university of Innsbruck two years later. On returning to Canada in 1868 Bégin was appointed professor of theology and church history at Laval University and held the chair until 1884 when he was appointed principal of the Laval normal school.

Bégin was raised to the episcopate as bishop of Chicoutimi, one of the suffragan sees of the province of Quebec, in 1888, and three years later returned to the city of Quebec as coadjutor to Cardinal Taschereau and titular archbishop of Cyrene. Owing to the state of the cardinal's health, Bégin was appointed administrator of the archdiocese in 1894, and succeeded Taschereau as archbishop of Quebec in 1898. While teaching at Laval, Bégin had published papers on the primacy and infallibility of the sovereign pontiffs and on scripture and the rule of faith. During his episcopate he brought out *La Chronologie de l'histoire des États Unis d'Amérique* (1895) and a *Catéchisme de controverse* (1902). His tenure of the see of Quebec was marked by the formation of many new parishes, the introduction of fresh religious communities, and, above all, by a campaign of social action. As bishop of Chicoutimi he had joined the other members of the Canadian hierarchy in their protests against the Manitoba school law of 1890. In 1907 he founded the organization known as L'Action Sociale Catholique with its publication *L'Action sociale.* He was greatly assisted in this work by Monseigneur Paul Eugène Roy who, at Bégin's request, was appointed titular bishop of Eleutheropolis in 1908. During the archbishop's later years much of the administrative work of the archdiocese of Quebec was undertaken by Monseigneur Roy, who became titular archbishop of Seleucia in 1914 and coadjutor with right of succession in 1920. Meanwhile, in May 1914, Archbishop Bégin had been created cardinal priest by Pope Pius X with the titular church of San Vitale. He lived to the age of eighty-five, and was only survived by a few months by his coadjutor, who was already suffering from an incurable disease at his succession. Cardinal Bégin died at Quebec 18 July 1925 and was buried in the crypt of his cathedral.

[A. Robert, *Le cardinal Bégin* in *Canada Française*, 1925; E. van Cauwenbergh in *Dictionnaire d'histoire et de géographie ecclésiastiques*, vol. vii, 1934.] D. Mathew.

BEILBY, Sir GEORGE THOMAS (1850–1924), industrial chemist, was born in Edinburgh 17 November 1850, the youngest son of George Thomas Beilby, M.D., by his wife, Rachel, daughter of the Rev. Jonathan Watson, minister of Dublin Street Baptist Church, Edinburgh. He was educated at private schools and at Edinburgh University. In 1869 he became associated with the Scottish paraffin shale industry, by joining the Oakbank Oil Company as chemist. Together with William Young he so improved the process of distillation of shale as to obtain a greatly increased recovery of ammonia, and the continuous retort introduced by them in 1881 brought about a large increase in the yield of paraffin and of ammonia. In 1890 Beilby turned his attention to the production of cyanides, in order to meet the new demand occasioned by the invention of the McArthur-Forrest process for the treatment of gold ores. He devised a process which involved the action of ammonia on a mixture of potassium carbonate and carbon, sufficient cyanide being always present to keep the mass fluid. The Cassel Gold Extracting Company, later called the Cassel Cyanide Company (of which Beilby became a director), used this process until 1906, when Beilby introduced a new process invented by Hamilton Castner, in which metallic sodium was employed. His association with Castner in the development of this process led him to become a director of the Castner-Kellner Alkali Company, which manufactured sodium at Runcorn, and now set up new works for the production of sodium at Newcastle-on-Tyne. With these branches of chemical industry Beilby remained closely connected throughout the rest of his life.

Having observed, in the course of manufacturing operations, the rapid destruction of metals by ammonia at high temperatures, Beilby was led to a detailed study of the flow of solids. As the result of very beautiful experiments with the microscope, carried out with the simplest of laboratory equipment, he concluded that when a solid is caused to flow, as in the polishing of its surface, the crystalline structure is partly broken down, and a layer is formed with the properties of a vitreous material. The fact that this layer is harder than the crystals seemed to provide a hypothetical explanation of the hardening of metals by cold-working. It was supposed that a vitreous layer was formed on surfaces of slip within the crystals, causing a decrease of density and an increased resistance to further flow. This hypothesis met with much criticism, especially from foreign chemists, but it accounted in a satisfactory way for a wide range of phenomena, and gave a great stimulus to research. Beilby's experiments on the crystalline and vitreous states, bearing the impress of a highly original mind, are collected in his only book, *Aggregation and Flow of Solids*, published in 1921.

Beilby's manufacturing experience led him to take great interest in the economical use of fuel, and in his presidential address to the Society of Chemical Industry in 1899 he reviewed the subject, this being the first of many such studies. He made a report to the royal commission on coal supplies and economy (1902–1904), and was a member of the royal commission on fuel oil engines for the navy (1912–1913). In 1906 he made a series of important experiments in the low-temperature carbonization of coal, and later carried out microscopical studies on the cell structure and properties of coke. His scientific knowledge proved of great value in the European War, and in 1917 he became the first chairman and director of the Fuel Research Board. It was under his direction that the Fuel Research Station at East Greenwich was designed and erected, and in the six years during which he was director of the Research Board attention was mainly directed to the production of oil from coal by carbonization and to a survey of British coal resources. To Beilby, also, is due the introduction of the 'therm' as the basis for reckoning the consumption of gas in towns.

Beilby was a man of high character and great modesty. He was keenly interested in educational matters, and from 1907 till 1923 was chairman of the governing body of the Royal Technical College, Glasgow, to which institution he was a generous benefactor as well as a wise counsellor. He was president of the Institute of Chemistry from 1909 to 1912 and of the Institute of Metals from 1916 to 1918. He received honorary degrees from the universities of Glasgow and Birmingham, and was president of the chemical section of the British Association at its meeting in South Africa in 1905. He was elected a fellow of the Royal Society in 1906 and knighted in 1916. He married in 1877 Emma Clarke, daughter of the Rev. Samuel Newman, and had one son and one daughter.

Beilby died at Hampstead 1 August 1924.

[*Proceedings* of the Royal Society, vol. cix, A, 1925; private information.]

C. H. Desch.

BEIT, Sir OTTO JOHN, first baronet (1865–1930), financier and philanthropist, was born at Altona 7 December 1865, the third son of Siegfried Beit, merchant, of Hamburg, by his wife, Laura Hahn. He was thus the brother, many years younger, of Alfred Beit [q.v.], the lifelong friend and associate of Cecil John Rhodes [q.v.]. Otto Beit's devotion to his elder brother Alfred during his life, and his reverence for his memory after his death, were perhaps the strongest influences in his life. Following in the footsteps of the brother who had linked himself so closely to the policy and fortunes of Rhodes, Otto Beit, who had been educated at Hamburg, came to England in 1888 and became naturalized as a British subject. In 1903 he entered the firm of L. Hirsch & Co., of London, a financial house closely connected with South African business. As it chanced, he was staying with Rhodes as his guest at Groote Schuur, Capetown, in December 1895 when the news arrived that (Sir) Leander Starr Jameson [q.v.] had started on his 'Raid' into the Transvaal.

On the death of Alfred Beit in 1906, Otto Beit succeeded to the bulk of his elder brother's great fortune and to his country house and estate at Tewin Water, Welwyn, Hertfordshire. Here and at his London house, 49 Belgrave Square, Otto Beit lived for the remainder of his life. He entertained hospitably; but his manner of living was, for a man of great wealth, as he had now become, simple and modest. He succeeded his brother not only as his residuary legatee, but also, in 1910, as a director of the British South Africa Company, and as one of the trustees under the will of Cecil Rhodes. He was also one of the trustees appointed under his brother's will to administer a fund of £2,000,000 bequeathed for the purpose of improving the means of communication in Africa, with special reference to the project (which had been dear to the heart of Rhodes) of a Cape to Cairo railway, or alternatively, for educational and charitable purposes in Rhodesia. Thenceforth the guiding motive of Otto Beit's life was that of using these and his own vast resources as his late brother would have wished. He took an active part in securing the realization of one of Rhodes's dreams, that of the establishment of a residential and teaching university for South African youths, whether of British or of Dutch descent, on the Groote Schuur estate; for this purpose both Sir Julius Charles Wernher [q.v.] and Alfred Beit had made liberal bequests. In recognition of his services in this matter Otto Beit received the honorary degree of LL.D. of the university of Capetown in 1920. He was also a munificent benefactor to the Imperial College of Science and Technology in London, and the founder, in memory of his brother, of the Beit memorial fellowships for medical research. For these and other acts of public generosity he was elected F.R.S., and was knighted K.C.M.G. in 1920. He was created a baronet in 1924, and received the honorary degree of LL.D. of the university of Edinburgh in 1930.

Beit married in 1897 Lilian, daughter of Thomas Lane Carter, who was connected with railway and telegraph business in New Orleans, U.S.A.; they had two sons (the younger of whom, Alfred Lane, succeeded to the baronetcy) and two daughters. He died in London 7 December 1930. He was a man of simple life and tastes, of unselfish ambitions, and of the strongest family affections and personal friendships.

[Private information; personal knowledge.]

D. O. MALCOLM.

BELL, ALEXANDER GRAHAM (1847–1922), inventor of the telephone and educator of the deaf, was born in Edinburgh 3 March 1847, the second of the three sons of Alexander Melville Bell (1819–1905), by his first wife, Eliza Grace, daughter of Samuel Symonds, surgeon in the royal navy. His grandfather, Alexander Bell (1790–1865), was professor of elocution in London, and his father was a distinguished authority on the physiology of the voice and on elocution. Bell was educated at McLauren's Academy, Edinburgh, and at Edinburgh High School, which he left at the age of thirteen. In 1863 he became a pupil-teacher of elocution and music at Weston House Academy, Elgin, Morayshire. After a year spent at Edinburgh University, he returned to Elgin, and from there went as a master to Somersetshire College, Bath. In 1867 he joined his father, who had taken up his grandfather's work in London, and became his assistant. The same year he matriculated at London University, where he studied anatomy and physiology. In 1870 his parents emigrated to Canada, and Bell accompanied them.

Before leaving England Bell had already begun the study of the two subjects which were to form his life-work. As early as 1865, while at Elgin, he had conceived the idea of the electrical transmission of speech; and in 1868 he began his work for the deaf by teaching his father's system of 'visible speech' at a school for deaf children in Kensington. Before leaving London, also, he had read Hermann Helmholtz's *The Sensations of Tone*, from which he gained knowledge of the physical principles underlying the theory of sound. Bell continued his work for the deaf, which was already becoming known in the United States, in Boston and Northampton, Massachusetts, and in Hartford, Connecticut (1871–1872). In 1873 he was appointed professor of vocal physiology and the mechanics of speech in the school of oratory of Boston University, a post which he held in conjunction with extensive private work. So great was the interest aroused by his lectures and so successful were his methods, that he was invited by the university of Oxford to deliver a course of lectures on 'Speech' at the Taylor Institution in October 1878. Bell's chief aim in life was, indeed, to promote the welfare of the deaf, and it was by this approach that he achieved his most important invention, the telephone.

It was in the summer of 1874 that Bell, while spending his vacation at his father's home, Brantford, Ontario, formulated the theory of the telephone which he was able shortly to put into practice and ultimately to perfect. He was simultaneously pursuing two lines of inquiry, the investigation of a tuned system of multiple telegraphy and the study of air waves in the ear of the human cadaver during the utterance of voice-sounds. The evolution of the telephone was due to the connecting up of these two pieces of research. Bell propounded his theory to the American physicist, Joseph Henry, who encouraged him to try to give practical effect to it. In June 1875 the first rough telephone was constructed in Boston; in March 1876 the first complete intelligible sentence was transmitted; and by April 1877 it was possible to conduct a partially successful telephone conversation between Boston and New York. The first telephone is thus described by Thomas A. Watson, Bell's assistant in his experiments: 'That first telephone was a very simple mechanism consisting of a wooden frame on which was mounted one of Bell's harmonic receivers, a tightly stretched parchment drumhead to the center of which the free end of the receiver reed was fastened and a mouthpiece arranged to direct the voice against the other side of the drumhead. It was designed to force the reed to follow the vibrations of the voice and so generate voice-shaped electric undulations.' [Thomas A. Watson, *Exploring Life*, p. 69, 1926.] In March 1876 Bell took out a patent for his invention and, although his claim was hotly and protractedly contested, it was eventually upheld by the United States Supreme Court.

In August 1877 Bell went to Europe in order to introduce the telephone into England and France. On his return to the United States in the autumn of 1878 he settled at Washington. In 1880 he was awarded the Volta prize of 50,000 francs by the French government for his invention of the telephone. With this money he financed the Volta Laboratory at Washington, afterwards converted into the Volta Bureau for the increase and diffusion of knowledge relating to the deaf. The Bureau worked in close co-operation with the American Association for the promotion of the teaching of speech to the deaf, organized in 1890, of which Bell was elected president. Among other scientific works he published a memoir *Upon a Formation of a Deaf Variety of the Human Race* (1884).

Bell's interest in the subject of the marriage of the deaf led him to study eugenics as a whole, and he was elected honorary president of the second International Congress of Eugenics. During the last twenty-five years of his life he showed a keen interest in aviation. He received many honours, including the legion of honour, the Hughes medal of the Royal Society (1913), the freedom of the city of Edinburgh (1920), and honorary degrees from several universities, including that of D.Sc. from the university of Oxford (1907). He was naturalized as an American citizen in 1874, but he never forgot his ties with Scotland; he owned a large estate in Nova Scotia, Beinn Bhreagh, near Baddeck, Cape Breton Island, where he spent his summers and where he died 2 August 1922.

Bell married in 1877 Mabel Gardiner, daughter of Gardiner G. Hubbard, who had given him much help in his work for the education of the deaf and in the commercial management of his inventions. Mrs. Bell had been entirely deaf from early childhood. Two daughters were born of the marriage.

[*The Times*, 3 August 1922; *Dictionary of American Biography*, vol. ii.]

M. R. Toynbee.

BELL, GERTRUDE MARGARET LOWTHIAN (1868 – 1926), traveller, archaeologist, and government servant, was born 14 July 1868 at Washington Hall, co. Durham, the elder child and only daughter of (Sir) Thomas Hugh Bell, ironmaster, afterwards second baronet, by his first wife, Mary, daughter of John Shield, of Newcastle. Sir Isaac Lowthian Bell, first baronet [q.v.], was her grandfather. Her mother dying in 1871, her father married secondly in 1876 Florence, daughter of Sir Joseph Francis Olliffe [q.v.], physician to the British embassy at Paris and sister-in-law of Sir Frank Cavendish Lascelles [q.v.], the diplomatist. She was educated at Queen's College, Harley Street, and at Lady Margaret Hall, Oxford, where her intellectual power and eager *naïveté* made an impression in a university still unused to women students of a serious type. In 1888, while still under twenty, she obtained a first class in modern history, being the first woman candidate to achieve that distinction.

The next ten years of Gertrude Bell's life were filled with various activities: social duties in her London and Yorkshire homes, a season's climbing in 1897, a voyage round the world, and long visits to Sir Frank and Lady Lascelles at Bucharest (1888–1889), Teheran (1892–1893), and Berlin (1897). She learned Persian, and in 1897 published an admirable verse translation of the Divan of Hafiz (*Poems from the Divan of Hafiz*); a volume of Persian sketches, *Safar Nameh*, had already appeared in 1894. But her true call to the East came in 1899, when she settled for the winter in Jerusalem in order to learn Arabic. Adventurous visits to Petra and Baalbek awoke in her an enthusiasm for desert travel and Syrian archaeology. Her first long journey, however, was delayed for five years. Meanwhile, in 1901, 1902, and 1904, with Ulrich Führer as guide, Gertrude Bell made her name as an Alpinist, her main achievements being an exploration of the Engelhörner group, an ascent of the Matterhorn from the Italian side, and an attempt, which nearly proved fatal, on the then unclimbed north-east face of the Finsteraarhorn, when her courage and endurance were the mainstay of the party, caught by bad weather near the summit and forced to spend forty-eight hours on the rope before reaching safety.

In January 1905 Gertrude Bell set out from Jerusalem on a journey through Syria and Cilicia to Konia in Asia Minor. Her vivid account of the Syrian portion, *The Desert and the Sown*, appeared in 1907; she described the later stages in the *Revue archéologique*, 1906 and 1907. She had by this time made herself, without formal apprenticeship, a competent field archaeologist. In 1907, in company with Sir W. M. Ramsay, she explored the Hittite and Byzantine site of Bin-bir-kilisse, near Isaura; the results of their work were described in a joint publication, *The Thousand and One Churches* (1909). In the latter year, journeying from Aleppo down the Euphrates, she was led to the almost unvisited site of Ukhaidír, a ruined early Islamic palace near Kerbela. She returned by way of Bagdad and Mosul to Asia Minor, and her account of this journey, *Amurath to Amurath* (1911), reflects her first impressions of the Young Turk revolution. She went back to explore Ukhaidír in 1911; and *The Palace and Mosque of Ukhaidír* (1914) is her most important archaeological publication.

Meanwhile, Gertrude Bell's thoughts had turned again to the project, which she had long nursed, of a journey into central Arabia proper, whither, of European women, only Lady Anne Blunt [see Blunt, Wilfrid Scawen] had preceded her. Starting from Damascus in December 1913, she reached Hail in safety, but could get no further. The emir of Hail was absent and on bad terms with his southern neighbour, Ibn Saud; his deputies, alarmed at her arrival amongst a fanatical population, kept her an honoured prisoner until, seeing no other way out, she agreed to make for Bagdad; thither she arrived, tired and suffering under a sense of failure, in April 1914. But she had gained, together with much new geographical material, a unique knowledge of north Arabian personalities and politics.

The outbreak of the European War in August 1914 did not at once send Gertrude Bell back to the East. In November 1914 she joined the Red Cross organization for tracing the missing, and after service at Boulogne, in February 1915 was called to reorganize the head-quarters in London—a task which she performed with fierce thoroughness. In the autumn of 1915, when an Arab movement against Turkish rule began to take shape, the military authorities in Cairo mobilized a number of British subjects with expert knowledge of pre-War Arabia for service with a newly-formed Arab intelligence bureau. Among them was Gertrude Bell. She reached Cairo on 30 November 1915 and was allotted the task of collecting and summarizing information about the Bedouin tribes and sheikhs of Northern Arabia. In January 1916 she undertook a mission of liaison to Delhi, where the government of India was preparing a gazetteer of Arabia. The viceroy, Lord Hardinge, asked her to visit Basra on her return journey in order to link up her tribal information with that coming in to the head-quarters of the Mesopotamian Expeditionary Force. Landing at Basra in March 1916, she was at first attached to the military intelligence staff; three months later she joined the secretariat of the chief political officer with the Expeditionary Force, Sir Percy Cox, was gazetted as an assistant political officer, and undertook the duties of Oriental secretary. In this capacity her special knowledge of Arab politics and her pre-War Arab friendships were of great value in the work of keeping friendly touch with the desert tribes on the left flank of the British force, and of explaining British intentions to the Arabs who ventured to head-quarters, while her energy, warm loyalty, and trained powers of statement and analysis made her a trusted and effective government servant and colleague. Moving to Bagdad soon after its capture in March 1917, she continued to act as Oriental secretary to Sir Percy Cox, now civil commissioner, and to his successor, Sir Arnold Wilson. In 1920 the latter commissioned her to prepare a *Review of the Civil Administration of Mesopotamia*, which was published in 1921 as a white paper, and acknowledged to be a masterpiece in its kind.

Liberal by instinct and upbringing, Gertrude Bell was a convinced believer in early political independence for the Arab people, and was out of sympathy with those who wished for some form of administration on British-Indian lines. With the return of Sir Percy Cox to Bagdad in 1920 as British high commissioner in Mesopotamia, charged with the task of setting up an Arab government, she found herself possessed of great influence; and in the following months that culminated in 1921 in the election of the Emir Feisal to the throne of Iraq, she was the adviser both of Sir Percy Cox and of the Arab ministers. The success of the new and doubtful venture was in large measure due to the trust which Feisal and the leading notables of Iraq placed in the British high commissioner and herself.

With the establishment of the new state, and as political negotiation gave way to administrative problems in which she claimed no special competence, one side of Gertrude Bell's work for Iraq was virtually accomplished. She remained at her post as Oriental secretary, but began to give her thoughts and few leisure hours to the organization of a service of antiquities. In 1918 she had been appointed honorary director of antiquities, and now she set herself to realize the project of a national museum at Bagdad. The museum was inaugurated in 1923, and installed in permanent quarters in 1926. While on sick leave in England in the summer of 1925, she spoke of coming back to England as soon as a permanent director of antiquities could be found; but first she was determined to pass one more summer in Iraq, and launch the museum on its course. Ten years in the country, however, broken only by three spells of leave in Europe and England, had worn down her reserves of strength. She died suddenly in her sleep in the night of 11–12 July 1926 at Bagdad, and was buried the following day. A large concourse, both Arab and British, followed her to the grave in the British cemetery, close to the south gate. At the suggestion of King Feisal in 1927, a wing of the Bagdad Museum was named after her.

Gertrude Bell was of middle height, slender, and erect, with auburn hair and piercing greenish-brown eyes set in finely cut features. Her look and manner conveyed an impression of intense vitality and high intelligence. No less characteristic were her loyalty to and affection for her friends and colleagues in archaeology and political service. A drawing of her by J. S. Sargent is in the possession of Sir Maurice Bell, Bart., at Mount Grace, Yorkshire, and a bust, executed by Anne Acheson, is in the Bagdad Museum.

[*The Times*, 13, 14, and 15 July 1926; *The Letters of Gertrude Bell*, selected and edited by Lady Bell, 2 vols., 1927; *Alpine Journal*, November 1922 and November 1926; *Geographical Journal*, July 1927; private information.] W. D. Hogarth.

BENSON, ARTHUR CHRISTOPHER (1862–1925), man of letters and master of Magdalene College, Cambridge, the second son of Edward White Benson [q.v.], afterwards archbishop of Canterbury, by his wife, Mary Sidgwick (a second cousin), was born 24 April 1862, at Wellington College, of which his father was the first headmaster. The eldest son, Martin, died as a scholar of Winchester, and Arthur thus became the eldest of a family of three brothers and two sisters. Robert Hugh Benson [q.v.] was his youngest brother. He went in 1872 to a well-known private school, Temple Grove, East Sheen, which he describes in a biography of the headmaster, O. C. Waterfield, in *Memories and Friends*. From there he gained a scholarship at Eton in 1874. He had there a happy and successful career, both in work and in games, and was elected to a scholarship at King's College, Cambridge, in 1881. At Cambridge, Benson's life began to broaden intellectually; he wrote for various university journals, read many essays before literary societies, and acted twice in Greek plays. He obtained a first class in the classical tripos in 1884, and returned to Eton as a master in the following year.

Benson soon began to write, his first publication being the imaginary *Memoirs of Arthur Hamilton*, written under the pseudonym of Christopher Carr in 1886. This was soon followed by three volumes of poems and one of essays, and by *Men of Might* (1892), a biographical book for boys written in collaboration with his friend, H. F. W. Tatham. In 1892 he became a house master, and was soon justly considered to be one of the best ever known at Eton. In *The Schoolmaster* (1902), Benson set forth the principles on which he acted, but not even his own book could describe his influence on his boys, which was above all of a humanizing character, and successful in making them do their best in all walks of life. Those boys especially who had literary inclinations found in him an encouragement quite exceptional in the public schools of the day. But in spite of his brilliant success, Benson found that schoolmastering took up too much time in a life which he wished to be devoted to writing. Having published in 1899 his excellent *Life* of his father and the *Fasti Etonenses*, he resigned his mastership in 1903 and went to live at Cambridge, intending to give himself up both to his own original work and to the editing, in collaboration with the second Viscount Esher [q.v.], of *Selections from the Correspondence of Queen Victoria*, which appeared in three volumes in 1907.

A chance then determined the course which the rest of Benson's life was to take. His friend, Stuart Alexander Donaldson, had been transferred from a mastership at Eton to become master of Magdalene College, Cambridge, and one day in the course of a walk mentioned to Benson that the college ought to elect a fellow, but would find it difficult, owing to its narrow resources at the time, to pay the fellowship dividend. 'Why not take me?' said Benson, who by that time could afford to accept a fellowship without emolument. The fellows of Magdalene were delighted to have so agreeable and distinguished an addition to their number, and he was elected in October 1904. He moved into rooms in college the next year, and in 1907 into the Old Lodge, a dwelling-house forming part of the college, to which he added some premises next door in Magdalene Street, making it a comfortable and even spacious house. There he remained for the rest of his life. On Donaldson's death in 1915 Benson was elected master of the college, as was hoped and expected by all. He died at the Old Lodge, from heart failure following pleurisy, 17 June 1925, having seen Magdalene rise from comparative insignificance to the position of one of the best and most sought-after among the smaller Cambridge colleges. At two periods during his Cambridge years, in 1907–1908 and 1917–

1922, he was troubled by deep and lasting fits of depression, a form of nervous breakdown which made it necessary for him to go away for a time: he was otherwise a healthy man, enjoying ordinary games in his youth, mountaineering as a young man, and shooting in middle age.

The literary activity which had begun in the busy years at Eton naturally broadened out when Benson had more leisure at Cambridge, and his published works amount to more than a hundred volumes. The essays were perhaps most widely read, and, curiously enough, gave him most pleasure to write; but they are somewhat tenuous in substance, and are unlikely to last. His literary criticisms—Rossetti, FitzGerald, Pater, Ruskin (the first three in the 'English Men of Letters' series, 1904–1906) are among his best subjects—are acute and sympathetic, and deserve the success which they attained. Towards the end of his life he published one or two novels, attractive in a quiet and cultured style. Short biographies (*The Leaves of the Tree*, 1911, *Memories and Friends*, 1924) show him at his very best. He has left in the custody of his college a voluminous diary, much more pungent than would be expected by all but the most intimate of his friends. A selection from it, edited by P. Lubbock, was published in 1926.

Benson will probably survive more by memory of personal contact than by any of his books, for he had a very wide and deep influence both at Eton and at Cambridge. He was a most attractive talker, and an almost perfect guide to young men with literary aspirations. He would hear and criticize the essays of nearly all the undergraduates of his college. Others, too, found in him a very ready and sympathetic adviser, and his was perhaps the strongest cultural influence at Cambridge during the twenty years before his death. His books had a wide popularity in all the English-speaking countries, and he was an indefatigable correspondent, always willing to reply to inquiries and to give counsel to unknown persons who wrote to him from all over the world.

Benson's name was freely mentioned as a possible and even probable successor to the headmastership of Eton when Dr. Edmond Warre retired in 1905. He was perhaps fortunate not to be appointed, for he had ideas of reform calculated to bring him into conflict with the other masters and with the traditions of the school. Although he owed all that he had and was to a classical education, and was a good specimen of what it could produce, he professed to believe that the right education for the upper-class youth of the day would be found in history and particularly in instruction in modern languages, of which he was himself curiously ignorant. Such views could do no harm at Cambridge, and were indeed welcomed by the 'liberals' in the academic world; but they would have been thought quite out of place at Eton.

Benson was never married. Faintly liberal in politics, in Church matters he was a keen conformist with some latitudinarian tendencies, but delighting in a well-ordered ceremonial. He had a tall, upright figure, growing a little bulky in middle age, with fair hair going grey, a ruddy complexion, and blue eyes. He generally dressed in grey flannel, with a double-breasted coat. There is a portrait of him by William Nicholson in the Fitzwilliam Museum, Cambridge, and another by R. E. Fuller Maitland in the combination room at Magdalene College. A cartoon by 'Spy' appeared in *Vanity Fair* 4 June 1903.

[*Arthur Christopher Benson as seen by some friends*, 1925; personal knowledge.]

S. Gaselee.

BENTON, Sir JOHN (1850–1927), civil engineer, born 5 August 1850 at Sheriffhaugh, Banffshire, was the second son of John Benton, of Sheriffhaugh, by his wife, Mary, daughter of Alexander Hay, of Edintore. He was educated at Aberdeen, attended lectures at the University, and in 1869 became a pupil of William Smith, a civil engineer in Aberdeen. In 1870 he entered Edinburgh University, but in 1871 he became one of the first students of the Royal Indian Engineering College at Cooper's Hill, which was opened in that year. In 1873 he was appointed a second-grade assistant engineer in the Indian Public Works Department. He was promoted to executive engineer, fourth grade, in 1881, to third grade in the same year, to second grade in 1885, and to first grade in 1892. During this period he had charge of heavy constructional work on the first division of the canal which irrigated the Upper Bari Doab and on the first and fourth divisions of the Sirhind canal. He also designed the auxiliary supply canal of the Upper Bari Doab canal.

In 1897 Benton became a superintending engineer and his services were lent to the government of Burma. Fresh from the

Punjab canals, he found irrigation in Burma in a primitive state, weirs being made of stakes and stones instead of masonry and brickwork; but by originality and resource, as well as by refusing to tolerate incompetence, he effected great reforms. On the Mandalay canal, his first work, opened in 1902, when he found that the standardized ten-foot openings could not take the amount of drift brought down by the floods, he substituted forty-foot openings, a practice which he followed later in the Shwebo and Ye-u canals, the former of which was opened in 1906. In the Thapaugaing aqueduct, spanning a flood-swept nullah, he converted the walls into folding shutters, so that the flood water might safely sweep over the whole structure. He remodelled the canals in the Kyaukse district, and improved the Meiktila lake works. He remained in Burma for five years, was made a chief engineer in 1900, and received the C.I.E. in 1902.

At the end of 1902 Benton returned to the Punjab in order to succeed Mr. Sidney Preston (with whom as a junior he had already been associated in his work on the Bari Doab and Sirhind canals) as chief engineer and secretary to government. He retired under the age limit in August 1905, but in January 1906 he was recalled by the viceroy, Lord Curzon, and appointed, in succession to Preston, inspector-general of irrigation for all India.

In these later periods of service Benton undertook two projects of the greatest importance, the Triple Canals scheme and the Upper Swat Valley canal. The former doubled the fertile area in the Punjab by distributing the surplus waters of the Jhelum across the province. The waters of the Jhelum (the most westerly of the five rivers of the Punjab) were drawn off at Mangla, not far from the Himalayas, and brought into the Chenab river below Kothala by the Upper Jhelum canal. This supply irrigates the Jech Doab in its passage and affords a surplus for irrigation to the Chenab river, which is drawn off some distance above Kothala by the Upper Chenab canal. This canal irrigates the Upper Rechna Doab, west of the Ravi river, and its tail waters are carried by a syphon under that river to irrigate the Lower Bari Doab to the east. The scheme, sanctioned in 1905 and completed in 1917 at a cost of eight million pounds, was the largest irrigation work hitherto carried out in India and served as an example for subsequent achievements. It was described by Benton in a paper read before the Institution of Civil Engineers in November 1915 (*Proceedings*, 1915–16, cci, 24) for which he received a Telford medal.

Benton's boldness of conception was manifested in his second great work of irrigation, nearer the Afghan frontier. He tapped the Swat river at Chakdarrah by a canal, which he carried in a tunnel more than two miles long, known as the Benton tunnel, under the Malakand Pass through the mountain barrier above Dargai. The area 'commanded' by this canal was two and a half times larger than that formerly served by the Swat River canal. The fall of four hundred feet from the mouth of the tunnel into the Dargai valley provided power for the electrification of the Nowshera-Dargai railway as well as for local purposes. Benton was created K.C.I.E. in 1911 and retired finally in 1912. He was elected a member of the Institution of Civil Engineers in 1893, and was a member of its council from 1906 to 1908. He died at Eastbourne 29 August 1927. He married in 1885 Margaret Forsyth, daughter of Robert Dick, provost of Rothes, Morayshire, by whom he had one son, who was killed in the European War, and two daughters.

[*The Times*, 31 August 1927; *Proceedings* of the Institution of Civil Engineers, 1927–1928, vol. ccxxv, 353.] E. I. Carlyle.

BERNARD, JOHN HENRY (1860–1927), archbishop of Dublin and provost of Trinity College, Dublin, was born 27 July 1860 at Sooree, Bengal, the only son of William Frederick Bernard, a civil engineer who worked in India for sixteen years and died there in 1862, by his wife, Martha Amelia Humphrys. He came of a family which had been settled in Kerry since the reign of Charles I. His grandfather was a naval surgeon, and three of his uncles served in the royal navy. His mother, left a widow with small means on which to rear her son and an infant daughter, returned to Ireland with the children, and settled in Bray, co. Wicklow, where the boy attended a small but efficient school. In 1875, being then little more than fifteen, he entered Trinity College, Dublin, where he held his own against older competitors, winning first a sizarship and then a scholarship of the House, and graduating in 1880 with second place of the first class in both mathematics and philosophy. He set to work at once to read for a fellowship. Success depended on gaining the highest total of marks at an exceedingly severe examination in which competitors who took different subjects were matched together. Besides being younger than most of his rivals, Bernard was under a further disadvantage: in order to help his mother's finances, he had been during his undergraduate course assistant master at a small school, and now while reading for fellowship he spent half the working day in giving private tuition. In spite of this handicap he was successful at his third attempt in 1884, defeating so formidable an opponent as the historian J. B. Bury. He won his fellowship mainly in mathematics, but his real interest lay in philosophy and theology; his college friends were mainly men of like tendencies. He took orders in 1886; two years later he was appointed to Archbishop King's lecturership, the second post in the divinity school of Trinity College. He was young for such a position, and looked even younger than he was, thanks to his fair complexion and alert carriage; but college opinion already recognized that these appearances belied a personality marked by concentration of purpose, cool judgement, and instinct for leadership.

There was at this time among the younger fellows much dissatisfaction with the management of college affairs, and Bernard soon became a leader of the malcontents. Reform was certainly needed. The college did not lack brilliant men on its staff; but a system which placed its government exclusively in the hands of the provost and the seven senior fellows was indefensible in principle and reactionary in practice. The reforms, however, which Bernard and a few others desired proved to be too radical for the majority, and the agitation expired in talk. Convinced by this fiasco that reform could only come from without, Bernard abjured college politics and thenceforth devoted his energies to the duties of his lecturership (which was converted into a professorship in 1906) and to literary activities. Under the influence of (Sir) John Pentland Mahaffy [q.v.] he set himself to interpret the Kantian philosophy to English readers; but he soon gravitated in the direction of biblical scholarship and theology. He worked at authorship with the same concentration and dispatch as in practical affairs; between 1889 and 1918 he scarcely let a year pass without its volume, maintaining always a high level of execution. Yet these occupations were never allowed to interfere with the business of his chair. He was an excellent teacher, clear and vigorous, and his dominating personality gave him exceptional influence with his students. Its effects in moulding the minds and characters of the young men who passed through his hands during his tenure of office (1888–1911) left a lasting impress on the Church of Ireland. His influence tended to liberalize the prevalent conception of churchmanship, and to emphasize the need for dignity and order in public worship. Judged by Irish standards he ranked as a high churchman, and he was accordingly a mark for the attacks of the extreme protestants in the General Synod; but he laid no excessive stress on ritual, and was entirely untouched by Romanizing tendencies.

Bernard's reputation in the church at large, especially among the clergy, increased steadily. He might have become bishop of Meath in 1897, but preferred to retain his academic post. In that year he was appointed treasurer of St. Patrick's cathedral, and in 1902 he accepted the deanery of St. Patrick's, a position which could be held along with his lecturership, although it involved the resignation of his fellowship. Without any remission of his college duties or literary work, he filled his new post with remarkable success, and took advantage of his position to invite visits from leading men in the Church of England. He was always anxious to maintain close relations with the larger community and to counteract the drift towards separatism in ecclesiastical as in secular policy. He was on terms of friendship with many prominent English churchmen, such as Archbishop Davidson and Armitage Robinson, dean of Westminster; he frequently preached at Westminster Abbey and was select preacher at Oxford and at Cambridge. 'No man', writes Archbishop Lang, 'has done more than he did to make links of understanding and sympathy between the Church of England and the Church of Ireland.'

In his double capacity at St. Patrick's and in Trinity College Bernard's influence reached its maximum. But he was needed on the episcopal bench, and in 1911 he accepted the see of Ossory, resigning his professorship, and severing for a time his connexion with Trinity College. In the palace at Kilkenny he spent four years of comparative rest, interrupted by one unusual event. A sermon which he preached in Westminster Abbey before the delegation from the Russian Duma which visited London in 1911 made so favourable an impression that Bernard was included in a party, organized by the Speaker of the House of Commons, which paid a return visit to Russia in 1912. An interesting record of these ten days is printed in Murray's *Life* of him.

In 1915 Bernard was elected archbishop of Dublin by the bench of bishops of the Church of Ireland. The office gave scope to his signal capacity for administration, and the condition of Irish affairs brought out also his higher gifts of statesmanship. In the year which followed the Easter rising of 1916 the British government summoned a convention representative of all Irish parties and laid upon it the task of framing 'a constitution for the future government of Ireland within the Empire'. The Church of Ireland was represented in the Convention by its two archbishops. Bernard had always been a convinced supporter of the Union, and had no sympathy with the self-centred nationalism of Sinn Fein, but he now joined the group of nine Southern unionists who were prepared for a compromise in the interests of peace. With the rest of the group he accepted the scheme of self-government for Ireland which was ultimately recommended by a majority of the Convention in the report presented to the British government in 1918. But the report fell dead: Ireland was then in no temper for compromise or conciliation.

Bernard had taken a prominent part in the debates of the Convention, and was chosen, along with Viscount Midleton, to speak for the Southern unionists in private negotiations with Mr. Lloyd George. The prime minister appreciated the archbishop's gifts as a public man, and it was not surprising that when the provostship of Trinity College fell vacant by the death of Sir John Mahaffy in 1919 it was offered to Bernard, who was fitted for the post no less by his talent for affairs than by his learning and academic experience. With some hesitation he decided to exchange his archbishopric for the provostship. It seemed at first that his new post would afford a field for his administrative gifts. A clause in the Government of Ireland Act of 1920 secured to Trinity College an annual grant of £30,000, charged upon the revenues of Southern Ireland. Had that clause become effective the income of the College would have been increased by more than a third, and expansion in many directions would have been possible. But the Act proved abortive so far as Southern Ireland was concerned, and the grant was never paid. Moreover, in the chaotic state of the country, it was impossible to collect the rents which formed a large part of the College's endowments; so that the hope of expansion gave place to the need of rigid economy. Nor was this the only cause of anxiety. When the Treaty of 6 December 1922 transferred the government of the country into new hands, the stability of the College, linked by its history and sympathies with the old régime, seemed to be in danger. Bernard was determined to give no handle for political attacks and he lost no time in declaring that Trinity College would loyally accept the new order of things. The Free State government showed no sign of hostility, and the College gradually recovered its buoyancy. Ambitious schemes of progress being out of the question, the provost applied himself to raising the efficiency of the College and improving its amenities. He took especial interest in the erection of a 'Hall of Honour' to commemorate those sons of the House who had fallen in the European War, in which he had himself lost a much-loved son. In May 1925 he undertook a short tour in Canada and the United States, but he had scarcely landed when he fell ill and was obliged to return home. He continued to discharge his college duties and strove to complete his *Commentary on St. John* while fighting a losing battle with cardiac disease, to which he finally succumbed in Dublin 29 August 1927.

Bernard's writings cover a wide range of subjects. Philosophy first engaged his attention. He collaborated with Mahaffy in the second edition of Mahaffy's book, *Kant's Critical Philosophy for English Readers* (1889), contributing a commentary on the *Dialectic of the Pure Reason*, which had been left unnoticed in the first edition; and in 1892 he published independently the first English translation of the *Kritik of the Judgment*. But he soon abandoned metaphysics for scholarship, although his four volumes of sermons often show evidence of his philosophical training. Between 1890 and 1894 he edited and translated for the Palestine Pilgrims' Texts Society a number of itineraries of the Holy Land, from the originals by Eusebius and several early travellers. He made an important contribution to Irish liturgiology in an edition of the *Liber Hymnorum*, published in collaboration with Robert Atkinson for the Henry Bradshaw Society (1898). Among several papers of Irish interest which appeared in the *Proceedings* of the Royal Irish Academy may be mentioned one on the *Domnach Airgid*, a Latin-Irish MS. of the Gospels, and another on the copy of St. John's Gospel in the Stowe Missal (1893). In the wider field of biblical learning his chief contributions were commentaries on the Pastoral Epistles (1899) and on Second Corinthians (1903), and two volumes in the *International Critical Commentaries* on the Gospel according to St. John (1928). On this last work, his most ambitious literary undertaking, he spent much labour, but did not live to see its publication. It is marked by the qualities which characterize all his writings: sound scholarship, terseness and lucidity of statement, well-balanced judgement, and a decidedly conservative point of view.

Bernard received the honorary degree of D.C.L. of Oxford University (1920) and of Durham University (1905), and the honorary D.D. degree of Aberdeen University (1906). He was an honorary fellow of Queen's College, Oxford (1919), and of the Royal College of Physicians, Ireland (1921), a privy councillor of Ireland (1919), president of the Royal Irish Academy (1916–1921), and warden of Alexandra College, Dublin (1905–1911).

Bernard married in 1885 his cousin Maud Nannie, second daughter of Robert Bernard, M.D., R.N., and had by her two sons and two daughters.

[R. H. Murray, *Life of Archbishop Bernard*, 1931; N. J. D. White, *John Henry Bernard. A Short Memoir*, 1928; J. H. Bernard, *The Bernards of Kerry*, 1922; personal knowledge.]

E. J. Gwynn.

BIGHAM, JOHN CHARLES, first Viscount Mersey (1840–1929), judge, was born 3 August 1840, the second son of John Bigham, a Liverpool merchant, by his wife, Helen, daughter of John East, of the same city. After passing through the Liverpool Institute he proceeded to London University where he matriculated; but he continued his education in Paris and Berlin. In 1870 he was called to the bar by the Middle Temple. Joining the Northern circuit, he found himself in a company of lawyers which included several men who later became eminent: among the juniors, William Rann Kennedy and Richard Henn Collins; among the leaders, Charles Russell, Farrer Herschell, and William Court Gully. The times were prosperous and there was an abundance of legal work for barristers in the North of England and in London. Bigham, who was learned, industrious, and full of confidence, obtained a large share of the commercial business in Liverpool, where his local connexions helped him, and at Westminster.

Having private means and ambition, Bigham took silk after he had been a junior for twelve years (1883). Henn Collins and Walter George Frank Phillimore became Queen's Counsel at the same time. This step added to his prosperity. Though surrounded by formidable competitors he was able to hold his own. He had no physical advantages to assist him; handicapped by small stature and a weak voice, he yet developed great powers of advocacy. Slow and concise of speech, he was lucid in statement and a skilful cross-examiner. Many learned lawyers fail with juries, but Bigham was no less successful when addressing a jury than he was when arguing a point of law before a judge. He was soon in request in every sort of case, but he was pre-eminent as a commercial lawyer owing to his familiarity with business methods. When the Commercial Court was established in 1895 Bigham shared with (Sir) Joseph Walton [q.v.] the briefs in cases of importance, and his name constantly recurs in the *Law Reports* and in the series of 'Commercial Cases' during the following two years. The rapid methods of Sir James Charles Mathew [q.v.], the first judge to preside over the court, suited Bigham, who was ever ready to accept an invitation to confine his argument to the essential points.

During his last decade at the bar Bigham's practice was enormous, and his income, though not comparable with the earnings of post-War leaders, was probably as large as that of any contemporary. A nimble and receptive mind enabled him to take up the threads of a case at any stage of its progress, and he was unruffled when required to hurry from the court in which he was engaged to another where his presence was more urgently needed.

In November 1885 Bigham stood unsuccessfully for parliament as liberal candidate for the Toxteth division of Liverpool, and he was again defeated in July 1892 when he stood for the Exchange division of Liverpool. In 1895 he was elected for the latter constituency as a liberal unionist. His interest in the political questions of the day was not great, and he made no figure in the House of Commons. One of his few interventions in debate was in support of a bill which in due course became the Liverpool Court of Passage Act, 1896; and he was a member of the parliamentary committee which inquired into the circumstances of the Jameson Raid.

In the course of 1897 five judgeships of the Queen's Bench division became vacant by death or retirement, and Bigham was appointed by Lord Halsbury to succeed Sir Lewis William Cave [q.v.]. The applause which greeted Bigham when he walked up the central hall of the Royal Courts of Justice on the first day of the Michaelmas sittings showed that the bar approved of the lord chancellor's choice. Bigham was at once placed upon the rota of judges in charge of the commercial list, and throughout his career as a judge of first instance he continued at intervals to preside in the court where he had played so prominent a part as counsel.

As a judge Bigham showed all the ability that was expected of him, though he was inclined to the failings of those whose minds work quickly. Disliking tedious arguments and full of robust common sense, he often took a short cut or forced the parties into a settlement. But his judicial worth was recognized by his appointment to preside over the court of the railway and canal commission (1904), to act as bankruptcy judge, and to assist the Court of Appeal and the Chancery division when a temporary member was wanted. In 1902, after the South African War, Bigham sat with Lord Alverstone, the lord chief justice, and Major-General Sir John Ardagh on a royal commission for the revision of martial law sentences.

As a criminal judge Bigham was occasionally criticized. In 1902 a Wiltshire lady, charged with the ill treatment of a child, was convicted before him at the Old Bailey. Bigham held that as the jury had acquitted her on the more serious charges in the indictment, a fine of £50 was the proper penalty. Some members of the public considered that he had been unduly lenient. In January 1904 it fell to Bigham to try Whitaker Wright [q.v.] for fraudulent dealings in connexion with company finance. The law-officers of the day had declined to advise criminal proceedings, and there was therefore some doubt whether the private prosecution which followed would be successful. Bigham's firm handling of the case helped to secure the conviction of the defendant; but counsel for the defence resented what they regarded as unjudicial hostility to their client.

In 1909 Bigham was appointed to succeed Sir Gorell Barnes (afterwards Lord Gorell) as president of the Probate, Divorce, and Admiralty division. Barnes had preserved the tradition of dignity and austerity which had been handed down by Lord Hannen, but Bigham brought to the trial of matrimonial cases the spirit of the commercial court. Giving evidence before the divorce commissioners in 1910 he explained that he did not look upon the question of divorce from a religious point of view at all. The divorce work of the division was not congenial to him, but with the admiralty business he was completely at home. His reign as president, however, was a short one. In March 1910 his retirement, for reasons of health, was announced. He had been a judge for less than fifteen years, but his 'permanent infirmity' (to quote the statute) entitled him to a pension, and he was raised to the peerage as Baron Mersey of Toxteth in the county of Lancaster.

During the following twenty years Bigham did much voluntary public and judicial work. As a peer who had held high judicial office he sat to hear appeals in the House of Lords, and he was a regular attendant at the Judicial Committee of the Privy Council. In 1912 he was appointed commissioner to inquire into the circumstances of the sinking of the S.S. *Titanic*; in 1913 he presided over the international conference on safety of life at sea; and in 1914 he held the court of inquiry in Canada on the loss of the S.S. *Empress of Ireland*. After the outbreak of the European War, when the Prize Court was established, he was invited to preside over the board of the Judicial Committee which heard appeals from that tribunal, and he continued to do so during the first two years of the War. The cases of the *Roumanian* (1916, as to the right to seize enemy property on land) and the *Odessa* (1916, as to the claims of pledgees of cargo seized as prize) were among those dealt with by him. In 1915 he inquired, as wreck commissioner, into the destruction of the S.S. *Falaba* and the S.S. *Lusitania*. He was created a viscount in 1916. Increasing deafness hampered him thereafter in the discharge of judicial duties, but in 1921, when there were heavy arrears in the divorce court, he helped to clear the lists with all his old efficiency.

Lord Mersey was a pleasant companion, and enjoyed social entertainment, both as host and guest. He was devoted to the Middle Temple, and in his extreme old age continued to dine with the benchers despite physical infirmities. He died at Littlehampton 3 September 1929.

Lord Mersey married in 1871 Georgina Sarah (died 1925), daughter of John Rogers, of Liverpool, and had three sons. He was succeeded in the viscounty by his eldest son, Charles Clive Bigham (born 1872). The drawing of Bigham by 'Spy' in *Vanity Fair* (3 February 1898) is a good likeness.

[*The Times*, 4 September 1929; *Law Journal*, 7 September 1929; personal knowledge.]

T. Mathew.

BIRKENHEAD, first Earl of (1872–1930), lord chancellor. [See Smith, Frederick Edwin.]

BLACKBURNE, JOSEPH HENRY (1841–1924), chess player, was born at Hulme, Manchester, 10 December 1841, the son of Joseph Blackburne, book-keeper, by his wife, Anne Pritchard. He was educated locally and subsequently entered the hosiery business. Blackburne became quite a proficient draughts player as a boy, until the visit of the young American chess player, Paul Morphy, to England in 1857–1859 turned his attention to chess. He won the first prize in the Manchester Chess Club's Tournament of 1861–1862, and competed in the London International Tournament of 1862, scoring only four games in a field of fourteen competitors. Yet one of Blackburne's victims on that occasion was the redoubtable Wilhelm Steinitz whom he was destined to meet many times in succeeding years. During this tournament Blackburne gave his first blindfold display, conducting ten games at the same time, winning five, drawing three, and losing two, a foretaste of his remarkable success in this branch of chess playing.

For the next forty years Blackburne was a constant competitor in international chess tournaments, having abandoned, probably with little regret, his position in the hosiery trade. His best performance during this period was the winning of the first prize in the Berlin Tournament of 1881, when the Germans nicknamed him 'The Black Death'. His name was generally to be found in the prize lists of other tournaments. By the end of the nineteenth century other players had come to the front, and Blackburne wisely realized that he could no longer expect to compete successfully with the younger generation. The formation of the British Chess Federation in 1904 led to his competing in the British Championship Tournaments, although he never succeeded in winning the title. He tied with F. D. Yates at the Chester Tournament of 1914, but resigned the title to Yates in the following winter as ill health prevented him from playing off the tie.

From the time of his first entry into the chess arena Blackburne made a feature of simultaneous displays, both with and without sight of the board, travelling all over England for this purpose until the last few years of his life. At one time he frequently walked the sixty odd miles from his home to the south coast, halting at intermediate towns where displays had been arranged. Probably he owed much of his good health to this practice, as that health only failed in the last three years of his life.

Blackburne was the most popular figure in the English chess world from the moment that he took up chess professionally. The subscription raised for his benefit when he completed fifty years of chess playing in 1911 was administered by Sir John Thursby and produced £100 per annum until Blackburne's death. One reason for his popularity was undoubtedly his prowess on the chess-board; the other was his attractive personality. Scrupulously correct in his attire and behaviour, Blackburne possessed a fund of humour which made him a most delightful companion. Added to that humour was an equally delightful wit, a combination which never failed to interest, whatever the subject under discussion. Moreover, although he would never have admitted it, Blackburne always had his country's reputation in mind, and his most severe criticisms were passed on those who appeared to think proficiency in sport an excuse for any departure from correct standards of behaviour.

Blackburne's last appearance at a tournament, and then only as a spectator, was at Hastings in 1919. When the great players of the world met for the London Tournament of 1922 he was too ill to attend. In the autumn of that year Señor J. R. Capablanca, the world champion, visited him at his bedside. He lingered on until 1 September 1924, dying at Lewisham. He was buried in Ladywell cemetery, Lewisham, in the same grave as his second wife, who had died in 1922. Blackburne married twice: first, Beatrice Lapham; secondly, Mary Jane Fox, by whom he had a son.

A cartoon of Blackburne appeared in *Vanity Fair* 2 June 1888.

[*The Times*, 2 September 1924; *The Times Literary Supplement*, 11 September 1924; *The*

Year Book of Chess, 1910; *Mr. Blackburne's Games at Chess*, selected, annotated, and arranged by J. H. Blackburne, edited by P. Anderson Graham, 1899; private information; personal knowledge.]

E. S. Tinsley.

BLAKE, Dame LOUISA BRANDRETH ALDRICH- (1865–1925), surgeon. [See Aldrich-Blake, Dame Louisa Brandreth.]

BLAND, EDITH, Mrs. Hubert Bland (1858–1924), writer of children's books, poet, and novelist, under the name E. Nesbit, the sixth child and youngest daughter of John Collis Nesbit [q.v.], agricultural chemist, and grand-daughter of Anthony Nesbit [q.v.], was born at 38 Lower Kennington Lane, London, 19 August 1858. Her father died in 1862 before she had reached her fourth birthday. She was educated at an Ursuline convent in France, for a short time in Germany, and at Brighton, after which she led an ordinary country life at Halstead Hall, Kent, which provided scenes for her stories later. She showed early aptitude for writing, and in 1876 took to it seriously: her first published piece, a poem, 'The Dawn', appeared in *The Sunday Magazine* in that year.

In 1880 Edith Nesbit married Hubert Bland: they both wrote for a living, chiefly in periodicals. Three volumes of her poetry (*Lays and Legends*, 1886; 2nd series, 1892; *A Pomander of Verse*, 1895)—sincere and accomplished, but hardly more—brought recognition and friendships, but not affluence. She took a keen interest in socialism and was one of the founders, in 1883, of a 'Fellowship of New Life', out of which, in 1884, sprang the Fabian Society. A later volume, *Ballads and Lyrics of Socialism* (1908), reveals this side of her interests.

It was not until 1899 that, with *The Story of the Treasure Seekers*, 'E. Nesbit' (she habitually wrote under this name) found her true bent and achieved financial success. In this and subsequent children's books, such as *The Would-be Goods* (1901) and *Five Children and It* (1902), she struck a new note. Her characters were neither heroes nor moral dummies, but real young human beings behaving naturally. This gift of character drawing, aided by the ease and humour of her style, place her in the highest rank among writers of books for children. For ten years or more these fresh, happy works appeared regularly and profitably. Her novels—*The Red House* (1903) was the best known—and artistic ventures like the irregularly produced *Neolith* (four numbers, 1907–8) were not lucrative. Her private life was difficult and unconventional. Her husband, a *poseur* by nature, was something more than a philanderer by habit, and his illegitimate children became part of their household, Mrs. Bland generously accepting the situation. At Well Hall, South Eltham, and at Dymchurch, they entertained lavishly: a vivid but gently malicious picture of their life appears in H. G. Wells's *Experiment in Autobiography* (vol. ii, 1934).

Hubert Bland died in 1914. The European War checked 'E. Nesbit's' output and reduced her income. In 1915 she was granted a civil list pension of £60. In 1917 she married Thomas Terry Tucker, a marine engineer. After trying vainly to maintain Well Hall as a guest-house she retired to a bungalow at Jesson St. Mary's, New Romney, Kent. She wrote little more; a last novel, *The Lark*, appeared in 1922. She died 4 May 1924. She had two sons and two daughters by her first marriage.

Edith Nesbit was a woman of striking appearance—in youth remarkably handsome—and of great personal charm. Her children's books reveal a natural genius which the circumstances of her life checked in other directions.

[D. L. Moore, *E. Nesbit, a Biography*, 1932; *Who Was Who, 1916–1928* (brief bibliography); Holbrook Jackson, *The Eighteen-Nineties*, 1913; E. R. Pease, *The History of the Fabian Society*, 1916; private information.]

F. J. H. Darton.

BLUNT, WILFRID SCAWEN (1840–1922), traveller, politician, and poet, was born at Petworth House, Sussex, 17 August 1840, the second son of Francis Scawen Blunt, of the Grenadier Guards, of Crabbet Park, Sussex, by his wife, Mary, daughter of the Rev. John Flutter Chandler, successively vicar of Witley and Woking, Surrey. Educated at Stonyhurst and at Oscott, he entered the diplomatic service at the age of eighteen (1858), and was successively a secretary of legation at Athens, Frankfort, Madrid, Paris, Lisbon, Buenos Aires, and Berne.

In 1869 Blunt married and left the service. Three years later, on the death of his elder brother, he inherited the Crabbet estates and began to travel. With his wife he visited Constantinople, rambled across Algeria and Egypt, explored Palestine, and made his way down the Euphrates from Aleppo to Bagdad. In 1878 the Blunts penetrated the mysterious territory of Nedj. At Hail the emir welcomed the travellers, presented them with his choicest brood mares, and provided their caravan with a safe conduct to Bagdad. Thence they went to Bushire, and took ship to India.

His visit to India—repeated in 1883–1884—had a decisive influence on Blunt's thought. It presented a new problem to him, and altered his political perspective. He could not reconcile the 'forward' policy favoured by Simla with the poverty of the people, and he attributed the inconsistency to the influence of imperialism. He thought empire synonymous with exploitation and he distrusted the connexion with trade and finance. These were the views put forth in *Ideas about India* which he published in 1885. In the meantime, the support lent by England to the khedive (Tewfik) of Egypt since 1882 had served to harden his convictions, and Blunt became a noisy critic of the Occupation. His endeavour to secure a fair trial for Arabi Pasha was chivalrous: his denunciation of the patient labour of Sir Evelyn Baring (afterwards Earl of Cromer, q.v.) less reasonable and less generous. Egypt stirred also his interest in Islam, and he indicated his beliefs in *The Future of Islam* (1882).

Blunt's sympathy with weak nations was not, however, confined to India and Egypt. His interest was catholic; but England, as the greatest colonizing power, was the chief object of his denunciation. The belief grew into an obsession, and Blunt came to speak and write as if England were always in the wrong, and her opponents invariably wise and reasonable men. He was perfectly sincere in this opinion; he genuinely believed that the pursuit of imperialism dishonoured his fellow countrymen.

Blunt next took up the cause of Ireland, standing for parliament as a tory Home Ruler at North Camberwell in 1885, and as a liberal Home Ruler at Kidderminster in the following year. Both elections went against him, and he thereupon went over to Ireland to exhort the tenantry of the Marquess of Clanricarde [q.v.] to resist eviction. In October 1887 he spoke at a meeting at Woodford, co. Galway (a proclaimed district), was arrested, and served a term of two months' imprisonment in Kilmainham and Galway gaols. *In Vinculis* (1889) records that gloomy experience.

Blunt will be remembered mainly for his poetry. If his verse is not of the highest rank, it is vivid, genuine, and spontaneous. His versatility was remarkable. He laid every human emotion and interest under contribution: he sang of romance, tragedy, politics, and religion with equal fervour and facility. His work is unequal in merit, and the more ambitious poems such as *Griselda* (1893), a novel in verse, are unlikely to survive: but his sonnets and lyrics, notably the *Sonnets and Songs of Proteus* (1875 and onwards) and *Esther* (1892), are of permanent value, and had considerable influence upon the younger generation of English poets of his day. A collected edition of Blunt's *Poems* appeared in 1914.

Blunt's prose-writings are on a lower plane, albeit in treatment rather than in style. He was constitutionally unfitted to write contemporary history. His discretion is questionable, his judgement superficial: he records gossip as fact, and allows prejudice to colour his narration. *The Secret History of the English Occupation of Egypt* (1907), *Gordon at Khartoum* (1911), and *My Diaries* (1919 and 1920) justify this verdict. These three works are interesting supplements to the impressions of more sober writers, but little else.

Blunt's life was full of interests. First and foremost he was an artist, a lover of beautiful and imperishable things: next he was a man of fashion, an agreeable host, and a brilliant talker; and lastly he was infected with the national passion for the horse. At Crabbet, his home in Sussex, he maintained a stud farm formed round the brood mares which he had acquired at Hail, and in 1884 he persuaded Newmarket to include in the July meeting a race for Arab horses. From Blunt's point of view the result was disappointing: his horses were outpaced, and thenceforth he bred for others to cross with.

About the same period Blunt created a social club, a little company of notable figures in the world of English politics and letters who came to Crabbet to play lawn-tennis and to talk. The club flourished until the host's political diatribes shocked and disconcerted the company, and the majority of the members ceased to attend. Blunt usually spent the winter in Egypt. In 1881 he purchased a small estate on the outskirts of Cairo, and there, round the tomb of a certain sheikh Obeyd, he built himself a comfortable house. In it he lived simply and patriarchally, dressing as an Arab, speaking the Bedouin dialect, and arbitrating in tribal disputes.

Illness crippled Blunt in his later years,

but his literary activity continued. His judgements remained unchanged: he was impenitent of his opinions to the end of his life. He died at Newbuildings Place, Southwater, Sussex, 10 September 1922, and was buried, according to his wishes, in Newbuildings Wood without religious rites.

Blunt's biography would be incomplete without mention of his wife. Lady Anne Isabella Noel (1837–1917), the only daughter of William, first Earl of Lovelace, by his first wife, the Hon. Ada Augusta Byron, the only child of Lord Byron, the poet (by his wife, Baroness Wentworth), was born in London 22 September 1837. She was a woman of high principles and Christian ideals: a devout Catholic, a staunch friend. She shared her husband's hatred of injustice, if not all his political beliefs, and she felt with him the attraction of the desert. Her knowledge of Arabic was profound: her fame among the Bedouin of Egypt surpassed that of Lord Cromer. She was an intrepid horsewoman, an accomplished musician, and an observant traveller. Her two books, *The Bedouin Tribes of the Euphrates* (2 vols., 1879) and *A Pilgrimage to Nedj* (2 vols., 1881) are admirable examples of their kind. She died at Cairo 15 December 1917 within a few months of succeeding to the barony of Wentworth.

The Blunts had one daughter, Judith Anne Dorothea (born 1873), who succeeded her mother as Baroness Wentworth. She married in 1899 the Hon. Neville Stephen Bulwer-Lytton, from whom she obtained a divorce in 1923.

[Blunt's writings, political pamphlets, and election addresses (see also Charles Meynell, *Proteus and Amadeus: a Correspondence*, 1878); *New Statesman*, 26 December 1914 and 10 May 1919; Hon. Neville Lytton, *The English Country Gentleman*, 1925; private information; personal knowledge.]

P. G. Elgood.

BOLS, Sir LOUIS JEAN (1867–1930), lieutenant-general, was born 23 November 1867, the second son of Louis Guillaume Bols, of the Belgian consular service, by his wife, Mary Wilhelmina, daughter of William Davidson, of Killyleigh, co. Down. Before entering Lancing College, Louis Bols had already been with his parents in Capetown, Sydney, Budapest, and Quebec. He was commissioned in 1887 to the Devonshire Regiment and entered upon what proved to be eleven years of routine work which included service in Burma (1891–1892) and in Chitral (1895). Promoted captain in 1897, he was sent to India on a station staff appointment in 1898, but the change was not altogether to his liking, and he much preferred the adjutancy at Aldershot (1899) of the 2nd battalion of his regiment. On the outbreak of the Boer War in October 1899 he sailed with this unit for South Africa, where he came under the influence of General Sir Henry Hildyard. As a result, and with the valuable experience, in addition, of the battles of Colenso and Spion Kop and the operations leading up to the relief of Ladysmith, Bols very quickly developed. He was thrice mentioned in dispatches, and was awarded the D.S.O. and the Queen's and King's medals. He studied deeply, and after passing through the Staff College in 1905, was given the command of a company of cadets at Sandhurst. In 1907 he was appointed brigade major, holding the post for just over two years, during which period he attended the German army manœuvres. A soldier whose name was to become famous a few years later, General von Mackensen, was the subject of a special report by Bols to the War Office.

In 1910 Bols received an appointment at the Staff College under Sir Henry Wilson [q.v.] and Sir William Robertson. There he quickly became very popular. The spring of 1914 found him at Belfast as lieutenant-colonel in command of the first battalion of the Dorset Regiment. Proceeding with his regiment to France on the outbreak of the European War, he took part in the field-fighting at the battles of Mons, Le Cateau, the Marne, and the Aisne. He was soon offered a staff appointment, but his corps commander refused to spare him, and he was still commanding the Dorsetshires at the battles of Givenchy and La Bassée. In November 1914 he was wounded and captured, but escaped back to his own lines, and by December was again in the field commanding the 15th, 13th, and 84th brigades in turn. While in the Ypres salient with the last-named brigade his rare spirit did much to keep up the hearts of those who fought with him in face of the dreadful losses incurred—some 5,600 out of a total strength of 7,000 under his command. He was awarded the C.B. in 1915. A high appointment on the staff of the XII Corps (brigadier-general, general staff) was followed in the same year (1915) by a still higher post with the Third Army (major-general, general staff), where he served under General (afterwards Lord) Allenby. In this appointment Bols was responsible for the plans of operations for the battles of the Somme and Arras. Promoted to the substantive rank of major-general in 1917, he was given the command of the 24th division, and with that division took a prominent part in the battle of Messines Ridge in June. Then followed his most important appointment and most conspicuous achievement. Accompanying General Allenby to Palestine as his chief of staff in June 1917, Bols's profound knowledge of the handling of troops, of their limitations, and their skilful use, enabled him to effect one of the most brilliant feats of the War, the capture of Jerusalem (9 December 1917) and the final defeat of the Turks in Syria. In 1918 he received the K.C.M.G. at the hands of the Duke of Connaught in Jerusalem, and in the following year was promoted K.C.B. After attending the Peace Conference in Paris in 1919 (January–March) he returned to Palestine later in that year as chief administrator of the province. He had been twelve times mentioned in dispatches, and besides his two military knighthoods had received many decorations from the Allied powers.

In 1920 Bols was appointed to command the 43rd Wessex division and the South-West area, and in 1921 became colonel of his own (the Dorset) Regiment and of the 12th London Regiment (the Rangers). Seven years later he was appointed governor and commander-in-chief of Bermuda. As an executive officer he had few equals in the service, and carried out the plans of others when that was his duty with the same enthusiasm and efficiency as he devoted to his own. He was of a kindly and sympathetic disposition, the possessor also of a keen sense of humour, these attributes attracting the admiration and affection of his comrades.

Bols married in 1897 Augusta Blanche, younger daughter of Captain Walter Cecil Strickland, by whom he had two sons. He died at Bath 13 September 1930.

[*The Times*, 15 September 1930; Sir J. F. Maurice and M. H. Grant, (Official) *History of the War in South Africa 1899–1902*, 1906–1910; Sir G. F. MacCunn and C. Falls, (Official) *History of the Great War. Military Operations. Egypt and Palestine*, 1928; private information.] C. V. Owen.

BONAR LAW, ANDREW (1858–1923), statesman. [See Law.]

BOND, Sir ROBERT (1857–1927), premier of Newfoundland, was born at St. John's, Newfoundland, 25 February 1857, the second son of John Bond, a native of Torquay, who founded the Newfoundland branch of William Hounsell & Co., of Bridport, a trading house of high reputation in the West of England, and who conducted an extensive mercantile business in St. John's for more than half a century. Robert Bond was sent to school in England, to Queen's College, Taunton, and to Edinburgh University, where he took honours in law. Afterwards he studied law in Newfoundland, but, owing to delicate health, gave up the course and, without being called to the bar, embarked upon a political career. In 1882 he was elected member of the Newfoundland house of assembly for Trinity Bay, and thereafter for Fortune Bay and Twillingate successively. His advancement was rapid and sustained. Two years after entering the house of assembly he was elected its speaker; and five years later, in 1889, he was given the portfolio of colonial secretary in the administration of Sir William Vallance Whiteway [q.v.], and held office, except for a short period from April 1894 to January 1895, until 1897.

At the outset of his term of office Bond encountered two difficult international problems with which he was to be closely concerned for the next twenty years—first, the fishery disputes between Newfoundland and France; and second, the negotiations between Newfoundland, Canada, and the United States about fishery rights and reciprocal trade. Bond's contact with the French disputes began in the summer of 1890 when he came to England on a deputation led by Whiteway to protest against a compromise which Great Britain had just arranged with France on the question of the lobster-fishery. France's claim to fishing rights on certain specified coasts of Newfoundland originated with the treaty of Utrecht in 1714, and had been reaffirmed, subject to modifications of coastline, in the treaties of Paris in 1763 and of Versailles in 1783. Broadly speaking, France contended that these treaties gave her an exclusive right of fishery on the specified coasts, and that all British fixed settlements, of whatever nature, on these coasts were illegal. Great Britain contended that her subjects had a concurrent right of fishery with the French and that the only fixed settlements on the specified coasts which were illegal were fixed fisher settlements. After many failures to settle these differences, a convention had been signed in 1885, but the Newfoundland legislature, of which Bond was then a member, refused to approve it. Instead, it prohibited the sale of bait to French fishing-vessels on all parts of the coasts not specified in the treaties. The French fishermen, thus hampered in their pursuit of the cod-fishery, established lobster factories on the coasts reserved to them, and contested the legality of the British lobster factories which had long been established there. In 1890 a compromise on this question was arranged between Great Britain and France without directly consulting Newfoundland, and it was against this arrangement that Bond joined with his colleagues in protesting. The agreement was not abandoned by Great Britain, but negotiations with France were resumed in an attempt to find a more satisfactory settlement.

In September 1890 Bond proceeded from England to the United States, authorized by the British government to communicate to (Lord) Pauncefote [q.v.], the British minister at Washington, the views of Newfoundland on reciprocal trade with the United States, with a view to the negotiation of a treaty. Thus Bond met his second problem. Proposals for reciprocal trade were closely associated with the United States' fishery rights in British North America. By a treaty of 1818, fishermen of the United States had been granted a concurrent right of fishery with British subjects on certain specified coasts of Canada and Newfoundland, and had renounced any right to fish within three marine miles of the remaining coasts, subject to the proviso that they might enter bays and harbours on such coasts to obtain shelter, or wood, or water, or to make repairs. In practice these treaty provisions had been interpreted most restrictively by the Colonial legislatures, and the United States had retaliated. From 1854 to 1866, however, Lord Elgin's Canadian-American reciprocity treaty, to which Newfoundland adhered, had solved the problem by linking the fisheries question with trade reciprocity. Briefly it provided for free fishing by British and American subjects on the coasts of both countries in exchange for reciprocal free trade in certain goods, the produce of both countries. It had proved impossible to renew this arrangement after 1866, but in 1890 Bond planned to negotiate a somewhat similar reciprocity treaty separately for Newfoundland, and not in association with Canada. His negotiations with the United States' secretary of state, Mr. Blaine, proceeded rapidly, and he was mainly instrumental in completing what is known as the Bond-Blaine convention. But Canada protested against the convention, alleging that it discriminated against her in favour of the United States, and Great Britain refused to authorize its signature. Bond was very angry, feeling, with some justification, that the British government had failed to give him the support he had been led to expect. In Newfoundland itself great hostility was manifested towards Great Britain and even more towards Canada. In an attempt to settle some of these difficulties with Canada, Bond went to Halifax in 1892 and met Canadian ministers, but no common policy emerged.

The great fire in St. John's of 1892, the bad fishery season of 1893, and the financial failure of 1894 led to the revival of the proposal that Newfoundland should enter the Canadian federation, and in March 1895 Bond was appointed chairman of a deputation sent by Newfoundland to a conference at Ottawa. The conference broke down, as Canada was unwilling to take over the whole of the public debt of the colony. Bond's courage in succeeding months saved Newfoundland from financial collapse. He undertook a mission to Montreal and New York in order to raise a loan. By pledging his own personal credit very heavily he obtained a temporary loan in Montreal. Finding that it was impossible to raise the larger loan in Canada, he went to New York, but failed. Finally he went to England in June 1895 and succeeded.

From 1900 to 1909 Bond was premier and colonial secretary. His first task as premier was to modify the 'Reid contract' which had resulted from the disasters of 1894. On Whiteway's defeat in 1897, the new premier, Sir James Winter, had sold the Newfoundland railways, telegraphs, and dock to R. G. Reid, a railway contractor. Bond had led the opposition to the contract and he had been returned to power on this issue. In 1901 the railways, telegraphs, and dock were bought back and then leased to a company controlled by Reid and his sons. It was not a thorough reform, and Bond's compromise was criticized. In external affairs, Bond had to deal with the French and American disputes. In 1901 he visited London, together with Sir Edward (afterwards Lord) Morris, in order to assist the Colonial Office in further negotiations with France. No settlement was possible, for Bond refused to remove the bait restrictions unless France modified her system of bounties on the export of fish, and this she was not yet prepared to do. In 1904, however, a settlement was reached as part of the *entente cordiale*. France agreed to abandon her right to land on the treaty shore, and in return the British government gave compensation in cash and inland concessions in Africa. Bond was consulted throughout and co-operated actively in framing the agreement. In 1902 Bond was authorized by the British government to reopen negotiations with the United States for a separate reciprocity treaty for Newfoundland. He succeeded in drawing up with the secretary of state, Mr. Hay, a draft treaty known as the Hay-Bond treaty, but it was not accepted by the American senate. In 1905, therefore, Bond announced a vigorous policy of retaliation. As embodied in legislation in 1905 and 1906, it was designed to prohibit fishermen of the United States from buying baits or supplies and from hiring crews in Newfoundland ports and further to restrict them in the exercise of their rights. Great Britain gave a measure of support to Bond, but declined to allow his more extreme legislation to come into operation. Instead she negotiated a *modus vivendi* with the United States, pending the reference of all the questions at issue to The Hague tribunal. Bond accepted the proposal to arbitrate but rejected the *modus vivendi*, and in the face of his most vigorous protests in the colony and at the Imperial Conference of 1907, it was enforced by imperial machinery. Bond's indignation with Great Britain was not endorsed by the entire colony, as the elections of 1908 and 1909 were to show. In 1910 the award of The Hague tribunal finally settled the disputes with the United States largely in favour of Newfoundland.

At the elections in 1908 Bond was involved in an extraordinary situation. The new house of assembly consisted of 18 government supporters and 18 opposition members. Bond asked for another dissolution; it was refused, and he resigned in March 1909. Sir Edward Morris formed a government, but at the meeting of the legislature Bond and his party held up proceedings and it was impossible even to elect a speaker. The governor attempted to form a coalition government, but failed, and granted a dissolution to Morris. At the election in May 1909 Bond's party was defeated. He continued as leader of the opposition until his resignation in 1914.

Bond was created K.C.M.G. in 1901; on his visit to the Colonial Conference in London in 1902 he was sworn of the Privy Council and received the freedom of the city of Edinburgh and the honorary degree of LL.D. from the university. On the occasion of the Imperial Conference in 1907 he received the freedom of the cities of London, Bristol, and Manchester. After his resignation from public life in 1914, he lived in retirement in Whitbourne, Newfoundland, where he died 16 March 1927.

Bond never married. He was a man of personal charm and culture, a good speaker, a careful administrator, and much respected by his political opponents.

[*The Times*, 17 March 1927; *Who's Who in Newfoundland; Cambridge History of the British Empire*, vol. vi, 1930; *British Documents on the Origins of the War*, vols. ii and iii, 1927 and 1928; *Newfoundland Royal Commission Report, 1933*, 1933; personal knowledge.] W. L. Grant.
K. C. Wheare.

BONNEY, THOMAS GEORGE (1833–1923), geologist, was born 27 July 1833 at Rugeley, Staffordshire, the eldest of the ten children of the Rev. Thomas Bonney, perpetual curate of Pipe Ridware, near Rugeley, and master of Rugeley grammar school. His mother was Eliza Ellen, daughter of Edward Smith, of Rugeley. The family was of French Huguenot origin, but had long been settled in Staffordshire. During his boyhood Bonney showed an inclination towards natural science, which seems to have been hereditary, as both his parents were keen botanists. The years which he spent at Uppingham School helped to increase this taste, and provided opportunities for fossil-collecting, thus awakening the interest in geology which dominated the rest of his life. On leaving Uppingham as head of the school in 1852, he proceeded to St. John's College, Cambridge, where he soon obtained a scholarship. He graduated in 1856 as twelfth wrangler, with a second class in the classical tripos. Shortly after, owing to a breakdown in health, he left Cambridge for a while, but a few months on the south coast and in the Alps restored him, and he became a mathematical master at Westminster School, at the same time preparing for holy orders, being ordained deacon in 1857 and priest in 1858.

In 1859 Bonney was elected to a fellowship at St. John's College, and in 1861 he returned to Cambridge as junior dean of his college, becoming tutor in 1868. In the last-named capacity he was eminently successful, combining firmness of discipline with abundance of human sympathy. But it was as lecturer in geology (1869) that he really made his mark, and it was owing to his influence that St. John's came to be recognized as the college to which students of that subject were especially attracted. During the years when the infirmities of age were weighing on Adam Sedgwick [q.v.], the Woodwardian professor, Bonney's lectures maintained the traditions of the Cambridge school of geology. Among the members of his own college whom he taught were: (Sir) Jethro Justinian Harris Teall [q.v.], (Professor) W. J. Sollas, (Sir) Aubrey Strahan, and (Professor) J. E. Marr, while members of other colleges who studied under him were Francis Maitland Balfour [q.v.] and (Professor) W. W. Watts.

In 1877 Bonney accepted the Yates-Goldsmid professorship of geology at University College, London, in addition to his work at St. John's College. In 1881, on being appointed assistant general secretary of the British Association, he left Cambridge, and went to live at Hampstead. He resigned his professorship in 1901 and returned to live in Cambridge in 1905, being a life fellow of St. John's. Although over seventy years of age, his scientific work was still in full activity, and its climax came in 1910 when he was elected president of the British Association for its meeting at Sheffield. His address dealt with the glacial history of the British Isles. It must be admitted, however, that the views then propounded by him were to some extent a championship of a lost cause.

Bonney held the Sc.D. degree of Cambridge University and the honorary D.Sc. degree of Dublin and Sheffield universities, and the honorary LL.D. of Montreal University: he was fellow and vice-president (1899) of the Royal Society, secretary and president (1884–1886) of the Geological Society of London, president of the Mineralogical Society and of the Alpine Club; he was also Whitehall preacher (1876–1878), Hulsean lecturer (1884), and Rede lecturer (1892) at Cambridge University, and an honorary canon of Manchester Cathedral.

Bonney's earliest publication seems to have been a contribution to an interminable subject, the study of palaeolithic flint implements; and the greater part of his writings, apart from theological works, have reference to geology, and especially to the study of rocks (petrology). In later life he took little or no interest in fossils, although his early Cambridge lectures on that subject are said to have been remarkably good and clear. It is a curious and perhaps instructive fact that Bonney as an undergraduate apparently never attended any lectures on geology. This may help to account for the originality and independence of his outlook, which was his most marked characteristic as a geologist. As things were at Cambridge in his time, it fell to him to give lectures rather than to listen to them: in the special branch of the subject to which he devoted himself little was then known, and he was essentially one of the pioneers. He was actually the first geologist to publish technical descriptions of a great number of British rocks, and he also described many specimens brought by travellers and climbers from distant parts of the earth. He especially treasured a small triangular lump of rock, which he said was the summit of the Matterhorn, 'collected' by himself.

The study of rocks, combined with an early love of the Alps, naturally led Bonney to attack the difficult problems of Alpine geology. He acquired an intimate personal knowledge of almost the whole of the Alpine chains, and, indeed, he was one of the pioneers in Dauphiné. From this it was an easy transition to the study of ice-work in all its forms, and this subject, perhaps even more than petrology, occupied the later years of his scientific life.

In addition to a vast number of purely scientific and technical papers on geology, Bonney wrote several books of a more popular character, including *The Story of our Planet* (1893); *Charles Lyell and Modern Geology* (1895); *Ice-Work* (1896); *Volcanoes* (1898, 3rd ed. 1912); *The Building of the Alps* (1912); *The Present Relations of Science and Religion* (1913); four volumes of sermons, and several writings on Alpine subjects. In 1921 there appeared a charmingly written little book of personal reminiscences entitled *Memories of a Long Life*, containing a wealth of anecdote about Cambridge in past days, travel, and climbing.

In spite of rather precarious health, Bonney was a man of extraordinary activity, both mental and physical, and in his day a famous climber. Even after his retirement to Cambridge in 1905, he led a very active life, and when over eighty years of age he was able to spend long, strenuous days on the hills of Cumberland and Yorkshire or scrambling about the cliffs of the Lizard. At this time also so great was his love of teaching that he spent many hours in assisting geological students in the Sedgwick Museum, enlivening his discourse with witty illustration and caustic comment. He died at Cambridge 9 December 1923, at the age of ninety. He was unmarried.

[T. G. Bonney, *Memories of a Long Life*, 1921; private information.]

R. H. Rastall.

BOOTH, WILLIAM BRAMWELL (1856–1929), Salvation Army leader, was born at Halifax, Yorkshire, 8 March 1856, the eldest son of William Booth [q.v.], the founder of the Salvation Army. Bramwell Booth saw the 'Army' grow from an obscure 'Christian Mission', established in Whitechapel in 1865, into an international organization with numerous and varied social activities. He was educated privately and at the City of London School. While still a lad, he went in 1870 to help in the management of his father's mission and in the cheap food kitchens established in its early days. There he had ample opportunities of studying human nature, and learned much that was invaluable to him in his later administrative work for the Salvation Army. He was greatly handicapped throughout his life by deafness, the result of sickness following injuries received while at school.

In 1882 Booth married Florence, eldest daughter of Dr. Isben Soper, of Blaina, Monmouthshire. Miss Soper had become a Salvation Army worker in 1880, and after her marriage took charge of the women's social work, becoming a commissioner in 1888. Two sons and five daughters were born of the marriage, all of whom became active workers in the 'Army'.

Bramwell Booth was chief of staff of the Salvation Army from 1880 until the death of the founder in August 1912. 'General' Booth had appointed Bramwell his successor. He held the position of 'general' until February 1929 when, by a resolution of a high council (of sixty-one leading officers) convened under the provisions of a deed poll (1904) supplemental to the foundation deed (1878), he was relieved of the generalship, and a successor was elected by a two-thirds vote of the council. He died at Hadley Wood a few months later (16 June).

As chief executive officer Booth was responsible for the preparation of *Orders and Regulations for Officers and Soldiers* and for the direction of the 'Army's' propaganda. He was the author of *Echoes and Memories* (1925), *These Fifty Years* (1929), and other books, as well as of many articles on Bible studies and social problems and frequent contributions to the press on prison reform, vagrancy, the homeless poor, and emigration.

In 1885 Booth was associated with William Thomas Stead [q.v.] in a campaign for the suppression of criminal vice, which resulted in the Criminal Law Amendment Act (1885) raising the age of consent to sixteen years. Owing to a technical breach of the law in their method of collecting evidence, Booth and Stead were arrested and tried at the Old Bailey. Booth was discharged.

It was through Booth's guidance that the right to hold open-air meetings—a matter which had brought the 'Army' into conflict with many local authorities—was firmly established, and certain local by-laws were declared by the High Court to be *ultra vires*. Booth did much to develop foreign missions, and both as chief of staff and as general of the 'Army' he visited most of the larger cities in Europe, where he conducted public meetings and officers' councils. During his generalship the 'Army' made rapid progress, nor was its international spirit impaired by the strain imposed upon it by the European War. He continued to visit European capitals after the War and to be received by their leading statesmen. He also travelled on behalf of the Salvation Army in India, Ceylon, Korea, Japan, the Dutch Indies, Australia, New Zealand, Canada, and the United States of America.

Bramwell Booth bore a strong facial likeness to his mother Catherine Booth [q.v.]. On the platform he presented a striking contrast to his father: the latter played upon the emotions of his hearers, his son relied for effect on calm and reasoned argument. He was something of a mystic; none the less he inherited his father's flair for questions concerned with finance and property. The strong position and influence which the Salvation Army maintains is largely due to Bramwell Booth's peculiar genius and to his devotion to the aims and ideals of his father.

[St. John Ervine, *God's Soldier*, 1934; Catherine Bramwell-Booth, *Bramwell Booth*, 1933; private information; personal knowledge.]

D. C. Lamb.

BOSANQUET, BERNARD (1848–1923), philosopher, was born 14 June 1848 at Rock Hall, near Alnwick, the fourth and youngest son of the Rev. Robert William Bosanquet, of Rock, sometime rector of Bolingbroke, Lincolnshire, by his second wife, Caroline, daughter of Colonel Day Hort Macdowall, of Walkinshaw, and of Castle Semple, Renfrewshire. The Bosanquets are an old Huguenot family, a younger branch of which has been in possession of the estate of Rock since 1804. Sir Frederick Albert Bosanquet, common serjeant [q.v.], was Bernard Bosanquet's second cousin. Bernard was sent to a preparatory school at Sherburn, Yorkshire, in 1856, to another at Elstree in 1860, and to Harrow in 1862. He was a classical scholar of Balliol College, Oxford, from 1866 to 1870. At Balliol he was chiefly influenced by Thomas Hill Green [q.v.] and Richard Lewis Nettleship [q.v.]. He obtained first classes both in classical moderations (1868) and in *literae humaniores* (1870), and was elected a fellow of University College in the latter year. At University College Bosanquet lectured both in Greek history and in philosophy. During the eleven years he was there he only published a translation of G. F. Schömann's *Constitutional History of Athens* (1878).

In 1881 Bosanquet resigned his fellowship and went to live in London, partly in order to have time for philosophical writing and partly in order to engage in social work. Without being a wealthy man he had sufficient independent means to live upon. He was an early and prominent member of the London Ethical Society which was founded in 1886, and of the London School of Ethics and Social Philosophy which carried on the Ethical Society's lecturing work from 1897 till 1900. Bosanquet did most of the popular lecturing on philosophy thus organized, and much of his published work grew out of those lectures—*The Essentials of Logic* (1895), *A Companion to Plato's Republic* (1895), *The Psychology of the Moral Self* (1897), and *The Philosophical Theory of the State* (1899).

Bosanquet also did much work for the Charity Organization Society. His half-brother Charles had been secretary to its council from 1870 to 1875, and his Balliol friend (Sir) Charles Stewart Loch [q.v.] had succeeded his brother in that post. Bosanquet served on district committees and on the administrative committee of the Society, frequently spoke at its public meetings and conferences, and gave lectures on its work. Many of these lectures were published in the *Charity Organization Review* and in his books of collected essays.

In all this time in London, however, philosophy was Bosanquet's predominant interest. He joined the Aristotelian Society in 1886 and contributed frequent papers to its proceedings. He was president of the Society from 1894 to 1898. He contributed a paper on *Logic as the Science of Knowledge* to a volume of *Essays in Philosophical Criticism* edited by R. B. (afterwards Viscount) Haldane and Andrew Seth Pringle-Pattison in 1883. In 1884 he edited and partly translated R. H. Lotze's *Logic*. In 1885 he published *Knowledge and Reality*, an appreciation and development of *The Principles of Logic* of Francis Herbert Bradley [q.v.] which had appeared in 1883. The book displays Bosanquet's characteristic power of criticism by appreciation. In 1886 he published a translation of the Introduction to Hegel's *Philosophy of Fine Art*, to which he prefixed an original essay *On the True Conception of Another World*. In 1888 his *Logic*, an important work in two volumes, appeared and in 1892 *A History of Aesthetic*. In 1895 he married Helen, daughter of the Rev. John Dendy, a Unitarian minister, of Manchester. She had worked with him in the Charity Organization Society and was afterwards on the Poor Law commission of 1906. In 1897 the Bosanquets left London and went to live at Caterham, and in 1899 they built a house at Oxshott, Surrey, which was their home until just before Bosanquet's death in 1923.

Bosanquet's next important publication was the *Philosophical Theory of the State* (1899). In 1903 he accepted an invitation to succeed Professor David George Ritchie [q.v.] in the chair of moral philosophy at St. Andrews University. He held this position until 1908, resigning because he found original work and the preparation of lectures incompatible. He resumed his old life at Oxshott, and produced the second edition of his *Logic* in 1911. He was Gifford lecturer at Edinburgh in 1911 and 1912 and published the two series of lectures, *The Principle of Individuality and Virtue* and *The Value and Destiny of the Individual*, in 1912 and 1913 respectively. These were the last of his large works. Of smaller works which he wrote subsequently mention may be made of *Some Suggestions in Ethics* (1918), *Implication and Linear Inference* (1920), which sets out more clearly than any other of his writings the essence of his logical theory, and *What Religion is* (1920). He had been gradually failing in health ever since 1915 and died at Hampstead 8 February 1923. He had no children.

Bosanquet and F. H. Bradley are ordinarily classed together as the last two great representatives of the nineteenth-century school of British Hegelianism. They both accepted from Hegel the view that science and morality as ordinarily understood involve abstractions and therefore inconsistencies; that neither abstract science nor abstract morality is consistent with itself nor with the other; that 'there is no truth but the whole', and that the test of man's attainment of truth is the progress of his knowledge towards that complete coherence and comprehensiveness which is found in the absolute. It is, indeed, in their occupation with the absolute that they are distinguished from the earlier members of the school. Bosanquet differed from Bradley in being more positive and less sceptical, in the wide range of his philosophical interests—tallying with the wider range of his practical interests—and above all in his greater concern with the concrete and individual.

These differences are partly connected with Bosanquet's devotion to Plato and with his interest in history and biology, but the most significant explanation of them is given in an article which he contributed to *Contemporary British Philosophy* (edited by J. H. Muirhead, 1924) where he sets out what he considers to be the main influences which have gone to the making of his philosophy. He puts first the experience of the practical working of the family estate which his father farmed himself. The lessons learned there were reinforced by Bosanquet's long work with the Charity Organization Society. These lessons, as they affected his philosophy, might be summarized in the statement that principles are only to be understood in relation to concrete individual situations and vice versa, and then only as the result of patient and unremitting work. He regarded as abstract the criticism that in spite of his schooling his social philosophy did less than justice to the individual, for he maintained that only those who are constantly occupied with individuals as individuals know how inseparable are individuality and social context. But the effect of those lessons was not confined to his social philosophy. Their influence is seen in his impatience with what he called 'philosophies of the first look', in the many-sidedness of his philosophical interests of which the titles of his books are sufficient evidence, and in his logical doctrine of the 'concrete universal'.

Another influence on Bosanquet's philosophy to which he attached importance was aesthetic experience. 'That', he says, 'gives us a present world, a world which is even one with the world we live in, but yet is twice-born, is at once its own truest self and the profoundest revelation which itself can convey.' Poetry gave him an assurance of the absolute, whose reality in other spheres we only gradually apprehend by patient and careful endeavour to understand.

All Bosanquet's writings, on aesthetic, on ethics, on social questions, on metaphysics, and on logic, show the same concern with principles seen in the concrete and the same insistence that understanding of reality is never immediate but always the outcome of the best and the most patient thinking. But these common characteristics are seen most strikingly in his logic. He takes a new view of the old distinction between knowledge and opinion. 'The necessity of knowledge depends upon its vitality. Axioms and dogmas, traditions and abstract principles are not knowledge but opinion. The life of knowledge is in the self-consciousness which systematically understands, and you cannot have it cheaper.' The essential nature of inference he regards as at all stages the same—an understanding of the individual by seeing its place in a system, and of system by seeing the individuals which it sustains. The differences between different stages of thought are for him differences in the thoroughness and richness of the apprehension involved. It is this remarkable combination of universality and concreteness which gives its distinctive value to all Bosanquet's philosophy, and, even if he sometimes does less than justice to those middle-distance distinctions with which theory is ordinarily occupied, makes him one of the most illuminating and wisest of modern philosophers.

This notice would be incomplete without a reference to the charm of Bosanquet's personality, his courtesy, and the wideness of his sympathies.

There is a portrait of Bosanquet by Hugh Glazebrook at Rock Hall.

[Helen Bosanquet, *Bernard Bosanquet: a short account of his life*, 1924; *Bernard Bosanquet and his Friends. Letters illustrating the Sources and the Development of his Philosophical Opinions*, edited by J. H. Muirhead, 1935.] A. D. Lindsay.

BOSANQUET, Sir FREDERICK ALBERT (1837–1923), common serjeant, was born at Lewes 8 February 1837, the fourth son of Samuel Richard Bosanquet [q.v.], of Forest House, Essex, and Dingestow Court, Monmouthshire, who belonged to an old Huguenot family. His mother was Emily, eldest daughter of George Courthope, of Whiligh, Sussex. His great-grandfather, Samuel Bosanquet, was governor of the Bank of England in 1792; Charles Bosanquet [q.v.], city merchant, and Sir John Bernard Bosanquet [q.v.], judge of the court of Common Pleas, were his great-uncles; James Whatman Bosanquet [q.v.], chronologist, was his uncle; and Bernard Bosanquet [q.v.], the philosopher, was his second cousin.

Bosanquet was a scholar of Eton, whence he proceeded to King's College, Cambridge. He obtained a first class in the classical tripos and was senior optime in 1860, becoming a fellow of his college in 1863. In the same year he was called to the bar by the Inner Temple (of which society he became a bencher in 1889 and treasurer in 1909) and joined the Oxford circuit. With J. G. N. Darby he wrote *A Practical Treatise on the Statutes of Limitations in England and Ireland*, which was published in 1867 and became the standard text-book on the subject. For some years he was junior counsel to the Admiralty, and he was appointed recorder of Worcester in 1879 and of Wolverhampton in 1891. In 1882 Bosanquet took silk and acquired a large practice both in London and on circuit, often appearing in local government and rating cases. His arguments, which were full and learned, were not always lively. But he was, in fact, a man of great humour and his after-dinner speeches at the bar mess were listened to with delight. To a colleague who told him that he was the dullest arguer at the bar he is said to have replied: 'Have you considered the case of Gainsford Bruce?' As a lawyer his reputation stood high and his elevation to the bench, always regarded as probable, seemed to be foreshadowed by his appointment on two occasions as commissioner of assize. But the times were not propitious for non-politicians, and a judgeship of the High Court was never offered to him.

On the promotion in 1900 of Sir Forrest Fulton to the recordership of London, Bosanquet was chosen by Lord Halsbury to succeed him as common serjeant. He at once proved himself to be worthy of higher judicial office. As common serjeant he had both civil and criminal jurisdiction, and was equally at home whether trying prisoners at the Central Criminal Court or cases in the mayor's court. Courteous to the bar, to which he was known as 'Bosey', he was able, when occasion required, to stand upon his dignity. He retired in 1917 after he had reached his eightieth birthday. After his retirement he was made an additional judge of the Central Criminal Court and he continued to act as chairman of the East Sussex quarter sessions until 1921. He was chairman of the Council of Law Reporting, 1909–1917; a member of the royal commission which in 1888, under the presidency of Lord Herschell, inquired into the old Metropolitan Board of Works; and a member of the Canterbury House of Laymen. He was knighted in 1907. He died in London 2 November 1923.

Bosanquet married twice; first, in 1871 Albinia Mary (died 1882), daughter of John Curtis-Hayward, of Quedgeley House, Gloucester, by whom he had two sons and two daughters; secondly, in 1885 Philippa Frances, daughter of William Bence-Jones, of Lisselan, co. Cork, by whom he had one son and one daughter. His youngest son, Captain William Sydney Bence Bosanquet, married a daughter of Grover Cleveland, twice president of the United States of America.

A cartoon of Bosanquet by 'Spy', which is a good likeness, appeared in *Vanity Fair* 21 November 1901.

[*The Times*, 5 November 1923; *Law Journal*, 10 November 1923; personal knowledge.]

T. Mathew.

BOUCICAULT, DION, the younger (1859–1929), actor-manager, whose full names were Dionysius George, was the second son of Dion Boucicault [q.v.], actor and dramatist, by his wife, Agnes Robertson, and was born in New York 23 May 1859. He came to England at an early age, and was educated at Esher, at Cuddington, Buckinghamshire, and later in Paris. He served for a short time in the militia. He made his first appearance on the stage at Booth's Theatre, New York, 11 October 1879 as the Dauphin in *Louis XI*, with his father. He appeared first in London, at the old Gaiety Theatre, 25 November 1880 in the title-role of *Andy Blake*. He played at the Court Theatre in 1881–1882, and in the following year toured with (Sir) Charles Hawtrey [q.v.], playing, among other parts, the original Harry Marsland in *The Private Secretary*, produced at Cambridge in November 1883. After appearing at the St. James's Theatre in *A Scrap of Paper* with William Hunter Kendal [q.v.] and Mrs. Kendal, he returned to America with his father and, after playing there for a year, accompanied him on a tour to Australia.

At the end of the tour the younger Boucicault decided to remain in Australia, and in October 1886 he entered into a partnership with Robert Brough, which lasted for ten years. They took the Bijou Theatre, Melbourne, and converted it into the most important theatre in that city, producing all the principal successes of the leading dramatists of the day. Later, they took over the management of the Criterion Theatre, Sydney.

Boucicault reappeared in London at the Court Theatre in October 1897 as the Minstrel in *The Children of the King*; and in January of the following year made a great success there as Sir William Gower in *Trelawny of the Wells* by (Sir) A. W. Pinero. He also appeared at the same theatre in *His Excellency the Governor*, *Wheels Within Wheels*, and *A Royal Family*.

In 1900 Boucicault went to the Criterion Theatre where he was associated with Arthur Bourchier [q.v.] and produced *Lady Huntworth's Experiment* by R. C. Carton and *The Noble Lord* by Robert Marshall. He appeared at the Garrick Theatre in September 1901 as Croker Harrington in Pinero's *Iris*, and subsequently joined Charles Frohman at the Duke of York's Theatre, as actor and producer. In 1901 he married Irene (the actress professionally known as Irene Vanbrugh), younger daughter of the Rev. Reginald Henry Barnes, vicar of Heavitree and prebendary of Exeter Cathedral.

Boucicault remained with Frohman until the latter's death in 1915, playing a variety of parts at the Duke of York's and elsewhere, and producing plays by Pinero, Carton, Anthony Hope, (Sir) J. M. Barrie, and others. He was the original producer of Barrie's *Peter Pan* in December 1904, and revived the play each Christmas until 1918; he was also responsible for the all-star revival of his father's play *London Assurance* at the St. James's Theatre in June 1913, the first of the annual productions given in aid of King George's pension fund for actors and actresses.

In December 1915 Boucicault entered on the management of the New Theatre in St. Martin's Lane, opening with a revival of *Peter Pan*. He produced a long series of plays there, including *Caroline* by W. Somerset Maugham, revivals of *His Excellency the Governor* and *Trelawny of the Wells*, *Belinda* by A. A. Milne, and *Mr. Pim Passes By* by the same author, in which he made the greatest success of his later years in the part of Carraway Pim. For a short period he was manager of the Duke of York's Theatre, where he produced *Miss Nell o' New Orleans* in February 1921. From December 1921 to July 1922 he was in management at the Globe Theatre, but was unsuccessful. In December 1922 he produced *Lilac Time* at the Lyric Theatre; this was his last successful production in London.

In February 1923, accompanied by his wife, Boucicault went to South Africa, playing in *His House in Order* and *The Second Mrs. Tanqueray* by Pinero, and in several of the plays which he had previously produced. Thence he travelled to Australia and New Zealand, where he appeared in *Aren't We All?* by Frederick Lonsdale, *The Notorious Mrs. Ebbsmith* by Pinero, and *The Truth about Blayds* by Milne. Returning to London in 1925, he produced *All the King's Horses* at the Globe Theatre, January 1926; later in the same year he played a further engagement in Australia, and in 1927 he again returned to South Africa, and then undertook still another tour in Australia and New Zealand. He returned to London in May 1929 suffering from a severe illness which had attacked him at the beginning of his return voyage. He died at his home, the Manor House, Hurley, Buckinghamshire, 25 June 1929.

Boucicault's most important work in the theatre was performed as producer. He was a brilliant stage-director, and he had the distinction of producing all the plays at the Duke of York's Theatre during his long engagement, lasting fourteen years, with Charles Frohman. As an actor he was handicapped by his short stature, but in many parts, such as Sir William Gower in *Trelawny of the Wells* and Mr. Pim in *Mr. Pim Passes By*, he gave performances which were unforgettable. He adapted two plays for the stage, *My Little Girl* (1882) and *Devotion* (1884), both produced at the Court Theatre.

[*The Times*, 26 June 1929; *Daily Telegraph*, 26 June 1929; *Who's Who in the Theatre*; personal knowledge.] J. Parker.

BOURCHIER, ARTHUR (1863–1927), actor-manager, born at Speen, Berkshire, 22 June 1863, was the only son of Charles John Bourchier, of Speen, sometime captain in the 8th Hussars, by his wife, Fanny, daughter of James Farr, a draper. In 1877 Bourchier went to Eton, where he excelled in theatricals and resolved to make acting his profession. Proceeding to Christ Church, Oxford, he matriculated in Trinity term 1882. He was at once put on the committee of the university dramatic club called the Philothespians, and acted Sir John Vesey in Bulwer Lytton's *Money*. In the summer term of 1883, Benjamin Jowett being vice-chancellor, the university formally recognized the club, of which Bourchier was then president. The next play chosen was *The Merchant of Venice*, in which Bourchier acted Shylock (December 1883). In Michaelmas term 1884 he was the prime mover in the foundation of the Oxford University Dramatic Society, which then superseded the Philothespians; and early in 1885 the society produced *King Henry IV, Part I*, with Bourchier as Hotspur. In February 1886 the New Theatre in Oxford was opened with a performance by the O.U.D.S. of *Twelfth Night*, in which Bourchier acted Feste. In 1887 he played Death in *Alcestis*; in 1888 Falstaff in *The Merry Wives of Windsor*; in 1889 Brutus in *Julius Caesar*. In the last-mentioned year he completed a somewhat roving academic career at Oxford by taking his M.A. degree, after having migrated from Christ Church to New Inn Hall in 1884, been attached to Balliol in 1887 (when New Inn Hall was incorporated in that college), and migrated again to Charsley's Hall in 1888, in which year he graduated B.A. from Christ Church.

In September 1889 Bourchier joined the theatrical company of Mrs. Lillie Langtry and made his first professional appearance at Wolverhampton as Jaques in *As You Like It*. In June 1890 he made a brief excursion into management at the St. James's Theatre, London. The next five years were occupied by engagements in England and (in 1892–1893) with Augustin Daly in the United States; until in September 1895 he began his own management of the Royalty Theatre. In 1894 he had married Violet Augusta Mary (the actress professionally known as Violet Vanbrugh), elder daughter of the Rev. Reginald Henry Barnes, prebendary of Exeter Cathedral; and she now became his leading lady in farces and comedies adapted (some by Bourchier himself, alone or in collaboration) from foreign sources.

Bourchier's management at the Royalty ended in 1896; and after a further tour in America he appeared again in London in one of his best performances, that of Dr. Johnson in a play of that name by Leo Trevor (Strand Theatre, 23 April 1897). In February 1900 he became joint manager with (Sir) Charles Wyndham [q.v.] of the Criterion Theatre. In September 1900 he became manager of the Garrick Theatre; and there during the next six years—the most stable and successful portion of his career—his productions included *The Merchant of Venice* (1905), in which he acted Shylock; *Macbeth* (1906), in which he acted Macbeth, and new plays by (Sir) A. W. Pinero, (Sir) W. S. Gilbert, Anthony Hope, Henry Arthur Jones, and Alfred Sutro, besides an adaptation from the French of Eugène Brieux, entitled *The Arm of the Law*. In September 1910 he joined Sir Herbert Beerbohm Tree [q.v.] at His Majesty's Theatre, where he acted the King in *King Henry VIII*, Bottom, and other Shakespearian parts.

Bourchier's remaining seventeen years of incessant activity and change included short spells of management of the Garrick Theatre (1912–1914), of His Majesty's Theatre (1916), and of the Strand Theatre (1919–1923), where in 1922 he staged *Treasure Island* and played the part of Long John Silver. Another of his best parts was Old Bill in *The Better 'Ole*, which in 1917–1918 had a long run at the Oxford music-hall. In 1927 he took a company to South Africa; he fell ill at Johannesburg, and died there on 14 September.

Bourchier was a devoted man of the theatre. He lectured on the drama at the Royal Institution, at Oxford, and at many other places, and he worked hard in organizing and supporting performances in aid of theatrical and other charities. He delighted in his work, and had considerable talent. In parts which required broad and hearty treatment he acted well. His Macbeth was merely a bluff and rugged warrior; his Shylock a man of intense malignity, displayed from the first moment to the last; his Iago (to the Othello of Matheson Lang, 1920) a naughty boy who thoroughly enjoyed being naughty. But as King Henry VIII, as Bottom, as Silver the pirate, as Old Bill the soldier, as the truculent judge in *The Arm of the Law*, he excelled. By nature impatient, he was so zealous for and devoted to the theatre that he hotly resented criticism. On 2 March 1903 A. B. Walkley [q.v.], the dramatic critic of *The Times*, was by his orders refused admission to the Garrick Theatre on a first night to which he had been invited; and this was not Bourchier's only attempt to browbeat his critics. His work both as actor and as producer was impaired by excess of the ardour and energy which gave life to it.

Bourchier's first wife, by whom he had one daughter, divorced him in 1917; in 1918 he married Violet Marion Kyrle Bellew, an actress, daughter of Louis Hance Falck and previously the wife of Allen Martin Reuben Nicholson, from whom she had obtained a divorce. Of Bourchier's second marriage there was no issue.

A cartoon of Bourchier by 'Spy' appeared in *Vanity Fair* 5 March 1896.

[*The Times*, 3, 7, and 9 March 1903, 15 September 1927; Alan Mackinnon, *The Oxford Amateurs*, 1910; *Who's Who in the Theatre*, 1925; personal knowledge.]

H. H. Child.

BOWLBY, Sir ANTHONY ALFRED, first baronet (1855–1929), surgeon, was born at Namur 10 May 1855, the third son of Thomas William Bowlby [q.v.], who was then in Belgium acting as correspondent of *The Times*, by his wife, Frances Marion, youngest daughter of Pulteney Mein, formerly surgeon in the 73rd Regiment, of Canonbie, Dumfriesshire.

Anthony Bowlby was educated at Durham School, and entered St. Bartholomew's Hospital in October 1876. He won the Brackenbury scholarship in surgery in 1880, and served as house-surgeon to Luther Holden and (Sir) Thomas Smith in 1881. Here also he filled in succession the offices of curator of the museum (1881–1884); surgical registrar (1884–1891); assistant surgeon (1891–1903); surgeon (1903–1920), and consulting surgeon (1919). In addition he acted as surgeon to the Alexandra Hospital for Diseases of the Hip in Queen Square, Bloomsbury (1885–1918), and as surgeon to the Foundling Hospital. At the Royal College of Surgeons of England Bowlby was admitted a member (1879) and a fellow (1881); he was a member of council (1904–1920); president, in succession to Sir George Makins (1920–1923), and Hunterian trustee (1925). He delivered the Bradshaw lecture in 1915, and was Hunterian orator in 1919.

When the South African War broke out in 1899 Bowlby went out as senior surgeon in charge of the Portland Hospital stationed first at Rondebosch and later at Bloemfontein; was mentioned in dispatches; and was invested with the C.M.G. in 1901. He accepted in 1908 a commission as major in the newly formed Territorial medical service, and on the outbreak of the European War in 1914 was called up with the First London General Hospital (Territorial Force). He served for a few days, and then offered his services to the War Office. These were accepted, and he was sent to France on 23 September 1914 as consulting surgeon to the British Expeditionary Force with the rank of colonel. He was appointed consulting surgeon to the Second Army (May 1915), and was afterwards general adviser to the director-general, Army Medical Service, and finally advisory consulting surgeon to the whole of the British forces in France, with the temporary rank of major-general. In these various positions Bowlby did excellent work. He insisted that more surgery should be done at the front, less at the base. He was thus instrumental in revolutionizing the practice of all former wars, and hospitals fully equipped with nurses and orderlies were established within four to six miles of the actual fighting line. His personality, also, did much to ensure harmonious co-operation between the civil and military medical officers.

Bowlby did not resume active practice at the end of the War, but he did much good work as a member of the executive committee of the British Red Cross Society and as chairman of the Radium Institute. In 1904 he had been appointed surgeon to the household of King Edward VII, and in 1910 gazetted surgeon-in-ordinary to King George V. He was knighted in 1911, and created K.C.M.G. (1915), K.C.V.O. (1916), K.C.B. (1919), and a baronet (1923). He married in 1898 Maria Bridget, eldest daughter of the Rev. the Hon. Hugh Wynne Mostyn, rector of Buckworth, Huntingdonshire, and honorary canon of Ely Cathedral. She survived him together with their three sons and three daughters. He died after a few days' illness whilst on a holiday at Stoney Cross, near Lyndhurst, 7 April 1929, and his body was cremated at Brookwood. He was succeeded as second baronet by his eldest son, Anthony Hugh Mostyn (born 1906).

Bowlby was a clear thinker and a dogmatic teacher; a first-rate organizer and a fine administrator. He had a genius for friendship and was extremely popular with students. Educated in the days before the value of Lister's work was recognized in London and without any training in science, he never excelled as a modern operating surgeon, but his large experience and his absolute honesty of purpose made him valuable as a consultant. His writings include *Wounds and other Injuries of Nerves* (Jacksonian prize essay), 1882; *Injuries and Diseases of the Nerves and their Surgical Treatment* (Astley Cooper prize essay 1886), 1889; a useful work on *Surgical Pathology and Morbid Anatomy* (1887, 7th ed. 1920), and he was joint editor with Sir William Grant Macpherson and others of *Medical Services: Surgery of the War*, 2 vols., 1922 (*History of the Great War based on official documents*).

A three-quarter length portrait in oils of Bowlby by Sir William Llewellyn, representing him in the uniform of a major-general, Army Medical Service, hangs in the great hall of St. Bartholomew's Hospital. He figures in a portrait-group by Moussa Ayoub of the council of the Royal College of Surgeons of England which hangs in the hall of the College in Lincoln's Inn Fields. Near it is a tablet, presented 'as a token of their esteem', by medical officers of the American Expeditionary Force who served with Bowlby in France. Bowlby's portrait is also included in the lower panel of the painting in the Royal Exchange by Frank O. Salisbury, representing King George V and Queen Mary visiting the battle-areas of France in 1917.

[V. G. Plarr, *Lives of the Fellows of the Royal College of Surgeons of England*, 2 vols., revised by Sir D'A. Power and others, 1930; W. Girling Ball in St. Bartholomew's Hospital *Reports*, vol. lxiii, 1930 (containing a complete list of Bowlby's writings and an excellent portrait); personal knowledge.] D'A. Power.

BOWLES, THOMAS GIBSON (1842–1922), politician, was born 15 January 1842. He was educated at King's College, London, and became an official of the inland revenue, but left the service early for journalism. He started in November 1868 a society paper, called *Vanity Fair*, which gave coloured cartoons, accompanied by racy biographical sketches, of public characters [see Ward, Sir Leslie]; he also owned other newspaper interests. These ventures proved profitable, and Bowles turned his attention to politics. At the general election in 1892 he was returned to parliament for King's Lynn as a conservative, and for three years sat on the opposition side of the House of Commons.

The budget of 1894, introduced by Sir William Harcourt, gave Bowles an opportunity of showing himself to be an able and well-informed critic of financial measures. He spoke well on other subjects, and when the conservatives were returned to office in 1895, seemed a likely candidate for some ministerial post. But he was passed over, and became henceforth a critic rather than a supporter of the government. He was virtually an independent member, and in the tariff reform controversy of 1903 he declared for free trade, attacking with bitterness both Mr. Chamberlain and Mr. Arthur Balfour, the leader of his party. The whips refused to recognize him, and put up another conservative candidate at King's Lynn in 1906. Bowles lost the seat, stood again as a conservative free-trader for the City of London against Mr. Balfour, but received little support, and before the end of the year joined the liberal party.

Bowles's association with liberalism was brief. In March 1909 he contested Central Glasgow as a liberal, and was beaten at the polls, but at the first of the two general elections of 1910, he was returned as a liberal for his old constituency of King's Lynn. This experience was rendered more curious by the fact that he won the seat as a supporter of Mr. Lloyd George's budget, a measure which seemed much at variance with his previous views on taxation. At the second general election in the same year he was turned out again, and this was the end of his political career. In December 1911 he announced his return to the conservative party, but he never sat in the House of Commons again, though he contested the Southern division of Leicester in 1916.

Bowles remained a vigilant guardian of the national purse. He felt so strongly on the question of the payment of members that in 1913 he contemplated taking action in the High Court in order to test the legality of this constitutional question. He was dissuaded from this course, and abandoned his intention with regret. In the same year he brought an action against the Bank of England for authorizing the deduction of income tax from dividend warrants on the strength of financial resolutions passed in the committee of ways and means, before the Finance Act of the year had given legal sanction to new taxation. The object of the practice which he challenged was to prevent forestalling in spirits, tea, and tobacco. Bowles won his case against the Bank; and this made necessary a change in the House of Commons procedure affecting finance; Mr. Lloyd George, the chancellor of the Exchequer, was obliged to get an Act passed making legal the provisional collection of taxes.

In February 1914 Bowles brought out the first number of a journal called the *Candid Quarterly Review*, the aim of which was 'to discover and denounce insincerity, dishonesty, corruption, or aught that may bring danger or dishonour to the State'. A second number of this periodical followed in May 1914, but there were no further issues. He was an authority on international and maritime law, and published, among other books, *Maritime Warfare* (1878), *The Declaration of Paris of 1856* (1900), and *Sea Law and Sea Power* (1910).

Bowles married in 1875 Jessica (died 1887), daughter of General Evans Gordon, of Kenmure. They had two sons and two daughters; the elder daughter married (1904) the Hon. David Freeman-Mitford, afterwards second Baron Redesdale.

Bowles died 12 January 1922 at Algeciras, and was buried at Gibraltar.

A cartoon of Bowles by 'Spy' appeared in *Vanity Fair* 19 October 1905. He was habitually nicknamed by *Punch* 'Captain Tommy Bowles' and represented with a wooden leg and hook arm.

[*The Times*, 13 January 1922.]

A. Cochrane.

BOYD, HENRY (1831–1922), principal of Hertford College, Oxford, the third son of William Clark Boyd, of Hackney, by his wife, Mary, daughter of William Steinmetz, was born in Holborn 26 February 1831. He was educated at Hackney School, and at the age of seventeen (1849) went up as a commoner to Exeter College, Oxford. He gained a second class in *literae humaniores* in 1852, the Ellerton theological essay prize in 1853, and the Denyer theological essay prize in 1856 and 1857. He was ordained in 1854 to the curacy of Bellean, Lincolnshire, and removed to that of Probus in Cornwall in 1856.

In 1862 Boyd came to London as perpetual curate of Saint Mark's, Victoria Docks. Here he worked with devotion for twelve years. He rebuilt his church, and his schools were a great source of pride to him. His interest in the social conditions of his parish made him an ardent pioneer of housing and sanitary reform. Eventually the strain of these exertions proved too much for his constitution, and he had a serious break-down, which brought on paralysis, so that for several months he was unable to move. He recovered, but was obliged to give up his work in the East End of London.

In 1874 a bill was passed through parliament whereby Magdalen Hall, Oxford, was dissolved, and its principal and scholars incorporated as a college of the university under the old name of Hertford College, the site and buildings of which had been occupied by the members of Magdalen Hall since their removal in 1822 from the original premises of the Hall contiguous to Magdalen College. The passage of this measure, which was initiated by Richard Michell [q.v.], principal of Magdalen Hall, was rendered easier by the munificence of Thomas Charles Baring, M.P., who offered an endowment for fellowships and scholarships, the benefits of which were to be restricted to members of the Church of England. This offer had been made first to Brasenose, Baring's old college, but had been declined, as it was thought that the proposed restriction was inconsistent with the University Tests Act of 1871. It was accepted by Hertford College, but the first examination for a fellowship on the new foundation was challenged by the nonconformists, who lost their case in the Court of Appeal. Baring retained under the Act of 1874 power to nominate for the first fellowships at Hertford, and he offered one of these to Boyd, who became also dean and divinity lecturer.

In March 1877, on the death of Michell, Boyd was appointed principal of the college, and from that day until his death, forty-five years later, the welfare of Hertford was his constant care. The college soon became popular, and made a reputation for itself, owed at first, perhaps, to successes on the river and the football field rather than in the schools. The principal, a notable figure in tall hat and frock coat, without an overcoat, followed the progress of the college in these matters with the closest interest.

In 1890 Boyd became vice-chancellor of the university, and began to give evidence of his capacity outside his college. His share in university affairs had not hitherto been important, but he now filled his high position with conspicuous success. His tact and courtesy enabled him to deal with men of all kinds, and to overcome many difficulties. His term of office ended, Boyd set his most permanent mark on Oxford. As master of the Drapers' Company (1896–1897) he exercised a great influence on the educational policy of that wealthy society, and he directed its benefactions in turn to Cambridge and to his own university. The chief monument of his activity is the Electrical Laboratory (for the use of the

Wykeham professor of physics), in Parks Road, designed by (Sir) T. G. Jackson [q.v.] and erected in 1910. Boyd also commissioned Jackson to enlarge and partly to rebuild Hertford College, for which additional accommodation and better premises were urgently needed. The result was, on the whole, successful, the new chapel (1907) being especially good, though the new hall (1889), owing to the impossibility of carrying out the original design, was scarcely so satisfactory. These improvements were completed in 1907. The supervision of them by the principal was valuable to the college, for Boyd was a man of much experience and taste in artistic and architectural subjects. He was an accomplished painter in water-colours, and filled portfolios with excellent sketches of cathedrals and churches in Spain, France, and Algeria. A collection of these sketches is preserved in the Taylor Institution at Oxford.

Boyd's interest in undergraduate recreations was the outcome of his own enjoyment of sports and games. A tall and active man, in his youth he was a climber and swimmer, while in middle life he spent much time on the golf links. He was one of the first to introduce golf at Oxford, and when he was vice-chancellor he reserved one afternoon a week for the game. He was also particularly fond of fishing, and for many years the long vacation found him on a salmon river in Norway. In 1914, when he was eighty-three, the outbreak of war interrupted this expedition, and obliged his return to Newcastle. The European War moved him deeply, and he was greatly concerned about its disruption of the university life with which he had been so long familiar. He felt doubts whether Oxford would ever recover from its effects—doubts which fortunately he lived long enough to see, in part at least, dispelled.

Boyd was a high churchman and an open-minded conservative, with a strong feeling for tradition and custom. In manner somewhat shy and reserved, he was a capable administrator of college and university affairs, and in private life a most attractive companion. His modesty, honesty of purpose, and humanity gained him the regard of men of varied type and conditions. He died at Oxford 4 March 1922. He was unmarried.

A portrait by Sir Hubert von Herkomer is in the hall of Hertford College.

[Private information; personal knowledge.]

A. Cochrane.

BRABAZON, REGINALD, twelfth Earl of Meath (1841–1929), was born in London 31 July 1841. He was the second son of William Brabazon, eleventh earl, by his wife, Harriot, second daughter of Sir Richard Brooke, sixth baronet, of Norton Priory, Cheshire. His elder brother died in childhood, and it was as Lord Brabazon that he entered the Rev. A. F. Birch's house at Eton in 1854. On leaving school he went for some years to Germany, and then passed into the Foreign Office as a clerk in 1863. Five years later he exchanged into the diplomatic service, his first appointment being to the embassy at Berlin. He was there during the Franco-Prussian War, and then, after a short time of service at The Hague, was transferred to the embassy at Paris in 1871. He was offered the position of second secretary at Athens in July 1873, but declined the promotion, and remained without pay at the disposal of the service, until he finally retired in 1877. He had married in 1868 Lady Mary Jane, daughter of Thomas Maitland, eleventh Earl of Lauderdale.

In 1873 Lord Brabazon, when his active work as a diplomat came to an end, went to live at Sunbury-on-Thames; thenceforth he and his wife devoted themselves to social and philanthropic work. His first undertaking was the foundation of the Hospital Saturday Fund Committee, of which he became honorary secretary. In the first year of the Fund (1874) the total sum raised for the hospitals by the working men of London was £6,463. By the time of the founder's death the amount had increased to over £100,000 annually. Lord Brabazon also started the Dublin Hospital Sunday movement for the benefit of the hospitals in that city. In 1879 he became the first chairman of the Young Men's Friendly Society, which grew into the Church of England Men's Society. In the following year he founded the Metropolitan Public Gardens Association, of which he was chairman until his death. He sat as an alderman of the London County Council from 1889 to 1892, and from 1898 to 1901, and was the first chairman of its parks committee. To his initiative and energetic action London is indebted for the preservation of many of its open spaces, and for the formation of parks, gardens, and playgrounds covering many thousands of acres. Among other social movements in which he took an active part were the Early Closing Association, and the National Association for promoting state-aided education and the teaching of physical exercises in schools. He twice without success brought a bill into parliament to make physical exercises compulsory in elementary schools, before the proposal was finally adopted in 1904. A full list of Lord Brabazon's philanthropic activities would be too long to give here. Among them may be mentioned the Ministering Children's League (founded by his wife) and the Lord Roberts Memorial Workshops.

His father died in 1887, and Lord Brabazon succeeded to the earldom of Meath and to the estate of Kilruddery in county Wicklow. A few years later he began to promote the movement, with which his name is chiefly associated, for the recognition of an Empire commemoration day. In 1893 he persuaded parliament to permit the union jack to be flown over the palace of Westminster. Some time afterwards his attention was attracted by a newspaper report of a ceremony at Hamilton, Ontario, at which the British flag was hoisted and the children sang the national anthem. His imagination was quick to see the possibilities of such a function. He wrote to colonial governors and prime ministers for their views, and eventually the idea of celebrating 24 May, the birthday of Queen Victoria, as 'Empire Day' was evolved. In promoting the Empire Day movement, Lord Meath expounded far and wide the idea of a lofty patriotism based on social service and civic duty.

Lord Meath was a staunch admirer of Lord Roberts, and a zealous supporter of his campaign for national military service. He was also the founder and first president of the Lads' Drill Association, afterwards incorporated in the National Service League, as well as chief commissioner for Ireland of the Boy Scouts organization. He wrote, or edited, several books on the subjects to which he devoted his life, among them being *Social Arrows* (1886) and *Social Aims* (1893). He was a frequent contributor to the *Nineteenth Century* and other reviews, and many letters in the newspapers appeared above his name. He also published two well-written volumes of reminiscences, *Memories of the Nineteenth Century* (1923) and *Memories of the Twentieth Century* (1924).

Lord Meath was created K.P. in 1905, G.B.E. in 1920, and G.C.V.O. in 1923. He was an Irish privy councillor, lord lieutenant for the city and county of Dublin, and a member, elected for Southern Ireland, of the senate of the Irish Free State. His wife, by whom he had four sons and two daughters, died in 1918. She not only supported her husband's schemes, but also herself devoted much time and money to philanthropic objects. Lord Meath died in London 11 October 1929, and was succeeded as thirteenth earl by his eldest son, Reginald Le Normand (born 1869).

A memorial to Lord Meath, showing a medallion portrait in relief, has been erected in Lancaster Gate, London.

[*The Times*, 12 October 1929.]

A. Cochrane.

BRADLEY, FRANCIS HERBERT (1846–1924), philosopher, was born at Clapham 30 January 1846. He was the fourth child and eldest surviving son of the Rev. Charles Bradley [q.v.], vicar of Glasbury, Brecknockshire, and incumbent of St. James's chapel, Clapham, by his second wife, Emma, daughter of John Linton. George Granville Bradley [q.v.], successively headmaster of Marlborough College, master of University College, Oxford, and dean of Westminster, was one of his six half-brothers. In 1854 his parents moved from Clapham to Cheltenham in the interests of his father's health. Bradley's schooling consequently began at Cheltenham College (1856–1861), and was continued at Marlborough College (1861–1863) under the headmastership of his brother. At Marlborough he was prominent as a football player and as an ardent member of the school rifle corps, until his schooldays were brought to an end by a dangerous attack of typhoid fever, followed by pneumonia. He had already begun the study of German at Cheltenham, and is said to have made acquaintance, while still a schoolboy, with Kant's *Critique of Pure Reason* (perhaps in Francis Haywood's English translation).

In 1865 Bradley went up to Oxford as a scholar of University College, where he worked hard, rowed, and took his full share in the social life of the college. He obtained a first class in classical moderations in 1867, but in *literae humaniores* in 1869 was placed only in the second class, as R. L. Nettleship had been earlier in that year. This reverse, and his consequent failure, more than once, to obtain a college fellowship, made it doubtful whether Bradley would be able to devote his life to philosophy; but in December 1870 he was elected at Merton College to a fellowship tenable for life but terminable by marriage. He never married, and Merton thus became his permanent home until his death more than half a century later.

In June 1871 Bradley was attacked by a violent inflammation of the kidneys which had lifelong effects. For the rest of his days cold, fatigue, or mental anxiety was apt to bring on severe illness; and he was compelled, for more than fifty years, to lead a singularly retired existence. From 1871 onwards the record of his career may almost be said to be given in the list of his published books and papers, the fruit of a meditation all the more intense by reason of his quiet life. Although he took no share in the teaching work of the college, he played a very active and unselfish part in the transaction of its general business, being as notable for sound, practical judgement in affairs as for wit and brilliance in conversation. He continued to live in college, fully occupied with his philosophical work until the late summer of 1924, when sudden symptoms of blood-poisoning led to his removal to an Oxford nursing home. Here he died, after an illness of a few days, 18 September 1924. He was buried in Holywell cemetery, Oxford, in the same grave as a younger brother who had been drowned in the Isis in 1866 when a freshman of New College. Bradley's very impressive features are preserved in a posthumously executed portrait by R. G. Eves which hangs in the fellows' common room of Merton College.

Bradley received many marks of public recognition during the course of his career. In 1883 the degree of LL.D. was conferred on him by the university of Glasgow; in 1921 he was elected member of the Royal Danish Academy, in 1922 of the Reale Accademia Nazionale dei Lincei, and in 1923 of the Reale Istituto Lombardo of Milan. The British Academy, which he had declined to join on its foundation on the ground that his health would not permit attendance at meetings, unanimously elected him an honorary fellow in 1923. In June 1914 he received the Order of Merit.

Bradley's contribution to philosophy is contained in four books and a great number of essays chiefly contributed to *Mind* (published as *Collected Essays*, 2 vols., 1935). The books, in order of publication, are *Ethical Studies* (1876, second edition revised with additional notes by the author, posthumous, 1927); *The Principles of Logic* (1883, second edition revised with commentary and terminal essays, 1922); *Appearance and Reality, a Metaphysical Essay* (1893, second edition with an appendix, 1897), and *Essays on Truth and Reality* (1914). Between them they cover the main departments of philosophy with the exception of aesthetics, a field in which Bradley did no special work. The essays in *Mind* are chiefly, although not exclusively, concerned with problems of general psychology.

The chief inspiration of Bradley's thought, as of that of Thomas Hill Green, Edward Caird, and other contemporaries, came from the study of Hegel. Bradley's writings probably did more than those of any other man to effect that naturalization of Hegelian thought in England which was so marked a feature of the close of the nineteenth century. Unlike Green, who was, moreover, cut off by death before he had brought his philosophy to maturity, he sat comparatively loose to the influence of Kant, and was not exclusively preoccupied with specifically ethical problems. Unlike Caird, being free from the burdens of university teaching, he felt no call to devote his best energies to the exegesis of a philosophy of the past. Over both Green and Caird he had the marked advantages of a racy and mordant humour, and a literary style of high individuality and rare distinction. Hence he naturally came to be looked upon by a younger generation as the head of a so-called 'Anglo-Hegelian' school, in spite of his protests that he neither had, nor desired to have, disciples, and that he dissented too profoundly from much which is fundamental in Hegel to regard himself as an Hegelian. Both contentions were, in fact, true. In philosophy a school presupposes a system, and system-making was alien to Bradley's temperament. His object was, on the one hand, to expose the hollowness of a pretended 'system', that combination of metaphysical scepticism, scientific empiricism, and ethical individualism represented by John Stuart Mill, and, on the other, to preach a single metaphysical principle, that of the thorough-going super-relational unity of all reality. The destructive part of this programme was, by general admission, fully effected. Individualism in ethics, 'conceptualism' in logic, associationism in the theory of knowledge, are not likely ever to recover from the blows dealt at them in *Ethical Studies* and *The Principles of Logic*. But a man need be no 'disciple' to admit this; it would probably be conceded by the 'pragmatists', 'humanists', and 'personal idealists' whose own philosophies have been largely created by the reaction against Bradley's positive doctrine.

Of that doctrine itself it is not quite easy to say how far it can really be called Hegelian. If it shows Hegelian inspiration, as it does, it no less clearly reveals the counterbalancing influence of Herbart, a thinker for whom Bradley had an exceptionally high regard, and, to a lesser degree, of Lotze and Schopenhauer. Something also has probably to be allowed for the subtle and all-pervading influence of that national psychological tradition in British philosophy against which Bradley was so largely in revolt. Bradley agreed heartily with Hegel in the doctrines that the universe is a single reality, that its unity is super-relational, and that it is in the life of self-conscious personality that we get the least inadequate clue to its character. Like Hegel, he is a 'spiritual monist', and like him, he holds that all attempts to conceive of the metaphysically real as a system of many inter-related 'things' or 'finite personalities' end in intellectual confusion and contradiction. But—and here it is, perhaps, that the influence of Herbart makes itself conspicuous—he wholly dissents from Hegel's most characteristic doctrine, the theory that the various 'partial' and 'contradictory' aspects of the supreme metaphysical reality can be arranged in a necessary serial order, and that the advance along the series is, in some sense, an evolution of the 'world-spirit' itself. There is nothing in Bradley corresponding to the 'objective logic' of Hegel, and this is, in fact, the reason why he always disclaimed the name of Hegelian. The 'dialectical' movement, in which Hegel had seen the secret of the history of the universe, becomes with Bradley simply a subjective process within the mind of the philosopher reflecting upon experience. As a consequence, sensation and unanalysed 'feeling' acquire with him, as the points of immediate contact between the mind and the given reality, an importance which they never seem to have had for Hegel. It is not surprising that the destructive and critical part of *Appearance and Reality* appears to have impressed more orthodox Hegelians as dangerously like Hume in its methods and conclusions. If Hegel's doctrine is correctly interpreted as a 'panlogism', Bernard Bosanquet [q.v.] and still more John McTaggart Ellis McTaggart [q.v.] are much better entitled to be described as Hegelians than Bradley.

[A. E. Taylor, *Francis Herbert Bradley, 1846–1924* (containing a bibliography of his works), in *Proceedings* of the British Academy, vol. xi, 1924–5; private information; personal knowledge.] A. E. Taylor.

BRADLEY, HENRY (1845–1923), philologist and lexicographer, born at Manchester 3 December 1845, was the only son of John Bradley, of Kirkby-in Ashfield, Nottinghamshire, by his second wife, Mary Spencer, of Middleton-by-Wirksworth, Derbyshire. From 1846 his father, who had been farmer and partner in a cloth-mill, resided at Brimington, near Chesterfield, and Bradley attended Chesterfield grammar school from 1855 to 1859. In the latter year his family moved to Sheffield, where in 1863 he became corresponding clerk to a cutlery firm. During the interval, circumstances had enabled him to pursue a wide course of miscellaneous reading and the study of languages, for which he had a great natural aptitude. His office-work gave him opportunities of developing this interest, and during the twenty years in which he remained in his post as clerk, he not only mastered a number of the modern European languages, but acquired a knowledge of the classical tongues which is rare except among trained scholars, as well as a considerable acquaintance with Hebrew.

In 1872 Bradley married Eleanor Kate, daughter of William Hides, of Sheffield, by whom he had one son and four daughters. In January 1884, partly for economic reasons and partly on account of his wife's health, he removed to London, where for some years he maintained himself by miscellaneous literary work, of which reviewing formed an important part. A review by him which appeared in the *Academy* for February and March 1884 of the first part of the *New English Dictionary*, drew attention to his unusual knowledge of English philology, and brought about a connexion with the *Dictionary* which led to his being appointed one of its editors in 1889, a position which he retained for the remainder of his life, becoming senior editor on the death of Sir James Augustus Murray [q.v.] in 1915. In 1891 he received the honorary degree of M.A. from Oxford University, and in 1914 that of D.Litt. To Oxford he removed permanently in 1896. At that date he was elected a member of Exeter College, and twenty years later (1916) a fellow of Magdalen

College. From 1892 he received a civil list pension in recognition of his services to learning. He was president of the Philological Society for three periods (1890–1893, 1900–1903, and 1909–1910) and was elected F.B.A. in 1907. From the time of his settling in Oxford the *Dictionary* became his main occupation, although he continued to write numerous articles and reviews, and produced two or three separate publications. With the exception of one or two short periods, he was able to carry on his work with great regularity during all these years, and his death, which took place at Oxford 23 May 1923, was very sudden.

During his first years in London, in addition to his extensive reviewing of philological and other books, Bradley wrote a number of articles for those volumes of the *Dictionary* which cover the letters B, C, and D. He also compiled the volume on *The Goths* (1888) for the 'Story of the Nations' series, a work written in a popular style, but based on a careful study of original sources. For the Oxford University Press he prepared a revised edition of F. H. Stratmann's *Middle English Dictionary*, which appeared in 1891 and still remains the most complete special dictionary for this period of the language. An edition of Caxton's *Dialogues* for the Early English Text Society (1900), the popular and highly successful *Making of English* (1904), and the British Academy paper on *Spoken and Written Language* (1913, issued in book form in 1919, the year in which he took part in finally instituting the Society for Pure English) complete the list of Bradley's separate works. In addition to these, however, his numerous articles and notes on both linguistic and literary points in Old and Middle English are important contributions in these fields, and give constant evidence of his wide knowledge, sound judgement, and originality of thought. Not a few of them contain brilliant discoveries or suggestions, which have been readily accepted by other scholars.

Bradley's earliest independent work arose from his interest in the history and origin of British place-names, and in later years his contributions to this subject were of great value in setting the study on a sounder philological and historical basis than it had previously possessed. Although he undertook no large detailed work of his own, his searching reviews of the publications of others not only exhibited the defects in their knowledge or methods, but made clear the principles on which the scientific investigation of place-names must be conducted. Of his special articles in this field the most important are those on *Ptolemy's Geography of the British Isles* (1885) and *English Place-names* (1910).

The share which Bradley took in the *Oxford English Dictionary*, from the date when he devoted most of his time to that work, was the editing of the letters E, F, G, L, M, S–Sh, St, and part of W, amounting in all to 4,590 pages out of a total of 15,487, and including several difficult portions of the vocabulary. The treatment of these, and the work as a whole, naturally gave opportunity for his unusual qualifications as a scholar—his extensive knowledge of ancient and modern languages, his thorough grasp of philological principles, his retentive and accurate memory, and his rare powers of analysis and definition. In some respects the *Dictionary* necessarily limited his range, and by its claims on the major part of his time restricted the possibilities of his contributing to the other fields of learning or literature in which he was equally fitted to excel. This was most evident to those who knew him most intimately, and by personal contact could realize that under a quiet and unassuming manner he possessed intellectual powers which transcended the ordinary bounds of scholarship and partook of the brilliancy of genius.

[*The Collected Papers of Henry Bradley.* With a memoir by Robert Bridges, 1928; Historical Introduction in the Supplement to the *Oxford English Dictionary*, 1933; personal knowledge.] W. A. Craigie.

BRANCKER, Sir WILLIAM SEFTON (1877–1930), major-general and air vice-marshal, was born at Woolwich 22 March 1877, the elder son of Colonel William Godeffroy Brancker, C.B., Royal Artillery, of Erbistock, North Wales, by his wife, Hester Adelaide, daughter of Major-general Henry Charles Russel, Royal Artillery. He was educated at Bedford School and at the Royal Military Academy, Woolwich, and was commissioned in the Royal Artillery in September 1896. He served in the South African War, 1900–1902, when he was wounded and mentioned in dispatches. He was promoted captain in 1902, and in the following year was sent to India, where he passed through the Staff College and served until 1912 chiefly in staff appointments.

Brancker had already had experience of ballooning—he had made an ascent at Lydd, Kent, in 1897—before opportunity for flying was presented to him in India. In 1910 a commercial aeroplane expedition arrived at Calcutta in order to give a demonstration to the general staff. Brancker was in charge of the disembarkation of the party, to which he at once attached himself and was given permission to fly unofficially, as an observer. He took part, as air observer, in the military manœuvres in the Deccan in 1911, and his air report impressed the many generals, including Sir Douglas Haig, who were present.

In 1912 Brancker returned to England, and continued his air experience by frequently flying as a passenger. He was promoted major in January 1913, and in the following April was given employment at the War Office. He now learned to fly at the Vickers Flying School, Brooklands, and, after qualifying for his Royal Aero Club certificate in June, passed through the Central Flying School at Upavon, Salisbury Plain. In October he was appointed to the staff of the director-general of military aeronautics, Sir David Henderson [q.v.]. He continued to fly whenever possible, and in June 1914 piloted the first aeroplane of the stable B.E. 2c. type from Farnborough to Upavon without using his hands except to throttle back before landing.

On the outbreak of the European War, when Henderson took command in August 1914 of the Royal Flying Corps in France, Brancker was appointed deputy-director of military aeronautics and virtually took charge of military aviation at the War Office, working directly under Lord Kitchener, the secretary of state for war. He was thus largely responsible for the early expansion of the Royal Flying Corps in personnel and equipment. In August 1915 Henderson returned to take control at the War Office, and Brancker, now a lieutenant-colonel, went to France in order to command the third wing, Royal Flying Corps, until December 1915, when he came back to England and took command of the Northern brigade, Royal Flying Corps, being promoted to brigadier-general. In March 1916 he was appointed director of air organization at the War Office, an appointment which he held until February 1917 when he became deputy director-general of military aeronautics. He was promoted major-general in June 1917 and continued in his appointment until October, when he left in order to command the Royal Flying Corps, Middle East, at Cairo; but he was recalled at the beginning of January 1918 to a seat on the newly-formed Air Council as controller-general of equipment. His duties took him in that year to the United States as head of a British aviation mission, and on his return he was appointed master-general of personnel, a post which he held until 1919. For his services in the war he was created K.C.B. (1919) and he was also the first to receive the Air Force Cross (1918).

Brancker retired from the Royal Air Force in 1919 in order to devote his energies to the encouragement of commercial flying. He joined George Holt Thomas [q.v.] in the Air Travel and Transport Company and helped to organize the first London to Paris air-line. In May 1922 he returned to the Air Ministry as director of civil aviation, and he held this appointment until his death. He was accorded the rank of air vice-marshal in 1925. On 4 October 1930 he set out in the airship R. 101, which was attempting to fly to India. In the early hours of the following morning the airship struck the ground at Allonne, near Beauvais, France, and was destroyed by fire, with the loss of forty-eight lives out of her total complement of fifty-four, crew and passengers. Brancker was among the victims of the disaster.

Short, dapper, monocled, high-spirited and charming, Sefton Brancker took life cheerfully, as he found it. He was an indifferent air pilot, but had a brilliant organizing capacity, and in the development of the national air service he played an outstanding part. He possessed just the necessary qualities, including unbounded energy, to compel attention to and consideration for the needs of the air service in the difficult war years when that service was young and competition in other quarters for material and men was most severe. To some, who judged him superficially, Brancker appeared to lack depth and poise. The truth is, he was gifted with unusual vision tempered by a shrewd common-sense.

Brancker married in 1907 May Wynne, daughter of Colonel Spencer Field, of the Royal Warwickshire Regiment, by whom he was survived with the one son of the marriage.

There is a portrait of Brancker by Captain E. Newling at the Royal Aero Club, and a bronze bust by L. F. Roslyn in the Imperial War Museum, South Kensington.

[W. A. Raleigh and H. A. Jones, *The War in*

the Air, 3 vols., 1922–1931; *The Aeroplane*, 8 October 1930; official records; private information; personal knowledge. A *Life* of Brancker by Norman Macmillan was published in 1935.] H. A. JONES.

BRAY, SIR REGINALD MORE (1842–1923), judge, was born at Shere, near Guildford, 26 September 1842, the elder son of Reginald Bray, J.P., of Shere, by his wife, Frances, daughter of Thomas Norton Longman [q.v.], the publisher. He eventually succeeded to the large estate in that part of Surrey which has been the property of the Bray family since the end of the fifteenth century, and throughout his life his interests, outside his profession, were centred in the neighbourhood. He was collaterally descended from his namesake, Sir Reginald Bray [q.v.], statesman and architect in the reign of Henry VII, and traced his ancestry in the direct line to Sir Thomas More. His paternal grandmother was a sister of T. R. Malthus, the economist.

From Harrow, Bray won a scholarship to Trinity College, Cambridge, and graduated as twelfth wrangler in 1865. He was called to the bar by the Inner Temple in 1868, having read in chambers with (Sir) Charles James Watkin Williams [q.v.]. He went the South-Eastern circuit, 'devilled' for J. P. Murphy, Q.C., and built up a respectable practice on the common law side. In 1891 he was made recorder of Guildford—a position which he held until 1904—and became a bencher of his Inn. He did not take silk until 1897. During his unusually long career as a junior he always had a full pupil room, and it is said that when his ex-pupils entertained him at dinner to celebrate his call within the bar, there were just over a hundred of them available. As a leader Bray was employed in many types of litigation. Thus in 1904, the year in which he became a judge, he was successful in obtaining the reversal by the House of Lords of three decisions of the Court of Appeal upon such diverse matters as local government law (*Caterham U.D.C.* v. *Godstone R.D.C.*), domicile in relation to liability for legacy duty (*Winans* v. *Attorney-General*), and the right to light (*Colls* v. *Home and Colonial Stores*) in which Lord Halsbury, lord chancellor, spoke of 'Mr. Bray's very able argument'.

Bray had served on several occasions as commissioner of assize, and in June 1904, at the age of sixty-one, upon the resignation of Mr. Justice Bruce, he was appointed by Lord Halsbury to be a judge of the King's Bench division and was knighted. Although this promotion came at an age when many men are seeking retirement, its wisdom was thoroughly justified, for Bray sat on the bench for nearly nineteen years, during the whole of which period he was considered one of the ablest of the puisne judges, being frequently called upon to sit in divisional courts and as a third member in the Court of Appeal. His knowledge of principles, his keen insight, and his robust common sense were exhibited in many reported judgments, examples of which are *Sanday* v. *British and Foreign Marine Co.* (1915, restraint of princes), the Slingsby legitimacy case (1916), in which his judgment took an hour and a half to deliver, and *Reeve* v. *Jennings* (1910, a novel point under the Statute of Frauds). He refused to assent to the admonition of Canon Henry Thompson for repelling from the sacrament of Holy Communion a man who had married his deceased wife's sister (*R.* v. *Dibdin*, 1909), and he favoured the exemption of Easter offerings from income-tax (*Cooper* v. *Blakiston*, 1907): in these two cases his opinion did not prevail in the higher courts, but in *R.* v. *West Riding C.C.* (1906) his view, expressed as a member of a divisional court, that the local education authority must pay for the cost of religious instruction in a non-provided school, was accepted by the House of Lords.

In March 1923 Bray was attacked by illness while sitting in his court, and he died, at the age of eighty, on the 22nd of that month, and was buried at Shere.

Bray married in 1868 Emily Octavia, fourth daughter of his neighbour, Arthur Kett Barclay, of Bury Hill, Dorking, and had four sons and four daughters. His younger brother, Sir Edward Bray, was for many years the learned and courtly judge of the Marylebone county court.

A portrait of Bray by the Hon. John Collier is at the Manor House, Shere. A cartoon by 'Spy' appeared in *Vanity Fair* 17 October 1906.

[Private information.] P. A. LANDON.

BRETT, REGINALD BALIOL, second VISCOUNT ESHER (1852–1930), government official, was born in London 30 June 1852, the elder son of William Baliol Brett, afterwards first Viscount Esher [q.v.], master of the Rolls, by his wife, Eugénie, daughter of Louis Mayer, an Alsatian. His mother, a step-daughter of

Colonel John Gurwood [q.v.], the editor of Wellington's dispatches, belonged to the D'Orsay-Blessington circle and also had influential friends in Paris. Reginald Brett was educated at Eton, where A. C. Ainger was his tutor, and where he came under the influence of William Johnson Cory [q.v.], and at Trinity College, Cambridge. At both he made important friendships and developed social as well as political and literary interests. In 1879 he married Eleanor, third daughter of Sylvain Van de Weyer, the Belgian minister in London, who was a close friend of Queen Victoria.

As private secretary to the Marquess of Hartington for seven years (1878–1885), the last three of them spent at the War Office, Brett lived in a society which still retained something of the Disraeli atmosphere; knowing 'everybody', handling confidential affairs touching great men, freely suggesting ideas and actions to ministers, generals, viceroys, and in touch also with literature and the stage. In 1880 he was elected to parliament in the liberal interest as one of the members for Penryn and Falmouth, but at the general election of 1885 he unsuccessfully contested Plymouth and never stood again. Maintaining his friendships, Brett withdrew to Orchard Lea near Windsor Forest, where he was admitted to the queen's private circle; entertained, wrote some minor books, mainly biographical, kept for a time a small racing stable and breeding stud, shot, and fished. But sport was never his passion, and after ten rather aimless years the civil service attracted him. In 1895 his school friend Lord Rosebery, then prime minister, after Brett had refused to enter diplomacy, made him secretary of the Office of Works. He showed such practical talents in improving the domestic arrangements of the royal residences and in superintending the diamond jubilee of 1897 (in which year he was made C.B.) that the queen held him to his post when he succeeded his father as second viscount in 1899, and again, when, in 1900, he was offered the permanent under-secretaryship at the War Office. Esher had already (1899) refused the same post at the Colonial Office under Mr. Chamberlain, and the governorship of Cape Colony, declining to work in leading-strings. The queen created him K.C.V.O. in December 1900 just before her death. After so long a reign, memories of a sovereign's funeral and coronation were dim; he mastered the precedents, and took charge of both ceremonies with complete success.

Queen Victoria had made Esher one of her intimate friends, and she often visited Orchard Lea informally. King Edward VII gave him close friendship and wider scope, in connexion with the new civil list, as secretary of the committee of the Queen Victoria Memorial fund, as deputy constable and lieutenant-governor of Windsor Castle (1901), and as editor, in collaboration with Arthur Christopher Benson [q.v.], of *Selections from the Correspondence of Queen Victoria* (1907). Esher also published *The Girlhood of Queen Victoria* in 1912. Whatever he touched succeeded, and the king's confidence seemed boundless.

In the universal anxiety about the state of the army, its reform became with Esher an obsession. He saw that the key to it lay in the rejected proposals of the Hartington commission of 1890: viz. no commander-in-chief, a War-Office council on the Admiralty model, and an inspector-general; and he at once sought the ear of the king. He retired from the Office of Works and was created K.C.B. in 1902. In the same year he was made a member of the royal commission appointed, under the chairmanship of the ninth Earl of Elgin [q.v.], to inquire into the military preparations for and conduct of the South African War. Esher commented on the commission's proceedings in daily letters to the king, who by the end of the year had accepted his views. Although general War Office reform was outside the commission's reference, Esher appended to its report (July 1903) a note formulating his proposals. The prime minister, Mr. Balfour, Esher's lifelong friend, assured of the king's support, definitely approved the policy without further debate, and asked Esher to become secretary of state for war in order to carry it through. Esher would not re-enter politics, but proposed to do the work as chairman of a prime minister's committee, independent of the secretary of state about to be appointed, Mr. Arnold-Forster. The War Office Reconstruction Committee, generally known as the Esher Committee, was set up accordingly, with Admiral Sir John (afterwards Baron) Fisher [q.v.] and Colonel Sir George Clarke (formerly secretary of the Hartington commission, and afterwards Baron Sydenham) as members and Lieutenant-Colonel (afterwards Lieutenant-General Sir) Gerald Ellison as secretary. On 11 January 1904, a fortnight after Clarke's return from the governorship of Victoria, Part I of the Report proposed in outline the creation of an Army Council on Admiralty lines, and an inspector-general of the forces. The Committee would go no further until this had been accepted. That done, and the Council formally constituted (6 February), it produced in quick succession Parts II (26 February) and III (9 March), containing detailed proposals, claiming that they followed logically from the action already taken, and insisting that the Report should be accepted as an organic whole, without any alteration. It was, in fact, approved as it stood. It made two important improvements on Esher's note, namely, the provision of a permanent naval and military secretariat for Mr. Balfour's Committee of Imperial Defence, on which political and service chiefs sat together under the prime minister, and the creation of a General Staff for the army. With the internal working of the War Office (of which Esher's experience was out of date and the other members had none) the Committee dealt less successfully, and many of its recommendations, designed to remove financial control, were founded on errors of fact, and after due trial abandoned within five years. Esher's note had put the adjutant-general first of the military members of the newly-formed Army Council, and the director-general of military intelligence, head of an incomplete thinking department, last. The Committee created a chief of the general staff, ranking first, charged with everything pertaining to operations of war and to training, and furnishing to commanders, in war and peace, staffs trained in such duties. This all-important change was a complete reversal of recent War Office evolution, in which peace and personal considerations had destroyed system. Under the Duke of Cambridge (who commanded in chief 1856–1895) the adjutant-general, as his chief staff officer, had been allowed to swallow whole the surveyor-general (Lord Cardwell's business head) and to eat the quartermaster-general (Wellington's right-hand man) leaf by leaf, that empty title being transferred to a soldier purveyor of transport and supplies. Operations had dropped out of sight. In the field, similarly, there had been a factotum chief staff officer; no clear line had been drawn between command and the business of supply; and no organized operations staff had existed. Accustomed in India to a quartermaster-general, in Wellington's sense of the term, at the head of the operations staff, and to an adjutant-general dealing with personnel and discipline, Lord Roberts [q.v.] had been shocked to find this state of things prevailing in South Africa. At the War Office, therefore, on becoming commander-in-chief (1901), he had overruled opposition and ordered the preparation of a staff manual on Wellingtonian lines. Colonel Ellison, who had worked out the ground-plan of this under Roberts's orders before being appointed secretary to the Esher Committee, produced it to the Committee, which adopted it entire and distributed War Office duties accordingly, only changing the title of Roberts's quartermaster-general to that of chief of the general staff. Thus Esher's uncompromising dictatorship combined with Roberts's initiative to produce a true General Staff which, expanded later by Lord Haldane [q.v.] into the Imperial General Staff, embracing India and the Dominions, built up the armies of the British Empire during the European War of 1914–1918.

His committee dissolved, Esher joined the Committee of Imperial Defence in its search for an improved army system, becoming a permanent member of it in 1905, just before political changes transferred the secretaryship of state for war to Lord Haldane. His support of Lord Fisher's case for a stronger navy brought upon him a personal attack by Kaiser Wilhelm II. A conscriptionist, Esher yet saw that the voluntary system must have full trial, and he gave Haldane invaluable support in his army reforms, commending them to the king as the best work accomplished since Cardwell's secretaryship (1868–1874); and he became the very active chairman (1909–1913) and later (1912–1921) president of the London County Territorial Force Association. His position at this period is perhaps best described as *liaison* between king and ministers. He gave advice freely, but all action was taken constitutionally by the responsible minister. Neither Sir Henry Campbell-Bannerman's succession as prime minister in December 1905 nor the accession of King George V in May 1910 caused any interruption of this relation.

An admirable committee man, Esher was in great demand for boards such as those of the British Museum (of which he was a king's trustee), the Imperial College of Science (of which he was governor), and the Wallace Collection; but after two years' trial of *haute finance* in the City he abandoned it as uncongenial (1904). He was created G.C.V.O. (1905) and G.C.B. (1908), sworn a privy councillor (1922), and appointed keeper of the king's archives (1910) and governor and constable of Windsor Castle (1928); but he refused the viceroyship of India in 1908 and an earldom at some date not known to his family. From September 1914 onwards he was in France on a confidential mission, at the request of Lord Kitchener, subsequently renewed by Mr. Asquith and by Mr. Lloyd George. The documents relating to it remain under seal in the British Museum until 1981 together with Esher's diaries for the first half of the War and other papers, but it is known that in 1917–1918 he was present at conferences with French ministers on military matters.

After the return of peace in 1919, Esher devoted much time to literature and published some more biographical books, including *Ionicus* (1923), an informal biography of William Johnson Cory. He died suddenly 22 January 1930 at his London house, leaving a widow, two sons, and two daughters. His family life was peculiarly happy, and, in particular, his relations with his younger son, Maurice, even while at Eton, as revealed in Esher's published *Journals and Letters*, were rather those of a brother than a father. He was succeeded as third viscount by his elder son, Oliver Sylvain Baliol (born 1881).

Inheriting marked ability, great social gifts, and influential connexions, Esher possessed all the qualifications for success in public life except the conviction that it was worth while. The first Viscount Esher had been spurred, by love and by lack of independent means, to set his foot on the path that led him to professional eminence; the second, whose dislike of the dust of the arena outweighed his liking for power, might have returned to the earlier Brett tradition of enjoying life as it came, without effort, had not his association with the royal family pointed a way to the power without the dust, and justified him in recording, when refusing the viceroyalty, that, with his opportunity of influencing vital decisions at the centre, India for him 'would be (it sounds vain, but it isn't) parochial'. This influence he exercised behind a curtain, seeking neither personal advancement nor the interests of a political party, but only the public good as he saw it—and his vision was acute. His work on the committee which goes by his name and his effective backing of Lord Haldane's army reforms at a critical juncture made no mean contribution to the Allied victory of 1918.

There are three portraits of Lord Esher at Watlington Park, Oxfordshire, painted by Julian Storey, Edmund Brock, and Glyn Philpot in or about 1885, 1905, and 1925 respectively.

[Maurice V. Brett, *Journals and Letters of Reginald Viscount Esher* (to 1910), 2 vols., 1934; C. H. Dudley Ward, *A Romance of the Nineteenth Century*, 1923; Sir Gerald Ellison, *Lord Roberts and the General Staff*, in the *Nineteenth Century*, December 1932; private information; personal knowledge.]

C. Harris.

BREWER, Sir ALFRED HERBERT (1865–1928), organist and composer, the eldest son of Alfred Brewer, hotel proprietor, of Gloucester, by his wife, Cordelia Dyer, was born 21 June 1865 at Gloucester. For three years (1877–1880) he was a chorister at the cathedral under Dr. Charles Harford Lloyd, whence he passed on to his earliest organistships, first at St. Catherine's church, then at St. Mary de Crypt. This early Gloucester phase ended in 1882.

Except for that part of the following year (1883) during which Brewer held the first 'open' organ scholarship ever given at the Royal College of Music in London (where he studied under (Sir) Walter Parratt, (Sir) Frederick Bridge, and (Sir) Charles Villiers Stanford), he was in Oxford from 1882 till 1885. There he succeeded Parratt as organist at St. Giles's church, and was, in addition, for two years organ scholar at Exeter College. Despite ill health, those Oxford days were rich in experience for him: new music helped with new friendships to further his development.

In 1885 a 'domestic' quarrel at Bristol Cathedral admitted young Brewer as organist there for a few weeks. But the episode scarcely counted for anything in his career. A more useful and permanent post came with his appointment in 1886 to St. Michael's, Coventry. For six years there he did his purely 'church' work brilliantly; characteristically rebuilt the organ (with the help of Henry Willis, q.v.), and reorganized the Coventry Choral Society. Then and there—as elsewhere later—he showed eagerness to improve upon things as he found them. He was always progressive. Tonbridge School next felt the stimulus of his presence, during the years (1892 to 1896) in which he was director of music there. There, too, he rebuilt the organ.

Brewer was the obvious choice for Gloucester when, in December 1896, (Dr.) Charles Lee Williams resigned the organistship of the cathedral. Brewer eagerly welcomed the return to his native city. He knew the tradition of the cathedral, its strength, and its weakness. He knew too—none more surely—where improvement was desirable. As successor to Harford Lloyd and Lee Williams he had to be a first-rate master of choristers: in the organ-loft the high technical standards of Samuel Sebastian Wesley [q.v.] had to be lived up to. In each sphere Brewer succeeded. Sound as a choir-trainer, he was superlative as a performer. His style, moulded under the influence of Parratt and Lloyd, was settled; and his sense of fitness never deserted him in his performances.

Any Gloucester Cathedral organist is tempted to think that his most important work is the conducting of the Three Choirs' Festival. Probably Brewer thought so, and certainly none of his precursors did the work with so much distinction. The record of his eight festivals (from 1898 onwards) reveals a finely progressive spirit. Under his hand, policy in relation to new works—by Verdi, Elgar, Parry, Sibelius, Vaughan-Williams, Holst, Goossens, Bliss, and others—was advanced and courageous, while his powers of organization were a safe insurance against the risks of that policy. Yet in the judgement of many people the quality and worth of Brewer's extra-festival work was finer still—as in the founding and maintenance of the Gloucestershire Orchestral Society (1905 onwards) and, more especially, in the establishment of recitals in the cathedral for elementary school children. In such new fields he worked with zeal and success.

As a composer Brewer was industrious, and touched upon many different styles. 'Emmaus' (1901) and 'The Holy Innocents' (1904) were oratorios of a seriousness and scope little suited either to his inclinations or his abilities. At the other extreme his songs often went dangerously far in concession to popularity. But between these diverse styles there was another, far more 'native' to him. It is found charmingly expressed in the 'Three Elizabethan Pastorals' (1906), in 'Summer Sports' (1910), and the song-cycle, 'Jillian of Berry' (1921), and in innumerable smaller works.

Brewer was elected F.R.C.O. in 1895 and became an honorary R.A.M. in 1906. He received the Dublin Mus. Bac. in 1897 and the Canterbury Mus. Doc. in 1905. He was widely known as an examiner and adjudicator. He was city high sheriff of Gloucester for the year 1922 to 1923, and was knighted in 1926.

Brewer married in 1894 Ethel Mary, daughter of Henry William Bruton, of Gloucester, and had two sons and one daughter. He died at Gloucester, after an illness of only a few hours, 1 March 1928.

[*Gloucester Journal*, 3 March 1928; A. H. Brewer, *Memories of Choirs and Cloisters*, 1931; personal knowledge.]

H. N. Howells.

BRIDGE, Sir CYPRIAN ARTHUR GEORGE (1839–1924), admiral, was born 13 March 1839, at St. John's, Newfoundland, the eldest son of the Ven. Thomas Finch Hobday Bridge, rector (afterwards archdeacon) of St. John's, Newfoundland, by his wife, Sarah Christiana, daughter of John Dunscomb, an aide-de-camp to the governor of Newfoundland. On his father's side Bridge was descended from a Flemish family settled in England in the twelfth century, and among his immediate predecessors he had associations with the sea service: two of his grandfather's brothers served in the navy, one of them under Rodney; his grandfather was a midshipman in the East India Company's and the Admiralty packet services; his father was only prevented by short sight from adopting a sea life, and became chaplain to Admiral Sir Thomas John Cochrane, governor of Newfoundland.

Bridge came to England first in 1851, with a nomination for the navy given him by Admiral Cochrane. He was sent to school at Walthamstow House, passed in January 1853 the entrance examination for the navy—a test then of a very simple nature—and was appointed at once to the paddle-wheel sloop *Medea*, 850 tons, and, later, to the flagship *Cumberland* on the North American station. Early in 1854 he was transferred to the *Brisk*, corvette, under Commander Beauchamp Seymour (afterwards Lord Alcester), and in her was sent into Northern waters on the outbreak of war with Russia, and was present at the operations in the White Sea of the squadron under Sir Erasmus Ommanney [q.v.].

In 1855 Bridge passed for midshipman, having served two years as cadet. 'I was still under sixteen years of age, but had been in three ships, had served on foreign stations, and had seen something of war.'

He was next appointed to the *Pelorus*, again under Seymour, for service in the East Indies. He took part in operations at Rangoon which continued for some years after the second Burmese War, and in the Bay of Bengal and the Red Sea made acquaintance with the old Indian navy, shortly afterwards dissolved, of the resuscitation of which as a fighting force he was a constant advocate in later years. He became a mate in 1858, and a lieutenant in 1859 at the age of twenty. Having passed the necessary examinations, he joined the *Algiers*, line of battle ship, and in her served in the Mediterranean under Sir William Fanshawe Martin [q.v.],whom later he described as 'the greatest flag officer since the Napoleonic Wars and an abler man than Lord St. Vincent.' His period of service in the *Algiers* was uneventful but highly instructive, for Admiral Martin conducted a continuous investigation into fleet evolutions and the tactics of battle. After three years in the Mediterranean Bridge served successively in the *Hawke* on the Irish station, and the *Fawn* (1864–1867) in the West Indies.

Being now of eight years' standing as a lieutenant, Bridge went to the *Excellent* in order to qualify in gunnery: he did not, however, serve as a gunnery specialist, for he was invited by Sir Alfred Ryder, second in command of the Channel fleet (1868–1869), to act as his flag-lieutenant. In April 1869, at the age of thirty, he was promoted to commander. He had now seen sixteen years of service, mostly at sea. In later life he contrasted the sea service of his younger days with that of more recent times. 'In the third quarter of the nineteenth century most officers and men were at sea from 250 to 300 days out of the 365. In the last quarter . . . there were not many officers and men who had been in blue water for 90 days in the year.' The importance of service at sea and of acquiring the habit of taking responsibility and risk was deeply impressed upon him. A service which has to take the risks of war must not, he considered, be nurtured delicately in peace; and he, when in command, never shrank from taking such risks.

After his promotion Bridge was appointed to the *Caledonia* in the Mediterranean. Two years of service in her were followed by a year in the *Cambridge*, gunnery ship, a year in the *Implacable*, and two and a half years in the *Audacious*, flagship of Admiral Ryder in China. In September 1877, with eight years' service as a commander, but not yet of command, he was promoted to captain. Four years on half pay followed. During this time Bridge's attention was drawn to the beginnings of the German navy, a subject on which he wrote two papers in the *Journal* of the Royal United Service Institution, *Estimates for the German Navy for the financial year 1877–1878* (vol. xxi, 1877) and *On the Organization and Strength of the German Navy* (vol. xxii, 1878). His close study of foreign affairs led him to foresee by many years the menace of this new maritime power, and also the need for that redistribution of the British fleet which it ultimately brought about.

During 1878 and 1879 Bridge served on Admiralty and War Office committees on heavy guns, on armour plates and projectiles, and on explosives; and for six months in 1881 he was a member of the ordnance committee. He was then offered command of the *Espiègle*, on the Australian station. In that appointment he was deputy commissioner for the Western Pacific, and rendered a series of reports on conditions in the islands which covered every field of activity and interest, political, social, ethnological, and commercial, and testify to the breadth of his mind and the acuteness of his perception. A note from the Admiralty hydrographic department in September 1884 remarked: 'The *Espiègle* sends us more information than any other dozen ships.'

Bridge returned from Australia in September 1885. After six months on half pay he was appointed to command the *Colossus*, the latest type of battleship, and while serving in her prepared and submitted to the Admiralty a scheme for the mobilization of the navy. He vacated this command in 1888, and in 1889 was made director of the recently established Intelligence department at the Admiralty. This department fulfilled, within limits, the functions of a naval staff, an institution to which Bridge in his later years was much opposed, holding the view that a staff of the military type was not adapted to the needs of sea service. After fourteen and a half years in the rank of captain, Bridge reached flag rank in 1892. He remained in his directorship for two and a half years longer, and on leaving the Admiralty in August 1894 was highly complimented by Lord George Hamilton, the first lord, on his 'stable and well thought out' work as director.

In November 1894 Bridge hoisted his flag as commander-in-chief of the Australian squadron. He held the command, with his flag on board the *Orlando*, until 1898. He was promoted vice-admiral in 1898, and was created K.C.B. in 1899, but he had no further command until April 1901 when he was appointed commander-in-chief in China. During the period of his command the Anglo-Japanese treaty was concluded (1902); Bridge's tact, ability, and firmness were important contributions to the successful issue of the negotiations. He strongly opposed the plan of establishing a permanent naval base at Wei-hai-wei, which had come into British hands in 1898, after the Chino-Japanese War. In a paper on 'The Supply and Communications of a Fleet' which he read at the Hong Kong United Service Institution in 1902, he demonstrated that the quantity of stores needed by a squadron in those waters was too great to be maintained in peace time, and that therefore, whether a permanent base were established or not, a chain of supplies would be needed. Flying bases, he explained, have always had to be maintained and are almost certain to be in better positions for strategical needs than permanent bases erected in peace. This reasoning appears to have been accepted by the Admiralty. Bridge reached the rank of admiral in 1903 and was promoted G.C.B. He remained in command in China until the spring of 1904, when he returned to England. He retired, having reached the age limit, 15 March 1904.

Bridge served as an assessor on the international commission of inquiry into the Dogger Bank 'incident' (October 1904), and as a member of the Mesopotamia commission of inquiry appointed in August 1916. During the European War he maintained a consistently optimistic attitude, and wrote many letters to the press rebuking pessimism and criticism of British action at sea. In the controversy which arose after the War concerning the size of fighting ships, Bridge was a strenuous advocate of a reduction in their size. He died at Coombe Pines (a house which he had built for himself on Kingston Hill, Surrey) 16 August 1924.

Bridge married in 1877 Eleanor, daughter of George Thornhill, of the Indian civil service; there were no children of the marriage.

Bridge was widely read in many languages. He read Latin, French, German, and Swedish with facility and was acquainted with Italian and Spanish. His study of war began early and continued throughout his life. It covered a wide period of modern history and thought and was by no means confined to naval affairs —one of his earliest papers was on 'Memoirs of the Marquis of Pombal' (*Edinburgh Review*, July 1872). The result of his wide reading was that his opinions were founded on a broad basis of recorded experience. This gave him at once clear vision and a consistency of view which never amounted to tenacious adherence to his own opinions. It was characteristic of his desire for truth that in the Trafalgar controversy (1911–1912), having been the most pronounced opponent of Sir Henry Newbolt's theory of the attack, he should have warmly congratulated him on the result of the inquiry and expressed his pleasure at signing the sentence against himself. With beliefs rooted in history and principles distilled from experience, and with a desire to arrive at truth only through honest investigation, Bridge disliked profoundly a naval policy which, in his view, not only conflicted with reason and experience but also suppressed all attempts at discussion. This, in his words, was a 'dictatorship of the materialate', meaning thereby a dictation of naval policy by men of a school of thought the dominating idea of which was the possession of instruments of war more powerful than those of any possible opponent —in short, the subordination of the strategical factor to the material. Naval architecture, Bridge held, should be 'the handmaid of tactics', and his views on ship-building policy were to a great extent compressed within two short objective paragraphs:

'Have the smallest fleet that can do the work which you want it to do: not the biggest that you can cajole or force the taxpayers into granting the money for.'

'Build the smallest and least costly ships that can play their part in war: not the biggest that naval architects and engineers are able to design and build' [*Current History*, New York, March 1921].

Bridge's political outlook was, conformably to his sentiments, liberal. His was one of the names proposed for a peerage in the Parliament Bill crisis of 1911. In 1910 Mr. Asquith spoke of him as one of our most distinguished admirals, 'a man absolutely detached from the various conflicting schools of the navy'. His social gifts were considerable. Very courteous, he was both a good listener and a good talker with a ready and sometimes caustic wit. He sought information at all times and was quick to discern those who possessed it.

Besides numerous contributions to the daily press, Bridge wrote, over a period of half a century (1872–1923), many articles on tactics, strategy, and naval policy in the reviews. His books were *The Art of Naval Warfare* (1907), *Sea Power and Other Studies* (1910), and *Some Recollections* (1918). He also edited a *History of the Russian Fleet during the reign of Peter the Great by a contemporary Englishman, 1724* (Navy Records Society, vol. xv, 1899), and wrote an important Admiralty paper on *British Port Defence Policy* (1901). His correspondence and journals are lodged in the Nautical Museum at Greenwich.

[*Some Recollections* (autobiography), 1918; private information; personal knowledge.]

H. W. Richmond.

BRIDGE, Sir JOHN FREDERICK (1844–1924), organist, composer, and musical antiquary, was born at Oldbury, Worcestershire, 5 December 1844, the eldest son of John Bridge, of Oldbury, by his wife, Rebecca Cox. Moving to Rochester, John Bridge was appointed a lay vicar in the cathedral choir. Frederick, at the age of six, was admitted probationer and began his education at the cathedral school. He remained in the choir until 1859, his musical training being under Dr. John Larkins Hopkins [q.v.], the cathedral organist, to whom later he was articled.

On leaving the choir school, Bridge was appointed organist of Shorne church, near Gravesend, about 1860, and of St. Nicholas church, Strood, near Rochester, in 1861. He studied composition under (Sir) John Goss for four years (1863–1867). In 1865, at the age of twenty, he was appointed organist of Holy Trinity church, Windsor, where he was influenced and encouraged by (Sir) George Job Elvey [q.v.], organist of St. George's chapel, Windsor. Mrs. Oliphant, the authoress [q.v.], who came to live at Windsor in 1866, also became interested in him, urging him to compose and in many ways preparing him for his career. A third fortunate friendship which Bridge formed at Windsor was with (Sir) John Stainer [q.v.], a friendship marked in after years by the marriage of Bridge's younger daughter to Stainer's son, Edward. Bridge used to give lessons at the Lower School, Eton, during these years; he studied hard, and was elected a fellow of the Royal College of Organists in 1867. He competed unsuccessfully for the organistship of Queen's College, Oxford, about 1867, but, spurred to further effort, graduated B.Mus. of Oxford in 1868 and D.Mus. in 1874.

In 1869, when only twenty-four, Bridge was appointed organist of Manchester Cathedral, later joining the teaching staff at Owens College. Owing to his enthusiasm, the standard of the cathedral music was improved, and his friend Sir William Houldsworth presented a new organ to the cathedral.

In 1875 Bridge was appointed permanent deputy organist of Westminster Abbey on the retirement of James Turle [q.v.] from active work; he succeeded to the full post on Turle's death in 1882. Bridge reformed many unsound traditions in the choir, and the services soon became renowned through his marked gifts as a trainer of boys' voices. Outstanding incidents in his work at the Abbey were the direction of the music at Queen Victoria's jubilee (1887), the Purcell commemoration (1895), King Edward VII's coronation (conductor-in-chief, 1902), the Orlando Gibbons commemoration (1907), the national memorial service on the occasion of King Edward's funeral (1910), the Samuel Sebastian Wesley commemoration (1910), King George V's coronation (conductor-in-chief, 1911), and the re-inauguration of Henry VII's chapel as the chapel of the Order of the Bath (1913).

In 1876 Bridge was appointed professor of organ-playing at the National Training School for Music, and on the opening of the Royal College of Music in 1883 was, on the nomination of the Prince of Wales, appointed professor of harmony and counterpoint, retaining this post until his death. In 1890 he was elected Gresham professor of music at Gresham College, London. His lectures commanded large audiences, to whom his genial style and illustrations made an intimate appeal. His antiquarian sympathies naturally influenced his choice of subjects, and he devoted untiring energy and research to the exposition of the works of Richard Dering, Henry Purcell, and others, and corrected many inaccuracies hitherto accepted. His course of lectures at the Royal Institution in 1903 on 'The musical references in Pepys's Diary' attracted the attention of Dr. H. B. Wheatley, editor of the standard edition of the *Diary*, and at his suggestion Bridge took a prominent part in the formation of the Pepys dining club in 1903. He was for many years a member of the Musicians' Company, becoming master in 1892. As conductor of the Royal Choral Society from 1896 to 1922 he was successful and popular.

Bridge composed much church and choral music, among the more important of his works being 'The Song of St. Francis of Assisi' (Worcester, 1884), 'Rock of Ages' (Birmingham, 1885), 'Callirhoe' (Birmingham, 1888), 'The Repentance of Nineveh' (Worcester, 1890), and a homage anthem for each coronation. The 'Centurion's Song' from his cantata, 'Boadicea' was given at a Royal Philharmonic concert in 1882. His overture 'Morte d'Arthur' was performed at Stockley's concert, Birmingham, in 1886. Bridge also composed and edited many carols, and was musical editor of the *Westminster Abbey Hymn-book* and the *Wesleyan Hymn-book*; his long experience of the needs of a congregation ensured the wide acceptance of these hymns, and although he was obliged to include in the Wesleyan book some tunes of which he did not much approve, his tact and good sense gained the goodwill of all concerned. Bridge's various primers on musical subjects became standard works, while his autobiography, *A Westminster Pilgrim* (1918), is widely known and esteemed.

Bridge was regarded with affection by friends in many walks of life, while his sympathy for those less fortunate in his profession finds expression in an admirable organization, the Organists' Benevolent League, founded by him in 1909.

Bridge was knighted in 1897, receiving the M.V.O. in 1902, and the C.V.O. in 1911. Durham University conferred on him the honorary degree of M.A. in 1905, and in 1908 the university of Toronto that of Mus.D. He was married three times: first, in 1872 to Constance Ellen (died 1879), daughter of John Lines Moore, of Hoxne, Suffolk; secondly, in 1883 to Helen Mary Flora (died 1906), daughter of Edward Amphlett, of Horsley, Staffordshire; and thirdly, in 1914 to Marjory Wedgwood (died 1929), daughter of Reginald Wood, of Bignall End, Staffordshire. By his first wife he had a son and a daughter, and by his second a daughter. He died at the Cloisters, Westminster Abbey, 18 March 1924.

A cartoon of Bridge by 'Spy' appeared in *Vanity Fair* 14 April 1904.

[Sir J. F. Bridge, *A Westminster Pilgrim*, 1918; private information; personal knowledge.] W. G. Alcock.

BRIDGEMAN, Sir FRANCIS CHARLES BRIDGEMAN (1848–1929), admiral of the fleet, the fourth son of the Rev. William Bridgeman Simpson, rector of Babworth, Nottinghamshire (who was nephew of Orlando Bridgeman, first Earl of Bradford), by his wife, Lady Frances Laura Fitzwilliam, daughter of Charles William, fifth Earl Fitzwilliam [q.v.], was born at Babworth 7 December 1848. He resumed the family name of Bridgeman in 1896. He entered the *Britannia* as a naval cadet in 1862, and after serving as midshipman in the Pacific and the Channel squadron, in 1868 went for nearly four years to the *Blanche* on the Australian station, being promoted sub-lieutenant in 1869. Bridgeman was promoted lieutenant in 1873, and, having taken up gunnery, served for nearly four years on the China station in the *Encounter* as gunnery lieutenant: while doing the same duty in the *Temeraire* in the Mediterranean he was promoted commander in 1884. In this rank he served in the *Triumph*, Sir Michael Culme-Seymour's flagship in the Pacific, from 1885 to 1888, and afterwards in the *Excellent* gunnery school until he was promoted captain in 1890.

Bridgeman's first ten years as captain were mainly employed as flag-captain to Sir Michael Culme-Seymour in the Channel squadron, the Mediterranean, and at Portsmouth. In October 1900 he went on half-pay until January 1903, when he commissioned the *Drake* and joined Admiral (Sir) W. H. Fawkes's cruiser squadron. In August of that year he was promoted rear-admiral. He hoisted his flag as second-in-command to Lord Charles Beresford in the Channel fleet for a year in June 1904, and in 1906 he again served as second-in-command to Beresford, this time in the Mediterranean fleet. In March 1907, having reached the rank of vice-admiral, he was selected as commander-in-chief of the newly formed home fleet, and held this command for two years with his flag in the new battleship *Dreadnought*. From 1910 until March 1911 he was second sea lord at the Admiralty under Mr. Reginald McKenna. He then returned as admiral to the command of the home fleet until December 1911, when he came back to the Admiralty as first sea lord under Mr. Winston Churchill, on the retirement of Admiral Sir Arthur Wilson. Twelve months later he resigned. On his resignation he was promoted G.C.B., having been created K.C.V.O. in 1907 and K.C.B. in

1908 and promoted G.C.V.O. in 1911. In another year he had reached the age limit of his rank and was placed on the retired list. On leaving the Admiralty he went to live at Copgrove Hall, near Leeds, his country seat, and rarely came to London except to attend court functions in his capacity as vice-admiral of the United Kingdom, to which he was appointed in 1920 in succession to his old chief, Sir Michael Culme-Seymour.

Bridgeman was a man of singularly handsome presence, and a fine sea officer with a great knowledge of the service. He was a strong supporter of the naval reforms and strategic schemes of Lord Fisher [q.v.], and gave him loyal and valuable support in the formation of the home fleet originally created out of the reserve divisions at the home ports. When Bridgeman returned to its command in March 1911, it had been combined with the Channel fleet, and he did fine work in organizing and training it for the duties which it was later to fulfil with the grand fleet during the European War.

Bridgeman had had no previous administrative experience at the Admiralty before he became second sea lord, but he was regarded as a man of sound judgement and commanded confidence in the fleet. When Mr. Churchill became first lord and reconstituted the Board of Admiralty, he chose Bridgeman as his first sea lord—a post of exacting responsibility at all times and especially so during the anxious naval situation of the years immediately preceding the European War. Bridgeman was a loyal supporter of Mr. Churchill in his plans for the constitution of a naval war staff, but his health became unsatisfactory, and at the end of a year the first lord found it necessary to require his resignation on that account. Bridgeman loyally accepted the decision, but the form in which it was communicated to him caused much resentment, and was the subject of an acrimonious debate in the House of Commons.

Bridgeman was popular in his home county of Yorkshire, and after his retirement devoted himself to the pursuits of a country squire. He married in 1889 Emily Charlotte (died 1922), daughter of Thomas Shiffner, of Westergate, Sussex; they had no children. He died at Nassau in the Bahamas 17 February 1929.

[*The Times*, 19 February 1929; Admiralty records; *Hansard's Parliamentary Debates*, 1912.] V. W. Baddeley.

BRIDGES, ROBERT SEYMOUR (1844–1930), poet laureate, was born at Walmer 23 October 1844, the fourth son and eighth of nine children of John Thomas Bridges, only son of John Bridges, of St. Nicholas Court, Isle of Thanet. His mother was Harriet Elizabeth, third daughter of the Rev. Sir Robert Affleck, at the time of the marriage (1829) vicar of Silkstone, Yorkshire, who in 1833 succeeded a cousin as fourth baronet and afterwards lived at Dalham Hall, Suffolk. The Bridges family had been substantial yeomen in the Isle of Thanet since the sixteenth century, descending from the Rev. John Bridges or Brydges (died 1590), rector of Harbledown 1579–1589. At the end of the eighteenth century the family belonged to the class of which Edward Hasted (*History . . . of Kent*, vol. iv, 291, 1799) says: 'The farms throughout the island are mostly large and considerable, and the farmers wealthy, insomuch that they are usually denominated *gentlemen farmers* on that account, as well as from their hospitable and substantial mode of living.' Most of the family property came into the hands of Robert Bridges's grandfather and so to his father, and was sold under the will of the latter, who died in 1853 at the age of forty-seven when Robert was only nine years old. Thus Robert grew up under no necessity of earning a livelihood.

During Bridges's childhood the family lived at his father's house, Roselands, Walmer, which afterwards became a convent. This period is recalled by two of his poems, 'The Summer House on the Mound' (*New Poems*, 1899) and 'Kate's Mother' written in 1921 (*New Verse*, 1926), and by many pictures and touches, especially in the *Shorter Poems*, of the sea, sky, cliffs, birds, and flowers of the south coast. The year after his father's death his mother became the second wife of the Rev. John Edward Nassau Molesworth [q.v.], vicar of Rochdale, Lancashire, and the vicarage was thenceforth Robert's home. Meantime, in September 1854, before he was ten years old, he had been sent to Eton, where he remained for nine years, and in his last winter played in the Oppidans' wall and field elevens. Eton, especially its river, trees, and meadows, St. George's chapel at Windsor with its music, and the companionship of eager, high-souled youth, fed and confirmed the inborn aesthetic sensibility and mental energy which distinguished Bridges throughout his life. During his later school years his mind was exercised by religious problems and drawn towards 'Puseyite' views, principally by his contemporary, Vincent Stuckey Stratton Coles [q.v.], 'pre-eminent' among his schoolboy friends 'for his precocious theological bent and devotion to *the cause*' [Bridges's memoir prefixed to *Poems of D. M. Dolben*, 1911]. In January 1862 Bridges's distant cousin, young Digby Mackworth Dolben, arrived at Eton, already passionately and poetically religious. Bridges was captain of his house and befriended Dolben, who in his turn both intensely admired his elder cousin and eagerly sought to convert him to his own enthusiasms, above all to the dream of founding an Anglican 'Brotherhood', of which Bridges writes: 'He was to decide everything, and I, who was to be the head of the community, could never of course disagree with him.'

Bridges was immune to theological dogmas, but equally alive both to the beauty of holiness and to the holiness of beauty; hence his affection for and at the same time independence of such friends as Dolben and Gerard Manley Hopkins, whose acquaintance he made at Oxford, whither he proceeded as a commoner of Corpus Christi College in October 1863. Hopkins entered Balliol College as an exhibitioner the same term, and they both took honours in *literae humaniores* in 1867; Hopkins obtained a first class in Trinity term, Bridges a second class in Michaelmas term. Bridges was a distinguished oarsman, stroked the Corpus boat as second on the river in 1867 and again the same summer in a regatta at Paris, which, to his distress, coincided with the death of Dolben from heart-failure while bathing in the river Welland.

During his undergraduate career Bridges was, as he records (*op. cit.*), 'drifting fast away' from 'the religious sympathies' of his Eton days, and becoming more interested in philosophy and natural science. In February 1866 his younger brother Edward died. They had been mutually devoted. Writing of Dolben's monastic dreams he says: 'The only definite plan of this kind which had seriously influenced me was an understanding between my younger brother and myself that we would always live together; and such was our affection that I think now [1909] that nothing but his early death could have prevented its realization.' Of this event he writes that it 'plunged me into deep sorrow at the time and considerably altered the hopes and prospects of my life'; and it was probably about this time that he resolved to study medicine. He had no intention of making this his lifelong profession; he pursued it mainly for the sake of knowledge and human experience; and he was so far from concentrating on his medical training that he spent much of his time both before and after being entered as a student at St. Bartholomew's Hospital (November 1869) in travel and literary studies abroad. Thus he travelled in Egypt and Syria and then, after an interval at home, spent eight months studying German in Germany with William Sanday [q.v.], who had entered Balliol as a commoner in 1862, became scholar of Corpus in 1863, and a fellow of Trinity College in 1866. He also made a tour in the Netherlands and was twice in France for some months, spending one winter in Paris. In 1874 he went to Italy for six months with his lifelong friend, Harry Ellis Wooldridge [q.v.], afterwards Slade professor of fine art at Oxford, an account of whom he contributed to this DICTIONARY, and to whose wide and accurate knowledge and discriminating taste in literature and the fine arts, especially music, Bridges gratefully acknowledged his indebtedness.

From his schooldays Bridges had been devoted to music and poetry; but, unlike most young poets, he was in no hurry to take the world into his confidence. He preserved affectionate letters from Hopkins, beginning in 1865, in which the latter writes of religion, music, and even his own poems. Yet apparently Hopkins was unaware that Bridges wrote poetry at all until, in January 1874, he came upon Andrew Lang's review of Bridges's first published volume [C. C. Abbott, *Letters of G. M. Hopkins*, i, 29]. Bridges writes of his later schooldays: 'My own boyish muse was being silenced [1862–3] by my reading of the great poets. . . . What had led me to poetry was the inexhaustible satisfaction of form, the magic of speech, lying as it seemed to me in the masterly control of the material: it was an art which I hoped to learn' [*Memoir* of Dolben]. The whole passage is most significant for any appreciation of Bridges as a poetic artist. Evidently this hope was one great motive in his studies of French, German, and Italian literature, and the last-named particularly left distinct traces upon his own poetry. But whatever verses he wrote before his thirtieth year, hardly any of them ever saw the light. Of his first volume, published in 1873, he himself wrote that he 'went to the seaside [Seaford] for two weeks and wrote it there'. It was greeted with a long and appreciative review by Andrew Lang in the *Academy* of 17 January 1874; but far from courting the *popularis aura* Bridges issued nothing more in his own name for ten years except a *jeu d'esprit* in Latin elegiacs for his friends at St. Bartholomew's Hospital in 1876 and a contribution to a brochure, *The Garland of Rachel*, privately printed in 1881 by his friend Charles Henry Olive Daniel [q.v.], afterwards provost of Worcester College, Oxford. Meantime, in 1876, he published anonymously *The Growth of Love; A Poem in Twenty-four Sonnets*, which was in great measure the fruit of his six months in Italy. Of these sonnets ten were dropped from subsequent editions, while six were much rewritten, and many new ones added.

Bridges actually began his medical course at St. Bartholomew's Hospital in 1871 and graduated M.B. in 1874. He was house physician for one year (1875–1876) to Dr. Patrick Black [q.v.], for whom he had great admiration and to whom he dedicated his Latin poem, of 558 lines, 'De Nosocomio Sti. Bartolomaei'. In 1877 he was appointed casualty physician, a post which he held for two years; and he contributed a trenchant 'Account of the Casualty Department' to the Hospital *Reports* of 1878, in which he recorded that he had seen 30,940 patients in the course of one year with an average of 1·28 minutes given to each case, and had ordered over 200,000 doses of medicine containing iron. In 1878 Bridges was appointed assistant physician to the Hospital for Sick Children, Great Ormond Street, and afterwards to the Great Northern Hospital in Holloway. His skill and acumen would have carried him far, but he intended to retire at the age of forty, and even while in medical practice must have found a good deal of time for his favourite studies. Thus he published in 1879 and 1880 two more sheaves of lyrical *Poems, by the author of the Growth of Love*, which were cordially, though not widely, noticed, the *Academy* reviewer complaining of his 'cryptic, scrappy' method of publication and, while praising his freshness and technical perfection, somewhat deprecating his 'experiments in a new prosody'.

In London Bridges lived first at 50 Maddox Street with Wooldridge, and after Dr. Molesworth's death in 1877 made a home for his mother at 52 Bedford Square. In June 1881 his medical career was ended by an attack of pneumonia and empyema, from the effects of which he did not recover for eighteen months. In November he went to spend the winter in Italy and Sicily, and on his return in 1882 took his mother to live at the Manor House, Yattendon, Berkshire. Here, in 1884, he married Monica, eldest daughter of his neighbour, the architect Alfred Waterhouse [q.v.]—a union in which the poet's charm and spiritual distinction were well mated with his wife's, and his welfare guarded by her unselfish devotion, a devotion extended to the careful editing of his prose writings after his death.

During the next few years Bridges's one son and two daughters were born; and at Yattendon he lived until 1904, pursuing poetry and music and congenial friendships with gusto, and producing, in collaboration with Wooldridge and with the friendly consent of the rector of Yattendon, Henry Charles Beeching, afterwards dean of Norwich [q.v], 'The Yattendon Hymnal' (1895–1899), which was influential in the contemporary reform of hymnody and the revival of sixteenth- and seventeenth-century music. Here, too, he wrote his eight dramas and quasi-dramas and his one long narrative poem, *Eros and Psyche* (1885), a version of Apuleius, as well as many lyrics, odes for music such as that in honour of Henry Purcell, and the first of his poems in quantitative verse, 'Now in wintry delights' and 'No ethical system' (1903). In 1887 he contributed an essay 'On the elements of Milton's Blank Verse in *Paradise Lost*' to Beeching's edition of the first book of that poem, and he followed this up in 1889 with a brief pamphlet *On the Prosody of Paradise Regained and Samson Agonistes*. Little noticed at the time, this masterly and original work was republished with additions in 1893, reviewed with insight by Laurence Binyon in the *Academy* of 10 March 1894 and, together with Bridges's practice as a poet, was the real inauguration of a new development of English verse, in which the natural accentuation of the phrase was to reassert itself, producing a fresh flexibility of rhythm, and requiring for success a highly sensitive discrimination of sounds. Bridges constantly discussed these matters with friends, most fruitfully in earlier years with Hopkins and afterwards with W. J. Stone, whose tract on *Classical Metres in English Verse* (1899) excited his keenest interest. After Stone's premature death,

Bridges added this tract, together with his own criticism, to an enlarged edition of *Milton's Prosody* (1901); and he further treated the subject in *Ibant Obscuri* (*New Quarterly*, ii, January 1909 and Clarendon Press 1916), in his edition of the *Poems* of G. M. Hopkins (1918), and elsewhere.

From the first Bridges was justly appreciated by contemporary and younger men of letters, as reviews by Andrew Lang, William Watson, and J. W. Mackail testify. In 1895 he was invited by a strong list of supporters to stand for election to the chair of poetry at Oxford. This he declined to do; and he made no efforts to get his plays acted, although he wrote *Demeter*, a masque, for the students of Somerville College, Oxford, to perform at the opening of their new library in June 1904. In 1905–1906 he spent nine months in Switzerland for the sake of his wife's health, and in 1907 settled at Chilswell House, which he built on Boar's Hill overlooking Oxford. He published little during his earlier years there, but a one-volume edition of his *Poems*, excluding the plays, was issued in 1912. When, in 1913, he was appointed poet laureate, the general reading public was surprised, although little interested in an office reduced again to insignificance by its last holder, Alfred Austin [q.v.], whose appointment had probably been a mere reward for political journalism. The prime minister, Mr. Asquith, unlike Lord Salisbury, was interested in literature; but certainly the popular voice would have acclaimed Rudyard Kipling—and still more so when only a year later the country was plunged into the European War. Bridges wrote about twenty poems concerned with the War, most of which were collected in his volume *October and other poems* (1920); few of them would be preserved apart from his more congenial work.

Bridges's artistic and musical bent had long inclined him to an interest in English pronunciation and spelling as well as prosody. He experimented in spelling in successive issues of his poetry, thereby delaying the recognition of its real poetic quality while proving the sincerity of his purpose. As early as 1900 he broached to Henry Bradley [q.v.] a scheme for introducing 'an aesthetic phonetic script so like our present literary spelling and writing that any one with common education could read it', and he published his scheme in 1910 (*English Association Essays*, vol. i). In 1926 he began to introduce his new 'symbols' in a series of reprints of his essays, which was continued by Mrs. Bridges after his death. In 1913 he founded the Society for Pure English in concert with Bradley, Sir Walter Raleigh, and Logan Pearsall Smith, though the War postponed its activity until 1919. For the rest of his life this was, after poetry, Bridges's principal public interest. 'From the beginning he planned its policy, chose its collaborators, and guided its destiny, and wrote its most important papers' [*S.P.E. Tracts*, no. xxxv, p. 500]. His principal confidants were Mrs. Bridges (in this as in other matters), Pearsall Smith, and Bradley, whom Bridges called the 'mainstay' of the Society, since 'though he never wrote any entire article for it, he passed and censored all its publications'.

These last words are quoted from a *Memoir* of Henry Bradley, one of the few but, in their kind, perfect appreciations which Bridges wrote. Three of these were memorials of intimate friends, R. W. Dixon (1909), D. M. Dolben (1911), and Bradley (1926), reissued in one volume, *Three Friends* (1932): another of special note was *John Keats, a critical essay*, written in 1894 (privately printed in 1895) as an introduction to G. Thorn Drury's edition of the *Poems* (1896). He wrote other occasional articles and lectures, always in a style which, without affectation, was strongly personal. In 1916 he compiled *The Spirit of Man*, a collection of passages in prose and verse 'designed to bring fortitude and peace of mind to his countrymen in war time'. This admirable and successful anthology was especially remarkable for the prominence given to Aristotle and Shelley, than whom no two authors influenced Bridges more, the one by his robust and magisterial reasoning, the other by his impassioned sense of beauty and joy.

In 1924 Bridges and his wife spent three months at Ann Arbor as guests of the university of Michigan, and in the same year his eightieth birthday was marked by the gift, from a distinguished group of admirers, of a clavichord made for the occasion by Arnold Dolmetsch. At the end of 1925 appeared *New Verse*, mostly written in 1921, 'a volume packed with beauty and humour' (Sir Henry Newbolt in *The Times*) and containing seven poems in the writer's latest manner, viz. 'Neo-Miltonic syllabics'. These are in themselves small masterpieces while serving as studies for the *magnum opus* upon which he embarked in July 1926. This was *The*

Testament of Beauty, which was published on the poet's eighty-fifth birthday in 1929, and achieved an instantaneous success both in England and the United States of America. *The Testament of Beauty* is a great poem, demanding too much intellectual effort ever to be popular, but full of passages which carry away any sensitive reader by their eloquence, wit, and beauty of sound and imagery. It is unique as the work of an octogenarian, able to sum up his aesthetic and spiritual experience in a poem surpassing all he had previously written, not only in scope and significance but in vigour and freshness. Fortunate to the end, Bridges had just revised his poem for the second English edition before he died at Chilswell 21 April 1930.

No better portrait could be given of Bridges than that contributed to *The Times* (22 April) by Sir Henry Newbolt: 'In presence Bridges was one of the most remarkable figures of his time; there is no company in which he would not have been distinguished. He had great stature and fine proportions, a leonine head, deep eyes, expressive lips, and a full-toned voice, made more effective by a slight occasional hesitation in his speech. His extraordinary personal charm was, however, due to something deeper than these: it lay in the transparent sincerity with which every word and motion expressed the whole of of his character, its greatness and its scarcely less memorable littlenesses . . . none would have wished these away: they were not the flaws but the "grotesque" ornaments of his character. Behind them was always visible the strength of a towering and many-sided nature, at once aristocratic and unconventional, virile and affectionate, fearlessly inquiring and profoundly religious.'

Bridges received the Order of Merit in 1929; he was also an honorary D.Litt. of Oxford University and an honorary LL.D. of St. Andrews, Harvard, and Michigan universities, and from 1895 an honorary fellow of Corpus Christi College, Oxford.

An oil portrait of Bridges, painted by Charles Furse in 1893, and a drawing by Anning Bell, are in the possession of Mrs. Bridges. An oil portrait painted by Lionel Muirhead from a photograph by F. Hollyer (1888), and another by Sir William Richmond (1911), are in the possession of Lt.-Colonel A. Muirhead, Haseley Court, Wallingford. A sketch by William Strang, gold point on pink paper, is in the National Portrait Gallery. Many drawings were made by Sir William Rothenstein, of which examples are published in his *English Portraits* (1897) and *Twenty-four Portraits* (1920), and in *The Portrait Drawings of W. Rothenstein 1899–1925* (1926). A drawing by Richard Troncy (1912) is prefixed to the Oxford one-volume edition of Bridges's *Poetical Works* (1913). A medallion profile was executed by Spicer Simson in 1922.

No complete edition of Bridges's works has yet appeared. The *Poetical Works of Robert Bridges* (1898–1905) contains poetry and plays previous to 1905.

[*The Times*, 22 April 1930; Bridges's published writings; *Letters of G. M. Hopkins*, edited by C. C. Abbott, 1935; private information.] N. C. Smith.

BROCK, Sir THOMAS (1847–1922), sculptor, was born at Worcester 1 March 1847, the only son of William Brock, of Worcester, by his wife, Catherine, daughter of William Marshall. Having received some teaching at the Government School of Design, Worcester, Brock in 1866 went up to London and became the pupil of the well-known sculptor John Henry Foley [q.v.]. He left Foley's studio, however, the next year in order to enter the Royal Academy Schools. In 1868 he exhibited for the first time at the Academy (a portrait bust of R. W. Binns, F.S.A.), and in 1869 he gained the Academy gold medal in sculpture for his group 'Hercules strangling Antaeus'; this was exhibited at the Academy in 1870, the year in which Brock also produced his first portrait statue, that of Richard Baxter at Kidderminster in the artist's native county. When, in 1874, his first master Foley died, Brock undertook to complete certain of Foley's unfinished works, such as the statues of Daniel O'Connell and Viscount Gough for Dublin, and the statue of Earl Canning for Calcutta. In a sense Brock thereby directly succeeded to Foley's practice as a much employed purveyor of monuments and official statuary; and for about half a century he was industriously active in a similar capacity.

Of Brock's public monuments, London possesses statues of Robert Raikes (1880) and Sir Bartle Frere (1888), both in the Victoria Embankment gardens; Sir J. E. Millais (statue) in the Tate Gallery grounds (1904); Sir Henry Tate, Brixton Oval gardens (a bronze bust, 1905); Sir Henry Irving (statue) in the space north of the National Portrait Gallery (1910); the huge memorial to Queen Victoria in front of Buckingham Palace (commissioned in 1901, carried out in conjunction with Sir Aston Webb [q.v.], and unveiled in May 1911); Captain Cook (statue) in the Mall East End (1914); and Lord Lister, Upper Portland Place (a bronze with bas-reliefs on the pedestal, unveiled after Brock's death in 1924). In London buildings there are the following statues: Sir Richard Owen in the Natural History Museum, South Kensington (1895), Gladstone in Westminster Hall (1902), Lord Russell of Killowen in the Law Courts (1904), and Gainsborough in the Tate Gallery (1906); while in St. Paul's Cathedral is Brock's monument of Lord Leighton (a recumbent effigy accompanied by allegorical figures of Painting and Sculpture).

Outside London the most notable public monument executed by Brock is his equestrian statue of the Black Prince at Leeds (1902). Kidderminster possesses by him, in addition to the Richard Baxter statue mentioned before, a statue of Rowland Hill (1882). In Worcester Cathedral is his seated marble figure of Henry Philpott, bishop of Worcester (1896). There are several portrait statues by Brock in India, including Sir Richard Temple (1884) and Lord Sydenham (1915) at Bombay, and Brigadier-General John Nicholson at Delhi (1904).

A long series of portrait busts was also produced by Brock: prominent among them is the bust of Queen Victoria which was exhibited at the Academy in the spring succeeding her death in 1901, and attracted much attention at the time; it is now at Christ Church, Oxford. There exist several other portrayals of Queen Victoria by him, including the head on the 1897 coinage, and a statue at Hove. Among Brock's works of an imaginative character may be mentioned 'The Moment of Peril', a Red Indian on horseback spearing a serpent (1880–1881, purchased by the Chantrey Trustees), and 'Eve' (marble, 1900), both in the Tate Gallery; and 'The Genius of Poetry' (1889).

Brock was elected A.R.A. in 1883 and R.A. in 1891, his diploma work being a bust of Lord Leighton (exhibited 1893). On the occasion of the unveiling of the Queen Victoria memorial in 1911 he was created K.C.B. Other honours came to him in considerable numbers: he was an honorary D.C.L. of Oxford University (1909); an honorary A.R.I.B.A. (1908); an honorary R.S.A. (1916); first president of the Royal Society of British Sculptors, founded in 1905; and membre d'honneur of the Société des Artistes Français.

Brock died in London after an operation 22 August 1922. He married in 1869 Mary Hannah (died 1927), only child of Richard Sumner, of Nottingham, and had six sons, one of whom is the painter Will Brock, and two daughters.

An artist of no great originality or inspiration, but capable at times of a vigorous and effective realism, Brock, as his immense output shows, adequately fulfilled the requirements of a very large circle of patrons. In his style he further exemplifies the departure from the neo-classic formula which had been initiated by his master Foley; and he has been well described as 'the English representative of the more conservative aspects of French sculpture in the second half of the nineteenth century'.

[*The Times*, 23 August 1922; Algernon Graves, *The Royal Academy of Arts, a complete dictionary of contributors and their work*, vol. i, 1905; subsequent Royal Academy Exhibition Catalogues; C. R. Post, *A History of European and American Sculpture*, vol. ii, 1921. Portrait, *Royal Academy Pictures*, 1920; cartoon by 'Spy', *Vanity Fair*, 21 September 1905.]

T. Borenius.

BROWN, HORATIO ROBERT FORBES (1854–1926), historian of Venice, the elder son of Hugh Horatio Brown, of Newhall House and Carlops, Midlothian, by his wife, Gulielmina Forbes, sixth daughter of Alexander Ranaldson Macdonell [q.v.], last chief of Glengarry, was born at Nice, then Italian territory, 16 February 1854. Mrs. Brown, who was considerably younger than her husband, after his death took a house at Clifton for the education of her two sons, Horatio and Allan. The boys were entered at Clifton College, then under the headmastership of Dr. John Percival [q.v.], in 1864. While at school Horatio Brown made the acquaintance of John Addington Symonds [q.v.], who was living at Clifton, and in 1869 gave lectures on the Greek poets to the Clifton College boys. The effect of these lectures on the boys is described in Brown's *Life* of Symonds [ii, 46–48]. Thus began an influence which Symonds, till his death in 1893, exercised over Brown's intellectual tastes.

From Clifton, Brown proceeded to New College, Oxford, with an exhibition which he forfeited owing to two failures to pass responsions. He was, however, encouraged to read for *literae humaniores*, in which he obtained a second class in 1877. He did not proceed to a degree, and consequently in the course of time became senior commoner of New College, a position which he used to say nothing but death or bankruptcy could take from him. He thought, however, that he would have made a good fellow of All Souls. The few surviving among his contemporaries remember him as 'pleasant and sociable . . . having artistic tastes which he could afford to indulge', and as 'a fair-haired, breezy out-of-doors person with a crisp Highland-Scottish speech'. Among his contemporaries was (Sir) Herbert Warren (also a Cliftonian), afterwards president of Magdalen College, who wrote Brown's obituary notice in *The Times*.

In 1877 Newhall House was let, and Brown's circumstances never allowed him to live there again. In the same year the Symonds family removed to Davos. It may have been this example which decided Brown and his mother to settle at Venice. This they did, after trying Florence (where Mrs. Brown's relatives, the Misses Forbes, lived), in 1879. The Browns first took an apartment on the Grand Canal, in the palazzo Balbi-Valier. Before long, however, they bought a block of buildings on the Zattere, inhabited by a number of tenants, whom they had difficulty in ejecting. They were left with a high, narrow building something like a ship. It commanded the shipping on the Giudecca canal and the Giudecca itself opposite. In the course of these migrations Brown had made the acquaintance of a gondolier, Antonio Salin, whom he now transported with his family to the back parts of his house, which he called Cà Torresella, from the name of the side-canal as given on an old map. Brown, unlike most tourists and literary men, saw Venice through the eyes of his gondolier and his gondolier's friends, with whom he spent much of his time, playing *tre sette* (a game of cards) and *bocce* (bowls) and drinking the wine of Padua at an *osteria* behind the house.

The result of this five years' experience was Brown's first book, *Life on the Lagoons* (1884). The qualities of this admirable account of Venetian life cannot be better expressed than in some lines of R. L. Stevenson, who had met Brown at Davos. The reference to 'your spirited and happy book . . . your pages clear as April air' is contained in *Underwoods*, xiii (1887). Brown answered Stevenson's epistle in verses of his own [*Drift*, p. 98, 1900]. In *Life on the Lagoons* the description of the view from Monte Pavione in the Venetian Alps and the 'Voyage of the *Beppi*', which caught Stevenson's eye, have perhaps most magic. In 1894 a new publisher cut the book down in order to adapt it for use as a guide-book; the omitted pieces were included by Brown in *In and Around Venice* (1905) with sketches of places in the Veneto, one of which, a description of the country-place of a Venetian patrician (where Brown went to buy wine), caused some talk.

In 1883 died Rawdon Lubbock Brown [q.v.], who had not left Venice since he came there in 1833, and who had in 1862 been commissioned by the British government to calendar such of the Venetian state papers, preserved at the Frari, as concern English history. His calendars, chiefly of the reports sent home by the Venetian ambassadors in London, had reached the year 1558 and were brought down to 1580 by his executor, G. Cavendish Bentinck. Horatio Brown—he was no connexion—was appointed to succeed him, and between 1894 and 1905 he compiled calendars covering the years 1581 to 1613. He occupied his mornings with the painful task of transcription and epitomization, and more or less liked the work. He would return home for lunch, and then set out on the *solito giro* in the *Fisolo* (his sandolo) with Antonio to the Lido, then a nearly deserted sandbank. His life was settled: the calendars, his servants and their interests, the English church in Venice, the consul's calls and messages, the English colony (of which Sir A. H. Layard [q.v.] and his wife were then leaders), and innumerable persons passing through with introductions—soldiers, diplomats, Indian officials, and simple tourists—gave him plenty to do. His Monday receptions were attended by Venetians as well as by members of the somewhat miscellaneous English colony. He was fond of climbing, belonged to the Venetian Alpine Club, and scaled peaks in Switzerland, the Tyrol, and the Friulan Alps.

Brown's appointment at the Frari had the result of turning his attention from literature to history. Sir Richard Lodge says: 'My impression is that Brown's original tastes and interests were literary rather than historical. His work in the archives compelled him to turn to history and to become a very competent historian. He had no academic training in modern history, and he never had to teach it. The result was that in his historical writings there was always a little of what some people would call "amateurishness", but which was really the freshness and vigour of one who was exploring hitherto rather unfamiliar fields—refreshing in contrast to the rather blasé treatment of most academic historians. There can be no doubt as to the value of his interpretation of Venetian history. No other Englishman could have written with equal authority and insight on the subject.' Brown produced *Venetian Studies* (1887), a collection of articles on historical subjects, a formal history, *Venice, an Historical Sketch* (1893, compressed as the *Venetian Republic*, 1902, which Edward Armstrong [q.v.] declared was his best book), some chapters in the *Cambridge Modern History* (vol. i, 1902, and vol. iv, 1905), and *Studies in the History of Venice* (2 vols., 1907), his most substantial work. Towards the end of his life he wrote a chapter for the *Cambridge Medieval History* (vol. iv, 1923). Although a professional researcher, he was not an antiquary; he used to say that the facts in his history came from the works of Samuele Romanin. His interest was in politics and political theory, as, for instance, the relations between the Serene Republic and the Holy See, and he projected a book on Paolo Sarpi, on whom he delivered the Taylorian lecture at Oxford in 1900. As a recognition the university of Edinburgh conferred on him the degree of LL.D., which he greatly appreciated.

Brown's researches at the Frari had another result. He discovered the registers of printed books, the laws of the Republic dealing with publishing, and other documents relating to the book trade—all unpublished. He had these transcribed, and prefixed to them chapters on the early printers and their production in *The Venetian Printing Press* (1891). The experts in possession of this field were not cordial to the newcomer, and Symonds disapproved of his spending time over bibliography. The value of the documents, however, cannot be denied.

In 1893 Symonds died in Rome, having appointed Brown his literary executor. In 1895 Brown's *John Addington Symonds, a Biography* appeared. It cost him pain as well as labour. Up till then he had paid yearly visits to Davos in the winter; and Symonds, who was often in Venice, rented the *mezzanino* of Cà Torresella.

During his first years in Venice, Brown had been something of a Bohemian. As time went on he went more into the world, both in Venice and in Midlothian. He visited England every summer, and spent some time in Oxford, looking up old friends and making new ones, such as Edward Armstrong and William Holden Hutton [q.v.]. With undergraduates he had an astonishing success, winning their confidence with ease. He continued to write, although hampered by failing sight. He brought out *Letters and Papers of John Addington Symonds* in 1923 and a book on *Dalmatia* as late as 1925. In 1909 he lost his remarkable and venerable mother. She was cremated, as he was in his turn, on the cemetery island of San Michele. He had long since acquired a position of influence in his quarter, San Gregorio, and he received a commendation from Pius X (who had been patriarch of Venice) when he and his gondolier and his gondolier's family knelt before the Pope in the Vatican.

The European War put an end to these occupations. For some time Brown stayed in Venice, opening his house as a refuge to the poor of the quarter when a bombardment was threatened. 'My duty', he said, 'is to appear at the top of the stairs and say *calma, calma, calma*.' As there are no Venetian cellars, the shelter was illusory. When the capture of Venice seemed imminent he said he could not face an Austrian prison, and went first to Florence and then to Scotland, where he lived among the military at the New Club in Edinburgh or in his own village of Carlops.

Brown returned to Venice in 1919, destined not to see England again. Venetian society was not cordial immediately after the War; his sight was failing, and required an operation at Zürich, and his income had diminished. Newhall was without a tenant, and he had to sell Cà Torresella, retaining the *mezzanino*. He assisted in the arrangements for the visit of King George V to the Asiago battlefields in 1923.

In March 1925 Brown had a severe heart attack, from which he recovered, thanks to the skill of his doctor and the devotion of his servants. His last year was serene; his estate had been sold, and he wrote: 'the doctor says I may be the same man again, but I doubt it, and am content to go on for two or three years, like Epicurus' Gods, neither giving nor taking trouble.' He was not allowed so long, and died 19 August 1926 at his doctor's house at Belluno, where he had gone to escape the heat. There is a monument to him in the English church at San Vio. He never married.

Brown was fond of his kind, had a strong faculty of admiration, and a large heart. He was a good scholar and read Greek fluently.

The books which he knew he absorbed; to write verse, he said, was the greatest pleasure in life; he had a tenderness for minor poets, saying that 'they were more like us' (such as T. E. Brown, his Clifton master, to whose works he contributed an introduction in 1908). In his last years he acquired a taste for Bossuet.

[*The Times*, 21 August 1926; *Scottish Historical Review* (containing an account by Brown of Newhall and Carlops), April 1919; private information; personal knowledge.]

T. W. ALLEN.

BROWNE, EDWARD GRANVILLE (1862–1926), Persian scholar and Orientalist, the eldest son of Sir Benjamin Chapman Browne, civil engineer, by his wife, Annie, daughter of Robert Thomas Atkinson, of High Cross House, Newcastle-upon-Tyne, was born at Uley, near Dursley, Gloucestershire, 7 February 1862. He was educated at Trinity College, Glenalmond, and at Eton. His sympathy with the Turks in their gallant struggle against Russia led him in 1877 to study Turkish, thereby awakening his interest in Oriental matters. On leaving Eton, he proceeded to Pembroke College, Cambridge, where he read for the natural sciences tripos with a view to taking up medicine, at the same time continuing his study of Oriental languages. He took the natural sciences tripos in 1882, and the Indian languages tripos in 1884. He spent the long vacation of 1884 in Constantinople, and on his return studied at St. Bartholomew's Hospital, London, until 1887, qualifying M.B. in that year.

In 1887 Browne was elected to a fellowship at Pembroke College, and this enabled him to pay his first and, as it turned out, his only visit to Persia (October 1887 to October 1888); this country became thenceforth the central object of his studies and the absorbing interest of his life. He visited Tabriz, Teheran, Isfahan, Shiraz, Jezd, and Kirman, avoiding European society as much as possible, and throwing himself with ever-increasing interest into the company of Persians, mystics, dervishes, and Kalandars, whose friendship and confidence he gained to a degree hitherto unparalleled. On his return from Persia in 1888, he was appointed university lecturer in Persian at Cambridge. In 1902 he was elected Sir Thomas Adams professor of Arabic. He lived in Pembroke, in the rooms once occupied by the younger Pitt; but on his marriage in 1906 to Alice Caroline, daughter of Francis Blackburne Daniell, he moved to a house in Trumpington Road, where he spent the remainder of his life.

On the eve of his departure for Persia, Browne had happened to come across the writings of Count Gobineau, and the description which he found there of the rise of the Babi movement gave him a new object for his journey. He was spellbound by the story of the courage and devotion shown by the Bab and his faithful followers, and at once resolved to make a special study of this movement. As he himself said, whereas he had previously wished to visit Shiraz because it was the home of Hafiz and Sa'di, he now wished to see it because it was the birth-place of Mirza Ali Muhammad, the Bab. He was eager to discover the nature of doctrines which could inspire so much heroism, and felt convinced that he would find among the Persians many still living who had known the Bab personally. The story down to 1852 had been adequately and eloquently told by Gobineau. It became Browne's object to continue the narrative from that date, and for some years after his return from Persia he contributed articles dealing with the Babis to the *Journal* of the Royal Asiatic Society, and published in 1891 *A Traveller's Narrative, written to illustrate the Episode of the Bab*, and in 1893 *The new history of Mirza Ali Muhammad, the Bab, translated from the Persian.* He also published in 1893 *A Year amongst the Persians*, which, although it is now included among the foremost classics of travel in English literature, did not at the time attract the attention which it deserved, and was not reprinted until 1926, after his death.

Having made excellent use of all the material gathered during his stay in Persia, Browne now turned his attention to the history of Persian literature, and, in a number of important contributions to the *Journal* of the Royal Asiatic Society, laid the foundations of his great *Literary History of Persia until the time of Firdausi*, of which the first volume appeared in 1902, and subsequent volumes in 1906, 1920, and 1924. The work marks a turning-point in the study of Persian history and literature, and is unlikely for many years to be superseded as the standard authority on the subject. Browne's greatest service lay in his exhaustive analysis of original sources. His knowledge of the Persian language was unrivalled, and his reading covered the whole field of Persian and Arabic literature. No man of his generation did more to enhance the prestige of his country in this field of scholarship.

Browne's early medical studies were often turned to good account in connexion with his Oriental researches. His Fitzpatrick lectures, delivered at the Royal College of Physicians in 1919 and 1920, and published in 1921 under the title of *Arabian Medicine*, form the most notable product of his combined studies in these two subjects.

Apart from the many books and articles which bore his name, Browne was responsible for the publication of many Persian texts, several of which he produced at his own expense. Among the most valuable and onerous of the tasks which he undertook was the editing of the *History of Ottoman Poetry*, written by his friend Elias John Wilkinson Gibb [q.v.]. Of this important work only one volume had appeared when Gibb died in 1901. The task of seeing through the press the five remaining volumes was one upon which few men would have had the unselfishness to embark. The most arduous part was the verification and identification of the Turkish originals of the many poems translated in the course of the five volumes. In order to perpetuate the memory of her son, Mrs. Jane Gibb left a sum of money to be used for the publication of texts and translations of Turkish, Arabic, and Persian books, and with this object in view Browne, with five other scholars, established in 1904 the E. J. W. Gibb memorial fund; he remained the moving spirit of the trust up to the time of his death.

From the days when Browne's sympathies with the Turks were first aroused, down to the end of his life, politics continued, in the midst of his academic studies, to engross much of his time and thought. When the Persian revolution broke out in 1905 he followed events in Persia with the greatest interest and sympathy. He was instrumental in forming the Persian Committee, consisting of members of both Houses of Parliament, which exercised considerable influence on public opinion. By utilizing the valuable material he had collected, and the information he had gathered from his extensive correspondence with Persian friends, he was able to publish *A Short Account of Recent Events in Persia* (1909), *A History of the Persian Revolution 1905–1909* (1910), and *The Press and Poetry of Modern Persia* (1914). His object in all these publications was to serve Persia by explaining to the West the new spirit of sound nationalism which had suddenly revealed itself in that country.

At Cambridge, as lecturer and professor, Browne quickly made his personality felt. He was able to achieve much for the promotion of Oriental studies in the university, and was mainly responsible for the creation of a school of living Oriental languages in Cambridge, in connexion with the training of candidates for the Sudan political service and the consular service in the Near East. He also undertook as a labour of love the wearisome task of cataloguing the Mohammedan manuscripts, both in the University Library and in the libraries of several of the colleges.

In middle life Browne became possessed of considerable wealth, and was then able to give full play to his natural generosity, especially in the direction of helping indigent—and it is to be feared at times quite undeserving—Orientals. He was without worldly ambition and was entirely absorbed in his work, though this did not prevent him from becoming a devoted husband and father. In politics he was a fearless upholder of the weak against the strong. He became, for example, an ardent champion of Irish Home Rule, and a bitter enemy of Russia because of her designs on Turkey and Persia. It thus often happened that he was opposed to the policy of the British government, and it was on this account that his unique knowledge of the Near and Middle East was not turned to better public account.

Browne's capacity for mastering Oriental languages was very remarkable, and he was among the very few Europeans who could write a correct letter with equal facility in Arabic, Persian, or Turkish. His memory was exceptional and his fund of quotation inexhaustible. He had the Boswellian gift of recalling whole conversations—a gift which contributed very largely to the value and interest of his *Year amongst the Persians*. The Persians themselves held him in the deepest affection and veneration, and his name is not likely to be soon forgotten in their country. On attaining his sixtieth birthday he received a number of remarkable tributes from leading men in Persia, and *A Volume of Oriental Studies*, edited by Sir T. W. Arnold and R. A. Nicholson, to which scholars of every country contributed articles, was presented to him.

In November 1924 Browne was suddenly stricken by a severe heart attack, which brought his intellectual activities to an end. In June 1925 his devoted wife, worn out with constant anxiety, suddenly collapsed and died. He never rallied from the blow, and survived her by only six months, dying at Cambridge 5 January 1926. He left two sons.

Browne was elected F.B.A. in 1903 and F.R.C.P. in 1911.

[*The Times*, 6 January 1926; *Introductory Memoir* by J. B. Atkins in *A Persian Anthology, being Translations from the Persian by Edward Granville Browne*, ed. Sir E. D. Ross, 1927; personal knowledge.] E. D. Ross.

BROWNE, GEORGE FORREST (1833–1930), bishop of Stepney and later of Bristol, elder son of George Browne, proctor of the ecclesiastical court at York, by his wife, Anne, daughter of the Rev. Robert Forrest, precentor of York, was born in that city 4 December 1833. He received his early education at St. Peter's School, York, afterwards proceeding to Catharine Hall, later called St. Catharine's College, Cambridge. Here he came under the influence of the master of the hall, Henry Philpott [q.v.], who combined personal charm with learning and remarkable capacity for business and administration. The two men were similar in character, and Philpott always remained Browne's ideal. In 1856 he graduated as thirtieth wrangler, and in the next year obtained a second class in the theological examination, which was not yet a tripos. In 1858 he was ordained, and in 1863 became a fellow and assistant tutor of St. Catharine's. Between degree and fellowship he went as a master to Trinity College, Glenalmond. There Browne was very happy, and in after life he often expressed his thankfulness for the opportunity of appreciating Cambridge from outside before returning to live there as a teacher.

In 1865 Browne vacated his fellowship on his marriage with Mary Louisa, eldest daughter of Sir John Stewart Richardson, thirteenth baronet, of Pitfour, Perthshire. Then began his most important work in the university. He was proctor, either junior or senior, three times between 1870 and 1881. In 1867 he was appointed chaplain of St. Catharine's, in 1869 rector of Ashley-cum-Silverley, Cambridgeshire (which living he held till 1875), and in 1871 secretary of the Local Examinations Syndicate. In the last capacity he showed his energy and skill as a pioneer, as he also showed it afterwards in promoting the higher education of women at Cambridge. He was the first editor, in 1870, of the *Cambridge University Reporter*, and in 1874 he began to serve on the council of the Senate, where his now matured business ability proved invaluable. The University Commission had the benefit of his services from 1877 to 1881, Browne proving an ideal secretary to that body, in its task of university reform. He also served on the Cambridge town council and on the bench. In 1887 there came to Browne a chance to develop his skill in archaeology, one of his many interests, for he was elected to the Disney professorship of archaeology in the university. In that year he was made an honorary fellow of St. Catharine's College. In 1892 he was appointed a canon of St. Paul's Cathedral; he received the honorary D.C.L. (1891) of Durham University; in 1893 he became secretary to the London Diocesan Home Mission. Two years later the new suffragan bishopric of Stepney found in Browne the right man to fill that not easy position. On his elevation to a bishopric he received the degree of D.D. at Cambridge. After two years at Stepney, Bishop Browne was translated (1897) to the diocese of Bristol. The times were difficult, but the new bishop was popular, successful, and happy. He resigned in 1914, and lived in retirement until his death, 1 June 1930. He received the honorary degree of D.D. from Oxford University in 1908, and he was elected a fellow of the British Academy on its foundation in 1903. He died, and was buried, at Bexhill-on-Sea. His wife, by whom he had two sons and three daughters, died in 1903.

Browne's published works include: *Ice-caves of France and Switzerland* (1865); *The Venerable Bede* (1879, new edition 1919); *Notes on Monk Wearmouth Church* (1886); *The Church in these Islands before Augustine* (1894); *Augustine and His Companions* (1895); *The Conversion of the Heptarchy* (1896); *Theodore and Wilfrith* (1897); *History of St. Catharine's College* (1902); *Boniface of Crediton* (1905); *The Recollections of a Bishop* (1915). He made a special study of runic stones, and published *The Ilam Crosses* (1889) and *The Ancient Cross Shafts of Bewcastle and Ruthwell* (1917). In 1923, when nearly ninety, he produced an edition of *Echt-Forbes Family Charters, 1345–1727*.

Browne was fond of fly-fishing and mountain-climbing, being president of the Alpine Club in 1905; but he found his best recreation in change of work. His versatility was remarkable; archaeology and history were to him a source of great pleasure, affording welcome and health-giving relief from the strain of administration. It is perhaps wrong to speak of 'strain', for Dr. Philpott had taught him to value and love official duties, and not to consider them a mere means to an end. For this reason his real life was his public work; but in spite of this, perhaps because of it, he won all hearts by his courtesy, sympathy, and lively personality.

[Browne's *Recollections of a Bishop*, 1915; private information; personal knowledge.]

W. H. S. Jones.

BROWNING, OSCAR (1837–1923), schoolmaster, fellow of King's College, Cambridge, and historian, was born in London 17 January 1837, the third son of William Shipton Browning, a merchant, by his wife, Mariana Margaret Bridge, aunt of Sir Cyprian A. G. Bridge [q.v.]. There is a tradition, unverifiable, but borne out by some of his characteristics, that an eighteenth-century ancestor on his mother's side had introduced a strain of Jewish blood. Six months after Browning's birth, his parents moved from London to one of the canons' houses in the precincts of Windsor Castle. In 1850 he was elected a scholar of Eton, his tutor being William Johnson Cory [q.v.]. In 1856 he was elected to a scholarship at King's College, Cambridge, and in 1859 to a fellowship. As a fellowship at that time was vacated only by marriage, Browning, who never married, remained a fellow of King's until his death. During his undergraduate days he was the friend of many men who were afterwards distinguished, such as Henry Sidgwick, R. C. Jebb, G. O. Trevelyan, and C. S. Calverley. He became president of the Union, and formed the ambition of becoming a statesman and a trainer of statesmen. He was placed fourth in the classical tripos of 1860, and in May of the same year accepted the offer of an assistant-mastership at Eton.

The years spent at Eton (1860–1875) were the most fruitful of Browning's life. His house, presided over by his beautiful, dignified, and accomplished mother, soon became the most popular in the school. He spent generously in the interests of the boys the large income which it provided. He arranged concerts by professionals from London, introduced singing competitions, encouraged private theatricals, and entertained famous men of letters. One thing only he discouraged—talk about athletics, to the cult of which, although not to the practice, he was resolutely opposed. A good classic himself, he believed at this time in classical education. But he also attached much importance to the teaching of history, by preference modern history. He presented to the royal commission on the public schools (1861–1864) a scheme of educational reform; and the commissioners' report, to a considerable degree, adopted his point of view. Unfortunately, although always a reformer, he was not a tactful one, and his activities involved him in a long series of disputes, controversies, and admonitions [see H. E. Wortham, *Oscar Browning*, 1927]. Moreover, his intimacy with the boys led to suspicions and charges which were never fairly and openly advanced in such a way that he could have refuted them. The result was his dismissal from Eton in 1875. The boys, their parents, and his friends rallied indignantly but vainly round him, and the matter was widely canvassed in the press and the clubs of London, and even debated in the House of Commons. But J. J. Hornby, then headmaster, was obdurate, and the governing body had no power except to dismiss the headmaster himself, which they were naturally unwilling to do.

Browning thus found himself at the age of thirty-eight deprived of £3,000 a year and the work to which he was devoted, and reduced to his fellowship at King's, then worth £300. Some men might have been broken, but Browning was always resilient. The work which had been interrupted at Eton he resolved to continue at King's, and he showed himself there as active, as provocative, as exasperating, and as right as he had been at Eton. He was welcomed with enthusiasm by his colleagues and friends, appointed a lecturer in history at King's in 1880, and a university lecturer in 1883. He founded the Political Society, of which most of the members were undergraduates, and where papers were read weekly, followed by discussion in which every one present had to take his part. He threw himself with his usual energy into the task of reforming and reorganizing the college. His ideal was laid down as follows, in a memorandum of 1897: 'I have always fancied to myself the King's of the future as a college of about 150 undergraduates reading for honours in the various faculties of the university, provided with the best teaching which the university can afford, which should be given to them to a great extent at the expense of the college, enjoying the stimulus of a very cultivated and energetic society, protected from the temptations of a larger college, and directed with a careful and sympathetic attention from the older men, which is at present little known in Cambridge, but which is one of the chief advantages of the sister university.' This ideal has in fact been largely attained, and part, at least, of the credit for it must be attributed to Browning's continuous insistence on it.

It was not, however, in the formal work of teaching that Browning's influence was most felt. His abundant energy overflowed into extremely varied fields. He was treasurer of the Union, president and treasurer of the Footlights Dramatic Club, and of the Bicycle Club (he once crossed the Alps on a tricycle), an officer of the Musical Club, the Swimming Club, and the Hockey Club. On Sunday evenings there assembled in his rooms every one of note in the university, and often distinguished strangers from outside. Admirable music was to be heard there by those who enjoyed it, while there lay about on the tables the latest literature of the newly-founded Society for Psychical Research. On these occasions Browning, who was anything but pompous or self-conscious, would himself perform comic songs with appropriate action. His vivacity, his contempt for dignity, his love of youth, and his frank devotion to the world delighted all undergraduates who were not prigs, and all dons who were not pedants. But it must not be supposed that he was not serious in his work. If he was not a great historian, he was a great educationalist, for he knew how to stimulate, to reprove, and to make men of boyish youths. Nor was his interest confined to undergraduates. He took a leading part in the foundation of the Cambridge University day training college for elementary teachers, of which he was principal from 1891 to 1909, made himself acquainted with a number of boys in the town and the neighbouring villages, and started them in their careers. He has been called a snob, but that innocent and common failing was compatible, in his case, with the warmest interest in any poor boy who showed promise.

Meantime Browning's activities at Cambridge did not interfere with his outside interests. He was always a keen radical, though with a strong tinge of imperialism. Three times he contested hopeless seats —Norwood (1886), East Worcestershire (1892), and West Derby (1895)—in the liberal interest, and once was invited to oppose Joseph Chamberlain. This opportunity, however, he declined—a decision which later he regretted. He had made the mistake, he said, of acting on reflection instead of on impulse. He never altered his political attitude nor allowed his natural optimism to be overclouded by the shadows of age. Even the European War left his ideals unshaken.

Browning's life at Cambridge came to an end in 1908, when he was over seventy. The last period was somewhat distressing, for he believed himself to have been badly treated by some of his colleagues at King's and by those who then controlled the day training college. But he bore little malice and never lost interest in King's and King's men. His latter years were spent in Rome, and he continued there his restless activities. He gave public lectures, sat on committees, and in 1921 became trustee and chairman of the British Academy of Arts in Rome. He resumed the classes on Dante which had been a feature of his life in Cambridge, and assisted young Italians, as he had done young Englishmen, towards the openings they desired. It was during these last years that he wrote several of his historical manuals: *A History of the Modern World, 1815–1910* (2 vols., 1912), *A General History of the World* (1913), and *A Short History of Italy, 375–1915* (1917). Among his earlier historical works may be mentioned *The Flight to Varennes and other historical essays* (1892). Contact with people and with life, however, meant more to him than book knowledge, and it is the influence of his stimulating personality, his friendships, and his practical philanthropy which form his real contribution to the life of his time. He died in Rome 6 October 1923, in his eighty-seventh year.

A portrait of Browning by — Teague is at Eton College. A cartoon appeared in *Vanity Fair* 24 November 1888.

[Browning's own reminiscences in *Impressions of Indian Travel*, 1903, *Memories of Sixty Years at Eton, Cambridge, and Elsewhere*, 1910, and *Memories of Later Years*, 1923; H. E. Wortham, *Oscar Browning*, 1927; personal knowledge.] G. Lowes Dickinson.

BRYCE, JAMES, Viscount Bryce (1838–1922), jurist, historian, and politician, born 10 May 1838 in Arthur Street, Belfast, was the eldest son of James Bryce the younger (1806–1877, q.v.), schoolmaster and geologist, and grandson of James Bryce the elder (1767–1857, q.v.), divine. His mother was Margaret, daughter of James Young, of Abbeyville, co. Antrim, a Belfast merchant. James Bryce spent the first eight years of his life in

Belfast and at the country house of his maternal grandfather, James Young, on the shores of Belfast Lough. The Bible, *The Arabian Nights*, and Baron von Humboldt's *Aspects of Nature* were among the books of his childhood. Already at the age of eight he was putting questions to his uncle, Reuben John Bryce, on the British constitution. In 1846 his father was appointed a master in the Glasgow high school. The family lived for some time in Lansdowne Crescent, Glasgow, and then removed to a house in the country at Blantyre. James attended the high school until the age of fourteen, when he went to live with his uncle Reuben, then headmaster of the Belfast Academy, attended classes at the Academy, and learnt from his uncle the elements of Erse. In 1854 he entered Glasgow University, where he studied Latin under William Ramsay [q.v.] and Greek under Edmund Law Lushington [q.v.]. In his second year he obtained the gold medal for Greek, besides a prize in mathematics. Among his college acquaintances were John Nichol [q.v.], afterwards professor of English at Glasgow, and George Monro Grant [q.v.], afterwards principal of Queen's University, Kingston, Ontario. Much of the vacation time was spent in rural wanderings in the west of Scotland and the north of Ireland, in which Bryce acquired a love of botany and a taste for climbing.

This taste for climbing endured in later life, and he pursued it in many places. Besides several peaks in the Alps and Dolomites, he ascended Hekla in Iceland with (Sir) Courtenay Ilbert in 1872, the Maladetta and the Vignemale in the Pyrenees with Ilbert in 1873, Mount Ararat with Aeneas Mackay in 1878, when he climbed the last 5,000 feet alone, the Tatra Ridge in the Carpathians in 1878 with (Sir) Leslie Stephen, Mauna Loa in Hawaii in 1883, when he nearly fell into the volcano, Machache in Basutoland in 1895, Etna in 1903, and Myogi-san in Japan in 1913. The triple-peaked Mount Bryce of the Canadian Rockies was named after him in 1898. When chief secretary for Ireland in 1906 he took his officials up Croagh Patrick and Croaghaun for exercise. He was elected in 1879 a member of the Alpine Club, of which he was president from 1899 to 1901. He wrote on *Mountaineering in Far-away Countries* in the Badminton Library (3rd ed. 1900).

In June 1857 Bryce was elected to a scholarship at Trinity College, Oxford. One of the competitors, George Gilbert Ramsay, who was also successful, described him as 'that awful Scotch fellow, who outwrote everybody'. With the sympathy of some of the younger fellows of Trinity he successfully resisted, on the ground that he was a presbyterian, an attempt of the president, John Wilson, to make him qualify for the scholarship by signing the Thirty-nine Articles, an episode which Lewis Campbell [q.v.], of Queen's College, characterized as 'the triumph of liberalism in Oxford'. He obtained a first class in classical moderations in 1859, and won the Gaisford prize for Greek prose in 1860. In 1861 he gained 'distinctly the best' of the two first classes in *literae humaniores* at Easter, a first class in the school of law and modern history at Michaelmas, the Gaisford prize for Greek verse, and the Vinerian law scholarship. In 1862 he obtained the Craven scholarship and the Chancellor's Latin essay prize. He was in succession librarian and president of the Union Society, although he spoke there comparatively seldom. He had many friends at Oxford. In 1857 he became a member of the Old Mortality Society, founded by his Glasgow contemporary, John Nichol, which included among its members A. V. Dicey, A. C. Swinburne, Birkbeck Hill, T. H. Green, T. E. Holland, Henry Nettleship, C. L. Shadwell, J. R. Magrath, Ingram Bywater, and Walter Pater. Dicey was for a few months his tutor and always his close friend. Other friends, outside the Old Mortality Society, were Arthur Butler, George Brodrick, and Aeneas Mackay. Among his seniors were Benjamin Jowett, Mark Pattison, and Matthew Arnold; slightly junior was Courtenay Ilbert. Bryce graduated B.A. in 1862, and D.C.L. in 1870, and was elected a fellow of Oriel College in 1862. He retained his fellowship until his marriage in 1889. He was re-elected professor fellow in 1890, resigned in 1893, and was made an honorary fellow in 1894. He was also elected an honorary fellow of Trinity College in the last-named year.

Bryce entered Lincoln's Inn in 1862. In 1863 he studied law at Heidelberg under Karl Adolf von Vangerow, and in 1864 he visited Florence, Rome, and Naples. At the opening of that year he began life in London, sharing rooms with Kenelm E. Digby and working in the chambers of (Sir) John Holker [q.v.]. While resident in London he attended the Saturday evenings of Dean Stanley at Westminster, where, among others, he met George Grote and William Whewell. His experience of London, he said, enabled him for the first time to understand *The Newcomes*. After being called to the bar in 1867 he joined the Northern circuit. He obtained a respectable practice as a junior and was engaged in some important commercial cases; but his real interests lay outside current litigation. He gave up his practice in 1882 as he found that it interfered with other activities and with his love of travel.

In 1863 Bryce won the Arnold historical essay prize at Oxford with his essay on the Holy Roman Empire, perhaps the most famous of prize essays, which was published in 1864 in so altered a form that Professor Freeman remarked: 'Mr. Bryce's book has been written since it gained the historical prize at Oxford.' The work has undergone less subsequent modification than some of his other writings because, as originally published, it was a carefully finished presentation of a primary medieval conception. Nowadays more attention might be given to the varied aspects of the ideal of the Holy Roman Empire at different periods, but the essay will always be an example of masterly lucidity and simplicity in the treatment of a highly complex subject. The book has been translated into German, French, and Italian. The last edition, enlarged, appeared in 1922. The work secured for Bryce the friendship of Freeman and a European reputation. About 1898 he and his wife fell into conversation, in an Alpine pass, with a group of Swiss professors. On learning his name 'the Professors all took off their hats exclaiming "Holy Roman Empire" and salaamed in the most impressive manner' [Fisher, i, 71].

In 1865 and 1866 Bryce was largely employed as an assistant commissioner in making a report on the schools of Lancashire, Shropshire, Worcestershire, Monmouthshire, and eight Welsh counties for the royal commission, known as the Schools Inquiry Commission (1864–1867), set up under the chairmanship of Henry Labouchere, first Baron Taunton, to report on the schools of England and Wales. In his report on Lancashire, published in 1867, Bryce emphasized the pressing need for educational co-ordination, and urged that any scheme for this purpose should be comprehensive and include universities and schools, boys' schools and girls' schools, elementary schools and secondary schools, as part of a single plan. He also urged the need for raising the standard of commercial education and of female education. In these recommendations he indicated three of the main lines of later development. He was himself associated with the beginnings of university education for women, being a friend of (Sarah) Emily Davies [q.v.] and an original member of Girton College. He was also associated with the development of university education at Manchester. In 1868 he accepted an invitation to lecture on law at Owens College, and continued to do so, first as lecturer, and then as professor until 1874. He also prepared the draft constitution for an enlarged college upon which was based the act of parliament for the incorporation of the college in 1871. In 1870 Bryce was appointed regius professor of civil law at Oxford, where he may be said to have begun the revival of the study of Roman law. He retained this post until 1893, when he was succeeded by Henry Goudy. Much of his teaching at Oxford, including his inaugural and valedictory lectures, is to be found in his *Studies in History and Jurisprudence*, published in 1901.

In the autumn of 1876 Bryce, with Aeneas Mackay, visited St. Petersburg and Moscow, proceeded down the Volga by steam-boat, and travelled through Southern Russia, the Caucasus, and Armenia. On his return he found England absorbed in the Eastern question, and in September 1877 he published *Transcaucasia and Ararat*, an account of his travels and of the state of the countries through which he had passed. The interest which the book aroused called forth three subsequent editions. Bryce's travels gave him a deep and lasting interest in the affairs of the Near East. He was impressed with the hopelessness of Turkish government and the responsibility of England for the protection of Eastern Christians. He joined the Eastern Questions Association, formed to combat Disraeli's policy, and helped to draft the popular appeal which led to the famous conference at St. James's Hall on 8 December in that year, and to draw up the memorial from the Armenians resident in London which was circulated at that meeting. He became the principal advocate of the Armenian nation in England, the founder and first president of the Anglo-Armenian Society and, when he entered parliament, the chief spokesman for Armenia in the House of Commons. On 23 July 1880 he urged in parliament the appointment of a Christian governor for Armenia. In 1896 the Armenian massacres moved him to strong protest [*The Times*, 22 January, 2 October 1896]. In 1915, when the massacres were renewed on a greater scale, he suggested the compilation of Mr. A. J. Toynbee's *Treatment of the Armenians in the Ottoman Empire*, procured for it material information, and contributed a preface. His last public appearance on 20 December 1921 was as chairman of a meeting summoned at the Mansion House to promote the liberation of Christian natives from Turkish rule.

The Eastern Question had a large share in drawing Bryce into political life. By heredity, as well as by bent of mind, he was a liberal. While an undergraduate he contemplated joining Garibaldi, but found it incompatible with the tenure of his scholarship. In the general election of 1874 he unsuccessfully contested the borough of Wick. In 1880 he was returned to parliament for the Tower Hamlets division, a region of East London with a working-class population including a number of German sugar-bakers, whom he addressed in their own tongue. In the general election of 1885 he abandoned this constituency, which had been transformed by the Redistribution Bill, and was returned by a large majority for South Aberdeen, a seat which he held until he retired from the House of Commons in 1906.

In parliament Bryce was not at first entirely successful as a speaker. His speeches were ordered, logical, and 'filled to overflowing with accurate information'. But he was fond of generalizations which, though fundamental, appeared to lesser minds irrelevant, and at any rate took up time. He had also the habit, dangerous in that assembly, of looking at both sides of the argument and meeting objections in advance instead of waiting for them to be raised. Joseph Chamberlain, to whom that kind of mind was antipathetic, termed him 'the Professor'. Nevertheless, Bryce had a considerable measure of parliamentary success. From the first he established himself as an authority on the Eastern Question, and he carried weight on many other subjects. He generally filled the House, although he could not always persuade it. But in spite of his membership of three Cabinets it is doubtful whether he ever gave the first place in his thoughts to politics, and he certainly never became absorbed in the political and social atmosphere of the House of Commons. In later years many of the defects of his oratory disappeared, largely perhaps as a result of his successful experience in America, and he became a public speaker of the first order. In the House of Lords he attained a position of great influence.

In 1881 Bryce refused the post of legal member of the viceroy's council of India. Much of his attention was taken up by the Irish question. Although he had reluctantly voted for the Coercion Bill of 1881, he afterwards thought that he had made a mistake, and he voted against the Crimes Act of 1882. He began to form the opinion that Home Rule for Ireland was inevitable as the only alternative to continuous coercion, and his election address in 1885 foreshadowed Irish self-government under an imperial parliament. When Gladstone came into office in February 1886 Bryce was offered the post of under-secretary for foreign affairs.

The defeat of the ministry three months later left Bryce free to resume his literary activities. Already in January 1883, while contemplating a work on Justinian, he had made a contribution to the study of medieval history by identifying in the Barberini library at Rome the text of a life of Justinian which Nicolaus Alemannus, in 1623, in his first edition of the *Anecdota* of Procopius, had ascribed to a certain Theophilus Abbas, said to have been Justinian's preceptor. Bryce published the text of the fragment in the *English Historical Review* for October 1887 with a commentary in which he maintained that the biographical details, though accepted by Gibbon, are drawn from late Slavonic tradition and are historically worthless, and that there is nothing to show that Theophilus Abbas ever existed. His views have been accepted by Professor J. B. Bury in his edition of Gibbon's *Decline and Fall* (Introduction, lix, lx).

Bryce was also at this time associated with the foundation of the *English Historical Review*. He had discussed the project with John Richard Green as far back as 1872, but financial support was lacking. In 1885 Messrs. Longman came to the rescue, and on 15 July the general policy of the *Review* was settled at a dinner given by Bryce in Bryanston Square at which were present, among others, Lord Acton, Dean Church, Mandell Creighton, Richard Garnett, (Sir) Adolphus Ward, and Robertson Smith. Bryce suggested Creighton as editor, and contributed a prefatory note to the first number which appeared in January 1886.

On his release from office in May 1886, Bryce turned to the completion of *The*

American Commonwealth which occupied him for the next two years. He had first visited the United States with Dicey in 1870. This visit was confined to the North-Eastern states and did not extend farther south than Washington. In 1881 he made a second tour, visiting the Pacific coast and the Southern states. He returned with his early impressions profoundly modified, and a third visit in 1883, when he crossed from San Francisco to Hawaii and back, further ripened his views. On his return he began writing *The American Commonwealth*, the first edition of which was published in 1888. A second edition, revised, appeared in 1889. In 1890 he paid his fourth visit, and a third edition, completely revised throughout, was issued in 1893 and 1895. A new edition, which was to some extent a new book, was published in 1910.

The aim of *The American Commonwealth* was to portray 'the whole political system of the country in its practice as well as its theory', to explain 'not only the National Government, but the State Governments, not only the constitution, but the party system, not only the party system, but the ideas, temper, habits of the sovereign people'. Apart from its grasp, its keen insight into American life, and its literary fascination, the striking feature of the work is that its author deliberately rejects the temptation, to which the acute forensic mind is liable, to set out his own general ideas. A vast mass of detail is presented with attractive lucidity and in such a manner that the reader is able, in a large measure, to make his generalizations for himself. Although the work of a visitor, the reputation of *The American Commonwealth* has stood very high in the United States. It has been continually quoted as a standard authority by contemporary American historians, and was used as a text-book throughout the country for over thirty years. It is much better known there than in England. When Edward Lawrence Godkin of the *New York Nation* was asked by an English member of parliament whether he had ever heard of a book called *The American Commonwealth* he answered 'You bet'.

During the concluding stage of his work on *The American Commonwealth* Bryce paid a visit to Egypt in December 1887 and January 1888. When the book had been finally published he started for India in October, returning in January 1889. In Egypt the past absorbed him, but he found that 'India is of the present', and that he could only get politics out of his head and discover the Arabian Nights in the native states of Rajputana.

When Gladstone formed his last administration in August 1892, Bryce was brought into the Cabinet as chancellor of the duchy of Lancaster and was a member of the Cabinet committee which prepared the Irish Home Rule Bill. He also took a substantial part in defending that measure in parliament. As chancellor of the duchy he provoked conservative criticism by insisting on an increased proportion of liberals among the magistrates of the duchy and by appointing some working men among the number. In March 1893 he accompanied Queen Victoria to Florence as minister in attendance. Randall Davidson, then bishop of Rochester, who was also in attendance, says that Bryce tried to talk with the queen quietly concerning Home Rule in Ireland, 'but found the pitch had been queered by Mr. Gladstone's sermonizing to her' on the subject [Fisher, i, 220]. But she had prepared herself by reading *The Holy Roman Empire*, and approved of Bryce who could, when required, talk to her fluently in German. 'I like Mr. Bryce. He knows so much and is so modest' [Ibid., i, 295].

In 1894, when Gladstone retired and a new administration was formed under Lord Rosebery, Bryce, with some misgivings as to his qualifications, became president of the Board of Trade. In this capacity he acted as chairman of the royal commission on secondary education, which sat from March 1894 until August 1895 and is generally known as the Bryce commission. He brought to its deliberations his experience of the work of the Schools Inquiry Commission of 1864–1867, and thus was enabled to maintain continuity of policy, particularly with regard to the co-ordination of primary and secondary education. The question really before this body, however, was whether there should be a state system of secondary education. It reported in effect that private endeavour had failed to produce an adequate supply of efficient secondary schools. It recommended the unification of the central authority by the creation of a general department of education under a responsible minister with a permanent secretary and a small council of experts to supervise, but not to supersede, local action. It also advocated the establishment of county and county borough educational authorities, a great extension of the scholarship system in secondary schools, the inspection of these schools, and the registration and training of teachers. 'The main findings of the Secondary Education commission became the foundation on which the new administrative structure of our secondary schools has risen' [Sir Michael Sadler in Fisher, i, 298].

In 1895 Bryce spent the autumn in South Africa. He travelled from Cape Town to Fort Salisbury in Mashonaland, passing through Bechuanaland and Matabeleland. He returned through Portuguese East Africa, traversed Natal, and visited the Transvaal, the Orange Free State, Basutoland, and the eastern province of Cape Colony. He had not travelled with the view of writing a book, but on his return, finding public interest excited by the Jameson Raid, he published in November 1897 his *Impressions of South Africa*, which was reprinted within the month, reaching a second edition in January 1898 and a third in October 1899. The book is chiefly valuable as an account of South Africa by an acute, trained mind at a time when it was on the verge of a great transformation. To the third edition Bryce added a prefatory chapter in which he explained his views on the situation. Briefly, he was of opinion that England was in the right on many of the points at issue, but that there was no conspiracy of the Dutch in South Africa to overthrow British power, and that a conflict with the Transvaal and the Orange Free State might yet be avoided.

Holding these opinions Bryce joined Sir Henry Campbell-Bannerman and (Lord) Morley, before the outbreak of war, in censuring the colonial secretary, Mr. Chamberlain, especially for raising the question of suzerainty, and in criticizing the handling of the situation by Sir Alfred (afterwards Lord) Milner at Cape Town. After hostilities had begun he held that the War should be fought until victory was obtained, but he denounced farm burning, the treatment of the Boers as rebels, and the establishment of concentration camps for the non-combatants. He also advocated the grant of liberal terms of peace and condemned the introduction of Crown Colony government. His attitude, which in certain respects was more uncompromising than that of Campbell-Bannerman though less extreme than that of Mr. Lloyd George, gained him much unpopularity in the country.

While the liberal party was divided on this question, Bryce was very closely associated with Campbell-Bannerman, as their correspondence shows, in the difficult task of maintaining parliamentary opposition without creating a permanent schism. When, however, the reunited liberal party came into power in December 1905, the best places went to the Liberal Imperialists, whom it was necessary to reconcile to Campbell-Bannerman's leadership, and Bryce reluctantly accepted the difficult office of chief secretary for Ireland [cf. J. A. Spender, *Life, Journalism, and Politics*, i, 30, 1927]. His under-secretary was Sir Antony MacDonnell (afterwards Baron MacDonnell, q.v.) with whom he worked in perfect accord. Both were impressed with the defects in the Irish administrative system, and both desired to introduce a measure for amending them. But the result of the general election of December 1905 had raised hopes in the Irish party which neither the government nor Bryce himself was prepared to satisfy. In February 1906 John Redmond [q.v.] found that Bryce was unwilling to pledge himself to the immediate repeal of the Coercion Act. Bryce also, in adopting MacDonnell's ideas with regard to Irish administration, fell far short of Redmond's demand for 'a complete scheme of Home Rule', and the Cabinet's proposals, when communicated to Redmond and John Dillon [q.v.], proved quite unacceptable. Bryce probably made a mistake in accepting too exclusively MacDonnell's views and in failing to get into touch with the Irish leaders. On 1 November Redmond was asked to discuss matters with Mr. Lloyd George who explained that Bryce was in despair and that the Cabinet had asked him to intervene. On 13 November Redmond wrote to Edward Blake, an Irish Canadian merchant, that the Irish administration of Mr. Bryce was lamentable in the extreme, that he was absolutely under the domination of MacDonnell, and that he should not be surprised to hear that Bryce had abandoned the task. Before the end of the month Redmond and Dillon got into touch with Campbell-Bannerman and Mr. Augustine Birrell, and in December Bryce succeeded Sir (Henry) Mortimer Durand [q.v.] as American ambassador [Denis Gwynn, *Life of John Redmond*, 119, 121–141, 1932].

Bryce's tenure of office in Ireland was not, however, altogether without achievement. He was responsible for the Labourers' (Ireland) Act, passed in 1906, for providing labourers' cottages with suitable plots of land to be owned by the rural district councils on land purchase terms. He was opposed to the dropping of the Peace Preservation (Ireland) Act, which had been passed by Gladstone in 1881, to restrict the possession of firearms, but found himself alone in the Cabinet in his opposition. The failure to renew this Act was afterwards criticized on the ground that it facilitated the arming both of the Ulster unionists and of the party of secession.

Perhaps Bryce's most notable achievement was to set up a commission to report on the organization of Irish university education. By a majority report it recommended the establishment of a single national state-aided university which was to comprise Catholic, Anglican, and Presbyterian colleges, including Trinity College, Dublin, and the existing Royal University. Almost the last act of Bryce as Irish secretary was unsuccessfully to urge the acceptance of this report in the House of Commons, in spite of the fact that it had not the general support of the Irish members and that his successor, Mr. Birrell, had a different plan. Balfour's comment was that Bryce 'had nailed his flag to another man's mast and then sailed for America'. Birrell suggested that in painting his picture Bryce had 'omitted to leave a few clouds on the horizon' [Fisher, i, 353].

As ambassador at Washington, an office which he filled from February 1907 until April 1913, Bryce was particularly successful in gaining the approval of the American people and in becoming an American institution. Whenever he attended the Old Presbyterian church at Washington he was as a matter of course ushered into Abraham Lincoln's pew. 'Old man Bryce is all right' was the reputed verdict of a miner in Nevada, and this popular sentiment gave him power in that great democracy which does not allow itself to be governed by the opinions of its politicians. One reason for his success was his assiduity in cultivating the acquaintance of the American public and in imparting instruction to a people which values instruction so highly. His activities were summarized in a volume, published in 1913, of *University and Historical Addresses* delivered during his six years' residence to American universities, bar associations, chambers of commerce, state teachers, farmers' congresses, religious conferences, and missionary congresses. He was capable also of masterly touches in diplomacy. When (Sir) Roger Casement [q.v.] was returning to England at the beginning of 1912 after his second visit to Peru to investigate the Putumayo rubber atrocities on which he had already drawn up a report which, when published, was likely to inflame humanitarian feeling in England and in America, Bryce had Casement intercepted by a cruiser and brought to Washington for an unofficial interview with President Taft and other leading statesmen, after which he was able to inform Sir Edward Grey that the American government would welcome the publication of the report [S. Gwynn, *Roger Casement*, 177–179, 1930], and Putumayo gave no more trouble in Washington. At the Pelagic Sealing conference, when the Russian and Japanese plenipotentiaries were on the verge of a rupture, Bryce expressed a desire to consider the point in its various aspects. By the time he had reached the seventeenth aspect the secretaries of the two embassies had been able to soothe their chiefs and retrieve the situation [Fisher, ii, 23–24].

Bryce's influence in America was not confined to the United States. By a visit to Canada in April 1907, and a speech to the Canadian Club at Ottawa, he created an atmosphere favourable to the removal of difficulties. The governor-general, Earl Grey, told him that his speech had won the confidence of Ottawa. This confidence assisted diplomatic action. On 4 April 1908 an Arbitration Convention was signed between Great Britain and the United States for referring a special class of disputes to the Hague Tribunal for settlement. Bryce's influence with Canada enabled him to obtain the consent of the Dominion to the employment of the machinery of this convention for the settlement of disputes with the United States, often of long standing, on such questions as boundaries, fishing rights, and private claims for pecuniary compensation.

During the last four months of 1910 Bryce paid a visit to Panama, South America, and Portugal. He gave an account of this journey in his book, *South America: Observations and Impressions*, published in 1912, interesting as a study of the South American peoples, but remarkable above all for its vivid impressions of form and colour in that continent. A new edition appeared in 1920.

Bryce had refused a peerage before going to America in 1907, and again in 1910, but after his return he was created Viscount Bryce, of Dechmont in Lanarkshire, on 1 January 1914. He was also made a member of the Hague Tribunal. In April and May he visited Palestine and Syria. He supported in the House of

Lords the Bill for excluding Ulster from the operation of the Home Rule Act. When the European War burst on the nation the invasion of Belgium led him to support the declaration against Germany. He presided over the commission, set up in September 1914, to consider the breaches of the laws and established usages of war alleged to have been committed by German troops, particularly in Belgium. The conclusion of the Bryce *Report* was that excesses had been committed in order to strike terror into the civil population and dishearten the Belgian army. Bryce was strongly opposed to any reprisals on the non-combatant population of Germany, and in the *Report* he urged the adoption of measures after the conclusion of peace to prevent 'the recurrence of such horrors'. This in fact became the leading aim of his life. In the autumn of 1914 he joined a small group formed to promote a League of Nations and corresponded on the subject with ex-President Taft and A. L. Lowell in America. But, convinced that the defeat of Germany was essential, he opposed the efforts to promote mediation which were popular in the United States in the early years of the War. On 8 August 1917 he forwarded to the English government a memorandum in which the structure of the League of Nations, as afterwards established, was substantially outlined. He regarded the inclusion of the United States as essential to the success of the League. In the last year of his life, in August 1921, he addressed a conference of political students from all parts of the United States, held at Williams College, Massachusetts, on the subject of international relations, and urged 'without venturing to prescribe the mode' that the American public should 'take their share in the great task of raising international relations to a higher plane'. The lectures were published in 1922.

In 1917 Bryce was appointed chairman of a joint conference, selected from members of the two houses of parliament, to report on the reform of the House of Lords. Owing to the wide differences of opinion in the conference the report took the unusual form of a letter from the chairman to the prime minister putting forward a somewhat complicated plan for constituting a second chamber of about 330 members by indirect election or nomination, and indicating the arguments for and against the more controversial parts of the plan.

From 1918 to 1921 Bryce was mainly engaged on his work on *Modern Democracies*, first projected in 1904, which became the central purpose of his visit to Australia in 1912 and to Switzerland in 1919. It was published in March 1921. This work may be regarded as in some respects complementary to *The American Commonwealth*, bringing the United States into comparison with the other great democracies of the present time. A special chapter was devoted to recent reforming movements in the United States. But the book is remarkable also for its treatment of novel developments in the other democracies and for its dispassionate justification of French republican policy and institutions.

In December 1921 Bryce addressed the House of Lords for the last time, supporting Lord Morley's motion for the adoption of the Irish Treaty and welcoming it as a sign of better times. He died in his sleep at Sidmouth 22 January 1922, and was buried in the Grange cemetery, Edinburgh. He married in 1889 Elizabeth Marion, daughter of Thomas Ashton, of Hyde and Fordbank, Didsbury. He had no children, and the peerage became extinct.

In spite of the high quality and great range of his historical learning, Bryce, with his boundless energy and his ubiquity, had the general characteristics of a man of action rather than of a scholar. Even his books were planned and sketched in the open air and on the move more than in the study. He possessed many of the essential qualities of a statesman; but he was wholly unfitted to be a party leader. Crowded with achievement as his life was, it leaves the impression that he possessed great reserve forces which were never called fully into action.

Bryce received degrees from thirty-one universities, of which fifteen were in the United States. He was elected a fellow of the Royal Society in 1893 and was an original member of the British Academy on its foundation in 1902, and president from 1913 to 1917. He was also made a foreign member of the Institut de France in 1904 and was a member of the academies of Brussels (1896), Turin (1896), Naples (1903), and Stockholm, and of the Imperial Academy of Sciences of St. Petersburg. In 1907 he received the Order of Merit and in 1917 was created G.C.V.O.

Besides the works already mentioned and numerous lectures, speeches, and contributions to journals, Bryce was the author of: 'The Historical Aspect of Democracy' in *Essays on Reform* (1867); 'The Judicature Act of 1873' in *Owens College Essays and Addresses* (1874); *The Trade Marks Registration Act and Trade Mark Law* (1877); *The Relations of the advanced and backward Races of Mankind* (Romanes lecture, 1902); *Studies in Contemporary Biography* (1903); *The Hindrances to Good Citizenship* (1909); *Neutral Nations and the War* (1914); *The Attitude of Great Britain in the War* (1916); *The Next Thirty Years* (1917); *Essays and Addresses in War Time* (1918), and *Memories of Travel* (1923). He also contributed a chapter on 'The Flora of the Island of Arran' to his father's *Geology of Clydesdale and Arran* (1859), an introduction to Helmolt's *The World's History* and the article on 'The Constitution of the United States' to the eleventh edition of the *Encyclopaedia Britannica*.

There are seven portraits of Bryce: (i) by Arthur Cope (1880 or 1881) in the possession of Lady Bryce, (ii) by A. Delécluse (about 1895–1899) in the possession of Mr. Roland Bryce, (iii) by F. Wilson Forster (about 1899) in the hall of Trinity College, Oxford, (iv) by Sir George Reid (1905) in the common room at Oriel College, (v) by Ernest Moore (1907) in the National Portrait Gallery, (vi) by Seymour Thomas (about 1912) in the National Liberal Club, (vii) by (Sir) William Orpen (1914) in the Aberdeen Art Gallery. A cartoon appeared in *Vanity Fair* 25 February 1893.

[*The Times*, 23 and 31 January 1922, 29 March 1927; *The Times Literary Supplement*, 31 March 1927; H. A. L. Fisher, *James Bryce*, 2 vols., 1927, and *Viscount Bryce of Dechmont, O.M., 1838–1922*, in *Proceedings* of the British Academy, vol. xii, 1926; J. A. Spender, *Life of Sir Henry Campbell-Bannerman*, 2 vols., 1923; Georges Lacour-Gayet, *Allocution à l'occasion du décès de M. le Vte James Bryce*, 1922; R. L. Archer, *Secondary Education in the Nineteenth Century*, 1921; Justin McCarthy, *British Political Leaders*, 1903; Lord Morley, *Recollections*, 2 vols., 1917.]

E. I. CARLYLE.

BUCHANAN, SIR GEORGE WILLIAM (1854–1924), diplomatist, was born at Copenhagen 25 November 1854, the fifth son of Sir Andrew Buchanan, first baronet, of Dunburgh [q.v.], by his wife, Frances Katharine, daughter of the Very Rev. Edward Mellish, dean of Hereford, and sister of Sir George Mellish [q.v.], lord justice of appeal. He was educated at Wellington College, and entered the diplomatic service in 1876. He served first under his father, who was then ambassador at Vienna, subsequently in the Foreign Office, and afterwards as third secretary at Rome in 1878. Promoted to be second secretary in 1879, he was appointed to Tokio, and travelled thither across America where he spent some time. He returned to Vienna in 1882, and, after periods in the Foreign Office and at Berne, became in 1893 chargé d'affaires at Darmstadt, at that time an important post of observation, since members of the Russian, German, and English royal families were frequent visitors to the grand duke, and valuable information was thus often obtainable. Buchanan was also brought into touch with Queen Victoria owing to her close relationship with the Darmstadt court. In 1898 he served as British agent on the Venezuela Boundary Arbitration tribunal at Paris, and in 1900 was promoted to be secretary of embassy (counsellor) at Rome, being transferred to Berlin in 1901. In 1903 Buchanan became agent and consul-general at Sofia, a difficult post, for much depended on his personal relations with Prince Ferdinand of Bulgaria. The period of his mission was an important one since it covered the declaration of Bulgarian independence and the recognition of Prince Ferdinand as king in 1908, whereby the agency became a legation and Buchanan became envoy-extraordinary. He was transferred to The Hague the same year.

Buchanan was appointed ambassador at St. Petersburg in 1910. Relations between England and Russia were cordial, but, in spite of the Anglo-Russian Agreement of 1907, misunderstandings, especially over Persia, were not infrequent. After a year or so the Balkan question became acute and the two countries co-operated for the maintenance of European peace. But there was always a strong pro-German party at St. Petersburg, and constant co-operation was necessary between Buchanan and M. Sazonoff, the foreign minister, in Russia, and between Sir Edward Grey, Sir Arthur Nicolson (Lord Carnock, q.v.), and the Russian ambassador, Count Benckendorff, in England, in order to prevent the wrecking of the Agreement: had they failed, history might have been entirely changed. From St. Petersburg Buchanan anxiously watched the progress of events in the Balkans during 1912 and 1913; the Serbo-Bulgarian alliance, the formation of the Balkan League, the first Balkan War, the Austro-Russian quarrel over Serbia which threatened to involve all Europe, the rupture of the Balkan alliance, the second Balkan War, and the Treaty of Bucharest. The events of these years intensified the rivalry between the Triple Alliance (Germany, Austria, and Italy) and the Triple Entente (Great Britain, France, and Russia), and Buchanan realized the greater solidarity of the former, since England's position in the Entente was always uncertain. Impracticable therefore though he knew it must be, owing to the hostility of English public opinion, he advocated in February 1914 an Anglo-Russian alliance on the ground that if Germany knew that France and Russia could count on the support of England she would never risk war.

It was not only over foreign affairs that there was cause for anxiety: internal discontent in Russia grew apace, and Buchanan agreed with the German ambassador's prediction that war would be followed by revolution. When the crisis of 1914 occurred Buchanan was just going on leave: his health was indifferent, and he had had serious thoughts of accepting the offer of a transfer to Vienna, but had been persuaded to remain at St. Petersburg. After the outbreak of war Buchanan's efforts were directed to obtaining the maximum of effort on the part of Russia, and later, to combating pro-German influences and demands for a separate peace. In so acting he was brought into constant touch with the emperor and empress, and he never hesitated to speak the truth to them, sometimes bluntly. Buchanan liked them both. The emperor he considered a lovable man, a true and loyal ally, and, despite appearances to the contrary, a ruler who, with the interests of his people at heart, was yet following a course which would lead his country and his family to ruin. He described the empress as a good woman, but considered that her reactionary influence on the emperor was instrumental in causing the final catastrophe. Owing to his outspokenness Buchanan made enemies, and he was later bitterly attacked by certain Russian exiles, though their charges against him were obviously absurd.

During the years 1914 to 1917 Buchanan watched the gradual decline of the Russian empire; first, the enthusiasm of the early days and the outbursts of loyalty, then the defeats of 1915, the utter incompetence of the administration and the weakness of the emperor. Buchanan attained a position of great personal influence in Russia, and in 1916 he was granted the freedom of the city of Moscow. In February 1917 he reported that the government and majority of the people were bent on fighting the war to a finish, but that the situation arising from the incompetence of the government was so serious that he doubted whether Russia could face a fourth winter campaign. The political and economic position was such that disagreeable surprises might be at hand. A month later they came, the revolution occurred, and the emperor abdicated (15 March). Buchanan was instructed to recognize the provisional government, but he took a pessimistic view of the situation and foretold a period of revolution and counter-revolution ; he did not think Russia ripe for democratic government. Although he abandoned hope of a successful Russian offensive, all his efforts were still concentrated against a separate peace. On behalf of the British government Mr. Arthur Henderson visited St. Petersburg in the spring of 1917 with the apparent intention of superseding Buchanan, but wiser counsels prevailed, and Henderson returned to England. Kerensky, who had become head of the provisional government, was overthrown in November 1917 and he was succeeded by the Bolsheviks, who concluded an armistice with Germany.

Buchanan left Russia for England in January 1918. He remained for a time unemployed, but his advice was sought on Russian questions. He consistently advocated armed intervention in Russia on the ground that to leave Russia to her fate might result in Germany obtaining control over her resources, while the consolidation of Bolshevik power would mean the dissemination of communism throughout Asia and Europe. In 1919 he was appointed ambassador at Rome. He retired in 1921.

Tall and handsome, an excellent linguist, with rather an elaborate manner, he was a typical example of the Victorian diplomatist. He had a very wide knowledge of foreign countries and foreign affairs, and great powers of observation and deduction. In his dealings with foreign governments he was always courteous, outspoken, and firm; and with his own government honest, straightforward, and loyal. He was a good shot and horseman, and was widely read in French, German, and Italian, as well as in English literature, and translated parts of Goethe's *Faust* and selections from Dante into English.

Buchanan married in 1885 Lady Georgina Meriel (died 1922), daughter of Allen Alexander, sixth Earl Bathurst, and had one daughter. Lady Georgina was a woman of remarkable individuality and of very great assistance to Buchanan in all his posts. She distinguished herself particularly during the War in the organization of the hospital provided for the Russian wounded by the British colony in St. Petersburg, and after returning to England in organizing relief for Russian refugees. When the women's battalion was seized by the Bolsheviks, after the defence of the Winter Palace in 1917, it was largely due to Lady Georgina's firmness and courage that its members were saved from outrage.

Buchanan was created K.C.M.G. in 1909, G.C.M.G. in 1913, and G.C.B. in 1915, besides receiving several foreign decorations. He was admitted a privy councillor in 1910. He died in London 20 December 1924.

[*The Times*, 22 December 1924; Sir George Buchanan, *My Mission to Russia, and other Diplomatic Memories*, 1923; private information; personal knowledge.] ONSLOW.

BURGE, HUBERT MURRAY (1862–1925), headmaster of Winchester College, bishop of Southwark, and afterwards of Oxford, was born 9 August 1862 at Kingston, Jamaica. He was the younger son of the Rev. Milward Rodon Burge, by his wife, Mary Louisa Raffaella, daughter of Matthew Guerrin Price, of Guernsey. His father was a chaplain in India from 1852 to 1869, first at Meerut, and later to Bishop Milman of Calcutta. Burge was sent to Marlborough College in September 1876, but left a year later to enter Bedford grammar school, which was at that time under the headmastership of James Surtees Phillpotts. He went up as a scholar to University College, Oxford, in 1882, and had a good all-round career as an undergraduate. He obtained a first class in classical moderations in 1883, and a second class in 1886 in *literae humaniores*. A big strong man, he was also a useful athlete, and, though not in the Oxford cricket eleven, batted and bowled with some success in trial games.

After leaving Oxford, Burge was appointed in 1887 sixth-form master at Wellington College, under the headmastership of Edward Charles Wickham. In 1890 he returned to Oxford on being elected fellow and tutor of University College. There he remained for the next ten years. His work as a tutor was successful, and he reached a position of great influence in the college. Popularity with the undergraduates was assured by his kindly sympathy with their interests and pursuits. He was appointed dean of the college in 1895. At the age of thirty-five Burge decided to take orders, and was ordained deacon in 1897 and priest in the following year by William Stubbs, bishop of Oxford.

In 1900 Burge was elected to succeed William Mordaunt Furneaux, afterwards dean of Winchester, as headmaster of Repton School, but he only held the office for two terms, and then, somewhat to the concern of the governors who had chosen him, resigned in order to become headmaster of Winchester College (1901). Burge was the first headmaster who had not been himself a Wykehamist. It was the expressed intention of those who appointed him that he should change the curriculum of Winchester in order to bring it more into line with modern views of public-school education. He took an early opportunity of making his views clear to the staff, but met with strong opposition. With characteristic tact he allowed his plan of reform to drop for the time being, and within twelve months found a strong body of opinion in favour of changes which had at first appeared impracticable. Burge's plan was to give boys, when they reached a certain age and a certain position in the school, a wide choice of alternatives upon which they might specialize, instead of devoting their attention to subjects for which they were unsuited. His headmastership was regarded as successful, and the alterations which he made as advantageous. At Winchester, as elsewhere, he was respected for his high character and his special gifts of personal sympathy.

After ten years' work at Winchester Burge's health broke down, and he was obliged to go away to recuperate. When he was about to return to work Mr. Asquith offered him the bishopric of Southwark (1911). He accepted the appointment, and although he had no experience at all of parochial work, he discharged the duties of the bishopric with remarkable efficiency. In some ways he was helped, rather than hampered, by the fact that he was new to the work. His strong common sense enabled him to take wide views, and his capacity for making friends stood him in good stead. He worked with great energy, and never spared himself. His duties were made more difficult by the constant necessity for raising money by subscriptions for the various organizations of his diocese, with its dense population and closely packed parishes, and the strain told severely upon his physical powers.

In 1919 Burge was appointed to succeed Charles Gore as bishop of Oxford. By this time his position was established, and his fitness for the episcopal bench had become clear to all. The only doubt was whether his health would be equal to his new duties. He was welcomed at Oxford, which his old connexion with the university made familiar to him. He was appointed to the see at a time when changes were impending both in the life of the Church and in that of the university. His influence in the inner circles of the Church grew, and he was more and more consulted by those in responsible positions in the state, especially upon questions of educational reform. Burge made himself beloved by his clergy because he combined the qualities of fairness, sympathy, and simplicity in a high degree. He had also a good memory for names and faces, and could pick up quickly the threads of conversation with people whom he had once met. He was an admirable counsellor, so that men naturally went to him for guidance, confident that they would secure his sympathetic attention. In the questions that from time to time caused divided opinions in the Church his attitude was marked by the same breadth of view. He took pains to understand the opinions of those with whom he was not in complete agreement, he was singularly free from prejudice, and was always willing to learn by experience.

In 1907 Burge was elected an honorary fellow of his college, and from 1911 he was sub-prelate of the Order of St. John of Jerusalem in England. In 1918 he was appointed clerk of the closet in ordinary to King George V; he was select preacher at Oxford from 1899 to 1902 and from 1920 to 1921.

Burge's health was undermined by repeated attacks of influenza, which weakened him, and during his latter years, although he never relaxed his labours, he was not a robust man. He died of pneumonia 10 June 1925.

Burge married in 1898 Evelyn, youngest daughter of Dr. James Franck Bright [q.v.], master of University College, Oxford, and had one son and one daughter.

An oil portrait of Burge, painted by George Harcourt in 1921, is at the Diocesan House, Carshalton; replicas are at Winchester College and the Old Rectory, Huish, Wiltshire. A posthumous oil portrait is at Cuddesdon College. A cartoon by 'Spy' appeared in *Vanity Fair* 2 July 1903.

[*The Times*, 11 June 1925; private information.] A. Cochrane.

BURNET, JOHN (1863–1928), classical scholar, was born at Edinburgh 9 December 1863, the eldest child of John Burnet, advocate, by his wife, Jessie, daughter of Dr. James Cleghorn Kay, R.N. He was educated at the Royal High School, Edinburgh, and was also for a few months at a school near Geneva. In October 1880 he matriculated at the university of Edinburgh, where he pursued the study of Latin and Greek, and began that of Sanskrit. He won there the Vans Dunlop scholarship in classics, and a little later the first open classical scholarship at Balliol College, Oxford. After paying a short visit to Paris, where he attended lectures at the Sorbonne and the Collège de France, Burnet went into residence at Oxford in October 1883. There, besides being placed in the first class in classical moderations (1884) and in *literae humaniores* (1887), he won the Taylorian scholarship in French (1885) and was *proxime accessit* for the Boden scholarship in Sanskrit. While he was an undergraduate he preferred to follow his own lines of study, even at the risk of leaving considerable gaps in the conventional programme of preparation for the schools. Like many of his contemporaries he was specially influenced by Richard Lewis Nettleship [q.v.], but he showed no particular interest in philosophy.

Burnet's first attempt to win a fellowship was not successful, and he left Oxford in order to become private assistant to Lewis Campbell [q.v.], professor of Greek at St. Andrews University. With his work there under Campbell began his lifelong concern with the philosophy of Plato. Campbell was a pioneer in the attempt to determine, largely upon 'stylometric' considerations, the chronological order of the Platonic Dialogues, and Burnet became convinced not only of the rightness of Campbell's methods, but of the correctness in the main of the results attained by them. After five months at St. Andrews he made a brief trial of school teaching at Harrow (1888), but did not find the work congenial. Fortunately, he was soon after elected to a prize fellowship at Merton

College, Oxford, and entered into residence there in 1889. The leisure which the position gave him was employed in increasing his knowledge of Aristotle, partly under the guidance of Ingram Bywater [q.v.], and in planning a commentary on the *Nicomachean Ethics*, which he did not complete until considerably later (1899).

After some experience of temporary professorial work at the universities of Edinburgh and St. Andrews in 1890 and 1891, Burnet was in 1891 elected professor of Greek at the latter university upon the resignation of Campbell, and occupied the chair there until he resigned it in 1926. He lived and worked at St. Andrews until his death. From the time of a grave illness in 1923 his health grew worse in spite of occasional rallies. In 1926 he was able to fulfil an engagement to deliver the Sather lectures in classical literature in the university of California; but the summer heat of Chicago, where he also lectured, exhausted his strength, and on his return to St. Andrews he was unable to continue his work as professor. He died at St. Andrews 26 May 1928.

Burnet married in 1894 Mary, daughter of John Farmer [q.v.], organist at Harrow and at Balliol College, and had one daughter.

During the whole tenure of his chair Burnet proved himself an exceptionally inspiring and successful teacher by his striking personality and his command of his whole subject, winning the affectionate admiration of generations of his students. He took a large part in the work of university administration. He had a wide knowledge of the systems of higher education in other countries, and held clear and firm views upon the proper methods of its organization. He occupied several important posts upon educational committees and boards, and was active in promoting the popularization of humanistic culture in Scotland through the Classical Association of Scotland. His services to education were not diminished by his occasional failures to secure the adoption of some of the policies which he advocated.

To the world of scholarship in the narrower sense Burnet's greatest contribution was his critical edition, in the 'Oxford Classical Texts' series, of the whole text of the works of Plato (1900–1913); this superseded all previous editions. It is based on a wide and soundly-estimated foundation of the manuscript evidence, and is guided by a close knowledge of Platonic vocabulary, idiom, and style. Burnet's judgements on disputed points are sober and sane, and the text is, upon the whole, a conservative one. The same characteristics mark his edition of the text of the *Nicomachean Ethics* of Aristotle, which is practically identical with that of Bywater. His commentaries on the *Phaedo* (1911), *Euthyphro*, *Apology*, and *Crito* (1924) are models of conciseness and lucidity, and are full of original observations upon Platonic usages. He designed a new *Lexicon Platonicum*, but although he laboured at it, did not proceed far in its construction. His commentary on the *Ethics* contains much that is fresh and enlightening, but his work on Aristotle, of whose philosophy he never acquired the same wide and intimate knowledge as he had of Plato's, perhaps scarcely reaches the same level as his work on Plato. The mind of Aristotle was never as congenial to him as that of Plato.

In his *Early Greek Philosophy* (1892, 3rd ed. 1920), Burnet did not carry his detailed study down beyond Aristotle, and indeed he gave no systematic account of the philosophy of Aristotle. On the other hand, he several times revised and restated his views on the Pre-Socratics, withdrawing some of his more venturesome speculations, but repeating his general results in a form which has won the acceptance of most scholars. In his account of these thinkers he keeps steadily in view and vividly expresses the historic background of their lives and thoughts. For the English reader he antiquated previous accounts, and effectively removed the misleading veil which had been cast over them by Hegel and the Hegelians. He utilized the contributions to this work of correction and interpretation made by Tannery, Baeumker, and Diels, but his agreement with them is the result of his own independent investigation of the evidence.

Burnet's *Greek Philosophy, Part I, Thales to Plato* (1914) adds to a summary statement of his views on these early cosmological thinkers an equally original account of the Sophists, Socrates, and Democritus. But its most valuable part is its masterly account of the life, character, and whole philosophy of Plato. It is brilliantly written, and is incomparably the best treatment in English of its subject. Burnet accepts as trustworthy evidence for the career and thought of Plato most of the Letters, and assumes as now ascertained facts the dates of composition of most of the Dialogues. In his account of the development of Plato's thought he draws a firm line between a Socratic period and a later period in which Plato is expounding his own philosophy; and he attributes to Plato a consciousness and acknowledgement of his passage from discipleship to independence. He regards Plato as in his later works criticizing his master's teaching on physics, theory of knowledge, metaphysics, and politics.

As Burnet continued his study of Plato, he became more and more convinced that the representation by Plato of the teaching of his master was intended by him as history, and that it in fact was so. Thus Burnet was led to ascribe to Socrates, and even to early Pythagoreans, much doctrine (including the 'theory of Forms') which previous scholars believed to have originated with Plato himself; and he threw back into the fifth century much that, according to them, belongs to the fourth. For this thesis or canon of interpretation Burnet never fully stated his case, and upon the whole it may be said that, while from some competent scholars it has won enthusiastic adherence, it is by most regarded as paradoxical and respectfully rejected.

Burnet's title to the fame which his work enjoys both at home and abroad rests securely upon his inspiring force as a teacher, upon his edition of the text of Plato, upon his classic and convincing account of the beginnings of Greek science and philosophy, upon his minute acquaintance with and vivid sense of the niceties of Platonic vocabulary and idiom, upon his long and deeply-meditated presentment of the philosophy of Plato, whom he admired and loved above all writers and thinkers, and upon the freshness of view and the distinction of style which mark all his writings.

[*Memoir* by Lord Charnwood in *Essays and Addresses by John Burnet* (with photograph portrait), 1929; W. L. Lorimer and A. E. Taylor, *John Burnet, 1863–1928*, in *Proceedings* of the British Academy (with bibliography), vol. xiv, 1928; personal knowledge.]

J. A. Smith.

BURNEY, Sir CECIL, first baronet (1858–1929), admiral of the fleet, was born in Jersey, 15 May 1858, the second son of Captain Charles Burney, R.N., for many years superintendent of Greenwich Hospital School, by his wife, Catherine Elizabeth, daughter of Charles Jones, of La Ferrière, Jersey. He was educated at the Royal Naval Academy, Gosport, and entered the *Britannia* as a naval cadet in July 1871. He went to sea as a midshipman in October 1873, served for three years in the flagships of the Pacific and American stations, and was promoted sub-lieutenant in October 1877. The next three years were spent in educational courses and in short appointments in the trooping ship *Serapis* and in the royal yacht, from which he was promoted to the rank of lieutenant. He then joined the *Carysfort*, corvette, one of the vessels of Lord Clanwilliam's detached squadron, which was afterwards merged into the Mediterranean fleet during the Egyptian campaign of 1882. This gave Burney an opportunity of war service ashore, and he was in charge of a Gatling gun at the actions of Mahatu and Kassassin in August 1882. In the same year he accompanied the mission led by (Sir) Charles Warren [q.v.] across the desert in order to capture the Arabs who had seized and murdered Professor Edward Henry Palmer [q.v.], Captain William John Gill [q.v.], and Lieutenant Harold Charrington; he also took part in the operations against Osman Digna near Suakin in 1884.

On returning to England Burney spent two years in the gunnery schools at Portsmouth and Devonport. Then followed over five and a half years' service as gunnery lieutenant in the North American Reserve and Channel squadrons. On promotion to commander in January 1893 he was appointed to the *Hawke* and served in the Mediterranean for three years; and in 1896 he went to Portland in command of the boys' training establishment in the *Boscawen* and *Minotaur* for three and a half years until September 1899, being promoted captain in January 1898. After commanding the *Hawke* in the naval manœuvres of 1900, he commissioned the *Sappho* for service on the south-east coast of America, but was soon transferred to the Cape station during the South African War. His ship struck the Durban bar when in charge of a pilot on 3 May 1901, and Burney had to bring her home. In May 1902 he became flag-captain to Rear-Admiral Atkinson-Willes in the Home fleet, and remained with him and his successor, Rear-Admiral Poë, until June 1904. He then spent a year (1904–1905) in command of the ex-Chilean battleship *Triumph* in the Channel fleet. His successful work in training boys at Portland led to his appointment in July 1905 to the *Impregnable* as inspecting captain of all boys' training ships, a post which he held until his promotion to flag rank in 1909. He thus spent, in all, six years in supervising the training of boys.

Burney's first appointment to flag rank was in the Plymouth division of the Home fleet for one year. From February 1911, when he took command of the fifth cruiser squadron, he was continuously on full pay for nine years. At the end of 1911 he took command of the Atlantic fleet, with the acting rank of vice-admiral, transferring to the third battle squadron in 1912, shortly before reaching confirmed vice-admiral's rank. This squadron was on special service in the Mediterranean, and the disturbances which arose in Montenegro and Albania at the close of the second Balkan War led to the dispatch, arranged by the British foreign secretary, Sir Edward Grey, of an international naval force to Antivari on the Montenegrin coast in April 1913. Burney's squadron was sent in order to secure that an Englishman should be senior officer of the combined fleet. Burney took command and handled the highly delicate and difficult situation, in which his firm manner and rugged mien stood him in good stead, with great ability, and he received a special commendation both from the Foreign Office and from the Admiralty. He had to secure unanimity of action between the naval forces of the five Powers represented, as well as resolve the differences between the turbulent Balkan States ashore. He established a pacific blockade of the coast during April and May of 1913, and then from May to November commanded the international force occupying Scutari, which the Montenegrins had captured, until the trouble was finally settled by the conclusion of peace. He was created K.C.B. in the summer of 1913, and on the termination of the Scutari affair he was gazetted K.C.M.G.

On his return to England at the end of 1913 Burney took over the command of the second and third fleets, then in partial reserve, and the early part of 1914 was occupied in preparing for the test mobilization of that summer. On the outbreak of the European War in August these fleets were organized as the Channel fleet, with the duty of protecting the Channel from enemy raids. In December 1914 Burney went to the first battle squadron of the grand fleet, being second in command under Lord Jellicoe. At the battle of Jutland (31 May 1916) his squadron was the rear of the line, and was more heavily engaged than the rest of the battleships of the main fleet. His flagship, the *Marlborough*, was torpedoed, and during the night he transferred his flag to the *Revenge*. He was promoted admiral a few days after the battle of Jutland, and was made G.C.M.G. for his services in the action.

In November 1916, when Jellicoe was appointed first sea lord, Burney joined the board of Admiralty as second sea lord. Sir Eric Geddes became first lord in July 1917, and on his reorganization of the board in the following September, Burney left the Admiralty and soon afterwards went to Rosyth as commander-in-chief, coast of Scotland; there he remained until appointed in March 1919 to be commander-in-chief at Portsmouth. A year later, owing to prolonged ill-health, he was relieved of the command at his own request. He was promoted admiral of the fleet in the following November, created a baronet for his war services in January 1921, and promoted to G.C.B. in 1922. He died at his home, Upham House, Hampshire, 5 June 1929.

Burney married in 1884 Lucinda Marion, second daughter of George Richards Burnett, of London, and had one son and two daughters. His son, Commander Charles Dennistoun Burney, R.N. (born 1888), who succeeded to the baronetcy, invented during the European War the paravane, a device for protecting ships against mines, which brought him a large fortune.

Burney was a fine seaman of the old school, with a deep sense of loyalty to his chiefs. In handling ships and fleets he had the natural ease and confidence of a born sailor. A man of powerful physique, in his early days he excelled in boxing and feats of strength. Although of somewhat austere demeanour, his patent sincerity won him the complete confidence and affection of those who served under him throughout his long sea service.

[Official records; private information.]

V. W. Baddeley.

BURNSIDE, WILLIAM (1852–1927), mathematician, was born in London 2 July 1852, the elder son of William Burnside, merchant, of 7 Howley Place, Paddington, London, by his wife, Emma Knight. His father was of Scottish ancestry; his grandfather, settling in London, had been a partner in the book-selling firm of Seeley and Burnside.

Left an orphan at the age of six, Burnside was educated at Christ's Hospital—then situated in Newgate Street—and achieved distinction in both the grammar school and the mathematical school. He won a mathematical scholarship at St. John's College, Cambridge, and began residence there in October 1871. In his day, all able mathematical students in the university were prepared for their tripos by private 'coaches', Burnside's 'coach' being W. H. Besant, one of the few rivals of the well-known Edward John Routh [q.v.]. Among his contemporaries were George Chrystal, of Peterhouse (afterwards professor of mathematics successively at the universities of St. Andrews and Edinburgh), and (Sir) Robert Forsyth Scott, also of St. John's College and afterwards its master. In April 1873 Burnside migrated to Pembroke College, and was enrolled a foundation scholar in June. In the mathematical tripos of 1875 he was bracketed second wrangler with Chrystal; in the immediately subsequent examination for the Smith's prizes, Burnside was first and Chrystal second.

Burnside was elected a fellow of Pembroke and appointed a lecturer at the college in 1875; he continued to be a fellow until 1886. College teaching at that time had slight influence upon the most capable students; and lectures by professors, not being directed towards the tripos, were attended by few, if any, undergraduates. A college usually provided the normal courses for average students; some more advanced courses were shared by colleges, in groups; and in addition to the usual college courses, Burnside lectured on hydrodynamics, a subject then developing into importance. He took a few private pupils, and examined occasionally for the tripos; but it soon became apparent that he was devoting himself to mathematical studies beyond the organized range of the tripos.

As an undergraduate, Burnside had proved an expert oar. While still a freshman, he had rowed in the St. John's (Lady Margaret) boat (with J. H. D. Goldie as stroke) when it went head of the river in 1872. After taking his degree, and as long as he continued in residence at Cambridge, he rowed in the Pembroke boat and had a large share in improving its position on the river; his reputation as an oar long survived in college circles. After leaving Cambridge his main recreation was found in fishing during holidays in Scotland, and in this also he developed marked skill. Through all his years his lithe frame retained an unusual power of physical endurance.

In 1885 Burnside was appointed professor of mathematics at the Royal Naval College at Greenwich; and the rest of his teaching life was spent in that post. He retired in 1919. His old college at one time invited him to return as tutor; and again, at a later date, on the death in 1903 of Sir George Gabriel Stokes [q.v.], Pembroke invited him to return as master. Both invitations were declined, mainly because (outside his teaching) the administrative and social details of official duty were irksome to his temperament.

At Greenwich Burnside's work consisted of three ranges. One section was concerned with ballistics, for gunnery and torpedo officers; a second section with mechanics and heat, for engineer officers; and a third with dynamics (especially hydrodynamics), for naval constructors. Both at Cambridge and at Greenwich he bore the reputation of being an excellent teacher. Also, he was in frequent demand as an external examiner for various bodies, and as a referee for papers submitted to the Royal Society and the London Mathematical Society. He was elected a fellow of the Royal Society in 1893, served on the council of the Society from 1901 to 1903, and was awarded a royal medal in 1904. He was president of the London Mathematical Society from 1906 to 1908, having received its De Morgan medal in 1899. In 1900 he was elected an honorary fellow of Pembroke College. He received the honorary degrees of Sc.D. from Dublin University and of LL.D. from Edinburgh University.

Burnside's name will be remembered by his original contributions to mathematics. He published over one hundred and fifty papers. His book, the *Theory of Groups* (1897), is now an acknowledged classic. He left a long manuscript on the *Theory of Probability*, which was published in 1928, after his death. His range of subjects, mainly in pure mathematics (although applied mathematics had been the Cambridge vogue of his earlier years), was extensive. Each of his papers dealt with a definite issue; nothing was elaborated beyond a main result; subsidiary developments were avoided. Even as an undergraduate he had been noted for his style. As a writer he was clear and definite in argument, lucid and terse in exposition. Thus his papers are always brief: many of them consist of only a few pages; the longest of them, which remains of special importance in the then new theory of automorphic functions (1892), and is really a combination of two distinct contributions, occupies only fifty-three pages.

Burnside wrote on hydrodynamics and on the theory of the potential, combining the established methods with the new analysis based on the complex variable. Not a few papers were devoted to elliptic functions; and several to differential geometry, at a time when the subject was receiving little attention in England. He passed from the automorphic functions and their groups of transformations to the general theory of discontinuous groups of finite order; and on this subject he produced some fifty papers, each of them containing some definite contribution to the theory, each marked by clarity and terseness.

With the coming of the European War in 1914 there was a comparative cessation in Burnside's output of papers. Its termination found him interested in the theory of mathematical probability; and he continued to produce fresh investigations. Ultimately, failing health interfered with creative work; but it did not cramp active interest, and he was able to draft an exposition of his views, so far as thought had framed them into systematic theory.

Burnside died at West Wickham, Kent, 21 August 1927, and is buried in the churchyard there. He married in 1886 Alexandrina, daughter of Kenneth Urquhart, of Poolewe, Ross-shire, and had two sons and three daughters.

[*Proceedings* of the Royal Society, vol. cxvii, A, 1928; personal knowledge.]

A. R. Forsyth.

BURT, THOMAS (1837–1922), trade-unionist and liberal politician, was born at Murton Row, a small hamlet in the south-east corner of Northumberland, 12 November 1837. He was the elder son of Peter Burt, a miner, who came of a long line of northern miners, by his wife, Rebecca, daughter of Thomas Weatherburn. To his maternal grandfather Burt always attributed much of his success in life. The old man took a great interest in the boy, and in their long walks together taught him many useful lessons. The Burts and Weatherburns were Primitive Methodists, a fact which had a great influence on Thomas Burt's character.

Burt had very little regular education. Out of four years nominally spent at village schools he did not attend for more than two, owing to the constant interruptions caused by strikes and stoppages and removals from one colliery to another. The day following his tenth birthday he began to work in a mine, and passed through almost every grade of pitwork with all its accompanying dangers. His father, Peter Burt, was an ardent trade-unionist, and was often the victim of his principles. This was the main cause of his frequent removals from one place to another. His son was thus nurtured in trade-unionism, and at the age of about sixteen began to take a part in the movement. He soon realized the need of education, and fortunately for him his father was a reader and had, for a working-man, a well-stocked library. From that time Thomas Burt became an ardent student. In later life he came to be recognized as one of the most cultured members of the House of Commons.

The Northumberland Miners' Mutual Confidence Association was established at the beginning of 1863, and in 1865 Burt was appointed general secretary, a post which he held until 1913. At the time of his appointment a strike was in progress at one of the largest groups of pits in the county. Burt never shirked a fight, but would never advise one until every means of reaching a reasonable settlement had been tried in vain. Throughout his whole career he was noted for his conciliatory methods in all trade disputes.

In 1873 Burt was adopted as liberal candidate for Morpeth, Northumberland, and in 1874 was returned to parliament. He retained this seat until his retirement in 1918, when he had become 'father' of the House of Commons. In his first election address Burt declared in favour of Home Rule for Ireland, adult franchise, payment of members of parliament, shorter parliaments, redistribution of seats, free and unsectarian national education, religious equality, disestablishment and disendowment of the Church, the Permissive Bill, abolition of the game laws, and land law reform. His maiden speech in parliament was in support of Mr. (afterwards Sir) George Trevelyan's Bill for household franchise. Burt spoke but seldom in the House, but when it was known that the member for Morpeth was on his feet, interest was immediately aroused. His name is associated with many reform measures, such as the Employers' Liability Act (1880), factory and workshop legislation, amendments to the Trades Union Acts, and improved Mines Acts for the greater safety of miners. He was secretary to the Board of Trade from 1892 to 1895 in the governments of Mr. Gladstone and Lord Rosebery. During his long membership of the House of Commons, which lasted nearly forty-five years, his goodness of heart and sincerity of purpose earned the affectionate esteem of all its members, irrespective of party.

Burt was one of the British representatives at the Berlin Labour Conference convened by the German Emperor in 1890. He was president of the Trades Union Congress held at Newcastle in 1891, and took part in many international miners' conferences. He was made a privy councillor in 1906, received the honorary degree of D.C.L. from the university of Durham in 1911, and was made a freeman of Newcastle in 1912. From 1882 to 1914 he was president of the International Peace League. During the whole of his life he was a staunch teetotaller.

During the last three years of his life Burt was mostly confined to bed, but he remained cheerful and full of hope for the future of the world. He died at Newcastle 13 April 1922.

Burt married in 1860 his cousin, Mary, daughter of Thomas Weatherburn, a retired colliery engineman. They had four sons and four daughters.

[*The Times*, 15 April 1922; personal knowledge.] W. Straker.

BURY, JOHN BAGNELL (1861–1927), classical scholar and historian, was born at Monaghan 16 October 1861. His father, the Rev. Edward John Bury, who came of the same south Irish stock as the Earls of Charleville, was curate of Monaghan and subsequently rector of Clontibret and canon of Clogher. He married Anna, daughter of Henry Rogers, of Monaghan, 'a very clever woman and a great reader'. John Bagnell was their eldest son.

Having learned the elements of Greek and Latin from his father, whose career as a student at Trinity College, Dublin, had been distinguished, Bury was sent to Foyle College, Londonderry, where Robert Yelverton Tyrrell [q.v.], in conducting an examination in Greek grammar, found that he was quite unable to puzzle the youth. From Foyle College Bury passed to Trinity College, Dublin, where he matriculated in 1878, produced (with (Sir) John Pentland Mahaffy [q.v.], at that time professor of ancient history) an edition of *The Hippolytus of Euripides* in 1881, and graduated in 1882 with a double first class, securing the top place in classics and fourth in mental and moral philosophy. In 1885 he became a fellow of Trinity College, Dublin, and in 1893 was elected to the Erasmus Smith professorship of modern history—a position which he was not required to vacate when in 1898 he was appointed regius professor of Greek. Four years later, in 1902, after it was known that F. W. Maitland did not desire the post, he was chosen to succeed the first Lord Acton as regius professor of modern history in the university of Cambridge; and this chair he retained until he died, at Rome, 1 June 1927, having also held a fellowship at King's College, Cambridge, since 1903. In 1885 Bury had married his second cousin, Jane, daughter of John Carleton Bury, physician, of Mitchelstown, co. Cork, and afterwards of Wisbech; one son was born of the marriage.

As a student in Dublin Bury showed interests of wide variety. His proper business was with classical philology and with philosophy; and among the philosophers none impressed him more strongly than Hegel, whose influence is plainly visible in much of his later work. But the occupations of his leisure were not less significant. Besides listening to music, in which he found an inexhaustible source of enjoyment, he was a voracious reader of poetry, much of which he learned by heart. Browning in particular, whose notice he attracted in 1882 by a paper on the poet's thought, appealed to the young Hegelian; and Swinburne touched another side of a mind whose admiration for pagan antiquity sprang from the convictions afterwards expressed in 'Anima naturaliter pagana' (*Fortnightly Review*, new series, vol. xlix, 1891) and *A History of Freedom of Thought* (1914). But, although he may well have believed, with Hegel, that 'a man ought to know, and can know, all the beautiful of the ancient and modern world', the most enduring mark of Bury's activities in these early days was left by his detailed studies in the field of classical scholarship; for his philological training exercised a powerful effect in later years on the formation of his view of history.

Between 1881 and 1892 Bury the philologist was rapidly becoming an historian. At first his published work was mainly concerned with the interpretation of classical texts and with the problems of comparative philology, a subject in which he moved with an assurance doubtless due in some degree to his study of Sanskrit under Theodor Benfey, as well as Hebrew and Syriac, to which he had devoted six months spent at Göttingen in 1880; but in 1886 four papers appeared, two of them in the first volume of the *English Historical Review*, which show that his mind was already turning to history, and in particular to the history of the later Roman Empire. Four years later, in 1890, he published *The Nemean Odes of Pindar*, which was followed in 1892 by *The Isthmian Odes of Pindar*—two books which are at once Bury's most notable contribution to classical scholarship in the narrower sense and the link between two periods in his own intellectual life. After this time he did not, indeed, lose interest in the language and literature of the ancient world. His translations into Greek and Latin verse, which he wrote with elegance and ease, continued to appear at intervals until 1895 in the magazine called *Kottabos*, of which from 1888 to 1891 he was editor; until the early years of the twentieth century, learned journals contained frequent communications from him on passages in classical authors, whose number and variety are a clue to the range of his reading; and in 1905 there was published (in the second volume of J. P. Postgate's *Corpus Poetarum Latinorum*) the recension of the *Argonautica* of Valerius Flaccus, which Bury had completed in 1900. Nevertheless, his reputation as an historian had been established in 1889, and to history he turned thenceforward with increasing concentration. In his editions of Pindar Bury was philologist and historian at once. The first of these volumes contains much ingenuity devoted to the development of the theory that in Pindar's poetry certain verbal echoes can be detected which reveal the sequence of thought within the odes—a theory in which criticism induced Bury to make drastic modifications before the publication of the second; but no small part of the value of these books lies in the sympathetic understanding with which a mind by nature and training attuned to the Hellenic mood interprets that view of life to which Pindar gives unrivalled expression.

For the study of later Roman history, in which his writings first reveal his interest in 1886, Bury improved his equipment by learning Russian in 1887 and Hungarian at latest by 1891; and in 1889 he produced what in some ways is his most striking contribution to historical literature—the *History of the Later Roman Empire from Arcadius to Irene* (2 vols). For sheer weight of knowledge it must not be compared with his later work; but the mastery of the original authorities and the maturity of judgement, at once sane and independent, with which through two long volumes he traced the tangled story of the period between A.D. 395 and A.D. 800, in a man of his years were not less than remarkable. At the age of twenty-eight Bury found himself welcomed as an equal by the leaders of historical study both at home and abroad.

After publishing in 1893 a revision of Freeman's *History of Federal Government*, vol. i, and his own *History of the Roman Empire from its foundation to the death of Marcus Aurelius*—his only book on Rome before the death of Theodosius I, and one which was written to order—Bury approached the task for which he was clearly marked. The right, gained by wide and incessant reading, to move, like Gibbon and Freeman, 'to and fro among the ages', and a special interest in the Roman Empire, which Freeman had convinced him was 'the key to European history', gave him peculiar qualifications to produce the long-needed edition of Gibbon's *Decline and Fall*, which, by the addition of notes and appendices, would put at the reader's disposal the accessions to knowledge gained since Gibbon wrote. The first two volumes of this distinguished achievement appeared in 1896, and the seventh and last in 1900. Meanwhile, Bury had been engaged on his *History of Greece to the death of Alexander the Great* (1900), which at once became a standard textbook, and this was followed, after several preliminary studies, by *The Life of St. Patrick and his place in history* (1905)—a work regarded by its author as essentially a chapter in the story of Roman influence in Europe.

It was now, with his powers at their height, that Bury began to publish the memorable series of papers which together form one of his most enduring monuments. 'The treatise De administrando imperio' (*Byzantinische Zeitschrift*, 1906), 'The Ceremonial Book of Constantine Porphyrogennetos' (*English Historical Review*, 1907), *The Constitution of the Later Roman Empire* (1910; the Creighton lecture for 1909), and, above all, *The Imperial Administrative System in the Ninth Century, with a Revised Text of The Kletorologion of Philotheos* (1911) were pronouncements which in six years raised the knowledge of public law and administration in the later Roman Empire to a new plane of precision, and rendered to these studies services comparable with those of Mommsen to the corresponding aspects of the Roman Republic and the Principate. In this period, too, Bury wrote his famous and controversial essay on 'The Chronological Cycle of the Bulgarians' (*Byzantinische Zeitschrift*, 1910; translated into Russian, 1912) and various articles in preparation for *A History of the Eastern Roman Empire from the fall of Irene to the accession of Basil I* (1912), one of his most impressive books, which reveals his scholarship in its full maturity.

Bury now began to be troubled by ill-health. From 1910, when the first warning came, his life was an increasing struggle against physical frailty; and travel, of which all his life he had been fond, now of necessity took more of his time. But his devotion to historical research was not affected; for seventeen years his own undaunted spirit and the sedulous encouragement of his wife enabled him to maintain his literary output at a rate not far below that of his prime. Nevertheless, although the quality of his thought was unimpaired, illness seems for a time to have had an influence on its course. Classical Greece had never lost its appeal to a mind which upheld 'the uncompromising assertion by Reason of her absolute rights throughout the whole domain of thought', and in 1908, despite other occupations, he had delivered at Harvard the lectures published as *The Ancient Greek Historians* (1909)—a work as valuable for the view of history adumbrated by the author as for the light it throws on the writers of whom he treats. But, with his hold on life precarious, Bury went straight to the point. *A History of Freedom of Thought* (1914) has a message, delivered with a fiery vigour which was usually repressed; but marks of the haste with which it was written are to be seen in slips which gave openings for criticism to those who sought for them. To a cognate theme he recurred in calmer mood and rose to what some held to be his greatest heights in attempting the history of an idea—*The Idea of Progress: an inquiry into its origin and growth* (1920). For the intelligible treatment of a subject so vast his learning and his philosophy were admirably combined; but in the narrower field covered by his last great work—the *History of the Later Roman Empire from the death of Theodosius I to the death of Justinian* (1923)—his overwhelming knowledge, though making these two volumes an unrivalled store, by the unconcealed minuteness of its detail produces a result which, as a synthetic interpretation, marks no advance on the far briefer account of the same period to be found in the work of 1889.

The *History* of 1923 is the last of Bury's major books, though it was followed by two volumes of lectures edited after his death—*The Invasion of Europe by the Barbarians* (1928) and a *History of the Papacy in the 19th Century* (*1864–1878*) (1930). In the closing years of his life the output of articles still continued, but such time as illness left free for study was largely claimed by his contributions to the *Cambridge Ancient History*, of which he was an editor. The published bibliography of his writings contains 369 entries.

Among undergraduate students Bury's influence was slight with all but a few: his main occupation in the professorial chairs which he held for thirty-four years was the conduct and encouragement of research. In the mind which he brought to this task two strands can be discerned, never wholly interwoven and both the outcome of his early training in philology and philosophy. As philologist, Bury found history in the first place a series of problems presented by the written sources, which at the start must be subjected to the treatment of the textual critic; but, even when the texts had been put in order and the historian came to elicit the tale they told, he was apt still to regard his material as no more than a succession of puzzles to be solved in turn. This tendency was accentuated by a belief, set out in his paper 'Cleopatra's Nose' (*R*(*ationalist*) *P*(*ress*) *A*(*ssociation's*) *Annual*, 1916), to which he held with increasing tenacity in later life—that, although the power of chance is reduced as civilization becomes more complex, in the past the course of history has so often been deflected by what may reasonably be described as accidents that it is idle to look for general causes to explain the trend of events throughout a period. The consequences of this emphasis on the element of contingency in human affairs were made still more noticeable by a reluctance on Bury's part, perhaps strengthened by the example of Kant, to let his own personality appear, or to put upon facts any interpretation which they do not inevitably yield of themselves. Better to leave the facts a mere sequence than present them as points in a logical development which, however probable, cannot be proved; and for this reason it was only in the modern age, for which evidence is abundant, that he believed it theoretically possible by legitimate means to display the inner nexus of events. In his inaugural lecture at Cambridge he had made a protest—of which the timeliness was demonstrated by the widespread misunderstanding with which it was received—against all attempts to treat history as the handmaid of other disciplines. The historian has a higher task than merely to supply a background to the great works of literature, or to provide guidance for the statesman and examples for the moral philosopher. 'History is a science, no less and no more', having a purpose and a method of its own; and among the other sciences it claims to move as an equal. But in Bury's hands, when applied to the scanty evidence for the periods which chiefly engaged his attention, the science yielded results which even in his longest books are enshrined in a series of monographs rather than in the related chapters of a coherent whole. With truth, so far at least as his most elaborate contributions to historical literature are concerned, Lord Morley observed that Bury did not 'cast his shadow on the page'; and the observation was not all praise.

Nevertheless, sceptical as Bury may often have been about the adequacy of the material for its attainment, he was clear about the end at which history should aim. Bury the philosopher had no doubt that European history is a unity, that the present is only to be explained by reference to the past, which it takes up and which—if progress is a fact, though Bury never admitted it to be more than a probable assumption—it transcends, and that the ultimate justification of all historical study is its essential service to generations present and to come in making them intelligible to themselves and so enabling them to act the more fully in accordance with the rules of reason. In practice, the clearest consequence of this belief was his emphasis on continuity, which he stressed with special vigour in his most familiar field. 'No "Byzantine Empire" ever began to exist; the Roman Empire did not come to an end until 1453' (*History*, 1889, i, v). But in this continuum he found the strongest thread in political institutions. Although he was well aware that all human experience is material for history, the life of the masses yielded less of relevance to his purpose; and religion did not attract him. Constantine had 'inaugurated a millennium in which reason was enchained, thought was enslaved, and knowledge made no progress' (*History of Freedom of Thought*, p. 52). It was public law and administration which offered the clearest evidence of the abiding influence of the past, and it is for his contributions to the study of these that Bury may well be remembered longest as an historian of New Rome. To New Rome he gave his best work, despite his lack of sympathy with the religion which dominates its history. This lack debarred him from the fullest understanding of the people with whom he had to deal; but his interest in the empire of Constantinople was well grounded. Although in his writings as a man Bury sternly repressed the poet that had been visible in his youth, the Hellenist was always unconcealed; and the later Roman Empire could justly claim him because its 'civilization . . . was the continuation of that of ancient Greece'.

Of medium height, slightly built, with reddish hair and a sanguine complexion, Bury long continued to look absurdly young; and of that youthful appearance, which enabled the professor to be mistaken for an undergraduate, many stories were told. He was a good talker: 'a talk with Bury was almost like being present at the making of history.' As he talked he grew absorbed in his subject; and a walk along the beach at Southwold, where for many years he had a cottage, was a leisurely affair, broken by long pauses while Bury elaborated a theme or marshalled his evidence. On his encyclopaedic knowledge he could always draw with astonishing readiness. In his younger days, before his life was clouded by the illness against which he fought with superb courage, he was happy and light-hearted; and to the last his courage never failed.

Bury was doctor *honoris causa* of the universities of Aberdeen, Dublin, Durham, Edinburgh, Glasgow, and Oxford, an honorary fellow of Oriel College, Oxford, a fellow of the British Academy, and a corresponding member of the Imperial Academy of Sciences, Petrograd, the Hungarian Academy of Science, the Massachusetts Historical Society, the Rumanian Academy, and the Russian Archaeological Institute at Constantinople.

A portrait is to be found in *Selected Essays of J. B. Bury*, edited by Harold Temperley (1930).

[*A Bibliography of the Works of J. B. Bury*, compiled, *with a Memoir*, by Norman H. Baynes, 1929; 'The Historical Ideas of J. B. Bury', editorial introduction to *Selected Essays of J. B. Bury*, edited by Harold Temperley, 1930; private information; personal knowledge.]

N. H. Baynes.
H. M. Last.

BUTLER, FRANK HEDGES (1855–1928), balloonist and pioneer of flying, was born in London 17 December 1855, the fifth son of James Butler, wine merchant, of Hollywood, Wimbledon Park, by his wife, Frances Mary, eldest daughter of William Hedges. He was educated at private schools at Brighton and Upper Clapton and, after travelling on the continent and in South America, entered the family business of Hedges & Butler (founded in 1667), Regent Street, London, in which he became a partner in 1882. He married in 1880 Ada (died 1905), daughter of Joseph Bartholomew Tickle, wool broker, of London and Sydney, and by her had one daughter, who shared many of his motoring and ballooning adventures.

Hedges Butler was one of the first persons in England to own a motor-car. He acquired a Benz car in 1897, and in the same year was appointed first honorary treasurer of the newly-formed Automobile Club of Great Britain, a post which he held until 1902. It was the shortcomings of a motor-car, and the consequent abandonment of a motor tour in Scotland in September 1901, which led Butler to turn his attention to the air. A balloon ascent was suggested instead of the tour, and Butler and his daughter, accompanied by the Hon. Charles Stewart Rolls [q.v.], went up in a balloon, the *City of York*, from the Crystal Palace, with Mr. Stanley Spencer in control. While in the air over London, Butler suggested the formation of an Aero Club as a branch of the Automobile Club. The suggestion bore fruit, and the Aero Club of the United Kingdom was registered at Somerset House in October 1901, and the first balloon ascent organized by the club took place in November.

The club (which in 1910 became the Royal Aero Club) brought together inventors and sportsmen, and supplied them with a ground at Shell Beach, Isle of Sheppey, suitable for their experiments. When the club was founded no power-driven aeroplane had yet been flown, and the members were chiefly interested in the balloon and the airship. When, however, the invention of flying became a reality, Hedges Butler took a keen interest in the early experiments, and in 1908, when the American inventor, Wilbur Wright, came over to France in order to demonstrate his aeroplane, Butler was one of the first two Englishmen to fly as passenger with him.

By 1907 Hedges Butler had completed one hundred balloon ascents, including a solo flight which established a record for distance in England (1902), and the world's longest cross-Channel balloon voyage (London to Caen, 1905).

As a result of the successful flights by Wilbur Wright in France in 1908, the Aero Club undertook the training of aeroplane pilots, to whom, from 1910 onwards, it issued its certificates; these were recognized by the government when it was decided to establish a national air service. The Aero Club, indeed, played an all-important part in fostering the early development of flying in England, and it was Hedges Butler who inspired the club's activity in this respect and supplied much practical help. Although he did little flying himself after 1908, his interest and enthusiasm never flagged.

Hedges Butler's concern with the air diminished in no way his interest in travel. In the course of his business he often visited the wine-producing countries of Europe, but these journeys only stimulated his enthusiasm, and with great enjoyment he moved widely about the world. He told the story of his adventures in *Five Thousand Miles in a Balloon* (1907), *Through Lapland with Skis and Reindeer* (1917), *Fifty Years of Travel by Land, Water, and Air* (1920), *Round the World* (1924), and *Wine and the Wine Lands of the World* (1926). He was elected F.R.G.S. in 1877.

Hedges Butler had still other interests. He was a violinist of merit, and in 1894 founded the Imperial Institute Orchestral Society, in which he played one of the first violins. He was a man of hospitable nature with a gift for friendship, who enjoyed splendid health, as well as ample means to indulge his many enthusiasms. He died in London 27 November 1928.

A cartoon of Hedges Butler by 'Spy' appeared in *Vanity Fair* 11 December 1907.

[*The Aeroplane*, 5 December 1928; Butler's published works; private information.]

H. A. JONES.

BUTLER, SIR (GEORGE) GEOFFREY (GILBERT) (1887–1929), historian, was born in London 15 August 1887. He was the eighth son and eleventh child of Spencer Perceval Butler, conveyancing counsel, Lincoln's Inn, by his wife, Mary Kendall. He was nephew of George Butler (1819–1890, q.v.), of Arthur Gray Butler [q.v.], and of Henry Montagu Butler [q.v.], and grandson of George Butler (1774–1853, q.v.).

Butler was educated at Clifton College, of the governing body of which he later was a member, and at Trinity College, Cambridge, whence he matriculated in 1906. He was placed in the first class of both parts of the historical tripos, and in his third year was elected by his college to a major scholarship. In his second year he won the chancellor's medal for English verse, and in the year after he had taken his degree (1909–1910) he edited the *Cambridge Review* and became president of the Union. At the end of that year, in June 1910, he was elected a fellow of Corpus Christi College, Cambridge, and was appointed lecturer in history. In 1912 he became librarian of the college, and the years from his election as a fellow until the outbreak of the European War were devoted partly to teaching modern history in his college and partly to familiarizing himself with the Parker manuscripts which were his chief charge as librarian.

From the first, Butler's main historical interest was modern diplomatic history. He regarded a European war in the near future as highly probable and, together with his brother Ralph, who became a fellow of Corpus in October 1913, he did his best to ensure that the undergraduates of his college should have some idea of what such a war would mean. When the War came, Butler, who was debarred by lameness from joining the army, went to the Foreign Office in the spring of 1915 and became a member of the News Department. He was well fitted alike by his historical training and by his literary ability and wit to present the English view of the diplomatic and other controversies. His department was of necessity largely concerned with opinion in the United States, and here again Butler had valuable experience. As an occasional lecturer before the university of Pennsylvania in 1913 and 1914, he had sought to overcome American prejudice in favour of a 'liberal party' and to expound the tory and conservative tradition. He lectured again at the same university in 1916, and in that year he married Elizabeth, eldest daughter of Joseph Levering Jones, a corporation lawyer of Philadelphia. Butler accompanied the Balfour mission to America in 1917, and from 1917–1919 he was director of the British Bureau of Information in the United States at New York. He did excellent work in that position, received the C.B.E. in 1918, and was created K.B.E. in 1919.

When Butler returned to Cambridge in 1919 he devoted himself to three things; to his duties as librarian of Corpus, and in particular to rearranging and cataloguing the incunabula and making the manuscripts more accessible; to his historical teaching; and to promoting conservative principles, as he understood these, among the undergraduates of the university. In 1920 he was appointed by his college praelector in diplomatic history, and as such it became his especial duty to encourage in the college and in the university this means of approach to the consideration of international relations and international law. He did so with marked success, the most notable feature of his teaching being his attitude to the League of Nations. A realist in international affairs, he found in this attitude ground for a firm belief in the importance of the League, insisting that the League could not and should not attempt very much in the first instance, but that provided it did not attempt too much, and judged justly, its influence and authority would necessarily spread. He showed the same realism in his politics. He was, and remained, a convinced conservative, but was intolerant of any conception of conservatism which was not concerned to secure reforms. He brought into being an undergraduate Conservative Association, threw immense energy into his work as its president, and made this body a considerable political force in Cambridge.

In 1923 Butler, to his great satisfaction, was elected burgess for his university. He gave up some of his college teaching, but continued both his university lectures and his work for his Conservative Association. At the same time he threw himself fully into his parliamentary work, giving more regular attendance than custom requires from university members. In 1925 he became parliamentary secretary to Sir Samuel Hoare, then secretary of state for air. In the same year he was a member of the Home Office committee on legal aid for poor persons. In 1927 he was nominated a member of the royal commission on the government of Ceylon, and he took a considerable part in the formulation of the commission's recommendations. The trip to Ceylon, which both Butler and his wife greatly enjoyed, afforded him a much needed rest and change: but undoubtedly his health had been affected by overwork, and the ill effects were aggravated by the fact that his physical disability made it difficult for him to take exercise. After his return he soon began to show signs of ill-health. He paid a short visit to America towards the end of 1928 in connexion with the work of the Employers' Liability Assurance Corporation, of which he was a director. By the time he returned he was seriously ill, and he died in London 2 May 1929. He had no children.

Butler's published works reflected his very varied interests. His work as librarian is represented by the *Edmondes Papers*, published for the Roxburghe Club in 1914, and by *Historical Manuscripts in the Library of Corpus Christi College, Cambridge* (1920). His political and historical studies were embodied in his Pennsylvanian lectures, published under the title of *The Tory Tradition* (1914); in a *Handbook to the League of Nations* (1919 and 1925); in *Studies in Statecraft* (1920); and in *The Development of International Law* (1928), this last being written in collaboration with a former pupil, S. Maccoby, and covering a wide field.

[Private information; personal knowledge.]

W. Spens.

CADBURY, GEORGE (1839–1922), cocoa and chocolate manufacturer and social reformer, was born at Edgbaston, Birmingham, 19 September 1839. He was the third son and fourth child of John Cadbury (1801–1889), tea and coffee dealer and founder of the firm of Cadbury Brothers, cocoa and chocolate manufacturers, by his wife, Candia, daughter of George Barrow, merchant and ship-owner, of Lancaster. The Cadbury family, of West country origin, had settled in Birmingham at the end of the eighteenth century, having been associated with the Society of Friends since the days of John Cadbury, of Burlescombe, Devon, great-great-grandfather of George Cadbury, in whose life the quaker influence remained one of the strongest motive forces.

George Cadbury was educated at home and as a day-boy at a quaker school at Edgbaston. His mother, an ardent temperance worker, died in 1855, and soon afterwards his schooling ended. His wish was to become a surgeon, but circumstances led him into commerce; and in 1856, after a period of employment in the grocery business of Joseph Rowntree [q.v.] at York, he joined his father's cocoa factory in Bridge Street. Birmingham. His elder brother, Richard, had been at work there since 1850. John Cadbury's health failed after his wife's death, with the result that the business declined very seriously, and in April 1861 Richard and George, aged respectively twenty-five and twenty-one, took entire control. It was only after a hard struggle and great personal sacrifice on the part of the two young partners that in 1864 prosperity began to return. George Cadbury was always an abstainer from alcohol and tobacco, but at this early period he also denied himself tea, coffee, and newspapers.

Once the tide had turned, the business expanded rapidly, chiefly because of the Cadburys' timely introduction in 1866, when the adulteration of food was being much discussed, of the first unadulterated British cocoa. In 1866, also, there arose quite naturally, out of the fact that they then usually breakfasted with their workpeople, the 'morning readings'—short religious services, with which work at the factory began for many years thereafter. The Cadburys were also the first employers in Birmingham to institute a weekly half-holiday for their workpeople, in whose welfare they took the closest interest, following the example set by their father. By 1879 the Bridge Street building was inadequate to the firm's needs, and the partners took the opportunity of making their greatest social and economic experiment—the moving of their works into the healthier rural surroundings of Bournville, four miles from Birmingham. The Cadburys were not the first to make a move of this kind, but they were the first to associate with it welfare and educational work in the factory, and, especially, the improvement of housing. Within the business it is scarcely possible to distinguish between the work of the two brothers, who acted in complete harmony until Richard's death in 1899, after which the firm was turned into a company, with George as chairman. The Bournville experiment in housing and town-planning was, however, George Cadbury's own. The success of the new factory made it likely that slum conditions would, if allowed, grow up in its neighbourhood. To avoid this, he bought, between the years 1893 and 1900, some 300 acres of adjoining land, on which he had built about 300 houses up to the date when he founded the Bournville Village Trust, in December 1900. The trust may hold land anywhere in Great Britain, and even the Bournville estate was never intended by George Cadbury to be solely for the benefit of employees of his own business. By 1931 the capital of the trust had increased from £170,000 to over £500,000, and its land to more than a thousand acres.

The Adult School movement was, however, the mainspring of Cadbury's social work. In 1849 he had begun as a teacher in an adult school in Birmingham, and he continued to teach until the age of seventy-two, riding, or latterly bicycling, into the city at six o'clock on Sunday mornings to take his bible class. Hundreds of Birmingham men learned from him to read and write. From the insight thus gained into working-class conditions arose his interest in housing and factory reform. His love of the country led him to attach special importance to the provision of gardens for working-class houses.

Cadbury's other social activities were many, and were mostly concerned with giving practical form to the opinions he held. A liberal in politics, he acquired in 1901 the controlling interest in the *Daily News*, in order that the views of men of his own stamp should have adequate expression in the press, particularly in regard to the South African War. He also owned four newspapers in the Birmingham district. In 1903 he handed over Woodbrooke, Selly Oak, a house which was for some years his home, to the Society of Friends, as a settlement for men and women engaged in religious or social work. He took a leading part in the campaign against sweated labour.

Cadbury was twice married: first, in 1873 to Mary (died 1887), daughter of Charles Tylor, writer and lecturer, of London; they had three sons and two daughters; secondly, in 1888 to Elizabeth Mary, daughter of John Taylor, a member of the London Stock Exchange and director of various City companies; three sons and three daughters were born of the second marriage. He died at the Manor House, Northfield, Birmingham, 24 October 1922.

[Helen C. Alexander, *Richard Cadbury of Birmingham*, 1906; *George Cadbury, 1839–1922*, memorial number of the Bournville Works Magazine, 1922; A. G. Gardiner, *Life of George Cadbury*, 1923; I. A. Williams, *The Firm of Cadbury*, 1931; private information.]

I. A. Williams.

CAILLARD, Sir VINCENT HENRY PENALVER (1856–1930), administrator, the eldest son of Camille Félix Desiré Caillard, of Wingfield House, Trowbridge, Wiltshire, a county court judge, by his wife, Emma Louisa, daughter of Vincent Stuckey Reynolds, J.P., of Canonsgrove, Somerset, was born in London 23 October 1856. His mother's mother was a first cousin of Lord Beaconsfield. He was sent in 1869 to Eton, where he was in Mr. Warre-Cornish's house, and after leaving school entered the Royal Military Academy, Woolwich, where he won the Pollock gold medal in 1872. He obtained a commission in the Royal Engineers in 1876.

In April 1879 Caillard was appointed assistant commissioner for England on the Montenegrin Frontier Commission, and in the following October he served in the same capacity on the Arab Tabia Bridge Commission. He rejoined the Montenegrin Commission in March 1880. In July of that year he was sent on special political duty to Epirus to make a report for the Berlin Congress. In September he was attached to the staff of Admiral Sir Beauchamp Seymour, afterwards Lord Alcester [q.v.], during the naval demonstration at Dulcigno consequent upon the Porte's reluctance to cede that town to Montenegro. Early in 1882 he was employed in the intelligence branch of the War Office; later in that year he was attached to the headquarters staff during the Egyptian campaign, and for his services received the medal and bronze star and the Medjidieh and Osmanieh orders.

In the following year, 1883, at the early age of twenty-six, Caillard entered upon the chief public work of his career. He succeeded (Sir) Edgar Vincent, afterwards Lord D'Abernon, as president of the council of administration of the Ottoman Public Debt, and financial representative of England, Holland, and Belgium in Constantinople. The selection of Caillard for this important position was due to his knowledge of the Near East and of Near Eastern languages, acquired when serving on the Montenegrin Frontier Commission. He was alternate president of the council, the other president being the French representative. The administration of the revenues assigned to the control of the council was in an incomplete state of organization when Caillard took up his post, and he was chiefly responsible for the success of the administration during its subsequent history. He reconstituted the silk-growing industry, which had very nearly perished, and largely increased the salt industry and viticulture. He devised the method of guarantees for Turkish railway construction, and secured British participation in the enterprise known later as the Bagdad Railway, the control of which subsequently passed into German hands. During the fourteen years while he was on the Debt council, Caillard held the British name high, and gained the confidence of the sultan, Abdul Hamid, acting at times as a confidential intermediary between the sultan and the British prime minister Lord Salisbury.

Caillard resigned his appointment at Constantinople in 1898, and left the public service in order to take up private employment. He joined the board of Messrs. Vickers, shipbuilders and armament manufacturers, and for many years rendered valuable assistance to that company. He was appointed financial director in 1906, and in that capacity had a large share in the control of the firm's foreign operations, an office for which his diplomatic training had well fitted him. Early in 1914 he negotiated for his firm and Messrs. Armstrong, Whitworth & Co. the reconstruction of the Turkish fleet as well as of the Turkish dockyards and arsenals. This contract was interrupted by the outbreak of the European War. During the War Caillard's organizing ability helped his company to make a substantial contribution to the national output of munitions and other material. He retired from the board in 1927.

When Joseph Chamberlain started in 1903 his campaign for tariff reform he found in Caillard an energetic supporter. Caillard was chairman, and afterwards president, of the tariff commission of 1904. As a tariff reformer he contested, unsuccessfully, the central division of Bradford in 1906. After the War he took a leading part in the Federation of British Industries, of which he was the third president in 1919. In addition to his work with Messrs. Vickers he was a director of several other business concerns. He wrote much on tariff reform and other economic subjects, was fond of music, and composed several songs.

Caillard was knighted in 1896, and was decorated by the Turkish government when he left Constantinople. He was twice married: first, in 1881 to Eliza Frances (died 1926), daughter of Captain John Hanham, of Dean's Court, Wimborne, Dorset, whose widow had married Caillard's father as his second wife; secondly, in 1927 to Zoe, daughter of Robert Ellis Dudgeon, M.D., and widow of John Oakley Maund. By his first wife he had a son and a daughter.

Caillard died in Paris 18 March 1930.

[*The Times*, 20 and 29 March 1930; private information.] A. COCHRANE.

CALLENDAR, HUGH LONGBOURNE (1863–1930), physicist, the eldest son of the Rev. Hugh Callendar, rector of Hatherop, Gloucestershire, by his wife, Anne Cecilia Longbourne, was born at Hatherop 18 April 1863. He was educated at Marlborough College and entered Trinity College, Cambridge, in 1882, obtaining a first class in the classical tripos at the end of his second year of residence and graduating as sixteenth wrangler in 1885. He was elected a fellow of his college in 1886, upon submission of a thesis on platinum thermometry. Not only intellectually gifted, he was also a tall, lithe, and skilful athlete, representing his university at lawn-tennis and other sports, and, with all his versatility, possessing exceptional modesty and charm.

Callendar was appointed professor of physics at the Royal Holloway College, Englefield Green, in 1888, and in 1893 to the chair of physics at McGill University, Montreal; he returned to England in 1898 as Quain professor of physics at University College, London. In 1902 he succeeded Sir Arthur Rücker as professor of physics at the Royal College of Science, London, and when it was incorporated in the Imperial College of Science and Technology in 1907, he continued to occupy the chair of physics until his death. He possessed an exceptional gift of exposition, and his dignified kindliness endeared him to his students. He was elected F.R.S. in 1894, and was awarded the Rumford medal of the Royal Society in 1906. He was president of the Physical Society of London in 1910, and was elected first Duddell memorial medallist of that society in 1924. He was president of Section A of the British Association in 1912, and was made C.B.E. in 1920.

Callendar married in 1894 Victoria Mary, eldest daughter of Alan Stewart, of Saundersfoot, Pembrokeshire, and had three sons and one daughter. He died at his home at Ealing 21 January 1930.

Callendar's achievements in physical research developed from his earliest thesis, which was to become of classic importance. Beginning where Sir William Siemens [q.v.] had left off, Callendar so improved the platinum resistance thermometer that it provided a standard for the establishment of the thermometric scale. He compared the behaviour of the resistance thermometer with the gas thermometer, and determined the boiling point of sulphur (with E. H. Griffiths, 1891), finding it 4° lower than the previously accepted value. He established a quadratic relation for the change of the resistance of pure platinum with temperature. The international temperature scale from 0° to 600° (agreed upon in Paris, 1927) is also based upon the resistance of a standard platinum thermometer at the ice point, the boiling point of water, and that of sulphur, from which the constants of the Callendar formula are determined. The sulphur point on the agreed international scale is only 0·07° different from that determined by Callendar and Griffiths, so that the present scale of temperature may be justly ascribed to Callendar's work.

Callendar was conspicuously ingenious and inventive; in connexion with his researches in thermometry he devised a compensated resistance bridge of great accuracy, an automatic recording bridge, a radio balance, a compensated constant volume gas thermometer, and numerous other instruments.

At McGill University, in collaboration with Professor H. T. Barnes, Callendar began the study of the calorimetric properties of water with the aid of his new methods of thermometry, and, with Professor J. T. Nicholson, he measured the temperature of dry steam expanding adiabatically, expressing the results by the simple equation $T/p^{3/13}$=constant. These investigations, coupled with those which Callendar was making in gas thermometry, culminated in an important paper by him on *Thermodynamic Properties of Gases and Vapours deduced from a modified form of the Joule-Thomson Equation* [*Proceedings* of the Royal Society, vol. lxvii, 1900]. This formed the basis of his subsequent work on steam, for in it he set himself the task of stating all the thermodynamic properties of steam by means of consistent thermodynamical formulae. His experiments on various substances at their critical points, and particularly those on the total heat of steam in the neighbourhood of the critical point, lent much support to his views as to molecular aggregation which were expressed in the Hawksley lecture delivered to the Institution of Mechanical Engineers a short time before his death. He held the view that the change of state between the liquid and the vapour was not always a continuous process.

Callendar also devised an equation which expressed remarkably well the total heat of water, and from which he deduced expressions for the entropy of saturated steam and for the saturation pressures of water. He modified these equations later to express the behaviour of steam at high pressures and temperatures. While developing this exceptionally comprehensive theoretical scheme for the representation of the properties of steam and water, Callendar devised methods by means of which those properties could be measured. The continuous flow method which he and Barnes had used for the determination of the specific heat of mercury and water, and by means of which many of the errors of the determination of calorimetric quantities can be avoided, was adapted to measure the total heat and (with J. H. Brinkworth) the specific heat of steam. Two types of calorimeter were devised, the differential throttling type for dry steam and the jacketed condenser type for wet or dry steam. The latter has enabled measurements to be made up to 4,000 lb. per square inch and to temperatures as high as 500°C.

Callendar took part in the first International Steam Tables Conference held in London in 1929 for the purpose of coordinating research work in various countries on the properties of steam, so that agreed values of those properties might eventually be achieved. He was the chief authority in this field: the rapid advance which the steam turbine has made is due in no small measure to his work, not only in the measurement and tabulation of the properties of steam but also in the discussion of flow through nozzles, with reference especially to super-saturation and friction.

In addition to these elaborate investigations into steam and thermometry, Callendar carried out and directed many other researches, such as those on the specific heat of gases, the temperature of gases in the cylinder of the gas engine, the expansion of silica, osmotic pressure, radiation, heat exchange, alternating currents, &c. During the last few years of his life he gave considerable attention to the phenomenon of 'knock' in the internal combustion engine, and directed research work on behalf of the Air Ministry which led to important results.

Callendar was the author of a treatise on *The Properties of Steam* (1920), of several editions of *Steam Tables* (1915, 1922, and 1927), of *A Manual of Cursive Shorthand* (1889), and of many scientific papers. Sir Joseph Larmor wrote of him 'as having a remarkable capacity for keeping personally in the background while giving at intervals his matured results to the world'. He was not only a man of genius, who has enriched the world as a result of patient, unhurried, and highly accurate work, but he was also an exceptionally simple-hearted and kindly man.

[*Proceedings* of the Royal Society, vol. cxxxiv, A, 1932; private information.]

A. C. EGERTON.

CALLWELL, SIR CHARLES EDWARD (1859–1928), major-general, was born in London 2 April 1859, the only son of Henry Callwell, of Lismoyne, Ballycastle, co. Antrim, by his wife, Maud, fourth daughter of James Martin, of Ross, Connemara. He was educated by a German governess, and then at Haileybury, whence he passed into the Royal Military Academy in 1876. Entering the Royal Field Artillery in January 1878, he joined a battery of the 3rd brigade, then stationed in India, and with that unit served in the closing stages of the second Afghan War. In January 1881 the battery was transferred to Natal, just in time to take part in the final operations of the ill-fated expedition against the Transvaal Boers. Shortly afterwards Callwell returned to Woolwich; then in 1884 he passed the entrance examination to the Staff College, where he was a student during 1885 and 1886. He was promoted captain in the latter year, and at the same time was awarded the gold medal of the Royal United Service Institution for an essay on 'Small Wars', a study based on the colonial campaigns of the British army since 1865. After gaining high commendation the essay was expanded into a book which was adopted as an official textbook in 1896 and won wide recognition not only in Britain but also abroad. In October 1887 Callwell, mainly by reason of his knowledge of foreign countries and of foreign languages, was appointed to the intelligence branch at the War Office, where he remained until September 1892. One year later he was appointed to the old Western district as brigade-major. In 1896 he was promoted major. Upon the outbreak of the Graeco-Turkish War in the following year, Callwell was attached to the Greek army and spent one year in the Near East.

In October 1899, when war was declared against the Boer Republics in South Africa, Callwell was appointed to the staff of Sir Redvers Buller [q.v.], and was present throughout the operations which ended with the relief of Ladysmith (28 February 1900). In 1900 he was rewarded with the brevet rank of lieutenant-colonel and entrusted with the command of a mobile column, with which he served in the Western Transvaal and in Cape Colony until the close of the War (1902). On returning home he was appointed a deputy-assistant-quartermaster-general in the mobilization branch of the War Office, being promoted brevet-colonel in October 1904 and made C.B. three years later. About this time several of Callwell's contemporaries were promoted to general officer over his head. Piqued at this apparent slight, as was comprehensible in view of his war service in South Africa, he retired from active service in the summer of 1909.

Writing now claimed Callwell's whole energy, and his literary craftsmanship improved rapidly in proportion to his output. In particular, he excelled in a form of story (*Service Yarns and Memories*, 1912) which was inspired by clever satire of army procedure and War Office routine; this had in truth contributed not a little to his being passed over for promotion.

On the outbreak of the European War in August 1914, Callwell was recalled to the active list, being appointed director of military operations and intelligence at the War Office with the temporary rank of major-general. In this capacity much important work fell to his lot, and he performed it with success. The most arduous part of his labours proved to be the preparation of various plans for organization of the Dardanelles campaign, an operation with which he was not at all in sympathy. He remained at the War Office until January 1916, when a complete reorganization of the general staff took place, following on the appointment of Sir William Robertson as chief of the Imperial General Staff. Callwell's twofold directorship of operations and of intelligence was divided into two independent branches placed under separate chiefs who were specially recalled from France for the reorganization entailed by the change. He himself was sent on a special mission to Russia in connexion with the supply of munitions to that country and with the general question of Russian co-operation in the War. On his return home in the autumn of 1916 he was given an important position in the Ministry of Munitions as an adviser on questions affecting the supplies of ammunition to the various armies. In 1917 he was promoted major-general and created K.C.B. for his services. After the end of the War he once more retired into private life and busied himself with literature and journalism. In 1921 he was awarded the Chesney medal of the Royal United Service Institution for his services to military literature. He died unmarried 16 May 1928 at the Queen Alexandra Military Hospital, Millbank.

Callwell was an exceptionally good linguist, a gifted intelligence officer, and in South Africa proved himself a competent column commander. It is perhaps due to his preference for literary work that he never rose to high command in the field. From the time of the publication of his first book, *Small Wars*, his reputation as a military writer was assured. His talent ran in two directions: first, in studies on tactics and on subjects connected with the European War; secondly, in stories and parodies where his native humour found free play. He excelled in the latter type of writing perhaps even more than in the former. His more serious work, from 1886 until 1914, included: *Small Wars; their Principles and Practice* (1896), *Tactics of To-day* (1900), *Military Operations and Maritime Preponderance* (1905), *The Tactics of Home Defence* (1908), *Tirah, 1897* (1911). After 1914 he wrote *The Dardanelles* (1919), *The Life of Sir Stanley Maude* (1920), *The Experiences of a Dug-Out 1914–1918* (1920), *Stray Recollections* (1923), *Field-Marshal Sir Henry Wilson, his life and diaries* (2 vols., 1927).

[*The Times*, 17 May 1928; Army Lists; Callwell's own writings mentioned above; private information; personal knowledge.]

H. DE WATTEVILLE.

CANTON, WILLIAM (1845–1926), poet and journalist, eldest son of Thomas Canton, of the Colonial civil service, by his wife, Mary, was born 27 October 1845 in the Chinese island of Chusan. His father died in Jamaica when the boy was nine. Canton's schooldays were spent in France, where 'the sudden discovery of a cromlech in a cornfield inspired him with a passion for antiquity', which became perhaps the most individual quality of his writing. His parents were Catholics, and for a while William studied for the priesthood at Douai. But in early manhood he left the Roman Catholic Church and became a protestant. Early friendships, and the estrangement inevitable from his change of faith, find utterance in such a lyric as *The Comrades* and in his beautiful story, 'The Lost Brother' (*A Child's Book of Saints*). From 1867 he engaged in teaching and journalism in London. In 1873 his long poem 'Through the Ages: the Legend of a Stone Axe', published in *The New Quarterly*, called out T. H. Huxley's enthusiasm as 'the first attempt to use the raw material of science' for poetry. In 1874 he married Emma, daughter of Charles Moore; she died in 1880. The only child of the marriage, a daughter, died in 1877 and was commemorated in *The Invisible Playmate* (1894), the first prose work which won him recognition.

In 1876 Canton entered on fifteen years of work for Glasgow papers, which made many assume him to be a Scot (and as such he was attacked in T. W. H. Crosland's diatribe, *The Unspeakable Scot*). In 1882 he married Annie Elizabeth, daughter of John Ingham Taylor, civil engineer, of Manchester; a daughter, Winifred Vida, was born in 1890, and a son, Guy Desmond, in 1896. In 1891 Canton came to London as general manager to Isbister and Co., the publishers, presently becoming sub-editor of *The Contemporary Review* and editor of *The Sunday Magazine*. He also wrote much prose and verse for *Good Words*. But he made his reputation by independent work of his own. *A Lost Epic and Other Poems* appeared in 1887 and won the admiration of Max Müller, T. E. Brown, and Walter Pater. The 'W. V.' (Winifred Vida) books—*The Invisible Playmate* (1894), *W. V. Her Book* (1896), *A Child's Book of Saints* (1898), *In Memory of W. V.* (1901)—gained him a large public.

His daughter Winifred Vida died in 1901, and Canton then accepted the task of writing the official *History of the British and Foreign Bible Society*, in the hope that the heavy work would prove an anodyne. It occupied nine years of conscientious labour; when he at last emerged to literary daylight he found himself forgotten. Thereafter, his work was all definitely commissioned. 'All my life I've *trudged*', he observed, shortly before his death, 'sometimes with satisfaction to myself, more often not.' Complaint was never on his lips; he merely stated truth. Much of his work was in small popular books for the Bible Society, the last being finished, with the exception of the final chapter, the night before he died. Imaginative relief came rarely, but did so notably in a retelling of *The Story of St. Elizabeth of Hungary* (1912). He was granted a civil list pension in 1912, and in 1925 his friends collected a sum to mark his eightieth birthday. He died at Hendon, where he had lived since 1912, on 2 May 1926.

Canton's verse lacks lyrical impulse, except in the elegiac poems included in *In Memory of W. V.*; another exception (in the same book) is the delightful 'L'Alouette', bilingual in diction (alternate lines are French) and in movement a happy marriage of Gallic grace and English directness and speed. An earlier generation considered Canton's poems of childhood his finest achievement. Some of these are admirable, but as a whole they fail to evoke enthusiasm to-day, when the work of that period seems often marred by a cult of the trivial, the domestic, or the merely pretty. His longer poems are of two kinds: classical, influenced, but remaining individual, by the Tennyson of *Œnone* and *Tithonus* and, still more, by the Browning of *Cleon* and *Artemis Prologises*; and what must be termed antiquarian. The latter are the best expression we have of the immense change in imaginative outlook which followed the mid-Victorian discovery of the almost immeasurable antiquity of man and of animal life generally. His prose suffered latterly from monotony of theme forced on him by circumstances. But the 'W. V.' books are likely to be read for many years. Here for once his style, whimsical, light (as if informed by French rhythm and idiom), allusive in a poetical and not merely scholarly fashion, often profoundly moving, had free play. For pity and solemnity, 'The Story of the Rheinfrid', and for imaginative power, 'The Ancient Gods Pursuing', are hard to surpass. His eager courageous spirit, whose expression in literature was so often clogged and jaded, showed itself in his private letters; very few who received his correspondence destroyed any of it.

[Foreword by his son to the *Poems of W. Canton*, 1927; note by James Ashcroft Noble in A. H. Miles's *The Poets and the Poetry of the Nineteenth Century*, 1906; private information; personal knowledge.]

E. J. Thompson.

CARDEN, Sir SACKVILLE HAMILTON (1857–1930), admiral, the third son of Captain Andrew Carden, of the 60th Rifles, by his first wife, Anne, eldest daughter of Lieutenant-General Sackville Hamilton Berkeley, was born at Templemore, co. Tipperary, 3 May 1857. He entered the royal navy in 1870. Early in his career he was fortunate in seeing a good deal of war service. Before he reached captain's rank he had taken part in the Egyptian and Sudan campaigns, 1882–1884, and, under Admiral Sir Harry Holdsworth Rawson [q.v.], one of the most efficient officers of his time, had served in the Benin expedition of 1897. Promoted captain in 1899, Carden was advanced to the rank of rear-admiral in 1908. He was for two years on half-pay, and then hoisted his flag in the battleship *London* as rear-admiral in the Atlantic fleet, an appointment which was only tenable for one year. This short period at sea was followed by special service at the Admiralty, and then, in August 1912, Carden was selected for the position of admiral superintendent of Malta dockyard, an appointment which is usually regarded as a precursor to retirement from service. But events conspired to defeat any such purpose, had it been officially entertained, for upon the outbreak of the European War in August 1914, Carden was forced into the forefront of the struggle by the circumstances which followed upon the escape of the German battle-cruiser *Goeben* from the Mediterranean into Turkish waters. Although Admiral Sir Berkeley Milne, the commander-in-chief in the Mediterranean, was held to have been blameless for this untoward incident, his continued presence in southern waters was incompatible, owing to his seniority, with the assumption by the French of the command of all the allied naval forces in the Mediterranean in accordance with a naval convention concluded between the Allies soon after the outbreak of the War. Carden, who had just attained the rank of vice-admiral, was thereupon chosen (20 September 1914) for the command of the British battle squadron which was associated with the French forces.

Following the closing of the Dardanelles by the Turks (27 September), war had been declared between Great Britain and Turkey on 5 November, and simultaneously French and British warships, under the command of Admiral Carden, had carried out a preliminary bombardment of the outer forts of the Straits. When, in January 1915, definite proposals to occupy the Gallipoli peninsula were being debated in the War Council on the initiative of the first lord of the Admiralty, Mr. Winston Churchill, Admiral Carden was asked by the Admiralty whether, in his opinion, the Dardanelles could be forced by naval action without military support. He replied that the Straits could not be 'rushed', but that the forts might be silenced by extended operations, employing a large number of men-of-war. He subsequently drew up a detailed plan, involving the systematic demolition of the fortifications and a subsequent invasion of the peninsula. Violent differences of opinion developed in the War Council as to the wisdom of undertaking operations in accordance with this plan and at that precise juncture in the War. Preparations for carrying out Carden's scheme were nevertheless begun, with the concurrence of the French and Russian governments. Strenuous opposition to this diversion of forces was subsequently offered by Lord Fisher [q.v.], the first sea lord; but, in spite of his objections, approval of the Dardanelles operations was given by the War Council on 28 January. Arrangements were accordingly made for the assembly of such men-of-war as were considered necessary, and the 29th division was eventually chosen (10 March) to co-operate with the naval forces.

The first phase of the operations against the Dardanelles, the systematic bombardment of the outer forts, was begun on 19 February with the support of a large force of ships of all classes, British and French, under the supreme command of Carden. Subsequently, it became known that successive bombardments of both the outer and intermediate defences (25 February—8 March) had proved in no sense decisive, as the Turks, warned by the preliminary attacks, had under German guidance greatly strengthened the defences on the peninsula, besides developing the mine-fields to a point of efficiency which exceeded the expectations of British naval officers. The attacks were undertaken under conditions of considerable embarrassment owing to the differences of opinion in the War Council; and the full responsibility of command rested with Carden, although he had the support of Admiral Guépratte, in command of the French squadron, and of two British flag officers, Rear-Admirals (Sir) J. M. de Robeck [q.v.] and Rosslyn E. Wemyss (afterwards Lord Wester-Wemyss). The strain on an officer who had not been employed at sea for several years and who was then nearly sixty years of age, rapidly undermined Carden's health. He was forced at length, on 16 March, to relinquish his command and to return home, being succeeded by Admiral de Robeck.

From April until June 1915 Carden was appointed to the Admiralty on special service, and in October 1917, after being on half-pay, he retired with the rank of admiral. He died at Lymington 6 May 1930. Though controversy continued as to the wisdom of the advice which he had given to the Admiralty on the practicability of forcing the Dardanelles, Carden took no part in it. He was content to leave the official records to exonerate or condemn him for the part which he had played. He was conscious that he had throughout been supported by the Admiralty, notwithstanding that the first sea lord had come to regard the attack on the Dardanelles as unwise in view of its reactions on projects of his own conception, and Lord Kitchener [q.v.] had wavered in his views on the desirability of a scheme which, it soon became apparent, required military co-operation on a considerable scale.

Carden, who was created K.C.M.G. in 1916, married twice: first, in 1879 Maria Louisa, daughter of Captain Loftus J. Nunn, of the 99th Foot; secondly, in 1909 Henrietta, daughter of William English Harrison, K.C., of Hitchin, Hertfordshire. He had one daughter, by his first marriage.

[Admiralty records; Sir Julian S. Corbett, (Official) *History of the Great War. Naval Operations*, vols. i, ii, 1920–1; Dardanelles dispatches.] A. Hurd.

CARMAN, WILLIAM BLISS (1861–1929), poet, was born at Fredericton, New Brunswick, Canada, 15 April 1861, the eldest son of William Carman, barrister, of Fredericton, by his second wife, Sophia Mary, daughter of George Bliss. He was descended on both parents' sides from loyalists who had removed from the United States to Canada after the American Revolution. On his mother's side he was related to Ralph Waldo Emerson. He was educated at the collegiate school at Fredericton, graduated from the university of New Brunswick in 1881, and studied at Edinburgh University in 1882–1883 and at Harvard University from 1886 to 1888.

From 1890 to 1892 Carman was office editor of the New York *Independent*, and he was afterwards on the staff of *Current Literature* and the *Atlantic Monthly*. His first book of poetry was *Low Tide on Grand Pré* (1893). In 1894 he won public attention by his contributions to *Songs from Vagabondia*, which he published in collaboration with Richard Hovey. This collection was followed by *More Songs from Vagabondia* (1896) and *Last Songs from Vagabondia* (1900), in both of which he continued to collaborate with Hovey. Carman's other noteworthy volumes of poetry are *Behind the Arras* (1895), *A Seamark* (1895), *Ballads of Lost Haven* (1897), *By the Aurelian Wall* (1898), *A Winter Holiday* (1899), *Sappho* (1902), *Pipes of Pan* in five volumes (1902–5), *Echoes from Vagabondia* (1912), *April Airs* (1916), and the posthumous collection *Wild Garden* (1929). He expounded his philosophy of life in several prose volumes, of which the more notable are *The Kinship of Nature* (1904) and *The Poetry of Life* (1905). He edited *The Oxford Book of American Verse* (1927). He died unmarried at New Canaan, Connecticut, 8 June 1929.

As a poet Carman is noteworthy for the infectious, lyrical spirit of his nature worship. His friendly contact with sun and rain, trees and grass was sung in natural, unpremeditated strains. Essentially a nature poet, he was not at his best in narrative ballads or in his efforts to interpret poetically the life of his own time. His later work was marred by diffuseness, but some of his lyrics written before the end of the nineteenth century, and many of those which he composed in his last years, have real charm and freshness. Historically his poetry is important as an influence on American poetry during the 'nineties. It inspired much creative energy in other poets.

[*The Times*, 10 June 1929; Odell Shepard, *Bliss Carman*, 1923; H. D. C. Lee, *Bliss Carman* (containing a bibliography of Carman's writings), 1912; private information.]

E. O'Brien.

CARMICHAEL, Sir THOMAS DAVID GIBSON-, eleventh baronet, Baron Carmichael, of Skirling (1859–1926), overseas administrator and art connoisseur, was born at Edinburgh 18 March 1859, the eldest son of the Rev. Sir William Henry Gibson-Carmichael, tenth baronet, by his wife, Eleanora Anne, daughter of David Anderson, of St. Germains, East Lothian. He was educated at the Rev. Cowley Powles's school at Wixenford in Hampshire, where he acquired a love of nature and a scientific inquisitiveness which remained with him throughout his life. In 1877 he entered St. John's College, Cambridge, whence he graduated B.A. in 1881. His Cambridge contemporaries bore testimony to the catholicity of his friendships—another lifelong trait. A visit to Italy in 1881–1882 turned his attention to that country and to art; and Lord Rosebery directed his mind to politics. By tradition a liberal, he became in 1886 private secretary to two successive secretaries for Scotland in Mr. Gladstone's administration, (Sir) George Otto Trevelyan and the Earl of Dalhousie. He succeeded his father in the baronetcy in 1891. After unsuccessfully contesting Peebles and Selkirk in 1892, Carmichael sat from 1895 to 1900 as liberal member for Midlothian in succession to Mr. Gladstone, and was chairman of the Scottish Liberal Association from 1892 to 1903. His liberalism was a habit of mind, not simply a political creed: his delight was to work behind the scenes rather than in the limelight.

In 1908 Carmichael was appointed governor of Victoria, Australia. His tenure of the office was very successful. He took part in every organization for the public welfare, fostered art and agriculture, and was quietly active for good in many minor ways. His dissolution of the state parliament on the defeat of the liberal ministry in 1908, instead of summoning the leader of either of the two minority parties, the dissentient liberals and the labour opposition, was strongly criticized; but the correctness of his judgement was afterwards admitted.

In 1911 Carmichael was summoned to the governorship of Madras. He assumed office on 3 November, but remained there only five months, for he was chosen to be the first governor of Bengal as reconstituted by the King-Emperor's announcement at the Delhi durbar. He took up his new duties on 1 April 1912, having been raised to the peerage on 7 February. It fell to Lord Carmichael to guide Bengal during troublous times. The shock due to the territorial readjustment and the removal of the capital from Calcutta to Delhi made the situation difficult from the first. The dislocation of trade and finance owing to the European War, and the local revolutionary movement with the consequent internment of suspects were added complications. Notwithstanding all this and his own indifferent health, Carmichael's administration was successful, and he was able to achieve progress in such important matters as public hygiene and education. His instinct prompted him to leave the larger issues to the influence of time, and an innate diffidence made him hesitate to impose his will upon others. His accessibility, hospitality, and kindliness made him personally very popular. He left India in 1917, and died in London

16 January 1926, after four years of failing health.

Lord Carmichael's appointment as trustee of the National Portrait Gallery (1904–1908), of the National Gallery (1906–1908, 1923–1926), and of the Wallace Collection (1918–1926) indicate the confidence placed in his artistic judgement. The sales of his collections in 1902 and 1926 were events in the art world. For him there were no limits in class, school, or period; but he had an unerring sense of the beautiful. His numerous public gifts included a bequest of a 'Virgin and Child' by Piero di Lorenzo to the National Gallery.

Lord Carmichael was one of the three members of the Scottish Churches Commission of 1904; and he held the highest office in freemasonry in Scotland, Victoria, and Bengal. He founded in 1891 the Scottish Bee-keepers' Association and was a keen agriculturist; he wrote a monograph on centipedes (*Proceedings* of the Royal Physical Society of Edinburgh, 1882, 1885). Personally, he inspired affection: he had a shrewd judgement, a quixotic philosophy, and a whimsical humour.

Carmichael was created K.C.M.G. in 1908, G.C.I.E. in 1911, G.C.S.I. in 1917, and appointed lord-lieutenant of Peeblesshire in 1921. He married in 1886 Mary Helen Elizabeth, lady of grace of St. John of Jerusalem (1917), daughter of Albert Llewellyn Nugent, younger brother of the second Baron Nugent. They had no children, and the peerage became extinct on Carmichael's death. He was succeeded in the baronetcy by his cousin, Henry Thomas Gibson-Craig (-Carmichael, born 1885), and on the latter's death in September 1926 by his kinsman Eardley Charles William Gibson-Craig (-Carmichael, born 1887).

[*Lord Carmichael of Skirling, A Memoir* prepared by his wife, 1929; private information; personal knowledge.] J. G. Cumming.

CARNARVON, fifth Earl of (1866–1923), Egyptologist. [See Herbert, George Edward Stanhope Molyneux.]

CARNOCK, first Baron (1849–1928), diplomatist. [See Nicolson, Sir Arthur.]

CARPENTER, EDWARD (1844–1929), writer on social subjects, the second son of Charles Carpenter, R.N., by his wife, daughter of Thomas Wilson, of Walthamstow, was born at 45 Brunswick Square, Brighton, 29 August 1844. His father, who came of a West country family long connected with the navy, had retired early from the service and settled at Brighton in 1843, where he read German philosophy, and enjoyed the friendship of F. W. Robertson and F. D. Maurice. Edward Carpenter was educated at Brighton College from 1854 to 1863, and after spending some months at Heidelberg entered Trinity Hall, Cambridge, in 1864, with a view to taking holy orders. He was tenth wrangler in 1868, became fellow of his college, and in 1869 won the Burney prize and was ordained.

When F. D. Maurice became incumbent of St. Edward's, Cambridge, in 1870, Carpenter joined him as his curate. He was, however, already becoming alienated from his profession. He was both writing and reading poetry, and Tennyson, Wordsworth, Shelley, and especially Walt Whitman, exerted a profound influence on his mind. His recoil from his orders was strengthened by a new enthusiasm for Greek sculpture, gained on a visit to Rome, Naples, and Florence about 1873, and by inspiring friendships, among others, with W. K. Clifford, Henry Fawcett, and Charles Dilke. He published a poem *Narcissus* in November 1873 and in the following summer relinquished his orders and resigned his fellowship at Trinity Hall. He joined the staff of the University Extension movement, founded in 1874 by Professor James Stuart, and lectured on astronomy in various industrial towns in the north of England, living at first at Leeds. He enjoyed the work, but found that his pupils were drawn less from the working class than he had hoped.

In April 1877, having finished a course of lectures at Nottingham, York, and Hull, Carpenter made a first visit to the United States and became acquainted with Emerson, Oliver Wendell Holmes, James Russell Lowell, William Cullen Bryant, and in particular Walt Whitman, in Carpenter's eyes the greatest of them all. In 1877 and 1878 he lectured at Sheffield and Chesterfield, and in the latter year made his home at Sheffield, whose rough, shrewd, and good-hearted people made a special appeal to him. But his work had injured his health, especially his eyesight; he craved for an open-air life and deeper affection, and he became to a large extent (though never completely) a vegetarian and teetotaller. In May 1880 he went to live, as a lodger, with the family of a working-class friend, Albert Fearnehough, at first at Totley, near Sheffield, and from March

1881 at Bradway, near Beauchief Abbey, a few miles away. He now entered on a year of great emotional excitement, devoting himself to the writing of an unrhymed poem, *Towards Democracy*. So much was he absorbed in this work that he resigned his post as University Extension lecturer, and joined his friends, the Fearnehoughs, in their farm-work in the afternoons, or went into Sheffield, among new associates, in the evenings, finding that every fresh experience added something to his poem. It was published at Manchester, a thin volume of 110 pages, in the early summer of 1883.

The death of his father in 1882 left Carpenter the master of some £6,000, much of which did not stay with him long. He purchased in 1883 seven acres of land at Millthorpe, a Derbyshire hamlet near Chesterfield, and built for himself and the Fearnehoughs a substantial cottage, with an orchard and market garden; this was his home for nearly forty years. In this country of hills and moorland Carpenter spent his days in literary work and market gardening, taking his fruit and vegetables to the market at Sheffield eight miles away, a heavy tax on his physical strength. But commercialism grew less congenial to him after he had read Thoreau's *Walden*, and had become interested in the socialist movements directed by H. M. Hyndman and William Morris. In 1884 he again visited America, travelling 'steerage'. He found Walt Whitman more self-centred than before, but was attracted by his henchman in Canada, R. M. Bucke. On his return he took up the strange occupation of sandal-making. In 1885 he started a socialist society in Sheffield, and for some years lectured frequently on the movement, there and elsewhere, collecting, in the meantime, 'Chants of Labour', which he set to music and published under that title in 1888.

In 1887 or 1888 Carpenter handed over the Millthorpe orchard to his friend Fearnehough in order to have more time for literary work. He next brought out, as supplementary to *Towards Democracy* (which had itself been much enlarged), two prose works, *England's Ideal* (first published 1885), essays showing some Marxist influence, and *Civilization, its Cause and Cure* (1889). These brought him many new friends. A visit to Ceylon in 1890 was recorded in *From Adam's Peak to Elephanta* (1892), part of which was reissued as *A Visit to a Gñani*, extolling the value of the Oriental peace of mind. Carpenter now felt that his development had been completed. His later books expressed his thoughts on art, *Angels' Wings* (1898) and *The Art of Creation* (1904), and on friendship and the relations of the sexes, *Love's Coming of Age* (1896), *Iolaus* (1902), and other works which had more vogue on the Continent than in England. Carpenter's attempts to analyse and interpret an emotional state which had been an element in his own development were liable to be misunderstood, but his friends saw nothing in him disordered or uncontrolled and never questioned his own claim to 'perfect healthiness of habit and general freedom from morbidity'. His remaining writings include a multitude of pamphlets upon vivisection, humanitarianism, prison reform, and the European War, together with many essays reprinted from periodicals.

In 1893 the Fearnehoughs left Millthorpe; in 1898 another family which had succeeded them also left, and a new companion, George Merrill, also of humble origin, became Carpenter's friend and fellow traveller for thirty years; market gardening and sandal-making now ceased to be part of his activities. With Merrill he kept open house for the immense number of friends in all ranks of life and from all countries who were attracted by his personal charm or by his books which by this time had been translated into many languages. Carpenter always humorously refused to be treated as a prophet; but he could not deny that, having 'liberated' himself, he had liberated many others from conventional ties and introduced them to a life nearer to nature. The Boer War he unhesitatingly condemned; his attitude towards the European War, expressed in more than one pamphlet, was much less definite. He took pride in the leading part played in the Zeebrugge affair by his nephew, Captain Francis Carpenter.

In 1922 Carpenter left Millthorpe and settled at The Mount, Guildford, where new friends sought him out. On his eightieth birthday he received an address from the Trades Union Congress. But deafness was growing on him, and his strength, which had been remarkable for his years, declined. After the death of his companion, Merrill, in 1928, he removed to a bungalow in Joseph's Road, Guildford, where he died, 28 June 1929. He was unmarried. An address was delivered over his grave at Guildford by Mr. H. W. Nevinson.

Carpenter's life was a reaction against Victorian convention and respectability, and he abjured his social class as a protest against what he regarded as the exploitation of the poor and the weak by the well-to-do. But he was neither a philosopher nor an economist, and political activity was, perhaps, a digression from his right path. He was not a very effective speaker. His gospel concerned something more personal and intimate than any doctrine of social reform. He detested all rules and systems, and demanded simplicity of life and the ordering of human relationships by no other code than that of charity and brotherly affection.

[Carpenter's works, especially *My Days and Dreams*, 1916, a volume of his reminiscences, with a bibliography of his writings; E. Lewis, *Edward Carpenter, an Exposition and an Appreciation*, 1915; *Edward Carpenter, in Appreciation*, by various contributors, ed. G. Beith, 1931; personal knowledge.]

G. C. Moore Smith.

CARPENTER, JOSEPH ESTLIN (1844–1927), Unitarian divine, was the second son of William Benjamin Carpenter, the biologist [q.v.], grandson of Lant Carpenter, Unitarian divine [q.v.], and nephew of Mary Carpenter, the philanthropist [q.v.]. His mother's name was Louisa Powell. He was born 5 October 1844 at Ripley, Surrey, whence his father soon afterwards removed to London. There Estlin Carpenter grew up in a home in which a puritan tradition of austere devotion to duty, a zeal for philanthropy, and a serene religious faith lived side by side with literary, musical, and scientific enthusiasm. After his schooldays at University College School he dedicated himself to the Unitarian ministry. He took his arts course at University College, London, graduating M.A. in 1863, second in mental and moral philosophy, with marks entitling him to the gold medal, and then entered on the three years' divinity course in Manchester New College, Gordon Square, London, spending his last summer vacation at Zürich University. Apart from a season of spiritual dryness, which was permanently cured by a mystical experience described in the *Memoir* cited below, his college years were a time of tranquil intellectual and religious development.

Carpenter became minister of Oakfield Road chapel, Clifton, Bristol, in November 1866; he resigned in April 1869 in order to take charge of Mill Hill chapel, Leeds, where once Joseph Priestley [q.v.] had ministered. At both places his ministry was marked by cultured preaching, often rising to prophetic fervour, and by efforts to popularize by means of public lectures critical views of biblical history. At Leeds he found time to translate and edit (1871) a large part (vols. 3–5) of G. H. A. von Ewald's *Geschichte des Volkes Israël*.

In 1875 Carpenter accepted rather unwillingly an invitation to become professor of ecclesiastical history, comparative religion, and Hebrew at Manchester New College. His heart was in his ministerial work, but a troublesome affliction of the voice made it prudent for him to give up preaching. His voice recovered after a few years and he frequently preached, but he remained in the service of the college. On the retirement of James Martineau [q.v.] from the principalship of the college in 1885, James Drummond [q.v.] became principal, and Carpenter vice-principal. In 1889 the college dropped 'New' from its title and was transferred from Gordon Square to Oxford where its successful establishment owed much to Carpenter's reputation and personality. He was known as the translator of Ewald, and as the collaborator with Thomas William Rhys Davids [q.v.] in the editing and translation of Pali texts, and as an expert in Old Testament criticism.

In 1899, after ten years of college work, Carpenter gave up the vice-principalship in order to devote himself to literary and denominational work, and for the next seven years he lectured only on comparative religion. On Drummond's retirement in 1906 he became principal, taking over, in addition to his own work, the New Testament department which had been in Drummond's hands. In 1914 the University of Oxford appointed him Wilde lecturer in comparative religion. In 1915, at the age of seventy, he retired from the principalship. He retained the Wilde lecturership until 1924. He died at Oxford 2 June 1927.

The bibliography of Carpenter's writings which is appended to C. H. Herford's *Memoir* contains over a hundred titles. They include lectures, articles, reviews, memorial sketches, and college addresses, and some of them represent substantial volumes. One of his most laborious works was *The Composition of the Hexateuch, an Introduction, with select list of words and phrases* (1902). This was a revision and expansion of his contribution to what is generally known as *The Oxford Hexateuch*, a co-operative work carried out by the

Society of Historical Theology and published in two quarto volumes in 1900 under the title *The Hexateuch according to the Revised Version arranged in its constituent documents by members of the Society of Historical Theology, Oxford. Edited with Introduction, Notes, Marginal References and Synoptical Tables by J. Estlin Carpenter and G. Harford Battersby.* Two manuals on New Testament subjects proved very popular, and were several times reprinted: *Life in Palestine when Jesus Lived* (1884) and *The First Three Gospels, Their Origin and Relations* (1890). Both Old and New Testament formed the subject of *The Bible in the Nineteenth Century* (1903), but he returned to the New Testament in his latest work, *The Johannine Writings, a Study of the Apocalypse and Fourth Gospel* (1927), published in his eighty-third year. Of Carpenter's other publications the more important are *The Place of Christianity among the Religions of the World* (1904), *Theism in Mediaeval India* (Hibbert lectures, 1921), and *Buddhism and Christianity, A Contrast and a Parallel* (Jowett lectures, 1923). He wrote an account of *Comparative Religion* (1913) for the 'Home University Library', a masterly example of compression; and showed a fine skill in biography both in *The Life and Work of Mary Carpenter* (1879) and in *James Martineau, Theologian and Teacher* (1905).

Carpenter's lectures and books established his reputation as a comprehensive scholar finely equipped in many fields of learning: especially able in his justifications of the higher criticism of the Old Testament, which he was one of the first to introduce into the curriculum of a theological college; reverent, if daring, in applying the same critical processes to the documents and history of Christianity; an enthusiastic pioneer in the study of comparative religions, and a judicious expounder and interpreter of Buddhism. He received honorary degrees from the universities of Glasgow, Jena, and Geneva; Oxford gave him the honorary degree of D.Litt. in 1906 and of D.D. in 1923; the public orator of the university described him when he died as 'a learned, gentle, and most Christian soul'. The Unitarian community revered him both as an outspoken defender of their faith and as a man of high integrity, kindliness, and humility.

Carpenter was a diligent promoter of congresses and summer schools of theology; he maintained a deep interest in churches of liberal religion in the East, and especially in India and Japan, and was a steadfast believer in the value of intellectual co-operation as a means towards international peace.

He married in 1878 Alice Mary (died 1931), daughter of George Buckton, of Leeds, and had no children. There is a portrait of him by Alfred Edward Emslie, in the possession of Sir Harold Carpenter at Wimbledon: there are two by Minna Tayler, one of which is at Essex Hall, London, and the other in possession of Dr. S. D. Hale Carpenter at Cumnor Hill, Oxford; and two by Howard Somerville, both in Manchester College, Oxford.

[C. H. Herford, *Joseph Estlin Carpenter, a Memoir* (with chapters by J. H. Weatherall, A. S. Peake, and L. R. Farnell), 1929; personal knowledge.]

J. H. Weatherall.

CARTON, RICHARD CLAUDE (1856–1928), dramatist, whose real surname was Critchett, was the younger son of George Critchett [q.v.], ophthalmic surgeon, by his wife, Martha Wilson, daughter of Captain Nathanael Brooker, R.N., of Bosham, Sussex, and younger brother of Sir George Anderson Critchett, first baronet, also an ophthalmic surgeon. He was born at 46 Finsbury Square, London, 10 May 1856. He first appeared on the stage at Bristol in 1875, and in June of that year acted Osric in *Hamlet* at the Lyceum Theatre, London. His undistinguished career as an actor ended in 1885, the year in which his first play, written in collaboration with Cecil Raleigh, was produced. This melodrama, *The Great Pink Pearl* (Olympic Theatre, May 1885), the authors followed with two more. In November 1890 a comedy, *Sunlight and Shadow*, the first play to be written by Carton alone, was successfully produced by (Sir) George Alexander [q.v.] at the Avenue Theatre. Carton wrote three more plays of the same kind, of which *Liberty Hall* (St. James's Theatre, 1892) was the most successful and was revived as recently as 1930. His model in those days was Dickens, and these comedies combine Dickensian sentiment and humour.

During the next five years Carton was feeling his way with plays of various kinds, of which only a witty drama called *The Tree of Knowledge* (St. James's Theatre, 1896) deserves to be remembered; but in 1898 he came into his own with a comedy, *Lord and Lady Algy*, in which the principal parts were acted by (Sir) Charles

Henry Hawtrey [q.v.] and an actress whom Carton married about this time, Katherine Mackenzie (known on the stage as Miss Compton), younger daughter of the actor Henry Compton [q.v.] and aunt of Miss Fay Compton, the actress, and of Compton Mackenzie, the novelist. Miss Compton was a great element in Carton's subsequent successes; she took the leading female part in most of his plays, her character being regularly that of a society woman of shrewd sense, a ready wit, a good heart, and few scruples.

Among the dozen or more plays by Carton which were staged between 1898 and his death, the most memorable were *Lady Huntworth's Experiment* (Criterion Theatre, 1900), *The Rich Mrs. Repton* (Duke of York's Theatre, 1904), *Mr. Hopkinson* (Avenue Theatre, 1905), *Mr. Preedy and the Countess* (Criterion Theatre, 1909), and *The Bear Leaders* (Comedy Theatre, 1912). These plays were comedies, tending towards farce, full of witty dialogue and mainly devoted to poking fun at the manners and foibles of the aristocracy. They appealed chiefly to the stalls, and owed much to their polished presentation by Hawtrey, James Welch, Weedon Grossmith, Lottie Venne, Henry Kemble, and other accomplished actors of the time.

Carton died at his house, the Red Lodge, Acton, Middlesex, 1 April 1928, his wife dying at the same place 16 May following. They had one daughter.

[*The Times*, 2 April and 17 May 1928; *Who's Who in the Theatre*, 1925; personal knowledge.] H. H. Child.

CASE, THOMAS (1844–1925), Waynflete professor of philosophy and president of Corpus Christi College, Oxford, was born at Liverpool 14 July 1844, the second son of Robert Case, stockbroker there, later of London, by his wife, Esther, daughter of Alexander MacMillan. From Rugby he entered in 1863 Balliol College, Oxford, obtained first classes in classical moderations (1865) and *literae humaniores* (1867), and was elected in 1869 fellow of Brasenose College. Pressed by his father, he joined the Stock Exchange for one year, but, finding it uncongenial, returned to Oxford in 1870. In that year he married Elizabeth Donn, daughter of Sir William Sterndale Bennett [q.v.]; they had two sons and one daughter. Invited by Jowett, just elected master, Case joined the staff of Balliol College, and lectured on Aristotle's *Ethics*, ancient history, and logic. Later he became lecturer at Corpus Christi College and in 1876, although Jowett wished to retain him, was persuaded to become a tutor of that college, adding Plato, English moral philosophy, Bacon, and Mill to his repertory. From 1883 to 1889 he also taught at Christ Church. In 1889, on the death of Henry William Chandler [q.v.], Case was elected Waynflete professor of moral and metaphysical philosophy and fellow of Magdalen College. In 1904 he succeeded Thomas Fowler [q.v.] as president of Corpus Christi College, holding the two posts until 1910 when he resigned the professorship. He was elected an honorary fellow of Magdalen in 1914. In 1924, resigning the presidency, he retired to Falmouth, where he died 31 October 1925.

Versatile and vigorous in body as in mind, Case was a distinguished cricketer, playing in the Oxford eleven from 1864 to 1867 and excelling in other games. Unsparing diligence, independence, and confidence in his own judgement, which Jowett, he said, taught him to use, thoroughness in detail, regard both to main and subsidiary issues, were his characteristics in general. His preference was for Aristotle among the ancients, Bacon and Newton among modern, and Clerk-Maxwell among recent thinkers. His own position, to reach which he studied both physics and physiology, was indicated in the titles of his works, *Realism in Morals* and *Physical Realism*. A 'laughing philosopher' of genial and at times even rollicking temper, understanding young men, and keen for their advancement, he was an excellent tutor and president, perhaps less successful as professor, because opposed alike to Descartes and Hegel and the idealism of Oxford of the day, and to Herbert Spencer. 'I am not a Tory, I am what I always was, a Palmerstonian liberal', he said in his seventieth year. As such he opposed alike liberal changes and tory concessions in church, state, and university. His notable letters to *The Times* punctuated his campaigns, especially those against the admission of women to Oxford and against the abolition of compulsory Greek. Both were 'thirty years wars', finally determined against him in 1920. His supporters, in 1911, after a signal success in the Greek question, presented him with two silver-gilt Homeric cups; his opponents recognized his fair and impersonal temper.

Case's latest letters to *The Times*, 1919–1922, criticized Einstein's theory of relativity. His skill in architecture was shown in the restoration of the hall roof at Magdalen, where he materially assisted G. F. Bodley, in that of the spire and pinnacles of St. Mary's, where he strove to control (Sir) Thomas Graham Jackson [q.v.], and in the new Lodgings at Corpus. In music a good pianist, his knowledge and taste were full and keen down to about the period of Mendelssohn. He loved the old English anthems and glees, and himself published two volumes of songs. His acquaintance with Shakespeare was exhaustive, and he was an ardent admirer of Nelson and a collector of Nelsoniana.

Beside playing, and writing on, cricket, Case persuaded the university, in the teeth of opposition, to admit that and other games into the University Park, and was a most popular and efficient treasurer of the University Cricket Club.

A benefactor himself, restoring the east window of the hall at Magdalen and rebuilding the Lodgings at Corpus, he showed an astonishing power of attracting to his college large gifts from others, notably those of Mr. C. M. Powell, Mr. E. P. Warren, and Miss Thomas.

Of Case's published writings the following deserve mention: *Materials for a History of the Athenian Democracy from Solon to Pericles* (1874), *Realism in Morals* (1877), *Physical Realism* (1888), *St. Mary's Clusters* (1893), 'Oxford University Cricket' (*The Jubilee Book of Cricket*, 1897), Preface to Bacon's *Advancement of Learning* (1906), articles on 'Metaphysics', 'Aristotle', and 'Logic' for the eleventh edition of the *Encyclopædia Britannica* (1910–1911), article on 'Jowett' for *Pitman's Encyclopædia of Education* (1921), and *Twelve Songs* (1918).

[*The Times*, 2 November 1925; *Thomas Case's Letters to 'The Times', 1884–1922*, edited, with Memoir, by R. B. Mowat (with portrait), 1927; private information; personal knowledge.]

T. H. Warren.

CAVE, GEORGE, Viscount Cave, of Richmond, Surrey (1856–1928), lawyer and statesman, was born in Cheapside, London, 23 February 1856, the second of the five sons of Thomas Cave, liberal member of parliament for Barnstaple 1865–1880 and a sheriff of the City of London 1863–1864, by his wife, Elizabeth (who died in her ninety-seventh year in 1925), daughter of Jasper Shallcrass, of Banstead, Surrey. He was educated at the *lycée* of Caen, at Merchant Taylors' School, and at St. John's College, Oxford, of which he was a scholar and eventually (1916) an honorary fellow. Leaving Oxford with first classes in classical moderations (1875) and *literae humaniores* (1878), he was called to the bar by the Inner Temple in 1880 and began practice on the Chancery side. In 1885 he married Anne Estella Sarah Penfold, daughter of William Withey Mathews, of Chard, Somerset, afterwards of Wolston Manor House, North Cadbury.

At the bar Cave's career was in no sense spectacular. He steadily earned and received in his earlier years the satisfactory rewards which industry and a genuine aptitude for legal work usually bring, but his professional advocacy, while thorough and methodical, was not brilliant or arresting. It was not until he had been twenty-four years a junior that he took silk in 1904, when he also became recorder of Guildford. By 1913, however, his merits had begun to receive fuller recognition, and in that year he was made a bencher of his inn and received the coveted appointment of standing counsel to the university of Oxford. In the following year he became attorney-general to the Prince of Wales.

Meantime Cave had been equipping himself elsewhere for the distinguished part which he was destined ultimately to play in the public life of the nation. From an early period he concerned himself actively with local government work, first at Richmond, where his parents had made their home, and later as a member of the Surrey county council. The remarkable efficiency in the conduct of business which he there displayed resulted in his appointment in 1893 as vice-chairman of the county council and in 1894 as chairman of quarter sessions, which office he retained until 1911. From local administration he naturally turned to the wider sphere of parliament, and in 1906 he was returned as unionist member for the Kingston division of Surrey, a seat which he held through successive elections until he entered the House of Lords in 1918.

In the House of Commons Cave soon acquired a position of unique influence. In the seething turmoil of the period which centred round the budget of 1909–10, the Parliament and Home Rule Bills (1911 and 1912), and the Marconi scandal (1913), his imperturbable moderation, his persuasive urbanity, and his calm lucidity, as well as the innate sense of fairness of which these were the outward expression, contrasted conspicuously with the prevailing tone of acrid political controversy and deservedly won for him the respect of all parties. In 1915 he was sworn a privy councillor, and later in the year he succeeded Sir F. E. Smith (afterwards Lord Birkenhead, q.v.) as solicitor-general in the first Coalition government and was knighted. In this capacity Cave dealt most competently with the many difficult and unfamiliar tasks which the European War laid upon the law officers of the crown, such as the conduct of prize cases and the trial for high treason in 1916 of Sir Roger Casement [q.v.]. When Mr. Lloyd George formed his government in 1916, Cave entered the Cabinet as home secretary, an office for which he was ideally suited. It was certainly to the public advantage that such matters as the introduction of compulsory military service, the control of aliens, the administration of the censorship, and the settlement of the police strike had the benefit of his wise guidance. When he quitted the House of Commons in 1918 to become a lord of appeal in ordinary, with the title of Viscount Cave, it was generally recognized that the alternative honour of the Speakership was at his disposal, such was the authority and popularity which he had acquired among his fellow members.

Lord Cave retained the seals of the Home Office until January 1919 and thereupon took up his judicial work in the place rendered vacant by the death of Lord Parker. Four years later, in October 1922, he was offered by Mr. Bonar Law, and accepted, the office of lord chancellor, thus attaining the summit of his career. This high office he held until within a few days of his death, with the brief interlude of less than twelve months in 1924 when Lord Haldane [q.v.] occupied the woolsack in the first labour government. During that interlude he relieved Lord Haldane, who was pre-occupied with the chairmanship of the Committee of Imperial Defence and other tasks, by undertaking his judicial duties for him.

To Lord Cave's temperament judicial work was eminently congenial, and he presided over the august tribunals of the House of Lords and the Privy Council with dignity and courtesy. The problems of the law interested him, and counsel always had the satisfaction of knowing that their arguments were addressed to an appreciative hearer. His judgments are of the sound and useful order and deal strictly with the matter in hand, avoiding, as in all his work he instinctively avoided, any tendency to the display of rhetoric or literary ornament. Probably the most important case on which he adjudicated was the reference to the Privy Council in 1927 of the rival claims of Canada and Newfoundland in regard to the boundary of their respective territories in Labrador, when the Judicial Committee in a lengthy judgment prepared by Cave advised the king that the 'coast' of Labrador extended far inland to the watershed, thus awarding a vast area of land to Great Britain's oldest colony.

Apart from law and politics, which formed the main occupations of his life, Lord Cave so obviously possessed the qualifications for the conduct of public inquiries that he was inevitably called upon to act as chairman of a series of very diverse commissions and committees. These included an inter-departmental committee on prisoners of war; a committee to examine the question of government machinery for dealing with trade and commerce (1919); the Southern Rhodesian commission (1919–20), which was the occasion of his visit to South Africa and of services for which he received the G.C.M.G. (1921); the munitions inquiry tribunal (1921); the committee on voluntary hospitals (1921); the committee on trade boards (1921–2); the British Empire cancer campaign (1924), and a committee on cruelty to animals (1924). He also took a share in the shaping of the legislation for the reform of conveyancing and the law of property, and was a member of the commission on land transfer (1908–1909). To all of these formidable tasks he brought the qualities of relevance and impartiality which lead to wise and practical conclusions.

Probably none of his many distinctions gave Cave more pleasure than his election in 1925 as chancellor of the university of Oxford, after a contest, which he would gladly have avoided, with Lord Oxford and Asquith. To the affairs of the university, which in the previous year (1924) had conferred on him the honorary degree of D.C.L., he devoted himself with special solicitude.

In the early part of 1928 Lord Cave showed signs that the long labours of his strenuous life had used up his strength. He confessed that he was 'tired', and a troublesome question which had arisen regarding a judgment of the Privy Council in a case from the Irish Free State greatly worried him. By the end of February he was gravely ill, and on 29 March he died at his Somerset home at Burnham-on-Sea. A few days before his death he had resigned the lord chancellorship and his advancement to an earldom had been announced. The title of countess was subsequently conferred on Lady Cave.

Lord Cave was a great public servant. If his distaste for every form of display and self-advertisement tended to give an appearance of conventionality and reserve to his public work, he had another side which he showed to those who enjoyed his friendship and whose affection he had won. He would not have wished any estimate of his career to be silent on the great debt which he owed to the lifelong companionship and constant inspiration of his wife. In Lady Cave's books the reader is able to share some of the intimacies of his life. In her *Three Journeys* (1928) she tells of their visits: in 1901 to Zanzibar, where her brother, General Sir Lloyd William Mathews [q.v.], was British minister and Lord Cave's brother, (Sir) Basil Cave, was consul; in 1919 to Rhodesia in connexion with the royal commission; and in 1920 to Canada and the United States when Lord Cave was the guest of the Canadian and American Bar Associations. In her *Memories of Old Richmond* (1922) and *Odds and Ends of My Life* (1929) some account will be found of the Caves' home at Wardrobe Court, Richmond, in the beauty and historical associations of which they took especial delight. They had no children.

There is a portrait of Cave by G. F. Kelly in the hall of Merchant Taylors' School; one by W. A. Symonds in the justices' room of the Surrey Quarter Sessions Court; a third by R. G. Eves in the benchers' rooms at the Inner Temple; and a fourth by Francis Dodd in the hall of St. John's College, Oxford. His published work was confined to some editions of legal treatises.

[*The Times*, 30 March 1928; Sir Charles Mallet, *Lord Cave, a Memoir*, 1931; Lady Cave's writings; personal knowledge.]

MACMILLAN.

CHALMERS, SIR MACKENZIE DALZELL (1847–1927), judge, parliamentary draftsman, and civil servant, the second son of the Rev. Frederick Skene Courtenay Chalmers, rector of Nonington, Kent, by his wife, Matilda, daughter of the Rev. William Marsh, honorary canon of Worcester Cathedral and perpetual curate of St. Mary's, Leamington, was born at Nonington 7 February 1847. He was educated at King's College, London, and at Trinity College, Oxford. He obtained a second class in classical moderations in 1866, but took only a pass degree in 1868. In 1869 he was called to the bar by the Inner Temple, and sailed for India as a member of the Indian civil service. In 1872 he resigned from that service, returned to London, went into chambers at 1 Paper Buildings, and joined the home circuit. His ability soon became known to Farrer Herschell (afterwards Lord Herschell, q.v.) who had taken silk in 1872, and he invited Chalmers to help him in his work. In 1875 Chalmers moved to Herschell's chambers at 3 Harcourt Buildings, and in 1881 they both moved to 11 New Court, Carey Street. In that year Chalmers was appointed a revising barrister.

It was with the encouragement of Herschell that Chalmers undertook his first task as a draftsman of Acts of Parliament. After labour which involved the study of about 2,500 cases and 17 statutes he published in 1878 his *Digest of the Law of Bills of Exchange*. It contained a series of numbered propositions substantially in the form of a bill, with an added commentary. In 1880 he read a paper on the project of codifying the law before the Institute of Bankers. The idea found favour, and he was instructed by that Institute and the Associated Chambers of Commerce to draft a bill: this practically reproduced his digest. It was introduced into the House of Commons by Sir John Lubbock, and referred to a committee of lawyers and bankers, of which Herschell was chairman. In 1882 it was passed.

In 1880 Herschell became solicitor-general, and through his influence Chalmers was appointed standing counsel to the Board of Trade in 1882. In that office Chalmers had much to do with the reform of the law of bankruptcy, which resulted in the Bankruptcy Act of 1883. In 1884 he was appointed county court judge at Birmingham, and he held this office with general approval until 1896, with an interlude as acting chief justice of Gibraltar in 1893. It is said that Herschell, who was lord chancellor for a few months in 1886, and again from 1892 to 1895, desired to promote Chalmers to the High Court, and he did appoint him a commissioner of assize in 1895. But the only occasion on which Herschell had to fill a vacancy in the Queen's Bench division was in October 1892, when Sir William Rann Kennedy was appointed: and it was left for Lord Birkenhead to recommend the first promotion from the county court to the High Court in 1920.

While at Birmingham Chalmers turned to the task of codifying the law of the sale of goods. In 1888 he completed his draft of a bill, and settled it in consultation with Herschell. The latter introduced it in the Lords, not to press it on, but to elicit criticisms of it. In 1891 it was again introduced in the same House, and was referred to a select committee consisting of Lords Herschell, Halsbury, Bramwell, and Watson. Delay then followed, because it was desired to make the bill apply to Scotland as well, and this involved some redrafting, with advice from Scots lawyers. Finally it was again introduced, and received the royal assent on 20 February 1894 as the Sale of Goods Act 1894.

In 1896 Chalmers was appointed legal member of the viceroy's council, and went for the second time to India. He was there concerned with the revision of the code of criminal procedure. He also drafted and passed an act to obviate the evil of legal touting, an endemic complaint which the act may have ameliorated but failed to destroy. In 1898 he was made a C.S.I., and on his leaving India Lord Curzon, the viceroy, paid a warm tribute to his services.

Chalmers returned home in the spring of 1899 upon his appointment as assistant parliamentary counsel, and in 1902 he succeeded Sir Courtenay Ilbert as first parliamentary counsel. In September 1903 he was transferred to yet another sphere of activity when he succeeded Sir Kenelm Digby as permanent under-secretary of state for the Home Department. From this post he retired in 1908. He was made a C.B. in 1904, and created K.C.B. in 1906.

Shortly before his retirement Chalmers saw the successful conclusion of his third great work of codification, when on 21 December 1906 the royal assent was given to the Marine Insurance Act 1906. He had completed the draft of a bill embodying the effect of multitudinous cases in 1894. In that year it was introduced in the Lords, and was then considered at length by a committee of lawyers, shipowners, underwriters, and average-adjusters, appointed by Lord Herschell. In 1900 it was again introduced in the Lords, and Lord Chancellor Halsbury had it again considered by a similar committee. It passed the House of Lords in 1900, but was blocked in the Commons until 1906, when Lord Chancellor Loreburn took it up, and it was passed. The drafting of this act is as excellent as that of the Bills of Exchange Act and the Sale of Goods Act: but the subject-matter is not so amenable to successful treatment in a code as is that of the other two, and for that reason only the Act is less valuable than its predecessors.

Despite his retirement from office in 1908, Chalmers remained a busy man. In 1910 and 1912 he was the British delegate at conferences at The Hague about the international unification of the law of bills of exchange. In 1911 he was a member of the royal commission on Maltese affairs, and in 1916 of the royal commission on the Easter rebellion in Ireland. Throughout the European War he was a member of the war risks commission, and he was chairman of the commission which investigated German violations of the laws of war in Belgium. Among many other activities he was a member of the council of the Royal Aeronautical Society and vice-president of the London Fever Hospital, and he was keenly interested in the affairs of the Order of St. John of Jerusalem.

Chalmers never married. In his later years he lived at Wimbledon, and was almost daily at the Athenaeum Club, where he had many friends. He was also a member of the Marylebone Cricket Club. In December 1927 he underwent a serious operation, and died at a nursing home in London on the 22nd of that month. He was buried at his birthplace, Nonington.

Chalmers retained from his undergraduate days that affection for Trinity College, Oxford, which is felt by all its sons. Upon the premature death of Professor H. F. Pelham in February 1907 it occurred to some members of the college that Chalmers, who had played so many parts with distinction, might be regarded as fit to succeed Pelham as president. Asked if he would entertain the idea, Chalmers replied that he had not thought, or even dreamed, of such a thing, but in fact there was nothing he could more desire. He knew that those who made the suggestion had no power to do more than suggest, and could have felt no surprise when nothing came of it. But any one who knew of the incident had an added reason to applaud his generosity when the terms of his will were published. He left more than £103,000 net personalty: subject to bequests to certain relations, and gifts of £3,500 to the London Fever Hospital and £500 each to the Athenaeum Club, the Order of St. John of Jerusalem, the Royal Aeronautical Society, and an old servant, he left his residuary estate, including his books, to Trinity. The college thus received the greatest individual benefaction made to it since its foundation by Sir Thomas Pope in 1555.

Chalmers published the following works: *A Digest of the Laws of Bills of Exchange* (1878; in the form of a commentary on the Act of 1882 this reached a 9th edition in 1927); *The Negotiable Instruments Act 1881* (*India*) (1882, 3rd edition 1902); *The Bills of Exchange Act 1882* (1882, 14th edition 1918; a briefer commentary than the *Digest*); *Local Government* (1883, in the 'English Citizens'' series); *The Bankruptcy Act 1883* (in collaboration with E. Hough, 1884); *The Sale of Goods* (1890; as *The Sale of Goods Act 1893* this reached an 11th edition in 1931); *Digest of the Law of Marine Insurance* (in collaboration with Douglas Owen, 1901; re-issued under Chalmers's name alone as a commentary on the Act of 1906, 3rd edition 1922). He also contributed articles to *The Encyclopœdia Britannica* and *The Dictionary of Political Economy*. In the Law Library of Trinity College there are the successive drafts of the three Acts which were his masterpieces, with many of his annotations.

A posthumous portrait by T. M. Ronaldson hangs in the senior common room of Trinity College.

[*The Times*, 23 December 1927, 13 February 1928; *Journal of Comparative Legislation*, vol. x, 124; prefaces or introductions to Chalmers's various books; *Law Lists*; personal knowledge; private information.]

F. D. MACKINNON.

CHAMBERLAIN, HOUSTON STEWART (1855–1927), political writer, was born at Southsea 9 September 1855, the third son of Rear-Admiral William Charles Chamberlain, by his first wife, Eliza Jane, daughter of Captain Basil Hall, R.N. [q.v.], and grand-daughter of Sir James Hall [q.v.]. He was nephew of Field-Marshal Sir Neville Bowles Chamberlain [q.v.], of General Sir Crawford Trotter Chamberlain [q.v.], and of Major-General Thomas Hardy Chamberlain. He had hoped to follow a military career, but was prevented by ill-health. Various influences contributed to his education—the Lycée Impérial at Versailles, Cheltenham College, a German tutor named Otto Kuntze, and the study of natural science at Geneva (1879–1884). In 1878 he married Anna Horst. From 1885 to 1889 he lived at Dresden, and, having fallen under the spell of Richard Wagner's music and philosophy, wrote in French his first book, *Notes sur Lohengrin* (1892). Later he published further studies of Wagnerian drama—including *Das Drama Richard Wagners* (1892)—and a biography of the master (1895). In 1889 he had removed to Vienna, where he resumed the study of natural science under Professor Julius Weisner, and published *Recherches sur la sève ascendante* (1897). At Vienna was published in 1899 his *magnum opus*, *Die Grundlagen des neunzehnten Jahrhunderts*, which he had written in that and the preceding year. Other important works were his studies of Kant (1905) and of Goethe (1912), and the autobiographical *Lebenswege meines Denkens* (1919). In 1908 he left Vienna and settled at Bayreuth, where he married in that year Wagner's only daughter, Eva, as his second wife, and where he died 9 January 1927. He had no children. Late in life he wrote that since 1872 his 'intercourse had been mainly with Germans', and the result was that he gradually cut himself adrift from his native moorings and regarded himself as German; but he became naturalized as a German only in August 1916, when the European War, which provoked him to the most unsparing censures on the land of his birth, seems to have made a complete severance with England expedient. He had received the German military cross in 1915.

It is upon the *Grundlagen*, published in English in two volumes in 1911 under the title *The Foundations of the Nineteenth Century*, with a sympathetic interpretation written at the author's request by the first Lord Redesdale, that Chamberlain's reputation as a thinker mainly rests. It is a broad survey of the entire field of European culture—philosophy, metaphysics, theology, history, ethnology, art, music, literature,—provocative of thought no less than of criticism and dissent. To regard it, as is commonly done, simply as a glorification of everything German, is to disparage unjustly a remarkable piece of scholarship. Such a description would also ignore Chamberlain's definition of the term 'German'. For his '*Germanen*' comprise the Greeks, Romans, Slavs, Teutons, Celts, and other European stocks contained in the western group of Aryans. It follows that the *Deutschen* of the present German Reich are not all Germans in his sense, and that large groups of his true Germans are found in other countries.

Chamberlain attributed the foundation-laying of European culture to Aryan Greeks and Latins, and in a lesser degree to Semitic Jews. An enthusiastic Hellene, he nevertheless held that Europe owes most to the Romans, since they gave it order and organization, law and constitutional life, and also threw off Semitic influence and changed Europe's cultural centre of gravity from the East to the West. He claimed, however, that when the Roman tradition of universalism was destroyed and nationalism triumphed, it became the mission of the Teutons from the thirteenth century onwards to rebuild Europe on new foundations, of which the principal were freedom and faith. For him the '*Germanen*' represent the dominant European race of the nineteenth century, and he could write: 'So long as there are true (*echte*) "*Germanen*" in the world, so long can and will we have confidence in the future of the human family.' He even annexed leading intellectual figures of other nations—Dante, Shakespeare, Milton, Descartes, Locke, Newton—as legitimate Teutonic booty. While admitting English to be 'a marvellous medium of human intercourse', he yet believed that the German language would one day become the universal idiom.

Much of Chamberlain's teaching was unquestionably in keeping with the contemporary spirit of Germany, although there is no justification for identifying him with the physical force cult, the grosser forms of anti-Semitic intolerance, or the extravagances of a certain type of neo-protestantism in that country. As to the Jews, he held with J. G. Herder that their entrance into European history was the intrusion of 'an element foreign to everything that Europe had hitherto been, and achieved, and had a call to achieve', and he complained that in appropriating the cultures of other races they ever make them 'something different', invariably to the loss of these races; but he dismissed as 'perfectly ridiculous and revolting' the idea of making the Jew 'the general scapegoat for all the vices of our time'. Again, remembering the destructive trend of much modern German theology, it is noteworthy that, while rejecting 'ecclesiastical' Christianity, he not only (in Browning's words) 'believed in soul and was very sure of God', but he wrote of 'Christ and the Cross' as the world's one centre of unity and its great hope. For him, however, God was Christ, instead of the reverse, and he did not allow that Christ was a Jew.

The *Grundlagen* at once established Chamberlain's reputation as a bold and original thinker. In Germany a large body of admirers acclaimed him as the revealer and interpreter of the German spirit, nature, character—everything connoted by the word *Wesen*—and the appearance of the work at a popular price in 1906 carried it to much wider circles; while many British and American readers, however much repelled by Chamberlain's narrow nationalist prejudices, were impressed by the range of his thought, by his undoubted sincerity, and, not least, by the grace and lucidity of his literary style, a characteristic which may be fairly claimed as part of his English inheritance.

[Leopold von Schroeder, *Houston Stewart Chamberlain*, 1918; Anna Chamberlain, *Meine Erinnerungen an Houston Stewart Chamberlain*, 1923; Christof Netzle, 'Chamberlains Stellung in der deutschen Literatur' ('Die Literatur', 26. Jahrg., *Literarisches Echo*), 1924; G. Schott, *Das Lebenswerk H. S. Chamberlains*, 1927; *The Times*, 10 January 1927.]

W. H. Dawson.

CHAMPNEYS, Sir FRANCIS HENRY, first baronet (1848–1930), obstetrician, born in Whitechapel 25 March 1848, was the fourth son of the Rev. William Weldon Champneys [q.v.], rector of St. Mary's church, Whitechapel, afterwards dean of Lichfield, by his wife, Mary Anne, fourth daughter of Paul Storr, of Beckenham, Kent. The third son was the architect, Basil Champneys. Francis Champneys was educated at Winchester, of which he was a scholar (1860–1866), and at Brasenose College, Oxford (1866–1870), where he obtained a first class in natural science in 1870 and was captain of boats. He then proceeded as a medical student to St. Bartholomew's Hospital, qualifying for the degrees of B.M. in 1875 and of D.M. in 1888. Elected to the Radcliffe travelling fellowship of Oxford University in 1872, Champneys spent half of each of the following three years in study at Vienna, Leipzig, and Dresden. In 1880 he was elected assistant obstetric physician to St. George's Hospital and obstetric physician to the General Lying-in Hospital, York Road. In 1885 he became obstetric physician to St. George's. In 1891 he succeeded James Matthews Duncan [q.v.] as physician accoucheur to St. Bartholomew's Hospital, where he remained until his retirement in 1913.

With very decided convictions and an inclination to conservatism, Champneys had yet an openness of mind and breadth of outlook that led to his counsel being much sought by his professional brethren. He maintained to the last a remarkable understanding of the aspirations of younger men, well shown by the enthusiasm with which, in 1929, he joined a junior group in founding the British College of Obstetricians and Gynaecologists, of which he was vice-patron and councillor at the time of his death. He made many contributions to medical literature, but his influence on practice in his own branch of medicine was nowise commensurate with his success as a consultant and teacher and his many public services. The mind of succeeding generations was too much preoccupied with the introduction of surgical procedures into obstetrics and gynaecology to heed one whose bias was towards the medical aspect of these subjects.

Among his public services the most prominent was the part which Champneys took in the controversies leading up to the Midwives Act of 1902 and the work which he did as chairman of the Central Midwives Board, the body set up under that Act. First as a member (1882) of the board for the examination of midwives of the Obstetrical Society of London, later as its chairman (1891–1895), and finally as president of the Society (1895), he advocated the legal recognition and registration of midwives, thereby arousing an agitation which led to the attention of the General Medical Council being drawn to the form of certificate issued under his signature, and to its revision after mutual discussion. When the functions carried on by the Obstetrical Society were taken over by the Central Midwives Board in 1903, Champneys became its first chairman and was annually re-elected until his death, twenty-seven years later. Controversy gradually died down, and under his guidance the Board assumed the place which it now holds in the health service of the nation. He was also crown nominee from 1911 to 1926 of the General Medical Council, where he strove to improve the training of medical students in practical midwifery.

Champneys found in music his chief relaxation from professional work and was regarded in his day as the finest musician in his profession in London. He had a wide knowledge of sacred music which he studied under Samuel Sebastian Wesley [q.v.] while at Winchester, and composed hymn tunes, anthems, and other metrical works. An organ which he installed in his house in London he took with him to Sussex, where it became the great solace of his later years.

Champneys married in 1876 Virginia Julian (died 1922), only daughter of Sir John Warrender Dalrymple, seventh baronet, of Luchie, North Berwick, by whom he had three sons and one daughter. He was created a baronet in 1910. He died at his home, Littlemead, Nutley, Sussex, 30 July 1930 at the age of eighty-two, and was succeeded as second baronet by his youngest and only surviving son, Weldon Dalrymple-Champneys (born 1892).

[*Journal of Obstetrics and Gynaecology of the British Empire*, vol. 27, 1930, containing memoirs and a list of Champneys's medical contributions and musical compositions; private information.] J. S. FAIRBAIRN.

CHANNELL, SIR ARTHUR MOSELEY (1838–1928), judge, was born in London 13 November 1838. He was the only child to survive infancy of Sir William Fry Channell, baron of the Exchequer [q.v.], by his wife, Martha, daughter of Richard Moseley, of Champion Hill, Camberwell, Surrey. He was educated at Harrow School, whence he proceeded as a scholar to Trinity College, Cambridge. He won the Colquhoun sculls in 1860, and in 1861 the University Pair oars, and was in the First Trinity crew which competed successfully at Henley for the Grand challenge cup and Ladies' plate. In the same year (1861) he was twenty-sixth wrangler and obtained a second class in the classical tripos. Channell was called to the bar by the Inner Temple in 1863 and joined the South-Eastern circuit. Both before and after he was called, his father would make him listen to the cases in his court and draft judgments, which the baron would criticize and revise.

Channell specialized in local government work, and his intellectual power, which was combined with common sense and industry, specially fitted him to thread his way through the tangle of statute and case law which surrounds this subject. His progress, however, was not rapid. He was unassuming and somewhat shy, and he had no turn for sensational advocacy. But he gradually acquired a substantial practice, and in 1885 became a Q.C. In 1888 he was appointed recorder of Rochester, an office which he held until 1897.

In 1897 Channell, who was then in his fifty-ninth year, was appointed a judge of the Queen's Bench division of the High

Court of Justice and was knighted. He proved an admirable judge—able, dignified, and patient, although not without a pleasantly astringent wit when this was needed. His summing up to juries gave them the necessary guidance without forcing the judge's own views upon them, and he showed himself a master of legal principle. He tried Richard Archer Prince, the murderer of the actor William Terriss [q.v.] in 1898, the jury finding Prince guilty but insane. In 1906 he tried the Great Yarmouth election petition case. Channell differed from his colleague, Sir William Grantham [q.v.], and the judgment of the latter was the subject of embittered debate in the House of Commons. Channell also tried the well-known libel action of *Jones* v. *Hulton* in which the plaintiff recovered damages in respect of statements in a newspaper article made about an imaginary person to whom the writer accidentally gave the plaintiff's name. Channell's direction to the jury was upheld by the Court of Appeal and the House of Lords. Among his noteworthy decisions on questions of law were *Dulaney* v. *Merry & Son* (1901), a case concerning the 'conflict of laws'; *Torkington* v. *Magee* (1902), in which he solved one of the many difficult problems connected with the assignment of choses in action; *Compania Naviera Vasconzada* v. *Churchill & Sim* (1905), which involved an important question as to the legal effect of statements in a bill of lading relating to the condition of the merchandise when shipped; *Oppenheimer* v. *Attenborough & Son* (1906), which concerned the authority of mercantile agents to pledge goods; *Andersen* v. *Marten* (1907), a case arising out of the Russo-Japanese War, in which Channell held that a ship which is captured and afterwards condemned by a prize court but is wrecked between capture and condemnation, is lost by capture and not by 'perils of the sea'; and *Carleton Illustrators* v. *Coleman & Co. Ltd.* (1910), which raised the question of the right of an artist to prevent the owner of the copyright from altering his work.

In 1914 Channell retired from the bench. In the same year he was sworn of the Privy Council, and during and after the European War he rendered distinguished service as a member of the Judicial Committee in prize-court appeals (1916–1921). His own experience as an amateur yachtsman and yacht-owner since 1876 doubtless assisted him in his masterly discussion of the nautical questions involved in the case of the *Ophelia* (1917), an appeal from the prize court in which the issue was whether the vessel was a genuine hospital ship or was really engaged in signalling to German submarines. In 1921, when Lord Birkenhead enlisted the services of retired judges in an effort to dispose of the arrears in the King's Bench division, Channell, who was then eighty-three years of age, sat for a few weeks in that division. As late as 1927 he sat in the Privy Council to hear the last prize appeal arising out of the European War. He died at Falmouth 4 October 1928 within a few weeks of his ninetieth birthday.

Channell was twice married: first, in 1865 to Beatrice Ernestine (died 1871), daughter of Captain Alexander Wadham Wyndham, of Blandford, Dorset, by whom he had one son and two daughters; secondly, in 1877 to Constance Helena, daughter of Walter Blackett Trevelyan, barrister-at-law, of Hendon, by whom he had four sons and one daughter.

[*The Times*, 5 October 1928; *Law Journal*, 13 October 1928; *Law Times*, 13 October 1928; *Law Reports*, 1897–1914; private information.] D. Davies.

CHAPLIN, HENRY, first Viscount Chaplin (1840–1923), politician and sportsman, was born 22 December 1840 at Ryhall Hall, near Stamford, the third son of Henry Chaplin, rector of the parish of Ryhall and lord of the manor, by his wife, Caroline Horatia, daughter of William Ellice, member of parliament for Great Grimsby, originally of Invergarry, Inverness, and niece of Edward Ellice the elder [q.v.], and of Horatio Ross [q.v.], Nelson's godson. John Chaplin (1658–1714), son of Sir Francis Chaplin, lord mayor of London, became squire of Tathwell, Lincolnshire, by his marriage with Elizabeth, only daughter and heiress of Sir John Hamby. In 1719 their fourth son, Thomas Chaplin (1684–1747), bought Blankney, Lincolnshire, which had formed part of the forfeited estates of Sir William Widdrington, fourth Baron Widdrington [q.v.]. Blankney Hall remained the Chaplin home until 1897.

After his father's death in March 1849, Henry Chaplin's mother and her family went to live at Blankney Hall with his uncle, Charles Chaplin, who, after the death of Henry's two elder brothers, brought him up as his heir. He was sent at the age of nine to a dame's school at Brighton, kept by a Mrs. Walker, spent two years at Harrow (1854–1856), studied with a private coach at Walton d'Eivile,

Warwickshire, and in 1858 matriculated from Christ Church as a gentleman commoner, going into residence in January 1859. At Christ Church he was contemporary with the Prince of Wales, with whom he made a lifelong friendship. In later days he was frequently at Sandringham. Queen Alexandra entrusted her daughters to his guidance in the hunting field and Queen Victoria telegraphed to him when her ponies had pink-eye.

Chaplin went down from Oxford in 1860, in order to take part in an expedition to the Rocky Mountains with (Sir) John Rae [q.v.]. The party landed at New York early in April 1861 whence they proceeded to Fort Garry (afterwards Winnipeg) but were turned back by the appearance of Black Foot Indians on the war path. Lake Chaplin, a salt lake in Saskatchewan, near the town of Moosejaw, was named after Chaplin by Rae.

On the death of his uncle in 1859 Chaplin became squire of Blankney, a title which he valued highly. 'No one', said Lord Willoughby de Broke, 'was half such a country gentleman as Henry Chaplin looked.' In his earlier days, if not throughout life, Chaplin's primary interests were hunting and racing. Politics, though important, were secondary. Hunting was more than a pastime, it was a study of absorbing scientific interest. His father brought him up with the Cottesmore and gave him his first lessons on a pony, and Lord Henry Bentinck, then master of the Burton hunt, completed his education. While at Oxford he hunted six days a week and had four hunters of his own, besides auxiliary mounts. It was hunting there that laid the foundation of his acquaintance with the Prince of Wales, who not infrequently stayed with him for hunting, at Burghersh Chantrey and at Blankney. In 1864 Chaplin purchased the Burton pack from Lord Henry Bentinck, and in 1865 succeeded Lord Doneraile as master of the Burton hunt, to which, like his uncle Charles, he contributed £1,200 a year. It had a famous whipper-in, Will Goodall, a description of whose methods, in a letter from Bentinck, was published by Chaplin in 1922 under the title of *Foxhounds and their handling in the Field*, with an introduction which is a literary masterpiece after the manner of Cobbett. While master, Chaplin kept four packs and hunted the country six days a week, mainly at his own expense. In 1871, when the country was divided, he retained the southern part, designated the Blankney hunt, with the greater part of the old pack. On account of his political duties he soon afterwards transferred the mastership to his brother Edward, but he acted again as master himself from 1877 to 1881. In 1883 he sold the pack to Lord Lonsdale. He continued to hunt until his latest days with the Cottesmore. In the opinion of the well-known jockey, Henry Custance [q.v.], he was 'the best big man that ever crossed a country'.

On the turf Chaplin's fortunes were chequered, but early in life he had a notable triumph. In June 1865, at the annual sale of William Blenkiron [q.v.], he purchased for a thousand guineas a yearling colt, which he named 'Hermit', and which in 1867 won the Derby by a neck at starting odds of 66 to 1 against, after breaking a blood vessel ten days before. Among the field was Mr. F. Pryor's 'Rake', and *Punch* improved the occasion by saying 'Who will dare say that racing is a sinful amusement? Think of £160,000 carried off from a Rake by a Hermit for the benefit of a Chaplin.' Chaplin was elected a member of the Jockey Club in 1865 and succeeded Lord Calthorpe as a steward in 1873.

In politics as in hunting Lord Henry Bentinck was Chaplin's instructor. Like him and his more famous brother, Lord George Bentinck [q.v.], Chaplin was a follower and admirer of Disraeli. He was born a protectionist and always retained the belief that protection meant fair play and that a tariff was the only means of restoring to the English farmer a satisfactory livelihood. Throughout life he was a force in the county constituencies, especially among farmers, whom he thoroughly understood. Accompanied by his agent he drove rapidly from one meeting to another in a dog-cart furnished with a magnum of champagne. At the general election of 1868 he was returned to parliament unopposed, for Mid-Lincolnshire, known after 1885 as the Sleaford division, and he continued to hold the seat until 1906, when he was defeated in the great liberal victory. In the following year he was returned at a by-election for Wimbledon, defeating the Hon. Bertrand Russell by a majority of seven thousand. He continued to hold this seat until he became a peer in 1916. He made his mark on 29 April 1869 in his maiden speech against the disestablishment of the Irish Church. He was congratulated by his leader, Disraeli, and complimented by Gladstone, whom he was criticizing. Although vehemently opposed to him in politics, Gladstone liked Chaplin, and retained to the end a kindly feeling for him. In April 1873 Disraeli put Chaplin on a small party committee of men of social influence to prepare the constituencies for the impending general election. Although not greatly devoted to the House of Commons, Chaplin, who was deeply interested in the Agricultural Holdings Bill, sacrificed Goodwood and a houseful of guests in order to support his leader in the minor political crisis caused by the protest made on 22 July 1875 by Samuel Plimsoll [q.v.] when Disraeli announced that he intended to drop the Merchant Shipping Bill in order to proceed with the agricultural measure.

In the following August Disraeli proposed to appoint Chaplin chief secretary for Ireland instead of Sir Michael Hicks Beach [q.v.], who was to go to the Board of Trade, but finally decided that he was 'not experienced enough for this nest of corruption'.

From 1880 to 1885 Chaplin was in opposition. In party matters he found himself in disagreement with Lord Randolph Churchill [q.v.]. The difference first manifested itself in 1878 when Chaplin, after listening to a speech by Lord Randolph, advised him, if such were his opinions, 'to lose not a moment in going over to the other side of the house'. When in 1880 Churchill and his 'Fourth Party' began to show themselves openly hostile to Sir Stafford Northcote [q.v.], Chaplin was one of those who rallied most warmly to Northcote's support, and in August 1883 Churchill wrote to Sir Henry Drummond Wolff [q.v.] that 'H. Chaplin and the Baron de Worms will soon make the tory party too hot to hold me'. When later in that year Churchill developed in the National Union of Conservative Associations his attack on the autocratic Central Committee set up by Lord Beaconsfield in 1880, Chaplin secured election to the council of the National Union and continued the battle there without great success. In Lord Salisbury's short administration Chaplin was chancellor of the Duchy of Lancaster from June 1885 to January 1886, and on Salisbury's return to power in July 1886 he was offered the presidency of the Local Government Board, but declined to take office without a seat in the Cabinet. In 1889 he entered the Cabinet as president of the newly formed Board of Agriculture. He had charge of the Small Holdings Act, which obtained the royal assent just before the ministry went out of office in July 1892.

On the return of the conservatives to power in 1895 Chaplin was included in the Cabinet as president of the Local Government Board, and he introduced the Agricultural Rating Act in 1896, the Vaccination Act in 1898, and the Housing Act in 1900. When Lord Salisbury reconstructed his Cabinet after the general election in 1900, Chaplin resigned office at Salisbury's request, because of the necessity for 'creating vacancies for others', but declined a peerage. At this period he had lost influence in the House of Commons. He was too pragmatical and not sufficiently supple in debate. His Agricultural Rating Bill roused fierce opposition, ably led by Sir William Harcourt. He was also addicted to advocating measures, such as bimetallism, which were not part of the party programme, the exact effect of which it was difficult to foresee. His advocacy of protection under the name of 'fair trade' was also at that time a serious disqualification for office.

Out of office Chaplin continued to speak in parliament on agricultural matters; served on several royal commissions; and was president of the old age pensions committee. But in the summer of 1903 when Joseph Chamberlain [q.v.] outlined his plans for a preferential tariff and exhorted the nation 'to think imperially', he found a larger field. At Chamberlain's request he became the representative of agriculture on the tariff reform commission, and he spoke frequently and with effect in the constituencies. According to his own statement it was his desire for an 'effective scheme of preference' that kept him in parliament. In the early months of 1914 he supported with equal zeal the cause of Ulster.

After the outbreak of the European War in August, Chaplin was active in advising on agricultural questions. He did not support the Coalition government formed in 1915, and became by common consent the leader of the opposition, but it was an opposition of suggestion and friendly criticism. When there was real hostility, as on the subject of the Military Service Bill, he would have nothing to do with it. In 1916 he was created Viscount Chaplin, of St. Oswald's, Blankney. He disapproved strongly of the continuance of the Coalition ministry after the War. When he went to the Carlton Club on 19 October 1922 to protest against its prolongation he was warmly cheered by the crowd in Pall Mall.

Chaplin's magnificent hospitality and the cost of his stables and kennels early impaired his fortune. His wife's uncle by marriage, the first Duke of Westminster, remarked, 'When our Harry is broke, which is only a matter of time, all the crowned heads of Europe ought to give him a hundred thousand a year in order that he may show them how to spend their money.' His family home, Blankney, was mortgaged, and in 1897 passed into the hands of Lord Londesborough, whose father had been one of the chief mortgagees. In later times Chaplin frequently made Stafford House, the London residence of his brother-in-law, the Duke of Sutherland, his head-quarters. After the duke's death in 1913, he lived in a flat in Charles Street, until October 1922, when his son-in-law, the Marquess of Londonderry, gave him a suite of rooms in Londonderry House. He died there 29 May 1923 and was buried at Blankney.

Chaplin was strikingly handsome as a young man; later on, as a well-known parliamentary figure his dignified appearance was a delight to the cartoonists of *Punch.* In 1864 Chaplin was engaged to be married to Lady Florence Paget, only daughter of the second Marquess of Anglesey, but within a few days of the date fixed for their wedding she eloped with and married the Marquess of Hastings, who subsequently lost approximately £120,000 at Chaplin's Derby in 1867. In 1876 Chaplin married Lady Florence Sutherland Leveson-Gower (died 1881), elder daughter of George, third Duke of Sutherland; by her he had one son, Eric (born 1877), who succeeded as second viscount, and two daughters.

[*The Times*, 30 May and 1 June 1923; Lady Londonderry, *Henry Chaplin*, 1926; *National Review*, July 1923; W. S. Churchill, *Lord Randolph Churchill*, 2 vols., 1906; W. F. Monypenny and G. E. Buckle, *Life of Benjamin Disraeli*, vols. v, vi, 1920; *Victoria County History of Lincolnshire*, vol. ii, 501–4; Sir H. W. Lucy, *Diaries of Parliament*, *passim*; Sir Sidney Lee, *Edward VII*, 1925, vol. i, index; Hon. G. Lambton, *Men and Horses I have known*, 1924; Henry Custance, *Riding Recollections*, 1894; H. H. Dixon, *The Druid*, 1880. Portrait, *Royal Academy Pictures*, 1909.]

E. I. CARLYLE.

CHASE, FREDERIC HENRY (1853–1925), bishop of Ely, the only son of the Rev. Charles Frederic Chase, rector of St. Andrew's-by-the-Wardrobe and St. Anne's, Blackfriars, by his wife, Susan, daughter of John Alliston, was born at St. Andrew's rectory, Blackfriars, 21 February 1853. He was educated at King's College School, London, and proceeded as a scholar to Christ's College, Cambridge, whence he graduated as eighth classic in the tripos of 1876. He was ordained deacon in 1876 and priest in 1877. Chase gained pastoral experience as curate of Sherborne, Dorset (1876–1879) and of St. Michael's, Cambridge (1879–1884). From 1881 to 1890 he was lecturer in theology at Pembroke College, Cambridge, and at Christ's College from 1893 to 1901. He was also principal of the Cambridge Clergy Training School from 1887 to 1901. In the latter year he was elected president of Queens' College and appointed Norrisian professor of divinity at Cambridge, a post which he held till 1905. He was vice-chancellor of the university from 1902 to 1904.

When Dr. Armitage Robinson founded in 1891 the important theological series entitled *Texts and Studies*, Chase contributed to the first volume a study of *The Lord's Prayer in the Early Church*—a valuable piece of work, in which ample use is made of the Greek and Latin Fathers and of the different versions, especially the Syriac. In 1900 he wrote for Hastings's *Dictionary of the Bible* three important articles—on St. Peter (Simon) and on the Petrine Epistles. These, like his earlier work, were marked by caution and completeness. His conclusion regarding 1 St. Peter was conservative, but it cannot be said that his judgement as a scholar was affected by theological prepossessions. After a full examination of 2 St. Peter he concludes that it 'is not the work of the apostle, but is a document which must be assigned to the second century'. Chase's Hulsean lectures on *The Credibility of the Book of the Acts*, delivered 1900–1901, were published in 1902 with important additions. These lectures are, perhaps, the most attractive of his works. His heart was in the Acts, and had leisure been granted him he would have edited the book for the *International Critical Commentary*. Even as bishop of Ely he continued to contribute articles on New Testament subjects to the *Journal of Theological Studies*.

Chase was appointed bishop of Ely in 1905, continuing to be president of Queens' College until 1906. He threw himself into his new work with great energy. His diocese was at first very large, including Cambridgeshire, Huntingdonshire, Bedfordshire, and the western half of Suffolk (565 benefices). But in 1914 Bedfordshire was transferred to the diocese of St.

Albans, and West Suffolk to the new diocese of St. Edmundsbury and Ipswich.

The bishop of Ely, however, still retained the oversight of 300 benefices and 360 of the clergy. Moreover, the revision of the Book of Common Prayer was in progress, and an important share in the work fell to Chase, who was trusted both for his learning and for his cautious judgement. In his primary visitation in 1910 he gave as his opinion that it was 'advisable that the Church should go forward slowly, cautiously, and deliberately in this confessedly difficult and anxious task'. Besides taking his share in the work as it came before the Convocations, Chase served on the three committees which revised respectively the Lectionary (of this he was chairman), the translation of the Prayer Book Psalter, and the Office for Holy Baptism; also on a fourth committee which drew up a 'Form and Manner of Making Deaconesses'. He took a special interest in the ministrations of women. His labour was not lost through the rejection by the House of Commons of the Prayer Book Measure of 1927–1928. The revised Psalter has been taken into the revised Prayer Book of the Church of Ireland, while the new Baptismal Office and the Form of Making Deaconesses are both used in England.

In the much debated question of an Alternative Office for Holy Communion, Chase again showed his Christian statesmanship. His speech in the Upper House of the Convocation of Canterbury on 11 February 1920 is a noteworthy utterance. He confesses that at first he was content with the present prayer of Consecration; he acknowledges that he once dreaded that if an alternative Communion Office were allowed, parishes would be divided between the old form and the new. But he goes on to say that he became increasingly conscious of a growing desire among English Churchmen for a form of the prayer of Consecration which approximates to that used in the old liturgies and in those of Scotland and the United States. He concludes by saying that he believes the new service 'to be true to liturgical principles, and to the thought and doctrine of the present Prayer Book' [*Chronicle of the Convocation of Canterbury*, sessions of February and April 1920, pp. 73–75].

Chase did not live to see the rejection of the book on which he had bestowed so much labour. In 1924 he resigned his see, and retired to Woking, where he sought a renewal of health. He died at Bexhill 23 September 1925, leaving behind him the reputation of a learned theologian, a conscientious administrator, and a faithful friend.

Chase married in 1877 Charlotte Elizabeth (died 1928), daughter of the Rev. George Armitage, vicar of St. Luke's, Gloucester, and had three sons and one daughter.

There are portraits of Chase by H. G. Riviere in Queens' College combination room and by George Henry at The Palace, Ely.

[*The Times*, 24 September 1925; personal knowledge.] W. E. Barnes.

CHAVASSE, FRANCIS JAMES (1846–1928), bishop of Liverpool, born at Sutton Coldfield 27 September 1846, was the eldest son of Thomas Chavasse, F.R.C.S., by his second wife, Miriam Sarah Wyld. As a child he was sent to Chesterfield grammar school, but a long illness supervened, and after private tuition he matriculated at Corpus Christi College, Oxford. He took his degree with a first class in the final school of law and modern history in 1869. He was ordained at Manchester in 1870, and after holding a curacy (1870–1873) at St. Paul's, Preston, became vicar of St. Paul's, Upper Holloway (1873–1877), and then rector of St. Peter-le-Bailey, Oxford (1877–1889). There the success of his Greek Testament readings for undergraduates and his widespread influence led to his being appointed principal of Wycliffe Hall in 1889. On the retirement of Bishop John Charles Ryle [q.v.] in 1900, Chavasse was nominated by Lord Salisbury to the see of Liverpool, and spent twenty-three years of untiring labour in that diocese.

By many Chavasse will be best remembered as the effective founder of Liverpool Cathedral: for although the project of a new cathedral had been mooted in his predecessor's time, the pressure of other work, the somewhat heated atmosphere of Liverpool churchmanship, and the controversy over the proposed site, led Bishop Ryle to stay his hand. He left the way open, however, for Chavasse, a man of training and conviction not unlike himself, but more open to the wider influences and tolerant charity of the time, and possessing the ability and persuasiveness necessary for the successful issue of so large an undertaking. After ten years the Lady Chapel of the new cathedral was opened for regular service (1910). Thirteen years later, when the first section of the main fabric, the choir and transepts, was nearing completion, Chavasse thought that the time had come for a younger man to replace him. He resigned and retired to Oxford, where he was elected an honorary fellow of Corpus, interested himself once more in undergraduate life, and meditated on the possibility of a new collegiate foundation in the university, which should make use of New Inn Hall with the adjacent buildings attached to his old parish church of St. Peter-le-Bailey, as a college or hall for undergraduates of moderate means and evangelical views. His scheme matured, and in February 1929 'St. Peter's Hall', which had been opened in 1928 as a hostel for undergraduates, in memory of him, was granted the status of a 'permanent private hall' within the university. At Liverpool his monument is not the cathedral only, where, in Founder's Plot his body was laid to rest, but a memorial church built in a new suburb, Christ Church, Norris Green.

Chavasse may fitly be regarded as the choicest spirit among the hard-working evangelical clergy of his time. His earlier teaching, both at St. Peter-le-Bailey and at Wycliffe Hall, was fruitful in the training of men who in their parochial work combined, after his example, the fervour of evangelical conviction with the system and order of sound churchmanship. In his prime he was an effective preacher; without very high academic qualifications, and aiming at no purely intellectual distinction, he could yet be listened to, week after week, by people of all ranks. Clearness of thought and arrangement, vigour and freshness of speech, sincerity of conviction—these were all his. But Chavasse's Christian life and example were his real message. His years in Liverpool included those of the European War and his errands of sympathy and messages of comfort to all who stood in need of them were never failing.

Chavasse married in 1881 Edith (died 1927), younger daughter of Canon Joseph Maude, sometime vicar of Chirk, Denbighshire, and had four sons and three daughters. The second and fourth sons lost their lives in the War, the former, Noel Godfrey, after gaining the V.C. with bar. Chavasse himself died at Oxford on 11 March 1928.

[J. B. Lancelot, *Francis James Chavasse*, 1929; personal knowledge.]

J. B. LANCELOT.

CHEATLE, ARTHUR HENRY (1866–1929), otologist, was born at Belvedere, Kent, 4 December 1866, the second son of George Cheatle, solicitor, of Featherstone Buildings, Holborn, of Belvedere, Kent, and of Burford, Oxfordshire, by his wife, Mary Anne, daughter of James Allen, of Dartford, Kent. He was educated at Merchant Taylors' School, at King's College Hospital, and in Vienna. After qualification he was one of (Lord) Lister's house surgeons at King's College Hospital. In 1899 he became assistant surgeon in aural surgery at King's College Hospital medical school, and in 1910 aural surgeon and lecturer in aural surgery at King's College Hospital.

Cheatle began practice in London when otology both in Great Britain and on the Continent was at a low ebb. By his original investigations he, perhaps more than any other man, transformed this branch of surgery into a scientific entity, and became himself a principal authority on the subject. In the middle years of the nineteenth century W. J. Wheeler and Sir William Wilde in Ireland, and Joseph Toynbee [q.v.] in England, had dissected specimens of the temporal bone and had commented on their application to treatment. Urban Pritchard had studied some points in the comparative anatomy of the internal ear. It was Cheatle's work which made a more general appeal both to British and foreign surgeons. Until his results became known little treatment was being given by otologists beyond what was included in very limited, empirical, and not altogether scientific methods. The so-called specialists did not then undertake operations on an extensive scale. General surgeons, notably (Sir) Arbuthnot Lane and (Sir) Charles Ballance, were beginning to perform with success extensive radical operations on the temporal bone and its surrounding structures. Cheatle's original investigations and publications gradually confined work of this kind to otological specialists only.

The chief aspect of Cheatle's original work was to correlate the anatomy of the temporal bone and its intimate pathological connexion with the spread of infective processes to mastoid cells, petrosquamosal and lateral sinuses, and the meninges of the skull and brain. At the sixth International Congress of Otology held in London in 1899, Cheatle was the curator of the museum. The specimens which he had collected from all over the world made a great impression on English and foreign visitors. This exhibition went a long way to impress upon surgeons the importance of otology as a special study worthy of a life's devotion.

At this congress Cheatle was awarded the Adam Politzer prize, which brought his name into international prominence. He was elected an honorary member of the New York Otological Society and of the Italian Otological Society. He was also elected Hunterian professor of the Royal College of Surgeons in 1906, and lectured on 'Points in the Surgical Anatomy of the Temporal Bone'. With Dr. Urban Pritchard he founded in 1899 the Otological Society of Great Britain, which became a special section of the Royal Society of Medicine. He was elected second president of this section in 1910.

On the outbreak of the European War in 1914, Cheatle was appointed lieutenant-colonel in the Royal Air Force, then in its infancy. Its officers, before his advent, were not subjected to crucial tests as to their fitness for the special work of aviation. The tests which Cheatle initiated and carried out are still employed upon all entrants into this service. For his work during the War he was awarded the C.B.E. in 1919.

In Cheatle's hospital and private practice, extensive operations on the temporal bone and its neighbouring structures became ordinary routine procedure. Old limited and useless operations were abandoned, and new ones were adopted which were guided by, and depended upon, the accurate knowledge gained by his work and that of international investigators, some of whom were not over scrupulous in adopting Cheatle's original observations as their own. He dissected and mounted hundreds of normal and abnormal temporal bones from both sexes of all ages, and based his practice and operations upon the evidence which they supplied. Other otologists followed his example. In 1911 Cheatle presented some 700 of these specimens to the Hunterian Museum of the Royal College of Surgeons, where they form a complete exhibition of the relation between the normal and abnormal anatomical formations of the temporal bone and the pathways of pathological processes arising and spreading therein. The collection, which was intended to supplement that of Joseph Toynbee, attracts aural surgeons from all countries. The choice of these specimens and Cheatle's descriptions of them in the catalogue testify to his industry and ability and form a lasting monument to his memory.

Cheatle, who was unmarried, died in London 11 May 1929. In addition to articles in the *Transactions* of various otological congresses and societies he published *Sight and Hearing in Childhood* (in collaboration with R. Brudenell Carter, 1903) and *Some Points in the Surgical Anatomy of the Temporal Bone* (Hunterian lectures, 1907).

[Personal knowledge.] G. L. Cheatle.

CHERMSIDE, Sir HERBERT CHARLES (1850–1929), lieutenant-general, was the second son of the Rev. Richard Seymour Conway Chermside, rector of Wilton, Wiltshire, by his wife, Emily Dawson, and grandson of Sir Robert Alexander Chermside [q.v.], army surgeon, who served in the Peninsular War and at the battle of Waterloo. Herbert Chermside was born at Wilton 31 July 1850, was educated at Eton, of which he was a scholar, and passed into the Royal Military Academy, Woolwich, at the head of the competitors. Nearly sixty candidates were successful in this examination, with Chermside, then aged seventeen, a thousand marks ahead of any of them. At the end of the course he passed out easily at the top of the list, and was commissioned to the Royal Engineers in 1870. He was a brilliant scholar, gifted with a remarkable memory which enabled him to apply his learning in unexpected ways as, for instance, when he corrected an interpreter in the middle of a proclamation in Crete. He was, moreover, an accomplished athlete, winning many prizes as a swimmer and oarsman, and emulating Leander and Byron by swimming the Hellespont.

In 1871 Chermside, with some other officers, received permission to visit Paris during the time when the communists were holding the city against French regular troops. He and another Englishman were arrested on a charge of assisting the insurgents, and next day were actually led out to be shot. They had, however, succeeded in getting in touch with the British ambassador, and after some difficulty managed to get out of Paris as queen's messengers carrying letters to the British government. Two years later Chermside's adventurous spirit found an outlet of a less exciting kind, for, after a period of ordinary duty in Ireland, he joined in 1873 Benjamin Leigh Smith's expedition to the Arctic regions in the ship *Pittsburg*, for which purpose he had obtained extended leave of absence. After this, a spell at Chatham on board H.M.S. *Hood* with submarine miners was followed by periods at Portsmouth and Devonport, where he learned the practical application of the method of coast defence by submarine mines.

Chermside's real career may be said to have begun in 1876 when he was ordered on foreign service; he did not return to England for twenty-three years, by which time he had risen to the rank of major-general. In that year (1876) he was specially employed in Turkey during the operations against Servia and Montenegro, and was acting as military attaché with the Turkish forces when Russia declared war on Turkey in 1877. The European powers intervened, the Russian march on Constantinople was stopped, and the Congress of Berlin settled the final terms of peace. Chermside remained attaché until June 1879, having spent the previous six months with the Turkish Boundary Commission. In July of that year he was appointed military vice-consul in Anatolia; while holding this appointment he was promoted captain (1882). In 1883 trouble in Egypt led to the dispatch there of a British expeditionary force, to the intelligence staff of which Chermside was appointed, although he was described as deputy assistant-adjutant and quarter-master-general. Here he came under the notice of Sir Evelyn Wood [q.v.], the first English sirdar, who gave him the command of the first battalion of the reconstituted Egyptian army. Now brevet major, Chermside stayed in Egypt for over four years, taking part in the Suakin expedition of 1884. He remained in Suakin with his command when the British force was withdrawn, until in October he was appointed governor-general of the Red Sea littoral, a post which carried the rank of brevet lieutenant-colonel, although he was still only a captain of Royal Engineers. In addition to continuous operations against surrounding Arabs, Chermside undertook difficult and delicate diplomatic negotiations with King John of Abyssinia, which he carried through successfully. Transferred to the command of the troops at Wadi Halfa in October 1886, he twice successfully repelled incursions of Dervishes at Sarras in that and the following year, whereupon a period of tranquillity ensued.

In 1887 Chermside was promoted brevet colonel, and in 1888 he returned to consular duties, this time in Kurdistan, where he remained for just over a year, when he went to Constantinople as military attaché. He spent nearly seven years in the Turkish capital, and was then sent to Crete as British delegate on the commission for the reorganization of the *gendarmerie*, and in March 1897 was appointed British military commissioner and commander of the British troops on the island. While there he did much good work, and was promoted from colonel to major-general in 1898, by which time he had spent over twenty years in Eastern Europe. On coming home from Crete in 1899 Chermside was immediately placed in command of the troops at the Curragh, but he was moved again in three months' time in order to take over command of the 14th brigade, 7th division, at Aldershot. On the outbreak of war in 1899 he went with his brigade to South Africa, where, in April 1900, he succeeded Sir William Forbes Gatacre [q.v.] as temporary lieutenant-general in command of the 3rd division. He was present at the actions of Paardeberg (27 February 1900), Poplar Grove (7 March), and Karee siding (29 March), and in the operations in the Transvaal, east and west of Pretoria, and in Cape Colony.

In January 1901 Chermside resumed command at the Curragh, and later in the same year was appointed governor of Queensland, assuming office in March 1902. Here he and his wife made many warm friendships throughout the state, which they toured to its remotest boundaries. He was friendly and sympathetic, approachable by every one, and proved himself also to be an administrator of sterling quality. His popularity was not lessened by his fearless expression of his own mind, and when he left Queensland he had established in the colony a reputation for high-mindedness, just dealing, and good sportsmanship. It was unfortunate that it became necessary for him to vacate the governorship after only two and a half years' service. The Australian parliament had been compelled, for economic reasons, to reduce the status and emoluments of state governors, and in order to afford an earlier opportunity for retrenchment Chermside resigned in September 1904, having previously surrendered voluntarily part of his official salary.

In 1907 Chermside retired from the army with the rank of lieutenant-general. Among the honours which he received were the C.M.G. (1880), C.B. (1886), K.C.M.G. (1897), and G.C M.G. (1899); in 1916 he was made colonel-commandant of his own corps, the Royal Engineers. He died in London 24 September 1929.

Chermside married twice; first, in 1899 Geraldine Katharine (died 1910), daughter of William Frederick Webb, of Newstead Abbey, Nottinghamshire; secondly, in 1920 Clementina Maria, second daughter of Paul Julius, first Baron de Reuter, and widow of Count Otto Stenbock. There were no children of either marriage.

[*The Times*, 26 September 1929; *Journal* of the Royal Engineers, June 1930; Sir J. F. Maurice and M. H. Grant, (Official) *History of the War in South Africa 1899–1902*, 1906–1910.] C. V. Owen.

CHEVALIER, ALBERT (1861–1923), comedian, the eldest son of Jean Onésime Chevalier, teacher of languages, by his wife, Ellen Louisa Mathews, was born at Notting Hill 21 March 1861. He received his early education at Clanricarde College, Bayswater, and at the early age of eight took part in 'penny readings' at the Cornwall Hall, Notting Hill. His parents were Roman Catholics, and at his mother's desire he was sent to St. Mary's College, Richmond, with a view to being trained for the priesthood. This did not appeal to the boy, who left school and became a junior clerk in a newspaper office. He was interested in amateur theatricals and at the age of fourteen joined the Roscius dramatic club. Subsequently, while engaged as pupil teacher at a school in Shepherd's Bush, he obtained, through his father, an introduction from the elder Dion Boucicault [q.v.] to a theatrical agent, and he made his first appearance on the professional stage on 29 September 1877, at the Prince of Wales's Theatre, Tottenham Street, then under the management of (Sir) Squire and (Lady) Bancroft [q.v.]. During the next twelve years Chevalier appeared at various London theatres and also went on tour, fulfilling engagements, among others, with William Hunter Kendal in *Diplomacy* (on tour, 1878), with (Sir) John Hare in *A Scrap of Paper* (Court Theatre, 1879), and with (Sir) George Alexander in *Dr. Bill* and *The Struggle for Life* (Avenue Theatre, 1890). He also appeared at the Court Theatre in two early plays by (Sir) A. W. Pinero, *The Magistrate* (1885) and *The Schoolmistress* (1886).

Chevalier, who had already made a hit with coster songs at provincial concert halls, appeared for the first time in a London music-hall at the London Pavilion on 5 February 1891, when he sang 'The Coster's Serenade', 'It's the Nasty Way 'e Sez It', and 'Funny Without being Vulgar'. He was immediately successful, and for the next seven years he was engaged in all the principal music-halls in London and the provinces. For months at a time he appeared at the Tivoli, the Oxford, and the London Pavilion, and occasionally he would be seen at as many as five halls in a single night. His songs were immensely popular, and in quick succession he introduced 'Wot Cher' or 'Knocked 'em in the Old Kent Road', 'The Future Mrs. 'Awkins', 'The Coster's Courtship', 'My Old Dutch', and others. He also began to give recitals in the country, frequently providing the whole entertainment himself. In 1893 he made an unfortunate venture into management, when, in conjunction with Hugh J. Didcott, he reopened the old Trocadero music-hall on 9 October; the venture lasted a few months only, and involved Chevalier in a loss of nearly £10,000. He went to America in 1896, and made his first appearance in New York at Koster and Bial's music-hall on 23 March. His success in New York was as great as it had been in London, and subsequently, under the management of Charles Frohman, he toured throughout the United States and Canada.

On his return to London, Chevalier began a series of recitals, first at the old St. James's Hall (May 1898) and subsequently (January 1899) at the small Queen's Hall. He gave these twice daily, and they proved so successful that he repeated them annually for many years, and in all gave over a thousand recitals. For a time he included in his entertainment 'The Follies' of Harry Gabriel Pélissier [q.v.]. He gave a selection of his songs before King Edward VII at Sandringham on 12 November 1902.

Chevalier appeared again several times on the regular stage, viz. at the Duke of York's Theatre in *Pantaloon* (June 1906), at Drury Lane in *The Sins of Society* (September 1907), at the Court Theatre in *The House* (December 1907), at the Hackett Theatre, New York, in *Daddy Dufard* (December 1910), at the Shaftesbury Theatre in *The Light Blues* (September 1916), and at the Lyceum (July 1920) in *My Old Dutch*, a play founded upon his successful song, with which he had already been on tour for nearly four years. At the Lyceum *My Old Dutch* was performed nearly 200 times, and there Chevalier made his last appearance in London on

9 December 1922. After a further short provincial tour, he was taken ill and died in London, after a severe operation, 10 July 1923.

Chevalier sang over one hundred songs, eighty of which he wrote himself. He also composed and appeared in numerous monologues, which proved equally popular. His work was always clever and highly finished, and, as he never sang an offensive song, his influence helped to make the music-hall of his time a more decent place. He wrote nearly twenty plays, but, with the exception of *My Old Dutch* (in which Arthur Shirley collaborated with him), none met with any striking success. He figured in several cinematograph film-plays, e.g. *The Middleman, My Old Dutch, The Bottle.*

Chevalier was rather under middle-height; he had extremely mobile features, expressive hands, and was a nimble dancer. He was a man of most affectionate and unassuming nature, and made many enduring friendships. He published more than one book of reminiscences. He married in 1895 Florence, daughter of George Leybourne, a well-known music-hall comedian.

[*The Times*, 12 July 1923; Albert Chevalier, *Before I Forget*, 1901; *Who's Who in the Theatre*; personal knowledge.] J. Parker.

CHEYLESMORE, third Baron (1848–1925), major-general. [See Eaton, Sir Herbert Francis.]

CHILDERS, ROBERT ERSKINE (1870–1922), author and politician, was born in London 25 June 1870, the second son of Robert Caesar Childers [q.v.], the Pali scholar, by his wife, Anna Mary Henrietta, daughter of Thomas Johnston Barton, of Glendalough House, co. Wicklow. From his father, the pioneer of Pali literary studies in England, who died of consumption, hastened by devotion to his beloved studies, at the early age of thirty-eight, Childers seems to have inherited his extraordinary powers of concentration on his work; from his mother, his intense love of Ireland, fostered by the fact that until his marriage Glendalough House was his only real home. He was educated at Haileybury and at Trinity College, Cambridge, taking the law tripos and his B.A. degree in 1893, and from 1895 to 1910 was a clerk in the House of Commons. Quiet and reserved in appearance, even in his early days he showed a singular power of rising to the occasion. At Cambridge his remarkable elocutionary efforts as a candidate for the presidency of the *Magpie and Stump* are still remembered as the occasion of the most delightful 'rag' there within living memory. Soon after he left Cambridge he began spending a large part of his holidays, either alone or with a friend or two, navigating some tiny little yacht through the storms of the Channel or the North Sea, or threading his way through the complicated shoals of the German, Danish, or Baltic coasts.

When, at the end of 1899, the call came for volunteers in the South African War, Childers was among the first to join the City Imperial Volunteer battery of the Honourable Artillery Company. As a result of this experience there came from his pen a vivid personal record of the war, *In the Ranks of the C.I.V.* (1900); he was also responsible, as a collaborator, for the official volume, *The H.A.C. in South Africa* (1903). But his most popular and lasting book, *The Riddle of the Sands* (1903), was the outcome of his yachting expeditions to the coast of Germany. The story, told with even more charm than his narrative about the C.I.V., and based on exact topographical observations of this coast, was a purely imaginary account of preparations for a German raid on England; but it at once touched the prevalent feeling of suspicion as to German plans, and became even more popular when it was republished in August 1914. In September 1903 he went to Boston with the Honourable Artillery Company on a visit to the Ancient and Honourable Artillery Company of Massachusetts, an offshoot of the London body, the first visit in peace time of an armed body of British soldiers to the United States. In the course of the celebrations he happened one day to sit next to Miss Mary Alden Osgood, of Boston: the two fell in love at first sight, and on 5 January 1904 were married at Boston. On his return to London in that month they established themselves in a Chelsea flat. Of this marriage Childers wrote some years later that it was 'the most wonderful happiness that I know'; indeed, in all his subsequent activities he and his wife were as one mind and soul. Two sons were born to them.

Childers's next literary work was vol. v of '*The Times*' *History of the War in South Africa* (1907)—a task which suggested to him a campaign against antiquated uses of cavalry, through his volumes *War and the Arme Blanche* (with a preface by Lord

Roberts, 1910) and *German Influence on British Cavalry* (1911). His summer holidays were, as before, spent yachting, chiefly in the Baltic in the yacht *Asgard*, modelled on the lines of Nansen's *Fram* by Colin Archer, of Larvig; the yacht was one of his wedding presents. In all these trips he was accompanied by his wife, who, though crippled, soon became almost as expert in seamanship as he was himself.

Meanwhile Childers's attention had been more and more concentrated on Irish affairs. Of unionist stock, he came back from the South African War with a growing inclination to liberalism; but in 1902 he still could write, 'I am not a Home Ruler'. It was not until 1908 that, after seeing much of Sir Horace Plunkett's work in Ireland, he wrote in a private letter, 'I have come back finally and immutably a convert to Home Rule'. Thenceforward he thought of little else but Ireland. In 1910 he resigned his clerkship in the House of Commons in order to devote himself to political work, appearing for a short time as liberal candidate for Devonport, a constituency which was little suited to him, and which he relinquished before the election came on. In London he joined a committee to discuss *Home Rule Problems* (the papers, including one of his, read before this committee being published under this title in 1911); and in his own book, *The Framework of Home Rule* (1911), he went farther than most Englishmen of the time in advocating full dominion status for Ireland. In July 1914, after the passage of Mr. Asquith's Home Rule Bill and the subsequent failure of the government to prevent the arming of the Ulster Volunteers, Childers and his wife undertook, on behalf of a small Anglo-Irish committee, to carry a cargo of arms in his yacht *Asgard* into Howth harbour, five miles north of Dublin, for the use of the National Volunteers—a task which he accomplished with complete success.

Immediately afterwards the European War broke out. Childers, with his knowledge of the German coast as displayed in *The Riddle of the Sands*, was naturally pitched upon by the Admiralty for reconnaissance work on the seaplane carrier H.M.S. *Engadine*. As an R.N.V.R. officer he took part in the Cuxhaven raid (November 1914), and during the rest of the War was employed as an intelligence officer and in training officers for reconnaissance work in the Royal Naval Air Service. He also did staff work at the Admiralty, and at the end of the War made an important report on the effects of enemy bombing on protected buildings. He was several times mentioned in dispatches, was promoted lieutenant-commander, and eventually, on amalgamation of the Naval Air Service with the Royal Air Force, held the rank of major; for his services in the War he received the D.S.C.

At the outset of the War Childers had joined up enthusiastically, in the belief that the rights of nationality promised by the Allies would be extended to Ireland; moreover, in 1917 he was seconded for service on the secretariat of the Irish Convention, which, however, failed to secure agreement on Home Rule. Bitterly disappointed in 1918 by the continued delay in giving any form of self-government to Ireland, he determined, on his demobilization in March 1919, to devote the rest of his life to securing, no longer dominion status, the time for which he believed had passed, but complete independence for Ireland as a republic. With this object, in the same year he accompanied the Irish republican envoys sent by Arthur Griffith [q.v.] to Paris to put the case for Ireland before the Versailles Conference, and in the following December settled with his family in Dublin in order to work in the Irish republican ranks. He wrote continually in the English, Irish, and foreign press to protest against the Dublin Castle methods of government and against the employment of the 'Black and Tans', some of his articles being reprinted as a pamphlet, *Military Rule in Ireland* (1920). In May 1921 he was elected to the self-constituted Dail Eireann as member for county Wicklow and was appointed minister of propaganda. After the truce of July in that year he went with Eamonn De Valera on the first delegation to London and was principal secretary to the subsequent Irish delegation which negotiated the Treaty with the British government (October–December 1921). But by this time Childers had become irreconcilable to any form of treaty which did not recognize an Irish republic, and in the Dail debates on the articles of agreement he vehemently opposed Arthur Griffith and Michael Collins, who were for acceptance of the Treaty.

After the establishment of the Irish Free State government, Childers joined the Republican army, and while actually serving in mobile columns in the south edited and published the Republican organ *Poblact na h-Eireann*. On 10 November 1922 his old home, Glendalough House, where he had taken passing refuge, was surrounded by Free State soldiers; he had a pistol, but did not fire it, as one of the women of the house threw herself between him and the soldiers. He was arrested, and court-martialled in Dublin on 17 November by a court which he refused to acknowledge; and on 24 November he was shot at Beggar's Bush barracks by a firing party, with each member of which he had first shaken hands.

At the time Childers's name was branded on both sides of the Channel as that of a traitor and renegade to both Ireland and England. But no one who knew the man believed that, whatever might be thought of his judgement, he had a particle of meanness or treachery in his nature, or that the course of action which he had adopted was based on anything but the prompting of his conscience and sense of honour. By his friends Childers will always be remembered as a man of indomitable courage, of winning modesty, of extraordinary generosity and, in his earlier and happier days, of a most engaging sense of humour.

[Basil Williams, *Erskine Childers* (a pamphlet privately printed), 1926; private information; personal knowledge.]

B. Williams.

CHILSTON, first Viscount (1851–1926), statesman. [See Akers-Douglas, Aretas.]

CHIROL, Sir (IGNATIUS) VALENTINE (1852–1929), traveller, journalist, and author, was the second (surviving) son of the Rev. Alexander Chirol, a member of a Huguenot family settled in England since the revocation of the edict of Nantes in 1685, by his wife, Harriet, daughter of the Rev. Denny Ashburnham, rector of Catsfield, near Battle, who came of well-known Sussex stock. Alexander Chirol took some part in the Tractarian movement in the English Church, but subsequently gave up his cure at Stoke Newington in order to be received, along with his wife, into the Roman communion. They went to the Continent, and while they were abroad Valentine was born 23 May 1852. Alexander Chirol reverted shortly afterwards to the Church of England, but his wife remained a Roman catholic. Valentine Chirol was brought up in his mother's faith, was educated mainly in France and Germany, and graduated at the Sorbonne.

Chirol served four years (1872–1876) as a clerk in the Foreign Office; and then spent the next sixteen years, from 1876 to 1892, in travel, mostly in the Near East, though he visited India and Persia in 1883, and Australia in 1890. In Egypt he witnessed from 1876 to 1879 the last years of Khedive Ismail's financial extravagance, Sir Garnet Wolseley's campaign against Arabi Pasha in 1882, the Sudan expedition of 1885–1886, and, at frequent intervals, the patient work of Sir Evelyn Baring (afterwards Lord Cromer) for the rehabilitation of the country. Chirol travelled much in the Turkish empire, then under the paralysing rule of Abdul Hamid. His first book, *'Twixt Greek and Turk* (1881), dealt with the question, left unsettled at the Congress of Berlin (1878), of the Turco-Greek frontier. He was present in Bulgaria during many of the stirring scenes in Prince Alexander of Battenberg's romantic career. He served a short apprenticeship to journalism at Constantinople in 1880 on the *Levant Herald*, and acted several times during his travels as an occasional correspondent, chiefly for the London *Standard*.

In 1892 Chirol was appointed correspondent in Berlin of *The Times*. Count Caprivi was then chancellor, and friendly relations existed between England and Germany, which Chirol did his best to preserve, as he held that there was no serious conflict of interests between the two countries. He was fortunate in establishing friendship with Friedrich von Holstein, the permanent official who for more than thirty years was the inspiring force in the German Foreign Office. After a close study of the country Chirol began to distrust the hard materialism of Berlin, and the impetuosity and vanity of Kaiser Wilhelm II; and he observed with anxiety the growing ill-will towards England shown in official quarters and in the press. The sudden dismissal of Caprivi in 1894 was disquieting; and in January 1896 came the Kaiser's telegram of congratulation to President Kruger after the Jameson Raid —a telegram which Baron Marschall von Bieberstein, the foreign secretary, told Chirol was an action of state, intended to be a lesson to England. Chirol explained the gravity of the situation to the readers of *The Times*; and would not unsay his words when British indignation and the mobilization of a naval flying squadron led the German government a few days later to minimize what it had originally emphasized. Thereupon Holstein closed the Foreign Office doors against Chirol for some weeks. The post-war publication of German state archives has disclosed a tribute paid to Chirol in 1899 by (Prince) Bülow, then German foreign secretary, afterwards chancellor, in a 'very secret' memorandum: 'Those Englishmen like Chirol and Saunders [Chirol's successor as *The Times* correspondent in Berlin] are most dangerous for us, who know from their own observation the depth and bitterness of German antipathy against England.'

Within a year of the Kruger telegram Chirol was recalled to England in order to take charge of the foreign department of *The Times* in London, at first as deputy for Sir Donald Mackenzie Wallace [q.v.], who in 1899 retired altogether. For the tenure of this post during a critical period Chirol was exceptionally fitted by his sound judgement and his wide knowledge of world politics and foreign statesmen. It was his practice, whenever possible, to visit personally the scene of any foreign complication. His influence was steadily exerted in favour of the Anglo-Japanese alliance (1905), the *entente* with France (1904), the subsequent understanding with Russia, and permanent good relations with the United States; and he constantly directed public attention to the grave features of German policy. In 1908 he became an original member of the board of *The Times* Publishing Company, resigning when he retired from the paper in 1912.

Two books published during Chirol's service on *The Times*, *The Far Eastern Question* (1896), and *The Middle Eastern Question* (1903) illustrate his visits to, and interest in Persia, China, and especially Japan, of whose remarkable progress he was a warm admirer; but India came gradually to hold the first place in his mind. He visited it seventeen times, and calculated that he had spent there altogether some six or seven years. Three of his most important books were about India: *Indian Unrest* (1910), *India Old and New* (1921), and *India* ('The Modern World' series, 1926). An admirer of the great achievements of the British Raj, he was also from the first a sympathizer with the native point of view, and in his writings strove to promote understanding and reconciliation between British and Indians. When he was at Printing House Square, Chirol helped to promote support for the Morley-Minto reforms of 1909, and he owed his knighthood (1912) to Lord Morley's appreciation of his services to India. When he left *The Times* he was appointed a member of the royal commission on the Indian public services (1912–1914), which reported in 1916; and the experience which he thus gained led him to approve the general spirit of the Montagu-Chelmsford reforms of 1919. *Indian Unrest* involved him in a libel action in the English High Court, brought by the Mahratta leader, Bal Gangadhar Tilak, to whom he ascribed in the book a large moral responsibility for outbreaks of violence and murder in India. At the trial in 1919 the verdict entirely vindicated Chirol.

In the summer of 1915 Chirol undertook for the Foreign Office a mission to the Balkan States on behalf of the Allied cause; but the miscarriage of the Gallipoli operations neutralized his efforts. He was present in Paris in 1919, during part of the peace negotiations, in order to keep the British government in touch with the French press. He frequently wrote on his own subjects for *The Times*, and continued his travels. *The Egyptian Problem* appeared in 1920 and *The Occident and the Orient* in 1924.

Chirol, who never married, had a wide circle of friends, both men and women, several of them among the most interesting figures of his day. A tribute to one such friendship is paid in his *Cecil Spring-Rice: In Memoriam* (1919). He was a water-colour artist of unusual merit for an amateur, as is shown by a volume published posthumously in 1929, *With Pen and Brush in Eastern Lands when I was young*. Never very robust, he died somewhat suddenly, 22 October 1929, at his house in Carlyle Square, Chelsea.

A portrait of Chirol by the Hon. John Collier belongs to Lady Margaret's School, Parson's Green, of which he was a governor.

[*The Times*, 23 October 1929; Sir Valentine Chirol, *Fifty Years in a Changing World*, 1927; private information; personal knowledge.] G. E. Buckle.

CHISHOLM, HUGH (1866–1924), journalist and editor of the *Encyclopædia Britannica*, the only son of Henry Williams Chisholm, successively chief clerk of the Exchequer and warden of the standards in the Board of Trade, by his wife, Anna Louisa, daughter of William Bell, of Aldersgate Street, wine merchant, and an official assignee in bankruptcy, was born in London 22 February 1866. He was educated at Felsted School, and proceeded as a scholar to Corpus Christi College, Oxford, where he obtained first classes in classical moderations (1886) and in *literae humaniores* (1888). He was called to the bar by the Middle Temple in 1892, but in the same year was appointed assistant editor of the *St. James's Gazette*, succeeding (Sir) Sidney Low as editor in 1897. In his work for the *St. James's* and in his contributions to weekly newspapers and monthly magazines, Chisholm gained a reputation as a literary critic and a sound conservative publicist. At the close of 1899 he left the *St. James's Gazette* and joined the *Standard* as chief leader-writer.

In 1900 Chisholm accepted an invitation from *The Times* to become joint-editor, with Sir Donald Mackenzie Wallace [q.v.] and President A. T. Hadley, of Yale University, of the new volumes of the *Encyclopædia Britannica*, which the success of the reprint in 1898 of the ninth edition had led the proprietors to have prepared. These eleven new supplementary volumes, which together with volumes 1–24 of the ninth edition constituted the tenth edition, were published in 1902–1903. The organization and the editorial work fell mainly upon Chisholm, and in 1903 he was appointed editor-in-chief in order to bring out another edition, which was to be an entirely new survey of the field of knowledge. The connexion of *The Times* with the *Encyclopædia Britannica* ceased in 1909; the Cambridge University Press took over the copyright, and the eleventh edition was published in twenty-nine volumes, under Chisholm's editorship, in 1910–1911. It was planned and executed as a whole so as to present the state of all departments of knowledge at the same period. This gave the work a unity conspicuously lacking in earlier encyclopædias. The *Britannica Year Book*, planned and edited by Chisholm in order to keep the *Encyclopædia Britannica* abreast of events, appeared in 1913.

In May 1913 Chisholm rejoined the staff of *The Times* as day editor, but from the end of that year until March 1920 he was City (financial) editor. He then resigned in order to resume the editorship of the *Encyclopædia Britannica*, the copyright of the work being now vested in the *Encyclopædia Britannica* Company, Ltd. The result was three volumes, supplementary to the eleventh edition, which with it constituted the twelfth edition, published in 1922. The new volumes gave the first impartial account of the War years. Chisholm died in London 29 September 1924. He married in 1893 Eliza Beatrix, daughter of Henry Harrison, J.P., landowner, of Holywood House and Arkdeen, co. Down, and had three sons.

Chisholm was physically a commanding figure, over six feet high, broad-shouldered, and with fine features. He had a kindly and generous nature, full of good fellowship, and he thoroughly enjoyed life. At school and college he was a keen cricketer and football player. He was musical, with a baritone voice. Intellectually also, Chisholm was a commanding figure. To scholarship he added special knowledge of modern English history, education, and English imaginative literature. He possessed great organizing ability and sound judgement. His work as editor of the *Encyclopædia Britannica* was brilliant, and the eleventh edition of it is his best memorial. Next in value was his City editorship of *The Times*: his seven years in that post included the War period, and he handled the new problems caused by the War with rare skill. His help in the raising of War loans was highly appreciated by the government. On trade questions, he was, from his *St. James's Gazette* days, a convinced believer in tariffs. Both in his writing and in the marshalling of his material he was lucid and orderly. In the United States he was looked upon as an excellent representative of English intellectual standards.

[*The Times*, 30 September 1924; Janet Courtney, *An Oxford Portrait Gallery*, 1931; *Encyclopædia Britannica*, vol. xxx, p. 669, 1922, and 14th ed., vol. v, p. 601, 1929; private information; personal knowledge.]

F. R. Cana.

CHRISTIE, Sir WILLIAM HENRY MAHONEY (1845–1922), astronomer, was born at Woolwich 1 October 1845. He was the eldest son of Samuel Hunter Christie [q.v.], professor of mathematics at the Royal Military Academy, Woolwich and secretary of the Royal Society from 1837 to 1854, by his second wife, Margaret Ellen, daughter of James Mahoney, of Killarney. James Christie the elder [q.v.] was his grandfather. Educated at King's College, London, and at Trinity College, Cambridge, he was fourth wrangler in 1868 and was elected a fellow of Trinity in 1869.

In the autumn of 1870, on the recommendation of (Sir) George Biddell Airy [q.v.], the astronomer royal, Christie was appointed chief assistant at the Royal Observatory, Greenwich. At that time observations were largely confined to determining the accurate positions of sun, moon, planets, and brighter stars. Christie entered heartily into this work, introduced several useful modifications into

Airy's transit circle, and in 1877 wrote an important paper on the declinations of stars as determined at Greenwich.

(Sir) William Huggins [q.v.] and Warren de la Rue [q.v.] found in Christie an enthusiastic advocate in persuading Airy to enlarge the scope of work at Greenwich by undertaking the regular observation of sun-spots and attempting the determination of the radial velocities of the brighter stars. With the assistance of Edward Walter Maunder [q.v.] the daily photography of the sun and measurements of the positions and areas of the spots were undertaken. This work has been continued to the present time and has yielded important information respecting the sun's rotation and the relationship of solar activity and the earth's magnetism. In the attempt to determine the radial velocities of stars Christie and his colleagues were not successful, as results of sufficient accuracy were not attainable with the equipment and methods then in use.

Christie succeeded Airy as astronomer royal in 1881. Photography and spectroscopy as applied to astronomy were at that time in their infancy but growing rapidly in importance. Larger telescopes were being made, and the silvering of glass was bringing large reflecting telescopes into use. Christie entered readily into these developments, and at the same time did not undervalue the importance of continuing the 'fundamental' astronomy which had been traditional at Greenwich since the foundation of the Observatory in 1675.

Considerable additions to the equipment of the Observatory were required before work in new fields could be undertaken. Christie obtained a large visual equatorial with an object-glass of 28-inches, a photographic refractor with visual guiding telescope so that Greenwich might take a part in the international photographic chart of the heavens, and an altazimuth to supplement the meridian observations of the moon. A great addition to the buildings was made between 1890 and 1897 for the accommodation of the larger staff, the library, and workshop. The new building is surmounted by a dome containing the Thompson equatorial, a gift of the surgeon Sir Henry Thompson [q.v.]. On one side of the declination axis of the equatorial is a photographic refractor with a glass of 26-inches diameter, and on the other side a 30-inch reflector. These new instruments were actively used during the whole of Christie's term of office, which ended in October 1910, when he retired at the age of sixty-five.

Christie made several expeditions to observe eclipses of the sun, and obtained beautiful large-scale photographs in 1898, 1900, and 1905. For many years he took an important share in the activities of the Royal Astronomical Society, being president from 1890 to 1892. He served three times on the council of the Royal Society, of which he was elected a fellow in 1881. He attended numerous international conferences of astronomers. While he considered the discussion of problems very valuable, he was cautious in adopting binding resolutions. He was an honorary D.Sc. of Oxford University, and a corresponding member of the Academy of Sciences of Paris and of St. Petersburg. He was created C.B. in 1897 and promoted K.C.B. in 1904.

Christie married in 1881 Violette Mary (died 1888), daughter of Sir Alfred Hickman, first baronet, of Wightwick, Wolverhampton, and had two sons, the younger of whom died in childhood. The elder, Captain Harold Christie, barrister-at-law, lived at the Observatory with his father until 1910, when they went to live at Downe in Kent. In 1922 Christie, apparently in fair health, started on a trip to Mogador; but he died at sea 22 January and was buried shortly before the ship reached Gibraltar. He was reserved in disposition, courteous, and hospitable. He was very determined in advocating what he believed to be for the good of the Observatory.

A photograph of the portrait of Christie by Jacomb Hood hangs in the octagon room at the Greenwich Observatory.

[*Monthly Notices* of the Royal Astronomical Society, vol. lxxxiii, p. 193; *Proceedings* of the Royal Society, vol. cii, A, 192.]

F. W. Dyson.

CHURCH, Sir WILLIAM SELBY, first baronet (1837–1928), physician, was the younger son of John Church, J.P., D.L., of Woodside Place, Hatfield, Hertfordshire, and Belshill, Northumberland, by his wife, Isabella, daughter of George Selby, of Beal and Twizell, Northumberland, and sister of Prideaux John Selby [q.v.], a field naturalist of note. Church was born at Woodside Place 4 December 1837. He entered Harrow in 1851, and in 1856 proceeded to University College, Oxford, his father's college, where he obtained a first class in the honour school of natural science in 1860. He then became Lee's reader in anatomy at Christ Church and a senior student of that college. He entered at St. Bartholomew's Hospital in 1862 and, adopting a medical career, resigned the Lee's readership in 1869. From that time until his resignation of the post of senior physician in 1902, he was continuously attached to St. Bartholomew's Hospital, where he held the usual series of intermediate posts and, for twenty-seven years (1875–1902), that of full physician. He qualified B.M. Oxon in 1864 and proceeded to the D.M. degree with a thesis on *Hydatid of the Liver* in 1868. In 1866 he was made assistant physician to the City of London Hospital for Diseases of the Chest, and during the epidemic of the same year was appointed to the charge of the cholera wards of St. Bartholomew's.

Church qualified M.R.C.P. in 1864 and was elected F.R.C.P. in 1870. On the death of his father in 1872 he inherited Woodside Place, his elder brother having died in 1867. Although a country life held many attractions for him, he decided to continue his professional career. Of the College of Physicians he was in turn examiner, councillor, censor and senior censor, and Harveian orator (1895). He was elected president of the college in 1899 and held that office with distinction for the exceptionally long period of six years. During his presidency he was appointed (1900) a member of the royal commission on the care and treatment of the sick and wounded during the South African campaign, which involved a visit to, and much travel in, the war areas. Shortly after his return (1901) he was appointed to the royal commission on arsenical poisoning in beer-drinkers.

As its treasurer, Church had rendered inestimable services to the medical school of St. Bartholomew's Hospital, and the reputation which he acquired for a remarkable business capacity led to his being called upon to perform a series of exacting tasks, both for the government and for the medical profession. These included membership of the royal commission on vivisection (1906) and chairmanship of the executive committee of the Imperial cancer research fund and of the distribution committees of the King Edward VII Hospital Fund for London and of the Hospital Sunday fund. He represented Oxford from 1889 to 1899 on the General Medical Council. He was also appointed chairman of a committee for the amalgamation of seventeen London medical societies, and, on the formation of the Royal Society of Medicine in 1907, he naturally became its first president, an office which he filled from 1908 to 1910.

Church's work met with recognition from various quarters; he was created a baronet in 1901, and after the appearance of the report of the South African commission a K.C.B. was conferred upon him in 1902. He was an honorary D.Sc. of the universities of Oxford and Manchester, a D.C.L. of Durham, and an LL.D. of Glasgow. After his retirement, Church continued to take an interest in the affairs of his county, as J.P. and county councillor.

Church was a man of handsome presence and innate courtesy which, combined with his decision and clear judgement, made him an ideal occupant of a presidential chair. His obvious uprightness inspired confidence in all who were brought in contact with him. As a physician he had a gift for accurate diagnosis which was seldom at fault. Oral teaching was not his method: his students learned most in watching his practice. He made no serious effort to obtain private practice, nor did he enter into the struggle of professional life. It would have been against all his instincts to push himself forward, but, if appealed to, he would give his considered opinion clearly and definitely, and he had the power of summing up a situation in a few terse phrases. Along with his other activities he had all the tastes of a country squire; he had played cricket in the Harrow eleven, was a member of the London Skating Club, and continued to shoot as an octogenarian. He died at Woodside Place 27 April 1928.

Church's chief contributions to medical literature were those relating to embolic aneurisms and the article on 'Acute Rheumatism' in (Sir) C. T. Allbutt's *System of Medicine* (vol. iii, 1897) which was based on a study of 700 cases.

Church married in 1875 his kinswoman Sybil Constance (died 1913), daughter of Charles John Bigge, of Linden, Northumberland, and had two sons and one daughter. His elder son, John William, having been killed in the European War (1918), he was succeeded as second baronet by his younger son, Major Geoffrey Selby Church, M.C., R.F.A. (born 1887).

[St. Bartholomew's Hospital *Reports*, vol. lxii, pp. 1–17, 1929; personal knowledge.]

A. E. Garrod.

CLAYTON, Sir GILBERT FALKINGHAM (1875–1929), soldier and administrator, was born 6 July 1875 at Ryde, Isle of Wight, the eldest son of Lieutenant-Colonel William Lewis Nicholl Clayton, of Sandown, Isle of Wight, by his wife, Maria Martha Pilkington. Educated at the Isle of Wight College, Ryde, and at the Royal Military Academy, Woolwich, Clayton received his commission in the Royal Artillery in 1895. He served under (Lord) Kitchener in the Nile expedition of 1898, being present at the battles of the Atbara and Omdurman, was mentioned in dispatches, and received British and Egyptian medals, the second with two clasps. He joined the Egyptian army in 1900, and was promoted captain in 1901. He was appointed deputy-assistant-adjutant-general in 1903 and private secretary to the governor-general of the Sudan in 1908. He retired from the army while still a captain in 1910, and was permanently transferred to the Sudan government service. In 1914 he became Sudan agent and director of intelligence in Cairo.

The outbreak of the European War recalled Clayton to active service. The forces in Egypt urgently needed reliable information, political no less than military, and Clayton's appointment (1914) as director of military intelligence at head-quarters was a happy inspiration. Owing to his knowledge of Arabian politics, he was in a position to assist the Arab revolt against the Turks, and by creating the Arab bureau in Cairo, to guide the course of the revolt throughout the War. In 1917 Clayton was promoted brigadier-general, and became chief political officer of the Egyptian expeditionary force which began the invasion of Palestine in that year. His first task was the administration of occupied Palestine territory. Later and more formidable tasks were to reconcile conflicting Allied interests in Syria and to soften the reaction of Zionism on Palestine. These and analogous duties severely tested his political capacity.

Clayton returned to Egypt in 1919 as adviser to the Ministry of the Interior. Anglo-Egyptian relations were passing through a critical phase. Egypt resented the protectorate: Great Britain would not withdraw it. Negotiation did not bridge the difference; and Clayton's task of maintaining order became difficult. Under pressure, his opinions shifted. In 1917 he had advocated annexation: in 1921, recognizing Egyptian aspirations, he courageously advised the concession to Egypt of political freedom. Following the declaration of Egypt's independence in 1922, Clayton resigned his appointment.

Thereafter Clayton was employed in Palestine as chief secretary from 1922 to 1925; in that capacity he assisted in negotiating a treaty between Great Britain and Transjordania (1922–1923), and held an even balance between Jew and Arab. He was next commissioned to settle various frontier disputes between Arabia and her neighbours Iraq and Transjordania. Negotiations at Kuwait (1924) had failed; but Clayton met Ibn Sa'ud, the ruler of the Hejaz, at Jeddah (1925), and succeeded in concluding the Bahra and Hadda agreements: then, travelling to Jerusalem and Bagdad, he obtained the assent of Transjordania and Iraq. From Bagdad he went to San'a (1926) in order to negotiate between the imam of Yemen and the Aden protectorate: but the imam was intractable, and Clayton abandoned the mission. He was compensated for this failure by negotiating with Ibn Sa'ud the treaty of Jeddah (1927), which finally disposed of differences between Great Britain and the Hejaz. This was Clayton's outstanding triumph in Arab diplomacy. Following his settlement of two minor issues in Arabia in the following year, he was appointed high commissioner of Iraq in 1929. He had barely recommended admission of Iraq to the League of Nations, when he died at Bagdad 11 September 1929.

Clayton's strongest instinct was caution, his supreme virtue patience; and to these qualities, so useful in the East, he added an unaffected and disarming manner. It was his habit before negotiation to consider a subject from every angle; and while very willing to concede unimportant points, he clung tenaciously to essentials. For the rest, he was an imperturbable and observant man, open to suggestion, and sympathetic with Oriental opinion.

Clayton was created C.M.G. (1915), C.B. (1917), K.B.E. (1919), and K.C.M.G. (1926); he was in possession of many Eastern decorations as well as the legion of honour. He married in 1912 Enid Caroline, second daughter of Frank Napier Thorowgood, civil engineer, of South Kensington, and had two sons and one daughter.

[Official documents for Egypt, Sudan, Palestine, and Iraq; *Report* by the British Government to the League of Nations of the progress of Iraq 1920–1931; Arnold J. Toynbee, *Survey of International Affairs 1925* (1927) and *1928* (1929); Sir G. F. MacMunn and Cyril Falls, *History of the Great War based on Official Documents. Military Operations. Egypt and*

Palestine, vols. i and ii, 1928; Lord Lloyd, *Egypt since Cromer*, vols. i and ii, 1933 and 1934; private information; personal knowledge.] P. G. Elgood.

CLERY, Sir CORNELIUS FRANCIS (1838–1926), major-general, was born at 2 Sidney Place, Cork, 13 February 1838, the fourth son of James Clery, wine merchant, of Cork, by his wife, Catherine Walsh. After being educated at Dublin and at the Royal Military College, Sandhurst, he was gazetted ensign in the 32nd Foot in March 1858. He was promoted lieutenant in June 1859, and in 1861 was appointed adjutant of his battalion, occupying that position until his promotion to captain in January 1866. Clery then turned his thoughts to military education, and in 1868 passed into the Staff College, Camberley, where he spent two years, graduating in 1870. The following year he was appointed an instructor at the Royal Military College, Sandhurst. In this post Clery proved an immediate success, and in September 1872 was appointed professor of tactics. On completing his term of office in May 1875, he published a treatise on *Minor Tactics*, the result of his teaching at Sandhurst, which for the next thirty years held the field as a textbook of the first importance: few British military handbooks can ever have exercised so much influence. The volume is now superseded by official publications; none the less, it is based on a valuable study of military history and it contains a wealth of historical illustrations which are not found in its successors.

Clery left Sandhurst in 1875 in order to join the administrative staff at army headquarters in Ireland; thence he was transferred to Aldershot in April 1877. A year later, when the attitude of the Zulus became threatening, he was sent to the Cape on special service as a major on half-pay. After the close of the Zulu War (January–July 1879), he returned home and was promoted brevet-lieutenant colonel in recognition of his services. In August 1882 he went out to Egypt as brigade-major in the expeditionary force dispatched under the command of Sir Garnet Wolseley against Arabi Pasha. After the battle of Tel-el-Kebir (13 September), Clery remained in Egypt on the headquarters staff, and subsequently acted as chief of staff in the Suakin expedition under Sir Gerald Graham [q.v.] in 1884, taking part in the fierce actions of El Teb (29 February) and Tamai (13 March). In these engagements he stood out as a conspicuous figure, for he had refused to adopt the new-fashioned khaki uniform and went through the campaign in a smartly cut scarlet jacket. For his services he was promoted brevet-colonel in May 1884 and was made C.B. He next served as deputy-adjutant and quartermaster-general in the Nile expedition for the relief of General Gordon in 1885, and was appointed chief of staff of the army of occupation in Egypt in March 1886. Having shown by his campaigning record that he was a fighting soldier, and no mere theorist, Clery was recalled from Egypt to the commandantship of the Staff College in August 1888. After five years' tenure of this position he reverted to half-pay until promoted major-general in December 1894. In 1896 he was appointed deputy-adjutant-general to the forces at the War Office. There he remained until, on the outbreak of the South African War in October 1899, he was appointed to command the 2nd division. These troops he led throughout the fighting which ended in the relief of Ladysmith (28 February 1900). For reasons never made known, he returned to England in October 1900, and retired in February 1901. It was rumoured that his recall from South Africa was occasioned by personal considerations in high places, and had no connexion with his professional ability. He was created K.C.B. in 1899 and K.C.M.G. in 1900. He died, unmarried, in London at the age of eighty-eight 25 June 1926.

Clery was a remarkable example of the mid-Victorian officer. Punctilious to a degree, a dandy of the old school (who dyed his whiskers), and an epicure, he was the embodiment of old-fashioned courtesy. Even in South Africa his dress was irreproachable; while his hospitality was renowned. Yet he was a fine soldier and gentleman, a brave man, and in his own way, a true student of war.

[*The Times*, 26 June 1926; personal knowledge.] H. de Watteville.

CLIFFORD, JOHN (1836–1923), Baptist leader, was born at Sawley, Derbyshire, 16 October 1836, the elder son of Samuel Clifford, a factory worker, by his wife, Mary Stenson. On his mother's side his ancestors were Baptists, and three of his uncles were preachers. His early educational opportunities were limited to elementary schools in Sawley and at Beeston and Lenton, Nottinghamshire. When eleven years old—at that time a twelve-hours' day for children was normal—he was set to work in a lace factory. At thirteen he was sufficiently expert to be able to read while occupied in mechanical work; and Emerson's *Essays*, which he absorbed in this way, became a decisive influence in his life.

Clifford's 'conversion' in November 1850 and his baptism on 16 June 1851 were associated with deep religious experiences and a definite mental awakening. The bible became the subject of his continuous study. The conviction of a call to the ministry followed, and in 1855 he entered the Midland Baptist College at Leicester. His student days were a period of severe intellectual questioning. The college course lasted three years, and at the age of twenty-two he accepted the pastorate of Praed Street Baptist church, in Paddington. He stipulated that he should be free to continue his studies, and this he did with such energy that, whilst fulfilling the duties of his ministry, he graduated in three faculties at the university of London: in arts, science, and law (1861–1866). Scholarship and omnivorous reading left their mark on the best of his literary work.

In settling at Praed Street, Clifford entered upon the one pastorate of his life. The congregation soon outgrew the small building; enlargements proved inadequate, and eventually Westbourne Park chapel was built and became a very well-known place of worship in London. Clifford's interests were unusually varied. He was an ardent evangelical, to whom a personal experience of redemption in Christ was the all-governing fact. But if his centre was fixed, his circumference was wide; he believed that religion had to do with the whole of life, economic, civic, national, and international, and that it claimed thought and will no less than heart. His boyhood had been passed among the workers at a time when Chartist ideas were prevalent, and although he abhorred 'class warfare', he was sensitive to the inequalities of opportunity under the existing social system. His sympathy with the masses was outspoken and unfailing; the radicalism of his outlook is expressed by his membership of the Fabian Society. For his readiness to take part in public agitation (e.g. by supporting the dock strike of 1889) he was often called a 'political parson', but he viewed it as a failure in duty for a minister to shrink from insisting on the social and political implications of religion. He was a formidable controversialist, but free of personal bitterness or self-seeking; and his moral insight had a certain detached and prophetic quality.

The service which Clifford rendered in directing the thought of free churchmen to the social aspects of religion is paralleled by his liberalizing influence in theology. He gloried in the fact that his own denomination, while definitely evangelical, had throughout its history refused to be bound by formal creeds, and claimed freedom to interpret the will of Christ in the light of growing knowledge and experience. He kept abreast of advances in science, and regarded such men as Charles Darwin as fellow workers in the kingdom of truth. Indeed, his responsiveness to modern ideas not infrequently troubled his fellow Baptists. Some were perplexed by a preacher who welcomed the principles of the 'higher criticism'. Those who took their stand upon the verbal, or 'plenary', inspiration of the Scriptures were uneasy at his acceptance of the evolutionary point of view. Others, again, resented his sympathetic attitude to non-Christian religions, in which, while firmly maintaining the unique authority of Christ, he found a *preparatio evangelica*. It was therefore natural that when Charles Haddon Spurgeon [q.v.] withdrew in 1887 from the Baptist Union of Great Britain and Ireland on the ground of its tolerance of 'down-grade' developments in theological outlook and of modern biblical criticism, Clifford, then vice-president of the Union, should have been foremost in its defence. For Spurgeon Clifford cherished respect and admiration, and his own evangelical outlook enabled him to understand Spurgeon's anxiety; but liberty was to him of such consequence that he firmly and successfully withstood Spurgeon's demand that the Union should adopt a definite creed, although he assented to the issue of a statement of 'things commonly believed'. This 'down-grade' controversy was more than merely a domestic concern of British Baptists. The outcome, for which Clifford was mainly responsible, was at once a vindication of the evangelical character of the Baptist Union, and a rejection of the idea that evangelicalism must 'run in blinkers'. In view of the position of the British Baptist Union as part of a fellowship represented in more than sixty countries and forming one of the largest Protestant communions, this stand for theological liberty was of far-reaching importance.

In another controversy Clifford was a protagonist. From the beginning of his ministry he displayed a close interest in popular education. He welcomed the Act of 1870 under which 'board schools' came into existence, and regarded the biblical instruction given in these schools under the safeguard of a conscience clause as a valuable element in general education and an arrangement fair to all the churches. It seemed to him only simple justice that denominational schools receiving grants from the taxes should, since their religious teaching represented 'sectional' views, be denied support from the rates. He held to the principle that no religious tests should be imposed upon board school teachers. Hence in 1893–1894, when an attempt was made, under the leadership of Mr. Athelstan Riley, to impose such tests in London, Clifford's polemic in the press was a factor in its defeat. A few years later (1902), the introduction of the Education Bill which sought to place denominational schools (henceforth called 'non-provided' schools) on the rates, and to secure for them maintenance grants on the same scale as the board schools (henceforth called 'provided' schools), although the non-provided schools were still to be left under denominational management, stirred Clifford to a vigorous campaign of protest. After the Bill had become an Act, he was the leader of the movement of 'passive resistance'. There can be no question that his influence, since at that time he was widely regarded as the most powerful platform speaker in the country, was an important factor in the defeat of the conservative party at the general election of 1906. Clifford took his stand on the ground of conscience, and maintained his position to the last.

In 1905 the first Baptist World Congress, attended by delegates from nearly thirty countries, assembled in London. The outstanding result of the congress was the formation of the Baptist World Alliance, with Clifford as its president. He held the office until 1911, and was afterwards deputy-president until the year of his death. His services during this period were very considerable, involving visits to the United States in 1911, and repeated visits to the Continent. An earlier journey round the world had occasioned the writing of *God's Greater Britain* (1899).

The extent of Clifford's literary output is remarkable. Much of it is occasional, e.g. his pamphlets on education; but a number of his works are of more permanent value. Some of the best are courses of sermons, such as *Is life worth living?* (1880). Archbishop Alexander, of Armagh, acknowledged his debt to Clifford as 'one whose depth of thought is mated with a singular majesty of expression'. Of his unhurried writing that judgement is true. Apart from his books—he wrote ninety-nine books and pamphlets—Clifford did much editorial work, and had a voluminous correspondence.

Clifford profoundly mistrusted movements for organic ecclesiastical reunion, believing that these involved sacrifices of truth and freedom which would enfeeble Christian witness before the world. All the honours which nonconformists were able to bestow were freely given to one who displayed a rare combination of leadership, integrity, unselfishness, and simplicity. His presidencies formed a remarkable and even unique series, including (in addition to the Baptist World Alliance) those of the London Baptist Association (1879), the General Baptist Association (1872 and 1891), the Baptist Union of Great Britain and Ireland (1888 and 1899), the National Council of Evangelical Free Churches (1898–1899), the Brotherhood Movement (1916–1918), and the World Brotherhood Federation (1919–1923). He was one of the first on whom King George V in 1921 conferred the Companionship of Honour.

Clifford died in the council chamber at the Baptist Church House in London 20 November 1923, a few minutes after delivering a brief and characteristically gracious speech. He married in 1862 Rebecca (died 1919), daughter of Dr. Thomas Carter, of Newbury, and had four sons and two daughters.

Clifford's portrait, by the Hon. John Collier, hangs in the National Portrait Gallery.

[Sir James Marchant, *Dr. John Clifford* (containing bibliography), 1924; C. T. Bateman, *John Clifford*, 1902; Memorial Supplement to *Baptist Times*, 30 November 1923; J. H. Rushbrooke, in *Baptist Year Book*, 1924; personal knowledge.]

J. H. RUSHBROOKE.

CLODD, EDWARD (1840–1930), banker and author, was born at Margate 1 July 1840, the eldest child of Edward Clodd, by his wife, Susan Parker. Of his six brothers and sisters four died in infancy and two did not survive childhood. Edward Clodd, senior, was a Trinity House pilot, and early in life was captain and part owner of a brig. Born at Aldeburgh, Suffolk, he lived for a time at Margate, whence his brig traded with the north, but he returned to Aldeburgh soon after his son's birth.

From his mother Clodd early acquired a love of reading. His parents, of Suffolk farming and fishing stock, were Baptists, and Edward was intended for the ministry. He attended Aldeburgh grammar school; but during a visit to London at the age of fourteen got work as a clerk and settled there. In 1862 he became a clerk at the London Joint Stock Bank, and ten years later was appointed secretary. From early days in London Clodd attended the Birkbeck Institute, read assiduously in the free libraries, and heard lectures. On Sundays he listened to the best-known preachers of every denomination and followed the controversies of the time with lively interest. His Baptist creed was exchanged for Congregationalism and he soon became friendly with many of the more liberal leaders of religious thought. The struggle over Darwinism quickened his early interest in science, and in 1869 (Sir) William Huggins [q.v.] got him admitted to the Royal Astronomical Society. Richard Anthony Proctor [q.v.] invited him to contribute to the weekly scientific periodical, *Knowledge*, of which for a time Clodd acted as sub-editor, and he gave occasional lectures on science or literature.

Clodd was a very industrious and disciplined reader, and he acquired a broad mind and, in the circumstances, a remarkably solid culture. His first work, *The Childhood of the World* (1873), quickly passed through four editions and was translated into six European and two African languages. In 1877 he joined the unconventional Century Club, where he met Samuel Butler, W. K. Clifford, John Tyndall, E. B. Tylor, and many other men of distinction in science and letters. In 1878 he resigned from the Royal Astronomical Society and joined the Folk-Lore Society. In 1880 appeared his book, *Jesus of Nazareth*, pronounced by the Unitarian *Inquirer* 'one of the best of its kind in the language'. It won for Clodd the friendship of T. H. Huxley, York Powell, John Collier, (Sir) Frederick Pollock, (Sir) Leslie Stephen, Mrs. Lynn Linton, and other well-known people.

Clodd's success had been laboriously won. Long hours of reading after an average of ten hours a day at work in the bank had strained his robust constitution. But the respect he had won in the banking world, his remarkable circle of friends, and the popularity of his books made him by his fiftieth year an esteemed and genial host. His *Story of Creation* (1888), a fine popular study of evolution, sold five thousand copies in three months, and publishers began to court him. At this time, under the influence of James Cotter Morison [q.v.], he had leanings towards the Positivist Society; but he found a corrective in his intimate friendship with Grant Allen [q.v.] and in the pagan wit of George Meredith. Clodd had a wonderful genius for friendship. Retaining the solidity of character which had brought him through his early struggles, he now revealed a fine sense of humour and a discriminating judgement—a combination of qualities which made him a magnetic personality.

In 1881 Clodd was elected to the Savile Club; he helped to found the Johnson Club in 1884 and the Omar Khayyám Club in 1892. The epicurean philosophy of the Persian poet best expressed his outlook from his fiftieth year onwards. In 1895 and 1896 he was president of the Folk-Lore Society and in 1895 of the Omar Khayyám Club. He lived chiefly at Aldeburgh, where his father's cottage facing the sea had been enlarged into 'Strafford House'. At Whitsuntide gatherings there and on his small yacht on the river Alde, he entertained nearly all the eminent later Victorians; besides the friends already mentioned, Thomas Hardy, Professor J. B. Bury, Sir Ray Lankester, Sir James Frazer, Sir Alfred Lyall, Sir Mortimer Durand, and George Haven Putnam, were often there. In 1900 thirty-two leading writers, including Herbert Spencer, subscribed for a birthday gift to him.

In 1906 Clodd became chairman of the Rationalist Press Association. He was by no means so combative as Mr. H. G. Wells represents him, under the name of 'Edwin Dodd' in *Boon*, although he was an agnostic from about 1887. Spiritualism was the only creed that found him aggressively critical. In 1915, on his seventy-fifth birthday, he retired from the Joint Stock Bank, and proceeded to write his *Memories*. A 'shrewd and excellent handler of credit', the *Investor's Review* said of him on his retirement. He was still vigorous in mind and body, lecturing at the Royal Institution in 1917 and 1921, and writing much on folk-lore and occultism. After 1922 he suffered occasional illness, sometimes severe, though his letters were still bright with humour and good stories. Only in time, as he saw his old friends pass away, did he begin to shed the optimism of his earlier years. In May 1928 he had a stroke, and for more than a year he suffered from aphasia, and could not read owing to cataract. He seemed to recover; but in the spring of 1930 he was prostrate with bronchial asthma. 'Death?' he asked quietly of the doctor shortly before the end. He died fully conscious and serene 16 March 1930, just three and a half months short of his ninetieth birthday. His body was cremated at Ipswich and the ashes were (as he had directed) scattered upon the sea off Aldeburgh.

Meredith called Clodd 'Sir Reynard', perhaps because of his shrewd expression; but on his native heath he looked like a sailor and radiated a bluff benevolence. He was essentially a man of generous and sociable disposition, who devoted unremitting attention to his guests, and showed himself a zealous humanitarian on all public issues.

Clodd's books, in order of date, were as follows: *The Childhood of the World* (1873, rewritten 1914), *The Childhood of Religions* (1875), *Jesus of Nazareth* (1880), *Myths and Dreams* (1885), *The Story of Creation* (1888), *The Story of Primitive Man* (1895), *A Primer of Evolution* (1895), 'Memoir of Henry Walter Bates' (preface to *The Naturalist on the Amazons*, 1892), *Pioneers of Evolution* (1897), *Tom Tit Tot, an Essay on Savage Philosophy in Folk-Tale* (1898), *Grant Allen, A Memoir* (1900), *Story of the Alphabet* (1900), *Thomas Henry Huxley* (1902), *Animism, the Seed of Religion* (1906), *Gibbon and Christianity* (1916), *Memories* (1916), *The Question—If a man die, shall he live again?* (1917), *Magic in Names* (1920), *Occultism* (Royal Institution Lectures, 1922). He also contributed articles to the *Encyclopædia Britannica*, *Chamber's Encyclopædia*, Hastings's *Encyclopædia of Religion and Ethics*, the *Quarterly Review*, and the *Fortnightly Review*. His literary remains are preserved in the Brotherton Library at Leeds; there is a portrait by the Hon. John Collier in the library of the Rationalist Press Association.

Clodd married twice: first, in 1862 Eliza (died 1911), daughter of Dr. Cornelius Garman, of Bow; they had six sons (of whom two died in childhood and one in youth) and two daughters; secondly, in 1914 Phyllis Maud, daughter of Arthur Mingay Rope, a farmer. There were no children of the second marriage.

[Joseph McCabe, *Edward Clodd, A Memoir*, 1932; personal knowledge.]

E. S. P. HAYNES.

CLUTTON-BROCK, ARTHUR (1868–1924), essayist, critic, and journalist, was born at Weybridge 23 March 1868, the third son of John Alan Clutton-Brock, a well-known banker, by his wife, Mary Alice, daughter of the Rev. H. J. Hill. He was sent to school at Summerfields, Oxford, and in 1882 gained a scholarship at Eton. From Eton he proceeded to New College, Oxford. At Eton, where he won an English verse prize with an ode in the manner of Shelley, and still more at Oxford, Clutton-Brock developed his love of literature and art, and the wit of his conversation and the brilliance of his circle at the university are attested by all who knew him. He obtained third classes in classical honour moderations and in *literae humaniores*. On leaving Oxford he was apprenticed for a short time in a stockbroker's office, but was called to the bar by the Inner Temple in 1895, and practised for some years. Meanwhile his natural bent for writing revealed itself in a number of early essays and poems. Some of the poems are printed in a posthumous collection, *The Miracle of Love and Other Poems* (1926).

Clutton-Brock married in 1903 Evelyn, daughter of Leveson Francis Vernon-Harcourt [q.v.], civil engineer, and settled down to a life of regular literary and critical work. From 1904 to 1906 he was literary editor of the *Speaker* and a frequent contributor to the *Times Literary Supplement*. To him this latter paper, which came into existence at the beginning of the twentieth century, owed much of its steady success and wide reputation: indeed, its editor went so far as to say that Clutton-Brock 'made it'. After being for a short time art critic on the *Tribune* and the *Morning Post*, in 1908 Clutton-Brock joined, as art critic, the staff of *The Times*, for which he worked as a writer on many subjects, ranging from gardening to religion, for the rest of his life. In 1909, at the age of forty-one, he wrote his first important book, which was also his best, *Shelley, the Man and the Poet* (materially revised in 1923; see also the introduction to his edition of Shelley's *Poems*, 1911). In this book Clutton-Brock combined a serious appreciation of Shelley's poetry with a sober survey of Shelley's life in a way which antagonized the whole-hearted worshippers of that poet.

The profound joy which Clutton-Brock took in his own daily work had led him to accept William Morris's aesthetic approach to socialism, and in 1909 he joined the Fabian Society. When the European War broke out in 1914 he had just completed an appreciation of Morris ('Home University Library', 1914). Morris, Shelley, and Swinburne were the favourite authors of his early literary years. The War wrought a considerable, if not a radical, change in his outlook. He may be said to have become less of an aesthete and more of a moralist. In a series of articles in *The Times Literary Supplement* (republished as *Thoughts on the War*, 2 vols., 1914–1915; see also *The Ultimate Belief*, 1916) he preached against turning patriotism into a religion, as he alleged the Germans had done. His outlook became more definitely Christian, and in articles and books from 1917 onwards he taught a religion of love, laughter, and beauty which, had he lived longer, might have won him fame as a religious philosopher. At the same time he continued to produce a series of essays on art, literature, and life, written more for pleasure than for profit, which represent his mature thought and culture. After three years of intermittent illness he died at Godalming 8 January 1924, leaving three sons.

The change from a broadly romantic to a more philosophic interest in the world in Clutton-Brock's later years may be gauged from the fact that whereas in his earlier writings the names of Shelley and Morris most frequently appear, in his later work the name of Christ, and those of Shakespeare and Mozart predominate. While, on the one hand, he repudiated the criticism of art in terms of morals which he found in men like Ruskin and Tolstoy, yet art, literature, religion, and politics were indissolubly linked in his philosophy of life. His opinions, always balanced, were far from rigid. In his *Studies in Christianity* (1918) religion had given him 'a buoyantly happy mood', but in 1919 he told his wife that 'he felt he had attained his religious optimism too easily', and at the time of his death he was still seeking a constructive philosophy of life. Hence his *Essays on Religion*, posthumously published in 1926, have been described as 'an unfinished torso' [B. H. Streeter, introduction]. But although his work in this field thus remained imperfect, and although we may suspect that the full flavour of his conversation never quite found its way into his books, Clutton-Brock must take a high place among that group of first-rate essayists which England produced in the first quarter of the twentieth century.

[*The Times*, 9 January 1924; *Observer*, 13 January 1924; J. L. Hammond, introduction to *Essays on Life*, 1925; (Mrs.) E. A. Clutton-Brock, introduction to *The Miracle of Love*, 1926; B. H. Streeter, *ut supra*; private information.]

M. P. ASHLEY.

COBDEN-SANDERSON, THOMAS JAMES (1840–1922), bookbinder and printer, was born 2 December 1840 at Alnwick, the only son of James Sanderson, district surveyor of taxes, by his wife, Mary Anne Rutherford How. He was educated at the grammar schools of Worcester, Hull, Pocklington, and Rochdale, at Owens College, Manchester, and at Trinity College, Cambridge, which he left voluntarily in 1863 without taking a degree. Sanderson then tried various occupations, and for a time studied medicine. In 1871 he was called to the bar by the Inner Temple. He worked seriously at the law, and carried out the heavy task of codifying the powers, rights, and obligations of the London and North-Western Railway Company. In 1881 at Siena, whither he had gone to recuperate from an illness produced by the strain of this work, he met Anne, fourth daughter of Richard Cobden [q.v.], the politician; and when he married her, in 1882, he prefixed her surname to his own.

It was at his wife's wish that, shortly after his marriage, Cobden-Sanderson abandoned the bar in order to seek self-expression in the work of his hands. He was in touch with the William Morris and Burne-Jones families, and shared the socialism and admiration for pure craftsmanship which were the central tenets of that group. It was Mrs. Morris, indeed, who in 1883 suggested that he should learn bookbinding. He became a pupil of Roger de Coverley; and in June 1884 opened a workshop of his own at Maiden Lane, Strand, moving a year later to Goodyers, Hendon. He rapidly established himself as a binder of admirable taste, fecund and versatile in decorative ideas, impeccable in technique, and scrupulous in finish. In March 1893 he opened, at Upper Mall, Hammersmith, the Doves bindery, which remained active until 1921.

William Morris issued his last book from the Kelmscott Press in March 1898. Cobden-Sanderson, although he had no technical knowledge of printing, then had the idea of founding a press. He was fortunate in securing as a partner the printer and engraver (Sir) Emery Walker. It was decided to revive the type used by the Frenchman Nicolas Jenson in the fifteenth century. Morris had adapted this as the foundation for his Golden type; but the Doves Press, as it was called, aimed at something lighter and more spare; and Walker enlarged the original photographically, re-drew it, and then reduced it again by photography. The first book printed was the *Agricola* of Tacitus, which appeared in January 1901. The second, a month later, was a tract by Cobden-Sanderson on *The Ideal Book or Book Beautiful*, which urged the close study of calligraphy by printers and laid stress upon the idea of unity in book-production. 'The whole duty of Typography', he wrote, 'as of Calligraphy, is to communicate to the imagination, without loss by the way, the thought or image intended to be communicated by the Author.'

The Doves Press issued fifty works in the course of its existence, which continued until 1916. Among the most notable were an English Bible (1903–1905) and a Milton (1905). Setting and presswork were done by hand. Only the one type was used throughout, and the lack of an italic fount was a disadvantage which could only be overcome by the use of red ink. The productions of the press are marked by a studious plainness, broken by this occasional red and, in certain books, by chastely designed red or blue initials. The books are in exquisite taste, though severely restricted in scope by the use of a single fount.

In the history of the arts and crafts movement, and indeed in the wider annals of British book-production, Cobden-Sanderson is an important figure. The very name 'arts and crafts' was his invention [J. W. Mackail, *Life of William Morris*, ii, 200], and in its beginnings had nothing of the slightly depreciatory meaning sometimes attached to it. Apart from its revolt against narrow academic tendencies and its preoccupation with handicraft, the movement had, in his view, a wider aim, 'to bring all the activities of the human spirit under the influence of one idea, the idea that life is creation, and should be creative in modes of art. . . .' [*Cosmic Vision*, p. 56]. The phrase may serve to describe the guiding principle to which, after many questionings, Cobden-Sanderson attained in middle life. His *Journals, 1879–1922* constitute a record of his spiritual development, and give him a place with such men as H. F. Amiel and W. N. P. Barbellion in the literature of self-revelation and introspection. Deeply philosophic in temperament, he constantly sought a unifying principle in life. His devotion to what he considered good and sound was uncompromising. He was very modest, and avoided publicity as far as possible. The drawing by (Sir) William Rothenstein in his *Twenty-Four Portraits* (later prefixed to the *Journals*) and the admirable photograph which forms the frontispiece to *Cosmic Vision* show a face which bespeaks great refinement of mind and high aspiration.

Cobden-Sanderson died in his sleep at his house at Hammersmith 7 September 1922. He had one son, who became a publisher, and one daughter.

[*The Times*, 8 September 1922; T. J. Cobden-Sanderson, *Cosmic Vision*, 1922, and *Journals, 1879–1922*, 2 vols., 1926; W. D. Orcutt, *Master Makers of the Book*, ch. ix, New York, 1928; *Cobden-Sanderson and the Doves Press* (articles by A. W. Pollard, E. Johnston, and T. J. Cobden-Sanderson), San Francisco, 1929; private information.]

H. B. Grimsditch.

COGHLAN, Sir CHARLES PATRICK JOHN (1863–1927), first premier of Southern Rhodesia, was born at King William's Town, Cape Colony, 24 June 1863, the fourth son of James Coghlan, J.P., of Cypherfontein and later of Clocolan, Orange Free State, who was at one time a member of the Imperial civil service, by his wife, Isabella Mary MacLaren, of Alice, Cape Colony. He was educated at St. Aidan's College Grahamstown, and at the South African College, Capetown. On leaving school he was articled to his brother, a solicitor at Kimberley, and in due course was admitted as solicitor, practising at Kimberley until 1900, when he moved to Bulawayo in Southern Rhodesia.

Coghlan, after establishing himself at Bulawayo, began to take an increasing interest in public affairs, and in 1908 was invited to stand for election to the legislative council. His decision to take an active part in politics did not commend itself to some of his more important clients. On Coghlan, however, on this as on other occasions, opposition acted merely as a stimulant. He decided without hesitation to risk the displeasure of clients and possible loss of business, and was duly elected to represent one of the divisions of Bulawayo, a connexion which he retained until his death.

At this time preparations were being made for the assembling of delegates from Cape Colony, Natal, Transvaal, and the Orange Free State at a national convention having for its object the formation of a South African Union, and it says much for the position which Coghlan had made for himself that when Southern Rhodesia was invited to send representatives to the convention, Coghlan should have been asked to attend in company with Sir William Milton, then administrator of the territory, and Sir Lewis Lloyd Michell [q.v.], who for many years acted as financial adviser to Cecil Rhodes. The minutes of the convention, which sat from October 1908 to May 1909, show that Coghlan was a member of committees appointed to consider questions relating to the franchise, the administration of justice, and the constitution of the provinces of the proposed Union. The South Africa Act, passed by the British parliament in 1910, in which the conclusions of the convention were embodied, contained a clause providing that the king might, on addresses from the houses of parliament of the Union, admit into the Union the territories then administered by the British South Africa Company, and it was generally assumed at the termination of the convention that the necessary steps would be taken to secure the inclusion of Southern Rhodesia. Coghlan himself was strongly in favour of this scheme. He soon found, however, that in Rhodesia there was little if any support for it, the Rhodesians feeling that they would be able to enter the Union on better terms when the population and resources of the territory were such as to warrant the establishment of responsible government. Coghlan, who was knighted in 1910 in recognition of his services at the convention, acquiesced in this decision, and thenceforward he supported the continuance of the British South Africa Company's administration until such time as the country could claim to be fit for self-government.

During the European War Coghlan, as leader of the elected members of the legislative council, gave general support to the administration until, in 1917, the directors of the British South Africa Company put forward the proposal that the two territories of Northern and Southern Rhodesia should be amalgamated under one administration. The scheme would have made possible a considerable economy in administrative expenditure, while a start would have been made with the building up of an important state which, as its population grew, would have had an increasing influence on South African affairs. Coghlan, however, considered that the backward condition of Northern Rhodesia, with its large native population, would, if amalgamation were effected, tend to postpone the grant of self-government to Southern Rhodesia. He therefore vigorously opposed the project of union with what he called 'the black North', and as his views were accepted by the majority of the elected members, the scheme fell through.

Meanwhile events were moving steadily in the direction of a change in the form of government in Southern Rhodesia. The Privy Council held that the unoccupied land was not the property of the British South Africa Company, but that the company was entitled to look to the Crown to secure to it the reimbursement of any outstanding balance of advances made for the administration of the territory, and it became evident that the territory must either enter the Union or be granted by the Crown sufficient assistance to make possible the establishment of responsible government. From that time Coghlan devoted his energies to justifying the claim of Southern Rhodesia to self-government. In 1921 he was the leader of a deputation which discussed in London a possible constitution. Between this scheme and entry into the Union (on terms proposed by General J. C. Smuts) it was arranged that the territory should choose by way of referendum. The referendum took place in October 1922. The verdict was a majority of three to two in favour of responsible government, and in October 1923 Coghlan became the head of the first ministry of Southern Rhodesia.

The first years of self-government were years of prosperity, and if the newly constituted government showed itself occasionally a little over-anxious to assert its authority, no great difficulties, financial or otherwise, were encountered.

Recognizing the value of the work which had been done by the British South Africa Company and its officials, Coghlan gave no encouragement to ill-advised attempts to pull up by the roots what had already been planted, so that in many respects, especially in regard to native affairs, administrative arrangements underwent but little change. He was at all times anxious to emphasize the close connexion between Rhodesia and Great Britain, and had no sympathy with the aims of the separatist party in the Union.

Coghlan died very suddenly at Salisbury, Southern Rhodesia, 28 August 1927, and was thus spared the difficulties arising from the economic crisis which since that date affected the world. The legislative assembly decided that, as one who in the terms of Cecil Rhodes's will had 'deserved well of his country', he should be buried in the Matoppo Hills, near Bulawayo, where he lies in close proximity to Rhodes himself and to Sir Leander Starr Jameson.

Coghlan married in 1899 Gertrude Mary, daughter of Colonel Frederic Schermbrucker, who for thirty years represented King William's Town in the Cape parliament. They had one daughter.

[Private information; personal knowledge.]

D. CHAPLIN.

COLERIDGE, BERNARD JOHN SEYMOUR, second BARON COLERIDGE (1851–1927), judge, is the fourteenth member of this distinguished Devonshire family to be noticed in this DICTIONARY. He was born at the family seat at Ottery St. Mary, Devon, 19 August 1851, the eldest son of John Duke (afterwards first Baron) Coleridge, lord chief-justice of England [q.v.], grandson of Sir John Taylor Coleridge, judge [q.v.], and great-grand-nephew of Samuel Taylor Coleridge, the poet and philosopher. His mother was Jane Fortescue, daughter of the Rev. George Turner Seymour, of Farringford, Isle of Wight. Bernard Coleridge was educated at Eton, where he was in F. W. Warre-Cornish's house, and at Trinity College, Oxford. He obtained a second class in modern history in 1875, and, amongst other athletic achievements, became captain of his college boat club. He was made an honorary fellow of the college in 1909.

After reading in chambers with the well-known special pleader, Baugh Allen, Coleridge was called to the bar in 1877 by the Middle Temple, of which he was later a bencher (1894) and treasurer (1919). He joined the Western circuit and there acquired a large local practice, chiefly in criminal cases. He was counsel for the defence in the Winford (1883) and Newton St. Cyres (1888) murder cases. In politics he inherited his father's liberalism, and was elected member of parliament for the Attercliffe division of Sheffield in 1885, as a follower of Mr. Gladstone, holding the seat for nine years. In 1892 he applied for silk and was granted it by Lord Halsbury.

On the death of his father in 1894 Coleridge succeeded to the peerage. He continued, however, to practise at the bar, being the first peer of the realm to pursue a regular forensic career. He not infrequently took part in debates in the House of Lords: thus he vehemently attacked Lord Milner's colonial policy and the system of Chinese indentured labour in the Transvaal, and he attempted to justify, from a legal standpoint, the Trades Disputes Bill of 1906. Not unnaturally, therefore, when the conservative land-slide occurred at the general election of 1906, he was marked out for early promotion, and in 1907 Lord Loreburn appointed him to a judgeship in the King's Bench division. As 'Lord Coleridge, J.', his name figures in the law reports from that date until his resignation in 1923. It was the first time in the annals of English law that father, son, and grandson successively became judges —a record which up to the present no other family can show.

As a judge, Coleridge neither sought nor attained brilliance or deep erudition, but he possessed the qualities of dignity, carefulness, and absolute fair-mindedness, and it is remarkable how seldom his decisions were reversed on appeal. He was at his best in jury cases, both civil and criminal. One of the most noted of these was the prosecution of the murderer, J. A. Dickman, at Newcastle-upon-Tyne assizes in 1910: a full report of the proceedings, edited by S. O. Rowan-Hamilton, was published in 1914 and may be regarded as a true picture of English criminal justice at its best. Coleridge also presided at the trials of the 'suffragettes', Mrs. Emmeline Pankhurst [q.v.] in 1912 and Mr. and Mrs. Pethick-Lawrence in 1913. In 1917 he sat with the archbishop of Canterbury in the first appeal under the Benefices Act of 1898 (*Rice* v. *Bishop of Oxford*).

Apart from his political and judicial career, Coleridge lived a busy and cultured life. He was chairman of Devon quarter-sessions and served regularly in that capacity even while he was a judge. From 1912 to 1918 he was chairman of the Coal Conciliation Board of the Federated Districts. He was a zealous humanitarian, a strong anti-vivisectionist, and an opponent of the punishment of flogging, although he favoured the retention of the capital sentence for the most heinous crimes. Loyalty to his birthplace led him to found and to become the first president of the Old Ottregian Society, and, being himself a talented musician, he composed 'The Ottery Song' which is sung at its gatherings. He published: *Ottery St. Mary and its Memories* (1904), *The Story of a Devonshire House* (1905), and *This for Remembrance* (1925).

Coleridge retired from the bench owing to ill-health in 1923 and, after living in retirement at his Devonshire home, The Chanter's House, Ottery St. Mary, for four years, died there 4 September 1927 at the age of seventy-six. He married in 1876 Mary Alethea, eldest daughter of John Fielder Mackarness, bishop of Oxford [q.v.], and had one son, Geoffrey Duke (born 1877), who succeeded him as third baron, and two daughters, the elder of whom predeceased her father.

There is a portrait of Coleridge by Giuseppe Anzino at The Chanter's House, Ottery St. Mary, and another by Dampier May in the hall of Trinity College, Oxford. A cartoon by 'Spy' appeared in *Vanity Fair* 13 January 1909.

[Private information.] P. A. LANDON.

COLES, CHARLES EDWARD [Pasha] (1853–1926), reformer of Egyptian prisons, was born at Buge, India, 17 November 1853, the only son of Major-General Thomas Gordon Coles, Indian army, by his wife, Maria, daughter of Colonel Charles D'Oyle Straker, Indian army. After private education at Bath, Coles entered the Indian police department in 1873, serving in the Bombay Residency. In 1883 his services were lent to the Egyptian government, which in 1884 appointed him deputy inspector-general of police. From 1894 to 1897 he held the post of commandant of the Cairo city police; and in the latter year, being promoted to the office of director-general of Egyptian prisons, Coles entered upon what was to prove his principal life work.

During the sixteen years (1897–1913) of his administration of the prison department, Coles transformed the Egyptian prisons from being a reproach to being a conspicuous credit to the government of that country. When he took up his task, the slowly improving finances of Egypt had not hitherto permitted more than a very insufficient budgetary provision being made for the prisons department. Prisoners were lodged in disused barracks, factories, and other completely unsuitable buildings, both inadequate and insanitary; while no regular provision was made either for the feeding or for the clothing of the inmates. Coles took up his duties with energy and enthusiasm, and with large ideas. He astonished the financial authorities by informing them that he should require £E500,000 for the rebuilding of all the prisons, and probably £E150,000 a year for their maintenance. Sixteen years later he was able to boast that he had spent £E473,738 on building, and that the budgetary provision for maintenance in the preceding year had been £E160,000.

Among other reforms achieved in the course of Coles's administration, arrangements were made for trades to be taught and practised in the prisons, and for short-sentence prisoners to work off their sentences in supervised work outside the prison-walls. Boys' and girls' reformatories, conducted on English principles of character training, were established; and a reformatory was created for adults under 'indeterminate sentences', which appears to have been the first institution of its kind in the world.

Having had, in the course of his service, to deal with two or three cases of serious mutiny in the convict prison, Coles made a point of relying largely upon his own personal influence with the prisoners to restore order. When shooting was unavoidable, he did it himself.

Spectacular as was the development of the Egyptian prison system under Coles's administration, he was by no means exclusively absorbed by his official duties; he took a keen interest in sport of all kinds, was a leading figure in Egyptian racing, and was the founder of the Alexandrian Sporting Club and of the Egyptian Jockey Club.

After his retirement in 1913, Coles, who had received the C.M.G. in 1900, lived in Somerset until 1921, when he moved to Biarritz, where he died 12 November 1926. His publications include *Recollections and Reflections* (1918) and *Occupational Franchise* (1922).

Coles married in 1881 Mary Emma Isabella, daughter of Crewe Alston, J.P., of Odell, Bedfordshire, and had four sons (two of whom were killed in the European War) and two daughters.

[*The Times*, 16 November 1926; C. E. Coles, *Recollections and Reflections*, 1918; private information.] M. S. AMOS.

COLES, VINCENT STUCKEY STRATTON (1845–1929), divine and hymn-writer, born 27 March 1845 at Shepton Beauchamp, Somerset, was the only son of the Rev. James Stratton Coles, rector of Shepton Beauchamp since 1836 and later rural dean and a prebendary of Wells Cathedral. His mother, from whom Coles learned the religious principles which inspired his long life, was Eliza, daughter of Vincent Stuckey, of Langport, banker and shipowner, who had been private secretary at the Treasury to Pitt and Huskisson. The Stuckey and Bagehot families had long dominated Langport; Walter Bagehot [q.v.], the economist, was Coles's cousin. Mrs. Coles had learned church principles from Keble's *Christian Year*; George Anthony Denison [q.v.], archdeacon of Taunton, was a neighbour and family friend, and the Puritan attack on Denison's exposition of Eucharistic doctrine in 1856, made an ineffaceable mark on Coles's mind. In 1858 he went to Eton, where he boarded with the Rev. C. C. James. Coles's moral courage and his genius for friendship triumphed over such disabilities as his stoutness, his awkwardness at games, and his uncompromising churchmanship. His intimate friends were Digby Mackworth Dolben, Robert Bridges, and Archibald Primrose, Lord Dalmeny (afterwards Earl of Rosebery).

In 1864 Coles entered Balliol College, Oxford. His Eton contemporary (Sir) W. R. Anson urged him to enter for an exhibition, which he won, but resigned from conscientious scruples on gaining only a third class in classical moderations in 1866. He obtained a third class in *literae humaniores* in 1868, and proceeded to Cuddesdon theological college, of which Edward King (q.v., afterwards bishop of Lincoln) was principal. Coles used to deplore his wasted time as an undergraduate; certainly his two third classes were no index to his intellectual power. He had been absorbed in church questions. Gerard Manley Hopkins was a close friend, and he came to know Henry Parry Liddon [q.v.], who heard his first confession and became his greatest friend.

Coles was ordained deacon at Winchester by Bishop Samuel Wilberforce at Advent 1869, and licensed to a curacy at Wantage under the Rev. William John Butler [q.v.], afterwards dean of Lincoln. He was ordained priest by Bishop Mackarness of Oxford in 1870. On his father's sudden death in 1872 he succeeded him as rector of Shepton Beauchamp. He resigned the living in October 1884 in order to become one of the librarians of the Pusey House, Oxford; Charles (afterwards Bishop) Gore and Frank Edward Brightman were the other two. Already Coles was widely known as a preacher, missioner, and spiritual guide; he had taken part in the second London Mission in 1874, made a preaching tour in the United States in 1876, and been appointed frequently by Dean Church and Dr. Liddon to preach in St. Paul's Cathedral. His abundant labours at Shepton Beauchamp had made it a model parish of the catholic revival in the English Church. In Oxford his genius for friendship found its true scope, and after Dr. King left Oxford for Lincoln in 1885, Coles carried on his apostolate to young men. His keen sense of fun, his discerning sympathy, and above all his holiness attracted undergraduates of every type and class, and his great energies were devoted to helping them. Consequently his greatest contribution to his age is hidden in the lives of other men. He was appointed principal of the Pusey House in 1897 and held the position until 1909, when he resigned from ill-health. In 1903 he undertook at the request of Bishop Wilkinson of St. Andrews a missionary tour through South Africa in preparation for the later 'mission of help'. From 1910 to 1920 Coles was warden of the community of the Epiphany at Truro, and in 1912 Bishop Gore made him honorary canon of Christ Church and his diocesan chaplain, in which capacity Coles worked indefatigably in the Oxford diocese until Bishop Gore resigned in 1919. Thenceforward he lived with one of his sisters at Shepton Beauchamp, where he died unmarried 9 June 1929 and is buried.

Coles published little: *Pastoral Work in Country Districts* (1906, being lectures delivered at Cambridge in Lent 1905), full of practical experience; *Lenten Meditations* (1899, 4th ed. 1905) and *Advent Meditations* (1899, new ed. 1901); and separate sermons. Some of his best hymns, notably 'We pray Thee, Heavenly Father', are in *Hymns Ancient and Modern* and the *English Hymnal*. Possessed of ample private means, he distributed them lavishly, living himself in severe simplicity. For many years his health was bad, but he never allowed it to hinder his activity. He had a fine presence and a beautiful voice: great spiritual beauty distinguished his kind and striking face. In early manhood one of his eyebrows became white through acute anxiety for the supposed loss of a sister. Coles's humility deceived many into taking him at his own valuation; actually his spiritual power influenced not Oxford only but penetrated the whole Anglican Communion.

[*V. S. S. Coles*, Letters, &c., with a Memoir, edited by J. F. Briscoe, 1930; *Life and Letters of W. J. Butler, D.D.*, edited by A. J. Butler, 1897; A. J. Mason, *A Memoir of George Howard Wilkinson*, 2 vols., 1909; F. J. Kinsman, *Salve Mater*, 1920; *A Dictionary of Hymnology*, edited by J. Julian, revised edition 1907; private information; personal knowledge.] S. L. Ollard.

COLLINS, MICHAEL (1890–1922), Irish revolutionary leader and chairman of the provisional government of the Irish Free State in 1922, was born 16 October 1890 at Woodfield, Clonakilty, co. Cork, the third son and youngest child in the family of eight children of Michael Collins, a farmer in humble circumstances but belonging to an old Irish family, by his wife, Mary Anne O'Brien. He was educated at the local primary school, where he was fortunate in having a teacher of unusual talents. He went to London when sixteen years of age and during ten years' residence there studied and read widely, acquiring a considerable general knowledge of business methods, economics, history, and contemporary politics, and developing a style of writing and speaking, at once easy and virile, which stood him in good stead in later times. His early years in London were uneventful; he was a boy clerk in the Post Office Savings Bank for some years, and subsequently (1910) held a minor post with a firm of London stock-brokers. He left this post during the moratorium following the outbreak of the European War in 1914, but soon afterwards found employment in the London office of the Guaranty Trust Co., of New York, where he remained until the end of 1915. He grew up a well-built man, about six feet in height, active and powerful, a good athlete, possessed of great physical endurance, with a pleasing open face, a genial and hearty manner, and a strong and self-assertive disposition. Generous in friendship, quick in temper, sparing in praise, and sharp in reproof, his strong character inspired extremes of affection and dislike, while his capacity for prompt decision and rapid action and his great physical bravery marked him as a leader in the revolutionary movement which grew rapidly in Ireland during the European War and which culminated in the establishment of an independent Irish state, of the first government of which he became head.

Collins first came into prominence on the political horizon about the year 1917. For many years prior to the outbreak of the European War, the dominant party in Irish politics was the Irish parliamentary party, which, under the leadership of John Redmond [q.v.], held a practical monopoly of the parliamentary representation of the country, save in the north-eastern portion of the province of Ulster, which was a unionist stronghold. A secret revolutionary nucleus known as the Irish Republican Brotherhood had remained in existence from the Fenian times, but its membership was small and its influence of little weight. In 1913, however, the anti-Home Rule movement in Ulster led by Sir Edward (afterwards Lord) Carson, opened the way for the organization of the Irish Volunteers. This body, avowedly military in its objects, was directed from the outset by the revolutionary group. For a short period Redmond succeeded in obtaining control, but the organization split and the militant party pursued its course until the Irish Rebellion of Easter week, 1916. The eventual release of the large number of men who had been imprisoned and interned after the Rebellion resulted in the re-constitution of the Irish Volunteers, to form a body which was later known popularly, though erroneously, as the 'Irish Republican Army'.

Prior to 1916 Collins had taken an active part in the Irish Republican Brotherhood in London. He returned to Ireland some months before the Rebellion, was in close association with the leaders of the revolt, and took part in the occupation of the General Post Office in Dublin during the fighting there. After the Rebellion he was deported to Stafford gaol, and subsequently interned in Frongoch camp, near Bala, Merionethshire, with a large number of fellow prisoners from all parts of the country. He was released shortly before Christmas 1916. He was consequently well known to most of the active members of the revolutionary organizations and was rapidly accepted as the organizing genius of the Volunteer and Sinn Fein movement. In April 1918 he was arrested in Dublin, tried at Granard, and imprisoned in Sligo gaol for a seditious speech. After his release he continued to be politically extremely active; north and south the country was searched for him, but he succeeded in eluding the vigilance of the police and the military authorities.

The Irish parliamentary party had now lost prestige, and at the general election in December 1918 was practically wiped out. The Sinn Fein party dominated Irish politics and captured 73 constituencies out of a total of 105. North-East Ulster remained unionist. The Sinn Fein members met in Dublin on 21 January 1919, adopted a declaration of independence and a provisional constitution, and elected a ministry. Collins, who had been elected for two constituencies, West Cork and Tyrone, was chosen as minister for home affairs. In February 1919 he took the principal part in planning and carrying out the escape of Mr. De Valera from Lincoln gaol, and in the consequent reorganization of the Sinn Fein ministry he became minister for finance. This portfolio he retained until his death.

Collins was now in a position to command. Besides being Sinn Fein minister for finance, he was director of organization and subsequently of intelligence for the Irish Volunteers, and member of the supreme council of the Irish Republican Brotherhood. His abundant energy and his mastery of detail enabled him to keep in close touch with every aspect of the revolutionary activities, and he enjoyed the respect and confidence of his colleagues. He became an almost legendary figure to the people, and his career during the three years which followed proved remarkable.

On 12 September 1919 Dail Eireann, the revolutionary parliament, and all the other Irish revolutionary organizations were declared illegal by the British government, and their activities were thereafter conducted mainly in secret. The British military and police forces were greatly augmented and kept up a constant and growing pressure by means of raids and arrests of prominent members of the organizations. Mr. De Valera, the president of Dail Eireann, having gone to the United States of America in the spring of 1919 in order to procure moral and financial support for the movement, it was decided by Dail Eireann to float an internal loan in Ireland and an external loan in the United States. Both ventures were highly successful, each loan being heavily over-subscribed. As minister for finance, Collins was responsible for the organization of the issue; in the case of the internal loan the greater part of the work fell on his shoulders, and as the British government took every possible step to disorganize and prevent its collection, the difficulties which had to be surmounted in getting in and safeguarding the funds were enormous. Collins was completely successful in his efforts, with the result that the various activities of the Dail were amply financed during the trying period prior to 1921.

In 1920 the Irish Volunteer organization, hitherto an independent body, proclaimed its allegiance to Dail Eireann. Its numbers were considerable, but its arms and equipment were very poor. The importation of arms was rigidly controlled, and the maintenance of a sufficiency of war material was a constant problem. The efforts made by the British forces to suppress the Dail and the Volunteers aroused great public resentment, and consequently when the Volunteers retaliated by attacks upon the police and the military, they were sheltered and succoured everywhere. The attacks gradually became more numerous and feelings grew progressively embittered, with the result that from the summer of 1920 until the truce of 11 July 1921 a state of guerrilla warfare existed. Collins organized the service through which arms and ammunition were provided. In addition he created an intelligence department which had contacts in the most unlikely quarters and kept him well informed of the plans and intentions of the British military and police.

During this period the normal administration of the country had largely ceased. The Dail ministry had set up its own judicial system in opposition to the existing courts. The local district and county councils refused to obey the directions of the Local Government Board for Ireland and attorned to the rival Dail department of local government. Almost every function of government was duplicated and the whole administration of former times was daily being rendered more impotent.

Negotiations for a settlement were initiated towards the end of 1920; they took definite shape in the formal cessation of hostilities on 11 July 1921, and in an invitation from the prime minister, Mr. Lloyd George, to Mr. De Valera to meet British ministers in a conference. A prolonged exchange of correspondence followed this invitation, and a conference was ultimately arranged 'with a view to ascertaining how the association of Ireland with the community of nations known as the British Commonwealth, may best be reconciled with Irish national aspirations'. Five Irish delegates, Arthur

Griffith [q.v.], Michael Collins, Eamonn Duggan, George Gavan Duffy, and Robert Barton, were selected by the Dail on 14 September 1921, and endowed with plenipotentiary powers. The outstanding figures among them were Griffith and Collins. Agreement was reached on 6 December, when articles of agreement for a Treaty between Great Britain and Ireland were signed. Ireland was recognized as having 'the same constitutional status in the community of nations known as the British Empire as the Dominion of Canada, the Commonwealth of Australia, the Dominion of New Zealand, and the Union of South Africa, with a Parliament having powers to make laws for the peace, order, and good government of Ireland and an executive responsible to that Parliament'.

Mr. De Valera, however, the president of the Dail cabinet, repudiated this agreement and was supported in his attitude by two of his colleagues, Cathal Brugha and Austin Stack. A sharp division of opinion manifested itself in the Dail, and the terms of the Treaty were accepted by only a small majority of that body. A provisional government was set up on 14 January 1922, with Collins as chairman and minister for finance. The provisional government immediately set to work to arrange to take over the machinery of government from the British departments and to frame a constitution for the Irish Free State. Meanwhile the opponents of the Treaty were actively organizing their forces. The Irish Volunteers were almost equally divided, and in March the section hostile to the Treaty seceded and adopted a policy of revolt. A bitter political campaign was also begun, and the occupation of various public buildings by armed irregular forces resulted in numerous clashes in various parts of the country. Collins made desperate efforts to heal the breach, and at one time appeared to have succeeded. He was able to arrange for a general election in June 1922, at which out of 128 deputies returned 94 were supporters of the Treaty. A parliament was summoned for July. Meanwhile the situation was growing rapidly more serious, and following the seizure by the irregular forces of an officer of the head-quarters staff of the regular army, an ultimatum was issued demanding the immediate evacuation of all buildings illegally occupied. This ultimatum expired on 28 June and a civil war began.

Collins immediately took over the command of the Free State army and speedily reduced the opposition in Dublin. The main strength of the irregular forces was broken towards the end of August, although sporadic attacks continued in isolated areas up to the spring of 1923. On 22 August 1922 Collins, accompanied by General Dalton and Commandant O'Connell and other members of his headquarters staff, was returning in the evening to Cork from a tour of inspection of military positions in that county, when he and his party were attacked by a small band of irregulars in the wild and hilly country around Macroom. A severe fight, lasting nearly an hour, ensued at Bealnablath, near Brandon. The irregulars, defeated, were on the point of retiring when Collins was mortally wounded by a bullet in the head. His body was taken to Dublin on 24 August and lay in state in the City Hall until the funeral at Glasnevin cemetery. Thus ended the short career of one of the most remarkable Irishmen of modern times. His dynamic energy and powerful personality played a leading part in the struggle for independence which resulted in the establishment of the Irish Free State.

[Dail Eireann: Official Reports; *Annual Register*; Piaros Béaslaí (Pierce Beasley), *Michael Collins and the Making of a New Ireland*, 2 vols., 1926; private information; personal knowledge.] W. T. Cosgrave.

COLVIN, Sir SIDNEY (1845–1927), critic of art and literature, was born at Norwood 18 June 1845, the third son of Bazett David Colvin, East India merchant, of The Grove, Little Bealings, Suffolk, by his wife, Mary Steuart, daughter of William Butterworth Bayley. The families of both parents had been connected with India for several generations. Colvin's boyhood was spent at Little Bealings; he was educated at home until he went in 1863 to Trinity College, Cambridge, of which he became a fellow in 1868. On taking his degree, after having been placed third in the first class of the classical tripos of 1867, he went to London, wrote for the *Pall Mall Gazette*, and contributed articles to magazines, especially from 1871 onwards to the *Portfolio*, founded in 1869 by Philip Gilbert Hamerton [q.v.]. In 1871 also he joined the Society of Dilettanti, of which he was from 1891 to 1896 honorary secretary. His membership of the New (afterwards the Savile) Club, which he joined in 1869, made him acquainted with many of the best intellects among his contemporaries; he was also a member from 1879 of the Athenaeum, and from 1893 of the Burlington Fine Arts Club.

In 1872 Colvin's *Portfolio* papers on *Children in Italian and English Design* appeared in book form, followed in 1873 by *Occasional Writings on Fine Art*. In January 1873 he was elected Slade professor of fine art at Cambridge, and held that appointment, several times renewed, until 1885. Among his more eminent pupils were Martin Conway (afterwards Lord Conway of Allington) and (Sir) Lionel Cust. He lectured on Florentine painting, on early Italian and German engraving, and on Greek sculpture with special reference to the recent discoveries in the Temple of Zeus at Olympia, which he visited with Sir Charles Newton [q.v.] in March 1875. In 1876 he was appointed director of the Fitzwilliam Museum, where he founded a collection of casts of Greek sculpture. He resigned the directorship in 1883 on taking up his duties at the British Museum, where he had been appointed by the principal trustees in July 1883 keeper of the department of prints and drawings in succession to George William Reid [q.v.].

Colvin, who held the keepership till June 1912, greatly improved the arrangement and mounting of the collection of prints and drawings, and superintended its removal from cramped quarters to the White wing, where a spacious gallery, adjoining the Students' room, was used for a series of exhibitions. To these he composed admirable guides, that of most permanent value being the guide to the exhibition in 1899 of Rembrandt's etchings, arranged for the first time in chronological order. About 1911–1912 he was once more planning a removal of the prints and drawings—to the new Edward VII galleries; but it was not carried out till 1913. Colvin's wide acquaintance with collectors and influential persons outside official circles was beneficial in many ways to the growth of the collection and its appreciation by the public. His greatest acquisition was that of the magnificent Malcolm collection of drawings and engravings, purchased in 1895 by a grant of £25,000 from the Treasury, a sum, even at that date, greatly below its actual value. Among important gifts or bequests secured by his influence were the Mitchell collection of early woodcuts (1895), the Henry Vaughan bequest of drawings, by Flaxman, Stothard, and others (1900), the Cheylesmore collection of mezzotints (1902), and George Salting's drawings and engravings by old masters (1910). The Reeve collection of drawings of the Norwich school (1902) was a purchase important for English art. Fine drawings were acquired separately from numerous sources. Colvin had wide knowledge, but his own preference was for the Italian school, in which he somewhat unduly depreciated any work that was later than the sixteenth century. He made a special study of engraving before Marcantonio (died *c.* 1534), and published his researches in the text accompanying *A Florentine Picture Chronicle* (1898, a book of drawings, bought from Ruskin, which Colvin attributed to Maso Finiguerra, 1426–1464, the reputed inventor of engraving) and in the official *Catalogue of Early Italian Engravings* (1910), in which he was assisted by Mr. A. M. Hind. An important piece of research, in which Mr. Hind also collaborated, was *Early Engraving and Engravers in England* (1905). Colvin wrote the text for a publication of drawings by old masters, selected by him from the University Galleries and Christ Church Library, Oxford (1902–1907).

During the last ten years of his keepership Colvin became keenly interested in the art of the Far East. He obtained for the Museum, between 1902 and 1909, four important private collections of Japanese woodcuts, and in 1910 the Wegener collection of Chinese paintings. On the retirement of Sir Edward Maunde Thompson [q.v.] in 1909, Colvin was a candidate for the directorship of the British Museum. He was knighted in 1911.

After his retirement from the British Museum Colvin returned with zest to the study of literature, from which he had been partially diverted during his busy years in Cambridge and Bloomsbury. In English literature he had a special love for Landor and Keats, and wrote volumes on both for the 'English Men of Letters' series (*Landor*, 1881, *Keats*, 1887). He also edited *Selections from Landor* (1882) in Macmillan's 'Golden Treasury' series. He devoted some years after 1912 to the preparation of a lengthy life of Keats, which appeared in 1917 as *John Keats, His Life and Poetry*, and is his most valuable contribution to literature. *Memories and Notes*, a collection of autobiographical fragments and reminiscences of Edward John Trelawny, George Eliot, Gambetta, and others, followed in 1921.

Of Colvin's many friendships with men

of letters the most famous is his attachment to R. L. Stevenson, which lasted from 1873 until his friend's death in 1894. When Stevenson left England for the Pacific in 1887, Colvin kept in touch with his writings and gave advice on their completion and publication. He published in 1895 the *Vailima Letters*, addressed to him by Stevenson from Samoa, and edited in 1899 and 1911 Stevenson's general correspondence; he was also editor of the Edinburgh edition of Stevenson's works (1894–1897). In later years, Stevenson's successor in Colvin's loving admiration was Joseph Conrad.

Colvin married in 1903 Frances, daughter of Cuthbert Fetherstonhaugh and widow of the Rev. Albert Hurt Sitwell. They had been close friends for more than thirty years, and Mrs. Sitwell had shared Colvin's intimacy with Stevenson. In their house at the British Museum, called by Stevenson 'the Monument', and afterwards at 35 Palace Gardens Terrace, Kensington, they were the centre of a literary and artistic circle into which youthful talent was ever welcomed. Lady Colvin died in 1924. This bereavement was a great blow to Colvin, whose last years were further saddened by deafness and loss of memory. He died in Kensington 11 May 1927. There were no children of the marriage.

Although he did little creative work, Colvin's scholarship and taste, and his knowledge of men as well as of books and prints, made of him a sound critic. Alike in his own professional writings, and in those which he deputed to assistants at the British Museum, Colvin insisted on a high standard of good English. An accomplished linguist, he was constantly in touch with continental critics and historians of art. He had more sympathy with modern movements in literature than in art. In person he was tall and thin, in manner animated and nervous, sometimes irritable, but charming in demeanour to those whom he liked. He walked with a slight limp after an accident in which his leg was broken. His portrait by T. Roussel (1908) is at the Savile Club; an earlier drawing by Alphonse Legros is in the British Museum.

[*The Times*, 12 May 1927; E. V. Lucas, *The Colvins and their Friends*, 1928; personal knowledge.]
C. Dodgson.

CONGREVE, Sir WALTER NORRIS (1862–1927), general, was born at Chatham 20 November 1862, the eldest son of Captain William Congreve, J.P., D.L., of Congreve Manor, Staffordshire, and of Burton Hall, Cheshire, by his wife, Fanny, daughter of Lee Porcher Townshend, of Wincham Hall, Cheshire. The family of Congreve claims to trace its descent from the thirteenth century, but it did not become well-known until the seventeenth century, its most famous representative being William Congreve, the playwright [q.v.]. The name also became known in the army, when Lieutenant-General Sir William Congreve rose to high distinction as an artilleryman during the eighteenth century and was created a baronet in 1812. His successor, also Sir William Congreve [q.v.], achieved greater renown as an inventor, chiefly through his production of the Congreve war rocket, which was adopted as a weapon of the Royal Artillery. Walter Congreve's father, William, a member of an elder branch of the family, served in the 9th and 29th Foot, but resigned his commission in order to become chief constable of Staffordshire.

Congreve was educated at Harrow and at Pembroke College, Oxford, where he matriculated in 1881. Having served for some years in the North Staffordshire Militia, he decided in 1883 to enter the army. After passing through the Royal Military College, Sandhurst, as was customary for university candidates at that period, he was gazetted into the Rifle Brigade in February 1885, whereupon he joined the 1st battalion in India. In 1889 he returned home with that unit, married in the following year, and became assistant adjutant for musketry. In this capacity his patience and faculty for methodical work first came to light and gained recognition. He was promoted captain in December 1893, and again served in India, returning two years later to his depot in England. In January 1898 he was appointed district inspector of musketry at Aldershot, an employment in which he again achieved excellent results.

On the outbreak of the South African War in October 1899, Congreve was ordered to the Cape, and thence on to Durban. After being attached to the staff of the 4th brigade he was appointed to Sir Redvers Buller's head-quarter staff as press censor. On 15 December Buller made his attempt to force the crossing of the River Tugela at Colenso. With a view to covering the infantry advance he ordered the 1st brigade Royal Field Artillery to a position near the river. Owing to the prevailing confusion the guns came into action within 1,000 yards of the enemy, where they became a target for such severe fire that, when their ammunition was expended, the detachments, unable to obtain any replenishment, sought cover in a hollow to the rear of the battery. Believing the guns to be abandoned, Buller ordered efforts to be made to withdraw them, and desired his staff to assist. Accordingly Congreve, with Buller's aidesde-camp, Captain H. N. Schofield, R.A., and Lieutenant Frederick Roberts, Lord Roberts's only son, galloped forward with the gun teams to bring in the batteries. Coming under very heavy fire, Congreve was hit many times, and with several others crawled into a hollow for cover. Some hours later, seeing Lieutenant Roberts lying severely wounded near the guns, Congreve, although barely able to walk, went out and brought him under cover. Roberts subsequently succumbed, and Congreve, for his gallantry throughout the day, was awarded the Victoria Cross.

After recuperating at Capetown, Congreve was ordered to join Kitchener's Horse, an irregular corps then in process of formation. This very raw regiment was not fortunate in the operations which terminated in General Piet Cronje's surrender at Paardeberg on 27 February 1900, so that Congreve readily accepted the appointment of brigade-major of the 18th Infantry brigade in the 6th division. He thus participated in Roberts's march to Pretoria, being present at Poplar Grove, Dreifontein, the surrender of Bloemfontein, and the subsequent operations in the Transvaal. In October he was appointed a deputy-assistant adjutant-general at head-quarters, and three weeks later was selected to act as assistant military secretary to Lord Kitchener, who succeeded Roberts as commander-in-chief at the beginning of 1901. In the multifarious duties that fell to his lot, Congreve's quiet courtesy, tact, and common sense gained Kitchener's high approbation. In December 1901 he was promoted major in his regiment, and on the following day received a brevet lieutenant-colonelcy for his war services. After his return home, in October 1902, he was selected for a personal appointment on the staff of the Duke of Connaught, who was then commander-in-chief in Ireland. In Dublin Congreve won golden opinions and was awarded the M.V.O. in 1903; accordingly it was not surprising that, when the duke was transferred to London as inspector-general to the forces in May 1904, Congreve accompanied him as secretary. The brevet of colonel was awarded him in June 1905.

After a spell of regimental duty and half pay, during which he received substantive colonel's rank, Congreve obtained the command of the School of Musketry at Hythe in September 1909. There he made a far-sighted but fruitless effort to obtain an increase in the establishment of machine-guns throughout the army. In spite of this set-back he was given the command of the 18th Infantry brigade, with the rank of brigadier-general, in 1911. At that time he also received the C.B. Essentially a regimental officer and an enthusiast for accurate rifle fire, Congreve brought a thoroughly practical mind to bear on the training of his brigade. He was hampered by constant asthma, but his unwavering courage surmounted all physical obstacles.

On the outbreak of the European War in August 1914, the 18th Infantry brigade was first sent to Edinburgh and then to Cambridge, but reached France in mid-September in time to take part in the battle on the River Aisne. After the deadlock on this front, the British troops were transferred to Flanders, and the 6th division, of which the 18th Infantry brigade formed part, came into action to the east of Hazebrouck on 13 October. On this front Congreve and his brigade fought stubbornly until mid-November. Congreve proved himself a good brigade commander, often incurring great personal risks while visiting the front line, though suffering much from bad health. In February 1915 he was specially promoted major-general, but continued with his brigade until selected to succeed to the command of the 6th division in the following May. This division was now ordered to take over part of the northern face of the Ypres salient, and there Congreve spent the next six months. His division during this period was not called upon to make any remarkable effort except for one particularly well-organized minor attack. On 15 November he was selected to command the newly formed XIII Army Corps, being given the temporary rank of lieutenant-general.

The XIII Corps at first formed part of the Third Army, but in the spring of 1916 it was allotted to Sir Henry Rawlinson's Fourth Army which had just been formed on the British right flank in preparation for the battle of the Somme. When the Fourth Army launched its great attack on 1 July, Congreve's troops, supported by a heavier concentration of artillery and encountering a weaker resistance, advanced on the extreme right between the British XV and French XX Corps. The success of the XIII Corps, which reached the Montauban ridge, was the outstanding feature of the day. But this great advantage was not followed up. Not until 14 July did Rawlinson advance again, when he tried the bold expedient of a night march; and Congreve successfully carried out this movement with two of his divisions. The battle then degenerated into a prolonged and dogged struggle. On 20 July his eldest son, William, a brilliant young soldier with a remarkable record of war service, was killed—a grievous blow to his father; in August, Congreve himself, undermined by hardship and grief, was struck down by an attack of cholera nostras. When he returned to his corps in late September he was ordered to move his troops into the First Army area, and saw no more fighting that year. In the spring of 1917, however, the XIII Corps was engaged in the battle of Arras almost continuously for about four weeks. During this fighting Congreve was hit by a shell when going to inspect his artillery below Vimy Ridge. His left hand was shattered and subsequently amputated, whereupon he was invalided home, being shortly afterwards created K.C.B.

On 1 January 1918 Congreve was promoted substantive lieutenant-general and assumed command of the VII Corps, which was then in France serving on the left of the Fifth Army, in the position where it abutted on the Third Army near Gouzeaucourt. The full weight of the German onslaught of 21 March 1918 thus included Congreve's corps. For ten days it fought gallantly in retreat before greatly superior forces. Congreve never gave way, but his health, sadly impaired by asthma, as well as by the results of his wound and of the loss of his son, was being tried beyond the limits of physical and mental endurance. Consequently he was transferred to the command of the X Corps, then resting near Crecy, and finally returned home in May 1918.

After being on half pay until August 1919 Congreve was sent to Haifa to command the troops there which formed part of the British forces in Egypt and Palestine. In October he was transferred to Cairo, there to command the entire British forces in Egypt. During this period his main task was the evacuation of Syria and the transfer of that territory to France, a duty which he accomplished with conspicuous tact. In 1922 he was promoted full general. Early the next year his appointment in Egypt came to an end—much to his regret, for the climate suited his health.

On return home Congreve was given the post of general commanding-in-chief, Southern command, at Salisbury, and appointed aide-de-camp general to the king. Feeling that his health was weakening, he allowed himself somewhat unwillingly to be persuaded into accepting the post of governor of Malta in June 1925. During his tenure of that office no incident of note occurred; he proved a popular governor and took a deep interest in the life of the island. But his health continued to fail, for his constitution had been undermined by the War. He died at Valetta 28 February 1927.

Although Congreve was not a deeply read or scientific soldier, he possessed qualities which made him a good and practical leader of men: clear insight into everyday difficulties, and exceptional self-control in moments of danger, the highest form of both moral and physical courage. In addition he was gifted with great personal charm and distinction. He hated pedants and despised all sham. His love of nature and knowledge of animals was profound; yet, although a fearless horseman, he began very early in life to lose interest in hunting, as his distaste for blood sports increased. Nevertheless, at heart he remained a true country gentleman of the old school.

Congreve married in 1890 Cecilia, daughter of Captain Charles Blount La Touche, of the Bombay army, and had three sons. His second son, Geoffrey (born 1897), was awarded in 1927 the baronetcy which had been destined for his father before the latter's death. Congreve was a J.P. and D.L. for the county of Stafford, and in 1922 was elected an honorary fellow of Pembroke College, Oxford, in recognition of his war services. He was also appointed a colonel commandant of the Rifle Brigade in the same year.

[*The Times*, 2 March 1927; L. H. Thornton and P. Fraser, *The Congreves—Father and Son*, 1930; Sir J. E. Edmonds, (Official) *History of the Great War. Military Operations. France and Belgium, 1914–1918*, 1922–1935; Army Lists; personal knowledge.]

H. de Watteville.

CONRAD, JOSEPH (1857–1924), master mariner and novelist, was of Polish birth and parentage. As Teodor Josef

Konrad Korzeniowski he was born near Mohilow in Poland 3 December 1857. He became a naturalized British subject under the name of Joseph Conrad in 1886. His father, Joseph Theodore Apollonius Korzeniowski, a member of a Polish landed family, was a well-known man of letters who translated Shakespeare into Polish. In 1862, when his son was only five years old, he was banished by the Russian government to Vologda on account of his implication in the Polish rebellion of that year. Accompanied by his wife (Evelina, daughter of Joseph Bobrowski, of Oratow, in Podolia) and child, he spent two or three years wandering about Russia, not actually destitute, but exposed to continual discomfort and in great spiritual misery; and to the anxieties and endurances of this period was in part due the premature death of Madame Korzeniowski in 1865. Not until 1867 was the widower permitted to leave Russia again and to take his little son to Lemberg in Austrian Galicia. There they settled, living quietly and in great intimacy, until in 1869 the father died. The twelve-year-old boy passed under the guardianship of an uncle, Thaddeus Bobrowski.

The influence on the mature Joseph Conrad of his early years, and particularly of his father's training and activities, was very great. On the one hand, such incidents of childhood as remained with him were later eagerly used in his novels, nearly all of which have an actuality beyond the average. On the other hand, Apollonius Korzeniowski, as Polish patriot, as student and translator of French literature and, incidentally, as teacher of the French language, brought his boy into direct contact with the nationalist aspirations of an oppressed people and, in the course of extensive readings in French literature, with the dangerously infectious work of Victor Hugo. To the translating by the father of Hugo's *Travailleurs de la Mer*, and to the boy's reading aloud of the translation, may be attributed in part Conrad's early desire for a seafaring life, and to a very large degree his later tendencies to literary rhetoric and to over-luxuriance of epithet. As for the fluent and admirable French which in youth he learned to speak, it was all his life a joy and an ally, but at the same time an intoxication.

After his father's death Conrad lived with his uncle and studied in Cracow. By 1872 the lad was already set on going to sea, and had begun the pleadings and arguments to which in 1874 the guardian-uncle finally yielded. In September of that year he set off to Marseilles, with all the ardour of his years, and with a few influential introductions in his pocket. In December, as a registered seaman in the French merchant marine, he sailed on his first voyage. His life from 1874 to 1878 was spent partly on the sea, partly in Marseilles. This period was fruitful in friendship and incident, later to be used in his writings. Among his acquaintance were several families of Spanish royalist sympathies; and the whole of *The Arrow of Gold* (published 1919), from the love-episode of 'Rita' and 'M. George' to the wildest of the Carlist escapades, as well as such prominent characters in other books as 'Tom Lingard', 'Nostromo', and 'Peyrol', owe their existence to the adventures of these impressionable years.

In April 1878 Conrad shipped on board the English vessel *Mavis*, and, after a voyage to Constantinople, first set foot on English soil when he landed at Lowestoft in June. Apart from a natural admiration for the British merchant marine, Conrad had not hitherto been conscious of any desire to visit England, much less to make her language his own. Even now he was to pass several strenuous years as a foreigner in English ships before the thought of naturalization came to him, and the impulse to write—whether in English or in any other tongue—was equally remote. His history from 1878 to 1886 was, from the point of view of incident, that of a hard-working and ambitious young seaman. He qualified as third mate in 1880, as second mate in 1881, and as first mate in July 1883. In August 1886 at the age of twenty-eight he assumed British nationality, and in November of the same year passed his final examination and became 'ship's master'. The voyages undertaken during these years brought experience which later, almost to the smallest detail, he used in his novels. The story of *Youth*, for example, was a reminiscence of his voyage as second mate from England to the East in the barque *Palestine*, while the events in *The Nigger of the 'Narcissus'* were taken almost literally from a memory of the year 1884.

As newly promoted 'ship's master', Conrad had the usual difficulty in obtaining a command. But employment, once secured, came readily, for he proved himself a skilled and resourceful seaman, passionately interested in his work and not less individual as a captain than later as a novelist. During 1887 and 1888 he sailed the Malay Archipelago, meeting the original of 'Almayer' (a half-caste Dutchman, who differed only in name from his fictional counterpart) and seeing the various places described in his novels and stories of life in and about the islands. The next two years took him to fresh places, and he discovered the regions up the Congo described in *Heart of Darkness* and *An Outpost of Progress*. It may be remarked that in the Congo he met and made passing acquaintance with Roger Casement [q.v.]. Conrad's inward sensations and heartburnings, at this as at other periods of his seafaring life, are described vividly and with feeling in his various volumes of avowed reminiscences. A brooding and melancholy temperament rendered more than normally acute his appreciation of his own changing moods, while his subsequent power of literary expression enabled him to describe his spiritual development in several passages of great poignancy. It was indeed from personal psychological experience that he contrived his most lasting contribution to English literature. Wherever he had an opportunity of describing in English words the reaction of an utterly un-English mind, either to ordinary English experiences or to emotions common to adult humanity, Conrad achieved an intensity all the more remarkable for its rarity.

In September 1889 Conrad had begun writing a story, rather as an alleviation of boredom than with any ambition toward authorship. The manuscript travelled about with him for several years, slowly increasing in length, twice lost and found once more. It was probably at this time that he developed the talent for verbal story-telling which John Galsworthy, who first made his acquaintance in March 1893 on board the *Torrens*, has recorded as one of his most striking qualities. Early in 1890 Conrad paid an overdue visit to his uncle and guardian in the Ukraine. He had not set foot in Poland for nearly twenty years, and the re-discovery of once familiar backgrounds by a man so travelled and so variously cosmopolitan was peculiarly vivid. When later he came to write of Poland and Russia, his vision was a queer blend of memories of childhood and the half-detached, half-romanticized impression gleaned on this later visit.

It was in January 1894 that Conrad made up his mind to leave the merchant service. He was making a hazardous decision, for he had little enough to live upon, and, although the idea of writing had taken a firm hold upon him, so far he had not published a single book. He spent a few months over the manuscript of his story and in June submitted it, under the title *Almayer's Folly*, to T. Fisher Unwin, who sent it for reading to Mr. Edward Garnett. This was for Conrad a most fortunate chance. Thanks to the perceptive sympathy of the first publisher's reader of his experience, Conrad achieved simultaneously first publication, a new and intimate friendship, and the appreciation of a small but discriminating section of the public. *Almayer's Folly*, published in April 1895, was welcomed by the connoisseurs and by those alert to new talent; even its sale was above the average for a first novel. A successor, *An Outcast of the Islands*, appeared within a year, and a third story, *The Nigger of the 'Narcissus'*, was running serially in the *New Review* during the latter half of 1897.

Conrad was now committed to the life of a man of letters. In March 1896 he had married Jessie, daughter of a bookseller, Alfred Henry George, and taken her to a remote spot on the coast of Brittany, where they stayed in happy discomfort, almost as sea-bound as if on board ship, and relying for such society as they needed on the seafaring population of neighbouring villages and on fortuitous visits from English friends. After their return to England in September they lived in various places in the eastern and southern counties. Money was scarce, for although Conrad's reputation with the elect was quickly established, he had many years to wait before the public became aware of his work. Two sons were born, and ill-health brought serious interruptions. Hard work was essential, and the strain and excitement of the new life, acting on a temperament predisposed to emotional extremes, exaggerated in Conrad the usual characteristics of the creative man. Although finely indifferent to the chances of popular applause, he was as susceptible as any artist to fluctuations of hope and resignation, and would fall into periods of despairing gloom when anticipation of disaster—a tendency to which he was always prone—would drive him to the bitterest pessimism. Strangely enough, anticipated failure affected him far more than actual disillusionment. The long indifference of the public to his work he bore with modest and humorous stoicism. It is recorded that only when the novel *Nostromo* (1904), over which he had spent two laborious years, failed to impress the world, did he betray a bitter chagrin; and certainly it is hard to understand why this magnificent story, unrivalled in Conrad's work for its richness, its cumulative excitement, and its vivid beauty, did not win for him the popularity he merited.

It was during the first decade of the new century that Conrad's troubles, spiritual and material, most nearly overwhelmed him. A tragic letter to a fellow writer, written in 1905, expresses the despair to which he was periodically subject, and at the same time a characteristic readiness to dramatize his own afflictions. 'I stick here fighting with disease and imbecility like a cornered rat, facing fate with a big stick which is sure to descend and crack my skull before many days are over. . . . As for working regularly in a decent, orderly, and industrious manner, I've given that up from sheer impossibility. The damned stuff comes out only by a sort of mental convulsion, which lasts for two, three, or more days up to a fortnight, which leaves me perfectly limp and not very happy.' Through years distracted by illnesses, money worries, discouragements of every kind he worked doggedly on. *The Mirror of the Sea*—a book of reminiscences to the making of which had gone, in his own words, 'the twenty best years' of his life—appeared in 1906 and perhaps, by its power to recall happier days, temporarily consoled him in the midst of his troubles. But whatever alleviations he had were private to himself. To outward appearance he was hardly gaining ground at all. In 1907 he published *The Secret Agent*, to be followed four years later by *Under Western Eyes* (1911), two novels compounded of distant memories of Russia and Russian folk, of the revised impression of Slavdom gained in 1890, and an angry irony born of his present discontents. These books, two more volumes of stories, and another instalment of reminiscences were all written with the anguish of a brain at once word-ridden but inarticulate, thronged with memories but balked by its own scrupulous artistry. What to say was never Conrad's difficulty: the torturing problem was how to say it. But although to the end of his life he had to struggle against the hindrance of his temperament, the companion obstacle of public neglect was abruptly and strangely to be removed.

Conrad's moment of emergence as one of the great novelists of the day came quite suddenly with the publication in New York, in 1914, of *Chance*, a book far less adapted to ready popularity than some of its predecessors and, it must be confessed, more characteristic of its author's affectations than of his qualities. The fact that *Chance* made Conrad's larger reputation is an ironic comment on the power of concerted publicity in modern life. It was felt by the friends and critics who had for long admired his genius that Conrad must be forced on an unreceptive world. A powerful American publisher, F. N. Doubleday, gave his co-operation, and *Chance* (which had first appeared in London in 1913) was 'put over' triumphantly. Materially speaking, Conrad was a made man. Money flowed in upon him; he was courted and fêted by admiring and inquisitive crowds.

From this date until his death in 1924 Conrad was more discussed, praised, and written about in England and America than any other living writer. But it is doubtful whether he was himself much the happier for this tardy recognition. Always an ironist, the sardonic hazard of his own life-story can only have increased his cynicism. And indeed there was both irony and pathos in this late arrival of a popularity not really suited to his genius. Just as once he had been neglected, so—from the moment of his acceptance by the English-speaking world—he was uncritically and therefore immoderately praised. He was doubtless aware that, although the real qualities of his work were not those of the best seller, he had become the idol of a literary fashion; and, being a student of literary history, he probably foresaw that when that fashion changed he would—at least temporarily—pay the penalty for a *Schwärmerei* which he had neither asked for nor deserved.

The years of the European War brought out in Conrad the fighting spirit which had made him so fine a seaman. He shared the anxieties of the thousands of parents whose sons were in the trenches and he toiled devotedly to raise funds for the refugees of his native Poland. By his visits to several of the northern naval bases he was allowed an inside view of the navy at work. In 1916 he went to sea for ten days in a 'Q' ship for trapping submarines. After peace came, he continued energetically his writing and his friendships—being happier now and free of the habit of foreboding which in earlier days had so miserably obsessed him. He died at Bishopsbourne, near Canterbury, 3 August 1924 in the sixty-eighth year of his age.

Conrad's work at its best achieved a synthesis of theme, treatment, and language of a kind without precedent in English literature; and it may well come to be admitted that, to a degree beyond the ordinary, he owed his fame to the good fortune of a remarkable life-story which enabled him to use as material for fiction many strange and picturesque experiences. Novelty of theme and the piquancy of a non-English origin rapidly established him—once a section of the public had become aware of his work—as a romantic, almost as a legendary, figure. His stories had excitement of a new kind, and his style, by its very queerness, could allure as powerfully as it could repel. Consequently the reputation of Conrad during his life and during the decade immediately following his death was inevitably a reputation of extremes, and it is not easy to forecast the probable measure of its survival.

That Conrad should have created so much fine prose in a language not his own must always be regarded as his most sensational achievement. Undeniably his very unfamiliarity with English forced him to an abnormally exigent study of its possibilities, and helped him to wring from it melodies of a rare and sonorous richness. Nor are these melodies mere Europeanisms translated into English terms; they are definitely individual, alike in their splendours and in their virtuosity. Stress has sometimes been laid on the French character of Conrad's writing; but it is doubtful whether the French influence, though superficially striking, was at all fundamental. Conrad himself denied a once prevalent rumour that he had hesitated between French and English as the language of his choice, and on the literary side, the surface grandiloquence of Victor Hugo rather than the deeper stylism of Flaubert seems to have remained with him from the years of companionship with his father. His language is not that of a man who came to English by the way of French, but rather that of a solitary and imaginative being who, having responded with rare sensitiveness to the drama of the sea and to the sinister beauty of tropical landscape, deliberately set himself to express in English words the emotions of a non-English soul.

The result is variously impressive. Where—as for example in the stories *Typhoon*, *Youth*, and *The Secret Sharer*, in *The Mirror of the Sea* and in *Nostromo*—remembered feeling or dramatic invention was strong enough to dominate the words used, Conrad achieved a perfect equilibrium of pictorial and narrative style. But often too great a part in the drama of Conrad's prose is played by language alone, which becomes in consequence self-conscious and obtrusive. Also, being a foreign language, its values are not always correctly judged, so that passages occur with words too emphatic for their context, and others where a curious equality of weight is given to words of varying significance.

Conrad's susceptibility to verbal experiment led him inevitably into another temptation, into prolonging a dramatic theme beyond its true narrative value. *The Nigger of the 'Narcissus'* and *Lord Jim* are the outstanding examples of this tendency to make a short novel of a short story, a long novel of a novelette. And the ingenuity with which he could elaborate a simple theme grew upon him, reaching in *Chance* and in one or two of the later books extremes of involution and criss-cross narrative which cause the basic themes of the books to be almost completely obscured by the machinery of their exploitation. But posterity will concern itself, not with Conrad's mannerisms, but with his fundamental qualities as a novelist. When, as time passes, the element of mere style in his reputation has faded to insignificance, his work will be treasured in proportion as it is simple and spontaneous. And it is simplest and most spontaneous when he writes of the sea and shows how sailors are leagued with their fellows in worship and in defiance of their mistress-tyrant. Although he himself tended to become more and more dramatically the literary man—'living his life as a novel', dreading above all things to be thought commonplace, phrasing his letters to friends and admirers with ever more of ornament and emotion—and although his books inevitably reflected this growing self-consciousness, they could never touch on the sea and on seafaring men without regaining immediately the fresh beauty of his youthful observations and experience. For the sea was always his real love; and as worshipper, interpreter, and prose-laureate of the sea his name will endure.

The principal works of Joseph Conrad are: *Almayer's Folly* (1895), *An Outcast of the Islands* (1896), *The Nigger of the 'Narcissus'* (1897), *Tales of Unrest* (stories, 1898), *Lord Jim* (1900), *The Inheritors* (with Ford Madox Hueffer (F. M. Ford), 1901), *Youth* (stories, 1902), *Romance* (with Ford Madox Hueffer, 1903), *Typhoon* (stories, 1903), *Nostromo* (1904), *The Mirror of the Sea* (reminiscences, 1906), *The Secret Agent* (1907, dramatized 1922), *A Set of Six* (stories, 1908), *Under Western Eyes* (1911), *'Twixt Land and Sea* (stories, 1912), *Some Reminiscences* (1912), *Chance* (1913), *Victory* (1915, dramatized 1919), *Within the Tides* (stories, 1915), *The Shadow-Line* (1917), *The Arrow of Gold* (1919), *The Rescue* (1920), *Notes on Life and Letters* (essays, 1921), *The Rover* (1922), *The Nature of a Crime* (with F. Madox Hueffer, 1924), *Laughing Anne* and *One Day More* (plays, 1924), *Suspense* (unfinished, 1925), *Tales of Hearsay* (stories, 1925), *Last Essays* (1926).

Conrad was also responsible for a number of pamphlets, privately issued on his own initiative or by his friend and bibliographer T. J. Wise; and for introductions to works by Maupassant, Stephen Crane, Thomas Beer, Edward Garnett, and Richard Curle. Details of all major and minor works will be found in the *Memorial Library of Joseph Conrad* by G. Keating (1929); the collection of T. J. Wise, up to 1921, is described in *A Conrad Library* (1928).

There are two drawings of Conrad in the National Portrait Gallery by Percy Anderson and (Sir) William Rothenstein.

[G. Jean Aubry, *Life and Letters of Joseph Conrad*, 2 vols., 1927; Jessie Conrad, *Joseph Conrad as I Knew Him*, 1926, and *Joseph Conrad and his Circle*, 1935; Richard Curle, *Joseph Conrad*, 1914, and *The Last Twelve Years of Joseph Conrad*, 1928; F. M. Ford, *Joseph Conrad*, 1924; Hugh Walpole, *Joseph Conrad*, 1916; *Letters of Joseph Conrad to Edward Garnett*, 1928; *Joseph Conrad's Letters to his Wife*, 1927; *Twenty Letters of Joseph Conrad*, 1926; Arthur Symons, *Notes on Joseph Conrad with some unpublished letters*, 1925; *One hundred and fifty Selected Letters from Joseph Conrad to Richard Curle*, 1928; also critical studies by Ruth M. Stauffer (1922), Ernest Bendy (1923), R. L. Megroz (1926), and others.] M. SADLEIR.

CONYBEARE, FREDERICK CORNWALLIS (1856–1924), Armenian scholar, was born at Coulsdon, Surrey, 14 September 1856, the third son of John Charles Conybeare, barrister-at-law, by his wife, Mary Catharine Vansittart. He was educated at Tonbridge School (his father having moved to Tonbridge), and in January 1876 proceeded with a scholarship to University College, Oxford. He obtained first classes in classical moderations (1877) and in *literae humaniores* (1879). He was elected a fellow of his college in 1880 and was made praelector in philosophy and, for one year only, in ancient history.

Being possessed of private means Conybeare resigned his college appointments in 1887 and devoted himself to research, studying, at the suggestion of a friend, the Armenian language (to which he afterwards added Georgian), at first with the idea of obtaining material for the textual criticism of Greek classics from ancient Armenian versions. The fruits of these studies appeared in his *Collation with the Ancient Armenian Versions of the Greek Text of Aristotle's Categories, &c.* (1892), and in articles, chiefly in the American *Journal of Philology* 1889–1924, dealing with the text of Plato; further, in comments on and translations of other Greek authors. In pursuit of these studies Conybeare travelled to various places where there are collections of Armenian manuscripts, and this literature being mainly religious he became interested in church history and in the textual criticism of the Septuagint and New Testament. The former study was one in which members of his family—notably Bishop John Conybeare [q.v.] and William John Conybeare [q.v.]—had previously won distinction. He made numerous discoveries, of which the most sensational was the ascription to the 'Presbyter Aristion' of the last twelve verses of St. Mark's gospel in a manuscript in the monastery library at Etchmiadzin, Transcaucasia. In a Vienna manuscript he discovered a translation of textual importance of the Commentary of Ephraem Syrus on the Acts of the Apostles. In the library of the Holy Synod in Moscow he unearthed *The Key of Truth*, the sole surviving monument of the Eastern Paulicians, in whose doctrines he became interested. He also brought to light from Armenian and Georgian printed books and manuscripts numerous documents bearing on the history of Christianity and its sects, and on general biblical and patristic literature. He was employed to catalogue the Armenian manuscripts in the British Museum (catalogue published 1913) and the Bodleian Library (catalogue published 1918).

The frankness with which Conybeare expressed his opinions, while endearing him to his friends, involved him in controversies. In 1904 he joined the Rationalist Press Association, which published his *Myth, Magic, and Morals, a Study of Christian Origins* (1909); its somewhat cynical scepticism elicited a rejoinder from Dr. William Sanday [q.v.] in *A New*

Marcion (1909). But he also attacked the school which denies the historicity of Jesus Christ in *The Historical Christ*, published by the same society in 1914. John MacKinnon Robertson, a leading writer of that school, was also a prominent member of the Rationalist Press Association, which Conybeare quitted in 1915, doubtless in consequence of the controversy evoked by his book.

When Alfred Dreyfus, an Alsatian Jew, attached to the French general army staff, had been declared guilty (1895) on the charge of delivering secret documents to Germany, Conybeare, having obtained private information about the affair, published in 1898 a book in defence of Dreyfus —*The Dreyfus Case*—which attracted notice in both England and France. Although Dreyfus was retried and reconvicted in the following year, he was immediately 'pardoned', but not reinstated until 1906.

Soon after the outbreak of the European War in 1914, Conybeare, against the advice of friends, wrote a letter in answer to Professor Kuno Meyer in which he threw the blame for the outbreak of war on Sir Edward Grey and Mr. Asquith. This letter Meyer, then in New York, published, in spite of a request from Conybeare to the contrary. The affair brought on Conybeare severe rebukes from the English press and alienated many of his friends. In 1917 he sold his Oxford house, and in 1921 took one at Folkestone, still spending much of his time in travel. In 1919 he visited the United States in order to deliver the Lowell lectures at Harvard. He died at Folkestone 9 January 1924. His valuable collection of Armenian books was given after his death to the London Library.

Conybeare was twice married: first, in 1883 to Mary Emily (died 1886), second daughter of Friedrich Max Müller, the philologist [q.v.]; she assisted him in translating R. H. Lotze's *Outlines of a Philosophy of Religion* (1892); secondly, in 1888 to Jane Macdowell, by whom he had one son and one daughter.

[A. C. Clark and J. Rendel Harris, *F. C. Conybeare, 1856–1924*, in *Proceedings* of the British Academy, vol. xi, 1923–5; *Revue des études Arméniennes* (containing bibliography of Conybeare's writings, extracts from reviews, and portrait), vol. vi, fasc. 2, Paris, 1926.]

D. S. Margoliouth.

COOLIDGE, WILLIAM AUGUSTUS BREVOORT (1850–1926), mountaineer and historian, was born near New York 28 August 1850, the elder son of Frederic William Skinner Coolidge, a merchant, of Boston, Massachusetts, by his wife, Elisabeth Neville Brevoort, who was of Dutch extraction. President Calvin Coolidge was a distant cousin. He was educated at St. Paul's School, Concord, New Hampshire, U.S.A., at Elizabeth College, Guernsey, and at Exeter College, Oxford. He obtained a first class in modern history in 1873 and a second class in jurisprudence in 1874. He was elected to a fellowship at Magdalen College in 1875 and, remaining unmarried, retained it until his death, which took place at Grindelwald 8 May 1926. A striking description of him near the end of his life is given by Henry Bordeaux in *Les Jeux dangereux* (1926).

Coolidge lectured and taught for some years in Oxford, and from 1880 to 1881 was professor of English history at St. David's College, Lampeter; but from 1885 Swiss pursuits claimed him almost entirely. These included mountaineering while his health allowed (for his training in this pursuit he regarded himself as indebted to his aunt, Miss Brevoort); the study of Swiss geography and history, especially of routes and passes; and the editorship and supervision of books on climbing and surveying. *A List of the Writings (not being Reviews of Books) dating from 1868 to 1912 and relating to the Alps or Switzerland of W. A. B. Coolidge* was compiled by Coolidge and privately printed in 1912; it occupies some thirty-five pages. A paper in the *Oberländisches Volksblatt* (Interlaken, 26 [*sic*] August 1920) in honour of his seventieth birthday gives an account of his achievement as a climber and of his first ascents, assigning to him, on the authority of a privately printed pamphlet, about 1,750 expeditions as having been carried out between 1865 and 1900, of which some 900 involved high ascents. He received recognition from the geographical and historical societies and Alpine clubs of many countries.

Coolidge's residence in Switzerland, which occupied every summer after he had grown up, and was continuous, except for one short visit to England in September 1901, for the last twenty-nine years of his life, and his rather small output on subjects unconnected with Swiss mountains has led to his being regarded only as a mountaineer. But his historical work is of high quality. His meticulous regard for accuracy of detail made it hard for him to satisfy himself. This went so far that he dismissed an important and scholarly book as 'worthless' on the ground that in it 'Grenoble' was printed with an accent. An editor once allowed him to review a study of his own for which no other competent critic could be found, and he increased the reputation of the journal by his severe exposure of certain minute errors which he thus took the opportunity of correcting.

Coolidge was ordained deacon in 1882 and priest in 1883. His known, though rarely expressed, theological opinions were those of a decided high churchman; and for a good many years, between 1883 and 1896, he regularly, when at Oxford, acted as honorary curate at South Hinksey. He chose a manner of life which made it for long intervals difficult to perform clerical functions; but those who came into contact with him at times of emotional experience could have no doubt as to his religious feeling or as to the value of the spiritual help which it enabled him to give.

[Private information; personal knowledge. Further details will be found in *Magdalen College Record*, 1934.] P. V. M. BENECKE.

COOPER, JAMES (1846–1922), Scottish divine, was born at Elgin 13 February 1846, the eldest son of John Alexander Cooper, merchant, afterwards farmer at Spynie, Elgin. His mother, Ann, daughter of James Stephen, of Old Keith, was descended from the Gordons and Stuarts of Birkenburn. Educated at Elgin Academy and at Aberdeen University, where he graduated M.A. in 1867, Cooper was licensed to preach in 1871. In 1873 he was ordained to St. Stephen's church, Broughty Ferry, in 1881 translated to the East Parish of St. Nicholas, Aberdeen, and in 1898 appointed to the regius professorship of ecclesiastical history at Glasgow University.

During his parochial ministry Cooper was indefatigable as pastor and preacher. At Aberdeen he revived the daily service, disused since the seventeenth century; he was also the first to institute a women's guild. Deeply interested in ecclesiology, he was instrumental in restoring the ancient St. Mary's chapel under the East Church; as founder of the Aberdeen Ecclesiological Society he was father of the Scottish Ecclesiological Society, of which he was four times president, and the *Transactions* of which he edited for many years. He also edited in 1888 the chartulary of the East Church for the New Spalding Club, supplying a translation and valuable liturgical notes.

Reared under the shadow of Elgin Cathedral and Spynie Castle (once the bishop of Moray's palace), Cooper early acquired zeal for catholic orthodoxy and a certain attachment to episcopacy. He was the first secretary of the Scottish Church Society, founded in 1892 to advance catholic doctrine, and he eventually became the leader of the 'Scoto-Catholic' party, which desired to see in Scotland a church both national and catholic and a reunion that should include episcopacy. His proudest moment came in 1917 when, suspicions allayed and misunderstandings removed, he was elected moderator of the General Assembly of the Church of Scotland.

As professor, Cooper exercised a remarkable personal influence over pupils and students by reason of his sincere and pious character; his cultured mind, varied interests, and affectionate nature brought him also a large circle of friends. He published many sermons, addresses, and pamphlets for the times, and was a frequent contributor to this DICTIONARY. He received the freedom of Elgin (1917) and honorary degrees from the universities of Dublin (1909), Oxford (1922), and Glasgow (1922). He died at Elgin 27 December 1922, and is buried in Urquhart churchyard.

Cooper married in 1912 Margaret, eldest daughter of George Williamson, farmer at Shempston in Moray; they had no children.

[H. J. Wotherspoon, *James Cooper, a Memoir*, 1926; W. Fulton in *The Aberdeen University Review*, March 1923.]
W. FULTON.

CORBETT, SIR JULIAN STAFFORD (1854–1922), naval historian, was the second son of Charles Joseph Corbett, architect, of Thames Ditton, Surrey, by his wife, Elizabeth, daughter of Philip Henry Byrne, of London. He was born at Imber Court, Thames Ditton, 12 November 1854, and was educated at Marlborough and Trinity College, Cambridge, where he gained a first class in the law tripos in 1875. In 1879 he was called to the bar by the Middle Temple, and continued to practise for five years, although the work from the first appears to have been irksome. In 1882 he abandoned it and, having private means, travelled extensively, visiting among other places India and the United States.

In 1886 Corbett found in fiction an outlet for literary ability which in his Cambridge days had occasioned remark. His first novel was *The Fall of Asgard*, and this was quickly followed by *For God and Gold* (1887) and *Kophetua the Thirteenth* (1889). By a natural process he was drawn towards biography, contributing to the 'English Men of Action' series the life of Monk in 1889, and in the following year Drake. It would, however, be a mistake to suppose that these volumes helped to shape his subsequent career. In 1895 he reverted to fiction, his next novel being *A Business in Great Waters*.

During this, the formative period of his life, Corbett continued to travel, visiting Norway frequently, and almost invariably spending the winter in Rome. It was his taste for sport and travel that induced him in 1896 to accompany the Dongola expedition as special correspondent of the *Pall Mall Gazette*. His experiences were much less exciting than he had anticipated, but the campaign undoubtedly set him thinking about the conduct of war as a subject for his pen. In 1898 he produced his first serious contribution to historical literature, *Drake and the Tudor Navy*. Corbett had already written two novels on this theme as well as a biography, and the choice was natural enough; but his experiences as a war correspondent had changed his outlook, and the two volumes may be taken as inaugurating a new chapter in his life. He was not quite sure, however, that he was pursuing the right course, even though his researches had brought him into touch with the Navy Records Society, recently founded by Sir John Knox Laughton [q.v.], who had persuaded him to edit a volume connected with Drake, *Papers Relating to the Navy during the Spanish War, 1585–1587* (1898). At forty-five Corbett was hesitating whether to follow his own preference and resume the role of the novelist or yield to the counsel of his friends and stand for parliament, when his marriage in 1899 with Edith, only daughter of George Alexander, cotton manufacturer, of Manchester, enabled him to make up his mind. At his wife's request he decided to devote himself to serious historical writing.

The first fruit of this decision was *The Successors of Drake* (1900), which may be regarded as continuing and concluding his work on the Tudor navy, although two years later (1902) he edited for the Navy Records Society Sir William Slyngsbie's contemporary *Relation of the Voyage to Cadiz, 1596*. On the strength of work already completed Corbett was appointed in 1902 lecturer in history to the Royal Naval War College, just established at Greenwich, and in 1903 was selected to deliver the Ford lectures at Oxford. In 1904 he presented the substance of the research which his two new spheres of work had involved in *England in the Mediterranean, 1603–1714*, a comprehensive study of naval strategy. Naval tactics next engaged his attention, and for the centenary of Trafalgar (1905) he prepared for the Navy Records Society a volume which he called *Fighting Instructions, 1530–1816*, a collection of documents illustrating the art of handling battle-fleets in the days of sail. But at the War College it was strategy rather than tactics that his audiences required, and in 1907 he completed another notable contribution to the subject, *England in the Seven Years' War*, a book which, more than any of its precursors, demonstrated the true relationship of naval power and national policy.

In 1908, almost by way of relaxation, Corbett edited for the Navy Records Society volumes dealing with *Views of the Battles of the Third Dutch War* and *Signals and Instructions, 1776–1794*, the latter a supplement to his *Fighting Instructions*. He found time, also, to write numerous articles and pamphlets, one of which, *The Capture of Private Property at Sea*, was reprinted by A. T. Mahan in *Some Neglected Aspects of War* (1907). But at this time Corbett was chiefly engaged upon a new study, *The Campaign of Trafalgar*, published in 1910. This, his most important work so far, disappointed the reviewers, who were expecting a controversial treatment of Nelson's tactics and received what may be called the first staff history of a naval campaign. The welcome which the book received from naval officers induced Corbett in the following year to present the essence of his doctrine in *Some Principles of Maritime Strategy*; while a paper on 'Staff Histories' which he read to the International Congress of Historical Studies in 1913 was reprinted in *Naval and Military Essays* (1914), the first volume of a series which was interrupted by the War. At this time (1913) he was editing for the Navy Records *Private Papers of George, second Earl Spencer*, which threw a flood of new light on naval administration in Nelson's day; and on the appearance of the second volume he was awarded the Chesney gold medal by the Royal United Service Institution (1914).

When the European War broke out, Corbett offered his services to the Admiralty and, in addition to organizing a bureau for the collection of material for the history of the struggle at sea, wrote pamphlets for the enlightenment of neutrals and supplied tabular statements of historical parallels for the assistance of the naval staff. In 1917 he was knighted.

Shortly before the War Corbett had undertaken to write an official history of the naval campaigns of 1904–1905; this was completed in 1915 under the title *Maritime Operations in the Russo-Japanese War* (for official use). The experience which he gained in the compilation of this work was invaluable. It showed him what was needed in the way of sources, and in conjunction with his labours at the war bureau accelerated the writing of *Naval Operations*, the official history of the European War at sea. The first volume appeared in 1920, and the second, carrying the narrative down to the resignation of Lord Fisher, appeared in the following year. In 1921 Corbett delivered the Creighton lecture at King's College, London, sketching in outline the subject which he had put aside to deal with the Russo-Japanese War and to which he always hoped to return—'Napoleon and the British Navy after Trafalgar' (published in the *Quarterly Review*, April 1922). But his plans were denied fruition; for he died quite suddenly at Stopham, Sussex, 21 September 1922, leaving one son and one daughter. He had just completed a third volume of *Naval Operations*, containing his account of the battle of Jutland, and this was printed posthumously (1923).

Corbett had a natural bent for antiquarian pursuits, collected rare books and manuscripts bearing on his chosen themes, and wrote in a cultured and arresting style; but left to himself, he would hardly have devoted himself so whole-heartedly to naval history. There was as much of the philosopher in him as the historian. It was the good fortune of his country that he had not committed himself to any definite line of inquiry when, at the opening of the new century, the Royal Naval War College was instituted and, finding in him the instrument it needed, inspired the series of monographs and histories which won for his original genius a wide measure of esteem.

[Letters and papers in possession of the family; personal knowledge.]

G. A. R. Callender.

CORELLI, MARIE (pseudonym), novelist. [See Mackay, Mary.]

CORYNDON, Sir ROBERT THORNE (1870–1925), South African administrator, was born at Queenstown, Cape Colony, 2 April 1870, the eldest son of Selby Coryndon, solicitor, of Plymouth, Devon, and of Kimberley, Cape Colony, by his wife, Emily, daughter of Charles Henry Caldecott, of Grahamstown, Cape Colony, a member of the legislative assembly of that colony. Coryndon was educated at St. Andrew's College, Grahamstown, and at Cheltenham College. It was intended that he should follow his father's profession of the law, and with that object he returned to South Africa at the age of nineteen (1889) in order to serve his articles with his uncle's firm, Caldecott and Bell, of Kimberley.

Of fine physique and ready for any kind of adventure, Coryndon was lured from office-work by rumours of the great schemes of Cecil Rhodes [q.v.] for exploration and development in the north under the charter recently granted by the Imperial government to the newly formed British South Africa Company. He was one of the twelve young Kimberley men who were chosen to form the nucleus of a civil service in the territories which Rhodes was planning to annex, and who were sent by him to Mafeking, there to be attached temporarily to the Bechuana border police as troopers. The rough and ready life of a frontiersman satisfied Coryndon's craving for an open air existence, and developed in him those powers of observation and quick decision which were to stand him in such good stead during the career that lay before him. He and his companions, who later became known as 'Rhodes's Apostles', were transferred to the pioneer column which entered Mashonaland in June 1890, and were present when the Union Jack was hoisted at Fort Salisbury on 14 September of that year. He made the first survey and drawings of the famous Zimbabwe ruins near Victoria, and presently became a clerk in the government survey department at Salisbury, now the capital of Southern Rhodesia.

Office routine, however, did not appeal to Coryndon. In 1892 he took up big-game hunting professionally, and secured two white rhinoceroses, one of which is now in the Natural History Museum, South Kensington, and the other in the Cape Town Museum. On the outbreak of the Matabele War in 1893, he joined the Salisbury Horse, and served as a sergeant under Major P. W. Forbes. After the war, he drove a post-cart between Salisbury and Kimberley, and on one occasion Rhodes was his passenger. The upshot of this meeting was that Rhodes, who was always attracted by men of the true pioneer type, engaged Coryndon as his private secretary. He accompanied Rhodes to England during the parliamentary inquiry into the Jameson Raid (1896). He returned to Rhodesia to take part in the suppression of the Matabele rebellion of 1896 which Rhodes brought to so dramatic a conclusion in the Matoppo hills.

With the pacification of the Matabele and Mashona tribes, Rhodes turned his attention to the vast territories which lay north of the Zambesi river, and in 1897 chose Coryndon to be the first British resident and British South Africa Company's representative with Lewanika, the paramount chief of the Barotse and other tribes inhabiting the Upper Zambesi basin. The choice was a good one. During his association with Rhodes Coryndon had assimilated much of that great man's broad outlook and dream of empire, and this, added to a hard life in the veldt, had made him the practical, purposeful man he showed himself to be throughout his administrative career. Coryndon proceeded to Lewanika's capital, Lealui, accompanied only by his secretary, Frank Worthington, and five policemen from Southern Rhodesia. Lewanika, who expected to receive a resident with an imposing retinue, was disappointed, and his suspicions were aroused by Coryndon's additional role of British South Africa Company's representative. However, by his personality, firmness, and fair dealing, Coryndon won the full confidence, not only of Lewanika and the Barotse, but also of the many tribes subject to them. He concluded a far-reaching agreement with the chief, which was mainly instrumental in bringing North-Western Rhodesia definitely within the sphere of the British South Africa Company's influence.

In 1900 Coryndon was appointed administrator of North-Western Rhodesia, a post which he held until 1907. During his comparatively short term of office he enrolled a native police force, established law and order, opened communications with the south and north, organized a civil service, subdivided the country into administrative districts, and made it safe for travel, legitimate trade, and land-settlement. He built wisely and well; upon the foundations which he laid has since arisen the prosperous crown colony of Northern Rhodesia. Meanwhile, affairs in Swaziland had reached a critical stage, the Swazis had become thoroughly out of hand, and rebellion was openly talked. Coryndon was appointed resident commissioner there in 1907, and quickly gained the respect and trust of Europeans and natives alike. To him is mainly due the regeneration of Swaziland. In 1914, while still resident commissioner of Swaziland, he was appointed chairman of a commission appointed by the Colonial Office to report upon the native reserves of Southern Rhodesia. His sympathy with the natives, and his knowledge of their customs and mode of living, enabled him to propose a scheme of settlement upon which the successful native policy of Southern Rhodesia to-day is mainly based. Coryndon stayed in Swaziland until January 1916, when he was appointed resident commissioner of Basutoland. There he remained for under two years, but even in that short time he left his mark by greatly improving means of communication and the natives' standard of living.

In 1917 Coryndon was appointed governor and commander-in-chief of Uganda. He had to deal with difficult racial and economic problems, and owed his great success to his policy of safeguarding and promoting the welfare of the natives, whilst not losing sight of the interests of the white settlers or the legitimate claims of the Indians. He encouraged the cultivation of cotton by native small-holders, stabilized the rate of exchange, and inaugurated a legislative council. In 1922 he was appointed governor and commander-in-chief of Kenya Colony and high commissioner of Zanzibar. Here he found European, Indian, and native interests in conflict, and was called upon to reconcile them. Again his efforts met with marked success, but his sudden death at Nairobi on 10 February 1925 brought to an end a remarkable career of thirty-five strenuous years spent in the service of his country.

Coryndon married in 1909 Phyllis Mary, daughter of James Worthington, of Lowestoft, Suffolk, and had three sons and one daughter. He was made C.M.G. in 1911 and K.C.M.G. in 1919. He was also a commander of the Belgian order of Leopold.

[Personal knowledge.]

F. V. Worthington.

COURTNEY, WILLIAM LEONARD (1850–1928), philosopher and journalist, was born at Poona 5 January 1850, the youngest son and child in the family of three sons and three daughters of William Courtney, of the Indian civil service, by his wife, Ann Edwardes, daughter of Captain Edward Scott, R.N., of Hoegarden House, Plymouth. His early years were profoundly influenced by his eldest sister, Emily (Minnie), a remarkable woman. Educated at Somersetshire College, Bath, under the Rev. Hay Sweet Escott, a stimulating teacher, he was elected scholar of University College, Oxford, the vigorous life of which he enjoyed from 1868 to 1872. After first classes in classical moderations (1870) and *literae humaniores* (1872) he won a fellowship at Merton College in the latter year, and shared the society of Mandell Creighton, William Wallace, R. J. Wilson, Andrew Lang, and Francis Herbert Bradley among the fellows. In 1873 Courtney was appointed headmaster of his old school, Somersetshire College, and in the following year (1874) married Cordelia Blanche, daughter of Commander Lionel Place, R.N., by whom he had four sons and three daughters.

Courtney returned to Oxford in 1876, having been elected to a fellowship and tutorship in philosophy at New College, where he remained until 1890. His lectures, especially those on Plato's *Republic*, were remarkable for their excellent form and clear presentation of philosophical problems, and many distinguished pupils acknowledged their debt to his teaching. Married life was beginning at the university, and the Courtneys with their social gifts and dramatic talent played an active part in it. Meanwhile he was writing on philosophy and, with Jowett's help, promoting the foundation of the New Theatre and assisting in the production of the *Agamemnon* in Balliol College hall in 1880 and of the early plays of the Oxford University Dramatic Society, founded in 1884. In this latter enterprise he was associated with amateurs who later achieved fame—Arthur Bourchier [q.v.], Ernest Holman Clark, and Harry Irving, whose father, (Sir) Henry Irving, Courtney brought to lecture in Oxford in 1886. He was treasurer of the University Boat Club, and a conspicuous figure on the tow-path. This versatility possibly stood in the way of his reputation as a philosopher.

Courtney was already writing for the *World* and for the *Fortnightly Review* and *Edinburgh Review*, and in 1882 he became assistant to T. H. S. Escott, who was then editing the *Fortnightly*. Divided between his devotion to philosophy and the call of a wider sphere, he accepted in 1890 a post on the staff of the *Daily Telegraph*, where he joined a group of able men, including (Sir) John Merry Le Sage, Henry Duff Traill, and Edward Levy-Lawson (afterwards Lord Burnham), from whom he learned much. He left many friends, not only in New College, which he had served with distinction, retaining there his fellowship for life, but in Oxford generally, chief among them being Edward Armstrong and Thomas Case.

In Fleet Street Courtney worked for thirty-eight years, writing general articles, and becoming in the mid-'nineties chief dramatic critic and literary editor of the *Daily Telegraph*, a post which he held until 1925, writing the weekly 'Book of the day', and always keeping in touch with dramatic, literary, and general society, at the Garrick Club (joined 1891), the Beefsteak Club (joined 1896), and elsewhere. His scholarly training and dramatic experience, his wide interests and resource in emergency, made him a first-rate journalist. In 1890–1891 he edited *Murray's Magazine*, but he found his great opportunity when he became editor of the *Fortnightly Review* in 1894. He kept it at a high level both on the literary and the political side to the end of his life, editing it with sympathy and judgement, and a wise regard for the highest interest of the public. He had an uncommon flair for choosing subjects and writers, and delighted in encouraging new talent. For many years he was chairman of the publishing firm of Chapman & Hall.

Courtney's first wife died in 1907, and in 1911 he married Janet Elizabeth Hogarth, an old pupil and friend, daughter of the Rev. George Hogarth, vicar of Barton-on-Humber, Lincolnshire, and sister of David George Hogarth [q.v.]. She had throughout been his assistant on the *Fortnightly*, and had done valuable work in the Bank of England, for *The Times* Book Club, and on the *Encyclopædia Britannica*. From this time forward she shared his life as editor and journalist, to the great happiness of both.

Although Courtney gave up writing on philosophy after leaving Oxford, philosophy and religion remained always near his heart, and most of his writing had a serious note, the outcome of a sane outlook and a high ideal. His influence did much to keep journalism steady at a time of shifting standards. His philosophical studies, *The Metaphysics of John Stuart Mill* (1879), *Studies in Philosophy* (1882), and *Constructive Ethics* (1886), were published in his Oxford period. These, together with his articles in the *Edinburgh Review*, won recognition from good judges. Of his later books, collected from his articles or written as holiday studies, the most original was *The Feminine Note in Fiction* (1904). His plays had little success.

Courtney had a tall and striking figure, resembling a soldier more than a philosopher. A portrait of him by Sir Hubert von Herkomer at New College is like him, but hardly does justice to his force of character. He was always a genial companion and a loyal friend. He died in London 1 November 1928.

[*The Times*, 2 November 1928; Janet Courtney, *The Making of an Editor, W. L. Courtney, 1850–1928*, 1930; W. L. Courtney, *The Passing Hour*, 1925; personal knowledge.]

P. E. Matheson.

COWDRAY, first Viscount (1856–1927), contractor. [See Pearson, Weetman Dickinson.]

CRAIK, Sir HENRY, first baronet (1846–1927), civil servant, politician, and man of letters, was born in Glasgow 18 October 1846, the fifth son and the ninth of the ten children of the Rev. James Craik, D.D., minister of St. George's church, Glasgow, and at one time moderator of the Church of Scotland, by his wife, Margaret, daughter of Walter Grieve, merchant, of Leith. From the high school of his native city he passed in 1860 to the university. In 1865 a Snell exhibition took him to Balliol College, Oxford, where he gained a first class in classical moderations (1867) and two years later a second class in *literae humaniores* and a first class in law and modern history. In 1870 he was appointed a junior examiner in the Education Department, and in due course was promoted to the senior grade (1878). His real opportunity, however, came in 1885, when the control of Scottish education was entrusted to a reorganized committee of the Privy Council. He was chosen for the secretaryship, and he continued to occupy the post with great distinction until he quitted the service in 1904. In the interval he had been created a C.B. (1887) and then a K.C.B. (1897).

Busy as he was, Craik had found leisure for authorship. He was a not infrequent contributor to the *Quarterly Review* and other periodicals, and in 1882 he published a *Life of Swift*. There followed *The State and Education* (1883), *Selections from Swift* (1893), *English Prose Selections* (1892–1896), and *A Century of Scottish History* (1901), the last written almost entirely at night, between the hours of 11 p.m. and 2.30 a.m. In 1906 he was returned to parliament in the conservative interest as one of the two members for the universities of Glasgow and Aberdeen. Books belonging to this period were *Impressions of India* (1908) and a *Life of Edward, First Earl of Clarendon* (1911). After the four Scottish universities were combined into a single constituency in 1918, he retained his seat as one of their three representatives, and he was still a member when he died in London 12 April 1927. A privy councillorship was conferred on him in 1918 and a baronetcy in 1926.

Craik's conspicuous success as a civil servant was not surprising, for he had a real aptitude for business and much practical sagacity, while his golden rule of 'Look ahead' made him a master in the art of correspondence. Temperamentally irascible, he did not always find it easy to appreciate an opposite point of view. But, if local administrators were sometimes prone to grumble at his 'dictatorial' methods, their underlying respect for his strong and capable guidance was never shaken. In his relations with his official chiefs he was a model of discretion and loyalty, and consequently his advice came to carry more and more weight with successive governments, whatever their political complexion.

When Craik laid down the reins of office, his influence had reached its zenith. Despite his well-stocked mind and his ripe experience, widened in later years by visits to South Africa (1903), Egypt and the Sudan (1907), India (1907–1908), and Canada (1912), he never overcame the disability attaching to one who begins parliamentary life at sixty with no previous practice in public speaking. Moreover, his relatively independent position as a university member induced a hardening of his innate conservatism. He sturdily refused to move with the times or to abate his dislike of new-fangled devices from type-writing machines to Cabinet secretariates, and he frequently chafed at having to stand idly by when his leaders preferred concessions and compromises to the courageous policies which he would himself have favoured. Nevertheless, the evening of his days was happy. Of a most likeable disposition, never forgetting a friend and never bearing a grudge, he was popular in all quarters of the House of Commons, of which he ultimately became in years the oldest member.

Craik was a man of exceptionally strong physique. His favourite recreation was hunting, and almost to the last he kept up the custom of taking morning exercise in the Row. It was characteristic of him that on the outbreak of war in 1914, although then verging on seventy, he was one of the first to volunteer as a special constable. When he retired in 1919 with the rank of sergeant ('I do not know that I ever valued any promotion more'), he was able to say that he had never missed a roll-call, except when detained at the House, and that he had been out in every air-raid over London.

Craik married in 1873 Fanny Esther (died 1923), daughter of Charles Duffield, of Manchester, and had three sons. He was succeeded as second baronet by his eldest son, George Lillie (1874–1929).

[Numerous autobiographical articles published in the *Glasgow Herald* between April 1922 and May 1925; private information; personal knowledge.] G. Macdonald.

CREAGH, Sir GARRETT O'MOORE (1848–1923), general, the seventh son of Captain James Creagh, R.N., by his wife, Grace Emily, daughter of Garrett O'Moore, of Cloghan Castle, co. Kerry, was born at Cahirbane, co. Clare, 2 April 1848. He was educated privately and at the Royal Naval School, New Cross, and finally at the Royal Military College, Sandhurst. In 1866 he was gazetted as an ensign to the 95th Foot (afterwards the Sherwood Foresters) and four years later transferred to the Indian army, taking up an appointment on the Bombay Staff Corps as a lieutenant. For nine years he remained on the staff, and then, having been promoted to captain in 1878, he saw active service in the Afghan War of 1879–1880. On 21 April 1879, at Kam Dakka, whither he had been detached with a small force to protect the village against the Mohmands, he won the Victoria Cross. With only 150 men he was repeatedly attacked by a force of 1,500, before which he retired to a position in a near-by cemetery. Here he repulsed every effort of the enemy, until relieved in the afternoon by another detachment. Finally the Mohmands were charged and broken by a troop of the 10th Bengal Lancers. The commander-in-chief in India, General Sir Frederick Haines, reported that 'but for the coolness, determination, and gallantry of the highest order, and the admirable conduct which Captain Creagh displayed, the detachment under his command would, in all probability, have been cut off and destroyed'. Creagh also received the medal for this campaign, was mentioned in dispatches, and awarded the brevet of major.

In 1882 Creagh was given command of the Merwara battalion. Passing on to the Indian Staff Corps in 1886 he was gazetted major in that year, and two years later joined the expedition which resulted in the annexation of the Zhob Valley, on the North-West Frontier (1884–1890). While still on the Indian Staff Corps he was promoted to lieutenant-colonel in 1892, and to colonel in 1896, when he was appointed assistant quartermaster-general at Bombay. In 1899 he was promoted to brigadier-general and became political resident and general officer in command at Aden. In 1900 he commanded the 2nd brigade in the China expedition, and in the following year became general officer commanding the British expeditionary force in China.

Returning to India, Creagh was given command of a first-class district and promoted major-general in 1903; in 1904 he took over the command of the 5th division (Western army corps). In that year he was promoted lieutenant-general, and in 1906 passed on to the command of the 2nd division (Northern command). In the following year he came home to England on special duty; in July he was appointed military secretary at the India Office, and in November promoted to the rank of full general. He held the India Office post until 1909, when he was appointed to succeed Lord Kitchener as commander-in-chief in India. In the five years of his administration in India General Creagh had no outstanding innovations to introduce; his predecessor had achieved all that was required of reorganization, and Creagh's tenure of office is marked by the assimilation of the many military reforms which Kitchener, with the support of the India Office and the War Office, had accomplished.

Creagh, who had been created K.C.B. in 1902, was promoted G.C.B. in 1909; in 1911 he received the G.C.S.I. and was made aide-de-camp to King George V. He married twice: first, in 1874 Mary Letitia Longfield (died 1876), daughter of John Brereton, of Oldcourt, co. Tipperary;

secondly, in 1891 Elizabeth, daughter of Edward Reade, of Kelverton, Buckinghamshire, by whom he had one son and one daughter. He died in London 9 August 1923.

[*The Times*, 10 August 1923; official records.] C. V. OWEN.

CROWE, SIR EYRE ALEXANDER BARBY WICHART (1864–1925), diplomat, the third son of Sir Joseph Archer Crowe, the historian of painting [q.v.], by his wife, Asta, daughter of Gustav von Barby, was born 30 July 1864 at Leipzig. He received his schooling at gymnasia at Düsseldorf and Berlin, subsequently preparing for the entrance examination of the Foreign Office at Wimbledon and in Paris (1881–1885). In 1885, when he entered the Foreign Office as junior clerk, he was equally fluent in English, French, and German.

At that time the junior clerks in the Foreign Office were allowed little initiative and little responsibility except for official secrecy. Crowe's ambition was to be master of his profession. He devoted himself to modern history, and in particular he acquired from State papers and from the Foreign Office records an intimate knowledge of the course of British diplomacy, especially in the nineteenth century. In 1890 he became a lieutenant in the first Volunteer battalion of the City of London Fusiliers and in 1894 was promoted captain. He made himself a thoroughly competent officer and read widely in the modern literature of tactics and strategy, but after volunteering for active service during the South African War and failing to pass the medical examination he resigned his commission in 1902. His health was always precarious, but his physical weakness was overruled by a strong will, concealed by a courtesy and cheerfulness which gave him a peculiar charm, although his personal dignity and self-possession made an impression of hardness on those who were not admitted to intimacy.

In 1896, on the death of his father, Crowe ceased to reside in the Foreign Office, as he had done for some ten years, and went to live with his mother in Chelsea. His ability, industry, and knowledge had already marked him out among his colleagues. He usually spent his vacations at his father's house in Paris or at that of his uncle, Professor Carl Gerhardt, at Gamburg, in Baden, but except for occasional walking tours in England, France, and Germany he travelled little, though on one occasion he went as queen's messenger to Constantinople. It was a great advantage to him that he enjoyed the freest confidence of German friends, although general aloofness from politics marked German scientific circles such as that of Gerhardt's house at Gamburg, where Crowe was attracted by Gerhardt's eldest daughter, Clema, widow of Eberhardt von Bonin. He married her in 1903, and she naturally came to share her husband's thoughts and feelings, his political ideas and his English patriotism.

During the years 1904 and 1905 Crowe took an active part in carrying out a scheme for the reorganization of the Foreign Office, one of the chief objects of which he had much at heart, namely the increased responsibility of the junior members of the staff. He also advocated a reform by which each of the missions abroad is required to make an annual report on the policy of the country to which it is accredited.

In January 1907 Crowe submitted to Sir Edward (afterwards Viscount) Grey a 'Memorandum on the present state of British relations with France and Germany' (printed in *British Documents on the Origins of the War*, vol. iii), in which he traced the history of those relations and showed the trend of German policy towards domination over Europe. He held that Bismarck's overbearing policy towards England had aimed at forcing her into becoming the subordinate ally of Germany; that it had been continued by Prince Bülow in order to estrange France from England; and that it ought to be met not by concessions but by 'the most unbending determination to uphold British rights and interests in every part of the globe'. Such a policy adopted in the past towards France had brought about a *rapprochement* between the two countries. Friendly relations with Germany were most desirable and could be attained in no other way. Crowe's memorandum made a great impression upon Sir Edward Grey, who submitted it to the prime minister and his principal colleagues.

In the following May Crowe acted as secretary to the British delegation at the second Peace Conference at The Hague. His services were recognized by the award of the C.B. In 1908 he was a British delegate at the International Maritime Conference held in London, at which was drawn up the abortive Declaration of London, intended as a codification of international law in regard to maritime warfare. Crowe's object was to safeguard every principle of vital importance to Great Britain and to oppose every proposal which would hamper her in the event of war. He secured the acceptance of all those points to which the British Admiralty attached importance; but after the Declaration had been approved by the conference, it was severely criticized by unofficial naval experts. The Admiralty made these criticisms its own, and they were echoed in parliament, with the result that the Declaration was never ratified. Crowe could at least feel that the failure was in no way attributable to him.

In 1911 Crowe acted as British agent in the arbitration at The Hague between the British and French governments in the Savarkar case. He succeeded in winning the case, which raised important questions of international law, by his broad and masterly statement of the facts. He was then created K.C.M.G., and in January 1912 became assistant under-secretary of state for foreign affairs.

In the crisis brought about by the Austrian ultimatum to Serbia in July 1914, Crowe promptly grasped the whole situation. His views are recorded in minutes which have been published [*British Documents on the Origins of the War*, vol. xi]. He wrote on 25 July: 'Our interests are tied up with those of France and Russia in this struggle, which is not for the possession of Servia, but one between Germany aiming at a political dictatorship in Europe, and the Powers who desire to retain individual freedom. If we can help to avoid a conflict by showing our naval strength, ready to be instantly used, it would be wrong not to make the effort.' On 27 July he pointed out that Austria's mobilization would necessarily be followed by that of Russia, Germany, and France, and therefore that 'within twenty-four hours His Majesty's Government will be faced with the question whether, in a quarrel so imposed by Austria on an unwilling France, Great Britain will stand idly aside or take sides'. On 31 July he wrote: 'If and when it is certain that France and Russia cannot avoid the war, and are going into it, my opinion, for what it is worth, is that British interests require us to take our place beside them as allies, and in that case our intervention should be immediate and decided.' The same day, in a memorandum for Sir Edward Grey, he wrote: 'The argument that there is no written bond binding us to France is strictly correct. There is no contractual obligation. But the *Entente* has been made, strengthened, put to the test, and celebrated in a manner justifying the belief that a moral bond was being forged. The whole policy of the *Entente* can have no meaning if it does not signify that in a just quarrel England would stand by her friends.'

Some time before the crisis Crowe had drawn up a plan, with a view to the possibility of war, for at once seizing German ships in British ports. When the War came, he was able, though not easily, to persuade the government to carry it out. Of his services during and after the War there is at present no accessible record; but it is certain that they were constant and increasingly important. In the autumn of 1915 he was attacked in a section of the press on the ground of his German connexions; but his integrity and position in the public service were vindicated in the House of Commons by Sir Edward Grey and in the House of Lords by Lord Robert Cecil.

In 1919 Crowe was one of the British plenipotentiaries at the Peace Conference at Versailles. In November 1920 he became permanent under-secretary of state for foreign affairs, that is, professional head of the Foreign Office—the position which, from the age of seventeen, had been the object of his ambition. His constant advice and assistance were so highly valued by the ministers whom he served in this capacity—Lord Curzon, Mr. Ramsay Macdonald, and Sir Austen Chamberlain—and he was so entirely devoted to his duties, that he denied himself the holidays indispensable for his health. When at length, in April 1925, he went for a brief rest to Swanage, it was too late; he died there 28 April after a few days' illness. He had one son and three daughters.

Sir J. W. Headlam-Morley, the historical adviser to the Foreign Office, who had exceptional opportunities of studying Crowe's work, wrote of him that he was 'one of the most distinguished public servants of the time'; the study of his minutes and memoranda revealed 'the remarkable faculty of seeing and stating the essential points in a highly complex and difficult situation, the quickness and sureness of judgement and expression, the power of bringing his exceptional knowledge and experience to bear upon the particular problem with which he had to deal, and, above all, the intense feeling of responsibility and the single-minded devotion to the honour of his country' [*British*

Documents, xi, pp. vii–viii]. The feelings of those who knew him were expressed by the prime minister, Mr. Baldwin, who, after hearing of Crowe's death, said: 'We have lost the ablest servant of the Crown.'

[G. P. Gooch and H. W. V. Temperley, *British Documents on the Origins of the War, 1898–1914*, vols. iii, xi, 1927–1928; private information; personal knowledge.]

S. WILKINSON.

CURZON, GEORGE NATHANIEL, MARQUESS CURZON OF KEDLESTON (1859–1925), statesman, was born at Kedleston Hall, Derbyshire, 11 January 1859. He was the eldest of the eleven children, four sons and seven daughters, of the Rev. Alfred Nathaniel Holden Curzon, fourth Baron Scarsdale, rector of Kedleston, by his wife, Blanche, daughter of Joseph Pocklington Senhouse, of Netherhall, Maryport, Cumberland. His father was of a reserved disposition, and his mother died when he was sixteen. The formative influences in his early life were those of his governess, Miss Paraman, and a private schoolmaster of the name of Dunbar. The discipline of Miss Paraman, at times ferocious, her exaggerated insistence on precision of detail, her morbid parsimony, her frequent injustice, while strengthening the combative qualities in Curzon, did not encourage the more gentle or elastic elements in his nature. At the age of ten he left the bleak nurseries of Kedleston for the private school of the Rev. Cowley Powles at Wixenford in Hampshire. Here again he was exposed to a strong and violent nature, and the harsh lessons learned from Miss Paraman, which during the holidays that lady would instil anew, were confirmed for him by the cramming of the assistant master, Mr. Dunbar. His capacity for acquiring knowledge was fully displayed during his three years at Wixenford. He became head of the school, and in his last term he carried off five prizes. Already at the age of twelve his letters had a touch of Gibbon.

In 1872 Curzon left Wixenford for Eton, where he remained until 1878. His first tutor was Mr. Wolley Dod; during his later years he was under the charge of Mr. E. D. Stone. His career at Eton was one of almost unbroken success. By 1877 he had risen to the position of captain of the Oppidans, was a member of 'Pop', had carried off seventeen prizes and been 'sent up for good' twenty-three times, was on the 'select' for the Newcastle scholarship, and was president of the Literary Society.

The precocity of Curzon at Eton had manifested itself in many forms. The influence of Oscar Browning [q.v.], who took him in the holidays to France and Italy, developed an early taste for history and for the historical, rather than the aesthetic, aspects of art. Already as an Eton boy he had begun, with that acquisitive instinct which never left him, to collect objects of interest and value. His love of rhetoric, both oral and written, was much encouraged by his proficiency in the Literary Society and at 'Speeches', and from his Eton days dated his abiding delusion that words, as the vehicle of thought, were more important than the thought itself. The doctrine of precision inculcated by Miss Paraman and Mr. Dunbar thus fused, towards his seventeenth year, with the doctrine of verbal elegance inculcated by Oscar Browning.

While still at Eton Curzon became absorbed, as the result of a chance lecture by Sir James Stephen, with a passion for the magnificent mystery of the East. The cold religion of Kedleston Hall had appealed only to his sense of fear and doom. This was no small constituent in his character, and there was always about him a touch of Calvinism. But the emotional aspects of his religion, which might in other circumstances have driven him towards the Roman Catholic Church, blended with his passion for travel and his almost mystic acceptance of the Oriental. Curzon's enthusiasm for Asia was, in its essence, a reaction against the chill protestantism of Kedleston. In other words it was a 'religious' passion.

In 1878 Curzon was assailed by the first symptoms of that curvature of the spine which was to torment him till the day of his death. His natural tendency to self-pity may at moments have tempted him to exaggerate the grave physical disability under which he suffered. It would be a mistake, however, to underestimate the effect upon his career and character of his spinal weakness. The presence of pain, always imminent and at times acute, was largely responsible for the tenseness of his mental energy, for that lack of elasticity which hampered his splendid activities of mind and soul. The steel corset which encased his frame and gave to his figure an aspect of unbending perpendicular, affected also the motions of his mind: there was no middle path for him between rigidity and collapse. Conversely, his determination not to be classed as a cripple led him to perform prodigies of industry which were often unnecessary and sometimes harmful. Finally, as is often the result of spinal afflictions, his disabilities, while constituting a constant drain upon his nervous system, affected him with abnormal suspicion of his fellow men.

In October 1878 Curzon went up to Balliol College, Oxford. Although he had failed to obtain a scholarship, a reputation for great gifts, fortified by even greater self-assurance, had preceded him. Less than a month after his arrival at Oxford he was declaiming to the Union upon the Afghan question, and within a few weeks he was the leading spirit in the group of young conservatives who formed the Canning Club. His friendships with St. John Brodrick (afterwards Lord Midleton), Lord Wolmer (afterwards Lord Selborne), and Lord Cranborne (afterwards Lord Salisbury) date from this period. His tutors were R. L. Nettleship and the benign and absent-minded Strachan-Davidson. In January 1880 he came of age. In May of that year he was elected president of the Union and gained a first class in honour moderations. On securing the secretaryship of the Canning Club he exercised over the meetings and minutes of that society an autocracy which filled his contemporaries with admiration and alarm. In 1882 he obtained a second class in *literae humaniores*: his mortification was intense. 'Now,' he exclaimed, 'I shall devote the rest of my life to showing the examiners that they have made a mistake.' At Balliol the unctuous adulation of Oscar Browning had been succeeded by the penetrating criticism of Jowett. The master suggested that Curzon should try to be less precocious, less prolix, less exclusive. His precocity in fact distressed his friends as much as his fluency: they feared that both these qualities might lead him to 'a superficiality of heart and mind'. But Curzon's only remedy for his lack of intellectual profundity was his great capacity for taking trouble. His political convictions during his Oxford period were those of tory democracy seasoned by a strong flavour of imperialism.

On leaving Oxford in 1882 Curzon joined Edward Lyttelton in a journey to Greece. The deference paid to his companion as being the nephew of Mr. Gladstone was somewhat irksome to Curzon, and he always retained a marked distaste for the Greek nation. In January 1883 he was in Egypt, visiting the battle-field of Tel-el-Kebir, genially assisting Lady Dufferin in her charity fêtes, and writing his Lothian prize essay in a dahabeeyah. In April he was in Constantinople, and in May, while stopping at Vienna, he learned that he had won the Lothian prize. He returned in delight to England. Further academic honours were still to come. In October 1883 he was elected a fellow of All Souls College, and in the same autumn he gained the Arnold essay prize. By these successes he felt that he had compensated for the mortification of his second in 'Greats'.

During 1884 Curzon, whose allowance from his father was far too meagre for his needs, endeavoured to increase his income by writing frequent articles for the reviews on current political questions. He had, while in Egypt, acquired some local knowledge of the Egyptian question, and this knowledge was of use to him in his journalistic work. He was at the same time adopted as prospective conservative candidate for South Derbyshire, and his first public speeches were devoted to the Egyptian problem.

The spring of 1885 was marked by a visit to Tunis, and by that strange meeting with General Boulanger which Curzon himself has admirably recorded in his *Tales of Travel* (1923). On 8 June 1885 Mr. Gladstone's administration was succeeded by that of Lord Salisbury. The new prime minister invited Curzon to become his assistant private secretary; but at the general election of that autumn Curzon was defeated for South Derbyshire by 2,090 votes in a poll of 10,280. On 1 February 1886 Mr. Gladstone returned to power pledged to the Home Rule Bill. Curzon decided to stand for the Southport division of Lancashire, and at the ensuing general election of June 1886 he was elected by a majority of 461 votes.

Curzon, as has been said, was at the outset of his career a believer in tory democracy. At Bradford in 1886 he came out openly as the pupil of Lord Randolph Churchill, whom he proclaimed to be 'instinct with life and fire'; he even clamoured for the reform of the Church and of the House of Lords. He happened, however, to be present at Hatfield on 20 December 1886 when the news was received of Lord Randolph's resignation, and the 'thanksgivings and hosannas' which arose on that occasion convinced him that, if there had been a mutiny, it would be preferable that there should be 'a solitary mutineer'. They also convinced him that, for a public man, it was sometimes a mistake to resign. From that moment tory democracy ceased to have any very potent attraction for Curzon: he spoke and wrote thereafter of 'respect for such institutions as reconcile a historic grandeur with the ability to meet the requirements of the age'; and his activities centred from that moment on obedience to Lord Salisbury, an intense interest in foreign and colonial policy, and the enjoyment of the social amenities of London.

'Society', wrote Curzon about this time, 'is passing through a phase of worshipping intellect.' Much has since then been written both about the Crabbet Club and the 'Souls'. The former, under the eccentric aegis of Wilfrid Scawen Blunt [q.v.], was a real stimulus. Curzon much enjoyed the annual symposia at Crabbet Park. The identity of the 'Souls', or 'the gang', as they called themselves, remains more questionable; their frontiers were fluid and undefined. Curzon was always fond of society and could prove the most genial of hosts: the hauteur of his platform and House of Commons manner, and the subsequent pomposity of his viceregal state, blinded many people to his convivial side, to the fact that, even if he possessed small wit and an uncertain sense of humour, he yet possessed a boundless sense of fun. In some ways Curzon never grew up; in other ways he never was a boy. For even in the early 'eighties he saw himself as the man with a career.

On 31 January 1887 Curzon delivered his maiden speech in the House of Commons. He spoke on the Irish question, and allowed himself to criticize Lord Randolph Churchill. The speech erred on the side of excessive proficiency: it was too polished, too eloquent, and too long. On 25 March his second speech, although 'a shade too petulant', was better received. During the spring of this year he gained for himself, at Manchester and elsewhere, a reputation as a platform speaker. There were those, indeed, who saw in Curzon the successor of Lord Randolph Churchill, but in actual fact his ambitions were not confined to Westminster.

The period of Curzon's great journeyings began in August 1887. It is convenient to anticipate the chronological narrative and to deal with these journeys by themselves. They can be summarized as follows: (1) 1887–1888: Canada — Chicago — Salt Lake City — San Francisco — Japan — Shanghai — Foochow — Hong-Kong — Canton — Singapore — Ceylon — Madras — Calcutta — Darjeeling — Benares — Agra — Delhi — Peshawar — Khyber Pass; (2) 1888–1889: St. Petersburg — Moscow — Tiflis — Baku — Askabad — Merv — Bokhara — Samarkand — Tashkent; (3) 1889–1890: Persia; (4) 1892: United States — Japan — China — Cochin China — Siam; (5) 1894: the Pamirs — Afghanistan—Kabul—the course of the Oxus. Apart from numerous articles in *The Times* and the reviews, the results of these travels were embodied in three books of importance, *Russia in Central Asia* (1889), *Persia and the Persian Question* (1892), and *Problems of the Far East* (1894). The industry, knowledge, and convictions embodied in these remarkable volumes rapidly earned for Curzon the reputation of being one of the leading authorities on Asiatic affairs. His Persian book, for instance, constitutes even to-day the most comprehensive textbook yet written upon that country. It may be true that much of its practical value and accuracy was due to the collaboration of (Sir) A. Houtum-Schindler, but the fact remains that Curzon's own knowledge was detailed and illuminating, and that it was his own genius for presentation which enabled him to transmute an inchoate mass of information into a form at once lucid, readable, and concise. It will be observed also that each of his journeys had drawn him in the end to the confines of India. By the age of thirty-five he had thus acquired an unequalled personal knowledge of the countries bordering upon British India. He had spoken face to face with Nasr-ed-Din of Persia; he had slept in satin sheets as the guest of Abdur Rahman of Afghanistan; he had seen the weakness of the French administration in Indo-China; he had gauged the inevitability of Russian infiltration on the north. His fervent, almost religious, faith in the imperial destiny of England had been confirmed for him upon the Yangtze and in the defiles of the Khyber Pass. Curzon had never been one of those who believed in the 'sordid policy of self-effacement'. His five great journeys rendered him at once a xenophobe and a nationalist. The rule of India and the defence of India became for him at once an ambition and a cause. It is not to be wondered at that the House of Commons thereafter appeared to him of minor importance.

The year 1889 and the early part of 1890 were spent in travelling. During the summer season of 1890 Curzon met, in a London ball-room, Mary Victoria Leiter, the daughter of an American millionaire, Levi Zeigler Leiter, of Chicago. She was a woman of outstanding beauty and great sweetness of character. They were not, however, engaged until the spring of 1893, and their engagement was not announced until Curzon's return from his expedition to Afghanistan and the Pamirs in March 1895. The following month they were married in Washington. It is impossible to exaggerate the humanizing effect exercised by this beautiful and unselfish woman upon Curzon's character. She became, indeed, the moral centre of his life.

During the intervals of this romance Curzon's career was centred upon his great voyages and the composition of the books and articles which they entailed. It was while he was intent upon the preparation of his book on Persia that he was offered, in November 1891, the post of under-secretary at the India Office. He had set his hopes on the under-secretaryship for foreign affairs, which had just been offered to and accepted by Mr. J. W. Lowther. The new post was almost as good, and his disappointment was allayed. Curzon entered the India Office with some trepidation. He adopted an attitude of 'virginal modesty' towards the permanent officials. But Lord Salisbury insisted, now that Curzon was a member of the administration, on certain modifications being introduced into the manuscript of his work on Persia. The passages regarding Nasr-ed-Din Shah were watered down, and in May 1892 the book was published. It met with an appreciative reception, but its permanent value was not fully realized at the time.

In March 1892 Curzon piloted the India Council Bill through the House of Commons. At the general election of July 1892 he retained his seat for Southport, but in the following August Lord Salisbury's government was defeated, and nine days later Curzon, again a private member, left England for Siam. The years 1893 and 1894 were occupied by his fierce battle with the authorities for permission to visit Afghanistan, and crowned by his final visit to Kabul and his repeated interviews with Abdur Rahman—'a great man and almost a friend'.

The year 1895 marked the end of Curzon's deliberate voyages of information: it also marked the beginning of his married life. Profiting by his wife's fortune he ceased to be the restless and often impoverished bachelor, and became the prosperous nobleman, renting castles in Scotland, country houses, and a mansion in Carlton House Terrace, purchasing works of art, and indulging his passion for stateliness. He began also early in 1895 to take his parliamentary career with greater seriousness. On Lord Wolmer's succession to the earldom of Selborne in May 1895 Curzon joined with St. John Brodrick in raising the constitutional issue whether a member of the House of Commons was obliged, on succeeding to a peerage, to take the Chiltern Hundreds. The issue was settled against him by the committee of privileges. On 24 June 1895 Lord Salisbury returned to office. He himself assumed the post of foreign secretary and offered Curzon the post of parliamentary under-secretary for foreign affairs. Curzon thus became charged with the duty of representing the Foreign Office in the House of Commons. The importance of his functions was signalized by his being sworn a member of the Privy Council at the early age of thirty-six.

Curzon's three years' service as under-secretary to Lord Salisbury were not wholly to his liking: by temperament he was ill suited to subordinate positions, and Lord Salisbury was too apt to ignore his under-secretary and to forget that he required information. Curzon, moreover, was a believer in dynamic diplomacy; he regarded the British Empire as 'a majestic responsibility' rather than as 'an irksome burden'; he desired the Empire to be 'strong in small things as in big'; and he regarded Lord Salisbury's policy of conciliating the concert of Europe as one of 'throwing bones to keep the various dogs quiet'. He thus saw himself obliged to accept, and even to defend, what he regarded as a policy of undue passivity in such matters as the Armenian atrocities, Venezuela, and the Cretan question. These subjects were, however, outside the Asiatic orbit, and as such possessed for him no intensely personal interest; similarly, his emotions were not stirred by the Jameson Raid or by the Kaiser's telegram to President Kruger. The German menace was for Curzon a purely European matter, and as he was no specialist on Europe it left him unmoved. It was otherwise with the French encroachments in Siam: he had been there; he had even seen the futility of French administration in Cochin China; on the Siamese question he felt very deeply indeed. Even more intense were his feelings on the subject of Kiao-chow. He urged that the occupation of that harbour by Germany in November 1897 would have as its corollary a Russian occupation of Port Arthur and a war in which he felt that Great Britain should take the side of the Japanese. In this, viewed as a matter of immediate expediency, Curzon was right; as also he was right in forcing on the Cabinet the lease of Wei-hai-wei. But a man of wider vision might have foreseen that it was not for a country possessing vast Asiatic responsibilities to desire or to assist the defeat of a Western by an Oriental power.

Confronted as he was by the well-informed criticism of Sir Charles Dilke and Henry Labouchere, Curzon did not find his task of defending Lord Salisbury in the House of Commons by any means a superficial one. The industry and the informative material which he brought to his speeches, while it sometimes irritated, also impressed. Labouchere might complain of his manner of 'a divinity addressing black-beetles', but the reputation of the under-secretary during these three years was established not only in the House but with the general public. He became, if not a popular, at least a public, figure: on his return to the House after a severe illness in the spring of 1898 he was greeted with sympathetic applause; his name and his features became familiar in the London press; and it was with no surprise that the public learned, on 10 August 1898, that this young man of thirty-nine had been chosen to succeed Lord Elgin as viceroy of India. On 11 November he was created Baron Curzon of Kedleston in the Irish peerage; he was unwilling to accept an English barony since he desired, so long as his father lived, to keep open the door of re-entry into the House of Commons. On 15 December he left England; on 30 December he landed at Bombay; and on 3 January 1899 he reached Calcutta and formally entered upon his term of office.

The seven years (December 1898 to November 1905) of Lord Curzon's viceroyalty fall into two main periods, divided from each other by the great Durbar of 1903. During the first period, in spite of the 'mingled bewilderment and pain' which he caused the local officials, he was admired in India and supported at home. During the second period his popularity in India began to wane, whereas his differences with 'the officials who rule and over-rule from Whitehall' became increasingly bitter.

On landing at Bombay Curzon created a good impression by his announcement that he 'would hold the scales even' between the manifold nationalities and interests committed to his rule; and that this was no figure of rhetoric was amply demonstrated by his firm attitude in the 'Rangoon outrage' of the following September, when he risked the resentment of British military circles by publicly disgracing a regiment in which an assault upon a native woman had occurred. On reaching Calcutta he at once proceeded to cut through the red tape which impeded administration. His constant battle against the departmental file earned him the name of 'a young man in a hurry', and within a few weeks of his arrival he had reversed the decision of the permanent officials in two important cases. He refused to sanction the Calcutta Municipal Act, which appeared to him to have been drafted 'partly in panic and partly in anger'. He further insisted on the imposition of countervailing duties to protect the sugar industry from the competition of bounty-fed sugar from other countries. He then turned his attention to external or frontier affairs. He at once curtailed the expenditure which it was proposed to devote to a policy of adventure upon the North-West Frontier, and decided in favour of retirement to defended positions covered by a screen of tribal levies. The administrative questions arising out of the political control exercised by the Punjab government were deferred for subsequent examination.

In the Persian Gulf Curzon was more adventurous. He concluded with Sheikh Mubarak of Koweit a treaty under which the latter agreed not to surrender his territory to any third power. He also obliged the sultan of Muscat to cancel a lease which he had accorded to the French government for the establishment of a coaling-station. Both these acts were high-handed. Sheikh Mubarak's own title to Koweit was at least questionable; and by the treaty of 1862 France was entitled to equal rights with Great Britain in Muscat. It is possible that in regard to Muscat the political agent went farther than Lord Curzon intended. In any case Lord Salisbury found himself exposed to embarrassing protests from the French ambassador. The government at home was therefore far from enthusiastic on receiving Curzon's famous dispatch of 1899 in which he claimed that the Persian Gulf, even at the risk of war, should be closed to all intruders.

On reaching Simla in the spring of 1899 Curzon, released from the social obligations of Calcutta, entered upon months of intensive labour. He endeavoured in vain to induce the home government to reduce the status of the Madras and Bombay presidencies; he waged renewed war on the departmental machinery; he flung himself with lavish energy into the question of famine relief; he completed the draft of the Calcutta Municipal Bill, although not in a form to satisfy native opinion; and he composed an encyclical on the duties of Indian ruling princes, which, while intended to discourage all 'absentee interests and amusements', was drafted in so hectoring a tone as to cause widespread consternation and alarm. It was doubtless in order to soothe the feelings which he had thus unintentionally inflamed, that Curzon set about drafting schemes for an imperial cadet corps in which Indian princes and gentlemen would have the opportunity of holding commissions.

The second year of Curzon's viceroyalty was darkened by the menace of a second famine, but the rains broke at the very moment when he journeyed to Guzerat for the purpose of himself supervising a campaign of relief. His timely arrival was taken by the natives as a sign of his miraculous powers. The second summer at Simla was devoted mainly to a study of the administration of the North-West Frontier, and after a stiff struggle with the local authorities he induced the home government to sanction the creation of a new North-West Frontier province under a chief commissioner responsible only to the government of India. This innovation was bitterly resented by Sir William Mackworth Young [q.v.], the lieutenant-governor of the Punjab, and the altercations which ensued 'embittered and rendered miserable' Curzon's life at Simla.

In the autumn of 1900 Curzon visited Bombay and Madras, and at the former place made a speech regarding the need of 'consulting and conciliating public opinion in India' which caused great, if transitory, satisfaction in Indian circles. The Simla season of 1901 was one of feverish and excessive activity. Lady Curzon had returned to England on account of her health, and the viceroy endeavoured by vast personal labour to numb his own loneliness. He plunged into an intensive study of the land assessment of India and produced a report thereon which was a model of detailed and lucid exposition; he re-examined every aspect of the educational problem, and himself arranged, and subsequently presided over, a great educational congress held in September. In spite of the enormous energy and vast knowledge which Curzon brought to this task, the educational problem was not, in fact, much advanced during his viceroyalty, although the main issues were formulated and the office of director of education established. After a short holiday in Burma Curzon returned to Calcutta, where he found both the Afghan and the Tibetan questions causing anxiety. In October 1901 the Amir Abdur Rahman had been succeeded by Habibullah, and Curzon endeavoured to induce his old acquaintance to visit him in India. The hesitation displayed by the new amir to accept this pressing invitation caused Curzon a certain amount of uneasiness. In Tibet also the Dalai Lama was proving recalcitrant: Curzon was indignant 'that a community of unarmed monks should set us perpetually at defiance', and suggested to the home government that an armed mission should be sent to Lhasa; the government, which had its hands full with the South African War, did not respond to this suggestion. In February 1902 Curzon visited the Khyber Pass, and in March he proceeded to Hyderabad, where he managed to conclude with the Nizam the basis of a settlement of the Berar question. This diplomatic adjustment, which removed a long-standing source of grievance between the Nizam and the government of India, was subsequently embodied in the treaty of 5 November 1902. It was hailed by Curzon as 'the biggest thing I have yet done in India'.

The spring and summer of 1902 were mainly occupied with the gigantic preparations for the Durbar of 1903. Curzon, who had a passion for organizing all forms of pageantry, took an autocratic interest in the arrangements, and there is evidence of constant friction between him and the home government on the question of expense. A further and even more acrimonious conflict with the India Office arose from Curzon's refusal to defray from Indian revenues the expenses of the Indian mission to King Edward VIIth's coronation. A third dispute arose over his desire to announce as a 'boon' at the Delhi Durbar a general remission of taxation. The Cabinet at home considered such a promise would furnish an awkward precedent, but Curzon threatened to resign if his views were not accepted. A private telegram from St. John Brodrick warned him that such a threat might be taken seriously; he therefore, with resentment in his soul, agreed to accept a compromise. The closing months of 1902 were further embittered by what became known as the

IXth Lancers incident. Curzon, having reason to suppose that officers of this regiment had endeavoured to hush up the circumstances of an assault by two troopers on a native, ordered an investigation, and as punishment stopped the leave of all officers. This action was much resented in military circles, and a demonstration in favour of the IXth Lancers at the Durbar review in January 1903 was exaggerated in England as evidence of Lord Curzon's growing unpopularity.

The Durbar of January 1903 marked the summit of Lord Curzon's viceregal splendour. From that moment the clouds began to gather. Lord Kitchener [q.v.] had arrived in India as commander-in-chief in November 1902; but before his final conflict with that masterful personality other and less pregnant issues had arisen between Curzon and the government at home. He had urged a forward policy in Afghanistan and Tibet: the home government desired to enter into no further commitments. Curzon also considered that Indian revenues were being unduly drawn upon in order to maintain troops in South Africa, a matter in which India could have only a contingent interest. Lady Curzon urged her husband to resign. 'Don't', she wrote to him, 'let us stay until the *joie de vivre* has died in us.' Curzon, unfortunately, did not follow this advice: his term of office was due to expire in January 1904; he hoped for a renewal; and the moment passed when resignation would have been dignified.

At Simla once again in the late spring of 1903 Curzon developed a passion for internal reforms, and commissions were constituted to deal with irrigation, railways, agricultural banks, and police questions. His financial reforms were already bearing fruit, and his currency reforms were widely applauded. His great work for Indian historical monuments, his restorations at Delhi and Agra, were already a source of personal satisfaction. Whatever Curzon may or may not have done in the administrative field, he set his stamp for ever upon the art and archaeology of India. The Victoria Memorial Hall at Calcutta was entirely due to his initiative and energy. Meanwhile the government at home had at last lent ear to his warnings about the Persian Gulf: not only did Lord Lansdowne himself make a public pronouncement that the British government would not tolerate any Russian encroachments in Southern Persia, but the viceroy was authorized to pay a state visit to the Persian Gulf. This visit, accompanied by every evidence of naval supremacy, took place in November 1903. From that moment, until the accession of Reza Khan to the throne of the Kadjars, British predominance in the Gulf remained unquestioned.

In January 1904 Curzon completed the first five years of his term of office. An extension of the period had been announced in the previous August: instead, however, of accompanying Lady Curzon to England on leave of absence, he decided to remain for a few months in India. His main occupation was the study of the partition of the Bengal province. His success in settling the Berar incident had convinced him that greater efficiency of administration could be secured by splitting up the more unwieldy provinces and creating smaller administrative districts from the parts thus detached. The scheme was sanctioned by the secretary of state in June 1905, and the formation of a new province, comprising 106,000 square miles with a population of eighteen million Moslems and twelve million Hindus, was formally inaugurated. This action, which was interpreted by the Bengalis as a revenge on the viceroy's part for the congress movement, cost him his popularity with that 'Indian opinion' which he had been the first to recognize and proclaim.

On 30 April 1904 Curzon sailed for England on leave of absence. Lord Ampthill remained in charge as acting governor-general. Curzon was offered and accepted the lord wardenship of the Cinque Ports and entered with enthusiasm on the tenancy of Walmer Castle. This enthusiasm was quickly damped: Lady Curzon fell ill at Walmer, and Curzon himself condemned it as 'an ancestral dog-hole'. Meanwhile, the India Office had at last sanctioned the mission of Sir Francis Younghusband to Tibet, and in September 1904 a treaty was extracted from the Tibetans. Curzon did not consider the terms of the Lhasa convention an adequate compensation for the effort made. His difference of opinion with St. John Brodrick on these matters did not improve their relations, and he was also angered at discovering that, in his absence, Lord Kitchener had addressed to the Committee of Imperial Defence a long memorandum condemning the system of dual control in force in the Indian army.

The Indian army possessed, in fact, two heads, the commander-in-chief and the military member of the viceroy's council.

The latter not only dealt with administrative matters, but was the sole channel through whom the commander-in-chief had access to the viceroy. It often happened, moreover, that the military member, while possessing these supervisory powers over the commander-in-chief, was his military junior. The anomalies of this position had impressed Lord Kitchener soon after his arrival, but Curzon had urged him to wait for a year before formulating his objections. The relations between the two men, during 1903, had been wholly amicable: Kitchener knew that it was Curzon himself who had pressed for his appointment. Curzon welcomed in Kitchener a reforming zeal equalled only by his own. It was thus during the summer of 1904, when Curzon was absent in England, that Kitchener first launched his attack. The government of Lord Ampthill could not support Kitchener's contention that the position of the military member should be rendered subsidiary to that of the commander-in-chief. Kitchener thereupon threatened to resign, and the home government, fearing that so dramatic a resignation would be unpopular in the country, asked Curzon for advice. Imagining that he would be better able to manage Kitchener himself, Curzon advised the home government to call for a report from the government of India and thus to postpone the issue until he himself had returned to Calcutta.

Curzon left for Bombay on 24 November 1904 and reached Calcutta on 13 December. Lady Curzon, who was seriously ill, did not accompany him: it would have been better if he had listened to her premonitions against his return. The dispatch calling for a report left London on 2 December 1904. On its receipt, Curzon asked for the comments both of Lord Kitchener and the military member. The latter defended the existing dual system; the former insisted that both functions should be fused in that of the commander-in-chief. Curzon then drew up his own minute of 6 February 1905, in which he decided in favour of the maintenance of the present dual system, mainly on the ground that the concentration of such powers in the hands of the commander-in-chief would create a military autocracy subversive of the supreme control of the civil government. On 10 March the matter came before the council: Curzon's opinion was endorsed by all the civilian members; Kitchener read a brief statement regretting that he was in a minority of one and refusing to discuss the matter further. The results of this meeting were conveyed to the India Office in a dispatch of 23 March. Kitchener at the same time took steps to see that his own views were placed before the home government and press. St. John Brodrick, faced with this deadlock, appointed a committee. The committee recommended a compromise by which the military member would in future deal only with the quasi-civilian side of army administration and be called the 'member in charge of the department of military supply'. All purely military matters would be under the commander-in-chief, who would have direct access to the viceroy and government. This compromise, under the style of a 'decision', was communicated in the India Office dispatch of 31 May 1905. On 25 June Curzon induced Kitchener to agree to some modifications in the compromise which would give the government of India a 'secondary military opinion' or, in other words, would enable the supply member also to be consulted on military matters. The home government was so startled by Kitchener's acquiescence in this modification that it asked for confirmation. This was given, and on 14 July the government telegraphed accepting the agreed modifications and congratulating Curzon on the settlement reached. Two days later Curzon heard that the new supply member had been chosen by the India Office without his being consulted. He had himself wished to propose (Sir) Edmund Barrow, to whom Kitchener had also agreed. Curzon telegraphed urging this appointment: it was refused, and Curzon tendered his resignation. On 22 August 1905 his resignation was accepted; it had, in fact, been published in London the day before, together with the announcement of Lord Minto's appointment as his successor. Curzon remained on in India in order to receive the Prince and Princess of Wales on 9 November. He left India, an angry and embittered man, on 18 November 1905.

It will be seen that Curzon's resignation came about, not as a result of the main conflict between himself and Kitchener, which had in fact been settled by a compromise, but on the subsidiary question whether his own nominee or that of the India Office should be selected as supply member of the viceroy's council. The home government, as is clear from its almost disappointed surprise when Kitchener agreed to Curzon's eleventh-hour modifications, had in fact determined that so turbulent a viceroy should be removed. It is indeed probable that the embittered relations which by then existed between Curzon and Brodrick rendered impossible all hope of smooth co-operation. The manner of his dismissal was, however, unnecessarily discourteous, and there was some foundation for Curzon's subsequent complaint that the Balfour-Brodrick combination had treated him with 'tortuous malignity'. There is a certain irony in the fact that the day after Curzon's return to London witnessed the fall of the Balfour administration and the return to power of a liberal Cabinet under Sir Henry Campbell-Bannerman.

There followed a period of eleven years' political disappointment and domestic sorrow. Curzon received no public recognition for his work in India. He retired in anger and mortification to the South of France. On 18 July 1906 Lady Curzon died. Curzon shut himself up with his three young daughters in Hackwood Park, Basingstoke, a prey to despair. In 1907 he was elected chancellor of Oxford University, and tried to find alleviation for his sorrows in the question of university reform. He visited Oxford in person and resided for some weeks at the Judge's Lodgings in St. Giles. His aim was to avoid a governmental commission into university finance by the passage of reforms from within. He succeeded in staving off a government inquiry for many years. During a visit to South Africa in 1909 he prepared with his own hand a long memorandum on university reform entitled *Principles and Methods of University Reform.* This was considered by the university authorities in April 1910, and a final report was ready by August of that year. Further reports followed until the outbreak of war put an end to all subsidiary efforts. Curzon's ardour in the cause of Oxford became his greatest solace during those lonely and inactive years.

Curzon refrained, largely in deference to the wishes of King Edward VII, from re-entering party politics, and did not seek re-election to the House of Commons. In January 1908 he entered the House of Lords as an Irish representative peer, and in February of that year he made a spirited and informed attack upon the Anglo-Russian convention of 1907. In the same year he was elected lord rector of Glasgow University. He flung himself with enthusiasm into Lord Roberts's agitation for universal military training, and he opposed Mr. Asquith's threats to the privilege of the House of Lords, urging his fellow members to fight to the last ditch. When he realized, however, that the liberal government was in deadly earnest, he had the wisdom to retreat, and it was Curzon's sensible advice which largely decided the debate of 8–10 August 1911 and secured for the liberal government a bare majority in support of its proposals.

Curzon's main activities during these years were not, however, of a political nature. His election in May 1911 as president of the Royal Geographical Society gave him an occasion for displaying his organizing talent, and within a few years he had collected sufficient money to purchase the fine premises in which the society is now housed. As a trustee of the National Gallery he drafted a report which to this day forms the main charter both of that gallery and of the Tate Gallery. His interest in architecture was also a great resource. He was elected an honorary fellow of the Royal Institute of British Architects, and his restoration of Tattershall Castle in Lincolnshire and subsequently of Bodiam Castle in Sussex (both of which he bequeathed to the nation) showed that his zeal for the preservation of ancient monuments was not confined to India. In November 1911, as a coronation honour, Curzon was created Earl Curzon of Kedleston, Viscount Scarsdale (with reversion to his father and heirs male), and Baron Ravensdale (with reversion to his daughters and heirs male). It was activities and honours such as these which, after a lapse of shrouded years, again rendered his name familiar to his countrymen. A second period of important public service was about to open before him.

On 27 May 1915, with the formation of the Coalition Cabinet, Lord Curzon was given the office of lord privy seal. He was not, however, accorded any important functions, and was, in fact, excluded from the war committee, established in the autumn of that year, until July 1916. He was bitterly opposed to the evacuation of Gallipoli, and addressed to his colleagues a cogent and vivid note protesting against any policy of retreat. He was strong also in pressing for compulsory service, and it was largely owing to his insistence that the national register was instituted in 1915. So deeply did he feel on this subject that when the Garter was offered him at the end of December 1915 he refused to accept this long-coveted honour until Mr. Asquith had pledged himself to introduce the Compulsory Service Bill into the House of Commons.

Early in 1916 Curzon was placed in charge of the Shipping Control Committee, and quickly realized that a drastic restriction of imports was essential if tonnage supplies were not to be exhausted. Throughout the year he struggled in vain to impose his opinion on the Cabinet, but it was only in March 1917 that his views were adopted and the necessary legislation passed. He also became president of the Air Board (May 1916), an organization established for the purpose of conciliating the conflicting requirements in aviation of the War Office and the Admiralty. He pressed strongly for the creation of an Air ministry, but it was not until January 1918 that his opinion prevailed.

With the fall of Mr. Asquith in December 1916 Curzon became a member of the inner War Cabinet under Mr. Lloyd George. In January 1917 he married, as his second wife, Grace, daughter of Joseph Monroe Hinds, at one time United States minister in Brazil, and widow of Alfred Duggan, of Buenos Aires. Once again 1 Carlton House Terrace became a social centre, and the loneliness of Curzon's middle age was succeeded by a second period of domestic happiness. He was intensely active. As member of the War Cabinet, leader in the House of Lords, and lord president of the Council, he could no longer complain of insufficient employment. Between December 1916 and November 1918 the Cabinet held as many as five hundred meetings, and at each of these Curzon would express his views with his customary trenchancy and conviction. He opposed, although in vain, the policy of Great Britain assuming any commitments towards the Jews in Palestine; he was, on the other hand, a strong supporter of a forward policy in Mesopotamia and of the creation of an Arab state. He was a bitter opponent of the Montagu-Chelmsford report (1918), feeling that it would lead to parliamentary government in the Indian Empire and thus shatter the basis of British rule. In this he showed some inconsistency, since it was he himself who had inserted into the announcement of 20 August 1917 the promise of 'the progressive realization of responsible government' in India. Nor was it in regard to India alone that Curzon found difficulty in reconciling his position as one of the leaders of the conservative party with his functions as the spokesman of a government pledged to liberal concessions. The Dublin rising of April 1916 revived the Home Rule controversy which had been shelved in September 1914. Curzon as a professed, although not convinced, unionist considered for a moment whether he should resign: he accepted instead the chairmanship of a Cabinet committee which prepared the draft of a bill for an Irish settlement. Mr. Lloyd George summarily rejected this draft in favour of his own scheme for an Irish Convention, and it fell to Curzon not merely to swallow this affront but to defend the Convention in the Upper House. Neither the Irish Convention nor the subsequent committee established under (Viscount) Long [q.v.] achieved a solution of the Irish problem, and in June 1918 Curzon had the melancholy satisfaction of announcing to the House of Lords that, in view of the spread of rebellion in Ireland, the government had been impelled to suspend all further proposals for Home Rule.

Curzon had never been a protagonist in the Irish question, and his subservience to Mr. Lloyd George in Irish matters, while it distressed his unionist friends, was no betrayal of deep personal conviction. His conduct in regard to the question of women's suffrage did, however, entail grave personal inconsistency, and contributed largely to his loss of prestige with the conservative party. For since February 1912 Curzon had been president of the Anti-Suffrage League, and when, in 1917, the House of Commons conferred the franchise upon women by a majority of 385 to 55 votes, the League looked to its president to oppose the Bill in the House of Lords. Curzon at this juncture did not manifest that firmness of decision which his rigid manner had led his supporters to expect. While leaving the Anti-Suffrage League under the impression that he would speak and vote against the Bill, he deserted it on the second reading and voted against Lord Loreburn's amendment on the ground that it would be imprudent for the Upper House to defy so strong a majority in the House of Commons.

With the conclusion of the Armistice in November 1918 it fell to Curzon to deliver a speech of victory in the House of Lords, and he was also charged with the task of organizing the peace celebrations. Meanwhile, Lord Balfour had accompanied Mr. Lloyd George to the Peace Conference in Paris, and Curzon was invited to take charge of the Foreign Office at home. From January to October 1919 he assumed the invidious role of foreign minister *ad interim*, and watched with growing dismay and resentful impotence what he felt to be the reckless policy pursued by Mr. Lloyd George in Paris. On 24 October 1919 Lord Balfour resigned the post of foreign secretary and Curzon was appointed in his place. But disillusionment was in store for him. Ever since the days when he had chafed under the dilatory caution of Lord Salisbury, Curzon had dreamed of the time when he himself would control the levers of British foreign policy. That time had now arrived; the levers were there, to all appearances under his hand: but the machine had altered and did not respond. Other hands than his were in control. The irony of it was that this functional change in the machine of imperial policy was brought home to him upon that very stretch of line with which he himself was most familiar. The end of the War saw British troops in occupation of large sections of Persian territory, and the general call for retrenchment and demobilization necessitated their recall. Curzon insisted, however, that the occasion should be seized to place British relations with Persia on a durable basis. After protracted negotiations a treaty was signed in August 1919 which placed Great Britain in control of the Persian army and finances. Curzon failed to realize the artificial nature of this agreement and acclaimed it as an outstanding triumph. The treaty in fact was never put into effect: no sooner had British troops evacuated Persian territory than the nationalists and the Majlis pronounced that the treaty had been secured by force and bribes, and refused to accept it. In February 1921 the nationalist government in Persia concluded with the Russian Soviet government a treaty diametrically opposed to that signed only eighteen months before between Vossuq-ed-Dowleh and Sir Percy Cox. The funeral oration of that instrument was preached by Curzon on 26 July 1921.

The failure of the Persian treaty appears to have shaken Curzon's confidence in the stability of his old Asiatic landmarks. In dealing with the Egyptian question he displayed a greater understanding of the post-war mentality of the East. In November 1919 the Milner commission had been dispatched to Egypt with the task of considering how the protectorate established in 1915 could be reconciled with the movement for self-government headed by Zaghlul Pasha. In the spring of 1920 the Milner report was submitted to Lord Curzon; it avowedly exceeded the terms of reference under which it had been framed. Curzon was quick to recognize the fact that Lord Milner had been wise in exceeding his instructions, and he agreed to receive an Egyptian mission under Adly and Zaghlul Pashas and to negotiate a treaty of alliance to supersede the existing protectorate. The mission arrived in June 1920, and by August of that year the heads of agreement had been initialed. In February 1921 these heads of agreement were approved by parliament, and an invitation was addressed to Egypt to send a mission to London with full powers to conclude a definitive treaty. This mission, under the leadership of Adly Pasha, arrived in July. In the interval, however, an Imperial Conference had been held in London, and great stress had been laid by the dominion delegates upon the importance of maintaining British control over the Suez Canal. The attitude of the Cabinet was thus less conciliatory than it had been at the time of the Zaghlul conversations of the previous year. Curzon was unable to induce his colleagues to consent to any terms which Adly could accept; the latter returned to Egypt without his treaty and immediately resigned. The British authorities at Cairo thereupon imposed martial law and deported Zaghlul. Curzon was able to assure the Cabinet that his own worst prognostications had been fulfilled.

This unsatisfactory situation continued till January 1922. Lord Allenby, the high commissioner, then suggested to Curzon the basis of an arrangement under which Sarwat Pasha would be prepared to form a ministry. The essence of this arrangement was that the protectorate should at once be abolished and Egypt be recognized as an independent kingdom. Curzon was able to induce the Cabinet to agree to this proposal, and a unilateral manifesto was thus published abolishing the protectorate while insisting upon certain reserved points. Under these reservations Great Britain safeguarded her position in regard to the Sudan, the Suez Canal, and the protection of Egypt against external interference. On 14 March 1922 the House of Commons approved this manifesto.

A more intense difference of opinion arose between Curzon (who was created a marquess in June 1921) and Mr. Lloyd George in regard to the Graeco-Turkish question. During the Paris Conference Curzon had repeatedly warned Mr. Lloyd George of the danger of any delay in concluding peace with the Turks, and of the more specific danger of allowing the Greeks to land at Smyrna. His own solution was the simpler one by which the Turks would be turned out of Europe and the Greeks would not be allowed into Asia. It is impossible here to trace the stages which led to the Treaty of Sèvres, the Kemalist movement in Turkey, the defeat of Venizelos in Greece, the return of King Constantine, and the final Greek debacle of August 1922. It may be said in general that Curzon's advice was not followed and that he was frequently not consulted in matters of policy, but that his assistance was evoked in meeting the difficulties to which the policy adopted gave rise. His renewed attempts to come to an agreement with the French in order to secure a basis for joint mediation between Greece and Turkey were constantly negatived by the intervention of Mr. Lloyd George, and thereby the conviction gained ground both in Paris and Athens that the ostensible impartiality of Curzon was but a cloak for the encouragement secretly given by the prime minister to Greece. This duality of purpose and lack of centralized responsibility led even to disorganization within the Cabinet at home. In 1922 Edwin Samuel Montagu [q.v.], secretary of state for India, authorized the viceroy to publish a pro-Turkish manifesto destined to appease the feelings of the Khalifat agitators. He was obliged to resign, but the spectacle of a Cabinet thus disunited and undisciplined in matters of foreign policy left Curzon embarrassed and weakened in face of M. Poincaré who, on assuming office in January 1922, embarked upon a concentrated and deliberate policy of siding with the Turks.

The inevitable crisis arrived in the early autumn of 1922. The Kemalist army, having flung the Greeks into the sea, now faced the Allied forces guarding the neutral zone of the Straits. At a Cabinet meeting of 15 September it was decided that the British forces at least should maintain their positions on the Asiatic side, although it was realized that M. Poincaré might well hold other views. On the following day, after Curzon had left London for Kedleston, certain members of the Cabinet, without his knowledge or consent, issued a *communiqué* in which the possibility of war with Turkey was foreshadowed. On 18 September Curzon returned to London, pointed out that this *communiqué* would enrage M. Poincaré, and insisted on proceeding alone to Paris to soothe the feelings of the French. On the following day M. Poincaré as a rejoinder to the *communiqué* withdrew the French detachment at Chanak on the Asiatic shore of the Dardanelles, leaving the British detachment to face the Kemalists alone. On 20 September Curzon reached Paris and after a series of scenes with M. Poincaré, one of which reduced the British foreign secretary to tears of rage, reached an agreement under which an armistice was to be negotiated with the Kemalists at Mudania.

Public opinion at home had been deeply alarmed by the Chanak crisis, and Mr. Lloyd George's position, in view of the disaster attending his phil-Hellene policy, was seriously shaken. Mr. Winston Churchill invited the leading members of the Coalition Cabinet to dinner at his house, and it was then decided that the Coalition should ask for an immediate dissolution and appeal to the electorate for a new lease of power. Curzon agreed to this procedure. On 15 October, however, Mr. Lloyd George, in spite of Curzon's entreaty, delivered an anti-Turkish speech at Manchester, and at the same time the foreign secretary was apprised of a further flagrant instance of negotiations conducted by the prime minister's secretariate behind his back. This incident convinced him that it would no longer be possible to support Mr. Lloyd George's Coalition: he refused to attend a second dinner party given by Mr. Churchill to the Coalition ministers; and on 19 October a meeting at the Carlton Club led to the fall of the Coalition Cabinet and the formation of a conservative ministry under Mr. Bonar Law. In this ministry, which was confirmed by the general election of 15 November 1922, Curzon retained the post of foreign secretary.

Within a few days Curzon was on his way to the European Conference at Lausanne. His complete domination of that assembly constitutes one of the most remarkable episodes in his career. The French and Italians imagined that British prestige had been so irretrievably shaken by the Greek disaster that it would be safe to leave to Curzon the invidious role of registering the defeat which Europe had suffered at the hands of Turkey. This was a miscalculation on their part. The retention of Chanak by Great Britain, in contrast with Poincaré's policy of retreat, had done much to inspire the Turks with respect for British determination. Curzon's own magnificent equipment of knowledge and rhetoric strengthened this impression. During the eleven weeks of the first Lausanne Conference he succeeded in impressing his personality upon Ismet Pasha and in securing his assent to the political clauses, and above all to the 'freedom of the Straits', which constituted the main British desiderata. Upon the question of Mosul the Turkish delegation found Curzon adamant, and his firm attitude on this point, in contrast with the weakness of the Cabinet at home, forced the conference to defer the matter for subsequent consideration. After the conference had been sitting for ten weeks the French realized that, whereas England had obtained as much as she had hoped for, the important financial, economic, and capitulatory chapters of the treaty, in which they themselves were mainly interested, had made no progress at all. On 30 January 1923 they issued through the Havas agency a statement to the effect that they did not consider the treaty as by then drafted to be more than 'a basis of discussion'. The Turks immediately refused to sign the treaty in the form which it had then reached. On the night of 4 February Curzon made a final appeal to Ismet Pasha to sign the treaty, and, on his refusal, broke off negotiations and left Lausanne on that very evening by the Orient express. It is true that he had not secured a treaty of peace: but he had secured those portions of it which were of chief interest to his own country, and he had broken off negotiations, not on a purely British issue, but on questions which were of equal, or even greater, interest to the Italians and French. Above all, he had restored British prestige in Turkey. The abortive Conference of Lausanne was the most striking of his diplomatic triumphs.

In dealing with Asia, even with the new Asia of post-war nationalism, Curzon had all the confidence of expert knowledge. His handling of European diplomacy was less certain and far less self-assured. For years the British and the French governments had envisaged the problems of security and reparation from a different standpoint. Much bickering had ensued. On 11 January 1923, while Curzon was still at Lausanne, these differences were brought to a head by M. Poincaré's occupation of the Ruhr Valley. During the period of *rupture cordiale* which then ensued between London and Paris, Curzon showed considerable skill in maintaining the British policy of benevolent neutrality, and it was his speech in April 1923 which formed the germ of what subsequently developed into the schemes of General C. G. Dawes and Mr. O. D. Young for reparation payments. For it was in this speech that the proposal of a jury of impartial experts was first mooted.

On 21 May 1923 Mr. Bonar Law, whose health had long been causing anxiety, resigned. On the following day Curzon, who was spending Whitsuntide at Montacute House, a seat which he had rented in Somerset, received from Lord Stamfordham, the king's private secretary, a letter asking for an immediate interview. He journeyed to London in the triumphant certainty that he had been designated as Bonar Law's successor. Lord Stamfordham informed him on his arrival that the king had decided to send for Mr. Stanley Baldwin. For several hours Curzon remained in a state of collapse under the crushing blow of this bewildering disappointment. He contemplated complete retirement from public life. His abiding sense of public duty asserted itself, however, and on the following day he wrote to Mr. Baldwin promising his support. Few actions in his public life were more magnanimous.

On resuming work at the Foreign Office Curzon embarked upon two acute controversies. He had never approved of Mr. Lloyd George's policy of recognizing the Soviet government in Russia, and by the early summer of 1923 it was clear that the trade agreement of 1921 had failed to work. Curzon prepared a long and detailed indictment of Russian evasions of that agreement and presented his demands in the form of an ultimatum. Somewhat to his own surprise the Soviet government replied giving him satisfaction on most of the points raised. His persistent endeavours to mediate between France and Germany met with less success: while urging the German government to abandon passive resistance, he endeavoured to obtain from the French their consent to an impartial inquiry into Germany's capacity to pay reparations; his failure to move M. Poincaré led to much acrimonious correspondence and to embittered interviews with the French ambassador. Realizing that further progress was impossible, Curzon caused a detailed statement of the British point of view to be prepared in the form of a note to the French and Belgian ambassadors. This note was delivered on 11 August 1923 and was thereafter published. The storm of indignation provoked in Paris by this indictment left Curzon unaffected: he journeyed to Bagnoles to nurse his phlebitis in peace.

In the autumn of 1923 Mr. Baldwin, against Curzon's urgent advice, decided to appeal to the electorate on the issue of protection. The government was placed in a minority and on 23 January 1924 Mr. Baldwin resigned. When the conservatives returned to power in November of the same year, Curzon was not invited to resume the post of foreign secretary. Once again he determined to retire from politics and to devote his closing years to the reconstruction of Kedleston. He was persuaded, however, to afford the government the moral support of his presence, and with great public spirit he again accepted the post of lord president of the Council.

In March 1925, while staying the night at Cambridge, Curzon recognized symptoms of grave internal disorder. He was taken next day to London and on 9 March an operation was performed. On 20 March he died. On 25 March his coffin was taken to Westminster Abbey, and on the following day he was buried by the side of his first wife in the church at Kedleston.

Curzon left three daughters by his first wife. In default of male heirs the marquessate became extinct on his death. He was succeeded in the viscounty of Scarsdale by his nephew, Richard Nathaniel (born 1898), and in the barony of Ravensdale by his eldest daughter, Mary Irene (born 1896).

Few men have experienced such extreme vicissitudes of triumph and defeat. Viceroy at thirty-nine, at forty-six it was his fate to be excluded from politics for eleven years; foreign secretary at a triumphant moment of his country's history, it fell to him not to fortify victory but to protect lassitude; and the supreme prize of his ambition was dashed at the last second from his lips. He acquired great possessions and resounding titles; he left his mark upon the art and literature of his country; and yet he achieved successes rather than success. Had his will been as forceful as his intellect, his determination as constant as his industry, he might have triumphed over his own anachronisms. But the tense self-preoccupation of the chronic invalid robbed him of all elasticity, and he failed to adapt himself to the needs of a transitional age which did not like him and which he did not like. He will live less by his achievements than by his endeavours: he will live as a man of great ambition, and some egoism, who was inspired by a mystic faith in the imperial destiny of his country, and devoted to that faith unexampled industry, great talents, and an abiding energy of soul.

The painted portraits of Lord Curzon are cold and statuesque representations, none of which is really life-like. The best, by J. S. Sargent (1914), is at the offices of the Royal Geographical Society, Kensington Gore. Another portrait, by P. A. de László (1913), is at All Souls College, Oxford, and copies of this are at Eton College and in the Carlton Club. The statues in Carlton Gardens, London, and at Calcutta bear little resemblance to the original. Curzon's personal appearance is better observed in the many photographs reproduced in published works.

[*The Times*, 21 March 1925; Lord Ronaldshay (now Marquess of Zetland), *Life of Lord Curzon*, 3 vols., 1928; H. Caldwell Lipsett, *Lord Curzon in India, 1898–1903*, 1906; Lord Curzon, *Speeches, 1898–1905*, 4 vols., Calcutta, 1900–1906, *British Government in India*, 2 vols., posthumous, 1925, *Bodiam Castle, Sussex*, 1926, *The Personal History of Walmer Castle and its Lords Warden*, 1927, *Tattershall Castle, Lincolnshire*, 1929; Winston Churchill, *The World Crisis, 1911–1914*, 1923; Wilfrid Scawen Blunt, *My Diaries*, 1919 and 1920; Lady Oxford, *The Autobiography of Margot Asquith*, 1922; private information; personal knowledge.] HAROLD NICOLSON.

CUSHNY, ARTHUR ROBERTSON (1866–1926), pharmacologist, was born at Speymouth, Morayshire, 6 March 1866, the fourth son of the Rev. John Cushny, minister of the Established Church successively at Fochabers, Speymouth, and Huntly, by his wife, Catherine Ogilvie, daughter of Alexander Brown, procurator fiscal of Elgin. He was educated at Fochabers Academy and Aberdeen University, where he graduated M.A. in 1886 and M.B., C.M. in 1889. As holder of the George Thompson fellowship, he worked for a year at Berne under Hugo Kronecker, and later at Strassburg under Oswald Schmiedeberg, then the most distinguished pharmacologist in Europe. From 1892 to 1893 he acted as Schmiedeberg's assistant, and in the latter year was appointed, at the age of twenty-seven, to the chair of pharmacology in the university of Michigan at Ann Arbor. In 1905 he returned to England in order to become the first occupant of the chair of pharmacology in University College, London, and in 1918 succeeded Sir Thomas Fraser [q.v.] as professor of *materia medica* and pharmacology at Edinburgh University. There he remained until his sudden death from cerebral haemorrhage 25 February 1926.

While at Ann Arbor Cushny continued researches, begun at Strassburg, on the action of the *digitalis glucosides*, which involved also an investigation of the physiology of the mammalian heart—subjects on which he wrote many papers, culminating in an exhaustive monograph, *The Action and Uses in Medicine of Digitalis and its Allies* (1925). In the course of these studies he incidentally suggested that the clinical condition known as *delirium cordis* might be identical with auricular fibrillation, a heterodox prediction which was verified ten years later as the result of the application of electrocardiographic methods to man. The condition now known as auricular fibrillation has proved to be one of the most important diseases of the heart.

While in America Cushny also began to study experimentally the functions of the kidneys and the action of diuretics. To this subject he made many valuable contributions, and published *The Secretion of Urine* (first edition 1917, second edition 1926), in which he co-ordinated the mass of contradictory evidence which had accumulated since Karl Ludwig's day; for which purpose, as he says in the preface, 'it was necessary to sift thoroughly this mass of printed matter of over 6,000 pages'. His account of kidney secretion not only was accepted as the most authoritative critical review of past work; it also put forward a novel view of the functions of the kidney which was to serve as a foundation for further research, and is specially associated with Cushny's name.

In 1903 Cushny published his first study of the pharmacological actions of optical isomers, in which he showed that *l*-hyoxyamine is about twenty times as active as the *d*-isomer, and about twice as active as the *dl*-compound (atropine). Later, he made similar quantitative studies of other optical isomers, which proved, as is now accepted, that two substances, identical in chemical composition and structure apart from their optical activity, may differ widely in pharmacological activity—a fact of fundamental importance for any theory of the ultimate nature of pharmacological action. Cushny summarized his own and other investigations on this subject in the Dohme lectures delivered at the Johns Hopkins University at Baltimore in 1925, and published as *Biological Relations of Optically Isomeric Substances* in 1926.

These three subjects formed, perhaps, Cushny's chief scientific interests, and his contributions to them constitute his main claim to a permanent position in the history of his science; but, in addition, he published a long and valuable series of monographs covering a wide field of pharmacological inquiry. In 1899 appeared the first edition of his *Textbook of Pharmacology and Therapeutics*, which went through eight editions in his lifetime. It was the first authoritative text-book to be written in English by an experimental pharmacologist, and it played an important part in guiding teaching and research during a period in which therapeutics was emerging from the mists of tradition and empiricism.

The originality of his researches, the authority of his writings, and his international friendships made Cushny perhaps the most influential single figure of his time in the field of pharmacology, the study of which was making such rapid advances. He was a man large of mind, heart, and stature, outwardly austere, inwardly kindly, generous in helping others. He served on many commissions and international conferences, notably the royal commission on whisky and other potable spirits (1908). He received honorary degrees from the universities of Aberdeen and Michigan and was elected F.R.S. in 1907.

Cushny married in 1896 Sarah, daughter of Ralph Firbank, railway engineer, and had one daughter.

[*Journal of Pharmacology and Experimental Therapeutics*, vol. xxvii, 1926 (with full bibliography); *Proceedings* of the Royal Society, vol. c, B, 1926; *Lancet*, 1926, vol. i, p. 519; *British Medical Journal*, 1926, vol. i, p. 455 (all with portraits); private information; personal knowledge.] J. A. Gunn.

CUST, Sir LIONEL HENRY (1859–1929), art historian, was born in London 25 January 1859, the only son of Sir Reginald John Cust, barrister-at-law, by his wife, Lady Elizabeth Caroline, elder daughter of Edward Bligh, fifth Earl of Darnley. He was a first cousin of Henry John Cockayne Cust [q.v.], the politician and journalist. Lionel Cust was educated at Eton, and matriculated at Trinity College, Cambridge, in 1877. He was elected a scholar of the college in 1880, and obtained a first class in the classical tripos of 1881. In the following year he entered the civil service, obtaining a post in the War Office; but the work was not congenial to him, and at the suggestion of (Sir) Sidney Colvin [q.v.] he was transferred in 1884 to the department of prints and drawings at the British Museum, of which Colvin had recently become keeper.

Here Cust's real interests were engaged. He had a good eye and an extremely retentive memory; his knowledge of pictures and prints had been enlarged by study on the Continent; he was methodical, enjoyed research, and had a scholar's conscience. His *Index* to the Dutch, Flemish, and German artists represented in the Print Room (1893), followed by an *Index* to the French artists (1896), was of great service to students, and the preparation of it made him familiar not only with the masters but with innumerable minor artists. Writers on art in England had hitherto mostly been attracted to the Italian schools; Cust's predilection was for the schools of Northern Europe. Of Van Dyck and also of Dürer he made a special study.

In 1895 Cust was appointed director of the National Portrait Gallery in succession to Sir George Scharf [q.v.]. His first task was the moving of the collection from its temporary home at Bethnal Green to the new gallery in St. Martin's Place. The study of portraiture in England appealed to his love of history and genealogy and to his interest in old English families. He had a wide knowledge of the collections in the great country houses. The biographies of artists, notable for their accuracy and painstaking research, contributed to this DICTIONARY made a fresh beginning in the study of English art. At the same time Cust maintained his former interests. An authoritative study of Dürer's paintings and engravings was published in 1897, followed in 1898 by a monograph on an early German engraver, *The Master 'E.S.' and the 'Ars Moriendi'*. In 1898 he produced a *History of the Society of Dilettanti* and in 1899 a *History of Eton College*. As a writer Cust lacked the graces of style, but he was always a master of facts. In 1900 he published his most important single book, a large and exhaustive work on Van Dyck. Two small monographs on the same master appeared in 1903 and 1906, and a *Further Study* in 1911.

In 1901 Cust was offered the post of surveyor of the king's pictures, and with the consent of the trustees was allowed to combine this with his directorship of the National Portrait Gallery. He resigned the directorship in 1909, but continued to hold the office of surveyor until 1927. In 1901 he was also appointed gentleman usher to the court. Cust's duties as surveyor involved the supervision of all the collections in the various royal palaces; and he was responsible for a good deal of rearrangement and rehanging of the pictures. His office brought him into personal relations with King Edward VII, who became his friend. He published a work on *The Royal Collection of Paintings: Buckingham Palace* (1905), *Windsor Castle* (1906). *Notes on the Authentic Portraits of Mary, Queen of Scots* had appeared in 1903 and a large illustrated work on *The Bridgewater House Gallery* in 1904.

From 1909 to 1919 Cust was joint editor with Roger Fry of the *Burlington Magazine*. Among his own contributions to the magazine was a series of *Notes on Pictures in the Royal Collections*, published in book form in 1911. In the long-neglected field of early portraiture in England his work was particularly valuable. He set himself to clear away the accumulations of legend, and to get to the facts, his most notable service being the rediscovery of the sixteenth-century painter 'H. E.' (Hans Eworth), long erroneously identified with Lucas d'Heere [q.v.]. His study of Eworth, which contains a full catalogue of the painter's works, was published in the Walpole Society's *Annual* (vol. ii, 1918). Cust was keenly interested in the movement for introducing good pictures into schools, and for many years, until its dissolution, was chairman of the Art for Schools Association, founded in 1883.

Cust's personal appearance hardly suggested his zest for scholarly research and his capacity for hard and rapid work. Inclined to plumpness, he gave the impression of one who enjoyed life to the full. He had a great love of music as well as of painting, and a gift for simple pleasures. The extraordinary accuracy of his memory enabled him to dispense with note-books. He married in 1895 Sybil, sixth daughter of George William, fourth Baron Lyttelton [q.v.], and half sister of Bishop Arthur Temple Lyttelton [q.v.] and of the statesman Alfred Lyttelton [q.v.]. They had one son. His wife contributed a memoir of Cust to his posthumously published volume on *Edward VII and his Court* (1930). This contains a reproduction of a photograph of Cust taken late in life. He was created K.C.V.O. in 1927. He died 12 October 1929 at Datchet, where his later married life was spent.

[*Memoir* by the Hon. Lady Cust, 1930; private information.] L. BINYON.

DALZIEL, DAVISON ALEXANDER, BARON DALZIEL, of Wooler, Northumberland (1854–1928), newspaper proprietor and financier, the youngest son of Davison

Octavian Dalziel (1825–1875) by his wife, Helen, daughter of Henry Gaulter, was born in London 17 October 1854. He was descended from a Northumbrian family distinguished alike for artistic and business ability. Of the eight sons of his paternal grandfather, Alexander Dalziel, of Wooler (1781–1832), seven were artists, and four of them, George [q.v.], Edward [q.v.], John, and Thomas Bolton Gilchrist Septimus [q.v.]—the Brothers Dalziel—produced as engravers, draughtsmen, and publishers a large proportion of the English woodcut illustrations issued between 1840 and 1880. The eighth son, Davison Dalziel's father, devoted himself to commerce.

As a young man Dalziel spent some years in the United States, and there gained experience of newspaper management. In 1893 he returned to London, and became one of the founders of Dalziel's News Agency. In 1910 he purchased from Sir Cyril Arthur Pearson [q.v.] a controlling interest in the *Standard* and the *Evening Standard* newspapers. The *Standard*, under Dalziel's management, attracted attention at a time of domestic controversy by opening its columns impartially to supporters and opponents of women's suffrage.

In 1916 Dalziel disposed of his newspaper interests, and soon became prominent as a director of public companies and notably of undertakings concerned with overland transport. He was chairman of the Pullman Car Company from its inception in 1915. He was a director of the International Sleeping Car Company for many years, and in 1919 was elected chairman of the directors and president of the managing committee. In 1927 Dalziel became chairman of the International Sleeping Car Share Trust Limited, a holding company which he formed with a capital of £5,250,000 in order to obtain a controlling interest in the International Sleeping Car Company: in 1928 he negotiated the purchase by the International Sleeping Car Company of the touring agency business of Thomas Cook & Son. He was also chairman of the General Motor-Cab Company, and in 1907 he was chiefly responsible for the introduction of motor-cabs in London. Dalziel was elected to parliament in the conservative interest as member for Brixton in 1910. He was an effective speaker and an able advocate of fiscal reform. Save for a short interval in 1923–1924 he continued to represent Brixton in the House of Commons until he was raised to the peerage as Baron Dalziel, of Wooler, in 1927. He had been created a baronet in 1919.

Dalziel was a man of unusual ability and energy: in negotiation he was forceful yet conciliatory, and much of his success in various enterprises was due to personal charm which, combined with business acumen, secured to him the loyalty of friends and associates in many walks of life both in Great Britain and abroad.

Dalziel married in 1876 Harriet, daughter of John Godfrey Dunning, of Edinburgh. Their only child, a daughter, predeceased her father in 1910, and on Dalziel's death, which took place in London 18 April 1928, the peerage and baronetcy became extinct. His estate was proved at £2,199,220 (net personalty £2,035,686).

[*The Times*, 19 April 1928; *Newcastle Journal*, 19 April 1928; *North Mail*, 19 April 1928; private information.]

A. E. Watkin.

DARWIN, Sir FRANCIS (1848–1925), botanist, the third son of Charles Darwin, the naturalist [q.v.], by his wife, Emma, daughter of Josiah Wedgwood and granddaughter of Josiah Wedgwood of Etruria [q.v.], was born at Down, Kent, 16 August 1848. He was educated at Clapham grammar school, of which Charles Pritchard [q.v.], afterwards Savilian professor of astronomy at Oxford, was until 1862 headmaster. He matriculated at Trinity College, Cambridge, in 1866, and took his degree with first class honours in the natural sciences tripos of 1870. He then studied medicine at St. George's Hospital, London. He took his Cambridge M.B. in 1875; but he never practised. He had already turned to botany, and in 1876 worked for a time under Julius von Sachs at the university of Würzburg. With this interval, for some years (1875–1882) he acted as his father's secretary and assistant in the researches at Down, living at first in the village, and after his first wife's death in 1876, with his parents at Down House. On Charles Darwin's death in 1882, Francis Darwin moved to Cambridge, where in 1884 he became university lecturer in botany, and in 1886 was elected to a fellowship at Christ's College. From 1888 to 1904 he was reader in botany, and, during the years 1892 to 1895 he acted as deputy to Professor Charles Cardale Babington [q.v.], devoting his share of the stipend of the chair to the improvement of botanical teaching in the university.

At the time when Francis Darwin began teaching in Cambridge, botanists were ceasing to be chiefly concerned with systematic description, and were turning to the study of the fundamental nature and mechanism of plants as living organisms —the study known as vegetable physiology. Thus he was teaching what was almost a new subject. Besides his more advanced lectures, for some years he gave the botanical part of the course in elementary biology for medical students, a heavy task. His pupils, both elementary and advanced, found that, while he was not an 'eloquent' lecturer, he had the important faculty of making the work interesting. To the surprise of some of those who came fresh from the infallibility of schoolmasters, Darwin never minded confessing that he did not know; his attitude to his students being, in essence, that of a joint searcher for truth. As a teacher, he left his mark on a generation, and a most pleasant memory among his pupils, who presented him with his portrait and an address on his resignation of the readership in 1904.

Francis Darwin's services to science can be grouped under two heads. First, as his father's biographer and editor, he recorded in an admirable way the history of one of the great epoch-making intellectual achievements of mankind. In 1887 he published in three volumes the *Life and Letters of Charles Darwin*, including an autobiographical chapter. This work has been well called 'one of the best of biographies'. As far as may be, the letters are left to tell their own tale of a man great indeed, but modest and lovable; yet the editor's part is necessary to complete the whole, and is extremely well done. In 1903, jointly with A. C. Seward, Francis Darwin brought out, as a sequel, *More Letters of Charles Darwin*; while in 1909, under the name *The Foundations of the Origin of Species*, he edited two essays written by his father in 1842 and 1844, and, in the same year, in the Darwin centenary volume, he published a chapter entitled *Darwin's Work on the Movement of Plants*.

Secondly, Francis Darwin increased our knowledge of vegetable physiology, especially by his researches on plant movements and the localization of their response to stimuli such as that of gravity, and again by his work on the transpiration of water through the openings on leaves known as stomata. This work, some of which needed the invention of new apparatus which he designed, sometimes helped by his brother Horace Darwin [q.v.], is recorded primarily in a series of papers in the *Transactions* of the Royal Society and elsewhere: those on plant movements between 1891 and 1904, and those on transpiration from 1897 to 1914. Jointly with E. H. Acton, Darwin published in 1894 *The Practical Physiology of Plants*, which set forth the new ideas which were transforming his subject. In 1895 he helped more elementary students by a textbook, *The Elements of Botany*.

But Darwin had many other interests. He edited in 1903 a *Naturalist's Calendar*, written between 1820 and 1831 by Leonard Blomefield [q.v.]; in 1917 he published *Rustic Sounds and other Studies in Literature and Natural History*, and in 1920 *Springtime and other Essays*. In these two last-named books his personality is well revealed. He was a good musician, playing the bassoon, flute, hautboy, and other instruments. He was devoted to dogs, and had a great love of the English countryside. A delightful sense of humour endeared him to his many friends and made him the best of company.

After the death of his second wife and his resignation of the readership in botany, Darwin gave up his house 'Wychfield' and had a short sojourn in London (1903–1904). But he soon returned to live in Cambridge. He was elected a fellow of the Royal Society in 1882, served on the council 1894–1895 and 1902–1908, and was foreign secretary 1903–1907. He was made an honorary fellow of Christ's College in 1908. In the latter year also he was president of the British Association when it met in Dublin, and delivered an address on the subject of his researches. He was knighted in 1913, and received honorary degrees from the universities of Dublin, St. Andrews, Upsala, and others. He died at Cambridge 19 September 1925.

Francis Darwin was thrice married: first, in 1874 to Amy (died 1876), daughter of Lawrence Ruck, of Pantlludw, Machynlleth, North Wales; secondly, in 1883 to Ellen Wordsworth (died 1903), daughter of John Crofts, of Leeds, and lecturer at Newnham College; and thirdly, in 1913 to Florence (died 1920), daughter of Herbert Fisher and widow of Professor Frederic William Maitland [q.v.]. By his first wife he had a son, and by his second a daughter.

There is a portrait of Francis Darwin by Sir William Rothenstein in the Botany School at Cambridge.

[*The Times*, 21 September 1925; *Nature*, 17 October 1925; *Year Books* of the Royal Society, 1883–1926; personal knowledge.]

W. C. D. Dampier.

DARWIN, Sir HORACE (1851–1928), civil engineer, was born at Down, Kent, 13 May 1851, the fifth son of Charles Darwin, the naturalist [q.v.], by his wife, Emma, daughter of Josiah Wedgwood, and younger brother of Sir George Howard Darwin [q.v.] and Sir Francis Darwin [q.v.]. He was educated at Trinity College, Cambridge, graduating B.A. in 1874. After an apprenticeship in the works of Messrs. Easton & Anderson, engineers, of Erith, Kent, he returned to Cambridge, where the rest of his life was spent.

During the years from 1875 to 1900 the natural science school at Cambridge grew rapidly. The laboratories which were erected needed apparatus, and in supplying this Darwin found his life work. At the suggestion of (Sir) Michael Foster, professor of physiology [q.v.], Darwin and A. G. Dew Smith joined partnership and began the design and manufacture of scientific instruments. At first attention was paid to the needs of the biological school. The physicists, however, soon realized the value of the work, and the reputation of the firm grew apace. In 1885 the Cambridge Scientific Instrument Company was established with Darwin as its chairman and chief shareholder. It was soon realized that at the head of the new firm there was a man with a genius for design and a knowledge of mechanics which enabled him to express his design in the most suitable form. 'Go and talk to Horace Darwin' was advice often given to a man seeking to work out some delicate apparatus.

Darwin's own views on design are expressed in his Wilbur Wright lecture delivered to the Royal Aeronautical Society (1913), and more fully in the article, 'The Design of Scientific Instruments', contributed by Darwin and his colleague, C. C. Mason, to the *Dictionary of Applied Physics*, vol. iii, 1923. They are also set out in the obituary notice of Darwin in the *Proceedings* of the Royal Society, vol. cxxii, A, 1929. According to Darwin the designer must be a mechanical engineer with much scientific knowledge, well acquainted with the available methods of manufacture. It was his habit to make himself thoroughly acquainted with the experimental details required; then, when satisfied with his problem, he would evolve, often with great rapidity, the suitable apparatus.

Measurement of the forces to which aircraft are subject is no easy matter. As a member of the Advisory Committee for Aeronautics, established by Mr. Asquith in 1909 on the suggestion of Lord Haldane, Darwin became the adviser of his colleagues on all questions relating to instruments. The navigation of an aeroplane, especially when in a cloud, raised a novel problem towards the solution of which he made valuable contributions; while during the War, as chairman of the Inventions Committee, his help was often sought and freely given.

The advance made in the design of British scientific instruments during the fifty years from 1880 to 1930 was very marked: Horace Darwin was a leader in this advance.

Darwin became an associate member of the Institution of Civil Engineers in 1877 and a member of the Institution of Mechanical Engineers in 1878. He was elected F.R.S. in 1903; his brothers George and Francis were already fellows. He was created K.B.E. in 1918.

Darwin married in 1880 the Hon. Emma Cecilia, daughter of Thomas Henry Farrer, first Baron Farrer [q.v.], and had one son, who was killed in action in 1915, and two daughters. He died at Cambridge 22 September 1928.

[*The Times*, 24 September 1928; *Proceedings* of the Royal Society, vol. cxxii, A, 1929; *The Cambridge Review*, 26 October 1928.]

R. T. Glazebrook.

DAVIDS, THOMAS WILLIAM RHYS (1843–1922), Oriental scholar, the eldest son of the Rev. Thomas William Davids, Congregational minister at Colchester, by his wife, Louisa Winter, was born at Colchester 12 May 1843. Educated privately, Rhys Davids, after studying Sanskrit at Breslau University, joined in 1866 the Ceylon civil service. He devoted his leisure to the study, under native teachers, of the Pali language and early Buddhism. Here he found his vocation. Quitting Ceylon after ten years, he was called to the bar by the Middle Temple in 1877 but practised little, devoting himself instead to the further study of Buddhism.

Rhys Davids's first publication was *Ancient Coins and Measures of Ceylon* (1877). This was followed in 1878 by *Buddhism*, written for the Society for Promoting Christian Knowledge, a work which, undertaken when few Pali texts were available in Europe, passed through twenty-three editions and laid sure foundations for the interpretation of early Buddhism without the stratigraphical confusion hitherto prevalent. In 1880 the publication of Victor Fausböll's *Jātakas* in Pali led Rhys Davids to contemplate a translation, but he abandoned this idea (after a notable first volume—*Buddhist Birth Stories*, 1880) in order to produce, for the series of 'Sacred Books of the East' (published by the Clarendon Press), *Buddhist Suttas from the Pali* (1881), which was followed in 1881–1885 by three volumes of translations (in collaboration with Hermann Oldenberg) of *Vinaya Texts* and in 1890–1894 by *Questions of King Milinda*.

In 1881 Rhys Davids founded the Pali Text Society, which has published (apart from two dozen volumes of translations) 117 volumes of Pali texts and a Pali-English dictionary. To this series he himself contributed, in collaboration with Joseph Estlin Carpenter [q.v.], the text of the *Dīgha Nikāya* in three volumes (1899–1910), vol. i of the *Commentary* thereon (1886), together with an admirable translation (partly in collaboration with his wife) also in three volumes, published in 1899, 1910, and 1921 as *Dialogues of the Buddha*. These *Dīgha* volumes constitute Rhys Davids's main contribution to the documented study of early Buddhism. Of his books about Buddhism not already mentioned, the chief are *The origin and growth of Religion as illustrated by . . . the history of Indian Buddhism* (Hibbert Lectures, 1881), *Buddhist India* (1903), and (his own favourite) *Early Buddhism* (1908).

Rhys Davids was honorary professor of Pali and Buddhist literature at University College, London, from 1882 to 1912. In 1904 he was appointed to the chair of comparative religion at the university of Manchester, a post which he held until 1915. He was secretary of the Royal Asiatic Society from 1888 to 1904, and was an original fellow of the British Academy, which he helped to found. In 1894 he was granted a civil list pension of £200 a year.

The production of a Pali dictionary, to garner the fruits of the Pali Text Society, was always in Rhys Davids's contemplation. Originally (1902) he had hoped to put the dictionary on an international footing, but difficulties arose and the European War finally stopped all idea of a co-operative enterprise. Although now over seventy, Rhys Davids in 1915 decided to launch a provisional dictionary himself. Quitting Manchester, he secured the whole-time services of Dr. William Stede as co-editor, and issued the first volume in 1921, and the second in 1922, the year of his death, which took place at his home at Chipstead, Surrey, 27 December 1922. The final instalment was published by Dr. Stede in 1925. Without Rhys Davids's energy this result could not have been achieved.

Rhys Davids was a lifelong liberal. He combined enthusiasm with a keen sense of humour, and was at his best when discussing religion, politics, and the historical evolution of ideas. He delighted in placing his materials and ideas at the disposal of his friends.

Rhys Davids married in 1894 Caroline Augusta, daughter of the Rev. John Foley, sometime fellow of Wadham College, Oxford, vicar of Wadhurst, Sussex, and had one son, who was killed in action during the European War, and two daughters. Mrs. Davids herself became a distinguished student of Buddhism.

[Private information; personal knowledge.]

Chalmers.

DAVIDSON, RANDALL THOMAS, Baron Davidson of Lambeth (1848–1930), archbishop of Canterbury, was born in Edinburgh 7 April 1848, the eldest of the four children of Henry Davidson, merchant, of Leith, by his wife, Henrietta, third daughter of John Campbell Swinton, of Kimmerghame, co. Berwick, who belonged to the Berwickshire family of the Swintons, of Swinton. He was of pure Scottish blood on both parents' sides. His father's great grandfather, the Rev. Thomas Davidson, of the Tron church, Edinburgh, was a chaplain to Queen Anne. Thomas Davidson's daughter married the Rev. Thomas Randall, whose son of the same name, also a minister, succeeded to the estate of Muirhouse, near Edinburgh, on the death of his mother's brother, in 1794, and as a condition of inheritance changed his name to Davidson. The second Thomas Randall's son was Henry Davidson (born 1810), the father of Randall Thomas Davidson. He was a keen sportsman, as well as literary, musical, and devout. His wife was deeply religious and also possessed a marked poetic gift. Both Henry and Henrietta Davidson were Presbyterians, and Randall Davidson was baptized at their home in Edinburgh by the minister of St. Stephen's church. His parents left Edinburgh in 1857 and settled at Muirhouse, where the three boys became adept at all country pursuits; Randall on one occasion narrowly escaped drowning. In 1862 he was sent to Harrow, and was confirmed in 1865. He had a second narrow escape from death from a shooting accident in the summer holidays of 1866. The accident affected his health for the whole of his life. He went up to Trinity College, Oxford, in 1867, but was constantly unwell, and in 1871 only obtained a third class in the school of law and modern history.

Davidson spent the next three years partly on Tweedside, partly in foreign tours, including visits to Rome (where he saw Pope Pius IX), Egypt, and Palestine; and partly in two spells of special training for holy orders under Dr. Charles John Vaughan [q.v.], master of the Temple. He was ordained deacon in 1874, and priest in 1875; and was curate at Dartford, Kent, from 1874 to 1877. He then became resident chaplain to the archbishop of Canterbury, Archibald Campbell Tait [q.v.], whose son Craufurd (died 1878) was Davidson's intimate friend. In November 1878 he married Edith Murdoch Tait, the archbishop's second daughter. They had no children. Until Tait's death (3 December 1882) he was the archbishop's indispensable assistant and 'true son'. On Tait's death he was summoned to see Queen Victoria, who wrote in her journal (9 December 1882): 'was seldom more struck than I have been by his personality. . . . I feel that Mr. Davidson is a man who may be of great use to me, for which I am truly thankful'. He was intimately concerned with the nomination of Tait's successor, being consulted by the queen both about Dr. Edward Harold Browne [q.v.], bishop of Winchester, aged seventy-two, whose health Davidson judged unequal to the task, and also about Dr. Edward White Benson [q.v.], who was appointed. He continued as Benson's chaplain at Lambeth for a few months until the queen secured his nomination by Mr. Gladstone as dean of Windsor. He was installed as dean in June 1883, at the age of thirty-five, and was also appointed the queen's domestic chaplain.

As dean of Windsor Davidson came into close personal relations with Queen Victoria who, partly through the death of her youngest son, Leopold, Duke of Albany, in March 1884, and other private sorrows, was led to turn to Davidson for religious consolation and thus to give him more and more of her confidence in a quite exceptional way. These confidential relations between the queen and Davidson were not, however, without occasions of conflict, when the dean felt obliged to offer distasteful advice or to make a remonstrance; but of these occasions he wrote, 'my belief is that she liked and trusted best those who occasionally incurred her wrath, provided that she had reason to think their motives good'. The queen also invariably consulted Davidson about all important Church appointments from 1883 to 1901.

As dean, Davidson continued to be the intimate counsellor of Archbishop Benson, who regularly turned to him for aid, sending daily packets of letters from Lambeth to Windsor for Davidson's annotation and advice. He was Benson's constant adviser on the conduct of the trial (1889–1890) of Edward King, bishop of Lincoln [q.v.], and he helped much behind the scenes through his contact with Viscount Halifax and other leading high churchmen.

Davidson's absorbing interest was the welfare of the Church; and the time came when he was clearly marked out for a bishopric. Although the queen was at first very reluctant to lose him from Windsor, she eventually agreed that he should be appointed to the bishopric of Rochester, then the third largest diocese in England. On 25 April 1891 he was consecrated in Westminster Abbey. Eleven days later he fell dangerously ill with haemorrhage, and was ill for six months—the first of three serious illnesses during his four years in South London. There he made his home and planned the new bishop's house, but it became clear that the conditions of the Rochester diocese were too severe for his health to stand the strain. During his first illness, however, his two-volume *Life* of Archbishop Tait, written while at Windsor, appeared, a masterly piece of work telling the story of Tait and of the last fifty years of the Church of England in a most thorough manner and with great lucidity. In connexion with the coal strike of 1893 he was prominent in pleading for the maintenance of a standard of decent living as an essential condition in the settlement of labour disputes. Appointed clerk of the closet immediately after consecration, he remained in the closest touch with Queen Victoria. He was also, as before, Archbishop Benson's right hand in the central work of the Church, and was largely concerned with his refusal in 1894–1895 of the request of Viscount Halifax and the Abbé Portal that he should negotiate with the Holy See with a view to the recognition of Anglican orders.

In 1895 Davidson was translated to the bishopric of Winchester. Residence at Farnham Castle, and in a country diocese, restored his health, and during the whole of his eight years' episcopate he had no serious illness. Within a week of taking up his duties he was confronted with his first and gravest ritual difficulty. The Rev. Robert William Radclyffe Dolling [q.v.], Winchester College missioner at Landport, had built a large new church, and only three days before the date of its opening for public worship Davidson was officially informed by the rural dean (Canon Edgar Jacob) that it contained a third altar which was to be used 'for the celebration of masses for the dead'. The bishop immediately saw Dolling, most enthusiastic of Irishmen; allowed the opening of the church without prejudice to the question of the third altar; and did his best to secure a mutual understanding. But he would not sanction a third altar which was avowedly to be used for the celebration of masses for the dead. Dolling immediately resigned. Davidson was vehemently attacked by Dolling's friends at that time; but he maintained that as bishop he was obliged to restrain Dolling 'from dealing absolutely at his will with the directions in our Prayer Book'.

On Benson's death (11 October 1896) it was the queen's desire that Davidson should succeed him as archbishop of Canterbury, but Lord Salisbury, with Davidson's whole-hearted approval, nominated Dr. Frederick Temple [q.v.]. When Salisbury then recommended Davidson for the see of London, vacated by Temple, the queen peremptorily forbade it, as impossible on grounds of health. Mandell Creighton [q.v.] was appointed instead; but on his death in 1901 Lord Salisbury, with King Edward VII's approval, made the offer to Davidson direct. Davidson declined on the same grounds. With Temple as archbishop, the old daily contact with Lambeth ceased, to the younger man's keen disappointment. During these years Davidson found his greatest happiness in diocesan work. But he also played a prominent part in public questions, speaking constantly in the House of Lords on social issues. He was particularly active in legislation to restrict the liquor trade. He was also one of Mr. Balfour's principal advisers and helpers with regard to public elementary schools in the Education Act of 1902. From 1898 to 1901 he was actively engaged in the ritual crisis in the Church: carried on a long correspondence on the subject with Sir William Harcourt [q.v.], that flail of high churchmen; spoke in the House of Lords; and treated the whole question comprehensively in his episcopal charge of 1899. He was always on the side of moderation, but was not perhaps sufficiently appreciative of the high churchman's basic principles. As bishop of Winchester he maintained the same close and confidential relationship with Queen Victoria as before. Her residence, Osborne House in the Isle of Wight, was in his diocese, and there he visited her constantly. On 19 January 1901 he was summoned to Osborne by telegram with the news that the queen was dying. He remained in close attendance until the end, and offered the commendatory prayer. On 23 December 1902 Temple died, and, as was generally expected, Davidson succeeded him (12 February 1903).

With Queen Victoria's death a new era began; and Mr. Balfour, the prime minister, when asking Davidson to accept the archbishopric told him that 'the occupant of that great post will have a task before him as critical as has fallen to the lot of any of the long line of his predecessors'. It might be said that Davidson's task during the twenty-five years of his primacy was alike to maintain the unity and to vindicate the comprehensiveness of the Church of England, and to strengthen the Church's witness in the life of the nation. In the former sphere he was at once confronted with a demand, made by a hundred unionist members of parliament on 11 March 1903, for drastic action against clergy who were guilty of flagrant and defiant illegality in the conduct of public worship. In replying to the deputation, while expressing his belief that the number of such clergy was small, Davidson agreed that with regard to them 'the sands have run out. Stern and drastic action is in my judgement quite essential. Speaking for myself, so far as in me lies, I assure you, using my words with a full sense of responsibility, I desire and intend that we should now act and act sternly.' The assurance was warmly welcomed. A royal commission on ecclesiastical discipline was appointed in 1904 under the chairmanship of Sir Michael Hicks Beach (afterwards first Earl St. Aldwyn), Davidson himself being a member and also a witness. In 1906 the commission issued a unanimous report: the principal recommendations being that (1) certain specified illegalities should at once be made to cease; (2) letters of business should be issued to the Convocations with instructions to consider the preparation of a new ornaments rubric 'with a view to its enactment by parliament' and to frame (also for enactment by parliament) such modifications in the existing law relating to the conduct of divine service and to the ornaments and fittings of churches 'as may tend to secure the greater elasticity which a reasonable recognition of the comprehensiveness of the Church of England and its present needs seem to demand'. In the same year letters of business were issued and the first step on the long road of Prayer Book revision was taken.

Davidson from the first had many opportunities of strengthening the Church's witness in the life of the nation. In 1903 he appealed to the prime minister for the Christians in Macedonia who were suffering at Turkish hands. In 1905 he gave public expression to his 'abhorrence of the blind and cruel spirit' which had led excited mobs to terrible acts of outrage against the Jews in Russia. In home politics he opposed the Deceased Wife's Sister Marriage Act (1907) on both social and religious grounds; but after its passing issued a letter to his diocese advising that (1) such marriages should take place elsewhere than in churches, but that (2) from men and women otherwise entitled to receive the privileges and ministrations of the Church they ought not to be withheld on the mere ground of such a marriage. He also opposed Mr. Augustine Birrell's Education Bill of 1906, which was the liberal government's reply to the Education Act of 1902 and was justly regarded as a radical attack on denominational elementary schools and the religious instruction for which they stood. Davidson was more conciliatory than was agreeable to the fiercer champions of the existing system, but he insisted on certain 'pretty far-reaching changes' in the Bill. The Lords' amendments produced a clash with the Commons, and in spite of Davidson's efforts at a later stage to mediate, the Bill perished. When, in 1908, Mr. Walter Runciman introduced an Education Bill of a much less drastic character, Davidson worked hard for a settlement and came to a provisional agreement with the government. But he was unable to secure the support of the main body of churchmen for what other Church leaders described as a complete surrender. The Representative Church Council passed an overwhelming vote against the Bill, which was then withdrawn. In 1908 Davidson presided over the fifth Lambeth Conference of bishops of the Anglican communion. He had attended every one of the series save the first (in 1867), having been present as Archbishop Tait's chaplain in 1878, as assistant secretary in 1888, and as episcopal secretary in 1897. In dealing at this conference (which followed a more popular Pan-Anglican Congress held a few weeks earlier) and throughout his primacy with a great variety of Church questions affecting the overseas as well as the home dioceses, Davidson gave remarkable evidence of his wide knowledge of missionary problems and his deep interest in the development of the Anglican Church abroad, an interest which caused overseas bishops again and again to turn to him for counsel. He was the first archbishop of Canterbury to pay an official visit to Canada and the United States of America (1904).

In 1909, when there was talk of war between England and Germany and a navy scare, Davidson strongly supported a mission of four bishops and other representatives to Berlin (where they were received by Kaiser Wilhelm II) to promote Anglo-German friendship; and he himself the following year held a reception for German church leaders at which he emphasized the ties of religion and brotherhood which bound the two countries together. At the same time he was called upon to play a full part in the political crisis at home, arising out of the budget introduced by Mr. Lloyd George in April 1909. When it came up to the House of Lords in November, it was clear that the division would be on party lines. Davidson, who with the majority of the bishops abstained from voting, justified abstention in a speech which emphasized the duty of bishops to take their share in social legislation but stated that ordinarily the bishops act rightly in 'sitting loose to party ties'. Party spirit, however, ran high, and on the Finance Bill being thrown out by the Lords, Davidson was attacked just as much by radicals for not voting for it as by unionists for not voting against it. The crisis grew more acute after the general election of January 1910 as the result of the threat by Mr. Asquith to force a bill through parliament severely limiting the powers of the Lords. But the sudden death of King Edward VII on 6 May changed the situation. There was another general election in December 1910, and in the consultations preceding the final division on the Parliament Bill in August 1911 Davidson played a very important part behind the scenes. On 7 August Mr. Asquith told the House of Commons that King George V had agreed to the creation of as many peers as might be necessary to secure the passing of the Bill. It was seen that much might depend on the voting of the bishops; and in the end Davidson, although condemning Asquith's tactics, decided that on this occasion they ought not to abstain. He spoke near the end of the debate, and Lord Morley paid a high tribute to the effect of his contribution, which recalled the House to the gravity of the issue and denounced the callousness, not to say levity, with which some seemed to contemplate the creation of five hundred peers. The Bill was passed (10 August). On 22 June 1911 the archbishop had crowned King George, and during the king's absence in India later in the year he was one of the three counsellors of state appointed to transact the business of the crown. During this year, when Davidson presented the German theologian, Adolf Harnack, and others to the king and queen at Buckingham Palace (5 February), and again in 1912, further advances were made in Anglo-German friendship through the medium of the Churches.

During the years immediately preceding the outbreak of the European War, Davidson had to face a strong attack on the Church in the Bill for the disestablishment of the Welsh Church; as well as grave menaces to its internal unity from two sides, one affecting credal orthodoxy, the other the Church's order and ministry. He resisted to the end the legislation (enacted in 1914, operative in 1920) which was to disestablish and disendow the four Welsh dioceses belonging to the province of Canterbury, and constantly spoke in parliament and outside, in Wales and elsewhere, as representing a practically united Church. His task in meeting the demands from Bishop Gore and others for new declarations of the Church's faith for the purpose of denouncing modernism, and from Bishop Frank Weston [q.v.] of Zanzibar for a condemnation of acts implying intercommunion with nonconformists, was more difficult, and required wise and careful statesmanship, as on both questions feeling ran high within the Church. After an anxious period of controversy, which threatened more than once to result either in Gore's resignation or his own, Davidson persuaded Convocation in April 1914 to adopt a Resolution, of which the crucial words declared that 'the denial of any of the historical facts stated in the Creeds goes beyond the limits of legitimate interpretation, and gravely imperils that sincerity of profession which is plainly incumbent on the ministers of the Word and Sacraments', and at the same time expressed an anxiety 'not to lay unnecessary burdens upon consciences, nor unduly to limit freedom of thought and inquiry, whether among clergy or among laity', and urged 'considerateness in dealing with that which is tentative and provisional in the thought and work of earnest and reverent students'. When Gore in January 1918 appealed to this Resolution and called upon the archbishop to refuse consecration to Dean Hensley Henson, the bishop-elect of Hereford, on account of his supposed statements on certain clauses of the Creed, a similar crisis arose; but Davidson, while affirming that, if he found himself called upon to consecrate to the episcopate one who was unworthy of that office or false to the Church's faith, he was prepared to refuse consecration and to abide the consequences, was able to show Gore, on Henson's own statement, that the latter repeated the words of the Apostles' Creed, including the clauses in question (on the Virgin Birth and the Resurrection of Christ), *ex animo*, and Gore accordingly withdrew his protest.

The other crisis in the field of Church order was concerned with Kikuyu in East Africa. In September 1913 Bishop Weston of Zanzibar denounced (1) a scheme devised at a conference held at Kikuyu in the previous June for federating the missionary societies in the dioceses of Mombasa and Uganda, whether Anglican or non-episcopal, and (2) a joint service of Holy Communion held at the close of the conference. The bishop of Zanzibar demanded either recantation on the part of the bishops of Mombasa and Uganda or their trial before the archbishop and twelve bishops of the province of Canterbury on the charge of propagating heresy and committing schism. A violent controversy broke out. The three bishops came to England. The archbishop refused a trial, and referred the matter to the consultative body of the Lambeth Conference which met 27–31 July 1914. Its report, which was unanimous, was by Davidson's wish not published until 1915, on account of the outbreak of war. The archbishop, guided by that report, in his final answer (Easter 1915) pointed out that the Church of England had never judged all non-episcopalians to be *extra ecclesiam*. He examined the scheme for federation and certain special difficulties which it contained. He asked that the scheme should be reviewed and brought up at the next Lambeth Conference; he held that (1) the admission of unconfirmed Christian men to Holy Communion, when out of reach of the ministrations of their own churches, was a matter within the discretion of the bishop of the diocese; (2) the preaching of non-episcopal ministers in Anglican pulpits in the mission field was similarly allowable on occasion; (3) Anglicans should not receive Holy Communion from non-episcopal ministers. He also expressed the opinion that the joint Communion service (although intelligible in the context of the Kikuyu Conference of 1913) should not be repeated. The archbishop's answer thus took a middle course, and although attacked by both sides, certainly upheld the comprehensiveness of the Anglican Church.

The outbreak of the European War was a grave shock to Davidson, who had earlier said that war between England and Germany was unthinkable. But he was clear that no other course than that taken by the British government was possible. In collaboration with a large number of other religious leaders he issued a reply to a manifesto of the German theologians which justified the action of the German government. The reply claimed that Great Britain's action was based on the paramount obligation of fidelity to plighted word and the duty of defending weaker nations against violence. Throughout the War by his sermons and other public utterances Davidson exercised a steadying influence; and while firm in his support of the Allies, felt the horror of war too keenly to indulge in anti-German rhetoric. He insisted on the spiritual responsibilities of the clergy, on the need of exercising a ministry of mercy and charity as well as of encouragement; and the prayers which he issued from time to time were in tune with his own precepts. It was largely with this spiritual purpose in view that in 1916 he authorized a National Mission of Repentance and Hope. In May of that year he spent ten days with the British troops in France. While allowing clergy, where they could be spared, to serve as noncombatants, he was opposed to their serving as combatants, though at the time of the last Military Service Act (1918) he would have acquiesced in combatant service on the part of clergy, in view of the gravity of the national emergency, had a demand for it been pressed. Throughout the War Davidson also from time to time publicly questioned or criticized the use of certain methods of warfare by British troops abroad—thereby incurring a good deal of odium. He protested against the use of poison gas in May 1915 and against reprisals by air in February 1916 and May 1917, and he did what he could to ensure kindness and considerate treatment for interned enemy aliens and their dependants as well as for prisoners of war. From very early in 1918 Davidson gave public support to the proposals for a League of Nations; and in 1922 he preached at Geneva just before the opening of the third assembly of the League. At the end of 1919 he published a selection of the addresses which he had given during the War under the title of *The Testing of a Nation*. Of this book Lord Haldane wrote to him that he wished that 'the standard of the government in action had been that laid down by the leader of the Church of England in the deliverances of this volume'.

After the end of the War, while continuing steadfast in his witness in the House of Lords on large moral issues, Davidson played a decisive part in the development of a corporate life, with real powers of self-government, in the Church of England, and in the movement towards reunion with other Churches. The passing of the Church of England Assembly (Powers) Act in 1919 was due to a combination of the enthusiasm of younger churchmen (notably Viscount Wolmer and the Rev. William Temple, afterwards archbishop of York), who organized a 'life and liberty' campaign, with the prudence and wisdom of Davidson. The Act was based on the recommendations of the archbishops' committee on Church and State (1913–1916). In its final form the Act gave wide powers to the National Assembly of the Church of England, consisting of three houses, bishops, clergy, and laity, to pass measures on any subject relating to the Church of England, with the proviso that before a measure could have the force of law, resolutions approving it must be adopted in both Houses of Parliament, after scrutiny of the measure by an ecclesiastical committee composed of representatives of both Houses. The archbishop asked parliament to pass the Bill so as 'to enable the Church of England to do its work properly', and emphasized the almost insuperable difficulty of procuring Church legislation by the existing process of Acts of Parliament; but he also made it plain that the Enabling Bill, as it was termed, definitely assumed the retention of the establishment, and that he 'would rather go on as we are if disestablishment were the only alternative'. On 23 December 1919 the Bill received the royal assent.

The sixth Lambeth Conference was held in 1920, with Davidson presiding. Its chief work was an appeal to all Christian people for the reunion of Christendom on a much wider basis than had been previously conceived possible. It was followed by a remarkable series of movements on the part of the Anglican Church towards unity with nonconformists in England; with the Orthodox Churches; and with the Roman Catholic Church. It may truthfully be claimed that no former archbishop of Canterbury had ever been so greatly trusted and admired by Free churchmen as was Davidson. With the Orthodox Churches also a much closer relationship was created during Davidson's primacy; this was no doubt partly due to the strong stand which the archbishop took by means of his appeal to Lord Curzon, the secretary of state for foreign affairs, and in other ways, for the retention of the oecumenical patriarchate in Constantinople (1922–1923) and on behalf of the Christian populations in the Near East suffering persecution at Turkish hands. But it was also due to the fuller theological and personal knowledge which the events of the period during and after the War brought about between the Greek, Serb, and Russian Orthodox Churches and the Church of England. In August 1922 the patriarch and holy synod of Constantinople issued a declaration recognizing the validity of Anglican ordinations, but until the rest of the Orthodox Churches accept the declaration action cannot be taken on its basis. The Russian Church had particular cause for gratitude to Davidson. On 31 May 1922 the archbishop telegraphed to Lenin, president of the Soviet Republic, a strong protest from Anglican and Free Church leaders against the attack on the Russian Church in the person of its Patriarch Tikhon. A reply, denying the attack, was received from Moscow on 6 June. The persecution increased; and on 13 April 1923 a still stronger protest appeared over the signatures of the Archbishops of Canterbury and York, Cardinal Bourne, the leaders of the Free Churches, and the chief Rabbi. Public opinion was deeply stirred by this action, which at once impressed the Soviet government with the widespread resentment caused in Great Britain by the persecution of religion, and assured religious people in Russia of the deep sympathy felt for them abroad.

The movement for a *rapprochement* with the Roman Catholic Church was renewed by Viscount Halifax and the Abbé Portal, and took the form of a series of conversations between Anglican and Roman theologians held at Malines in the years 1921 to 1925 under the chairmanship of Cardinal Mercier. The first conversation (December 1921) was of a purely private character; but the archbishop of Canterbury agreed to give friendly cognizance to the conversations after learning from the cardinal that Pope Pius XI was giving a similar cognizance. Three further conversations took place, the personnel being strengthened on each side for the last two. It was made clear by Davidson and Mercier that there was no question of negotiations, but simply an attempt at 'some re-statement of controversial questions and some elucidation of perplexities'. After the death of Cardinal Mercier in January 1926, a fifth meeting was held to arrange about the reports, which were published in January 1928. Further conversations were immediately forbidden by the pope, who about the same time issued his encyclical *Mortalium animos*, which was directed against reunion movements in general. But although the dogmatic differences remained unbridged, a real step forward in actual understanding and charity had been made at Malines.

Few actions in the whole of his life made so much stir as the appeal which Archbishop Davidson issued during the General Strike which began on 3 May 1926. While condemning the strike as an act, he from the start urged that every possible effort should be made for a settlement in a spirit of co-operation and not dictated as the result of force. At the request of certain churchmen and Free churchmen he consulted with other leaders of the Churches, and ultimately issued on 7 May a strong appeal for the resumption of negotiations, involving 'simultaneously and concurrently' (1) the cancellation of the strike by the Trades Union Congress; (2) the renewal by the government of a subsidy to the coal industry for a short period; (3) the withdrawal by the mine owners of the new wages scales. The appeal represented a different policy from that of the government, which insisted that the strike must be cancelled before negotiations could begin. The British Broadcasting Corporation refused to broadcast, and the official *British Gazette* to publish, the appeal; and great excitement was caused. Davidson's action was much criticized at the time, but the labour world generally was deeply encouraged by his sympathy. On 17 May the strike was terminated unconditionally; but in the opinion of many the archbishop had given a great lead to the forces of peace.

During Davidson's last years of office

the question of the revision of the Prayer Book was brought to a head. By 1920 Convocation had finished the work begun in 1906. Its recommendations were larger than had been contemplated in the early days, and included difficult new proposals relating, in particular, to Reservation of the Sacrament, the outcome, in part, of war needs. From 1920 to 1927 the proposals were thoroughly reconsidered by the new Church Assembly in the first flush of youth, to the accompaniment of a flood of criticisms and suggestions. In the end a measure was produced with a revision on a still more ambitious scale. But the measure was only intended to authorize the permissive use of the revised Prayer Book; and the Prayer Book of 1662 remained as before. As the final stages drew near, controversy became more and more acute. It centred on Reservation for the sick and on an alternative Order of Holy Communion. The archbishop was challenged publicly by the evangelical leaders to say whether, if the Prayer Book measure were adopted, he would insist on obedience. His reply was not sufficiently definite to satisfy his critics; nor were they convinced by his statement that the revised Prayer Book involved no change in doctrine, but only a change of emphasis. The Church Assembly, after a vigorous debate, in June 1927 finally approved the measure by 517 votes to 133. The ecclesiastical committee of parliament in a lengthy report advised that the measure should proceed for the royal assent. On 14 December the Lords, after three days' debate, approved it by 241 votes to 88. But on the following day (15 December) the Commons, after an emotional debate in which the 'No Popery' cry was the dominant note, rejected the measure by 238 votes to 205. The archbishop, although deeply disappointed, decided with the bishops on a reintroduction of the measure with a clearer statement as to the limitations within which continuous Reservation would be allowed, and *inter alia* caused the insertion of the Black Rubric at the end of the Alternative Order of Holy Communion. But, after the Church Assembly had passed it with smaller majorities, the Book was again rejected by the Commons on 14 June 1928, by 266 votes to 220. The archbishop took the defeat bravely, but too calmly for those who wished at once to challenge the action of parliament. He knew that the Church was divided with regard to the revised Prayer Book, and that its most influential opponents in parliament were earnest evangelical churchmen.

On 12 November 1928 Davidson resigned, not because of the Prayer Book failure, but in order to give his successor time to prepare for the Lambeth Conference of 1930. He had been archbishop of Canterbury longer than any of his predecessors since William Warham (1504–1532). On his resignation he was created Baron Davidson of Lambeth on 14 November. The affection and sympathy of the public were expressed in the gift of over £17,000 presented to him to mark the completion of his twenty-five years' primacy, his eightieth birthday, and his golden wedding. He died at Chelsea 25 May 1930 at the age of eighty-two. Burial in Westminster Abbey was offered, but by his own wish he was buried in the cloister garth of Canterbury Cathedral.

In addition to the works already mentioned Davidson published *The Lambeth Conferences of 1867, 1878, and 1888* (1896), *The Christian Opportunity* (1904), *Captains and Comrades in the Faith* (1911), and *The Character and Call of the Church of England* (1912).

Primate during a most difficult period, Davidson certainly succeeded in giving a strong Christian witness in national life, and in maintaining the comprehensiveness of the Church of England, and especially freedom for scholarship and inquiry. He did not succeed in solving the ritual crisis —and this was partly due to the fact that the subject of ritual and Prayer Book revision was not one in which his whole soul was engaged. He was not therefore able to establish a basis for the exercise of lawful authority which the different parties in the Anglican Church were willing to accept. On the other hand, he immensely increased the influence of the Anglican communion in Christendom, and he saw the Church of England taking far more of a world view than it had taken previously. His own personal hold on the affection of Church people grew steadily. Regarded as a courtier and little known when he became archbishop, by the end of his life he was a popular figure: this was greatly due to the way in which his chairmanship of the Church Assembly (1920–1928) had revealed him to the rank and file of Church members. In his general policy he pursued a middle course; and he was often criticized for not giving a clear enough lead, and for being too ready to wait on circumstances. His capacities were essentially those of a chairman, and a chairman of extraordinary fairness. He was a most able administrator, while at the same time a man of great simplicity of character, and this won him the friendship and trust of men of widely different points of view.

There are portraits of Davidson by A. S. Cope at Wolvesey Palace, Winchester; by J. S. Sargent at Lambeth Palace; by P. A. de László at the Church House, Westminster; and by H. Riviere at Trinity College, Oxford, of which Davidson was elected an honorary fellow in 1903. A cartoon by 'Spy' appeared in *Vanity Fair* 19 December 1901.

[R. T. Davidson and W. Benham, *Life of Archbishop Tait*, 2 vols., 1891; G. K. A. Bell, *Life of Archbishop Davidson*, 2 vols., 1935.]

G. K. A. Bell.

DAVIS, HENRY WILLIAM CARLESS (1874–1928), historian, and editor of the Dictionary of National Biography from 1919 to 1928, was born at Ebley, near Stroud, Gloucestershire, 13 January 1874, the eldest of the five children—three sons and two daughters—of Henry Frederick Alexander Davis, solicitor, of Ebley, by his wife, Jessie Anna, third daughter of William Carless, M.D., of Stroud. He and his brothers and sisters were brought up in somewhat straitened circumstances by their mother, who was a woman of character and ability. She removed in 1884 to Weymouth, opened there a school for young children, including her own, and managed it so successfully that she was subsequently (1903) appointed first headmistress of Weymouth College preparatory school. Henry Davis entered Weymouth College in 1886, made his mark there as a boy of unusual capacity, and in 1891 proceeded to Balliol College, Oxford, with a Brackenbury history scholarship. Except to his close friends, who admired his qualities, and to his tutors, who recognized his promise, he was not well known in college; but he came to the front when, after gaining first classes in classical moderations (1893) and *literae humaniores* (1895) as well as the Jenkyns exhibition, he was elected in 1895 to a fellowship at All Souls College.

Davis's interest in history had been awakened at school by the teaching of the Rev. Thomas Brace Waitt; and at Oxford, under the guidance of Arthur Lionel Smith [q.v.], of Balliol, he found in that subject his true bent. He therefore abandoned his intention of entering the civil service, and settled down to the career of a student and teacher of history and especially of medieval history. Save for a short spell of teaching at University College, Bangor (1896–1897), he lived in All Souls from 1895 to 1902, where among his friends and contemporaries were Herbert Hensley Henson, afterwards bishop of Durham, (Sir) John Simon, and (Sir) C. Grant Robertson. In 1897 he won the Lothian prize. In the same year he was appointed to a lecturership at New College, and thus began his twenty years' experience as a college tutor at Oxford, in the course of which he built up a great reputation as a scholar and teacher of the most exacting standard. In 1899 he exchanged his post at New College for a lecturership at Balliol, and on the expiry of his All Souls fellowship in 1902 he was appointed an official fellow of his old college.

Davis had already published *Balliol College* (1899) in the series of 'College Histories', a life of *Charlemagne* (1900) for the 'Heroes of the Nations' series, as well as articles, from 1901, in the *English Historical Review*. But it was the appearance in 1905 of his book *England under the Normans and Angevins* which revealed the full measure of his gifts as an historian and made his name. The book at once became a standard authority and by 1930 had reached a tenth edition; but it remains the only substantial contribution to narrative medieval history which Davis made. He wrote in 1911 a masterly little summary, *Medieval Europe*, in the 'Home University Library' series, and many articles and reviews in historical journals, but after 1905 he devoted a great part of his literary energies to editorial work, preparing an edition of Jowett's translation of Aristotle's *Politics* (1905), a revision of Bishop Stubbs's *Select Charters* (1913), and embarking upon a valuable, if ambitious, calendar of royal charters, *Regesta Regum Anglo-Normannorum* (vol. i, 1913), which, as events proved, he was never able to complete.

Davis's influence as a teacher, however, was of greater moment than his reputation as a writer. Few Oxford tutors can have inspired in their pupils more genuine respect and regard. If his austere manner, steady gaze, and precise speech compelled attention and a touch of awe, closer acquaintance revealed behind the reserve a friendly soul, much quiet humour, and above all an unstinting devotion to his pupils' needs. He lacked entirely the infectious enthusiasm of a teacher like A. L. Smith, but he set an example of hard work and fine scholarship which won immediate response from almost every one whom he taught. His lectures were very carefully prepared and delivered, and largely attended, but he made no effort to draw big audiences. With his writing and teaching he combined much examining and administrative work. He was junior dean of Balliol from 1906 to 1910, an examiner in the final school of modern history from 1907 to 1909 (and again 1919–1921), and Chichele lecturer in foreign history in 1913; he served on the board of his faculty from 1905, on the general board of the faculties from 1913, and became a curator of the Bodleian Library in 1914. He was much interested in women's education and joined the council of Somerville College in 1908.

The years of the European War, 1914–1918, made a complete break in Davis's university activities and came near to deflecting the whole course of his career. After collaborating in the production of the series of 'Oxford Pamphlets' on the War, and publishing a dispassionate analysis of the *Political Thought of Heinrich von Treitschke* (1914), he went to London early in 1915 and helped to organize the 'Trade Clearing House', a bureau of commercial intelligence arising out of the Postal Censorship, sponsored by the Admiralty and the Board of Trade. By the following summer the Trade Clearing House had expanded into the 'War Trade Intelligence Department', forming a constituent part of the Ministry of Blockade under the ultimate control of the Foreign Office. Of this department Davis was the vice-chairman for three and a half years. Davis himself wrote subsequently an official, but unfinished, *History of the Blockade* (1920), which describes in detail the elaborate departmental machinery which was devised to put the blockade of the enemy Powers into execution. In his own department his organizing ability, power of rapid decision, and almost limitless capacity for work, backed by his fine personal qualities, were a source of inspiration to his colleagues, and attracted the notice of the Cabinet. After the Armistice he served on the large British delegation to the Peace Conference in Paris from December 1918 till March 1919, and then for a few weeks, at the invitation of Sir Arthur Steel-Maitland, undertook the duties of acting-director of the Department of Overseas Trade in London. He received the C.B.E. in the new year honours of that year.

An opportunity of high appointment in the public service was now presented to Davis, had his ambition lain in that direction; but he decided otherwise, and in April 1919 returned to Oxford, where for two years he resumed the routine of college and university work. It was at this time that he undertook the editorial direction of the DICTIONARY OF NATIONAL BIOGRAPHY, which had been conveyed in 1917 to the university of Oxford to be continued by the Clarendon Press [see SMITH, Reginald John]. Arrangements had to be made for the continuation of the Dictionary from 1911, to which year it had been brought down by the previous editor, Sir Sidney Lee [q.v.]. The names to be included in the Dictionary, and contributors of the biographical notices, were selected by Davis and his co-editor in consultation with an Oxford committee and a number of external advisers. Alike in his dealings with contributors and in his conscientious treatment of the material Davis was an exemplary editor. He had a deft and skilful touch, and although he worked with great rapidity he never spared himself the more laborious part of the routine. The volume for which he was responsible appeared in 1927, bringing the Dictionary down to the end of the year 1921. He wrote a short preface and contributed several articles.

In 1921, shortly after he had embarked on the editorship of the Dictionary, and in the midst of the heavy routine of Oxford teaching after the War, Davis accepted an invitation to occupy the chair of modern history at Manchester University. His health had suffered from the strain of his war-work, and the new post promised him more leisure for his own studies. He settled at Bowdon, and spent there three and a half busy but quiet years. His studies now took a modern turn—due partly to the requirements of his professorship and partly to his interest in post-war political questions. When, therefore, he was elected Ford's lecturer at Oxford for 1924–1925, he took as his subject *The Age of Grey and Peel* (posthumously published 1930). He gave the lectures in Hilary Term 1925, and in the course of that term he was appointed to succeed Sir Charles Firth as regius professor of modern history at Oxford. He thereby became a fellow of Oriel College. In the same year he was elected an honorary fellow of Balliol College and a fellow of the British Academy.

Davis returned to Oxford as regius professor in the summer of 1925. In addition to the duties of his chair he undertook much committee work, both for his new college and for the university. As a curator of the Bodleian Library he was called upon to take a prominent part in the discussions on the question of the extension of the Library and to move in Congregation, in May 1928, the official proposals for Bodleian extension in their earliest form (subsequently modified by the report of the Bodleian Commission, and finally adopted by the university in 1931). Outside his university activities he was appointed in 1925 to serve on the Unemployment Insurance Committee under the chairmanship of Lord Blanesburgh, and in 1927 he went to Geneva as British representative on a committee of experts who were charged by the International Labour Office to investigate and report upon factory legislation in several European countries. These public services—the aftermath of his war-time reputation—made heavy demands on his time and energies during 1926 and 1927.

Davis succeeded to the regius chair of modern history at Oxford at a time when changes in the syllabus were deemed desirable, but as it turned out he had not time to initiate reforms. His ideas on the needs of the school would probably have taken shape in accordance with the views expressed in his inaugural lecture on *The Study of History*, delivered in November 1925. For the moment his commitments were heavy enough. He was getting ready for press his Ford lectures, the *Dictionary of National Biography, 1912–1921*, and the *Report* of the Blanesburgh Committee, editing *Essays in History presented to Reginald Lane Poole* (1926), and preparing his Raleigh lecture for the British Academy, *The Great Game in Asia* (delivered November 1926)—one of the liveliest of his writings. In the midst of such activities, while engaged in examining at Edinburgh University, he died of pneumonia, at Edinburgh, after a few days' illness, 28 June 1928. He was buried at Wolvercote cemetery, Oxford.

Davis married in 1912 Jennie, only daughter of Walter Lindup, of Bampton Grange, Oxfordshire; three sons were born of the marriage.

Davis was a young-looking man, whose features and reddish hair changed little during middle age. His expression was rather grave, his manner reserved but modest, his gaze singularly penetrating, in spite of short sight, and his words ever to the point. His learning, never paraded, was very great in range and depth. But, as his career shows, he was not in the least the don or scholar of convention. Men of the most diverse types found his qualities of mind and heart peculiarly attractive, and his circle of friends in Oxford and outside was very large. Few who met him failed to feel the impress of his high intelligence and unsullied character. His influence upon the Oxford of his time was very great; yet his comparatively early death seemed to many to have left his fullest powers unrevealed and his greatest work unaccomplished.

[*The Times*, 29 June 1928; F. M. Powicke in *The English Historical Review*, October 1928; J. R. H. Weaver and A. L. Poole, *Henry William Carless Davis, A Memoir, and a Selection of his Historical Papers* (with portrait and bibliography), 1933.]

J. R. H. Weaver.

DAWKINS, Sir WILLIAM BOYD (1837–1929), geologist, palaeontologist, and antiquary, was born 26 December 1837 at Buttington, near Welshpool, the only son of the Rev. Richard Dawkins, vicar of Buttington, by his wife, Mary Ann Youngman. He was educated at Rossall School and at Jesus College, Oxford, where he graduated in 1860 with a first class in natural science. In 1861 he was the first recipient of the Burdett-Coutts scholarship, which had just been founded at Oxford in order to promote the study of geology; and thenceforth he devoted his life to this and allied sciences. For eight years (1861–1869) Dawkins was a member of the Geological Survey of Great Britain, and mapped parts of Kent and the Thames valley. In 1869 he was appointed curator of the Manchester Museum, and in 1874 first professor of geology at Owens College, which became the Victoria University of Manchester in 1880. He occupied the chair until his retirement in 1908.

At the time when Dawkins began his researches there was widespread interest in the subject of the antiquity of man and in the possible occurrence of human implements associated with the remains of extinct animals in Western Europe. He was thus led to study these problems, and he soon became a pioneer in the modern methods of dealing with them. So early as 1859 and the two following years he examined the deposits on the floor of Wookey Hole, the cave near Wells in Somerset; and in his first paper communicated to the Geological Society, in 1862, he showed that the cave had been occupied during the Pleistocene period at times by hyenas, at other times by man. The stone and bone implements of primitive (Palaeolithic) man were clearly associated with remains of the mammoth and other Pleistocene mammals. In 1875–1878 Dawkins joined the Rev. John Magens Mello, rector of St. Thomas, Brampton, Derbyshire, in making similar excavations in caves in the Cresswell Crags, near Worksop, on the border of Derbyshire. Here the evidence for the contemporaneity of man with extinct mammals proved to be still more abundant, and Dawkins was able to recognize a definite succession of faunas and clear progression in the handiwork of successive human races. In the latest Pleistocene deposit he discovered a piece of bone bearing an incised figure of the head of a horse—the first example of cave man's art met with in Britain. After long experience he concluded that none of the existing caves could be older than the beginning of the Pleistocene period, because the land surface was always being worn away so rapidly by natural agencies that the open caves of earlier date had been destroyed. In 1903, however, he ended his researches on the subject by discovering in an old fissure in the limestone at Dove Holes, Derbyshire, some bones and teeth of Pliocene mammals which had evidently been washed out of a hyena den of that earlier period. There were no accompanying traces of man.

In 1874 Dawkins summarized his results in a volume entitled *Cave Hunting*, and in 1880 he published another work of wider scope, *Early Man in Britain and his Place in the Tertiary Period*. The latter work will long remain a classic, for it definitely marks an era in the progress of geological knowledge.

While occupied with the excavation of caves Dawkins realized that a more precise knowledge of the mammalian bones and teeth was needed to determine the relative age of the various Palaeolithic and Neolithic deposits in which human remains occurred. He accordingly made numerous studies of these fossils, and as an illustration of his thoroughness special reference may be made to his monograph on the cave lion, which was written in co-operation with William Ayshford Sanford for the Palaeontographical Society in 1866–1872 (*British Pleistocene Mammalia*, vol. i). He also studied fossil mammals in general, and he was one of the first to point out that they could be used as well as shells for dividing the Tertiary rocks into successive well-marked stages.

In his later years Dawkins was much occupied with economic geology, and was often consulted about water-supply and engineering projects. While engaged on plans for a Channel tunnel in 1882 onwards he suggested that the shaft which had been sunk at the Dover end would be a suitable spot for boring to find the buried coal-field which must underlie south-east England. This boring, which was made in 1890, reached productive coal measures at a depth of 1,100 feet, and inaugurated the exploitation of the Kent coal-field.

Apart from his scientific work Dawkins had very wide interests, and he took an active part in the life of his adopted city, Manchester. His personal charm and gift of simple exposition attracted large audiences to his popular lectures at the Museum, and he was always a welcome speaker at public meetings. At Oxford he had become an accomplished classical scholar, and in 1875 he widened his experience by travelling round the world, going direct to Australia and New Zealand and returning across North America. In later years he paid other visits to the United States and Canada, and he also travelled much in France, Switzerland, and Italy, where he visited the museums to examine material for his various researches. Before the European War he made a hobby of deep-sea fishing.

Dawkins was elected F.R.S. in 1867 and an honorary fellow of Jesus College, Oxford, in 1882, and was knighted in 1919. The Geological Society of London awarded him the Lyell medal in 1889 and the Prestwich medal in 1918. He married twice: first, in 1866 Frances (died 1921), daughter of Robert Speke Evans, clerk to the Admiralty, and had one daughter; secondly, in 1922 Mary, daughter of William Poole, of Leamington, and widow of Hubert Congreve, civil engineer. He died at Bowdon, Cheshire, 15 January 1929.

[*Proceedings* of the Royal Society, vol. cvii, B, 1931 (portrait); *Geological Magazine* (containing list of writings and portrait), December 1909.] A. S. Woodward.

DE FERRANTI, SEBASTIAN ZIANI (1864–1930), electrical engineer and inventor. [See Ferranti.]

DENT, JOSEPH MALABY (1849–1926), publisher, was born at Darlington 30 August 1849, the fourth son and tenth child of George Dent, house-painter, by his wife, Isabella, daughter of Hugh Railton, of Staindrop, co. Durham. George

Dent's chief interest lay in music, and when his business failed in 1859 he took to music-teaching and the sale of musical instruments for a living. Joseph was sent to an elementary school in Darlington, and had already grown fond of books and of reading Scott's novels before he was eleven. At the age of thirteen he left school, and began his working career, being apprenticed to a printer as 'all-round workman'. But he was much more attracted by the bookbinding in the workshop, and soon transferred his apprenticeship to that craft to which all his life he remained devoted. He next went to work with a Mr. Rutherford, a bookbinder in Darlington. During his boyhood Dent suffered a good deal from lameness due to an accident, and was unable to play games, but as a consequence he developed his taste for reading, which included books like Macaulay's *Essays* and Boswell's *Life of Johnson*.

When his employer failed, Dent tried to get jobs in Darlington which he could do for himself, and set up a hand-press in his bedroom. But this was not enough for a livelihood, so in August 1867, when nearly eighteen, he joined an elder brother in London. He secured work with a bookbinder in Bucklersbury and steadily made his way, working from eight in the morning till eight, sometimes ten, at night. In 1870 Dent married Hannah, daughter of George Wiggins, and, having finished his London apprenticeship, in 1872 opened business on his own account in a workshop in Hoxton. He gradually built up a business there and, finding a toy-shop to let in East Road, took it, and was able to employ a man and boy.

Four sons and two daughters were born to Dent, and it was a struggle for the young bookbinder to pay his way. About 1881 he moved to 69 Great Eastern Street, but at the end of 1887, just after he had lost his wife, his bookbinding factory was burnt, and it seemed that the results of fifteen years' struggle would be wasted. However, with the insurance money and a friend's help, he was able to buy a bookbinder's plant and to set up in a larger way in the rebuilt factory. His first experiments in publishing soon followed. In the autumn of 1888 he published his first two books in the 'Temple Library'—Lamb's *Essays of Elia* and *The Last Essays of Elia*, edited by Augustine Birrell. About this time, too, he became an outside member of Toynbee Hall. In 1890 Dent married as his second wife Alexandra Campbell, daughter of Thomas Burnett Main, by whom he had two sons and four daughters. A voyage to Italy with the Toynbee Travellers' Club in 1890 led him to project the 'Medieval Towns' series, the volumes of which were designed to reveal 'the personalities of towns', through their architectural and other features.

A series of eighteenth-century novelists, from Henry Fielding to Jane Austen, followed, and by the early 'nineties Dent was fairly established as publisher. Meanwhile he was gaining an American market and made the first of many voyages to the United States in 1893. In the same year he produced a 'Temple' (pocket) Shakespeare in a special format, and secured an expert editor in (Sir) Israel Gollancz [q.v.]. A translation of Balzac's novels, edited by George Saintsbury, was produced simultaneously. Dent's friend, Frederick H. Evans, a Cheapside bookseller, who was a man of remarkable literary taste, was of much service in all these earlier adventures. Another pocket series, the 'Temple Classics', begun in 1896, strengthened Dent's reputation as a publisher with original ideas.

In 1898 Dent moved from Great Eastern Street to larger premises at 29–30 Bedford Street, Strand. This meant an increased outlay, but, nothing daunted, he projected a 'Haddon Hall Library'—books dealing with outdoor life and sporting subjects—a larger 'Temple' Shakespeare, and a complete edition of Lamb, over which, unluckily, there were some copyright difficulties.

In 1904 Dent planned a still more ambitious scheme—a working library of the world's literature, within the means of every book-buyer, to be sold at a shilling a volume. When it came to estimating the cost of such a series, it was clear that a greater capital would be required than the firm could command. Eventually this difficulty was overcome, and Dent found a good lieutenant in his son, Hugh Dent, and, on the literary side, a collaborator in Ernest Rhys, who became editor and suggested the title 'Everyman's Library'. A scheme of a thousand volumes was projected, and in the first twelve months 153 volumes were produced. Dent showed great enthusiasm and courage in working out the scheme with a very meagre staff and in the face of obstacles which would have put a strain on any publisher's resources. The huge equipment required for the series involved the finding of a site outside London, and in 1907 a model factory was opened at Garden City, Letchworth, where the printing and binding could be carried on under a single control. In 1911 Dent was able to secure a corner site on the other side of Bedford Street, and put up the spacious building, Aldine House, which remains the head-quarters of the firm. A weekly paper, literary and critical, with the title of *Everyman* was among his ventures at this busy period. Through his Paris branch he started the 'Collection Gallia', and from London the 'Wayfarer's Library' of popular fiction and holiday literature.

Two of Dent's younger sons who had entered the firm in 1913 went on active service at the outbreak of the War in 1914, and both were killed. The War involved a long pause in the production of 'Everyman's Library', and Dent's hope of living to see a thousand volumes completed had to be given up. However, the 'Library' maintained its hold, even at an increased price, and, with the aid of a branch in Canada and of Australian agents, widened its inter-Colonial market.

Dent did not confine his activities to publishing. He wrote, besides his *Memoirs* (1928), introductions to sundry volumes of 'Everyman's Library', including Mrs. Gaskell's *Cranford*, and several characteristic essays and pamphlets on the making and printing of books. An enthusiastic educationist, he joined the council of the British and Foreign School Society, and also helped Miss Margaret McMillan in her nursery school movement.

Dent died at his house in Croydon 9 May 1926, in his seventy-seventh year, and was buried at Sanderstead near that town. The most life-like portraits of him are a drawing by Dora Noyes, reproduced as frontispiece to his *Memoirs*, and a photograph by Frederick H. Evans.

[J. M. Dent, *Memoirs*, 1928; private information; personal knowledge.]

E. Rhys.

DE ROBECK, Sir JOHN MICHAEL, baronet (1862–1928), admiral of the fleet, was born at Gowran Grange, Naas, co. Kildare, 10 June 1862. He was the second son of John Henry Edward Fock, fourth Baron de Robeck, of Gowran Grange, an Irishman of Swedish descent, and the only British subject holding a Swedish title of nobility. John's great-grandfather fought with the French army in the American War of Independence, but was subsequently naturalized as a British subject and settled in Ireland; his grandfather served in Spain under Sir John Moore. His mother was Sophia Charlotte, daughter of William Fitzwilliam Burton, of Burton Hall, co. Carlow. Entering the *Britannia* as a naval cadet in 1875, De Robeck was less interested in the mechanical aspects of his profession, at a time when engines and high-powered guns were exciting attention, than in seamanship. His only first-class certificate on passing out of the *Britannia* was in that subject, but it was apparent that he had the makings of a leader of men as well as of a good seaman. His early career, when he served first in China waters and then on the Newfoundland coast, with periods in home waters, was at first uneventful. Between the time when he left the *Britannia* in 1877 and his promotion to commander twenty years later, he was appointed to no fewer than twenty-four ships, including two spells of duty in the *Britannia*, which suggested, as was, in fact, the case, that the Admiralty regarded him as peculiarly well fitted to assist in the difficult task of training boys for the naval service, by reason of his open and attractive character and his keen interest in all forms of sport and athletics.

As a commander De Robeck's first independent command was the destroyer *Desperate*. In 1900 he was given the cruiser *Pyramus*, a unit of the Mediterranean squadron. He was serving in this ship when, two years later, he was posted to captain. Although he remained inspecting-captain of training ships until his promotion to rear-admiral in 1911, he had been marked out for the command of small craft; and when, early in 1912, the new post of admiral of patrols was created, as part of a scheme of reorganization of the naval forces in home waters, De Robeck proved fully equal to the position. He had under his orders four flotillas of destroyers, with cruisers as 'leaders', and he not only brought this force to a high standard of efficiency, but also laid the foundations of a reserve of motor-boats, which proved of the greatest value during the European War. After accomplishing this dual task to the satisfaction of the Admiralty, he went on half-pay, with the result that when war broke out in August 1914 he was unemployed.

De Robeck was, however, an officer whose services could not be dispensed with, and on the mobilization of the naval forces he was immediately chosen to command the ninth cruiser squadron, which was commissioned from the reserve. This squadron was ordered to patrol one of the mid-Atlantic areas, with its base at Finisterre. The new admiral's special duty was to protect British merchant ships and to harry those of the enemy. During his period of duty on that station he captured first the North German Lloyd liner *Schlesien* and then the *Græcia*.

As soon as the decision of the War Cabinet to send a naval expedition to the Dardanelles was communicated to the Admiralty early in 1915, De Robeck was appointed as second-in-command to Vice-Admiral (Sir) Sackville Carden [q.v.], to whom this difficult enterprise had been confided. He hoisted his flag in the battleship *Vengeance* in time to take part in the bombardment of the outer forts of the Dardanelles, an operation which was made in the middle of February and lasted several days. The bombardment was quite ineffective, as has since been revealed, but plans for further naval operations were immediately drawn up. The two officers co-operated with conspicuous success in this task, and when Carden had to return home in March owing to ill-health De Robeck, with the full concurrence of Vice-Admiral Rosslyn Wemyss, who was also on the station and was his senior, was chosen to take over the command of all the naval forces engaged in the operations against the Dardanelles. So complete had been the confidence between Carden and De Robeck that when the former had gone home, the latter expressed himself well satisfied with Carden's plans for the reduction of the forts at the Narrows. This movement was carried out on 18 March. Owing to the prolonged opportunity for mine-laying which the enemy had enjoyed, the three battleships *Irresistible*, *Ocean*, and *Bouvet* (French) were sunk, and little progress was made towards the admiral's objective. The ill success of this plan was not without its effect on the mind of De Robeck, who, with a clear appreciation of the situation, resisted strenuously the proposal that a further attempt should be made to force the Straits with naval forces, unsupported by the army which had been assembled under General Sir Ian Hamilton. Events had convinced him that military co-operation was essential. Unfortunately a month elapsed before the joint operation could be carried out (25 April). The military expedition, which was placed under the command of General Sir Charles Carmichael Monro [q.v.], proved a failure in spite of the loyal co-operation of the fleet; and its ill success was subsequently the matter of a controversy in which, however, De Robeck, who had shown marked ability as a leader, was in no way involved. His work and that of the forces under his command was in fact highly praised, and by none more unreservedly than by Sir Ian Hamilton, who wrote in his first dispatch (20 May 1915): 'Throughout the events I have chronicled, the Royal Navy has been father and mother to the Army. Not one of us but realizes how much he owes to Vice-Admiral de Robeck; to the warships, French and British; to the destroyers, mine-sweepers, picket-boats, and to all their dauntless crews, who took no thought of themselves, but risked everything to give their soldier comrades a fair run in at the enemy.' De Robeck was indeed fortunate in winning the approval of all who were in any way associated with the disastrous attempt to force the Dardanelles, and when the withdrawal of the army was decided upon he retained the supreme command of the Allied naval forces which carried out on the night of 8–9 January 1916, with consummate success and with relatively small loss of life, this most difficult operation. For his services at Gallipoli he was created K.C.B. in 1916.

The abandonment of the Dardanelles coincided with a number of changes in the command of the grand fleet, owing to the recall of Admiral Sir John Jellicoe to the Admiralty as first sea lord and his relief by Admiral Sir David Beatty, who had hitherto commanded the battle-cruiser fleet. This reorganization of the high command in the North Sea offered an opportunity of giving De Robeck further employment, and he was made vice-admiral commanding the second battle squadron, hoisting his flag in the *George V* on 3 December 1916. He retained his command on being promoted to the substantive rank of vice-admiral in 1917, and his association with the grand fleet continued until May 1919, when it ceased to exist as a unified command.

De Robeck was one of the senior officers who subsequently received the special thanks of parliament for his war services, being given a grant of £10,000 and created a baronet in 1919, besides being gazetted G.C.M.G. (1919) and G.C.B. (1921). In 1919 De Robeck was chosen as commander-in-chief of the Mediterranean fleet, hoisting his flag in the *Iron Duke*, which had been the flagship of Admiral Jellicoe at the battle of Jutland. It was an appropriate appointment, for no one of his rank was better qualified to act as high commissioner at Constantinople, the additional duty which was assigned to him pending the conclusion of a separate treaty of peace with Turkey. His period of duty in the Mediterranean was otherwise uneventful. On relinquishing this command in April 1922 he was appointed in August commander-in-chief of the Atlantic fleet, his flagship being the *Queen Elizabeth*, which had been Admiral Beatty's flagship when he took over the command of the grand fleet.

De Robeck's resignation of this command in 1924 marked the end of his sea career, although he remained on the active list and was promoted to admiral of the fleet in November 1925, having become admiral five years before. On coming ashore De Robeck was able once more to take part in sport of all kinds. He was a keen follower of hounds, as well as a good shot, and owing to his sustained interest in cricket he was elected president of the Marylebone Cricket Club in 1925, being the first naval officer to hold that position.

De Robeck married in 1922 Hilda Maud, daughter of Colonel Augustus Henry Macdonald-Moreton, Coldstream Guards, of Hillgrove, Bembridge, Isle of Wight, and widow of Colonel Sir Simon Macdonald Lockhart, fifth baronet. There were no children of the marriage, and the baronetcy became extinct on the death of De Robeck, which took place suddenly at his house in London 20 January 1928.

There is a portrait-drawing of De Robeck by Francis Dodd in the Imperial War Museum, South Kensington.

[*The Times*, 21 January 1928; Navy Lists; personal knowledge.] A. Hurd.

DEWAR, Sir JAMES (1842–1923), natural philosopher, was born at Kincardine-on-Forth, Scotland, 20 September 1842, the youngest son of Thomas Dewar, vintner, of that town, by his wife, Ann Eadie, daughter of a shipowner. At the age of ten his schooling was interrupted by an attack of rheumatic fever, caused by a fall through the ice, and during the period of incapacity that followed he found occupation in making fiddles—an exercise to which he was wont to attribute his manipulative skill. On recovering from his illness he was sent to Dollar Academy, and thence, about 1858, to Edinburgh University. There he worked successively under James David Forbes [q.v.], the professor of natural philosophy, under Lyon (Lord) Playfair [q.v.], the professor of chemistry, whose demonstrator he was, and, on Playfair's resignation, under his successor Alexander Crum Brown. In 1869 he was appointed lecturer on chemistry (later professor) in the Royal (Dick) Veterinary College, and from 1873 he was also assistant chemist to the Highland and Agricultural Society, with the duty of delivering what he called 'peripatetic lectures'. In 1875 he left Edinburgh for Cambridge, on his election to the Jacksonian chair of natural experimental philosophy. Two years later he was elected Fullerian professor of chemistry at the Royal Institution of Great Britain, London. Both these chairs he held until his death, which took place in London 27 March 1923. While at Edinburgh he married in 1871 Helen Rose, daughter of William Banks, of that city. They had no children.

Dewar's first published paper, presented to the Royal Society of Edinburgh in 1867, described a 'simple mechanical arrangement' for illustrating the structure of the non-saturated hydrocarbons, and showed how it could be used to represent seven different formulae for benzene. The device was sent by Playfair to the German chemist F. A. Kekulé, the author of the well-known ring formula for that substance, who in consequence invited Dewar to spend the summer of 1867 in the laboratory at Ghent. Other subjects on which Dewar worked while at Edinburgh were chlorosulphuric acid, the oxidation products of picoline, the thermal equivalents of the oxides of chlorine, the temperature of the sun and of the electric spark, and the specific heat of Graham's hydrogenium. The last-mentioned investigation is noteworthy because in it, in order to prevent the influx of heat into his calorimeter, Dewar employed, in 1872, the vacuum jacket which later proved indispensable for the liquefaction of gases, and became, though not in his hands, the 'Thermos' flask of commerce. Similarly, the use of coco-nut charcoal for absorbing gases, which also played a most important part in his later work, was mentioned in a paper published with Professor Peter Guthrie Tait [q.v.], in 1874, on a 'new method of obtaining very perfect vacua'. Dewar's interest in biological subjects, which repeatedly appeared in his subsequent researches, was shown by his investigation with Dr. Arthur Gamgee [q.v.] of the constitution and physiological relations of cystine (1871), and by the elaborate studies conducted from 1873 onwards with John Gray M'Kendrick, professor of physiology in Glasgow University from 1876 to 1906, on the physiological action of light on the eye.

Soon after coming south Dewar joined George Downing Liveing [q.v.], then the professor of chemistry at Cambridge, in a series of spectroscopic investigations the results of which were published at intervals over a quarter of a century. Some of this work was done at Cambridge: but the Royal Institution, where he had better laboratory facilities, became the chief centre of Dewar's experimental activities, and, indeed, of his whole life, and it was there that his work on the liquefaction of gases was carried out. In 1878, at a Friday evening lecture, he showed in operation the apparatus by which L. P. Cailletet had effected the partial liquefaction of oxygen; and at another lecture, in 1884, he exhibited the gas in the form of a true liquid by the aid of a modification of the apparatus of Z. F. Wroblewski and K. S. Olszewski. In 1891, using essentially improved methods, he discovered that both it and liquid ozone are attracted by the magnet. Hydrogen, the only one of Faraday's 'permanent' gases which had not been liquefied, was for the first time collected by Dewar as a liquid in an open vessel in 1898, and in the following year he obtained it as a transparent ice. For this work he built a large machine, weighing a couple of tons, in which he made use of the Joule-Thomson effect by continuously expanding the highly compressed gas through a fine orifice. His success was largely due to the inclusion of two novel features—the vacuum jacket as a means of heat-insulation, and a device consisting of a coiled tube which gave sufficient elasticity to enable the liquid gas to be drawn off without fracture of the glass by the intense cold. He also essayed the liquefaction of helium, the only known gas not reduced to the liquid state, but had not succeeded when, in 1908, H. Kamerlingh Onnes, working at Leyden along the general lines which Dewar had marked out, obtained the liquid.

In 1902, the year in which he was president at Belfast of the British Association, Dewar again turned his attention to charcoal, studying the conditions under which it must be prepared in order to develop the greatest activity, and finding that its power of absorbing gases is enormously increased by cold. He used it for the liquefaction of gases, the analysis of gaseous mixtures without liquefaction, and, above all, for the production of very high vacua; this last application probably contributed more than any other single agency to the advances made by atomic physics in immediately succeeding years. Charcoal also enabled him to make vacuum storage vessels of metal larger and stronger than was possible with glass; for he found that a portion of charcoal placed in the vacuous space absorbed occluded gas escaping from the metal and thus maintained the vacuum.

In producing liquid gases Dewar always had in view their utilization in opening up new fields to research. Thus as soon as he commanded them in quantity, besides devising methods for their thermometry and making determinations of their physical constants, he applied them to a wide range of pioneer explorations of the properties of matter at very low temperatures—chemical and photographic action, phosphorescence, the cohesion and strength of materials, and, with Professor (afterwards Sir) John Ambrose Fleming, of University College, London, electric and magnetic effects such as conduction, thermo-electricity, dielectric constants, and magnetic permeability. With Henri Moissan, Dewar liquefied (1897) and solidified (1903) fluorine; and he made several researches on radium, investigating with Sir William Crookes [q.v.] the effect of extreme cold on its emanations (1903), examining with Pierre Curie the gases occluded or given off by it (1904), and determining the rate at which it evolves helium (1908). A notable research, published in 1913, showed that the mean atomic specific heats of the elements between the boiling-points of liquid nitrogen and hydrogen exhibit, when plotted in terms of their atomic weights, a definite periodic variation instead of being approximately uniform as they are at ordinary temperatures. Similar observations, published posthumously, of the molecular specific heats of many series or homologous groups of inorganic and organic compounds revealed some striking relations.

Reverting during the European War, 'in the restricted time left for research after meeting the demands of government departments', to the soap bubble, which had been the subject of the first (1878–1879) of the nine courses of Christmas lectures for juveniles which he delivered at the Royal Institution, Dewar elucidated the conditions necessary for the production of long-lived bubbles and flat films, and studied the interference colours displayed when a jet of air was made to play upon their surface. At this period also he made from the roof of the Institution a series of observations of sky radiation with a delicate charcoal thermoscope.

The papers recording the spectroscopic researches which Dewar made with Liveing were published in collected form in 1915, and the rest of his papers in 1927, both by the Cambridge University Press. Although these volumes contain some 2,000 pages they leave untouched many aspects of his work. They tell nothing, for example, of the experiments resulting in the invention of cordite which he and Sir Frederick Augustus Abel [q.v.] carried out as members of the government committee on explosives (1888–1891), nor of the special chemical and other researches entailed by his large practice as an expert witness; and they do not suggest that he was an authority on sewage disposal and water-supply, and a member of the Balfour commission on London water-supply (1893–1894), and that for many years he and Crookes made daily chemical and bacteriological analyses of the water distributed to the metropolis.

Dewar, who was elected F.R.S. in 1877, knighted in 1904, and received many honours from scientific societies in Europe and America, was essentially an artist. Well read in English literature, especially poetry, he was devoted to music, and a little violin-playing, with his wife as accompanist, often ended the day's work in the small hours of the morning. His rooms at the Royal Institution and his house at Cambridge were filled with *objets d'art* of all kinds, and he was a fine judge of wine and tobacco. Though sometimes choleric and prone to vigour of expression, he was a kindly and generous man, and while impatient of pretension and of dishonesty, whether mental or material, he was always ready to help the genuine inquirer. His contributions to science lay rather in the discovery of new facts than in the elaboration of theory: as an experimenter he was unsurpassed, as daring and imaginative in conception as he was brilliant and sure in execution.

Peterhouse, Cambridge, of which Dewar was a fellow, possesses a portrait of him by Sir W. Q. Orchardson; the Royal Institution a bronze portrait panel by Sir Bertram McKennal; the Chemical Society a portrait by René de l'Hôpital; the National Portrait Gallery a bronze bust by G. D. Macdougald and a bronze statuette by C. Melilli; and the Scottish National Portrait Gallery a portrait by his nephew Dr. Thomas W. Dewar and a copy of the Orchardson portrait.

[Agnes M. Clerke in *Proceedings* of the Royal Institution, vol. xvi, 699–718; H. E. Armstrong, *ibid.* vol. xix, 354–412, vol. xxi, 735-785, and *James Dewar* (a lecture given at the Royal Institution 18 January 1924); J. D. Hamilton Dickson in *Peterhouse Magazine*, 1923 (privately printed); personal knowledge.]

H. M. Ross.

DE WET, CHRISTIAAN RUDOLPH (1854–1922), Boer general and politician, was born at Leeuwkop, Smithfield district, in the former Orange Free State republic 7 October 1854. He was the sixth son of Jacobus Ignatius De Wet, of De Wetsdorp, by his wife, Aletta Susanna Margaretha, daughter of Gert Cornelis Strijdom. Of his early years little is known save that he was privately educated and lived the roving life common to the nomad Boers of the period. During the Transvaal War of 1880–1881 De Wet served with the republican forces, taking part in the various engagements which culminated in the British disaster on Majuba Hill (27 February 1881). After the retrocession of the Transvaal he remained in that country farming for some years, in the course of which he was elected (1885) to represent Lydenburg in the republican Volksraad. But ordered routine did not suit him. He resigned his seat and took to his old life once more, ultimately returning to the Free State.

In 1889 De Wet achieved some local notoriety by collecting an armed force and riding with it to Bloemfontein, the seat of government, to protest against the building of a railway line from the coast, for he and his followers looked upon this as a dangerous innovation calculated to throw the country open to foreign invasion. His vigorous political methods were so much in keeping with the times that, in consequence of his exploit, he became a member of the Free State Volksraad; but after an unsuccessful attempt to prohibit the use of mail-coaches and other vehicles on Sunday, he left law-making to others and although he remained a member of the Raad until 1898 he returned to his former roving.

On the outbreak of the South African War in October 1899 De Wet was called up for service as an ordinary burgher and sent to the Natal frontier, where he participated in various preliminary encounters with the British troops. Then came his great chance in life. A British force had marched out of Ladysmith at night, intending to strike at the rear of the Boer army, but plans miscarried and daylight (30 October) found the troops isolated on the flat-topped summit of Nicholson's Nek. Here De Wet attacked them with a few hundred men whom he had hurriedly collected, and so determined was the assault that he captured the whole force, taking over a thousand prisoners and scoring the first important success of the campaign. This exploit was his making. There was a dearth of leaders among the Boers, and he was immediately promoted to the rank of general and sent to the western borders of the Free State, where British troops were massing for the relief of Kimberley.

General Piet Cronje was in supreme command of this front, and De Wet made strenuous but unsuccessful efforts to prevent him from committing the series of blunders that led to his capture by Lord Roberts [q.v.] at Paardeberg on 27 February 1900. De Wet had further distinguished himself by his capture of Roberts's convoy at Waterval on 13 February, so that it is not surprising that when he escaped from the *débâcle* of Paardeberg he found himself appointed commander-in-chief of the Free State forces. His post was a thorny one. The effects of Cronje's surrender, coinciding as it did with the Boer defeats in Natal, proved disastrous to the republican cause. The commandos were melting away, and on every hand were discouragement and wholesale desertions.

De Wet, however, rose superior to these misfortunes. Ably seconded by Martinus Steyn, president of the Orange Free State, a man as indomitable as himself, he set to work to rally his demoralized army. On 31 March he ambushed Colonel R. G. Broadwood's mounted brigade at Sanna's Post, outside Bloemfontein, and on 4 April defeated a British detachment at Reddersburg. As the tide of war rolled northwards to the Transvaal, he remained in the rear of the invading British forces and by immense efforts succeeded in re-establishing the fighting spirit of his men. Realizing that the Boers could no longer resist in the open field, he now decided, in conjunction with the Boer leaders in the Transvaal, to resort to guerrilla tactics. Of this form of warfare he became one of the greatest exponents in modern times. With a few thousand hard-bitten followers he kept the field for the next two years against tremendous odds, to the despair and admiration of his opponents. No detailed account can be given here of his innumerable exploits, his hairbreadth escapes, and his many successes and failures. Suffice it to say that when the long drawn-out contest came at last to an end in June 1902, De Wet was still holding his own. By that time he had won an international reputation for his daring and courage, a reputation generously endorsed by his former enemies.

After the war De Wet, who had taken part in the peace negotiations, visited Europe with the other Boer generals. On the granting of responsible government to South Africa, he entered the political arena. He was elected a member of the first parliament of the Orange River Colony (1907) and appointed minister of agriculture. He was a delegate to the Union Convention of 1908–1909 and a member of the Union Defence council under General Louis Botha [q.v.].

For a time there was peace and material progress in South Africa; but in 1911 there sprang up a bitter feud between the followers of General Botha on the one side and those of General J. B. M. Hertzog on the other. De Wet flung himself into the fray with characteristic energy on the side of Hertzog. He became a strong supporter of a movement that was set on foot which aimed at secession from the British Empire and the re-establishment of the republics of the Orange Free State and Transvaal.

The outbreak of the European War in August 1914 found De Wet in the midst of this agitation, and when, immediately afterwards, Botha announced his intention of invading German South-West African territory with South African troops, De Wet expressed great hostility to the expedition. On 15 September there followed the accidental shooting of General J. H. De la Rey by the police during the operation of rounding up a gang of desperadoes which had been terrorizing the suburbs of Johannesburg. This event profoundly influenced De Wet's subsequent conduct. General De la Rey and he had both played a great part during the Boer War, and they were close personal friends. He mistakenly assumed that De la Rey had been killed by order of Botha's government, and this goaded him into action.

In conjunction with General C. F. Beyers, the leader of the Transvaal malcontents, De Wet planned an armed revolt. On 24 October Beyers raised the standard of rebellion in the north, and two days later De Wet followed suit in the Free State.

Both men speedily collected thousands of adherents, and the insurrection assumed formidable proportions. Botha, however, took prompt action against his former companions-in-arms. Summoning his supporters, he took the field in person, and within a week he fell on Beyers and signally defeated him (27 October). Then he turned upon De Wet. He found him at Mushroom valley in the central Free State at the head of 6,000 men, and in a pitched battle drove him in headlong rout (12 November). De Wet now attempted to resort to the old guerrilla tactics that had served him so well in former days, but he had met his master. Botha understood the art of mobile warfare even better than De Wet himself, and, in addition, the era of the motor-car had set in, which made it impossible for the mounted commandos of the Boers to play hide-and-seek across the veld as they had done in the past. Botha was the first to demonstrate this. By the skilful use of motor detachments he harried and hustled the rebels, giving them and their horses no rest. So hot was the pursuit that within ten days De Wet was a mere fugitive fleeing westward with less than a dozen men for the sanctuary of the Kalahari desert, whence he hoped to escape into German territory. But Botha's men were hot on his trail, and on 2 December the old *condottiere* was run to earth and captured on the farm Waterberg in the Kuruman district. A week before, Beyers had met his death while trying to cross the Vaal river, and with both its leaders accounted for the rebellion was soon stamped out.

De Wet was arraigned before a special tribunal at Bloemfontein on 9 June 1915, and tried for high treason. On 21 June he was found guilty on eight of the ten counts against him, and sentenced to six years' imprisonment and a fine of £2,000. In the following December, however, he was released on parole by Botha and allowed to return to his farm in the Free State. Here he lived quietly until his death which took place on the farm Klipfontein, district De Wetsdorp, 3 February 1922. He was buried at the Women's monument at Bloemfontein beside his old leader President Steyn.

De Wet married in 1873 Cornelia Margaretta, daughter of Isaak Johannes Christian Kruger, of Bloemfontein. They had five sons and one daughter. He wrote an account of his campaigns of 1899–1902 which appeared in an English version as *Three Years' War* (1902).

A cartoon of De Wet appeared in *Vanity Fair* 31 July 1902.

[*'The Times' History of the War in South Africa*, 1900–1909; Sir Arthur Conan Doyle, *The Great Boer War*, 1900; Sir J. F. Maurice and M. H. Grant, (Official) *History of the War in South Africa, 1899–1902*, 1906–1910; F. H. E. Cunliffe, *History of the Boer War*, 2 vols., 1901–1904; Louis Creswicke, *South Africa and the Transvaal War*, 6 vols., 1900–1902.]

D. Reitz.

DICEY, ALBERT VENN (1835–1922), jurist, was the third son of Thomas Edward Dicey, proprietor of the *Northampton Mercury*, by his wife, Anne Mary, younger daughter of James Stephen [q.v.], master in chancery. An elder brother was Edward James Stephen Dicey [q.v.], author and journalist. Albert Dicey was born at the family home, Claybrook Hall, near Lutterworth, 4 February 1835; the name Venn was given to him in honour of John Venn [q.v.], the leader of the Clapham Evangelicals, whose daughter Jane had married Mrs. Dicey's brother, Sir James Stephen [q.v.]. He was brought up in the Clapham tradition, and his memory was rich in reminiscences of the movement. A lack of control over his muscles hampered him in childhood, and, indeed, throughout life, and it was not until 1852 that he was sent to King's College School, then situated in the Strand. He entered Balliol College, Oxford, in 1854, and obtained a first class in classical moderations in 1856 and in *literae humaniores* in 1858. His abilities as a debater were recognized by his election as president of the Union for Lent Term, 1859, and to his Oxford years he owed most of the friendships which constituted much of the happiness of his life. He was one of the founders of perhaps the most remarkable of the smaller Oxford clubs, the Old Mortality, which during a brief existence included a singularly large number of men who afterwards attained distinction. Among them were Thomas Hill Green [q.v.], Edward Caird [q.v.], G. Birkbeck Hill [q.v.], A. C. Swinburne [q.v.], John Nichol [q.v.], and James (afterwards Viscount) Bryce [q.v.]; with the two last-mentioned Dicey made the most intimate of his lifelong friendships.

In 1860 Dicey was successful in an examination for a fellowship at Trinity College, and in the same year he was awarded the Arnold prize for an essay on the Privy Council, to the composition of which he attributed the origin of his interest in constitutional law and history.

He remained a fellow of Trinity until his fellowship was vacated in 1872 by his marriage to Elinor Mary, youngest daughter of John Bonham-Carter (M.P. for Portsmouth from 1830 to 1841); but he ceased to reside in Oxford in 1861. From that year until 1882 he lived in London, practising at the bar, having been called in 1863 as a member of the Inner Temple, and contributing to the *Northampton Mercury* (of which he occasionally acted as temporary editor), the *Spectator*, and the New York *Nation.* Dicey acquired a considerable practice at the bar, was appointed junior counsel to the commissioners of Inland Revenue in 1876, and published in 1870 a *Treatise on the Rules for the Selection of the Parties to an Action* and in 1879 *The Law of Domicil.* Changes in the law have rendered the first of these books obsolete, and the second was afterwards incorporated in a larger work covering a wider field, but it was in virtue of the reputation acquired by these volumes that he was elected in 1882 to the Vinerian professorship of English law at Oxford. Dicey held this chair, to which a fellowship at All Souls College is attached, for twenty-seven years. After his resignation in 1909, the college elected him to a fellowship without emolument, which he held until his death. From 1910 to 1913 he also held a lecturership in private international law established by All Souls College.

During his long tenure of the Vinerian professorship, Dicey published the three books which give him a permanent place among historians of English law. His *Introduction to the Study of the Law of the Constitution*, originally published in 1885, was at once recognized to be no mere technical discussion but a literary contribution to the analysis and interpretation of the fundamental ideas which underlie the political thought and life of the nation. To the eighth edition (1915) he prefixed an introduction dealing with the development of the constitution and of constitutional theory during the preceding thirty years. His *Digest of the Law of England with Reference to the Conflict of Laws* (1896)—an expansion of his *Law of Domicil*—in the words of his successor in the Vinerian chair, William Martin Geldart, 'not only reduced to order one of the most intricate and technical branches of law . . . but exerted a potent influence on its development'. The third book was the result of an invitation to give a course of lectures at the Harvard law school. In 1870 Dicey had accompanied Bryce on a visit to the United States and had brought back an abiding interest in the American people and friendships with some distinguished Americans, especially Edwin Lawrence Godkin, founder of the *Nation*, Charles William Eliot, president of Harvard, and Chief Justice Holmes. He visited Harvard again in 1898 and lectured on 'The Development of English Law during the nineteenth century in connexion with the Course of Public Opinion in England', delivering also a series of Lowell lectures on comparative constitutions. *Lectures on the relation between Law and Public Opinion in England during the Nineteenth Century* was published in 1905 and was received as a notable contribution to political philosophy—'the *esprit des lois* of our times'.

During these years Dicey took a prominent part in political controversy. A liberal up to 1885, he became, after Gladstone's conversion to Home Rule, the most ardent defender of the Union outside the Houses of Parliament, and published *England's Case against Home Rule* (1886), *Letters on Unionist Delusions* (1887), *A Leap in the Dark* (1893), and, at a later stage of the controversy, *A Fool's Paradise* (1913). He wrote much, up to the end of his life, on the political questions of the day. His interest in social problems led in 1899 to his election to the principalship of the Working Men's College in London, founded in 1854 by Frederick Denison Maurice [q.v.]. He held the post until 1912.

After his resignation of the Vinerian professorship, Dicey revised his three chief works and published a number of lesser books. The events of the European War suggested an edition (1915) of Wordsworth's *Tract on the Convention of Cintra* (1809) and a volume on *The Statesmanship of Wordsworth* (1917), designed to emphasize the intensity of the poet's effort to persuade his countrymen to continue the struggle for 'a peace grounded on the destruction of despotism'. The suggestions, made during and at the end of the War, for a reconstitution of the United Kingdom on a federal basis led him to fulfil an old intention of collaborating with the present writer in a book upon the Union between England and Scotland, which he believed to be the greatest achievement of British statesmanship. It was published in 1920 under the title of *Thoughts on the Union between England and Scotland.* He had resigned his post as counsel for the Inland Revenue in 1890, but took silk in the same year, and did not retire from practice until 1916. Among the distinctions of his later years were honorary fellowships at Trinity College (1894) and Balliol College (1921), and honorary degrees from the universities of Glasgow (1883), Princeton (1898), and Oxford (1907).

Dicey's intellectual and critical powers were accompanied by a lovable simplicity of character and a lively wit. 'It is better to be flippant than dull' he used to tell his pupils, and it was the force of his epigrams that made his early reputation as a speaker in the Oxford Union. His remarkable faculty of exposition, acquired by persistent revision of his compositions, was sometimes marred by a tendency to redundancy of which he could not rid himself.

Dicey died at Oxford 7 April 1922 and was buried in St. Sepulchre's cemetery. His wife died in 1923. They had no children. A portrait of Dicey as a young man, by D. Laugée, hangs in the hall of Trinity College, Oxford.

[W. Knight, *Memoir of John Nichol*, 1896; R. S. Rait, *Memorials of Albert Venn Dicey*, 1925; private information; personal knowledge.] R. S. Rait.

DICKSEE, Sir FRANCIS BERNARD (FRANK) (1853–1928), painter, was born in London 27 November 1853, the elder son of the painter and illustrator Thomas Francis Dicksee (1819–1895), by his wife, Eliza, daughter of John Bernard, of Church Place, Piccadilly. His uncle, John Robert Dicksee (1817–1905), was also a painter; thus Frank Dicksee had from the outset close family associations with art. Having been educated at the Rev. George Henslow's school, Bloomsbury, Dicksee received his first training in art under his father and subsequently, from 1870 to 1875, studied in the Royal Academy Schools. Among leading academicians of the day with whom he was brought into contact during his student period were (Lord) Leighton and, to a lesser degree, (Sir) J. E. Millais. Dicksee had a successful career as a student, eventually in 1875 being awarded the Academy gold medal for his picture 'Elijah confronting Ahab and Jezebel in Naboth's Vineyard', which, in 1876, became his first contribution to an Academy exhibition. For some years previously Dicksee had been making drawings for book and magazine illustrations and he continued to do so for a considerable period, his later work in this category including illustrations for *Evangeline* (1882), *Romeo and Juliet* (1884), and *Othello* (1889), the two latter for Messrs. Cassell's 'royal' edition of Shakespeare. The department of engraving, illustration, and design in the Victoria and Albert Museum possesses several drawings made by Dicksee for woodcut illustrations in the *Cornhill Magazine* between 1876 and 1879. Among the formative influences of Dicksee's earlier years must also be mentioned Henry Holiday [q.v.], under whom he worked for some time.

Dicksee's first great popular success was achieved at the Royal Academy exhibition of 1877 through his picture 'Harmony', which represents a girl in medieval costume playing the organ, while a youth listens in rapt attention. This elaborate effort to create a highly sentimental, pseudo-medieval atmosphere made an instant appeal, and the picture was purchased by the Chantrey trustees for 350 guineas; it is now in the Tate Gallery. The quasi-historical, romantic, and sentimental vein, or else the vein of melodrama in modern setting, was thenceforth actively exploited by Dicksee, who thus gratified a taste which for many years to come was very widespread. Among his more resounding Academy successes (often hailed as 'the picture of the year') may be mentioned: 'The Symbol' (1881); 'A Love Story' (1882); 'Too Late' (1883; this was bought for £997 10*s*. at the A. Shuttleworth sale at Christie's, 3 May 1890, the auction 'record' for Dicksee); 'Romeo and Juliet' (1884); 'Memories' (1886); 'Within the Shadow of the Church' (1888); 'The Passing of Arthur' (1889); 'The Redemption of Tannhäuser' (1890); 'The Crisis' (1891; through a pure coincidence the subject—a father with his sick girl—presented a certain similarity to that of Luke Fildes's 'The Doctor' exhibited in the same year; Dicksee's picture is now in the Melbourne Art Gallery); 'The Mountain of the Winds' (1891); 'The Funeral of a Viking' (1893); 'The Magic Crystal' (1894, now in the Lady Lever Art Gallery, Port Sunlight); 'Paolo and Francesca' (1895); 'A Reverie' (1895, now in the Walker Art Gallery, Liverpool); 'The Mirror' (1896); 'An Offering' (1898); 'The Two Crowns' (1900, now in the Tate Gallery; purchased by the Chantrey trustees for £2,000); 'The Ideal' (1905); 'The Shadowed Face' (1909); 'The Light Incarnate' (1922), and 'This for Remembrance' (1924, now the property of the Liverpool Corporation). The popularity of many of these pictures was increased by their being engraved soon after exhibition.

For a time Dicksee was also a fashionable portrait-painter, being especially in demand for female sitters; leading examples are his portraits of the Duchess of Buckingham and Chandos (1901), Mrs. W. K. D'Arcy (1902), Lady Aird (1903), Mrs. Frank Shuttleworth (1904), Lady Hillingdon (1905), the Marchioness of Ailesbury (1911), and Mrs. Frank S. Pershouse (1928, the last portrait painted by the artist). A portrait group, reflecting the taste of a whole period, is 'The House Builders', which portrays Sir W. E. and the Hon. Lady Welby-Gregory (1880). Landscape painting was also practised by Dicksee, but forms only a minor section of his work.

Academic and other honours were not slow in coming to Dicksee. In 1881 he was elected A.R.A. and in 1891 R.A., his diploma work 'Startled' being deposited in 1892. In 1924, on the retirement of Sir Aston Webb [q.v.] under the new age limit, he was elected president of the Royal Academy. He was knighted in 1925 and created K.C.V.O. in 1927. In 1926 he was nominated by the newly elected chancellor of Oxford University, Viscount Cave, for the honorary degree of D.C.L. He was also a trustee of the British Museum and the National Portrait Gallery and president of the Artists' General Benevolent Association. He died, unmarried, 17 October 1928, at his house in St. John's Wood, which had been his home for over thirty years. A retrospective selection of his works formed part of the Royal Academy Winter Exhibition in 1933.

As an artist Dicksee can scarcely be said to have undergone any notable evolution. In subject he remained to the end essentially wedded to sentimental or melodramatic anecdote. He is at times vaguely reminiscent, in attitude and *mise-en-scène*, of certain pre-Raphaelites, although expressing himself in a more realistic, 'up-to-date' manner, the introduction of tremulous twilight being a favourite device. At times again he suggests an approximation to the manner of Watts or of Leighton, enfeebled in the process of prettified imitation. ·Qualities of more solid, strictly artistic, worth may be said to be conspicuous by their absence in his work; and even its popular appeal has now almost entirely waned. As a man Dicksee was noted for his kindliness and courtesy. During his short tenure of the presidency of the Royal Academy he creditably acquitted himself of the more ceremonious functions of the post. When, on the other hand, in his public speeches he felt called upon to venture into the realm of aesthetic discussion, he did not succeed in being either profound or stimulating.

A self-portrait by Dicksee is in the Aberdeen Art Gallery.

[Edward Rimbault Dibdin, *Frank Dicksee, R.A., his life and work* (the Christmas number of the *Art Journal*, 1905); Algernon Graves, *The Royal Academy of Arts, a complete dictionary of contributors and their work*, vol. ii, 1905; subsequent Royal Academy Exhibition Catalogues.] T. Borenius.

DILL, Sir SAMUEL (1844–1924), classical scholar, historian, and educationist, was born 26 March 1844 at Hillsborough, co. Down, the eldest son of the Rev. Samuel Marcus Dill, D.D., Presbyterian minister of Hillsborough, later professor of systematic theology and first president of Magee College, Londonderry, by his wife, Anna Harrison, daughter of James Cowan Moreland, of Hillsborough. The family of which he came was founded by a soldier of Dutch descent in William III's army, and gave noted ministers, writers, and controversialists to Irish Presbyterianism.

Dill was educated at the Royal Academical Institution and at the Queen's College, Belfast, where he took his degree in arts in 1864. He then went, as a scholar, to Lincoln College, Oxford, and obtained first classes in classical moderations (1867) and in *literae humaniores* (1869). In 1869 he was elected fellow and tutor of Corpus Christi College, Oxford. Later he became librarian and dean of the college, and was made an honorary fellow in 1903. In 1877 Dill was appointed high master of Manchester grammar school—this being the last appointment to that post made by a president of Corpus. During his headmastership the school was reorganized; new buildings were erected and school societies developed. Dill was equally effective as administrator and teacher. His liberal conception of education is illustrated by his development of the modern side, and by the connexion which he established between the school and working boys' clubs. Among his pupils were J. A. Hamilton, afterwards Viscount Sumner, and Gordon (afterwards Baron) Hewart. The latter, who records Dill's gift for inspiring his pupils and the combination in his teaching of breadth of interest with precision of scholarship, has described him as 'a striking personality, equally magnificent in form and shy and reserved in speech . . . one of the very few men who appear to the boy to be heroes, and throughout life never lose that character'.

Dill resigned his headmastership in 1888 and devoted himself to the preparation of his first book. In 1890 he returned to Queen's College, Belfast, as professor of Greek. As a member of the Belfast university commission, he took a large share in transforming the college into a university in 1909. He was chairman of the viceregal committee of inquiry into primary education (1913–1914), which achieved the feat, uncommon in Ireland, of producing a unanimous report. He also influenced Irish education by his work as a member, and later as chairman, of the Intermediate Board of Education. He was a man of strong religious feeling. A Presbyterian by birth, in his later years he became more identified with the Church of Ireland. His views were unionist, but he took no part in politics.

Dill was even better known as a writer. If literary power and productiveness are considered, he ranks high among the ancient historians of his day and country. In 1898 he published *Roman Society in the Last Century of the Western Empire*, which was followed in 1904 by *Roman Society from Nero to Marcus Aurelius*. Then at the age of sixty he turned to a wide and ill-mapped field. His *Roman Society in Gaul in the Merovingian Age*, edited and published posthumously in 1926 by his son-in-law, the Rev. C. B. Armstrong, shows much of his old gift but also the lack of his *manus summa*. Although not research in the technical sense, Dill's works are founded on a thorough study both of the primary and secondary sources. Less histories of a period than studies of the life of societies in dissolution or in spiritual crisis or decay, they reveal his moral and religious sympathies. Their interest, combined with the lucidity and charm of their style, attracted the general reader as well as the scholar.

Dill's services to education were recognized by a knighthood in 1909, and he received the honorary degrees of Litt.D. from the university of Dublin, and of LL.D. from Edinburgh and St. Andrews. He resigned his professorship in 1924, and died at Belfast 26 May of that year.

Dill married in 1884 Fanny Elizabeth, daughter of Richard Cadwallader Morgan, of Shrewsbury, and had three daughters.

[*The Times*, 27 and 29 May 1924; J. R. Dill, *The Dill Worthies*, 2nd ed., 1892; A. A. Mumford, *The Manchester Grammar School, 1515–1915*, 1919.] R. W. Livingstone.

DILLON, JOHN (1851–1927), Irish nationalist politician, the second son of John Blake Dillon [q.v.], the Irish politician, by his wife, Adelaide, daughter of William Hart, a Dublin solicitor, was born at Blackrock, near Dublin, 4 September 1851. He was first educated at the University School in Harcourt Street, Dublin, which was connected with the Catholic University founded by (Cardinal) Newman. He entered the university in 1865 and was an arts student until 1870, when he went to Manchester for apprenticeship in a cotton-broker's warehouse. Disliking the life, he returned to Dublin and entered the Catholic University medical school in 1878 and graduated as licentiate of the College of Surgeons, Ireland. He was a demonstrator in anatomy at the Cecilia Street medical school when the call came to a political career.

In 1875, when his father's friend and fellow rebel, John Mitchel [q.v.], returned to Ireland and was proposed as member of parliament for Tipperary (which from 1865 to 1866 had been represented by John Blake Dillon), Dillon went down to support him and was at the old rebel's death-bed a month after his election. He was at the time a close adherent of Mitchel and therefore an advocate of physical force; but he had never joined the Fenian movement, probably because his father was opposed to it. With the rise of Charles Stewart Parnell [q.v.] he saw hope for an effective constitutional movement, and as the struggle between Isaac Butt [q.v.] and Parnell for leadership developed he made a fierce speech against Butt in the Molesworth Hall, Dublin, on 5 February 1879, the old leader's last public appearance. On 21 October of that year, when the Land League was founded, it was resolved that Parnell, as its president, should go to America to obtain assistance, and Dillon was selected to accompany him. Before the American campaign was completed Parnell was hurried home by news of the impending dissolution of parliament, and Dillon was left to complete the organization of the League in America. In his absence Tipperary elected him member of parliament.

The distinction which he enjoyed in Irish politics as a rebel's son was enhanced by Dillon's own striking personality and eloquence, and in the first years of the Land League he was the most prominent of Parnell's colleagues. Perhaps he was also the most extreme in advocating agrarian agitation, and although he denounced the shooting of men from behind hedges he gave his entire support to boycotting and to every form of agrarian combination, holding that unless the tenants were so organized assassination would continue.

When, in November 1880, the Irish chief secretary, W. E. Forster, decided to prosecute the chiefs of the Land League, Dillon was one of five members of parliament (with Parnell at their head) among the 'traversers'. The failure of this prosecution led up to Forster's Coercion Act, which Dillon violently denounced everywhere, till he was himself arrested in May 1881 and sent to Kilmainham jail. On grounds of ill-health he was released later; but in October, when Parnell and all the chief officials of the League were taken to Kilmainham as 'suspects', he was again imprisoned. On 2 May 1882, Parnell, Dillon, and James O'Kelly were released as part of the Kilmainham Treaty, although Dillon denied all knowledge of the arrangement. Four days later came the Phoenix Park murders, and the manifesto denouncing them was signed by Parnell, Dillon, and Michael Davitt.

Parnell was now inclined to mitigate the fierceness of agrarian agitation. Dillon disagreed; and the more readily submitted to medical advice and went to Colorado, where his elder brother William was established. His physique was never strong; indeed, its delicacy contributed to the romantic beauty of his appearance—the pale, oval face and long, black hair, the tall, slender, but upright body, and the long, fine hands. He did not return until the general election of 1885 under the new franchise was at hand, and then by Parnell's wish, and against his own, he stood for East Mayo instead of Tipperary.

Up to this period Dillon was accounted by English politicians as a separatist who accepted Parnell's policy as a second best. During his absence in America other men, notably T. M. Healy, had come to the front, and thenceforward his position was in a sense less individually outstanding; on the other hand it was now strengthened by the closest personal alliance with William O'Brien [q.v.]. After the defeat of Mr. Gladstone's first Home Rule Bill in 1885, when the tories came in, Dillon and O'Brien jointly promulgated, on the notorious Clanricarde [see CLANRICARDE, Second Marquess of] estate in county Galway, the 'plan of campaign' under which tenants on an estate pledged themselves to offer to the landlord what they considered a fair rent as settlement in full, and, if he refused, to lodge the money with trustees as a fund for supporting ejected tenants. In 1887 Dillon was prosecuted for collecting these 'rents', but the jury disagreed. On 9 September in that year, while he was addressing a demonstration at Mitchelstown in the presence of a huge crowd, the police, seeking to force their way to the platform, were driven back to the barracks, and from that cover fired, killing three persons. 'Remember Mitchelstown' became a war-cry. Dillon's personal courage and coolness prevented even worse consequences; he walked straight up to the barracks and checked the firing. During the following winter O'Brien was imprisoned, and the task of carrying on the 'plan' fell to Dillon, who was in his turn sentenced to six months' imprisonment. During the chief secretaryship (1887–1891) of Mr. A. J. (afterwards the first Earl of) Balfour [q.v.] political prisoners were treated as ordinary criminals, and Dillon's health suffered. He was released in September 1888. Early in 1889 he went, by his doctor's orders, with other colleagues to Australia and New Zealand on a fund-raising mission. After his return in 1890 he was again active in agitation; and in September of that year, when he and O'Brien were on the point of starting for an American tour, both were arrested on a charge of criminal conspiracy. Being allowed out on bail they (with the consent of their sureties) escaped to France in a fishing-boat and went on to the United States—being sentenced in their absence to six months' imprisonment. Thus when, two months later, the Parnell divorce proceedings took Ireland by surprise, these two men, whose joint influence was second only to that of the leader, were out of reach, and could return only to be arrested. Both men were unwilling to forsake Parnell's leadership, and both cabled to the Leinster hall meeting in Dublin (20 November) a tribute to his services. But both agreed that Parnell's subsequent manifesto in reply to Mr. Gladstone made his retirement from the chairmanship essential. Parnell offered to retire if O'Brien should succeed him. O'Brien refused, but proposed Dillon, and Parnell, whose preference for O'Brien was marked, unwillingly assented. Yet the project broke down because of some details—one being Dillon's claim that Parnell should liberate from the party funds then held in Paris as much as would finance the party for twelve months. After this failure of negotiations

Dillon and O'Brien went to Folkestone, were arrested, and sent to Galway jail (February 1891). On coming out after six months they declared unconditionally for the anti-Parnellites—the decision, according to O'Brien, being Dillon's.

In 1895, after the close of Mr. Gladstone's last parliament, Dillon at length felt free to marry a lady to whom he had long been attached, Elizabeth, daughter of Lord Justice Sir James Charles Mathew [q.v.]. Thenceforward he no longer habitually courted the risk of imprisonment; but his directing activity was undiminished. In 1896 he was chosen chairman of the group of seventy anti-Parnellites, and his activities were much engaged in a struggle against T. M. Healy, always a dissident. This was the period of 'killing Home Rule with kindness' under the chief secretaryship of Mr. Gerald Balfour. (Sir) Horace Plunkett, also, began to develop a propaganda of co-operation; to this Dillon was hostile because he held that it diverted attention from the main object of extirpating landlord power. When the Department of Agriculture and Technical Instruction was established, with Plunkett as its minister, Dillon persistently opposed the grant of any subsidy to the Irish Agricultural Organization Society founded by Plunkett, on the ground that the taxpayers' money should not be used to subsidize associations which competed against individual shopkeepers who were taxpayers. It did not lessen his opposition that the class in question, to which he belonged, was, in his opinion, unfairly accused of usury. Again, when local government on the English plan was extended to Ireland, Dillon and O'Brien resisted the proposal, which John Redmond [q.v.] favoured, of associating the old landlord class with the elected local authorities.

From 1898 onwards a move for unity was made, Dillon amongst others advocating it. Early in 1899 he insisted on retiring from the chairmanship of the party, which remained vacant for a year until, at the beginning of 1900, Redmond, leader of the few Parnellites, was chosen chairman of the united party. Dillon did not cordially accept this choice, but he promised Redmond 'strict fair play', and gave it, and up till Redmond's death he was in fact his main ally. The situation was strangely altered by the Land Conference and the resulting Land Purchase Bill of George Wyndham [q.v.]—both of which had O'Brien's enthusiastic support. Dillon, who had gone to America in October 1902 on a mission in support of the new United Irish League, returned distrustful of the conclusions of the conference, and finally, after Wyndham's Bill had passed (1903), attacked it in his own constituency at Swinford on 25 August 1904. Others followed his lead, and the result was a threatened split in the party, avoided only by a breach in the intimate friendship between Dillon and his closest ally. O'Brien retired from public life for some years and the quarrel was never appeased.

The devolution proposals put forward by the fourth Earl of Dunraven [q.v.] in consultation with Sir Antony (afterwards Baron) MacDonnell [q.v.] seemed to Dillon insidious. But when the liberals came into power in 1906 with a huge independent majority pledged to introduce a Home Rule Bill, Redmond and he went into consultation with the chief secretaries, first with (Viscount) Bryce [q.v.], and then with Mr. Augustine Birrell, on the Irish Council Bill, which reached its sudden end in 1907. At this period and until Redmond's death Dillon was the chief member of the Irish leader's 'cabinet', which included also Joseph Devlin and T. P. O'Connor. Moreover Dillon, who lived in Dublin and was an untiring worker, virtually controlled the organization in Ireland, Redmond limiting himself in the main to the parliamentary leadership.

The rejection by an Irish convention of the Council Bill was a rebuff both to Redmond and to Dillon; moreover, at this moment (May 1907), Mrs. Dillon died. The loss of this gifted companion and comrade, who had made his house one of the most attractive centres of hospitality in Dublin, cut Dillon off from general society.

In 1908 a long-standing difficulty was solved, largely by Dillon's help. Bryce's University Bill, which proposed to incorporate Trinity College, Dublin, and the Royal University in a single state-aided national university, had met with violent opposition and had been withdrawn. Mr. Birrell, who succeeded Bryce as chief secretary, returned to the proposal originally sketched by Dillon, of linking the Queen's Colleges with University College, Dublin (the survival of Newman's foundation), in a National University, and the scheme went through. Dillon's delight in its success was somewhat damped when he found himself overruled in his opposition to the proposal that Irish should be a compulsory subject for matriculation.

From 1909 onwards, as the struggle for Home Rule became involved with the question of the powers of the House of Lords, the perilous task of stating the Irish view in parliament was seldom entrusted to any one but Redmond, Dillon, or O'Connor. To these men, and to Healy and O'Brien (now leaders of a dissident faction), the House instinctively accorded the status which is by courtesy given to ministers and to important ex-ministers. In the last stage, at the Buckingham Palace Conference on the Ulster question, which sat from 21 to 24 July 1914, Dillon was joined with Redmond as representative of the Irish Nationalists. Then came the outbreak of the European War. Dillon, who was in Dublin when the House of Commons met on 3 August and Redmond's famous speech on Sir Edward Grey's statement was made, avowed later that he would not have dared to approve in advance what he had come to recognize as a great stroke of statesmanship. But he abstained from any public part in Redmond's recruiting campaign, although the Allied cause appealed strongly to his sympathies as a nationalist and liberal in the European sense. But after the Dublin rebellion in Easter week 1916, Dillon, protesting against the nature of the repressive measures which ensued, was taunted with undue tenderness for the rebels, and broke into a passionate outburst in defence of them. He acted with Redmond and Devlin in an attempt made in July of that year to bring Home Rule into operation by agreement; but, after the consent of Nationalists in the north to a temporary partition had been obtained, members of the Coalition Cabinet refused to accept the written terms laid down by Mr. Asquith and Mr. Lloyd George. Dillon then virtually washed his hands of further attempts at settlement, and in 1917 refused to serve on the Irish convention set up under the chairmanship of Sir Horace Plunkett. On Redmond's death in 1918 Dillon was unanimously elected to the vacant chairmanship of the Irish party. But it was a hopeless position. A few weeks later the proposal to extend conscription to Ireland against the will of her representatives united Nationalists of all shades, and Dillon with Healy joined Mr. De Valera and other Sinn Fein leaders in a committee to organize resistance. The effect was to put the country into the hands of the Sinn Fein volunteers, and when the government, in order to avoid civil war, postponed the application of conscription, the credit went to Sinn Fein. In the general election which followed the Armistice the Irish party was virtually wiped out of existence, and Dillon himself was defeated by Mr. De Valera in East Mayo. After this he withdrew from public life and abstained from public criticism of Sinn Fein activities.

Dillon died in London after an operation 4 August 1927. All his children, five sons and one daughter, survived him.

Dillon owed his position as a political leader in the first instance to the quality of his oratory which, although often lacking in form, had the power of arousing passion and of convincing the audience of his own passionate sincerity. Secondly, his knowledge was enormous and his labour endless. No other man had so minute and so extensive a personal knowledge of nationalist Ireland; and he was always accessible. His mind was stored with reading of every kind; in the House of Commons he followed not only Irish affairs but every matter of general policy. His interest in foreign politics was notable, and was always inspired by the Gladstonian tradition. His usefulness for the peculiar task of an Irish leader was perhaps lessened because his personal sympathies, unlike Redmond's, were engaged with the liberals as liberals; and his hereditary antipathy to the landlord class in Ireland was a disability. He had great gifts in counsel, but his long foresight was ever tempered by an excessive pessimism. The breach between him and O'Brien, who counterbalanced this defect, was a great misfortune for Ireland.

Unlike nearly all his chief colleagues, although in many ways the most lettered and bookish among them, Dillon never wrote for publication, and all of O'Brien's books of reminiscences were written after the quarrel between these old intimates. This adds to the difficulty of judging one who was very diversely judged. But it is safe to say that from 1878 to 1918 no Irishman except Parnell (and possibly Davitt) played a more important part in Irish history than John Dillon.

[*The Times*, 5 August 1927; T. P. O'Connor, *The Parnell Movement*, 1886; William O'Brien, *Recollections*, 1906, *An Olive Branch in Ireland and its History*, *Evening Memories*, 1920; private information; personal knowledge.]

S. GWYNN.

DINES, WILLIAM HENRY (1855–1927), meteorologist, was born in Pimlico, London, 5 August 1855, the youngest child and only surviving son of George Dines, a builder's foreman. His father had begun life in humble circumstances, but became the leading member of a successful firm of builders in Pimlico. Later in life he moved to Hersham, Walton-on-Thames, became a prominent member of the Meteorological Society, and was recognized as an authority on scientific questions relating to dew, dew-points, and dew-point instruments. His wife, Louisa Sara Coke, was connected with the Cokes of Norfolk.

William Henry Dines was educated at Woodcote House School, Windlesham, Surrey, and was then apprenticed as an engineering pupil at the Nine Elms works of the London and South Western Railway. On the completion of his articles in 1877 he entered Corpus Christi College, Cambridge. The choice of Corpus at that time would suggest an evangelical upbringing. Dines read for the mathematical tripos and took his degree as twentieth wrangler in 1881. He remained in residence as mathematical coach for a year.

Thenceforward Dines's profession, so far as he could be said to have one, was private tuition in mathematics by correspondence. Tall, spare, not very robust or athletic, reticent and retiring, somewhat austere although not by any means devoid of humour, scrupulously accurate and trustworthy, with an innate capacity for making things work, he could scarcely be taken for a bustling man of action. He objected to the granting of the M.A. degree at Cambridge without examination, and thereby debarred himself from the degree of doctor of science, for which the M.A. was a necessary qualification.

As a young Cambridge graduate with some assurance of private means Dines devoted his spare time, and from the age of fifty or thereabouts until his death at the age of seventy-two his whole time, to the dynamical and physical sides of the science of meteorology. He became the leading exponent of experimental meteorology in England and the interpreter of its collected observations. He will be remembered for his work on anemometry, on the investigation of the upper air, and on solar and terrestrial radiation.

Combining the practical skill of an engineer with the precision of thought of a competent mathematician, Dines was able in any subject to concentrate his attention on the elements which matter. His first achievement, after taking his degree, was an apparatus for determining directly the pressure of water-vapour in the atmosphere, as a help to his father's work on humidity. He next took up the subject of wind-force, which had become an urgent matter in consequence of the Tay Bridge disaster on 28 December 1879. His efforts resulted in the development of the pressure-tube anemometer, the records from which are now becoming recognized all over the world as setting out in the most effective way possible the dynamical problem of meteorology. The difficulties encountered were many; but they are all circumvented in the final form of the instrument, which records direction as well as velocity. In the course of the work a proper formula for wind-force in terms of wind-velocity was established in place of previous imperfect ones.

There followed next investigation of the upper air by means of kites, begun by Dines in 1902 under the auspices of the British Association and the Royal Meteorological Society; eventually, in 1905, Dines was appointed to direct work on the upper air for the British Meteorological Office with the co-operation of a number of volunteer helpers in different parts of the country. The work is summarized in *The Characteristics of the Free Atmosphere*, published as a geophysical memoir by the Government Meteorological Committee in 1919.

Lastly, Dines undertook a searching examination of the problems of solar and terrestrial radiation, with the help of apparatus which is described in a number of papers contributed to the Royal Meteorological Society.

These investigations, in addition to various duties in connexion with the Society, of which he was president in 1901 and 1902, occupied Dines's time until his health failed in 1927. He died 24 December 1927 at his home at Benson, Oxfordshire, a property which he had acquired in 1914 for the work of the investigation of the upper air. Previously he had conducted his experiments at Pyrton Hill, near Watlington, Oxfordshire, which he had rented since 1906 when he found the neighbourhood of Oxshott, where he had been living, had become so populous that flying kites with several miles of invisible steel wire was no longer practicable.

Dines was elected a fellow of the Royal Society in 1905, and received the Symons medal of the Royal Meteorological Society in 1914 and the Buchan prize in 1924. His contributions to the science of meteorology are commemorated by the Meteorological Society in a special memorial volume. His real services to the science will find increasing expression as his work becomes gradually absorbed into the working ideals of the subject.

Dines married in 1882 Catharine Emma, daughter of the Rev. Frederic Tugwell, vicar of St. Andrew's, Lambeth, and sister of the Rev. Herbert Tugwell, subsequently bishop of Western Equatorial Africa, who was also at Corpus. It was an ideal marriage: without the encouragement and stimulus of his wife Dines would probably not have fulfilled the promises of his genius. They had two sons, both of whom entered the national meteorological service.

[*Proceedings* of the Royal Society, vol. cxix, A, 1928 (portrait); Official records of the Royal Meteorological Society and Meteorological Office; private information; personal knowledge.] N. Shaw.

DORRIEN, Sir **HORACE LOCKWOOD SMITH-** (1858–1930), general. [See Smith-Dorrien.]

DOUGHTY, CHARLES MONTAGU (1843–1926), poet and traveller, was born 19 August 1843 at Theberton Hall, Suffolk, the younger son of the Rev. Charles Montagu Doughty, landowner, by his wife, Frederica, daughter of the Hon. Frederick Hotham, prebendary of Rochester and rector of Dennington, Suffolk, and a granddaughter of Beaumont, second Baron Hotham [q.v.]. Charles Hotham Montagu Doughty-Wylie [q.v.] was the son of his elder brother. He was prepared at Beach House School, Portsmouth, for the royal navy, but was rejected at the medical examination, and after some private tuition he matriculated in 1861 at Cambridge as a pensioner of Gonville and Caius College. Here he read geology, but finding his college unwilling to let him work in his own fashion, he migrated after two years to Downing College, and proceeded to spend some nine months of 1863–1864 alone in Norway studying glacier action. A paper on the Jostedal-Brae glaciers in Norway, read at the 1864 meeting of the British Association, was the result of this expedition. In 1865 he was placed second in the second class of the natural sciences tripos, returned to Caius, and took his degree.

Reserved and serious, with strong antiquarian tastes, Doughty had already begun to read sixteenth-century literature and to study Teutonic languages. A deep enthusiasm awoke in him that was at once literary and patriotic. He resolved that it should be his life's task to serve his country and his mother tongue as a poet; to recall the legendary beginnings of the British race in verse which should revive the diction of Chaucer and of Spenser. Leaving Cambridge in 1865 he settled down to linguistic and antiquarian studies in long preparation for this task. In 1870, partly for the sake of economy and partly that he might visit the cradles of European civilization, Doughty began his travels as a poor student: first to Holland and Louvain, and on through Provence to Italy; thence to Spain by way of Sicily and North Africa; next, in the summer of 1873, to Italy again, and on to Greece. An ardent geologist, he climbed Vesuvius during the eruption of August 1872, an experience which he described twelve years later in *Travels in Arabia Deserta* [i, 420–421]. In February 1874 he reached Acre, and spent the summer and autumn wandering on foot through the Holy Land and Syria. A visit to Egypt followed, and early in 1875 he set out on a camel-journey through Sinai which brought him in May to Maan and Petra. Here he heard tales of other rock-monuments, unseen by western eyes, at Medain Salih on the pilgrim road to Medina, and he determined to explore them. His interest had been aroused not less in the geology and the life of Arabia than in its ancient remains, and he proposed a survey of the Wadi Arabah region as a second object of his expedition.

At Damascus, however, Doughty found the Turkish authorities unwilling to let him join the Meccan pilgrim caravan; and the British Association and the Royal Geographical Society, to both of which he appealed for support, declined to aid him. So rebuffed, he made up his mind to enter Arabia at his own risk and charges. His original plan, however, was modified: instead of returning northwards from Medain Salih, he would join the Bedouin and live with them, if he might, as a wandering physician. Adopting the name Khalil and the dress of an Arab Christian, he settled down at Damascus for a year to learn Arabic. In November 1876 he slipped out and quietly joined the pilgrim caravan.

The journey thus begun led Doughty from Medain Salih to Hail, Kheybar, and the Kasim in central Arabia: it ended twenty-one months later, on 2 August 1878, at Jiddah on the Red Sea. Its first object, the investigation of the Nabathaean remains of Medain Salih and El Ala, did not furnish its most important results. Doughty's records of those monuments were, indeed, the first to reach Europe, and, edited by Ernest Renan, were published in 1884 by the Académie des Inscriptions as *Documents épigraphiques recueillis dans le nord de l'Arabie*. But as a spectacle Medain Salih is no rival to Petra, and within a few years its inscriptions were recopied by scholars who were expert, as Doughty did not profess to be, in Semitic archaeology. The unique value of his journey began with its second stage, when, alone, with small funds, and stubbornly proclaiming himself an Englishman and a Christian, Doughty had to endure not only the fatigue and privation of desert life, but also, in a measure spared to those travellers who have enjoyed powerful support or gone in disguise as Moslems, the suspicion and occasionally the violence of the Arab society to which he had entrusted himself. In these circumstances of difficulty he gathered a vast amount of new information about the geography and geology of north-western Arabia, being the first to record accurately the true direction of the great watercourses of Wadi Hamd and Wadi er-Rumma. Of still greater value was the understanding which he gained of Arab character and the conditions of nomad life. In these respects his contribution to western knowledge of Arabia was, taken as a whole, the greatest which had yet been made; and the acuteness and the wisdom of his observation made him the acknowledged master of all later travellers.

Doughty reached England at the end of 1878, broken in health by his ordeal. Continued weakness delayed publication of his results, and the first geographical summary appeared only in 1880–1881 in the German periodical *Globus*. He addressed the Royal Geographical Society on 26 November 1883, his paper being printed in the *Proceedings* for July 1884; but he did not receive the founder's gold medal until 1912.

Meanwhile Doughty was at work upon a fuller narrative, designed to be not only a faithful record of all that he had learned and suffered in Arabia, but the vehicle of his first experiment in Elizabethan English. *Travels in Arabia Deserta*, finished in 1884, was issued in 1888 by the Cambridge University Press, after it had been refused by four publishers, of whom one wrote that it ought to be 'practically rewritten by a practised literary man'. Scholars at once recognized its value to Arabian studies, and reviewers praised it as the story of a wonderful feat: few readers, but among them William Morris and Robert Bridges, discerned its literary qualities. To the public at large it remained almost unknown until, in 1908, an abridgement by Mr. Edward Garnett, under the title *Wanderings in Arabia*, immediately gained for Doughty a host of admirers. In 1921 *Travels in Arabia Deserta*, long since out of print, was reissued with a new preface by Doughty and an introduction by T. E. Lawrence. A new generation of readers accepted it as a classic of travel.

With the completion of *Arabia Deserta* Doughty was set free to return to his long meditated epic of the British race, and the rest of his life was given up to poetry. In 1886 he married Caroline Amelia, daughter of General Sir William Montagu Scott McMurdo [q.v.], and went to live first on the Riviera and after 1899 at Tunbridge Wells and Eastbourne, practising everywhere a rigid self-discipline of study which almost wholly cut him off from the outer world. *The Dawn in Britain* appeared in six volumes in 1906–1907; it was followed by *Adam Cast Forth* (1908), *The Cliffs* (1909), *The Clouds* (1912), *The Titans* (1916), and *Mansoul* (1920; a second edition, corrected and enlarged, appeared in 1923). In 1900 Doughty privately issued *Under Arms, 1900*, a slim volume of verses addressed to the troops in South Africa.

Doughty considered his poetry more important than his prose. Conceived and shaped on a noble scale, and composed from first to last in a peculiarly stressed blank verse, with many archaisms of usage and word-form, it did not reveal its character to a glancing reader, or lend itself to anthologists. Some good judges among reviewers acclaimed *The Dawn in Britain* as a major achievement, and its great qualities showed again in *Adam Cast Forth*, in which Doughty returned with magnificent effect to an Arabian theme and setting. The characteristic excellences of Doughty's verse—its strong and nervous diction, its concrete imagery, its power to express epic themes, and its frequent passages of lyrical beauty—gradually came to be recognized by a small but elect circle of admirers. Yet the success of Doughty's poetry with the public at large could not be compared with that of his one work in prose.

During his earlier life, ill-health and temperamental ignorance of the ways of officials sometimes made Doughty intolerant in his dealings with learned societies and publishers who did not understand the value of his journey or who tried to reform his English: 'I am by nature self-willed, headstrong, and fierce with opponents,' he wrote in 1886, 'but my better reason and suffering in the world have bridled these faults and in part extinguished them.' His true nature and familiar aspect were well described by Mr. Edward Garnett who, meeting him for the first time in 1902, was 'captivated by his curiously abstracted gaze and by his sweet and benevolent smiles. He radiated courtesy, goodness, and modesty when he spoke.' Unconcerned with the contemporary world of letters, Doughty did not easily make close friendships; and perhaps only his wife and his two daughters knew the full depth and affection of his character.

Tall and strongly, though not heavily, built, with aquiline features and a thick beard which was reddish in early and middle life, Doughty in old age looked the hermit-patriarch of letters for which the world had come to take him. His health, which gradually improved after the Arabian adventure, failed during the last few years of his life, and he died 20 January 1926 at Sissinghurst, Kent, to which place he had migrated from Eastbourne in 1923.

Doughty was an honorary doctor of letters of both Oxford and Cambridge universities, and an honorary fellow of the British Academy. A portrait by Eric Kennington, painted in 1921, is in the National Portrait Gallery; a good medallion in bronze by T. Spicer Simson, reproduced, with other photographs, in the *Life* by D. G. Hogarth, is in the cloister-wall of the crematorium at Golders Green.

[D. G. Hogarth, *The Life of Charles M. Doughty*, 1928; Barker Fairley, *Charles M. Doughty, A Critical Study*, 1927; private information.] W. D. Hogarth.

DOUGLAS-SCOTT-MONTAGU, JOHN WALTER EDWARD, second Baron Montagu of Beaulieu (1866–1929), pioneer of motoring, was born at 3 Tilney Street, London, 10 June 1866. He was the elder son of Lord Henry John Douglas-Scott-Montagu, first Baron Montagu of Beaulieu, who was the second son of Walter Francis Scott, fifth Duke of Buccleuch [q.v.]. After sitting in the House of Commons for twenty-three years, first as member for Selkirkshire (1861–1868) and then for South Hampshire (1868–1884), Lord Henry Scott-Montagu was raised to the peerage in 1885. He married the Hon. Cecily Susan, younger daughter of John Stuart-Wortley, second Baron Wharncliffe [q.v.].

John Scott-Montagu was sent in 1880 to Eton, where he was in Mr. Marindin's house and was one of the school shooting eight in 1884 and 1885. From Eton he proceeded to New College, Oxford, and stroked the college boat in 1887 and 1888. In the first of these years New College went head of the river, but in the second lost two places. After leaving the university Scott-Montagu worked for some time in the shops of the London and South Western Railway Company at Nine Elms, and made himself a competent mechanic and engine-driver. He then travelled in Canada, the United States of America, South Africa, and the East. At the general election of 1892 he entered the House of Commons as conservative member for the New Forest division of Hampshire. He represented this constituency until, on the death of his father in 1905, he succeeded to the peerage.

Lord Montagu was one of the pioneers of motoring in England. He was always ready to adopt new ideas, and the motor-car made a special appeal to his engineering tastes. He was a firm believer in the internal combustion engine as the engine of the future for road traffic. In the opening years of the twentieth century he travelled all over England, explaining the advantages of the new system of locomotion and combating the prejudice against it. Among other feats he took King Edward VII for his first trip in a motor-car in 1900, and he was the first motorist to drive into Palace Yard. He also founded and edited for many years a weekly periodical, *The Car Illustrated*, with its associated publications of maps and road-books. He wrote numbers of articles and letters to the press on motoring and the use of the highways, dealing with the subject rather, it must be admitted, from the motorist's than from the pedestrian's point of view. There can be no doubt that Montagu's energetic advocacy played no small part in the extension of motoring and in the development of the modern motor-car.

Lord Montagu's intimate acquaintance with the technical side of mechanical transport made his assistance of great value in all problems connected with the subject. He spoke both in the House of Commons and in the House of Lords with the authority of a recognized expert, defending the motor industry from needless restrictions and from the attacks of vested interests. He served as a member of the Road Board from 1909 to 1919.

When the European War broke out in

1914 Lord Montagu at once rejoined his old militia regiment, the 7th battalion of the Hampshire Regiment, and was sent out to India. In 1915 he was appointed adviser on mechanical transport services to the government of India, a post which he held until 1919. Here again his knowledge and experience admirably fitted him for the position, and his efficiency was rewarded by a C.S.I. in 1916 and a K.C.I.E. in 1919. During the War he had a remarkable escape from drowning, for he was on board the *Persia* when in 1916 she was torpedoed by a German submarine in the Mediterranean. He was rescued from a partially submerged boat, after being many hours in the water and suffering terrible hardships. He was at first reported to be lost, and he had the unusual experience of reading obituary notices of himself.

The progress of aviation interested Lord Montagu greatly. In 1916 he called the attention of the House of Lords to the importance of air policy, and in the following year he visited Canada in order to lecture on aviation. He believed in the future of the seaplane as the best defence against submarines.

A man of vigorous and inquiring mind, Lord Montagu did not confine his activities to mechanical pursuits. He was a landowner in Hampshire and verderer of the New Forest, as his father had been before him. He made himself master of the details of estate management; he was fond of natural history, and an authority on the fauna and flora of the Forest; and there were few branches of rural life on which he was not full of information. He made great numbers of friends in all classes, friends who, even if some of them were occasionally amused by the wide range of his enthusiasms, found in him a most attractive companion.

Lord Montagu married twice: first, in 1889 Lady Cecil Victoria Constance (died 1919), eldest daughter of Schomberg Henry Kerr, ninth Marquess of Lothian [q.v.]; secondly, in 1920 Alice Pearl, daughter of Major Edward Barrington Crake, Rifle Brigade. By his first wife he had two daughters, and by his second a son, Edward John Barrington (born 1926), who succeeded his father as third baron, and three daughters. Lord Montagu died in London 30 March 1929.

A cartoon of Lord Montagu by 'Spy' appeared in *Vanity Fair* 8 October 1896.

[*The Times*, 1 April 1929; Lady Troubridge and Archibald Marshall, *John, Lord Montagu of Beaulieu*, 1930.] A. Cochrane.

DOYLE, Sir ARTHUR CONAN (1859–1930), author, the eldest son of Charles Altamont Doyle, clerk in the Board of Works and artist, by his wife, Mary Foley, was born in Edinburgh 22 May 1859. He came of an Irish Roman Catholic family, and one well known in art and letters. His grandfather was John Doyle [q.v.], the portrait-painter and caricaturist, and his uncle was Richard Doyle [q.v.], the black-and-white artist who drew for *Punch* in the early years of that journal and designed its well-known cover.

Arthur Conan Doyle was educated at Stonyhurst and at Edinburgh University. He qualified M.B. in 1881 and M.D. in 1885, and practised at Southsea from 1882 to 1890. In 1887 he published his first book, *A Study in Scarlet*—a novel, of a not more than moderately thrilling type, which is chiefly noteworthy for introducing to the public a character, Sherlock Holmes, who became a famous figure in detective fiction. Conan Doyle followed this tale with *Micah Clarke* (1887), *The Captain of the Polestar* (1889), *The White Company* (1890), *The Sign of Four* (1890, another Holmes story), and other novels of general or historical interest.

But what attracted more attention than these complete works was a series of short stories which came out under the title *The Adventures of Sherlock Holmes*. The first of these, 'A Scandal in Bohemia', appeared in the *Strand Magazine* for July 1891, and for many months the stories formed an attractive feature of that periodical. The hero of these exploits was now handled with greater sureness and fertility of invention. Sherlock Holmes was represented as a private detective, living in Baker Street with a friend, Doctor Watson, who describes the cases brought to them by distracted clients, and the manner in which Holmes solved mysteries which baffled every one else, including the leading officials of Scotland Yard. Holmes's methods consisted in the careful and systematic examination of minute details, and a process of deduction from the points observed. The character is said to have been suggested to Doyle by his recollection of an eminent Edinburgh surgeon, Dr. Joseph Bell, under whom he had worked as a medical student. It was Bell's custom to impress upon his pupils the value in diagnosis of the faculty of close observation of facts and the intelligent interpretation of them.

Conan Doyle made free use of this creation of his fancy in many stories both short and long. Sherlock Holmes, with his clean-shaven face and penetrating eyes, his spare yet muscular frame, his pipe, his dressing-gown, his violin, and the cocaine syringe with which he soothed his nerves, became a familiar figure to millions of readers. Equally appreciated, and in striking contrast, was the simplicity of Doctor Watson, who could be trusted to put the questions necessary for displaying to the best advantage his leader's unusual gifts. All too soon, however, the association of Holmes and Watson was cut short by a fatality which befell the great detective, when he shared the fate of a master-criminal whom he at last brought to account in a life and death struggle on the brink of a precipice. The public was deeply distressed. The Sherlock Holmes stories which had begun, as stated, in July 1891, in the *Strand Magazine*, continued with a break of a few months only until December 1893, when this tragedy occurred. Fortunately, after some time had passed it was discovered that, although in grave peril, Holmes had escaped with his life and was able to embark upon a new series of exploits. These short stories began in October 1903, and the adventures continued to appear at irregular intervals until within a year or two of the author's death. He had published, besides, a longer and rather more elaborate Sherlock Holmes tale *The Hound of the Baskervilles*, which ran in the *Strand* from August 1901 to April 1902, and was afterwards published as a separate volume. Whatever rank may be assigned to Conan Doyle among English novelists, he at least earned the distinction of having created a figure whose name has passed into the language as a synonym for the qualities with which the author invested him.

Conan Doyle did not confine his energies to literature. He was distinguished by a spirit of genuine patriotism, and any Imperial cause attracted him. During the South African War of 1899–1902 he placed his medical knowledge and experience at the disposal of the government, and acted as senior physician to the field hospital maintained and equipped by Sir John Langman. He wrote an account of the earlier stages of the campaign in his book *The Great Boer War* (1900). More important than this book was his pamphlet, *The War in South Africa. Its Cause and Conduct* (1902), which had as its object the justification of England's action in declaring war against the Boers, and the vindication of her method of conducting the campaign. Some exposition of the facts had become essential in order to correct misconceptions industriously spread over the Continent. The pamphlet was translated into twelve European languages, and more than a hundred thousand copies of it were given away. Shortly after the conclusion of the War, Conan Doyle came out as a warm supporter of the proposals put forward in 1903 by Joseph Chamberlain for tariff reform and Colonial preference. He had already stood for parliament in 1900 as liberal unionist candidate for Central Edinburgh, without success; and in 1906 he stood again—this time for the Hawick Burghs as a tariff reformer. Though a capable speaker on his own subjects, and a most vigorous electioneer, he failed to obtain a seat in parliament. He was an active propagandist in fields other than political, and devoted much labour to championing the cause of a man named Oscar Slater, who was sentenced to death (commuted afterwards to penal servitude) for murder and robbery at Glasgow in May 1909. Actuated by a firm belief that this was a case of mistaken identity, Doyle published in 1912 a criticism of the judgment, which led to an official inquiry in 1914. As a result it was announced that no grounds for interference with Slater's sentence had been found, and this announcement was repeated by the secretary for Scotland in 1925. Two years later the introduction of fresh evidence led to the case being remitted to the Scottish court of criminal appeal, and upon 20 July 1928 the sentence was quashed, and Slater, who had already been released from gaol, received an *ex gratia* payment of £6,000 as compensation.

For nearly forty years Conan Doyle continued to write and publish regularly. He chose a hero, Brigadier Gerard, for several stories of Napoleonic times, and his lively imagination played with many different forms of sensation, as in *The Lost World* (1912) and *The Poison Belt* (1913). He also wrote several more books dealing with public topics, such as *The Crime of the Congo* (1910). During the European War he was engaged upon a *History of the British Campaign in France and Flanders* (6 vols., 1916–1920), and he also wrote *A Visit to Three Fronts* (1916). He made a few essays in dramatic authorship, the most successful being *A Story of Waterloo* (1894); in this, a one-act play, Sir Henry Irving gave a remarkable representation of a veteran soldier.

In the later years of his life Conan Doyle

became absorbed by the subject of spiritualism, upon which he wrote and lectured not only in England, but in South Africa and Australia. Among his books on this subject are *The Wanderings of a Spiritualist* (1921) and a *History of Spiritualism* (2 vols., 1926), and most of the writing that he undertook in this period was coloured by his views on the evidence for spirit communication.

Conan Doyle was a big man, strong, and heavily built. He was fond of all sports and games. He was a fair cricketer, and played in many good second-class matches for the Marylebone and other clubs. He was also a regular patron of boxing, and brought the subject of pugilism into one of the best of his novels, *Rodney Stone* (1896). His writings were in keeping with his character. His novels, with no claim to literary distinction, are for the most part capital stories told in a straightforward and vigorous style.

Conan Doyle was knighted after the South African War, in 1902. He received the honorary degree of LL.D. from the university of Edinburgh in 1905 and was a knight of grace of the order of St. John of Jerusalem. He married twice: first, in 1885 Louise (died 1906), daughter of J. Hawkins, of Minsterworth, Gloucestershire, by whom he had one son and one daughter; secondly, in 1907 Jean, daughter of James Blyth Leckie, of Glebe House, Blackheath, by whom he had two sons and one daughter. He died at his home at Crowborough, Sussex, 7 July 1930.

[*The Times*, 8 July 1930.]

A. Cochrane.

DREYER, JOHN LOUIS EMIL (1852–1926), astronomer, was born at Copenhagen 13 February 1852, the third son of John Christopher Dreyer, lieutenant-general in the Danish army, by his wife, Ida Nicoline Margarethe Rangrup. His father served with distinction in the Schleswig-Holstein War in 1864, and his grandfather was a staff officer in Napoleon's army under Marshal Davoust. As a boy at school Dreyer was deeply interested in the story of Tycho Brahe and his observatories on the Danish island of Hven, and decided that he would be an astronomer. He was encouraged in this resolution by Schjellerup, an assistant at the Copenhagen observatory. He entered the university of Copenhagen in 1869 and studied mathematics and astronomy. A little later he made observations at the observatory and acquired a practical knowledge of meridian astronomy. In 1874 he was awarded a gold medal by the university for an essay on 'Personal Errors in Observations', one of the great difficulties in meridian astronomy of that time, but now largely eliminated.

In 1874 Dreyer succeeded Dr. Ralph Copeland [q.v.] as assistant in the Earl of Rosse's observatory at Birr Castle, Parsonstown, Ireland. Here he made with Lord Rosse's great reflecting telescope many observations of nebulae and clusters, which are incorporated in a memoir presented by Lord Rosse to the Royal Dublin Society recording the observations made at Birr from 1848 to 1878. In 1877 Dreyer published a supplement to Sir John Herschel's *Catalogue of Nebulae*, containing 1,136 nebulae discovered by D'Arrest, Marth, Stephan, and Tempel.

In 1878 Dreyer left Lord Rosse's observatory and became an assistant at the Dublin University observatory at Dunsink, near Dublin. Here he returned to the meridian observing with which he had been familiar at Copenhagen. In 1881 he published *A New Determination of the Constant of Precession*—the result of comparing the observations of Lalande made in 1800 with those of Schjellerup in 1865, prefaced by a valuable historical account of previous determinations of this important astronomical constant. In 1882 he left Dunsink in order to become director of the Armagh observatory in succession to Dr. Thomas Romney Robinson [q.v.]. Here he collected and reduced observations made since 1859, supplemented them by many of his own, and published the results in the *Second Armagh Catalogue of 3,300 Stars* (1886).

In 1886 Dreyer submitted to the council of the Royal Astronomical Society a second supplementary catalogue of nebulae. The council suggested that as Herschel's catalogue was out of print it would be better to make a complete catalogue of all known nebulae. Dreyer accordingly undertook this laborious task, and published in the *Memoirs* of the Society a *New General Catalogue of Nebulae and Clusters of Stars, being the Catalogue of Sir John Herschel, revised, corrected, and enlarged* (1888). This contains the positions and descriptions of 7,840 nebulae and clusters, as discovered up to the year 1888. He subsequently published, in 1895 and 1908 respectively, descriptions and positions of 1,529 nebulae and clusters found in the period 1888 to 1894, and 3,857 nebulae and clusters found in the period 1895 to 1907. These have been accepted by astronomers as standard works of reference.

Dreyer now returned to a subject which had interested him since his boyhood, and in 1890 published a life of *Tycho Brahe*. His knowledge of Danish as well as French, German, and Italian made it possible for him to read all that had been written about the great astronomer, as well as the original manuscripts of observations in the library of Copenhagen. The work is, as stated in the sub-title, 'a picture of scientific life and work in the sixteenth century', and describes the by-paths and blind alleys into which the great pioneers of astronomy strayed in their search for truth, as well as the roads along which advances have been made.

Dreyer's next book was a *History of the Planetary Systems from Thales to Kepler* (1906). In this learned work he unfolds man's conception of the universe from the earliest historical ages to the completion of the Copernican system by Kepler. He points out that the spherical form of the Earth was taught by Parmenides about 500 B.C., and that scientific astronomy may be dated from Eudoxus of Cnidus and Calippus about 350 B.C., with the homocentric spheres which made observation agree with theory and freed the science from mere philosophical speculation. He explains why the heliocentric theory of Aristarchus of Samos (250 B.C.) failed to find acceptance. He next gives an account of the theory of epicycles originating with Apollonius of Perga (230 B.C.) and developed by Hipparchus (130 B.C.) and Ptolemy (A.D. 140); how Eratosthenes (230 B.C.) determined the size of the Earth, and Hipparchus its distance from the Moon. Finally, Greek astronomy was summed up in the second century A.D. by Ptolemy in the *Almagest*, which remained the authoritative word until Copernicus wrote the *De Revolutionibus Orbium Coelestium* in 1543. The book concludes with chapters on Copernicus, Tycho Brahe, and Kepler.

In 1908 Dreyer began preparations for a complete edition of the observations of Tycho Brahe, under the auspices of the Carlsberg Institute. Later, through the munificence of G. A. Hagemann, of Copenhagen, it was made possible to include all the works of Tycho Brahe, and his correspondence, from manuscripts as well as from published sources. The work occupies no less than fourteen volumes including two long prolegomena by Dreyer which were translated into Latin by Dr. Raeder of the university of Copenhagen. The last proofs of the *Tychonis Brahe Opera Omnia* (1913–1926) were read just before Dreyer's death.

In 1910 Dreyer was invited by the councils of the Royal Society and the Royal Astronomical Society to edit a complete edition of the works of Sir William Herschel. Although engaged upon the life of Tycho Brahe he undertook the task and contributed a memoir on Herschel's life and work. The *Scientific Papers of Sir William Herschel* appeared in 1912.

In 1916 Dreyer left Armagh and settled in Oxford. In the same year the gold medal of the Royal Astronomical Society was awarded to him for his work on the history of astronomy and his catalogues of nebulae. His residence in England brought him into closer touch with fellow-astronomers. He served on the council of the Royal Astronomical Society from 1917 and was president in 1923 and 1924. In 1923 he collaborated with Professor H. H. Turner in publishing a *History of the Royal Astronomical Society, 1820–1920* in commemoration of the society's centenary.

Dreyer's great erudition was accompanied by a single-mindedness in the purpose of his life and an unsparing devotion to the science of astronomy. He was endeared to many friends by his gentle and amiable disposition. Near the end of 1925 his health showed signs of breaking down, but he was able to do some reading and to correct proofs. He died at Oxford 14 September 1926 at the age of seventy-four.

Dreyer married in 1875 Katherine Hannah (died 1923), daughter of John Tuthill, of Kilmore, co. Limerick. They had three sons and one daughter.

[*The Times*, 15 September 1926; *Monthly Notices* of the Royal Astronomical Society, vol. lxxxvii, 1927; *The Observatory*, October 1926; Dr. Dreyer's published works.]

F. W. Dyson.

DUCKWORTH, Sir DYCE, first baronet (1840–1928), physician, the fourth and youngest son of Robinson Duckworth, a Liverpool merchant, by his wife, Elizabeth Forbes, daughter of William Nicol, M.D., of Stonehaven, Kincardineshire, was born in Liverpool 24 November 1840. He was educated at the Royal Institution School, Liverpool, and at the university of Edinburgh, where he took the M.D. degree with honours in 1863. He was awarded a gold medal for his thesis, which embodied work done by him on the anatomy of the suprarenal capsules.

After graduation Duckworth held the post of resident physician (house physician) at the Royal Infirmary, Edinburgh, but relinquished it a year later (1864) in order to enter the naval medical service, in which his maternal grandfather, Dr. Nicol, had served. Duckworth left the service in 1865. The premature death, in December 1864, of Dr. William Stenhouse Kirkes [q.v.] had caused a vacancy in the office of medical tutor at St. Bartholomew's Hospital, and to this post Duckworth was appointed. But through life he retained a special affection for the senior service.

Thenceforward Duckworth followed the career of a teacher of medicine and consulting physician in London. He held a series of posts at St. Bartholomew's Hospital, and ultimately those of full physician to the Hospital (1883–1905) and joint lecturer on medicine (1890–1901). On his retirement he became consulting physician to, and governor of, the Hospital.

The Royal College of Physicians also claimed Duckworth's devoted services. He was elected member in 1865 and fellow in 1870, and served in turn as councillor, examiner, censor, and senior censor. He was treasurer to the college for almost forty years, and on his retirement from that office in 1923 was elected emeritus treasurer. He delivered the Lumleian lectures in 1896 on *The Sequels of Diseases*, and the Harveian oration in 1898, when he took as his subject *The Influence of Character and Right Judgement in Medicine*.

Always interested in the nursing profession, Duckworth was for some years vice-president of the Royal British Nurses' Association and he was a knight of justice and almoner of the Order of St. John of Jerusalem in England. He was president of the Clinical Society (1891–1893). He acted as examiner in medicine at the universities of Edinburgh, Durham, and Manchester, for the royal naval medical service and for the Conjoint Board.

On his retirement from St. Bartholomew's in 1905 at the age of sixty-five, Duckworth was appointed physician to the Seamen's (Dreadnought) Hospital, Greenwich, and lectured in its school. He was consulting physician to the Italian Hospital, Queen Square, medical referee to the Treasury (1905–1911), and member of the Pensions Commutation Board (1900–1910).

Duckworth received many honours: he was knighted in 1886 and created a baronet in 1909; he was accorded the honorary degrees of LL.D. of Liverpool and Edinburgh universities and M.D. of Belfast, of the Royal University of Ireland, and of Cincinnati, U.S.A.; he was also honorary F.R.C.P. of Ireland and corresponding member of the Académie de Médecine of Paris.

Duckworth had all the attributes of the courtly physician of former days. He was characterized by a courteous though somewhat formal manner and by a strong sense of propriety. He liked everything done in order and with due ceremonial. He did not suffer fools gladly and had no patience with fads, but he had a sense of humour and could laugh at his own expense. On many subjects he held strong views and expressed them with emphasis; and a conservative outlook permeated his attitude towards life. He was a cultured man, widely travelled, and a linguist. He had a good knowledge of French and great sympathy with the ideas of French medicine, especially as regards diathesis, in which his early teacher, Thomas Laycock [q.v.], had first awakened his interest.

As a physician Duckworth was above all an exponent of the art of medicine, and feared that this art might be lost in what he regarded as 'the futile effort to make medicine into an exact science'. His pupils learned more from example than from precept, and to watch his handling of a case of acute illness, his resource in emergencies, his foresight of possible accidents, and his meticulous care of all details of medical treatment and nursing was a valuable training in the art of medicine. He made many minor contributions to medical literature, and delivered many addresses on temperance and other social subjects; but his chief monument is his *Treatise on Gout*, published in 1889.

Duckworth married twice: first, in 1870 Annie Alicia (died 1889), daughter of Alexander Hopkins, of Limavady, co. Antrim, and widow of John Smith, East India merchant, of Mickleham Hall, Dorking, by whom he had a son and two daughters; secondly, in 1890 Ada Emily, daughter of George Arthur Fuller, of Dorking, by whom he had two sons. He died in London 20 January 1928 and was succeeded as second baronet by the son of his first marriage, Edward Dyce (born 1875), sometime a judge of the High Court of Judicature in Rangoon.

[Memoir in St. Bartholomew's Hospital *Reports*, vol. lxii, 1929; private information; personal knowledge.] A. E. Garrod.

DUKE, Sir FREDERICK WILLIAM (1863–1924), Indian civil servant, born at

Arbroath 8 December 1863, was the eldest son of the Rev. William Duke, D.D., parish minister of St. Vigean's, Forfarshire, by his wife, Annie, daughter of Surgeon Peter Alexander Leonard, R.N., inspector-general of hospitals. Duke came of an old Angus family; an ancester fought in the Rebellion of 1745. Educated as a child at a dame's school at Norwood, he returned to Scotland and spent seven years at the Arbroath high school, whence he went to Messrs. Wren and Gurney's to be coached for the Indian civil service examination, which he passed, eleventh on the list, in 1882. His two years probation was passed at University College, London.

Assigned to Bengal, where he remained throughout his Indian career, Duke had, unlike most members of his service who have risen to high office, no secretariate experience until, after twenty-four years service in districts, he became chief secretary to the government of Bengal in 1909. But this long apprenticeship gave him a very thorough knowledge of district administration and of the people of Bengal; and his modesty and lack of ambition saved him from disappointment at the promotion of others before him. Duke was, indeed, a public servant whose good and unobtrusive work came little into notice; so that his selection for his first high appointment was made after considerable hesitation. But, once chosen for a post of great responsibility, he fully justified the choice by his qualities of sound judgement, tact, and industry, and by his high standard of personal and political uprightness. Quiet and reserved in manner and utterance, he was a shrewd though kindly judge of men. While he possessed political imagination to a degree unsuspected by those who did not know him intimately, his temperament was cautious, and when he came in later years to be closely concerned in the deliberations which led to the transmutation of the Indian political system by the Montagu-Chelmsford reforms (1918–1919), the disadvantage of never having served inside the government of India was to some extent counterbalanced by his intimate knowledge of those fundamental facts of provincial and district administration which are sometimes forgotten at Simla and hardly discernible from Whitehall.

Duke's earlier years were spent for the most part in remote and politically unimportant districts of Bengal, Bihar, and Orissa (then undivided); but the tenure from 1897 to 1902 of the magistracy at Howrah, which carried with it the chairmanship of its municipality, introduced him to a new and difficult phase of administration, and brought him into personal touch with members of the business and mercantile European community of Calcutta, among whom he made many friends. He restored the disordered finances of the Howrah municipality, and for a short time acted as chairman of the Calcutta corporation. His promotion in 1905 to be commissioner of Orissa enlarged his experience and increased his reputation among his colleagues. In Sir Andrew Fraser [q.v.] he found a sympathetic lieutenant-governor; and his appointment to officiate as chief secretary in 1908, which came as somewhat of a surprise, was continued by Sir Edward Baker, a brilliant but difficult chief, whom Duke's imperturbable good temper and quiet loyalty gradually impressed. Thus, when an executive council under the lieutenant-governor was created in 1910, Duke became one of its members, and, on Baker's going home on leave in July 1911, acting lieutenant-governor. Baker retired in the following September, and Duke continued to rule the province, until the spectacular changes, announced at the royal durbar at Delhi (12 December 1911), reunited Eastern and Western Bengal into a presidency (cutting off Bihar and Orissa), with a governor brought, as in Madras and Bombay, from political circles in England. Sir William Duke (he was knighted in 1911) was thus the last of the lieutenant-governors who for more than half a century had ruled Bengal, and the last official occupant of Belvedere, Warren Hastings's house in Alipur (Calcutta).

When Lord Carmichael of Skirling [q.v.] was transferred from Madras to Bengal in April 1912 to be the first governor, Duke became his senior member of council. His expert knowledge was placed unreservedly at the disposal of a governor ignorant of local conditions and with but short experience of India. He was especially useful in bringing together again the officers and the administrative systems of the two provinces which had been severed by Lord Curzon.

In November 1914 Duke retired from the Indian civil service, and was appointed a member of the Council of India. Though the ordinary work of the Council in Whitehall was diminished by war conditions, the political problems of India became increasingly insistent. In London Duke met the group of students of Imperial questions associated with the *Round Table* quarterly review, and with these, and some of the senior officials of the India Office, engaged in discussions on the framework of Indian government in the course of which the novel idea of 'dyarchy' was hatched, though in a form very different from that established by the Government of India Act of 1919. In a memorandum, in the composition of which Duke took the leading part, an attempt was made to sketch the way in which an Indian province might be governed under a scheme of partial 'responsibility'. This unofficial document, read by the viceroy, Lord Chelmsford, acquired an importance that its authors had not foreseen: and when the secretary of state, Mr. Edwin Samuel Montagu [q.v.], went to India in 1917 after the momentous declaration of his new policy, he chose Sir William Duke from among his council to accompany him. But Duke's own preference had been for a modest beginning of self-government in territorial units smaller than the existing provinces of India. In the consultations held in India in the cold weather of 1917–1918 between the secretary of state's delegation and the governments of India and of the provinces, Montagu relied upon Duke to a far greater extent than is likely to be conveyed by the sometimes petulant extracts from his unrevised private diary, published after his death. In January 1920, on the retirement of Sir Thomas Holderness (q.v., the only other Indian civilian to hold the office) Montagu made Duke permanent under-secretary of state at the India Office. In this post, confronted by the difficult task of adjusting the degree of control exercised by the secretary of state in council to the new conditions in India, as well as by the un-unfamiliar duties of the head of the major office in the home civil service, Duke earned the confidence of Montagu's successors, Lord Peel and Lord Olivier, as well as the regard of the permanent staff. On 11 June 1924 he died suddenly in London of a heart attack due to arteriosclerosis.

Duke thoroughly enjoyed Indian life, especially in its outdoor aspects, was a fair shot, and acquired a good field-knowledge of the fauna and flora of Bengal. An indefatigable walker, he liked to explore his districts and to get to know the villagers, by whom he was called 'the sahib who does all his *daks* (journeys) on foot'. Genuinely interested in Indian archaeology, he was able to do useful work at Gaza in the conservation of Buddhist remains.

Duke married in 1889 Mary, daughter of James Addison Scott, of Newton of Arbirlot, near Arbroath, who with their two sons and one daughter survived him. He was awarded the C.S.I. in 1910, the K.C.I.E. in 1911, the K.C.S.I. in 1915, and the G.C.I.E. in 1918. An unofficial distinction which he valued highly was his election to the Athenaeum Club under rule II in 1922.

[Lionel Curtis, *Dyarchy*, 1920; *Lord Carmichael of Skirling: a Memoir*, 1929; Edwin S. Montagu, *An Indian Diary*, 1930; private information.] M. C. C. Seton.

DUNRAVEN AND MOUNT-EARL, fourth Earl of (1841–1926), Irish politician. [See Quin, Windham Thomas Wyndham-.]

DURAND, Sir HENRY MORTIMER (1850–1924), Indian civil servant and diplomat, was born at Sehore, Bhopal State, India, 14 February 1850, the second son of General Sir Henry Marion Durand (1812–1871, q.v.), by his first wife, Anne, daughter of Major-General Sir John McCaskill. After being educated at Blackheath Proprietary School and at Eton House, Tonbridge, he passed into the Indian civil service in 1870. He was called to the bar by Lincoln's Inn in 1872. He arrived in India early in 1873, and after serving in Bengal for eighteen months was appointed attaché in the Foreign Office. He was proficient in Oriental languages, and rose rapidly in the political or diplomatic department, serving under (Sir) Alfred Lyall in Rajputana and as political secretary to Sir Frederick (afterwards Earl) Roberts in Afghanistan in 1879–1880. He was shut up with Roberts's force in the Sherpur cantonment, and assisted his brother-in-law, Sir Charles Metcalfe MacGregor [q.v.], in recapturing some guns which had fallen into the enemy's hands. He was mentioned in dispatches for conspicuous gallantry and was awarded the Afghan war medal with two clasps.

Returning to Calcutta, Durand rejoined the Foreign Office and soon rose to be its head. In 1885 he was confirmed as foreign secretary by the governor-general, the Earl of Dufferin, who considered him 'about the ablest civil servant we have, and certainly the loftiest-minded man I have met in India—brave, cool, proud, and absolutely disinterested, very industrious and with a tremendous sense of the obligations and of the dignity which should attach to an English gentleman'. As foreign secretary and head of the political department, Durand accomplished the best work of his life. He enjoyed the complete confidence of Lord Dufferin (whom he accompanied to Mandalay in 1886) and of his successor, Lord Lansdowne. He exercised a powerful permanent influence on frontier policy, on the settlement with Russia after the Panjdeh affair of 1885, on the annexation of Upper Burma, and on the critical negotiations with Ameer Abdur Rahman, which led up to the final settlement of boundaries between Afghanistan and Russia on one side, and Afghanistan, British India, and Persia on the other. In 1893 he negotiated with the ameer at Kabul an agreement whereby the British Indian Empire acquired a frontier of actual and definite responsibility in advance of its administrative border. The 'Durand line', which was subsequently demarcated, divides tribes under British political control from those under Afghan influence for the entire distance from Chitral to Seistan, thereby removing a source of constant misunderstanding and friction. A northern border had already been secured for the ameer, which has marked a definite barrier against Russia's advance towards India, and may therefore be said to have prepared the way for the Anglo-Russian agreement of 1907 and for Anglo-Russian co-operation in the European War of 1914. Durand also planned and carried through the establishment of the Imperial service troops of the Indian princes, whereby 26,000 trained men were added to the number of combatants sent from India in the European War.

The main secret of Durand's success was his enthusiasm and the confidence which he inspired in his subordinates and in the Asiatic rulers with whom he came into contact. His object was to meet men face to face, to discuss all problems with local experts, to visit all outposts of empire. 'I have never forgotten', wrote Sir West Ridgeway [q.v.], on the successful conclusion of the labours of the Russia-Afghan boundary commission, 'what I owe to your generous friendship and appreciation.' 'Sir Mortimer Durand', says Ameer Abdur Rahman in his autobiography, 'being a clever statesman, realized that confidence begets confidence; hearts have intercourse with hearts; affection creates affection; and hatred creates hatred.' Anxious to promote good relations between all classes in Simla, Durand organized Association football there in 1886, and in 1888 presented a silver football to be competed for annually. The game speedily became exceedingly popular.

Durand was created K.C.I.E. in 1889, and K.C.S.I. in 1894, after his return from Kabul. In the spring of the latter year he was offered by Lord Rosebery the post of minister-plenipotentiary at Teheran, and prematurely retired from the Indian civil service. His services were acknowledged in the *Gazette of India* as 'rarely equalled and never excelled during the first twenty years of an Indian career'. He remained in Persia from 1894 to 1900, but in spite of his fine qualities and exceptional ability to speak Persian easily, was not particularly successful, largely because he could not induce Lord Salisbury's government to give substantial countenance to capitalists prepared to find the two million loan for which the shah's government insistently begged. He handled with conspicuous judgement the difficult situation which resulted from the assassination of Shah Nasir-ud-din and made useful suggestions, which were afterwards carried out, for the establishment of British consulates at important centres; but, as may be learned from the friendly testimony of Sir Cecil Spring-Rice, who served under him and afterwards succeeded him as chargé d'affaires, he was hardly on speaking terms with any of the Persian ministers. His manners were stiff, but his whole work was obstructed by peculiar difficulties which were no fault of his. The position at Teheran after his departure has been pithily described by Spring-Rice: 'Order in this town is kept by a Russian colonel and his Russian-drilled troops, by the guns given by the Czar, and by the advice which the Russians are giving. Finances have been for a time set in order by a Russian loan. Corn is brought into the starving city by a Russian road. We have done nothing and given nothing, and cannot expect to get anything.'

On being promoted ambassador at Madrid, Durand received the G.C.M.G. In 1901 he was made a privy councillor. He was liked and respected in Spain, and Spanish feeling towards Great Britain improved during his term of office. In 1903, upon the sudden death of Sir Michael Herbert, he was offered by Lord Lansdowne the Washington embassy. He accepted with alacrity, and began work in this new sphere with the eager ambition to promote British and American friendship, and with a strong admiration for President Roosevelt. But Roosevelt was anxious to have Spring-Rice as ambassador, as was also

Senator Cabot Lodge, who stood at the president's elbow. To both of these men Spring-Rice was an intimate friend of many years' standing. Durand was temperamentally unsuited to America; he was not a professional diplomat, and was stiff and unyielding in upholding British and Canadian rights and claims. His embassy was not strongly equipped; and his deeply-rooted patriotism made him very sensitive to rough-and-ready criticisms of British methods and ideas. Roosevelt, too, was much annoyed by the refusal of Mr. Balfour's government to advise their ally Japan 'to be reasonable' in the negotiations with Russia in 1905. With a change of government in England came an opportunity for a change of ambassadors at Washington. In October 1905 Durand was recalled, to his own surprise, on the ground that his temperament prevented him from keeping in personal touch with the president and the foreign secretary, and that consequently the British embassy was placed at a considerable disadvantage. Sir Edward Grey's letter held out no hope of another diplomatic appointment.

Deeply hurt, Durand returned to England in 1906. He was offered and refused the governorship of Bombay. He contested Plymouth in the conservative interest in 1910, but was unsuccessful, and retired into private life, occupying himself largely with literary pursuits. He emerged during the War, first as a vigorous recruiter in the West of England, and then as chairman of a committee whose duty it was to revise exemptions from military service. He died 8 June 1924 at Polden, Minehead, Somerset, where he was buried.

Durand's literary output was considerable. In 1879 he edited his father's *History of the First Afghan War* and in 1883 he published a biography of his father. His other works were *Helen Treveryan, or the Ruling Race* (first published anonymously in 1891), *Nadir Shah*, an historical novel (1908), the life of Sir Alfred Lyall, perhaps the best of his books (1913), a biography of Sir George White (1915), *A Holiday in South Africa* (1911), and *The Thirteenth Hussars in the Great War* (1921). He was a director of the Royal Asiatic Society from 1911 to 1919 and president of the Central Asian Society from 1914 to 1917.

Durand was a man of fine appearance and physique. He rode, shot, and played games well. But he suffered from shyness and nervousness, and for this reason was apt to assume a somewhat rigid official demeanour. Those who served under him in India, however, appreciated his uncompromising rectitude and essential simplicity of nature; and a close observer at Washington spoke of him in 1905 in a letter to Spring-Rice as possessing a fine mind and character. 'No man ever struggled with greater adversity.' He seems to have been mistaken both in abandoning his Indian career prematurely and in declining to return to it as a governor later on. At heart he was a soldier and would have adopted a military career but for his father's dissuasion.

Durand married in 1875 Ella (died 1913), daughter of Teignmouth Sandys, of the Bengal civil service. They had a son and a daughter. A portrait of Durand by W. Thomas Smith (1904) is in the National Portrait Gallery, and a cartoon by 'Spy' appeared in *Vanity Fair* 12 May 1904.

[Sir Percy Sykes, *The Life of Sir Mortimer Durand*, 1926; Stephen Gwynn, *The Letters and Friendships of Sir Cecil Spring-Rice*, 2 vols., 1929; *The Life of Abdur Rahman, Amir of Afghanistan*, edited by Mir Munshi Sultan Mahomed Khan, 1900; Sir Frederick Maurice, *The Life of General Lord Rawlinson of Trent*, 1928; private information; personal knowledge.]

H. V. Lovett.

DURNFORD, Sir WALTER (1847–1926), provost of King's College, Cambridge, was born 21 February 1847 at Middleton, Lancashire, the younger son of the Rev. Richard Durnford [q.v.], rector of Middleton, and afterwards bishop of Chichester, by his wife, Emma, daughter of the Rev. John Keate, D.D. [q.v.], headmaster of Eton from 1809 to 1834. Durnford entered Eton in 1859 as an oppidan at a dame's house (T. H. Stevens) but was soon elected a king's scholar. His tutors were, at first his uncle, F. E. Durnford (lower master), and later Mr. A. C. James. In 1865 he was admitted scholar of King's College, Cambridge, where he obtained a first class (as fourth classic) in the classical tripos of 1869, becoming, on graduation, a fellow of his college in the same year.

In 1870 Durnford returned to Eton as an assistant master under the Rev. James John Hornby, D.D. [q.v.], and remained there till 1899, having been for many years a housemaster. Throughout he was a very successful teacher and a beloved and popular tutor. Among the many useful functions which he discharged were the management of the army class and the command of the Volunteer corps. His house was always in high repute. In 1899 he was compelled by persistent attacks of gout to retire.

As he had never married, Durnford still held his fellowship at King's College under the statutes of 1861, and to King's he returned. He speedily became an important and influential member of many boards and syndicates, including the council of the senate and the town council. In 1909 he was mayor of Cambridge, and from 1909 until his death principal of the Cambridge University day training college for elementary teachers. In 1909 he also became vice-provost of King's, and in 1910 a fellow of Eton. On the outbreak of the European War in 1914 Durnford threw himself into the task of selecting candidates for commissions, and alike in this and in the many other new tasks entailed by the situation his services were invaluable. These were recognized in 1919 when he was created G.B.E. In 1918, on the succession of Dr. M. R. James to the provostship of Eton, Durnford was elected provost of King's, an office which he held until his death, which took place at Cambridge 7 April 1926 at the age of seventy-nine.

Durnford was a man of great sweetness of character, which he masked under a humorous incisiveness of manner. There is some truth in the kindly description of him by his old friend Canon Hugh Pearson of Windsor: 'He forms opinions hastily and expresses them strongly.' He was not without a certain family resemblance to his grandfather, Dr. Keate. In every circle which he entered—and his acquaintance was extensive—he was loved; especially, perhaps, by his pupils at Eton and his undergraduate friends at Cambridge, in whose pursuits (not least those connected with the drama) he took a vivid interest. As an administrator, both at Eton and King's, he was greatly valued for his sane views and his helpfulness.

There are portraits of Durnford by Sir A. S. Cope (1914) and Sir William Orpen (1924) at Eton and King's respectively. A quasi-caricature by 'Spy' appeared in *Vanity Fair* 4 December 1902.

[*The Times*, 8 April 1926; *Memoir of Sir Walter Durnford*, printed for King's College, 1926; personal knowledge.]

M. R. James.

DYER, REGINALD EDWARD HARRY (1864–1927), brigadier-general, was born at Murree, a hill station in the Punjab, 9 October 1864, the youngest son and sixth child of Edward Dyer, by his wife, Mary Passmore, of Barnstaple. His father, the son of a pilot of Devonshire descent in the East India Company's service, was the first to brew beer successfully in India, and at the time of his youngest son's birth was managing partner in the Murree Brewery Company. After education at Bishop Cotton School, Simla, Middleton College, co. Cork, and the Royal Military College, Sandhurst, Dyer received in 1885 a commission in the Queen's Royal Regiment. In 1888 he transferred to the Indian army, in which the rest of his military career was spent. He saw active service in the Burma campaign of 1886–1887, the Hazara expedition (1888), the relief of Chitral (1895), the Waziristan blockade (1901–1902), and the Zakka Khel operations (1908). But in the European War his opportunity of putting to the test the experience thus gained did not come until 1916, when he was placed in command of operations in South-Eastern Persia. Here, by energy, courage, and bluff, he achieved a notable success; and the C.B., which he received, was well earned.

Having completed this task, Dyer returned to India to be posted to the command of a training brigade at Jullundur; but in the spring of 1917 he met with a serious riding accident. This incapacitated him for a whole year and necessitated sick leave to England: indeed, it is probable that, had the times been less strenuous or Dyer a less determined character, he would have been invalided out of the service. Always a full-blooded man, and liable to attacks of gout in the head, he suffered for the rest of his life from frequent and severe headaches; while the internal injuries which he received may account for the gradual loss of power over his lower limbs. But he returned to India and resumed his command at Jullundur in April 1918.

A year later, grave civil disorders broke out in the Punjab and in many other parts of India. What was probably the most violent of these outbreaks occurred on 10 April 1919 at Amritsar, within the territorial area of Dyer's brigade. There, without provocation, a mob killed five Englishmen, gutted several public buildings, looted two banks, and beat a lady missionary, leaving her for dead. Dyer arrived on the scene the next day at 9 p.m., when the local civil authority appears to have relinquished all control into his hands. Dyer acted with great vigour and restored order. Three of his actions, however, gave rise to the bitterest controversy. First, on 13 April, when a dense crowd of several thousand persons had assembled contrary to his orders in a confined space in the city (the 'Jalianwala Bagh'), he marched a small force of fifty rifles to the spot and opened fire without warning. The panic-stricken mob endeavoured to disperse: the exits were inadequate; and Dyer, thinking apparently that the mob was massing to attack him, did not give the order to cease fire until 1,650 rounds had been expended. 379 persons are known to have been killed; the wounded are estimated at three times this number; and it is widely supposed that the casualties were higher still. Secondly, on 19 April, Dyer issued an order that no Indian should be permitted to pass except in a crawling posture along the street in which the lady missionary had been assaulted. Thirdly, on the spot where that assault took place he caused to be whipped, after conviction on an entirely different charge, six persons whom he believed to have been also guilty of committing the assault, although it was not until later that they were actually convicted of it.

Whatever view may be taken of these proceedings, there is no doubt that Dyer's actions during the ensuing three weeks were excellent. His pacification of the district earned for him from the guardians of the Golden Temple (the central shrine of the Sikh faith), who may reasonably have feared pillage by the mob, the signal honour of investiture in that temple as a Sikh. Barely was his task in Amritsar completed, when Dyer was appointed to command a brigade on active service in the third Afghan War (May 1919). Again, in spite of continuous physical pain which would have prostrated a less determined man, he distinguished himself, notably in the relief of the small fort of Thal, which was threatened by the Afghan commander-in-chief (afterwards King Nadir Shah) with a force greatly exceeding his own.

Meanwhile, racial ill-feeling over the events at Amritsar had been growing apace in an atmosphere of general ignorance, rumours, and suspicions. At length, on 14 October 1919, the government of India appointed a committee, of which Lord Hunter, a Scottish judge, was chairman, 'to investigate the recent disturbances . . . their causes and the measures taken to cope with them'. Before this committee Dyer was summoned as an official witness, and gave evidence. The strictures which the committee, in its report, passed upon his conduct led the commander-in-chief in India, Sir Charles Carmichael Monro [q.v.], to revoke Dyer's officiating promotion to a divisional command and to insist on his resignation from the service (March 1920). He was, in fact, within a few months of the age limit for retirement. The home government, although it permitted Dyer to submit a further statement, upheld the action of the commander-in-chief.

The publication of certain passages in Dyer's evidence added fresh fuel to Indian resentment and, coupled with the treatment accorded to him, rekindled controversy among Englishmen. For, while admitting that he could probably have dispersed the crowd at Jalianwala Bagh without the use of force, he had attempted to justify the severity shown by reference to eventualities which had not yet arisen and to the impression which he hoped to produce in other parts of India. Much that he said, moreover, appeared to be tinged with racial arrogance. Debates took place in both houses of parliament. It was widely felt that Dyer's actions at Amritsar and his attitude must be officially repudiated. On the other hand there were many who insisted, with equal reason, that he had been condemned, not only without a properly constituted trial, but after being put in a position in which, according to the essential principles of English legal procedure, no accused person should be placed. Estimates of Dyer's conduct will probably continue to differ. This much at least is certain: the crawling order was indefensible; the firing on the crowd in the Jalianwala Bagh was a great tragedy; and the effect of both incidents in alienating responsible Indian opinion from England was lamentable. Nor was ill-feeling allowed to die a natural death. Interested parties bought the Bagh in order to preserve it as a shrine of race hatred; while the *Morning Post* newspaper raised a testimonial in favour of Dyer and collected £26,000, which Dyer accepted.

After resigning the service Dyer's health rapidly failed. In November 1921 he was stricken with paralysis, and never recovered. He died at Long Ashton, near Bristol, 23 July 1927, of arterio-sclerosis and cerebral haemorrhage.

Although a strict disciplinarian with a strong sense of his own authority, Dyer was always well known for the care which he took, and insisted on others taking, for the comfort of the Indian rank and file under his command; with them he was popular, not only on that account, but as a simple and courageous soldier. No one ever questioned his statement that his action at Amritsar was dictated by a stern sense of duty.

Dyer married in 1888 Anne, daughter of Colonel Edmund Pippon Ommaney, Indian Staff Corps, who survived him with two sons.

[*The Times*, 25 July 1927; Ian Colvin, *Life of General Dyer*, 1929; Sir G. de S. Barrow, *Life of Sir Charles Carmichael Monro*, 1931; Hansard, *Parliamentary Debates*, 5th series, House of Lords, vol. 41, 19 and 20 July 1920, House of Commons, vol. 131, 8 July 1920; *Report* of the Committee appointed to investigate the disturbances in the Punjab (Lord Hunter's Committee), Cd. 681, 1920 (evidence before the same committee, vol. iii, Amritsar, 1920); full shorthand report of the summing-up of McCardie J. in *O'Dwyer* v. *Nair*, King's Bench Division, 4 and 5 June 1924; private information.] S. V. FitzGerald.

DYER, Sir WILLIAM TURNER THISELTON- (1843–1928), botanist. [See Thiselton-Dyer.]

EARDLEY-WILMOT, Sir SAINT-HILL (1852–1929), forester. [See Wilmot.]

EATON, HERBERT FRANCIS, third Baron Cheylesmore (1848–1925), major-general, was born in London 25 January 1848, the third son of Henry William Eaton, created in 1887 Baron Cheylesmore, of Cheylesmore, Coventry, by his wife, Charlotte Gorham, daughter of Thomas Leader Harman, of New Orleans. He succeeded his brother, William Meriton, in the barony in 1902. He was educated at Eton, and joined the Grenadier Guards in 1867. All his life the welfare of the Guards was of primary interest to him. He commanded the 2nd battalion for four years, 1890–1894, having the special responsibility of taking it to Bermuda for a year in 1890, following on an act of insubordination in the battalion. He retired as a major-general in 1899, after commanding the regiment, but without having seen active service. He returned to military work during the European War as president of courts martial in espionage and other cases, and as chairman of various boards; he was also commandant of the National Rifle Association's school of musketry at Bisley. He was created C.V.O. in 1905, K.C.V.O. in 1909, K.C.M.G. in 1919, and G.B.E. in 1925.

As an Eton boy Lord Cheylesmore shot at Wimbledon in the match for the Ashburton shield in 1866, and he always retained a great interest in rifle-shooting, being closely associated with the National Rifle Association for some years before he joined its council in 1899. He was its chairman from 1903 until the time of his death, and was enthusiastic in developing rifle-shooting overseas and among the boys of the Empire. Under his chairmanship Bisley developed into the best shooting centre in the Empire, and produced a company of expert marksmen, who, formed into a school of musketry, played an important part in training instructors for the new armies raised during the European War.

The confidence inspired by Cheylesmore's attractive and open personality, his tact, and his human sympathies led him into public work in many directions, and he proved himself a diligent committee man. He was chairman of the Middlesex Territorial Army Association from its inception in 1908 until his death. He did much for the welfare of the ex-service man, being chairman for twenty-three years of the Soldiers' and Sailors' Help Society. He was also vice-chairman of the British Red Cross Society and an active worker for it for many years, and was a knight of grace of the order of St. John of Jerusalem. He was at various times honorary colonel or commandant of Queen Victoria's Rifles, of the Middlesex Volunteer Regiment, and of the County of London Royal Engineers. His philanthropic work as a civilian included twenty-one years as chairman of the Brompton Hospital for consumption, and many years' service on the board of the Middlesex Hospital, during five of which he was chairman. He was also chairman of the board of governors of Dulwich College, and served as master of the Salters' Company. His municipal work also was important; he was for twenty-three years an alderman, and for two years (1904–1906) mayor of Westminster; from 1907 to 1919 he represented St. George's, Hanover Square, on the London County Council, and was chairman of the Council in 1912–1913. He stood, unsuccessfully, for parliament in 1887, when he contested Coventry in the conservative interest, on the elevation to the peerage of his father, who had held the seat for many years.

Lord Cheylesmore formed a large collection of military medals, and in 1897 published *Naval and Military Medals of*

Great Britain. He lived mainly in London, but at one time rented Hughenden Manor, and resided later at Cooper's Hill.

Dignified, courteous, considerate, experienced in affairs, Lord Cheylesmore was an ideal chairman. He was everywhere popular, and by his brother officers was affectionately nicknamed 'Brown'. He married in 1892 Elizabeth Richardson, daughter of Francis Ormond French, of New York, and left two sons. He died at Englefield Green, 29 July 1925, from injuries received in a motor accident, and was succeeded in the barony by his elder son, Francis Ormond Henry (born 1893).

A cartoon of Lord Cheylesmore appeared in *Vanity Fair* 17 July 1912.

[*The Times*, 30 July 1925; *The National Rifle Association Journal*, August 1925; private information; personal knowledge.]

COTTESLOE.

EDGE, Sir JOHN (1841–1926), Indian judge, was born 28 July 1841 at Clonbrock, Queen's County, Ireland, the only child of Benjamin Booker Edge, J.P., of Clonbrock, by his wife, Esther Anne, only child of Thomas Allen, of the Park, co. Wicklow. The family, which originated from Malpas, in Cheshire, had settled in Ireland in Stuart times. Like his father before him, Benjamin Edge possessed qualifications as a mining engineer, an unusual accomplishment among the Irish gentry of that day, and worked coal mines in the Queen's County and elsewhere.

John Edge was educated at Trinity College, Dublin, where he took the degrees of B.A. (1861) and LL.B. (1862). He was called to the Irish bar by the King's Inns, Dublin, in 1864, and to the English bar by the Middle Temple in 1866, and went the Northern and North-Eastern circuits. In 1886 he took silk; and the same year was appointed chief justice of the high court of judicature for the North-Western Provinces of India (as they were then styled) at Allahabad, being knighted on appointment. As chief justice it was Edge's good fortune to preside over an exceptionally strong court, several of his colleagues being men of marked ability. But he quickly showed himself worthy to be their leader. A good example of his quality may be found in the judgment in *Bhagwansingh* v. *Bhagwansingh* (1895), in which he held that the adoption of certain near relatives is not invalid in Hindu law. In the appeal from this decision which came before the Privy Council in 1898, Lord Hobhouse [q.v.], although differing from his conclusions, complimented Edge on the 'elaborate fullness' of his judgment, and it remains worthy of study. In fact, although the law is now settled in the opposite sense, the general opinion of scholars inclines to Edge's view, and it has been found necessary to engraft on the prohibition laid down by Lord Hobhouse a large body of customary exceptions.

In addition to his judicial work Edge found scope for his administrative ability. On his initiative the rules and orders of the high court were codified. From 1887 to 1893 he was the first vice-chancellor of the newly created university of Allahabad and did much to lay the foundations of that institution on right lines. His services were recognized by an honorary doctorate in laws. In 1896 he was chairman of the famine relief committee which dispensed charitable relief in the great famine of that year.

Retiring from the chief justiceship in 1898, Edge was appointed in January 1899 judicial member of the Council of India, being elected at the same time to the bench of the Middle Temple, where he subsequently served the office of treasurer (1919). His duties on the Council of India were not onerous, and it was possible for him to sit as a member of the royal commission on the South African War (1902) and to serve on the committee of inquiry into the case of Adolph Beck (1905), who had been convicted and sentenced for an offence of which he was subsequently proved not to have been guilty. The report of this committee helped to secure the establishment in 1907 of the Court of Criminal Appeal.

Edge retired from the Council of India in 1908, and in January 1909 was sworn of the Privy Council and appointed a member of the judicial committee. From 1916 till his retirement in May 1926, two months before his eighty-fifth birthday, he was constant in the hearing of Indian appeals. He maintained his great reputation for care and thoroughness, and the tribute paid to him by the lord chancellor, Viscount Cave, in moving the second reading of the Judicial Committee Bill in 1923 was well deserved. In the case of *Arumilli* v. *Subharayadu* (1921), though loyally accepting the decision in *Bhagwansingh* v. *Bhagwansingh*, Edge had the satisfaction of pointing out limitations to the principles laid down by Lord Hobhouse. His judgments remained to the last models of clear and cogent reasoning: but towards the end of his career his knowledge of the lacunae in the law occasionally tempted him into elaborate *obiter dicta* intended to settle doubtful points which did not really arise in the case before him. He survived his retirement barely two months, dying suddenly at his house in Kensington 30 July 1926.

Of quiet and unassuming presence, Edge was a man of wide interests. As chief justice of Allahabad he fully lived up to the responsibilities of his position in the matter of hospitality; as a sportsman he was equally proficient with rod, rifle, and gun, and he was also a keen alpinist. In freemasonry he held high rank. He was an enthusiastic volunteer both in the Inns of Court Rifles during his early days at the bar and later in India, where he commanded a battalion of the Allahabad Rifle Volunteers and was honorary aide-de-camp to the viceroy. For many years he made a hobby of the study of genealogy; and four stout volumes dealing with the pedigree and connexions of his own family were bequeathed by him to the William Salt Library at Stafford.

Edge married in 1867 Laura, younger daughter of Thomas Loughborough, solicitor, of Tulse Hill, Surrey. They had one son and three daughters.

[*The Times*, 2 August 1926; *Indian Law Reports*, Allahabad Series, 1886–1898; *Law Reports, Indian Appeals*, 1912–1926; Burke's *Landed Gentry*, vol. ii (1908 edition); official records; private information.]

S. V. FitzGerald.

EDGEWORTH, FRANCIS YSIDRO [originally Ysidro Francis] (1845–1926), economist and statistician, was born at Edgeworthstown, co. Longford, 8 February 1845, the fifth son of Francis Beaufort Edgeworth, by his Spanish wife, Rosa Florentina Eroles. His father was the sixth son of the author Richard Lovell Edgeworth [q.v.], and half-brother of the novelist Maria Edgeworth [q.v.] and of Anna Edgeworth, who married Thomas Beddoes [q.v.]. Francis Ysidro Edgeworth thus had an aunt (Maria) born in 1767 and already well known in the eighteenth century, and a first cousin—Thomas Lovell Beddoes, the poet [q.v.]—born in 1803. Apart from descendants of the eldest son of Richard Lovell Edgeworth living in the United States, Edgeworth, who was himself unmarried, was the last representative of his grandfather in the male line, and succeeded in 1911 to the family estate of Edgeworthstown.

Edgeworth, whose father died when he was two years old. was educated at home until he went, at the age of seventeen, to Trinity College, Dublin. Thence he passed to Oxford as a scholar of Magdalen Hall, proceeding from there to Balliol College, where he obtained a first class in *literae humaniores* in 1869. After taking his degree, he spent some years in London with straitened means, studying and writing and lecturing on the moral sciences at King's College, London, where, in 1888, he was appointed professor of political economy, becoming Tooke professor of economic science and statistics in 1890. Meanwhile, he had been called to the bar by the Inner Temple in 1877, but never practised. In 1891 he succeeded J. E. Thorold Rogers [q.v.] as Drummond professor of political economy at Oxford and was elected a fellow of All Souls College, which became his principal home for the rest of his life. He resigned his chair in 1922, and was then made emeritus professor.

It seems likely that Edgeworth's interest in the moral sciences was first stimulated at Balliol by Benjamin Jowett, of whom he had been a favourite pupil. But the most important and definite influences on his economic thought were first of all William Stanley Jevons [q.v.], who was a near neighbour in Hampstead in Edgeworth's early years in London, and subsequently Alfred Marshall [q.v.].

Edgeworth approached the moral sciences with a strong mathematical bias, and his main contributions to these subjects were along formal and highly abstract lines. His first book, *New and Old Methods of Ethics*, mainly a commentary on Henry Sidgwick's *Methods of Ethics* (1874), was published in 1877. His second volume, entitled *Mathematical Psychics, an Essay on the Application of Mathematics to the Moral Sciences* (1881), was not only one of his most original and important contributions to science, but indicated in its title the field to be occupied by nearly all his work. Apart from *Metretike, or the Method of Measuring Probability and Utility* (1887), Edgeworth published no book during the remaining thirty-nine years of his life, but contented himself with a long series of contributions to learned journals and some pamphlets published during the European War. A list of twenty-five publications between 1877 and 1887 is given in an appendix to *Metretike*; twenty-nine items bearing on the theory of probability, published between 1883 and 1921, are given in the bibliographical appendix to J. M. Keynes's *Treatise on Probability* (1921). His principal contributions to economics, amounting to thirty-four papers and seventy-five reviews, were reprinted in his *Papers relating to Political Economy*, published by the Royal Economic Society in 1925; and seventy-four papers and nine reviews on statistical theory are cited in A. L. Bowley's memoir entitled *Edgeworth's Contributions to Mathematical Statistics*, published after his death by the Royal Statistical Society (1928).

A great part of Edgeworth's time for the last thirty-five years of his life was occupied with the editorship of the *Economic Journal*, the quarterly organ of the Royal Economic Society. He was its first editor from its commencement in 1891, and designed and moulded the form which the *Journal* took during subsequent years. He was continuously connected with it, first as editor, then as chairman of the editorial board, and finally as joint editor with J. M. Keynes, from the first issue in March 1891 down to the day of his death, which took place at Oxford, 13 February 1926. This work kept him in close touch not only with English but also with continental and American economists. For many years he played a large part in maintaining the contacts of the world of economic science in various countries. He was president of the economics section of the British Association in 1889 and president of the Royal Statistical Society from 1912 to 1914. He was elected F.B.A. in 1903.

Since Edgeworth never attempted a systematic treatise on economics, his influence was overshadowed by that of Alfred Marshall. But, whereas Marshall deliberately shrank from highly abstract attempts to formalize the main propositions of the subject, Edgeworth became in many directions the parent of the strictly formal and mathematical treatment of economic theory in English-speaking countries. He was principally interested in those parts of the subject which were susceptible to development somewhat on the lines of symbolic logic, and in the metrical aspects of the moral sciences which seemed to lend themselves to a quasi-mathematical treatment. He was very fond of elaborate arithmetical illustrations, drawn so far as possible from actual facts, of highly abstract economic and statistical theories. The greater part of his work can be classified under five applications of mathematical psychics (to use his own term): to the measurement of utility or ethical value; to the algebraic or diagrammatic determination of economic equilibriums; to the measurement of belief or probability; to the measurement of evidence or statistics; and to the measurement of economic value or index numbers.

That Edgeworth never systematized his numerous and important contributions to these various subjects may perhaps be attributed not wholly to his temperament, but also to a gradually growing doubt as to the validity of pushing too far the analogy between psychics and physics which had seemed to him so attractive and fruitful at the opening of his scientific life.

Edgeworth spent most of his life in college and in clubs. Although much in the company of his fellow men, he was essentially reserved and recluse. He mingled an old-fashioned classical culture with his highly abstract technique, and his style of writing, although sometimes eccentric and sometimes obscure, often has much aesthetic attraction. He was fond of appealing to authority and preferred to state his opinions inconclusively. This inconclusiveness, together with his reserve and his obscurity, detracted from his value as a teacher, and he developed no school of economists during his long tenure of the Oxford chair. He was a man of the highest gifts and greatness of nature which failed in some way of complete fruition.

[J. M. Keynes, *Memoir of F. Y. Edgeworth*, first published in the *Economic Journal*, March 1926, and republished with some revision in *Essays in Biography*, 1933; A. L. Bowley, *Francis Ysidro Edgeworth* in *Econometrica*, April 1934; personal knowledge.]

J. M. Keynes.

EGERTON, HUGH EDWARD (1855–1927), historian, was born in London 19 April 1855, the younger son of Edward Christopher Egerton, of Mountfield Court, Robertsbridge, Sussex, member of parliament for Macclesfield 1852–1868, and for East Cheshire 1868–1869, under-secretary of state for foreign affairs. His mother was Lady Mary Frances, elder daughter of Charles Pierrepont, second Earl Manvers. He was descended from Thomas Egerton, Baron Ellesmere [q.v.], lord chancellor, and from the first and second Earls of Bridgewater [q.v.].

Egerton was educated at Rugby and at Corpus Christi College, Oxford. He obtained a second class in classical moderations (1874) and a first class in *literae humaniores* (1876). He was called to the bar by the Inner Temple in 1880, and joined the North Wales and Chester circuit. In 1885 he became assistant private secretary to his first cousin by marriage, Edward Stanhope [q.v.], and it was his chief's promotion to be secretary of state for the Colonies in 1886 which introduced Egerton to the field in which his life's work was to be done. Just at this time a strong interest in the overseas Empire had been awakened in England; and Egerton was one of those on whom the publication of (Sir) J. R. Seeley's *Expansion of England* in 1883 and the Imperial character of Queen Victoria's jubilee of 1887 made a lifelong impression. By nature a scholar rather than a politician, he might have found no means of service to the British Empire had he not, as a member of the newly-created (1886) Emigrants Information Office (later merged in the Overseas Settlement Office), taken part in the preparation of an official handbook on the Colonies and thereby discovered the urgent need for an authoritative account of the growth of the Empire in the light of the political and economic ideas which had directed it. Thenceforward Egerton gave all his leisure to the study of colonial history, and in 1897 his *Short History of British Colonial Policy* was published. It was a pioneer work, concealing under its modest title the fruits of prolonged first-hand research in a neglected field. It was widely read in the Dominions as well as in England, reaching a ninth edition in 1932, and with its publication Egerton found his *métier* and made his name.

A short biography of Sir Stamford Raffles (1900) and a collection of the speeches of Sir William Molesworth (1903) on Colonial policy enhanced Egerton's reputation; and when, in 1905, a new chair of colonial history was founded at Oxford by Alfred Beit [q.v.], there was no doubt as to who should be its first occupant. Egerton was never a popular lecturer, but serious students recognized him as a master of his field, and his objective judgement and high standard of historical scholarship were of especial value in the teaching of a subject which easily lends itself to tendentious interpretation. His useful handbook, *Federations and Unions within the British Empire* (1911) was quickly made a prescribed authority in the modern history syllabus at Oxford. He was at his best, however, on controversial issues, and his *Causes and Character of the American Revolution*, published in 1923, three years after his resignation of the chair, was a masterpiece of clarity and learning. His last piece of work was a valuable account of Joseph Chamberlain contributed to this DICTIONARY.

Egerton was a fellow of All Souls College from 1905 onwards, and he held the office of sub-warden shortly before his death, which took place at Oxford 21 May 1927 after a long illness. He married in 1886 Margaret Alice, daughter of Alexander Trotter, stockbroker, of Dreghorn, Midlothian, and had two sons and two daughters. His wife was a great granddaughter of Sir Robert Strange [q.v.], engraver, and sister of Coutts Trotter [q.v.], vice-master of Trinity College, Cambridge.

[*The Times*, 23 May 1927; personal knowledge.] R. COUPLAND.

ELLIOT, ARTHUR RALPH DOUGLAS (1846–1923), politician, was born at 27 Eaton Place, London, 17 December 1846, the second son of William Hugh Elliot, third Earl of Minto, by his wife, Emma, only daughter of General Sir Thomas Hislop, first baronet [q.v.]. He was younger brother of Gilbert John Murray Kynynmond Elliot, fourth Earl of Minto [q.v.], governor-general of Canada and viceroy of India. At the age of four his leg had to be amputated as the result of a fall. This prevented him from going to school, but his spirit was such that he climbed, shot, rode to hounds, and learned to swim. He went to Edinburgh University in 1863, before proceeding to Trinity College, Cambridge, in 1864, as a fellow commoner, and, in spite of the loss of a year due to a serious illness in 1866, graduated B.A. in 1868 as third junior optime in the mathematical tripos.

After leaving Cambridge, Elliot was called to the bar by the Inner Temple in 1870 and joined the Northern circuit. In 1878 he published a pamphlet on *Criminal Procedure in England and Scotland*. At the general election of 1880 he was elected member of parliament for Roxburghshire in the liberal interest. He declared against Mr. Gladstone's Home Rule policy in 1886 in a notable speech, was again elected for Roxburghshire, as a liberal-unionist, in that year, and founded the Liberal Union Club. He lost the seat in 1892; and was defeated (by one vote) in 1895 for the city of Durham, where, however, he was successful at a by-election in 1898, and held the seat until 1906. In April 1903 Elliot was appointed financial secretary to the

Treasury by Mr. A. J. (afterwards Earl of) Balfour. Almost immediately the Free Trade controversy became acute; and when Mr. C. T. Ritchie (afterwards Lord Ritchie, of Dundee), the chancellor of the Exchequer, left the government in September 1903, Elliot, who was a strong free trader, felt it his duty to resign also. For some years afterwards he took part in the campaign for free trade, and founded the Unionist Free Trade Club. But when he was defeated at Durham in the general election of 1906, he left politics, in which, as unionist and Free Trader, he had no place, sacrificing his political future in order to preserve his independence.

Elliot had succeeded Henry Reeve as editor of the *Edinburgh Review* in 1895, and his policy was to make the *Review* an organ of moderate and responsible opinion representing the modern developments of the old whig tradition. Under his careful management—he remained editor until 1912—the principle of anonymity was maintained, and the importance of the political side of the *Review* emphasized. For Elliot was chiefly a politician, with strong convictions coloured by the whig tradition—he was sometimes called the last of the whigs—combined with ardent patriotism. He did not, however, neglect the literary side of the *Review*, for he had great knowledge of literature, and himself wrote several books. In 1882 he contributed *The State and the Church* to the 'English Citizen' series. In 1911 he published the *Life of George Joachim Goschen, first Viscount Goschen* (2 vols.), valuable for its authentic account of the Home Rule split, with the history of which he was intimately connected; and, in 1918, before the Armistice, *The Traditions of British Statesmanship*.

A man of great personal charm and kindliness, and popular with all conditions of men, Elliot married in 1888 Madeleine Harriet Dagmar, daughter of Sir Charles Lister Ryan, of Ascot, sometime comptroller and auditor-general, and had two sons. Only the younger son survived him, and at his house at Romsey he died on 12 February 1923. For some years Elliot lived at Freshwater, Isle of Wight, in the house formerly occupied by Mrs. Julia Margaret Cameron, the early photographer.

The best portrait of Elliot is a sketch by Barbara Leighton at the Grillion Club.

[*The Times*, 13 February 1923; *Edinburgh Review*, April 1923; private information.]

M. F. Headlam.

ELWES, HENRY JOHN (1846–1922), traveller, botanist, and entomologist, was born 16 May 1846, the eldest son of John Henry Elwes, of Colesbourne, Gloucestershire, by his wife, Mary, fourth daughter of Admiral Sir Robert Howe Bromley, third baronet, of Stoke Hall, Newark. One of his sisters, Caroline Susan, was the first wife of Sir Michael Edward Hicks Beach, ninth baronet and first Earl St. Aldwyn [q.v.]; another, Edith Mary, was the first wife of Frederick du Cane Godman, F.R.S., who shared all Elwes's botanical and zoological interests and was his best friend. He was great-great-grandson of the eccentric miser, John Elwes (1714–1789, q.v.), of Marcham, Berkshire, on whose Marylebone property Portman Square and Portland Place were built. His great-grandfather, John Elwes, bought the Colesbourne estate.

Elwes was educated at Eton, and entered the Scots Guards in 1865, retiring with the rank of captain five years later. The rest of his life was devoted to natural history and sport. In 1869 his first publication, 'The Bird Stations of the Outer Hebrides', appeared in the *Ibis*, but it was in the *Proceedings* of the Zoological Society for June 1873 that his remarkable paper on 'The Geographical Distribution of Asiatic Birds' was published, and to it he attributed his election to the fellowship of the Royal Society in 1897. In 1880 he produced his folio *Monograph of the Genus Lilium*, and fifty-five years later it remains the authoritative work on that subject. He was a frequent contributor to the *Transactions* of the Zoological and Entomological Societies. He collected birds, butterflies, and moths wherever he travelled, and he discovered many new species. The British Museum has been greatly enriched by the 30,000 picked specimens of his Lepidoptera which Elwes presented to the nation. Although he retained his interest in these throughout his life, his preoccupation was the collecting of plants. Few amateur gardeners have grown successfully more new and rare plants than Elwes. No less than ninety-eight species, for a great part collected by Elwes and first flowered by him, have been figured and described in the *Botanical Magazine*. Several bear his name, of which the first—*Galanthus Elwesii*, the snowdrop which he gathered near Smyrna in 1874—is perhaps the most familiar. Sir Joseph Dalton Hooker [q.v.] dedicated to Elwes the volume of the *Botanical Magazine* published in 1877.

Elwes's travels were made in Turkey, Asia Minor, India (four times), Tibet; in Mexico and North America (thrice); in Chile; in Russia and Siberia (thrice); in Formosa, China, and Japan (twice). He was an ardent hunter of big game. For several years he stalked chamois, roe, and red deer in the Vorarlberg and Styria; also elk, reindeer, and bear in Norway; and for some years he was a member of a boar-shooting syndicate in the Ardennes. In his expedition to Central Asia in 1898 he secured specimens of Ovis ammon, the great sheep of the Altai. Elwes was the British official representative at the Botanical and Horticultural Congresses held at Amsterdam in 1877 and at St. Petersburg in 1884. In 1886 he was appointed scientific member of the embassy to Tibet which, however, never crossed the frontier. It is probably true that no naturalist ever travelled more widely—indeed such long-continued journeying was only possible to one of Elwes's ample means and remarkable bodily health; in him the boyish love of adventure persisted throughout his life. He spoke French and German with facility and wrote English with a terse clearness and vigour rarely matched in scientific literature.

The most important work of Elwes's life was begun in 1903 when, in collaboration with his friend Augustine Henry, he undertook the production of *Trees of Great Britain and Ireland*. The first volume appeared in 1906 and the seventh and last in 1913. The labour was happily divided between the authors; Henry, the trained botanist, was responsible for the botanical descriptions, while Elwes spared neither time nor money in visiting six hundred of the best tree collections in Great Britain and Ireland and on the Continent. He was already familiar, by reason of his previous extensive journeys, with an immense number of species in their native habitat.

In his home Elwes lived the life of a Gloucestershire squire. His handsome bearded face and burly figure were well known in the hunting-field; he was an admirable host, generous alike of his knowledge and his plants. He was keenly interested in the management of his estate and in the formation of his plantations. Unfortunately, the oolitic soil of the Cotswolds precluded his making the fine arboretum which would certainly have resulted from the enormous number of tree seeds which he sowed at Colesbourne, had it been situated on greensand or old red sandstone. In 1912 and 1913 he published papers on primitive breeds of sheep, of which he kept small flocks; he was greatly interested in the wools produced by crossing these.

Elwes was president or served on the councils of many scientific societies, and in 1897, the year in which it was instituted, he received the Victoria medal of honour of the Royal Horticultural Society. He died at Colesbourne 26 November 1922.

Elwes married in 1871 Margaret Susan, second daughter of William Charles Lowndes-Stone, of Brightwell Park, Oxfordshire; they had one son and one daughter, Susan Margaret, the wife of Major-General Sir Frederick Carrington [q.v.], who predeceased her father.

[H. J. Elwes, *Memoirs of Travel, Sport, and Natural History*, edited by E. G. Hawke, 1930; *Royal Society Catalogue of Scientific Papers*, vol. xiv, 1915; *Royal Botanical Garden, Kew, Bulletin*, No. 1, 1923; *Société Dendrologique de France, Bulletin*, No. 47, May 1923.] F. R. S. Balfour.

EMMOTT, ALFRED, first Baron Emmott, of Oldham (1858–1926), politician and cotton spinner, was born at Chadderton, near Oldham, 8 May 1858, the third son of Thomas Emmott, cotton spinner, of Brookfield, Oldham, by his wife, Hannah, daughter of John Barlow, of Chorley, Cheshire. Educated at the Friends' School, Kendal, where he became a good cricketer, and at Grove House, Tottenham, he graduated B.A. of London University in 1880, having entered his father's firm in 1879. In 1881 Emmott joined the Oldham town council and in 1891 became mayor. He took a prominent part in the committee work of the town council, and for forty-three years was a member of the Oldham chamber of commerce and for long its president. He was also president of the Oldham Master Cotton Spinners Association. He was active on the local bench, and all his life was closely identified with Oldham, not only as its most prominent citizen, but also as one of the leading men of the Lancashire cotton industry.

In 1899 Emmott entered parliament, winning Oldham from the conservatives, and holding the seat until he became a peer in 1911. He became chairman of committees of the House of Commons in 1906 when Sir Henry Campbell-Bannerman came into power, and he presided in committee during the stormy debates on the budget of 1909. Tall and striking in appearance, quiet, if somewhat stern in manner with a considerable sense of humour and an essentially fair and judicial mind, Emmott carried out the difficult duties of his position during five years (1906–1911) with complete success. During this time he also served on the royal commission on food supply in time of war and as chairman of a committee on technical education. In 1911 he was raised to the peerage as Baron Emmott, of Oldham, and became under-secretary of state for the Colonies, an office which was specially congenial to him. He had been sworn a privy councillor in 1908. In 1913 he was chairman of the first delegation of the Empire Parliamentary Association to proceed overseas. It visited Australia, Canada, New Zealand, and South Africa. Interchange of views took place between the English delegates and the members of the parliaments of the countries visited, and the delegation inaugurated the system of parliamentary conferences throughout the Empire, now a prominent feature of the work of the Parliamentary Association.

On returning to England Emmott was created G.C.M.G. (1914), and in the same year entered the Cabinet as first commissioner of works. He was a strong supporter of Mr. Asquith during the early months of the European War, but left office in 1915 on the formation of the first Coalition government. He then began what was perhaps the most important work of his life, namely the creation of the War Trade Department, which he directed until 1919. The principal duty of the department was the issue of licences designed to maintain British export trade without weakening the blockade. As the War proceeded, the department created a system of statistics whereby exports from England to countries conterminous with Germany were rationed on the basis of the average figures for such exports before the War. This rationing was negotiated with the countries concerned and in return certain necessary imports were received from them. In order to eliminate the chance of export licences being granted to persons likely to trade with the enemy, a list of reliable consignees was prepared. Later, other considerations came before the department, such as the conservation of supplies for home use and for military needs. Thus the department gradually became a clearing-house dealing with all questions of blockade requirements, domestic and military necessities, and the prevention of the total loss of British export trade, which was largely falling into the hands of America and Japan. Committees were established for the granting of the export licences, with an appeal to Emmott, whose decision was final. His commercial knowledge and judicial temper gained for him the respect of the exporting firms and enabled the country to safeguard a large part of its overseas trade during the War. For his war services he was created G.B.E. in 1917.

In 1920 Emmott was appointed chairman of a commission to inquire into the political and economic conditions of Russia and the usage of British subjects by the Bolsheviks. The report of the commission contained a severe indictment of the brutality with which British subjects were treated. He also served as chairman of a commission to inquire into the desirability of a decimal coinage, and signed the majority report against the scheme. About this time he resumed the direction of the family firm, which had become Emmotts and Walkshaw, and also became a director of the textile engineering firm of Platt Brothers, of Oldham, the Lancashire and Yorkshire Bank, the National Boiler General Insurance Company, and the Calico Printers Association. In 1921 he was president of the World Cotton Congress at Manchester and Liverpool, after which he advocated a scientific investigation into the cost of cotton manufacture in Lancashire and in the competing countries, having been struck by the relatively lower cost prevailing in the latter.

Emmott was deeply interested in education and served as chairman of the governors of the Hulme grammar school at Oldham, and was a member of the court of governors of Owens College, and later when the College became the Victoria University of Manchester. He was also chairman of the committee charged with examining the working of teachers' superannuation, as the result of which the Superannuation Act of 1925 was passed. From 1922 to 1924 he was president of the Royal Statistical Society, and in 1922 he became president of the National Association of Building Societies, presiding at the annual meeting at York in 1923. He was active in the management, and for many years president, of the Lancashire and Cheshire Young Men's Christian Association, and a founder of the Anglo-Belgian Union (1917). During the War his wife had worked hard for the Belgian refugees, and he was thus brought into close touch with Belgium. In 1923 he laid the foundation-stone of the British memorial at Zeebrugge, and attended its unveiling by King Albert two years later, receiving the order of the Belgian Crown.

All these activities left Emmott little time for politics, but he spoke frequently in the House of Lords as a consistent supporter of Mr. Asquith and a critic of the post-war coalition government. Emmott was a churchman, but his education and ancestry led him to understand and sympathize with nonconformist views. A strong free trader, he was nevertheless attracted by Imperial preference and was a supporter of the Liberal League, in the principles of which he believed as firmly as he did in the Empire. But although in the House of Commons he was a man on whom the party whips could firmly rely, he did not always vote with them, and in the House of Lords he was conspicuous for his independence of view. He was a keen sportsman, a good shot and golfer, and always interested in cricket.

Emmott died very suddenly from angina pectoris at his London house 13 December 1926, the day on which he was engaged to speak at a liberal party gathering. He married in 1887 Mary Gertrude, daughter of John William Lees, of Waterhead, Oldham, by whom he had two daughters. As he left no son, the barony became extinct.

A cartoon of Emmott appeared in *Vanity Fair* 19 October 1910.

[*The Times*, 14 December 1926; Hansard, *Parliamentary Debates*; Lord Ullswater, *A Speaker's Commentaries*, 1925; *Journal* of Royal Statistical Society, 1927; private information; personal knowledge.] ONSLOW.

ESHER, second VISCOUNT (1852–1930), government official. [See BRETT, REGINALD BALIOL.]

ESMOND, HENRY VERNON (1869–1922), actor and dramatist, whose original name was Henry Jack, was the fourth son in the family of fourteen children of Richard George Jack, physician, by his wife, Mary Rynd. He was born at Bridge House, Hampton Court, Middlesex, 30 November 1869. Educated privately, he went on the stage in 1885, acting mainly in the provinces for four years. In the spring of 1889 he made a hit in a small part in *The Panel Picture* by W. O. Tristram at the Opera Comique in London, and was afterwards engaged by E. S. Willard and by Edward Terry, chiefly in the parts of old men.

In 1893 (Sir) George Alexander [q.v.] engaged Esmond to act Cayley Drummle (an elderly man) in (Sir) A. W. Pinero's *The Second Mrs. Tanqueray* at the St. James's Theatre; and for the next seven years most of his work was done at that theatre, where he had opportunities to show his versatility as well as his accomplishment. Clement Scott called him 'perfect', and A. B. Walkley 'diabolically clever'. His best work was done in parts which gave scope either for boyishness, such as Little Billee in *Trilby* by George du Maurier, which he played at the Haymarket Theatre with (Sir) Herbert Beerbohm Tree [q.v.] in 1895, or for fantasy, such as Touchstone, Mercutio, the young Eddie Remon in *The Masqueraders* by Henry Arthur Jones, or Widgery Blake in W. J. Locke's *The Palace of Puck*. After leaving Alexander in 1900, Esmond acted less than before, being more engaged in writing and producing plays.

Esmond wrote about thirty plays. In 1894 he and his wife took the St. James's Theatre for a few weeks in order to produce there his comedy, *Bogey*, which, although not successful, brought him into notice as a playwright. In 1895 *The Divided Way*, a more serious play, was also produced at the St. James's, and in 1897 his success was assured when (Sir) Charles Hawtrey [q.v.] produced and acted his comedy, *One Summer's Day* (Comedy Theatre). In 1899 *Grierson's Way* (Haymarket Theatre) showed him in gloomy mood; but in 1901 *When We Were Twenty-one* (Comedy Theatre) revealed his best vein, that of light, rather sentimental comedy, gay but touched with pathos—the vein in which he also wrote *Eliza Comes to Stay* (Criterion Theatre, 1913), and *The Law Divine* (Wyndham's Theatre, 1918). Less agreeable were two cleverly conceived and written plays, *Billy's Little Love Affair* (Criterion Theatre, 1903) and *The Dangerous Age* (Vaudeville Theatre, 1914).

In 1900 and 1914 Esmond visited the United States, and in 1920 Canada, in order to produce and act in his own plays. On the last two visits he was accompanied by his wife, Eva Moore, actress, eighth child and seventh daughter of Edward Henry Moore, public analyst for the county of Sussex, whom he married in 1891, and by whom he had a son and a daughter. In private life Esmond, who had Irish blood in him, was an amusing, excitable, wilful man of much charm. He died suddenly at an hotel in Paris 17 April 1922.

[*The Times*, 18 April 1922; Eva Moore, *Exits and Entrances*, 1923; personal knowledge.] H. H. CHILD.

EVAN-THOMAS, Sir **HUGH** (1862–1928), admiral, was born 27 October 1862, the fifth son of Charles Evan-Thomas, J.P., D.L., of Gnoll, Glamorganshire, a member of a prominent Welsh family, by his wife, Cara, eldest daughter of Henry Shepherd Pearson, of the East India Company's service.

Evan-Thomas entered the *Britannia* as a naval cadet in 1876. In the following year the Princes Albert Victor and George (afterwards King George V) also joined the ship, and when they were sent on their three years' cruise in the *Bacchante*, Evan-Thomas was chosen as one of the midshipmen to join them in the gun-room. Before the cruise was over he was promoted sub-lieutenant, and at the end of 1883 was sent to the *Sultan* on the China station until July 1886, being promoted lieutenant at the end of 1884. He was for a short time flag-lieutenant to Admiral Sir Algernon Lyons in the *Bellerophon* on the North America station, and he served for two years (1890-1892) in the ill-fated *Victoria* in the Mediterranean [see Tryon, Sir George], after which he was appointed to the royal yacht *Osborne*. From January 1894 he was for three years flag-lieutenant to Admiral Sir Michael Culme-Seymour in the *Ramillies*, Mediterranean, and was promoted commander in 1897. In 1898 his experience as flag-lieutenant justified his appointment in charge of the Signal School at Portsmouth for two years. After another two years in command of the *Pioneer* in the Mediterranean, he was promoted captain (1902), and was then employed at the Admiralty in assisting the development of Lord Fisher's reforms of the naval personnel. He was flag-captain to Lord Charles Beresford in the Channel for two years, and in May 1905 he was chosen for the command of the Admiralty yacht *Enchantress*.

In the autumn of 1905 Evan-Thomas was appointed to act as temporary naval secretary to the first lord of the Admiralty, Earl Cawdor, during the absence of the naval secretary, Captain Tyrwhitt, in command of the *Medina*, which took the Prince of Wales to India for the Durbar. In the meantime Mr. Balfour's government fell, but the new first lord confirmed Evan-Thomas as naval secretary, and he continued to hold the office until the end of 1908, under Lord Tweedmouth and Mr. Reginald McKenna successively. It was thus accidental that this important office, the holder of which is responsible to the first lord for advice on all naval promotions and appointments to command, should be held by so junior a captain; but Evan-Thomas's charm of manner, knowledge of the service, and honesty of purpose made him a very acceptable and successful naval secretary.

Evan-Thomas then took command of the *Bellerophon* in the home fleet until August 1910, when he was appointed captain of the Naval College at Dartmouth. He was promoted to flag-rank in July 1912. After a year on half-pay he was appointed second in command of the first battle squadron with his flag in the *St. Vincent*. The outbreak of the European War in 1914 found him still in this command, which he retained until August 1915, when he was transferred to the command of the fifth battle squadron, flying his flag in the *Barham* (Captain A. W. Craig). In this post he took a notable part in the battle of Jutland (31 May 1916).

Evan-Thomas's splendid squadron, consisting of the *Barham*, *Valiant*, *Warspite*, and *Malaya* (*Queen Elizabeth* was refitting), sister ships, armed with eight 15-inch guns and capable of 25 knots speed, was at the time acting with the battle cruiser fleet under the command of Admiral Sir David Beatty. The combined force, which cleared the Forth at 11 p.m. on 30 May, reached the appointed rendezvous off the Danish coast at 2.15 p.m. on the 31st, and turned to the northward to meet Admiral Jellicoe coming with the British battle fleet from Scapa Flow. The fifth battle squadron was stationed five miles NNW. from Beatty's flagship, the *Lion*, and directed to look out for the battle fleet, when at 2.32 Beatty, acting on the *Galatea*'s report of enemy ships in sight, turned to the east, signalling the course to the *Barham*. This signal was not received until 2.37, and at 2.38 the fifth battle squadron turned to SSE. and increased to full speed in order to close Beatty who was now eight miles ahead. The distance of the fifth battle squadron from the *Lion*, coupled with the delay in transmitting the 'alter course' signal, prevented Evan-Thomas from giving the battle cruisers full support during the opening stages of the action, when they suffered severely with the loss of the *Indefatigable* and *Queen Mary*. Much controversy has arisen over this since the War, but there can be no doubt that Evan-Thomas, as soon as he was aware of Beatty's intentions and movements, acted with prompt decision and brought his squadron effectively into action at the earliest possible moment. The *Lion* opened fire at 3.49 p.m., and eleven minutes later the fifth battle squadron engaged the rear ships of the German line at 20,000 yards, and, following in the wake of the British battle cruisers at 24½ knots, inflicted serious damage on the *Von der Tann* and *Moltke*, with the result that the fire of the Germans weakened perceptibly. When Vice-Admiral Scheer's battle fleet was sighted coming north, the fifth battle squadron turned 16 points in the wake of the British battle cruisers and thus covered them during the period between 5 p.m. and 6 p.m. when the whole German force was closing the British battle fleet. In Beatty's words the fifth battle squadron supported him brilliantly and effectively. The *Barham*, *Warspite*, and *Malaya* were all hit by heavy shell at this time from the *König* and other ships of the fifth division of the German fleet, in return getting hits home on the *Grosser Kurfürst* and *Markgraf* and putting the wireless of the *Lützow* out of action. It was the *Barham* at 6.10 p.m. which signalled to Jellicoe the position of Scheer's battle fleet, and at 6.14, when the British battle fleet deployed, Evan-Thomas manœuvred skilfully under heavy fire to form astern of Jellicoe's ships and followed the movements of the commander-in-chief during the subsequent course of the action. The fine force which he commanded saw some of the heaviest fighting of the day: his flagship was hit six times and his wireless was wrecked, and the *Warspite* and *Malaya* suffered heavily. The squadron inflicted equally heavy injury on the enemy, and its work and the notable services of its admiral on that momentous day, which wrecked Scheer's hopes of success, are best summed up in the words of Jellicoe: 'The magnificent squadron commanded by Rear-Admiral Evan-Thomas formed a support of great value to Sir David Beatty during the afternoon and was brought into action in rear of the battle fleet in the most judicious manner in the evening.'

For his services in the battle Evan-Thomas was awarded the C.B. (1916), and immediately afterwards promoted K.C.B., and was given the French legion of honour, the first class of the Russian order of St. Anne, the second class of the Japanese order of the Rising Sun, and the order of the Crown of Italy.

Evan-Thomas was promoted vice-admiral in September 1917. He retained the command of the fifth battle squadron until October 1918. In 1919 he was created K.C.M.G. He remained unemployed until March 1921, when, having been promoted admiral in October 1920, he was appointed commander-in-chief at the Nore. In 1924 he retired at his own request. In the same year he was promoted G.C.B. He married in 1894 Hilda, daughter of Thomas Barnard, of Cople House, Bedfordshire. They had no children. After his retirement he lived at Charlton, near Shaftesbury, where he died 13 August 1928.

During the last four years of his life Evan-Thomas suffered much from ill-health, which was accentuated by the distress which he felt at the animadversions on his handling of the fifth battle squadron at Jutland as expressed in Mr. Winston Churchill's book *The World Crisis, 1916–1918*, Part I, 1927. Although he hated publicity, he felt compelled to send to *The Times* (16 February 1927) a letter containing an effective and dignified defence of his conduct in the battle.

[Sir Julian Corbett, *Official History of the Great War, Naval Operations*, 3 vols., 1920–1923; personal knowledge.]

V. W. Baddeley.

EVANS, JOHN GWENOGVRYN (1852–1930), Welsh palaeographer, was born at Ffynnon Velved, Llanybydder, Carmarthenshire, 20 March 1852, the only son of Thomas Evans, farmer, by his wife, Margaret Rees. When he was a year old, his parents moved to Cadabowen, Llanwenog, Cardiganshire. Up to the age of fourteen he attended the local school, and then spent four years in business at Llanbedr Pont Stephan. As the life did not suit him, he made a fresh start, first at Carmarthen school, then at the old Pont Siân grammar school, and in 1872 was admitted, as a candidate for the ministry, to the Presbyterian College, Carmarthen, where he stayed till 1875. After acting for a short period as assistant master at Milton College, near Rugby, he returned to Carmarthen as pastor of the Unitarian church, Park-y-velved (1876). In the following year he accepted a call to Preston, Lancashire, where he remained till 1880, when ill-health and voice failure compelled him to give up the ministry. He entered Owens College, Manchester, but before the end of the year left for Oxford. A complete break-down in health, however, prevented him from working for a degree; pulmonary tuberculosis set in and made it necessary for him to take a sea-voyage to Australia and South Africa, followed by some months at Davos Platz.

On his return to Oxford in 1882, Evans, in spite of extreme weakness, attended the lectures of Professor (Sir) John Rhŷs [q.v.], and the intense interest in Welsh palaeography which was aroused in him at this time enabled him to cast off his depression and to some extent to conquer his illness. 'A Collection of Welsh Proverbs', compiled in part from the columns of the Red Book of Hergest, the famous manuscript belonging to Jesus College, Oxford, secured for him the prize at the Liverpool National Eisteddfod in 1884 and the commendation of Rhŷs. The deficiencies of the edition of the Mabinogion published by Lady Charlotte Guest [q.v.] in 1838–1849 spurred him on to make a transcript of these tales from the Red Book, and later from the White Book of Rhydderch—a copy meticulously faithful to the original, letter for letter, line for line, even spacing for spacing. Rhŷs consented to act as co-editor, and the Oxford University Press was willing to print it. Thus the series of Old Welsh Texts began with the *Red Book Mabinogion*, a diplomatic reproduction of the original, beautifully executed (1887). Evans brought out by himself in 1888 a *Facsimile of the Black Book of Carmarthen*, reproduced by the autotype process; also a reprint of the Welsh translation of the *Book of Job* made by (Bishop) William Morgan [q.v.] in 1588. Both editors produced the *Red Book Bruts* (1890), Evans contributing a valuable account of all the manuscripts then known of the Welsh Bruts. In 1893 appeared the *Book of Llan Dâv* (edited by Rhŷs and Evans) reproduced from the Gwysaney manuscript, Latin and Old Welsh, together with the Welsh entries in the Book of St. Chad. This was followed by the text of the *Black Book of Carmarthen*, edited by Evans alone (1906); *White Book Mabinogion* (1907); *Book of Aneirin* (text and facsimile, 1907); *Kymdeithas Amlyn ac Amic* (1909); *Chirk Codex of the Welsh Laws* (facsimile only, 1909); *Book of Taliesin* (text and facsimile, 1910); *Red Book Poetry* (1911); complete editions of the *Taliesin* with introduction and notes, together with a companion volume, a 'restored' text of the poems (1915); a complete *Aneirin* on similar lines (1922); and lastly, *Poetry by Medieval Welsh Bards* (1926). In the 'Guild of Graduates' series Evans published a reprint of the 1546 (?) edition of *Oll Synnwyr Pen Kembero* of William Salesbury [q.v.] with an introduction (1902); and in the *Revue Celtique*, vols. xl, xli, the oldest text of the Gogynfeirdd.

Side by side with his editing of texts, Evans from 1894 onwards served as inspector for the Historical Manuscripts Commission, and was responsible for the *Report on Manuscripts in the Welsh Language* preserved in various public and private libraries: it appeared in seven parts, the first in 1898 and the last in 1910, and is a monumental work, dealing succinctly with the contents of some 900 manuscripts ranging in date from about 1100 to 1800.

This list shows the magnitude of Evans's contribution to Welsh scholarship. For over forty years, in spite of great bodily weakness, he toiled over manuscripts and proofs, and even set type with his own hand, in order to provide scholars with texts as perfect as possible in every detail and absolutely reliable as a basis for linguistic research. It was his devotion and indomitable courage which kept him to his task. The honorary doctorates which the university of Oxford (1903) and the university of Wales (1905) conferred upon him were fully deserved.

Unfortunately, in his introductions and notes to the Taliesin and Aneirin poems Evans left his own field and ventured to formulate theories as to their nature and date which were uncritical and even fantastic. Sir John Morris-Jones [q.v.] dealt fully and fiercely with the Taliesin in *Y Cymmrodor* (1918), Evans retorted with equal fury in the same periodical (1924). His Aneirin was even worse, and received similar treatment.

Evans married in 1877 Edith, youngest daughter of the Rev. Stephenson Hunter, principal of the Presbyterian College, Carmarthen, and had two sons and one daughter. She died in 1923, and was buried in the grounds of Tremvan, Llanbedrog, Carnarvonshire, his Welsh home. He survived her seven years, dying at Tremvan 25 March 1930, and was buried in the same grave.

[R. J. J. in *The Unitarian Students at the Presbyterian College, Carmarthen*, 1907; *The Welsh Weekly*, 1 July 1892; *Revue Celtique*, vol. xlvii, 1930; *Cymru*, vol. iv, 1893.]

I. WILLIAMS.

EVERSLEY, BARON (1831–1928), statesman. [See SHAW-LEFEVRE, GEORGE JOHN.]

EWART, SIR JOHN SPENCER (1861–1930), lieutenant-general, was born at

Langholm, Dumfriesshire, 22 March 1861, the eldest son of General Sir John Alexander Ewart [q.v.], a veteran of the Crimean War and the Indian Mutiny, by his wife, Frances, daughter of Spencer Stone, of Callingwood Hall, Stafford. His grandfather was Lieutenant-General John Frederick Ewart, colonel of the 67th Foot, a Peninsular veteran; Lieutenant-General Charles Brisbane Ewart [q.v.], colonel-commandant of the Royal Engineers, and Vice-Admiral C. J. F. Ewart were his uncles; and Admiral Arthur Wartensleben Ewart was his brother. Among his kinsmen were the politician William Ewart [q.v.] who was godfather to William Ewart Gladstone, and Colonel John Ewart who was murdered at Cawnpore with his wife and daughter in 1857. It may truly be said that John Spencer Ewart was born a soldier. He received his early education at Marlborough, where he made a reputation as a fine footballer and a cricketer above the average, and thence passed into the Royal Military College, Sandhurst, which he left with the sword of honour. He joined the Queen's Own Cameron Highlanders in 1881, and so early as the following year was on active service in the Egyptian War, being present at the battle of Tel-el-Kebir (13 September 1882). Ewart was also with his regiment throughout the Nile expedition of 1884–1885, and with the Sudan Frontier field force in 1885–1886. In the latter expedition he was adjutant of the battalion and also acted as garrison adjutant, was staff officer at Kosheh during its investment (12–29 December 1885), and fought in the engagement at Giniss (30 December), being mentioned in dispatches and awarded the order of the Medjidie (5th class). In 1893, having passed out of the Staff College two years previously, Ewart was appointed aide-de-camp to the general-officer-commanding-in-chief, Scottish command, which office he himself was destined to fill later. For five years from 1893 he was military secretary to the governor of Malta, rejoining his battalion in 1898 in order to take part in Lord Kitchener's Sudan campaign. He was present at the battle of Omdurman (2 September) and at the capture of Khartoum (4 September) and, besides being again mentioned in dispatches, was awarded the brevet of lieutenant-colonel.

After a short time as deputy assistant-adjutant-general, Western district, the war in South Africa called Ewart to further active service. He was at first base-commandant at East London and of the lines of communication to Stormberg. He later took part in the advance to the relief of Kimberley as brigade-major of the 3rd (Highland) brigade, and in the battle of Magersfontein (11–12 December 1899), where he gained considerable distinction by his admirable rallying of the brigade when it was unexpectedly attacked while in the act of deploying into fighting formation at the foot of Magersfontein hill. Again in action at Koodoosberg (2–4 February 1900), Ewart was shortly afterwards appointed assistant adjutant-general of the 9th division, with which he was present at the actions of Paardeburg (27 February 1900), Poplar Grove (7 March), and Driefontein (10 March). He also took part in the occupation of Bloemfontein (13 March) and the engagements at Waterval Drift (30–31 March), Vet River (5 May), Blaauwberg (26 May), and Roodepoort (30 May). Passing on to the 10th division Ewart served in the same capacity in the operations in Wittebergen (20–21 July), and at Retief's Nek (23 July) and Slaapkranz (28 July), ending up as quarter-master-general at Pretoria, where he remained until May 1902. For his services in this campaign he was twice mentioned in dispatches, awarded the C.B. (1902), and promoted brevet-colonel.

Ewart now entered on a long career at the War Office, where he spent almost all the ensuing years until the outbreak of the European War. He began in October 1902 as assistant military secretary. In 1903 he became deputy military secretary, and in March of the following year military secretary to Mr. (afterwards Viscount) Haldane and secretary of the Selection Board. Following a period as director of military operations at head-quarters (1906–1910), Ewart was appointed in the latter year director-general of the Territorial Force in succession to Sir William Henry Mackinnon [q.v.]. A few months later he was appointed adjutant-general to the forces and second military member of the Army Council. In the same year he became aide-de-camp-general to King George V and held that position until 1914. In 1911 he was promoted lieutenant-general and created K.C.B. As a result of the Curragh incident in the spring of 1914 Ewart, together with the secretary of state for war, Colonel J. E. B. Seely, and the chief of the Imperial General Staff, Sir John French, resigned his office in April. This temporary retirement, however, lasted a very short time, for within a few days he was appointed to succeed Sir James Wolfe Murray [q.v.] as general-officer-commanding-in-chief, Scottish command. Ewart held this appointment until his retirement in 1918. In that year he became honorary colonel of the 4th battalion of his own regiment, and he was colonel of the regiment from 1914 to 1929.

Although Ewart never held high command in the field, he experienced a full share of active service, and at the War Office accomplished much in helping forward the reorganization of the British army and the perfecting of the plans which stood the severest possible test at the outbreak of the European War.

Ewart married in 1891 Frances, daughter of Major George William Platt, of Dunallan, Stirlingshire, and had one daughter. He died at Langholm, Dumfriesshire, 19 September 1930.

[*The Times*, 20 September 1930; *Scotsman*, 20 September 1930; Major F. R. Wingate, *Mahdism and the Egyptian Sudan*, 1891; Sir J. F. Maurice and M. H. Grant, (Official) *History of the War in South Africa, 1899–1902*, 1906–1910; the *79th News* (journal of the Queen's Own Cameron Highlanders), October 1930.] C. V. OWEN.

FAIRBRIDGE, KINGSLEY OGILVIE (1885–1924), founder of farm schools overseas, the elder son of Rhys Seymour Fairbridge, surveyor to the government of Cape Colony and later to the British South Africa Company, by his wife, Rosalie Ogilvie, was born 5 May 1885 at Grahamstown, Cape Colony. At the age of eight he was sent to St. Andrew's preparatory school, Grahamstown. When he was eleven his parents moved to Rhodesia, and that ended his schooling. His father said that he must make himself useful. An old wagon, raised on stones, provided an office; a tent on the top a bedroom. There Kingsley Fairbridge slept and worked, making calculations for his father. Sometimes, for weeks together, he camped on the veld, 'dragging Dad's survey chain'. He was only twelve, he relates in his *Autobiography*, when he first asked himself, 'Why are there no farms here?', and then said to himself, 'Some day I will bring farmers here.' The idea which thus sprang up in his mind stayed there: it came in time to possess him.

Meanwhile Fairbridge helped his father; he was also, at different times, bank clerk, market-gardener, and journalist. He educated himself as best he could, reading, scribbling verses, translating native folk-lore stories. At the age of seventeen he spent a year in England. In London he went down to the East End, and saw women fight and men beat their wives. He visited other cities, too, noting things. He returned to Rhodesia with a clearer vision of what he would attempt. Not clerks or mill-hands should be his emigrants, nor men soiled by life in slums: but children. Caught young, they should be trained, under decent and kindly conditions, in the new land where they were to spend their lives.

In 1906 Fairbridge was promised a Rhodes scholarship at Oxford if he passed Responsions. He sailed for England, passed Responsions at the fourth attempt, and entered Exeter College in October 1908. One year later, at a meeting of the Oxford Colonial Club, the Child Emigration Society was founded, to forward Fairbridge's idea. He remained at Oxford until 1911, studying forestry, in which he obtained a diploma, entering vigorously into the life of the university, and devoting much time to nursing the infant Society.

A grant from the Rhodes trustees enabled Fairbridge to carry on his emigration work after leaving Oxford. In December 1911 he married Ruby Ethel, daughter of Harry Whitmore, of Edenbridge, Kent, and the following March he and his wife sailed for Western Australia—Rhodesia having dropped out of the scheme. They settled on a farm near Pinjarra, in the neighbourhood of Perth, where they opened a school. Early in 1913 twelve children were sent out to them: twenty-two more followed five months later. It was a desperate struggle. In 1915 the home committee instructed Fairbridge to close the school. He protested, and his protest was backed by the Perth committee. The school survived, and after the War, on a new site, grew rapidly in numbers. In 1935 it has 365 children, and is the accepted model for similar institutions in other Dominions.

Fairbridge died at Perth, Western Australia, 19 July 1924, worn out at the age of thirty-nine, leaving a widow, two sons, and two daughters. He published a volume of poems, *Veld Verse*, in 1909; and an incomplete but very interesting *Autobiography* appeared posthumously in 1927.

[*The Times*, 23 July 1924; *The Autobiography of Kingsley Fairbridge*, with an epilogue by Sir Arthur Lawley, 1927; private information; personal knowledge.]

F. J. WYLIE.

FARQUHAR, JOHN NICOL (1861–1929), missionary and Oriental scholar, was born at Aberdeen 6 April 1861, the eldest child and only son of George Farquhar, of that city, by his wife, Christian Alexander. He was educated first at the grammar school and university of Aberdeen, and proceeded to Christ Church, Oxford, with a classical exhibition in 1885. He obtained first classes in classical moderations (1887) and in *literae humaniores* (1889). He received the degree of D.Litt. from the university of Oxford in 1916, and he was also an honorary D.D. of Aberdeen University.

In 1891 Farquhar went out to India as a professor in the college of the London Missionary Society in Calcutta. In 1902 he became a secretary of the Young Men's Christian Association in the same city, and presently he found in the study of Oriental religions his true vocation. It may be claimed for Farquhar that he, more than any other individual, brought about a new orientation of the whole missionary outlook towards the non-Christian systems. He was not alone in realizing the implications for missionary methods of the facts which the comparative study of religions has made known, but he translated these implications into action and induced others to join him in the work.

Farquhar's pioneer publication for this end was his *Primer of Hinduism* (1912). This was followed by *The Crown of Hinduism* (1913), which suggests by its title what he held to be the relation of Christianity to the faith, the religious life and practice of which he there investigates, and *Modern Religious Movements in India* (1915). But the ripe fruit of his long years of careful research is to be found in his last book, *An Outline of the Religious Literature of India* (1920), a book which, by the accuracy of its learning and the balance of its judgement, is likely to retain for long a notable position.

No less significant than Farquhar's own contributions to learning were those which he inspired other scholars to make. The various series of books which he projected and which, in collaboration with other writers, he edited, remain a monument to the influence which he exercised and the unwearied patience with which he guided fellow workers in the same field. The scope of these series is indicated by their titles—*The Religious Quest of India*, *The Religious Life of India*, and *The Heritage of India*. The last two series were produced in India at popular prices.

The state of his health compelled Farquhar in 1923 to return to England, where he was appointed professor of comparative religion in Manchester University, succeeding, after an interval of eight years, the distinguished Buddhist scholar, T. W. Rhys Davids [q.v.]. He died 17 July 1929 at Withington, Manchester.

Farquhar married in Calcutta in 1891 Euphemia Neil Miller, eldest daughter of James Watson, of Aberdeen, and had one son and one daughter.

[*The Times*, 19 July 1929; private information; personal knowledge.] N. MACNICOL.

FARRER, WILLIAM (1861–1924), historian of Lancashire and feudal genealogist, born at Little Marsden, near Burnley, Lancashire, 28 February 1861, was the second son of William Farrer Ecroyd, a stuff manufacturer and merchant, and one of the leaders of the 'Fair Trade' movement of the early 'eighties of last century. The son changed his surname to Farrer in 1896 in compliance with the will of a great-uncle, William Farrer, a Liverpool merchant. His mother was Mary, elder daughter of Thomas Backhouse, of York. After his school days at Rugby Farrer entered the family business, but found it uncongenial, and retiring in 1896 settled down to a country life, first at Marton, near Skipton, then at Thornburgh House, Leyburn, later at Hall Garth, Over Kellet, and finally at Whitbarrow, Westmorland. An interest in his yeoman ancestry widened into a taste for local history; and the acquisition in 1895 of the collections for a new history of Lancashire made by John Parsons Earwaker [q.v.] induced him to take up this unfinished task. He spent large sums on the transcription and local publication of unprinted materials, unravelled the obscure problems of the Domesday survey of North-Western England in papers contributed to the *Transactions* of the Lancashire and Cheshire Antiquarian Society, and in 1903 published the first instalment of the work in the *History of the Parish of North Meols*. It was on so large a scale that it may be counted as fortunate that Farrer was presently persuaded to take part in the more manageable scheme of the Victoria County Histories. With the appointment of a co-editor, Mr. John Brownbill, the work was pushed forward rapidly, and the *Victoria History of the County of Lancaster* appeared in eight volumes between 1906 and 1914. It is specially full and thorough for the medieval period, and has almost entirely superseded the older county history of Edward Baines [q.v.].

Turning his investigations to Yorkshire, the original home of the Ecroyds, Farrer contributed a searching analysis of the Domesday survey of Yorkshire to the Victoria history of the county, and between 1914 and 1916 published privately three volumes of what was planned to be an almost complete collection of *Early Yorkshire Charters* before the thirteenth century. Unfortunately, the War and other adverse circumstances put an end to this valuable undertaking when some 1,900 charters had been printed, most of them for the first time. The arrangement by fiefs which Farrer had chosen for this work perhaps suggested the history of fiefs which he began as soon as the War was over. Started on a county basis in *Feudal Cambridgeshire* (1920) it was continued on a more logical and time-saving plan in his general history of *Honors and Knights' Fees*, in which the fees of each honour are dealt with together, irrespective of the counties in which they lay. Farrer died 17 August 1924 at Forsjord, Mosjoën, Norway, where he was spending his annual fishing holiday, when only two volumes of this ambitious work had been published (1923–1924). A third appeared in 1925, and the history of the honour of Warden has been printed by the Bedfordshire Historical Society (1927); but several others still remain in manuscript.

Farrer had the appearance of a man of the open air rather than of the study; he loved rural quiet and sports, and disliked towns and publicity. He received the honorary degree of Litt.D. from the university of Manchester and he was an honorary lecturer in local history in the university of Liverpool. He was twice married: first, in 1895 to Ellen Jane, daughter of Henry Ward, of Rodbaston, Staffordshire, by whom he had one daughter; secondly, in 1900 to Eliza, daughter of John Boyce, of Redgrave, Suffolk, by whom he had one son and two daughters.

Among Farrer's more important publications, besides those mentioned above, are: *Court Rolls of the Honor of Clitheroe* (3 vols., 1897–1913); *The Chartulary of Cockersand Abbey* (3 vols., Chetham Society, 1898–1909); *Final Concords of the County of Lancaster* (4 parts, Record Society of Lancashire and Cheshire, 1899–1910); *Court Rolls of Thomas, Earl of Lancaster in the County of Lancaster* (*ibid.*, 1901); *Lancashire Pipe Rolls and Early Charters* (1902); *Lancashire Inquests, Extents, and Feudal Aids* (3 parts, Record Society, 1903–1915); *An Outline Itinerary of King Henry I* (*English Historical Review*, vol. xxxiv, (July) 1919, and reprint, Oxford); *Records relating to the Barony of Kendale* (with J. F. Curwen, 2 vols., Cumberland and Westmorland Antiquarian Society, 1923–1924).

[Memoir by the present writer in *English Historical Review*, vol. xl, (January), 1925; Burke, *Landed Gentry*, 1921; private information; personal knowledge.] J. Tait.

FAWCETT, Dame MILLICENT (1847–1929), better known as Mrs. Henry Fawcett, leader of the women's suffrage movement, was born at Aldeburgh, Suffolk, 11 June 1847, the fifth daughter and seventh child of Newson Garrett, merchant, of Aldeburgh, by his wife, Louisa, daughter of John Dunnell. She was descended on both sides from families of the Eastern counties, and was much influenced by the characteristic independence and humour of the people among whom she grew up. At the age of twelve she was sent to a school at Blackheath, kept by Miss Browning, an aunt of the poet, Robert Browning, but she was taken away at fifteen, and had no other regular instruction. During Millicent's childhood her sister Elizabeth (afterwards Mrs. Garrett Anderson, q.v.) was trying to obtain professional qualification as a medical practitioner. The difficulties which she met with in this novel enterprise made Millicent indignant, and strengthened her natural inclination to work for an improvement in the position of women: Elizabeth's friendship with Sarah Emily Davies [q.v.], then embarking on her efforts to secure secondary education for girls, strengthened this determination.

In 1865 Millicent Garrett met Henry Fawcett [q.v.], the blind professor of economics at Cambridge and member of parliament for Brighton. In April 1867 they were married, and in the following year their only child, Philippa, was born. Mrs. Fawcett's marriage brought her into contact with the radical thinkers of the day, John Stuart Mill being among the close friends of herself and her husband. At Cambridge, where the Fawcetts lived for half the year, their circle included such men as (Sir) Leslie Stephen and James Stuart, and they were active in schemes for university reform, including the founding of colleges for women. It was in their drawing-room in 1869 that the lecture scheme, which later developed into Newnham College, was launched, and Mrs.

Fawcett became an active member of the council by which the college was managed, and took a detailed interest in its affairs and in those of the students.

Owing to her husband's blindness Mrs. Fawcett worked in closest co-operation with him, reading to him, summarizing documents, and writing speeches and articles, and this political training reinforced the natural bent of her own mind, and deepened her interest in problems of political theory and economics. In 1870 she published a little text-book, *Political Economy for Beginners*, which immediately became popular, was often reprinted, and was still in use by students at the time of her death. But these interests and occupations did not prevent Mrs. Fawcett from working for women's suffrage, which throughout her life seemed to her to be the key question in regard to the position of women. In 1867 she became a member of the first women's suffrage committee, and in 1868 she made her first public speech on the subject. Thereafter she took a large share in the pioneer efforts to bring the question before the country. She encountered ridicule and opposition, but was encouraged by the steady support of her husband as well as by her own convictions. The effort to secure to married women the legal right to their own property was another cause for which she worked hard, until its success was achieved by the Married Women's Property Act in 1882.

Mrs. Fawcett's life was a full and happy one. In 1884, however, its course was interrupted by the sudden death of her husband. This was a crushing sorrow; but she did not allow it to weaken her efforts for the causes in which they had both believed. She devoted herself more than ever to her work. The publication in 1885 of *The Maiden Tribute of Modern Babylon* by William Thomas Stead [q.v.] awakened her interest in the problem of the protection of girls, and for many years she took an active part in the work of the Vigilance Society. But she came to believe that neither this nor any other reform touching women would advance satisfactorily without the parliamentary vote. During the 'eighties and 'nineties the movement for women's suffrage made slow progress, but Mrs. Fawcett was not discouraged. In 1887 she joined the liberal-unionist group, and became an active member of the women's committee, which, however, she left in 1903 on the tariff reform issue. Between 1887 and 1895 she visited Ireland repeatedly, and made many speeches in opposition to Home Rule, becoming known as a leading political figure of the day. In 1890 her daughter, Philippa, then a student at Newnham College, was placed above the senior wrangler in the mathematical tripos list, an achievement which materially advanced the cause of higher education for women and naturally gave her mother the greatest satisfaction. When the South African War broke out in 1899, Mrs. Fawcett very strongly supported the patriotic side, and in July 1901 she was sent to South Africa as the leader of the commission of ladies to inquire into conditions in the concentration camps. She effected great reforms, but was subjected to bitter criticism from the pro-Boer party in England.

After the War, Mrs. Fawcett resumed her work for women's suffrage, and within a few years a revival of public interest in the subject was apparent. By 1905 the formation of the Women's Social and Political Union (popularly known as the Suffragettes) with its unconventional methods rapidly hastened the pace. Mrs. Fawcett did not join the leaders of the new 'militant' movement, Mrs. Emmeline Pankhurst [q.v.] and her daughter Christabel, although at first she did not altogether disapprove of their methods. Later, however, their policy of sensational activity merged into one of positive violence, and she then thought it right publicly to dissociate herself and her constitutional organization from them. Between 1905 and 1914 Mrs. Fawcett's societies grew fast in size and importance. She had become in 1897 the president of a National Union of Women's Suffrage Societies, which was composed of independent societies in all parts of the country, co-operating in a common policy and in propaganda, and formed with the sole object of obtaining the vote for women on 'the same terms as it is or may be granted to men'. This union became an exceedingly efficient and determined political force: it enrolled thousands of intelligent and active men and women, and pursued its way by lawful and constitutional methods, unperturbed by the militant activities which were simultaneously going on.

Mrs. Fawcett, as the president of this large organization, was incessantly at work, taking part in processions and demonstrations, speaking in all parts of the country, directing policy and tactics. The difficulties were great, owing to the prevailing prejudice, the organized opposition, and the intricacies of the party system. Through all the ups and down Mrs. Fawcett remained wise and steadfast, and kept her followers to the paths of reason and reality. In 1914, when the European War broke out, the suffrage societies, under her leadership, suspended their propaganda and devoted themselves to the task of 'sustaining the vital forces of the nation' 'Let us prove ourselves worthy of citizenship, whether our claim be recognized or not', Mrs. Fawcett wrote; and while the War lasted this remained their policy. In 1916, however, the question of the registration of soldiers and sailors brought franchise matters again before parliament, and Mrs. Fawcett strongly urged that if any change was to be made the women's claim must be considered at the same time. This was admitted by the government, and a conference, of which the Speaker was chairman, was set up which, in February 1917, recommended a limited measure of women's suffrage. In the following June this was passed by the House of Commons, and in January 1918 by the House of Lords.

All through her life Mrs. Fawcett worked unremittingly. She was invariably punctual and exact, never broke engagements, always answered her letters, left nothing unattended to, and was eminently reasonable in all her ways. As a speaker she was clear and cogent, but not eloquent; she impressed the mind rather than the emotions, but her devotion to her cause and her profound faith in it were plain. During all the vicissitudes of the long campaign she never wavered in her belief that women's suffrage must ultimately triumph, and she took each reverse as a call to further effort.

After the first victory in 1918 Mrs. Fawcett retired from the presidency of the National Union, but continued to be actively interested in the many improvements in the position of women which followed the granting of the vote. She took a prominent part in the efforts to secure full equal franchise, which came in 1928, and also in the successful attempts to open the legal profession and the civil service to women, to equalize the law as to divorce and guardianship, and to raise the age of marriage.

In 1905 Mrs. Fawcett had been given an honorary LL.D. degree by St. Andrews University, and in 1925 she was made D.B.E. During the last years of her life she travelled often, visiting Palestine four times, and going to Ceylon. She also took advantage of her comparative leisure to write several books, including her own reminiscences, and she much enjoyed attending meetings at which she did not have to speak. She found time also to listen to a great deal of music, which had been one of her lifelong interests. She died at her home in London 5 August 1929 after a very short illness.

Three portraits of Dame Millicent Fawcett were painted: the first, executed in 1874, showing her as a young woman with her husband, is by Ford Madox Brown, and was placed in the National Portrait Gallery after Henry Fawcett's death; the second, showing her in middle life, was painted by Mrs. Annie Swynnerton, and was bought by the nation for the Tate Gallery; the third, painted in 1927, is by Mr. Lionel Ellis, and is at Newnham College, Cambridge. A memorial was placed in Westminster Abbey in 1932, being added to the monument to the memory of Henry Fawcett, which stands in the chapel of the Holy Cross.

[M. G. Fawcett, *What I Remember*, 1924; Ray Strachey, *Millicent Garrett Fawcett*, 1931; records of the suffrage societies; private information.] R. Strachey.

FELKIN, ELLEN THORNEYCROFT (1860–1929), better known as Ellen Thorneycroft Fowler, novelist, was born at Chapel Ash, Wolverhampton, 9 April 1860. She was the elder daughter of Henry Hartley Fowler, first Viscount Wolverhampton [q.v.], of Chapel Ash, by his wife, Ellen, youngest daughter of George Benjamin Thorneycroft. She was educated at home for the most part, but at the age of seventeen attended Laleham School, Middlesex, for about one year. Until her marriage with Alfred Laurence Felkin, an inspector of schools, in 1903, she lived at home with her parents at Woodthorne, Wolverhampton, a house built by her father shortly after her birth. She spent three months in London with them every year. Her first publication, *Songs and Sonnets* (1888), was followed by *Verses, Grave and Gay* (1891) and *Verses, Wise or Otherwise* (1895). It was not, however, until 1898 that she won wide public commendation by her novel *Concerning Isabel Carnaby*. Her gifts as a writer of fiction were perceived from the first by (Sir) William Robertson Nicoll [q.v.], who encouraged her to devote herself to novel-writing. Her best-known books followed one another in quick succession: *A Double Thread* (1899), *The Farringdons* (1900), *Fuel of Fire* (1902), *Place and Power*

(1903), and *Kate of Kate Hall* (1904), the last-named written in collaboration with her husband. She wrote several other novels and numerous short stories which showed her talent, without attracting much further public attention. Her last book was *Signs and Wonders* (1926).

After her marriage Mrs. Felkin lived at Eltham, Kent, until 1916, when she removed to Bournemouth, where she died 22 June 1929. Her marriage was childless and her husband survived her. She left practically no literary remains. During her later years failing health curtailed her writing. While it is true that she was brought up in a Methodist household, the general supposition that she was a Methodist is incorrect. She was a member of the Church of England from childhood.

Ellen Thorneycroft Fowler was a brilliant and witty conversationalist; generous, tolerant, and unaffected in every kind of company. As a novelist, she was a quiet and faithful chronicler of simple society. Her sense of character was firm and her dialogue lively. Her place in English fiction would have been higher had the construction of her novels been more vigorous and their range less narrow; but she was a solid writer in her quiet way.

[*The Times*, 24 June 1929; private information.] E. O'Brien.

FERRANTI, SEBASTIAN ZIANI DE (1864–1930), electrical engineer and inventor, born at Liverpool 9 April 1864, was the second son of César Ziani de Ferranti, by his wife, Juliana, daughter of William Scott, portrait-painter, and widow of a Polish musician, Count Szczepanowski. César's father, Marc Aurelio Ziani, who in later years added 'de Ferranti' to his name, resided in earlier life at Bologna and afterwards became guitarist to Leopold I, king of the Belgians. César was educated on the Continent, but settled in England and established a photographic art-studio in Bold Street, Liverpool. Sebastian's passion for invention and machinery showed itself very early. After a few months spent at the age of eight at Arlon in Luxemburg, where his uncle, George de Ferranti, was professor of English at the university, he was sent to St. Stanislas's School at Hampstead, kept by Mlle Flon, where he remained until the summer of 1877, when he entered the Roman Catholic college of St. Augustine at Ramsgate. The principal, Abbot Egan, wisely encouraged his taste for electrical experiments, and allowed him to fit up the school with electric bells entirely designed by himself. He remained there until the summer of 1881. His technical knowledge up to this time, according to his own statement, had been derived mainly from *The Boy's Playbook of Science* by John Henry Pepper [q.v.] and from Edmund Atkinson's translation of Adolphe Ganot's *Elementary Treatise on Physics*. In July 1881 he obtained work with Siemens Brothers at Charlton, near Woolwich, and assisted (Sir) William Siemens [q.v.] in experiments with an electric furnace for making steel. 'There', he said, 'I really got what I wanted. I was surrounded by dynamos and everything electrical. I felt entirely happy.' While there he attended for a short time evening classes at University College, London, where he heard lectures by (Sir) Oliver Lodge, George Carey Foster, and (Sir) Alexander Kennedy [q.v.].

At the age of thirteen Ferranti had made an arc-light with the aid of a bichromate battery, and in 1878, while at St. Augustine's College, he had made a dynamo, which he afterwards improved. It was constructed on the Paccinotti principle; though, as he did not know of Paccinotti, the Siemens flat-coil alternator may be considered its progenitor. In 1882 he patented it as the Ferranti alternator [see *Engineering*, 1 December 1882]. The first Ferranti dynamo with its coreless disk was installed in the arches under Cannon Street railway station. It had an output for its size greatly in advance of any existing machines, and achieved a success which tided its inventor over hard times and won him recognition among electrical engineers of the day. It was, however, discovered that the idea of using a zigzag winding, which was an essential feature of the machine, had occurred independently to Sir William Thomson (afterwards Lord Kelvin, q.v.). This made it necessary to take out a joint patent in 1884 for the Thomson and Ferranti alternator and to guarantee Thomson a minimum royalty of £500 a year.

In order to place his dynamo on the market Ferranti in 1882 went into a short-lived partnership with Alfred Thompson, an engineer, and Francis Ince, a solicitor (whose daughter he afterwards married). In 1883, assisted by Ince, he started an independent business at 57B Charterhouse Square for the manufacture of electrical apparatus. This brought him into connexion with the Grosvenor Gallery Electric Supply Corporation, formed by Sir Coutts

Lindsay, the Earl of Crawford, and others, to supply the Grosvenor Gallery and its neighbourhood with electric light, using overhead mains. In 1883 they installed one of Ferranti's alternators under the Grosvenor Gallery. But Ferranti shortly afterwards designed and made small transformers of a greatly improved type, which he patented in 1885. He convinced the directors of the superiority of his system, comprising dynamo, transformer, and meter, and in 1886 he was appointed engineer to the company. The meters, motors, and switches required were designed by Ferranti as part of his ordinary work. He installed two 750 h.p. generators working at a pressure of 2,500 volts, and by means of five overhead circuits he provided a supply to an area extending at first from Lincoln's Inn Fields to the Albert Gate and from Regent's Park to Charing Cross, and later as far as the City, where entry was barred, and well into Chelsea on the south-west.

Experience at the Grosvenor Gallery showed that it was inconvenient to have an electric generating station in a crowded area, on account of noise and dirt. Ferranti aimed at supplying all London, north of the Thames, and he selected Deptford as more suitable for a power-station because, being less populous, it would enable him to use high-tension feeders without causing inconvenience, and because it was more accessible to sea-borne coal and provided river water for condensing. The London Electric Supply Corporation was registered on 26 August 1887 with Ferranti as chief electrician. The erection of a station, the whole of which except the roof was planned by Ferranti, was begun at Deptfor in 1888 and finished early in 1890. The station was intended to have an ultimate capacity of 65,000 h.p., and two generators, each of 10,000 h.p., were designed to begin with. In constructing the station Ferranti in fact conceived and intended to carry out the methods by which the generation and distribution of electricity on a large scale have been accomplished in recent times; but these methods were opposed to the ideas of contemporary engineers, who sought to put low-power generating stations in the middle of small areas. But in order successfully to carry out work on such a scale in opposition to prevailing expert opinion it was necessary to have parliamentary powers over the area to be supplied, and these the London Electric Supply Corporation failed to obtain. A government committee of inquiry, presided over by Major Francis Arthur Marindin, crippled Ferranti's scheme by promoting the Electricity Lighting Act of 1888, which not only drastically reduced the area which Ferranti intended to supply, but also permitted the competition of low-power-stations with small initial expenses in every part of the area which he already supplied. In face of this situation the equipment of Deptford was reduced to two generators of 1,250 h.p., though later Ferranti built a 2,000 h.p. alternator for the station. Nevertheless, he had to solve a variety of novel problems. For main transmission he determined to employ a current of 10,000 volts. To step up the current to this voltage from the generators he built a transformer, of which he characteristically remarked later, 'curiously enough, it worked'. There were then no instruments which could measure so high a pressure, and he had to gauge the current by joining a hundred 100-volt lamps in a series. It was difficult to procure cables that would carry the current, and finally, after repeated breakdowns, he designed and made his own cables, employing concentric tubes of copper separated by brown paper soaked in ozokerit wax. These were made in lengths of 20 feet, so that over 7,000 joins were necessary in the 28 miles laid. A clever mechanical device brought the ends of the tubes into intimate electrical contact. Though these cables were contrary to the Board of Trade regulations, they proved satisfactory, and some were still in use thirty-five years later. The main ideas of Ferranti's scheme were realized more than thirty years later by the London Power Company, which was registered as a public company in August 1925 under powers conferred by the London Electricity Act of 1925. The companies then supplying the metropolitan area, including the London Electric Supply Corporation, became shareholders of the London Power Company and were confined to distribution. The Deptford (now the East Deptford) power station was purchased by the Company 1 January 1928.

In 1892 Ferranti gave up his post at Deptford with the London Electric Supply Corporation and devoted his attention to his private business as a manufacturing engineer and to his inventions. His first conspicuous achievement was obtaining the contract for lighting Portsmouth in 1894. In a short time his reputation was European and American, and he was compelled to make repeated journeys in order to supervise his plant abroad. In 1896 he established a factory at Hollinwood near Oldham in Lancashire, which became the head-quarters of Ferranti Limited, finally registered on 27 February 1905. After reconstruction in earlier days the firm made the whole range of plant required for electric lighting, but later it concentrated attention on transforming and measuring machines. Ferranti's own inventions were numerous and varied. Between 1882 and 1927 he took out 176 patents, ranging from vacuum-pumps to loud-speakers and including an electrolytic lighting arrestor for overhead wires, an induction furnace, afterwards developed by Kjellin, and a mercury meter which became one of the most successful products of the firm. His activities were not confined to electricity. From 1895 onwards he worked on the gas-turbine, and in 1902 took out a patent for working on an isothermal expansion cycle, heat being supplied at stages during the expansion by the use of superheaters. This procedure, as well as some other of his devices, has become standard practice in steam-turbine work, and his method of reheating, to which he again called attention in his James Watt lecture in 1913, afterwards came into extensive use. From 1906 he was also occupied with the production of textile yarns. By new processes he succeeded in improving the speed of production and the quality of the yarn spun by the continuous process first devised by Arkwright. His inventions were taken up by Mr. Ernest Coats, of Paisley, and he was still carrying on experiments at the time of his death.

In 1910 Ferranti's presidential address to the Institution of Electrical Engineers attracted much attention (*Journal* of the Institution, February 1911). It dealt with coal conservation, and urged that the only effective solution of the problems presented was to convert the whole of the coal needed for heat and power into electricity, to be distributed from large generating stations, and to apply electricity universally for all services. Lighting, heating, motive power for every purpose, whether domestic, factory, or transport, was to be electrical. Thereafter Ferranti urged this ideal by reason and argument and by practical example in his own home, and by his contrivances for household distribution did much to realize it. His idea was regarded by many as impracticable, but it differs little in general conception and even in detail from the 'grid' scheme inaugurated by the Electricity Act of 1926.

From 1913 Ferranti resided at the Hall, Baslow, Derbyshire. In 1891 he became a member of the present Institution of Electrical Engineers, of which he was president in 1910 and 1911. In 1912 he received the honorary degree of D.Sc. from the university of Manchester. He was also a member of the Institution of Civil and Mechanical Engineers, and he was elected a fellow of the Royal Society in 1927. He died at Zurich, after an operation, 13 January 1930, and was buried at Hampstead. Ferranti married in 1888 Gertrude Ruth, second daughter of Francis Ince, a member of the firm of Ingledew, Ince, and Colt, solicitors. By her he had three sons and four daughters. He was a man of charming personality and inspired with enthusiasm and affection those who worked with him. He was a pioneer in high-voltage systems and may be considered the originator of long-distance transmission of high-power electrical current. The full value of his work and ideas has hardly yet been fully appreciated.

[*The Times*, 14 and 16 January 1930; Mrs. G. R. Ferranti and Richard Ince, *Life and Letters of Sebastian Ziani de Ferranti*, 1934; *Journal* of Institution of Electrical Engineers, February 1922 and November 1930; *Engineer*, 17 January 1930; *Engineering*, 17 January 1930; *Proceedings* of the Institution of Mechanical Engineers, May 1930; *Nature*, 1 and 15 February 1930; *Echo*, 9 December 1891.] E. I. Carlyle.

FERRIER, Sir DAVID (1843–1928), physician, the sixth child and second son of David Ferrier, by his wife, Hannah, daughter of Alexander Bell, of Brechin. was born 13 January 1843 at Woodside near Aberdeen, where his father was in business. He was sent to Aberdeen grammar school, proceeding thence to Aberdeen University (King's College), where he read classics and philosophy and was a pupil of Alexander Bain [q.v.]. He graduated M.A. in 1863 with first-class honours in classics and philosophy. In the following year he travelled on the Continent for six months. In 1865 he entered on the formal study of medicine at the university of Edinburgh. By the end of 1868 he had graduated M.B. The next two years Ferrier spent at Bury St. Edmunds as assistant to Dr. W. E. Image, a general practitioner there, an accomplished man, who came of a family well known for scholarship and scientific pursuits. While with Image, Ferrier prepared his M.D. thesis which was awarded a gold medal. In 1870 he moved to London, and was appointed lecturer on physiology at the Middlesex Hospital school. The following year (1871) he began his long service with King's College, London, at first as demonstrator of physiology. He was successively appointed assistant physician, physician, and consultant physician; the post of professor of neuropathology was specially created for him in 1889; on retirement in 1908 he was made emeritus professor.

It was early in 1873, after a visit to his friend and fellow graduate, Dr. (afterwards Sir) James Crichton-Browne, at the West Riding Asylum, Wakefield, of which Browne was then director, that Ferrier began his memorable researches on electrical excitation of the brain (*Report* of the West Riding Asylum, 1873). This work, continued at King's College, he prosecuted steadily by his method of faradic stimulation until the brain had been explored systematically in a series of vertebrate types up to and inclusive of the monkey. Ferrier's observations gave to the hitherto disputed existence of 'localization' of cerebral functions a solid basis of proved experimental fact. This research formed the subject of his Croonian lectures at the Royal Society in 1874 and 1875, as also of his treatise *The Functions of the Brain* (1876, 2nd edition 1886), which was translated into several languages.

The positions on the brain-surface of excitable points evoking movements of the limbs, face, &c., were determined by Ferrier much as they are now known. He showed the combined area of these points to be more extensive and the movements elicitable through them more detailed in the ape than in animals less akin to man. He proved that the destruction of this area produces in the ape paralysis similar to that characteristic of cerebral 'stroke' in man. By continental physiologists, who did not use for experiment animals so close to the human type, his observations were received for a time with much reserve. He did not himself enter into controversy willingly; but at the International Medical Congress held in London in 1881 he gave to a large gathering of physicians and others there assembled a convincing demonstration of his discoveries. His findings carried the day. The distinguished French physician present, J. M. Charcot, exclaimed, as one of Ferrier's animals was led forward, 'C'est un malade!'

Ferrier, from the experience of his work on monkeys, drew the further inference that, with Listerian precautions against sepsis, such as he was himself following for his experiments—Lord Lister [q.v.] was his colleague at King's College—conditions of disease in the brain could be effectively dealt with surgically to an extent not hitherto attempted. Ferrier reiterated this belief; and after his Marshall Hall oration at the College of Physicians of London in 1883 (Sir) William McEwen [q.v.], of Glasgow, operated in that year for intracranial disease, and in London the next year (Sir) Rickman Godlee [q.v.], Lister's nephew, removed a brain-tumour, the seat of which within the brain had been correctly 'localized'. Sir Charles Ballance, himself distinguished in brain surgery and versed in the history of its development, has said with penetration and generosity that to Ferrier not less than to the surgeons themselves the origination of modern cerebral surgery is primarily due. One result, among others, traceable to Ferrier's experiments on the monkey, has therefore been the relief now widely given by surgery to patients suffering from certain forms of brain-tumour and brain injury. The fact touches with irony one sequel to his beneficent research, namely, his prosecution at law by anti-vivisectionists. The attack, however, failed, their main accusation proving untrue.

Despite increasing claims upon him of hospital and consulting practice, Ferrier made time to conduct experiments in the laboratory assiduously far into later life; but his early work in that direction is the more important. It wrought a great change in cerebral diagnosis and treatment. It is difficult now to think back to a time when the cerebral cortex was pictured as an uncharted sea of featureless uniformity.

Ferrier was knighted in 1911, and he received many academic and professional distinctions. The Royal Society elected him a fellow in 1876, and it awarded him in 1890 a royal medal. In the year following his death a lecture bearing his name was endowed at the Society. At the Royal Society of Medicine a Ferrier memorial library has been founded and endowed.

In figure slight and erect, genial and alert in bearing, the burden of years weighed lightly on Ferrier. A reflective quietude of voice and manner went far to veil the underlying energy which was no less a part of his nature. Keenly alive to men and things, and turning with enjoyment to classical literature, his talk had a charm and humour enhanced by the trace of Aberdeen accent. Sensitive to natural beauty, for his summer holidays he preferred the sea-coast, often Cornwall; it was with the seascape that he most indulged his love of pictures.

Ferrier died in London, where had been his home for nearly sixty years, on 19 March 1928. He married in 1874 Constance, daughter of Albert Crakell Waterlow, of London, and niece of Sir Sydney Hedley Waterlow, first baronet [q.v.]. Lady Ferrier survived her husband, together with their son and daughter.

[*Proceedings* of the Royal Society, vol. ciii, B, 1928 (portrait); private information; personal knowledge.] C. S. SHERRINGTON.

FILDES, SIR (SAMUEL) LUKE (1844–1927), painter, was born at Liverpool 18 October 1844, the son of James Fildes, of Chester, by his wife, *née* Fogg. Educated privately at Chester, he studied art successively at Warrington, at the South Kensington Art School, and the Royal Academy Schools. Towards the end of the 'sixties he began practising book and magazine illustration, working for the *Cornhill Magazine*, *Once a Week*, and the *Graphic*; to the first number of the *Graphic* he contributed in 1869 a drawing, 'The Casuals', which anticipates the subject of one of his most famous pictures, painted five years later. Through (Sir) J. E. Millais Fildes was brought into contact with Charles Dickens, and produced the set of illustrations which in August 1870 appeared in the volume containing Dickens's unfinished novel *The Mystery of Edwin Drood*. His first exhibit at the Royal Academy, in 1868, was a drawing, 'Nightfall'; in 1872 he exhibited for the first time a picture, 'Fair Quiet and Sweet Rest' (now belonging to the Corporation of Warrington), which was followed in 1873 by 'Simpletons' and in 1874 by 'Applicants for admission to a Casual Ward'. The last of these was Fildes's first great public success in the then popular anecdotal and melodramatic vein, which for a considerable period he continued to exploit: the picture, the significance of which was emphasized by a quotation from Dickens, is now at the Royal Holloway College. 1874 was also the year of Fildes's marriage to Fanny, daughter of William Woods, of Warrington, and sister of the painter Henry Woods, R.A. (1846–1921). Fildes's brother-in-law soon afterwards settled permanently in Venice, and as a result, Fildes was brought into frequent contact with that city, being also to some extent influenced by certain contemporary painters working there, notably an Austrian artist who at the time enjoyed a great vogue, Cecil von Haanen. Scenes from Venetian life were thenceforth for a while frequently treated by Fildes alongside of those anecdotal subjects in an English setting by which he had established his position as a popular painter. Among his pictures in the former category 'An Alfresco Toilet' (1889; now in the Lady Lever Art Gallery, Port Sunlight) was an immense success; and in the latter group there should further be mentioned 'The Widower' (1876; this and the 'Casual Ward', already mentioned, each realized £2,100 at Christie's, 28 April 1883); 'The Return of the Penitent' (1879); 'The Village Wedding' (1883); and, Fildes's most widely known painting, 'The Doctor' (1891; now in the Tate Gallery). Meanwhile, Fildes had in 1879 been elected A.R.A. and in 1887 R.A., his diploma work being 'A School Girl', exhibited in 1888. He soon became an influential member of the Academy council; and he was also for many years chairman of the Arts Club.

The portrait of his wife exhibited by Fildes at the Academy in 1887 attracted much attention, and gradually the artist was led to devote himself almost exclusively to portraiture, gaining a large and fashionable clientele. In 1901 he was commissioned to paint a state portrait of King Edward VII (exhibited in 1902) followed by one of Queen Alexandra (exhibited in 1905; both are in the Blue Drawing Room at Buckingham Palace); and in 1912 the task of painting a state portrait of King George V was also allotted to him. A fluent, facile realism is characteristic of Fildes's work as a portrait-painter and may be regarded as the keynote of his art generally, explaining its wide popularity at the time. Pictorially, Fildes stands for that average modernity of handling which gained ground in European painting as the conquests of French impressionism were gradually absorbed.

Fildes, who was knighted in 1906 and created K.C.V.O. in 1918, died 27 February 1927 at his house, 11 Melbury Road, Kensington, built by Richard Norman Shaw. His wife, who also practised painting, and exhibited at the Academy in 1878 and 1883, died in April 1927; they had four sons and two daughters. A selection of Fildes's works was exhibited at the Royal Academy Winter Exhibition in 1928.

[*The Times*, 28 February 1928; Algernon Graves, *The Royal Academy of Arts, a complete dictionary of contributors and their work*, vol. ii, 1905; subsequent Royal Academy Exhibition Catalogues, including that of the Memorial Exhibition of 1928.]

T. BORENIUS.

FINLAY, ROBERT BANNATYNE, first VISCOUNT FINLAY (1842–1929), lord chancellor, was born 11 July 1842 at Newhaven, near Edinburgh, the eldest son and child in the family of eleven of William Finlay, F.R.C.P.E., who practised medicine in Newhaven and Trinity, by his wife, Ann, daughter of Robert Bannatyne, of Leith. He was educated at Edinburgh Academy, where he became 'dux', and at Edinburgh University, where he graduated M.D. in 1864.

Although he left school at the age of sixteen and graduated only in medicine, Finlay was a fine classical scholar. He also made himself proficient in French and German and acquired a reading knowledge of Italian and Spanish. His classics he kept up to the end of his life. In 1924, when he was eighty-two years of age, he delivered as president of the Scottish Classical Association an address in defence of classical education, as rich in classical lore as it was attractive in method.

Finlay practised medicine for a few months only. He was called to the bar by the Middle Temple in 1867 and took silk in 1882. As a Q.C. he soon came to the front. He had at one time a large jury practice, appearing in many *causes célèbres*, including at least one famous divorce case. Gradually, however, he gravitated to a weightier and less showy class of business. He was briefed on special occasions in the Admiralty and Chancery divisions, in patent cases, and, with increasing frequency, before the House of Lords and Privy Council. By the time he became solicitor-general in 1895, he held a leading position in this class of work.

Before a jury Finlay made no display of rhetoric, but he managed his case with excellent judgement, was effective in cross-examination, and made a convincing speech. He lost nothing by the fairness and courtesy which he always displayed. In heavier cases and before appellate tribunals his strength lay in the clearness and directness of his presentation. If a case called for the investigation of first principles, he would embark on research with the avidity of a scholar.

In appearance Finlay had the advantage of a good stature, striking features, and fine, deep-set eyes. Accustomed to work with method and rapidity, he was able to avoid working late at night. He never worked on Sundays, and he never worried. He preserved practically to the end an appearance of freshness and vigour which, in combination with a singular serenity of demeanour, was no unimportant element in his personality. He enjoyed golf, and in 1903 was captain of the Royal and Ancient golf club at St. Andrews.

After an unsuccessful contest in East Lothian in 1882, Finlay entered parliament in 1885 as liberal member for the Inverness Burghs. He made a well-reasoned speech against Mr. Gladstone's Home Rule Bill, and retained his seat, as a liberal-unionist, in the election of 1886. In 1892 he was defeated, but was again returned in 1895 when he became solicitor-general and was knighted. In 1900, still sitting for the same constituency, he became attorney-general, retaining this position until the fall of Mr. Balfour's government at the end of 1905. In the election of 1906 he was defeated.

Between 1895 and 1905 the law officers of the crown, as advisers of the government, were involved to an unprecedented extent in matters of international law. Apart from minor questions, there were the difficulties arising in connexion with three important wars in which Great Britain occupied the position alternately of neutral and belligerent, namely, the Spanish-American, the South African, and the Russo-Japanese wars. The last-named gave rise in 1904 to the famous Dogger Bank incident, when the Russian Baltic fleet fired upon British trawlers in the North Sea. In addition there were several important international arbitrations: the Venezuelan boundary arbitration in 1899, in which Finlay, as solicitor-general, assisted in preparing the British case, although he took no part in the argument; the Alaska boundary arbitration in 1903 in which, as attorney-general, he led for Great Britain and Canada; and, most interesting of all, the Venezuelan claims arbitration in 1903. The last mentioned was the first case of importance to come before the recently established Permanent Court of Arbitration at The Hague, and ten Powers were represented. In this, too, Finlay led for Great Britain. In 1902, as lord rector of Edinburgh University, he had delivered a lecture on international arbitration, pointing out its limitations as well as its possibilities.

When he ceased to be attorney-general in 1905 Finlay returned to private work at the bar. Although he had been absent for ten years, he stepped immediately into an even larger practice than that which he had left when he took office. He was almost continuously before the House of Lords or Privy Council. He won a great reputation among Dominion lawyers, and in 1910 was briefed to lead for Canada in the Newfoundland fisheries arbitration. His opening speech, which occupied sixteen sittings, on a subject of extreme difficulty, was the crowning effort of his career.

Upon the formation in 1916 of Mr. Lloyd George's government Finlay, who had re-entered parliament in 1910 as member for Edinburgh and St. Andrews universities, became lord chancellor and was raised to the peerage as Baron Finlay, of Nairn. In the reconstructed Cabinet of 1919 he did not again obtain office. He was advanced to a viscounty on retirement, but received no pension: he had waived the usual arrangement for one at the time of his appointment. Notwithstanding this, he continued for some time to give his services in judicial business in the House of Lords and Privy Council.

In 1920 Lord Finlay became a member of the Permanent Court of Arbitration, and in 1921 one of the first judges of the Permanent Court of International Justice at The Hague. In spite of his years he possessed incomparable qualifications for this post. In a speech made after his death by M. Anzilotti, the president of the court, who referred to him as the most beloved and respected of its judges, stress was laid upon the unique combination in Finlay's experience of the study and application of both municipal and international law, upon his knowledge of languages, and his classical and literary culture. The speaker recalled how in private conversation Finlay had tersely disposed of an argument heard in the court by an apposite citation from the *Divina Commedia*. Quite apart from the advantage to the newly established court of Finlay's learning and high character, it was widely recognized as being of the greatest value to Great Britain to have sent there as its first representative a personality of so much culture and distinction.

During the seven years of his membership of the court, Lord Finlay only missed one of the fifteen sessions held. In 1928 his eyes became affected with cataract, and the operation which he underwent for its removal proved too much for his strength. He died at his house in Kensington 9 March 1929 at the age of eighty-six.

Finlay was created G.C.M.G. in 1904 and was sworn of the Privy Council in 1905. He received the honorary degree of LL.D. from the universities of Cambridge, Edinburgh, and St. Andrews.

Finlay married in 1874 Mary (died 1911), daughter of Cosmo Innes [q.v.], principal clerk of session and professor of constitutional law and history at Edinburgh University. He had one son, William (born 1875), who before his father's death had become a judge of the King's Bench division, and who succeeded him as second viscount.

There are portraits of Finlay by Fiddes Watt, in the robes of lord chancellor, in the benchers' room in the Middle Temple (a replica is in the Peace Palace at The Hague); by H. T. Wells (a crayon drawing, 1898) in the possession of the family; by Sir Hubert von Herkomer (1908), also in the possession of the family; and by Antoon van Welie (painted at The Hague *c.* 1925), in the hall of the Edinburgh Academy.

[*The Times*, 11 March 1929; *Journal of Comparative Legislation*, vol. xvi, 1916; *British Year Book of International Law*, 1929; private information; personal knowledge.]

S. A. T. Rowlatt.

FISHER, ANDREW (1862–1928), Australian statesman, born 29 August 1862 at Crosshouse, near Kilmarnock, Ayrshire, was the second son of Robert Fisher, coal-miner and bee-keeper, by his wife, Jean Garven, daughter of an Ayrshire blacksmith. The father, described by his neighbours as 'like Carlyle, gey ill to put up with', ruled his family of seven with great strictness, and took the boys early from school to work in the local mines, where in the early 'seventies wages were high. The family savings he invested in a co-operative society of which he was treasurer, and the boys were set to study Carlyle and Emerson in the society's library. Andrew left school before he was twelve years old, and worked in the mines for the next eleven years. From boyhood he devoted his spare time to the study of public affairs, and in 1884, when Gladstone's campaign for the extension of the franchise was arousing great excitement in southern Scotland, he took the chair at a Crosshouse meeting which protested vehemently against the opposition of the House of Lords.

In 1885 Fisher, with one of his brothers and several other Crosshouse youths, migrated to Queensland, where for a time he worked in the Burrum collieries, and later became an engine-driver on the Gympie goldfield. At Gympie in 1901 he married Margaret Jane, daughter of Henry Irvine, the local mine-manager. Five sons and one daughter were born of the marriage.

The labour movement in Australia was still inchoate in the early 'eighties, but in 1886 an attempt was made to send to the Queensland parliament direct representatives of labour. Fisher—already spoken of as 'exceptionally well read in the literature of reform, and an impressive and courageous personality'—plunged into the fight, although his first active political campaign, on behalf of a Saturday half-holiday for miners, led to his being promptly ostracised by the mine-owners. In 1893 the labour leaders determined to constitute a political party, and Fisher became member for Gympie. He lost the seat, however, in 1896 (elections in Queensland are triennial); and finding re-employment at the mines blocked to him, earned a little by bookbinding, and soon got together enough capital to found a labour newspaper, *Gympie Truth*, which still flourishes. At the 1899 elections he regained his seat, rapidly establishing himself as the most level-headed member of the labour group, and in December joined the seven-days' ministry of Anderson Dawson—the first labour ministry in Australia, and, indeed, in the world—as secretary for railways and public works.

Queensland was not, however, a favourable *milieu* for labour politicians; the squatters' interests were still powerful, and their memories of the 1891 strike made them hostile to the whole labour movement. It was Fisher's election in 1901 to the first Commonwealth parliament as member for Wide Bay (which included the Gympie district) that really opened the way for him to a political career. He came to federal politics with a reputation for high principles, sound and sober thoughtfulness, and unshakable determination. His ability was at that time considered mediocre, but the leader of the federal labour party, Christian Watson, appeared to have all the ability needed, and he welcomed Fisher as an ideal second-in-command. Many of the labour members were unaccustomed to responsibility and inclined to hot-headedness, and only by Watson's tact and Fisher's earnestness was the party gradually moulded into a reliable instrument of government. Fisher himself, meanwhile, was fast acquiring political wisdom from Alfred Deakin [q.v.], attorney-general and subsequently (1903–1904 and 1905–1908) premier of the Commonwealth; in all matters not directly affecting labour he valued highly Deakin's judgement and sought to follow it. In October 1907 Watson was forced by ill health to resign the party-leadership, and Fisher, succeeding him, held the party together in support of Deakin's ministry for a further eighteen months until the new federal protective tariff, giving a substantial preference to British imports, and thus establishing Deakin's principles of preferential Imperial tariffs, was secured. Then the dissatisfaction among labour members outgrew restraint, the party formally withdrew its support from the government, Deakin resigned, and on 13 November 1908 Fisher rather unwillingly became prime minister. The restiveness of his party betrayed itself at once in a decision that the rest of the Cabinet should be chosen by the caucus, though Fisher insisted on deciding which department each of his colleagues should administer.

Fisher's first tenure of office was short, lasting only until 2 June 1909; Deakin, who for the remainder of the current session had kept his personal following behind the new ministry, during the summer of 1909 was persuaded to join a fusion of the anti-labour elements, and he took office, in coalition with (Sir) Joseph Cook, as head of a party most of whose members had always been bitterly opposed to him. This disgusted the electors, who at the polls of April 1910 returned a strong labour majority and put Fisher back into power. During the next three years Fisher was able to place on the statute-book measures which embodied the considered policy of the labour party—land taxation designed to break up big estates and replace sheep with crops; a Commonwealth bank intended to destroy the political dominance of the existing private banks; the readjustment of state and federal finances in favour of the Commonwealth; and a defence policy which included compulsory training for the land forces and a locally controlled Australian naval squadron for guarding the neighbouring seas. The defence measures were in principle non-party; the 'fusion' had inaugurated both the training and the squadron; but Fisher carried out the measures with vigour, stiffened and extended the land training, and paid for the squadron out of revenue rather than by means of loans. He also inaugurated the building of the trans-continental railway, and of the new capital at Canberra. He visited London in 1911 for King George V's coronation and the Imperial conferences, on which occasion he was made a privy councillor. In England he made his mark, notably by refusing, in spite of great pressure from British ministers, to vote for the confirmation of the Declaration of London (1908–1909)—a refusal which strengthened the House of Lords in its decision to reject the Declaration; so that when the European War broke out Great Britain remained unfettered by its provisions.

In 1913 the elections gave the liberal party a majority of one, but after a year in opposition Fisher returned to power (September 1914) soon after war had broken out in Europe. He announced that Australia 'would stand beside Britain to the last man and to the last shilling', and he proceeded to administer the affairs of the Commonwealth in this spirit, placing the Australian squadron at the disposal of the Admiralty and dispatching two divisions of Australian troops to Egypt and Gallipoli. Presently the strain of many years' work without a respite began to tell on him; he felt that a younger and more vigorous man was needed to handle the war situation, and in 1915 he handed over the premiership to his ablest colleague, William Morris Hughes, the attorney-general. He was thereupon appointed to the post of high commissioner of the Commonwealth in London. The simple administrative duties to which this office was necessarily confined during the War he carried out adequately; but on account of ill-health he gradually withdrew from active life, and in 1921 resigned the post, thereafter living a secluded life at Hampstead, where he died 22 October 1928.

Fisher's career is a triumph of character. But three of his qualities need particular emphasis: his personal modesty, which caused him for long to refuse a privy councillorship on the ground that Alfred Deakin, a much greater man, had not been so honoured; his exact knowledge of his own limitations, which led him to seek eagerly the advice of better-informed men on the details of any policy he was pledged to carry out; and his strong devotion to the Empire as a whole, which made him declare six years before the outbreak of war that 'in the event of any emergency the resources of the Commonwealth would be immediately placed at the disposal of the mother country'. British publicists, accustomed to the vagaries of labour leaders at home, found it hard to believe that Australian labour could be in the best sense imperialist: Fisher convinced them; and it was not till he was wholly removed from influence in the Commonwealth that the anti-British extremists—most of them immigrants—ventured to lift their heads in Australian labour circles.

[*The Australian Encyclopædia*; private information; personal knowledge.]

A. W. JOSE.

FITZMAURICE, SIR MAURICE (1861–1924), civil engineer, born 11 May 1861 at Cloghers, Tralee, co. Kerry, was the son of Dr. Robert Fitzmaurice, of Cloghers, Tralee. At the age of nineteen (1880) he began a three years' course of study under Professors Samuel Downing and Robert Crawford at Trinity College, Dublin, and graduated B.A. in 1882 and M.A.I. (Master of Engineering) in 1903. From 1883 to 1885 Fitzmaurice was articled to Sir Benjamin Baker [q.v.], and on the termination of his articles was engaged, until 1888, under Baker and Sir John Fowler [q.v.] in the construction of the Forth Bridge and the approach railways on each side of the Forth. From 1888 until 1891 Fitzmaurice was engaged on work in connexion with the Chignecto ship railway (for which Baker and Fowler were consulting engineers) on the peninsula between Nova Scotia and New Brunswick. On his return to England he superintended the renewal in steel of several cast-iron bridges on the London, Brighton, and South Coast Railway. In 1892 he resigned his position under Baker and entered the service of the London County Council under Sir Alexander Richardson Binnie [q.v.], and was appointed joint resident engineer with David Hay for the construction of the Blackwall Tunnel.

In 1898 Fitzmaurice was appointed chief resident engineer to the Egyptian government, and was placed in charge of the construction of the Assuan dam, which was begun in that year [see BAKER, Sir Benjamin, and GARSTIN, Sir William]. He was engaged on this work for three years, and in recognition of his services received the order of the Medjidie (second class) in 1901 and the C.M.G. in the following year.

On Binnie's retirement in 1901 Fitzmaurice succeeded him as chief engineer to the London County Council. In this position he completed many works begun by his predecessor. The most important of these was the improvement of the main drainage of London, which involved eighty-seven miles of additional sewers and an increase in the daily discharging capacity from seven hundred million to two thousand one hundred million gallons. Fitzmaurice also carried out the engineering works connected with the Kingsway and Aldwych improvement scheme, including the tramway tunnel from the embankment to Holborn. The reconstruction of the London tramways for electrical traction formed another important part of his work, over two hundred and fifty miles of single track being electrified under his charge. The new Vauxhall bridge was completed under his supervision, and the Rotherhithe tunnel constructed and opened in 1908. Other important works were the Woolwich passenger tunnel, the extension of the Thames embankment to the west of the Houses of Parliament, and the embankment of the river at the site of the London County Hall. At the end of his period of office in 1912 he was knighted on the occasion of the laying of the foundation stone of the County Hall.

When he retired Fitzmaurice became a partner in the firm of Coode, Son, & Matthews, which afterwards became Coode, Fitzmaurice, Wilson, & Mitchell. He took an active part in the business of the firm. In 1913 he visited Australia in order to advise the Commonwealth government on naval harbours and works. His professional work also included the construction of the Prai wharves (Burma), the Johor Causeway, in the Malay Peninsula, and harbours and docks at Singapore, Colombo, Lagos, Kilindini (Mombasa), Dover, and Peterhead. From 1922 until his death Fitzmaurice was associated with the work on the Sennar dam on the Blue Nile as consulting engineer [*Proceedings* of the Institution of Civil Engineers, 1925–1926, vol. ccxxii, 96, 106].

During the European War and afterwards Fitzmaurice served on numerous committees and commissions. From 1912 to 1918 he was chairman of the advisory committee of the Admiralty on naval works, from 1914 to 1919 chairman of the War Office committee on civilian labour on London defences, in 1919 chairman of the Treasury committee on aerodrome accounts, from 1917 to 1919 chairman of the Canal Control committee of the Board of Trade, and during 1918 and 1919 chairman of the Nile projects committee of the Foreign Office. For many years he was an officer of the Engineers and Railway Staff corps, of which he was colonel-commandant at the time of his death.

Fitzmaurice was admitted a student of the Institution of Civil Engineers in 1883, elected an associate in 1887, and became a member in 1893. He served on the council of that body from 1905, and was president in the session 1916–1917. In 1919 he was elected a fellow of the Royal Society. He was an honorary member of the American Society of Civil Engineers and of the Royal Engineers Institution, and an honorary fellow of the Society of Engineers. He received the honorary degree of LL.D. from the university of Birmingham in 1909. He married in 1911 Ida, eldest daughter of Colonel Edward Dickinson, R.E., of West Lavington Hill, Midhurst, Sussex, and had two daughters. He died at his home, 54 Onslow Square, London, 17 November 1924, and was buried at Brookwood.

Fitzmaurice published a book on *Plate-Girder Railway Bridges* (1895) and contributed to the *Proceedings* of the Institution of Civil Engineers a paper on 'The Nile Reservoir, Assuan' (1902–1903, vol. clii, 71) and with David Hay a paper on 'The Blackwall Tunnel' (1896–1897, vol. cxxx, 50).

[*The Times*, 18 November 1924; *Proceedings* of the Institution of Civil Engineers, 1902–1903, vol. clii, 124–125, 138, 151–154, and 1924–1925, vol. ccxix, 285.]

E. I. Carlyle.

FITZMAURICE-KELLY, JAMES (1857–1923), historian of Spanish literature, was born at Glasgow 20 June 1857, the eldest son of Colonel Thomas Kelly, then of the 40th Foot but formerly of the Egyptian police, by his wife, Catherine Fitzmaurice. Catholic and three-parts Irish, he inherited sociability, wit, and sympathy with a profoundly Catholic civilization like that of Spain. From his French maternal grandmother he obtained an exact command of French and the discipline of French literary taste. His mother, who died abroad while he was still a boy, remained a powerful influence in his life; a circumstance which he later acknowledged by prefixing her surname to his own. Educated at St. Charles's College, Kensington, he learned some Spanish from a school-fellow of that nationality, and later taught himself to read *Don Quixote*. At first destined for the priesthood, he was deterred partly through the study of Pascal, although he retained the affectionate esteem of leading Catholics. Some medical studies equally revealed want of vocation. Literature, art, and music exerted on him a powerful attraction, which was variously manifested before love of Cervantes gave him to Spain. He was in Spain in 1885, acting as tutor to Don Ventura Misa in Jerez de la Frontera and there formed friendships with Juan Valera, Gaspar Núñez de Arce, and other leading men of letters.

Returning to London in 1886, Fitzmaurice-Kelly began to make a name for himself as an authority on Spain and as a reviewer for the *Spectator*, *Athenæum*, and *Pall Mall Gazette*. He was influenced by William Ernest Henley [q.v.], who was one of the first to recognize his quality. In 1892 he made his mark on Spanish studies with his *Life of Miguel de Cervantes Saavedra*; but it was with the issue of his *History of Spanish Literature*, in 1898, that he came to occupy a position of authority in this subject, not seriously challenged before his death. He was contemporary with, and kept abreast of, a decisive advance in the knowledge of Spanish literature; and by his friendship with M. Raymond Foulché-Delbosc and Mr. Archer Huntington (of New York) he constituted one of a triumvirate of foreign scholars influential in guiding the new studies. For many years Fitzmaurice-Kelly maintained himself by his pen; until, in 1909, he was chosen by the university of Liverpool as its first Gilmour professor of Spanish language and literature. He held the chair with distinction, and entered actively into the life of the university for seven years. In 1916 he accepted the Cervantes chair of Spanish language and literature at King's College, London. His health began to fail in 1920, and he retired from teaching, although continuing his literary work. He died at his house at Sydenham 30 November 1923. He married in 1918 Julia, third daughter of the Rev. William Henry Sanders, curate of St. Nicholas's church, Nottingham, herself a gifted Spanish scholar. They had no children.

The value of Fitzmaurice-Kelly's work was early recognized by learned bodies. He was elected a fellow of the British Academy in 1906, a corresponding member of the Spanish Academy (1895), and a member of the academy of history (Madrid, 1912), of buenas letras (Barcelona, 1914), and of sciences (Lisbon, 1922). He was member of council and medallist of the Hispanic Society of America (1904), and was created a knight of the order of Alfonso XII in 1905.

Fitzmaurice-Kelly's contributions to Spanish studies form three groups. General works include the *History*, twice remodelled (1913 and 1926), *Chapters on Spanish Literature* (1908), thirty-nine articles on Spanish literature and authors in the *Encyclopædia Britannica* (11th edition, 1910), *The Oxford Book of Spanish Verse* (1913), and *Cambridge Readings in Spanish Literature* (1920). They brought into focus the great advance in Spanish studies made since the days of the American scholar, George Ticknor, and in particular the gains due to the creative criticism of Don Marcelino Menéndez y Pelayo; they also served as platforms for fresh investigation. Omnivorous reading, wide sympathy, French proportion, and Irish wit made Fitzmaurice-Kelly's *History* as unique as it was convenient. Its accuracy caused the author to develop it in the direction of factual and bibliographical precision in the French *rifacimento* of 1913, finding an outlet for his delight in varied styles of great literature in the more informal *Chapters*. The *New History* (1926) is a return to the simpler and more genial manner of 1898, with fresh information. A second group of studies is formed by miscellaneous essays, chiefly essays of revision. Fitzmaurice-Kelly did not research very deeply or evolve new theories; but he had a remarkable gift for extracting from often disproportioned and over-enthusiastic theses what represented a permanent gain for knowledge, and for ascertaining in what degree it intensified enjoyment of literature. His devotion to Cervantes gave rise to a third group. *Miguel de Cervantes Saavedra* (1913, the older *Life* rewritten in the light of Señor Pérez Pastor's documents) remains definitive. He collaborated with John Ormsby in a monumental edition of *Don Quixote* (1898–1899), and edited the English *Complete Works* of Cervantes (only the *Galatea*, *Exemplary Novels*, and *Don Quixote*, numbered vols. ii–viii) in 1901–1903. He summarized Cervantine studies for the *Year Book of Modern Languages* (1920) and delivered tercentenary addresses before the British Academy on *Cervantes in England* (1905) and *Cervantes and Shakespeare* (1916). In 1902 he delivered a Taylorian lecture at Oxford on Lope de Vega. A selection from his delightful letters appeared in the *Revue Hispanique*, vol. lxxiv, 1928. All his principal works were translated into Spanish, and serve as standards in Spain.

A portrait of Fitzmaurice-Kelly, painted by Sir John Lavery in 1898, is in the National Portrait Gallery. He also figures in a group of some members of the faculty of Arts of Liverpool University, painted in 1917, which hangs in the staff common-room of the university.

[*The Times*, 1 December 1923; *Manchester Guardian*, 5 December 1923; Oliver Elton, A. F. G. Bell, and Julia Fitzmaurice-Kelly in *Revue Hispanique*, vol. lx, 1924, containing bibliography; E. Mérimée in *Bulletin of Spanish Studies*, vol. i, 1924; A. Bonilla in *El Debate*, 9 February 1924; B. Sanin Cano in *La Nación*, Buenos Aires, reprinted in *La Civilización Manual y otros ensayos*, 1925; private information.] W. J. Entwistle.

FORDHAM, Sir HERBERT GEORGE (1854–1929), writer on cartography, the eldest son of Herbert Fordham, brewer, of Odsey, Ashwell, Hertfordshire, by his wife, Constantia Elizabeth, daughter of his uncle, Edward George Fordham, of Odsey, was born at Odsey 9 May 1854. Educated at home, at private schools, and at University College, London, he early showed an ability for scientific research, and was a member of the Geological Society at nineteen and a life member of the British Association at twenty-one. Between 1874 and 1892 he published several papers on the geology, natural history, and botany of Cambridgeshire and Hertfordshire, two of which on 'The Level of Water in Chalk Wells' (*Transactions* of the Hertfordshire Natural History Society, vol. v, 1890, vol. vi, 1892) have since proved useful in investigations into the water-supply of the London basin. After leaving college he entered the family brewery at Ashwell, of which his father was managing partner; but in 1882 he left it, and in 1885 was called to the bar by the Inner Temple, joining the South-Eastern circuit. The legal side of local government soon began to interest him, and in 1887 he published *Rural Municipalities and the Reform of Local Government*, a study which showed much independence and originality of thought. When, on the death of his father in 1891, he went to live at the family seat at Odsey, he devoted his energies to local administration; and the sense of duty and sound understanding of rural and agricultural problems which he brought to the service of the Cambridgeshire County Council, of which he was chairman from 1904 to 1919, were rewarded with a knighthood in 1908.

Although busy with the management of his estate, Fordham soon found fresh material for research. In 1900 he was studying old local maps and road-books and in 1901–1905 published *Hertfordshire Maps; a descriptive catalogue, 1579–1900* (*Transactions*, Herts. Nat. Hist. Soc.). This was reprinted separately in 1908, when he completed a similar catalogue of Cambridgeshire maps (*Communications* of the Cambridgeshire Antiquarian Society). Between 1908 and 1914 he published several bibliographical studies of the early maps of both France and England, which were later collected as *Studies in Carto-Bibliography* (1914). These studies were largely based on his own map collection, which he had increased by many purchases in France. During this period he found time also to write many articles, letters, and pamphlets on Cambridgeshire antiquities, rural education, parish councils, and district midwifery, and took an energetic part in opposing the creation of a county borough of Cambridge. In 1918 he contested West Fulham as a liberal, but was defeated, partly owing to his opposition to conscription.

After 1920 Fordham, though active as a deputy lieutenant of Cambridgeshire and a magistrate of Cambridgeshire and Hertfordshire, devoted himself more and more to the study of cartography, publishing a succession of valuable books and articles on the development of road-making and map-making during the sixteenth, seventeenth, and eighteenth centuries. In these he gathered together for the first time all the available information about such pioneer English surveyors as Christopher Saxton [q.v.], John Norden [q.v.], John Ogilby [q.v.], and John Cary, and brought to light many new facts in the early history of surveying, communications, geodesy, and economics, as well as of engraving and publishing, in England and France. He was frequently called upon to deliver addresses, generally illustrated by exhibits from his collections, to the British Association and to other learned bodies, both at home and in France and Belgium. These established his reputation as one of the foremost authorities in Europe on cartography and allied subjects. They brought, too, what Fordham most desired, a recognition of the importance of historical geography in school and university education. Fordham presented some rare maps and atlases to the British Museum and to Cambridge University Library, and bequeathed his collection of geographical works, numbering some 1,300 volumes and including many rare road-books and itineraries, to the Royal Geographical Society. To the same institution he gave, in 1928, the sum of £200, to provide a fund for the encouragement of carto-bibliography.

Fordham died at Cambridge 20 February 1929. He married twice: first, in 1877 Fanny Osler (died 1911), third daughter of William Blake, of South Petherton, Somerset, by whom he had two sons and three daughters; secondly, in 1914 Ethel Maud Elizabeth (died 1917), daughter of the Rev. Thomas Brodbelt Berry and widow of Commander Stewart Carnac Weigall, R.N.

Although Fordham distributed his energies among too many interests, his publications, which number some fifty in all, show a mind in many ways ahead of the time. Before he died he had the satisfaction of seeing research in the subject of cartography and carto-bibliography, in which he had worked as a pioneer, taken up by the universities and by many learned societies.

[Catalogues of the British Museum; private information; personal knowledge.]

E. Lynam.

FORREST, Sir GEORGE WILLIAM DAVID STARCK (1845–1926), historian of India, the second son of Captain George Forrest, Bengal Artillery, one of the officers who received the Victoria Cross for the defence of the magazine at Delhi on 11 May 1857, by his wife, Anne O'Schonessey, was born at Nusseerabad, India, 8 January 1845. His father did not long survive wounds received at Delhi, and the widow returned to England with her children. Her elder son, Robert Edward Trexton Forrest (died 1914) entered the Public Works Department of India, and was the author of a well-known novel relating to the mutiny, entitled *Eight Days*. George Forrest was educated privately until he entered St. John's College, Cambridge, as a pensioner in 1866. He took his B.A. degree as twenty-third junior optime in the mathematical tripos of 1870, and thereafter read for the bar as a member of the Inner Temple, contributing at the same time to the *Saturday Review* and other periodicals. He was appointed to the Bombay educational service in 1872, and was promoted to a professorship of mathematics in the Deccan College, Poona, in 1879. For many years he was a correspondent for *The Times*, and he used to relate how he sent to London the earliest news of the battle of Maiwand.

Neither teaching, which he disliked, nor journalism was, however, the chief concern of Forrest's many years in India. He was frequently seconded for special duty, his first important appointment of this kind being as census commissioner in Bombay in 1882. Two years later he entered upon the real work of his life. The publication of his *Selections from the Official Writings of Mountstuart Elphinstone* in 1884 was followed by his appointment for work upon the records preserved in the secretariate of the Presidency. He published two series of records in 1885 and 1887, and in the latter year exchanged his post at Poona for the chair of English history in Elphinstone College, Bombay. His services and his enthusiasm were rewarded by the creation in 1888 of the post of director of records, Bombay, and a year later he was summoned to Calcutta to investigate the records of the government of India. There he repeated the achievement of his Bombay period, for, after the publication of his first volume of *Selections from the State Papers in the Foreign Department* (1890), an Imperial Record Office was established at Calcutta, and Forrest held the post of director from 1891 to 1900, acting also as assistant secretary in the patents branch from 1894 to 1900, and as assistant secretary to the government of India in 1898. He was made C.I.E. in 1899 and knighted in 1913.

After his retirement in 1900, Forrest rewrote and enlarged his Introductions to the volumes of State Papers which he had edited, and published them as separate contributions to Indian history. In this way he produced his *History of the Indian Mutiny* (3 vols., 1904 and 1912), and his *Selections from the State Papers of the Governors-General of India: Warren Hastings* (2 vols., 1910), intended as the first instalment of a long series. The second instalment dealing with the rule of Lord Cornwallis (2 vols., 1926) was published a few months after his death. He also wrote a biography of Lord Clive (2 vols., 1918), based upon his own researches on India and upon the manuscripts in the possession of the Earl of Powis. His *Life of Lord Roberts* (1914) was the result of an intimate friendship with that distinguished soldier, who, knowing Forrest's work in India, asked him, on undertaking the command in South Africa at the close of 1899, to prepare a memorandum on previous hostilities in that country. Forrest's contributions to Indian history, if sometimes liable to the imperfections of what was, in the main, pioneer work, represent a great advance in the investigation of the subject and entitle him to remembrance both as a preserver and as an exponent of Indian history. He used a vigorous style, and his narrative is often picturesque and animated. Outside Indian topics, he wrote little, except for magazine articles on the Irish controversy. An Irishman on both sides, although never resident in Ireland, he held the views of a moderate unionist.

Forrest married in 1877 Emma Georgina, daughter of Thomas Viner, of Bradfield, Crawley, Sussex, by whom he had a son and a daughter. He died at Iffley Turn House, Oxford, where he had resided since 1904, 28 January 1926 and was buried at Iffley.

[*The Times*, 29 January 1926; records of St. John's College, Cambridge, from Forrest's own entry in which the date of his birth is taken. In later life he believed he was born in 1846. Private information; personal knowledge.] R. S. Rait.

FOWLER, ELLEN THORNEYCROFT (1860–1929), novelist. [See Felkin, Ellen Thorneycroft.]

FOX, Sir FRANCIS (1844–1927), civil engineer, born in Paddington 29 June 1844, was the second son of Sir Charles Fox [q.v.], by his wife, Mary, second daughter of Joseph Brookhouse. In 1855 he was sent to school at Cavendish House, Sherwood, Nottinghamshire, under the Rev. Thomas Gascoigne, where he remained until 1861. In that year he began his career as a partner with his father and elder brother (Sir) Charles Douglas Fox (1840–1921) in the firm of Sir Charles Fox & Sons, civil and consulting engineers. He was brought early into a responsible position in consequence of a serious accident which befell his father and incapacitated him from the more active duties of an engineer. From 1864 to 1867 Francis Fox was employed as assistant to the resident engineer, Edmund Wragge, in widening the Pimlico railway bridge over the Thames to Victoria station. In 1872 he was appointed manager of an iron-mine in Cleveland, Yorkshire, and in 1880 he and his brother Douglas, together with (Sir) James Brunlees [q.v.], were the engineers placed in charge of the construction of the Mersey tunnel, which was completed in 1886; Fox described the tunnel in a paper contributed to the *Proceedings* of the Institution of Civil Engineers [vol. lxxxvi, 40]. During its construction the British fleet inadvertently anchored over the tunnel and was alarmed, but not damaged, by the blasting operations, which caused the crews to be called to quarters.

In 1882 Fox accepted an invitation to become engineer to the Manchester, Sheffield, and Lincolnshire Railway. One of the first works which he had to execute was the erection of a swing bridge over the river Dee below Chester. From 1887 to 1893 he was one of the engineers in charge of the works for the Liverpool Overhead Railway, and from 1894 to 1896 he and his brother Douglas were employed in the construction of the Snowdon Rack Railway. In 1894 his firm was entrusted with the Rugby to Marylebone section of the Great Central Railway's extension to London. The first sod was cut 13 November 1894 and the railway was opened for traffic 9 March 1899. Francis and Douglas Fox were also associated, as joint engineers with James H. Greathead, in the construction of two tube railways in London, the Great Northern and City line, begun in 1898, and the Charing Cross, Golders Green, and Highgate line, opened for traffic 22 June 1907.

In his later years Fox was largely employed in superintending the treatment and preservation of ancient buildings. For this purpose he made great use of the grouting machine invented by James H. Greathead for the purpose of filling in the concentric cavity between the cast-iron segments of the London tube railways and the tunnel walls. By this machine a liquid mixture of cement, sand, and water can be forced into the cracks and crevices of decayed masonry, which is thereby formed into a solid monolithic structure. The most important buildings thus treated by Fox were the cathedrals of Winchester and Lincoln. At Winchester not only was the stonework disintegrated, but the foundations were unsound, resting on clay, peat, and quicksand. After the walls had been grouted, the building was underpinned and the foundations carried down to a solid bed of gravel and flints. As the condition of the fabric did not permit pile-driving, and as pumping would have drawn away the silt from beneath the whole cathedral, Fox adopted the ingenious plan of employing a diver to replace the existing substratum with concrete. The diver, William A. Walker, did the whole of the work single-handed in five and a half years. The work of preservation was begun in 1905 and completed in 1912 at a cost of £114,000.

At Lincoln Cathedral the foundations were perfectly sound, but the walls were greatly decayed. About the end of 1921 Fox was requested to collaborate with the consulting architect, Sir Charles Nicholson, and to advise what steps should be taken to preserve the stone-work. He afterwards superintended the work on the walls of the north-west, south-west, and central towers as well as in the south transept. He was also consulted about the repair of Peterborough Cathedral in 1897, St. Paul's Cathedral in 1912, and Exeter Cathedral about 1923. At St. Paul's he personally explored the foundations (in diver's dress) and certified the existence of an adjacent quicksand. Fox was concerned with the preservation of many other buildings, including the Saxon church at Corhampton, Hampshire, in 1906, the church at Bletsoe, Bedfordshire, in 1907, the sea-wall at Lyme Regis, and Ashbourne church, Derbyshire (described by George Eliot) between 1912 and 1919.

Fox was elected an associate of the Institution of Civil Engineers in 1870 and member in 1874. In 1894 he was nominated by the British government as one of an international commission of three experts to report on the plans for the Simplon tunnel (completed in 1906); and he and his brother Douglas were associated for many years with Sir Charles Metcalfe [q.v.] in the development of South African railways, including the construction of the railway bridge over the Zambesi at the Victoria Falls in 1903. He was knighted in 1912. Fox was a man of strong evangelical piety, and with his brother Douglas devoted much of his spare time to mission work in London from 1867 onwards. His eldest daughter, Selina Fox, M.D., founded the Bermondsey hospital and medical mission in 1904.

From 1887 to 1893, while engaged on the Liverpool Overhead Railway, Fox lived at Mount Alyn, Rossett, Denbighshire. In 1894 he removed to Alyn Bank, Wimbledon, where he died 7 January 1927. He was buried at Putney Vale cemetery. He married twice: first, in 1869 Selina (died 1900), third daughter of Francis Wright, of Osmaston Manor, Derbyshire, by whom he had two sons and three daughters; secondly, in 1901 Agnes, younger daughter of Henry King Horne, of Guerres, Normandy.

In addition to two or three short articles and pamphlets, Fox was the author of *River, Road, and Rail* (1904) and *Sixty-Three Years of Engineering* (1924). Both these works are mainly autobiographical and show considerable literary ability.

[*The Times*, 8 and 11 January 1927; Fox's writings.] E. I. Carlyle.

FRAMPTON, Sir GEORGE JAMES (1860–1928), sculptor and craftsman, was born 16 June 1860, the second son of James Frampton, of London, by his wife *née* Ilanfield. He received his first artistic training at the Lambeth School of Art, under the sculptor, W. S. Frith, and studied between 1881 and 1887 at the Royal Academy Schools, producing all the while decorative and ornamental sculpture for a variety of customers. His first exhibit at the Royal Academy was 'Socrates teaching the people in the Agora', which was shown in 1884; in 1887 'An Act of Mercy' won for him the Academy gold medal and travelling studentship. The years from 1888 to 1890 Frampton spent in Paris studying sculpture under Antonin Mercié, a master of far-reaching influence at the time, and also painting under P. A. J. Dagnan-Bouveret and Gustave Courtois. His 'Angel of Death' gained him a medal at the Salon of 1889. The last notable work of Frampton's earlier manner is a group, 'The Children of the Wolf', contributed to the Academy exhibition of 1892 in plaster (in bronze, 1893).

At the beginning of the 'nineties, Frampton felt powerfully attracted towards the 'arts and crafts' movement, and before long took to producing works in which the element of craftsmanship is strongly accentuated and which largely belong to the category of applied art. The influence of contemporary French symbolism was also strongly felt by him, as witness his bas-relief 'Mysteriarch' (1893), now in the Walker Art Gallery, Liverpool, which was awarded the *médaille d'honneur* at the Paris exposition of 1900. Frampton was closely associated with the art magazine *The Studio* from its inception in 1893, and he contributed to it several articles on subjects such as enamelling, goldsmiths' work, wood-carving, and polychrome sculpture. More particularly through *The Studio* he wielded very great influence on the rise of the late nineteenth-century style of decorative design in Germany, which, from the title of the magazine which sponsored it, has become known as the *Jugendstil*. Peculiarly characteristic of

Frampton from this time onwards is the combination of different materials in one work, as, for instance, bronze and marble in his statue (one of his best works) of Mrs. Alice Owen (died 1613) for Owen's School, Islington (1897), and ivory and bronze adorned with jewels in his bust 'Lamia' (1900).

The technical excellence of Frampton's work cannot, however, obscure the qualities of preciosity and affectation which characterize most of his productions: and, generally speaking, they 'date' by now emphatically and in the derogatory sense of the word. His career, however, was for long one of unbroken and resounding success; he was elected A.R.A. in 1894 and R.A. in 1902, his diploma work being a marble bust of the Marchioness of Granby; in 1908 he was knighted; and numerous other honours came to him—the honorary LL.D. of St. Andrews University (1894), the position of master of the Artworkers' Guild, and president of the Royal Society of British Sculptors (1911–1912), and membership of the Fine Arts Commission from its foundation in 1924.

Among Frampton's more important works may be mentioned, in addition to those already noticed: a series of statues of Queen Victoria at Calcutta, Southend, St. Helens, Newcastle-upon-Tyne, Leeds, and Winnipeg; in London, several public monuments, notably statues of Quintin Hogg in Langham Place (1906), of 'Peter Pan' in Kensington Gardens (1912), and of Edith Cavell in St. Martin's Place (1920), the last being one of Frampton's most conspicuous failures; in the Victoria Embankment wall, on the north side of Waterloo Bridge, a characteristic bronze bas-relief memorial to Sir W. S. Gilbert (1913). Mention should also be made of the sculptures in the spandrels of the main entrance to the Victoria and Albert Museum (1909) and of the two couchant stone lions in front of the new wing of the British Museum (1914). Among other works worthy of notice are the terra-cotta decorations of the Constitutional Club, Northumberland Avenue, London; the sculptured decoration on the front of Lloyd's Register in the City; the portrait-busts of King George V and Queen Mary in the Guildhall; the saints on the chantry of William of Wykeham in Winchester Cathedral; some figures on the spire of St. Mary's church, Oxford; the figure of St. George on the South African War memorial at Radley College; the statue of Edward VI at Giggleswick School; the monument to Charles Mitchell, the shipbuilder, at Newcastle-upon-Tyne; the sculpture decoration on the façade of Glasgow Art Gallery; and the statues of Queen Mary in the Victoria Memorial Hall, Calcutta, and Government House, Delhi. The Tate Gallery possesses, by Frampton, a posthumous bas-relief portrait in bronze of Charles Keene, the draughtsman. Among medals modelled by Frampton may be mentioned the City Imperial Volunteers medal for the Corporation of the City of London (1901), and the coronation medal of King Edward VII (1902).

Frampton died in London 21 May 1928. He married in 1893 Christabel, daughter of George Russell Cockerell, of London, and had one son, the painter Meredith Frampton.

A portrait of Frampton by Solomon J. Solomon was lent by the sitter to the Winter Exhibition of the Royal Academy in 1928.

[*The Times*, 22 May 1928; H. Muthesius in *Zeitschrift für bildende Kunst*, 1903; H. C. Marillier in *Dekorative Kunst*, vol. vii, 1904; Algernon Graves, *The Royal Academy of Arts, a complete dictionary of contributors and their works*, vol. iii, 1905; subsequent Academy Exhibition Catalogues.] T. Borenius.

FREEMAN, JOHN (1880–1929), poet and critic, was born at Dalston, Middlesex, during a great snowstorm on 29 January 1880, the elder son of John Freeman, commercial traveller, by his wife, Catherine Botham. His paternal grandfather came from Liddington in Wiltshire to London as a young man and married a Miss Mitchell, of Lewes, and these country origins counted for much in Freeman's life and poetry. His great-grandfather on the mother's side was a captain in a regiment of the Guards, and was wounded at Talavera. At the age of three an attack of scarlet fever left him with heart trouble, which declared itself when he began to grow rapidly, and was a constant danger in mature life. He was educated at Hackney. Just before his thirteenth birthday he left school and entered the head office of the Liverpool Victoria Friendly Society as a junior clerk. His exceptional ability soon showed itself and marked him out for promotion. He rose rapidly, and finally, in 1927, was made secretary and director, in which position he was (in the words of a colleague) 'the chief executive officer, directing very successfully and efficiently the operations of a staff of over 7,000 engaged in the business of industrial and national health insurance with many millions of contracts and funds of £20,000,000'.

In the early years of his business life Freeman set about remedying the defects of his education, teaching himself Greek and reading widely and passionately in English literature. His early loves in poetry were Swinburne, Coventry Patmore, and Matthew Arnold, and of these Coventry Patmore made the deepest and most lasting impression. He married in 1902 Gertrude, daughter of Samuel Farren, originally of Colchester, later of Dalston, and her sedulous care provided the ideally happy home life which was the condition of all his work. They had two daughters.

Freeman began to write when he was about eighteen, and his life was thenceforward divided into two parts, carefully kept distinct so that his literary and business associates were equally ignorant of the other side of his activity. Among his earliest literary friends were Roger Ingpen and Walter de la Mare. Later he did critical work for the *Academy* during Lord Alfred Douglas's editorship, and for the *New Statesman* and the *London Mercury*. An article on Patmore in the *Academy* gained him the friendship of Alice Meynell [q.v.], which he valued highly. His first publications in poetry were two booklets, *Twenty Poems* (1909) and *Fifty Poems* (1911), but recognition only came to him on the publication of *Stone Trees* in 1916. After this there followed rapidly *Presage of Victory* (1916), *Memories of Childhood* (1919), *Poems New and Old* (1920), *Music* (1921), *The Grove* (1924), *Collected Poems* (1928), and (posthumously) *Last Poems* (1930). *Prince Absalom* (1925) was his only drama, dealing with one of the biblical themes which constantly haunted his mind. *Solomon and Balkis* (1926) is a delightful fantasy based on the Oriental legends of the Queen of Sheba and King Solomon. In prose he published *The Moderns* (1916), *Portrait of George Moore* (1922), *English Portraits* (1924), and *Herman Melville* (1926, in the 'English Men of Letters' series). He was awarded the Hawthornden prize in 1920.

This is a remarkable output of work for a man engaged in an exacting business life and at all times struggling against ill-health. It was only made possible by rigid system and unremitting self-control. He died at Anerley, London, where he had lived for twenty-seven years, 23 September 1929 at the age of forty-nine, and was buried in the churchyard at Thursley, Surrey. His friends subscribed to dedicate to his memory a field adjoining the churchyard, the maintenance of which was accepted by the National Trust.

Freeman was best known to a discriminating public as a poet of that Nature which had been for him since his childhood an abiding passion. But the range of his work was far wider than this. In grave and quiet rhythms, subtly varied to match changing emotions born of the immediate experience of life, he embodied a developing philosophy based upon a restless investigation of human personality at grips with the issues of life and death. His early end prevented the full realization of this pattern, which becomes clear when his work is considered as a whole. His mode was one of lyrical meditation, expressed in rhythms and phrases of an unobtrusive beauty governed by a constant sense of appropriate form. In direct narrative verse he was not successful, but in such poems as 'The Pigeons' and 'The Grove', where the incidents were implicit in the lyrical situation, he did some of his most characteristic work.

Freeman's prose showed the same character in another mode. He would often say that modern prose was addressed rather to the eye than the ear, and tended to eschew imagery. His own practice was the opposite of this. He was drawn to Herman Melville by his rich prose and metaphysical intensity and to George Moore by the artistic conscience which ruled the development of his style. In his other studies he sought always to discover the artistic personality of his subject and to express it in terms of his style and the development of his work. He was an admirable and discursive letter-writer. In appearance Freeman was tall, slow-moving, and grave, with large eyes and full lips; in conversation reserved, but capable of eloquence, and with a constant shimmer of kindly humour. As host in his own house or as companion at a luncheon table or on a walking tour, those who knew him best found no one to replace him.

Reproductions of portraits by William Rothenstein and Laura Knight are prefixed to *Music* and *Collected Poems* respectively. The original portrait by Laura Knight belongs to Mrs. Freeman.

[Introduction, by J. C. Squire, to *Last Poems*, 1930; *Insurance Mail*, 5 October 1929; private information; personal knowledge. See also *John Freeman's Letters* edited by G. Freeman and Sir J. Squire, 1936.]

R. Flower.

FREMANTLE, Sir EDMUND ROBERT (1836–1929), admiral, the fourth son of Thomas Francis Fremantle, first Baron Cottesloe [q.v.], by his wife, Louisa Elizabeth, eldest daughter of Field-Marshal Sir George Nugent, first baronet [q.v.], was born in London 15 June 1836. When he was old enough to know his own mind he had no doubt as to the profession he should follow. His great-grandfather, Sir Thomas Francis Fremantle [q.v.], had been Nelson's friend, and he had two uncles who were then post-captains in the navy, so that he felt himself 'bound to enter the naval service'. After going to Mr. Tabor's school at Cheam in Surrey, where great stress was laid on punctuality and correctness of demeanour, he obtained a nomination from the first sea lord, Sir James Whitley Deans Dundas. He went to Portsmouth in 1849 for his entrance examination, and after a correct answer to the question 'If a yard of cloth costs 1*s.* 4*d.* how much will three yards cost?' and a correctly written 'dictation' was told that he had passed 'a very good examination'.

Fremantle's first appointment was to the *Queen*, 116 guns, Captain Charles Wise, flying the flag of Admiral Sir William Parker, the 'last of Nelson's captains'. Having spent three years in the Mediterranean, he came home and was appointed to the *Spartan* frigate, 26 guns, Captain Sir William Hoste, for service on the China station. There he had his first taste of war in the Burmese War of 1852.

The six years' service then required to qualify for mate's rank were completed by Fremantle in June 1855. In December of the same year he was made acting lieutenant, but he was not confirmed as lieutenant until 14 January 1857 at the age of twenty. The *Spartan*'s commission lasted five and a half years, Sir William Hoste remaining throughout in command. During this long service Fremantle acquired a taste for serious reading. 'In my midshipman's days in the *Spartan* I read through Gibbon, . . . Alison's *History of Europe*, Shakespeare, Byron, and many standard works; while James's *Naval History*, over which I talked and argued with some of my messmates, became a household word with us . . . In this way many naval officers of my day did much to make up for defective early education, and I think our knowledge of naval history was generally superior to that of our better instructed successors. . . .' Of these early years of service he wrote: 'If I took my lessons as a naval officer from the *Queen*, my time in the *Spartan* gave me my real sea experience and I believe to a great extent formed my character.'

On his return to England in 1857 Fremantle spent eight months on half pay. In July 1858 he was appointed flag lieutenant to his uncle, Admiral Sir Charles Fremantle, who was then commanding the Channel squadron, and served with his flag in the *Renown* (July–October 1858) and the *Royal Albert* (October 1858–October 1860). As his uncle did not complete the full three years in command, Fremantle did not at once obtain his promotion on hauling down the flag, but a fortnight later (25 October 1860) he was appointed as fifth lieutenant to the *Neptune* in the Mediterranean, later commanded by Captain (afterwards Admiral Sir) Geoffrey Thomas Phipps Hornby [q.v.]. Nine months later he obtained his promotion to commander (August 1861) and, as a necessary consequence, a long period of half pay. This time was not, in his opinion, wasted. He agreed with what his former captain, Hornby, had remarked, that, given a sound grounding on naval matters, a man's mind was enlarged, and he became a more capable officer, through mixing in civil society and affairs. For much the same reason Fremantle favoured early promotion, even at the expense of 'favouritism', for the reason that men who serve long in the junior ranks may become 'deeply immersed in the routine of the service and perhaps too full of details' to acquire the qualities more needed in a great commander than mere technical knowledge. This by no means implied that he considered technical knowledge unnecessary. On the occasions on which he was on half pay he seized the opportunities to study, as a commander, steam engineering, mathematics, and nautical astronomy, and, as a captain, gunnery. He then made the acquaintance of that distinguished naval thinker, Captain (afterwards Admiral) Philip Howard Colomb [q.v.], and attended lectures at the Royal United Service Institution; thus he kept in touch with both the technique and the theory of naval science.

The Maori War in New Zealand was in progress in 1864, and Fremantle, seeing that the commander of the *Eclipse* had been severely wounded in the fighting, went to London and applied for the vacancy. A few days later he received notice of his appointment and that he must sail by the next mail; this he did, although he had been rather seriously injured in a hunting accident, and joined his ship in New Zealand in April 1864. The *Eclipse* was a 700-ton steamer, 4 guns, barque-rigged; Fremantle commanded her for three years, and although he 'saw little real fighting' in the New Zealand War he had a not uneventful commission of varied and valuable experience in command. In 1866 he married, at Sydney, Barberina Rogers (died 1923), eldest daughter of the Hon. Robert McIntosh Isaacs, of Sydney. They had six sons, the fourth of whom died as a child.

Returning home in February 1867, Fremantle was promoted to captain in April. Appointments for captains were few, and he now spent no less than six years on half pay. This was a very hard time for a married officer with scanty private means and a family of four boys; but he lived in a small house of his father's at Swanbourne, in Buckinghamshire, and devoted his time to local interests, to taking part in discussions at the United Service Institution, and to writing on naval subjects—occupation which 'had its uses in keeping me in touch with the service'; he observed, however, that in the navy there was some prejudice against officers writing to the papers. He spent some time in 1871–1872 at the Royal Naval College at Portsmouth, where he passed the examination in gunnery—an unusual thing for a captain, for which he received the thanks of the Admiralty. It was not, however, until March 1873 that he obtained the command of the paddle-steamer *Barracouta*.

In May 1873 the ports in the Gold Coast Protectorate were threatened by an Ashanti army, and the *Barracouta* was sent with a reinforcement of 100 marines for Cape Coast Castle, where Fremantle found himself senior officer of a squadron of seven small vessels. He took part in the operations for the defence of Elmina, in protecting Cape Coast Castle and Sekondi, Dix Cove, and Axim, and in various affairs on the coast, including Sir Garnet Wolseley's first operations. He was severely wounded in the advance on Kumassi. In November a severe bout of fever obliged him temporarily to leave the coast to recover at St. Helena; and he finally came home in May 1874. He was made C.B. and C.M.G. in that year, and was mentioned in the vote of thanks in parliament.

In September 1874 Fremantle took command of the *Doris*, frigate, 32 guns, one of a detached squadron cruising under sail. Paying her off in September 1876 he spent nine months on half pay, again attending lectures and writing articles for naval and other papers. On 15 May 1877 he was appointed to command the *Lord Warden*, ironclad, 7,800 tons, in the Channel squadron, but saw little sea-service in her, as she passed into the reserve in the following year. The command lasted till November 1879, when he transferred to the *Invincible*, ironclad, 6,000 tons, one of the squadron in the Mediterranean under Admiral Hornby. While in command of these ships he saved life on two occasions. When leaving Plymouth Sound in June 1877 he jumped overboard after a boy who had fallen from aloft, and in Alexandria harbour in February 1880, his ship being under way, he dived off the bridge and rescued with great difficulty, and nearly at the cost of his own life, a man who had fallen overboard. For the first of these acts he received the bronze medal of the Royal Humane Society, and for the second the Stanhope gold medal for 1880, the silver medal of the Royal Humane Society, and the gold medal of the Shipwrecked Fishermen and Mariners' Royal Benevolent Society. In 1880 he was awarded the gold medal of the Royal United Service Institution for a prize essay on 'Naval Tactics'.

In January 1881 Fremantle was appointed senior naval officer at Gibraltar. There he spent three years, 'probably the most pleasant service of my career', although it galled him to witness, as an onlooker, the transports and men-of-war on their way to the war in Egypt. His next ship was the *Dreadnought*, 10,800 tons, which he commanded from August 1884 until April 1885, when he became rear-admiral at the age of forty-nine: he was then, with the exception of the Duke of Edinburgh, the youngest officer on the flag list. Fifteen months on half pay followed. Shortly before this time the torpedo boat had made its appearance, and a school of French naval thought, which had adherents also in England, contended that the days of great ships were over. Fremantle strongly opposed this view in two articles on 'Ironclads and Torpedo Flotillas' and 'Are Ironclads Doomed?' in the *Nineteenth Century* and *Blackwood's Magazine* respectively. Many years later he maintained the same view in the controversy which was conducted in *The Times* in 1920–1921 between those who believed that the submarine had abolished the 'battleship' and their opponents. The problems of shipbuilding policy in relation to strategical needs was, in fact, the unceasing study of his active mind. His view, in 1903, was that 'we should build battleships of medium size, not more than 11,000 or 12,000 tons . . . which would be far more useful than our 15,000 ton battleships'. He wrote much in these years on the problems of trade defence and the need which it imposed for extensive cruiser forces ('Our Food Supply and Raw Material in War', *Fortnightly Review*, February 1903; 'Oversea Trade in War', Navy League, 1909).

From August 1886 until August 1887 Fremantle flew his flag on board the *Agincourt* as second in command of the Channel squadron. In February 1888 he was appointed to the command on the East India station, with his flag on board the *Bacchante* and, later, the *Boadicea*. During his command a blockade on the East coast of Africa was conducted with the object of stamping out the slave trade. In January 1890, in expectation of a rupture with Portugal, his command was increased by vessels from the Cape, Australia, and China, but action proved unnecessary. In October 1890 an expedition was prepared for the punishment of the Sultan of Vitu, in British East Africa, who had murdered nine Europeans. The sultan's forces numbered some 7,000 to 8,000 men, though not more than 1,500 had fire-arms. Fremantle's force, consisting of 700 seamen and marines, 400 troops from Lamu, and 150 Indian police, with 400 porters, marched against the sultan and carried the operation to a successful end. In August of that year Fremantle was promoted to vice-admiral.

In February 1892 Fremantle was appointed commander-in-chief in China, flying his flag successively on board the *Impérieuse* and *Centurion*. He held the command until July 1895. During the Chino-Japanese War of 1894–1895 he had the delicate task of preventing as far as possible British trade with China. In June 1896 he succeeded Admiral Sir Algernon Lyons as commander-in-chief at Devonport, and held the post for the customary three years. In October 1896 he was promoted to admiral. On 15 June 1901, having reached the age limit, he retired. During the years between his retirement and his death, which took place in London 10 February 1929, he both read and wrote on current naval matters. His principal contributions to naval literature were his prize essay on 'Naval Tactics on the open sea with the existing types of vessels and weapons' (1880), the lives of Hawke and Boscawen in (Sir) John Laughton's *From Howard to Nelson* (1899), and an autobiographical volume, *The Navy as I have known it* (1904). He was buried at Swanbourne.

A cartoon of Fremantle appeared in *Vanity Fair* 29 November 1894.

[Admiralty record of service; Navy Lists; Sir E. R. Fremantle, *The Navy as I have known it*, 1904; private information.]

H. W. Richmond.

FRENCH, JOHN DENTON PINKSTONE, first Earl of Ypres (1852–1925), field-marshal, was born 28 September 1852 at Ripple, Kent. He was the only son and the youngest of the seven children of Commander John Tracy William French, R.N., J.P. and D.L. for the county of Kent, by his wife, Margaret, daughter of William Eccles, of Glasgow. Both his parents died while John French was still a child, so that he was brought up by his sisters, who intended him to enter his father's profession. To that end he was educated at Eastman's Naval Academy, Portsmouth, and entered H.M.S. *Britannia* in 1866, whence he passed out as a midshipman in 1868. But he never took kindly to the sea, and hankered after a military career. In 1870 he therefore left the navy to join the Suffolk Artillery Militia, serving with that regiment until he succeeded in passing into the regular army. In 1874 he was gazetted to the 8th Hussars, being transferred to the 19th Hussars a few weeks later.

French's advancement proved rapid. After serving as adjutant for a few months he was promoted captain in October 1880, and obtained his majority in April 1883. His career during these years differed in no wise from that of many of his colleagues. He learnt to ride well, played polo, and took great interest in the training of his men. In addition he developed a taste for books and showed anxiety to acquire some knowledge of the science of war. This was the more noteworthy in that he subsequently never displayed any bent for abstract knowledge nor even aspired to pass into the Staff College. In 1881 he had been appointed adjutant of the Northumberland Hussars (yeomanry), but relinquished that post in September 1884 when offered the opportunity of going to Egypt, where Lord Wolseley was organizing an expedition for the relief of General Gordon, then besieged in Khartoum. On arrival, French assumed command of the detachment of the 19th Hussars which was allotted to the column of Sir Herbert Stewart [q.v.]. This column crossed the Bayuda desert from Korti to Metemmeh. But long before coming within sight of Khartoum Stewart learnt that the place had been captured and Gordon killed. Thereupon he decided to retreat by the way he had advanced. Throughout this withdrawal French displayed courage and resource, covering every movement with success. During this campaign he was present at the actions of Abu Klea, Gubat, and Metemmeh, and on one occasion was all but cut off by the pursuing enemy. On return home, after being specially commended for his work, he was awarded a brevet lieutenant-colonelcy in February 1885.

After three years' home service, in September 1888 French was promoted to the command of the 19th Hussars. As he was then thirty-six years of age and had only fourteen years service to his credit he had every prospect of rising high in a profession where seniority counted for so much. His Egyptian experience, together with a practical grasp of minor tactics, stood him in good stead. In February 1889 he was advanced to the rank of brevet-colonel, and shortly afterwards took his regiment to India, where it gained a name for efficiency. At the end of his period of command, in the spring of 1893, French was placed on half pay, and, in spite of early promise, there seemed some prospect of his being forgotten. But the adjutant-general, Sir Redvers Buller, mindful of French's work in the Sudan, offered him the appointment of assistant-adjutant-general at the War Office; this post he accepted in August 1895, being simultaneously promoted full colonel. In his new employment French was occupied in the production of a new *Cavalry Manual*, in the formation of cavalry brigades, and in other reforms, long overdue, in the mounted branch. In May 1897 he was transferred from the War Office to Canterbury in order to assume the duty of colonel on the staff, an appointment which carried with it the command of the newly formed 2nd Cavalry brigade with the rank of brigadier-general. Eighteen months later he was again transferred—to the 1st Cavalry brigade at Aldershot, a move which gave him the temporary rank of major-general.

The outbreak of the South African War proved the great opportunity of French's career. In September 1899 he was despatched to Natal to command the mounted troops under Sir George Stuart White [q.v.]. Almost on arrival he was sent forward to assist the retirement of Major-General Penn Symons from Dundee to Ladysmith. After the death of Penn Symons at Talana Hill the command devolved on Major-General Yule, who was greatly assisted in his retreat by French. The latter had succeeded in dislodging the enemy from a strongly held position at Elandslaagte on 21 October. It was French's first opportunity of commanding a force of all arms in the field, and he was highly commended for his share in the operations. Shortly afterwards White's troops were concentrated in Ladysmith, and it became obvious that a siege was inevitable, so that mounted troops would find no employment there. French and his staff accordingly managed to escape in the last train that succeeded in leaving the town.

French was now sent to the Cape, where he was confronted with a menacing situation. Lord Methuen was advancing along the railway towards the Orange Free State in an endeavour to relieve Kimberley, and encountering serious opposition. Further east Major-General Sir William Forbes Gatacre [q.v.] was attempting to prevent the disaffected Dutch from joining the Boer commandos. Between the two British forces lay an invading Boer column whose farther advance must gravely threaten Methuen's communications. French thereupon led all available mounted troops to Naauwpoort junction in order to check any further Boer movements. While he was able to keep the enemy at bay in the region of Colesberg, the general situation was made more difficult by the successive defeats of Methuen and Gatacre in Cape Colony and of Buller in Natal. In spite of these complications French continued to work round his opponents with such success that he virtually cleared Cape Colony of invaders before the arrival of Lord Roberts [q.v.] in South Africa in January 1900.

With his mounted troops French was next ordered by Roberts to turn the Boer left on the River Modder, where Methuen was facing the enemy. By forcing the passage of the River Riet French achieved this object. Then, by launching against the Boers two whole cavalry brigades in open order at the gallop, he cleared the road to Kimberley, and relieved the town on 15 February. His further movements enabled him to seize Koodoesrand Drift on the Orange River, thereby holding up the Boer retreat from Kimberley towards Bloemfontein. This check resulted in the surrender of 4,000 Boers at Paardeberg on 27 February. During the subsequent advance on Pretoria, French, by turning the Boer front at Poplar Grove (7 March) and again at Driefontein (10 March), greatly assisted the advance, and on 13 March Bloemfontein was occupied. But French's next manœuvres at Karee Siding on 29 March and at Thaba Nchu on 28 April were not so conspicuously successful. After the fall of Pretoria on 5 June French followed up the Boers until they retreated over the Portuguese frontier at Koomati Poort. Finally during July he carried out some skilful movements which led to the occupation of Middelburg, and in September he took Barberton as the result of a clever manœuvre. For his noteworthy share in the campaign his rank of major-general was made substantive and he was created K.C.B.

The remainder of French's service in South Africa does not require detailed record. After losing the services of his two brilliant staff officers, Major (later Sir) Herbert Lawrence and Major (later Field-Marshal Earl) Haig, he assumed command of the Johannesburg district in November 1900. In June 1901 he was transferred to Cape Colony in order to hunt down the last Boer commandos active in that district. His movements during these two years, if sadly lacking the characteristics of his earlier operations, were slowly brought to a satisfactory conclusion. In August 1902 he was promoted lieutenant-general and created K.C.M.G.

Shortly after his return home French was appointed commander-in-chief at Aldershot, and held that post until November 1907. The reform of army-training on the basis of South African experiences was then to the fore, while the troops themselves were being regrouped according to a new plan of divisional organization. French found himself fully occupied with these tasks; but he held very conservative views as to any tactical innovations in his own arm, the cavalry. Before vacating his position he was promoted general in February 1907, and created G.C.V.O. A few months later, on leaving Aldershot, he was appointed inspector-general of the forces. In this capacity he was responsible for a total reform in the conduct of military manœuvres; he visited Canada; and he was engaged in supervising the training of the higher commands of the army generally. In March 1912, when he was close on sixty years of age, he succeeded Field-Marshal Lord Nicholson as chief of the Imperial General Staff. In June 1913 he was promoted field-marshal.

The principal interest in French's tenure of the headship of the general staff centres round what is known as the Curragh incident. This arose out of the declaration made by a number of officers stationed at the Curragh in county Kildare that they would resign their commissions rather than participate in any armed coercion of Ulster into the acceptance of Home Rule for Ireland. A written pledge that they would not be thus employed was handed to the representatives of these officers by the secretary of state for war, Colonel Seely, after the document had been initialed by French in his capacity of chief of the general staff and by Sir Spencer Ewart in that of adjutant-general. The Cabinet, however, repudiated this undertaking, whereupon both French and Ewart resigned their appointments.

It had long been an open secret that in the event of a European war French would command any British forces dispatched to the Continent. His appointment as commander-in-chief of the British Expeditionary Force followed the declaration of war against Germany on 4 August 1914. On 14 August he landed at Boulogne at the head of one cavalry and four infantry divisions. On the 21st he met General Lanrezac, commanding the French Fifth Army, which formed the extreme left of the French forces, and he conceived an antipathy for this officer which produced grave results. The British troops, after concentrating round Maubeuge, began moving forward in prolongation of Lanrezac's advance with a view to gaining touch with the Belgian forces. The British came into contact with the Germans near Mons, where French, dissatisfied with the information supplied by his allies, decided to give battle. On the morning of the 23rd the German First Army there attacked the British. The blow fell upon the II Corps under General Sir Horace Lockwood Smith-Dorrien [q.v.], who was left virtually unsupported by the I Corps under Sir Douglas Haig, which was on the inner flank. The full significance of the German movement then began to dawn upon French. On 24 August, realizing that he was threatened with a total envelopment of his left, he began to retreat, following the similar French movement. In so doing he allowed his army to separate, the II Corps retiring to the west of the forest of Mormal, the I Corps keeping to the east of it.

The Germans pressed forward, with the result that on 26 August Smith-Dorrien, in view of the fatigue of his troops, and after consulting Major-General Allenby, then commanding the cavalry, decided to contest the enemy's advance. Smith-Dorrien informed French of this decision and received his written approval. The battle of Le Cateau resulted, and the German advance was effectually checked, though at the cost of severe loss in men and guns. Thereupon French, convinced that the II Corps had met with disaster, motored forty miles back to Noyon, thinking only of saving what he could of his army; accordingly he prevented Haig from going to assist Lanrezac when the latter fought a rear-guard action at Guise on the 30th, and finally informed the Cabinet of his intention of retreating south-westwards to St. Nazaire, regardless of his allies' movements. The situation grew so critical that Lord Kitchener, then secretary of state for war, travelled to Paris, met French on 1 September, and enjoined him to conform to the French plan of action. French did so, but after suggesting a stand on the River Marne, on the 3rd, continued to retreat on the 4th and 5th, although he must have learnt from General Gallieni, the governor of Paris, that the French armies were about to turn.

By this time a new French Sixth Army was being formed near Amiens. On 5 September General Joffre, the French commander-in-chief, gave the order for a general attack. On the 6th French thereupon advanced northwards. On the 9th he recrossed the River Marne and entered a gap of thirty miles that had been allowed to form between the German First and Second Armies. This threat, combined with the pressure of the new French Sixth Army, was really instrumental in bringing about the German retreat to the River Aisne, where they held fast to a strongly entrenched position. French, now as optimistic as he had been pessimistic before, and imagining the enemy to be still in retreat, ordered several attacks on the German line that were carried out with great gallantry. In spite of them, by the 15 September a stalemate resulted which led to a succession of attempts made by both armies to outflank each other farther to the north-west; this was the so-called 'race to the sea'.

The British Expeditionary Force was now transferred to Flanders. The first troops left the Aisne on 1 October, and arrived in the region of Bethune a week later; the rest continued to detrain in Flanders until the 19th. On the 14th the II Corps was heavily engaged at La Bassée. On the 20th the Germans began a series of violent attacks on the Allied left that only grew fiercer as they proved to be inconclusive. On the 22nd French reported to Kitchener that the enemy were 'playing their last card'. Two days later, in spite of a grave shortage of munitions, he was writing that the battle was 'practically won'. Yet the crisis was not reached until the 31st in front of Ypres, where the British stood flanked on either side by the French. No commander-in-chief could exercise much influence on the course of such a struggle. The valour of the men in the ranks and the efforts of their direct leaders could alone affect the ebb and flow of the battle, while the French troops, themselves heavily engaged, lent precious aid to their British allies. By the middle of November the fighting died down into the comparative quiet of trench warfare.

Throughout the winter French continued in optimistic mood, maintaining that he could break the German line provided he were given adequate forces and a sufficiency of high-explosive ammunition. Accordingly on 10–13 March he made his attempt at Neuve Chapelle. In spite of an auspicious opening the effort proved fruitless. It had been planned on too small a scale and was inadequately supported. French next combined with the Allies in elaborating a greater project. But before this could be put into effect the Germans again attacked at Ypres on 22 April. The infantry assault was preceded by the first discharge of chlorine gas released in the War, which drove back the French on the British left in wild disorder. Failing to exploit this somewhat unexpected success the Germans yet succeeded in placing the British flank, then commanded by Smith-Dorrien, in jeopardy. French, now swayed by alternate hope and fear, succeeded in holding his own, but subsequently vented his resentment on Smith-Dorrien so strongly that the latter resigned his command on 6 May. The battle of Frezenberg Ridge followed, involving severe fighting from the 8th to the 13th of May, while there was a final attack on Bellewarde Farm on the 24th.

Meanwhile, in compliance with his allies' plans, French attempted to seize the Aubers Ridge on 9 May, hoping thereby to facilitate the capture of Lille. As the operation failed, renewed attempts were made at Festubert from the 15th to the

27th, and, on the failure of these, yet a third attack was launched at Givenchy on 15 June. In each of these French failed in his purpose. The attacks were delivered with inadequate forces, while on every occasion the enemy, being well prepared to meet the British tactics, parried the assault.

At length a more ambitious plan was put forward by the French—a combined attack against both fronts of the great German salient in France. This time French was not so confident of success. Only with reluctance was he induced, on the grounds of reasons of state, to participate in the operation, the British share of which became the battle of Loos (25–28 September 1915). This opened with a British attempt, under cover of a gas attack, to carry the Lens coal-field, a difficult area strongly fortified by the enemy. On the right the attempt at first made headway. But the gains could not be held. Moreover, French's handling of his general reserves, composed of raw 'new army' divisions, has since given rise to much criticism that may be regarded as justified. No real success was ever attained, and the fighting dragged on in a forlorn manner until 14 October.

Dissatisfaction with the conduct of the operations in France now became more pronounced. French himself was beginning to show signs of strain. Doubts were being freely expressed as to his fitness to cope with the intellectual and physical exigencies imposed by modern warfare on the high command. It is difficult not to sympathize with a leader who for fourteen months had filled a most unenviable position to the best of his ability. At the very outset he had found himself involved in a plan of campaign which was practically unknown to him. The plan failed; whereupon he had been compelled to carry out a retreat difficult and hazardous in the extreme. He did not have a fair opportunity of understanding his allies; they did not even try to understand him; worse still, they underrated the quality of the British troops and of their leaders. Grave difficulties arose in the conduct of the War as a whole. Inadequate provision had been made to meet the needs of such a campaign. Weaknesses became evident even in French's own head-quarters staff. Nevertheless, when all these unforeseen and immense obstacles are taken into account, the fact remains that French revealed defects not only of temperament but also of military aptitude, which must preclude him, in spite of his military qualities, from ever ranking with any of the great generals of the past. In particular, his protracted quarrel with Sir Horace Smith-Dorrien, and its grave sequel, together with the eventual publication of its details in an ill-judged book, *1914* (1919), can only be regarded as deplorable.

On 4 December 1915 French resigned his position as commander-in-chief, being succeeded on 19 December by his former staff-officer, Sir Douglas Haig. He had received the Order of Merit in December 1914; in January 1916 he was created Viscount French of Ypres and of High Lake, county Roscommon, and appointed commander-in-chief of the Home Forces. The constitution of this office was urgently needed, since the high command of all troops in the United Kingdom had so far been vested in the War Office, while the training of troops for overseas required much closer supervision and simplification than was thus possible. In this new capacity French achieved satisfactory results. More difficult was the protection of Great Britain against the air attacks which were threatening to impede the flow of munitions to the armies overseas. This complicated problem was assigned to French in the spring of 1916 and finally solved by the organization of special staffs and troops to deal with the raiders, so that by October 1916 the menace of the enemy's attacks by Zeppelin air-ships had been effectively countered. But during the summer and autumn of 1917 a series of hostile aeroplane raids revived the danger in a more acute form. Thanks to the vigorous efforts of the British aviation and anti-aircraft services these attacks were also overcome and French's task was thus achieved. No other enemy activity, save a few insignificant coastal bombardments, disturbed the United Kingdom down to the close of the War. French's reorganization of the system of home defence, whereby any possible enemy landings were to be resisted on the spot, was consequently never put to the test.

In Ireland, however, a situation of real gravity arose at Easter 1916, when the Sinn Fein party rose in arms in Dublin (24 April), seized certain points of the city, and proclaimed a republic. Fighting ensued, and French dispatched two Territorial divisions to Dublin. He also appointed General Sir John Maxwell [q.v.] to be commander-in-chief in Ireland. Within a short time the Rebellion was crushed and certain of its leaders shot after trial by court-martial. But Ireland remained a hotbed of acute discontent and a source of considerable anxiety until long after the end of the War.

In May 1918 French was appointed lord-lieutenant of Ireland. It was then thought that his Irish extraction and military reputation might win for him both respect and obedience among the Irish. As a result of the Irish Convention, which had just concluded its labours, it was still imagined that Ireland might accept some form of conscription in return for the grant of Home Rule. All such hopes were doomed to speedy disappointment. French next attempted to raise 50,000 voluntary recruits, but scarcely 10,000 could be obtained. Matters went from bad to worse, until the country could only be governed by military authority based on special regulations for the restoration of order. Nevertheless, the troops, supported by the Irish Constabulary and assisted by newly formed auxiliary police units, were hampered by restrictions of every kind. The struggle degenerated into a campaign of aggression and punishment, of outrages and of reprisals. In December 1919 a serious attempt was made on French's life, when a bomb and a volley of shots were aimed at the cortège of cars in which he travelled. French escaped unharmed, but his position only grew more unsatisfactory with the lapse of time. As a soldier there was no opening for him to command; as an administrator he was never able to enforce the law. On 30 April 1921 he resigned his post, after the passing of the Government of Ireland Act, which by its nature entailed a change of viceroy. French thereupon retired into private life, and was created Earl of Ypres for his services in June 1922. Thereafter much of his time was spent in France, mainly in Paris, until in August 1923 he was appointed captain of Deal Castle by the lord warden of the Cinque Ports. There he decided to make his home, and there he died, after a severe operation, on 22 May 1925.

French married in 1880 Eleanora, daughter of Richard William Selby-Lowndes, of Elmers, Bletchley, Buckinghamshire. He had two sons and one daughter; both his sons served in the European War. He was succeeded as second earl by his elder son, John Richard Lowndes (born 1881), who had retired from the Royal Artillery some years before the War, as the result of a hunting accident.

French figures in the picture 'Some General Officers of the Great War' by J. S. Sargent, which is hung in the National Portrait Gallery. A portrait of him by J. St. H. Lander belongs to the Cavalry Club, Piccadilly. A cartoon appeared in *Vanity Fair* 12 July 1900. There is a monument to him in the rebuilt cathedral at Ypres and a memorial tablet in Canterbury Cathedral.

[*The Times*, 23 May 1925; Sir J. E. Edmonds, (Official) *History of the Great War. Military Operations, France and Belgium, 1914–1915*, 1922–1928; Edward Gerald French, *Field-Marshal Lord French*, 1931; Lord French, *1914*, 1919; E. L. Spiers, *Liaison*, 1930; personal knowledge.]

H. de Watteville.

FROWDE, HENRY (1841–1927), publisher, was born at Southsea 8 February 1841, the son of James Frowde, who came of an old Devonshire family said to have some connexion with James Anthony Froude, by his wife, Catherine Branscombe, of Kingsbridge, Devon. He began work at the age of sixteen, and after holding various posts in bookselling and publishing firms in London, and finally that of manager of the London Bible Warehouse, in February 1874 was offered and accepted the management of the London office of the Oxford University Press. In 1883 he took over the publication of all Clarendon Press books, and was formally entitled 'Publisher to the University of Oxford'. He retired from this position in March 1913. Frowde's administration was marked by the publication on 17 May 1881 of the Revised New Testament, and the distribution, by a small staff in cramped premises, of over a million copies in one day—an achievement which was repeated in 1885 with the complete Revised Bible; by the discovery and use of Oxford India paper, the first book issued on this paper being a Bible in August 1875; and by a general expansion of the business of the Press. He was given the honorary degree of M.A. by the university of Oxford in 1897.

Frowde married in 1874 Mary Blanche Foster, daughter of Joel Foster Earle, and had three daughters and a son who died as a child. He died at Croydon 3 March 1927.

[*The Times*, 4 March 1927; personal knowledge.]

H. S. Milford.

FRY, THOMAS CHARLES (1846–1930), schoolmaster and dean of Lincoln, was born at Forest Hill, Sydenham, 16

April 1846, the only son and youngest child of Peter Samuel Fry, solicitor, by his wife, Katherine Eliza Ann, daughter of the Rev. John Charles Williams. His grandfather, the Rev. Thomas Fry, of Axbridge, was a fellow of Lincoln College, Oxford, and rector of Emberton, Buckinghamshire. Fry was educated at Bedford grammar school, and at Pembroke College, Cambridge, where he gained a scholarship, and obtained a second class in the classical tripos of 1868. After two years at Durham School as assistant master, he was appointed an assistant master at Cheltenham College, and was ordained deacon in 1871 and priest in 1873. In 1883 he was appointed headmaster of Oundle School, but in the following year, owing to a serious illness, he resigned, under doctors' orders, and went to the Riviera. In 1886 he took charge of the parish of Wyke Regis, Dorset.

In 1887 Fry was appointed headmaster of Berkhamstead School. He proved himself a great headmaster. By his initiative the school was provided with modern equipment, additional class-rooms, a new hall, and a beautiful chapel, to which he and his wife contributed generously. He inspired his staff with his own enthusiasm, and, although a strict disciplinarian, he won the esteem of the boys by his devotion and singleness of aim. The educational standard was raised, the numbers grew, and the school which he had found as a country grammar school attained a recognized position among the public schools of the country.

A man of wide interests, Fry did not confine himself to the routine of school work. A radical in politics and a liberal high churchman, he threw himself with unbounded energy into the task of presenting the Church's spiritual and social message to the age. In sermons and in addresses at meetings and Church congresses he delivered his mind on such questions as the drink traffic, purity, the sanctity of marriage, the housing question, and economic and industrial problems, with impassioned earnestness, entire fearlessness, and at times with biting severity. He was one of the pioneers in the work of the Christian Social Union, and also chairman of the Church Reform League.

In 1910 Fry was appointed dean of Lincoln. Here he played a conspicuous part in the life of the city and of the diocese, and showed a keen interest in adult, no less than in elementary and secondary education. The Workers' Educational Association found in him ready sympathy and active help, and his addresses to working men, school teachers, and others were illumined by striking epigrams and flashes of humour. His colleagues in the chapter found him at first somewhat of the schoolmaster, but soon recognized his singleness of purpose and devotion to the cathedral and all that affected its life and worship. The greatest test of Fry's powers came in 1921, when the fabric of the cathedral was found to be in serious danger. To the task of restoration he brought gifts of imagination and good business capacity, and soon enlisted the interest not only of England but of the British Colonies and the United States of America. Twice he crossed the Atlantic on visits to Canada and the United States to collect funds. His third and last visit overseas, in his eighty-fourth year in 1929, to South America, was cut short by illness, and he was brought back to England, and died at the deanery at Lincoln 10 February 1930. He had raised nearly £100,000 for the cathedral restoration fund. Although his task was not actually completed, it was due to his heroic efforts that the fabric had been saved.

Fry's chief recreations were fishing and climbing, and he was a member of the Alpine Club. He was a great traveller and had a facility in acquiring foreign languages. He married in 1876 Julia Isabella (died 1928), third daughter of Edward Greene, of Nether Hall, Bury St. Edmunds, member of parliament for that place from 1865 to 1885, and had two sons.

[*The Times*, 11 February 1930; private information; personal knowledge.]

J. H. Srawley.

FURNEAUX, WILLIAM MORDAUNT (1848–1928), schoolmaster and dean of Winchester, was the eldest son of the Rev. William Duckworth Furneaux, by his wife, Louisa, eldest daughter of William Dickins, of Cherrington, Warwickshire. His father, who owned a family estate at Swilly, Devonshire, was rector of Berkeley, Somerset, from 1860 until his death in 1874. William Mordaunt Furneaux was born at Walton D'Eiville, a village near Stratford-on-Avon, of which his father was then perpetual curate, 29 July 1848. When he was ten years old he was sent to St. Peter's College, Radley, of which Dr. William Sewell [q.v.] was warden. In 1861, possibly because the future of Radley was somewhat uncertain, he was transferred to Marlborough College, where he had a successful school career under Dr. George Granville Bradley [q.v.], afterwards dean of Westminster. He was a junior scholar in 1862, and Cotton scholar and an exhibitioner in 1867. He was also in the school football team for two seasons. He went up to Oxford as a scholar of Corpus Christi College in 1868. He obtained a first class in classical moderations in 1870, being in the same year *proxime accessit* for the Hertford scholarship, and graduated in 1872 with a first class in *literae humaniores*.

On leaving Oxford Furneaux accepted an assistant mastership at Clifton College. He remained there only two years, returning in 1874 to his old school, Marlborough, of which Dr. Frederic William Farrar [q.v.] had become headmaster. He was ordained deacon in 1874 and priest in 1875. At Marlborough he remained for eight years, until in 1882, at the age of thirty-four, he was appointed headmaster of Repton School.

At Repton for eighteen years Furneaux did excellent work, and proved an admirable headmaster. His business capacity was considerable and enabled him to overcome the financial and other difficulties which at the date of his appointment confronted the school. By judicious negotiation he obtained a secure tenure of the land which it occupied, and this point having been settled, he added to the advantages of the school by many new buildings. Chief among these was the hall erected by subscription as a memorial to Dr. Steuart Adolphus Pears [q.v.], headmaster from 1854 to 1874, who had raised the ancient foundation of Repton to its present public-school status. The block of buildings, consisting of a large speech-room with class-rooms underneath, was completed and opened in the summer of 1886. In other departments of the school life Furneaux was equally effective. A vigorous and inspiring teacher, he infected his pupils with much of his own enthusiasm for both classical and English literature.

Furneaux resigned the headmastership of Repton in 1900, and in 1903 he was appointed dean of Winchester, an office which he held for sixteen years. His term as dean will be remembered chiefly for the successful renovation of the foundations of Winchester Cathedral. In 1905 it was found that the subsidence of the fabric had become so serious that, unless measures were taken at once to arrest it, the building was in danger of collapse. The magnitude of the necessary operations was such that doubts were expressed whether the saving of the fabric would be possible or was worth attempting. The dean, however, laboured unceasingly to raise the necessary funds. The final accomplishment of the restoration may fairly be described as due to his energy and perseverance. After seven years the new foundations were completed in 1912 at a cost of £120,000 [see Fox, Sir Francis].

Furneaux retired from the deanery in 1919. He was an honorary canon of Southwell Cathedral from 1891 to 1901, and the Lambeth degree of D.D. was conferred on him in 1903. He acted as examining chaplain successively to the bishops of Southwell and Winchester. His writings include *A Commentary on the Acts of the Apostles* (1912). He married in 1877 Caroline Octavia, youngest daughter of Joseph Mortimer, of Weymouth, and had three daughters. His wife died in 1904, shortly after his appointment to Winchester. Furneaux died at White Cottage, New Milton, 10 April 1928.

[*The Times*, 11 April 1928; personal knowledge.] A. COCHRANE.

FURNISS, HARRY (1854–1925), caricaturist and illustrator, was born at Wexford 26 March 1854, the youngest son of James Furniss, civil engineer, by his second wife, Isabella Cornelia, daughter of Eneas Mackenzie [q.v.], topographer, of Newcastle-upon-Tyne. James Furniss came from Hathersage, Derbyshire, and had settled in Ireland in the practice of his profession. Although his parents were not Wesleyans, Harry Furniss was educated at the Wesleyan Connexional School (afterwards the Wesleyan College), St. Stephen's Green, Dublin, to which city his family had moved in 1864. His talent as a draughtsman showed itself at a very early age, and while still at school he produced in manuscript a monthly magazine called 'The Schoolboy's *Punch*'. His several experiences of formal instruction in drawing were short, and gave him nothing of value; he was essentially self-taught, and by the time he had reached the age of seventeen was already busily contributing to *Zozimus* (the Dublin '*Punch*') and illustrating books of varied character.

In the summer of 1873 Furniss went to London. He received his first commission from Miss Florence Marryat [q.v.], then editor of *London Society*; and he rapidly made his way as a caricaturist and illustrator. Within a year he was contributing regularly to the *Illustrated Sporting and*

Dramatic News; in 1876 he joined the staff of the *Illustrated London News*; and on 30 October 1880 his first sketch appeared in *Punch*. In the following year (Sir) Henry Lucy [q.v.], who, as 'Toby, M.P.', had just taken over *Punch's* 'Essence of Parliament', chose Furniss as his illustrator. Furniss's parliamentary sketches proved a welcome innovation, giving the public rapid impressions of the interior life of St. Stephen's; and in 1884 the seal was set on his success by his being 'called to the Table' at the *Punch* office. He remained a member of the staff of that journal until March 1894, when he resigned in order to take up other work.

Cartoons and caricatures, however, formed but a part of Furniss's enormous activity. In 1887, after three years' work in secret, he gave an amusing exhibition at the Gainsborough Gallery, Bond Street, of eighty-seven large monochrome works parodying the styles and subjects of leading exhibitors at Burlington House. In 1888 he travelled through England on the first of many successful lecture-tours which, in the 'Humours of Parliament' series (1891), became exercises in mimicry and entertainment. In 1889 he began a long association with Lewis Carroll (Charles Lutwidge Dodgson, q.v.) by illustrating *Sylvie and Bruno*. *Royal Academy Antics* (1890), which he both wrote and illustrated, was an historical sketch and a far from temperate indictment of that institution. In 1892 he paid the first of several visits to the United States. In 1894 he embarked on a big journalistic venture—the publication of a threepenny humorous weekly paper, *Lika Joko*, of which 140,000 copies were sold on the first day. Next year he merged this with William Waldorf Astor's *Pall Mall Budget*, which he renamed the *New Budget* and conducted from April to October 1895, when heavy commitments on the advertising side forced him to cease publication.

For another thirty years Furniss maintained an untiring and prolific output as a cartoonist, illustrator, journalist, author, and lecturer. His parliamentary illustrations for the *Daily News* (1896) were a novel feature in daily journalism. In 1912, at the age of fifty-eight, he took up with zest the new art of the cinematograph, working for Thomas Alva Edison in New York as a writer, actor, and producer, transferring his activities to London in 1913, and writing *Our Lady Cinema* (his hopes and plans for the craft) in 1914. Shortly before this two of his most notable works as an illustrator had appeared—complete editions of Dickens (1910) and of Thackeray (1911). Ten years before (1901) he had begun a series of books of reminiscences and anecdotes with *Confessions of a Caricaturist*. He wrote, among other books, several manuals of instruction in drawing, a novel, *Poverty Bay* (1905), and studies (illustrated by himself) of *Some Victorian Women* (1922) and *Some Victorian Men* (1924). He died at his home at Hastings 14 January 1925.

Furniss was one of those talented humorous artists who, like Phil May, Linley Sambourne, and Sir John Tenniel, found in *Punch* a fruitful field of expression. He was never of that order of caricaturists, of whom Thomas Rowlandson is the chief English exemplar, who employ considerable distortion as a satiric weapon. His genius lay largely in the rapid seizing of an idiosyncrasy (like the famous Gladstone collar), in whimsies (like the insertion of modern and Western personages in the willow-pattern plate), and in his (unpopular) series of composite portrait-heads. He never possessed the monumental quality of Tenniel, and began work before that tightening of design which became *de rigueur* after Aubrey Beardsley. An accomplished and versatile draughtsman, a rapid and industrious worker, a jovial and friendly personality, he made few enemies despite a satirical turn which was often scathing. His illustrations to Dickens are among his most noteworthy achievements, and hold their own well even in the company of George Cruikshank and Hablot Browne (Phiz). His writings, which are unduly jocose and addicted to clichés, are only noteworthy for the mass of interesting anecdote about nearly all the famous figures of his age. Furniss 'knew every one' in a less hyperbolical sense than is usually understood, and was an excellent *raconteur*.

Furniss married in 1877 Marian, eldest daughter of Alfred Rogers, the London manager of Whitehead Brothers, felt manufacturers. He had three sons and one daughter.

[Harry Furniss, *Confessions of a Caricaturist*, 2 vols., 1901; M. H. Spielmann, *The History of Punch*, 1895, and an article in the *Magazine of Art*, vol. xxiii, 1899; private information. For details of his numerous works see the British Museum *Catalogue of Printed Books*. A memoir of Furniss by his daughter, Miss Dorothy Furniss, is in course of preparation.]

H. B. Grimsditch.

GALLOWAY, Sir WILLIAM (1840–1927), mining engineer, born 12 February 1840, was the eldest son of William Galloway, J.P., of Paisley, owner of a Paisley shawl factory and colliery-owner, by his second wife, Margaret Lindsay. He was educated at a private school, the university of Giessen, the Bergakademie at Freiberg, Saxony, and University College, London. He became a junior inspector of mines in West Scotland; later he was transferred to South Wales. He early directed his attention to the causes of explosions in mines, and in 1873 won a prize offered by Edward Hermon, M.P., for the best essay on this subject, being bracketed equal with Wilfred Creswick. His essay was included among the Hermon Prize Essays (1874). Although at this time Galloway still accepted the orthodox view that the most serious explosions are occasioned by the combustion of fire-damp, he subsequently altered this opinion, and in a series of papers published in the *Proceedings* of the Royal Society between 1875 and 1887 contended that floating coal dust was the means of extending the area of explosions. From an analysis of the evidence afforded by actual explosions he demonstrated that fire-damp could not have been present in appreciable quantities along most of the track in the cases examined. He also conducted experiments in galleries specially constructed for the purpose, whereby he was able to get ignition and very violent explosions from coal dust without the presence of fire-damp.

For many years, however, Galloway's conclusions were received with scepticism, and, owing to the conflict of views between him and his senior colleagues he was compelled to resign his inspectorship. Eventually, however, his theory was confirmed by the testimony of mining engineers and of junior inspectors of mines, particularly by the brothers Atkinson [see W. N. and J. B. Atkinson's *Explosions in Coal Mines*, 1886], and by (Sir) Henry Hall, who was appointed to experiment and report to the royal commission of 1893 on coal dust explosions in mines. As a preventive of such explosions Galloway first recommended the wetting of the roads in mines, a method which was not found to be wholly effective; later, in 1896, he advocated the use of stone dust. This method, which was independently initiated and developed by (Sir) William Garforth, proved very successful and has been generally adopted since 1908, with the result that the death-rate resulting from colliery explosions has been lowered to ten per cent. of the figure prevailing when Galloway began his investigations.

From 1891 to 1902 Galloway was professor of mining at University College, Cardiff. He also carried on until his death an extensive business at Cardiff as a consulting mining engineer. He received many awards for his investigations, was president of the South Wales Institute of Civil Engineers in 1912, and was knighted in 1924. He died 2 November 1927 at his residence, 17 Park Place, Cardiff.

Galloway married twice: first, in 1874 Christiana Maud Mary, daughter of William Francis Gordon, of Milrig, Ayrshire, by whom he had two sons; secondly, in 1900 Mary Gwenap Douglas, daughter of Captain James Wood, Royal Marines, of Nunlands, Surrey. He published twenty-one papers on his researches into the causes of colliery explosions, eight of which appeared in the *Transactions* of the Royal Society, and nineteen other papers mainly on subjects related to mining.

[*The Times*, 4 November 1927; *Nature*, 26 November 1927; *Journal of Education*, December 1927.] E. I. Carlyle.

GARSTIN, Sir WILLIAM EDMUND (1849–1925), engineer, born in India 29 January 1849, was the second son of Charles Garstin, of the Bengal civil service, by his wife, Agnes Helen, daughter of W. Mackenzie, of the East India Company's service. He was educated at Cheltenham College (1864–1866) and at King's College, London, where he studied engineering. In 1872 he entered the Indian public works department.

In 1885, while still in the Indian service, Garstin was invited by (Sir) Colin Campbell Scott-Moncrieff, under-secretary of state in the ministry of public works at Cairo, to join the small group of Indian engineers who were to reorganize the irrigation system of Egypt, at that time in complete disorder. Garstin was placed in charge of the circle of irrigation which included the eastern part of the Nile Delta, and he laboured there for seven years, until, on the retirement of Colonel Justin Charles Ross, he was appointed in May 1892 inspector-general of irrigation in Egypt, at the same time definitely retiring from the Indian service. In the following September he succeeded Sir Colin Scott-Moncrieff as under-secretary of state in the ministry of public works.

According to Lord Cromer, the chief

needs of Egypt at that time were justice and water. Garstin, during his term of office as under-secretary, was largely responsible for giving her water. Cromer wrote: 'It would be difficult to exaggerate the debt of gratitude which the people of Egypt owe to Sir William Garstin' [*Modern Egypt*, i, 686]. On another occasion Cromer asserted that Garstin had 'raised himself to the rank of the greatest hydraulic engineer in this or any other country', while the Egyptian nationalist press styled him 'the treasure of Egypt'.

Great improvements in the Egyptian water system had already been made by Garstin's predecessor, Colonel Ross. These mainly consisted in the substitution in suitable districts of perennial for basin irrigation, that is, of irrigation from canals which run during the whole year, instead of from canals which run only during the Nile flood. As the perennial system required a greater volume of water for a given area and also made it possible to bring large additional areas under cultivation, it made necessary an extensive control of the flow of the Nile. The work of control, although still far from complete, was carried out mainly under Garstin's administration and in accordance with his plans. It comprised the construction of the great dam at Assuan and the barrages at Assiut and Esna—notable achievements which were all parts of one system of water storage and control. The subsequent heightening of the Assuan dam and the construction of the Esna barrage were planned and begun under Garstin's administration, but were not completed when he retired.

The problem of water storage was forced on the British engineers by the regular exhaustion of the Nile between 1890 and 1902 in the months of May and June, as well as by the needs of perennial irrigation. In 1894 (Sir) William Willcocks wrote his report on *Perennial Irrigation and Flood Protection for Egypt*, in which he suggested the construction of a reservoir at Assuan. Garstin referred the question to a commission composed of Sir Benjamin Baker [q.v.], M. Boulé, and Signor Torricelli. The commission reported in favour of Assuan by a majority composed of Baker and Torricelli. Four years later (Sir) Ernest Joseph Cassel [q.v.] offered to advance the necessary funds, and on Garstin's advice the offer was accepted. With Sir John Aird [q.v.] as the contractor, Baker as consulting engineer, and (Sir) Maurice Fitzmaurice [q.v.] as chief engineer in charge, the dam was finished by December 1902, at a cost of £2,400,000. Protective works downstream were completed in 1906.

As early as 1904, however, the whole of the water stored at Assuan had been appropriated to particular tracts and there was still a large demand for an additional supply [Willcocks, *The Assuan Reservoir and Lake Moeris*, 6, 1904]. In that year Garstin published his *Report on the Basin of the Upper Nile*, in which he recommended the heightening of the Assuan dam. The work was begun in 1907, in accordance with plans drawn up by Baker, and completed in December 1912. By this means the cubic capacity of the storage-lake was increased about two and a half times. As the construction and subsequent raising of the Assuan dam involved the complete submersion of the temples on the island of Philae, a short distance above Assuan, except from August to December, Garstin took measures for the safety of the temples by underpinning those that were not founded upon rock; he also obtained a grant for an archaeological survey of the part of the Nile valley affected.

The Assiut barrage was intended to secure to Middle Egypt its share of the reservoir water in the summer and to improve the water-supply of the Ibrahamiya canal by raising the level of the river. The barrage was constructed, according to Garstin's directions, from the original design of (Sir) William Willcocks, with Baker as consulting engineer, and Aird and Co. as contractors. It was begun at the end of 1898 and finished by the middle of February 1902 at a cost of nearly £900,000. After the completion of the Assiut barrage it was decided to improve the irrigation of the Kena province during flood by the construction of another barrage across the Nile immediately north of Esna town. The structure was designed by (Sir) Arthur Lewis Webb and built by (Sir) Murdoch Macdonald. It was begun in April 1906 and completed at the end of December 1908 at a cost of £1,000,000.

In addition to the Assuan dam and its subsidiaries, the Zifta barrage was also constructed on the Damietta branch of the lower Nile between 5 May 1901 and 27 December 1902 at a cost of £420,000, from the design of Sir Hanbury Brown, in order to improve the water-supply of the northern part of the Delta.

After the battle of Omdurman (2 September 1898), as soon as the Sudan had been freed from Dervish rule, Garstin took measures to clear the Bahr el Jebel and the Bahr el Ghazal from the 'sudd', that is, blocks of drift and growing vegetation, which had closed many channels. The Bahr el Jebel was cleared by 1905. Garstin also made a series of journeys throughout the regions of the upper Nile with a view to utilizing its waters for Egypt and the Sudan. In 1902–1903 he travelled up the White Nile to Lake Albert Edward, and proceeded along the north shore of Lake Victoria as far as the railway head at Kisumu. The Sudan irrigation service was formed, and from that time the river flow has been carefully observed and measured at various seasons. Garstin's own observations, forming the basis of a mass of hydrographical information of great value, appeared in two reports, the first of which is contained in the Foreign Office Blue Book, Egypt (No. 2), 1901, while the second was published at Cairo in 1904 under the title *Report upon the Basin of the Upper Nile, with proposals for the improvement of that River*. The execution of the proposals contained in the latter report and also in a more general form in Garstin's article on 'Some Problems of the Upper Nile' (*Nineteenth Century and After*, September 1905), although begun in 1913, was interrupted by the European War and is still incomplete.

Irrigation was only one of Garstin's responsibilities. As under-secretary in the department of public works, the buildings and antiquities of Egypt came under his supervision. The present buildings of the National Museum of Egyptian Antiquities at Cairo, opened 15 November 1902, were due to his efforts to house the ever-increasing collections. In 1896, on his recommendation, a geological reconnaissance of Egyptian territory was begun, and soon developed into the present Geological Survey.

At the close of 1904, in consequence of the development of the public works service, the department was reorganized. On 1 January 1905 two new offices were created—namely, under-secretaryships for irrigation and for buildings and towns, while Garstin became adviser to the department. He retired from the Egyptian service in 1908, but often revisited the country in order to give advice on irrigation questions and to act as a British director of the Suez Canal Company. On a farewell tour in the Delta before his retirement, Garstin was enthusiastically greeted by people of all ranks, nationalities, and politics, and by thronging crowds of the fellahin. For his services he was created C.M.G. in 1894, K.C.M.G. in 1897, and G.C.M.G. on the opening of the Assuan reservoir in 1902. He was also a chevalier of the legion of honour and held the grand cordons of the Medjidie and Osmanie orders. In 1905 he received a gift of £15,000 from the Egyptian government.

During the War Garstin devoted himself to work with the St. John's Ambulance and on the Council of the Red Cross Society, for which he was awarded the G.B.E. in 1918. He died in London at his residence, 17 Welbeck House, Wigmore Street, 8 January 1925. He married in 1888 Mary Isabella, daughter of Charles Augustus North, and granddaughter of Brownlow North (1810–1875, q.v.). He obtained a divorce from her in 1902. They had a son and a daughter both of whom predeceased their father.

[*The Times*, 9 January 1925; *Journal* of the Royal Geographical Society, vol. lxv, 279, 1925; *Nature*, 17 January 1925; Annual Reports on the Administration of the Public Works Department in Egypt; Lord Cromer's Report on Egypt in 1902; Note by Garstin to Willcocks's *Report on Perennial Irrigation and Flood Protection for Egypt*, 1894; H. G. Lyons, *Physiography of the River Nile*, 132–144, 1906; Preface by Garstin to H. G. Lyons's *Report on the Island and Temples of Philae*, 1896; *Encyclopaedia Britannica*, 14th edition, s.v. Nile; W. Willcocks and J. I. Craig, *Egyptian Irrigation*, 1913; *Proceedings* of the Institution of Civil Engineers, 1902–1903, vol. clii, 71, 108, 1904, vol. clviii, 26; Mary A. Hollings, *Life of Sir Colin Campbell Scott-Moncrieff*, 1917; A. B. Lloyd, *Uganda to Khartoum*, 1906.]

E. I. CARLYLE.

GASQUET, FRANCIS NEIL (in religion DOM AIDAN) (1846–1929), cardinal and historian, was born in London 5 October 1846, the third son of Raymond Gasquet, M.D., by his wife, Mary Apollonia, daughter of Thomas Kay, of York. The Gasquets were of Provençal origin. Francis Gasquet's grandfather was vice-admiral of the French fleet at Toulon when Napoleon Bonaparte took the town for the Republic in 1793. Being a strong royalist, he escaped with his family on a British warship to England. Thus Francis's father came to England as a child, and he never returned to France.

In 1862 Gasquet was sent to the school attached to the Benedictine priory at Downside, near Bath, and in 1866 he entered the Benedictine novitiate, taking the 'religious' name of Aidan. After four years of training and theological studies at St. Michael's Priory, Hereford, he returned to Downside as a master in the school. A man of slight build, but overflowing with energy, he threw himself into every phase of the school life, including games and music, and was a successful teacher of history and mathematics. He was ordained priest in 1874, and soon afterwards was put in charge of the studies of the school, and exercised considerable influence over the elder boys. His influence in the monastery was no less; he was regular in the observance of the monastic life, earnest, with much good-humoured enthusiasm. In 1878 the community elected him prior, he being just thirty-two years of age.

Gasquet's priorship of seven years was the turning-point in the history of Downside. In 1878 Downside was a small place—a community of some twelve monks and a school of sixty or seventy boys. As prior, Gasquet took the first steps in the modernization of the school, and in the monastery he promoted a policy of enlargement of outlook and growth. These ideas were symbolized in the new church, of which he built the first portion—the transepts—thus laying down the lines of the present abbey church.

Gasquet at that time enjoyed robust health, but he taxed it severely: he would sit up late at night, at work or reading, and yet was always first down for the early morning office in choir. He was consumed with activity in every aspect of the life both of the community and of the school. His energy and industry were contagious, and he infused his ideals and his zeal into the young monks around him. He was not a strong ruler; but he ruled well by the power of his personal charm and understanding sympathy. Seven years of this energetic life undermined Gasquet's strong constitution; he was threatened with serious heart trouble, and warned that he must give up office and take a prolonged rest. In the summer of 1885, therefore, he resigned the post of prior.

Gasquet's idea of rest took the form of work at the British Museum and Public Record Office. After a couple of years of assiduous spade-work the first-fruits of his labours were seen in the two volumes of *Henry VIII and the English Monasteries* (1888–1889). The book had a great reception and won for Gasquet at once a recognized position among English historians. James Gairdner [q.v.] wrote that the charges against the English monks and nuns at the time of the Reformation 'are now dispelled for ever'. It was followed by a long series of works, great and small, the output of twenty years' unflagging industry, the effect of which was to make Gasquet a leading authority on the ecclesiastical history of the English later Middle Ages and Tudor period.

During these years Gasquet lived in London, near the British Museum, and he became a popular and respected figure in historical and archaeological circles, owing to his charm and fund of humour, ever religious, industrious, human. In 1903 he was elected a member of the Athenaeum Club under rule II.

In 1896 Gasquet was called to Rome in order to take part in the investigation into the question of Anglican orders. In 1899 Pope Leo XIII put into his hands the execution of the Bull whereby the old English Benedictine Congregation was released from the conditions imposed since penal times, and reorganized on more traditional Benedictine lines, the monasteries being raised to the rank of abbeys. The Pope named Gasquet chairman of the papal commission appointed to carry through this reform and to draw up revised constitutions. In 1900 the general chapter of the Congregation elected him abbot president, to give effect to the new order of things; and to this office he was re-elected up till 1914. On the death of Cardinal Vaughan in 1903, Gasquet's name was one of three submitted to Rome by the canons of Westminster for nomination to the vacant archbishopric.

In 1907 Pope Pius X entrusted to the Benedictine Order the task of preparing a critical revision of the text of the Vulgate, and appointed Gasquet president of the commission for carrying through the work. This necessitated his residing in Rome, in the Benedictine College of Sant' Anselmo. He and the monks of divers nationalities associated with him worked assiduously, rotographing the chief Vulgate manuscripts in many countries, collating the texts with the Clementine Vulgate, and tabulating the readings. The expense of the work was heavy, and although the Pope subsidized it, Gasquet in 1913 made a lecturing tour in the United States to arouse interest and raise funds.

On 25 May 1914 Pope Pius X created Abbot Gasquet cardinal deacon, with the *diaconia* of San Giorgio in Velabro which he exchanged for that of S. Maria in Campitelli in December 1915. The appointment was received with appreciation in England. The new cardinal came to England, and had solemn public receptions at Downside, his own monastery, and elsewhere. In August came the outbreak of the European War and the death of Pius X, and Cardinal Gasquet, with Cardinal Bourne, had to hurry to Rome for the conclave which elected Pope Benedict XV. The Vatican had not yet settled down into the attitude of firm neutrality maintained by the Pope, and the English cardinals found strong pro-German influences at work. On Cardinal Gasquet, as the resident English cardinal, fell the task of countering the anti-English and anti-Allies propaganda of the Central Powers. His success was fully recognized by leading English statesmen; and on his death the public press, *The Times* conspicuously, paid tribute to his effective service to the Allied cause. He took a leading part in negotiating the appointment of a British minister to the Vatican in December 1914.

On his return to Rome in August 1914, Cardinal Gasquet resided in the Palazzo San Calisto in the Trastevere, where the Vulgate commission was established. During the War the Vulgate revision was suspended, the workers joining the armies as chaplains; after the Peace it was resumed. Not only did Gasquet himself work at the Vulgate text, inspiring his collaborators and holding together by his personality the diverse national elements among them, but he took his full part in the work of the Roman Congregations—Propaganda, Rites, Religious; and here his historical training and experience in dealing with documents gave special value to his *vota* or 'opinions'. But what gave him keenest satisfaction as cardinal was his appointment in 1917 as prefect of the archives of the Holy See, and in 1919 as librarian of the Holy Roman Church. In these offices he devoted great attention to the organization of the library and the archives, effecting marked improvements in both departments.

As the English cardinal *in Curia* Gasquet was the centre of English life and influence in Rome, and all English visitors of note came to see him. In 1924 he received King George V and Queen Mary at the library and showed them its treasures. In 1924, also, he was raised to the rank of cardinal priest.

Gasquet lived and worked in Rome for twelve years, the centre of a wide circle of friends of many nations. Shortly after his eightieth birthday he had a slight stroke from which he never fully recovered. He lived on a couple of years more, infirmities closing in upon him. He died in Rome 5 April 1929, leaving to the monks around his bed as his last bequest the motto 'Ora et labora', which fitly sums up his own life. He was buried, according to his wish, in the abbey church at Downside, where a monument, designed by Sir Giles Gilbert Scott, is erected over his remains.

[*The Times*, 6 April 1929; *Downside Review* (containing a bibliography of Gasquet's works), May 1929; personal knowledge.]

E. C. Butler.

GEIKIE, Sir ARCHIBALD (1835–1924), geologist, born at Edinburgh 28 December 1835, was the eldest son of James Stuart Geikie, musician, of Edinburgh, by his wife, Isabella, daughter of Captain Thom, of the mercantile marine, of Dunbar. Educated at Edinburgh High School and University he received a classical and literary training which made itself evident in all his writings, but his love of nature and his youthful enthusiasm for geology determined for him a scientific career. The geological observations which, as a boy, he made round Edinburgh, in Arran, Skye, and elsewhere, first attracted the notice and friendship of Hugh Miller [q.v.], and later of Sir Roderick Impey Murchison [q.v.], director-general of the Geological Survey. At the age of twenty (1855) Murchison appointed Geikie a member of the Scottish branch of the Survey. He became director in Scotland in 1867, director-general for Great Britain in 1882, and retired in 1901, after over thirty years of able administration. For a portion of this period (1871–1881) he occupied with great success the newly founded Murchison chair of geology and mineralogy at Edinburgh University.

Geikie began his official duties by surveying first in Haddington and then in Midlothian and Fife. His study of the igneous rocks of these districts, especially of Arthur's Seat and the Pentland and Bathgate hills, laid the foundation of his greatest contributions to geological science, namely those concerning the past volcanic history of Great Britain. He extended his knowledge by studies in the Western Isles and other parts of Scotland and by excursions to foreign regions such as the Auvergne, the Eifel, the active volcanic regions of Italy, the Faröe Islands, Iceland, and the lava-fields of Idaho. He published (1861) a paper on the *Chronology of the Trap Rocks of Scotland*, suggested (1867) the Tertiary age of the *Basaltic Plateaux of Ireland, West of Scotland and Iceland*, and wrote on the *Carboniferous Volcanic Rocks of the Firth of Forth* (1879). In 1888 his first great memoir on the *History of Volcanic Action during the Tertiary Period in Britain* was published by the Royal Society of Edinburgh. Later (1891–1892) he delivered presidential addresses to the Geological Society of London on past volcanic activity in Britain, and this synopsis he subsequently expanded into his great work on the *Ancient Volcanoes of Great Britain* (2 vols., 1897).

A confirmed glacialist, Geikie did much to further the study of glacial deposits in Scotland and wrote an important paper on the *Glacial Drift of Scotland* for the Geological Society of Glasgow (1863). As the result of his own work on the Old Red Sandstone of the central valley of Scotland, and by the far-sighted interpretation of observations made by his colleagues, he established the existence of an upper and lower series, each characterized by its particular fish-fauna and separated by an unconformity. Traverses made in other parts of Scotland resulted in the publication of an elaborate paper on the *Old Red Sandstone of Western Europe* (1878) which was, without question, his greatest original contribution to stratigraphical geology. His appreciation of the natural beauty of his country and the geological significance of its physiography found expression in a charming work on the *Scenery of Scotland* (1865), in which, as on his maps and in other publications, his deftness with pen and pencil is exemplified by original sketches of exceptional merit.

Geikie's early acquired literary ability, coupled with sound judgement and a kindliness of treatment, enabled him to present true and sympathetic biographies of some of his many distinguished friends —*Edward Forbes* (with Professor G. Wilson, 1861), *James David Forbes* (1869), *Sir Roderick Murchison* (2 vols., 1875), and *Sir Andrew Ramsay* (1895). His *Founders of Geology* (lectures delivered at Johns Hopkins University, 1897) is a delightful series of biographical studies with the progress of geology as the theme, and his *Geological Sketches at Home and Abroad* (1882) a volume full of scientific value and of great human interest. Geikie's appreciation of the humorous and his charm as a raconteur are well displayed in a collection of *Scottish Reminiscences* published in 1904. Although he had a great volume of original scientific work to his credit his *Text-Book of Geology* (1882) and other publications destined for the student did much to enhance his reputation by their lucid, orderly, and attractive presentation of geological facts and principles. His last publication was his autobiography, *A Long Life's Work* (1924).

Geikie's work for the learned societies was one of the outstanding features of his life: he made to them many of his most important scientific communications, and took great interest in their affairs. He was elected a fellow of the Royal Society of Edinburgh in 1861, and a fellow of the Royal Society of London in 1865; of the latter society he was the 'father' at the time of his death (1924), having been foreign secretary 1889–1893, secretary 1903–1908, and president 1908–1912. The Geological Society of London elected him a fellow in 1859. He was president 1891–1892 and again, on the occasion of the centenary of the Society, 1906–1908. He filled the office of foreign secretary from 1908 until the time of his death. For all these societies he spared no labour to further their interests. His sympathy with education showed itself in his being appointed a governor of Harrow School (1892–1922), chairman of the royal commission on Trinity College, Dublin (1920), a member of the 1851 Exhibition commission, and of the council of the British School at Rome, and a trustee of the British Museum.

Geikie was the recipient of many academic distinctions and other awards. He was knighted in 1891, created K.C.B. in 1907, and received the Order of Merit and the cross of the legion of honour in 1913. He held honorary degrees of almost every English and Scottish university as well as many from foreign universities. He received, in recognition of his services to geological science, the gold medals of the Geological Society of London, the Royal Geographical Society of Scotland, the Royal Society of Edinburgh, and the Royal Society of London, as well as others from abroad.

Geikie was a man of untiring industry and directness of purpose, tenacious of his opinions, and possessed of a strength of personality which showed itself in every task he undertook.

Geikie married in 1871 Alice Gabrielle Anne Marie (died 1916), youngest daughter of Eugène Pignatel, of Lyons, by whom he had one son and three daughters. The son and youngest daughter predeceased their father. He died at his home, Shepherd's Down, Haslemere, 10 November 1924, in his eighty-ninth year.

A portrait in oils of Geikie by R. G. Eves hangs in the apartments of the Royal Society, Burlington House, London. A marble bust executed by Edouard Lantéri is in the Museum of Practical Geology, South Kensington, and a replica in plaster is in the possession of the Geological Society of London.

[Sir A. Geikie, *A Long Life's Work, an Autobiography*, 1924; 'Eminent Living Geologists' in the *Geological Magazine*, vol. vii, 1890; *Proceedings* of the Royal Society of London, vol. xcix, B, 1926; *Proceedings* of the Geological Society of London, vol. lxxxi, 1925.]

H. H. Thomas.

GEORGE, Sir ERNEST (1839–1922), architect, was born in London 13 June 1839, the second son of John George, of Streatham, who, in the son's own words, was 'a man of Kent engaged in the wholesale iron trade in Southwark'. His mother was Mary Elizabeth, daughter of William Higgs. The boy's education appears to have had little continuity; schools at Clapham, Brighton, and Reading were all tried in turn. While he was at Reading, where he filled his headmaster with enthusiasm by his marked aptitude for sketching, George realized what he wanted to do in life, and begged his father to allow him to become an architect. He had his wish, and began his architectural education in the way which was customary at that time, by being articled. His master was a Mr. Samuel Hewitt, of Buckingham Street, Adelphi, of whom little is known. It was while he was in Hewitt's office that he joined the Royal Academy Schools, where he soon achieved an outstanding success, winning the gold medal for architecture in 1859 when he was just twenty years old.

In the meantime George had formed a friendship with Thomas Vaughan, a fellow student in the Royal Academy Schools. This led to a partnership being formed in 1861. The young men began by taking a City office. A City practice, however, was not for them, for it soon became evident that George's talents, at any rate, lay in the direction of domestic rather than of civic architecture, with the result that a move was made into more fashionable quarters, in Maddox Street, Regent Street. The partnership was not destined to last long, however, for Vaughan died in 1871, but not before George had met with his first important patron. This was Sir Henry Peek, who commissioned him to build at Rousdon, in Devonshire, the first of a long series of great country houses, which were to make their designer's name almost, if not quite, as well known as that of his contemporary, Richard Norman Shaw [q.v.].

Successful as the work at Rousdon undoubtedly was, it was not until George had thrown in his lot with his second partner, Harold Peto, that his career became really assured. Peto was the son of a well-known building contractor, Sir Samuel Morton Peto [q.v.], whose activities were of the greatest assistance to the pair. Apart from this advantage, however, Harold Peto was a great acquisition to the partnership, for he was a man of considerable culture, which he combined with business acumen, admirable taste, and a love of society. George, on the other hand, was of a retiring disposition, preferring to remain in the quiet of his room in Maddox Street, where he designed the work for which his partner had obtained commissions in the world outside. It was an ideal combination, and it succeeded brilliantly. Commissions began to pour into the office, nearly always of the same type—elaborate domestic architecture where cost was a negligible consideration. The clientele for these mansions was drawn from the most highly placed and the richest in the land. Young men scrambled to get into the office of 'George & Peto', which soon began to be known all over the kingdom as a fashionable training-ground. It must have been a good one, for many of those who passed through it, either as articled pupils or assistants, lived to distinguish themselves. Sir Edwin Lutyens, Sir Herbert Baker, Sir E. Guy Dawber, Arnold Mitchell, J. J. Joass all at one time or another worked under 'E. G.', as George was invariably known in his office.

Shortly after the formation of his partnership with Peto, George, who was certainly one of the most brilliant and rapid draughtsmen of his day, can be said to have 'discovered' the Netherlands for the nineteenth century, in just the same way and for the same purpose as Robert Adam [q.v.] 'discovered' Dalmatia for the eighteenth century. He brought back from his visits sketch-books packed with details of Flemish and Dutch work of the early renaissance, and these he adapted with the utmost skill for use in London. The results can be seen in a colony of town houses in Harrington and Collingham Gardens, South Kensington, the best-known example, perhaps, being the house which he built for Sir W. S. Gilbert. George soon began to have his imitators, but it is only necessary to glance at their work in order to realize that he stood head and shoulders above them.

While all this activity was going on in the town, George was busily designing one great house after another in the country. The home counties and the West both contain many mansions designed by him, the best-known of which are Motcombe (Dorset), Batsford (Gloucestershire), West Dean (Sussex), Shiplake (Oxfordshire), and North Mimms (Hertfordshire). These houses are not in the manners either of the Dutch or of the Flemish renaissance, which he kept for his urban architecture, but are carried out with great splendour of detail in the more elaborate phases of the Tudor and Jacobean styles.

By 1893 Harold Peto had retired and the famous partnership was at an end. George, however, continued to carry on the business. He had no thought of retirement, for he was much too happy in his work. He took as his third and last partner A. B. Yeates, who was working as chief assistant in his office at the time of Peto's retirement. George's position was by then so well assured and his work so much liked that Peto's retirement made no material difference to the new partnership. The influx of commissions for great country houses continued. Crathorne Hall (Yorkshire), Eynsham Hall (Oxfordshire), Ruckley Grange (Shropshire), the partial rebuilding of Welbeck Abbey after the fire in 1902 all belong to the 'George & Yeates' period and were completed by 1906. They were the last of their kind, for soon afterwards the liberal party came into power, and the democratic legislation with which it heralded its advent meant the ruin of this side of George's practice. But other work came to occupy the place of the great country houses. The Royal Exchange Insurance Building, the Royal Academy of Music in Marylebone, Southwark Bridge, and a palace at Shaipur in India are among the more notable commissions of the last years of his life.

In 1920, at the age of eighty-one, George retired. He was knighted in 1911, elected R.A. in 1917, awarded the king's gold medal for architecture in 1896, and was president of the Royal Institute of British Architects 1908–1910. He died 8 December 1922 at his home at Kensington. He was cremated at the crematorium at Golders Green which he had himself designed.

George was not in any sense an intellectual artist, but an intuitive one, keenly sensitive to the pictorial, the scenic side of architecture. Gifted as he was with all the qualities of a brilliant draughtsman and water-colour artist, able to transfer to paper with the utmost sureness and rapidity the first transient idea for a design, he never felt the necessity for looking deeply into any problem set before him. This almost certainly explains his lack of success when he attempted, as he occasionally did, the larger forms of monumental architecture. Although he cannot be said to have been a truly great architect, he was a first-class designer of houses. He always built well and planned well, and he understood the mechanism of life as it was lived in great households. He had no confessed 'credo', but was content to adapt for the usage of his own time the architectural scenery of the past, with illustrations of which he had filled so many sketch-books.

George married in 1865 Mary Allan, daughter of Robert Burn, of Epsom, and had three sons and two daughters.

[*The Times*, 9 December 1922; *Builder*, 18 May and 15 December 1922; *Architect's Journal*, 20 December 1922; *Architect*, 15 December 1922.] DARCY BRADDELL.

GILSON, JULIUS PARNELL (1868–1929), palaeographer and scholar, was born at Worksop, Nottinghamshire, 23 June 1868, the younger son of Henry Robert Gilson, of Worksop, by his wife, Mary Anne, daughter of the Rev. George Quilter, vicar of Canwick, near Lincoln. He was educated at Haileybury and at Trinity College, Cambridge, of which he was a scholar. He was placed in the first class of both parts of the classical tripos (1889 and 1890). After a period of study at Cambridge, Bonn, Hanover, and elsewhere, and a brief trial of teaching at Sherborne School under (the Ven.) F. B. Westcott, he was appointed assistant in the department of manuscripts at the British Museum in 1894, and was promoted assistant keeper (a title afterwards changed to deputy keeper) in 1909, and keeper of the department and Egerton librarian on the retirement of Sir George Frederic Warner in 1911.

Gilson's external life was uneventful; but his intellectual travels were by no means only 'from the blue bed to the brown'. To fine classical and particularly Greek scholarship he added a wide knowledge of the medieval world and thought and he was also a first-rate palaeographer.

The fruits of Gilson's learning make no

great show in catalogues. From 1903 he edited the *Facsimiles of Ancient Manuscripts* published by the New Paleographical Society, of the publications of which he became one of the joint-editors in 1910. In 1905 he edited the *Mozarabic Psalter* for the Henry Bradshaw Society; in 1906 *Gulliver's Travels and other Works* of Swift; in 1910, for the Roxburghe Club, *The Correspondence of Edmund Burke and William Windham*; and in 1916, for the same club, *Lives of Lady Anne Clifford and of her Parents*. In 1907 he contributed to the *Transactions* of the Bibliographical Society an account of 'The Library of Sir Henry Savile of Banke' (*Transactions*, vol. ix, 1908), and in 1920 he wrote the small but admirable *Guide to the Manuscripts of the British Museum* in the 'Helps for Students of History' series. His largest work, the result of a great part of his official life, appeared in 1921 (produced in conjunction with the former keeper of his department, Sir George Warner), *A Catalogue of Western Manuscripts in the Old Royal and King's Collections*. Gilson contributed not only many of the descriptions, but also the important introduction, in which his range and power are well shown. In 1925 he wrote a *Description of the Saxon Manuscript of the Four Gospels in The Library of York Minster* (privately printed); he also began to edit, with Dr. W. W. Greg, the series of *English Literary Autographs*; and before his death had just produced for the Museum trustees, in honour of the Monte Cassino celebrations, a reproduction of *An Exultet Roll* (1929). For several years before his death Gilson had been preparing for a work on manorial history; and in 1933 there was produced, in memory of him, a publication of a thirteenth-century legal formulary for the bailiff of a manor from a manuscript (Add. MS. 41,201) acquired by the Museum during his keepership.

Gilson had a notable gift of silence, but one which could never be mistaken for misanthropy. He probably inherited this quality from his mother, a woman of great ability and force of character. He possessed unbounded patience and charity in putting his great learning at the disposal of the students, whether profound or trivial, who sought it in the Museum; and it is in fact in the writings of others, whether or not acknowledged, as well as in the catalogues of his department, that much of his contribution to knowledge is to be found. He was a skilled Alpine climber.

Gilson married in 1899 Helena Georgina, fourth daughter of Frank Joseph Pearce, of Ledwell House, Oxfordshire: they had no children. He never sat for his portrait, but a good photograph appears in the memorial volume. He died rather suddenly at Weybridge 16 June 1929.

[*The Times*, 17 June 1929; private information.] A. J. K. Esdaile.

GLADSTONE, HERBERT JOHN, Viscount Gladstone (1854–1930), statesman, the youngest of four sons in the family of eight children of William Ewart Gladstone [q.v.], prime minister, by his wife, Catherine, elder daughter of Sir Stephen Glynne, eighth baronet, of Hawarden, Cheshire, was born 7 January 1854 at 12 Downing Street (now known as No. 11), which his father then occupied as chancellor of the Exchequer. He went in 1866 to Miss Evans's house at Eton, where also were his brothers and his cousins, sons of the fourth Baron Lyttelton [q.v.]. At Eton he was popular, high-spirited, and a fair football player, but did not greatly distinguish himself. Proceeding in 1872 to University College, Oxford, he obtained a third class in classical moderations in 1874, and a first class in modern history in 1876, and from 1877 to 1880 was history lecturer at Keble College under Edward Stuart Talbot, the first warden.

Herbert Gladstone began his political career in April 1880, when he unsuccessfully contested, as a liberal, the strongly conservative county constituency of Middlesex. In May he was elected for Leeds, a seat which was vacant because his father, having been elected there as well as for Midlothian, chose to represent the latter constituency. Herbert Gladstone sat for Leeds until 1885, and thereafter for West Leeds, a constituency formed at the redistribution of seats in that year, until he became a peer in 1910. He acted as one of his father's private secretaries until 1881, when he was appointed a liberal whip and a junior lord of the Treasury. In that year he paid his first visit to Ireland, which was then in a highly disturbed condition. It was the year of Mr. Gladstone's second Land Act, to be followed in 1882 by the Crimes Act. In December 1885 Herbert Gladstone came in for scarcely deserved blame when a journalist made use of a conversation, which he had intended to be confidential, about his father's intention of supporting Home Rule. Mr. Gladstone's mind was, in fact, made up, but he believed that Lord Salisbury's government, with the Earl of Carnarvon [q.v.] as lord-lieutenant in Dublin, was about to produce a scheme of limited self-government; and he proposed to make no pronouncement at the moment of his own intentions. He vigorously denied that such intentions were attributed to him with any authority. This incident of the 'Hawarden kite', as it was called, gave Herbert Gladstone a lesson in the need for discretion in high politics. In his father's governments of 1886 and 1892 respectively he was financial secretary at the War Office and under-secretary at the Home Office. This early connexion with the Home Office, then under Mr. Asquith, foreshadowed some of his most important work when he himself was home secretary. He became a privy councillor in 1894 and first commissioner of works in Lord Rosebery's government, 1894–1895. The liberal party went into opposition in 1895 and Herbert Gladstone became chief liberal whip in 1899. It is high testimony to his tact that there was no parliamentary rupture in the party during the South African War, when some liberals were 'imperialists' and others were called 'pro-Boers'. He himself was strongly attached to Sir Henry Campbell-Bannerman [q.v.], who deplored the war; but he preserved a complete neutrality within the party. The liberals had full confidence in him and allowed him the chief authority in making the party arrangements for the general election of 1906, when their representation rose to 377 members; with the support of the Irish nationalists and the labour party they came into power stronger than they had been since 1832.

In the government of Sir Henry Campbell-Bannerman Herbert Gladstone was appointed secretary of state for home affairs and held office for four years. The liberals in opposition had promised large measures of domestic reform, and he carried through parliament twenty-two bills of varied importance. These were not, on the whole, conceived in the spirit of 'Gladstonian' liberalism, which had promoted personal freedom together with economy and non-interference on the part of the state. They showed a growing tendency towards bureaucracy, which is inevitable when the details of legislation are largely influenced by departmental officials, and they marked the approximation of liberal aims to those of the labour party and the socialists. Herbert Gladstone was certainly active in the preparation of these measures and very successful in piloting them through the House of Commons. His earliest Acts of major importance were the Workmen's Compensation Act (1906), the Eight Hours Act (Coal Mines Regulation Act, 1908), and the Trade Boards Act (1909). The Court of Criminal Appeal was established in 1907 and in criminal legislation he was responsible for the Probation of Offenders Act (1907), the Prevention of Crime Act (1908), and the Children Act (1908); these instituted the Borstal system and the children's courts. Gladstone was deeply interested in the problem of young offenders, and subsequent legislation affecting this question may fairly be described as the extension of experiments first tried by him and his advisers, such as Sir Evelyn Ruggles-Brise. He was a conscientious administrator of justice throughout his term of office, which was made especially uneasy by the advocates of female suffrage, who indulged in rioting, assault, and arson, and often in schemes devised particularly to embarrass the Home Office and the police. The home secretary gave unflinching support to the police and vindicated the law without giving cause for accusations of vindictiveness against political offenders.

In December 1909 Gladstone was appointed to be the first governor-general and high commissioner of the Union of South Africa. He had been a warm supporter of the policy of granting responsible government to South Africa as soon as possible, and his name was certain to commend him to those of the Dutch population who remembered the first Boer War. In the following March he was created G.C.M.G. and raised to the peerage as Viscount Gladstone, of the county of Lanark. He arrived in Capetown in May 1910 accompanied by Lady Gladstone. She was Dorothy Mary, youngest daughter of Sir Richard Horner Paget, first baronet, of Cranmore Hall, Somerset, and they had been married in 1901. Since the passing of the South Africa Act in 1909 the South African colonies had settled down, and commercial prosperity was already returning. The most influential men in South Africa at the moment were Sir Leander Starr Jameson [q.v.], John Xavier Merriman [q.v.], premier of Cape Colony, General Louis Botha [q.v.], Generals Smuts and Hertzog, ex-President Steyn, and the chief justice, Lord de Villiers [q.v.]. From all these the new governor-general sought advice. Gladstone's first important decision was to call upon General Botha to form a constitutional government for the Union; and in the following November he received the Duke of Connaught, who came, on behalf of King George V, to open the first parliament of the Union. Gladstone worked in full harmony with General Botha. He was anxious that the first prime minister should not seem too dependent on the governor-general, and he wisely left Botha to fill the public eye as much as possible; but he did not fail in his duties on behalf of the Imperial government, nor as a ready mediator between British and Dutch. He also visited the native protectorates, for which, as high commissioner, he was directly responsible. For two years all went smoothly. In 1912 Botha resigned owing to differences in the cabinet with General Hertzog, the minister of justice. Lord Gladstone asked Botha to form a new government. He therefore reconstituted the ministry, excluding Hertzog. This was the only serious political crisis during Gladstone's term of office; but in 1913 industrial trouble spread over the Rand, threatening such violent disturbance that the governor-general declared martial law in and around Johannesburg, and enforced it until order was restored. His term came to an end in July 1914, and he left South Africa amid the regrets alike of British and Dutch, whose confidence he had fully won. He received the G.C.B. in recognition of his successful work.

Gladstone arrived in England at the outbreak of the European War. He became treasurer of the War Refugees Committee, and with Lady Gladstone devoted himself to the charge of Belgian refugees in this country. For this service he received the G.B.E. (1917) and was made a grand officer of the crown of Belgium and a knight of grace of the order of St. John of Jerusalem.

This was Gladstone's last public work of importance. He had been out of party politics since 1909, and the time was not congenial to him to re-enter them. He held that the old liberal party had been betrayed by its new leaders, and throttled within the coalition government formed in 1916. He was still, as always, a hearty controversialist. He attacked the government at intervals, particularly over its policy in the Near East, which he considered faithless to his father's principles of safeguarding the Christian minorities. He visited Bulgaria in 1924 and was given a reception which showed a very lively remembrance of his father's championship of that nation. With the approval of Mr. Asquith he worked at the liberal headquarters through 1922 and 1923 to reorganize the liberal party, and later he supported Lord Grey of Falloden in the Liberal Council formed in December 1926. He also took up work for the League of Nations Union.

But Gladstone had no more taste for politics, and infinitely preferred to cultivate his garden at Dane End, a property of his wife's family near Ware, in Hertfordshire. He had written in 1918 a memoir of his nephew, W. G. C. Gladstone (the only son of his eldest brother William Henry Gladstone), who had been killed in the War. He was now anxious to write a book in honour of his father, both as a man and as a statesman. In 1928 he published a volume, *After Thirty Years*, which contains delightful pictures of the home life of the Gladstones. The political chapters vindicate his father's Eastern policy. Those devoted to Irish politics are thrown somewhat out of balance by his strong criticism of the editing of the second series (vol. iii, published in 1928) of *The Letters of Queen Victoria*. He suspected that letters could have been included, in fairness to his father, which would have shown that Lord Salisbury's government at one time contemplated a measure of Home Rule for Ireland. There was a violent correspondence in *The Times* with the editor of the *Letters*, Mr. G. E. Buckle, whose denials Lord Gladstone had to accept. The same pious pugnacity on behalf of his father's reputation led him and his surviving brother in 1928 to bring into the Law Courts a writer who had impugned Mr. Gladstone's moral character. They won the case handsomely.

Lord Gladstone was a man of middle height and sturdy build, who enjoyed excellent health and spirits throughout his life. He played golf for some years, and shot and fished all his life. He appreciated music highly and was fond of glee-singing. He died at Dane End 6 March 1930. Lady Gladstone survived him without issue, and the peerage became extinct.

At Hawarden Castle there are three portraits of Lord Gladstone: a water-colour portrait of him as a child by Ann Mary Severn, an oil-painting of him as a young man by J. R. Herbert, and a posthumous portrait by C. H. Thompson, based on a water-colour, by Arthur Garratt, at Dane End. A portrait by P. Tennyson Cole is the property of the government of the Union of South Africa.

[Sir C. E. Mallet, *Herbert Gladstone. A Memoir*, 1932; *The Times*, 7 March 1930; personal knowledge.] W. V. Cooper.

GLAISHER, JAMES WHITBREAD LEE (1848–1928), mathematician, astronomer, and collector, was born at Lewisham, Kent, 5 November 1848, the elder son of James Glaisher [q.v.], astronomer and meteorologist. He was sent to St. Paul's School, London, in 1858 and remained there for nine years, leaving it as Campden exhibitioner. In 1867 he went into residence at Trinity College, Cambridge, and was elected a scholar in the following year. In 1871 he graduated as second wrangler, John Hopkinson [q.v.], also of Trinity, being senior wrangler. He was elected a fellow of the college in the October of that year; and he was at once appointed a lecturer and assistant tutor. He remained in residence at Trinity for the rest of his life, being the senior on the roll of fellows at the time of his death. His lecturership continued for thirty years (1871–1901), a special extension having been made by the college council; and he was a tutor of the college from 1883 to 1893, for the then customary period of tenure. He proceeded to the newly established Cambridge degree of Sc.D. in 1887, and he ultimately became the senior doctor in the faculty. He received the honorary degree of Sc.D. from Trinity College, Dublin (1892), and from the Victoria University of Manchester (1902), and was an honorary fellow of the Royal Society of Edinburgh as also of the Manchester Literary and Philosophical Society; he was also a foreign member of the National Academy of Sciences of Washington.

Glaisher never held any permanent appointment outside Cambridge. He refused the official invitation to become astronomer royal in 1881 on the retirement of Sir George Airy, an invitation which was a recognition of his eminence as a mathematical astronomer. He had joined the Royal Astronomical Society in 1871, became a member of the council in 1874, and was re-elected continuously for the rest of his life; and for two periods (1886–1888, 1901–1903) he was president. His personal charm was such that for thirty-three years he was president of the Royal Astronomical Society club.

In 1875, at the early age of twenty-seven, Glaisher was elected a fellow of the Royal Society. His earliest original paper, dealing with numerical tables of some non-evaluable integrals, was written while he was still an undergraduate and was communicated to the Society in 1870 by Arthur Cayley [q.v.]. He served on the council of the Society for three periods (1883–1884, 1890–1892, 1917–1919), during the last of which he was vice-president; and he was awarded the Sylvester medal in 1913.

Throughout his scientific life Glaisher was closely connected with the work of the London Mathematical Society. Joining that body in 1872, he became a member of the council in the same year; and he was re-elected every year until his retirement in 1906, being president in 1884–1886. He was awarded the De Morgan medal in 1908. His presidential address is a valuable monograph on the history of the Mathematical Tripos down to the date of delivery (1886); and some of his remarks are a virtual anticipation of the changes adopted in 1909, when the order of merit and the title of senior wrangler were abolished. An address which he gave when the Society celebrated a belated jubilee in 1925 is an excellent record of the work of the Society.

For a number of years Glaisher, like his father before him, had a considerable share in the work of the British Association. He was secretary of Section A for a number of years, and was president of the section at the Leeds meeting in 1890, his address being a plea for the fuller recognition of pure mathematics, at a time when it still was necessary to plead in England for that cause. He was a member of many of the committees of the Association dealing with numerical tables and with special reports upon the progress of branches of mathematical science. He was also, as a matter of course, a member of the Cambridge Philosophical Society, frequently contributing papers and serving as president in 1882–1884.

The main part of Glaisher's published work consists of his papers on mathematics and astronomy. He wrote a few isolated papers on ceramics; and he contributed an appendix on Wrotham ware to B. Rackham and H. Read's *English Pottery* (1924). But most of his writings relate to pure mathematics or to such astronomical topics as the use of the method of least squares. The tale of his papers amounts to nearly four hundred. Among them mention should be made of his contributions to definite integrals, differential equations, elliptic functions and their developments, and especially to the theory of numbers particularly in connexion with elliptic functions. He devoted much attention to the calculation of mathematical tables such as those of the Theta-functions; and from the beginning to the end of all his work he maintained a productive interest in the history of mathematics. His papers appeared in the transactions of learned societies and in various mathematical journals; and for many of the later years of his life he was the pecuniary mainstay of the *Messenger of Mathematics* and the *Quarterly Journal of Pure and Applied Mathematics*, both of which ceased to exist at Cambridge after his death.

About the middle of his life Glaisher took up a hobby which developed into the dominant pursuit of his remaining years —the study of pottery. While still actively engaged in maintaining his scientific interests he began collecting. At first it was Delft ware; then followed kindred wares, of the pre-industrial period, made in London and Bristol during the seventeenth and eighteenth centuries. Then he turned to slip-ware, as made over a wide range in England. Afterwards he passed to the collection of English porcelain, specializing in early productions from Chelsea, Bow, and Derby. Later his not infrequent continental holidays were devoted to the search for additions to his ever-growing collections, which had even begun to include productions of nearer Asia. By systematic devotion and untiring diligence he became one of the leading collectors of his day. As his possessions grew, he kept a faithful record of their story; his elaborate catalogue, in forty manuscript volumes, is a valuable addition to the literature of the subject. The whole of his collection (together with a substantial cash legacy) he bequeathed to the Fitzwilliam Museum, Cambridge, where it is a visible monument to his memory.

Beyond his teaching, research, administration of several learned societies, and his rare zest in collecting pottery, Glaisher's personal pursuits were varied. Very tall, and spare in frame to the end, he was fond of walking. He was elected president of the Cambridge University Bicycle Club while the bicycle was still in its 'penny farthing' days. He paid many visits to the United States and travelled much in Europe. Even in his early seventies he maintained the vitality and the geniality of youth; and it was only in the last years of his life that his health gave way. He died in his college rooms 7 December 1928 and is buried at Cambridge. He never married.

Glaisher attained eminence in three branches of the activities of human thought. In the prime of his life he was one of the outstanding English pure mathematicians. His astronomical devotion was lifelong; and his work was of acknowledged significance in the domain of mathematical astronomy. He also became a recognized authority on pottery; the collection which he made remains of permanent value in the study of ceramics.

A pencil drawing of Glaisher, made by Francis Dodd in 1927, is at Trinity College, Cambridge.

[Sir J. J. Thomson in *The Cambridge Review*, vol. l, 1929; G. H. Hardy, 'Dr. Glaisher and the *Messenger of Mathematics*', *Messenger of Mathematics*, vol. lviii, 1929; H. H. Turner in *Monthly Notices of the Royal Astronomical Society*, vol. lxxxix, 1929; A. R. Forsyth in *Proceedings* of the Royal Society, vol. cxxvi, A, 1930, and in *Journal* of the London Mathematical Society, vol. iv, 1929, including a note by Bernard Rackham; Bernard Rackham, *The Glaisher Bequest*, a Fitzwilliam Museum pamphlet, 1931; personal knowledge.]

A. R. Forsyth.

GLAZEBROOK, MICHAEL GEORGE (1853–1926), schoolmaster, the eldest of the five children of Michael George Glazebrook, merchant, a member of an old Lancashire family, by his wife, Margaret Elizabeth, daughter of Alfred Tapson, was born in London 4 August 1853. He was educated at Brentford grammar school, Blackheath proprietary school, and Dulwich College, where he became head of the school, and in 1872 entered Balliol College, Oxford, as a mathematical scholar. He obtained first classes in mathematical and classical moderations in 1873 and 1874 respectively, a second class in the final mathematical school (1876), and a first class in *literae humaniores* (1877). He represented Oxford against Cambridge in the hundred yards and high jump: at the latter in 1875 he was amateur champion. At Balliol he was a close friend of Arnold Toynbee [q.v.], of whose social work he was afterwards a strong supporter.

After a year of adventurous travel in Mexico and elsewhere Glazebrook in 1878 accepted an invitation from Dr. H. M. Butler to go to Harrow as an assistant master. In 1888 he was appointed high master of Manchester grammar school. There he set himself the task of planting the corporate activities of public boarding schools in soil which was hardly ready for them. Perhaps Glazebrook was rather too conscious of being a disciple of Jowett and Butler, but the later developments of this great school owe much to his energy and organizing ability. In 1891 he was appointed headmaster of Clifton College. Under (Bishop) John Percival [q.v.] and (Canon) J. M. Wilson Clifton had gone from strength to strength, but the original impetus was beginning to die down. The masters of the heroic age of Percival were leaving or else passing their prime. Without waiting to get public opinion on his side, Glazebrook began his work of reorganization and development. His stern manner and almost brutal candour prevented his ever being popular. But although there was a considerable decline in numbers, there was none in efficiency. He strengthened the staff where it had before been weak, especially in modern languages and music. In music he made Clifton a pioneer school by appointing A. H. Peppin director of music and giving him a free hand. The encouragement which he gave to music was perhaps Glazebrook's most important contribution to English education. He resigned in 1905.

The same year Glazebrook, who had been ordained deacon and priest at Manchester in 1890, was appointed canon of Ely Cathedral, where he became a leader of the 'Modern Churchmen' movement. His passion for sincerity and truth found a congenial task in the interpretation of the Bible and the Christian religion to a scientific age. Already he had written a school edition of the Old Testament—*Lessons from the Old Testament* (1890, revised edition 1922)—which was widely used. It enabled many schoolmasters to teach the Old Testament with a new sincerity. He himself regarded his Warburton lectures at Lincoln's Inn (1907–1911) as most fully representing his mature views. They were collected under the title *The End of the Law* (1911). His *Faith of a Modern Churchman* (1918), although it brought him into conflict with his diocesan bishop, Frederic Henry Chase [q.v.], made clear to the ordinary layman the results of other men's researches in biblical scholarship. In 1914 Glazebrook became chairman of the Churchmen's Union. He took an active part in the annual conferences of 'Modern Churchmen', where his firmness and moderation made him an admirable chairman. He was elected chairman of the council of Ripon Hall when it opened at Oxford in 1919. In his later days Glazebrook found it much easier to show the humanity and sympathy which some had always discerned behind his rather frigid public manner. He was especially loved by and devoted to children.

Glazebrook married in 1880 Ethel, fourth daughter of the chemist Sir Benjamin Collins Brodie, second baronet [q.v.], and elder sister of the wife of his Balliol contemporary, Sir Thomas Herbert Warren [q.v.]. They had no children. She shared his life and his work, and it was her fatal illness that brought on his own death, which took place at Ely 1 May 1926, fifteen days before hers. He was buried at Ely.

A memorial to Glazebrook and his wife is in Ely Cathedral, and there are portraits of him by his brother, H. de T. Glazebrook, at Dulwich College, and by William Strang at Clifton College.

[*The Times*, 3 May 1926; *The Cliftonian*, June and July 1926; private information.]

N. Whatley.

GLEICHEN, LADY FEODORA GEORGINA MAUD (1861–1922), sculptor, was born in London 20 December 1861, the eldest daughter of Admiral Prince Victor of Hohenlohe-Langenburg [q.v.], the son of Prince Ernest of Hohenlohe-Langenburg and Queen Victoria's half-sister Feodora (*née* Princess of Leiningen), by his wife, Laura Williamina, youngest daughter of Admiral of the Fleet Sir George Francis Seymour [q.v.] and sister of Francis George Hugh Seymour, fifth Marquess of Hertford. The daughter of a man who, in addition to his naval activities, had practised sculpture with success, Lady Feodora (who until 1917 was known as H.S.H. Countess Feodora Gleichen, from the second title in the family, assumed by her father on his marriage in 1861 and borne by him until 1885) studied art under Professor Alphonse Legros [q.v.], the celebrated teacher at the Slade School of Art, University College, London, remaining under his tuition for four years. A serious and industrious worker, Lady Feodora was from 1892 onwards a regular exhibitor at the Royal Academy, and produced a large number of sculptures which, while not disclosing any great originality, yet are very decidedly above the amateur standard. Examples of them may be found all over the world. Among works on a monumental scale may be instanced the life-size group of Queen Victoria surrounded by children for the Children's Hospital in Montreal (1895); a fountain in the garden of the

Comtesse de Béarn, Paris (1901); the external decoration of the Foundling Hospital at Cairo (1904); a panel for the exterior of the National Art Gallery at Sydney (1907); the Edward VII memorial at Windsor (1912); the Florence Nightingale memorial at Derby (1914); the Kitchener memorial in Khartoum Cathedral (1920), and the memorial to the fallen of the 37th (British) Division (which had been commanded by Lady Feodora's brother, Lord Edward Gleichen) at Monchy-le-Preux in France, unveiled in October 1921. In London her only work of this character to be seen in public is the Diana fountain in Rotten Row, Hyde Park, surmounted by a bronze figure of the nude goddess discharging an arrow; this was executed for Sir Walter Palmer and set up at Frognal, Ascot, in 1899, being presented to Hyde Park by Lady Palmer in 1906. Lady Feodora also produced a number of portrait busts, including two of Queen Victoria; among her last works was a head of King Feisal of Iraq. She, moreover, executed some work in combined and complicated techniques, such as bronze with enamel and ivory (a looking-glass exhibited at the Royal Academy in 1897) and mosaic with silver (a shrine with the Madonna and Child exhibited at the Academy in 1898). At the Paris Exhibition in 1900 Lady Feodora gained a bronze medal for her sculpture; and shortly before her death the French government, in recognition of her work at Monchy, conferred upon her the order of the legion of honour. She died 22 February 1922 in the suite of rooms in Engine Court, St. James's Palace, which had been placed at the disposal of her father and mother by Queen Victoria. She never married. She was made a posthumous member of the Royal Society of British Sculptors, being the first woman to receive that honour.

[*The Times*, 23 February 1922; *Life and Work of Feodora Gleichen*, privately printed, 1934; Algernon Graves, *The Royal Academy of Arts, a complete dictionary of contributors and their work*, vol. iii, 1905; subsequent Royal Academy Exhibition Catalogues.]

T. Borenius.

GODLEE, Sir RICKMAN JOHN, baronet (1849–1925), surgeon, was born 15 April 1849 at 5 Queen Square, London, the second son of Rickman Godlee, barrister-at-law, by his wife, Mary, eldest daughter of Joseph Jackson Lister, F.R.S., wine merchant and microscopist [q.v.], and sister of Joseph (afterwards Lord) Lister [q.v.]. The Godlees and the Listers belonged to the Society of Friends, a circumstance which exerted a powerful influence on Rickman John Godlee. After education at Grove House School, Tottenham, where he took up field botany and ornithology, he entered University College, London, in 1866, and in the next year graduated B.A. of the university of London. Entering the faculty of medical sciences, he soon attracted attention as a skilled dissector, and, like his uncle, Lord Lister, and his cousin and future colleague, Marcus Beck, was house surgeon to (Sir) John Eric Erichsen [q.v.] at University College Hospital. He took the degrees of M.B. (1872) and M.S. (1873), receiving a gold medal in surgery at each examination, and spent part of a year from the autumn of 1872 in Edinburgh, living with his uncle, who was then professor of clinical surgery at the university. The impressions thus gained of the antiseptic method he published in the *Lancet* (1873).

Godlee returned to University College Hospital as surgical registrar in 1873, and in the following year made drawings of 'curious minute bodies arranged in rows or chains' in the contents of an abscess connected with bone; these bacteria (streptococci) were not further recognized until 1881. Marcus Beck and H. G. Howse of Guy's Hospital were in the 'seventies the first London surgeons to carry out properly Lister's technique, and Godlee was a keen follower of their methods in the face of the by no means passive opposition of the senior surgeons. In 1876 he was appointed assistant surgeon to Charing Cross Hospital and lecturer on anatomy in the medical school, a post at that time practically always held by a surgeon. A year later, however, Godlee was elected assistant surgeon at his old hospital; this was a new post which carried with it a demonstratorship in the anatomical department of University College. After having been elected F.R.C.S. in 1876 he had begun working at an *Atlas of Human Anatomy* with an explanatory text. For this he made drawings, with distinctive colours for vessels and nerves, from more than a hundred dissections, mainly made by his own hand. The title-page states that the book illustrates 'most of the ordinary dissections and many not usually practised by the student'. It was published in 1880, but did not receive the attention which it deserved. Godlee's drawings were presented to the Royal

College of Surgeons. He was much in demand as an illustrator; some of his work adorned Quain's *Anatomy* (10th edition, 1896), two editions of Erichsen's *Surgery*, and his own contribution to *Diseases of the Lungs* (1898, mentioned below).

Although a general surgeon, Godlee was a pioneer in branches which have since become specialized; on 25 November 1884 he performed the first operation for the removal of a tumour from the brain, the accurate 'localization' of which had been rendered possible by recent physiological (experimental) and clinical research including that of two spectators, (Sir) David Ferrier [q.v.] and John Hughlings Jackson [q.v.]. This turning-point in surgery provoked a storm of controversy with the antivivisectionists in *The Times*. In the same year (1884) Godlee was appointed surgeon to the Brompton Hospital for Consumption and Diseases of the Chest: he published lectures on the surgical treatment of a number of chest diseases, and was joint author, with (Sir) James Kingston Fowler, of *Diseases of the Lungs* (1898), a work which stimulated the development of thoracic surgery, then in its infancy. In 1876 Godlee had also joined the staff of the North-Eastern (now the Queen's) Hospital for Children, in Hackney Road. He was appointed full surgeon at University College Hospital in 1885, professor of clinical surgery in 1892, and Holme professor of clinical surgery in 1900. In April 1914, shortly before attaining the age-limit of sixty-five, he resigned his appointments, becoming emeritus professor of clinical surgery. An extremely clear and successful teacher, he was, even in his busiest period, most conscientiously punctual in his hospital visits.

During and after the European War Godlee was extremely active on the Central Medical War Committee and was chairman of the Belgian doctors and pharmacists relief fund. Earlier in his career he had been secretary of three leading medical societies—the Royal Medical and Chirurgical, the Pathological, and the Clinical—being also honorary librarian of the first-named (1895–1907); on the amalgamation of these and other societies into the Royal Society of Medicine, he was librarian (1907–1916) and president (1916–1918). At the Royal College of Surgeons he held many offices, including those of president (1911–1913) and Hunterian orator ('Hunter and Lister', 1913); in November 1913 he delivered an address at the first convocation of the American College of Surgeons at Chicago, presented an illuminated address of greeting from the Royal College of Surgeons of England, and was made an honorary fellow.

A man of wide interests, Godlee was a collector of etchings, a good linguist, a book lover, had an extensive knowledge of old London and of biography, wrote, although he never published, verse, and had an excellent idiomatic style of English. With Sir (William) Watson Cheyne he had assisted Lord Lister throughout his active practice in London, and scientific problems were constantly discussed between them. No one else had so intimate a personal knowledge of Lister, and, in addition, Godlee had seen the results of the old system of surgery in London and so was able to compare them with those of Lister in Edinburgh. In 1917, five years after Lister's death, he brought out the *Life*, which was an immediate success—it reached a third and revised edition in 1924—and is probably, as the importance of the subject fully entitles it to be, the outstanding biography of a medical man in modern times. It gives a graphic account of the state of medicine in the second half of the nineteenth century in Edinburgh, Glasgow, London, and abroad, and of the reactions to the antiseptic system. Godlee took an essential part in bringing out *The Collected Papers of Joseph, Baron Lister* in two volumes (1909), and as acting executor presented to the Royal College of Surgeons, where he assisted in their arrangement, all his uncle's scientific and surgical possessions, including manuscripts and instruments.

Godlee was reserved, high-minded, inwardly humble though outwardly dignified, approachable, and well able to hold his own. He married in 1891 Juliet Mary, eldest daughter of Frederic Seebohm [q.v.], banker and historian, of The Hermitage, Hitchin, but had no children. In London he lived first in Henrietta Street, then at 81, and finally at 19 Wimpole Street. For many years he had owned Coombe End Farm, Whitchurch, near Reading; here he settled down after his retirement from London in 1920, and was happy in the simple pleasures of farming, carpentering, and writing essays about the village, which appeared posthumously as *A Village on the Thames: Whitchurch Yesterday and To-day* (1926). He died at Whitchurch after a few hours' illness 20 April 1925 and was buried there.

Godlee received many honours. He was surgeon to the household of Queen Victoria, and honorary surgeon to King Edward VII and King George V. He was created a baronet in 1912 and K.C.V.O. in 1914, and received the Belgian médaille du Roi Albert in 1919. He was a fellow of University College, London, and held honorary degrees of the universities of Toronto and Dublin. The baronetcy became extinct on his death.

A portrait of Godlee by Alan Beeton was presented to the Royal College of Surgeons by Lady Godlee in 1925.

[V. G. Plarr, *Lives of the Fellows of the Royal College of Surgeons of England*, 2 vols., revised by Sir D'A. Power and others, 1930; *British Medical Journal*, 1925, vol. i, pp. 809–10; private information; personal knowledge.]

H. D. Rolleston.

GODLEY, ALFRED DENIS (1856–1925), classical scholar and man of letters, was born at Ashfield, co. Cavan, 22 January 1856. His father was the Rev. James Godley, rector of Carrigallen, co. Leitrim, brother of John Robert Godley [q.v.], the friend of Gibbon Wakefield. His mother was Eliza Frances, daughter of Peter La Touche, of Bellevue, co. Wicklow. Alfred Godley was the eldest surviving son. After a year at a well-known preparatory school, Mr. Bassett's, in Dublin, he went, with a scholarship, to Harrow, where his powers were noted and encouraged by Dr. Montagu Butler, then headmaster. At sixteen Godley won a classical exhibition, and at seventeen a scholarship, both at Balliol College, Oxford; but he did not go into residence until the following year (1874). He obtained a first class in classical moderations in 1875 and a second class in *literae humaniores* in 1878. His honours at the university included the Gaisford prize for Greek verse, the Chancellor's Latin verse and Latin essay prizes, and the Craven scholarship. In 1879 he accepted the post of assistant classical master at Bradfield College. Four years later (1883), Godley returned to Oxford as a tutor and fellow of Magdalen College, a post which he occupied till his retirement in 1912. In 1910 he was elected public orator of the university, and held the office till his death. The honorary degree of doctor of letters was conferred on him in 1919; he had already received a similar degree from Princeton University when he visited the United States in 1913. He was elected an honorary fellow of Magdalen in 1912. He married in 1894 Amy, daughter of Charles Hope Cay, fellow of Gonville and Caius College, Cambridge. They had no children. In the spring of 1925 Godley went on a tour in the Levant, in the course of which he contracted a malignant fever which, after some weeks, proved fatal. He died at Oxford on 27 June of that year.

Godley's reputation as a writer of light humorous or satiric verse and prose dates from his association with the *Oxford Magazine*. He became a contributor in 1883, and editor in 1890. His first published collection of poems was *Verses to Order*, some of them reprinted from the *Oxford Magazine*, in 1892. Later publications were *Lyra Frivola* (1899), *Second Strings* (1902), a second (enlarged) edition of *Verses to Order*, 1904, and *The Casual Ward* (1912). Several pieces also appeared in *Echoes from the Oxford Magazine* (1890), *More Echoes* (1896), in the posthumous *Reliquiae* (1926), and in *Fifty Poems* (1927). The unfailing ease, ingenuity, and point of Godley's writings have caused his verse to be considered, by the most competent critics, not inferior to that of C. S. Calverley; his political ballad *The Arrest* has become a classic of the unionist party in Ireland. His work as a commentator on and translator of Herodotus, Tacitus, and Horace, and as joint-editor of the *Classical Review* from 1910 to 1920, made him prominent among contemporary classical scholars in Oxford; while the nine Creweian orations delivered by him as public orator have been described as 'perhaps his best title to fame as an almost perfect writer of elegant Latin'. He was also the author of *Socrates, and Athenian Society in his Age* (1896), *Aspects of Modern Oxford* (1894), and *Oxford in the Eighteenth Century* (1908). In 1909 he published an edition of selected poems of Praed and in 1910 an edition of the poetical works of Thomas Moore.

Godley's marked personality, conversational gifts, and high character made him, notwithstanding his shyness, a leading figure in the life of the university and of the town; he was an alderman, and had he lived another year, would have been mayor of Oxford. Conservative by nature, as well as in politics, he staunchly advocated such losing causes as the compulsory study of Greek at Oxford and the exclusion of women students; but to the tenacity of the Northern Irish race he joined a philosophic temperament which preserved him from bitterness, even where he felt most strongly. He was an ardent supporter of the Volunteer movement, and the patriotism which was one of his deepest feelings found practical expression in his very efficient training and organization of a volunteer force during the European War. Although generally indifferent to games, he was a lover of active life, and a distinguished member of the Alpine Club; he was also joint-founder of an Oxford and Cambridge dining club.

[C. R. L. Fletcher, *Memoir* included in *Reliquiae A. D. Godley*, 1926; personal knowledge.] E. C. Godley.

GODWIN-AUSTEN, HENRY HAVERSHAM (1834–1923), explorer and geologist, was born at Teignmouth 6 July 1834, the eldest son of Robert Alfred Cloyne Godwin-Austen [q.v.], the geologist, of Shalford House, near Guildford, Surrey, by his wife, Maria, only daughter of Major-General Sir Henry Thomas Godwin [q.v.]. He entered in 1848 the Royal Military College, Sandhurst, where he was a contemporary and friend of Frederick Sleigh Roberts (afterwards Earl Roberts of Kandahar). At Sandhurst he learnt the art of topographical pen-drawing from Captain Petley, a master of the old French pictorial school. In December 1851 he obtained his commission in the old 24th Foot, afterwards the South Wales Borderers, and as early as 1852 served in the second Burmese War as aide-de-camp to his grandfather, General Godwin, who was in command of the British force. It was in Burma that he first surveyed unknown ground by mapping the creeks and navigable waterways of the Irrawaddy delta. From Burma he was transferred to the Peshawar division as aide-de-camp to Major-General Sir Thomas Reed [q.v.].

Towards the end of 1856, on the application of Sir Andrew Scott Waugh [q.v.], the surveyor-general of India, Godwin-Austen was attached to the Great Trigonometrical Survey of India in order to assist with the first survey of Kashmir under Colonel Thomas George Montgomerie [q.v.], and it was on Manganwar in Kashmir that the latter first pointed out the great Karakoram summits with which Godwin-Austen's name was afterwards associated. Throughout the Indian Mutiny the surveyors continued their explorations, with some disturbance from marauding bands of rebels, but without serious interruption. After working in the Kazi Nag and Pir Panjal ranges, Godwin-Austen surveyed, during 1858 and 1859, the Marau-Warwan valley and Northern Jammu. In 1860 he was appointed to a permanent post as topographical assistant in the Trigonometrical Survey and mapped the Shigar and lower Saltoro valleys of Baltistan. The following year he crossed the Skoro La, beyond Skardu and Shigar, and surveyed the great Karakoram glaciers, the Baltoro (36 miles), the Punmah (28 miles), the Biafo (37 miles), and the Hispar (38 miles), together with the giant mountains that enclose them. He was the discoverer of this great glacier system, the greatest outside Polar and sub-Polar regions. During the surveys of such remote districts, officers were instructed not to waste time over the details of uninhabited tracts over 16,000 feet. Godwin-Austen refused to be bound by these instructions; slight and hardy, with little to carry, he was ideally built for mountaineering; and he possessed intense enthusiasm. At a time when mountaineering technique had not been developed he set no altitude limit to his climbs, and he made several ascents above 20,000 feet. His surveys of those regions are beautiful examples of the surveyor's art of his day; subsequent travellers have remarked on the accuracy with which they reveal the structure and topography of the ranges. In 1862 he explored the upper Changchenmo and mapped the northern border of the Pangong district on the western edge of the Tibetan plateau, while towards the end of the season he was surveying the upper valleys of the Zaskar ranges, including the numerous glaciers of the Sutlej-Zaskar watershed. The following year he completed the survey of the Pangong lake and district as far as the Rudok Tibetans permitted. His journal, published as a special paper (*Notes on the Pangong Lake District of Ladakh . . .*) by the government of India in 1864, gives an account of the morphology of the region, which is most valuable to scientists to-day.

Late in 1863 Godwin-Austen was appointed to serve on the political mission of (Sir) Ashley Eden [q.v.] to Bhutan, in the Eastern Himalaya. His topographical surveys carried out in the following year between Sikkim and Punakha, and his reconnaissance surveys made later with the Bhutan field force, remained the only maps of this country for over thirty years. He next commanded the party engaged in the survey of the Garo, Khasi, and Jaintia hills, and of the Naugong and Kachar districts of Assam. In 1873–1874 he was exploring the Naga hills, previously unvisited by Europeans, and in 1875 accompanied the first Dafla expedition, surveying 1,700 square miles of previously unexplored country in the Eastern Himalaya. This work on the northern frontier of

Assam was of great geographical importance and threw much light on, though it did not finally solve, the vexed question of the identity of the Assam Brahmaputra with the Tibetan Tsangpo, while the course of the Subansiri river was placed on the map.

In the intervals between this active pioneer exploration Godwin-Austen was engaged on geological investigations of considerable importance, especially in the outer Himalaya. He was one of the first to search the Siwalik range of Himalayan foothills for fossil evidence of their formation, and there was no greater authority in his day on the structure of the Karakoram and other ranges beyond the Great Himalayan axis. Godwin-Austen was not the discoverer of K², the highest of the Karakoram summits and the second highest mountain on the earth (28,250 ft.). This peak was first observed by Montgomerie in 1856 from Haramukh in Kashmir; the designations K¹, K², K³, &c., were given to peaks in the direction of the Karakoram observed by him by theodolite from hills in Kashmir. But Godwin-Austen was the first to discover the setting of the great peak and the first to explore and survey its precipitous sides and the glaciers at its base; he was also the first to investigate the geological structure of this region. Various names have been proposed for the peak: *Dapsang*, *Chiring*, *Chogo Ri*, *Lanfafahad*; none are known to the natives, and objection has been raised to all of them. In 1888 General J. T. Walker, a former surveyor-general of India, proposed that the name *Godwin-Austen* should be given to the peak to commemorate the exploration of the region, but the government and survey of India did not adopt the suggestion, on the general principle that personal names are unsuitable for Himalayan summits. The official designation therefore remains K², now corrupted by the local people to *Kechu* or *Cheku*, although Godwin-Austen's name is to be found on some unofficial maps.

Fever contracted on survey work in the Eastern Himalaya undermined Godwin-Austen's health, and caused his premature retirement from the service in June 1877; but in England he rapidly recovered, and set himself to study natural science in all its branches; in several of these he obtained distinction. He was elected F.R.S. in 1880 for his contributions to geography and geology, became president of section E (geography) of the British Association in 1883, of the Malacological Society from 1897 to 1899, and of the Conchological Society in 1908–1909, and received the founder's gold medal of the Royal Geographical Society in 1910. He retained a lasting interest in the survey of India and kept up a constant correspondence with young officers serving in the Himalaya, interesting them in the natural history of their surroundings, and obtaining from them specimens, which he dissected, examined under the microscope, sketched, and described when nearly ninety years of age. He published in scientific journals more than 130 papers on his geographical, geological, and ethnographical studies, besides important works on the mollusca and fauna of India (*The Land and Fresh-Water Mollusca of India*, 1882–1914; *The Fauna of British India*, vol. i of *Mollusca*, 1908).

Godwin-Austen married twice: first, in 1861 Pauline Georgiana (died 1871), daughter of Lieutenant-Colonel Arthur Wellesley Chichele Plowden, and had one son; secondly, in 1881 Jessie (died 1913), daughter of John Harding Robinson, examiner in the House of Lords. Godwin-Austen died at Nore, Godalming, 2 December 1923.

[*The Times*, 5 December 1923; *General Reports* and *Synoptical Volume VII* of the Survey of India; Sir Clements Markham, *A Memoir of the Indian Surveys*, 2nd ed., 1878; *Transactions* of the Royal Geographical Society 1861, 1864; *Geographical Journal*, February 1924; private information; personal knowledge.]

K. Mason.

GOLDIE, Sir GEORGE DASHWOOD TAUBMAN (1846–1925), founder of Nigeria, was born at The Nunnery, Isle of Man, 20 May 1846, the fourth and youngest son of Lieutenant-Colonel John Taubman Goldie-Taubman, of the Scots Guards, and speaker of the House of Keys, by his second wife, Caroline, daughter of John Eykin Hovenden, of Hemingford, Cambridgeshire. Goldie's father was of mixed Scottish and Manx descent, the paternal line being originally named Goldie (of Dumfriesshire), the maternal, Taubman (Isle of Man). George Goldie reverted to the paternal name by royal licence in 1887.

Goldie, after passing through the Royal Military Academy at Woolwich, obtained a commission in the Royal Engineers in 1865, which he resigned in 1867. He then travelled for several years, principally in upper Egypt and the Sudan. In 1877 he first visited West Africa, primarily in order to look into the affairs of a trading company on the Niger in which a member of his family was interested, and secondly with the intention of crossing Africa from the Niger to the Nile. The illness of his brother, who accompanied him, obliged to him abandon the latter project. In this visit to the basin of the Niger the seed was sown which developed into Goldie's life's work.

In 1830 the brothers Richard Lemon Lander [q.v.] and John Lander [q.v.] had discovered the outlet of the river Niger in the Gulf of Guinea, thereby demonstrating to Europe the existence of a great navigable waterway leading from the sea into the heart of the African continent and giving access to the Mohammedan states lying to the west of Lake Tchad. Two years later Macgregor Laird [q.v.] had made the first attempt to open up the river to British trade. He was followed by others, with varying success; a consular agent was appointed, and after some trouble friendly relations were established with the natives. Meanwhile opinion in Great Britain was strongly averse from undertaking any responsibilities in the interior of Equatorial Africa; and following the report of a committee appointed to investigate the affairs of British West African possessions, the House of Commons in June 1865 adopted a resolution deprecating any further extension of activities and intimating a desire to reduce responsibilities 'with the view to ultimate withdrawal from all, except probably Sierra Leone'. Three years later the consular agent was withdrawn from the Niger in pursuance of this policy, and a period of stagnation followed.

When Goldie arrived in 1877 he found some British firms trading in the Niger delta, engaged in cut-throat competition, and making no attempt to open up trade with the rich interior. Then it was that he conceived the idea of securing under a royal charter the whole valley of the Niger for Great Britain. He had a fair field, for there was at that time no foreigner, whether trader, soldier, missionary, or traveller, in the entire basins of the Niger and Lake Tchad, between the French colony of Senegal on the extreme west of Africa and the valley of the Nile on the extreme east. His first step was to amalgamate the various trading interests in the river. This took him two years to accomplish, and in 1879 the United African Company was formed. In 1881 the first application for a charter was made, when Goldie was informed that a largely increased capital would be an essential preliminary. The National African Company was then launched with a capital of a million sterling. Meanwhile two French companies, supported by the French government, had established themselves in the river; this made the granting of a charter impossible for the time. Goldie at once opened negotiations with a view to amalgamating the French companies with the National African Company under the British flag. This was accomplished in 1884 after a determined struggle, and the way seemed clear for the grant of a charter. Then suddenly, to the surprise of the world, Germany launched out as a colonizing power, and summoned the West African Conference in Berlin (1884–1885), thus inaugurating the real scramble for Africa. The buying out of the French companies was achieved only just in time to enable the British plenipotentiary, Lord Salisbury, with Goldie by his side, to state at the Conference that 'the whole trade of the Niger basin is at the present moment exclusively in British hands'. This fact gave to Great Britain a recognized position of predominance upon the principal waterway of that portion of West Africa. For the very considerable services rendered on this occasion Goldie was created K.C.M.G. in 1887.

In the same year that Germany appeared on the scene as a competitor, Togoland and the Cameroons became German colonies. France was pushing east from Senegal, and Goldie was advancing up the Niger and was busily engaged in entering into commercial treaties with the native rulers in the interior. All had the same objective—the establishment of relations with the Mohammedan empires of Gandu and Sokoto: so the race began. But Goldie was handicapped because, as a commercial concern, the National African Company had as competitors two powerful foreign governments with all the advantages of public revenue at their command. This disadvantage forced a decision on the issue of a charter which would give to the British Company the same political standing in relation to treaties with natives as that of its competing neighbours. The hesitation of the British government was overcome, and a royal charter was granted (July 1886). The Company again changed its name to that of the Royal Niger Company Chartered & Limited. Under the charter the Company was empowered to govern, to keep in order, and to protect the territories of the chiefs with whom it had concluded treaties and, subject to the sanction of the secretary of state for the

Colonies, to acquire new territories. It was authorized to levy customs duties in order to defray the cost of administration. It was given jurisdiction over British subjects and foreigners throughout its territories. It was to discourage and gradually to abolish slavery, to tolerate the religion of the inhabitants, and to uphold as far as possible their native laws and customs. It was a peculiarity of this charter that the Company remained a trading concern in addition to being charged with administrative duties. It was controlled by a governor and council in England; Lord Aberdare (home secretary, 1868–1873) was appointed governor, and Goldie political administrator and deputy-governor. On Lord Aberdare's death in 1895 Goldie himself became governor. From the date of the charter all the Company's treaties with native chiefs contained a clause by which the native parties recognized that 'the Company as a government represents Her Majesty the Queen of Great Britain and Ireland and agree to place their territories, if and when called upon to do so by the Company, under the protection of the British flag'.

Equipped with this charter the Company found the struggle with France and Germany for supremacy in the interior a less unequal one. Both foreign powers launched repeated expeditions with a view to cutting off the Chartered Company from the hinterland, and it was not until the signing of conventions with Germany in 1893 and with France in 1898—both initiated by Goldie—that an end was put to the struggle and the respective spheres were finally defined. The British sphere was far smaller than Goldie had originally aimed at; nevertheless, he was able to secure for Great Britain a territory covering half a million square miles of the most fertile, highly mineralized, and thickly populated portion of West Africa. This territory, consisting of an agglomeration of pagan and Mohammedan states brought by the exertions of the Chartered Company within the confines of a British protectorate, came to be known generally by the name of Nigeria (1897), this differentiating it from the British colony of Lagos and the Niger Protectorate on the coast, the hinterlands of which had been secured by Goldie's foresight and determination.

While the Company had been engaged in these dangerous international complications, difficulties had arisen on its own borders. Its stations on the Middle Niger had brought the Company into close communication with the powerful Mohammedan emir of Nupé, with whom it had negotiated treaties. But the emir persisted in slave-raiding expeditions across the river. In 1892 Goldie visited the emir in his capital at Bida: he presented him with a letter of greeting from the queen, and impressed upon him that the Company came to Nupé for trade and friendly intercourse only; that it must have security for the lives of its officials; that its stations and goods must not be molested, and that slave-raiding expeditions across the river, where the pagan inhabitants were under the Company's protection, must cease; otherwise force would have to be used. Assurances of good behaviour were given, but they were short-lived. Before long, slave-raiding expeditions across the river were resumed, and Goldie realized that the Company's obligations as a government could only be carried out by force of arms. The Company had at its disposal a small but well-trained and well-armed body of native troops under British officers. Goldie acted swiftly and silently. Taking advantage of the Nupé army being divided (half of it was across the river, raiding for slaves) he assembled his force of 800 men at Lokoja and, accompanying it in person, advanced (6 January 1897) straight on the Nupé capital, while the Company's fleet policed the river and prevented the slave-raiding portion of the emir's army from recrossing. Outside the walls of Bida Goldie was assailed by the Nupé army, estimated at some 15,000 men, mostly mounted, led by the emir himself. The Nupés were completely defeated, and the Company's troops entered the capital the following morning. The emir, who had fled, was declared deposed and the heir apparent, who had accepted the Company's terms, was installed in his place. Subsequently the smaller Mohammedan state of Ilorin, west of the Middle Niger, which had given similar trouble, was subjugated after two days' fighting, and the town of Ilorin captured. This most admirably planned and executed campaign was followed immediately by a decree of the Company abolishing the legal status of slavery throughout its territories.

The final definition of boundaries between the sphere of the Company and those of France and Germany (referred to above), and the great responsibilities thereby involved, led the British government to decide that it was desirable to revoke the charter on grounds of national policy and to assume direct control over the frontier and fiscal policy of British Nigeria. A bill was introduced in the House of Commons making provision for terms and conditions in connexion with the surrender of the charter; this passed both Houses in July 1899. The ceremony of the transfer (for the sum of £865,000) of the political and territorial powers of the Royal Niger Company to the British Crown took place at Lokoja on 1 January 1900 in the presence of Colonel (afterwards Lord) Lugard, who had been appointed high commissioner. Another ceremony took place in England at the final meeting of the Chartered Company, when the shareholders presented to Sir George Goldie, 'The Founder of Nigeria', a portrait of himself by Sir Hubert von Herkomer (afterwards presented to the National Portrait Gallery) in token of their unbounded admiration and gratitude. In acknowledging the gift Goldie said that the inscription on the portrait vividly recalled to him a thrill of emotion when, twenty-two years before, on the Niger, the conception, which had doubtless long been floating in his mind, and which was only the revival of an earlier dream of his in another part of Africa, suddenly crystallized into a firm conviction that the only possible way of preventing a recurrence of the fiascos which had terminated all the earlier enterprises for opening up the Niger—the only feasible means of dealing with inner Equatorial Africa as a whole—was political acquisition, or, in other words, the formation of a civilized government there. They were all Imperialists now, and this conception might not appear to some to be a very original one: but things were very different in 1877. Between the formation of that conception and its partial realization by the granting of the charter in July 1886 there were years of heart-breaking struggle, when every one had to be convinced from the merchant on the Niger to the statesman in Downing Street. Although the West African merchant was in those days just as enterprising as he was to-day, yet he was not at that early period alive to the fundamental doctrine that political acquisition could alone give permanent security to his commerce, that it alone could prevent foreign annexation, with disastrous consequences to British trade, and that it alone could bring about a great development of commerce by giving to the native peace, justice, and liberty, instead of the incessant inter-tribal wars and fetish barbarism of pagan Africa and the incessant slave-raiding and disturbances in the northern territories. The 'castle in the air' of 1877 had now become an impregnable fortress. Five international agreements had secured to Great Britain absolute rights over her sphere in Nigeria. These agreements were not only rendered possible by, but were entirely based upon, the political treaties of the Company with native states and tribes—treaties exceeding four hundred in number. In both the southern and northern regions of Nigeria there remained to be done a vast amount of commercial development, which could not be properly commenced until the political situation had been assured. Meanwhile it was satisfactory to know that what Lord Salisbury aptly called the work of preparation was completed and that the political foundation of Nigeria was securely laid (*The Times*, 28 October 1899).

Goldie's connexion with West Africa then ceased. In 1900–1901 he visited China. In 1902–1903 he served on the royal commission on the military preparations for the South African War, and in 1905–1906 on that on the disposal of South African War stores. In 1903–1904 he went to Rhodesia at the request of the Chartered Company to examine the question of self-government. In 1905 he was elected president of the Royal Geographical Society. In 1908 he was chosen an alderman of the London County Council, and he was chairman of the finance committee until 1919. From then onwards his state of health compelled him to live chiefly in southern Europe until his death, which took place in London on 20 August 1925 at the age of seventy-nine.

Goldie married in 1870 Matilda Catherine (died 1898), daughter of John William Elliott, of Wakefield, and had one son and one daughter. He was admitted a privy councillor in 1898, elected F.R.S. in 1902, received honorary degrees from the universities of Oxford and Cambridge in 1897, and was awarded the Livingstone gold medal of the Royal Scottish Geographical Society in 1906.

Goldie's personality was remarkable. He was 'a slim, fair, blue-eyed man, with piercing eyes which seemed to bore holes into one'. Throughout his life he shunned publicity for his work and for himself: for his work he was a firm believer in what he called 'the Chinese policy of silence'; for himself, in reply to repeated requests that his biography should be undertaken, he wrote: 'Although deeply grateful for these delicate compliments, I have throughout refused compliance. I daresay it has been partly due to excessive sensitiveness; and if this were all I should try to conquer it. But, behind that, lies a principle which has remained unaltered ever since I began to think, nearly half a century ago. That principle is "L'œuvre, c'est tout: l'homme n'est rien". We (not I) bring our children up to think that fame, position, recognition by the public, are proper objects of human ambition. I loathe them all. I do not believe that the world will make any great advance until children generally are brought up with the idea that real happiness is only to be found in doing good work, in however small or great a sphere. . . . Having all my life regarded self-advertisers, from Caesar to Napoleon, as the worst enemies of human progress, I cannot in my old age foreswear my principles and join the array of notoriety hunters. When my active work is over I want, before I die, to write on this subject. "Una voce poco fa", but the sea is made up of drops, and I may be able to help the world to see in which direction true happiness lies.'

[Private information; personal knowledge. See also Dorothy Wellesley and Stephen Gwynn, *Sir George Goldie. Founder of Nigeria*, 1934.] SCARBROUGH.

GOLLANCZ, SIR HERMANN (1852–1930), rabbi, Semitic scholar, was born at Bremen 30 November 1852, the eldest son of the Rev. Samuel Marcus Gollancz, minister of the Hambro' synagogue, then in Leadenhall Street, London, by his wife, Johanna Koppel. He had three sisters and three brothers, his youngest brother being Sir Israel Gollancz [q.v.]. At the age of ten he passed from the Whitechapel Foundation School to the school attached to the Jews' College, then in Finsbury Square; he entered the Jews' College itself and also University College, London, in 1869. He graduated B.A. with honours in classics and philosophy in 1873, and M.A. in Hebrew, Syriac, and German in 1889. From 1872 to 1876 he assisted his father at the Hambro' synagogue as assistant preacher. Thereafter he was preacher successively at the synagogues in St. John's Wood (1876–1881) and Great St. Helen's, E.C. (1881–1882), and minister at Manchester (1882–1885) and Dalston (1885–1892). In 1892 he succeeded the chief rabbi, Dr. Hermann Adler [q.v.], as first minister at the Bayswater synagogue, Harrow Road, where he remained for thirty-one years, completing, in 1923, a unique record of fifty-one years' service in the Jewish ministry. On his retirement a special salaried post of emeritus minister was created for him.

Gollancz's main work falls under three heads, pastoral, scholarly, and philanthropic. His congregations naturally had the first claim on his energies, but he undertook many duties outside his parish, and worked zealously for the foundation of new synagogues at South Hackney, New Cross, Walthamstow, Reading, Hanley, Hull, Sunderland, and Cardiff.

In 1897 Gollancz obtained the rabbinic degree. His action raised and decided an important principle. Hitherto the requirements for the rabbinic degree, which any qualified rabbi can grant to a suitable candidate, had not been definitely specified in England, and the degree had, in fact, never been conferred in this country. It was therefore necessary for Gollancz to go abroad—he went to Galicia—in order to obtain his certificate of rabbinical competence. The chief rabbi, Dr. Hermann Adler, however, felt that the time was not yet opportune for increasing the number of qualified rabbis in England. The Anglo-Jewish clergy had consisted hitherto of rabbis and precentors (chazanim) and the sermon was not a regular institution in every synagogue. He considered that the status of minister-preacher, a comparatively recent innovation, needed a further period of development, and that a generation should pass before minister-preachers should attain to full rabbinic status. He therefore refused to recognize Gollancz as a rabbi and an acrimonious controversy began in the *Jewish Chronicle*. The questions at issue were not merely personal, whether Gollancz was or was not a rabbi or whether Dr. Adler's position as chief rabbi was impugned. Two matters of principle were involved. First, should the rabbinic degree be given in England? secondly, should rabbinic degrees gained abroad be recognized in England? The reasoned arguments of 'Historicus' (Israel Gollancz) stated the case for an enlarged rabbinate so cogently that in the end Dr. Adler gave way. Gollancz was publicly recognized as rabbi and the requirements of Hebrew and rabbinics necessary to obtain the diploma of rabbi in this country were formally defined. To-day theological students at Jews' College are encouraged to work for this degree before entering the ministry. These satisfactory results are due to the arduous struggle carried on by Gollancz and his brother Israel in the face of great opposition and much personal inconvenience.

Dr. Adler died in 1911. Gollancz's claims to succeed him as chief rabbi were overruled by the imperative need for a younger man to fill the position. Gollancz therefore remained at the Bayswater synagogue for another eleven years, during the trying period of the European War. He published in 1915 a special translation of Joseph Kimchi's *Foundation of Religious Fear*, of which he presented in 1918 an edition of 10,000 copies for the use of members of the Jewish faith in the British forces. His wife received the Belgian order of Queen Elisabeth in recognition of her war-work.

Gollancz undertook much public work outside the special interests of the Jewish community. In 1880, in conjunction with the Rev. Samuel Augustus Barnett [q.v.], he promoted the first of the Whitechapel loan exhibitions; he took part in the several movements which secured Clissold Park as an open space (1888), created the North London Technical Institute (1889), and saved Moyse's Hall, Bury St. Edmunds (1896). He served on the royal commissions which inquired into the birthrate (1913–1916) and the cinema (1917), and on the special committee appointed to report on venereal disease and adolescence (1920–1921); he was vice-president and treasurer of the National Council of Public Morals and vice-chairman of the Paddington Social Service Council. In 1917 he received an illuminated address, signed by representatives of many educational and philanthropic bodies, on the occasion of his completing forty-five years' service as a Jewish minister and public worker.

Gollancz, who was the first Jew to obtain the degree of D.Litt. at London University (in 1899), was elected in 1902 Goldsmid professor of Hebrew at University College, London, in succession to Professor Schechter. On his retirement in 1923 the senate of the university accorded him the title of emeritus professor, and in order to commemorate his twenty-one years' tenure of the chair of Hebrew he presented his valuable library of *Hebraica* and *Judaica* to University College; he had previously been largely responsible for the acquisition by University College of the library of Jewish history bequeathed to public uses in 1905 by Frederic David Mocatta [q.v.]. Gollancz was president of the Jewish Drama League, of the Jewish Historical Society (1905), and of the Union of Jewish Literary Societies (1925–1926). In 1922 he celebrated his golden jubilee and was the recipient of many marks of esteem. In 1923 he was knighted, being the first British rabbi to receive this honour.

Gollancz married in 1884 Thérèse, daughter of Samuel Henry Wilner, merchant, of Manchester, and by her had three sons. The close of his life was saddened by domestic sorrows. In September 1929 he lost successively his youngest son Leonard, his wife, and his sister Emma, within ten days; his brother Israel died in June of the next year. Gollancz died in London 15 October 1930.

Gollancz's literary output was very great. A bibliography of his works, which, besides extensive translations from Hebrew and Aramaic texts, comprise contributions to Jewish history, sermons and addresses, and personal reminiscences, is given in his *Personalia* (1928).

[Sir H. Gollancz, *Personalia*, 1928.]

H. M. J. Loewe.

GOLLANCZ, Sir ISRAEL (1863–1930), scholar and man of letters, the fourth and youngest son of the Rev. Samuel Marcus Gollancz, minister of the Hambro' synagogue, London, by his wife, Johanna Koppel, was born in London 13 July 1863. His eldest brother was Sir Hermann Gollancz [q.v.], Goldsmid professor of Hebrew at University College, London. He was educated at the City of London School, at University College, London, and at Christ's College, Cambridge, of which he was a scholar (1883–1887). After taking his degree (1887) with a second class in the medieval and modern languages tripos he lectured for some years in English at Cambridge before the establishment of a school of English there, and in 1896 was appointed the first lecturer in English at the university. Previously, in 1892, he had been appointed Quain English student and lecturer at University College, London, and this post he held until 1895. Some years later, in 1903, Gollancz was appointed to the chair of English language and literature at King's College, London, a post which he held until his death. In 1906 he resigned his Cambridge appointment, and on leaving Cambridge took the degree of Litt.D.

In his new post it fell to Gollancz to supervise and direct the development of the English department of the university of London from a small and relatively unimportant faculty to that of one of the principal faculties of the university. In 1910 Gollancz was selected as one of the first two recipients of the Albert Kahn travelling fellowships, but was unable to take up the fellowship. In 1919 he was elected a corresponding member of the Royal Spanish Academy, and in 1927 of the Medieval Academy of America. He was also Leofric lecturer in Old English at University College, Exeter, honorary director of the Early English Text Society, president of the Philological Society, chairman of the Shakespeare Association, an honorary freeman of the Stationers' Company, and honorary secretary of the Shakespeare Tercentenary Committee (1916).

Apart, however, from his literary work and teaching Gollancz is best known in connexion with the British Academy, of which he was one of the founders and original fellows, and the secretary from its formation in 1902 until his death. To his initiative, as secretary of the Academy, was largely due the foundation of the Schweich lectures, the Cervantes chair of Spanish and the Camoens chair of Portuguese at King's College, London, and the British School of Archaeology in Jerusalem. Another of Gollancz's special interests was the project for a national theatre. He was honorary secretary of the committee whose task it was to frame a scheme for the foundation and endowment of such a theatre. He also organized the first Anglo-American conference of professors of English in London in 1921, and two years later headed the English delegation to the similar conference in New York. He took advantage of his visit to America in that year to lecture at several American universities.

As an English and Shakespearian scholar Gollancz was in the first rank. His first publication, an edition of the Early English poem *Pearl*, appeared in 1891. In 1892 appeared Cynewulf's *Christ* and in 1895 *The Exeter Book of Anglo-Saxon Poetry*. Other publications of his in the same or a related field include *The Parlement of the Three Ages* (1897), *The Tragical History of Doctor Faustus* (1897), *Hamlet in Iceland* (1898), *The Quatrefoil of Love* (1901), Boccaccio's *Olympia* (1913), *Ich Dene: some observations on a manuscript of the life and feats of arms of Edward, Prince of Wales* (1921), *The Sources of Hamlet* (1926), and *The Caedmon Manuscript of Anglo-Saxon Biblical Poetry* (on the occasion of the twenty-fifth anniversary of the British Academy, 1927). In 1916 he edited *The Book of Homage to Shakespeare* and in 1893 he issued *Charles Lamb's Specimens of English Dramatic Poets*. Gollancz was also the general editor of the 'Temple' *Shakespeare*, the 'Temple Classics', 'The King's Library', 'The King's Novels', 'The Medieval Library', and the *Shakespeare Survey*.

In the Anglo-Jewish community, of which he was one of the most distinguished members of his generation, Gollancz interested himself specially in the training and qualifications of rabbis. To this object he devoted himself on the council of the Jews' College, the Anglo-Jewish theological seminary of which he was for many years a member; and the curriculum for the rabbinical diploma granted by that institution was to a large extent his work. He was the second president of the Union of Jewish Literary Societies and he also served for a term as president of the Maccabaeans and honorary president of the Inter-University Jewish Federation.

Gollancz won wide recognition for his scholarship both at home and abroad, and in 1919 he was knighted. He was an excellent lecturer, and his charm of manner, his readiness to help other scholars, and his fondness for children brought him many friends. He married in 1910 Alide, daughter of Adolphus Goldschmidt, and by her he had one son and one daughter. He died at his residence in Brondesbury, London, 23 June 1930, and a lecturership was founded at the British Academy in his memory.

[*The Times*, 24 June 1930; *Jewish Chronicle*, 27 June 1930; *Jewish Guardian*, 27 June 1930; personal knowledge.] A. M. Hyamson.

GOSLING, HARRY (1861–1930), trade-union leader, born in Lambeth 9 June 1861, was the second son of William Gosling, master lighterman, by his wife, Sarah Louisa Rowe, school-teacher, who continued to follow her profession after her marriage. He attended an elementary school until the age of thirteen, when he began, as an office boy, his wage-earning career. In the following year (1875) he was bound apprentice to the trade of waterman of the river Thames, the occupation of his family for four generations. Although Gosling was not physically fit for the arduous calling, he followed it until 1887, when a break-down in health made it necessary for him to seek less laborious employment as timber, clothes, and general salesman. Nevertheless he kept in contact with the river, and in 1889 he joined the Amalgamated Society of Watermen and Lightermen of the River Thames. In 1893 he was elected general secretary of the Society.

Thenceforward Gosling was in the forefront of the long struggle to improve the working conditions of dock and river labour throughout the country, which began with the great dock strike of 1889. In 1910 he was elected president of the National Transport Workers' Federation, of which his own organization was a section. In 1921 the Transport and General Workers' Union replaced the federation, and Gosling retained the office of president. He attended the annual Trades Union Congress as a delegate without a break from 1893 until his death. He was elected to the parliamentary committee of the Congress in 1908 and was chairman of the Congress in 1916. In the revision of the constitution of the Congress and the creation of the general council of the Congress (1920) with larger powers and functions than those of the parliamentary committee, he took a prominent part. He was a member of the general council until 1923.

In addition to his trade-union activities Gosling engaged in both municipal and national politics. He was elected alderman of the London County Council in 1898 and was a member of that body for twenty-seven years. On the establishment of the Port of London Authority in 1908 he was appointed a member and served for the remainder of his life. In 1923 he was elected member of parliament in the labour interest for Whitechapel and St. George's, and sat for that constituency until he died. During the administration of the labour government, in 1924, he was minister of transport and paymaster-general, and was responsible for the London Traffic Act (1924). Gosling's long trade-union experience and high reputation for skill and tact in negotiations connected with industrial disputes brought, during the European War of 1914–1918, many calls upon him by the government to assist in the settlement of the multifarious labour difficulties which then arose. He was a member of several important government committees, notably the Port and Transit Executive committee which co-ordinated and regulated the transport of men, munitions, and food supplies, and the Civil Service Arbitration board, set up to adjust the salaries of lower-grade civil servants. In 1917 he was appointed to the Imperial War Graves commission. His many public services during the war period were recognized by his being created C.H. in 1917.

Gosling's views were those of a socialist whose faith was tempered by intimate acquaintance with the difficulties of social and industrial organization arising from the intractableness of the human factor. His shrewdness, common sense, and moderation, combined with his equable temper, earned the respect and esteem of both foes and friends in the industrial and political spheres; while in labour circles he was regarded with sincere affection owing to his loyalty, courtesy, kindliness, and gentle humour.

Gosling married in 1884 Helen Martin, daughter of Joseph Low Duff, engineer, and had no children. He died at Twickenham 24 October 1930.

[Harry Gosling, *Up and Down Stream*, 1927; private information; personal knowledge.] W. S. Sanders.

GOSSE, Sir EDMUND WILLIAM (1849–1928), poet and man of letters, born in Hackney 21 September 1849, was the only child of Philip Henry Gosse [q.v.], the distinguished writer on zoology, by his first wife, Emily, daughter of William Bowes, of Boston, Massachusetts [see Gosse, Emily]. His childhood was spent in Hackney until the death of his mother in 1857, when he was taken by his father to live at St. Marychurch, South Devon. His parents were devout members of the Plymouth Brotherhood, and Gosse was brought up in an atmosphere of rigid piety. His reading was restricted to a narrow repertory of religious literature, and until his seventeenth year his only knowledge of poetry and fiction was gained surreptitiously, or during his attendance at neighbouring schools, the first of which was called Mount Veden.

In 1865, when Charles Kingsley, a friend of Philip Gosse, secured for Edmund an appointment in the cataloguing section of the British Museum, he had already some knowledge of French, German, Italian, and Swedish. Freed from the mental bondage imposed on him at home, he gave himself up to the study of literature. He made the acquaintance of leading writers, often introducing himself to an author by a letter expressing admiration for his work. In this way he became acquainted with William Bell Scott [q.v.], and through him with the pre-Raphaelites. In 1870 he published *Madrigals, Songs, and Sonnets*, with

John Blaikie as joint author. Gosse's contributions to the volume showed him to be a writer of graceful and accomplished verse, but without notable inventive power. His maturer poetry bears the same stamp of elegance and delicacy of expression, best seen in the lyrics contained in his volume of *Collected Poems* (1911). Perhaps the best example of his careful, clear-cut, perspicuous verse is to be found in his poem *Revelation*, printed in *The Oxford Book of English Verse*, or again in *Melancholy in the Garden*, *The Suppliant*, *The Return of the Swallows*, and *Epilogue*.

In 1871 Gosse paid a visit to the Lofoden Islands. In a bookshop at Trondjhem he bought a copy of a recent work of Henrik Ibsen. He at once set to work with the help of a dictionary to study the Norwegian dramatist, and subsequently in articles and reviews became the first writer to introduce him to the English public. Gosse himself translated Ibsen's *Hedda Gabler* (1891) and *The Master-Builder* (with William Archer, 1893). His first published article, 'The Lofoden Islands', appeared in *Fraser's Magazine* in 1871. He was an omnivorous reader, and by means of immense industry, a clear and vivid style, and a discriminating taste quickly earned the reputation of a sound critic. He wrote for the *Spectator*, the *Academy*, and other periodicals. In 1873 his first independent volume of verse, *On Viol and Flute*, was well received. *Studies in the Literature of Northern Europe* (1879) established him as one of the leading authorities on Scandinavian and Dutch literature.

In 1875 Gosse gave up his post at the British Museum, on being appointed translator to the Board of Trade, where he was attached to the commercial department. (Henry) Austin Dobson [q.v.], William Cosmo Monkhouse [q.v.], and Samuel Waddington were serving in the marine department at the time. In 1882 he published his life of Gray, in the 'English Men of Letters' series, one of his most popular books, and in 1884 a complete edition of Gray's works. *Seventeenth Century Studies* appeared in 1883, and was followed, at irregular intervals, by numerous volumes of poetry, criticism, and biography, including a *Life of William Congreve* (1888), *A History of Eighteenth Century Literature* (1889), *Life of P. H. Gosse* (1890), *Life and Letters of Dr. John Donne* (1899), a life of Jeremy Taylor ('English Men of Letters' series, 1904), *Coventry Patmore* (1905), *Life of Sir Thomas Browne* (1905), *Henrik Ibsen* (1907), and *Life of Algernon Charles Swinburne* (1917). His *Collected Essays* were published in five volumes in 1913.

In 1884 to 1885 Gosse carried out a successful lecturing tour in the United States, at the conclusion of which he was offered, but declined, the professorship of English literature at Harvard University. On his return to England, having been appointed to succeed (Sir) Leslie Stephen as Clark lecturer in English literature at Trinity College, Cambridge, a post which he held until 1890, he repeated at Cambridge the lectures which he had delivered in America, subsequently (1885) publishing them under the title *From Shakespeare to Pope*. In October 1886 a bitter and damaging article by John Churton Collins [q.v.], entitled 'English Literature at the Universities', in which Gosse's teaching was denounced, appeared in the *Quarterly Review*. Gosse replied in the *Academy*, but was unable to dispose of many of the charges of inaccuracy which Churton Collins had brought against him. His reputation suffered, and the controversy, in which A. C. Swinburne joined in his defence, deeply affected him.

In 1904 Gosse was appointed librarian to the House of Lords, a post which he held for ten years. This gave him independence and financial security, 'under conditions favourable to leisurely and extended thought'. In 1907 he published anonymously *Father and Son*, his most notable contribution to English literature. The book, which describes his own childhood passed in the religious atmosphere created by his father, was written with a creative and imaginative power which surprised his warmest admirers and raised his reputation to a high level. It was crowned by the French Academy in 1913. This book was a turning-point in Gosse's career, and when, eleven years later (1918), he began in the *Sunday Times* a series of weekly articles which continued until his death, he wrote with a prestige enjoyed by scarcely any critic of the day. Selections from these articles were reprinted in *Books on the Table* (1921), *More Books on the Table* (1923), and other volumes.

Gosse's model was Sainte-Beuve, and his weekly criticisms will bear comparison with the *Causeries du Lundi*. From his 'pulpit', as he called the *Sunday Times*, he covered a varied and extensive range of literary topics. The light which he shed was diffused rather than penetrating, but his volumes of criticism, often marked by wit, humour, and a delicate irony, and always by a style of conspicuous lucidity and charm, are eminently readable and enlightening. He claimed that he wrote to please rather than to instruct, and to spread abroad his own enjoyment in reading. This may be seen in his earlier works, *Gossip in a Library* (1891) and *Questions at Issue* (1893), but is perhaps more noticeable in some of his later publications, *Inter Arma* (1916), *Books on the Table*, and *Silhouettes* (1925).

Gosse excelled in literary portraiture. In his youth he had not allowed his reverence for celebrities to interfere with his powers of critical observation. He was fitted by temperament, as he said, to notice 'the little fireside ways that distinguish men from one another', and at an early stage of his career he had been urged by R. L. Stevenson to cultivate this gift. Vivid and intimate records of the leading literary figures of his time lie scattered through his volumes of criticism, and form a lasting, and in many ways unique, contribution to one aspect of the history of the period.

In spite of an element of sparkling malice apparent at times in his conversation and a proneness to take offence, Gosse was benevolent in disposition and generous in the pecuniary and literary help which he gave to others. Socially he was genial and inspiriting, and in conversation he was seldom outshone. To quickness of wit and high spirits he added genuine love of companionship; in talk his wide knowledge of literature was used with a deft and easy mastery, and then only to lighten and enliven the occasion. R. L. Stevenson has described Gosse's conversation in *Talk and Talkers*, in which Gosse appears under the sobriquet of Purcel.

Gosse was of medium height, quick in movement, and rather Scandinavian in colouring—fair with piercing blue eyes under a fine forehead. He was an accomplished and persuasive lecturer, and in much request as an after-dinner speaker. His gift for friendship was remarkable, and among his many friends were Swinburne, Thomas Hardy, Austin Dobson, R. L. Stevenson, George Moore, Henry James, Lord Haldane, and Sir Hamo Thornycroft.

Gosse was the recipient of numerous honours. He was made C.B. in 1912 and knighted in 1925. Honorary degrees from the universities of St. Andrews (1899), Cambridge (1920), Strasburg (1920), Gothenburg (1923), and the Sorbonne (1925), and the orders of St. Olaf in Norway (1901), of the Polar Star in Sweden (1908), of the Dannebrog in Denmark (1912), and the legion of honour in France (1925) testified to his wide recognition as a man of letters. He died 16 May 1928 at a nursing-home in London, where he had continued to the last to write his weekly articles with unabated skill and vivacity. He married in 1875 Ellen, daughter of George Napoleon Epps [q.v.], and sister of the second wife of Sir Lawrence Alma Tadema [q.v.]. They had one son and two daughters.

Gosse was twice painted by John Sargent in 1886; one of these portraits hangs in the National Portrait Gallery, the other is in the possession of the family. There is also a drawing of him by William Rothenstein in the National Portrait Gallery.

[*The Times*, 17 May 1928; Evan Charteris, *Life and Letters of Sir Edmund Gosse*, 1931; private information.] E. Charteris.

GOULD, Sir FRANCIS CARRUTHERS (1844–1925), cartoonist, was born at Barnstaple 2 December 1844, the second son of Richard Davie Gould, architect, by his wife, Judith Carruthers, daughter of William Ford. Educated at private schools in Barnstaple, he entered a local bank at the age of sixteen. From childhood he had been ready with the pencil, chiefly making studies of birds and animals; and while at the bank he drew, purely for amusement, caricatures of various colleagues, customers, and well-known persons in the town. In 1865 he went up to London to work in a stock-broker's office, and after a few years became a member of the stock exchange, operating first as a broker and later as a jobber. Here, too, his pencil was busily at work, and his caricatures were in great demand among business acquaintances and friends. Large numbers of them were issued for private circulation. Gould found the 'House' (i.e. the stock exchange) an excellent school, for, in his own words, 'there was every variety of personality and very marked individuality among the members'; but for many years he looked upon these drawings solely as distractions and had no idea of embarking on the career of a professional cartoonist.

In 1879, however, Gould was asked by Horace Voules to illustrate the Christmas number of *Truth*, and his work therein was so much appreciated that his services were regularly engaged for the subsequent

Christmas issues of that journal up to the year 1895. From 1887 onwards he became a fairly constant contributor of cartoons and sketches to the *Pall Mall Gazette*. In 1890, when W. T. Stead was succeeded in the editorship by (Sir) Edward Tyas Cook [q.v.], Gould became a member of the staff; and early in 1893, after the paper had passed under the control of Mr. William Waldorf (afterwards Viscount) Astor (changing its politics from liberal to conservative in the process), Gould joined, with Cook and Mr. J. A. Spender, the staff of the newly founded *Westminster Gazette*. With that paper he remained until 1914. He was not only a draughtsman but a capable journalist. A keen radical, he devoted himself by word and line to the attack on conservative principles and policies; and in 1896 he was appointed assistant editor. Lively accounts of parliamentary debates came from his pen; and he lectured on parliamentary matters in various parts of England and Scotland. On the accession of the liberal party to power in 1906 he was knighted in recognition of his political services. From 1894 to 1914 he edited a paper of his own, *Picture Politics*, and in 1903 and 1904 collections of his political cartoons were issued in folio form. From 1914 onwards he lived in retirement at Porlock, Somerset, where he died, at the age of eighty, 1 January 1925.

Gould was a doughty fighter and a power among the liberals in the stormy days of the Irish question, the South African War, and the great fiscal controversy which raged in the late nineteenth century and on into the twentieth. He was once described by Lord Rosebery as 'one of the few remaining political assets of the party'. Extremely modest in his opinion of his work, Gould laid no claim to the title of artist in the serious sense. 'I accentuate', he said, 'the salient features of the political situation of the moment.' His drawing was uncertain and his line undistinguished; but if there is one branch of pictorial art in which content heavily outweighs style that branch is the political cartoon. For this Gould undoubtedly possessed three essential qualities—wit, a wealth of ideas, and a faculty for seizing the likenesses of his victims. He held his political faith very sincerely, and was fertile and resourceful, if not very profound, in notions calculated to bring his opponents into ridicule. If the main function of such work be to effect changes of opinion and to sway policies, then Gould was the most successful cartoonist of his day. His effects were not produced by distortion or extreme exaggeration, but by a sense of character and of humorous situation.

Gould's lifelong interest in animals, and above all in birds, was reflected in his cartoons. His favourite subject was Mr. Joseph Chamberlain, whom he caricatured in innumerable guises. (Lord) Balfour, the eighth Duke of Devonshire, and (Lord) Morley also figured largely in his work. He made considerable use of the works of Dickens, of *Alice in Wonderland* and *Alice through the Looking-Glass*, and of J. C. Harris's *Uncle Remus* as vehicles for his satire. Occasionally the Bible or Shakespeare supplied him with a text, or a celebrated painting—such as Sir W. Q. Orchardson's 'Napoleon aboard the Bellerophon'—was parodied in line. He was very urbane (in his own phrase, 'I etch with vinegar, not with vitriol'), and rarely or never caused heartburning or annoyance to his subjects.

Among Gould's many books, one of the most amusing was *Froissart's Modern Chronicles*, which appeared in three parts in 1902, 1903, and 1908, a political history of the day, written in a style parodying that of Froissart, and illustrated with caricatures of prominent politicians clad as knights, Chaucerian characters, and so forth.

Gould married in 1869 Emily (died 1920), daughter of Hugh Ballment, of Barnstaple, first a ship-builder and shipowner, and later a tanner. They had three sons and two daughters.

[*The Times*, 2 January 1925; *The Studio*, vol. xxiii, 1901; Aaron Watson, '*F. C. G.*', *Caricaturist* (a pamphlet), 1903; S. M. Phinne in *Magazine of Art*, new series, vol. i, 1903; private information.] H. B. GRIMSDITCH.

GRAY, GEORGE BUCHANAN (1865–1922), Congregational minister and Hebrew scholar, was born at Blandford, Dorset, 13 January 1865, the second son of the Rev. Benjamin Gray, Congregational minister at Blandford, by his wife, Emma Jane, daughter of George Buchanan Kirkman. He was educated at private schools at Blandford and Exeter, after which he acted as a schoolmaster at Blandford for several years, during which he studied for matriculation at London University, passing that examination in 1882. He continued in the same way while studying for his degree at New College, Hampstead, and University College, London, where he read Greek and Latin and began working at Hebrew, and took the degree of B.A. in 1886. He then began working for the degree of M.A., but left London before finishing the course in order to go to Oxford, where, as a non-collegiate student, he studied Semitic languages at Mansfield College, and obtained a first class in the school of Oriental studies in 1891. He also won the Pusey and Ellerton Hebrew scholarship (1889), the junior Hall-Houghton Septuagint prize (1890), and the junior (1891) and senior (1893) Kennicott Hebrew scholarships. He completed his studies at the university of Marburg.

On taking his Oxford degree in 1891 Gray was appointed a tutor at Mansfield College, and in 1893 was ordained to the Congregational ministry. Seven years later (1900) he was promoted to be professor of Hebrew and the exegesis of the Old Testament at Mansfield College, where he remained for the rest of his life. He married in the same year Frances Lilian, only daughter of Alfred Williams, the artist [q.v.], and had one son and one daughter.

Gray was both a teacher and an original investigator. As a teacher, he encouraged a succession of students, both inside and outside his own college, to pursue Hebrew studies, showing himself no dry scholar in spite of his profound learning, but very human in his wide and manifold interests. Moreover, although his mind was calm and critical and his nature neither sentimental nor demonstrative, he won the affection and often lifelong devotion of his pupils, who remembered him as a real power in their intellectual and spiritual life. He had a great suspicion of all attempts to escape from facts by emotional side-tracks; he cared above all things for the truth, and sought only to guide his students to an interpretation of the Bible which would not afterwards fail them. As an investigator, he produced numerous original articles on Semitic and biblical subjects in learned and religious publications, and several books, of which six may be mentioned as works of outstanding merit and importance. These are *Studies in Hebrew Proper Names* (1896), in which he showed that the Hebrews tended to employ different types of personal names at different periods of their history and that these may therefore be of importance in the critical examination of the documentary sources of the Old Testament; a *Commentary on Numbers* (1903); a *Commentary on Isaiah I–XXVII* (1912) in the *International Critical Commentaries*, in which he also completed in two volumes the *Commentary on Job* (1921) of Samuel Rolles Driver [q.v.]; the *Forms of Hebrew Poetry* (1915), in which he proved that there is a real distinction between Hebrew prose and poetry, consisting, in respect to poetical form, in a combination of parallelism and rhythm, although he also admitted the possibility of a third form of composition which might be called 'parallelistic prose', not unlike the early Arabic 'rhymed prose'; and lastly, a more or less complete set of lectures on Hebrew ritual practices, published after his death under the title *Sacrifice in the Old Testament* (1925), in which he discussed exhaustively everything connected with the altar and sacrifice, the festal calendar, and the priesthood.

These works show Gray to have been a follower of the school of biblical criticism represented in Germany by Julius Wellhausen and in England by S. R. Driver, but he was an independent thinker with a positive and constructive aim essentially his own. He loved the writings of the Old Testament, their history, theology, and poetry, and dedicated his life to leading others to a right understanding of them. On critical questions his judgement was shrewd and sane; he distrusted extreme views and advanced cautiously to his conclusions, but, so soon as he was sure of his ground, he could not be shaken. His books were learned but sagacious, lively but reverent. At the same time he regarded it as part of his mission to spread modern knowledge about the Bible beyond the narrow bounds of select classes of advanced students or future ministers; he lectured freely to schools and meetings, to societies of the Friends, and ministerial gatherings. In preaching he generally took his text from the Old Testament and showed how deeply he was permeated by its devotional spirit.

Apart from his biblical studies, Gray was much interested in problems of social welfare; he frequently visited the Mansfield College settlement in Canning Town and for many years was an active member of its committee. In politics he was a liberal in both Imperial and municipal affairs; ecclesiastically, he was a convinced free churchman and an old-fashioned Independent, keenly interested in chapels in country districts and their ministers, amongst whom he had been brought up. He was a loyal and devoted friend and colleague, a vigorous personality full of the joy of life and endowed with a richly furnished mind, capable of showing himself learned without pedantry and controversial without bitterness, and withal possessed of a strong sense of humour. In his younger days he had been an Alpine climber, and in later life he took to lawn-tennis and to bicycling both in France and in England, which enabled him to gratify his love of the countryside.

Gray paid one visit to Palestine and Syria for purposes of study (1904) and served for many years on the committee of the Palestine Exploration Fund. He also made two journeys to the United States of America, the first at the request of the Council of Mansfield College on a tour of inquiry concerning a possible successor to Dr. A. M. Fairbairn as principal of the college (1908), and the second to give a course of lectures at the university of Chicago (1919). Amongst the honours which he received were the honorary degree of D.D. of Aberdeen University (1903) and the degree of D.Litt. of Oxford University (1905). At Oxford he held also the offices of Speaker's lecturer in biblical studies (1914–1919) and Grinfield lecturer on the Septuagint (1919–1921). He died suddenly at a meeting of the board of theological studies at Oxford 2 November 1922, on the afternoon of the day on which he was expected in the evening to deliver his inaugural address as president of the Society of Historical Theology.

[*The Times*, 3 November 1922; bibliography in Gray's posthumous *Sacrifice in the Old Testament*, 1925; private information.]

G. R. Driver.

GRAY, HERBERT BRANSTON (1851–1929), schoolmaster, was born at Putney 22 April 1851, the second son of Thomas Gray, of St. Peter's, Isle of Thanet, by his wife, Emily Mary, daughter of William Heath, of Pennsylvania Castle, Isle of Portland. In 1865 he went to Winchester College where, in the following year, he gained an exhibition. He proceeded in 1870 with a classical scholarship to Queen's College, Oxford, and obtained a first class in classical moderations in 1872 and a second class in *literae humaniores* in 1874.

In 1875 Gray joined the staff of Westminster School, where he came under the influence of Dean Stanley. Of Stanley Gray wrote that he 'instilled into me whatever inspiration I have had in life'. He was ordained deacon in 1877 and priest in 1878 and, while retaining his mastership at Westminster, gained some parochial experience in London. In 1878 he was appointed headmaster of Louth grammar school, and went there in 1879. Gray raised the numbers and developed the school, but when, in 1880, he was offered the headmastership of St. Andrew's College at Bradfield in Berkshire, he decided to accept a position which, however unpromising at the time, seemed to him to offer more scope for his abilities.

The rebuilding of Bradfield proved to be the main work of Gray's life. The expectations formed at the time of the foundation of the school in 1850 had not been realized. During the first ten years the numbers had risen to 120, but decline followed, and when Gray came, the boys numbered barely 50, only a few were paying fees, and the end was in sight. When he retired thirty years later, the number of boys exceeded 300, which is now the normal figure. In 1880 Bradfield needed rebuilding, in two senses. Gray supplied the necessary skill and enthusiasm. A new constitution on modern lines succeeded the patriarchal rule of Thomas Stevens, the founder, rector of Bradfield and lord of the manor; and new buildings were added from time to time to supplement an old country house. Gray's energy, mental and physical, was exceptional, and it had full scope. Though short in stature, he was very muscular; he played fives with picked boys and beat them, until quite late in life; his lawn-tennis was of a quality not often seen at that time, and he rarely seemed to be walking at less than five miles an hour. When he retired, Bradfield was fully equipped in the many branches which are now thought necessary for a leading public school. He also instituted a navy class, and engineering workshops at a time when the value of what is now called practical work was little recognized; and in 1909 he established a ranch in Alberta, Canada, where boys leaving Bradfield could learn local conditions of agriculture. Although the ranch did not prove permanent, it was pioneer work in a valuable direction.

Outside Bradfield, Gray was best known as the founder of the Bradfield Greek Play, and of the open-air theatre near the school, built in 1890, partly by the boys themselves, on the model of the Greek theatre at Epidaurus. Here, every third year, the boys give either the *Antigone*, the *Alcestis*, or the *Agamemnon* before large audiences. Gray himself more than once acted as the *coryphaeus*. A strong point was made that, while such training had much educational value, it was never allowed to interfere with the general work of the school; but the success and almost world-wide fame of the Bradfield Greek Play was naturally a source of pride to its founder and a distinction to the school.

After his retirement in 1910 Gray travelled widely, and published several books on educational and Imperial questions: *The Public Schools and the Empire* (1913), *Eclipse or Empire?* (1916), and *America at School and at Work* (1918). In 1918 he became vicar of St. Mary's church, Bury St. Edmunds, and in 1926 rector of Lynton, Devonshire. He died at Southampton 5 April 1929.

Gray married in 1882 Selina, youngest daughter of the Rev. Wharton Booth Marriott [q.v.], assistant-master at Eton, and a cousin of the Rev. Charles Marriott [q.v.]. They had two sons.

A medallion portrait of Gray by Lady Harris, executed in 1905, and a drawing by John Pettie, representing him as *coryphaeus*, are in the possession of Mrs. Gray.

[*The Times*, 6 April 1929; Selina Gray, *Gray of Bradfield*, 1931; A. F. Leach, *History of Bradfield College*, 1900; private information.] G. S. FREEMAN.

GREAVES, WALTER (1846–1930), painter, the son of a Chelsea waterman and boat-builder, was born 4 July 1846 in Chelsea and lived as a boy at 10 (afterwards 3) Lindsey Row, Chelsea. A few doors away was the first home in London of the painter, James Abbott McNeill Whistler [q.v.], at 7 Lindsey Row (afterwards 101 Cheyne Walk). Whistler went to live there in 1863, and at that date, or earlier, the two brothers Walter and Harry Greaves used to row him about the Thames as their father had rowed J. M. W. Turner. They also worked for Whistler in his studio, buying materials, preparing canvas and colours, making his frames, and they attended an art class in his company. In late life, and possibly with imperfect recollection, Walter Greaves stated that his brother and himself were painting pictures of the Thames and Cremorne Gardens, both day and night effects, before they knew Whistler. Whistler spoke of them as his 'first pupils', and Walter Greaves said: 'He taught us to paint and we taught him the waterman's jerk.'

Of the two brothers, Walter showed more accomplishment as a painter. He knew Carlyle and painted more than one portrait of him at about the time (1870) when Carlyle was sitting for Whistler. Most of his portraits and landscape subjects painted in the Chelsea district show strongly the influence of Whistler in their outlook and tonality, but in his early days Greaves, in his own words, 'was accustomed to fill pictures with numerous details'; to this class belong his two largest pictures in oil, 'Chelsea Regatta', now in the City Art Gallery, Manchester, and the unsophisticated and brilliant 'Boat-race Day, Hammersmith Bridge', bought by the Chantrey Trustees in 1922 and now at the Tate Gallery. These pictures, and many of his water-colour drawings of old Chelsea, the busy water-front, the picturesque streets and courtyards, the bygone gaiety of Cremorne Gardens, show an originality and a profound interest in detail which were lost in his later work done under the dominating influence of Whistler. Greaves once said: 'To Mr. Whistler a boat was always a tone, to us it was always a boat.'

For many years Greaves practised the art of painting patiently and disinterestedly, without receiving rewards or recognition, disposing of his work to local patrons and dealers; but in 1911 he was 'discovered' by Mr. W. S. Marchant, of the Goupil Gallery, who became his friend and loyal supporter. An exhibition of Greaves's work held at the Goupil Gallery in 1911 helped to establish his reputation as a painter, and later exhibitions took place in 1922 and 1931. He was elected an honorary member of the Chelsea Arts Club in 1921. In 1922, through the efforts of the rector of Chelsea and several distinguished artists, Greaves was admitted to the Charterhouse. He died in hospital as the result of an accident 23 November 1930. He was unmarried.

A portrait of Greaves by William Nicholson is in the Manchester Art Gallery. Greaves's full-length portrait of his sister 'Tinnie' (Alice Greaves, died 1921) is in the Johannesburg Art Gallery.

[*The Times*, 29 November 1930; E. R. and J. Pennell, *Life of J. McNeill Whistler*, 2 vols., 1908; Catalogues of Goupil Gallery Exhibitions; *Walter Greaves, Catalogue of Paintings, etc., exhibited at the Cottier Gallery, New York* (with an introduction by Christian Brinton), 1912; private information.] M. HARDIE.

GREEN, ALICE SOPHIA AMELIA (1847–1929), better known as MRS. STOPFORD GREEN, historian, wife of John Richard Green, the historian [q.v.], was the seventh child of the Rev. Edward Adderley Stopford, archdeacon of Meath, by his wife, Anne Catherine Duke. She was born 30 May 1847 at Kells, co. Meath. Her mother was a rigid protestant of an almost Calvinist type, and brought up her children in the stern tenets of that creed. Alice imbibed the religious atmosphere of her parents and also inherited some of the political ability of her father, who, though opposed to the disestablishment of the Church of Ireland, saw that Gladstone was determined upon it, and eventually assisted him in drafting the bill (1869). She taught herself Greek in order to help her father in his biblical studies, but at the age of seventeen she was stricken with semiblindness and for seven years could only read for fifteen minutes a day. In 1871 an operation restored her sight. By a self-imposed system of mental training she emerged from her long ordeal with a mind well stored and a remarkably retentive memory.

On the death of Archdeacon Stopford in 1874 the family migrated to England, and Alice, at that time deeply interested in ecclesiastical history, came to live in London with her cousins, the children of Stopford Augustus Brooke [q.v.]. It was here that she met John Richard Green, just becoming famous as the author of the *Short History of the English People* (1874), and the two were married in June 1877. Their short married life was spent in a gallant struggle with her husband's increasing ill-health in the endeavour to carry out his design of writing the history of England on a larger scale. When J. R. Green died in March 1883, he had bequeathed to his wife his own enthusiasm for historical writing as well as a sound training in historical method. She completed and brought out his *Conquest of England* in the year of his death, and was occupied for many years in the production of new and revised editions of his various works. Her first independent book was a biography of Henry II, undertaken at the urgent request of John Morley for his 'English Statesmen' series; this appeared in 1888. She then plunged into a study of the development of English towns, in fulfilment of a promise made to her husband, and brought out her *Town Life in the Fifteenth Century* (2 vols.) in 1894. This book marked her possession of an assured literary style—in which, however, a tendency to generalization had already established itself—and its appearance enhanced her growing reputation as an historian.

During these years Mrs. Green's house in Kensington Square became the centre of a brilliant group of friends, including Florence Nightingale, Mary Kingsley, Bishop and Mrs. Creighton, Mr. and Mrs. Humphry Ward, Bishop Stubbs, John Morley, R. B. Haldane, H. A. L. Fisher, Winston Churchill, and many others. Politicians, writers, and young people met here freely in one of the most interesting salons of the day in London. Following in her husband's footsteps, Mrs. Green became an ardent radical and home ruler, and her conversational powers and mordant wit made her formidable in argument.

Towards the end of the century Mrs. Green came, politically, under the influence of an Irish journalist, John Francis Taylor, whose study of Owen Roe O'Neill (1896) attracted some attention. Her views became anti-English and anti-Imperial on nearly every question, and she presently determined to devote herself to a study of early Irish history, in order to refute the widespread assumption that before the Tudor conquest the Irish clans had had no civilization of their own. As the result of her labours her book, *The Making of Ireland and its Undoing*, appeared in 1908, and provoked much controversy. It was violently attacked in the *Quarterly Review* (January 1909) for inaccuracy. But on the whole her work has stood the test of time: if she deduced too much from the new facts that she discovered, it was high time that these facts should be recognized and interpreted by an historian with sympathy and critical intelligence. This book was followed in 1911 by *Irish Nationality* (the 'Home University Library' series), a little volume that had a large circulation among young Irishmen during the troubled and critical years from 1913 to 1921. Mrs. Green took an active interest in the counterblast to Sir Edward Carson's importation of arms—the gun-running at Howth. She was at this time a close personal friend of Sir Roger Casement [q.v.], but she did not approve of the Easter Rebellion. Still, the tragedies of 1916 went very deep with her, so that she decided to leave her pleasant home in London (36 Grosvenor Road) and to spend her remaining years in Ireland. She settled at 90 St. Stephen's Green, Dublin, and there continued her role of intellectual leader and friend of Young Ireland. In 1918 she published an incisive pamphlet, *Ourselves Alone in Ulster*, attacking Sir Edward Carson's proceedings there; but during the post-War 'troubles', although her house was repeatedly searched by the authorities, her influence was in reality exerted in favour of peace and she was a strong supporter of the Treaty of December 1921. Her name was on the first list of Irish senators nominated by President Cosgrave in December 1922.

Meanwhile Mrs. Green was working indefatigably at her last considerable book, *A History of the Irish State to 1014*, basing it to a large extent on the research of her friend Professor John McNeill. Here she carried her study of the social life of Celtic Ireland very much farther than she had been able to do in the earlier work. It was published in 1925. Although she never learnt to read Irish, Mrs. Green always had the work of original scholars at her disposal, and her two principal books form an important and permanent contribution to the knowledge of Irish civilization. She received the honorary degree of Litt.D. from the university of Liverpool in 1913. Mrs. Green died in Dublin 28 May 1929, two days before her eighty-second birthday.

[*The Times*, 29 May and 7 June 1929; *Manchester Guardian*, 29 and 30 May 1929; *Irish Times* and *Irish Independent*, 29 May 1929; *Irish Statesman*, 8 June 1929; *The Nation* (Dublin), 8 June 1929; *The Letters of J. R. Green*, edited by Leslie Stephen, 1902; private information; personal knowledge.]

J. P. Trevelyan.

GRENFELL, BERNARD PYNE (1869–1926), papyrologist, was born at Birmingham 16 December 1869, the eldest and only surviving son of John Granville Grenfell, F.G.S., a member of the junior branch of the Cornish and Buckinghamshire family of that name, by his wife, Alice, daughter of Henry Pyne. His father, at first (1861–1866) assistant in the department of Greek and Roman antiquities at the British Museum, and later a master successively at King Edward's School, Birmingham, and Clifton College, which he left in 1889, died abroad in 1897. Both parents showed intellectual tastes and wide interests; Mrs. Grenfell in later life took up the study of mythological and amuletic scarabs, on which she contributed articles to learned journals.

As a child Grenfell was delicate and required special treatment at Clifton College, of which he was a scholar; but his health improved at Queen's College, Oxford, where he obtained a scholarship in 1888. He obtained first classes in classical moderations (1890) and *literae humaniores* (1892), and during a fifth year at Oxford turned his attention to the study of Greek papyri, a subject which was then coming into prominence. Elected in 1893 to the Craven travelling fellowship, Grenfell went in the winter of 1893–1894 to Egypt, where he joined Professor (afterwards Sir) Flinders Petrie at Guft (Coptos) in order to learn something of the excavator's art. Purchasing in the course of the winter a long Greek papyrus roll of the third century B.C., Petrie entrusted the task of editing it to Grenfell, who, after publishing in the *Journal of Philology* (vol. xxii, 1894) three seventh-century contracts from Apollonopolis Magna, began work upon it in June 1894. From November until the following April, having been elected a research fellow of his college, Grenfell was again in Egypt, and while there had the good fortune to acquire a second roll containing the remainder of Petrie's text, which consisted of fiscal regulations by Ptolemy II. In 1896 he published the whole under the title *The Revenue Laws of Ptolemy Philadelphus*. Although he had the help of other scholars, the work was essentially Grenfell's own and gave convincing proof of his exceptional gifts alike as decipherer and as commentator. It was almost immediately followed by a slim volume of texts, literary and documentary, acquired in the two previous winters, *An Alexandrian Erotic Fragment and other Greek Papyri* (1896); and a year later appeared a second which bore for the first time, together with Grenfell's name, that of Arthur Surridge Hunt, a junior contemporary at Queen's and a personal friend. Thus was formed a partnership destined to be fruitful in the annals of scholarship; and thenceforth, save in the temporary absence of one or the other, most of their work until Grenfell's death was done in collaboration.

During 1895 the Egypt Exploration Fund (afterwards Society) decided to embrace in its scope the Graeco-Roman period; and in the winter of 1895–1896 Grenfell and David George Hogarth [q.v.], joined in January by Hunt, were sent to the Fayum in order to examine likely sites. Excavations in various places, although not very systematic, were fruitful enough to justify the continuance of the experiment, and next winter Grenfell and Hunt began work at a site some distance south of the Fayum, Behneseh, the ancient Oxyrhynchus, with sensational results. Works of Christian literature, among them the 'Sayings of Jesus', many classical fragments, including a new poem of Sappho, and important documents, ranging from before the Roman conquest to the Arab period, were discovered; and the result was the formation of the Graeco-Roman branch of the Egypt Exploration Fund in 1897.

After further excavations in the Fayum (1898–1902), some of which were undertaken for the university of California at Ûmm el-Baragât (Tebtunis), operations were transferred in March 1902 to El-Hibeh and were continued there during the first part of the next season, after which a return was made to Behneseh. There, in successive campaigns until 1906, vast quantities of papyri were found; and publication followed with commendable promptness in the annual volumes of the Fund (*The Oxyrhynchus Papyri*, 17 volumes, 1898–1927), besides which the two scholars were engaged in editing *The Amherst Papyri* (vol. i, 1900, vol. ii, 1901) and *The Tebtunis Papyri* (vol. i, 1902, vol. ii, 1907). This achievement was rendered the more remarkable by the high standard of scholarship maintained. In the accuracy of their texts and the quality of their commentary, evading no difficulty but free from superfluity, Grenfell and Hunt's editions have never been surpassed, and their methods served as a model to other editors.

Honours were showered on both scholars by universities and academies, alike at home and abroad. Grenfell was elected a fellow of the British Academy in 1905, and in 1908 was appointed to the professorship of papyrology at Oxford, a chair specially created for him. Unfortunately, signs of mental trouble had already appeared. From a break-down in 1906–1907, while in Egypt, he quickly recovered, but a more serious attack in the autumn of 1908 incapacitated him for over four years. The devoted attention of his mother was rewarded by his complete recovery and return to work, with energy and mental power unimpaired, in the spring of 1913. His professorship having meantime lapsed, Hunt was appointed to the vacant chair in 1913, but Grenfell became honorary professor in 1916 and joint professor in 1919. During most of the War years (1914–1918), when Hunt was on military service, Grenfell worked single-handed at the preparation for press of Parts xii–xv of the *Oxyrhynchus Papyri*, besides doing some work on vol. iii of *The Tebtunis Papyri* and collecting materials for a comprehensive study of the geography of Egypt. Early in 1920 he revisited Egypt in order to collate at Cairo the texts of certain papyri intended for Part xvi of the *Oxyrhynchus Papyri*. He returned in April, apparently in good health and spirits, but the old symptoms soon afterwards reappeared, and after a partial recovery a relapse made it necessary for him to go first to a sanatorium at St. Andrews and thence to Murray's Royal Mental Hospital, near Perth. This time he lacked the care of his mother, who had died in 1917, and despite occasional rallies, he never really recovered. He died 18 May 1926, and was buried with his mother in Holywell cemetery, Oxford. He never married. Hunt survived his fellow scholar eight years, dying in 1934.

Grenfell was peculiarly gifted for his life's work. To excellent eyesight and a gift for the marshalling and lucid exposition of a complex mass of evidence he united energy, enthusiasm, and a brain at once imaginative and critical. A very rapid worker, he spared no pains to correct first impressions by later revision. As a man he had a singularly attractive personality. Ardent, generous, and affectionate, he made friends easily and retained them when made; and he won the trust and affection no less than the respect of his Egyptian workmen.

[A. S. Hunt, *Bernard Pyne Grenfell, 1869–1926*, in *Proceedings* of the British Academy, vol. xii, 1926; *Aegyptus*, vol. viii, 1927; *Gnomon*, vol. ii, 1926; publications of the Egypt Exploration Society; personal knowledge.] H. I. Bell.

GRENFELL, FRANCIS WALLACE, first Baron Grenfell, of Kilvey, Glamorganshire (1841–1925), field-marshal, the fourth son of Pascoe St. Leger Grenfell, J.P., D.L., of Maesteg House, Swansea, Glamorganshire, by his first wife, Catherine Anne, daughter of James Du Pré, M.P., of Wilton Park, Beaconsfield, Buckinghamshire, was born at Maesteg House 29 April 1841. The Grenfells are an old Buckinghamshire family, well known as bankers in the City of London and also as sportsmen, foremost among the latter being the present Lord Desborough. An aunt of Francis Grenfell, Frances Eliza Grenfell, married Charles Kingsley in 1844. The Du Prés also are an old Buckinghamshire family.

Grenfell was educated at Milton Abbas School, Dorset, but left school early, and after passing the army entrance examination, purchased his commission into the third battalion of the 60th Rifles (later the King's Royal Rifle Corps) in 1859. His early service was uneventful and advancement slow; he actually purchased his commission as captain in 1873 in the last gazette in which purchase was allowed. Then in 1874 he decided to leave the army, going so far as to send in his papers and give away his uniform. At that instant he was unexpectedly invited to become aide-de-camp to General Sir Arthur Cunynghame [q.v.] in South Africa, and accepted the offer at the last moment. Thereafter Grenfell's prospects improved rapidly. In 1875 he took part in the bloodless Diamond Fields expedition in Griqualand West. Again in 1878 he acted as staff officer during the last of the Kaffir wars. A successful expedition was undertaken against the Galeka tribe during which Grenfell was present at the action of Quintana Mountain; this was followed by a march against the rebellious Gaika tribe, in the north-east of Cape Colony, and ended with their complete rout in the Gwili Gwili Mountains. For his services Grenfell received a brevet majority. Next, the Zulus began to trespass on British territory, committing many provocative acts; these, early in 1879, led to the invasion of Zululand. Grenfell was then given an appointment on the head-quarters staff, and so took part in the final defeat of the Zulus at Ulundi on 4 July 1879. Returning home he was appointed brigadier-major at Shorncliffe, receiving a brevet-lieutenant-colonelcy, for his war services.

Early in 1881, when the first Boer War broke out, Grenfell returned to Natal to act as deputy-assistant-quartermaster-general, but saw no fighting, as peace was made soon after his arrival. In 1882 he was again selected for staff service, this time as assistant-adjutant-general to Sir Garnet (afterwards Viscount) Wolseley [q.v.] in the Egyptian expedition of that summer; he was thus present at the battle of Tel-el-Kebir (13 September). After the close of that campaign he remained in Egypt as assistant-adjutant-general to the permanent garrison, and was at the same time promoted brevet-colonel and aide-de-camp to Queen Victoria. Desiring to continue serving in Egypt he accepted the appointment under Sir Evelyn Wood [q.v.] as second in command of the Egyptian forces, which were then placed under British tutelage. At that time the revolt of the Mahdi was making great headway in the Sudan, so that General Gordon was dispatched to Khartoum in January 1884 in order to extricate the Egyptian subjects and garrisons from the Sudan. By the autumn of 1884 Gordon's position had become grave, and Lord Wolseley was sent out to rescue him. Grenfell thereupon proceeded to Assuan in order to command the Egyptian troops on the Nile and the communications of the whole expedition. After the failure of the attempted relief (January 1885), Grenfell remained at Assuan in command of the Egyptian detachments, being finally appointed sirdar of the Egyptian army in succession to Sir Evelyn Wood in April 1885. He thus came to play an important part in the operations undertaken for the defence of the frontiers of Egypt against the Dervishes during the next few years. He commanded a division of the Anglo-Egyptian forces at the battle of Ginnis on 30 December 1885, for which action he received the C.B. and the grand cordon of the Medjidie, while next year he was created a K.C.B. and promoted major-general. Shortly after, he assumed sole command of the Egyptian forces which repulsed Osman Digna's attack on Suakin at Gamaiza (20 December 1888) and then signally defeated the amir of Kordofan at Toski (3 August 1889). Two years later (1891) he consolidated the Egyptian hold on Suakin. On the death of the Khedive Tewfik, in the ensuing spring (1892), Grenfell reluctantly resigned the sirdarship. His tenure of office was memorable for the reorganization of the Egyptian forces which were to prove of such value during Lord Kitchener's subsequent re-conquest of the Sudan. Without ever giving proof of any outstanding gifts of generalship, which indeed were not required at this period, Grenfell had completed his task in Egypt with rare common sense and to excellent purpose.

On his return home, and after being rewarded with the G.C.M.G., Grenfell was appointed deputy-adjutant-general for reserve forces at the War Office, a post which involved the supervision of reserves, militia, yeomanry, and volunteers. In 1894 he was raised to the position of inspector-general. During 1896 he was dispatched to Moscow to attend the coronation festivities of the young Tsar Nicholas II, and in 1897 figured prominently at the celebration of Queen Victoria's diamond jubilee. Shortly afterwards he was appointed to the command of the British garrison in Egypt. This new position was not easy, since (Lord) Kitchener [q.v.] was now in command of the expedition which had been working up the Nile since the spring of 1896. But

Grenfell, with great self-effacement, refrained from the slightest act that might hinder Kitchener; indeed, although he was the latter's senior in rank—having been promoted lieutenant-general in 1898—he subordinated his own authority to that of the sirdar in very generous fashion. After Kitchener's victory of Omdurman (2 September 1898), Grenfell in the following January was appointed governor and commander-in-chief of Malta. There he proved a successful governor, displaying much interest in the antiquities of the island and in the methods of cultivation in use. Finally, at the coronation of King Edward VII in 1902, he was raised to the peerage as Baron Grenfell, of Kilvey, co. Glamorgan. In 1903 he was selected for the command of the newly created fourth Army Corps and, on promotion to full general in 1904, was appointed commander-in-chief in Ireland, a post which he held until 1908 when he was promoted field-marshal. During the remainder of his life he devoted himself to work on behalf of the Church Lads' Brigade, the Royal Horticultural Society, of which he was president, and to various other voluntary services. He died at Windlesham, Surrey, 27 January 1925.

Lord Grenfell was a man of wide and deep sympathies, taking a profound interest, wherever he served, in the daily life and history of the people around him. He was an Egyptologist and an antiquary of no small attainments. His popularity, both in the army and in society generally, never waned.

Grenfell was the recipient of many honours: he was a colonel commandant of the 60th Rifles from 1899 until his death and colonel of the 2nd Life Guards from 1898 to 1907, when he exchanged this colonelcy for that of the 1st Life Guards. He received the honorary LL.D. degree of Edinburgh University in 1902 and of Cambridge University in 1903. He was sworn of the privy council of Ireland in 1909.

Grenfell was twice married: first, in 1887 to Evelyn (died without issue 1899), daughter of Major-General Robert Blucher Wood; secondly, in 1903 to the Hon. Margaret (died 1911), daughter of Lewis Asshunt Majendie, M.P., J.P., of Hedingham, Essex, by whom he had two sons and a daughter. He was succeeded as second baron by his elder son, Pascoe Christian Victor Francis (born 1905).

[*The Times*, 28 January 1925; Lord Grenfell, *Memoirs*, 1925; Army Lists.]

H. DE WATTEVILLE.

GRIFFITH, ARTHUR (1872–1922), Irish political leader, was born at 4 Dominick Street, Dublin, 31 March 1872, the second son of Arthur Griffith, printer, by his wife, Mary Phelan. He was educated at the Christian Brothers schools, Strand Street and St. Mary's Place, and later he served his apprenticeship as a compositor and worked for a short time at the printing trade. At an early age he associated himself with the Irish national movement. As a boy in his teens he was a follower of Charles Stewart Parnell in his last campaign.

The fall of Parnell in November 1890 led to a disruption of the nationalist ranks, rent the Irish Home Rule movement from end to end, and caused widespread disillusionment and pessimism. Arthur Griffith with certain other young men, inspired by an ardent patriotism, felt that the time had come to rally the Irish people, and especially the youth, to a heroic national effort. They resented as a humiliation the fact that representatives in the Westminster parliament, elected to secure Irish rights, should enter into close association with English political parties. Irish nationalist opinion had hitherto accepted a Home Rule bill as the only measure of freedom immediately attainable and therefore worth working for. With the fall of Parnell, however, it had become clear that years must pass before even that modified measure of freedom could be realized. Before this time Griffith had been interested in various clubs and organizations which had maintained the Fenian and separatist tradition, and were the precursors of the Sinn Fein organization of later days. Among the societies founded at the time, of which Griffith was a member or with which he had connexions, were, in addition to the Gaelic League, the Young Ireland Society, the Celtic Literary Society in Cork and Dublin, and Cumann na Gaedheal. He also joined the Irish Republican Brotherhood, a secret organization which carried on the activist traditions of the Fenians. These various societies, however, of small but enthusiastic membership, remained an apparently negligible force in Irish politics.

In 1896 Griffith went to the Transvaal, where he was employed for a time in the diamond mines at Langlaagthe, and later spent about a year in Johannesburg, where he joined a fellow countryman in publishing a small newspaper. Before he left Ireland it had already been recognized that his intense patriotism, his strength of character, his capacity for clear constructive thought, and his gifts as a journalist, marked him out as a leader. In 1898 the celebration in Ireland of the centenary of the Rising of 1798 was looked to by the minority nationalists as a means of overcoming apathy and of founding a new movement which would enlist the enthusiasm of Irish youth. '’98 clubs' with a frankly separatist object were formed. Griffith returned to Ireland in January 1899 in order to take part in the founding of a weekly paper which was to be the organ of this new movement. Of this paper, *The United Irishman*, the first issue of which was published on 4 March 1899, he was editor until 1906. The power of his articles was quickly recognized, not only by the more ardent supporters of the separatist idea, but also by a new body of readers which was varied and intelligent, though comparatively small in number. He preached the doctrine that Irish self-government could never be won through parliamentary action at Westminster, where national aspirations were made a pawn in English party politics. But at that time the vast majority of the Irish people were not prepared to forsake parliamentary action.

In 1904 Griffith wrote in the *United Irishman* a series of articles, which later in the same year were published as a pamphlet entitled *The Resurrection of Hungary, a Parallel for Ireland.* This dealt with the movement of Kossuth and Déak in Hungary in the period following 1848, and proposed the adoption of a similar policy towards the British administration in Ireland. The aim was the setting up of a national assembly functioning by the goodwill and co-operation of patriotic citizens united in their resolve not to recognize foreign institutions. Passive resistance to British administration was to follow. Thus, when Irishmen were elected to parliament, instead of going to Westminster to plead, they would assemble in Dublin as the representatives of the Irish people, who would treat the decisions arrived at in this assembly as the equivalent of national laws. By this popular corporate action it was proposed to make British rule impotent. The 'National Council', hitherto a group rather than an organization, which had been in existence for some years, held a convention in the Rotunda, Dublin, on 28 November 1905. At this convention Griffith elaborated his adaptation of the Hungarian method to Irish conditions under the title of the 'Sinn Fein' policy.

The foundation of Sinn Fein was an event of the first importance in the social and political history of modern Ireland. Its importance lay in its clear enunciation of, and energetic efforts to put into practice, the doctrine of national self-help and self-reliance. The words *sinn fein* mean simply 'We Ourselves'. They were chosen as summing up the attitude of Griffith and his followers in the face of the accepted policy of the majority of nationalists, who looked chiefly to the liberal party in England, or to the persuasion of the English electorate, or to the interplay of English party politics for the realization of Home Rule. In contrast with the latter policy Griffith set out to impress upon the Irish public the necessity for self-reliance and for direct though peaceful action on their part in order to achieve self-government. This was the core of his 'Hungarian' policy, and indeed of all his proposals for the improvement of Irish conditions, social, cultural, political, or economic. His principal objective was an independent self-governing Ireland. His practical genius sought the attainment of this aim by those means which lay nearest to hand and which best served the interests of his country. In all his efforts he was actuated primarily by a steady realism, which made him put the welfare of his countrymen before more abstract and less immediate considerations. He was a believer in physical force as a method which on a suitable opportunity might prove serviceable, and he only severed his connexion with the Irish Republican Brotherhood in 1906 because of its rule that its members must act as a body and as directed by their leaders. As a member of the new Sinn Fein organization, he could not hold himself so bound. His 'Hungarian' policy, moreover, gave a definite programme of action to those who were advocating a merely theoretical physical force policy. Griffith put forward as something which might unite all Irishmen the policy of the kingdom of Ireland, or as it was sometimes called, the policy of the King, Lords, and Commons. In his view no constitutional nationalist could ask for more, and no separatist could take less.

Griffith's movement soon gathered support, though apparently it was not sufficiently strong to be a menace to the constitutional nationalist party. Already by 1906 there was a significant group of Sinn Feiners in the Dublin corporation. But the overwhelming victory of the liberal party in the general election held at the beginning of that year reawakened hopes of an immediate Home Rule bill. Griffith hardly shared these hopes. Nevertheless, he agreed that the nationalist party should be given a chance to get the promises made to them fulfilled. In the meantime the action of Sinn Fein should be directed to ensuring that the proposed measures of Home Rule should not be whittled down, but should be sufficiently wide to give the contemplated Irish government real power to legislate and govern in accordance with the opinion of the Irish people and with their consent. The hopes, however, of a substantial measure of Irish self-government were soon disappointed. Instead of a Home Rule bill, an 'Irish Council's' bill was introduced in parliament in May 1907; but criticism by Griffith and his party and the general lack of support for it in the country forced the bill's withdrawal. Home Rule once more became the issue. The Sinn Fein party, of which Griffith was elected president in 1910, maintained its attitude of critical watchfulness. Confronted with the threat of force on the part of the Ulster Volunteers—a body formed in 1912 in order to oppose Home Rule—the British government wavered. In the face of this weakness the Irish National Volunteers were established in November 1913, in an atmosphere of enthusiasm unknown since the days of Parnell. Nationalist young men all over Ireland enrolled in large numbers. The Volunteer organization was declared to be strictly non-party and its objects were declared to be: (1) to secure and maintain the rights and liberties common to all the people of Ireland; (2) to train, discipline, arm, and equip, a body of Irish volunteers for that purpose; and (3) to unite in these aims Irishmen of every creed and of every party and class. Griffith associated himself with this new movement and drilled as a volunteer. In July 1914 he took part in the Howth gun-running incident, when the Irish Volunteers succeeded in taking possession of a quantity of arms and ammunition landed for them from a yacht belonging to Robert Erskine Childers [q.v.]. He marched in from Howth to Dublin with a gun on his shoulder.

The outbreak of the European War in August 1914 found Griffith strongly opposed to any Irishman joining the British army or serving under any conditions in an expeditionary force. His constant opposition to England and his advocacy of Irish claims brought the ban of the military authorities upon his paper *Eire*, which along with its contemporary *Sinn Féin* (also edited by Griffith) was suppressed in December 1914. He immediately brought out a newspaper called *Scissors and Paste*, the title of which disclosed the principle on which the paper was edited; it consisted of extracts tending to show that all was not well with the Allied cause in the War. *Scissors and Paste* was suppressed in its turn, in 1915, to be followed by *Nationality*. Griffith's earlier papers had been almost as unfortunate. *The United Irishman*, published at irregular intervals, ceased publication in 1906 as the result of a libel action. Within a month *Sinn Féin* appeared, and ran for a while as a daily newspaper, the first issue in this form appearing on 28 August 1909. The policy of all these papers was the same, but even in 1914 that policy had not yet reached and won the approval of the majority, and tens of thousands of young Irishmen joined the British army. Griffith, however, did not waver in his opposition to this course, nor in his hope that in the readjustments which would inevitably follow the War, Ireland would at last come into her own. That section of the Irish Volunteers which believed in his doctrines was often called the Sinn Fein Volunteers.

Griffith's twenty years of apparently thankless work began at last to have its effect on the national consciousness. Whatever his personal attitude may have been towards the policy of insurrection, it was but natural that the rising of Easter 1916 should be called the Sinn Fein Rebellion. There was in this the recognition of its spiritual parentage. The leaders of the Rebellion were all members of the Irish Republican Brotherhood. Griffith, who had left that organization several years before, was probably not one of those who had previous knowledge of the Rebellion, and he took no part in it. In the summer of 1916, following the execution of the leaders of the Rebellion, it was recognized that the country was impressed by Griffith's work, and that support of Sinn Fein was rapidly growing. That party contested by-elections, and except in special constituencies was sensationally successful. Griffith himself was elected a member for East Cavan in June 1918. The Sinn Fein members elected were pledged not to attend the parliament at Westminster.

In the years following 1916 Griffith led a life of strain and difficulty, both physically and mentally. He had been arrested on 3 May 1916, after the Rebellion, and had been imprisoned first at Wandsworth and later at Reading, being released just before Christmas. On 17 May 1918 he was again arrested in connexion with a German plot scare in Ireland and was imprisoned at Gloucester, where he was detained until March of the following year. On 24 November 1920 he was again arrested and imprisoned in Mountjoy, Dublin, not being set free until the signature of the Anglo-Irish truce (11 July 1921). During this period of imprisonment, in December 1920, he was visited by Archbishop Clune, of Perth, with certain proposals for a peace with the British government. He was himself certain that these interviews would lead to a settlement, and was even hopeful of a general release before Christmas of that year. The negotiations were broken off by Mr. Lloyd George, following upon what he considered, wrongly as it proved, to be signs of a weakening in the Sinn Fein movement in the country. In the intervals of freedom allowed him in these years, Griffith carried on his campaign on behalf of Sinn Fein.

During these years events had marched quickly in Ireland. On 25 October 1917 the Sinn Fein organization held a convention at the Mansion House, Dublin, at which the growing strength of the movement was clearly demonstrated. At this convention, which declared in favour of an Irish republic, Griffith resigned his presidency of the party in favour of Mr. Eamon de Valera, becoming instead one of the vice-presidents. Griffith himself did not possess the romantic personality which moves crowds, and although a forceful speaker, was no spell-binding orator. Mr. de Valera had taken part in the Rebellion, had been a commandant, and had narrowly escaped execution. He had a fine public presence and the capacity to move large audiences. Griffith believed that in him he saw a leader who could sweep the country, and accordingly resigned in Mr. de Valera's favour. That decision was strongly opposed by those of his supporters who had followed him from the beginning, but he persisted in his determination to resign.

In the general election held in December 1918 the Sinn Fein party obtained an overwhelming success, and on 21 January 1919, Dail Eireann was formed, and proclaimed itself the legitimate parliament of Ireland. Mr. de Valera, on his escape from Lincoln jail, was made the head of the Dail government with the title of prime minister, and Griffith (vice-president) minister for home affairs. Mr. de Valera went to the United States in June 1919, and Griffith was acting-president during the greater part of the critical years 1919 and 1920. During that period Griffith enjoyed the confidence and affection of colleagues like Michael Collins [q.v.] and Richard Mulcahy, who were responsible for the active resistance to British forces throughout the country. The real policy of Sinn Fein, enunciated by Griffith years before, was now as far as possible put into practice. The town and county councils refused to acknowledge Dublin Castle; Sinn Fein courts were set up and administered justice; and civil departments of the Dail government functioned as far as circumstances would allow.

At the end of 1920 Mr. de Valera returned from America. Six months later (11 July 1921) a truce was signed by Sir Nevil Macready, the commander-in-chief of British troops in Ireland, and by Richard Mulcahy as chief of staff of the Irish Volunteers. Proposals for negotiations were discussed between representatives of the British government and the Irish leaders. Informal conversations were followed by correspondence between Mr. Lloyd George and Mr. de Valera, until the stage was reached for formal negotiations. Mr. de Valera himself did not wish to participate directly in these negotiations, and he proposed that Dail Eireann should send plenipotentiaries under the chairmanship of Griffith. Griffith accepted this position and, accompanied by Michael Collins and three other plenipotentiaries, carried on negotiations with the British government and eventually secured the agreement incorporated in the Treaty of 6 December 1921.

Mr. de Valera, on the return of the plenipotentiaries, endeavoured to secure the rejection of the Treaty, but was defeated in the Dail; and on 10 January 1922 Griffith was elected president of Dail Eireann. On 14 January a provisional government was elected, with Michael Collins as chairman. A general election held in the following June resulted in an overwhelming victory for the Treaty. The anti-Treaty party then resorted to civil war. Before the new Dail, which was to act as the constituent assembly of the newly created Irish Free State, could meet, Griffith, whose health had been severely taxed by the strain of the preceding six months, died suddenly, 12 August, in a private nursing home in Leeson Street, Dublin, as he was about to leave for his office at Government Buildings. His death came as a signal shock to a troubled country, and his funeral was the occasion of remarkable demonstrations of grief on the part of the people. Thousands filed past his bier during the days that his body lay in state in the City Hall, Dublin. He was buried in Glasnevin cemetery.

Arthur Griffith was a shy and retiring man, but he had brought a new soul into Ireland. His writing, distinguished by its clarity and simplicity, reflected his burning earnestness and selfless devotion to his country and people. He spent his life in comparative poverty, sometimes receiving for his work scarcely as much as the wages of a hired labourer. In the summer of 1901 he refused an offer of £1,000 a year to go to New York and take up a post on one of the leading newspapers. He often wrote, set up in type, and distributed, practically unaided, individual issues of his papers, making as the result of his toil as little as 30*s*. for a week's work. In spite of his literary gifts, wide reading, and extensive knowledge of men and affairs, Griffith was a true representative of the Dublin working man. He had a real and intimate sympathy with the people in their aspirations, in their poverty, and in their patience. He was always in touch with reality. He was a man of great moral and physical courage. No task was too small for him—no risk too great. It might be said of Griffith that his qualities asserted themselves in spite of him. He always preferred to stay in the background, but was always ready to come forward in order to take over a thankless task. It was in this spirit that he agreed to accept the position of chief plenipotentiary for the negotiations with the British government. When he was told by the man whom he had urged the Irish people to elect as leader, that it might be necessary to 'have a scapegoat', he said he was ready to take that position. During his earlier struggles he had to meet with indifference and contempt. When at last he had led his movement to the eve of success, it was the claims of others to leadership that he advocated to the neglect of his own. He declared in August 1922 that it was his intention to move that Collins be made president, when the Dail met in September. These two men, so dissimilar in many ways, had formed a sure friendship based on mutual respect. During the last six months of his life the nation which he had served was daily urged to renounce him, but the people had come to recognize that during her long history their country had known no more noble and devoted servant.

Griffith died before he could see the Irish people reap the full fruit of his labours on their behalf. But even in his troubled last days it had become evident that in the comparatively short space of one lifetime, and largely through his efforts and the spirit which he infused into those around him, and ultimately into the Irish nation, a record of enduring achievement had been established. An autonomous Irish State remains as his best monument.

Griffith married in 1910 Mary, second daughter of Peter Sheehan, of Dublin, and had a son and a daughter.

There are portraits of Griffith by Sir John Lavery and Lily Williams in the Municipal Gallery of Modern Art, Dublin.

[Official *Reports* of Dail Eireann; private information; personal knowledge.]

W. T. Cosgrave.

GRIFFITHS, Sir JOHN NORTON-, first baronet (1871–1930), engineer. [See Norton-Griffiths.]

GUGGISBERG, Sir FREDERICK GORDON (1869–1930), soldier and administrator, was born at Toronto 20 July 1869, the eldest son of Frederick Guggesburg, merchant, of Galt, Ontario (of German-Swiss origin), by his wife, Dora Louise Wilson, who came originally from the United States of America. Coming to England about 1879, Guggisberg was educated at Burney's school, near Portsmouth; entered the Royal Military Academy, Woolwich, in 1887, and was commissioned in the Royal Engineers in 1889. He served at Singapore from 1893 to 1896, and became instructor in fortification at Woolwich in 1897. In this office he distinguished himself by reforming the methods and syllabus of instruction. In 1900 he published *The Shop; The Story of the Royal Military Academy*, and, under the pseudonym 'Ubique', *Modern Warfare*, in 1903.

In 1902 Guggisberg was employed under the Colonial Office on a special survey of the Gold Coast Colony and Ashanti, and in 1905 was appointed director of surveys in that colony. In 1908 he returned to Chatham for regimental work; but in 1910 was appointed director of surveys in Southern Nigeria. Here he found full scope for his energies and capacity for organization and for the guidance of his assistants compiled *The Handbook of the Southern Nigeria Survey* (1911). Of this work the director-general of the ordnance survey wrote: 'The duties of all members of the staff were strictly defined and, in particular, sensible rules were laid down as to the relations of the staff with the civil administration. Much attention was paid to the treatment of villagers; unpaid labour was forbidden; all goods bought were to be paid for at the recognized rate, and great care was to be exercised not to damage the crops. . . . They were model instructions and the survey of Nigeria was a model survey.'

On the union of Southern and Northern Nigeria in 1913 Guggisberg was appointed surveyor-general of Nigeria. In 1914 he was appointed director of public works on the Gold Coast, but on the outbreak of the European War rejoined the army, and commanded the 94th field company, Royal Engineers, from 1915 to 1916; he was in command of the Royal Engineers in the 8th division during the battle of the Somme (July 1916), and in the 66th division from November 1916. He was brigadier-general commanding the 170th infantry brigade 1917–1918, assistant-inspector-general of training, general headquarters, France, in 1918; and in command of the 100th infantry brigade in 1918. He was mentioned in dispatches five times, and was awarded the D.S.O. (1918).

In 1919 Guggisberg was appointed governor of the Gold Coast. There he energetically undertook works of development and extension of railways, and created the deep water harbour of Takoradi superseding the use of surf-boats for handling traffic. Close association with native Africans during his survey work convinced Guggisberg that the African races are capable of eventually attaining the mental development of the European. Toward the close of his life he wrote: 'My practical experience . . . during the last twenty-seven years has convinced me that what individuals have achieved, in spite of ill-selected systems of education, can be achieved by the race generally, provided we alter our educational methods' [G. Guggisberg and A. G. Fraser, *The Future of the Negro*, 1929]. In order to carry out that purpose he founded Achimota College for the training of native teachers and instructors; it is now the largest and most complete establishment for the education of native Africans. The aim of Guggisberg's whole policy was the development of the country by and for the native rather than for the benefit of European capitalists.

In 1928 Guggisberg was appointed governor of British Guiana, but owing to failing health he was obliged to leave the colony in 1929, and soon afterwards resigned the appointment. He introduced drastic administrative reforms and devoted himself energetically to the problems of maintaining and improving the system of drainage and irrigation upon which the sugar and rice cultivation of the colony depends. He also promoted immigration and peasant settlement and the development of the production and marketing of rice. These activities were cut short by his illness and resignation in 1929. He died at Bexhill 21 April 1930.

During his last illness Guggisberg addressed to his personal friends a remarkable letter setting forth the aims which he had had in view in his administrative work in British Guiana, his confidence in divine guidance and in the spirit of Christianity, and his hope of being able to return to Africa 'to try to do some more work for the African races. . . . As you know', he concluded, 'my heart is in Africa, and I believe that away from the trammels of the Colonial Office, there is opportunity for me to do something useful both for the Empire and for the natives of Africa.'

Guggisberg was of tall and athletic figure, as a young man very handsome, and always of impressive and dignified presence. His personality was attractive and inspiriting. He was for some years captain of the Royal Engineers' cricket eleven, and was a fine player of polo, racquets, golf, and football. He was created C.M.G. in 1908 and K.C.M.G. in 1922, and was made a chevalier of the legion of honour in 1917.

Guggisberg was twice married: first, in 1895 to Ethel Way, whom he divorced in 1904 and by whom he had two daughters; secondly, in 1905 to (Lilian) Decima Moore, the actress, daughter of Edward Henry Moore, of Brighton, county analyst. She accompanied him on his survey journeys, and their joint book, *We Two in West Africa* (1909), is an interesting study of a transitional phase in West African development.

[*The Royal Engineers' Journal*, March 1931; private information; personal knowledge.]

OLIVIER.

GUINNESS, EDWARD CECIL, first EARL OF IVEAGH (1847–1927), philanthropist, was born at St. Anne's, Clontarf, county Dublin, 10 November 1847, the youngest of the three sons of Sir Benjamin Lee Guinness [q.v.], brewer, of Dublin, by his wife, Elizabeth, third daughter of

Edward Guinness, of Dublin. His eldest brother, Arthur, was raised to the peerage as Baron Ardilaun in 1880. Edward Cecil Guinness was not sent to any public school, but was prepared by a tutor for entrance to Trinity College, Dublin, where he took his degree in 1870. His father died in 1868, leaving him a share in the Guinness brewery at St. James's Gate, Dublin. The brewery had been bought by his great-grandfather, Arthur Guinness, in 1759 from Mark Rainsford, and in 1855 Sir Benjamin Guinness had become the sole proprietor. A large export trade was developed, and the business became famous all over the world. After leaving the university Edward Guinness took up his part in the management of this great concern, and showed administrative and financial ability of a very high order. He also interested himself in public affairs, and from early manhood was a prominent figure in Dublin municipal life. He was high sheriff of the city in 1876, and of the county in 1885.

In 1886 the Guinness brewery was incorporated as Arthur Guinness, Son, & Co., Ltd. When the public company was formed the capital required by the vendors was subscribed many times over. Indeed the applications received amounted to more than a hundred million pounds, so anxious was the public to acquire shares. Edward Guinness became chairman.

Three years later Guinness retired from active management of the company, though he retained the chairmanship. In November of that year (1889), in order to mark his retirement, he placed in trust the sum of £250,000, to be expended in the erection of dwellings which could be let at such rents as would place them within reach of the poorest of the labouring population. £200,000 was to be spent in London, and the remainder in Dublin. Guinness followed up this gift by presenting another quarter of a million pounds to Dublin for the purpose of pulling down slum property in the Bull Alley district. As a result seven acres which had been covered with squalid dwellings were cleared. This was one of the greatest benefits that Guinness ever conferred upon his native city. Among later instances of his munificence was a contribution of £250,000 to the Lister Institute of Preventive Medicine in London for the endowment of bacteriological research.

In 1885 Guinness was created a baronet, and in 1891 he was raised to the peerage of the United Kingdom as Baron Iveagh, of Iveagh, county Down. During the South African War he equipped and maintained an Irish field hospital. In 1903, when King Edward VII and Queen Alexandra visited Ireland for the first time after their coronation, Lord Iveagh gave £5,000 to the Dublin hospitals, and he repeated this act of liberality on the occasion of the visit of King George V and Queen Mary in 1911.

In 1905 Lord Iveagh was raised to a viscounty. By this time he lived chiefly in England, where he had bought Elveden Hall, in Suffolk, a well-known sporting estate. Here he entertained both King Edward and King George for pheasant and partridge shooting. But his interest in Ireland did not diminish. The Iveagh markets, which were opened in Dublin in 1907, were due chiefly to his generosity. In 1908 he was elected chancellor of Dublin University in succession to the fourth Earl of Rosse—an appropriate honour, for his services to his old university had been both liberal and judicious. In September 1909 he received a striking compliment, when the nationalist corporation of the city of Dublin presented him with an address of thanks for his many and lavish gifts to Dublin, gifts which, in the words of the address, 'constitute the noblest monuments of your generosity and civic patriotism'. About the same time there was a movement among the nationalists to offer him, notwithstanding his strong and openly expressed unionist views, the lord mayoralty of Dublin; but, with a tact which was characteristic and which left behind no ill feeling, he declined to allow his name to be put forward.

The disturbances in Ireland during and immediately after the European War caused much distress to Lord Iveagh. He took no active part in the settlement of 1922, but he maintained his connexion with the Irish Free State, and continued his many charities under the new régime. In 1919 he was advanced to the dignity of an earldom, becoming Earl of Iveagh and Viscount Elveden. In March 1925, when the Ken Wood preservation committee had come to the end of its resources, he purchased the remainder of the Ken Wood estate to the north of Hampstead Heath, about seventy-six acres, and arranged that this area should become public property in ten years' time, or at his death should it occur before that term. The estate was thus saved from being sold for building purposes.

Iveagh was a man of quiet and unassuming manner, impressing all who came into contact with him by his courtesy and genuine kindness no less than by his high sense of public duty and undoubted ability. He certainly took the utmost care that his great benefactions should be used to the best advantage of those whom they were intended to benefit. In addition to his other honours he was created a knight of St. Patrick in 1896 and received the G.C.V.O. in 1910. He was elected F.R.S. in 1906 and was granted honorary doctorates by the universities of Dublin and Aberdeen. He married in 1873 his cousin Adelaide Maud (died 1916), daughter of Richard Samuel Guinness, M.P., of Deepwell, co. Dublin, and had three sons. He died at his London house in Grosvenor Place, 7 October 1927, and was succeeded as second earl by his eldest son, Rupert Edward Cecil Lee (born 1874).

Lord Iveagh's estate at his death was valued provisionally at £11,000,000. He bequeathed to the nation a valuable collection of pictures, including twenty-four examples by Reynolds and Romney. It was his intention that these should form the nucleus of an art gallery at the house at Ken Wood which he endowed with the sum of £5,000 for this purpose.

[*The Times*, 8 October 1927.]

A. Cochrane.

GUTHRIE, Sir JAMES (1859–1930), portrait-painter and president of the Royal Scottish Academy, was born at Greenock, 10 June 1859, the third son and fourth and youngest child of the Rev. John Guthrie, D.D., a minister of the Evangelical Union who had charges in London and Glasgow, by his wife, Ann, daughter of Thomas Orr. He was educated at Glasgow High School and University, but, having determined to be an artist, left college without taking a degree. He never attended an art school, and except for advice from John Pettie [q.v.] in London in 1879–1881, when the future animal-painter, Joseph Crawhall, junior, was with him, he was entirely self-trained. Pictures by Guthrie attracted attention at the Royal Academy in 1882 and 1883, but he had become associated with the group of young rebel artists then coming together in Glasgow, and his earlier development is related to that of the 'Glasgow School'. After painting figure and landscape pictures at Cockburnspath, Berwickshire, which during his residence there (1883–1885) was the country centre of the new movement, Guthrie returned to Glasgow, where he painted chiefly portraits at once realistic and pictorial. Some of these, with one or two of his rustic subjects, were very favourably noticed in Paris before the first great success of the 'Glasgow School' at Munich in 1890. He was elected A.R.S.A. (1888) and R.S.A. (1892), and was also a member of several foreign art societies and was awarded many medals abroad.

Settling down as a portrait-painter, Guthrie had for a few years a studio in London as well as in Glasgow, but in 1902 he was elected president of the Royal Scottish Academy and removed to Edinburgh. Academy affairs were in a critical state, and the position of the other national art institutions of Scotland was unsatisfactory and was being investigated by a government commission. Under Guthrie's guidance the differences within the Academy were composed and, in a considerable degree through his influence, new galleries for the Academy were inaugurated in 1911 and improved conditions obtained for the National Galleries of Scotland. He was knighted in 1903.

Meanwhile Guthrie's art had been developing. During the 'nineties there were occasions when purely decorative qualities and Whistlerian tone had attracted him; but from about 1897 he was completely himself, and the portraits painted after that date possess a depth of insight and a nobility of outlook and style which make them perhaps the most distinguished of their period.

Having filled the position of president with conspicuous success, Guthrie resigned early in 1919 with the intention of devoting himself quietly to his own work, but a few weeks later was induced to accept a commission, from the National Portrait Gallery, London, to paint the large portrait group 'Some Statesmen of the Great War' now in that gallery. A very notable work, remarkable in both portraiture and design, it occupied most of his last decade, and had just been finished when he died 6 September 1930 at Rowmore on the Gareloch, Dumbartonshire, where he had resided for many years. The series of studies from life made for his 'Statesmen' was presented to the Scottish National Portrait Gallery, Edinburgh.

Guthrie was a man of singular refinement and personal distinction, as well as a highly gifted artist and a very able president of the Royal Scottish Academy. He married in 1897 Helen Newton (died 1912), second daughter of Alexander Whitelaw, of Rowmore, and had one son.

There are good photographs but no painted portrait of Guthrie. A drawing of him made in 1888 by E. A. Walton is in the Scottish National Portrait Gallery, Edinburgh.

[Sir James L. Caw, *Sir James Guthrie, P.R.S.A., LL.D.* (with contributions by Sir D. Y. Cameron, Frank Rinder, and John Warrack), 1932; F. Rinder and W. D. McKay, *The Royal Scottish Academy 1826–1916*, 1917; Royal Scottish Academy *Annual Reports*, 1918, 1919, and 1930; *Scotsman* and *Glasgow Herald*, 8 September 1930; personal knowledge.] J. L. Caw.

HAGGARD, Sir **HENRY RIDER** (1856–1925), novelist, was born 22 June 1856 at West Bradenham Hall, Norfolk, the sixth son of William Meybohm Rider Haggard, of West Bradenham, barrister-at-law, by his wife, Ella, elder daughter and co-heir of Bazett Doveton, of the East India Company's service. He was educated at Ipswich grammar school and by private tutors. In 1875, at the age of nineteen, he went out to South Africa as secretary Sir Henry Bulwer, governor of Natal. At the time of the first annexation of the Transvaal (1877) he was on the staff of the special commissioner, Sir Theophilus Shepstone [q.v.], and hoisted the Union flag in the square at Pretoria. In 1878 he became a master and registrar of the high court of the Transvaal. In 1879 he returned to England, and married in 1880 a Norfolk heiress, Mariana Louisa, daughter of Major John Margitson, 19th Regiment, of Ditchingham House, Norfolk. They had one son (who died young) and three daughters. On going back to the Transvaal he witnessed its surrender to the Boers and the overthrow of Shepstone's policy. He returned again to England shortly afterwards.

Haggard, like many other writers, read for the bar—he was called by Lincoln's Inn in 1884—but soon discovered that literature was to be his career. In 1882 he had published *Cetywayo and his White Neighbours*, a defence of Shepstone's policy. The interests of his life may be said to have been two—agriculture and romantic writing. In both of these he showed very much the same qualities—a sharp attention to detail, an accurate survey of facts, and an optimistic geniality which made his pictures whether of real agriculture or of imagined romance vivid and memorable.

In 1895 Haggard unsuccessfully contested the East Norfolk parliamentary division in the unionist interest. In 1899 he published his principal contribution to agriculture, *The Farmer's Year Book*, a sensible and reliable summary of facts by one who had practical experience of agricultural questions. During the years 1901 and 1902 he journeyed through England investigating the condition of agriculture and of the rural population. The result of his researches appeared in *Rural England* (2 vols., 1902) in which he exposed the evils of depopulation in country districts.

In 1905 Haggard was appointed by the Colonial Office special commissioner to inquire into the Salvation Army settlements in the United States with a view to the establishment of similar colonies in South Africa. His report on the subject was first published as a blue book, and afterwards, in an enlarged form, as *The Poor and the Land* (1905), with suggestions for a scheme of national land settlement in Great Britain itself. In later years much of Haggard's time was occupied with matters concerning the welfare of the British Empire. From 1912 to 1917 he travelled round the world as a member of the Dominions royal commission; in 1916 he visited all the Overseas Dominions as honorary representative of the Royal Colonial Institute in connexion with the after-War settlement of ex-service men; in 1918, as a member of the Empire Settlement committee, he visited various parts of the Empire. He was knighted in 1912 and created K.B.E. in 1919. He died in London 14 May 1925.

It is, however, on his romances that Haggard's reputation rests. There were very many of these. He attempted every kind of fiction—the modern analytical novel in such books as *Mr. Meeson's Will* (1888) and *Joan Haste* (1895), the novel of South Africa in *Jess* (1887) and *Swallow* (1889), the modern fantastic in *Stella Fregelius* (1903), the historical in *Cleopatra* (1889) and *Lysbeth* (1901), and the sheer romantic in *King Solomon's Mines* (1885), *She* (1887), *Ayesha* (1905), and many more.

It is for these last novels that Haggard will be remembered. *King Solomon's Mines* and *She* are by far his most remarkable works. In these he showed his gifts at their finest, surest, and strongest. They had many successors from his own hand and from the hands of others, but neither he nor any other has quite recaptured that same magic. These two books have delighted generations of schoolboys and will delight generations more, but they are not to be dismissed, any more than the stories of Captain Marryat, as only books for boys. They show astonishing imaginative vigour and a power of constructing a world which, although it may be impossible, is nevertheless credible. Their principal quality, however, is their remarkable zest in narrative. This gift Haggard never lost altogether, although it comparatively failed him towards the close of his life. He had the advantage of living and writing at a time when narrative was considered a very important part of the novelist's equipment, before it had yielded to a passion for psycho-analysis in the novel.

Haggard's characters are vivid and strong, but they express themselves in action rather than in thought and are moved by the simplest and most enduring motives—love, hatred, loyalty, curiosity, and fidelity. In the creation of Umslopogaas in *Allan Quatermain* (1887) he achieved an almost symbolic power. He was fortunate, too, in writing during a period when romance was taken seriously by criticism as a legitimate inspiration for art, when Stevenson and Kipling led the way, when he was surrounded by such men as Maurice Hewlett, Sir Arthur Quiller-Couch, Stanley Weyman, H. B. Marriott-Watson, and Sir Arthur Conan Doyle. He excelled all of these writers in the 'robustness' of his narrative. *King Solomon's Mines* and *She* read as though they had rock for their foundations. His real knowledge of the countries about which he wrote—for, as has been seen, he was a great traveller—assisted him, and it must not be forgotten that he believed implicitly in the virtues of his heroes and heroines. Their way was, it seemed to him, the way that life should be lived. This sincerity is to be felt in every page of his work.

[Rider Haggard, *The Days of my Life: An Autobiography*, edited by C. J. Longman, 2 vols., 1926.] H. Walpole.

HAIG, DOUGLAS, first Earl Haig (1861–1928), field-marshal, the youngest son of John Haig, of Cameron Bridge, Fife, by his wife, Rachael, daughter and coheiress of Hugh Veitch, of Stewartfield, Midlothian, was born in Edinburgh 19 June 1861. John Haig belonged to a younger branch of a famous Border family, the Haigs of Bemersyde, Berwickshire. Douglas, after some schooling in Edinburgh and at Mr. Hanbury's preparatory school in Warwickshire, was sent to Clifton, and proceeded in 1880 to Brasenose College, Oxford. In 1883 he passed into the Royal Military College, Sandhurst, which he left in the winter of 1884 as senior under-officer, first in order of merit of his year, with the Anson memorial sword, to be gazetted (February 1885) to the 7th Hussars, then in India.

Devoted to horses, Haig had shown some skill at polo both at Oxford and at Sandhurst, and although the 7th Hussars was then the crack polo team in India, he was soon playing for the regiment. In 1888 he was made adjutant and began to study French and German, spending much of his leave in France and Germany. His knowledge of German and of the German army brought him his first staff appointment, as aide-de-camp to the inspector-general of cavalry in England. While in that position he passed the entrance examination for the Staff College, but was rejected for colour blindness, a decision which was fortunately reversed on appeal. He was promoted captain in 1891.

Haig entered the Staff College in 1896, Edmund (afterwards Viscount) Allenby being amongst his contemporaries there, and came under the influence of Colonel George Francis Robert Henderson [q.v.], who was on the staff of the college. Henderson prophesied of Haig that he 'one of these days will be commander-in-chief', an indication of the impression which the young cavalry captain made at the college. To that impression he owed his first chance of active service, for (Earl) Kitchener [q.v.], who was engaged in the reconquest of the Sudan, applied to the college at the end of 1897 for some special service officers, and Haig was one of those chosen. He was employed with the Egyptian cavalry during the advance to Omdurman, and distinguished himself in the reconnaissance before that battle. For his services he received the brevet of major, and on his return home was appointed brigade-major of the 1st Cavalry brigade at Aldershot, then under the command of Major-General French (afterwards Field-Marshal the Earl of Ypres, q.v.).

Haig was holding that position when, in October 1899, war broke out with the South African republics. French was given command of the cavalry division in the army sent out under Sir Redvers Buller [q.v.], and Haig accompanied him as his staff officer. Owing to the critical situation in Natal, Buller sent French, who had arrived before his division, to take charge of the mounted troops in that colony, and on 21 October French defeated the Boer force in the battle of Elandslaagte, the plan of which was in the main Haig's. When it became clear that Ladysmith would be invested, French and Haig escaped in the last train to leave the town, and returned to Cape Town to meet the cavalry division, which was arriving. French was then sent to Naauwpoort to cover that railway junction. He established himself in a position on the heights round Colesberg, holding in check a superior force of Boers, and in this successful work at a critical time Haig's ingenuity, enterprise, and brilliant staff work played an important part. On the arrival of Lord Roberts [q.v.] with reinforcements, the cavalry division was secretly moved to the Modder River, and played a leading part in the relief of Kimberley, the battle of Paardeberg, and the occupation of Bloemfontein and Pretoria (February–June 1900). Towards the end of 1900 when the war became almost entirely of the guerrilla type, Haig received his first independent command, that of a column, and he continued to serve with distinction as a column commander until the end of the war (31 May 1902).

For his services in the South African War, Haig received the brevet of colonel and the C.B., and was appointed aide-de-camp to the king; he was also given command of the 17th Lancers, then in South Africa, and brought the regiment home to Edinburgh. Haig's work in the Sudan and South Africa had attracted the notice of Kitchener, who was commander-in-chief in India in 1903, and in that year had Haig appointed as his inspector-general of cavalry. Haig was promoted major-general in 1904 at the age of forty-three. During a short period of leave in 1905, while the guest of King Edward VII at Windsor, he met his future wife, the Hon. Dorothy Vivian, daughter of Hussey Crespigny, third Baron Vivian, one of the queen's ladies in waiting, whom he married in that year, and thus began a family life of unclouded happiness.

A year later (1906) Haig was summoned home by Mr. (afterwards Viscount) Haldane [q.v.], then secretary of state for war, to aid him, in his military reorganization, as a director on the general staff at the War Office. Haig was responsible for the scheme of the Imperial General Staff, under which the Dominions accepted establishments and methods of training uniform with those of the British regular army, and for the drafting of the first British field service regulations, which defined the principles of military organization and tactics—measures which in the main stood the test of the European War. This experience caused Haig to appreciate, as few soldiers did at the time, how much the country owed to Haldane's courage, ability, and foresight, and one of his first acts on returning home after the European War was to call on Haldane and present him with a copy of his dispatches inscribed 'To Viscount Haldane of Cloan, the greatest Secretary of State for War England has ever had'.

In 1909 Lord Kitchener completed his term of office as commander-in-chief in India. His successor, Sir O'Moore Creagh [q.v.], was an officer of the Indian army, and custom required that his chief of staff should be of the British service. Haig was offered and eagerly accepted the appointment. His primary object was to complete Kitchener's plan for enabling the Indian army to take part in the great struggle which both predicted. This plan was strenuously opposed by many in high places, who maintained that a European war would not concern India. Haig's energy and ability, however, overcame all obstacles, and it was due to the work which he built upon Kitchener's foundations that India was able to give Great Britain prompt assistance at the time of crisis in 1914.

In the autumn of 1911 Haig, who had been created K.C.V.O. in 1909 and promoted lieutenant-general in 1910, was appointed to the Aldershot command, a post which carried with it the command of the first army corps in the event of the mobilization of a British expeditionary force. Thus in August 1914 Haig (now K.C.B., 1913, and aide-de-camp general, 1914), took to France the I Army Corps, mainly composed of the Aldershot troops which he had been training for nearly three years.

Haig did not share the cheerful optimism which prevailed with Sir John French and many of the head-quarters staff. He had continued the close study which he had begun as a young man of the French and German armies, and one of his first acts was to urge upon Lord Kitchener that the War would last for years, and that Great Britain must set about the creation of a great national army. How far the two men simultaneously and independently arrived at the same conclusion is uncertain; but there is no doubt that Haig held these views, which were not shared by most military authorities either at home or in France, and on the outbreak of war he pressed them on the secretary of state for war, who first gave public expression to them in his call to the nation for men issued in the second week of August. During the battle of Mons (23–24 August) Haig's corps was on the inner flank and was but lightly engaged. Having expected the great German turning movement through Belgium, he was not surprised when the order came for retreat, and having his plans ready he got his corps away without difficulty.

On 25 August the retreating British troops reached the forest of Mormal; this entailed a separation of the I and II Corps, the I Corps making a detour to the east of the forest, which left it in an isolated position that night. Consequently, chance collisions with the Germans at Landrecies and Maroilles created considerable, but as it turned out, unnecessary alarm. On 1 September Haig's rearguards were heavily engaged in the forest of Villars-Cottérêts, but the long retreat came to an end on 5 September without further fighting, and with the morale and efficiency of the I Corps unimpaired.

Turning northwards in pursuit of the retreating Germans on 6 September, the I Corps reached and began to cross the Marne early on the morning of 9 September, well ahead of the French on its right. The corps had struck a gap in the German front, and the opportunity presented itself of separating von Kluck's First Army from von Bulow's Second Army. By an unlucky chance Haig at this moment received an air report that a strong force of the enemy was posted on his right front. The commander-in-chief had cautioned him against getting ahead of the French on his right, and fearful of being attacked in the act of crossing the river, Haig stopped his advance and directed his troops to entrench. The German troops reported to be menacing Haig's flank shortly afterwards moved off to support von Kluck's right, but this was not discovered until too late.

Continuing the advance on 10, 11, and 12 September, the I Corps on the 13th reached and began to cross the Aisne. Once again his corps had struck a gap, and Haig pressed forward with all energy to secure the important Chemin des Dames ridge, but was just anticipated by the arrival of German reinforcements at the critical point. Thus twice the hopes of a resounding success were disappointed, but Haig by his handling of his men had won both their confidence and that of his commander-in-chief. The battle of the Aisne then settled down into trench warfare, in which numerous attempts of the Germans to drive the British forces over the river were defeated.

At the end of September French had arranged with General Joffre that the British army should be relieved on the Aisne and should move round to Flanders in order to attempt to turn the German right. The I Corps was the last to leave the Aisne, and on 19 October was approaching Ypres, where the corps commanded by Sir Henry (afterwards Baron) Rawlinson [q.v.], after the abortive attempt to relieve Antwerp, had already arrived. Already the British I and II Cavalry Corps were engaged in a fierce struggle extending from La Bassée through Armentières to the Messines ridge, and the Belgian army, retiring from Antwerp, was arriving on the Yser on Haig's left. Then suddenly a new crisis developed with the appearance of four new German army corps, which endeavoured to drive in and turn the Allied left. In the first battle of Ypres (19 October–22 November) Haig's magnificent defence, his imperturbable calm, and tactical skill made him a national figure. Like Wellington at Waterloo he was on the spot at every crisis, during a period of weeks instead of hours, and the successful defence of Ypres was due as much to his personal influence as to the dogged gallantry of his men.

Early in 1915 the arrival of reinforcements in France brought about the organization of the British forces into two armies, and Haig at Ypres had earned the right to the command of the First, which was composed of his own I Corps, the Indian Corps, and the IV Corps. In February the commander-in-chief called for plans for attack from his army commanders, and selected Haig's proposal for the battle of Neuve Chapelle (10–13 March). Haig's plan was original in that it comprised a short and intense bombardment, followed by an infantry assault. In the attack Neuve Chapelle was quickly captured, but the difficulty of getting up reserves and of overcoming the German machine-guns, quickly put a stop to progress. Neuve Chapelle none the less marked the beginning of a new epoch in the War, for the first success gained convinced both the French and British that, given a sufficiency of guns and shells, the German front could be broken.

Joffre had planned an offensive campaign in Artois for the spring of 1915 to be conducted by General Foch, and to assist this effort Haig's First Army was directed to attack the Aubers ridge. The attack on the Aubers ridge, begun on 9 May, failed from lack of heavy guns and high explosive shell, but as the French, on the British right, were making progress and pressed for co-operation, the battle was renewed on the Festubert front (15–25 May). Again, however, owing to lack of the requisite munitions, the gains were small and the losses heavy. During the summer of 1915 the arrival of divisions of the new army created by Kitchener enabled the British to extend their front, and Haig's right was prolonged across the plain of Loos. The French army had then reached its maximum strength, and its supply of guns and munitions had been greatly increased. This decided Joffre to make a great effort to break through the German lines by attacks in Champagne and Artois, the latter again under the direction of Foch. Joffre desired the British army to attack on Foch's left across the plain of Loos, but both French and Haig objected that the ground there was such as to present little prospect of success. Joffre thereupon appealed to his government, with the result that the British Cabinet directed French to fall in with Joffre's plans. Again the attack was entrusted to Haig who, finding that the supply of guns and munitions would still be inadequate, determined to use gas, with which the British had been experimenting ever since the first German gas attack in April 1915. The attack on Loos began on 25 September, and was at first successful, but owing to an unfortunate misunderstanding between French and Haig the general reserve did not arrive in time to improve the first success, while Foch's attack on the Vimy ridge failed. Consequently the battle of Loos resolved itself into bitter trench warfare in which some of the first British gains were lost. The battle dragged on until 14 October.

One of the results of the battle of Loos was to determine the British government to change the commander-in-chief, and on 19 December Haig succeeded French. Meanwhile the British forces in France, now organized in three armies, were steadily increasing in strength, while the evacuation of the Gallipoli Peninsula, completed early in January 1916, made further reinforcements available. Thus, when on 21 February 1916, the Germans began the battle of Verdun, Haig was able to respond at once to Joffre's appeal to extend the British front and set free French reinforcements for Verdun. Gradually during the summer the British front was extended southwards to the Somme, and a Fourth Army was created. At Joffre's request Haig set about preparing for a counter-offensive on the Somme to relieve Verdun. On 23 June the Germans captured Fort Thiaumont and Joffre therefore called upon Haig to make his effort; thus on 1 July began the battle of the Somme, with a combined British and French attack astride that river. Only on the French front and on the British right was the first attack successful, but the situation at Verdun was such that no cessation of effort was possible, and Haig determined to follow up the success gained by his right. In a prolonged struggle which lasted until the middle of November the Germans were slowly driven from the uplands north of the Somme and compelled to concentrate their efforts on resisting British attacks, with the result that before the end of the year the French were able to regain most of the ground which they had lost in the battle of Verdun.

This failure at Verdun and their heavy losses in the Somme fighting alarmed the Germans: General von Falkenhayn was dismissed and replaced by General von Hindenburg with General Ludendorff as his chief of staff. Both Joffre and Haig, realizing the exhaustion of the enemy, wished to continue their efforts, but the French and British governments had been equally alarmed at the cost in life of the Somme battle—the British casualties had amounted to 343,000 of whom about 90,000 were killed. General Nivelle had in two attacks at Verdun won important successes at comparatively small cost, and it was hoped that his methods could be applied on a larger scale. So Joffre was made a marshal of France, and given an honorific position in Paris, and Nivelle was made commander-in-chief of the French armies. Nivelle's plan involved a further extension of the British front, and considerable delay in order to complete his preparations. At an Allied conference held at Calais at the end of February 1917 Haig was directed to conform to Nivelle's instructions, which comprised, in addition to the extension of the front, a British attack in the neighbourhood of Arras in combination with a secondary French attack on the St. Quentin front, and a main French effort in Champagne. Profiting by the delay which Nivelle's plans involved, the Germans on 14 March began a retreat from the Somme to their 'Hindenburg' lines, a retreat of which, owing to the weakening of their front by extension, the British were unable to take full advantage. Despite this radical change in the situation Nivelle adhered to his plans, and his campaign began on 9 April with a British attack on the Vimy ridge and on the German lines in front of Arras. This attack was successful, and the Vimy ridge, which in two campaigns had resisted Foch's efforts, was captured.

The French attacks failed, however, with heavy loss. Nivelle had rashly held out hopes of speedy and complete success, and the reaction was severe. There followed a series of mutinies in the French armies and general depression in France, and it became essential for the British army to gain time for the French to recover. The fighting in front of Arras was therefore continued until 15 May, several weeks longer than had been projected, and on 7 June Haig began an offensive campaign in Flanders, his Second Army under Sir Herbert Plumer capturing the Messines ridge, thus eliminating the greater part of the Ypres salient, which had been a weakness in the British lines since the winter of 1914. General Pétain, who had taken Nivelle's place as commander-in-chief of the French armies on 15 May, urged Haig to continue his attacks that he might have time to restore the *moral* of the French armies, and Haig therefore on 31 July began an attack on the Ypres front.

Haig's reasons for choosing this front were that this appeared to him to be the only part of the front on which the Germans could not, without great sacrifices, repeat the manœuvre of retreat to the Hindenburg lines, that the Admiralty was pressing for an attempt to capture Ostend and Zeebrugge, which the Germans were using as submarine bases, and lastly that there was a prospect, if the attack progressed, of making effective use of naval co-operation against the Belgian coast. Unfortunately, at the very beginning of August the weather broke, and the country to the east of Ypres became a sea of mud. In view of the state of the French army and of Pétain's request that there should be no relaxation of pressure on the enemy, it was impossible to change the front of attack, and the British army was committed to an even more exhausting effort than the battle of the Somme. Slowly and painfully it forced its way up the Ypres ridges, and on 6 November captured Passchendaele. It had early become apparent that there was no prospect of driving the Germans from the Belgian coast, but the second purpose of the battle was attained. Pétain was given time to nurse the French army back to health, and on 23 October at Malmaison and on 3 November on the Ailette it signalized its recovery by two successful attacks.

By the middle of October Haig had decided to take advantage of the effect upon the Germans of the long struggle in front of Ypres by delivering a surprise attack with the aid of 'tanks' which, first used in September 1916 in the battle of the Somme, were then available in considerable numbers. This attack was made on the Cambrai front on 20 November, and a considerable initial success was won. But, before it was made, a severe crisis had arisen in Italy owing to the defeat on 24 October of the Italian army at Caporetto. Accordingly, the British and French governments decided that each should send five divisions from France to Italy. This made a serious diminution of the reserves available to follow up the success won at Cambrai, and the Germans were able in a counter-attack to recover a considerable part of the ground which they had lost. The situation in the winter of 1917–1918 was critical for the Allies. The French and British armies were weakened by the detachments sent to Italy, and in both countries man power was approaching exhaustion. It became necessary to reduce in each British division the number of battalions in a brigade from twelve to nine. The United States had joined the Allies in April 1917, but it was improbable that American troops could take the field in strength before the late summer of 1918. On the other side, the collapse of Russia had released the German armies on the Eastern front, and German divisions were arriving in a steady stream in France and Belgium. Under pressure from the French government Haig was compelled reluctantly to agree to a further extension of his front, and his Fifth Army under General Sir Hubert Gough prolonged his right as far south as the Oise. The crisis in Italy had caused the Allied governments to create the Supreme War Council for the better co-ordination of Allied efforts, and at a meeting of this body held at Versailles at the end of January 1918 it was decided to meet the danger of the expected German attack by creating a general reserve to be controlled by an executive committee with Foch as chairman. This committee required Haig to contribute eight British divisions to the reserve, and to this request he at once replied that, in view of the masses of German divisions on his front, he could not provide more than two divisions which were to be returned to him from Italy. At a further meeting of the Supreme War Council in London early in March 1918 Haig's views were upheld, and the proposal to create the general reserve collapsed, Haig being left to concert with Pétain arrangements for mutual support.

The expected German blow fell upon the British Third and Fifth Armies on 21 March. The right of both armies was driven in, and this involved a general retreat which threatened a rupture of the junction of the British and French armies in the neighbourhood of Amiens. Haig's reserves were quickly exhausted, and Pétain was disposed to consider it of greater importance to cover Paris than to maintain connexion with the British. In these circumstances Haig telegraphed to Lord Milner, the secretary of state for war, to come over with the chief of the Imperial General Staff, Sir Henry Wilson [q.v.], with the object of getting Foch appointed to control operations on the Western front. This object was achieved in a conference at Doullens on 26 March. On coming out of this conference Haig said: 'I can deal with a man, but not with a committee.' Foch set to work energetically to fill the gap in the Allied front which was opening in the neighbourhood of Amiens; but before his efforts could take effect a great German attack on the left of the British Third Army and the right of the British First Army on the Arras front, intended to recapture the Vimy ridge, was shattered—a result which fully justified Haig's policy of keeping the bulk of his reserves north of the Somme, leaving the Fifth Army south of that river to be supported by the French.

Hardly had this first crisis of the year been resolved when a second arose. On 9 April the Germans attacked in Flanders, and broke through a portion of the line near Neuve Chapelle held by a Portuguese division. This opened a dangerous gap and involved another general withdrawal on the British front, which appeared to endanger the security of the Channel ports. As at Ypres in 1914, so in April 1918 with an immeasurably greater burden of responsibility on his shoulders, Haig's calm courage and resolution called forth all that was best in his men. In a memorable order issued on 11 April he told them: 'With our backs to the wall and believing in the justice of our cause, each one of us must fight to the end. The safety of our homes and the freedom of mankind depend upon the conduct of each one of us at this crisis.'

On 29 April the second great German effort petered out; but five weeks of the severest fighting against heavy odds had wofully reduced the British army in France, and no less than twenty divisions had to be broken up. Fortunately the Germans gave Haig a respite, of which he took full advantage. Reinforcements were hurried to France from Palestine and Salonika, and more man power was made available from home. Thus, while in May and June the Germans were seeking to break through the French front, Haig was able to make good most of the losses of the spring. Thrice during this period Foch appealed to Haig for help, and on each occasion the British authorities at home warned Haig of the danger of weakening his front; but each time Haig ignored the warning and loyally supported Foch.

At length the tide turned. Foch's counter-attack begun on 18 July had by the first week of August driven the Germans from the great salient which in their May attack on the Chemin des Dames had brought them a second time to the Marne. By this time the preparations of the American army were well advanced and the Allies were assured of superior power on the Western front. Already, by the middle of July, Haig had become convinced that the German strength was diminishing, and before Foch's counter-attack was delivered he had begun preparations for an attack on the Amiens front. This attack delivered by the British Fourth Army with the help of the French First Army on 8 August was completely successful. Foch, delighted with this success, urged Haig to press forward across the Somme and to capture Péronne; but on 12 August Haig had found that the German resistance was hardening in ground much broken up in earlier battles, and having now sufficient guns and munitions to be able to extend rapidly the front of attack, he refused to risk renewal of the experience of prolonging the fighting on the original front of battle, with the probable result of small gains in return for heavy losses. Instead, on 21 August, he attacked with his Third Army across the Somme battlefield of 1916, and proposed to extend gradually the front of battle right up to Arras. This change proved decisive. It altered Foch's plan of limited attacks, designed to free the Allied lines of railway communications, into a general advance against the enemy. In fact, Haig was the first to envisage the possibility of victory before the end of 1918. In a general order issued to his armies in the third week of August, he told them that the situation had changed decisively, and that the time had come to press the enemy everywhere with the utmost energy. At that time Foch himself was looking for a victory in 1919, and the British government was considering plans for a final effort in 1920.

Under Haig's inspiration the British armies pressed forward, and by the third week in September the Germans had everywhere on their front been driven into the shelter of their great 'Hindenburg' defensive system. The responsibility of assaulting these formidable defences was great, but Haig, confident that his judgement was right, and that the time had come for a supreme effort, unhesitatingly assumed it, despite authoritative warnings from home. By 12 October the British troops had broken clean through the 'Hindenburg' lines, the Germans were in retreat to their last organized system of defence behind Lille, and Hindenburg had advised his government to seek terms of peace. On 11 November, when the enemy accepted terms of armistice which left them militarily helpless, Haig's judgement was triumphantly vindicated. It was his decision that made victory in 1918 possible.

After leading his armies to the Rhine, Haig came home in July 1919 in order to take up the post of commander-in-chief of the Home Forces, to which he had been appointed in the previous April, and to superintend the demobilization of the nation in arms. In the following year he turned to a work which was very near his heart. In the last year of the War he had been perturbed to learn of the grave distress amongst those who had been disabled in the War, and while still commanding in France he had, with the help of Lady Haig, taken steps to provide remedies. After the Armistice he informed the government that he would accept no further honours until parliament had made better provision for those who had served under him. When this was done, he received the thanks of both Houses of Parliament and a grant of £100,000. The king created him Earl Haig and conferred on him the Order of Merit. He had been awarded the G.C.B. in 1915, the G.C.V.O. in 1916, and in 1917 had been made a knight of the Thistle.

On giving up the chief command of the Home Forces in January 1921, Haig devoted himself entirely to the cause of the men who had served under him in the War. In 1921 he succeeded in uniting the various organizations of ex-service men which had been created to deal with their grievances into one body, the British Legion, of which he became president. In this he rendered an inestimable service, not only to those who had fought but to the nation at large, by removing causes of discontent which at one time threatened to become dangerous. He also became chairman of the United Services Fund, created to administer for the benefit of ex-service men and their dependents the large profits made by the canteens during the War. Together the United Services Fund and the British Legion formed the largest benevolent organization ever created in Great Britain, and to its administration Haig gave himself unsparingly.

Always somewhat reserved, and with no gifts of speech, Haig, as a commander in the field, never aroused in his men the enthusiasm and affection inspired by a Marlborough or a Roberts, but his devoted services to their cause won for him from those who had fought for their country a measure of esteem such as few British commanders-in-chief have ever enjoyed. He undoubtedly shortened his life by denying himself rest; and when he died suddenly in London 30 January 1928 and was awarded a national funeral, the most striking tribute to him came from the thousands of ex-service men who lined the route of the procession.

In 1921 Haig was presented with the ancestral home of the Haigs, Bemersyde, purchased by public subscription. He was at his own request buried hard by Bemersyde in Dryburgh Abbey. A statue of him was erected in Edinburgh, and another at his old head-quarters, Montreuil, the cost of which was defrayed by public subscription in France; parliament granted the sum of £5,000 for the erection of a third statue in Whitehall. A national memorial fund provided groups of Haig Homes for disabled ex-service men in various parts of the country. A portrait of Haig is included in J. S. Sargent's picture, 'Some General Officers of the Great War', painted in 1922, in the National Portrait Gallery. There are also portraits of him in the Imperial War Museum, South Kensington, by Sir W. Orpen and Solomon J. Solomon, the Cavalry Club by Oswald Birley, the Royal and Ancient Golf Club of St. Andrews by Sir J. Guthrie, and Brasenose College, Oxford, by Sir William Orpen. In 1916 he had been elected rector of St. Andrews University and two years later he became its chancellor. He received the honorary degree of D.C.L. from the University of Oxford in 1919.

Haig had one son, George Alexander Eugene Douglas (born 1918), who succeeded him as second earl, and two daughters.

[Sir J. F. Maurice and M. H. Grant, (Official) *History of the War in South Africa 1899–1902*, 1906–1910; Sir J. E. Edmonds, (Official) *History of the Great War. Military Operations, France and Belgium, 1914–1916*, 1922–1931; G. A. B. Dewar and J. H. Boraston, *Sir Douglas Haig's Command, 1915–1918*, 1922; *Sir Douglas Haig's Despatches*, ed. J. H. Boraston, 1919; J. Charteris, *Field-Marshal Earl Haig*, 1929; British Legion *Journal*, Earl Haig Memorial Number, 1928. See also Duff Cooper, *Haig*, 2 vols., 1935, 1936.]

F. Maurice.

HALDANE, RICHARD BURDON, Viscount Haldane, of Cloan (1856–1928), statesman, lawyer, and philosopher, was born in Edinburgh 30 July 1856. He was the second son of Robert Haldane, writer to the signet, by his second wife, Mary Elizabeth, second daughter of Richard Burdon-Sanderson, of West Jesmond and Otterburn Dene, Northumberland. Robert Haldane, who lived in Charlotte Square, Edinburgh, and at Cloanden (later called Cloan), Auchterarder, Perthshire, was descended from an old Perthshire family, the Haldanes of Gleneagles. Amongst his relatives were many men distinguished in naval and military life, such as Adam, first Viscount Duncan, of Camperdown, and Sir Ralph Abercromby, of Aboukir. Richard Haldane's grandfather, James Alexander Haldane [q.v.], and his great-uncle, Robert Haldane [q.v.], were, however, best known as having given up their naval careers in order to carry on evangelical propaganda in Scotland. On his mother's side Haldane was great-great-nephew of the eminent lawyers Lord Eldon and Lord Stowell; but his grandfather, Richard Burdon-Sanderson, a man of learning and a fellow of Oriel College, Oxford, gave up his profession as a barrister for country life and the pursuit of religion. Thus there was a tradition of evangelical piety on both sides of the house. Sir John Burdon-Sanderson, the physiologist [q.v.], was the brother of Haldane's mother; she died in 1925 in her 101st year.

According to the Scottish fashion of the time, Haldane was sent to a day school, the Edinburgh Academy. He did not look back on his school-days with complete satisfaction, although he held his class-master, Dr. James Clyde, in the deepest respect. From Clyde he first learned that stoical regard for truth which continued with him throughout his life. On leaving school he passed to the university of Edinburgh at the age of sixteen. It was matter of discussion whether he should go on to Balliol College, Oxford, but finally, on the advice of Professor John Stuart Blackie [q.v.], of Edinburgh, he went to Göttingen University in 1874, returning to Edinburgh in order to complete his studies and graduate. There were other reasons than those advanced by Blackie to cause Haldane's parents to object to his going to Oxford. They had adopted the extreme form of evangelicalism advocated by their respective families, and to his mother's father this implied a violent distrust of the Church of England as he had known it at Oxford in his youth.

From the beginning of his university career Haldane was attracted to the study of philosophy, and associated with others interested in the same subject. Edinburgh University at that time possessed a distinguished set of professors, including William Young Sellar, David Masson, Alexander Campbell Fraser, and Peter Guthrie Tait. At Göttingen Haldane came under the influence of R. H. Lotze and gradually adopted, through the study of Berkeley, Fichte, Kant, and Hegel, the idealistic outlook to which, with various modifications, he adhered to the end.

When he returned to Scotland, Haldane applied himself to his studies with renewed vigour, inspired, to a remarkable degree for so young a man, by what he had imbibed in a few months' stay in a foreign land. He graduated M.A. at Edinburgh in 1876 with first-class honours in philosophy, won the Bruce of Grangehill prize for philosophy, and was awarded both the Gray scholarship and also the Ferguson scholarship in philosophy, the latter being in competition with students from the four Scottish universities. He was an active member of the Edinburgh University Philosophical Society, and found congenial fellow students, such as Andrew Seth Pringle-Pattison and W. R. Sorley. His studies had the effect of separating Haldane to a considerable degree from the tenets of his father, who died in 1877. Nevertheless, there was sufficient understanding between the two to make their relationship happy during the older man's last years.

After his father's death, Haldane, who was the eldest surviving child of his mother's family, went to London in order to read for the bar. He was called by Lincoln's Inn in 1879, after having read in equity drafting and conveyancing with William Barber. While so reading, he became imbued with a passion for the law which never left him, although it was associated with a similar passion for philosophy. The two studies seemed, indeed, in Haldane's case to be complementary to one another. The consequence of his double allegiance was that the type of legal work which he dealt with most successfully was that which involved the consideration of legal principles, however intricate they might be, rather than the mere interpretation of facts. In later life it was in the House of Lords and the Judicial Committee of the Privy Council that these powers of his were most fully developed. After working for a year with Barber, Haldane entered as pupil with Lumley Smith and remained with him until the end of 1879, when he took chambers. There, until work came, he read authorities and edited J. H. Dart's *Compendium of the Law of Vendors and Purchasers of Real Estate* together with William Robert Sheldon in 1888.

Work came in but slowly, although each year it increased, assisted by the fact that the young barrister remained in London during part of the long vacation. In 1882 he was taken by Horace (afterwards Lord) Davey [q.v.] as a junior to read his briefs and 'devil' up his authorities for him. This work, which was mostly for the supreme tribunals, was thoroughly congenial to Haldane, and through it he obtained his first chance of showing his powers in a case before the Privy Council concerning the government of Quebec. Davey was summoned to appear in another case before the House of Lords, and, to the dismay of the solicitors and clients, left the matter to be dealt with by a young man who appeared before the Judicial Committee for the first time. The result, however, was satisfactory for Haldane's reputation, as it led to his appearance in another great case of Davey's, known as the Scottish petroleum case (1883), although this time judgment was not given in his favour.

Haldane remained for ten years a junior before taking silk in 1890. He carried on his work at the bar until 1905, when he accepted office in the liberal government formed at the end of that year. He had stood for parliament in the liberal interest in December 1885, as a junior, and had been elected as member for East Lothian. He held the seat until he was raised to the peerage as Viscount Haldane, of Cloan, in 1911, a period of twenty-six years.

As a Q.C. Haldane attached himself to the court of Mr. Justice Kay in the chancery division, and then to that of his successor Mr. Justice Romer (Sir Robert Romer, q.v.); but by 1897 he felt justified in 'going special', and began to be employed very largely in Canadian cases, as also in Indian and other appeals before the Privy Council. He also dealt with a considerable number of Scottish appeals to the House of Lords. One of the most important of these concerned the millions of money claimed by the small minority of members of the Free Church of Scotland, who declined to concur in the union of the Free Church with the United Presbyterian Church which took place in 1900 under the name of the United Free Church of Scotland, and in which Haldane argued for the defendants. The claimants argued that the union was invalid since it involved the sacrifice of an essential principle of the constitution of the Free Church. The case was much to Haldane's mind, implying as it did discussions of a doctrinal nature (involving the doctrines of free will and predestination) in which he was quite at home. The decision was adverse to the United Free Church as regarded its trust deed, and the Church was left stripped of its property and condemned to pay all costs. Haldane at once offered to contribute £1,000, and before many hours had passed £150,000 was subscribed. A Bill had to be passed by parliament in order to rectify an intolerable state of affairs. Later on, in 1922, Haldane presided over an expert committee appointed by the government, the report of which was embodied in a statute which helped to restore harmony between the religious bodies in Scotland.

Another legal matter in which Haldane was specially interested was the law relating to real property and conveyancing. After he became lord chancellor he introduced a bill for the recasting and codification of much of the law in this regard, but the European War put an end to consideration of it. After the War the matter was dealt with by his successors, and by himself when again lord chancellor in 1924.

Haldane was twice lord chancellor: on the first occasion he succeeded Lord Loreburn in 1912, and remained on the woolsack until 1915. He held office during a period of great political stress and quitted it on the reconstruction of the Cabinet in the latter year. His second tenure of the chancellorship was during the nine months' existence of the labour government of 1924.

When Haldane first took office as lord chancellor he believed that the supreme tribunal of the British Empire, whether it performed its function as the House of Lords or as the Judicial Committee of the Privy Council, was weak in numbers, and the latter body, he held, was lacking in the attributes of dignity needful to command the respect of the Dominions and Colonies. The body of lords of appeal was, through his efforts, increased in number, and he set himself to impress upon those concerned the importance of the duties of the Judicial Committee. His ideal was to combine the two supreme tribunals into one supreme Imperial court. He also took the view that those who had held the office of lord chancellor, and drew the regulated pension of the post, should sit regularly in their judicial capacity; and he himself endeavoured to sit in any Dominion appeal case which raised a constitutional point.

Haldane's mind was essentially an administrative one, and the office of lord chancellor offered scope for reorganization: the working parts, he considered, required co-ordination, and the whole should be run in a just relation to the constitution, to parliament, and to the other departments of state. There existed, in his view, many anomalies in its organization, and the complete solution of the problem was to be found, he considered, in a ministry of justice and a separation of the judicial from the administrative duties of the lord chancellor. This plan he adumbrated in a scheme for a reformed House of Lords, which, however, did not develop.

In considering the value of the work done by Haldane in respect of law, education, and philosophy, army reform and other public administration, it will probably be held that his services under the last two heads rank highest. Haldane himself used to say that his interests had been almost too varied for concentration on any one branch of his activities, and this probably applied to his legal work. He was diverted from the law by political work too early in his career to make the mark in it which he might have made, and he had the unusual experience of never having held a legal office under the government, or occupied a seat on the bench, until he came to occupy the supreme position of lord chancellor. As he himself said, a judge, if he is to reach the highest level, must devote himself, not to many subjects, but to passionate absorption in the law; whereas his own time and energies had been demanded by other things. His judgments in the House of Lords, however, attained a high standard, and he raised the Judicial Committee of the Privy Council to a position in which it commanded increasing confidence at home and in the Dominions. His pronouncements were always received with deep respect, and thus he was able to exercise a lasting influence on the development of English law.

By temperament Haldane was a liberal in politics. He took part as a young man in founding the Eighty Club, and later on he became a prominent member of the band of liberal-imperialists who worked for the Liberal League under the leadership of Lord Rosebery [q.v.] during the Boer War and after it. Sir Edward Grey and H. H. Asquith were associated with him in these efforts. In the early part of his political life he was an ardent supporter of Free Trade; he also helped Sir William Harcourt in drafting and defending the bill which, as the Finance Act of 1894, established the estate duty.

When Sir Henry Campbell-Bannerman was forming the liberal government of 1905, Haldane decided, after some hesitation, to accept office in it as secretary of state for war, and for the next seven years his most important work was done in refashioning the army. He took office under very difficult conditions, for at first he had not the full confidence of the prime minister, and the only interest which most members of the liberal party took in the army was in the reduction of its cost, and that at a time when Lord Roberts and others were pressing for national service. Haldane made an extensive study of the whole problem of the organization of the army, which was far from satisfactory, while there were gathering clouds on the political horizon. An 'Expeditionary Force' was shaped to meet the demands which might be made upon the country under the conditions then existing in Europe; and a few years later this force met those demands to the full. Haldane's view was that the army must be a real whole, complete with a due proportion of the various arms, and equipped with its requirements in transport and supply services. He also considered that means must be provided for a scientific expansion of the regular army in the event of a national emergency.

On the report of Lord Esher's committee in 1904 [see Brett, Reginald

Balliol] it had been decided to create, in the General Staff, an effective thinking and training department, and one free from the daily cares of administration. This matter was further developed in 1909 when, at a Dominions conference, it was agreed to form an Imperial General Staff, so that the Dominions should adopt the same organization and principles of training as the home regular army. In this way the contingents sent out by the Dominions when the European War broke out, fell at once easily and readily into their places in the armies of the British Empire [see Haig, Douglas, first Earl Haig].

In addition to this work within the War Office Haldane carried through the House of Commons, with great courage and energy, the legislation necessary to give effect to his schemes of army reform (1907). The Militia was converted into a special reserve which on mobilization was legally embodied in the regular army as a part of its reserves. The volunteers, whose formerly haphazard establishments had to be pruned and built up in order to conform with the divisional organization (in the same way as the regulars but on a much larger scale), were then transformed into a field army for home defence, organized on the same pattern as the regular divisions which were then liberated to go abroad as the Expeditionary Force. The formation of the Officers' Training Corps provided from the secondary schools and universities a recruiting ground for officers.

Not only did Haldane placate his own party by adding economy to increased efficiency, but, by giving the lords-lieutenant and landed gentry of counties, as well as employers of labour and county councils, representation on the County Association formed to administer the units of the Territorial army, he succeeded in interesting his political opponents in its success. There was not the slightest chance that the liberal government could have been induced to accept a proposal for national service, and the general staff in the War Office found against it. It was also believed by those in power that its introduction at that juncture, instead of preserving peace, would most probably have precipitated war.

In 1911 Haldane felt that his work at the War Office was nearing completion, and he went to the House of Lords in order to help in leading the House during the absence in India of Lord Crewe. In the following year he left the War Office and became lord chancellor.

In 1906 Haldane had accepted an invitation to visit the annual manœuvres of the German army. Besides coming into touch with many distinguished Germans he was able to make a study of German military organization, which proved of great use in the development of his scheme of army reform. In 1912, before actually quitting the War Office, Haldane was sent by the Cabinet on a mission to Germany in order to see if the political tension between that country and Great Britain, which had become acute over various matters and particularly over the projected great increase in the German navy, could be allayed. The mission failed, inasmuch as the war party in Germany, headed by Admiral von Tirpitz, insisted on the policy of building up the strength of the German navy, and left Great Britain with no alternative but to proceed with counter-preparations. Other discussions were carried on during Haldane's visit, in all of which he took part as one who spoke German fluently, often visited that country for pleasure, and was anxious for better relations with it. It was owing to this visit that, a few months after the outbreak of the European War in August 1914, a violent agitation arose against Lord Haldane, mainly in a section of the press, which accused him of pro-German sympathies; and when the liberal government was reconstituted as a coalition under Asquith in 1915, the prime minister felt himself unable to retain Haldane's services. Haldane bore the often absurd attacks made on him with great dignity and absolute silence; his only regret being that a considerable part of his scheme of army reform, more especially that which concerned the full use of the Territorial force as a machinery of expansion, was not utilized as it might have been. In other respects Lord Kitchener had freely made use of Haldane's knowledge and experience, and their relations had been cordial.

It is in respect of his work for the army and its administration that Haldane will be chiefly remembered, and that not alone because of the actual work carried out by him, but because it was carried out in time to be of vital significance to the country. He gave infinite thought to the details of the scheme, and the result was seen, for example, in the improvement in the rationing of the army, and perhaps almost more impressively in the organization of the medical and nursing services. The improved organization of these services under the Territorial system had as result that when war broke out there were men and women (hitherto civilians) ready to take their places as doctors, nurses, and stretcher-bearers, without a hitch, and the transport system was equally efficient. The secret of this success lay in the fact that Haldane relegated to those immediately responsible the duty of finding men competent to carry out the complicated duties required. The Territorial system was devised to make use of the latent power which was to be found in civil life, and this it did most effectively.

In August 1913 Lord Haldane paid a brief visit to the United States and Canada in order to deliver an address to the American and Canadian Bar Associations at Montreal, where he had a warm reception. His address was published in the same year under the title of *The Higher Nationality*.

Throughout his life one of Haldane's main interests as a public man lay in the field of higher education and administration, and of this subject he made a full study in Germany and elsewhere. His ideas on the matter found expression in the War Office, but he applied them elsewhere with equal effect. As a young man he lectured at the Working Men's College in Great Ormond Street; later he became for a time a member of the council of University College, London, and he took a leading part in the negotiations which preceded the University of London Act (1898). In association with Mr. and Mrs. Sidney Webb he was also one of the founders of the London School of Economics in 1895, and later (from 1919 until his death) presided over Birkbeck College.

One of Haldane's principal efforts on behalf of university organization was directed towards the establishment of universities in the provinces—what he called 'civic' universities. In 1902 he appeared as counsel for University College, Liverpool, in support of a petition to the Privy Council for the grant of a university charter. It was his desire to extend university and higher education in England to that large class of people who could not obtain it, that made him devote much of his maturer life to assisting proposals for the creation of new universities; and on behalf of those who could not become regular students, he applied his utmost energies in the support of the Workers' Educational Association and the British Institute of Adult Education. In 1904 he was made chairman of a small committee whose recommendations resulted in the creation of the Universities Grants Committee—a body which advises the government on the allocation of state grants to the universities and university colleges of Great Britain. His next interest was in a committee on the constitution of the Imperial College of Science and Technology, South Kensington, of which he served as chairman. In 1909 he was appointed chairman of the royal commission on university education in London, which sat for four years, during which time he was successively secretary of state for war and lord chancellor. The European War delayed the carrying out of the commission's recommendations, but, after many difficulties, they were in substance adopted. The site which the Haldane commission recommended and which was actually bought by the government, was re-sold by the university; but it was re-purchased in 1928 with government assistance and became the site adopted. Lord Haldane was also chairman of the royal commission on university education in Wales (which reported in 1918). Until his last illness, indeed, adult education in its various forms (university and non-university) continued to engross his attention, and he constantly spoke in its favour.

In 1917 Haldane was made chairman of a committee on the machinery of government, appointed by the reconstruction committee of the Cabinet. The conclusions reached by the committee and reported in 1918 were that the number and function of government departments had grown in a haphazard fashion and that their efficiency might be greatly increased. Some of the committee's suggestions, which were of great value, have been adopted. Haldane was also interested in the establishment of the department, under the committee of the Privy Council, for scientific and industrial research, and in early days was a constant attendant at the committee's meetings. The improving of the efficiency of public administration was always a matter in which he was concerned, and he was anxious that the civil administration should be better adapted to modern conditions. He was the first president of the Institute of Public Administration (founded 1922), a body formed voluntarily amongst civil servants and local government officers to carry out this object. As regards his own administrative work, the secret of Haldane's success, as stated by those who worked under him, lay in the fact that he expected his subordinates to take responsibility and was willing to devolve responsibility on them.

After he left office in 1915 Lord Haldane found it increasingly difficult to work with the liberal party, especially as its interest in educational policy appeared to him to be of the slightest. He found in the party no sympathy with his early endeavours either to bridge over the nonconformist difficulties in regard to elementary and secondary schools, or to promote university education; still less did it co-operate with him in his work for non-university adult education. He therefore became more and more estranged from official liberalism. The labour party, on the other hand, seemed to show both readiness to second his efforts and an idealism which was entirely lacking in his own party. Hence he began to attend labour meetings when educational matters were under discussion; and when the labour party first came into power in 1924 he held again the office of lord chancellor for the nine months during which it carried on the government of the country with the tacit assistance of the liberals. Haldane always believed that this experience was a valuable one both to ministers and to people, although there was not time to do much towards realizing the ideals which he had in view. When the labour party went into opposition in 1925 he was asked to lead the small number of labour peers who formed the official opposition in the House of Lords, and this he did until his death.

Lord Haldane was not by temperament or tradition a member of the labour party, nor did he join its organizations; but he held many of its leaders in deep regard, and as the only member of the 1924 ministry with Cabinet experience, he was a valuable asset to the party in the difficult task of forming a government for the first time in its history.

Lord Haldane's intense interest in philosophy is clearly derivable from his early traditions and training. On both sides of his family, as has been seen, he had inherited an almost exclusive concern with matters of religion and with the dogmas from which that religion proceeded. After 1877, when he went to London, he translated together with a friend, John Kemp, Schopenhauer's *The World as Will and Idea* (3 vols., 1883–1886), but his first independent paper of a philosophical nature was contributed to a volume of *Essays in Philosophical Criticism* which appeared in 1883, dedicated to the memory of T. H. Green. The essays were written by a number of young men—all of them distinguished in later life—who were interested in philosophy of an idealistic kind, such as was opened up by Kant and developed by Hegel. The preface to the *Essays* was written by Edward Caird. Another essay in the volume was written by Haldane in conjunction with his brother, (Professor) J. S. Haldane, who had begun to work out the conclusions as to the nature of life with which his name is associated. The idea in these early essays of a sort of scale of modes of existence with a corresponding series of categories rising from those of mathematics and mechanism to those of organic life and then to conscious personality, is developed in Haldane's Gifford lectures delivered at St. Andrews in 1902–1903 and published as *The Pathway to Reality* (1903). To him philosophy gave back what science threatened to take away, namely faith in the reality of the spiritual world. It was to the reading of philosophy, and more especially to the reading of Hegel, that Haldane turned for relaxation at the end of a hard day's work. The abstract thought of the latter philosopher expressed in a difficult style which itself required interpretation, tended to make Haldane's exposition of his philosophical views difficult and obscure to any reader unfamiliar with the special terminology used. *The Pathway to Reality*, the text of which was taken down from Haldane's extempore lecturing (in itself a remarkable feat) suffers less from this difficulty than his other writings. Haldane, however, never ceased to realize that the poet, the artist, or the simple religious person, each expressing himself in images or in appeal to the emotions, is capable of reaching, in his own way, the highest result of speculative thinking. 'Abstract reasoning', he says, 'has no monopoly of the means of access to reality, although I hold it to be the only competent guardian of the pathway.'

A later book, *The Reign of Relativity* (1921), presented the same philosophical position, but it was connected with the theories of relativity put forward by Einstein, which were matter of intense interest to Haldane. The subject was one of eager debate when the book was published and it had a large circulation. His last philosophical works were *The Philosophy of Humanism* (1922) and *Human Experience* (1926). The latter, like *The Reign of Relativity*, is a philosophical discussion of the new ideas in modern science.

Lord Haldane, who never married, died

at Cloan 19 August 1928 and was buried in the private burial place of his family at Gleneagles. The peerage became extinct on his death. Haldane was admitted a privy councillor in 1902, was created K.T. in 1913, and received the Order of Merit in 1915. He was elected F.R.S. in 1906 and fellow of the British Academy in 1914, and served on the council of the latter from 1919 to the year of his death. He was elected lord rector of Edinburgh University in 1905, and shortly afterwards delivered his rectorial address to the students under the title of 'The Dedicated Life'. In 1912 he was made chancellor of the university of Bristol, one of the newer universities in whose welfare he was deeply interested and which he visited as long as he was able to do so. Shortly before his death in 1928 he was elected chancellor of the university of St. Andrews, but was unable to be present in order to be installed. Haldane received honorary degrees from Oxford, Cambridge, and many other universities, including that of Göttingen.

There are portraits of Haldane in the National Portrait Gallery (P. A. de László), Lincoln's Inn (G. Fiddes Watt), the office of the Judicial Committee of the Privy Council (C. W. Cope), and elsewhere. A cartoon by 'Spy' appeared in *Vanity Fair* 13 February 1896.

[*The Times*, 20 August 1928; Richard Burdon Haldane, *An Autobiography*, 1929; Viscount Grey of Fallodon, Sir Charles Harris, Sir H. Frank Heath, and Sir Claud Schuster, *Viscount Haldane of Cloan, O.M.*, 1928; A. Seth Pringle-Pattison and Viscount Dunedin, *Richard Burdon Haldane, Viscount Haldane of Cloan, 1856–1928*, in *Proceedings* of the British Academy, vol. xiv, 1928; Viscount Haldane, *Before the War*, 1920; The Haldane Memorial Lectures for 1929, 1931, and 1933 delivered respectively by Lord Justice Sankey, Sir Henry Hadow, and Major-General Sir Frederick Maurice at Birkbeck College; private information; personal knowledge.]

E. S. Haldane.

HALL, Sir EDWARD MARSHALL (1858–1927), lawyer, was born at Brighton, where his father, Alfred Hall, was a well-known doctor, 16 September 1858, the youngest of ten children. His mother was Julia Elizabeth, daughter of James Sebright, an official in the postal service. After two years at Rugby he became a clerk in a tea merchant's office, with the entire approval of his house-master, who thought it a suitable occupation for an unpromising pupil. His father was wiser, and after a period of probation sent his son to St. John's College, Cambridge, in 1880. His studies were varied by a year in Paris and a visit to Australia. Thus it was not until 1882 that he took a pass degree.

An early marriage made a profession essential, and in accordance with his father's wishes Marshall Hall was called to the bar by the Inner Temple in 1888. He became a bencher in 1910. Time had not been altogether wasted. From his father he had acquired a knowledge of medicine; the tea-trade had given him some insight into business methods; and a precocious knowledge of the world was not without its uses to the future advocate. The local connexion helped him on the South-Eastern circuit and the Sussex sessions, and briefs began to come in.

Marshall Hall's personality was much to his advantage. A handsome man with a commanding presence, he always appealed to the lay client, as solicitors were not slow to appreciate, and he had an instinct for making the most of his qualities. It was eleven years, however, before a real opportunity came. He was retained in a squalid and repulsive murder case (*Rex* v. *Hermann*), with an uncongenial client. Against him were (Sir) Charles Willie Mathews [q.v.] and (Sir) Archibald Bodkin, two deadly prosecutors. But, after a long trial, Marshall Hall obtained a verdict of manslaughter. It was a fine performance and attracted both public and professional attention.

Although Marshall Hall never practised regularly in the criminal courts, the publicity which such cases entail kept him well in the public eye, and materially assisted him at *nisi prius*. His practice rapidly increased, and at the early age of thirty-nine justified him in taking silk. The result was never in doubt. He soon became a fashionable leader in cases where fact rather than law was the predominant issue.

Success introduced Marshall Hall to politics, and in 1900 he was returned to parliament as conservative member for the Southport division of Lancashire; he retained the seat until 1906. From 1910 to 1916 he represented the East Toxteth division of Liverpool. Although a member for eleven years, he made no mark. He was handicapped by an unfortunate maiden speech, his knowledge of politics was superficial, and his speeches, effective on a platform, made no appeal to the House of Commons. Professionally he seemed on the crest of the wave; his success had, perhaps, been too easy. A certain irresponsibility and a tendency to quarrel with authority became apparent.

In a libel case against the *Daily Mail* in 1901 Marshall Hall procured very large damages by suggesting that an adjournment had been obtained for the purpose of finding out something detrimental to the character of his client, an attractive young actress. There was no foundation for this suggestion, and his conduct was severely criticized in the Court of Appeal. His explanation did not improve matters, and the press was uniformly hostile. For a time he seemed to lose balance, and his differences with the judges became so marked that it affected his practice, and a fine professional income was reduced to a mere pittance. It was the crisis of Marshall Hall's career, but he met the reverse with great courage, and he not merely built up a new and sounder practice on the ruins of the old, but showed that there were solid qualities behind what unkind critics had deemed a mere façade. A brilliant and successful defence in 1907 of a young artist charged with murder did much to help him, and before long few sensational cases seemed complete without him.

Marshall Hall's greatest triumph was the Russell divorce case in 1923, which he won for the petitioner in the court of first instance after two such redoubtable advocates as (Sir) John Simon and (Sir) Douglas Hogg had failed. Unable to appear in the second trial Sir Douglas Hogg said to his client: 'There is only one man at the bar who might pull it off for you. He might win you a brilliant victory and he might make a terrible mess of it.' It was an apt description of Marshall Hall's advocacy, but the brilliant victory came about, only to be upset on appeal upon a point of law.

For some time before his death Marshall Hall's health had been failing. An attack of pneumonia years before had weakened his constitution, and it became obvious that he was often working under physical disabilities. Yet he went on with undaunted courage. When he died at his home at Brook, near Godalming, 23 February 1927, he was engaged in a part-heard case. His death was a great shock to the bar, which realized that with all his limitations Marshall Hall had been a unique figure. If his reputation was more public than professional, at his best he was a powerful advocate, and always the kindest and most generous of leaders. In many ways there was much of the child in him. He had a passion for showing off, tempered by an attractive simplicity and combined with a love of the marvellous, which made him on questions of fact somewhat of an impressionist. But there was about his personality something which even his most austere critics found hard to resist.

Marshall Hall was twice married: first, in 1882 to Ethel (died 1890), daughter of Henry Moon, M.D., of Brighton; secondly, in 1896 to Henriette, daughter of Hans Kroeger, of Altona, Schleswig-Holstein, by whom he had one daughter. He was appointed recorder of Guildford in 1916 and knighted in 1917.

A cartoon of Marshall Hall by 'Spy' appeared in *Vanity Fair* 24 September 1903.

[Edward Marjoribanks, *Life of Sir Edward Marshall Hall*, 1929; *Law Reports* (civil and criminal); personal knowledge.] C. Biron.

HALL, HARRY REGINALD HOLLAND (1873–1930), archaeologist, was born at Fulham 30 September 1873, the only child of Sydney Prior Hall, artist, of Fulham (later of Hampstead), by his wife, Hannah Holland. He entered Merchant Taylors' School in 1886, and proceeded to St. John's College, Oxford, in 1891 with a scholarship in modern history. As a boy he had shown an interest in antiquities, more particularly in those of Egypt, and a definite archaeological turn was given to his career when he offered the history and language of Ancient Egypt as a special subject in *literae humaniores*, in which he gained a second class in 1895. This qualification won him his entry to the British Museum, where in 1896 he was appointed an assistant in the department of Egyptian and Assyrian antiquities. Here it was that he gained that familiarity with Near Eastern antiquities which, along with an inherited artistic taste, made him a foremost authority on the date, style, and authenticity of any object that came from the Near East. As part of his duties in the department he produced three of the official catalogues: *Coptic and Greek Texts of the Christian Period* (1905), *Egyptian Scarabs* (1913), and *Hieroglyphic Texts from Egyptian Stelae*, vols. ii to vii (1912–1925).

Fortunately for Hall the trustees of the Museum believed in the advisability of field-work for their younger men, and in the winter of 1903–1904 he was allowed to take part in the excavations of the Egypt Exploration Fund at Dêr el-Bahrî. So valuable did he prove himself here that he was released again in the two following winters for the same work. The volumes in which this excavation is reported, *The XIth Dynasty Temple at Deir el-Bahari* (vols. i–iii), are largely the work of his hand. In 1910 and again in 1925 he took part in the excavations of the same society at Abydos.

In 1901 Hall showed his courage by publishing *The Oldest Civilization of Greece*, the first attempt made to harmonize the new discoveries in Crete with what had previously been known of the Aegean area. Coming from one whose studies might reasonably have been confined to Egypt and Mesopotamia, this work was a revelation, and it established its author as a kind of chief liaison officer between the archaeology of three widely separated areas, a position which he continued to occupy unchallenged until his death. A later book, *The Ancient History of the Near East* (1913, seventh edition 1927), consolidated this reputation.

During the European War Hall was employed first in the military section of the Press Bureau, later in the intelligence department of the War Office, and subsequently on political service in Mesopotamia, where he held the rank of captain. In 1918 he was sent to Iraq by the British Museum with a mandate to protect the antiquities of the country from damage and to take advantage of any opportunity of profitable excavation. In 1919 he directed the British Museum excavation at Ur of the Chaldees and Abu Shahrain and discovered a new site at Al-'Ubaid. The results were described in *A Season's Work at Ur*, which appeared in 1930, a short time after Hall's death.

Hall had acquired a first-hand acquaintance with the three countries in which his main archaeological interests lay, and could speak of the Near East with an authority that few could equal. In 1919 he was made deputy keeper in the department of Egyptian and Assyrian antiquities, and in 1924 keeper. From this time onward his main concern was with the collections in his charge, in the arrangement of which his artistic eye and his ability to understand and sympathize with the popular as well as the academic aspect of a museum stood him in good stead. Yet the other sides of his work were not neglected. During these years he poured out a stream of valuable articles on Egypt, Babylonia, and the Aegean, and was also engaged on larger works. A handbook called *Ægean Archæology* had already appeared in 1915. The Rhind lectures on *The Civilization of Greece in the Bronze Age*, which he delivered at Edinburgh in 1923, were published in that year and reissued with new material in 1928.

Hall was an influential member of the councils of many archaeological societies; in particular, of the Royal Asiatic Society, the Egypt Exploration Society, and the Society for the Promotion of Hellenic Studies; he was chairman of the Palestine Exploration Fund (1922) and a vice-president of the Society of Antiquaries. On all these bodies he was valued not only for the soundness of his judgement but also for the energy with which he would enter into and push forward any scheme in which he believed. He received the honorary degree of D.Litt. from Oxford University in 1920, and was elected a fellow of the British Academy in 1926. But among the honours which fell to him he appreciated most his election in 1929 to an honorary fellowship at his own college of St. John's.

Hall died in London 13 October 1930, after a few days' illness. He was unmarried.

[*The Times*, 14 October 1930; *Journal of Egyptian Archaeology*, vol. xvii, Parts i and ii, May 1931; R. Campbell Thompson, *Harry Reginald Hall, 1873–1930*, in *Proceedings* of the British Academy, vol. xvi, 1930; personal knowledge.] T. E. Peet.

HAMBLEDEN, second Viscount (1868–1928), philanthropist. [See Smith, William Frederick Danvers.]

HAMILTON, Lord **GEORGE FRANCIS** (1845–1927), statesman, was born at Brighton 17 December 1845, the third son of James Hamilton, first Duke of Abercorn [q.v.], by his wife, Lady Louisa Jane, second daughter of John Russell, sixth Duke of Bedford. James Hamilton, second Duke of Abercorn [q.v.], was his eldest brother. He was educated at Harrow, and entered the Rifle Brigade, exchanging later into the Coldstream Guards.

While still a subaltern Hamilton was returned to parliament, in the conservative interest, for Middlesex at the general election of 1868, defeating Henry Labouchere. He represented Middlesex until the Reform Act of 1884, after which he sat for the Ealing division of the county (1885–1906). Hamilton was fortunate in attracting the attention of Disraeli by his maiden speech on the Irish Church Bill and by a motion condemning the action of the government in 1873 over the interpretation of the Treaty of Oregon. After Gladstone's defeat in 1874, Disraeli offered Hamilton the under-secretaryship for foreign affairs; he refused it on the score of ignorance of French, but accepted the under-secretaryship for India. As his chief, Lord Salisbury, was a peer, the duty of representing India in the Commons devolved upon Hamilton. He distinguished himself at once in introducing the Indian Loans Bill (1874), and during his term of office presented several Indian budgets and assisted in piloting the Royal Titles Bill (1876), whereby the queen assumed the title of Empress of India. From 1878 to 1880 he was vice-president of the council, the minister responsible for education. While in opposition from 1880 to 1885 he devoted much attention to Irish affairs, and in 1883 brought in a motion in favour of land purchase, which Gladstone was somewhat reluctantly obliged to accept. In 1885 he became first lord of the Admiralty, and held that office, except for a few months in 1886, until 1892.

Hamilton's administration was a period of extensive naval reform, during which the principles which were to govern organization of the fleet were formulated. Some great defects in departmental administration had been revealed, particularly in connexion with finance, repairs, and shipbuilding. Hamilton's first step in 1885 was to appoint practically a complete new Board and to define clearly the duties and departments of each lord.

Naval construction also required immediate attention. There was a vast programme of uncompleted ships of different varieties. The building programme was overhauled, and Hamilton introduced a Naval Defence Act (1889), providing for the construction, in five years, of eight first-class and two second-class battleships, nine large and twenty-nine small cruisers, four fast gunboats, and twenty-four torpedo boats. The supply of naval guns and ammunition was transferred from the War Office to the Admiralty. A complete reform of dockyard administration was instituted, in order to ensure more effective construction and repair. Provision was made for the care and maintenance of ships in reserve; and reserves of officers, men, guns, ammunition, and supplies were prepared to facilitate mobilization. The men in reserve were transferred from the hulls in which they had hitherto been quartered to naval barracks built on shore, and Portsmouth, Devonport, and Sheerness were made self-supporting for mobilization, each under its commander-in-chief. Between 1886 and 1892 heavy guns were increased from 499 to 1,868, quick-firers from 33 to 1,715, torpedoes from 820 to 2,874, tonnage from 342,000 to 544,000, and personnel from 61,400 to 74,100. Arrangements were made for arming fast merchantmen in time of war, and an agreement was concluded with the Australian colonies for the provision of a squadron, which was to be paid for in part by their governments. More open to criticism, perhaps, was the cession of Heligoland to Germany in 1890.

In 1894 Hamilton became chairman of the London School Board. On the return of the conservatives to power in 1895, he was appointed secretary of state for India, an office which he held until 1903. He was at once faced with the necessity of deciding whether or not to evacuate the state of Chitral, whither a relief expedition had recently been sent to extricate a British mission, headed by Surgeon-Major (Sir) George Scott Robertson [q.v.], which had been dispatched there to restore order. To hold it necessitated keeping the road open; to abandon it would have rendered it almost impossible to carry out Great Britain's treaty obligations regarding the tranquillity of this part of her sphere of influence. The Indian government recommended the former course, but the liberal government had decided to evacuate. Hamilton, however, on the advice of Lord Lansdowne [q.v.], the retiring viceroy, decided to accept the recommendations of the Indian government. In 1897 a more formidable situation was created by the revolt of the Waziris. They were joined by the Afridis, and the Indian government had to dispatch an army of 70,000 men to quell the revolt. Hamilton's Frontier policy was bitterly attacked by his opponents, but he persisted with it, and in a long dispatch to the Indian government laid down a series of principles which experience had proved to be essential to the peace of the districts concerned.

Famine and plague had to be dealt with as well as Frontier trouble. Hamilton and Lord Elgin [q.v.], the new viceroy, were severely criticized for their famine relief administration, but when the relief operations were reviewed after the crisis was over it was generally admitted that they had been effective. Measures against plague were equally successful, though they were used as a grievance by the extremist native press. A campaign of misrepresentation began, culminating in a series of murderous outrages all over India, which it took two years to punish and stamp out.

When the South African War broke out in October 1899, Hamilton suggested that troops from India should be sent to the Cape. Lord Wolseley demurred, but Lord Lansdowne supported Hamilton, and the force arrived just in time to save Natal. After the War, tariff reform became a question of supreme importance. It was obvious from the outset that there was a serious difference of opinion between Mr. Chamberlain's supporters and the free-traders, of whom Hamilton was one. The Cabinet was unable to agree upon a common definition of its fiscal views: resignations ensued, among them that of Hamilton, who finally left the front bench, after being a member of it for thirty-three years. He explained his reasons at length to his constituents in a speech at Ealing on 22 October 1903.

Hamilton did not offer himself for reelection to parliament in 1906, but he continued in public life. In 1905 he became chairman of the royal commission on poor law and unemployment, a task which taxed his capacity in the highest degree. The commission sat until 1909 and the evidence covered 7,000 pages of printed matter. The members were mainly experts and advocates of different and conflicting schools of thought. Hamilton's endeavour was to preserve as large a measure of agreement as was practicable. Although the report was not unanimous, common ground was found upon the outstanding question of the abolition of the boards of guardians and the transfer of their functions to local authorities, and much credit is due to Hamilton for securing it. The soundness of the main lines of the royal commission's recommendation has been generally recognized by successive governments, and was given effect to by the provisions of the Local Government Act of 1929.

During the European War Hamilton served as chairman (1916–1917) of the royal commission on the Mesopotamia campaign, which reported in 1917, and he also undertook other public duties. He published two volumes of reminiscences in 1916 and 1922.

All his life Hamilton maintained his connexion with his old school and served as a governor and eventually as chairman of the governors of Harrow (1913–1924). He was a prominent freemason, and was for more than thirty years provincial grand master of Middlesex. Outside politics Hamilton found his occupation in sport and society; he was a good shot and a keen golf player. He was sworn a privy councillor in 1878, created G.C.S.I. in 1903, and was an honorary D.C.L. of Oxford University, and an honorary LL.D. of Glasgow University. He was captain of Deal Castle, where he spent a good deal of his leisure time, from 1899 to 1923. He married in 1871 Lady Maud Caroline, youngest daughter of Henry Lascelles, third Earl of Harewood, by whom he had three sons. He died in London 22 September 1927 in his eighty-second year.

[Lord George Hamilton, *Parliamentary Reminiscences and Reflections, 1868–1885*, 1916, *1886–1906*, 1922; W. F. Monypenny and G. E. Buckle, *Life of Benjamin Disraeli*, 6 vols., 1910–1920; B. H. Holland, *Life of Spencer Compton, Eighth Duke of Devonshire*, 2 vols., 1911; W. S. Churchill, *Lord Randolph Churchill*, 2 vols., 2nd ed., 1907; Hon. A. R. G. Elliot, *Life of George Joachim Goschen, First Viscount Goschen*, 2 vols., 1911; Dispatches of the Government of India; Lord Ronaldshay (now Marquess of Zetland), *Life of Lord Curzon*, 3 vols., 1928; Speech of Lord George Hamilton at Ealing, 22 October 1903; *Reports* of the royal commissions on poor law and unemployment, 1909, and on Mesopotamia, 1917; private information.] ONSLOW.

HARCOURT, LEWIS, first VISCOUNT HARCOURT (1863–1922), politician, the younger and only surviving son of Sir William Harcourt [q.v.], by his first wife, Marie Thérèse, daughter of Thomas Henry Lister [q.v.], of Armytage Park, Staffordshire, novelist, was born in London 31 January 1863. His mother died at his birth, and he remained throughout his life his father's close and constant companion. He was educated at Eton, but ill-health prevented him from going to Cambridge and obliged him to spend some time abroad. From 1881 to 1885 he acted as his father's private secretary at the Home Office, at the Treasury (1886, and 1892 to 1895), and in opposition from 1895 to 1904, refusing to leave his father either to enter parliament or to accept the post of secretary to the commissioners of woods and forests in 1893. Harcourt devoted himself to party organization, being active on the Home Counties Liberal Federation from its foundation in 1887. During the South African War he strenuously opposed the government and the liberal Imperialists.

In 1904 Harcourt was elected member of parliament for the Rossendale division of Lancashire, a seat which he held until 1916. When Joseph Chamberlain launched his tariff reform proposals Harcourt took part in founding the Free Trade Union, raising £10,000, and arranging that liberals should not oppose socialist free-traders as candidates for parliament. He joined Sir Henry Campbell-Bannerman's Cabinet in 1905 as first commissioner of works, a congenial post, for he had always been interested in art and archaeology, and was at various times a trustee of the Wallace Collection, of the National Portrait Gallery, and of the British Museum, as well as being an honorary fellow of the Royal Institute of British Architects, a member of the advisory committee of the Victoria and Albert Museum, and of the council and executive of the British School at Rome. With Viscount Esher [q.v.] he founded the London Museum in 1911, and his knowledge of gardening enabled him to make extensive improvements in the London parks. He also did much for the embellishment and comfort of the Houses of Parliament. He did not, however, confine himself to the duties of his own office. He introduced the Plural Voting Bill in 1906 and, representing the Board of Agriculture, a Small Holdings and Allotments Bill in 1907. At first a determined opponent of women's suffrage, he later withdrew his opposition and voted in the House of Lords in 1918 for the Representation of the People Bill (which granted the vote to women of thirty and over). In 1910 he became secretary of state for the Colonies.

Harcourt's years at the Colonial Office were the most fortunate of his career. There was general prosperity throughout the Empire, self-government in South Africa was proving successful, and there were few disturbances elsewhere. Anglo-German and Anglo-Belgian-Portuguese frontier delimitation agreements were reached in West and Central Africa, and in 1912 the political union of Northern and Southern Nigeria was accomplished. Harcourt's main interest was in economic and scientific development. In West Africa a new Eastern railway was planned from the junction with the Western line at Kadina to Port Harcourt, which was named after the colonial secretary. In East Africa the Jinja Kakinda railway linked Lake Victoria Nyanza with the navigable Nile. A new railway from Belgian territory to Lake Albert Edward helped to open up Central Africa, a light railway was built out of British funds from Nairobi to the Thihar River, and Kilindini harbour was constructed. Questions of land tenure were settled on the Gold Coast and in British East Africa, but in the latter colony discontent arose among the European settlers over Harcourt's discouragement of colonial self-government. In the West Indies there was also much disappointment at the withdrawal of Great Britain from the Brussels Sugar Convention in 1913. At the Imperial Conference of 1911 questions of imperial defence were mainly considered, and Harcourt established a standing committee consisting of the Colonial Office representatives and the high commissioners of the various colonies. He devoted much time to promoting medical research in British colonies, and in 1911 reached an agreement with Germany for the investigation of sleeping sickness.

Harcourt believed that the relations of Great Britain with Germany could be improved, and that a spirit of goodwill towards England existed at Berlin. In July 1914 he at first supported Viscount Morley [q.v.] in his pacific attitude, and proposed to resign from the Cabinet. But after the invasion of Belgium by Germany on 3 August he altered his mind, and thereafter, adhering to the views of Mr. Asquith and Sir Edward Grey, was active in helping to prosecute the War. In 1915 he returned to the Office of Works, but he resigned in December 1916 when Mr. Asquith withdrew from the premiership. He was raised to the peerage as Viscount Harcourt in January 1917. On leaving office Harcourt became chairman of the Army Agricultural Committee which dealt with food supply in England, France, and Mesopotamia, and later of the Empire Oil Resources Committee. His interest in Empire development continued after leaving the Colonial Office, and he was associated with the Imperial Institute, especially in the bureaux of mycology, entomology, and imperial resources. He was also an ecclesiastical commissioner and a commissioner for the 1851 Exhibition.

Harcourt succeeded to his father's Oxfordshire estate of Nuneham Courtenay in 1904, and did much to improve the place, especially the gardens. Besides gardening, his favourite recreations were shooting and fishing; he was also a collector, especially of books about Eton. In later years his ill-health increased. He died suddenly 24 February 1922 at Nuneham, and was buried there. An inquest followed at which a verdict of death by misadventure was returned. He was admitted a privy councillor in 1905 and made an honorary D.C.L. of Oxford in 1911.

Harcourt married in 1899 Mary Ethel, daughter of Walter Hayes Burns, of New York and North Mymms Park, Hertfordshire, and had one son and three daughters. He was succeeded as second viscount by his son, William Edward (born 1908).

[*The Times*, 25 February 1922; A. G. Gardiner, *Life of Sir William Harcourt*, 2 vols., 1923; Lord Ullswater, *A Speaker's Commentaries*, 1925; Lord Morley, *Memorandum on Resignation*, 1928; private information.]

ONSLOW.

HARDY, THOMAS (1840–1928), poet and novelist, was born 2 June 1840 at Higher Bockhampton, a hamlet near Stinsford in Dorset. On both sides he came of the native Dorset stock. Although his father's people no doubt originally sprang from the Jersey family of Le Hardy, they had for centuries belonged to the Frome valley: a numerous clan which had given several worthies to the county, among them Vice-Admiral Sir Thomas Masterman Hardy [q.v.], Nelson's flag-captain. His mother's ancestors, mostly small-holders in the north of the county, bore Saxon names—Swetman and Childs and Hand or Hann. There was strong character on both sides; and also decided talent, although not of a kind to achieve more than local fame. Both his maternal grandmother and his mother, Jemima, daughter of George Hand, of Melbury Osmund, were notable women of vigorous and lively minds, and from them perhaps Hardy drew his keen sensitivity and his tenacious intellectual curiosity. But in depth of character—and especially in his quiet, unassuming determination, wholly unambitious in worldly affairs—he seems more to have resembled his father; who also, moreover, had one conspicuous talent which had proved heritable in the family, and which was obviously important in Hardy's early experience and must have done something to shape his genius. For his father, Thomas Hardy the elder, like his grandfather (also a Thomas Hardy), had a consuming passion for music. The Hardys, indeed, had made Stinsford parish church celebrated for the instrumental music which they contributed to the services there; and they were always ready to provide the music for secular festivities also. In his boyhood Thomas Hardy very willingly fell in with this family tradition of rural music, sacred and profane. His father, too, was not unwilling to show himself an expert dancer in the rustic style, and was profoundly attached to the manners of Dorset life as well as to the wild nature of the country-side: he liked to lie on a bank in hot weather 'with the grasshoppers leaping over him'. He was a builder by trade, and for that business his out-of-the-way house in Bockhampton was most unsuitably placed; but he refused to leave it, and the woods and heaths he inarticulately loved; neither would he let business interfere with music. That such a man was the father of the author of the Wessex novels is clearly significant. He was not, naturally, very successful in his trade; but did good work, and was always sound financially. It is of some importance to note that his son, although he had to make his own way, was never in immediate need of money, and always knew, while his father lived, that he could have assistance if required, unwilling though he was to be dependent.

Hardy was the eldest of four children—two sons and two daughters. He was the only one of them who married, and he had no children himself. The surgeon thought that he was stillborn, but the midwife roused the life in him; and he grew to healthy childhood, though of slight physique, rather dangerously precocious, and of unstable emotions, being strangely sensitive to the music of his father's indefatigable fiddle. Of his babyhood one incident, which in ancient days would have been considered ominous, may be mentioned: his mother found him one hot day asleep in his cot with a sleeping snake coiled on his breast (or, in another version, on the floor beside him). At eight years old he began his schooling in the village, but went next year as a day boy to an unusually good private school, kept by a nonconformist master, in Dorchester; there he was soon well grounded in Latin and French, to which he afterwards added some study of German on his own account. Later on he made himself fairly proficient in Greek. Of his schooldays a characteristic trait was that, while his amiable nature made him generally liked, he himself secretly disliked the familiarities of schoolboy companionship, and resented the touch of arm-in-arm affection.

Out of school, Hardy's life at home, and in rural society round about, gave him many experiences of which it would be impossible to exaggerate the importance;

for his deeply retentive nature kept them vividly alive in his mind, and from them, more or less transformed, supplied many years later rich material for his art. Thus, by good fortune, as a very small boy he attended one of the last of the old-fashioned harvest-home suppers at which the full tradition of these celebrations was still unimpaired, to the inestimable advantage of *Far from the Madding Crowd*; and when we learn that some of the military were there too, it is impossible not to think of Sergeant Troy. Hardy frequently acted as the fiddler at local dance-parties, and to the wealth of experience which he gained thereby both his prose and his verse bear witness throughout; as they also do to his equally lively familiarity with church services, church music, and the habits and personages of church choirs. It was the same with experiences of purely subjective importance. A capital instance is the lyric, 'To Louisa in the Lane', written shortly before his death, in which he completely resumes a shy romance of his early boyhood—an affair of childish sentimental reverie almost without any incident, but preserved intact into old age. But this vivid preserving of experience was a trait which continued long after boyhood, and is an essential characteristic of Hardy's genius. Thus the famous lines 'In Time of the Breaking of Nations' were written in 1915, but the experience which they record came to him in 1870, when the battle of Gravelotte was fought. So, too, the mummers' play of 1923, *The Famous Tragedy of the Queen of Cornwall*, releases and gives form to feelings and dreams which, ever since as a young man he had visited Tintagel with the lady whom he was to marry, he had retained for fifty years.

In 1856, when he was sixteen, Hardy was placed as a pupil with John Hicks, an ecclesiastical architect in Dorchester for whom his father had worked as a builder. He continued to study Latin and Greek; he did not read many authors, but those he read he knew well, especially Virgil; the Greek tragedians, too, strongly attracted him, and Homer. About this time he became acquainted with the Rev. William Barnes [q.v.], the Dorset poet, whom he occasionally consulted in his classical studies; long afterwards (1908) he edited a selection of Barnes's poems. Another friend and helper of this time was Horace Moule, of Queens' College, Cambridge, a good Grecian, and a miscellaneous writer: he it was who first decisively encouraged Hardy to continue his own experiments—it is impossible to say when they began—in prose and verse. A somewhat odd cause moved Hardy also to intense study of the New Testament in Greek. A fellow pupil in Hicks's office was a strong Baptist, and insisted on discussing paedobaptism, supported by two young friends from Aberdeen University, sons of the local Baptist minister, whose ready knowledge of the Greek Testament gave them an advantage which Hardy was determined to reduce. The topic of paedobaptism reappears in *A Laodicean*, along with a portrait of the minister; and the two young Scotsmen perhaps gave some suggestions for the character of Farfrae in *The Mayor of Casterbridge*.

By the time he was twenty, Hardy was proficient enough in his architecture to be employed by Hicks on the disastrous restoration of old churches then in vogue. As may be supposed, he later came to regret this; but the work which it gave him must have been of the greatest value in the unconscious education of his art. He used to speak later of the 'three strands' in his life at this time—architecture, study of the classics, and participation (musical and otherwise) in the rural society of Bockhampton. Hardy, with more book-learning, might have become a scholar; but for the man he was to become, the poet and novelist, it is difficult to imagine an education more suitable than the intertwining of these 'three strands'. However, believing that he ought to advance himself in his profession, he decided, on his friend Moule's advice, not to go on exploring Greek tragedy, but to give all his mind to architecture; and he seems to have become an expert Gothic draughtsman. In 1862, at the age of twenty-two, in accordance with his father's wish that he should by then be earning his own living, he sought work in London, with naïve prudence taking a return-ticket. The return-half was not needed; he almost at once found employment with (Sir) Arthur William Blomfield [q.v.], to whom Hardy's training in Gothic was a strong recommendation.

Hardy remained five years in London, and got to know the town well. He worked hard at architecture, in 1863 winning the essay prize offered by the Royal Institute of British Architects. He worked hard, too, at educating himself generally, reading systematically in ancient and modern literature, and attending evening classes for a while at King's College in order to improve himself in French. It was not long before he was writing again; and in March 1865 *Chambers's Journal* took a mildly humorous article, 'How I Built Myself a House.' But his interest at this time was almost entirely in poetry. That Walter Scott, after such a 'Homeric' performance as *Marmion*, should have taken to novels, he thought deplorable. His letters to his sister Mary mention Thackeray, Lytton, and Trollope as writers of repute, but, except for some approval of 'truthful representation of actual life' in Thackeray, without any sign of being personally interested. Meanwhile he was quite unsuccessfully trying the magazines with poems, many of which, however, he preserved and some thirty years and more afterwards published, slightly revised, in *Wessex Poems* and later volumes. The literary life of London was unknown to him; but he made a very methodical study of pictures in the National Gallery, and was impressed by the acting of Samuel Phelps [q.v.] in Shakespeare, by Dickens in his readings, and, as would be expected, by the oratorios at Exeter Hall. It must have been about this time that he read, with enthusiasm, *The Origin of Species*. This may have had something to do with his change from the orthodoxy of his youth; but the steady progress of his mind towards the very individual determinism of *The Dynasts* seems to have been largely the evolution of his own nature, independently of external influences.

Ill-health in London made Hardy return in 1867 to Dorchester, and to architectural practice with Hicks again. But by this time he was bent on writing; now, however, determined, for purely practical reasons, to try his hand at prose fiction. *The Poor Man and the Lady* was the result, a comprehensive satire of socialist tendency, said to resemble Defoe in style. Alexander Macmillan rejected it as being too ferocious a view of society, but expressed both his own admiration and that of John Morley, who praised the rustic part. Chapman & Hall accepted it in 1869; but their reader requested an interview. This reader was no other than George Meredith, who advised against publication, and urged on Hardy the importance of 'plot'. Hardy was completely unaware of the formidable nature of his first novel, the loss of which is very regrettable. The manuscript was destroyed, but a shortened and, apparently, much modified version of the story was published in the *New Quarterly Magazine* for July 1878, as *An Indiscretion in the Life of an Heiress*. The quality of the original work can scarcely be judged from this mildly charming novelette which, however, occasionally foreshadows, in setting and psychology, the art of his mature fiction. It was reprinted by Mrs. Hardy for private distribution in October 1934, and independently published in America, with an introduction by Professor Carl Weber, of Colby College, in 1935.

Too faithfully following Meredith's recommendation of plot, Hardy wrote *Desperate Remedies*, and submitted it in 1870 to Macmillan, who refused it. Hicks having died meanwhile, his practice was taken over by one Crickmay, of Weymouth, who sent Hardy as his deputy to make surveys for the restoration of the remote church of St. Juliot, near Boscastle in Cornwall. This expedition was the source of *A Pair of Blue Eyes*; and it was at St. Juliot that he met his first wife, the rector's sister-in-law, Emma Lavinia, daughter of John Attersoll Gifford, a Plymouth lawyer, and niece of Edwin Hamilton Gifford [q.v.], archdeacon of London.

The St. Juliot restoration was Hardy's last work of any importance in Gothic. For a couple of years more he accepted temporary architectural engagements in London and Weymouth, but, in spite of some discouragement and uncertainty at first, gave himself chiefly to fiction. *Desperate Remedies* was published anonymously in 1871 by William Tinsley [q.v.], to whom Hardy had to pay £75; it received some good reviews, but was bludgeoned by the *Spectator*. Yet the sales were such that Hardy recovered £60 of his outlay. In the summer of this year, following the advice implied in Morley's criticism of *The Poor Man and the Lady*, he found his true vein and wrote *Under the Greenwood Tree*, which Tinsley bought for £30 and brought out in 1872. It was well received, and Tinsley suggested a serial for his *Magazine*. Hardy agreed, made much better terms, and wrote *A Pair of Blue Eyes*, which, when published in book form (1873), had considerable success. While he was busy with this last novel (Sir) Leslie Stephen, strongly attracted by *Under the Greenwood Tree*, wrote proposing a serial for the *Cornhill*, of which he was then editor. Still hoping to get back to poetry, and regarding prose fiction chiefly as a means of livelihood, Hardy, with no more immediate ambition than to be 'considered a good hand at a serial', sent Stephen some chapters of *Far from the Madding Crowd*. It was accepted and began to appear (anonymously) in the *Cornhill* for January 1874; and was at once recognized as something remarkable. Hardy finished the book at Bockhampton during the summer, close to the district where the scene of the story was laid, which, he said, he found a 'great advantage'. In September he and Miss Gifford were married. *Far from the Madding Crowd* was published in two volumes in November, and had great success—a fact imperfectly appreciated by Hardy himself, then living at Surbiton with his wife after a honeymoon abroad.

It might be supposed that, with the publication of this masterpiece, so richly confirming the promise of *Under the Greenwood Tree*, Hardy had found past mistake the right road for him as a novelist. But he had a curious faculty of being unaware of his own powers. His next book, *The Hand of Ethelberta* (1875), also a *Cornhill* serial, might well disconcert his admirers then, as it still does now, not so much by the difference of its subject, as by its lapse in quality, although that was doubtless due to the subject. But in 1878 *The Return of the Native* appeared; and thenceforth for close on twenty years his fiction was not only his profession (a fact which he still at times regretted), but an art of noble form, amazing wealth of substance, and profound significance. There is variety, and no doubt inequality, in the series of his novels. *The Trumpet-Major* (1880), a story in an historical setting, may, for all its charm and good-humour, be ranked below, if only just below, his highest achievements. *A Laodicean* (1881) and *Two on a Tower* (1882) show that his art was not confined to rural society, though plainly at its best there; and *The Romantic Adventures of a Milkmaid* (summer number of the *Graphic*, 1883) is a pleasant modern fairy-tale. But *The Mayor of Casterbridge* (1886) and *The Woodlanders* (1887) must be grouped with the earlier *Far from the Madding Crowd* and *The Return of the Native*, their prelude *Under the Greenwood Tree*, and with the two later novels of more extended, more epic, structure, *Tess of the D'Urbervilles* (1891) and *Jude the Obscure* (1895), as together forming one of the supreme and most individual achievements of the art of fiction in English. Between these two last came the strange experiment of *The Well-Beloved* (serially, 1892; revised and published in book form, 1897); and interspersed among the series of the novels were several collections of admirable short stories, *Wessex Tales* (1888) and *Life's Little Ironies* (1894), and two sets of tales linked together by the occasion of their telling, *A Group of Noble Dames* (1891; incomplete in Christmas number of the *Graphic*, 1890) and—a minor masterpiece—*A Few Crusted Characters* (1891). A collection of stories not hitherto published, *A Changed Man and Other Tales*, was made in 1913. All the novels except the first two had come out serially; *Tess* and *Jude* were deliberately modified to suit the delicacy of editors, while the final form of *The Mayor of Casterbridge* was a drastic revision of the more sensational serial version.

Hardy's career as a writer of prose fiction was now at an end. He had never himself required more of it than a means of modest subsistence; but now at long last he could devote himself to poetry, which he had, in fact, been writing off and on during his work as a novelist. In spite of his practical attitude to the business of novel-writing, he had made his fiction, both in its conduct and its substance (his own Wessex life, for instance), as personal an expression of his artistic genius and of his deepest convictions as poetry could well be. But with *Jude the Obscure* it seemed that he had exhausted the possibilities of the novel as a vehicle for his artistic and intellectual idiosyncrasy. He was perhaps subconsciously aware of this; if so, the feeling was doubtless confirmed by some stupid, and some malignant, abuse of *Tess* and *Jude*. That he was nettled by the outcry is certain; and some impatient remarks of his ascribe his abandonment of fiction to this strident noise of journalistic disapproval. In itself the reason seems inadequate, especially considering the immense success of both books, and the splendid praise of such men as Swinburne. The truth is that the novel had served Hardy's turn, both practically and artistically. He was now free of the profession which he had served so long, and secure, and could be without interruption what he had always wanted to be—a poet. After living in several places—Sturminster Newton (1876), Upper Tooting (Trinity Road, near Wandsworth Common, 1878), Wimborne (1881, after a long and severe illness)—he had settled finally (1883) near Dorchester in a house, Max Gate, which he had built for himself (1885); but he made regular visits to London, attended functions, was a good clubman, and knew and frequently met most of the people worth knowing in his day. He had always been a man of large and varied culture, and throughout his life continued to read widely in all kinds of imaginative literature, and in history and philosophy. His delighted interest in his own Wessex people, needless to say, never changed.

Hardy's first task, in his new and specifically poetic career, was to collect in two volumes (*Wessex Poems*, 1898, and *Poems of Past and Present*, 1901) lyrics composed from the time when he first began seriously to write at all down to the time when he had broken with the profession of fiction. They elaborate and concentrate moods and thoughts discoverable, no doubt, in the novels, but in a remarkably original poetic style, which now is seen clearly to announce the revolutionary lyrical art of his last years. But a grand project had long been gradually taking shape in his mind, and was now ripe for execution. Hardy's imagination was full of local memories and traditions of Napoleonic times, and he had drawn on these for *The Trumpet-Major* and several poems and stories; but from quite early years the vast theme of the Napoleonic wars as a whole had presented itself to his poetic ambition. Already in 1875, as his note-books testify, he had thought of 'an Iliad of Europe from 1789 to 1815' in the form of a ballad-epic; later on the project defined itself as a 'grand drama' or chronicle-play. In 1892 he is considering 'methods for the Napoleon drama. Forces; emotions; tendencies. The characters do not act under the influence of reason'; and by 1896 (when he visited Waterloo with the poem in his mind) the drama is planned as 'three parts, five acts each'—almost in its present form. The three parts of *The Dynasts* were published in 1903, 1906, and 1908 respectively, the whole in one volume in 1910. 'The Spectacle here presented' (to quote the preface) 'in the likeness of a Drama' is, then, although dramatic in manner, epic in progress and proportion. The colossal historical theme is both enlarged and unified by the invention of a symbolic supernatural world contemplating and commenting on earthly events. By this invention Hardy was enabled to present history as epic with a success which no previous attempt at any such thing (Lucan's or Ercilla's, for instance) had ever come near: he kept the substantial accuracy of his history, but he gave it the emotional scope and imaginative reverberation of epic. Moreover, he was thereby enabled to give explicit artistic form to the 'metaphysic' implicit in his fiction and progressively becoming more and more insistent as the series of the novels advanced. *The Dynasts* is thus by far his greatest single achievement, and the fullest and most complete expression of his genius. A work of such dimensions, and so unprecedented both in content and in style, was not unnaturally somewhat coolly received at first. But it was not very long before it made its way, and in its grand exhibition of absolute determinism—the 'Immanent Will' ruthlessly and purposelessly working itself out through the welter of human affairs—has seemed to many the one modern English poem which fulfils the nature of the great epics of the past: it shapes a spectacle of large action so as to convey a significance characteristic of its time.

This was the climax of Hardy's whole career, and a noble justification of his jealously preserved poetic ambition. But in that extraordinary career nothing is more extraordinary than what followed. Soon after *The Dynasts* came (1909) *Time's Laughingstocks*, a collection of lyrics, some (previously overlooked) from very early years, some of recent composition. This inaugurates the third period of his art, the period of wholly lyrical activity, except for the mummers' play of Tristran and Iseult, *The Famous Tragedy of the Queen of Cornwall* (1923): *Satires of Circumstance* (1914), *Moments of Vision* (1917), *Late Lyrics and Earlier* (1922, including a further gathering of poems from former years), *Human Shows, Far Fantasies* (1925), and *Winter Words* (1928, published after his death). It is of course completely mistaken to regard Hardy as having turned to poetry in his last years. He had been writing poetry all his life, and if he had never written a line after he had finished his work as a novelist he would still have been a very considerable poet. But in both bulk and quality his lyrical poetry is chiefly the work of his old age, from his seventieth year until his death at eighty-seven. It is all surprisingly original in theme and manner, with a diction throughout wholly unlike any other poet's, while keeping as a rule to orthodox forms or kinds of form; and it ranges from extremely subtle subjectivity to vigorously objective balladry. From his earliest efforts in the 'sixties down to his last poems the general character of his poetic style is quite continuous; but the full expansion and most daring development of his lyrical art belongs to the third and last phase of his life.

Hardy's first wife died in 1912. In 1914 he married Florence Emily, daughter of Edward Dugdale, of Enfield (but of a Dorset family). He received the Order of Merit in 1910, and, what especially pleased him, the freedom of Dorchester in the same year. In 1909 he succeeded Meredith as president of the Society of Authors. He received honorary doctorates from the universities of Aberdeen, Cambridge, and Oxford, and was an honorary fellow of Magdalene College, Cambridge, and of Queen's College, Oxford. He died at Max Gate 11 January 1928. His ashes were buried in Westminster Abbey, but his heart was interred in the churchyard of Stinsford.

There are several portraits of Hardy in public collections: in the National Portrait Gallery, oil paintings by W. W. Ouless (1922) and R. G. Eves (1923), a pencil drawing by William Strang (1919), and a bronze bust by Sir Hamo Thornycroft (1917); in the Tate Gallery, another portrait in oils by R. G. Eves (1924); in the Fitzwilliam Museum, an oil painting by Augustus John (1923) with the pencil study that preceded it, and another pencil drawing by William Strang (1910); in the Dorset County Museum, Dorchester, an oil painting by (Sir) Hubert von Herkomer (1906), and a bronze bust by Mrs. M. R. Mitchell (1923). In the possession of Mrs. Hardy at Max Gate are two portraits earlier than any of these—viz. oil paintings by Winifred Hope Thomson (*c.* 1891), and by William Strang (1893), who about the same time also did the etching published in the first edition (1894) of Lionel Johnson's book (see below).

[The sole authority for Hardy's biography is the invaluable memoir by his second wife, *The Early Life* (1928) and *The Later Years* (1930), which contain some letters and many extracts from his note-books. His literary career has been studied by Lionel Johnson, *The Art of Thomas Hardy* (1894); F. A. Hedgcock, *Thomas Hardy, penseur et artiste* (1911); Lascelles Abercrombie, *Thomas Hardy, a critical study* (1912); Harold Child, *Thomas Hardy* (1916); H. C. Duffin, *Thomas Hardy. A Study of the Wessex Novels* (1916); S. C. Chew, *Thomas Hardy, Poet and Novelist* (1921); R. E. Zachrisson, *Thomas Hardy as Man, Writer, and Philosopher* (1928); W. H. Gardner, *Some Thoughts on 'The Mayor of Casterbridge'* (1930). F. A. Hedgcock's work contains a valuable detailed bibliography of the fiction and the early poems. See also the bibliography by John Lane (revised and brought down to date 1923) appended to Lionel Johnson's book; and A. P. Webb, *A Bibliography of the Works of Thomas Hardy, 1865–1915*, 1916.] L. Abercrombie.

HARMSWORTH, ALFRED CHARLES WILLIAM, Viscount Northcliffe (1865–1922), journalist and newspaper proprietor, was the eldest son of Alfred Harmsworth, barrister, of Dublin and the Middle Temple, by his wife, Geraldine Mary, daughter of William Maffett, a land agent in county Down. Born at Chapelizod, near Dublin, 15 July 1865, he was brought to London two years later on the decision of his father to exchange the Irish for the English bar. In 1876 he was sent to Stamford grammar school, and in 1878 as a day boy to Henley House, Hampstead (then kept by John Vine Milne, father of Mr. A. A. Milne), near his parents' new home. Harmsworth was, however, largely self-educated, for his father's health broke down when he was only fifteen and left him responsible, with his remarkably capable mother, for the upbringing of a family which now numbered seven sons and three daughters. For his mother, who survived him (she died in 1925) and from whom he inherited all that was best in his character, he had a lifelong and very touching devotion. In spite of all his activities there was hardly a day, down to his last illness, on which he did not either visit her or, during his absences, write or telegraph to her. Of the future of his brothers it may be recorded here that Harold eventually became first Viscount Rothermere and the successor to most of the Harmsworth enterprises; Cecil, entering the House of Commons as a liberal in 1906, was under-secretary for foreign affairs from 1919 to 1922; Leicester, a liberal member of parliament from 1900, and Hildebrand were both interested in newspapers and were both created baronets; while St. John, who was crippled at an early age by a motor accident, had already shown great promise in business and was the principal proprietor of the 'Perrier' table-water. All owed their start in life to the young head of the family.

There was never any question about Alfred Harmsworth's choice of a profession. At the age of thirteen he founded for his schoolfellows the *Henley House Magazine*, at first typewritten and later printed, often by his own hand. By 1880 he was acting on occasion as reporter for the *Hampstead and Highgate Express*. A year later, when the prospect of his going to Cambridge was under discussion, he was placed under a tutor, but spent most of his time in composing articles for the *Bicycling News*, the *Globe*, and the various boys' and girls' papers produced by James Henderson, a shrewd old Scotsman who was afterwards described by Harmsworth as 'his first journalistic sponsor', and whose other claim to fame is that he was the original publisher of *Treasure Island*. He then travelled extensively on the continent as companion and secretary to a son of the third Lord Lilford, and throughout the tour kept up a continuous bombardment of the newspapers. The result, when he returned, was a growing personal acquaintance with many of the leading journalists of the day—Sir William Ingram of the *Illustrated London News* (who made him assistant editor of *Youth* at a guinea and a half a week), Frederick Greenwood [q.v.], J. M. le Sage, Sir William Hardman, and George Augustus Sala [q.v.]. In 1882 he took rooms in the Temple at 6 Pump Court, abandoned all thoughts of Cambridge, resisted suggestions that he should go to the bar, and gave himself up entirely to free-lance journalism. The papers for which he wrote at this time included the *Globe*, the *Morning Post*, the *St. James's Gazette*, and the various publications of Messrs. Cassell and (Sir) George Newnes [q.v.]. Meanwhile he was becoming an industrious reader, chiefly of the classical English novelists and of the latest discoveries of science, and was contriving also to see a good deal of England as an ardent bicyclist.

It was owing to an attack of pneumonia brought on by one of his bicycle expeditions—he had ridden from Bristol to London in pouring rain and without food—that young Harmsworth was initiated into other branches of journalism; for in 1885 he was ordered by his doctor to live out of London for a time, and proceeded to obtain employment with the firm of Iliffe & Sons, of Coventry, a publishing house which owned among other journals the *Midland Daily Telegraph* and the *Bicycling News*, and in which he took part in the whole business of editing, circulation, and management. Meanwhile Harmsworth retained his connexion with London, and found time to write for Messrs. Newnes two books of popular information which are sufficiently described by their titles—*One Thousand Ways to Earn a Living* and *All About Our Railways*. Mr. Iliffe offered him a partnership before he was twenty-one; but by this time he had recovered his health, had saved £1,000, and had other fields to conquer.

Accordingly, returning to London in 1887, Harmsworth formed a general publishing business of his own at 26 Paternoster Square, and issued from it a growing number of periodical journals, of which the best known was *Answers*—founded in 1888—a popular weekly suggested by the success of Messrs. Newnes with *Tit-Bits*. In this he was joined by his brother Harold, whose financial ability was thenceforward to be combined with Alfred's imagination in a partnership for which the nearest parallel is the contemporary co-operation of Cecil Rhodes and Alfred Beit. The making of money for its own sake was never of great interest to Alfred, but the business, which was the nucleus of the great Amalgamated Press, prospered amazingly. Its profits soon reached £50,000 a year, and in five years *Answers* alone was able to record net weekly sales of more than a million copies.

The Harmsworths made their first incursion into daily journalism in 1894, when Mr. Kennedy Jones persuaded them to acquire for £25,000 the then derelict *Evening News* (on which the conservative party had vainly squandered a fortune), and joined them in restoring it to prosperity. Two years later (4 May 1896) came the foundation of the *Daily Mail*, an elaborately planned halfpenny morning newspaper, which may fairly be said to have opened a new epoch in Fleet Street. Its advent coincided with a period both of awakening popular interest in the stirring events of the world, and particularly of the British Empire, and also of singular inertia on the part of its older rivals. As originally conceived and laboriously rehearsed for many months, the *Daily Mail* completely fulfilled its purpose of presenting 'all the news in the smallest space'. It was comprehensive, alert, and concise. The services of a number of brilliant writers—including George Warrington Steevens [q.v.], who was too soon to die in Ladysmith—were enlisted on its staff. Leading articles were reduced to paragraphs. Immense attention was paid to what were regarded as the interests of the new reading public, and especially to those of women. (It may be recalled that the *Daily Mirror*, which was added to the Harmsworth publications in 1903, began its career with a complete failure as a journal devoted exclusively to women's interests.) Meanwhile the inventions of the day—motoring, flying, wireless, came in turn—were advertised and stimulated; schemes of exploration—the *Evening News* had already broken the ground in 1894 with the Jackson-Harmsworth expedition to Franz Josef Land under Mr. F. G. Jackson—were financed; prizes were offered for household and gardening skill. The rewards which came to be offered later for the first great feats of aviation which followed M. Blériot's first crossing of the Channel in 1909—£10,000 was won in 1910 by M. Paulhan for his flight from London to Manchester and £10,000 in 1919 by Sir John William Alcock [q.v.] and Sir Arthur Whitten Brown for their non-stop flight across the Atlantic—were indeed on a princely scale, and, with the many other marks of encouragement which he gave, justify Harmsworth's claim to a place among the pioneers of applied science. This variety of enthusiasms was perhaps as important for the new venture as any definite policy.

The *Daily Mail* became firmly established between the second Jubilee (1897) and the outbreak of the South African War (1899). A robust imperialism was imposed as much by its instinct for the popular sentiment of the moment as by the natural bent of its founder. Nevertheless, the paper as it was in its original form —as distinguished from its subsequent vagaries—must be regarded in retrospect as Harmsworth's greatest achievement in creative journalism and its foundation an event which deeply affected every newspaper in the land. 'There has been nothing in the story of English journalism,' wrote a none too friendly critic long afterwards, 'comparable with the apparition of the *Daily Mail*. It found a vast territory unchallenged, which it proceeded to occupy with an efficiency and completeness that left little room for competition.'

More breaches with tradition followed. During the South African War, when the value of the telephone in journalism was becoming established, the *Daily Mail* issued a duplicate edition in Manchester, an innovation which gradually compelled its imitators to set up printing presses in Leeds and elsewhere. In 1905 a continental version was established in Paris, and thus the flying start in circulation which had been won in North Britain and Ireland was extended to the whole of Europe. In 1905 also the *Observer* passed under Harmsworth's control, which he eventually abandoned in 1912. Meanwhile all these activities had led to a search by the two brothers for a sure supply of the raw material of newspapers. Pioneering in Newfoundland was begun in 1904. Two years later 3,000 square miles of forest land were acquired at Grand Falls on the Exploit River, and the Anglo-Newfoundland Development Company was formed. The mills for paper-making were opened in 1909, and another great constructive enterprise, including a considerable town and port, private railways, and ocean steamers, was added to the Harmsworth business.

This first decade of the twentieth century must be counted the zenith of Alfred Harmsworth's career. His initial struggles were over. The clouds of his later years were not yet in sight. By his own efforts as a journalist he had won a remarkable position in English life. The support of his newspapers was courted by statesmen: he was surrounded by friends who were not mere sycophants: he was rich beyond the dreams of avarice. In 1888 he had married Mary Elizabeth, daughter of Robert Milner, of Kidlington, Oxfordshire, a West India merchant; she shared all his early trials and now presided with charm and great capacity over a series of beautiful houses. The first home, to which he clung as a working retreat to the end of his life, was Elmwood, an enlarged farm-house at St. Peter's, Thanet. In London, after various experiments in rented houses, he purchased first 36 Berkeley Square (a transaction which led to a close friendship with his next door neighbour, Lord Rosebery); then 22 St. James's Place; then, after an interval during the European War, 1 Carlton Gardens. But his best-known home during all this period was Sutton Place, the famous Tudor mansion in Surrey, which he held on lease from 1899 to 1917 and where he entertained an unending stream of British and foreign visitors. He was an admirable host and, at his best, a delightful companion. There were no children of the marriage and in a sense Harmsworth had no domestic life, for his restless energy turned every incident of his waking hours to account in his journalistic work. He was devoted from boyhood to the English country-side and especially to birds—one of his interests at Sutton was an attempt to acclimatize the North American robin—and made himself a skilful dry-fly fisherman, as he afterwards by incessant practice became a competent golfer. These recreations, however, came more and more to be undertaken as a deliberate means of maintaining his health. His eyes and his throat gave him trouble at different times and led to periodical sojourns abroad. These anxieties were partly the explanation and partly the result of the high pressure at which he worked and lived. In spite of all his opportunities for escaping the strain of his work, few men can have been more consistently engrossed in their profession and few professions can admit of so much absorption.

Harmsworth was created a baronet in 1903, and was raised to the peerage as Baron Northcliffe, of the Isle of Thanet, in 1905, in each case on the recommendation of Mr. Balfour, with whom he had a friendship remarkable for the fact that it remained unbroken to the end. In 1908 he achieved the summit of his ambition in the newspaper world by becoming chief proprietor of *The Times*. For various reasons—the distraction of its hereditary proprietors, the Walters, by their landowning and parliamentary interests; a comfortable sense of supremacy, the growing but unsuspected competition of other journals, the great cost of the legal proceedings resulting from the articles on 'Parnellism and Crime'—*The Times* had come at this time to a financial crisis from which its manager, Charles Frederic Moberly Bell [q.v.], was endeavouring to save it by a number of desperate expedients. He it was who, notwithstanding a similar arrangement already practically concluded with (Sir) Cyril Arthur Pearson [q.v.], eventually carried through (23 March 1908) negotiations by which Northcliffe became principal shareholder in the company which was now formed to take over the business, the chairmanship remaining with Mr. A. F. Walter throughout his lifetime and passing at his death in 1910 to his son.

The new proprietor exercised his influence gradually. He had an intimate knowledge of the history of *The Times* and a great respect for its traditions. In these early days his name never appeared in its columns. To the old staff, who remained for the most part, he was known mysteriously as 'Mr. X'. But new machinery was ordered at once and new men were added by degrees. The 'make-up' of the paper soon became more attractive, special features were introduced into its columns, suggestions of all sorts for organization, for news gathering, and to a smaller extent for comment, were made in numberless bulletins and interviews. Northcliffe probably never had a more difficult task than his struggle to put *The Times* on its feet, for there was no question of the untrodden field and the free hand which he had enjoyed in the case of the *Daily Mail*. To give no other example, the question of price was a constant anxiety to him, and it is significant of the uncertainty of his views on this subject that he changed it no fewer than seven times in little more than as many years—from 3*d.* to 2*d.* in May 1913, to 1*d.* in March 1914, to 1½*d.* in November 1916, to 2*d.* in March 1917, back to 3*d.* in March 1918, to 2*d.*, with a special price of 1½*d.* for regular readers, in March 1922, and finally to a flat rate of 1½*d.* later in the same month. It is also significant of the peculiar position and public of *The Times* that most of these changes in themselves made no more than a temporary impression on its circulation. It had sunk to its lowest point, 38,000, when Northcliffe assumed control, and the price was still 3*d.* It rose very rapidly at 1*d.* to a high-water mark of 318,000 after the outbreak of the War, which, like all great national events, brought a host of new readers. But the tale thenceforward was one of steady decline in numbers through all the vicissitudes of price, and at Northcliffe's death both circulation and finance were once more seriously imperilled by the instability of his later years.

That decline, however, forms another chapter of Harmsworth's life. During the period 1908 to 1914 the restoration of *The Times* was his main preoccupation, and a series of almost daily notes to the editor illustrated both the range of his interests and the wisdom of his journalistic advice. They were written from his houses in London and the country, from Paris and the South of France, from Scotland, Canada, Newfoundland, wherever he might be. They dealt almost indiscriminately—to pick out a few topics at random—with the hours and health of a newspaper staff; with the coming influence of such portents as the Panama Canal, the Diesel engine, the aeronautical experiments of Orville Wright; with food taxes, the Marconi case, the warlike preparations of Europe; with what he held to be the special concerns of women, such as dress and dancing; with the improvement of the *Literary Supplement*; above all, and running through all, with the presentation of news in the paper, the importance of 'topicality', the need for incessant vigilance in watching competitors. In the light of these notes the hasty verdict that Northcliffe 'ruined *The Times*' is manifestly grotesque. The truth is that at a critical moment he was wholly responsible for saving it from extinction; but it is also true that his association with it had lasted long enough when he died and that another change of proprietorship was needed to add steadiness to vitality.

The European War transformed Northcliffe from the anxious newspaper proprietor, working in the background, into the public figure seeking the limelight of the stage. He felt that he had been right about its imminence when others were wrong, and in December 1914, soon after its outbreak, a volume of quotations entitled *Scaremongerings from the Daily Mail* set out, not unjustly, to belaud 'the paper that foretold the War'. He placed himself at the head of all the popular movements of the moment—the preposterous attack on Lord Haldane's presence in Whitehall, the demand for the prompt dispatch of the Expeditionary Force, the clamour for more news from the Front. He also initiated and watched over the great fund for the sick and wounded which *The Times* raised, to the eventual total of nearly £17,000,000, and entrusted to the joint administration of the Red Cross Society and the Order of St. John of Jerusalem. In the spring of 1915 he shocked public opinion for the moment by his strong personal criticism of Lord Kitchener, whose appointment to the War Office he had demanded, for supplying the army with inefficient and obsolete shells. A campaign for a Ministry of Munitions and for compulsory national service followed. The two successive coalition governments (of Mr. Asquith, May 1915, and of Mr. Lloyd George, December 1916) were welcomed, and subsequently denounced, in turn. All these developments were due to public pressure in which Northcliffe, through his command of publicity, was able to play a more and more conspicuous part, but which he caused to be attributed too exclusively to his own influence. Meanwhile he paid several visits to the armies in France and Italy—notably to Verdun during the great German attack of March 1916—busied himself as a special correspondent, and republished some of his dispatches in *At The War* (1916).

In May 1917 Mr. Lloyd George, now firmly established as prime minister, invited Northcliffe to undertake the direction of the British war mission in the United States, and from June to November he was engaged in this task, devoting himself rather to the establishment of personal contacts than to the actual business of purchases and finance, which already occupied a large and capable staff. He visited the Middle West during this period, went to Canada more than once, and found time to write a series of circular letters to his friends, which remain on record (unpublished) as an admirable first-hand account of the problems and personalities that he encountered. On his return to England Northcliffe was created a viscount as a reward for his services. He was also at once offered the position of secretary of state for air—the prime minister was doubtless anxious to keep him occupied—and seized the opportunity to publish a letter (*The Times*, 16 November 1917) in which he not only declined any office in the government but expressed the gravest dissatisfaction with the attitude of some of his prospective colleagues. In February 1918, however, he accepted the direction of propaganda in enemy countries, an office which he could combine with his newspaper work; and this he retained, supervising intermittently the large organization at Crewe House, until the end of the War.

The Armistice brought a new set of personal campaigns—an irrelevant attack in the *Daily Mail* on Lord Milner, then secretary of state for war; an embarrassing demand for the immediate demobilization of the vast armies still in the field; above all, an insistent pursuit of the prime minister throughout the general election which followed. The policies and predictions to which Mr. Lloyd George—quite unnecessarily—committed himself at this time may be traced almost precisely to the daily vociferation of the 'Northcliffe press' that the Kaiser should be brought to trial and that Germany should pay for the War. The breach between the two men was no longer to be bridged when Mr. Lloyd George finally declined to gratify Northcliffe's ambition to be an official delegate to the Peace Conference at Versailles; and their growing estrangement culminated in a scathing indictment by the prime minister in the House of Commons on 16 April 1919.

The exaggerated sense of his own influence which grew on Northcliffe during the War was attributable partly, no doubt, to increasing ill-health. His throat began to trouble him again; in June 1919 he underwent a serious but successful operation for the removal of an adenoma; much of the rest of his life was spent abroad in search of a milder climate. But he continued to throw himself into fresh campaigns in which a persistent anxiety to keep his name before the public was still combined with, though it tended to weaken, his support of causes which were essentially sound. Thus he tilted against waste and excessive public expenditure, against the misunderstanding between capital and labour, and, in particular, against the futility of perpetuating the Irish quarrel. The backing of *The Times* was a potent influence in bringing about the Irish settlement of 1921.

In May of that year Northcliffe's increasing obsession with the size of the organization under his control—the same obsession which had produced his elaborate *Who's Who of the American Mission*—led him to celebrate the twenty-fifth birthday of the *Daily Mail* by a luncheon at Olympia (the only building in London large enough for the purpose) given to 7,000 members of the staffs of his various newspapers. The occasion is worth noting, not only for its magnitude, but for the spirit of the hour which permitted an admiring clergyman to offer a thanksgiving that 'Thou hast endued thy servant Alfred with many singular and excellent gifts' and to describe his host in prayer as 'guiding aright the destinies of this great Empire'. Nothing less, indeed, had by this time come to be Northcliffe's own conception of his mission in life. Two months later he started on a long-projected tour of the world, and visited in turn Canada, New Zealand, Australia, the Philippines, Japan, China, Singapore, Siam, India, Egypt, and Palestine. The guest throughout of viceroys and governors, he attracted immense attention wherever he went, displayed all his old interest in the various problems that he encountered, and proved himself, as on previous occasions, the ideal special correspondent in a series of articles and circular letters which were collected by two of his brothers after his death under the title *My Journey Round the World* (1922). No one better understood the knack of conveying to stay-at-homes the life and atmosphere of a foreign land or of impressing in picturesque language the vital importance of such manifest dangers as the great empty spaces of Australia and the cramped ambitions of Japan, the rising tide of nationalism in India, the conflict of races and religions in Palestine.

Northcliffe's world tour was his last great effort. He was a sick man when he reached Marseilles in February 1922 and, although he appeared again in London at several public functions in his honour, and paid a brief private visit to Germany (where he became convinced that his enemies had poisoned him), the next few months showed that his powers were failing rapidly. He died 14 August at 1 Carlton Gardens of infective endocarditis, and was accorded a funeral service in Westminster Abbey, for the restoration of which a large fund had recently been raised by *The Times*, before the interment at Finchley. On his death his title became extinct.

The influence which Northcliffe exercised on his generation was profound; but it was of a totally different kind from that which towards the end of his life he was apt to ascribe to himself, and which his biographers, taking their cue from him, recorded in the various memoirs which followed his death. Too much stress has been laid in nearly every published account of him on the public work which he undertook during the European War—the direction of propaganda in enemy countries and of the British mission to the United States—and on the statesmanlike qualities which were held to have inspired his earlier distrust of German intentions and his support of Lord Roberts's campaign for national service, or his later enthusiasm for a settlement in Ireland. There was never any question about his patriotism or about the wisdom of the main policies to which he gave his support. But it was neither as a statesman nor as a public administrator that he was primarily distinguished. The driving-power which he displayed in his own business was better adapted to dictatorship than to team-work. Given the same resources other men could have done the work in Washington and at Crewe House as well as he. The public offices which he held were those in which he was the unquestioned head of a body of subordinates, and he prudently declined the offer which would have shackled him as one of a group of Cabinet ministers. Nor did his capacity for taking pains in consulting experts ever compensate altogether for that initial lack of education (which he often regretted) and of a grasp of first principles which is the foundation of statesmanship. In spite of all that has been written about it the period during which Northcliffe emerged from his newspapers (and attempted to play other parts in public affairs) was perhaps the least conspicuously successful of his life. He was passionately anxious to throw his whole weight both into the conduct of the War and into the discussion of the Peace; and yet he felt himself perpetually frustrated. The truth is that he never quite understood the rooted objection of his countrymen to the exercise of power without responsibility. There was no means of fitting the position of an independent proprietor of newspapers, who naturally clung to the source of his strength, into the accepted scheme of government in England, or even into the national delegation to Versailles. Mr. Lloyd George might perhaps have won his continued support, instead of his bitter enmity, if he had seen his way to include him as an official member in the peace conference; but the violence of the feud which followed was itself the measure of the difficulty of combining a press autocracy with Cabinet cohesion.

Northcliffe's real claim to fame is that he was a consummate journalist, who changed the whole course of English journalism. He was endowed in a pre-eminent degree with two of the journalist's essential qualities—an intense interest in everything that was happening in the world around him and an uncanny prescience of what was likely to attract the public next. That was the true secret of his success in a profession which he entered at a peculiarly favourable moment. He owed something of it to the American model, which he studied incessantly, and particularly to the methods of Joseph Pulitzer; but his impact on English journalism was due mainly to his own qualities. He woke it up and made it alive. He also made it prosperous. The great fortune which he accumulated for himself and for others was reflected throughout the newspaper world. The prizes of journalism were multiplied a hundredfold. Salaries and wages were raised to scales which were unknown in Fleet Street before his arrival. New schemes for pensions, hospitals, and homes of rest for journalists were put into effective operation. For the first time journalism took rank with the recognized professions in the range of opportunities which it could offer to young men. The best and most enduring monument of Northcliffe's life-work was the final demolition of Grub Street.

There was another side to the picture, no doubt, in the vast amalgamations of newspaper interests and the dictatorial habits of their proprietors, of which he set the example. It was a new experience to the working journalist that some legitimate difference of opinion with his employers might mean his permanent exclusion from a whole series of allied publications. Nor was it to the national advantage that a number of independent newspapers, each with its individual point of view, should be crushed out of existence in the process. But these developments, which began with Northcliffe, reached their climax after his death.

Northcliffe's portrait (a replica) by P. A. de László hangs in the board-room of the office of *The Times*. A cartoon by 'Spy' appeared in *Vanity Fair* 16 May 1895. A posthumous bust by Lady Hilton Young (Lady Kennet) faces Fleet Street from the churchyard of St. Dunstan's in the West. Lady Northcliffe married, as her second husband, in 1923, Sir Robert Arundell Hudson [q.v.].

[*The Times*, 15 August 1922; Max Pemberton, *Lord Northcliffe: a Memoir*, 1922; R. Macnair Wilson, *Lord Northcliffe: A Study*, 1927; H. Hamilton Fyfe, *Northcliffe, An Intimate Biography*, 1930; Tom Clarke, *My Northcliffe Diary*, 1931; private information; personal knowledge.] G. DAWSON.

HARPER, SIR GEORGE MONTAGUE (1865–1922), lieutenant-general, youngest son of Charles Harper, R.N., physician and surgeon, by his wife, Emma, daughter of John Skinner, of independent means, was born at his father's home, Manor House, Batheaston, Somerset, 11 January 1865. After being educated at Bath College and the Royal Military Academy, he entered the Royal Engineers in July 1884. He was promoted captain in 1892 and appointed adjutant of the 2nd Yorkshire (West Riding) Royal Engineer Volunteers at Leeds. In 1898 he returned to his regiment, and on the outbreak of the South African War in October 1899 proceeded on active service to South Africa. He took part in the operations in Natal which culminated in the relief of Ladysmith, being present at the action at Spion Kop in February 1900. In the following summer he was engaged in the Transvaal, but he there contracted enteric fever and was invalided home in October, when he was rewarded with the D.S.O. He passed into the Staff College and spent the year 1901 at Camberley, being promoted major in April. On leaving the college he proceeded directly to the mobilization branch of the War Office, where he served until October 1906. In recognition of his work, which was mainly connected with imperial defence problems, he received a brevet lieutenant-colonelcy in January 1907, and at the same time was selected by Brigadier-General (later Field-Marshal Sir Henry) Wilson [q.v.] as an instructor at the Staff College. In this position he proved a popular and versatile teacher and made many friends. In July 1911 he was again selected by Wilson, who had become director of military operations at the War Office, to serve as his deputy-director. At the same time he was promoted substantive colonel.

On the outbreak of the European War Harper proceeded to France as general staff officer, first grade, for operations, on the army head-quarters staff. After the first fighting at Ypres he was advanced, in November 1914, to the temporary rank of brigadier-general, and in the following February given the command of the 17th infantry brigade. He was also created C.B. In his new position Harper did well, particularly at the minor action of Epinette (11–12 March). In September 1915 he was promoted to the temporary rank of major-general, with command of the 51st (Highland) division, Territorial Force, and he was confirmed in this rank in January 1916. He soon proved a successful leader in battle as well as a capable instructor of troops. Gifted with a cheerful, optimistic, placid temperament, caring only for the essentials of life and inspired with an oddly fatalistic outlook as to his own destiny, Harper quickly established a reputation for command, and his division the name of a hard-fighting formation. His first opportunity came during the battle of the Somme, when the division was given the thankless task of capturing High Wood (20 July 1916). Although this attack ended in failure, Harper had learnt his lesson to good effect, for on 13 November his men carried Beaumont Hamel village in brilliant fashion.

In April 1917 the 51st division took part in the battle of Arras: first, in the bitter fighting of 9–12 April; again on 23 April, when the Highlanders captured the ill-famed chemical works at Roeux; lastly, in the severe struggle of 12–13 May. The division then went into reserve and moved north. Then at the opening of the third battle of Ypres on 31 July, it distinguished itself by carrying the line of the Steenbeek brook. On 20 September it made considerable progress at Poelcapelle and effectively repulsed the enemy's counter attacks. Harper's troops then moved southwards again and were engaged in the battle of Cambrai; on 21 November they advanced as far as Bourlon Wood, by the village of Flesquières, but were then drawn out of action. The successes of the 51st division in the fighting of the previous two years may be ascribed largely to Harper's cool leadership in action as well as to the methodical and reasoned manner in which he invariably prepared his troops for the next operation in view. Early in March 1918 Harper was advanced to the command of the IV Army Corps, of which the 51st division formed part, being then promoted temporary lieutenant-general.

Harper's corps formed part of the Third Army, and bore the full weight of the great German onslaught of 21 March 1918 and the following days. Though slowly beaten back, the IV Corps fought stubbornly to the end, although Harper himself was much shaken by the severe losses sustained by his old division. Nevertheless he recovered himself and had the satisfaction of leading his corps throughout the closing stages of the War until the final German retreat; the corps particularly distinguished itself in the fighting round Miraumont, north of the river Ancre, in the following August.

Harper continued to hold his command until after the Armistice, being created K.C.B. at the close of the year 1918 and awarded the substantive rank of lieutenant-general in January 1919. In the following June he was transferred from the IV Corps to the post of commander-in-chief, Southern command, at home. In that appointment he continued to do good work at Salisbury until he was killed in a motor-car accident in Dorsetshire 15 December 1922.

Harper married in 1893 the Hon. Ella Constance Jackson, second daughter of the first Baron Allerton [q.v.]. They had no children. Harper is commemorated by a relief portrait in bronze in the north aisle of Salisbury Cathedral.

[*The Times*, 16 December 1922; Army lists; F. W. Bewsher, *History of the 51st* (*Highland*) *Division*, 1921; personal knowledge.]

H. de Watteville.

HARRIS, FREDERICK LEVERTON (1864–1926), politician and art collector, the eldest son of Frederick William Harris, of Norwood, by his wife, Elizabeth Rachel, daughter of Peter Macleod Wylie, was born at Norwood 17 December 1864. He came of Quaker stock. At the age of twelve he went to Winchester, and at seventeen to Gonville and Caius College, Cambridge, where he gained a second class in the natural science tripos in 1884. He then joined his father's firm, Harris & Dixon, ship-owners in London for the past hundred years. Two years later he married Gertrude, daughter of John G. Richardson, of Moyallon, co. Down, and Bessbrook, co. Armagh; they had no children.

In 1900 Leverton Harris entered parliament as conservative member for Tynemouth, and held the seat for six years. He next sat for Stepney as a unionist from 1907 to 1910, and after that for East Worcestershire from 1914 to 1918. He was a member of the tariff commission, a body which met in 1904 at the invitation of Joseph Chamberlain [q.v.] to consider the principles on which a tariff should be based, and of the London county council from 1907 to 1910. But the subject which engaged his liveliest interest was the Declaration of London (1909), a proposal to limit the right of search at sea of neutral vessels carrying contraband; and it was in great measure owing to his foresight and the energy of his opposition that the bill which embodied this document was defeated in 1911.

Thus, when the European War began, Leverton Harris's path was marked out for him; and he was destined to play an important part, aided as he was by the insight and imaginative drive of the artistic temperament, in devising and directing the policy which led to the successful blockade of Germany. Early in August 1914 he joined the trade division of the Admiralty with the honorary rank of lieutenant, R.N.V.R. He was made adviser in commerce and promoted commander in February 1915, and in 1916 was sworn of the Privy Council. In June of that year he was placed in control of the Restriction of Enemy Supplies Department under the Foreign Office; and from December 1916 to January 1919 he was under-secretary to the Ministry of Blockade. He was active in promoting measures for diverting supplies of cotton from Germany before it had been declared contraband, and for stopping her imports of copper and meat. After visiting Norway in July 1916 and meeting in congress the leading fish exporters, he succeeded in obtaining for England 85 per cent. of all the fish and fish-oil landed on Norwegian shores. The American ambassador of that time wrote of Leverton Harris as follows: 'The man who really makes the blockade, lives around the corner (you never heard of him, a man named Harris . . .). He and Lloyd George are the two most energetic men that I know of in this kingdom. . . . This gentle, resolute, quiet man sits guardian at all the gates of Germany' (*Life and Letters of Walter Hines Page*, vol. iii, p. 311). In 1919 Leverton Harris succeeded Lord Robert Cecil as chairman of the economic council in Paris; he was made an officer of the legion of honour (France), and of the order of SS. Maurice and Lazarus (Italy), and was confirmed in the rank of honorary captain, R.N.V.R., for the Tyne division. He then retired from political life.

So much for Leverton Harris's public career. There was, however, another side to his activities, for he was one of the most discerning art connoisseurs of his time. During his business career he had already amassed a considerable fortune, and on his succession in 1906, by bequest from his uncle, James L. Wylie, to Camilla Lacey, the home of Fanny Burney, he continued the collection of antiques which his uncle had begun, and also made a 'grangerized' life of Fanny Burney, many of whose possessions and manuscripts had been sold with the house when his uncle purchased it in the 'sixties. The great bulk of his collection, including the Fanny Burney engravings, was burnt in 1919, but with astounding perseverance he at once set about reconstituting the grangerized Fanny Burney (subsequently bequeathed by him to the National Portrait Gallery), and forming another collection of antiques, which at his death enriched through his bequest the Victoria and Albert Museum, the National Portrait Gallery, the British Museum, and the Fitzwilliam Museum at Cambridge. His collection of majolica, which he left to the Fitzwilliam Museum, together with £10,000, illustrates with singular completeness the whole development of Italian majolica and maintains a very high standard of artistic excellence.

Leverton Harris was elected honorary secretary of the Contemporary Art Society in 1923, holding this post until his death, and he served on the sites committee of the Office of Works from 1922 to 1924. During the last six years of his life, by a surprising development, he became a painter. He studied at the Slade School, and in 1926 he held an exhibition of his work at the Goupil Gallery. He had already achieved a distinct personal style by the time of his death, which took place in London, from angina pectoris, 14 November 1926.

Leverton Harris was an attractive, eager, accomplished man; quick of intellect, skilled in negotiation, he had a burning patriotism and an immense zest for life.

A cartoon of Leverton Harris by 'Spy' appeared in *Vanity Fair* 30 December 1909.

[*Manchester Guardian*, 17 November 1926; T. Borenius, *The Leverton Harris Collection*, 1931.]

H. S. Ede.

HARRISON, FREDERIC (1831–1923), author and positivist, was born at 17 Euston Square, London, 18 October 1831, the eldest son of Frederick Harrison, of Threadneedle Street, by his wife, Jane, only daughter of Alexander Brice, of Belfast. His father, a prosperous London merchant who came of Leicestershire yeoman stock, went to live, shortly after his son's birth, at Muswell Hill, and afterwards moved to Oxford Square, Paddington, and then to Lancaster Gate. His country house was Sutton Place, Guildford. It was of Sutton Place that his son wrote a description in his *Annals of an old Manor House* (1893).

At the age of eleven (1842) Harrison went to King's College School, London, and when he left in 1849 he had risen to be second in the school. Among his schoolfellows was Henry Parry Liddon, with whom, although their paths in life followed widely different lines, he maintained a friendship, and for whom he had a strong regard. Harrison won a scholarship at Wadham College, Oxford, in 1848 and went up to the university in the autumn of the following year. In 1852 he obtained a second class in the first examination ever held for classical honour moderations, and in 1853 a first class in the final school of *literae humaniores* and a fourth class in that of law and history. In 1854 he was elected a fellow of his college. He held his fellowship for two years, and his active connexion with Oxford ended in 1856. He was called to the bar by Lincoln's Inn in 1858 and followed the profession of the law, according to his own statement, for some fifteen years with little zest and with no ambition.

Harrison considered his seven years (1849–1856) at Oxford as the formative period of his life and of his opinions. He went there, as he says in an autobiographical note written long afterwards, as something of a neo-catholic, and took the Sacrament with a leaning towards belief in Transubstantiation. He found the dominant type of thought presented to him at Oxford positive rather than catholic, and liberalism in the ascendant. His religious beliefs were unsettled, and it was not until some time later that he found a new faith to satisfy him in the Comtist doctrine of positivism. In politics he was attracted by the tenets of the liberal party. Those were days when liberalism made a strong appeal to ardent and active-minded young men, not only by its claim to a monopoly of political enlightenment, but also by its claim to a monopoly of sympathy with classes less fortunate than those to which they themselves belonged. Harrison, under the influence of John Stuart Mill, George Grote, Thomas Arnold of Rugby, and others, became a liberal, and remained one long after the outlook of both the great political parties had altered out of all recognition.

It was also at Oxford that Harrison was first attracted by the doctrines of positivism, as enunciated by Auguste Comte (1798–1857). This was chiefly due to the influence of a fellow and tutor of Wadham, Richard Congreve [q.v.], who is generally regarded as the founder of positivism in England. Comte's teaching, centred as it was upon the phenomena of human life, fell in with the views of those who were dissatisfied with social conditions, and anxious to promote reforms. Harrison, like a few others, eventually accepted positivism as a religion and as a substitute for belief in the supernatural. It was defined as a 'reorganization of life, at once intellectual, moral, and social, by faith in our common humanity'. There was a meeting-house in Chapel Street, London, where services were held and addresses given. Differences arose in 1878, when Congreve's claim to be head of the Positivist community was contested by a section who supported the authority of Pierre Laffitte, Comte's literary executor. Among those who refused to follow Congreve was Harrison, now considered one of the leaders of the movement. They opened Newton Hall, Fetter Lane, as a place of meeting in 1881 and founded the *Positivist Review* in 1893.

Under the auspices of Harrison, who was president of the English Positivist Committee from 1880 to 1905, the positivist society led an active religious life, but in his later years the stress which came to be laid upon the sacerdotal side of positivism to some extent alienated his sympathy. It cannot be said that at the end of his life these questions possessed much general interest. The *Review* came to an end about the time that he died, and a few years later hardly any trace of the movement remained. As a religion positivism never met with wide acceptance, while as a system of social ethics its part had been played. The daring theories of its early days were the commonplaces of twentieth-century politics, and the practical effect given to many of them had created new problems to deal with which other organizations were required.

Harrison influenced the life and thought of his time, less by his activity as a missionary of positivism, than by his vigour as a man of practical purpose. The eagerness, or vehemence, of his political and social sympathies impressed persons who neither professed nor knew anything about his positivist faith. He influenced by example, and not by precept only, for he worked industriously to give what assistance he could in applying the principles which he preached. His outside interests were many, and he was never able either to give up religion or philosophy for politics, or to drop politics for the sake of books. He was always anxious to study movements on the spot. For some years he taught at the Working Men's College in Great Ormond Street in the company of Frederick Denison Maurice [q.v.] and Tom Hughes [q.v.]. He also served on the royal commission on Trades Unions (1867–1869), and was secretary of the royal commission for digesting the law (1869–1870). In 1869 he was appointed examiner in jurisprudence, Roman law, and constitutional history for the Council of Legal Education, a post which he held for some years. From 1877 to 1889 he was professor of jurisprudence, constitutional and international law for the Council of Legal Education. When the first London county council, of which Lord Rosebery was the chairman, was formed in 1888, Harrison was nominated as one of the aldermen in the following year. His one attempt to enter parliament was his unsuccessful candidature for London University as a supporter of Home Rule at the general election of 1886.

Harrison travelled much and was a prolific writer on historical and literary subjects. He acted as the special correspondent of *The Times* in France during the constitutional crisis which preceded the fall of Marshal MacMahon in 1877. For a long time he refused to describe himself as a man of letters, but as he grew older his literary activity increased, especially in fields where there was less scope for controversy and more for the use of his well-stored mind and remarkable memory. He contributed *Cromwell* (1888) and *Chatham* (1905) to the popular series of 'Twelve English Statesmen'; published a biography of *William the Silent* (1897); and wrote a short life of *Ruskin* (1902) for the 'English Men of Letters' series. He made many studies and criticisms of his own contemporaries, and collected them in a volume of *Studies in Early Victorian Literature* (1895). He edited in 1892 *The New Calendar of Great Men*, biographies of the 538 worthies of all ages included in the positivist calendar of Comte, and contributed largely to its pages. During the European War, in which he lost one of his sons, Harrison published *The German Peril* (1915). He had long regarded German imperialism as a menace to England and to civilization, and much of this book was a repetition of his earlier warnings. He was strongly opposed to the Allies making any terms with the Hohenzollerns, or with any other ruling house in Germany.

Up to 1904 most of Harrison's literary work had consisted of historical, political, or critical studies. In that year, yielding to what he termed a senile weakness, he brought out a romance entitled *Theophano: the Crusade of the Tenth Century*. He had given prolonged study to Byzantine history and its influence on the modern world, choosing this as the subject of his Rede lecture at Cambridge in 1900. This book, which is one of Harrison's most important works, is described by its author as a romantic monograph. His aim was to paint a general picture of the South and East of Europe in the tenth century, and of the relations of that part of Christendom with the advancing power of Islam. Harrison's special knowledge of the subject gives to this romance a considerable value, and, although as a story it may be thought over-long in places, the perspective of history is carefully preserved. He followed this book up with the publication in 1906 of *Nicephorus, a Tragedy*, written in blank verse which is stately without elaboration. The characters in the tragedy are taken from *Theophano*.

Until his marriage in 1870 Harrison lived with his parents, and for thirty years after his marriage he continued to live in London, during the greater part of the time in Westbourne Terrace, Paddington. He left London in 1902 and lived at Elm Hill, Hawkhurst, Kent, until 1912, when he went to live at Bath, a city which attracted him by the charm of its eighteenth-century architecture and associations. His house was No. 10 in the Royal Crescent, a block of buildings which is one of the chief beauties of Bath. He maintained remarkable vitality to the end of his life, writing, reading, and talking with the energy and eagerness of a much younger man. His appreciation of Bath was reciprocated and in November 1921 the honorary freedom of the city was conferred upon him.

Harrison was a man of masculine temper and powerful intellect. He was a student of many literatures, much-travelled, and widely read. As a writer, he was described by Lord Morley as a master of language, his style, although not wholly free from excess, being direct and plain. He delighted in controversy and championed many generous causes. The conviction that his own view was the right one lent emphasis to the exposition of his case.

Harrison was Rede lecturer at Cambridge (1900), Washington lecturer at Chicago (1901), Herbert Spencer lecturer at Oxford (1905), and a vice-president of the Royal Historical Society and of the London Library. He received honorary degrees from the universities of Oxford, Cambridge, and Aberdeen, and in 1899 was elected an honorary fellow of his old college, Wadham.

Harrison married in 1870 his cousin, Ethel (died 1916), only daughter of William Harrison, of Craven Hill Gardens, London, and had four sons and one daughter. He died at his house in Bath 14 January 1923, in his ninety-second year.

[*The Times*, 15 January 1923; Frederic Harrison, *Autobiographic Memoirs*, 1911; Austin Harrison, *Frederic Harrison: Thoughts and Memories*, 1925; private information.]

A. COCHRANE.

HARRISON, JANE ELLEN (1850–1928), classical scholar, born at Cottingham, Yorkshire, 9 September 1850, was the third daughter of Charles Harrison, timber merchant, by his first wife, Elizabeth Hawksley, daughter of Thomas Nelson, of Limber Grange, Lincolnshire. Shortly after her birth, her mother, 'a silent woman of singular gentleness and serenity', died; and her father entrusted her education to a succession of governesses. Only one of these proved willing to indulge Jane Harrison's passion for languages by learning with her to read German, Latin, the Greek Testament, and even a little Hebrew. Another of her governesses, a conscientious and fervently religious woman, became her stepmother. An old-fashioned and strict upbringing at Scalby in Yorkshire and Hendre Mynach in North Wales was broken off when her stepmother sent her to be 'finished' at Cheltenham College, then (1868–1870) under the rule of Miss Dorothea Beale. Thanks chiefly to her own unshakeable resolution to learn what she wanted to learn, she obtained honours in the London University examination for women in 1870.

When she won a scholarship on the results of the Cambridge higher local examination, Miss Harrison's father consented to her becoming a student at Cambridge. At Newnham College from October 1874 to June 1879 she was the centre of a group of friends which included Mary Paley (afterwards Mrs. Alfred Marshall), Margaret Merrifield (afterwards Mrs. A. W. Verrall), Ellen Crofts (afterwards Mrs. Francis Darwin), and Alice Lloyd (afterwards Mrs. Dew-Smith). Henry Sidgwick persuaded her to read classics rather than moral sciences. After being placed in the second class of the classical tripos in 1879, she settled in London in order to study archaeology under Sir Charles Newton at the British Museum. Among scholars who, then and later, shared in her work and enjoyed her vivid friendship were Dr. and Mrs. Verrall, S. H. Butcher, Mr. D. S. MacColl, and Professor Gilbert Murray.

In London (1880–1898) Miss Harrison lectured on Greek art in the galleries of the British Museum and even at boys' schools, an adventure which some Victorians thought rather bold. Three visits to Greece and a study of the topography of Athens under Dr. Wilhelm Dörpfeld inspired the most substantial of her writings in this period, *The Mythology and Monuments of Ancient Athens* (1890), a commentary on Pausanias, Book I, with a translation by Mrs. Verrall. Before leaving London she had won recognition as a scholar of the first rank. The universities of Aberdeen and Durham gave her honorary degrees, and the Berlin Classical Archaeological Institute made her a corresponding member in 1896.

In 1898 Miss Harrison returned to Cambridge as lecturer in classical archaeology at Newnham College, which remained her home until 1922. A lecture was, both to her and to her audience, a dramatic event. Once she enlisted two friends to swing bull-roarers at the back of the darkened lecture-room in order that the audience might learn from the 'awe-inspiring and truly religious' sound what Aeschylus meant by 'bull-voices roaring from somewhere out of the unseen'. A pupil has recorded that, as a teacher, 'she never sought or desired influence; indeed, she regarded a consciously exerted influence as an insult to personality. And since she had no sense of age she felt no special responsibility to youth. She treated everybody alike, and talked perfectly freely on all subjects. The influence which she did exert, if it can be limited by such a term, was of course all the more profound because it was so subtle and unselfconscious.' She was never happier than when teaching the rudiments of Greek or other languages to beginners, whose co-operation she easily won by her infectious enthusiasm.

Miss Harrison's two most important books were published between the opening of the twentieth century and the outbreak of the European War. The *Prolegomena to the Study of Greek Religion* (1903) marked the end of her tenure (1900–1903) of a research fellowship at Newnham, a position which she was the first to occupy. Following a principle already illustrated in *Mythology and Monuments* and fundamental to all her work, that myths to a large extent took their rise 'not in poetic imagination but in primitive, often savage, and, I think, always *practical* ritual', she concentrated attention on the older Chthonic ritual of the aversion and purgation of evil, underlying the Olympian rites whose formula is *do ut des*, and on Orphism as a spiritual mysticism developed out of primitive ceremonies of purification. In 1907, when a new edition of the *Prolegomena* was called for, she felt the need to reconsider her attitude to religion in the light of two ideas due respectively to Henri Bergson and Emile Durkheim: 'first, that the mystery-god and the Olympians express respectively, the one *durée*, life, and the other the action of conscious intelligence which reflects on and analyses life; and secondly that, among primitive peoples, religion reflects *collective* feeling and *collective* thinking.' The results of this re-examination were given in *Themis, a Study of the Social Origins of Greek Religion* (1912). In the preface to the second edition of this work (1927) Miss Harrison was able to claim that most of her old heresies, condemned as rash by her contemporaries, were now accepted as commonplaces by a younger school of anthropologists.

In the same preface Miss Harrison wrote: 'Between the two editions lies the Great War, which shattered much of academic tradition, scattered my fellow-workers all over Europe to be killed or drilled, and drove me, for I am no Archimedes, to fly from Greece and seek sanctuary in other languages and civilizations —Russian, Oriental, and, finally, Scandinavian—bringing with them no bitter tang of remembrance. For nearly ten years I never opened a Greek book.' After studying Russian in Paris (1915) she came back to Newnham (1917) and lectured on Russian until, at the age of seventy-two, she dispersed her classical library and finally left Cambridge for Paris and London 'to see things', as she wrote, 'more freely and more widely'.

Miss Harrison took life as a series of adventures; and, although belonging to the first generation of women who, in vindicating their claim to the highest education, were tempted to imitate the masculine approach to learning, she worked, as she lived, with a passion that was distinctively feminine. In her last years a young novelist, Miss Hope Mirrlees, gave her the devotion of an adopted daughter. She died in London 5 April 1928. A portrait by Augustus John (1909) is at Newnham College.

[Jane Harrison, *Reminiscences of a Student's Life*, 1925; *Newnham College Letter*, January 1929; J. L. Myres, *Jane Harrison Memorial Lecture*, 1933; personal knowledge.]

F. M. Cornford.

HASTINGS, JAMES (1852–1922), editor and divine, was born at Huntly, Aberdeenshire, 26 March 1852, the second son and fifth child of James Hastings, miller, of the Mill of Huntly, by his wife, Hope Ross. He was educated at the public school at Huntly, Old Aberdeen grammar school, Aberdeen University (where he graduated M.A. in 1876 and of which he received the honorary degree of D.D. in 1897), and the Free Church Divinity College, Aberdeen. In 1884 he was ordained and became pastor of Kinneff Free church, Kincardineshire. At Kinneff Hastings early gave evidence of those qualities which made him an eminently suitable recipient, in 1913, of the Dyke Acland medal, which is awarded biennially to a distinguished scholar whose work is especially directed to the popularization of exact knowledge of the Bible. Here, in face of difficulties which would have deterred most men, he founded in 1889 a monthly magazine, *The Expository Times*, editing it continuously and writing much of it himself from 1889 until his death. In 1898, within a year of his moving (1897) to Willison church, Dundee, appeared volume i of his *Dictionary of the Bible*; in 1902 the fourth volume was published, an extra volume completing the work in 1904. Hastings, who was incapable of neglecting any duties which he had undertaken, found the demands of a city charge too exacting, and in 1901 accepted a call to the United Free church, St. Cyrus, Kincardineshire, a country parish, where he remained until he retired from pastoral work to Aberdeen in 1911.

No year found Hastings without some large enterprise in train. In addition to numerous series of expository publications he published a *Dictionary of Christ and the Gospels* (2 volumes, 1906–7), a single-volume *Dictionary of the Bible*, an entirely new compilation (1908), a *Dictionary of the Apostolic Church* (vol. i, 1915, vol. ii, 1918), and the work by which his name will probably be remembered longest—the *Encyclopaedia of Religion and Ethics*, the twelve volumes of which (1908–1921) he saw completed, and the index volume of which he had planned.

Hastings's lively Christian faith and love of learning, his discernment, his rare skill in planning large works of reference, his eye for the right contributor of whatever nationality or 'confession', his scholarly accuracy which quickly convicted a careless writer, his unhurried energy, his firmness and courtesy—these qualities equipped him for his life's unique achievement in the promotion of religious knowledge. He was a notable preacher, simple and direct, and an eager worker for social welfare. Puritan in temper, he was of catholic tastes in literature, happy in the possession of a private library which can have had few rivals in Scotland. Games he played keenly, and test matches drew him south of the Border.

Hastings died at Aberdeen 15 October 1922. At his bedside were the revised proofs of the November number of *The Expository Times*. He married in 1884 Ann Wilson, daughter of Alexander Forsyth, of Elgin, by whom he had a son and a daughter. *The Expository Times* continued to be published under the joint editorship of his children.

[*Aberdeen Free Press*, 28 June 1913 and 16 October 1922; *Aberdeen Daily Journal*, 16 October 1922; *Elgin Courant and Courier*, 20 October 1922; *Glasgow Herald*, 17 October 1922; *British Weekly*, 19 October 1922; *Expository Times*, December 1922; private information.] E. R. Micklem.

HAWTREY, Sir CHARLES HENRY

HAWTREY, Sir CHARLES HENRY (1858–1923), actor, the fifth son and eighth of the ten children of the Rev. John William Hawtrey, by his first wife, Frances Mary Anne, daughter of Lieutenant-Colonel George Procter, historical writer and superintendent of studies at the Royal Military College, Sandhurst, was born at Eton 21 December 1858. His father, a first cousin once removed of Edward Craven Hawtrey [q.v.], provost of Eton, was then a house master at Eton, the lower school of which Charles Hawtrey entered at eight years old. In 1869 his father left Eton and founded St. Michael's School, Aldin House, Slough; and there Hawtrey was educated until he returned to Eton in 1872. In 1873 he left Eton for Rugby, where he played cricket for the school. Intended for the army, he went in 1875 to a crammer's in London, but he abandoned the intention, and from 1876 to 1879 was a private tutor. In February 1881 he matriculated at Pembroke College, Oxford, but in November following his name was taken off the books, since in October he had gone on the stage.

Hawtrey made his first appearance under the name of Charles Bankes at the Prince of Wales's Theatre, London, in the part of Edward Langton in *The Colonel* by (Sir) Francis Cowley Burnand [q.v.]. With his brother William, who had also gone on the stage (as did another brother, George), Hawtrey took a company on tour in the spring of 1883; but he had been a professional actor for less than two years when he came upon the play which began his very successful career in farce and comedy. This was an English version of a German farce, *Der Bibliothekar*, by Gustav von Moser. Re-written by Hawtrey, who entitled it *The Private Secretary* and later revised it, the play was first staged at the Prince's Theatre on 29 March 1884, and transferred on 19 May 1884 to the Globe Theatre, where W. S. Penley succeeded (Sir) Herbert Beerbohm Tree in the title-part, and Hawtrey, under his own name, took the part of Douglas Cattermole. The play ran for two years, and Hawtrey claimed that he inaugurated the 'queue' for pit and gallery in order to control the crowds which came to see it.

Thereafter for nearly forty years Hawtrey worked hard at his profession. He managed the Globe Theatre till the autumn of 1887; then the Comedy Theatre till the beginning of 1893 and again from April 1896 to April 1898. At one time and another he managed sixteen other London theatres and produced about one hundred plays. Of these the most memorable by reason of their success and of his performances in them, were two more adaptations from von Moser, *The Pickpocket* by George Hawtrey, and *The Arabian Nights* by Sydney Grundy; *Jane* by Harry Nicholls and William Lestocq; *One Summer's Day* by H. V. Esmond; *Lord and Lady Algy* by R. C. Carton; *A Message from Mars* by Richard Ganthony; *The Man from Blankley's* by 'F. Anstey'; *Dear Old Charlie* by C. H. Brookfield; *Jack Straw* by W. S. Maugham; *The Little Damozel* by Monckton Hoffe; *General John Regan* by 'George Birmingham', and *Ambrose Applejohn's Adventure* by W. Hackett.

Hawtrey was a good producer of plays and teacher of acting. In staging farce and light comedy he showed a mastery of fine shades and the polish which belonged to the school of the Bancrofts and W. S. Gilbert; but now and then he proved himself efficient in producing more serious drama. As actor, he had the wit to make his greatest strength out of what had been the bane of his youth, his immobility of face. He learned so to charge that immobility with expression that he excelled in the characters of liars, selfish men, and erring husbands, in which imperturbability was necessary, and any break in it came with great effect. Better than any of his contemporaries he achieved by art an air of being entirely natural. He seldom attempted the pathetic; but in *One Summer's Day* he showed that his method was capable of giving a signal moment of it.

In 1901 and in 1903 to 1904 Hawtrey paid professional visits to the United States. He was knighted in 1922. He was twice married: first, in 1886 to Madeline Harriet, daughter of Thomas Sheriffe, of Henstead Hall, Suffolk, who divorced him in 1893 and died in 1905; and secondly, in 1919 to Katherine Elsie, daughter of the Rev. William Robinson Clarke, and widow of the Hon. Albert Henry Petre, son of William Henry Francis, eleventh Baron Petre. He had no children by either marriage. He died in London 30 July 1923.

Off the stage and on, Hawtrey was a charming man, and had many friends of both sexes. He was a good cricketer and golfer; but the chief interest of his life (an interest shared by his father) was horse-racing. He began betting when at Eton; in 1885 he won £14,000 on a single race, and in 1885 and 1886 he had horses of his own in training.

[*The Times*, 31 July 1923; Charles Hawtrey, *The Truth at Last*, 1924; Florence Molesworth Hawtrey, *The History of the Hawtrey Family*, 1903; *Who's Who in the Theatre*, 1912.]

H. H. Child.

HEADLAM-MORLEY, Sir JAMES WYCLIFFE (1863–1929), political historian, was born at Whorlton, near Barnard Castle, Durham, 24 December 1863. He was the second son of the Rev. Arthur William Headlam, successively vicar of Whorlton, vicar of St. Oswald's, Durham, and rector of Gainford, honorary canon of Durham Cathedral, by his wife, Agnes Sarah, daughter of James Favell, of Normanton, Yorkshire. He was nephew of Thomas Emerson Headlam, judge advocate-general [q.v.], and cousin of Walter George Headlam, scholar and poet [q.v.]. His elder brother, Arthur Cayley Headlam, became bishop of Gloucester in 1923. In 1918 James Headlam assumed by royal licence the additional surname (and arms) of Morley, on inheriting the property of the last member of the West Riding family from which he was descended through the wife of his paternal grandfather.

Headlam was educated at Eton, where he was a King's scholar, and at King's College, Cambridge. He was placed in the first class of both parts of the classical tripos (1885 and 1887), and elected a fellow of his college in 1890, a position which he held until 1896. The dissertation on which he obtained his fellowship was 'Election by Lot at Athens', which had gained the Prince Consort prize at Cambridge in 1890 and was published in 1891 (reissued in 1933).

Headlam had meanwhile visited Germany, first staying in families in order to learn German, and then studying at the university of Berlin under Treitschke and Hans Delbrück. During this period he first met (about Christmas 1887) the lady whom he married in 1893, Elisabeth (Else), youngest child of August Sonntag, doctor of medicine, of Lüneburg, then resident at Dresden. They had a son and a daughter.

Both before and after gaining his fellowship, Headlam was engaged in writing, teaching, and lecturing, gradually turning from classical to historical studies. From 1894 to 1900 he was professor of Greek and ancient history at Queen's College, London. He served as an honorary assistant commissioner on the royal commission on secondary education which sat from March 1894 to August 1895 under the presidency of (Viscount) Bryce [q.v.]. The commission had as result the Board of Education Act of 1899 and the Education Act of 1902. From 1902 until the European War Headlam was a staff inspector of secondary schools for the Board of Education.

Before the European War Headlam had become known as an expert on German history. He had published in 1899 *Bismarck and the German Empire* in the

'Heroes of the Nations' series, and collaborated in 1914 with W. Alison Phillips and A. W. Holland in *A Short History of Germany and her Colonies*. A few days after the outbreak of the War in August 1914, the prime minister, Mr. Asquith, sent for Charles F. G. Masterman [q.v.] and instructed him to get together the nucleus of a propaganda organization, as it was already clear that the enemy was going to make full use of this weapon. As a result, the propaganda department at Wellington House came into existence. The secretary of Masterman's committee, Sir Claud Schuster, at once sent for Headlam and asked for his help; and on the first day he entered the new office Headlam began to write his book *The History of Twelve Days* (1915), which may be considered as the foundation of his future work and reputation. This is a close and detailed study, based on the diplomatic correspondence, of the political situation in Europe at the outbreak of the War, and remained by far the most valuable contribution to the history of that short and agitated period until the fuller publication of the records which became possible after the War was over.

For the next three years Headlam remained as the adviser on all historical matters to Wellington House, publishing several controversial books and pamphlets on subjects connected with the origins of the War. He served as assistant director, under Lord Edward Gleichen, of the political intelligence bureau in the Department of Information 1917–1918, and when British governmental propaganda was transferred to a separate ministry under Lord Beaverbrook in the latter year, Headlam went to the Foreign Office, becoming assistant director of a newly formed political intelligence department of the Office, where his services were found of the highest value.

In 1919 Headlam-Morley (as he had now become) went to the Peace Conference at Paris as a member of the political section of the British delegation, where he served on several of the more important committees, dealing with Belgian and Danish problems, Danzig, the Saar Valley, Alsace-Lorraine, 'Minorities', and the Eastern frontiers of Germany.

On his return to England in 1920, Headlam-Morley was appointed historical adviser to the Foreign Office (a post which was specially created for him and which did not survive his retirement in 1928) and settled down to write a history of the peace settlement for official use. This was mostly—but not entirely—completed at the time of his death. He also composed many other memoranda on various historical subjects on which he was consulted, and a selection of these was published in 1930 under the title *Studies in Diplomatic History*.

When, in 1924, Mr. Ramsay MacDonald (whose decision was confirmed by his successor at the Foreign Office, Sir Austen Chamberlain) entrusted to Dr. G. P. Gooch and Mr. H. W. V. Temperley the publication of the complete series of British documents dealing with the origins of the War, from 1898 to 1914, the editors found that Headlam-Morley had already made a very complete collection of documents for the period immediately preceding the outbreak of war, with a view to publishing a third edition of the *History of Twelve Days*. They accordingly arranged with him to issue first what was chronologically the last (vol. xi) of the volumes of *British Documents on the Origins of the War*, and this appeared in 1926 with the title *The Outbreak of War: Foreign Office Documents, June 28th–August 4th, 1914*.

This was Headlam-Morley's last published work of importance. He retired from the public service in December 1928, received a knighthood in June 1929, and died in a nursing home at Wimbledon 6 September of the same year. He had not yet received the accolade, but his widow was allowed by royal licence to assume the style of a knight's widow.

Headlam-Morley was tall, clean-shaven, with a keen and pale intellectual face. There is a portrait of him—a photogravure by Sir Emery Walker from a photograph—at the Royal Institute of International Affairs, St. James's Square, London.

[Personal knowledge.] S. Gaselee.

HEAVISIDE, OLIVER (1850–1925), mathematical physicist and electrician, was born 18 May 1850 at 55 King Street, Camden Town, the youngest of the four sons of Thomas Heaviside, a wood-engraver and water-colour artist. His mother was Rachel Elizabeth, daughter of John Hook West, and sister of Emma West, who married in 1847 Sir Charles Wheatstone [q.v.]. Although drawings produced by Heaviside at the age of eleven showed promise, his early inclinations were soon diverted from art to science. He went neither to public school nor to university, but by self-training he acquired remarkable skill in the application of mathematics to electro-dynamics. From 1870 to 1874 he was in the service of the Great Northern Telegraph Company as a telegraph operator at Newcastle-upon-Tyne. Later he returned to London, where from 1876 to 1889, in a room in his father's house in Camden Town, he pursued his rigorous studies in seclusion. By athletic exercises he kept himself fit. He suffered, however, from partial deafness, a circumstance that accounts for many apparent eccentricities.

So far as is known, Wheatstone took no direct part in shaping the career of his nephew Oliver Heaviside. Charles Heaviside, an elder brother, after having been employed in Wheatstone's musical-instrument shop at 128 Pall Mall, set up business for himself at Torquay, with a branch at Paignton, where, in 1889, he invited his aged parents and Oliver to make their home. At Paignton Oliver passed many happy days; he was always willing to break off his work to play with his brother's children, and he retained enough power of hearing to find his greatest pleasure in listening to his mother playing upon the piano the sonatas of Beethoven. He was somewhat below medium height, rufous, reserved, witty, and autocratic. He never married.

Heaviside's mother died in 1894, and his father in 1896. Thereafter until 1909 he lived at Newton Abbot, Devon, and subsequently in a lonely house in Lower Warberry Road, Torquay, which afterwards became his property. Towards the end of his days he led a hermit-like existence in some discomfort. From men of science in universities and elsewhere he constantly received appeals for aid in the solution of intricate mathematical problems, and he responded generously. His financial means were restricted, but he was never destitute. He accepted a civil list pension, and there were not lacking friends who sought to assist him with funds. Their success was small, for he was hard to help. Loneliness brought with it poor health, which culminated in serious illness. At the last he was moved to a nursing home in Torquay, where on 3 February 1925 he died. He was buried in the local cemetery at Paignton.

Heaviside was a disciple of Michael Faraday [q.v.] and of James Clerk Maxwell [q.v.]. In the sequence of great electricians his place is between Maxwell and Heinrich Hertz. As early as 1868 he was engaged upon electrical experiments. His first technical article was published in *The English Mechanic* when he was twenty-two years of age. To the *Philosophical Magazine* in 1873 and 1876 he contributed proposals for rendering duplex telegraphy practicable. It was, however, his series of papers in *The Electrician* from 1885 to 1887 which established his reputation, though there were but few mathematicians at that time who could penetrate the obscurity of his mode of presenting his ideas. Certain opponents whom he branded as 'scienticulists' were sorely perplexed by his satire. His prejudices were undisguised; they were accompanied, however, by invincible logic and by mirthful wit.

In 1886 David Edward Hughes [q.v.], in an inaugural address to the Society of Telegraph Engineers and Electricians, described experiments which confirmed Heaviside's theory that when an electric current starts in a wire it begins on its boundary and is propagated inward. Thus, in the language of Heaviside, such a transient current is 'in layers, strong at the boundary, weak in the middle' [see Heaviside's *Electrical Papers*, vol. ii, pp. 170–171.] Heaviside referred to this phenomenon briefly as 'surface conduction', and in 1887–1889 Hertz gave further support to that theory. Meanwhile, by the exercise of his onomastic genius, Heaviside enriched and clarified the language of electro-dynamics. In addition, he proposed a change of electro-magnetic units, to be based upon his suggested convention that the outward flux of force due to unit charge from a closed surface in air should be unity. In his pioneer work he introduced his 'Expansion Theorem', or operational calculus, for the investigation particularly of transient phenomena such as determine the shape of transmitted waves in telegraphy. He predicted that advantage would follow from inductive 'loading' of telegraph cables, and he thus introduced a new era in their design. He discovered that by proper proportioning of the electrical resistance, capacity, inductance, and 'leakance' of an electrical circuit, it is possible to obtain 'a kind of propagation of unique simplicity' in which a wave may suffer attenuation without distortion—this being his 'distortionless' case. It proved to be of wide application in general dynamics. In 1902 he remarked, with regard to 'wireless' waves, that there might possibly be a sufficiently conducting 'layer' in the atmosphere to aid their transmission. This useful conception, which has not yet descended from hypothesis to established reality, is known as the 'Heaviside layer'. The library of the Institution of Electrical Engineers contains a collection of Heaviside's manuscripts, books, and correspondence. Heaviside was elected a fellow of the Royal Society in 1891. He was Faraday medallist of the Institution of Electrical Engineers; he received the honorary degree of Ph.D. from Göttingen University, and was an honorary member of the American Academy of Arts and Sciences.

[O. Heaviside, *Electrical Papers,* 2 vols., 1892, and *Electromagnetic Theory,* 3 vols., 1893, 1899, 1912.] R. Appleyard.

HERBERT, GEORGE EDWARD STANHOPE MOLYNEUX, fifth Earl of Carnarvon (1866–1923), Egyptologist, was born at Highclere Castle, near Newbury, 26 June 1866, the only son of the statesman, Henry Howard Molyneux Herbert, fourth Earl of Carnarvon [q.v.], by his first wife, Lady Evelyn, only daughter of George Augustus Frederick Stanhope, sixth Earl of Chesterfield. He was a first cousin of Auberon Thomas Herbert, eighth Baron Lucas and eleventh Baron Dingwall [q.v.]. From his mother, who died in 1875, he inherited Bretby and other Stanhope estates, to which she had succeeded on the death of her brother, the seventh Earl of Chesterfield.

Lord Porchester—the title by which he was known during his father's lifetime—was educated at Eton, which he left early in order to study modern subjects with tutors at home and abroad, with a view to entering the army. This project, however, came to nothing, and in 1885 he proceeded to Trinity College, Cambridge. There he developed what were to be the two main interests of his life—archaeology and sport. On leaving Cambridge in 1887 he set out on a yachting cruise round the world, but he was unable to complete the full tour. He next paid visits to South Africa, Australia, and Japan. In 1890 he succeeded his father as fifth earl.

In the course of the next few years Lord Carnarvon continued to indulge his love of travel. He also took up racing, and later won some of the important races, including the Ascot Stakes, the Steward's Cup at Goodwood, and the Doncaster Cup. In 1895 he married Almina, only daughter of Frederick Charles Wombwell, fourth son of Sir George Wombwell, third baronet; one son and one daughter were born of the marriage.

In 1901 Lord Carnarvon met with a serious motoring accident, the effects of which prevented him from entering public life and necessitated his spending his winters abroad. Accordingly, in 1903 he went to Egypt. As far back as 1889 he had been captivated by the idea of carrying out excavations, and in 1906, with the aid of Sir William Edmund Garstin [q.v.], the adviser to the ministry of public works in Egypt, he began excavating in Thebes. As an amateur, Carnarvon soon felt the need of expert advice, and on the advice of (Sir) Gaston Maspero, the director of Egyptian excavations, he approached Mr. Howard Carter, formerly an inspector-in-chief of the antiquities department of the Egyptian government at Luxor. Thenceforth, for sixteen years, the two men worked together in the closest collaboration. An account of the work accomplished by Lord Carnarvon and Mr. Carter during the years 1907 to 1912 was published by them in *Five Years' Exploration at Thebes* (1912). It included the discovery of the tomb of a 'king's son' of Dynasty XVIII (1908); a small funerary temple of Queen Hatshepsut (1909); and a rich tomb of Dynasty XII, containing a precious casket and gaming board (1910).

The outbreak of the European War in 1914 temporarily brought Lord Carnarvon's work of excavation to a close. To his great disappointment he was unable to go on active service abroad, but he and Lady Carnarvon converted their house, Highclere Castle, near Newbury, into an officers' hospital, which was subsequently transferred to 38 Bryanston Square, London.

After the end of the War Lord Carnarvon applied for, and obtained, a concession to excavate in the Valley of the Tombs of the Kings near Thebes. As soon as possible he rejoined Mr. Carter, who, in the intervals of his war work at general headquarters in Cairo, had begun preliminary investigations in the valley. Previous excavators, who had employed the system of making pits in rubbish in the hope of finding a tomb entrance, had failed in their objective. Lord Carnarvon and Mr. Carter decided to try another method. They realized that they must excavate down to actual bedrock, but in order to do this satisfactorily it was first necessary to clear away the rubbish dumps left by their predecessors. This involved the removal of some 150,000 to 200,000 tons of rubbish, but for some time no finds of importance were brought to light. It was not until 4 November 1922, in the first days of what Lord Carnarvon had decided should be their last season in the Valley of the Kings, that the perseverance of the excavators was rewarded by the great discovery, unique in the annals of excavation, of the tomb of King Tutankhamūn, with which Lord Carnarvon's name will always be associated.

It was actually Mr. Carter who, shortly before Lord Carnarvon's arrival from England, came upon the steps cut in the rock which led down to the tomb for which they had been searching for six years. An entrance passage, filled with stone and rubble, led to a sealed antechamber containing part of a royal funerary equipment, including statues, chariots, boxes, and vases piled in confused heaps. The fact that most of the objects bore the name of King Tutankhamūn, of Dynasty XVIII, who ascended the throne about 1350 B.C., put the identity of the occupant beyond a doubt. Leading out of the antechamber was the sealed doorway of a second chamber, which, it was surmised, contained the burial itself. In December, before the opening of this sealed chamber was undertaken, Lord Carnarvon and his daughter, Lady Evelyn Herbert, returned to England, and he was received by King George V. At the end of January 1923 they returned to Egypt in order to take part in the opening of the inner chamber, which was accomplished, in the presence of a number of officials of the Egyptian government and archaeologists, on 17 February. It was found to be almost completely filled by a vast gilded wooden shrine, which later proved to contain three other similar shrines and the coffins and mummy of the king. Out of the burial chamber an open doorway led to the store-chamber of the sepulchre; in this an extraordinary wealth of treasures of both artistic and archaeological importance was to be seen. At the end of February the tomb was closed and the entrance filled in, as it had been decided to devote the remainder of the season to the preservation and transport to Cairo of the objects removed from the antechamber, leaving the clearance of the burial chamber and store-chamber for the following season.

Early in March 1923, while he was in the Valley of the Kings, Lord Carnarvon was bitten on the cheek by a mosquito. The bite became infected, and he left for Cairo, where later in the month erysipelas and blood-poisoning set in. Pneumonia subsequently supervened, and after several rallies he died 5 April 1923. His body was brought to England, and he was buried, as he had wished, on the top of Beacon Hill overlooking Highclere.

Lord Carnarvon was a man of great versatility, marked individuality, and much personal charm. He was succeeded as sixth earl by his only son, Henry George Alfred Marius Victor Francis (born 1898).

[*The Times*, 6 April 1923; Introduction by Lady Burghclere to Howard Carter and A. C. Mace, *The Tomb of Tut-ankh-amen*, vol. i, 1923.]

HERDMAN, Sir WILLIAM ABBOTT (1858–1924), marine naturalist, was born in Edinburgh 8 September 1858, the eldest son of Robert Herdman, R.S.A., by his wife Emma Abbott, of Maryborough, Queen's County, Ireland. He was educated at Edinburgh Academy and the university of Edinburgh. After graduating in 1879 he was chosen as one of the assistants of Sir Charles Wyville Thomson [q.v.] in working on the collections made during the voyage of the *Challenger*. Herdman took as his special study the Tunicata, a group of marine organisms, on which he became in time the leading authority. He was also interested in marine dredging and collected materials for papers on the fauna of the Firth of Forth. After being secretary of the *Challenger* expedition committee and, from 1880, demonstrator in zoology in the university of Edinburgh, he was appointed in 1881 first Derby professor of natural history in the university of Liverpool. There he devoted much attention to the co-ordination of the fishery industry with scientific research. His first step was the foundation in 1885 of the Liverpool Marine Biology Committee, which two years later opened a research laboratory at Puffin Island, off Anglesey. Herdman's enthusiasm inspired many amateur naturalists besides his own students, and led to a series of publications on the fauna of Liverpool Bay and the Irish Sea. In 1892 the station was moved from Puffin Island to a more central position at Port Erin, Isle of Man, where it was from time to time enlarged to meet the growing demands of research workers. Herdman also took a great interest in the archaeology of the Isle of Man and was largely instrumental in the foundation of the government museum at Douglas.

In 1891 the recently founded Lancashire

Sea Fisheries Committee secured Herdman's services in the organization of a marine research laboratory in the university of Liverpool; in 1897 Herdman was also instrumental in helping to establish a fish hatchery at Piel Island in Barrow Strait. The latter soon grew into a general biological station and a centre of instruction for fishermen in biology, navigation, and seamanship. Much faunistic and statistical work was carried out at Piel. Specially noteworthy were the researches into plankton which were carried out in collaboration with the Irish fishery authorities.

In 1901 Herdman went to Ceylon, at the request of the Colonial Office, in order to investigate and report on the pearl oyster fisheries of the Gulf of Manaar. His work resulted in various recommendations made to the government of Ceylon regarding the future of the fisheries, and led to the establishment of a marine research station at Trincomalee [see *Report to the Government of Ceylon on the Pearl Oyster Fisheries of the Gulf of Manaar*, 1903–1906].

Returning to his investigations in the Irish Sea, Herdman assisted the plankton survey by the use of his small steam yachts, and extended the survey northwards to the west coast of Scotland. When the European War restricted work at sea, he became chairman of the grain pests committee of the Royal Society. In 1916, with his wife, he founded the George Herdman chair of geology in the university of Liverpool in memory of his son who was killed at the battle of the Somme; and in 1919 he endowed a chair of oceanography in the same university, of which he became the holder for one year, after resigning in 1919 the chair of natural history.

Herdman was a general secretary of the British Association from 1903 to 1919, and he was president at the Cardiff meeting of 1920, when the theme of his address was a plea for a new *Challenger* expedition. He received honorary degrees from several universities, and was elected a fellow of the Royal Society in 1892, served on its council from 1898 to 1910, and was foreign secretary from 1916 to 1920. He was president of the Linnean Society from 1904 to 1908. He received the C.B.E. in 1920 and was knighted in 1922.

Apart from numerous scientific papers and the section on Ascidia in the *Cambridge Natural History*, Herdman's only published work of general interest was *The Founders of Oceanography* (1923). He married twice: first, in 1882 Sarah (died 1886), daughter of David Douglas, bookseller and publisher, of Edinburgh, by whom he had two daughters; secondly, in 1893 Jane Brandeth (died 1922), daughter of Alfred Holt, shipowner, of Liverpool, by whom he had one son and one daughter. He died suddenly in London 21 July 1924.

[*Proceedings* of the Royal Society, vol. xcviii, B, 1925; *Proceedings* of the Linnean Society of London, October 1925, 137th session; *Annual Report* of the Liverpool Marine Biological Committee, 1919; private information.] R. N. Rudmose Brown.

HESELTINE, PHILIP ARNOLD (1894–1930), writer on music, and musical composer under the pseudonym Peter Warlock, was born in London 30 October 1894, the only child of Arnold Heseltine, solicitor, of London, by his wife, Edith Covernton. His father died when the boy was two years of age. He was sent to a private school at Broadstairs when he was about nine, and thence to Eton (1908–1911). In 1910 he made the acquaintance of Frederick Delius, with whom there followed a remarkable interchange of letters, and whose music became the chief formative influence on Heseltine's own compositions. The two years after Eton found Heseltine in Germany, where he spent some months at Cologne, and at his mother's home, Cefn Bryntalch, Abermule, Montgomeryshire. He went up to Christ Church, Oxford, in the autumn of 1913, but left at the end of the summer term of 1914. Thereafter, for a few years, he lived principally in London. He had liked neither Eton nor Oxford, and liked still less the patriotic attitude to the European War. His letters to Delius about this time reveal him a brooding, melancholy, yet passionate soul, an 'apparent misfit in any surroundings'. In November 1915 Heseltine met David Herbert Lawrence [q.v.], whose personality and philosophy affected his music, and he stayed with Lawrence in Cornwall in the spring of 1916. About this time he also met Bernard van Dieren, the influence of whose music upon him was second only to that of Delius and ultimately became greater. In December 1916 he married Minnie Lucy, daughter of Robert Stuart Channing, a mechanical engineer. They had one son. From August 1917 to August 1918 he was in Dublin, and after that in London again. He first used the pseudonym 'Peter Warlock' as the signature to certain songs published in 1919. He founded *The Sackbut* (incorporating *The Organist*), a musical journal, in May 1920, and edited it until June 1921. During these two years he was abroad for long periods in France and North Africa. He settled at Cefn Bryntalch in the autumn of 1921, but, having separated from his wife in or about the year 1923, he left Wales in 1924 and after a few months in London went to live, early in 1925, at Eynsford, Kent. There he stayed until October 1928. After returning to Wales for a short time, he went again to London and lived there till his death, which took place at Chelsea, 17 December 1930, as the result of gas poisoning. At the inquest the jury were unable to determine whether he had committed suicide.

Heseltine left about a hundred songs with pianoforte accompaniment; *The Curlew*, a song cycle for tenor voice, flute, cor anglais, and string quartet (1920–1922); *Serenade* for string orchestra, in homage to Delius (1923); and other instrumental compositions, besides numerous choral works and part songs. He edited a large body of Elizabethan and Jacobean music, Purcell's *Thirteen Fantasies for strings*, and transcriptions of many works by Delius. He was the author, among other books, of *Frederick Delius* (written under his own name, 1923), *The English Ayre* (1926), and, in collaboration with Cecil Gray, *Carlo Gesualdo, Musician and Murderer* (1926).

Heseltine's music is that of a belated Elizabethan. His best songs—described by a writer in *The Times* as 'some of the most exquisite and original songs of our day'—have unusual purity of tone, a delicate clarity of utterance, and a learned simplicity. His books are scholarly contributions to their subjects.

[Cecil Gray, *Peter Warlock: A Memoir of Philip Heseltine* (containing a complete list of his works musical and literary), 1934; private information.] E. O'Brien.

HEWLETT, MAURICE HENRY (1861–1923), novelist, poet, and essayist, was born at Oatlands Park, Weybridge, Surrey, 22 January 1861. His father, Henry Gay Hewlett, was of French extraction and his ancestors were in all probability Huguenot refugees. The original name was Hulotte, afterwards corrupted into Hulet. The family appears to have settled in Dorsetshire, but is to be traced in a number of other counties. Hewlett's father had the civil service appointment of keeper of His Majesty's land revenue records. He married Emmeline Mary, daughter of James Thomas Knowles, an architect, and sister of (Sir) James Thomas Knowles [q.v.], founder and editor of the *Nineteenth Century*. They had eight children, of whom Maurice was the eldest. In 1872 his parents moved to Farningham in Kent, and Maurice became a day-boy at Sevenoaks grammar school. In 1874 he went as a boarder to Palace School, Enfield, and in 1875 to the International College, Spring Grove, Isleworth. In 1878 he joined his cousin, W. O. Hewlett, in the family law business at 2 Raymond Buildings, Lincoln's Inn. He married in 1888 Hilda Beatrice, daughter of the Rev. George William Herbert, vicar of St. Peter's, Vauxhall, by whom he had one son and one daughter. He was called to the bar by the Inner Temple in 1890, and in 1897 he succeeded his father as keeper of land revenue records, a post which he held until 1901.

The year 1898 was the turning-point in Hewlett's career, for it saw the publication of *The Forest Lovers*. The success was great and immediate, and he was now, at the age of thirty-seven, widely famous. It may be said without exaggeration that the rest of his life was spent in combating this fame which he always felt to be, in its origin and proportion, unbalanced and stultifying to his proper reputation. Hewlett now gave up his life to his writing, which may be divided into three periods. During the first, from 1898 to 1904, he produced mainly Italian and historical romances. The most important of these, after *The Forest Lovers*, are *The Life of Richard Yea-and-Nay* (1900) and *The Queen's Quair* (1904). The second period, which lasted roughly until the outbreak of war in 1914, was occupied with Regency novels and stories of modern life, such as *Rest Harrow* (1910). During the third period, from 1914 until his death at Broadchalke, Salisbury, 15 June 1923, he was in the main poet and essayist, and it was in this period that he wrote what was perhaps his greatest work, *The Song of the Plow* (1916). A typical volume of essays was *Wiltshire Essays* (1921).

Hewlett was a man of sardonic speech with an exceedingly warm heart. His own description of himself remains the best: 'If I am to deal with life it must be in my own way, for there's no escape from one's character. I may be a good poet or a bad one—that's not for me to say: but I am a poet of sorts.' It was as poet that he regarded himself, first, last, and all the time. It was as poet that he wrote his Italian romances, his historical novels, his modern fiction, his *Song of the Plow*, his essays, and it was as poet that he made in his last years his passionate declarations of belief in the English peasantry as the only hope for England. But he had made his name as the author of romantic fiction, and the public refused to take him seriously in any other aspect. So, sardonically, humorously, and sometimes bitterly he tiraded, all his later life, against what he considered his false position. Nevertheless, in *The Queen's Quair* and *Richard Yea-and-Nay* he did great things for the English historical novel, bringing lyrical poetry into it without robbing it of its actuality and drama. And in his *Song of the Plow* he wrote one of the five epics of English poetry—a work as likely to survive as anything else in English contemporary literature. It must be said also that he was a splendid friend, fiery in his loyalty, indulgent in his patience, and a great open-air companion.

[Maurice Hewlett's *Letters*, edited by Laurence Binyon with an introductory memoir by Edward Hewlett, 1926; private information.] H. Walpole.

HICKS, ROBERT DREW (1850–1929), classical scholar, was born at Aust, Gloucestershire, 29 June 1850, the eldest son of William Hicks, a head clerk in the post office at Bristol, by his wife, Frances Oldland. He was educated at Bristol grammar school, and in 1870 entered Trinity College, Cambridge, of which he was elected a scholar in 1872. He was bracketed sixth classic in the tripos of 1874, and in the same year obtained a second class in the moral sciences tripos. In 1876 he was elected fellow of his college, a position which he held until his death, and from 1884 to 1900 was lecturer in classics. Hicks married in 1894 Bertha Mary, daughter of Samuel Heath, farmer, of Thornton Curtis, Lincolnshire, and sister of Sir Thomas Little Heath and Robert Samuel Heath, the mathematicians. They had one son and one daughter. In 1900 he became blind; but, helped by his wife and by a few friends, he continued with indomitable courage to pursue his laborious and fruitful studies in the classics. In 1928 the honorary degree of D.Litt. was conferred on him by Manchester University. He died at Cambridge 8 March 1929.

In 1894 Hicks published an edition of five books of Aristotle's *Politics*, based on the edition of the German scholar, Franz Susemihl, but including much original work of his own. In 1899 he edited, in collaboration with Richard Dacre Archer-Hind [q.v.], a volume of *Cambridge Compositions* in Greek and Latin. He contributed the section on chronology and on the later philosophical schools to the Cambridge *Companion to Greek Studies* (1905) and that on philosophy to the *Companion to Latin Studies* (1910). In 1907 appeared Hicks's chief book, a monumental edition of Aristotle's *De Anima*. In 1910 he published *Stoic and Epicurean*, and in 1925 a text and translation of Diogenes Laertius. In 1921 he prepared a *Concise Latin Dictionary* in braille type.

Hicks must be accounted one of the most learned students of Greek philosophy in his generation. His *magnum opus*, packed as it is with detailed discussions of the text and interpretation of the *De Anima*, and showing knowledge of the whole literature of the subject, would have been a remarkable achievement for any one; considered as the work of a blind man, it is much more remarkable. His other works are slighter in character, but are models of clear and judicious presentation, and worthy of the high reputation for scholarship which Hicks enjoyed. As a teacher, he would take endless trouble to deal with the difficulties of his students, and his wide reading and tenacious memory made him an oracle to whom they seldom appealed in vain. When he had become blind, he wrote out many of his favourite philosophical works in braille, and a friend relates how he found him in bed reading Aristotle with his fingers under the bed-clothes. It may be added that, although no performer, he was passionately devoted to music.

[*The Times*, 9 March 1929; private information.] W. D. Ross.

HILLS, ARNOLD FRANK (1857–1927), shipbuilder and philanthropist, was born at Denmark Hill, London, 12 March 1857, the youngest son of Frank Clarke Hills, a manufacturing chemist, who made a fortune, and acquired a large interest in the Thames Ironworks and Shipbuilding Company at Blackwall, by his wife, Anne Ellen, daughter of James Rawlings.

Hills entered Mr. Bushell's house at Harrow in 1871, and in 1876 went up to University College, Oxford. Both at school and at the university he was a good football player and long-distance runner. He was the captain of football at Harrow, and he represented Oxford twice under Association rules. At the athletic sports he ran the mile twice for Oxford, and, although he did not win against Cambridge, he was amateur champion over that distance in 1878. In the following spring he won the three miles' race at the inter-university sports in creditable time. He obtained a second class in classical moderations in 1877, and a second class in modern history in 1879.

Almost immediately after taking his degree Hills joined the directorate of the Thames Ironworks. The company owned a shipyard on the Thames, and it was from this yard that the *Warrior*, the first British sea-going iron-clad battleship, had been ordered in 1859, as well as a second large vessel, the *Minotaur*, two years later. The Thames Ironworks was at one time one of the leading shipyards in the country, but at the date when Hills became associated with it competition with more modern establishments on the Clyde and the Tyne was becoming acute. The general trend of heavy industries was to Scotland or the North of England, where the necessary steel and iron could be obtained more conveniently and handled more economically. On the Thames it became more and more difficult to find work for the shipbuilding yards.

Hills was a student of social problems, and he recognized the importance of this question for the industrial population of South-East London and the riverside. For five years (1880–1885) he lived in Canning Town close by his work, devoting his days to the shipyard and his evenings to the improvement and recreation of his workpeople. Large sums were spent by the firm in organizing clubs of all kinds, and in arranging lectures, concerts, and other entertainments. Unfortunately, Hills found himself involved in disputes with the trade unions, chiefly on the subject of employing non-union labour. He maintained his right to engage whom he wished, and, although in the end his point was gained, it was only after heavy losses had been incurred through strikes. In an endeavour to improve the relations with his workmen he instituted a profit-sharing scheme, and introduced also an eight-hour day.

After the settlement of these differences a period of prosperity followed, and during the last decade of the nineteenth century the Thames Ironworks enjoyed considerable custom. At one time there were in hand four first-class battleships, including one for the Japanese navy. To meet this pressure various steps were taken. The engine works of Messrs. John Penn and company at Greenwich were bought, so that marine engines as well as hulls could be built. The plant of the yard was modernized, the ship-repairing and civil engineering departments were extended, and an electrical department was opened. Hills also tried to re-establish a popular service of river steam-boats.

Circumstances proved too much for this activity to continue. The northern shipyards were able to undersell the Thames, and the unequal competition could not be maintained. When about 1909 the Admiralty considered placing the order for the battleship *Thunderer* with the Thames Ironworks, protracted negotiations took place before the contract was finally decided. There was a strong body of opinion against the abandonment of shipbuilding on the Thames, and no doubt weight was given to this view. The order required costly additions to the company's resources, but Hills faced these conditions with unfailing spirit. The *Thunderer* was laid down on the same slip from which the *Warrior* had been launched fifty years before, though the slip had been strengthened and lengthened in the interval. The contract was quickly and efficiently carried out, but it proved to be the last effort of the yard. Not long afterwards the Thames Ironworks was compelled to close down from lack of work. On 17 November 1911 a receiver for the debenture-holders was appointed, and the sale of the property was completed early in 1914.

This long fight in a losing cause would in any case have been worthy of notice, but it was rendered more remarkable by the fact that for some years it had been carried on by Hills under physical disability. The strain and anxiety of his incessant labours proved too severe for his strength. His health was gradually affected by an illness which made him in 1906 a complete cripple. His mind was as vigorous as ever, but he was unable to move hand or foot. He was carried about in an invalid chair, and it was from this that he continued to direct his affairs. At the launch of the *Thunderer* he spoke from his chair for half an hour with much eloquence. Outside his business as manager of a shipbuilding firm Hills had a number of other interests. He was an ardent advocate of total abstinence as well as of vegetarianism, and his philanthropic activities were many.

Hills married in 1886 Mary Elizabeth, daughter of Alfred Lafone, of Hanworth Park, Middlesex, and had one son and four daughters. He died 7 March 1927 at his home, Hammerfield, Penshurst, Kent.

[*The Times*, 8 March 1927.]

A. Cochrane.

HOBHOUSE, LEONARD TRELAWNY (1864–1929), philosopher and journalist, was born at St. Ive, near Liskeard, 8 September 1864, the youngest of the seven children of the Rev. Reginald Hobhouse, rector of St. Ive for fifty-one years, and archdeacon of Bodmin from 1877 to 1892. His mother was Caroline, daughter of Sir William Lewis Salusbury-Trelawny, eighth baronet, of Trelawny, Cornwall. She was a gifted woman, who read French, German, and Italian with ease, and taught him Latin before he went to school. He went to a preparatory school at Exmouth and in 1877 to Marlborough, where he developed slowly and not without difficulty, though he was a clever boy. 'It was his own line of private reading that marked the future man', as one of his masters has said. He read J. S. Mill, Herbert Spencer, and Mazzini's *Essays*, and these writers confirmed his natural bent for thinking for himself. He went up to Oxford in 1883 with a scholarship at Corpus Christi College, gained first classes in classical moderations (1884) and *literae humaniores* (1887) and in the latter year obtained a prize fellowship at Merton College. In 1890 he was appointed assistant-tutor at Corpus, and in 1894 was elected a fellow of that college.

Hobhouse's chief interest at Oxford lay in philosophy, which was the subject of his teaching, but he had already enlarged his knowledge by studying science at the University Museum. In 1889 he took up the cause of the movement known as the 'New Unionism'. This brought him in contact with the world of labour, which appealed to him emotionally, as philosophy did intellectually, and he sought to combine them in the study of sociology.

In 1891 Hobhouse married Nora, daughter of George Burgess Hadwen, a mill-owner of Sowerby Bridge, who lived at Kelroyde, and entered on a happy married life. A son and two daughters were born of the marriage. In 1893 he published his first book, *The Labour Movement*; it dealt with trade unions, co-operation, and the control of industry, and went through several editions. Then he went back to philosophy and in 1896 published *The Theory of Knowledge*. This work revealed him as an original thinker. It was opposed to the Idealism then dominant in philosophical circles at Oxford, and was coldly received. The fact increased in Hobhouse a certain restlessness, which had been growing for some time. He felt that the life of an Oxford don was too academic for him, too far removed from the real world. He wanted to go to London; but, on the invitation of Mr. C. P. Scott, he actually went in 1897 to Manchester in order to work on the staff of the *Manchester Guardian*. He had been recommended by Dr. Arthur Sidgwick, whom Scott had consulted, as 'quite the ablest of our younger Greats men and a strong liberal and progressive of the best type'.

Hobhouse's interest in politics dated from his school days, when he read Mill and became a radical with a marked tendency towards the left. It was a real interest, which lasted throughout his life until the closing years, when the turn of party politics disappointed him and he cut himself adrift from all party associations. In Manchester he remained for five years, working at a philosophical book in the daytime and writing for the *Manchester Guardian* at night. He had an extraordinary facility in writing leading articles, as in speaking; but the double work exhausted him, and in 1902 he gave it up and left Manchester for London. His association with the *Manchester Guardian* did not cease, however; he became a director of the paper in 1911, contributed frequently to it, especially from 1915 to 1925, and in 1921 acted as deputy editor.

In the meantime Hobhouse's philosophical study had been published in 1901, under the title of *Mind in Evolution*. In 1903 he took an active part in forming the Sociological Society, and thenceforward sociology was his chief preoccupation; but he still continued his journalistic work. In the following year he published *Democracy and Reaction*, in which he protested against imperialism and the negative social policy of the liberal party. From 1903 to 1905 he was secretary of the Free Trade Union, and he acted for some time as the editor of its organ, the *Sociological Review*; for eighteen months (1906–1907) he was political editor of *The Tribune*. In 1906 his *Morals in Evolution* appeared, and marked a new departure in the study of sociology. In 1907 he was appointed the first professor of sociology in London University on the Martin White foundation, and he held the post until his death. In 1911 he published *Social Evolution and Political Theory* and *Liberalism* (in the 'Home University Library'), and in 1913, *Development and Purpose*; he also wrote, with G. C. Wheeler and M. Ginsberg, *The Material Culture and Social Institutions of the Simpler People* (1915). During the European War he took the patriotic side, but he advocated an agreed peace in 1917. Afterwards he was made chairman of several trade boards, in the working of which he had taken a keen interest from their first formation.

In the decade following the War Hobhouse published *The Rational Good* (1921), *The Elements of Social Justice* (1922), and *Social Development* (1924); these three books developed his sociology into a complete system. He also wrote *The Metaphysical Theory of the State* (1918), and in 1927 published a revised and largely rewritten edition of his *Development and Purpose*. The death of his wife in 1925 was a heavy blow to him, and his own prolonged illness which began in 1924 increased a tendency to depression. He died 21 June 1929 at Alençon in Normandy, and was buried at Wimbledon. His sociological works were more appreciated in America than in England, and he had many requests to lecture from American universities. He received honorary degrees from the universities of St. Andrews (1919) and Durham (1913). The Hobhouse Memorial Trust, which provides for an annual lecture to be delivered in rotation at the London School of Economics, University College, King's College, and Bedford College, and also for a memorial prize to be awarded annually to a student who shows conspicuous merit in sociology, was founded in 1930.

[*The Times*, 24 and 27 June 1929; H. Carter, *The Social Theories of L. T. Hobhouse*, 1927; E. Barker, *Leonard Trelawny Hobhouse, 1864–1929*, in *Proceedings* of the British Academy, vol. xv, 1929; J. A. Hobson and Morris Ginsberg, *L. T. Hobhouse, His Life and Work*, 1931.] A. Shadwell.

HOGARTH, DAVID GEORGE (1862–1927), scholar and traveller, was born at Barton-on-Humber, Lincolnshire, 23 May 1862, the eldest son of the Rev. George Hogarth, vicar of that parish for nearly forty years, by his wife, Jane Elizabeth, daughter of John Uppleby, of Scarborough. He was educated at Winchester, where he was a commoner from 1876 to 1881, not exerting himself in his progress up the school, but gaining distinction as a runner (in his last year he won the mile, half-mile, and quarter-mile) and acquiring a reputation for greater ability than he cared to show. His own observation, written when he had a son at Winchester, was 'At Winchester I learned how to learn things, and that was a great deal'. In October 1881, he went up to Oxford as a demy of Magdalen College, where his career was similar. Ostensibly more interested in horse-racing and athletics, he obtained first classes both in classical moderations (1882) and in *literae humaniores* (1885), was president of junior common room, and was generally recognized as a man of outstanding ability. After taking his degree in 1885, a year of uncertainty followed, when the possibilities of fellowships, of the bar, and of the British Museum were contemplated without much enthusiasm. His chance came in 1886 when he was elected to the Craven travelling fellowship, then first instituted. By this means he embarked on the career of a travelling archaeologist, in which he made his name, and acquired the experience which was afterwards used in other fields.

Hogarth's apprenticeship to archaeology is described in the early chapters of his *Accidents of an Antiquary's Life* (1910). It included travelling with (Sir) William Mitchell Ramsay [q.v.] in Asia Minor in 1887—'an arduous apprenticeship to the best epigraphist in Europe'—excavating at Paphos in Cyprus in 1888, another journey with Ramsay in Asia Minor in 1890 and with another companion in 1891, and three seasons in Egypt, working for the Egypt Exploration Fund at Deir-el-bahri, Alexandria, and the Fayum from 1894 to 1896. In Egypt he perfected his knowledge of the technique of excavation, but he never acquired any enthusiasm for Egyptian archaeology. His taste was always distinctly classical. Meanwhile he had been elected a fellow of Magdalen in 1886, and in 1894 he married Laura Violet, daughter of Charles Uppleby, of Barrow Hall, a distant relative of his mother. They had one son.

In 1897 Hogarth was appointed director of the British School of Archaeology at Athens; but before taking up the duties of the post he had an exciting interlude as correspondent for *The Times* in Crete during the revolution and in Thessaly on the eve of the Greco-Turkish War of that year, of which he has left a lively account [see *Accidents of an Antiquary's Life*, ch. 1].

He held the directorship for only three years. He had great administrative capacity, but at this period his passion was for travel, and for a still wider field of experience. The principal episodes of his directorship were the excavation of Phylakopi in Melos, and a season at Naucratis in 1899. In 1900 he left the School, and joined (Sir) Arthur Evans in his first campaign in Crete after the revolution, in which a beginning was made on the epoch-making excavations of Cnossos, while Hogarth in particular undertook the clearing of the Dictaean cave. In the following year a season at Zakro, in the east of the island, was cut short by a disastrous flood.

After leaving Athens, Hogarth had his head-quarters at Oxford, his activities being mainly divided between literature and sporadic archaeological expeditions. He had made his name as a brilliant and picturesque narrator of travel by his little book *A Wandering Scholar in the Levant*, published in 1896; and in 1897 he published his *Philip and Alexander of Macedon*, a subject to which he had been attracted ever since his undergraduate days. He did not take the time necessary to make it a full-scale work of research and history; but it remains a brilliant and original essay. To this same period belong *Authority and Archaeology* (1899), a collection of essays of which he was the editor, an admirable book on *The Nearer East* (1902), and *The Penetration of Arabia* (1904). He had never visited Arabia (indeed, a mission to Jiddah in 1917 was his only first-hand experience of the country on which he became a recognized authority), but he had studied the literature minutely. He was one of the discoverers and champions of Charles Montagu Doughty [q.v.], whose life he subsequently wrote; and his knowledge of the country and the people proved of vital importance to the British government during the European War.

Meanwhile, Hogarth paid another visit to Naucratis in 1903, and in 1904–1905 he conducted a campaign of excavation on behalf of the British Museum on the site of the temple of Artemis at Ephesus. It was also on behalf of the Museum that in 1908 he visited the upper Euphrates, and prospected the sites of Jerablus (Carchemish) and Tell Bashar. He visited the United States as a lecturer in the winter of 1907–1908, and again in 1909 and 1921. In 1908, however, his life as a 'wandering scholar' came to an end. Domestic reasons made a settled home and a regular income desirable, and in that year he accepted the appointment of keeper of the Ashmolean Museum at Oxford, and he held the post until his death. His only archaeological expedition after this date was in 1911, when the plans made three years earlier for the excavation of Carchemish fructified. Hogarth planned and started this work for the British Museum, but his duties at Oxford precluded him from carrying it through, though he visited the site again in 1912 and 1914, when the work was being continued by (Sir) C. L. Woolley and T. E. Lawrence.

The life of a museum director has few outstanding details; but under Hogarth the Ashmolean grew markedly in importance, especially in the departments of Cretan and Hittite archaeology. The latter was, in fact, his own principal interest, and his contributions to the subject were substantial and important. The routine details of his office he conducted efficiently and without fuss, and he combined with his museum duties other work for the university, particularly as a delegate of the Clarendon Press, where his knowledge and his practical sense were of great value. The orderly train of a settled life in the university was, however, broken by the outbreak of the European War. Hogarth at once offered to put his knowledge of the East at the service of the government, and in 1915 he was sent out to Cairo and Athens. There, perhaps for the only time, he found full scope for his powers in work of the first importance. After various vicissitudes he was made director of the Arab Bureau at Cairo, with the rank of commander in the Royal Naval Volunteer Reserve, and in this position he was largely responsible for the difficult and delicate diplomacy which underlay the Arab campaign so brilliantly conducted in the field by his former archaeological disciple (whom he had recruited for this work), T. E. Lawrence. With Lawrence, Sir G. F. Clayton, (Sir) Wyndham Deedes, (Sir) George Lloyd, (Sir) Mark Sykes, and one or two others, he formed a loose group which probably was mainly responsible for the development of the British-Egyptian (as opposed to the British-Mesopotamian) point of view about the aims and policy of operations in Arabia, Palestine, and Syria. It was for the home government to decide how far such aims should be adopted and carried out. The details are not public property; but all concerned with the work have borne testimony to Hogarth's level-headed ability, his patience, his knowledge, and his sound judgement of men. Here he found administrative and organizing work of a scale and importance to call forth his full powers. It is the great period of his life, but one of which little can be written. He received the C.M.G. for his services in 1918.

After the War Hogarth was a member of the British delegation at the Peace Conference at Versailles, and then returned to his work at Oxford. His health had suffered from the strain of the War, but his powers were not yet affected, and during this period he served on the hebdomadal council, and was an active member of the statutory commission on Oxford University. In 1917 he had received the gold medal of the Royal Geographical Society, and in 1925 he became its president, in which capacity he carried out much administrative work with his usual efficiency. In 1926 his health definitely began to cause alarm, and he died suddenly in his sleep 6 November 1927 at Oxford.

In person Hogarth was somewhat above middle height, well set-up, dark in colouring, with a rather sardonic expression which suited a cynicism of phrase characteristic of him. It was only a superficial and good-natured cynicism, quite compatible with readiness to serve and help others. The outstanding impression given by him was that of mastery of his work. Indeed, except during the War, he never seemed to have a task which called out his full powers. He disliked routine and a fixed employment; hence he passed from one piece of work to another, and settled down to nothing till past middle life. He was a wise adviser, because he was full of knowledge and experience without being led astray by unbalanced enthusiasm, and because he was quite free of envy or jealousy. He was not a fighter or self-assertive, but he generally succeeded in attaining his end, for he knew his own mind and was trusted. He was a vivid descriptive writer, and his books rank among the best in the literature of travel. It was in travel that he was probably happiest. He had a keen eye both for geography and for national character, and excelled in relating both to their historical background, and in interpreting history in their light.

Hogarth was elected F.B.A. in 1905, obtained the degree of D.Litt. of Oxford in 1918, and received the honorary degree of Litt.D. of Cambridge in 1924.

In addition to the works already mentioned, and not including articles in periodicals, Hogarth was the author of *Devia Cypria* (1889); *The Archaic Artemisia of Ephesus* (1908); *Ionia and the East* (1909); *The Ancient East* (1914); *Carchemish*, Part I (1914); *The Balkans* (1915); *Hittite Seals* (1920); *Arabia* (1922); *Kings of the Hittites* (1926, being the British Academy Schweich lectures for 1924); *C. M. Doughty, A Memoir* (1928, seen through the press by his son after his death); he also wrote several chapters in the *Cambridge Ancient History*, particularly on Hittite history and archaeology. He was a contributor to this DICTIONARY, and gave its editors much valuable advice and active help.

[A. H. Sayce, *David George Hogarth, 1862–1927*, in *Proceedings* of the British Academy, vol. xiii, 1927; Mrs. Courtney (Hogarth's sister) in the *Fortnightly Review*, January 1928; C. R. L. Fletcher in the *Geographical Journal*, April 1928; Hogarth's letters and writings; personal knowledge.]

F. G. KENYON.

HOLDERNESS, SIR THOMAS WILLIAM, first baronet (1849–1924), Indian civil servant, came of a Yorkshire family, of Sutton-in-Holderness, his grandfather, Thomas Holderness, being a timber merchant in Hull. His father, John William Holderness, settled for a time in New Brunswick, where he married Mary Ann Macleod and where, at St. John's, Thomas Holderness, the eldest son, was born 11 June 1849. Soon after his birth his parents returned to England, and in 1867 he was sent to Cheltenham College to be educated. The untimely death of his father two years previously (1865), left the family in straitened circumstances, but Holderness was able to maintain himself at Cheltenham by means of scholarships and prizes, and in 1869 he went as a scholar to University College, Oxford. In 1869 and again in 1870 he passed the open competitive examination for the Indian civil service, on the later occasion obtaining a place high enough to give him a choice of his province. In those days it was comparatively rare for Indian civil service probationers to pursue their university studies simultaneously with their preparation for India, but Holderness continued to read for classical honour moderations, in which he obtained a second class in 1871. Next year he obtained a second class in law and modern history.

Proceeding to India in the winter of

1872–1873, Holderness spent his first three years in the seclusion of the small stations of Bijnor, Fatehpur, and Muzaffarnagar in what were then called the North-West Provinces. As many others have done who have risen to distinction in the Indian service, he began to contribute to the press, and it was probably his writings as well as his exceptional administrative ability that attracted the notice of the lieutenant-governor, Sir John Strachey [q.v.], and led to his being called in 1876 to the provincial capital, Allahabad, for secretarial duties in the offices of the government and the board of revenue. It is a coincidence that in later years he was entrusted with the work of revising and reissuing (4th ed., 1911) Sir John Strachey's classic work on *India, its administration and progress*. As a secretary he showed a capacity so obvious and outstanding that, during the rest of his Indian career, he never, except for one short interval, returned to executive work in the districts. At Allahabad he laid the foundations of a comprehensive knowledge of the revenue systems of India and learned to appreciate their bearing on the welfare of the peasantry. After five years' apprenticeship in the provincial offices, Holderness was selected in 1881 to be under-secretary to the government of India in the revenue department, and there he remained, occasionally acting as secretary, until 1885. In this year he married Lucy Shepherd, daughter of George Robert Elsmie, C.S.I. [q.v.], a civilian of note in the Punjab, and paid a visit to England. In 1888, after being for a short time in charge of the district of Pilibhit, he was appointed director of land records and agriculture, and later, secretary to the government of the United Provinces in both judicial and financial departments.

Holderness was now recognized as marked out for a distinguished career, and his promotion was accelerated by the work which he carried through successfully in dealing with measures of relief in the disastrous series of famines with which the nineteenth century closed. The United Provinces were gravely affected as early as 1896, and Sir Antony (afterwards Lord) MacDonnell [q.v.], who, as lieutenant-governor, directed the relief operations, summoned Holderness to assist him. Owing to the experience so gained, when the distress later on spread to other provinces, he was called by the viceroy, Lord Curzon, to Simla, as adviser to the Imperial government in the emergency. For his services he was rewarded by the C.S.I. (1898), and by the Kaiser-i-Hind gold medal (1901). In 1898 he became secretary to the government of India, revenue and agricultural department, and was now in the recognized line of succession to the headship of a province. He was, in fact, offered such a post, but in order not to continue separated from his family, then resident in England, declined.

In 1901 Holderness retired from the Indian civil service and accepted the post of secretary in the revenue, statistics, and commerce department at the India Office, where Lord George Hamilton was at the time the secretary of state. He was now in the wider stream of the world's affairs. International conferences on the sugar trade and on problems of sanitation claimed his attention, and the selection of the experts required by the great expansion of the scientific services, especially those connected with agriculture, during Lord Curzon's viceroyalty, came into his hands. In recognition of his work as secretary he was created K.C.S.I. in 1907, and in 1912, on the death of Sir Richmond Ritchie [q.v.], the permanent under-secretary of state, he was promoted to the vacant post, a unique distinction for an officer of the Indian services.

In June 1914 Holderness had reached the full retiring age of sixty-five, but he was granted an extended term of office, and after the outbreak of war his great experience and soundness of judgement made him an invaluable adviser, first in connexion with the organization of munition supplies and the utilization of civil officers for war work, and later in connexion with discussions on the Rowlatt Bills and the Montague reforms. Accordingly, the further retention of his services was considered indispensable, and his term of office was extended by successive secretaries of state until 1919. To the Montague reforms he gave his cordial support, being convinced that a liberal measure of political advance should be conceded in India.

In 1917 Holderness was given the G.C.B. (having received the K.C.B. in 1914), and in 1920, after his retirement, a baronetcy was conferred on him. His mental vigour being unimpaired, he devoted his retirement to reading, writing, and business in the City, where his keenness and sound judgement impressed his new colleagues. Sanity of judgement was, indeed, his predominant trait; moreover, he had considerable literary gifts, and the works which he wrote or edited on Indian questions, in a lucid and persuasive style, commanded wide attention. He was of studious character, grave in demeanour, and simple, almost ascetic, in his habits of life.

Holderness died very suddenly 16 September 1924, while walking on the golf-links near his home at Tadworth in Surrey. He left a widow and two children, Ernest William Elsmie (born 1890), who succeeded to the baronetcy, and Helen Alice, who married C. M. Page, F.R.C.S.

Besides his edition of Strachey's *India*, Holderness wrote the official *Narratives of the Indian Famine, 1896–1897*, *Peoples and Problems of India* (1912, revised edition 1920), and *India's Arduous Journey in These Eventful Years* (1924).

[*The Times*, 17 September 1924; *India Office List* and Histories of Services of United Provinces; private information.]

J. O. Miller.

HOLDICH, Sir THOMAS HUNGERFORD (1843–1929), Anglo-Indian frontier surveyor, was born at Dingley, Northamptonshire, 13 February 1843, the eldest son of the Rev. Thomas Peach Holdich, rector of that parish, by his wife, Susan, daughter of William Atherton Garrard, of Carisbrooke, Isle of Wight, and Olney, Buckinghamshire. He was educated at the Godolphin grammar school, Hammersmith, whence he proceeded to the East India Company's Military College at Addiscombe, where in 1860 he gained the sword of honour. His intention had been to join the Bengal Engineers, but on the abolition of that corps he entered the Royal Military Academy at Woolwich and, passing out high, was duly commissioned in 1862 in the corps of Royal Engineers.

After completing various instructional courses, Holdich was sent out to India in 1865. At that period the government of India was sadly behindhand in its knowledge of those important terrains that lay on and beyond its borders, especially on the critical North-West Frontier, and there was almost unlimited scope for the scientifically trained surveyor of adventurous spirit. Serious political developments were afoot, and it was all-important that the government should have exact information about these regions. There were local tribal problems; more serious problems with the kingdom of Afghanistan; and the paramount problem of Russia's expansion to the east. Borders had to be explored, distant mountain ranges and rivers accurately located, and frontiers defined. For this work scientific training was not all that was required. Men were wanted who had the taste and the physique for adventure, and could endure both the fierce heat of the desert plains and the arctic cold of the Central Asian highland; who were prepared, moreover, to face the very real danger of attacks from wild and fanatical tribesmen, and who had the tact and personality to handle delicate situations and to disarm suspicion. That Holdich possessed these qualities is amply attested by his remarkable record of service for twenty years in that rough borderland.

Holdich began his career in India as temporary assistant surveyor with the Bhutan expedition in 1865–1866. This led to his permanent appointment to the Survey Department, and in 1867 he was lent for survey work on the Abyssinian campaign. In 1878 he began his long connexion with the North-West Frontier, as a survey officer with the Southern Afghanistan field force. He served through both Afghan campaigns with distinction, being mentioned in dispatches and promoted brevet-major in 1881. Then followed some years of useful work in Baluchistan, Waziristan, and other parts of that vexed border, until in 1884 he was appointed to serve on the Russo-Afghan Boundary Commission. In spite of an inadequate staff and countless local difficulties, the results obtained were remarkable, and the frontier then laid down—admittedly based to a large extent on Holdich's advice—has been respected to this day. In 1892 Holdich, who had been promoted brevet-colonel in 1891, was appointed superintendent of frontier surveys, a post which he held until 1898. In 1895 he was once more deputed to deal with the Russo-Afghan border—this time in the remote Pamirs. In 1896, when a commission was appointed to demarcate the Perso-Baluch boundary, Holdich was chosen as chief commissioner, and his local knowledge proved highly useful. In 1897, when there was a general conflagration on the North-West Frontier, he did valuable service by supplying each column with suitable survey officers, and directing their efforts to the best advantage.

This was the close of Holdich's Indian career. But in 1902 his services were utilized for an important purpose elsewhere. A dispute between the governments of Chile and Argentina regarding their common frontier in Patagonia had been dragging on, until both parties agreed to invite the British government to appoint a tribunal to arbitrate on the matter. Holdich was invited to be a member of the tribunal. Thanks in a great measure to his technical experience, his powers of conciliation, and his arduous examination of the actual ground, the tribunal was enabled to give an award entirely satisfactory to both sides.

One of Holdich's hobbies was painting in water-colours. A sketch-book and battered paint-box were always in his haversack. Wandering as he did in wild places, often amidst the most impressive scenery, he had unique opportunities for this pursuit, long before the days of the kodak. His talent is attested by the fact that he twice won the viceroy's cup in the Simla Fine Arts Exhibition. But the really absorbing interest of Holdich's life was geography. To him a blank space on the map was simply an incentive to go and find out and show accurately what was there. Accuracy was almost an obsession with him, and he had no sympathy with the amateur explorer and his sloppy 'intelligence'. Throughout, his work was marked by meticulous exactitude—and more than this—by broad-minded common sense. He refused to be hidebound by theoretical principles, 'believing', to use his own words, 'that the first and greatest object of a national frontier is to ensure peace and goodwill between contiguous peoples, by putting a definite edge to the national political horizon, so as to limit unauthorized expansion and trespass'.

Holdich contributed a volume, *India* (with 114 maps and diagrams, 1904) to the 'Regions of the World' series, and was also the author of *The Indian Borderland* (1901), *The Countries of the King's Award* (1904), *The Gates of India* (1909), and *Political Frontiers and Boundary Making* (1916).

Holdich was created C.B. in 1894, C.I.E. in 1897, and K.C.I.E. and K.C.M.G. in 1902. He was an active member of the Royal Geographical Society, of which he was gold medallist in 1887 and president 1916–1918.

Holdich married in 1873 Ada Maria, daughter of Captain John Heyning Vanrenen, of the East India Company's service, and had two sons and two daughters, the elder son being Brigadier-General Harold Adrian Holdich. He died at Merrow, near Guildford, 2 November 1929.

[*The Times*, 4 November 1929; *Geographical Journal*, March 1930; Holdich's own writings, especially *Political Frontiers and Boundary Making*; private information.]

A. Hamilton Grant.

HOLIDAY, HENRY (1839–1927), painter and worker in stained glass, was born in London 17 June 1839, the eldest son of George Henry Holiday, teacher of classics and mathematics, by his wife, Climène Gerber, of Mulhouse, Alsace. He was educated at home, and in 1854 began his training as an artist at Leigh's School of Art, Newman Street. At the end of 1854, at the early age of fifteen and a half, he was admitted as a student to the Royal Academy Schools, and he contributed to the Academy exhibition of 1857 two pictures, 'Darlestone Bay, near Swanage' and 'Swanage, Dorsetshire'. Holiday soon became a close friend and associate of several of the leading pre-Raphaelites: his picture 'The Burgess of Calais', exhibited at the Academy in 1859 and now in the Guildhall Art Gallery, bears striking witness to the tendencies which he developed as a result. Holiday continued to practise painting for a long time, his best-known work probably being his 'Dante and Beatrice', first exhibited in 1883 at the Grosvenor Gallery and now in the Walker Art Gallery, Liverpool; the title is not to be confused with that of an earlier picture by him of Dante and Beatrice first meeting as children, exhibited at the Academy in 1861.

From 1863 onwards, Holiday was principally active as a designer of cartoons for stained glass, having been invited at the end of 1862 to become the successor of (Sir) Edward Burne-Jones at Messrs. James Powell & Sons' glass-works at Whitefriars, London. The stained glass executed under Holiday's direction constitutes a life's work of remarkable extent, and may be studied in various buildings not only all over England but on the continent of Europe and also in the United States. Among his chief productions may be mentioned the memorial window to Lord Frederick Cavendish set up in St. Margaret's, Westminster, by the House of Commons; windows in Salisbury Cathedral, Ormskirk church, Lancashire, and St. Saviour's, Southwark; and, of examples abroad, windows in the church of the Epiphany, Washington, St. Paul's church, Richmond, Virginia, St. Luke's Hospital, New York, and the Children's Hospital, Toronto.

Although he worked with an unflagging seriousness of purpose and possessed considerable mastery of his craft, Holiday nevertheless, as an artist, lacks life and originality, remaining essentially a minor figure, tinged by academism. His name, however, is of permanent historical importance in the annals of nineteenth-century glass-painting, and many valuable observations are contained in his book *Stained Glass as an Art* (1896). Holiday made experiments in various crafts and techniques, inventing a new form of enamel on metal in relief for the purpose of extending the use of the material to work on a large scale; he also produced a number of sculptures. He was a man of remarkably wide interests, which embraced mountain-climbing in England, music, science, social questions, female suffrage, and dress-reform; the last of these entailed the editorship of *Aglaia*, the journal of the Healthy and Artistic Dress Union. He accompanied the solar eclipse expedition of (Sir) Norman Lockyer [q.v.] to India in 1871, and was otherwise widely travelled. His *Reminiscences of my Life*, published in 1914, convey a vivid impression of his exceptional personality and undoubted gifts, even if his mind cannot be described as having been either profound or original.

Holiday died 15 April 1927 at his house at Hampstead, which had long been the centre of a wide circle of devoted friends. He married in 1864 Catherine (died 1924), daughter of the Rev. Thomas Raven, incumbent of Holy Trinity, Preston, and sister of the landscape-painter, John Samuel Raven [q.v.]. She was an accomplished embroideress and talented musician, who in particular did much pioneer work towards gaining appreciation in England for the music of Wagner. They had one daughter, the violinist Winifred Holiday.

[*The Times*, 16 April 1927; Henry Holiday, *Reminiscences of my Life*, 1914; Algernon Graves, *The Royal Academy of Arts, a complete dictionary of contributors and their works*, vol. iv, 1906.] T. Borenius.

HOLLAND, Sir THOMAS ERSKINE (1835–1926), jurist, was born at Brighton 17 July 1835, the eldest son of the Rev. Thomas Agar Holland [q.v.], poet, and rector of Poynings, Sussex, from 1846 to 1888, who was a grandson of Thomas Erskine, first Baron Erskine, lord chancellor [q.v.]. His mother was Madalena, daughter of Major Philip Stewart. He was educated at Brighton College from 1847—the year in which the school was opened—until 1853. In 1854 he matriculated at Balliol College, Oxford, but in the following year migrated to Magdalen College with a demyship. He obtained a second class in classical moderations in 1856 and a first class in *literae humaniores* in 1858. He was elected to a fellowship at Exeter College in 1859, and for a short time taught philosophy there. In 1860 he won the chancellor's prize for an English essay.

Holland soon turned from philosophy to law, and going to London, read in chambers with W. H. Butterworth, the special pleader, with G. De Morgan, the conveyancer, with H. T. Erskine, and with A. Kekewich (in equity). In 1863 he was called to the bar by Lincoln's Inn and joined the home circuit. After some years of practice at the bar, combined with journalism and lecturing, he was elected Vinerian reader in English law at Oxford in 1874, but later in the same year was elected to the Chichele chair of international law and diplomacy in succession to its first occupant, Mountague Bernard [q.v.]. In the following year he was elected to a fellowship at All Souls College, and held it until his death fifty-one years later. He resigned the Chichele chair in 1910, receiving the title of emeritus professor, but continued to live at Oxford, working at his subject almost to the end. He died at Oxford 24 May 1926, in his ninety-first year.

Holland won an immediate reputation in his subject by his inaugural lecture on the life and work of Alberico Gentili [q.v.], the Italian civilian who taught at Oxford in the reign of Elizabeth; he showed how much the work of Grotius owed to that of this hitherto neglected predecessor. The lecture led to a general revival of interest in Gentili, and in 1877 Holland published an edition of the text of Gentili's *De Jure Belli*. *The European Concert in the Eastern Question* appeared in 1885, and a volume of *Studies in International Law* in 1898. He rewrote for the Admiralty the official *Manual of Naval Prize Law* in 1888 and he prepared a handbook on the *Laws and Customs of War on Land* which was issued to the army in 1904.

From 1903 to 1905 Holland served on the royal commission on the supply of food and raw material in time of war, and in 1906 he was one of the British plenipotentiaries to the conference at Geneva at which the Geneva Convention of 1864, dealing with the sick and wounded in land warfare, was revised. He also collaborated actively for many years in the scientific work of the Institut de droit international, of which he became associate in 1875, member in 1878, and honorary member in 1925, and he presided over the session of that body which was held at Oxford in 1913. But it was as a vigorous and independent commentator on contemporary events of international legal interest that Holland became best known to the public. In a long series of letters to *The Times* (first reprinted, 1881–1909, in 1909, 3rd edition, 1881–1920, in 1921 under the title *Letters to 'The Times' on War and Neutrality*) he was in the habit of contributing to the formation of a sound public opinion by exposing the true issues of a complicated situation. In later life he returned to his early interest in the history of international law, and published editions of the *Jus et Judicium Feciale* of Richard Zouche [q.v.] in 1911, and of the *De Bello, de Represaliis, et de Duello* of Giovanni da Legnano in 1917. A volume of lectures on *International Law*, edited by T. A. Walker and W. L. Walker, was published posthumously in 1933.

It is, however, as the author of perhaps the most successful book on jurisprudence ever written that Holland's name is most familiar to many generations of law students. He first published *The Elements of Jurisprudence* in 1880, and he revised it for a thirteenth edition in 1924, when in his eighty-ninth year. It gained for him in 1894 the Swiney prize and silver cup. The book belongs to the school of English analytical jurisprudence founded by John Austin [q.v.], and attempts to construct 'a formal science of positive law' based on 'those comparatively few and simple ideas which underlie the infinite variety of legal rules'. It is free from the repetitions and inconsistencies which make Austin's own work, with all its merits, so wearisome to the reader, and is, indeed, probably in part responsible for the long-continued vitality of the Austinian tradition in English-speaking countries.

Both in its merits and in its defects the *Elements of Jurisprudence* is characteristic of all Holland's work. He wrote once of his own 'morbid hatred of disorder', and the phrase expresses, with humorous exaggeration, the salient quality of his work. It is always clear, vigorous, exact, and if its premisses be accepted its conclusions are generally irresistible. Its weakness is that the premisses are sometimes over-simplified, and the conclusions have a finality of which the subject-matter does not always admit. Moreover, Holland was not easily moved by argument or by the later researches of other students to modify a conclusion which he had once reached.

Throughout his Oxford life Holland was deeply interested in university business, and especially in the formal organization of the university, both past and present. He published a number of articles on the origins of the university, in the Oxford Historical Society's *Collectanea*, vol. ii (1890), in the *English Historical Review*, vol. vi (1891), and elsewhere. In 1884 he persuaded the university to reform its statute book by co-ordinating the recent legislation of the nineteenth century with the remnants of the Laudian code. He was assessor (sole judge) of the Chancellor's Court from 1876 to 1910, and during his tenure of the office secured a thorough reform of the then antiquated procedure of that tribunal. In current problems of university administration he hardly obtained the influence to which his learning and his industry entitled him. His natural conservatism and his disinclination to compromise even on matters which seemed unimportant to others, impaired his effectiveness in debate, and too often ranged him on the losing side.

To the end of his life Holland remained active and alert in body as well as mind. He was a great walker, and visited the Eggishorn every summer from the late 'sixties until 1925, except for the period of the European War. Behind a slightly formal manner he had a real kindliness of heart and a readiness to place the resources of his well-stored mind at the service of younger men.

Holland was one of the founders (1885) of, and a regular contributor to, the *Law Quarterly Review*. He became a K.C. in 1901, a bencher of his Inn in 1907, and was an original fellow of the British Academy. In addition to the degree of D.C.L. of Oxford University his academic honours included doctorates of Bologna, Glasgow, Dublin, and Brussels. He was knighted in 1917.

Holland was twice married: first, in 1871 to Louise Henriette (died 1891), daughter of Jean Delessert, of Passy, and by her had six sons, two of whom predeceased him, and one daughter; secondly, in 1895 to Ellen, daughter of David Edwardes, M.R.C.S., of Wimbledon, and widow of the Rev. Stephen Edwardes, fellow of Merton College, Oxford; there were no children of the second marriage.

A portrait of Holland by Hugh Goldwin Riviere was presented to him by friends at home and abroad in 1914, and is in the possession of the family.

[*The Times*, 25 May 1926; *Law Quarterly Review*, October 1926; Sir W. S. Holdsworth,

Sir Thomas Erskine Holland, 1835–1926, in *Proceedings* of the British Academy, vol. xii, 1926; T. E. Holland, *A Valedictory Retrospect*, 1910, and *The Hollands of Conway*, privately printed, 1915.] J. L. Brierly.

HOLME, CHARLES (1848–1923), founder and editor of *The Studio* magazine, was born 7 October 1848 at Derby, the younger son of George Holme, silk-manufacturer, by his wife, Anne Brentnall. Educated at a private school in Derby, he was put to his father's trade, but at about the age of twenty-three he went to Bradford and set up for himself in the woollen business. His sound commercial instinct brought him material success, and it was the extension of his business to the East which developed in him an absorbing interest in art. A lecture by Robert Barkley Shaw [q.v.], the Oriental traveller, at the Bradford Chamber of Commerce about 1873, led him to exchange Bradford goods against the products of Turkestan, and later of India, China, and Japan. He was profoundly struck by the perfection of Japanese craftsmanship. When he made a tour round the world in 1889 he spent some months in Japan, and two years later he became one of the founders of the Japan Society.

Meanwhile, another potent influence in his life had been that of William Morris, into whose Red House at Bexley Heath, Kent, Holme moved in 1889. It was not long after this that Holme began the work by which he will be remembered. In 1893, having retired from business a year earlier, he founded *The Studio*, a magazine of fine and applied art. In this his primary aim was not commercial, but the illustration and furtherance of good design. Holme had remarkable taste and prescience, and in his first issue he introduced to the public the works of two young men, then unknown—Aubrey Vincent Beardsley [q.v.] and Frank Brangwyn. *The Studio* (the first few numbers of which were produced in collaboration with Gleeson White) appeared at a time when photo-process engraving was opening up new possibilities in reproduction. A cardinal principle of Holme's artistic creed was that architecture and the applied arts are not to be regarded as intrinsically inferior to the fine arts—a salutary doctrine in an age when everyday objects were so often designed in the worst taste. *The Studio* soon attained a very wide circulation and influence at home and abroad. It set itself a very high standard of production, and Holme added lavishly illustrated special numbers, which were in effect books, and he became a respected and successful publisher. He continued to take an active part in this work until 1922, when ill-health compelled him to retire. He died at his house, Upton Grey, near Basingstoke, Hampshire, 14 March 1923.

Holme's special gift as an editor and publisher was his catholic and sensitive taste. To this he added courage, modesty, geniality, and the faculty for carrying on a business with dignity and humanity. He wrote little or nothing, and had no literary interests. He was content to exercise influence by choosing and illustrating works of art which he instinctively felt to be good.

Holme married in 1873 Clara, daughter of George Benton, brass-founder, of Birmingham, by whom he had one son and three daughters. The son, Geoffrey Holme, succeeded to the editorship of *The Studio*. An admirable portrait of Holme by P. A. de László, painted in 1908, is at present in the house of his widow.

[*The Studio*, January 1928 (portrait); private information.] H. B. Grimsditch.

HORNE, HENRY SINCLAIR, Baron Horne of Stirkoke, co. Caithness (1861–1929), general, the third son of Major James Horne, of Stirkoke, by his wife, Constance Mary, daughter of Edward Warner, of Cheltenham, was born at Stirkoke 19 February 1861. He was educated at Harrow and at the Royal Military Academy, Woolwich, from which, in May 1880, he received a commission in the Royal Artillery. He was at first posted to the garrison artillery, from which in 1883 he was transferred to the mounted branch, and after serving as adjutant of artillery brigades in both branches, he was promoted captain in 1888. In September 1890 he was appointed staff captain, Royal Artillery, at Meerut, and two years later became adjutant of Royal Horse Artillery at Kirkee. Returning to England in 1896 he was soon afterwards posted to 'J' battery, Royal Horse Artillery, with which he remained until he was promoted major in 1898.

On the outbreak of the South African War in 1899 Horne was given command of an ammunition column and landed in Natal on 15 November of that year, to be soon afterwards moved to Cape Colony in order to join the cavalry division under Major-General (Sir) John French [q.v.]. With the cavalry division Horne took part in the operations which resulted in the relief of Kimberley (15 February 1900), the occupation of Bloemfontein (13 March), and in the advance from Bloemfontein into the Transvaal. In May 1900 he was given command of 'R' battery, Royal Horse Artillery, which was attached to French's 3rd cavalry brigade, and with that battery he took part in the occupation of Johannesburg (31 May), the battle of Diamond Hill (11–12 June), and the operations in the Wittebergen, which resulted in the surrender of General M. Prinsloo (25–29 July). From that time until the end of 1901 Horne was employed with mounted columns in the Orange River Colony and Cape Colony, and from January 1902 he was in command of remount depots. For his services he was mentioned in dispatches and received the brevet of lieutenant-colonel and the queen's medal with five clasps, and the king's medal with two clasps.

After three years in charge of the artillery depot at Weedon, Horne was promoted regimental lieutenant-colonel in November 1905, and was given successively the command of field artillery and horse artillery brigades in Ireland. He was gazetted brevet-colonel in May 1906, and in the following September was appointed staff officer for horse and field artillery at Aldershot. In May 1912 he was appointed inspector of horse and field artillery with the rank of brigadier-general, and on the outbreak of the European War in August 1914 he proceeded to France as brigadier-general commanding the Royal Artillery, I Army Corps, under Sir Douglas (afterwards Earl) Haig [q.v.].

At the beginning of the retreat from Mons (24 August 1914) Horne was appointed by Haig to command his rear-guard. He rendered conspicuous service throughout the retreat, in the battle of the Marne (5–9 September), the battle of the Aisne (12–15 September), and in the first battle of Ypres (19 October–22 November). In October he was promoted major-general as a reward for distinguished service in the field, and at the end of the year he was made C.B. In January 1915 Horne was placed in command of the 2nd division of the I Corps, and he led it in the operations about Givenchy in March 1915, in the battle of Festubert (15–25 May), and in the battle of Loos (25 September–8 October). It was on his suggestion that as a result of experience gained at Festubert the system of command of the artillery was changed.

In November 1915 Horne was chosen by Lord Kitchener [q.v.] to accompany him to the Dardanelles, when the question of the evacuation of the Gallipoli peninsula was at issue. After the evacuation had been successfully carried out he was again employed by Lord Kitchener to devise a scheme for the defence of the Suez Canal, and when that task was completed he was given command in January 1916, with the temporary rank of lieutenant-general, of the new XV Corps in the northern sector of the Canal defences. In March 1916 the XV Corps was moved to France, where it joined the Fourth Army, commanded by Sir Henry (afterwards Lord) Rawlinson [q.v.], which was preparing for the battle of the Somme (1 July–30 September). The chief achievements of Horne's corps in that battle were the capture of Fricourt (2 July) and of Flers (15 September). In September he was created K.C.B., and after the capture of Flers he was promoted to the command of the First Army with the temporary rank of general.

As part of the campaign designed by General Nivelle, the commander-in-chief of the French armies, for the spring of 1917, the British army undertook the battle of Arras, in which the most important share, the assault on the Vimy ridge, fell to the First Army. In 1915 repeated attempts by French troops to capture the ridge had failed, and General Nivelle's staff was sceptical of a British success and openly critical of Horne's plans. Horne was also harassed at this critical time by the pain from a broken bone in his leg caused by a fall from his horse, but he triumphed over these difficulties and stuck to his plans, and the capture of the Vimy ridge (9–10 April), in which the Canadian Corps took the chief part, was the outstanding success won by the British army up to that time in the War. Owing to the failure of Nivelle's attack the operations on the Arras front had to be continued until well into May, several weeks beyond the period which had been proposed. Thereafter Haig began to transfer troops to his northern flank in preparation for the battles of Messines and Passchendaele, and the role of the First Army became one of attracting the attention of the Germans to itself with reduced effectives, a part which Horne skilfully played until October 1917, when the Canadian Corps was taken from him for the battle of Passchendaele.

The winter of 1917–1918 was devoted to preparations for meeting the great German attack expected in the spring. The brunt of the German effort fell on the armies further south, but on 28 March a heavy German attack was made on the Vimy ridge and successfully beaten off. On 9 April another German attack on the Lys front fell on the Portuguese divisions attached to Horne's army, just at the time when arrangements for the relief of those divisions had been completed. The Germans broke through, and the situation again became highly critical, but the resolute stand of the 55th division of the First Army at Givenchy saved the Vimy ridge, and Horne was the only British army commander who was not forced by the German offensive to move his headquarters to the rear.

After May 1918 the German efforts were directed against the French, and the First Army was given a breathing space in which to recover and prepare for attack in its turn. After Rawlinson's victory at Amiens on 8 August, the Germans began to withdraw from the great salient which they had created in the north in the spring, and towards the end of August the First Army began an advance which was to be continuous until the signing of the Armistice on 11 November. On 2 September Horne's army, in co-operation with the Third Army on its right, broke through the Drocourt-Quéant section of the Hindenburg line. This brilliant success was followed on 27 September by the forcing of the Canal du Nord. Then in swift succession Lens (3 October), Douai (17 October), and Valenciennes (2 November) were captured, and the advance of the First Army ended with the occupation of Mons two and a half hours before the Armistice became effective.

Horne was promoted substantive lieutenant-general in 1917, and substantive general in 1919. He was created K.C.M.G. in 1918 and G.C.B. in 1919. For his services in the War he received the thanks of both Houses of Parliament, was raised to the peerage as Baron Horne of Stirkoke, and given a grant of £30,000. He also received many foreign decorations, including the legion of honour. The university of Oxford conferred on him the honorary degree of D.C.L., the universities of Cambridge and of Edinburgh that of LL.D., and the borough of Northampton made him a freeman. In 1918 he was made colonel commandant of the Royal Artillery.

Soon after his return to England Horne was appointed general officer commanding-in-chief, Eastern command, in which capacity he was actively concerned with the problems of demobilization and of the reorganization of the army. In 1920 he was appointed aide-de-camp general to King George V. Refusing offers of governorships abroad, he retired from the army in May 1926, and in the same month he was appointed master gunner, St. James's Park. He interested himself actively in service charities, particularly in those of the Royal Artillery, the British Legion, and the National Association for the Employment of Soldiers, Sailors, and Airmen. He became governor and commandant of the Church Lads Brigade, and took a prominent part in the affairs of his county, Caithness, of which he was deputy lieutenant. In 1929 he was made colonel of the Highland Light Infantry, in which his father had served. He died suddenly while shooting on his estate at Stirkoke 14 August 1929, and was buried at Wick.

Horne married in 1897 Kate, daughter of George McCorquodale, of Newton-le-Willows, Lancashire, and Gladlys, Anglesey, and widow of William John Sinclair Blacklock. They had one daughter, and the peerage became extinct on his death.

There are portraits of Horne by J. H. Lander (*c.* 1908) and Oswald Birley (painted during the War) at Stirkoke House, at the Royal Artillery Mess, Woolwich, and at the Harrow School War Museum, both by Oswald Birley.

[Major-General Sir H. Uniacke in the *Journal* of the Royal Artillery, October 1929; Lieutenant-General Sir Hastings Anderson in the *Army Quarterly*, January 1930; Lord Horne, *Diaries of the South African War*, privately printed, 1900.] F. MAURICE.

HOSE, CHARLES (1863–1929), civil servant in Sarawak, ethnologist, and naturalist, was born at Willian, Hertfordshire, 12 October 1863, the son of the Rev. Thomas Charles Hose, perpetual curate of Little Wymondley, Hertfordshire, by his wife, Fanny, daughter of Thomas Goodfellow, of Hall O'Wood and Tunstall, Staffordshire. He was educated at Felsted School, and in 1882 matriculated at Jesus College, Cambridge. He did not take a degree, as he left Cambridge during his second year, having been offered, through the influence of his uncle, George Frederick Hose, bishop of Singapore, a cadetship in the Sarawak civil service, under the second raja, Sir Charles Anthony Johnson Brooke [q.v.]. Hose accepted the post with enthusiasm, as likely to fulfil his keenest aspirations. Leaving England in 1884, he reached Kuching, the capital of Sarawak, in April of that year, and his active association with the administration of that independent state lasted until his retirement from the service in 1907, by which time he had risen to the position of divisional resident and had been appointed a member of the supreme council and a judge of the supreme court of Sarawak (1904). His official connexion with Borneo did not cease entirely on his retirement, for he was appointed a member of the Sarawak State advisory council at Westminster (1919); and in 1909 he was sent on a special mission to Sarawak, with Dr. Erb, a Swiss geologist, in order to investigate the potentialities of the oil (petroleum) fields of the Miri district. From his earlier surveys he had felt confident of the oil-yielding capacity of these fields, and the renewed investigations amply justified his predictions.

During the period of his official administrative work, mainly in the Baram district, Hose held positions of much responsibility; he was appointed officer-in-charge in 1888 and resident (2nd class) in 1891, and resident (1st class) in 1904. The area was occupied by warlike natives, who had not as yet been brought under effective control. Raiding and head-hunting were still rife, and constant local feuds prevailed. Interference by an intrusive government was not welcomed and was frequently opposed with vigour. Hose was the right man to deal with the situation. By his tact, fairness, and sympathetic understanding of their customs he succeeded in establishing friendly relations with the natives. His firmness, constancy, and determination impressed them no less than his physical powers, pluck, and endurance. As resident, he had from time to time to organize punitive expeditions and penetrate far into disturbed areas, largely unexplored; but the expeditions, though successful, were usually carried through without bloodshed, and many of the more turbulent chiefs became his loyal friends. Head-hunting was gradually suppressed and a state of peace was inaugurated, with recognition of the beneficent intentions of the raja's administration. When Hose retired from the service in 1907, he left the areas of his administration settled and peaceful with a developing trade. A visit which he paid in 1920 to the scenes of his official labours, accompanied by his wife and children, became a veritable triumphal progress up the Baram river, when he was welcomed by hosts of natives, many of whom had travelled hundreds of miles to greet their old administrator.

In the course of his official work in Sarawak, Hose was able to pursue his lifelong hobby, natural history, a keen taste for which he had inherited from his father. In addition to his general field observations, he enriched zoological and botanical records with many new species and subspecies, and, at least, three new genera. The British national collections benefited greatly from his enthusiasm and success as a scientific collector. Early in his period of residence in Borneo he became interested in the perplexing problem of the cause of the dreaded disease, beriberi, which was very prevalent in Malaysia and Japan, and frequently fatal. He studied closely the habits of the natives, paying special attention to their diet and to the effects of rice upon its consumers under varying conditions. He noted the effects produced by freshly husked home-grown rice, and by the milled imported rice, the latter being liable to become mouldy in the trade bags, and infected by a minute fungoid growth; and he ascertained that there was a far higher incidence of the disease among consumers of the imported cereal. Hose himself contracted the disease and recovered from it, and his personal experience helped to confirm his views. His researches, together with those of other investigators, finally established the fact that the principal cause was to be found in the milled or 'polished' rice, and that the complete elimination of the husk, or pericarp, which was found to contain important vitamins, was the prime causative factor in the genesis of beriberi.

Most important of all Hose's scientific works was ethnographical research among the tribes of Sarawak. He made full use of his opportunities. Owing to his success in winning the confidence of the natives to an unusual extent, he gained a valuable knowledge of their ethnological relationships and culture. No one has done more for the study of Bornean anthropology; and his researches have proved not only of value to ethnological science, but have a practical bearing upon the administration of native affairs. The knowledge which Hose acquired at first hand was freely placed at the disposal of others. Much of the material contained in H. L. Roth's *The Natives of Sarawak and British North Borneo* (1896), and W. H. Furness's *The Home-Life of Borneo Head-Hunters, its Festivals and Folk-lore* (1902), was derived from Hose; while the assistance which he gave to the Cambridge Anthropological expedition in 1898–1899 resulted in his co-operating with (Professor) William M'Dougall in the production of a valuable monograph upon *The Pagan Tribes of Borneo* (1912), a standard work of high merit. Early training in surveying equipped Hose for another noteworthy achievement, namely the making of the first reliable map of the whole of Sarawak (scale, 1/500,000), showing, besides the geographical features, the distribution of the tribes. Much of the area had previously been unsurveyed.

Hose's varied activities brought him recognition from many different sources. He received the order of the White Falcon of Saxe-Weimar for his zoological researches (1890), the order of merit of the Netherlands government (1893), and the order of the Prussian crown (1896), and he was elected officier de l'Académie Française (1898). For his survey work he was awarded the Cuthbert Peek grant by the Royal Geographical Society in 1893. His researches into the cause of beriberi were recognized by the award of the Emperor's cup by the Japanese government in 1909. Cambridge University conferred on him the honorary degree of Sc.D. in 1900, and he was elected an honorary fellow of Jesus College, Cambridge, in 1926. He was also made a freeman of the City of London in 1929.

Hose married in 1905 Emilie Ellen, daughter of John Peter Ravn, and had one son and one daughter. He died, after an operation, in a nursing-home at South Croydon 14 November 1929. A full list of his published works is given in an appendix to his book, *Fifty Years of Romance and Research* (1927). To that list should be added two other books, *Natural Man. A record from Borneo* (1926) and *The Field-Book of a Jungle Wallah* (1929).

[*The Times*, 15 November 1929; Charles Hose, *Fifty Years of Romance and Research*, 1927.] H. Balfour.

HOSIE, Sir ALEXANDER (1853–1925), diplomatist and Chinese explorer, was born at Inverurie, Aberdeenshire, 16 January 1853, the elder son and second child of Alexander Hosie, by his wife, Jean, daughter of James Anderson. He came of farmer stock on both parents' sides. His father's farm did not prosper, and the family moved to Aberdeen, where the elder Alexander Hosie was accidentally killed when his elder son was sixteen years old. Together with his mother, to whom he was devoted, young Hosie set himself to keep the household and to bring up his younger brother. He was educated at Old Aberdeen grammar school and at King's College, Aberdeen. He worked his way through the university by taking pupils, graduated in 1872, and was appointed sub-librarian of the university. His eyes, however, were turned to the East. In 1876 he joined the Chinese consular service, and sailed for China in company with a young man who was to be his lifelong friend and future chief, Sir John Newell Jordan [q.v.].

Hosie's first post, after he had finished his student interpretership at Peking, was in Shanghai, where he met General Gordon and was given the task of tabulating for the official archives his numerous memoranda and suggestions to the legation on British policy in China. At that time Edward Colborne Baber [q.v.] was the chief consular traveller of innermost China; and at his suggestion Hosie was sent in 1882 on special service to Chungking. Isolated and lonely in this far western province of Szechwan, he soon realized the need, and the opportunity, of devoting himself to some absorbing preoccupation. At much risk, he set out on a series of travels in the interior, making full notes as he journeyed of the geography and products of the country. This resulted in his first book, *Three Years in Western China* (1889), which passed through two editions. In it he described for the first time the trade and showed the potentialities of those little-known regions. He next saw service in Canton, Wenchow, Chefoo, Amoy, Tamsui, Wuhu, and in 1894 went north to take charge of the consulate at Newchwang during the difficult days of the Chinese-Japanese War. In 1897 he was sent south to Pagoda Anchorage and then Wuchow, a port the trade of which was much harassed by river-pirates. After the Boxer Rising (1900), during which he was on home-leave, he went north to take charge again at Newchwang. He travelled extensively in the Three Provinces of Manchuria, and in 1901 produced his book *Manchuria: Its People, Resources, and Recent History*, which also passed through two editions. His official duties were concerned with the defence of British trade in Manchuria against the diplomatic and military inroads on Chinese sovereignty of Russia and Japan; but he was always proud that he on one occasion received the thanks of the Chinese government for his effective defence of the Chinese maritime customs on behalf of China, at a time when Chinese officials had fled before Japanese troops.

In 1903 Hosie was appointed first consul-general at Chengtu in Szechwan. The boat which took him up the Yangtsze-kiang was wrecked, he narrowly escaped with his life, many of his goods were lost, and his books had ten days' soaking at the bottom of the river. He used his term at Chengtu to compile an invaluable 'white paper' on the products of the province, which in 1922 he republished in book form as *Szechwan: Its Industries and Resources*. He journeyed to the verge of the forbidden land of Tibet, and brought to official notice the boundary-stone which was to figure largely in the tripartite boundary *pourparlers* at Darjeeling in 1914. From 1908 to 1912 Hosie was given the rank of consul-general at Tientsin, but did not proceed to that post; and from 1905 to 1909 was retained as acting commercial attaché to the legation at Peking, in which post he did much pioneer work on behalf of trade.

In 1908 the government of India offered to stop the export of opium to China *pari passu* with the abandonment by China of the cultivation of the opium poppy. Hosie was appointed commissioner to arrange proceedings, and in 1909 was British delegate at the Shanghai International Opium Commission, where the Chinese delegates admitted that 'the annual production of opium in China was eight (or more) times the quantity annually imported from India'. This led to his being sent in the following year, at the request of the Indian government, to visit the chief opium-growing provinces of China in order to discover whether the Chinese were fulfilling their part of the bargain. During these long overland journeys he underwent many hardships, made daily copious notes in his diary, and published an account in his book, *On the Trail of the Opium Poppy* (2 vols., 1914), which included much information on agricultural and other economic products. He found that certain provinces, notably Shansi and Szechwan, had signally succeeded in their task, but others still lagged behind. It may be added that since 1913 India has ceased to export opium to China.

Hosie retired in 1912, having travelled in each of the twenty-two provinces of China, except Sinkiang. He settled at Sandown, Isle of Wight, where he was active in public affairs. In 1919 he revisited China on a trade commission, and was retained as special attaché in Peking till early in 1920. In 1922, as a result of his many hardships, his right foot was amputated. Aided by his second wife, herself a writer on China, he edited Philips's *Commercial Map of China*, published in 1922, the authoritative economic map of China, a work of great accuracy and research.

Tall, broad-shouldered, deep-chested, Hosie was a man of striking appearance and personality. Gifted with extraordinary powers of observation, unfailing patience and industry, he was *facile princeps* in his knowledge and presentation of the possibilities of Chinese trade, and his trade reports are models of their kind. He contributed numerous articles to learned journals. Interested in botany, he sent thousands of specimens to Kew, Hongkong, and Singapore especially from Szechwan. About 1905 or 1906 the Kew authorities requested Sir Ernest Satow, then minister in Peking, that his services might be specially requisitioned for this work, and they named an order, *Ormosia Hosiei*, after him. He lectured in 1886 before the Royal Geographical Society; in 1885 he had been proposed as the recipient of its medal, which was, however, awarded to H. M. Stanley, who found Dr. Livingstone in that year. He was knighted in 1907. In 1913 Aberdeen University conferred on him the honorary degree of LL.D.

Hosie was twice married: first, in 1887 to Florence (died 1907), daughter of John Lindsay, corn factor, of Aberdeen; secondly, in 1913 to Dorothea, daughter of the Rev. William Edward Soothill, missionary first of the United Methodist Church at Wenchow, then president of the Government University at Shansi, and afterwards professor of Chinese at Oxford University. One son was born of the first marriage. Hosie died at Sandown 10 March 1925.

[Hosie's published works; private information; personal knowledge.] W. E. Soothill.

HOWARD, Sir EBENEZER (1850–1928), originator of the garden city movement and founder of Letchworth and Welwyn garden cities, was born at 62 Fore Street in the City of London 29 January 1850, the third child and only son of Ebenezer Howard, confectioner, who owned several shops in and near the City, by his wife, Ann Tow, of Colsterworth, Lincolnshire. He was educated from the age of four to the age of fifteen at private boarding schools, first at Sudbury, Suffolk, then at Cheshunt, Hertfordshire, and finally at Ipswich. After leaving school, he earned his living as a clerk in the City of London, obtaining a varied experience in the offices of a firm of stockbrokers, a firm of merchants, and two firms of solicitors. He taught himself shorthand in his spare time. He was employed for a short period as private secretary by Dr. Joseph Parker [q.v.], the well-known Congregationalist preacher (afterwards of the City Temple, Holborn), whose powerful personality exercised a considerable influence on Howard.

In 1872, at the age of twenty-two, Howard sailed for New York. After spending a few months working on a farm in Howard county, Nebraska, he went to Chicago and joined the staff of the official stenographers to the Law Courts. The religious outlook of the society in which he found himself, the outcome of the teaching of R. W. Emerson, J. R. Lowell, Walt Whitman, and other unprofessional religious teachers, had great influence on his life, helping him greatly, to quote his own words, 'to a clear perception that all values, to be rightly estimated, must be assessed mainly by their influence on the spiritual elements of our nature: thus only can material conditions be widely and permanently improved'.

In 1877 Howard returned to England and obtained employment as a shorthand writer from Gurney & Sons, the official reporters to the Houses of Parliament: in addition to his work in parliament, he carried on a business of his own as shorthand writer in the Law Courts. A few years later he became a partner of William Treadwell, with an office near the Law Courts, and upon the termination of that partnership he continued to carry on the business and office until his retirement in 1920.

In 1898 Howard read Edward Bellamy's *Looking Backward*, which had been published in America ten years previously. This book describes the experiences of a Bostonian who falls into a trance and wakes up in the year 2000 to find the United States transformed into an ideal community under a system of state socialism. It made a strong appeal to Howard, and he determined to take such part as he could in helping to bring into being a new civilization, based on service to the community, and not on self-interest. As a first step he wrote *Tomorrow. A Peaceful Path to Real Reform*. Parts of this book he circulated among friends, and he lectured about it, chiefly in London. But it was only with the help of £50 given him by a friend that he was able to publish it in October 1898. The book was republished in 1902 under the title *Garden Cities of Tomorrow*.

The aim which Howard set before himself was to find a remedy, on the one hand for the overcrowding and unhealthy conditions which were produced by the excessive growth of large cities, and on the other hand for the depopulation of the country-side. Believing access to the country-side and to nature to be necessary for the full development of man's moral and spiritual qualities, he regarded the conditions under which large sections of the British nation were living in the towns as no less harmful to their moral and spiritual life than it undoubtedly was to their physique. He saw that the evils arising from the existing system of urban development were due to such development being left to the unregulated enterprise of landowners working for private profit. He proposed to remedy this, not by legislating against landowners, but by the building of new towns, not for the profit of individuals, but in the interest of their inhabitants. Such towns, which were to be both residential and industrial, were to be well planned, of limited size, and surrounded by a rural belt, so as to place within reach of the inhabitants the advantages alike of a civilized town life and of access to and knowledge of the country and of nature. The population of the rural belt would also benefit by having a market for their produce close to their farms and easy access to the advantages of the town. He called the towns which he proposed to create 'garden cities', not so much on account of their open development, as because, being surrounded by a rural belt, each town would be set in a garden.

An essential part of Howard's scheme was that the town should directly or indirectly own the land on which it was situate. He suggested that trustees should purchase the land with borrowed money, and should hold it in trust in the first place to pay interest on and fulfil the other obligations of the loans, and, subject thereto, in trust for the community. He believed that the value of the land would rapidly increase, and at an early date would produce a surplus applicable to purposes beneficial to the town. In order that the town should obtain the benefit of the increased value, he proposed that the land should be leased, and that ground rents should be revised at short intervals.

After publishing his book, Howard set to work to obtain backing in order to carry his proposals into effect. In 1899 he formed the Garden City Association. Although a poor man, possessing neither social nor financial influence, he had by 1903 obtained enough support to form a company with the object of creating a garden city and with sufficient capital to buy and to begin the development of a large estate at Letchworth in Hertfordshire. While some of his proposals were modified to meet practical requirements, his general principles were maintained. The principle that the town should directly or indirectly own the land was adopted in a modified form in the provision that the dividends on the shares of the developing company are limited to a cumulative dividend not exceeding 5 per cent. per annum and that any surplus is applicable to purposes of benefit to the town. Although its growth was less rapid than Howard anticipated, Letchworth developed into a thriving residential and industrial town with a population exceeding in 1934 15,000 persons. Since the year 1923 the company has paid each year the full authorized dividend on its shares, but a considerable sum is still due for arrears of dividend accruing in the early years of the company.

In 1919 Howard, learning that an estate at Welwyn, also in Hertfordshire, which he had noted as a suitable site for a garden city, was about to be put up to auction, hastily collected sufficient money from a few friends to pay the deposit, attended the sale, and bought the property. A company was formed to take over the estate and to develop it as a garden city. In twelve years Welwyn Garden City was transformed from a purely agricultural estate into a flourishing town of nearly 10,000 inhabitants.

A further stage in the garden city movement was reached when the corporation of the city of Manchester decided to develop the Wytenshawe estate as a satellite town in accordance with Howard's principles. Wytenshawe differs from Letchworth and Welwyn Garden City in two important respects. It is financed and managed by a powerful city corporation and not by a company; and its cottages are being provided by the city corporation as part of its housing operations for the people of Manchester. Although active development was begun in 1931 only, the population in 1934 exceeded 20,000.

Garden Cities of Tomorrow was translated into many languages, and societies for the purpose of encouraging the formation of garden cities were established in many countries in Europe and in the United States of America. In 1909 the International Garden Cities and Town Planning Association was formed with Howard as president, a position which he held until his death. So-called garden cities have been built in many countries. Generally speaking, they consist of specially planned suburbs of existing towns, which have few of the characteristics of Howard's garden city, except open development. The town of Radburn, New Jersey, however, is being built definitely in accordance with Howard's principles, with the interesting modification that it is specially planned to minimize the danger and inconvenience arising from motor traffic.

After the European War of 1914–1918, London and other great cities grew with unprecedented rapidity, and the objections which Howard urged against the indefinite growth of large cities became increasingly apparent. Successive governments consequently considered the possibility of guiding some of the development into garden cities. Provisions were inserted in the Housing (Additional Powers) Act (1919) and in subsequent housing and town planning Acts in order to facilitate the establishment and development of garden cities, and a departmental committee appointed by the minister of health is now (1934) sitting to consider whether further measures can or should be taken for the purpose of encouraging the establishment of garden cities or satellite towns.

Howard's influence was not limited to the formation of garden cities: it has had important effects on the more general problem of town planning. His teaching drew people's attention to the haphazard growth of existing towns, and provided a stimulus to the increasing demand that all urban development should be planned. Letchworth and Welwyn Garden City demonstrated the benefits obtainable from planning, and it was obvious that many of their features could be adopted with advantage in the new development of existing towns. Hence Howard's influence can be traced in many town planning schemes, both at home and abroad. In particular, the spacious lay-out and the character of the buildings of many municipal cottage estates erected since the War derived their inspiration from Letchworth.

It is given to few idealists to see during their lifetime such practical results from their ideas as Howard did. His ultimate object, however, the provision of a new form of urban development, which would put a stop to and take the place of the continuous growth of large cities, has not yet been attained. This failure has been due in the main to two difficulties, neither of which Howard foresaw: the first is that of attracting residents and industries to an entirely new town; the second is that of financing the development of a garden city during its early stages. The example of the Manchester corporation in developing Wytenshawe points to a more hopeful method than those adopted in the case of Letchworth and Welwyn Garden City; but it is improbable that the local authorities of many large cities will accept the responsibility of establishing satellite towns.

Howard remained a poor man all his life. The fees which he received from his directorships of the Letchworth and Welwyn schemes were inconsiderable, and he continued until the age of seventy to practise his profession of shorthand writer in order to meet the modest needs of himself and his family. Money presented little attraction to him, and he was singularly free from personal ambition or self-seeking. Being absolutely convinced of the rightness of his ideas, he was animated by an ardent enthusiasm. He had a remarkable gift of inspiring other people: his zeal infected them and his transparent honesty of purpose gave them complete confidence. He was neither a professional town-planner nor a financier, but he convinced town-planners and financiers that his ideas were practical, and had the modesty and good sense to accept their advice when carrying his ideas into practice. His public work and his profession allowed him little leisure for other interests. As a young man he spent much time in inventing improvements to the typewriting machine, and during the last years of his life he was engaged in constructing a typewriter for shorthand writing. The international side of his work brought him into touch with many foreigners. This led him to study Esperanto, in which he became proficient. As a young man he enjoyed watching cricket at Kennington Oval. In later life he was a fair chess player.

In recognition of his public services Howard was made O.B.E. in 1924 and was knighted in 1927. He married twice: first, in 1879 Elizabeth Ann (died 1904), daughter of Thomas Bills, of Nuneaton, by whom he had one son and three daughters; she helped him indefatigably in his early schemes; secondly, in 1907 Edith Annie, daughter of William Knight Hayward, of Highfield House, Wellingore, Lincoln, who survived him. He died 1 May 1928 at his home in Welwyn Garden City. His height was about 5 feet 5 inches, his hair and complexion fair, and his eyes blue and animated. A good portrait of him by Spencer Pryse belonging to Lady Howard is deposited on loan at the Letchworth Museum.

[*The Times*, 2 May 1928; Dugald Macfadyen, *Sir Ebenezer Howard and the Town Planning Movement*, 1933; private information; personal knowledge.]

E. Bonham Carter.

HUDSON, Sir ROBERT ARUNDELL (1864–1927), political organizer, was born at Lapworth, Warwickshire, 30 August 1864, the eldest son of Robert Hudson, of Lapworth, by his wife, Jessie, daughter of John Kynoch, of Peterhead. He was a delicate boy, and his education at Ludlow grammar school was cut short at the age of sixteen, when he was sent to South Africa for his health. A year later (1881) he was put to an office in Birmingham, where it is supposed that he came under the spell of Bright and Chamberlain. He obtained at eighteen a post in the National Liberal Federation, which had been founded in Birmingham five years earlier. Hudson quickly attracted the notice of the secretary, Francis Schnadhorst [q.v.], and was appointed assistant secretary in 1886, in which year, as a result of the defection of Chamberlain, and therefore of Birmingham, on the Home Rule question, the offices of the Federation were transferred to London. Here Hudson was intimately associated with the left-wing liberals, notably Sir Arthur H. D. Acland [q.v.], who in 1892 became vice-president of the Committee of Council on Education, Thomas Edward Ellis, later chief whip, and Mr. J. A. Spender, afterwards editor of the *Westminster Gazette*. Hudson had a share with these men in planning the social legislation advocated (1891) in the Newcastle 'programme'. Succeeding Schnadhorst in 1893 he became secretary both of the Federation and of the Liberal Central Association. These institutions had offices under one roof in Parliament Street, and their joint-secretary was the link between the confidential organization of the parliamentary party and the autonomous machine which represented the liberalism of the constituencies. In this capacity Hudson was influential in guiding the party through the many troubles of the next twelve years. His chief coadjutors were Herbert (afterwards Viscount) Gladstone [q.v.], who became chief whip in 1899, and successive presidents of the federation, Robert Spence Watson [q.v.], and Augustine Birrell. Although himself a strong churchman, he came to be regarded as keeper of the nonconformist conscience. After the liberal triumph of 1906 the labour of years was recognized; Hudson was hailed as the 'organizer of victory', and was knighted. The liberal organization maintained its efficiency in power, as the two elections of 1910 showed.

In 1914 Hudson offered his services to the Red Cross, and became chairman of the joint finance committee of the British Red Cross Society and the Order of St. John of Jerusalem. This brought him into co-operation with Lord Northcliffe [q.v.], and made him responsible for *The Times* fund for the British Red Cross, and so ultimately for the collection and administration of nearly £17,000,000 subscribed to relieve the sick and wounded. In 1916 he was offered high office by Mr. Lloyd George, an offer which he at once refused. In 1918 he was given the G.B.E. and the legion of honour.

On returning to party politics in 1919 Hudson continued to act with the independent liberals under Mr. Asquith; but not even he could make bricks without straw, and in 1927 he resigned.

Both in his political work before the War, and in his war-work Hudson's success was complete. In 1906 it was officially declared that in twenty-five years of political work he had made 'countless friends and no enemies'. For the Red Cross he earned the reputation of an irresistible beggar and an impeccable administrator. He was a man of great energy and practical ability. One of the secrets of his political success was his extraordinary knowledge of the persons and local conditions in every constituency. An acute observer wrote that he had 'more common sense and a shrewder judgement of men than any one I ever met'. But by general consent the greatness of his achievement was due less to his intellectual powers than to his qualities of character; to a rare union of strength and sweetness, which found expression in his keen, hard features, lit up by an unforgettable smile. He was a man of varied interests; religion, philanthropy, sport, travel, and society all had a share in his time. The number of his friends and acquaintance was enormous. But it did not seem possible to exhaust his sympathy or his inventive kindliness.

Hudson was twice married: first, in 1889 to Ada (died 1895), daughter of Henry Hammerton, of Coventry, by whom he had one daughter; secondly, in 1923 to Mary Elizabeth, widow of Viscount Northcliffe, who survived him without issue. He died in London 25 November 1927.

[J. A. Spender, *Sir Robert Hudson, a Memoir*, 1930; personal knowledge.]

R. W. Chapman.

HUDSON, WILLIAM HENRY (1841–1922), naturalist and writer, was born 4 August 1841 at Quilmes, ten miles from Buenos Aires. His paternal grandfather came from Clyst Hydon, Devonshire. He was the third son in the family of six children of Daniel Hudson, who was born at Marblehead, Massachusetts, about 1804, by his wife, Catherine Kemble, of Maine, U.S.A., a descendant of one of the pilgrim fathers. Daniel Hudson, being threatened with tuberculosis, migrated with his wife to the Argentine. William Henry Hudson was brought up on the farms and ranches of the Rio de la Plata. His schooling was haphazard. In his own words, he 'ran wild in a wild land'. His father was a generous and hospitable man, but unbusiness-like and, in the choice of tutors for his children, limited by the conditions of the country to a very narrow field. A first tutor was dismissed owing to his violent temper; a second tutor was ignorant and idle; a third tutor was a clever ne'er-do-well. Hudson was allowed to ride his own pony at will when he was six years old and to spend hour after hour watching the bird life of the great plains. He grew up a strong boy; but his career was entirely changed at the end of his fifteenth year by an attack of typhus fever after a holiday spent in Buenos Aires. Before he had fully recovered from this attack he caught rheumatic fever. His heart was affected. He could do no active work, and was told by doctors that his case was hopeless. His physical weakness, and the passivity of his life in surroundings where nearly every one was engaged in hard outdoor work, affected a mind already filled with the exaggerated consciousness and fear of death common to many men of great artistic sensibility and love of external nature. He read a great deal, and, before he was twenty-one, endangered his sight by overstrain. His first apprehension of the Darwinian theory of natural selection, which was supported by his own acute observation, left a lasting and, in a sense, a saddening impression upon his mind. After some years of wandering from place to place in South America, he went to England in 1869, and never saw the pampas again. One of the reasons which kept him from going back to his home in later life was his belief that the increase of immigration, especially the immigration of Italians, had been destructive of the bird life which he had studied with such care and passion.

Hudson lived in London for some years in poverty and loneliness. For a time he was secretary to Chester Waters, an archaeologist who was often without money to pay an assistant. In 1876 he married Emily Wingrave (died 1921), a woman some fifteen years older than himself. His wife kept a boarding-house at 11 Leinster Square until 1884, when the house failed. The Hudsons then moved to another boarding-house in Southwick Crescent. In 1886, after a second failure, they gave up boarding-house keeping, and lived in lodgings in Ravenscourt Park. Finally they settled at 40 St. Luke's Road, Westbourne Park, in a house left to Mrs. Hudson by her sister. This period was one of continual worry over the needs of existence, with little or no chance of leading the kind of life for which Hudson's temperament was suited. A description given of him about the year 1880 shows a man peculiarly unfitted for the drabness of London boarding-houses. He was six feet three inches in height, broad-shouldered, of great muscular strength, though sallow in complexion and with a slight stoop of the head. His eyes were hazel in colour, keen and deeply set, under a heavily ridged brow and well-marked eyebrows.

During these years Hudson wrote a great deal, but he did not find a wide public. One of his best books, *The Purple Land that England Lost: Travels and Adventures in the Bandu Oriental*, was published in two volumes in 1885. His first book on bird life was an *Argentine Ornithology*, written in collaboration with Dr. P. L. Sclater, and published in two volumes in 1888–1889. In 1887 Hudson published anonymously his Utopian romance, *A Crystal Age*. This book, like Richard Jefferies's *After London* and William Morris's *News from Nowhere*, was a reaction against the dreary and unsatisfying life of a great city. Jefferies was almost savagely content to see the destruction of the ugly houses and the return of the trees; Morris soon left his socialist propaganda to take delight in a dream of untroubled summer; but Hudson followed a curious speculation suggested by his scientific reading and observation, and took as the theme of his book a belief that there could be no rest or peace in human society until the sexual impulse had burned itself out over a long period of time. The book attracted little attention at the time, and has received little notice since.

The first of Hudson's works to bring him into prominence was *The Naturalist in La Plata* (1892). This book, which was praised by Alfred Russel Wallace and other well-known naturalists, was written a year before Hudson's first essays on bird life in England, *Birds in a Village* (1893). Thenceforward his books had an increasing sale; but the demand for them was still comparatively small. As late as 1900 a member of parliament (probably Sir Edward Grey, afterwards Lord Grey of Fallodon), finding that Hudson had not enough money to allow him to travel even in his own frugal way over the wild country in the south and west of England, suggested to Mr. Balfour that Hudson might be given a civil list pension. A pension of £150 a year was awarded him in 1901. Thenceforward Hudson was able to leave London for long periods and to write the series of books and articles on birds and the descriptions of country life which followed in rapid succession from 1902 until his death. Mr. Edward Garnett, whom Hudson met in 1901, also helped a great deal towards making his work known. There was a break in Hudson's writing about 1910 owing to a return of heart trouble, and in 1911 owing to the long illness of his wife. In 1918, during the European War, while he was being nursed in a convent hospital at Brighton, Hudson wrote what is probably his best and certainly his most interesting work, *Far Away and Long Ago: a history of my early childhood*. Hudson's own view was that the interest of the book lay only in its 'feeling for nature and wild life, and *that* only appeals to those who have it in them, in whom it is a passion and more to them than interest in human character and affairs'.

After 1918 there was a continuous decline in Hudson's strength, although he went on writing books and articles. The War had perhaps less effect upon him than upon most men of his sensitiveness. His life and interests were entirely remote from politics. A sudden reversion to violence was neither perplexing nor numbing to a man whose childhood had been spent among men quick to use the knife in moments of anger, and among stories of recent South American warfare. Hudson's own philosophy of life was based upon observation of the animal world, and took account of the biological importance of conflict and even of fear. He notices, for example, the part played by awareness of danger in keeping birds healthy and alert. He was too much absorbed by the external world to understand that his view of war as a natural purge and purification did not apply to the conditions of a modern European battle-field.

Hudson described himself as 'a naturalist in the old, original sense of the word, one who is mainly concerned with the "life and conversation of animals"'. He wrote a great deal; his collected works (published in 1923) fill twenty-five volumes, and he was a quick and frequent letter-writer. In later life he destroyed as many of his letters as he could find. The greater part of his writings deal with animal life, and particularly with the life of birds; he was hardly less interested in snakes. He did not care overmuch for domestic animals. He had lived in a country where dogs ran wild, and where horses were taken for granted as among the necessaries of life. His eyes and ears were too sharp for him to miss anything which came within his view or hearing. His curiosity was unspoiled by premature bookishness, and kept to the end a certain naïve and child-like quality. Hudson's experience of the natural life of two widely different countries gave him unusual opportunities for comparison, although in other respects his experience was limited. He could describe natural scenery with great vividness; but he knew little of mountains or great woods; and while he wrote of the sea in a business-like way, it remained to him literally the 'gannet's home', never the most moving sight in the world.

Hudson's stories of romance and adventure fill several volumes. They were written at different periods of his life, but their theme shows little variation. For the most part they are nature stories in which human figures appear. The women are more living than the men because Hudson himself was at his best in describing the wisdom of instinct or the charm of physical beauty. The plots are always simple, and in nearly every case belong to the imaginative history of his South American life. There is a certain Spanish influence in his work, particularly in the earlier romances. Hudson had a low opinion of his own tales; he wrote of *Green Mansions* (1904): 'the story doesn't move—it simmers placidly away.' A few unsuccessful experiments in verse, and one three-volume novel, *Fan* (1892), may be ignored in an estimate of his work.

Hudson's style is simple and direct, though at times a little clumsy. One of his critics has said that he 'wrote like a peasant'. Another critic has blamed the 'dead level' of his work; a third is nearer to the mark in pointing out that he wrote 'always like a provincial, without regard for the fashion of his time'. How, then, is his popularity, long in coming, but very wide in his last years, to be explained? It may be said that, while the times were favourable in 1900 for Hudson's nature books, the public was unprepared for them twenty years earlier. By 1900 the great cities, especially London, had increased enormously in size. Access to the country was becoming yearly more difficult for the large middle-class public which formed the bulk of Hudson's readers; the motor-car had not yet made 'unspoiled' and sparsely inhabited districts easily accessible. On the other hand, the changes in the educational system had awakened in town-bred people a new interest in nature and in a natural life from which they seemed to be irrecoverably cut off save for a few weeks of holiday in the year. After 1900 a turn in literary fashion and the beginning of the revolt against reason which was to develop in strength twenty years later, helped the popularity of Hudson's romances and of his studies of the life and thought of country folk. The background of Hudson's early life, and the setting of his stories were so very different from the environment of most professional literary men that Hudson was able without effort to 'add strangeness to beauty' in his work.

These factors gave Hudson the success which never came to him in the different popular moods of the eighteen-eighties; they would not have been enough if he had himself not been a man of strong imaginative power as well as a talented observer of bird and animal life. The best appreciation of Hudson's peculiar gifts has been made by Lord Grey of Fallodon in a preface (in the collected edition of Hudson's works) to *Dead Man's Plack* (first published 1920). Grey mentions Hudson's fine taste in reading and great literary knowledge, and notices his 'gift for pure observation . . . the power of being moved to think and feel, without any desire to interfere'. Hudson 'belonged to no class and to no one country'. He was 'a man of high culture, but people of little culture felt no reserve with him'. Foreigners would not notice in talk with him any of the barriers of nationality. 'This absence of class feeling, political prejudice, national traditions, gave him an absolute freedom of spirit and detachment', qualities rarely combined with great sensitiveness and receptivity. To this analysis must be added Hudson's almost mystical sense of natural beauty.

No philosophical terms actually fit Hudson's view of the world, since his philosophy was not worked out in logical phrases or the language of the schools. He used the word animism to describe the intensity of his love of the visible world. He knew that he was more sensitive than most men to the many colours and forms of life, although he was wise enough to realize that the difference between himself and others was one of degree rather than of kind. He hated cruelty, and disliked 'sport' as much as he disliked 'specimen-collectors', but there was nothing of the pathetic fallacy about his attitude towards the natural world. Hudson, who read Fabre with pleasure, thought Maeterlinck unreal. 'For me Maeterlinck makes his bees human and all false.' Yet he found and, in an age of religious disintegration, confirmed in the minds of many of his readers a belief in the ultimate value and significance of life. He once wrote, apparently to Grey at a moment of great political trouble, that he was sure that 'his friend would be able to find the central peace subsisting at the heart of endless agitation'. This sense of the 'everlasting rightness' of things distinguished Hudson's writings, and his faithfulness to this central theme is the measure of his artistic attainment and of the permanence of his finest work.

Hudson died in London 18 August 1922. A bird sanctuary, with decorative work by J. Epstein, was established in Hyde Park as a memorial to him in 1925.

[W. H. Hudson, *Far Away and Long Ago*, 1918; Edward Garnett, *A Hundred and Fifty Three Letters from W. H. Hudson*, 1923, republished as *Letters from W. H. Hudson to Edward Garnett*, 1925; Morley Roberts, *W. H. Hudson: A Portrait*, 1924.]

E. L. Woodward.

HÜGEL, FRIEDRICH VON, Baron of the Holy Roman Empire (1852–1925), theologian. [See Von Hügel.]

HULTON, Sir EDWARD (1869–1925), newspaper proprietor, was born at 4 Fir Street, Hulme, Lancashire, 3 March 1869. He was the second son of Edward Hulton by his wife, Mary Mosley. The elder Hulton, who started the business with which his son's name is associated, began his career as a compositor on the *Manchester Guardian*. In 1871 he went into the newspaper trade on his own account, and established the *Sporting Chronicle*, a daily issue. This was followed by the *Athletic News* (1875), a weekly periodical, and the *Sunday Chronicle* (1885). In later life he lived at Oakfield House, Ashton-on-Mersey, and he died in 1904, leaving a considerable fortune.

Edward Hulton, the son, was educated at St. Bede's College, Manchester. He was taken away from school when he was sixteen, and set by his father to learn the business of newspaper management. After serving an apprenticeship in the various departments of his father's offices, he was able by the time he was twenty-five to relieve his father of a large share of control. As soon as he became an active partner in the concern he set about enlarging its activities. In 1897 he founded a new halfpenny evening paper in Manchester called the *Manchester Evening Chronicle*. This was an immediate success, and he followed it in 1900 with the *Daily Dispatch*, a general morning paper.

Five years after his father's death Hulton produced the *Daily Sketch* (1909), an illustrated morning paper. This enterprise, like his earlier ventures, originated in Manchester, but as it was found that London was a better centre for news of pictorial interest, the paper was transferred to Fleet Street, and succeeded in establishing itself there after some initial difficulties. Later, Hulton started the *Illustrated Sunday Herald* (1915), and made further additions to his newspaper interests, including the purchase and development of the *Evening Standard* in 1915.

Hulton's health was for many years unsatisfactory, but he was reluctant to give up the personal direction of his business, and it was not until 1923 that he acted upon medical advice and decided to retire. In that year the Hulton periodicals, fourteen in all, were taken over by a company called Allied Newspapers Limited. It is stated that the price which Hulton obtained for his trade properties amounted to £6,000,000.

Hulton's interests as a newspaper proprietor were purely commercial. In an age when the political influence of large press syndicates is so marked this limitation may perhaps be considered rather to his credit than otherwise. His newspapers, if they were without literary merit, were at least free from the charge of political interference. He recognized that the public wanted news, and set himself to supply it in its simplest form, garnished with prize competitions, puzzles, serial stories, and other harmless aids to popularity. He was always ready to lend the aid of his newspapers in raising money for public causes.

Apart from his business occupations Hulton was interested in racing and coursing. In 1906 he registered his colours on the turf under the name of 'H. Lytham', and laid out large sums in the purchase of yearlings, chiefly on the advice of Richard Wootton, whom he appointed his trainer. He never won the Derby, but in 1916 he carried off the Newmarket race substituted, during the war years, for the Derby, and in 1924 he won the Oaks with Straitlace, a filly which won upwards of £25,000 in stakes. In coursing he won the Waterloo Cup in 1908 and 1918.

Hulton was created a baronet in 1921. About the time that some of his newspaper business was transferred to London, he went to live in the south of England, and in his patent he is described as of Downside, Leatherhead. Hulton was twice married: first to Miss Turnbull, the daughter of a Manchester solicitor; she obtained a divorce, and he married, secondly, Millicent, daughter of John Warriss. Hulton died at his home near Leatherhead 23 May 1925, and the baronetcy became extinct.

[*The Times*, 25 May 1925.]

A. Cochrane.

HUTTON, WILLIAM HOLDEN (1860–1930), historian and dean of Winchester, was born at Gate Burton, Lincolnshire, 24 May 1860, the younger son of the Rev. George Hutton, rector of Gate Burton, by his wife, Caroline, daughter of Robert Holden, of Nuttall Temple, Nottinghamshire. His mother was sister to Sophia Holden, wife of the Hon. and Rev. Alfred Curzon, grandfather of George Nathaniel Curzon, first Marquess Curzon of Kedleston. Although belonging to different generations, William Hutton and George Curzon were almost exact contemporaries and lifelong friends.

William Hutton was rather a delicate boy. He was sent to a well-known preparatory school at Bengeo in Hertfordshire, but for reasons of health to no public school, and began his secondary education only when he matriculated at Magdalen College, Oxford, in 1879. He came, however, of a family which was both clerical and 'bookish', and his rooms in Oxford were adorned with portraits of several bewigged divines, and a fine collection of leather-bound volumes of eighteenth-century literature, theological and historical. He was not, as was natural from his physique, one of the prominent undergraduate members of what was then an athletic rather than a 'reading' college; he found his friends outside Magdalen, among those who were interested in literature and history. He was one of the original members of the society of young students of history founded by (Bishop) Stubbs, regius professor of modern history, in 1880. Nearly every member of Stubbs's little flock achieved distinction in one way or another. Hutton obtained the Stanhope essay prize in 1881—the subject was 'The political disturbances which accompanied the early period of the Reformation in Germany'—and was placed, as all his friends expected, in the first class of the honour school of modern history in December 1882. In 1884 he was elected to a fellowship at St. John's College, which he was destined to hold for nearly forty years (until 1923). He was ordained deacon in 1885 and priest in 1886. For twenty-five years he taught modern history at St. John's to an ever-increasing number of pupils, and for seven years (1913–1920) was university reader in Indian history. He had the advantage of a personal knowledge of India from a long stay which he made with his cousin, George Curzon, the viceroy, when the latter was at the height of his career.

Hutton's beautiful, if somewhat secluded, rooms in the little side-quadrangle of St. John's were the centre of a happy group of literary friends, mostly of the conservative way of thinking; still more so was the splendid Queen Anne house at Burford—capable of sheltering many guests—which he acquired in 1895. He became a specialist in local Cotswold history, and the many traditions which he acquired at Burford from old residents took permanent shape in two of his pleasant books of essays—*By Thames and Cotswold* (1903) and *Burford Papers* (a series of letters from Cotswold worthies, 1905)—and occasionally in magazine articles, always of the most attractive kind.

Considering that Hutton was in full

university work for twenty continuous years—he was proctor in 1891–1892, examiner in the modern history school 1892–1895 and 1908–1910, and select preacher in 1898–1900—his literary output was prodigious. Among other works he produced histories of *St. John Baptist College* (1891 and 1898), lives of *The Marquess of Wellesley* (1893), *Sir Thomas More* (1895), and *William Laud* (1895), a study of *Philip Augustus* ('Foreign Statesmen' series, 1896), a monograph on *Hampton Court* (1897), a study of *Constantinople* (1900), *A Short History of the Church in Great Britain* (1900), *The English Church from the Accession of Charles I to the death of Anne, 1625–1714* (vol. vi of W. R. W. Stephens and W. Hunt, *The History of the English Church*, 1903), and *The Church and the Barbarians* (1906). In addition he wrote many articles and reviews for learned periodicals. The only regret of his friends was that his works, though full of research, were of moderate dimensions, for he never set himself to produce a *magnum opus*: yet all his books were well-rounded and complete units.

When the venerable Dr. James Bellamy [q.v.], after holding the presidency of St. John's College for thirty-eight years, resigned in 1909, there was a general expectation among those who did not belong to that college that Hutton would be elected as his successor. But a younger race of fellows had grown up in the twentieth century, mostly of a less conservative mentality than that of Bellamy and Hutton, and he was not chosen. In 1909 he gave up the history tutorship which he had held for just twenty years, and two years later (1911) was appointed archdeacon of Northampton and canon residentiary of Peterborough Cathedral—posts for which his tried administrative work in Oxford as well as his literary distinction recommended him. To the grief of his friends in the university he had to give up the beautiful house at Burford which all of them knew so happily, and to remove to a close in the Fenland. Peterborough is not a literary centre, nor very accessible to Oxford residents. His administration of the archdeaconry was exact, and his sermons drew the townsfolk to the cathedral —as might have been expected from one who had been select preacher at Oxford, Cambridge, and Dublin, and who had filled St. Mary's with his Bampton lectures of 1903 on 'Lives and Legends of the English Saints' (published as *Lives of the English Saints* the same year).

In 1919 Hutton was promoted to the deanery of Winchester—one of the few posts which would satisfy his historical and ecclesiastical aspirations. In the beautiful old deanery he dwelt for eleven years (1919–1930), much visited by friends of his old Oxford circle, as well as by many other literary acquaintances. The panelled rooms, the long Caroline library, and the garden with its rushing stream were a perfect setting for his later years, and those who remember him think of him always as installed in surroundings even more appropriate to his genial temperament than those of The Great House at Burford. In 1928 he began to be troubled with rheumatic and nervous complaints, which gradually sapped his activity and vitality, and after a prolonged illness he died while under medical treatment at Freiburg im Breisgau 24 October 1930. He was unmarried, and at his death his valuable collection of books and works of art was dispersed—some by bequest to his own college and friends, others among his numerous but distant relatives.

[Personal knowledge.] C. W. C. Oman.

ILBERT, Sir COURTENAY PEREGRINE (1841–1924), parliamentary draftsman, was born at Kingsbridge, Devonshire, 12 June 1841, the eldest of the six sons of the Rev. Peregrine Arthur Ilbert, rector of Thurlestone, Devonshire, by his wife, Rose Anne, daughter of George Welsh Owen, of Lowman Green, Tiverton. The Ilberts are an old Devonshire family, who acquired the estates of Bowringsleigh and Horswell at the end of the seventeenth century.

Ilbert was sent to Marlborough in 1852, and was there for eight years, under the headmasterships of George Edward Lynch Cotton and George Granville Bradley. He and T. L. Papillon, his contemporary at Marlborough, both won scholarships at Balliol College, Oxford, in 1859. Going up to Oxford in 1860, Ilbert had a brilliant university career. He won the Hertford, Ireland, and Craven scholarships in 1861, 1862, and 1864 respectively, as well as the Eldon law scholarship in 1867. He obtained first classes in classical moderations (1862) and in *literae humaniores* (1864). He was elected a fellow of Balliol in 1864, and for a few years (1871–1874) was bursar of the college. He became an intimate friend of Benjamin Jowett, master of Balliol, and acted as his literary executor.

Ilbert was called to the bar by Lincoln's Inn in 1869. It was about this time that the arrangements for drafting parliamentary bills were revised, and a special department was formed for the purpose. The head of his department was Sir Henry (afterwards first Baron) Thring [q.v.], with the title of parliamentary counsel to the Treasury. Thring availed himself of the assistance of Ilbert, whose wide study of legal systems and principles enabled him to render valuable services as a parliamentary draftsman. He had a large share in preparing the Statute Law Revision Act of 1881 and the Civil Procedure Act of 1883. In this way he obtained experience in a department of which he was to become in later years a principal official.

In 1882 Ilbert was offered by Lord Hartington, secretary of state for India, the position of law member of the governor-general's council. He was at first doubtful about accepting this appointment, for his practice was increasing and his position at the bar favourable. But the prospect of work in India attracted him, and finally overcame his hesitation.

The first Marquess of Ripon [q.v.] had succeeded the first Earl of Lytton as viceroy of India when Mr. Gladstone's second ministry took office in 1880. A man of advanced opinions, Ripon was inclined to deal with Indian affairs upon principles for which the time was not yet ripe. Many years were to pass before the idea of extending self-government to India took practical shape. The viceroy raised the dangerous question of the jurisdiction of Indian judges over Europeans, and early in 1883 it fell to Ilbert, as law member, to propose and to pilot through the council a measure to remove from the code at once and completely every judicial disqualification based merely upon race distinctions. Ilbert himself, while approving of the principle, doubted the expediency of introducing this Bill, owing to the state of Anglo-Indian feeling and the bitter racial dispute which it was certain to arouse. The result fully justified these forebodings. A storm of opposition arose, and the cleavage between English and educated Indian opinion was acute. The conditions, from being unpleasant—for Government House was boycotted and Indian administration was threatened with disastrous divisions—became obviously impossible. There was no other course open to the council but to withdraw, and a compromise was effected under which the main principles of the measure were given up.

Ilbert was also responsible for the Bengal Tenancy Act, a measure which reviewed the relations between landlord and tenant, and was the subject of much discussion. Upon the annexation of Burma in 1885 he prepared for Lord Dufferin, who had succeeded Lord Ripon as viceroy, a general system of law and procedure for the new province.

At the end of 1886 Ilbert returned to England and was appointed assistant parliamentary counsel to the Treasury. He proved himself a first-rate parliamentary draftsman, with an unfailing grasp of law and legal principles. He retained his interest in Indian legislation, and in 1898 published *The Government of India*, an attempt to codify Indian law from the time of Warren Hastings. This book has thrice been reprinted with additional matter. Upon the death of Sir Henry Jenkyns in 1899 Ilbert became head of the department; but he only held the office of parliamentary counsel to the Treasury a short time, for in 1902 he exchanged it for that of clerk of the House of Commons. He was popular in this position, for members found him courteous and considerate, while his knowledge of procedure was great. Upon his resignation in 1921 he received the special thanks of the House for his services.

In addition to his book on Indian legislation, Ilbert wrote *Legislative Methods and Forms* (1901), a short work on *Parliament, its history, constitution, and practice* (1911), and *The Mechanics of Law-making* (1914). He was created K.C.S.I. in 1895, K.C.B. in 1908, and G.C.B. in 1911. He married in 1874 Jessie, daughter of the Rev. Charles Bradley, and niece of his old headmaster at Marlborough and of Francis Henry Bradley [q.v.]. Lady Ilbert died only a few months before her husband. There were five daughters of the marriage. He died at his country home, Troutwells, Penn, Buckinghamshire, 14 May 1924.

Ilbert was a man of intellectual gifts, a master of his own subjects and able to express himself clearly about them in writing. An inclination to examine questions from every point of view made him as a rule reluctant to press his own opinions, and it was curious that circumstances should have caused his name to be associated with a bitter political controversy.

[Sir Frederick Pollock, *Sir Courtenay Peregrine Ilbert, G.C.B., 1841–1924*, in *Proceedings* of the British Academy, vol. xi, 1924–1925; private information.] A. COCHRANE.

IMAGE, SELWYN (1849–1930), artist, was born at Bodiam, Sussex, 17 February 1849, the second son of the Rev. John Image, vicar of Bodiam, by his wife, Mary Hinds. The family had emigrated from France on the revocation of the Edict of Nantes in 1685. Image was educated at Marlborough, and proceeded to New College, Oxford, as an exhibitioner in 1868, graduating B.A. in 1872, and M.A. in 1875. For the rest of his life he worked in London.

At Oxford Image became an enthusiastic disciple of John Ruskin, who in 1870 was appointed the first Slade professor of fine art, and studied drawing under him. His artistic bent had already shown itself at school. He was ordained deacon in 1872, and priest in the following year. He was successively curate of All Hallows, Tottenham (1872–1877), and of St. Anne's, Soho (1877–1880). In taking orders he had suppressed the desire, strong in him at Oxford, to become a professional artist: in 1883 this desire was fulfilled, and he relinquished his orders. Image's interest was in design of all sorts, but he became best known by his designs for stained glass, remarkable for their austere dignity and a rare feeling for the capacities and limitations of the medium. The west window of St. Luke's, Camberwell, four archangels in a window of Morthoe church, Devon, two windows in Marlborough College chapel, and one in memory of Bishop Lancelot Andrewes in Gray's Inn chapel, are his most important works in this kind. He also designed decorative panels for the Century Guild, founded by his friend A. H. Mackmurdo in 1883, which undertook the designing of houses and furniture, and published a magazine, *The Century Guild Hobby-Horse*, for which Image designed the cover (1886) and to which he contributed tail pieces as well as poems and essays. During the eighteen-nineties he designed a number of decorative title-pages and covers for books. In 1892–1893 he designed a fine Greek type for Messrs. Macmillan, the publishers.

In later life Image gave much time to lecturing on art; also to landscape drawings and water-colours. He found his favourite motives in Epping Forest, which he also frequented on moth-hunting expeditions, for he was an ardent entomologist and made a collection of British butterflies, exquisitely arranged and labelled, now in the Hope Collection at Oxford. In 1894 he published *Poems and Carols*, and he continued writing occasional poems, of a simple grace and directness, until his death. In 1900 he was elected master of the Art Workers' Guild, and in 1910 Slade professor of fine art at Oxford, holding the latter post until 1916. He was happiest in lecturing on English artists, such as Thomas Bewick and Thomas Rowlandson, for whom he had an especial admiration.

Image would have produced more original work had he not always been at the service of his friends and ready to undertake labours of love. A selection of his *Poems* and a selection of his *Letters* were published in 1932, after his death, both edited by A. H. Mackmurdo, and both containing a photographic portrait. His beautiful penmanship added to the charm of his letters. In conversation the wisdom and sweetness of his nature, his zest in life, and the fervour of his convictions, were even more intimately revealed. There was choiceness and a sense of beauty in all he wrote, said, and produced. Drawings by him are in the British, the Victoria and Albert, and the Ashmolean museums: cartoons for stained glass are in public collections at Birmingham, Glasgow, Newcastle, Nottingham, Bristol, Dublin, and Melbourne.

Image married in 1901 Janet, youngest daughter of Thomas Hanwell, of London, and had no children. He died at his home in Holloway 21 August 1930.

A portrait bust of Image by W. H. Frith belongs to the Art Workers' Guild.

[Private information; personal knowledge.]

L. Binyon.

IVEAGH, first Earl of (1847–1927), philanthropist. [See Guinness, Edward Cecil.]

JACKSON, Sir CYRIL (1863–1924), educationist, was born at Highgate 6 February 1863, the elder son of Laurence Morris Jackson, of South Park, Bodiam, Sussex, a member of the Stock Exchange, by his wife, Louisa Elizabeth Craven. He was educated at Charterhouse and at New College, Oxford, where he obtained second classes in classical moderations (1883) and in *literae humaniores* (1885).

Inspired by home influence and by the Oxford movement for a university settlement in London, Jackson took up residence at Toynbee Hall in 1885, soon after its establishment. Here he remained until 1895. In the life of an industrial community, as a member of the London School Board (1891–1896), as secretary of the

Children's Country Holiday fund (1888–1896), and particularly at his boys' club at Northey Street School (now the Cyril Jackson School), moulding Limehouse street boys into self-respecting citizens, he found congenial and absorbing work.

In 1896 Jackson accepted an invitation to go to Western Australia as inspector-general of schools and permanent head of the education department. Between 1896 and 1903 he reorganized the system so completely that it was soon recognized throughout the Commonwealth as equal to, if not, the best system in Australia. To himself the concession of the 'right of entry' to schools of all denominations was especially gratifying. He returned to England in 1903 as chief inspector in the Board of Education, a post which he resigned in 1906.

On the one hand, Jackson now acted as investigator for the poor law commission (1906) and served on numerous commissions and committees (often as chairman) on unemployment, relief works, and boy labour, and also as vice-chairman, under the Prince of Wales, of the statutory committee on war pensions (1916–1917). On the other hand, he became immersed in municipal work as elected member of the London County Council, Limehouse division, 1907–1913, alderman (1913–1916 and 1919), twice chairman of the education committee (1908–1910 and 1922), leader of the municipal reform party, and later chairman of the Council (1915).

When war broke out in August 1914 Jackson took full charge of, and responsibility for, the Council. A week later he was appointed chairman of the emergency committee. He served also on the senate of London University (1908–1921), on the Port of London Authority (1915–1916 and 1919), on the royal commission on the superior civil services in India (1923), and as member of the memorial committee which presented to London the King Edward park in Shadwell in 1922.

Unceasing work, regardless of health, resulted in inevitable break-downs. At such times Jackson suffered much from insomnia and was not easy to get on with. He sought relief in sea voyages. Possessed of a quick mind, he was instant in puncturing defective proposals or arguments. In municipal politics he was in advance of his party, whose feelings towards him were perhaps more those of admiration than of affection. An economist, an Anglican churchman, and a believer in voluntary agencies, he opposed unnecessary expenditure, and supported non-provided schools. More than any one else he was responsible for co-operation between existing institutions in the medical treatment of school children, and for the creation of care committees of voluntary workers in London. While he was chairman of the education committee, the London County Council adopted a far-reaching scheme for reducing the size of elementary school classes, and established central schools. He gave enthusiastic support to the reorganization of evening education and to the compulsory day continuation system.

Jackson was called to the bar by the Inner Temple in 1893 but never practised. He was created K.B.E. in 1917. He died unmarried at his beautiful home, Ballards Shaw, Limpsfield, 3 September 1924.

Jackson did not wear his heart on his sleeve: he never talked about the motive of his work; but his papers clearly confirm the impression left by the record of his work—namely, that he regarded life as definitely service and renunciation of self.

Jackson published the following books: *Unemployment and Trades Unions* (1910), *Outlines of Education in England* (1913), and *The Religious Question in Public Education* (1911, jointly with (Sir) Michael Sadler and Mr. Athelstan Riley).

[Private information; personal knowledge. Portrait, *Royal Academy Pictures*, 1917.]

R. Blair.

JACKSON, Sir FREDERICK JOHN (1860–1929), explorer, naturalist, and administrator, was born at Oran Hall, Yorkshire, 17 February 1860, the only son of John Jackson, of Oran, by his wife, Jane Outhwaite. He was educated at Shrewsbury School and Jesus College, Cambridge (1879–1881). He rowed for his college, but he took no university degree. After leaving Cambridge, he went on shooting expeditions, first to Kashmir and in 1884 to East Africa. He spent nearly two years in the region of Lamu, with occasional trips to Zanzibar, and during his wanderings learned much about native life which stood him in good stead later on. In 1886 he organized a hunting and collecting expedition to the Kilimanjaro region. This period of sport and collecting was, however, shortly afterwards interrupted, when serious financial losses, among other reasons, made Jackson decide to embark upon a career of public service.

In 1888 Jackson joined the service of the newly incorporated Imperial British East Africa Company, and early in 1889 was dispatched with Ernest Gedge, James Martin, and Dr. Archibald Donald Mackinnon to explore the hinterland of the company's territory, to establish friendly relations with the various tribes, and if possible to make contact with (Sir) Henry Morton Stanley [q.v.], who was returning from his expedition to Lake Albert Nyanza for the relief of Emin Pasha. Upon reaching Mumias, Jackson received an appeal from Mwanga, the kabaka or, as some styled it, 'king', of Uganda, asking for his support in the civil war against his brother Kalema and his Mohammedan supporters. Jackson was reluctant to accede to the request, having had instructions not to enter Uganda; he therefore proceeded north in order to explore Mount Elgon and to obtain news of Stanley. During his absence, the notorious German agent, Dr. Karl Peters, arrived from the coast in February 1890 with an expedition the ostensible object of which was the relief of Emin Pasha, but the real object the acquisition of territory for Germany. Having rifled Jackson's mail at Mumias and found a further appeal from Mwanga, Peters hurried into Uganda and persuaded Mwanga to conclude a treaty by which the country was placed within the sphere of German influence. Becoming aware of these proceedings on his return to Mumias in March, Jackson took immediate steps to safeguard British interests in Uganda, and fortunately the activities of Peters were brought to nought by the Anglo-German Agreement of 1 July 1890.

In June 1894 the kingdom of Uganda was declared a British Protectorate, and in July Jackson was appointed by the Foreign Office as a first-class administrative assistant in that country. He was successively vice-consul (1895), deputy commissioner (1896), and was on occasion acting commissioner at Entebbe for the Protectorate. While he was stationed at Eldama Ravine in 1897, a serious mutiny of the Sudanese troops, which had been employed in Uganda since 1892, took place. At great personal risk Jackson tried, without avail, to persuade the troops to return to duty, and thereafter assisted Major (afterwards Sir) James Ronald Leslie Macdonald [q.v.] to collect a force of Zanzibaris and to beat back the mutineers near Lubwa's Station. During the fighting which ensued Jackson was seriously wounded (19 October). In 1900 he acted as political officer in the operations against the Nandi tribe.

In 1902 Jackson was appointed deputy commissioner of the East Africa Protectorate under Sir Charles N. E. Eliot. It was not a happy period of his service, for unfortunately he did not see eye to eye with his chief on questions of policy relating to the Masai tribe and white colonization. The natures of the two men were antipathetic; but the position was relieved by Eliot's resignation in 1904. Three years later (1907) Jackson became lieutenant-governor of the Protectorate, and in 1911 he was appointed governor of Uganda, a position which he held until his retirement in 1917. His governorship was not marked by any striking reforms, but the general prosperity of Uganda was well maintained during the period of the European War, and Jackson was justly popular with all sections of the people. He received the C.B. (1898) for his services in the Uganda mutiny; in 1902 he was awarded the C.M.G and in 1913 was promoted K.C.M.G.

Second only to his official duties were Jackson's interests as a naturalist. He studied mammals, butterflies, and birds, but as time went on concentrated his attention on birds. He was handicapped by short sight, yet there can have been few field observers possessed of such powers of acute perception. His collection of birds numbered over 12,000 specimens, representing 774 species. From 1888 onwards he contributed articles to *The Ibis* on his bird collections. In 1897 he wrote the East African section of the volume of the 'Badminton library' on *Big Game Shooting*. In 1926 he published *Notes on the Game Birds of Kenya and Uganda*, and at the time of his death he had practically finished a complete history of the remaining avifauna of those countries. In 1930 a book of reminiscences dealing with the earlier part of his service, entitled *Early days in East Africa*, was published posthumously.

Jackson was a man of engaging personality and had a large circle of friends; he was blessed with many natural gifts, but was often too diffident to make the best of them. He had a wide influence for good, and was an energetic, wise, and sympathetic administrator both of native races and of white colonists.

In 1904 Jackson married Aline Louise, daughter of William Wallace Cooper, a Dublin barrister. He had no children. He died 3 February 1929 at Beaulieu-sur Mer, and was buried there.

[Sir F. J. Jackson, *Early Days in East Africa*, 1930; official publications; private information.] C. W. Hobley.

JACKSON, Sir HENRY BRADWARDINE (1855–1929), admiral of the fleet and pioneer of wireless telegraphy, was born at Barnsley 21 January 1855, the eldest son of Henry Jackson, farmer, of Cudworth, Yorkshire, by his wife, Jane, daughter of Charles Tee, of Barnsley. He was educated at Chester and at Stubbington House, Fareham, and joined the royal navy at the age of thirteen in December 1868. From the outset Jackson was interested in the more scientific aspects of his work, and at first specialized in navigation. In 1878–1879 he was junior lieutenant on board the *Active* on the African station, and took part in the Zulu War. In 1881 he was appointed to H.M.S. *Vernon*, torpedo-school ship at Portsmouth, and became intensely interested in the mechanism of the torpedo, finally qualifying as a torpedo lieutenant. He served in the *Vernon* for three and a half years. In January 1890 he was promoted to the rank of commander, and in the same year he conceived the idea of employing wireless waves to announce to a capital ship the approach of a friendly torpedo boat. Opportunities to experiment were few and progress was very slow until 1895 when, while in command of the *Defiance*, Jackson became aware of the experiments of Dr. Jagadis Chunder Bose on coherers. Jackson made, and experimented with, many types of coherer, the form finally adopted for his comparatively long distance experiments consisting of a tube of metal filings between two metal plugs. The coherer was tapped by hand and the receiving circuit was a simple loop of wire. With such a receiver Jackson succeeded in effecting communication by electromagnetic radiation from one end of the *Defiance* to the other, the signals transmitted over the length of the ship being sufficiently intense to ring an electric bell of high resistance inserted in the receiving circuit. Tapping the coherer with the bell was the next development, and towards the end of 1896, using the ship's inductance coil, which under favourable conditions gave a spark of two inches, he succeeded in receiving strong signals over distances of several hundreds of yards.

In June 1896 Jackson was promoted to the rank of captain, and in September of the same year he met Signor Guglielmo Marconi at a conference at the War Office. These two pioneers had been working on parallel lines, but whereas Marconi was aiming at long distance wireless communication over land and sea, Jackson's main objective was to improve the efficiency of the communication service of the fleet. In 1897 Jackson was appointed naval attaché in Paris, and in 1899 was given command of the torpedo depot-ship *Vulcan*, in which he continued his wireless experiments. He felt well rewarded for his labours when in 1900 a contract was placed with the Marconi Company for the supply of wireless installations to many ships of the royal navy, an event which was regarded by Jackson's friends as the culmination of his strenuous efforts to introduce this new means of communication into the service.

In 1901 Jackson's scientific work was recognized by his election as a fellow of the Royal Society, and in 1902 he communicated his most important scientific paper to the *Proceedings* of that body. The title of this was *On Some Phenomena Affecting the Transmission of Electric Waves over the Surface of the Sea and Earth*, and the paper described signalling experiments at sea over distances up to 140 nautical miles. Intervening land of any kind was found to reduce the signalling range between two ships by a distance which varied with the height, thickness, contour, and nature of the land. Jackson observed the disturbing effect of lightning flashes, and particularly noted that whenever any electrical disturbances were present in the atmosphere the travel of the wireless waves was affected, the intensities of received signals being from 30 to 80 per cent. of those obtained in fine weather. He appears to have been the first to observe the mutual interference of two wireless waves of the same wave-length arriving at the same point with varying phase difference. His own words were: 'The phenomenon manifests itself by the gradual weakening and occasionally by the total cessation of signals as the distance between the two ships (one transmitting and the other receiving) increases, up to a certain point, and then reappears as the distance is still further increased.' At that time Jackson could only assign the effect to a want of synchronism in the oscillatory discharge between the spark balls of the transmitter; many years later he remarked that had he had the advantage of cathode ray receivers his conclusions might have been very different.

In 1902 Jackson was appointed assistant director of torpedoes at the Admiralty, and in 1904 captain of the *Vernon*. In February 1905 he was appointed third sea lord of the Admiralty and controller of the navy. He stood then, as always, for the application of science to the practical work of the navy, and it was during his years of control that recommendations were approved for building the first turbine battleship, *Dreadnought*, and the famous *Invincible* class of battle-cruiser. Among other types of warships designed under the general direction of Jackson were the *Frobisher* and *Hawkins* class. He served as controller until 1908, when he was appointed to command the third (afterwards known as the sixth) cruiser squadron in the Mediterranean. In 1910 he represented the Admiralty at the International Conference on Aerial Navigation in Paris, and in 1911 he assumed the direction of the newly created Royal Naval War College at Portsmouth, where he had the task of training the first War Staff officers. In February 1913 he was appointed chief of the War Staff of the Admiralty.

When the European War broke out in August 1914 Jackson had been nominated to be commander-in-chief in the Mediterranean, but instead of taking over that command, he was retained at the Admiralty. Among his other duties were those of president of a sub-committee of the Committee of Imperial Defence which, in co-operation with the War Staff, developed schemes of attack on German colonial possessions. On the resignation of Lord Fisher from the post of first sea lord in May 1915, Mr. Arthur (afterwards Earl of) Balfour, then first lord of the admiralty, selected Jackson to succeed him. It was a period of great anxiety, largely caused by Germany's adoption of ruthless submarine warfare, and Jackson, by reason of his high scientific achievements, his intimate knowledge of the technical services, and his absolute fearlessness in all matters, was obviously well suited for the post. A new mining policy was initiated and an attack on the mole of Zeebrugge was planned, but the latter had to be abandoned owing to the difficulty, at that time, of setting up an effective smoke screen. Means of combating the submarine menace were under constant survey, but the destruction of merchant shipping continued to increase, and in December 1916 Jackson was appointed president of the Royal Naval College at Greenwich and Admiral (afterwards Earl) Jellicoe became first sea lord. During Jackson's period of office as first sea lord the battle of Jutland (31 May 1916) was fought, and he afterwards stated that the evidence which had convinced him that the German high fleet was coming out for action was the result of observations made by a radio direction-finding station, a change of five degrees being shown in the angular position of a German warship. Jackson filled his new post as president of the Royal Naval College with great distinction, and did not vacate it until July 1919, when he was advanced to the rank of admiral of the fleet. From 1917 to 1919 he was first and principal naval aide-de-camp to King George V. In July 1924 he retired from the navy.

In 1920 Jackson was appointed the first chairman of the Radio Research Board of the Department of Scientific and Industrial Research. The task of once more taking up experimental work in wireless telegraphy was most welcome to him. Under his guidance experiments were carried out dealing with the propagation of wireless waves, the nature of atmospherics, radio direction-finding, and precise radio frequency measurements. It was during his tenure of office that methods were developed for determining the height of the Kennelly-Heaviside layer [see Heaviside, Oliver]. He gave his personal attention to the work, spending much time in visiting the laboratories and discussing aspects of the investigations with the staff. Under his guidance more than a hundred important papers were published, but his modesty was such that he always disclaimed credit for any of the results obtained. In 1926 the Royal Society awarded him the Hughes medal in recognition of the great merit of his work; although many honours came his way, it is probable that Jackson prized this one the most highly. He was secretary, and later chairman, of the British National Committee on Radio Telegraphy formed in connexion with the International Union for Scientific Radio Telegraphy, and he regularly attended the meetings of the general assemblies of the Union. It is no exaggeration to say that British prestige in the scientific aspects of radio telegraphy owes much to his guidance.

Among the numerous honours which Jackson received were the K.C.V.O. (1906), the K.C.B. (1910), and the G.C.B. (1916). He also received honorary degrees from the universities of Oxford, Cambridge, and Leeds. Of foreign honours he received the grand cross of the Spanish order of naval merit in 1909, the Japanese order of the Rising Sun, and the Russian order of the White Eagle (first class), and he was a grand officer of the legion of honour. He was a member of the Institution of Electrical Engineers and honorary vice-president of the Institution of Naval Architects. He was also vice-president of the Seamen's Hospital Society. He died at his home, Salterns House, Hayling Island, 14 December 1929, and is buried in the neighbouring churchyard.

Jackson married in 1890 Alice Mary Florence, eldest daughter of Samuel Hawksley Burbury, F.R.S. [q.v.]: they had no children. Many of Jackson's early experiments were carried out in co-operation with Burbury's son, H. H. T. Burbury, who was also an enthusiastic investigator in radio telegraphy.

[*The Times*, 16 December 1929; *Proceedings* of the Royal Society, vol. lxx, A, 1901–2, and vol. cxxvii, A, 1930; *Nature*, 11 January 1930; personal knowledge.] F. E. Smith.

JACKSON, Sir THOMAS GRAHAM, first baronet (1835–1924), architect, the only son of Hugh Jackson, solicitor, of Hampstead, by his wife, Eliza, daughter of Thomas Graham Arnold, M.D., of Stamford, was born at Hampstead 21 December 1835. He was educated at Brighton College and matriculated at Corpus Christi College, Oxford, in 1854, but in the same year was awarded a scholarship at Wadham College. He graduated in 1858 with a third class in *literae humaniores*. He was elected to a non-resident fellowship at Wadham in 1864 and was made an honorary fellow in 1882.

Jackson entered the office of (Sir) George Gilbert Scott [q.v.] in 1858, and, having served his articles, set up as an architect in London in 1862. Among his earlier designs is the Ellesmere monument on Walkden Moor, the commission for which he won in competition in 1868. No other man has altered the appearance of Oxford in modern times so greatly as Jackson, and there is much of his work at Cambridge and at numerous public schools. His Oxford employment began with his success in a competition limited to five architects for the design of the New Examination Schools, the foundations of which were laid in 1876. He was architect of the High School for Girls in 1879, of the High School for Boys in 1881, and later designed the Grove Buildings at Lincoln College (1882), the new buildings at Trinity College (1883–1887), the restoration of the chapel at Oriel College (1884), the annexe at Corpus Christi College (1884–1885), the new buildings at Brasenose College (1886–1889 and 1909–1911), the offices for Non-Collegiate students 1887–1888, new buildings at Hertford College (1887–1890 and 1903–1913, including the new chapel finished in 1908), the remodelling of the spire of St. Mary's church (1893–1896), the refitting of All Saints church (1896), additions to the Acland nursing home (1897), the restoration of Wadham College (1900–1908), the Schools of Rural Economy and Forestry (1907–1908), and the Electrical Laboratory (1910). He also designed a Tutor's House in Mansfield Road for Balliol College, the circular tower in the grounds of the Radcliffe Observatory, and a small block of buildings at Somerville College. Of these buildings the New Examination Schools is the largest, the chapel of Hertford College that which he is said himself to have preferred, and the front of Brasenose College that which has met with most general approval. In various parts of the country he built about a dozen churches, and added to or restored many more. He designed the campanile of Zara Cathedral in Dalmatia (1892), and his numerous restorations of old buildings include his collaboration with Sir Francis Fox [q.v.] in the underpinning and stabilizing of Winchester Cathedral (1905–1912).

Early associated with the Arts and Crafts movement, Jackson soon became recognized as an accomplished adapter of ornament, and in the many buildings he designed throughout his career it is the ornament that is likely to entitle them to any permanent esteem. In middle life he gave particular attention to the re-use of Renaissance detail, although he constantly returned, upon appropriate occasions, to the Gothic of his training and first practice. In either style he was wont to employ unusual processes and materials: Hornblotton church, Somerset (1872–1873), is decorated internally with sgraffito plaster work, the town hall at Tipperary has some coloured decoration externally, and the new buildings at Brighton College have flint walling mingled with terra-cotta dressings which are imitated from Sutton Place. In the chapel of Giggleswick School—his outstanding achievement in buildings connected with schools—very many different processes and materials are characteristically combined.

Jackson had little skill as a planner, and was unsuccessful in the important public competitions for which he entered, notably those for the Admiralty and War Office, for the Imperial Institute, for the Queen Victoria Memorial, and for the London County Hall. He was a good draughtsman, and in an age when architecture was commonly regarded as an art of stylistic decoration, deserved and won many distinctions. He was elected R.A. in 1896, received the royal gold medal for architecture in 1910, and in 1913 was created a baronet. The universities of Oxford and Cambridge conferred upon him honorary degrees in 1911 and 1910 respectively.

Jackson's reception of the royal gold medal was the sign of a reconciliation between him and the Royal Institute of British Architects, on the recommendation of which the medal is awarded. Distrusting professionalism in architecture, he had taken a prominent part in the secession from the Institute in 1891 of those who opposed the policy of official registration for which the Institute was then pressing. As time went on, however, his opposition abated. In his first attacks upon the policy of the Institute he was associated with many of his most distinguished confrères, and was joint-editor with Richard Norman Shaw [q.v.] of a volume of protesting essays entitled *Architecture, a Profession or an Art?* (1891).

Jackson had already written several books when he embarked, at the age of seventy-seven, upon a series of architectural histories, of which he lived to complete seven volumes: *Byzantine and Romanesque Architecture* (2 vols., 1913, 2nd ed., 1920), *Gothic Architecture in France, England, and Italy* (2 vols., 1915), and *The Renaissance of Roman Architecture* (3 vols., 1921–1922).

Jackson married in 1880 Alice Mary (died 1900), daughter of William Lambarde, J.P., D.L., of Sevenoaks, and had two sons. He died in London in his eighty-ninth year 7 November 1924, and was succeeded as second baronet by his elder son, Hugh Nicholas (born 1881).

[*Builder*, 14 November 1924; *Architects' Journal*, 19 November 1924; *Journal* of the Royal Institute of British Architects, 22 November 1924 and 26 June 1926; private information.] H. S. Goodhart-Rendel.

JEBB, EGLANTYNE (1876–1928), philanthropist, was born 25 August 1876, at Ellesmere, Shropshire. She was the third daughter and fourth child in a family of seven of Arthur Trevor Jebb, of Ellesmere, by his wife, Eglantyne Jebb (who was a distant cousin of her husband), and niece of Sir Richard Claverhouse Jebb [q.v.]. She was educated at home, and in 1895 she went up to Lady Margaret Hall, Oxford, where she obtained a second class in the honour school of modern history in 1898. On leaving college Miss Jebb spent a year at Stockwell training college in order to prepare for teaching in an elementary school, and in 1899 she went to St. Peter's church school, Marlborough, remaining there rather more than a year. She was obliged to give up this post for reasons of health, and returned to live with her mother, who had settled in Cambridge after her father's death in 1894. There she immediately interested herself in social work, and compiled a register of the charities of the town, which was published and became a model survey.

From 1900 until 1914 Miss Jebb was busy with charitable work, with poetry, and with travel. She visited Egypt and spent several winters in Italy, always taking a close interest in the people of the country. In 1913, after the second Balkan War, she went to Macedonia in order to do relief work among the peasants, and on her return threw herself into the task of speaking and collecting for the Macedonian relief fund. In these years, too, she was actively associated with her sister, Mrs. Roland Wilkins, in the work of the Agricultural Organization Society for the encouragement of small holdings.

During the European War Miss Jebb helped another sister, Mrs. C. R. Buxton, in editing weekly 'Notes from the Foreign Press' in the *Cambridge Magazine*. As she studied the war news she came to realize more clearly the ruthless effects of war upon the defenceless and innocent in belligerent countries, and when, after the Armistice, it became evident that there were between four and five millions of children in Europe who were literally starving, she felt that it was impossible to remain inactive. With Mrs. Buxton she started an organization for investigation and propaganda called the 'Fight-the-Famine' Council. This led in 1919 to the initiation of the 'Save the Children' Fund, to the work of which Miss Jebb devoted the rest of her life. At the time of the formation of the fund there was much prejudice and opposition; but she broke her way through every obstacle, and forced her movement upon the notice of the world. It rapidly spread into forty countries, while the sums contributed rose to five and a half millions. In 1919 Miss Jebb was received in special private audience by Pope Benedict XV.

During the years between 1919 and 1922 the 'Save the Children' International Union became responsible for an immense amount of detailed relief administration, the problems of which extended from the daily feeding of hundreds of thousands of children in Greece, Bulgaria, Rumania, Armenia, Poland, and Russia, to the provision of hospitals, educational facilities, and the care of blind and crippled orphans. 'Often', said Miss Jebb, 'we were tempted to shrink back from the magnitude and complexity of the problems . . . but . . . we learnt to realize how marvellous is the response when a little love and a little money go with a well-thought-out plan.'

In this great international work many persons took a share; but Eglantyne Jebb was in a real sense the inspirer of them all. Her constructive imagination and her intensity of passion led the movement into ever wider fields; and after the emergency of the post-War period she turned the work into permanent channels. The vast problems of child life in non-European lands, child labour, child marriage, and child suffering all the world over made an irresistible appeal to her, and the work of child protection seemed to her the most productive and most necessary of all social tasks.

'Every generation of children', she wrote to a friend, 'offers mankind a new possibility of rebuilding this ruin of a world.' With this hope and inspiration she worked out in 1923 the text of the 'Children's Charter', based upon the principle that 'every child is born with the inalienable right to have the opportunity of full physical, mental, and spiritual development'; and at the meeting of the Assembly of the League of Nations on 26 September 1924 the charter was unanimously adopted under the name of the Declaration of Geneva. It is printed in the *International Handbook of Child Care and Protection*. Upon this international agreement Miss Jebb at once began to build the lasting work of the 'Save the Children International', and a year later she was made an assessor to the League of Nations advisory council for the protection of children. Thenceforth much of her work was done from Geneva. In the years which followed she spared no personal effort to raise support and money for the development of the children's movement, and worked for it without ceasing. But the sensational period of horrors and emergencies was over, and the task was very hard. She was herself, moreover, exhausted and weakened by the strain of all the suffering which she had witnessed, and felt about so keenly. She toiled as hard and as bravely as ever; but she wore herself out. In July 1928 she fell ill, and she died at Geneva 17 December 1928.

There is a monument to Miss Jebb's name in the Save the Children Fund's model village in Albania which was called after her, Xheba; but the best memorial, and the one which most truly expresses the value of her life and work, is the international movement for the care of children which she founded and inspired.

[*The Times*, 19 December 1928; Mrs. C. R. Buxton and Edward Fuller, *The White Flame*, 1931; private information.] R. Strachey.

JENKINS, Sir LAWRENCE HUGH (1857–1928), Indian judge, was born at the Priory, Cardigan, 22 December 1857, the younger son of Richard David Jenkins, solicitor, of Cilbronnau, Cardiganshire, and the only issue of his second marriage with Elizabeth, daughter of Thomas Lewis, of Machynlleth, a surgeon in the royal navy. He was educated at Cheltenham College and University College, Oxford, obtaining a first class in the honour school of jurisprudence in 1881. In 1883 he was called to the bar by Lincoln's Inn and practised on the chancery side until 1896, when he accepted a judgeship of the high court at Calcutta. In 1899 he was promoted to be chief justice of the high court of judicature, Bombay. During his tenure of this office he was an active member of the committee, which, under Sir Henry Erle Richards, successfully revised and redrafted the code of civil procedure, the new draft receiving legislative approval in 1908. In that year, at Lord Morley's invitation, Jenkins returned to England to take his seat on the Council of India. On the Council his strong liberal sympathies gave him an exceptional position in the confidence of his chief, and he had a large share in the drafting of the Morley-Minto reforms of 1909. He returned to India in that year as chief justice of Bengal at the earnest request of the viceroy, Lord Minto.

Shortly after Jenkins's appointment as chief justice, there was a serious recrudescence of revolutionary terrorism and outrage in Bengal. Very difficult and complicated conspiracy cases came before him, and in view of his well-known sympathy with constitutional reform, his judicial conduct did not escape both ignorant criticism and undiscerning praise. But it is to his honour that he was always anxious to temper justice with mercy, particularly to youthful offenders, whom he felt were often but the tools of older men. A conspicuous example of this was the Khulna conspiracy case (1911), in which he released on probation some schoolboys and university students who had been convicted of an offence more serious than those for which such a course was provided in the criminal procedure code. There can be little doubt that the initiative on this occasion came from Jenkins, though that fact does not appear in the report. When government, alarmed at the impossibility of getting convictions in face of the terrorization of witnesses, took powers under the Defence of India Act to intern suspects without trial, it applied to Jenkins for the services of a high court judge to advise on the evidence which appeared in confidential reports; but this course Jenkins steadily refused to permit, holding that it would compromise the judicial office. At the same time he realized that judicial criticism of the executive might be very unjust to officials who from the circumstances cannot be heard in their own defence. A notable example of this may be seen on comparing Jenkins's judgment with those of his two brother judges in the Musalmanpara bomb case (1915). In this case the police evidence, which all three judges legitimately suspected, but the other two unsparingly condemned, was subsequently shown to be substantially true. Jenkins enjoyed, indeed throughout this period the personal confidence of thoughtful men of all shades of opinion and in all positions from the governor downwards.

In 1915 Jenkins retired, and in 1916 was appointed, though without allowances, to a seat on the Judicial Committee of the Privy Council. In the work of that tribunal he took but little part, and the judgments of the board delivered by him are disappointingly few. But he usually attended the autumn session of the committee, and his judicial eminence received public recognition in 1924 when he was selected to be a member of the board, under Lord Dunedin, to which was referred the delimitation of the boundary between Northern Ireland and the Irish Free State. Failing health and the fogs of London made him more and more prefer the occupations of a country gentleman at his home in Cardiganshire, where he was elected chairman of quarter sessions. He died at Ealing 21 October 1928.

Jenkins's legal equipment when he first went to India was a keen dialectical mind, a thorough grasp of English equity principles, and a power of expressing himself in clear and forcible English. To this he soon added a mastery of Indian law and custom astonishing in one who did not visit India till his thirty-ninth year, and then served only in Presidency towns; many of his finest judgments enlighten dark questions of Hindu law. The same power to acquire rapidly a complete grasp of unfamiliar legal principles was again exemplified when the outbreak of war in 1914 brought before him a large crop of cases in prize. His unpublished official opinions as chief justice on proposals for improvement of the law and similar topics are also noteworthy. He was business-like in the administrative side of his duties; and the men whom he singled out for high responsibility justified his choice. A man of strong social tastes and a keen freemason, Jenkins also devoted himself with success to breaking down the barriers which at that time separated Englishmen and Indians, especially in the Presidency towns. He thus came to know intimately the leading Indian politicians, and sympathized with their aims. It was his advice which led the national congress to elect (Lord) Sinha [q.v.] to its presidency in 1915.

Jenkins married in 1892 Catherine Minna, daughter of Andrew Brown Kennedy, sugar planter, of Sea Cow Lake, Natal. She survived him with one son who died unmarried in 1930: a daughter had died in infancy. His official honours were few: a knighthood on becoming chief justice of Bombay in 1899, and the K.C.I.E. in 1903. His masonic honours included the district grand masterships of Bengal and Bombay.

[*The Times*, 3 October 1928; *Calcutta Weekly Notes*: notes portion, April 1911 and November 1928, reports, 1915, vol. xix, p. 923; private information.] S. V. FitzGerald.

JENKINSON, FRANCIS JOHN HENRY (1853–1923), librarian, born at Forres, Morayshire, 20 August 1853, was the elder son of John Henry Jenkinson, younger brother of Sir George Samuel Jenkinson, eleventh baronet, of Hawkesbury, Gloucestershire, by his wife, Alice Henrietta, daughter of Sir William Gordon Gordon-Cumming, second baronet, of Altyre and Gordonstown, Elginshire, and sister of Roualeyn George Gordon-Cumming [q.v.], the African lion-hunter. Jenkinson was educated at a private school at Woodcote, near Henley-on-Thames, and at Marlborough, and entered Trinity College, Cambridge, as a minor scholar in 1872. After obtaining a first class in the classical tripos of 1876, he was elected a fellow of his college in 1878, becoming lecturer in classics (1881) and assistant tutor (1882). He was also curator in zoology in the university from 1878 to 1879, for he was all his life an expert on *Lepidoptera*.

Jenkinson soon came, however, under the influence of the university librarian, Henry Bradshaw [q.v.], and entered upon the bibliographical studies, with extensions into liturgiology, palaeography, archaeology, and Celtic philology, to which he was to devote the remainder of his life. Bradshaw died in 1886; and, after a three years' tenure of the librarianship by William Robertson Smith [q.v.], Jenkinson succeeded to the post in 1889 and held it until his death thirty-four years later.

Jenkinson began to specialize about this time in the study of *Incunabula*, in which he was much encouraged by his friendship and interchange of ideas with two younger men who were working on Bradshaw's methods, Edward Gordon Duff and Robert Proctor [q.v.]. The 'natural history method', as Bradshaw called it, of studying these books, that is, their classification according to their fount and the names of their printers, towns, and countries of origin, as opposed to mere descriptive cataloguing, appealed especially to one whose other great interest was the identification and scientific arrangement of *Lepidoptera*. The acquisition of fifteenth-century books for the University Library, and the analytical study of them when acquired, remained Jenkinson's chief professional pursuit: his hawk-like vision was unerring in seizing, remembering, and comparing early types; and little as he published, he was an acknowledged master of this study, and the inspirer of many who afterwards pursued and systematized the subject.

Few librarians excel both as scholars and administrators, and Jenkinson cared less for the administrative side of his work; but he was much loved by all his assistants, and adequately carried on the duties of the librarianship during what may be termed a period of consolidation—acquiring and cataloguing books in an old-fashioned but perfectly satisfactory manner, as yet untroubled by problems of collection and storage which later made new and enlarged accommodation a necessity. He died, after an operation, in a nursing home at Hampstead 21 September 1923.

Jenkinson's literary output was small. In 1889 he edited Bradshaw's *Collected Papers*, and in 1908 published an edition of the *Hisperica Famina*, a curious and extremely difficult low-Latin poem, probably of Irish origin, of about the sixth century, on which Bradshaw had been at work at the time of his death. His writings, bibliographical and entomological, were contributed to periodicals (a list of them is given in the memoir cited below), but the lecture on the early Cologne printer, Ulric Zell, which he delivered as Sandars reader in bibliography in 1907–1908, is still unprinted.

A character of extraordinary sweetness and charm, Jenkinson will be remembered for the help, often amounting to inspiration, which he gave to other scholars during three generations, as well as for his lasting influence on the developing study of early printing, and for his extension of the collections of the University Library. After books and flies, his chief interest lay in music, of which he was an accomplished connoisseur. He was tall and handsome, and there is an admirable portrait of him by J. S. Sargent, painted in 1915, in the Fitzwilliam Museum at Cambridge.

Jenkinson married twice: first, in 1887 Marian Sydney (died 1888), daughter of Champion Wetton, of Joldwynds, Surrey, a sister-in-law of Sir Charles Villiers Stanford [q.v.]; secondly, in 1902 Margaret Clifford, daughter of Surgeon-General Ludovick Charles Stewart, of Drummin. There were no children by either marriage.

[Rev. H. F. Stewart, *Francis Jenkinson* (containing a bibliography of his writings), 1926; personal knowledge.] S. Gaselee.

JEROME, JEROME KLAPKA (1859–1927), novelist and playwright, was born at Walsall 2 May 1859, the younger son of Jerome Clapp Jerome, a colliery proprietor and nonconformist preacher, by his wife, Marguerite Jones, elder daughter of a Swansea solicitor. The colliery business proving unsuccessful, Jerome's father left Walsall and set up as a wholesale ironmonger in the East end of London. Jerome was educated at Marylebone grammar school until, at the age of fourteen, he began to make his own way. He obtained work, first as a railway clerk, and later as a schoolmaster; then he went on the stage, and finally took to journalism. It was his experience as an actor which led to the publication in 1888 of his first book, *On the Stage and Off*. In 1889 followed *The Idle Thoughts of an Idle Fellow* and *Three Men in a Boat*. Both these achieved considerable success; the latter has been translated into a great number of languages and, curiously enough, had an enormous circulation in Russia. The blending of farcical humour with somewhat naïve sentiment, and of pretty descriptive writing with simple philosophizing, suited the taste of the period, and brought Jerome immediate popularity.

In 1892, with Robert Barr and George Brown Burgin, Jerome founded *The Idler*, an illustrated monthly magazine which owing to its humour and originality had for some years a remarkable success. With the exception of Bret Harte, Mark Twain, and W. L. Alden the contributors were nearly all young men, notably Israel Zangwill [q.v.], Eden Phillpotts, and W. W. Jacobs. Features of the magazine were the informal discussions of the 'Idlers' Club', and *The Idler* monthly teas, where the editors met their contributors—an innovation at that time regarded as imperilling the sanctity of editorship. In 1893 Jerome founded a twopenny weekly paper, *To-day*, in which with characteristic vigour he constantly attacked Kaiser Wilhelm II and warned his readers to beware of his over-weening ambition. Jerome's connexion with this publication was ended in 1897 by a costly lawsuit.

After producing several volumes of tales and sketches, Jerome published in 1900 *Three Men on the Bummel*, a humorous account of a tour in Germany, and in 1902 *Paul Kelver*, a long autobiographical novel which he himself thought his best work.

Jerome had always been anxious to write for the stage, and an early play of his, *Barbara*, was accepted by Sir Charles Hawtrey and produced at the Globe Theatre in London 19 June 1886. It was not, however, until 1908 that he won fame as a dramatist by *The Passing of the Third Floor Back*, produced at the St. James's Theatre with Sir Johnston Forbes-Robertson playing the chief part. This has several times been revived. His other plays include *Miss Hobbs* (1899), *Fanny and the Servant Problem* (1908), *The Master of Mrs. Chilvers* (1911), on the woman suffrage problem, and *The Great Gamble*, a study of German life produced shortly before the outbreak of war in 1914. He wrote many other novels, plays, and sketches, and in 1926 published a volume of reminiscences, entitled *My Life and Times*.

Jerome, who was a good rider and oarsman, served during the European War as driver of a French motor ambulance on the Western front. During the last years of his life he lived at Belsize Park. In 1927, although in failing health, he decided to make a long motoring tour through England; he was taken ill, and died in Northampton general hospital 14 June 1927. His body was cremated, and his ashes subsequently buried in the churchyard of Ewelme, Oxfordshire. A tablet to his memory has been placed on the house at Walsall where he was born.

Jerome married in 1888 Georgina Henrietta Stanley, daughter of Lieutenant Nesza, of the Spanish army. They had one daughter.

[*The Times*, 15 June 1927; J. K. Jerome, *My Life and Times*, 1926; Alfred Moss, *Jerome K. Jerome: his Life and Work*, 1929.]

G. B. Burgin.

JOHNSON, WILLIAM PERCIVAL (1854–1928), archdeacon of Nyasa, was born at St. Helen's, Isle of Wight, 12 March 1854, the third son of John Johnson, solicitor, of Ryde, by his second wife, Mary Percival. He was educated at Bedford grammar school where he won an appointment to the Indian civil service, and at University College, Oxford, of which he was an exhibitioner. In 1874 and in 1875 he stroked his college boat to the head of the river. As an undergraduate Johnson became the firm friend of Chauncy Maples, afterwards second bishop of Nyasaland, and in 1874 he determined to renounce his prospects of a career in India, and to join the Universities' Mission to Central Africa under Bishop Edward Steere [q.v.]. He therefore abandoned his Oriental studies, and after obtaining a second class in the honour school of theology in 1876 sailed for Zanzibar in August of the same year.

Johnson was ordained deacon in September 1876 by Bishop Steere at Zanzibar, and priest two years later; but it was not until 1881 that he reached Lake Nyasa on the waters and by the shores of which he worked unremittingly for the next forty-seven years. His cool courage in meeting attacks of wild beasts and wilder men became proverbial, and his undaunted struggles against difficulties were heroic. A violent attack of ophthalmia in 1884 rendered him totally blind for a time, and although an iridectomy performed in London gave partial sight to one eye, he could thenceforward read only in a strong light through the narrow slit formed by putting two fingers together. Yet to the end he remained a keen student, and his translations formed the beginning of a literature in several African languages.

Johnson's most considerable work as a

translator was done in Nyanja, into which language he translated the whole of the Bible including the Apocrypha, the Book of Common Prayer, *The Pilgrim's Progress*, commentaries on the Acts and other portions of the New Testament, a short church history, and a short life of Mohammed. After he was fifty he began work in Mpoto, Manda, and Pangwa, and produced translations of considerable portions of the New Testament in all three languages.

The two mission steamers *Charles Janson* and *Chauncy Maples* were both the result of Johnson's efforts and the means of much of his work, the *Chauncy Maples* serving for a time as a floating theological college under his care. He was appointed archdeacon of Nyasa in 1896. In 1911 he received the honorary degree of D.D. from the university of Oxford, and in 1926 he was made an honorary fellow of his college. After a five weeks' illness he died at Liuli on the shores of Lake Nyasa 11 October 1928. His two books *Nyasa the Great Water* (1922) and *My African Reminiscences* (1924) recount much of the early history of Nyasaland: he had seen the end of the East African slave-trade, the advent of ordered government, and the development of missionary pioneering into an organized diocese; but he always looked back rather regretfully to the early days of difficulty and danger when he was laying the foundations on which others might build.

[B. H. Barnes, *Johnson of Nyasaland*, 1933; A. E. M. Anderson-Morshead, *History of the Universities' Mission to Central Africa*, 1909; personal knowledge.] E. F. Spanton.

JOHNSTON, Sir HARRY HAMILTON (1858–1927), explorer and administrator, was born at Kennington 12 June 1858, the third son of John Brookes Johnston, secretary of the Royal Exchange Assurance Company, by his second wife, Esther Laetitia, daughter of Robert Hamilton, of Bloomfield, Norwood, formerly a jewel merchant in India. Both his parents came of gifted Scottish families. At four years of age Johnston became engrossed in drawing and in bird-life. His early education by very intelligent and enlightened women (his grandmother, mother, and schoolmistresses) stimulated his interests in natural history, art, and humanity. When ten years old he was given a year's rest from school work, and spent the time in pursuing freely his own tastes in reading, in learning to paint at the Lambeth School of Art, in studying animals at the Zoological Gardens, and in frequenting the British Museum. These precocious adventures of a very intelligent and attractive boy brought him into early contact with several men of distinction in the world of natural science, whose interest and friendship he retained in later life.

From 1870 to 1875 Johnston was a day scholar at Stockwell grammar school, where the headmaster and staff allowed and encouraged him to follow the bent of his scientific and linguistic interests. In 1875 he entered King's College, London. There he worked at modern languages (he did not, however, take a degree) while qualifying himself for a studentship in painting at the Royal Academy Schools, and continuing to study zoology in Regent's Park and anatomy in the museum of the Royal College of Surgeons. Meanwhile he travelled adventurously, and sketched in Majorca, Spain, and France.

In 1879, in consequence of fears for his health, Johnston spent eight months in Tunis. Here, while painting and exploring, he learnt Arabic and came into contact with the problem, in its early stages, of the partition of Africa. He began a life-long connexion with English journalism by means of illustrated contributions which he sent to the *Graphic*, and articles in the *Globe* on the subject of French designs on Tunis; in appreciation of the latter he received from the Bey of Tunis his first political decoration, the order of the Nizam.

Increasingly interested in the international problem of Africa and in the extension of British influence in that continent, Johnston abandoned his aim of making a career as an artist, and, in 1882, on the recommendation of W. A. Forbes, prosector of the Zoological Gardens, joined the seventh Earl of Mayo in an expedition through Southern Angola. Thence Johnston penetrated alone, with great intrepidity and resource, into the Congo basin, where in 1883 he won the friendship and encouragement of (Sir) Henry Morton Stanley [q.v.], who was then engaged in organizing the Congo Free State. On the strength of his reports on his observations, Johnston was invited, in 1884, on behalf of the Royal Society, to undertake a scientific mission to explore Mount Kilimanjaro and its surroundings. The mission had also covert political objects; and Johnston was accredited by the Foreign Office to (Sir) John Kirk [q.v.], the British agent and consul-general at Zanzibar. On this expedition he made valuable contributions to scientific knowledge, and effected treaties with the chiefs of local native tribes by which they accepted British protection. These treaties formed the basis of the subsequent foundation of the British East Africa Protectorate (1895), now represented by Kenya Colony and Uganda.

In 1885 Johnston entered the service of the Foreign Office and was appointed vice-consul in Cameroon and the Niger Delta. Here he not only displayed and perfected his great natural talent for conciliatory dealing with African natives, but did valuable service in helping to open the navigable mouths of the Niger to legitimate trade. His action in inducing the chief, **Ja Ja**, of Opobo, who had established armed control of these waterways, to submit himself to a trial by the British admiral on the station, which resulted in Ja Ja's deportation, was sharply attacked in parliament. The case was made the subject of an official inquiry, and Johnston was absolved of all blame. His name was thus brought into public notice, and Lord Salisbury, impressed by the energy and ability of his work in East Africa and Cameroon, employed him in 1889 to assist in the (abortive) negotiations at Lisbon for a settlement of the respective spheres of influence of Great Britain and Portugal in South Central Africa. In this connexion Johnston had already formed a friendly alliance with Cecil Rhodes [q.v.] in the endeavour to secure an 'all-red' (British) route 'from the Cape to Cairo'—a phrase of which Johnston claimed to be the author.

On his return from Lisbon in 1889 Johnston was appointed to Mozambique as British consul in Portuguese East Africa. Scottish settlers were already established in the Shiré Highlands and at the south end of Lake Nyasa. They were at that time in armed conflict with Arab slavers. In 1889 a Portuguese force entered the Highlands, and its commander, Major Serpa Pinto, laid claim to the country; but after he had been defeated in an encounter with native forces, a British protectorate was proclaimed over the Shiré Highlands. Johnston, with the help of his vice-consul, T. Buchanan, (Sir) Alfred Sharpe, Captain Alfred J. Swann, and Cecil Rhodes (who provided funds), repressed the Arab slavers, made treaties with many native tribes, and within twelve months extended the British Protectorate to include Nyasaland, the greater part of what is now Northern Rhodesia, and the country adjoining Lake Tanganyika (with Mount Kilimanjaro) which was subsequently (1890) ceded to Germany.

In 1891 Johnston was appointed British commissioner for South Central Africa, and he remained in Nyasaland till the end of 1896—six fruitful years of good government, restoration of peace, suppression of slave-raiding, and economic development. During this period he gave offence to Cecil Rhodes by declining to co-operate with him in an attack upon the Portuguese, in the course of Rhodes's attempt to overrun Manika-land (lying south of the Mozambique Company's territory between the coast and what is now Southern Rhodesia). Rhodes never forgave Johnston for this, and withdrew the financial help which he had promised to Johnston for the completion of the campaign against the Arab slavers.

Fever having impaired his health, Johnston, who had been created K.C.B. in 1896, was transferred to Tunisia as consul-general in 1897. Here he actively pursued his archaeological, linguistic, and anthropological studies. In 1899 he was sent to Uganda as special commissioner. The country was distracted by political and religious faction-fighting, and the Sudanese armed police had mutinied. Johnston handled this difficult situation with great ability, and in 1901 left the Protectorate pacified, contented, and friendly to the British connexion, as it has ever since remained. During his administration he gained the personal friendship of the leading men of this progressive African state, and succeeded in his work largely by reason of his tact and sympathetic understanding of the people with whom he had to deal. But in the land settlement which he made for the protection of native property against European land-grabbing, he fell into the error of vesting in the personal ownership of the chiefs and about two thousand minor landlords exclusive rights in lands which were traditionally the common endowment of their tribes—a mistake which has sown the seeds of later difficulties. He explored Mount Ruwenzori, and added considerably to recorded knowledge of the flora, fauna, and ethnology of all that part of Africa. He discovered two animals new to British zoology—the okapi and the five-horned giraffe, and he made interesting studies of the pygmies of the Congo forest. His book, *The Uganda Protectorate* (1902), profusely illustrated by himself, is one of the most notable of his many valuable works dealing with African regions. He was created G.C.M.G. in 1901, and retired from the consular service in 1902.

From 1904 to 1906, at the request of the government of Liberia and with the encouragement of the secretary of state for foreign affairs, the Marquess of Lansdowne, Johnston was principally occupied in elaborating, in concert with President Barclay of Liberia, a promising scheme for improving and strengthening, by the employment of British officials, the financial, judicial, and defensive administration of that republic. This beneficent project was supported by (Sir) Austen Chamberlain, then chancellor of the Exchequer, but under French pressure the whole scheme was jettisoned by Sir Edward Grey when he became foreign minister, and the affairs of Liberia relapsed into anarchy. During three visits Johnston explored the country, and embodied in a valuable book, *Liberia* (1906), his observations of the sociology of the cannibal tribes which formed the uncivilized mass of its population.

Subsequently, in 1908 at the invitation of President Theodore Roosevelt, he visited the United States in order to study the development in that country of the transplanted Africans and their descendants. This work he extended by travelling through Haiti, the West Indies, Cuba, Central America, and Brazil, and on the results of his observations produced his last important volume, *The Negro in the New World* (1910)—a document of great penetration and admirable humanitarian intelligence.

After his retirement from the consular service Johnston twice stood for parliament in the liberal interest, in 1903 and 1906, but was defeated. He wrote five novels and an autobiography, was ceaselessly active, especially in connexion with African interests, and completed for the Oxford University Press his important *Comparative Study of the Bantu and semi-Bantu Languages* (1919–1922).

Johnston married in 1896 the Hon. Winifred, daughter of Florance George Henry Irby, fifth Baron Boston. He died at Woodsetts House, near Worksop, 31 August 1927, leaving no issue. He was awarded the gold medal of the Royal Geographical Society in 1904, and received the honorary degree of D.Sc. of Cambridge University in 1902, and many other distinctions. He was president of the African Society in 1902–1903.

Johnston was a man of small stature, of extraordinarily active and versatile intelligence, untiring industry, and great personal energy and courage. He was a witty talker, with acute powers of observation and lucidity of exposition. He was actively instrumental in adding about 400,000 square miles of the African continent to the British Empire, and in suppressing the curse of slavery and laying the foundations of good government in the new protectorates. Nearly fifty volumes, many of them profusely illustrated, attest his abilities as a researcher and writer. Many of his paintings have been exhibited at the Royal Academy.

A bust of Johnston was executed by Henry Pegram in 1904.

[Sir Harry Johnston, *The Story of my Life*, 1923; Alexander Johnston, *The Life and Letters of Sir H. H. Johnston*, 1929; private information; personal knowledge.] OLIVIER.

JONES, SIR HENRY (1852–1922), philosopher, born at Llangernyw, Denbighshire, 30 November 1852, was the eldest son of Elias Jones, by his wife, Elizabeth, daughter of William Williams. His father, the village shoemaker, was a man of unusual qualities, uniting deep and tender religious feeling with gaiety of humour and firmness of character. His lineaments, physical and moral, appeared again in his son; and certainly his influence was one of the strongest in Jones's life.

Jones left school at twelve years of age, to be apprenticed to his father. But after some four years the general ferment of the Welsh religious life of the time awakened new ambitions within him, so that in 1869 he returned half-time to school. He had nearly two years of desperate and doubting preparation, working most nights for half the hours of sleep, until in November 1870 he qualified for admission to the Bangor Normal College. His course showed no special distinction; but without difficulty he gained his 'teacher's certificate'. In 1873 he was appointed master of the Ironworks School at Brynamman, in South Wales; there in two years he raised the numbers of the school from 200 to 400 pupils, and left a vivid and long-enduring impression both upon his pupils and upon the town. At this time also he was received as a preacher into the Calvinistic Methodist denomination, and was encouraged to prepare himself for the regular vocation of the ministry. In 1875, therefore, after a summer of hard study, he matriculated, with a Dr. Williams scholarship, in the university of

Glasgow. His interests lay chiefly in the field of philosophy, to which John Nichol [q.v.] and especially Edward Caird [q.v.] —by far the strongest intellectual influence of Jones's life—introduced him. On graduation he won the G. A. Clark fellowship, which gave him four years of leisured study in Germany and in Glasgow. In 1882 he married Annie, daughter of James Walker, manufacturer, of Kilbirnie, Ayrshire.

By this time, under Caird's guidance, Jones had decided to seek a career in philosophical teaching. In 1882 he was appointed to a lecturership in philosophy at the University College, Aberystwyth. Two years later, he was elected to the professorship of philosophy and political economy in the new University College of North Wales at Bangor; thence in 1891 to the chair of logic, rhetoric, and metaphysics at St. Andrews; and finally, in 1894, to succeed Caird in the chair of moral philosophy in Glasgow, which he held until his death.

In principle, Jones's doctrine did not depart from the Hegelian idealism which he had received from Caird. He called himself a 'spiritual realist'. But his own philosophical position was reached from an analysis rather of the postulates of moral experience than of the conditions of knowledge; and the fundamental groundwork of all his thinking was a faith in the reality and reliability of moral values. From that premiss he deduced the permanent significance of the individual subject of experience, and of his contribution to historic progress; and correspondingly he controverted those renderings of Idealism which assigned a 'static' perfection to the Absolute. The fullest statement of his metaphysic is given in his last volume, *A Faith that Enquires* (1922), the substance of the Gifford lectures delivered at Glasgow in 1920 and 1921. But his earlier writings had developed one or other of the several aspects of his view. His studies of Browning (1891) and of Lotze (1895) were critical interpretations of two Idealist teachers, the former from the point of view of religion and ethics, the latter from that of logic and epistemology. In later books, *Idealism as a Practical Creed* (1909)—a series of lectures delivered in the university of Sydney in 1908, *Philosophical Landmarks* (1917)—lectures given at the Rice Institute, Houston, Texas, in 1912, *The Working Faith of a Social Reformer* (1910), *Social Powers* (1913), and the *Principles of Citizenship* (1919)—a book written for the soldiers' classes in France during the War, he expounded especially the ethical and political consequences of his philosophy. With Professor J. H. Muirhead he wrote *The Life and Philosophy of Edward Caird* (1921); and in the last few months of his life, in *Old Memories* (edited by Thomas Jones, 1923), he gave an account of his own youth. He published also a large number of papers and pamphlets on philosophical and public questions; and he was at all times an eager and helpful correspondent. But his greatest contribution to contemporary philosophy was undoubtedly his own teaching. His rich and radiant personality gave him a remarkable influence over his students; and in the years between 1900 and 1915 he was unmistakably the dominant force in the speculative life both of the west of Scotland and of Wales.

Apart from his professorial work, Jones was profoundly interested in educational reform. He took a leading part in the movement which culminated in the Welsh Intermediate Education Act of 1889. He was a member of the royal commission on the university of Wales in 1916–1917, and of the 1918 departmental committee on adult education. For years, too, he was an ardent liberal. His interventions in politics concerned chiefly the free trade issue, and the budget of 1909 with its ensuing controversies. On the outbreak of the European War, he devoted his energies to two long campaigns on behalf of recruiting and of national savings. He served on many committees and public bodies, and finally, in 1918 visited the United States as a member of the British university mission to that country. This last work tried him greatly. A severe operation for cancer in 1913 had impaired his strength, and only his unshakable courage carried him through the days of public and private anxiety that followed. Of his six children, one son and one daughter had died in youth; his three remaining sons went on active service in the War, and the youngest died in France.

Soon after the end of the War, the cancer returned, and after three years of much suffering, though also of much productive work, Jones died in his country home at Tighnabruaich, in the Kyles of Bute, 4 February 1922. He was knighted in 1912; he received honorary doctorates from the universities of St. Andrews (1895) and Wales (1905), and was elected a fellow of the British Academy in 1904. In January 1922, a few weeks before his death, he was made a Companion of Honour. There are portraits of him in the University College, Bangor, and in the university of Glasgow.

[Sir Henry Jones, *Old Memories*, 1923; H. J. W. Hetherington, *The Life and Letters of Sir Henry Jones*, 1924; J. H. Muirhead, *Sir Henry Jones, 1852–1922*, in *Proceedings* of the British Academy, vol. x, 1921–1923; personal knowledge.] H. J. W. HETHERINGTON.

JONES, HENRY ARTHUR (1851–1929), dramatist, was born 20 September 1851 at Grandborough, Buckinghamshire, the eldest son of Silvanus Jones, a farmer of Welsh descent, by his wife, Elizabeth, daughter of John Stephens, also a farmer. At the age of twelve Jones was withdrawn from John Grace's Commercial Academy at Winslow and sent to work for his uncle, a Ramsgate draper. Three and a half years later he passed into the service of another draper, at Gravesend; thence, in 1869, to a warehouse in London. For the next ten years he worked as a commercial traveller in the London, Bradford, and Exeter districts.

Jones read widely and intelligently in his leisure hours. During his first year in London he wrote several one-act plays (all rejected) and followed these with a novel, which was also unsuccessful. The first of his plays to be produced was *It's Only Round the Corner*, which was put on at the Theatre Royal, Exeter, 11 December 1878. Thereafter he gave up his employment and relied for a livelihood solely on the writing of plays. His first London production was the comedietta, *A Clerical Error*, which was played 16 October 1879 at the Court Theatre, just opened under the management of Wilson Barrett [q.v.]. The same actor-manager produced and took the principal part in the melodrama, *The Silver King* (Princess's Theatre, 16 November 1882) which ran for 289 nights, made Jones's name widely known, and banished all his pecuniary anxieties. Henry Herman [q.v.] and Wilson Barrett both had some share in shaping this play, but in later years Jones repudiated in acrimonious terms Barrett's claim to its authorship. In 1905 an arbitration vindicated Jones as sole author. Matthew Arnold saw the play, and described it as 'a sensational drama in which the diction and sentiments do not overstep the modesty of nature'.

Jones was now fairly launched on his career as a dramatist. *Saints and Sinners* (Vaudeville Theatre, September 1884) had a successful run, although a section of the audience on the first night resented its use of biblical quotations. In 1887 (Sir) Herbert Beerbohm Tree played in *Hard Hit* at the Haymarket Theatre; *The Middleman*, produced at the Shaftesbury Theatre in 1889, was the beginning of a long association with E. S. Willard; and *Judah* (Shaftesbury Theatre, May 1890) was generally hailed as a distinct advance in thought and technique. An even greater success was *The Dancing Girl* (Haymarket Theatre, January 1891), in which Tree took the part of the Duke of Guisebury, and which ran for 310 nights. An allusion in this play to the teaching of Herbert Spencer led to a meeting with the philosopher which greatly gratified Jones, who had long been a close student of Spencer's works and acknowledged a deep intellectual debt to him.

The Bauble Shop (Criterion Theatre, January 1893) was Jones's first play under the management of (Sir) Charles Wyndham [q.v.]. In the same year he broke new ground with *The Tempter*, a tragedy in blank verse with incidental music by (Sir) Edward German, which was produced by Tree at the Haymarket Theatre in September, with Julia Neilson, Fred Terry, and Irene Vanbrugh in the cast. In Jones's own judgement, given shortly before his death, this was one of his five best plays, the other four being *The Case of Rebellious Susan* (1894), *Michael and his Lost Angel* (1896), *The Liars* (1897), and *The Divine Gift* (1913, never produced). The consensus of critical opinion considers *The Liars* to be his best work. *The Triumph of the Philistines* (St. James's Theatre, May 1895) and *Michael and his Lost Angel* (Lyceum Theatre, January 1896) both caused controversy—the first because of its criticism of Victorian prudery, and the second because it contained a church scene and showed a clergyman guilty of adultery. *Truth* found the very title 'as silly as it is objectionable', (Sir) Johnston Forbes-Robertson wanted the title altered, and Mrs. Patrick Campbell, after rehearsing for seven weeks, abandoned the part of Audrie because she disliked the church scene. But Jones, as was his invariable practice, refused to alter a line. *The Liars* (1897) and *Mrs. Dane's Defence* (1900) showed at their highest the dramatist's constructive power, stagecraft, and command of dialogue. *The Hypocrites* (produced by Charles Frohman at the Hudson Theatre, New York, in 1906) was strong in action and social criticism, and *The Lie*, which had been played in New York in 1914, was produced at the New Theatre, London, in October 1923, with (Dame) Sybil Thorndike as leading lady, and had a *succès fou*.

From the time of the outbreak of the European War in 1914, Jones unfortunately frittered away much energy in ill-tempered and somewhat incoherent political controversy. In his early days he had been proud to meet William Morris; and under Morris's influence and that of (Sir) Emery Walker, a lifelong friend, he had shown some interest in socialistic theories. But material success, coupled with constant fear of confiscatory legislation, drove him to the opposite extreme. His diatribes against Mr. H. G. Wells, Mr. Bernard Shaw, and advanced thought in general (e.g. *Patriotism and Popular Education*, 1919, and *My Dear Wells*, 1921), added nothing to his reputation. Always a vigorous controversialist, Jones wrote many articles in periodicals on subjects connected with the drama, a number of which were collected in volume form as *The Renascence of the English Drama* (1895) and *The Foundations of a National Drama* (1913). He played a prominent part in the agitation for the abolition of the censorship. In his latest years he suffered grievously in health and underwent several surgical operations. He survived undaunted, however, to the age of seventy-seven, and died at his home in Hampstead, of pneumonia, 7 January 1929.

Jones married in 1875 Jane Eliza (died 1924), daughter of Richard Seeley, manufacturer of artificial flowers, by whom he had three sons and four daughters.

In the revival of the English drama Jones played an important part. Thomas William Robertson [q.v.] had shown some stirrings of a returning sense of responsibility, but it was Jones and Sir Arthur Pinero who really initiated the renaissance of dramatic art in England. Jones approached his work with a sense of high purpose and, although he once said that very rarely had he been able to write exactly as he would have wished, he never failed to envisage the drama as a branch of literature—in his view, the highest and most difficult. He had neither the highly polished wit of an Oscar Wilde, nor the intellectual force of Bernard Shaw, but as a craftsman he was perhaps superior to both. From the rise of the curtain his plays fulfil the primary purpose of arousing interest in the characters and the dramatic situation, and Jones knew how to sustain that interest. Many of his subjects seem, after thirty or forty years, a little tame; but one glance at a photograph of the actresses in the costume of those days brings a realization of how revolutionary Jones's views appeared to many, and of how far the drama has travelled since. In Mr. Percy Allen's phrase, Jones was 'always a shrewd observer rather than a deep philosopher'. He strongly repudiated the idea that he had been influenced by Ibsen. In point of fact he did not cut so deeply; yet, within his limitations, he has claims to be a pioneer. He had a genuine sense of comedy, and excelled in creating parts in which a middle-aged character draws the threads together and brings erring and emotional youth back to reality. That such parts were ideal for the established actor-manager may go a long way towards explaining his brilliant material success. Jones made many friends in the literary and social world. He also made not a few enemies, for his sincerity and strength of feeling often led him to express himself in violent terms. His work was keenly appreciated both in America and in France. In 1907 Harvard University conferred an honorary degree upon him, and the French government offered him the ribbon of the legion of honour.

A portrait of Jones by H. G. Riviere is in the possession of Jones's daughter, Mrs. Irving Albery, of the Manor House, Farningham, Kent.

[Jenny Doris Jones, *The Life and Letters of Henry Arthur Jones*, 1930 (contains the only full list of his works): P. P. Howe, 'Henry Arthur Jones', in *Dramatic Portraits*, 1913; Percy Allen, 'Henry Arthur Jones', in the *Fortnightly Review*, new series, vol. cxxv, 1929; R. A. Cordell, *Henry Arthur Jones and The Modern Drama*, New York, 1932.]

H. B. Grimsditch.

JONES, Sir JOHN MORRIS- (1864–1929), Welsh poet and grammarian. [See Morris-Jones.]

JORDAN, Sir JOHN NEWELL (1852–1925), diplomatist, was born at Balloo, co. Down, Ireland, 5 September 1852, the second son of John Jordan, of Balloo, by his wife, Mary Newell. He came of substantial Presbyterian farmer stock on both parents' sides. He owed much to his mother, to whom he was devoted, and who imbued him with her own steadfast sense of duty. He was educated at the Royal Academical Institution, and at Queen's

College, Belfast, where he obtained first-class honours (B.A. 1873, M.A. 1881). In 1874 he went to Queen's College, Cork, where he was senior classical scholar, and subsequently junior classical tutor. He was made a freeman of Belfast in 1910, an honour of which he was particularly proud.

In 1876 Jordan joined the China consular service as student interpreter in Peking, and passed his Chinese language examinations with credit. The next nine years were spent in Peking and various ports where he learned the routine of the consular work which, owing to the peculiar conditions prevailing in the Far East, entails judicial and political duties not usually included elsewhere. Thus he came into constant contact with Chinese officials of the old obstructive diplomacy, who entertained suspicions of all foreigners and, when possible, pursued the policy of masterly inactivity. It was a school of patience and tact, by which Jordan amply profited. He acquired a deep insight into Chinese character and ways of conducting affairs, tempered with considerable sympathy: qualities which made him in the long run an outstanding public servant. While in Canton (1882) he reaffirmed the principle, then lapsing into abeyance, that British citizens in the service of China, such as the commissioners of maritime customs, are nevertheless amenable to British jurisdiction.

The pay was small and promotion seemed far off; but in 1886 Jordan was appointed to the legation in Peking and showed his value. He became assistant Chinese secretary in 1889, and full Chinese secretary in 1891, his versatility and energy combining with his practical experience to add distinction to a post always requiring great abilities, but especially in those years when other foreign nations were beginning to dispute the British tradition of the 'Open Door'. In 1896 Jordan was appointed consul-general at Seoul, the capital of Korea; he received the jubilee medal in 1897, was promoted to be chargé d'affaires in 1898, and minister resident in 1901. He was created K.C.M.G. in 1904. Korea was in the throes of contention between her old overlord China, and Russia and Japan. As a result of China's defeat by Japan in 1894–1895, Korea declared her independence of China, but only to fall more fully into the grasp of Japan. In 1895 the Queen of Korea, the sole hope of her people, was murdered by Japanese invaders, Korea turned to Russia for sympathy, and there began the struggle between Japan and Russia over the Korean promontory. During this period Jordan made lasting friendships with the Chinese commissioners at Seoul, notably Tang Shao-yi, who later became one of the elder statesmen of the Chinese Republic, and Yuan Shih-k'ai, who became president. These friendships were to be of service in later years in promoting understanding of high diplomatic problems. In 1906, after the defeat of Russia by Japan, the legation at Seoul was withdrawn in consequence of the establishment of a Japanese general and resident, and Jordan was appointed envoy extraordinary and minister plenipotentiary to the court of Peking, in succession to Sir Ernest Satow [q.v.].

After the tragic upheaval of the anti-foreign Boxer Riots in 1900, a new era dawned in China, and the Chinese people now turned with eagerness to learn from the foreigner. Jordan had married in 1885 Annie Howe, daughter of Dr. Robert Cromie, of Clough, co. Down, and he and his wife showed much hospitality to both Western and Chinese guests alike in the beautiful old Chinese palace which is the British legation. In 1908, with Sir Alexander Hosie [q.v.], and Tang Shao-yi, his friend of Korean days, Jordan forwarded the negotiations begun in 1906, which had for their aim the cessation of the export to China of Indian opium, *pari passu* with the abandonment by China of her large cultivation of poppy. Their efforts were so successful that by 1913 the export of Indian opium to China had ceased entirely, despite the loss to Indian finances, and although in the prolonged chaos following the Revolution unlimited poppy-growing began in China again. But that blot on British trade was removed.

In November 1911, the revolt against the dynasty plunged China into civil war. The Northern anti-republican army, under the half-hearted direction of Yuan Shih-k'ai was, nevertheless, hard pressing the revolutionaries until Jordan, distressed at such fratricidal war, unknown since the Taiping Rebellion of 1853, persuaded Yuan to cease fighting and open negotiations. Throughout the remainder of his service, Jordan equally set his face against war-making in China, strongly deprecating any loan or advance which would eventually mean the purchase of war-munitions and materials. During the European War of 1914–1918 he used all his influence towards bringing China on to the side of the Allies. The Germans in China, as a result, lost the extra-territorial rights which all foreigners in China then possessed, and became subject to Chinese jurisdiction; but since then the whole question has been opened up.

Jordan was made a privy councillor in 1915, created K.C.B. in 1909, G.C.I.E. in 1911, and G.C.M.G. in 1920. He retired in 1920 and lived at Putney. In November 1921 he accompanied Mr. (afterwards the Earl of) Balfour to the United States for the Washington Conference, at which the Powers undertook to respect China's territorial sovereignty, and to allow her to impose her own customs dues. These dues had been originally settled by treaties now considered out of date.

Jordan died in London 14 September 1925, leaving three sons. His only daughter predeceased him.

Jordan had an admirable gift of style, and his dispatches are models of conciseness, interest, and lucidity. Of a kind and cheerful nature, he won the affection and esteem of Chinese officials who realized that he never supported a cause unless he was convinced of its justice to Chinese as well as to British.

There is a pencil-sketch of Jordan from a photograph in the library of Queen's College, Belfast.

[*The Times*, 15 September 1925; private information; personal knowledge.]

D. Hosie.

JOYCE, Sir MATTHEW INGLE (1839–1930), judge, was born 17 July 1839 at Breedon-on-the-Hill, Leicestershire, the fourth son of John Hall Joyce, yeoman farmer, of Blackfordby, Leicestershire, by his wife, Mary, daughter of Matthew Ingle, of Ashby-de-la-Zouch. He was educated at Ashby-de-la-Zouch grammar school and at Gonville and Caius College, Cambridge. He graduated as eighth wrangler in the mathematical tripos of 1862, and in that year was elected a fellow of his college, a position which he held until 1875. He was called to the bar by Lincoln's Inn in 1865, and was junior equity counsel to the Treasury from 1886 to 1900; in the latter year he was appointed a judge of the High Court and was knighted. He remained on the bench until 1915. On his resignation he was sworn a member of the Privy Council. His college made him an honorary fellow on his appointment as a judge. He married in 1891 Miriam Bertha (died 1922), eighth daughter of Sir William Jackson, first baronet, a well-known contractor, and had one daughter. He died at Liverpool 10 March 1930.

The outstanding characteristic which marked the judicial as the private life of Joyce was sincerity. One who had exceptional knowledge of him said that 'he never said anything he did not mean, and rarely refrained from saying what he did mean'. A somewhat brusque manner concealed the kindest of hearts, and no one who deserved help or encouragement failed to obtain it from him. Joyce never attempted to garnish his judgments with a display of learning. Perhaps the most important was *Colls* v. *Home and Colonial Stores* (1904), concerned with the nature and extent of the easement of light. His decision in this case was reversed by the Court of Appeal, but restored by the House of Lords. In *Grierson* v. *National Provincial Bank* (1913) he made a notable contribution to the mass of learned decisions on priorities among different mortgagees of the same land. In his whole judicial career Joyce showed himself to be a sound lawyer with a wide knowledge of real property and equity jurisprudence. He valued above everything simplicity and common sense, distrusting any subtlety or technicality. Although not one of the more profound lawyers in the history of the bench, he was in the highest sense a just and upright judge. He knew well how to impart his knowledge, for during his practice at the bar his pupil room was very popular and produced some distinguished lawyers, notably Lord Parker of Waddington and the younger Lord Russell of Killowen.

A cartoon of Joyce by 'Spy' appeared in *Vanity Fair* 23 January 1902.

[*The Times*, 12 March 1930; private information.]

H. G. Hanbury.

KELLY, JAMES FITZMAURICE- (1857–1923), historian of Spanish literature. [See Fitzmaurice-Kelly.]

KELTIE, Sir JOHN SCOTT (1840–1927), geographer, was born at Dundee 29 March 1840, the elder son of David Keltie, builder and stone mason, by his wife, Christian, daughter of William Scott, of Crieff. Soon after his birth his parents moved to Perth, where Keltie was educated until he entered the university of St. Andrews at the age of nineteen. He left the university before taking his degree in order to study in Edinburgh for the United Presbyterian Church; but although he completed his course he did not enter the ministry. While still a student he began journalistic work, and in 1861 joined the staff of Messrs. W. & R. Chambers, and worked on *Chambers's Encyclopædia* and other publications, including *A History of the Scottish Highlands, Highland Clans and Highland Regiments* (1874). In 1871 he came to London to join the editorial staff of Messrs. Macmillan, and became sub-editor of *Nature* in 1873. In 1884 he undertook for this firm the editorship of the *Statesman's Year Book*, which he retained to the end of his life, being associated from 1919 with Mr. M. Epstein. In 1875 he began to write for *The Times* on biographical, statistical, and geographical topics, principally relating to Africa, which at that time was being actively explored and rapidly divided among the European powers.

Keltie's long association with the Royal Geographical Society began in 1884, when the Society, anxious to further geographical teaching, appointed him inspector of geographical education. After a year spent in visiting the universities and schools of Europe he presented an exhaustive report on the subject (*Report on Geographical Education*, 1886), which may be regarded as inaugurating the scientific study of geography in the schools and universities of Great Britain. Meantime (1885) Keltie had become librarian of the Society, and in 1892 he succeeded Henry Walter Bates [q.v.] as assistant secretary, a title changed in 1896 to that of secretary. As years went on the work of the Society occupied an increasing amount of Keltie's time and thought, and the high prestige which it gained was due in large measure to his wide interests, genial sympathy, and sound judgement, exercised over the long period of his service. Among his activities was the reorganization of the Society's publications. The new monthly *Geographical Journal* appeared in 1893, and was under Keltie's editorship until 1915 and joint editorship until 1917. In 1895 he was one of the chief organizers of the sixth international geographical congress in London, and in 1897, at Toronto, he was president of the geographical section of the British Association, on the council of which he afterwards served from 1919 to 1924. His editorial work included the geographical section of the tenth edition of the *Encyclopædia Britannica*, the *World's Great Explorer* series, the *Story of Exploration* series; and his principal books were *Applied Geography* (1890), *The Partition of Africa* (1893), and *The History of Geography* (with O. J. R. Howarth, 1913). He resigned the secretaryship of the Royal Geographical Society in 1915, was elected to the council in 1917, and became a vice-president in 1921.

Keltie was knighted in 1918, and was also made a commander of the Swedish order of the North Star, the Norwegian order of St. Olaf, and the Finnish order of the White Rose. Other honours he held were the honorary LL.D. of St. Andrews University (1897), the Cullum gold medal of the American Geographical Society (1914), the gold medal of the Royal Scottish Geographical Society (1915), the medal of the Paris Geographical Society (1915), and the Victoria medal of the Royal Geographical Society (1917). He was an honorary member of the chief geographical societies of the world.

Keltie married in 1865 Margaret, daughter of Captain John Scott, of Kirkwall (died 1922), and had one daughter. He died in London 12 January 1927.

[J. S. Keltie, 'Thirty Years' Work of the Royal Geographical Society', in the *Geographical Journal*, May 1917; *The Times*, 13 January 1927; *Geographical Journal*, March 1927; H. R. Mill, *Record of the Royal Geographical Society*, 1930; private information.]

R. N. Rudmose Brown.

KENNEDY, Sir ALEXANDER BLACKIE WILLIAM (1847–1928), engineer, born in Stepney 17 March 1847, was the eldest son of the Rev. John Kennedy, congregational minister, by his wife, Helen Stodart, daughter of Alexander Blackie, bank manager, of Aberdeen, and sister of John Stuart Blackie [q.v.]. He was educated at the City of London School and the School of Mines, which was then in Jermyn Street. At the age of sixteen he was apprenticed for five and a half years to the firm of J. and W. Dudgeon at Millwall, and gained his first experience in marine engine construction. In 1868 he was made leading draughtsman in the engine works established by Sir Charles Mark Palmer [q.v.], at Jarrow-on-Tyne, and here he worked out the designs for the first compound marine engines built on Tyneside. In 1870 he became chief draughtsman to the firm of T. M. Tennant & Co., of Leith, working under Wilson Hartnell. He remained there until in 1871 he went into partnership with H. G. Bennett, a consulting marine engineer of Edinburgh and Glasgow. In 1873, at the request of William Henry Maw, editor of *Engineering*, he went to Vienna and in conjunction with Maw and James Dredge [q.v.] contributed to *Engineering* (vols. xv, xvi) reports of the engineering exhibits in the Vienna Universal Exhibition. He continued to contribute regularly to *Engineering* until 1887.

In 1874 Kennedy was appointed professor of engineering at University College, London, at a salary of less than two hundred a year, and there founded a school of engineering teaching, the principles of which have been widely followed in England and the United States of America. His teaching was based on Franz Reuleaux's *Theoretische Kinematik*, which he translated and edited in 1876 with the title *Kinematics of Machinery: Outlines of a Theory of Machines*. He also established in University College in 1878 an engineering laboratory, the first of its kind in England. It was described by him in a paper which he read before the Institution of Civil Engineers in December 1886. In this laboratory between 1881 and 1892 he carried out experiments on the strength and elasticity of materials, on the strength of riveted joints, and on marine engines. While professor he designed the steel arch pier at Trouville and the steel and concrete internal structure of the Hotel Cecil and of the Alhambra Theatre, the latter being probably the first building in which concrete slabs were used on a large scale to carry heavy weights. Between 1887 and 1889, in collaboration with Bryan Donkin (1835–1902, q.v.), he made exhaustive tests of different kinds of boilers, the results of which were published in *Engineering*, and afterwards edited by Donkin under the title *Experiments on Steam Boilers* (1897).

In 1889 Kennedy resigned his professorship and began practice as a consulting engineer at Westminster, in partnership with Bernard Maxwell Jenkin, son of Henry Charles Fleeming Jenkin [q.v.], and on Jenkin's retirement in 1908, with his own son, John Macfarlane Kennedy, and Sydney Bryan Donkin, son of Bryan Donkin. In 1900 Kennedy was appointed by Lord Goschen a member of the Belleville boiler committee.

From 1889 or 1890, however, Kennedy directed his attention particularly to electrical engineering, which was becoming important, and in which his interest had been aroused in 1887 by trials of motors for electric lighting carried out by him with John Hopkinson [q.v.] and Beauchamp Tower for the Society of Arts (*Journal* of the Society of Arts, February 1889). For this work he showed remarkable ability for one whose previous training had been in mechanical engineering; and without the aid of his splendid talents the establishment of low power electric stations in opposition to Ferranti's great project for supplying London might have been less successful [see FERRANTI, Sebastian Ziani de]. In a few years he built up one of the largest practices in the country. He was engineer to the Westminster Electric Supply Corporation from its foundation in 1889, and planned the whole system and works. Similarly he planned the system and was chief engineer of the Central Electric Supply Company from the start in 1899, and was also engineer to the St. James' and Pall Mall Electric Light Company, registered in 1888.

Kennedy was also closely connected with the development of electric transport. On the death of James Henry Greathead in 1896, he became joint engineer with W. R. Galbraith for the Waterloo and City Railway and prepared the whole of the electrical work, substituting for locomotives, motors in the front and rear ends of the train, a plan which afterwards came into general use where practicable. In 1899 the London County Council consulted him as to the electrical working of its tramways, and adopted his recommendation of a conduit system for the central district with overhead wiring for the outlying suburbs. As consulting engineer to the Great Western Railway, he prepared the plans for the work of electrification west of Paddington on the Great Western, and Hammersmith and City railways. His firm were consulting electrical engineers to the London and North Western, and London and South Western railways for their schemes of suburban electrification round London, and later on he carried out similar work for the South Eastern and Chatham railway. He was consulting engineer to the Calcutta Electric Supply Corporation until 1928, and to the Corporation of Edinburgh. He was also concerned with the construction of electrical stations in Manchester and many other English and Scottish towns, and also in Japan.

Kennedy did work in other fields. From June 1909 he was an associated civil member of the Ordnance Committee, and in 1913 served on Lord Parker's committee on wireless telegraphy. During the European War he served on the panel of the Munitions Invention department, was chairman of the committee on gun-sights and range-finders, and was vice-chairman of the committees on ordnance and ammunition and on anti-aircraft equipment. In 1920 he was chairman of the Ministry of Transport's committee on electrical railways. He was also closely associated with the formation of the London Power Company.

After the War Kennedy was desirous of preserving a record of the scenes of devastation. He therefore made a survey of the Western front, and in 1921 he published his observations and photographs under the title *From Ypres to Verdun*. In 1922, at the age of seventy-five, he undertook the exploration of Petra with a view to giving a full description of the remains there. He made a short preliminary visit in 1922 and two long visits in the years following. Husain, king of Nedj and Hejaz, received him kindly, afforded him help, and gave him the title of pasha in 1924. In 1925 he published *Petra; Its History and Monuments*, the most complete monograph on the subject, the value of which is considerably enhanced by the photographs, taken by himself. He was a musical amateur of taste and enthusiasm, and at his rooms in The Albany, Piccadilly, gave private concerts at which chamber music was performed by leading professional musicians. He was president of the London Camera Club, and a member of the Alpine Club, and in 1902 edited and published Adolphus Warburton Moore's diary under the title *The Alps in 1864*. In addition to the works already mentioned, he wrote a text-book, *The Mechanics of Machinery* (1886, 4th edition 1902).

Kennedy became a member of the Institution of Civil Engineers in 1879, and president in 1906, a member of the Institution of Mechanical Engineers in 1879, and president in 1894, and a member of the Institution of Electrical Engineers (originally the Society of Telegraph Engineers) in 1890. He was elected F.R.S. in 1887, and was knighted in 1905. He received honorary degrees from the universities of Glasgow (1894), Birmingham (1909), and Liverpool (1913). He retired from business early in 1928 and died in London 1 November of that year at The Albany, Piccadilly. He married in 1874 Elizabeth Verralls (died 1911), eldest daughter of William Smith (1816–1896, q.v.), actuary, of Edinburgh, and the translator of Fichte. He had two sons and one daughter.

[*The Times*, 2 November 1928; *The Engineer*, 9 November 1928; *Engineering*, 9 November 1928; *Proceedings* of the Institution of Civil Engineers, 1928–1929, vol. ccxxi, pp. 269–275; *Proceedings* of the Institution of Electrical Engineers, April 1922 and December 1927.] E. I. Carlyle.

KENNY, COURTNEY STANHOPE (1847–1930), legal scholar, was born at Halifax, Yorkshire, 18 March 1847, the elder son of William Fenton Kenny, a solicitor of that town, by his wife, Agnes Ramsden Ralph, of Halifax. On his father's side Kenny was descended from a family of French Huguenots named Du Quesne, who had fled to Connaught in the seventeenth century. He was educated in Yorkshire at the Heath and the Hipperholme grammar schools, and in 1863 was articled to a Halifax firm of conveyancing solicitors. After his admission to practice in 1869, he worked for two years as a partner in the firm, but in 1871 he decided to leave practice and acquire a university education. He entered Downing College, Cambridge, in that year and was elected to a foundation scholarship in 1872. His career as a student was brilliant. In 1874 he was senior in the law and history tripos, won the Winchester reading prize, and was elected president of the Union. In 1875 he won the Chancellor's medal for legal studies.

Kenny was elected a fellow of Downing College in 1875, being appointed to a lecturership in law and moral science. In three successive years, 1877, 1878, 1879, he won the Yorke prize with essays on *The History of the Law of Primogeniture in England and its Effect upon Landed Property*, *The History of the Law of England as to the Effects of Marriage on Property and on the Wife's Legal Capacity*, and *The True Principles of Legislation with Regard to Property Given for Charitable or other Public Uses*. In all of these works Kenny wrote both as a legal historian and as a reformer, his book on charities exercising a direct influence in bringing about the introduction in 1891 of the Mortmain and Charitable Uses Bill, which Lord Herschell piloted through parliament.

In 1881 Kenny was called to the bar by Lincoln's Inn and joined the South-Eastern circuit. In 1885 he was elected member of parliament for the Barnsley division of Yorkshire, as a follower of Mr. Gladstone, and at the general election of June 1886 he was again returned. While in parliament he introduced bills for the abolition of primogeniture and for the amendment of the law relating to blasphemy, demanding the repeal of the laws restricting the expression of religious opinion.

In 1888, on the election of Frederic William Maitland [q.v.] to the Downing professorship of the laws of England, Kenny succeeded him as university reader in English law, and retired from parliament in order to devote himself exclusively to his academic duties. He took part, however, in local affairs, serving for several years as vice-chairman of the Cambridgeshire county council and for a long period as chairman of the Cambridgeshire quarter sessions. The practical experience thus gained proved of great value to him as a lecturer and writer on law. In 1907, on Maitland's death, Kenny was elected to succeed him as Downing professor, and he held the chair until his resignation in 1918.

Kenny was unquestionably the most successful of all the Cambridge law teachers of his time. He did more than any one else to raise the standard of lecturing, for, as Professor Winfield has said, 'His lectures flame like a beacon in the memories of those who have attended them, and have been the altar at which younger instructors have sought to kindle their own more humble torches.' Kenny's contributions to legal literature cover a wide range, and are distinguished by sound scholarship, lucid expression, and charm of style. He was one of the first to edit collections of judicial decisions, his *Cases on Criminal Law* (1901, 7th edition 1928) and his *Cases on the Law of Torts* (1904, 5th edition 1928) being recognized as models of their kind. Of the former Maitland once said that he could not imagine a book better fitted to give the freshman his first ideas about law. Kenny's three articles, 'What an Old Reporter Told me', in the *Law Quarterly Review* (vol. xliii, 1927) illustrate his lively interest in the human side of the law, a characteristic which distinguishes all his writings.

Kenny's most important work is his *Outlines of Criminal Law* (1902, 14th edition 1932; American edition by J. H. Webb, 1907; French edition by A. Poulian, 1921). It has become a legal classic, being an indispensable text-book used not only by students but also by the bench and bar. It contains a clear and penetrating exposition of fundamental principles, illustrated by novel and vivid examples, many of them borrowed from Continental legal literature, for Kenny had made a study of French, German, and Italian criminal law. Of the *Outlines* Professor A. V. Dicey wrote that it 'proves conclusively that the art of treating legal topics with the literary skill which makes a legal text-book a work, full not only of instruction but of interest, may be displayed to-day quite as markedly as in the time of Blackstone'. In 1910 Kenny published his essay on *The Law of the Air*, which was one of the pioneer contributions to this subject; and in 1927 he brought out an edition, with introduction and notes, of *Parliamentary Logic*, the title under which the works of William Gerard Hamilton [q.v.], 'Single-speech Hamilton', were published in 1808 by Edmund Malone.

Kenny was elected a fellow of the British Academy in 1909, and later served as a member of its council. He married in 1876 Emily Gertrude, daughter of William Wood Wiseman, surgeon, of Osset, Yorkshire, and had two daughters. He died at Cambridge 18 March 1930. There is a portrait of him by Clegg Wilkinson in the hall of Downing College, and a pair of wrought iron gates, known as the Kenny memorial gates, have been presented to the college by his daughters.

[*The Times*, 19 March 1930; H. D. Hazeltine, *Courtney Stanhope Kenny, 1847–1930*, in *Proceedings* of the British Academy, vol. xviii, 1932; P. H. Winfield, Biographical Note, with portrait, in *Cambridge Legal Essays*, 1926; *Cambridge Review*, 25 April 1930; private information; personal knowledge.]

A. L. Goodhart.

KER, WILLIAM PATON (1855–1923), scholar and author, was born at Glasgow 30 August 1855, the eldest son of William Ker, merchant, of that city, by his wife, Caroline Agnes Paton. He passed from Glasgow Academy to Glasgow University, and proceeded thence in 1874 with a Snell exhibition to Balliol College, Oxford, of which Benjamin Jowett was then master. He obtained a first class in classical moderations (1876) and a second class in *literae humaniores* (1878). He was awarded the Taylorian scholarship in the latter year, and was elected to a fellowship at All Souls College in November 1879. In 1878 he was appointed assistant to William Young Sellar [q.v.], professor of humanity in the university of Edinburgh. This assistantship was one of the most valued experiences of his life.

In 1883, at the age of twenty-eight, Ker was appointed professor of English literature and history in the new university college of South Wales, Cardiff. It was hard, pioneering work, and he looked back on it with keen pleasure. Six years later, in

1889, he succeeded Henry Morley [q.v.] in the Quain chair of English language and literature in University College, London. Until his resignation of that chair in 1922 he spent most of the long London terms at his house, 95 Gower Street. He gave every week a great number of lectures and classes—in the early years of his professorship as many as a dozen. When the university of London was reorganized in 1900, Ker was appointed chairman of the modern languages board, and later of the English board, and he took the leading part in moulding English studies throughout the university. It was not always an easy task. He was inflexible in his hatred of any officialdom which seemed likely to hamper the school, and, on the other hand, of any slackness on the part of his colleagues on the board. But the building up of an honours school of English was only one of Ker's labours. He threw himself into the general work of the university, as a member of the senate, the academic council, and the faculty of arts, and of the professorial board of his college. He attended meetings assiduously, spoke seldom, and then always very briefly, but with extraordinary effect. He was conservative in politics and in every habit of his daily life, but his conservatism was combined with a readiness for any development upon sound lines. His eagerness for new adventure was shown by the energy with which, even during the distractions of the European War, he undertook the work of organizing Scandinavian studies in London University. He had been teaching Icelandic to his students for years, but that was not enough: largely through his initiative and energy a department of Scandinavian studies was founded in 1917, and he became its first director.

Such was the 'ubiquitariness' of Ker's mind that he could attend to all the literatures of Western Europe, and to the affairs of more than one university, with a thoroughness which made it difficult to believe that each of these interests was not first in his mind. He retained his fellowship at All Souls for forty-four years, until his death, for he never married; indeed, the college, quite as much as his house in Gower Street, was his home. His position at All Souls was unique. He was at once a wit, a sage, and an institution. He held at different times various offices in the college; he was assiduous in his attendance at its meetings, sparing of speech but rich in wise counsel; above all, he was the very centre of the college's social life. As a talker he was unequalled; his very silence, frequent enough, breathed sympathy. His kindness to the young Fellows was unbounded: the rich stores of his learning, never displayed, were always at their disposal; and many of his happiest hours were spent in taking them for long walks in the country or in sitting with them in the common room in the evening. Almost every week-end in term time was spent in Oxford, and he kept throughout in the closest touch with Oxford affairs. In 1920 he was elected to the chair of poetry at Oxford—a distinction which might have been his earlier had he wished, and one which he retained when he resigned his London chair. His directorship of Scandinavian studies he also retained to the end.

Ker was slow to publish. He was forty-two when *Epic and Romance* appeared in 1897; until then he had printed hardly anything, except an essay on 'The Philosophy of Art', which appeared in *Essays in Philosophical Criticism* in 1883. It was not at once realized how great was the light which *Epic and Romance* threw on problems which had been puzzling scholars for many years. In 1900 Ker selected and edited *The Essays of John Dryden* (2 vols.), and from 1901 to 1903 he edited Lord Berners' translation of Froissart's *Chronicles* (6 vols.) with a characteristic Introduction. In *The Dark Ages* (1904) and *English Literature: Medieval* (1912) he compressed into small volumes much of the result of his vast reading. His lectures as professor of poetry were issued in 1923 (*The Art of Poetry: Seven Lectures, 1920–1922*); most of his shorter writings have been reprinted in *Essays on Medieval Literature* (1905) and in the two volumes of *Collected Essays of W. P. Ker* (1925) edited by Charles Whibley [q.v.] after Ker's death. *Form and Style in Poetry* (edited by R. W. Chambers, 1928) includes lectures delivered in Cambridge and London on the history of poetic forms and the relation of form and substance, subjects which he had made peculiarly his own.

Ker's wide reading in many languages, his critical acumen, and strength of imagination enabled him to see farther into things than most people, and so to throw fresh light on problems of literary relationships and to bring out the essential in the books and authors with which he dealt. His best-known work, perhaps, is concerned with questions of literary form and medieval literature, but his lectures on writers of later centuries, French, Italian,

Spanish, Scandinavian, as well as English, are no less valuable.

Immense as was the range of Ker's knowledge, he always kept the spirit of an adventurer, wandering far afield when the spirit really prompted, carrying his students with him by his power of mind and temper. Towards the end of his life he gave *Nos manet Oceanus* as his favourite motto; it was in this spirit that in his farewell speech at University College he gave his students the advice of the abbey of Thelema, 'Do what you like'. Few men liked more things, or got more out of life in all its aspects than Ker. The love of books and the love of nature were the two passions of his life; he loved children also, and animals, climbing, walking, rowing, dancing, good wine, and good fellowship. He had a keen wit and a strong sense of humour, and a firm belief in the virtue of cheerfulness. Above all, he had the instinct for friendship in a most uncommon degree; students and friends alike found him full of generous sympathy and understanding.

Ker's vacations were mostly spent walking or climbing, boating or swimming, in Scotland, Switzerland, and elsewhere. During the European War he was doing confidential work for the Admiralty: after the War he returned to the Alps, doing, at the age of sixty-five, strenuous climbs in quick succession, in a way which might have tried a young and very strong man. His first and last year of complete freedom, after the resignation of his London chair in 1922, was passed in this way, in the spirit of an explorer, until, on 17 July 1923, he fell dead from heart failure on the Pizzo Bianco, which he had just described as 'the most beautiful spot in the world'. He was buried in the old churchyard at Macugnaga, Italy.

A portrait of Ker by Wilson Steer is at University College, London, which also possesses a bronze bust by his lifelong friend John Tweed; another bust by Tweed is at All Souls College, Oxford, and a replica is at the university of Glasgow.

[*The Times*, 20, 21, 23, 25 July 1923; R. W. Chambers (with contributions from J. MacCunn and J. W. Mackail), *W. P. Ker, 1855–1923* in *Proceedings* of the British Academy, vol. xi, 1924–1925; T. Gregory Foster in *English Studies*, October 1923; A. D. Godley in *The Alpine Journal*, November 1923, René Galland in *Revue Anglo-Américaine*, February 1926; J. and F. MacCunn, *Recollections of W. P. Ker by two friends*, privately printed, 1924; private information.]

R. W. Chambers.

KERR, Lord WALTER TALBOT (1839–1927), admiral of the fleet, was born at Newbattle Abbey, Midlothian, 28 September 1839, the fourth son of John William Robert Kerr, seventh Marquess of Lothian, by his wife, Lady Cecil Chetwynd Talbot, daughter of Charles Chetwynd, second Earl Talbot [q.v.]. Their second son was Schomberg Henry Kerr, ninth Marquess of Lothian [q.v.]. He was educated at Radley School from 1851 till 1853, when he joined H.M.S. *Prince Regent* as a naval cadet. During the Baltic operations of the Crimean War, 1854–1855, he served in the *Neptune* and *Cornwallis* and earned the Baltic medal, being promoted midshipman in August 1855. The next year Kerr was appointed to the *Shannon*, China station. On the outbreak of the Indian Mutiny in 1857 his ship was ordered to Calcutta, and his captain, (Sir) William Peel [q.v.], third son of Sir Robert Peel, the statesman, landed with most of his ship's company as a naval brigade. Kerr served with it throughout the Mutiny, was wounded in an action near Cawnpore, and was given an independent command at the siege and capture of Lucknow. For this service he was specially rated mate for the rest of the *Shannon*'s commission, and in the following year served for a few months in the same rank in the *Victoria and Albert*, and was promoted lieutenant in September 1859. In 1860 he was appointed to the *Emerald* for three years' service in the Channel, and in 1864 he went to the *Princess Royal*, flagship on the East Indies and Cape station, for another three years. Kerr was promoted commander in 1868 and served in that rank in the *Hercules*, Channel squadron, until 1871, and afterwards in the *Lord Warden*, Mediterranean flagship, until promotion to captain in November 1872. While in the *Hercules* he was given the silver medal of the Royal Humane Society for jumping overboard from a height of thirty feet into the Tagus in order to rescue a man who had fallen from the rigging.

During his first eleven years on the captains' list, four of which were spent on half-pay, Kerr's principal commands were as flag-captain to Sir Beauchamp Seymour (afterwards Lord Alcester) in the Channel squadron 1874–1877, and in the Mediterranean 1880–1881. In September 1880 he was sent by Seymour, who was in command of the combined fleet of the five naval powers assembled to enforce, under the terms of the Treaty of Berlin, the surrender of Dulcigno to Montenegro by

Turkey, on a special mission to Riza Pasha, the Turkish governor of Albania. He then had a shore appointment as captain of the Medway steam reserve until 1885, when Lord George Hamilton [q.v.], on becoming first lord of the Admiralty, appointed him as his naval private secretary.

Kerr retained this appointment at the Admiralty until nearly a year after his promotion to rear-admiral in January 1889. He then hoisted his flag in the *Trafalgar*, as second in command in the Mediterranean until 1892, when he returned to the Admiralty as junior naval lord, the fifth Earl Spencer, on taking office, including him in his Board for the duties of fourth naval lord, although he was actually senior to (Sir) John Fisher [q.v.], who was third naval lord and controller of the navy. In November 1893 he became second naval lord until May 1895, when, having been promoted vice-admiral in the preceding February, he was appointed vice-admiral commanding the Channel squadron, with his flag in the *Majestic*, for two years. In June 1895 he took part with his squadron in the celebration of the opening of the Kiel canal. In May 1899 Mr. Goschen brought him back to his former post on the Board of Admiralty, preparatory to succeeding Sir Frederick Richards [q.v.] as senior naval lord in the following August. He retained the latter office, being promoted admiral in March 1900, and by a special order in council admiral of the fleet in June 1904, until Trafalgar day (21 October) of that year, when Lord Selborne brought Sir John Fisher back from Portsmouth to succeed him. He remained on half-pay until he retired on account of age in September 1909.

Kerr's early promotions made him a senior captain when he came to the Admiralty as private secretary, but although some naval members of the Board were his juniors, he did not presume upon his seniority to take a too prominent part in the administration, while his high rank enabled him to be of good service to the first lord in the course of certain troubles with members of the Board, notably in connexion with the difference between Lord Charles Beresford [q.v.], junior or fourth naval lord, and Sir Arthur Hood, senior or first naval lord. By temperament Kerr was unassuming and not opinionative and therefore got on well with all his colleagues, naval and civilian, while his moderation and judgement ensured respect for his opinions. He was a thorough seaman and had a great love of the service, and although conservative at heart, he recognized the necessity of advancing with the times. He was not a man to initiate change, but when he recognized its necessity, he at once adopted it and gave it his firm support. His service at the Admiralty as private secretary coincided with the beginning of the shipbuilding activity which continued with only one brief interruption up to the outbreak of war in 1914, and his sound common sense and knowledge of the service were of great help to Lord George Hamilton in carrying out the programme of the Naval Defence Act of 1889. Again, as fourth naval lord and second naval lord from 1892 to 1895, his moderation and firmness were of much help to Lord Spencer, when confronted with Cabinet difficulties in the carrying out of the second shipbuilding programme. Finally, in his last period of service at the Admiralty as senior naval lord from 1899 to 1904, under Lords Goschen and Selborne, he was able to give wise advice in the carrying out of the far-reaching changes in the training and organization of the personnel of the navy, for which Lord Fisher was primarily responsible. He ably held the balance between the exuberance of the reformers and the hostility of their opponents. During Fisher's absence as commander-in-chief at Portsmouth (1903–1904) the carrying on of the new scheme rested largely with Kerr, and it was due to his firmness that things proceeded without a hitch during the interval until Fisher returned as first sea lord himself. Kerr had no share in the changes made in the organization of the fleet in 1905, but it would not have been so easy to make those reforms if he had been less convinced of the necessity of the changes to come. His was not a creative mind, but his character was such that he enjoyed in the highest degree the esteem of his fellow officers and of all who knew him. In Lord George Hamilton's own words, he might well be termed the *Preux Chevalier* of the royal navy. He was created K.C.B. in 1896 and G.C.B. in 1902.

Soon after Kerr entered the navy, his widowed mother became, with her younger children, a Roman Catholic, and Kerr was thenceforth a devoted adherent of that faith. He married in 1873 Lady Amabel Cowper (died 1906), the youngest daughter of George Augustus Frederick, sixth Earl Cowper, and sister of Francis Thomas De Grey, seventh Earl Cowper [q.v.]. They had four sons and two daughters. On the seventh earl's death in 1905, Lady Amabel succeeded to the properties of Brocket Hall, Hertfordshire, and Melbourne Hall, Derbyshire, and became co-heiress, with Lady Desborough and Lord Lucas, of the barony of Butler. After his retirement, Kerr resided at Melbourne Hall, and died there 12 May 1927. His grandson, Peter Francis Walter (born 1922), is the heir presumptive to the Marquess of Lothian.

A cartoon of Kerr by 'Spy' appeared in *Vanity Fair* 8 November 1900.

[*The Times*, 13 May 1927; Admiralty records; private information; personal knowledge.] V. W. BADDELEY.

KINGSFORD, CHARLES LETHBRIDGE (1862–1926), historian and topographer, was born at Ludlow 25 December 1862. He was the third son of the Rev. Sampson Kingsford, headmaster of the grammar school there, by his wife, Helen, daughter of William Lethbridge, of Kilworthy, Tavistock. He received his education at Rossall and at St. John's College, Oxford (1881–1886), where he gained a first class in *literae humaniores*, a second class in modern history, and the Arnold essay prize (1888). After a year's experience of sub-editorial work on the DICTIONARY OF NATIONAL BIOGRAPHY, he published a scholarly edition of the *Song of Lewes* (1890) and in the same year he became a junior examiner at the Board of Education. Kingsford rose to the position of assistant secretary (1905); but the Education Act of 1902 had led to changes in the office which he found uncongenial. In 1912 he voluntarily resigned and thenceforth devoted his whole time to historical research. No radical change of habits was involved, for the record of his publications between 1890 and 1912 shows how fully the leisure hours of his official life must have been occupied in such studies. He contributed nearly four hundred biographies to this DICTIONARY and more than thirty to the *Encyclopædia Britannica*. At first, his main interests lay in the twelfth, thirteenth, and fourteenth centuries, and in 1894 he published, with T. A. Archer, a volume on *The Crusades: the Story of the Latin Kingdom of Jerusalem*; but his attention was diverted to the last century of the Middle Ages by the task of writing for this DICTIONARY the life of Henry V. The article (1891) was expanded into a book in 1901 (2nd ed. 1923), which was followed by a study of the early biographies of Henry (*English Historical Review*, January 1910) and an edition of the *First English Life of Henry V* (1911).

Kingsford's discovery of the importance of city chronicles for Henry's reign led him into a new and fruitful field of study, that of London history and topography. His edition of three unprinted *Chronicles of London* in 1905 was pioneer work which he and others afterwards carried much further. An important outcome of these investigations was a new edition of John Stow's *Survey of London* (1908), freed from the accretions due to earlier editors and furnished with admirable introduction, notes, and indices. It has placed the study of London history and topography upon a new footing. The first fruit of Kingsford's increased leisure after his retirement from the Board of Education was the expansion of a course of lectures delivered at Oxford in 1910 into a volume on *English Historical Literature in the Fifteenth Century* (1913), an illuminating survey which has no parallel for any other century of English history. The outbreak of war, during which he served first as a special constable and afterwards in the Ministry of Pensions, interrupted most of his historical activities, but he was able to some extent to continue his work on medieval London, and, in another field, he wrote *The Story of the Middlesex Regiment* (1916).

With the return of peace, Kingsford fell to work again. Two volumes of the medieval letters and papers of the Stonor family appeared in the Camden Series of the Royal Historical Society in 1919; *The Story of the Royal Warwickshire Regiment* followed in1921; in 1923–1924 he delivered the Ford lectures at Oxford, and in 1925, besides printing these as *Prejudice and Promise in Fifteenth-Century England*, an able plea for a fairer estimate of that century of our history, he brought out his most striking contribution to London topography, *The Early History of Piccadilly, Leicester Square, Soho, and their Neighbourhood.* His services to history were recognized in 1924 by his election as a fellow of the British Academy. Meanwhile, he was busy preparing reports on the manuscripts of Lord De L'Isle and Dudley for the Historical Manuscripts Commission, and on those at Madresfield Court for Earl Beauchamp. His contributions to historical periodicals and to the transactions of the many learned societies of which he was a member, and often an officer, make a long list; and one paper at least was in proof at the time of the sudden seizure which ended in his death at his house in Kensington 27 November 1926.

Kingsford married in 1892 Alys, daughter of Charles Thomas Hudson [q.v.], naturalist. They had no children. He was above the middle height, of sturdy build, and in later years looked 'like a country squire, not a Londoner'. He was rather reserved, but a good friend and colleague, very conscientious in all he undertook, and an exceptionally methodical and accurate worker. Something of this he may have owed to his official training. He had a vein of humour which does not often appear in his books and an occasional causticity of speech to which he seems to have given much freer rein in official circles than in the more congenial surroundings of his later life.

[*The Times*, 29 November 1926; A. G. Little, *Charles Lethbridge Kingsford, 1862–1926*, in *Proceedings* of the British Academy, vol. xii, 1926; E. Jeffries Davis, 'The Work of C. L. Kingsford in London History and Topography' in *The London Topographical Record*, vol. xiv, 1928.] J. Tait.

KIRK, Sir JOHN (1832–1922), naturalist and administrator, was born at Barry, Forfarshire, 19 December 1832, the second son of the Rev. John Kirk, at that time minister of the parish, by his wife, Christian Carnegie, who was descended from a cadet branch of the Southesk family. From Arbroath high school he passed in 1847 to the university of Edinburgh, where he took his M.D. degree in 1854. After a year as a physician in the Edinburgh Royal Infirmary, Kirk volunteered for the Crimean War and served in the Erenkevi hospital on the Dardanelles (1855–1856), giving his spare time to the study of the botany of Asia Minor. On his return to England in 1857 he gave up the idea of teaching natural history on being appointed to accompany David Livingstone [q.v.], as physician and naturalist, on his second Zambezi expedition. For five years (1858–1863) Kirk was Livingstone's chief assistant and proved an unqualified success. The expedition first explored the Shiré valley and highlands, and made the earliest investigation of Lake Nyasa and its surroundings; the Zambezi was then ascended as far as Sasheke, and a thorough examination made of the Victoria Falls. On the return journey Kirk was nearly drowned (November 1860) in the Kebra-basa rapids, and early in 1863 he was attacked by dysentery and ordered home. His botanical collections were considerable and laid the foundations of the *Flora of Tropical Africa* which was published under government auspices 1868–1917.

His experiences turned Kirk's interests definitely towards Africa, and he refused an important post at the Royal Gardens, Kew, in order to accept one as medical officer to the Zanzibar agency in 1866. Later in that year he was made vice-consul, and in 1868 assistant political agent, in 1873 consul-general, and in 1880 political agent.

When Kirk came to Zanzibar the Sayyid or Sultan, fortified by the guarantee of Great Britain and France (1862) of his rights in tropical Africa, saw no reason to interfere with the lucrative slave-trade. Kirk, however, soon gained a position of authority and persuaded the Sayyid that his interests lay in abolishing the trade. Accordingly in 1873 the Sayyid made slavery illegal in his dominions. The prosperity of the coast towns was adversely affected, but Kirk found a partial remedy in the establishment of the East African rubber trade (1878), the outcome of his discovery of the rubber-yielding vine (landolphia). British influence was in the ascendant and Kirk had become virtual ruler of Zanzibar when, in 1885, Friedrich Gerhard Rohlfs, the explorer, arrived as first German consul. Previously Kirk had been consul for Hamburg as well as for Portugal and Italy. Two years later (1887) the German East Africa Company was founded and acquired from native chiefs much of the territory over which the Sayyid claimed nominal authority. Kirk was instructed by the British government to mollify the Sayyid (who had dispatched forces to the disputed territories) and to discourage opposition to German claims. At the same time he checkmated German designs on Zanzibar and, as his crowning work in Africa, was instrumental in persuading the Sayyid to make great concessions from the rest of his mainland territories to the East African Association (1887), which in the next year became the Imperial British East Africa Company.

In 1887 Kirk retired from the consular service but continued to serve the state in several capacities in African affairs. He was British plenipotentiary to the African slave-trade conference at Brussels (1889–1890). In 1895 he was sent to Nigeria to inquire into a dispute, which had resulted in considerable fighting and loss of life, between the Brass natives and the Royal Niger Company; and the subsequent *Report by Sir John Kirk on the Disturbances at Brass* (1896) supplied important information about the country and people. From 1895 he was chairman of the government committee for the construction of the Uganda railway, and in 1896 he was appointed to the Royal Society's tsetse fly committee. Kirk's many valuable contributions to the botany and zoology of Zanzibar and East Africa were communicated in various papers to the Linnean, Zoological, and other societies. Several were of an important economic nature, and his experimental garden at Mgweni may be regarded as the precursor of several botanic gardens which have materially helped the economic development of East Africa.

Kirk was awarded the patron's medal of the Royal Geographical Society in 1882, was a vice-president of the society from 1891 to 1894, and foreign secretary from 1894 to 1911. In 1887 he was elected a fellow of the Royal Society and in 1894–1895 he was a vice-president. He was also a vice-president of the Linnean Society 1882–1883. He was awarded the C.M.G. in 1879, and was created K.C.M.G. in 1881, G.C.M.G. in 1886, and K.C.B. in 1890. He received decorations from Portugal and Italy, and was an honorary LL.D. of Edinburgh (1890), Sc.D. of Cambridge (1897), and D.C.L. of Oxford (1898). His name is perpetuated in Nyasaland in the Kirk Range, west of the Shiré river.

Kirk married in 1867 Helen (died 1914), daughter of Charles Cooke, of Ledbury, Herefordshire, and had one son and three daughters. He died 15 January 1922 at Sevenoaks.

A portrait of Kirk by his nephew, A. H. Kirk, hangs in the National Portrait Gallery.

[*The Times*, 16 January 1922; D. Livingstone, *Narrative of an Expedition to the Zambesi and its Tributaries*, 1865; W. G. Blackie, *Personal Life of David Livingstone*, 1880, 6th edition 1925; R. Coupland, *Kirk on the Zambesi*, 1928; *Geographical Journal*, March 1922; *Proceedings* of the Royal Society, vol. xciv, B, 1923.] R. N. Rudmose Brown.

KIRK, Sir JOHN (1847–1922), philanthropist, the second son of Alfred Kirk, tinsmith and brazier, of Kegworth, Leicestershire, by his wife, Mary, daughter of Harry Wilkins, was born at Kegworth 10 June 1847. He was educated at Castle Donington grammar school, Leicestershire. Part of his boyhood was spent in France, but at the age of sixteen, after his father's death, he went to London and was appointed clerk to the Pure Literature Society.

In 1867 Kirk entered the service of the Ragged School Union, then housed in 'two rooms and a cupboard' in Exeter Hall, Strand. He acted as evening schools visitor from 1873 to 1879, during which period he was secretary of the Open Air Mission, but in 1879 he was appointed secretary of the Ragged School Union. He thus became closely associated with Antony Ashley Cooper, seventh Earl of Shaftesbury [q.v.], president of the Union from 1844 until his death in 1885. It was largely owing to Kirk's power of adaptation, his gift of seizing opportunities, and his determination, that the Union survived the critical years following the passage of the Education Act of 1870. Thereafter ragged schools were transformed into mission Sunday schools with multiplying activities: country holiday homes, the cripple mission, and clothing guilds were developed.

Kirk was knighted in 1907 and a public testimonial was presented to him at the Mansion House; his title was altered from secretary to director. His jubilee of service was celebrated in 1917, also at the Mansion House, when he took the opportunity of presenting a cheque for £1,000, which he had raised privately, for the establishment of a Shaftesbury Foundation Fund. The same year he delivered the first Shaftesbury lecture, a notable review and forecast of child welfare.

During Kirk's period of service the annual income of the Union increased from £6,000 to £60,000. In 1914 its title, as an incorporated body, was changed to the Shaftesbury Society and Ragged School Union. Kirk resigned the position of director in 1919, but accepted the post of honorary treasurer, which he held until his death, which took place at his home at Westcott, Surrey, 3 April 1922. The freehold quarters of the Society in John Street, Bloomsbury, bear Kirk's name, but the best tribute to his philanthropic career is the great expansion of the work of the Society which he guided for fifty years.

In 1892 Kirk helped (Sir) Cyril Arthur Pearson [q.v.] to start the Pearson 'fresh air fund', and in 1909 he founded the National Federation of Christian Workers among Poor Children.

Kirk travelled widely. He visited the United States and Canada four times, also South Africa, and in 1911 went on a world tour which included America, Australia, and New Zealand. He was a modest man, open-minded, observant, and possessed of a great capacity for the service of others. In religion he was a devout evangelical.

Kirk married in 1872 Elizabeth (died 1934), daughter of George Ayris, of Witney, Oxfordshire, and had four sons and three daughters.

There is a portrait of Kirk by Fred Stratton at John Kirk House.

[*The Times*, 5 April 1922; John Stuart, *Mr. John Kirk; the children's friend*, 1907; David Williamson, *Sir John Kirk*, 1922.]

A. BLACK.

KNOLLYS, FRANCIS, first VISCOUNT KNOLLYS, of Caversham (1837–1924), private secretary to King Edward VII, was born in London 16 July 1837, the second son of General Sir William Thomas Knollys [q.v.], by his wife, Elizabeth, daughter of Sir John St. Aubyn, fifth baronet [q.v.]. He was educated in Guernsey, and proceeded in 1851 to the Royal Military College at Sandhurst. Although he received a commission as ensign in the 23rd regiment of Foot in 1854, Knollys decided to abandon a military career and to enter the civil service. He became junior examiner in the department of the Commissioners of Audit in 1855. When his father was appointed treasurer and comptroller of the household to Albert Edward, Prince of Wales, in 1862, Knollys helped him with his work, and in 1870 was appointed private secretary to the prince.

The Prince of Wales's interests were very varied, and although he relied on experts to advise him in many matters, it was to his private secretary that he usually turned for information and counsel. He soon found that he could rely on Knollys's sound judgement and carefully considered advice. In cases like the Mordaunt divorce suit (1870), when the Prince of Wales was brought in quite unnecessarily, and the baccarat scandal (1891), which was grossly mishandled at the start, the advantage of having some one with whom he could talk freely, some one who would tell him the whole truth, however unpalatable, was incalculable. Knollys's tact and discretion could always be relied upon, and his knowledge of men, and of the motives which actuated them when they put forward requests, enabled the Prince of Wales to deal successfully with many difficult problems. In 1868 Queen Victoria, in order to show her appreciation of Knollys's services, appointed him gentleman usher in her household. In 1875 he accompanied the Prince of Wales on his Indian tour as private secretary, and was the pivot of a large staff which had been chosen to go with the prince.

When the Prince of Wales ascended the throne as King Edward VII in 1901, Knollys naturally continued to be his private secretary, and was raised to the peerage as Baron Knollys, of Caversham, in 1902. In accordance with tradition, the Prince of Wales had become more and more liberal as Queen Victoria became more and more conservative, but this suited Knollys, as his instincts were wholly liberal. During the reign of King Edward, however, the fact that Knollys was so strong an adherent of the liberal party was the subject of much criticism among conservatives, who considered that the private secretary to the sovereign should be as unbiassed as a civil servant. None the less, his absolute impartiality was recognized by Mr. Balfour, who was prime minister at the beginning of the reign, and by the other ministers of the conservative government.

Knollys was a past master at letter writing, and had the gift of expressing himself concisely without omitting anything of importance. He usually wrote his letters standing up at a high desk and considered a stenographer unnecessary and tiresome, but after King Edward's accession the number of letters and telegrams increased so much that Knollys was forced to dictate most of his answers, although he continued to write all political letters with his own hand up to the end. He was an omnivorous reader, and his grasp of political questions combined with a quaint sense of humour made him a delightful companion. He had a certain contempt for orders and decorations, both British and foreign—a trait in his character which was quite unintelligible to King Edward. He was created K.C.M.G. in 1886, K.C.B. in 1897, G.C.V.O. in 1901, I.S.O. in 1903, G.C.B. in 1908, and received many foreign orders. He was made a privy councillor in 1910, and was advanced to a viscounty in 1911.

On the death of King Edward in 1910 Knollys was pressed by King George V to remain as joint private secretary with Lord Stamfordham. This he did for three years, but in 1913 he asked to be allowed to retire. In 1910 he became lord-in-waiting to Queen Alexandra, a purely honorary post which he accepted in order that he might be of some assistance to the queen in her retirement. He died at Rickmansworth 15 August 1924.

Knollys married in 1887 the Hon. Ardyn Mary, daughter of Sir Henry Thomas Tyrwhitt, third baronet, and had one son, Edward George William Tyrwhitt (born 1895), who succeeded his father as second viscount, and one daughter.

[Private information; personal knowledge.]
F. E. G. Ponsonby.

KNOTT, RALPH (1878–1929), architect, was born at Whitheads Grove, Chelsea, 3 May 1878. He was the eighth child and youngest son of Samuel Knott, tailor, of Pont Street, London, by his wife, Elizabeth Ann White, formerly of Portland, Dorset. He was educated at the City of London School and later articled to Messrs. Woodd & Ainslie, architects, of London. During this period he also studied at the Architectural Association, and was taught etching by Frank Brangwyn, R.A. After the completion of his articles he entered the office of Sir Aston Webb [q.v.] as a draughtsman. Here he gained experience of large architectural work and of architectural competitions, which stood him in good stead later on. Among the latter was the competition for the design of the layout of the Queen Victoria Memorial, for which Knott made many beautiful drawings under Sir Aston Webb's guidance. He was an architectural draughtsman of no mean order and an able water-colourist; he was left-handed and could draw equally well with either hand. In 1908 he entered into partnership with E. Stone Collins; they had offices in Adelphi Terrace.

When in 1908 the London County Council announced a public competition in two stages for the design of the new County Hall on the south side of the river at Westminster, Ralph Knott entered for it and was placed amongst the successful competitors in the first stage. For the second stage some of the most successful architects of the day sent in designs, but Knott, at the age of twenty-nine, won the competition. The building was modified somewhat from his competitive design, which in one respect at least was twenty years ahead of its time; in Knott's design the offices in the cross blocks were planned on both sides of the corridors—an almost universal practice to-day in office building both in England and in America. In the first portion of the County Hall to be built, this arrangement was abandoned, but it was adopted in a modified form in the last section of the building. The outbreak of the European War interrupted the progress of the building, and Knott spent three years of this period in the designing shops of the Royal Air Force. In 1919 on his return to civil life the work on the County Hall went rapidly forward, and about two-thirds of the building—the centre and one wing—were completed and opened by King George V in 1922. Posterity must be the final judge of this great building; but by contemporaries it is considered to be one of the most successful public buildings of its time, a signal addition to the architecture of London, and not unworthy of the Houses of Parliament on the other side of the river.

From this time to his death, Knott did no work of great importance architecturally, but the vigour of his style can be seen in No. 21 Upper Grosvenor Street; its simplicity and directness of purpose in a delightful little house in Mallord Street, Chelsea, and in commercial work for Messrs. W. T. Henley's Telegraph Works Company at Gravesend. He made the sketch plans for the remaining portions of the County Hall in 1928 and 1929, which were completed by his partner, Mr. E. S. Collins, after his death.

In 1923 Knott was instructed by the British government to design the speaker's residence and the two blocks of departmental offices, forming part of the Parliament Buildings for Northern Ireland at Belfast. (Sir) Arnold Thornely was appointed architect of the Parliament House proper, and Knott's office blocks were to be in the form of two buildings flanking the central Parliament House. Later it was decided that Thornely should re-design the Parliament House in order to include the departmental offices and the Upper and Lower Chambers under one roof. Knott was compensated, and to his great disappointment his agreement terminated.

Knott was elected fellow of the Royal Institute of British Architects in 1921. In 1919 he married Ada, widow of Sidney James Longden, and daughter of Richard Brown. He left no issue. He died 25 January 1929 at West Lodge, East Sheen.

[Private information; personal knowledge.]
M. E. Webb.

KNOX, Sir GEORGE EDWARD (1845–1922), Indian civil servant and judge, was born at Madras 14 November 1845, the eldest son and child of the Rev. George Knox (an Irishman who was at that time chaplain in the East India Company's service and afterwards vicar of Exton, Rutland) by his wife, Frances Mary Anne, daughter of Thomas Forbes Reynolds, M.D., of Wallington, Surrey. His younger brother, Edmund Arbuthnott Knox, was bishop of Manchester from 1903 to 1921. He was educated at Merchant Taylors' School, where he laid the foundation of his linguistic attainments by acquiring the rudiments of Hebrew in addition to the usual classical training; and while still at school he became also an evening student at University College, London, where he gained a first prize in Sanskrit. In 1864 he passed the open examination for the Indian civil service; and, continuing a member of University College for his probationary year, again secured a first prize in Sanskrit. He proceeded to India in the autumn of 1865 and was almost the last member of the Indian civil service to be posted for further study to Fort William College, Calcutta—a course which, in his case, proved to be abundantly justified. In eighteen months, in addition to the usual examination in Hindi, he passed the high proficiency tests both in Urdu and Sanskrit. Urdu he spoke and read throughout his career with fluency and ease. He also acquired a knowledge of Persian, and learned Arabic sufficiently well to be able to consult the classical authorities of Mohammedan law in the original texts. The latter accomplishment is exceptional for English and even for Indian judges, and combined with proficiency in Sanskrit law texts almost unique.

On completing his training in 1867 Knox was posted to Meerut, and for nearly ten years carried out the ordinary duties of an executive officer. In 1877 he joined the judicial department as judge of the small causes court at Allahabad, a post which provides valuable insight into the details of the daily life of humble folk. After two years he began to hold posts as district and sessions judge, involving responsibilities which correspond roughly with those of a high court judge in England. In 1885 he was chosen legal remembrancer to the local government of the North-Western Provinces and Oudh, a post which combined the functions of principal law officer and draftsman, and carried with it a seat in the local legislature. In 1890 Knox was appointed a judge of the high court of judicature at Allahabad; and, as at the time of his appointment there was no retiring limit for judges appointed to the high courts from the Indian civil service, he continued on the bench for the next thirty years, acting as chief justice on no less than thirteen different occasions. He received a knighthood in 1906. Failing health compelled him to take long leave in January 1921; and while still on leave he died, 20 July 1922, at Naini Tal, the official hill station of the United Provinces.

Long before his death, Knox had become an almost legendary figure. In fifty-six years' service he had only taken one day's furlough, and that through an accident for which he was not responsible; he served for longer than any other civil servant since the time of John Company and was senior by over a quarter of a century to the next member of the service on the active list in the United Provinces. His patriarchal appearance and long white beard were in keeping with the fact that he had a son and a grandson on the active list of the service in his own province. But he was much more than a picturesque figure: his legal, no less than his linguistic, equipment for judicial office was outstanding; and his great experience was always ready to the need of the moment. Even more noteworthy was his industry: as a junior officer he had edited a number of legal works, and during the greater part of his time in the high court he not only dealt with a volume of judicial work equal to if not larger than that of any of his colleagues, but also had the supervision and control of the subordinate judiciary and establishments in some forty districts. His complete independence of official translators contributed greatly to the dispatch of business. He also took an active interest in the affairs of Allahabad University, serving the office of vice-chancellor on more than one occasion. His services were recognized by the honorary degree of LL.D.

Knox was a devout churchman of the evangelical school. He gave generously both time and money to missionary, educational, and other activities of the Church; and, if his rigid sabbatarianism occasionally involved him in controversy, it in no way diminished the respect in which he was universally held. To the bar in general and specially to its Indian members he was endeared by his unfailing courtesy and patience on the bench.

Knox married in 1868 Katharine Anne Louise, younger daughter of Major William Loch, 1st Bombay Lancers. She survived him with five sons and two daughters. Four of his sons attained distinction in the Indian services.

[*The Times*, 22 July 1922; *The Leader* (Allahabad), 19 January 1921; *The Pioneer* (Allahabad), 21 July 1922; *Indian Law Reports*, Allahabad series, 1890–1921; official records; private information.]

S. V. FitzGerald.

LAMBOURNE, first BARON (1847–1928), politician. [See LOCKWOOD, AMELIUS MARK RICHARD.]

LANE, JOHN (1854–1925), publisher, born 14 March 1854 at West Putford, Devon, was the only son of Lewis Lane, yeoman, by his wife, Mary Grace, daughter of John Jenn, miller and corn merchant, of Cory Mill, in the same parish. He went first to the national school at Hartland, whither his family had removed when he was three years old, and was afterwards sent to a school at Chulmleigh, near South Molton. In 1869 he was appointed to a junior clerkship in the Railway Clearing House. He is described by one of those who knew him in his earliest London days as shy, rustic in appearance, and speaking with a strong Devonshire accent. These characteristics he exchanged in time for a debonair exterior and a very urbane manner.

During the eighteen years that Lane was forced to spend in the Railway Clearing House, the idea of becoming a publisher was slowly taking shape in his mind. It was not, however, until 1887 that, having chanced upon suitable premises in Vigo Street, Piccadilly, he began business in association with Elkin Mathews, an antiquarian bookseller from Exeter. Lane was a born antiquary, and his passion for collecting books, prints, china, glass, samplers, fans, pewter, pictures—in short any and every historical relic that came to his hand—won him a number of friends among persons of similar tastes. When, therefore, he set up in business, first as a vendor of rare editions, and, soon afterwards, as a publisher, he had a clientèle ready to his hand.

Appropriately enough, the name of Sir Thomas Bodley, one of the most illustrious of Devonians, was chosen as the tutelary genius of the business. In 1889 appeared the first book under the imprint of the 'Bodley Head'; this was *Volumes in Folio* by Richard Le Gallienne. From this modest beginning, in a tiny office, with an absurdly small capital, most of it borrowed, sprang a publishing house which soon became well known. Almost at once, indeed, the new firm gained a high reputation, not only for the quality of its publications, but also for the taste and elegance with which they were produced. In no long time the Bodley Head became a favourite haunt of the Muses, 'a nest of singing birds'. Among the poets whose work appeared under its imprint were William Watson, John Davidson, Francis Thompson, Ernest Dowson, and Richard Le Gallienne. If the artist in John Lane had cause for pride in being the means of giving good poetry to the world, the man-of-business in him had no less reason to be contented, because the poetry paid.

No publishing house ever took on a more personal and intimate character than the Bodley Head. It was, in fact, much more like a club than a place of business; and to a degree that no other firm could rival, it became the centre of that extraordinary ferment in art and letters which is associated with the 'nineties. Writers and artists offering the strongest contrasts in character and aim were found equally patient of Lane's yoke. This result Lane achieved largely by means of *The Yellow Book*, an illustrated quarterly into which all his flock—poets, essayists, dramatists, story-tellers, artists—poured their multifarious, and often startling, contributions. The literary contents of the new periodical were under the control of Henry Harland [q.v.]; while for its artistic side Aubrey Beardsley [q.v.] was responsible. Among the most noted writers who contributed to *The Yellow Book* were Max Beerbohm, John Davidson, 'Baron Corvo', Ernest Dowson, (Sir) Edmund Gosse [q.v.], Kenneth Grahame, Henry James, Richard Le Gallienne, Anatole France, George Moore, George Saintsbury, Maurice Baring, (Sir) William Watson, Netta Syrett, Ella D'Arcy, and Arthur Waugh. Its artists included (Lord) Leighton, Joseph Pennell, (Sir) William Rothenstein, R. Anning Bell, D. Y. Cameron, Walter Sickert, C. W. Furse, P. Wilson Steer, and, of course, Aubrey Beardsley. When, after the fourth number, Beardsley gave up the post of art-editor, Lane himself took it over. *The Yellow Book* lasted a little over three years, the first number appearing in April 1894 and the last in April 1897.

The seven years' partnership with Elkin Mathews came to an end in 1894 and, taking with him the sign of the Bodley Head and most of the young poets and artists who had gathered around it, Lane moved across Vigo Street to The Albany where, with undiminished ardour and success, he continued his search for new, distinguished, and sometimes daring, writers and artists. One of his achievements was the collected edition of the works of Anatole France in English. Another name indissolubly associated with the firm is that of William John Locke [q.v.], some thirty of whose novels appeared under its imprint.

As early as 1896 Lane opened a branch of his business in the United States, the John Lane Company of New York, which endured with varying success until the spring of 1922 when, chiefly owing to the difficulties arising from the tariff on imported books, he brought it to an end. Before that, in the spring of 1921, Lane had converted his London business into a private limited liability company.

If anything exceeded Lane's antiquarian and artistic ardour, it was his passionate love of his native county, Devon, and particularly of Hartland, the home of his childhood. When, therefore, he succumbed to an attack of pneumonia at his London house 2 February 1925, it was fitting that Hartland should receive his remains, and there, on the seaward side of the church of St. Nectan, his ashes repose.

Lane married in 1898 Annie, daughter of Julius Eichberg, director of the conservatory of Music at Boston, U.S.A., and widow of Tyler Batcheller King, LL.D., of Boston. They had no children. Mrs. John Lane who, as a girl of sixteen, wrote the words of the American national hymn 'To Thee, O Country', for music composed by her father, was the author of *The Champagne Standard*, *According to Maria*, and several other books published by the Bodley Head, to which she also acted as an unofficial literary adviser.

[Holbrook Jackson, *The Eighteen Nineties*, 1913; Osbert Burdett, *The Beardsley Period*, 1925; personal knowledge.]

J. Lewis May.

LANGLEY, JOHN NEWPORT (1852–1925), physiologist, was born at Newbury 2 November 1852, the second son of John Langley, a private schoolmaster there, by his wife, Mary, eldest daughter of Richard Groom. He was educated first at home, and later at Exeter grammar school, where his uncle by marriage, the Rev. Henry Newport, was headmaster. In October 1871 he proceeded with a sizarship to St. John's College, Cambridge, where he was subsequently awarded a scholarship. He was reading mathematics and history with a view to entering the Indian civil service when, late in his second year at Cambridge, he began, under the tuition of (Sir) Michael Foster [q.v.], praelector of physiology at Trinity College, a course in biology. Attracted by that subject and by its teacher, Langley relinquished mathematics and history, and began to read for the natural sciences tripos, in which he gained a first class in 1874. In the following year Foster appointed him a demonstrator in succession to H. Newell Martin. In 1877 he was elected to an open fellowship at Trinity College. He resided at Trinity until his marriage in 1902.

At Foster's suggestion, Langley began experimental research even before taking his degree. Foster had handed him a new drug, pilocarpine, to examine; its action as tested on the frog's heart formed Langley's earliest subject of research. The work was published in the newly started 'Papers from the Cambridge Physiological Laboratory' along with contributions by a group of young researchers, most of whom became well known, and with most of whom Langley formed enduring friendships. They included F. M. Balfour, Milnes Marshall, S. H. Vines, W. H. Gaskell, and James Ward.

The course of his work on pilocarpine led Langley to the study of secretion. He passed from the frog's heart to the mammalian salivary glands. It was characteristic of him to seek a field where with skilled technique he could hope to deal quantitatively with fundamental factors. He found that the new drug exerted a specific influence on the secretory process. He took this reaction as the point of departure for a study of secretion in general; he followed it with a precision which had never before been approached. He soon showed that the accepted view, based on statements made by Rudolf Heidenhain, of Breslau, that gland-cells become more granular as secretion proceeds, is actually the reverse of what obtains. He demonstrated that the secretory granules accumulate when the gland is not secreting, and when secretion ensues the granules are discharged from the cell. Along with strictly quantitative secretory experiments he conducted careful microscopical examination of the gland-cells which were actually under experiment. He further checked his microscopical observations of the 'fixed' and 'stained' gland-cells by observations on the living cells themselves, sampled from the glands at various stages of experiment. Langley investigated also the nervous influence exerted on the gland-cells; he distinguished between the 'loaded' and the 'exhausted' states of the gland. He showed that the belief in the existence of specific 'trophic' nerve-fibres for the salivary glands rested on evidence which could be explained by vascular effects concurrently produced in the local blood-circulation. Besides the fundamental information his papers furnished, the form and style in which the papers themselves were cast were generally recognized as setting an exceptionally high standard of effectiveness, clearness, and precision of statement, with absolute freedom from all merely speculative argument.

Langley's systematic exploration of the secretory process occupied the first fifteen years of his career in research. In 1883 he was appointed a lecturer at Trinity College, and the same year university lecturer in physiology. He was thus confirmed, both in college and university, as assistant to Foster who, in 1883, had been appointed professor of physiology. In 1900 Langley became deputy to Foster, and in 1903 succeeded him in the professorship. He wrote the notice of Foster for this DICTIONARY. As far back as 1878 Foster had founded the *Journal of Physiology*, in order to supply a medium for publication of English and American research in what was already a rapidly growing study. This *Journal* had established its reputation, but it did not pay its way. It was saddled with a very extensive free-list to professors and laboratories on the continent of Europe. By 1894, it had become greatly embarrassed by running expenses and by debt; it seemed doomed to extinction. Langley then came forward, and arranged to pay off the very considerable debt and to receive the unsold stock. Thenceforward until his death he both owned and edited the *Journal*, though Foster's name was retained upon the cover during Foster's lifetime. This taking over of the *Journal* by Langley proved a decisive event not only for the *Journal* itself but indeed for British physiology. Langley saw to it that every paper issued in his *Journal* made not only a solid contribution to knowledge, but maintained the standard of form and style desired, saying what it had to say with succinctness, perfect lucidity, and a minimum of speculative discussion. He would, where he judged fit, almost entirely recast a paper, even of a distinguished contributor. He shrank from no labour or difficulty in that respect. His strictness annoyed many of his collaborators; some it alienated altogether. Many, however, came ultimately to recognize his assistance with gratitude. He declined unalterably any published acknowledgement of the unselfish labour which he thus put upon himself. In the course of time not only the English-speaking world but the international scientific world came to recognize that in doing what he did he was accomplishing a reform and setting a pattern in the presentation of scientific work which soon proved a boon to every reader wherever such literature was used. To-day it is generally felt that the diffuse publications of Central Europe must eventually follow the example which he set, and attain greater intelligibility and lessened monetary charge to their subscribers.

As an investigator, the climax of Langley's achievement was perhaps his research (1890–1906) into the sympathetic nervous system. William Henry Gaskell [q.v.], likewise working in Foster's laboratory, had in the preceding decade shown that that system is wholly of spinal origin, and with unexpectedly restricted spinal segmental connexions. Langley carried this analytic inquiry further. Proceeding from the discovery, made by himself and his pupil, W. Lee Dickinson, in 1889, that nicotine 'paralyses' the nerve-cells in sympathetic ganglia, he used that procedure as a method, and subjected the whole of the sympathetic ganglionic system to exhaustive analysis, determining for each ganglion whence its paths come and whither they lead. Previously the belief had been that sympathetic nerve-paths vary greatly, and differ greatly between themselves; thus that some have one and some many nerve-cells intercalated along their course. Langley made clear that in the sympathetic from its spinal to its distal goal, wherever this latter be, whether in muscle, gland, or other peripheral tissue, one nerve-cell and one only is interposed in each and every path. Each ganglion forms the one and only relay station for the fibres interrupted there. Langley showed further that the sympathetic ganglia belong entirely to efferent paths. It became clear, therefore, that the pain so common and formidable an accompaniment of visceral disease, is not due to the ganglia, predominantly visceral though they are. It had been thought that the true reflex actions could be obtained from sympathetic ganglia, but Langley showed that spread of conduction along merely branched nerve-fibres (axon-reflexes) would explain the seemingly reflex phenomena. Indeed, the functional anatomy of a portion of the nervous system, knowledge of which had previously been a sheer confusion of obscurities and mistakes, he left perhaps the most clearly elucidated in the body, so simple indeed that the smallest text-book, after he had made his investigation, provided the student with a key diagram of its arrangement. This work will always remain a landmark in the history of physiology. Of it Langley furnished an excellent summary in 1901 for (Sir) E. A. Sharpey-Schafer's *Advanced Text-book of Physiology*, vol. ii.

In 1907 Langley turned to another field, there again using the selective action of drugs as a means of analysis. He noticed that adrenaline stimulates the cells of the sympathetic after degeneration of the spinal fibre which conveys to them their normal stimulation. He found that the same holds good for nicotine. Nicotine causes also a local contraction of muscle which has its seat at the point of nerve-entry into the muscle-fibre; this local contraction is prevented by curari. Langley inferred from observations of this kind that the mechanism of excitation of one cell by another consists in a locally developed 'receptive' substance which sensitizes the cell for the stimulus which it receives from the cell to which it reacts. The cells of different tissues he supposed to have different and specific 'receptive' substances.

This work was interrupted by the outbreak of the European War in 1914. Earlier in that year, owing to the generosity of the Drapers' Company, a fine new physiological laboratory had been completed from designs by Sir Thomas Graham Jackson [q.v.] in consultation with Langley. The War at once depleted it of staff and students. Langley therefore directed the energies of its remaining workers into channels of direct value for medical application in time of war. He was himself sixty-two years of age, but he performed service of national importance by collaborating with foreign visitors to his laboratory, mainly Japanese, in investigations especially connected with the trophic changes ensuing in muscle and nerve from traumatic injury and during recovery from such injury.

When the War was over Langley quickly returned to his former routine of research and teaching. His reputation had for many years past attracted to Cambridge young men who wished to work at physiology, and his school now grew larger than ever. The results of his later research were collected in his *Autonomic Nervous System*, Part I (1921); no further Part appeared. As for himself, the progress of years seemed to affect but little his well-knit frame and brisk, athletic step. His personal touch with his students and junior staff did, however, perhaps grow less constant. At the beginning of November 1925 he was apparently in his usual health, when he was suddenly attacked by pneumonia, which in a few days proved fatal. He died at his home at Cambridge 5 November.

Langley married in 1902 Vera Kathleen (died 1932), daughter of Frederick G. Forsythe-Grant, of Ecclesgreig, Kincardineshire, and had one daughter. From his marriage onward he lived at Hedgerley Lodge, a house just outside Cambridge in the direction of Madingley. All his life he had a keen interest in outdoor games. With years he passed from rowing to lawn-tennis, from lawn-tennis to gardening. He had been a first-rate skater. Physically, he was of middle stature, and his steel-blue eyes, habitually rather widely opened, lent an arresting trait to his regular-featured face otherwise chiefly remarkable for its firmness. He showed considerable power as a hypnotist, when, for a time, the subject of mesmerism had engaged his attention.

Langley was elected a fellow of the Royal Society in 1883, was vice-president in 1904–1905, delivered the Croonian lecture in 1906, and received the royal medal of the Society in 1892. He was president of the Neurological Society of Great Britain in 1893, and of the physiological section of the British Association in 1899. He was awarded the Baly medal of the Royal College of Physicians in 1903, and the Andreas Retzius medal of the Swedish Society of Physicians in 1912. Among the other honours which he received were honorary degrees from several British and foreign universities.

During Langley's tenure of the chair of physiology at Cambridge his school was remarkably productive of physiologists of distinction, several of whose names already find place in this DICTIONARY. His own direct influence as a teacher was, however, largely confined to those whom he met in the research rooms; in the lecture room he was less effective. His accuracy in experimental observation, his scrupulous fidelity of statement, and the untiring pains which he took to obtain objective data were a byword not only in his own laboratory, but wherever physiology was studied. He was a member of the international committee of the International Congresses of Physiology from 1904 until the outbreak of the War. His name is ensured a lasting place in the annals of experimental biology; the *Journal* to whose development, character, and practical success he gave so much time and care, bears the lasting impress of his public-spirited devotion and of his fearless service in the cause of an ideal.

[*The Times*, 6 November 1925; *Proceedings* of the Royal Society, vol. ci, B, 1926 (portrait); personal knowledge.]

C. S. Sherrington.

LANKESTER, Sir EDWIN RAY (1847–1929), zoologist, was born at 22 Old Burlington Street, London, 15 May 1847, the eldest son of Dr. Edwin Lankester [q.v.] by his wife, Phebe, eldest daughter of Samuel Pope, of Highbury (formerly a mill-owner in Manchester), and sister of Samuel Pope [q.v.], barrister. His father, a physician and coroner for Central Middlesex, was a scientist of distinction, particularly interested in microscopy, and one of the founders and editors of the *Quarterly Journal of Microscopical Science*; his mother was an accomplished writer on wild flowers. Lankester's boyhood was spent at home, where he met Darwin, Huxley, and other eminent men of the day. Educated at St. Paul's School, he obtained a scholarship at Downing College, Cambridge, at the age of seventeen; but migrated in his second year to Oxford, where Professor George Rolleston [q.v.] was giving courses of lectures and practical work in zoology in the newly built University Museum. Having entered Christ Church as a junior student (1866) Lankester gained a first class in the honour school of natural science (1868), the Burdett Coutts scholarship in geology (1869), and the Radcliffe travelling fellowship (1870). He then visited Vienna and Jena, and studied marine zoology in Naples (1871–1872). There he met Anton Dohrn, the founder of the Stazione Zoologica, in which famous laboratory he and Francis Maitland Balfour [q.v.] were among the first students to work. Returning to Oxford in 1872 Lankester became a fellow and tutor at Exeter College. In 1874 he was appointed to the Jodrell chair of zoology at University College, London, and in 1875 he was elected F.R.S. In 1882 he accepted the regius professorship of natural history at Edinburgh University; but, finding the conditions of the appointment to be other than he supposed, he resigned in a fortnight and returned to University College. There he remained until 1891, when he succeeded his friend Henry Nottidge Moseley [q.v.] in the Linacre chair of comparative anatomy at Oxford, to which a fellowship at Merton College was attached.

At Oxford Lankester took great interest in the reorganization of the zoological exhibits in the University Museum, and he made good use of his experience when, in 1898, he was appointed director of the natural history departments and keeper of zoology in the British Museum, South Kensington. In the same year he was appointed Fullerian professor of physiology and comparative anatomy in the Royal Institution—a post which he held until 1900. On his retirement from his posts at the British Museum at the age of sixty he was created K.C.B. (1907). He was awarded the royal medal of the Royal Society in 1885, the Copley medal in 1913, and the Darwin-Wallace medal of the Linnean Society in 1908, and he received numerous honours from other societies at home and abroad. He was vice-president of the Royal Society in 1882 and 1896, and in 1906 presided over the meeting of the British Association at York. He was elected an honorary fellow of Exeter College in 1889 and an honorary student of Christ Church in 1912.

Endowed with a powerful intellect and a commanding presence, Lankester soon became recognized as the leading British authority in zoology. He had a great love for the wonders and beauties of nature, a knowledge ranging over the whole field of biology, an insatiable scientific curiosity which lasted to the very end of his life. A keen observer, a skilful manipulator, he was also a great teacher and master of exposition, who could rouse the interest and stir the imagination of his hearers. Pupils and colleagues owed much to his help and advice in research. He was a quick worker and prolific writer. Some two hundred scientific papers stand to his credit—most of them short, written without waste of words, and often admirably illustrated by his own hand. He was no specialist; his researches extended over almost every group of the animal kingdom; but it was as a morphologist that he gained most distinction. His first publication was a letter on Pteraspis (*The Geologist*, 1862), one of the remarkable group of early fossil fishes on which he later wrote a classical monograph (*Proceedings* of the Palaeontological Society, 1868–1870). He was no more than a schoolboy when he began writing on the earthworm (1863), and later he made important contributions to the knowledge of other Oligochaeta, the Mollusca and the

Arthropoda. These and other studies helped much towards the understanding of the general morphology and phylogenetic relationships of the Invertebrata. More particularly did they explain the nature of the body cavities in animals, and the distinction between the coelom in worms and vertebrates and the enlarged blood-space, or haemocaele, in Mollusca and Arthropoda; also the unique structure of the heart, and the segmental nature of the head and brain in arthropods.

Lankester's famous memoir on 'Limulus an Arachnid' (*Quarterly Journal of Microscopical Science*, new series, vol. xxi, 1881) not only proved that remarkable animal, the king crab, to be closely allied to the scorpion, but permanently removed it from the class Crustacea in which it had previously been placed. His pioneer researches on the embryology of the Mollusca led to the publication of two important essays, *The Primitive Cell-layers of the Embryo* (1873) and *Notes on the Embryology and Classification of the Animal Kingdom* (1877), which have had a lasting influence on the science of embryology. It was in these essays that he introduced many new terms, such as 'invagination', 'nephridium', 'blastopore', 'stomodaeum', 'proctodaeum', which have since been universally adopted.

The Protozoa had a great fascination for one so devoted to the microscope. Lankester was among the first, in 1871, to describe protozoan parasites in the blood of vertebrates. These early researches, and C. L. Laveran's later discovery of the malarial parasite in man, led to a great advance in the knowledge of the cause and prevention of disease. Both at home and abroad Lankester did much to encourage the study of this important branch of parasitology. He also worked on various interesting bacteria, and put forth a theory of 'pleomorphism', maintaining that various cocci, bacilli, and vibrios, may be but form-phases of the same protean species found under different conditions. Another line of microscopical research dealt with the corpuscles or cells which float in the blood and other fluids of animals, and with the respiratory and other pigments of invertebrates.

Of Lankester's later works on vertebrates may be mentioned papers on Lepidosiren, Okapia, the heart of various fishes, and more particularly on Amphioxus; while of a more general character were his essays *On Comparative Longevity in Man and the Lower Animals* (1870), *On the use of the term Homology* (1870), *Degeneration: a chapter in Darwinism* (published 1880, reprinted in *The Advancement of Science*, 1890), and a letter on Lamarckism (*Nature*, 1894); all these were contributions of value, remarkable for common sense and sound judgement. Scientific imagination and penetrating insight distinguished all his work: for speculation remote from facts he had no liking.

So early as 1865 Lankester wrote on the brain of the monkey, semnopithecus, and later (1899) on *The Significance of the increased size of the Cerebrum in Recent as compared with Extinct Animals* (Jubilee volume of the Société de Biologie, Paris), pointing out the importance of inherited educability as opposed to acquired responses in the evolution of man, a theme which he developed further in the Romanes lecture which he delivered in Oxford in 1905. In his later years he became keenly interested in pre-history and the flint implements of the Pliocene age. It was greatly due to his influence that the rough 'rostro-carinate' implements were accepted as artifacts by many archaeologists. To the ninth edition of the *Encyclopædia Britannica* he contributed masterly articles on Protozoa, Hydrozoa, Mollusca, Polyzoa, and Vertebrata; in the tenth edition he wrote on Arachnida and Arthropoda, and in the eleventh the article on zoology. He was the author of interesting introductions to parts I and II of *A Treatise on Zoology* (1900–1909), of which he was general editor, while among his more popular writings may be mentioned *Extinct Animals* (1905), *The Kingdom of Man* (1907), *Science from an Easy Chair* (1910), and *Great and Small Things* (1923).

From 1869 to 1878 Lankester was joint-editor with his father of the *Quarterly Journal of Microscopical Science*. Under his sole editorship from 1878 to 1920 it became the leading British journal of zoology and acquired a world-wide reputation.

Among the great services rendered by Lankester to zoological science must be mentioned the founding of the Marine Biological Association in 1884. It was greatly owing to him that the necessary funds were raised for erecting its laboratory at Plymouth, and that the undertaking became an institution of national importance to which the government contributed its support. For long, as its president, Lankester took an active interest in the welfare of the Association, and helped to raise its laboratory to the position which it now holds as a centre of zoological research.

Lankester received the honorary degree of D.Sc. from the universities of Oxford and Leeds, and the honorary LL.D. degree from the university of St. Andrews. He died in London 15 August 1929. There is a portrait of him by Sir William Orpen at Messrs. Knoedler's, 15 Old Bond Street, London. A cartoon of him by 'Spy' appeared in *Vanity Fair* 12 January 1905. He was unmarried.

Lankester was a man of strong feelings which he did not hesitate to express. Any form of sham, fraud, or injustice roused his anger. As an instance may be given his ruthless exposure of the fashionable medium Slade in 1876. Though generally in the right, his impetuous temperament sometimes led him into regrettable quarrels and difficulties. He had many interests, artistic and literary as well as scientific, and could talk well on almost any subject. His tall and massive frame, his mobile expressive face, his deep booming voice made up a vivid and impressive personality. Eager, direct, humorous and sympathetic in conversation, sociable in habit, steadfast in friendship, he possessed a personal charm which endeared him to a wide circle of friends at home and abroad.

[*The Times*, 16 August 1929; *Proceedings* of the Royal Society, vol. cvi, B, 1930 (portrait); *Nature*, 24 August 1929; *Journal* of the Marine Biological Association, vol. xvi, 1930; *Journal* of the Royal Microscopical Society, vol. xxxix, 1929; *Quarterly Journal of Microscopical Science*, vol. lxxiv, 1931.] E. S. Goodrich.

LANSDOWNE, fifth Marquess of (1845–1927). [See Petty-Fitzmaurice, Henry Charles Keith.]

LAW, ANDREW BONAR (1858–1923), statesman, born 16 September 1858 at Kingston, near Richibucto, New Brunswick, Canada, was the first man of colonial birth to become prime minister of Great Britain. His father, the Rev. James Law, a Presbyterian minister, was an Ulsterman who came of farming stock from the neighbourhood of Portrush. His mother, a native of Halifax, Nova Scotia, was Elizabeth, daughter of William Kidston, a Glasgow iron-merchant. They had four sons, of whom Bonar was the youngest, and one daughter. The manse was a lonely wooden farm-house, four or five miles above the mouth of the Richibucto river. The Sunday congregation consisted of settlers drawn largely from Dumfries and Galloway. The pastor was a man of intellectual gifts and an eloquent preacher. But he was the victim of a brooding melancholy which increased as the years advanced, and the memory of this affliction sometimes depressed his youngest son and made him fear a similar fate. Bonar Law's mother died when he was two years old, and in his twelfth year he was brought by an aunt from Canada to Scotland. He now found himself in affluent surroundings, but the lessons of his simple home, where the tasks of the kitchen and the farm were shared by all, were not lost upon him. After a short period at Gilbertfield School, Hamilton, he was sent to Glasgow high school, where James Bryce and Henry Campbell-Bannerman had been educated a few years earlier. He had a quick and energetic mind, but neither there nor at lectures which he attended later at the university, did he show unusual promise. He was an omnivorous reader, and delighted in recalling the fact that before he was twenty-one he had read Gibbon's *Decline and Fall of the Roman Empire* three times. But undoubtedly the author who gripped him at this period was Thomas Carlyle, from whose pages he later drew the literary quotations with which he occasionally graced his political speeches: his favourite quotations were figures from blue books.

Bonar Law's relatives, William, Richard, and Charles Kidston, were partners in a Glasgow firm of merchant bankers. Their business had been mainly concerned with financing trade in iron and steel, but at this time they were in the autumn of their commercial careers, nursing their investments rather than actively trading with them. From these conservative cousins he imbibed his earliest political impressions, including dislike of Mr. Gladstone and admiration of Mr. Disraeli. At the age of sixteen he entered the family business and had leisure and means to visit France, Germany, and Italy, to learn to read French and German, and to speak French. His speech in French, as in English, betrayed his ancestry and upbringing. In 1885, at the age of twenty-eight, he joined the Glasgow firm of William Jacks & Co., iron-merchants, as a junior partner. The business of the Kidstons was merged in the Clydesdale Bank, of which, later, Bonar Law became a director. Other directorships and the chairmanship of the Glasgow Iron Trade Association followed. He lived with the Kidstons at Helensburgh and there met

Annie Pitcairn, daughter of Harrington Robley, of Glasgow, whom he married in 1891, and by whom he had four sons and two daughters. He continued after his marriage to travel daily between Helensburgh and Glasgow.

When about twenty years of age Bonar Law had joined the Glasgow Parliamentary Debating Association, the procedure of which was closely modelled on that of the House of Commons. As member for 'North Staffordshire' of this local 'parliament' for many years, he rehearsed his later triumphs as a debater and made himself thoroughly familiar with parliamentary procedure. It is probable that during these debates was born the ambition to exchange the local for the national forum, and the way was made possible not only by such means as he acquired in business, but also by the receipt of two legacies of £30,000 each, from Miss Catherine Kidston and Mrs. Janet Kidston, the childless widow of Charles Kidston. The abilities which he displayed at the Debating Association impressed officials of the Conservative and Liberal Unionist Associations, and in 1898 he was adopted as their candidate for the Blackfriars and Hutchesontown division of Glasgow. It was and had long been a radical seat, but in the general election of 1900 the liberal candidate deserted his party on the question of Home Rule. The Irish voters preferred to support the unionist, and with their help Bonar Law was returned by a majority of 1,000 and entered parliament at the age of forty-two.

In February 1901, in a debate on the Address, Bonar Law delivered his maiden speech—a defence of Joseph Chamberlain and Cecil Rhodes, who had been attacked on the previous day by Mr. Lloyd George. It was ignored by the press, which was more interested in the maiden speech made during the same sitting by Mr. Winston Churchill. The speech which singled out Bonar Law for special notice by the government was made on 22 April 1902 in favour of the corn duty proposed by the chancellor of the Exchequer (Sir Michael Hicks Beach). This speech was widely praised, and led to Bonar Law's appointment as parliamentary secretary to the Board of Trade, after a parliamentary apprenticeship of barely eighteen months. He soon distinguished himself in a twenty-minutes' speech on the Sugar Bounty Convention, the colonial secretary (Mr. Chamberlain) describing it as 'one of the most admirable short speeches he had ever listened to in the House of Commons'. These early speeches were closely reasoned and delivered without notes, but they were marred by a too rapid delivery. Their strength lay in the speaker's familiarity with the intricacies of imperial and foreign trade, and it was these matters which were to become in the immediate future the warp and woof of party warfare. In May 1903 Chamberlain launched his scheme of colonial preference and tariff reform. Nothing could have better suited the retired Glasgow iron-merchant, and he advanced steadily to the front rank of the exponents of the new policy. On 16 September 1903 Chamberlain resigned from Mr. Balfour's administration in order to be free to carry on his campaign in the country. This and the simultaneous resignation of free-trade ministers weakened the government, and in the general election of January 1906 it suffered overwhelming defeat. The conservative party was reduced to 157 members, who were divided into Balfourites, Chamberlainites, and unionist 'free-fooders'. At Blackfriars (Glasgow) Bonar Law was defeated by Mr. G. N. Barnes, a labour candidate, but on 15 May 1906 he was returned for Dulwich at a by-election. In the summer of 1906 Chamberlain's health broke down. Balfour's attitude to tariff reform, however clear to himself, was incomprehensible to the multitude. Bonar Law, on the other hand, was sure of himself and his utterances bore no trace of philosophic doubt. He was a merchant. He and Mr. Austen Chamberlain were now recognized as the most effective advocates of fiscal change in the unionist party. Bonar Law delivered innumerable speeches on the one subject, buttressed by an array of statistics which impressed those less skilful in their use.

The mantle of Joseph Chamberlain, now aged seventy, passed quietly to Bonar Law. Their careers were similar. Both were metal merchants, who entered parliament in middle age after succeeding in business; both found office at the Board of Trade; both were fighting men and effective speakers in and outside the House of Commons; both were ardent advocates of imperial preference. In origin and outlook they were both middle class. Neither belonged to the Church of England.

On 29 April 1909 Mr. Lloyd George, as chancellor of the Exchequer, made his first budget statement. Bonar Law denounced it as socialism 'pure and unadulterated'. Nor was he enamoured of the chancellor's schemes for health and unemployment insurance. 'It was the success of tariff reform,' he argued, 'which had made the German insurance system possible.' Also he would have made the scheme for old age pensions contributory. The struggle over the budget had been preceded by a demand on the part of the conservatives for the construction of battleships of the *Dreadnought* class in reply to the German naval programme. Throughout this and the following year party feeling ran high. Joseph Chamberlain, from his retirement, declared that the fate of the budget involved the fate of tariff reform, and called upon the House of Lords to reject the measure. The Lords did so, and on 1 December Mr. Asquith moved that the action of the House of Lords was a usurpation of the rights of the Commons.

At the general election which followed, in January 1910, Bonar Law was again returned for Dulwich, but at that of December 1910, at the bidding of his party, he gave up a safe seat and essayed to win North-West Manchester. This fight aroused intense interest, as the seat had been wrested from Mr. Winston Churchill in 1908 by Mr. William Joynson-Hicks (afterwards Viscount Brentford), and had been lost again to the liberals in January 1910. Bonar Law failed to capture it, but he reduced the liberal majority from 783 to 445. In March 1911, however, he was returned for the Bootle division of Lancashire at a by-election. Throughout these contests his main themes were: 'naval supremacy and not merely naval superiority over Germany'; 'the defence of the loyal minority in Ireland against the imposition of a tyranny'; and tariff reform as 'the greatest of all social reforms'. 'We propose two things: to raise part of our revenue by the imposition of a duty on foreign manufactured goods that compete with those made in this country, and we propose also so to readjust our taxation as to obtain the largest possible amount of preference for the work of our own people in the overseas markets of the Empire' (Manchester, December 1910).

Disaffection in the conservative party over the questions of tariff reform and the Parliament Bill had undermined Mr. Balfour's prestige as leader. Bonar Law supported Lord Lansdowne and Mr. Balfour in their decision to accept the Parliament Bill rather than proceed to extreme courses with Lord Halsbury and the 'diehards'. On 8 November 1911 Balfour resigned, and on 13 November Bonar Law was elected leader in the Commons. The party was pretty evenly divided between supporters of Mr. Walter (afterwards Viscount) Long [q.v.] and (Sir) Austen Chamberlain. These two respectively proposed and seconded, as a compromise, the election of a man much their junior in parliamentary experience and public recognition, who had never held Cabinet office. 'The fools have stumbled on their best man by accident' was Mr. Lloyd George's comment at the time.

When his wife died in 1909 Bonar Law was desolate; old associations were ended and never renewed. Into the void came Mr. William Maxwell Aitken, a young Canadian man of business, full of energy and confidence. A strong and lasting friendship sprang up between the two men. In Lord Beaverbrook, as Aitken became in 1916, Bonar Law found the kind of assistance which is given to a minister by a first-rate parliamentary secretary in whose judgement the minister has confidence and who can be used as a sounding-board for ventilation of ideas and criticism of persons, and for the expansion of the minister's influence.

On 23 November 1911 the new leader of the opposition addressed a conference of the National Union of Conservatives at Leeds, where he denounced Home Rule, the disestablishment of the Welsh Church, and free trade with a stinging directness which contrasted sharply with Balfourian subtleties. 'The waters of Marah were not more bitter than his speeches' wrote a contemporary. This bitterness found its most tart expression in his handling of the Irish question which, with tariff reform, almost monopolized the attention of politicians in the years preceding the European War. With Sir Edward Carson he shared the leadership of the section which repeatedly postponed and paralysed a succession of Home Rule Bills, carrying their opposition to the brink of civil war. At vast demonstrations in 1912 at Belfast (Easter) and at Blenheim (27 July) and in the House of Commons itself Bonar Law imported into his speeches a deliberate note of defiance of authority. To the organizers of the Orange celebrations (12 July 1913) he sent a message declaring that 'whatever steps they might feel compelled to take, whether they were constitutional, or whether in the long run they were unconstitutional, they had the whole of the Unionist Party under his leadership behind them'. At Wallsend (29 October) he indicated the various courses which were open to the government. Either it must go on as it was doing and provoke unionists to resist—that was madness; or it could consult the electorate, whose decisions would be accepted by the unionist party as a whole; or thirdly, it could try to arrange a settlement which would at least avert civil war. When parliament met in February 1914, the prime minister, Mr. Asquith, struck a conciliatory note and promised to introduce a proposal which would 'consult . . . the susceptibilities of all concerned'. This proved to be county option with a time limit of six years. In an Amending Bill to the Home Rule Bill which the Commons had passed (25 May) the Lords substituted the permanent exclusion of the whole province of Ulster for the proposed county option with a time limit (8 July). But instead of introducing the Amending Bill in the altered form in which it had left the Upper House, Asquith announced the meeting of a conference at Buckingham Palace to discuss the Irish situation. Lord Lansdowne and Bonar Law represented the unionist party. The conference failed to reach agreement on the portion of Ulster which should be excluded from the jurisdiction of the Dublin parliament. On 30 July the prime minister, prompted by Bonar Law and Carson, said that the Amending Bill would be indefinitely postponed in order that the country might present a united front to the threatened outbreak of war in Europe.

The rest of the Irish story may be outlined here before Bonar Law's services during the War are described. On 18 September the Home Rule Bill received the royal assent, and a Suspensory Bill simultaneously provided that it should remain in abeyance until after the end of the War. Bonar Law denounced this as a breach of faith, left the House with his followers in protest, and crossed to Belfast in order to renew and even to extend the pledges of the unionist party to Ulster (28 September). Abortive negotiations for a settlement proceeded intermittently throughout 1915 and 1916, and in 1917 (16 May), when Bonar Law was chancellor of the Exchequer, Mr. Lloyd George offered Ireland the alternative of a bill for the immediate application of the Home Rule Act to Ireland, excluding the six counties of North-East Ulster, or the summoning of a convention of Irishmen of all shades of opinion for the purpose of drafting a constitution. The latter was accepted, but its report (8 April 1918) showed that the 'substantial agreement' laid down by the prime minister as the condition precedent to legislation had not been reached. Ten days later the Military Service (No. 2) Act, 1918, extended conscription to Ireland, and in announcing that the government intended to enforce it, Bonar Law announced also the introduction of a further Home Rule Bill. This was never produced owing to the discovery in May of a widespread mutinous intrigue in Ireland and the arrest of Arthur Griffith [q.v.] and Mr. Eamon de Valera. Conscription remained a dead letter. On the eve of the general election of December 1918, Mr. Lloyd George and Bonar Law issued a joint letter which declared: 'Two paths are closed: the one leading to a complete severance of Ireland from the British Empire, and the other to the forcible submission of the six counties of Ulster to a Home Rule Parliament against their will.' The policy of alternating repression with conciliation continued. At the end of 1919 the government introduced the last Home Rule Bill, providing a parliament for Northern Ireland (the six counties), a parliament for the rest of Ireland, and a federal council for all Ireland. Bonar Law supported the Bill in a speech in which he condemned Dominion Home Rule as tantamount to giving the right to set up an Irish republic. On 17 March 1921, his health undermined, Bonar Law resigned the leadership of the House of Commons and of the unionist party after filling the one post for over four years and the other for nearly ten. He was thus not a member of the Coalition ministry which concluded the Irish Treaty (6 December 1921). But he was frequently consulted by the government and by Sir James Craig (afterwards Lord Craigavon), who spoke for Ulster, and he emerged unexpectedly from his temporary retirement in order to recommend the treaty to the House of Commons. Had he opposed the negotiations there would have been no treaty.

On the outbreak of the European War Bonar Law tendered the liberal prime minister (Mr. Asquith) the support of the unionist party in resisting German aggression (2 August 1914). During the opening months of the War this support was loyally given, but with growing impatience on the part of the opposition. Traces of the conflict over Ireland still remained and made co-operation difficult. Finally, on the resignation of Lord Fisher from the Admiralty, Bonar Law informed the prime minister (17 May 1915) that a change in the composition of the government had become inevitable. Two days later the formation of the first Coalition ministry was announced, and the leader of the unionist party found himself relegated to the insignificant position of secretary for the Colonies, an appointment which not only reflected Bonar Law's self-abnegation but also Asquith's preference for Balliol men to business men as close colleagues. In the autumn of 1915 Bonar Law led the group in the Cabinet which pressed for the evacuation of the Dardanelles, carrying his own opposition to the verge of resignation, at which point Asquith surrendered. In January 1916 he took charge of the Compulsory Military Service Bill. He resisted its application to Ireland as, on balance, unprofitable, and skilfully surmounted amendments dealing with conscientious objection. The third reading was carried by 383 votes to 36. In June 1916 he attended an economic conference in Paris and agreed to the policy of joint economic action by the Allies during the War and permanent defensive collaboration thereafter. It was not until April 1917 that he had the satisfaction of announcing that the Imperial War Cabinet had accepted the principle of imperial preference for the British Empire.

As early as March 1916 Bonar Law had expressed the view to John Redmond that while Asquith was then the best possible prime minister, he would probably eventually be replaced by Mr. Lloyd George. This actually happened in December 1916. The devious operations by which Bonar Law's mistrust of Mr. Lloyd George was changed into active co-operation have been described by Lord Beaverbrook, who largely engineered them, by the biographers of Mr. Asquith, and by Mr. Lloyd George in his *War Memoirs*. They cannot be disentangled here. On 3 December, after a meeting of conservative ministers, Bonar Law saw the prime minister at Downing Street and demanded the resignation of Asquith's government. Mr. Lloyd George resigned on 5 December and Asquith a few hours later on the same day. On the same evening King George V invited Bonar Law to form an administration. He first sought the co-operation of Mr. Lloyd George and then that of Asquith, and when this was not forthcoming he advised the king to call on Mr. Lloyd George. On 7 December Mr. Lloyd George became prime minister. In the new government Bonar Law became chancellor of the Exchequer and leader of the House of Commons. He was also a member of the War Cabinet, but he was not expected to take the same active part in it as the other four members. At the Treasury and in the House Bonar Law quickly revealed abilities which had been fatally underestimated by Asquith. He reversed the prevailing policy of high money rates and short-term indebtedness and issued a series of War Loans, on a lower interest basis for long terms, which rank among the greatest achievements in the history of British finance. In October 1917 he launched a campaign for national war bonds to an unlimited amount on terms which ingeniously combined the advantages of short- and long-dated securities. This was remarkably successful and provided the state with a continuous flow of money until the end of the War.

The fifth war budget was introduced by Bonar Law on 2 May 1917. He recounted with pride the great success of the war loan which he had floated in a memorable appeal at the Guildhall on 11 January. By 31 March the total yield, including conversions, amounted to £2,067 millions. In fixing the low terms of this loan he had defied the advice of the City and of his own officials, and the public response amply supported his judgement. He now added no new taxes, but increased the excess profits duty from 60 to 80 per cent. and the tobacco duties and entertainments tax were also increased. Critics denounced the budget for 'its miserably small addition to taxation' and the needless burden which would cripple industry in the post-War years. The chancellor argued that no belligerent country had provided, as Great Britain had done, 26 per cent. out of revenue to meet expenditure during the War. Replying to those who desired conscription of wealth as of men, he said: 'If we can get the money we need by voluntary methods, by unsettling as little as possible the existing machinery, then I am certain you will get more of it and for a longer time than by an attempt at conscription.'

On 22 April 1918 Bonar Law submitted the sixth war budget, 'a financial statement on a scale far exceeding any that had ever been known at any time or in any country'. The revenue for 1918–1919 he estimated at £842 millions, expenditure at £2,972 millions. New taxes were expected to produce £114 millions in a full year. Income tax was placed at 6*s.* in the £ at £2,500 a year, and super-tax at 4*s.* 6*d.* in the £ on excess over £10,000 a year. Farmers' tax was doubled. A proposal to tax luxuries, a French fiscal device, was later withdrawn as impracticable. The balance to be borrowed, roughly £2,000 millions, was more than three times the pre-War national debt. The chancellor declared himself to be guided by the rule of his predecessor, Mr. Reginald M'Kenna, that 'on the assumption that the War came to an end at the close of the year for which the financial statement was made, there would be a sufficient revenue without new borrowing or new taxation to make sure that not only the expenditure left after the War, but the debt charge could be met'. This unparalleled budget coincided with some of the most desperate struggles of the War, and it passed very easily and with so little change that the chancellor's revenue proposals were modified only in respect of two million pounds.

Throughout these years of vast and anxious responsibility the chancellor, while confident of the ultimate victory of the Allies, deprecated optimism and pessimism alike, and couched his appeals for sacrifice in speeches of marked sobriety. These were in sharp contrast to the flamboyant manifesto issued by Mr. Lloyd George and himself on the eve of the general election of December 1918, which followed the Armistice (11 November). Bonar Law justified the continuance of the Coalition as the one condition of ensuring peace abroad, and preventing revolution at home. The 'orgy of chauvinism' which characterized the election was not his doing, and he discouraged extravagant hopes of the financial terms to be imposed upon Germany. But he was a consenting party to the device of issuing 'coupons' to approved unionist and coalition liberal candidates, whereby the sacrifice of seats to labour candidates and independent liberals was avoided. The result was a coalition majority of nearly 250, and a large accession of unionist members. Bonar Law himself was returned for Central Glasgow, the division in which his business life had been spent. He took the office of lord privy seal and leader of the House of Commons, and during the prolonged absences of Mr. Lloyd George while attending conferences abroad he acted as prime minister. Only when his presence was absolutely necessary did he attend the Peace Conference at Paris, travelling by air whenever possible. He was one of the signatories to the Treaty of Versailles. At home, during the years 1919 and 1920, he was absorbed in the problems of demobilization and resettlement, the removal of war-time restrictions, and the transfer of industries from a war-time to a peace basis. And there was always the Irish question. When delivering his address as lord rector of Glasgow University on 11 March 1921, he betrayed signs of momentary collapse, and on 17 March, broken down by years of incessant labour and by personal sorrows, he resigned office and sought rest in the south of France. His health improved and he returned home in the autumn, emerging from his retirement to recommend the Irish Treaty.

Meanwhile a growing section of conservatives was chafing under the dominance of Mr. Lloyd George and the Coalition. Matters came to a head over 'the Chanak crisis'—the fear that the prime minister and certain of his colleagues were bent on resuming war against Mustapha Kemal, who was threatening the neutral zones by which Constantinople, the Bosphorus, and the Dardanelles were then protected. This policy aroused widespread opposition in the country among all parties, but conflict was avoided by the tactful attitude of Sir Charles Harington, the Allied commander-in-chief at Constantinople. At the Carlton Club on 19 October 1922 a speech by Mr. Stanley Baldwin, and the declaration of Bonar Law that the unity of his party could only be saved by withdrawing from the Coalition, combined to bring about the fall of the government. Mr. Lloyd George resigned, and on 23 October Bonar Law became prime minister with a purely conservative Cabinet. On the same day he was unanimously elected to the leadership of the party in place of Mr. Austen Chamberlain. The new prime minister at once struck the note of his policy: tranquillity and stability, 'leaving the recovery to come, not so much by action from above, as by the free play and energy of our own people. . . . There are times when it is good to sit still and go slowly.' This programme of negation secured him an independent majority of 75 at the general election in November. Nevertheless, unemployment, housing, and foreign affairs gave the prime minister little of the 'freedom from disturbance at home and abroad' for which he yearned.

During 1922 British and French 'reparations' policies, which had hitherto been in general accord, showed signs of increasing divergence. At the conference held at Cannes in January, and indeed throughout that year, British influence was being used to mitigate and postpone payment of reparations by Germany in face of the vigorous and literal demands of M. Poincaré, and to question the right of independent action by France in the event of default. The German mark fell in the course of the year from about 800 to 34,000 to the £. Inter-allied debts, reparations, the co-operation of the United States of America in the affairs of Europe, and the mounting figures of unemployment had been treated by the Coalition Cabinet as interlocked problems, and the solution of none of them was in sight when Bonar Law took office. He presided over a conference of Allied prime ministers in London, 9–11 December, which was adjourned to Paris until January 1923. Between the two sessions Bonar Law announced that on certain conditions Great Britain 'would be willing to run the risk in the end of paying more to the United States than she would receive from the Allies and Germany', and the Reparations Commission, the British member dissenting, declared that Germany's failure to deliver timber to France during 1922 constituted a default and that this paved the way for the imposition of sanctions. In Paris (2 January 1923) Poincaré and Bonar Law tabled proposals too complicated for summary here; in essence their differences were accentuated. Great Britain wished to fix figures within the reasonable capacity of Germany to pay, on condition that she should stabilize the mark and balance her budget under supervision. France would agree to no policy which did not involve strict control of Germany's finances, together with the taking of extensive 'productive pledges' of material assets guaranteeing future payments. At the close of the first session of the conference Bonar Law was convinced that compromise was impossible, and but for the demands of courtesy and the pressure of advisers he would have returned to London at once. On 4 January he declared that 'the ditch was one which no bridge could span', and the conference broke down. Within a week the French and Belgian governments announced their intention of occupying the Ruhr, the policy against which Bonar Law had protested in vain. It is difficult to imagine him conducting international conferences extending over many weeks, like Lord Curzon at Lausanne, or Mr. Lloyd George on several occasions. He was quick to understand a situation, deliberate and dexterous in handling it, lucid and accurate in his statement of it, but his patience and resource were very limited. He never practised self-deception, and of two views he chose the one less favourable to himself. He did not preen himself, delivering elaborate pronouncements after the manner of Lord Curzon, nor revel in a battle of bargaining wits like Mr. Lloyd George. He was free of the vanity which clothes failure in a formula, and, like Mr. Asquith, he 'disdained the minor arts of popularity'.

One of the major questions which called for immediate action by the new conservative administration was that of the funding of the American debt. The parts played respectively by the prime minister and the chancellor of the Exchequer (Mr. Baldwin) in the settlement ultimately concluded have been the subject of much debate, and until contemporary state documents are available in Great Britain and in the United States no final judgement is possible. Reluctance to surrender office and disperse colleagues newly assembled in a purely conservative Cabinet after seventeen years in opposition or coalition, must have weighed heavily with the prime minister. Mr. Richard Law, member of parliament for South-West Hull, in a speech delivered in the House of Commons on 13 June 1933, stated it as his view that, but for the fact that his father was at the time a very sick man, he would not have accepted the settlement, and would sooner have broken up his own government, fresh as it then was.

As early as November 1918, Bonar Law, then chancellor of the Exchequer, had considered the possibility of the entire cancellation of inter-Allied debts, and throughout the years of negotiation which followed, this idea persisted in the minds of some British ministers, despite recurrent and emphatic discouragement from Washington. Another body of opinion, considering the economic restoration of Europe to be the matter of chief urgency, favoured the funding of the debt without delay and on such terms as were then obtainable. There were also those who, while willing to forgo Great Britain's reparation claims as part of a general settlement, were unwilling that the United States should play off debtors against each other, and insisted on a most-favoured-nation clause as a condition of agreement. After protracted debate and delay the Cabinet succeeded in harmonizing its views in the Balfour Note (1 August 1922). It had already agreed to dispatch a delegation to Washington. Certain other antecedent facts must be borne in mind in judging the position as it stood when Bonar Law became premier. On 31 January 1922 the American senate had passed an Act establishing a World War Debt Funding Commission, closely defining its powers, fixing the minimum rate of interest at 4¼ per cent. and the period of debt repayment at twenty-five years. On 20 February 1922 the financial secretary to the British Treasury had announced that £25,000,000 would be provided in the budget estimates for 1922–1923 to cover one half-year's interest, and on 21 March the chancellor of the Exchequer (Sir Robert Horne) told the House of Commons that he did not propose 'to make any conditions to the United States for the payment of our due obligations'. The absence of hostile criticism of this announcement suggests that the prevailing opinion was that, whatever other nations might do, Great Britain meant to pay. Speaking in New York (4 October 1922) Mr. Reginald M'Kenna, a leading banker and former chancellor of the Exchequer, declared that Great Britain had both means and determination to pay the debt in full. The effect of the Balfour Note on American opinion was bad, and would have been worse but for the good will engendered by the signature of the agreement constituting the Irish Free State (6 December 1921) and of the Washington Naval Treaty (13 December 1921 and 6 February 1922).

The British delegates, the chancellor of the Exchequer (Mr. Baldwin) and the governor of the Bank of England (Mr. Montagu Norman), arrived in Washington on 4 January 1923. They had been given no written instructions, but they knew that the annuity envisaged by the prime minister was in the neighbourhood of £25,000,000 and a rate of interest of 2½ per cent. Even lower figures than these had been hinted at by the American ambassador to Great Britain (Mr. George Harvey) as likely to satisfy Congress, and this had coloured Bonar Law's views. This optimism had no basis in fact. Negotiations between the British and American commissions proceeded and were reported to the prime minister, who grew increasingly despondent. On 14 January the American commission offered a settlement on the basis of 3 per cent. interest for the first ten years and 3½ per cent. thereafter; a sinking fund at ½ per cent. throughout, and back interest to be calculated at 4¼ per cent. This offer was equivalent to annual payments of $161,000,000 for ten years, and of $184,000,000 for fifty-two years, and was in reply to Mr. Baldwin's provisional suggestion of 3 per cent. throughout. Its acceptance was strongly pressed upon the Cabinet by the delegation and by the British ambassador to the United States (Sir Auckland Geddes) as the best obtainable, and on 21 January Sir Robert Horne, then in New York and in consultation with interests friendly to England, cabled the same advice. Bonar Law denounced the terms as exceedingly harsh and unfair; they would inflict a crippling burden of taxation on the British people for two generations and would severely strain their relations with the people of the United States. The French were in occupation of the Ruhr, and he saw little hope of payments being made to England from Europe. Mr. M'Kenna and Lord Beaverbrook, two of his closest friends, and also Mr. J. M. Keynes, the economist, confirmed the prime minister in his opposition. A meeting to adjourn the Washington negotiations and to permit consultations in London was fixed for 18 January, but on 16 January the respective offers of the two commissions appeared in the American press and the result was to stabilize the American offer. Some observations made by Mr. Baldwin to pressmen on his arrival at Southampton on 27 January stiffened opinion in the United States against any further concession. The British Cabinet met on 30 January, and Bonar Law made it clear that he would resign rather than be a party to the proposed terms. He refused to believe that a day would not come when the rank and file of Americans would share what he knew to be the mind of their more enlightened compatriots. The discussion was inconclusive and was adjourned to the following afternoon. In the interval certain ministers indicated that they were not prepared even to appear to repudiate acknowledged obligations. This became the dominant view of the large majority of ministers. On the morning of 31 January Mr. M'Kenna, convinced that the City favoured acceptance, advised Bonar Law to yield. In the afternoon the Cabinet decided to accept the American terms and the crisis ended. Whether Bonar Law yielded because he was at the time a very sick man, or whether, but for his sickness, he would have shared the views of his colleagues, no one can say.

When Bonar Law had left office in March 1921 he had told the prime minister that he was 'quite worn out'. Before returning to office on 23 October 1922 he had 'hesitated up to the last moment'. He was prime minister for 209 days only, resigning on Whitsunday, 20 May 1923. When, on 30 October following, he died, there could be no doubt that, in the words of his successor, Mr. Baldwin, Bonar Law had given his life for his country, just as much as if he had fallen in the European War. He died at 24 Onslow Gardens, London, and was buried in Westminster Abbey on 5 November. Two of his sons were killed in the War, Charles in Palestine, and James in France. He was survived by two sons and two daughters.

No one will claim for Bonar Law a place among the greatest of England's prime ministers. Posterity indeed may give him a lower rank than is his due, not only because of his own indifference to fame but also because his solid qualities made no popular appeal. When he reached the top he was a tired man. He had filled the highest offices in the state with great ability and sagacity in years of unparalleled strain and anxiety. His mind worked rapidly; he grasped clearly the most technical memoranda submitted to him; his criticism was swift, acute, and extremely practical; his memory was abnormally retentive and accurate. His industry was concentrated and his curiosity severely restricted. He had none of Lord Curzon's insatiable appetite for information. Literature and art had no interest for him; to music he was deaf and to scenery blind. His sceptical outlook was tinged with melancholy. He lived simply, smoked excessively, and shunned society. He rarely left London and made no use of Chequers Court in Buckinghamshire, the official country residence of the prime minister. All this is true, but it gives a completely misleading picture of the man. Bonar Law united a character 'honest to the verge of simplicity' with a disposition 'sweet and kind' and a manner so gentle and charming as to prove irresistible to his associates. Diffident about his own powers, he could, when roused, show a stubborn firmness and decision. But his normal attitude was one of repose and quiet friendliness, which kindled a loving loyalty in all who became intimate with him. In human affection and hard work, he told the Glasgow students, he had found the best that life could offer. He played chess and bridge, lawn-tennis and golf, and was proficient in all, but parliament absorbed his energies. He was supreme as leader of the House of Commons, and his ascendancy has been compared with that of Walpole in the eighteenth century and of Peel in the nineteenth. He conducted its business with easy mastery from day to day, judging bills primarily by the smoothness of their passage, and untroubled by dreams of millennial achievement. For him, as for his hero, Joseph Chamberlain, a fortnight's future sufficed in politics. By Ulster alone was he stirred to the depths as by some primitive passion. Tariff reform was a paying business proposition. For the rest, he was open to argument, and it was parliamentary expediency which was apt to turn the scale. In the election of November 1922, where his was the determining voice, he envisaged 'as little legislation as possible'. This was doubtless in part reaction from the methods of December 1918, but it was also in harmony with the speaker's native caution and distrust of glittering promises.

Bonar Law's speeches are no longer read, but if judged by their fitness for their immediate purpose they must be given high rank. Speaking with engaging candour, his lucidity, moderation, and plain sense were perfectly adapted to convince and unite those who listened to him and to dissolve opposition. During the years of the War his fairness in debate, his modesty in demeanour, his freedom from envy and all uncharitableness, no less than the purity of his patriotism, made him beloved of all parties in the House of Commons. A passage from Macaulay's description of William Pitt the younger as a speaker can be applied to Bonar Law:

> 'He could with ease present to his audience, not perhaps an exact or profound, but a clear, popular, and plausible view of the most extensive and complicated subject. Nothing was out of place; nothing was forgotten; minute details, dates, sums of money were all faithfully preserved in his memory. Even intricate questions of finance, when explained by him, seemed clear to the plainest man among his hearers. . . . He was the only man who could open a Budget without notes.'

In December 1916 it was Bonar Law's action which made possible the second Coalition government and which brought Mr. Lloyd George to the premiership. The partnership of the two men—'the most perfect partnership in political history'—with their humble origin and austere upbringing, with their complementary gifts and divergent temperaments, profoundly affected the fortunes of the War. For over four years the one never took an important step without conferring with the other, and to compute the contribution of Bonar

Law to the partnership it would be necessary to know not only the policies and projects of his sanguine colleague which he approved, but also those which he resisted, modified, or defeated. That colleague has placed on record his sense of the value of Bonar Law's searching criticism and his real courage when together they were responsible for the momentous decisions of the European War.

There is a portrait of Bonar Law by Sir James Guthrie in the National Portrait Gallery; a second by René de l'Hôpital at the Carlton Club; a third, outlined by Sir James Guthrie and painted by J. B. Anderson, at the Constitutional Club; a fourth by J. B. Anderson at the Conservative Club, Glasgow; a cartoon by 'Spy' appeared in *Vanity Fair* 2 March 1905, and an anonymous one 10 April 1912.

[Lord Beaverbrook, *Politicians and the War 1914–1916*, 2 vols., 1928 and 1932; J. A. Spender and Cyril Asquith, *Life of Lord Oxford and Asquith*, 1932; *War Memoirs of David Lloyd George*, vol. ii, 1933; H. A. Taylor, *The Strange Case of Andrew Bonar Law*, 1932; Sir Austen Chamberlain, *Down the Years*, 1935; private information; personal knowledge.]

T. Jones.

LAWRENCE, DAVID HERBERT (1885–1930), poet, novelist, and essayist, born 11 September 1885 at Eastwood, near Nottingham, was the fourth child and third son of John Arthur Lawrence, a coal-miner, by his wife, Lydia Beardsall. As a child Lawrence had pneumonia, and became susceptible to consumption. Later in life he contracted the disease, and eventually died of it. Life as a collier was therefore out of the question. At the age of thirteen, however, he won a scholarship at Nottingham high school, and, after a short period as a clerk, went to the British school at Eastwood as a pupil teacher. At the age of eighteen he entered Nottingham University College, matriculated, and two years later took his teacher's certificate, and was appointed to the Davidson Road School, Croydon. This education was made possible by the self-sacrifice of his mother, to whom he was passionately devoted; and it is possible that her example influenced his literary pursuits, since she had been a school teacher, had a taste for reading, and had written poetry. Mr. Ford Madox Hueffer, at that time editor of *The English Review*, encouraged Lawrence to write, published contributions by him, and introduced him to his first publisher. Lawrence was also assisted by the friendship and advice of Mr. Edward Garnett. After the publication of his novel, *The White Peacock*, in 1911, Lawrence resigned his post (receiving very honourable certificates from his superiors), and determined to live by his writing.

The circumstances of his early life made a deep impression on Lawrence's sensitive nature. The conditions of life in a mining community filled him with bitter hatred of industrialism and machinery, because he believed that men were degraded by them. Fortunately, he was able to escape to the open country on long walks, and the poet in him awoke as he responded to the rhythm of natural life with a passionate sensibility which is apparent throughout his writings. He felt the universe as a living thing, a mystic inspiration ('Not me, not me, but the wind which blows through me'), and his life might be explained as the passionate and fruitless quest for a society where men 'lived breast to breast with the cosmos'. His human sympathies were no less vivid, stimulated by contact with miners and farm people and by his profound filial love for his mother. From them Lawrence learned to value quality of feelings more than intellectual distinction, sensibility more than agreeable manners, vitality more than success.

After *The White Peacock*, Lawrence wrote *The Trespasser* (1912) and one of the most widely read of all his books, *Sons and Lovers* (1913), which appeared soon after his first book of poems, *Love Poems and Others* (1913). Meanwhile he had gone abroad for the first time, to Germany in May 1912. There he lived in a small cottage in the Isar valley; then he moved into Austria, and went on foot over the Brenner Pass to Lake Garda, where he stayed (at Gargnano) until April 1913. After a brief return to Germany and thence to England, he lived at Lerici, in Italy, from September 1913 until June 1914. In July 1914 he was married in England to Frieda von Richthofen, after her divorce from her first husband, Professor Ernest Weekley. She was the daughter of Baron von Richthofen, military governor of Metz. It is entirely erroneous to suppose that Lawrence either practised or countenanced 'free love'. He placed the sanctity of marriage in the reality of the human relationship and not in its social or legal aspect. For the poetry of this period, see his *Amores* (published 1916) and *Look, We Have Come Through* (published 1917).

Like most people who achieve anything,

Lawrence had gambled on the future, by abandoning teaching and by assuming the responsibilities of marriage. It was not so imprudent as might be thought. In 1914 he had already won a certain reputation as an author, and was welcomed in London by distinguished members of his own profession as well as by people in society. And he was in no danger of being spoiled by success. He was a man of frugal, even austere habits, to which he owed the preservation of his always delicate health. To spare his lungs, he never smoked; he drank little, and lived on the plainest food, which he frequently prepared himself; all his tastes were simple. He was indifferent to material success and to all the usual rewards; but he did ardently desire a sympathetic response to his writings and was convinced that what he had to say was of value to mankind. Here he was defeated by the disarray and hectic psychology of the years of the European War.

During the early part of the War, Lawrence lived in or near London, and in December 1914 he published a volume of short stories, *The Prussian Officer*. The topical title was not his. Active service was impossible for a man so fragile, even if his views had allowed him to serve willingly; but though he could not be a conscientious objector, and was twice rejected for service, he held that the War was wholly evil. Something of this attitude is expressed in the latter part of *The Rainbow*, a novel which he published in 1915, though the war there denounced is the Boer War. This book, perhaps the most profound and poetical of Lawrence's novels, was the subject of a prosecution, and was condemned as indecent. The blow to Lawrence was far more staggering than is generally realized. It involved him in pecuniary difficulties which he did not escape for years; it marked him with a disgrace which he felt keenly, and believed to be undeserved; it was a severe rebuff to his idealistic beliefs. All this was mingled with acute suffering over the continuance of the War and its destructiveness.

Lawrence's chief desire now was to leave England, and he applied for passports for himself and his wife to America. Lack of money for the passage frustrated his project, and he retired to a small cottage at Zennor, Cornwall, where he worked on *Women in Love* (privately printed in New York, 1920; published in London, 1921). For reasons unknown to him, he and his wife (who was cousin to the well-known German airman, von Richthofen) were ordered to leave Zennor in October 1917, and not to enter any prohibited area. He went first to London; then lived in small cottages, at Hermitage near Newbury, and at Middleton-by-Wirksworth in Derbyshire. His sufferings during this period are related in two long chapters, headed 'The Nightmare', in his Australian novel, *Kangaroo* (1923).

Towards the end of 1919 Lawrence scraped together a few pounds and left England, to which he never returned except on very brief visits. While resentment at the treatment he had received may have had something to do with this, the chief motive of his exile was despair at the hostile attitude displayed in England towards himself and his writings. For the remainder of his life he was a wanderer, and only the main outline of his pilgrimage can or need be traced here. He went first to Florence (see the Florentine chapters in *Aaron's Rod*, 1922), then to Picinisco in the Abruzzi (see the latter part of *The Lost Girl*, 1920). He fled from the intense cold of the Abruzzi to Capri, liked and disliked it, and then settled for a time at Fontana Vecchia, near Taormina, where he remained until February 1922, except for short excursions. In *Sea and Sardinia* (1921) he produced the second of his remarkable travel books—the first was *Twilight in Italy* (1916), describing a walking tour through Switzerland to Italy—and accomplished the feat of making an interesting book out of the impressions and experiences of a few days.

The chronology of Lawrence's writings cannot at present be precisely determined; what is certain is that the order of composition does not correspond with the dates of publication. Among the books published at this time may be mentioned *Psychoanalysis and the Unconscious* (New York, 1921), *Fantasia of the Unconscious* (1922), and the short stories entitled *England, My England* (New York, 1922). Traces of his life in Sicily will be found in his beautifully written introduction to *Memoirs of the Foreign Legion* by 'M. M.' (London, 1924) and in the poems, *Birds, Beasts and Flowers* (1923). *Studies in Classical American Literature* was issued in America in the same year (1923).

Early in 1922 Lawrence left Sicily for America, by way of Ceylon and of Australia, where he stayed for a time. He reached San Francisco in September 1922, travelled in the United States and in Mexico, and settled on a small mountain ranch near

Taos, New Mexico. Between December 1923 and March 1924 he paid a flying visit to England and the Continent, returning to Taos, from which he moved in October 1924 to Oaxaca, Mexico. Experiences there are recorded in his novel *The Plumed Serpent* (1926) and in *Mornings in Mexico* (1927). In 1925 he was seriously ill with malaria, and nearly died; this may have been the basis of his imaginative story, 'The Man Who Died', published in 1929 under the title *The Escaped Cock*. His illness compelled him to leave Mexico in October 1925. He lived at Spotorno, Italy, until March 1926, and then settled at the Villa Mirenda, Scandicci, near Florence. There he wrote *Lady Chatterley's Lover* (Florence, 1928) and remained until May 1928. No less than three manuscript versions of this novel are extant, showing the pains which he took over its composition; yet in many ways it is one of the least satisfactory of his books.

Lawrence's last years were agitated by the police prosecution of *Lady Chatterley's Lover*, the confiscation of the original manuscript of his poems, *Pansies* (1929), police action over an exhibition of his pictures held in London in 1928, and the suppression of the book containing facsimile reproductions of these paintings. It is an ironical fact that far more attention was drawn to Lawrence by these unfortunate scandals than by the excellence of his other and very varied productions; while his private edition of *Lady Chatterley's Lover* brought him more substantial earnings than any of his previous books. While living near Florence Lawrence had more than once been seriously ill and near death, yet he had found energy to visit Etruscan towns, and produced the unfinished *Sketches of Etruscan Places*, published posthumously. After leaving Florence, he lived at Bandol, near Toulon, and visited Spain. Early in 1930 his condition became so serious that he was moved to a clinic at Vence, where he died on 2 March 1930. His grave there is marked by a mosaic of the risen phoenix, which he had long before chosen as his emblem. His literary activity continued to the very end, and an unfinished poem was written only a few days before he died. Among the posthumous books the most important are: the *Letters* (1932); *Apocalypse* (Florence, 1931), a statement of his attitude to life; and *Last Poems* (Florence, 1932), which contains, among pieces of slighter interest, the poignant record of his feelings and thoughts as he faced the reality and certainty of death. His spiritual loneliness was complete.

Since his death Lawrence's reputation has grown with astonishing swiftness, and, though opinion is far from unanimous, he is now widely recognized in many countries as one of the most original and gifted English writers of his age. The misunderstanding which original genius often meets with from contemporaries is gradually being cleared away, and his reputation cannot but gain by closer and more serious study of his books.

[*Letters of D. H. Lawrence*, edited by Aldous Huxley, with photographs, 1932; Ada Lawrence (sister), *Young Lorenzo*, with photographs, 1932; *Bibliography of the Writings of D. H. Lawrence*, Philadelphia, 1925; private information; personal knowledge.]

R. Aldington.

LEADER, BENJAMIN WILLIAMS (1831–1923), painter, was born at Worcester 12 March 1831, the second son in the family of eleven children of Edward Leader Williams, chief engineer to the Severn Navigation Commission. The eldest son was Sir Edward Leader Williams [q.v.], the engineer of the Manchester ship canal and of Shoreham harbour and Dover docks. Having been educated at Worcester grammar school, Benjamin Leader Williams worked for a time in his father's office, studying also at the Government School of Design at Worcester; in 1854 he entered the Royal Academy Schools. At this period of his career he felt greatly attracted towards the pre-Raphaelites, and began by painting figure subjects which are definite essays in the pre-Raphaelite manner. The first picture exhibited by him at the Royal Academy, in the year of his admission (1854), was 'Cottage Children blowing Bubbles', and this was followed in 1855 by 'The Bird Trap' (bought by Mr. Arden, who from the same exhibition acquired (Sir) J. E. Millais's 'Order of Release'), and in 1856 by 'The Young Mother'. The following year, in order to avoid confusion with the many painters of the name of Williams, he transposed his surname and second christian name, adopting the latter as his surname.

In 1862 Leader settled at Whittington, near Worcester, henceforth devoting himself mainly to landscape painting, choosing his subjects from Worcestershire and Wales. After a long period of steady work and fair, but not conspicuous success, Leader for the first time came prominently into the public eye with his large Worcestershire landscape 'February Fill-Dyke', contributed to the Academy exhibition 1881. Scarcely inferior was the success of his landscape entitled 'In the Evening there shall be Light', exhibited at the Academy in 1882, and in 1889 at the Paris Salon, where it gained the gold medal. In 1883 Leader, by now well established as one of the most successful landscape-painters of the day, was elected an A.R.A., becoming R.A. in 1898; his diploma work was 'The Sandpit, Burroughs Cross'. In the meantime he had moved to Surrey, settling in 1890 at Burrow's Cross, Shere, near Guildford, a house built by Richard Norman Shaw for the painter Frank Holl.

Until the very end of his long life Leader went on painting, contributing, indeed, three pictures to the Academy exhibition of 1922, the year preceding that of his death at the age of ninety-two. His style as a landscape painter tends to be overemphatic in design and commonplace in colour. He betrays, indeed, little of that connexion with Constable which one might feel inclined to deduce from the fact that Constable was a friend of the Williams family and deposited some of his pictures at their house. However, the popular appeal of Leader's art was enormous for a time, and was exercised not only through the originals but also through a large number of engraved reproductions. In June 1914 Leader was presented with the freedom of the city of Worcester; he had been made a chevalier of the legion of honour by the French government in 1889.

Leader died at his Surrey home 22 March 1923. He married in 1876 Mary, daughter of William Eastlake, of Plymouth, and niece of Sir Charles Lock Eastlake, president of the Royal Academy [q.v.], herself a painter of flowers. They had two sons, the elder of whom was the painter, Eastlake Leader, who was killed in action in 1916; they also had three daughters.

[*The Times*, 23 March 1923; Lewis Lusk, *The Life and Work of B. W. Leader, R.A.* (the Christmas number of the *Art Journal*, 1901); Algernon Graves, *The Royal Academy of Arts, a complete dictionary of contributors and their work*, vol. v, 1906; subsequent Royal Academy Exhibition Catalogues.] T. Borenius.

LEAF, WALTER (1852–1927), classical scholar and banker, was born at Upper Norwood 28 November 1852, the elder son of Charles John Leaf, who was a partner in the firm of Leaf, Sons, and Co., dealers in silks and ribbons, of Old Change, London. His mother was Isabella Ellen, daughter of John Tyas, a fine classical scholar, who was for twenty years on the staff of *The Times* and had been an important witness of the 'Peterloo massacre' in 1819. Leaf was tutored at home by Dr. Charles Mayo and won an entrance scholarship at Winchester, but was not sent there as his parents wished him to continue living at home. For that purpose they sold their house in Norwood and moved to Harrow, where in 1866 he entered the school as a 'home boarder'. He was very short-sighted, and since, according to the custom of the time, no one thought of providing him with spectacles, he was at a great disadvantage in sports and games. He quickly became a favourite with his teachers, and in 1867 was taken by two of them, E. M. Young and Edward Ernest Bowen [q.v.], on a trip to Rome and Naples. In 1868 his tutor, Frederic William (afterwards Dean) Farrar [q.v.], took over a house, The Park, which had got into a bad state of discipline, and asked Leaf to come to it as head boy. The ordeal for a small, short-sighted, and scholarly boy was terrifying, but Leaf faced it, insisted on order, caned a miscreant twice his size, and conquered. In March 1869 he won a classical scholarship at Trinity College, Cambridge, but as he was not much over sixteen did not reside until October 1870. The year between was spent in deliberate coaching for the tripos, five years distant, for which he and F. H. Rawlins, of King's College, were early marked as the favourites. At Cambridge he was a member of the select society known as the 'Apostles', which included F. W. Maitland, S. H. Butcher, and A. W. Verrall; he became an adept at figure-skating and mountaineering; won the Craven scholarship in 1873; and in 1874 was bracketed senior classic with Rawlins, with whom he also tied for the chancellor's classical medals. In the following year he was elected a fellow of Trinity. In the meantime, however, the family business was in need of help; in 1874 Leaf's father had a severe illness, and his grandfather and his uncle Frederick died; his uncle William had died three years before. Leaf felt it his duty to abandon Cambridge and his intended career at the bar, and enter the 'rag business', in which two years later (1877) he was made a partner.

In spite of his first distaste for Old Change, Leaf's clear head and firm character were in due course to make him a power in the City. During the time that he remained with his firm it was converted into a limited liability company, of which he was chairman from 1888 to 1892. When, in the latter year, the company was amalgamated with a kindred business, Leaf retired in order to devote more attention to banking. In 1891 he had been elected a director of the London and Westminster Bank; in 1918 he became chairman of the bank and in 1919 of the Institute of Bankers. He wrote for the 'Home University Library' an admirable little handbook on *Banking* (1926), and his speeches on financial subjects were greatly admired by a severe critic, Mr. Asquith. After the European War he supported the League of Nations movement, and in 1926, as president (elected in 1924) of the International Chamber of Commerce, he made an important and successful visit to Germany with a view to economic reconciliation. It was immediately after this effort that his health failed, and, after a voyage to South Africa, he died at Torquay 8 March 1927. He married in 1894 Charlotte Mary, daughter of John Addington Symonds [q.v.], and had one son and one daughter.

Leaf was a man of extraordinary intellectual range. His list of languages included—besides perfect French and German—Italian, Russian, and Persian. He was a fine musician, an authority on political economy, and an important, though sceptical, member of the Society for Psychical Research. On other subjects, such as mathematics, astronomy, and botany, he was generally 'the best informed person in the room'. He was also one of the founders in 1876 of the University Extension movement, a leading member of the London County Council—he represented East Marylebone from 1901 to 1904—and was active in various forms of social work. It is recorded that he had a quite peculiar power of restoring confidence in the 'down and out'. People could not help trusting him and drawing, as it were, on his own stores of integrity and courage.

But Leaf's reputation rests chiefly on his work as a Greek, and particularly as a Homeric, scholar. His first book, produced in 1882 in co-operation with Andrew Lang [q.v.] and Ernest James Myers [q.v.], was a translation of the *Iliad* into archaic and poetical prose, a delicate task successfully carried through. On the death in 1878 of J. H. Pratt, of Trinity College, Cambridge, he was invited by Messrs. Macmillan to undertake the large edition of the *Iliad* which Pratt had promised, and from 1886 to 1888 he produced his first edition in two volumes with a commentary. The second edition (1900–1902) was enlarged and improved, particularly by the collation of five important manuscripts. This remains by far the best edition of the *Iliad* in English, and perhaps the best in any language. Its lasting goodness is the more remarkable because Leaf had adopted, and followed with scrupulous consistency, a hypothesis which is now generally abandoned —that of a 'genuine' story of Achilles by 'Homer', expanded by later 'interpolations' into our present *Iliad*. Leaf had such mastery of his subject, and such a clear and exact way of treating his problems, that this error of theory hardly affects the value of the book.

In 1912 Leaf published *Troy, a Study in Homeric Geography*, based on his own explorations and those of Wilhelm Dörpfeld, and arguing that the catalogue of Trojan allies contained in the *Iliad* proves the existence of ancient trade routes converging on Troy as a centre. He thus agreed with V. Bérard that Troy shut off the trade of the Hellespont, and hence the war against her was commercial in origin. In *Homer and History* (1915) he argued that the Greek catalogue was a late addition, describing a division of territory inconsistent with the rest of the *Iliad*, which, for the purposes of argument, he treated as a consistent unity. He accepted the conclusions of H. M. Chadwick's *Heroic Age* (1912) and Dörpfeld's more doubtful identification of Ithaca with Leucas. Finally in *Strabo on the Troad* (1923) he edited with translation and commentary Strabo's discussion of that territory. The book is a masterly chapter, as it were, of that edition of the whole of Strabo which he had long contemplated as a joint enterprise to be undertaken by the Hellenic Society.

Leaf said of himself that he tried to combine 'scholarship with reality'. That explains the great qualities of his work. He never lost his sense of reality and proportion; all that he wrote was interesting, alive, and businesslike. He was admirably fair in controversy and clear in sustained argument. His fine scholarship was combined with a vigilant common sense. On the other hand, it may be thought that this desire for 'reality' made him try to find historical and geographical 'realities' where they did not exist, and not allow sufficiently for the elements of myth, fiction, and mere conventional ornament in

Homeric poetry. Not that he lacked poetical sense; his translations of the *Greek Anthology* are of high quality, and there is real beauty in his Greek elegiacs: for example, those prefixed to *Homer and History*.

A drawing of Leaf by William Rothenstein (1910) is reproduced in *Portrait Drawings of William Rothenstein, 1889–1925* (1926).

[Leaf's published works; Charlotte M. Leaf, *Walter Leaf*, containing a fragment of autobiography, 1932; personal knowledge.]

G. Murray.

LEE, Sir SIDNEY (1859–1926), Shakespearian scholar and editor of the Dictionary of National Biography, born in Keppel Street, Russell Square, London, 5 December 1859, was the elder son of Lazarus Lee, a London merchant, by his wife, Jessie Davis. He was originally named Solomon Lazarus, but early in 1890 he adopted the name Sidney instead of Solomon, and shortly afterwards dropped the name Lazarus. He was educated at the City of London School, then situated in Milk Street, Cheapside, under Dr. Edwin A. Abbott [q.v.]. Abbott's predecessor, Dr. G. F. W. Mortimer [q.v.], had encouraged the study of English, and Abbott, by his teaching and influence, stimulated interest in Elizabethan literature. The Elizabethan scholar, Arthur Henry Bullen [q.v.], and Henry Charles Beeching [q.v.], the poet and writer, were Lee's contemporaries at school and friends in later life. Lee matriculated from Balliol College, Oxford, as a commoner, in October 1878. In November 1879 he was *proxime accessit* for the Brackenbury history scholarship and was awarded a minor exhibition. He obtained a third class in classical moderations in 1880 and a second class in modern history in 1882, graduating B.A. in the same year. Among his contemporaries at Balliol, though two years senior, was his lifelong friend (Sir) Charles Harding Firth, who afterwards gave valuable advice and assistance to the Dictionary of National Biography.

Lee's Shakespearian studies began early. While an undergraduate he wrote two articles in the *Gentleman's Magazine* which attracted notice from Shakespearian scholars, especially from J. O. Halliwell-Phillipps and F. J. Furnivall. The first of these articles, *The Original of Shylock*, which appeared in February 1880, suggested that the reputation of Roderigo Lopez [q.v.] and the popular excitement caused by his trial and execution in 1594, incited Shakespeare to a subtler study of Jewish character than had been essayed before (cf. *English Historical Review*, vol. ix, 1894, pp. 470–472). The second article, which appeared in October 1880, called attention to the topical character of *Love's Labour's Lost*, the relation of its nomenclature to Henry of Navarre and his circle, and its references to contemporary France. Lee afterwards expanded these two articles. The first formed the basis of a paper, dealing with Jewish life in Elizabethan England, which he read to the New Shakespere Society on 10 February 1888 (*Transactions*, 1887–1892, p. 143). The topical aspect of Elizabethan drama was made the subject of two papers read by him to the same society on 8 February 1884 and 22 October 1886 (*ibid.*, 1880–1886, p. 80; 1887–1892, p. 1).

About May 1882 Lee was offered a professorship of English which was about to be founded in the university of Groningen; but before the matter was finally arranged he became sub-editor to (Sir) Leslie Stephen [q.v.] when George Smith founded the Dictionary of National Biography [see the memoir of Smith now prefixed to the first volume]. Dr. F. J. Furnivall, who had already commissioned Lee to edit for the Early English Text Society the translation by Lord Berners of *The Boke of Duke Huon of Burdeux*, which appeared in four volumes between 1882 and 1887, recommended him to Stephen, and he became assistant editor in March 1883 at a salary of £300 a year [see the memoir of Lee prefixed to the volume for 1912–1921]. From the beginning Lee gained Stephen's confidence by his industry and discretion, and this confidence ripened into intimacy and lifelong friendship. In 1903 Stephen wrote: 'My greatest piece of good fortune was that from the first I had the co-operation of Mr. Sidney Lee as my sub-editor. Always calm and confident when I was tearing my hair over the delay of some article urgently required for the timely production of our next volume, always ready to undertake any amount of thankless drudgery, and most thoroughly conscientious in his work, he was an invaluable helpmate' [*Some Early Impressions*, ed. 1924, p. 160]. In fact, Stephen and Lee were admirably fitted to co-operate in the work in hand. Stephen's position among men of letters enabled him to choose and control the contributors, while Lee's exact and scholarly methods were well fitted for organizing the editorial work and raising the general standard of the articles by adding necessary detail and excluding what was redundant. The latter function was later summarized by Canon Alfred Ainger [q.v.] at the dinner given by George Smith to the contributors at the Hotel Métropole on 8 July 1897 in the phrase, 'No flowers by request'.

In the autumn of 1889 Stephen had a serious break-down, and Lee became joint editor at the beginning of 1890. A recurrence of Stephen's illness led him to resign his editorship in April 1891, whereupon Lee became sole editor. He held this post until the DICTIONARY and its FIRST SUPPLEMENT were completed in 1901, and he resumed it from October 1910 to December 1912, while editing the SECOND SUPPLEMENT. But he retained throughout the years 1901 to 1916 the general oversight of the Dictionary, receiving and incorporating corrections, and adding fresh information. Lee set out his views on biography and biographical work, as they evolved, in his lecture on 'National Biography' delivered at the Royal Institution on 31 January 1896, in his Leslie Stephen lecture given at Cambridge on *Principles of Biography* (1911), and in his address delivered to the English Association in 1918 on *The Perspective of Biography* (English Association pamphlet no. 41). As editor, however, his greatest asset was his personality. Leslie Stephen said that the editor ought to be a 'considerate autocrat' (*Athenæum*, 23 December 1883), but Lee was not more autocratic than was necessary for the smooth running of the machine up to time. He preserved the balance and uniformity of the Dictionary, and realized that its value depended on the general standard of the articles and not chiefly on the merits of the more important lives. He kept in close personal touch with most of the regular contributors, frequently entertaining them at his house in Lexham Gardens and at his clubs. His popularity with them was evinced in a presentation of silver plate which they made to him in 1900. His relations with his staff were far from autocratic, although he believed in a good day's work, and his own powers of prolonged work at a pinch were remarkable. A four-hour afternoon without tea was the main trial to his Oxford assistants. Hospitable, kindly, and considerate, Lee made the period of service a happy memory to the present writer. The Dictionary was completed in sixty-three volumes in October 1900, and the First Supplement, including the lives of persons accidentally omitted and of those who, while the work was coming out, had died too late for admission, was issued in three volumes in 1901.

Out of two of his articles in the Dictionary Lee developed his *Life of William Shakespeare* and his *Queen Victoria, a biography*. The article on Shakespeare appeared in July 1897 and the book in November 1898. It was received enthusiastically, and went through four editions in two months. Although the book was based on the article, the changes and additions were sufficient to make it an independent production. After it had passed through six editions Lee published in October 1915 a rewritten and enlarged edition in anticipation of Shakespeare's tercentenary; in this he gave a much fuller account of the development of the Elizabethan drama and its presentation on the London stage, and incorporated many of the results of his own subsequent work and of his discoveries in the archives at Stratford-on-Avon and the wills at Somerset House of Shakespeare's Stratford friends. The *Life* reached a thirteenth edition in his lifetime (1925), and was translated into German in 1899 under the direction of Professor Richard Paul Wülcker, of Leipzig. The copyright was left by Lee to the Faculty of English Language and Literature at Oxford, and a fourteenth edition was published in 1931 under the supervision of that body.

In his preface to the *Life* Lee modestly claimed to have provided students of Shakespeare with 'a full record of the duly attested facts and dates of their master's career' and with 'verifiable references to all the original sources of information'. But with more than eighteen years of Elizabethan study behind him he did much more than this. By treating the life and writings of Shakespeare in close connexion with each other and with the literature and history of the time, he produced a work of exegesis of the first order; and although he asserted that he 'avoided merely aesthetic criticism', he furnished a reliable basis for sound aesthetic appreciation by his study of the origin and formation of Shakespeare's text and of the influence of foreign literature on Shakespeare's subject-matter. These two themes, especially the second, he proceeded to develop subsequently. He followed up the former in 1902 in his introduction to the Clarendon Press facsimile of the first folio of Shakespeare's Plays, where he described the methods by which publishers at that time procured their 'copy', and discussed the sources and value of the text of the folio. In 1905 he brought out for the Clarendon Press facsimiles of the earliest editions of *Venus and Adonis*, *Lucrece*, the *Passionate Pilgrim*, the Sonnets, and *Pericles*, with introductions dealing in the case of the Sonnets mainly with the text, but in that of the others with the literary origin and subject-matter also. In 1908 he reprinted at Stratford-on-Avon the quarto editions of *The Merchant of Venice*, *A Midsummer Night's Dream*, *King Lear*, and *The Merry Wives of Windsor*. In 1909 he edited a facsimile of *The Chronicle History of King Leir*, which, if compared with Shakespeare's play, affords an interesting illustration of the poet's treatment of raw material.

The question of Shakespeare's subject-matter led Lee to deal with the wider issue of the extent of foreign influence on Elizabethan literature, and to insist on the need for the comparative study of national literatures. In his *Life* of Shakespeare, while examining the influence of France on Shakespeare's poems, sonnets, and early plays, he had contended that the subject-matter and even the thought, particularly of the sonnets, was mainly conventional and that the poet, while improving what he touched, had borrowed abroad from Ovid, Petrarch, Ronsard, and Desportes, as well as from Sidney, Thomas Watson, and others at home. In his introduction to the two volumes of Elizabethan sonnets in Thomas Seccombe's revised edition of Edward Arber's *English Garner* in 1904, and in his article on 'The Elizabethan Sonnet' in the *Cambridge History of English Literature*, vol. iii (1909) he demonstrated more generally the close dependence of Elizabethan sonnets on foreign models. In the facsimiles of 1905, already mentioned, he dealt similarly with the Poems and with *Pericles*. In April 1909, in an article in the *Quarterly Review* on *Ovid and Shakespeare's Sonnets*, he worked out in detail the debt of the Sonnets to the *Metamorphoses*, and in his lecture delivered in June to the English Association on 'The Impersonal Aspect of Shakespeare's Art' (English Association leaflet no. 13), he denied that Shakespeare's personal life was reflected in his plays. In 1910 Lee enlarged and published some lectures which he had given at Oxford in 1909 under the auspices of the Common University Fund, under the title of *The French Renaissance in England*. In these he dealt with the debt of Tudor culture to French grammarians, prose-writers, and dramatists, while in a lecture delivered to the British Academy in 1915 on *Shakespeare and the Italian Renaissance* he indicated the channels through which the 'new faith in beauty and reason' filtered from Italy through France to England, where it found disciples in Sidney, Spenser, and Shakespeare. Finally, he published a paper in the *Anglo-Italian Review* for September 1918 on *Tasso and Shakespeare's England*. With these studies on international literary relations, which demanded an extraordinarily accurate knowledge of the great body of literature from which they were drawn, may be mentioned *The Call of the West*, four articles published in *Scribner's Magazine* during 1907, setting forth the knowledge of America in Shakespeare's time and its influence on current thought in Spain, France, and England. On 19 October 1918, in his inaugural address to the Modern Language Research Association (now the Modern Humanities Research Association), he emphasized the pacific influence of the international element in literature.

The other book developed from the Dictionary, *Queen Victoria*, was to some extent unpremeditated. When the First Supplement of the Dictionary was planned it was intended to carry it down to the end of the nineteenth century, but when the queen died twenty-two days later, it was resolved to include the whole period of her reign. With some misgiving with regard to its difficulties Lee undertook the article on the queen at the earnest request of George Smith. The article appeared in October 1901, and in response to a widespread wish the book followed in November 1902. It was the first serious attempt to present the queen's public and private life as a whole. The book was expanded to contain more biographical detail than had been given in the article and more explanatory comment on events. Lee aimed at making the queen's personality the principal study, and with space at his disposal he was able to use more fully references to public affairs in her diary and letters, so far as these were available, and 'to let the Queen speak for herself'. Victoria's influence on events after the death of the Prince Consort in 1861 was very imperfectly known, and became increasingly difficult to elucidate as her reign drew nearer to its close. Although Lee's reputation as an editor for discretion and care assisted him to get information otherwise unattainable, the latter part of the biography is distinctly slighter than the rest. But as a pioneer piece of work it was remarkably successful. A fourth edition appeared in 1907.

Lee suffered financially when his full employment as editor ceased in 1901. He did some further work for the Dictionary before the commencement of the Second Supplement, superintending a summary which appeared in March 1903 as the INDEX AND EPITOME, a volume of ERRATA in 1904, and a reissue of the Dictionary and First Supplement in 1909. But as these were not very remunerative, he also engaged in lecturing and writing. As a lecturer Lee was sometimes diffuse, but he improved very much in later years. He was Clark lecturer in English literature at Trinity College, Cambridge, in 1901–1902, he made a successful tour through the universities and colleges of the United States of America in 1903, and in October 1904 he published his lectures delivered at the Lowell Institute, Boston, on *Great Englishmen of the Sixteenth Century* (new ed. 1925). He edited for the university press of Cambridge, U.S.A., between 1907 and 1910 the *Renaissance Shakespeare*, using William Aldis Wright's text, and contributing a general introduction and notes, as well as separate introductions to several plays. This work was reissued in England in 1910 as the *Caxton Shakespeare*. In 1909 he undertook to edit for the Clarendon Press *Shakespeare's England*, a collection of articles describing the habits and life of the time. Although Lee contributed only one article, he planned the work and enlisted most of the writers, but in 1914 he gave up the editorship of the volume, which was brought out by (Dr.) C. T. Onions in 1916.

From October 1910 to December 1912 Lee was engaged in editing the Second Supplement of the Dictionary. George Smith had intended to continue the work by means of a supplement at the end of each decade, and Mrs. Smith, to whom he bequeathed the Dictionary, proceeded to carry out his plan. This principle of quick biography has met with criticism, but it was advocated by Leslie Stephen on account of the rapid disappearance of material, and defended by Lee in December 1912 in the *Nineteenth Century and After* in an article entitled 'A Journey's End', in which he instanced Boswell's *Johnson* and Lockhart's *Scott* in support of his view.

Neither the First nor the Second Supplement preserved exactly the standard of selection maintained in the main work. The First Supplement tended to restrict admission, particularly in certain classes; the Second Supplement, on the other hand, was far more inclusive than the main Dictionary. The work of editing was undoubtedly more arduous, as Lee had to train a new staff and to supply the place of contributors no longer available after ten years. Nevertheless, the rate of production was maintained and the work appeared less than a year after the close of the period which it covered. Lee wrote few articles, but among them were those on King Edward VII, Leslie Stephen, Goldwin Smith, F. J. Furnivall, and John Churton Collins. After its issue Lee, as before, carried on a general editorial supervision until the death of Reginald John Smith [q.v.] in December 1916. The Dictionary was soon afterwards presented to Oxford University, which transferred it to the Clarendon Press, and Lee's connexion with it came to an end. Lee felt that the Dictionary should be carried on in accordance with George Smith's plan and on traditional lines, and insisted on this with considerable and natural earnestness. Though it was impossible, while the War continued, for the Clarendon Press to make definitive pledges, a volume covering the years 1912–1921, with Henry William Carless Davis [q.v.] and J. R. H. Weaver as editors, was begun soon after the conclusion of peace.

Lee became a university professor comparatively late in life. From early days he had been an unofficial teacher and had devoted much of his spare time to popularizing English studies. He took part in the University Extension summer meetings at Oxford and Cambridge, and in London he lectured on Saturday evenings at the Working Men's College in Mile End Road. But the institution with which he was most closely connected was Toynbee Hall, for which in early days he arranged concerts and lectures, and where from 1890 he was president of the Elizabethan Literary Society. This society was founded in London on 8 March 1884 by the Rev. W. Bartlett, was given head-quarters at Toynbee Hall in 1886 by Samuel Augustus Barnett [q.v.], and in 1913 removed to King's College, Strand. Lee was included in the first list of vice-presidents and he and Frederick Rogers, who began life as an errand boy, were largely responsible for developing it as a centre of Elizabethan study. Especially Lee brought it into touch with contemporary research and secured the active support of leading Elizabethans of the day. In January 1925, at the annual supper, he induced the Society to set itself to complete the Marlowe memorial at Canterbury, designed by Edward Onslow Ford [q.v.] and completed by Charles Hartwell. It had been projected by two members of the Society, Rogers and J. E. Baker, was erected in the Canterbury butter-market in 1891, and removed still incomplete in 1924 to the Dane John park, where it now stands, and finally completed and unveiled on 1 November 1928. Lee was also one of the founders of the English Association in 1906 and was its president in 1917; he compiled for it in 1910 a catalogue for *A Shakespeare Reference Library* (English Association leaflet no. 15; 2nd ed., with Sir E. K. Chambers, 1925, English Association pamphlet no. 61). In 1913 Lee was appointed to the new chair of English language and literature at the East London College in the university of London. His lectures attracted serious students. 'He took great personal interest in his pupils and was never weary of advising and helping them, especially if they were ex-service men' [Firth, *Sir Sidney Lee*, p. 10]. The death on 10 July 1920 of his sister, Elizabeth Lee, who shared his interests and to whom he was much attached, was a great sorrow to him. In 1921 he had a serious operation, and in 1924 impaired health and pressure of other work led him to give up his professorship.

Lee's last work of importance was his *Life of King Edward VII*, undertaken at the request of King George V. Unlike the *Queen Victoria* it was not made difficult by scarcity of material. The documents in the royal archives at Windsor Castle and Buckingham Palace were placed at his disposal, as well as several private collections of King Edward's letters. Controversies concerning the diplomatic origin of the European War had led to the publication of much British and foreign official material relating to the period, and the marked decrease in Great Britain and in other countries of the reticence of public men with regard to recent public affairs was also not without its advantages. King George, who made the work feasible, left the plan and the execution entirely to Lee's discretion. As with Victoria, Lee made Edward VII's personality and influence the central study, and therefore gave considerable space to international affairs. The first volume appeared in March 1925, but its production overtaxed Lee's failing strength and the second volume, which dealt with the reign, was far from completely written at the time of his death. It was finished by his secretary, Mr. F. S. Markham, with some assistance noticed in the preface, and appeared in 1927. In the autumn of 1925 Lee's health steadily gave way, and he died, unmarried, 3 March 1926 at his residence, 108A Lexham Gardens, Kensington. After cremation his remains were interred, as he had requested, in the cemetery at Stratford-on-Avon.

All through life Lee had many warm friends. It was said of him in *The Times* that 'those who knew him best know best how genial and generous he was, and how unselfishly he gave himself, both publicly and privately in service to others'. Beside this may be recorded George Saintsbury's testimony, given two days later in the same paper: 'He is about the only man, I think, of the whole lot of us (including myself) from whom I have never heard an unkind speech about a fellow craftsman.' Lee's portrait, drawn in the last months of his life, by William Rothenstein, is at East London College; but some of the photographs of him, especially that reproduced in Professor Boas's collection of Lee's *Essays* (opposite p. 84), recall him better to those who knew him earlier.

Lee held many offices. He was chairman of the executive of Shakespeare's Birthplace Trust from 1903 until his death, and worked hard on its behalf. He was registrar of the Royal Literary Fund from 1907. In 1910 he was appointed a member of the royal commission on the public records and elected a fellow of the British Academy. He was appointed a trustee of the National Portrait Gallery in 1924. He was a foreign member of the American Academy of Arts and Sciences and a corresponding member of the Massachusetts Historical Society. He was knighted in 1911, was elected to the Athenaeum Club in 1901 under Rule II, and received honorary degrees from the universities of Manchester (1900), Oxford (1907), and Glasgow (1907).

Besides the books and articles already mentioned, Lee wrote a *History of Stratford-on-Avon from the Earliest Times to the Death of Shakespeare* (1885, new ed. 1907); edited the *Autobiography* of Edward, first Baron Herbert of Cherbury [q.v.] with a continuation of his life (1886, new ed. 1906); compiled a *Census of Extant Copies of the First Folio* of Shakespeare's Plays as a companion to the *Facsimile* (1902), and gave an account of fourteen more copies in *The Library*, April 1906 (reprinted as *Notes and Additions to the Census*, 1906); contributed in 1904 to vol. iii of the *Cambridge Modern History*, chapters x and xi, on 'The Last Years of Elizabeth', of which period he contemplated writing a detailed history, and 'The Elizabethan Age of English Literature'; and published in 1906 eleven articles on *Shakespeare and the Modern Stage and other Essays*. In 1929 Professor F. S. Boas published a selection of Lee's lectures and essays under the title of *Elizabethan and Other Essays*. Lee left a number of his books to the Birthplace Museum at Stratford-on-Avon, and his annotated working copy of the reissue of the Dictionary of National Biography to the London Library for the use of the librarian and staff. The bulk of his English library belongs by bequest and purchase to East London College, to which he also left £5,000 with which to endow two bursaries.

[*The Times*, 4 and 6 March 1926; Sir C. H. Firth, *Sir Sidney Lee, 1859–1926*, in *Proceedings* of the British Academy, vol. xv, 1929, and *Memoir of Sir Sidney Lee* prefixed to the *Dictionary of National Biography, Twentieth Century, 1912–1921*, 1927; F. S. Boas in the English Association *Bulletin*, No.56, April 1926, in *Review of English Studies*, July 1926, and in his introduction to *Elizabethan and other Essays*, 1929; A. F. Pollard, 'Sir Sidney Lee and the Dictionary of National Biography', in the *Bulletin* of the Institute of Historical Research, June 1926; F. S. Boas, *The Elizabethan Literary Society*, reprinted from the *Quarterly Review*, April 1934; F. Rogers, *Labour, Life, and Literature*, 1913; *The Toynbee Record*, 1890 et seqq.; *History and Description of the Marlowe Memorial, Canterbury*, 1928; Sir Leslie Stephen, *Early Impressions*, ed. 1924, and *Studies of a Biographer*, 1898; *Jewish Guardian*, 5 March 1926; private information; personal knowledge.] E. I. Carlyle.

LEISHMAN, Sir WILLIAM BOOG (1865–1926), bacteriologist, born in Glasgow 6 November 1865, was the fourth child and youngest of three sons in the family of six children of William Leishman (1833–1894), regius professor of midwifery in the university of Glasgow, by his wife, Augusta Selina, eldest daughter of George Drevar, of Rosehill, Blackrock, co. Dublin. Educated at Westminster School and at the university of Glasgow, where he graduated M.B., C.M. in 1886, he entered the Army Medical Service in 1887, passing fifth into the Army Medical School at Netley. After home service for three years, he proceeded to India and served until 1897 with a year's sick leave (1892–1893); he went through the Waziristan campaign of 1894–1895. Promoted major in the Royal Army Medical Corps in 1899, he was posted to Netley in order to take charge of the medical wards, spending his spare time in the pathological department then under the direction of (Sir) Almroth Wright, and in the following year succeeded Major (Sir) David Semple as assistant professor of pathology.

Although he had been exceptional in taking a microscope with him to India in 1890 and had worked at bacteriology when staff surgeon to Sir George Wolseley at Lahore, this appointment at the Army Medical School was Leishman's first real opportunity for original work, and came a little late in his career. At Netley he was able to watch the early development of Almroth Wright's anti-typhoid vaccination, in which he later took so important a part. During this period Leishman elaborated the stain for blood—a modification of Romanowsky's—which is known by his name and was employed by him in the detection of the parasite of kala-azar, also called Dum-Dum fever. This parasite, now known as the Leishman-Donovan body (*Leishmania donovani*), Leishman detected in 1900, but he did not publish his observations until 1903, the year in which Lieut.-Col. Charles Donovan, of the Indian Medical Service, confirmed the discovery. The name Leishmania was introduced in 1903 by Sir Ronald Ross; the term Leishmaniasis also covers Oriental sore, a disease due to the closely allied protozoan parasite *Leishmania tropica*.

When the Army Medical School was transferred from Netley to Millbank, London, in 1903, Leishman became professor of pathology, and held this post until 1913. During these ten years he continued his work on kala-azar and perfected the protective vaccine against typhoid fever, a large reserve store of which was kept at the Royal Army Medical College, so that within two weeks of the outbreak of war in August 1914 170,000 doses were issued to the troops. It has been estimated that without its use in the European War there would have been about 551,000 cases of this disease, with more than 77,000 deaths; actually there were 21,139 cases and 1,191 deaths only. Leishman also spent much time on a difficult piece of research, for which his masterly technique fully qualified him, namely, the life cycle of the *Spironema duttoni* of relapsing fever, conveyed by the tick *Ornithodoros moubata*; in 1920 he gave the Horace Dobell research lecture before the Royal College of Physicians of London, taking as his subject 'An experimental investigation of the Parasite of Tick Fever'.

When Leishman's professorship terminated at the end of January 1914, he became War Office expert on tropical diseases on the army medical advisory board, but he was able to continue for a time his own research work in the laboratories at the Royal Army Medical College. In October 1914 he joined the British Expeditionary Force in France as adviser in pathology, and was chairman of the committees on 'trench fever' and 'trench nephritis', new aspects of disease consequent on stationary warfare. In April 1918 he was brought back to duty at the War Office; in the following October he was gazetted major-general; and in June 1919 he became the first director of pathology at the War Office, a post which he retained until, in July 1923, he was appointed medical director-general, Army Medical Services, with the rank of lieutenant-general—promotion which showed that an officer who has devoted his life to the scientific aspects of medicine can obtain the highest position in his branch of the service. Leishman had shown his administrative ability at Netley and also in connexion with the organization of anti-typhoid inoculation; he had proved a very successful teacher and promoter of research, who had won the confidence of the members of his corps. A fellow officer wrote that 'he made potential rivals into friends and friends into brothers'.

Leishman was knighted in 1909, created C.B. in 1915, K.C.B. (military) in 1924, and K.C.M.G. in 1918. He was made honorary physician to King George V in 1912, commander (1915) and grand officer (1925) of the legion of honour, and he received the distinguished service medal of the United States of America. He was elected a fellow of the Royal Society in 1910 and later served on the council and on many committees. In 1914 he was elected a fellow of the Royal College of Physicians of London under the special by-law xl (6), and in 1925 a member of the Athenaeum Club under Rule II. He was an original member of the Medical Research Committee (later Council) from 1913 to 1923 and was re-elected in 1926. He was president of the Society of Tropical Medicine and Hygiene (1911–1912), of the section of comparative medicine of the Royal Society of Medicine (1926), and chairman of the foot-and-mouth disease research committee, Ministry of Agriculture (1924). The universities of Glasgow and McGill conferred on him the honorary degree of LL.D. He delivered the Harben lecture (1910) on anti-typhoid inoculation, and the Linacre lecture at St. John's College, Cambridge, on health in the tropics (1925).

Leishman had many interests outside his profession and was an accomplished landscape artist and musician. He married in 1902 Maud Elizabeth, eldest daughter of Lieut.-Col. Edward Gunter, East Lancashire Regiment, and had one son and three daughters. He died after a short illness 2 June 1926 at Queen Alexandra's Military Hospital, Millbank. Memorial tablets were placed in the chapel of the Hospital and in the pathological laboratory of the Royal Army Medical College, Millbank.

[*Journal of Pathology and Bacteriology*, 1926, vol. xxix, pp. 515–528; *British Medical Journal*, 1926, vol. i, pp. 1013–1016; private information; personal knowledge.]

H. D. Rolleston.

LE SAGE, Sir JOHN MERRY (1837–1926), journalist and managing editor of the *Daily Telegraph*, was born at Clifton 23 April 1837, the only son of John Sage, of that town, by his wife, Elizabeth Godfrey. He adopted the name of Le Sage in middle life. Educated at Bristol, Le Sage became a reporter on the *Torquay Directory* and the *Western Morning News* at Plymouth before obtaining an appointment in London on the *Daily Telegraph*. His connexion with that paper, begun in 1863, remained unbroken until his retirement sixty years later.

Le Sage's principal journalistic feat as a special correspondent consisted of getting through to London, hours ahead of his rivals, an account of the entry of the German army into Paris in January 1871. He remained in Paris throughout the Commune. He attended the coronations at St. Petersburg of Alexander III (1881) and Nicholas II (1894), was in Egypt in 1882 at the time of Sir Garnet Wolseley's expedition against Arabi Pasha, and was received in audience by Pope Leo XIII and by Sultan Abdul Hamid. Le Sage did not, however, achieve marked distinction as a writer on a paper which had on its literary staff such well-known journalists as (Sir) Edwin Arnold, George Augustus Sala, W. Beatty Kingston, W. J. Prowse. George Hooper, Frederick Greenwood,

Edward Blanchard, and, at a later date, H. D. Traill, E. J. Dillon, and W. L. Courtney.

Le Sage's talents were best displayed in an executive capacity. He enjoyed the confidence in turn of Joseph Moses Levy [q.v.], the original proprietor of the *Daily Telegraph*, and that of his son, Edward Levy-Lawson, first Baron Burnham [q.v.]. The latter was in full direction and control of the paper for more than thirty years before he was raised to the peerage in 1903, and Le Sage was his trusted right-hand man. Later, when the Hon. Harry Lawson, afterwards second Baron Burnham, took charge, Le Sage served the son as loyally as he had served both the father and the grandfather. For practically forty years Le Sage was managing editor, and, in his contacts with the staff in the daily conduct of the paper, the autocrat of Peterborough Court. He strongly maintained the traditions by which the *Daily Telegraph* had established its special position, which Edmund Yates once described as 'the organ of the knife-board of the omnibus'. Le Sage regarded the middle-class as the backbone of the country, and had little sympathy with the later developments of democracy. To let well alone was one of his working principles. News interested him more deeply than politics. The minutiae of any political controversy bored him. He liked it presented, as he said, 'in six lines'.

Le Sage made up his mind quickly—a sovereign editorial virtue. A good judge of men, he reposed great faith in what he called his 'journalistic instinct', which worked 'in flashes'. The criticism of outsiders he met with imperturbability. It was a fixed article of his creed that enemies of the *Daily Telegraph* always came, sooner or later, to a bad end.

Unquestionably, Le Sage's special gifts were better suited to the last two decades of the nineteenth century than to the first two of the twentieth. The rapid rise of the new journalism, just before and after the turn of the century, shook him. He responded gamely to the challenge, but with ever-increasing effort. Yet the anxieties and responsibilities of the European War of 1914–1918 served to give him new vigour. He did the day's work with unshaken resolution, and nothing but illness or holidays kept him, even when past his eightieth year, from his usual office routine. For many years he had rooms in Clement's Inn, and punctual to the minute, twice a day, he trod the Fleet Street pavement—an erect, imposing, and well-groomed figure.

Outside Fleet Street Le Sage was hardly known. He never attended meetings: he cultivated few social and no political relationships: he never wrote a letter except under compulsion; and he never made speeches. He was a lieutenant of the City of London, but the only public recognition which he received was the knighthood bestowed upon him in 1918 in recognition of his long services to journalism and more especially of the *Daily Telegraph's* steady support of the national policy during the War.

In his younger days Le Sage travelled widely: in later life he enjoyed the gossip of the Garrick Club. An hour at Lord's on a sunny afternoon, with W. G. Grace at the wicket and scoring freely, was for years his ideal of recreation.

Le Sage retired from the *Daily Telegraph* in June 1923 and died 1 January 1926 at his home at Hurlingham. He married three times: the record of his first marriage is not available; he married secondly, in 1868, Clara Ellen (died 1873), daughter of Charles Henderson Scott, legal reporter, by whom he had one son and one daughter; thirdly, in 1874 Elizabeth Lord (died 1933), daughter of John Burton Martin, of London, by whom he had two sons.

[*Daily Telegraph*, 2 January 1926; personal knowledge.] J. B. Firth.

LESLIE, Sir BRADFORD (1831–1926), civil engineer, was born in London 18 August 1831, the second son of the painter, Charles Robert Leslie [q.v.], by his wife, Harriet Stone. He was named after Samuel T. Bradford, the senior partner of the publishing firm of Bradford & Inskeep, of Philadelphia, to which his father had been bound apprentice in 1808. He was educated at the Mercers' School, London, and at the age of sixteen was apprenticed for five years to the civil engineer, Isambard Kingdom Brunel [q.v.], who waived his fee of one thousand guineas in consideration of C. R. Leslie's painting him a picture or two. In 1851, while still an apprentice, Leslie was employed, as assistant engineer, on the construction of the bridge over the Wye at Chepstow on the Gloucester and Dean Forest Railway, and afterwards until 1853 on the Royal Albert bridge over the Tamar at Saltash. He also supervised for Brunel the erection of the Stony Creek and Salt

Water River railway bridges in Victoria, Australia, and assisted him in the construction of material for the *Great Eastern* and in the launch of that steamship on 31 January 1858.

In the same year Leslie entered the service of the Eastern Bengal Railway Company (to which Brunel was consulting engineer), acting under William Purdon in the capacity of resident engineer in charge of large bridges and viaducts. There he superintended the erection of the bridges in the Ganges delta over the Ichamati river and over the Kumar river at Alumdanga, on caissons founded by the pneumatic process. While employed on these he had to teach the native labourers how to rivet by hand, there being no machine tools, and at times he had himself to work in the cylinders. Leslie returned to England in 1862 and was appointed chief engineer of the Ogmore (or Ogwr) Valley Railway in Glamorganshire. After completing this work he re-entered the service of the Eastern Bengal Railway in 1865 as chief resident engineer for the extension of the line in the northern delta to the neighbourhood of Goalundo, begun in November 1867 and opened for service on 1 January 1871. The undertaking included Leslie's first great achievement in India, the bridge over the Gorai, the largest and most important deltaic branch of the Ganges. The bridge was supported on eight piers having two iron cylinders each, and was remarkable for the ingenious boring gear of his own invention by means of which the caissons were sunk in the shifting bed of the Gorai to a depth of nearly one hundred feet. For his paper describing this work, read before the Institution of Civil Engineers in February 1872 in the course of a short visit to England [*Proceedings* of the Institution of Civil Engineers, vol. xxxiv, 1871–1872], he was awarded a Telford medal and premium.

During his stay in England Leslie was appointed consulting engineer to the Oudh and Rohilkhund Railway Company, and in the same year he returned to India, at the invitation of the secretary of state, in order to inquire into the condition of the bridges over the rivers Beas, Jumna, and Sutlej on the Sind, Punjab, and Delhi Railway. At this time he became concerned in the construction of a bridge of a highly original character, which he had designed, crossing the Hugli between Calcutta and Howrah. The Hugli is a deep and rapid river, subject to big fluctuations of level from tides and floods, with a large and varied ocean and river traffic, through which a bridge would be exposed to damage from shipping breaking adrift in cyclone and storm waves. In 1868 Leslie had designed and modelled parts of a floating bridge, which could be more cheaply and quickly built in the first instance, and more readily repaired in case of accident, than a fixed structure. His design and model were seen and approved by the viceroy, the Earl of Mayo, at the opening of the Gorai bridge. The viceroy tested the stability of the design by standing on the floating model, while the coolies agitated the water in which it was floating. In spite of some adverse official opinion the floating bridge was begun in January 1873 and opened for traffic in October 1874, when the assembled crowds sang ballads and hymns in praise of Leslie for having given them a means of crossing the sacred river. The floating portion of the bridge, which was 1,530 feet long and 60 feet wide, was carried on fourteen pairs of rectangular iron pontoons, and an opening of two hundred feet was provided in the centre for the passage of the larger vessels by making the two central pairs movable, so that they and their superstructure could be dropped downstream and hauled sideways out of the fairway. For his paper describing the structure read before the Institution of Civil Engineers on 5 March 1878 [*Proceedings*, vol. liii, 1878] Leslie was awarded a Watt medal and another Telford premium. In 1899, realizing that the bridge though structurally sound was becoming inadequate for the traffic, he visited India in order to induce the government to take up the question of its replacement. But it was only in 1910 that a bridge committee was appointed. In 1918, by request, he submitted a design for two larger one-way bridges on the same plan, but this was not accepted, and at the time of his death he had almost completed a design for a single cantilever bridge. Thus Leslie's original bridge is still standing (1934).

While the Hugli floating bridge was being constructed, the municipal engineer of Calcutta, William Clarke, was invalided home, and Leslie succeeded him, resigning his position of consulting engineer to the Oudh and Rohilkhund Railway Company. In consequence, the floating bridge was for the most part constructed under his own supervision. He also completed the Calcutta city water supply and drainage schemes initiated by Clarke, besides taking an active part in many other schemes. Leslie held this post until 1876, when he was appointed agent and chief engineer of the East Indian Railway Company.

This new appointment carried with it wide administrative duties. Leslie carried out a thorough inspection of the railway, replaced wooden wagons by iron ones of larger capacity, introduced cast-iron sleepers, and employed native drivers for goods trains, though the advisability of this last measure has been questioned. In order to bring the producers of the Ganges valley into direct touch with Calcutta, it was resolved to carry the railway over the Hugli at Naihati. Although Leslie's design for the necessary bridge, a model of which he presented afterwards to the Institution of Civil Engineers, was not accepted, he supervised the construction of the new bridge as consulting engineer. On 24 January 1888 he read a paper describing it to the Institution of Civil Engineers [*Proceedings*, vol. xcii, 1888], for which he was awarded a George Stephenson medal and a third Telford premium. The structure, known as the Jubilee bridge, was opened in 1887, when Leslie was created K.C.I.E. Almost immediately afterwards he was invalided home on account of malaria. During his long residence in India he distinguished himself not only by his originality, thoroughness, and resource, but by his constant care for the well-being of his assistants and subordinates, and by carrying out personally arduous and dangerous inspection work.

On his way to England in the *Tasmania* Leslie was shipwrecked off Corsica and received a permanent injury to his knee. In London, within three months, he began to practise as a consulting engineer, and in 1895 he was made chairman and engineering adviser to the Southern Punjab Railway Company and presided at the board meetings until October 1925. He never retired from work, but continued to practise and lecture to the end. He died in London, at his home, 171 Maida Vale, 21 March 1926, in his ninety-fifth year.

Leslie married in 1855 Mary Jane Eliza (died 1886), daughter of William Honey, civil engineer, of Plymouth, and had one son and four daughters; three of his daughters predeceased him.

Besides the three papers already mentioned, Leslie contributed to the Institution of Civil Engineers a communication, 'On an improved method of lighting vessels under way at night' [*Proceedings*, vol. lxxxiii, 1886].

Leslie's portrait, painted by his younger brother, George Dunlop Leslie, is in the possession of his granddaughter, Miss Lydia Spence.

[*The Times*, 22 and 23 March 1926; *The Engineer*, 26 March 1926; *Proceedings* of the Institution of Civil Engineers, vol. ccxxiv, 1926–1927; private information.]

E. I. Carlyle.

LEVER, WILLIAM HESKETH, first Viscount Leverhulme (1851–1925), soap manufacturer, was born in Wood Street, Bolton, Lancashire, 19 September 1851, the elder son of James Lever, wholesale and retail grocer, of Bolton, by his wife, Eliza, daughter of William Hesketh, a cotton-mill manager, of Manchester. After being for a time at a private school in Bolton, he became, at the age of thirteen, a pupil at the Church Institute. His father, although a nonconformist, was attracted by the teaching and influence of the headmaster of the Institute, William Tate Mason. It was his mother's wish that William Lever should study medicine, but it was decided that he should enter the family business, and in 1867, when he was sixteen, he began his commercial training.

The grocery firm, of which James Lever had, in 1864, become the sole proprietor, prospered and increased. When William Lever was admitted to a share in the undertaking in 1872 his partnership was worth £800 a year. At the same time he became engaged to Elizabeth Ellen, daughter of Crompton Hulme, linen-draper, a neighbour in Wood Street. The marriage took place in 1874, and the newly wedded couple went to live in Park Street, Bolton. The junior partner soon began to show that ardour for development which marked his career. A branch of the grocery business was opened at Wigan by the purchase of another firm, reforms in the organization were made, larger premises were built, and new commitments undertaken. The elder Lever, with the conservatism of age, was inclined to view with anxiety some of this progress, but its success disarmed opposition.

It was in 1884 that Lever decided to begin trading on his own account, and to specialize in soap. There was no particular reason, as he used to admit, for choosing this commodity, and he might just as well have chosen anything else. His brother, James Darcy Lever, agreed to join him, but his father hesitated to support the scheme, although he eventually assisted the new firm with some additional capital. Lever himself withdrew some of his money from the grocery company, and got together about £4,000 for the establishment of his new business. One of his earliest steps was to find for his new soap a name which would look and sound well in advertisements. The name 'Sunlight' was chosen and registered. The new soap was made largely from vegetable oils, instead of almost entirely from tallow, and in the first instance was supplied by other manufacturers for sale by Lever Brothers. But in 1885 the new firm purchased the soapworks of Winser & Co. at Warrington, and in the following January began to make its own soap.

The demand for Sunlight soap grew rapidly. The output, which in the first year had been 20 tons a week, had increased in the second year to 450 tons a week, and the need for larger works became pressing. In 1887 the idea of founding a centre, where his works should be, and where his work-people should live, took shape in Lever's mind. He bought 52 acres of land—subsequently extended to 500 acres—conveniently situated on the Mersey, near Bebington, Cheshire, and on 3 March 1888 the first sod of the new town of Port Sunlight was cut by Mrs. Lever. Manufacture began in the new surroundings in January 1889.

About this time Lever travelled much, spreading his business overseas, opening branches or agencies in the colonies, the United States, and various European countries. In 1892 he contributed some articles on his tour round the world to a Birkenhead newspaper, and these were afterwards republished in book form under the title of *Following the Flag* (1893). Some of his foreign ventures made slow and disappointing progress at the start, but generally speaking, the profitable development of his affairs was continuous.

In 1890 Lever Brothers was made a limited company, and in 1894 this company was made public with a capital of £1,500,000, divided equally into preference and ordinary shares. The first issue of a portion of the preference capital was heavily over-subscribed. No ordinary shares were offered to the public, and Lever, who became chairman of the company, gradually acquired all these. It was his view that as the chief risk of the new enterprises would fall on the ordinary shares, he himself should carry that risk.

After the formation of the public company, a definite policy of amalgamation with other soap-making firms was followed. The first business acquired was that of Benjamin Brooke & Co. in 1899, and the production of the soap was transferred to Port Sunlight. Other transactions, either by purchase or by interchange of shares, resulted in Lever exercising, during the opening years of the twentieth century, a wide control over the soap-making trade, and occupying the most prominent position in that industry.

In 1906 the increase in the cost of raw material, and the necessity for advancing prices, suggested to Lever further efforts in the direction of amalgamation. The proposed combine attracted the hostile attention of the *Daily Mail* and other newspapers under the management of Lord Northcliffe [q.v.]. For some months during the autumn of 1906 these newspapers indulged in violent criticism of Lever, against whom all kinds of startling accusations were launched, including that of fraudulent trading and bad treatment of his workpeople. The Sunlight soap business was seriously affected by these attacks, and certain firms which had agreed provisionally to a pooling of interests were alarmed into abandoning the arrangement. Counsel's opinion was taken, and an action for libel was brought by Lever Brothers against the newspapers concerned. The case came before the assize court at Liverpool on 15 July 1907. Lever was the first witness called for the plaintiffs, and in the course of examination and cross-examination had no difficulty in establishing that the charges brought against his company and himself were wholly unfounded, and had occasioned great harm to his trade. After this evidence it became clear that the only question left was the extent of the damages to which Lever Brothers were entitled, and rather than leave this to the jury the defendants offered a settlement. Lever consented to accept £50,000—the highest award ever made in a libel case—and he obtained a further £91,000 from certain Scottish newspapers owned by the defendants. He used a part of this sum for the purchase of the old Blue Coat school in Liverpool, and gave the balance to Liverpool University as an endowment for the school of tropical medicine and other educational objects.

Holding the position that he did, Lever naturally received several invitations to enter political life. He contested Birkenhead as a liberal three times without success, in 1892, 1894, and 1895. In 1900 he failed again in the Wirrall division of

Cheshire, but in 1906, when there was a general reaction in favour of liberal views, he was returned for that constituency. He found the additional work too heavy, and retired in December 1909. He came forward, however, once more in the following month for the Ormskirk division of Lancashire, but did not win the seat. Although unsuited by temperament for party politics, he seems to have enjoyed electioneering, and, by practice on many platforms, he became a competent speaker. He was liked by his fellow members of parliament, and a striking incident in his short career in the House was the warm welcome which he received when he returned after winning his libel action.

When the European War broke out in 1914, Lever supported the recruiting activities of the government in his own district, and served himself for a time in the ranks of the Birkenhead battalion of the Cheshire regiment. Fulfilling duties more suitable for a man of his age (sixty-three), he was a member of several important committees, and acted as honorary treasurer of the Star and Garter Home for disabled soldiers at Richmond. In 1918 he was appointed honorary commandant of his battalion of the Cheshire regiment.

In pursuance of his aim to provide the raw materials for his own trade, Lever became interested in the supply of palm-oil and palm-kernel oil from West Africa. He began at once to experiment with modern machinery which should supersede the primitive methods used by the natives for obtaining these oils. In 1910 he established crushing mills in Nigeria, and, as large areas of forest were essential to secure continuity of supply, he obtained in the following year a concession of land and works in the Belgian Congo. After the War he extended his African policy, and was instrumental in the purchase of the shares of the Niger Company. The high price paid for these shares was unfortunate, for the transaction was followed by a disastrous fall in values, due to trade depression.

In his care for Port Sunlight, the model township of his own foundation, Lever was assiduous. However much his politics leaned to *laisser-faire* liberalism, and however much he disliked state interference, his government in practice was a benevolent autocracy. He introduced profit-sharing and benefit schemes, he planned houses and gardens, and inaugurated all kinds of social and sporting amenities for the benefit of those employed by his company. Later in his career he attempted something of the same kind in another part of the kingdom. In 1917 he bought from Colonel Duncan Matheson the island of Lewis, and followed this up by the purchase in 1919 of the islands of North and South Harris. He hoped to be able, by a substantial outlay of capital, to develop the fishing industry and in this way to improve the circumstances of the crofter population. But difficulties arose, chiefly in connexion with the tenure and occupation of the land, and in 1923 he decided to abandon the scheme. When he left Lewis he offered as a gift to the town of Stornoway a considerable acreage of the land which he had acquired.

Lever was interested in architecture and in art generally. He was an enthusiastic collector, with resources that did not oblige him to be discriminating, of pictures, pottery, and old furniture. After his death there was a sale lasting fifteen days of the contents of the houses which he had filled with his purchases. His public munificence was constant. An important instance of this was his gift to the nation of Stafford House, St. James's, a house built by James Wyatt for the Duke of York, second son of George III, and afterwards the London residence of the Dukes of Sutherland. This building, under the name of Lancaster House, was opened to the public in 1914 as the London Museum, and contains exhibits relating to the history of the City. To Liverpool University he was a generous benefactor, and he also gave largely to his native town of Bolton, of which he was mayor in 1918–1919. On Port Sunlight he lavished many gifts, including an art gallery in memory of his wife.

The extent of Lever's business undertakings may be judged from the fact that in 1924 the capital of Lever Brothers amounted to nearly £57,000,000, and it had grown to be the largest commercial undertaking of its kind in the world. The controller of these vast interests was in some ways an exceptional figure among industrial leaders of the time. He had courage, foresight, and an untiring capacity for working himself, as well as the gift of obtaining loyal and effective service from others. But the interest of Lever's character and career lies as much in his few failures as in his many successes. His restless imagination seemed quite unable to contemplate inefficiency in any department of life without a burning desire to correct it regardless of cost or trouble to himself. To say that there was a commercial motive behind his enterprises is a comment that might well have gratified him, for, although responsive to the claims of charity, he maintained, by precept as well as by example, that the best service to humanity was to give men the opportunity of improving their conditions by their own efforts.

Lever was created a baronet in 1911 and in 1917 was raised to the peerage as Baron Leverhulme. His title was a combination of his own and his wife's names. In 1922 he was advanced to a viscounty, and added to his title 'of the Western Isles'. His wife was a woman of character and of much kindness, and her support was of great value to her husband. She died in July 1913. In that year she went with him on an adventurous journey through central Africa, and shortly before her death she was elected a fellow of the Royal Geographical Society. There was one child of the marriage, a son, William Hulme Lever (born 1888), who succeeded his father as second viscount. Lord Leverhulme died at his house in Hampstead 7 May 1925.

[*The Times*, 8 May 1925; *Viscount Leverhulme, by his son*, 1927. Portrait, *Royal Academy Pictures*, 1916.] A. Cochrane.

LEVERHULME, first Viscount (1851–1925), soap manufacturer. [See Lever, William Hesketh.]

LEWIS, AGNES (1843–1926), discoverer of the *Sinai Palimpsest*, the elder twin daughter of John Smith, solicitor, of Irvine, Ayrshire, was born at Irvine in 1843, and educated at Irvine Academy and at private schools in Birkenhead and London. In 1868 she travelled, with her sister Margaret Dunlop Smith, in Egypt and Palestine, and in 1870 published *Eastern Pilgrims*, an account of their experiences. In 1883 her sister married the Spanish translator, James Young Gibson [q.v.]; he died in 1886. In 1887 Agnes Smith married the antiquary, Samuel Savage Lewis [q.v.], librarian of Corpus Christi College, Cambridge. Her husband died suddenly in 1891. The twin sisters were very much alike, and after the deaths of their husbands always lived and travelled together, visiting Cyprus, Greece, and other Oriental lands. They had considerable proficiency in modern Greek.

In 1892 Mrs. Lewis and her sister were persuaded by Dr. James Rendel Harris to visit the convent of St. Catherine on Mount Sinai, which Harris had visited in 1889 and where he had discovered a Syriac manuscript of the hitherto lost early Christian *Apology of Aristides*. It was in this convent that Tischendorf had discovered the famous Greek *Codex Sinaiticus*, but the room or closet which contained Syriac manuscripts had hitherto remained unknown to scholars. When Agnes Lewis and Margaret Gibson went to Sinai, their knowledge of conversational Greek was a passport to the good graces of the *hegumenos* (or prior), Galakteon, and he brought out the Syriac manuscripts for the inspection of the Western ladies. One manuscript specially struck them: it was written in A.D. 778, but underneath the eighth-century script older effaced writing was visible here and there, and from the headlines it was clearly a text of the Gospels. Thinking that so ancient a manuscript might be interesting, Agnes Lewis photographed several pages. When the sisters returned to Cambridge (Professor) F. C. Burkitt, of Trinity College, offered to try to read the photographs, and with the help of Professor Robert Lubbock Bensley [q.v.] a few pages were deciphered, enough to show that the manuscript was akin to those fragments in the British Museum which were discovered by and called after William Cureton [q.v.]. In 1893 Agnes Lewis and her sister, accompanied by Bensley, Rendel Harris, and Burkitt, with Mrs. Bensley and Mrs. Burkitt, visited Sinai and made a transcript of the Gospel from the manuscript, together with a better set of photographs, the result being published at Cambridge in 1894.

Agnes Lewis and her sister made two further visits to Sinai in the following years, copying manuscripts and taking photographs; good copies of those of the *Sinai Palimpsest* (as the manuscript is called) being presented by them to the University Library, Cambridge, and to Westminster College, Cambridge. She and her sister published a considerable number of Syriac and Christian Arabic texts in the following years, some of value; but nothing equalled the importance of their first discovery. Agnes Lewis received the gold medal of the Royal Asiatic Society in 1915, and obtained honorary doctor's degrees from the university of Halle, St. Andrews, Heidelberg, and Dublin. She and her sister were generous benefactors to Westminster College, where their portraits hang in the Hall.

Agnes Lewis died at her house, Castle Brae, Cambridge, 29 March 1926, having been for some years entirely incapacitated by paralysis. Her sister predeceased her 11 January 1920.

[Private information; personal knowledge.]
F. C. BURKITT.

LINCOLNSHIRE, MARQUESS OF (1843–1928), politician. [See WYNN-CARRINGTON, CHARLES ROBERT.]

LINDSAY, DAVID (1856–1922), explorer, was born at Goolwa, South Australia, 20 June 1856, the younger son of John Scott Lindsay, master mariner, of Dundee, Scotland, and of Goolwa, by his wife, Catherine Reid. His father had come to Australia two years before Lindsay's birth in command of a schooner destined for the coasting trade. Lindsay was educated privately at Port Elliott, near Goolwa, and in 1873 entered the South Australian survey department, where he remained until 1882. He held the post of junior surveyor in the Northern Territory from 1878 to 1882. In 1883 he led an expedition across the north of Arnhem Land from Palmerston (Port Darwin) to Blue Mud Bay, and found land suitable for settlement. In 1885–1886 he continued his explorations in Central Australia between the Georgina river in Western Queensland and the Hay and Finke rivers to the east of the Macdonnell ranges and reported deposits of rubies in the Macdonnell ranges. Two years later he rode across Australia from north to south, and his report threw some light on unknown geographical features of the interior.

When in 1891 Sir Thomas Elder, of Adelaide, provided funds for a scientific exploration of the interior of Western Australia, Lindsay was chosen to command the expedition. The projected route was from Peake, on the railway, to the west of Lake Eyre, over the Everard range and the Great Victoria Desert to Lake Barlee, and thence to the Murchison river and the West coast, with a return journey across the Western desert to the Kimberley district of the North-West and thence to Tennants Creek (Northern Territory) on the overland telegraph line. The expedition was organized by the Royal Geographical Society of Australasia and its patron spared no expense. The results, however, largely because of a season of severe drought, fell far short of the ambitious programme. With the help of camels the expedition, starting in May 1891, crossed the north of the Great Victoria Desert via the Everard and Blyth ranges, traversing 550 miles in 35 days to Lake Lefroy; thence it proceeded north-west to Geraldton. In January 1893 Lindsay left the expedition, handing over the command to L. A. Wells, who for two months continued explorations to Lake Wells and the Virginia range. The criticism of Lindsay's leadership, made by some of his staff, proved on investigation by the Royal Geographical Society of Australasia to have no foundation and he was completely exonerated. His journey revealed the existence of an auriferous area, and led to the opening up of the West Australian goldfield.

For the next few years Lindsay continued his explorations in Western Australia with the object of investigating the mineral resources, and his discoveries led to further prospecting and development. In 1895 he again explored in Arnhem Land. In 1913 he was appointed to serve on the Commonwealth royal commission, the object of which was to advise on the development of ports and railways in the Northern Territory, and in 1920 he reported good pastoral and agricultural land in Arnhem Land. It was in connexion with this work that he was engaged at Port Darwin when he died there 18 December 1922.

Lindsay married in 1881 Annie Theresa Stuart, daughter of Arthur Lindsay, civil servant, of Adelaide; four sons and one daughter were born of the marriage.

[*The Times*, 19 December 1922; *Journal of the Elder Scientific Exploring Expedition, 1891–2*, 1893; *Geographical Journal*, January 1893; *South Australian Register*, 11 July 1878; private information.] R. N. RUDMOSE BROWN.

LIVEING, GEORGE DOWNING (1827–1924), chemist, the eldest son of Edward Liveing, surgeon, of Nayland, Suffolk, by his wife Catherine, the only daughter of George Downing, of Lincoln's Inn, barrister-at-law, was born at Nayland 21 December 1827. He was admitted to St. John's College, Cambridge, in 1847, and was eleventh wrangler in the mathematical tripos of 1850. He then read for the newly established natural sciences tripos, and was placed at the head of six successful candidates in the first year of that tripos, 1851, with distinction in chemistry and mineralogy. Next he studied for a while with Karl Rammelsberg at Berlin, but soon returned to Cambridge. In 1852 he started the first course of practical chemistry for medical students in a primitive laboratory fitted up in a cottage in Corn Exchange Street.

In 1853 Liveing was elected a fellow of St. John's College, and the college founded for him a lecturership in chemistry, and built a laboratory for his use. That he was an active and courageous junior fellow is clear from a pamphlet which he printed in 1857, attacking the existing system of government of the college and advocating measures of reform which almost exactly foreshadow those put into force many years later. In 1860 Liveing became professor of chemistry at the Staff College and at the Royal Military College, Sandhurst, though he continued to teach in Cambridge also. In the same year he married Catherine, second daughter of the Rev. Rowland Ingram, rector of Little Ellingham, Norfolk. He thereby vacated his fellowship at St. John's, though he retained his lecturership.

On the death in 1861 of the Rev. James Cumming [q.v.], professor of chemistry at Cambridge, Liveing was elected to succeed him. The salary was about £100 a year, and the material provision made by the university for the subject was meagre, consisting of one lecture room, which the professor of chemistry had to share with the professor of botany and the Jacksonian professor of experimental philosophy, and two small empty rooms which might be used for other purposes. But in 1863, after much controversy, the university began building laboratories, thus initiating the great development in experimental science which has transformed modern Cambridge. The first buildings were raised on land which, acquired in 1762, had been used as a botanic garden; and in the course of the years 1864 and 1865 accommodation was provided successively for zoology, anatomy, chemistry, mineralogy, and botany. In 1865 Liveing began to announce regular experimental courses in chemistry and, until physics were otherwise provided for, in heat. In 1875 (Sir) James Dewar [q.v.], was elected Jacksonian professor of experimental philosophy and directed the work of that chair to chemistry. He was thus brought into close association with Liveing. Collaboration cannot have been easy. As a colleague wrote in 1925: 'Liveing and Dewar were men of widely different temperaments and widely different ideals; and they were both quick-tempered. Nevertheless, a lifelong friendship was formed between them.' In 1878 they began a long series of spectroscopic investigations which continued till 1900. Their joint papers were republished as a single volume by the Cambridge University Press in 1915. This is the chief record of Liveing's scientific labours.

When Liveing and Dewar began their spectroscopic researches the subject was comparatively new. In ignorance of a previous experiment of J. B. L. Foucault, von Bunsen and G. R. Kirchoff in 1859, in the course of the work which first put spectrum analysis on a sound footing, passed the continuous light from incandescent lime through an alcohol flame in which common salt was vaporized, and found that a dark line appeared in the spectrum coinciding with the sodium line and with the corresponding dark line, Frauenhofer's D, in the solar spectrum. The dynamical explanation of this phenomenon was given by Sir George Gabriel Stokes [q.v.], who pointed out that a vibrating system absorbs energy of the same period of oscillation that it can itself emit. By these several investigations, the examination of the chemical composition of the sun and stars was made possible, for dark lines in the spectra of light from their interiors which passes through their cooler envelopes coincide with the bright lines of terrestrial elements. Most of the earlier work of Liveing and Dewar was concerned with this important point, eight papers 'On the Reversal of the Lines of Metallic Vapours' appearing in the *Proceedings* of the Royal Society between the years 1878 and 1881. After publishing in 1882 some work on the spectrum of carbon, they turned to ultra-violet spectra, on which a paper appeared in the *Philosophical Transactions* of the Royal Society in 1883. Two papers on sun spots followed, while Dewar's tastes may be traced in 'Spectroscopic Studies of Gaseous Explosions', in 'The Influence of Pressure on the Spectra of Flames', and in a series of papers on the spectra of the constituents of liquefied gases at very low temperatures. Finally, papers appeared between 1899 and 1904 on the absorption spectra of solutions, and on the spectra at the anode and cathode when an electric discharge is passed through gases. If these seventy-eight joint papers cannot be said to disclose any epoch-making discovery, they certainly chronicle careful, exact, and useful contributions to knowledge.

The only book published by Liveing was a thin volume on *Chemical Equilibrium the result of the Dissipation of Energy*, which appeared in 1885. This early recognition of the importance of thermodynamics to chemistry clearly showed Liveing's insight into the fundamental principles of his science. It is worthy of note that he returned to this subject in later years, his last paper, read to the Cambridge Philosophical Society on 7 May 1923 (when he was ninety-six), being entitled 'The Recuperation of Energy in the Universe'.

In the 'eighties and early 'nineties Liveing was in the middle period of his career. Year by year he delivered lectures both to elementary and advanced students. To the former, he taught general chemistry, and to the latter, principles of chemistry and spectroscopy. The rest of the teaching was shared among an increasing staff, both in the university laboratory and in several college laboratories. Liveing's elementary lectures were attended by men conspicuous more for light-heartedness than love of learning. The lectures were illustrated with experiments, and his impatience with the laboratory attendants when the experiments went wrong was eagerly watched for by his youthful class. His advanced students found him somewhat difficult of approach; but when the approach was made he took great trouble and gave them individual attention: many distinguished chemists owe much to his teaching. By 1885 the number of students and staff had made the original university chemical laboratory, on the east side of the old botanic garden site, quite inadequate, and in 1888 the present laboratory was begun. Liveing took endless trouble over the plans, and the success of the building was largely due to his examination of other laboratories and careful studies of the whole problem. In 1888 also he arranged a course of lectures on agricultural chemistry, thus inaugurating activities which ultimately developed into the successful Cambridge school of agriculture. For many years that school owed much to Liveing's help and support.

In 1889 Liveing was elected a professorial fellow of St. John's College, and thus again brought into close association with his college. He was elected a fellow of the Royal Society in 1879, served on the council in 1891–1892 and again in 1903–1904, and was awarded the Davy medal in 1901. For many years he acted as the Cambridge correspondent of the chancellor of the university. He also took part in local affairs, and did good work as a county and borough magistrate.

In the year 1908, at the age of eighty-one, Liveing resigned the professorship of chemistry, though he remained to the end of his life in touch with the laboratory and with research. Throughout his tenure of the chair he took full financial responsibilities for the maintenance of the laboratory, which in its early years must have caused a heavy drain on his private income. On retiring he was at once re-elected a fellow of St. John's, and in 1911 became president, an office corresponding to that of vice-master. In this final phase of his career he found, in some ways, his truest expression. He still lived a busy life between his house and garden at The Pightle (now Pytell), Newnham, the laboratory, and St. John's College. His character seemed to mellow with age, his asperities softened, and the patriarch of ninety seemed easier of access than the professor of fifty or sixty. His memories of days long past were of historic interest, both to chemists and to other members of the university. In 1923 he gave up his house at Newnham, and, after a short sojourn at the University Arms hotel, moved to Maid's Causeway. It seemed almost certain that he would complete his hundredth year, but, one October day, while walking to the laboratory, he was knocked down by a bicyclist, and, some two months later, 26 December 1924, he died of his injuries. His wife died in 1888. They had no children.

There is a portrait of Liveing by Sir George Reid at St. John's College.

[*The Times*, 27 December 1924; *Nature*, 24 January 1925; *Proceedings* of the Royal Society, vol. cix, A, 1925; *Year Books* of the Royal Society, 1880–1925; personal knowledge.]

W. C. D. Dampier.

LLOYD, MARIE (pseudonym), music-hall comedian. [See Wood, Matilda Alice Victoria.]

LOCH, Sir CHARLES STEWART (1849–1923), social worker, was born 4 September 1849 at Baghalpur, Bengal, the fifth son of George Loch, judge of the High Court, Calcutta, by his first wife, Louisa Gordon. He was educated at Trinity College, Glenalmond, and proceeded to Balliol College, Oxford, in 1869. Ill-health, which had interrupted his work at school, continued to handicap him at the university. He obtained a third class in classical moderations in 1870 and a second class in the final school of modern history in 1873. His tutors were Professor Edwin Palmer and Thomas Hill Green. Loch was profoundly influenced by Green's character and philosophy, and the two men remained intimate for life. Loch's chief friends at Balliol were Andrew Bradley, Bernard Bosanquet, and A. L. Smith. In 1874, during a period of residence at Oxford, while employed in London, he formed one of the gang of university men who constructed the 'Ruskin road' from Ferry Hinksey to Botley.

It had been Loch's original intention to enter the Indian civil service, but considerations of health stood in the way. Also, while at Balliol, he had been attracted to ideals of social service, both through Green's teaching and through the influence of Arnold Toynbee [q.v.]. Loch accordingly resolved to make his career in London, and in 1873 became clerk to the Royal College of Surgeons. He held the position for two years.

While engaged at the College of Surgeons, Loch maintained his interest in social questions, and became honorary secretary of the Islington branch of the Charity Organisation Society. In 1875 he was appointed secretary to the council of the Charity Organisation Society. This institution was founded in 1869. Small and unimportant at first, it steadily gained support. Its principal aims were to assist the needy to help themselves, to improve the conditions of the poor, and to promote the ideal of co-operative charity. Its administrative object was the co-ordination of charitable effort throughout London, and the prevention of 'overlapping' among the authorities and societies. Loch was a very successful administrator. Working with a small staff and extreme economy, he maintained an office which conducted a large amount of business with great efficiency. He was an enthusiastic idealist, whose idealism was accompanied by strong common sense. The charitable system of the Society was based on the principle of dealing with the individual. Help was given only after most careful inquiry concerning every single application for assistance. A file was kept for each 'case', and maintained as a permanent record. Branches of the Charity Organisation Society came into existence in every London borough; and new or already established societies were affiliated to it throughout the rest of the country. Contact was maintained with similar bodies overseas, especially in the United States, and with the French group of P. G. F. Le Play and Edmond Demolins.

Although the charitable work of the Society was carried on upon scientific principles, it was anything but impersonal. Loch's method was to deal with all applications for relief through voluntary workers. Very soon he gathered together a large corps of volunteers, chiefly men and women of education, many of them of the leisured class, who devoted a large part of their time to investigation, and to visiting work for the Society. A man of great personal charm and lofty enthusiasm, Loch aroused like enthusiasm in all his associates, so that the work of the Society, both inside the office among the staff and outside among the volunteers, proceeded with extraordinary cheerfulness and zeal.

The influence of the Charity Organisation Society made itself felt in legislation. Loch was very active in writing pamphlets and letters to the press, in speaking in public, and in approaching central and local authorities. He also obtained the co-operation of influential people on the committee of the Society. The outcome of these efforts can be traced in a number of Acts of parliament concerned with social matters, such as the Mental Deficiency Act of 1913 and the Maternity and Child Welfare Act of 1918. Another practical result was the institution of almoners in hospitals whose function was to ensure that patients should contribute according to their ability. This system, which Loch regarded as a revival of a wholesome medieval practice, has been almost universally adopted.

In 1896 Loch spent three months in the United States, visiting the social groups called 'Associated Charities'—bodies similar to the London Charity Organisation Society. The contact thus made with American charitable work was maintained throughout Loch's life. He was an active member of certain royal commissions: on the aged poor (1893–1895), the care and control of the feeble-minded (1904–1908), and the poor laws (1906–1909). Loch signed the majority report on the poor laws which, in fact, was very largely his own work. The recommendations of the majority report, although at first neglected, were subsequently put into effect, partially at any rate, in the Local Government Act of 1929 and the Poor Law Act of 1930.

Although a liberal in politics, Loch had little sympathy with the social legislation of the liberal government of 1906–1914, which he criticized as placing responsibility upon the bureaucracy and the public treasury rather than upon the individual or the family. His position as a thinker and teacher, as well as a worker in social affairs, was widely recognized. He held the position of Tooke professor of economic science and statistics at King's College, London, from 1904 to 1908. In 1905 the university of Oxford conferred upon him the honorary degree of D.C.L.

In October 1914, Loch retired, on account of illness, from the secretaryship of the Charity Organisation Society after thirty-nine years' service, refusing the pension which the Society voted to him. He was knighted in 1915. He died at Little Bookham, Surrey, 23 January 1923.

Loch was a man of powerful intellect and dominating personality, combined with great sweetness of disposition and complete tolerance of other people's point of view. At Oxford he had studied art under Ruskin; and throughout life he had a strong interest and catholic taste in schools of painting. He was essentially a philosophic radical of the school of John Stuart Mill, and he represented, on its most intellectual and practical plane, the great philanthropic effort of the Victorian age. He lived successively at Chelsea, Chiswick, Oxshott, and Little Bookham. He had a large circle of friends, including, besides friends from Balliol days, Frederick York Powell and Octavia Hill.

Loch's chief published works are: *How to help Cases of Distress* (1883) and *Charity and the Social Life* (1910), which is based on his long article on 'Charity and Charities' in the *Encyclopædia Britannica* (tenth edition, 1902). Some of his articles and addresses have been collected in a volume entitled *A Great Ideal and its Champion*, edited by Sir Arthur Clay (1923). He also published a volume of poems, *Things Within* (1922).

Loch married in 1876 Sophia Emma (died 1934), daughter of Edward Peters, of the Indian civil service, and had one son and one daughter.

A portrait of Loch by J. S. Sargent hangs in the offices of the Charity Organisation Society, Denison House, Vauxhall Bridge Road, London.

[Private information.] R. B. Mowat.

LOCKE, WILLIAM JOHN (1863–1930), novelist, was born at Demerara, British Guiana, 20 March 1863, the elder son of John Locke, banker, of Barbados, by his wife, Sarah Elizabeth. His parents were English. In 1864 his family went to Trinidad, where he was educated at the Queen's Royal College, and won an exhibition to St. John's College, Cambridge. He matriculated at Cambridge in 1881, and graduated with honours in the mathematical tripos of 1884. After leaving Cambridge he became a schoolmaster. His reticence in after years makes it difficult to trace his career as a teacher, but he is known to have been a master at the Oxford Military College at Temple Cowley in 1889 and 1890 and at Clifton College, Bristol, in 1890, and from 1891 to 1897 he was modern languages master at Trinity College, Glenalmond. He disliked teaching; and in 1890 he had a serious illness, which left him tuberculous for the rest of his life. From 1897 to 1907 he was secretary of the Royal Institute of British Architects, and lived in London. He resigned this position when his writings began to afford him a substantial income.

The earliest of Locke's numerous novels, *At the Gate of Samaria*, was published in 1895; but it was his ninth novel, *The Morals of Marcus Ordeyne* (1905), which first won him wide recognition. *The Beloved Vagabond* (1906), *Septimus* (1909), and *Simon the Jester* (1910) consolidated his reputation. His first venture in playwriting was a dramatization of *The Morals of Marcus Ordeyne* (1906); five other plays, some of which are based on his novels, followed in rapid succession between 1907 and 1912. They were all staged in London. In 1912 he published *The Joyous Adventures of Aristide Pujol*, perhaps the last of his more notable books. During the ensuing eighteen years, novels and short stories flowed rapidly from his pen. Scarcely a year passed without a novel, and sometimes he published two books in a year; but to the last he held the interest of his public.

From 1914 to 1918 Locke, at his own expense, converted his house at Hemel Hempstead into a hospital for soldiers from the ranks. He was also engaged untiringly in helping Belgian refugees; for this service he was made chevalier of the Belgian order of the crown. His health, always fragile, suffered from his overwork during these years, and in 1921 it became necessary for him to settle at Cannes. He regarded the remaining years of his life as years of exile in which he eagerly gathered round him a social circle of English and American visitors to the French Riviera. He died of cancer in Paris 15 May 1930. One novel from his pen was published posthumously.

Locke can hardly be said to have left

any notable literary achievements, but the general quality of his novels and short stories is worthy of respect. Such books as *The Morals of Marcus Ordeyne*, *The Beloved Vagabond*, *The Glory of Clementina Wing*, and *The Joyous Adventures of Aristide Pujol* have a clear, sparkling gaiety and gentle charm which made an instant appeal. Moreover, his scenes and characters were looked upon as idealized presentments of the England of the time, and, if unappreciated by foreigners, they found a romantically minded and very sympathetic public in England and America both before and during the European War. Many of his books, however, especially the later ones, suffer from the extreme facility of his pen and are unsatisfying and artistically incomplete.

Locke was an attractive conversationalist, sympathetic, modest, and unassuming; yet his easy gaiety masked much patient suffering. In early life as a teacher he had had a hard struggle, and when wealth came to him, his sympathy with others less fortunate made him generous and self-effacing. His interest in architecture was lifelong, and he was a corresponding member of various British, Dutch, Spanish, Portuguese, and American architectural societies.

Locke married in 1911 Aimée Maxwell, daughter of Theodore Heath. The marriage was childless.

[*The Times*, 17, 19, 20, 21 May 1930; *The Glenalmond Register*, 1929; private information.] E. O'Brien.

LOCKWOOD, AMELIUS MARK RICHARD, first Baron Lambourne (1847–1928), politician, was born in London 17 August 1847, the eldest son of Lieutenant-General William Mark Wood, who had changed his name from Lockwood in 1838 on inheriting the property of his maternal uncle, Sir Mark Wood, of Gatton, Surrey, by his wife, Amelia Jane, daughter of Sir Robert Williams, ninth baronet, of Penrhyn, co. Carnarvon. Their son reverted to the original name of Lockwood in 1876. He was educated at Eton, first at Mr. Sam Evans's and then at Warre's. Entering the Coldstream Guards in 1866, he served as adjutant and as aide-de-camp to John Poyntz, fifth Earl Spencer [q.v.], lord-lieutenant of Ireland, retiring with the rank of lieutenant-colonel in 1883. In 1892 Lockwood entered parliament in the conservative interest as member for Epping, which constituency he represented until 1917, when he was raised to the peerage as Baron Lambourne, of Lambourne, co. Essex. He was for many years chairman of the kitchen committee, and was very popular with all parties in the House of Commons, where he was known as 'Uncle Mark'. Afterwards he was equally popular in the House of Lords.

Although Lockwood took no very prominent part in politics and never held office, he came to be regarded as the typical country squire member of parliament, and exercised a considerable independent influence in the House of Commons. He never cared for racing, but was a keen sportsman and lover of horses and dogs, being for many years an active member of the Royal Society for the Prevention of Cruelty to Animals, of which he was vice-president.

Lockwood served on the royal commission on vivisection (1906–1908), a practice which he strongly disliked, although his views were not extreme. He was instrumental in securing the abolition of pigeon-shooting in England, and introduced, but failed to carry, a bill to stop the export of worn-out horses. He was a great horticulturalist and was for many years president of the Royal Horticultural Society, and a successful exhibitor at many shows. He was specially known for his carnations and his collection of flowering shrubs at his house, Bishop's Hall, near Romford. A well-known connoisseur of china, especially majolica, and of books, his library contained a valuable collection of county histories and topographical works. He was a prominent freemason both in grand lodge and in Essex, of which he was provincial grand master from 1902 until his death. He was interested in the prevention of corruption, and succeeded Sir Edward Fry as president of the Bribery and Secret Commissions Prevention League in 1918. He was a director of the London and North-Western Railway Company and a member of the council of the Railway Association.

Well known and popular as he was in London, Lord Lambourne was still more so in his native county, of which he became lord-lieutenant in 1919. At Bishop's Hall he was the most hospitable of hosts and entertained King Edward there in 1904. Besides holding the lord-lieutenancy of Essex, he was associated with almost all the activities of the county, being president of the Territorial Association, honorary colonel of the 4th Essex Regiment, president of the Essex Hunt Club, and of the Essex Automobile Club, and a J.P. In 1928 Lord Lambourne refused to support the appeal for King George's Hospital at Becontree on the ground that this was a new town created by the London County Council without consulting Essex, but he withdrew his opposition immediately at the wish of the king.

Lord Lambourne died at Bishop's Hall, Romford, 26 December 1928 and was buried at Lambourne. He was sworn a privy councillor in 1905. He was created C.V.O. in 1905 and promoted G.C.V.O. in 1927. He married in 1876 Isabella (died 1923), daughter of Sir John Ralph Milbanke-Huskisson, eighth baronet. They had no children and the peerage became extinct on his death.

A cartoon of Lord Lambourne by 'Spy' appeared in *Vanity Fair* 6 September 1894.

[*The Times* and *Daily Telegraph*, 28 December 1928; *Essex County Standard*, 28 December 1928; *Report* of the royal commission on vivisection, 1908; Army Lists; Hansard, *Parliamentary Debates*; private information.]

ONSLOW.

LOGUE, MICHAEL (1840–1924), cardinal, was born at Carrigart, co. Donegal, 1 October 1840, the second in the family of six children of Michael Logue, innkeeper, of Carrigart, by his wife, Catherine Durnan. He was educated, first at Carrigart by a hedge-schoolmaster (to whom he owed a love of ships and a knowledge of sailing), and later at Kilmacrenan by Mr. Craig, a former scholar of Trinity College, Dublin (who taught him Latin), and (1854–1857) at a private school at Buncrana under Mr. Campbell. Having decided to study for the priesthood, he entered Maynooth College in 1857, became leader of his class and a prizeman, and was ordained deacon in 1864. He was nominated to the Dunboyne establishment for advanced studies in 1865, but before completing the course he was appointed, in 1866, to the chair of dogmatic theology at the Irish College in Paris, receiving priest's orders in that year. He remained in Paris until 1874, having attended imperial levées at the Tuileries and having seen the Irish College converted into a hospital under the British flag during the siege of Paris in 1871.

In 1874 Logue, having failed to obtain a chair of theology at Maynooth, was sent as curate to Glenswilly parish, co. Donegal. There he laboured for two years, often preaching in Irish, as he was bilingual. In 1876 he was appointed dean in Maynooth College, and was given the honorary chair of Irish, and, two years later, a chair of theology. In the following year (1879) he was elected bishop of Raphoe, and consecrated in the old cathedral at Letterkenny by Archbishop McGettigan, of Armagh. As bishop, Logue proved very active and influential. He raised funds in America in order to forestall and relieve the famine of 1880 in his diocese; he studied emigration and afforestation, planting 25,000 trees around Glenswilly; he collected the nucleus of a fund for building a new cathedral at Letterkenny; preached total abstinence in the endeavour to stamp out poteen-drinking; and took pains to examine personally every candidate for confirmation. Politically, his counsel and criticism carried much weight with the Irish nationalist party; while at Rome, which he visited in 1881 and 1885, he made his influence felt in the conferences of the Irish bishops held there in those years.

Early in 1887 Bishop Logue was elected coadjutor to Archbishop McGettigan. On the latter's death at the end of that year Logue succeeded to the archbishopric of Armagh. Five years later, in January 1893, he was created cardinal by Pope Leo XIII, with the title of Santa Maria della Pace.

As archbishop and cardinal, Logue continued to exercise great influence in Irish politics. At the time of the crisis in the nationalist party over the O'Shea divorce case, he denounced unsparingly both Parnell himself and a number of priests who still supported him; with the result that Parnell was eventually deposed from the leadership of the party. Logue remained suspicious of the Irish parliamentary party; disliked its alliance with the liberals, thinking that it endangered the position of Catholic schools in England; and kept a strong check on the party behind the scenes. He favoured the secession from the party of T. M. Healy, and supported him until he allied himself with William O'Brien [q.v.], whose 'plan of campaign' in the land agitation Logue regarded as a tactical mistake. Logue's support being withdrawn, Healy lost his seat in North Louth (1909). The cardinal's politics were national rather than nationalist. He was a patron of the Gaelic League and attended its *feiseanna*, and criticized the Intermediate Board of Education for not helping to promote the Irish language.

As primate, Logue was very regular in attending meetings whether of bishops, or of the Maynooth Union, or of the Catholic Truth Society. He generally had his way with the bishops, and he made a habit of talking down, humorously, proposals of which he disapproved. Educational questions, however, he usually left to be dealt with by Archbishop Walsh. He was on cordial terms with the English sovereigns, dining with Queen Victoria at the Viceregal Lodge in 1900, and receiving at Maynooth King Edward VII and King George V and Queen Mary on the occasion of their Irish visits in 1903 and 1911 respectively. In 1904 he celebrated his episcopal silver jubilee and witnessed the consecration by the papal delegate, Cardinal Vanutelli, of Armagh Cathedral; the foundation stone had been laid in the year of Logue's birth, but the decoration of the interior and the completion of the sacristy, library, and synod-hall were due to his labours in collecting a fund of £50,000. He was a great builder, and promoted the erection of fifteen new churches in his archdiocese. He visited the United States in 1908, and attended Eucharistic congresses in London (1908), Montreal (1910), Vienna (1912), and Lourdes (1914). At Rome he took part in three conclaves—for the election of Popes Pius X, Benedict XV, and Pius XI.

During and after the European War Cardinal Logue had a very difficult task. In a characteristic letter to Sir Horace Plunkett he denied that the Irish Catholic bishops were 'pro-German', adding that 'they preferred the tyrants they knew to the tyrants they knew not'. He exerted himself to help the Belgian refugees in Ireland, and to procure chaplains for Irish soldiers; but he opposed conscription on moral grounds. He denounced the Sinn Fein movement when it became a fighting force; but he criticized British methods and reprisals. During the troubles of the years 1919–1921 he endeavoured to mediate between the Irish people and the British government, and a letter addressed by him to Bishop Amigo of Southwark was quoted in the House of Lords by the archbishop of Canterbury (1921) and helped to pave the way to the peace of 1921. Logue accepted the terms of the treaty, having already made vigorous protest against partition. With the coming of peace in Ireland he began to set his house in order and, without consultation, indicated Bishop (afterwards Cardinal) O'Donnell, of Raphoe, as his successor. Rome acquiesced, and he thereby again 'secured the red hat for Armagh'. He died 19 November 1924, and was buried at Armagh.

Logue had an Irish temper but was devoid of rancour. He was of the old school, loved telling his stories, and could quote Horace and Virgil to suit the occasion. He interpreted canon law very strictly for himself, but very liberally for others. He lived to consecrate the bishops of the Northern province two or three times over. In church ceremony he was described as 'slovenly but not careless, awkward but accurate'. He was a keen yachtsman, a good swimmer, and a fine shot, once defeating the musketry instructor at Dundalk. His love of birds—small birds would feed from his hand—induced him as a youth to give up wild-duck shooting. He enjoyed remarkable health, never spending a day of his life in bed. He published nothing except pastorals and an article in French in *Le Monde* (3 April 1870), refuting the view of Bishop Dupanloup on the subject of papal infallibility. His portrait by Sir John Lavery hangs in the Belfast Gallery.

[*Memoir* by Cardinal MacRory in *Centenary History of Maynooth*, 1895; *Life* (in preparation) by P. J. Toner; private information.]

S. LESLIE.

LONG, WALTER HUME, first VISCOUNT LONG OF WRAXALL (1854–1924), statesman, was born at Bath 13 July 1854, the eldest son of Richard Penruddocke Long, M.P., of Rood Ashton, Wiltshire, by his wife, Charlotte Anna, daughter of the Rt. Hon. William Wentworth Fitzwilliam Dick (formerly Hume), M.P., of Humewood, co. Wicklow. His ancestors had been Wiltshire landowners since the end of the fourteenth century; he had four brothers, of whom the eldest was created Baron Gisborough in 1917, and five sisters.

Walter Long was country born and bred, and a typical West country gentleman he remained until the end of his life. As a child he was brought up in a rural atmosphere, where he learned to ride horses, milk cows, look after hounds, and mix as an equal with his father's tenants and employees, with whose outlook and interests he identified himself from a very early age. From a private school he proceeded to Harrow, where he reached the sixth form, and played for the school both at football and cricket, distinguishing himself at Lord's in the Eton and Harrow match of 1873. In that year he went up to Christ Church, Oxford, which he left without taking a degree. In his charming (and only) book, *My Memories* (1923), he gives vivid pictures of the life of an undergraduate of the time, commenting on the opportunities that it offered for every kind of manly sport, and dwelling with proper satisfaction upon the part that he was able to play in reducing the amount of drinking and gambling, which in his day was risking the reputation of the 'House'.

Even at Oxford Long was a politician, a conservative, of course. He took so prominent and useful a part in a by-election for Oxford city that the conservative party invited him, even as an undergraduate, to contest the seat at the next election. Equally flattering was the offer, during this period, of the mastership of the Vale of White Horse hounds. However, he accepted neither of these tributes to his political and sporting instincts, which nevertheless developed until he was elected to parliament as member for North Wiltshire at the general election of 1880. He now abandoned coaching, gave up polo, and, apart from an odd day's hunting in the winter or a cricket match in the summer, devoted himself for the next forty years to his duties as a member of parliament. During that long period he had ample opportunity of making himself acquainted with the needs and interests of all classes of his fellow citizens in town and country, and he took the fullest advantage of it. He sat for North Wiltshire from 1880 to 1885 and for East Wiltshire from 1885 to 1892; for the West Derby division of Liverpool from 1893 to 1900; for South Bristol from 1900 to 1906; for South County Dublin from 1906 to 1910; for the Strand division of Middlesex from 1910 to 1918 and, finally, for St. George's, Westminster, from 1918 to 1921, when he was raised to the peerage: a long, varied, but unbroken chain of parliamentary service worthy of his inherited tradition.

The parliament of 1880 contained many men of the same type as Walter Long; they were called 'the country party', and no name could have suited them better. Whole-hearted advocates of Disraelian imperialism, champions of law and order, they welcomed the addition to their ranks of this new recruit from the West country. Long did nothing of note during Mr. Gladstone's second parliament, but was recognized as a good, hard-working party man who knew everything about agriculture and English country life. It was a matter of no surprise, therefore, to anybody except himself, when in 1886 Lord Salisbury invited him to join the government as parliamentary secretary to the Local Government Board. For this post he was very well suited, as his chief, Mr. Ritchie (afterwards Lord Ritchie of Dundee, q.v.), soon discovered. To Long was delegated the whole management of poor-law work both in and out of parliament. This experience proved of the greatest service to Long when, later in the same parliament, it fell to him to take a large part in framing and in getting through the House of Commons the Local Government Act of 1888, which created county councils throughout Great Britain. The London County Council Bill followed, though Long assumed no responsibility for that. His speeches, however, combined with the tact and skill that he exhibited in piloting these two important measures through parliament, brought him at once into the front rank of parliamentarians and marked him as a man who would soon reach Cabinet rank. This impression was deepened by his work in opposition during the following parliament, when he gave discriminating but invaluable assistance to the liberal president of the Local Government Board, Mr. G. J. Shaw-Lefevre (afterwards Lord Eversley, q.v.), in carrying through the Local Government Bill of 1894 which established parish councils.

When, in 1895, Lord Salisbury formed his third administration, Long was appointed president of the Board of Agriculture, with a seat in the Cabinet, at the age of forty, a very early age in those days. The selection of Long for this office was warmly applauded throughout the agricultural community. The farmers felt that they now had a 'man in possession' who was a complete master of their problems and requirements, one who would carry on Mr. Chaplin's wise policy of protecting British herds and flocks from infection at home and from imported disease. But Long's popularity was soon seriously impaired by his rigorous policy in combating the alarming spread of hydrophobia (*rabies*) throughout the country. After a scientific investigation in 1897, a diagnosis of the disease was officially declared and immediate preventive steps were ordered to be taken. Muzzling, quarantine for imported dogs, detention, and (where necessary) destruction were among the measures universally enforced and ruthlessly executed in the teeth of violent organized opposition; Long himself was subjected to the fiercest criticism by hundreds of his hitherto warmest admirers. But he stuck to his guns, pursued his policy, and, as a result, rabies was stamped out of the country at the end of five years, and Long's reputation established as a fearless and just administrator. In 1900, after the general election and in the midst of the Boer War, he returned at Lord Salisbury's request to the Local Government Board as president; to the department in which he had served his official apprenticeship eleven years previously. Here, once more, his knowledge of administrative detail, his skill in debate, and above all his 'hands' in driving a very unruly team, were talents that required the fullest exercise in order to secure the passing of the Metropolitan Water Act (1902) against a sustained and bitter opposition, some of it coming from members of his own political party. The Bill was debated with great expert knowledge on both sides and with a pertinacity worthy of a measure fraught with important consequences. But it was characteristic of Walter Long that, however fiercely he fought in debate, he never overstepped the limits of parliamentary courtesy; and when his Bill passed into law, he had not lost a single friend among his former opponents but, on the contrary, was presented by some of them with a valuable souvenir of the occasion.

In 1902 Lord Salisbury retired; and Mr. Balfour became prime minister (1902–1905) during the troublous years which saw the birth of tariff reform, of which Walter Long was a moderate but convinced supporter. In 1905, when Lord Selborne, then first lord of the Admiralty, was appointed to be high commissioner for South Africa, Mr. Balfour was most anxious that Long should take promotion to the Admiralty, leaving the Local Government Board to which he was very much attached. The proposal was flattering, but Long preferred to remain where he was, and suggested the name of Lord Cawdor for the Admiralty. Long's career at the Local Government Board was, however, soon closed. Within a few weeks came the resignation of George Wyndham [q.v.] from the post of chief secretary for Ireland owing to a break-down in health and a serious disagreement with the government. It was a difficult and thankless post for the prime minister to offer to any of his colleagues at that moment. In offering it to Walter Long, Mr. Balfour said: 'I do not *ask* you to go to Ireland; but if you accept the office of chief secretary you will be doing me a great service and rendering a still greater one to your country.' Such a message from his leader, for whom Long had high regard and great affection, was sufficient. He went to the chief secretary's lodge, Dublin, and remained there for nine important months, until the general election of 1906. During that time he restored harmony in the unionist party, confidence throughout the Irish constabulary and all branches of the administration, and law and order throughout Ireland, so effectively that his liberal successor in office, Mr. Birrell, declared that he arrived to find Ireland more peaceful, more contented, and more free from internal trouble than she had been for six hundred years. From beginning to end of this short but eventful term of office, in spite of threatening letters, plots, and police protection, there was no more popular personality in Ireland than Walter Long. He had all the qualities that endeared themselves to Irishmen; he was accessible to all classes; genial, courageous, firm, and just in administration; an agriculturist by instinct and training, and an all-round sportsman. It was a tribute to his universal popularity that at the general election of 1906 he should have been elected as the unionist member for South County Dublin and, a few weeks later, as leader of the Irish unionists in the House of Commons.

When the new parliament met in 1906 it was clearly recognized that Home Rule, of which nothing had been heard since 1893, would soon be resuscitated in one form or another, and Walter Long took immediate steps to deal with the situation. He created in 1907 the Union Defence League, an organization whose activities and influence grew steadily until the agitation against the Home Rule Bill of 1912 was suspended by the outbreak of the European War.

In 1909 Long went on a visit to South Africa. On his return he was immediately elected president of the Budget Protest League, formed in order to fight Mr. Lloyd George's budget of that year. Here again he exerted himself to the uttermost, even though his health was a matter of grave concern to his friends. Two general elections followed in 1910, and in the following year Mr. Balfour retired from the leadership of the unionist party. The choice of his successor lay between Walter Long and (Sir) Austen Chamberlain; the one, a tory, a moderate tariff reformer, and the leader of the older men of the conservative party; the other, a liberal unionist, an extreme tariff reformer, and the leader of the younger generation. Between the supporters of the two candidates, though never between the candidates themselves, there were the makings of a bitter faction fight which would have gravely impaired the future usefulness of the unionist party. Recognizing this, Long offered to withdraw if Chamberlain would do likewise, and if they could find another man whom the whole party would consent to follow. Mr. Bonar Law was then proposed by Walter Long, seconded by Austen Chamberlain, and unanimously elected leader at a party meeting held in the Carlton Club.

Throughout the difficulties and political struggles of the next three years, when the House of Lords and the Union seemed to be in jeopardy, Walter Long took a foremost part by the side of his new leader. Then, after the outbreak of war, when Mr. Asquith formed the first Coalition government in 1915, Long was asked to return to the Local Government Board with Cabinet rank, a post which he felt bound to accept, against his doctor's advice. To his office was assigned the duty of framing the Conscription Acts, and also of caring for the thousands of Belgian refugees who landed in Great Britain; these duties the president carried out with complete success until the second Coalition government was formed in 1916, when he was appointed secretary of state for the Colonies. In this post, also, he made his mark as a statesman by organizing the Imperial War Conferences of 1917 and 1918; by introducing a system of weekly cables to the overseas prime ministers, giving them full accounts of what was happening in all the theatres of war; and by co-ordinating and controlling, with the help of Sir John Cadman, the oil supplies of the British Empire and of the Allies, which were in grave peril. Although previously an opponent of women's suffrage, Long introduced the Franchise Bill of 1917, which became law in the following year, and under which women over thirty were given the vote. It is probable that only those who were working with him during this desperately anxious period of the War knew how exacting and exhausting were the duties cast upon Long, at a time when his health was patently failing every day. In 1918 came the Armistice and a reconstruction of the Cabinet. Long had hoped to be allowed to put off his official harness, but it was not to be—yet. In the new administration he became first lord of the Admiralty, the post which he had declined in 1905, and there he remained until he resigned through ill-health in 1921, having reduced the British navy from a war to a peace footing, and having secured for its officers and men a substantial increase in the rates of pay previously existing. He was created a viscount for his services, and few men can ever have deserved or received more sincere congratulations.

Long, who was lord-lieutenant of Wiltshire and president of the Marylebone Cricket Club, was elected a fellow of the Royal Society in 1902, and received the honorary LL.D. of Birmingham University. He died at Rood Ashton 26 September 1924.

Long married in 1878 Lady Dorothy (Doreen) Blanche, fourth daughter of Richard Edmund St. Lawrence Boyle, ninth Earl of Cork and Orrery, and had two sons and three daughters. The eldest son, Brigadier-General Walter Long, C.M.G., D.S.O. (2nd Dragoons), was killed in action in 1917. His son, Walter Francis David (born 1911), succeeded his grandfather as second viscount in 1924.

A portrait of Lord Long by A. H. Collins (1918) hangs at Rood Ashton, and a replica by the same artist in the Harrow war memorial hall.

[*The Times*, 27 September 1924; Viscount Long of Wraxall, *My Memories*, 1923; private information; personal knowledge.]

I. Malcolm.

LOREBURN, Earl (1846–1923), lord chancellor. [See Reid, Robert Threshie.]

LORIMER, Sir ROBERT STODART (1864–1929), architect, was born in Edinburgh 4 November 1864, the third and youngest son of James Lorimer [q.v.], regius professor of public law at Edinburgh University, by his wife, Hannah, daughter of John Riddell Stodart, writer to the signet. The latter's father, Robert Stodart, a celebrated piano-maker, invented the 'upright grand', and it was from the maternal side that Lorimer inherited much of his artistic and musical bent, though his father, too, was a competent amateur artist. He first showed an enthusiasm for building and for the companionship of craftsmen at the age of thirteen when his father bought and began to restore Kellie Castle, Fife. Educated at Edinburgh Academy and University, where he cheerfully 'shirked his books', he was in 1885 apprenticed to the architect, Sir Rowand Anderson, with whom he remained for four and a half years. In 1889 he entered the office of George Frederick Bodley [q.v.] in London, where his romantic bias towards craftsmanship was encouraged and directed by Bodley's Gothic revival ideals.

In 1892 Lorimer returned to Edinburgh in order to take up his first notable commission, the restoration of Earlshall, Fife, for his parents' friend, R. W. Mackenzie. This was the first of a long series of restorations which were among his most pleasing works, and in which he showed a faculty for the sympathetic preservation of the character of old buildings. Thenceforward Lorimer was well established as an architect in Scotland, engaged during the ensuing decade on small and medium-sized country houses, at first in the neighbourhood of Edinburgh, but after 1901 in England as well.

In 1903 Lorimer received his first commission for a large Scottish country house, Rowallan, Ayrshire, for Lord Rowallan (never finished), and in 1906 that for Ardkinglas, Argyll, for Sir Andrew Noble. In the latter house he remedied a certain lack of cohesion apparent in the former by adapting traditional Scottish features to a picturesque but compact style which became characteristic of him. The most successful example is at Formakin, Renfrewshire (1912–1914, unfinished) where he had much help from his client, Mr. J. A. Holms. Other notable houses of this period are Hill of Tarvit, Fife (1907), and Woodhill, Barry (1908), both in a version of the Scottish Georgian style. In 1907–1909 and again in 1911–1912 he was engaged on the restoration, with additions, of Lympne Castle, Kent, and on the reconstruction after fire of Monzie Castle, Crieff.

In 1906 Lorimer designed his first important church, St. Peter's Roman Catholic church, Morningside, Edinburgh (completed 1929), together with a priest's house and school. It had to be built cheaply, and for the interior he used brick, whitewashed above, in a simple, direct style which makes it the most original of his non-traditional works. In contrast, however, with St. Andrews University Library Annexe (1907) in the classical style, came a commission for the chapel of the Order of the Thistle, added to St. Giles's Cathedral, Edinburgh (1909–1911); this established his reputation thereafter as essentially a Gothic architect.

The Thistle chapel is a remarkable example of a true revival of the medieval crafts. Into a setting of vigorous native Gothic, massively simple up to the flamboyant groining of the vault, Lorimer introduced the sculpture, wood-carving, and stained glass of a group of artificers whom he had been training to his requirements for some years. For the stone carving he employed Joseph Hayes, for the woodwork the brothers Clow, for the windows Louis Davis (the east window is by Douglas Strachan). In recognition of his work, the whole of which was performed within the estimated cost, Lorimer was knighted in 1911.

In 1911–1912 Sir Andrew Noble commissioned Lorimer to restore the ruined castle of Dunderave on Loch Fyne, Argyllshire. Other reconstructions at this time were Pittencrief House and Lennoxlove (1912). In addition to Formakin, new houses were the Corner House, Gullane, and Laverockdale, Colinton. A town-planning scheme, involving a 'town centre' of strikingly romantic appearance, Cornmill Square, was instituted at Galashiels, and the restoration of Dunblane Cathedral was put in hand, notable especially for the rich woodwork introduced.

The War years (1914–1918) coincided with, although they largely hindered, the recognition of Lorimer as the leading architect of Scotland. He was occupied on the remodelling for Mr. R. F. McEwen of the William Adam mansion of Marchmont, Berwickshire, including a large music room adorned with an organ case which is one of the best works of the brothers Clow; on the building of Midfield, Lasswade, a Georgian style house; on the redecoration of Dunrobin Castle, Sutherland, after a fire; and on the restoration of Balmanno Castle, Perthshire, for Mr. W. S. Millar. The last, which Lorimer regarded as his most successful restoration, included the complete furnishing from his designs by Whytock and Reid, of Edinburgh, and much of the best plasterwork, which was executed for him by Samuel Wilson and Thomas Beattie.

After the War Lorimer was chiefly occupied on memorials, including, besides numerous personal monuments, those for Loretto and Westminster Schools, Edinburgh University, Galashiels, and Paisley (with Mrs. Meredith Williams as sculptor). For the Imperial War Graves Commission he visited the Italian front (designing all the cemeteries there), Egypt, and Macedonia. In Macedonia he was responsible for all the principal cemeteries, the chief being the memorial to the missing at Lake Doiran. He also designed several cemeteries in Germany, including that at Cologne. In England he designed the naval war memorials at Chatham, Portsmouth, and Plymouth.

Lorimer's absorbing occupation between 1918 and 1927 was the Scottish National War Memorial, for the building of which his whole development proved to have been a preparation. His first scheme was for a Gothic memorial cloister attached by a low passage to a lofty octagonal shrine crowning the highest point of the Edinburgh Castle rock. This design is attached to the report (July 1919) of a committee appointed to consider the utilization of the castle for a national war memorial; the committee recommended using the site of part of a disused eighteenth-century barracks forming the north side of Crown Square. By 1922 the proposed cloister had been altered to a long low 'hall of the regiments' but, on a full-sized model being erected, a storm of protest was aroused by the height of the shrine and its alteration of the familiar skyline. Thereupon Lorimer, within a few days, produced the existing design, which uses the shell of the barracks as the hall, with the shrine, bisected and only half its former height, attached to it. Work was begun early in 1924 and the memorial was dedicated 14 July 1927. The combination of styles adopted is not unexceptionable to the purist; but, by inspiring his craftsmen with his own enthusiasm Lorimer succeeded in carrying out, in the face of many checks, a conception which fulfils to a remarkable degree the emotional requirements of a national war memorial. The popular response was profound and immediate. In 1928 Lorimer was made K.B.E.

Subsequent important works by Lorimer were the restorations of Paisley abbey and St. John's church, Perth (1923–1928); the building of Stowe School chapel (1927–1930) in which the pillars of an eighteenth-century temple were incorporated; and St. Andrew's church, Aldershot, which returns to the earlier simplicity of St. Peter's, Edinburgh.

In appearance Lorimer was handsome and alert, with large, keen eyes of grey-blue. Latterly he felt some resentment that he was not more fully employed, particularly in connexion with the Calton Hill site at Edinburgh. His strength as an architect lay in an obstinate idealism and an instinctive perception of the elements on which the character and psychological effect of a design depended. Having little intellectual sense of form, he disliked and avoided classicism, but appreciated the more romantic aspects of functional modernism. Fundamentally a craftsman, his vigorous encouragement of fine handwork constitutes him the saviour of the crafts in Scotland, which he found rapidly dying out but left as a flourishing school. Based on these and on national tradition, it was his achievement to restore to Scotland a vital and characteristic architecture.

Lorimer married in 1903 Violet, daughter of Edward Wyld, of Denham, Buckinghamshire, by whom he had three sons and one daughter. He was elected A.R.S.A. in 1903, A.R.A. in 1920, and R.S.A. in 1921. He died suddenly in Edinburgh after an operation 13 September 1929, and his ashes were placed in the family burial ground at Newburn, Fife.

[Architectural Supplement to *Country Life*, 27 September 1913; Sir Lawrence Weaver, *The Scottish National War Memorial*, 1928; *Journal* of the Royal Institute of British Architects, 21 February 1931; *Edinburgh Academy Chronicle*, December 1929; *Quarterly of Incorporation of Architects in Scotland*, No. 31, 1929; Christopher Hussey, *The Work of Sir Robert Lorimer*, 1931.] C. Hussey.

LUCY, Sir HENRY WILLIAM (1843–1924), journalist, was born at Crosby, Lancashire, the son of Robert Lucy, a rose-engine turner in the watch trade, by his wife, Margaret Ellen Kemp. The date of his birth is probably towards the end of March 1843, for he was baptized (as William Henry) on 23 April of that year. While he was still an infant the family removed to Everton, Liverpool, and he attended a private school called the Crescent School until August 1856; thereafter until 1864 he was junior clerk to Robert Smith, hide merchant, of Redcross Street, Liverpool.

Lucy began to write at an early age. During his clerkship he contributed verse to the *Liverpool Mercury*, and, having taught himself shorthand, he sought a post as reporter on one of the Liverpool papers. Eventually, without experience, but with a testimonial from (Sir) Edward Russell, then assistant editor of the *Liverpool Post*, he became in July 1864 chief reporter to the *Shrewsbury Chronicle*. He soon began to contribute leader-notes to the local

Observer and the *Shropshire News*. For a short time in 1865 he was editor and part-proprietor of the former. Then he became secretary to Richard Samuel France, railway contractor, and at the same time greatly enlarged his experience as a free-lance journalist.

From May to December 1869 Lucy lived in Paris, learning French; thereafter he was for a short time (January to June 1870) in London as a sub-editor on the newly founded morning edition of the *Pall Mall Gazette*, and for eighteen months (June 1870 to January 1872) in Exeter as assistant editor of the *Exeter Gazette*. Returning to London he was a free-lance for some months, until he secured a regular engagement on the *Daily News* in October 1872. He was soon in the full tide of success. (Sir) John Richard Robinson [q.v.] made him manager of the *Daily News* parliamentary staff and writer of its parliamentary summary; in addition he contributed London letters to several provincial papers. A journalistic venture of his own, *Mayfair*, started in December 1877, never paid its way, and after two years collapsed. In 1880 he began a connexion with *The Observer* which lasted for twenty-nine years, and in 1881 he succeeded Shirley Brooks as the writer of 'Essence of Parliament' for *Punch*, continuing to write as 'Toby, M.P.' until February 1916.

Lucy's industry, fertility, humour, and remarkable *flair* for politics and parliamentary affairs soon brought him to the front rank of his profession. Two further promotions were in store for him. In July 1885 Henry Labouchere offered him the editorship of the *Daily News*. He refused, out of loyalty to Frank Harrison Hill [q.v.], who was then editor; but in December, Hill having had his *congé*, Lucy took the post. He found editing distasteful, however, and in June 1887 resigned, and returned to the press gallery. Ten years later (April 1897) he again showed his loyalty, this time to (Sir) F. C. Burnand [q.v.], by refusing the editorship of *Punch*, offered to him by (Sir) William Agnew. Notwithstanding his copious output as a journalist, Lucy found time to write two novels and a collection of short stories, a study of W. E. Gladstone (1895, 2nd ed. 1898), popular handbooks on *Parliamentary Procedure* (1880) and the *Law and Practice of General Elections* (1900), six volumes of parliamentary diaries, and several of personal reminiscences. He was knighted in 1909. He died 20 February 1924 at Whitethorn, a country house which he had built near Hythe in 1883, and at which he spent most of his week-ends. In London he lived at 42 Ashley Gardens, Westminster.

Lucy owed his rapid rise in his profession solely to his own ability and hard work. He was the most urbane, well-informed, and indefatigable of parliamentary chroniclers, and claimed that he was the first journalist to establish close personal relations with prominent politicians. This contact gave his work a first-hand quality which, combined with his lambent humour and undoubted probity, made him *persona grata* with men of all parties.

Lucy married in 1873 Emily Anne, daughter of his old schoolmaster at Liverpool, John White. There were no children of the marriage.

A portrait of Lucy by J. S. Sargent was bequeathed by Lucy to the *Punch* dining-room, with the proviso that after ten years it should be offered to the National Portrait Gallery. A cartoon by 'Spy' appeared in *Vanity Fair* 31 August 1905.

[*The Times*, 22 February 1924; *The Nation* (New York), 12 March 1924; Sir H. W. Lucy, *Sixty Years in the Wilderness* (autobiography), 1909; M. H. Spielmann, *The History of 'Punch'*, 1895; Great Crosby baptismal registers; various allusions in J. McCarthy and Sir J. R. Robinson, *The 'Daily News' Jubilee*, 1896; F. M. Thomas, *Fifty Years of Fleet Street: being the Life and Recollections of Sir John R. Robinson*, 1904; and E. V. Lucas, *Reading, Writing, and Remembering*, 1932.]

H. B. Grimsditch.

LUKIN, Sir HENRY TIMSON (1860–1925), major-general, was born at Fulham 24 May 1860, the only son of Robert Henry Lukin, barrister-at-law, of St. Peter's-in-Thanet, by his wife, Ellen, daughter of Richard Watson, of Northampton. He was educated at Merchant Taylors' School from 1869 to 1875. The family had distinguished military associations, and the boy ardently desired to become a soldier, but failed to pass into the Royal Military College. It was typical of him that, on the prospect of war with the Zulus, he sailed for Durban in January 1879. He obtained a commission in Bengough's Horse, a native cavalry contingent, thus entering by a 'side-door' the profession for which he was so well fitted. Severely wounded at the battle of Ulundi (4 July), Lukin saw no more of that campaign, but on 23 March 1881 he was gazetted lieutenant in the Cape Mounted Riflemen, and he served with that regiment in Basutoland in 1881 and, as field adjutant in the Bechuanaland field force through the Langeberg operations, 1896–1897, which completely crushed the Bechuana rebellion. In the course of these services he was several times decorated and mentioned in dispatches.

In the South African War (1899–1902), Lukin particularly distinguished himself in command of the Cape Mounted Rifles' artillery in the defence of Wepener, Orange Free State, in April 1900, and was awarded the D.S.O. Subsequently, he commanded a mounted column in Cape Colony. When, in December 1901, the Cape government formed a colonial division, Lukin was given command of it. After the War he received the C.M.G. (1902). In 1904 he was appointed commandant-general of the Cape Colonial forces. In 1912 he was made inspector-general of the permanent force, Union of South Africa.

In the European War, Lukin was first given command of a mixed force in the operations in German South-West Africa (March to July 1915). On the conclusion of that campaign he organized and commanded the 1st South African Infantry brigade. After a few months in England this brigade was dispatched to Egypt in January 1916. The commander-in-chief in Egypt, Lieut.-General Sir John Maxwell [q.v.], had been obliged, largely for lack of experienced troops, to evacuate the coast between Matruh and Sollum in November 1915 on the threat of an invasion of Egypt by the Senussi. With the South African brigade available, he adopted a forward policy. At Agagiya on 26 February 1916 Lukin gained a remarkable victory over the enemy, capturing their able Turkish commander, Ja'far Pasha, and on 14 March he reoccupied Sollum. It was a brilliant desert campaign.

Under Lukin's command the South African brigade proceeded to France in April 1916, replacing the 28th brigade in the 9th (Scottish) division. In the battle of the Somme the brigade greatly distinguished itself in the capture of Delville Wood on 15 July. In December Lukin, promoted major-general, took command of the 9th division, thus keeping under his orders the brigade which he had raised and trained. He commanded the division in the battle of Arras in April 1917, and in the 'third battle' of Ypres in the following September and October. In January 1918 he was created K.C.B. He returned to England in February 1918, and was in command of the 64th division at home until the end of the War.

After his retirement in 1919, Lukin returned to South Africa and lived there until his death at Muizenburg, Cape Colony, 15 December 1925. Strong, independent, modest, and a born leader of men, he had become one of the most popular figures in the Union.

Lukin married in 1891 Lily, daughter of Michael Herbert Quinn, landowner, of Fort Hare, Victoria East, Cape Colony; there were no children of the marriage.

[*The Times*, 17 December 1925; R. E. Johnston, *Ulundi to Delville Wood, the Life Story of Major-General Sir Henry Timson Lukin*, 1931; Sir George MacMunn and Cyril Falls, (Official) *History of the Great War. Military Operations. Egypt and Palestine*, vol. i, 1928; John Ewing, *The History of the 9th (Scottish) Division*, 1921.] C. B. Falls.

LUSH, Sir CHARLES MONTAGUE (1853–1930), judge, the fourth son of Sir Robert Lush [q.v.], lord justice of appeal, by his wife, Elizabeth Ann, daughter of the Rev. Christopher Woollacott, a London Baptist minister, was born in London 7 December 1853. Educated at Westminster and at Trinity Hall, Cambridge, he obtained a first class in the classical tripos of 1876. Lush was called to the bar by Gray's Inn in 1879, and joined the North-Eastern circuit. On the passing of the Married Women's Property Act (1882) he produced an excellent treatise on *The Law of Husband and Wife*, which became and remains the standard work on the subject for students and practitioners. His progress at first was slow, but he gradually acquired a leading position at the common-law bar in London, and in 1902 he took silk.

Lush was generally recognized as a sound lawyer, and it was as such, rather than as an advocate, that he was expected to succeed. His small stature and his gentle tones seemed to disqualify him for a jury practice. But, to the surprise of his friends, he developed unsuspected gifts of advocacy, and for eight years was in great request in actions of all descriptions, and in particular in those coming before juries. Surrounded by formidable competitors, he held his own with such great leaders as Edward Carson, Rufus Isaacs, H. E. Duke, and John Lawson Walton; his 'lachrymatory eloquence'—as it was once described by Lord Birkenhead—combined with an appearance of complete simplicity and candour, often secured unexpected verdicts. The clashing of appointments did not disturb him, and he could be relied upon to be on the spot in time to cross-examine the important witness or to make the final speech. In the Court of Appeal Lush was no less successful than in courts of first instance. He appeared in, amongst other notable actions, *Paquin Ltd.* v. *Beauclerk* (1906, husband's liability for goods supplied to his wife) and *Hulton & Co.* v. *Jones* (1910, liability for unintentional defamation).

In October 1910 Lush was appointed to a judgeship of the King's Bench division under the Additional Judges Act of that year, and received a knighthood. The bar warmly approved of his promotion. He seemed to possess all the qualifications necessary to ensure a great judicial career. But on the bench he hardly fulfilled the expectations formed of him by the profession. Courageous to a fault as a barrister, he appeared to lose confidence in himself as a judge. His anxiety to do justice was so great that he hesitated to arrive at a decision, and his subtle mind was inclined to detect difficult problems in cases which to others seemed simple enough. Sometimes he allowed his feelings to master his judgement. In the case which is reported in the House of Lords as *Harnett* v. *Bond* (1925) Lush was the trial judge. His sympathy with the plaintiff, who alleged that he had been wrongly detained as a lunatic, resulted in a verdict for £25,000 damages against the two defendants. The order for a new trial by the Court of Appeal was affirmed by the House of Lords.

Always careful and courteous, Lush was personally popular with the bar, and he was a kindly criminal judge. He sat occasionally as a temporary member of the Court of Appeal, and in 1915 he was appointed president of the railway and canal commission. Increasing deafness compelled him to retire in 1925. Although he was sworn a member of the Privy Council in that year he never sat as a member of the Judicial Committee. He was a bencher of Gray's Inn and an honorary fellow (1911) of his college. Lush died 22 June 1930 at Stanmore, Middlesex. He married in 1893 Margaret Abbie (died 1925), daughter of Sir Charles Brodie Locock, second baronet, and had four sons and two daughters.

[*The Times*, 23 June 1930; personal knowledge.] T. Mathew.

MACARA, Sir CHARLES WRIGHT, first baronet (1845–1929), cotton spinner, was born at Strathmiglo, Fife, 11 January 1845, the only child of the Rev. William Macara, minister of the Free Church of Scotland, by his wife, Charlotte Grace, daughter of Thomas Cowpar, of Memus, Kerriemuir, Forfarshire, and niece of Sir Archibald Galloway [q.v.], sometime chairman of the East India Company. Macara's father was a Scottish divine of the old school, whose life, writes Macara in his *Recollections*, 'was a standing exhortation to me to find out what was good and hold on to it'. He refers also to the influence of his mother, an equally vivid personality.

Educated in his native village and at Edinburgh, Macara began work in 1862, at the age of seventeen, with a Scottish merchant in Manchester. In 1875 he married Marion, daughter of William Young, of Bournemouth, and granddaughter of one of the founders of the firm of Henry Bannerman & Sons, cotton spinners and merchants of Manchester, and cousin to Sir Henry Campbell-Bannerman. In 1880 Macara was made managing partner in this firm. In 1884 he fought a strike with ruthless success, and soon afterwards took a leading part in establishing the Manchester Cotton Employers' Association; but he also claims to have been 'one of the forces which have extended and solidified the operatives' unions'. His belief was that all workers and all employers should join their respective unions and organizations and that between employers and employees, so organized, there need be no ill feeling. In the famous twenty weeks' strike in the cotton-spinning industry in 1892–1893, which was ended by the signing of the Brooklands Agreement (March 1893), Macara had to fight the workers on the question of wages, which had originated the strike, and his fellow employers on the wider issue of full recognition of the workers' right to have a say in industry. The Brooklands Agreement provided rules for the settlement of future disputes by conciliatory methods and, in Macara's view, inaugurated a new era 'not in the cotton industry alone, but in all industry'.

In 1894 Macara was elected president of the Federation of Master Cotton Spinners' Associations, and he held this position till 1914. During all that time there occurred only one strike concerning wages (in 1910) which affected the whole industry; whereas before his presidency the industry was known as the cockpit of industrial strife. Macara took a leading part in all public movements connected with the cotton trade, including the inauguration (1894) of the Manchester Cotton Association, which had for its object the direct importation of raw cotton to Manchester by the Ship Canal, and of the British Cotton Growing Association. In 1902 he headed a delegation, equally representative of capital and labour, to the China Shipping Conference, and succeeded in securing a reduction in freights which is calculated to have saved the Lancashire trade about £100,000 a year. Spurred on by the cotton crisis of 1903–1904, Macara founded in 1904 the International Federation of Master Cotton Spinners' and Manufacturers' Associations, of which he was chairman from 1904 to 1915, and which he regarded as one of the most important movements in the history of international co-operation. He also did much to assist the establishment of the International Institute of Agriculture.

Macara was created a baronet in 1911, and received many foreign decorations. He died at his home at Hale, Cheshire, 2 January 1929, leaving one son, who succeeded to the baronetcy, and four daughters.

Macara was the author of *Social and Industrial Reform* (1918), *In Search of a Peaceful World* (1921), *Recollections* (1921), *Getting the World to Work* (1922); and numerous articles on labour questions, organization of trade, philanthropic movements, and lifeboat work.

A cartoon of Macara appeared in *Vanity Fair* 13 March 1912.

[*The Times*, 3 January 1929; Sir C. W. Macara, *Recollections* (with portrait), 1921; private information.] H. Withers.

McCLURE, Sir JOHN DAVID (1860–1922), schoolmaster, was born at Wigan 9 February 1860, the eldest son of John McClure, of Wigan, a Congregationalist business man, whose ancestors came originally from Skye. His mother was Elizabeth, daughter of James Hyslop, who came from Kirkcudbrightshire and who lived for a time at Wigan. He was educated at Holly Mount College, near Bury (1874–1876), Owens College, Manchester (1876–1877), and Trinity College, Cambridge (1882–1886). In the intervening years he taught as an assistant master at Holly Mount (1877–1878) and at Hinckley grammar school, Leicestershire (1878–1882), and graduated B.A. of London University in 1878. During this period music became, as it remained, one of the dominant influences in his life. At Cambridge McClure read for the mathematical tripos, and gave much time to the work of the Nonconformist Union, to lay preaching in neighbouring free churches, and to music; he took his degree with a second class in 1885, but remaining a further year at Trinity (as Walker prizeman), took his LL.B. in 1886, his M.A. in 1889, and entered the Inner Temple. At that time the Free Church ministry, the law, music, or education were all open to him as professions: he chose the last, and after five years of Extension lecturing was appointed headmaster of Mill Hill School in 1891. He also held, from 1889 to 1894, the chair of astronomy at Queen's College, London. Meanwhile, in 1889 he had married Mary, the daughter of James Johnstone, a Scotch business man living at Holcombe, near Bury; by her he had one son and two daughters.

McClure remained at Mill Hill until the end of his life, and saw it grow from a comparatively unknown Nonconformist school of sixty boys to a successful public school, with over three hundred names on its books. His impressive personality, his remarkable memory for names and faces, his sense of humour, and his unfailing fund of stories, of which he was a born raconteur, made him a popular and effective figure not only in the school, but in wide circles outside. He moved in many such circles, as an educationist, a musician, and one of the leading free churchmen of his time. He was called to the bar in 1890 and took the LL.D. degree at Cambridge in 1897. In 1900 he was elected a member of the senate of London University, and in 1902 a member of the council of Mansfield College, Oxford; he was joint honorary secretary of the Incorporated Association of Headmasters from 1904 to 1912, president in 1914–1915, and treasurer from 1920 to 1922. He became a Mus.B. of London University in 1903, a D.Mus. in 1909, was elected to the corporation of the Trinity College of Music in 1906, and became its chairman in 1920. The Congregational Union elected him to the chairmanship in 1919, and he was largely responsible for the compilation of its new hymnal between 1909 and 1916. He received the freedom of the borough of Wigan in 1920. The Teachers' Registration Council (now the Royal Society of Teachers) owes its foundation mainly to his work. For his services to education he was knighted in 1913. During the European War he served on many local committees, and did valuable work in the interests of teachers on the Professional Classes War Relief Council, of which he was a founder. In 1921 he was invited to stand as a university representative in the House of Commons, but his health was beginning to fail. He died at Mill Hill, after a week's illness, 18 February 1922.

McClure's chief work was the making of Mill Hill School. But he made, also, important contributions to the educational, musical, and religious life of his time, all marked by a broad-mindedness and a devotion to truth which were characteristic; the former, indeed, sometimes tended to alienate him from the stricter Free Church circles, but made him an effective advocate of the cause of reunion and, in a different field, of the League of Nations, after the War. Sociable and of ready sympathies, he was much in demand for committee work; while his power of marshalling facts and of presenting a balanced and reasoned case made him a telling advocate, and some of his most effective public work was done as a mediator in difficult situations. He wrote no books, but contributed an article on 'Preparation for Practical Life' to *Cambridge Essays on Education*, edited by A. C. Benson; as he said in a speech addressed to the old boys of Mill Hill School: 'If I have written no books . . . my writings are happily more lasting, and they are round about me.'

[K. M. J. Ousey, *McClure of Mill Hill. A Memoir by his daughter*, 1927; private information.] M. L. Jacks.

McCORMICK, Sir WILLIAM SYMINGTON (1859–1930), scholar and administrator, was born at Dumfries 29 April 1859, the elder son of William McCormick, an ironmonger and maker of agricultural implements in that town, by his wife, Agnes Ann, daughter of the Rev. William Symington [q.v.], professor of divinity in the Reformed Presbyterian Church of Scotland (the Cameronians), and niece of Andrew Symington [q.v.]. He was educated at Dumfries high school and at Glasgow University, graduating in 1880. For a short time he lectured in mathematics at Glasgow as assistant to Professor Hugh Blackburn; afterwards he went to the universities of Göttingen and Marburg in order to study literature. On his return to Glasgow, McCormick became in 1884 assistant to John Nichol [q.v.], professor of English literature, and after the transference of Queen Margaret College for women to the university in 1893 he was put in charge of the department of English language and literature. For a time he was also in partnership with a Mr. Wilson in a publishing business.

In 1890 McCormick was appointed to the chair of English literature at University College, Dundee, to which was added later a lecturership in English at the university of St. Andrews, whither he transferred his home. He was an admirable lecturer, and he was continuously engaged in literary work and in university administration throughout this period of his life. He published a volume of *Three Lectures on Literature* (1889), edited *Troilus and Cressida* for the Globe edition of Chaucer's works (1901), and formulated his theory of English rhythms, based on the continuity of the Old English four-beat line, which, unfortunately, was never published. He also prepared a valuable *Report* for the General Medical Council on preliminary examinations for medical students (1900).

In 1901 McCormick was invited by Andrew Carnegie [q.v.] to become the first secretary of the Trust for the Universities of Scotland which he had endowed with a fund of £2,000,000. This changed the whole course of McCormick's life, for thenceforth he was to become primarily an administrator, although he never lost his interest in literature, especially in Chaucer. In his last years he prepared for the Clarendon Press, on the basis of photostat copies presented to him by the university of Chicago, a critical description of the known MSS. (57 complete and 28 fragmentary) of the *Canterbury Tales*, which shows the nature and order of the contents of each manuscript, with the divisions marked and headings supplied by the scribe, together with all additions, omissions, transpositions, and other structural variants from the text adopted as standard. McCormick was led to undertake this work (published in 1933 as *The MSS. of Chaucer's Canterbury Tales, a critical description*) in preparation for a full critical edition of the *Tales*, by a study of the Pardoner's Tale which he had made in 1900, which was printed but not published.

On his appointment as secretary of the Carnegie Trust, McCormick moved to Edinburgh, where he lived until he came to London in 1920. The new work revealed his administrative ability, and when the liberal government came into power in 1906, (Lord) Haldane, one of the Carnegie trustees, secured McCormick's appointment as a member of the Advisory

Committee set up 'to advise the Treasury as to the distribution of grants in aid of colleges furnishing education of a university standard'. From 1906 onwards McCormick was intimately connected with every important step taken by the government to aid university education. In 1907 he served on the departmental committee on the university of Wales and the Welsh colleges. From 1909 to 1913 he was a member of the royal commission on university education in London. In 1911 the Treasury Advisory Committee was transferred to the Board of Education, and McCormick became its chairman, in which office he was confirmed when it became the Treasury University Grants Committee in 1919. He held this post until his death.

In 1915 McCormick also became chairman of the Advisory Council for Scientific and Industrial Research, at first attached to the Board of Education, but transferred in 1916 to a new Department under the lord president. The experience gained in the European War, and the study made of the universities by McCormick and his committee, had convinced the government that systematic encouragement of scientific research was urgently needed in the national no less than in the industrial interest. McCormick was trusted by the universities, and his chairmanship of the Advisory Council mitigated from the beginning their suspicions of this bold undertaking and soon won their confidence and support. The industrial firms were more difficult to move, but the fund of a million sterling granted by the government, on McCormick's initiative, to the new Department towards the maintenance of co-operative research associations to be established and run by the industries themselves, greatly helped to overcome apathy. When McCormick died fifteen years later, the Department controlled an annual expenditure of over £700,000 upon a series of large national research stations and in support of research conducted in the universities and by industry. The Royal Society in 1928 admitted McCormick to be a fellow as a person who, in the opinion of the council, 'had rendered conspicuous service to the cause of science'.

McCormick was an original trustee of the Carnegie United Kingdom Trust, formed in 1913, and chairman of its music committee, which published Tudor and Elizabethan church music and the work of modern British composers, assisted the musical competition festivals, and helped to save the 'Old Vic' Theatre. As a member of its library committee, he was active in the development of the rural libraries, the formation of the Central Library for Students, now the National Central Library in Malet Place, London, and the School of Librarianship at University College, London. He also became chairman of the British National Opera Company and a member of the committee of management of the 'Old Vic'. He was knighted in 1911 and created G.B.E. in 1929. He died at sea 23 March 1930.

McCormick married in 1897 Mabel Emily, younger daughter of Sir Frederick Lucas Cook, second baronet, head of the firm of Cook, Son & Co., warehousemen, St. Paul's Churchyard, and had one son and two daughters. A vivid portrait by his friend Sir William Orpen hangs in the Tate Gallery.

[*Proceedings* of the Royal Society, vol. cxxxii, A, 1931; private information; personal knowledge.] H. F. Heath.

MACDONALD, Sir JAMES RONALD LESLIE (1862–1927), major-general, the eldest son of Surgeon-Major James Macdonald, M.D., was born 8 February 1862. He was educated at the grammar school and the university of Aberdeen, and proceeded thence to the Royal Military Academy, Woolwich. There he quickly made his mark, and passed out in 1882 well ahead of the rest of his year, having gained many prizes, the Pollock medal, and the sword of merit. In November of the same year he was gazetted, as lieutenant, to the Royal Engineers, and entered upon the two years' course at Chatham. He spent part of his leisure in yachting and racquets, displaying in all that he did an energy and concentration which characterized his subsequent military career.

Macdonald sailed for India in 1884, and after a short period of attachment to the Bengal Sappers and Miners, was posted for duty to the Military Works Department. From 1885 to 1887 he was employed on survey work for the construction of the Harnai Railway in Baluchistan. The Hazara expedition of 1888 gave him his first experience of active service; for his part in it he was mentioned in dispatches and received the India frontier medal with clasp. Two years later he was promoted captain, and carried out the survey for the Kabul River Railway. He was next employed (1891) in the Zhob Valley Railway survey, and later in the same year returned home on leave. Soon after reaching England he was offered and accepted the appointment of chief engineer on the preliminary survey for the projected railway between Mombasa and Lake Victoria Nyanza—the Uganda Railway. He had just completed this long and very arduous survey and was on his way back to the coast when he received urgent orders to return to Uganda, where civil war had broken out. During the next two years Macdonald was successively engaged in quelling a rebellion of Mohammedans, in expeditions by lake against the Wavuma, and in operations in Unyoro, when he acted as chief of staff to (Sir) Henry Edward Colvile [q.v.] during the expedition against King Kabarega, the slave-raider. He was made acting commissioner of the Uganda Protectorate in 1893. The story of these exciting and strenuous years is told by Macdonald in his *Soldiering and Surveying in British East Africa, 1891–1894* (1897). For his services he was rewarded with the brevet of major, and he also received two medals and the brilliant star of Zanzibar, second class.

Resuming duty in the Military Works Department, India, in 1894, Macdonald was attached to the head-quarters staff at Simla. In 1896 he returned to Chatham for the 'refresher' course for Royal Engineers serving in India. In 1897, while (Lord) Kitchener's conquest of the Sudan was in progress, it was decided to dispatch a British exploring expedition, under Macdonald's command, from Mombasa through East Africa to Fashoda. Macdonald landed at Mombasa early in July, but, owing to the mutiny of the Sudanese troops under his command and the revolt of Buganda Mohammedans, was unable to achieve his object. He was engaged for many months in operations against the mutineers and rebels over a very wide stretch of country. He laid siege to Luba's Fort in Usoga (18 October 1897), fought against and defeated King Mwanga in Ankole (19 January 1898), conducted successful operations near Lake Choga (23 January), and fought several other minor engagements which finally freed Uganda of the mutineers and assured the safety of that Protectorate. His expedition returned to the coast in April 1899, and for his valuable services Macdonald was made a C.B. (1900), gazetted brevet lieutenant-colonel, and received a medal with two clasps.

Shortly after the beginning of the South African War (October 1899) Macdonald, now a major in the corps of Engineers, was put in charge of the balloon factory at Aldershot; but on the outbreak of the Boxer rebellion in the summer of 1900, he was sent out to China with a staff appointment as director of balloons. This post, however, provided insufficient scope for one of his experience and ability, and he was shortly given the post of director of railways for the China expeditionary force. His services in China were rewarded by a mention in dispatches, the China medal, and the brevet of colonel. On the disbanding of the China force Macdonald returned to India, where he was employed in military works at Quetta until 1903. In that year the government of India decided to dispatch a political mission to Tibet under (Sir) Francis Younghusband, in order to counter Russian intrigues and to stabilize relations with Tibet by means of a treaty. Lord Kitchener, commander-in-chief in India, selected Macdonald to command the military escort. The party crossed the Jelep pass and entered Tibet on 12 December 1903. The journey was broken by several engagements with the Tibetans, who resisted the advance of the mission during the next four months, especially in the neighbourhood of Gyantse. Gyantse fort itself was the scene of severe encounters and, although it surrendered without resistance on 12 April, the capture was not finally consolidated until 7 July, when the monastery and the rest of Gyantse were secured. The last stage of the march began on 13 July 1904, and on 3 August the mission arrived at Lhasa, where a treaty was duly concluded. For this arduous campaign, Macdonald was awarded the K.C.I.E. and received the medal and clasp of the expedition.

In 1905 Macdonald was promoted colonel and given the command of the presidency brigade at Calcutta, passing on two years later to the command of the Lucknow infantry brigade. In the following year (1908) he was made major-general, and in 1909 was appointed general officer commanding in Mauritius. He held this post until 1912, when under medical advice he resigned and returned to England. He was compelled, owing to failing health, to retire in the following year, and, although he offered his services immediately on the outbreak of the European War in 1914, he was unable to satisfy the medical authorities. Later, he was appointed military member of the Aberdeen District Emergency Committee, and he served on that body with untiring zeal until the end of the War. In 1924 he was appointed colonel commandant of his own corps, the Royal Engineers. He also served as deputy-lieutenant for Aberdeenshire.

Macdonald married in 1894 Alice Margaret, youngest daughter of General George Pringle, Indian Staff Corps. They had no children. He died at Bournemouth 27 June 1927.

[*The Times*, 28 June 1927; *Journal* of the Royal Engineers, September 1927; Official records.] C. V. OWEN.

MACDONELL, ARTHUR ANTHONY (1854–1930), Sanskrit scholar, born 11 May 1854 at Muzaffarpur in Tirhut, North Bihar, India, was the elder son of Colonel Alexander Anthony Macdonell, of the 40th Bengal Native Infantry, by his wife, Margaret Jane Lachlan, of Rum. Sent to England with his mother in 1861, he was placed in a school in Dresden (Neustadt, 1866–1869), where a boyish adventure resulted in a permanent weakness of his lower limbs and led to the stimulation of his intellectual interests. After four years at the Göttingen gymnasium he matriculated (1875) in the university of that city, and under Professor Theodor Benfey began the study of Sanskrit and comparative philology. At Oxford, as an exhibitioner (1876) of Corpus Christi College, he obtained a second class in honour moderations (1878) and a third class in *literae humaniores* (1880). He also won the Taylorian scholarship in German (1876), the Davis Chinese scholarship (1877), and the Boden Sanskrit scholarship (1878), besides rowing in his college eight and taking an active share in the life of the college.

Having worked with Professor Friedrich Max Müller [q.v.], and having been appointed Taylorian lecturer in German (1880) and lecturer in Sanskrit to Indian civil service probationers in Balliol College (1884), Macdonell revisited Germany for the purpose of reading with the distinguished Sanskrit scholar Professor Rudolf von Roth, and graduated Ph.D. of Leipzig University. In 1888 he was appointed deputy to Sir Monier Monier-Williams [q.v.], the Boden professor of Sanskrit at Oxford and keeper of the Indian Institute. Upon that scholar's death in 1899 Macdonell was appointed his successor in both those offices and also in a professorial fellowship at Balliol College. Retiring in 1926, he received the title of emeritus professor, and in 1928 he was elected an honorary fellow of Balliol. His connexion with Corpus Christi College had been restored in 1921 by his election to an honorary fellowship there.

As keeper of the Indian Institute, Macdonell was charged with the general administration, superintendence of the staff, library, and museum, correspondence, and provision for lectures, regular and occasional. With a succession of librarians he interested himself effectually in the development of the library: more occasional, and partly volunteer, assistants attended to the arrangement and classification of the museum, the growth of which was arrested about 1911. He also occupied himself with the administration of the Max Müller memorial fund, which he had raised in 1900, with the object of providing for subventions, acquisitions, and publications.

Outside Oxford, Macdonell was active in various ways. Elected in 1906 a fellow of the British Academy, he represented it from 1911 to 1913 upon a committee of the International Union of Academies which was concerned with promoting a critical edition of the great Sanskrit epic, the *Mahā-Bhārata*: he was a signatory to an appeal for funds, addressed to the princes and nobles of India, and subsequently, by means of an independent appeal in conjunction with a colleague, he elicited contributions amounting to about £1,500. He served on the council of the Royal Asiatic Society, being vice-president 1921–1924. In the quasi-triennial International Congresses of Orientalists Macdonell was usually, from 1881 to 1912, a participant; on the last of these occasions he secured assent for an Oxford congress, which, frustrated in 1915 by the European War, was realized in 1928, when he was no longer able to take an active part in it. Of two visits which he made to India, the first (1907–1908) led to the acquisition by the Bodleian Library of a large collection of Sanskrit manuscripts and produced some hundreds of mainly archaeological photographs, subsequently presented to the Indian Institute; it also inspired some comprehensive views regarding Indian temple architecture and iconic sculpture, which Macdonell expounded in lectures (1909) before the British Academy and the Royal Society of Arts. The second visit (1922–1923) was for the purpose of delivering in the Calcutta University a course of 'Stephanos Nirmalendu' lectures on comparative religion. In 1904 Macdonell represented the

Sanskrit language and literature at a Congress of Arts and Sciences held at St. Louis, Missouri, and in 1912 he visited Canada. His War service (1915–1920) was performed in the Intelligence Department of the Admiralty, for which he compiled three historical memoirs.

Macdonell received various honorary distinctions and degrees, and in 1913 he was chosen by the Bombay branch of the Royal Asiatic Society to receive its Campbell memorial medal, in which connexion he propounded, at a gathering in the rooms of the Society in London, the idea of an institute of research in India on the lines of the British School at Athens.

As a Sanskrit scholar Macdonell worked chiefly in the Vedic field, to which appertain his most important publications, namely his editions of two 'control' texts: *Sarvānukramaṇī* (1886) and *Bṛhad-devatā* (2 vols., 1904), his *Vedic Mythology* (1897), *Vedic Grammar* (1910), *Vedic Index of Names and Subjects* (in collaboration with A. B. Keith, 2 vols., 1912), and one or two of his educational publications. But his *History of Sanskrit Literature* (1900), his *Lectures on Comparative Religion* (1925), and his *India's Past, a study of the Literatures, Languages, Religions, and Antiquities* (1927) contemplated a wider subject and public.

As a young man, Macdonell was distinguished by an abounding vitality, which made his various activities a proverb in Corpus Christi College. His physical defect was not incompatible with prowess as an oarsman: a love of aquatic adventure persisted into middle life and is attested by two published brochures (*Camping Voyages on German Rivers*, 1890, and *Camping Out*, 1892, 1893), while his humour and fondness for jocular anecdote enlivened both his conversation and the earnestness of his teaching. A stroke, following upon the exertions of his second Indian journey, resulted in his retirement (1926) from his professorship and seriously curtailed his powers of work; a second stroke, during the summer of 1930, was a premonition of the end, which came at Oxford on 28 December of that year.

Macdonell married in 1890 Marie Louise, youngest daughter of William Lowson, J.P., D.L., of Balthayock, Perthshire, who survived him with their two daughters. Their only son was killed in the European War in 1915.

[*The Times*, 29 December 1930 and 2 January 1931; *Oxford Mail*, 29 December 1930; *Oxford Magazine*, 29 January 1931; *Proceedings* of the British Academy, vol. xvii, 1931.]

F. W. Thomas.

MacDONNELL, ANTONY PATRICK, Baron MacDonnell, of Swinford (1844–1925), statesman, the eldest son of Mark Garvey MacDonnell, landowner, of Shragh, co. Mayo, by his wife, Bedelia, daughter of Michael O'Hara, of Springtown, co. Roscommon, was born at Shragh 7 March 1844. He was educated at the Roman Catholic College, Summerhill, Athlone, and at Queen's College, Galway, where he won high honours in French and German and, in the words of the most distinguished of his teachers, gave evidence in the college debating society 'of high logical capacity, prompt argumentative resource, and a copious fund of picturesque and impassioned rhetoric'. In 1864 he graduated with honours, winning the Peel gold medal, and in the same year competed successfully for appointment to the Indian civil service. He was posted to Bengal, and passing out after a year's probation, arrived at Calcutta in November 1865. MacDonnell served in the executive line in various districts of Bengal and Bihar, and in Tirhut in 1873–1874 so distinguished himself in famine operations that he was complimented by the lieutenant-governor, Sir Richard Temple [q.v.], and was afterwards placed on special duty in the distressed districts. His book, *Food-Grain Supply and Famine Relief in Bihar and Bengal*, published by the government in 1876, increased his reputation. His health breaking down, he took furlough, and married in 1878 Henrietta, younger daughter of Ewen MacDonell, chief of the Keppoch branch of the clan Macdonald, who helped and supported him throughout all the difficulties and trials of his subsequent career.

After his return to India in 1881 MacDonnell served first as accountant-general and then as revenue secretary to the provincial government at Calcutta. In 1884 he took a prominent part in preparing legislation for the protection of the tenants of Bengal from rack-renting and arbitrary ejectment. The Tenancy Act of 1885, strongly opposed by the landlords, was largely his work. His sympathies throughout his public life were with the peasants who live on and by the land. Agrarian discontent too often provides a fertile field for political agitation; and convinced of this fact, MacDonnell laboured for its removal from Bengal with a zeal and fiery energy which commanded the admiration of the anonymous author of *Letters to Eminent Indians*, published at Calcutta in 1885, who testifies that although his temper was 'very hot', his judgement was always cool. In 1886 Lord Dufferin appointed him home secretary to the central government, and on leaving India in 1888, commended him to Lord Lansdowne as a man 'without reproach, who could safely be conferred with on most delicate questions, and was likely to render invaluable service'. In the same year he had received the C.S.I.

In 1889 MacDonnell was selected to officiate for three months as chief commissioner of Burma, and in 1890 to be chief commissioner of the Central Provinces. While holding this post, he was in 1893 chosen to act for six months as lieutenant-governor of Bengal, and later on was called to a seat on the viceroy's executive council. In a letter to Lady MacDonnell, written after her husband's death more than thirty years later, Lord Lansdowne wrote: 'I look back wistfully to my five years in India, and there is no chapter of my Indian experience to which my thoughts turn with more satisfaction than that which brought me into close relations with your husband. There was no one with whom I liked better to work.' In January 1893 MacDonnell was created K.C.S.I.

In 1895 MacDonnell was nominated by Lord Elgin to be lieutenant-governor of the North-Western Provinces and Oudh, soon afterwards to be known as the United Provinces of Agra and Oudh. His period of administration was marked by severe visitations of plague and famine. At such times the people are prone to blame their rulers, and in particular they regarded with resentful suspicion measures taken to check and combat outbreaks of plague, such as disinfection and evacuation of dwellings. The opportunity was seized by political malcontents; and two British officers in anti-plague operations were murdered at Poona in 1897. Misunderstanding and discontent spread gradually, in the wake of plague, to the United Provinces, and eventually in April 1900 produced serious rioting and murders of policemen at Cawnpore. Times were anxious from the beginning of MacDonnell's administration, for the rains of 1895 had fallen short, and those of 1896 largely failed. Fears of famine were speedily justified. Though new to the people and to their language, and hardly at first appreciating the degree to which conditions differ from those in Bengal, MacDonnell went everywhere, and was over-inclined to gather all authority into his own hands, ignoring the susceptibilities of his commissioners. When he gave his confidence, he was an inspiring and considerate chief. But he was slow to give it; and the younger men were better able than the older to appreciate his indefatigable energy and anxious enthusiasm. His secretaries were driven hard, but appreciated his great ability and knew that he never spared himself. The people respected and feared him. When famine came in November 1896, he took personal charge of relief operations instead of appointing a special commissioner, and travelled indefatigably to all distressed districts. The energy and ability of his famine administration was recognized by his appointment in June 1898 to be G.C.S.I., an honour hitherto unique for a lieutenant-governor while still in office. In March 1898 he refused a pressing invitation from Lord Elgin to take charge of Bengal. The transfer would have meant an extra three years of active service, and for that reason would have been welcome. But partly on account of Lady MacDonnell's indifferent health and partly because of his devotion to the tasks on which he was then engaged, he decided to stay in the United Provinces.

After six months' leave in Europe on medical certificate, MacDonnell began his second term of office, which was prolonged for an additional year on the recommendation of the viceroy, Lord Curzon, and ended in October 1901. He initiated and carried through his legislative council an Agra Tenancy Act, which afforded wider opportunities to cultivators of gaining and keeping occupancy rights, and was therefore vigorously opposed by the landholders. Another measure which provoked passing controversy was a government order permitting the presentation of petitions to the law courts in either the Nagari (Hindi) or the Persian Urdu character and directing that legal summonses and proclamations were to be bilingual. Court officials had henceforth to be able to read and write Hindi as well as Urdu. Until then Urdu alone had been employed for such purposes, a legacy of Moslem supremacy resented by a section of literary Hindus. The innovation was vehemently protested against by Mohammedans, but not for long, as in fact the concession appeased an unreal demand. The point once gained, no one cared to present

Hindi petitions, and the order became a dead letter.

At the beginning of 1901 MacDonnell was requested by the viceroy to undertake the chairmanship of an important famine commission. He consented, refusing an offer of relief from his ordinary responsibilities, and after making a rapid tour with his colleagues through various provinces, produced a report which remains the standard authority on famine prevention and relief. Before MacDonnell resigned office in November 1901 Lord Curzon wrote to him: 'It has been a great pleasure as well as an advantage to me to have had as one of my lieutenants, for nearly three years, an administrator of your unique experience and ability. . . . You are about to leave India with a record unapproached at the present moment, and equal to that of the most illustrious of Indian administrators in the past.' The tribute was not extravagant. Firmly resolved to maintain order, yet sympathetic towards Indian feeling and wishes, MacDonnell's energies had never flagged. An impetuous manner and a quick temper could not conceal his kindness of heart, and his qualities of character and leadership were recognized by all.

In September 1902 after being sworn of the Privy Council, MacDonnell accepted from the secretary of state a nomination to the Council of India, but soon afterwards was called to a new sphere of action. Much to his surprise, he was invited by George Wyndham [q.v.], chief secretary for Ireland in Mr. Balfour's government, to take the place of Sir David Harrel as permanent under-secretary at Dublin Castle. In a letter dated 22 September 1902 MacDonnell set forth the only conditions which, subject to his obligations to the India Office, would induce him to accept the appointment. Although he was an Irishman, a Roman Catholic, and a liberal, and did not see eye to eye with Wyndham on certain matters, there was a substantial measure of agreement between them, and he was greatly attracted by the chance of renewing ties with, and working for, his native Ireland. If appointed, his aims would be the maintenance of order, the solution of the land question on the basis of voluntary sale, the co-ordination, control, and direction of the detached and semi-detached boards into which the government of Ireland was then subdivided, and the promotion of education, economic reform, and administrative conciliation. He would require 'adequate opportunities of influencing the policy and acts of administration'. His best friends warned him that he was deluding himself. He would be abused by Orangemen as a Home Ruler and by Home Rulers as a renegade, and would retire disgusted within a year.

But MacDonnell had made up his mind. If his conditions were agreed to, he would 'try the business'. He had been recommended to Wyndham by Lord Lansdowne; and with the approval of the prime minister, his conditions were enthusiastically accepted. Wyndham considered that Ireland was 'now more plastic than at any time since 1887; many there were growing weary of barren conflict'. King Edward VII, Sir Sidney Lee has said, discovered in MacDonnell an influence for lifting the long-standing Irish quarrel above the bitterness of party warfare. This was indeed MacDonnell's aim; but, as his friends anticipated, his administration was regarded with suspicion by both parties in Ireland. He was able, however, to render valuable service to Wyndham in preparing and shaping the Irish Land Purchase Bill (1903), and on the occasion of the visit of the king and queen to Ireland in July 1903 he received the K.C.V.O. He had been informed by the chief secretary that he was wanted by Lord Curzon for the governorship of Bombay but could not be spared from Ireland. King Edward, too, was 'most earnest and emphatic' on this point and impressed his wishes personally on MacDonnell. So, at a heavy pecuniary sacrifice, MacDonnell stayed. Then the prospect clouded. The assistance which he gave to Lord Dunraven and the Irish Reform Association in preparing as a basis for discussion a scheme of 'devolution' which they had launched, led to a storm of Orange and Unionist protest. The scheme allowed Ireland a semi-elective financial board and a substantial measure of legislative control over her own affairs; and for these reasons was denounced as an insidious breach in the Unionist defences. It was repudiated by Wyndham; and a weak-kneed censure was passed by the Cabinet on MacDonnell. The latter, however, whose action had met with the full approval of the lord-lieutenant, Earl Dudley, and was vigorously defended by Lord Lansdowne in the House of Lords, resigned the lien on the India Council which till then he had retained, and resolutely stayed where he was. He had certainly been given ample grounds for supposing that such action as he had taken would not be considered *ultra vires*. This was the expressed opinion of Wyndham's successor, Mr. (afterwards Viscount) Long.

With the advent of the liberals to power at the close of 1905, James (afterwards Viscount) Bryce [q.v.] became chief secretary for Ireland. The two men became friends for life. A scheme of devolution, prepared by MacDonnell, was approved by Bryce and formed the basis of the Irish Council Bill of 1907. But Bryce was transferred to Washington and was succeeded by Mr. Augustine Birrell, who in April 1907 described Ireland as being 'in a more peaceful condition than it had been in for 600 years'. Then the Council Bill was dropped as unwelcome to the Irish party in parliament. A university measure was indefinitely postponed, and MacDonnell found no support for his policy of firmly repressing the disorder which accompanied a grave recrudescence of cattle-driving agitation. In correspondence with the chief secretary he had expressed his faith in devolution, both administrative and financial, 'as a practical measure of regeneration which need not block the larger issue'. But to fail in stopping disorder could only result in measures which must 'accentuate that antagonistic state of feeling between the two countries which it is the incessant aim of certain agitators to promote'. He resigned office in July 1908 and was raised to the peerage as Baron MacDonnell, of Swinford, a town close to Shragh. In 1907 he had received the honorary degree of D.C.L. from Oxford University. Throughout his tenure of office at Dublin Castle he had retained King Edward's full confidence.

MacDonnell thus passed from public employment, but not from public life. From 1912 to 1914 he served as chairman of a royal commission on the civil service. In 1917 and 1918 he was an influential member of the Irish Convention. On 6 October 1918 he addressed a powerful and closely reasoned confidential letter to Lord French, then lord-lieutenant, on the necessity of abandoning conscription in Ireland. In 1921 he was offered, but refused with deep regret, a seat on the senate of Southern Ireland. He was consulted by Lord Morley [q.v.] on the Indian constitutional reforms of 1909, and by Edwin Montagu [q.v.] on those of 1919. He took exception to the former on two points only which he regarded as concessions tending to weaken executive authority in India. He also desired that the opportunity should be seized for reconsideration of the Partition of Bengal, a measure which he had always regarded with disfavour. He considered Montagu's proposals dangerously crude and hasty, and denounced them vigorously in the House of Lords on 12 December 1919. His interest in Indian and Irish affairs only ceased with his life.

MacDonnell was offered many directorships of companies but accepted only two: those of the Midland Great Western Railway of Ireland, and the National Bank. In 1923 he was offered the chairmanship of the latter and accepted the vice-chairmanship. His assiduity in business and shrewd judgement were highly appreciated by his fellow directors. He died in London after a brief illness 9 June 1925. The strain of his last days was relieved for his family by the attentive sympathy of two of the most distinguished of his old Indian officials.

For the theoretic perfection of political institutions MacDonnell cared little; for the peace and social order which alone can give happiness to the masses he cared a great deal. He pursued his ideals inflexibly. The outlines of his character were firmly drawn. From childhood he was a convinced Roman Catholic. In private life he was generous and hospitable, always welcoming warmly his old lieutenants in India. He possessed an impressive literary style, but wrote two books only, *Food-grain Supply and Famine Relief in Bihar and Bengal* (Calcutta, 1876), already mentioned, and *Agricultural and Administrative Reform in Bengal, by a Bengal Civilian*, published anonymously in 1883.

MacDonnell was survived by his wife and their only surviving child, the Hon. Anne MacDonnell. On his death the barony became extinct. He was of medium height, squarely built, with light hair, a heavy moustache, and a fair complexion. His features were rugged, his eyebrows bushy, and his chin firm. His forehead was fine and massive, his eyes were hazel and his glance penetrating. His expression was keen, masterful, and intellectual. A portrait of MacDonnell by Sir William Orpen is in the Municipal Gallery of Modern Art, Dublin. Another, by H. Harris Brown, was exhibited at the Royal Academy in 1916. A cartoon of him by 'Spy' appeared in *Vanity Fair* 3 August 1905. A statue of MacDonnell by (Sir) George Frampton was erected at Lucknow by the Talukdars of Oudh in 1907.

[*Report of Her Majesty's Civil Service Commissioners for the year 1865*; *History of Gazetted Officers of the United Provinces of Agra and Oudh for the year 1901*; *Report* of the Indian Famine Commission of 1901; *Letters to Eminent Indians by Sadyk Dost* (reprinted from the *Indian Daily News*), Calcutta, 1885; Hansard, *Parliamentary Debates* (*Lords*, 17 February 1905, 4 May 1909, 12 December 1919; *Commons*, 21, 22 February 1905, 9 May 1905); Sir Sidney Lee, *Life of King Edward VII*, vol. ii, 1927; J. W. Mackail and Guy Wyndham, *Life and Letters of George Wyndham*, 1924; H. A. L. Fisher, *James Bryce*, 2 vols., 1927; Lord Newton, *Lord Lansdowne*, 1929; family papers; private information; personal knowledge.] H. V. LOVETT.

McEVOY, ARTHUR AMBROSE (1878–1927), painter, was born in Wiltshire 12 August 1878, the elder son of Captain Charles Ambrose McEvoy, by his wife, Jane Mary. The younger son, Charles, gained some distinction as a playwright. Their father was an Irish-American soldier of fortune, who after serving in the Confederate army in the American civil war, became an authority on submarine warfare, making many successful inventions, including an anti-submarine hydrophone in 1893, and later settled in England. Captain McEvoy was in close touch in London with the painter James McNeill Whistler (one of whose brothers had served with him in the Confederate army), and Whistler joined with him in encouraging Ambrose McEvoy's ambition to become a painter. At the age of fifteen McEvoy entered the Slade School of Fine Art, then under the direction of Professor Frederick Brown; with him, as fellow students, were (Sir) William Orpen and Augustus John. While at the Slade School he worked in the National Gallery, copying one work of each of the painters Titian, Rembrandt, Velasquez, Hogarth, and Gainsborough. He spent sketching holidays in Wales with Augustus John, and in 1909 was at Dieppe with Walter Sickert. By 1912 his painting began to show signs of the broader, looser treatment which was characteristic of his later work.

Beginning as a painter of poetical landscapes and of restful interiors ('The Engraving', 1901, 'The Book', 1903, and 'The Earring', 1911, the last-named being in the Tate Gallery), McEvoy became popular as a portrait-painter after exhibiting 'Madame' (Mrs. A. McEvoy, 1915, now in the Musée du Luxembourg, Paris) and 'Mrs. Walter Russell' (1916). In obtaining the flower-like fragrance, the freshness, and the dewy quality which are characteristic of his work, McEvoy was prepared to sacrifice detail, but he never lost the underlying sense of form. His delicate and fluttering brush-work, his experiments in colour, tone, and surface quality, his preoccupation with lighting effects, his device of using mixed daylight and artificial lighting thrown up from below, all give strong individuality to every portrait, although the likeness may be more spiritual than actual. In his use of water-colour, a medium which made a distinct appeal to the emotional side of his nature, he would draw and paint solidly, then put his picture under running water, then scrub and scrape, adding accents in chalk or ink, and floating on colours which fused into delicate opalescent harmonies.

During the European War McEvoy was attached to the Royal Naval Division, spent three months on the Western front, and later was with the fleet in the North Sea. This accounts for a series of portraits, now in the Imperial War Museum at South Kensington, of which 'Lieutenant R. D. Sandford, R.N., V.C.' is a notable example. That he could render masculine qualities successfully is shown also in his striking studies of Lord D'Abernon (1916), Claude Johnson (1917), and Augustine Birrell (1918). But it is his subjective treatment of women's portraits which gives McEvoy a unique place among contemporary English portrait-painters. Further notable examples are 'The Artist's Mother' (1915), 'Silver and Grey' (Mrs. Charles McEvoy, 1915), 'Consuelo, Duchess of Marlborough' (1916), 'Blue and Gold' (Mrs. Claude Johnson, 1916), 'Mrs. Walter Rosen' (1921), 'The Viscountess Henri de Janzé' (1926), and 'Anna' (his daughter, 1926), the last picture he painted.

McEvoy was a member of the New English Art Club and of the International Society of Painters; he was elected A.R.A. in 1924, a member of the Royal Society of Portrait Painters in 1924, and an associate of the Royal Society of Painters in Water-Colours in 1926. Examples of his work are to be found in the Tate Gallery, British Museum, and Victoria and Albert Museum, and in the public galleries at Manchester, Dublin, Cork, Belfast, Ottawa, Johannesburg, and Pittsburg, as well as in the Musée du Luxembourg. An exhibition of his water-colours was held at the Leicester Galleries in 1927 and memorial exhibitions of his oils and water-colours took place at the Royal Academy Winter Exhibition in 1928, and at Manchester in 1933.

McEvoy married in 1902 Mary, daughter of Colonel Spencer Edwards, of Abbotsleigh, Freshford, Bath, by whom he had a son and a daughter. From 1906 until his death he lived at 107 Grosvenor Road, on the Embankment. He died of pneumonia, after a week's illness, at a nursing-home in London 4 January 1927, and his ashes are buried in the wall of All Saints' church, Grosvenor Road.

A self-portrait in oil of McEvoy, from the Claude Johnson collection, is owned by Mrs. Archibald Douglas, and an earlier self-portrait in pencil belongs to his widow.

[*The Times*, 5 January 1927; *The Year's Art*, 1928; *Ambrose McEvoy Exhibition*, Duveen Galleries, New York (with an introduction by Christian Brinton), 1920; *The Works of Ambrose McEvoy, 1900–1919* (privately printed for Claude Johnson, 163 illustrations, 16 copies), 1919; R. M. Y. Gleadowe, *Ambrose McEvoy*, 1924; *Old Water-Colour Society's Club*, 7th annual volume, 1929–1930; catalogues of exhibitions mentioned above; private information.] M. Hardie.

MACEWEN, Sir WILLIAM (1848–1924), surgeon, was born at Rothesay, Isle of Bute, Scotland, 22 June 1848, the youngest son of John Macewen, marine trader, of Bute, by his wife, Janet Stevenson. John Macewen gave his children such education as was then available in Rothesay. In 1865, at the age of seventeen, William Macewen, after having attended the Collegiate School in Glasgow for a brief period, entered the university of Glasgow as a student of medicine. He obtained the degree M.B., C.M., in 1869, at the early age of twenty-one. He had grown into a man of very fine physique—tall, well-proportioned, with clearly chiselled features and deep-set grey eyes, the characteristics of a stock which is found in the Western Highlands of Scotland. In his student days he was noted for his athletic attainments and gave no apparent promise of the great originality which he was afterwards to manifest. He came, however, under the influence of (Lord) Lister [q.v.], then regius professor of surgery in the university.

In the year in which Macewen began his medical studies Lister first applied his antiseptic method to the treatment of wounds in the wards of the Old Royal Infirmary of Glasgow, and in due time Macewen became a leading exponent of Listerism. When Macewen graduated in 1869 Lister succeeded James Syme [q.v.] as professor of clinical surgery in the university of Edinburgh, his post in Glasgow being filled by his pupil (Sir) George H. B. Macleod [q.v.]. Macewen became house-surgeon to Macleod in the Old Infirmary, and twenty-two years later (1892) succeeded him as regius professor of surgery in the university and surgeon to the Royal Infirmary. On his appointment to the chair of surgery, he had to transfer his surgical activities from the Royal to the Western Infirmary. He retained his chair and surgeoncy until his death, which took place at Glasgow, 22 March 1924. Although then in his seventy-sixth year, he was still erect in carriage and vigorous in mind and body.

Macewen's surgical career began in 1875 when he was appointed assistant surgeon to the Royal Infirmary at Glasgow, becoming a full surgeon in 1877. In the years which elapsed before his appointment to the Royal Infirmary he had taken the degree of M.D. (1872), held several appointments, including the superintendentship of a fever hospital (Belvidere), and had built up a nucleus of private practice. On his appointment to the Infirmary he devoted himself solely to surgery. By his thirtieth year he had made important advances in two branches of surgery—brain surgery and bone surgery. He was the first deliberately to operate for the relief of brain disorders. In 1876 he diagnosed the presence of an abscess in the frontal lobe of a boy, but was not permitted to operate; after the boy's death his diagnosis was found to be correct and an operation might have saved the lad's life. In 1878 he removed a tumour from the brain; in 1879 he operated for the relief of subdural haemorrhage. He thus laid the basis of modern brain surgery. His next great advance was the result of his recognition that disease of the middle ear was the commonest cause of abscess of the brain. He introduced and perfected the methods of operating on cases of mastoid disease. His experience of this branch of surgery is summarized in *Pyogenic Infective Disease of the Brain and Spinal Cord* (1893) and the anatomical basis of his surgical procedure in an *Atlas of Head Sections* (1893).

Macewen was also a pioneer in bone surgery. He looked upon bone as a living tissue, and introduced the method of implanting small grafts to replace missing parts of limb-bones. In 1880 he sowed such grafts in the arm of a lad to replace the shaft of the humerus which had been destroyed by disease. The operation was successful, and the lad regained a useful arm. In 1877 he introduced a new method of rectifying knock-knee by cutting through the thigh-bone just above the knee by a subcutaneous operation—a practice which has been followed by surgeons in all lands. Macewen became interested in the biology of bone and carried out a long and critical series of experiments on animals in order to determine the manner in which bones grow and the conditions underlying their repair. He came to the conclusion that the membrane which covers bone (periosteum) cannot produce bone. He published an account of his inquiries in *The Growth of Bone* (1912), reserving his observations on the natural history of bone for *The Growth and Shedding of the Antler of the Deer* which appeared in 1921.

These are the chief contributions which Macewen made to surgery, but there are also many minor improvements which stand to his credit. He was a pioneer in opening up the chest to surgical procedure. He proved that the fear of the human lung collapsing when the chest is opened was groundless, and he successfully resected the entire lung. He was one of the first to 'intubate' the larynx in order to keep the airway open instead of resorting to tracheotomy. He introduced and perfected a method of operating for the radical cure of inguinal hernia. He invented his own surgical tools and made his own catgut.

Macewen was a man of independent outlook, paying little attention to books or to accepted opinions. His teaching and practice were based on his own experience and on observations made by his own eyes. His personality was forceful and masterful; he pursued his career with fiery zeal and resolution. On Lord Lister's death in 1912 he became in the eyes of his fellows the leader amongst British surgeons. Glasgow University conferred on him the degree of LL.D. in 1890; he was elected a fellow of the Royal Society in 1895, and was made an honorary fellow of the Royal College of Surgeons of England in 1900. The universities of Oxford, Dublin, Liverpool, and Durham conferred honorary degrees on him; he received recognition from the leading surgical societies and academies of France, Italy, Germany, Russia, Hungary, and America. He was knighted in 1902. He rendered many public services, being consulting surgeon for naval forces in Scotland during the European War and training a band of pattern-makers to become expert in the difficult art of fashioning artificial limbs for disabled men.

Macewen married in 1873 Mary Watson, daughter of Hugh Allen, of Crosshill, Glasgow, and had three sons and three daughters.

[*Proceedings* of the Royal Society, vol. xcvi, B, 1924; *British Medical Journal*, 1924, vol. i, p. 603; *Lancet*, 1924, vol. i, p. 676; *Nature*, 26 April 1924; *Glasgow Medical Journal*, April 1924. Portrait, *Royal Academy Pictures*, 1901.]

A. Keith.

McGRATH, Sir PATRICK THOMAS (1868–1929), statesman and journalist, was born at St. John's, Newfoundland, 16 December 1868, the eldest son of William McGrath by his wife, Mary Bermingham. He was educated at the Christian Brothers Schools in St. John's, which he left at the age of fourteen. For seven years he was employed in a chemist's shop in St. John's; and when failing health made an outdoor occupation necessary, he joined the reporting staff of the Newfoundland *Evening Herald*. Thenceforth McGrath's career developed along two parallel lines, the one journalistic, the other political. In 1893 he became acting-editor of the *Evening Herald*, and from 1894 to 1907 he was its editor. He then established a journal called the *Evening Chronicle*, and in 1912, when the *Chronicle* and *Herald* were combined, he became the president of the newly formed company. From 1894 until his death he was Newfoundland correspondent for *The Times*, and he wrote extensively for British and American periodicals.

From 1897 to 1900 McGrath was assistant clerk in the Newfoundland House of Assembly, and from 1900 to 1911 chief clerk. In 1912 he retired in order to become a member of the Legislative Council, of which he was president from 1915 to 1919 and from 1925 until his death. At the Anglo-American conference held at Quebec in 1898 he acted as private secretary to Sir James Spearman Winter [q.v.], the premier of Newfoundland. McGrath assisted in preparing Newfoundland's case in the various fishery disputes with the United States and France; and he was Newfoundland's agent in the dispute with Canada over the boundary of Labrador, which was tried before the Privy Council in 1926–1927 and resulted in a decisive victory for Newfoundland. In 1914 he acted as secretary for Newfoundland in connexion with the visit of the Dominions royal commission to the colony. During the European War he acted as honorary secretary of the Newfoundland Patriotic Fund, the Newfoundland Regiment Finance Committee, and the Newfoundland War Pensions Board, which he organized. In 1917 he was made chairman of the Cost-of-Living Commission.

In addition to many pamphlets on Newfoundland, McGrath wrote *From Ocean to Ocean, an account of a trip across Canada in 1911* (1911) and *Newfoundland in 1911* (a history and guide-book of the colony, 1911); he also contributed chapters on Newfoundland to the volume on *British America* (1923) in the 'Nations of To-day' series edited by John Buchan, and to Volume II of Sir Charles Lucas's *The Empire at War* (1923).

McGrath was created K.B.E. in 1918. He died, unmarried, at St. John's, Newfoundland, 14 June 1929. In spite of defects in his early education, he was both a reader and a thinker. He was a man of infinite humour, full of good stories, and to the last had a touch of the Irish gamin. More than once he won an election by his shrewd and biting tongue and pen, but neither in victory nor in defeat did he bear malice.

[*The Times*, 15 June 1929; *Who's Who in Newfoundland*; private information.]

W. L. Grant.

MacGREGOR, Sir EVAN (1842–1926), civil servant, was born 31 March 1842 at Fernie Castle, Fife, the third son of Sir John Atholl Bannatyne Murray MacGregor, third baronet, of Lanrick and Balquhidder, and great grandson of Lieutenant-General Sir John Murray MacGregor (1745–1822). The clan MacGregor had been under a ban during the greater part of the seventeenth and eighteenth centuries, and the use of the name was forbidden by penal statutes, repealed in 1661 and reimposed in 1693. When the penal Acts were finally repealed in 1774, the members of the clan acknowledged General John Murray as their chief, and he was created a baronet in 1795, resuming the name of MacGregor in 1822.

When Evan MacGregor was nine years old his father died at Tortola in the West Indies, as lieutenant-governor of the Virgin Islands. His mother, who was Mary Charlotte, youngest daughter and co-heir of Admiral Sir Thomas Masterman Hardy, first baronet [q.v.], who commanded the *Victory* at Trafalgar, was given by Queen Victoria a residence at Hampton Court, and went to live there with her young family and her twice-widowed mother. MacGregor was sent to Mr. Walton's school at Hampton, and afterwards as a boarder to the Charterhouse, then in the City. In August 1860 his father's first cousin, Captain the Hon. James Drummond, R.N., procured for him a nomination from the Duke of Somerset (then first lord) to a temporary clerkship in the Admiralty.

MacGregor entered the Admiralty service thoroughly imbued with the traditions of the royal navy. Captain Drummond himself joined the board of Admiralty as junior naval lord in June 1861, and in the following year appointed his young cousin as his private secretary. On Drummond going to sea in 1866 Lord John Hay and Sir John Dalrymple Hay, who in succession filled the post of junior naval lord within a few months, both appointed MacGregor as their private secretary. In January 1869 he became private secretary to the senior naval lord, Admiral Sir Sidney Dacres. During the next ten years he continued as private secretary to successive senior naval lords, Sir Sidney Dacres, Sir Alexander Milne, Sir Hastings Yelverton, and Sir George Wellesley. In the meantime, he had been advanced through the various ranks of the department until, in January 1880, he was promoted to be principal clerk in the secretariat and was appointed head of the military branch which dealt with fleet operations and political work, and came directly under the supervision of the senior naval lord. Having reached this important position at the early age of thirty-seven, MacGregor soon had opportunity of proving his merit.

In 1880 a combined naval demonstration by the principal naval powers, under the command of the English admiral, Sir Beauchamp Seymour, was undertaken off the coast of Albania in order to compel the Porte to surrender Dulcigno to Montenegro, in accordance with the terms of the Treaty of Berlin. At the end of the year the Boer War broke out, and naval assistance was rendered by the landing at Durban of a naval brigade which served throughout the War. In 1882 the Egyptian War began, and the Admiralty was closely occupied with the naval operations involved by the bombardment of Alexandria, the subsequent landing of a naval brigade, and the steamboat work up the Nile. The head-quarters' administration of all this business under the direction of the board fell upon MacGregor's branch, and his energy and efficiency was rewarded by the grant of the C.B. in 1882.

In 1877 the ancient office of permanent secretary of the Admiralty, which had been held continuously by civilians since Samuel Pepys was first appointed to it in 1673, was abolished by Mr. W. H. Smith, and a naval secretary took over the duties. This office was in turn abolished in May 1882 by Lord Northbrook, and (Sir) Robert Hamilton, accountant-general of the navy, was appointed permanent secretary. But almost immediately Hamilton was lent to the Irish government as permanent under-secretary, after the murder of Mr. T. H. Burke, and Captain (afterwards Admiral Sir) George Tryon was appointed to act during his absence. Hamilton never returned to the Admiralty, and Captain Tryon resigned in order to go to sea in 1884. Lord Northbrook then chose MacGregor to fill the post of permanent secretary, and he held the office for twenty-three years, with Lords Northbrook, Ripon, George Hamilton, Spencer, Goschen, Selborne, Cawdor, and Tweedmouth as his Cabinet chiefs.

The period 1884 to 1907 was one of immense development both in the fleet itself and in the administration of the navy. Under the Naval Defence Act (1889) of Lord George Hamilton [q.v.] the navy was almost entirely rebuilt, and under the Naval Works Acts from 1895 onwards new harbours, barracks, and dockyards were constructed all over the world; while before MacGregor retired, the reforms in naval education and training and in the distribution and organization of the fleet, promoted by Lord Fisher [q.v.], had been carried through, and the construction of the new great fleet, which was to determine the issue of the European War, had begun.

MacGregor saw great changes during his career both in the navy and in the Admiralty. When he joined the office, all the members of the board occupied residences in the Whitehall building, which also housed a total staff of 124, and the navy estimates amounted to £12,800,000; nearly a third of the ships afloat were still sailing-ships. When he retired the navy estimates had reached nearly £32,000,000, and the departmental staff under his control in Whitehall had grown to 1,089, and great new buildings had been constructed to house them, partly owing to the transfer of the subordinate navy departments from Somerset House.

MacGregor's early training and associations made him a faithful guardian of the interests of the naval service and a promoter of the policy of the sea lords with whom he served; he had little experience of, or interest in, finance or the civil side of his office, which he was content to leave in the hands of trusted colleagues and subordinates. He could not, in consequence, fill the role of close personal adviser to the Cabinet minister at the head of the department, which is usually the function of a permanent secretary in the public service; but his retentive memory and previous experience made him an invaluable ally, especially of the first sea lords who wished to introduce any new line of policy. He had the faculty of clear and incisive writing, and his letters and minutes were models of official correspondence. Endowed with a power of concentration on the business before him, he set to his rapidly growing staff an example of punctuality and thoroughness in the dispatch of official work and of single-minded devotion to the service. He was impartial in his own decisions and loyally accepted any overruling of his advice by superior authority. He neither was, nor wished to be the initiator of important reforms, but his shrewd counsel and loyal assistance were of the greatest advantage to successive naval administrators with whom he served.

MacGregor was promoted K.C.B. in 1892 and G.C.B. in 1906, and was one of the first to receive the Imperial Service Order when it was created in 1903. He married in 1884 Annie Louise (died 1922), daughter of Colonel William Alexander Middleton, C.B., and had one daughter.

Personally, MacGregor had an intense dislike of publicity and inherited the Scottish reserve, but he was devoted to his family and genial to friends of whatever rank of life. In his early days at Hampton Court rowing was his chief recreation, and he made many canoeing trips on the rivers of Central Europe, and even to the Norwegian fjords, where in later years he went annually for salmon fishing.

[*The Times*, 23 March 1926; Admiralty records; private information; personal knowledge.] V. W. Baddeley.

MACKAY, MARY (1855–1924), novelist, known as Marie Corelli, was born in Gloucester Terrace, Bayswater, the only child of Charles Mackay, LL.D. [q.v.], by Mary Ellen Mills, who became his second wife. While she was still a child, her parents moved from London to Fern Dell, a house under Box Hill, Surrey, with a garden abutting on that of Flint Cottage, recently acquired by George Meredith. Charles Mackay became friendly with Meredith, who took an interest in Mary Mackay, particularly encouraging her to persevere with her piano-playing, for which she showed a precocious talent. In 1876 Mrs. Mackay died, and to the household at Fern Dell was added Miss Bertha Vyver, a contemporary of Mary's and her friend since childhood. From that time onward these two were never separated. In 1883, for reasons of health, Charles Mackay left Box Hill and returned to London, taking a lease of 47 Longridge Road, Kensington.

Mary Mackay's pseudonym 'Marie Corelli' had been devised during the last years at Fern Dell for use in the musical career which she had planned for herself. She sang, and played both harp and mandolin, but her taste and gifts were for the piano, on which she came to improvise with a brilliance which astonished her hearers. The move to London suggested a beginning of professional activity, and in December 1884 she gave a successful concert of improvisations at a friend's house. This concert was followed by other public appearances; but for various reasons she did not pursue professional piano-playing, and in *Temple Bar* for July 1885 appeared her first published article. It was called 'One of the World's Wonders' and was signed 'Marie Corelli'. In February 1886 her first novel, *The Romance of Two Worlds*, was issued by the firm of Bentley.

Writing many years later [prologue to *The Life Everlasting*, 1911] of her debut as a novelist, Marie Corelli declared that 'it was solely on account of a strange psychical experience which chanced to myself when I stood upon the threshold of what is called "life" that I found myself producing my first book. . . . It was a rash experiment, but it was the direct result of an initiation into some few of the truths behind the veil of the Seeming Real. I did not then know why I was selected for such an initiation—and I do not know even now. . . . I was not compelled or persuaded into it, for being alone in the world and more or less friendless, I had no opportunity to seek advice or assistance . . .' This extract is typical of Marie Corelli's inveterate tendency to dramatize her own life, personality, and achievement. She was, in fact, thirty years of age when she wrote her first novel; was living with her father, her half-brother, Eric Mackay, and Miss Vyver; and had numerous friends on every side.

Neither her first book nor her second (*Vendetta*, 1886) made much impression on the public, but with her third novel, *Thelma*, published in 1887, Marie Corelli made a mark. The story's rather naïve romanticism, its delineation of smart society, and the overwhelming rhetoric of its description of the 'land of the midnight sun', attracted wide, if uncritical, attention. In 1889 came *Ardath: The Story of a Dead Self*, which enchanted Mr. Gladstone, but left the public cold. *Wormwood* (1890), with its lurid picture of absinthe-sodden Paris, was more generally acceptable, although neither it, nor *The Soul of Lilith* (1892), nor an anonymous novel *The Silver Domino*, seemed to foretell the imminent emergence of a novelist destined to outsell all her competitors. But in 1893 came a book which for the first time achieved a popularity of inescapable significance. *Barabbas: A Dream of the World's Tragedy* seemed to the author's former publishers an over-daring treatment of the story of the Crucifixion; but the book was accepted by the comparatively new firm founded by (Sir) Algernon Methuen [q.v.], and its reception proved that Marie Corelli, if not a better judge of mass-taste in fiction than Messrs. Bentley, was instinctively more in sympathy with it. *Barabbas*, with its gorgeous scene-painting and its fervent religiosity, thrilled a vast public from the Prince of Wales downwards.

The popularity of *Barabbas* was, however, a mere desultory shouting beside the hysterical triumph of its successor, *The Sorrows of Satan* (1895). Everything conspired to give this book an immediate sale greater than that of any previous English novel. The story was at once topical, daring, and transcendental; it lashed the vices of the rich, while describing their manner of life in savoury detail; and it dealt melodramatically with a semi-sacred theme. Nevertheless, it may be doubted if *The Sorrows of Satan* would have attained a popularity which broke all records, but for the accident of its date in publishing history. It was among the early books of fiction which appeared in a single six-shilling volume, and in consequence benefited to an incalculable degree from public excitement over the collapse of the three-decker.

The appearance of *The Sorrows of Satan*

was in more than one respect the climax of Marie Corelli's career. It established her in the position she was to hold for a dozen years—that of the most popular novelist in Great Britain. Secondly, it marked her determination to flout the literary critics, who had been increasingly hostile toward her, and in their reviews of *Barabbas* had frankly expressed their low opinion of her literary quality. Their words shocked Marie Corelli rather than hurt her. She regarded hostile criticism of work which she genuinely believed to be inspired as a kind of blasphemy. Wherefore, when *The Sorrows of Satan* was published she caused to be printed at the head of the first chapter a statement that no copies had been or would be sent for review. The third element in *The Sorrows of Satan* which made the book a landmark in its author's life, related to this inward conviction of her own authority and message. An important part in the story is played by a woman writer, 'Mavis Clare', whose wonderful doings and serene spiritual personality are the chief opponents of the devil on earth. When, the very next year (1896), Marie Corelli in her new novel, *The Murder of Delicia*, created an almost similar character, whispers became open mockery, and she was accused of a vanity so irrational that it permitted her to describe herself in terms more divine than human. She indignantly denied the charge; and the denial, coming from one with her strange power of self-deception, was doubtless sincere. But, although she may not have known it, both 'Mavis Clare' and 'Delicia' were expressions of the ideal of womanly nobility to which she believed herself to have attained.

In 1901 Marie Corelli settled in Stratford-on-Avon, in which town she was to spend the rest of her life and a great deal of her now abundant wealth. Adoration of Shakespeare and a somewhat obstinate idealization of the antique for its own sake brought her into frequent conflict with the powers and personalities of the place. A little unwisely she counter-attacked in *God's Good Man* (1904), which was her only full-dress *roman-à-clé*. The book did not silence her local opponents, but merely blended anger with their ridicule. But her services to Stratford were undoubted. She was generous in her benefactions and, within the limits of her own taste, saved the town from reckless 'modernization' at a period when modernization was most disastrous.

When the European War began, Marie Corelli threw herself into patriotic activity of a characteristically confused and emotional kind. Her warm-heartedness moved her to deep and practical sympathy towards soldiers and their dependants; her love of an attitude tempted her to speech and writing which suggested a collaboration between Niobe and Britannia. Nevertheless, and cruelly enough, her local enemies caused her to be prosecuted in 1917 for food hoarding; and although she protested that her heavy sugar purchases were for jam-making and the jam destined for public consumption, she was convicted. She told her story in *My Little Bit* (1919), and one cannot doubt that her intentions had been above reproach.

Already before the War Marie Corelli had begun to lose her hold on the public. She continued to write, but sales steadily decreased. When, on 21 April 1924, she died at her home in Stratford, the public merely noted that a once popular novelist was dead.

The tragedy of Marie Corelli was her inability to understand either why she was popular or why she was unpopular. A warm-hearted, high-principled, and industrious woman, she thought herself a chosen vessel; a woman of talent, she thought herself a genius. Her great popularity, which she accepted as the inevitable tribute to her gifts and inspiration, was in fact due to her complete conformity to the middle-class type of her day. The hostility shown towards her in other quarters was the natural mixture of scorn and irritation provoked in critical minds by what seemed to be the pretentious mannerisms and autocratic ways of a woman fundamentally commonplace. Both as an individual and as a writer she was the victim of her own incompetence for self-criticism. Essentially emotional, but without the mental capacity to control emotion or test the suitability of its expression, she could only appreciate the excellence of her own motives, and was incapable of realizing that to others her fervour might seem either exhibitionist or ridiculous. For a time her sincerity, her aggressive morality, and her lavish use of scientific, philosophical, and religious jargon hypnotized the pre-War bourgeoisie, whose prejudices, sentimentalities, gentilities, and muddled well-meaning she so thoroughly shared. But as a new generation grew to maturity, with bigotries and sham refinements of its own, the work of Marie Corelli lost most of its meaning and therefore its lure. For it had little intrinsic quality, but merely voiced the mass-sentiment of a particular class at a particular period.

Marie Corelli's principal works, in addition to those already mentioned, are: *The Mighty Atom* (1896), *Boy* (1900), *The Master Christian* (1900), *Temporal Power* (1902), *The Treasure of Heaven* (1906), *Holy Orders* (1908), *The Secret Power* (1921).

[Bertha Vyver, *Memoirs of Marie Corelli*, 1930; private information.] M. SADLEIR.

McKECHNIE, WILLIAM SHARP (1863–1930), constitutional historian, was born at Paisley 2 September 1863, the third and youngest son of William McKechnie, M.D., of Paisley, by his wife, Helen Landale Balfour. He was educated at Greenock Academy, and at the age of sixteen entered the university of Glasgow, where he graduated M.A. in 1883 with first-class honours in philosophy. Destined for the legal profession, he served his apprenticeship at Glasgow in the office of Sir James Roberton, whom he ultimately succeeded in the chair of conveyancing at Glasgow University. After being first prizeman in the classes of constitutional law, public law, and conveyancing, he proceeded in 1887 to the degree of LL.B. Forgoing his original intention of being called to the Scottish bar, he set up in business in Glasgow with a friend as solicitors under the name of McKechnie and Gray, a partnership which lasted from 1890 to 1915.

McKechnie's interests, however, were definitely academic, and his opportunity of satisfying them came in 1894, when he was appointed lecturer in constitutional law and history at Glasgow University. His students were drawn from the two faculties of law and arts. He gave far more than the allotted number of lectures in his ordinary course, and made possible the establishment of an honours group in history by voluntarily offering an honours course in his own subject. The only chair in constitutional law in Scotland is in Edinburgh University, and when that became vacant in 1909, McKechnie submitted his name. But the wide reputation which he had gained by this time from his published work did not avail to break the monopoly in an office hitherto reserved for members of the faculty of advocates.

In 1916 the chair of conveyancing in his own university fell vacant, and McKechnie was persuaded to stand for it. His election meant the abandonment of the work with which he had especially identified his name, although he never gave up the hope of returning to it after retirement. A considerable part of the duty of his chair was that of acting as a kind of official referee in cases of disputed interpretations of deeds of conveyancing. McKechnie's lectures were prepared with a care similar to that which he had lavished on his course in constitutional history. But he had never built up a large practice nor specialized in the intricacies of the Scottish land law, and his anxious nature suffered under the strain. He fell into ill-health and resigned the chair in 1927. On his retirement the university conferred on him the degree of LL.D. He had already moved from Elderslie, where he had resided since 1879, into the neighbourhood of the university in Glasgow, and there he died 2 July 1930. He was buried in Woodside cemetery, Paisley.

McKechnie was modest and retiring by nature, and although a man of decided opinions, never made himself prominent in public life. He was in frequent correspondence with scholars in his own subject at home and abroad, but felt most at home in a small circle of intimate friends. He married in 1894 Elizabeth Cochrane, daughter of John Malloch, J.P., of Elderslie, and they had one son and one daughter.

McKechnie's published work falls into three categories. As a student of political philosophy his earliest book on *The State and the Individual*, written as a thesis for the degree of doctor of philosophy which was conferred on him in 1895, was published in 1896 and was very favourably received. In 1906 he made another excursion into the same domain with an article on George Buchanan's tractate *De Jure Regni*, contributed to *George Buchanan: Glasgow Quatercentenary Studies*. Holding strong political views, he felt that an historian of the British constitution should express an opinion on the important constitutional question at issue in 1908–1909. A series of articles contributed to the *Glasgow Herald* (there was a later series in the *Morning Post*) appeared in book form in 1909, entitled *The Reform of the House of Lords*. It was admitted even by opponents of his views to be 'an informing and suggestive little book'. In 1912 his alarm at the alteration in the balance of the British constitution wrought by the measures of the liberal party, wrung from him a confession of political faith in a book entitled *The New Democracy and the Constitution.* His work as a constitutional historian is represented by his great volume on *Magna Carta,* which appeared in 1905 and was greeted both at home and abroad with almost universal praise. It represents the reaction from Bishop Stubbs's view that 'the Great Charter is the first public act of the nation, after it has realized its own identity'. To McKechnie the Charter is, rather, a feudal document only accidentally serving the interests of others than the baronial class. Its fame rests on sentiment, on what later generations read into it. The most serious criticism of the book pointed to its neglect of some important work of foreign writers on the period. This and other defects were rectified in the second edition issued in 1914, in which, without any change in the main thesis, the book was subjected to a thorough revision. The most emphatic tribute to its merits was the invitation to the author from the Royal Historical Society to deliver the introductory lecture at the commemoration in 1915 of the seven hundredth anniversary of the grant of the Charter.

[*The Times,* 5 July 1930; private information; personal knowledge.] D. J. MEDLEY.

MACKENZIE, SIR JAMES (1853–1925), physician and clinical researcher, was the second son of Robert Mackenzie by his wife, Jean Campbell Menzies. He was born at his father's farm of Pickstonhill at Scone, Perthshire, 12 April 1853. Educated at Perth Academy and at the university of Edinburgh, he graduated in 1878 and became doctor of medicine in 1882. In 1879 he settled in general practice at Burnley, Lancashire, and was appointed physician to the Victoria Hospital. At Burnley he married in 1887 Frances Bellamy, daughter of George Jackson, of Boston, Lincolnshire, by whom he had two daughters. While at Burnley he began the patient and exhaustive clinical studies which were to be continued fruitfully until his death. In 1907 he moved to London and entered consulting practice in which he won unusual success. He became consulting physician to the London Hospital (1913), was elected a fellow of the Royal Society (1915), was knighted (1915), and received many other honours.

During the European War Mackenzie acted as consulting physician to the Military Heart Hospital, an institution formed chiefly at his suggestion. In 1918 he moved to St. Andrews, there to found a clinical institute in which the development of disease was to be studied; but he was already in ill-health, and the cold of the North drove him back to London after a few years and before his self-appointed task was done.

Mackenzie's earliest work was upon herpes zoster (shingles); he made use of the phenomena displayed by this disease to map out areas of the skin supplied by the spinal nerves. Out of these observations in large part grew his later observations upon *pain* and *tenderness,* and upon symptoms viewed more generally; these were collected and published in a monograph of remarkable originality, *Symptoms and their Interpretation* (1909, 3rd ed. 1918). From the same basal observations were developed his studies and views of angina pectoris, published in a book of that title in 1923. He is best known, however, for his long-continued researches into the nature of irregularities of the heart's rhythm; for these studies first aroused widespread interest in the man and his work. He graphically recorded the movements of the jugular veins and used these records in conjunction with others in an elaborate and acute analysis of the movements of the heart's separate chambers. His 'polygraph', an instrument devised to take his records, was invented with the aid of a Lancashire watchmaker. His book *The Study of the Pulse* (1902), in which the earlier observations were collected, gave the impetus to much work of the same kind by others. The fuller studies of the pulsations, his rich experiences of cardiovascular disease from other points of view, and the general philosophy underlying his work, were displayed in *Diseases of the Heart* (1908), a book which quickly ran through several editions, and which, like *Symptoms and their Interpretation,* was translated into several languages. Mackenzie provided striking examples of exact observation upon patients and of simple and accurate deductions from these. He was intensely interested in the mechanism of disease and of the symptoms displayed by disease. He did more, perhaps, than any other man before him to place upon a rational basis forecasts of the course of heart disease in individual patients, and the treatment of heart disease by digitalis.

Mackenzie's vigorous and impressive personality, blunt but enlivening humour, combative form of argumentation, and clear vision of essentials, combined to make him a teacher of great stimulating power. An uncommon faculty of criticism, a deep-rooted distrust of authoritative statement, gave him rare discrimination between the known and the unknown; this, associated in unusual degree with originality of mind, a retentive memory, and determined purpose, underlay his success as an investigator. A true appreciation of his character and of his work can be obtained only if it is remembered that his chief discoveries were made in time snatched during the routine of a heavy industrial practice, and that during the last fifteen years of his life he suffered much from the malady angina pectoris, which he had done so much to elucidate, and from which he eventually died in London, 26 January 1925, in his seventy-second year.

[*Heart*, vol. xii, 1925–1926 (portrait); personal knowledge.] T. Lewis.

MACKENZIE, Sir WILLIAM (1849–1923), Canadian financier and railway builder, was born in Kirkfield, Upper Canada (now Ontario) 30 October 1849, the fifth son of John Mackenzie, farmer, by his wife, Mary, daughter of John Maclaughlin, who had come after their marriage from Inverness-shire, Scotland. He was educated at the local primary school and at the Lindsay grammar school. In his early days he was a primary school teacher, but soon became a carpenter and lumber-merchant, and ultimately in 1871 a contractor. He constructed part of the Victoria Railway (afterwards the midland division of the Canadian National Railways), and part of the mountain division of the Canadian Pacific Railway.

In 1886 Mackenzie entered into partnership with (Sir) Donald Mann. Their first line was the Lake Manitoba Railway and Canal Company, 125 miles in length, from Gladstone through Dauphin to Winnipegosis, built to connect with existing lines, and to carry part of the rapidly increasing grain crop. The first train was operated on this line in December 1896, and its success fired the partners' ambition. In 1899 the Canadian Northern Railway Company was incorporated: all through Canada other lines were gradually bought or built, and connected. On 1 January 1902 the line was completed from Port Arthur to Winnipeg; in December 1905 from Winnipeg to Edmonton; and in November 1915 trains were running from Montreal to Vancouver. In one year over 600 miles of track were laid, and in all, including branches, the system comprised not less than 9,500 miles of railway. Mackenzie was the financier of these operations, and gradually succeeded in selling about £65,000,000 of bonds in Great Britain, while retaining practically all the common stock in the hands of his partner and himself. In most cases the guarantees of either the Dominion or of provincial governments were secured, and in addition large subsidies were obtained. This was an era of great building activity in Canada; between 1900 and 1915 the railway mileage increased from 17,657 miles to 34,882 miles.

In 1903 the Grand Trunk Railway entered into arrangements with the Canadian government under Sir Wilfrid Laurier [q.v.] to build in co-operation the Grand Trunk Pacific and National Transcontinental Railways. An attempt was made to bring together Mackenzie and the Grand Trunk directors, but this failed through the fault of the grandees of the older company, who greatly underestimated the ability and constructive genius of Mackenzie. In 1911, disappointed in his attempt to obtain from Laurier the promise of a subsidy for his Rocky Mountains section, Mackenzie threw all his weight into the conservative scale, and was partly responsible for the defeat of Laurier in the general election of that year. With the conservatives in power, the subsidy was granted, and in 1915 Mackenzie saw his ambition fulfilled. But the European War threw everything into confusion: the influx of settlers and capital from Europe ceased abruptly; the profits of the prairie section of the line, although considerable, were insufficient to carry the vast expense of the mountain section; and in 1917–1918 the Canadian Northern was taken over by the Dominion government and eventually merged in the National Railways. Little was paid for the common stock, but every British bondholder was paid in full.

Mackenzie's enterprise had long before sought other directions. In 1889 he founded the São Paulo Tramway, Light and Power Company, the first of numerous Canadian enterprises in Brazil. In 1891 he obtained the franchise for the Toronto Street Railway, which proved to be very profitable; but he quarrelled with the city, and on the expiry of the franchise in 1921 the line was taken over by the city and placed under a commission. In 1910 a line of steamers from Montreal to Bristol was established in connexion with the Canadian National Railways.

Mackenzie married in 1872 Margaret (died 1917), daughter of John Merry, of Kirkfield, Ontario; one son and six daughters survived him, two other sons predeceasing their father. He and his partner, Mann, were created knights bachelor on 1 January 1911. He died at Toronto of pneumonia 5 December 1923.

Mackenzie was of medium height, thickset, dark and vivid in colouring, with deep blue, restless eyes. No man in Canadian life has been more variously judged. By his enemies he was accused of never hesitating either to bribe a newspaper or to corrupt a legislature [W. T. R. Preston, *My Generation of Politics and Politicians*, 1927, chap. xxxiv]. To his friends he was the trail-blazer, the nation-builder. 'For sheer tenacity, for courage which attacked the most formidable obstacles without a quail: for capacity to bring things to pass, I think Canada has not yet begotten his equal' [D. B. Hanna and Arthur Hawkes, *Trains of Recollection*, 1924, p. 241]. Like his Highland ancestors he was both dreamer and freebooter; but his passion for construction made him one of the great railway builders of North America.

[H. J. Morgan, *Canadian Men and Women of the Time* (editions of 1898 and 1912); Hanna, *op. cit.*; Toronto *Daily Globe* and *Daily Mail and Empire*, 6 December 1923; private information.] W. L. Grant.

MACKINNON, Sir WILLIAM HENRY (1852–1929), general, was born in London 15 December 1852, the younger son of William Alexander Mackinnon, F.R.S., of Acryse Park, Kent, the thirty-fourth chief of clan Fingon (Mackinnon) and member of parliament for Rye 1852–1853 and for Lymington 1857–1868. His mother was Margaret Sophia, daughter of Francis Willes. William Henry Mackinnon was educated at Harrow, and while still there was appointed to the Grenadier Guards in 1870. Six years later he became adjutant to his regiment, and held the post until 1880. In 1884 he was appointed military secretary to the governor of Malta (General Sir John Lintorn Simmons), and in the following year went on to India in order to become private secretary to the governor of Madras (Sir Mountstuart Grant Duff). He was promoted colonel in 1889. From July 1893, Mackinnon spent five years as assistant adjutant-general, London district, vacating the post, after the usual period of duty, in 1898. When, however, the South African War broke out in October of the following year, he returned to the appointment as a temporary expedient.

The City of London Imperial Volunteers, with which Mackinnon's name will always be associated, were formed in December 1899, and Mackinnon was appointed colonel commandant. The unit, which consisted of three parts, an infantry battalion, mounted infantry, and a field artillery battery, went out to South Africa in January 1900, and took part in various engagements in the Orange Free State and the Transvaal. The mounted infantry, attached with other units as divisional troops to the 9th division, played a minor part in the movements which led to the relief of Kimberley on 15 February 1900, and assisted in the capture of Jacobsdal, which post was held as a strategic position in the investment of General Piet Cronje's laager. In the following month the same detachment played its part in the action at Karee siding which restored to the British troops the use of the railway bridge over the Modder river. During the advance from Bloemfontein to Kroonstad the City Imperial Volunteers battalion was in support of the 21st brigade, and, in the advance from Kroonstad to Pretoria, it led the way in the battle of Doornkop on 29 May, carrying a hill after a sharp fight, and putting to flight about 500 of the enemy. In this brilliant affair the City Imperial Volunteers acquitted themselves well, but a much sterner task lay before them when, in the following month, they were called upon to attack Kleinfontein ridge as a preliminary to the battle of Diamond Hill. With the help of the Royal Sussex Regiment, the ridge was captured on 11 June, and next day Diamond Hill itself was carried. In Western Transvaal the C.I.V. (as the unit was habitually styled) formed part of the force commanded by (Sir) Horace Smith-Dorrien [q.v.] in pursuit of the elusive General Christiaan De Wet [q.v.], while in the Orange River Colony their battery assisted in the holding of Bloemfontein, and they were represented in July at the affair of Bakenkop, where they were very heavily engaged. The mounted infantry, still with Smith-Dorrien's brigade, took part in the advance to Komati Poort in September, while in the previous month the battalion arrived for the third time at Pretoria. The most outstanding of the City Imperial Volunteers' experiences were the battles of Doornkop and Diamond Hill, but all their achievements completely justified the faith of their commandant, Mackinnon, whose own military reputation was enhanced by the exploits of his splendid unit. The City Imperial Volunteers left South Africa early in October 1900, and on reaching England received an enthusiastic welcome on their march through London to a special thanksgiving service at St. Paul's Cathedral. Mackinnon was mentioned in dispatches and awarded the C.B. for his services in this campaign; he subsequently published *The Journal of the C.I.V. in South Africa* (1901).

Mackinnon, now a major-general, on returning to England was appointed to command the Imperial Yeomanry at Aldershot in 1901. Three years later he was made director of auxiliary forces, and in 1908 was chosen to fill the post of director-general of the newly formed Territorial Force. In that year he was promoted lieutenant-general, and two years later (1910) went to the Western command as general officer commanding-in-chief. He was promoted full general in 1913. In February 1916, in the middle of the European War, he was appointed director of recruiting at the War Office, but was succeeded in that post by Sir Auckland Geddes in the following May.

Mackinnon, whose honours included the C.V.O. (1903), K.C.B. and K.C.V.O. (1908), G.C.B. (1916), and the colonelcy of the Liverpool Regiment, retired in 1919, but although his distinguished and useful career in the army then came to an end, his activities by no means abated, for he took up or continued to hold many important positions in philanthropic institutions and movements in which he showed a deep and, indeed, lifelong interest. He was, for instance, chairman of the Heatherwood Hospital, Weybridge, and of the Royal Soldiers' Daughters' Home, Hampstead, vice-president of the Officers' Association, British Legion, a member of the councils of the United Service Fund, the Royal United Kingdom Beneficent Association, and the Gordon Boys' Home, a trustee of the Guards' Home, and the senior churchwarden of the Guards' chapel, Wellington barracks. He was possessed of high ideals and was incapable of a mean thought or an unkind word—a simple, unassuming, and charming personality.

Mackinnon's term of service at the War Office before the European War coincided with the important reforms of Mr. (afterwards Viscount) Haldane [q.v.]; and when the formation of a Territorial Force was under consideration, the advice of so experienced a commander of volunteers, both in the field and as director-general in peace time, was of the highest value. When the Territorial Force came into being in 1908 Mackinnon, by his fairness and courtesy, was able to smooth away many difficulties which his experience as a citizen-soldier enabled him to foresee and to appreciate. A more self-assertive or apparently strong soldier might easily have failed where the kindly tact of the first director-general of the Territorial Force ensured success.

Mackinnon married in 1881 Madeleine Frances, daughter of Villiers La Touche Hatton, of Clonard, by whom he had one daughter. He died in London 17 March 1929.

A cartoon of Mackinnon by 'Spy' appeared in *Vanity Fair* 7 February 1901.

[*The Times*, 18 March 1929; *Household Brigade Magazine*, Spring 1929; Sir J. F. Maurice and M. H. Grant, (Official) *History of the War in South Africa 1899–1902*, 1906–1910; (Sir) W. H. Mackinnon, *The Journal of the C.I.V. in South Africa*, 1901.]

C. V. OWEN.

MACKINTOSH, CHARLES RENNIE (1868–1928), architect and painter, was born 7 January 1868 in Dennistoun, Glasgow, the second son of William Mackintosh, superintendent of police, by his wife, Margaret Rennie. From Allan Glen's school he went in 1885 to the Glasgow School of Art, where he studied under Francis Newbery until 1892, though he was apprenticed for two years to John Hutchinson, a local architect, in 1887, before joining the Glasgow firm of Honeyman and Keppie, of which he became a partner in 1902. The Alexander (Greek) Thomson travelling scholarship which he gained in 1890 enabled him to visit France and Italy. He was awarded the Soane gold medal of the Royal Institute of British Architects in 1902, and was elected a fellow of that body in 1906.

Mackintosh's designs won the limited competition held in 1894 for the new building of the Glasgow School of Art, which was partly opened in 1899 but not completed until 1909. Though his first independent work, it evinced a consummate originality which owed nothing to any traditional style. It remains his most abiding title to fame as an architect. This building, the Scotland Street school (finished by another architect), Queen's Cross ehurch, and two or three houses outside Glasgow represent almost the sum total of Mackintosh's structural work, since his intense conscientiousness and sensitive individuality made him difficult for anybody to deal with who did not understand his temperament. In 1897 Mackintosh and George Walton undertook the complete decoration and furnishing of the first of their four celebrated Miss Cranston's Tea-Rooms in Glasgow. These were in the order of their dates of opening: 98 Buchanan Street (April 1898); 144 Argyle Street (1899); 205 Ingram Street, the only one that now survives (1900); and 'The Willow Tea-Rooms', 217 Sauchiehall Street (1904). The result was the earliest, though an entirely mature, embodiment of the curiously elongated formalism which in Germany was soon hailed as the 'Glasgow School style'.

In 1900 Mackintosh was invited to exhibit at the Wiener Sezession. While in Vienna Fritz Wärndorfer, of the 'Wiener Werkstätte,' commissioned him to design 'A Room for a Music-Lover'. This was included in the set of plans and drawings by Mackintosh, *Charles Rennie Mackintosh, Glasgow, The House of an Art Lover*, published in 1902 by Alexander Koch, of Darmstadt, with Hermann Muthesius's enthusiastic introduction. The Scottish Pavilion at the Turin Exhibition of 1902, which Mackintosh designed and virtually filled, led to Mackintosh exhibitions in Venice, Munich, Dresden, Budapest, and Moscow, where everything he showed was eagerly bought up. Mackintosh's influence on Continental design during the pre-War decade can hardly be exaggerated.

After 1910, when he finished his most important house, The Hill House, Helensburgh, Mackintosh's architectural work was really over. He resigned his partnership in Glasgow in 1913, and moved to London. During the European War he lived partly in Chelsea, making designs for textiles, and partly in Suffolk, where he worked at landscape-painting and flower studies. Subsequently he devoted himself to water-colours, spending much of his time round Port Vendres in the Eastern Pyrenees. 'La Rue du Soleil' and 'Le Fort Maillet' (1927) are perhaps the ripest achievements of a man who will probably rank among the greatest British water-colour painters and as the first master of modern abstract design.

By an irony of fate, Mackintosh, who had no followers in Great Britain, founded a foreign school (the so-called *Jugendstil*), and was the first British architect since Robert Adam whose name was a household word abroad. Himself a pioneer of *art nouveau*, Mackintosh was the first anywhere to translate its mannerisms into an architectural idiom, and so to free architecture from the last remnants of historical reminiscence. But as his essentially decorative genius knew no development, there is no direct link between his modernism and the structural evolution of modern architecture.

Mackintosh married in 1900 a fellow art student, Margaret, daughter of John Macdonald, consulting engineer, of Glasgow, but had no children. His wife, though of decidedly inferior artistic calibre, was his constant inspiration and his collaborator in all his decorative work. Mackintosh died, almost forgotten, in London 10 December 1928.

[Introduction to the Catalogue of the Mackintosh Exhibition in Glasgow, May 1933; *Art Work*, Spring 1930; *Architectural Review*, January 1935; *Quarterly of Incorporation of Architects in Scotland*, Spring 1932; *The Studio*, June 1933; private information.]

P. Morton Shand.

MacMAHON, PERCY ALEXANDER (1854–1929), mathematician, was born in Malta 26 September 1854, the second son of Colonel Patrick William MacMahon by his wife, Ellen, daughter of George Savage Curtis, of Teignmouth. He was sent to Cheltenham College, whence he proceeded early in 1871 to the Royal Military Academy, Woolwich. He joined the Royal Artillery at Madras in 1873 as lieutenant, and was promoted captain in 1881 and major in 1889. His battery took part in 1877 with the Punjab frontier force in a punitive expedition against the Jawaki Afridis, penetrating into their country and capturing several villages.

MacMahon left India on medical certificate in 1877, was posted to the 9th brigade at Dover, and in 1882 returned to the Royal Military Academy, Woolwich, as instructor in mathematics. This post brought him into touch with (Sir) George Greenhill, then professor of mathematics at the Artillery College, Woolwich, whose friendship changed the current of MacMahon's life. In 1890 he was appointed professor of physics at the Ordnance College, and he held this post until 1897. He retired from the army in 1898, and thereafter devoted himself to mathematical and scientific pursuits. From 1904 to 1920 he was deputy warden of the standards under the Board of Trade, a post which brought in due course membership from 1920 onwards of the Conférence Générale and of the Comité Internationale des Poids et Mesures which were held in Paris. For twelve years (1902–1914) he was one of the general secretaries of the British Association. His easy address and power in extempore talk upon a mathematical theme made him a welcome and prominent member of learned societies. He was elected a fellow of the Royal Society in 1890, and he received the Society's highest honours, the royal medal (1900) and the Sylvester medal (1919). The London Mathematical Society, of which he was president 1894–1896, awarded him the De Morgan medal in 1923. He received honorary degrees from several universities, was president of the Royal Astronomical Society (1917), and was a member of the Permanent Eclipse Committee and of the council of the Royal Society of Arts.

On his return to Woolwich in 1882 MacMahon entered into a mathematical heritage peculiarly fitted to his powers. The theory of algebraic forms was in the full flight of development owing to the activities of Arthur Cayley [q.v.], James Joseph Sylvester [q.v.], and George Salmon [q.v.], this being the one predominantly British domain in the vast range of modern abstract mathematics. From the outset MacMahon was captivated: the subject came to him as a kind of chess algebra, demanding lightness of touch and a daring playfulness combined with an abiding sense of form. So complete was his absorption that his military friends would refer to him in chaff as 'a good soldier spoiled'. But he won their admiration, as, indeed, he did that of the scientific world into which he had so thoroughly forced an entrance.

MacMahon's writings are scattered through journals and volumes of transactions of scientific societies, covering a period of nearly fifty years. While they adhere closely to combinatory analysis, that department of abstract algebra which his genius so conspicuously developed, they continually show the writer to be no isolated philosopher. 'I do not believe in any branch of science being destitute of connexion with other branches,' he said at a meeting of the British Association in Glasgow (1901). This isolation was particularly characteristic of a certain tract of pure mathematics which appeared to be in a 'forlorn condition'. The timeliness of MacMahon's masterly rescue of this department, which includes problems of the nature of the magic squares of the ancients, has become the more evident as the twentieth century has advanced, in its capital significance for the theory of groups and the quantum theory.

For many years MacMahon resided in London. In 1907 he married Grace Elizabeth, daughter of C. R. Howard, of 32 Gloucester Place, London: they had no children. His charming personality, his human sympathy, and the hospitality of his home in Westminster endeared him to a wide circle of friends. He was also an expert billiards player at the Athenæum Club, of which he was elected a member under Rule II in 1903. In 1922 MacMahon gave up most of his London associations and retired to Cambridge, becoming a member of St. John's College, to which, on receiving from Cambridge University the honorary degree of Sc.D. in 1904, he had attached himself by invitation. Although his absorption in scientific problems became more pronounced in later life, he mixed very willingly in social gatherings, until ill-health compelled his retirement to Bognor; there he died on Christmas Day 1929.

In 1915 MacMahon brought together the substance of his principal discoveries in a two-volume work *Combinatory Analysis*, a ripe and penetrating account of a favourite theme, which retains throughout the impress of his personality. There followed *An Introduction to Combinatory Analysis* (1920) and *New Mathematical Pastimes* (1921). This last is in lighter vein, a book which gives the geometrical by-products of his characteristic algebra, as manifested in the construction of repeated patterns. The whole subject of mathematics was enriched and adorned by the contributions made to it by MacMahon, who proved a worthy successor to Cayley and Sylvester, and encouraged many a younger mathematician by his infectious enthusiasm for algebra.

[*The Times*, 28 and 31 December 1929; *Monthly Notices* of the Royal Astronomical Society, vol. xc, no. 4, 1930; *Proceedings* of the Royal Society, vol. cxxvii, A, 1930 (portrait).] H. W. Turnbull.

MacNEILL, JOHN GORDON SWIFT (1849–1926), Irish politician and jurist, was born in Dublin 11 March 1849, the only son of the Rev. John Gordon Swift MacNeill, curate of St. James's church, Dublin, by his wife, Susan Colpoys, daughter of the Rev. Henry Tweedy. His father's mother, Anna Maria Swift, was the daughter of Godwin Swift, grandson of Godwin Smith who was uncle and guardian of Jonathan Swift. Thus all Swift MacNeill's connexions were with protestant Ireland. His nationalism was Irish in much the same sense as Swift's was, and neither his interest in Irish history nor his knowledge of it went back far beyond the reign of William III. In 1866 he went to Trinity College, Dublin, but after a year migrated to Oxford, where he gained an exhibition at Christ Church, and obtained second classes in classical moderations (1870) and the final school of law and modern history (1872). He then proceeded to read for the Irish bar, was called in 1875, and in 1882 was elected professor of constitutional and criminal law at the King's Inns, Dublin, a post which he held until 1888. He took silk in 1893.

MacNeill's taste for politics and public speaking had made him active in the Historical Society at Trinity and at the Union at Oxford, and in 1875, he became auditor of the Law Students' Debating Society. He joined the Home Government Association founded by Isaac Butt [q.v.] in 1870 and became a member of its council, being present at its meeting in 1874 when the offer made by Charles Stewart Parnell [q.v.] to contest county Dublin at his own expense was adopted, and at the subsequent meeting in the Rotunda when Parnell made his first public appearance and broke down in speaking. MacNeill himself records that in 1879 he was asked by Parnell to enter the House of Commons, and that he could have been returned for an Irish constituency before that date if he had wished. But, although a seat in the House of Commons was the ambition of his life, he 'thought the time premature' until Mr. Gladstone was definitely committed to Home Rule in 1886. No seat being available at the general election of that year, he was chosen at a by-election to represent South Donegal, and he remained member for that constituency during thirty-one years (1887–1918). He had already published a propagandist work, *The Irish Parliament: what it was, and what it did* (1885), which earned Mr. Gladstone's commendation; and he was recognized from the first as an addition to the nationalist party by his knowledge of constitutional history. Three of its members, already prominent, T. M. Healy and the two Redmonds, had attended his lectures at the King's Inns. But MacNeill found a new object for his erudition in a close study of the rules of parliament. This knowledge was necessary for the business of obstruction, the chief object of the Irish members in the parliament of 1886 to 1892. MacNeill became conspicuous in the art, and his oddities of appearance and manner kept caricaturists busy. But when Mr. Harry Furniss published an especially outrageous drawing, the victim, although a confirmed pacifist, retorted by a physical assault in the lobby.

MacNeill differed from almost all his colleagues in having a real veneration for parliament, and a desire to uphold its best traditions. He fought a long fight, ultimately successful, to establish the principle that ministers must not be the directors of public companies. In March 1892 Lord Salisbury's government was defeated on a motion of MacNeill's that the votes of three members in favour of a grant to the British East Africa Company of which they were directors should be disallowed. In 1906, when the flogging of boys in the navy was finally abolished, Sir Henry Campbell-Bannerman paid a tribute to MacNeill's long efforts for this reform. The last of the personal achievements on which he prided himself was the passing in 1917 of an Act to take from the princes of hostile countries the British titles which they held.

On the establishment of the National University in Ireland in 1909 MacNeill was appointed professor of constitutional law, and in 1910 he became clerk to convocation. At the end of 1918, after the Sinn Fein movement had begun to sweep over Ireland, he did not stand again for South Donegal, and the House lost one of its best-known figures. He accepted the Irish Free State without enthusiasm, but his latest historical work, *Studies in the Constitution of the Irish Free State* (1925), was a distinct service to Mr. Cosgrave's government. The last years of his life, spent at his home in Dublin, in the society of his sister, his lifelong companion—for he never married—and of their cats and dogs, among his mass of books and curiosities, were chiefly occupied in completing his amusing memoirs, *What I have Seen and Heard* (1925). He died in Dublin 24 August 1926.

Whether in public speech or private conversation, MacNeill was an exuberant and untidy talker; enthusiasms, information, and gossip tumbled pell-mell from a loose-hung mouth set between a ragged beard and prominent, excited light-blue eyes. But his good nature, his courtesy, and his outflowing humanity made him widely beloved. Nobody delighted more to do the honours of parliament; and his erudition there and elsewhere, though not always exact, was generously available. Few figures in the House of Commons were better known or better liked than this eccentric, warm-hearted Irish protestant gentleman.

A cartoon of MacNeill by 'Spy' appeared in *Vanity Fair* 13 March 1902.

[*The Times*, 25 August 1926; J. G. S. MacNeill, *What I have Seen and Heard*, 1925; private information; personal knowledge.]

S. Gwynn.

M'TAGGART, JOHN M'TAGGART ELLIS (1866–1925), philosopher, was born at 28 Norfolk Square, London, 3 September 1866, the second son of Francis Ellis M'Taggart, county court judge, by his wife, Caroline Ellis. He was educated at Clifton College and Trinity College, Cambridge. At Cambridge he studied the moral sciences under Henry Sidgwick [q.v.] and James Ward [q.v.] and was placed alone in the first class of the moral sciences tripos in 1888. He was an active member of the Union Society, of which he was elected president in 1890. He continued to be a member of the library committee of this society until his death, and his long connexion with it is commemorated in the library by a bookcase of eighteenth-century memoirs, purchased by subscription, and by a brass memorial plate. In 1891 he was elected to a prize fellowship at Trinity, and in 1897 he was appointed college lecturer in the moral sciences.

M'Taggart's writings fall into three groups. His earlier work was devoted to expounding and defending the method, and some of the results, of Hegel's *Logic*. The dissertation by which M'Taggart gained his fellowship dealt with the dialectical method, and his first book, *Studies in the Hegelian Dialectic* (1896), was an expanded form of this dissertation. This was followed in 1901 by *Studies in Hegelian Cosmology*. In this book M'Taggart discusses and criticizes certain applications which Hegel and others had made of Hegelianism to ethics, politics, and religion. He also attempts to determine by Hegelian methods, more definitely than Hegel himself had done, the nature and structure of the Absolute. In 1910 M'Taggart published his *Commentary on Hegel's Logic*. In this he takes the detailed argument of Hegel's *Greater Logic* category by category from Pure Being to the Absolute Idea. He tries to expound in intelligible English the characteristic content of each category, and to explain and criticize the transitions from one category to another. M'Taggart considered that the dialectical method, within the *Logic*, can be defended, both as to its validity and its fruitfulness, if it be regarded as a means of gradually making explicit what is implicit in every rational mind. He also held that Hegel's transition from Logic, through Nature, to Spirit can be defended on similar lines. He was convinced that the Absolute Idea, the highest category of the Logic, as interpreted by himself, expresses the complete nature of reality, so far as this can be determined by purely *a priori* reasoning. But he rejected many of Hegel's particular steps; he thought that Hegel often deceived himself and his readers by giving to his categories names taken from concrete empirical facts; and he rejected almost all the applications which have been made of Hegelianism to ethics, politics, and religion.

The second group of M'Taggart's writings contains only one book—*Some Dogmas of Religion*, published in 1906. This is the only popular philosophical work which he wrote. M'Taggart was at once an atheist and a convinced believer in human immortality. He held, on philosophical grounds which he developed in his *Hegelian Cosmology* and his *Nature of Existence* (1921 and 1927), that the Absolute is a perfect society of spirits, each of whom loves one or more of the others. He also held that each of these spirits is eternal, and that each human mind, as it really is, is one of these spirits. He thought it most probable that the eternal and timeless existence of these spirits would appear, under the partly delusive form of time, as a series of successive lives of finite duration. In *Some Dogmas of Religion* he takes the doctrine of pre-existence, rebirth, and post-existence as an hypothesis, and defends it with great ingenuity against the more obvious objections. In this book he also discusses Free Will and Determinism, arriving at a completely deterministic conclusion, and the Omnipotence of God. On the latter subject he concludes that the existence of a non-omnipotent and non-creative God is the utmost that can be granted to be philosophically possible. In *The Nature of Existence* his conclusions are even more definitely atheistic.

The later years of M'Taggart's life were spent in elaborating his own system of constructive metaphysics. This is contained in *The Nature of Existence*, the first volume of which appeared in 1921, the second and concluding volume being published posthumously in 1927. This is a complete system of deductive philosophy of extreme acuteness and ingenuity. It arrives at much the same conclusions as the writings of the Hegelian period by an entirely different method. The turning-point of the argument is a principle about the endless divisibility of substance, which M'Taggart called the Principle of Determining Correspondence. The work is remarkable for the strenuous attempt which the author makes to deal satisfactorily with the existence of error and illusion, particularly the illusion of time and change, in a world of eternal beings perfectly related to each other. A clear but highly condensed account of the system will be found in M'Taggart's contribution to *Contemporary British Philosophy* (edited by J. H. Muirhead, vol. i, 1924).

M'Taggart married in 1899 Margaret Elizabeth, daughter of Joseph Bird, civil servant, of Taranaki, New Zealand. They had no children. He retired from his lecturership at Trinity College in 1923, after completing twenty-five years' service. He continued to give some of his courses of lectures until his death, which took place, after a short illness, 18 January 1925 in a nursing home in London.

M'Taggart was a man of great wit and great business ability. He felt a passionate affection for his friends, for his country, and for his school and college. He was for many years an active member of the governing body of Clifton College, and he gave great help to Trinity College in drawing up the new statutes imposed upon it by the statutory commission. Although an atheist, he was a keen supporter of the Church of England, being in ecclesiastical matters an Erastian whig. In national politics he was a free-trade unionist, in university politics a strong feminist. He had an extraordinary knowledge of English novels, both past and contemporary, and of eighteenth-century memoirs. The honorary degree of LL.D. was conferred on him by the university of St. Andrews in 1911 and he was elected a fellow of the British Academy in 1906. A portrait of M'Taggart by his friend, Roger Fry, was presented to Trinity College by his widow, and hangs in his old lecture-room. In the college chapel there is a brass to his memory, near to those of Sidgwick and Ward, with his favourite quotation—*Homo liber de nulla re minus quam de morte cogitat; et ejus sapientia non mortis sed vitae meditatio est*—from Spinoza and an inscription by his friend, Nathaniel Wedd, of King's College.

[C. D. Broad, *J. M. E. M'Taggart, 1866–1925*, in *Proceedings* of the British Academy, vol. xiii, 1927.] C. D. Broad.

MAGRATH, JOHN RICHARD (1839–1930), provost of Queen's College, Oxford, was born at St. Peter Port in Guernsey 29 January 1839, the third son of Nicholas Magrath, surgeon in the royal navy, by his wife, Sarah Mauger Monk. He was educated at Elizabeth College, Guernsey, whence he won, at the age of seventeen, a classical scholarship at Oriel College, Oxford. At Oxford he followed a custom then not unusual, of reading both classics and mathematics, with the result that he obtained a first class in *literae humaniores* and a fourth class in mathematics in 1860. The same year he won the Stanhope essay prize, his subject being 'The Fall of the Republic of Florence', and was elected a fellow of Queen's College. In 1861 he began to read theology, and won the Johnson theological scholarship, finding time also to be president of the Union. He was ordained deacon in 1863 and priest in 1864. His tastes lay mainly in the direction of *literae humaniores*, especially Aristotelian philosophy, and for some years he was well known as a 'Greats' tutor, numbering amongst his pupils Edward Talbot, afterwards warden of Keble College and bishop of Winchester, and W. G. F. (afterwards Lord) Phillimore. These, and many more, looked back with gratitude to Magrath's long vacation reading parties at Beddgelert.

In 1864 Magrath succeeded to a tutorship at Queen's College, and thenceforward for many years he confined his academic activities to that college. From 1864 till 1877 he held the office of dean, and drastically, but with tact and patience, reformed the discipline of the college. He was also chaplain of the college from 1867 to 1878, and in 1874 he assumed the office of bursar, which then combined the work which is now divided between the estates and the domestic bursars. But although he was bursar only for four years, he retained to the end of his life a knowledge of the college estates of which successive bursars were glad to avail themselves. As if this were not enough, in 1876 he became senior proctor. Magrath brought to this last office the same industry and efficiency and the same combination of firmness and geniality which had made him such a success as dean and tutor of his college.

In the following year (1877) Dr. William Jackson, the provost of Queen's, appointed Magrath to assist him as pro-provost, and a year later Magrath succeeded Jackson as provost. Thenceforth his whole time was taken up with college administration and with university business. He was elected a member of the Hebdomadal Council in 1878, and served on it for twenty-one years. He was curator of the University Chest from 1885 to 1908, and was for many years also a curator of the Sheldonian Theatre, and a delegate of the Common University Fund and of the University Museum (1903–1912). He did particularly valuable work as a delegate of the University Press from 1894 to 1920. It was during his chairmanship of this body that he made himself responsible for the authorization of the proposal made by Henry Frowde [q.v.] in 1896 for the foundation of a branch of the Press in New York, a courageous measure from which the Press has reaped substantial benefits. In 1894 Magrath became vice-chancellor of the university, and for four years he carried out the duties and maintained the traditions of this office with dignity and ability. He was now at the height of his powers, and made a picturesque figure, with his flowing beard, his keen but kindly eyes, and his courtly bearing.

Throughout his life Magrath took a keen interest in municipal affairs, and was, in fact, the first Oxford don to accept civic office, first as a member of the Oxford local board, of which he was chairman from 1882 to 1887, and then, on its dissolution and the reconstitution of the city council, as alderman from 1889 to 1895. He was a J.P. for Oxfordshire from 1883. In Magrath's earlier days, when Oxford was still a country town, the city was decidedly dominated by the university, and somewhat resented its subservience. There was often unpleasant friction between 'town and gown', and there is no doubt that Magrath did good and lasting work in mediating between them.

In politics Magrath was a liberal, a supporter and personal friend of Lord Rosebery, and a devoted admirer of Mr. Gladstone. In education, also, he was progressive up to a point. He was wholeheartedly in favour of the movement for the higher education of women. Miss Dorothea Beale [q.v.], in her pioneer work at Cheltenham Ladies' College, found in him her chief supporter, and he was among the earliest friends of Somerville and St. Hilda's Colleges at Oxford. He also had a deep sympathy with the poor scholar. In the foundation of Lady Elizabeth Hastings [q.v.], which linked Queen's College by valuable exhibitions to a number of schools in Yorkshire, Cumberland, and Westmorland, he found an instrument ready to his hand. With the cordial support of the fellows of Queen's he gradually raised the status of these exhibitioners and the standard of the examination by which they were elected. Moreover, he visited the northern schools in person, accompanied by some fellow of the college, and it is not too much to say that these visits saved from extinction some distant outposts of the 'humanities'. Especially great were his services to St. Bees School, Cumberland; he was chairman of the governors for many years and was largely responsible for a policy of expansion by which the school was developed from a small country grammar school into a public school with some three hundred boarders.

At Oxford Magrath generally identified himself with the reforms of the Statutory Commission of 1877. These included the gradual absorption of the halls into the colleges. St. Alban Hall was taken into Merton College, St. Mary Hall into Oriel College, New Inn Hall into Balliol College, and in 1882 the commissioners made a statute for the absorption of St. Edmund Hall into Queen's College, which was to take effect at the next vacancy of the principalship. When therefore Dr. Edward Moore [q.v.] was nominated to a canonry in Canterbury Cathedral in 1903, Magrath sought to put the statute into operation. To this proposal, however, there was strong opposition, which came as much from Queen's College as from the Hall, and a short but sharp contention took place between old friends. But eventually, owing in large measure to the mediation of Lord Curzon as chancellor, and to the influence of the Hebdomadal Council, Magrath withdrew his scheme. St. Edmund Hall was finally secured in its separate identity in 1913 by a university statute which received the approval of the King in Council in that year, and no one rejoiced more unfeignedly than Magrath at the subsequent development and increasing success of the Hall. One other modern development at Oxford was strongly supported by Magrath, namely, the school of medicine; he was a valued member of the board of that faculty from 1890 to 1912.

There was, however, much in the trend of modern education which Magrath viewed with apprehension. Particularly he feared that the classics were being gradually ousted by other subjects from their position at Oxford as the chief instrument of education, and he was strongly opposed to the abolition of Greek as a compulsory subject for admission to the university. He believed, in fact, that without such a support, Greek would not survive in the northern grammar schools for more than a generation. Moreover, he dreaded lest the 'Huxley ladder' from the elementary school to the university should be made too easy. He also deplored what seemed to him the excessive interference of local education authorities with the independence of schools and schoolmasters and their governing bodies. These views he expressed with no uncertain voice from time to time in his annual progress round the northern schools, and however much people might disagree with and criticize them, his utterances on education created a profound impression in the North of England.

As a writer, Magrath will chiefly be remembered by his history of *The Queen's College* (2 vols., 1921), at which he worked for many years, assisted by Mr. Charles Stainer. He also edited *The Flemings in Oxford* (vol. i, 1904, vol. ii, 1913, vol. iii, 1924) for the Oxford Historical Society, and contributed the section on Queen's College to Andrew Clark's *Colleges of Oxford* (1891). He published in 1910 a sumptuous edition of the *Liber Obituarius Aulae Reginae in Oxonia*, and presented a copy to every member of the college past and present.

Magrath was a sportsman in the truest sense of the word, but his innate conservatism limited his activities to rowing and to the kindred sport of swimming. He had a distant respect for cricketers, but none for spectators of games, and for this reason he took little interest in football, until his college gained prestige on the football field as well as on the cricket field and on the river. He himself as a fellow both rowed for the college and was captain of the boats, and for many years he was a conspicuous figure in the 'Ancient Mariners' crew, stroked by W. L. Courtney, and comprising among its members A. L. Smith, L. R. Farnell, and W. E. Sherwood. Magrath was a familiar sight, too, at 'Parsons' Pleasure', diving from a tree rather taller than himself, and instructing Magdalen schoolboys to do the same. He was one of the earliest and keenest supporters of the Volunteer movement, and for seventeen years held the rank of sergeant in the university corps.

Magrath married in 1887 Georgiana (died 1899), third daughter of his predecessor in the provostship, the Ven. William Jackson. They had no children. On his wife's death his niece, Miss Eva Lefroy, kept house for him and carried on his tradition of hospitality. He was a most entertaining host, and Queen's men of all generations enjoyed his conversation on things grave and gay and his tales of bygone Oxford.

In 1911, at Magrath's request, a pro-provost of Queen's was appointed, first the well-known historian, Edward Armstrong [q.v.], a clever man of affairs, and one of the most popular figures in Oxford society; and, on his resignation in 1922, the Rev. E. M. Walker, who served with unswerving loyalty and conspicuous ability until, on Magrath's death, which occurred at Oxford at the age of ninety-one, 1 August 1930, he succeeded to the position of provost.

A portrait of Magrath, painted by the Hon. John Collier in 1898, and presented by some old members of Queen's College, hangs in the college hall.

[Personal knowledge.] H. A. P. Sawyer.

MAGUIRE, JAMES ROCHFORT (1855–1925), sometime president of the British South Africa Company, was born at Kilkeedy, county Limerick, 4 October 1855, the second son of the Rev. John Mulock Maguire by his wife, Anne Jane Humphries. He was educated at Cheltenham College and at Merton College, Oxford, where he obtained first classes in mathematical moderations (1875) and mathematical finals (1877) and also in jurisprudence (1879). In the last-mentioned year he was elected to a fellowship at All Souls College. He was called to the bar by the Inner Temple in 1883.

While at Merton, Maguire became a close friend of Cecil John Rhodes [q.v.], then an undergraduate of Oriel College. This friendship was destined to last until Rhodes's death in 1902, and to determine the whole course of Maguire's career. Maguire became associated with Rhodes's projects for the federation and extension of the British Empire, and, in particular, with his scheme for securing for the British Empire, through the medium of a powerful British commercial corporation, that part of South Central Africa which lay to the north of the Transvaal Republic and is now named Rhodesia, then a savage territory under native rulers, of whom the most powerful was the Matabele chief, Lobengula.

Rhodes, who was in sympathy with the Irish nationalist party's demand for Home Rule, but was opposed to Gladstone's Home Rule Bill of 1886 because it would have excluded Irish representatives from the House of Commons, was at that time in frequent communication with Charles Stewart Parnell [q.v.]. Maguire, who shared Rhodes's admiration for Parnell, became the chief connecting link between Rhodes and the nationalist party. In 1890 he was returned unopposed to the House of Commons as Parnellite member for North Donegal. At the general election of 1892 he was elected for West Clare, but was defeated in 1895, and did not again enter parliament.

Meanwhile Rhodes's schemes of British expansion in South Africa were being carried through. A concession granted by Lobengula over all the minerals in his territory formed the basis for Rhodes's projected company. This concession was obtained, not without great difficulty and considerable personal danger, by Maguire and two other emissaries, C. D. Rudd and F. R. Thompson, who were sent up by Rhodes for the purpose to Lobengula's kraal at Bulawayo in 1888. After the grant of the concession, Maguire had to remain in Bulawayo lest Lobengula should be persuaded to revoke his action. The ever-increasing danger of his position forced Maguire to leave for the south in April 1889, but by this time Rhodes's purpose was achieved, and in the following October the British South Africa Company was incorporated by royal charter with governmental as well as commercial powers.

In 1895 Maguire married the Hon. Julia Peel, eldest daughter of Arthur Wellesley, first Viscount Peel [q.v.], formerly Speaker of the House of Commons. At the end of the same year (29 December) the Jameson Raid took place. It is probable that Rhodes had made Maguire privy to his plans in connexion with the revolutionary 'reform movement' in Johannesburg, but Maguire was no party to the actual incursion of (Sir) Leander Starr Jameson [q.v.] into the Transvaal, and he strongly disapproved of it. With Rhodes, and accompanied by his wife, Maguire went through the siege of Kimberley in the South African War (October 1899–February 1900). This was the last of his active adventures.

After the death of Rhodes in March 1902, Maguire devoted himself to the business of the British South Africa Company, of which he became vice-president in 1906 and president in 1923, and of its associated railway companies, of which he was chairman. It was largely through his efforts that these companies were brought through great difficulties to a position of sound prosperity; and it was under his presidency, in October 1923, that the present colonial governments of Southern and Northern Rhodesia succeeded to the administration of the British South Africa Company.

Maguire died in London 18 April 1925, leaving no children.

[*Reports* of the British South Africa Company; private information; personal knowledge.] D. O. MALCOLM.

MAHON, SIR BRYAN THOMAS (1862–1930), general, the eldest son of Henry Blake Mahon, of Belleville, county Galway, by his wife, Matilda, second daughter of Colonel Thomas Seymour, of Ballymore Castle, county Galway, was born at Belleville 2 April 1862. He was educated in Ireland, and joined the fourth (militia) battalion, Connaught Rangers, whence he was gazetted lieutenant in the 21st Hussars in January 1883. Three weeks later he was transferred to the 8th (King's Royal Irish) Hussars. After five years' service in India, he returned to England in 1888 and was promoted captain. Two years later he was appointed adjutant of his regiment, but resigned in 1893, when he obtained employment with the Egyptian army. For the next seven years he served in Egypt, playing an active part in the operations which led to the final destruction of Dervish power (1896–1899). As staff officer of mounted troops, Mahon shared in the campaign which ended in the recovery of the province of Dongola in the summer of 1896, and was awarded the D.S.O. He served in the operations in the Nile valley early in 1897, being promoted major in that year, and was present at the battles of Atbara (8 April 1898) and Omdurman (2 September 1898); in the latter engagement he was erroneously reported killed. He remained at the front after (Lord) Kitchener's occupation of Khartoum, holding the appointment of assistant adjutant-general. He was also head of the intelligence branch of the flying column which finally defeated the Khalifa in Kordofan in November 1899. For his services in the campaign he received the brevet of lieutenant-colonel in 1898 and the brevet-colonelcy in 1899.

In January 1900, three months after the outbreak of the South African War, Mahon left Egypt for South Africa on special service. He first received the command of the colonial mounted troops of the Kimberley relief force. In May, with the rank of brigadier-general, he was given the command of a column and entrusted with the task of directing the movements for the relief of Mafeking, where Colonel (afterwards Lord) Baden-Powell, with a small force, had shut himself up in order to detain in comparative inactivity as large a number of the enemy as possible. The town had been closely invested since 13 October 1899 by a Boer force of about 6,750 men. The British garrison, even with the town guard and railway employees and others who volunteered their services, numbered only about twelve hundred effectives; but Baden-Powell improvised such a spirited defence that it withstood all the efforts of the enemy. On 15 May news reached the town that a relief column was on its way from the south. This was Mahon's column, consisting of two colonial mounted corps, one hundred British infantry, four field-guns, and two pom-poms—a fighting force about eleven hundred strong. Starting from Barkly West on 4 May, Mahon, by the afternoon of 15 May, had covered 230 miles and reached Massibi to the west and abreast of Mafeking, having been forced to make a detour by the presence of a body of the enemy. The Boers had discovered his change of direction and sharply attacked him, but did not succeed in delaying his advance for more than an hour. At Massibi, Mahon effected a junction with a force of Rhodesian levies under Lieutenant-Colonel (afterwards Lord) Plumer, and joint operations were undertaken the next day for the immediate relief of Mafeking. The combined force was divided into two brigades, one under Plumer and the other under Lt.-Colonel A. H. M. Edwards, of the Imperial Light Horse, with Mahon in command. The enemy was now alive to the new situation, and General De la Rey, who had just assumed command, interposed a strong Boer force between Mafeking and the relieving columns. The latter came under fire soon after noon on 16 May, and although their progress was slow, it was never really checked. Edwards on the left broke up all opposition before him, and a patrol of the Imperial Light Horse rode into Mafeking shortly before 6 p.m. Plumer on the right, had to meet sterner opposition, especially at Israel's Farm, where he was temporarily checked. Mahon organized a successful attack on the place, and soon all opposition ceased. Collecting his forces, Mahon finally advanced on Mafeking, seven miles distant, and at 3.30 a.m. on 17 May entered the town. Thus was achieved the relief of Mafeking—a notable operation upon which Mahon's reputation chiefly rests. The event was hailed at home with extraordinary enthusiasm, and in London especially occasioned scenes of almost delirious rejoicing.

Mahon was engaged in further operations in the Transvaal during the ensuing summer, acting successively under the orders of Lieutenant-Generals Sir Archibald Hunter and (Lord) French. In August 1900 he was gazetted to the command of the 12th Lancers, but he never actively served with that unit. Late in that year he returned to England, being awarded the C.B. for his services.

After one year's absence, Mahon arrived back in Egypt in January 1901, and was appointed to the governorship of Kordofan, a post which he held for just over three years. In April 1904 he was promoted to the substantive rank of colonel, and left Egypt for India in order to take command of the district of Belgaum. Two years later he was advanced to major-general, and in 1909 was given the command of the Lucknow division. At the end of his term in that command he returned to England (1913), was promoted lieutenant-general, and created K.C.V.O.

Mahon was holding no appointment when the European War broke out, but his services were soon engaged, for he was appointed to command the 10th (Irish) division of the new armies. In a history of that division it is recorded of Mahon that 'everything about him appealed to them (the Irishmen)—his great reputation, the horse he rode, his Irish name, and his Irish nature all went to their hearts' [Bryan Cooper, *The 10th (Irish) Division in Gallipoli*, 1918, p. 5]. In July 1915 the 10th division, under the command of Mahon, was dispatched to Gallipoli, after completing its training first at the Curragh and then at Basingstoke. In the following month the division took part in the severe fighting at Suvla. So heavily was it engaged there that dispersion of his troops left Mahon at one time with only a single brigade. Continuous fighting throughout September preceded the withdrawal of the division to Mudros, whence it was transferred to Salonika for the new campaign against the Bulgarians (5 October 1915). At Salonika Mahon and his division were joined shortly afterwards by three French divisions, and General Sarrail was placed in chief command of the Allied force. The first attempt to save the Serbian army was not successful; the French were driven back and the British, faced by heavy odds, were forced to retire, after a very gallant struggle, to the south of the line Guevgheli–Doiran. The next four months were spent in establishing the ever increasing British army, in organizing the 'entrenched camp' of Salonika, and in maintaining contact with the enemy nearer the Greek frontier. In May 1916, after accomplishing all that was possible in most difficult circumstances, Mahon was succeeded as British commander-in-chief by Sir George Milne.

Once more Mahon went to Egypt, and there commanded for a month the Western Frontier force. He then returned to England, and towards the end of 1916 was sent to Ireland as commander-in-chief. This appointment was made in the hope that Mahon's knowledge of his fellow countrymen and his long established popularity would help to relieve the situation in Ireland after the bitterness aroused by the Easter Rebellion. The appointment was fully justified, but Mahon was not destined to hold it long, for when Lord French was appointed viceroy of Ireland in May 1918, he requested that Sir Frederick Shaw should be appointed commander-in-chief. Mahon therefore returned to England, and in the following October took over the duties of military commander at Lille. Here he remained in what proved to be his last active appointment, until March 1919.

Retiring in 1921, Mahon went to live in Ireland, and in the following year became a senator of the newly formed Irish Free State. He was sworn of the Privy Council of Ireland in 1917, became colonel of his own regiment, and received the K.C.B. in 1922. He was a grand officer of the legion of honour, and held the grand cross of the white eagle of Serbia.

Mahon married in 1920 Amelia (died 1927), daughter of the Hon. Charles Frederick Crichton, and widow of Lieutenant-Colonel Sir John Milbanke, tenth baronet. He had no children.

Mahon was essentially a cavalry leader. He was fond of shooting, hunting, pig-sticking, and polo, and was a fine steeplechase rider. In 1925 he took over the management of the Punchestown race meeting, and showed himself a very efficient administrator of turf affairs. He also became chairman of the committee for the control of mechanical betting in Ireland. He died in Dublin 24 September 1930.

[*The Times*, 25 September 1930; Sir J. F. Maurice and M. H. Grant, (Official) *History of the War in South Africa 1899–1902*, 1906–1910; (Official) *History of the Great War. Military Operations*: C. F. Aspinall-Oglander, *Gallipoli*, vol. ii, 1932, and C. Falls, *Macedonia*, vol. i, 1933; Bryan Cooper, *History of the 10th (Irish) Division in Gallipoli*, 1918; *The Cross-belts* (Journal of the VIIIth King's Royal Irish Hussars), January 1931.] C. V. Owen.

MALLOCK, WILLIAM HURRELL (1849–1923), author, was born at Cheriton Bishop, near Crediton, Devonshire, 2 February 1849. He was the eldest son of the Rev. William Mallock, rector of Cheriton Bishop, who belonged to an old Devonshire family, the Mallocks of Cockington Court, near Torquay. His mother was Margaret, daughter of the Ven. Robert Hurrell Froude, archdeacon of Totnes, and sister of Richard Hurrell Froude [q.v.], William Froude [q.v.], and James Anthony Froude [q.v.].

Mallock was not sent to a public school, but went from a private tutor, the Rev. W. B. Philpot, of Littlehampton, to Balliol College, Oxford, in 1869. At Oxford he won the Newdigate prize in 1871 with a poem on the Isthmus of Suez. Although fond of the classics, Mallock only obtained a third class in honour moderations (1871) and a second class in *literae humaniores* (1874). Benjamin Jowett, then master of Balliol, thought little of him, regarding him as a mere dilettante.

Shortly after leaving the university, Mallock published *The New Republic* (1877), a book which had a considerable success. He had found the orthodox views in which he had been brought up disturbed by the religious liberalism of Oxford. In *The New Republic* a number of friends are gathered at a country-house party and discuss, in the manner of Plato's dialogues, problems of religion and society. The principal speakers are drawn without disguise from well-known men—Jowett, Ruskin, Matthew Arnold, Pater, and others. The arguments of most of these leaders of thought are pushed to lengths and conclusions which, in the author's view, demonstrate the impossible position of undogmatic belief. He applies in fact the method of *reductio ad absurdum* to everything. Mallock followed this book with *The New Paul and Virginia, or Positivism on an Island* (1878), a short satirical sketch which is considered by many to be the most amusing of his works, and *Is Life worth Living?* (1879), a treatise in which the values of life and their connexion with religious faith are submitted to scientific analysis.

His writings had attracted attention, and as a clever young man Mallock found an immediate welcome in fashionable society, a mode of life which to the end of his days he appreciated and enjoyed. He spent much of his time in London, on the Riviera, and in country-house visits, but in spite of these distractions he worked with industry, and was continually engaged upon different subjects. He wrote philosophical and political treatises as well as several novels. In these works of fiction of which, perhaps, *The Old Order Changes* (1886) was the most popular, he usually attempted to illustrate some particular view or theory of human life, and to rouse interest rather by the development of character than by intricate plot or dramatic episode. He also produced a small volume of *Poems* (1880), and *Lucretius on Life and Death in the Metre of* [FitzGerald's] *Omar Khayyám* (1900). He had already (1878) published a handbook on Lucretius in Blackwood's 'Ancient Classics for English Readers' series, including some translations of his own.

Mallock combined with his satires, novels, and philosophical books, some political literature of a different kind. About 1881 his attention was attracted by the spread of revolutionary views about the distribution of wealth, and he became convinced, to quote his own words, that such views were based upon a serious distortion of historical facts and figures. He published a short book called *Social Equality* (1882) in which his object was to show that the various efforts which produce wealth are not only essentially unequal in themselves, but can only be stimulated by unequal circumstances. Especially as regards the ownership of land did he set himself to refute erroneous statements by statistical evidence which he collected and tabulated with much labour. When, as a result of his *Social Equality*, he accepted provisionally an invitation to stand as a conservative for a Scottish constituency, he held a number of meetings at which large diagrams were exhibited contrasting the amounts of rentals, as they were represented by Henry George and other opponents of the land system, with the amounts as they actually were. Although in the end he withdrew in favour of another candidate, and did not himself attempt to enter parliament, he continued for many years his careful study of political problems. His *Labour and the Popular Welfare* (1893) was followed by *Aristocracy and Evolution* (1898), and much of the information which he gathered was circulated in leaflet form for the instruction of speakers and audiences. In 1907 he went to the United States on a lecturing tour, and delivered a series of addresses which he afterwards collected and published in a book called *A Critical Examination of Socialism* (1908). Occupied as he was with these inquiries, he maintained a constant interest in religion and religious discussion. He published *Doctrine and Doctrinal Disruption* (1900), *Religion as a Credible Doctrine* (1903), and *The Reconstruction of Belief* (1905).

Towards the end of his life, Mallock wrote his autobiography—*Memoirs of Life and Literature* (1920)—in which he described the progress of his opinions from youth to age. From this retrospect it may be learned how extensive and varied was his literary output. He always wrote well, putting his points with clearness, and often with humour. He took great pains with his style, and would rewrite sentences until their rhythm satisfied him.

Mallock, who was never married, died at Wincanton, Somerset, 2 April 1923. On his death-bed he accepted the ministrations of the Roman Catholic Church.

[W. H. Mallock, *Memoirs of Life and Literature*, 1920; personal knowledge.]

A. Cochrane.

MALLORY, GEORGE LEIGH (1886–1924), mountaineer, was born at Mobberley, Cheshire, 18 June 1886, the elder son of the Rev. Herbert Leigh Mallory by his wife, Annie Beridge Jebb. The Mallorys had for several generations been squire-parsons at Mobberley, owners of the advowson of the living as well as of the manorial rights of the parish. George Mallory, the eldest of a family of four, two sons and two daughters, intended to take orders. From a preparatory school at Eastbourne he won a scholarship to Winchester College in 1900, whence he proceeded as an exhibitioner in history to Magdalene College, Cambridge, in 1905. Arthur Christopher Benson [q.v.] had recently been elected a fellow of Magdalene, and Mallory came much under his influence. While at Cambridge, Mallory abandoned the intention of taking orders. His tastes were strongly literary and historical, and under Benson's influence he turned eagerly to the idea of teaching such subjects at a public school. In 1909 he published a study of James Boswell, the biographer, and in the following year was appointed an assistant master at Charterhouse, where he remained until he joined the army in 1915. He returned to Charterhouse in 1919, but although still keenly interested in the wider aspects of education, he decided after a few years to give up being a schoolmaster. He had married in 1914 Ruth, second daughter of Hugh Thackeray Turner, architect, of Godalming. After the interruption of his school work caused by his joining the expeditions to the Himalayas in 1921 and 1922, he moved in 1923 with his wife and three children, two daughters and a son, to Cambridge, and took up a post as lecturer and assistant-secretary for the Board of Extra-Mural Studies in the university.

While still at school Mallory had been introduced by a Winchester master, R. L. G. Irving, to the sport of climbing in the high Alps. He rapidly made his mark among expert mountaineers, both as a rock-climber in Great Britain and on ice and snow in the Alps. Almost every holiday he returned to the mountains, and when away from them he would talk, think, and dream about them. By the year 1920 Mallory was known as one of the leading young mountaineers of the day, and when the project of climbing Mount Everest took shape, he was invited to form one of the party chosen for the attempt. On the first expedition, organized by the Mount Everest Committee and led by Lieutenant-Colonel C. K. Howard-Bury in 1921, the climbing party for the preliminary survey of the mountain was a small one, and it fell to Mallory and his companion, G. H. Bullock, to carry through the main reconnaissance almost unassisted, except by eighteen native porters whose language they could not speak. As the natural sequel to this pioneer work, Mallory took part in the first main attempt to reach the summit in the following year. The route followed was the one discovered and surveyed by him and his small party the year before. On 21 May 1922, in company with Major E. F. Norton and Dr. T. H. Somervell, Mallory reached the record height of 26,985 feet, but any further ascent was prevented by the early arrival of the monsoon. In 1924 he found himself for the third time at the Rongbuk glacier, the base of the expedition, preparing for the great climb. This year all seemed propitious for success. The party was ideally composed, the equipment very complete, and the stages of the climb had been thought out in the minutest detail. Hopes of success ran high, if only the weather should be reasonably good. But this was not to be. The Himalayas that year were repeatedly swept by storms in a way unknown in living memory. Twice the whole expedition had to retire to their base-camp to recuperate after the most terrible hardships from snow and icy winds. For the third advance, the party was much depleted and all the carefully laid plans had to be given up for lack of men to carry them out. Two attempts upon the summit were made. On the first, Mallory's companions, Lieutenant-Colonel E. F. Norton and Dr. Somervell, reached the highest recorded point, 28,126 feet (4 June). From the second, made on 8 June, Mallory and his companion, the young climber, A. C. Irvine, of Merton College, Oxford, never returned. They had slept at a height of 26,000 feet and were last seen at 12.50 p.m. the next day, going well, and about 800 feet below the summit. Then the clouds gathered round and hid the final scene of Mallory's greatest mountaineering achievement.

[David Pye, *George Leigh Mallory*, 1927; personal knowledge.] D. R. Pye.

MANN, ARTHUR HENRY (1850–1929), organist, was born at Norwich 16 May 1850, the youngest child, in a family of three sons and two daughters, of Henry James Mann, musician, of Norwich, by his wife, Anne Couzens. He entered the choir of Norwich Cathedral as a very small boy. His ability was early apparent, for at the age of eight he played a service at the cathedral. The choirmaster was Zachariah Buck [q.v.], who used the cane freely on boys who omitted to practise the 'shake', and encouraged the open mouth by a curious apparatus 'placed between the teeth during singing exercise'. Mann was appointed organist of St. Peter's, Wolverhampton, in 1870 and of Tettenhall parish church in 1871. He matriculated at New College, Oxford, in 1872, and took the degree of B.Mus. in 1874 and that of D.Mus in 1882. He was appointed organist of Beverley Minster in 1875, and after a few months there went to King's College, Cambridge, in 1876 and stayed there fifty-three years.

At this time the choir of King's College chapel consisted of lay clerks and boys from the town, like that of a cathedral. By degrees, and with Mann's active co-operation, this was changed. Choral scholars replaced the lay clerks, and a residential school for the boys opened the door to a wider source of supply. Mann had ideas of his own about vocal quality, speed, and style, with which some critics did not agree; but he understood what sounded best in that wonderful building, and the standard of performance was always high, sometimes remarkably so. He was an excellent organist, and played the best music from Bach to C. M. Widor, with fluency and good taste. His extempore voluntary at the beginning of a service was unique. It was impossible either to imitate it, or remember it. There was no tune, no form, no development, but it seemed to be part of the chapel, as it rose to a climax, and died down on a solitary note of extreme depth.

Mann's relation with the choir, boys and men, was strongly personal. The rehearsals were not easy occasions, but kindly goodwill reigned. To members of the choir, as to all his friends, Mann was 'Daddy', but he was not to be trifled with. During the European War it was touching to see young officers, on a few days' leave from France, coming back to Cambridge just to sing once more, and for the last time it might be, in a service at King's.

Mann conducted many fine performances of great works on a larger scale in King's chapel. His Festival Choir was established in 1887, and continued under his name until 1912. This chorus with a large London orchestra—often the London Symphony Orchestra—presented a fine series of works, such as Elgar's 'Apostles' (12 June 1906), 'The Kingdom' (11 June 1907), 'Dream of Gerontius' (15 June 1909); Beethoven's Mass in D (16 June 1908); Brahms's Requiem (14 June 1910, for King Edward VII), to which may be added Beethoven's 'Choral Symphony', played in the Guildhall at Cambridge 16 March 1911. Another interesting production was Tallis's great motet in 40 vocal parts—'Spem in alium'—which Mann printed on his own responsibility, and conducted in London (1898) and in Cambridge (1899). Besides these efforts, he gave eight symphony concerts in Cambridge during the years 1910 to 1912, when three London orchestras were conducted by Sir Edward Elgar, (Sir) Landon Ronald, Sir Henry Wood, and (Sir) Thomas Beecham. The programmes consisted of works by Mozart, Debussy, Berlioz, Wagner, Beethoven, Tschaikowsky, Brahms, Haydn, Elgar, Schubert, Bizet, and included twelve symphonies by seven composers. Thus it is clear that Mann's view of music was broad and deep, and by no means confined to Handel, as some people thought.

Mann was choirmaster of the Norwich Festival in and after 1902, and director of music at Leys School, Cambridge, from 1894 to 1922. He became organist to the university of Cambridge in 1897 and received the honorary degree of M.A. in 1910. In 1892 he became a freeman of the city of Norwich. He was an early member of the Royal College of Organists. An institution very near his heart was the Incorporated Society of Musicians, of which he was a moving spirit for many years.

A valuable work of an entirely different sort was the rearrangement by Mann of the Handel MSS. at the Fitzwilliam Museum. The manuscripts were kept partly in parcels, partly in six bound volumes of 'sketches', in no sort of order. Mann spent much time and labour from 1889 to 1892 in putting them into shape, and, as far as possible, identifying the numberless scraps, sometimes consisting only of a few notes, with the corresponding passages in Handel's complete works. His work fills 70 pages of the printed catalogue. In 1894 Mann conducted a performance of the 'Messiah' in King's chapel with a reconstructed score including the original wind parts which had been discovered at the Foundling Hospital.

Mann was a great collector of early hymn books, concert programmes and tickets, and other *miscellanea* connected with music. He possessed a mass of remains connected with Dr. William Crotch [q.v.], first principal of the Royal Academy of Music, including water-colours painted by Crotch himself.

After his wife's death, which occurred in 1918, when he was nearly 70, Mann lived in King's College, and became a great favourite with all the residents, some of whom had not known him intimately before. In 1922 he was elected a fellow of the college. Mann's life was happy, and his death no less so. His eightieth year half over, he sang in the Latin motet for

Advent on Sunday afternoon 17 November 1929. He died early on the Tuesday following (19 November).

Mann married in 1874 Sarah, daughter of John Ransford, a yeoman farmer, and had one son (who died in infancy) and three daughters.

[*The Times*, 20 and 23 November 1929; *Cambridge Review*, 29 November 1929 and 17 January 1930; The Rev. A. E. Brooke (Provost of King's) and others, *Arthur Henry Mann* (with portrait), 1930; private information; personal knowledge.]

E. W. NAYLOR.

MANSFIELD, KATHERINE (pseudonym), writer. [See MURRY, KATHLEEN.]

MANSON, SIR PATRICK (1844–1922), physician and parasitologist, was born 3 October 1844, the second son of John Manson, of Cromlet Hill, Oldmeldrum, Aberdeenshire, laird of Fingask and manager of the local branch of the British Linen Bank, by his wife, Elizabeth, daughter of Patrick Blaikie. Mrs. Manson was a woman of very happy and resourceful disposition and of artistic temperament. Manson was educated at the Gymnasium and later at the West End Academy, both in Aberdeen, whither his parents had moved in 1857. He was at first apprenticed to an engineering firm in Aberdeen, but convalescence from an illness gave him the opportunity of gratifying his taste for natural history, and this soon led him to abandon engineering and take up the study of medicine. He entered Aberdeen University in 1860, and in 1865 graduated M.B. and C.M., taking his M.D. degree in 1866. In this year, through the interest of his elder brother who was already in Shanghai, Manson was appointed medical officer for Formosa to the Chinese Imperial Maritime Customs.

Owing to the political unrest in Formosa, Manson left the island in 1871 and went to Amoy. It was there, while in charge of a missionary society's hospital and dispensary, and busy with his private practice, that he made those observations which were to bring him fame in the future.

His surgical work in the removal of the massive tumours of elephantiasis, and the prevalence of this and allied conditions among the Chinese, impressed Manson with the importance of these diseases, the cause of which at that date was unknown. While in England in 1875 he heard of the discovery in Calcutta in 1870 and 1872 by Timothy Richards Lewis (1841–1886) of microscopic nematode worms (*micro-filariae*) in the blood of patients suffering from diseases allied to elephantiasis; later discoveries, in 1876 by Joseph Bancroft, of Brisbane, and in 1877 by Lewis in Calcutta, revealed the adult worms corresponding to the embryonic blood forms.

On his return to China early in 1876 Manson made a series of observations which convinced him of the causal relationship of *filaria* worms to elephantoid diseases, and he brought to light the remarkable fact that the embryonic forms of the worm do not appear in the blood until sunset, that they increase in number until midnight, and then decrease, disappearing about 9–10 a.m. He began now to speculate on the fate of these embryonic blood *filariae*—how they get out of the body. By a fortunate accident, thinking at that time—erroneously, as is now known—that the geographical range of mosquitoes and of filarial disease is identical, Manson selected mosquitoes as the probable means by which the embryos escaped. He consequently proceeded to feed mosquitoes on a patient whose blood teemed with embryo *filariae*. 'After many months of work', he wrote in the China Customs *Medical Reports* for September 1877, 'often following up false scents, I ultimately succeeded in tracing the filaria through the stomach wall into the abdominal cavity, and then into the thoracic muscles, of the mosquito. I ascertained that during this passage the little parasite increased enormously in size. It developed a mouth, an alimentary canal and other organs. . . . Manifestly it was on the road to a new human host.'

Unfortunately here Manson took the wrong turning. 'A regrettable mistake, the result of a want of books, was my belief that the mosquito died soon after laying her eggs' [*Life*, 57]. He had not, before leaving England in 1883, seen the suggestion of an anonymous reviewer in the *Veterinarian* [vol. lvi, p. 178, 1883] that 'the parent worm is in the first instance introduced into the body from without, and it may be deposited by the mosquito in the act of biting'. He conjectured that the filarial larva got into water at the death of the 'short-lived' mosquito, and thence in some unknown way back to man. This unfortunate error just prevented Manson from rounding off his investigation as a perfect piece of research. But none the less, this great and fundamental discovery of a developmental phase in the life of a parasite in the tissues of a blood-sucking insect, was to have important results.

In December 1883 Manson left Amoy and settled in Hong Kong, where he soon built up a large private practice, became a leader in public work, and instituted a school of medicine which developed into the university and medical school of Hong Kong. In 1886 he received the honorary LL.D. degree of Aberdeen University—the first official recognition of his scientific work.

Manson retired from practice in 1889, left China, and went to live in Scotland. A year later, however, he was compelled, through financial losses, to take up practice again in London. His appointment in 1892 as physician to the Seamen's Hospital Society gave him the opportunity of continuing his researches into tropical diseases. It was while holding this post that he first observed the malaria parasite, which had been discovered by A. Laveran in 1880. Before the discovery of the malaria parasite, many writers had expressed the view that mosquitoes might be concerned in the transmission of malaria; but Manson's discovery, in the case of *filaria*, that the development of a blood worm occurred in the body of a mosquito led him to argue, by analogy, that the malaria parasite had a similar intermediate host. He was now familiar with certain forms of the malaria parasite which behaved in a peculiar manner when examined under the microscope. Motile filaments developed on some of these, and the filaments broke loose and moved through the blood fluid. The importance of this phenomenon was not lost on Manson. He would not have it that these motile bodies were functionless, but inferred that they were meant by nature to occur while the parasite was in the body of an intermediate host, e.g. in the stomach of a mosquito. This was the essence of Manson's mosquito-malaria theory. In 1897 W. G. MacCallum, of Baltimore, discovered what these motile filaments really were, viz. male elements prepared to fertilize female forms, similar in appearance, but without motile filaments [*Lancet*, 1897, vol. ii, p. 1240]. Thus Manson's induction became firmly established. Though the function of the motile filaments was now known, there was still no clue as to what happened next. It was (Sir) Ronald Ross who traced the subsequent steps. 'His brilliant induction', Ross writes of Manson, 'so accurately indicated the true line of research, that it has been my part merely to follow its direction.'

In 1894 Manson began to give public lectures in London on the subject of tropical diseases, and in 1897 he was appointed physician and medical adviser to the Colonial Office. He was thereby brought into close association with Joseph Chamberlain [q.v.], at that time secretary of state for the Colonies, in the reform of the system of medical reports from the Colonies, in the reorganization of the West African medical service, and finally in the foundation (1899) of the London School of Tropical Medicine. The last-named was the outcome of a scheme drawn up by Manson in 1897 for systematic instruction in the diagnosis, treatment, and prevention of tropical disease; he had been appalled at the ignorance of, and the lack of training in, the subject with which practitioners had hitherto proceeded to the tropics.

In 1896 Manson delivered the Goulstonian lectures on 'The Life History of the Malarial Germ outside the Body' [*British Medical Journal*, 1896, vol. i, pp. 641, 712, 774; *Lancet*, 1896, vol. i, pp. 695, 751, 831], and in 1898 was published his *Tropical Diseases: a Manual of the Diseases of Warm Climates*, a work founded on his large experience and numerous original researches made while in China. Later important contributions to the subject were his *Lectures on Tropical Diseases* (the Lane lectures delivered at San Francisco, 1905) and in 1908 (with C. W. Daniels) *Diet in the Diseases of Hot Climates*.

Manson, who had been elected a fellow of the Royal Society in 1900, was created K.C.M.G. in 1903, and promoted G.C.M.G. on his retirement from the Colonial Office in 1912. He received the honorary degree of D.Sc. from the university of Oxford in 1904. At the International Congress of Medicine held in London in 1913 he was described as the 'father of tropical medicine'—a recognition of his achievement which can hardly fail to be endorsed by future generations. He died in London 9 April 1922, and was buried in Allenvale cemetery, Aberdeen.

Manson married in 1875 Henrietta Isabella, second daughter of Captain James Ptolemy Thurburn, R.N., of Norwood, and had three sons and three daughters. There is a portrait of Manson at Manson House, 26 Portland Place, in oil, by J. Young Hunter (1911), and another at the London School of Hygiene and Tropical Medicine, in water-colour, by M. Lucy Gee [Mrs. Coxeter].

[P. H. Manson-Bahr and A. Alcock, *The Life and Work of Sir Patrick Manson*, 1927.]

J. W. W. STEPHENS.

MARSHALL, ALFRED (1842–1924), economist, was born at Clapham 26 July 1842, the second son of William Marshall, a cashier in the Bank of England, by his wife, Rebecca Oliver. The Marshalls were a West of England family, many members of which since the seventeenth century had been clergymen. His great-grandfather was the Rev. John Marshall, headmaster of Exeter grammar school, who married Mary, daughter of Charles Hawtrey, canon of Exeter, and aunt of Edward Craven Hawtrey, provost of Eton. At the age of nine he was sent to Merchant Taylors' School with a nomination obtained by his father from a director of the Bank of England, and, rising to be third monitor, he became entitled in 1861 to a scholarship at St. John's College, Oxford, in the last year of the old statutes, which would have qualified him to proceed in due course to a fellowship. This would have meant his continuing to work at the classics, as the first step towards ordination, which was his father's wish. But Marshall was determined to turn towards mathematics, for which he had already shown at school some genius; and a small loan from an Australian uncle made it possible for him to go to St. John's College, Cambridge, with the Parkin's exhibition of £40 a year. He graduated as second wrangler in 1865, the year in which J. W. Strutt (afterwards Lord Rayleigh) was senior wrangler, and was immediately elected to a fellowship at his college. He proposed at that time to devote himself to the study of molecular physics. Meanwhile he earned his living for a short period as a mathematical master at Clifton College, and afterwards by coaching at Cambridge for the mathematical tripos.

It was at about this time (1867) that Marshall first came into the intellectual circle of which Henry Sidgwick [q.v.] was the centre. As a member of the Grote and Eranus clubs he came into contact not only with Sidgwick, but with F. D. Maurice, John Venn, J. R. Mozley, W. K. Clifford, Henry Fawcett, Henry Jackson, and J. F. Moulton. Under these influences there came a crisis in his mental development, of which he often spoke in later years as the turning-point in his life. His design to study physics was, in his own words, 'cut short by the sudden rise of a deep interest in the philosophical foundation of knowledge, especially in relation to theology'. At that time the philosophical world of Cambridge was passing, with painful doubts and hesitations, away from the Christian dogma, which a few years previously had in that atmosphere been scarcely questioned. Then, or a little earlier, Leslie Stephen was an Anglican clergyman, James Ward a nonconformist minister, Alfred Marshall a candidate for holy orders, W. K. Clifford a high churchman. A little later none of these could have been called Christians. But Marshall continued in sympathy with Christian morals and Christian ideals and incentives, and little or nothing is to be found in his writings or teaching of a tendency to influence his readers or pupils one way or the other in matters of belief. After a short metaphysical period, Marshall turned his mind to ethics. He accepted, on the whole, the Utilitarian ideas which had dominated the previous generation of economists, but with great caution and qualifications. Whilst his work was much concerned with ideals of social service, his treatment neither of economic theory nor even of economic motive is linked up with, or dependent upon, any particular ethical theory. His final transition to the choice of economics as the subject of his life's study is described in his own words in an unpublished autobiographical fragment written about 1917: 'I gave myself for a time to the study of metaphysics; but soon passed to what seemed to be the more progressive study of psychology. Its fascinating inquiries into the possibilities of the higher and more rapid development of human faculties brought me into touch with the question: how far do the conditions of life of the British (and other) working classes generally suffice for fullness of life? Older and wiser men told me that the resources of production do not suffice for affording to the great body of the people the leisure and the opportunity for study; and they told me that I needed to study political economy.'

In 1868 Marshall was appointed to a lecturership in moral science at St. John's College, and was soon able to specialize in economics. For nine years he remained fellow and lecturer of the college, laying the foundations of his subsequent work but publishing nothing beyond one or two occasional articles. Meanwhile, he was helping Henry Fawcett [q.v.], the professor of political economy, and Henry Sidgwick to establish political economy as a serious study in the university of Cambridge.

After returning from a visit to the United States (1875), Marshall married in 1877 Mary, daughter of the Rev. Thomas Paley, and great granddaughter of Archdeacon William Paley [q.v.]. Miss Paley, who was a former pupil of his and a lecturer in economics at Newnham College, was one of the small band of five pioneers who in 1871, before the foundation of Newnham, came into lodgings in Cambridge under the control of Miss A. J. Clough [q.v.]. Marshall's first book, *The Economics of Industry* (1879), was written in collaboration with his wife. For forty-seven years of married life he was completely dependent on her devotion and understanding. His marriage involved the loss of his fellowship and made it necessary for him to find a new means of livelihood. Accordingly he went to Bristol in 1877 as the first principal of University College and as professor of political economy. Soon after his marriage his health and nerves began to break down, chiefly as a result of stone in the kidney, and he resigned the position of principal in 1881. After nearly a year spent in Italy, he returned to Bristol, where he still held his professorship, with his health much restored. But he remained for the rest of his life somewhat hypochondriacal. His nervous equilibrium was easily upset by unusual exertion or excitement or by controversy, and he never felt his physical strength equal to the claims which the activity of his mind put upon it. In 1883, on the death of Arnold Toynbee, Marshall was invited by Balliol College to succeed him as fellow and lecturer in political economy. In 1884 Marshall returned to Cambridge as the successor of Fawcett in the chair of political economy, which he held until his retirement in 1908 at the age of sixty-six. He continued thereafter to reside in Cambridge and to keep in close touch with the school of economics up to his death, which took place at Cambridge 13 July 1924, a fortnight before his eighty-second birthday. He had no children.

The progress of Marshall's most characteristic contributions to economic theory is a little obscure, owing to the long periods between the dates at which much of his most original work was carried out and the dates at which it was published. His serious study of the subject began in 1867; many of his characteristic doctrines had been shaped by 1875; and by 1883 they were taking their final form. No part of his work was published in any adequate form until the appearance of his *Principles of Economics* in 1890, whilst his *Money, Credit and Commerce* did not appear until 1923. But long before they were formally made public, Marshall was in the habit of sharing his ideas without reserve in lecture and in talk with friends and pupils. In 1879 a pamphlet was privately printed in which some fundamental principles were briefly outlined, while some of his most characteristic contributions to economic theory first found their way into print in the evidence which he gave before royal commissions. Thus, by the time Marshall's doctrines were actually published, they were already in a sense familiar and their influence was already observable in the work of his English pupils and contemporaries. None the less, when at length it saw the light, his *Principles of Economics* was readily accepted as the greatest economic treatise of his generation; and for more than thirty years most serious work on the subject was built on his foundations. By the end of 1928 some forty thousand copies of the book had been sold in English, it had been translated into many languages, and its influence had penetrated to all schools of economic thought in every part of the world.

Marshall served on the royal commission on labour (1891–1894), and he spent much time on the preparation of evidence for the royal commission on the aged poor (1893), the Indian currency committee (1899), and the royal commission on local taxation (1899). In 1903, during the tariff reform controversy, he wrote a *Memorandum on the Fiscal Policy of International Trade* at the request of the Treasury, which was printed in 1908 as a White Paper. But it was not until 1919 that the next section of his main life's work, *Industry and Trade*, was given to the world. Finally in 1923 there appeared the third section, *Money, Credit and Commerce*. The postponement of his only treatise on money until after he was eighty years of age was an extraordinary example of Marshall's hesitation in allowing his work to reach the world; for the theory of money had been one of his earliest subjects of study, much of the material published in 1923 having been nearly complete forty years earlier, and some of it going back quite fifty years.

Some explanation of these long delays is to be found in the great pains which

Marshall took with his more promising pupils. The number of students of economics at Cambridge in his time was never great. But there were generally a few of good quality, and in these Marshall was nearly always successful in developing what was strongest and most fruitful. The development of the school of economics at Cambridge was carried by him a stage farther, shortly before his retirement, by the foundation of the economics tripos in 1903. As early as 1888 Professor Foxwell was able to claim that Marshall's pupils already occupied half the economic chairs in the United Kingdom, and that the share taken by them in general economic instruction in England was even more preponderant. At the time of his death he was recognized as the father of economic science as it then existed in England.

Marshall's letters and scattered writings have been collected in *Memorials of Alfred Marshall* (edited by A. C. Pigou, 1925), and his contributions to the reports of royal commissions in *Official Papers of Alfred Marshall* (edited by J. M. Keynes, 1926). A portrait by William Rothenstein hangs in the hall of St. John's College, Cambridge; and a replica in the Marshall Library, Cambridge, an extensive library for students of economics, the nucleus of which was formed by Marshall's bequest of his own books and later increased by Mrs. Marshall's benefactions in accordance with his wishes.

[Obituary notices reprinted in *Memorials of Alfred Marshall* (with bibliographical list of his writings) and in J. M. Keynes's *Essays in Biography*, 1933; private information; personal knowledge.] J. M. Keynes.

MARSHALL HALL, Sir EDWARD (1858–1929), lawyer. [See Hall.]

MASON, ARTHUR JAMES (1851–1928), theological scholar and preacher, was born at Langherne, Carmarthenshire, 4 May 1851, the third son and fifth child of George William Mason, of Morton Hall, Retford, D.L., J.P. for Nottinghamshire and sometime high sheriff of the county, by his wife, Marianne Atherton, daughter of Captain Joseph George Mitford, of the East India Company's Service. He was educated at Repton School, and proceeded as a scholar to Trinity College, Cambridge, where he graduated as eighth classic in the tripos of 1872, and was elected a fellow in 1873. A short time spent as assistant master at Wellington College was notable chiefly as the beginning of his devoted, almost romantic, friendship with the headmaster, Edward White Benson [q.v.], afterwards successively bishop of Truro and archbishop of Canterbury—a friendship which greatly influenced Mason's future career. In 1874 he returned to Cambridge as assistant tutor of Trinity, and in the following year accepted from his college the charge of St. Michael's church, Cambridge. This was really a preachership, and here Mason, a man of graceful figure, attractive face, voice, and manner, at once weighty and persuasive, found scope for his pastoral and devotional instincts. He showed an unusual power and quality of preaching, which was still further developed when, in 1878, Dr. Benson drew him to Cornwall as honorary canon of Truro Cathedral and diocesan missioner without stipend. Mason's missionary work in the new diocese was of lasting value. Years afterwards Archbishop Davidson, speaking in Canterbury Cathedral, recalled 'the lithe, spare figure' which 'passed to and fro among the wind-swept villages of Cornwall . . . as if a mission priest had stepped out from the Celtic centuries into our own'.

In 1884 Dr. Benson, who had become archbishop of Canterbury in 1882, invited Mason to All Hallows, Barking-by-the-Tower—a benefice with few parishioners and large endowment—in order to establish there a kind of college of mission-preachers for work in London among the more educated classes. This was a new idea, justified by success at least as regards Mason himself, for he was in great request as lecturer and preacher all the eleven years he was there. In 1893 he was appointed an honorary canon of Canterbury Cathedral (resigning Truro), and examining chaplain to the archbishop.

In 1895 the scholarship and wide theological learning which he was known to possess led to Mason's election as Lady Margaret's professor of divinity at Cambridge, where he accepted a professorial fellowship at Jesus College: in the same year Dr. Benson appointed him a residentiary canon of Canterbury. In earlier life he had been closely connected with religious activities of an ascetic type, but in 1899 he married. His wife was Mary Margaret, daughter of the Rev. George John Blore, D.D., headmaster of the King's School and honorary canon of Canterbury; they had two sons and two daughters.

In 1903, while retaining his canonry

at Canterbury, Mason resigned his professorship at Cambridge in order to become master of Pembroke College. As master of the college and as vice-chancellor of the university (1908–1910) he showed himself well able to deal with administrative affairs and an excellent representative of the college and the university on all occasions; he also gave free play, by benefactions to the college and in other ways, to his natural generosity and love of hospitality. But all this work was exacting, and Mason could not leave any of it undone. Canterbury stood first in his affections, both because Benson had, as he said, 'put' him there, and because its historical associations attracted his own ecclesiastical and artistic interests. In 1912, therefore, finding the responsibilities of the two offices too much for his strength, he resigned the mastership (he was at once elected an honorary fellow of the college) and withdrew to Canterbury. Except for six months (1915–1916) during the European War, when he went to Alexandria on a preaching and lecturing mission, he lived at Canterbury for the rest of his life, taking an active part in all the work of the cathedral and in matters affecting the religious, educational, and social welfare of the city.

All the offices which Mason held he filled with distinction. If he produced no literary work of outstanding importance, his many published writings show delicate scholarship and insight and an easy command of historical, theological, and antiquarian learning. Among them are: on early Christian history, *The Persecution of Diocletian* (1876) and *The Historic Martyrs of the Primitive Church* (1905); on Christian theology, *The Faith of the Gospel* (1888) and *The Five Theological Orations of Gregory of Nazianzus* (1899, in the series of Cambridge Patristic Texts, of which he was editor); on the Reformation settlement of the Church of England, *Thomas Cranmer* (1898), *The Church of England and Episcopacy* (1914), and *What became of the bones of St. Thomas?* (1920); and memoirs of two of his friends, Bishop G. H. Wilkinson (1909) and Bishop W. E. Collins (1912), the latter of whom owed much in his earlier life to Mason's beneficence, teaching, and example. He also wrote short articles of a specialist character, for example, on the ancient glass of Canterbury Cathedral and on the hymns of St. Hilary. Five hymns of his own composition are included in *Hymns Ancient and Modern*, and several volumes of verse show the poetical outlook which was one of his characteristics.

Throughout his life much of Mason's time and energy was given to current ecclesiastical affairs behind the scenes, e.g. in connexion with the archbishop's mission to the Assyrian Christians, the discussions on reunion with the Church of Rome and with other Churches (such as that of Sweden, whose language he knew), the archbishop's commissions on 'spiritual healing' and 'the ministry of women', and the questions raised in the Kikuyu controversy. In all these matters Mason was the trusted adviser and helper of successive archbishops. He was appointed an honorary chaplain to the king in 1911.

Ecclesiastically Mason was in line with the older school of 'high' churchmen, avowedly both catholic and protestant, convinced that the Church of England with its Prayer Book as settled at the Restoration retained the true catholic faith and tradition. None the less, he favoured wider use in the Church of England of practices and institutions such as private confession and community life. Orthodoxy, ancient custom, stately worship, picturesque ceremonial—all these appealed to him. He shrank from 'modernity' of any kind. Learning and scholarship were used by him to elucidate and confirm the historical tradition, and his great gifts as a preacher to bring learned and simple folk alike to an evangelical trust in Christ. He died at Canterbury after a short illness 24 April 1928.

[*The Times*, 25 April 1928; *Kentish Gazette and Canterbury Press*, 28 April 1928; private information; personal knowledge.]

J. F. Bethune-Baker.

MASSEY, WILLIAM FERGUSON (1856–1925), prime minister of New Zealand, was born at Limavady, co. Londonderry, 26 March 1856, the eldest son of John Massey, farmer, by his wife, Marian, daughter of William Ferguson. He was educated first at the national school and later at a private school at Londonderry. He lived with his grandmother, and subsequently with his uncle, his parents having emigrated to New Zealand in 1862.

Massey joined his parents in New Zealand in 1870, and took up farming, after gaining some experience in Canterbury, at Mangere, near Auckland. He soon began to take a prominent part in the local affairs of the district. He was an active member of the farmers' club, the local road board, the school committee, and other bodies, and became president of the Auckland Agricultural and Pastoral Association in 1891. He was defeated by a narrow majority in his first contest for a seat in the New Zealand house of representatives in 1893, but was elected member in the conservative interest for Waitemata in 1894. He held that seat until 1896, when he was elected for Franklin, which seat he held until his death in 1925.

Massey's first important political post was that of chief opposition whip, which he held from 1895 to 1903. From 1903 to 1912 he was leader of the conservative opposition to Richard John Seddon [q.v.] and Sir Joseph George Ward [q.v.] in succession to Sir William Russell. In 1904 the opposition adopted the name 'reform party', and it was as leader of the reform party that Massey, on the defeat of the ministry of (Sir) Thomas Mackenzie, became prime minister of New Zealand in July 1912. He held office until his death thirteen years later, his term including the exacting period of the European War. Of the many offices which he held, the departments of lands and agriculture were the most congenial to him. Massey was a sincere and persistent advocate of freehold tenure in New Zealand, and in its first session the reform government passed the necessary legislation to enable holders of Crown leases in perpetuity to acquire the freehold on favourable terms. In 1913 his government dealt successfully with a great strike of transport workers, seamen, and miners.

In August 1915 Massey formed a national government, composed of the two chief parties, reform and liberal. He was joined, among other colleagues, by Sir Joseph Ward, as minister of finance and postmaster-general, and he led New Zealand through the War with great ability and firmness. His attendances at the Imperial War Cabinet and Conference of 1917–1918, at the Imperial Conference of 1921, and at the Imperial and Economic Conferences of 1923, gave him opportunities of getting to know intimately the leading statesmen of the British Empire, and New Zealand benefited in no small degree by the knowledge which he thus gained. He was also a plenipotentiary to the Paris Peace Conference of 1919, and he signed the Treaty of Versailles on behalf of New Zealand.

Massey was admitted a privy councillor in 1914. He was granted the freedom of ten cities, including London, Edinburgh, Glasgow, Belfast, York, Cardiff, and Manchester. He received honorary degrees from the universities of Cambridge, Edinburgh, and Belfast, and he was the first overseas statesman to receive the freedom of the city of Londonderry. He was also the first colonial freeman to exercise his right and privilege to vote at an election of sheriffs for the city of London.

Massey's health failed after the Imperial Conference of 1923, and although he recovered sufficiently to be able to continue his work for a time, he died at Wellington 10 May 1925. He married in 1882 Christina, eldest daughter of Walter Paul, farmer, of Mangere, and had three sons and two daughters.

Physically, Massey was a very strong man; mentally, he was alert, capable, and ready for a political encounter at all times. His opponents always found him a fair, if vigorous, antagonist, and although he cannot be said to have been a great speaker, he was fluent in his delivery, with a natural power of repartee and very ready with biblical quotations, and definite in his opinions. But the greatest interest of his life was politics. He will be remembered, both in England and in New Zealand, as a strong purposeful man, who, once having come to a decision, never faltered.

[*The Times*, 11 May 1925; New Zealand Parliamentary Record, 1840–1925.]

T. M. Wilford.

MASSINGHAM, HENRY WILLIAM (1860–1924), journalist, was born 25 May 1860 at Old Catton, Norwich, the second son of Joseph Massingham, private secretary to a member of the Gurney family, and a methodist preacher, by his wife, Marianne Riches. He was educated at King Edward VI's School, Norwich, under Dr. Augustus Jessopp [q.v.], from whose teaching and influence he acquired his lifelong love and critical judgement of literature.

At the age of seventeen Massingham joined the staff of the *Eastern Daily Press* as a reporter. There he met 'Mark Rutherford' (William Hale White, q.v.), whom he greatly admired, and whom, on coming to London in 1883, he succeeded as 'London letter' writer for the same paper. For a short time Massingham was a contributor to and then editor of the *National Press Agency*, and in 1888 he joined the staff of the *Star*, recently founded by T. P. O'Connor [q.v], becoming editor for a few months in 1890. He next became editor of the *Labour World* in 1891. Early in the following year, Massingham entered a wider sphere of influence as successively literary editor, special parliamentary representative, assistant editor, and finally editor, after the resignation of A. E. Fletcher in 1895, of the *Daily Chronicle*. He edited that paper for four years, raising it to a position of great influence as the exponent of advanced liberal opinions in home and foreign politics, while maintaining the high level of its daily literary page. In November 1899, however, he was driven to resign owing to the unpopularity of his strong opposition to the South African War. For a time he worked in London for the *Manchester Guardian*, and then for the *Daily News*, writing the 'Pictures in Parliament' in succession to (Sir) Henry William Lucy [q.v.], and contributing a series of articles upon South Africa, which he visited in 1905.

In March 1907 Massingham was appointed editor of the *Nation*, a liberal weekly journal which had been developed out of the *Speaker*. During the European War he strongly advocated an earlier peace, in support of the letter written by Lord Lansdowne [q.v.] in November 1917. He remained editor until April 1923, when he resigned owing to a change in the political aspect of the paper on its sale to other proprietors. He definitely joined the labour party in November 1923, and transferred his 'Wayfarer's Diary' to the *New Statesman*. But he deeply, although silently, lamented the loss of the editorship of the *Nation*, the paper which he had created and formed into a powerful organ of advanced but independent opinion. The sixteen years of his editorship of the *Nation* must be accounted the most effective period of Massingham's journalistic career, although his impetuous spirit would have preferred the medium of a daily paper, such as the old *Daily Chronicle*, in which he could get in his successive blows more rapidly. The objection to a weekly publication was even stronger in regard to the *Christian Science Monitor* (published in Boston, U.S.A.), to which for a time he contributed a weekly 'London letter'.

Massingham used to say, with a shade of regret, that he had given up everything for journalism, and certainly he found in journalism the expression of his ardent and impatient spirit. His interests were versatile, and as a journalist he wrote with eager appreciation of everything in which he discerned excellence, whether in literature, drama, or pictorial art. As far as self-expression goes, his literary and dramatic criticisms are among his best work. In all the arts he was indifferent to precise refinements of thought and word, but he delighted in virile writers who could move and influence mankind in general. Like Tolstoy, whom he greatly admired, he was always on the look-out for the ethical rather than the strictly artistic, and the same was true of his own style in writing. His articles, whether 'leaders' or 'middles', were written with intense vigour and breadth. He cared nothing for epigrams or delicate subtleties. Every sentence had to seize the reader at once; none the less, his care for minute accuracy, even to the last comma, was as remarkable as it was unexpected.

His passionate energy for human welfare was Massingham's highest distinction. Even as an advanced liberal he never worked for party, and he was never guided by theory. He appreciated fine personality in any party, and would choose one hero after another, usually to be disappointed in each. Regarding official tories and liberals as hidebound by obsolete dogmas, he turned to the labour party and a kind of 'practicable socialism', but there, too, he was disappointed by the narrow, material aims of the Trade Unionists. His hatred of what he deemed injustice to a subordinate race lost him the editorship of the *Daily Chronicle*; his hatred of injustice to the working people lost him that of the *Nation*; and to the service of these two papers his existence had been devoted. At the well-known *Nation* lunches, attended by his permanent staff and a visitor or two, he would listen quietly to a debate upon some leading question of the day, and then would strike at the very centre of the problem. With all his humour and sympathetic attractiveness, he kept a veil drawn over his inmost self, and although friends and admirers surrounded him, few, if any, felt themselves really intimate with him.

Massingham was the author of two pamphlets, *The Gweedore Hunt* (dealing with the Irish land war, 1889) and *Humphrey's Orchard* (dealing with an English eviction, 1894). He also wrote 'The London Daily Press' (articles for the *Leisure Hour*, 1892), and introductions to *Labour and Protection* (a symposium, 1903), to Winston Churchill's *Liberalism and the Social Problem* (1909), and to the memorial edition of the *Works of 'Mark Rutherford'* (1923), a notice of whom Massingham contributed to this DICTIONARY.

Massingham married twice: first, in 1887 Emma Jane (died 1905), daughter of Henry Snowdon, of Norwich; secondly, in 1907, her sister, Ellen. He had five sons and one daughter by his first wife. He died suddenly at Tintagel, Cornwall, 28 August 1924.

[*H. W. M.: a Selection from the Writings of H. W. Massingham*, edited by H. J. Massingham, with introductory essays by J. L. Hammond, H. N. Brailsford, H. M. Tomlinson, H. W. Nevinson (members of the *Nation* staff), Vaughan Nash (of the *Daily Chronicle*), and G. Bernard Shaw, 1925; personal knowledge.]

H. W. NEVINSON.

MASTERMAN, CHARLES FREDERICK GURNEY (1874–1927), politician, author, and journalist, the fourth son of Thomas William Masterman, of Rotherfield Hall, Sussex, by his wife, Margaret Hanson, daughter of Thomas Gurney, of New Park Lodge, Brixton Hill, was born at Spencer Hill, Wimbledon, 25 October 1874. He was educated at Weymouth College and at Christ's College, Cambridge. His career at Cambridge was a brilliant one. He obtained first classes both in the natural science tripos (1895) and in the moral science tripos, part II (1896). He was one of the best speakers at the Cambridge Union, and became president of the Society in 1896. In 1900 he was elected a fellow of his college. At Cambridge Masterman associated chiefly with members of the liberal and progressive school of thought which found expression in *The Heart of the Empire* (1901), a collection of essays by Masterman, G. M. Trevelyan, Noel Buxton, G. P. Gooch, and others.

Masterman's liberalism was strongly tinged with Christian socialism, then under the leadership of men like Bishop Westcott, Canon Scott Holland, and (Bishop) Gore. The appalling contrast between the squalor of the slums and the luxury of Mayfair stirred his emotional nature, and an indignant pessimism inspired his next two books, *From the Abyss* (1902) and *In Peril of Change* (1905). These writings and his success as a platform speaker made Masterman a welcome recruit to the political liberalism which began to dominate England after the Boer War. He soon gained a footing in Fleet Street, and contributed to the *Independent Review*, the *Pilot*, the *Commonwealth*, the *Daily News*, of which he became literary editor, the *Speaker*, then under the editorship of J. L. Hammond, and afterwards to the *Nation* under the editorship of H. W. Massingham [q.v.]. At the well-known *Nation* lunches his witty and often cynical sayings found an appreciative audience.

In 1903 Masterman stood for parliament, contesting Dulwich unsuccessfully. With the assistance, however, of Mr. John Burns, then a power in London, he was returned for West Ham (North) in 1906. At first, Masterman was fortunate in his political career. His party had an unprecedented majority and his talents were recognized by Mr. Asquith, who succeeded Sir Henry Campbell-Bannerman as prime minister in April 1908 and offered Masterman the under-secretaryship of the Local Government Board, of which Mr. Burns was then president. Masterman accepted the office, and in his new capacity helped Mr. Burns to carry the important Housing and Town Planning Act of 1909. But the two men did not always work in harmony, and in July 1909 Masterman was appointed under-secretary of state for the Home department, where, in 1910, Mr. Winston Churchill became his political chief. In 1912 he was promoted to be financial secretary to the Treasury. Masterman had laboured indefatigably on Mr. Lloyd George's national insurance scheme, under the fire of bitter opposition from die-hard conservatives; and after the Insurance Act became law in 1911, he was appointed first chairman of the national insurance commission and guided a difficult and complicated measure into smooth waters.

For his conspicuous support of the National Insurance Bill, Masterman suffered; for in February 1914, when he was appointed chancellor of the duchy of Lancaster with a seat in the Cabinet, and had to seek re-election, the whole artillery of the opposition was turned upon him. In 1911 he had been unseated on petition at West Ham (North), owing to irregularities committed by his agent in the election of 1910, and had subsequently been elected member for South-West Bethnal Green. He was now defeated there by twenty-four votes. In spite of his ability as a platform speaker, he was not a good electioneer. He lacked the knack of either winning or retaining a seat. Perhaps his failure was partly due to ill luck, or perhaps it was that his high churchmanship repelled the nonconformists, who formed the backbone of the liberal party even in the days of its supremacy. However that may be, for nearly ten months after joining the Cabinet Masterman had to suffer the mortification of being unable to find a seat. He was, none the less, a member of the Cabinet which took the fateful resolution of declaring war in August 1914. He was proud, as he wrote afterwards in a letter to the prime minister, to be associated with a government which had faced the situation and had chosen war as the only alternative to dishonour.

When, after disappointments at several by-elections, Masterman was passed over for a vacancy in the Shipley division of the West Riding of Yorkshire, Mr. Asquith in February 1915 reluctantly accepted his resignation, requesting him to remain on the war committees to which he was attached. He was director of Wellington House (propaganda department) from 1914 to 1918, and in the latter year was made director of the literary department of the Ministry of Information.

After the War, Masterman continued his attempts to re-enter parliament and was at last successful for the Rusholme division of Manchester in 1923, but lost his seat at the general election in the following year. After this his health, which had begun to fail, became gradually worse, and he died in London 17 November 1927. He married in 1908 Lucy Blanche, daughter of General Sir Neville Lyttelton, and had one son and two daughters.

As a writer Masterman may be judged by his most popular book, *The Condition of England*, which appeared in 1909. His style at its best was vigorous and fluent, resembling in many ways the ease and energy of his conversation.

[*The Times*, 18 November 1927; private information; personal knowledge.]

F. W. Hirst.

MATTHEWS, Sir WILLIAM (1844–1922), civil engineer, born at Penzance 8 March 1844, was the eldest son of John Matthews, borough surveyor of Penzance, by his wife, Alice, daughter of Thomas Richards, of Penzance. He was educated locally at a school kept by a Mr. Teague, and on leaving served a short part of his apprenticeship in the engineering works of Sandys, Vivian, & Co., near Hayle, Cornwall. Later he entered his father's office, where he worked for some years. When he was about twenty, he executed for the use of (Sir) John Coode [q.v.], the harbour engineer, a survey of Penzance harbour, and as a result was invited to become a pupil in Coode's London office, and later was given a post on his staff. Matthews speedily rose to be chief assistant, and he was entrusted in time with the control of the office and home connexion when Coode was abroad. In 1892, the year of Coode's death, Matthews was made a partner of Sir John and his son, J. C. Coode, the firm taking the style of Coode, Son, & Matthews. It was subsequently reconstructed in 1912 and 1921.

The firm, of which Matthews was senior consulting engineer for nearly forty years, acted as consulting engineers to the Crown agents for the Colonies. They were frequently employed by the Admiralty in connexion with works at naval bases. Thus, they were chief engineers for the naval harbour at Dover, a work which occupied thirteen years (1896–1909). They were also consulted by the Board of Trade, the India Office, the Mersey Conservancy, the Humber Conservancy, the Tyne Commissioners, and other public bodies. Matthews was engaged in the construction of a wet dock and a graving-dock at Singapore, and in the reconstruction of the main wharf. He visited and inspected these works in 1901 and 1905. At the same time he advised the Straits Settlements administration as to the advisability of taking over the works of the Tanjong Pagar Dock Company. Matthews was also appointed by the Admiralty in 1900 to report upon the naval harbour in Malta, and he served on a committee appointed by the Admiralty in 1901 to inquire into the naval works at Gibraltar. He also visited and inspected harbour works in progress in Ceylon, Hong Kong, Cyprus, and at the Cape. For his services in connexion with colonial harbours he was awarded the C.M.G. in 1901, and created K.C.M.G. in 1906. He was also made an officer of the order of Leopold for services in connexion with the harbour of Zeebrugge in 1894.

Matthews was a member of the royal commission on coast erosion (1906), of the International Technical Commission on the Suez Canal (1908), and of the royal commission on oil fuel and engines (1912), and he acted as chairman of the British Standards Cement Committee (1912). He retired from active work at the end of 1917. He died, unmarried, at his home at Hampstead 8 January 1922.

Matthews became an associate of the Institution of Civil Engineers in 1870 and a member in 1876, and was elected president in 1907.

A portrait of Matthews by Stanhope

Alexander Forbes is in the gallery of the Institution of Civil Engineers.

[*The Times*, 10 January 1922; *Proceedings* of the Institution of Civil Engineers, 1922, vol. ccxiii, 418; G. C. Boase and W. P. Courtney, *Bibliotheca Cornubiensis*, vol. iii, 1882.]

E. I. Carlyle.

MAXWELL, Sir JOHN GRENFELL (1859–1929), general, was born at Aigburth, Liverpool, 11 July 1859, the second son of Robert Maxwell, senior partner in the firm of A. F. and R. Maxwell, merchants, of Liverpool, by his wife, Maria Emma, daughter of Vice-Admiral John Pascoe Grenfell [q.v.] and cousin of Field-Marshal Francis Wallace Grenfell, first Baron Grenfell [q.v.]. The marriage of Mrs. Maxwell's sister Sophia to Pascoe Grenfell, Lord Grenfell's eldest brother, greatly strengthened the intimacy which arose between young Maxwell and the field-marshal. John spent his boyhood with his father's parents and was educated at Cheltenham College, whence he entered the Royal Military College, Sandhurst, in 1878, and was gazetted into the 42nd Foot (Royal Highlanders, now 1st Battalion, the Black Watch) in 1879. When Sir Garnet Wolseley went to Egypt in 1882, the 42nd formed part of the expeditionary force, and Maxwell was chosen by Major-General Sir Archibald Alison [q.v.] to act as his aide-de-camp for the battle of Tel-el-Kebir (13 September), remaining in that position until Alison's departure for England in 1883. But Maxwell then stayed in Egypt with Sir Evelyn Wood as assistant-provost-marshal. In that capacity, and as camp commandant, he spent the winter of 1884–1885 up the Nile with Wolseley in the latter's fruitless attempt to relieve General Gordon, then besieged in Khartoum. When, in April 1885, Sir Francis Grenfell succeeded Wood as sirdar of the Egyptian army, he summoned his young kinsman to his staff, first as aide-de-camp and then as assistant military-secretary, although the appointment was not to be made permanent until September 1886. In that capacity Maxwell took part in the Sudan frontier operations, being present at the action of Giniss (30 December 1885), for which he received the D.S.O., at the engagement at Gamaiza, outside Suakin (20 December 1888), which brought him the order of Osmanieh, and lastly (3 August 1889) at the more decisive battle of Toski, after which he was awarded a brevet-majority.

When Sir Herbert (afterwards Earl) Kitchener [q.v.] succeeded Grenfell as sirdar in 1892, he retained Maxwell on his own staff, and there sprang up a close association and lasting friendship between the two men. The next few years were spent in planning the re-conquest of the Sudan, until the crushing defeat of the Italians by the Abyssinians at Adowa on 1 March 1896 necessitated a hastening of the advance. This straightway led to the battle of Firket (7 June) in which Maxwell commanded the third Egyptian infantry brigade, retaining this position until the recapture of Dongola on 23 September. During 1897 he acted as 'governor of Nubia', and in this office administered the area in which the railway was being pushed forward. Finally, during the operations of 1898, he commanded the 1st Sudanese brigade at the battle of Atbara (8 April), and was transferred to the 2nd brigade for the battle of Omdurman (2 September). He was mentioned in dispatches and received the thanks of parliament. After the Dervish collapse he filled the onerous position of governor of Omdurman, receiving the brevet of lieutenant-colonel for his services.

On the outbreak of war in South Africa in October 1899, Maxwell was still in the Sudan, but in February 1900 he proceeded to the Cape. There he received command of the 14th infantry brigade, which he led to Pretoria, distinguishing himself on the Zand River. After the capture of the Boer capital (5 June) he was appointed military governor of Pretoria and thus administered a large area of the Transvaal. He fulfilled this task with tact and humanity, being created K.C.B. for his services and appointed temporary major-general in 1900; subsequently, in 1902, he received a brevet colonelcy and the C.M.G. In the latter year, before the end of hostilities, he was given the command of a column based on Vryburg, where he remained after the conclusion of peace on 31 May.

In the autumn of 1902 Maxwell was chosen by the Duke of Connaught, then acting as commander-in-chief in Ireland, to be his chief staff officer at Dublin. There he remained until May 1904, when the duke became inspector-general of the forces, and Maxwell followed his chief to London. At the end of 1907 the duke was transferred to Malta as commander-in-chief and chief commissioner in the Mediterranean; Maxwell once more accompanied him, and served with him until

September 1908. He had been promoted major-general at the end of 1906.

Maxwell left Malta in order to assume command of the British troops in Egypt, a position which fell to him as a reward for his service with the duke. His tenure of office in Egypt lasted until November 1912, that is, shortly after his promotion to lieutenant-general. It was not marked by any incident of note, although the Italo-Turkish War of 1912 caused him some preoccupation. After leaving this appointment he went on half-pay.

On the outbreak of the European War Maxwell was dispatched to French headquarters as head of the British military mission. There he served until the opening of the battle of the Marne, when, finding little scope for his activities, he was glad to resume command in September 1914 of all the troops in Egypt. The position proved to be both important and exacting. In February 1915 the Turks appeared on the Suez Canal after an arduous desert march, and were easily driven back. Events, however, rapidly increased Maxwell's responsibilities. Egypt became the base for the Gallipoli operations during 1915; subsequently, after the evacuation of the peninsula, the troops were withdrawn to Egypt in order to be refitted before being sent to the Salonika front. The Palestine expedition of 1916 was also based on Egypt. Maxwell's personal position was further complicated by the system of command which grew up around him. No less than 400,000 men were quartered in or based on Egypt, whilst three different groups of higher authorities were concerned in their command and administration. After repelling an attack by the fanatic Senussi in the Western desert in January 1916, Maxwell pressed for his own recall home in March. He had been created K.C.M.G. in 1915.

Shortly after Maxwell's return to England, on Easter Monday, 24 April 1916, the Sinn Fein rebellion broke out in Dublin. He was thereupon appointed commander-in-chief in Ireland with very extensive powers for the purpose of re-establishing order. This he accomplished in the course of a few days, during which thirteen rebels were shot by sentence of court martial. For the next few months Maxwell virtually governed Ireland through the army and the Royal Irish Constabulary under a proclamation of martial law. His administration proved just and humane, but the situation was far from easy and exposed him to fierce criticism both in Ireland and in England. He received the G.C.B. as his reward in November 1916, when he was appointed commander-in-chief, Northern command, at York. There he remained until after the end of the War, when he was sent to Egypt as a member of Lord Milner's mission (December 1919 to March 1920) which was to define the future relations of Great Britain with that country. He had been promoted general in June 1919, but was not re-employed, and went on retired pay in 1922. He died at Cape Town 20 February 1929.

Maxwell, although not a student nor a deeply read man, possessed an uncommon sense of proportion in dealing with concrete matters, and he excelled in handling administrative problems. His career never afforded him an opportunity of showing himself a great leader in the field, but his readiness to take action on his own responsibility never forsook him in any emergency. In private life he was a sincere and staunch friend, generous as far as his purse allowed. He was also an Egyptologist of considerable repute.

Maxwell married in 1892 Louise, daughter of Charles William Bonynge, of New York and Dublin, and had one daughter.

[*The Times*, 22 February 1929; Sir George Arthur, *General Sir John Maxwell*, 1932; Army Lists; personal knowledge.]

H. de Watteville.

MAY, Sir WILLIAM HENRY (1849–1930), admiral of the fleet, was born at Liscard, Cheshire, 31 July 1849, the third son in the family of ten children of Job William Seaburne May, by his wife, Anne Jane Freckleton. Since the seventeenth century the family had lived in Holland, where an ancestor, John May, had settled in the profession of naval architect. William Henry May's grandfather, an admiral in the Dutch navy and at the same time captain in the British navy, had assisted in restoring Prince William of Orange to the throne of Holland in 1813. His father left Holland in 1840 and established himself in business on the stock exchange in Liverpool, where he acted as consul for the Netherlands.

May was educated first at the Royal Institution School, Liverpool, and later, when he had decided to enter the royal navy, at Mr. Eastman's academy at Portsea. Passing into the training ship *Britannia* in the twenty-second place out of fifty entrants in 1863, he passed out a year later in the fourth place, and embarked at once, at the age of fifteen, on board the *Victoria*, flagship of the Mediterranean fleet. After three years he was transferred to the frigate *Liffey*, in which he served the remaining eighteen months of his midshipman's time. A sub-lieutenant in 1869, May passed his examinations in that rank with so much credit that, as a reward, he was appointed, after a few months in the *Hercules*, to the royal yacht *Victoria and Albert*. He was advanced to lieutenant after two and a half years, gaining promotion before many of his seniors. Returning to the *Hercules*, he served on board her for two years (1872–1874) and was then appointed to the gunnery-school ship *Excellent* to qualify as a specialist in gunnery. So far his career had been on the usual lines, but now an opportunity was presented of taking part in the Arctic expedition fitting out (1875) under Captain (Sir) George Strong Nares [q.v.]. May at once volunteered, and was accepted for this service as navigating officer of H.M.S. *Alert*. He served throughout the expedition until its return in 1876, having taken part in the sledging expeditions to Lincoln Bay and in relief of the party led by Commander (Sir) Albert Hastings Markham [q.v.] and in the search for a practicable overland route to Cape Prevost. He was engaged in much surveying work, for which he was commended by Sir George Nares in his official report.

On his return from the Arctic expedition May joined the torpedo-school ship *Vernon*. There he played a prominent and important part in developing the Whitehead torpedo and an underwater discharging apparatus. After three and a half years (1877–1880) in the *Vernon* and a few months in the frigate *Inconstant*, he was promoted to commander, after only nine and a half year's service in lieutenant's rank, and was at once given command of the new torpedo-ram ship *Polyphemus*. He held this command for two and a half years (1881–1884) and for the next three years was second in command of the royal yacht. At the age of thirty-eight he was promoted to captain.

In March 1888 May went to China as flag captain to Admiral Sir Nowell Salmon in the *Impérieuse*. On the voyage to the East he took possession, acting on secret orders, of Christmas Island. He returned to England at the end of the commission in December 1890, and received the appointment of naval attaché to the European states. Two and a half years were spent in this service, principally in France, Russia, and Germany, followed, without any intermission, by appointment to the Admiralty as assistant director of torpedoes. In January 1895 he went as chief of staff to Admiral Sir Michael Culme Seymour [q.v.] on the Mediterranean station, where he gave evidence of a very high degree of organizing ability. After two years' service in the Mediterranean he returned to England and was at once appointed flag captain to Admiral Sir Nowell Salmon, commander-in-chief at Portsmouth, acting as chief of staff during the jubilee celebrations of 1897. On the conclusion of the celebrations, May went to the gunnery school *Excellent*, which he commanded until January 1901. He was then appointed director of naval ordnance and torpedoes.

In April 1901, at the age of fifty-one, May reached flag rank, having a month earlier been made third sea lord and controller of the navy. During the four years of his controllership many far-reaching changes in naval construction and dockyard administration took place. The *Dreadnought* policy [see Watts, Sir Philip] was initiated, though May was not a member of the 'committee of design' appointed in October 1904 to consider the characteristics of the new type; a greater seagoing capacity was given to the torpedo-boat destroyer class; the use of oil sprayed upon coal was introduced, and ships' machinery underwent great alterations. In February 1905 May, who had been created K.C.V.O. in 1904, was appointed to the command of the recently formed Atlantic fleet with his flag on board the *King Edward VII*. In July it fell to him to take the fleet to Brest, where a naval demonstration of the *entente cordiale* took place. May's presence and personality, his knowledge of French, and his able handling of the fleet in entering and leaving Brest harbour left a very good impression upon French naval officers.

After two years in command of the Atlantic fleet, May returned to the Admiralty as second sea lord. At this time (1907) great efforts were being made to cut down naval expenditure, and a reduction of £1,000,000 was ordered by the Cabinet of Sir H. Campbell-Bannerman. When a further reduction of three-quarters of a million was proposed, May, together with the third and fourth sea lords, sent a memorandum to the first sea lord, Sir John (afterwards Lord) Fisher [q.v.], intimating that if this was done they must resign. The reduction was not carried out.

In 1909 May was appointed to the command of the Home fleet with his flag in the *Dreadnought*. This command included all the ships in home waters, and was, in May's opinion, too large. He concentrated his attention upon the investigation of the many tactical problems which the recent growth of the fleet in numbers and size, and the addition to the sea-going fleet of a fighting flotilla, had brought into existence. Gunnery, under the impulse of (Sir) Percy Moreton Scott [q.v.], had made great advances, though it still was far short of what came to be demanded of it in 1914. The torpedo had increased in both range and speed, and presented a new element in tactics. Many officers serving under May's command were dissatisfied with the existing tactical doctrines, and advocated new systems of handling the large and heterogeneous body of ships which formed a modern fleet command. May was always open to receive new ideas, to discuss them, and to try them. He initiated an extensive series of tactical exercises on a scale and with a comprehensiveness not hitherto attempted; the cruising formations from which deployment into battle formation could most rapidly be made; the use of flotillas in a tactical offensive; the employment of fast squadrons in action; the alternative of squadronal command in place of the single line under one command—these were prominent among the tactical matters to which May devoted attention. A man of an essentially practical turn of mind, he submitted to trial new theories and suggestions 'on the scale of twelve inches to the foot'. On hauling down his flag in March 1911 May was appointed commander-in-chief at Devonport. He held this command until promoted admiral of the fleet in March 1913, when his flag came down for the last time.

During the European War May served as a member of the Dardanelles Commission (1916–1917) which sat under the chairmanship of the Earl of Cromer, as chairman of the Reconstruction Committee which dealt, in anticipation, with the problems of the reductions to be made after the war, and on a sub-committee on fisheries. After his retirement he lived at Coldstream, where he took an active part in all local affairs. He died 7 October 1930 in his eighty-second year.

Few flag officers of his time had more continuous employment than Sir William May. In the forty-four years of his service he spent but twenty months in all on half pay, and at no time was longer unemployed than seven months. In person he was tall, strikingly handsome, and physically active and powerful. He rowed in a race in a fleet regatta in his sixty-first year; he hunted until his horses were taken for the War; he shot, and played golf until within ten days of his death. He possessed the great gift of eliciting the opinions and theories of his officers, encouraging their suggestions, and giving them his unbiased consideration.

May married in 1878 Kinbarra Swene, daughter of William John Marrow, merchant, and had two sons. He received the legion of honour in 1905, the K.C.B. in 1906, and was promoted G.C.V.O. in 1909 and G.C.B. in 1911. A private memoir prepared for the immediate circle of his friends is the only hitherto published record of his career.

A cartoon of May by 'Spy' appeared in *Vanity Fair* 26 March 1903.

[Admiralty records; Sir W. H. May, *The Life of a Sailor* (memoirs privately printed 1934); private information; personal knowledge.] H. W. Richmond.

MEATH, twelfth Earl of (1841–1929). [See Brabazon, Reginald.]

MELCHETT, first Baron (1868–1930), industrialist, financier, and politician. [See Mond, Alfred Moritz.]

MEREDITH, Sir WILLIAM RALPH (1840–1923), Canadian politician, was born in the township of Westminster, Middlesex, Upper Canada (now Ontario), 31 March 1840, the eldest son of John Walsingham Cooke Meredith, of London, Ontario, by his wife, Sarah, daughter of Anthony Pegler, of the same town. His father was of Irish birth, and a graduate of Trinity College, Dublin. Meredith was educated at the London district grammar school; in 1859 he won a two-year scholarship in the Toronto law school, and in 1861 was called to the bar of Upper Canada. He soon rose in his profession, but found time to study for and take the degree of LL.B. at the university of Toronto (1867). He practised law in London, Ontario, becoming Q.C. in 1875, and a bencher of the Law Society of Upper Canada in 1876. In 1888 he moved to Toronto, where from February to October 1894 he held the office of corporation counsel and head of the legal department of the city.

Meanwhile, in 1872, Meredith had been elected to represent London as a conservative in the legislative assembly of Ontario, and in 1878 he became leader of the opposition in that body. Although a distinguished speaker and a man of great powers of work, Meredith was not wholly a success in politics. He had not the political subtlety of (Sir) Oliver Mowat [q.v.], the liberal leader in the provincial house, and his opinions were really much more radical than conservative. As early as 1875 he advocated manhood suffrage, and soon after made the compensation of working-men for accidents a plank in his platform. He had too much independence of mind to see eye to eye with Sir John Alexander Macdonald [q.v.], the conservative leader in the federal house. At the same time he was compelled to support Macdonald in his fight with Mowat on the question of provincial rights and the ownership of the Crown lands. By doing so, Meredith lessened his local popularity; for Mowat was fighting for the importance of the province, and was ultimately successful, after the question had been taken before the Judicial Committee of the Privy Council.

In education Meredith opposed the liberal policy of placing the department of education under a political minister, with a seat in the cabinet, and urged that control should be given to a non-political superintendent. He also came into conflict with the Catholic Church over educational policy, since he wished to curtail the power of the clergy over the separate (Catholic) schools. His dialectical triumph in 1894 in a conflict with an ultramontane bishop was not very agreeable to his federal leader, who depended largely upon the support of an ultramontane Quebec.

In 1894 Meredith retired from political life, and was appointed by the federal (conservative) government to be chief justice of the common pleas division of the high court of justice of Ontario. During the break-up of the federal (conservative) government in 1895–1896, repeated efforts were made, especially by Sir Charles Tupper [q.v.], to induce him to leave the bench and to take a portfolio in the ministry, but without success [J. S. Willison, *Sir Wilfred Laurier*, ii. 222, 253]. In 1912 he became chief justice of Ontario and thereby president *ex officio* of the appellate division. As a judge, Meredith took an important part in codifying the laws of the province. In 1896 he had been appointed a member of the commission for the revision of the provincial statutes, and did most of the work upon it. In 1910 he was the chairman of a provincial commission on whose report was based the existing provincial statute awarding compensation to working-men for injuries.

Meredith also played an important part in educational affairs. In 1895 he was appointed to the senate of the university of Toronto, and in 1900 was elected its chancellor, a position which he held until his death. In 1904 the conservatives came into power in the province, after thirty-three years of opposition, and one of their first acts was to appoint a commission under Meredith's chairmanship to look into the affairs of the provincial university (known as the university of Toronto), which had long been hampered by undue political interference. The report of the commission, which was largely due to Meredith, took shape in the Act of 1906, by which the university was placed under an independent board of governors, and given greatly increased financial support. Since then its growth has been steady and rapid, and until his death Meredith was the power behind the scenes, and the adviser of the government in all matters relating to the university.

Meredith was knighted in 1896. He was a man of fine presence, great industry, and unblemished integrity, with an extraordinary grasp both of the details and the principles of the law in a great variety of subjects. In religion he was an Anglican. He died in Montreal 21 August 1923, of a chill brought on by sea-bathing.

Meredith married in 1862 Mary (died 1930), daughter of Marcus Holmes, of London, Ontario. His only son died on active service during the European War; three daughters survived him. He belonged to a very able family: his brother, Sir Vincent Meredith, first baronet (1850–1929), became president of the Bank of Montreal, and another brother, Richard Martin (born 1847), was also chief justice of the common pleas and president of the high court division of the Supreme Court of Ontario.

[H. J. Morgan, *Canadian Men and Women of the Time* (editions of 1898 and 1912); W. S. Wallace, *Dictionary of Canadian Biography*, 1926; Toronto *Daily Globe* and *Daily Mail and Empire*, 22 August 1923; private information.]

W. L. Grant.

MERRIMAN, JOHN XAVIER (1841–1926), South African statesman, the eldest son of Nathaniel James Merriman [q.v.], vicar of Street, Somerset, and later bishop of Grahamstown, by his wife, Julia Potter, was born at Street 15 March 1841. His parents removed in 1848 to South Africa, where Merriman received his early education at the diocesan school at Rondebosch. Later he was sent to Radley College, where he rowed in the race of 1858 against Eton, and gained a proficiency in the classics which he retained to the end of his life. After a year or two spent in a London business house, Merriman returned to the Cape in 1861, became qualified, and practised as a land surveyor. In 1869 he was elected to the Cape house of assembly as member for Aliwal North, and he soon distinguished himself as a leading opponent of responsible government, for which he thought the country was not yet ripe. After the Cape had obtained self-government in 1872, however, Merriman became its staunchest upholder, and was soon to show his dislike for imperial interference in any form. In 1871 he became a diamond dealer in Kimberley as the representative of a Cape Town syndicate, and at the diamond fields he met, and soon became on the closest terms of friendship with, Cecil Rhodes. During the years 1874 to 1875 he carried on business as a wine merchant in Cape Town, and also was the first to experiment in the canning of the Cape lobster or crayfish.

Merriman gave up this occupation in 1875 when (Sir) John C. Molteno [q.v.], who had formed the first Cape ministry in 1872, invited him to join his cabinet as commissioner of Crown lands and public works. From the outset Merriman became Molteno's chief lieutenant in opposition to the scheme of confederation for South Africa proposed by the British colonial secretary, the fourth Earl of Carnarvon [q.v.]. His lively and mordant pen was useful in framing the cabinet's replies to the Colonial Office; in fact, he got into trouble for a speech at Uitenhage in which he described the activities of J. A. Froude [q.v.] in Cape Colony and the Orange Free State in 1875 as an 'agitation by an imperial agent which was very embarrassing to the government'. At this time a correspondence was begun with Goldwin Smith [q.v.] at Toronto on the working of the Canadian constitution, a correspondence which went far to convince Merriman of the superiority of the unitary principle which he was to advocate so strongly at the National Union Convention over thirty years later.

Meantime a constitutional issue of more immediate importance arose. The Kaffir War of 1877–1878 had broken out, and to Merriman the cabinet deputed the duties of a secretary for war. The governor of the Cape, Sir Bartle Frere [q.v.], demanded that the colonial levies should be placed under the British officer commanding at the Cape, and expressed doubts whether the commissioner of public works could legally exercise powers which normally belonged to the colonial secretary. Molteno and Merriman put forward a view of ministerial responsibility in advance of the time, and the cabinet was summarily dismissed. When parliament met, Merriman moved a vote of censure on the new ministry for accepting office.

Merriman now began a long association with Jacobus Wilhelmus Sauer which lasted until the death of the latter in 1913. Together they served in the ministries of (Sir) C. T. Scanlen (1881–1884), Cecil Rhodes (1890–1893), W. P. Schreiner (1898–1900), and in Merriman's own ministry (1908–1910). Merriman's interest in the relations between the Cape Colony and her neighbours began during the Scanlen ministry, in which he was again commissioner of public works. Unlike Rhodes, who believed that in the possession of the hinterland lay the key to hegemony in South Africa, Merriman was anxious to see the ports in British hands. His was the chief influence behind Scanlen in urging Lord Derby to proclaim a protectorate over South-West Africa in 1883–1884, and, in the Rhodes ministry, he made tentative efforts to secure the sale or lease of the Portuguese possessions south of Sofala, but especially of Delagoa Bay. In 1890 Merriman took the treasurer's portfolio, which he retained in each subsequent term of office. Always finding a deficit and the stocks depressed, he was always successful in leaving the finances in order and the Cape's credit high.

Out of office, Merriman was back in Kimberley in 1885, first straightening the affairs of the Mining Board for the banks, and then attempting the amalgamation of the mines on behalf of French interests. On the opening of the Transvaal goldfields he engaged in mining. In 1892 he bought the wine and fruit farm 'Schoongezicht' at Stellenbosch, becoming a pioneer in the export of fresh deciduous fruit. Sympathizing with the Uitlanders on the Rand in their grievances, Merriman strongly disapproved of their methods. He drafted the report of the Cape select committee which inquired into the Jameson Raid in 1896, and moved the address calling for the revocation of the charter of the British South Africa Company. He used all his influence with President Steyn, of the Orange Free State, and other leaders in the northern republics to avert the Boer War. He differed with the premier, W. P. Schreiner [q.v.], over the treatment of the Cape rebels, desiring a complete amnesty after the Canadian precedent. This caused a split in the cabinet and led to its resignation in 1900.

In 1901 Merriman and Sauer went on a fruitless mission to try to persuade the English government and people to grant the Boer republics autonomy under their own flags coupled with a scheme of general confederation for South Africa. In 1904 Merriman was defeated at Wodehouse through the disfranchisement of many of his supporters, and was out of parliament for a few weeks—the only break in a parliamentary career extending over fifty-five years. He was returned for Victoria West at a by-election. When the new colonies gained responsible governments, he entered on a correspondence (1907–1908) with President Steyn and General Smuts in anticipation of the union which the Boers were ready to welcome as soon as there were similar governments in the Cape Colony, Transvaal, and Orange River Colony.

In February 1908 Merriman succeeded (Sir) L. S. Jameson as prime minister, and immediately set about the twofold task of hastening forward union and extricating the finances of Cape Colony from the chaos into which they had fallen since the Boer War. In May the Customs Conference at Pretoria appointed him convener of the National Convention which was to meet in Durban. As leader of the Cape delegation, Merriman played a notable part in the discussions which led to union. He moved the resolution which adopted the unitary principle as against the federal, and sacrificed much for the sake of safeguarding the Cape native franchise. He formed one of the delegation which took the Union Bill to England in 1909. Passed over when the first Union prime minister was chosen, Merriman refused General Botha's invitation to join his cabinet, preferring to remain a candid friend of the administration. On the secession of General Hertzog and the formation of the nationalist party, Merriman gave fuller support to the administration, and during the European War assisted Generals Botha and Smuts with advice and all the eloquence at his command. He died at Schoongezicht 2 August 1926, his last years being clouded by a stroke which had seized him on the death of his wife in September 1923.

Merriman was responsible for the Cape Irrigation (1877) and Banking (1891) laws; but his chief political service to South Africa was the promotion of a high standard of financial and public rectitude. He also took a leading part in the cultural development of South Africa. During his first period of office he had moved for a select committee to investigate the Cape archives, and as prime minister he appointed an archives commission; subsequently he himself accepted membership of a commission appointed by the Union government. He was one of the chief movers in the foundation of the South African Philosophical Society and was cofounder and first president of the Van Riebeeck Society for the publication of South African historical documents.

Merriman married in 1874 Agnes, daughter of Joseph Vintcent, a member of the Cape legislative council. There were no children of the marriage.

[Merriman MSS. in the South African Library, Cape Town; Sir Perceval Laurence, *Life of John Xavier Merriman*, 1930; E. A. Walker, *Lord De Villiers and his Times*, 1925, and *A History of South Africa*, 1928; personal knowledge.] A. C. G. Lloyd.

MERRY DEL VAL, RAFAEL (1865–1930), cardinal, was born in London 10 October 1865, the second of the four sons of Don Rafael Merry del Val, then secretary of the Spanish legation in London, afterwards Spanish ambassador in Vienna and to the Holy See, by his wife, Sofia Josefina, daughter of Pedro José de Zulueta, second Count de Torre Diaz. Their eldest son, Alfonso, was Spanish ambassador in London 1913–1931. Merry del Val belonged on his father's side to a family of Irish origin which had emigrated to Spain and become completely Spanish. His maternal grandmother was Scottish. He was educated at Bayliss House, near Slough (1874–1876), and at the Jesuit colleges in Namur and Brussels (1876–1883), but the strong English influence on his early development was shown by the choice of Ushaw College, Durham, for his first priestly studies (1883–1885). Thence he passed to the Roman Pontificia Accademia dei Nobili Ecclesiastici (1885–1891), and attended classes at the Gregorian

University. He was ordained priest, of the diocese of Westminster, in December 1888 and graduated doctor of theology in 1890.

Merry del Val's desire had been to become a simple priest, if not a religious, in England, but from his first arrival in Rome he was singled out for the papal service by Leo XIII, who insisted on his immediate transference from the Scots College, for which he had been entered, to the Accademia. Even before ordination he was sent on complimentary missions, in 1887 to London for Queen Victoria's jubilee, and in 1888 to Berlin; his studies completed, he was in December 1891 moved to the Vatican as *cameriere segreto partecipante*. In 1896 he was appointed secretary to the historic papal commission of inquiry on Anglican orders, and in 1897 he was sent to Canada, as apostolic delegate, to report on the controversy which had arisen over the Catholic schools. On his report the Holy See accepted concessions which previously had not satisfied Catholics. In 1898 he became president of the Accademia, and in 1900 was consecrated titular archbishop of Nicea.

During the last illness of Leo XIII in 1903 the secretary of the College of Cardinals died suddenly; Merry del Val succeeded him. His conduct of the conclave and of the interregnum in the secretariate of state brought him into contact with the new pope, Pius X, who retained him, most exceptionally, as secretary of state. In November 1903, when he was just thirty-eight, he was created cardinal priest with the titular church of Santa Prassede. The critical questions of this pontificate (1903–1914) were political anticlericalism and modernism. Anti-clericalism came to a head in France with the unilateral renunciation of the concordat and the *Loi de Séparation* (1905). Acceptance of the *Associations Cultuelles* would have destroyed the hierarchical constitution of the Church. Similarly, failure to condemn modernism (1907) would have been an abandonment by Rome of her secular tradition. To both questions the papal answer was an utterly uncompromising assertion of principle. It was the right answer, as is now admitted, but at the time it was much criticized, and the secretary of state was held responsible. This was to misunderstand both his personal and his official relation to the pope; but doubtless he was at one with Pius X in recognizing the sharpness of the issues and the necessity for heroic measures. The integral Catholicism for which chiefly he had been chosen left him no alternative.

In January 1914 Merry del Val was appointed archpriest of St. Peter's, but on Pius X's death in August of that year he ceased, as a matter of course, to be secretary of state. From October 1914 until his own sudden death at Rome 26 February 1930 he was, under Benedict XV and Pius XI, secretary of the Holy Office. Charged with the discipline of the whole Church, as an exceptionally experienced and senior, though in years comparatively young, member of the principal Congregations, he exercised great, if unobtrusive, influence. But although he was freely spoken of as a possible successor of Benedict XV, his election was never probable. His conduct of the ceremonies at St. Peter's was deeply impressive.

This career thwarted Merry del Val's constant pastoral aspirations. Yet by lifelong direction he developed into an important institution a boys' and men's club which he had, as a young priest, founded in a poor district of Rome, the Association of the Sacred Heart in Trastevere. His charity to the poor was boundless. The confessional, the sermons, and retreats of his earlier years had to be abandoned, but all his life he pursued an active apostolate by personal intercourse and correspondence. His knowledge of England remained intimate, and his special affection for English people never waned. He was the author of a small controversial book, *The Truth of Papal Claims* (1902), and composed the popular prayer for the conversion of England. On his tomb in the crypt of St. Peter's are inscribed, by his desire, the fitting words: *Da mihi animas. Caetera tolle.*

There are portraits of Merry del Val by B. Georgiev in the Treasury of St. Peter's and by F. D' Ignazio in the Holy Office.

[P. Cenci, *Il Cardinale Raffaele Merry del Val*, Rome, 1933; F. A. Forbes, *Rafael, Cardinal Merry del Val*, 1932; personal knowledge.]

F. de Zulueta.

MERSEY, first Viscount (1840–1929), judge. [See Bigham, John Charles.]

METCALFE, Sir CHARLES HERBERT THEOPHILUS, sixth baronet (1853–1928), civil engineer, born at Simla 8 September 1853, was the only child of Sir Theophilus John Metcalfe, fifth baronet [q.v.], and great-nephew of Charles Theophilus Metcalfe, Baron Metcalfe [q.v.]. His mother, Charlotte (died 26 September

1853), daughter of Lieutenant-General Sir John Low [q.v.], was his father's first wife. His great-grandfather, Sir Thomas Theophilus Metcalfe, a director of the East India Company, was created a baronet in 1802. In 1867 Charles Metcalfe was sent to Harrow, where he was in Mr. Bull's house, and he matriculated from University College, Oxford, in 1874. He obtained a third class in classical moderations in 1876 and a second class in law and history in 1877, graduating B.A. and M.A. in 1881. He played in the university rugby football team in 1875 and ran for Oxford in the quarter-mile in 1876 and 1877. He succeeded to the baronetcy on his father's death in 1883.

Metcalfe served his articles to the engineering firm of Fox and Sons [see Fox, Sir Charles, and Fox Sir Francis] from 1878 to 1881, and was then engaged as their assistant engineer in the construction of the Southern Railway of Ireland and on the West Lancashire Railway. In 1882 and 1883 he was resident engineer on the Southport and Cheshire Lines Railway and for the reclamation of the Hesketh Marsh, and in 1884 on the Liverpool, Southport, and Preston Junction Railway. In 1886 he and (Sir) Douglas Fox, second son of Sir Charles Fox, were jointly appointed consulting engineers for the Liverpool and St. Helens and South Lancashire Railway.

Metcalfe's most important work was accomplished in South Africa. From 1882 to 1914 he lived there more and more continuously, personally locating projected railway lines, and taking charge of their construction. Much of the work was done on foot, sometimes from necessity, sometimes from choice. He and Douglas Fox were engineers for the continuation of the Cape Town Railway through Bechuanaland from Kimberley to Vryberg, and Metcalfe was in charge of the survey from 1888 to 1891. This work brought him into touch with Cecil Rhodes [q.v.], with whom he had been friendly at Oxford. He accompanied Rhodes on the campaign against the Matabele in 1896, and remained closely associated with him until Rhodes's death in 1902. Metcalfe was one of the two or three friends who were present at Rhodes's funeral in the Matoppos. It was Metcalfe's railway work which converted into reality Rhodes's dreams of northward expansion in Africa; for in laying out his routes Metcalfe had in mind not only physical facilities but also the economic development of the country.

Metcalfe and the firm of Sir Douglas Fox and Partners acted jointly as consulting engineers for the various lines constituting the Rhodesia railway system, which links up northwards with the Belgian Congo railways, and southwards with the railways of the Union of South Africa, providing through communication with Cape Town, and forming the centre of a trans-continental connexion joining east to west. The system was inaugurated on 24 May 1893 with the registration of the Bechuanaland Railway Company, the name being changed to Rhodesia Railways on 1 June 1899. The line was begun at Vryberg in May 1893, reached Mafeking in October 1894, and Buluwayo in October 1897. It was intended at that time to carry the railway via Gwelo to the southern end of Lake Tanganyika. Work on the section from Buluwayo to Gwelo was begun in June 1899, but suspended on the outbreak of the Boer War in October. A more detailed survey and the discovery of coal at Wankie led Metcalfe to recommend that, for commercial reasons, the main line should be diverted westward to the Victoria Falls. The Falls were reached in April 1904. The Zambesi was crossed below the falls by the Victoria Falls bridge and in January 1906 the line was opened to the copper mines of Broken Hill. Thence it was carried to the frontier of the Belgian Congo by the Rhodesia–Katanga Junction Railway, completed in 1909, but this section was purchased in 1928 by the Rhodesia and Mashona Railway Company. The eastern branch line was completed from Salisbury to Umtali, on the Portuguese frontier, in May 1899 and from Buluwayo to Salisbury in October 1902.

Metcalfe and Sir Douglas Fox's firm also acted as consulting engineers for the Benguela Railway through Portuguese West Africa, a development which was due to the enterprise of Rhodes's friend, (Sir) Robert Williams. The company was constituted in Lisbon on 28 May 1903 under a concession granted by the Portuguese government in November 1902. The railway was begun from Lobito Bay in 1903 and was completed to the Congo frontier on 28 August 1928. This line is important not only because it is a western outlet for Northern Rhodesia and for the Katanga copper fields, but also because it is designed to be a section of a trans-continental system of which the Rhodesian railways will form the centre, Lobito Bay and Walvis Bay the western, and Beira and Dar-es-Salaam the eastern ports.

Metcalfe was also very largely concerned in establishing communication by rail between British Nyasaland and the port of Beira in Portuguese East Africa. He was joint consulting engineer for the construction of the Shiré Highlands Railway, from Blantyre to Port Herald, which was registered on 25 April 1895, begun in 1904, completed in 1908, and incorporated, together with the Central Africa Railway from Port Herald to Chindio on the Zambesi, in the Nyasaland Railways Company in 1931; and for the survey of the Trans-Zambesia Railway from Beira to Muracca on the Zambesi, which was not completed until 1922, eight years after Metcalfe had left Africa. Since the completion, early in 1935, of the Zambesi bridge on the Lower Zambesi, through railway communication has been established between Blantyre and Beira.

Metcalfe was elected an associate of the Institution of Civil Engineers in 1885, and a member in 1897, and served on the council from 1904 to 1906. He was a director of the Victoria Falls Power Company (which in 1909 became the Victoria Falls and Transvaal Company) from its registration on 17 October 1906. After retiring from Africa in 1914 he took up his residence at Winkworth Hill, Hascombe, near Godalming, Surrey, where he cultivated his hobby of gardening and successfully experimented in colour photography. In 1919 he visited Palestine in order to report to the Zionist organization on the future development of the country. He died, unmarried, at Winkworth Hill 29 December 1928, and was buried at Busbridge, Godalming. He was a bon-vivant, loved good company, and shone in it. Yet most of his life was arduous and solitary. In an emergency he was cool and resourceful. He was succeeded as seventh baronet by his cousin, Theophilus John Massie Metcalfe (born 1866).

[*The Times*, 1 January 1929; *Proceedings* of the Institution of Civil Engineers, 1929, vol. ccxxviii, 352; Union Castle Company's *South and East Africa Year Book and Guide.*]

E. I. Carlyle.

METHUEN, Sir ALGERNON METHUEN MARSHALL, baronet (1856–1924), publisher, was born at 171 Union Street, Southwark, 23 February 1856, the third son of John Buck Stedman, F.R.C.S., of Godalming, at one time mayor of that town, by his wife, Jane Elizabeth, daughter of Richard Marshall, of King's Lynn. He changed his surname from Stedman to Methuen in 1899. He was educated at Berkhamsted School and at Wadham College, Oxford, where he took his B.A. degree in 1878 and proceeded M.A. in 1881. While at Oxford he wrote a book about the University, entitled *Oxford Life*, which was not very favourably received by the authorities. On leaving Oxford he acted for a while as tutor in a coaching establishment, and in 1880 opened a private school of his own at Milford, Surrey. In 1884 he married Emily Caroline, daughter of Edwin Bedford, solicitor, of Ladbroke Terrace, London. They had no children. During his period as a schoolmaster he wrote a number of text-books of elementary Latin, Greek, and French, of which some twenty are still in print. It was primarily with the idea that he might handle these little books more profitably himself that, in June 1889, under the style Methuen & Co., he opened a small publishing office in Bury Street, London, with a manager in charge. From the beginning educational works were an important part of his production, but the business of the firm was gradually extended to every department of letters.

The first important success of the firm of Methuen was the publication in 1892 of Rudyard Kipling's *Barrack-Room Ballads*. In 1895 Stedman gave up his school and concentrated on publishing. Kipling's poetry continued to be published by him, and the popularity of the novels of Marie Corelli [q.v.], most of which bore the Methuen imprint, was another source of profit. Others of the firm's successful authors were F. W. Bain, Hilaire Belloc, 'George Birmingham', A. G. Bradley, J. B. Bury (with his edition of Gibbon), G. K. Chesterton, A. Clutton Brock, Joseph Conrad, Kenneth Grahame, A. P. Herbert, 'Anthony Hope', Edward Hutton, W. W. Jacobs, E. V. Knox, Sir E. Ray Lankester, Sir Oliver Lodge, E. V. Lucas (with his edition of Charles Lamb and miscellaneous works), Robert Lynd, Maurice Maeterlinck, Sir John Marriott, John Masefield, A. A. Milne, Sir Charles Oman, Sir Gilbert Parker, Sir Flinders Petrie, R. L. Stevenson, and Oscar Wilde. The firm also issued a *History of England* in seven volumes (1904–1913) by leading historians, which met with marked success. Methuen's range was catholic, but if he may be said to have had one special leaning it was towards topography. He was particular that every book and every edition issued by his firm should bear the year of publication. The office of the firm was moved to Essex Street, Strand, in 1895, and the business was turned into a limited liability company in 1910.

In politics, of which he was a constant observer, Methuen was at one time a tariff reformer and follower of Joseph Chamberlain; he changed his mind, however, and in 1905 wrote, under the title *England's Ruin*, a pamphlet in favour of free trade. In 1910 he contested the Guildford division of Surrey as a liberal, but was unsuccessful. Two other political works from his pen were, in 1901, a pamphlet on the Boer War, called *Peace or War in South Africa*, afterwards expanded into *The Tragedy of South Africa* (1905), and in 1911, *A Simple Plan for a New House of Lords*. In 1921 he compiled *An Anthology of English Verse*, following it in 1922 with a sequel, *Shakespeare to Hardy*, both of which met with a warm welcome. His only other non-political work was a little book on rock plants, entitled *An Alpine A.B.C.* (1922), gardening being the constant delight of his spare hours. He was created a baronet in 1916. He died 20 September 1924 at Haslemere, where he was buried.

In business Methuen was vigilant, imaginative, and constructive, concealing under a diffident and even detached manner great shrewdness. In private life he was urbane and philanthropic, much concerned in schemes for social welfare. By his will he left large sums to Berkhamsted School and to Wadham College.

[*Sir Algernon Methuen, Baronet: a Memoir*, privately issued in 1925; private information.]

E. V. Lucas.

MEUX (formerly LAMBTON), Sir HEDWORTH (1856–1929), admiral of the fleet, was born in London 5 July 1856, the third son of George Frederick D'Arcy Lambton, second Earl of Durham, by his wife, Lady Beatrix Frances, second daughter of James Hamilton, first Duke of Abercorn [q.v.]. He was educated at Cheam School and entered the *Britannia* as a naval cadet in 1870. He went to sea in December 1871 in the *Endymion*, frigate, of the Channel squadron, being transferred to the flagship *Agincourt*, under Sir Beauchamp Seymour, in August 1874. At the beginning of 1875 he went to the *Undaunted*, flagship, in the East Indies until his promotion to sub-lieutenant at the end of that year. From the end of 1876 to March 1879 he served in the *Alexandra*, flagship, in the Mediterranean under Sir Geoffrey Hornby. He was promoted lieutenant in February 1879, and in 1880 returned to the *Alexandra* as flag-lieutenant to his old chief, Sir Beauchamp Seymour, under whom he was present at the bombardment of Alexandria (11 July 1882) and took part in the ensuing operations on the coast of Egypt. Admiral Seymour (created Lord Alcester for his services), on leaving his command to join the board of Admiralty in March 1883, secured a 'haul-down' promotion for his flag-lieutenant. On returning home, Commander Lambton went to Dublin as aide-de-camp to the lord-lieutenant, the fifth Earl Spencer. In July 1886 he returned to the Mediterranean in command of the *Dolphin*, sloop; and in February 1888 he was appointed to the command of the royal yacht *Osborne*, a post which he held until his promotion to captain in 1889. From 1890 to 1892 he was flag-captain to (Sir) Charles Hotham in the *Warspite* on the Pacific station.

In July 1894 Earl Spencer, then first lord of the Admiralty, appointed Lambton his naval private secretary, and Lambton retained the post under Spencer's successor, Viscount Goschen, until 1897. In this important office both ministers placed the greatest reliance on his independent and fearless judgement on the claims of senior officers for appointments; indeed, on more than one occasion Lambton advised his chief to make high appointments to which the sea lords objected, but which in the event were fully justified. He failed, however, to make himself popular with the officers with whom he had to deal through the lack of consideration which he showed them, although he was far junior to most of them in rank and to all of them in age.

In 1897 Lambton went to the China station in command of the cruiser *Powerful*, and on his voyage home in her in October 1899 he was sent to Durban, at a critical moment in the early stages of the South African War. On his way thither he called at Mauritius, and on his own initiative embarked the 2nd battalion of the South Yorkshire Regiment. Sir George Stuart White [q.v.], in command of the defence of Ladysmith, had been sending urgent messages for the supply of more powerful guns. Captain (Sir) Percy Scott [q.v.] in the cruiser *Terrible*, which had arrived at the Cape on its way to replace the *Powerful* on the China station, devised gun-carriages for 12-pounder and 4·7 naval guns, and with these powerful reinforcements Lambton landed with a naval brigade and arrived at Ladysmith on 30

October just in time. The naval guns kept down the Boer artillery throughout the subsequent siege; and Lambton was, in Sir George White's words, 'the life of the garrison' until its ultimate relief (28 February). Lambton was awarded a C.B. for his services, and on the arrival of the *Powerful* in England was welcomed with great popular enthusiasm. At the end of that year he was persuaded by Lord Rosebery and by his brother, Lord Durham, to stand at the general election, in the liberal interest, for Newcastle-upon-Tyne; but he was unsuccessful. In April 1901 he was appointed to the command of the royal yacht *Victoria and Albert*, and three months later he was made commodore in charge of the king's yachts; he retained this command until April 1903, having been promoted to rear-admiral in October 1902. From June 1903 he had a year's service afloat as second in command to Lord Charles Beresford in the Channel fleet, and from November 1904 to December 1906 he commanded the cruiser division of the Mediterranean fleet. In January 1908 he was appointed vice-admiral and commander-in-chief in China, returning home in April 1910.

At this stage in Lambton's career occurred a great change in his private affairs. A few days after hauling down his flag he married Mildred, third daughter of the first Baron Alington [q.v.] and widow of Viscount Chelsea (died 1908), second son of the fifth Earl Cadogan [q.v.]. In the following December he came into a large fortune under the will of Valerie Susie, widow of Sir Henry Brent Meux, brewer, third baronet, of Theobald's Park, Waltham Cross. During the South African War Lady Meux, on hearing of the landing of the naval guns for the defence of Ladysmith, had ordered six naval 12-pounder guns, mounted on travelling carriages, to be made at Elswick and sent out to the commander-in-chief in South Africa, Lord Roberts. They were known as the Elswick battery. On his return to England later in that year, Lambton had called upon Lady Meux, described the work of his guns at Ladysmith, and praised her patriotic action in sending similar guns to the front. Touched by this tribute, Lady Meux, after making many wills, decided to make Lambton her heir on the sole condition that he changed his name to Meux. This he did by royal licence in September 1911. He was promoted admiral in March 1911 and remained on half-pay until his appointment in July 1912 to be commander-in-chief at Portsmouth, an office which he retained until February 1916, having been selected for the rank of admiral of the fleet in March 1915.

On the outbreak of the European War, Meux's principal duty was to secure the safe passage of the transports conveying the British Expeditionary Force to France, and to guard the army's main line of communication from Southampton to Havre. This anxious work was carried out with complete success; moreover, on his own initiative, Meux organized a life-saving patrol service composed of yachts and other small craft, sailing under the blue ensign with a red cross at the main. On giving up his command he was persuaded to enter parliament, without contest, as conservative member for Portsmouth, in the vacancy caused by Lord Charles Beresford's elevation to the peerage. He was a popular figure in the House of Commons and several times intervened with vigorous speeches on naval subjects; but he was not really interested in parliamentary work, and retired at the general election of 1918.

Meux was now free to devote himself to the turf, which since his boyhood had been his greatest interest outside the navy. He had started breeding blood stock in 1882, and had had some good horses trained by Tom Green at Stapleton Park, Pontefract. He won the Grand Military gold cup with 'Ruy Lopez' in 1895, and was elected to the Jockey Club in 1906. On inheriting Theobald's Park, where Lady Meux had a racing stable, he bred his own horses there, and with them won the Hardwicke stakes at Ascot three times, the Manchester November Handicap (top weight), the Liverpool cup, the Chester cup, and many other races. He was a very shrewd judge of racing and breeding and of all turf matters, and would have been an even more successful owner had he not been too fond of his horses to part with them.

Meux was a man of strong and independent character, though by no means a typical naval officer; in fact, the service was for him an interest rather than a profession. He carried out his duties with marked ability and won the confidence not only of King Edward VII but of all his associates in the service. He was created C.V.O. in 1901 and K.C.V.O. in 1906. He was promoted K.C.B. in 1908 and G.C.B. in 1913. He died 20 September 1929 at Danebury, an estate which he had bought near Stockbridge. His will was proved at £910,465 gross, with net personalty £734,265. He had no children, and he left his fortune, subject to his widow's interest, to her grandson, Ian Hedworth Gilmour.

There are portraits of Meux, painted by P. A. de Lászlό and Ambrose McEvoy, in the possession of his widow, who subsequently married Lord Charles Montagu. A cartoon of him by 'Spy' appeared in *Vanity Fair* 28 June 1900.

[Official records; private information.]

V. W. BADDELEY.

MEW, CHARLOTTE MARY (1869–1928), poet, the eldest daughter of Frederick Mew, an architect, by his wife, Anne, daughter of Henry Edward Kendall, an architect well known in the middle of the nineteenth century, was born in Doughty Street, London, 15 November 1869. She was educated privately, and later attended lectures at University College, London. She passed almost the whole of her life in Bloomsbury, and lived for over thirty years at 9 Gordon Street. In 1923 she was awarded a civil list pension of £75. Shortly afterwards her much loved sister and companion, Anne Mew, was smitten with a mortal illness of which she died in 1927. From this blow Charlotte Mew was unable to rally, and she died by her own hand in a nursing home in London 24 March 1928.

Early in her life Charlotte Mew showed an unusual talent for writing verse and prose, and from her twentieth to her thirtieth year she was a regular contributor to *Temple Bar*. She published one excellent story, 'Passed', in the *Yellow Book*, July 1894. Her poems, stories, essays, and studies appeared in periodicals from time to time, mainly in *The Nation*, *The New Statesman*, *The Englishwoman*, and *The Chap-book*. Her work was admired by her contemporaries, notably by Thomas Hardy, who greatly valued it and considered her to be the best woman poet of her day.

Although Charlotte Mew continued to write throughout her life, only two small books of her verse have been published—*The Farmer's Bride* (1915) and *The Rambling Sailor*, which appeared posthumously in 1929. Her fastidious self-criticism prevented her even from preserving anything that did not conform to the standard which she had set for herself. The appearance of her first book brought her immediate recognition. The title poem exhibits to the full her peculiar powers of condensation and her dramatic and psychological insight. She had a particularly individual manner and mode of expression. Her verse is characterized by a tense fine-drawn rhythm which varies according to the emotion of the poem. It is clear, concise, and remarkably direct. Her passionate insistence on facing the truth is particularly evident in *Madeleine in Church*; her uncanny power of arousing in her readers the same emotion as had inspired her own poem makes *In Nunhead Cemetery* almost too piercing; and *Sea Love* is a notable example of lyrical condensation.

[*The Times*, 29 March 1928; personal knowledge.]

A. MONRO.

MEYER, FREDERICK BROTHERTON (1847–1929), Baptist divine, the only son of Frederick Meyer, merchant, of London, and great-grandson of John Sebastian Meyer, who migrated from Worms to London early in the eighteenth century, was born at Clapham 8 April 1847. His mother was Ann, daughter of Henry Sturt, of London. He was educated at Brighton College. Home influences and associations with Baptist churches in Bloomsbury and afterwards in New Park Road, London, where he was baptized in 1864, awakened in Meyer a desire to become a minister. Before entering upon special training he spent two years in an office in Billiter Square. In 1866 he entered Regent's Park (Baptist) College, and in 1869 graduated B.A. of London University. In 1870 he became assistant to the Rev. Charles Mitchell Birrell, of Liverpool, the father of Augustine Birrell, and a man of considerable culture. In May 1872 he was called to the ministry of the Baptist chapel in York, where he came into contact with the well-known American evangelist Dwight Lyman Moody, whose influence proved deep and lasting. In 1874 Meyer became pastor of Victoria Road Baptist church, Leicester, but 'the amalgam of Birrell and Moody' was unable to find in its forms of service adequate scope for his powers, and he therefore resigned in 1878. Melbourne Hall, Leicester, was then built for him as the centre of the social and religious activities of a new pastorate, and it is still the home of a flourishing community. Meyer's later London ministry was exercised in two churches—Regent's Park chapel (1888–1892 and 1909–1915) and Christ Church, Westminster Bridge Road (1892–1907 and 1915–1921). He remained 'pastor emeritus' of the latter until his death. In

1911 the McMaster University of Canada conferred upon him the honorary degree of D.D.

For more than half a century Meyer carried on a unique ministry. His industry was extraordinary, and he served in many capacities with distinction. In 1904–1905 and in 1920–1921 he was president of the National Free Church Council; in 1906–1907 president of the Baptist Union; he presided at the World's Sunday School Convention held at Washington in 1908, and he served other movements with similar energy and ability. He was a prolific writer of devotional and expository books, sermons, pamphlets, and articles. Some seventy volumes came from his pen, and of these several have been published in other languages. It has been estimated that at the time of Meyer's death 5,000,000 copies of his books and tracts had been circulated. He travelled widely, visiting Germany, Canada, North and Central America, the Near and Far East, South Africa, and Australia, always with a religious purpose. He took a large part in social and philanthropic work, and his outspoken protests against public evils occasionally exposed him to severe criticism. But he lived the gospel that he preached. His deep sincerity, his emphasis upon the experience of the Holy Spirit, and his frank unveiling of his inner life in the effort to help others impressed his contemporaries, and made him widely respected outside nonconformist circles. In conferences such as those held at Keswick and at Northfield, Massachusetts, he was an ever-welcome figure. He died 28 March 1929 at Bournemouth.

Meyer married in 1871 Jane Eliza Jones, of Birkenhead (died January 1929), and had one daughter.

[*The Times*, 30 March 1929; *The Baptist Year Book*, 1930; W. Y. Fullerton, *F. B. Meyer, a Biography*, 1929.]

J. H. Rushbrooke.

MEYER, Sir WILLIAM STEVENSON (1860–1922), Indian civil servant, was born at Galatz, Moldavia, during a temporary visit of his parents, 13 February 1860. He was the elder son of the Rev. Theodore Jonah Meyer, a minister of the Presbyterian Church of England, who was naturalized as a British subject in 1855, by his wife, Jane Ann, daughter of William Stevenson. He was educated at a mission school at Blackheath, at University College School, and at University College, London; and in the open competition for the Indian civil service held in 1879 he obtained the third place. Two years later Meyer joined the service in Madras. His first post outside the Presidency, where his ability and industry had soon been marked, was that of deputy secretary, finance department, government of India (1898). Throughout his long connexion with that department, Meyer's work was distinguished by great critical power, which sometimes offended through its mordancy, and by a comprehensive grasp of detail which never obscured his perception of the broad features of a case.

In 1902 Meyer succeeded Sir Herbert Risley as Indian editor of the *Imperial Gazetteer of India* (third edition), a post which he held till 1905. Although he was not an Oriental scholar, his clear historical sense, based on wide study of ancient and modern history, enabled him to guide on right lines a number of contributors of unequal merit. After he had become financial secretary, government of India, in 1905, the controversy between Lord Curzon [q.v.] as viceroy and Lord Kitchener [q.v.] as commander-in-chief led to the abolition of the post of military member of the viceroy's council. Meyer was appointed in 1906 to the newly created post of secretary of military finance, which involved important and delicate duties as *liaison* officer between the civil and military departments. Here his knowledge of finance and powers of organization were especially useful during Lord Kitchener's rearrangement of the army in India. He was subsequently (1907–1909) a member of a royal commission which inquired into the possibility of decentralizing control in almost all departments of the civil administration of India, and had important results in freeing local bodies from official restraint.

After serving (1912–1913) on a small committee, presided over by Field-Marshal Lord Nicholson, which inquired into military expenditure in India, Meyer succeeded Sir Guy Fleetwood Wilson in 1913 as finance member of the government of India, and held that post throughout the European War. His administration of military finance was charged with parsimony leading to disaster, especially in the *Report* of the royal commission on the Mesopotamia Campaign (1917), which referred to 'indications of reluctance on the part of the Indian government to recognize the indisputable fact, that war means extra expenditure' (p. 106). But the criticisms were largely unjust so far as Meyer was concerned, for in India real and final responsibility attaches to the viceroy and commander-in-chief whose policy binds the finance member. The Government of India Act (1858) had contemplated an army in India organized only for internal security and for frontier defence, and during fifty years successive secretaries of state had resisted expenditure beyond what they considered sufficient for those purposes. In spite of restriction, expenditure had risen from 16 million sterling at the time of the Boer War to nearly 20 million in 1913–1914, and was regularly challenged as excessive by Indian politicians. The measures which Meyer took to reduce the dislocation caused by the War through fluctuating exchange, deficiency of currency, loss of confidence, diminished trade, and increased expenditure were generally approved. He changed the system of income tax by introducing a sliding scale instead of flat rates; and when the customs tariff had to be raised, he framed it, in accordance with Indian desires, so as to give some preference to Indian industries, especially cotton and iron. His services as first president of the central recruiting board were also notable, and he enlarged the field of recruitment by changing it from a regimental to a civil agency.

Towards Indian aspirations for a larger share in the control of their own affairs Meyer's attitude was liberal and optimistic, though cautious, especially in the matter of finance. He is reported to have coined the term 'dyarchy' in reference to the method of administration introduced by the Government of India Act (1919) in which a provincial government includes both members appointed by the crown and ministers chosen from elected members of the legislative council.

Meyer, who retired from the Indian civil service in 1918, was appointed in October 1920 first high commissioner of India, to take over from the secretary of state functions of agency analogous to those performed by the high commissioners of the Dominions. His organization of this important and difficult office was very successful. Mainly at his suggestion, the Indian government has declared an open market, without preference for British manufactures, for its requirements of material not available in India.

Meyer now took some part in international affairs. He represented the British and Indian governments at the International Opium Conference at The Hague (1911–1912), and he headed the Indian delegations at the first and second assemblies of the League of Nations (1920–1921). His financial experience prompted the decision that an external committee should control the estimates and accounts of the League, and his plea that India should be represented on the governing body of the International Labour Organization was accepted later. He was also chairman of the finance sub-committee of Earl Haig's Officers' Association and a member of the Imperial Shipping Committee.

During the early years of his service Meyer was interested in the affairs of the Madras University, to which he left a legacy; and he translated and revised J. Chailley's *L'Inde Britannique* as *Administrative Problems of British India* (1910). His ready wit in private life made him an attractive companion to those who escaped his caustic judgements. In recognition of his public services he was made K.C.I.E. (1909), K.C.S.I. (1915), and G.C.I.E. (1918). He married in 1895 Mabel Henrietta (died 1914), daughter of Major William W. Jackson, Indian army. Their son and daughter predeceased him, the deaths of both being due to tragic accidents. His own death, which occurred in London 19 October 1922, was sudden. A crayon portrait by 'Spy Junior' is at India House, the office of the high commissioner for India, Aldwych, London.

[*The Times*, 20 October 1922; *India Office List*, 1922; *Mesopotamia Commission Report*, 1917, Cd. 8610; private information; personal knowledge.] R. Burn.

MEYNELL, ALICE CHRISTIANA GERTRUDE (1847–1922), poet, essayist and journalist, was born at Barnes 11 October 1847, the younger of the two daughters of Thomas James Thompson, by his wife, Christiana, daughter of Thomas Edward Weller. The elder daughter, Elizabeth, well known later as a painter of battle-scenes, married Lieutenant-General Sir William Francis Butler [q.v.]. The Thompsons lived almost as much in Italy and France as in England. Mr. Thompson, a Cambridge man, a friend of Charles Dickens (by whom he was introduced to Christiana Weller), and a lifelong dilettante, devoted himself to his daughters' education, and Alice Meynell has recorded in a memorable essay and in a poem her indebtedness to his intellect and character. Mrs. Thompson became a Roman Catholic about 1870; her example was followed by Alice about 1872, by Elizabeth a year later, and by their father shortly before his death in 1881. Their change of religion brought Alice into touch with the circle that included Aubrey de Vere, who introduced her to Tennyson and encouraged her to publish; and her first volume of poems, *Preludes*, appeared in 1875, when she was twenty-eight.

In 1877 Alice Thompson married Wilfrid Meynell, and became his helpmate in journalism, the births of eight children between 1879 and 1891 still leaving her time for much writing. In 1880 the Meynells took over a short-lived magazine, *The Pen*, and here are to be found essays on Tennyson, Ruskin, Browning, Rossetti, and Swinburne, which anticipate the convictions and style of Alice Meynell's later writing. From 1881 to 1898 Wilfrid Meynell, with his wife's help, edited *The Weekly Register*. From 1883 to 1895 they edited *Merry England*, a monthly, and this, too, is full of writing recognizable as Alice Meynell's even when unsigned or pseudonymous, including essays on Trollope, Charles Reade, George Eliot, the Carlyles, Coventry Patmore, and Aubrey de Vere. (Another source for her unreprinted prose is the *Dublin Review* from 1906 to 1922.) She also contributed to the *Scots Observer* (after 1891 the *National Observer*) from 1889 to 1894 during the editorship of W. E. Henley [q.v.], and her first volume of essays, *The Rhythm of Life* (1893), was almost entirely reprinted from these two periodicals. About 1892 she became personally acquainted with Coventry Patmore, whose genius she had long recognized, and who now proclaimed her genius with equal ardour. In 1894 she undertook to write a weekly article in the *Pall Mall Gazette*, at first anonymously, and afterwards under the initials 'A. M.' George Meredith sought out the acquaintance of the writer of these articles, and her second volume of essays, *The Colour of Life* (1896), all, except one, reprinted from the *Pall Mall Gazette*, was reviewed both by Patmore and Meredith. Their championship, and Francis Thompson's poems to her, 'Love in Dian's Lap' (*Poems*, 1893), did much to secure for her writing that prestige which its own depth and reticence might have longer delayed.

In 1893 a collection of Alice Meynell's *Poems* was published at the same time as her first volume of essays. The former comprised mostly the *Preludes* of 1875. This volume was followed by *Other Poems* (privately printed, 1896), *Later Poems* (1902), *A Father of Women and other Poems* (1917), and posthumously, *Last Poems* (1923). It is likely that Alice Meynell will rank among women poets with Emily Brontë, Elizabeth Barrett Browning, and Christina Rossetti. There is a marked difference between her earlier and later poems, and her public will often be divided into admirers of one or the other. She herself depreciated her earlier work, with its mournful sweetness. Her later verse is generally (as her prose always) packed close with subtle and original thought.

Further volumes of reprinted essays are *The Children* (1897), *The Spirit of Place* (1899), *Ceres' Runaway* (1909), *Hearts of Controversy* (1917: essays on Tennyson, Swinburne, Dickens, and the Brontës), and *The Second Person Singular* (1921). In 1901–1902, during a visit to the United States, she lectured on Dickens, the Brontës, and seventeenth-century poetry.

Of her volumes of prose only one or two were written as books: the first was *John Ruskin* (1900), a discussion of his teachings and contentions, considered book by book. The other was *Mary, The Mother of Jesus* (1912), essays on the Blessed Virgin in theology, tradition, morality, art, and poetry. Even these were commissioned by publishers, not spontaneously undertaken by herself; which is no more than to say that her life was conditioned by necessity: almost all her prose was journalism, but all her journalism was literature.

Two enterprises, however, she must have undertaken with all her heart: the first, an anthology from Patmore, *The Poetry of Pathos and Delight* (1895); the second, an anthology of English lyric poetry, *The Flower of the Mind* (1897), with notes which are sometimes miniature essays. She also wrote prefaces to over a dozen volumes of selections from individual poets, and to one seventeenth-century anthology (The Red Letter Library, 1902–1906). Her last work, published posthumously, was *The School of Poetry*, an anthology for children, with delightful notes. All these bear witness to her passion for poetry, and pre-eminently for the poetry of the seventeenth century.

The rareness of Alice Meynell's prose and later verse arose from her exact use of words, and her subtle senses. Her eyes and ears were extraordinarily acute; her sense of justice insatiable—with some very human lapses. Her Christianity meant not 'the uneasy certainties of the bigot' (her own phrase), nor the certitude of the mystic; it meant firm but difficult faith.

'Thou art the Way.
Hadst Thou been nothing but the goal
I cannot say
If Thou hadst ever met my soul.'
(*Later Poems*, 'I am the Way.')

Religion, with whatever innocent alleviations of 'the burthen of the mystery', makes the thought of much of her poetry and provides the subjects of many of her essays. The alleviations being most real, she has appreciations, a delight, and a most unusual gaiety of spirit. And every one who knew her—the non-Christian Meredith no less than the Catholic Patmore—testified to her evident sanctity.

Alice Meynell died in London 27 November 1922. A water-colour sketch of her, made by Adrian Stokes in 1877, is in the possession of Mr. Wilfrid Meynell. An etching of this made by Tristram Ellis has been much reproduced. A nearly full-length pencil-drawing of her by John Sargent (1895) is in the National Portrait Gallery.

[Viola Meynell, *Alice Meynell, a Memoir*, 1929; Anne Kimbell Tuell, *Mrs. Meynell and her Literary Generation*, 1925; personal knowledge; private information.] F. Page.

MICHELL, Sir LEWIS LOYD (1842–1928), South African banker and politician, was born at Plymouth 11 August 1842, the second son of John Michell, solicitor, of Ilfracombe, a member of an old Cornish family, by his wife, Mary Bryan. He was named after Lewis Loyd, the banker (father of Samuel Jones Loyd, first Baron Overstone, q.v.), through whose instrumentality he was sent to school at Christ's Hospital, then situated in Newgate Street, London. In 1859 he entered Bolitho's Bank at Penzance, and after four years' training there was transferred to the London and South African Bank. In 1864 he was sent to Port Elizabeth, Cape Colony, where he was destined to remain for twenty-one years. About 1872 he left the London and South African Bank in order to become manager of the Standard Bank of South Africa at Port Elizabeth. His life at Port Elizabeth seems to have been peaceful enough, until the outbreak in 1880 of the first Boer War, at the conclusion of which, in 1881, he met Presidents Kruger and Brand and secured the insertion in the convention then made with the British government of a clause safeguarding banking interests in the Transvaal. In 1885 he was transferred to Cape Town, which then became his permanent head-quarters.

About this time Michell made the acquaintance of Cecil Rhodes [q.v.], who was then engaged in trying to convince the British government of the necessity of preventing the Boer republics from occupying Bechuanaland and closing the trade route to the North. Michell was deeply impressed with the views and character of Rhodes. 'I loved Rhodes', he said, 'as I have never loved any other man'; and Rhodes, on his side, had implicit faith in Michell's judgement. For ten years before Rhodes's death in 1902 Michell held his general power of attorney and, during Rhodes's frequent periods of absence from South Africa, acted for him in matters relating to the affairs of the British South Africa Company. In 1897 Rhodes asked Michell to become one of his executors, and obtained from him a promise that on his death he would retire from the Standard Bank and succeed him as chairman of De Beers Consolidated Mines, and become a director of the British South Africa Company.

Meanwhile Michell's influence in the banking world steadily increased. In 1893 he attended a conference called to consider the adoption of a single coinage for South Africa. The conference broke down, as Dr. Leyds, who represented the Transvaal, insisted that the proposed coinage should bear the head of President Kruger. It was on the occasion of this conference that Kruger asked Michell why he could not speak Dutch, an attack which Michell countered by suggesting that, as the president had been born at Colesberg, in British territory, he should be familiar with the English language. In recognition of his services at this conference Michell was presented by the Cape government with a silver salver, and in 1895 he became sole general manager in South Africa of the Standard Bank.

Michell's account, in his *Life* of Rhodes, of the events connected with the Jameson Raid (29 December 1895) shows that it was not until Rhodes saw him shortly after the Raid that Rhodes explained how his policy of federation had been marred by 'the precipitancy of the Raid, the unpreparedness of the Rand and the timidity of Mr. Hofmeyr'. In Michell's view the Raid was not the cause of the War which broke out in 1899, but was 'a picturesque and irregular episode in the long duel between Republican aspirations and the settled convictions of those who preferred British institutions'. The Raid, he argued, retarded rather than accelerated the final struggle, in that it tied for a while the hands of the paramount power.

Throughout the South African War, on behalf of the British War Office, Michell directed the financing of the army's requirements in South Africa, and at the close of the War, after attending Rhodes's funeral in the Matoppo Hills, near Bulawayo, in March 1902, in fulfilment of his promise, he retired from the Standard Bank, receiving a grant of £5,000 from a grateful board of directors, and was appointed chairman of De Beers Consolidated Mines and a director of the British South Africa Company. At this time (1902) Michell was knighted in recognition of his services as chairman of the Cape martial law board, which had been appointed to consider the cases of British subjects who had been guilty of treasonable practices during the War.

Michell was now elected a member of the Cape House of Assembly, and in 1903 became minister without portfolio in (Sir) Leander Starr Jameson's cabinet. Parliamentary life, however, in no way appealed to him, and in 1905 he resigned his seat, and also the chairmanship of De Beers. From this time his attention was chiefly concentrated on the business of the Rhodes Trust and of the British South Africa Company, which entailed frequent visits to London and Rhodesia, although his interest in public affairs was by no means diminished. Together with Sir William Milton and Sir Charles Coghlan [q.v.] he represented Rhodesia at the national convention (October 1908–May 1909) which preceded the formation of the Union of South Africa. In 1910 he published his *Life* of Rhodes, with the object, as he said, of showing that Rhodes was a great Englishman.

At this period Michell's health was giving him cause for anxiety, and in 1917 he resigned his position of Rhodes trustee. With advancing age his activities naturally decreased, but he retained to the last his directorship of the British South Africa Company and his close connexion with all Rhodesian affairs. He died at Cape Town 29 October 1928.

Michell married in 1871 Maria Agnes, daughter of Edward Philpott, magistrate at Uitenhage, and they had four sons and three daughters.

[Sir Lewis Michell, *Life of Cecil J. Rhodes*, 2 vols., 1910; private information; personal knowledge.] D. Chaplin.

MILLIGAN, Sir WILLIAM (1864–1929), laryngologist and otologist, was born at Aberdeen 24 August 1864, the son of the Very Rev. William Milligan [q.v.], professor of biblical criticism, Aberdeen University, 1860–1893, by his wife, Annie Mary, daughter of David Macbeth Moir [q.v.], physician and author. He was educated at Aberdeen University, graduating M.B., C.M., in 1886 and M.D. with the highest honours in 1892. He was demonstrator of anatomy in the Aberdeen medical school, and subsequently served for a time as house surgeon at the Northern Hospital, Liverpool. He then proceeded to study oto-laryngology at Göttingen and Vienna, finally settling in Manchester, then at the zenith of its prosperity.

Milligan had the opportunity of introducing more scientific methods, especially those of pathology, into a subject which was then in the stage of primitive empiricism. He became aural surgeon to the Manchester Ear Hospital, aurist and laryngologist to the Royal Infirmary and Christie Hospital, Manchester, and lecturer on diseases of the ear and throat to the Victoria University. He was president of the laryngological and otological sections of the Royal Society of Medicine (1911 and 1921). He possessed all the attributes of the successful surgeon—impressive personality, sound judgement born of ripe experience, and the power of putting his opinion into action with his hands. He was eager in trying new methods, and was a firm believer in the employment of radium. He delighted in a carpenter's shop, but cared little for sport. His interests were wide and were justified by his ability. They extended from the Radium Institute at Manchester to a financial trust which he founded in Edinburgh and of which he was chairman. A lifelong liberal, he unsuccessfully contested the West division of Salford in 1922.

During the War Milligan was appointed consulting surgeon for the throat and ear in the North-Western area, serving with the rank of major in the Royal Army Medical Corps (Territorial Force). In 1914 he was knighted for his work in the investigation of cancer. His publications include *A Practical Handbook of the Diseases of the Ear* (1911). He married in 1890 Bertha Warden, daughter of James Anderson, of Frognal Park, Hampstead, and Hilton House, Aberdeenshire, and had one son and one daughter. He died of pneumonia in a nursing home in Manchester 19 December 1929.

Milligan was a distinguished-looking man, well-built, with slightly aquiline features and fair hair. Well-dressed, with charming and dignified manners, he was as successful in the financial world as in medicine: he left some £100,000 at his death.

[Personal knowledge.] E. A. Peters.

MILNER, ALFRED, Viscount Milner (1854–1925), statesman, was born at Giessen, Hesse-Darmstadt, 23 March 1854, the only son of Charles Milner, M.D., by his wife, Mary Ierne, daughter of Major-General John Ready, successively governor of Prince Edward's Island and of the Isle of Man, and widow of St. George Cromie. His father, coming of a Lancashire business family, was a man of brilliant parts—'twice my brains', Milner said of him—but with interests too varied to make him a success in his chosen profession. His mother, nearly twenty years older than her second husband, was a woman of rare elevation of character, noted, too, for her frank and joyous laugh; she died when her son was only fifteen, yet old enough to remember her always as an inspiration for his own life.

Milner's first four years were spent with his parents in Germany; then, after eight years in Chelsea, where his father set up with moderate success as a doctor, he returned with his family to Germany and was sent to school for three years at the gymnasium of Tübingen. These three years at school at Tübingen, of which Milner always spoke with appreciation, and the fact that his paternal grandmother, Sophie von Rappard, was a German, gave a handle to his detractors in after-life for reproaching him with being more German than English in his outlook. But, although he always had in him something of the German precision and logical consistency, in the main his education and outlook were thoroughly English. By his mother's wish he was brought back to England after her death and put in special charge of her brother, Colonel Charles Ready; and at the early age of fifteen he was entered as a student at King's College, London. There he did brilliantly, carrying off nearly every available prize in classics, history, and literature, as well as making his mark in the debating society: so great, indeed, was his reputation there that in 1878, six years after he had left, the professor of classics, J. B. Mayor, invited him to take over some of his classes. But it was a hard and lonely life: his means were very slender, and, as his father had gone back to live in Germany, he was boarded with a cousin, Mr. Malcolm. Yet there were compensations: he and his cousin's daughter, Marianne, struck up a close friendship, never broken in after-life; and during the holidays he often went for long walking tours with his father. The most memorable of these was in 1870, during the Franco-Prussian War, when they followed in the wake of the German army and actually saw something of the siege of Strasburg: the impression then made on young Milner by what he saw of the military and political preparedness of the Germans, as contrasted with the chaotic state of the French, was lasting and greatly influenced his whole political outlook.

Two years later (1872) Milner won the first scholarship at Balliol College, and for the next four years his nature could unfold itself in the genial atmosphere of Oxford; it may, in fact, be said that during these pregnant four years he formed or developed the principles on which his whole future life was to be based. The Oxford to which he came, as he himself once said, was marked by 'a very striking change in the social and political philosophy of the place, a change which has since reproduced itself on the larger stage of the world'. The rector of Lincoln College, Mark Pattison, it is true, still represented among the dons the cynicism of an older generation, with its uses, perhaps, as a corrective of youth's exuberant enthusiasm; but at Balliol there were R. L. Nettleship, 'so great in his humility and humble in his greatness', as has been well said of him, T. H. Green, afterwards Whyte's professor of moral philosophy, Francis de Paravacini, Milner's special tutor, sympathetic guides in drawing out the best of youth's generous instincts and giving them a basis of scholarship and deep thought; and, above all, the master, Benjamin Jowett, with his catholic outlook on life and his bracing Socratic irony. Balliol, in Milner's first year, was at the height of its fame and achievement, with seven out of ten university scholarships and prizes to its credit. Milner himself soon took no small part in these triumphs, obtaining a first class in classical moderations (1874) and winning successively the Hertford (1874), the Craven (1877), the Eldon (1878), and the Derby (1878) scholarships, and narrowly missing the Ireland scholarship owing to his diffidence. At the Union he spoke rarely and then only on matters which deeply interested him, then and thereafter, such as the subject of imperial relations. But although his speeches were infrequent and not marked by great eloquence, they carried more weight, says a contemporary, than those of any other man of his time: and he was accordingly elected president in 1875. It is also recorded that at a meeting of the Palmerston Club he attacked Gladstone to his face for his 'Little-England' views. In 1876 he obtained a first class in *literae humaniores* and was elected to a fellowship at New College.

Academic honours, however, were the least part of what Milner gained from Oxford: far more came to him from such friends and contemporaries as H. H. Asquith, Herbert Warren, Sidney Ball, Charles Gore, E. B. Iwan-Müller, Leonard Montefiore, J. M. Rendel, and, especially, Arnold Toynbee. In this earnest, stimulating society Milner found just the sympathy he needed with the passion already latent in him for public work, political and social. Even there, however, he sometimes seemed precociously aloof, precociously master of his own counsel, and already in his third year the young president of the Union is described by a visitor to Oxford as 'tall, dignified, and grave beyond his years, weighing evidence on every subject, anxious for the maintenance of absolute justice, eager to organize rather than to influence, and fearful to give generous impulses full rein'. At any rate at Oxford, by his scholarships and his fellowship, Milner gained freedom from the grinding fear of poverty which had haunted him in the past, lost his sense of loneliness, profited to the full from friendships and leisure for thought, and developed a saving sense of humour and enjoyment of life. Oxford, and in Oxford Balliol and especially New College, his home there after 1876, always remained especially dear to him. When, in later life, he sought for young men to help him in his South African labours, it was from Oxford almost entirely that he drew them. And Oxford responded to his affection. In 1906, when he had returned to England to find a coldly critical attitude in many of his old supporters, she showed her faith in him by conferring upon him the honorary degree of D.C.L., and in the last month of his life elected him, without opposition, to the chancellorship of the University.

Yet, devoted son as he was of Oxford, after taking his degree Milner had ambitions beyond that of the tutorship offered him by New College. He was already conscious that his bent was for a life of 'public usefulness', as he expressed it in his diary; so in 1879 he betook himself to London, staying at first with the Malcolms in Claverton Street, ate dinners at the Inner Temple, and was called to the bar in 1881. But briefs were scarce, and he turned to journalism as a means of livelihood, working on the old *Pall Mall Gazette*, first under John (afterwards Viscount) Morley [q.v.] and in 1883 as assistant editor to William Thomas Stead [q.v.], a chief with whose imperialist views on foreign and colonial policy and enthusiasm for social reform he was in complete accord. At first he even entered into the fun of Stead's revolutionary escapades in journalism, but their crude sensationalism became more than he could stomach, and in 1885 he resigned his connexion with the *Pall Mall*. Journalism, in fact, as he himself used to say, 'neither suited him nor he it'.

More important, however, for Milner's ultimate purpose in life than journalism or any other method of earning a livelihood during these early days in London was the association which he maintained with some of his old Oxford friends and with a few new-comers of the same stamp. It is a tribute to Milner's persistence and to the core of warm affection, veiled to outsiders by his somewhat cold exterior, that his deepest friendships were enduring and were nearly all made during his Oxford days or in the early years in London. Such friends were Arnold Toynbee [q.v.], first and foremost, (Sir) Edward Tyas Cook [q.v.], whom he brought on to the *Pall Mall Gazette*, Henry Birchenough, with whom he set up in rooms in St. James's in 1884, Iwan-Müller, Clinton Dawkins, the Montefiores, Lyttelton Gell, and a few others. Some of these used to continue the *noctes Oxonienses* at a little discussion society in the Temple founded by Arnold Toynbee, who of all Milner's friends exercised the most decisive influence upon him, no less after his premature death in 1883 than during the brief years of their friendship. 'In spite of the lapse of years', Milner said in an address eleven years later, 'his thought, his aspirations, his manner of speech, yea, the very expression of his countenance and the tone of his voice, are so vividly present to me, and seem to me still, though I am long past the age of illusions, no less noble and inspiring than they did in the radiant days of youthful idealism, when we first were friends.' By Toynbee Milner and his friends at Oxford or at the Temple 'were deeply impressed', to quote Milner's own words again, 'with their individual duty as citizens and filled with enthusiasm for social equality, which led them to bridge the gulf between the educated and the wage-earning class'. Under this influence and that of Samuel Augustus Barnett [q.v.], 'one of the best men that ever lived, a really noble and beautiful character', as Milner wrote of him in 1913, one of the first things Milner did when he came to London was to take a large part in the then novel University Extension Society founded by Barnett and his wife in Whitechapel, acting as its joint secretary and giving several courses of lectures. In the list of lecturers at Whitechapel on behalf of this society, besides the names of William Stubbs, James Bryce, and Arnold Toynbee, appears that of Milner with a course on 'The State and the duties of Rulers'; and two years later (1882) he gave six lectures on 'Socialism', posthumously published in the *National Review* in 1931. In 1884, as a result of a meeting in Sidney Ball's rooms at St. John's College, Oxford, addressed by Barnett on the subject of founding a university settlement in East London 'to bring the classes into relation' and 'to enable University men to live with the poor', the well-known settlement named after Milner's closest friend, Toynbee, was inaugurated in Whitechapel. Milner himself eagerly cooperated in its foundation, and for the rest of his life was one of its most devoted supporters. Even after his return from South Africa he lectured there on trade boards, and from 1911 until his death was chairman of the governing body. To commemorate his connexion with Toynbee Hall and the friend who inspired him and its other founders, plaques of Milner and Arnold Toynbee were unveiled there in 1931.

In the same year that Toynbee Hall was founded Milner, while still retaining his post on the *Pall Mall Gazette*, became private secretary to Mr. G. J. (afterwards Viscount) Goschen [q.v.] and thus came into touch with the man destined to start him on the career for which he was most fitted. Goschen, although he had been a member of Lord Russell's last and Mr. Gladstone's first ministries, was never a strong party man and had refused to join Gladstone's second ministry: convinced of the great part which England should play in the world, he was bitterly opposed to Gladstone's foreign and imperial policy, and in domestic affairs was antagonized by the doctrine of 'ransom', with its implied class warfare, propounded by Joseph Chamberlain [q.v.]. At the same time he was deeply interested in such new social experiments as were being made by the Barnetts in Whitechapel, where in 1879 he had proclaimed the principle implicit in the future Toynbee Hall, 'to provide people with the means of life rather than of livelihood'. Thus there was a natural affinity between Goschen and Milner, whose interests, then and throughout his life, were mainly social reform as expounded by his friend Toynbee and as exemplified by the whole conception of Toynbee Hall, and England's paramount duty of leadership in foreign and colonial affairs, so vociferously proclaimed in the *Pall Mall Gazette* under W. T. Stead. During the year of this first intimate connexion between Goschen and Milner, the secretary was more 'a colleague and adviser' [Hon. A. R. D. Elliot, *Life of G. J. Goschen*, i, 289] than a subordinate, urging Goschen on to deliver, and with infectious enthusiasm collaborating in the preparation of, the two notable speeches which won him the seat at Edinburgh in November 1885. At the same time, however, Milner had to give up this secretaryship, partly because he himself stood as liberal candidate for Harrow. In this election Milner made over ninety speeches, all excellently reasoned, but, as he prided himself, without once mentioning Gladstone's name, and not impassioned enough to rouse electoral audiences; it was said of him that he could not speak with real effect until he was 'hit in the eye'. At any rate, in spite of a gallant fight, he was beaten by 1,000 votes, in this his first and last attempt to enter the House of Commons. But this was not the end of his connexion with Goschen and with party politics. In 1886 Gladstone had finally disrupted the old liberal party by his Home Rule proposals, and Goschen was one of the most active in forming the new Liberal Unionist Association; but for sheer hard work in organizing and obtaining recruits to the new Association Milner was unsurpassed. At the inaugural meeting he was elected to the general committee, and to him was due the general supervision of the arrangements by services 'impossible', said one of the members, 'to over-estimate'. He himself, describing his own zeal and that of such helpers as Albert (afterwards fourth Earl) Grey [q.v.] and Alexander Craig Sellar [q.v.] at this crisis, declared that 'for the Liberal-Unionist propaganda we slaved ourselves to shreds. We poured out pamphlets and leaflets. When we were all nearly dead, we used to say to each other, "Never mind; go on; Dagon must be thrown down."'

When Lord Randolph Churchill, on his sudden resignation of the chancellorship of the Exchequer in December 1886, 'had forgotten Goschen', Milner was one of the foremost in urging his friend to put the country's interests above old party ties and take Churchill's place in a conservative government. The new chancellor of the Exchequer at once made him his official private secretary. In this post Milner was in his element: he had the rare capacity of assimilating figures even quicker than words: as he said of himself, 'when I have once read a balance sheet or a budget, the figures seem to be written on the wall in front of my eyes'; and he had a gift also for the wider aspects of national finance. Thus he proved an invaluable helper to Goschen, especially during the famous conversion of the National Debt from 3 per cent. to 2½ per cent. in 1888.

In the following year Goschen, who felt in parting with Milner that he had 'lost his right hand', gave him his chance of independent work by procuring for him the post of director-general of accounts in Egypt, where six months later, in 1890, he was promoted to the office of under-secretary in the finance ministry of Khedive Tewfik. Here, wrote his chief, Sir Evelyn Baring (afterwards Lord Cromer, q.v.), Milner proved himself 'one of the most able Englishmen who have served the Egyptian government; not only was he versed in all the technicalities of his own department, but he had a wide grasp of the larger aspects of Egyptian affairs.' He revelled in his financial work for a country where, as he wrote himself, 'economic causes produce their theoretically correct result with a swiftness and exactitude not easily visible in other lands', and where the connexion of 'economics with politics and with morality' was so apparent. But probably the greatest service that Milner rendered to his country's task in Egypt was by his book *England in Egypt*, written in six months and published shortly after his return home in 1892. In this book he for the first time gave a vivid and convincing account of the complicated problems of Egyptian government, for the solution of which Great Britain had assumed responsibility. He made it clear why the British were there, why they must remain there till their task was accomplished, and what were the prospects of Egypt being able eventually to stand on her own feet. The book is written with a deep sense of responsibility, albeit with a light touch, illuminated by sympathy and kindly humour; above all, he puts the temporary presence of the British in Egypt upon the only justifiable ground: 'It is not only, or principally, upon what Englishmen do for Egypt that the case for England rests. It is upon what England is helping the Egyptians to do for themselves.'

Milner was called back to England by Goschen in 1892 in order to take over the chairmanship of the Board of Inland Revenue, a post bringing him into the closest touch with the chancellor of the Exchequer in his most important duty of preparing the budget. But in this duty Milner was not to serve his old friend, for in the same year the conservative government was defeated and Sir William Harcourt [q.v.] took Goschen's place. Milner accordingly had the chief part in putting into shape Harcourt's ideas for his budget of 1894, introducing the new form of death duties, which have been continued, and increased far beyond the conception of the original framers, to the present day. Harcourt was enthusiastic over Milner's work, speaking of him as 'a man deserving of all praise and affection', while Harcourt's successor, Sir Michael Hicks Beach (afterwards Earl St. Aldwyn, q.v.), was so fully convinced of his merits that he even had thoughts of opposing Mr. Chamberlain's choice of Milner for a higher post on the ground that he could not be spared from the Board. For his services there Milner was created C.B. in 1894 and K.C.B. in 1895.

In 1897 the difficulties created by President Kruger's illiberal policy on the Rand and accentuated by the Jameson Raid of 1895 showed no sign of solution: Lord Rosmead [q.v.] as high commissioner for South Africa, responsible for dealings with the South African Republic (Transvaal), had not proved a success, and was due to retire; it was therefore essential to find a successor eminently qualified for this difficult post by strength of character and diplomatic gifts. Chamberlain, the secretary of state for the Colonies, had met Milner in Egypt, and had been impressed by his ability, as he was later by the wide and conciliatory outlook revealed in *England in Egypt*. Accordingly in January 1897 he summoned him to the Colonial Office. Would Milner, he first asked, to try the ground, accept the post of under-secretary for the Colonies about to be vacated by Sir Robert Meade? To this Milner unhesitatingly replied, 'No'. 'Well then,' said Chamberlain, 'will you go to South Africa?' After a moment's reflection Milner replied, 'I'll do it.' Lord Salisbury had already approved of the suggestion, Queen Victoria gave her consent, Hicks Beach's objection to the loss of so valuable a financial expert was tactfully overcome, and the appointment was enthusiastically welcomed by friends and statesmen of all parties, who gave Milner a send-off dinner marked by extraordinary warmth of affection and confidence. This confidence was strengthened by Milner's own speech declaring his passionate devotion to the conception of imperial union: to succeed in forwarding such an ideal, 'to render any substantial service to any part of our world-wide state, would', he said, 'be all that in my most audacious dreams I had ever ventured to aspire to'; and no less by his definition of the task immediately awaiting him: 'to reconcile and to persuade to live together in peace and goodwill two races whose common interests are immeasurably greater than any differences that unfortunately exist.' Earlier he had written to his friend R. B. Brett (afterwards Viscount Esher) with almost boyish enthusiasm for the great task: '"There is many a slip"; so I shall believe in the thing when I land at Cape Town. But I hope there will be no slip, for, though I know perfectly well that I may break my neck over it, I am wild to go'; and in a graver tone to his old friend Iwan-Müller: 'I run a great risk of growing conceited, and, if I had not such a profound σέβας of the High Gods, on whose knees it all lies, I might be exposed to the danger of failure from over-confidence.'

When Milner landed at Cape Town on 5 May 1897, he came with an open mind as to the rights in the dispute between Boers and Britons and resolved to form his own judgement on the spot. Indeed, it is characteristic of him that on the eve of his departure, when an old friend had wished to impress upon him his very strong anti-Boer views, he refused even to discuss the matter; and for nearly a year he gave no public indication of his opinions, 'struggling', as he said, 'successfully against the temptation to say anything of substantial importance'. He learned Dutch, in order that he might be able to read the Dutch as well as the English newspapers, and also the *taal* which enabled him to talk to the Boer country folk; he made tours through Cape Colony, Bechuanaland, Rhodesia, and Basutoland; with the help of J. H. (afterwards Lord) de Villiers [q.v.], the great chief justice of Cape Colony, he tried to enter into friendly and informal relations with Kruger; with Cecil Rhodes, the other dominating figure in South Africa, although at first very much on his guard, he gradually came to an understanding, when he had made it plain that the high commissioner was second to none in South Africa. But, while non-committal in his public utterances, he had been thinking the more. Although before his arrival Chamberlain had induced Kruger to withdraw the Aliens Immigration Act as contrary to the Convention of London (1884), Milner soon began to realize that the difficulties of the Uitlanders in Johannesburg were no nearer solution. They were still without any voice even in their own municipal affairs; Kotze, the one judge with independence of character, was summarily dismissed; large sums, almost entirely obtained from taxation of the Uitlanders, were spent in arming the Transvaal for a conflict which could only be against Great Britain; above all, the re-election of Kruger to the presidency in February 1898 had taken away all hope of a more conciliatory and reforming spirit in the republic. In addition there were difficulties in Cape Colony, where many of the Dutch, in enjoyment of the full liberties denied to the Uitlanders in the Transvaal, almost openly sympathized with Kruger's despotic and anti-British policy.

By the end of February 1898 Milner had come to the grave conclusion that 'there is no way out of the political troubles of South Africa except reform in the Transvaal, or war. And at present the chances of reform in the Transvaal are worse than ever.' So he wrote in a private letter to Chamberlain on 23 February. Ten days later he for the first time gave public expression to his belief in his famous speech at Graaff Reinet, which was not so much an attack on the Transvaal as a warning to the Cape Dutch against disloyalty. This speech came almost as a thunderclap in a clear sky. In South Africa the British in Cape Colony and the Uitlanders in the Transvaal realized that in Milner they had at last found a champion who meant business: at home, however, doubts began to assail some of those who had lately been most enthusiastic about 'the safe man with a cross-bench mind', when they discovered in him, as was said, at once the queen's representative and 'a great party-leader of the British race against the Dutch'. Milner was slow and deliberate in forming his convictions; but once he had formed them he was immovable. Not only that, but he became rigid in his methods of attaining his object. Here for the first time appears a difference between him and his chief Chamberlain. The objects of both were identical: to secure justice and reasonable liberty for the Uitlanders, such as were enjoyed by the Dutch in the Cape, and to ensure that Great Britain's right under the London Convention to be alone responsible for the whole of South Africa's external relations should not be impaired. But Chamberlain at the centre had to take account of the political situation in England and of her difficulties with foreign powers no less than those in South Africa; he was also more elastic and adaptable in diplomacy, and more inclined to display patience and restraint in the details of negotiation until some overwhelmingly important issue had to be faced. Milner, on the other hand, immersed as he was in his own extraordinarily difficult task, was naturally not so conscious of external difficulties, nor had he, at this stage of his career, schooled his mind to exercise the patience and elasticity of method quite compatible with an unyielding grasp of the main objects of policy; and accordingly he was more inclined to rush the issue. Shortly after the Graaff Reinet speech Milner's difficulties were increased by a hotly contested general election at the Cape, in which the prime minister, Sir John Gordon Sprigg [q.v.], lost his majority and in October 1898 gave place to William Philip Schreiner [q.v.] with a ministry largely Afrikander Bond in complexion.

Immediately after the installation of Schreiner, Milner returned to England for a couple of months, partly to rest from the strain of his first eighteen months, but chiefly to discuss with Chamberlain the question—as he put it in an interview with a journalist—'Am I to work a passive and dilatory policy with the best credit I can, or am I to go back to pursue an active and resolute policy even at the risk of its leading to war?' But although the laconic entry in his diary on the day of his arrival was 'Home, happy!', he got little satisfaction for his more forward policy from Chamberlain or the Cabinet, and he returned to the Cape at the end of January 1899 convinced that it was useless to 'force his views upon others at this stage'. By a strange irony of fate, too, during his absence in England General Sir William Butler [q.v.], acting in his place as high commissioner, having been appointed to the command by the War Office against the wish of Milner and even of Chamberlain, had been pursuing a policy diametrically opposed to his own and representing the grievances of the Uitlanders as artificially exaggerated by the capitalists for their own purposes.

But without any interference from Milner events soon began to move rapidly to a crisis. Already in December the shooting of an Englishman, named Edgar, by one of the Boer policemen in Johannesburg had stirred up bitter resentment among the rank and file of Uitlanders; and grievances were accumulating without sign of redress. Lippert's dynamite monopoly, involving outrageous costs for one of the essentials of gold-mining, the refusal of representation in the volksraad to the Johannesburg community, which contributed most of the state's taxation, or even of a representative municipality, at last convinced the Uitlanders that they could not hope for redress without a direct appeal to the Crown. Accordingly on 24 March 1899 a petition signed by over 20,000 people on the Rand was sent to Milner for submission to the queen. It recounted the grievances of the Uitlanders, deprived of all rights as citizens, at the mercy of a hostile police-force and hostile juries, overawed by a ring of forts round Johannesburg, and hampered in their daily lives, even to the education of their children, by vexatious legislation. Milner at once forwarded the petition to Chamberlain, who asked him to send by cable a dispatch summing up the position for publication at the same time as the petition. The result was Milner's famous cable of 4 May in which, with words of burning indignation, he set forth all the grievances against the Transvaal government. The most salient passages are: 'South Africa can prosper under two, three, or six governments, though the fewer the better, but not under two absolutely conflicting social and political systems, perfect equality for Dutch and British in the British Colonies, side by side with permanent subjection of British to Dutch in one of the Republics. . . . The spectacle of thousands of British subjects kept permanently in the position of helots, constantly chafing under undoubted grievances, and calling vainly to H.M. Government for redress, does steadily undermine the influence and reputation of Great Britain and the respect for the British Government within its own dominions;' and lastly, 'The case for intervention is overwhelming.'

So downright a dispatch was perhaps hardly what Chamberlain wanted, since he still hoped to achieve his ends by negotiation, so he delayed its publication and eagerly seized on a hint sent by Milner six days later that Kruger might be willing to discuss the whole question in conference with himself. As a result Milner met Kruger in conference at Bloemfontein on 31 May in order to discuss proposals put forward by the Transvaal government for dealing with the Uitlanders' grievances. But the conference was doomed to failure from the outset, for the two negotiators were men unyielding on any matter on which they had made up their minds. Milner made the initial mistake of ignoring Chamberlain's suggestion that he should take with him Schreiner, the Cape prime minister, who understood and could rival Boer methods of arguing almost interminably round a question before coming to a decision, whereas Milner, with his clear-cut and decisive mind, could not brook such shilly-shallying. The whole discussion turned on how far Kruger was willing to give immediate and genuine effect to proposals made for representation of the Uitlanders in the volksraad: he was all for whittling down and delaying the concession, for he feared that a large Uitlander vote would give them control of his beloved country. Milner, equally rigid in his determination to procure them their full rights of suffrage without delay, would accept no compromise. Finally, after five days' discussion (5 June), Kruger, with tears in his eyes, said, 'It is my country you want.' Milner broke off with the fateful words, 'This conference is absolutely at an end, and there is no obligation on either side arising out of it.' The two great antagonists never met again. This abrupt ending disappointed Chamberlain, and he urged that further attempts should be made to attain their common aim by peaceful means, while Milner himself admitted, 'I think I was wrong in breaking off the conference quite as quickly as I did.' Accordingly negotiations still continued, at times with some prospects of success, especially when Johannes Smuts, the new attorney-general of the Transvaal, intervened; but at the last moment Kruger always withdrew any temporary concession. Finally, after a categorical demand from Chamberlain that he should remedy the Uitlanders' grievances, Kruger, hoping to strike a decisive blow before British reinforcements had landed, on 9 October sent an ultimatum which amounted to a declaration of war.

At the outbreak of war, whereas the Boers had been accumulating armaments for months and were prepared for an immediate invasion of British territory, the British colonies, in spite of Milner's urgent representations, were almost defenceless. Happily the arrival in September of Sir George Stuart White [q.v.] with troops enabled Natal to put herself in a posture of defence, and, largely owing to Milner's insistence, Kimberley and Mafeking were able to hold out. But the arrival of Sir Redvers Buller [q.v.] on 31 October, followed by an army corps in the latter part of November, owing to that general's ill-judged strategy and ineffective tactics, did little to relieve the situation. Milner's anxieties were increased by risings in Cape Colony in support of the republics and by the hardly disguised sympathy with the Boer cause of some of Schreiner's ministers: nor was the home government always sympathetic to his suggestions. A proposal of his to cut off the Transvaal's source of supplies by a blockade of the Portuguese port of Delagoa Bay was emphatically rejected, as was his remedy for domestic difficulties in the Cape by suspending the Cape constitution and substituting for it Crown Colony government. On this proposal Chamberlain minuted at the time that 'the drastic views of Sir Alfred Milner seem to me impolitic and unnecessary', and he explained to Milner himself that such a policy would not only create a storm in parliament but also alarm in Canada and Australia. But Milner was not to be shaken, and reverted twice to this unfortunate suggestion. However, with the arrival of Lord Roberts [q.v.] in January 1900, followed by his victorious march up country and the capture of Pretoria on 5 June, many of Milner's difficulties vanished. His troubles at the Cape were greatly relieved in the same month by the resignation of Schreiner's ministry.

Schreiner himself, as Milner admitted, had 'honesty, sincerity, and courage', but his 'interminable sermons' were a trouble to a harassed governor, while his ministry was difficult, if not dangerous in war time: Sprigg's platitudes and his more docile cabinet gave far less trouble. By the beginning of October 1900, when the last compact and centrally organized Boer force seemed to have been dispersed, Roberts was of opinion that the War was practically concluded. How erroneous was that belief soon appeared by the resumption of guerrilla warfare which continued for another eighteen months.

Almost from the beginning of the War Milner had been in consultation with Chamberlain as to the government of the two Boer states now formally annexed to the British Empire, and on 8 October 1900 he was appointed administrator of the Orange River Colony and the Transvaal. Milner was anxious at the earliest possible moment to begin to create the fabric of civil administration. In March 1901 he took up his residence at Sunnyside on the outskirts of Johannesburg, where he encouraged the return of the civil population and the resumption of work on the mines; he also appointed a small executive council for the Transvaal and a town council for Johannesburg. In the Orange River Colony his deputy, (Sir) Hamilton Goold-Adams, carried out a similar policy. He linked the two new colonies by amalgamating their railways under one management and by creating a common police force, the South African constabulary. But while the War lasted the military were in supreme command in the area of hostilities, and Milner was hampered by military necessities and to some extent by military policy. He disapproved of the indiscriminate farm-burning ordered by Lord Roberts as a warning against guerrilla warfare, and of (Lord) Kitchener's scheme of concentration camps for the Boer fighters' women and children, both of which policies aroused opposition in England. On the other hand, Milner was not prepared to go as far as Kitchener in concessions to the Boers at the abortive Middelburg negotiations of February–March 1901.

Having done all he could for the time being, in the following May Milner went to England on leave for four months. There, as an answer to the violent campaign for his recall made by Bond partisans at the Cape and a section of the liberals in England, he was received with extraordinary honour; he was welcomed on arrival by the Cabinet and immediately taken to see King Edward VII, who raised him to the peerage as Baron Milner, of St. James's, London, and Cape Town; a few weeks later he received the freedom of the City. But strict business was his chief object. He arranged with Chamberlain that a grant of £5,500,000 should be voted for the cost of administration in the new colonies, for railway repairs, and for land purchase for English settlers, that the railways should ultimately be bought by the government, and, lastly, that a war indemnity of £50,000,000 (in 1903 reduced to £30,000,000 and in 1907 abandoned altogether) should be a charge on the Transvaal mines. He also chose a band of able and keen young men, fresh from Oxford or Toynbee Hall, soon to be famous as 'Milner's kindergarten', to help him in starting his schemes of reorganization and social reform in the new colonies. On his return to South Africa in August he was thus enabled to perfect his preparations for peace. A beginning was made with education by sending out teachers to hold classes for the Boer children in the concentration camps; and schemes for the rehabilitation of the new colonies were carefully planned.

At last in March 1902 the Boer leaders made fresh overtures for peace. Negotiations, however, dragged on for another three months. Milner himself would have preferred that the War should end by the process of attrition, and he distrusted Kitchener, with whom he was associated in the negotiations, as willing to be content with much less precise and stringent terms than he himself thought advisable. The actual treaty of Vereeniging was signed by Kitchener and Milner and ten of the Boer leaders on 31 May 1902: 'It has been an awful ten days, but I saved more than I expected', was Milner's report to a friend. After the peace Kitchener returned to England; and Milner, advanced to a viscounty on 15 July, assumed full powers, not only as high commissioner, but as governor of the Transvaal and Orange River Colony, where his lieutenant-governors, Goold-Adams at Bloemfontein and (Sir) Arthur Lawley a few months later at Pretoria, relieved him of some of the details of administration. Milner and Kitchener were poles apart in character and methods. Kitchener concentrated on his object and was comparatively indifferent to the methods by which he attained it, and so was more rough and ready in his procedure and more inclined to compromise on what seemed to him unessentials. Milner, at this stage of his career—although later he became more adaptable—was more rigid, from his habit of not only planning the result but also every step by which it was logically to be attained, and so was impatient of loose ends and anything in the nature of a compromise; he also had in mind the fact that he, not Kitchener, would have to give effect to the terms of the treaty and work the new régime. But, although they had their differences, each could appreciate the other's qualities, and twelve years later, on an even greater emergency, Milner was one of the first to insist on the necessity of securing Kitchener's services.

'People think the War decided that South Africa should remain for good and all part of the British Empire. I never took that view. . . . It only made that result possible—at most probable. To make it certain requires years of strong, patient policy.' So wrote Milner in 1905, and by his actions after Vereeniging he showed that he already had his 'strong, patient policy' mapped out. The first business was to repatriate the Boers on their farms. This was not merely a question of bringing back to their homes the prisoners of war from Ceylon and elsewhere, the burghers left in the field, and their women and children from the concentration camps, but of rebuilding those homes, sowing crops to feed the population, providing them with horses and cattle and ploughs, in a country devastated by three years' war; and to add to the difficulties there was an unusually prolonged drought in 1902. In spite of all this, however, within exactly a year of the peace the main work of repatriation had been accomplished and a population of some 200,000 burghers had been replaced on their farms and given the means of living. Simultaneously with repatriation a permanent system of education was organized. The teachers from the concentration camps, reinforced by others from various parts of the Empire, were sent out to the country districts to establish schools, at first, until building materials became accessible, often in marquees, to which the children could be brought from their farms. High schools were established in some of the larger towns and an advanced technical college in Johannesburg and another college at Bloemfontein. The chief difficulty was found to be with regard to the language. Milner was determined to establish English as the medium of instruction, with concessions to the *taal* in the elementary stages; he thereby roused opposition from some of the Boer leaders and most of the *predikants* (Dutch clergy), who insisted on equality for both languages. Otherwise, the Boers were very well satisfied with the methods of instruction given them, far superior to any which they had enjoyed before. Two years after peace Milner was able to record that in the Transvaal schools there were 29,000 children as compared with only 14,000 under the Boer government. Roads, prisons, the treatment of lunatics, were improved, a new and badly needed water-supply was made for Johannesburg, which was also cleared of some disgraceful slums, and in the principal towns self-governing municipalities were established.

Two matters very dear to Milner's heart were agriculture and land settlement. To encourage better methods and results in farming he brought from overseas a small band of experts to improve the breeds of cattle, to make suggestions for better scientific methods of crop-raising and for exterminating the pests and diseases rife in the country, and to start irrigation schemes and experimental farms. Land settlement by British farmers he was anxious to stimulate mainly in order to introduce English ideas to the country districts, which were almost entirely Boer preserves. But owing to the limited amount of money available and the difficulty of securing the most suitable settlers, his land settlement schemes were not as successful as he had hoped, although a few farms, some government-owned, some privately owned, have proved permanent and beneficial to their neighbours, especially in the Orange River Colony. Always, too, Milner had as an ultimate aim the union of all the South African colonies. In order to prepare the way for this he set up an Inter-Colonial Council for dealing with affairs common to the two new colonies, such as the railways and the constabulary; and within a year of the peace he was presiding at Bloemfontein over a conference of all the South African colonies, old and new, which resulted in a customs union and other co-operative measures, notably in a commission for securing a uniform policy in dealing with the natives throughout South Africa. In this tremendous task of re-making a country laid waste by war and introducing higher standards of public work, Milner's financial ability was not the least of his gifts. Already in three years from the peace he had provided for the interest and sinking fund charge on a loan of £30,000,000 advanced by the British government for development, without impairing the recuperative powers of the country by increased taxation.

On two matters, however, Milner's action aroused acute controversy. The first was on the old question of suspending the Cape constitution. Shortly after the end of the War the progressive party at the Cape sent to Milner a petition for suspension: he replied unofficially in sympathetic terms and his reply was published in the *Cape Times*. Chamberlain was naturally annoyed at Milner's public encouragement of a policy which he had himself already rejected, but after a frank admission of regret by Milner and a magnanimous defence of him by Chamberlain in the House of Commons, the affair blew over. At the end of 1902 Chamberlain himself went out to South Africa, and the two men found themselves in general accord on South African policy. This visit was the last time they met officially, for after his return to England (March 1903) Chamberlain resigned from the Cabinet on the tariff question. The loss to Milner was great, for no man could have been a more considerate, a more loyal chief than Chamberlain, who also had that sound instinct for the politically possible as a corrective to Milner's more unbending logic. Chamberlain, too, for his part, although sometimes differing from Milner in method, was fortunate in having such an agent to carry out the policy, on the main lines of which both agreed. As has been well said, 'It is doubtful if any two strong men, separated by 6,000 miles, ever worked so well together at a time of appalling strain and difficulties.'

The second extremely controversial matter was the question of Chinese labour in the mines. Milner was convinced that the success of the new colonies depended largely on the rapid recovery of the mining industry, so that what he called the 'overspill' of a prosperous Rand should fructify the whole country, just as Rhodesia owed its foundation to the 'overspill' of Kimberley. But the mines were seriously handicapped by the deficiency of native labour; white labour to take its place was found impracticable; so, at first reluctantly, Milner agreed to supply the deficiency by importing labourers under indenture from China. So urgent did the need appear to him that in September 1903 he paid a flying visit to England in order to try to convince not only the government but his old liberal friends Sir Edward Grey, Mr. Asquith, and (Lord) Haldane. Chamberlain was opposed to the proposal, but had just left office. The prime minister, Mr. Balfour, at once urged Milner to take Chamberlain's place at the Colonial Office. The offer was tempting, for the post would have given him full scope for his ideas of imperial development and would not have been so arduous as his position in South Africa: nevertheless, Milner characteristically and decisively rejected the offer because, tired as he was, he felt that his paramount duty was to complete the South African work to which he had set his hand. Failing him, Alfred Lyttelton [q.v.] was appointed, and from him Milner obtained consent for the importation of Chinese labour. The scheme, however, aroused intense opposition from a large section of opinion in England; the whole liberal party joined in the anti-Chinese campaign; and it was one of the causes of the rout of the conservatives at the general election of 1906.

The last great question which occupied Milner in South Africa was that of a constitution for the two new colonies. Both he and Alfred Lyttelton had come to the conclusion that a step forward must be made towards the responsible government promised at Vereeniging as the ultimate goal. Milner, however, felt very strongly that the final step must be delayed for some time, especially in the Orange River Colony where the population was overwhelmingly Boer, and at least until the Boers had acquiesced in membership of the British Empire; but that representative institutions might safely be given as a first step to the Transvaal. As these views coincided with those of the home government, letters patent establishing an elective legislative assembly to take the place of Milner's nominated legislature for the Transvaal were issued on 10 May 1905.

By this time Milner himself had left South Africa. He had been working continuously at the highest pressure for eight years in circumstances as difficult as any man could well be faced with for so long. In his farewell speech at Johannesburg on 31 March 1905 he said: 'I shall live in the memories of people here . . . in connexion with the great struggle to keep this country within the limits of the British Empire . . . I was from head to foot one glowing mass of conviction of the rightness of our cause. . . . But', he added, 'I should prefer to be remembered for the tremendous effort . . . made after the war, not only to repair its ravages, but also to re-start the new colonies on a far higher plane of civilization than they had ever previously attained.' This was a noble aspiration, but the way in which it was expressed helps perhaps to indicate why Milner himself became disappointed with the result. He sought to impose a new order on a very dogged people, with whom he was never entirely in sympathy. His ideals were high indeed, but he had thought them out by himself, and he had not the faculty possessed by other less candid and direct people of inducing those for whom he was working to think that his ideals coincided with their own wishes. Materially he had given the new colonies such a standard of civilization as they had never had before and which had proved lasting: moreover, he had not only proclaimed the need of South African union; he had also shown the way to its accomplishment. It is true also that he had touched the hearts and fired the imagination of the British in South Africa, who regarded him as their bulwark. But he had not touched the hearts or won the confidence of his Boer fellow citizens: perhaps no one who had fought so strenuously against them as he had early in his South African career could have done so. Yet they respected him as one who in the end had their interests at heart, even if it was not in their own way.

In April 1905 Milner sailed from South Africa by the east coast route, visiting Zanzibar, Mombasa, and Nairobi, and paying a long visit to his old chief, Lord Cromer, in Egypt. Thence he returned to England in July—an England strangely altered for him from that whence he had sailed eight years before for South Africa with the confidence and good wishes of every party in the state. The government which had supported him throughout was now tottering; many of his old liberal friends looked askance at him; posters about 'Chinese slavery' met him on every hoarding; and in January 1906 Sir Henry Campbell-Bannerman's new ministry obtained a record majority in parliament. It was not long before Milner's adversaries attacked him openly. Before he left South Africa he had sanctioned the flogging of Chinese coolies in certain cases, and some instances of ill treatment had occurred under the regulation, which was rescinded by the colonial secretary as soon as he heard of it; on 27 February 1906 Milner himself in the House of Lords had, characteristically, taken full responsibility for the error he now admitted. On 21 March a radical member seized on the incident for a motion of censure on Milner, a motion passed in a modified form by the House of Commons. A week later, however, the House of Lords recorded 'its high appreciation of the services rendered by Lord Milner to South Africa and the Empire'. Already he had protested in the House of Lords against the declared intention of the new government to grant full responsible government forthwith to both of the new colonies. When this promise took effect he regarded it as the death-blow to all his hopes for South Africa, and to the end of his life he never ceased to regret it as premature. But he never showed a trace of personal bitterness.

For some time after his return Milner took little part in politics. He was impoverished by his expenses in South Africa and refused to ask for a pension or grant, which would assuredly have been bestowed on him—he even declined the gift of a country house offered him by his friends—so that he was obliged to take up remunerative work in the City, where his financial ability was invaluable, especially in his management of the Rio Tinto Company's affairs. But he did not refuse such public work as that of member of the Port of London Authority; and he devoted himself especially to the congenial work of the Rhodes Trust, of which he had been named by Rhodes an original member. For the rest of his life he was the most influential trustee, working out with his old Oxford friend, Sir George Robert Parkin [q.v.], the best method of selecting scholars, managing the Trust's finances, and making grants out of the surplus revenue for such objects as imperial forestry, the study of tropical medicine, and other educational purposes. He was always ready to discuss national questions on a non-party basis, joining with former members of his South African 'kindergarten' in their 'moot', from which originated the political review, *The Round Table*, and in a more heterogeneous society, the 'Coefficients', where he discussed social and imperial problems with such curiously assorted members as L. S. Amery, H. G. Wells, (Lord) Haldane, Sir Edward Grey, (Sir) Michael Sadler, Bernard Shaw, J. L. Garvin, William Pember Reeves, and W. A. S. Hewins.

Of all the members Wells 'oddly enough, found Milner the most satisfactory intelligence among us. He knew we had to make a new world. . . . so that he fell into Imperialistic Monarchist forms, which a partly German education may have made easier for him. But upon many minor issues we were apt to agree' [H. G. Wells, *Experiment in Biography*, ii, 765].

'Always avowedly a free lance,' as Milner said of himself, 'and unhampered by the obligation to adhere strictly to the limits of any "authorized programme", I could afford to devote myself to those subjects on which I really felt strongly.' Thus he warmly supported Lord Roberts in his campaign in favour of national service, as necessary for the defence of the British Empire, and Chamberlain's tariff reform movement, as an essential measure for drawing the different parts of Empire into closer relations. He had, indeed, managed to introduce a preference to the mother country in his South African customs union in support of that movement. Anything, too, which stimulated a better apprehension of Great Britain's imperial responsibilities appealed to him. He took up warmly a suggestion made by (Sir) Sidney Low for promoting imperial studies, then almost entirely ignored in the universities, and presided over a committee set up by the university of London with that object. As a result of its work a scheme of public lectures on those and similar topics was inaugurated, and the Rhodes chair of imperial studies was established at King's College in 1919. Even the Institute of Historical Research partly owes its genesis to this committee, which Milner guided in so broad-minded a spirit that it incidentally tended to smooth away many of the inter-collegiate rivalries and jealousies which had in the past been so great a bane to London University.

On only two definite issues separating the great political parties did Milner take a decisive line. The first was Mr. Lloyd George's budget of 1909, which he advised the Lords to reject and not flinch from the consequences, and its outcome the Parliament Bill of 1911, which he strenuously opposed. The second was Home Rule, which, as in 1886, he abhorred as disruptive of the Empire; in order to combat it he offered his services to Sir Edward Carson and helped to organize in England a league of 'Covenanters' pledged to support Ulster's resistance to separation. Throughout this period, between 1906 and 1912, he made many speeches, chiefly on imperial subjects but also on social questions such as sweated industries and industrial law, not only in Great Britain but also during two tours in Canada (1908 and 1912), speeches which he published in 1913 in a volume entitled *The Nation and the Empire*. He even arranged to write a life of Chamberlain in collaboration with his friend L. S. Amery, a plan stopped by the outbreak of the European War in 1914.

When, half-way through the War, it was suggested that Milner should become prime minister, a diarist commented on this as a stupid suggestion, for 'rightly or wrongly few men in the country are more distrusted than Milner'. The diarist lived to see his mistake; but already Milner had been proving that he was well prepared for the tasks awaiting Great Britain. In fact the country's danger and the need of definite action seemed to give him a fresh lease of youthful energy. In the first year of the War he presided over a committee to increase the food production of the country, and within a month of its formation, so deeply had he thought out the question beforehand, the committee produced a scheme for putting a million more acres under wheat with a promise of a guaranteed price to the farmer. Although Mr. Asquith's government rejected the scheme, it was put into operation in 1917 with surprisingly successful results. Milner was next asked to tackle the problem of coal production and to secure some harmony between the conflicting interests of miners, exporters, and government and home producers. When Mr. Lloyd George became prime minister at the end of 1916, he at once picked out Milner to be a member of his small War Cabinet, whose principal business it was not only to deal with big questions on the general conduct of the War, but also with matters affecting several departments of state. With a man of Milner's administrative capacity and his long preparedness for such a crisis this system worked well; and whenever a difficult problem presented itself, Milner, 'the only synoptic person in the Cabinet', as he said of himself, was called upon to solve it. He had to settle the allocation of shipping tonnage between various contending departments; the amount of beer to be brewed, the 'buying out' of the spirit trade in order to secure alcohol for munitions; a programme for the reduction of imports owing to the losses of shipping; and he also took a part in getting the convoy system established. He was chairman of the committee on post-war reconstruction, and was chiefly responsible for the establishment of the new Ministry of Health in 1919, with an enlightened programme for dealing with social questions hitherto neglected. He, too, was mainly responsible for the inclusion in the War Cabinet of the prime ministers of the Dominions and a representative of India as regular members, an important step which secured not only closer co-operation between the constituent parts of the Empire, but also complete unity in war plans and peace aims.

Milner was often called upon to undertake missions to various seats of war; he went with Mr. Lloyd George to the Allied Conference in Rome in January 1917 and thence he was sent to Russia in order to arrange about munition supplies, unfortunately on the eve of the Russian revolution, the drastic nature of which he hardly foresaw; but his most notable mission was to France at the blackest period of the War. When, by 23 March 1918, the Germans in their last great attack had pierced the British lines near Amiens and so broken the connexion between them and the French, Milner was sent to the Amiens front in order to report on the serious state of affairs and on the break-down of co-operation between the two Allied commands. Attempts had already been made to pool the reserves available for either army, but there was no directing mind to allocate this reserve in an emergency, especially as Sir Douglas (afterwards Earl) Haig [q.v.] and General Pétain, the French commander-in-chief, did not always see eye to eye, while General Foch's committee of the Supreme War Council, nominally charged with the duty, had little real power of making decisions. Milner reached France on the evening of 24 March and, realizing the imperative need of immediate action, took upon himself full responsibility for the momentous decision for enforcing unity of command. It was plain to him that one man should be responsible for co-ordinating the efforts of the Allies, but who should it be? Pétain was perhaps the obvious man, as being in command of the largest force on the Western front, but in the conferences which took place he seemed too cautious and niggardly of his reserves, and, indeed, too pessimistic at such a crisis, whereas Foch, whom Milner had hardly known before, appeared to him to possess just the right spirit. A short talk with M. Clemenceau, an old friend of Milner's, who had hitherto been inclined to favour Pétain rather than Foch, and the thing was done. The decision, to which Haig gave his hearty support and Pétain his loyal assent, is recorded in the two terse sentences of the agreement reached at the Allied conference held at the Hôtel de Ville, Doullens, north of Amiens, on 26 March:

'Le général Foch est chargé par les gouvernements britanniques et français de coordonner l'action des armées alliées sur le front ouest. Il s'entendra à cet effet avec les généraux en chef, qui sont invités à lui fournir tous les renseignements nécessaires.

Doullens, le 26 Mars 1918

G. Clemenceau. Milner.'

This little bit of paper, entirely due to Milner's initiative, securing thereafter the harmonious co-operation of the Allied forces, marks the turning-point in the War.

This was the last of Milner's great services as a member of the small War Cabinet, for on 19 April he was induced reluctantly to accept the post of secretary of state for war. At the War Office his tact and good sense in smoothing out difficulties and appeasing jealousies had already proved invaluable. He was still in the closest touch with Mr. Lloyd George in planning the last great efforts of the War, and the combination of the latter's resiliency with Milner's balance and grasp of essentials proved invincible. In administration Milner's great reform was to inaugurate a carefully thought-out Army Education branch, primarily to train the soldiers both at the front and at home for civilian employment on their discharge at the end of the War, but also as a permanent institution for the same object in peace time.

In all his great and manifold war-work Milner hardly appeared before the public at all; and only those at the centre could fully appreciate its value. Only once did he attract public attention and then to his great credit. About a month before the signing of the Armistice on 11 November 1918 he was questioned by a journalist as to his conception of complete victory and of the best form of peace. Before all other forms of victory he put the destruction of Prussian militarism and the disappearance of the Hohenzollern régime for ever. This, he said, could best be attained by an armistice admitting the complete military superiority of the Allies, without the tremendous losses and time involved in marching to Berlin. At the same time he protested against the 'fulminations . . . denouncing the whole German nation as monsters of iniquity', and indicated that in his view peace should not be made an instrument for 'punishing Germany or gratifying our own feelings of anger or indignation against her, however justified'. In the excited feelings of the time, this sane and prudent utterance drew down upon Milner much vituperative criticism from persons who cited his remote family connexion with, and his early schooling in, Germany in order to dub him as 'pro-German'. Milner could afford to despise calumny, but he was nevertheless pleased when the whole band of men who had learned under him in South Africa to appreciate his patriotism united to testify to him their affectionate respect.

In December 1918, on the reconstruction of the ministry, Milner was transferred, again with considerable reluctance, to the Colonial Office. He was then worn out, and as the negotiations for peace proceeded, felt less and less in sympathy with Mr. Lloyd George. At Versailles he was unfortunately not one of the chief British delegates, and attended only to speak on matters affecting his department: but when he did appear, his influence and great weight, General Smuts has said, were 'all for a fair and generous peace, a peace of understanding which might be lasting, and which would heal the dreadful wounds the war had caused'. Had he been a constant delegate his profound knowledge and his mellow sanity might have helped to make a better business of the treaty.

At the Colonial Office Milner had too short a term to make a deep impression, but, with the help of his under-secretary, Mr. Amery, he was able to promote several of the schemes which he had at heart, such as the development of imperial resources in Africa and in the West Indies, where he inaugurated an Imperial College of Agriculture at Trinidad, inter-imperial migration, and the new dyarchic constitution for Malta. While he was colonial secretary he was entrusted with the task of reporting on the future relations of Great Britain with Egypt, and had to spend over four months (November 1919 to March 1920) in that country and afterwards to conduct in London long negotiations with Zaghlul Pasha and other nationalist leaders. He reported in favour of independence for Egypt in alliance with Great Britain, with certain safeguards for British interests solemnly guaranteed by an Egyptian national assembly. This report was rejected by the Cabinet, although it was subsequently accepted without even the national assembly's guarantee. Partly owing to its rejection, partly too from exhaustion after another spell of seven years' exacting labours, Milner resigned on 7 February 1921, and so brought his official career to a close. To mark the value of his services he was created K.G.

Milner had never married, for quite early in life he had decided that he must choose between marriage which might bring private happiness and the public usefulness which he had most at heart. Now, however, less than three weeks after his final resignation, when he was nearing seventy, he married, on 26 February, Violet Georgina, younger daughter of his old friend Admiral Frederick Augustus Maxse [q.v.] and widow of Lord Edward Herbert Gascoyne-Cecil [q.v.]. This marriage opened the way to four years of happiness which they shared with their friends, in London and at their country home, Sturry Court, near Canterbury. This property was given by Lady Milner after her husband's death to the King's School, Canterbury.

Yet even after his marriage Milner did not take the rest which he had earned. He resumed his work in the City, consented to preside over a tariff committee which Mr. Stanley Baldwin had proposed to set up in 1924, had he returned to power, but, above all, devoted himself to writing on the social and imperial questions which had been his main interest through life. These essays were published in book form as *Questions of the Hour* in 1923 and reissued (1925) by Lady Milner after his death, with the addition of his 'Credo', found among his papers and embodying his imperialist creed.

In the autumn of 1924 Lord and Lady Milner paid a visit to South Africa, where he had some joy in seeing some results of his great recuperative schemes for the country, but still more disappointment at the conviction that much of his political work had been thrown away by the action of a liberal government in 1906. Shortly after his return he was attacked by sleepy sickness, probably caught in South Africa. His illness was mercifully short, and he died at Sturry Court, with the knowledge that his name had been accepted as chancellor-elect of Oxford University, 13 May 1925. He was buried at Saleshurst, near Robertsbridge, after a service conducted by Archbishop Davidson in Canterbury Cathedral, where the chapel of St. Martin of Tours was subsequently restored in his memory. The peerage became extinct on his death without heir.

Milner was a great public servant—few more devoted have appeared in British annals—most in his element when he had some definite task to perform, as in the finance ministry in Egypt, in concentrating on the issues between Great Britain and the Boer Republics, or in trying to realize a plan of reorganization thought-out to the minutest details for the new Colonies, and lastly, during the War, in his clear grasp of the essential objectives and his consummate ability in carrying out the measures required to attain them. His chief contribution to the political thought of his generation is to be found in his passionate conviction of the need for imperial unity, a conviction not divorced from a sympathetic understanding of distinctive national feelings in each of the Empire's widely scattered parts. This passionate feeling is expressed or implicit in all his public action, in his speeches, in his writings, but, above all, in the influence which he exercised privately on all, especially the young, who looked up to him as mentor. He had not, however, the qualities of a great political leader, partly because he stood outside any political party and so could never have gained an effective political following to carry out his ideas; but chiefly owing to a want of elasticity in his temperament, which made it impossible for him to yield a point or be satisfied with less than the whole, which is rarely attainable in politics. Curiously enough he realized this defect in Mr. Gladstone, whom he criticized for disregarding Hesiod's maxim *πλέον ἥμισυ παντός*, without recognizing it in himself. On the other hand, these very defects, which denied him the gift to rule debates and lead the multitude, arose from one of his noblest characteristics, a deep sincerity which made it impossible for him to compromise on what he regarded as the truth. To this quality above all he owed his superlative gift of making and keeping friends and attracting loyalties. As one would expect in a man so determined to think out a policy in all its aspects and implications for himself, he worked best with young men, ready to take their cue from him; even they often found it difficult to relieve him of the drudgery of small details; but he inspired them with his ideals of work and high ambition and made of them a notable band for influencing public life long after they had left his service. His chief friends were nearly all friends of youth and were lifelong. He had, too, one characteristic rare in most men, rarer still in those of his temperament, that he was never soured by disappointments, even over his most cherished objects: indeed the older he grew the more tolerant of opposition he became. General Smuts, one of his most effective opponents in South Africa, noted, after meeting him once more in war-time, twelve years later, besides 'his great personal modesty and reserve', which he always had, how he had found him in spite, or because, of cares and sorrows, 'matured and deepened . . . broadened in outlook and sympathy' [*The Times*, 15 May 1925].

There is a bronze bust of Milner by François Sicard at Doullens, another casting of which is also at Doullens, and a third in the possession of Lady Milner; a posthumous bust by Lady (Hilton) Young (afterwards Lady Kennet) is at Rhodes House, Oxford; and a portrait plaque is in Westminster Abbey, a replica being at Toynbee Hall, Whitechapel. There are portraits by Max Balfour (said to be the best likeness) at New College, Oxford, by Theodore Roussel at Johannesburg, by Hugh Glazebrook in the National Portrait Gallery, and by Sir William Orpen, painted for Sir Abe Bailey; a drawing of him was also made by J. S. Sargent. A cartoon of him by 'Spy' appeared in *Vanity Fair* 15 April 1897.

[*The Milner Papers*, edited by Cecil Headlam, 2 vols., 1931–1933 (deals almost exclusively with the South African period: Milner's original South African papers are at New College); W. Basil Worsfold, *Lord Milner's Work in South Africa*, 1906, and *Reconstruction of the New Colonies under Lord Milner*, 2 vols., 1913; E. B. Iwan-Müller, *Lord Milner and South Africa*, 1902; Blue Books relating to South Africa 1897–1905; *War Memoirs of David Lloyd George*, vol. iii, 1934; J. L. Garvin, *Life of Joseph Chamberlain*, vol. iii, 1934; Dr. Christopher Addison, *Four and a Half Years (1914–1919)*, 2 vols., 1934; '*The Times*' *History of the War in South Africa*, edited by L. C. M. S. Amery, 7 vols., 1900–1909 (especially vols. i and vi); private information; personal knowledge.]

B. Williams.

MOND, ALFRED MORITZ, first Baron Melchett (1868–1930), industrialist, financier, and politician, was born at Farnworth, Lancashire, 23 October 1868, the younger son of Ludwig Mond [q.v.], a gifted Jew who had come to England from Cassel in 1862 and with (Sir) John Tomlinson Brunner had founded and built up the great chemical industry which in 1881 was formed into a public joint-stock company as Brunner, Mond & Co. His mother was Frida, daughter of Adolph Meyer Löwenthal, of Cologne, a cousin of his father and a highly cultivated woman.

Mond was educated at Cheltenham College, St. John's College, Cambridge (where he was ploughed in the natural science tripos), and Edinburgh University. He was called to the bar by the Inner Temple in 1894 and practised for a time on the North Wales and Cheshire circuit. Up to this time his ambitions had been entirely political, and he looked upon the law as the high way to a parliamentary career. His father's business, however, had stronger claims on his energies, and in 1895 he became a director and, a little later, managing director.

It was in his capacity of active manager of a great manufacturing corporation that Mond made a deep mark on the industrial history of his time as an earnest exponent of the need for organization and research, later as a successful champion of the process of rationalization and amalgamation, and finally as a strenuous advocate of close co-operation between employers and employed. His width of vision and imagination, applied to industrial problems, showed him that the way to success in production lay through control of raw material, diversity of enterprise, and harmonious relations between all parties at work on the process of supply. Contemptuous of the doctrine of *laisser-faire* and of all that it implied, he was convinced that the planning of great enterprises, to be carried out by big industrial battalions, was the only line of future development; and that the competition of a number of small units was less effective, even from the point of view of the consumer, than co-operative effort which aimed at procuring cheap supplies of materials by large-scale buying and at providing cheap articles by large-scale distribution. 'The trend of all modern industry', he wrote, 'is towards greater units, greater co-ordination for the more effective use of resources' [*Industry and Politics*, p. 9].

While thus eagerly advocating combination rather than competition as the basis of industrial enterprise, Mond was equally emphatic on the need for the abolition of the lock-out and strike as methods of settling disputes between capital and labour, and for the development of measures, such as profit-sharing and employee-shareholding, by which the essential partnership between proprietors and workers might be made more apparent and binding and the divergence of their interests less wide. In the introduction to his *Industry and Politics*, published in 1927, he gives the results of his personal contact with workers, in an executive capacity, over more than a generation. 'In the industry in which I am mainly interested', he writes, 'we have succeeded in avoiding for a period of over fifty years any serious industrial dispute. This has been largely due to a liberal, far-seeing policy, which did not consist in waiting for claims to be made and then yielding them reluctantly, but in foreseeing reasonable demands and in granting them even before they were asked' [*ibid.*, p. 3].

Working persistently to further these principles of co-ordination and co-operation, Mond was prominent not only on account of the number and importance of the enterprises with which he was connected, but also by reason of the vast—perhaps grandiose—scale of the amalgamations which were eventually (1926) consolidated in the firm of Imperial Chemical Industries, Ltd., with its £95,000,000 of authorized capital and its immense ramifications and alliances. He was also chairman of the Amalgamated Anthracite Colleries, a company in which he had embodied the control of the greater part of the Welsh anthracite field, and a director of the International Nickel Company of Canada (formed in 1928), the Mond Nickel Company, the South Staffordshire Mond Gas (Power and Heating) Company, the Westminster Bank, and the Industrial Financial Investment Corporation.

It is noteworthy that Mond himself in his criticism of nationalized industry pointed to the self-same weakness that has been alleged against the vastness of his own conceptions. 'One of your chief difficulties', he said, apostrophizing the socialists in a speech mentioned below [*ibid.*, p. 314], 'is magnitude. I have deliberately come to the conclusion that it is quite impossible for human beings to control any industry beyond a certain magnitude.' Time will show whether, under his leadership, industry made the mistake with which he charged the schemes of the socialists. Whatever may be the ultimate verdict on Mond's industrial and financial ideals, there can be no question that his work for conciliation between capital and labour, and the admirable arrangements for the comfort and welfare of employees at the Brunner-Mond works at Northwich, at the Imperial Chemicals head-quarters at Westminster, and at other factories where he was able to have a say in this matter, successfully promoted the harmony and goodwill which are essential to prosperous industry. His most notable effort for this end was the formation of a committee of employers to meet representatives of the general council of the Trades Union Congress in 1927, when the Mond-Turner conferences, as they were called (Mr. Ben Turner being the Trades Union Congress chairman at the time) endeavoured, in the light of the bitter lessons of the strikes of 1926, to open a new chapter in the history of the relations between employers and employed. These conferences have since been followed by discussion and joint action between the general council of the Trades Unions and the two chief bodies representing the industrial employers.

Mond's success in dealing with the representatives of labour was a remarkable tribute to his sincerity, for he had many difficulties to overcome. A typical Jew in appearance, with a harsh half-German voice and accent, he had none of the suave Hebrew adroitness that often disarms opposition. Blunt, direct, sometimes rather blustering, and occasionally distinctly ill mannered, he carried his point by his strength of character and by his power of getting down to essentials. These qualities also finally gained for him the ear of the House of Commons, where his career began in 1906 as liberal member for Chester. From 1910 to 1923 he represented Swansea, and from 1924 to 1928, when he was raised to the peerage, Carmarthen. Neither his virtues nor his disadvantages were conducive to success as a party politician, but he applied his business capacity as first commissioner of works from 1916 to 1921 in Mr. Lloyd George's coalition ministry, and as minister of health from 1921 to 1922 in the next ministry he effectively cleared up the confused condition into which the housing problem had been allowed to fall.

In the House of Commons Mond was listened to at first critically and with impatience, but finally with the attention which is always paid to those who show that they know their subject, talk in the light of first-hand experience, and keep to the point. His outstanding parliamentary success was a speech on socialism, delivered on 20 March 1923 in answer to an indictment of the capitalist system uttered by (Viscount) Snowden. This speech was considered by many to have been one of the most damaging criticisms of the socialist ideal ever heard in the House. Perhaps the most telling passage in it was the account of the daring and determination with which, in the teeth of immense risks and discouragements, his father and his partner had created their business and given work to thousands—an enterprise which could 'never have been commenced under any Socialist system that I have ever known' (printed in Mond's *Industry and Politics*, p. 313).

Having begun his political life as a liberal, and a highly effective exponent of the blessings of free trade, Mond, like many other free traders, was converted by after-war conditions to the view that, with economic nationalism rampant all over the world, it was no longer possible to keep England's market open as the general dumping ground. In 1926 his objections to Mr. Lloyd George's land policy drove him into the ranks of the conservatives, but he was invited by his constituents at Carmarthen to remain their representative, and did so until he became a peer. His zeal as a newly converted protectionist expressed itself chiefly in the ardour and thoroughness with which he threw himself into the campaign for imperial economic unity. In his *Imperial Economic Unity* (1930) he urged the application of the principles of rationalization to inter-imperial business relations. He became chairman of the Empire Economic Union, and a visit to South Africa in the course of the same year (1930) confirmed his determination to work for the cause of trade co-operation within the Empire. But his premature death, which took place at his London house in Lowndes Square 27 December 1930, at the age of sixty-two, robbed this cause of one of its most effective advocates.

Business and political activities by no means exhausted Mond's energies, or rather, his capacity for getting things done without apparent effort; for, thanks to his power of concentrating on essentials, he gave the impression of one who took life easily and had plenty of time for appreciation of its amenities. Although his manner with strangers was shy and by no means genial, he was extremely kind and charitable, and his keen sense of humour enabled him to enjoy and collect the numerous caricatures which his features invited. As an enthusiastic Zionist, he visited Palestine in 1921, contributed £100,000 to the Jewish

Colonization Corporation for Palestine, and wrote sundry articles for Zionist publications. He had a genuine love of art and music, and took a deep and practical interest in his father's bequest of forty-two pictures to the National Gallery (1924) and provided a large part of the cost of the room in which it is housed. In 1929 he bought a piece of ground in Chelsea for the Chelsea Health Society, of which his wife was president.

Mond was created a baronet in 1910, sworn of the Privy Council in 1913, and raised to the peerage in 1928 as Baron Melchett, of Landford, co. Southampton. He was elected a fellow of the Royal Society in 1928, and received honorary degrees from several universities, including Oxford and Paris. He married in 1894 Violet Florence Mabel, daughter of James Henry Goetze, coffee merchant, of Mincing Lane, London, and had one son, Henry Ludwig (born 1898), who succeeded him as second baron, and three daughters.

There is a portrait of Mond by Sir John Lavery in the possession of Violet, Lady Melchett.

[*The Times*, 29 December 1930; H. H. Bolitho, *Alfred Mond, first Lord Melchett*, 1932; Melchett's own writings; private information.]

H. Withers.

MONRO, Sir CHARLES CARMICHAEL, baronet (1860–1929), general, was born at sea in ss. *Maid of Judah* 15 June 1860, the sixth son of Henry Monro, of Craiglochart, near Edinburgh, who had gone to Australia as a young man, by his wife, Catherine, daughter of Alexander Power, of Clonmult, co. Cork. He belonged to an old Scottish family, best known in the medical world, his grandfather having been Alexander Monro, tertius (1773–1859, q.v.), the last of the distinguished trio of that name who, from father to son, had held the chair of anatomy at the university of Edinburgh from 1720 down to 1846. Charles Monro was educated at Sherborne School and at Sandhurst, whence he was gazetted in August 1879 into the 2nd Foot, now 1st battalion The Queen's (West Surrey) Regiment. In 1881 he was appointed adjutant, and held that office for five years. He obtained his company in July 1889, having just passed the entrance examination into the Staff College, where he was a student during the years 1889–1890. His chief distinction at Camberley was his captaincy of the cricket eleven. He next spent some time in Malta, acting first as aide-de-camp to the governor and then as brigade-major. In 1897 he went to India, where he served with his battalion in the Malakand Field Force, next with the expedition into the Mohmand country, and finally with the Tirah Expeditionary Force. In February 1898 he was promoted major, and in November received the appointment of brigade-major at Gibraltar. In April 1899, however, he was advanced to the post of deputy assistant adjutant-general in Guernsey.

On the outbreak of the South African War in 1899 Monro was transferred to Aldershot in order to continue his appointment with the 6th division, which began to mobilize on receipt of the news of Lord Methuen's reverse at Magersfontein (11 December). He arrived in Africa in time to take part in Lord Roberts's march to Pretoria, and was present at General Piet Cronje's surrender at Paardeberg on 27 February 1900 and also at the actions of Poplar Grove (7 March) and Dreifontein (10 March). After the capture of Pretoria he continued working with his division in Cape Colony south of the Orange river until the close of the year. He had already been rewarded with a brevet lieutenant-colonelcy.

Monro's services were now required at the Hythe School of Musketry, and he returned home to assume the appointment of chief instructor there in February 1901. It was at Hythe that his abilities were first measured at their true worth. Fresh from South Africa and the Indian frontier where he had learnt to appreciate the value of rifle fire in war, he set to work to reform the methods of teaching musketry in the army. But his work did not end there and he became virtually responsible for the evolution of a new system of infantry fire-tactics. Monro remained at Hythe six years, the last four being spent as commandant of the school, and during that period was promoted substantive colonel in November 1903. He left Hythe in March 1907, having radically reformed army musketry; target-shooting was henceforth to become battle-shooting. The reputation which he had acquired at Hythe brought about his selection, two months later, to the command of the 13th Infantry Brigade, then stationed in Ireland. His tenure of that command was marked by the same practical outlook which had distinguished his work at Hythe. In October 1910 he was promoted major-general, but he remained with his brigade until January 1912. Two months later he was appointed to command the 2nd London Division of the Territorial Force; in this capacity he proved a sympathetic and successful chief.

On the outbreak of the War with Germany in August 1914, Monro was transferred to the command of the regular 2nd division at Aldershot, and proceeded with the British Expeditionary Force to France on 12 August. He thus participated in all the early fighting of the War. He led his division, which formed part of the I Corps, under Sir Douglas Haig, back from Mons to the Marne; and he advanced from the Marne to the Aisne, where his troops played a distinguished part in the battle. The 2nd division was then transferred to Flanders and fought throughout the latter part of October and the beginning of November in the first battle of Ypres. On 31 October, when the combined staffs of the 1st and 2nd divisions were assembled at Hooge Château, the building was struck by an enemy shell, and nearly all the assembled officers were killed; but Monro escaped with a severe shock. At the end of the year he received the command of the I Corps in succession to Sir Douglas Haig, with the temporary rank of lieutenant-general, and in March 1915 was created K.C.B. for his war services. During the early summer he commanded the I Corps through the battles of Aubers Ridge, Festubert, and Givenchy, until in July 1915 he was given the command of the newly raised Third Army with the rank of general. But his tenure of that position, was not long, for in October 1915 he was ordered to take over the command of the Mediterranean Expeditionary Force at Gallipoli, in succession to Sir Ian Hamilton.

Monro arrived at Gallipoli on 27 October and proceeded to examine the situation. By the 31st he had communicated his views to the Cabinet, recommending instant evacuation. Lord Kitchener demurred, and left London on 4 November in order to investigate the situation for himself. Monro and other naval and military officers met Kitchener on 9 November and discussed the position, after which meeting Kitchener went round the British lines. On the 15th, before returning to London, Kitchener telegraphed to the Cabinet, supporting Monro's opinion as to evacuation. The view was then put forward in the Cabinet that the Peninsula should be evacuated except for the footing at Cape Helles; and this view gained ground. But Monro stood firm in his advocacy of a complete withdrawal, and this decision was finally adopted on 23 December. The positions at Suvla Bay and Anzac Cove were evacuated between 8 and 19 December, the Cape Helles position in the first week of January 1916. By 9 January 1916 not a single British soldier remained in Gallipoli. The successful embarkation of so large a force at a cost of virtually no casualties and a relatively small sacrifice of material may be regarded as one of the most remarkable operations of the War.

Monro returned to France in January 1916 in order to assume the command of the First Army and held this post until 1 August of that year. His army did not play any notable part in the events of the summer, although the IV Corps, under Sir Henry Wilson [q.v.], sustained a somewhat nasty reverse at Vimy; Monro, however, would not sanction any attempt being made to recapture the lost ground.

On 1 October 1916 Monro was appointed commander-in-chief in India. By that time India had already placed in the field several divisions, which fought in France, Egypt, East Africa, and Mesopotamia, in addition to smaller contingents. But the Indian army was now required to undergo a further considerable expansion mainly for service in Palestine and Mesopotamia. In order to achieve this end it was found necessary to raise new classes of native soldiers and—an infinitely more difficult problem—efficient officers, British and native, to lead them. Proportionate expansion was required in the supply and medical services, while mechanical transport units had to be created. Lastly, supplies of war material and munitions adequate for the needs of these greatly augmented forces had to be found and organized. Throughout 1917 and 1918 Monro worked ceaselessly to overcome the difficulties of this colossal task. In addition, he was constantly engaged on inspection work, and even visited Mesopotamia. With the viceroy, Lord Chelmsford, Monro remained on the best of terms, so that the co-operation of these two able men made for success. At the time of the Armistice (11 November 1918) the Indian troops totalled nearly 600,000 men—nearly a fourfold expansion of the Indian establishment of August 1914.

The aftermath of the War, however, gave rise to events in India which caused Monro even greater anxiety than the development of Indian military power. Unrest in the Punjab culminating in the

Amritsar incident in April 1919, and events in Afghanistan leading to the so-called third Afghan War in the summer of that year, were followed by a difficult campaign in Waziristan during the winter of 1919 to 1920. The disturbances in the Punjab had for a time assumed serious dimensions. On 30 March there occurred an outbreak of mob violence at Delhi. At Lahore and at other towns similar incidents took place. At Amritsar on 11 April the officer in command, Brigadier-General R. E. H. Dyer [q.v.], ordered the troops to fire on a riotous crowd, with the result that 379 persons are known to have been killed and some 1,200 wounded; the incident aroused acute controversy. After the holding of an inquiry Dyer was eventually relieved of his command. From the first Monro had regarded Dyer's action as not showing the wisdom and sense of proportion which should be expected of officers of his position, and he never altered his opinion throughout the long agitation which ensued.

The Afghan and Waziristan campaigns were brought to a successful issue, the former in a few weeks; the latter after some laborious and protracted fighting. In spite of minor adverse criticism, both undertakings can be regarded as having been thoroughly well handled by Monro.

Eventually, however, the heavy cares of office began to tell on an over-worked man; Monro therefore resigned his appointment in August 1920 and went to live on half-pay in London. He was appointed governor of Gibraltar in September 1923, in which post he proved popular and efficient until his retirement in 1928. He died at his home in London 7 December 1929.

Monro may be regarded as a fine representative of the best type of British officer who fought in the European War. His cool common sense in battle was matched by true humanity; he was deliberate in council, determined in action. He possessed a great knowledge of warfare and remarkable insight into the reactions of men in battle. In addition to the K.C.B. he received the G.C.M.G. (1916), the G.C.S.I. (1919), and the G.C.B. (1919). He was created a baronet and appointed Bath King-of-Arms in 1921. He was an aide-de-camp general to King George V, 1918–1922, colonel of his old regiment, The Queen's, and a trustee of the Imperial War Museum.

Monro married in 1912 the Hon. Mary Caroline Towneley O'Hagan, daughter of Thomas, first Baron O'Hagan [q.v.], lord chancellor of Ireland. There were no children of the marriage, and the baronetcy became extinct on his death.

[*The Times*, 9 December 1929; Sir G. de S. Barrow, *The Life of General Sir Charles Carmichael Monro*, 1931; Sir J. E. Edmonds, (Official) *History of the Great War. Military Operations. France and Belgium, 1914–1915*, 1922–1928; (Official) *History of the Great War. Gallipoli*, ed. C. F. Aspinall-Oglander, vol. ii, 1932; Army Lists.]

H. DE WATTEVILLE.

MONTAGU OF BEAULIEU, second BARON (1866–1929), pioneer of motoring. [See DOUGLAS-SCOTT-MONTAGU, JOHN WALTER EDWARD.]

MONTAGU, EDWIN SAMUEL (1879–1924), statesman, the second son of Samuel Montagu, first Baron Swaythling [q.v.], by his wife, Ellen, daughter of Louis Cohen, was born in London 6 February 1879. His boyhood was undistinguished. He was educated for two years at Clifton College, until ill-health necessitated a sea-voyage, after which he spent two and a half years at the City of London School. But he made no mark until his undergraduate days at Trinity College, Cambridge, which he entered in 1898. As a young liberal politician he became president of the Union in 1902. He graduated B.A. in 1902 and M.A. in 1905.

Lord Swaythling was well known and respected as an unswerving upholder of Judaism, and his son, Edwin, remained a member of the Jewish community, but he did not inherit his father's rigid convictions. The Zionist movement appealed little to him, and national ties counted with him far more than the bond of race. But his racial antecedents may have quickened his Indian sympathies, and saved him from the sense of the colour bar in his personal relations with Indians. He notes in his Indian diary that 'there might be some truth in the allegation that I am an Oriental. Certainly that social relationship which English people find so difficult comes quite easily to me'.

Entering into politics when the liberal tide was running full flood, Montagu won, at the general election of 1906, the Chesterton division of Cambridgeshire, and remained member for that division until 1922. His foot was on the ladder as soon as he entered the House of Commons. He sought and obtained a private secretaryship to Mr. Asquith, then chancellor of the Exchequer, retaining the post when his chief became prime minister. Promotion to the minor posts of government soon followed. He was for four years (1910–1914) parliamentary under-secretary of state for India, serving, during a period of considerable Indian change, under Viscount Morley and the Marquess of Crewe. In 1912 he paid a cold-weather visit to India, and his last Indian budget speech in 1913 showed the first-hand knowledge which enabled him to handle with easy and fluent mastery a wide range of Indian subjects.

In February 1914 Montagu became financial secretary to the Treasury, and during the first two years of the European War he held a succession of minor posts in the rapid ministerial changes which the War entailed. He won the coveted honour of a privy councillorship in February 1915, and entered the Cabinet at the unusually early age of thirty-six as chancellor of the duchy of Lancaster. He did good work in popularizing the first war loans, and in establishing voluntary war-saving associations and the scheme of war-saving certificates (February 1916). In various offices he showed administrative ability and financial instinct which might have made him a good chancellor of the Exchequer, had he lived.

In June 1916 Montagu was made minister of munitions. An arrangement made by him with Messrs. J. P. Morgan & Co. saved the Allies many hundreds of millions on their American purchases. His loss of this office on the fall of Mr. Asquith's ministry in the following December was a heavy blow to his ambition. He had been in close personal touch with his chief; felt, as he says in his diary, 'hero-worship' for him, and owed to him his rapid promotion. He did in the end resign with most of Mr. Asquith's liberal colleagues, but he had no intention of being permanently entangled in the fallen fortunes of the prime minister. He felt it proper to give general support to the new government in the conduct of the War, and in June 1917 his chance came again when Mr. Lloyd George offered him the post of secretary of state for India on the resignation of (Sir) Austen Chamberlain.

Montagu accepted the office at a critical time. The need for constitutional change in India at the close of the War had been foreseen, and at the end of 1915 the viceroy, Lord Hardinge, had sent home a memorandum advocating a large programme of reform, so that the conclusion of peace might not find the home government unprepared. The building of a new political structure in war time being impossible, an announcement of the goal of British policy in India might suffice for the moment, and it was the first task of Montagu to make this declaration on behalf of the Coalition government on 20 August 1917. The goal of British policy was declared to be the 'progressive realization of responsible government' in India as an integral part of the British Empire, to be attained in successive stages as might be determined by the Imperial parliament. Unexpectedly, the announcement was made, not in Montagu's language, but in terms drafted by Lord Curzon [q.v.], who was at that time a conservative member of the inner War Cabinet under Mr. Lloyd George [see Lord Ronaldshay's *Life of Lord Curzon*, iii, 127, for the two drafts]. Curiously enough, Lord Curzon's draft, by introducing the term 'responsible government', pointed more definitely than Montagu's to the familiar British model of an executive responsible to an elected legislature. No liberal, in Montagu's view, could question that parliamentary institutions had the same value for Indians as for Englishmen, and he was determined to introduce an adequate instalment forthwith into British India.

In order to determine on the spot the first step towards the announced goal, Montagu, with a small delegation, half of civil servants and half of politicians, toured round the provinces of India from November 1917 to May 1918. It was decided not merely to frame a scheme for submission to parliament, but to compile a report on the lines of the historic Durham report which led up to Canadian self-government. The task of drafting this report, *Report on Indian Constitutional Reforms* [Cmd. 9109 of 1918], under severe time limits, was carried through by (Sir) William Marris, joint secretary to the government of India.

Montagu's diary of this tour, published twelve years afterwards by his wife [*An Indian Diary*, edited by Venetia Montagu 1930], is an uncensored document which reveals the part played by him in the construction of the proposed scheme of reform. Written or dictated from day to day, and not meant for publication, the diary gives a vivid picture of the varying moods of a mind prone to ups and downs of feeling. Many of the statements in the diary, therefore, need not be treated as considered or deliberate judgements. Montagu is often unjust to the viceroy, Lord Chelmsford, though in the end he does recognize the loyal and generous support which the viceroy gave him; and the picture drawn of the statesman playing a lone hand, dragging forward a reluctant viceroy and wrestling day by day unaided with the narrow obstinacy of all around him, can hardly be accepted. The scheme of the *Report* was not, in fact, the emanation of his own or, indeed, of any single brain. It was a composite structure, built up laboriously from the suggestions of many minds, and such strength as it possessed was due to this pooling of ideas. But if Montagu was not the sole author of the scheme, the diary makes two points clear. First, it reveals his own mental method, which he describes as 'framing conclusions and training himself to discard them, without prejudice, for better ones'. There were no precedents for a scheme of reform to serve a transitional period, such as he sought to find; and if there had been any, they would have required modifications to suit the wholly exceptional conditions of India. Montagu handled his problem with elasticity and resilience of mind, but the flexibility with which he entertained and discarded expedients was not without its embarrassments, even for himself. Secondly, the diary reveals the untiring pains which he took personally to persuade, convince, and even to cajole doubters or opponents, both British and Indian. He resented the Olympian airs of the government of India, and consulted Indian opinion as it had never been consulted before. If the scheme went through with goodwill, or at least acquiescence, it was largely due to the pertinacity, drive, and determination with which the secretary of state had previously rallied the bulk of opinion to his side.

Montagu had the satisfaction of seeing the scheme of constitutional reform accepted, with important amendments made by the joint select committee of both Houses of Parliament, but without opposition in parliament except from a determined group of retired Indian civilians. It passed into law in the Government of India Act (1919). Lord Curzon, then foreign secretary, in spite of his part in the declaration of 20 August 1917, suffered a violent revulsion of feeling. Speaking in the House of Lords, 12 December 1919, he said that 'the act was a great experiment—a daring experiment—he would not cavil at the word 'rash' being applied to it.' But he acquiesced in its passage. Space only suffices to point out where the scheme broke new ground; its details must be sought in the *Report* itself. The central feature was a substantial but duly safeguarded extension of self-government in the nine major provinces, operating through the novel and much criticized expedient, incorrectly nicknamed 'dyarchy', whereby the governor of the province was to administer certain 'reserved' services through his executive council, and other 'transferred' services through Indian ministers responsible to the elected legislature of the province. Lord Morley in defending the Minto-Morley reforms had expressly disclaimed any intention of introducing parliamentary institutions into India. Up to 1919 a chain of responsibility reached from the district officer, personally administering his district in India, through the head of the province to the governor-general, who being subordinate to the secretary of state, was through him responsible to parliament. Montagu's plan broke this chain of responsibility to a definite but limited extent. Henceforth there would be a sphere of provincial government in which Indian ministers would be responsible, not to the British parliament, but through an Indian legislature to an Indian electorate.

Meanwhile, however, divergence widened between Montagu's views and those of the government of which he was a member. The treatment of conquered Turkey was bound to excite strong feeling among the ninety million Moslems of India. They resented the disintegration of the last great Mohammedan power and what seemed to them the desecration of the holy places of their religion. Mr. Lloyd George, following the Gladstonian tradition, wished to overthrow Turkish power in Europe, and cared nothing for pledges given in the opposite sense. The government of India was bound to represent the dangerous reaction of this policy on disturbed Indian opinion, and Montagu caused growing irritation among his colleagues by supporting the Indian view. The final breach came over a technicality; at a critical moment (March 1922) in the negotiations with Turkey and Greece, the government of India asked leave to publish its protest against the Treaty of Sèvres. Without obtaining permission from the Cabinet, Montagu sanctioned publication. The doctrine of Cabinet responsibility had worn thin under coalition government, but the constitutional impropriety of his action could not be disputed. Lord Curzon at the Foreign Office was indignant, and Mr. Lloyd George promptly required Montagu's resignation.

For Montagu, this proved to be the end of his political career. He took it hard, violently attacking Lord Curzon and the Coalition in a speech at Cambridge (11 March 1922). His speech in vindication of his action in the House of Commons closed with the words: 'this is the unhappiest moment of my life.' In the general election of 1922 his Cambridgeshire constituency turned against him, and in a three-cornered contest, in which he was opposed both by a conservative and a labour candidate, he was left at the bottom of the poll. He broke away from politics, took business posts in the City, went on a financial mission to Brazil (1923–1924) and died in London 15 November 1924, at the early age of forty-five. Montagu had married in 1915 the Hon. Beatrice Venetia, youngest daughter of Edward Lyulph Stanley, fourth Baron Sheffield [q.v.], and left an only child, a daughter.

A word may be added about Montagu's main recreation, the passion for shooting to which his Indian diary bears eloquent testimony. He cared for shooting for its own sake, but in India he did, in fact, get more out of it than the satisfaction of the deep-seated instinct of pride in efficient killing. It brought him into easy personal touch alike with British administrators and with maharajas, who glory in their tiger preserves. Nor did he wholly sink the naturalist of his early days in the sportsman; he delighted to shoot pochard in Norfolk or sandgrouse in Gujner, but he and Lord Grey of Fallodon established a bird sanctuary near his Norfolk home at Breckles Hall.

Speaking in the chamber of princes after Montagu's death, the Maharaja of Alwar applied to him a slightly altered quotation, 'He was our friend, faithful and just to us', and Indian nationalists have reason to echo that judgement.

For the measure of success attained by Montagu's scheme of Indian reform in the first years of its working, reference may be made to the report of Sir John Simon's commission [*Report of the Indian Statutory Commission of 1930:* Cmd. 3568]; but time alone can decide on the ultimate wisdom of the introduction of parliamentary institutions into India, towards which he gave the deciding impulse.

A portrait of Montagu is included in the painting by Sir William Orpen of the signature of the Peace of Versailles at the Imperial War Museum, South Kensington. There is a statue of him by Lady (Hilton) Young (afterwards Lady Kennet) in Calcutta, and another by E. Riccardi at Jamnagar.

[*The Times*, 17 November 1924; *Edwin S. Montagu: a memoir*, privately printed; *An Indian Diary*, edited by Venetia Montagu, 1930.]

C. Roberts.

MONTAGUE, CHARLES EDWARD (1867–1928), man of letters and journalist, was born at Ealing 1 January 1867, the third of the four sons of Francis Montague, by his wife, Rosa McCabe, daughter of a Drogheda merchant. The father was an Irish priest from county Tyrone who had renounced his orders owing to scruples of conscience and had settled in England. Montague was educated at the City of London School under Edwin Abbott Abbott, and at Balliol College, Oxford, where he matriculated as an exhibitioner in 1885, and where he was deeply influenced by Richard Lewis Nettleship [q.v.]. He obtained a first class in classical moderations in 1887 and a second in *literae humaniores* in 1889. Next year (1890) he joined the staff of the *Manchester Guardian*, on which he remained, except during the European War, until 1925. In 1898 he married Madeline, daughter of the editor, Charles Prestwich Scott. Trained by Scott, and also by William Thomas Arnold [q.v.], his chief lieutenant, Montague became a brilliant and many-sided journalist, writing for home rule, free trade, women's rights, and all the liberal causes, and taking, with his paper, the unpopular side in the Boer War. He also made his mark as a dramatic critic by articles which were reprinted in *The Manchester Stage* (reviews by Arnold, Montague, Allan Monkhouse, and Oliver Elton, 1900) and by his *Dramatic Values* (1911). In time, after Arnold's retirement in 1898 from the *Manchester Guardian*, Montague became second in command. He contributed the section 'Middle Life' to Mrs. Humphry Ward's memoir of his friend Arnold. This memoir was prefixed to Arnold's posthumously published *Studies of Roman Imperialism* (1906). In 1910 appeared Montague's witty skit on low journalism, *A Hind Let Loose*, and in 1913 *The Morning's War*, a tale full of the poetry of mountaineering, his favourite recreation.

On the outbreak of the European War in 1914, despite his age and family ties, Montague dyed his hair, which had been grey from his youth, and enlisted. He was hurt by an explosion while training as a bomber, but in November 1915 crossed to France as a private in the 24th battalion of the Royal Fusiliers. After three weeks in the line he was invalided home, but in June 1916 was commissioned and entered the intelligence service on the Western front. For a year he was a 'conductor' of distinguished guests of the army; in June 1917 he became an assistant press censor. He saw most of the front in France and Flanders, and in 1918 went with the advance to Cologne.

Montague kept a war diary [see *Memoir*] which contains some of his best and simplest writing. He also wrote, while on service, vivid notes and introductions to the drawings by Muirhead Bone entitled *The Western Front* (1916–1917), and to those by various other hands (*British Artists at the Front, 1918*.)

On being demobilized in 1919 Montague returned to the *Manchester Guardian*. Thereafter he published *Disenchantment* (1922), a series of fierce and notable essays on the War, which greatly widened his reputation; *Fiery Particles* (1923), short stories in which the War again figures; *The Right Place* (1924), gay holiday essays; *Rough Justice* (1926), a war novel with much personal reminiscence, and *Right off the Map* (1927), a fantasia full of anti-militarism. Posthumously published were *Action* (1928), more short stories, and *A Writer's Notes on his Trade* (1930), chiefly on the niceties of style and cadence. An unfinished paper, 'Inexpert Approaches to Religion' [see *Memoir*, appendix], reveals the movement of Montague's mind towards an undogmatic and partly mystical faith. In 1925 he retired from journalism and settled at Burford, Oxfordshire. In 1926 he received the honorary degree of Litt.D. from the university of Manchester. He died of pneumonia at Manchester 28 May 1928, leaving five sons and two daughters. His death was noticed with regret, and his career with pride, by journalists in most of the English-speaking countries.

In spite of a shy address, which covered great native courage, and of a certain film of reserve, Montague was at home in many companies, and not least with working people. His associates in the press and in the War, including the war correspondents, have paid him many tributes. As a journalist he had, when occasion demanded, an excellent fighting style. He also acquired a peculiar artistry in prose. His letters and diaries written without study, show a great delicacy in the use of plain language. In his books the style, although never flat or commonplace and often most eloquent and beautiful, is not seldom over-conscious; it can also be unadorned and direct. All his gifts are seen in his longer novels, but on these his reputation will hardly rest; he found construction difficult, and the characters are not all equally real. Many of the shorter tales are admirably built and told, and are peopled by humorists, Irish or English, whose idiom is happily reproduced. As an essayist, whether polemical and satirical (*Disenchantment*), or buoyant and free of care (*The Right Place*), or aesthetic (*A Writer's Notes*), Montague excels and is likely to be remembered.

[Oliver Elton, *C. E. Montague, a Memoir* (including extracts from the Diary and 'Inexpert Approaches to Religion', &c.), 1929; personal knowledge.] OLIVER ELTON.

MONTEATH, SIR JAMES (1847–1929), Indian civil servant, was born at Guileburn, Lockerbie, Dumfriesshire, 7 September 1847, the fourth son of Thomas Monteath, of the Bank of Scotland, who came of an old Perthshire family, by his wife, Hannah Johnstone. After early education at Lockerbie, Monteath went to the Royal Academical Institution, Belfast, and thence to Queen's College, Belfast, where he graduated M.A. He passed the open examination for the Indian civil service in 1868, and was appointed to the Bombay Presidency in August 1870.

Monteath's early service was in the south of the Presidency, and his interest in this part of the province was shown by his contributions to the *Bombay Gazetteer* of the North Kanara district. His abilities, however, soon marked him for work at head-quarters, and he was transferred to Bombay in 1873. Here, after holding the posts of under-secretary and secretary to government and private secretary to the governor, Lord Reay, he became, in July 1896, chief secretary to the government of Bombay. In that capacity he had to deal with the great Bombay famine of 1896–1897. He handled the situation with such success that the Bombay government justly claimed that no previous failure of crops of equal magnitude had left so little mark on the agricultural community. Monteath received the C.S.I. in June 1897. The famine of 1896–1897 was followed, after two seasons of indifferent harvests, by the still more disastrous famine of 1899–1902, which affected fifteen districts and ten million people. Monteath was placed in special charge of famine relief, and the famine commission of 1901 referred appreciatively to his work, in support of the recommendation for the regular appointment of a famine commissioner upon similar occasions in the future.

Monteath became revenue member of the Bombay executive council in August 1900, and was acting-governor of Bombay from 6 September to 13 December 1903. In January of that year he was promoted K.C.S.I. As member of the council he initiated, with lasting benefit to the agriculturists of Bombay, his important reforms of land-revenue law. The famine commission of 1901 had criticized the existing system of land tenure in Bombay, where, it alleged, at least one-quarter of the cultivators had lost their land and less than one-fifth were free from debt. The new and restricted tenure introduced by Monteath in the Land Revenue Code Amendment Bill of 1901 aimed at reducing agricultural indebtedness by restricting, on state lands, the tenants' power to alienate their land. The Bill met with heated opposition in the Bombay Legislative Council, but Monteath, with characteristic firmness, declined to yield.

Monteath left India in August 1905, taking with him the respect of every one, even of those who were most opposed to his policy, for his ability, determination, and unfailing devotion to duty. A man of reserved disposition, he was a great reader, especially of classical literature, the love of which he had acquired from 'dominie' Ferguson of Lockerbie, and retained to the end of his life. After retirement Monteath lived at Buckerell Lodge, near Honiton, where he died 18 April 1929. He married in 1872 Amelia (died 1927), daughter of Thomas Hunter, of Belfast, a member of a Scottish family long settled in Ireland. They had five sons and three daughters. Two of the sons followed their father in the Bombay civil service, a third was in the Indian forest service, while a fourth entered the India Office and became private secretary to the secretary of state—an unusual family record of service for India.

Monteath's reputation rests on his success as a famine administrator, and as an agrarian reformer whose policy has left an enduring mark on the land-revenue system in Bombay.

[*The Times*, 22 April 1929; *Reports* of Indian Famine Commissions of 1898 and 1901; official records; personal knowledge.]

A. C. McWatters.

MOOR, Sir FREDERICK ROBERT (1853–1927), South African statesman, was born at Pietermaritzburg, Natal, 12 May 1853, the eldest son of Frederick William Moor, a settler under the Byrne immigration scheme of 1850, by his wife, Sarah Annabella, daughter of Robert Ralfe. He was educated at Hermannsburg School, near Greytown, Natal. The discovery of the diamond fields attracted him, as a young man of nineteen, to the dry diggings at Kimberley. Here he met, and in 1878 married, Charlotte, daughter of William James Dunbar-Moodie and granddaughter of Donald Moodie [q.v.], first colonial secretary of Natal. Three sons and four daughters were born of the marriage. Moor remained at the diggings for seven years. With the arrival of Barnet Isaacs, better known as Barney Barnato [q.v.], and Alfred Beit [q.v.], Moor realized that it would be increasingly difficult for the individual digger to make a fortune. Like many others, he sold out his claims, and in 1879 returned to Natal, settling down as a farmer near the small town of Estcourt.

Moor's experiences in Kimberley, where he had twice been elected to the mining board, fostered an inclination towards public life; and in 1886 he began his political career in Natal as member, for Weenen county, of the legislative assembly. He attached himself to the party which advocated self-government for Natal; and in 1893, when responsible government was conceded, he was offered the portfolio of native affairs. This office he held for four years. His eloquence made him one of the most formidable members of the country party, and he possessed the full confidence of the native inhabitants of the colony. Two years in opposition (1897–1899) were followed by a further tenure of office as minister for native affairs. During this period (1899–1903) the two most important political issues were the maintenance of the Bantu tribal system, and the serious financial and administrative problems arising from the divergent policies of the four British South African colonies with regard to customs and railway rates. As minister for native affairs, Moor was disposed to modify the traditional policy of Sir Theophilus Shepstone [q.v.] of maintaining communal customs and upholding the authority of the Bantu chiefs. He favoured the grant of land titles to natives on individual tenure, but failed to carry a bill to that effect through the colonial legislature. He retired with his chief,

Sir Albert Hime, on the defeat of the ministry in August 1903.

As leader of the opposition to the ministry of C. J. Smythe (1905–1906), Moor trenchantly criticized the increase in the taxation of natives, and particularly the ill-advised poll tax which provoked the native rebellion of February 1906. On the larger question of the political future of South Africa, he consistently urged the necessity for some measure of political and economic unification. As delegate for Natal to the inaugural ceremonies of the Australian Commonwealth in 1901, he had been profoundly impressed by the enthusiasm of Australian statesmen, and by their confident anticipation that federation would lead to an immense expansion of the resources of their country.

In November 1906 Moor succeeded Smythe as prime minister, and the opportunity to throw the weight of Natal into the scales in favour of a movement for the unification of South Africa came in the critical years 1908–1910. In 1908 he went to Pretoria to attend the conference on customs and railway rates, and identified himself whole-heartedly with the proposal that immediate steps should be taken to assemble a national convention for the purpose of preparing a draft union constitution. Opinion in Natal was extremely sympathetic towards federation, but hostile to the suggestion of a unitary constitution. On this issue, Moor and his colleagues were outvoted in the National Convention which met at Durban in October 1908. Eventually Moor acquiesced in the grant of large discretionary powers to the Union government, believing that public opinion would safeguard the essential rights of the provinces. He informed the Natal legislature that a strong central government was essential for the immediate future in order to develop the resources of South Africa. He predicted, however, that the powers granted to provincial councils would ultimately be enlarged. His insistence that isolation would be suicidal brought round the bulk of his followers, and at a referendum in June 1909 Natal accepted the Union constitution by an unexpectedly large majority.

In General Botha's federal ministry of 1910, Moor took the portfolio of commerce and customs; but he was defeated at the first election following the Union. His previous experience as minister for native affairs in Natal qualified him to serve as a senator with special knowledge of native requirements and he was nominated in this capacity, retaining his seat for ten years (1910–1920). He then retired to his farm, Greystone, at Estcourt, where he died 18 March 1927.

Moor was not a great parliamentary leader, but he was a fluent speaker and a man of genuine breadth of view. He was entirely devoid of racial prejudice, personally popular with Dutch-speaking colonists, and a sincere friend of the native population. Even political opponents acknowledged his deep attachment to the interests of Natal. In private life, he was a keen sportsman, and an excellent big-game shot. His political services were rewarded with a privy councillorship on the occasion of the Imperial Conference of 1907, which he attended as premier of a self-governing colony. He was knighted in 1911.

[*The Natal Witness*, 19 March 1927; *Debates of the Legislative Assembly of the Colony of Natal*, vols. xlv–xlviii, 1908–1909; *Sports and Sportsmen: South Africa*, n.d.; private information.] A. F. Hattersley.

MORESBY, JOHN (1830–1922), admiral and explorer, was born at Allerton, Somerset, 15 March 1830, the second son of Admiral of the Fleet Sir Fairfax Moresby [q.v.], by his wife, Eliza Louisa, youngest daughter of John Williams, of Bakewell, Derbyshire. He was educated at a private school until the age of twelve when he joined the royal navy in the *Caledonia*, then the flagship at Devonport. In 1845 he sailed as a midshipman in the frigate *America* for the Pacific via Cape Horn. The *America* returned to England the next year with a freight of specie which it was then the custom to send home in naval ships. Moresby next served with the Channel fleet, and in the paddle frigate *Odin* was at Palermo during the rising of 1848. The following year he joined the *Excellent* for gunnery instruction, and subsequently was appointed gunnery mate of the frigate *Amphitrite* and sailed for the west coast of South America in 1850. Shortly afterwards he was transferred to the frigate *Thetis* as gunnery lieutenant, and in 1853 was in command of a punitive expedition against the Indians of Vancouver Island. Returning home on promotion, Moresby joined the paddle sloop *Driver* as first lieutenant in 1854 on the eve of war with Russia. For two summers he was on reconnaissance work in the Baltic, and took part in the storming of the Bomarsund forts and the abortive attack on Riga.

On the conclusion of peace with Russia Moresby was appointed flag-lieutenant to the admiral in command of the Irish station and was given leave to accompany his father to Austria when Sir Fairfax Moresby represented the British navy at the centenary of the order of Maria Theresa. In 1858 he became commander, and after a period on half pay was appointed in 1861 to command the *Snake* on the China station, where he took part in the suppression of the Taiping rebellion and was in action at Shanghai. The *Snake* was subsequently engaged in the suppression of piracy on the coasts of southern China and in safeguarding the rights of English ships engaged in the opium trade. In the sloop *Argus*, of which he took command in 1863, Moresby went to Japan and took part in the international attack on the Shimonoseki forts in 1864 and in the subsequent naval demonstration in Japanese waters.

In 1865 Moresby was promoted captain and, sharing the fate of many officers of his rank at that time, went on half pay until 1871 when he was given command of the paddle sloop *Basilisk* for service on the Australian station. The *Basilisk* was not a survey vessel and carried no officers specially trained for such work, but the chances of exploration which her area of cruising afforded, led Moresby to apply successfully for a small outfit of surveying instruments. Between 1872 and 1874, except for two cruises to New Zealand and among the South Sea Islands respectively, the ship was in Torres Strait and along the coasts of New Guinea; and although primarily concerned with the suppression of the kidnapping of native labour, she carried out a long series of important explorations, adding to the charts some of the coast lines which were still unknown outside polar regions.

The Queensland government lent the services of a survey officer, but otherwise Moresby received scant encouragement until, at the end of its commission, the *Basilisk* was ordered to return home by the north coast of New Guinea in order that the survey work might be continued. In those days the south-east coast of New Guinea, though visited by a few missionaries, was scarcely known. The work of Luis Vaes de Torres in 1606 at the eastern end of the island was revealed only in 1878 by the discovery of his map in Madrid. Moresby surveyed, on the south coast, Hall Sound and Redscar Bay, discovered Port Moresby, Fairfax Harbour (which he named after his father), and Discovery Bay, as well as their approaches, and various islets and reefs in Torres Strait. By Hilda and Ethel rivers he tried to penetrate the unknown interior. He next discovered at the east end Hayter, Basilisk, and Moresby Islands and China and Fortescue Straits, and took possession of the islands in the name of Queen Victoria (1873). Of the eastern part of the north coast nothing was known at the time except a few vague landfalls of J. A. B. d'Entrecasteaux in 1793. Moresby mapped the whole coast westward to Astrolabe Bay as well as the islands of the d'Entrecasteaux group—Normanby, Ferguson, and Goodenough. In all, his surveys covered 1,200 miles of unknown coastline and about a hundred islands.

Moresby returned home at the end of 1874 to find that while geographers realized the value of his work, the Admiralty had become strangely indifferent and the government of the day had no anxiety to establish British claims in eastern New Guinea. It was not until 1884 that the hand of the government was forced by the action of Queensland, and a British protectorate, with its capital at Port Moresby, was proclaimed in the south-east of the island. The greater part of Moresby's discoveries eventually fell into German hands, but on 17 September 1914 Kaiser Wilhelm land, as the territory had been called, surrendered to an Australian force, and since 1920 has been administered by Australia under a mandate from the League of Nations.

After a short spell in charge of the coastguards between Cromer and St. Abb's Head, Moresby was senior naval officer in charge of the Bermuda dockyard from 1878 to 1881; there he effected many improvements. In 1881 he became a rear-admiral and was appointed assessor to the Board of Trade. He retired in 1888 with the rank of vice-admiral and became admiral on the retired list in 1893.

Moresby married in 1859 Jane Willis (died 1876), eldest daughter of Philip Scott, J.P., of Queenstown, Ireland, and had one son and four daughters. He enjoyed the unique distinction of having his name bestowed, during his lifetime, on a destroyer built in 1916, in recognition of his discoveries in New Guinea. He died at Fareham, Hampshire, 12 July 1922.

[*The Times*, 13 July 1922; J. Moresby, *Two Admirals* (an autobiography with some account of his father's career), 1909, and *Discoveries and Surveys in New Guinea,* 1876; private information.]

R. N. Rudmose Brown.

MORLAND, Sir THOMAS LETHBRIDGE NAPIER (1865–1925), general, was born 9 August 1865 at Montreal, Canada, the eldest son of Thomas Morland, a manufacturing engineer, who, after emigrating to Canada as a young man, played an important part in the construction of the Canadian Pacific Railway, by his wife, Helen Elizabeth, daughter of General Henry Servante. On losing both parents when still a child, Morland was brought to England to be educated, and sent to Charterhouse and subsequently to the Royal Military College, Sandhurst. Thence he was gazetted into the King's Royal Rifle Corps in August 1884. Whilst still a subaltern he passed in 1890 into the Staff College, Camberley, where he spent two years, graduating in December 1892. After being promoted captain in April 1893, he was appointed aide-de-camp to General Sir A. J. Lyon Fremantle, commander-in-chief in Malta, in February 1895.

Being of an adventurous disposition, and a good horseman, Morland desired more active employment. This he found in Nigeria, being transferred in February 1898 to the West African Frontier Force, which he joined in time to take part in the operations which were then in progress in the river Niger valley and hinterland. This was the first of six minor campaigns in those regions in which he participated with credit. In recognition of his earliest service Morland was promoted brevet-major in July 1899 and given command of the 1st battalion West African Frontier Force with the temporary rank of lieutenant-colonel. Early in 1900 he commanded the little column engaged in the Kaduna expedition in Northern Nigeria; later in the same year he took part in the Ashanti operations, after which he obtained the brevet of lieutenant-colonel. In 1901 he conducted the operations against the emir of Yola, when he was slightly wounded, subsequently receiving the D.S.O. (1902). In the latter year he was given the command of the small Bornu expedition. Finally, in 1903, he was engaged in the campaign against the rulers of Kano and Sokoto. In the following March (1904) he was awarded the C.B. After a spell of leave Morland was promoted colonel in September 1905 and returned to Africa as inspector-general of the West African Frontier Force with the temporary rank of brigadier-general. No more fighting fell to his lot, and he finally returned home in 1909. He did not obtain further employment until the following June (1910), when he was given command of the 2nd brigade at Aldershot, where he remained for three years. He then gave up his command (June 1913), having been promoted major-general three months earlier.

Morland now remained on half pay for over a year. On the outbreak of the European War, he was appointed (August 1914) to the command of the 2nd London division of the Territorial Force, but he was very soon transferred to the command of the newly created 14th division of the New Armies. Two months later he was again transferred, to the vacant command of the 5th division. Arriving in Flanders on 18 October, he led part of his new command at La Bassée during the first battle of Ypres. In July 1915 he was advanced to the command of the X Army Corps, with the temporary rank of lieutenant-general, and was created K.C.B. The X Corps was then in process of formation, and so did not participate in any important engagement until it was allotted to the Fourth Army before the opening of the battle of the Somme (1 July 1916). It then fought in the arduous actions at Bazentin and on Pozières Ridge (14–31 July). For some weeks during the following August and September Morland commanded the XIV Army Corps in the absence of Lord Cavan.

The X Corps was next moved into the Second Army, and thus came to take a full share in the battle of Messines (June 1917). It continued to fight in the operations that ensued to the east of Messines in the third battle of Ypres. For the closing stages of that battle Morland's Corps was transferred to the Fifth Army and took part in the sanguinary struggle of Passchendaele (September–October). Morland was then rewarded with the K.C.M.G. (1917). After this the X Corps was again brought south, and was virtually used up for reinforcements during the German offensive in March 1918. Morland himself, in April, was given the command of the XIII Army Corps, a position which he held until March 1919. During that period he commanded his troops with some success in the fighting round Cambrai in August 1918. His Corps was again heavily engaged on the river Selle, and at the date of the Armistice (11 November) was standing on the river Sambre.

Morland was promoted substantive lieutenant-general in January 1919. But he was then struck down by an attack of the prevalent influenza, and never really recovered good health. In March 1919 he returned to the command of his former troops, the reconstituted X Corps, in the army of occupation at Cologne. A year later he succeeded Sir William Robertson as commander-in-chief of that army, and became temporary general. In March 1922 he returned home in order to assume the chief command at Aldershot in succession to Lord Cavan, and in November of that year he was promoted full general. Owing, however, to his impaired health he vacated his appointment at the end of February 1923. He never obtained further employment, and died rather suddenly at Montreux, Switzerland, 21 May 1925. He was appointed colonel of the Suffolk Regiment in 1919, and an aide-de-camp general to King George V in 1922.

Morland married in 1890 Mabel Elinor Rowena (died 1901), daughter of Admiral Henry Craven St. John, of Stokefield, Thornbury, Gloucester, and had two daughters.

[*The Times*, 25 May 1925; Army Lists; private information.] H. de Watteville.

MORLEY, JOHN, Viscount Morley of Blackburn (1838–1923), statesman and man of letters, was born at Blackburn on 24 December 1838. His father, Jonathan Morley, a surgeon, who came from Mytholmroyd in the West Riding of Yorkshire, was the son of a small clothier. Morley's mother, Priscilla Mary Donkin, belonged to a shipowning family in North Shields. There were three sons, Edward, John, and William. Grace, the only daughter, was John's favourite companion and they were deeply attached to one another. The father, a man of strong character and quick temper, was a lover of books. Originally a Wesleyan, he joined the Church of England after settling as a surgeon in Blackburn. Blackburn, the chief centre of the cotton-weaving industry, was, in common with the whole North of England, suffering from trade depression during Morley's childhood. Distress often approached famine during the 'hungry forties'. The people were overcrowded and badly housed; there was much brutality, and rioting was frequent in the town.

John Morley's studious tastes were encouraged by his father, and by the headmaster of an excellent local school, known as Hoole's Academy, which he attended. There he attained such proficiency that his father sent him to University College School, London, and thence to Cheltenham College. There he took no part in sports but worked steadily, and in 1856 won an open scholarship at Lincoln College, Oxford. In an essay on Mark Pattison [q.v.], written long afterwards, Morley described the 'intellectual dilapidation' into which Lincoln College had fallen about this time. When, in 1851, the Fellows had elected as their rector not Pattison, but an obscure and unlearned person, Pattison, in consequence of this rebuff, had become a misanthorpe who took no part in college life; Morley, therefore, only came to know the great scholar in after years. But he won the esteem of a young tutor, Thomas Fowler [q.v.], afterwards president of Corpus Christi College, and took a prominent part in the social life of the college as well as in the debates at the Union Society. His chief friend in college was James Augustus Cotter Morison [q.v.], then senior commoner, wealthy, brilliant, independent, who was already at work on his life of St. Bernard, and 'brought our young souls into vivid and edifying contact' with great contemporaries like Carlyle and wise teachers like Emerson. Morley had been destined for holy orders, but Oxford life gradually disinclined him for a religious vocation, and a quarrel with his father forced him, after obtaining a second class in honour moderations, to relinquish 'Greats' in his third year, and to leave Oxford with only a pass degree.

For the next three or four years (1860–1863) Morley had a hard struggle as a free-lance journalist in London. Of his experiences at this time he wrote to Frederic Harrison [q.v.] in 1873: 'I was a scrawler when I first came to town, and I have scribbled many a day before now with a hungry paunch, but 'twas all honest and honourable.' At last, after much ill-paid hack work, his contributions to the *Saturday Review* so impressed John Douglas Cook [q.v.], its almost illiterate but highly successful managing editor, that he sent for Morley (who was then lodging in King's Bench Walk) and commissioned him to write 'middle' articles and reviews, giving him at the same time a handsome retaining fee. Among others on the *Saturday's* staff at that time were Robert Cecil, afterwards third Marquess of Salisbury and prime minister, and (Sir) Leslie Stephen, with whom Morley now formed a lifelong friendship.

In the same year (1863) Morley became acquainted with George Meredith, and later, through Meredith and Cotter Morison, with Frederick Augustus Maxse [q.v.], William Hardman, Frederic Chapman [q.v.], the publisher, and a set of bohemians at the Garrick Club. In those days, George Meredith lived in a cottage near Esher. Morley recalls [*Recollections*, i, p. 36] what Meredith's friendship and personality meant to a young journalist with an ambition for 'letters in their broadest sense—letters in terms of life, and in relation to life'. Besides being a poet and a novelist, Meredith was an ardent radical, though he did not always hold party views; and by this time, Morley, by nature an idealist, was open to the ideas and impulses of liberalism. He had no taste for the slashing toryism of the *Saturday Review*, and never contributed to its political effusions. In 1865 he thought it worth while to republish some of his 'middles' in an anonymous volume entitled *Modern Characteristics*. The book made no mark, and in after life the author never claimed it as his own. Only here and there can be detected the originality of thought and style which appears two years later in his first book on Burke. But one of his *Saturday* essays—on 'New Ideas'—arrested the attention of John Stuart Mill, and brought Morley into personal contact and lasting friendship with the great teacher and philosopher of liberalism. After this, until Mill's death in 1873, Morley was a constant visitor at Blackheath; and never in after life forgot his debt to the 'saint of rationalism'. At Mill's house he met George Grote, Herbert Spencer, Leonard Courtney, Henry Fawcett, John Elliot Cairnes, and others of Mill's school. Another of Morley's articles, a review of *Toilers of the Sea*, written in 1866, brought him a much prized letter from Victor Hugo, then an exile in Guernsey.

By this time Morley's gifts were beginning to impress a widening circle of notable men and women, whose ideas were penetrated by progressive thought in science, religion, morals, and politics. In 1866, a criticism of her novels in *Macmillan's Magazine* gained him the friendship of George Eliot; and in January 1867, largely through the influence of Cotter Morison, he was appointed editor of the *Fortnightly Review*, a venture which had been launched in the previous year by Frederic Chapman in conjunction with Cotter Morison, George Henry Lewes, and Anthony Trollope. In Morley's hands, the *Fortnightly* soon became an influential organ of liberal opinion, distinguished by the boldness and originality of its views, and by a happy variety of signed contributions from many brilliant writers and scientific men, such as Meredith, Trollope, Mill, Huxley, Herbert Spencer, Matthew Arnold, Swinburne, Mark Pattison, Walter Bagehot, and Leslie Stephen. At this time Morley was in close sympathy with Frederic Harrison and the leading positivists; but, like George Eliot, he never identified himself with the religion of Comte. In Frederic Harrison's chambers at Lincoln's Inn he read a little law. He was called to the bar in 1873, and, although he never practised, was elected in 1891 a bencher of Lincoln's Inn, where he often dined.

Morley held the editorship of the *Fortnightly Review* for fifteen years, and maintained throughout, with a few exceptions, the policy, then an innovation, of the signed article. Morley discussed and planned almost every number of the *Review* with Frederic Harrison, who virtually acted as assistant-editor. Up to a point, Harrison's positivism and Morley's agnosticism harmonized well enough, for both were enthusiastic opponents of established dogma, and eager champions of the new humanitarian rationalism which, it was thought, would take its place. Of Morley's published letters some of the liveliest are those which, in the early 'seventies, he wrote to Harrison.

Much of the best work published in the *Fortnightly Review* came from Morley's own pen. His first real contributions to English literature, a series of essays on Burke, began in the *Fortnightly* for February 1867. They were republished in the same year with some additions in book form by Messrs. Macmillan, who had just appointed him their reader and literary adviser. In this, his first study of Burke, are many faults; but there are passages to show that he had just begun to form a prose style of the first order. The book is also interesting for the light which it throws thus early on his political ideals, and for the characteristic blend of conservatism with liberal or radical doctrines, which he was ready to apply to problems of government and society. In these early days, his masters were Adam Smith, the Physiocrats, Bentham, Austin, Maine, Comte, Mill, and Turgot. 'But', he says, 'I owed more to Burke for practical principles in the strategy and tactics of public life than to the others.' Comte's philosophy and his calendar of the great men who had contributed to human improvement made a lasting impression on Morley, but the influence of Mill and Huxley, as well as his own strong anti-sectarian instincts, prevented him from joining the English Positivist church, though he had much in common at this time with the three Wadham disciples of Comte—Frederic Harrison, E. S. Beesly, and J. H. Bridges.

For Huxley, ablest of the scientific agnostics and their most powerful controversialist, Morley entertained a lively admiration. Of all the articles published in the *Fortnightly* that of Huxley on the *Physical Basis of Life*, which appeared in February 1869, made, perhaps, the most stir. At a time when the Old Testament account of the origin of the world and even its chronology were still defended by orthodox theologians, Huxley was allowed and encouraged by the editor of the *Fortnightly* to substitute evolution for the Book of Genesis. A few months later, reviewing Lecky's *History of European Morals*, Morley combined in a constructive criticism utilitarian conceptions of ethics and politics with the new evolutionary interpretation of life, using Mill's refinement of Bentham's 'greatest happiness' formula to show how such virtues as mercy, humanity, and kindness to animals are useful and advantageous to society. From Mill, and from another of his favourite writers, Condorcet, Morley learned the desirability of raising the status of women, though it was long before he came to support, and even then without much enthusiasm, their political enfranchisement.

Towards the end of 1867 Morley had paid a brief visit to the United States, where he met Walt Whitman, Emerson, Charles Sumner, and E. L. Godkin. The antipathy of the American Irish to England made a painful impression on his mind; and soon after his return in May 1868, in an address at Blackburn on Ireland's rights and duties, he drew from his observations in America, as well as from the state of Ireland, a strong argument for the redress of Irish grievances, especially those connected with the position of the Established Church and with the land. A general election was not far off, and Morley's political ambitions were stirred. After some unsuccessful negotiations with Preston, he turned to Blackburn, but there also was disappointed. It happened, however, that the two victorious conservative candidates were unseated on petition, and in March 1869, when new writs were issued, the Blackburn liberals chose Morley as their second candidate. The proceedings only lasted a few days. There was open voting, and the liberal candidates were heavily defeated, Morley being bottom of the poll. It was complained that many voters had been intimidated by conservative mill-owners, and the experience converted Morley into a strong supporter of the ballot. His radical opinions were now well known, and in June 1869 he was appointed editor of the *Morning Star*, a paper which had been started by Cobden and Bright to promote peace, retrenchment, and reform. But when Morley took over the paper it was already moribund, and was absorbed a few months later by its liberal rival, the *Daily News*.

After this double repulse from parliament and daily journalism Morley returned to the *Fortnightly Review*. In May 1870 he married Mary, daughter of Thomas Ayling, of Abbey Road, London, and took a short lease (in 1870) of Flexford House, near Guildford. He now devoted himself to a new task on which he had embarked after finishing his life of Burke. This was an attempt, in a series of biographical essays, to interpret the Frenchmen of the Revolution and to make their ideas known and serviceable to a new generation of English radicals. His *De Maistre*, *Condorcet*, and *Turgot* appeared first in the pages of the *Fortnightly*. These studies were interrupted, however, by the outbreak of the Franco-German War in 1870, which led to a sharp difference of opinion between certain of his friends. Harrison and several others favoured intervention on behalf of the French, especially after the fall of the Second Empire in 1871. Cotter Morison was equally ardent for Germany, while Morley and Meredith did their best, as Meredith wrote, 'to preserve an even balance'. In November 1870 Mill congratulated Morley on not having yielded to the 'utterly false and mistaken sympathy with France'; but Morley would not endorse Mill's advocacy of compulsory service, and printed in the *Fortnightly* an outspoken attack by Harrison on the Bismarckian policy of 'blood and iron'.

In 1871 Morley gave up Flexford, and

bought the lease of a small farm-house on the Hog's Back, just above Puttenham. Here he lived happily for a couple of years. The view from Pitfield, as it was called, was declared by Mill to be the finest in the south of England. At Pitfield, Morley completed his *Voltaire* in 1871 and his *Rousseau* in 1873—two masterly studies. In the spring of 1873 Mill visited Mr. and Mrs. Morley at Pitfield. 'He is the one living person', wrote Morley to his sister at the time, 'for whom I have an absolutely unalloyed veneration and attachment, and of whose kindness I am most proud.' A few weeks later his friend and master passed away; and thereupon Morley wrote for the *Fortnightly* (June 1873) a very beautiful *éloge* on the 'Death of Mr. Mill'.

Morley's style, usually restrained, but often rich in colour, and sometimes vibrating with passion, gave distinction to his French studies. In the art of mingling meditative and critical reflections with narrative and description he had come to excel. In depicting the Frenchmen of the Revolution and their precursors, interpreting their minds, and expounding their doctrines, he found means to convey a message of rationalism and progress well adapted to catch the ear and move the hearts of a generation fired with new ideas and already advancing towards radicalism in politics and Darwinism in science. His writings often reflect the fierce indignation against moral and social wrongs which surged up within him. This was for him the attraction of Rousseau—a character in other ways rather repellent to one who held that great thoughts, though they spring from the heart, should go round by the head. Morley's own mind found expression sometimes in the critical and destructive rationalism of Voltaire, sometimes in the sentimental dreams of Rousseau. In Turgot he hailed his ideal philosopher-statesman.

About this time radical opinions verging on republicanism and a coincidence of view about national education—then a burning subject—brought Morley into political alliance and intimate friendship with a rising statesman, whose character, methods, and ways of approach to the problems of the day were strangely unlike his own. Joseph Chamberlain [q.v.] was a practical man of business, who had made his mark as a municipal reformer in Birmingham. A Unitarian and a radical, he was glad to lead nonconformists who resented denominational teaching at public expense, and agnostics, like Morley, who demanded a national system of purely secular education, free to all. A National Education League was formed, with Morley's support, under the political guidance of Chamberlain. In 1873 Morley wrote four articles for the *Fortnightly*, and republished them in the same year with additions in a volume entitled *The Struggle for National Education*. This was a vigorous polemic against the Education Act of 1870, in the course of which the Church of England is denounced as 'the ally of tyranny, the organ of social oppression, the champion of intellectual bondage' at every great crisis except one in English history. Against this indictment is set the record of the nonconformists, who had always stood forth against privilege, and had even 'shed their blood for law and ordered freedom'. Morley was as fearless in attack as Chamberlain. In commenting on one of Gladstone's arguments for Anglican claims and voluntary schools, he wrote: 'A poorer sophism was never coined even in that busy mint of logical counterfeits.'

For the next twelve years Morley worked with Chamberlain; and they formed, together with Sir Charles Dilke [q.v.], a radical triumvirate whose programme of disestablishment, secular education, land reform, and progressive taxation gradually took strong hold on a large section of the liberal party. It was little liked by Mr. Gladstone, and still less by Lord Hartington. After 1875 the *Fortnightly* became the recognized organ of political radicalism. It was a severe critic of Disraeli's imperialist aims in India and South Africa. It supported Gladstone's policy during the Russo-Turkish War (1877) and denounced the second Afghan War (1879). Morley's attacks on Sir Bartle Frere, whom he dubbed 'a prancing Proconsul' for his action in South Africa, were especially bitter. His outlook on foreign and imperial policy was becoming definitely and notoriously pacific. He was again anxious to be in parliament; but at the general election of 1880, standing for Westminster, he received another rebuff. In the same year he accepted the editorship of the *Pall Mall Gazette*, a position which greatly augmented his influence in politics. He swung the paper round from conservatism to radicalism and from Imperialism to Cobdenism. At that time William Edward Forster [q.v.] was chief secretary for Ireland, and recollections of the Education Act of 1870 did not make

Forster's coercive policy any the more palatable to Morley, who maintained in a series of brilliant articles that Ireland had real grievances, for which force was no remedy. In May 1882 Morley's views prevailed. The Cabinet decided that the Irish Coercion Bill should not be renewed, and that Parnell, with John Dillon and Michael Davitt, should be released from Kilmainham jail. Forster resigned; but the murder of his successor, Lord Frederick Cavendish, in Phoenix Park (6 May), made it clear that coercion had to be resumed.

In the early 'eighties Morley had his hands very full. He had undertaken in 1879 to write the life of Cobden. His defeat at Westminster was fortunate; for it enabled him to finish the task in the autumn of 1881. The *Life of Cobden* (dedicated to John Bright) is one of the best of his writings and holds its place as a classic among English political biographies; it had, moreover, a very much larger sale than any of his previous books, and made Morley's name widely known, especially in the North, where Cobden and Bright were still the political idols of radical nonconformity. The study of Cobden's unselfish character and international statesmanship left impressions on Morley's mind which were never effaced. Most of the principles which guided him thenceforth as critic or director of public policy were essentially those of Cobden.

Just before the *Life of Cobden* appeared, Morley's connexion with the *Fortnightly Review* came to an end. A valedictory article in October 1882 (reprinted in his *Essays*) describes very happily the methods and aims of his editorship. He hinted that the radical programme had excited far more wrath than unorthodox theology. But he made no claim to have founded a new system of political thought. The liberals and radicals of the early 'eighties might have a party programme in common, but it could not be pretended that they surveyed society and institutions in a comprehensive and philosophic way, like the Benthamites or Philosophic Radicals. Morley was now entering party politics, and he would soon have to be content with compromises and second bests; but party politics never meant for him a relinquishment of doctrine; and it is significant that, in bidding good-bye to readers of the *Fortnightly*, he paused to tell them that in 1882 Englishmen were not less in need of systematic politics than their fathers: 'We shall need to see great schools before we can make sure of powerful parties.' Indeed, by temperament, Morley was far better qualified to found a school than to lead a party.

After his two unsuccessful attempts, at Blackburn in 1867 and at Westminster in 1880, Morley's parliamentary ambitions were at last gratified early in 1883, when he was returned at a by-election for Newcastle-upon-Tyne, then a two-member constituency.

His fellow member was Joseph Cowen [q.v.], a jingo radical, editor and proprietor of the *Newcastle Chronicle*, who, although at first friendly enough, proved himself eventually a formidable if not an open foe. In the House of Commons Morley was only moderately successful. His set speeches were generally adequate to the occasion; but in the cut and thrust of debate he was inferior to many men of less talent. The charm of voice and gesture, the felicities of thought and expression, which made his conversation the delight of private society, found little play in parliament. But he had the gift of moral leadership, and his powerful protests against military intervention in Egypt, wars in South Africa, and coercion in Ireland soon gave him a position of independence and influence. In the summer of 1885 he was still an ally of Chamberlain and Dilke, and joint author with them of the radical programme. But when Chamberlain's negotiations with Parnell fell through, the Birmingham leader began to reconsider his Irish policy, and this change of view was confirmed when he saw the Irish vote in England and Scotland transferred to the conservatives. Morley refused to abandon Irish claims, and began to remonstrate with Chamberlain, reminding him, 'I have thought, read and written about Ireland all my life'.

When the general election of 1885 was over, the liberals and conservatives were equal, and the Irish Nationalists under Parnell held the balance. Though second to Cowen, Morley held his seat at Newcastle. Gladstone announced his conversion to Home Rule; but Lord Salisbury, whose short administration had been conciliatory towards the Irish Nationalists, drew back, and when a combination of liberals and Irish defeated him on a radical amendment to the address on 27 January 1886, he resigned, leaving Gladstone to form a government. To the chagrin of Chamberlain, Morley received what was obviously a post of honour and danger in becoming chief secretary for Ireland. The rupture with Chamberlain was painful, but Morley had no doubts or qualms; for to him the conciliation of Ireland seemed a far grander policy than the material reforms on which Chamberlain's mind was set. Gladstone's choice was justified by the fidelity and loyalty of his new colleague, and their friendship continued unbroken until Gladstone's death more than twelve year later.

Gladstone formed his third administration at the beginning of February 1886. It was necessary to draft the first Home Rule bill very rapidly, and Morley shared with his new chief the difficult and (as it proved) hopeless task of framing a measure which would satisfy the Irish nationalists without completely alienating Chamberlain and the 'liberal-unionists'. Lord Hartington, (Lord) Goschen, and a small group of whigs were already in opposition, and the fate of the bill was practically sealed on 26 March, when Chamberlain and Sir George Otto Trevelyan [q.v.] left the government. Over ninety dissentient liberals or liberal-unionists headed by Hartington, Bright, and Chamberlain determined to vote against the second reading, which was thereby defeated by 341 votes to 311. The general election in July resulted in a large unionist majority; but at Newcastle Morley was returned at the head of the poll. In the following year (January–February 1887) he took a leading part in the Round Table Conference, at which it was hoped to bring about a concordat with Chamberlain and Trevelyan on the Irish question; but the breach between Chamberlain on the one hand, and Gladstone, Morley, and Parnell on the other could not be healed, although Trevelyan and several other liberal-unionists returned to the Gladstonian fold.

During these years of opposition Morley's energies were largely absorbed by politics. In parliament and on the platform he was constantly opposing and denouncing Lord Salisbury's policy of coercion which was pursued with persistence and defended with dexterity by Arthur Balfour, the chief secretary for Ireland. In February 1888 Morley visited Dublin and received the freedom of the city. By this time he was, next to Gladstone, with the possible exception of Sir William Harcourt, the most popular orator on liberal platforms. By-elections were going against the government, and Home Rule seemed to be coming into favour when in 1890 the Parnell divorce suit, and the nationalist split which followed, made the cause desperate. In the autumn of 1891 a large programme of reform was adopted by the liberal party at Newcastle, and the general election of 1892 yielded a composite liberal and nationalist majority of 40. Meanwhile, Morley supported himself by his pen. He was editing the 'English Men of Letters' series, and found time to write *Walpole* (1889) for the 'Twelve English Statesmen' series, to which he persuaded Lord Rosebery to contribute *Pitt*.

Morley kept his seat for Newcastle in 1892, but this time he was only second. Although he had assented to the Newcastle programme of October 1891, he had steadily refused to support an Eight Hours' Bill which was being hotly demanded by some of the younger trade union leaders. Consequently the socialists worked against him, and his poll fell far below expectations. It looked as if he would be defeated at the by-election when he took office for the second time as chief secretary for Ireland; but although he was again opposed by the socialists, there was a great revulsion of local feeling in his favour, and he was returned with a handsome majority over his conservative opponent.

From the beginning of Gladstone's fourth administration it was obvious that Home Rule could not be carried without the consent of the House of Lords, and for two years the liberal government was mainly occupied in ploughing the sands. Morley's Irish administration, during his three years of office from 1892 to 1895, involved many real difficulties and more petty vexations. He had to deal not only with the Orangemen, but with the two factions of Irish nationalists, and with many personal jealousies. One of his admirers described him in the office of chief secretary as over-cautious, slow in taking decisions, and too much afraid of acting on the advice of the Irish leaders. He might perhaps have done more to decentralize Dublin Castle administration; but at any rate he avoided serious blunders, and achieved his main task of helping Gladstone to prepare and carry through the House of Commons the second Home Rule Bill. He also reduced the protestant ascendancy among the county justices of Ireland, and modified the Crimes Act by a partial suspension of its operations. In the Cabinet he had many difficulties with Harcourt, whose temper at this time exasperated nearly all his colleagues. Hence it was that, on Gladstone's retirement in March 1894, Morley played a leading part in the choice of Lord Rosebery to succeed Gladstone as prime minister. The decision was unpopular with rank and file liberals, who resented the supersession of Harcourt in favour of a young and comparatively inexperienced peer. Morley quickly regretted on grounds of policy a course which he had taken for personal reasons, and soon found himself co-operating with Harcourt in the Cabinet on questions of foreign and colonial policy against the liberal imperialism of Rosebery. The government struggled on until the middle of 1895, when it was defeated on a snap division, and resigned rather ignominiously. At the general election the conservative and unionist party gained a sweeping majority, and Morley lost his seat. For a time he cultivated the pleasure and leisure of retirement; but Harcourt and other liberals of the Gladstonian school were anxious for his return to the House of Commons, and early in 1896 Morley was elected for the Montrose Burghs.

With Chamberlain at the Colonial Office, imperialism was now in the saddle, although Lord Salisbury did his best to preserve moderation in foreign policy. Morley and Harcourt resisted to the utmost the policy which found expression in Kitchener's conquest of the Sudan, and later on in the Boer War. At the end of 1898 a crisis occurred in the liberal party, owing to the sharp division between the friends of Harcourt and those of Rosebery. Harcourt resigned the leadership of the opposition in the House of Commons, and a correspondence between him and Morley was published, in which Morley complained of cross-currents and agreed that Harcourt's position had become intolerable. Fortunately for the party Sir Henry Campbell-Bannerman was chosen to fill the vacancy.

Meanwhile the death of Gladstone in May 1898 led Morley to undertake the most important and arduous literary task of his life—the official biography of his old chief. It was while he was engaged in August 1899 in examining and selecting the vast mass of letters and documents then assembled in the 'Temple of Peace' at Hawarden Castle that the negotiations between Sir Alfred (afterwards Viscount) Milner [q.v.] and President Kruger took an unfavourable turn. Morley was deeply concerned at the prospect of a war against the two South African republics, and made several speeches of protest in the hope of averting it. One of these, perhaps the finest of all his orations, was delivered on 17 September 1899 to a crowded and excited audience in St. James's Hall, Manchester.

Once war had broken out there was no more to be done; Morley, therefore, withdrew and devoted himself to the *Life of Gladstone*. He had finished a biography of Oliver Cromwell in the autumn of 1899 —a book of balanced criticism, abounding in aphorisms and reflections on government, which, as he often recalled with pleasure, was read and highly praised by the prime minister, Lord Salisbury. His *Gladstone* proved a Herculean task, but its progress was assisted by a doctor's mandate which for a long time debarred him, owing to an affection of the throat, from speaking either in the House of Commons or on public platforms. In spite of this disability he was re-elected for Montrose at the general election of October 1900. As the Boer War dragged on it became unpopular, and public opinion began to turn in favour of Campbell-Bannerman and Morley, who favoured a settlement by negotiation rather than the unconditional surrender which Milner wanted. Eventually Milner was overruled and the War was brought to an end by Lord Kitchener in 1902. In the same year King Edward VII conferred upon Morley the newly created Order of Merit, and Andrew Carnegie [q.v.] presented him with the library of Lord Acton [q.v.], which Morley, in his turn, presented to the university of Cambridge.

The *Life of Gladstone* was completed and published in three volumes in October 1903. Its reception by the public surpassed all expectations. Thirty thousand copies were sold in the first year, and a hundred thousand more in the ten years that followed. As literature it is perhaps less attractive than Morley's earlier biographies; but as the tribute of a colleague to the greatest English statesman of his age, a tribute of admiring but not uncritical friendship, it is unique; and Morley had a right to say, as he did, that the years of labour devoted to this commemoration of Gladstone were not ill employed.

Towards the end of 1904 Morley paid a visit to Canada and the United States, where he made many friends, and stayed for a few days at the White House with President Roosevelt. By this time the long reign of conservatism and liberal-unionism was coming to an end. In 1905 the fiscal question united the liberal party and broke up the conservative Cabinet.

On Balfour's resignation in the autumn of that year Campbell-Bannerman formed a government in which Morley took office as secretary of state for India. Thereafter Morley had the satisfaction of assisting in the restoration of self-government in South Africa, and also of laying the foundations of a series of reforms in the administration of India, on which he bestowed infinite pains. He listened to experience, read deeply, and formed his plans with an admirable mixture of caution and courage. The story of these reforms, which aimed at gradually associating the people of India with the civil administration and government, is told in his letters to the viceroy, the fourth Earl of Minto [q.v.], which Morley published in the second volume of his *Recollections*. Under the new system of government, experience would have tested the capacity of Indian public men, and in the course of a generation or two would have shown in what directions further advance might safely be made. This was the intention of Morley and his advisers. But during the European War a new secretary of state, Edwin Samuel Montagu [q.v.], with a rash precipitancy which Morley deplored, introduced 'the dyarchy' and gave further pledges, upon the theory (always rejected by Morley) that India is a nation, and as such is capable of a complete system of responsible government.

Sympathy was the keynote of Morley's policy. He repudiated the idea that India, with its diversities of races, religions, languages, and castes, was fitted for a democratic constitution; but by appointing Indian members to the viceroy's council and to the India council in London, as well as by enlarging the representative element on the viceroy's legislative council and on the provincial councils, he associated many more Indians with the work of government. The strain of office, combined with attendance in the House of Commons, told on Morley's health; and in 1908, when, on the death of Campbell-Bannerman, Mr. Asquith became premier, he was transferred at his own request to the House of Lords, being raised to the peerage as Viscount Morley of Blackburn. In November 1910, when his reforms were completed, he resigned his post at the India Office, but remained in the Cabinet as lord president of the Council. Afterwards Lord Crewe, who had succeeded him, fell ill; whereupon Morley returned to the India Office for a few months. He helped to conduct through the Upper House the Parliament Bill limiting the Lords' veto. It fell to him to read the famous paper stating that in the event of rejection by the Lords King George V would assent to a creation of peers sufficient to prevent the Parliament Bill being exposed a second time to defeat. On the night of the division in the House of Lords Morley felt the strain even more intensely than on the occasion, twenty-five years before, when the House of Commons threw out the first Home Rule Bill. It was only by abstentions that the government gained a narrow majority of seventeen (August 1911).

Morley was in friendly intercourse with Sir Edward Grey during the years from 1906 to 1914, and shared responsibility for the *entente* with Russia, which, by relieving him from anxiety about the Indian frontier, made much easier the paths to economy and reform in India. At times, and especially during the Agadir crisis in 1911, he was persuaded that peace might be endangered by the *ententes* with France and Russia, and he asked for assurances that Great Britain was in no way committed to war in support of France and Russia against Germany and Austria. After Agadir these assurances were given to the Cabinet and repeated in the House of Commons. But the expansion of continental armies and navies went on apace, and in July 1914 the Asquith Cabinet had to decide between intervention and neutrality.

At first, under Morley's lead, a majority of the Cabinet (at least three-quarters, according to Mr. Winston Churchill) was determined not to be drawn into war unless Great Britain were attacked. How the peace group diminished until only four, and finally only two (Morley and John Burns), were left to resign, is told in the *Memorandum on Resignation* which Morley wrote to be published after his death. In a few dramatic pages he sketches the drift of the Cabinet towards intervention between 24 July and 4 August, when his resignation took effect. The *entente*, he felt, had proved even more dangerous than an alliance. When the question of Belgian neutrality arose, Belgium took 'the place that had been taken before, as pleas for war, by Morocco and Agadir'. Morley held that Grey should have taken advantage of his conversation (1 August) with the German ambassador about Belgian neutrality as an occasion for more talk and negotiation, instead of closing the door by refusing to consider conditions on which Britain might remain neutral. But his resignation was based on wider grounds. He could not and would not share the responsibility for a war which he foresaw would be disastrous to Great Britain and to Europe. Nothing that happened afterwards made him regret his decision. He retained his interest in politics to the end, watching the course of the struggle with melancholy forebodings. The decline of the liberal party, whose doctrines and ideals, which he still cherished, had been thrown on the scrap-heap of war, occasioned him more grief than surprise. His loyalty indeed was to the faith rather than to the party.

Morley's last return to public life was during the brief parliamentary session of December 1921 after the treaty of peace with Ireland. On that occasion, in his eighty-fourth year, he expressed in the Lords his satisfaction that the British government, by consenting to the creation of the Irish Free State, had saved Great Britain and Ireland from an irreparable disaster. He remarked that Mr. Gladstone, 'who toiled so long to change our Irish policy, would have welcomed this settlement by a coalition Government, seeing that in 1885 he had proposed to Lord Salisbury a coalition for the purpose'.

For the rest of his life Lord Morley lived in retirement with his wife at Flowermead, Wimbledon Park, enjoying visits from congenial friends, reading books, new and old, and busying himself in the affairs of Manchester University, of which he had been elected chancellor in 1908. His interest in men and women, politics, history, and letters remained with him to the end, although his physical powers gradually yielded to the infirmities of age. The later writings of his old teacher Mill show how that 'saint of rationalism' and high priest of individual liberty was beginning to lean towards theism and socialism. On these subjects Morley's opinions also ripened and mellowed. They lost the asperities of his *Fortnightly* days, but he remained to the end of his life an agnostic, a liberal, and an individualist, as uncompromising on essentials as when he wrote *On Compromise* (1874), a book of which a witty critic remarked, 'I can find no sign of compromise except on the title page'. Agnostic though he remained to the end, Morley cared less and less about religious and metaphysical polemics, and his attitude towards religion revealed a sense of piety, holiness, and of the mystery of life and death not always found among orthodox church-goers. That he should have combined consistency with success in public life, and with practical achievements in constructive statesmanship, is a tribute not only to his own character but to that of his countrymen. During a long public career he kept his course from first to last, remaining constant to the faith that he had reasoned out in early manhood. This consistency of thought and conduct gave moral weight to his opinions and helped to raise the standards of public life. He died, childless, at Wimbledon 23 September 1923, and his viscounty became extinct.

The following is a list of Lord Morley's published works, excluding his Essays which have been published and republished in several volumes: *Modern Characteristics* (anonymous, 1865); *Edmund Burke* (1867); *Voltaire* (1872); *Rousseau* (1873); *On Compromise* (1874); *Diderot, and the Encyclopaedists* (1878); *Burke* ('English Men of Letters' series, 1879); *Life of Richard Cobden* (1881); *Walpole* (1889); *Oliver Cromwell* (1900); *Life of Gladstone* (1903); *Notes on Politics and History* (1913); *Recollections* (1917), and *Memorandum on Resignation* (posthumous, 1928). An edition of his works in fifteen volumes, with corrections by himself, was published in 1921.

A portrait of Morley by the Hon. John Collier hangs in the hall of Lincoln College, Oxford, and there is a replica of it at the National Liberal Club.

[Lord Morley, *Recollections*, 2 vols., 1917; F. W. Hirst, *Early Life and Letters of John Morley*, 1928; A. G. Gardiner, *Life of Sir William Harcourt*, 2 vols., 1923; Lord Morley's *Indian Speeches*, 1909.] F. W. Hirst.

MORRIS-JONES, Sir JOHN (1864–1929), Welsh poet and grammarian, was born at Trefor, Llandrygarn, Anglesey, 17 October 1864, the eldest son of Morris Jones, shopkeeper, by his wife, Elizabeth Roberts, both originally of Llanrug, Carnarvonshire. When he was three years old his parents moved to Llanfairpwll, Anglesey, and he was sent to the local school, the 'Duchess of Kent's', and the board school. From 1876 to January 1879 he attended the Friars' School, Bangor, under the headmastership of Daniel Lewis Lloyd (afterwards bishop of Bangor), and when Lloyd left for Christ College, Brecon, Jones, like many other Friars' boys, went with him. His father died at Christmas 1879, and his help was now required at home. He assisted his mother for a year in the shop, but somehow managed to find time to read a considerable amount of

Welsh literature, especially poetry, and the beauty of the old *cywyddau* and *englynion* captured his imagination so completely that he could barely tolerate any other kind of verse as long as he lived. Lloyd had a high opinion of his old pupil's gifts as a mathematician, and made it possible for Jones to return to Brecon early in 1881, in order to read for a mathematical scholarship at Oxford. But the old zest had gone. The year at home had roused in him such an interest in Welsh poetry that mathematics had to take second place. He won a scholarship, indeed, and went up to Jesus College, Oxford, in October 1883, but obtained only a third class in the final school of mathematics in 1887. A Meyricke scholarship from his college, tenable for a year, then enabled him to follow his real bent. He had already attended the lectures of (Sir) John Rhŷs [q.v.] on Celtic; he now devoted himself wholly to Welsh, and began to prepare an edition of *The Elucidarium* and other tracts in Welsh from *Llyvyr Agkyr Llandewivrevi*, which appeared under his name and that of Rhŷs in 1894.

Jones and six others had already (May 1886) founded the 'Dafydd ap Gwilym' Society in Oxford for the discussion of Welsh problems. Two of the first members, Jones himself and (Sir) Owen Morgan Edwards [q.v.], were to play the leading parts in the revival of Welsh literature. Edwards turned to history and Welsh prose; Morris-Jones to philology and Welsh verse. Both felt the need of a more regular and scientific orthography; both loved purity of idiom and diction, although the former found his models in the living dialect and the latter in the medieval poetry. Vigorous discussions at the 'Dafydd' paved the way for the work of the Orthographical Committee of the Society for Utilizing the Welsh language, whose *Report on Welsh Orthography* was published in 1893, Jones being the secretary. It is admitted that he did most of the work, and for years afterwards in controversy after controversy he defended this Oxford Welsh, as it was called, against all comers.

Jones's chance came when he was appointed lecturer in Welsh at Bangor University College in January 1889; he was elected professor of Welsh in 1895, and held the post until his death. The new university of Wales gave him students in plenty, and through them his lectures on Welsh grammar became known throughout Wales. He studied the versification of the medieval poets, and dealt faithfully, if not tenderly, with Joseph Loth's *Métrique Galloise* in the *Zeitschrift für Celtische Philologie* (vol. iv, 1903). His own skill in the ancient technique of the bards was proved by the ode 'Cymru Fu, Cymru Fydd', published in *Cymru* (1892) and republished with other poems in his *Caniadau* (1907). Jones's exposure of the falsity of the claims made by Iolo Morganwg on behalf of the 'Gorsedd' appeared in *Cymru* for 1896, and in the same year, curiously enough, he gave his adjudication on the odes, the chief poetic competition, at the National Eisteddfod held at Llandudno. This was the first of a series of pronouncements, continuing until 1927, on correct Welsh and correct prosody given by him at this popular assembly, which made his name famous throughout Wales and helped to spread his doctrines. All slovenly work he castigated with ruthless severity; no man did more, no man did as much, to raise the standard of poetic diction in the Eisteddfod poetry. Although Jones's chief interest lay in the strict alliterative metres, he also helped to perfect the form of the free lyric by his translations from Heine, J. L. Uhland, and others; in particular his translation of Omar Khayyám ought to be mentioned. His chief contribution to the study of Welsh prosody and, in the opinion of many, his best work, is his *Cerdd Dafod* (1925), a full account of Welsh metric art. Modern critics assert that his poetry is too cold and formal: it may be so, but there is real satiric strength in his *Salm i Famon* and parts of *Cymru Fu, Cymru Fydd*, and his songs to Wales came from the heart.

Jones's chief contribution to Welsh prose is the masterly introduction to Ellis Wynne's *Bardd Cwsc* (1898). He edited *Y Beirniad* from start to finish (1911–1920), but wrote little himself for that periodical, although he spent a great deal of time in correcting the work of others. Occasional articles from his pen appeared in various magazines; his 'Tudur Aled' in the *Transactions* of the Cymmrodorion, 1908–1909, should be noticed, and the review in English in *Cymmrodor*, vol. xxviii, 1918, of the edition of the Taliesin by John Gwenogvryn Evans [q.v.], which, although too acrimonious in spirit, contains much valuable material for the student of early Welsh poetry.

Jones's *Welsh Grammar* (1913) has been both overrated and underrated: it deals only with the phonology and accidence. An unfinished draft on *Welsh Syntax*, written in 1907, was printed posthumously (1931), and it is to be regretted that its author did not live to revise and finish it, for he had a remarkable gift of lucid exposition, and skill in the clear arrangement and presentation of grammatical facts. These qualities are evident in *A Welsh Grammar*. As a descriptive grammar it is unrivalled, and will remain a worthy memorial of years of devoted research into the history of the Welsh language.

Jones married in 1897 Mary, second daughter of William Hughes, of Siglan, Llanfairpwll, by whom he had four daughters. He was knighted in 1918, when he began to style himself Morris-Jones. In 1919 Glasgow University conferred on him the honorary degree of LL.D., and in 1927 the National University of Ireland that of D.Litt.Celt. He died after a brief illness at his home at Llanfairpwll 16 April 1929.

A bust of Morris-Jones, by R. L. Gapper, has been placed in the University Library of Bangor.

[*Transactions* of the Cymmrodorion, 1919–1920; *Y Cymmrodor*, vol. xl, 1929; *Wales*, 1896 and 1912; *Welsh Leader*, 28 January 1904; personal knowledge.] I. Williams.

MOTT, Sir FREDERICK WALKER (1853–1926), neuro-pathologist, was born at Brighton 23 October 1853. He was the only son of Henry Mott, of Brighton, who came of Huguenot stock, by his wife, Caroline, daughter of William Fuller, of Pulborough.

Both father and mother died whilst he was a child. He studied medicine at University College, London, where he graduated M.B., B.Sc. in 1881 and M.D. in 1886, and obtained many distinctions. In 1883 he was appointed assistant professor of physiology at Liverpool University, but in the following year returned to London in order to take up the post of lecturer on physiology at Charing Cross Hospital medical school, where he became in succession lecturer on pathology, assistant physician, physician, and lecturer on medicine. He was elected fellow of the Royal College of Physicians in 1892 and fellow of the Royal Society in 1896.

Mott laid the foundation for his subsequent study of the diseases of the nervous system by researches into its normal structure and functions. Most of his earlier work was carried on in Professor Schafer's laboratory at University College, some of it in conjunction with other workers. These investigations included the paths of conduction in the spinal cord, localization in the cerebral cortex (especially relating to movements of the eyes), and the effect of acute anaemia on the brain. The influence of these studies upon his later work is manifest.

In 1895 the London County Council decided to appoint a pathologist in charge of the laboratory which it was proposing to establish at Claybury: all indications pointed to Mott as the most suitable occupant of the post. He stipulated, however, that he should retain his clinical appointment at Charing Cross Hospital, considering it essential that the study of diseased conditions should be combined with clinical observation. The Council consented, and was thus able to secure Mott's services, which were rendered whole-heartedly for a long period of years, during which time a vast amount of research work was carried out by him and his pupils and assistants. Most of this is published in a series of important volumes to which the title *Archives of Neurology and Psychiatry* was given.

Subsequently, when the Maudsley Hospital for mental diseases was established at Denmark Hill, Mott's pathological work for the Council was transferred to the newer and better-equipped laboratory attached to that institution, and was continued there until his final resignation from the post of pathologist to the London County Council asylums in 1923, the age limit having been stretched in order that his services might be continued as long as possible. But his activities were by no means at an end, for he continued to teach at the Maudsley Hospital, and also accepted the post of lecturer on morbid psychology at the university of Birmingham. This position he held up to the time of his death.

Besides the articles in the *Archives of Neurology*, Mott contributed numerous papers on the nervous system to the *Philosophical Transactions* and *Proceedings* of the Royal Society, to *Brain*, to the *Journal of Physiology*, to the *Proceedings* of the Royal Society of Medicine, and to other scientific and medical periodicals.

Largely owing to Mott's researches it became definitely established that the hitherto obscure disease of the nervous system, known under the designation 'general paralysis of the insane', is, in fact, a manifestation of syphilis, and is associated with the presence of the specific spirochaete. The determination of the association between syphilitic infection and this and other mental disorders is the achievement by which Mott's name will probably be best known. But it was by no means his only important contribution to neuro-pathology, for he further demonstrated the close relation between the nervous system and the sexual organs manifested in dementia praecox, as well as the association of deficient mental condition with degeneration of the thyroid and other endocrine organs.

As the result of these researches Mott firmly and insistently supported the view, which had hitherto been strangely ignored, that mental disorders are, for the most part, correlated with bodily changes. Indeed, all his work tended to uphold this doctrine, which may be said to have dispelled the obscurity which had hitherto invested the causation of diseases of the mind. Even in the affection known as 'asylum dysentery' the cause used to be ascribed to a hypothetical nervous affection of the intestine, instead of to infection associated with micro-organisms, which was indicated by Mott to be its true causation. He wrote a report on his *Histological Observations on Sleeping Sickness and other Trypanosome Infections* which was published as No. VII of the *Reports of the Sleeping Sickness Commission* of the Royal Society in December 1906.

Mott received numerous honours and prizes, as well as appointment to lecturerships, in recognition of his scientific work. He was awarded the Stewart prize of the Medical Association (1903), the Fothergill gold medal and prize of the Medical Society of London (1911), and the Moxon gold medal of the Royal College of Physicians (1919). He was Croonian lecturer (1900), Oliver-Sharpey lecturer (1910), Lettsomian lecturer (1916) and Harveian orator (1925) to the Royal College of Physicians, London, Morrison lecturer to the Royal College of Physicians, Edinburgh (1921), Huxley lecturer at Charing Cross Hospital (1910), Bowman lecturer to the Ophthalmological Society (1904), and Fullerian lecturer at the Royal Institution. He delivered the Chadwick lecture at the university of Liverpool in 1917 and 1926. At the time of his death he was president of the Royal Medico-Psychological Association.

Himself an accomplished singer, Mott was devoted to music, especially to vocal music, upon which he published two works. His interest in this was recognized by his election as president of the Society of English Singers in 1923. In 1919 he was created K.B.E. in acknowledgement of his war services as lieutenant-colonel, Royal Army Medical Corps. His work on shell-shock was especially notable. In the same year he received the honorary degree of LL.D. from Edinburgh University. He was a good lecturer, always speaking to the point, and an honest investigator, his one desire being to arrive at truth.

Mott married in 1885 Georgina Alexandra, daughter of George Thomas Soley, shipowner, of Liverpool, and had four daughters. He died at Birmingham as a result of cerebral haemorrhage 8 June 1926. His friends and colleagues dedicated to his memory a volume containing original articles on the subjects to which he had himself contributed. This book, published in 1929, contains an appreciation of the man and his work by his lifelong friend, Professor W. D. Halliburton, as well as a complete list of his published writings.

[*Proceedings* of the Royal Society, vol. c, B, 1926 (portrait); *Birmingham Medical Review*, vol. i, no. 6, 1926; *Lancet*, 1926, vol. i, p. 1228; *British Medical Journal*, 1926, vol. i, p. 1063; Memorial Volume, *ut supra*; personal knowledge.]

E. A. Sharpey-Schafer.

MUDDIMAN, Sir ALEXANDER PHILLIPS (1875–1928), Indian civil servant, was born at Leighton Buzzard 14 February 1875, the second son of Alexander Phillips Muddiman, bookseller and publisher, of that place and afterwards of Duffield House, near Derby, by his wife, Anne Griffiths. He was educated at Wimborne School and at University College, London, passed the open examination for the Indian civil service in 1897, and joined that service in 1899.

From the outset Muddiman's ability attracted attention, and his promotion was exceptionally rapid: but he lacked the normal training of an Indian civil servant. After barely three years of district work, he became under-secretary to the Bengal government in 1903: two years later he was selected to be registrar of the appellate side, Calcutta high court. In this post, in spite of his lack of judicial experience, Muddiman gave such satisfaction that, in 1910, he was promoted to be deputy secretary to the government of India in the legislative department. There he remained for the next ten years, becoming in 1915 secretary to government and a nominated official member of the central legislature. No enactment of outstanding importance was passed by the Indian legislature during this period; nor did Muddiman play any considerable part in drawing up the policy of the Montagu-Chelmsford reforms. But he was one of the two additional members appointed by the government of India to serve on Lord Southborough's committee on the franchises (1918–1919); in this capacity he came to England on deputation, and his experience and skilful draftsmanship were of great value in framing the rules for the conduct of business in the legislatures.

Nevertheless, there was general surprise when in January 1921 Muddiman was appointed president of the council of state, the newly-created upper house of the Indian legislature. The appointment, however, was soon seen to be fully justified. Muddiman made an ideal chairman, courteous, imperturbable, and conciliatory. In March 1924 he was promoted to be ordinary member of the governor-general's council in charge of the home department, an appointment which made him the official leader of the assembly, or lower house. Here the same qualities stood him in good stead; and the affection with which he was personally regarded by the Indian members of all shades of opinion contributed not a little to the growth of a healthy parliamentary tradition in which political acrimony was mitigated by personal good feeling. The brilliant debating power and even the occasionally virulent invective of a strong opposition were effectively parried by Muddiman's unfailing serenity of temper. In the administrative work of his post he had the gift of being able to leave details to subordinates without losing his grasp of essentials.

Muddiman was knighted in 1922 and created K.C.S.I. in 1926. In 1928 he was appointed governor of the United Provinces. But, though his natural gaiety and zest for life never deserted him, he was already a very sick man; and on 17 July 1928 he died at Naini Tal of heart failure after barely six months of office. He was unmarried.

In the work of legislative draftsman Muddiman had an elegant and clear style: he never had the opportunity to become a profound or learned lawyer. His *bonhomie* and high spirits led him to take a larger part in the social life of Simla and Delhi than is usual with high officials in the government of India: in particular, though no gambler, he was (often till late hours) a brilliant bridge-player; and superficial observers found it difficult to believe that the same man could be efficiently discharging onerous official duties. But in fact the double strain contributed not a little to his early death.

[*The Times*, 18 June 1928; official records; private information.] S. V. FitzGerald.

MURRAY, Sir JOHN (1851–1928), publisher, was born in London 18 December 1851, the eldest son of John Murray (1808–1892, q.v.), of 50 Albemarle Street, London, and Newstead, Wimbledon, by his wife, Marion, daughter of Alexander Smith, banker, of Edinburgh. His father was the third of his name to be head in succession of the publishing house founded in 1768 by John Murray the first, who was followed by John Murray the second (1778–1843, q.v.), the friend of Byron and Scott. Publishing, therefore, was to him an hereditary profession, and in due course he became John Murray the fourth. He was educated at Eton and at Magdalen College, Oxford, and then entered the firm's house in Albemarle Street, passing through all its departments until, in 1892, he succeeded his father as its head.

Throughout his life Murray laboured with unceasing concentration at the work of his publishing house; but few publishers have so harmoniously combined such concentration with freshness of outlook, unfailing courtesy, and sympathy with the strivings and ambitions of young authors, added to wide interest in social and literary life. He was a staunch churchman and conservative, and was resolute to maintain the high standards of the past in the midst of a rapidly changing world. But this did not mean a stereotyped or reactionary outlook: his home was, as it had been in the days of his father and grandfather, the resort of many leaders both of literary and political thought, and he was the centre, the guide, philosopher, and friend.

In 1917 Murray's house acquired the publishing business of Smith, Elder & Co., and this enabled him, late in life, to take a personal interest in many of the younger school of novelists. From 1922 until his death in 1928 he edited the *Quarterly Review* and surveyed politics from an interested and yet detached point of view. His friendships were legion: from the earliest days, when he could recall Livingstone and Borrow, and was a friend of Darwin, down to his death he was able to make friends with authors, and to retain their friendship.

In Byron, Murray took an hereditary

interest, editing his *Correspondence* in 1922; and it was in honour of the Byron centenary in 1924 that he received the D.Ph. degree of the university of Athens and was created a commander of the order of the Redeemer (of Greece). In recognition of his publication of the first and second series of volumes of the *Letters of Queen Victoria* he was created C.V.O. in 1912 and K.C.V.O. in 1926. He found time not only to edit Gibbon's *Autobiography* (1897) and to write *John Murray III: a Memoir* (1919), but to be chairman of the Publishers' Association in 1898–1899, when his knowledge of copyright proved of great service, and for many years to be an active J.P. in London, of which he was also a D.L. and high sheriff in 1908. In addition, he was for forty-two years a member of the board of the Hospital for Sick Children, Great Ormond Street, and for thirty-seven years its vice-president.

Murray married in 1878 Evelyn, daughter of William Leslie, of Warthill, Aberdeenshire, sometime M.P. for Aberdeenshire, and had one son (John Murray the fifth), and three daughters, two of whom died young. He died at Hove 30 November 1928.

[*The Times*, 1 December 1928; personal knowledge.] GORELL.

MURRY, KATHLEEN (1888–1923), writer under the pseudonym of KATHERINE MANSFIELD, was born at Wellington, New Zealand, 14 October 1888, the third daughter of (Sir) Harold Beauchamp, banker and company director, by his first wife, Annie Burnell, daughter of Joseph Dyer, secretary of a provident society. Her early childhood was passed for the most part at Karori, a village near Wellington. Her first story was published at the age of nine. In 1903 she was taken to England, and was a resident student for three years at Queen's College, Harley Street, London, where she edited the college magazine. In 1906 she returned unwillingly to New Zealand, but came back to England two years later on a modest allowance from her father. She married in London in 1909 George Bowden, from whom she parted soon after. In 1910 and 1911 she contributed regularly to a weekly paper, *The New Age*, and in 1911 published, under the pseudonym of 'Katherine Mansfield', her first collection of short stories, *In a German Pension*, based on experiences which she underwent in Woerishofen in Bavaria.

In 1911 Katherine Mansfield met John Middleton Murry, the critic, eldest son of John Murry, of the Inland Revenue Department. They lived together from April 1912 until their marriage in 1918. From 1911 to 1913 she published short stories and poems in *Rhythm* and *The Blue Review*, two periodicals of which Mr. Murry was associate editor. In 1915 she compiled and edited, with the help of Mr. Murry and D. H. Lawrence [q.v.], a magazine called *The Signature*.

Nervous strain due to the European War, a physical constitution weakened by operations and recurrent pleurisy, and the loss of her only brother, Leslie Heron Beauchamp, who was killed in France in 1915, led Katherine Mansfield to withdraw herself for a time into memories of her childhood, and she now sought to frame these memories in collections of short stories. *Prelude* was published in 1918 and *Je ne parle pas français* printed privately in 1919. Katherine Mansfield was divorced from George Bowden in 1918 and married John Middleton Murry in London in the May of that year. In April 1919 her husband was appointed editor of the *Athenaeum*, and she began to review current novels in its pages. These reviews were collected and published as *Novels and Novelists* in 1930.

Bliss, a volume of short stories, published in 1920, established Katherine Mansfield's reputation. Another volume, *The Garden Party* (1922), was the last of her books to be published in her lifetime. In December 1917 she had been found to be consumptive, and thereafter her life was marked by chronic illness. She travelled from place to place in Italy, Switzerland, and the south of France, returning infrequently to England. Her letters and journals describe her physical and spiritual conflict in poignant detail. She now came to feel that her attitude to life had been unduly rebellious, and she sought, during the days that remained to her, to renew and compose her spiritual life. With this object in view she entered on 17 October 1922 the Gurdjieff Institute, near Fontainebleau, which aimed at achieving physical, mental, and spiritual health by esoteric methods. She died there of pulmonary haemorrhage 9 January 1923, and was buried in the communal cemetery at Avon, near Fontainebleau.

The Doves' Nest (1923) and *Something Childish* (1924) are posthumous collections of Katherine Mansfield's stories. Her *Poems* were collected in 1923, her *Journal* edited in 1927, and her *Letters* published in

1928. *The Aloe*, an early draft of *Prelude*, appeared in 1930.

As a short story writer Katherine Mansfield is closely akin to Tchehov. Their sensitiveness of perception is similar, their grasp of significant detail, their sense of quiet pattern, and their insistence on the poetic quality of simple homely familiarities. Katherine Mansfield broke completely with the older tradition of English tale-telling. Her influence on her own generation, which has been great, has served to render it conscious of the possibility of the short story as an art form presenting life at an arrested moment. Her *Journal* and her *Letters* belong to the permanent literature of self-revelation. They record with integrity the sensitive response of her generation to the War, and to the difficult years of transition after it, when youth, after a shattering experience, was endeavouring to formulate new values. Her *Poems* show promise rather than achievement.

[Ruth Elvish Mantz, *The Critical Bibliography of Katherine Mansfield*, 1931; Ruth Elvish Mantz and J. Middleton Murry, *The Life of Katherine Mansfield*, 1933; Katherine Mansfield, *Journal*, 1927, and *Letters*, 2 vols., 1928; *Letters of D. H. Lawrence*, ed. Aldous Huxley, 1932; private information.]

E. O'Brien.

NEILSON, GEORGE (1858–1923), historian and antiquary, was born at Ruthwell, Dumfriesshire, 7 December 1858, the only child of Edward Neilson, captain in the mercantile marine, by his wife, Janet Paterson. He was educated at Cummertrees parish school and at King William's College, Isle of Man. After serving an apprenticeship at Dumfries, he attended law classes at Glasgow University, and qualified as a solicitor in 1881. After seven years of private practice in Glasgow, he was appointed procurator fiscal of police there in 1891, and in 1910 he became stipendiary police magistrate of Glasgow. He held this office until a few months before his death.

Neilson was endowed with an eager and alert mind and an insatiable ardour for investigation. He was eager to direct the attention of others to subjects which interested him and to place at their disposal the fruits of his studies. By his thirtieth year he had gained a first-hand knowledge of the sources of early Scottish history and of the antiquities of Scots law. As time passed he became a charter scholar and expert palaeographer. The reading of *Bracton's Notebook*, edited by Frederic William Maitland [q.v.] in 1887, led him to send to Maitland in 1889 the manuscript of a study which he had made of the origin and early history of the duel. Maitland was enthusiastic, and Neilson's *Trial by Combat* was published at Glasgow in 1890. It was favourably received and, after forty years, is still the final word on the subject in English. Terse, pointed, and illuminating, it provides an admirable examination of an obscure field, and in particular makes clear the distinction between the judicial duel and the duel of chivalry. Its value was recognized by Maitland in the *History of English Law before the Time of Edward I*.

Up to the date of his death (1906) Maitland was in close correspondence with Neilson, and they met from time to time. Maitland constantly applied to him for guidance and information on questions of Scottish law and history. Neilson formed similar, though less intimate, relations with other scholars, especially Mary Bateson, J. H. Round, Andrew Lang, F. J. Haverfield, H. C. Lea, and F. Liebermann. It might be said that in the field of medieval studies he represented Scotland in the eyes of students south of the Border. He had real scholarship and most infectious enthusiasm, and much of his time was devoted to solving the problems of others. In 1894 he published *Peel, its meaning and derivation* and in 1899 *Annals of the Solway*, both admirable examples of the work of a learned antiquary, whose numerous papers are to be found in many volumes of transactions. He also edited *The Antonine Wall Report* of the Glasgow Archaeological Society (1899).

Neilson devoted many years to the study of middle Scots verse. His principal writings in this field are *John Barbour, Poet and Translator* (1900) and *Huchown of the Awle Ryale, the Alliterative Poet* (1902). He was not a philologist, and his interests were historical. He sought to claim for Barbour the authorship of a series of alliterative poems and to identify Huchown with Sir Hugh of Eglinton and to assign certain poems to him. He carried on a controversy about these matters in the pages of the *Athenaeum* and elsewhere for years, and in the course of it formed relations with Henry Bradley, F. J. Furnivall, W. P. Ker, W. W. Skeat, and others. These were of the friendliest character, for Neilson had the gift of inspiring liking even in opponents. His arguments for the thesis which he maintained were ingenious rather than convincing, and the debate is still open. It may be claimed, however, that his writings and the replies which they called forth revived an interest in a literature which had fallen into neglect and supported the view that Scotland was the place of origin of a considerable body of verse which had not been attributed to her previously.

In 1903, on the invitation of the university of Glasgow, he delivered a course of lectures on early Scottish literature, and in the same year the university conferred on him the honorary degree of LL.D. In 1913, at the invitation of the Society of Antiquaries of Scotland, he delivered the Rhind lectures in archaeology on 'Scottish Feudal Traits'.

In 1918, after delay due to the European War, the record commissioners issued the *Acta Dominorum Concilii, 1496–1501*, edited by Neilson and Mr. Henry Paton. The substantial introduction was Neilson's work. It contains many interesting suggestions and speculations, but it is somewhat lacking in cohesion and precision.

From 1903 to his death, much of Neilson's time was devoted to the *Scottish Historical Review*; no issue of the journal was without contributions, signed or anonymous, from his pen, and he had a large share in its direction.

After some months of illness Neilson died in Glasgow 15 November 1923, to the sorrow of a wide circle of friends and correspondents. He married in 1892 Jane, daughter of Thomas Richardson, of Hexham, by whom he had one son, who died in infancy, and one daughter. Neilson was slight and of medium height. He had a long thin face and large eager melancholy eyes. His portrait, etched by William Strang, R.A., is in the possession of Mrs. Neilson.

[*The Times*, 17 November 1923; private information; personal knowledge.]

D. Baird-Smith.

NESBIT, EDITH (1858–1924), writer of children's books, poet, and novelist. [See Bland, Edith.]

NEWBOLT, WILLIAM CHARLES EDMUND (1844–1930), divine and preacher, was born at Somerton, Somerset, 14 August 1844, the youngest son of the Rev. William Robert Newbolt, rector of Somerton, by his wife, Ann Frances Dorrien, daughter of Magens Dorrien Magens, of Hammerwood, East Grinstead. Newbolt was educated at Uppingham, where the teaching and character of the headmaster, Edward Thring [q.v.], exercised a strong and permanent influence on him. He proceeded to Oxford as an Oades scholar of Pembroke College in 1863, obtained a second class in classical moderations (1865) and a third class in *literae humaniores* (1867). He was never a scholar in the academic sense of the word.

In 1868 Newbolt was ordained deacon for the parish of Wantage, of which the vicar was William John Butler [q.v.], the friend of John Keble, and afterwards dean of Lincoln. The parish was admirably administered on strong and original lines, and Newbolt was always loyal to the principles and methods which he learned from Butler. After two years at Wantage he became vicar of Dymock, Gloucestershire, on the nomination of Frederick, sixth Earl Beauchamp [q.v.]. There he did patient and persevering work, and on the whole was able to commend new ways of church life in a parish of slow and conservative country people. In 1877 Lord Beauchamp nominated Newbolt for the parish of Malvern Link, and there again he did excellent parochial work, besides rebuilding the church.

At Malvern Link Newbolt was in close touch with Worcester. In 1886 the dean of Worcester, Lord Alwyne Frederick Compton [q.v.], became bishop of Ely, and in 1887 invited Newbolt to succeed Dr. H. M. Luckock as principal of Ely Theological College. This was for Newbolt the beginning of the most important work of his life. The theological college at Ely had been founded by Bishop Woodford [q.v.] on the pattern of Bishop Wilberforce's college at Cuddesdon, with the aim of providing for ordinands a spiritual and professional training in accordance with Tractarian ideals of the priestly life. In 1856 and 1857 Dr. H. P. Liddon had published in the periodical *Ecclesiastic and Theologian* an essay, 'The Priest in his inner life', which suggested the lines along which the devotional life of the clergy should be developed, and it was on these lines that Newbolt worked at Ely. He brought to his task the knowledge of and sympathy with human nature gained by nineteen years of pastoral work, besides the example of his own strong and disciplined character.

On the death, in 1890, of Dr. Liddon, Lord Salisbury asked Liddon's brother whom he thought Liddon would have wished to succeed him as canon of St. Paul's. The answer was 'the principal of Ely'. The same year Newbolt was installed at St. Paul's, and he held the canonry until his death forty years later. At that time St. Paul's held a great place in the religious life of London and England generally. Richard William Church [q.v.], with his unique distinction of intellect and character, was still dean; crowds had surrounded the pulpit when Liddon preached, and the eloquence of Henry Scott Holland [q.v.] was only less popular and persuasive; another canon was Robert Gregory [q.v.], a man of first-rate administrative ability, soon to be dean; the services were performed with great reverence and dignity; Sir John Stainer [q.v.] was the organist. Newbolt entered enthusiastically into the spirit and plans of the chapter; he wished to make the cathedral the central church of London, the spiritual home of the metropolis and of the British Empire, where the liturgy of the Church of England was perfectly rendered throughout the year.

Newbolt was a fluent and facile, but painstaking, preacher. His sermons were always carefully prepared; excellently phrased, and delivered with ease and grace; they were always interesting and fresh, and gave proof of wide reading and generous culture. For many years they reached a wide public through the medium of the *Church Times*. Newbolt made no attempt to grapple with the intellectual and social problems of the time; he was content to commend goodness and faithfulness and the Tractarian piety which he had known all his life. He was an unswerving champion of Tractarian orthodoxy, and of views about the inspiration of the Bible and the observance of Sunday which were becoming obsolete.

Large business houses stand round St. Paul's, and Newbolt was anxious to help the young men employed in them and living on the premises. With this object he founded in 1893 the St. Paul's Lecture Society, which provided courses of lectures and retreats, and later on the Amen Court Guild, which had about 400 members and associates.

Newbolt is chiefly to be remembered for the work which he did for the spiritual life of the clergy. During the whole time he was at St. Paul's he continued and developed the ministry which he had begun at Ely. Every year he conducted retreats for priests and heard their confessions; he published many books of counsel and admonition containing the meditations which he had given in retreat. *Speculum Sacerdotum* (1893) was the most characteristic and successful of these books. He also edited, with Dr. Darwell Stone, the *Oxford Library of Practical Theology*. Newbolt's theological standpoint changed very little during his long life. He was true to the end to the ideals of Butler and Liddon. He was so thoroughly convinced of the excellence of the standard of religious life implied in the Prayer Book of 1662 that he felt some hesitation in following modern developments which went beyond what the Prayer Book enjoined. In his prime he was a leading speaker in Convocation, and for some years he was returned at the head of the poll as representative of the clergy of the London diocese in Convocation and the Church Assembly.

Newbolt's life was shadowed by a great sorrow. He married in 1870 Fanny Charlotte, fourth daughter of William Weld Wren, of 27 Gower Street, London; she was afflicted with mental illness for thirty years before her death in 1923. They had one son and two daughters. He died in London 12 September 1930.

[W. C. E. Newbolt, *Years that are passed*, 1921; personal knowledge.] J. F. Briscoe.

NEWMAN, WILLIAM LAMBERT (1834–1923), scholar and philosopher, the second son of Edmund Lambert Newman, solicitor, of Cheltenham, was born at Cheltenham 21 August 1834. He was educated at Cheltenham College and at Balliol College, Oxford, which he entered as a scholar in 1851. Among his contemporaries at Balliol were the future scholars William Walter Merry, Robinson Ellis, and David Binning Monro, and the three future great lawyers, Charles Synge Christopher (afterwards Lord) Bowen, (Sir) Thomas Erskine Holland, and Albert Venn Dicey: his tutors were Benjamin Jowett, James Riddell, Edwin Palmer, and Henry Smith. He won the Hertford scholarship (1853) and the Ireland scholarship (1854), obtained first classes in classical moderations (1853) and in *literae humaniores* (1855), and while still an undergraduate was elected a fellow of his college (1854). As lecturer in history for the schools of *literae humaniores* and of law and modern history from 1858 to 1870, Newman exercised a unique influence on the teaching of history and political philosophy at Oxford; those who attended his lectures describe them with great unanimity as the best they ever heard. There was then no regular system of inter-collegiate lectures, but Balliol was constantly asked by other colleges to permit their students to attend Newman. Among those who heard him were the philosophers T. H. Green (afterwards his close friend and colleague), Thomas Case, Edward Caird, and R. L. Nettleship; the historians, J. L. Strachan-Davidson and Evelyn Abbott; the lawyers, R. T. Reid (afterwards Lord Loreburn) and (Sir) W. R. Anson; and among others, Andrew Lang, John Addington Symonds, F. Y. Edgeworth, and the Earl of Kerry (afterwards fifth Marquess of Lansdowne). In spite of frequent absences owing to ill-health, and of a weak voice and rapid delivery, Newman's importance as a teacher was quite equal to that of Jowett and Green. His treatment of ancient history (the principal subject of his lectures) was then a new thing in its independence and imagination, in the wide range of modern history and law from which he drew his illustrations, and in the connexion between history and philosophy which he always maintained and which became characteristic of *literae humaniores*. In 1868 he was appointed university reader in ancient history, but in 1870 ill-health obliged him finally to leave Oxford. Thenceforward Newman lived in retirement at Cheltenham, preparing the edition of Aristotle's *Politics*, which is his principal monument, reading everything that bore upon the subjects of his interest, making endless notes on odd scraps of paper in his tiny handwriting, and corresponding with other scholars. Although partially lame, he took his country walk almost daily, and was a keen observer of birds.

While at Oxford Newman published only an essay on the land-laws in a volume entitled *Problems for a Reformed Parliament* (1867). Other contributors were (Sir) Godfrey Lushington, Frederic Harrison, and Thorold Rogers. Newman's essay deserves still to be read not only for the insight which in the retrospect seems almost prophetic, but as a masterpiece of noble English. While he has always in view the ethical principles which should govern the tenure of land, he never forgets historical and practical considerations; and in thus holding the balance between philosophy and practice this early work exhibits a notable quality of his edition of the *Politics*, of which the first two volumes were published in 1887. The first is occupied by an introductory essay which is virtually a treatise on political philosophy. The third and fourth volumes appeared in 1902. The whole work belongs to the grand, leisurely type of scholarship, in which even notes have a literary quality, and the views of others (sometimes even when they do not deserve it) are discussed with courteous fullness. The hurried or perfunctory student finds little in Newman's work to encourage him; the minute pedant who has no sense of proportion may speak slightingly of it; but for soundness of interpretation, copiousness of illustration, and mature wisdom its value is permanent.

Newman died at Cheltenham 23 May 1923. He was unmarried. He retained his fellowship of Balliol until his death, but for many years refused to accept the stipend, and left a considerable benefaction to the college in his will.

[Private information; personal knowledge.]
A. W. Pickard-Cambridge.

NEWTON, ERNEST (1856–1922), architect, was born in London 12 September 1856, the fourth son of Henry Newton, then resident agent for the Sturt property in Hoxton, by his wife, Mary Lockyer. Educated at Uppingham, under Edward Thring [q.v.], he entered the office of Richard Norman Shaw [q.v.] in June 1873, and after three years as a pupil and three as an assistant, began to work independently in 1879. In Shaw's office he came into contact with E. S. Prior, Mervyn Macartney, G. C. Horsley, and, later, with W. R. Lethaby: the early meetings of this group for discussion of architectural matters ultimately developed into the Art Workers' Guild. To Shaw himself Newton owed a conception of architecture as an art, an adventure, a mode of personal expression, rather than an exercise in archaeology or a professional occupation. His own work is almost from the first marked by a serenity which is in marked contrast with his master's somewhat dramatic vigour.

Newton's earliest important work was the House of Retreat, Lloyd Square, Clerkenwell (1880), a building in the Shaw manner; but for the first ten years of his career he was working mainly on small suburban houses, hitherto the almost undisputed province of the speculating builder, and showing how orderliness of plan and unity of materials could give an effect of breadth even to minor works, a lesson which was not lost upon the next generation of architects. His small books, *A Book of Houses* (1890) and *A Book of Country Houses* (1903), illustrate a number of his earlier buildings. Bullers Wood (Chislehurst, Kent, 1889) was his next large work (altered by another hand in 1932). Here a stucco house was cased and enlarged into what is in effect a new house, of substantial dignity, built in brick and tile. It is not only a departure from contemporary pseudo-Gothic, but a marked advance on the stylistic tendency of good work of the time. It is thought of in terms of wall and window, roof and chimney, while others were still thinking in terms of style and period. This is important, because it throws light on all Newton's subsequent work. Although a lover of old things, he was in advance of his times in that he was always profoundly conscious of the future use of a building: he was sensitive enough to put himself in the place of master and mistress and maid; and out of their various points of view the shape of the house would grow, as an embodiment of the home-life as it was to be lived.

Newton's work of the next fifteen years is peculiarly fresh and personal, notably the chapel for the House of Retreat, Lloyd Square, Clerkenwell (1891), Red Court, Haslemere (1894), Martin's Bank, Bromley (1898), Steep Hill, Jersey (1899), and many smaller works. The handling of the materials, lead, brick, rough-cast, granite, metal-work, plaster, and wood-work, reflects the contemporary interest in crafts.

In the spire of St. George's church, Bickley, Kent (1904), and in Ardenrun Place, Blindley Heath, Surrey (built in 1906 and burned down in 1932), appeared work more obviously referable to tradition. Perhaps most characteristic of Newton's maturity are seven houses, which are all based upon the same plan-idea —a long low house, with short projecting wings embracing a paved southern terrace. Of these Luckley, Wokingham (1907), Feathercombe, near Godalming (1908), and Logmore, Dorking (1913), are in brick, with wood cornice and tiled roof; Ludwick Corner, Hertfordshire (1907), Scotman's Field, Church Stretton (1908), and Brand Lodge, on the Malvern Hills (1911), are in rough-cast or stucco; and Flint House, above Goring (1913), is in flint, with stone dressings. All have peacefulness, a spacious handling of plan, and many small touches of charm in detail. Three large houses in a more traditional manner at Burgh Heath, Banstead, Kingswood, Surrey, and Abbotsbury, Dorset, were being built when the European War broke out in 1914; and a house near Versailles was abandoned unfinished.

Works of importance by Newton, in addition to those already mentioned, include the following houses: Glebelands, Wokingham (1897), Dawn House, Winchester (1907), Lukyns, Ewhurst (1910), and a house in Holland (1914); a number of cottages and small buildings at Overbury, Worcestershire (between 1899 and 1910), and a portion of the Whiteley Homes, Burhill, Surrey (1914); a dozen type houses for the development of the Bickley Park estate (1902–1905); major alterations at Shavington, Shropshire (1903), Field Place, Begbroke, Oxfordshire (1906), Upton Grey, Hampshire (1907), The Greenway, Shurdington, Gloucestershire (1910), and Oldcastle, Dallington, Sussex (1910); the church of St. Swithun, Hither Green (1892), office for the Alliance Assurance Company, St. James's Street, London (in collaboration with Norman Shaw, 1904), a Carmelite convent at Caen (1920), and the initial scheme, carried out by his son, W. G. Newton, for a memorial Hall at Uppingham School (1921).

Newton was elected president of the Royal Institute of British Architects in 1914. In 1916 he voluntarily undertook onerous public work in connexion with the issue of building licences. In 1918 he was awarded the royal gold medal on the recommendation of the council of the Royal Institute of British Architects. He was elected A.R.A. in 1911 and R.A. in 1919, and created C.B.E. in 1920. He married in 1881 Antoinette Johanna, the eldest daughter of William Hoyack, merchant, of Rotterdam, and had three sons. He died in London 25 January 1922.

As an architect Newton was thoroughly conversant with the building crafts, and more happy with intimate than with monumental problems. His work was at once too sane and too personal for the growth of a school of disciples, but the serenity of his touch evidently influenced English domestic architecture during the first quarter of the twentieth century.

As a man Newton had a peculiar faculty for making friends in every walk of life. He was from early years a freemason; and at various times keenly pursued the study of the Dutch language, the violin, acting, French conversation and literature, and the technique of water-colour. He had a notably candid mind and an unusually frank admiration for attainments which he lacked himself. He had a very great capacity for taking pains, and a cordial dislike of pedantry and fanaticism.

There is a portrait of Newton by Arthur

Hacker at the head-quarters of the Royal Institute of British Architects in Portland Place, London.

[W. G. Newton, *The Work of Ernest Newton, R.A.* (containing a complete list of his works), 1925; personal knowledge.]

W. G. Newton.

NICHOLSON, JOSEPH SHIELD (1850–1927), economist, the only son of the Rev. Thomas Nicholson, Independent minister at Banbury, by his wife, Mary Anne Grant, was born at Wrawby, Lincolnshire, 9 November 1850. His education began at a preparatory school at Lewisham. After attending classes at King's College, London, he matriculated there in 1867, and gained his B.A. with high honours in 1870. From 1872 to 1873 he studied at Edinburgh University. In 1873 he went to Trinity College, Cambridge, where he graduated with a first class in the moral science tripos in 1876. In 1877, the year of its institution, and again in 1880, Nicholson was awarded the Cobden (triennial) prize. The earlier of his prize essays, published in 1878 under the title of *The Effects of Machinery on Wages*, gained for him the Cambridge degree of Sc.D. In 1877 he was placed first in the London M.A. examination (philosophy branch), obtaining the Gerstenberg prize for special distinction in political economy. Subsequently, accompanied by his friend (Sir) James George Frazer, he went to Heidelberg, where he attended lectures, chiefly on law, at the university.

From 1876 to 1880 Nicholson was a private tutor at Cambridge; he lectured on English history at Trinity College, and took an active part in the extra-mural teaching of the university. For two years (1878–1880) he lectured on political economy for the Association for the Higher Education of Women in Cambridge. In the early days of the Cambridge Chess Club (founded 1871) Nicholson was an outstanding player, and a member of the team which, in 1874, defeated Oxford for the first time. In later years he became widely known through the chess column of *The Times* as a subtle composer and solver of chess problems. Nicholson was devoted to boating and fishing, and he was an accomplished swimmer. His vacations at this period were usually spent in the north of Scotland and his daring exploits in the seas around Cape Wrath and in the lochs of Sutherland became a tradition of the district.

In 1880, before he was thirty, Nicholson was elected to the chair of political economy and mercantile law at the university of Edinburgh. He came to Edinburgh from Cambridge with a reputation as a hard worker and as a teacher of great ability who could expound economic principles with lucidity and bring them into close and intelligible relation with the problems of the day. This reputation he fully justified throughout the whole period of forty-five years during which he held the chair. As professor he maintained the highest Scottish traditions. His teachings and his writings played a definite and important part in the formation of public opinion. On questions of imperial economic policy and of currency and banking he attained a position of exceptional authority. In the difficult period of war finance his counsel and consistent teaching did much to keep depreciation of currency within remediable limits. There were few teachers of his time in Scotland who did more to bring academic life into touch with that of the community. He was the pioneer of economic history in Scotland, and during his professorship his department grew until it included nearly half as many teachers as there had been students when it was opened.

As a writer Nicholson possessed a lucid and happy style. His main work, *Principles of Political Economy* (vol. i, 1893, vol. ii, 1897, vol. iii, 1901), may be said to complete the nineteenth-century tradition of a great system of economics. The general standpoint is that of the classical school, extended, humanized, and endowed with vitality. Especially is the attempt made to unite in one organic whole the tendencies of the historical and mathematical methods.

The numerous minor writings of Nicholson may be said to constitute an adequate guide to the economic controversies of the half-century ending in 1925. They begin with *Tenant's Gain not Landlord's Loss* (1883), which was followed by many articles and lectures relating to currency and bimetallism, the most important being included in *The Silver Question* (1886), *Money and Monetary Problems* (1888), and *Bankers' Money* (1902). To the *Economic Journal* Nicholson contributed articles on 'The Use and Abuse of Authority in Economics' (1893), 'Historical Progress and Ideal Socialism' (1894), and 'Strikes and Social Problems' (1896). Related to the tariff controversy are the following: *The Tariff Question* (1903),

History of the English Corn Laws (1904), *Rates and Taxes as Affecting Agriculture* (1905), *Rents, Wages, and Profits in Agriculture* and *Rural Depopulation* (1906), *A Project of Empire* (1909—translated into Japanese), and 'Economics of Imperialism' (*Economic Journal*, 1910). The War resulted in a new series of articles and essays, of which no less than forty-six were reprinted in *War Finance* (1917, enlarged edition 1918), and *Inflation* (1919), a volume of lectures given, on the invitation of Barclays Bank, to its London staff. His chief contribution to post-war problems is represented by *The Revival of Marxism* (1920—translated into Japanese). Of a less topical character were his editions of *The Wealth of Nations* (1884), a short treatise on economics entitled *The Elements of Political Economy* (1903), and *Lectures on Public Finance* (1906).

No estimate of Nicholson's personality would be complete without a reference to his literary activities of a lighter kind. His romance *A Dreamer of Dreams* (1889) is very revealing as a human document, while the other two—*Thoth* (1888) and *Toxar* (1890)—in their allegorical undertones give many of his views on life and its problems. The link between these and his books on Ariosto—*Tales from Ariosto* (1913), and *Life and Genius of Ariosto* (1914)—is to be found in the position assigned to Ariosto as 'the father of modern romance'.

Nicholson was an honorary LL.D. of the universities of St. Andrews (1911) and Edinburgh (1916), F.R.S.E. (1884), F.B.A. (1903), and medallist of the Statistical Society (1918). In 1885 he married Jeanie, daughter of William Ballantyne Hodgson [q.v.], his predecessor in the chair of political economy at Edinburgh. They had one son (who died of wounds in the European War) and two daughters. In *Quasi Cursores*, the tercentenary album of the university of Edinburgh (1884), there is an etching of Nicholson by William Hole, in which he is represented as seated in his class-room, lecturing, with volumes of the works of Adam Smith and John Stuart Mill on the table at his hand. In the presentation portrait painted by Henry Lintott in 1927, which is in the possession of Nicholson's family, the Tassie medallion of Adam Smith is reproduced to mark Nicholson's influence and success as an interpreter of Smith's genius and spirit. In 1925 he resigned his chair owing to an illness. In 1927 an operation became necessary, and he died at Edinburgh 12 May of that year.

[*The Times*, 13 May 1927; *University of Edinburgh Journal*, autumn issue, 1927; W. R. Scott, *Joseph Shield Nicholson, 1850–1927*, in *Proceedings* of the British Academy, vol. xiv, 1928; private information; personal knowledge.] W. R. Scott.

NICOLL, Sir WILLIAM ROBERTSON (1851–1923), journalist and man of letters, was born at Lumsden, Aberdeenshire, 10 October 1851, the elder son of the Rev. Harry Nicoll, Free Church minister of Auchindoir, Aberdeenshire, by his wife, Jane Robertson. The manse at Auchindoir contained one of the largest private libraries in northern Scotland, for although the minister's stipend was less than £200 a year, Nicoll's father collected 17,000 volumes. His children had access to the shelves, and there young Nicoll formed and fostered a love for books which influenced his whole career. He attended the parish school of Auchindoir, and the Aberdeen grammar school. At fifteen he entered Aberdeen University, graduating M.A. in 1870. At the Free Church Divinity Hall he received the customary four years' theological training. During this period he contributed regularly to the *Aberdeen Journal*, writing reviews and literary notes. In 1874 he was ordained to his first charge at Dufftown, Banffshire. Three years later, in September 1877, he was inducted minister of the Free Church, Kelso, where he was second in succession to the hymn-writer, Horatius Bonar. In 1878 Nicoll married Isa, the only child of Peter Dunlop, a prosperous Berwickshire farmer. Two children, a daughter and a son, were born in the manse at Kelso.

During seven-and-a-half years' ministry at Kelso Nicoll established his reputation as a preacher, and a brilliant future seemed to be opening for him when, at the close of 1885, serious ill-health compelled him to resign his charge. His mother, a sister, and his only brother had died of consumption, and now he himself was 'ordered south'. Leaving Kelso, he went to live at Norwood in South-East London. Fortunately he had begun at Kelso a connexion with the publishing firm of Hodder & Stoughton which was to last, with ever-increasing confidence on both sides, to the end of his life. The firm appointed him editor of their monthly theological magazine, *The Expositor*, and he directed it from January 1885 until his death thirty-eight years later. His list of contributors included many of the most distinguished names in Biblical scholarship at home and abroad.

A new opening came to Nicoll soon after his settlement in London. On 5 November 1886 appeared the first number of *The British Weekly: A Journal of Social and Christian Progress*, with Hodder & Stoughton as proprietors and publishers, and Nicoll as editor. Nicoll's aim was to establish a penny religious journal of the best sort, in which, to quote his own words, 'everything should be treated in a Christian spirit'. In view of the precarious state of his health, the enterprise was a venture of faith; but the publishers showed their confidence in Nicoll by supplying the whole capital and business organization, while leaving him an entirely free hand in the management and circulation of the paper. In the course of a few years Nicoll raised the *British Weekly* to a position of wide influence, and in due course to a circulation perhaps unrivalled among publications of its kind. (Sir) J. M. Barrie was a frequent contributor to the journal from the first year of its foundation, and Nicoll himself wrote for thirty years, with few interruptions, a well-known series of weekly letters, signed 'Claudius Clear', from which were published: *Letters on Life* (1901), *The Daybook of Claudius Clear* (1905), and *A Bookman's Letters* (1913).

In 1891 Nicoll founded *The Bookman*, a literary monthly which proved very successful. Two years later he established *The Woman at Home*, an illustrated magazine, to which the Scottish novelist, Annie S. Swan (Mrs. Burnett Smith), was one of the chief contributors. In 1892 he removed with his family from Norwood to Bay Tree Lodge, Hampstead, an old Georgian house to which he added a library with room for 24,000 volumes. In 1894 his wife died after an operation, and he was left alone with his two children, and an ever-increasing load of work. In 1896 he paid a visit to the United States, accompanied by his friend J. M. Barrie. This was his only visit to America, but he kept in constant touch with American authors, politicians, and preachers. In the following year he married Catherine, daughter of Joseph Pollard, of Highdown, Hitchin, Hertfordshire. By his second marriage he had one daughter.

At the turn of the century Nicoll's health had greatly improved, and through the medium of his paper he threw himself vigorously into the political controversies of the next twenty years. In addition to his editorial work, he was able from time to time to preach and address meetings. He was one of the champions of the movement of 'passive resistance' to Mr. Balfour's Education Bill of 1902; he became an ardent supporter of the social legislation identified with the name of Mr. Lloyd George; and he made the *British Weekly* a focus of Nonconformist support for the government during the European War. The political influence which he was in a position to exercise was thus considerable, and he was for long in touch with liberal members of the Cabinet. He was knighted for his political services in 1909, and in 1921 was made C.H. After 1920 Nicoll's health began to fail, but he continued to write until a few weeks before the end. He died 4 May 1923 at his Hampstead home, and was buried in Highgate cemetery.

In addition to many theological writings of a popular character, Nicoll edited (with T. J. Wise) *Literary Anecdotes of the Nineteenth Century* (2 vols., 1895, 1896), and wrote biographies of James Macdonell of *The Times* (1890) and of Ian Maclaren (Dr. John Watson, 1908); he also published an edition of the works of Charlotte Brontë (1902).

[T. H. Darlow, *William Robertson Nicoll: Life and Letters*, 1925; personal knowledge.]

J. T. Stoddart.

NICOLSON, Sir ARTHUR, eleventh baronet, and first Baron Carnock (1849–1928), diplomatist, was born in London 19 September 1849, the younger son of Admiral Sir Frederick Nicolson, tenth baronet, by his first wife, Mary Clementina Marian, daughter of James Loch, of Drylaw, member of parliament for St. Germains and the Northern Burghs. Intended for the navy, he passed through H.M.S. *Britannia*, but changed his mind and proceeded to Rugby and Brasenose College, Oxford. He entered the Foreign Office in 1870. In 1872 Lord Granville, the secretary of state for foreign affairs, made Nicolson his assistant private secretary. In 1874 he went as third secretary to Berlin under Lord Odo Russell, and shortly afterwards exchanged permanently into the diplomatic service. From Berlin he went to Peking in 1876, returning to his former post in 1878, just after the Berlin Conference. Thence he was transferred in 1879 as second secretary to Constantinople, where he served under Sir Austen Henry Layard, (Viscount) Goschen, and Lord Dufferin, and became superintendent of student interpreters. Nicolson was also chosen to inspect the consulates in Asia Minor in 1881, and accompanied Lord Dufferin to Cairo in 1882. He served as chargé d'affaires at Athens from 1884 to 1885 and was then transferred as secretary of legation to Teheran, where he was in charge for three years, and succeeded in beginning the revival of British influence in Persia. For his services he was created C.M.G. in 1886 and K.C.I.E. in 1888.

From 1888 to 1893 Nicolson was consul-general at Budapest; in 1893 he became secretary of embassy at Constantinople, where he was in charge for most of the time during Sir Clare Ford's absence. In 1894 he went as agent to Sofia and in 1895 as minister to Tangier.

Nicolson's first years in Morocco were uneventful, but in 1901 serious unrest broke out. There had long been traditional rivalry between English and French, but the position of the latter in North Africa had become predominant. Germany also was beginning steadily to push her interests there. Nicolson saw that it was impossible successfully to continue rivalry with France, and he advocated a policy of agreement. In 1905 Germany promoted a conference on Morocco. This took place at Algeciras, and Nicolson, who had gone as ambassador to Madrid in 1904, was appointed British delegate. England and Russia steadily supported France against Germany. The conference nearly broke down, but, largely owing to Nicolson's patience, the French view prevailed, and the Treaty of Algeciras was signed on 7 April 1906. For his work in the conference Nicolson received the G.C.M.G. (1906). He was transferred to St. Petersburg the same year.

The Anglo-French *Entente* had been concluded in 1904, and now the peace between Russia and Japan encouraged the resumption of negotiations for an *entente* with Russia, which had been postponed on the outbreak of the Russo-Japanese War. These were carried to a successful conclusion by Nicolson, and an agreement was signed in 1907. For this service he received the G.C.B. (1907).

In 1910 Nicolson succeeded Lord Hardinge of Penshurst as under-secretary of state for foreign affairs. Nicolson's St. Petersburg experience made him aware of Russian limitations. He knew that Russia was the weak link in the *Entente*, but that without her England and France could not successfully resist German pretensions. For him the cardinal point of British policy was to keep Russia in the *Entente*, but there were many, both in St. Petersburg and London, who did not agree with him. Nicolson and Sir Edward Grey wished to terminate the friction which had so long embittered Anglo-Russian relations, and to trust Russia to co-operate. Their policy was successful.

In 1914, when trouble first arose between Servia and Austria, Nicolson did not think that it would have serious results, but the moment it appeared that Germany was behind Austria, he realized the full gravity of the situation. He did everything possible to second Grey's efforts to avert war. Impressed by the effect produced on Germany by firmness during the Agadir crisis in 1911, he thought that a clear declaration by England of her intention to support her friends was the best chance of avoiding war. On 26 July he suggested that England should invite a conference between Germany, France, Italy, and herself, and Grey accordingly made the proposal. On 31 July and 1 August he officially recommended the mobilization of the fleet and the army.

Nicolson had been the intended successor of (Lord) Bertie [q.v.] as ambassador at Paris, but the outbreak of war made this impossible, and he remained at the Foreign Office as under-secretary until his retirement in 1916, when he was succeeded by Lord Hardinge. For a time he acted as liaison officer between the Foreign Office and Buckingham Palace, but important City interests offered him employment, and to these he devoted himself for the rest of his life.

Nicolson had been created a privy councillor and a G.C.V.O. in 1905. On his retirement he was raised to the peerage as Baron Carnock, of Carnock, Stirlingshire. Among the honours which he received were the grand cross of the legion of honour, the Russian order of Alexander Nevsky, and the Spanish order of Charles III. He succeeded his father as eleventh baronet in 1899, his elder brother having predeceased him. He married at Constantinople in 1882 Mary Katherine, daughter of Captain Archibald Rowan-Hamilton, of Killyleagh Castle, co. Down, and had three sons and one daughter. Nicolson died 5 November 1928 at his London house, and was succeeded as second baron by his eldest son, Frederick Archibald (born 1883). A portrait by P. A. de László is in possession of the family.

[Harold Nicolson, *Sir Arthur Nicolson . . . first Lord Carnock*, 1930; (Lord) Curzon, *Persia and the Persian Question,* 1892; Stephen Gwynn, *The Letters and Friendships of Sir Cecil Spring-Rice,* 2 vols., 1929; Lord Grey, *Twenty-five Years, 1892–1916,* 2 vols., 1925; Lady Dufferin, *My Russian and Turkish Journals,* 1916; G. P. Gooch and H. Temperley, *British Documents on the Origins of the War 1898–1914,* vols. iii–vi, xi, 1927–8; Prince Karl Lichnowsky, *My Mission to London, 1912–1914* (translated), 1918; B. von Siebert, *Diplomatische Aktenstücke zur Geschichte d. Ententepolitik d. Vorkriegsjahre,* 1921 and *Graf Benckendorffs diplomatischer Schriftwechsel,* 1928; Sir George Buchanan, *My Mission to Russia, and other Diplomatic Memories,* 1923; Lord Newton, *Lord Lansdowne,* 1929; H. von Eckardstein, *Lebenserinnerungen,* translated by Sir George Young as *Ten Years at the Court of St. James, 1895–1905,* 1921; *Slavonic Review,* March 1929; private information.] ONSLOW.

NORTHCLIFFE, VISCOUNT (1865–1922), journalist and newspaper proprietor. [See HARMSWORTH, ALFRED CHARLES WILLIAM.]

NORTHUMBERLAND, eighth DUKE OF (1880–1930). [See PERCY, ALAN IAN.]

NORTON-GRIFFITHS, SIR JOHN, first baronet (1871–1930), engineer, was born 13 July 1871 in Somerset, the only surviving son of John Griffiths, of The Watton, Brecon, by his second wife, Juliet, daughter of Richard William Avery, of London. He had an unsettled youth and at the age of seventeen signed on as a seaman before the mast on a windjammer bound for Australia. On arrival in that country he was employed in engineering, excavating, and tunnelling in remote mining areas. Later he went to South Africa, where he practised as an engineer. In the Matabele War of 1896–1897 Griffiths commanded a body of scouts. On the outbreak of the South African War in 1899 he volunteered, and served as squadron leader in the second (colonial) division of the South African Field Force under (Sir) Edward Yewd Brabant, and later, from 1900 to 1902, as captain and adjutant of Lord Roberts's body-guard on the head-quarters staff. He took part in the Paardeberg, Modder River, and other engagements, was thrice mentioned in dispatches, and was awarded the queen's medal and clasp.

After the conclusion of peace in 1902, Griffiths built up a business as an engineering contractor, and in 1905 he constructed the first section of the Benguela railway in Portuguese West Africa, about one hundred miles in length. He also carried out works in America, and in England he founded the firm of Griffiths & Co., public works contractors, of which he was managing director. He also became senior partner of the firm of Norton, Griffiths, Bruce, Marriott & Co. He represented Wednesbury in parliament in the conservative interest from 1910 to 1918, and Wandsworth Central from December 1918 to October 1924. He was an untiring advocate of 'Imperial' projects and ideas, contemplated founding a town in Canada for British emigrants, and was known in the House of Commons as 'Empire Jack'.

On the outbreak of the European War in August 1914, Griffiths, at his own expense, organized and equipped the second regiment of King Edward's Horse, which was entirely distinct from the first regiment [L. James, *History of King Edward's Horse,* 1921, 71–72]. In December 1914 he suggested to the War Office that coal-miners and other underground workers should be specially enlisted for military mining purposes. In February 1915 he was authorized to enlist a party of these workers for service in France, and it was determined that they should form distinct units with their own establishment. Griffiths went to work with the most remarkable energy. The War Office approved the formation of eight companies on 19 February, and next day the first party of miners arrived in France to form the nucleus of the 170th company of Royal Engineers. Five days previously the men had been employed on sewer work at Liverpool. Within a fortnight four companies existed in embryo, and were engaged in active mining. By the end of June 1916 there were twenty-five Imperial companies and seven Overseas companies actively employed, the total force in existence being about 25,000 men in addition to the temporary employment of detachments from infantry battalions [*Work of the Royal Engineers in the European War. Military Mining,* 1922, 1–3]. Griffiths himself, with the rank of major, was attached to the staff of the engineer-in-chief at general head-quarters in France. He was mainly responsible for the planning and carrying out of the tunnelling operations under the Messines ridge, which successfully destroyed that German vantage-point on 7 June 1917. For his services he was three times mentioned in dispatches, and awarded the D.S.O. and the temporary rank of lieutenant-colonel in 1916.

The same year Griffiths was appointed general service officer, first grade, and sent on a special mission to Rumania. After the retirement of the Rumanian forces it became important for the Allies to prevent the supplies of oil and corn, left exposed, from falling into the hands of the Austro-German troops. Griffiths succeeded in wrecking the oil works and in destroying the standing corn with such completeness as to earn for himself a second nickname, that of 'Angel of Destruction'. It was a dangerous task, and for his daring and technical skill in carrying it out he was created K.C.B. in 1917 and officer of the legion of honour, and was awarded the star of Rumania and the order of St. Vladimir of Russia (third class). In 1917 he assumed by deed-poll the additional surname of Norton, and he was created a baronet in 1922.

In February 1929 the Egyptian government, in consequence of the report of an international commission, decided to raise the height of the Assuan dam [see Baker, Sir Benjamin, and Garstin, Sir William], by twenty-three feet, and the firm of Norton-Griffiths & Co. obtained the contract for the work. The contractors, however, stopped work on 21 September 1930, notifying the Egyptian government that the resident Egyptian engineering inspectors were inexperienced and incompetent, and that by their persistent obstruction they had made it impossible to continue. The Egyptian government in reply complained that the work had not been carried on at the proper rate, and stated that the contractors were in need of financial assistance, implying that this was the real reason of the stoppage. Norton-Griffiths in a further statement said that the suspension was irrespective of the financial position, but that the obstruction complained of had made further expenditure by the company difficult [*The Engineer*, 26 September 1930]. On the morning of 27 September 1930 Norton-Griffiths shot himself while alone in a surf boat at a short distance from the Casino hotel at San Stefano, a sea-side resort near Alexandria. His body was embalmed and sent to England.

Norton-Griffiths married in 1901 Gwladys, daughter of Thomas Wood, head of the engineering firm of Browning, Wood, & Fox. By her he had two sons and two daughters. He was succeeded as second baronet by his elder son, Peter (born 1905).

Norton-Griffiths was a member of the Institute of Mining and Metallurgy and a fellow of the Geological Society. He founded the Veterans of the Grand Army Association, afterwards called Comrades of the Great War.

[*The Times*, 29 September 1930; *The Engineer*, 3 October 1930.] E. I. Carlyle.

O'BRIEN, IGNATIUS JOHN, Baron Shandon (1857–1930), lord chancellor of Ireland, was born at Cork 31 July 1857, the ninth child and youngest son of Mark Joseph O'Brien, merchant, and freeman of Cork, by his wife, Jane, daughter of William Dunne, of Cork. He was educated at the Vincentian School, Cork, and then privately; and at the age of sixteen entered the Catholic University of Ireland, Dublin, a moribund institution which had no power to award recognized degrees. There he remained for only two years, for the circumstances of his family were straitened, and it became necessary for him to earn his own living immediately. He obtained a post first as junior reporter on *Saunders' Newsletter*, a Dublin conservative daily paper, and subsequently on the *Freeman's Journal*. Meantime he was studying for the bar, to which he was called in 1881.

Success came slowly, and O'Brien had to maintain himself by means of free-lance journalism. In his first year at the bar he made six guineas, in his second twenty-nine; in his third he began to acquire a small practice on the Munster circuit. Despairing of any real success, he was about to emigrate to New South Wales when a lucky opportunity brought his name before the public. In 1887 Canon Keller, the parish priest of Youghal, had been examined in the Court of Bankruptcy as to the means of certain of his parishioners, and, on his refusal to disclose knowledge which he had acquired in his capacity of priest, had been committed to prison for unsatisfactory answering. On the suggestion of Mr. T. M. Healy, and supported by the Land League, O'Brien brought a motion of habeas corpus to secure Canon Keller's release, and after being unsuccessful in the Court of Queen's Bench, secured an order of release from the Court of Appeal. Popular interest had been greatly stirred, O'Brien was the hero of the hour, and his solid attainments began to be realized. His practice now steadily increased. He gave up circuit business and devoted himself to cases in chancery and bankruptcy, becoming a leading authority in the latter branch of law. In 1899 he took silk, and his income suffered no decrease by this step.

Thenceforward events combined to ensure O'Brien's success. The long liberal régime which began in 1906 found few liberals among the more eminent men at the Irish bar. O'Brien had always held liberal views and, although he never contested a seat, he had helped and continued to give help at elections. In 1907 he became a bencher of King's Inns, and in 1910 his services were recognized by promotion to the dignity of serjeant-at-law. In 1911 he was appointed solicitor-general for Ireland; in 1912 he became attorney-general and was admitted a privy councillor for Ireland. In 1913 the offices of lord chancellor and of lord chief justice of Ireland became vacant at the same time, and O'Brien as attorney-general sought for and obtained the chancellorship.

O'Brien's tenure of office was uneasy, for the political intrigues in England were reflected in attempts to oust him from his position. When the first Coalition government was formed in 1915, he was on the verge of being superseded in favour of the unionist (Sir) James Henry Mussen Campbell, a former solicitor-general and attorney-general for Ireland; but the weight of American and Irish nationalist opinion was too heavy for a government which feared a popular outcry. In 1916 O'Brien was created a baronet, and in 1917, when his rival, Sir James Campbell, was made lord chief justice, his position seemed safe. But in 1918 the conservative pressure was again felt; he received notice that his services were no longer required, and Campbell was appointed lord chancellor in his stead.

As some consolation for his summary dismissal, O'Brien was offered a peerage of the United Kingdom; this he accepted, choosing the title of Baron Shandon from childhood memories of the chimes which had inspired the poem 'The Shandon Bells' by 'Father Prout' (Francis Sylvester Mahony, q.v.). His work in Ireland was finished. Disgusted and disappointed with the violence and excesses of Sinn Fein, of which he had personal experience in a raid on his house, he sold his Irish property and went to live at St. Lawrence in the Isle of Wight. He was called to the English bar by the Middle Temple in 1923. In the House of Lords he found unexpected solace. The quiet, restrained atmosphere was strange to him, but he grew to appreciate it, and even became reconciled to the hereditary system. While the abortive Government of Ireland Act (1920) was before parliament, Shandon took a prominent part in negotiation and debate, but thereafter spoke less and less frequently, confining himself to matters affecting Ireland, and to topics on which his legal experience might be of value. His last speech was delivered in 1927, on the Law of Libel Amendment Bill, which he opposed. He never returned to live in Ireland, and died in London 10 September 1930.

Shandon was not in the first rank whether as advocate, judge, or statesman, but he was always hardworking and pertinacious. During the troubled times when he was in office he exercised a moderating influence, aiming at securing a wide measure of Home Rule combined with preservation of the Imperial tie. Unfortunately he possessed neither the force of personality nor the skill in diplomacy necessary to make his advice effective, and he was overborne by abler and more subtle men.

Shandon married in 1886 Anne, daughter of John Talbot Scallan, a well-known Dublin solicitor. They had no children, and the peerage became extinct on his death.

[*The Times*, 12 September 1930; an unpublished autobiography and the private papers of Lord Shandon; Hansard, *Parliamentary Debates* (House of Lords); private information; personal knowledge.]

T. C. Kingsmill Moore.

O'BRIEN, WILLIAM (1852–1928), Irish nationalist leader, was born at Mallow, co. Cork, 2 October 1852, the second son of James O'Brien, of Mallow, a solicitor's clerk, by his wife, Kate, daughter of James Nagle, a local shopkeeper. Although his parents were Roman Catholics, O'Brien was educated at Cloyne Diocesan College, the Protestant high school of the district, and at Queen's College, Cork. In 1869 he became a reporter on the Cork *Daily Herald*; and in 1875 he joined the *Freeman's Journal*, Dublin, as a special correspondent. In 1881 Charles Stewart Parnell [q.v.] appointed him editor of *United Ireland*, the weekly organ of the Land League movement, the first number of which appeared on 13 August of that year. O'Brien made it the most militant political journal ever published in Ireland. In October it was suppressed by the chief secretary for Ireland, William Edward Forster [q.v.], and O'Brien was committed to Kilmainham jail, in which Parnell and other land leaguers had already been lodged, without trial, being 'reasonably suspected' of treasonable designs.

On his first day in prison O'Brien (as he relates in his *Recollections*) wrote, at Parnell's request, the 'No Rent' manifesto appealing to the farmers to stop paying rent until the land question was settled; and it was the reading of this document at a meeting of the Land League in Dublin that led, on 20 October, to the proclamation of the League as an illegal and criminal organization. *United Ireland* continued to appear, however, being printed secretly in London and Liverpool, and ultimately in Paris, whence it was distributed in Great Britain and Ireland. Parnell and other suspects were released on 2 May 1882 under the Kilmainham treaty, *United Ireland* was issued again in Dublin, and O'Brien, still editor, was elected nationalist member of parliament for Mallow in 1883. His remarkable powers as a speaker and writer made O'Brien second only to Parnell as a nationalist leader.

The rejection of Gladstone's Home Rule bill in 1886, followed by the first unionist government under Lord Salisbury, with Mr. A. J. (afterwards first Earl of) Balfour as chief secretary for Ireland, led to renewed Irish land agitation in a form as intense as ever. O'Brien and his colleague John Dillon [q.v.] started the 'plan of campaign' (1886), under which the tenants of estates whose landlords refused abatements paid their rents into a common fund for the purposes of defence and support in case of eviction. This step was taken without consulting Parnell, and he made known that he did not approve of it. The plan was declared illegal in February 1887, and O'Brien, after a visit to Canada for the purpose of agitation against the governor-general, Lord Lansdowne (on whose Irish estates evictions had taken place), was convicted on a charge of conspiracy in order to intimidate tenants to refuse to pay their rents, and sent to Tullamore jail for six months. His claim to be treated as a political prisoner having been ignored, he declined to wear the prison uniform. He lay naked on his plank bed for several weeks, until one morning he was found clad in a suit of Blarney tweed which had been smuggled in by a warder. On his release, O'Brien reappeared in the House of Commons, as member for North-East Cork (in which Mallow had been absorbed in a redistribution of constituencies), and was the central figure of some stormy debates on the subject of his prison treatment, which Balfour dealt with in an exasperatingly cool and ironic manner.

In September 1890 O'Brien and Dillon were arrested on a charge of criminal conspiracy. Being admitted to bail during the trial, they escaped to France and thence to the United States. There they were engaged in conducting a political mission when the split in the Irish party occurred (November 1890) on the question of Parnell's leadership after the O'Shea divorce case. They immediately returned, and at Boulogne O'Brien conducted protracted negotiations intended to restore unity to the party by making Dillon temporarily leader until the feeling against Parnell had subsided. Nothing came of his efforts. Parnell consented to retire only if O'Brien would take his place as leader; and this O'Brien, in an excess of self-distrust, refused to do. In February 1891 Dillon and he returned to Ireland and served the imprisonment of six months in Galway jail to which they had been sentenced. Not until 1900 was the Irish party re-united, through the influence of O'Brien, under the leadership of John Redmond [q.v.].

O'Brien, in the general election of 1892, was returned as nationalist member both for Cork city and the North-East division of the county, and chose to sit for the city. He soon started on a new career. He who had been the most extreme exponent of the nationalist policy, and the founder (1898) of the United Irish League, the object of which was to break up the great grazing farms by methods akin to those of the former Land League, had now come to the conclusion that Ireland's regeneration must be sought for on different lines. Her social troubles could be remedied and her national demand satisfied only by the conciliation and union of all classes, creeds, and political parties in Ireland. His first move in this direction was the Land Conference of 1902, representative of landlords and tenants. This had remarkable success. It led to the Land Purchase Act of 1903 brought in by George Wyndham [q.v.], the chief secretary, by which agricultural Ireland was to be transformed from a land of tenant occupiers to a land of occupying owners. It meant the abolition of Irish landlordism. O'Brien's next aim was the settlement of the 'national' question by agreement between unionists and nationalists. In this he was opposed by the majority of the Irish parliamentary party, who held that the concessions to Ulster which his policy involved would curtail the powers of a Home Rule parliament. O'Brien thereupon left the party. After some years of retirement from public life, he was again elected for Cork city in 1910 and founded the 'All for Ireland' League, which was supported by an independent parliamentary party under his own leadership, consisting of seven members (including T. M. Healy) returned by Cork constituencies in the general election of 1910. The motto of the League was 'Conference, Conciliation, Consent'. To this policy of combining all elements of the Irish population in a spirit of mutual tolerance and patriotic goodwill, O'Brien remained true to the end. He ascribed the rise of Sinn Fein to the blunders of the Irish party under John Redmond in their relations with the liberal government in the years before the European War. At the general election of 1918, O'Brien and his 'All for Ireland' followers retired, so as to leave the field clear for the contest between Sinn Fein and the Irish party. O'Brien saw the complete extinction of that great party, of which he had been a member at its rise under Parnell. He opposed the treaty which set up the Free State, because it divided Ireland.

O'Brien was the author of two novels, *When we were Boys* (1890), a story of the Fenian movement, and *A Queen of Men* (1898), dealing with the exploits of Grace O'Malley, a heroine of ancient Ireland. He also wrote *Recollections* (1906), *Evening Memories* (1920), *The Irish Revolution* (1923), *Edmund Burke as an Irishman* (1924), *The Parnell of Real Life* (1926), and other works. He married in 1890 Sophie, daughter of Hermann Raffalovich, of Paris, a French and Russian banker. They had no children. O'Brien died suddenly in London 25 February 1928, and was buried at Mallow.

There are portraits of O'Brien by Henry Holiday (1887) in the National Gallery, Dublin, by H. J. Thaddeus (1890) in Cork University, and by Sir William Orpen (1904) in the Municipal Gallery of Modern Art, Dublin.

[William O'Brien, *Recollections*, 1906, and *Evening Memories*, 1920; Michael Macdonagh, *Life of William O'Brien*, 1928; Mrs. William O'Brien, *Golden Memories*, 1929–1930.]

M. MACDONAGH.

O'CONNOR, THOMAS POWER (1848–1929), journalist and politician, was born at Athlone 5 October 1848, the eldest son of Thomas O'Connor, shopkeeper, by his wife, Theresa Power, daughter of a non-commissioned officer of the Connaught Rangers. He was educated at the College of the Immaculate Conception, Athlone, and at the Queen's College, Galway, where he took his B.A. degree in 1866. In the following year he began his career in journalism as a reporter on the staff of *Saunders' Newsletter*, a Dublin conservative daily paper. In 1870 he went to London in search of work, and at the outbreak of the Franco-German War his mastery of French and German led to his appointment as sub-editor, dealing with war news, on the *Daily Telegraph*. He next became a free-lance journalist, and endured much hardship in the years during which he followed this precarious calling until he found settled employment in the London office of the *New York Herald*.

It was at this period that O'Connor wrote his first book, a *Life of Lord Beaconsfield*, which appeared anonymously in serial numbers during 1876. It was so unsparing an attack on the prime minister that it attracted considerable notice, and when it appeared in book form, with the author's name, in 1879, it brought O'Connor into public notice. In the general election of 1880 he won the borough of Galway as a supporter of Parnell, and was one of the most voluble and pertinacious talkers among the Parnellites who opposed the liberal government of Mr. Gladstone. At the general election of 1885 he wrote an address from the Irish party to the nationalist voters in Great Britain, urging them to defeat the liberal oppressors of Ireland by supporting the conservative candidates; and at the general election of 1886, when Gladstone had adopted Home Rule, he wrote another address to the same electors, exhorting them in even more moving terms to vote liberal.

Throughout his long life O'Connor combined journalism with politics and was better known, perhaps, as a journalist than as a politician. John (afterwards Viscount) Morley [q.v.], editor of the *Pall Mall Gazette* in the early 'eighties, engaged him to write a nightly sketch of the proceedings in parliament, and thought him unrivalled in depicting the personalities of the party fight of that day and its dramatic episodes. In 1887 O'Connor founded *The Star*, an evening journal noted both for its radicalism and for its inauguration of 'the new journalism', characterized by what was called the 'human touch'. After three years of O'Connor's editorship, differences arose between him and the proprietor, and O'Connor was bought out for £15,000, subject to the condition that he should not start another evening paper in London for three years. In 1891 he brought out the *Sunday Sun*, which was subsequently called the *Weekly Sun*. *The Sun*, which he founded in 1893 when he was free to start another evening paper, failed to outshine his earlier luminary. His next venture, *T.P.'s Weekly* (he was known familiarly as T.P.), a penny literary paper of more than ordinary merit, which he set going in 1902, flourished for many years. He started other weekly papers, such as *M.A.P.* ('Mainly about People') and *P.T.O.* ('Please Turn Over'), both devoted chiefly to personal gossip, and tried his hand also at a monthly called *T.P.'s Magazine*. Of his books the more important are *The Parnell Movement* (1886) and *Memoirs of an Old Parliamentarian* (1929). As a journalist he was not a publicist in the sense that he wrote leading articles of weight and influence on public affairs. He was content rather to be an observer of life and its chronicler in an easy and agreeable style, reminiscent and anecdotal. Nor as a parliamentarian did he ever aspire to leadership. To the end he was only a subordinate member of the Irish party, but very useful by reason of his ready pen, great popularity, and wide circle of influential acquaintance.

In 1917 O'Connor became the first president of the Board of Film Censors—a salaried appointment in the gift of the cinematograph trade, but independent of trade control or influence. O'Connor's signature on the Censors' certificate which preceded the presentation of every film thus became familiar to millions. His censorship was successful in that it excited no controversy. In 1924 he was made a member of the Privy Council by the first labour government. He was also for many years 'father' of the House of Commons by right of the longest unbroken period of service, having sat continuously for the Scotland division of Liverpool since 1885.

O'Connor loved the House of Commons for its history, its customs, and its sociabilities, and wrote innumerable articles about its more prominent members, their fortunes and fates. In his later years there was more than one demonstration of the regard in which he was held by his fellow members. On his seventy-fifth birthday they presented him with a Georgian gold snuff-box, he being one of the few members who continued the practice of snuff-taking; and on his eightieth birthday he was entertained at a dinner, King George V sending to him his 'heartiest congratulations'. O'Connor died 18 November 1929, and was buried in the Roman Catholic cemetery, Kensal Green.

He married in 1885 Elizabeth Paschal (died 1931), daughter of a judge of the supreme court of Texas, U.S.A. They had no children.

There is a portrait of O'Connor by Sir John Lavery in the National Gallery, Dublin, and another by J. F. Bacon in the Walker Art Gallery, Liverpool.

[*The Times*, 19 November 1929; T. P. O'Connor, *Memoirs of an Old Parliamentarian*, 1929; Elizabeth O'Connor, *I Myself*, 1910.]

M. Macdonagh.

O'DONNELL, PATRICK (1856–1927), cardinal, was born at Kilraine, near Glenties, co. Donegal, 28 November 1856, the second son in the family of nine children of Daniel O'Donnell, of Kilraine, who claimed direct descent from the famous O'Donnell clan, by his wife, Mary Breslin, of Gortlosk. His father was a very small tenant farmer, who still wore the old-fashioned cut-away coat and white stock. The family was Gaelic-speaking, and Patrick O'Donnell remained all his life a fluent speaker of Gaelic, and, as bishop and cardinal, strongly supported the Irish language revival and for years issued his pastorals in Gaelic as well as English. Educated at the local national school and at the high school at Letterkenny, he gained first place in 1873 at a concursus for nomination to the Propaganda College in Rome, but Dr. James MacDevitt, bishop of Raphoe, sent him to Maynooth, where, after completing his studies with a year in the Dunboyne Establishment, he was ordained priest in 1880. He was appointed professor of theology there in the same year, and prefect of the Dunboyne Establishment in 1884.

In 1888, at the age of thirty-two, O'Donnell was consecrated bishop of Raphoe, and for thirty-five years laboured to improve the condition of his extremely poor diocese. He built many churches and schools in county Donegal, including a large industrial school at Killybegs and a diocesan college at Letterkenny, and he opened the new cathedral of St. Eunan at Letterkenny in 1901. In 1922 he was appointed by Pope Pius XI coadjutor, with the title of archbishop of Attalia, to Cardinal Michael Logue [q.v.], archbishop of Armagh, whom he succeeded as primate of all Ireland in 1924. He was created cardinal by Pope Pius XI, with the title of Santa Maria della Pace, in 1925. He attended the International Eucharistic Congress at Chicago in 1926. In the summer of 1927 he held a plenary synod of the Irish hierarchy at Maynooth, which introduced a large number of reforms concerning the clergy and ecclesiastical organization.

A man of great energy and courage and of charming personality, O'Donnell devoted his brilliant gifts to public life. An early supporter of the agitation for Irish land reform, he helped to promote reunion among the Irish nationalists after Parnell's death in 1891, and presided at the national convention (1900) which elected John Redmond [q.v.] leader of the Irish nationalist party. As the intimate friend of Redmond and John Dillon [q.v.] he became one of the three trustees of the Irish national fund. He supported Redmond's policy during the European War, and was an active member of the Irish convention of 1917–1918; but his final disagreement with Redmond on fiscal questions made the failure of the convention inevitable.

O'Donnell had been a champion of the Ulster catholics in opposing the partition of Ireland; but as archbishop of Armagh with his see in Northern Ireland, he accepted partition as an accomplished fact, and strove to promote better relations between catholics and protestants. In long service on many public bodies and commissions, especially on the Congested Districts Board, and by his work concerning education and in the founding of the National University of Ireland, O'Donnell gained wide experience; his courageous sincerity, shrewd judgement, and moderation commanded general respect and affection. He died at his summer residence at Carlingford, co. Louth, 22 October 1927.

[Walter McDonald, *Reminiscences of a Maynooth Professor*, edited by Denis Gwynn, 1925; Denis Gwynn, *Life of John Redmond*, 1932; P. J. Walsh, *William Joseph Walsh, Archbishop of Dublin*, 1928; private information.]

D. Gwynn.

O'HIGGINS, KEVIN CHRISTOPHER (1892–1927), Irish statesman, born at Stradbally, Queen's County, 7 June 1892, was the fourth son of Thomas Francis Higgins, physician, by his wife, Anne, daughter of Timothy Daniel Sullivan, M.P., the nationalist poet. His mother's sister was the wife of Timothy Michael Healy, K.C., first governor-general of the Irish Free State. He was educated at Clongowes Wood College, Knockley College, Carlow, St. Patrick's College, Maynooth, and at the National University of Ireland, Dublin. Having joined the Sinn Fein movement when a student in Dublin, he was imprisoned for six months in 1917 for a seditious speech. In December 1918 he was elected M.P. (Sinn Fein) for Queen's County, but was pledged not to attend parliament at Westminster and for the next three years led the fugitive existence of a revolutionary organizer and journalist. Meanwhile Arthur Griffith [q.v.] made him assistant minister for local government in the (revolutionary) ministry which the Sinn Fein party set up in January 1919; and with Mr. W. T. Cosgrave, minister for local government, O'Higgins secured control over local affairs. At the close of the year 1921, however, he came to the fore as the most effective advocate of the Treaty by which the Irish Free State was established (6 December), and in January 1922 he was appointed minister for economic affairs in the provisional government formed by Arthur Griffith, the president of Dail Eireann, under the chairmanship of Michael Collins [q.v.].

Early in the civil war which broke out at the end of June 1922 between the Free State government and the republican party, after the death of Arthur Griffith (13 August) and Michael Collins (22 August), O'Higgins stepped into the breach as vice-president of the executive council and minister for justice. He saw in the civil war primarily a struggle for parliamentary democracy. His uncompromising policy, which resulted in the execution of 77 republicans in the year 1922–1923, mercifully shortened that struggle, but concentrated on him the resentment of the defeated party. The murder of his father, in the course of a raid by the insurgents on his house on 11 February 1923, foreshadowed his own fate. With the coming of peace in May 1923 more direct opportunities for statesmanship presented themselves. Already in the previous autumn O'Higgins had skilfully piloted the new Free State constitution through the Dail. In 1924 he established the new judiciary, and his confidence in the sound instincts of the people was justified by the success of the new unarmed police force, the Civic Guard, which he established in 1922. His handling of a military mutiny in March 1924 was a further effective demonstration of democratic rule. Nevertheless he scarcely gauged the depth of the revolutionary spirit in Ireland, and he made little progress towards allaying it.

As a negotiator, however, O'Higgins revealed the essentials of his political outlook. He aimed not at a republic, but at a free and undivided Ireland within the British Commonwealth of nations. He had been the chief factor in reconciling the Southern unionists to the establishment of the Free State, and it was his cherished ambition to reconcile Ulster. With the failure of the boundary commission in 1925, he refused to press the issue, securing, instead, remission of the Free State's share of the National Debt. At the Imperial Conference of 1926 he took a leading part in formulating the conception of equality within the British Commonwealth.

O'Higgins was assassinated near Dublin on 10 July 1927 while on his way to attend Mass at Booterstown church. During his short political career he had proved himself one of the outstanding personalities of modern Ireland. He possessed a rare grasp of essentials and breadth of vision, combined with a passion for first principles and justice. His ruthless integrity made him at once the most admired and hated man of his time. 'A figure out of antiquity cast in bronze' is Mr. Winston Churchill's pen picture of him. To his fellow countrymen he appeared the embodiment of Spartan virtue.

O'Higgins married in 1921 Bridget Mary, daughter of Andrew Cole, of Drumlish, co. Longford, and had one son and two daughters.

[*Irish Times*, 11 July 1927; Dail Eireann, *Official Reports*, 1922–1927; Winston S. Churchill, *The World Crisis*, vol. v, 1929; private information.] J. Hogan.

OWEN, JOHN (1854–1926), bishop of St. David's, was born in the parish of Llanengan, Carnarvonshire, 24 August 1854. He was the only son of Griffith Owen, by his wife, Ann Jones. His father, a working weaver and afterwards a wool-merchant, was a man of strong character and deep piety. Both his parents were staunch Calvinistic Methodists, and their son was brought up as a member of that denomination. Educated first at the local British school, and later at the old grammar school of Bottwnog, Owen developed quickly. At the age of fifteen the headmaster made him his assistant. In 1872 he proceeded with a mathematical scholarship to Jesus College, Oxford. He obtained second classes in both classical (1873) and mathematical (1874) moderations, and graduated in 1876 with a second class in the final school of mathematics. He began reading for *literae humaniores*, but abandoned the idea of taking the examination. At Oxford, Owen came under the influence of (Canon) A. M. W. Christopher, rector of St. Aldate's church, in whose Sunday school he was, for a time, a teacher, although he had not yet been confirmed. From 1877 to 1879 he was an assistant master at Appleby grammar school. There his inclinations towards the Church of England, fostered years before by his friend and patron, Canon James Rowlands, rector of Llanbedrog (incumbent of Bottwnog 1860–1877), led to his confirmation in 1879.

In 1879 Owen was appointed professor of Welsh and lecturer in classics at St. David's College, Lampeter. He was ordained deacon in 1879 and priest in 1880 by Bishop Basil Jones, of St. David's. At Lampeter, Owen began a remarkable career of service to Wales and to the Welsh Church. The principal of the college, Francis John Jayne [q.v.], afterwards bishop of Chester, immediately recognized his character and gifts, and helped to develop them. In 1881 Thomas Frederick Tout [q.v.] joined the staff as professor of modern history, and Lampeter thus came to possess a trio of really able men in its service. Owen remained at Lampeter for six years as a diligent and stimulating teacher. During these years the attack on the established and endowed position of the Welsh Church was renewed, and he soon became one of her most skilful defenders. Under the pseudonym of 'Einion' he wrote for the Welsh press a series of articles which established his reputation as a controversialist.

In 1885 Owen left Lampeter to become warden and headmaster of Llandovery College, in succession to the Rev. Alfred George Edwards, afterwards first archbishop of Wales. He found Llandovery a small school of about eighty boys. During the four years of his headmastership the number was more than doubled, and Llandovery reached a respectable place among public schools, with a good record at the universities.

In 1889 the Rev. A. G. Edwards, vicar of Carmarthen and Owen's predecessor at Llandovery, was consecrated bishop of St. Asaph, and one of his first bold acts was to appoint Owen, at the age of thirty-four, to the deanery. The appointment seemed startling and aroused criticism, but events speedily justified it. The bishop and dean proved themselves to be a very able pair of organizers, and especially strong in controversy, in which both had been engaged for some years. The 'tithe war' in North Wales, and especially in Denbighshire, caused many unpleasant disturbances, and friendly relations between different political parties and religious denominations became increasingly difficult to maintain. The dean's letters to *The Times* in 1890, and a series of articles which he contributed to the weekly Welsh newspaper *Baner ac Amserau Cymru*, compelled attention. He successfully sought to prove that the agitation was not due to the injustice of tithe as a charge upon land, or even to the acute agricultural depression, but that it was being used as a lever (trosol) to bring about the disestablishment of the Welsh Church. The backbone of the agitation was soon broken, and the Tithe Rent-Charge Recovery Act was passed in 1891, making the owner and not the occupier of land responsible for the payment of tithe.

In the same year (1889) in which Owen was appointed dean of St. Asaph, the Welsh Intermediate Education Act, providing for the creation in every county in Wales (including Monmouthshire) of joint education committees, was passed, and although it was far from being satisfactory to churchmen, Owen, a keen and competent educationist, saw in it great possibilities for Welsh children. A member of the Flintshire committee, as well as of the joint committee for Wales and Monmouthshire, his experience in education, both secondary and higher, made his services invaluable in the work of establishing the Central Welsh Board and in the founding of schools in different parts of Wales.

In 1892, at the urgent request of the college board, and with the cordial approval of Bishop Basil Jones, Owen was induced to accept appointment as principal of St. David's College, Lampeter, with which he had kept in close touch since 1879. He relinquished the office of dean, but maintained his connexion with St. Asaph Cathedral through his preferment to a residentiary canonry, which he retained from 1892 to 1897. He was also sinecure rector of Llangeler, Carmarthenshire, for the same period. During his tenure of the principalship Owen took an active part in establishing the university of Wales and in drafting its charter (1893). One difficulty arose. St. David's College, Lampeter, had hitherto been the only degree-conferring body in Wales, and Owen fought strenuously for its inclusion as a constituent college of the new university. When his efforts proved unavailing he accepted the situation and set himself to reform the constitution of his college, by drafting for it a new charter. This charter was granted in 1896, and resulted in the transfer of government to a council representative of the Welsh Church and of the Welsh university colleges. Hitherto the appointment of the principal had been the prerogative of certain officials of the universities of Oxford and Cambridge, while the other members of the college staff had been appointed by the college board. By the new charter the right of all appointments was vested in the new council. Owen was always mindful of the fact that, while it opened its doors freely and without test to all, the primary object of the college was to educate men for the ministry of the Church, and he was intensely anxious that this object should be attained.

The years 1892–1897 were not free from ecclesiastical controversy. In 1893 a Suspensory Bill was introduced into parliament, designed to prevent persons appointed to offices in the Church in Wales from acquiring any vested interest in their emoluments. The bill was not passed, but in 1895 another bill was introduced by Mr. Asquith, the object of which was to disestablish and disendow the Church in Wales and to sever her long organic union with the Church of England. The opposition to this bill was short and sharp, and as usual Owen was prominent in the struggle. But Lord Rosebery's ministry fell, and for a time Owen was set free to do the work that appealed most to his heart, namely, to raise the spiritual tone of his college.

In January 1897 Bishop Basil Jones died, and the hopes of Welsh churchmen were fulfilled when Owen became his successor. At that time St. David's was, in area, the largest diocese in the province of Canterbury, presenting many difficulties in administration—geographical, linguistic, and economic. Extending from Presteign, on the borders of Radnor and Herefordshire, westward to the city of St. David's, with parts of it populated by monoglot Welsh, parts by monoglot English, and parts of it bilingual, it was also poorly endowed. Owen set himself at once to improve conditions all round and, by reviving the diocesan fund established by his predecessor, he achieved a large measure of success. His efforts were greatly helped by the recently established Queen Victoria Clergy Fund. Between 1898 and 1913 a total sum of more than £100,000 was raised, but even then the ideal of a minimum stipend of £200 for every incumbent had not been reached.

The year 1902 saw the passing of the new Education Act introduced by Mr. A. J. (afterwards first Earl of) Balfour [q.v.]. This Act transferred the maintenance of elementary education from local school boards to county councils, which were empowered to levy rates for the purpose of maintaining the schools. The Act also sought to improve the condition of church schools, which were now to be rate-aided on condition that they were kept in repair by those responsible for them. Definite religious instruction was secured. The liberals were strongly opposed to the measure, and a Welsh 'revolt' ensued, led by Mr. David Lloyd George. Some Welsh county councils refused to maintain church schools, and that of Carmarthen, in which the bishop's palace at Abergwili is situated, was stubborn in its refusal. An official inquiry was held in August 1904, and was followed by the passing of a parliamentary Default Bill, largely at the instigation of the bishop. The result was that the county council accepted the Act of 1902 and put it into operation.

In 1906 there began the sittings of the royal commission on the Welsh Church and on the general condition of religion in Wales. This commission, presided over by Sir Roland Bowdler Vaughan Williams [q.v.], continued in being for over four years, and issued a voluminous report in December 1910. The bishop's palace at Abergwili remained during all this time a centre of activity where evidence on behalf of the Church's case was collected and sifted. Owen himself gave evidence in 1908, occupying the witness chair for four days. His testimony fills about seventy pages of the report, and is elaborate and exhaustive. The findings of the commission were not unanimous, several minority reports being appended. Owen maintained that one result of the inquiry was finally to explode the statistical argument for disestablishment [*Report* of the Welsh Church Commission, 1910]. A new Disestablishment Bill was introduced in 1909, which formed the basis of a series of measures brought forward until, by the operation of the Parliament Act of 1911, a bill was successfully passed on 18 September 1914, which disestablished the Church in Wales and Monmouthshire.

Throughout these years the labours of Owen in opposition to disestablishment were strenuous and incessant. He toured the greater part of England as well as of Wales, appealing everywhere to reason and judgement instead of to emotion and prejudice. But when the die was cast he counselled the acceptance of the position. In spite of considerable differences of opinion within the Welsh Church, Owen's view was finally accepted, and the Church set herself to meet the new situation and to prepare for the future. An Act of parliament passed in 1915 postponed the operation of the original Act until after the end of the European War, and the years 1915–1919 were used by churchmen in refashioning the Church's constitution. A meeting held at Shrewsbury in December 1914, followed by another held in London in January 1915, led to the formation of committees which sat in London for the purpose of drafting an appropriate constitution for the disestablished Church. In October 1917 the work of these committees was reviewed by a representative convention summoned at Cardiff, at which it was resolved to form a governing body and a representative body, the former to be the ruling power, and the latter to manage the finances of the Church. A general constitution, previously drafted in committee, was also amended and approved. The Church had set her house in order when, after the end of the War, fresh negotiations were opened with the government, which resulted, in August 1919, in the passing of the Welsh Church Temporalities Act, which greatly mitigated the severity of the Act of 1914. Owen was active in procuring the passing of this measure, and afterwards justified his acceptance of it in a pamphlet entitled *The Acceptance of the Welsh Church Temporalities Act*, issued to his diocese on 1 November 1919.

Owen, in conjunction with his leader, Bishop Edwards of St. Asaph, was both active and effective in all this work of reconstruction, his great ambition being to see the Church once more resuming her place as the national church in Wales. Throughout his life the religious divisions in his country were a source of great grief to him. He yearned for religious re-union without hoping to see it. Although sometimes called a 'fighting bishop', he disliked fighting and longed for peace, national and international. As early as 1888 he had formed one of a small band of distinguished Welshmen, which included Thomas Charles Edwards [q.v.], A. G. Edwards, and F. J. Jayne, who met together to discuss the religious situation. After the War he was an ardent supporter of world peace, and he became Welsh president of the League of Nations Union. A man of many activities in many parts of the country, Owen never at any time neglected his own diocese and work. He knew every corner of his vast diocese, and was personally acquainted with every one of his clergy.

When the day came for the disestablishment of the Welsh Church (31 March 1920) Owen acquiesced, after some doubt, in the formation of an ecclesiastical province of Wales, and himself conducted the proceedings in the parish church of Llandrindod, when the bishop of St. Asaph was elected the first archbishop and metropolitan of Wales.

From 1920 to 1926 Owen devoted his time and energy to the work of building up the Church in Wales and to facing the new conditions, especially in his own diocese, which on 1 July 1923 was divided into two by the creation of the new diocese of Swansea and Brecon. Although the old diocese was unwieldy, he was reluctant to part with any portion of it, especially Swansea, where his influence had always been great. For about half of this time Owen was obviously in failing health, but he never ceased his manifold activities. In 1924, when the governing body of the Welsh Church appointed a committee to confer with a number of representatives of nonconformist bodies in order to consider afresh the question of religious education, his hope of a settlement revived. Although there were no immediate results, the work then accomplished paved the way to an ultimate settlement of a vexed question. In 1925 Owen was appointed chairman of a departmental committee of the Board of Education in order to inquire into the use of the Welsh language in education. But his waning physical strength was over-taxed by his exertions, and he did not live to see the report of the committee completed and published [*Welsh in Education and Life*]. He died in London, after an illness which lasted several weeks, 4 November 1926, and was buried in the churchyard of Abergwili, hard by the house in which he had lived for over twenty-nine years.

Few churchmen of his time were better known throughout England and Wales than Bishop Owen. He frequently addressed meetings of the English Church Congress, notably those held at Manchester in 1908 and at Stoke-on-Trent in 1911. In 1909 he presided at Swansea over the fourth meeting of the Congress to be held in Wales; there he was as usual a central and impressive figure. After his death an old pupil wrote of Owen: 'Endowed with a power of work far surpassing that of ordinary men, burning with enthusiasm, he had an extraordinary faculty for organization and for selecting the right men to work out the details of a policy with which he was always able to keep in touch in spite of his multifarious activities' [*Welsh Outlook*, December 1928].

Owen married in 1882 Amelia Mary Elizabeth, daughter of Joseph Longstaff, of Appleby, and had four sons and six daughters. As a memorial to him in the diocese of St. David's a recumbent effigy was placed in the Lady chapel of the cathedral, and a sum of money was set aside to help widows and orphans of the clergy of the diocese. No portrait of him was ever painted.

[*The Times*, 5 November 1926; *Report* of Welsh Church Commission, 1910; Owen's published charges and addresses; reminiscences contributed by him to *Y Llan*; private information; personal knowledge.]

R. Williams.

OXFORD AND ASQUITH, first Earl of (1852–1928), statesman. [See Asquith, Herbert Henry.]

PAGET, STEPHEN (1855–1926), biographer and essayist, was born in London 17 July 1855, the fourth and youngest son of the surgeon Sir James Paget, first baronet [q.v.], by his wife, Lydia, second daughter of the Rev. Henry North, domestic chaplain to Edward, Duke of Kent. He was nephew of Sir George Edward Paget [q.v.], physician, and younger brother of Francis Paget [q.v.], bishop of Oxford. He was educated at Marylebone grammar school, Shrewsbury School, and Christ Church, Oxford, where he obtained second classes in classical moderations (1875) and *literae humaniores* (1878). In October 1878 he entered the school of St. Bartholomew's Hospital, London, where his father had become a consulting surgeon in 1871. He qualified as F.R.C.S. in 1885 and proceeded to practise surgery, serving on the staffs of three London hospitals, the Middlesex, the Metropolitan, and the West London. He found himself, however, in some ways unsuited for surgical work, and in 1897 he abandoned general surgery, although retaining some medical practice until 1910. He was thus earlier freed for literary work and for the propaganda which he had much at heart in the social struggle against disease.

This propagandist activity, which remained an aspect of his life until its very close, may be summarized before turning to Paget's more enduring work as a man of letters. An Act of parliament to regulate the performance, for scientific purposes, of experiments on animals had come into force in 1877. An association was formed by leading physicians and surgeons to watch and submit advice to the government on the working of this Act. Paget was appointed (1888) its secretary, a post demanding tact and courage. His success in it was complete. His fairness of view and unimpeachable integrity of statement won the confidence of all open-minded adherents of both the parties opposed in the controversy. In this post he could gauge the public needs of the question, and he determined to marshal in a book for the general public the facts bearing on the position of animal experimentation as an auxiliary in man's struggle against disease. He produced in 1900 *Experiments on Animals*, with an introduction by Lord Lister, a book with no pretence to literary appeal. In it Paget characteristically suppressed himself for his cause, often admitting descriptions of the crudest kind because they were written by actual experimenters, whereas he himself was not one. The book proved effective despite its drawbacks.

In 1908 Paget founded the Research Defence Society, its inaugural meeting being held on 27 January in his own house, 70 Harley Street. As its honorary secretary he conducted an unwearying campaign in justification of animal experimentation. Furthermore, in the early days of the European War protective inoculation of the troops against tetanus and the typhoid fevers was imperilled by prejudice and violent agitation. Paget volunteered to deliver lectures to the soldiers, and succeeded in removing the misconceptions which obstructed the measures for their safety. His career of devotion to public enlightenment in the cause of modern medicine is commemorated by the Research Defence Society in an annual lecture bearing his name.

Yet Paget was essentially a man of letters, and above all an essayist. He contributed in some measure to biography, and in that field made his somewhat tardy literary début (1897) with a sketch of *John Hunter* [q.v.], the anatomist. The same year appeared his *Ambroise Paré and his Times, 1510–1590*, an account of the famous surgeon of the French renaissance. Four years later (1901), following on his father's death in 1899, he produced the *Memoirs and Letters of Sir James Paget*. An autobiographical sketch left by his father, completed as to the concluding years of his life and amplified by letters, is made to portray with delightful intimacy the simple and cultured family life and upright professional leadership of the surgeon who more than any other personified to the Victorian community the beneficence of his calling. Paget also collaborated with the Rev. J. M. C. Crum in 1912 in a memoir of *Francis Paget, Bishop of Oxford*. Much later, when already well known as an essayist, Paget returned incidentally to biography. His *Henry Scott Holland, Memoir and Letters* (1921) presents admirably some memorable correspondence. Less successful is the *Study* of the life and work (1919) of the surgeon Sir Victor Horsley [q.v.], undertaken in response to a request.

Paget's career as an essayist began in 1906 with *The Young People*, a slim volume which obtained immediate success. There followed a series of essays, which appealed to an ever increasing public—*Confessio Medici* (1908), *Essays for the Young People* (an enlarged issue of *The Young People*, 1910), *I Wonder* (1911), *I Sometimes Think* (1916), and *I have Reason to Believe* (1921). These offer a forceful and graceful criticism of life, commenting on social ways and views. With a delicate, half judicial humour they mingle enthusiasms and regrets. They follow the eager advances towards manhood and womanhood of young people whose lot is cast with youngish parents in a refined home in a great city, observing the poignant contrasts around them, poverty and wealth, religion and the lack of it, toil and leisure, well-being and disease. The style, individual and flexible, ranges securely over wit and pathos. Precepts are softened of didacticism by the fathering of them upon great masters, from Homer onwards, quoted as familiar friends. There is gentle tolerance of other men's tastes. The reader feels in contact with a character actuated by strong convictions but rich in judgement and sympathy, and broad with sane knowledge of the world. One of the last of the series was *Essays for Boys and Girls* (1916). The European War had come and Paget had at once perceived the full measure of its issues. His book deals with it, and records the facts and impressions of those opening two years, with a fidelity and Bunyan-like simplicity which furnish an ineffaceable picture. His indictment to boys and girls of the German violation of Belgian neutrality and the atrocities of its violators reveals a power not before exerted; it marks the summit of his literary achievement.

Exhausting efforts among the troops at home and among the sick and wounded in Russia (1917), as surgeon to Lady Muriel Paget's hospital in Petrograd, gradually overtaxed a constitution never robust. Paget had to give up work; he retired to Limpsfield, Surrey; there at his house, Furzedown, he died 8 May 1926. In stature somewhat short, and plain of feature, he had a pleasing resonant voice and unfailing charm of manner. He married in 1885 Eleanor Mary (died 1933), second daughter of Edward Burd, M.D., a physician in practice at Shrewsbury; by her he had two daughters.

[*The Times*, 20 May 1926; V. G. Plarr, *Lives of the Fellows of the Royal College of Surgeons of England*, revised by Sir D'A. Power and others, 2 vols., 1930; personal knowledge.] C. S. Sherrington.

PAIN, BARRY ERIC ODELL (1864–1928), humorist, was born at Cambridge 28 September 1864, the son of John Odell Pain, linen-draper, of Cambridge, by his wife, Maria Pain. He was educated at Sedbergh School from 1879 to 1883, and in the latter year proceeded to Corpus Christi College, Cambridge, where he was awarded a scholarship in 1884, graduating in 1886 after obtaining a third class in the first part of the classical tripos.

From 1886 to 1890 Pain practised as an army coach at Guildford. He had contributed to the Sedbergh school magazine and with much success to the *Granta* while he was at Cambridge; he now decided to devote himself to writing. Settling in London in 1890, he obtained regular work from the *Daily Chronicle* and *Black and White*. His first book, *In a Canadian Canoe* (compiled from his contributions to the *Granta*), appeared in 1891. Shortly afterwards he was invited by James Payn [q.v.], the editor of the *Cornhill Magazine*, to become a contributor to that journal. In a very few years he became well known as a novelist and writer of short stories, mainly of a humorous character. In 1897 he succeeded Jerome K. Jerome [q.v.] as editor of *To-day*. In 1900 he moved from Pinner, where he had lived for several years, to Hogarth House, Bushey, where he remained until about 1908; thereafter, until 1917, he lived at St. John's Wood.

In the autumn of 1914 Pain made a tour in the United States; but he felt the claims of war-work, and in April 1915 he joined the anti-aircraft section of the Royal Naval Volunteer Reserve; he was posted to the searchlight station on Parliament Hill, and quickly attained the rank of chief petty officer. Eye-strain caused by this work eventually compelled him to abandon it, and in 1917 he became a member of the London Appeal Tribunal, adjudicating on claims to exemption from military service. At this time, and until 1920, he lived at Farnham Royal, Buckinghamshire. His last home was at Watford, where he died 5 May 1928. Pain married in 1892 Amelia Nina Anna (died 1920), daughter of the portrait painter Rudolf Lehmann [q.v.], and sister of Liza Lehmann, the composer. They had two daughters.

Pain was a man of varied gifts. His interests included subjects so diverse as drawing, Georgian literature, occult lore, and precious stones, and his books range from a philosophic religious treatise to a detective novel. Some of his stories of the supernatural happily combine poetry with that *frisson* which is expected in tales of this kind. Early in his career he was advised by W. E. Henley to devote himself to 'serious' work, but his sense of fun being the most highly developed faculty in him, his humorous works predominate, and it is by these that he is best known. *Eliza* (1900) was the first of a successful series of books (continued until 1913) purporting to be written by a pretentious and ridiculous suburban clerk, describing incidents in his home life. The detail and descriptions are realistically exact, and the whole recital mordant in its irony, even if somewhat overdone. Other typical characters drawn by Pain are the charwoman, *Mrs. Murphy* (1913), and the jobbing gardener, *Edwards* (1915). These books are comedies of manners based on keen insight into the character of humble people, but their humour, if high-spirited and satirical, is not without sympathy and restraint.

[*The Times*, 7 May 1928; 'Mr. Barry Pain at Home' in *Sylvia's Journal*, February 1894; *The Bookman*, December 1927; *London Mercury*, June 1928; private information.]

H. B. Grimsditch.

PALMER, GEORGE HERBERT (1846–1926), musician, was born at Grantchester 9 August 1846, the elder son of Jonathan Palmer, master-printer, of Cambridge, by his wife, Elizabeth, daughter of Thomas Stevenson, of Rainton, Yorkshire. He was cousin to the printer and bibliographer William Blades [q.v.] and to Sir George Grove [q.v.], the musical critic and historian.

Brought up at Cambridge, Palmer was greatly influenced by his father's friend the liturgiologist John Mason Neale [q.v.]; and after graduating B.A. at Trinity College, Cambridge, in 1869, was ordained deacon in 1869 and priest in 1871 at Chester. His first curacy was at St. Margaret's, Toxteth Park, Liverpool, where his organ-playing attracted the sympathetic admiration of the musician William Thomas Best [q.v.].

From 1876 to 1883 Palmer, as priest-organist at St. Barnabas's church, Pimlico, came to know the Rev. Thomas Helmore [q.v.], precentor of St. Mark's College, Chelsea, 1846–1877, and one of the pioneers of the Gregorian revival; and also the Rev. G. R. Woodward, curate of St. Barnabas, with whom he began his life-work in the rediscovery of the true plain chant tradition and the adaptation of the ancient melodies to English texts. To this task Palmer brought a fine musical perception and a natural gift for language; but it was from the manuscripts themselves that he learned the principles of the art of adaptation. The preservation of the Latin *cursus* necessitated at times a somewhat free translation, but he admitted no word alien to the authorized version of the Bible. He kept in touch with the researches of the Benedictine community at Solesmes near Le Mans, where his musical scholarship was held in great respect.

In 1888 Palmer co-operated in the foundation of the Plainsong and Medieval Music Society, to which he subsequently made several contributions. He also did a great work in the training of English religious communities in the liturgical music of the Church, issuing through St. Mary's Press, Wantage, *The Sarum Psalter* (1894, 5th ed. 1916), *The Order of Vespers from the Sarum Breviary* (1899, latest ed. 1934), *The Offices or Introits* (1908, 3rd ed. 1927), and *Grails, Alleluyas and Tracts from the Sarum Gradale* (1908), as well as many other adaptations of the music of the Mass and Divine Office.

In 1917 the archbishop of Canterbury, Dr. Randall Davidson, on a petition from a number of influential musicians, conferred upon Palmer a Lambeth degree of doctor of music. He was presented for the degree by (Sir) Richard Terry, organist of Westminster Cathedral, this being further evidence of the esteem in which Palmer's learning was held outside the Anglican communion. The same year he went to Oxford, taking over for a time the direction of the music at the church of the Society of St. John the Evangelist, Cowley, where he had founded the plain chant tradition many years before. He now had the opportunity of concentrating on his most important work, *The Diurnal Noted*, the text of which appeared in 1921 under the title *The Diurnal after the Use of the illustrious Church of Salisbury*. The manuscript of the music was completed just before his death: Part i was published in 1926 and Part ii in 1929; the remainder is in the press. He died at Oxford 20 June 1926, and was buried in the churchyard of St. Mary and St. John.

Palmer was a true son of the catholic revival, a scholar-saint of gracious courtesy, lavish in bestowing on others the fruits of his labours, who welcomed criticism and bore disappointment as they alone can who are completely single-minded.

[*Church Times*, 25 June 1926; private information; personal knowledge.]

J. M. Close.

PANKHURST, EMMELINE (1858–1928), leader of the militant movement for women's suffrage, was born at Manchester 4 July 1858. She was the eldest daughter and third of the eleven children of Robert Goulden, owner of calico printing and bleach works, by his wife, Sophia Jane Craine. Her parents were actively interested in radicalism and reform movements, and Emmeline was only fourteen when, with her mother, she attended her first women's suffrage meeting. She was first sent to a 'ladylike' school in Manchester as a weekly boarder, and at fifteen to a much more efficient one in Paris. At eighteen she was considered 'finished'; she returned home, and shortly afterwards, in 1879, married Richard Marsden Pankhurst, LL.D., a barrister, many years older than herself. A radical, passionately interested in social reform, Dr. Pankhurst had long been a prominent advocate of women's suffrage. With Sir John Duke Coleridge he had been counsel for the claimants in the case of *Chorlton* v. *Lings* in 1868, when 5,346 women householders of Manchester unsuccessfully claimed to vote under the existing law. His wife at once began suffrage work, and became a member of the Manchester women's suffrage committee; later, when differences of policy arose, she and Mrs. Jacob Bright formed a separate committee of their own. Dr. and Mrs. Pankhurst also supported the Married Women's Property Bill—Dr. Pankhurst drafted the Act of 1882—and their house was a centre for political reformers, Keir Hardie, Mrs. Besant, Sir Charles Dilke, and William Morris being among their friends. They both left the liberal party after Mr. Gladstone's refusal to put women's suffrage into the Reform Bill of 1884, and joined the Fabian Society. Five children were born to them, two sons and three daughters, of whom the eldest, Christabel, later became her mother's chief collaborator.

The death of Dr. Pankhurst in 1898 put an end to an exceptionally close and congenial companionship, and left Mrs. Pankhurst with four young children (the eldest boy having died) in straitened circumstances. She procured the post of registrar of births and deaths at Rusholme, which brought her a small income, and she held this office until 1907 when her increasing preoccupation with the suffrage movement caused her to resign and forfeit her claim to a pension. Having been for some years an active member of the independent labour party, she made efforts to press women's suffrage upon that body, but thinking that insufficient attention was given to it, she resigned in 1900. In 1903 she and her daughter, with a few friends, founded a new women's suffrage society, the Women's Social and Political Union, which began with propaganda among Lancashire working-women. In 1905 they decided on the adoption of more strident methods. At a liberal election meeting held in Manchester in October 1905, Christabel Pankhurst and Annie Kenney asked Sir Edward Grey what would be the new government's policy about votes for women; getting no answer they asked again, and were forcibly ejected from the hall amid great disturbance. A protest meeting in the street was followed by their arrest and imprisonment, and the resulting commotion in the newspapers revealed to Mrs. Pankhurst the uses of publicity.

From that moment Mrs. Pankhurst adopted sensational methods of propaganda: interruptions at meetings were followed by importunate deputations, by processions to the House of Commons, and by original and unexpected devices to secure notoriety for the cause. The Suffragettes, as they were called, seemed to be ubiquitous. They appeared in all sorts of disguises, they chained themselves to railings, and from every point of vantage they waved their flags in the faces of Cabinet ministers and shouted 'Votes for Women'. They were repeatedly arrested and imprisoned; but each attempt at suppression brought more converts and more money to the Union, which grew rapidly. In 1908 Mrs. Pankhurst was herself arrested and charged with others at Bow Street with 'conduct likely to provoke a breach of the peace'. Mrs. Pankhurst spoke in her own defence. She was a true orator, quiet in manner and clear in substance, but with a quality of restrained emotion which moved even the police-court audience to tears. Oratory, however, was unavailing, and she was sentenced to three months' imprisonment in Holloway jail.

This militant campaign was intensified in 1909 by definitely illegal acts, such as window-breaking and destruction of property. More arrests followed, and the prisoners then adopted a policy of hunger-striking which, in spite of attempts at forcible feeding, obliged the authorities to release them after a short time. In this year Mrs. Pankhurst made a tour in the United States to arouse interest in the movement and to raise money for her work. In 1910, when an all-party committee of members of parliament brought forward a Women's Suffrage Bill which seemed to offer some chance of success, Mrs. Pankhurst consented to a truce to militancy; but, when the liberal government went to the country in November of that year promising nothing more than an adult male franchise bill, militancy broke out with renewed violence. Mrs. Pankhurst visited America again in 1911, but returned to carry on the campaign. In 1912 a police raid was made upon the head-quarters of the Women's Social and Political Union, and Mrs. Pankhurst and others were again arrested. After a trial at the Central Criminal Courts they were convicted on the charge of conspiracy.

In Holloway Mrs. Pankhurst adopted the hunger-strike and, when it had lasted until her condition was serious, she was released. In 1913 she was again arrested and sentenced to three years' penal servitude for incitement to violence. By that time a special Act had been passed to deal with hunger-strikers, under which they could be re-arrested and sent back to continue their sentences as soon as their health was sufficiently restored. Mrs. Pankhurst had therefore to face a very serious ordeal. To work off a sentence of three years by repeated weeks of starvation seemed likely to break down the strongest constitution; but she did not hesitate. She even added to her hunger-strike a refusal to sleep or drink, with the result that the periods of imprisonment before her condition became critical were very short. In the course of the next twelve months she was re-arrested twelve times, serving in all for thirty days. Each of her releases was marked by demonstrations, and ingenious plans were devised to trick the police and delay re-arrest, and more than once she managed to appear on public platforms, even though she was too ill to speak. In 1913, while still under sentence, Mrs. Pankhurst paid a third visit to the United States, and on her return was arrested in Plymouth harbour, and the intermittent imprisonment was resumed.

The outbreak of the European War, however, ended the women's suffrage agitation, and all the pending sentences were remitted. Mrs. Pankhurst devoted herself to recruiting, organized a procession of munition workers at the request of the government, and also went to the United States and to Russia on propaganda missions. When the question of women's suffrage again became prominent in 1916 Mrs. Pankhurst decided to maintain the truce to militancy, and she took little part in the final stages of the agitation which led to the first instalment of women's suffrage in 1918. Soon after the War she went to Canada, and took up work as a speaker on social hygiene and child welfare. In 1926 she returned to England and joined the conservative party. She was adopted as prospective candidate for Whitechapel and St. George's in the East, and worked there with great energy and devotion. She was, however, worn out by the hardships of her life, and died in London 14 June 1928, just after the passing of the second Representation of the People Act which gave full and equal suffrage to men and women. A bronze memorial statue was erected in the Victoria Tower Gardens, under the shadow of those Houses of Parliament to the opening of which to women she had devoted her energies and her life.

[*The Times*, 15 June 1928; E. Sylvia Pankhurst, *The Suffragette Movement*, 1931, and *The Life of Emmeline Pankhurst*, 1935; Emmeline Pankhurst, *My Own Story*, 1914; Dame Ethel Smyth, *Female Pipings in Eden*, 1933; private information.] R. Strachey.

PARKIN, Sir GEORGE ROBERT (1846–1922), educationist and Imperialist, was born at Salisbury, Westmoreland county, New Brunswick, Canada, 8 February 1846, the youngest of the thirteen children of John Parkin, a farmer who had emigrated from Yorkshire, by his wife, Elizabeth McLean, of Nova-Scotian birth and loyalist descent. He attended the village school at Salisbury, and in 1863 went for further training to the normal school at St. John. After teaching for a year in the primary schools at Buctouche and on the island of Campobello, he entered the university of New Brunswick at Fredericton in 1864 and graduated in 1867. In the latter year he was appointed headmaster of the Gloucester grammar school at Bathurst, and in 1871 of the collegiate school at Fredericton. Here he greatly influenced such pupils as Bliss Carman [q.v.] and Charles Roberts, probably the two most distinguished Canadian poets. He came under the influence of John Medley [q.v.], the Anglican bishop of Fredericton, and soon became known as a speaker on religious and educational subjects, and as a fervid opponent of the liquor traffic, the evils of which were rampant in the province.

In 1873 Parkin came to England with a year's leave of absence, and matriculated at Oxford as a non-collegiate student. He spoke at the Union in behalf of Imperial federation, and was elected secretary, an honour almost unique for a freshman. He came into close touch with a brilliant group at Balliol, of whom the chief were H. H. Asquith, Alfred Milner, and (Sir) Thomas Raleigh. Even more influential in his life was a friendship formed with Edward Thring [q.v.], headmaster of Uppingham. In 1898 Parkin published the official *Life and Letters of Edward Thring*, a task confided to him by Thring shortly before his death.

Returning to Canada in 1874, Parkin resumed his headmastership in Fredericton until January 1889, when he resigned in order to devote himself to the cause of the Imperial Federation League, organized in England in 1884, and in Canada in 1885. As its representative he visited Australia from March to November 1889, and spoke with great effect. From December 1889 until 1895 he lived in England, mainly at Harwich, lecturing in every county, and writing on Imperial questions with such effect that *The Times* said that he had 'shifted the mind of England'. In 1892 he published *Imperial Federation, or The Problem of National Unity* and *Round the Empire*, an admirable text-book which had a wide circulation. In the same year he visited Canada as special correspondent for *The Times*, and his letters were published in the next year with the title *The Great Dominion* (revised edition, 1895). In 1895 he was appointed principal of Upper Canada College in Toronto, an old foundation which had fallen on evil days, and which he soon made into the leading school in the Dominion. He held this post until 1902.

In 1902 Parkin was chosen to be the first organizing secretary of the Rhodes Scholarship Trust and settled permanently in England. The spiritual side of Rhodes's bequest [see Rhodes, Cecil John], the transforming of Oxford from an English into an Imperial university, appealed strongly to his imagination, and in 1903–1904 he visited every portion of the Empire and of the United States. His home at Goring-on-Thames became a meeting-place for the Rhodes scholars and for innumerable other visitors, and until 1920 he wrote and talked, travelled and organized, indefatigably. In 1908 he published a *Life of Sir John A. Macdonald*, and in 1912 *The Rhodes Scholarships*. In a tour of the United States in 1917–1918 during the European War he spoke with remarkable effect. In 1920 he retired, and he died suddenly in London 25 June 1922. He was buried at Goring.

Parkin was tall and loose-limbed, of great physical energy, and with a rare capacity for friendship. He was a convinced but broad-minded Anglican, singularly unworldly, and looking on all questions rather from the moral than the political point of view. In 1911 the honorary degree of D.C.L. was conferred on him by Oxford University, and in 1920 he was created K.C.M.G.

Parkin married in 1878 Annie Connell (died 1931), eldest daughter of William Fisher, of Fredericton, a provincial civil servant, and member of a well-known loyalist family, which had long been prominent in the public service of New Brunswick. Parkin was survived by one son and four daughters.

[*The Times*, 26 June 1922; Sir John Willison, *Sir George Parkin*, 1929.]

W. L. Grant.

PARRATT, Sir WALTER (1841–1924), organist and composer, was born at Huddersfield 10 February 1841, the second son and fifth child of Thomas Parratt, organist, of Huddersfield, by his wife, Sarah Elizabeth, daughter of William Perkins. Thomas Parratt was a classical scholar, and greatly esteemed as organist of the parish church, Huddersfield, where for ninety-two successive Christmas Days the services were played either by him or by his elder son. Walter Parratt received his early education at home, where he was taught by his parents, and for a short time at Huddersfield Collegiate School. At the age of eleven he succeeded his elder brother Henry as organist of Armitage Bridge church, near Huddersfield. Later in the same year (1852) he was sent to the choir school attached to St. Peter's chapel, Palace Street, S.W. There he acted as organist. This arrangement proved unsatisfactory except in so far as it afforded him the opportunity of taking organ lessons from George Cooper [q.v.], assistant organist of St. Paul's Cathedral. He returned home two years later (1854) and succeeded his brother as organist at St. Paul's church, Huddersfield.

In 1864 Parratt married Emma, daughter of Luke Gledhill, manufacturer, of Huddersfield, and left Huddersfield in order to become organist of Great Witley church, Worcestershire, and private organist to William, first Earl of Dudley, at Witley Court. Witley did not afford much scope for Parratt's powers, but he frequently visited St. Michael's College, Tenbury, where he enjoyed the friendship of its founder, the musician and composer, Sir Frederick Arthur Gore Ouseley [q.v.]. The warden of the college has left on record Parratt's feats of memory in music and chess performed with another guest, Adolf von Holst, father of the well-known composer, Gustav Holst. Life at Witley did not long satisfy Parratt and his wife, so that he accepted an invitation which he received in 1868 to go to Wigan as organist of the parish church.

In 1872 (Sir) John Stainer [q.v.] was appointed organist of St. Paul's Cathedral, and he advised Parratt to apply for the post of organist of Magdalen College, Oxford, which he himself was vacating. Parratt applied and was at once elected, and his name immediately became closely associated with Oxford and its music, remaining so until his death. He spent ten happy years at Oxford, and entered fully into the musical life of the university, conducting various college musical societies, and taking a prominent part in the activities of the University Musical Club. He was also president of the University Chess Club.

In 1882 Parratt received a command invitation from Queen Victoria to succeed Sir George Job Elvey [q.v.] as organist of St. George's chapel, Windsor. Windsor was thenceforth to be the centre from which radiated all the activities of Parratt's maturing powers. Elvey's legacy to his successor was a fully equipped choir, the services of an apprentice assistant organist—Hubert Walter Hunt, afterwards organist of Bristol Cathedral—and an extensive repertory from the works of Thomas Tallis to those of S. S. Wesley, on which to graft works by the younger British school of Church musicians, notably those of (Sir) Charles Villiers Stanford [q.v.]. Many of Stanford's works were first performed, before publication, in St. George's chapel. But by no means the least important item of Elvey's legacy was the Windsor and Eton Madrigal Society, an admirably equipped body wellnigh one hundred strong, founded by himself. This society, in conjunction with the choir of St. George's chapel, made the annual performance of the 'St. Matthew Passion' an important part of the musical life of the neighbourhood. The founding by Parratt of the Windsor Orchestral Society left his successors similarly indebted.

Almost immediately after his removal to Windsor, Sir George Grove [q.v.] invited Parratt to become chief professor of the organ at the recently founded Royal College of Music, of which Grove was the first director. This appointment made the opportunity of learning to play the organ under one of its foremost living exponents available to a greater number of pupils than had hitherto been possible, and in July 1902 several hundreds of these entertained their master at a banquet in London and presented him with a piece of old silver. Parratt's influence as a teacher of the organ is evidenced by the 'school of organ playing' which he founded. His insistence on attention being paid to the minutiae of the text, cleanness of technique in its delivery, and crystal-clear phrasing are noted by all whom he taught. The services at St. George's chapel became the focus point of organists all over the country, as a very large number of important organistships came to be filled by Parratt's pupils.

In appreciation of Parratt's work as teacher and organist and of his responsibility for music connected with public services as well as with the more intimate ones of the royal family, Queen Victoria knighted him and made him her private organist in August 1892, and a year later appointed him master of the queen's music. Both of these offices were confirmed by King Edward VII, who awarded Parratt the M.V.O. (1901), and also by King George V, from whom he received the C.V.O. (1917) and the K.C.V.O. (1921). At Oxford his appointment in 1908 as successor to Sir Charles Hubert Hastings Parry [q.v.] in the professorship of music, a post which he held until his resignation in 1918, the award of the honorary degree of Mus. Doc. in 1894, as well as his election to an honorary fellowship at Magdalen College in 1906, testify to the university's appreciation of his distinction as a musician. The universities of Cambridge and Durham awarded him honorary degrees in 1910 and 1912 respectively.

For Parratt's organ playing no term seems more adequate than 'statuesque', to which 'poetical' must be added when considering his powers as an accompanist. He had no set rules, but taste always; no set interpretation, but dullness never. His work as a composer must not be left unrecorded. General acclamation greeted his 'Confortare', the anthem written for the coronation of King Edward in 1902, and again performed at that of King George in 1911. 'The Face of Death' (words by Tennyson), at its first public performance at the Windsor Festival in 1934, made a deep impression. His madrigal, 'Long Live Victoria' (words by Sir Herbert Warren), was written for and performed at the open air aubade on the occasion of the queen's eightieth birthday in 1899, by the combined musical societies of Windsor. As a composer of church music, considered solely as the author of the impressive and dramatic setting of the 'Obiit' and its preceding hymn (words by A. C. Benson), and the music for the special service for the investiture of a knight of the Garter in St. George's chapel, revived for the investiture of Edward, Prince of Wales, in 1911, Parratt is worthy of respect.

Parratt's only serious illness, which began a few months before he died, did not interfere very materially with his conduct of the services in St. George's chapel, and he was still carrying out the duties of his position when the end came at his house in the cloisters at Windsor 27 March 1924. His ashes are buried at the foot of the stair under the shadow of the loft and the organ console on which he played for forty-two years. Of his five children, one son and four daughters, all save his eldest daughter survive him.

There are portraits of Parratt by Gerald Moira (1892) in the practice-room of Magdalen College, Oxford, and by J. S. Sargent (1914), presented to Lady Parratt by her husband's friends, and now in the possession of his daughters.

[Private information; personal knowledge.]

R. F. M. Akerman.

PATON, DIARMID NOËL (1859–1928), physiologist, was born in Edinburgh 19 March 1859, the eldest son of Sir Joseph Noël Paton, artist [q.v.], by his wife, Margaret, daughter of Alexander Ferrier, of Bloomhill, Dumbartonshire. He was educated at Edinburgh Academy and at Edinburgh University. He graduated B.Sc. in 1881 and M.B., C.M., with first class honours, in 1882, and in the same year was elected Baxter scholar in natural science.

Originally attracted to botany, Paton carried out his first research in this field. In the study of medicine, however, he found his true vocation, and, after a brief period of study in Vienna and Paris, he was awarded in 1884 a biological fellowship in the Edinburgh physiological department under Professor William Rutherford [q.v.]. Then began a steady output of research which only ended with his retirement four months before his death. In 1886 Paton was elected lecturer in physiology at Surgeons' Hall (School of Medicine of Royal Colleges, Edinburgh), and three years later (1889), was appointed superintendent of the research laboratory of the Royal College of Physicians, Edinburgh. His whole time was then devoted to teaching and research, and the output from the laboratory under his control was remarkable for its excellence and diversity. This office he vacated in 1906 for the regius professorship of physiology in Glasgow University, a post which he held until his retirement in 1928. As professor he was a stimulating teacher, a helpful colleague, and an enthusiastic researcher.

Attracted from the first by the chemical aspects of physiology, Paton was one of the earliest workers in Great Britain to take up the study of metabolism and nutrition. Some of his most original work was done in this field. Of his several dietary investigations the most outstanding was the valuable report, produced in conjunction with Dr. Leonard Findlay, on *Poverty, Nutrition and Growth*, published by the Medical Research Council (1926). He was also intensely interested in the endocrine glands, and published in 1913 a very stimulating book on the *Nervous and Chemical Regulators of Metabolism*. Interested also in heredity, he published (1926) *The Physiology of the Continuity of Life*, a book in which he vigorously attacked many of the orthodox views on the subject. In all he published some ninety papers, as well as text-books for medical and veterinary students.

Paton was appointed a member of the royal commission on salmon fisheries (1900) and of the Medical Research Council (1918–1923). Elected a fellow of the Royal Society in 1914, he was on its council from 1922 to 1924. He was also a fellow of the Royal Society of Edinburgh (1886), and a fellow of the Royal College of Physicians, Edinburgh (1886). He received an honorary LL.D. degree from Edinburgh University in 1919. He married in 1898 Agatha, daughter of Alexander Balfour, merchant, of Dawyck, Peeblesshire, and had one son and one daughter. He died at his home, Stobo, Peeblesshire, 30 September 1928.

[*Proceedings* of the Royal Society, vol. civ, B, 1929; personal knowledge.]

E. P. Cathcart.

PEAKE, ARTHUR SAMUEL (1865–1929), theologian and biblical scholar, was born at Leek, Staffordshire, 24 November 1865, the second son and third child in a family of seven of the Rev. Samuel Peake, a Primitive Methodist minister, by his wife, Rosabella Smith, the daughter of a Herefordshire farmer. In accordance with the custom of the Methodist ministry, his father moved frequently from one 'circuit' to another, and Peake was educated at various day schools, ultimately going up in 1883 with a classical scholarship from King Henry VIII grammar school, Coventry, to St. John's College, Oxford. After classical honour moderations he read for the honour school of theology, with a view to taking orders in the Church of England. He obtained a first class in 1887, and continued to reside after graduation, winning the Denyer and Johnson scholarship in 1889 and the Ellerton essay in 1890. He was not, however, ordained, but remained to the end a Methodist layman.

In 1890 Peake was elected to a theological fellowship at Merton College, a position which he held for seven years. Earlier in the same year he had begun teaching at Mansfield College, which had been established at Oxford in 1886 for the training of candidates for the ministry of the Free Churches. His work here was mainly in the field of the Old Testament, though his interest in the New Testament was probably equally great, and his distinctive contribution to biblical studies was possible only to one who was a master in both fields.

Peake's career was soon given a decisive turn by a call from his own Church. Up to this time the Primitive Methodists had been backward in providing for the theological training of their ministry. A group of reformers, with the financial backing of (Sir) William Hartley, a wealthy manufacturer of Aintree, formed a plan to turn the existing Theological Institute at Manchester, with its one-year course and antiquated methods, into a college with a full theological curriculum on modern lines. On the foundation of Hartley Primitive Methodist College at Manchester, Peake was asked to take responsibility for the curriculum, with the position of tutor in the college. After some hesitation, and against the advice of some of his friends, he accepted the post. He went to Manchester in 1892, and for the remaining thirty-seven years of his life he was identified with Hartley College. At the beginning, his theological position was looked upon with suspicion by many as being dangerously 'advanced'; but his personal qualities won confidence even where his views were disliked, and at his death he held a position of almost unique authority in his Church. The higher intellectual standard of its ministry, and the broader outlook of its members in general, were largely the result of Peake's teaching and influence.

Peake's work at Manchester was not confined to a denominational college. In 1904 it was decided to form a faculty of theology in the university of Manchester. This was the first theological faculty to be established in any of the modern, 'secular' universities, and had from the outset an interdenominational character. Peake took a leading part in working out the scheme, and when the faculty was set up, he became the first occupant of the Rylands chair of biblical criticism and exegesis, while retaining his appointment at Hartley College.

In addition to his strictly academic work, Peake rendered important service on the council of the John Rylands Library from its foundation in 1899 to his death as chairman of the council. He edited the *Holborn Review* from 1919 until his death. He took an active part in the ecclesiastical affairs of his own Church, and of the Free Churches in general, and was a leader in the movement for reunion, both among the Methodist bodies and beyond them. His numerous activities were carried out under the handicap of uncertain health, and the amount which he accomplished was astonishing to those who knew him.

Peake's knowledge of current literature, both native and foreign, in the field of biblical studies, was as nearly exhaustive as one man's knowledge can be. His original contributions to biblical learning were marked by accurate scholarship and a severe and balanced judgement, leaning to the side of caution in critical questions. But the works of scholarship on a large scale which he was known to have had in hand for many years remained as fragments on his premature death. His distinctive achievement lay in the diffusion of the methods and results of sound biblical learning. Such books as *The Bible: Its Origin, its Significance, and its Abiding Worth* (1913), and *The Problem of Suffering in the Old Testament* (1904), together with a *Commentary on the Bible* (1919) which he planned and edited, have had a wide circulation and very great influence. He helped a generation of Christian laity, brought up in the older tradition, to make the difficult transition to a modern outlook without loss of balance, and his work did much to save the Free Churches of Great Britain from the baneful effects of 'Fundamentalist' controversies.

Peake married in 1892 Harriet Mary, daughter of John Sillman, of Oxford, who survived him together with their three sons. He received the honorary degree of D.D. from the university of Aberdeen in 1907, and from the university of Oxford in 1920. He died at Manchester 19 August 1929.

[*The Times*, 20 August 1929; L. S. Peake, *Arthur Samuel Peake: A Memoir*, 1930; personal knowledge.]

C. H. Dodd.

PEARCE, ERNEST HAROLD (1865–1930), bishop of Worcester, the eldest son of James Pearce, was born 23 July 1865 at 48 Great Marlborough Street, London, which then housed the West branch of the Young Men's Christian Association, of which his father was the secretary. His mother, Jane Courtenay, was the eldest daughter of Walter Edmonds, of Penzance, and sister of the Rev. Walter John Edmonds, chancellor of Exeter Cathedral. A severe attack of rheumatic fever at the age of seven seriously affected Pearce's heart and conditioned his habits throughout his life, so that he was always aware of the possibility of a sudden end, which ultimately came.

In 1874, on the presentation of the banker F. A. Bevan, Pearce was admitted to Christ's Hospital, and thus began his connexion with that foundation which was, in one form or another, to last all his life: he was exhibitioner, assistant master, governor, almoner, chairman of the education committee, and vice-chairman of the council of almoners. He also became its historian in *The Annals of Christ's Hospital* (1901, 2nd ed. 1908). In 1884 Pearce, who was a Grecian at Christ's Hospital, entered Peterhouse, Cambridge, as a classical scholar and choral exhibitioner, and obtained second classes in the first division of the classical tripos (1887) and in the second part of the theological tripos (1888), graduating B.A. in 1887 and M.A. in 1891. He was ordained deacon in 1889 and priest in 1890 by Archbishop Benson, his title to orders being an assistant-mastership at the South Eastern College (now St. Lawrence College), Ramsgate. In 1891 he returned to Christ's Hospital as an assistant master, but in 1892 accepted the post of metropolitan district secretary of the British and Foreign Bible Society, of which he ultimately became a life governor and vice-president (1914).

In 1895 there occurred a vacancy in the living of Christ Church, Newgate Street (held in conjunction with that of St. Leonard, Foster Lane), where the boys of Christ's Hospital attended the Sunday morning service; and the patrons for that turn, the governors of St. Bartholomew's Hospital, appointed Pearce to fill it. He soon re-seated the church and brought the boys down from uncomfortable galleries to the floor of the building. Pearce's appointment to the living led to his becoming chaplain in 1896–1897 to the lord mayor of London, Sir George Faudel-Phillips, the alderman of his ward, and to a close connexion for many years with the Mansion House and the life of the City. His life while he held his City living (that is, until 1912) was full of activities of all kinds: he became a freeman on the roll of the Musicians' Company and served as its chaplain; he was professor of biblical history at Queen's College, Harley Street (1899–1905); for four years he was secretary of the London Diocesan Church Reading Union; he was elected on to the court of Sion College, became treasurer and president, and in 1913 published its history, *Sion College and Library*; he was a member of the court of assistants of the Corporation of the Sons of the Clergy, was twenty-nine times a steward of its festival, and for ten years a treasurer, and wrote an account of the charity, *The Sons of the Clergy* (1904, 2nd ed. 1928).

In 1899 Pearce joined the staff of *The Times* as its ecclesiastical correspondent and was in Printing House Square every night, except Saturday, in order to write up the news and to provide obituaries. Newspapers usually keep a 'graveyard' in stock, but from time to time a gap has suddenly to be filled; on one occasion the obituary notice of a very eminent scientist had to be compiled on a Sunday night by the joint efforts of the ecclesiastical and military correspondents. Pearce's facility of composition and sound common sense soon led to leader-writing as well. About this time he came into close contact with the prime minister's office and became an unofficial adviser in the allocation of ecclesiastical patronage. Since he possessed the gift of knowing men and of holding his tongue, he was passed on from one prime minister to another, and was still 'looking in at Downing Street' to the day of his death.

In 1911 Pearce was appointed by Mr. Asquith to a canonry at Westminster Abbey, for, in addition to his work for the prime minister's office, he was becoming known as a thoughtful and acceptable preacher, and Bishop Ryle, as dean of Westminster, had suggested his name for the post. At Westminster Pearce became in due course treasurer (1912–1916), archdeacon (1916–1918), and sub-dean (1918–1919). Whatever position he held, he at once wanted to research into its history: Christ's Hospital, Sion College, the Sons of the Clergy, had given him the opportunity. At Westminster much investigation had been carried out by Dean Armitage Robinson and his predecessors; but Pearce spent a large amount of time in the muniment room and produced a work of great importance for ecclesiastical and monastic history in *The Monks of Westminster: being a Register of the Brethren of the Convent from the time of the Confessor to the Dissolution* (1916). He also produced *William de Colchester, Abbot of Westminster* (1915), and *Walter de Wenlok, Abbot of Westminster* (1920). By this original research he qualified for the Cambridge degrees of Litt.D. (1917), B.D. (1920), and D.D. (1924).

In the course of the European War Pearce's activities were strangely diverted into quite a different channel. During his time at Cambridge he had served in the Volunteers, and in the City he had been chaplain to the 8th battalion, London Regiment (Post Office Rifles), and had gained the Territorial decoration. The chaplains' department of the War Office, sufficient for peace time, was in need of assistance to deal with the new situation created by the War. Pearce was appointed assistant chaplain-general (1915–1919), with the substantive rank of brigadier, and greatly helped to secure the smoother and more orderly working of the department. He was a chaplain to King George V in 1918 and 1919, and in 1919, at the close of the War, received the C.B.E.

In 1919 Pearce was nominated by Mr. Lloyd George to the bishopric of Worcester, and was consecrated in Westminster Abbey 24 February. It was something of an experiment to send a Londoner born and bred to a rural diocese, with Hartlebury Castle as his residence; but Pearce's country clergy soon got to know and to respect him. London was still the scene of part of his labours; for, as a director of the London Life Association, which had incorporated the Clergy Mutual Office, he was there every week and was thus able to keep up his regular attendances at the board meetings of Christ's Hospital, the Ecclesiastical Commission, Queen Anne's Bounty, and other bodies where his capacity for business was valued. But Hartlebury Castle was his home; and, *more suo*, he wrote a book about it, *Hartlebury Castle* (1926). His antiquarian interests (he was elected F.S.A. in 1918) led him to work upon the Worcester Cathedral muniments and to edit for the Worcestershire Historical Society *The Register of Thomas de Cobham, 1317–1327* (1930); on his knowledge of the Register he had already published a life of *Thomas de Cobham, Bishop of Worcester* (1923).

In the controversies over the Prayer Book (1927–1928) Pearce always took the conservative side, and he spoke and voted in the House of Lords against the approval of the 'Deposited Book'. But this attitude did not in any way affect the regard of the Worcestershire people for him; they had found him to be a just and generous ruler of his diocese.

Pearce's own college, Peterhouse, elected him an honorary fellow in 1919 and, on his incorporating at Oxford and proceeding to the degree of D.Litt. in 1929, Worcester College, Oxford, paid him the like honour. Among his writings not previously mentioned are *The Book of God's Kingdom* (1902), *English Christianity in its Beginnings* (1908), *The Laws of the Earliest Gospel* (1913), and a posthumous work, *The Correspondence of Richard Hurd and William Mason*, completed and edited by Leonard Whibley (1930).

Pearce died suddenly, within the precincts of Westminster, while on his way to attend the opening of parliament 28 October 1930; his ashes are buried in Worcester Cathedral at the foot of the monument of Bishop Hurd. He was unmarried.

There is a portrait of Pearce by Solomon J. Solomon at Hartlebury Castle, and another by A. Hyndman hangs in the hall of Christ's Hospital, Horsham; there is also a memorial tablet to him in the cloisters of the Hospital.

[Personal knowledge.] E. C. Pearce.

PEARSON, WEETMAN DICKINSON, first Viscount Cowdray (1856–1927), contractor, was born at Shelley Woodhouse, Yorkshire, 15 July 1856, the eldest son of George Pearson, of Brickendonbury, near Hertford, by his wife, Sarah, daughter of Weetman Dickinson, of High Hoyland, Yorkshire. He was educated privately at Harrogate. His grandfather, Samuel Pearson, had founded a firm of contractors, and of this firm Weetman Pearson, after serving a short apprenticeship, became a partner in 1875, at the early age of nineteen. When he joined, the head-quarters of the business were at Bradford, and its operations were carried out chiefly in the North of England. The firm was suffering at the time from the high price of coal, and the moment was favourable for new developments. Young Pearson decided to extend its sphere of activity by finding openings abroad, and he visited both Spain and the United States, where contracts of all kinds were undertaken. These brought prosperity to the company, and in 1884 the head offices were moved from Bradford to London.

In 1889 Pearson went to Mexico, and there established for his firm a valuable business connexion. The first contract which he secured was for a big drainage scheme; this was followed by contracts for railways, electric lines, harbours, and waterworks. In the course of these operations he acquired extensive tracts of land rich in oil. Pearson's position in Mexico was for some time one of predominant authority, although he had not the field to himself. Subsidiary branches of the American Standard Oil Company were already at work there, and the struggle between contending interests was carried on vigorously and not without exciting episodes. In July 1908 the Dos Bocas well, the largest oil gush on record, was opened by Pearson, and burst forth in overwhelming volume. Unfortunately for the contractors, the column of oil caught fire, and the crater, flaming up to an immense height, burned for weeks, an accident which caused heavy loss. Another well, the Polvero, yielded a hundred thousand barrels of oil a day. Pearson was the first to fill oil-tankers at sea through pipes. After the European War he relinquished his controlling interests in the Mexican oil-fields to the Royal Dutch Shell group.

Apart from their special connexion with Mexico, Pearson and his firm carried out, as contractors, works of great importance in many parts of the world. In 1894 they completed the Blackwall tunnel under the Thames, and at the opening ceremony Pearson was created a baronet. They extended Dover harbour, a difficult task which occupied many years, as the requirements of the Admiralty were eventually included in the original scheme. In America they constructed four tunnels under the East River for the Pennsylvania railway. One of the greatest of their contracts was for the building of the dam across the Blue Nile above Khartoum: this dam was inaugurated in 1926.

Pearson made his first attempt to enter political life in 1892, when he stood for Colchester in the liberal interest and was defeated. But he won that seat at the general election of 1895, and held it for fifteen years. He was raised to the peerage in 1910 as Baron Cowdray, of Midhurst, Sussex. During the War he supervised the construction of an important munition factory at Gretna Green, and early in 1917 he was invited to become president of the Air Board. His duty was to consider how the air forces could be brought harmoniously under a single ministry, and how the supply of aircraft could be increased. When his work came to an end in the following November, he was able to point to a considerable increase in the effective air forces of the country.

After the War Lord Cowdray made occasional appearances upon political platforms, and took some part in the discussion of current questions. But in public life generally he was little known, although his business ability was recognized by those who came in contact with him. A point of some interest in his career is the fact that his earliest business triumphs were gained when he was a boy, with hardly any education or technical training. In later life he used to emphasize the necessity of a contractor having an expert's knowledge of every detail of the work which he undertook, a praiseworthy maxim to which he himself had proved a striking exception.

Lord Cowdray's gifts to public objects were numerous and often substantial. He maintained his interest in the Air Force, contributing in 1918 the sum of £100,000 for the endowment of the Royal Air Force Club, and at a later date another large sum to the Force's memorial fund. Aberdeen in particular was indebted to him and Lady Cowdray for many benefactions. The Cowdray memorial hall bears his name, while the university, of which he was rector from 1918 to 1921, the hospitals, and other institutions of the city owed much to his support. He owned extensive estates in Aberdeenshire and Kincardineshire, and took trouble to improve the conditions of those living on his property.

Lord Cowdray was promoted to a viscounty in 1917, and was created G.C.V.O. in 1925. He died at Dunecht House, Aberdeenshire (formerly the property of the Earls of Crawford), 1 May 1927. He married in 1881 Annie, daughter of Sir John Cass, of Bradford, Yorkshire, and had three sons, the youngest of whom was killed in action, and one daughter. He was succeeded as second viscount by his eldest son, Weetman Harold Miller (born 1882).

[*The Times*, 2 May 1927.] A. Cochrane.

PEASE, Sir ARTHUR FRANCIS, first baronet, of Hummersknott (1866–1927), coalowner and industrialist, was born at Hummersknott, Darlington, 11

March 1866, the eldest son of Arthur Pease, M.P. for Whitby 1880–1885 and for Darlington 1895–1898, by his wife, Mary Lecky, daughter of Ebenezer Pike, of Bessborough, co. Cork. He came of a quaker family which had long been associated with industrial development in Durham and Yorkshire. He was great-grandson of Edward Pease [q.v.], railway projector, grandson of Joseph Pease [q.v.], also a railway projector, and the first quaker to sit in parliament, and nephew of Sir Joseph Whitwell Pease [q.v.], first baronet of Hutton Lowcross and Pinchinthorpe, who for nearly forty years represented a Durham constituency in the House of Commons. Pease was educated at Brighton College and Trinity College, Cambridge, and received a business training in the offices at Darlington of Pease and Partners. In 1906 he became chairman and managing director of that company. In course of time Pease became associated as chairman or director with numerous coal-mining and other industrial undertakings in the north of England: he was also a director of Lloyds Bank and of the London and North-Eastern Railway Company.

Pease became known to the public as a prominent negotiator when an organized demand arose among miners for a minimum wage. He was one of three representatives of the Durham owners who served on the committee of coalowners which was appointed in 1912 to meet the government and the Miners' Federation. Subsequently, when the Joint District Board for Durham was set up under the Minimum Wage Act of 1912, he was called upon to state the case for the owners. On the outbreak of the European War in 1914, Pease's great experience of industrial affairs was at once available for the government, and during the years 1914–1921 he was an active member of many government committees. He held office as second civil lord of the Admiralty in 1918–1919, and was created a baronet in 1920.

Although Pease did not originate any definite policy in relation to the coal-mining industry of Great Britain, yet his intimate knowledge of that industry, his powers of conciliatory exposition, and his personal popularity even among those to whom his views were unacceptable, combined to make him an acknowledged leader and the chosen spokesman of a large section of the coal-mining community. He was one of the leaders of British industry from whom successive administrations sought and received expert advice and service during the many and great emergencies in the European War.

Pease devoted much time to the affairs of his native county. He was elected chairman of the Durham county council in 1922 and took an especial interest in education. He was a J.P. and deputy-lieutenant for the county of Durham, and in 1920 he served as high sheriff. During the European War he assisted in the raising of the 18th battalion of the Durham Light Infantry. Preoccupation with business affairs prevented Pease from seeking election to the House of Commons, but his strong political sympathies induced him to act as president of the Durham Unionist Association from the time of its formation in 1910. He was devoted to all forms of sport and was a regular follower of the Zetland hounds. On 23 November 1927 Pease, whose health had become precarious as a result of overwork, was seized with sudden illness at a meeting of directors, and on the same day he died at his home, Middleton Lodge, near Darlington.

Pease married in 1889 Laura Matilda Ethelwyn, daughter of Charles Peter Allix, of Swaffham Prior House, Cambridgeshire. She survived him with one son, Richard Arthur (born 1890), who succeeded his father as second baronet, and three daughters.

[*The Times*, 24 November 1927; *Darlington and Stockton Times*, 26 November 1927; private information.] A. E. WATKIN.

PENTLAND, first BARON (1860–1925), politician. [See SINCLAIR, JOHN.]

PERCY, ALAN IAN, eighth DUKE OF NORTHUMBERLAND (1880–1930), was born in London 17 April 1880, the fourth of the seven sons of Henry George Percy, Earl Percy, afterwards seventh Duke of Northumberland, by his wife, Lady Edith, eldest daughter of George Douglas Campbell, eighth Duke of Argyll, and sister of John Douglas Sutherland Campbell [q.v.], ninth Duke of Argyll. The second and third sons died young, and on the death of the eldest son, Henry Algernon George Percy, Earl Percy [q.v.], in 1909, Lord Alan Percy became heir to the dukedom as Earl Percy, and held the courtesy title for nine years. He was educated at Eton and at Christ Church, Oxford (1897–1899), and joined the Grenadier Guards in January 1900. He served in the South African

War from 1901 to 1902, and with the Egyptian army from 1907 to 1910, retiring from the army with the rank of major in 1912. On the outbreak of the European War he rejoined his regiment, and served in France as one of the official 'eye-witnesses' from 1914 to 1916. Subsequently he was appointed to the general staff (Intelligence department) at the War Office, being promoted temporary lieutenant-colonel in 1916, and brevet lieutenant-colonel two years later.

After his succession to the title in 1918 the duke played a prominent part in public life. He was lord-lieutenant of the county of Northumberland, president of the Territorial Army Association, and an alderman of the Northumberland county council. He became president of the Royal Institution in 1919 and chancellor of Durham University in 1929, and was still holding those offices at the time of his death.

Politically the duke was a conservative, belonging to the extreme right wing of the party and often at variance with the policy of its leaders after the War. But the sincerity and fearlessness with which he expressed his views gained him universal respect, even his political opponents recognizing his integrity of purpose and intense faith in the ideals which he had at heart. He was a gifted speaker and writer, and a skilful debater, who always showed complete mastery of his subject. His political and military essays and articles, notably *The Writing on the Wall*, published under the pseudonym of 'Daniel' in 1911, conveyed a warning from the events of that year; and articles on the military weakness of Great Britain and the inadequacy of the proposed British Expeditionary Force, written in 1913, expressed his point of view in a clear and concise manner and are remarkable for their accurate knowledge and logical deduction. His two short stories, *The Shadow on the Moor* and *La Salamandre, the Story of a Vivandière*, published after his death in 1931 and 1934 respectively, show that he also possessed a real power of dramatic description.

In his younger days the Duke of Northumberland was conspicuous for his love of adventure and light-heartedness, but as he grew older he became far more serious-minded, and his deep-rooted religious and political convictions sometimes seemed to weigh unduly on his spirits. His patriotism and faith in the historic traditions of his country were such that he could never reconcile himself to any course of policy which appeared to him to lower its prestige or to be out of keeping with its imperial status. To him the settlement effected in Ireland by Mr. Lloyd George's coalition government in 1922 and the opening of relations between Great Britain and the Russian Soviet government in 1924 were utterly repugnant, because he considered the former to be a surrender to lawlessness, and the latter a recognition of an intolerable and anti-Christian system of government. The word expediency did not exist in his vocabulary, and any form of compromise or surrender of principle was abhorrent to him. In a sense it was unfortunate that he was so rigid in his adherence to his particular political beliefs; for, had he been more ready to appreciate that new social and economic conditions must inevitably necessitate new policies, he might, had he lived, have played a leading part in English politics, for he had high courage, conspicuous ability, and, above all, the power of leadership.

The duke's death, which took place at his London house 23 August 1930 at the comparatively early age of fifty, was an especial loss to the north of England where, at his seat of Alnwick Castle, his kindness of heart, his keen sense of the duties of his position, and his love of sport made him popular with all sorts and conditions of men.

The Duke of Northumberland married in 1911 Lady Helen Magdalen, youngest daughter of Charles Henry Gordon-Lennox, seventh Duke of Richmond and second Duke of Gordon, and had four sons and two daughters. He was succeeded as ninth duke by his eldest son, Henry George Alan (born 1912).

[*The Times*, 25 August 1930; privately printed biography of the Duke of Northumberland by his wife.] C. M. Headlam.

PEREIRA, GEORGE EDWARD (1865–1923), soldier and traveller, was born in London 26 January 1865, the eldest son of Edward Pereira, of 23 Grosvenor Square, by his wife, the Hon. Margaret Anne Stonor, eighth daughter of Thomas Stonor, third Baron Camoys. Educated at the Oratory School, Edgbaston, under Cardinal Newman, where he showed a characteristic determination to succeed, Pereira joined the Grenadier Guards in 1884. A hunting accident that winter left him with a permanent limp, and threatened to impede the fulfilment of the two great ambitions of his life—to see active service and to win fame as an explorer; but in the event he achieved both.

From 1884 to 1899 Pereira served at home. In the latter year he was seconded for service with the Chinese regiment recently formed at Wei-hai-wei. He took part in 1900 in the fighting at Tientsin and in the relief of the legations at Peking, and was slightly wounded. He was awarded the D.S.O. After a year spent in touring the provinces of North-East China, he rejoined his battalion in South Africa in 1902 towards the close of the Boer War.

In January 1904 Pereira was appointed a temporary military attaché to the British minister at Seoul in Korea, and on 11 February, from aboard H.M.S. *Talbot*, he saw the Japanese fleet attack and sink two Russian ships, the *Varyak* and the *Koreetz*, which were sheltering at Chemulpo. In 1905, as military attaché with the Japanese army, he witnessed the Manchurian campaign, and at its close became military attaché at Peking. He spent the following years mainly in making a series of long journeys in every part of China. He remained attaché at Peking until 1910. Being at home on the outbreak of the European War in 1914, Pereira immediately rejoined the service, first serving on the staff of the 47th London division, and in June 1915 taking over command of the 4th Royal Welch Fusiliers, the pioneer battalion of the 1st division. From January 1916 until November 1917 he commanded the 47th brigade of the 16th division. He always won the absolute confidence of the troops under his command by his complete disregard of danger. He retired at the end of the War with the rank of brigadier-general.

Since the two French Lazarist missionaries, Évariste Huc and Joseph Gabet, had visited Lhasa in 1846, seventy-six years previously, all attempts by European travellers to reach that city from the east had been frustrated by the Tibetan authorities. Pereira had long desired to accomplish this journey, and after the end of the War, although over fifty-four years of age, lame, and in indifferent health, he set out. Leaving Peking in January 1921 he crossed the famine-stricken provinces of Chihli, Western Shensi, and Honan. He went to Honan Fu (Loyang) at the invitation of General Wu-pei-fu in order to visit his model army and establishments. From the end of July to October Pereira undertook three most arduous shooting-trips in the wild mountainous district of Muping in Szechwan in the hope of shooting a giant pandar, a rare animal that no European had ever shot. He failed to get one, but secured a pandar cat, equally rare in China, which is now in the Natural History Museum at South Kensington. After this he was laid up, suffering from frost-bitten feet. Leaving Tangar in Kansu in May 1922, Pereira reached Jyekundo on 23 June, after crossing an area devoid of food, with very little grazing, and waterless in places. During this journey he lost most of his transport animals, but was fortunate in procuring assistance from passing caravans. Chamdo was reached on 28 July after eighteen days of difficult travelling. On 3 September he received the anxiously awaited permission to proceed to Lhasa. The next six weeks were spent in a succession of journeys following valleys and crossing numerous passes, varying in height from 14,500 to 16,800 feet, scrambling over tracks covered with large boulders where the height above sea-level made every step an exertion. Pereira arrived at Lhasa on 17 October, completely exhausted by hardships and suffering from thrombosis. There he was comfortably housed by the Tibetan commander-in-chief, and he had an interview with the Dalai Lama. He reached Calcutta early in December, and went to hospital to be treated for thrombosis. Since leaving Peking he had travelled nearly 7,000 miles, more than half of them on foot.

In January 1923 Pereira left Calcutta on his last journey, in order to explore the wild Tibetan–Szechwan border; but after covering 4,000 miles he died at Kanze, in Szechwan, about thirty miles from the Tibetan border, 20 October 1923. It is known that, had he lived, he would have been recommended for the award of the gold medal of the Royal Geographical Society.

Pereira's journeys on foot in China covered almost 45,000 miles. He could never have ventured upon such travels had he not possessed a knowledge of Chinese which made him independent of interpreters, a familiarity with Chinese etiquette which saved him from imposition, and a personal liking for the Chinese, among whom he numbered many friends; but without his iron will and indifference to danger, discomfort, and fatigue he could assuredly never have accomplished them. He carried out much important survey work, and his reports and new maps were of great value to the British government.

Pereira was made C.M.G. in 1905 and C.B. in 1917. He was unmarried.

[Personal knowledge.] C. E. Pereira.

PERKIN, WILLIAM HENRY (1860–1929), organic chemist, born at Sudbury, Middlesex, 17 June 1860, was the elder son of the chemist (Sir) William Henry Perkin [q.v.], by his first wife, Jemima Harriet (died 1862), youngest daughter of John Lissett, who was of Huguenot descent. From 1870 to 1877 he attended the City of London School where, according to Sir Walter A. Raleigh (in the School magazine), 'two boys fought with an abandon and a fury that I have never seen surpassed at the business of taking and rescuing prisoners. They were a West Indian . . . and W. H. Perkin, now my colleague at Oxford.' At school Perkin concentrated so fully on mathematics to the detriment of the classics that he failed to pass the matriculation examination of London University.

Perkin's early years were passed in the most favourable environment possible, for his father maintained a private laboratory and allowed his sons, William and Arthur, to assist him in experimental work while refraining from any attempt to give them systematic instruction. The whole atmosphere of the home was one of devotion to the cause of the advance of chemical science. The most important recreation was music; all the members of the family had executive ability, in several cases far above the average, and an effective orchestra of eight or ten players practised weekly and occasionally gave concerts. This interest remained lifelong with Perkin; at first a pianist, he then took to the violin, and used a fine Joseph Guarnerius, the property of his uncle, Thomas D. Perkin. Later, on going to Germany, he found that ordinary violins were unsatisfying, and he returned to the pianoforte. Perkin was ever hospitable, and later in his life the chamber music concerts held at his house, in which distinguished musicians frequently participated, were memorable occasions.

In 1877 Perkin entered the Royal College of Chemistry at South Kensington, and studied under Professor (afterwards Sir) Edward Frankland [q.v.] and Dr. W. R. E. Hodgkinson. Mr. A. J. Greenaway, who was one of the demonstrators, has testified that Perkin's special aptitude for practical chemistry was the astonishment of his teachers and that his organic preparations were marvels of purity and yield. After some hesitations on the part of his father, who as an evangelical churchman regarded Germany as a dangerous centre of free thought, Perkin proceeded in 1880 to Würzburg, where he studied under Professor Johannes Wislicenus, a great chemist and a great leader. Two years later Perkin migrated to Munich, where he found his real scientific hero in the person of Adolf von Baeyer. It was not entirely a question of the influence of a senior on a junior, although Perkin regarded himself as the pupil, almost the disciple, of Baeyer. Much that Perkin has written of Baeyer is equally true of himself, as for instance in the Baeyer memorial lecture delivered before the Chemical Society in 1923: 'It was only necessary for the commanding figure of Baeyer to stroll through the research laboratories every day, and for him to chat with the various workers, criticize their results, and admire their preparations, to make it out of the question for any one to forget for a moment that research was the only thing that really mattered.' And so, in the company of a famous galaxy of organic chemists—Philip Otto Fischer, Wilhelm Koenigs, Theodor Curtius, Hans von Pechmann, Eugen Bamberger, Paul Friedländer, and others—Perkin untiringly gathered material for his systematic building. As a *Privatdozent* in the department of chemistry at Munich University from 1883 and later as a private assistant of Baeyer, he took part in many of the latter's original studies, including the classical work on the polyacetylenes, and outside the laboratory entered into all the normal activities of German students in a large university city.

In 1887 Perkin was appointed professor of chemistry at the Heriot-Watt College, Edinburgh, and on the last day of that year married Mina, eldest daughter of William Thomas Holland, of Bridgwater, who survived him and whose charm and graciousness made as strong an impression as Perkin's power and geniality. They had no children. Elected a fellow of the Royal Society in 1890, he succeeded Carl Schorlemmer [q.v.] as professor of organic chemistry at Owens College, Manchester, in 1892. His colleague on the side of inorganic chemistry was H. B. Dixon, whom he first met on the occasion of the visit of the British Association to Canada in 1884.

This step was destined to have important consequences, not only for Perkin, but also for the future of chemistry in Great Britain. The opportunity was presented of organizing a school of organic chemical research and Perkin took full advantage of it, first, in prosecuting analytic and synthetic investigations with unflagging zeal; secondly, in directing and encouraging the work of others; and thirdly, in providing the necessary facilities. A man of considerable administrative ability, he understood exactly how to advance the case for expansion, with the result that he was able to supervise the construction of fine laboratories first in Manchester and later in Oxford. It is credibly stated that Perkin was once invited by the curators of the university chest at Oxford to offer an explanation of the overspending of his grant, and that the result of the interview was that the curators were induced to part with a considerable further sum.

Perkin's first pupil was Frederic Stanley Kipping, who studied under him at Munich and was his assistant at Edinburgh. Kipping collaborated with Perkin in writing three books: *A Course of Practical Chemistry* (1890), *Organic Chemistry* (1894–1895), and *Inorganic Chemistry* (1909, 1911). He married Perkin's sister-in-law and later became a notable investigator and professor of chemistry at University College, Nottingham. At Manchester Perkin trained a succession of distinguished organic chemists, who have occupied more than twenty chairs in the universities of Great Britain and of the British Empire.

In 1912 Perkin accepted the offer of the Waynflete professorship of chemistry at Oxford University. A new laboratory was erected in the museum area with a frontage to South Parks Road in 1915. A substantial part of the cost was borne by the university, but the completion of the building and the endowment were rendered possible by the munificence of Mr. Charles William Dyson Perrins, whose father, Mr. J. D. Perrins, had carried out early work on the derivatives of berberine. Perkin's studies of berberine were initiated in Edinburgh and completed in the Dyson Perrins laboratory. The work which Perkin did in Oxford is second in importance only to that of his Manchester period; he established a strong school of original research, trained pupils who have done the same elsewhere, and brought about a minor revolution in the attitude of Oxford to chemistry. As Waynflete professor he was a fellow of Magdalen and greatly appreciated his connexion with the college, to which he left, as a reversionary bequest and to found research scholarships, the larger part of his fortune.

As a teacher Perkin was the personification of lucidity; his success was partly due to clear thinking and direct expression, and partly to the atmosphere which he created. The audiences which listened to his lectures felt that the subject was being developed then and there. 'Pa Perkin' was indeed beloved of his students, who respected his achievements, admired his great experimental skill, and had confidence in his fairness and in his judgement. He had many personal friends and was regarded for a generation as the first organic chemist of his country and one of the outstanding scientific figures of his age. After music, his chief recreation was gardening; he was very successful at Oxford in the culture of roses, delphiniums, and carnations. He enjoyed travel, particularly in the Alps and Dolomites, a visit to which was often combined with a call on Baeyer in Munich.

When Perkin died at Oxford 17 September 1929 after a visit to Switzerland, it was generally recognized that something more than the usual obituary was called for, and a memorial notice of 138 pages was published by the Chemical Society as a separate issue. Only a very brief summary of his work can be attempted here. Perkin was not regarded as a great theoretician, but his practical skill at the bench amounted to genius. In Munich he began a long series of researches on the formation of rings of carbon atoms; this was pioneering work of the first order, and it would be hard to overstate its importance. He made rings of three, four, five, six, and seven carbon atoms and emerged triumphant from a controversy in regard to the three and four rings; even the acute and brilliant Victor Meyer did not at first credit the possibility of their existence. At Edinburgh Perkin attacked an entirely different problem, that of the molecular structure of the yellow plant-base, berberine. This interest in complex alkaloids continued to the end; he synthesized many of them and threw light on the intricate transformations of strychnine. In this field he was not alone, but practically the whole of our knowledge of cryptopine and protopine is due to Perkin's single-handed efforts. At Manchester he made his renowned syntheses of camphoric acid, limonene, sylvestrene, terpineol, and other members of the terpene group of constituents of essential oils. He also placed the chemistry of brazilin and haematoxylin on a firm basis, discovering in these substances a protean character rivalling that of camphor. The periods of research overlapped, and there are very many significant discoveries which cannot be placed in the above-mentioned categories. Unquestionably Perkin's scientific interests were narrow, but this constitutes no valid criticism of his pre-eminence as an organic chemist. Hardly anything he did was superfluous; his results have stood the tests of time and repetition.

In addition to his purely scientific work Perkin had many contacts with industry. As befitted the son of the discoverer of 'mauve', he made valuable contributions to the establishment of the manufacture of dyes in Great Britain both in his laboratory work and in an administrative capacity.

Perkin received many academic honours. He was awarded the Longstaff medal of the Chemical Society (1900), and the Davy and Royal medals of the Royal Society (1904 and 1925). Honorary degrees of the universities of Cambridge (1910), Edinburgh (1910), St. Andrews (1911), and others were conferred upon him, and he received corresponding or foreign membership of scientific academies of Bavaria, Göttingen, Edinburgh, Washington, Belgium, and Sweden, and of the Institute of France. He was the president of Section B of the British Association in 1900 and of the Chemical Society in 1913–1915.

Many interesting photographs of Perkin are accessible, and some of these formed the basis of the bronze plaques which were presented by his colleagues and pupils to the Chemical Society and to the universities of Oxford and Manchester. Two of these mementoes (by E. G. Gillick) adorn the walls of laboratories which owe their existence largely to him and in which he laboured to such good purpose.

[*The Times*, 18 September 1929; A. J. Greenaway, J. F. Thorpe, and R. Robinson, *Life and Work of W. H. Perkin*, Chemical Society, 1932 (containing an account of Perkin's scientific work embodied in over 275 original memoirs); personal knowledge.]

R. Robinson.

PETTY-FITZMAURICE, HENRY CHARLES KEITH, fifth Marquess of Lansdowne (1845–1927), was born at Lansdowne House, Berkeley Square, 14 January 1845, the elder son of Henry Thomas, fourth Marquess of Lansdowne [q.v.], by his second wife, Emily Jane Mercer Elphinstone de Flahault, Baroness Nairne, daughter of the Comte de Flahault and the Baroness Keith and Nairne. During the lifetime of his grandfather, the third marquess, he was known as Viscount Clanmaurice and his father as Earl of Shelburne—the latter title having been called into use when Henry Fitzmaurice, by the death of his elder brother, William, Earl of Kerry, became heir to the Lansdowne estates. The Kerry title has, however, since been resumed by the eldest son, and was borne by the fifth marquess during the three years (1863–1866) in which his father held the marquessate.

From 1855 to 1858 Clanmaurice was educated at a private school at Woodcote, near Reading, kept by the Rev. P. H. Nind, vicar of South Stoke with Woodcote. From there, at the age of thirteen, he went to Eton, where, with several boys who remained his friends in after years, he 'boarded' at the house of the Rev. Augustus Birch. Towards the end of his Eton career he was 'fag master' to Arthur James Balfour, who was some three years his junior. As a 'wet bob' Clanmaurice rowed for two years in the 'boats'; in the field of scholarship he showed no marked pre-eminence, although his masters appear to have had a high opinion of his abilities. It was at his tutor's suggestion that, in order to be suitably prepared for Oxford, he was removed from Eton and its distractions in his final year. The Rev. Lewis Campbell [q.v.], the collaborator of Jowett in his edition of Plato's *Republic*, and at that time vicar of Milford in Hampshire, was the coach chosen. It was through Campbell's influence that Lord Kerry, as he now was, proceeded to Balliol College, Oxford, instead of to Christ Church, and that Jowett eventually became his tutor. Though not yet master, Jowett was already a leading figure at Balliol, and Kerry was one of those pupils on whom, foreseeing future possibilities, he delighted to use his influence. His debt to Jowett was freely acknowledged by Lansdowne in after years. At the moment, however, Kerry somewhat neglected his work in favour of the lighter side of Oxford life: the river, the drag, and the society of friends all claimed their share of his time. He obtained a second class in classical moderations in 1865, and, in spite of a serious effort in his last year to retrieve the situation, disappointed expectations by leaving Oxford in 1867 with only a second class in *literae humaniores*. His father had died suddenly in 1866, and he thus found himself at the age of twenty-one a member of the House of Lords and one of the largest landowners in the country.

It would seem that at this period Lansdowne had displayed no marked political ambitions. Interested in agriculture and forestry, a keen rider to hounds, a good shot, and an expert angler, he found plenty of occupation, and had it not been for Jowett he might have rested content with the life of a country gentleman. As the representative of a family with Whig traditions of long standing he was, however, soon called upon to take his part in public affairs, and his response was such that for the remainder of his active life he was seldom free from political or administrative responsibility.

Lansdowne's public career may be conveniently divided into four periods. First (1868–1883), when as a liberal he held minor posts in two Gladstonian administrations and acted with his party in opposition to Lord Beaconsfield's government of 1874 to 1880; secondly (1883–1894), as governor-general of Canada and viceroy of India; thirdly (1895–1906), as secretary of state for war and foreign secretary in two consecutive unionist administrations; and fourthly (1906–1916), as leader of the conservative opposition in the House of Lords.

Owing to the liberal traditions of his family Lansdowne was not without friends in the inner councils of that party. Lord Granville had long been intimate with his family, and Lansdowne's earlier appointments were probably in part due to the influence which that statesman exerted with Mr. Gladstone. In 1869, within two years of leaving Oxford, he was appointed a junior lord of the Treasury, a post in which he acquitted himself so creditably that he was transferred in 1872, in succession to Lord Northbrook, to that of under-secretary for war. Two years later, however, Gladstone resigned, and Lansdowne, with the rest of his party, found himself in opposition.

Lansdowne married in 1869 Lady Maud Evelyn Hamilton, the youngest of the seven beautiful daughters of James, first Duke of Abercorn [q.v.], and the next six years were spent with his wife and children at his various homes—Lansdowne House in Berkeley Square, Bowood near Calne in Wiltshire, and Derreen near Kenmare in county Kerry. The last of these homes was largely Lansdowne's own creation. Although his Irish ancestry reached back to the Norman Conquest, his family had for upwards of a century been non-resident in Ireland. Derreen, commemorated by J. A. Froude in his *Fortnight in Kerry* (1869), was little more than a cottage when Lansdowne decided to make it his Irish home in 1870. In the years which followed it was enlarged, the surrounding country, then destitute of trees, was planted, and under Lansdowne's personal supervision gardens were laid out and filled with the sub-tropical vegetation which now constitutes their great attraction. The love of this Irish home was one of the dominant features of Lansdowne's life, and its destruction in 1922 was to him a devastating blow.

On the return of the liberals to power in 1880, Lansdowne was appointed under-secretary of state for India. Gladstone was now developing his new Irish policy, and although Home Rule was still distant, Lansdowne, as an Irish landlord, at once found himself out of sympathy with the legislation of his chief. Matters came to a head over the Compensation for Disturbance Bill, which Lansdowne, having first resigned his office, effectively opposed in the House of Lords (3 August 1880). Although he continued thereafter to give general support to his party, he now found himself a target for radical and nationalist attacks. He was assailed in the newspapers by Mr. Charles Russell (afterwards Lord Russell of Killowen, q.v.) in respect of the management of his Kerry estates, but he successfully replied to the charges brought against him. Later on he became the object of one of the most determined manifestations of the Land League in a 'plan of campaign' for the wholesale withholding of Irish rents at another of his estates, Luggacurran, in Queen's County. He continued none the less to spend a portion of each year at Derreen.

In the summer of 1883 Lansdowne was offered by Mr. Gladstone the governor-generalship of Canada in succession to the Marquess of Lorne. His numerous home interests made him unwilling to absent himself for five years, but he was feeling the strain of administering a large estate on an income depleted by the non-payment of Irish rents as well as by some heavy charges to which it was then subject. Financial considerations, therefore, largely determined his acceptance of this post.

Lansdowne's tenure of office in Canada

(1883–1888), broken only by a visit of a few months to England in the autumn of 1886, passed smoothly and successfully. He worked throughout in complete and friendly accord with the prime minister, Sir John Alexander Macdonald [q.v.]. The principal Canadian achievement during the period, and one which owed not a little to the backing of the governor-general, was the completion of the Canadian Pacific Railway in June 1886. Lansdowne himself had travelled over the new line to British Columbia, riding along the unfinished portion, in the previous autumn, and was greatly impressed by all he saw. Another matter of moment was the long-drawn-out dispute with the United States over the delimitation of the Newfoundland fisheries, a quarrel which more than once threatened to become acute, and was not finally settled until after his return to England. It was in this connexion that Lansdowne first met Mr. Joseph Chamberlain [q.v.], who was sent out to Canada as British commissioner in the autumn of 1887. In the summer of 1885 there took place in the North-West Provinces the second rebellion of Louis Riel [q.v.], a half-breed who had already given trouble in 1870. The rising caused much anxiety at the time, but it was successfully put down by Canadian troops with scarcely any bloodshed, Riel being sentenced to death.

A more personal incident took the form of an attack by the Irish nationalist, William O'Brien [q.v.], who came over in 1887 for the express purpose of stirring up feeling against Lansdowne in Canada. His ill success was a tribute to the popularity which the governor-general had already established, and showed that Canadians were not prepared for the importation of the Irish land-war into their country.

In January 1887 Lansdowne had been offered, and had refused, a post in Lord Salisbury's government. A year later Salisbury suggested that he should succeed Lord Dufferin as viceroy of India. This Lansdowne agreed to do, stipulating, however, that he should be allowed a few months in England between the two appointments. His Canadian governorship had thus to be cut short. He embarked for England in June 1888 and spent a short time in London, at Bowood, and at his beloved Derreen, where, in spite of all that had passed, he received an address of welcome from his tenants. He left for India in November and was sworn in at Calcutta on 10 December.

In India, Lansdowne's term of office as viceroy passed without any sensational incidents. Although the national congress was becoming increasingly active, the demand for self-government had scarcely been formulated, and the prosperity of the country, which had been steadily enhanced by the policy of railway extension and irrigation work, made its administration, in comparison with more recent times, a matter of no great difficulty or anxiety.

Lansdowne found in his council a body of singularly able men with whom he worked in complete harmony, and in the commander-in-chief, Sir Frederick (afterwards Earl) Roberts, one who became and remained through life a close personal friend. With few exceptions also he was well supported by the home government. Problems, however, arose of sufficient magnitude to become dangerous if injudiciously handled, and it must be reckoned to Lansdowne's credit that none of them were allowed to reach the acute stage. A long dispute, as to frontiers and trade, with Abdur Rahman, the ameer of Afghanistan, was after several years adjusted through the agency of Sir Henry Mortimer Durand [q.v.], who was dispatched for the purpose to Kabul in 1893. A sudden rising in 1890 in Manipur, a small native state on the borders of Burma, resulted in the murder of the British resident there and of the chief commissioner of Assam. It was quickly put down, and its instigator, a native official known as the senapati, executed; but in securing the extreme penalty for the offender the viceroy had to meet considerable opposition at home. On another matter, the Juries Bill (1893), a measure designed to remove criminal cases in some parts of Bengal from the purview of juries who were notoriously afraid to convict, Lansdowne was definitely overruled by the home government. His Indian Councils Bill, which sought to introduce for the first time the elective principle into Indian affairs, failed also in the first instance (1890) to obtain the necessary backing at home, although it was eventually placed upon the statute-book two years later in a somewhat altered form.

A very troublesome position arose during Lansdowne's term of office in connexion with the Indian currency. Owing to the depreciation of silver the exchange value of the rupee, which had been nominally two shillings, had shrunk to half that amount and remained very unstable from day to day. Remittances from the government as well as the hard-earned savings of civil servants and army officers, when sent home in terms of gold currency, were thus greatly diminished in value. After protracted and anxious consultation Lansdowne in 1893 took the drastic step—by many considered foredoomed to failure—of restricting the supply of the currency by the closing of the Indian mints to free coinage. The rupee at once gained in price and in stability, and a few years afterwards (1899) it became possible to fix its value at 1*s*. 4*d*. by legal enactment.

Some anxiety was also caused to the government of India by the anti-opium agitation which arose in England in 1892. A considerable portion of the Indian revenue had for long been derived from the growth and sale of this drug, and it was officially urged that, since it would be impossible to prevent its use, it was better that the traffic should remain in government hands rather than fall into those of private individuals by whom it would be exploited. There were some excited debates in the House of Commons, but the question was finally referred (1893) to an opium commission under the chairmanship of Lord Brassey. The commission's report went far to maintain the position of the Indian government.

As regards the social side of the viceregal office, it is enough to say that both Lord and Lady Lansdowne earned in India an exceptional measure of popularity, and left behind them many friends, Indian as well as British. Amongst numerous distinguished persons whom it fell to their lot to entertain were the Duke of Clarence, the Archduke Franz Ferdinand of Austria (who was murdered at Serajevo in 1914), and the Tsarevitch, afterwards Tsar Nicholas II.

An additional four months were added to Lansdowne's viceroyalty owing to the failure of his successor designate, Sir Henry Wylie Norman [q.v.], to take up the office. A substitute was eventually found in the person of Lord Elgin [q.v.], and Lansdowne returned to England in January 1894. In the interval which elapsed before his next appointment he was offered, but declined, the embassy at St. Petersburg. At this time he was created K.G., received an honorary D.C.L. from the university of Oxford, and was appointed lord-lieutenant of Wiltshire. By the death of his mother in 1895 he added two Scottish properties to those which he already possessed in England and in Ireland.

On the formation of Lord Salisbury's government in 1895, Lansdowne was appointed secretary of state for war, a more than usually difficult post at the moment, since it involved, not only the selection of a commander-in-chief, but the initiation of an entirely new system in the place of that which had so long centred in the person of the Duke of Cambridge. The claims of Viscount Wolseley [q.v.] to the reversion, which were backed by the new secretary of state, proved successful, and the reorganization of the office, long overdue, was then proceeded with on the lines which had been recommended by the Hartington commission of 1890. The effect of the reforms introduced in 1896 was to transfer to the secretary of state much of the administrative power previously exercised, without parliamentary control, by the commander-in-chief, though the conduct of operations in time of war remained as before in the hands of the military staff of the office. All went well at the outset, Wolseley being from the first conspicuously supported by the secretary of state, who on one occasion went so far as to threaten resignation if the commander-in-chief's demands were not complied with.

After the Jameson Raid (December 1895), war in South Africa was generally regarded as inevitable sooner or later; it was, indeed, within measurable distance about eighteen months afterwards. Not, however, until October 1899 was war finally precipitated as the result of President Kruger's famous ultimatum. An efficient and well-equipped expeditionary force was at once dispatched to the scene of action, under Sir Redvers Buller [q.v.] as commander-in-chief, but met with no success. The failures of the British army created consternation at home, and it was generally believed that the system under which they had occurred must be at fault. Lansdowne thus found himself the target for public criticism. Essentially loyal to his office, he made no attempt to clear himself, as he might have done, at the expense of his military colleagues, but in the light of subsequent knowledge it is clear that the responsibility for the mistakes which had been made lay with the military rather than with the civilian side of the War Office. The difficulties of the military situation in South Africa had been, indeed, gravely underestimated by Lansdowne's advisers, the prevalent military opinion being that the war would be over in a few months. But the numbers, the fighting powers, and the mobility of the enemy had been underrated; the assistance of troops from India had been refused; while the Colonies were encouraged to send infantry instead of mounted men. The fighting, moreover, was of a sort new to British generals in the field, whose lesson had to be learned at a heavy cost. In the earlier operations the commander-in-chief himself had not only been notably unsuccessful in effecting the relief of Ladysmith, but had succeeded in entangling the major portion of the British forces among the fastnesses of Natal. These were matters over which Lansdowne, since military operations could not be directed from Whitehall, had no control. It is, however, on record that throughout the War every demand for men, money, and material was met with the minimum of delay by the office which he controlled. With the supersession of Sir Redvers Buller and the advent of Lord Roberts as commander-in-chief in January 1900, matters immediately began to improve, although it was not until nearly two years after Lansdowne had relinquished his office that the War was brought, under Lord Kitchener, to a successful conclusion.

Foreseeing that a further reorganization of the War Office would be called for, Lansdowne had, in August 1900, intimated his readiness to make room for a new secretary of state. After the general election in November he was offered the post of secretary of state for foreign affairs by Lord Salisbury, who no longer felt able to combine control of the Foreign Office with his duties as prime minister. Lansdowne accepted the position, for which it soon became evident that he possessed exceptional qualifications.

To a courteous manner Lansdowne joined an intimate knowledge of the French language. Diplomatic conversations were to him a pleasure rather than an effort. He was correct and discreet almost to a fault, and although naturally diffident, had the gift of making friends with those with whom he came into personal contact. He never betrayed a confidence nor promised more than he intended or was able to perform. His position gave him every opportunity for entertaining, which he did at this time lavishly, both in town and country. He was soon on the best of terms with the whole diplomatic corps in London.

Lansdowne's term of office will be chiefly remembered for the two great alliances—with Japan and with France—for the negotiation of which he was responsible. Japan had long been seeking to strengthen her position in Europe, and, with the full consent of her government, the ground had been prepared between Lansdowne and the Japanese ambassador, Baron Hayashi, in 1901. The negotiations were, however, gravely endangered at the last moment by the arrival in Russia of the Marquess Ito, a Japanese statesman whose preferences inclined towards an alliance with that country. It was not until Ito had been persuaded to come to England and to pay a visit to Bowood that all was satisfactorily settled and the treaty signed (30 January 1902). England was at the time in a position of complete isolation, and the community of interests which this treaty established between her and the most virile power of the East did much to strengthen her position, as well as that of Japan, in the eyes of the world. This was to become apparent in the Russo-Japanese War of 1905.

The Anglo-French *Entente* of 1904, which paved the way for the alliance of 1914, had its origin in the difficulties which were constantly recurring between England and France in various parts of the world. These had been most acute in Egypt, and Lord Cromer [q.v.], whose administration had been gravely hampered, lent the full weight of his influence towards a general settlement. Lansdowne found a friendly and able coadjutor in the person of M. Cambon, the French ambassador in London, and together they worked out the numerous details of a difficult and lengthy agreement. In the event all was settled—in Egypt, in Morocco, in Newfoundland, and in Siam—at one stroke, and by this securing of the friendship, instead of the potential enmity of Great Britain's nearest neighbour, the whole orientation of European diplomacy was changed. King Edward VII by his tact and his well-known love of France did much to create the necessary atmosphere for the *Entente*, although his share in its actual formation seems to have been somewhat overrated in popular estimation.

With other countries the relations of Great Britain during Lansdowne's term of office sensibly improved, but in view of after events the diplomatic exchanges with Germany have since attracted the most attention. Germany's policy of naval expansion, joined to the Kaiser Wilhelm II's unconcealed jealousy of his royal uncle and of all things English, had for some time been a source of anxiety. Nevertheless, private *pourparlers* for an alliance between England and Germany took place in 1901, and made considerable progress, although they were eventually allowed to drop. Later (in 1903) Lansdowne was amongst those who were desirous that Great Britain should, in view of her interests in the Persian Gulf, cooperate with Germany in the project of the Bagdad Railway. Strong public feeling was, however, manifested against any association with that country, and the foreign secretary was obliged to yield to it.

With the United States there were two incidents which required careful handling during Lansdowne's period as foreign secretary. The blockade of Venezuela which, after persistent flouting of diplomatic representations, Great Britain, in co-operation with Germany and Italy, had deemed it necessary to establish (at the beginning of 1903) was considered by President Theodore Roosevelt to be an interference with the American sphere of action, and provoked representations to which the British government was eventually forced to yield. The principal objects had, however, been obtained before the blockade was lifted in deference to American opinion. The government of the United States also showed itself obdurate over the question of the Alaskan boundary. This had long been a subject of dispute, and when President Roosevelt demanded that it should be decided by arbitration, the British Foreign Office had perforce to agree (January 1903). There was considerable feeling, both in Canada and in England, over the appointment of the American members of the tribunal, who hardly satisfied the agreed condition of being 'impartial jurists', as well as over the eventual award (October 1903), which did scant justice to the strength of the Canadian claims. Lansdowne's position was rendered the more difficult by the fact that the American president had privately informed the British government that he would accept no result which did not satisfy the American claims.

When Lord Salisbury died in 1903 and Mr. Balfour succeeded him as prime minister, the leadership of the conservative party in the House of Lords devolved upon Lansdowne as of right. A general election took place in December 1905 and resulted in an overwhelming victory for the liberal party, which had long been out of office and was pledged to legislation of a drastic nature. In the House of Lords there was, as always, a large conservative majority, and collisions of opinion between the two Houses upon almost every subject were inevitable. It fell in the main to Lansdowne to decide the delicate question how far the revisionary powers of the Upper House should in these circumstances be exercised, though he acted throughout in close consultation with his colleagues in the House of Commons.

The first clash came over the Education Bill of 1906. The Commons refused to accept the Lords' amendments to this measure which, after the failure of an attempt at compromise, was dropped by the government. In the same year the Plural Voting Bill was summarily rejected by the Lords on second reading; though the Trades Disputes Bill, a much more far-reaching measure, was allowed to go through. In recommending this course Lansdowne was much criticized for openly stating that he considered that the latter bill afforded 'unfavourable' ground on which to fight. The Old Age Pensions Bill (1908) was passed under protest, since the Lords' amendments thereto were ruled to be privileged. The Licensing Bill, after a strenuous fight in the Commons, was thrown out on second reading, and the same fate befell the Scottish Land Bill and another Education Bill. Thus the process of 'filling up the cup' against the House of Lords had already gone far when the climax was reached in the famous 'People's Budget' of 1909. This measure sought to introduce *inter alia* a variety of land taxes (all to be afterwards repealed by common consent); after strenuous opposition in the Commons it was, on Lansdowne's advice, summarily dismissed in the Lords (1 December 1909). The prime minister (Mr. Asquith) immediately appealed to the country (January 1910). The action of the Lords was so far endorsed by the electorate as to transfer some hundred seats from the liberal to the conservative side, but the liberals with the help of the Irish vote were still in a position to get their way. They lost no time in preparing a measure to curtail the powers of the second chamber, while in the Lords Lansdowne gave notice of a measure for the internal reform of that body. The death of King Edward then occurred, and an attempt to settle the question by consent was made in the Constitutional Conference which assembled in the summer. This having proved abortive, the Parliament Bill, limiting the Lords' veto to a period of two years, was introduced and a fresh election held (December 1910). The strength of parties emerged much as it was before, and it became clear that if the government could make sure of the Irish vote it would be able to dictate its terms. This object it achieved by giving a definite promise of Home Rule, and the Parliament Bill was soon passed in the House of Commons, the government making no secret of the fact that, in the event of the Lords proving obdurate, the consent of the new king had been obtained in advance to the creation of a sufficient number of new peers to ensure the passage of the Bill into law. Meanwhile Lansdowne's Bill for the reform of the House of Lords had been introduced and framed in that chamber. It was in these circumstances that the Parliament Bill, after heated controversy amongst conservative peers, was finally passed in the upper house. Lansdowne, although he abstained from voting himself, and advised others to do the same, failed for the first time to carry with him the whole of his followers. Some thought that they could not be expected to subscribe to so drastic a curtailment of the legislative powers of their own house; others believed that the threat of a wholesale creation of peers could not and would not be carried out, or that at all events it should be put to the test of execution. In the result 114 'die hards' recorded their votes against the measure, which was only carried by the narrow margin of seventeen votes, a number of conservative peers having given way at the last moment (9 August 1911).

In the following year Mr. Balfour, with whom Lansdowne had now worked in the closest harmony and friendship for eight years, resigned his position as leader of the conservative party and was succeeded by Mr. Bonar Law. The new leader was expected to be more acceptable to the extremist advocates of tariff reform than his predecessor, who had always been a lukewarm supporter of that policy. Lansdowne himself had throughout occupied a central position between the 'food taxers' and 'free fooders' within the party. It was now attempted to bring these two sections into line on the basis of a policy for the taxation of foreign wheat only; but this proved so far from satisfactory that both Bonar Law and Lansdowne for a time contemplated resignation, nor was it until all food taxes had been definitely dropped that harmony was restored. The imminence of Home Rule with the threatened resistance of Ulster now dominated the political situation. It culminated in the abortive conference which met, with Lansdowne among its members, in July 1914 at Buckingham Palace in an endeavour to avoid civil strife in Ireland. But the European War was now imminent.

It was on Sunday 2 August 1914 that the historic meeting took place at Lansdowne House between Bonar Law, Lansdowne, and a few hurriedly summoned colleagues, at which it was agreed to pledge the unionist party to the support of France, already at war with Germany. This decision was immediately communicated to Mr. Asquith, whose Cabinet was known to be at variance on the subject of Great Britain's entry into the War; and it turned the scale. Two days later England declared war on Germany.

In May 1915, with other conservative colleagues, Lansdowne joined the first Coalition administration, in which, though himself without portfolio, he was a member of the inner committee responsible for the conduct of the War. He soon became profoundly disquieted by the trend of events, and like many others at the time feared that the War, if fought 'to a finish', would result in such mutual exhaustion that the fruits of victory would not be worth having. In response to an invitation from the prime minister in November 1916 he set out at length in a private memorandum his views as to the possibility of a peace 'of accommodation'. With this document Mr. Asquith, in a short note, expressed his 'complete concurrence'; it was circulated to the Cabinet, and no one who saw it seems to have shown any signs of disapproval. At a later date, however, Lord Crewe, one of Lansdowne's colleagues, put it on record that this memorandum was the prime cause of the break-up of the first Coalition government [Earl of Oxford and Asquith, *Memories and Reflections*, vol. i, c. 14, 1928]. Asquith's dilatory methods had for some time been the subject of violent newspaper attacks, and it would seem that it was the fear of his colleagues supporting Lansdowne's plea for peace that led Mr. Lloyd George to take the steps which brought Asquith's ministry to a speedy end and placed Lloyd George in control of the situation as prime minister in the second Coalition government (December 1916).

In the new ministry Lansdowne did not find a place; it is doubtful whether in the circumstances he would have accepted one had it been offered him. Although he continued to attend and not infrequently spoke in the House of Lords, he was thenceforth without personal responsibility in affairs of state. Living now in partial retirement, he grew increasingly uneasy as to the results of a continued war of attrition. He had long been anxious that, in the hopes of shortening hostilities, the war aims of the Allies should be more definitely stated, and he had thought of initiating a debate in parliament to that end. Ultimately he propounded his views in his famous letter to the *Daily Telegraph* (29 November 1917). It was for long generally supposed, even by those who were in his closest confidence, that Lansdowne took this step without consulting any of his friends or former colleagues. It did not transpire until some years after his death that the matter had been fully discussed between him and the foreign secretary (Mr. Balfour) who, although he did not himself see the letter before publication, made no attempt to dissuade Lansdowne from publishing it, and was content to refer the whole matter to the permanent under-secretary, Lord Hardinge [Lord Riddell's *War Diary, 1914–1918* (1933) and correspondence in *The Times*, 1 August 1933]. The argument of the letter was practically identical with that of the memorandum of 1916 and in its essence was unassailable. That argument Lansdowne summed up at the conclusion of the letter as follows: 'An immense stimulus', he wrote, 'would probably be given to the peace party in Germany if it were understood: (1) that we do not desire the annihilation of Germany as a Great Power; (2) that we do not seek to impose upon her people any form of government other than that of their own choice; (3) that, except as a legitimate war measure, we have no desire to deny to Germany her place among the great commercial communities of the world; (4) that we are prepared, when the war is over, to examine in concert with other powers the group of international problems, some of them of recent origin, which are connected with the question of "the freedom of the seas"; (5) that we are prepared to enter into an international pact under which ample opportunities would be afforded for the settlement of international disputes by peaceful means.'

It seems, however, that Lansdowne and those who had knowledge of his intention did not realize that a communication of this kind broadcast throughout the world was calculated to raise in Great Britain's friends fears, and in her enemies hopes, of a weakening purpose on the part of the principal partner amongst the Allies. The moment also was inopportune. A negotiated peace might conceivably have been possible in 1916, but, as subsequent knowledge of Germany's inner counsels has proved, would have been impossible in 1917, except on terms which could not have been contemplated by the Allies. Lansdowne's letter was at once violently repudiated by the government and in the press. His previous record as a tried servant of the state was forgotten in a moment, his argument was misrepresented, and he was bitterly reproached with disloyalty to the Allied cause. At a conservative meeting addressed by Mr. Bonar Law on 30 November he was, to use his own expression, 'excommunicated' from the party. True to his character he vouchsafed no answer to these attacks, and his respect for official secrecy was so ingrained that he never made the slightest allusion in public or in private to his memorandum of 1916 or to the communications with the Foreign Office which had preceded the publication of his letter. But he felt most keenly the absence of any support or countenance from those who were aware of his intentions. He did not, however, give up his efforts to work for peace. Two more letters from him were published in the same strain on 5 March and 31 July 1918; but the armies in France and elsewhere were by that time at death-grips, and, with the German collapse, the peace which had seemed so unattainable soon came in sight.

Lansdowne was now in his seventy-fourth year. Although scarcely to be described as a strong man, he had hitherto on the whole enjoyed good health, but in May 1919 he was struck down by a severe attack of rheumatic fever from which he did not recover for nearly two years. During this time he ceased to attend parliament, and his bodily activity, which had been very striking for one of his age, was thenceforth markedly impaired.

Lansdowne spent most of these later years at Bowood. Already in 1921 the condition of affairs in Ireland had become such as to make residence in a remote corner of that country undesirable. In 1922 it became for Lansdowne impossible; all communication with Derreen was cut off, and after being looted by the 'Irregulars' the house was destroyed by fire in September. This was to him a bitter blow, for there seemed little prospect of reconstruction during his lifetime. The work, however, was pushed forward as soon as circumstances permitted, and in 1925 he was able to return to Derreen once more. At the end of 1926 his health again gave cause for anxiety, but he had sufficiently recovered in May to start on his annual visit to Ireland. On his way to Derreen he stopped at Newtown Anner, Clonmel, the home of his youngest daughter; an aneurism of the heart supervened, and he died there rather suddenly 3 June 1927.

Of a modest and even retiring disposition, Lansdowne was no seeker after high office. His personal predilections inclined him towards a domestic life, and he was at his best when he found himself in the midst of his friends and family. But his strong sense of duty impelled him to accept the great responsibilities which fell to his lot. His habit of reticence was always marked, and it no doubt increased owing to the fact that at a comparatively early age he occupied positions in which its exercise was essential. Politics, which formed so large a part of his life, were scarcely mentioned, and never discussed, in his home circle, nor did he often open his heart except to a few intimate friends. Although he was an excellent speaker and ready debater, he took little pleasure in speech-making. He was quick at getting at the heart of a question and in expressing his conclusions clearly and concisely. His minutes on official as well as on private papers were models of lucidity and terseness. His ability, his probity, and his straightforwardness were never called in question by friend or foe, but he abhorred publicity in any form and was thus little known or understood by the public. To the world he seemed to be the typical aristocrat—aloof, severe, and unbending—a conception of the conservative leader in the House of Lords which it suited political opponents to foster. To those who really knew him, on the other hand, he was a kind friend, a lover of nature and of poetry, a good classical scholar with a remarkable store of knowledge on all kinds of subjects, and not without a saving sense of humour—in short, a man full of human sympathies.

Lansdowne had two sons and two daughters. He was succeeded as sixth marquess by his elder son, Henry William Edmond (1872–1935). His younger son, Charles, who had assumed the name of Mercer Nairne when Lansdowne made over to him his Scottish estates in 1913, was killed in action in 1914.

There are portraits of Lansdowne by P. A. de László in the National Portrait Gallery and at Bowood; by Fiddes Watt at Balliol College, Oxford; and by Frank Holl in the possession of Lady Emily Digby. There is an equestrian statue by Harry Bates at Calcutta (Maidan).

[Lord Newton, *Lord Lansdowne: A Biography*, 1929; *The Nineteenth Century and After*, March 1934; personal knowledge.]

LANSDOWNE.

PHILLIMORE, JOHN SWINNERTON (1873–1926), classical scholar and poet, was born at Boconnoc, Cornwall, 26 February 1873, the fourth son of Vice-Admiral Sir Augustus Phillimore, of Shedfield, Hampshire, by his wife, Harriet Eleanor, second daughter of the Hon. George Matthew Fortescue, of Boconnoc, M.P. for Hindon, Wiltshire, 1826–1831. He was a first cousin of Sir Walter George Frank Phillimore, first Baron Phillimore [q.v.]. He was educated at Westminster, and proceeded with a scholarship to Christ Church, Oxford. At Westminster his talent was recognized and fostered by William Gunion Rutherford, and at Oxford he proved himself the best classical scholar of his time. He obtained first classes in classical moderations (1893) and in *literae humaniores* (1895), and won the Hertford and Craven scholarships (1892), the Ireland scholarship (1893), and the chancellor's prize for Latin verse (1894). He was already writing distinguished verse, and, like his friend Hilaire Belloc, he was a leading figure at the Union, of which he became president in 1895. Christ Church appointed him a lecturer in that year, student in 1896, and tutor in 1898. With one of his colleagues, S. G. Owen, he published in 1898, under the title *Musa Clauda*, a collection of versions from English into Latin elegiac verse. He took up the study of Russian, and wrote a translation of Mikhail Lermontov's novel *A Hero of Nowadays* (not published until 1921). In politics also he took a serious interest at this period, and he was one of the contributors to a volume of *Essays in Liberalism by Six Oxford Men* (1897). In the vacation much of his time was spent in mountaineering in the Dolomites. In recognition of his skill and daring the guides and president of the Club Alpino decided that 'one of the fine ascents he had made should bear his name'.

In 1899, at the age of twenty-six, Phillimore was appointed to succeed Professor Gilbert Murray in the chair of Greek in the university of Glasgow. For some years he took a prominent part in the political life of the West of Scotland as a liberal imperialist, but his interests were steadily concentrating on his work as a scholar and teacher. In 1902 he published a translation in rhymed verse of three plays of Sophocles, but the texts of Propertius (1901) and of Statius's *Silvae* (1905), which he revised for the Clarendon Press at this period, showed where his real bent lay. It was a great satisfaction to him when in 1906 he was transferred from the chair of Greek to that of Humanity, rendered vacant by the retirement of Professor George Gilbert Ramsay. Thenceforward he contributed to the *Classical Quarterly*, the *Classical Review*, *Mnemosyne*, and other periodicals a steady stream of notes, linguistic and textual, on Latin authors. He published a translation and an *Index Verborum* of Propertius (1906), and he set to work upon a large-scale edition of that poet. His facility in Greek now exercised itself in studies of the intellectual and religious life of the Roman Imperial period; and a translation of Philostratus's *Apollonius of Tyana*, introduced by a characteristic essay, appeared in two volumes in 1912. From time to time he published papers and addresses on classical subjects, notably 'The Greek Romances' (in *English Literature and the Classics*, 1912), *Some Remarks on Translation and Translators* (1919), *The Revival of Criticism* (1919), '*Ille Ego*' (1920), and *Pastoral and Allegory* (1925). His growing reputation at home and abroad was shown by the conferment upon him of the honorary degree of LL.D. by the university of St. Andrews (1917) and of that of Litt.D. by Trinity College, Dublin (1921); by the dedication to him, as 'philologue, humaniste, poète', of Frédéric Plessis's edition of the *Odes* of Horace (1924); and by his appointment for the year 1914–1915 to the Sather professorship in classics in the university of California. This appointment he was prevented from taking up by the outbreak of the European War.

In 1902 Phillimore published a volume of *Poems* containing a selection of the verse which he had written up to that year. In 1918 he issued a second volume under the title *Things New and Old*. A change of mind visible in his poems is explained by the fact that in 1906 he was received into the Roman Catholic Church. He wrote occasionally for the *Dublin Review*, his contributions including a notable essay on 'Blessed Thomas More and the Arrest of Humanism in England' (1913). A substantial work on Christian Latin poetry he left unfinished. In the year of his death he published in a popular series a selection of *The Hundred Best Latin Hymns* (1926). It was characteristic of his versatility that in the same year he wrote an introduction to a reprint of Francis Hickes's translation of the *Vera Historia* of Lucian.

Phillimore was an occasional contributor to the *Eye Witness*, to its successor the *New Witness*, and to *G. K.'s Weekly*. As his sympathetic association with those reviews indicated, Phillimore no longer concerned himself with party politics, but he maintained from a new angle his interest in national affairs and international relations, and he welcomed the opportunity to go to France towards the close of the War as a representative of the Franco-Scottish Society. At the universities of Bordeaux and Toulouse and at the Sorbonne he delivered addresses on the cultural relations of Great Britain with France and with Germany. In the public life of the West of Scotland he held a position of his own as a witty speaker and an admired lecturer on a wide variety of topics, among which he once ventured to include the national poet (speech printed by the Govan Burns Club, 1905). But Phillimore's main concern was with his duties at the university. He was scrupulously diligent in attendance at academic committees, and he took his full share in the routine of his chair. Most of the work he published was a by-product of his careful preparation of his lectures. The regard in which he was held by his students found expression in January 1925, when, in their name, a portrait of him painted by Maurice Greiffenhagen was presented to the university. Yet Phillimore's influence was not confined to the Latin class-room. When the students of Glasgow first decided to issue a volume of *University Verses* (1910), and when all four Scottish universities later combined to publish a volume of *Scottish University Verses* (1923), he was invited on each occasion to supply the preface introducing the volume to the public. As professor of humanity he exercised a profound influence upon the student body as a whole, and through it upon the cultural life of Scotland.

Phillimore married in 1900 Cecily, only daughter of the Rev. Spencer Compton Spencer-Smith, vicar of Kingston, Dorset, and had one son and one daughter. He died at Shedfield 16 November 1926.

[Phillimore's published writings and private papers; personal knowledge.]

S. N. Miller.

PHILLIMORE, Sir WALTER GEORGE FRANK, second baronet, and first Baron Phillimore, of Shiplake (1845–1929), judge, ecclesiastical lawyer, and international jurist, was born in London 21 November 1845, the only son of Sir Robert Joseph Phillimore, first baronet [q.v.], the last of the judges of the ancient High Court of Admiralty. He was grandson of Joseph Phillimore [q.v.], regius professor of civil law at Oxford University, and first cousin of John Swinnerton Phillimore [q.v.]. His mother was Charlotte, third daughter of John Denison, of Ossington Hall, Nottinghamshire, and sister of John Evelyn Denison, Viscount Ossington [q.v.], Speaker of the House of Commons, and Edward Denison [q.v.], bishop of Salisbury. Phillimore was sent to Westminster, where he found his family name carved amongst those of many distinguished old boys on the porch leading to the famous schoolroom. He became captain of the school, and won a studentship at Christ Church, Oxford, in 1863. He obtained first classes in classical moderations in 1865, in *literae humaniores* in 1866, and in law and modern history in 1867. He was secretary and treasurer of the Union. In the interval between the two final schools he was elected to a fellowship at All Souls College, and he subsequently (1868) won the Vinerian (law) scholarship. He entered the Middle Temple, was called to the bar in 1868, and joined the western circuit.

Phillimore was counsel in many famous ecclesiastical cases, amongst them being *Boyd* v. *Philpotts* (the Exeter reredos case, 1874) and *Reed* v. *the Bishop of Lincoln* (1891) in the court of the archbishop of Canterbury. He was also counsel in other cases in which questions of ritual were under discussion, such as the use of lighted candles on the Communion Table, the wearing of certain ecclesiastical vestments, the eastward position during the prayer of Consecration, the singing of the 'Agnus Dei', and the legality of a reredos with sculptural representations of the Transfiguration and Ascension. In 1872 he became chancellor of the diocese of Lincoln. In that office he held that a nonconformist minister was not entitled to describe himself by the title of 'Reverend' on the tombstone erected to his daughter (*Keet* v. *Smith*, 1876). The decision was upheld by his father, Sir Robert Phillimore, but reversed by the Privy Council. Phillimore never took silk, but in December 1883 a patent of precedence was conferred upon him which enabled him to be ranked with Her Majesty's counsel. In 1885 he succeeded to his father's baronetcy. Apart from ecclesiastical cases he was almost entirely engaged in the Admiralty Court, of which for many years he was the leader.

As a politician Phillimore was not successful. An admirer of Mr. Gladstone, he was unable to persuade the electors of St. George's, Hanover Square, to return him as a liberal in 1885, and a similar fate befell him when he contested the Henley division of Oxfordshire in 1886 and again in 1902.

Phillimore was seldom seen in common law courts, and some surprise was felt when, in December 1897, he was appointed a judge of the Queen's Bench division. He remained a judge of first instance for sixteen years. His lack of experience of criminal law exposed him to considerable criticism when presiding as the red judge at assizes. It was thought that his sentences were too severe, especially in sexual cases. As the years passed he modified the severity of his outlook. Again, on the civil side of his work, he was not always happy in trial of an ordinary *nisi prius* case before a jury, and was wont to interrupt cross-examination of counsel. In cases tried before himself alone, he was more at home and excelled in the difficult task of interpreting confusing and apparently conflicting Acts of parliament, although here also he was apt to be somewhat precise and pedantic in his ways and methods. His decision on facts was not as sound as his determination of the law, where his classical education enabled him to express his judgments in language of exceptional brevity and lucidity. An example of his versatility was shown when he was appointed to administer the bankruptcy jurisdiction of the King's Bench. He was a rapid judge in whose court no time was wasted, and it was the admiration of spectators to watch him taking notes of the evidence sometimes with his right and sometimes with his left hand, with equal facility. His courtesy to everybody and his kindness to the junior bar were recognized on all sides. In summing up his career as a judge of first instance, a place cannot be found for him among the inner circle of great common law judges, but he became a better judge every year he sat. Always a man of great public spirit, even during his occupancy of the bench he devoted his spare time to public work. He was an alderman of the borough of Kensington, where he lived, and mayor from 1909 to 1911.

In 1913 Phillimore was made a lord justice of appeal and admitted to the Privy Council. Again the appointment was not altogether expected, but it was at once justified by results, and it was from this time onward that his legal capacities bore their best and most abundant fruit. It was fortunate that the Court of Appeal should, during the European War, have had as one of its members so distinguished an international lawyer as he was. He was party to the judgment in the *Continental Tyre Co.* v. *Daimler Co.* (1915), where the issue was the status of an English company controlled by Germans resident in Germany. He was one of those who decided the case of *The King* v. *Speyer* (1916) as to whether naturalized British subjects were eligible for membership of the Privy Council; and his judgment in *Beal* v. *Horlock* (1915) on the effect under the Merchant Shipping Act of the detention of a British ship in a German port at the outbreak of war was subsequently affirmed in the House of Lords.

Phillimore retired from the bench in 1916, and two years later (1918) was raised to the peerage under the title of Baron Phillimore, of Shiplake, co. Oxford. He gave regular assistance to the judicial proceedings of the House of Lords and the Privy Council for the next ten years, bringing to the help of his colleagues a ripe experience, a memory which seemed never to forget any case in which he had been engaged at the bar or which had been cited to him as a judge, and, in addition, a great knowledge of Roman and canon law. The manner in which his native ability, enriched by all this learning and experience, enabled him to deal with other codes and new problems was seen in his masterly treatment of Burmese, Hindu, and Mohammedan law in the Judicial Committee. Here the facts had been found and his duty was to apply the law to them. By the Naval Prize Act (1918) he was appointed chairman of the Naval Prize Tribunal. Summing up his career as a lord justice and in the highest tribunals of the land, his work justified his claim to be considered as one of the great lawyers of his generation.

As an international jurist, Phillimore acquired a European reputation. He was a constant attendant at the meetings of the International Law Association at Grenoble, Stockholm, Vienna, and Warsaw. He was president of the Association in 1919–1920. At the request of the secretary of state for foreign affairs, he had, in the years 1917 and 1918, been appointed chairman of a committee to consider early schemes for the League of Nations. His report was sent to the Cabinet, taken up by General Smuts, and communicated to President Woodrow Wilson. The president deputed Colonel E. M. House to work upon Phillimore's draft, and his name thus links up the British Empire with the institution of the League. In 1917 he published *Three Centuries of Treaties of Peace and Their Teaching*, and in 1920 was a member of the committee which drew up the statute constituting the Permanent Court of International Justice at The Hague.

Like other busy men, Phillimore found time for many activities outside his profession. He was seldom absent from the meetings of the governing body of his old school, of which he was a member from 1885 until his death, and he took a prominent part in the affairs of the Middle Temple, of which he was reader (1898) and treasurer (1907). He joined the English Church Union in 1865 and was president in 1919. For many years he was treasurer of the Pusey House at Oxford, and after his retirement from the Court of Appeal, he took part in the sessions of the Church Assembly, especially in the controversies which arose in connexion with the revision of the Prayer Book (1927–1928). He was one of the chief authors of the scheme for clergy pensions.

In the House of Lords Phillimore's speeches were not persuasive, but he took a large share in the debates upon the Legitimacy Bill (1926) and the Guardianship of Infants Bill (1925). Those who heard him will always remember him as a man who had decided though rather narrow views, which were always advanced with the greatest courtesy and the greatest consideration for the opinions of others.

Phillimore was responsible for the second edition of his father's *Ecclesiastical Law of the Church of England* (2 vols., 1895), for the third edition of vol. iv of his father's *Commentaries on International Law* (1889), and for many editions (1872–1905) of J. H. Blunt's *Book of Church Law*.

In his private life Phillimore was a charming host who frequently engaged in argument with his visitors and was accustomed to verify his views by immediate reference to one of the many books in his well-stocked library. It remains to record what was perhaps his greatest good fortune. In 1870 he married Agnes, eldest daughter of Charles Manners Lushington, M.P. for Canterbury, and had four sons and three daughters. She died in January 1929, but for nearly sixty years Phillimore spent with her a life of unalloyed happiness. He himself seemed to be in league with time, for to the end he preserved his youthful appearance and quick and incisive manner of speech and walk. He died at his house in Kensington 13 March 1929, and was succeeded as second baron by his third (the elder surviving) son, Godfrey Walter (born 1879).

There is a portrait of Phillimore by George Henry in the Kensington Town Hall, but it is not a very satisfactory likeness. A cartoon of him by 'Spy' appeared in *Vanity Fair* 24 November 1898.

[*The Times*, 14 March 1929; *Law Journal*, 16 March 1929; W. P. W. Phillimore and Lord Phillimore, *Genealogy of the Family of Phillimore*, 1922; *Law Reports*, *passim*; private information; personal knowledge.]

SANKEY.

PHILLIPS, SIR CLAUDE (1846–1924), art critic, was born in London 29 January 1846, the second son of Robert Abraham Phillips, court-jeweller, by his wife, Helen, daughter of Moses Lionel Levy, and sister of Joseph Moses Levy [q.v.], founder of the *Daily Telegraph*. He was educated chiefly in France and Germany, and graduated B.A. at London University. He was admitted a solicitor, but subsequently entered the Inner Temple and was called to the bar in 1883. Phillips's practice involved visits to Italy, of which he took full advantage for artistic study. This was extended by travel in other European countries, and systematic visits to their galleries, churches, and private collections. His knowledge and love of music came only second to this leading interest, and his first contributions to the *Daily Telegraph* in the later 'eighties dealt with that subject. Articles on painting followed, growing in number, and in 1897 Phillips was given ample scope for his abilities when he was appointed regular art-critic to that paper—a post which he filled until the end of his working life, devoting to it his main energies, and a high sense of the responsibilities of his task.

In the same year (1897) Phillips's authority as a scholar was recognized by his appointment to the keepership of the Wallace Collection, which was then being prepared for its opening at Hertford House in 1900. In the arrangement of the collection a committee of the trustees played a controlling part, but the cataloguing fell to Phillips, and in the course of it he identified as an original Titian the 'Perseus and Andromeda', which had been neglected as a school piece.

In addition to journalistic work, Phillips was the author of *Sir Joshua Reynolds* (1894) and of five valuable numbers of the *Portfolio* monographs inaugurated by Philip Gilbert Hamerton [q.v.]—*Frederick Walker* (1894), *Antoine Watteau* (1895), *The Picture Gallery of Charles I* (1896), *The Early Work of Titian* (1897), and *The Later Work of Titian* (1898). His unsurpassed knowledge of pictures, old and new, and his retentive memory furnished him with a copious and even embarrassing wealth of illustration for any given topic. Phillips's approach to painting reflected a fervently emotional nature. If his sense of painter's quality was not so strong, he was anxiously wide-minded, honourably and fiercely independent of personal influence or any taint of commerce. He was unmarried, but found satisfaction in social life and activities, and had deep family affection. He was knighted on retirement from the keepership of the Wallace Collection in 1911, and died at his home in Kensington 9 August 1924. He left a bequest of money and pictures to the National Gallery.

[Preface by Maurice Brockwell to Claude Phillips's posthumous collection of essays, *Emotion in Art*, 1925; personal knowledge.]

D. S. MACCOLL.

PICKFORD, WILLIAM, BARON STERNDALE (1848–1923), judge, was born at Manchester 1 October 1848, the second son of Thomas Edward Pickford, merchant, of that city, by his wife, Georgina, daughter of Jeremiah Todd-Naylor, of Liverpool. The Pickfords came from Prestbury in Cheshire. James Pickford, who died in 1768, was a wagoner between Manchester and London. His son Matthew, and his grandson Thomas (who was Lord Sterndale's grandfather) developed a big carrier's business, and the latter took Joseph Baxendale into partnership. The Baxendales eventually took over the concern, but the name of Pickford is still connected with it. When William Pickford was made a peer he said in conversation that he had been told that he ought to provide himself with supporters for his arms. 'You had better choose Hadley and Baxendale both proper', said one of his colleagues on the bench: lawyers will appreciate the point.

Soon after the death of Pickford's father, which took place in 1859, his mother moved to Liverpool, and he was educated at Liverpool College. In 1867 he entered Exeter College, Oxford, where he obtained second classes in classical moderations (1870) and in *literae humaniores* (1872). The college elected him an honorary fellow in 1916. In 1871 he entered as a student of the Inner Temple, was a pupil of Thomas Henry Baylis [q.v.], and was called to the bar in 1874. In 1875 he joined the northern circuit, and began as a 'local' at Liverpool, having his chambers for a few years at 22 North John Street, and from 1879 at Commerce Chambers, Harrington Street. He had to wait some years before he got much work; he then acquired a sound and increasing practice, largely in commercial affairs, but with the diversity that a provincial practice usually involves. The most sensational case he had was in 1889 as counsel for Mrs. Maybrick at the police court, and as her junior counsel at the assizes.

Pickford married in 1880 Alice Mary, daughter of John William Brooke, of Sibton Park, Yoxford, Suffolk: she died in 1884, leaving him with two daughters. Her death was the one great misfortune of his successful and otherwise happy life.

In 1892 Pickford moved to London. He had been for some time increasingly engaged there. In particular, he was sent up to conduct in the Admiralty Court almost all the collision and salvage cases in which Liverpool shipowners or solicitors were concerned. He accordingly made London his head-quarters, with his chambers at 2 Mitre Court Buildings, Temple. Of this Admiralty work he continued to enjoy a large share while he remained at the bar. In 1893 he took silk: another Queen's Counsel created at the same time was Charles Swinfen Eady (afterwards first Baron Swinfen) whom Pickford was to succeed as master of the Rolls twenty-six years later.

At first, after these changes, Pickford still went the northern circuit, of which he soon became the *de facto* leader. But the growth of his business in London made his visits to the north more and more infrequent to the great loss of the circuit bar mess, where he was very popular. 'His gaiety and vivacity as a young man', one of his oldest circuit companions has said, 'are not easy to realize for those who only knew the temperate dignity and reserve of the master of the Rolls.' Another friend, who first knew Pickford shortly after he lost his wife, says, 'I can hardly believe that description, except that I know how deeply her loss changed him.' As an advocate he had never the brilliance of Charles Russell, or the learning of Lord Herschell or Sir Joseph Walton—great names on that circuit; but he could get what he wanted from a jury as well as, or better than, any of them. One who knew him well says that in the tradition of the circuit he was the lineal successor of James Scarlett (Lord Abinger) and Sir John Holker. But he was not merely a jury advocate: references to the earlier volumes of the *Commercial Cases* will show that he had a large share of the work of the Commercial Court from its foundation in 1895 until he became a judge, which was the period of its busiest days.

In 1901 Pickford was made recorder of Oldham, and in 1904 recorder of Liverpool. In 1902 he became a bencher of the Inner Temple. In 1905 he was leading counsel for Great Britain at the inquiry held in Paris into the affair of the attack by the Russian fleet upon the Hull trawlers at the Dogger Bank. In 1906 he was sent as commissioner of assize on the north-eastern circuit, an appointment which, for a man with so leading a practice, is usually the prelude to promotion to the King's Bench.

In 1907, parliament having sanctioned the appointment of an additional judge of the High Court, King's Bench division, Pickford was selected for the post by Lord Loreburn, and received the usual knighthood. It was that lord chancellor's first judicial appointment, and none could have met with more universal approval. Nor was expectation disappointed, for Pickford proved an ideal judge. He was not a very learned lawyer, and he had no brilliancy of style or expression; but in the substance of his decisions he was almost invariably right. Moreover, he possessed that quality which in a judge is of the first importance for efficiency—not to mention his own happiness—the power of making up his mind without being worried, and of forgetting all about a case immediately it is finished. Whether he was trying criminals, or civil cases with a jury, or sitting alone, as he often did, in the Commercial Court, he was equally successful. Nor has any judge more deservedly earned the respect of the bar for his kindly but dignified courtesy.

When at the bar Pickford had been active in the proceedings of the International Maritime Committee and other movements for the unification of maritime law, and he continued so to be interested after he became a judge. In 1905 he had been the senior British representative at the Brussels Conference which formulated the conventions as to collision and salvage: these were given legal force in England by the Maritime Conventions Act of 1911. He took a prominent part in the later conferences which formulated conventions about limitation of liability and mortgages and maritime liens. He also presided in 1923 over a select committee of both houses of parliament to which was referred the bill which became the Sea Carriage of Goods Act of 1924.

In 1914, upon the resignation of Sir Roland Bowdler Vaughan Williams [q.v.], Pickford was promoted to the Court of Appeal as lord justice, and sworn of the Privy Council. It would be hard to find two men more unlike in every respect than Vaughan Williams and his successor. Pickford had little of the erudition of his predecessor, but he was a much more efficient judge, and proved as successful in the Court of Appeal as he had been in the inferior court.

In July 1916 the bill to set up a commission 'to inquire into the origin, inception, and conduct of operations in the Dardanelles' was introduced. In the House of Lords Lord Cromer [q.v.], the designated chairman, proposed that some one of judicial experience should be added to the commissioners named in the bill as it came from the Commons, and, as a result, Pickford's name appears in the Act (6 and 7 Geo. V cap. 34) which received the royal assent on 17 August. He attended diligently at the laborious meetings of the commission. An interim report was issued before the death of Lord Cromer on 29 January 1917. Lord Justice Pickford was then selected by his colleagues to succeed Lord Cromer as chairman. The final report signed by him as chairman was published 8 March 1917. Another additional task which Pickford undertook during the European War was to preside over a 'conscientious objectors' tribunal in Chelsea. He did the work, as some in a similar position did not, judicially.

In 1918, upon the death in September of Sir Samuel Thomas Evans [q.v.], there was still much work to be done in the prize court, and it was important to find a man to carry on the task which Evans had done so well. Pickford was obviously the man for this, and, with some reluctance, but with a characteristically high sense of duty, he accepted the post of president of the probate, divorce, and admiralty division of the High Court, and was raised to the peerage as a baron. A few years earlier he had inherited a small estate at King Sterndale, near Buxton, in Derbyshire (which had been first purchased by his great-grandfather), and he therefore took the title of Lord Sterndale. In London he lived first at 92 Elm Park Gardens, and from 1910 onwards at the fine Queen Anne house in Cheyne Walk called 'Queen's House'.

The War ended about two months after Pickford's appointment to the Admiralty Court, and in a year most of the important prize cases had been disposed of. In October 1919, upon the resignation of Swinfen Eady very shortly before his death, Lord Sterndale was appointed master of the Rolls. The prospect, now that the prize work was ending, of trying divorce suits, and, by the strange variety of that court, collision and salvage cases, was not attractive, and he gladly returned to the Court of Appeal as its president. For four years he presided there, and did his work as admirably, and with as much apparent ease, as he had done everything before. On 16 August 1923 he spent an active day in a hayfield at King Sterndale, and went to bed seemingly in the excellent health which he had always enjoyed: next morning it was found that he had died in his sleep. The front page of *The Times* announced his death as on 17 August, i.e. after midnight. He was buried at King Sterndale on 22 August. As he had no son, the barony became extinct.

Pickford was a very tall, handsome man. When he presided in the Court of Appeal, and his colleagues were Lord Justice Bankes and Lord Justice Scrutton, he overtopped them, but there must have been nearly nineteen feet of them altogether. In his younger days he was an ardent bicyclist, a cricketer, and a follower of a Cheshire pack of beagles. He was also a keen climber, and, despite his great weight, an accomplished one. He was elected a member of the Alpine Club in 1894, and was its president from 1914 to 1916. He was also a member of the Athenaeum Club and of the United University Club, and served on the committee of the latter. His service was in one respect especially valuable to his fellow members: for he was as good a judge of port as he was of men and things. He was also a prominent freemason. He took no part in politics, and never contested a constituency.

There is a portrait of Lord Sterndale, in his robes as master of the Rolls, by Fred Stratton, in the possession of his daughter, the Hon. Dorothy Pickford. An engraving of this was made as a private plate. There is also a copy of this portrait in the Parliament Chamber at the Inner Temple. To those benchers who, in that friendliest of fraternities, remember him as they knew him, it does not do justice to his great and kindly personality.

[*The Times*, 18 and 22 August 1923; *Law Journal*, 25 August 1923; *Law Lists*; Memoranda in *Law Reports*; A. J. Ashton, *As I Went On My Way*, pp. 216–219, 1924; *Alpine Journal*, vol. xxxv, pp. 267–271; private information; personal knowledge.]

F. D. MACKINNON.

PIRRIE, WILLIAM JAMES, VISCOUNT PIRRIE (1847–1924), shipbuilder, was born at Quebec 31 May 1847. He was of Irish parentage, being the only son of James Alexander Pirrie, of Little Clandeboye, county Down, by his wife, Eliza, daughter of Alexander Montgomery, of Dundesart, county Antrim. He was brought up at Conlig, county Down, near Belfast, and educated at the Royal Belfast Academical Institution. In 1862, at the age of fifteen, he entered as a pupil the shipbuilding firm of Messrs. Harland & Wolff, and made such rapid progress in his profession that he became a partner in 1874, when he was only twenty-seven. He remained for the rest of his life with Harland & Wolff, and after the firm was converted into a limited company he was chairman of the board for many years.

Pirrie's career was contemporaneous with the introduction of modern steel-shipbuilding, and for half a century he was identified with all the important developments which took place in naval architecture and marine engineering. A practical constructor himself, he was also a shrewd man of business, and under his administration Harland & Wolff became one of the leading shipbuilding companies in Great Britain. In a sense he may be said to have been the creator of the big ship. The tendency of his firm was to increase the size of vessels built by them, the 10,000-ton ship of the 'eighties being succeeded by larger vessels, and culminating in the *Olympic* of 46,000 tons (1911), and the *Britannic* of 48,000 tons (1914). The latter was used as a hospital-ship during the European War, and was torpedoed and lost in the Mediterranean. Harland & Wolff were the sole builders for the White Star line and the Bibby line, and they also supplied important ships for the Peninsular & Oriental Company, the Royal Mail Steam Packet Company, and other leading lines.

Many of the improvements, both in the design of ships and in their machinery, during this period of progress were due to the suggestions of his company or of Pirrie himself. With the increase in the size of ships he was alive to the importance of securing additional strength and rigidity by improved methods of construction. His firm was also the first to arrange passenger accommodation amidships, and to provide many of the amenities of modern ocean travel. Great as were the changes which Pirrie witnessed in the building of ships, the concurrent advance in the science of marine engineering was even greater. Balanced engines reduced vibration to a minimum; quadruple expansion engines, coupled with a low-pressure turbine, gave the greatest economy of steam; the adoption of oil fuel owed much to his foresight; and he did valuable pioneer work in connexion with the introduction of Diesel internal-combustion engines.

Pirrie built up the firm of Harland & Wolff into a very large organization. The works at Belfast alone covered 230 acres, and he established other yards on the Clyde, as well as ship-repairing works at Liverpool and other ports. In busy times the enterprises under his direct control must have employed about 50,000 men.

During the European War, like other leaders of industry, Pirrie placed the resources of his establishments at the service of the Admiralty. Warships were constructed in his yards with rapidity, and liners were converted into cruisers. An extensive aeroplane department was also inaugurated. In March 1918 Pirrie was appointed comptroller-general of merchant shipbuilding, and his energy in this capacity was of value in making up as quickly as possible the shortage caused by submarine warfare. His influence was continually used in favour of harbour and dock development, and he was one of the moving spirits in the promotion of the Atlantic shipping combine, which was formed at the beginning of the twentieth century. As a result of these negotiations various British and American shipping interests were brought into one organization in 1902 under the title of the International Mercantile Marine Company.

Pirrie's whole career was bound up with Belfast, and most of his interests were centred in that city. His philanthropic activities were considerable, and he devoted special attention to education. He supported the practice, which is now followed by most engineering and shipbuilding firms, of encouraging apprentices in his employment to continue their education by attending classes at technical schools.

Pirrie's prominent place in the life of the city was recognized by his election in 1898 as the first honorary freeman of Belfast. He served as lord mayor in 1896–1897, and was appointed His Majesty's lieutenant for the city in 1911. Honorary degrees were conferred upon him by the Royal University of Ireland (1899), and by Trinity College, Dublin (1903). He was raised to the peerage as Baron Pirrie, of Belfast, in 1906, and when King George V visited Belfast in 1921, to open the first parliament of Northern Ireland, he received a viscounty. He was admitted privy councillor in 1897, and created K.P. in 1909.

Pirrie died at sea 6 June 1924 while on a business tour, one of the objects of which was to inspect the ports of South America and to impress on their authorities the necessity of increasing and extending facilities in order to meet the growing commerce of the world.

Pirrie married in 1879 Margaret Montgomery, daughter of John Carlisle, of Belfast, but left no issue, and the peerage became extinct at his death.

[*The Times*, 9 June 1924; *Transactions* of the Institute of Naval Architects, vol. lxvi, 1924.] A. Cochrane.

POLAND, Sir HARRY BODKIN (1829–1928), criminal lawyer, was born in London 9 July 1829. He was the sixth son of Peter Poland, furrier, of Bread Street and Winchester Hall, Highgate, by his wife, Sarah Selina, daughter of Edward Matless Jackson, of London. He was educated at St. Paul's School from 1841 to 1846 and was called to the bar by the Inner Temple in 1851. He became a bencher in 1879. He took chambers first at 7 King's Bench Walk and afterwards at 5 Paper Buildings with his friend Hardinge Giffard (afterwards Lord Halsbury, q.v.). The two friends shared these chambers until Giffard became lord chancellor in 1885. At the time of Poland's call his uncle by marriage, (Sir) William Henry Bodkin [q.v.], was in large practice as a criminal lawyer, and this fact doubtless contributed to Poland's decision to try his fortunes at the criminal bar and assisted him to make a start at the Old Bailey and at the Middlesex sessions at Clerkenwell. But it was his own qualities of untiring industry, lucidity, and accuracy which enabled him to build up a good practice.

In 1855 Poland appeared for the Crown in the successful prosecution of the bankers Sir John Dean Paul [q.v.], William Strahan, and Robert Makin Bates for misappropriation of securities. This case, according to Poland's own account, 'made his fortune'. In 1865 he was appointed counsel to the Treasury at the Central Criminal Court (the 'Old Bailey') and adviser to the Home Office in criminal matters; he held these offices for the unequalled period of twenty-three years. Poland proved an ideal prosecutor, eschewing all appeals to passion or prejudice but presenting the case for the Crown with a completeness, lucidity, and force which were all the more effective because they were combined with scrupulous fairness. The phrase 'Poland at whose name Freedom shrieks' (an adaptation of Campbell's 'And Freedom shriek'd when Kosciusko fell') was applied to him in jesting appreciation of the terror which he inspired in malefactors.

During his term of office Poland was necessarily engaged for the Crown in most of the important criminal trials of the day. In 1876 he appeared for the Crown against the *Lennie* mutineers who were tried for the murder of the captain and two mates of their ship. In this case he came to the conclusion that one of the prisoners, an Austrian named Giuseppe Lettis, was not a party to the murder. He therefore withdrew the case against him and accepted his evidence for the Crown. After the conclusion of the case the Austrian consul inquired whether Poland would accept a decoration from the Austrian government as an expression of its appreciation of his fairness to this prisoner. Poland declined the honour. Other noteworthy murder trials in which he appeared for the Crown were those of the Wainwrights (1876) and the Stauntons (1877).

Poland was also engaged for the Crown

in the *Franconia* case (*R.* v. *Keyn*, 1876) which raised the question of the jurisdiction of the English courts as regards crimes committed at sea. He also appeared on occasion for the defence—thus in 1868 he appeared for Edward John Eyre [q.v.], governor of Jamaica, in both the criminal and the civil proceedings. The case of *R.* v. *Willoughby* illustrates Poland's fairness. The prisoner (who had been previously convicted several times) was indicted for stealing chickens and also for a serious assault on their owner committed (as was alleged) immediately after the theft. The indictment for assault (as being the more serious of the two) was tried first. The defence was an alibi, and the prisoner asserted that two persons who were not called as witnesses might have established this defence. The judge summed up against the prisoner and the jury convicted. In view of this conviction the Crown did not proceed with the minor charge of stealing. Poland, however, was not satisfied of the man's guilt, and he caused inquiries to be made as a result of which the two witnesses were found. Poland then arranged that the prisoner should be tried on the indictment for stealing the chickens. The prisoner again set up his alibi and, as he was not represented by counsel, Poland, at the suggestion of the judge and with the consent of the prisoner, examined the two new witnesses as well as all the other witnesses for the defence. The result was an acquittal and a free pardon for the assault of which the prisoner had been previously convicted.

Besides his criminal work, Poland had acquired a considerable practice in other common law work, especially rating and licensing. He became a bencher of the Inner Temple in 1879. In 1888 he took silk and relinquished his appointment as Treasury counsel. He now appeared as leading counsel for the defence in criminal cases. His methods in this novel capacity remained unchanged, but his quiet and unimpassioned style was by no means unsuccessful with juries, and he was probably assisted by the reputation for fairness which he had acquired as a prosecutor. He is said to have been one of the earliest exponents of the defence of kleptomania. In 1895 he retired from practice and was knighted. It is said that he had intimated his unwillingness to accept a High Court judgeship when approached by Lord Halsbury. In 1874 he had succeeded Sir W. H. Bodkin in the recordership of Dover, an office which he retained until 1901 when he was succeeded by his cousin, Sir Archibald Henry Bodkin, afterwards director of public prosecutions.

Poland's retirement from his absorbing work at the bar had no adverse effect on his health, for he survived until his ninety-ninth year and his faculties remained almost unimpaired until he had long passed his ninetieth year. During his retirement he was a frequent correspondent of *The Times* on matters of legal and antiquarian interest, and he was a familiar and picturesque figure, in his black skull cap and slightly old-fashioned garb, in the library of the Inner Temple, where he spent much time verifying his references. There he was wont to converse in sonorous tones which aroused the affectionate interest of the other readers and which his deafness doubtless caused him to suppose were no louder than the customary discreet whisper.

Poland never married. His main interest in life until his retirement had always been his practice, although in his earlier years he had been fond of the theatre and of swimming. He was, however, an alderman of the London County Council from 1893 to 1901, and he gave useful evidence at governmental inquiries into the law of licensing and rating and the defence of poor prisoners. He was also an influential advocate of the reform which was ultimately achieved by the Criminal Evidence Act of 1898 under which accused persons and their wives or husbands are permitted to give evidence for the defence. He was, however, an opponent of the creation of a Court of Criminal Appeal. In 1862 he published a handbook on the Merchandise Marks Act 1862 entitled *Trade Marks. The Merchandise Marks Act 1862.* In 1900 he contributed a lecture on changes in criminal law to a series of lectures entitled 'Changes in the law of England during the Nineteenth Century' organized by the Council of Legal Education and published in 1901 under the title *A Century of Law Reform.*

Poland died in his sleep at his house in Sloane Gardens, London, 2 March 1928. An excellent photograph of him in his old age and a reproduction of a cartoon by 'Spy' will be found in Mr. E. Bowen-Rowlands's *Seventy-two Years at the Bar* (1924).

[*The Times*, 5 March 1928; *Law Journal*, 10 March 1928; *Law Times*, 10 March 1928; E. B. Bowen-Rowlands, *Seventy-two Years at the Bar*, 1924.] D. Davies.

POSTGATE, JOHN PERCIVAL (1853–1926), classical scholar, was born at Birmingham 24 October 1853, the eldest son of John Postgate, F.R.C.S., of Scarborough, by his wife, Mary Ann, daughter of Joshua Horwood, of Driffield, a surgeon in the royal navy; he was thus of purely Yorkshire stock. His father had had his own way to make, but had succeeded in qualifying as a medical practitioner before his thirtieth year, and subsequently won an honourable position in Birmingham, where he showed keen interest in the public side of his profession. Postgate was sent to King Edward's School, Birmingham, of which A. R. Vardy, a distinguished classic, was then headmaster; and in 1872 he was elected a scholar of Trinity College, Cambridge. He was placed eighth in the first class of the classical tripos of 1876, having won one of the chancellor's medals in the same year. In 1878 he was elected to a fellowship at his college, and in 1884 he was appointed a classical lecturer, an office which continued the fellowship; and, since he held the lecturership for the requisite twenty-five years, he remained a fellow until his death.

Postgate's first book, an edition of all the best-known elegies of Propertius (*Select Elegies of Propertius*, 1881), was hardly surpassed in scholarship and literary power by any of his later work; the discriminating enthusiasm and poetic feeling which appear in this volume, and no less in his editions of Books VII and VIII of Lucan (1896 and 1917) and in his text and translation of Tibullus (Loeb Library, 1913), show Postgate at his best; and it is mainly these qualities which constitute his peculiar contribution to English scholarship.

In 1880 Postgate was appointed to the professorship of comparative philology in University College, London, a post which he held till 1910. Although he wrote little on this subject apart from Latin, it gave a special degree of breadth and precision to his grammatical writing. Hence came his *New Latin Primer* in 1888, a short but admirable Latin grammar which had lasting success; hence, too, his enthusiasm for the correct pronunciation of Latin, the establishment of which perhaps owed more to him than to any other single scholar; and hence the delicate sense of Latin diction which inspired his own writing and teaching of Latin prose (see especially his *Sermo Latinus*, 1889 and 1913). It is not possible here to enumerate the thirty or forty books and booklets which Postgate devoted to one or other aspect of classical study; still less, the scores of articles which he contributed to the *Classical Review* and the *Classical Quarterly* before, during, and after his own editorship of those journals. His greatest undertaking was one which demanded twenty years of labour—his edition, with a critical commentary, of the *Corpus Poetarum Latinorum* in two quarto volumes (1893–1894 and 1904–1905). No such enterprise had been previously undertaken by any British scholar, and few other scholars, perhaps, could have carried it through with such distinction.

The *Corpus* has been seriously criticized in two points only. First, for its exclusion of the *Appendix Vergiliana* and several later poets, *e.g.* Ausonius and Claudian, as well as those commonly known as the *poetae minores*: omissions which, although it is perhaps ungrateful to resent them, do leave something substantial to be added by a succeeding generation. The other admitted failure is the result of Postgate's too sanguine attempt to rearrange the couplets and poems of Propertius merely by internal evidence, a task which he might have known was hopeless.

Postgate's editorial services were not confined to the *Corpus Poetarum*. He was in charge of the *Classical Review* from 1899 to 1907, and of the *Classical Quarterly* from 1907 to 1911. It may be doubted whether the contributions to any other learned journal ever received more careful editing. Even a second-rate article might be transformed into a first-class piece of work by his painstaking comments and suggestions. In questions of procedure, no doubt, he sometimes made mistakes which he afterwards regretted; but as a rule he was open to argument, although he clung to points on which he felt sure that he had reached the facts.

In the collation and criticism of manuscript evidence Postgate's work was hard to surpass; so rarely was his selective judgement of readings at fault. On the other hand, his own emendations, though often very clever, were rarely convincing. Those who did not know him imagined wrongly that it was only the smaller points of a case which he recognized. He was, in fact, deeply interested in questions of literature, politics, and philosophy. But his acute perception was always alive to the dangers of premature generalization, and he instinctively looked first to any points of fact, however small, that were in debate;

and if the evidence on these seemed to him adverse to some theory he was apt to reject that theory outright.

Thus it was that those who knew Postgate only at a distance were not a little surprised to find that his enthusiasm, embodied in an eloquent article in the *Fortnightly Review* in 1902 entitled 'Are the Classics to go?', followed up by a large and prolonged correspondence, brought to birth, in 1903, one of the most interesting and typical of English institutions, the Classical Association. He and Professor Edward Adolf Sonnenschein [q.v.] were its first honorary secretaries, and it still continues active work with twenty-four branches in Great Britain alone. Postgate was president of the Association in 1924–1925. Meanwhile his merits as a scholar had been recognized by honorary Litt.D. degrees from the universities of Manchester (1906) and Dublin (1907). He was elected a fellow of the British Academy in 1907.

In 1909 Postgate accepted the chair of Latin in the university of Liverpool. He held it for eleven years, and carried out its varied duties with resourcefulness, good humour, and enthusiasm. In addition to his translation of Tibullus and his edition of Lucan VIII, already mentioned, he published an edition of the *Fables* of Phaedrus (1920), during this period.

One of Postgate's last adventures in scholarship was his effort to reform both the teaching and the practice of Greek accentuation ('Ancient Greek Accentuation', *Proceedings* of the British Academy, vol. xi, 1924–1925). He contended with justice that the new evidence of the papyri showed that the traditional system, though correct in the main, is incorrect in some important details; secondly, that teachers of Greek had no right to force upon their pupils the labour of acquiring any rules which were ill founded; and thirdly, that it was to be seriously considered whether English teachers ought not to follow the example of other nations and give to the accents a proper spoken value. This fearless attempt at the age of seventy-one to reform what seemed to him fundamentally wrong was most characteristic and is probably destined to bear fruit.

Postgate's last essay was on a famous passage of Lucretius alleging and describing the use of wild animals in battle by primitive tribes—a passage which scholars have long defended, and some still defend, as being a pardonable poetic exaggeration. Postgate's frank declaration that it was the work of a brilliant mind which for the time had been unable to distinguish between dream and reality, and that it must be attributed to one of the fits of dementia to which we know the poet was liable, has won cordial assent from many Latin scholars. ('New Light on Lucretius', John Rylands Library *Bulletin*, January 1926).

A few months after this article had appeared Postgate met with a serious bicycle accident a few yards from his own home in Cambridge. He died from grave injuries the next day, 15 July 1926, leaving behind him memories of keen disputation, lively friendship, and whole-hearted devotion to knowledge.

Postgate married in 1891 a former pupil of his at Girton College, Edith, daughter of T. B. Allen, tea-merchant, and had four sons and two daughters.

[S. G. Owen in *Proceedings* of the British Academy, vol. xii, 1926; personal knowledge.]

R. S. Conway.

POWELL, Sir RICHARD DOUGLAS, first baronet (1842–1925), physician, born at Walthamstow 25 September 1842, was the second son of Captain Scott Powell, of the 23rd Royal Welch Fusiliers, by his wife, Eliza, daughter of Richard Meeke. Much of his boyhood was spent at Toft, near Cambridge, and there he laid the foundations of the interest in natural history and sport (fishing and shooting) which were the chief relaxations of his later life. Educated privately at Streatham, he gave up his wish to follow his father's profession and entered University College, London, with the object of studying medicine. He continued his course at University College Hospital, becoming physician's assistant (now termed house physician) to Sir William Jenner [q.v.], to whom he owed much in his early professional career.

A brilliant student with first class honours in the M.B. (1865) and qualifying for the gold medal at the M.D. (1866) examinations of the university of London, Powell was appointed in 1867 to take temporary charge of out-patients, and in 1869 he applied unsuccessfully for a vacancy as assistant physician at University College Hospital. Two years later (1871) he was elected assistant physician to Charing Cross Hospital where, five years afterwards (1876), he was joined by two other colleagues from his old medical school, (Sir) Thomas Barlow, who followed him as president of the Royal College of Physicians of London, and (Sir) Rickman John Godlee [q.v.], subsequently president of the Royal College of Surgeons of England. In 1878 Powell was elected assistant physician to the Middlesex Hospital, becoming physician in 1880 and consulting physician in 1900. Thus for nearly thirty years he taught medical students, being a stimulus to the thoughtful rather than a source of dogmatic answers for those interested only in satisfying examiners. As resident clinical assistant, assistant physician (1868), physician (1875), and consulting physician (1889) he was attached to the Brompton Hospital for Consumption and Diseases of the Chest, and was much in demand as a consultant in thoracic disease. For thirty-eight years he was connected with the court, being appointed physician-extraordinary (1887) in the place of Wilson Fox [q.v.], whom in some respects he much resembled, and physician-in-ordinary (1899) to Queen Victoria, whom he attended in her last illness (1901); he continued to serve in the latter capacity King Edward VII and King George V.

A hard worker, Powell's published writings extended over a period of fifty-six years and included articles on diseases of the chest contributed to Russell Reynolds's *System of Medicine* (1879), and to the two editions (1898–1899 and 1909) of its successor, Sir T. C. Allbutt's *System.* He also wrote a text-book on *Pulmonary Tuberculosis* in 1872 which, with altered titles, went through six editions, the last two appearing in 1911 and 1921 respectively in collaboration with Sir Percival Horton-Smith Hartley. He also published his Lumleian lectures, delivered in 1898 at the Royal College of Physicians of London, in an expanded form as *The Principles which govern Treatment in Diseases and Disorders of the Heart* (1899).

In the medical life of London Powell was continuously at work from the time when he was a junior at the Pathological Society, of which he was secretary (1877–1879). Later he was successively president of the Medical Society of London (1891), the Clinical Society of London (1899–1901), and the Royal Medical and Chirurgical Society (1904–1906), being in the chair at the centenary banquet (22 May 1905) of the last-named society, and taking a full share in the arrangements, occupying two years, necessary for its amalgamation with seventeen other medical societies into the Royal Society of Medicine (1907). Powell also lent his help to the formation, initiated by Sir William Osler [q.v.], of the Association of Physicians of Great Britain and Ireland, and was its first president (1907). At the Royal College of Physicians of London he became a member (1867), a fellow (1873), held several offices, was president (1905–1910), and delivered the Harveian oration in 1914. He was deputy-chairman (1899–1925) of the Clerical, Medical, and General Life Assurance Society, and in 1896 was president of the Life Assurance Medical Officers' Association. With the Conservative and Unionist Association of the university of London he was closely connected for more than thirty years, and was its president 1909–1919. He was created a baronet in 1897 and K.C.V.O. in 1901, and received several honorary degrees from English, Scottish, and Irish universities.

Powell was a striking personality. Tall, slight, with an ascetic, clean-shaven, pale face, charming in manner and voice, reticent, correct, cautious, dignified, and kindly, he was widely recognized as an impressive leader. He married twice: first, in 1873 Juliet (died 1909), second daughter of Sir John Bennett [q.v.], sheriff of London and Middlesex, and niece of William Cox Bennett [q.v.], miscellaneous writer; secondly, in 1917 Edith Mary Burke (died 1935), younger daughter of Henry Wood, of Cleveland Square, Hyde Park, London. By his first wife he had three sons and two daughters. He died in London after a short illness 15 December 1925, contributions from his pen to the medical press appearing three days before and two weeks after his death. He was succeeded as second baronet by his eldest son Douglas (1874–1932,) brevet lieutenant-colonel, Royal Welch Fusiliers. The second son was killed in the South African War; the third in the European War.

A portrait of Powell by Spencer Watson belongs to his grandson, Sir Richard Powell, third baronet; a replica is in the possession of the Royal College of Physicians of London. A cartoon of him by 'Spy' appeared in *Vanity Fair* 28 April 1904.

[*British Medical Journal*, 1925, vol. ii, p. 1201; personal knowledge.]

H. D. Rolleston.

PRIMROSE, ARCHIBALD PHILIP, fifth Earl of Rosebery (1847–1929), statesman and author, was born at 20 Charles Street, Berkeley Square, London, 7 May 1847, the elder son and third child of Archibald Primrose, Lord Dalmeny, and grandson of Archibald John Primrose, fourth Earl of Rosebery [q.v.]. His mother was Catherine Lucy Wilhelmina, the only daughter of Philip Henry Stanhope, fourth Earl Stanhope, the sister of Philip Henry Stanhope, fifth Earl Stanhope, the historian [q.v.]. Lord Dalmeny died in 1850. Fours years later his widow married Harry George Vane, fourth Duke of Cleveland.

Archibald Philip Primrose was educated first at Bayford, near Hertford, and then at Mr. Lee's school at Brighton. In 1860 he went to Eton. His tutor, William Johnson, better known as William Johnson Cory [q.v.], formed a high opinion of his ability, writing of him as 'surely the wisest boy that ever lived'. In 1862 a privately printed volume of verse indicated Lord Dalmeny's literary bent, and when in 1864 he was elected to 'Pop' he showed exceptional gifts as a speaker. He made no mark as a scholar, but reading where his inclination led him and to no specified end, he acquired a wide general culture. In later years he declared that he owed 'whatever ambitions or aspirations I ever indulged in to Macaulay's *Essays*'. In spite of a 'shade of constraint' in his bearing and a precocious maturity which made him difficult of approach, he was popular at school. Among his contemporaries at Eton were Arthur James Balfour, Lord Randolph Churchill, and the fifth Marquess of Lansdowne.

In January 1866 Dalmeny matriculated at Christ Church, Oxford. In the following year, in reply to a suggestion that he should enter parliament, he declared that he had no politics, adding that 'in any case it is not the time for a young man to commit himself in any way on either side'. A year later (March 1868) on the death of his grandfather he succeeded to the earldom and estates which included Dalmeny Park, near Edinburgh, and other properties in Scotland.

Before the opening of parliament in 1869 Rosebery was invited by Lord Granville to second the address in the House of Lords. In declining the offer he announced his adhesion to the liberal cause. In the same year he began his career as an owner of racehorses, buying and entering for the Derby a colt called Ladas. The university authorities took exception to an undergraduate figuring on the turf and, on his refusal to give up his stud, his name was removed from the books. Rosebery, therefore, left Oxford without a degree. In 1870 he was elected to the Jockey Club, and in February 1871, in seconding the address, made his first speech in the House of Lords. The encomiums which the speech evoked were more than customary. Rosebery himself noted in his diary: 'Great congratulations, very ill deserved'. In November of the same year he read to the Edinburgh Philosophical Institution a striking paper on the Union of England and Scotland, which confirmed the opinions already formed of his talents. His speeches, which showed increasing study and reflection, his territorial possessions, his association with the most popular British sport, an established reputation for wit, and the charm of his personality, combined to make him at the age of twenty-four an outstanding figure among his contemporaries, with a future of great expectation.

In the House of Lords in the session of 1872 in committee on the Scottish Education Bill, Rosebery moved an amendment against denominationalism. At Queensferry in September, when presented with the freedom of the burgh, he spoke at length on the same topic. At this time Scottish interests were prominent in his speeches, and he was continually urging that they should receive fuller consideration by parliament. In the same year Mr. Gladstone offered him a household appointment with the duty of answering for the Poor Law Board in the House of Lords. The offer was declined, but refusal to accept the lord-lieutenancy of Linlithgow was withdrawn in deference to pressure from Lord Granville.

On 4 June 1872 Rosebery intervened for the first time in foreign affairs in a debate on the terms of the arbitration between the United States and Great Britain for damage done in the American Civil War. It was proposed as a condition precedent to arbitration that the United States should be invited to withdraw certain heads of claim. Rosebery urged that nothing should be done which could have the appearance of dictation to America or disturb the relations between the two countries. There was no division, and before the arbitration America withdrew the claims in question.

In the autumn of 1873 Rosebery paid his first visit to North America, including a flying visit to Canada. His notes written at the time record his close observation of the American outlook on home and foreign affairs. He returned to the United States in 1874 and 1876 and again in 1882 with Lady Rosebery on their way to Australia.

In parliament during these years Rosebery spoke seldom, but always with effect. A speech in the House of Lords against creating the title of Empress of India (1876), and speeches in Scotland in defence of liberal principles marked him out as a force in political life. But the Eastern question was now growing acute, and he became an active critic of Lord Beaconsfield's policy, attacking the government for failing to satisfy the claims of Greece and for undertaking to defend the Asiatic dominions of Turkey, as to which he declared 'that one may pay too great a price even for the preservation of India'. He was opposed then, as he was opposed thirty years later in the case of France, to incurring obligations which might involve Great Britain in war, and in October 1878, at Aberdeen, he charged the government with having, by the Treaty of Berlin, 'incurred responsibilities of a vast and unknown kind' without consulting the British parliament and the British people.

In the autumn of 1878 Rosebery was elected lord rector of Aberdeen University, delivering his inaugural address, a characteristic and powerful plea for the study of Scottish history, on 5 November 1880. On the day following his Aberdeen address he was elected lord rector of Edinburgh University, but it was not until 4 November 1882 that he delivered his rectorial address on patriotism.

In 1878 Rosebery married Hannah, only daughter and heiress of Baron Meyer Amschel de Rothschild [q.v.], of Mentmore, Buckinghamshire. Baron Meyer having died in 1874 and his wife in 1877, Hannah de Rothschild had succeeded to the family fortune, which comprised Mentmore and its famous works of art. In 1879 Rosebery, who had risen to a position of eminence and authority in Scotland second only to that of the Duke of Argyll, and was now regarded as the future leader of the Scottish liberals, invited Mr. Gladstone to make Dalmeny the head-quarters for his Midlothian campaign. The course of the contest, which resulted in the return of Gladstone as member for Midlothian, brought Rosebery into spectacular prominence and bound him to Gladstonian liberalism. On the formation of his second ministry in 1880 Gladstone offered Rosebery the under-secretaryship of the India Office. In a letter of 25 April, acting on a characteristic scruple, Rosebery declined the offer, saying that in accepting he would 'lose the certainty that what I have done in the matter of the elections, however slight, has been disinterested'. The offer was renewed in July, but again declined on account of the state of his health. In the new parliament he was active in pressing Scottish claims, and the desirability of appointing a minister for Scottish affairs.

In August 1881 Rosebery was offered and accepted the under-secretaryship of the Home Office with special charge of Scottish business in the House of Lords, thus coming into official relations with Sir William Harcourt [q.v.], then home secretary. In Scotland, especially, the office was regarded as far from commensurate with the position which Rosebery had acquired in the country and in parliament. While generally supporting Gladstone's Irish measures Rosebery was by no means satisfied, and he wrote in his diary (6 May 1882): 'I am clear that I disagree with the policy of government, but am almost clear that I ought not to resign', adding an intention to ask Gladstone 'what is the exact position of a subordinate like myself with reference to Cabinet policy?' The next day his doubts were resolved by the news of the assassinations of Lord Frederick Cavendish and T. H. Burke. The government must be supported. But the close of 1882 found him dissatisfied with the delay in dealing with Scottish affairs, and in the spring of 1883—nothing having been done in the meantime, notwithstanding his protests to Gladstone—he resigned. In July he was offered the Scottish Office, should the bill creating it be passed, but he declined, stating that his advocacy of the office debarred him from accepting.

In September 1883 Lord and Lady Rosebery visited New Zealand and Australia, where, in the course of a series of public speeches, Rosebery developed his view of Imperial relations. On 18 January 1884, speaking at Adelaide, he asked the question whether the fact of Australia being a nation implied separation from the Empire. 'God forbid', he continued, 'there is no need for any nation, however great, leaving the Empire, because the Empire is a *Commonwealth of Nations*.' He returned to England (by way of Ceylon, March 1884) with the Imperial idea deeply rooted in his mind, and convinced of the need for a new outlook on the development of empire, broadly comprehended in the phrase 'commonwealth of nations', with 'mutual self-respect and mutual independence' as basic conditions. In Scotland he was given the freedom of Dundee, his reception showing the commanding position which he now held in Scottish opinion.

On 20 June 1884 Rosebery took his first step towards reform of the House of Lords, moving 'that a select committee be appointed to consider the best means of promoting the efficiency of this House'. In a speech praised for its eloquence and wit, he urged the necessity for increasing the representative character of the House, and enlarged on the danger of delay. The defeat of the motion was made decisive by Lord Granville and his colleagues walking out. Rosebery's speech in support of the second reading of the Representation Bill in July established his reputation as one of the best speakers of the day. The Prince of Wales (afterwards King Edward VII) wrote to express his admiration, and T. H. S. Escott described it as 'incomparably the best speech in the whole debate'. In November Gladstone offered him the post of first commissioner of works with a seat in the Cabinet. The offer was less perhaps than that to which Rosebery's position entitled him, but it was declined on other grounds. In February 1885, however, the political situation was rendered critical by the fall of Khartoum. Rosebery at once informed Gladstone of his willingness to take office. 'The question', he wrote, 'now is one less of policy than of patriotism', and he was thereupon appointed to the Board of Works with a seat in the Cabinet as lord privy seal. The government early in April decided to abandon the Sudan. In reply to a letter from Sir Henry Ponsonby inviting his opinion, Rosebery wrote justifying government action: 'It is a choice of great evils, I admit, but I am sure we chose the least.' The situation had been altered in March by the Penjdeh incident, which brought Great Britain to the verge of war with Russia, and rendered imperative the suspension of military operations in the Sudan.

In May Rosebery visited Count Herbert Bismarck, a lifelong friend, in Berlin, and was introduced to his father, the chancellor, with whom he discussed informally the attitude of Germany with regard to the Egyptian loan, the Afghan frontier question, Turkey, and the African colonies, all which matters were causing friction between Great Britain and Germany. Meanwhile, the Irish question had reached an acute stage in the Cabinet. Joseph Chamberlain [q.v.], supported by Sir Charles Dilke [q.v.], was opposed to 'coercion' and in favour of a large measure of local government; Rosebery, while favouring local government, held that the lord-lieutenant, Lord Spencer, should be granted such powers as he claimed were essential for the maintenance of law and order. On 8 June the government was defeated on an amendment to the budget. Upon the resignation of Mr. Gladstone, Queen Victoria sent for Lord Salisbury, who consented to form a government pending the dissolution of parliament in November.

In the autumn, at Paisley, Rosebery, after an effective attack on the conservative policy of general conciliation towards Ireland and on the negotiations between the lord-lieutenant, Lord Carnarvon [q.v.], and Parnell, dealt with the Irish leader's recent demands. 'What is proposed', he continued, 'is that Ireland should be treated as a colony. . . . If I had the power and if I were convinced that Ireland were loyal to the connexion with this country, there would be no limits to the concessions that I would offer to Ireland.' At Sheffield he dealt with social subjects, favouring shorter hours and state-aided emigration. At Slaithwaite (near Huddersfield) he outlined a land policy advocating the abolition of primogeniture, more equitable distribution of interests, simplification of transfer, and extension of allotments. In November, at a banquet given to him by the Scottish liberals, he returned to the Irish question and said: 'If you can obtain from the representatives of Ireland a clear and constitutional demand which will represent the wishes of the people of Ireland, and which will not conflict with the unity or the supremacy of this country, then by satisfying that demand Ireland might see in this country her best ally.'

At the general election of November 1885 the conservatives and the followers of Parnell exactly balanced the liberals, but on 26 January 1886 the government was defeated on an amendment to the address, and Lord Salisbury resigned the next day. Mr. Gladstone was sent for by the queen, and in the new administration Rosebery accepted the foreign secretaryship. To the queen he said of his new office: 'It was too much.' But the queen herself described it as 'the only good appointment'. At his official visit to Lord Salisbury, Rosebery expressed his intention of maintaining the continuity of policy in foreign affairs. The outlook had recently improved: danger of war with Russia had been removed by the protocol of 10 September 1885 which secured the Zulfikar pass to the ameer of Afghanistan; a better understanding with Germany had eased the situation in Egypt; and Lord Salisbury had given a warning that a threatened war between Greece and Turkey would not be tolerated by Great Britain. In April Rosebery, in continuation of his predecessor's policy, joined in an ultimatum addressed by the Powers to Greece. In May notice of blockade by the combined squadrons was presented, and Greece capitulated. Anticipations freely entertained that a liberal government would mean a new policy in South-Eastern Europe were thus falsified.

In his foreign policy Rosebery showed that he could be decided and firm. The attempt of the French to occupy the New Hebrides formed the subject of a strongly worded dispatch to Lord Lyons [q.v.], ambassador at Paris; a failure on the part of Sir Robert Morier [q.v.], ambassador at St. Petersburg, to adhere to his instructions called forth a severe reprimand; while later, a declaration by Russia that Batum was no longer to be a free port, was met by a dispatch from Rosebery in which he said: 'H.M. government are compelled to place on record their view that this proceeding of the Russian government constitutes a violation of the Treaty of Berlin.... In no case can H.M. government have any share in it. It must rest on the responsibility of its authors.' The Tsar was painfully affected by the terms of the document, while the Russian chancellor, M. de Giers, described it as 'the most wounding communication that has ever been addressed to one Power by another'. In Egypt Rosebery recognized that a respite was needed from 'projects, reports, and conventions', and gave whole-hearted support to Sir Evelyn Baring (afterwards first Earl of Cromer, q.v.).

The defeat of Mr. Gladstone's Home Rule Bill in June 1886 resulted in another general election and the return of the conservatives and liberal-unionists to power with a majority of 113. Rosebery left the Foreign Office with his reputation as a statesman greatly strengthened. He had kept foreign affairs free of the fluctuations of domestic politics, and in distrusting Russia, in maintaining an attitude of firmness towards France, and in laying stress on the common interests of Germany and Great Britain, he had secured continuity with the policy of Lord Salisbury. Speaking at Manchester in August, Gladstone told the liberal party that in Rosebery they saw 'the man of the future'.

In October 1886 Rosebery left England for a visit to India, returning in the spring of 1887. During his absence the Round Table Conference had shown that no agreement between Home Rulers and liberal-unionists was possible. Rosebery in speeches up and down the country declared his adherence to Gladstonian liberalism and to the general principle that 'Ireland should be allowed to manage her own affairs in the way of domestic legislation'. To Lord Randolph Churchill he expressed his satisfaction with the state of the liberal party, 'no longer a flabby disconnected majority but a compact minority united by a principle'. As chairman at this time of the Imperial Federation League, Rosebery was constantly bringing before the country the question of Imperial Federation, 'the closest possible union of the various self-governing states ruled by the British Crown, consistently with the free national development which is the birthright of British subjects all over the world—the closest union in sympathy, in external action, and in defence'. Describing it as 'the dominant passion of his public life', he probably did more than any statesman of his time to advance the cause of cohesion as against disintegration, to dissociate the idea of empire from aggrandizement, and to reconcile liberal opinion to a new conception of Imperial relations. While refraining from specifying the form of the relationship which should exist, he advocated recurrent colonial conferences and the admission to the Privy Council of colonial ministers and colonial judges.

In 1888 Rosebery again brought forward his motion for a select committee to inquire into the constitution of the House of Lords. His definite proposals included curtailment of the hereditary right to a seat in the House, election of peers by county councils and municipalities, representation of the colonies, and, in the event of disagreement, a joint meeting of both Houses with decisions dependent upon certain fixed majorities. The motion was defeated by 97 votes to 50. In 1889 Rosebery was returned for the City in the election for the new London County Council and was chosen as chairman by 104 votes to 17. He held the office for a year and threw himself into the work with devoted public spirit. His authority and experience gave distinction to the new body, and his aptitude for detail, by many unsuspected, proved invaluable in guiding the proceedings. Time, however, has not endorsed two items of his municipal programme, namely, the control of the police by the Council and the merging of the Corporation of the City and the London County Council. For a short period in 1892 he again accepted the chairmanship of the Council.

In November 1890 Rosebery's life was darkened by the death of his wife. This was a blow from which it is doubtful if he ever wholly recovered. Her wisdom and rare serenity of character had been invaluable elements both in his domestic and in his public life. For the next eighteen months he withdrew from politics and, with his health affected, spent much of his time on the continent.

In June 1892 parliament was dissolved. The election which followed showed a majority of forty for Home Rule, and Mr. Gladstone became prime minister for the fourth time. Rosebery was reluctant to take office: he had the gravest doubt if 'his long loneliness and sleeplessness' had not unfitted him for public life, and expressed to Gladstone his 'loathing of politics' [Lord Crewe, *Life*, ii, p. 402]. This attitude excited impatience among some of his colleagues. Harcourt regarded it as 'pretty Fanny's way'; Morley wrote: 'How tiresome all this sort of thing is.' But it was only after a moving appeal from Mr. Gladstone and a strongly worded letter from the Prince of Wales indicating the wishes of the queen, that Rosebery's distaste for office was overcome. On 15 August he again became secretary for foreign affairs, and in October he was created K.G.

The question of British withdrawal from Uganda at once revealed differences in the Cabinet. Harcourt was in favour of immediate evacuation. To this Rosebery was opposed. A crisis was only averted by a compromise suspending withdrawal for three months, the question to be investigated by a commissioner on the spot. Some eighteen months later (June 1894), as the result of the mission of Sir Gerald Portal [q.v.], a British protectorate was declared, and Uganda, in accordance with Rosebery's policy, became part of the British Empire. In January 1893 there was again disagreement over Egypt. The dismissal by the young khedive Abbas of ministers friendly to England was objected to by Lord Cromer. Rosebery supported the action of Cromer, but Harcourt, who was in favour of withdrawal from Egypt, was strongly opposed to the interference involved. A protest by France against British action was met by instructions from Rosebery to the British ambassador in Paris to the effect that so long as the British flag was flying in Egypt such action on the part of the khedive would not be tolerated. Appointments were thereupon made in conformity with the wishes of Cromer, and in February, the British garrison having been reinforced, fear of a Mohammedan outbreak ended. In July a French ultimatum to Siam and a rumour that the French had ordered British gunboats to leave Bangkok, created a grave crisis. The rumour proved to be false, and the handling of the crisis by the foreign secretary resulted in a settlement of the differences between the two countries. In answer to a communication from the queen, Rosebery in a memorandum of 9 June dealt with his attitude towards Home Rule. He viewed it with guarded approval 'as the most practicable or the least impracticable method of governing the country'. In the House of Lords he spoke at length on the second reading of the second Home Rule Bill, which was defeated on 8 September by 419 votes to 41.

On 17 November Rosebery intervened in the great coal strike of 1893 and, presiding at the Foreign Office over a meeting of owners and men's leaders, succeeded in bringing about a settlement. Towards the end of the year there was disagreement in the Cabinet over the naval estimates. The controversy dragged on; Rosebery supporting Lord Spencer, then first lord of the Admiralty, Gladstone and Harcourt protesting against the increase asked for. Harcourt finally accepted some minor amendments; but Gladstone was inflexible, and burdened with his weight of years and threatened with loss of sight, he resigned on 3 March 1894. On the same day, acting on her own initiative, the queen offered the premiership to Rosebery. Anticipating that the policy which he had inherited and intended to pursue might disturb his relations of confidence with the queen, he accepted with hesitation.

The Cabinet as a whole approved the appointment, but differences soon became apparent. Harcourt, whose claims to the succession had received strong support in the liberal party and in the radical press, was at variance with his chief on a number of questions. The foreign secretaryship, which a section of the Cabinet held should be in the House of Commons, was given to Lord Kimberley. On 11 March a pronouncement by Rosebery in his speech on the address 'that before Irish Home Rule is concluded by the Imperial parliament, England as the predominant member of the partnership of the three kingdoms will have to be convinced of its justice and equity', which was interpreted as meaning that Home Rule could only be passed by purely English votes, created consternation in the party and exasperated the Irish. Two days later an amendment to the address, abolishing the veto of the Lords, was carried by two votes. A new address had to be substituted. Friction in the Cabinet increased as the session advanced. Harcourt's famous death-duties budget evoked criticism from the premier and gave rise to an exchange of embittered memoranda between the two ministers. Further, an Anglo-Belgian agreement for the lease to the king of the Belgians of territory on the Upper Nile, negotiated by Rosebery and Kimberley, was bitterly opposed by Harcourt without whose knowledge the preliminaries had been adjusted. Protests to Belgium from Germany and France led to the abandonment of the lease by the king.

On 27 October 1894 Rosebery at Bradford opened his campaign for reform of the House of Lords, but beyond the audience of 4,500 whom he addressed, the proposals aroused little enthusiasm. The rejection of the Home Rule Bill had strengthened the position of the upper chamber in the country. The queen wrote (30 October) to protest against the policy which Rosebery had announced. In a letter in reply, Rosebery on 1 November justified his policy, claiming that it was conservative in its ultimate tendency and deprecating the suggestion put forward by the queen that she should have been consulted before the policy was announced [*Letters of Queen Victoria*, third series, vol. ii, pp. 432–444]. Before a large audience at Glasgow on 14 November, Rosebery again spoke on House of Lords reform, and declared himself in favour both of Welsh and of Scottish disestablishment. In the same month, by summoning a conference at Downing Street on the co-ordination of the fighting services, he may be said to have taken the first step towards the formation of the Committee of Imperial Defence. In January 1895 at a meeting of the National Liberal Federation he paid a generous tribute to the work done by Harcourt as leader of the House of Commons, and renewed his plea for reform of the House of Lords and disestablishment of the Welsh Church.

Early in 1895 Rosebery suffered from a severe attack of influenza which left him seriously weakened and a victim of insomnia. The strain of office, the difficulties which beset him within the Cabinet, and the attacks to which he was subjected in a portion of the radical press were undoubtedly at this time affecting his health. The session opened on 5 February. The party programme included plural voting, Welsh disestablishment, and a liquor control bill. But the Parnellite group under the leadership of John Redmond [q.v.] was hostile, and the government could only count on a majority of fifteen. Against the advice of Rosebery, the question of the House of Lords was relegated to the background. On 21 June the government was defeated by 132 votes against 125 in the House of Commons on the question of the supply of cordite, and Rosebery at once resigned, receiving from the queen as a mark of special favour the order of the Thistle. Cabinet differences were reflected in the election which followed, Rosebery, Harcourt, and Morley putting in the forefront respectively reform of the House of Lords, local option, and Home Rule. The unionists were returned with a majority of 152. On 12 August Rosebery wrote to Harcourt a formal intimation that their official connexion must be regarded as at an end.

In 1895–1896 the Armenian massacres drew Mr. Gladstone from his retirement. In a speech at Liverpool in August 1896 he suggested that the British ambassador should be recalled from Constantinople and the Turkish ambassador in London be given his passports. This policy was supported by a section of the liberals. To Rosebery, who saw in isolated action the likelihood of war, this proved the 'last straw on his back', and on 8 October he resigned the leadership of the liberal party. The following day at the Empire Theatre, Edinburgh, to a tense and crowded audience he made his farewell speech as leader. 'Home to supper. What a relief', is the entry in his diary for that evening. Inability to act in partnership with Harcourt, the fact that his lead had been disregarded at the general election, and lastly, the intervention of Mr. Gladstone with a policy to which he could not subscribe, combined to make a further continuance of his harassed term of leadership impossible. In 1897 by the purchase of the Villa Delahante at Posilipo, near Naples, a locality to which he was devoted, he secured a retreat remote from the arena of politics.

The death of Gladstone in 1898 brought Rosebery back to the House of Lords to deliver a fine panegyric on his chief. His retirement had failed to effect any semblance of unity in the liberal ranks, and in 1899, Sir Henry Campbell-Bannerman having succeeded Harcourt in the leadership of the party, Rosebery emerged from his seclusion, and in May, at the City Liberal Club, urged the party to return to liberalism as it had been before 1886, and to seek a combination of the old liberal spirit with the new Imperial spirit. In November he delivered an eloquent and memorable rectorial address on Imperial questions at Glasgow University.

The outbreak of the South African War in 1899 accentuated the cleavage in the liberal party. In 1901 a new organization, the Liberal Imperial Council, was formed of the followers of Rosebery with the object of supporting his leadership and promoting his Imperial policy. But on 17 July in a letter to *The Times*, while pointing out that there were now two schools of liberal statesmanship, the insular and the Imperial, pulling in opposite directions, Rosebery stated that he could never voluntarily return to the arena of party politics. Two days later (19 July) at the City Liberal Club, he referred to 'ploughing his lonely furrow'. A speech at Chesterfield in December in which he called for 'a clean slate' and advocated discussion of peace terms with the Boers led to a visit from Campbell-Bannerman in search of agreement. But co-operation was not to be attained, and in February 1902 the formation of the Liberal League with Rosebery as president and H. H. Asquith, Sir Edward Grey, and Sir Henry Fowler as vice-presidents, denoted a definite split between the two wings of the party. But in May 1903 the opening of Chamberlain's tariff reform campaign brought about a change in the situation, and supplied the liberal party with a common ground in defence of free trade. Rosebery in the course of the year spoke at a number of meetings in opposition to Chamberlain's proposals, but mindful of the way in which his own policy had been received, he held aloof from formal co-operation with the official leader of the party.

In 1905 Rosebery spoke at the City Liberal Club and in the country in criticism of the Anglo-French agreement, anticipating that it was more likely to lead to complications than to peace, and in a speech at Bodmin he emphatically dissociated himself from Home Rule, which had once more been brought to the front by Campbell-Bannerman. But his independence brought with it an inevitable decline in influence, and when Campbell-Bannerman became prime minister in December and was joined by the vice-presidents of the Liberal League, Rosebery finally severed himself from official liberalism. In the years immediately following he was much at his house at Posilipo. At home he took little part in politics beyond presiding at the annual meetings of the Liberal League. In the House of Lords he thenceforward occupied a seat on the cross benches. In Scotland he spoke on a number of ceremonial occasions, and among his most notable utterances must be included his speech when unveiling a memorial to the Scots Greys at Edinburgh on 16 November 1906 and his address as chancellor of the university of Glasgow on 12 June 1908 on the influence of national universities on Scottish character.

In 1909 the budget introduced by Mr. Lloyd George recalled him once more into the political field, and in a letter to the press (21 June 1909) and at a meeting in Glasgow (10 September 1909) he denounced the financial provisions dealing with land as revolutionary and leading directly to socialism. In November the Finance Bill reached the House of Lords, and he again spoke in condemnation of its proposals, but warned the House against rejecting the measure. This attitude was much criticized, yet his Glasgow speech had indicated that he was not prepared to stake the existence of the House of Lords on such an issue. The rejection of the budget by the peers was followed by the general election of January 1910. In the parliament which succeeded on 14 March Rosebery brought forward in the House of Lords resolutions in favour of reform and reconstitution. The resolutions were passed, but the death of King Edward VII on 6 May prevented their being further dealt with at the moment. On 15 November the conference dealing with the constitutional crisis between Lords and Commons having meanwhile broken down, Rosebery again brought forward his resolutions, which were again passed without a division. Before the general election of December 1910 he spoke at Manchester and Edinburgh, condemning the Parliament Bill as 'ill-judged, revolutionary, and partisan'. On 9 August 1911 the Bill, which had been drastically amended by the Lords, was again returned from the House of Commons, and Rosebery, who had not supported the amendments, denounced the measure but declared that great as were its evils he considered them less disastrous than the creation of sufficient peers to ensure the passing of the Bill. He therefore voted with the government, afterwards drawing up a protest, signed by fourteen other peers, to be recorded in the journals of the House. It was the end of his work in the House of Lords. At the coronation of King George V in June he had been created Earl of Midlothian in the peerage of the United Kingdom. In September he delivered his rectorial address at St. Andrews University—one of the happiest of all his notable non-political utterances.

The outbreak of the European War in 1914 led to Rosebery's appearance on many platforms, and in a series of stirring speeches he spoke on empire, the calls of patriotism, the need for recruits, and confidence in final victory. In December 1916 he was offered high office in the second Coalition government, but refused. The following year his younger son, Neil Primrose, was killed in action. Rosebery continued his war speeches from time to time, but he was a stricken man. In November 1918 he was prostrated by the circulation of an embolism, and thenceforward remained partially crippled, but maintaining his interest in current affairs, in books, and in the society of his friends. He died 21 May 1929 at his home, The Durdans, Epsom, and was buried in the church at Dalmeny. Since 1887 his town house had been 38 Berkeley Square.

In 1891 Rosebery published a small volume on William Pitt for the 'Twelve English Statesmen' series edited by John Morley. The work is a judicial exposition of the known facts of Pitt's career, written with consummate felicity and charm. It met with an instant success. It was followed in 1900 by *Napoleon: the Last Phase*, and in 1910 by *Chatham: his Early Life and Connections*. The reputation of the three books is based less on research or even revelation than on Rosebery's power to give life and colour to historical portraits. The volumes abound with evidence of this special gift, and although limited in scope, they reveal the loss suffered by literature and historical writing when their author gave himself to a political career. In 1906 Rosebery published a monograph on *Lord Randolph Churchill*, the most completely successful of his writings. The combination was unusual. Contemporaries at Eton and close friends at Oxford, and later occupying positions of eminence in the state, the two men, although differing in politics, retained to the end the sympathy and affection of their early days. The appreciation is written with lightness and charm and an intimate comprehension of Churchill's character and genius. In the same vein of portraiture Rosebery's sketches of *Sir Robert Peel* (1899), *Oliver Cromwell* (1899), and *William Windham* (1913) stand out among his numerous occasional essays and addresses.

Few men have had a more successful career as an owner of racehorses than Lord Rosebery. He won the principal classic events of the turf, including the Derby three times, with Ladas the second in 1894, with Sir Visto in 1895, and with Cicero in 1905. He was no amateur owner, but a highly versed student of breeding and form. The Durdans (which he purchased in 1874) is celebrated for its collection of pictures of famous horses of the past, and in the extensive library is included a section dealing with the horse in all its aspects. He was the last to use in London a cabriolet, driving a high-stepping horse with a 'tiger' standing on a platform at the back. In later years he made a habit of driving in the country at night after dinner in an open victoria with a pair of horses and a postilion.

Rosebery was of middle height, strongly built, and of active habits. His head was massive, with a fine intellectual forehead and regular features. His eyes were light blue, and normally enigmatic in the quiescence of their expression, but readily breaking into animation and a smile of singular radiance which illuminated his whole countenance. His general appearance altered little with age. He found pleasure in long walks in the country, and in shooting, at which he was proficient. But yachting, regardless of weather, and racing were his principal pastimes. He disliked games, saying, 'Balfour prefers any game to no game, I prefer no game to any game'. He was a born talker, varied, witty, and informed, master of ironic banter and humour, passing easily from light to shade, from gaiety to earnestness, and appearing always to give his best. In society he was liable to disconcerting moments of silence and was at little pains to disguise when he was bored. He was at his happiest when in company of his own choosing, at Dalmeny, or The Durdans, on his yacht, or at his villa at Posilipo.

Although Rosebery inherited works of art of the highest quality, his interest lay in the associations rather than in the beauty of his possessions. He was a noted collector of portraits and relics of historical characters. Every year his outlay on books for the libraries at Barnbougle, the castle adjoining Dalmeny, and The Durdans was considerable, and his gift (1927) to the National Library in Edinburgh of Scottish books and pamphlets is remarkable for the range and rarity of its contents. He was an omnivorous reader in the field of biography, history, and memoirs, and of these, with the aid of a strong and accurate memory, his knowledge was profound. But he eschewed science and philosophy, and, indeed, speculative writing of all kinds, and concerned himself little with modern literature save in so far as it threw light on aspects of the past.

As an orator Rosebery enjoyed a period of unequalled prestige. His speeches were studiously prepared, and the contrivance of his effects, if sometimes too elaborate, was often masterly. His voice was strong, flexible, and harmonious; his vocabulary authentic and direct rather than subtle or rare. In speaking he would emphasize a passage with an up and down movement of both arms bent, or sink his voice to a note so deep as to appear at times almost painfully mannered. He delighted in the exercise of his gift of oratory, and passages in his speech to the press of the Empire (5 June 1909), in his rectorial addresses at Glasgow (16 November 1900) and St. Andrews (14 September 1911), and in his address on Robert Burns (21 July 1896) have been ranked with the greatest masterpieces of British eloquence.

Rosebery held that he had been drawn into politics largely by force of circumstances and was wont to declare that they were hateful to him. But he was far from insensible to the gratifications of celebrity and high position. He wanted office on his own terms with freedom to carry out his own policy. As foreign minister he approached most nearly to the conditions which he required. As such he acted with judgement and distinction, showing firmness and restraint, brooking little interference from his colleagues, and winning a position of authority among the statesmen of Europe. As prime minister he was faced with the conditions which he was least qualified to control, by a powerful leader of the House of Commons definitely hostile to him, and a party of which a large section regarded Imperialism, and reform of the House of Lords as a means to the creation of a strong second chamber, with open disfavour. At the same time in Home Rule he was inheritor of a policy as to the expediency of which his doubts steadily increased. 'I never did have power', he said of himself as premier. He wrote of William Windham: 'His self-conscious, self-tormenting nature was indeed wholly unsuited for public life.' For similar reasons Rosebery was unsuited, not indeed for public life as such, but for public life as he had the misfortune to find it. Thus situated, his sensitiveness to criticism, his dislike of contradiction, his hatred of political intrigue, and, above all, a dread of failure tended to aggravate the difficulties of his position as leader. His name is not associated with any notable parliamentary measure, and he proved unequal to the desperate task of re-uniting a party shattered by Home Rule; but as a missionary of Imperial ideals he left a deep and lasting influence on the political thought of his time. His earliest and his latest parliamentary activities were directed to reform of the House of Lords, a cause which he did more to bring before the country than any other statesman of his time. Later years may be said to have completed his alienation from the party which he had led, while a growing fear of socialism drove him more and more to sympathize with other political views.

Lord Rosebery had two sons and two daughters. Of the sons the elder, Albert Edward Harry Mayer Archibald (born 1882), was M.P. for Midlothian in the liberal interest 1906–1910, and succeeded his father as sixth earl. The younger, Neil James Archibald, was under-secretary of state for foreign affairs in 1915 and joint parliamentary secretary to the Treasury 1916–1917.

A portrait of Rosebery by Sir John Millais and a bust by Sir Edgar Boehm are both in the possession of the sixth earl. A cartoon of him by 'Spy' appeared in *Vanity Fair* 14 March 1901.

[*The Times*, 22 May 1929; Marquess of Crewe, *Lord Rosebery*, 2 vols., 1931; E. T. Raymond, *The Man of Promise, Lord Rosebery; a critical study*, 1923; T. F. G. Coates, *Lord Rosebery, his Life and Speeches*, 2 vols., 1900; John Buchan, *Lord Rosebery, 1847–1930* in *Proceedings* of the British Academy, vol. xvi, 1930; Lord Rosebery, *Miscellanies Literary and Historical*, 2 vols., 1921; personal knowledge.]

E. Charteris.

PRIMROSE, Sir HENRY WILLIAM (1846–1923), civil servant, was born in Edinburgh 22 August 1846, the second of the six sons of the Hon. Bouverie Francis

Primrose, by his wife, Frederica Sophia, daughter of Thomas Anson, first Viscount Anson, and sister of Thomas William Anson, first Earl of Lichfield. His father was the second son of Archibald John Primrose, fourth Earl of Rosebery [q.v.], and uncle of Archibald Philip Primrose, fifth Earl of Rosebery [q.v.], the statesman. Henry Primrose was educated at Trinity College, Glenalmond, and Balliol College, Oxford. He obtained second classes in classical moderations (1867) and in the final honour school of law and modern history (1869). From Oxford he passed into the home civil service, entering the Treasury in 1869.

Primrose was in India from 1880 to 1884 as private secretary to the viceroy, Lord Ripon; in 1886 he became private secretary to Mr. Gladstone. It is said that he drafted the financial proposals for the Irish Home Rule Bill which the prime minister introduced that year in the House of Commons. In 1887 Primrose was appointed secretary to H.M. Office of Works, and held that post until 1895, when he was appointed chairman of the Board of Customs. In 1899 he became chairman of the Board of Inland Revenue, a position which he occupied until his retirement from the civil service in 1907.

Useful as his official career had been, the duties which Primrose undertook after he retired were no less valuable. In the same year that he left the civil service he was appointed chairman of the Pacific Cable Board. This body contains Dominion representatives whose interests are at times divergent, and control of it is not easy. Primrose presided over its deliberations with tact and courtesy, so that the seven years of his chairmanship resulted in the accomplishment of much good work. In 1912 he was nominated a member of the royal commission on the civil service, a commission of which Lord MacDonnell [q.v.] was chairman, and in the same year was appointed chairman of the committee to consider the financial position of Ireland before the introduction of the new Home Rule Bill. The government did not, however, act upon the report of his committee. In 1913 he served under the chairmanship of Lord Loreburn on a royal commission upon railways, a body whose labours were interrupted by the European War. In 1914 Primrose accepted the chairmanship of the Welsh Church Commission. During the War he was chairman of the Sugar Commission, and in 1918 was a member of Sir John (afterwards Baron) Bradbury's committee on the reduction of staffs in government offices.

Primrose's record of public service was distinguished, and his sound judgement and extremely business-like methods well qualified him for the various important positions which he held. He also had considerable gifts of writing, and his reports and minutes are models of clear statement. He was created K.C.B. in 1899, and was sworn a member of the Privy Council in 1912.

The end of Primrose's useful life came tragically by his own hand. He suffered much from insomnia, and the depression consequent upon loss of sleep unhinged his mind. Early in the morning of 17 June 1923 he was missed from his house. He was found to have shot himself in Kensington Gardens, and was taken to St. George's Hospital, where he died almost immediately upon arrival.

Primrose married in 1888 Helen Mary (died 1919), eldest daughter of Gilbert McMicking, of Miltonise, Wigtownshire, and formerly the wife of James Montgomery Walker. They had one son.

[*The Times*, 19 June 1923; private information.] A. COCHRANE.

PRINGLE, WILLIAM MATHER RUTHERFORD (1874–1928), politician, was born at Gordon, Berwickshire, 22 January 1874, the third and youngest son of George Pringle, of Gordon, by his wife, Elizabeth Mather. He was educated at Garnethill School, Glasgow, and at Glasgow University, where he graduated with honours in classics and history.

He was called to the bar by the Middle Temple in 1904. His opinions matured early, and he never changed them. Alert, intelligent, hardworking, vigorous in private and eloquent in public, he seemed to be marked out for promotion when, after unsuccessfully contesting the Camlachie division of Glasgow in 1906 in the liberal interest, he entered parliament as member for North-West Lanarkshire at the general election of January 1910: he retained the seat until 1918. He had time to make his mark but not to attain office before the break-up of the liberal party. He swiftly won a reputation for exhaustive knowledge of parliamentary procedure, and in collaboration with James Myles Hogge, liberal member for East Edinburgh 1912–1924, was not slow to take advantage of the opportunities which this knowledge afforded of promoting the interests of his party. Pringle was certainly the abler and more popular member of the partnership, but 'Pringle and Hogge' achieved a fame which neither alone was able to sustain. Pringle was passionately loyal to Mr. Asquith, and this loyalty led him into the wilderness, in which he gained a new but not less deserved reputation for tenacity and for optimism. He contested the Springburn division of Glasgow at the general election of December 1918 but, in common with all except a handful of 'Wee Free' liberals, failed to be elected. He returned to parliament, in company with another small liberal band, in 1922, when he stood successfully for the Penistone division of Yorkshire. He held this seat in the election of 1923, but only to lose it at the end of the succeeding short-lived parliament in 1924.

Mr. Asquith said of Pringle in 1922 that he was the 'first man' in parliament, and that there was no position in the state which he was not fitted to fill. Pringle never had the chance to justify this opinion. Events brought him disappointment after disappointment. But he never lost hope of being one of the architects of a real liberal revival. His ability was recognized when he was invited, in 1924, to join the liberal 'shadow Cabinet' under Mr. Asquith, and he was one of the chief movers of its open rebuff to Mr. Lloyd George after the General Strike in May 1926. Pringle was certainly expressing his characteristic feelings when he signed the letter describing Mr. Lloyd George as 'one whose instability destroys confidence'. Mr. Lloyd George's well-known readiness to co-operate with other parties and the existence of the 'Lloyd George Fund' were alike repugnant to one so wholly devoted to the conception of independent and locally financed liberalism.

Although it seemed almost impossible for the breach in an already diminished party to be healed, Pringle relaxed neither hope nor energy. The loss of his seat was a great handicap to one who delighted in the House of Commons, and it cut short the most effective display of his special gifts, which he had given as a critic in parliament of the first labour government. But he founded and was first chairman of the Liberal and Radical Candidates Association in 1924, and at the time of his death was prospective liberal candidate for Paisley, whither he had gone in the hope of winning back a seat once held by his leader, Mr. Asquith. He was also a keen supporter of the formation of the Liberal Council in 1927. Pringle takes a place in political history as a member of the invaluable band of those who have never held office but who have, nevertheless, exercised a considerable influence upon any House of Commons of which they were members.

Pringle died suddenly at his home in Southfields 1 April 1928. He married in 1906 Lilias Patrick, daughter of Joseph Somerville, of Glasgow. They had four sons and one daughter.

[*The Times*, 2 April 1928; private information.] W. E. Elliot.

PROTHERO, Sir GEORGE WALTER (1848–1922), historian, was born at Charlton, Wiltshire, 14 October 1848. He was the eldest of the four sons of the Rev. George Prothero, vicar of Clifton-upon-Teme, Worcestershire, afterwards rector of Whippingham, Isle of Wight, and canon of Westminster, by his wife, Emma, daughter of the Rev. William Money Kyrle, of Homme House, Herefordshire, and Whetham House, Wiltshire. The third son, Rowland Edmund, was president of the Board of Agriculture from 1916 to 1919 and was raised to the peerage as Baron Ernle in the latter year.

George Prothero was educated on the foundation at Eton and became head of the school. In 1868 he went with a scholarship to King's College, Cambridge, where he had an equally distinguished career. He was awarded the Bell scholarship in 1869, was sixth classic in the tripos of 1872, and was elected a fellow of King's in the same year. He also captained his college boat (1870–1871). After acting for a short time as assistant-master at Eton, Prothero studied at Bonn University, where he became familiar with the work of the great German historians of the time, contracting a special admiration for Ranke, the first volume of whose *Weltgeschichte* he translated in 1883.

Returning to Cambridge in 1875, Prothero was appointed history tutor at King's in 1876, and in 1884 university lecturer in history. With these appointments, his publications indicated the trend of his aims and interests. In 1877 appeared his *Life and Times of Simon de Montfort* and in 1894 his valuable collection of *Select Statutes and other Documents Illustrative of the Reigns of Elizabeth and James I.* His own wise, generous, and sympathetic outlook on life is, however, perhaps most clearly shown in his *Memoir* (1889) of his friend Henry Bradshaw [q.v.].

In 1894 Prothero was appointed to the

newly created chair of modern history at Edinburgh University. Whilst resident at Edinburgh he lived at 2 Eton Terrace, a house with a charming view over the Water of Leith. He found his new work entirely congenial. He liked the raw Scottish students with their passion for knowledge and their sacrifices to get it; and they returned his affection.

In 1899, however, there came to Prothero the offer of the editorship of the *Quarterly Review* resigned by his brother Rowland. He accepted the offer, moved to London, and held the editorship until his death. Changes such as the European War produced elsewhere have modified the administration of the *Quarterly*, and Prothero might, perhaps, be reckoned the last in the old editorial tradition. His position as editor of the famous periodical was sustained by many academic distinctions. He was president of the Royal Historical Society (1901–1905), fellow of the British Academy (1903), Rede lecturer at Cambridge (1903), Lowell lecturer at Boston and Schouler lecturer at Johns Hopkins University, U.S.A. (1910), and Chichele lecturer at Oxford (1915, lectures delivered 1920). Thus he had a definite place in the social and intellectual life of the London of his time. He entertained generously, and those who were privileged to be his guests at 24 Bedford Square were sensible of the quiet charm of their host not less than of the vivacious charm of their hostess. In touch with representative men in political and diplomatic as well as in historical and literary circles, Prothero had good company at his command; and the talk at his table was enriched by his own balanced and sympathetic contributions.

Whether Prothero would have been well-advised to exchange, as he might have done, his work and interests in London for the perhaps more dignified but also less public post of provost of King's College is open to debate. Howbeit, he decided to refuse the offer of the provostship, and it is primarily as an editor that he left his mark upon the intellectual life of his time. Those who worked with him on the *Quarterly Review* were conscious of his scrupulous regard for careful English and considered opinion. Prothero had further opportunity of showing his patience and thoroughness as co-editor of the *Cambridge Modern History* (1901–1912) and as general editor of the Cambridge Historical Series and of the handbooks designed to supply the British delegates at the Peace Conference at Versailles in 1919 with the requisite historical, geographical, and economic information. These last were prepared between 1917 and 1919 jointly in the Intelligence division of the Admiralty, in the War Trade Intelligence Department, and in a specially created historical section of the Foreign Office. In his capacity as historical adviser to the Foreign Office Prothero attended the Peace Conference in 1919, and in 1920 was created K.B.E. as a reward for his services. The work, however, had overtaxed his strength, and he died in London 10 July 1922.

Prothero married in 1882 Mary Frances, daughter of Samuel Butcher [q.v.], bishop of Meath, and sister of Samuel Henry Butcher [q.v.] and of John George Butcher, afterwards Lord Danesfort. They had no children.

[*The Times*, 12 July 1922; *Quarterly Review*, October 1922; personal knowledge.]

A. Cecil.

QUIN, WINDHAM THOMAS WYNDHAM-, fourth Earl of Dunraven and Mount-Earl in the peerage of Ireland and second Baron Kenry of the United Kingdom (1841–1926), Irish politician, was born at Adare, co. Limerick, 12 February 1841. He was the only son of Edwin Richard Windham Wyndham-Quin, third Earl [q.v.], by his first wife, Augusta, daughter of Thomas Goold [q.v.], master in chancery in Ireland. During his boyhood his father, who had been under the influence of the Tractarian movement, joined the Roman Church. Lady Dunraven, however, remained strongly Protestant, and the boy was accordingly sent to Rome for education, and forbidden to communicate with his mother. This produced an obstinate resistance. Lord Adare, as he then was, after some tuition in Paris, went to Christ Church, Oxford, in 1858 without having had any public-school education.

After three idle years at Oxford Adare entered the army in 1862, as cornet in the first Life Guards, and with his troop saw the 'battle of Hyde Park' on 23 July 1866, when the mob threw down the railings as a protest against the Cabinet's prohibition of a meeting of the Reform League. He rode steeplechases, being a very light weight, and raced a little; but already the passion of his life was sailing, and his leaves were mostly spent on a yacht. In 1867, when the military expedition to Abyssinia was announced, no volunteers from England were accepted for Sir Robert Napier's force, but Adare contrived to get the post of war-correspondent for the *Daily Telegraph*, and was present at the capture of Magdala. He again acted for the *Daily Telegraph* in the war of 1870 between France and Prussia, and witnessed the earlier battles from the Crown Prince's head-quarters. He spent the winter of 1870 to 1871 at Versailles, and was present when the king of Prussia was proclaimed German emperor in the Galerie des Glaces. There, half a century later, he saw the signing of the peace between the Allies and defeated Germany, being the only person who was present on both occasions.

In 1871 Adare succeeded to the earldom and to the seat in the House of Lords; but his wandering instinct was not sated, and he went immediately to America (which he had visited with his wife in 1869) for big game shooting. He was introduced by General Sheridan to 'Buffalo Bill' (William Cody) and 'Texas Jack', and with these famous scouts he shot buffalo and wapiti about the Platte River in the days of Indian war. In 1874 he again went to the United States, accompanied Dr. George Henry Kingsley [q.v.], and explored the Yellowstone region, in special pursuit of mountain sheep. His observations were written in *The Great Divide*, published in 1876. From this time on for sixteen years he yearly crossed to America for sport, especially in Canada and Newfoundland.

Unlike his predecessors, who had lived chiefly at Dunraven Castle in Glamorganshire, Dunraven made his home at Adare, county Limerick, and in 1880 published the first of his many pamphlets on Irish public affairs, *The Irish Question*. In 1885–1886 and again in 1886–1887 he was under-secretary for the Colonies in Lord Salisbury's administration, but resigned because he thought the government unfair to Newfoundland in the controversy with France over the fishery question, and also in general too ultra-tory. He had, as he says himself, 'a cross-bench mind', interested in politics but not in party politics. Turning his attention to social subjects, Dunraven moved in the House of Lords for the appointment of a committee on sweated labour, carried his motion, and was appointed chairman (1888–1890). He considered that much later legislation sprang from its recommendations. A different task was the chairmanship in 1896 of the commission on Irish horse-breeding. His stud at Adare was famous and successful. He raced a good deal, but his interest lay chiefly in breeding, 'Desmond' being the most famous of his sires.

In the years before 1900, however, Dunraven was chiefly known to the public as a yachtsman. He competed for the America's Cup in 1893 and 1895 with two specially built yachts, *Valkyrie II* and *III*—both times unsuccessfully. In the second contest against the American *Defender*, after two races out of three had been sailed, he withdrew from the third race, being dissatisfied with the keeping of the course. His subsequent protest in a pamphlet created much acrimonious international controversy, and he was struck off the membership of the New York Yacht Club. Dunraven took out his certificate as master and extra master, and in 1900 published *Self-Instruction in the Practice and Theory of Navigation* primarily for the use of yachtsmen. This training enabled him in the European War to take command of the steam yacht *Grianaig* (bought and run at his own expense) for service as a hospital ship, navigating both Channel and Mediterranean among mines and submarines. Thus he continued the life of active adventure until close upon his eightieth year.

But the service by which Dunraven will be best remembered was connected with Ireland. In 1902 George Wyndham [q.v.], as chief secretary, was contending with a renewed outburst of land agitation, when the idea of a conference between representatives of landlords and tenants was suggested in a public letter by Captain John Shawe Taylor, a young Galway squire. An official communication from the chief secretary supported the suggestion, which was accepted by the Nationalist leaders, but repudiated by the Irish Landlords' Convention. Lord Dudley, the viceroy, however, joined in advocating the plan, and a group of powerful landlords, of whom Dunraven was chief, set up an organization which polled the lieutenants and deputy-lieutenants of Ireland on the question and secured 103 votes for conference against 33 opposing. After further proceedings, the Landlords' Convention having renewed its refusal, a poll of individual landlords nominated four representatives, Lord Mayo, Colonel Sir Hutcheson Poë, Colonel (afterwards Sir) Nugent Everard, and Lord Dunraven. When the conference of eight assembled, Dunraven was named chairman on the motion of Mr. Redmond. After long and difficult negotiation a unanimous report recommended a general policy of land purchase, and specified terms. This became the basis of the Wyndham Land Act (1903) which settled the policy that Irish landlords should, without exception, be bought out and the occupier become the owner. 'For the first time', William O'Brien [q.v.] wrote in his book *An Olive Branch in Ireland* (1910), 'both parties in the state were brought to vie with one another in acclaiming an Irish compact which brought honour to both of them.'

This achievement was the great success of Dunraven's life, and naturally led him to attempt more. The Land Conference was revived as the Irish Reform Committee, which advocated the policy that came to be known as 'devolution', a partial transfer of Irish administration and legislation to an Irish assembly. Sir Antony (afterwards Lord) MacDonnell [q.v.], under-secretary to the lord-lieutenant, helped to draft the proposals which, when published in 1905, were denounced by extreme Nationalists and Unionists alike, with the result that the scheme broke down and Wyndham was forced into resigning the chief secretaryship. On the other hand, a split among the Nationalists occasioned the temporary withdrawal of William O'Brien, Dunraven's most ardent admirer. Later, in 1910, when O'Brien returned to active political life and launched a new organization, the All for Ireland League, Dunraven gave it public support.

In the struggle over the Home Rule Bill and the Parliament Act Dunraven played a cross-bench part. His last opportunity to forward what he always believed in, a settlement of the Irish difficulty by conciliation between different sections of Irishmen, came when the Irish Convention was set up in 1917; and in that assembly he advocated, what he had preached in many pamphlets and public letters, a solution on federal lines. But there, as elsewhere, he lacked one of the main qualifications of a political leader; he had neither the equipment nor the temperament of an orator. He lived to see, after the European War, a period of savage turmoil in Ireland, which profoundly saddened him. Yet the postscript to his book of memoirs, *Past Times and Pastimes*, published in 1922, ends on a note of hope, declaring that 'by acceptance of the Treaty the foundations of a great and desirable peace had been laid', and paying a tribute to the 'governing qualities displayed by the leaders of the provisional government' in Ireland. He was among the members nominated by President Cosgrave to serve on the first senate of the Irish Free State in June 1921.

Dunraven married in 1869 Florence Elizabeth (died 1916), daughter of Lord Charles Lennox Kerr, and had three daughters, two of whom predeceased him. He was succeeded in all his Irish titles by his cousin, Windham Henry Wyndham-Quin (born 1857). He died at his London residence 14 June 1926.

Few of his contemporaries touched life at more points than Dunraven, and although he experimented in many directions, he dropped nothing that interested him, while his physical endurance permitted. A large experiment in tobacco growing at Adare was checked by the accidental burning of his factory in 1916; but even so he continued to grow as much Turkish leaf as would supply the cigarette factory which he had established. Fishing in all its forms was one of his main interests; and he constantly advocated the serious development of fish supply by hatcheries, both fresh water and marine, for the British Isles. Adare under his ægis continued to be what perhaps his forerunners had first made it—one of the few villages in Ireland having beauty as well as historic interest, a place not of ruins but of ancient churches and buildings nobly preserved for use. He was never officially in a position to have enthusiastic followers, and circumstances never called on him to make important sacrifices: but few men in his day brought more intelligent goodwill to the service of Ireland, and few Irish politicians have done so little mischief to offset their work for good.

[*The Times*, 15 June 1926; Lord Dunraven, *Past Times and Pastimes*, 1922; *Report* of New York Yacht Club's Special Committee on certain charges made by the Earl of Dunraven, 1896. Portrait, *Royal Academy Pictures*, 1921.]

S. Gwynn.

RALEIGH, Sir WALTER ALEXANDER (1861–1922), critic and essayist, was born at 4 Highbury Quadrant, London, 5 September 1861, the fifth child and only son of Alexander Raleigh [q.v.], then Congregationalist minister of Hare Court chapel, Canonbury, by his wife, Mary Darling, only daughter of James Gifford, of Edinburgh. After a short time at the City of London School, he was sent in 1876 to Edinburgh, where he lived with his uncle, Adam Gifford, Lord Gifford [q.v.], and he became a pupil at the Edinburgh Academy. On his return to London in 1877 he attended University College

School, whence he proceeded to University College, London, graduating B.A. in 1881. In October 1881 he entered King's College, Cambridge, and obtained a second class in the historical tripos of 1885. His residence had been interrupted in the Lent Term of 1883 by a sea voyage to Italy. Since childhood he had been subject to a nervous tremor in both arms, which he never wholly overcame, and he had shot up to the height of six feet six inches. For some time he edited the *Cambridge Review*, and in Michaelmas Term 1884 he was president of the Union.

In the autumn of 1885 Raleigh went out to India on being appointed the first professor of English literature in the Mohammedan Anglo-Oriental College, Aligarh, but he was invalided home in April 1887. His letters give a vivid picture of his Indian experience [*Letters*, i, 28–107], and he always spoke of it with enthusiasm. Forbidden by his doctors to return to India, he had thoughts of becoming a journalist. During the winter of 1888–1889 he lectured for the Oxford University Extension Delegacy, and in March 1889 became personal assistant to Professor (Sir) Adolphus William Ward [q.v.] at the Victoria University, Manchester. In November of the same year he was appointed professor of modern literature at University College, Liverpool, in succession to A. C. Bradley, beginning his work there in January 1890.

At Liverpool Raleigh played a spirited part in college affairs, at a time when the college was developing into the university; and he began to write, his chief publication hitherto having been a paper read to the Browning Society while he was still at Cambridge (Browning Society's *Papers*, No. 25, 1884). His first book was *The English Novel* (1894), which he soon came to regard as ''prentice' work, but it exhibits his gift of lucid and lively narrative. It was followed by *Robert Louis Stevenson: an Essay* (1895), a brief appreciation based on a lecture delivered at the Royal Institution, and by *Style* (1897), the gayest of his longer publications, which he wrote with enthusiasm but afterwards disparaged as 'stuck up'. He was Clark lecturer in English literature at Trinity College, Cambridge, in 1899, and embodied his lectures in his *Milton* (1900), his first substantial study of a poet. The same year he edited, with a long introduction which breaks new ground, Sir Thomas Hoby's *Book of the Courtier, from the Italian of Count Baldassare Castiglione*, for 'The Tudor Translations', a series of reprints projected by W. E. Henley [q.v.]. These five books belong to the ten years of Raleigh's professorship at Liverpool, and in addition he had contributed to *English Prose Selections*, edited by (Sir) Henry Craik [q.v.], and to periodicals such as the *New Review* and the *Yellow Book*. His appointment in 1890 had been a risk taken on his promise; in 1900 he was winning recognition as the most original and stimulating of the younger critics.

In June 1900 Raleigh was appointed by the Crown to the chair of English language and literature at Glasgow University, again in succession to A. C. Bradley, and for the next four years was one of the outstanding personalities there. As a member of the university court he was involved in academic affairs to an extent which those who knew his apparent indifference to them in later years would not have credited. Daily lectures to hundreds of students and continual meetings left him less time for writing than he had enjoyed at Liverpool. But in the summer vacation of 1902, while staying at Stanford-in-the-Vale, Berkshire, he wrote his *Wordsworth* (published 1903), a companion to his *Milton*, and a surprise to admirers of Wordsworth, who had not expected the author of *Style* to state their faith for them so loyally. He intended that his next book should be on Chaucer, whom, in contrast to Milton and Wordsworth, he called 'my man', but only disjointed lecture-notes remain. Having been consulted by the publishing firm of MacLehose, of Glasgow, about their projected series of English voyages, Raleigh promised an essay for their edition of Richard Hakluyt's *Voyages*. This he wrote at Uffington, Berkshire, in the summer of 1904, and it was published under the title of *The English Voyages of the Sixteenth Century* (*Hakluyt's Voyages*, vol. xii, 1905, published separately, 1906); and more than once he said that it was his 'best book'. In 1903 he had also undertaken to write the long desired volume on *Shakespeare* for the 'English Men of Letters' series.

In June 1904 Raleigh became the first holder of the new chair of English literature at Oxford, with a fellowship at Magdalen College. The school of English language and literature had been established in 1894, but its steady development began with Raleigh's appointment. His usual method as a lecturer was informal—a few facts, the reading of passages (admirably interpreted), and a running commentary. Much depended on his mood at the time, but when he was at his best no student forgot the impression he had made. Believing that system and dogma are not trusty servants in the study of literature, he invited his listeners to read and think for themselves. His audience contained men of all ages—during one term Robert Bridges attended regularly—and to one and all he seemed to speak as an equal. To this rare attitude in a professorial teacher was largely attributable his remarkable power of arousing enthusiasm. In directing enthusiasm he was not so successful; here his indifference to system sometimes told unfavourably.

Raleigh's first essay written at Oxford was on Blake (*Lyrical Poems of William Blake*, 1905). He wrote his *Shakespeare* during the latter half of 1906 (published in 1907); and none of his books was he more pleased to have finished. 'I think Falstaff is good,' he said, 'so are Shakespeare's women.' He realized the book's inequalities; but it would not be easy to find more vivid criticism of Shakespeare than the chapter on 'Story and Character'. He welcomed the relaxation offered by a voyage to South Africa in 1907, although during his two months there he lectured at Pretoria, Johannesburg, Durban, Grahamstown, Cape Town, and Stellenbosch. On his return he made a collection of Samuel Johnson's essays and notes on Shakespeare (*Johnson on Shakespeare*, 1908). Two years later (1910) he brought out his *Six Essays on Johnson*. This was his last book on a single author, and there are many critics who consider it his best. He was knighted in 1911 on the occasion of the coronation of King George V.

Raleigh had never overrated the importance of the academic study of literature, and from his first years at Oxford, and even earlier, he had an increasing desire to write on men and things directly. It was significant of this changing interest that his next book should have been an edition of the *Complete Works of George Savile, first Marquess of Halifax* (1912). His Henry Sidgwick memorial lecture on Dryden, delivered at Newnham College, Cambridge, in 1913, was largely on politics and the application of Dryden's satire to the present day. His essay on Burns (contributed to W. S. Douglas's edition of J. G. Lockhart's *Life of Burns*, 1914) he thought as good as anything he had written 'on a man'. But he had no heart for further literary criticism after the outbreak of the European War in 1914. He wrote only one more critical essay on a new subject, 'Don Quixote' (*The Times Literary Supplement*, 27 April 1916), and it was on the moods of Quixote and Sancho, which 'seem to divide between them most of the splendours and most of the comforts of human life'. In October 1914, when his Oxford professorship was reconstituted as the Merton chair of English literature, he became a fellow of Merton College.

The War occupied Raleigh's thoughts for the rest of his life. *Might is Right*, written for the series of Oxford Pamphlets (October 1914), was followed by addresses on *The War of Ideas* (December 1916), *The Faith of England* (March 1917), *Some Gains of the War* (February 1918), and *The War and the Press* (March 1918), and by his British Academy lecture on *Shakespeare and England* (July 1918). Together these form a volume entitled *England and the War* (1918), the main subject of which is the English character. In 1915 Raleigh was responsible for '*The Times* Broadsheets for Soldiers and Sailors'. In that year he went to the United States of America in order to deliver at Princeton the two lectures published under the title of *Romance* (1915); they were based on old material and delivered in the intervals of speaking about England and the War. His introduction to *Shakespeare's England* (1916), a book which he had planned many years earlier, is a glorification of the Elizabethan spirit and ends on a patriotic note. He found a new interest in his lectures at Oxford after 1918, when men who had fought in the War crowded to hear him, and at no time was he more sought after by the younger members of the university. These post-War years were busy, for in July 1918 he had accepted the invitation of the Air Ministry to write the official history of the Royal Air Force.

Raleigh was able to complete only the first volume of *The War in the Air* (*History of the Great War based on official documents*, 1922), but it remains his longest work. It was his first experience of writing history on a large scale. The assistance of a skilled staff in sifting details and explaining technicalities enabled him to work with sustained zest. 'The writer of this history', he said in his preface, 'has endeavoured to make his narrative intelligible to those who, like himself, are outsiders.' It is the most readable of official histories, and it contains some of his best writing. His style is here at its simplest, but the fervour of his admiration for the heroism of the air is everywhere apparent, and finds memorable expression in the introduction. The volume was published a few weeks after his death. On 16 March 1922 Raleigh set out for the East in preparation for his second volume. When he returned to London on 25 April he was in the grip of typhoid fever, contracted when his aeroplane was marooned for four or five days in the desert between Jerusalem and Bagdad. He died at the Acland Home, Oxford, 13 May. He was buried at Ferry Hinksey, the village near Oxford where he had lived since 1909 at The Hangings, the house designed for him by his friend A. H. Clough, the son of the poet. He married in 1890 Lucie Gertrude, only daughter of Mason Jackson, art editor of the *Illustrated London News*, and had four sons and one daughter.

Raleigh could be equally at his ease in very different kinds of company, and many thought of his talk as the best that they could ever hope to hear. Something of its quality is preserved in his letters, which show a wide range of mood and often disguise their purpose in their gaiety. As a critic he came to write most freely when dealing with an author's character and outlook. His aim, he once said briefly, was 'to explain people'. General questions he preferred to treat incidentally when dealing with 'live men'. He was more interested in men than in movements or theories. Yet he taught the continuity of literature and maintained that the English school at Oxford must be a school of the history of English literature and language. An important part of his work at Oxford was done as adviser to the Clarendon Press.

At Cambridge Raleigh was Clark lecturer at Trinity College again in 1911 and Leslie Stephen lecturer in 1907, and he was elected an honorary fellow of King's College in 1912. He received honorary degrees from the universities of Glasgow and Durham. He was elected an honorary fellow of Magdalen College in 1916.

A selection from Raleigh's lighter pieces in verse and prose, among them three 'little plays', was edited by his second son, Hilary Raleigh, in 1923 under the title *Laughter from a Cloud*, and in the same year fourteen of his occasional essays and addresses, written between 1896 and 1916, were collected in *Some Authors*, a volume which he had roughly planned. The longer passages in his notes for his lectures were edited in 1926 by George Gordon under the title *On Writing and Writers*. His *Letters* (2 vols.), edited by Lady Raleigh, also appeared in 1926.

A portrait in oils of Raleigh by Francis Dodd, which belongs to Lady Raleigh, is reproduced in *Laughter from a Cloud*, and a drawing by William Rothenstein, also in the possession of Lady Raleigh, is reproduced in the *Letters*. A memorial window by Anning Bell is in the library of Merton College. The larger portion of the fund which was raised in memory of Raleigh provides an income for the purchase of rare books for the library of the English school at Oxford.

[*The Letters of Sir W. Raleigh, 1879–1922*, edited by Lady Raleigh with a biographical preface by D. Nichol Smith, 2 vols. 1926; O. Elton in *Liverpool Post*, 15 May 1922; H. W. Garrod in *Oxford Chronicle*, 19 May 1922; G. S. Gordon in *The Times Literary Supplement*, 8 June 1922; R. W. Chapman, *Walter Raleigh*, privately printed 1922; H. A. Jones, *Sir Walter Raleigh and the Air History, a personal recollection*, 1922; Violet Crum, *Sir Walter Alexander Raleigh*, 1923. A full bibliography of Raleigh's writings is printed in the *Periodical* for September 1922, and is reprinted in abstract in the *Letters*, vol. ii.]

D. Nichol Smith.

RAMSAY, Sir JAMES HENRY, tenth baronet, of Bamff (1832–1925), historian, was the eldest son of Sir George Ramsay, ninth baronet [q.v.], a voluminous writer on philosophy, by his wife, Emily Eugenia, daughter of Captain Henry Lennon, of West Meath. William Ramsay [q.v.], professor of humanity in the university of Glasgow, was his uncle. James Ramsay was born at Versailles 21 May 1832. He was educated at Rugby and at Christ Church, Oxford. He obtained a second class in classical moderations in 1853 and a first class in *literae humaniores* in 1854. He also obtained a first class in the school of law and modern history in 1855. He was elected a student of Christ Church in 1854, but lost that position in 1861 on his marriage to Mary, daughter of William Scott Kerr, of Chatto and Sunlaws, Roxburgh. Although he abandoned an academic career, Ramsay remained all his life a loyal and devoted member of his college. He was called to the bar by Lincoln's Inn in 1863, but, although he continued to reside in London until 1871, he does not appear to have practised. During these years he lost his first wife, who died in 1868 leaving three daughters.

The first important event of Ramsay's life as a scholar was his appointment as an examiner (1867–1869) in the Oxford school of law and modern history. This experience convinced him that the current books on English political history were unsatisfactory. He records in his diary that in December 1869 he consulted Dean Liddell, of Christ Church, on the advisability of his writing a new history of England. The leisure and the means necessary were supplied in 1871 when he succeeded to the baronetcy and estates of Bamff, near Alyth in Perthshire. For a moment he was tempted to enter the political arena, and in 1872 he stood for Forfarshire in the liberal interest. Fortunately, he was unsuccessful, and, although he continued to take a keen interest in politics (after 1886 as a liberal unionist), his activity was limited to membership of local associations and to the writing of occasional letters to the *Scotsman*. He had by this time settled down to his life's work, the writing of the history of England down to the end of the Middle Ages—the period covered, from a different angle, by another eminent scholar, William Stubbs [q.v.]. The difference between the two men was that Stubbs lived an active academic and ecclesiastical life, in constant touch with other scholars and with practical problems, whereas Ramsay was, as a scholar, comparatively solitary. The distractions from his work were the ordinary occupations of a landowner, visits to London for the purposes of research in the Public Record Office, and occasional trips abroad. French he knew well from boyhood, and spoke fluently; but he never mastered German, and this was a serious handicap to his researches, especially in dealing with the early history of England.

Ramsay's second marriage in 1873 to Charlotte Fanning (died 1904), daughter of Major William Stewart, of Ardvorlich, gave him a renewal of a happy home life. A young family of two sons and three more daughters grew up around him at Bamff. As time went on, his elder daughters were able to give him valuable assistance in his *magnum opus*, which was at all times his primary occupation.

Although as a student Ramsay was essentially solitary, and very few outside his family, except the officials at the Record Office, knew about his literary occupations, he was no pallid indoor scholar. Like his younger brother, George, who had succeeded his uncle William as professor of humanity at Glasgow, and whose successive country homes were within easy reach of Bamff, he exulted and excelled in out-door recreations. With a short sturdy figure, he was an admirable walker, skater, and mountaineer. Both brothers were keen members of the Alpine Club, and Sir James was a pioneer in ascending Mont Blanc from the Italian side. The physical vigour which enabled him to continue his long spell of work was largely due to his habit of regular bodily exercise.

Twenty years of solid and almost unsuspected labour had elapsed when the first instalment of Ramsay's work was issued in two volumes by the Clarendon Press in 1892. Rather curiously this instalment was the concluding part, dealing with the fifteenth century, and was entitled *Lancaster and York: A Century of English History: 1399–1485*. No such elaborate and carefully documented work on this period had yet appeared, and it at once attracted the attention of scholars, although it failed to find many readers among the general public. Six years later, in 1898, two more volumes were issued by a different publisher, Swan Sonnenschein & Co., under the title *The Foundations of England*. These volumes, which had been partially rewritten during the interval, covered the years from 55 B.C. to A.D. 1154. The same publisher issued the succeeding volumes, *The Angevin Empire, 1154–1216*, in 1903, and *The Dawn of the Constitution, 1216–1307*, in 1908. The last two volumes, however, *The Genesis of Lancaster, 1307–1399*, were published, like the first two, by the Clarendon Press in 1913. The Clarendon Press made amends for its temporary defection by taking the whole work under its ægis, and re-issuing it in eight volumes under the general title *The Scholar's History of England*.

After the completion of his great book, Ramsay found occupation for his unfamiliar leisure in editing *The Bamff Charters and Papers*, which was published by the Clarendon Press in 1915. He lived for ten more years, and died at Bamff 17 February 1925. In these later years he put together his researches into medieval finance, which had attracted considerable attention in his previous volumes, and they were issued in collected form under the title of *A History of the Revenues of the Kings of England, 1066–1399*, by the Clarendon Press in 1925, a few months after the author's death.

There can be no doubt that Ramsay's reputation as a historian will rest upon the eight solid volumes of his consecutive narrative. His financial conclusions, although they represent his most original research in manuscript records, are not likely to be accepted as conclusive. Ramsay had insufficient training in accountancy to grasp fully all the problems that he set himself to solve, and he had not explored all the available material. This was one of the results of his comparative isolation. If he had been in more intimate and constant touch with other workers in the same field, he would have been more critical than he was, both of his method and of the value of his results. On the other hand, it is difficult to overpraise the narrative part of his work. Nowhere else is it possible to find so orderly an account in chronological order of the facts of English history, or such a careful series of references to the available sources. It is not only a quarry in itself, but it is a guide to the bigger quarry from which historians have to extract their materials. It may be said that his mind was that of a chronicler rather than historian, that he was more concerned to show when and how a thing happened than why it happened. But a trustworthy narrative history, covering fifteen centuries and compiled with no aim but the desire to ascertain the truth, is a possession which few other countries enjoy.

Apart from his historical work, Ramsay's chief interest was in his family. He was a resolute advocate of the education of women, and an eager supporter of St. Leonard's girls' school at St. Andrews, to which he sent four of his daughters. He was immensely gratified by the success of his third daughter by his first marriage, Agnata Frances, who was placed by the examiners above the senior classic at Cambridge in 1887, and who subsequently married, as his second wife, Henry Montagu Butler [q.v.], master of Trinity College, and became the mother of very able sons. His eldest daughter by his second marriage, Katharine, Duchess of Atholl, not only entered the House of Commons in 1923 as member for Kinross and West Perthshire, but was also promoted to hold political office under the conservative government in 1924. Ramsay's last appearance at a political meeting took place when his daughter was nominated as candidate for the division. He was succeeded as eleventh baronet by his only surviving son, James Douglas (born 1878). His elder son, Nigel Neis, was killed at Magersfontein in 1899 while serving with the Black Watch.

Ramsay's work received a measure, but only a measure, of public recognition. The first came from his brother's university of Glasgow, which conferred upon him the honorary degree of LL.D. in 1906. Cambridge gave him an honorary D.Litt. two years later, and he was elected a fellow of the British Academy in 1915. But he missed what he would have valued most. He was never a D.C.L. of Oxford nor an honorary student of Christ Church.

[T. F. Tout, *Sir James Henry Ramsay, 1832–1925*, in *Proceedings* of the British Academy, vol. xi, 1924–1925; private information; personal knowledge. Portrait, *Royal Academy Pictures*, 1922.] R. Lodge.

RASHDALL, HASTINGS (1858–1924), moral philosopher, theologian, and historian of universities, was born in London 24 June 1858. He was the elder son of the Rev. John Rashdall, incumbent of Eaton Chapel, Eaton Square, London, previously vicar of the Priory Church, Malvern, and afterwards (1864) of Dawlish, a friend of the Tennyson family, by his wife, Emily, daughter of Thomas Hankey, banker, and sister of Kate Hankey, author of the mission hymn 'Tell me the old, old story'. His father died in 1869, but his mother only six months before himself, at the age of ninety-two in 1923. In September 1871 he went to Harrow, to the house of the headmaster, Montagu Butler, whom he always greatly admired, and who in his turn is said to have replied, when asked in later years whom he considered his most distinguished pupil: 'It is not easy to say, but, if you press me, I think—Rashdall.' In 1877 Rashdall passed with a scholarship to New College, Oxford, where he read for classical honours, and obtained a second class both in moderations (1878) and in *literae humaniores* (1881). In 1879 he won the Stanhope essay prize with an essay on John Huss. He twice failed to obtain a fellowship by examination, but won the chancellor's prize for an English essay in 1883 with an essay on the universities of the middle ages. This was eventually expanded into the work entitled *The Universities of Europe in the Middle Ages*, published in three volumes by the Clarendon Press in 1895, which established his reputation as an historical scholar. It will long be the standard work on the subject in English, and this contribution to learning would by itself entitle Rashdall to a place in this Dictionary. A new edition, prepared by F. M. Powicke and A. B.

Emden, was issued by the Clarendon Press in 1936.

Between the winning of the prize and the publication of the book, Rashdall had passed through a varied experience of teaching, first at St. David's College, Lampeter, in 1883, next at University College, Durham (1884–1888), and lastly at Hertford College, Oxford, of which he was elected a fellow at the end of 1888, thus returning to Oxford, to fulfil for the next twenty-seven years what he had already decided was his real vocation—teaching philosophy for the school of *literae humaniores*. At Hertford College he remained for six years; during the last of these (1894–1895), however, he resided in Balliol College as divinity tutor and chaplain—he had been ordained deacon in 1884, and priest in 1886—while retaining his fellowship and philosophical teaching at Hertford. In 1895 he accepted a fellowship as tutor in philosophy at his first college, New College, which he retained during the remaining years of his residence in Oxford. Two volumes on *The Theory of Good and Evil*, which appeared in 1907, embody the teaching on moral philosophy imparted during the preceding years to those who attended his lectures. The 'ideal utilitarianism' expounded in this work 'combines the utilitarian principle that ethics must be teleological with a non-hedonistic view of the ethical end.' In this view 'actions are right or wrong according as they tend to produce for all mankind an ideal end or good which includes, but is not limited to pleasure' [i. 184]. Whatever criticisms may be urged against this theory, the exposition 'bears the impress of a philosopher who makes a valiant attempt to grapple with ethical problems, and who illuminates his ideas by vivid and arresting practical illustrations' [*Life*, 117]. There is perhaps no English book to be preferred to Rashdall's as an introduction to ethics, covering the ground and giving to the student a sense of being engaged with real issues.

Among Rashdall's other writings of this period, during which he produced a volume of university sermons (*Doctrine and Development*, 1898), are a number of articles and reviews, as well as contributions to two notable volumes, one of philosophical, the other of theological essays, *Personal Idealism* and *Contentio Veritatis*, both published in 1902. Specially noteworthy is his article on 'The Ethics of Religious Conformity' in the *International Journal of Ethics* for January 1897, written in answer to Henry Sidgwick (a philosopher for whom Rashdall had a special admiration), and in defence of Anglican clergymen who did not personally assent to every article of the creeds taken in its literal sense. Rashdall's interest in the same cause found expression also in his active participation in the work of the Churchmen's Union, of which he was a vice-president from its foundation in 1898. He also joined the Synthetic Society for philosophical and theological discussion, established by Arthur Balfour, Wilfrid Ward, and Bishop E. S. Talbot 'to consider existing Agnostic tendencies and to contribute towards a working philosophy of religious belief', which in 1896 arose from the ashes of the older Metaphysical Society [see KNOWLES, Sir J. T.]. He was a member of the Christian Social Union from its inception in 1890, and from 1892 to 1910 one of the editors of the organ of the Oxford University branch, *The Economic Review*. He was preacher at Lincoln's Inn for two years from 1898, and was elected a fellow of the British Academy in 1909. In 1905 he married Constance, daughter of Henry Francis Makins. The union was a very happy one; his wife (who survived him) was 'one who shared his interests and helped him in every way' [*Life*, 114]. They had no children.

In 1909 Rashdall was appointed by Bishop Percival to a canonry at Hereford, with a share in the teaching of candidates for holy orders. He was installed in 1910 and for seven years divided his time between Hereford and Oxford, where he retained his New College fellowship with a reduced amount of teaching and lecturing. He was elected Bampton lecturer in 1914 and delivered in 1915 eight sermons, published in 1919 as *The Idea of Atonement in Christian Theology*. This is an important contribution to the history of one of the central doctrines of Christianity, and a powerful defence of the theory, associated with the name of Abelard, that the passion and death of Christ 'justifies' man by enkindling in him the love of God, which expresses itself in regeneration of life. Rashdall was now recognized as being no less distinguished in the field of theology than in history and moral philosophy.

When the European War broke out Rashdall was wholeheartedly in sympathy with the national cause, and while in Oxford, although in his fifty-seventh year, joined the volunteer training corps commanded by his old schoolfellow Alfred

Denis Godley. In 1917 he was appointed dean of Carlisle, and resigned his canonry and fellowship. He was, however, elected three years later, to his great satisfaction, an honorary fellow of New College. Rashdall's six years at Carlisle were remarkable for his encouragement of friendly relations between the Anglican clergy and nonconformist ministers, and for the generous hospitality to city and diocese of which he and his wife made the deanery the centre. The cathedral owed much to his zealous care for the dignity and beauty of its fabric and services.

In the spring of 1921 Rashdall visited Spain in search of information to be used in a second edition of his *Universities*. The report of a paper read by him in August to a conference of modern churchmen at Cambridge gave rise to attacks upon him for denying the divinity of Christ. These attacks he felt deeply, since this doctrine, his interpretation of which he believed to satisfy the most exacting standards of orthodoxy, lay at the heart of both his personal religion and his theology. His sensitiveness to these criticisms was probably increased by the inroads of the disease which was within two years to bring his life to an end. An operation in 1922 revealed the presence of cancer; and the fortitude with which he bore the period of weakness and suffering which followed was the admiration of all who witnessed it. He went abroad for the last time in August 1923, preached regularly in his cathedral until within two months of his death, and kept up to the last his keen interest in the matters which had been the chief preoccupation of his life. He died 9 February 1924 at Worthing, whither he had been taken to recruit his strength after an operation, and was buried in Holywell cemetery at Oxford. A memorial tablet was placed in New College cloister by the warden and fellows; and another, with a medallion portrait, in the south aisle of Carlisle Cathedral by his widow, who also gave two bells to complete a peal to be rung annually on his birthday. He is also commemorated at Carlisle by an exhibition founded by his friends for boys and girls from the diocese of Carlisle who have been awarded scholarships or exhibitions at Oxford. A portrait painted in 1923 by Oswald Birley, and now in the possession of Mrs. Rashdall, gives a good likeness of him, although showing evident traces of the pain which he was then suffering.

Rashdall was a figure of real importance in the recent history of English religious thought. His candour and courage, profound earnestness, unquestioned learning, and attachment to historical tradition fitted him to be a leader of the liberal school of Anglicanism; while his gift of clear and interesting exposition extended his influence to a much wider circle. He had little sympathy with 'the mystical element in religion'. His historical studies had led him to suspect it of being morally dangerous; and he was before all things a moralist. He had no love for the phrase 'religious experience' and disclaimed an immediate knowledge of God, whose existence, he held, was postulated by morality and could be inferred from the impossibility of supposing the material world to exist except as the object of some consciousness. This conviction, however, no more interfered with the fervour of his devotional life than his parallel conviction that we only infer by analogy the existence of other minds than our own was inconsistent with a great capacity for warm and intimate friendship. His general *Weltanschauung* was that of 'personal idealism'. Individual and mutually exclusive consciousnesses or spirits were ultimately real, and indeed the only ultimate reality, although they were not all alike eternal, one personal God being the cause of the existence of the rest. Belief in individual immortality was bound up with this view; for denial of it was incompatible with a wholehearted acknowledgement of the standards implied in that acceptance of Christ's life and teaching as the supreme revelation of God to man which was to Rashdall essential Christianity.

As often happens with remarkable personalities in universities, Rashdall became the hero of a cycle of legends, many of them turning upon a notable absentmindedness which did but endear him the more to those who knew him. His strongly held political views were in general of a liberal cast; he was a unionist, but always a liberal unionist, and rejoiced when the free trade controversy of 1902 ranged him again with the majority of the liberal party. In ecclesiastical matters he was, although not Anglo-catholic in his theory of sacraments or ministry, a thorough churchman, caring greatly for the historical institutions of religion, and for continuity and tradition even in the smallest details; in his own practice he set great store by frequent communion and regular attendance at public worship.

Since the publication of Rashdall's *Life*,

which contains a bibliography up to date, two further collections of pieces from his pen have appeared, *Ideas and Ideals* (1928) and *God and Man* (1930).

[P. E. Matheson, *Life of Hastings Rashdall*, 1928; H. W. B. Joseph in *Oxford Magazine*, 14 February 1924; P. J. Kirkby in *The Modern Churchman*, October 1927; personal knowledge.] C. C. J. Webb.

RAWLINSON, Sir HENRY SEYMOUR, second baronet and Baron Rawlinson, of Trent (1864–1925), general, the elder son of Sir Henry Creswicke Rawlinson [q.v.], first baronet, by his wife, Louisa, daughter of Henry Seymour, of Knoyle House, Wiltshire, and of Trent Manor, Dorset, was born at Trent Manor 20 February 1864. He was educated at Eton and Sandhurst, and on his twentieth birthday (1884) was gazetted to the King's Royal Rifles, joining the fourth battalion of that regiment in India. In 1886, thanks to the friendship between his father and Sir Frederick (afterwards Lord) Roberts [q.v.], then commander-in-chief in India, the latter appointed him to be one of his aides-de-camp. Rawlinson accompanied Roberts to Burma, and there, in the guerrilla warfare which followed the capture of Mandalay by (Sir) Harry N. D. Prendergast [q.v.], saw his first active service, being attached to the mounted infantry of the Rifle Brigade, and earning the Burma medal and a mention in dispatches.

In 1889 Rawlinson was called home by the serious illness of his mother, who died in October, her death making him heir-presumptive to the Seymour property of Trent Manor. In the following year (1890) he married Meredith, daughter of Coleridge John Kennard, of Fernhill, Hampshire. In order to be near his father he resigned his appointment on Lord Roberts's staff, and on his promotion to captain in 1891 obtained a transfer to the Coldstream Guards, being gazetted captain in that regiment in July 1892. In the following year he passed into the Staff College, Camberley, amongst his fellow students there being J. H. G. (afterwards Viscount) Byng and (Sir) Henry Wilson; the latter he had already met in Burma. After passing through the Staff College Rawlinson was appointed brigade-major at Aldershot in November 1895. In the previous spring his father, to whom he had been devoted, died, and he succeeded to the baronetcy.

In the winter of 1897 Rawlinson took his wife to Egypt for her health, and he was in Cairo when (Lord) Kitchener [q.v.] was preparing for his advance to Omdurman. Kitchener offered him an appointment on his staff, which was eagerly accepted, and in that capacity Rawlinson served at the battles of Atbara and Omdurman. He was mentioned in dispatches and promised the brevet of lieutenant-colonel on promotion to major. He received his majority in the Coldstream Guards in January 1899, and the next day was gazetted brevet lieutenant-colonel, at the age of thirty-five.

In the autumn of that year, when the crisis in South Africa came to a head and Sir George White [q.v.] was sent out to Natal with reinforcements, Rawlinson was given an appointment on his staff and was with him throughout the siege of Ladysmith. It was at Rawlinson's suggestion that the naval guns which played such an important part in the defence were brought up from Durban just before the Boers completed the investment. On the relief of Ladysmith Rawlinson was appointed assistant adjutant-general on Lord Roberts's staff, and joined him in March 1900 at Bloemfontein. In November of that year, when all the chief Boer towns had been occupied and the War seemed to be drawing to a close, he accompanied Lord Roberts to England. But it was soon discovered that the British had been too optimistic, and within three weeks of coming to England he had sailed again for South Africa, to join Lord Kitchener in Pretoria. Within a month Kitchener appointed him to the command of a mobile column, and in that capacity he served until the end of the War in May 1902, proving himself one of the most energetic and successful of the younger commanders. For his services in the South African War, during which he had been five times mentioned in dispatches, he was made C.B., and in June 1902 a brevet-colonel.

After eight months' service at the War Office, Rawlinson was in December 1903 promoted brigadier-general and made commandant of the Staff College, and there for three years his experience of staff work in peace and in war enabled him to make the course of instruction more practical than it had been. On leaving the Staff College he was given the command of a brigade at Aldershot, which he gave up on promotion to major-general in May 1909. In June of the following year he was made commander of the 3rd division and spent four happy and strenuous years in its training. His time of command came to an end in May 1914, and to his distress there was no place for him in the Expeditionary Force which went to France in the following August. But he had not long to wait, for in the third week of September he was given command of the 4th division, then on the Aisne, and thence early in October he was sent to Belgium to take command of the 7th division and the 3rd cavalry division, which were landing at Ostend and Zeebrugge in order to attempt the relief of Antwerp.

Antwerp fell before Rawlinson's force was ready for action, and he then had the difficult task of covering the right flank of the retreating Belgian army and of retiring on Ypres to join the British army, which was moving into Flanders from the Aisne. He reached Ypres on 14 October. There his command soon became involved in the struggle for the defence of the Channel ports. His 7th division was absorbed in the I Corps, under Sir Douglas Haig [q.v.], and the 3rd cavalry division joined the Cavalry Corps. On this break up of his command Rawlinson returned to England in order to bring out the 8th division, destined with the 7th division to form the IV Corps, under his command. Towards the end of the year the IV Corps went into the line on the Neuve Chapelle front, and on 10 March took a leading part in the battle of Neuve Chapelle. Throughout 1915 Rawlinson commanded the IV Corps, leading it in the battles of Aubers Ridge, Festubert, and Loos. His experiences of those battles made him a strong advocate of the method of attack with limited objectives; but that method was not then generally accepted, and fate decided that he should be the protagonist in the first of the prolonged battles which were the outstanding feature of trench warfare on the Western front.

In December 1915 when Sir Charles Carmichael Monro [q.v.] left France to recommend and organize the evacuation of the Gallipoli Peninsula, Rawlinson was given temporary command of the First Army, and early in the next year he was promoted lieutenant-general and chosen to command the newly created Fourth Army. This army was given the task of preparing for the counter-offensive on the Somme, which was to disengage Verdun. Rawlinson strongly advocated that the battle of the Somme should be begun with limited attacks, but he was overruled and set himself loyally to carry out Haig's plan, which aimed at breaking through the German first and second systems of defence at one blow. The attempt to do this on 1 July failed, only the attacks of the French on the British right and of the right of Rawlinson's army succeeding. Haig's plan then became one of exploiting the success of the right and of gradually forcing the Germans back from the Somme ridges.

By the end of the first week of July Rawlinson had driven the Germans from their first defensive system. He then proposed to attack the second system by night with four divisions. A night attack on this scale had never before been attempted in war, and Haig at first hesitated to accept the risk of such a novel experiment; but, won over by Rawlinson's insistence and by the perfection of his arrangements, Haig in the end consented, and the attack was successfully made on 14 July. Unfortunately in the interval the Germans had been reinforced, and it is at least probable that if the attack had been made 48 hours earlier, as Rawlinson had wished, the results would have been far greater. The battle dragged on until the middle of November, when bad weather and mutual exhaustion brought it to a close. In the following January Rawlinson was promoted general.

During the early months of 1917 the British Fourth Army was occupied in extending its front in order to set free the French troops required for the operations planned by the new French commander-in-chief, General Nivelle. The Fourth Army was thus too much extended to take full advantage of the German retreat to the Hindenburg line, which began in March 1917; it thus took no part in the battles of Arras and Messines. In July, when Haig was preparing to attack the Germans at Ypres, he chose Rawlinson to take charge of the secret preparations for a combined naval and military attack on the Belgian coast; but this, owing to the failure of the Ypres attack to make sufficient progress, came to nothing. In November 1917, towards the close of the battle of Passchendaele, Rawlinson took over the command of the British left, and he was in that position when in February 1918 he was appointed British military representative on the Supreme War Council in succession to his old friend Sir Henry Wilson, who had been recalled to the War Office. From that position he was removed at the end of March 1918 to take command of the remnants of the British

Fifth Army, which had been shattered in the great German attack launched on 21 March. These he reconstituted as the Fourth Army, while fully occupied with the defence of Amiens. The last German effort to drive the British from that vital railway junction ended with the recapture by the Fourth Army of Villers-Brettoneux on 25 April, and Rawlinson was then left a period of comparative leisure in which to fill the gaps in his army and perfect its training.

A part of this training consisted of practice in co-operation between infantry and the latest pattern of 'tank'. A test of this carried out on 4 July in an attack on a small scale on Hamel was completely successful, and Rawlinson then prepared to apply his methods on a larger scale. His plans being approved by Haig and Foch, he attacked astride the Somme on the Amiens front on 8 August and at once gained the most important success which up till then had been won by the British army. General Ludendorff has, indeed, described that day, 8 August, as 'the black day in the history of the German army'. Following on this victory Haig extended the front of battle northwards from the Somme, and while the Third and First Armies on his left were pressing back the Germans, Rawlinson's Fourth Army crossed the Somme, captured Peronne (31 August), and by the middle of September had driven the Germans into the shelter of the Hindenburg line. The attack of the Fourth Army, reinforced by an American Corps of two divisions, on those formidable defences began on 29 September, when the St. Quentin canal was crossed, and by 8 October the army had forced its way through the Hindenburg system. Nine days later it attacked in the battle of the Selle the Germans who had made a stand behind that river. On 4 November the army again attacked, forced its way across the Sambre canal, and drove the enemy through the Mormal forest. When the Armistice became effective on 11 November, the Fourth Army had reached a point south-east of Maubeuge, a few miles west of Beaumont, having, since 8 August, fought and won four great battles and eighteen actions, as the result of which the enemy had been driven back 60 miles with the loss of 79,743 prisoners and 1,108 guns. It had engaged 24 British, Australian, Canadian, and American divisions against 67 German divisions; but it had suffered 122,427 casualties.

After the Armistice the Fourth Army remained in occupation in Belgium, and on its dissolution Rawlinson came home in March 1919, to be appointed, at the end of July, to carry out the evacuation of Northern Russia by the Allied forces. On his way to Archangel he received the news that he had been accorded the thanks of both Houses of parliament, with a grant of £30,000, and had been created a baron. He was back in England in October 1919, having successfully accomplished his mission, and after a short period of command at Aldershot he was, in November 1920, appointed commander-in-chief in India.

The major problems which Rawlinson set himself to solve in India were: (1) the reorganization of army head-quarters and of its relation with the military member of the viceroy's council, a question which had been the subject of long and bitter dispute between Lord Curzon and Lord Kitchener; (2) the reorganization of the Indian army and the improvement of its equipment, consistently with the urgent demand for economy; (3) the introduction of the process of Indianization; and (4), most important of all, the application of a new policy on the North-West Frontier. Rawlinson's father had been one of the earliest advocates of the policy of opening up Baluchistan, as successfully initiated by Sir Robert Groves Sandeman [q.v.]; and despite considerable, and at times somewhat acrimonious, opposition Rawlinson applied the same policy to Waziristan, opening up the country by constructing roads and establishing an important military station at Razmak in the midst of the Waziris. That policy has since stood the test of disturbed conditions on the Frontier. The other items of his programme he carried through with equal success, and he could claim in 1925 that while the military budget had been reduced from 82 crores of rupees in 1921 to 56 crores in 1925, the British garrison from 75,300 to 57,000 men and the Indian army from 159,000 to 140,000, the general standard of efficiency had been raised. He achieved the difficult task of gaining the admiration and affection of the army while making these reductions, and the even more difficult task of winning the respect of the legislative assembly. A fine horseman and brilliant polo player, Rawlinson exercised a healthy influence upon the development of the game both at home and in India. It was after taking part in a hard game of polo on his sixty-first birthday and soon after making 21 runs at cricket against the boys of the new Dehra Dun military school, that he was taken ill at Delhi, and died of the after effects of an operation 28 March 1925. His body was brought home and buried at Trent. He had no children, and on his death the barony became extinct. He was succeeded as third baronet by his brother Alfred (born 1867).

There are portraits of Lord Rawlinson by Oswald Birley in the possession of Lady Rawlinson and at the Staff College, Camberley. He figures in J. S. Sargent's group 'Some General Officers of the Great War' (painted in 1922), in the National Portrait Gallery, and there is a portrait of him by Sir William Orpen in the Imperial War Museum.

[Sir J. F. Maurice and M. H. Grant, (Official) *History of the War in South Africa, 1899–1902*, 1906–1910; Sir J. E. Edmonds, (Official) *History of the Great War. Military Operations. France and Belgium, 1914–1918*, 1922–1935; Sir F. Maurice, *Life of Lord Rawlinson of Trent*, 1928.] F. MAURICE.

RAWLINSON, WILLIAM GEORGE (1840–1928), art collector and writer on Turner, was born 23 December 1840 at Taunton, the only son of William Rawlinson, who owned a silk mill there. His mother's name was Harriet Jeboult. About 1865 young Rawlinson joined a London silk firm which handled the produce of the mill at Taunton. Later, as a partner in that business (James Pearsall & Co.) he helped to create the English embroidery-silk trade, until then a German monopoly. In conjunction with Sir Thomas Wardle [q.v.], of Leek, he reintroduced old methods of dyeing silk with the natural dyes of the East. He retired from this business in 1908.

Rawlinson's chief claim to remembrance is the zeal and precision with which he collected and studied the drawings and engraved work of Turner. In 1878 he produced a catalogue of the *Liber Studiorum*, describing for the first time the states of the engravings comprised in that work. Its revised edition (1906) remained the standard catalogue of the *Liber* until the publication, in 1924, of Mr. A. J. Finberg's more exhaustive description.

Rawlinson then studied closely the miscellaneous engravings after Turner, produced during the painter's lifetime and under his supervision, or shortly after his death. He based on this research another detailed catalogue, *The Engraved Work of J. M. W. Turner, R.A.*, of which vol. I (1908) described the engravings on copper, vol. II (1913) the engravings on steel and prints by other processes. In 1909 he wrote on Turner's water-colours for a special number of *The Studio*. He contributed technical notes in 1902 for the catalogue of an exhibition of English mezzotint portraits held at the Burlington Fine Arts Club, of which he was a keen and active member from 1872 to 1921.

These researches grew out of Rawlinson's activity as a collector. His choice cabinet of Turner water-colours was sold in 1917 to R. A. Tatton, after whose death it was dispersed at Christie's on 14 December 1928. His collection of *Liber* proofs, of which he issued a privately printed catalogue in 1887 (a revised edition, November 1912, cites additions bought at the J. E. Taylor sale at Christie's, 15–16 July 1912) was sold late in 1912 to Francis Bullard, of Boston, Massachusetts, whose entire *Liber* collection, in which Rawlinson's proofs were incorporated, was bequeathed at his death in 1913 to the Boston Museum of Fine Arts. Rawlinson's fine collection of other engravings after Turner was bought, as a whole, in September 1919 by Mr. S. L. Courtauld. Rawlinson also became interested, late in his career as a collector, in coloured aquatints of the early nineteenth century, which were then beginning to enjoy a revival of popularity. Another of his hobbies was the collection of blue and white Chinese porcelain.

For many years until he left it in 1919, subsequently taking a flat in Chelsea, Hill Lodge, Rawlinson's residence on Campden Hill, was the centre of a large circle of friends, especially writers and artists. By his marriage in 1867 to Mary Margherita, daughter of the Rev. Alexander Cridland, incumbent of Hensall-cum-Heck, Snaith, Yorkshire, he had one son and three daughters. Rawlinson died in London 13 May 1928.

[*The Times*, 15 May 1928; private information; personal knowledge.] C. DODGSON.

READ, SIR CHARLES HERCULES (1857–1929), antiquary and art connoisseur, was born at Gillingham, Kent, 6 July 1857, the third son of John Finsbury Read, by his wife, Catherine, daughter of Hercules Angus, of Shetland. He was educated privately. His first official appointment was as ethnographical assistant in the collection of prehistory and ethnography formed by Henry Christy [q.v.], then housed in Victoria Street, Westminster, but transferred in 1883 to the British Museum. There Read was appointed assistant in the Department of British and Medieval Antiquities and Ethnography in 1880. In 1896, at the early age of thirty-nine, he succeeded Sir Augustus Wollaston Franks [q.v.] as keeper of the department, and he held the post until his retirement in 1921. Read owed much to the training and friendship of Franks, a notice of whom he contributed to this DICTIONARY. Of the many valuable gifts acquired for the department during his keepership, the most important were reproduced in a volume which was presented to him as a parting gift. These benefactions included the Waddesdon bequest (the collection of Baron Ferdinand de Rothschild, q.v., 1898); the Greenwell collection of prehistoric bronzes, presented by Mr. J. Pierpont Morgan in 1909; the collection of painted enamels bequeathed by the Rev. A. H. S. Barwell in 1913; and that of plaquettes given by Mr. T. Whitcombe Greene in 1915.

Read's connexion with the Society of Antiquaries was also exceptionally long and useful, as he became successively secretary (1892–1908) and president (1908–1914 and 1919–1924); and he claimed that his knighthood in 1912 was meant as a compliment to the Society with which he was identified. An ideal chairman, he held various offices, such as president of the Royal Anthropological Institute (1899–1901 and 1917–1919) and of Section H of the British Association (1899). The university of St. Andrews conferred on him the honorary degree of LL.D. in 1908, and he was elected F.B.A. in 1913. He also received many distinctions from foreign academies and learned societies.

Read's main official publications were catalogues of the *Waddesdon Bequest* (1899 and 1902) and of the *Antiquities from Benin* (with O. M. Dalton, 1899). He also contributed the introduction to the *Catalogue of the Faience of Persia and the Nearer East* (1907), and prefaces to those of *Early Chinese Pottery and Porcelain* (1910) and *Chinese Art* (1915). His contributions to the publications of learned societies were numerous, the Society of Antiquaries receiving no less than 115. He was a member of the Society of Dilettanti and of the Gentlemen of Spalding; and his social gifts enabled him to form a group of 'Friends of the British Museum', to supplement with gifts the inadequate purchase grant of his department. These benefactors formed the nucleus of the National Art Collections Fund, which, with its thousands of subscribers, can conduct operations on a grander scale.

A fluent speaker and an imposing figure, Read also possessed a most retentive memory of things he had seen, together with artistic feeling and capacity of no mean order, which made him a useful member of the Burlington Fine Arts Club, and justified his appointment in 1920 as vice-chairman of the National Art Collections Fund. As keeper of a miscellaneous department of national antiquities he acquired a most extensive knowledge of ancient material. On his retirement from the Museum, his department was divided into two, ceramics and ethnography being separated from prehistoric and medieval antiquities.

Read died after a lingering illness 11 February 1929 at Rapallo, where he was buried. He married in 1880 Helen Mary, elder daughter of Frederick George Smith, of Chelsea, and had two daughters. His striking features are preserved in Seymour Lucas's drawing of 1912 (reproduced as frontispiece to the presentation volume of 1921). Augustus John's painting of 1921 shows him in declining years.

[*The Times*, 13 February 1929; O. M. Dalton, *Sir Charles Hercules Read, 1857–1929*, in *Proceedings* of the British Academy, vol. xv, 1929; *Antiquaries Journal*, vol. ix, 1929.]

R. A. SMITH.

REID, JAMES SMITH (1846–1926), classical scholar and ancient historian, was born at Sorn, Ayrshire, 3 May 1846, the eldest son of John Reid, schoolmaster, by his wife, Mary Smith. Among collateral relatives on his mother's side he reckoned Adam Smith, the author of *The Wealth of Nations*. He was educated at the City of London School, and entered Christ's College, Cambridge, as a scholar in 1865. Three years later (1868) he was bracketed senior classic, and was awarded the Browne medal for a Latin epigram. He was senior chancellor's medallist in 1869, and the same year was elected a fellow of his college. Concurrently with his classical work Reid had been studying law, and was Whewell scholar in 1870 and graduated LL.M. in 1872.

From 1873 to 1878 and again from 1880 to 1885 Reid was classical lecturer at Pembroke College, and in 1878, having ceased to be a fellow of Christ's on his marriage in 1872, he was elected to a fellowship at Gonville and Caius College, of which society he remained a member for forty-four years. Here, together with the Rev. E. S. Roberts (master of the college, 1903–1912), he built up a brilliant classical school. In 1899 he was elected first professor of ancient history in the university, and held this chair until 1925. He received the honorary degrees of Litt.D. of Dublin University and LL.D. of St. Andrews University, and in 1917 he was elected a fellow of the British Academy. He was also an honorary fellow of Christ's College.

Reid's main interests were in Latin studies, and he early took a foremost place among Ciceronian scholars, bringing to the establishment and elucidation of the texts a mastery of idiom which has had few rivals. His forerunner and model was the Danish philologist, Johan Nicolai Madvig, for whose lightest word Cambridge men of that day manifested a respect little short of idolatry. He produced a smaller and a larger edition of the *Academica* (in 1874 and 1885), and editions of the *Pro Archia* (1877), the *Pro Balbo* (1878), *De Amicitia* (1879), *De Senectute* (1879), *Pro Sulla* (1882), and *Pro Milone* (1894). The first volume of his edition of the *De Finibus*, containing Books I and II, appeared in 1925, forty-two years after the publication of his translation of the whole work. The text was constructed too early to do full justice to the manuscript tradition available at the time of publication. In this and in the *Academica* Reid showed himself a master of later Greek philosophy. This list does not, however, exhaust his contribution to Ciceronian studies, for his knowledge was at the disposal of his friends, and it was freely utilized and acknowledged by them. Reid's erudition in Latin literature of the republic and early empire was wide as well as deep. As professor of ancient history he was most concerned with questions of Roman constitutional history, in which his training in law stood him in good stead. Even when his suggestions on much-debated topics did not wholly win assent, his command of the evidence and a natural instinct for Roman ways of thinking were recognized. It may indeed be said that he viewed Roman history as a Roman would have viewed it. To his command of literary evidence he added a great knowledge of inscriptions, so that the absence of documentation in his *Municipalities of the Roman Empire* (1913) is to be deplored.

Reid played a large part in the foundation in 1910 of the Society for the Promotion of Roman Studies, of which he succeeded F. J. Haverfield as president in 1916, and in his own university he was both accessible and indefatigable in giving encouragement and help. For fifteen years he was a tutor of Caius, but his forte was in scholarship and teaching rather than in administration. For university affairs he had little taste. In politics he was a liberal of the old school, and was for some years chairman of the party in the town of Cambridge. His personality, in which the desire to shine found no place, was gentle and kindly. He retired from his chair on the ground of failing health in 1925, and died at Cambridge 1 April 1926.

Reid married in 1872 Ruth, daughter of Thomas Gardner, of the Stock Exchange, and sister of Professor Percy Gardner, Professor Ernest Gardner, and Miss Alice Gardner. He had three sons, two of whom survived him, and one daughter.

[A. Souter, A. C. Clark, and F. E. Adcock, *James Smith Reid, 1846–1926*, in *Proceedings* of the British Academy, vol. xiii, 1927; memoir by Peter Giles in *The Caian*, 1926–1927; private information; personal knowledge.] F. E. Adcock.

REID, ROBERT THRESHIE, Earl Loreburn (1846–1923), lord chancellor, was born 3 April 1846 at Corfu, the second son of Sir James John Reid, of Mouswald Place, Dumfries, sometime chief justice of the Ionian Islands protectorate, by his wife, Mary, daughter of Robert Threshie, of Barnbarroch, Kirkcudbrightshire. He was educated at Cheltenham College, where he distinguished himself both as a scholar and as an athlete. He rose to be head of the school, he was for three years (1862–1864) in the cricket eleven, and he was the best racket-player. From Cheltenham he won a demyship at Magdalen College, Oxford, but threw it up, and entered for a scholarship at Balliol College, to which he was elected in 1864. His Oxford career was very successful, and few better all-round men have passed through the university. He obtained first classes in classical moderations (1866) and in *literae humaniores* (1868), winning the Ireland scholarship in the latter year. He played for Oxford for three seasons at cricket, and, although he did little as a batsman, he was in the front rank as a wicket-keeper. He played rackets, both doubles and singles, against Cambridge in 1865 and 1867, and he was a fair short-distance runner. His busy life allowed him little leisure in later years for athletics, but his reputation as an expert at games remained with him throughout his career, and gained him many friends. He always kept up his interest in cricket, and served as president of the Marylebone Cricket Club in 1907.

Reid's ancestry and associations were legal, and immediately upon leaving the university he prepared for the English bar. He was called by the Inner Temple in 1871, and went the Oxford circuit. It is related of him that with characteristic honesty he broke through the established convention that barristers on circuit should travel first-class, admitting that he could not afford the luxury, and that he was indifferent to what the bar mess might say. His rise at the bar was rapid. For a time he 'devilled' for Sir Henry James (afterwards Lord James of Hereford, q.v.). James was himself an old Cheltonian, having been one of the first boys at the college, and he was glad to help a prominent younger member of his old school by every means in his power. Reid's practice, however, soon increased so much that he had enough work of his own. His advance was chiefly due to his quick mastery of the salient points of a case. He was particularly effective in commercial suits, and as a junior contributed to several legal questions of importance. An interesting appeal in which he was led by Sir Charles Russell, afterwards Lord Russell of Killowen, was that of the *Capital and Counties Bank* v. *Henty* (1882) on the doctrine of innuendo in a libel action. The issue of a circular among the respondents' (the bank's) customers to the effect that the respondents would not accept the appellant's cheques in payment of accounts, was held not necessarily to imply a doubt of the appellant's solvency.

Before many years Reid turned his attention to politics. At the general election held in the spring of 1880, when Mr. Gladstone was returned to power, Reid entered the House of Commons as the second liberal member for the borough of Hereford. He was again fortunate in receiving help from Sir Henry James, who had influence in the constituency. After he became a member of parliament, Reid's interest in politics to some extent diverted his thoughts from legal work. He took silk in 1882, but his practice as a leader scarcely fulfilled his early promise. He found constant employment before the House of Lords and the Judicial Committee of the Privy Council, but, as an advocate, he never rose to the first class. As a politician he was a loyal and ardent supporter of Mr. Gladstone, and was always an effective speaker on the platform. In the House of Commons he confined himself chiefly to the discussion of bills in committee, and made no special mark in the early stages of his career.

After the passing of the Redistribution Bill of 1885, the borough of Hereford became a single-member constituency, and Reid had to look elsewhere for a seat. At the general election of December 1885 he stood for Dumbartonshire and was defeated. This election was followed by the division in the liberal party over the question of Home Rule for Ireland. Another appeal to the country became necessary in June 1886, and, although the Gladstonian liberals were decisively defeated, Reid managed to win the seat of Dumfries as a supporter of the prime minister's Irish policy. He continued to sit for this constituency until 1905, when he became lord chancellor.

In 1892 the verdict of the electors was reversed, and the Home Rule section of the liberal party came into power. Less than two years later, when Gladstone had retired and Lord Rosebery had become prime minister, some rapid changes in the law offices of the Crown brought about the promotion of Reid. In May 1894 Sir Charles Russell was made a lord of appeal, his place as attorney-general was taken by Sir John Rigby [q.v.], and Reid became solicitor-general and was knighted. In the debates on Sir William Harcourt's Finance Bill of 1894 Reid took an active part, though the defence of the measure was mainly entrusted to Rigby as a Chancery lawyer. Rigby was promoted a few weeks later to be a judge of the Court of Appeal, and Reid became attorney-general. His tenure of the attorney-generalship was also short, for in June 1895 the liberal government was defeated in the House on a technical question of War Office administration. Although the division appeared unimportant, the increasing difficulties of the government rendered the dissolution of parliament advisable. At the general election which followed, the small liberal majority was turned into a substantial majority for their opponents, and the unionists remained in office for the next ten years. Reid retained his seat for the Dumfries district both at the 1895 election and at that of 1900.

Out of office Reid dropped much of his

practice, but other appointments followed. In 1899 he was chosen by the unionist government to act as arbitrator in the boundary dispute between Venezuela and British Guiana, and for his services in arranging a settlement he received the G.C.M.G. In the same year (1899) he was appointed standing counsel for Oxford University, a position which he held until 1906.

During the period of the South African War Reid, without regard to his professional or political prospects, took the unpopular side and supported the cause of the Boers. The unionists had obtained a further lease of power at the election of 1900, but three years later Mr. Chamberlain's tariff proposals revived the controversy between supporters of free trade and of protection, and this became again the party question of the day. In December 1905 Mr. Balfour's ministry resigned, and the liberals under Sir Henry Campbell-Bannerman took office. There were two other eminent lawyers whose claims to the woolsack were thought to be considerable, but Reid was preferred to them. As lord chancellor he assumed the title of Baron Loreburn (really 'lower-burn', a war-cry in faction fights at the old burgh in which his father had lived, and which he had himself represented in parliament). Immediately after Sir Henry Campbell-Bannerman had taken office parliament was dissolved. At the general election which followed, in January 1906, the liberals won many seats all over the country, and in the new parliament had a large majority.

Lord Loreburn's principal legal achievement as lord chancellor was the establishment of the Court of Criminal Appeal in 1907. This reform, which before it had long been in operation came to be looked upon as an obvious necessity, had met with strong opposition from many lawyers, whose prophecies proved to be signally mistaken. Another change which Loreburn advocated consistently was the extension of the jurisdiction of the county courts. From the first he set his face against long and rambling judgments. His own were clear and concise, and his gift of lucid expression made them easy reading. There may not have been much in them which was novel or illuminating to lawyers, but to the lay mind they were convincing proof that every effort had been made to secure justice. He was courteous and patient in hearing appeals, listening to counsel and not interrupting them.

In the duty of presiding over the House of Lords no chancellor has ever been so uncomfortably placed as was Loreburn, and it is a remarkable tribute to his personal qualities that he came through the ordeal with so much credit. He found an assembly almost united in its hostility to his party, and himself the spokesman of a government whose measures were received with suspicion and dislike. The climax was reached when in 1909, owing to the rejection by the House of Lords of the budget introduced by Mr. Lloyd George as chancellor of the Exchequer, the question of the relations of the two Houses was raised in the country. Two general elections were held in 1910—in January and in December—and at both the liberals were returned with majorities, which, although much reduced from the 1906 figures, were held to justify the policy of curtailing the powers of the upper chamber. Under the Parliament Bill, which was sent up from the House of Commons in May 1911, it was proposed that a measure passed by the House of Commons in three consecutive sessions should become law with or without the assent of the House of Lords. The crisis occasioned by this constitutional change was settled by the final withdrawal of unionist opposition after long and heated controversy. Loreburn spoke on the second reading, on 24 May, not, indeed, arguing with much force on the constitutional advantages of the Bill, but pleading with sincerity the disheartening effect from the liberal point of view of the conservative preponderance in the chamber over which he was presiding. Throughout the discussion, although he was tactful in his management of the House, he never made any attempt to disguise his own complete approval of the proposed reform, or to disarm resistance with conciliatory phrases. There is no doubt that his straightforward support impressed favourably political adversaries, many of whom were personal friends. On the occasion of his second marriage in 1907 a large number of peers on both sides of the house subscribed for his portrait, painted by Sir George Reid, as a wedding gift.

Generally speaking Loreburn was more effective as a debater in the House of Lords than he had been in the House of Commons. As lord chancellor, and throughout his public career, he showed himself a man of inflexible integrity. Liberals found fault with him for refusing to take into account political services in the appointment of new magistrates. But he would not be influenced by party considerations, and insisted on fitness for the bench as the sole test. Although nothing could move him, it was characteristic of him that this controversy troubled him, for he was sensitive to criticism and easily depressed. Overwork and the anxieties of office told upon his health. He had not been long on the woolsack before some weakness of the heart showed itself, and he was obliged to rest from time to time. This eventually brought about his resignation, and he was succeeded as lord chancellor by Lord Haldane in June 1912. It was significant of his sense of public duty that he insisted on a substantial reduction of the life-pension to which he was entitled.

In 1911 Loreburn was advanced to an earldom, and in the same year was named one of the four councillors of state during the absence of King George V in India. He received the honorary degree of D.C.L. of Oxford University in 1907, and in 1912 his old college, Balliol, exercising its unique privilege, appointed him visitor. In the latter year he defrayed the cost of replacing the medieval glass in the windows of the college chapel, as a memorial to his first wife.

After his retirement Loreburn lived at Dover. He occupied his leisure in writing two books, *Capture at Sea* (1913) and *How the War Came* (1919). His health had failed for some time before his death, which took place at Dover 30 November 1923.

Loreburn married twice: first, in 1871 Emily Douglas (died 1904), daughter of Captain Arthur Cecil Fleming, first Dragoon Guards; secondly, in 1907 Violet Elizabeth, eldest daughter of William Frederick Hicks-Beach, of Witcombe Park, Gloucestershire, and niece of Sir Michael Edward Hicks-Beach, first Earl St. Aldwyn [q.v.], the conservative statesman. There was no issue of either marriage, and on his death the peerage became extinct.

The portrait of Loreburn by Reid now hangs in the council chamber of the Privy Council. There are also portraits of him by Fiddes Watt at Balliol College, Oxford, and by Ruth Garnett at Cheltenham College. A cartoon of him by 'Spy' appeared in *Vanity Fair* 10 January 1895.

[*The Times*, 1 December 1923; private information.] A. Cochrane.

REPINGTON, CHARLES à COURT (1858–1925), soldier and military writer, was born at Heytesbury, Wiltshire, 29 January 1858, the elder son of Charles Henry Wyndham à Court (afterwards Repington), of Amington Hall, near Tamworth, Warwickshire, M.P. for Wilton 1852–1855, by his wife, Emily, eldest daughter of Henry Currie, banker, of West Horsley Place, Surrey. In 1903 he assumed the additional surname of Repington, according to the custom established by a great-uncle, on succeeding to the family property of Amington Hall. His grandfather was a general, one great-uncle an admiral, and another the diplomatist William à Court, first Baron Heytesbury [q.v.]. He was educated at Eton and Sandhurst, and joined the Rifle Brigade in 1878. After seeing active service in Afghanistan, he entered the Staff College, Camberley, by competition in 1887. His fellow students included (Field-Marshal Lord) Plumer, (General Sir) Horace Smith-Dorrien, and many other officers who rose high in the service; but all regarded Captain à Court as the most brilliant man of his year.

à Court left Camberley in time to take part in the Burma campaign of 1888–1889. Then, after duty in the Intelligence Department of the War Office and on the staff in the Atbara and Omdurman campaigns in the Sudan, having been promoted brevet lieutenant-colonel, he was in 1898 appointed military attaché at Brussels and The Hague. He proceeded, however, to South Africa in 1899 on the head-quarters staff of Sir Redvers Buller [q.v.]. After the relief of Ladysmith he was invalided home, and resumed his post of attaché. He was awarded the C.M.G. in 1900. In 1902 his military career came to an end owing to personal indiscretion. Whilst he was in Egypt à Court had carried on an intrigue with the wife of a British official. The affair had been condoned; but it had been brought to the notice of the military authorities, and before he had been allowed to take up his post in Brussels he had been called upon to give his word of honour to the military secretary that there should be no recurrence of the liaison. Nevertheless, it was renewed; the husband instituted divorce proceedings; and à Court was forced to resign his commission. He had married in 1882 Mellony Catherine, daughter of Colonel Henry Sales Scobell, of Pershore, and sister of Henry Jenner Scobell, an eminent cavalry general. As she refused to divorce him, he was unable to regularize the position of the lady whom he had compromised.

Repington (as he now became) turned

to his pen, obtained employment on the *Morning Post*, and then, from 1904, as a military correspondent of *The Times*. His articles in the columns of the latter paper on the Russo-Japanese War brought him international fame. There was some thought of reinstating him in the army, and as a step towards this he was in 1911 appointed editor of the *Army Review*, a pre-War General Staff quarterly. But the fact that he had divulged, in a letter to *The Times* in March 1908, private correspondence between Lord Tweedmouth, first lord of the Admiralty, and Kaiser Wilhelm II, of which he had obtained cognizance, caused the project of his reinstatement to be dropped. His influence on public opinion, however, continued to increase.

During the European War of 1914–1918 Repington served on recruiting and exemption tribunals, but went on with his work for *The Times*, frequently visiting France. The views which he expressed in 1917 did not, however, coincide with those of Viscount Northcliffe [see Harmsworth, Alfred Charles William], who had gained control of the paper, and in January 1918 he left *The Times* and returned to the *Morning Post*. He had already on several occasions made public more than was discreet in war time, and on 22 March, in consequence of having alluded in the *Morning Post* to the formation of an Allied General Reserve, he, with the editor, was charged with contravention of the Defence of the Realm regulations. Both men were found guilty and fined. After the War Repington became military correspondent of the *Daily Telegraph*, a post which he held until his death. His finances being in a desperate condition, he set about writing a record of his life, publishing in 1919 *Vestigia*, which carried his story as far as the Tweedmouth incident. This he followed up with *The First World War* (1920) and *After the War* (1922), in which he divulged a mass of private conversations and correspondence and dinner-table scandal. The books had a considerable success, but lost him his social position. His last book, *Policy and Arms* (1924), attracted no attention. He died 25 May 1925 at Hove, having some time previously been reconciled to his wife. He left two daughters.

[Repington's writings; personal knowledge.] J. E. Edmonds.

RIDGEWAY, Sir JOSEPH WEST (1844–1930), soldier and administrator, the second son of the Rev. Joseph Ridgeway, rector of High Roothing, Essex, by his wife, Eliza Letitia Chambers, was born at High Roothing 16 May 1844. Charles John Ridgeway (1841–1927), bishop of Chichester, and Frederick Edward Ridgeway (1848–1921), bishop of Salisbury, were his brothers. He was educated at St. Paul's School, London, and obtained a commission in the Bengal Infantry at the age of sixteen. In 1869 the viceroy, Lord Mayo, selected him for civil employment in the Central India and Rajputana agencies, and in 1873 he became an attaché in the Indian foreign department. He returned to Rajputana in 1875, serving as assistant agent to the governor-general and later as political agent of the Eastern States. Late in 1879 he succeeded (Sir) Henry Mortimer Durand [q.v.] as political secretary to Major-General Frederick Roberts (afterwards Earl Roberts, q.v.), and accompanied him on his march to Kandahar in August 1880. He was twice mentioned in dispatches, received the brevet rank of lieutenant-colonel, and was appointed junior foreign secretary to the government of India.

In 1884, owing to the occupation of Merv by the Russians in March and the continuous southward advance of Cossack outposts towards Herat, a serious position arose, and England and Russia agreed to send commissions to determine on the spot the ill-defined northern boundary of Afghanistan. This gave Ridgeway opportunity for important service. He was placed in command of the Indian section of the commission, a force of about a thousand men, and ordered to join the chief commissioner, Sir Peter Stark Lumsden, at Herat. Starting from the Pishin district, near Quetta, at the end of August 1884, Ridgeway conveyed his force across an arid desert to Kwajeh Ali on the Helmand without a single casualty and accomplished the remainder of the march through Seistan and its fanatical tribes with rapidity and success, joining Lumsden at Kuhsan, north-west of Herat, on 19 November. Lumsden and Ridgeway had been told to expect a Russian boundary commission with a small military escort: they found, instead, a considerable military force hastening to occupy the territory in dispute. In consequence, the work of the commission was held up, and Ridgeway remained for the winter with a small escort to keep the Turcoman population quiet and to give moral support to an Afghan force which was occupying the district of Panjdeh, due south of Merv. By a combination of diplomacy and firmness he made friends with the Turcomans and held the Russians back throughout the winter; but on 29 March 1885, while he had gone to Herat to report to Lumsden, the Russians under General Komarow attacked and defeated the Afghans at Panjdeh. This incident brought England and Russia to the brink of war. Ultimately, the work of the commission was resumed in November, Ridgeway succeeding Lumsden as chief commissioner. By June 1886 the boundary had been settled as far as Dukchi, thirty miles from the Oxus, but the line to the Oxus could not be agreed upon. In August the commission was recalled, and the English and Russian cabinets decided to determine for themselves the remaining frontier line. Ridgeway on his return to India was invested with the K.C.S.I. in November 1886. In April 1887 he was sent from England to St. Petersburg in order to resume negotiations. He found the military party in Russia hostile, and on returning home to report progress 'was positively shocked to find that Lord Salisbury and his Cabinet wished to let the whole thing slide', and it was only with the assistance of Sir Edward Bradford and the under-secretary at the Foreign Office, Sir Philip Currie (Lord Currie), that he induced the government to continue negotiations. Fortunately he found the Tsar Nicholas II in favour of a settlement, and a final agreement was arrived at in July 1887, defining the whole north-western frontier of Afghanistan between the Hari Rud and Oxus rivers. The treaty contented the ameer Abdur Rahman and pleased the tribesmen by securing them their northern pasture-lands. It has proved permanent as well as satisfactory. In 1887 Ridgeway was promoted colonel for distinguished service.

On his return from Russia in 1887 Ridgeway was appointed under-secretary for Ireland, and in 1889 was sworn of the Irish Privy Council. He held office under Mr. Balfour and his successor, Lord Allerton, and materially assisted in framing Balfour's Land Purchase Act of 1891. He was created K.C.B. in the same year. Although Ridgeway's office was non-political it was thought advisable, when the liberals came back to power in 1892, to remove an under-secretary so closely associated with Balfour's policy. After being sent by Lord Rosebery on a special mission to the sultan of Morocco, he was appointed governor of the Isle of Man from 1893 to 1895, and of Ceylon from 1896 to 1903. In Ceylon he reorganized the civil service, and by the Waste Lands Ordinance protected crown-lands from encroachment, and crown-forests from promiscuous timber-cutting. In 1900 he was made G.C.M.G., and on retiring he published a review of affairs in Ceylon during his administration.

On returning to England Ridgeway, who held free-trade principles, identified himself with the liberal party and stood as candidate for parliament for the City of London in January 1906 and for London University in 1910, in each case unsuccessfully. After the liberals came into office in December 1905, they set aside the limited measure of representative government proposed for the Transvaal by the Lyttelton constitution [see Lyttelton, Alfred], and in March 1906 appointed Ridgeway chairman of a committee of inquiry to proceed to Africa and consider in detail the constitutions to be given to the Transvaal and Orange River Colony. Lord Selborne, the high commissioner, was at first opposed to granting responsible government, but Ridgeway was conciliatory, the home government supported him by telegram, and by the end of May he and Selborne reported in a joint telegram that a settlement was in sight. The commission easily gained the confidence of the Boer leaders, and General Botha [q.v.], who had insisted on negotiating in Dutch, with General Smuts as interpreter, began to converse in English. The committee reported in favour of immediate responsible government for both States. The Transvaal constitution was announced in parliament by Mr. Winston Churchill on 31 July and that of the Orange River Colony on 17 December—measures which prepared the way for the Union of South Africa effected by the Act of 1909. In November 1906 Ridgeway was promoted G.C.B.

In 1910 Ridgeway became president of the British North Borneo Company. After inducing Sir Richard Dane to visit Borneo and make a report, he took steps to reorganize the civil service and to improve the railway management there. In 1927 members of the civil service of North Borneo made an address and presentation to him in recognition of the progress made under his administration.

Ridgeway was an honorary LL.D. of Cambridge and Edinburgh Universities and a vice-president of the Royal

Geographical Society. He died suddenly in London 16 May 1930. He married in 1881 Carolina Ellen (Lina), younger daughter of Robert Calverley Bewicke, of Coulby Manor, Middlesbrough. She died in 1907, leaving one daughter.

[*The Times*, 17 May 1930; A. C. Yate, *Travels with the Afghan Boundary Commission*, 1887; C. E. Yate, *Northern Afghanistan*, 1888, and *Khurasan and Sistan*, 1900; *Annual Register*, 1884, pp. 340–350, 1885, pp. 309–314, 1886, pp. 413–417; J. A. Spender, *Life of Sir Henry Campbell-Bannerman*, vol. ii, 1923.]

E. I. Carlyle.

RIDGEWAY, Sir WILLIAM (1853–1926), classical scholar, was born 6 August 1853, the youngest son of the Rev. John Henry Ridgeway, of Ballydermot, King's County. His mother was Marianna, only daughter of Samuel Ridgeway, of Aghanvilla, King's County. The Ridgeways were a Devon family, which settled in Ulster under James I and intermarried with Cromwellian settlers in King's County—in his own words 'all first-class fighting men'—and with Huguenot families round Portarlington. He belonged, therefore, to 'the Pale', and believed that he had 'not a drop of Gaelic blood in his veins'. But from his earliest years he was surrounded by those who had plenty; and they contributed much to his personality and outlook. He was educated at Portarlington School and at Trinity College, Dublin, where he won all the chief classical prizes, studied Sanskrit, and graduated as senior moderator in both classics and modern literature. From Dublin he proceeded in 1876 to St. Peter's College, Cambridge, whence he migrated to Gonville and Caius College in 1878, subsequently being elected a scholar of the college. He was bracketed fifth in the classical tripos of 1880, and was elected a fellow of his college in the same year. In 1881 a vacancy occurred on the classical staff of the college, but Ridgeway was not chosen. His disappointment was severe, and the partisan feeling then engendered delayed the recognition of his originality.

In 1883 Ridgeway was appointed to the chair of Greek at University College, Cork. This left him free to spend five months of every year in Cambridge. He published essays on the historical interpretation of Aristotle, on the size of the Homeric horse, and on the origin of the mathematical element in the teaching of Pythagoras. He was among the first English scholars to recognize the new scientific school of comparative philology in Germany, in marked contrast with the attitude prevailing at Cambridge as late as 1890. But he was deeply indebted to the Cambridge Philological Society and to the encouragement of Dr. Henry Jackson [q.v.]. His discoveries, fiercely resisted, passed quickly into currency, and his fearless inquiry emancipated classical study in England from an unintelligent orthodoxy.

The turning-point of Ridgeway's career was his appointment in 1892, after the publication of his first substantial book, to the Disney chair of archaeology at Cambridge and his re-election to a fellowship at his own college. Although the Disney chair was then poorly endowed, he resigned his chair at Cork, in which he had rendered important services to Irish education. But his appointment in 1907 to the Brereton readership in classics established his position in Cambridge. The university was passing through a period of dissension, and Ridgeway's affection for the Anglican Church and for the traditions of Cambridge scholarship limited his enthusiasm for reform. The bitter struggle about women's degrees separated him from some of his oldest friends. In the controversy on compulsory Greek he was again one of the opponents of change. Yet after the end of the European War he was clear-sighted enough to discourage further resistance, a step since justified by steady increase in the study of Greek.

Ridgeway's first book, *The Origin of Metallic Currency and Weight Standards* (1892) attacked current theories of the purely religious origin of Greek coin-types, and threw a flood of light on the early life of the Mediterranean lands: thus, the tunny-fish, the plant silphium, or the ox (on early Athenian issues) were not objects of some unknown worship, but recognized tokens of local commerce. In the first volume of his *Early Age of Greece* (1901) he enforced the fundamental distinction between the authors of the Mycenaean culture with bronze weapons, figure-of-eight shields, and southern ways of life, and the Achaeans of Homer, whom he proposed to identify with warrior immigrants of the Early Iron Age bringing with them the round shields and long iron swords of central Europe and the sterner morals of the North. This work was never completed; of the second volume, parts already in type at his death (dealing with kinship and ancestor-worship in early Europe, and with Ireland in the Heroic

Age) were published by friends in 1931, with an introduction exhibiting later developments of Ridgeway's doctrine. This book is Ridgeway's chief contribution to history. Its main doctrine secured wide acceptance, even among those who attacked it in detail. But the bitterness of the controversy took a tragic colour in Ridgeway's memory, and he retained the conviction that in certain quarters he would never be fairly treated.

In strict logic Ridgeway was weak. In support of a theory, of the truth of which he was convinced, he would use all kinds of evidence, strong and weak alike. Nor did he always give enough consideration to difficulties. But (to quote his pupil Professor D. S. Robertson) 'his mind's eye surveyed so vast a range of facts that he saw in a flash the great lines of their connexion, and his lively knowledge of human nature kept him always within the limits of reasonableness and good sense. He did not love the bizarre or the exotic, and some delicate beauty escaped him. But his enjoyment of masterpieces was suffused with a glow of enthusiasm. Nor was it only poetry that stirred him to eloquence. In a lecture on ancient gems, he would suddenly break into a paean on the extraordinary beauty of jewels. His words had a rough splendour that stamped them imperishably on his listeners' minds. He did not like formal lecturing; but round a table, with half a dozen students, he was incomparable. His vivid imagination, his width of view, his unbroken contact with reality kept one spellbound, as gems, coins, axeheads, totem-spoons tumbled on to the table from his inexhaustible pockets. He must always have had sensitive fingers, and as his sight failed he depended more and more upon touch. And he knew at once from the way in which new pupils handled and spoke of the stuff which he passed round the table, whether or no they had the makings of real archaeologists.'

In *The Origin and Influence of the Thoroughbred Horse* (1905) Ridgeway showed the development of the horse from its small Homeric ancestor through admixture of zebraic blood by the horse-breeding Greeks of North Africa and their Mohammedan successors. This conclusion he reached almost simultaneously with, and independently of, the zoologists, J. C. Ewart and H. F. Osborn, completing their zoological results by his historical study. His British Academy paper *Who were the Romans?* (1907) revived by fresh evidence Schwegler's view of the racial distinction between the Sabine or Patrician element in Rome, and the Latin or Plebeian (cf. *Cambridge Ancient History*, vol. iv, c. xiii, 1926). In *The Origin of Tragedy, with special reference to Greek Tragedians* (1910) Ridgeway argued that tragedy arose from the commemoration of local heroes at their tombs, the representations being later drawn into the ritual of Dionysus and combined with the Satyric plays. In *Dramas and Dramatic Dances of Non-European Races* (1915) he confirmed his theory by comprehensive induction from China to Bolivia and Japan, from Australia and Central Africa to the Alaskan Eskimos. Other interests of his are represented by his studies of *Cuchulain* (1905 and 1907) and unpublished papers on the (Danish) 'Origin of the Scots', and on the 'Origin of Ballads' in the praises of popular heroes (lecture delivered in 1926).

In later years Ridgeway was a frequent and valued correspondent of *The Times*, remarkable both for range of subject and vigour of style. His trenchant but genial criticism made him also a speaker in great request at such learned gatherings as had a popular side. To the last his enthusiasm for the great social ends of classical study remained unabated, and none of the honours that fell to him gave him more pleasure than his election as president of the Classical Association for 1914. The establishment of the Cambridge school of anthropology is a monument to another side of his influence. The general recognition of his work was marked on his sixtieth birthday (1913) by the presentation of a volume of *Essays and Studies* in his honour. Ridgeway was elected F.B.A. in 1904, was president of the Royal Anthropological Institute from 1908 to 1910, and received honorary doctorates from the universities of Dublin (1902), Manchester (1906), Aberdeen (1908), and Edinburgh (1921). He was knighted in 1919.

No picture of Ridgeway's life would be complete which did not indicate the extraordinary stimulus which he exerted upon others, and his untiring interest in the research and the prospects of younger men. His home at Fen Ditton, about four miles from Cambridge, with its pleasant garden, was the constant resort of scholars engaged in many kinds of research, not merely in classical or antiquarian learning. To all his visitors he gave the same unselfish and penetrating attention; no one went away without some new point of view. Yet his intercourse with scholars and students was only a part of his cordial acquaintance with all sorts and conditions of men.

The last months of Ridgeway's life were darkened by the sudden death of his wife in May 1926. She was Lucy, eldest daughter of Arthur Samuels, of Kingstown, and sister of Arthur Warren Samuels, judge of the High Court of Justice in Ireland. His companion almost since his boyhood, he had married her in 1880; she shared his ideals and was hardly less interested than he was in his work. They had one daughter. His own death occurred suddenly at Fen Ditton 12 August 1926, not quite three months after that of his wife.

[R. S. Conway, *Sir William Ridgeway, 1853–1926*, in *Proceedings* of the British Academy, vol. xii, 1926. Portrait, *Royal Academy Pictures*, 1921.] R. S. Conway.

RIGG, JAMES McMULLEN (1855–1926), biographer, historian, and translator, the eldest son of James Harrison Rigg [q.v.], principal of the Wesleyan College, Westminster, by his wife, Caroline, daughter of John Smith, alderman of Worcester, was born at Brentford 28 September 1855. He was educated at the City of London School under Dr. E. A. Abbott [q.v.] and at St. John's College, Oxford, of which he was a scholar. He obtained a second class in classical moderations in 1876 and a third class in *literae humaniores* in 1878. Two years after leaving Oxford he entered Lincoln's Inn, and was called to the bar in November 1881. Although he enjoyed a small practice for a few years, he soon abandoned law entirely, and devoted the rest of his life to literary work.

Rigg's first book, published in 1884, was an edition of *The Bankruptcy Act, 1883*. It was carefully compiled, but contained little discussion of legal principles. In the following year he began to write articles for this Dictionary, to every volume of which, with one exception, he made contributions, upwards of 600 in all. A large number of his notices were of famous judges, ancient and modern. All were accurate and sufficient, but in some of the modern biographies he was thought to be rather daring in his criticism. Rigg's next work was an edition of Sir Thomas More's translation of the Latin life of Pico della Mirandola, which appeared in 'The Tudor Library' in 1890. Its luminous introduction has perhaps received less attention than it deserves. This was followed in 1896 by *St. Anselm of Canterbury*, the book by which Rigg will be chiefly remembered. Although it treats Anselm as a thinker and writer rather than as a man of affairs, it remains a valuable contribution to ecclesiastical biography and to the history of medieval thought. In 1902 Rigg's *Select Pleas . . . from the rolls of the Exchequer of the Jews, 1220–1284*, with a translation and well-written introduction, was published by the Selden Society. The first two volumes of *A Calendar of the Plea Rolls of the Exchequer of the Jews* (vol. i, Henry III, 1218–1272; vol. ii, Edward I, 1273–1275), edited by Rigg, were published by the Jewish Historical Society in 1905 and 1910 respectively. In 1909 Rigg was appointed by the deputy-keeper of the records to make researches in the Vatican archives, and spent nine months of each of the years 1909 to 1915 in Rome. He edited two volumes of *A Calendar of State Papers, . . . Rome* (vol. i, 1558–1571, vol. ii, 1572–1578), partly from transcripts made by W. H. Bliss, who had recently died. They were published in 1916 and 1926 respectively. All Rigg's editorial work was distinguished by accuracy and scholarly expression. In addition to the books already mentioned, he published in 1903 a translation in two volumes of Boccaccio's *Decameron*, which has been several times reprinted, and in 1909 the section on 'The King's Friends' in chapter xiii of volume vi of the *Cambridge Modern History*.

In appearance Rigg was spare and ascetic; in manner shy and reserved. He usually spoke abruptly and very emphatically. Yet in friendly surroundings he was an excellent talker. His greatest interest in life was probably the history and philosophy of religion. In spite of his Wesleyan birth he seemed to be pleased when anybody referred to him, as sometimes happened, as a Roman catholic, although he was never in fact a member of that communion. He died at Brixton Hill 14 April 1926. Rigg was unmarried, and he lived with the elder of his two sisters, Miss Caroline Edith Rigg, headmistress for forty-one years of the Mary Datchelor School, Camberwell.

[Private information; personal knowledge.] G. J. Turner.

RIVAZ, Sir CHARLES MONTGOMERY (1845–1926), Anglo-Indian administrator, the second son of John Theophilus Rivaz, of Watford Hall, Watford, by his wife, Mary, daughter of William Lambert, was born at Tirlings Park, Essex, 11 March 1845. His father served for thirty years in the Indian civil service, his maternal grandfather belonged to the same service, and through his mother he was also related to Sir Robert Montgomery [q.v.], a distinguished Indian civilian. Charles Rivaz himself accordingly, after a successful career at Blackheath Proprietary School, entered the Indian civil service in 1864, and was almost immediately appointed to the Punjab, the land of the five rivers. In after times three of his brothers were also serving in various capacities in the same province, a circumstance which went far to justify the local witticism which alluded to the family as 'the five Rivaz of the Punjab'.

After six years of district work Rivaz spent five years (1871–1876) in the provincial secretariat, and was then appointed to be superintendent of the Kapurthala State during the minority of the ruling chief. The autocratic powers which this post conferred were suited to his temperament, and he conducted the affairs of this important State with much success for nine years (1876–1885). In 1885 he received the C.S.I., and after two years (1885–1887) in the Kangra district was made commissioner of Lahore (1887–1892), and subsequently promoted to be financial commissioner of the Punjab—a post which he held from 1892 to 1897.

In October 1897 Rivaz was appointed to the executive council of the governor-general to serve as member in charge of the home department and of the revenue and agricultural departments. With the arrival of Lord Curzon [q.v.] as viceroy in December 1898 the work in these and in the other departments of the government of India became very strenuous, and Rivaz entered on a period of heavy and responsible duty. It was not in his nature to initiate large reforms, but he responded readily to all reasonable suggestions for administrative progress and gave them his vigorous support. In one direction, indeed, he may be considered an initiator, namely in the treatment of landed indebtedness in the Punjab. The alarming expropriation of the peasants by the commercial classes had long engaged the attention of the Punjab officials, but many of them hesitated to advocate the drastic remedy of restricting by law the power to alienate the land. With the support of Lord Curzon, however, and the assistance of (Sir) Denzil Ibbetson [q.v.], the secretary of the revenue department, Rivaz prepared a measure which had this for its object, and took the extraordinary course of passing it through the Indian legislature (the Punjab Land Alienation Act, 1900) in opposition to the wishes of the head of the province. This courageous step has been justified by the subsequent history of the problem.

Rivaz was promoted K.C.S.I. in 1901, and early in the following year left the governor-general's council in order to become lieutenant-governor of the Punjab. He held the post until March 1907. He was indefatigable in visiting every place of interest in his province and he did much to improve the appearance and amenities of its capital, Lahore. During his term of office the province developed steadily. There were some recurrences of plague, and a terrible earthquake at Kangra on 4 April 1905, but assistance and relief were energetically organized by the lieutenant-governor. Large irrigation schemes were being carried through at this time; and the bold experiment of colonizing the newly irrigated wastes of the province proved eminently successful. Had it not been for threatenings of discontent, caused by the over-regulation of these colonies, which clouded the last few weeks of Rivaz's régime and led subsequently to popular disturbances, his tenure of the lieutenant-governorship could have been described as a triumph of firm and progressive administration.

As an Indian administrator Rivaz represented the best characteristics of the official class of his own period. He was not brought much into contact with, nor did he attempt to solve, problems connected with Indian nationalism. His interest lay rather in ensuring for the population, and more especially for the agricultural population, a just and efficient official rule, adapted to the needs and ideals of the people themselves. He had a wide acquaintance with the notables of his own province, and earned their respect by dealing with them searchingly and justly. By his own officials he was warmly esteemed, reposing, as he did, a full measure of confidence in his advisers and inspiring them with a sense of their responsibility. While never slackening his grasp on the course of events, he avoided all but the most necessary interference, and his orders were in every case decisive and brief, seizing the essential point and neglecting minor issues. Probably no Anglo-Indian official has ever exercised such effective control of affairs with so little recourse to writing; among the voluminous records connected with the passing of the Punjab Land Alienation Act in 1900, for instance, there are probably few pages where more than five consecutive lines could be found in Rivaz's bold and characteristic handwriting, and yet he was the controlling spirit of the measure, fully cognizant throughout not only of the principles but also of the details under discussion.

Rivaz was a man of spare build and refined features, with an upright carriage, a penetrating eye, and a quick, slightly nervous temperament, coupled with great modesty and restraint; scornful of all pretence and yet contemptuously tolerant of much that would offend others. Although reserved in general society he was a cordial host, and to his intimates he was a genial companion and a good friend.

Rivaz married in 1874 Emily, daughter of Major-General Agnew, of the Bengal Staff Corps, and had three sons. After completing his service in India he settled in London and lived a retired life, seeing his personal friends but refraining from public connexion with Indian questions. He died in London 7 October 1926, and was buried at Walton-on-the-Hill.

[*The Times*, 12 October 1926; official records; personal knowledge.]

E. D. MACLAGAN.

ROBECK, SIR JOHN MICHAEL DE, baronet (1862–1928), admiral of the fleet. [See DE ROBECK.]

ROBERTS, GEORGE HENRY (1869–1928), politician and labour leader, the only child of George Henry Roberts, by his wife, Ann Larkman, was born 27 July 1869 at Chedgrave, Norfolk, where his father was the village shoemaker. At the age of five he was taken to live in Norwich, and attended St. Stephen's national school, in which he rose in his eleventh year to the position of monitor; but he left school at fourteen and was apprenticed to the printing trade, continuing his education at evening classes in the higher grade and technical schools in the city. He completed his apprenticeship in 1889. As a journeyman printer he worked for a few years in London and joined the trade union of his craft, the Typographical Association. He returned to Norwich in 1894 to work first as a compositor on a local weekly journal and then as foreman printer, and by taking an active part in the local branch of his union as president for some years and later as secretary, from 1899 to 1904, he found his way, through the Norwich trades council, into public life at a comparatively early age.

Roberts was active in local politics just at the beginning of the political organization of labour in the trade unions and the socialist societies. The focus of this activity in Norwich was the Independent Labour Party, in which he was soon recognized as a leader. He was the first labour member to be elected (in 1899) to the Norwich school board, and fought, unsuccessfully, his first contest as parliamentary labour candidate at a by-election in Norwich in 1904, in which year he also became the national organizer of his union and was adopted as its nominee for parliament. He entered parliament as labour member for Norwich in the general election of 1906. He was by this time widely known in the labour movement as a vigorous propagandist on the Independent Labour Party platform and as an able, well-informed politician; his standing in the party was attested by his immediate election as one of its whips in the House of Commons. He was a member of the party's executive committee; and he was, although an outspoken critic of extremist tendencies in socialist policy, an influential member of the group of Independent Labour Party leaders who practically controlled the labour political movement in those years.

In general politics, however, as well as in relation to labour and socialist policy, Roberts moved steadily towards the right wing. He parted company with the Independent Labour Party at the outbreak of the European War in 1914, and widened the breach with his old associates when he entered the Asquith Coalition ministry in 1915 as a lord commissioner of the Treasury; in the second Coalition ministry, formed by Mr. Lloyd George in December 1916, he became parliamentary secretary to the Board of Trade; and in the reorganization of the Lloyd George government, in the summer of 1917, he was given the post of minister of labour with a seat in the Cabinet. But in June 1918 the labour party withdrew its support of the Coalition government and terminated the political truce which had been observed by all parties during the War. This brought to a head the antagonism that had been developing between Roberts and the labour party. His relations with the local party organization had already been strained for some years, and they had reached the stage of open rupture in 1917 when the Norwich labour party opposed him in the by-election necessitated by his acceptance of office in the government. He now broke finally with the labour party by refusing, with two or three other labour ministers, to withdraw from the Coalition, emphasizing his defiance by accepting in January 1919 the office of food controller vacated by his colleague, J. R. Clynes, in obedience to the party's decision. He held this office until February 1920, when he resigned from the government.

In the general election of 1918 Roberts had stood as an independent and had retained his seat at Norwich against the challenge of a local labour candidate; and he successfully resisted the labour attack in the following general election of 1922. But in August of the following year he avowed himself a supporter of the conservative government and applied for official recognition by that party. His conversion to conservatism, however, marked the end of his political career, for, standing as a unionist, he lost his seat at Norwich in the general election of December 1923, and thereupon withdrew from politics and turned his attention to business, becoming a director of several companies and taking an active interest in the development of the English beet sugar industry.

Roberts's political evolution was conditioned, in some measure, by his temperament, which did not permit him to brook rivalry within or criticism by the party organization at Norwich. But he was also genuinely opposed to what he regarded as manifestations of the labour party's sympathy with the doctrine of class-war and the method of revolutionary violence. He belonged essentially to that group of trade union politicians whose moderating influence in the labour party has counteracted the strong left wing tendencies of the socialist societies within it, especially those fostered by the Independent Labour Party. In the formative period of the labour party's history Roberts was, curiously enough, identified more closely with the Independent Labour Party than with the trade union elements in the party, but in the closing years of his political career he added the weight of his influence to the trade union side of the alliance. What drove him finally into conservatism was his conviction that trade unionism, too, had become corrupted by the propaganda of direct action and social rebellion, derived, as he believed, from the socialist teaching of the Independent Labour Party.

Roberts died at Sevenoaks from heart failure 25 April 1928. He had become a privy councillor upon his acceptance of a position in the first Coalition ministry (1915), and in 1918 he had received the freedom of Norwich, where he resided for nearly the whole of his life. He married in 1895 Anne, daughter of Horace Marshall, of Norwich, and had two sons and one daughter.

[*Reformers' Year Book* (1905); *Reports* of annual labour party conferences, 1900–1918; private information; personal knowledge.]

H. T. Tracey.

ROBINSON, Sir JOSEPH BENJAMIN, first baronet (1840–1929), South African mine-owner, was born at Cradock, Cape Colony, 3 August 1840, the youngest son of Robert John Robinson, by his wife, Martha Emily, daughter of William Henry Strutt. His father had emigrated from England twenty years earlier, and had become a farmer on a large scale. While still a lad, Robinson set up for himself as a wool-buyer, travelling among the Boers from farm to farm. In 1865 he fought with the Free State Dutch in their war against the Basuto. Three years later, at the rumour of a discovery of diamonds, he at once made for the Vaal river, and began digging at Hebron. His claims proved immensely rich. In 1871 he secured further valuable diamond claims in the area which was to become famous as Kimberley. It was mainly Robinson's vigorous denunciation of the illicit diamond traffic which secured the passing by the Cape parliament of the Diamond Trade Act (1882) which, by a strange inversion of British principles of justice, laid upon an accused person found in possession of an uncut stone the onus of proving his innocence.

Robinson was among the first adventurers to reach the Rand gold-field in 1886. Outspanning on the farm Langlaagte, he looked about for the outcrop, found it, panned it, and got gold. Thereupon he sank the first shaft on the Rand. He had already bought the farm for £7,000, which was considered an immense sum. Sceptics called it Robinson's 'cabbage-patch'. In 1889 he acquired the vast Randfontein block on the far West Rand. The development of this area, some 40,000 acres in which the reef outcropped for nearly ten miles, was to be his life's work.

Robinson was one of those uneasy people who must quarrel, and could not co-operate. At various times he ran his own chamber of mines, his own bank, his own newspaper; but none of them lasted. His pugnacity, intolerance, and harshness isolated him. He had, moreover, the misfortune to be very deaf. As an employer he was exacting, though not unfair.

In politics Robinson sided with the reactionary Dutch (at his persuasion President Kruger actually descended the Langlaagte shaft). In the Uitlander agitation which culminated in the South African War (1899–1902) Robinson took no part. By his own success in recruiting mine labourers in South Africa he proved that the Chinese labour imported under the ordinance of 1904 was not indispensable. The demonstration was of timely service to the liberal government of 1906, which had pledged itself to repatriate the Chinese coolies from the Rand, and fulfilled its promise. Robinson's baronetcy, granted on General Botha's recommendation in 1908, was the reward of his advocacy of a generous measure of self-government to the conquered South African colonies.

In 1922 the announcement of the government's intention to confer a peerage on Robinson provoked a vehement and unprecedented protest in the House of Lords. In the course of the debate, attention was drawn to a case in the Supreme Court of South Africa arising out of Robinson's sale of his Randfontein interests, in which he was condemned to pay a sum, including costs, of over half a million, and petition to the Judicial Committee of the Privy Council for leave to appeal was dismissed. The matter was settled by the lord chancellor reading out a letter in which Robinson requested the king's permission to decline the proposed honour.

Robinson left no business partners. When, at the age of seventy-six, he wished to retire, he had no option but to sell out everything. His undoubted power lay in his boldness, his foresight, his invincible energy, and, not least, in his exceptional flair for finance. He was a man, unlovable certainly, whose qualities and success place him in the front rank of the pioneers of industrial development in South Africa.

Robinson died at Cape Town 30 October 1929. He married in 1877 Elizabeth Rebecca, eldest daughter of James Ferguson, a Kimberley merchant, and had four sons and five daughters. He was succeeded as second baronet by his eldest son, Joseph Benjamin (born 1887).

[*The Times*, 31 October 1929; Leo Weinthal, *Memories, Mines, and Millions*, 1929; private information.] D. Pollock.

RONAN, STEPHEN (1848–1925), lord justice of appeal in Ireland, was born at Cork 13 April 1848, the second son of Walter Ronan, solicitor, of Cork, by his wife, Sarah McNamara. The family at one time had owned considerable property, and its head was entitled to the ancient privilege of being met at the bounds of the city of Limerick by the mayor, corporation, and garrison with regalia, arms, and music. Ronan was educated at a day school in Cork, and then for three years at a school in France, where he acquired the interest in French literature which endured throughout his life. In 1864 he entered Queen's College, Cork, where he gained distinctions in science and mathematics, and graduated in 1867 with honours in logic, metaphysics, and political economy.

In Michaelmas Term, 1870, Ronan was called to the Irish bar, and worked under Christopher Palles [q.v.], the greatest Irish lawyer of the nineteenth century, with whom he formed a lifelong friendship. Palles, who became attorney-general in 1872, appointed Ronan in 1873 to be junior Crown prosecutor for the disturbed county of Kerry, and experience in this post laid the foundations of his future extensive practice as a prosecutor, and of his knowledge of criminal law. In 1881 he acted as junior prosecutor at the famous Cork winter assizes, which lasted for five weeks owing to the numerous cases of intimidation and outrage of that uneasy year.

Then, as now, there was little specialization at the Irish bar, and Ronan sought and accepted legal work of all kinds and in every court, becoming a good pleader, conveyancer, draftsman, and advocate. His legal subtlety gradually came to be appreciated, and in 1883, when John Naish [q.v.] became attorney-general, he chose Ronan to be his counsel or 'attorney-general's devil', and for four years Ronan's time was largely occupied with the mass of Crown briefs which this appointment entailed. In 1887, with the promotion of J. G. Gibson to be attorney-general, (Sir) Edward Carson (afterwards Lord Carson) became the new 'devil', and took over most of the government work. But Ronan had given so much satisfaction that he was still employed in many of the more important cases. His reputation was now established. In 1888 he was called to the English bar by the Inner Temple, and for the greater part of that year, as one of the junior counsel for *The Times*, was engaged on the work of the Parnell commission. His leader, (Sir) Richard Webster (afterwards Viscount Alverstone, q.v.), attorney-general for England, acknowledged the exceptional value of Ronan's assistance by the gift of a silver cup.

In 1889 Ronan took silk in Ireland; in 1891 he was appointed senior Crown prosecutor for Cork city and county; in 1892 he became a bencher of King's Inns, Dublin, and in the same year his eminence in the Admiralty Court was recognized by his appointment as queen's advocate-general for Ireland. Thereafter no official preferment came his way for more than twenty years. Had he chosen to involve himself in politics, he would soon have gained a seat on the bench. Although he was in favour of the Union, he held radical views. But he had a shrinking from public life, a distaste for politics, and a large contempt for politicians. He devoted himself entirely to the practice of his profession. Concentrating more and more on the Chancery side of the courts, and on cases of purely legal argument, he came to be recognized as the most subtle if not the most profound lawyer at the Irish bar. He was briefed in every important case of the types he favoured, and was a frequent pleader before the bar of the House of Lords. He took silk in England in 1909.

For over a quarter of a century after he became a senior counsel, Ronan's history is to be found within the covers of the Irish Law Reports and nowhere else. He continued to carve his deep, narrow, and solitary groove. At last, in 1915, when he was sixty-seven years of age, he was made lord justice of appeal and was sworn of the Irish Privy Council. The appointment was non-political, and was a tribute to his pre-eminent position. Everyone expected great things from him. But the appointment came too late. He had been overlong an advocate easily to forsake the active for the passive role. As an assize judge he was prone to take the case out of the hands of counsel, and even in the Court of Appeal his impatient intellect led him continually to interrupt the course of the argument with questions on points which eventually proved to be unimportant. His judgments, clear, erudite, and lengthy, smacked too much of special pleading, and laboured under the tyranny of multitudinous decisions. He lacked the temper of a great judge, the capacity to ground himself on broad principles, rather than on their exposition in decided cases, and to adapt the essence of those principles to the changing needs of the times. In 1924, when the new judicial system was established in the Irish Free State, Ronan retired. He died at his house, 45 FitzWilliam Square, Dublin, 3 October 1925.

Ronan's title to fame is that he was a great advocate. Although small and of the most fragile physique—he weighed only eight stone—his prominent nose, restless eyes, and long, aggressive beard gave him an unusual, but impressive, appearance; and his voice, clear and light, with the wide modulations of Cork, commanded instant attention. From his experience as a prosecutor he brought to the Chancery bar great skill in cross-examination, and he was able to overwhelm a witness with a hail of questions, delivered with great rapidity and capable of being answered with the unqualified 'yes' or 'no' upon which he insisted. Tensely strung to the point of pugnacity, he dominated both witness and judge. In a legal argument his powers reached their fullest development. He sifted and combined into a close pattern the mass of authority which his industry had collected, and presented it with a force of personality which seemed to paralyse opposition. Only at *nisi prius* was he a failure, having neither the instinct to penetrate the mind of a civil jury, nor the urbanity to attract it.

Outside his profession Ronan had few interests. In earlier life he was fond of cricket and yachting, and spent his vacations in travel, usually by sea; but in later days he lived as a recluse. Kindly to all, he had few intimate friends. He was unmarried.

[*The Times*, 5 October 1925; *Journal* of the Cork Historical and Archaeological Society, vol. xxx, p. 62, 1925 and vol. xxxvi, p. 35 n., 1931; Irish Law Reports; *Irish Law Times*, *passim*; private information; personal knowledge.] T. C. Kingsmill Moore.

ROSEBERY, fifth Earl of (1847–1929), statesman and author. [See Primrose, Archibald Philip.]

ROUND, JOHN HORACE (1854–1928), historian, the eldest child and only son of John Round, by his wife, Laura, daughter of Horatio (Horace) Smith, the poet [q.v.], was born at Brighton 22

February 1854. His father's family had been connected with Essex since the early part of the eighteenth century, and to the end of his life Round showed especial interest in the history of that county. He was a delicate child, and was educated privately, living at Brighton with his father and younger sister after his mother's death in 1864. He entered Balliol College, Oxford, in 1874, obtaining a second class in classical moderations in 1876 and a first class in the final honour school of modern history in 1878. He had developed an interest in history and genealogy during his isolated boyhood, and at Oxford he was fortunate in coming into personal relationship with William Stubbs [q.v.], then regius professor of modern history, who acted as tutor to a small number of pupils reading for the history school. The influence of Stubbs, a historian who was also a genealogist, was very important in determining the direction of Round's work, and his subsequent attitude towards Stubbs was always that of a pupil towards his master.

It was unnecessary for Round to follow any definite profession. After taking his degree he returned to Brighton, and lived with his father, whose health was failing, until he died in 1887. For the next sixteen years Round's head-quarters were in London, but in 1903 he returned to Brighton, where he spent the remainder of his life. He began to write for publication soon after leaving Oxford, and quickly developed the nervous, controversial style characteristic of his later work. Politically he was a strong conservative, and he first became known beyond the circle of his friends and fellow-students through an attack upon E. A. Freeman's paper of 1884 on the *Nature and Origin of the House of Lords.* These articles aroused considerable interest, but Freeman made no reply to Round's assaults, and the attack subsided. At this date, although a quick worker, and eager to engage in controversy, Round had not yet found himself as a scholar. His interests were beginning to centre round the Anglo-Norman period, but he was also attracted by the sixteenth century, and in 1886, in his *Early Life of Anne Boleyn*, he entered into a detailed criticism of J. S. Brewer's and J. Gairdner's *Calendar of Letters and Papers of the Reign of Henry VIII.* He had reached his thirty-second year before he gave any real promise of the work on which his reputation as a historian was to rest.

In 1886 the eight-hundredth anniversary of the Domesday Survey was marked by the preparation of papers by various scholars, published under the title *Domesday Studies* (vol. i, 1888, vol. ii, 1891). For this occasion Round wrote three essays, two of which are of especial importance as emphasizing the principle that the clue to the understanding of Domesday Book lies in the contemporary system of assessment to the Danegeld. In 1888 the Pipe Roll Society issued a volume of *Ancient Charters, Royal and Private, Prior to A.D. 1200*, with notes by Round on each document. These works, with which Round made his first important contribution to Anglo-Norman studies, were the forerunners of a succession of articles, notes, and reviews, which continued to appear at very short intervals throughout the next twenty-five years. The establishment of the *English Historical Review* in 1886 gave a new opportunity for the publication of detailed work, of which Round took full advantage, but his writings appeared in many different quarters. The volume of his work is very imperfectly represented by the actual books which he produced. He was a contributor to the *Encyclopædia Britannica*, to this DICTIONARY, and to many periodicals of general interest. He supplied articles to the *Genealogist*, the *Ancestor*, the Essex Archaeological Society's *Transactions*, and the Sussex Archaeological Society's *Collections*; he wrote introductions to the Domesday surveys of twelve counties for the *Victoria History of the Counties of England*, and prefaces to the Pipe Rolls of twelve consecutive years of the reign of Henry II. Although Round never founded a school of history, and, indeed, can hardly be said to have belonged to one, few scholars have supported a larger number of co-operative enterprises.

In 1892 Round published a book which gave him at last a place among the leading historians of the day. As an example of new methods applied to old materials, *Geoffrey de Mandeville, a Study of the Anarchy*, opened a fresh line of approach to Anglo-Norman history. The biographical narrative promised by the title is by no means a model of composition. Round was always unwilling to repeat what was well known, and the reader who hopes for a consecutive biography of the first Earl of Essex will be disappointed. The strength of the book lies in the use of charters as sources of information supplementing and sometimes correcting the statements of chroniclers. These documents, which previous scholars had used primarily as sources of genealogical fact, became in Round's hands materials of the first importance for administrative and even political history. The central theme of the book is the process by which an ambitious baron increased his power by offering his support, alternately, to each of two rival claimants to the English throne. The study of this process involved the investigation of many incidental problems, such as the number and character of the earldoms created by Stephen and the Empress Matilda, the government of London in the twelfth century, and the nature of Anglo-Norman castellation. Some of these problems have been brought nearer solution by subsequent writers, and with others Round himself dealt more fully in later life. His articles on 'The Castles of the Conquest' and 'Castle Guard', published respectively in *Archaeologia* and the *Archaeological Journal* in 1902, carry the study of Norman defensive methods far beyond the point reached in *Geoffrey de Mandeville*; but that book marks a turning-point in the study of the relations between the baronage and the Crown, and it remains a model of investigation.

Three years later (1895) Round published under the title *Feudal England* a collection of essays bearing on English history in the eleventh and twelfth centuries. To the reader interested in the general history of the period this is probably the most important of all Round's books, for it contains his convincing description of the methods by which Danegeld was assessed in the eleventh century, and his demonstration that the English system of tenure by knight-service, regarded by most writers of the previous generation as a gradual development, was in reality the creation of William the Conqueror. It includes the text of a feudal survey of Leicestershire, which made an important addition to the existing materials for the reign of Henry I, and an article on Richard I's change of seal—a brilliant example of Round's method—proving from a large collection of royal charters that the king's second seal was put into use in 1198, not, as previous writers had believed, in 1194. In curious contrast to these studies, which are as fresh to-day as on their first appearance, the volume contains a number of essays directed against Freeman's *History of the Norman Conquest*, of which the interest has certainly faded. Already in July 1892 an article by Round, challenging, in particular, Freeman's account of the battle of Hastings, had appeared in the *Quarterly Review*. The fact that Freeman had died in the interval between the writing of the article and its publication naturally intensified the controversy which followed. Freeman's narrative was defended by other scholars, to whom Round replied, and the debate was by no means over when *Feudal England* appeared. Apart from the political differences which first set Round in opposition to Freeman, the two writers represent very different types of historian. To Freeman the criticism of sources and the investigation of their origins, although an essential part of the historian's duty, were subordinate to the writing of an interesting narrative. Round had little gift of narration; his distinctive work was done through the discovery and combination of scattered pieces of evidence, and he was fundamentally out of sympathy with Freeman's methods. On most of the points at issue Round's was undoubtedly the better opinion; but he never undertook a complete investigation of the materials for the history of the battle of Hastings, and it was left for a German scholar, Dr. Wilhelm Spatz, to show that they were inadequate to support a detailed narrative on the scale attempted by Freeman [*Die Schlacht von Hastings*, Berlin, 1896].

Echoes of this controversy are still to be heard in Round's next volume of essays, *The Commune of London*, published in 1899, but the volume as a whole relates to the twelfth rather than to the eleventh century. It covers a wide range of subjects, beginning with an essay on the settlement of the South and East Saxons, and ending with a paper on the Marshalship of England, but its chief importance lies in a study of the origin of the Exchequer and in two contributions to the early history of London. In the first of these London studies Round brought together many facts illustrating the government of the city in Stephen's reign, a subject with which he had already dealt in *Geoffrey de Mandeville*, and in the second he entered more fully than any previous writer into the origins of the commune of 1191. In a brilliant paper on the struggle between John and William of Longchamp, Round compiled from the various contemporary authorities a convincing account of a series of events which previous writers had confused. This, the last of Round's books in which matters of general history predominate, appeared almost simultaneously with a volume of very different character, the *Calendar of Documents preserved in France illustrative of the History of Great Britain and Ireland.* This volume arose from an invitation from the Public Record Office that he should prepare a calendar of a large collection of transcripts from documents in French archives, which had been made for the original Record Commission. Round devoted much time and energy to this work, travelling widely in order to secure accurate texts. The conditions of publication did not allow of any elaborate notes or discussions of problems, but Round was able to illustrate the interest of his materials in a long introduction, and the dates which he assigned to each document represent much investigation which is not set out in detail. Although some parts of the calendar have been superseded by the publication of documents *in extenso*, it remains a very valuable guide to these important and scattered texts.

The next book to appear was a series of essays, mostly of genealogical interest, entitled *Studies in Peerage and Family History* (1901). It contains some of Round's most characteristic work, and the three articles on 'The Origin of the Stewarts', 'The Counts of Boulogne as English Lords', and 'The Family of Ballon and the Conquest of South Wales' are admirable illustrations of the services which genealogical studies can render to history. The book attracted general attention through its destructive criticism of the alleged descents of a number of families, and this side of Round's work was carried much further in two volumes published in 1910 and called *Peerage and Pedigree.* In the following year there appeared the last of Round's books to be published in his lifetime, *The King's Serjeants and Officers of State.* The coronation of King George V had aroused interest in the services centred round the person of a medieval sovereign, and Round's book illustrates their variety and their place in the general scheme of English tenures. It does not offer an exhaustive account of these services, but it shows the true nature of many half-forgotten forms of tenure, and it was the first modern work to emphasize the historical interest of the medieval king's household.

These studies on the king's serjeants may be regarded as representing the general trend of Round's later work. He had always felt the interest of the survival, in England, of ancient institutions such as the medieval offices of state and the peerage. He was anxious that their historic continuity should be preserved, and, in particular, that every claim to hold one of these offices at a coronation, or to succeed to a dormant peerage, should be decided in accordance with the principles governing the treatment of historical evidence. He had already given advice on the complicated case of the Lord Great Chamberlainship to the Court of Claims established in preparation for the coronation of King Edward VII in 1902, and in the early years of the twentieth century he wrote a series of reports on individual claims to peerages. His work in this direction was recognized by his appointment in 1914 as honorary historical adviser to the Crown in peerage cases, and he held this position until the beginning of 1922. The work was heavy, but he found it attractive, and although his opinion was not always adopted, his appointment meant that the historical issues underlying claims to peerages were not likely to be forgotten.

These official duties, combined with failing health, prevented Round during these years from carrying through any elaborate work on general history. His health had been uncertain from childhood, and it was only during the middle years of his life that he could mingle freely with other scholars. As time went on, it became difficult for him, at first, to leave home, and then to receive visitors, and long before the end, with few exceptions, his friends could only keep in touch with him by correspondence. He preserved his interest in history to the last. He gave valuable help when the English Place-Name Society was founded in 1923, supported the scheme for the publication of the early records of Lincoln Cathedral in 1925, and within a week of his death, wrote a long letter to the editor of the Pipe Roll Society on the volume then passing through the press. Despite the isolation of his last years, those who were working in the same field of study had never ceased to regard him as an active scholar, and it was with surprise that they learned of his death, which took place at Brighton 25 June 1928.

Round's life was marked by few notable incidents, and its character never underwent any sudden change after his father's death in 1887. He never married, or held any appointment involving routine association with other men. He received the honorary degree of LL.D. from Edinburgh

University in 1905, but declined other academic recognition. Apart from occasional intervention in local politics in youth, almost his only direct connexion with the world of affairs came through his investigations of claims to peerages and honorary offices of state. To an extent unusual even among scholars, his life was in his writings, and the form which they took was influenced by the uncertain health which always tended to isolate him. He was naturally unfitted for the task of large-scale writing, and his strength was given to a long succession of studies, each complete in itself, and dealing with some definite problem. Ill-health, moreover, goes far to explain the least attractive quality in his writings, the violence with which he attacked other scholars of whose work he disapproved. Most of those against whom he wrote deserved his criticism, and he warned his contemporaries against the acceptance of many ill-founded opinions and much unsatisfactory work. Unfortunately, in pursuit of error he sometimes lost all sense of proportion. His criticisms were often expressed immoderately, and he would return again and again to an attack which his earlier writings had made unnecessary. It should, however, be added that most of the objects of these attacks were writers of established position, and that Round could be very generous to the work of young scholars. His criticism might be severe, but it was never simply magisterial, and it was always written from the worker's standpoint.

Round's occasional aberrations in criticism are insignificant in comparison with his positive achievement. He founded the modern study of Domesday Book. His insistence on the importance of family history gave a new value to genealogical studies, and it is probable that no other scholar has made so many or such valuable contributions to this subject. He was the first modern historian to base a narrative on charters, and all subsequent use of these materials has been influenced directly or indirectly by his work. He showed the aristocratic character of the Anglo-Norman constitution, and effectively challenged previous assumptions of the continuity of English governmental institutions from Anglo-Saxon into Norman times. His work gave a new direction and precision to the studies which he had followed, and its permanent value is becoming clearer as the controversies in which he engaged are fading out of memory.

In 1930 a collection of papers which Round had intended to publish but had never revised for press appeared in a volume entitled *Family Origins and Other Studies*, edited by Dr. William Page. As the title implies, most of the essays relate to matters of genealogy, but the volume contains several historical studies recalling Round's earlier work, and, in particular, an illuminating article on the Bayeux Inquest of 1133. Dr. Page prefaced the volume with a portrait and memoir of Round and a bibliography of his writings. The bibliography, which fills twenty-six pages, first made it possible to appreciate the range and volume of Round's work, and the memoir, written with intimate knowledge, gives a vivid impression of his remarkable personality.

[*Memoir* by W. Page prefixed to *Family Origins*, 1930; article by James Tait in *English Historical Review*, October 1928; personal knowledge.] F. M. STENTON.

ROWNTREE, JOSEPH (1836–1925), cocoa manufacturer and philanthropist, was born at York 24 May 1836, the second son of Joseph Rowntree (1801–1859, q.v.), quaker educationist, by his wife, Sarah, daughter of Isaac Stephenson, of Manchester. He was educated at Bootham School, York, and at the age of fifteen joined his father in the grocery business which he had established at York in 1822. In 1869 Rowntree entered into partnership with his elder brother Henry Isaac, who in 1862 had acquired from the quaker grocers, Tuke & Co., the cocoa-manufacturing portion of their business. When his brother died in 1883, Joseph Rowntree became the sole owner of this business, known as H. I. Rowntree & Co., which in 1897 became a limited company. He acted as chairman until his retirement in 1923.

Rowntree was an industrial and social reformer who devoted wealth and business ability to practical philanthropy. Brought up as an earnest quaker, he was deeply conscious of the unhappy conditions imposed by the industrial revolution on many of his fellow countrymen, and he became convinced that such conditions were the result of improvised development and were not by any means a necessary accompaniment of industrial progress. He determined that his employees should work for reasonable hours and receive adequate wages, that they should be consulted about working conditions, and that provision should be made for periods of unemployment and for old age and for widows' pensions. In 1891 he introduced social workers into his factory, and from that time onwards he gradually built up the welfare organizations associated with his name. He established three trusts—the Joseph Rowntree Village Trust, the Joseph Rowntree Social Service Trust, and the Joseph Rowntree Charitable Trust. The New Earswick model village was founded in 1904 under the management of the Joseph Rowntree Village Trust: in it well-designed houses and carefully provided resources for social and intellectual activities fulfilled Rowntree's intentions towards his employees. Rowntree's philanthropic undertakings were always the outcome of systematically prepared plans, the guiding principle of which he indicated in a memorandum written in 1904 for the direction of the trustees of the three charitable foundations already mentioned. 'I feel', he wrote 'that much current philanthropic effort is directed to remedying the more superficial manifestations of weakness or evil, while little thought or effort is directed to searching out their underlying causes.'

Rowntree was a man of gentle ways but of strong convictions. He was an ardent temperance reformer, and in collaboration with Arthur Sherwell wrote four books on temperance questions. In his later years he did much to promote adult education, especially within the Society of Friends. He was also a strong supporter of the League of Nations. From 1868 to 1874 he was an alderman of the city of York, and in 1911 he was made an honorary freeman of the city. The directors of his firm gave to the citizens of York Rowntree Park in memory of their employees who fell in the European War. He died 24 February 1925 at York, and was buried there.

Rowntree was twice married: first, in 1862 to Julia Eliza (died 1863), daughter of Benjamin Seebohm and sister of Frederic Seebohm [q.v.], the historian, and of Henry Seebohm [q.v.], the ornithologist, and by her had a daughter who did not survive infancy; secondly, in 1867 to Emma Antoinette (died 1924), daughter of Wilhelm Seebohm and cousin to his first wife; by her he had four sons and two daughters.

[*The Times*, 25 February 1925; private information.] A. E. Watkin.

RUSSELL, Sir CHARLES, first baronet (1863–1928), solicitor, born in London 8 July 1863, was the second son of Charles Russell, afterwards Lord Russell of Killowen [q.v.], lord chief justice of England, by his wife, Ellen, daughter of Joseph Stevenson Mulholland, M.D., of Belfast. Educated at Beaumont College, Windsor, he was admitted a solicitor in 1888, having served his articles with the firm of Hollams, Son, and Coward, of Mincing Lane, E.C. After a few years of partnership with Edward Francis Day, a son of Sir John Day [q.v.], he set up an independent practice in Norfolk Street, Strand, under the firm name of Charles Russell & Co.

In 1893 Russell acted as solicitor to the British agent in the Behring Sea arbitration, the arbitrators being Lord Hannen and Sir John Thompson (for Great Britain and Canada) and representatives of France, Italy, Sweden, and the United States. In that capacity he instructed his father, then attorney-general. As the representative of the eighth Marquess of Queensberry [q.v.] in the proceedings for criminal libel brought against him by Oscar Wilde [q.v.] in 1895, Russell had a further opportunity of showing his ability; and his industry resulted in the accumulation of a body of evidence which brought about the break-down of the prosecution and the subsequent criminal proceedings against the prosecutor. In 1896 Russell was appointed solicitor for the government of the Dominion of Canada, and thereafter he had the conduct of the many cases in the Privy Council in which the Dominion government was interested. He was appointed solicitor to the Stewards of the Jockey Club in 1903.

For some thirty years Russell had a large and varied litigating business in the Common Law and Chancery division and in the Divorce Court. He was essentially a man of the world, and his advice was sought by persons in every station of life. Full of shrewdness and common sense, he was able to foretell what view a jury would be likely to take upon a given set of facts, and he was discriminating in his choice of counsel. He was the first solicitor of standing to instruct (Sir) Edward (afterwards Lord) Carson when he began to practise at the English bar in 1893.

A liberal in politics, Russell stood unsuccessfully for Central Hackney in 1895 and for South Salford in 1910; he sat on the London County Council from 1910 to 1913; and he was on the political committee of the Eighty Club. Actively interested in Roman Catholic charities, he was chairman of the board of management of the Hospital of St. John and St. Elizabeth, and during the European War he was chairman of the collections committee of the British Red Cross Society, of which Sir Robert Arundell Hudson [q.v.] was a member. In 1916 he was created a baronet with a special remainder to his brothers and their sons, and in 1921 K.C.V.O. and a knight of grace of the order of St. John of Jerusalem. He was a good public speaker, a pleasant companion, and an accomplished host. An enthusiastic member of the Johnson Club, he was a discriminating buyer of Johnsonian relics, and his collection of mezzotint portraits of Dr. Johnson's contemporaries was large and valuable. He died in London after an operation 27 March 1928.

Russell married in 1889 Adah Walmsley, daughter of William Williams, of Glanmawddach, Dolgelley, and granddaughter of Sir Joshua Walmsley [q.v.]. His only daughter, Monica, married her first cousin, Alec Charles Russell (born 1894, the eldest son of his younger brother, Cyril), who succeeded him as second baronet.

An admirable caricature of Russell by 'Spy' appeared in *Vanity Fair* 10 April 1907, and a portrait by P. A. de László is in the possession of his family.

[*The Times*, 28 March 1928; personal knowledge.] T. Mathew.

RYLE, HERBERT EDWARD (1856–1925), successively bishop of Exeter and of Winchester and afterwards dean of Westminster, was born in London 25 May 1856, the second son of the Rev. John Charles Ryle [q.v.], bishop of Liverpool from 1880 to 1900, by his second wife, Jessy, eldest daughter of John Walker, of Crawfordton, Dumfriesshire. She died when Herbert Ryle was three years old, and in 1861 his father married Henrietta, daughter of Lieutenant-Colonel William Legh Clowes, of Broughton Old Hall, Lancashire, who proved a true mother to her stepchildren. Ryle and his brothers and sisters were brought up in their father's country parishes in Suffolk, first at Helmingham and after 1861 at Stradbroke. Throughout his life Ryle bore the marks of his upbringing in his love of country sights and sounds; and although he outgrew the somewhat narrow evangelical traditions of his home, he remained bound to his father by the closest ties of affection and admiration.

After a year at Eton as an oppidan, Ryle entered college in 1869. In 1875 he won the Newcastle scholarship, and proceeded to King's College, Cambridge, as a scholar in the same year. An accident at football in 1877 not only deprived him of the chance of running against Oxford in the quarter mile, but also compelled him to take an *aegrotat* degree in 1879. Between 1879 and 1881, however, he won every distinction open at Cambridge to students of theology, including a first class in the theological tripos in the latter year. He was elected a fellow of King's College in April 1881, and thus entered upon twenty years of work as a teacher. He was ordained deacon in 1882 and priest in 1883. An interlude of eighteen months (September 1886–March 1888) spent as principal of St. David's College, Lampeter, enabled him to make proof of his administrative powers; but, apart from this, Ryle's work until 1901 lay at Cambridge, whither he returned from Lampeter on his election (1887) to the Hulsean professorship of divinity.

Ryle's main interest was in the study of the Old Testament, and he strove to commend to successive generations of students the methods and the more assured results of the higher criticism. His lecture-room was crowded. In the words of one of his pupils, 'As a teacher he was so clear and direct and so easy to follow; never any sort of parade of learning, but giving us all the greater impression of real knowledge, and at the same time stimulating us to dig for ourselves' [*Memoir*, p. 93]. During these years Ryle published a number of books connected with his special studies, including *The Early Narratives of Genesis* (1892), *The Canon of the Old Testament* (1892), and *Philo and Holy Scripture* (1895). After his election as president of Queens' College, Cambridge, in 1896 he found little leisure for literary work. Thenceforward, indeed, his Old Testament studies bore scanty fruit, save for his admirable edition of *Genesis* in the 'Cambridge Bible', published in 1914, when he was dean of Westminster.

In these books Ryle revealed the qualities of his mind. They exhibit a painstaking and accurate scholarship; a sound and balanced judgement, inclined to caution rather than yielding to the temptations of specious, but questionable, theories; and a stimulating freshness of treatment. While Ryle was at Cambridge the methods of the higher criticism still provoked widespread misunderstanding and suspicion. But in the face of opposition which was sometimes both unreasonable and bitter, he took a leading part in laying a sound foundation for the historical study of the Old Testament in England, and in commending to a wider audience the work of other scholars of eminence in the same field. His influence over his pupils was increased by the friendly relations which he established with them; for he was sympathetic and sociable, and almost to the end retained much of the happy spirit of a boy. In all his social intercourse he was greatly helped by his marriage in 1883 to Nea, daughter of Major-General George Hewish Adams.

In December 1900 Ryle was appointed bishop of Exeter, and was consecrated in Westminster Abbey in January 1901. His time at Exeter was short, for he was translated to Winchester in the spring of 1903; but he was indefatigable in his endeavours to get into touch with both clergy and laity, and won their trust and affection in a singular degree. At Winchester he was less fortunate. He had been greatly overworked at Exeter, and in January 1904 the strain showed itself in an attack of *angina pectoris* followed by appendicitis. Unfortunately, within six weeks of his enthronement at Winchester he had issued a letter to the diocese which alarmed high churchmen by the peremptory tone in which it forbade certain ritual practices. This step, together with a mistaken impression that his health rendered him unequal to the burden of his episcopal duties, undoubtedly hindered him in winning the confidence which had been given him so readily at Exeter. Nevertheless, he steadily wore down initial prejudice, and his resignation of the see in 1911 was received with great regret throughout the diocese. As an administrator Ryle was strong, patient, and scrupulously fair. The organization of the diocese was steadily consolidated under his rule, and he left it, as was generally admitted, in a higher state of efficiency than it had ever attained before. His reputation at large may be judged from his appointment as chairman of the commission sent to Sweden in 1909 by the archbishop of Canterbury to investigate the possibility of closer relations between the English and Swedish Churches.

In December 1910 Ryle accepted the offer of the deanery of Westminster. For several months he had been crippled by an affection of the foot, and he reluctantly decided that it was his duty to exchange episcopal work for less exacting duties. He was installed in the Abbey in April 1911, at a time when the building was being prepared for the coronation of King George V. As it proved, his lot was cast in times which never allowed him leisure to resume a scholar's life. The years which he spent at Westminster were, in fact, among the most fruitful of his career. Under his guidance, and with the help of his advisers, the dignity and the beauty of the Abbey services were notably enhanced; and his name is commemorated in the 'Dean Ryle fund', a sum of £170,000 raised for the maintenance of the Abbey in response to an appeal issued by him in 1920. During the European War Ryle himself used to take the daily noontide service of intercession, and was responsible for the many special services held during those anxious years. His carefully prepared sermons were simple in form and direct in style, but of peculiar power. Archbishop William Temple has written of them: 'I do not think I have ever heard such exquisitely beautiful preaching of the simple Gospel' [*Memoir*, p. 295].

Apart from his duties as dean, Ryle's time was much occupied by committee work. As chairman of the so-called 'Grand Committee' of the Representative Church Council, he did much to prepare the way for the passing of the Enabling Act of 1920, while from 1919 to 1925 he was prolocutor of the lower house of the Canterbury Convocation, and there presided over the prolonged debates on the revision of the Prayer Book. His margin of strength was always slender, and in the autumn of 1924 his health broke down completely. After five months in a nursing-home at Bournemouth he returned to the deanery in May 1925; and he died there 20 August. He was buried in the Abbey in a spot close to the tomb of the 'unknown warrior'.

Ryle was a man of fine presence and a gracious courtesy of manner, and was possessed of a quick sense of humour and a wide and ready sympathy. But there was in his nature a strong element of reserve, and he had a scholar's dislike of pretention or self-advertisement. In ecclesiastical matters his standpoint was that of a 'central churchman'. His character was conspicuous for sanity of judgement and strong simplicity of faith. Bishop Francis Paget described him as 'a past master in equity'; and Archbishop Davidson bore witness to 'that gift of lucid vision and Christian common sense which gained for him the quite exceptional confidence of his brother Bishops' [*Memoir*, pp. xi and xii].

Ryle was created C.V.O. in 1911 and K.C.V.O. in 1921. He had three sons, of whom the eldest died at birth, and the youngest at the age of eight in 1897.

A cartoon of Ryle appeared in *Vanity Fair* 27 March 1912.

[M. H. FitzGerald, *A Memoir of Herbert Edward Ryle*, 1928; private information; personal knowledge.] M. H. FitzGerald.

SALTER, Sir ARTHUR CLAVELL (1859–1928), judge, was born in London 30 October 1859, the eldest son of Henry Hyde Salter, M.D., F.R.S., of Harley Street, London, by his wife, Henrietta Laura, eldest daughter of the Rev. Edward Powlett Blunt, vicar of Spetisbury, Dorset. He was educated at Wimborne grammar school and King's College, London, and graduated in arts and law. He was called to the bar by the Middle Temple in 1885, and joined the Western circuit in 1886. He took silk in 1904, and was recorder of Poole from 1904 to 1917. Salter unsuccessfully contested West Southwark in the conservative interest at the general election of January 1906, but he was elected at a by-election in the same year for the Basingstoke division of Hampshire, which he continued to represent until 1917. In the latter year he was appointed a judge of the King's Bench division of the High Court and was knighted. He was appointed chairman of the railway and canal commission in February 1928. He died in London 30 November 1928. Salter married twice: first, in 1894 Mary Dorothea (died 1917), daughter of Major John Henry Lloyd, Royal Artillery, by whom he had one son, who was killed in action in the European War; secondly, in 1920 Nora Constance, eldest daughter of Lieutenant-Colonel Thomas Heathcote Ouchterlony, of The Guynd, Arbroath, Forfarshire.

Salter kept steadily before his mind the view that the sole function of a judge is to adjudicate. In his civil judgments he eschewed irrelevant prolixity; so in his conduct of criminal cases he rigorously abstained from attempting to edify the prisoner or the public with moral aphorisms. He was at once too modest and too high-minded to wish to attract attention to himself by brilliant epigram or startling opinion. His brain was of the highest calibre, and he displayed an almost uncanny power of illuminating the dark recesses of a complicated case, and separating the vital from the non-essential. His judgments contain no unnecessary word, and no word out of place. He saw no useful purpose in the elaborate enumeration of a chain of authorities; reserving his speech for the results, rather than the process of his thought. Having considered a problem from every angle, he would be content with a brief statement of his solution, delivered without circumlocution.

Perhaps Salter's most conspicuous criminal case was the trial of Horatio Bottomley for fraudulent conversion (1922). The case was a very difficult one, involving a search into the most intricate facts and figures, but Salter emerged from it with signal success. He presided with the utmost dignity and ability. His summing-up was masterly, marked by lucidity and conciseness of expression, a narrative in itself complete. Another trial over which he presided, the dramatic circumstances of which arrested public attention, was that of Colonel Rutherford for murder (1919). This case was far from simple in that the prisoner's action seemed to lie in the debatable border-land between hysteria and insanity; but Salter's admirable common sense overcame all difficulties, and directed the case to its just and logical conclusion.

Salter's civil judgments may in some sense be said to be an acquired taste. Their brevity is to be explained by the fact that he desired for them not the admiration of posterity, but the advancement of the law. This understood, they will be found to be replete with the concentrated essence of juristic wisdom. His judgments were seldom reversed, and in most of the cases in which they were reversed much remains to be said in favour of his opinion. A notable illustration of this is the case of *Blundell-Leigh* v. *Attenborough* (1921). Salter here annexed a qualification to the doctrine that an improper sub-pledge by a pledgee does not determine the bailment as between the pledgee and pledgor so as to entitle the pledgor to demand the return of the chattel pledged without a tender of the amount due on the sub-pledge. But in this case he found a series of facts which seemed to him to fall outside the ambit either of this doctrine or of the Factors Act, a bailee having parted with the actual possession of the chattel prior to entering into an agreement with the bailor to take it on a contract of pledge. In these circumstances Salter held that the bailor was entitled to the unconditional return of the chattel. His decision was reversed by the Court of Appeal on a different view of the facts, but a considerable body of contemporary learned opinion regarded Salter's reasoning as the more convincing. Previously, in *Whiteley* v. *Hilt* (1918), Salter took a view of the nature of the contract of hire-purchase which has strong claim to approval. He regarded the act of a hirer who sells the chattel prior to the discharge of all instalments due upon it as a simple determination of a bailment, which confers no right whatsoever in the chattel to the purchaser. The Court of Appeal regarded it as an assignment of a chose in action, entitling the purchaser to keep the chattel on doing what should have been done by the hirer, that is to say, paying the unpaid instalments.

It is, however, because of their very rarity that cases in which Salter met with reversal recur to the memory, for in general the Court of Appeal, as also the Court of Criminal Appeal, regarded his decisions with the utmost respect. A bold paraphrase of Othello's estimate of himself might be applied to Salter—he did the law some service, but owing to his great modesty and devotion to truth few outside the profession which admired and honoured him can know it.

[*The Times*, 8 December 1928; private information.] H. G. Hanbury.

SALVIDGE, Sir ARCHIBALD TUTTON JAMES (1863–1928), political organizer, was born at Birkenhead 4 August 1863, the second son of Archibald Tutton Salvidge, of Sunnyside, West Kirby, by his wife, Sarah, daughter of William Croxton, of Hoylake, Cheshire. He was educated at a local Wesleyan school and at the Liverpool Institute. He entered as a youth the service of Bent's Brewery Company, Liverpool, of which in due course he rose to be the managing director.

Salvidge first came into notice as being interested in politics in 1892, when he was chosen leader of the local conservative democratic party. He built up the Liverpool Working-men's Conservative Association, and ultimately became leader of the party in the city council. He was returned unopposed to the Liverpool council in 1896, and was elected an alderman two years later. In the face of some prejudice, he gradually obtained recognition by his energy and organizing ability as the principal figure in Liverpool conservatism. Nominally he shared the leadership with Sir Charles Petrie, but it was generally admitted that Salvidge was the real head, commanding as he did the confidence of the party workers in the divisions and wards. His approval was sought for all conservative candidates in the district, whether parliamentary or municipal.

Salvidge turned the Working-men's Conservative Association into a powerful electoral machine, and the value of his assistance was fully appreciated by his party. In 1913 his standing in national politics was such that he was elected chairman of the National Union of Conservative and Unionist Associations. More than once efforts were made to induce him to contest a parliamentary division, but he declined, pleading business as his excuse. He was equally resolute in his refusal to become lord mayor of Liverpool in 1910.

On the outbreak of the European War in 1914 Salvidge abandoned politics and became chairman of the Liverpool advisory committee on recruiting. He supported Mr. Asquith's government, and afterwards the Coalition, to the break-up of which he was opposed. After the general election of 1923, at which a number of Mersey-side conservative seats were lost, he criticized the party leadership, and protested against the country being plunged unprepared into a contest on what he held to be a forlorn issue. This remonstrance was followed by Mr. Baldwin's pledge against the introduction of a general tariff; and, as a result, a number of conservative gains ensued on the appeal to the constituencies in the following year. During the later part of his life Salvidge devoted much time and effort to opposing the labour movement in politics.

Apart from political work, Salvidge was a consistent advocate of the scheme for the Mersey road tunnel, which at the time of his death was in course of construction. Although the idea was not his, he saw the possibilities of the tunnel, and he deserves credit for helping to pilot the scheme through many difficulties.

Salvidge was knighted in 1916, created K.B.E. in 1920, and sworn of the Privy Council in 1922. He was awarded the honorary freedom of Liverpool in 1925, and the honorary degree of LL.D. was conferred on him by the university in 1928.

Salvidge married in 1885 Alice Margaret, daughter of Thomas McKernan, of Liverpool, and had two sons and one daughter. He died at Braxted, Hoylake, 11 December 1928.

[*The Times*, 12 December 1928.]

A. Cochrane.

SAMUEL, MARCUS, first VISCOUNT BEARSTED, of Maidstone (1853–1927), joint-founder of the Shell Transport and Trading Company, was born in London 5 November 1853, the second son of Marcus Samuel, a London merchant, by his wife, Abigail, daughter of Abraham Moss, of London. He was educated privately, and began his commercial career as the owner of a small business in Houndsditch, trading principally in painted shells. Other lines were afterwards added, such as curios of all kinds, general produce, and rice. It was during a visit to Japan on behalf of this undertaking that Samuel first became acquainted with the petroleum industry. He took up the business of shipping oil from Russia to the Far East. The chief difficulty of transport up to that time was that steamers could only obtain freights one way: owing to the fact that it was considered impossible to clean them thoroughly, no attempt was made to carry merchandise on the return voyage. Samuel overcame this obstacle by adopting the system of cleaning out the hull with steam, a plan which was suggested to him by a captain in the merchant service. He was thus able to send his steamers home laden with rice and other Eastern commodities. Assisted by the financial support of the Rothschilds, the business became a success, and in 1897 a combination was formed of several firms trading with the East. The concern thus established was called the Shell Transport and Trading Company, the name being taken from Samuel's original business. When the company was formed the capital was £1,800,000: at the time of Samuel's death thirty years later this had increased to more than 26 millions.

For a time the British combination encountered a serious rival in the Dutch Petroleum Company, which obtained its oil from Java and Borneo, as the difference in freight-rates enabled the latter firm to undersell the Russian oil supplies. In consequence the Shell Company turned its attention to Borneo, and began to operate properties there on its own account. This undertaking proved much more costly than had been anticipated, and for a time the Shell Company had an arduous struggle. The issue of additional capital, however, enabled it to bring its new sources of supply to the producing stage. At this point, realizing the future importance of oil both for the navy and for the merchant service, the Shell Company invited the co-operation of the British government in its schemes, but these overtures met with no response. The success of the Borneo developments caused the Dutch Company to prefer partnership to competitive trading, and in 1907 the important step was taken of amalgamating the British and Dutch interests into a single large oil-producing, refining, and distributing organization.

Samuel was knighted in 1898 for services rendered in the salvage of H.M.S. *Victorious*. In February of that year this vessel grounded off Port Said, and she was pulled off by two of the Shell Company's tugs. Owing to the resources of his company, he was of assistance to Great Britain in the European War. Not only was every form of petroleum made available wherever it was required either for the land or the sea forces, but a petroleum distillate, which formed the basis of the high explosive T.N.T. (trinitrotoluene), was provided in large quantities. A refinery was established near Bristol for this purpose, the erection of the works being carried out, owing to Samuel's energy, in a few weeks.

Although he was one of the first to appreciate the value of oil fuel as a substitute for coal, Samuel's contention was that the burning of oil under boilers was a waste of power. He was always an advocate of the internal combustion engine for ships, and his efforts were directed to proving that this type of propulsion could be made suitable for large vessels. During the War he formed a company to test this possibility by experiment and inquiry.

Samuel was at one time a prominent figure in the life of the city of London. His municipal career began in 1891 when he was elected alderman of the Portsoken ward. He was chosen as sheriff in 1894, and was lord mayor of London in 1902–1903. In this capacity he presided over the committee which formulated the scheme for the Port of London authority. He carried out his duties as lord mayor with zest, paying a state visit to Brussels and other places, as well as entertaining the French president at the Guildhall. When his year of office came to an end he was created a baronet for his municipal and other services.

Samuel's benefactions to hospitals and other philanthropic schemes were considerable. In 1895 he bought for his residence the Mote, near Maidstone. When the European War broke out, he turned this house into a hospital for non-commissioned officers, continuing to live there and interesting himself in the welfare the patients.

In 1921 Samuel was raised to the peerage as Baron Bearsted, of Maidstone, and in 1925 was advanced to a viscounty. He received the freedom of Sheffield and of Maidstone and honorary degrees from the universities of Cambridge and Sheffield in 1925 and 1924 respectively.

Samuel married in 1881 Fanny Elizabeth, only daughter of Benjamin Benjamin, and had two sons and two daughters. The younger son was killed in the War; the elder, Walter Horace (born 1882), succeeded his father as second viscount. His wife died 16 January 1927, and he only survived her by a few hours, dying at his home in London 17 January 1927.

[*The Times*, 18 January 1927.]

A. Cochrane.

SANDERSON, FREDERICK WILLIAM (1857–1922), schoolmaster, was born at Brancepeth, co. Durham, 13 May 1857, the youngest son of Thomas Sanderson, of Brancepeth, who was employed in the estate office of Viscount Boyne, by his wife, Margaret Andrews. He received his early education at the village school of his native place, but later he became a student teacher in the neighbouring village of Tudhoe. In 1876 he entered Durham University as a theological student, was awarded the Van Mildert theological scholarship in 1877, and obtained a first class in mathematics and physical science in the B.A. examination in the same year. In 1881 he was elected fellow of the university. In 1879 he gained an open mathematical scholarship at Christ's College, Cambridge, was bracketed eleventh wrangler in 1882, and, in the same year, his performance in the examination for Smith's prizes, in which he was bracketed third, was highly commended.

Sanderson remained at Cambridge for some years, coaching and lecturing at Girton College, until, in 1885, he was appointed an assistant master at Dulwich College. The instructions he received were to develop the teaching of chemistry and to introduce the study of physics, but a year or two after his appointment he began an experiment which was to prove one of his most successful ventures, namely, the formation of what was called the engineering side of the school. The syllabus of work for this side included applied mechanics and physics, workshop practice, and mechanical drawing. The work was not that of a technical school, but the experiments performed were on a larger scale than usual in public schools, and the apparatus consisted of actual working engines, dynamos, and testing machines, and not mere models.

In 1892 Sanderson was elected headmaster of Oundle School. From the day of his appointment he so completely identified himself with the school that it is impossible to separate the life of the man from the life of the school. The school, an old foundation dating back to the fifteenth century, had, like most of the old schools, experienced vicissitudes. In 1876 the Grocers' Company, its governing body, had brought out a new scheme for the working of the school which for some years had been very successful. But a period of depression had followed, and there were only 92 boys at the time of Sanderson's appointment. He was appointed with the definite object of reorganizing the teaching, introducing fresh subjects of study, and, if possible, not only checking the decline but also raising the status of the school and giving it fresh life. In this he was completely successful. The numbers in the school rose to 500 by 1920 and, by the time of his death, the reputation of Oundle was secure.

Immediately on his appointment Sanderson began his reforms. Science and engineering sides were established, at first consisting of only a few boys; but it was soon found that more and more boys took to these subjects and that many who found no interest in, and showed no capacity for classics, were by no means deficient in intelligence when confronted with the problems and inspiration of science. New laboratories and workshops were fitted up; and when after a few years Oundle boys gained open scholarships in science at the universities, and those who entered engineering professions found the work they had done at school was of real value, the new subjects began to assume an established position in the school.

As numbers increased fresh subjects were added. What was more important, as it was found possible to have whole forms of boys working on the same lines, the stimulus of numbers produced a very marked effect. New laboratories and workshops were built, machinery of a heavier type was installed, and it was found possible in 1905 to build a reversing engine for a 4,000 h.p. marine engine. The rough castings were supplied by a firm of marine engineers, but the whole of the fitting and erecting was done in the school workshops. Finally, a full working test was carried out and, when this proved satisfactory, the engine was dispatched to the ship-yard and, without any alteration, installed in its appointed place. Other work of a similar nature followed. The system adopted was that of ordinary engineering shops, except that the staff (of boys) employed in testing and erecting was the same as that employed for fitting. Each boy had his job for which he alone was responsible; but the result of his efforts had to be combined with that of all the others, and the final success depended upon the independent work of each individual. This co-operative work appealed very strongly to Sanderson, and he attempted to introduce the method in other subjects. In the library it was notably successful. A subject for study was chosen, the boys in a form were divided into small groups each of which studied one aspect of the subject, and the results of their work were collected and combined into one whole. Each small group gained a detailed knowledge of that aspect of the subject which was its particular care, but each knew that its work was only a part, though an essential part, of the whole. Each was naturally interested in the work of all the other groups and gained a good general grasp of the whole subject. By this method it was possible to tackle a much bigger subject than would have been practicable if all the boys had done exactly the same work.

During the European War the school workshops were converted into munition shops and many schemes were tried in order to increase 'output'. The experience gained of running one department of the school on factory lines was most instructive, and many of the lessons learnt were afterwards applied to other departments.

After the War some portion of Sanderson's time was devoted to lecturing and addressing various societies, explaining his views on education and the part that schools and education should take in the work of national reconstruction; the subjects were often controversial and gave rise to much discussion. It was at the close of such an address, delivered in London on 15 June 1922, that Sanderson died from a sudden heart attack.

Sanderson married in 1885 Jane, daughter of Tom Hodgson, of Broughton Hall, Cumberland, and had two sons and one daughter. A portrait in oils, painted from a photograph, hangs in the hall of Oundle School.

[*Sanderson of Oundle*, 1923; H. G. Wells, *The Story of a Great Schoolmaster . . . Sanderson of Oundle*, 1924; private information; personal knowledge.]

H. M. King.
A. D. Nightingale.

SANDERSON, THOMAS HENRY, Baron Sanderson, of Armthorpe, Yorkshire (1841–1923), civil servant, was born 11 January 1841 at Gunton Park, Norfolk, which had been rented from Lord Suffield by his father. He was the second son of Richard Sanderson, for many years conservative member of parliament for Colchester, by his wife, the Hon. Charlotte Matilda, elder daughter of Charles Manners-Sutton, first Viscount Canterbury [q.v.], Speaker of the House of Commons 1817–1835. The Sandersons were a Yorkshire yeoman family whose head-quarters were at Armthorpe, near Doncaster. Thomas Sanderson was sent to Eton, but in 1857 his father failed in business, dying not long afterwards, and he had to leave school when only sixteen years old. In 1859, after passing the recently instituted competitive examination, he was appointed to a junior clerkship in the Foreign Office.

Sanderson remained at the Foreign Office for forty-seven years, his only service abroad being with Lord Wodehouse's mission to King Christian IX of Denmark in 1863–1864, and at Geneva during the Alabama arbitration in 1871. His qualities are well described in a dispatch addressed to Lord Granville by Lord Chief Justice Cockburn, the British arbitrator: 'His perfect mastery of the subject of the Alabama claims, extending even to the most minute details; his general information, his great intelligence, his indefatigable industry, his readiness, only excelled by his ability, to afford assistance, have excited my warmest admiration and deserve my sincerest acknowledgements.'

These qualities, enriched by long experience, and coupled with an admirable gift for the composition of official dispatches, made Sanderson an invaluable public servant. He was private secretary to two secretaries of state for foreign affairs, the fifteenth Earl of Derby from 1866 to 1868 and from 1874 to 1878, and the second Earl Granville from 1880 to 1885. He was promoted senior clerk in 1885 and appointed assistant under-secretary in 1889 and permanent under-secretary in 1894, a post which he held until 1906. He was created C.B. (1880), K.C.M.G. (1887), K.C.B. (1893), and G.C.B. (1900). He was raised to the peerage as Baron Sanderson, of Armthorpe, co. York, in 1905.

As permanent under-secretary, Sanderson was an efficient administrator of the old school. He took care that work should be done with accuracy and rapidity, and he insisted successfully on good and clear drafting, setting up as a model for his juniors Wellington's dispatches. He even issued in 1891, in pamphlet form for the instruction of juniors, *Observations on the Use and Abuse of Red Tape*. The views expressed are sound, especially as regards the use of ordinary official language, and there is some humour about them, but the writer obviously did not contemplate any change of system.

Sanderson's conception of his own duties made him slow to offer opinions, but it is true that, while his colleagues generally considered this a serious defect, Lord Salisbury certainly, and Lord Lansdowne probably, would not have welcomed any great forwardness in this respect. It was natural, therefore, that he should not easily realize that reforms of organization were necessary, and it was only a short time before his retirement that he consented to appoint a committee of inquiry. The revolution, by which the diplomatic staff were relieved of the routine duties which occupied the whole time of all but a very few, and were allowed the use of their brains, only bore fruit after Sanderson's departure.

As a chief, Sanderson's justice and real kindness of heart were sometimes obscured by an irritability due probably to poor physique, and his popularity was consequently somewhat impaired. Nevertheless, he was a great official.

Although Sanderson served all secretaries of state alike with complete loyalty, his ties were closest with Lord Derby. After their official connexion had ended (1878) he continued to act as Lord Derby's general adviser, and by the earl's will he was appointed co-executor with Lady Derby and received a legacy of £10,000. In 1893 Sanderson published a volume of Lord Derby's speeches, prefixing an introduction in which he praised his friend's wisdom, impartial judgement, and devotion to the cause of international peace.

In private life 'Lamps', to give him the name by which he was universally known throughout the service, was distinguished by a great gift for friendship and a very conscientious recognition of its claims. He was never married, but was a devoted son and brother. Like all men high up in the Foreign Office he was obliged to work many hours at home as well as in Downing Street, but he found time to entertain a good deal and to read widely. He also, rather surprisingly, played the flute. 'This', Lord Cromer used to say, when he thought that some dispatch would disturb the Foreign Office, 'will send Lamps's flute into a minor key.'

After his retirement Lord Sanderson served on various committees, such as the committee on Indian emigration to the Crown colonies, of which he was chairman (1909–1910), but increasing blindness made much public work impossible. He died in London 21 March 1923, when the barony became extinct.

[*The Times*, 22 March 1923; Foreign Office records; private information; personal knowledge.] J. Tilley.

SANDERSON, THOMAS JAMES COBDEN- (1840–1922), bookbinder and printer. [See Cobden-Sanderson.]

SANDYS, Sir JOHN EDWIN (1844–1922), classical scholar, was born at Leicester 19 May 1844, the fourth son of the Rev. Timothy Sandys, of the Church Missionary Society, Calcutta, by his wife, Rebecca, daughter of Joseph Swain, of Leicester. He was educated at Repton, whence he won a scholarship at St. John's College, Cambridge, in 1863. His academic career was distinguished. He obtained a Bell scholarship (1864) and a Browne medal for Greek ode (1865), was twice Porson prizeman (1865, 1866), twice Members' prizeman for Latin essay (1866, 1867), and in 1867 was senior classic. He was elected fellow of his college in the last-mentioned year, when he was also appointed to a lecturership at St. John's, which post he held until 1907. Sandys's official connexion with his college was always close, for he was appointed to a tutorship in 1870, and held the office until 1900. In the university, his scholarship was early recognized by election to the post of public orator in 1876 and, after his retirement in 1919, he was given the title of orator emeritus.

In the academic world, Sandys was accorded a full share of honours, including honorary doctorates of Dublin (1892), Edinburgh (1909), Athens (1912), and

Oxford (1920). From Cambridge, where he had already taken the Litt.D. degree in 1886, he received the honorary degree of LL.D. in 1920. Added to these distinctions was a fellowship of the British Academy (1909), and a commandership in the order of the Saviour (1914)—an honour which gave him especial pleasure, as a recognition by modern Greece of his services to classical literature and archaeology.

For Greece was always Sandys's spiritual home; and, although his main interest lay in Greek oratory and poetry, he emphasized, both in his lectures and editions, the value of Greek art. But Sandys was much more than a Grecian; he exercised his great knowledge of the classics in papers on such subjects as *The Literary Sources of Milton's Lycidas* (for the Royal Society of Literature, 1914) and *Roger Bacon* (for the British Academy, 1914). No less than Sir John Cheke and Roger Ascham, of his own college, he was a great humanist.

Sandys's published work was remarkable in both quantity and quality. He worked rapidly, without loss of accuracy—indeed, his scholarship may be called impeccable. In his early years, he devoted his chief study to the Greek orators, his first edition being Isocrates, *Ad Demonicum et Panegyricus* (1868), followed by *Select Private Orations of Demosthenes* (1875). A succession of editions of the *Leptines* (1890), *Philippics* (1897 and 1900), and other Demosthenic speeches, brought him a reputation as the foremost editor of Greek orators; and to these he added Cicero's *Orator* (1885), besides valuable work on Aristotle's *Rhetoric* in editing the *Commentary* by E. M. Cope (3 vols., 1877) and the *Translation* by Sir R. C. Jebb (1909). His interest, however, was by no means confined to rhetoric: one of his early editions was the *Bacchae* of Euripides (1880), the illustrations of which showed the editor's archaeological taste and knowledge. This work passed into a fourth edition twenty years after (1900). In 1903 he edited the newly discovered *Constitution of Athens* by Aristotle—an edition which has been ranked very high by competent scholars; and, towards the end of his life, he contributed a translation of Pindar to the Loeb classical library.

Sandys's greatest book, however, was undoubtedly the *History of Classical Scholarship*, which he began in 1900, and finished in 1908, although a book of such magnitude and learning might well have been the lifework of an ordinary man. The three volumes embrace the history of all scholarship from the sixth century B.C. to the year of publication, ending with an appreciative notice of Walter George Headlam [q.v.], who died in 1908. They are not only marked by great erudition, but are eminently readable, and likely to interest many who are outside the circle of classical scholars. His *Harvard Lectures on the Revival of Learning* (1905) show equal learning, on a different scale.

The academic public knew Sandys best as the orator who during more than forty years had presented nearly 700 distinguished men for honorary degrees, with speeches which, of their kind, were almost perfect. His style was modelled on Cicero, and could well pass the most stringent test of Latinity both in rhythm and language; but his speeches were as remarkable for their matter as for their manner. However eulogistic, Sandys went straight to the point, picking out the real merits of the person presented. He himself was honoured by a knighthood in 1911.

Sandys was known to many, but intimate, perhaps, with few. His pupils were apt to think of him as 'donnish', cold and impassive, unapproachable, and unsympathetic. This was largely a form of self-protection: he was extremely shy, and never able to take, or simulate, any great interest in the daily life and amusements of the average undergraduate. But beneath a rather frigid exterior, his friends and many of his pupils recognized the generosity of the man, and his warmth of affection for those whom he liked and trusted.

Sandys married in 1880 Mary Grainger, daughter of the Rev. Henry Hall, vicar of St. Paul's church, Cambridge; there were no children of the marriage. He died at Cambridge 6 July 1922. By his will, he left over £8,000 to Cambridge University for the purpose of founding a studentship for research in the language, literature, or other branches of classical study. He was also, in various ways, a benefactor of his college, to which he was loyally devoted.

[*The Times*, 7 July 1922; J. S. Reid, *Sir John Edwin Sandys, 1844–1922*, in *Proceedings* of the British Academy, vol. x, 1921–1923; N. G. L. Hammond, *Sir John Edwin Sandys*, 1933; personal knowledge.]

E. E. Sikes.

SANTLEY, Sir **CHARLES** (1834–1922), singer, was born at Liverpool 28 February 1834, the elder son of William

Santley, an official in the employ of the Liverpool corporation and an organist and wood-wind player, the descendant of an old Welsh family, by his wife, Margaret Fletcher, who came of Cumberland stock. Santley was educated at the Liverpool Institute. As a boy he sang alto in the choir of the Unitarian Ancient Chapel, Toxteth Park. He passed the examination for admission among second tenors (later he transferred to the basses) of the Liverpool Philharmonic Society on his fifteenth birthday, and in the same year (1849) took part in the concerts at the opening of the Philharmonic Hall. Within a few years he was singing as an equal with the best-known soloists of the day, with the exception, perhaps, of Luigi Lablache [q.v.] who was shortly to retire. He also learned the piano and later the violin, on which he obtained such proficiency as to become leader of the second violins in a symphony orchestra.

As a youth, working for a living in the book-keeping department of large wholesale provision and leather merchants' houses in Liverpool, Santley devoted all his spare time to music, and his voice early developed into a fine baritone. The elder Santley, urged by the violoncellist Joseph Lidel, allowed his son to abandon commerce and become a professional singer. After giving a farewell concert on 15 October 1855, he left Liverpool for Milan, where he placed himself under Gaetano Nava, who later bequeathed to Santley his library. Santley made his début in opera at Pavia in 1857, in the part of the Doctor in *Traviata*. He also appeared at the Santa Radegonda Theatre at Milan in the same year. On the advice, however, of Henry Fothergill Chorley [q.v.], whom he met in Milan, he returned to England in October 1857. Arriving in London, Santley was engaged by John Pyke Hullah [q.v.] to sing the part of Adam in *The Creation* at St. Martin's Hall, Long Acre, on 16 November 1857, and made an immediate impression. After further studies in singing with Manuel Garcia [q.v.] and in acting with Walter Lacy [q.v.], he entered on a career as a singer probably unparalleled for length, versatility, and distinction. He appeared in opera in English (Pyne and Harrison Company), at Her Majesty's Theatre, in 1859, and in Italian opera (*Il Trovatore*) at Covent Garden, in 1862. Thereafter he sang in English and Italian opera, in London, Manchester, and elsewhere in England, in Dublin, Milan (La Scala Theatre), Barcelona, and in America, vindicating his right to rank with such artists as Thérèse Tietjens and Ilma de Murska, and being a tower of strength to the Carl Rosa and Pyne and Harrison companies, as well as to John Hollingshead [q.v.] in an important English season at the Old Gaiety Theatre in 1870.

Among Santley's notable appearances may be mentioned Valentine in the first performance (1863) of *Faust* in England, which was so successful that Gounod wrote especially for him, at his suggestion, the air 'Even bravest heart'; the title-role in Ambroise Thomas's opera *Hamlet*, with Christine Nilsson as Ophelia (1869); and Vanderdecken in the *Flying Dutchman* (1870), the first Wagner opera ever given in the English-speaking world. His last appearance in opera was in this part in 1876. Santley's first festival engagement was at Birmingham in 1861, and from that time he was a prominent figure at all festivals, where his singing of Handelian numbers was always a noteworthy feature, as also was his dramatization of the title-role in *Elijah*, which he sustained for over half a century. He also made tours in Australia (1898–1890), New Zealand, South Africa (1893, 1903), and Canada. No sort of vocal music on any concert platform came amiss to him, whether Italian airs, with Grisi and Mario as colleagues, or *lieder* with Madame Schumann and Joachim, or French songs, or English, Irish, and Scotch ballads, homely, dramatic, or humorous —he excelled in them all.

In 1871 Santley received the gold medal of the Royal Philharmonic Society. His artistic jubilee was celebrated on 1 May 1907 by a concert at the Royal Albert Hall. When upwards of eighty years of age he sang with much of his old mastery at a concert at the Mansion House in aid of the Belgian Refugees' fund in February 1915.

Santley's voice was one of great beauty and carrying power, of extensive compass, and perfectly even. His technique in scales, roulades, &c., was remarkable, his enunciation in various languages and in dialect singularly clear, and his declamation, which showed complete realization of the meaning of the text, eloquent, and in accordance with the canons of the art of singing. As a man, while outspoken where inefficiency or anything that did not 'ring true' was concerned, he was a staunch and generous friend and ever ready to hold out a helping hand. A late instance of this was his active interest in arrangements for concerts for the troops during the European War.

Santley published three books: *Student and Singer* (1892), *The Art of Singing* (1908), and *Reminiscences of my Life* (1909), written with characteristic humour and containing criticisms and advice of value. He also composed some works for services of the Roman Catholic Church, and a berceuse for orchestra was produced during his Australian tour. A collection of Santley relics—early letters, programmes of state concerts, &c.—is preserved in the Liverpool Corporation Library.

Santley joined the Church of Rome in 1880. In 1887 Pope Leo XIII made him knight commander of the order of St. Gregory the Great. He was knighted in 1907. He died in London 22 September 1922. A leading article in *The Times* (23 September) referred to him as a great singer, creator of a classical epoch, to whom the English people had granted the respect due to a high-minded gentleman and a simple, devout Christian.

Santley was twice married: first, in 1858 to Gertrude (died 1882), daughter of John Mitchell Kemble [q.v.], the historian; by her he had two sons and three daughters; secondly, in 1884 to Elizabeth Mary, daughter of George Rose-Innes, by whom he had one son. His eldest daughter, Edith, was well known as a concert singer.

[*The Times*, 23 September 1922; Grove's *Dictionary of Music and Musicians*, 3rd edition, vol. iv, edited by H. C. Colles; J. A. Fuller-Maitland, *A Doorkeeper of Music*, 1929; Herman Klein, *Thirty Years of Musical Life in London*, 1903, *Musicians and Mummers*, 1925, and *The Golden Age of Opera*, 1933; George Bernard Shaw, *Music in London, 1890–1894*, 1931; J. M. Levien, *Sir Charles Santley*, 1930; personal knowledge. Portrait, *Royal Academy Pictures*, 1909.]

J. M. Levien.

SARGEAUNT, JOHN (1857–1922), teacher and scholar, was born at Irthlingborough, Northamptonshire, 12 August 1857, the eldest son of John Barneby Sargeaunt, barrister-at-law, by his wife, Elizabeth, daughter of the Rev. William Drake, curate-in-charge of St. Giles's church, Northampton. He was educated at Bedford grammar school under James Surtees Phillpotts, and in 1876 went up with a classical scholarship to University College, Oxford, of which George Granville Bradley was then master and Samuel Henry Butcher senior classical tutor. He obtained a first class in classical moderations (1878) and a second class in *literae humaniores* (1880). He was president of the Union Society in 1881.

On leaving Oxford, Sargeaunt went as a master to Inverness College, and in 1885 became master of the classical sixth form at Felsted School. Five years later, on the recommendation of Dr. Bradley, then dean of Westminster, Dr. William Gunion Rutherford [q.v.], headmaster of Westminster School, offered Sargeaunt a place on his staff, and in January 1890 Sargeaunt began his work there as master of the classical sixth form. That form is not the highest division in the school, for Westminster preserves the seventh form of Dr. Busby's day. Sargeaunt held his post for nearly twenty-nine years with a distinction which made him one of the select company of schoolmasters who enjoy a reputation and a memory far wider than the field of their main work.

Sargeaunt's exceptional capacity as a teacher was founded not only upon the versatility of his learning but also upon the breadth of his tastes. Fisherman, mountaineer, botanist, and gardener, he was also archer, amateur actor, and devotee of the chessboard and bridge-table. He was an antiquary and an ardent genealogist. He had a wide and thorough command of Greek and Latin literature, a lifelong passion for poetry, and a skilled and sensitive appreciation of English letters. He was most at home in the eighteenth century. It almost follows that he was first and foremost a Virgilian. The chief of his familiars was Dr. Johnson, whose distaste for music he shared, though not his toryism. All Sargeaunt's resources were at the command of a masterly memory, and all contributed copiously to his teaching. It was true in a narrow sense that he taught without method or discipline. He could afford to indulge his unpedagogic aversion from penalties, for he enjoyed an effortless hold upon boys and their interest, and boys were eager to justify his quiet assumption that they were responsible fellow-learners. The method was equally free. Sargeaunt taught by digression: there was no saying where the play of illustration, quotation, and parallel, not without dramatic impersonation and declamation at times, might not carry a lesson. It was not a system at work, but a personality, and the end was attained when a boy became fired with the determination to seek out Sargeaunt's treasures for himself.

Sargeaunt was a bachelor and, with his

easy, humorous temperament, a clubbable man. He availed himself fully of the social and literary opportunities which London offers. He was a member of the Literary Society, sometime 'prior' of the Johnson Club, and an original member of the Pepys Club.

Sargeaunt, claiming that 'boys have a right not to be taught by a sexagenarian', retired at Christmas 1918 to a small house which he had built near Fairwarp in Sussex. He intended to employ his leisure as an additional inspector under the Board of Education, in local government, and in writing. But in little more than three years a sudden illness cut short his life. He died at Hove 20 March 1922, and was buried in Brighton cemetery.

Sargeaunt's published output, like that of many who have given their lives to teaching, leaves too scanty a memorial of his scholarship. His principal works were the *Annals of Westminster School* (1898), an excellent example of lightly borne erudition, and an edition of the restored text of *Dryden's Poems* (1910). His observation of the annual Latin play on the Westminster stage is reflected in the translation and edition of the plays of Terence, which he contributed to the Loeb classical library in 1912. He contributed two essays to the Johnson Club *Papers* in 1899, and was joint-editor with Mr. George Whale of two volumes of the Club's *Papers* (1899 and 1920). He was also the author of *Virgil's Pastorals in English Verse* (1900), an edition of Pope's *Essay on Criticism* (1909), a little book on the *Trees, Shrubs and Plants of Virgil* (1920), an important tract on *The Pronunciation of English Words derived from the Latin* (1920), and of various school text-books of the Latin and English classics. At the time of his death he had completed a selection of his poems, posthumously published under the title of *Westminster Verses* (1922), and a translation of the Odyssey into English hexameters.

[*The Times*, 23 and 24 March 1922; Memoir by Dr. James Gow, prefixed to *Westminster Verses*, 1922; *The Elizabethan* (magazine of Westminster School), April and November 1922; personal knowledge.]

R. M. Barrington-Ward.

SARGENT, JOHN SINGER (1856–1925), painter, was born at the Casa Arretini in Florence 12 January 1856, the second (but eldest surviving) child and only son of FitzWilliam Sargent, of Gloucester, Massachusetts, and Boston, a distinguished surgeon attached to Wills Hospital, Philadelphia, from 1844 to 1854, by his wife, Mary Newbold, only child of John Singer, of Philadelphia. The Sargent family is descended from William Sargent who emigrated from Gloucester, England, to America in the seventeenth century and is first mentioned in 1678, as a resident of Gloucester, Massachusetts; while the descent of the Singer family can be traced from Caspar Singer, a native of Alsace-Lorraine, who settled in America in 1730. Mrs. FitzWilliam Sargent was a highly cultured woman, artistic as well as musical; and it was owing to her influence that in 1854 her husband, at the early age of thirty-four, gave up his practice—which had already brought him independent means, supplemented after his marriage by his wife's personal fortune—and went to live with her in Europe, settling first in Florence. After the birth of their only son, three daughters were born to Dr. and Mrs. Sargent, two of whom survived infancy.

John Sargent's early life was spent with his parents in making sojourns of varying length in different countries of Europe, chiefly however in Italy and France. Much care was expended on his education, and especially on his musical training. Originally intended for a naval career, his artistic inclinations were not slow in declaring themselves. Among those who first gave them guidance were, during a stay at Mürren in the summer of 1868, Joseph Farquharson, R.A., who was then a young artist some ten years older than Sargent; and, during the winter of 1868–1869 in Rome, the landscape painter Feodor Karl Welsch (1829–1904), a pupil of Felix Ziem and Alexandre Calame, who had lived for eight years in America. During the winter of 1870–1871 Sargent studied at the Accademia delle Belle Arti at Florence, which was pronounced by him shortly afterwards to be 'the most unsatisfactory institution imaginable'; but although by now it had been decided that he was to follow the career of a painter, it was not until May 1874 that his artistic training was taken seriously in hand. As shown by a letter from him to Heath Wilson, written almost three weeks later (12 June 1874), he at that time (not, as has been stated, in October), entered the studio, in Paris, of Carolus Duran, one of the leading portrait-painters of the time and the artist who was to have the most far-reaching influence on Sargent's development. Later in the same year, he was also admitted to work at the École des Beaux-Arts under Adolphe Yvon. To the next year (1875) belongs Sargent's first serious effort as a portrait-painter in oils, his portrait of Mr. Benjamin P. Kissam (now in the possession of Mrs. A. C. Train, U.S.A.). In May 1876 he sailed with his mother and sister Emily for his first visit to America, returning to Paris in October; and the next year (1877) he sent his first contribution to the Salon, a portrait of Miss Watts, which brought Sargent much praise. In the Salon of 1878 he followed up this success with his picture 'En route pour la pêche' (now in the Corcoran Gallery of Art, Washington), which was awarded the *mention honorable*.

Sargent had by now established for himself a recognized position among the younger artists of Paris. To his more notable works during the next few years belong, among portraits, that of Carolus Duran (Salon, 1879), 'Madame R. S.' ('a Chilian lady', Salon, 1881, awarded the second class medal), the 'Lady with the Rose' (Miss Burckhardt, also Salon, 1881), 'Mrs. Valle Austin' (Salon, 1882), and the 'Daughters of Edward Boit' (Salon, 1883, now in the Museum of Fine Arts, Boston, U.S.A.). Among subject pictures are the 'Fumée d'Ambre Gris' (Salon, 1880) and 'El Jaleo' (Salon, 1882, now in the Isabella Stewart Gardner Museum, Boston), which reflect the artist's experiences during a journey to Spain and Morocco in 1879–1880. While in Spain, Sargent executed many copies of works by Velazquez; and in the spring of 1880 he copied paintings by Frans Hals at Haarlem. For all this interest in the study of the old masters, he was yet enthusiastically identified with the art movements of his day; and it is on record that during his Paris years, in 1881, he described himself as an impressionist and an 'intransigeant', entirely given up to the faithful reproduction of 'les valeurs'. His admiration for Claude Monet was, on the testimony of that painter himself, forcibly expressed as far back as about the year 1876.

The year 1884 was fraught with destiny for Sargent, for in the spring he exhibited at the Salon his portrait (begun in 1883) of Madame Gautreau, a celebrated Paris beauty; and the picture, daringly conceived in a spirit of simplification which is, perhaps, not untinged with sophistication, achieved on the occasion of its public exhibition a veritable *succès de scandale*. The picture is now in the Metropolitan Museum of Art, New York, and an unfinished life-size variant hangs in the Tate Gallery. The storm of vituperative criticism which it met with had to some extent the effect of making Paris uncongenial to Sargent; he spent the summer of 1884 in England, which he had visited twice before and where, in 1882, he had first exhibited at the Royal Academy. The main artistic result of his sojourn in England was a portrait group, 'The Misses Vickers' (Salon, 1885, Royal Academy, 1886). After a brief return to Paris he settled in London at the beginning of 1885, taking J. M. Whistler's former studio at 13 Tite Street, Chelsea (subsequently renumbered 33 Tite Street), the house which was to remain his permanent home for the rest of his life. The central achievement of Sargent's early English days is his study of childhood, 'Carnation, Lily, Lily, Rose', painted at Broadway, Worcestershire, during the autumn of 1885 and the summer of 1886. The picture, exhibited at the Royal Academy in 1887 and immediately purchased by the Chantrey trustees, was Sargent's first considerable public success in England. In September 1887 he went to America in order to carry out a commission for a portrait of Mrs. Henry G. Marquand; he spent the winter of 1887–1888 mainly at Boston where, in December 1887, the first public exhibition of pictures by him held in America took place at the St. Botolph Club.

After his return to England in 1888 Sargent, with untiring energy and industry, continued his work as a portrait-painter, eventually gaining among his contemporaries in that department of painting an international prestige which is almost without parallel. He was a regular exhibitor at the Royal Academy, and was elected A.R.A. in 1894 and R.A. in 1897, his diploma work being 'Interior in Venice' (1899). Among his more outstanding successes as a portrait-painter during the period of his life which came to a close with the outbreak of the European War in 1914, there may be mentioned 'Miss Ellen Terry as Lady Macbeth' (1889, now in the Tate Gallery), the Spanish dancer 'Carmencita' (1890, now in the Musée du Luxembourg, Paris), 'Lady Agnew of Lochaw' (1893, now in the National Gallery of Scotland), 'Coventry Patmore' (1894, now in the National Portrait Gallery), 'W. Graham Robertson' (1894), 'Mrs. Carl Meyer and Children' (1896, now in the Tate Gallery), '(General Sir) Ian Hamilton' (1898), 'Lady Elcho, Mrs.

Adeane and Mrs. Tennant' (1900), 'The Misses Hunter' (1902, now in the Tate Gallery), 'Lord Ribblesdale' (1902, now in the Tate Gallery), 'The Marlborough Family' (1905), 'Cora, Countess of Strafford' (1908), 'The Earl of Wemyss' (1909), and 'Henry James' (1913, now in the National Portrait Gallery). In this connexion mention should also be made of the series of nine portraits of Mr. Asher Wertheimer, the well-known Bond Street art-dealer, and his family which Sargent began in 1898 and which is now in the Tate Gallery.

Although Sargent during the period under review mainly devoted himself to portrait-painting he undertook, as far back as 1890—as part of an ambitious scheme with which other painters were also associated—to decorate the special libraries floor in the Boston Public Library with a series of paintings which it was eventually decided were to have as their subject 'The development of religious thought from paganism through Judaism to Christianity'. This great undertaking absorbed a considerable part of Sargent's energies for more than a quarter of a century, and was not finished until 1916. Sargent having made provision for the inclusion of a number of reliefs in his scheme of decoration, carried these out himself: to this series belongs a 'Crucifixion' of which the original bronze was presented by his two surviving sisters, as a memorial of their brother, to St. Paul's Cathedral, London, while another version is in the Tate Gallery. Sketching in oil and water-colour during his holidays in England and abroad still further added to the activities of Sargent's well-filled life. His work as a water-colour painter owed much to the inspiration of Hercules Brabazon Brabazon [q.v.], with whom he became acquainted in 1886 or 1887.

When the European War broke out Sargent was on a painting tour in the Austrian Tyrol; as an American citizen, and so at that time a neutral, his personal freedom was not interfered with, and it was not until November 1914 that he returned to London. The year 1915 was spent by him in England, but early in 1916 he went to America and stayed there for about a year. It was during this sojourn that his work for the Boston Library was finished; and he also now undertook to carry out the decoration of the rotunda of the Museum of Fine Arts in Boston—a work which continued until 1921 and was followed by the decoration of the main staircase and library of the same building, which was completed by the time of his death. In June 1918 Sargent, in the company of Henry Tonks, Slade professor of fine art in the university of London, paid a visit to the war zone in France which lasted until the end of October. During this visit he witnessed in August at a dressing station near Arras the scene which provided the subject for his great picture 'Gassed', which was completed the same year, exhibited at the Academy in 1919, and is now in the Imperial War Museum, South Kensington. His work in connexion with the War also includes a large portrait-group 'Some General Officers of the Great War' (1922, now in the National Portrait Gallery) and two decorative panels in the Widener Memorial Library, Harvard University, Cambridge, Massachusetts (1922). Sargent never wholly gave up portrait-painting, although his output in that province became much restricted towards the end of his career; and to the very last he continued to produce rapid portrait-sketches in charcoal.

Official and academic recognition was extended to Sargent in large measure and from numerous quarters. He received the honorary degrees of D.C.L. from Oxford University in 1904 and of LL.D. from Cambridge University in 1913. He was a member of a large number of academies, including the Académie des Beaux-Arts of France, and he was awarded the Prussian order 'pour le mérite' in 1909. For the famous series of artists' self-portraits which hangs in the Uffizi Gallery at Florence, Sargent painted his own portrait in 1907. In the same year he was offered by the prime minister, Sir Henry Campbell-Bannerman, a knighthood, which he declined, pleading as an excuse his American citizenship, which he retained all his life. When in 1918 the presidency of the Royal Academy fell vacant, Sargent would undoubtedly have been elected to that position, had he allowed his candidature to be put forward: but his innate shyness and disinclination to appear in public caused him to decline all requests to that effect. Nevertheless, the influence of his forceful and highly cultured personality inevitably made itself felt in wide circles, entirely irrespective of any official position; and his personal kindness and sympathy, when he felt that they were needed, would at times go to quite unaccustomed lengths.

Sargent, who never married, died in his

sleep in his London house in the early hours of 15 April 1925, just as he was about to start on a voyage to America. A sale of the contents of his studio was held at Messrs. Christie's rooms 24 and 27 July 1925, and the pictures and drawings by Sargent included in it realized the huge total of £175,260. The entire Winter Exhibition of the Royal Academy in 1926 was devoted to a retrospective collection of his works [see *Illustrations of the Sargent Exhibition, Royal Academy 1926*, 1926]; it had been preceded by a memorial exhibition held at the Museum of Fine Arts at Boston in 1925.

It would be idle not to recognize the immense accomplishment of Sargent in many directions; the imposing series of portraits painted by him will doubtless retain permanent importance as a vivid commentary on the chapter of human history to which it relates. A certain essential lack of sensitiveness may, however, be said to detract from the value of his work as a whole; coupled with this defect is a disposition towards what is somewhat obviously bizarre or sophisticatedly eloquent. The result is that in his imaginative compositions Sargent's true limitations as an artist become only too plainly apparent.

A cartoon of Sargent appeared in *Vanity Fair* 24 February 1909.

[William Howe Downes, *John S. Sargent, his Life and Work*, 1926; the Hon. Sir Evan Charteris, *John Sargent*, 1927. For critical estimates of Sargent as an artist see *The Work of J. S. Sargent*, with an introductory note by Alice Meynell, 1903, re-issued with additional plates, and an additional introduction by J. B. Manson, 1927; Jacques-Émile Blanche in *La Revue de Paris*, 1 April 1926; Roger Fry in *Transformations*, 1926; and Henry James in *Harper's Magazine*, October 1887. On the comparatively little known circle of Sargent's student years in Paris, valuable information is contained in the letters (in Swedish) of his friend and fellow-student, the Finnish painter, Albert Edelfelt, notably those published by W. Söderhjelm in *Profiler ur finskt kulturliv*, 1913. The beginning of Sargent's training under Carolus Duran is fully elucidated by him in two letters, unknown to his previous biographers and written to Heath Wilson 23 May and 12 June 1874; they are entered under No. 201 in the catalogue (No. 605) of autograph letters and historical documents offered for sale in the spring of 1935 by Messrs. Maggs Ltd., 34 and 35 Conduit Street, London, W.]

T. Borenius.

SATOW, Sir ERNEST MASON (1843–1929), diplomatist and historian, was born at Clapton 30 June 1843. He was the fourth son of Hans David Christopher Satow, a Swedish merchant, who came from Riga to settle in London in 1825. His mother, Margaret Mason, was English. Ernest Satow was brought up in protestant traditions and had a stiff, puritan education at Mill Hill School. But his studies at University College, London, which he entered in 1859, and where he graduated B.A. in 1861, widened his outlook. His desire to see Asia was fired by reading a book of travel, and he seized the opportunity to compete for a student interpretership to the Far East (1861). He was placed first in the examination and assigned to the consular service in Japan.

Since 1858 the process of opening up Japan to the West had begun. The first years of transition proved dangerous for foreigners. Satow arrived in Japan on 8 September 1862, and six days later an Englishman was cut to pieces and two others severely wounded by the retainers of a Japanese nobleman called Saburo. Satow was on board a ship of the British flotilla which bombarded Saburo's castle in August 1863, and he was also with the Franco-British fleet when it fought the battle of the Shimonoseki Straits a year later. This defeat discredited the rule of the shogun, or prime minister, and induced the mikado to accept the terms of the Western powers and to open up the country. On the accession of a new mikado, Mutsu Hito, in 1867, the shogun finally abdicated. During these years Satow, who had learned the Japanese language, had become the indispensable interpreter at the legation, to which he was finally appointed Japanese secretary in 1868. On 23 March of the same year the minister, Sir Harry Smith Parkes [q.v.], and Satow were attacked by men with swords when proceeding to an audience with the mikado at Kyoto. The assassins missed their blows, and the mikado's horror at this incident ended the period of danger for foreigners. Internal unrest and rebellion continued for another ten years, and the work of adjustment for a generation longer. Satow received the C.M.G. in 1883 as a recognition of his services. He had not only learned the language but had got to know all the leading Japanese personalities, notably the Marquess Ito, the leader of reform, with whom his friendship began so early as 1864. In after days he was wont to say that the Far East was not mysterious to those who knew the languages and cultures of China and Japan.

Satow himself is, in fact, the only Englishman who hitherto has represented his country in both China and Japan, and spoken the language of each.

In 1884 Satow was appointed consul-general at Bangkok. He so distinguished himself that he was promoted to the rank of minister in 1885. But Siam did not suit his health, and in 1888 he became minister at Montevideo, an earthly paradise in which he found nothing to do. When transferred to Morocco as envoy extraordinary and minister plenipotentiary in 1893 he showed great ability in negotiating with the Sultan Mulai Hassan, and visited his successor, Abdul Aziz, at Fez in 1894. In June 1895 he received the K.C.M.G. and was appointed minister plenipotentiary at Tokio. He remained there until 1900.

The years during which Satow was at Tokio were of crucial importance in the Far East. No Englishman was so fitted as he to understand what was taking place or to warn his government as to the consequences of the growing power of Japan. During the years 1894–1895 Japan defeated China and forced her to surrender Korea. But she suffered a severe set-back when Russia combined with Germany and France to force her to give back Port Arthur to China. Still severer was the blow when Germany seized Kiaochaow at the end of 1897 and Russia followed this up by occupying Port Arthur for herself and obtaining China's consent thereto in March 1898. Great Britain followed suit by occupying Wei-hai-wei. Satow had long foreseen the results of Russian aggression. Even in 1896 he had predicted that Japan was preparing to be revenged on Russia. Russian expansion at Port Arthur and in Korea only illustrated his warnings.

In 1900 the Boxer rebellion broke out in China, and the foreign legations were besieged in Peking. After much trouble they were relieved by an international force. In October Satow replaced Sir Claude Maxwell Macdonald [q.v.], the existing minister at Peking, who was transferred to Tokio. On his arrival at Peking Satow undertook the difficult task of inducing the Chinese government to submit and to pay indemnities, and the still more difficult task of reconciling the claims of the various Allies, and of managing Count Waldersee, the German generalissimo of the Inter-Allied forces. During this negotiation Satow showed knowledge of the West as well as of the East, of commerce and finance as well as of diplomacy, and combined suavity and charm of manner with great firmness and resolution. The agreement between China and the Powers, signed at Peking in September 1901, was one for which Satow deserved, and obtained, the credit.

Early in 1902 the Anglo-Japanese Treaty of Alliance was signed. Satow was not consulted about it beforehand, and he did not agree with the view of Sir Thomas (afterwards Lord) Sanderson [q.v.] that it would enable Great Britain to prevent Japan from making war upon Russia. He continued to point out the increasing danger of a Russo-Japanese war, and his predictions were finally realized in February 1904. Satow followed the course of the war with inside knowledge and, through his confidential intercourse with some Japanese statesmen, gave the first true accounts of the Japanese reasons for ending the war with Russia by the peace of Portsmouth (New Hampshire) on 23 August 1905. Satow was recalled from Peking in 1906. He had been made G.C.M.G. in 1902. He now became a privy councillor, and was also appointed for six years British member of the Court of Arbitration at The Hague. His last diplomatic service was to act as the second British delegate to the Second Hague Peace Conference in 1907. He came away with the belief that foreign nations generally expected a naval war between England and Germany, and by 1909 he had come to expect it himself.

Satow never married, and he spent the remainder of his life on his property at Ottery St. Mary, Devonshire. His splendid intellect remained quite unimpaired until within a few months of his death, which took place at Ottery St. Mary 26 August 1929 at the age of eighty-six. Originally a pronounced sceptic, he became converted to a personal form of Christianity in 1887 and was thereafter deeply religious. He was happy with his flowers and his books in retirement, and kept in touch with the outside world and with personal friends. He read deeply in the literatures of England, France, Germany, Spain, and Italy as well as of Japan and China.

Satow is one of the few British ministers abroad who have shown themselves as accomplished in the theory as in the practice of diplomacy, and of the still fewer who have written history. He received the honorary degree of D.C.L. from the university of Oxford and that of LL.D. from the university of Cambridge, and gave the Rede lecture at the latter in 1908. He wrote various studies on international law and history, and delivered his final message in a work full of practical wisdom, legal acumen, and antiquarian knowledge, entitled *A Guide to Diplomatic Practice* (1917, 2nd edition 1922. The 3rd edition, 1932, is much altered and was not revised or authorized by Satow). He contributed a chapter on 'The Far East 1815–1871' to volume xi of the *Cambridge Modern History* (1909). Many articles by him on phases of the language, history, and literature of Japan, Korea, and Siam are contained in the *Transactions* of the Asiatic Society of Japan (1872–1899). His two most notable historico-legal articles are 'Private Property at Sea in Time of War' (*Nineteenth Century and After*, February 1913), and 'Pacta sunt servanda' (*Cambridge Historical Journal*, vol. i, no. 3, 1925). His own account of his early years in Japan (*A Diplomat in Japan*, 1921) is historically of high value.

Satow's comments on history and politics are difficult to find in his published works, as he remained invariably discreet. But some judgements known to his friends are worth recording. Castlereagh and Canning he considered the greatest British foreign ministers. He preferred the latter because of his handling of public opinion, and in view of the wonderful clearness of his dispatches. He condemned Palmerston for his policy in the Chinese War, but acknowledged the force of his character. Of his own chiefs he admired the massive character of Lord Salisbury, the worldly wisdom of Lord Lansdowne, and the integrity of Sir Edward Grey. A. J. Balfour and Sir Henry Campbell-Bannerman he thought too amateur to excel in foreign politics. He deplored the former's handling of the Port Arthur question in March 1898; he considered the latter had failed at the Second Hague Peace Conference, for he had not been clear in his views over disarmament and in respect of the capture of private property at sea. At The Hague he detected the rising abilities of (Sir) Eyre Crowe [q.v.], and he had a warm personal regard for Lord Curzon. Of ministers abroad in the past he thought Lord Stratford de Redcliffe the most powerful and the first Earl of Malmesbury the wisest. He thought Lord Lyons the most prudent and Lord Dufferin the most adroit of the diplomats of his own day. As regards the methods of diplomacy, he adhered to confidential intercourse but stipulated that honesty and integrity should accompany it. He was a believer in constitutionalism and in parliaments and had a great suspicion of dictatorships. He sought to apply the rule of law to international politics, but, being a realist, knew the dangers of pressing it too far. He was at first inclined to question the usefulness of the League of Nations, but ended by acknowledging its value. The permanent Court at The Hague in especial appealed to him as laying down, for the first time, a standard of international justice. He believed that the future of international relations would represent a compromise between the pre-1914 diplomacy and the subsequent diplomacy of publicity and discussion.

A cartoon of Satow by 'Spy' appeared in *Vanity Fair* 23 April 1903.

[B. M. Allen, *The Rt. Hon. Sir Ernest Satow. A Memoir* (containing a portrait and a complete list of his writings), 1933; Sir Ernest Satow, *A Diplomat in Japan*, 1921. Satow's private papers are in the Public Record Office. Many of his dispatches, together with a selection of his private papers, are published in *British Documents on the Origins of the War*, edited by G. P. Gooch and H. W. V. Temperley, vols. i, p. 345, ii, p. 417, iv, p. 639, and viii, p. 750.] H. W. V. Temperley.

SCHARLIEB, Dame MARY ANN DACOMB (1845–1930), gynaecological surgeon, was born in London 18 June 1845, the only daughter of William Candler Bird, later of the Hollies, Kersal, Manchester, by his first wife, Mary Dacomb, who died ten days after the birth of her child. Five years later Mary Bird's father married again, and owing to the influence of an enlightened stepmother, she received an education unusually good for the time, first at a boarding-school in Manchester, then at a school in New Brighton, where she showed her aptitude for science, and later, at a school in St. John's Wood, where she again showed her interest in science and also in music, an interest which she preserved all her life. She was fond of riding, but never joined in games and disliked dances and parties.

In 1865, Mary Bird met her future husband, William Mason Scharlieb, son of Charles Scharlieb, of Madras; he was in England reading for the bar, and in December of that year they were married. Early in 1866 Mary Scharlieb and her husband, who had been called to the bar by the Middle Temple, sailed for Madras. Their elder son was born there in 1866, their younger son in 1868, and their daughter in 1870. From her husband's clients and clerks Mary Scharlieb heard much of the sufferings of Hindu and Mohammedan women, and thus became aware of the urgent need of qualified medical women to attend and help them. After much delay and opposition, she, together with three other women, secured entrance to the Madras Medical School, where, after three years, in 1877 she duly became qualified. Then, early in 1878, for the sake of the health and education of her children, and also for her own health, she returned to England. She had determined to obtain medical qualification in the university of London, and during the the voyage home, in the intervals of looking after her children, she studied mathematics with one of the engineers of the ship, and read the other necessary subjects in preparation for the London matriculation examination. In 1878 she entered as a student at the London School of Medicine for Women and the Royal Free Hospital. In 1882 she passed the M.B. examination, being awarded the gold medal and scholarship in obstetrics.

In 1883 Mary Scharlieb went to Vienna in order to gain practice in operative midwifery, after which she and her husband, whom she joined in Brindisi, came to England to spend the Easter vacation with their children. In the autumn they returned to India, but before they left Mrs. Scharlieb was received by Queen Victoria and on the day before their departure by the Prince and Princess of Wales. The queen insisted on hearing details of the difficulties and sufferings of the caste and Gosha women, and finally said: 'How can they tell me that there is no need for medical women in India?' She sent Mary Scharlieb back with a message for her future patients: 'Tell them how deeply their queen sympathises with them, and how glad she is that they should have medical women to help them in their hour of need.' Back in India, Mary Scharlieb soon realized the necessity for hospital treatment for her patients, and the outcome of her work was the establishment about 1884–1886 of the Royal Victoria Hospital for Caste and Gosha Women in Madras. She built up a very large private practice, but, her health once more failing, she left Madras in February 1887, and came again to London. In 1888 she graduated M.D. of London University—being the first woman to do so—and in 1889 was appointed lecturer on diseases of women at the School of Medicine for Women. Two years later (1891) her husband died, only a short time after he had returned to England.

After her husband's death Mary Scharlieb remained in England, and there followed a period full of work and recognition. From 1892 to 1903 she was senior surgeon at the New Hospital for Women (afterwards the Elizabeth Garrett Anderson Hospital), and was a member of its consultant staff until her death. She obtained the M.S. degree in 1897, and in 1902 she was appointed gynaecologist at the Royal Free Hospital, thus becoming the first woman to hold a staff appointment in a London general hospital. In 1913 she was appointed to serve on the royal commission on venereal diseases. In 1917 she was made C.B.E. and was also elected president of the London (Royal Free Hospital) School of Medicine for Women, and in 1926 she was created D.B.E. In 1920 she was appointed one of the first women magistrates, serving in one of the children's courts. She was a commissioner in lunacy for Marylebone, and one of the visiting magistrates for Holloway Gaol. In 1928 she received the honorary degree of LL.D. from Edinburgh University. She died in London at the house of her younger son 21 November 1930, having seen patients until within ten days of her death.

Dame Mary Scharlieb was an indefatigable worker and a remarkably skilful operator, and although she never had an operating knife in her hand until she was forty years of age she soon became one of the great abdominal surgeons of her day. She was not only a great surgeon but also a great physician. A keen sense of humour and a deep vein of common sense running through her thorough knowledge of human nature equipped her for dealing with the mental as well as the physical difficulties of her patients. She was interested in life from many angles and had the gift of true friendship. She was a woman of deep religious conviction, her faith dominating her life.

By her surgical skill and by her powers of diagnosis as well as by the sanity and charm of a remarkable and vigorous personality, Dame Mary Scharlieb secured for herself a very honoured place in the medical world of her day, and probably more than any one other woman she familiarized the general public with the work of medical women in Great Britain. The name of 'Mrs. Scharlieb' was a household word and, for many, she became the embodiment of their idea of medical women.

[Mary Scharlieb, *Reminiscences*, 1924; private information; personal knowledge.]

W. C. Cullis.

SCHLICH, Sir WILLIAM (1840–1925), forester, was born at Flonheim in Rheinhessen, Germany, 28 February 1840, the sixth son of Kirchenrat Daniel Schlich, a Lutheran pastor, of Hesse-Darmstadt, by his wife, Charlotte Frank. He was educated at Darmstadt, Karlsruhe, and at the university of Giessen, where he took his degree of Ph.D. in 1866. The same year he accepted an appointment in the Indian Forest department, and was posted to Burma, where he served until 1870, when he was transferred to Sind. In 1872 he was again transferred, on promotion, to the conservatorship of forests of Bengal, which at that time included not only Bengal proper but also Bihar and Orissa as well as Assam. Schlich administered this heavy charge until 1879, when he proceeded to Europe on furlough. On his return to India in 1880 he was posted to the Punjab as conservator of forests, but the following year he was appointed to act as inspector-general of forests to the government of India in place of Sir Dietrich Brandis [q.v.]. He was confirmed in this appointment in April 1883, when Brandis retired from the service, and held it until February 1885, when he finally left India in order to organize the forestry branch at the Royal Indian Engineering College at Coopers Hill, Englefield Green. Perhaps the most important measure passed during Schlich's term of office as inspector-general of forests was the formation of the Imperial Working Plans branch, which ensured the preparation of forest working plans on approved lines and their scrutiny by a central authority. Although he left India in 1885, he did not actually retire from the service until 1 January 1889. He became a naturalized British subject in 1886.

Valuable as had been Schlich's services in the Indian Forest department, his subsequent services in the cause of forestry were even more distinguished. His appointment in 1885 to the professorship of forestry at Coopers Hill gave him full scope for the display of those qualities which marked him out as an unusually successful teacher. Combining sound knowledge, judgement, and enthusiasm for his subject with a keen sense of humour, he succeeded in winning to a remarkable degree the confidence and affection of his pupils. His duties at Coopers Hill were concerned primarily with the training of recruits for the Indian Forest service, although a few of his pupils obtained appointments in other parts of the British Empire.

On the decision, taken in 1905, to close the college, its forestry branch was transferred to Oxford, and although he had then reached the age of sixty-five, Schlich succeeded in building up a school of forestry worthy of the university which had adopted it. In its earlier years the Oxford school continued the tradition of Coopers Hill in being primarily a training centre for the Indian Forest service, and Schlich maintained an official connexion with the India Office until 1911, when the necessity for this connexion had ceased to exist; the university then appointed him reader with the status of professor of forestry. By this time, owing to the demand for trained forest officers in other parts of the Empire, the scope of the school had become considerably widened. Schlich's services to India, which were rewarded in 1891 with the C.I.E. and in 1909 with the K.C.I.E., may be realized from the fact that he was responsible, while at Coopers Hill and at Oxford, for the training of no fewer than 272 out of a total of 283 officers who joined the Indian Forest service during that period. At Oxford he worked strenuously to obtain full recognition for forestry as a branch of scientific learning in the university, first, by having it included among the subjects of the B.A. degree, and secondly, by securing the endowment of a permanent professorship. In 1919 he had the satisfaction of seeing his efforts crowned with success. He retired from his university post 1 January 1920, but continued to reside in Oxford, occupying himself with writing until his death five years later.

Schlich's activities were by no means confined to academic work. His advice on matters concerning forestry was widely sought, and the British Empire as a whole has reason to be grateful for the services rendered by him. Among other things, he constantly urged on the British government the importance of increasing the supplies of home-grown timber by afforestation and by improving the condition of British woodlands. He was a member of the forestry sub-committee of the Reconstruction Committee which was appointed in 1916 to consider this question, and whose final report, issued in 1918, led to an extensive scheme of state afforestation. He was elected a fellow of the Royal Society in 1901, and an honorary fellow of St. John's College, Oxford, in 1909. He was president of the Royal English Arboricultural Society in 1913–1914, and was on the governing council of the Empire Forestry Association at the time of his death.

Among his published writings, Schlich's *Manual of Forestry*, in five volumes—three by himself and two by his colleague W. R. Fisher—ranks as a standard work. The first edition appeared from 1889 (vol. 1) to 1896 (vol. 5), and each volume went through two or more editions, the last (vol. 3, fifth edition) being published in 1925, when he was eighty-five years of age. His other publications include *Forestry in the United Kingdom* (1904), and numerous papers and reports. He was the first honorary editor of *The Indian Forester*, a professional journal started in 1875, and was a contributor to its pages until the year of his death.

Schlich died at Oxford 28 September 1925. He was twice married: first, in 1874 to Mary Margaret (died 1878), daughter of William Smith, civil engineer; secondly, in 1886 to Adèle Emilie Mathilde, daughter of Hermann Marsily, of Antwerp. By his first wife he had one son, who died in childhood, and one daughter, and by his second, one son and three daughters.

[*The Times*, 1 October 1925; *Nature*, 24 October 1925; *Empire Forestry Journal*, 1925; private information.] R. S. Troup.

SCOTT, GEORGE HERBERT (1888–1930), airship commander, was born in Lewisham, London, 25 May 1888, the eldest son of George Hall Scott, civil engineer, by his wife, Margaret Wilkinson. He was educated at Alton School, Plymouth, at Richmond School, Yorkshire, and at the Royal Naval Engineering College, Keyham. From 1908 onwards he was engaged in general engineering, and just before the European War he was employed on the building of naval vessels in the yards of the Sociedad Española de Construccion, at Ferrol, Spain.

Soon after the outbreak of the European War in 1914 Scott joined the Royal Naval Air Service as a flight sub-lieutenant and was sent for training to the airship stations at Farnborough and Kingsnorth, Kent. In May 1915 he was appointed to the airship station at Barrow-in-Furness, and he remained there until October 1916 when he left in order to take command of the airship station at Anglesea. In March of the following year he was back at Barrow as captain of the Parseval airship P. 4.

In April 1917 the first British rigid airship to fly, No. 9, which had been built by Messrs. Vickers at Barrow, was taken into service at Howden, Yorkshire, and Squadron Commander Scott was posted to Howden to take command of her. In July he took the ship on patrol off the north-east coast and was in the air for twenty-seven hours, a notable flight for a British 'rigid' at the time. He subsequently commanded the same airship at Cranwell, Lincolnshire, and at Pulham, Norfolk, and it was while he was at the latter station that he developed the system—with which his name is associated—of mooring airships at the head of a mast or tower.

On the formation of the Royal Air Force in April 1918, Scott was gazetted to the rank of major. In November 1918, soon after the signing of the Armistice, he went to Inchinnan, Renfrewshire, where Messrs. William Beardmore were building the 'rigid' R. 34, a copy of the Zeppelin airship L. 33 which had landed, owing to damage by anti-aircraft gun-fire, near Mersea Island in September 1916. He was given command of the R. 34 on her completion and received orders to prepare for a voyage to the United States of America. The journey was made in July 1919. The R. 34 left East Fortune, East Lothian, at 1.42 a.m. on 2 July and returned to Pulham, where she landed, at 6.57 a.m. on 13 July. The outward journey to Mineola, east of New York, during which mails were dropped at Newfoundland, was made in 108 hours 12 minutes, and the homeward journey, after circling New York, was completed in 75 hours 3 minutes. During her whole flight of some 6,000 miles, the R. 34 was in wireless touch with the Air Ministry in London. She encountered severe electrical storms, particularly off St. John's, and she was much thrown about; but the cool, alert, and expert handling of Scott brought the ship safely through the ordeal. This was the first airship flight across the Atlantic, and for his achievement Scott was awarded the C.B.E. He had already received the Air Force cross in 1918 for his work on airships during the War.

In October 1919 Scott retired from the Royal Air Force, but in 1920 he was appointed to the technical staff of the Royal Airship Works at Cardington, Bedford. Airship development in England, however, after being stimulated by the War, began to languish in peace time, and soon ceased altogether, although a nucleus staff, including Scott, was retained at Pulham. About 1924, the government once again took up the problem of the airship, and Scott was appointed to the Air Ministry as officer in charge of flying and training in the directorate of airship development. The project was to open up airship communications throughout the British Empire, and in 1927 Scott visited Canada in order to advise the Canadian government on the selection of a site for an airship base. As a result of his visit a mooring tower was built at St. Hubert, Montreal.

In January 1930 Scott was appointed assistant director for airship development with responsibility for all airship flying operations and for the training of airship crews. He was also responsible for the trials of the new British 'rigids', the R. 100 and R. 101. He made his second flight across the Atlantic, although not in command, in the R. 100, which left Cardington, at 3.48 a.m. on 29 July 1930 and reached St. Hubert, Montreal, at 2.25 a.m. on 1 August after a journey of 3,364 miles. On 4 October 1930 he set out as a passenger in the R. 101 on a flight to India, and he was among the forty-eight victims when the ship crashed and caught fire at 2 a.m. on 5 October at Allonne, near Beauvais, France. He had been responsible with Lieutenant-Colonel V. C. Richmond, the designer of the R. 101, for the unbraced transverse frame, first used in that ship and regarded as one of the most important developments in airship construction.

Scott was a quiet, conscientious, and hard-working officer. A trained and experienced engineer, he had a firm belief in the future of the airship, and his life was devoted to the establishment of the airship as a safe and reliable form of transport. His pioneering efforts he regarded solely as incidental to this end, and in no sense as record-breaking achievements. He was, without doubt, the foremost British airship commander of his time.

Scott married in 1919 Jessie, the eldest daughter of Archibald Jack Campbell, general manager of Messrs. William Beardmore's shipbuilding yards, Dalmuir, and had one son and three daughters.

[Private information; personal knowledge.]

H. A. Jones.

SCOTT, Sir PERCY MORETON, first baronet (1853–1924), admiral, the son of Montagu Scott, solicitor, by his wife, Laura Kezia Snelling, was born in Canonbury, North London, 10 July 1853. He was educated at Eastman's Naval Academy, Southsea, and entered the *Britannia* as a naval cadet in September 1866. In December 1867 he was appointed to the *Forte* frigate and sailed in her to the East Indies, where she became flagship of Commodore Sir Leopold Heath. He was rated midshipman in June 1868, and returned to England at the end of a three and a half years' commission in February 1872. After a year's service in the new armoured battleship *Hercules*, having been promoted sub-lieutenant in December 1872, he joined the *Excellent* gunnery school ship in order to complete examinations. When the Ashanti War broke out Scott volunteered for service on the West coast of Africa and was appointed to the *Active*, flagship of (Sir) William Hewett. He arrived too late for active service in the campaign. He remained in the *Active* until April 1877—a memorable commission covering a number of minor operations on the West coast of Africa. Scott was promoted lieutenant in November 1875, and recommended in dispatches for services in the Congo expedition of that year. In September 1877, he was appointed to the *Excellent* for a gunnery course, and remained in the school as junior staff officer until July 1880.

Scott was then appointed gunnery lieutenant of the *Inconstant*, flagship of Lord Clanwilliam's squadron, which was commissioned for a voyage round the world, was detained on the way for service at the Cape during the Boer War, and on the completion of the cruise was sent to the Mediterranean for the Egyptian campaign at Alexandra in 1882. Scott did valuable service in mounting some heavy Egyptian guns for the army, for which he was praised in military dispatches. In November 1882 he was appointed to the *Cambridge* gunnery school at Devonport as senior staff officer, and in April 1883 was again sent to the *Excellent*, where he remained until promoted commander in September 1886. From September 1887 until February 1890 he was commander of the *Edinburgh*, Mediterranean station, and then returned to the *Excellent* for another three years, during which he was very active in converting the gunnery school at Whale Island into a model naval barracks and training establishment. Scott was promoted captain in January 1893, and after two and a half years' service on the ordnance committee at Woolwich, was in command of the *Scylla* in the Mediterranean from May 1896 to July 1899. While in that ship he developed and introduced a number of valuable inventions in signal apparatus and gunnery appliances. By the latter means he became a pioneer in the improvement of gunnery practice in the fleet and established a record for marksmanship and rate of fire in the firing of his own ship.

In September 1899 Scott was appointed captain of the *Terrible* for service on the China station; but owing to the trouble impending in South Africa, the ship proceeded via the Cape, and was detained there until March 1900. On the outbreak of the South African War, Scott rendered valuable service by devising land mountings and carriages for the heavy 4.7-inch naval guns which were landed for the defence of Ladysmith and undoubtedly saved the situation. He also mounted on mobile mountings a number of 4.7-inch and 6-inch guns which accompanied the naval brigades attached to the armies. For these very valuable services he received the C.B. (1900). For a short time Scott acted as military commandant at Durban. He reached the China station at the time of the Boxer rebellion, and once again he was able to devise mountings and to land heavy guns, which were used in the international operations against the Boxers. On the conclusion of the land operations Scott devoted himself with ardour to improving the gunnery efficiency of his own ship, and by example that of the whole squadron. The *Terrible* achieved remarkable success in her firings, and as a result Scott's methods were adopted throughout the service, thereby raising the standard of shooting to a far higher level. On returning home in 1902 Scott received a great public welcome, and was awarded the C.V.O. by King Edward VII.

In April 1903 Scott was appointed captain of the *Excellent*, and during the two years until his promotion to flag rank in 1905, made full use of his opportunities for improving the gunnery appliances and training of the fleet. As flag officer he was immediately given the new appointment of inspector of target practice, which he held until July 1907. The duties required him to attend the firing practices of the fleet, report on them, and make suggestions for improvements. Scott showed characteristic energy, inventiveness, and originality of mind in this task, with the result that the efficiency of the firing practice of the fleet was doubled during these two years. The gunlayer's test and battle practice at towed targets were two of the methods which he instituted. In July 1906, on the occasion of the launch of the *Dreadnought*, he was created K.C.V.O. by King Edward. In July 1907 he was given his first and only flag appointment at sea in command of the second cruiser squadron (flagship H.M.S. *Good Hope*) of the Channel fleet, then under the command of Lord Charles Beresford [q.v.]. During the first year the personal relations between the two admirals became badly strained: both were naturally impulsive and critical of higher authority, and after an unfortunate incident in which Scott hoisted what Beresford considered an insubordinate signal, the Admiralty decided to remove the second cruiser squadron from the Channel fleet, and sent it under Scott on a special cruise to South Africa in connexion with the Convention of the Union of that Dominion, and to South America to show the flag. Scott was highly successful in this Imperial mission, and, having been promoted to vice-admiral in December 1908, hauled down his flag in February 1909. He spent the next four years, until promotion to admiral and retirement in March 1913, in developing and pressing for the introduction of various improvements in gunnery apparatus, particularly his invention of the director firing system. In 1910 he was promoted K.C.B., and given an award of £2,000 by the government for his various inventions and appliances, having had a previous award of £8,000 in 1905. He obtained considerable financial advantage from the arrangements which he made with armament firms for the production of his inventions. This enabled him to accept the offer of a baronetcy which was conferred on him in February 1913.

Soon after the outbreak of the European War, Scott was appointed to the Admiralty for special service, and continued on duty until May 1918. His first work was to fit out a fleet of dummy battleships by converting sixteen merchant steamers so as to give them with fair accuracy the appearance of some of the most important units of the British navy. He was then employed on various duties as adviser on the gunnery efficiency of the fleet and on measures for coping with the submarine danger, which, as he had prophesied some months before the War, had become very serious. In September 1915, when the zeppelins had begun their raids over England, he was appointed by Mr. Balfour, then first lord, to undertake the gunnery defence of London against air attack until the army should be ready to take over the work, which it did in the following February. The Anti-Aircraft Corps which Scott created laid the foundations of the elaborate system of anti-aircraft defence which in the end largely defeated the zeppelin danger.

After the War was over Scott wrote a series of letters to *The Times*, reiterating the theory, which he had first propounded in June 1914, that the day of the battleship was over owing to the development of submarines and aircraft; he urged that Great Britain should no longer build battleships, but rely in future on smaller craft and submarines. He died in London 18 October 1924.

Scott was a man of very remarkable inventive power, and his numerous devices, inventions, and methods for improving the gunnery of the fleet, especially after he had obtained the powerful support of his senior, Admiral of the Fleet Lord Fisher [q.v.], for their adoption in the service, were of immense advantage to the royal navy in the European War. His methods and apparatus for improving gun drill and thereby the rate of loading, and also for training gun layers in accurately and rapidly aligning their weapons, have been adopted in all the navies of the world. The Scott director system for laying and firing numbers of guns from one gunsight was of particular value in the War, and has also been universally adopted. Scott's persistence in pressing his views, and his contempt for officers of the older school, continually brought him into conflict with the authorities, and, although he was popular with the lower deck, his equals and superiors in rank did not always find him easy to work with. He was a fine seaman, but his judgement in tactical matters was frequently at fault; and it is upon his inventive genius and the services which it enabled him to render to his country that his claim to fame principally rests.

Scott was twice married: first, in 1894 to Teresa Roma, daughter of Sir Frederick Dixon-Hartland, baronet, whom he divorced in 1911; secondly, in 1914 to Fanny Vaughan Johnston, daughter of Thomas Ramsay Dennis and formerly wife of Colonel A. P. Welman. He had two sons and a daughter by his first wife. The elder son was lost as a midshipman in the *Defence* at the battle of Jutland (1916). The younger son, Douglas Winchester (born 1907), succeeded as second baronet.

A cartoon of Scott by 'Spy' appeared in *Vanity Fair* 17 September 1903.

[Admiralty Records; Sir P. Scott, *Fifty Years in the Royal Navy*, 1919; private information.] V. W. BADDELEY.

SECCOMBE, THOMAS (1866–1923), critic and biographer, born at Terrington St. Clement, Norfolk, 18 June 1866, was the eldest son of John Thomas Seccombe, a country doctor, and grandson of Sir Thomas Lawrence Seccombe, of the India Office. His mother was Elizabeth Margaret, daughter of Thomas Clout, of Lambeth. He was educated at Felsted School, and proceeded to Balliol College, Oxford, in October 1885. He won the Stanhope prize in 1887 with an essay on 'Political Satire in England in the Eighteenth Century', and obtained a first class in the school of modern history in 1889. He graduated B.A. in 1889 and M.A. in 1895.

In 1891 (Sir) Sidney Lee [q.v.], who had just succeeded (Sir) Leslie Stephen as editor of the DICTIONARY OF NATIONAL BIOGRAPHY, chose Seccombe as assistant editor, and he continued in that position until the editorial staff was disbanded on 31 December 1900 on the completion of the main work. In this post Seccombe's kindliness and courtesy made him a favourite with the contributors and assisted materially to maintain those friendly relations among editors and contributors which characterized the whole period of publication. He himself contributed to the DICTIONARY over seven hundred biographies, mainly of eighteenth-century writers, and also of sportsmen and athletes. Among them may be mentioned particularly his articles on Smollett and Sir John Vanbrugh. Later he wrote a number of articles for the 1901–1911 SUPPLEMENT of the Dictionary, including a memoir of George Meredith, an example of his best work.

After giving up his post on the Dictionary, Seccombe devoted most of his time to literary work. He had already edited *The Lives of Twelve Bad Men* in 1894, and had published in 1900 *The Age of Johnson*, an excellent summary of the literature of the later eighteenth century. After 1901 he collaborated for some time with (Sir) William Robertson Nicoll [q.v.] on the '*Bookman' History of English Literature*, which appeared in 1905 and 1906. He edited, with introductory prefaces, many reprints of well-known authors, including

George Borrow, George Gissing, Mrs. Gaskell, Francis Parkman, W. H. Prescott, and Smollett's *Travels through France and Italy*. From 1907 to 1912 Seccombe was lecturer in modern history at the East London College in the university of London; from 1912 to 1919 he was professor of English at the Royal Military College, Sandhurst; and during the same period he lectured on history at the Staff College, Camberley. From 1919 to 1921 he was a lecturer in the school of English language and literature at Oxford, and in 1921 he accepted the chair of English literature at Queen's University, Kingston, Ontario. Illness compelled him to resign this post in the spring of 1923 and to return to England. He died at Torquay 20 June, within a month of his return.

Seccombe married in 1896 Elizabeth Jane, daughter of Henry Goddard, farmer, of St. Mary Bourne, Hampshire, and had a son and two daughters.

[*The Times*, 21 June 1923; *The Bookman*, July 1923; private information; personal knowledge.] E. I. Carlyle.

SEYMOUR, Sir EDWARD HOBART (1840–1929), admiral of the fleet, born at Kinwarton, Warwickshire, 30 April 1840, was the second son of the Rev. Richard Seymour, rector of Kinwarton, by his wife, Frances, third daughter of Charles Smith, M.P., of Suttons, Essex. He was grandson of Rear-Admiral Sir Michael Seymour [q.v.], first baronet, and nephew of Admiral Sir Michael Seymour [q.v.]. He was sent to school at Radley, then under the headmastership of the Rev. W. B. Heathcote, where among his schoolfellows were two other future admirals, Lord Walter Talbot Kerr and Lord Charles Thomas Montagu-Douglas-Scott. Seymour had little difficulty in choosing his profession: 'As soon as I had sense enough to form a real wish, it was to go to sea.' Having been offered a nomination for the royal navy, he was sent to Eastman's Naval Academy at Southsea in the autumn of 1852, and two months later passed the entrance examination at the Royal Naval College, Portsmouth. A sum in the rule of three and a 'dictation' of twenty lines from the *Spectator* comprised the test. The next day he joined the *Encounter*, screw corvette. He served in her for eight months and was then appointed to the *Terrible*, in the Mediterranean, a paddle-wheel frigate of 21 guns, which was one of the ships of the allied fleet which was sent to make a demonstration in the Black Sea in January 1854. In the *Terrible* Seymour sailed for Odessa on the declaration of war with Russia in the following April, and thereafter he served in all the operations in the Black Sea until the final evacuation of the Crimea in 1856.

At the end of the War in 1857, Seymour, still a midshipman, was appointed to the *Calcutta*, flagship of his uncle, Sir Michael Seymour, on the China station. He took passage in the sloop *Cruiser*, and his experience in that vessel he afterwards described as 'a first-rate specimen of how youngsters were disregarded and neglected as to their instruction or care of any sort'. He reached China in time to take part in the operations which resulted from the *Arrow* incident [see Parkes, Sir Harry Smith]. Canton was being blockaded and an attack upon a Chinese fleet of about a hundred junks was in preparation. Seymour took part in the attack, during which the launch on board of which he was serving was sunk by a round shot. After the destruction of the fleet of junks the expedition moved up the Canton river to take the city, and Seymour served with the battery of the naval brigade; the other midshipman of the battery was (Sir) Arthur Knyvet Wilson [q.v.], afterwards admiral of the fleet. After the capture of Canton (December 1857) the squadron moved to the gulf of Pechili in order to get in touch with the Chinese government at Peking. Seymour took part in the severe engagement in which the mouth of the Peiho river, protected by the Taku forts, was forced (May 1858). This was his last service in that war, for shortly afterwards he was invalided home as a result of sunstroke.

On his return to England Seymour passed his examinations and was promoted mate (1859). Hearing that war had again broken out in China, he applied for a ship of that station and sailed for the East in the frigate *Impérieuse*. In Rhio Straits, on the way out, he went overboard to rescue a seaman in waters infested with sharks, and for this exploit he received the silver medal of the Royal Humane Society.

The commander-in-chief on the China station, Sir James Hope [q.v.], having a blank commission for a lieutenant, gave it to Seymour and took him into his flagship, the *Chesapeake*. In her, Seymour took part in the combined attack by British and French forces on the Taku forts in September 1860. An expedition up the Yang-tse river in a flotilla of light craft and paddle-wheel vessels gave him a new experience; he served first as executive officer, and later was given command of the paddle-steamer *Waterman* on the Canton river. He returned to the flagship in 1861 and took part in the operations against the Tai-ping rebels (1862), in the capture of Ningpo and Kahding, commanding small-arm parties. In 1863 he returned to England. He was now twenty-three, and had seen ten years' continuous active service, afloat and ashore.

On his return to England Seymour served for three years as flag-lieutenant to his uncle, Sir Michael Seymour, commander-in-chief at Portsmouth. He then received a 'haul-down' promotion to commander at the age of twenty-six (1866). Posts for commanders were few, and Seymour was on half pay for two years. Anxious to take part in a projected Arctic expedition, he took a cruise in northern waters in a Peterhead whaler, in order to gain experience of the ice. In 1868 he was appointed to the coastguard in Ireland, a position which, although enjoyable, was uncongenial to one whose whole desire was to serve at sea. In June 1869 he obtained his wish as commander of the gunboat *Growler* on the West coast of Africa. In the course of operations on the Congo in 1870 he was shot in the leg. The wound was severe and he was invalided: consequently, when he applied in 1875 for the command of the *Discovery* in the Polar expedition under (Sir) George Nares, he was rejected on medical grounds.

An enforced leisure of eighteen months on half pay was used by Seymour to improve his French by visiting France and Switzerland. In January 1872 he was given command of the paddle-wheel dispatch vessel *Vigilant* for service in the Channel fleet. In March 1873, at the age of thirty-three, he was promoted to post captain. A further period on shore followed, but caused him no deep regret. He spent a year at the Royal Naval College and then travelled in France and Italy. Normally, officers at that time spent at least five years on half pay on promotion, but the Admiralty, taking into consideration Seymour's loss of the command of the *Discovery* in the Arctic expedition, appointed him at his own request to the troopship *Orontes*. Three years' experience, in his own words, 'greatly enlarged my knowledge of that seemingly volatile yet really constant element called "human nature"'. Although he considered that 'trooping was not proper naval work', he saw value in it for the contact which it promoted between the services.

In 1879 Seymour found himself once more on half pay, and used the opportunity to study at the torpedo school and, as before, to travel abroad and refresh his knowledge of French. His service in combined operations with foreign officers in his early days, and later in China as commander-in-chief, impressed him greatly with the need for naval officers to have a knowledge of foreign languages. 'I should make it a rule', he wrote in his memoirs, 'that no boy might become a naval cadet unless he could hold an ordinary conversation in at least one foreign language.' In April 1880 Seymour commissioned the cruiser *Iris* in the Mediterranean, and in the following July joined the fleet commanded by Sir Beauchamp Seymour (afterwards Lord Alcester, q.v.). When the rioting took place at Alexandria in July 1882, Seymour was detached to guard the Suez Canal. Later, he dismantled the forts on the Rosetta mouth of the Nile. In November he succeeded Captain J. A. Fisher (afterwards Lord Fisher) in command of the battleship *Inflexible*; he hauled down his pennant in February 1885. Three months later, when war threatened with Russia, he was placed in command of the Cunard liner *Oregon*, commissioned as an auxiliary cruiser—an experience which convinced him that the fighting value of such vessels is very small.

Ten months on half pay followed. From May 1886 to December 1887 Seymour served as flag-captain to Admiral Sir George Willes, commander-in-chief at Portsmouth, and was then made assistant to the admiral-superintendent of naval reserves; this post he held until his promotion to flag rank at the age of forty-nine (1889). A long period of half pay was then employed in again visiting foreign countries: he travelled in France, Russia, the West Indies, and the United States. In July 1892 he hoisted his flag for the first time on board the *Swiftsure* for the annual manœuvres, after which he became second-in-command of the Channel squadron with his flag on board the *Anson*. It fell to him to take part in the raising of the *Howe* when she grounded at Ferrol, but apart from that particular service the command gave him less work than his energetic mind required. More active work followed when he was appointed, for three years, admiral-superintendent of the reserves.

In December 1897 Seymour was appointed commander-in-chief on the China station. Service there was peaceful until the Boxer rising in 1900. On 31 May he received news from the British minister, Sir Claude Macdonald, that the situation at Peking was precarious. Having already detached a small force for the defence of the legations, Seymour proceeded at once to the Taku forts. A naval force of ships of several nations shortly assembled, of which, as senior admiral, Seymour assumed command. At a consultation with the foreign commanders it was decided to form a naval brigade under the command of Seymour, to march, if necessary, to Peking. Matters moved fast. Immediate help was urgently called for from the legations on 9 June; the next day the brigade—a mixed force of 2,000 marines and bluejackets—was landed, and a sharp encounter with the Boxers took place on the 11 June at Lang Fang, about half way to Peking. Seymour then found himself unable to proceed. He was faced by considerable forces, the railway was cut, and he had no other means of transport. He held on for a week, but was then forced to retire on Tientsin, his short-rationed force harassed by the enemy. At Hsika, an important arsenal, he was attacked by regulars of the Chinese army. He stormed the arsenal and there defended himself against continued assaults until relieved by a body of Russian troops, when he withdrew his brigade and left the operations in the hands of military forces. Seymour's conduct throughout these difficult operations was highly commended, and his command was extended for a further six months. In March 1901 he was promoted to admiral and returned to England, hauling down his flag on 21 August.

In 1902 Seymour accompanied the Duke of Connaught on his mission to Madrid for the coronation of King Alfonso XIII. In the same year he served on Sir Edward Grey's committee on the manning of the navy. In 1903 he was appointed to the command at Devonport, which he held until February 1905, when he was made admiral of the fleet. In accordance with custom, he would have then hauled down his flag, but an exception was made on account of his distinguished service, and he kept his flag flying for another month. In 1906 Seymour accompanied Prince Arthur of Connaught on his state visit to Japan, and in 1909 he had the unusual honour of re-hoisting the flag of an admiral of the fleet on board the *Inflexible* when he commanded a squadron sent to Boston, Massachusetts, for the Hudson-Fulton celebrations. He retired in 1910 and took no further part in public affairs. He died at his home at Maidenhead 2 March 1929. His honours included the Order of Merit (1902), the G.C.B. (1901), and the G.C.V.O. (1906); he was a privy councillor (1909), and received the honorary degree of LL.D. from the university of Cambridge.

Seymour was a man of a singularly broad and humane outlook, with a particular capacity for appreciating the point of view of others; this contributed largely to the harmony of his relations with foreign officers serving under him. He was widely read and a good linguist. He described his services with great modesty and a total lack of self-consciousness in *My Naval Career and Travels* (1911). He was unmarried.

There are portraits of Seymour by H. G. Herkomer (1906) and by P. F. Spence (1907).

A cartoon of him by 'Spy' appeared in *Vanity Fair* 31 October 1901.

[Admiralty records; Sir E. H. Seymour, *My Naval Career and Travels*, 1911; private information.] H. W. Richmond.

SHACKLETON, Sir ERNEST HENRY (1874–1922), explorer, was born at Kilkee, co. Kildare, 15 February 1874, the second child and eldest son of Henry Shackleton, M.D., by his wife, Henrietta Letitia Sophia, daughter of Henry John Gavan, inspector-general of police in Ceylon and formerly of the Royal Irish Constabulary. Shackleton's descent from north of England Quaker stock on his father's side and his Irish ancestry on his mother's may have accounted for the mingling of caution, perseverance, reckless courage, and strong idealism which were his leading characteristics. After private education in Ireland he was sent to a preparatory school at Sydenham, and thence to Dulwich College (1887–1890), where he was described as 'backward for his age'. In 1890 he went to sea as an apprentice in the mercantile marine, serving in the *Hoghton Tower*, a sailing ship of the White Star line, until 1894 when he transferred to steamers of the Shire line, qualifying as first mate in 1896 and master in 1898. Shackleton then joined the Union Castle line, and when third officer in the *Tintagel Castle* collaborated with Dr. W. McLean in a book entitled *O.H.M.S.* (1900), describing experiences in carrying troops to the South

African War. In 1901 he became a sub-lieutenant in the Royal Naval Reserve.

Desire for adventure, not unmixed with the hope of fame, led Shackleton to apply successfully for a post on the National Antarctic expedition under Commander Robert Falcon Scott [q.v.] in the *Discovery* in 1901. As junior officer, an appointment due largely to his knowledge of sails, he took a leading part in the expedition and was one of the two men chosen to accompany the leader in his long southern sledge journey over the Ross barrier to lat. 82° 16′ 33″ S. On the return journey, although weakened by scurvy, he refused to give in and struggled back on foot with the others. After being invalided home in the relief ship *Morning* in 1903, Shackleton left the sea as a profession and took up various engagements, each of which in turn attracted his optimistic mind and in turn was abandoned. From 1904 to 1905 he was secretary of the Royal Scottish Geographical Society where his enterprise was quickly felt. After standing unsuccessfully for parliament as liberal-unionist candidate at Dundee in January 1906, he entered Messrs. W. Beardmore's engineering works in Glasgow, but was already busy maturing plans for returning to the Antarctic. One of his main objects was to reach the South Pole, but he laid stress also on the importance of exploring the Barrier, discovering its southern limits, and solving the problem of its origin, as well as tracing to the south the lofty mountain ranges discovered by Scott, ascending the high plateau to the west and reaching the South Magnetic Pole. He hoped also to explore King Edward Land.

His plans, announced in 1907, showed characteristic daring in conception with admirable foresight in methods, equipment, and choice of staff. Funds were obtained largely by guarantees to be redeemed on the return of the expedition by the proceeds of lectures and the narrative of the voyage, a financial undertaking which appealed to Shackleton's sanguine temperament. Shackleton sailed in the small whaler *Nimrod* in August 1907, and reached the Ross barrier in the following January. Forced by pack ice to abandon his intention to land on King Edward Land, he made his base in McMurdo Sound, and accompanied by Dr. Eric Marshall, Lieutenant Jameson Boyd Adams, R.N.R., and Frank Wild, R.N., by way of the Barrier and the Beardmore glacier, which he discovered, succeeded in reaching lat. 88° 23′ S. on the Antarctic plateau (9 January 1909). The expedition also sent a party under Professor (Sir) T. W. Edgeworth David to the South Magnetic Pole, which was reached 16 January 1909, and another to the summit of Mount Erebus (13,200 ft.), which was gained 10 March 1908. On his return in March 1909 Shackleton was the hero of the hour and enjoyed to the full his well-merited popularity. He received the C.V.O. and a knighthood, was elected a younger brother of Trinity House, and was awarded a score of medals from the leading geographical societies of the world, including a special gold medal from the Royal Geographical Society and the Livingstone gold medal of the Royal Scottish Geographical Society. Parliament voted £20,000 to defray the liabilities of the expedition, and Shackleton paid other costs by a prolonged lecturing tour in Europe and America. The expedition is described in his *The Heart of the Antarctic* (1909).

After various attempts to enter business in his persistent dream of making a fortune with which to endow his family, Shackleton began to plan an even more ambitious Antarctic expedition which was to solve the problem of the extent of the Weddell Sea and the relation of the ranges of Graham Land with those of Victoria Land. A proposal to cross the Antarctic continent with this end in view had been made in April 1908 by William Speirs Bruce [q.v.], who had, however, failed to raise the funds required. Shackleton was more successful, and his scheme for an imperial trans-Antarctic expedition involved the use of two ships, one, the *Endurance*, to land a sledging party in the Weddell Sea and another, the *Aurora*, to land a depot-laying party at McMurdo Sound in the Ross Sea to meet the trans-polar party. Funds were supplied chiefly by (Sir) James Caird, (Dame) Janet Stancomb-Wills, and a government grant of £10,000. All was ready in August 1914, when war broke out. Shackleton's offer to the Admiralty of his ships and men for war service was refused and he was told to proceed. Reaching South Georgia, the *Endurance* left for the south in what proved to be a bad ice year. Bruce's Coats Land was passed and Caird Coast was discovered (11 January 1915) when the ship was beset on 18 January in heavy pack ice in lat. 76° 34′ S. long. 31° 30′ W. After drifting for nine months she was crushed in the ice on 27 October 1915 about 200 miles from the nearest land and 1,000 miles from human help. Shackleton now showed his supreme qualities of leadership. In the face of difficulty and danger he was always at his best. Proceeding by sledges and boats the party eventually reached Elephant Island on 15 April 1916 and camped on the small ice-free area of a forbidding land. Realizing that no search expedition would be likely to visit Elephant Island, Shackleton determined to reach South Georgia in an effort to bring help. With five companions he made a voyage of 800 miles in a twenty-two foot boat through some of the stormiest seas in the world, crossed the unknown lofty interior of South Georgia, and reached a Norwegian whaling station on the north coast. After three attempts in different vessels Shackleton succeeded (30 August 1916) in rescuing the rest of the *Endurance* party and bringing them to South America. He then went to New Zealand and sailed in the *Aurora* to rescue his Ross Sea party. An account of the whole expedition is given by Shackleton in *South* (1919).

In 1917 Shackleton was sent by the British government on a special mission to South America in order to explain to neutral countries the war aims of the Allies. On his return he spent the winter of 1918–1919 with the North Russian expeditionary force, with the rank of major, organizing the winter equipment. In February 1919 he resigned his commission and turned again to various commercial projects, none of which led him far. A plan to explore the Beaufort Sea under Canadian government auspices did not mature, and once more he planned an Antarctic expedition. This expedition, largely financed by John Quiller Rowett, was designed chiefly to explore the little known region round Enderby Land. The *Quest* sailed in September 1921, and after several delays due to faulty engines, reached South Georgia on 4 January 1922. On the following morning Shackleton died suddenly of *angina pectoris*. He was buried at the whaling station at Grytviken on South Georgia Island. On 2 March a memorial service was held in St. Paul's Cathedral and was attended by King George V and Queen Mary.

In addition to his knighthood and C.V.O., Shackleton received the O.B.E. (military) in 1919. He held the Polar medal with three clasps and many foreign decorations. The university of Glasgow conferred on him the honorary degree of LL.D. in 1914. A statue of Shackleton by Charles Sargeant Jagger was placed as a memorial outside the Royal Geographical Society's house in Exhibition Road, South Kensington. His name is perpetuated in Mount Shackleton in the Canadian Rockies, Shackleton Inlet and Shackleton Ice Shelf in the Antarctic, and Mount Shackleton in East Greenland.

Shackleton married in 1904 Emily Mary, daughter of Charles Dorman, of Wadhurst, Sussex, and had two sons and one daughter.

Shackleton found in polar exploration an outlet for his restless energy, love of adventure, and zest for life. In the more ordered walks of civilization his lack of convention, his intolerance of shams, and his impetuous candour made him less easy to satisfy. His success as an explorer lay in the boldness of his conceptions, his resourcefulness, and his good leadership. Apart from his considerable discoveries and the scientific results of his expeditions, he left his mark on Antarctic exploration by his adoption of a new technique in sledge travelling and his abandonment of many of the old traditions of polar exploration.

A cartoon of Shackleton appeared in *Vanity Fair* 6 October 1909.

[H. R. Mill, *The Life of Sir Ernest Shackleton*, 1923; R. F. Scott, *The Voyage of the 'Discovery'*, 1905; F. R. Worsley, *Endurance*, 1931; F. Wild, *Shackleton's Last Voyage*, 1923; *Geographical Journal*, March 1923.]

R. N. Rudmose Brown.

SHANDON, Baron (1857–1930), lord chancellor of Ireland. [See O'Brien, Ignatius John.]

SHANNON, Sir JAMES JEBUSA (1862–1923), painter, was born at Auburn in the state of New York 3 February 1862, the third son of Patrick Shannon, a contractor and railway builder. Both his parents were Irish. At the age of sixteen (1878), having received some slight tuition in art, Shannon left America for England, where he studied for three years at the National Art Training Schools, South Kensington (afterwards the Royal College of Art), his teacher in painting being (Sir) Edward John Poynter [q.v.]. Shannon's record as a student was a creditable one; and in 1881, at the early age of nineteen, he received an unusual honour: his portrait of the Hon. Horatia Stopford, maid-of-honour to Queen Victoria, painted for the queen, was exhibited at the Royal Academy by royal command. This was Shannon's first appearance at Burlington House, where he subsequently became a regular contributor to the Academy exhibitions, eventually gaining a very widespread clientele for his portraits. His first outstanding success was his full-length portrait of Mr. Henry Vigne, master of the Epping Forest harriers, in hunting dress, exhibited at the Grosvenor Gallery Summer Exhibition in 1888.

Shannon's portraits constitute the bulk of his production, and while certainly not the work of a master of the first rank, possess undeniable qualities of colour and arrangement. In style, like so many other artists of his generation, he had a tendency towards what may be termed a modified impressionism. He received many medals at exhibitions held on the Continent and in the United States. He was elected A.R.A. in 1897 and R.A. in 1909, his diploma work being a portrait of a lady with a dog, entitled 'Black and Silver'. He was a foundation member of the New English Art Club (1885), although his association with it did not last long; and he held successfully the office of president of the Royal Society of Portrait Painters from 1910 until his death. At the Tate Gallery Shannon is represented by three pictures, among them being 'The Flower Girl' (exhibited at the Royal Academy in 1901, and purchased in the same year by the Chantrey trustees), and a portrait of Phil May (exhibited at the Royal Academy in 1902, purchased by the Chantrey trustees in 1923).

Shannon, who was knighted in 1922, died in London 6 March 1923. He married in 1886 Florence Mary Cartwright. She survived him together with their only child, a daughter. A memorial collection of his works was hung in the Burlington House Winter Exhibition in 1928; this collection included (No. 38) a self-portrait of Shannon, lent by Lady Shannon.

[*The Times*, 7 March 1923; Kitty Shannon, *For My Children*, 1933; Mentle Fielding, *Dictionary of American Painters, Sculptors, and Engravers*, 1926; Algernon Graves, *The Royal Academy of Arts, a complete dictionary of contributors and their work*, vol. vii, 1906; subsequent Royal Academy Exhibition Catalogues, including that of the Memorial Exhibition of 1928.] T. Borenius.

SHARP, CECIL JAMES (1859–1924), musician, author, and collector and arranger of English folk-songs and dances, was born in London 22 November 1859, the eldest son of John James Sharp, slate-merchant, by his wife, Jane Bloyd. He was educated at Uppingham School and at Clare College, Cambridge. He had inherited a love of music from his father, and in his early days had studied music, practically and theoretically. While at Cambridge he entered fully into the musical activities of the university. After taking his degree (a third class in the mathematical tripos), Sharp went in 1882 to Adelaide, where he held the legal post of associate to the chief justice of South Australia. He was also during this period assistant organist of the cathedral and conductor of the Philharmonic Society. From 1889 to 1891 he was co-director of the Adelaide College of Music. While in Australia he composed two light operas and some smaller pieces. Early in 1892 he returned to England. In 1893 he married Constance Dorothea (died 1928), daughter of Priestley Birch, of Woolston, near Kingsbridge, Devon, and had one son and three daughters. He became conductor of the Finsbury Choral Association (1893–1897), music master at Ludgrove School (1893–1910), and principal of the Hampstead Conservatoire of Music (1896–1905). From 1910 to 1912 he held no official position. From 1912 to 1924 he was director of the English Folk-Dance Society. From 1919 to 1923 he held the post of occasional inspector to the Board of Education with special reference to the teaching of folk-dance. In 1923 he received the honorary degree of Mus.M. of Cambridge University. He died at Hampstead 23 June 1924, after a short illness.

Such are the external facts of Sharp's career, but interest centres in the last twenty-five years of his life and in the gradual growth under his influence of the knowledge of the English traditional arts of music and dancing. In 1902 his experience as singing-teacher at Ludgrove School led him to prepare and publish *A Book of British Song*. This contains both traditional melodies (gleaned from William Chappell's *Popular Music of the Olden Time*, 1838, and other printed sources) and 'composed' music of a simple kind. It was probably his work on this book which led Sharp to realize the essential importance of traditional art, and in 1903 he decided to find out for himself how far traditional music survived in England and what was its quality. His first experiment was made in September 1903 at Hambridge, in Somerset, where, with the help of the vicar, the Rev. C. L. Marson, he made an exhaustive search of the neighbourhood with surprising results. A selection from the songs which he discovered, called *Folk-Songs from Somerset*, was published in 1904 and aroused great interest. That such beautiful and vital melodies should have been sung for generations in 'unmusical' England was indeed a remarkable discovery.

Opinion had, however, been ripening. (Sir) Hubert Parry [q.v.] had in 1893 published his *Art of Music*, in which he applied the theory of evolution to music and showed the line of succession from the simplest of folk-tunes to the most elaborate symphony. Already, also, a certain number of traditional melodies had been collected. In 1898 the Folk-Song Society had been founded, and in 1904 Sharp was elected on to its committee. Nevertheless, his ideas were not cordially welcomed by the leading members of the society, whose ideal was that of quiet research, while Sharp was above all a teacher and a propagandist. He used scholarship and research as a means to an end; for he believed in folk-song, not as a relic of the past, but as a thing of living beauty. These simple and lovely melodies have awakened in thousands of people a musical consciousness hitherto dormant. In 1906, after the Board of Education had published a list of recommended songs for children in which no distinction was made between songs which were traditional and those which were merely popular, Sharp vainly urged the Folk-Song Society to make a protest.

Meanwhile Sharp persistently pressed the claims of folk-song by lectures, articles, and letters to the newspapers, thereby arousing some bitter opposition. In 1907 he tabulated his experiences in his book *English Folk-Song: some Conclusions*. The theories set out therein are not new, nor do they pretend to be so. They are the logical conclusions of the evolutionary theory of music and that of the communal authorship of folk-song already vaguely formulated by others. It should be noted that Sharp claimed communal authorship, but not communal origin, for the folk-song. He held, together with Jacob Grimm and others, that folk-music, developing as it does by purely oral tradition without being stereotyped by print or writing, tends to evolve as it passes through the minds of generations of singers; that therefore no individual singer can at any given moment be said to be the author of the song, but that it truly represents the communal mind of those to whom it belongs. Moreover, he held that the law of the survival of the fittest applies here, and that the process is one not of disintegration but of evolution.

All this time Sharp was collecting more songs and publishing the cream of them in further volumes of *Folk-Songs from Somerset* (five series, 1904, 1905, 1906, 1908, and 1909). His example fired others, and it soon appeared that there was hardly a village in England where this native art did not survive.

Sharp's final adventure in search of songs was his visits to the Southern Appalachian Mountains in North Carolina, Tennessee, Kentucky, and Virginia in 1916 to 1918. In these remote parts of the United States there lives a people descended from early English colonists segregated by natural surroundings from the rest of the world. They have preserved the customs, speech, and above all the songs, which they brought with them from England in the early eighteenth century. When Sharp heard of this community he characteristically determined to get at the facts of the alleged survivals, and he paid several visits (lasting forty-six weeks in all) to the Appalachian Mountains, although he was in indifferent health and had to make his investigations in circumstances of the most primitive discomfort.

Sharp noted down altogether nearly five thousand tunes and variants, about one-third being collected in the Appalachian Mountains. Of these he published some five hundred for use with pianoforte accompaniment, and a further thousand are printed in the *Journal of the Folk-Song Society* and other scientific publications. The rest remain in his manuscript books which he left to Clare College, Cambridge. These figures conclusively dispel the idea that Sharp imagined that all folk-songs were of equal value.

The other main subject of Sharp's activities was the folk-dance, in which he was practically first in the field. This was a much more difficult problem than the folk-song, for it takes only one man to sing a song while it takes six to dance a morris, and by the time Sharp began to collect there were few complete morris 'sides' left. Most of the dances had, therefore, to be reconstructed from the explanations and partial demonstrations of old and infirm men. Further, there is no recognized notation of the dance as there is of the song; so the only thing to do was to invent a notation for the purpose. Sharp's first dance researches, dating from 1905 (he had previously, in 1899, noted the tunes of several morris-dances from Headington, Oxfordshire), were in the Midlands, the home of the morris-dance.

In 1910 he turned his attention to the corresponding ceremonial dance of northern England, the sword-dance. Less artistically important, but, as it proved, socially more far-reaching, was the country dance. This is not a ceremonial dance for experts, but a form of social enjoyment; moreover it is danced by both sexes, whereas the morris and sword dances are traditionally danced by men only. Sharp collected some examples of the country dance from living tradition, but most of those which he published were transcribed by him from the seventeen editions of John Playford's *Dancing Master* (1650–1728). Here his unfailing instinct enabled him to select those dances which reflect the spirit of tradition, even though some of them have no doubt been consciously worked on by individuals.

Sharp was, of course, not content merely to collect; he also wanted to teach, and between 1907 and 1914 he published over three hundred dances with their tunes. He recognized, however, that these things cannot be learned from books only. In 1905 he had come into contact with Mary Neal and her Espérance club for working-girls in Cumberland Market, London; and it was here that practical folk-dance teaching was first undertaken. For a time Sharp and Miss Neal worked together; but the object of the Espérance club was social regeneration rather than artistic excellence. Miss Neal held that Sharp's interpretation of the dances was formal and pedantic and robbed them of the joyousness which it was the object of her club to encourage: Sharp considered that the joy of doing a good thing well was the ultimate object to be secured. So the two parted company, and Sharp found new allies in the Chelsea College of Physical Training, where he established a school of folk-dance in 1909.

In 1911 Sharp founded the English Folk-Dance Society, the object of which was to 'preserve and promote the practice of English folk-dances in their true traditional forms'. From this time forward his life became that of an inspiring teacher and an efficient and autocratic organizer, and with the exception of a few flying visits to discover new folk-songs and dances and the expeditions to America already recorded, the rest of his life was devoted to the society which he founded. The English Folk-Dance Society prospered far beyond his expectations, and since his death it has gone on growing. In 1931 the membership was 1,689, besides fifty-two local branches (including two in the United States) with a membership of over twenty-two thousand, and early in 1932 an amalgamation with the Folk-Song Society was effected.

On Sharp's death a fund was opened to build a house where his memory could be kept alive by preserving, practising, and teaching folk-songs and dances. In June 1930 Cecil Sharp House in Regent's Park Road, London, was opened, and on its foundation-stone are inscribed the words: 'This building is erected in memory of Cecil Sharp who restored to the English people the songs and dances of their country.'

Sharp won the admiration of all who came into contact with him, even those whom his uncompromising methods of controversy had antagonized before they got to know him. His absorption in his mission did not prevent him from taking an intelligent interest in all that was going on in the world, about which he always had something pregnant to say. In politics he inclined to the Fabian socialist view. His favourite composers were Beethoven, Wagner, and Handel. He suffered all his life from ill-health, but this only added to the energy with which he worked for the causes that he loved.

A portrait by Sir William Rothenstein hangs in the library at Cecil Sharp House.

[*The Times*, 27 June 1924; *Journal* of the Folk-Song Society, December 1924; *English Folk-Dance Society News*, November 1924; A. H. Fox Strangways, *Cecil Sharp*, 1933; private information; personal knowledge.]

R. Vaughan Williams.

SHATTOCK, SAMUEL GEORGE (1852–1924), pathologist, was born 3 November 1852 in Mornington Street, Regent's Park, London, the son of Samuel Chapman Betty, chemist, by his wife, Jane Betty, née Brown. Some thirty years later he changed his name to Shattock. He married Emily Lucy Wood, and had three sons and one daughter. He died at Wimbledon 11 May 1924.

Shattock was educated at University College, first at the boys' school and afterwards as a medical student, qualifying in 1874. After a few years as curator of the museum at his own school, he moved to St. Thomas's Hospital, where he rearranged the museum and was one of the teachers of pathology for the rest of his life. Shattock's connexion with the Royal College of Surgeons began informally soon after he graduated. In 1897 he became curator of the pathological museum and he gave it devoted service for twenty-seven years, reorganizing the whole collection on improved and original lines. From 1880 onwards he was one of the mainstays of the Pathological Society of London and its successor, the section of pathology of the Royal Society of Medicine, editing its *Transactions* and *Proceedings* for many years and himself contributing about 150 papers. He was elected a fellow of University College in 1910 and a fellow of the Royal Society in 1917.

For forty years Shattock was one of the chief influences in London which moulded the course which pathology was to take in a time of transition. As he came to maturity, it was just beginning to be recognized that pathology was a science with its own methods and results and that it could no longer be dealt with satisfactorily as a casual interest of men engaged in medical practice. Its scope was also being greatly enlarged by the development of bacteriology and by the appreciation of the importance of experimental and chemical methods of investigation. Shattock was one of the first to give his whole time to pathology and was able to play an important part in this revolution of outlook. He was a devoted and industrious student who made it his first business in life to have a scholar's knowledge of his subject, and he became the most erudite pathologist of his time. He had also a catholic conception of the content of pathology: he was an acknowledged authority on morbid anatomy, and he investigated the virulence of bacteria, the healing of wounds in plants, the microbic origin of cancer, and secondary sexual characters. His teaching was clear and dramatic, and although he was too aloof to make intimate personal contact with his students, his influence was durable.

Shattock was a strangely shy and reserved man with curious fads and habits. His immense knowledge was cordially at the disposal of any serious student, but apart from his work he was a difficult man to know. He was a devout Roman Catholic, and the posthumous publication of his *Thoughts on Religion* (1926) revealed an aspect of his life of which few of his associates had been aware.

[*The Lancet*, 1924, vol. i, p. 1028; *British Medical Journal* 1924, vol. i, p. 889; *Proceedings* of the Royal Society, vol. xcvi, B, 1924; *Journal of Pathology and Bacteriology*, vol. xxvii, 1924 (portrait); personal knowledge.]

A. E. Boycott.

SHAUGHNESSY, THOMAS GEORGE, first Baron Shaughnessy, of Montreal, and of Ashford, co. Limerick (1853–1923), Canadian railway administrator, was born 6 October 1853 at Milwaukee, Wisconsin, U.S.A. He was the son of Thomas Shaughnessy, an officer in the Milwaukee detective police, a native of Ashford, co. Limerick. His mother was also of Irish birth. He was educated in the common schools of Milwaukee, where he showed a special aptitude for mathematics. In 1869 he obtained employment in the purchasing department of the Milwaukee and St. Paul Railway. For some time he studied law privately, hoping to escape into the legal profession; but as his energy and enterprise gained him promotion, he became reconciled to his calling. Shaughnessy attracted the favourable notice of (Sir) William Cornelius Van Horne [q.v.], the general superintendent of the railway company, at whose instance he was in 1879 appointed its general storekeeper. In 1882, however, Van Horne, now general manager of the lately formed Canadian Pacific Railway company, persuaded Shaughnessy to accept the post of general purchasing agent to that undertaking. He thereupon settled in Montreal, where he resided for the rest of his life.

During Shaughnessy's first years in Canada the financial situation of the Canadian Pacific Railway was often extremely precarious, and he rendered invaluable service in placating and reassuring alarmed and importunate creditors. Van Horne's biographer, Walter Vaughan, goes so far as to say that in the early months of 1885, when the very difficult section of the line along Lake Superior was being built 'on faith and credit', 'the one bright spot in the darkness was the success of the indefatigable and resourceful Shaughnessy'. In 1885 he was appointed assistant-general manager; in 1891 he became vice-president, and in 1899 president in succession to Van Horne, who had relied much on his business acumen and organizing ability.

The period of Shaughnessy's presidency saw the Canadian Pacific at the height of its prosperity and renown. It is true that the general condition of Canada during the first years of the twentieth century was strongly in its favour; but much of its progress and success was undoubtedly due to Shaughnessy. He seldom missed a chance of applying the policy of his predecessors to new ventures. Perhaps his most notable achievement was the creation, partly by purchase, partly by new construction, of the company's Atlantic fleet, which for the first time attracted large numbers of well-to-do passengers to the St. Lawrence route to North America. On the collapse of the long-continued boom in 1913—a misfortune aggravated by the outbreak of the European War—Shaughnessy showed that his old resourcefulness had not left him, and his shrewd and daring financial measures enabled the company to weather the crisis with astonishing success and, alone among the important railways of Canada, to continue as a private undertaking. He resigned the presidency in 1918, becoming chairman of the board of directors.

Shaughnessy was knighted in 1901 and created K.C.V.O. in 1907. In 1916 he was raised to the peerage of the United Kingdom. In 1911 he received the honorary degree of D.C.L. from Trinity College, Dublin. The public honours bestowed on him were a recognition of his contribution to the economic development of Canada. He would never accept any political post or associate himself definitely with any political party. Soon after he joined the staff of the Canadian Pacific Railway he was naturalized as a British subject, and in his later years his Canadian patriotism led him now and then to take a strong line on political questions. He was, for instance, very hostile to the liberal government on the Reciprocity issue of 1911, although when he cried, 'Fix the channels of Canadian trade eastward and westward', his critics naturally pointed out that such advice was in striking accord with the interests of the shareholders of the Canadian Pacific Railway. During the European War Shaughnessy turned his experience and energy to the promotion of his country's cause: he was freely consulted by both the Dominion and the Imperial governments; he rendered very valuable service in negotiations between the British government and big financial interests in America, and his counsel carried especial weight with Mr. Lloyd George's Coalition ministry.

Shaughnessy married in 1880 Elizabeth Bridget Nagle, of Milwaukee, by whom he had two sons and three daughters. He died at Montreal 10 December 1923 after a very short illness. He was succeeded as second baron by his elder son, William James (born 1883). His younger son was killed in the European War.

Although not obstinate or arrogant, Shaughnessy was wont to place great trust in his own judgement. He had a quick wit and a keen sense of humour. Despite the defects of his early education, he was a well-informed man and an omnivorous reader. He was fond of music, but he cared little for pictorial art. Much of his success was due to his faculty of detaching his mind from his work when business hours were over. For many years he habitually drank a pint of champagne with his dinner; he was fond of billiards and bridge; for some time he owned one or two race-horses; but he took no exercise whatever until, when quite elderly, he became interested in golf. His vigour was astonishing, and his health remained very good until a few hours before his death. In religion he was a Roman Catholic.

A cartoon of Shaughnessy by 'Spy' appeared in *Vanity Fair* 26 August 1908.

[Notices in the Montreal press; *Canadian Men and Women of the Time* (second edition), 1912; Walter Vaughan, *Sir William Van Horne*, 1920; private information.]

W. T. Waugh.

SHAW-LEFEVRE, GEORGE JOHN, Baron Eversley (1831–1928), statesman, the only son of Sir John George Shaw-Lefevre [q.v.], and nephew of Charles Shaw-Lefevre, Viscount Eversley [q.v.], was born in London 12 June 1831. His mother was Rachel Emily, daughter of Ichabod Wright, of Mapperley Hall, Nottingham, and sister of Ichabod Charles Wright [q.v.], the translator of Dante. From his father, a man of great ability, who was reputed to know fourteen languages, Shaw-Lefevre imbibed a keen interest in politics and a taste for foreign travel, as well as great industry, considerable powers of observation, and a memory which was especially retentive of curious and often grotesque stories about strange characters and persons of note whom he had met. Few could match his experience and knowledge of pubiic affairs. He had known personally—he was heard to say—thirteen prime ministers, seventeen lord chancellors, and seven archbishops of Canterbury. As clerk of the parliaments, his father was acquainted with most of the public men of his day, and thus from his boyhood young Shaw-Lefevre was familiar, like his friend and contemporary, Sir George Otto Trevelyan [q.v.], with political society. Like Trevelyan, he was by tradition and upbringing a whig, but like Trevelyan also, he rapidly developed strong liberal, and even radical, leanings. He was educated at Eton and at Trinity College Cambridge, taking his degree in 1853. In the previous year he carried the coronet at the Duke of Wellington's funeral.

After leaving Cambridge in the summer of 1853, Shaw-Lefevre visited the United States, and saw the slave market at Richmond, Virginia. In the following year he was called to the bar by the Inner Temple, and in the spring of 1855 went on circuit. In September 1855 he sailed in Sir Edward Colebrooke's yacht to the Crimea, taking with him an early form of photographic camera. His photographs from the lines before Sebastopol are still in the possession of his family. In 1857 Shaw-Lefevre rode on horseback from Vienna to Constantinople, and afterwards visited Athens. This journey gave him an abiding interest in the Eastern problem and in the declining fortunes of the Turkish Empire.

After contesting Winchester unsuccessfully at the general election of 1859, Shaw-Lefevre was elected member for Reading in the liberal interest in 1863, and held the seat until 1885. In the House of Commons he soon made his mark. His maiden speech, delivered in 1864—inspired by a then unfashionable sympathy for the North in the American Civil War—was a plea for the stopping of the *Alabama* before she left port. Most of his friends tried to dissuade him from his motion, but Cobden urged him to persevere. It was, of course, unsuccessful, although its wisdom and foresight were speedily proved. His second speech (March 1865) was directed against the fortification of Quebec. The motion, although defeated, eventually took effect, and the scheme was dropped. His third speech (also in 1865) aimed at establishing public rights over all commons. This was a principle for which he contended all his life, and he had the satisfaction in 1925 of seeing it embodied in a statute, although even then it was only applied to commons in urban districts.

On 19 July 1866 Shaw-Lefevre invited a number of friends to a meeting, at which it was decided to form a new society called the Commons Preservation Society, for the immediate purpose of organizing resistance to the threatened enclosure of commons. Among its first members were Edward North Buxton, John Stuart Mill, Thomas Hughes, Leslie Stephen, George Grote, Henry Fawcett, Thomas Farrer, and James Bryce. Shaw-Lefevre was appointed chairman, and held the office, with a few brief intervals, down to his death. To the exertions of this society England owes the preservation, from the enclosing landlord and the encroaching builder, of Hampstead Heath, Wimbledon Common, Epping Forest, and many other famous common lands. The Commons Preservation Society and its achievements constitute a lasting memorial to the industry and public spirit of its founder. His exertions in this cause never flagged. The story of what he accomplished is well told in his own book, *Commons, Forests, and Footpaths* (1894), which remains a standard work on the subject.

In the same year (April 1866) Shaw-Lefevre joined the government of Lord John Russell as civil lord of the Admiralty, but it fell two months later. His next success was in opposition, when, in 1868, he carried a resolution in favour of submitting the *Alabama* claims to arbitration. After the general election of 1868, Mr. Gladstone appointed him secretary to the Board of Trade, of which John Bright was president. After carrying the General Tramways Act (1870), he was transferred in 1871 to the Home Office as under-secretary, and later in that year to the Admiralty as secretary; this post he held until 1874, when Mr. Gladstone's first ministry fell.

On the formation of the second Gladstone administration in 1880, Shaw-Lefevre was appointed first commissioner of works, an office which gave him considerable scope, although it did not carry Cabinet rank. He was responsible for several important public works, including improvements at Hyde Park Corner and at the Tower of London, the restoration of the front of Westminster Hall, and the removal of the old Law Courts from Westminster to the new buildings in the Strand. After a long controversy with the Treasury and Office of Works, Shaw-Lefevre also succeeded, by personally arguing the case before Mr. Gladstone, in throwing open to the public a number of private enclosures in Regent's Park, thus affording access along the whole length of the lake. In 1883 he was appointed postmaster-general with a seat in the Cabinet. While in office he initiated the sixpenny telegram.

Probably the most bitter disappointment of Shaw-Lefevre's public career was his defeat, at Reading, in the general election of 1885, which wrecked his natural expectation of a seat in Mr. Gladstone's Home Rule Cabinet. A strong supporter of Home Rule for Ireland, he wrote several books and pamphlets on the subject. At the election of 1886 he was returned for Central Bradford, and retained the seat until 1895. In Mr. Gladstone's fourth administration (1892–1894) he was again appointed first commissioner of works, this time with a seat in the Cabinet. During his second term of office he obtained the queen's consent to the throwing open of Hampton Court Park, and also of Kew Palace, with consequent valuable additions to Kew Gardens. He was the only Cabinet minister who fully supported Mr. Gladstone's opposition in 1893–1894 to the increased naval estimates. After his own resignation in 1894, Mr. Gladstone regretted that he had not appointed Shaw-Lefevre, instead of Lord Spencer, first lord of the Admiralty. In that position, Shaw-Lefevre, whose passion for public economy and objection to increased armaments were as strong as Mr. Gladstone's, would indubitably not have acquiesced in the demands of the naval lords, and the sharp crisis which ended Mr. Gladstone's fourth administration, with disastrous consequences to the liberal party, would almost certainly have been avoided. In the brief administration of Lord Rosebery (1894–1895) Shaw-Lefevre remained in the Cabinet as president of the Local Government Board. In that capacity he took the initiative in the Equalization of Rates (London) Act (1894), and in a very useful measure providing that disused burial grounds should be converted into public gardens.

Like several of his colleagues, Shaw-Lefevre suffered defeat at the general election of 1895, and decided not to re-enter the House of Commons. His devotion to public administrative work, however, found scope on the London County Council. He was elected as a progressive for the Haggerston division in 1897, and acted as chairman of the improvements committee until 1901. In that capacity he brought about the Kingsway and Aldwych Street improvements and the extension of the Thames embankment to Lambeth bridge, as well as the removal of many slums.

In 1912 increasing deafness induced Shaw-Lefevre to retire to his country home, Abbotsworthy, near Kingsworthy, a pleasant seat on the Itchen, where he lived, with occasional visits to London, for the rest of his life. In 1906, at the instance of his old colleague, Sir Henry Campbell-Bannerman, he was raised to the peerage as Baron Eversley, of Old Ford; but he seldom attended the House of Lords or intervened in its debates.

In addition to his work for the Commons Preservation Society, Lord Eversley was a very active member of the Cobden Club, and took a leading part in the preparation of several of its publications, notably *Fact v. Fiction*, a reply to Joseph Chamberlain's Tariff Reform speeches, in 1904, and *The Burden of Armaments*, a plea for the reduction of military and naval expenditure, in 1905. During the European War his interests reverted to foreign policy, and in 1915 he published a book on *The Partitions of Poland*, and in 1917 another on *The Turkish Empire, its Growth and Decay*. He found diversion later in a series of reminiscences, which appeared in the *Cornhill Magazine*; and until a few weeks before his death, which took place at Abbotsworthy 19 April 1928, he retained a keen interest in politics, reading, or having read aloud to him, the daily newspapers and most of the important debates in Hansard. He kept up almost to the end a vigorous and animated correspondence on public affairs with friends who shared his views on public economy, fiscal policy, and other subjects.

Lord Eversley married in 1874 Lady Constance Emily (died 1929), only daughter of Henry John Moreton, third Earl of Ducie. They had no children, and on his death the barony became extinct.

Shaw-Lefevre was a statesman and administrator of extraordinary industry and public spirit. At one time in the 'sixties, he was spoken of as a future prime minister. That he did not fulfil these high expectations is perhaps attributable in part to a lack of personal magnetism, and to a certain self-absorption which alienated sympathy and prevented others from appreciating fully the value and real disinterestedness of his public work. It may be added that he never deserted, or failed to support, any of the principles, causes, and ideals with which his public life is associated. As a speaker and debater he was competent but not brilliant, and the same may be said of his style as a writer.

[Private information; personal knowledge.]

F. W. Hirst.

SHEARMAN, Sir MONTAGUE (1857–1930), judge, was born 7 April 1857 at Wimbledon, the second son of Montagu Shearman, solicitor, of Wimbledon, by his wife, Mary, daughter of Frederic Adam Catty, whose father, a royalist refugee from France, was French master at the Royal Military Academy, Woolwich. He went from Merchant Taylors' School, where he was head-monitor and captain of the rugby football XV in 1874–1875, with a scholarship to St. John's College, Oxford. At the university he was distinguished both as a scholar and as an athlete. He obtained first classes in classical moderations (1877) and in *literae humaniores* (1879). He played in the university rugby football XV both as a forward and three-quarter; he was president of the university athletic club in 1878 and represented the university between 1876 and 1879 in the hundred yards—the 'classic perfection' of his style was noted in 1876—the quarter-mile, and putting the weight; he was a good long jumper; and he rowed in his college eight. Shearman was also amateur champion for the hundred yards (1876) and the quarter-mile (1880): he played rugby football for the South of England, and twice was 'reserve' for England; and in 1881 he swam the Niagara River below the Falls. In 1915 he succeeded Lord Alverstone as president of the Amateur Athletic Association. He was joint author with J. E. Vincent of *Football: its history for five centuries* (1885), and author of *Athletics and Football* (Badminton Library, 1887).

After taking his degree in 1879, Shearman read in chambers with C. M. Warmington, then a flourishing chancery junior, and was called to the bar by the Inner Temple in 1881. He was soon busy in London, on the Midland circuit, and at the Birmingham sessions. A fluent speaker, with a good appearance and an even temper, he got on well with his tribunal. For the most part his cases demanded skilful advocacy rather than deep knowledge of the law, and he relied much on his tact and common sense. Shearman thoroughly understood the mentality of jurymen, who appreciated addresses which, if sometimes unpolished, were always plausible. Money-lenders, especially, recognized his qualities as an advocate and for some years he was standing counsel to the leading firms. Taking silk in 1903, he acquired a substantial practice in the front row at a time when competition at the bar was keen.

On the retirement of Lord Justice Vaughan Williams and Mr. Justice Channell in 1914, Lord Haldane chose Shearman to fill one of the vacant judgeships in the King's Bench division, and he was knighted. His wide experience in the courts made him a useful judge of first instance. Although he never pretended to be a profound jurist, he was not afraid of grappling with legal problems or of making up his mind. Shortly after his appointment he presided over the trial of Nicholaus Ahlers, the German consul at Sunderland, who was charged with 'adhering to, aiding and comforting the King's enemies'. The evidence for the prosecution showed that Ahlers had assisted German subjects of military age with money and information in order that they might return from England to Germany. The conviction of the accused man at the Durham autumn assizes in 1914 for high treason was subsequently set aside by the Court of Criminal Appeal. In 1916 Shearman served with Lord Hardinge of Penshurst and Sir Mackenzie Chalmers on the committee appointed to inquire into the origin and causes of the Easter Rebellion in Ireland. He was the judge of assize at Carmarthen in November 1920, when Harold Greenwood, after a seven days' trial, was acquitted on a charge of having poisoned his wife; and in 1922, at the Central Criminal Court, he tried Frederick Bywaters and Mrs. Edith Thompson who were convicted of the murder of Mrs. Thompson's husband: after an unsuccessful appeal both were hanged. During the same year he tried at the Central Criminal Court and sentenced to death the murderers of Field-Marshal Sir Henry Wilson [q.v.]. An operation necessitated by an old injury in the football field gravely impaired his powers of speech, and he struggled against this disability for some two years before his retirement in October 1929. He died at his London residence 6 January 1930.

Shearman married in 1884 Mary Louise, daughter of Job Long, of New York, by whom he had two sons, the younger of whom died from wounds received in the European War.

A cartoon of Shearman appeared in *Vanity Fair* 4 July 1895, and an oil painting by Miss May Clifford is in the possession of his family.

[*The Times*, 7 January 1930; *Law Journal*, 11 January 1930; personal knowledge.]

T. Mathew.

SHEFFIELD, fourth Baron (1839–1925). [See Stanley, Edward Lyulph.]

SHIPLEY, Sir ARTHUR EVERETT (1861–1927), zoologist, was born at Walton-on-Thames 10 March 1861, the second son of Alexander Shipley, of The Hall, Datchet, Buckinghamshire, by his wife, Amelia, daughter of William Henry

Burge, of Windsor. In 1877 he was sent to University College School, London. Two years later he entered St. Bartholomew's Hospital as a medical student. In 1880 he proceeded with a scholarship in natural sciences to Christ's College, Cambridge, where he resided continuously until his death forty-seven years later. He obtained first classes in both parts of the natural sciences tripos (1882 and 1884); in the second part he took zoology as his subject. He received encouragement in his scientific studies from S. H. Vines, who was then a fellow of Christ's College and Shipley's director of studies, but it was undoubtedly the influence of Francis Maitland Balfour [q.v.], professor of animal morphology at Cambridge, which led Shipley to devote himself to the study of zoology. Balfour's work on *Comparative Embryology* had appeared in 1880–1881 and had revealed a new field for zoological research. Moreover, the study of the morphology of the smaller animals and embryos had been greatly facilitated by the invention in 1883 by W. H. Caldwell and R. Threlfall in the zoological laboratory at Cambridge of the rocking microtome, which enabled a series of microscopic sections to be cut and mounted. This invention was fully employed by Shipley and his contemporaries. Shipley's early interest in zoology and his capacity for research were shown by a visit to the Stazione Zoologica at Naples, and by the publication of the results of his work there in a paper on the structure and development of the Brachiopoda before he had taken the second part of his tripos. His next publication was an account of the development of the river lamprey, which appeared in 1887. Shipley's early publications give little indication of the lines of work which established his reputation as a zoologist. After the publication of an important memoir on one of the Gephyrean worms (*Quarterly Journal of Microscopical Science*, vol. xxxi, 1890), he turned his attention to the study of parasitic worms. His published work on parasitic worms, which eventually extended to nearly fifty papers in scientific journals, gradually built up his scientific reputation as a competent and successful researcher, and led, in 1904, to his election as a fellow of the Royal Society.

At Cambridge Shipley successively held the posts of university demonstrator in comparative anatomy (1886), lecturer in the advanced morphology of the Invertebrata (1894), and reader in zoology (1908). This last post he resigned in 1920, after which he held no official teaching post in the university. Shipley's teaching was enlivened by many touches of humour, which are also present in all his writings. In addition to his scientific papers, he produced in 1893 a text-book, *The Zoology of the Invertebrata*, which was much used by students. He collaborated with Professor E. W. MacBride in writing a *Text-book of Zoology*, which was published in 1901 and passed through four editions, the last in 1920. He also collaborated with (Sir) S. F. Harmer in editing the *Cambridge Natural History*, a work in ten volumes which appeared between 1895 and 1909, and of which Shipley himself wrote several sections. He edited the biological series of the Pitt Press Natural Science Manuals and, for a time, the 'Fauna of British India' series. He was co-editor with Professor G. H. F. Nuttall of the journal *Parasitology* from 1908 to 1914, and he also assisted in editing the *Journal of Economic Biology* from 1905 to 1913.

Shipley was perhaps at his best when writing as a popular exponent of zoology. His first book of this nature was a collection of essays entitled *Pearls and Parasites*, published in 1908. It was about this time that he gave up active research in zoology, and turned to literary work. In 1913 he published a memoir of his friend, John Willis Clark [q.v.], under the title of *'J', a Memoir of John Willis Clark*. *The Minor Horrors of War* (1915) passed rapidly through three editions and was so successful that a year later he wrote *More Minor Horrors*. These two books introduced parasitology to a public which had, at the time, practical experience of the parasites therein described. *Studies in Insect Life* appeared in 1917, and in 1923 Shipley published a small book entitled *Life*, which he had written at the request of the Cambridge University Press in order to serve as an introduction to the study of elementary biology. This book had a very wide circulation and encouraged the teaching of this subject in schools. In 1924 appeared *Cambridge Cameos* and *Islands—West Indian and Aegean*. Shipley's last book, *Hunting under the Microscope*, was posthumously published in 1928, being prepared for publication by his friend and former pupil, C. F. A. Pantin. Shipley was for many years Cambridge University correspondent of *The Times*, and he contributed numerous articles to that paper, as well as to many other papers, encyclopaedias, and reviews, on a great diversity of subjects.

Shipley had been elected a fellow of Christ's College in 1887. At the time of his election the study of natural sciences in Cambridge was beginning to make great strides. Contemporary teachers of science were J. G. Adami, William Bateson, (Sir) S. F. Harmer, (Sir) Henry Head, (Sir) C. S. Sherrington, and D'Arcy Thompson, all of whom achieved distinction as biologists in later life. Shipley's reputation as a scientist is overshadowed by some of his contemporaries, but it must be remembered that his intellect was essentially versatile. As early as 1887 he was sent by the Colonial Office to the Bermudas in order to investigate a plant disease. This was the beginning of a connexion with the Colonial Office which lasted until his death. In the administration of the affairs of his college and of the university Shipley played a leading part. In 1891 he was appointed secretary to the museums and lecture rooms syndicate, a post which constituted him virtually business manager of the university laboratories and museums. In the following year he became tutor in natural sciences at Christ's College. From 1896 to 1908 he was a member of the council of the senate of the university, besides serving on many other boards and syndicates. Shipley's life was a successful combination of scientific research and administration. He made administration easy by an unusual sympathy with all sorts and conditions of men, and by a gift for entertaining which made his hospitality a notable feature of Cambridge during his period of residence. He travelled a great deal, frequently visiting the United States of America. It was on one of these visits that he received the honorary degree of D.Sc. from Princeton University (1906), and on another occasion (1909) he visited Canada in order to preside over the zoological section of the British Association which was holding its meeting in Winnipeg. He was an excellent talker, and could always entertain a large company with a good story well told.

Outside the university Shipley accomplished a notable amount of public work. He was chairman of the Marine Biological Association, treasurer and vice-president of the Research Defence Society, a member of the Central Medical War Committee and of the managing committee of the Imperial Bureau of Entomology. He was also a member of the royal commissions on the civil service (1912), on Trinity College, Dublin (1920), and on the importation of store cattle (1921). He was consulted by Lord Milner about the foundation of a college of agriculture in the tropics, and in 1919 was appointed chairman of a Tropical Agriculture Committee. When the Imperial College of Tropical Agriculture was established in Trinidad in 1921, Shipley was appointed chairman of the governing body.

In 1910 Shipley was elected master of Christ's College, in succession to John Peile [q.v.]. The Master's Lodge, which was to be his home for the rest of his life, was an old portion of the college which had undergone many previous internal alterations. Under Shipley's direction the Lodge was largely restored to its original condition, and became one of the most interesting of the older buildings in Cambridge. He furnished it with great taste, and at his own expense panelled one of the larger rooms, which served as his study. The ampler quarters of the Lodge provided Shipley with additional opportunities for entertaining. To his frequent lunch and dinner parties he invited not only men of distinction, but also undergraduates; and it was remarkable how he was able to bring together people of dissimilar ages and vocations. During the European War, when ordinary entertaining was suspended, he entertained at the Lodge a long succession of wounded officers, who were convalescing after discharge from hospital.

From 1917 to 1919 Shipley was vice-chancellor of the university. During his period of office he visited the United States as a member of the British university mission, which was sent out in 1918 by the Foreign Office on the invitation of the Council of Defence at Washington in order to counteract German propaganda in American universities, and to make known the facilities for postgraduate work in British universities. He was in America when the Armistice was signed on 11 November. He afterwards wrote an amusing account of this visit in his book *The Voyage of a Vice-Chancellor* (1919).

In 1920 Shipley was created G.B.E. in recognition of his public services. After the end of the War he took no further part in university administration. But he still continued to entertain and to write, and he also retained his interest in the affairs of his college. Moreover, he did not retire from public work outside the university, and in 1924 he visited Trinidad in order to lay the foundation stone of the new buildings of the College of Tropical Agriculture. It was probably due to principle that Shipley withdrew from university administration at this time in order to make way for the younger generation which had returned to Cambridge after the War. He had always urged that younger men should interest themselves in administration, believing that the university would be best administered by those who combined, as he did, administrative skill with academic distinction. The university was preparing for the royal commission which was appointed in 1923, and which eventually made far-reaching changes in the administration of the colleges and of the university as a whole. This work of reorganization Shipley left to others. He lived to see the new statutes come into operation in 1926, but before this there were signs that his health was beginning to fail. He suffered during the early part of 1927 from a serious illness, from which he recovered, but a second attack later in the same year proved fatal, and he died at the Master's Lodge 22 September. He was not married.

In appearance Shipley was dark and short, and, in later life, he was decidedly stout. In his early years at Cambridge, although he never played games and showed little interest in them, he took regular exercise, walking, bicycling, and riding, but latterly he gave this up and became, as he himself expressed it, 'quite rotund'. He was a person of most regular habits, who maintained a high standard of private and public duty. He was both punctual and punctilious, and it was an ideal of his to answer all his correspondence by return of post. In spite of the fact that he was always occupied with administrative and social duties, Shipley's output of literary work was considerable, if account be taken of all his scientific papers, articles, and reviews. That he could accomplish so much was due to his power of being able to write both articles and books at odd moments, even when others were talking in the room, as was often the case during the War, when convalescent officers were staying in his Lodge. He had no appreciation of music, and he attended the theatre only on rare occasions, but he had a keen appreciation of painting and architecture. He also collected furniture, and he filled his rooms in college and, later his Lodge, with many valuable pieces, which he delighted to show to his visitors.

There is a portrait of Shipley by P. A. de László in the hall of Christ's College, and another by J. Nicholson at the Imperial College of Agriculture, Trinidad.

[*The Times*, 23 September 1927; *Proceedings* of the Royal Society, vol. ciii, B, 1928; personal knowledge.] J. T. Saunders.

SHORTER, CLEMENT KING (1857–1926), journalist and author, was born in Southwark 19 July 1857, the youngest of the three sons of Richard Shorter, who came of Huntingdonshire and Norfolk stock, by his wife, Elizabeth Clemenson, who had some Spanish blood. Richard Shorter, of the historic Bull Inn, Bishopsgate, was a carrier between London and Cambridge, who was ruined by the competition of the Great Eastern Railway and emigrated to Australia, dying in poverty at Melbourne while his son Clement was still a child. Clement Shorter was sent to school at Downham Market, Norfolk, from 1863 to 1871. On leaving school he went to London and filled three different situations in four years with booksellers and publishers in Paternoster Row. He then returned to school for three months in order to study for the junior branch of the civil service. From 1877 to 1890 he was a clerk in the Exchequer and Audit department at Somerset House. At first he continued his education by attending evening classes at the Birkbeck Institution, where he had lessons in French and German, and 'had a try at Latin and Italian'. His adolescent reading was chiefly in the works of Carlyle, Emerson, Ruskin, and the English historians. By running two annual holidays into one, he was once able to spend three months in the family of a Lutheran pastor at Mecklenburg-Schwerin, where he improved his German. He writes in his *Autobiography* that he knew all the best German fiction, was enthusiastic over Goethe and Schiller, and was much influenced by Lessing, especially by his *Nathan der Weise*. In 1890 he annotated, very briefly, a reprint of *Wilhelm Meister*, and in 1892 he prefixed 'The Private Life of Ferdinand Lassalle' to a revised edition of George Meredith's novel, *The Tragic Comedians*. In the same year he issued a selection of Wordsworth's lyrics and sonnets.

In 1888 Shorter was writing twice weekly a column of gossip about books for the *Star* newspaper, as well as, a little later, a weekly column for the *Queen*. In 1890 he left Somerset House in order to become, at the invitation of (Sir) William James Ingram, editor both of the *Illustrated London News* (in 1891) and of the *English Illustrated Magazine*. He had already been sub-editing, for Ingram, the *Penny Illustrated Paper* in his evenings. In 1893 Shorter founded, and edited for the *Illustrated London News* Company, the *Sketch*, 'on less serious lines': he called this his one positive achievement in journalism, because in it he was the pioneer of the use of half-tone blocks in newspaper production. He writes: 'I knew nothing about art and cared less', and much later he wondered whether he had not done some harm to the national intellect, quoting against himself Wordsworth's sonnet on illustrated books and newspapers:

'Now prose and verse sunk into disrepute
Must lacquey a dumb Art that best can suit
The taste of this once-intellectual Land.'

Shorter's journalism was, for himself, a joyous adventure, out of which he made much less profit than he might have done if money had been his main object. In 1897 he was editing five papers at once—the three already mentioned, together with the *Album* and *Pick-me-up*. In 1900 he parted from Ingram, in pique over a criticism of the *Sketch*, and founded the *Sphere*. Shorter remained editor of this paper until his death, contributing every week from 27 January 1900 (its first number) to 17 April 1926 a literary letter, always lively but often controversial and even personal, and much concerned with his hobbies—the Brontës, George Borrow, Samuel Johnson, and Napoleon. In 1901 he founded the *Tatler*, 'on more frivolous lines'—again it is his own description.

As early as 1889 Shorter had written an introduction to *Jane Eyre*. His first book, *Charlotte Brontë and her Circle*, appeared in 1896 (re-issued in 1914 as *The Brontës and their Circle*). This was followed by *Charlotte Brontë and her Sisters* (1905), *The Brontës: Life and Letters* (2 vols., 1908), an attempt to present a full and final record of the lives of the three sisters, from the biographies of Mrs. Gaskell and others, and from numerous hitherto unpublished manuscripts and letters. He edited Mrs. Gaskell's *Life of Charlotte Brontë* (incorporating many new letters) in 1899 and again (for 'The World's Classics') in 1919, and in 1910–1911 the *Complete Poems of Emily Brontë* and *Wuthering Heights*, in texts which left much work to be done by later editors. *George Borrow and his Circle* appeared in 1913, containing hitherto unpublished letters of Borrow and his friends; and in 1923 he edited Borrow's *Complete Works*, in sixteen volumes. In 1908 he published *Napoleon and his Fellow-Travellers*, narratives of the emperor's voyages on the *Bellerophon* and *Northumberland* to exile in St. Helena, with an introduction; and in 1910 appeared *Napoleon in his own Defence*, with notes and an essay on Napoleon as a man of letters. Shorter's biographies of the Brontës and of George Borrow were compilations of facts, governed much more by the novelty of their discovery than by their importance, set forth with no literary grace, and with hardly any attempt at critical appreciation. He himself was conscious of this, and excused his own abstention from literature on the score of his all-exacting journalism.

Shorter, who was a very contentious man, was much satirized in his lifetime, but *C.K.S., an Autobiography*, a fragment posthumously published in 1926, shows him to have been a happy man, happy in his unthinking energy, enjoying controversy, naïve, and affectionate. He was an industrious collector of books, manuscripts, and literary material of all kinds; he possessed unique Brontë manuscripts and a valuable collection of grangerized books.

Shorter married twice: first, in 1896 the poet, Dora Sigerson (died 1918), daughter of George Sigerson, M.D., of Dublin; secondly, in 1920 Annie Doris, daughter of John Banfield, shipowner, of Penzance, who survived him with their daughter. He died at his home at Great Missenden, Buckinghamshire, 19 November 1926, and was cremated at Golders Green.

Among Shorter's writings not previously mentioned are *Victorian Literature: sixty years of books and bookmen* (1897), *Immortal Memories: Essays and Addresses* (1907, Lassalle, Cowper, Borrow, Crabbe, Johnson, &c.), and *Highways and Byways in Buckinghamshire* (1910). He also produced editions of the novels of Henry Kingsley (1894–1895, with a note on Kingsley in *Geoffrey Hamlyn* and a note on Old Chelsea church in *The Hillyars and Burtons*), of the novels and tales of Mrs. Gaskell (1907–1915, with introductions to each volume), and of Boswell's *Life of Johnson* (1924).

A cartoon of Shorter by 'Spy' appeared in *Vanity Fair* 20 December 1894.

[*The Times*, 20 November 1926; *C.K.S., an Autobiography*, edited by J. M. Bulloch, 1926; private information.] F. PAGE.

SIFTON, Sir CLIFFORD (1861–1929), Canadian statesman, was born 10 March 1861 at St. John's, Middlesex, Ontario, the second son of John Wright Sifton by his wife, Kate Watkin. He came of Irish Protestant stock, his great grandfather, Charles Sifton, having emigrated from Clonmel, Ireland, to Upper Canada in 1819. His father built the first section of the Canadian Pacific Railway in Manitoba, and was afterwards active in public life, becoming speaker of the Manitoba legislative assembly. Sifton was educated at the High School, London, Ontario, and the Boys' College, Dundas, and graduated from Victoria University, Cobourg, in 1880, as gold medallist in mathematics. In 1882 he was called to the bar and began the practice of law in Brandon, Manitoba. Elected to the Manitoba legislature for North Brandon in 1888 as a liberal, he became attorney-general and minister of education in 1891. His activities in defence of the school law of 1890, which abolished denominational schools in the province and established a non-sectarian system, made him a national figure at an early age. The remedial order issued by the federal government instructing the province to restore Roman Catholic schools was rejected by the Manitoba legislature and by the electors of Manitoba under the leadership of Sifton; and after the defeat of the conservative federal government of Sir Charles Tupper [q.v.] upon this issue in 1896, Sifton entered (17 November 1896) the liberal government of Sir Wilfrid Laurier [q.v.] as minister of the interior. As the representative of Western Canada he took charge of the developmental programme of the government, and his policies with respect to immigration, colonization and land settlement, railway building, and the administration of the Yukon goldfields became the major political issues of the time. His methods were effective in inducing immigration and settlement, and during his nine years of office the prairie west, which had long suffered from stagnation, underwent an almost magical transformation. The yield of wheat in Western Canada was multiplied tenfold during these nine years, the population was trebled, and nearly three thousand miles of railway were built. His immigration policies were particularly successful in inducing farmers in the United States to remove to Canada.

Sifton's resignation from the government in March 1905 was the result of a disagreement with the prime minister, Sir Wilfrid Laurier, over the educational clauses in the constitutions of the new provinces, Alberta and Saskatchewan. He organized an opposition which was successful in forcing a modification of these provisions, as a result of which the rights of the minority were limited to those which they had enjoyed under the territorial ordinances. He continued to sit in parliament as a liberal; but in the session of 1911 he joined with the conservatives in opposing the reciprocity agreement made with the United States by the liberal government. In the general election which followed he conducted a vigorous campaign against the agreement and was a prime agent in bringing about the government's defeat. He did not offer himself for re-election, and thereafter was not officially in public life; but he continued until the end of his life to be an influential figure in politics. He retained a strong influence in the liberal party; and this was manifested in 1917 when, again in opposition to Laurier, he was chiefly instrumental in bringing about a coalition, for war purposes, between the conservatives and those liberals who favoured conscription.

In 1909 Sifton organized the commission for the conservation of natural resources, and was for nine years its chairman. His tenure of the chairmanship was notable for the successful defence of the water-power of the St. Lawrence against attempts at alienation by private interests; this led to the formulation of a Dominion policy which preserved the public ownership of the water-power permanently. Sifton gave his name to a number of places in Canada: Lake Sifton in the province of Quebec; Mount Sifton in the Selkirk Mountains, British Columbia; Sifton Mountains and Sifton Pass in the Tukon district; and the town of Sifton in Manitoba.

Sifton was prominent in the nationalist movement which sought to have the relationship of Great Britain and Canada within the British Commonwealth defined in terms of constitutional and legislative equality. His interest in this question dated from 1903 when, as British agent, he had charge of the Canadian case in the Alaskan boundary arbitration. He supported the two Canadian commissioners in their protest against the finding by their British associate, Lord Alverstone [q.v.], in favour of the United States; thereafter he held the view that Canada should have control of her external affairs—a claim in which the policy of constitutional equality with Great Britain was implicit. From 1915 onwards he publicly advocated a restatement of the relationship between Great Britain and the Dominions, giving formal recognition to the already conceded principle of equality.

During the last decade of his life Sifton had a recognized position in Canada as an elder statesman, and his views on public issues exercised great influence. As he advanced in life he regained, in his own words, his 'pristine radicalism' and on public questions, such as control of transportation rates, the tariff, banking and credit policies, he was accepted as an unofficial exponent of left-wing liberal opinion.

Upon his retirement from the government in 1905 Sifton did not resume the practice of law; but he was thereafter extensively engaged in business operations. He was the principal proprietor of a group of Canadian newspapers, chief of which was the *Free Press* of Winnipeg; and he was actively associated with their editorial management.

Sifton was created K.C.M.G. in 1915 for public and war services. He married in 1884 Elizabeth Arminella (died 1925), daughter of Henry Joel Burrows, of Ottawa. Five sons were born of the marriage.

Portraits of Sifton by Kenneth Forbes and Wyly Grier are in the possession of the family.

[J. W. Dafoe, *Clifford Sifton in relation to his Times*, 1931; family papers; private information; personal knowledge.]

J. W. Dafoe.

SIMS, CHARLES (1873–1928), painter, was born 28 January 1873 in Islington, the elder son of Stephen Sims, costume manufacturer, by his wife, Alice Metcalfe. He became lame in the right leg in early infancy, probably as the result of a fall. He was put to school at the age of three, at Margate; later he went to school in London. In 1887 he was placed in the office of a commission agent in Paris, with the idea of learning French and commercial practice; in the following year he entered the counting house of a drapery firm in Holloway; but his heart was not in office work. He had taken violin lessons in Paris from John Tiplady Carrodus [q.v.], and showed considerable promise as a musician. At this time also he drew a great deal, but without showing special ability; and about 1887 he sought employment with a firm of engravers. In 1890 he became a pupil at the National Art Training Schools, South Kensington (afterwards the Royal College of Art), and in 1891–1892 he studied at the Académie Julian, in Paris, under Jules Lefebvre and Benjamin Constant.

On his return to England, Sims spent a year in vainly trying to earn a living as a landscape painter; then, in 1893, he joined the Royal Academy Schools. There he did well, winning the silver medal for drawing, and the Landseer scholarship. In 1895, however, he and four other students were expelled from the Schools for a trivial breach of discipline. None the less, Sims had two paintings in the next year's Academy exhibition, and one of them, 'The Vine', aroused critical interest. In January 1897 Sims married Agnes Helen, elder daughter of the landscape painter, John MacWhirter [q.v.]. A few months later he exhibited at the Academy a picture called 'Childhood', which was shown at the Paris Salon of 1900, whence it was bought for the Musée du Luxembourg. In 1900 Sims took a cottage at St. Lawrence, Essex, and began the outdoor figure-painting of which he was to do so much. The next year, when his eldest son began to walk, he began the delightful, sympathetic series of mother-and-child pictures which are associated with his name. The first of these, 'Top o' the Hill', was exhibited at the Academy of 1902, and was bought by the Sydney Art Gallery. For the next few years Sims spent his holidays in Arran, while he was living first in London and later at Étaples and Bruges. His first 'one-man' show, at the Leicester galleries, in February 1906, resulted in the immediate sale of thirty out of fifty-four pictures. His period of economic struggle was now at an end, and he was able to settle securely to work at Fittleworth, Sussex.

Sims's subsequent career was a record of success broken only by the production of works in which originality of conception outran public and academic taste. 'An Island Festival', exhibited at the Academy of 1907, was highly praised; 'The Fountain' (1908) was bought for the Tate Gallery by the Chantrey trustees; and in 1910 he held his second 'one-man' exhibition. In 1907 he had been elected A.R.A. In 1912 he won the gold medal of the Carnegie Institute, Pittsburg, and also that of the international exhibition held at Amsterdam. 'The Wood Beyond the World' (1913), the second of his pictures in the Tate Gallery, was purchased the same year, again by the Chantrey trustees. During the last year of the European War (1918), Sims was an official artist in France. His Canadian War Memorial panel is in the Parliament House at Ottawa; two more of his War pictures are in the Imperial War Museum, South Kensington. He was elected R.A. in 1915; and in 1920 he was appointed keeper of the Royal Academy Schools—a position which he resigned six years later, owing to heavy pressure of engagements in New York, following a successful exhibition at Knoedler's galleries.

In April 1928 Sims was staying with friends at Ravenswood, St. Boswell's, Roxburghshire, and on the morning of 13 April his body was recovered from the river Tweed, after the finding of a letter in which he expressed the intention of taking his life. The nature of the mental affliction which brought about his tragic end is known, if known at all, only to his intimates. It is certain that some profound mystical apprehension ruled him in his latter days; for the six 'spirituals' which he painted in 1928 (and which were exhibited posthumously at the Royal Academy of that year) are in a style and temper totally alien from any former manner of his. They are impressive but somewhat obscure records of spiritual states, executed in a technique which includes some use of cubist formulae, and bizarre colours; they show, despite vital differences, some affinity with the predominant mood of William Blake. They are in the possession of various owners, notably Mrs. William Younger.

Both his work itself and his posthumously published book *Picture Making: Technique and Inspiration* reveal Sims as one of the most assiduous and fertile technical experimenters of his day. His method of using tempera and oil together, which is his most interesting personal technique, is seen to advantage in 'The Countess of Rocksavage and her Son' (1922), a most attractive rendering of feminine beauty and childish grace, executed without the least trace of sentimentality. His joy in breezy, sunny, open-air portraits and landscapes, and in playful action, is explained by his son and biographer as a sublimation arising out of his lameness, which, although it became less severe than had been at first feared, remained a serious disability throughout his life. The best of these open-air lyrics, like 'The Kite' (1905) and 'The Fountain' (1908), are delightfully loose and free as records of exuberant joy in sunlight and movement and fresh air. As a portrait-painter Sims eschewed conventional arrangement and painted with sympathy and penetration; the official royal portrait (1924) was deemed unacceptable, however, and was destroyed by the artist. His colour, in general, is bright and joyous, but in composition he is less sure, several of his pictures betraying a lack of coordination and balance.

Sims was a close student of the masters, old and modern, and his book *Picture Making* contains valuable observations on their methods and results. The various influences to which he was subject from time to time can be detected in such works as 'The Wood Beyond the World', where Perugino and Puvis de Chavannes provide the dominant inspiration, and 'The Seven Sacraments of Holy Church' (1917), which shows clear traces of the influence of Italian primitives. These pictures are more purely decorative than most of his work. In addition to his large oil-paintings, Sims was expert in water-colour, and made the most of the airiness and transparency to which that medium lends itself. He did a good deal of mural work, a notable example being at Sir Philip Sassoon's house in Park Lane; but his official efforts in this kind (in St. Stephen's Hall and the House of Commons) caused much controversy, largely on extra-aesthetic issues.

Sims's wife survived him. The eldest of their three sons was killed in action in the European War.

[*The Times*, 17 April 1928; *Daily Telegraph*, 18 April 1928; *Daily Express*, 18 April 1928; *Saturday Review*, 5 May 1928; *New Statesman*, 12 May 1928; Charles Sims, *Picture Making: Technique and Inspiration*, with a Critical Survey of his Work and Life by Alan Sims 1934; private information.]

H. B. Grimsditch.

SINCLAIR, JOHN, first Baron Pentland (1860–1925), politician, was born at 6 Moray Place, Edinburgh, 7 July 1860, the eldest son of Captain George Sinclair, an officer of the Bengal army, by his wife and cousin, Agnes, daughter of John Learmonth, of Dean, Edinburgh, who built and presented to the city of Edinburgh the Dean bridge. His grandfather was Sir John Sinclair, sixth baronet, of Dunbeath, in Caithness, where this branch of the family had been settled since about 1680.

Sinclair was educated first at Edinburgh Academy, then at Wellington College, and entered Sandhurst in 1878. He passed out fifth, and joined the 5th Royal Irish Lancers in 1879. He hunted regularly in England and Ireland, rode in point-to-point races, and played polo for his regiment. He served with the Sudan expedition of 1885, earning the medal and clasp. Returning home with his regiment, he was appointed aide-de-camp to the lord-lieutenant of Ireland, the Earl of Aberdeen, in 1886. He contested the Ayr Burghs as a liberal, without success, in the second general election of that year.

Early in 1887 Sinclair left the army, and began to read law and study economics, becoming a resident at the recently founded Toynbee Hall. In 1889 he was elected a member of the first London County Council, as a progressive, for East Finsbury. In that capacity he did much work on committees; he also founded the London Playing Fields Society. He was returned as member of parliament for Dumbartonshire at the general election of 1892; and the secretary of state for war, (Sir) Henry Campbell-Bannerman, made him his assistant private secretary. At the general election of 1895 Sinclair lost his seat. But after serving for a year (1896–1897) as private secretary to Lord Aberdeen, who was at that time governor-general of Canada, he was elected to parliament in 1897 for Forfarshire, winning a critical by-election for the liberals. This seat he retained until he became a peer in 1909; and during the ministries of Lord Salisbury and Mr. Balfour he was closely associated, from 1900 to 1905, as Scottish liberal whip, with the leaders of the opposition, when his universal popularity helped to keep the party together.

After Mr. Balfour's resignation in 1905 Sinclair was appointed secretary for Scotland. In office, his intimate relations with Campbell-Bannerman (who made him his executor and left him his papers) enabled him to exercise considerable influence upon the general policy of the liberal party. His secretaryship was marked by several measures of importance to Scotland. In the first session (1906) he carried through the National Galleries (Scotland) Act; and the improvements in the accommodation of the Scottish galleries, as well as in the various collections, are largely due to his reorganization. As political head of the Scottish education department Sinclair was responsible for the Scottish Education Act of 1908, which provided for better physical care of children, improved the training of teachers and the secondary school system, and gave greater facilities for continued instruction after school age. His Small Landholders' (Scotland) Bill, the object of which was to extend to small-holders in the rest of Scotland the security of tenure already granted to the crofter counties, was rejected by the Lords in 1907 and 1908; but it became law in 1911, Sinclair having been raised to the peerage (as Baron Pentland, of Lyth, Caithness) in February 1909 in order to take charge of the Bill.

In 1912 Lord Pentland was appointed governor of Madras, where he took special interest in the administrative, educational, and economic development of the Presidency. His tenure was extended, owing to the European War, until 1919, the additional period being largely occupied by the discussions on the Montagu-Chelmsford reforms. After his return to England he did much public and philanthropic work.

Lord Pentland, who was sworn of the Privy Council in 1905, and created G.C.I.E. in 1912 and G.C.S.I. in 1918, died of pneumonia at his home at Hampstead 11 January 1925. He married in 1904 Lady Marjorie, daughter of John Campbell Gordon, seventh Earl and first Marquess of Aberdeen. He left a son, Henry John (born 1907), who succeeded him as second baron, and a daughter.

[Lady Pentland, *The Rt. Hon. John Sinclair, Lord Pentland. A Memoir*, 1928; Scottish Office records; family records.]

M. F. Headlam.

SINHA, SATYENDRA PRASANNO, first Baron Sinha, of Raipur (1864–1928), Indian statesman, was born in June 1864 at the village of Raipur in the Birbhum district of Bengal, the youngest son of Babu Siti Kantha Sinha, a small Kayastha landowner. At the age of fourteen (1878), on leaving Birbhum Zilla school, Sinha matriculated in the university of Calcutta, entering Presidency College with a scholarship. He left in 1881, however, without taking a degree, and came to England to be called to the bar. Owing to the prejudice which still prevailed against travel oversea, Sinha's preparations for departure had to be made in secret, and he arrived in England with insufficient means; but the scholarships and prizes which he won relieved him from financial difficulty. In 1886 he was called to the bar by Lincoln's Inn, and returned to Calcutta.

As a barrister Sinha built up a large

practice, and in 1903 was appointed standing counsel to the government of Bengal. His personality made the appointment popular even with many who felt that the claims of a senior candidate, an English barrister, had been slighted. In 1905 he was promoted to officiate as advocate-general of Bengal, and he was confirmed in the post in 1908. He was the first Indian to fill the position. He was thus the constitutional legal adviser of the governments both of India and Bengal during the troubled years of the anti-partition agitation, in which many of his associates were taking a leading and even an extreme part. Nevertheless, he was able to command the confidence of government without forfeiting the intimacy of his friends or the trust of his fellow countrymen.

In 1909 Lord Morley, in pursuance of his policy, appointed Sinha to be legal member of the governor-general's council. No Indian had previously been a member of the government of India. The acceptance of this post involved great pecuniary and other sacrifices: the duties are not purely legal in character but involve a joint responsibility, like that of an English Cabinet minister, for the policy of government. There were those who doubted the wisdom of the appointment, for the post had never before been filled except by an English barrister appointed from practice in England: but of the universal satisfaction with which Sinha discharged the duties the viceroy, Lord Minto, bore testimony in a letter to King Edward VII. Differing from his colleagues over certain clauses of a bill for the control of the press, Sinha resigned: but of his own motion withdrew his resignation rather than desert his post at a time when political assassination was rife. Returning to the bar in 1910 he immediately recovered all his old practice.

In 1915 Sinha was elected to the presidency of the Indian National Congress. This incursion into the realm of controversial politics was due to the influence of two men: Sir Lawrence Hugh Jenkins [q.v.], who persuaded the congress leaders that the cause of Indian self-government would be advanced by the election of an Indian so universally trusted and liked by the English both in India and Whitehall, and Mr. B. N. Basu, who with some difficulty persuaded Sinha that it was his duty to accept the task thus thrust upon him. The result was as Jenkins and Basu had anticipated; in a closely reasoned address Sinha claimed an authoritative definition of the ultimate goal of British policy for India, and the claim was met by the historic declaration made in parliament 20 August 1917 [See Montagu, Edwin Samuel].

With the carrying out of that policy the next period of Sinha's career is closely connected. In 1917 he became a member of the Bengal executive council; but, together with the Maharaja of Bikaner, he was summoned to England almost at once, and until 1919 was in the closest association with the secretary of state, E. S. Montagu, first as an assistant, and then as a member of the Imperial War Cabinet and Conference, sharing the inter-allied deliberations at the close of the European War and in the settlement of peace terms. In 1919 he was made parliamentary under-secretary of state for India and was raised to the peerage as Baron Sinha, of Raipur. He piloted the Government of India Act (1919) through the House of Lords.

Sinha returned to India in 1920 in order to take up the post of governor of Bihar and Orissa under the constitution which he had largely helped to create. This position he held for eleven months (1920–1921). On broad questions of policy his judgement was probably as sound as ever; but he felt acutely his lack of training for the detailed administration and innumerable minor decisions, of which a governor's work largely consists. The strain on a constitution never very strong was too great and he was compelled to take a prolonged rest. Towards the close of 1925 Sinha again began to interest himself in public life, contributing to the editorial columns of the *Bengalee* a series of articles embodying his faith in the association of England and India and pleading with his countrymen for patience, moderation, and goodwill. By his welcome to the Indian Statutory Commission under Sir John Simon (1927) he strove to give a lead and to smooth the path of that body in India. In 1926 he was appointed to the Judicial Committee of the Privy Council: but he was twice compelled by his health to winter in his own country, and during the second of these trips he died 4 March 1928 at Berhampore in Bengal.

Lord Sinha's interests lay in his own profession of the law: he was never so happy as at the bar, and although probably he preferred the position of advocate, his short tenure of a seat on the Judicial Committee gave proof of high judicial capacity. The most individual achievement of his career, his congress address, was a triumph of careful advocacy as well as a statement of deep convictions. Socially he appeared to all who knew him a perfect combination of the culture of East and West; and this favourable opinion was heightened by an absence of self-seeking and by a modesty which no success could spoil. He came to be the accepted type of the educated Indian whom British politicians could summon to a share in the government of India and the councils of the Empire. Hence the numerous honours and official positions (1909 to 1921) which he was the first Indian to hold. Many of these he would have preferred to refuse, but his sense of duty to his countrymen compelled acceptance.

Sinha was knighted in 1914 and created K.C.S.I. in 1921. He took silk (the first Indian to do so) in 1918. He was sworn of the Privy Council in 1919 and received the freedom of the City of London in 1917. In 1926 he was made a bencher of Lincoln's Inn. He married in 1880 Gobinda Mohini, daughter of K. C. Mitter, a landowner; and the conversion about 1886 of himself and his wife to the *Sadharan Brahmo Samaj* rendered this in law what it always was in fact, a monogamous marriage. His wife survived him with four sons and three daughters.

[*The Times*, 6 March 1928; *Calcutta Weekly Notes*, 12 March 1928; private information.]

S. V. FitzGerald.

SMARTT, Sir THOMAS WILLIAM (1858–1929), South African politician, was born at Trim, co. Meath, Ireland, 22 February 1858, the son of Thomas William Smartt, by his wife, Sarah Rerdon, of Kilcooly, co. Meath. He studied medicine at Trinity College, Dublin, qualifying L.R.C.S., Ireland, and went to South Africa in 1880. There he settled in Britstown, Cape Colony, where he began practice as a doctor.

Smartt speedily established himself in his profession and became one of the most popular medical men in that very large, sparsely populated area. He was genial in disposition, a good 'mixer', devoted to his work, and impulsively self-sacrificing in the cause of others; these qualities won for him prosperity and the affection of those whom he served, just as their support afterwards became invaluable to him as a political leader. He gathered, too, a wide knowledge of agriculture, learned the language of the Dutch among whom his practice lay, and was soon persuaded to embark on a political career, entering the house of assembly, the lower house of the Cape parliament, as member for Wodehouse in 1893.

Smartt, in addition to his other qualities, had an Irishman's eloquence and a magnificent voice. He was a powerful platform speaker, revelling in the cut-and-thrust of political controversy. A retentive and ready memory completed his equipment for a political career. He soon made his mark in Cape politics, becoming a member of the Afrikander Bond, which, under the leadership of Jan Hendrik Hofmeyr [q.v.], the *éminence grise* of the Cape Colony, was at that time in close alliance with Cecil Rhodes [q.v.]. The Jameson Raid (29 December 1895) broke this alliance for ever, and threw Smartt into personal association with Rhodes, although their political ties were not yet close, as Smartt became colonial secretary in the ministry of Sir John Gordon Sprigg [q.v.], which came into power when Rhodes fell in 1896. When the Sprigg cabinet fell in 1898 Smartt returned to parliament as member for Cathcart, in an opposition which was loosely knit, a section of it being in increasing sympathy with Rhodes. Of this section Smartt was the natural leader. When war with the Boers became inevitable he and Rhodes took train for Kimberley, arriving just before it was surrounded by the Boer commandos. Smartt and Rhodes became bosom friends during the siege, and the friendship profoundly influenced the rest of Smartt's career.

Through Rhodes's last illness—he died in March 1902—Smartt shared with (Sir) Leander Starr Jameson [q.v.] a devoted attendance on the dying man; and for the rest of their lives both held themselves pledged to fight for Rhodes's plans and ideals in South Africa.

In the course of the Boer War Sprigg again became prime minister of the Cape Colony (June 1900), and Smartt took office under him with the portfolio of public works. They split on the question of the suspension of the constitution, and Smartt became the leader of the progressives in opposition to Sprigg. When the Sprigg ministry fell in 1904, Smartt had every right to expect to be called upon to form a ministry. But he saw that Jameson was the man for the leadership, and, resigning his claims, became the loyal lieutenant of his friend.

The Jameson cabinet lasted till 1908,

with Smartt commissioner of crown lands and public works. He and Jameson together attended the Imperial Conference held in London in 1907, when Alfred Deakin [q.v.], prime minister of Australia, urged the policy of Imperial preference. Smartt and Jameson strongly supported Deakin. They returned home to certain defeat, but they had laid the foundations, in alliance with General Louis Botha [q.v.], prime minister of the Transvaal, of that Union of the four states of South Africa which came into being in 1909. Jameson and Smartt were members of the National Convention which drafted the South Africa Act, and at the suggestion of Botha, the first prime minister of the Union, Smartt received the K.C.M.G. in January 1911.

When the Union was accomplished there were hopes that the political antagonism between Dutch and English South Africans, which was the legacy of the Boer War, might be buried for good. But Botha found himself unable to form the first Union cabinet on those lines. Jameson and Smartt then organized the unionist party, whose policy was to help Botha against the extremists on his side and at the same time to fight for the traditional policy of Cecil Rhodes. Failing health forced Jameson to resign the unionist leadership in 1912 and Smartt succeeded him. The split between General Botha and General Hertzog, followed two years later by the outbreak of the European War, made Smartt's task one of great delicacy. Although not a born leader, he came through the trial unshaken and with enhanced personal prestige. When Botha died in 1919 and was succeeded as prime minister by General Smuts, the Hertzog nationalists gained rapidly in political strength, and the election of 1920 left Smuts without a majority. Labour had won seats from the unionists, and Hertzog's nationalists were the strongest single party in the house of assembly. If the republican nationalists were to be kept at bay, a combination between the parties of Smuts and Smartt was essential. This combination took place in 1920. Smartt once more stepped down from the leadership of a party and became as loyal a lieutenant to Smuts as he had been to Jameson. He received the office of secretary of agriculture, which he held from 1921 to 1924. He was invaluable to Smuts as a colleague, both in the cabinet and in the opposition, for the rest of his parliamentary career, which ended with his retirement, owing to sudden failure of health, in March 1929. He died a month later, 17 April 1929, at Cape Town, and was buried on his farm, Glenban, in the Stellenbosch district.

Smartt was conspicuous among the many men from Great Britain who have made South Africa their home. He won the affection of the Dutch—not a very common achievement. To his own people he was almost an idol. Although not in the very front rank of South African leaders, he excelled them all, with the single exception of Botha, in his power of commanding the loyalty and affection of a political party. He was an ideal political lieutenant, loyal, disinterested, and always ready to throw himself, without display, into the thick of political fighting.

Smartt married in 1891 Sybil Anna, daughter of Edmond Lombard Swan, of Allworth, Abbeyleix, Ireland. They had one son, who died in infancy, and two daughters.

[*The Times*, 17 April 1929; *Cape Times*, *passim*.]

B. K. Long.

SMITH, ARTHUR LIONEL (1850–1924), historian, the second son of William Henry Smith, civil engineer, by his wife, Alice Elizabeth, daughter of Jacob George Strutt [q.v.], painter and etcher, was born in London 4 December 1850. His father was at one time employed on the Blackwall Tunnel and was the author of several ingenious but unsuccessful inventions: he died at the age of thirty-seven, leaving his family in difficult circumstances. A nomination for Christ's Hospital was offered to Mrs. Smith by a friend and accepted on behalf of the second son, as the eldest boy decided to go to sea. Smith went to the school at the age of six, and remained there continuously for over twelve years, his mother, with the younger children, having settled in Italy. She afterwards married again, was again widowed, and lived for many years in Chicago, where her son visited her in 1910, shortly before her death. At Christ's Hospital Smith was second Grecian in 1868, and in the same year he won an exhibition at Balliol College, Oxford. He came into residence in 1869, his chief school friend, R. H. Roe, afterwards headmaster of Brisbane grammar school, Australia, being his exact contemporary in college. He obtained first classes in classical moderations (1871) and *literae humaniores* (1873), and in the latter year divided the Jenkyns exhibition, the chief Balliol prize for classical men. He then read modern history in one year and obtained a second class in 1874. In the same year he won the Lothian prize with an essay on Erasmus. He rowed bow in the college eight which went head of the river in 1873.

In 1874 Smith was elected a fellow and lecturer of Trinity College, Oxford. He retained his fellowship until it was vacated in 1879 by his marriage: he resided and taught at Trinity and rowed in the college eight until 1876, but in that year he began to read for the bar at Lincoln's Inn. The offer of a tutorship in modern history from Balliol brought him back to Oxford in 1879, and in 1882 he was elected a fellow of the college. The same year he was elected junior proctor, his colleague being Henry Scott Holland [q.v.], then a student of Christ Church. He first examined in the final school of modern history in 1884—continuing until 1887 and examining again in 1895 and from 1901 to 1903—and he was one of the small band of tutors, including Arthur Johnson, Edward Armstrong, (Sir) Richard Lodge, and C. R. L. Fletcher, who were active in building up the position of the school in the university. He found time to contribute some incisive articles to *Social England*, edited by H. D. Traill, the *Dictionary of Political Economy*, and the *Dictionary of English History*, and in 1905 he published the *Notes on Stubbs's Charters* which he had compiled for his pupils. But Smith's main work in these years was that of a college tutor. He was absent for only one term, in 1902, when he went to Egypt after an attack of rheumatism. During the last years of the mastership of Benjamin Jowett [q.v.] he was an enthusiastic champion of the master's ideas and projects, and enjoyed much of his confidence. He developed a distinctive style as a teacher of history, and his sympathy, humour, and generosity won him the loyalty and affection of many generations of undergraduates. A succession of resident pupils, most of them preparing for entrance to Balliol, shared with his growing family first his small house in Crick Road and subsequently The King's Mound, Mansfield Road, built for him by the college, whither he moved in 1893. In the same year he took a house at his wife's old home at Bamburgh, Northumberland, which became the scene of many reading parties. From 1879, when he coached the college crew which went head of the river, he maintained a close interest in the Boat Club; he was an advocate and for many years an exponent of hockey from its first appearance at Oxford, an early champion of the bicycle, and a propagandist of the theory and practice of skating. Believing as he did—and claiming to have made a convert of Jowett—in the value of athletics as a solvent of social barriers in college, he gave much time to raising funds for the college field and to organizing a system which brought games within the means of the poorer undergraduates. The movement initiated in 1904 by his pupil and friend, the Hon. T. A. Brassey (afterwards second Earl Brassey), to put the finances of the college on a better footing owed much to his influence and encouragement.

In 1905 Smith's work for the history school was recognized by his appointment as Ford's lecturer in English history. He took as his subject 'Some Sidelights on English History in the Thirteenth Century'. The lectures were published in 1913 under the less suitable title of *Church and State in the Middle Ages*. In 1908 Smith published two lectures of generous appreciation of the work of the historian Frederic William Maitland [q.v.], together with a bibliography of his works, and in 1909 he contributed a chapter on 'English Political Philosophy in the Seventeenth and Eighteenth Centuries' to volume vi of the *Cambridge Modern History*. But the increased leisure which he obtained by his appointment in 1906 as one of the first two Jowett fellows, on the foundation of his Balliol contemporary, Lord Newlands, was largely absorbed by a new interest.

In 1907 Smith was nominated by the vice-chancellor as one of the seven representatives of the university of Oxford appointed to form a joint committee with representatives of the Workers' Educational Association and to prepare a report on the higher education of workpeople, and in 1908 he began his membership of the standing joint committee of the University Extension Delegacy set up as a result of that report. For the rest of his life he threw himself eagerly into every stage of the movement for the establishment and extension of tutorial classes for working men, devoting, in particular, much attention to the summer school held each year at Balliol by the Workers' Educational Association.

It was this sympathy with and understanding of working-class people which brought Smith his main opportunity for useful work during the European War. At its outbreak he had been dean of the college and senior resident fellow for seven years, since the retirement from the mastership in 1907 of Edward Caird [q.v.]. In April 1916 he succeeded James Leigh Strachan-Davidson [q.v.] as master. He was thus occupied throughout the War with the task of keeping the college in being, and he also showed much kindness to the cadet officers in training who soon came to form the main body of residents in the college. But the bulk of his time was given to lecturing all over the country, largely to working-class audiences, and, particularly after his appointment as master, to active membership of various public or semi-public bodies concerned with industrial and social questions. He was appointed early in 1914 to the Archbishops' Committee on Church and State under the chairmanship of Lord Selborne, and with Sir Lewis Dibdin wrote the section of its report, published in 1917, dealing with the history of the relations of church and state in England. In 1916–1917 he served on one of the five committees appointed by the archbishops in 1916, that concerned with 'Christianity and Industrial Problems', and was responsible for the section of its report, published in 1918, which dealt with 'historical illustrations'. In July 1917 he was appointed chairman of the Adult Education Committee set up by the Ministry of Reconstruction, the final report of which was published in 1919.

During the last five years of his life Smith was in failing health, and in October 1921 he underwent an operation. He exerted himself, however, to play an active part in the revival of Balliol and of the university after the War. He served on the Hebdomadal Council, acted as a curator of the Bodleian Library, and as a trustee of the University Endowment Fund, and continued to teach and lecture in college. In February 1924 he was taken suddenly ill, and he died at the Master's Lodgings 12 April. He is buried in Holywell cemetery.

Smith was an almoner of Christ's Hospital, and in 1919 he received the honorary degree of LL.D. from the university of St. Andrews. He married in 1879 Mary Florence, eldest daughter of John Forster Baird, of Bowmont Hill, Northumberland, who survived him together with their two sons and seven daughters. After his death a fund for the endowment of an A. L. Smith fellowship at Balliol was subscribed by friends and pupils.

Smith's portrait by Fiddes Watt hangs in the hall of Balliol College, and a memorial tablet to him is in the college chapel.

[*The Times*, 14 April 1924; *Arthur Lionel Smith, Master of Balliol (1916–1924), a Biography and some Reminiscences, by his Wife*, 1928; personal knowledge.] K. N. Bell.

SMITH, Sir FREDERICK (1857–1929), major-general, Army Veterinary Service, was born at Hull, the elder of twins, 19 April 1857. His father, Joseph Smith, a quartermaster who had served in the Crimean War, died while Smith was at school, leaving a widow (Ellen, *née* McCaffery), and three younger children, the other twin having died.

At the age of sixteen (1873) Smith entered the Royal Veterinary College, London. In April 1876 he obtained his diploma 'with great credit', gaining prizes in physiology and cattle pathology, and the Coleman medal for an essay on specific ophthalmia. Having passed his army veterinary examination in December 1876, he was commissioned to the Artillery (veterinary captain 1880, major 1896, lieutenant-colonel 1899, colonel 1905, major-general 1907), and in October 1877 sailed for India, but came home for medical treatment early in 1879. The same year he married Mary Ann, daughter of Arthur Samuel Briggs, of Spigot Lodge, Middleham, Yorkshire, a trainer of racehorses. They had a son and a daughter.

Returning to India at the end of 1879, Smith investigated the cause of sore backs among the 480 horses of his new regiment, the 12th Lancers. Contrary to prevailing opinion, he showed that the main cause was ill-fitting saddles and not errors of riding. In 1882, with J. H. Steel, he established the *Quarterly Journal of Veterinary Science in India*, which lasted seven years.

In 1886 Smith was appointed professor at the Army Veterinary School at Aldershot, where he spent five years of strenuous work, only relieved by a tour of the continental veterinary schools, one consequence of which was the establishment at Aldershot in 1888 of a Vaccine Institute which supplied all the calf lymph required for the army. From Aldershot he wrote forty-nine original papers for the professional journals, besides his *Manual of Veterinary Hygiene* (1887, 3rd edition 1905), *Manual of Veterinary Physiology* (1892, 5th edition 1921), and *Manual of Sore Backs* (1891, subsequently embodied in the army *Manual on the Care and Management of Horses*). The first two became the recognized text-books for all English-speaking veterinary students.

Among the many papers which Smith published between 1893 and 1898 may be mentioned *The Physiology of the Horse's Eye*, *The Loss of Horses in War*, and *The Physiology of the Horse's Foot*. He also worked at the control of strangles and pneumonia.

Smith served in the Nile campaign of 1898, and in the following year went on active service to South Africa. After the War he was for two and a half years principal veterinary officer in South Africa, and then returned to England as principal veterinary officer, Eastern command. In 1907, at the age of fifty, he was appointed director-general of the Army Veterinary Service with the rank of honorary major-general.

An Army Veterinary Corps having already been created, Smith reorganized the system of veterinary stores. He also succeeded in obtaining the inclusion of veterinary cadres in the organization of Viscount Haldane's Territorial Force, and strove to get the veterinary service, then subordinate to the remount department, placed directly under the quartermaster-general. The claim was not conceded until 1911, and Smith had retired in 1910. It can be said, however, that the subsequent development of the Service, culminating in its conspicuous efficiency during the European War, followed naturally on the reforms introduced at Smith's instigation.

Save for the years of the War, when he was re-employed, first as deputy director of veterinary services, Southern command, and then as assistant director-general, the remainder of Smith's life was devoted unremittingly to the completion of his historical works. *The History of the Royal Army Veterinary Corps* (1927) and *The Veterinary History of the War in South Africa* (1919) are of the highest interest and importance for this branch of the army. He saw through the press two volumes of his *History of Veterinary Literature* (i, 1919, ii, 1924), and passed the proofs of the third volume (issued 1930). The fourth volume he left in manuscript to the writer of this notice together with all his other papers.

Smith died at St. Leonards-on-Sea 27 July 1929; his body was cremated at Golders Green, and his ashes are preserved, together with his heart, at the Royal Veterinary College. His fortune of about £12,000 he left, after the life interests of his widow and two children, to the Royal College of Veterinary Surgeons for the establishment of a fund for veterinary research. No man of his generation deserved better of his profession or rendered it greater service. His portrait by Dorsfield Hardy hangs in the council chamber of the Royal College of Veterinary Surgeons.

[A. G. Todd, 'The Royal Army Veterinary School', in *Veterinary Journal*, vol. lxxxiii, pp. 14–30, 1927, gives a fuller account of Smith's work at Aldershot; personal knowledge.]

F. Bullock.

SMITH, FREDERICK EDWIN, first Earl of Birkenhead (1872–1930), lord chancellor, was born at Birkenhead 12 July 1872, the eldest son of Frederick Smith, of Birkenhead, by his wife, Elizabeth, daughter of Edwin Taylor, of Birkenhead. His father, after an adventurous early manhood, had settled down to the family business of an estate agent, in which he prospered. He took part in local politics, was called to the bar by the Middle Temple, and became mayor of Birkenhead. He died in early middle age (1887), leaving his widow with three sons and two daughters. Frederick Edwin Smith always acknowledged that he inherited from his father his rhetorical gifts, his inclination to the bar as a profession, and his ambition. From his mother, perhaps, came the more stable elements in his character. Mrs. Smith's financial resources were slender, though in later years her son was disposed to exaggerate the poverty of the family. She, with help from a relation, was able to provide a good education for her children. F. E. Smith was sent to Birkenhead School, whence, in 1891, he obtained a scholarship at Wadham College, Oxford.

Wadham was then a small college and of no great reputation in the university, but among Smith's contemporaries were several men who attained eminence in after life: of these the most distinguished were J. A. (afterwards Sir John) Simon, C. B. Fry (outstanding in every field of athletics), A. A. (afterwards Lord Justice) Roche, F. W. Hirst, the economist, and H. M. Giveen, afterwards junior counsel to the Treasury on the common law side. Smith plunged with zest into the social life of the undergraduate. He played Rugby football, coming within measurable distance of a place in the university XV; he achieved fame at the Union, of which he was elected president (1893); he read widely, though not the books necessary for success in the schools; he ran into debt; he reached the second class in classical moderations (1893); then, taking up law instead of reading for *literae humaniores*, after a burst of intensive reading, gained a first class in jurisprudence (1895). He remained at Oxford in order to read for the Vinerian scholarship, which he was awarded in 1896, and the same year he was elected a fellow of Merton College. There, and at Oriel College from 1897, Smith taught law for the next three years, adding to his income by delivering university extension lectures on modern history. During part of this time also he passed his vacations as a pupil in the chambers of Mr. (afterwards Sir) Leslie Scott, who carried on a large practice in Liverpool. During this period also, Smith made the acquaintance of the lady who afterwards became his wife, Margaret Eleanor, second daughter of the Rev. Henry Furneaux, fellow of Corpus Christi College and editor of Tacitus. Further, he acquired that love of horses and of horsemanship which was one of the main pleasures of his life, and that love of Oxford as a place and of the university as an institution, which remained his passion.

Smith entered as a student at Gray's Inn in 1894. In 1899 he was called to the bar and began to practise in Liverpool. He was already well known there. His father's memory still lingered, and his own successes at the Oxford Union had attracted the attention of Mr. (afterwards Sir) Archibald Salvidge [q.v.], the leader of the conservative party on the Liverpool city council. As early as 1894, while still an undergraduate, Smith was addressing important political meetings. Liverpool politics at this time turned on the Irish question. The Irish population commanded the representation of one of the parliamentary divisions of the city and formed an important element in another. Thus, the natural tendency of local toryism was to assume an Orange colour, and Smith found a congenial place in the conservative ranks. Sympathy with Ulster, engendered at his entrance into politics, remained with him throughout his career.

Smith's first chance at the bar came to him in the shape of a number of briefs at licensing sessions owing to Scott's absence during the long vacation of 1899. In his first complete calendar year he earned more than £500. His next year showed a further advance, and on the strength of it he married (1901). In 1902 came his first *cause célèbre*, the defence at the Central Criminal Court of Goudie, a Liverpool bank clerk, who was indicted, together with a number of confederates, for frauds on the bank in which he was employed. Goudie's case was hopeless and he pleaded guilty. But Smith greatly increased an already growing reputation by his speech for the mitigation of sentence. During the next few years he was engaged in several cases which attracted public attention: the defence of a girl named Rollinson from the charge of a peculiarly cold-blooded murder (1902); the long and complicated litigation arising from the trade war between the Imperial Tobacco Company and an American combine (1902–1906); the prosecution of the youth John McKeeven, charged with the manslaughter of John Kensit [q.v.], the protestant agitator (1902), and that of the murderers of the master and members of the crew of the *Veronica* (1903). By the end of 1905 he was firmly established in a large local practice, and was well known to bench and bar generally by his occasional visits to London.

In January 1906 Smith was elected member of parliament for the Walton division of Liverpool. He at once moved his chambers to London. But his forensic success was unchecked and was indeed accelerated. His most lucrative employment about this time was in the series of actions brought in 1907 by Lever Brothers against the newspapers under the control of Lord Northcliffe [see Lever, William Hesketh, first Viscount Leverhulme]; his most famous case, the defence of Ethel le Neve, the mistress of the murderer Crippen (1910). But Smith had now reached the stage of his career at which, having attained a secure place in his profession and the certainty of earning a substantial income, he was able to employ his ambition more fully in the wider field of politics. Unfortunately, by this time he had acquired habits of extravagance which he never shook off. Probably he had never possessed any sense of the value of money: he had always spent what he was about to earn. Thenceforth he acted on the theory that he could earn to-morrow whatever he spent to-day.

Smith was fortunate in the moment of his entry into parliament. His party had suffered a crushing disaster at the polls. At St. Stephen's there was nothing to lose and everything to gain. On 12 March 1906 he made his maiden speech. He spoke for an hour. The subject of the debate was fiscal policy. He poured forth invective and epigram; he kept the House amused; he put new heart into his friends; he exasperated his opponents. The effect was exactly what was required by a beaten and dispirited party. Smith sat down having achieved a parliamentary reputation.

During the remaining years of the 1906 parliament Smith maintained with energy the fight against overwhelming odds. At the same time he formed enduring friendships not only with members of his own party but among his opponents, and particularly with Mr. Winston Churchill. But the brilliance of his first appearance, the rapidity of his wit, and the ferocity of his attack caused men to take a false view of his character and of his attainments. He was regarded as a swashbuckler, witty and courageous, but headstrong and superficial—in the courts, as the man for a crushing cross-examination or a speech to a jury rather than for a serious legal argument, and in the House, for the brilliance, raillery, and rhetorical display of a partisan rather than for the measured view and wise counsel of the statesman. His appearance and his manner of life contributed to this view. He was strikingly handsome, six feet one inch in height, of a distinguished figure, slightly marred by sloping shoulders. His clothes, although not in any one particular out of the ordinary, gave the impression that he was over-dressed. The hat worn on the back of his head, the red flower in his buttonhole, the very long cigar always carried in his mouth, made him a ready subject for the caricaturist. The great houses in which he stayed, the late hours which he kept, his fondness for gaiety and for gay people, for cards, for horses, and for all the bright and expensive things of life, confirmed the opinion that he was a reckless partisan, fighting hard for his own side, grasping at his own enjoyment and advantage, not a responsible or serious person either as a lawyer or as a parliamentarian. Furthermore, his sharp tongue, his aggressive demeanour, and the cynical attitude which he at times assumed made many enemies and not only among his political foes.

Smith was in part conscious of the effect which he produced, and having moral as well as physical courage he intensified these traits, which were rather of outward conduct than of inward character. Regarding ambition as one of the most powerful spurs to fine action, he gloried in it. He had an artist's pleasure in getting the most out of life as he conceived it. And knowing that he could stir masses of men and that he enjoyed the affection of those who knew him best, he unduly disregarded the dislike which he inspired among the soberminded. Without any pretence at black-letter learning, Smith knew that he possessed a firm grasp of legal principles and could apprehend the most subtle doctrine. In politics he seemed to be dazzled by his own fireworks. Inwardly he felt a deep and sincere sense of responsibility. He looked upon the mass of attempted liberal legislation as a mean revenge upon the enemies of the party in power (as in the Education and Licensing Bills), or as an unprincipled concession to electioneering needs (as in the Trades Disputes Bill). He therefore attacked these measures and their promoters with passionate violence, spurred on the more because, nonconformist though he was by upbringing, he did not understand the sincerity of some at least of their supporters. On these matters he was content to be a partisan and to fight with every weapon in his armoury. But beyond these conflicts, which seemed to him ephemeral, more vital issues loomed in his vision. He believed that these could be faced only by a government comprising men of all the constitutional parties.

An opportunity for putting this theory into action soon arose. The chief parliamentary event of 1909 was the passage through the Commons of Mr. Lloyd George's land valuation budget. Smith fought it fiercely in that House, but when the Bill reached the Lords, he did his utmost to persuade his friends there to allow it to pass. To reject it seemed to him to be to present the liberals with the opportunity which they desired. As a party manager he was unquestionably right. The decision against him was of momentous historical consequence. But in his own career the controversy with his friends was of even greater import. It showed to himself and to others on what side he would be found when the strain between immediate party loyalties and national interests became acute. For the moment his party forgave his lukewarmness.

The general election of January 1910 justified Smith's fears. The government majority fell from 356 to 126. But for the opposition to fail by so much was to fail altogether. The government at once launched its direct attack on the Lords' veto. The eventual result was the Parliament Act, and, as its inevitable consequences, the disestablishment of the Welsh Church and Home Rule. Smith's attitude was consistent and courageous. In parliament and in the country he continued his opposition unabated. But when the leaders of both parties, recognizing that party passions were driving them to an end which they could not foresee, entered into a conference (June 1910), he was instant openly for the party truce, and in secret negotiation, for a settlement and for the formation of a national government which should include moderate men of both shades of opinion. The conference failed and Smith's efforts proved futile. Once again (December 1910) Mr. Asquith went to the country, and with the same result. In May 1911 the Bill for the Parliament Act passed the Commons. The Lords amended it, but the government refused to accept their amendments.

The strife now shifted from parliament to the councils of the unionist party. Should the Lords give way, or should they stand fast and leave to the government the final stroke of advising the creation of peers sufficient in number to pass the Bill? Smith was unhesitatingly for the latter course. He did not believe that the government would dare to carry out its threat, and to the end of his life he held the same opinion. All the evidence which has come to light in recent years is against that opinion. His own party leaders, with the exception of Lord Halsbury [q.v.], were against him at the time. The extreme right wing was voted down, though by a small majority (10 August 1911). It was the only occasion in Smith's political career when, bearing responsibility, he threw the weight of his authority on to the side of extreme measures. The full consequences of the Parliament Act and of the Lords' surrender are not yet discernible. Years must pass before a final judgement can be pronounced on his action.

For the moment, the crisis had the effect of confirming Smith in the affection of the more unbending tories. It also effected a revolution in the party itself. In November Mr. Balfour resigned the leadership and Mr. Bonar Law was elected in his room. At the coronation of King George V, Mr. Asquith had recommended that a privy councillorship for Smith should be included in the honours list. Mr. Balfour, who had not been consulted, objected and did not invite Smith to take his seat on the front opposition bench. Mr. Bonar Law repaired the omission, and Smith found himself at the age of thirty-nine, after less than six years' service in parliament, one of the accredited leaders of the unionist party.

The next two-and-a-half years were occupied in the struggle which raged round the Home Rule Bill. Smith seemed absorbed in the preparations for resistance in Ulster. He visited Belfast with Sir Edward Carson in 1912 and addressed a great audience on the anniversary of the battle of the Boyne (12 July). In the following year he 'galloped for Carson' at a review of the Belfast volunteers. But in the same month (September 1913) Smith was endeavouring first to bring his own friends to consider the question of an accommodation, and secondly to open some communication with the other side. Then, as nine years later, he took his stand on the security of Ulster. If this end could be attained, he was prepared to make sacrifices and to recommend them to his friends. 'It was impossible', he wrote, 'to ignore the unbroken parliamentary representation of that part of Ireland which was in favour of Home Rule.' Having opened the matter to Sir Edward Carson, and received a response which was not wholly discouraging, he began to discuss it with Mr. Lloyd George, who was equally willing. Mr. Churchill was of the same mind. In October Smith, with his leader's unacknowledged authority, in a public speech proposed a settlement, with Ulster excluded. Negotiations, both open and secret, went on through the first half of 1914. They broke down again and again, but were resumed at a conference at Buckingham Palace and finally broke down in the last week of July. In August party passions were suddenly stilled by the outbreak of war.

During the exciting events which crowded the years of Smith's life as a private member of parliament, he had carried on an ever-increasing practice at the bar. He took silk in 1908. By 1914 he was in the front rank of fashionable advocates and was making an income which was, by the standards of those days, prodigious. He was also spending as much as he earned. The European War changed his life. Thenceforth, except for the short periods when he was out of office, he was continually engaged on constructive work for the government. In the days immediately preceding 4 August 1914 his friendship with Mr. Churchill and his qualities of courage and resolution made him a suitable go-between through whom the government might be assured of the support of the opposition in any measures necessary for the safety and honour of the country. He then accepted the post of head of the Press Bureau, a thankless and indeed well-nigh impossible task. The chief incident of this interlude was his emendation of the bulletin describing the retreat of the British forces from Mons, still a matter of controversy. His next employment was in France as a descriptive writer attached to the Indian Corps. The experiment was not a success. He did not understand soldiers, nor they him. On the formation of the first Coalition government in May 1915, Smith returned to England in order to become solicitor-general. In November he succeeded Sir Edward Carson as attorney-general. This year he was knighted.

The office of attorney-general, in peace perhaps the most laborious in the public service, becomes in war almost unbearably burdensome. The attorney-general was necessarily consulted on the enormous mass of legislation passed or authorized by parliament. The law of prize, which must necessarily occupy the attention of the law officers during any war, had to be developed and adapted to modern needs. The necessary interference of government with the business and private affairs of the individual incessantly raised new problems. It would have been impossible for any man efficiently to discharge the duties of the office if he had not possessed, as Smith did, the power of delegation to a most unusual degree. He absorbed instructions very quickly. Confident in his judgement of men, he was prepared to rely upon the help of others. He chose his instruments carefully and, where he gave his trust, he gave also his complete loyalty and support.

The most famous cases in which Smith was engaged in court were, perhaps, those of the S.S. *Zamora* (1916) and the S.S. *Ophelia* (1916), both heard on appeal in the Judicial Committee of the Privy Council sitting as an appellate court in prize; the trial of Sir Roger Casement [q.v.] for high treason (1916); the trial of the Wheeldons for a conspiracy to murder the prime minister (1917); and the Rhodesian land case before the Judicial Committee (1918). During this time also, and until the end of the War, Smith had a seat in the Cabinet. He found time towards the end of 1917 to pay a lightning visit to the United States of America and to Canada, where he expounded to crowded audiences the Allied case against Germany. Before he went he had been elected treasurer of Gray's Inn for the year 1917–1918, and, during his absence, in the New Year honours list of 1918, he received a baronetcy. At the general election of 1918 Smith abandoned his old constituency and was returned for the West Derby division of Liverpool. He held the seat for a month only, for, upon the reconstruction of the government, Mr. Lloyd George offered him either continuance in office as attorney-general without a seat in the Cabinet or advancement to the woolsack. The choice was painful, but it was not difficult. Although the chancellorship had always been among the objects of his ambition, Smith did not wish to leave the Commons or to cut off the possibility of his eventual return to the bar. But he could not deprive himself of the opportunity of taking part in the work of government in the dangerous days which he foresaw, nor could he, without Cabinet rank, identify himself with a policy in the shaping of which he could have only a minor share. He inevitably took the course which, however splendid, was the more disagreeable to him. It was not rendered more agreeable by the public reception of the announcement. Except among his private friends, who welcomed it with some regret, the appointment was unpopular.

Smith received the Great Seal on 14 January 1919, and on 31 January he presided as lord chancellor at the hearing of his first cause. On 3 February the patent creating him Baron Birkenhead passed the Great Seal, and on the following day he was 'introduced' as a peer. During his chancellorship, Lord Birkenhead sat regularly as Speaker of the House of Lords for judicial business or as chairman of the Judicial Committee of the Privy Council. He soon acquired great authority among his legal colleagues. The time had come when he could bring into play the learning which he had acquired as a teacher and as a practitioner. His demeanour as a judge was dignified and impressive. He kept the court together, and strove earnestly to do justice and to make it clear that justice was being done. His judgments were composed with great care and after close consultation with his colleagues. In style they were vigorous and often witty. His most famous cases, while he held the Great Seal, were *Bourne* v. *Keane* (legality of a bequest for Masses for the dead, 1919); *Sutters* v. *Briggs* (Gaming Act [1835], 1921); *Admiralty* v. S.S. *Volute* (contributory negligence in a maritime collision, 1921); *Rutherford* v. *Richardson* (an illustration of his methods when considering conflicts of testimony on fact, 1922). All these cases were heard by the House of Lords in the exercise of its ordinary appellate jurisdiction. In the Judicial Committee Smith presided at the hearing of two cases raising constitutional points of importance—one from British Columbia (*Canadian Pacific Company* v. *Tuley*, 1921), the other from Australia (*McCawley* v. *the King*, 1920). *The Director of Public Prosecutions* v. *Beard* (1920) was an appeal to the House of Lords, under section 1 (6) of the Criminal Appeal Act (1907), involving an examination of the doctrines as to the effect of drunkenness on criminal responsibility; *Wakeford* v. *the Bishop of Lincoln* (1921) was a case turning purely on fact heard by the Judicial Committee with ecclesiastical assessors on appeal from the consistory court of Lincoln under the Clergy Discipline Act (1892); *C.* (*otherwise H.*) v. *C.* (1921) and *Gaskill* v. *Gaskill* (1921) were cases heard before him sitting to try matrimonial causes as an additional judge of the Probate, Divorce, and Admiralty division of the High Court when that division was hard pressed. In the Rhondda peerage case (1922), sitting under the chairmanship of the lord chairman (Lord Donoughmore) in the Committee for Privileges, Birkenhead delivered the very elaborate leading judgment. After he had left office in 1922 and before he became secretary of state for India in 1924, he sat in a few cases. In *Russell* v. *Russell* (1924), a case heard on appeal from the decision of the Court of Appeal in England, he held, with the majority, that a husband's evidence of non-access was not admissible on his petition for divorce in a case in which the only evidence of adultery consisted in the birth of a child.

Birkenhead, who avowed himself to be eager for posthumous fame, was inclined to rest his claim to remembrance on the part played by him as a law reformer. The heaviest task which he set himself in this capacity was the amendment of the law relating to the transfer of land. Renewing the efforts made by Lord Haldane [q.v.], he caused to be prepared and passed through parliament the gigantic piece of legislation which reached the statute book as the Law of Property Act (1922). The work was accomplished in the face of many difficulties. It was highly technical; its details were of no great interest either to the public or to parliament; and it had to withstand the force of some persistent professional opposition. Using, as he always did, the learning of others, Smith had many ready helpers. But the successful passage of the bill was due to his energy and parliamentary skill. In other fields of legal administration he worked hard. He prepared the way for the Supreme Court of Judicature (Consolidation) Act (1925), by the passage of a number of minor measures dealing with the administration of justice in the Supreme Court. With the assistance of the Supreme Court Rule Committee he remodelled the Rules relating to the conduct of litigation by and against poor persons, and caused provision to be made for the trial on circuit of poor persons' divorce cases. He effected considerable improvements in the tenure of office of county court judges and, by inaugurating an inquiry into the administrative machinery of the county courts, laid the foundation for the County Courts Act (1924).

In the administration of his patronage Birkenhead was entirely free from political bias. Six judges of the High Court (of whom one afterwards became a lord of appeal in ordinary and two became members of the Court of Appeal) were appointed on his recommendation. He appointed ten judges to the county court bench.

Throughout his tenure of office Birkenhead was a vigorous and impressive exponent and defender of the government's general policy. On occasion he allowed himself to speak on matters which were not the subject of political controversies of the moment. His most famous effort was his speech upon the bill designed to give effect to the majority report of Lord Gorell's committee on divorce. No one who heard the speech could doubt his ability as a parliamentary orator; but most of those who heard it were surprised not so much at its eloquence as at its deep moral earnestness and at its evidence of mature consideration of the social question involved.

Birkenhead's place as one of the statesmen of the third Coalition government must stand or fall, however, by his attitude on the Irish question. Once more, as in the days preceding the War, that question formed the major problem. So long as the only course open to the government seemed to be that of resistance to a criminal conspiracy, Birkenhead was for the maintenance of the struggle. So late as 21 June 1921, he delivered in the House of Lords a speech which gave no indication of any intent to seek peace. But negotiations had already begun between the British government and the Irish republican leaders. On 10 August Birkenhead spoke in the House advocating a settlement by consent. He maintained then, and afterwards, that there was no inconsistency in his attitude. It was, as he thought, the natural development of the views which he had held in 1913–1914. He desired to save the effusion of English blood and the waste of English treasure in Southern Ireland provided only that he could secure the independence of Ulster. In this spirit he attended the Gairloch meeting in August and entered upon the London conference in October. As soon as he met the Irish negotiators he became convinced of their sincerity, and of the possibility of healing the long quarrel between Southern Ireland and Great Britain. He acquired a respect which amounted almost to affection for Arthur Griffith [q.v.] and Michael Collins [q.v.], and it was in the spirit not of one who had been defeated but of a statesman bent on securing a long-desired aim that he supported the proposals of the government to give effect to the Irish Treaty (6 December 1921) and to the bill confirming the Free State constitution (1922).

These efforts, however, laid a heavy strain upon the ties between Birkenhead and many of his political and personal friends. For other reasons, certain sections of the conservative party were impatient at the continued existence of the Coalition. Birkenhead strove for its safety. As in past years, he still believed that the country required a national government and a national party. He was unsuccessful, and the Coalition fell in October 1922. It would be idle to deny his feeling of extreme bitterness towards those who had destroyed the work which he had in hand. He expressed himself in the country with acrimony and in the House of Lords in speeches which were regarded as vindictive and flippant. He doubted the wisdom wherewith affairs were conducted under Mr. Stanley Baldwin's first administration, and he anticipated the catastrophe which followed.

On the fall of Mr. Ramsay MacDonald's government in October 1924 Birkenhead was ready to be reconciled to his friends and to accept office as secretary of state for India. His main work there was to prepare for the examination of the constitution granted to that country by the Government of India Act (1919), which had been foreshadowed in the preamble to that Act. He induced Sir John Simon to undertake the task of presiding over the commission which was to investigate the matter. Before that commission had reported Birkenhead had left office. He was not in sympathy with any attempt to anticipate the findings of the commission, and before he had ceased to be secretary of state signs were apparent that his mind was not moving upon the same lines as that of Lord Irwin, whose appointment to the viceroyalty in November 1925 he had approved. It is impossible to tell what view he would have taken upon the proceedings of the successive Round Table Conferences and of the Government of India Bill (1935).

Early in his lord chancellorship, Lord Birkenhead showed signs that his health was beginning to suffer from the excessive strain which he put upon it. He had for long been burning the candle at both ends. With prodigious labours both within and without his office he combined every form of physical activity. Meanwhile he had taken little care of his financial position. During his absence from office and after his return to it he had made money as a writer for the press and of books having a popular appeal. While he was secretary of state for India, public opinion in the Commons was adverse to these activities. He found himself under the necessity of increasing his income, and in 1928 he resigned and took up work in the City. By now even his magnificent powers were failing. His last speeches in the House of Lords sounded forced and hollow. In the spring of 1930 he fell seriously ill. He died in London 30 September, aged fifty-eight.

Birkenhead was advanced to a viscounty in June 1921, and on the fall of Mr. Lloyd George's government in 1922 he was, in November, created Earl of Birkenhead and Viscount Furneaux, taking his second title from his wife's maiden name. He was created G.C.S.I. on leaving office in 1928, and he held the grand cordon of the order of Leopold, conferred upon him by Albert, King of the Belgians. In 1922 he received the honorary degree of D.C.L. from the university of Oxford, of which he was appointed high steward the same year. He was lord rector of Glasgow University (1922) and lord rector of Aberdeen University (1926).

Lord Birkenhead had one son, Frederick Winston Furneaux (born 1907), who succeeded him as second earl, and two daughters.

Birkenhead was often painted. His most famous, and on the whole most satisfactory portrait, is that by Glyn Philpot, which hangs in Gray's Inn hall. The cartoon by 'Spy' (*Vanity Fair*, 16 January 1907), reproduced in colour as the frontispiece to Vol. i of his son's *Life*, gives a faithful representation of him as he was when he was emerging into fame. Another, anonymous, cartoon also appeared in *Vanity Fair* 9 August 1911.

[*Frederick Edwin, Earl of Birkenhead, by his son* (the Earl of Birkenhead), 2 vols., 1933–1935; personal knowledge.] C. Schuster.

SMITH, Sir HENRY BABINGTON (1863–1923), civil servant and financier, was born 29 January 1863 at Riverbank, Putney, the London house of his father, Archibald Smith [q.v.], mathematician, of Jordanhill, Renfrewshire. This branch of Smiths was long settled at Craigend in Stirlingshire as farmers and armourers. In 1800, a younger son, Archibald Smith, having succeeded as a West India merchant, bought the estate of Jordanhill, then a country place, but now a suburb of Glasgow. He was the father of James Smith [q.v.], geologist and man of letters, and grandfather of Archibald Smith, Henry's father. Henry Smith's mother was Susan Emma, daughter of Vice-Chancellor Sir James Parker [q.v.], and granddaughter of Thomas Babington, of Rothley Temple, Leicestershire. He was thus related to Babingtons and Macaulays, since Thomas Babington married Jean, sister of Zachary Macaulay [q.v.].

Smith was the fifth son in a family of six sons and two daughters, of whom all the sons obtained distinction, his eldest brother, James Parker Smith, sometime M.P. for Partick, Lanarkshire, being the best known.

After attending a private school (Dr. Spyers's) at Weybridge, Henry Smith was elected king's scholar at Eton in 1875, third on the list. He won the Tomlin mathematical prize in 1880, was Newcastle medallist in 1882, and obtained a minor scholarship at Trinity College, Cambridge, in the same year. As captain of the school he delivered to Queen Victoria an address from the Eton boys after the attempt on her life at Windsor in 1882. He was very competent at football and in the boats. Already he had a reputation for quiet efficiency and sober sanity of judgement, a calmness of mind and a sweetness of temper which inspired confidence; and these qualities remained with him through life. Eton also had its effect on him, for he valued few of his honours more than his election, in later life, as a fellow of Eton, in which capacity he proved invaluable to the college in educational and financial business. At Cambridge, where he was a member of the 'Apostles', he gained a first class in both parts of the classical tripos, was second chancellor's medallist, obtained the Browne medal three times, and finally (1889) was elected a fellow of his college.

Already in 1887 Smith had entered the Education Office as an examiner. His inclination, however, was rather to administration and finance than to educational subjects. His chance came when, in 1891, Mr. Goschen, then chancellor of the Exchequer, appointed him his private secretary. In 1892 he was transferred to the Treasury establishment. Here he had his first taste of international finance, in which he was to play so large a part, as secretary to the British delegates at the Brussels Silver Conference in that year. But he was not allowed to develop under the Treasury routine. In 1894 he was chosen by Lord Elgin, the new viceroy of India, as his private secretary. On his return from India, at the beginning of the South African War, he was diverted to inquire into the finances of Natal, which were feeling the strain of the War. Another appointment followed when he was made British representative on the council of administration of the Ottoman Public Debt in 1900, and president in 1901. In 1903 he returned to home service as secretary to the Post Office, where he remained until 1909, administering that department with success, and representing it at various international congresses with dignity and efficiency. He received the C.S.I. in 1897, the C.B. in 1905, and in 1908 was created K.C.B.

Smith's conspicuous ability in finance had attracted the attention of Sir Ernest Cassel [q.v.]. Largely through the latter's influence he was, in 1909, appointed administrateur directeur-général of the National Bank of Turkey and consequently left the civil service. Other directorships followed. As chairman of the Pacific Cable Board (1913) he was still closely in touch with government work, and during the European War his wide financial experience was freely called upon.

He went twice to the United States—with the Anglo-French Commission in 1915, and as assistant high commissioner under Lord Reading in 1918. He helped to found the British Italian Corporation and the British Trade Corporation, and he served on many of the more important financial committees of that critical time. He was also chairman of the royal commission on the Civil Service in 1915, and after the War (1919) chairman of the Indian Currency and Finance Commission, and chairman of the Railways Amalgamation Tribunal (1921–1923). He was made a director of the Bank of England in 1920. He died at Vineyards, Saffron Walden, 29 September 1923, and was buried at Eton.

Smith married in 1898 Lady Elizabeth Mary, eldest daughter of Victor Alexander Bruce, ninth Earl of Elgin [q.v.], and had four sons and five daughters.

[*The Times*, 1 October 1923; family records; private information.] M. F. Headlam.

SMITH, Sir ROSS MACPHERSON (1892–1922), airman, was born at Adelaide, South Australia, 4 December 1892, the second son of Andrew Smith, pastoralist, of that city (a native of Dumfries, Scotland), by his wife, Jessie Macpherson. He was educated at Warriston School, Moffat, Scotland, and at Queen's School, Adelaide. In 1910 he made a tour round the world with a party of Australian mounted cadets, who were received by King George V. While he was in England, Ross Smith visited Lord Roberts, who showed the young man his medals, and impressed him with the danger of Great Britain becoming involved in a European war and of her reliance upon Australia's support.

Ross Smith was one of three brothers, all of whom were expected in due time to join the business, an estate of three million acres, of which their father was managing director. Meanwhile they each sought experience in other employment. Keith, the eldest (afterwards Sir Keith Smith), joined a firm of wool brokers; Colin, the youngest (who died of wounds received at Passchendaele in 1917), went into a bank; and Ross entered a firm of hardware merchants.

On the outbreak of the European War in August 1914, Ross Smith enlisted as a trooper in the 3rd Australian Light Horse. He sailed with the first Australian expeditionary force, and landed in Egypt in December 1914. After four months' service on the Gallipoli Peninsula in 1915, he received a commission, but was shortly afterwards invalided to England. He rejoined his regiment in March 1916 and took part in August in the battle of Romani during the last attack made by the Turks on the Suez Canal.

In October 1916 Ross Smith was transferred to the Royal Flying Corps, and joined No. 67 (Australian) Squadron as an observer. He served with the squadron in Palestine, and gained valuable knowledge of the country. In July 1917 he qualified as a pilot at the training schools in Egypt, and rejoined his squadron in Southern Palestine. He was one of the most successful pilots of the squadron, engaged in many combats with German aeroplanes, and took a leading part in the bombing attack, 19 September 1918, on the Turkish central telephone exchange at 'Affule, the successful prelude to the offensive which put an end to Turkey's part in the War.

Ross Smith served in his squadron until the end of the War. On the conclusion of peace he at once began a series of long-distance flights which made his name famous. At the end of November 1918 he piloted Brigadier-General A. E. Borton on the first flight made from Cairo to Calcutta, for which he received the Air Force cross. He subsequently accompanied Borton on a series of reconnaissances for suitable aerodrome sites in Burma, Siam, the Malay States, and the Dutch East Indies. In 1919 Ross Smith undertook the first flight from England to Australia. The Commonwealth government had offered a prize of £10,000 for a flight from Great Britain to Australia to be performed in 720 consecutive hours by an Australian airman. The prize was won by Ross Smith and his brother Keith who, with Sergeants W. H. Shiers and J. M. Bennett, left Hounslow on 12 November and reached Port Darwin on 10 December after a journey of 11,294 miles. Their aeroplane was a Vickers Vimy machine fitted with Rolls Royce engines, and the journey was handicapped by bad weather and inadequate aerodrome facilities. The flight was continued to Melbourne and, at its conclusion, the Smith brothers were each created K.B.E.

In 1922 Sir Ross Smith arranged to make a flight round the world in a Vickers Vimy amphibian. He was making a first trial flight at Brooklands on 13 April, when the amphibian spun out of control and the pilot with his sole passenger, Lieutenant J. M. Bennett, was killed. Sir Keith Smith, who was to have accompanied them on the trial flight, had been delayed by fog in reaching Brooklands in time to join them.

Ross Smith was a rugged, determined character. He was very level-headed and took no foolish risks. The plans for his long flights were made only after the most exhaustive study of every aspect of the journey. Although he will be chiefly remembered for his pioneer flight from England to Australia, his service record earned great distinction for the Australian Flying Corps.

Ross Smith received the M.C. and bar, the D.F.C. and two bars, and the order of El Nahda, fourth class, conferred upon him by the King of the Hejaz. He was unmarried.

[F. M. Cutlack, *The Australian Flying Corps*, 1923; private information; personal knowledge.] H. A. Jones.

SMITH, WILLIAM FREDERICK DANVERS, second Viscount Hambleden (1868–1928), philanthropist, was born at Filey, Yorkshire, 12 August 1868. He was the younger and only surviving son of William Henry Smith [q.v.], the well-known statesman, by his wife, Emily, daughter of Frederick Dawes Danvers, of Bushey, Hertfordshire, clerk of the council of the duchy of Lancaster. On the death of W. H. Smith in 1891, his widow was raised to the peerage as Viscountess Hambleden, in recognition of her husband's public services. Frederick Smith, as he was usually called, succeeded to his father's business and estate, and to his mother's title on her death in 1913.

Smith entered Dr. Warre's house at Eton in 1882, and went up to New College, Oxford, in the autumn of 1887. A good oarsman, he was in the Eton College eight, and stroked the New College boat, but under medical orders was obliged to abandon the attempt to secure a place in the university crew. Always a man of many friends, he later became, at his Henley home, the popular host of generations of university oarsmen. He left Oxford with a third class in modern history in 1890. In the following year his father's death placed him at the head of the newspaper-distributing business of W. H. Smith and Son. At the same time he was invited to succeed his father as conservative member of parliament for the Strand division of Westminster, and was returned by a substantial majority in October 1891. He held the seat until the general election of January 1910, when he resigned. Neither in the House of Commons nor in the House of Lords, which he entered three years later, did he make much figure as a politician. The chief interests of his useful life lay elsewhere.

Smith devoted constant attention to the business of W. H. Smith and Son, which his grandfather had founded and his father had developed. He was proud of the traditions of the firm, and showed himself devoted in many ways to the welfare of its employees. One of his first acts was the establishment of a benefit society for his workpeople, and his sympathetic outlook earned him the regard of all who served with him or under him. When in 1905 a crisis occurred in reference to the firm's book-stall contracts with the railway companies, and two of the most important of these contracts were given up, Smith was prepared to risk all his resources in organizing a book-shop branch, and by 1 January 1906, two hundred new shops of this kind had been opened. The new departure was in the end fully justified, and under his able management the business generally increased and prospered.

The other chief interest of Lord Hambleden lay in philanthropic work, and especially in the administration of voluntary hospitals. He was closely connected with King's College Hospital, of which for many years he was chairman. He was the prime mover in the transfer of that institution from the neighbourhood of Clare market to its new site on Denmark Hill. His experience gave him a wide knowledge of the problems of hospital management, and he was chairman of the London regional committee of the British Hospitals Association as well as treasurer of the association itself. He was the founder (1922) and first chairman of the Hospital Savings Association, and also chairman of the King Edward's fund pay beds committee.

Coming as a young man into great wealth, Smith regarded his riches as a trust to be administered for the benefit of others. He was a sincere churchman, and there was no good cause which he was not ready to assist with wise generosity, and sometimes, as in the case of the hospitals, with valuable personal service as well.

During the European War Lord Hambleden served in Gallipoli and in Egypt (1915–1916) with the Royal first Devon Yeomanry, of which he was lieutenant-colonel.

Lord Hambleden married in 1894 Lady Esther, third daughter of Arthur Gore, fifth Earl of Arran, and had three sons and two daughters. He died at Henley-on-Thames 16 June 1928, and was succeeded as third viscount by his eldest son, William Henry (born 1903).

[*The Times*, 18 June 1928; private information.] A. Cochrane.

SMITH-DORRIEN, Sir HORACE LOCKWOOD (1858–1930), general, the sixth son of Colonel Robert Algernon Smith-Dorrien, J.P., of Haresfoot, Hertfordshire, by his wife, Mary Anne, daughter of Thomas Driver, M.D., was born at Haresfoot 26 May 1858. After passing through Harrow School and the Royal Military College, Sandhurst, he was gazetted as lieutenant in the 95th Foot in January 1877.

Smith-Dorrien's first experience of active service was in the Zulu War of 1879, where he was one of the five officers who escaped from the disaster at Isandhlwana (22 January). On 4 July he saw the final defeat of the Zulus at Ulundi. In 1882 he went with his regiment to Egypt, at the time of Arabi Pasha's rebellion, and took part in some skirmishes outside Alexandria. The regiment then went on to Lucknow, where Smith-Dorrien won the first of his many successes on the race-course and polo-field. But during a shooting expedition he wrenched his knee so badly that he had to be invalided home. In January 1884 he joined the newly raised Egyptian army under the sirdar, Sir Evelyn Wood. But the trouble with his knee broke out again, and he remained at the base, unable to take active part in Lord Wolseley's attempt to relieve General Gordon at Khartoum. He recovered in time, however, to command the Egyptian cavalry at the battle of Ginniss on 30 December 1885.

After passing through the Staff College —where he chiefly distinguished himself as master of the draghounds—Smith-Dorrien returned to his regiment in India, and served there for nearly ten years (1889–1898). He kept a large stud for polo and racing, and was greatly delighted when his horse 'Shannon' won the army cup; it was ridden by Captain (afterwards General Sir) Hubert Gough. He held staff appointments at Lucknow and Umballa, and spent five months (1897–1898) on the Tirah expedition against the unruly tribes of the North-West Frontier.

While Smith-Dorrien was on leave at home in June 1898, the sirdar, Sir H. H. Kitchener, telegraphed for him to come to Egypt. He hastened out in time to take command of the 13th Sudanese battalion at the battle of Omdurman (2 September). Immediately afterwards he was selected to command the troops which accompanied Kitchener to Fashoda to meet the column under Major Marchand. The appearance of the French expedition in territory which was held to be under British control gave rise to an extraordinary outburst of feeling in the press. But although the trip was full of interest, Smith-Dorrien declared that he had little knowledge of what was going on, as Kitchener did not confide his intentions to subordinates.

On the outbreak of war with the Boer republics in 1899, Smith-Dorrien went to South Africa with his regiment and was at once given command of the 19th brigade. With this he distinguished himself at the battle of Paardeberg (18 February 1900), and in the advance to Pretoria. Another year was spent with the columns hunting Generals Botha and De Wet. But before peace was declared he had been promoted major-general, and Lord Roberts, who was then commander-in-chief at the War Office, insisted on sending him to India as adjutant-general (November 1901).

In those days the post of adjutant-general was regarded as the most important staff appointment in the whole army. Smith-Dorrien found it far from easy. Between the viceroy, Lord Curzon [q.v.], and army head-quarters there arose serious differences, which became so acute that the adjutant-general found his position intolerable. He asked to be allowed to resign. At that moment, however, Lord Kitchener arrived in India as commander-in-chief (December 1902), and insisted that Smith-Dorrien should remain in office for a few months; after this he was transferred to the 4th division at Quetta. This was his first important command, and he thoroughly enjoyed every day of the five years which he spent in it. With the commander-in-chief he made extended tours along the North-West Frontier; they studied the various problems connected with possible operations in Afghanistan, and the best system of training for war.

Kitchener gave Smith-Dorrien a very free hand in instituting many reforms on which the young general had set his heart. Chief among these were contrivances for promoting the health and comfort of his troops; soldiers' clubs and recreation grounds were provided in every station. As was his custom he entered zealously into every form of sport, and at one race meeting he won two steeplechases and a hurdle race on his own horses. In 1902 he had married Olive Crofton, daughter of Colonel John Schneider, of Oak Lee, Furness Abbey, and she acted as hostess in entertaining many distinguished guests, including the Prince and Princess of Wales. In every way Smith-Dorrien's tenure of the appointment was a success, and perhaps it did even more than his previous services in the field to enhance his reputation. The 4th division became known as a happy one in which to serve, for although the commander occasionally gave vent to an outburst of wrath, it never fell on innocent shoulders. His popularity arose from his close interest in the personality of his officers; it was commonly said that he knew by sight every subaltern in the division, and every subaltern's pony.

In December 1907 Smith-Dorrien went on to the command at Aldershot, and, after four years there, to the Southern command at Salisbury (1912). Here for the first time he found himself in touch with the Territorial forces, and formed a very high estimate of their value. Being convinced of the probability of a European war, he studied the problem of increasing the strength of the British army; more than once he came into conflict with Cabinet ministers by suggesting some system of universal training. He drew up a scheme for expansion on the basis of the Territorial associations which were already in existence, and in August 1914 he submitted it to Lord Kitchener when the latter went to the War Office as secretary of state. Kitchener, however, had determined to make his new armies independent of any existing organization, and Smith-Dorrien's proposals were rejected.

The dispatch of the British Expeditionary Force to France in August 1914 marks the beginning of the outstanding period of Smith-Dorrien's career, when, after the sudden death of Sir J. M. Grierson [q.v.] on the 17th of the month, he succeeded to the command of the II Corps. He later commanded the Second Army in France. Controversy has been aroused by the events which in the end led to his resignation.

After bearing the brunt of the fighting at Mons, the II Corps retired, on 25 August, to a selected position at Le Cateau. Then the commander-in-chief, Sir John French (afterwards Earl of Ypres, q.v.), found that the French Fifth Army on his right was continuing the retreat; he therefore decided to conform to its movement, and issued orders for another march southward on the following day. Smith-Dorrien had every intention of complying with these orders, but during the course of the night he became aware that the difficulties were increasing. The few roads were hopelessly blocked by country carts of fugitives; a heavy thunderstorm made some of the steeper gradients impassable; in the darkness the scene was one of unavoidable confusion. Half the troops had been delayed by a rearguard action, and many of them were wandering about until dawn next morning. Throughout the night the commander of the II Corps was engaged in consultation with his generals, and in trying to collect reports from his scattered units. At 2 a.m. Major-General Allenby came in to say that the German cavalry had pressed up to within two miles of the British position, and would be on the top of the II Corps unless it could march before dawn. Major-General Hubert Hamilton was then consulted, and he stated definitely that the 3rd division, on the left of the II Corps, would not be ready to move before 9 a.m. As the commander-in-chief and his staff had gone on to St. Quentin, 26 miles to the south, Smith-Dorrien was forced to take responsibility on his own shoulders. He issued orders to stand fast and await the German attack. This led to the battle of Le Cateau (26 August). By 2 p.m. the block on the roads had been cleared, and Smith-Dorrien determined to resume the retreat. It is evident that he chose the right moment, for the enemy had suffered too much to make any attempt at pursuit. The official *History* says: 'In fact, the whole of Smith-Dorrien's troops had done what was thought to be impossible. With both flanks more or less in the air, they had turned upon an enemy of at least twice their strength; had struck him hard, and had withdrawn, except on the right front of the 5th division, practically without interference, with neither flank enveloped, having suffered losses certainly severe, but, considering the circumstances, by no means extravagant' [*Military Operations. France and Belgium. 1914*, 1922, pp. 181–182]. The total casualties amounted to 7,812 men and 38 guns.

Sir John French's first dispatches on the battle were full of praise. Later on, however, he changed his opinion and took a very gloomy view of what he called 'the shattered condition of the Second Corps'. His book *1914* passes adverse comment on Smith-Dorrien's decision. But the generals on the spot believed that that decision saved the day; for unless the troops had been ordered to stand and fight an extremely dangerous situation would have ensued. Practically all military historians have now accepted this view. Far from being shattered, the II Corps went on to win fresh laurels on the Marne, the Aisne, and in the first terrible battles near Ypres.

By the end of the year (1914) the trench line stretched from the North Sea to the Alps, and the deadlock which followed gave rise to wide divergences of opinion regarding strategy. The French, with their system of compulsory service, had already mobilized all available men; they had little faith in the value of Kitchener's new armies; they were naturally impatient to drive the invaders out of their country, and they believed that it could be done by vigorous offensive action. Sir John French shared this belief. Smith-Dorrien, on the other hand, put a high value on the new armies, and, although fully convinced that the struggle would end in victory for the Allies, was content to await the time when British resources, in men and munitions, would be more fully developed. In the meanwhile he wanted to husband the few regulars who still remained.

During the first months of 1915 Smith-Dorrien gradually became aware of the differences of opinion between himself and general head-quarters. The British forces had been reorganized into two armies, of which he commanded the second. In April this Second Army relieved French troops in the southern half of the big salient round Ypres. German guns from north, east, and south made the position dangerous and very uncomfortable; every day showed a heavy roll of casualties; transport and fatigue parties, carrying ammunition and rations to the front line, suffered terribly from concentrated fire. Smith-Dorrien was in favour of withdrawing to a position some two miles back which would be less exposed and could be prepared beforehand. French refused to allow any voluntary surrender of ground, since that to his mind would be a confession of weakness.

On 22 April the matter was brought to a head by the first German gas attack. This burst in full force on the northern half of the salient, which was held by an Algerian division and some second line French territorials. They were swept back in confusion, evacuating the whole of their sector. This retreat exposed the left flank of the Royal Canadians, who, less affected by the gas, were still holding the apex. Orders were issued for immediate counter-attacks to retake the former French position, but although they were continued throughout the next five days, the only result was heavy loss, especially to British and Indian troops. The French were unable to afford any material assistance; they had lost nearly all their guns in the salient, and reinforcements were slow in arriving.

On 27 April Smith-Dorrien wrote a long and important letter to head-quarters; he said that unless the French could render more help, further attacks by the British would only cause useless loss of life; although he was not pessimistic, he thought that a scheme should be prepared for a withdrawal to a line nearer Ypres. The same afternoon a telegram came from head-quarters directing him to hand over command of all troops in the salient to General Sir Herbert (afterwards Lord) Plumer. This drove Smith-Dorrien to the conclusion that the relations between himself and the commander-in-chief were so much strained that they constituted a weak link in the chain of responsibility. On 1 May he sent a message asking for an interview, and, as no answer was received, he followed it up on 6 May by a second letter offering to resign. The same evening he was handed a telegram ordering him to return to England. The official *History* says: 'No reason or explanation was vouchsafed.' After his departure steps were taken to carry out the withdrawal which he had recommended. This was the end of Smith-Dorrien's active service in the field.

Lord Kitchener wished to make Smith-Dorrien inspector-general of all troops in the United Kingdom, but the prime minister, Mr. Asquith, insisted on keeping this appointment open for French, who came back from France a few months later. Smith-Dorrien was given command of the First Army for home defence, and he held this post for six months (June–November 1915).

In December 1915 Smith-Dorrien was selected for command of an expedition in German East Africa, but an attack of pneumonia, which necessitated three serious operations, caused him to be invalided home from Cape Town. The War was over before he had fully recovered his health.

In September 1918 Smith-Dorrien went to Gibraltar as governor, and spent five years there, after which he retired. He devoted much time to work for his old regiment (originally the 45th and 95th Foot, now the Sherwood Foresters), of which he was colonel for over twenty-five years.

On 11 August 1930 Smith-Dorrien was terribly injured in a motor accident on the Bath Road, and he died the next day in Chippenham hospital without recovering consciousness. His wife and three sons survived him.

Smith-Dorrien's autobiography, *Memories of Forty-Eight Years' Service* (1925), gives a full and lively account of his early experiences, but he always refused to discuss questions connected with his resignation.

Smith-Dorrien had a total of nineteen military decorations, of which ten were war medals; the others included the K.C.B. (1907), G.C.B. (1913), G.C.M.G. (1915), D.S.O. (1886), and the Legion of Honour (1915).

Smith-Dorrien was of medium height and build, with a very active figure which he kept in hard condition by constant exercise. A square chin gave a look of determination which was emphasized by a clear and decided manner of speaking.

A cartoon of Smith-Dorrien by 'Spy' appeared in *Vanity Fair* 5 December 1901.

[*The Times*, 13 August 1930; Sir H. L. Smith-Dorrien, *Memories of Forty-Eight Years' Service*, 1925; C. R. Ballard, *Smith-Dorrien*, 1931; Sir J. E. Edmonds, (Official) *History of the Great War. Military Operations. France and Belgium. 1914* and *1915*, 1922–1927. Portrait, *Royal Academy Pictures*, 1910.]

C. R. Ballard.

SOLOMON, SOLOMON JOSEPH (1860–1927), painter, was born in the Borough, London, 16 September 1860, the fourth son of Joseph Solomon, leather merchant, by his wife, Helena Lichtenstadt, of Prague. He was educated at Thomas Whitford's South London School, Great Dover Street, and received instruction in Hebrew and German from the Rev. Simeon Singer, minister of the Borough synagogue. Having shown an artistic bent, Solomon was sent at the age of sixteen to Heatherley's art school in Newman Street, where Samuel Butler [q.v.], then a man of mature years, was a fellow-student: after a year's study there he proceeded to the Royal Academy schools, where (Lord) Leighton, (Sir) J. E. Millais, and (Sir) Lawrence Alma Tadema were among his teachers. A short period at the École des Beaux Arts, Paris, under Alexandre Cabanel, made a great impression on him; but the Munich Academy, where he continued his studies, did not attract him, and he stayed only some three months.

After a journey to Spain, Italy, and Morocco with his friend, the painter Arthur Hacker [q.v.], in 1880, Solomon settled in London, where he gradually made a name as a painter of portraits and classical and biblical scenes. His first exhibit at Burlington House was a portrait in 1881, but his first outstanding success was 'Samson' (1887), a dramatic representation of strong emotion and violent action, which now hangs in the Walker Art Gallery, Liverpool. 'Niobe' (1888) and 'Echo and Narcissus' (1895) are notable exercises in flesh-painting, and 'Your Health' (1893) is a genre painting in which problems of lighting are the main technical preoccupation. 'The Birth of Love' (1896), although an allegory, shows a movement towards a more formal decorative quality than had been evident in Solomon's earlier works. In portraiture, he did his best work when he was genuinely interested in the personality of the sitter: thus 'Israel Zangwill' (1894) is one of his most successful portraits, although 'Mrs. Patrick Campbell as the Second Mrs. Tanqueray' (1894) also shows incisive reading of character and real decorative skill.

Solomon was elected A.R.A. in 1896 and R.A. ten years later (1906). In the latter year he took a house at Birchington-on-Sea, Kent, which thenceforward became his home. His later work includes portraits of Mr. Asquith (1909) and of Mr. Ramsay MacDonald (1912). In 1910 he published a book on *The Practice of Oil Painting*. He was elected president of the Royal Society of British Artists in 1918.

Shortly after the outbreak of the European War in 1914 Solomon was impressed by the need for the use of 'camouflage'—the masking of trenches and other military objectives in such a way as to reduce their visibility to enemy aircraft. He communicated his views on the subject to the War Office, and in January 1916 was sent to France, with the rank of lieutenant-colonel in the Royal Engineers, in order to help to organize this work. In 1920 he published a book entitled *Strategic Camouflage*. He died at his home at Birchington 27 July 1927.

In an age of technical innovation in painting Solomon remained faithful to traditional methods. He was a good average portrait-painter and an exceedingly conscientious craftsman; and the critic who is not contemptuous of all emotional content in painting finds considerable poetic power in his subject pictures. He was keenly interested in Jewish social and religious life, and was one of the founders in 1891 of the Maccabeans Society, of which he was a vice-president.

Solomon married in 1897 Ella, daughter of Hyman Montagu, F.S.A., solicitor and numismatist, sometime lord-lieutenant of the City of London; they had one son and two daughters.

[Olga S. Phillips, *Solomon J. Solomon: a Memoir of Peace and War*, 1933; *The Idler*, vol. x, 1896; *The Studio*, vol. viii, 1896; S. L. Bensusan, 'Solomon J. Solomon' in *Jüdische Künstler*, edited by M. Buber, Berlin, 1903; private information.] H. B. Grimsditch.

SONNENSCHEIN, EDWARD ADOLF (1851–1929), classical scholar and writer on comparative grammar and metre, was born in Holloway, London, 20 November 1851, the eldest son of Adolf Sonnenschein, an Austrian supporter of the Hungarian patriot, Louis Kossuth, who settled in England and became well known as a teacher and writer of school-books, by his wife, Sarah Robinson, daughter of the Rev. Edward Stallybrass, who was for many years a missionary in Siberia. A younger son was William Swan Sonnenschein, founder of the publishing house of that name.

Sonnenschein was educated at University College School and at University College, London, whence he proceeded as a scholar to University College, Oxford, where he obtained first classes in classical moderations (1873) and *literae humaniores* (1875). On the recommendation of the master of his college, G. G. Bradley, he became assistant (1877–1881) to G. G. Ramsay, professor of humanity at Glasgow. After two years as headmaster of Kelvinside Academy, Glasgow, he was appointed in 1883 professor of Greek and Latin at the newly founded Mason College, Birmingham (afterwards Birmingham University), where he spent the rest of his active teaching life. In 1884 he married Edith Annesley, daughter of Ogden Bolton, barrister-at-law, of Liverpool, who survived him with two of their three sons.

Sonnenschein had long been interested in Plautus, and as early as 1879 had published an edition of the *Captivi*, based on the German edition of Julius Brix, and notable for an account of Richard Bentley's emendations on all the plays, which he discovered in the British Museum, in the margin of Bentley's copy of Pareus's edition of the works of Plautus. This account Sonnenschein afterwards elaborated into a volume of the *Anecdota Oxoniensia* (1883). A more independent edition was his *Mostellaria* of Plautus (1884), containing contributions from his former London teacher, Robinson Ellis [q.v.], who became a lifelong friend. This book led to his long friendship with Oskar Seyffert, of Berlin, who spoke of Sonnenschein as his 'literary heir'. Seyffert's influence is seen in the edition of the *Rudens* of Plautus (1891), up to that date the best English edition of any of the plays, and perhaps the best Plautine text in any country. In Sonnenschein's later years Plautine criticism was thrust into the background by more urgent calls, but he never slackened in his study, and wrote many articles in journals, besides contributing the article on Plautus to the eleventh and later editions of the *Encyclopædia Britannica.*

Meanwhile Sonnenschein had been developing his ideas on the reform of the prevalent chaotic and unscientific manner of teaching of grammar by treating all Indo-European languages on the same plan, with a common terminology. His efforts gave rise to the 'Parallel Grammar' series, of which he was editor and his brother publisher. The series was welcomed with acclamation not only in Great Britain, but on the Continent, where nothing like it was to be found. Sonnenschein's own contributions marked an advance on previous grammars, not only in their logical and scientific accuracy and happy expression (e.g., 'prospective subjunctive'), but in external presentation, to which he gave much thought, being probably the first editor to use marginal lines in order to indicate essentials, as he was among the first to interleave a school-text (the *editio minor* of the *Rudens*, 1901). Other pioneer work in teaching Latin is to be found in his two Latin stories for schools, *Ora Maritima* (1902) and *Pro Patria* (1903), with their ingenious Latin equivalents for modern appliances.

Sonnenschein's interest in the teaching of the classics led him to join John Percival Postgate [q.v.] in forming the

Classical Association (1903), to which he devoted much time and enthusiasm, ever insisting on the claims of the classics and the reform of their teaching. As chairman (1904–1909) of the Curricula Committee he issued four reports (1906–1909), and as chairman (1909–1911) of the Joint Committee on grammatical terminology, representing eight associations, two further reports (1909–1910), which have in substance been adopted by all bodies concerned with language teaching, including the Board of Education. His views appear in the Joint Committee's pamphlet of 1911, and are exemplified in *A New Latin Grammar* (1912), *A New French Grammar* (1912), and *A New English Grammar* (1916).

Besides his contributions to periodicals, for many years Sonnenschein wrote the chapter on 'Grammar, Lexicography and Metric' for *The Year's Work in Classical Studies* (founded in 1906). He was much interested in the evidence for Shakespeare's classical reading (which he was perhaps inclined to overstrain), and the later influence of Stoicism, on which he wrote in the *Hibbert Journal* (1907) and the *Contemporary Review* (1923). Much of his grammatical research was summed up in *The Unity of the Latin Subjunctive* (1910) and *The Soul of Grammar* (1927), the latter being a readable exposition, by the comparative method, of the unity in framework of the Aryan languages, intended, in his own words, to 'demolish the arch-enemy, Jespersen' (Otto Jespersen, of Copenhagen), and widely accepted by competent judges as having done so. His projected *magnum opus* on Plautine metre never saw the light, but the results of his wider metrical studies appeared in *What is Rhythm?* (1925).

Sonnenschein's brilliance as a grammarian tended to obscure in popular estimation his other qualities, and the inevitable references to Browning's Grammarian at his retirement and after his death, however apposite, tended to fix this one-sided view. He was in demand at college functions for his social qualities, and was a good talker with a fund of humour, which, as it never appeared on public occasions, never received due recognition. In Birmingham he lived in a house said to have belonged to David Cox, the painter, where he bestowed much hospitality of a quiet and intimate kind. He showed a growing interest in philosophy, and both at Birmingham and at Lansdown, Bath, where he lived from his retirement in 1918 to his death, which took place there 2 September 1929, he formed 'Socratic' societies for the discussion of philosophical and other problems.

One of Sonnenschein's foremost claims to remembrance has been strangely passed over. He had always insisted upon the humanities taking their proper place in the modern university. Before the university of Birmingham received its charter in March 1900 (largely through the activities of Joseph Chamberlain), Sonnenschein, both in the press and in interviews with Chamberlain and others, had urged that liberal policy which was adopted by Birmingham, and following Birmingham's lead, by the other modern universities which date from the decision of the Privy Council of 10 February 1903. In the teeth of strong opposition he secured a much improved organization of the faculties, each being represented by its dean on the governing body along with the lay members, with complete autonomy for professors, security of tenure, and the recognition of research as an essential part of their functions.

During the European War, besides being, with his wife, prominent among those who organized relief for Belgian refugees, Sonnenschein was the first to call attention to the manifesto of the German professors on war-guilt, which led to the publication of a rejoinder by representative English scholars, circulated both in English and German. He also wrote two of the Oxford war pamphlets, *Through German Eyes* (1914) and *Idols of Peace and War* (1915), and numerous letters in the press on the question of war-guilt.

In scholarship, as in other things, Sonnenschein prided himself on being 'a conservative of the right sort'. He was minutely accurate, and averse to loose quotations and incorrect innovations in language; for instance, he objected to the expression 'post-graduate'. He was a loyal friend, but uncompromising in condemning anything which fell short of his own exacting standards. As a correspondent, he was most conscientious in answering questions or discussing difficulties, and never spared himself in promoting the cause of good scholarship or helping fellow students. A certain absent-mindedness in society and indifference to correctness in dress only served to endear him the more to several generations of pupils. There is a small portrait by Charles Gere in the possession of the family.

[*The Times*, 3 and 7 September 1929; *Classical Review*, November 1929; private information. For Sonnenschein's share in fixing the constitution of the modern university, see his letters to the *Birmingham Daily Post*, 26 April, 1 and 8 May 1899, his correction of the statement in Lord Haldane's *Autobiography* (p. 146), *The Times*, 28 June 1929, and particularly a pamphlet by E. J. Somerset, *The Birth of a University*, 1934.]

W. B. Sedgwick.

SPENCER, Sir WALTER BALDWIN (1860–1929), biologist and ethnographer, was born 23 June 1860 at Stretford, Lancashire. He was the second son in the family of thirteen of Reuben Spencer, himself one of twelve, a Derbyshire lad who had worked his way up to be head of Rylands and Sons, Ltd., a Manchester firm of textile merchants. His mother's name was Martha Circuit. He was sent as a day-boy to Old Trafford School, where his inherited vigour showed itself alike in examinations and in athletic sports. Thence he went for a year to the Manchester School of Art, where he acquired a graphic touch which later on adorned and vivified his demonstrations in the lecture-room as well as the copious records of his studies in the field. To study good pictures and, within his means, to collect them, ever remained the chief of his hobbies. Spencer's true vocation was discovered when he entered Owens College, Manchester; there, under the able tuition of Professor Arthur Milnes Marshall [q.v.], who later described him as 'the best student I ever had', he became fired with an enthusiasm for biology. In 1881 he won an open scholarship in that subject at Exeter College, Oxford. There two of the fellows, Henry Nottidge Moseley and Edwin Ray Lankester, were eminently qualified not only to train him in research but to secure the recognition of his talents. After gaining a first class in natural science in 1884, Spencer became assistant to Moseley in April 1885, and was elected a fellow of Lincoln College in January 1886. At Moseley's suggestion, he assisted Edward Burnett Tylor, then reader in anthropology at Oxford, to arrange the ethnological material presented to the university in 1883 by General Pitt-Rivers [q.v.]—an experience which inspired Spencer with a second interest, whence so much of his future reputation was to come.

In June 1886 Spencer read a paper before the Royal Society on the median, or pineal, eye in lizards—a palaeontological mystery to which he provided the evolutionary key. The paper won him instant recognition. Within six months he was elected to the chair of biology in the university of Melbourne. Accompanied by his wife, Mary Elizabeth, the daughter of Richard Bowman, whom he married in January 1887, Spencer sailed immediately afterwards to the Antipodes, of all possible regions the richest in forms of arrested life.

Spencer held his professorship at Melbourne for thirty-two years. He proved an admirable and energetic teacher and organizer, and was rewarded with many honours. He was elected a fellow of the Royal Society in 1900, and an honorary fellow of Exeter College in 1906, and of Lincoln College in 1916. He received the C.M.G. in 1904, and was created K.C.M.G. in 1916.

But it is what Spencer did for uncivilized rather than for civilized Australia that demands special mention, for, as Sir James Frazer has well said, 'the record of Central Australian savagery, which we owe primarily to the genius of Baldwin Spencer, is likely to remain for all time the standard by reference to which, more than to any other documents, future inquirers will attempt to estimate the comparative antiquity of forms of society and to trace them to their origin in times which lie far beyond the reach of history' [Preface to *Spencer's Last Journey*, p. 8].

Attached as zoologist to the expedition organized in 1894 by W. A. Horn to carry out scientific investigation in Central Australia, Spencer, at Alice Springs, near the very centre of the continent, fell in with Francis James Gillen, who was stationed there as telegraphist among absolutely primitive natives. With these natives Gillen, a genial Irishman, had become so friendly as to be regarded by them as one of the tribe and a party to its most intimate secrets. Grasping the anthropological possibilities of a unique situation, Spencer brought his trained method to the aid of Gillen's experience; and as a result of this collaboration, of repeated explorations on Spencer's part, and of a subsequent journey undertaken by them both right across the continent to the gulf of Carpentaria (1901–1902), a quite unknown world of authentic stone-age folk was brought to light and vividly described. Under their joint names there appeared *Native Tribes of Central Australia* (1889), and *Northern Tribes of Central*

Australia (1904), each of them anthropological classics. After Gillen's death in 1912, Spencer more than once revisited the regions explored by them and published in 1927 under their joint authorship (a pious fiction) *The Arunta, a study of a Stone Age People*; this was meant to be a final effort to verify their findings, and it proved feasible with a minimum of substantial modification. Readable as they are, these digests of severely controlled evidence are meant for the expert. Covering the same ground, however, two other works, more popular in character, *Across Australia* (1912) and *Wanderings in Wild Australia* (1928), the first written by the partners, the second by the survivor, reveal the personal side of a close contact with what almost amounts to another order of humanity.

In 1911–1912 Spencer, who held the position of special commissioner for the Commonwealth government and chief protector of aborigines in the Northern Territory, explored wide spaces of the Northern Territory, partly on his own account and partly at the instance of the government. Here he amassed much fresh material with the insight and thoroughness that mark all his field observations, and in 1914 was published *Native Tribes of the Northern Territory of Australia*. He resigned his chair at Melbourne University in 1919, retaining the title as professor emeritus.

It had always been one of Spencer's dreams to follow up Darwin's study of the Fuegians, another derelict race. Accordingly in 1929, at the age of sixty-nine, with the threat of *angina* upon him, he braved a winter at Cape Horn; but he died suddenly on 14 July of that year in a snow-bound hut at Hoste Island, off Tierra del Fuego. His venture was not in vain, since he left behind him valuable notes which are incorporated in *Spencer's Last Journey* (1931). His grave is at Magellanes. He had one daughter.

There are two portraits of Spencer by W. B. McInnes, an Australian artist, one in the possession of the university of Melbourne, the other hanging in the hall of Exeter College, where his name appears also in a memorial window.

[R. R. Marett and T. K. Penniman, *Spencer's Last Journey*, with memoir and bibliography, 1931. *Spencer's Scientific Correspondence*, 1933, by the same editors, throws light on his intellectual friendships, and especially on his constant literary intercourse with Sir J. G. Frazer.] R. R. Marett.

SPOFFORTH, FREDERICK ROBERT (1853–1926), Australian cricketer, was born at Balmain, Sydney, 9 September 1853, the fourth child and second son of Edward Spofforth, a Yorkshireman who had emigrated to Australia in 1828, by his wife, Anna McDonnell. Spofforth was educated at Eglinton College, Sydney, where he learned his cricket. On 31 March 1877 he formed one of the Australian eleven at Melbourne against the team of English professionals captained by James Lillywhite [q.v.]. This fixture, in which Spofforth took 4 wickets for 115 runs, is usually counted the second in the series of test matches between England and Australia. Spofforth came to England in 1878 with the first Australian team which visited this country. Though the batting of the Australians was weak, the strength and variety of the bowling came as a revelation to English cricketers. At Lord's on 27 May a good Marylebone Cricket Club eleven, which included William Gilbert Grace [q.v.], was dismissed for 33 and 19. Owing to rain, the ground was difficult, but Spofforth's performance of taking 11 wickets for 20 runs was amazing. Throughout the tour he was successful, and in the first-class matches took 107 wickets at a cost of 11 runs each. When he came again to England in 1880, his bowling seemed as good as ever, but an injury kept him out of the only test match that was arranged. It was on his third visit to England, in 1882, that Spofforth accomplished the most famous feat of his career: this was at the Oval on 28 and 29 August when the Australians won their first victory in international cricket on English soil. England, with 80 runs to win, was put out, chiefly by Spofforth, for 72, and lost by 7 runs. Although the conditions were against the batting side, it was generally admitted that more formidable bowling had never been seen, and the public gave Spofforth the name of the 'demon bowler'. He paid two more visits to England, in 1884 and 1886, but found no opportunity in test matches of repeating his sensational achievement. Early in the 1886 tour, when he was bowling very well, his hand was hurt by a ball driven back at him, and he himself fancied that he lost something of his skill owing to this injury.

Spofforth was a tall, lean man, with long arms, and he delivered the ball at his full height. In his younger days he was a fast bowler, but afterwards he owed most of his success to clever variations of length and pace, and his best ball was of medium pace with a break from the off. His name will always be associated not only with the development of Australian cricket, but also with a marked advance in the art of bowling.

In 1886 Spofforth settled in England. Thereafter he was a member of the Derbyshire county eleven on several occasions, and played in a few other first-class fixtures. In Australia he had been a bank-manager, but in England he entered a tea-merchant's business, which he directed with energy and success. He married in 1886 Phyllis Marsh, daughter of Joseph Cadman, of Breadsall, Derbyshire, and had two sons and two daughters. He died at Ditton Hill Lodge, Surrey, 4 June 1926.

[*The Times*, 5 June 1926; private information.] A. Cochrane.

SPOONER, WILLIAM ARCHIBALD (1844–1930), warden of New College, Oxford, the eldest son of William Spooner, barrister, county court judge for North Staffordshire, of Walton Lodge, Stafford, by his wife, Jane Lydia, daughter of John Wilson, of Seacroft Hall, Leeds, was born 22 July 1844 at 17 Chapel Street, Grosvenor Place, London. Archibald Campbell Tait [q.v.], afterwards archbishop of Canterbury, who had married his father's sister, Catherine Spooner, was his godfather. Though robust in general, he suffered as an albino from defects of eyesight and taste, but triumphed over them by sheer force of character. Educated at Oswestry School, he won an open scholarship at New College, Oxford, in 1862, being the first scholar elected from outside Winchester College.

From this time onward Spooner's life was bound up with New College as successively scholar, fellow, and warden, and after his retirement as honorary fellow, in a period which saw its conspicuous growth in numbers, buildings, and importance. In this process of expansion the leading spirits were Edward Charles Wickham [q.v.], to whose tuition Spooner owed much, and Alfred Robinson, who came from University College in 1865. Spooner helped to carry out their policy. As a freshman, he was welcomed by the small Wykehamist society for his alert and cheerful spirit and for his connexions, through his family and friends, with other colleges. He had many noteworthy contemporaries: in college, W. A. Fearon, John Wordsworth, W. J. Courthope, Edgar Jacob, and R. C. Moberly, and among those outside, R. W. Raper, F. H. Jeune, W. R. Anson, E. S. Talbot, Mandell Creighton, J. L. Strachan-Davidson, Evelyn Abbott, and W. G. F. Phillimore. He showed independence by going to Henry Wall's logic lectures at Balliol College, and getting some tuition from Benjamin Jowett. After obtaining first classes in classical moderations (1864) and *literae humaniores* (1866), Spooner was elected fellow of his college in 1867, lecturer in 1868, and tutor in 1869, and for thirteen years (1876–1889) held the office of dean. He lectured on ancient history, philosophy, especially on Aristotle's *Ethics*, and divinity; and many generations of undergraduates were grateful for his tuition. He was ordained deacon in 1872 and priest in 1875, and the college became his lifelong parish. He was examining chaplain to Edward Carr Glyn, bishop of Peterborough, from 1902 to 1916, and was made honorary canon of Christ Church by Bishop Stubbs in 1899. He took his D.D. degree in 1903. His sermons, good in substance, suffered from his difficulty in reading. His fine eloquence found expression in his *extempore* speeches at the college Gaudy, which went to the hearts of his hearers by their mingled wisdom, humour, and love of the college.

On the death in 1903 of James Edwards Sewell [q.v.], who had been warden of New College since 1860, Spooner was unanimously elected warden, and entered on the happiest period of his life. The Lodgings, long neglected, were reconstructed with his generous assistance, and became a hospitable centre where he discharged with zest every duty of his office, making himself the friend of all, high or low, connected with the college: in this he had the gracious co-operation of his wife. No duty came amiss to him, but he excelled on such human occasions as a Gaudy or a Choir School prize-giving. He had an extensive knowledge of his undergraduates, who could count on his interest and good-will, but if they presumed on his good nature, were surprised by some pungent phrase which they never forgot. Considerate to his colleagues, he took them into his confidence and won their affection. He loved the ties with Winchester, and enjoyed his visits there as *ex-officio* fellow. He did not take a very active part in university affairs; he was a pro-vice-chancellor, but declined the vice-chancellorship and entered the Hebdomadal Council too late to make a mark. But he did valuable service as a first-rate examiner in 'Greats', and his judgement as an awarding examiner in Scripture knowledge for the Oxford and Cambridge Joint Board was highly esteemed, and his opinion on university affairs carried weight. He supported the promotion of natural science studies, and welcomed the foundation in 1901 of the Wykeham chair of physics at New College. He was also chairman of the council of Lady Margaret Hall, Oxford (1901–1907) and of that of the Oxford House in Bethnal Green (1908–1920), and for many years was a poor law guardian, an active member of the Charity Organisation Society in Oxford, and chairman of the council of the Warneford Hospital. He was an ardent member of the Political Economy Club and for many years its secretary. He retired from the wardenship at the end of 1924, but continued to live in Oxford until his death, which took place there 29 August 1930.

Spooner's weak eyesight limited both his reading and his studies, but he published in 1891 an edition of *The Histories of Tacitus* which was widely used, and small volumes on *Bishop Butler* (1901) and *William of Wykeham* (1909). His letters to *The Times* on public affairs were distinguished by clarity and sound sense. In politics and churchmanship he belonged to the centre, and disliked extremes; his inner life was one of simple piety, undisturbed by outside storms. A tendency to lapse of speech led to the association of his name with one form of slip which gave a new word, 'Spoonerism', to the English language ('Kinquering kongs their titles take' is the best-known example); but this had no relation to his general conversation, which was fluent, vigorous, often witty, and was enjoyed by all who shared it. His death left Oxford a duller place: for nearly seventy years, except for a dangerous illness in 1915–1916, he was a familiar figure in its streets, and had become a 'character' respected for great personal qualities, and for long and loyal service to the university. As he wrote himself of William of Wykeham, 'he accomplished more than many able and more masterful men'.

Spooner married in 1878 Frances Wycliffe, third daughter of Harvey Goodwin [q.v.], bishop of Carlisle, and had two sons and five daughters.

Spooner's grave is at Grasmere, where his wife's house, How Foot, had for many years been a beloved holiday home. His portrait by Hugh Riviere in New College hall is an excellent likeness. There is also a cartoon by 'Spy' in *Vanity Fair* (21 April 1898), the original of which is at New College.

[*The Times*, 1 September 1930; *Oxford Magazine*, 16 October 1930; private information; personal knowledge.]

P. E. Matheson.

SPY (pseudonym) (1851–1922), cartoonist. [See Ward, Sir Leslie.]

SQUIRE, WILLIAM BARCLAY (1855–1927), musical antiquary, was born in London 16 October 1855. He was the only son of William Squire, of Feltham Hill, Middlesex, merchant of the City of London, by his wife, Elizabeth Ogden. He was educated privately, at Frankfurt-am-Main, and at Pembroke College. Cambridge, where he graduated B.A. in 1879, having obtained a third class in the historical tripos. He practised as a solicitor in London from 1883 to 1885, and in the latter year was appointed an assistant in the department of printed books in the British Museum, and in 1912 was made an assistant keeper, with special charge of the printed music. Although Squire retired from this office under the age limit in 1920, he was in 1924 appointed honorary curator of the King's music library which is permanently on loan to the Museum, and this bore valuable fruit in the publication of a catalogue of this collection. Part I, dealing with the Handel MSS., appeared in 1927; Part III, the printed music and musical literature, in 1929. The second portion had not been begun by Squire when he died, and is the work of Miss Hilda Andrews.

From 1890 to 1904 Squire acted as music critic for the *Saturday Review, Westminster Gazette, Globe*, and *Pilot* in succession. He wrote the libretto of (Sir) C. V. Stanford's opera, *The Veiled Prophet of Khorassan* (1881) and of (Sir) F. Bridge's cantata, 'Callirrhoe' (1888). Squire contributed many articles to all three editions of Grove's *Dictionary of Music*, and in the third edition, which is illustrated, his special interest in portraits of musicians proved of great service. He was also a contributor to the *Encyclopædia Britannica*, to this Dictionary, and to other publications. He compiled catalogues of old printed music in the British Museum (2 vols., 1912), of the music in the chapter library of Westminster Abbey (*Monatshefte* for 1903), and of the printed music in the Royal College of Music (1909), of which he had been librarian since 1885. He also collaborated with Helen, Countess of Radnor in the *Catalogue of the Pictures in the Collection of the Earl of Radnor* (1909).

Squire did much valuable editorial work on English madrigals and old keyboard music, the most important of which, the *Fitzwilliam Virginal Book*, was done in co-operation with his brother-in-law, J. A. Fuller-Maitland, and was published in 1894–1899. He edited a reprint of the words of Robert Jones's *Muses' Gardin for Delights* (1901), and for the Purcell Society, of which he was honorary secretary, he edited Purcell's harpsichord music (4 vols., 1918).

During the European War, Squire worked for the Intelligence Department of the Admiralty (1916–1918), and from 1918 to 1920 he served in the historical section of the Foreign Office. His report on the *Tribes of Tunisia* (1916) was officially adopted by the French government. He died, unmarried, in London 13 January 1927.

Squire became a fellow of the Society of Antiquaries in 1888 and of the Royal Geographical Society in 1894. He was elected an honorary fellow of Pembroke College, Cambridge, in 1925. In 1918 he became a knight of grace of the order of St. John of Jerusalem, and in 1926 received the C.V.O.

As an historian and archaeologist Squire's habitual care and accuracy made him regarded as a sound authority, and his readiness to place his great knowledge, not only of music, but of matters artistic and genealogical, at the disposal of all genuine applicants for information, will not be readily forgotten by students in the British Museum Library and elsewhere.

[Private information; personal knowledge.]

H. Thompson.

STACK, Sir LEE OLIVER FITZMAURICE (1868–1924), soldier and administrator, was born at Darjeeling, India, 15 May 1868, the only son of Oliver Stokes Stack, inspector-general of police, Bengal, by his wife, Emily Dickson. Educated at Clifton College and the Royal Military College, Sandhurst, he was commissioned to the Border Regiment in 1888, promoted captain in 1896, and appointed staff officer to the British commissioner and commander in Crete in 1899.

Eager for experience, Stack turned his eyes to the Sudan, at that time administered by British officers attached to the Egyptian army. He joined that army in 1899, served in the adjutant-general's department, and in 1902 commanded the Shambé field force operating in the Shambé district of the Bahr el Ghazal, being awarded the medal and clasp. His discreet handling of this mission attracted the notice of the authorities, and Stack was chosen for service with the Sudan government. He was appointed private secretary to the governor-general in 1904, and Sudan agent and director of military intelligence in Cairo in 1908. Two years later he retired from the British army, and threw in his lot permanently with the Sudan service.

Following the transfer from the Sudan of the governor-general, Sir Reginald Wingate, to be high commissioner in Egypt in 1917, Stack, who had become civil secretary to the Sudan government in 1914, was gazetted (1917) acting sirdar of the Egyptian army and governor-general of the Sudan. It was an obvious choice: his military credentials were ample, his acquaintance with the Sudan was intimate. He succeeded to an inheritance unhampered by embarrassing legacies. The Sudan was tranquil, trade was reviving, revenue expanding. Fortified by this knowledge, Stack urged the expediency of carrying out proposals, already approved in principle by the Treasury, to develop cotton production in the area lying between the Blue and White Niles. But the business proved more protracted than he had anticipated: erroneous estimates and technical disputes so delayed making a beginning with the enterprise that Stack did not live to witness its completion.

Meanwhile his appointments had been confirmed (1919), and sensible of wider responsibility, Stack began a cautious experiment in decentralization. Up till then, the post-War fever of disruptive nationalism had not penetrated the Sudan, but, too shrewd to expect such immunity to last, Stack hoped to forestall the menace by providing existing tribal organizations with a definite place in the government of the state. He sanctioned and extended the judicial and administrative powers exercised hitherto unofficially by sheikhs, and he encouraged the admission of young Sudanese into the executive. In these and other ways he laid the foundations of a wholesome national consciousness.

Stack was present at the Anglo-Egyptian negotiations in London in 1924 in order to watch the interests of the Sudan, and when negotiations broke down, returned to Cairo. The situation was disquieting. Mutiny was afoot in the Sudan, murder being hatched in Egypt. Tragedy drew near. On 19 November 1924 Stack was waylaid in the streets of Cairo and shot through the body. He died the following day.

Stack was an attractive personality: sympathetic and unaffected, inclining to advise rather than to command, finding reward in the simple performance of duty. No conspicuous achievement stands to his credit, but his administration was always constructive, his judgement cool and balanced. He piloted the Sudan without mishaps through seven difficult years, and he laboured unceasingly for the welfare of its people.

Stack married in 1902 Flora Center, daughter of Edwin Ramsay Moodie, commodore captain of the Cunard Company, and had one daughter.

Stack was a temporary major-general of the British army (1917) and a ferik of the Egyptian army. He was created C.M.G. (1914), K.B.E. (1918), and G.B.E. (1923). He was also in possession of the fourth class Osmanie (1902), third class Medjidie (1910), grand cordon of the Nile (1917), and first class El Nahda of the Hejaz (1920).

[Egyptian and Sudan governments' *Reports*; private information; personal knowledge.]

P. G. Elgood.

STANFORD, Sir CHARLES VILLIERS (1852–1924), composer, conductor, and teacher of music, was born in Dublin 30 September 1852, the only child of John Stanford, of Dublin, examiner in the court of Chancery and clerk of the crown, co. Meath, by his wife, Mary, daughter of William Henn, of Dublin, master in Chancery. He was educated at Henry Tilney Bassett's school in Dublin. His early Dublin life was spent in a favourable intellectual atmosphere. His father was an enthusiastic amateur vocalist and violoncellist. His music teachers, Arthur O'Leary (under whom he studied in London), Michael Quarry, and Sir Robert Prescott Stewart [q.v.], were all of them able musicians and all of them Irishmen. Quarry, in particular, exercised a great influence upon Stanford by instilling into him a love for the music of Bach, Schumann, and Brahms, little of which had, in those days, penetrated to Ireland. These early influences never lost their spell and can be traced in Stanford's works up to the last.

Stanford did not definitely decide to adopt music as a profession until 1870, when he was eighteen years of age. His father, in accepting the situation, insisted upon a general university education first and a specifically musical study abroad afterwards. This plan was carried out, but not without some difficulty. Stanford went up to Queens' College, Cambridge, as choral scholar in 1870, but he achieved such distinction in the musical life of Cambridge as an undergraduate that in 1873 he was appointed organist of Trinity College, and his university activities prevented any prolonged musical study abroad. Nevertheless, from 1874—the year in which he took his degree with a third class in the classical tripos—to 1876 he was given leave of absence for considerable periods in order to visit Germany for musical instruction. He studied first with Carl H. C. Reinecke in Leipzig and afterwards with Friedrich Kiel in Berlin. Stanford's reputation as a composer soon extended beyond Cambridge. As early as 1876 he attracted attention in London by his music to Tennyson's *Queen Mary*, written, at the poet's suggestion, for the Lyceum production, and by a symphony which gained a prize in a competition organized by the Alexandra Palace authorities. In 1877 his name figured in the Gloucester Festival programme with an overture. In 1882 a second symphony appeared, and his orchestral serenade was produced at the Birmingham Festival. His music to the *Eumenides* of Aeschylus (1885) took Cambridge by storm, and had much to do with consolidating his position as a musician of distinction.

It is surprising that with his manifold and varied activities, which increased when he settled in London in 1892, Stanford's output as a composer was so continuous. Whatever else claimed his attention—and he touched nothing timidly or half-heartedly—the time reserved for creative work was seldom allowed to be disturbed. He was a rapid worker. He scarcely ever made a sketch. Even complicated works were written straight into score, in ink, without previous preparation. Stanford was certainly the most versatile British composer of the latter half of the nineteenth century. There was no department of music in which he did not seek to challenge comparison with the foremost composers of his age, and there were few departments in which he failed to achieve some measure of distinction.

Stanford's efforts in the cause of English

opera deserve special mention. If he gained only temporary successes with his stage works his fate in this respect must in part be attributed to the difficult conditions which beset operatic production in England. His first opera, *The Veiled Prophet of Khorassan* (1881), enjoyed only two performances, one in Hanover, and one in London. *Savonarola* (1884), *The Canterbury Pilgrims* (1884), *Much Ado about Nothing* (1901), and *The Critic* (1915), in which Sheridan's 'tragedy rehearsed' became an 'opera rehearsed', fared little better. His last opera, *The Travelling Companion*, published by the Carnegie Trust in 1919, has not up to the present time (1934) received an adequate professional presentation. The nearest approach to a popular success which Stanford secured on the stage was with his *Shamus O'Brien*, a romantic light opera, which had a run of several weeks at the old Opera Comique Theatre, London, in 1896.

Stanford's large-scale choral works, although many of them are forgotten, were highly esteemed in their day, and certainly left their influence upon the work of later writers. 'The Three Holy Children' (1885) and 'Eden' (1891) have not been heard in recent years, but his 'Requiem' (1897) and especially his 'Stabat Mater' (1907) created a more lasting impression, and may be regarded as representing his finest work for chorus and orchestra. On a smaller scale, in the form of secular ballads, his 'The Revenge' (1886), 'Phaudrig Crohoore' (1896), and 'The Last Post' (1900) remain conspicuous examples of the best type of British choral writing, and have won both professional and popular acceptance.

For orchestra alone Stanford completed seven symphonies, the best-known of which are No. 3, 'The Irish' (1887), and No. 5, 'L'Allegro ed il Penseroso', inspired by Milton's poems (1895). His six 'Irish Rhapsodies' are, however, more representative of his genius, and their national character, combined with the imperishable poetic beauty of the native melodies from which the main themes are derived, give them a place of special significance in modern music. No. 1 (1902) is the most obstinately popular, but No. 2 (1903) is a finer work, and No. 4, 'The Fisherman of Lough Neagh' (1913), is probably the most satisfying example of Stanford's orchestral writing which exists.

Stanford was also a prolific writer of chamber music—skilfully wrought, but mostly of a severely classical type which seldom reflected his personality attractively. There are eight string quartets; two string quintets; a pianoforte quintet and quartet; several trios and duet sonatas for various combinations, &c. None of these are publicly performed with any regularity, although many of them are in the repertories of amateur players.

Stanford's church music, on the other hand, has established itself firmly in the services of all English cathedrals and important churches. His settings of the canticles are healthy, vigorous, and far superior in quality to those of most of his contemporaries. No religious music is better loved in Great Britain than 'Stanford in B flat' (1879), whilst his four later services, and several anthems, have almost equal claims upon the affection of church musicians. Medievalists have taken exception to some of his methods, and complained that this music is not always devout in style, but Stanford took a liberal view of the Church's needs for various occasions.

The mastery of design and fluency which distinguish Stanford's services and anthems are features also in his secular part-songs, notably the 'Elizabethan Pastorals', of which there are three sets; in the infinitely charming vocal pieces for children; in the much-esteemed compositions for organ, as well as in his smaller instrumental solos, too numerous to mention in detail. Fleeting trifles many of them are, but sometimes they reveal his individuality with greater clearness than more elaborate works.

It is, however, as a writer of solo songs that Stanford's reputation appears to be most securely established. Through the art of his friend, Plunket Greene, he won especial fame for his settings for baritone voice with choral and orchestral accompaniment. Early and brilliant examples are the 'Three Cavalier Songs', settings of Browning's poems, with male chorus (1882), but his 'Songs of the Sea' (1905) and 'Songs of the Fleet' (1910) are his finest essays in a form which he made peculiarly his own. They strike a note of romantic patriotism at once stirring and dignified. In writing for solo voice with pianoforte he excelled in settings of modern Irish poems, several collections of which won wide acceptance. The high-water mark in this type of song is reached with 'An Irish Idyll' (1901), but the succeeding collections, 'Cushendall' (1910), 'A Fire of Turf' (1913), and 'Songs from Leinster' (1914), all maintain an excellent standard and contain many of his happiest thoughts.

As a conductor Stanford gained extensive experience with the Cambridge University Musical Society (1872–1893), but he will chiefly be remembered as director of the Bach Choir, London (1885–1902), and of the Leeds Festival, where he succeeded Sir Arthur Sullivan and officiated from 1901 to 1910. He also had chief charge of the Royal College of Music orchestra during the period of his professorship at that institution. It has been well said by one of his pupils, George Dyson, that 'Stanford was never a virtuoso conductor. Virtuosity of every kind was alien to his temperament. Contrasted with the more exuberant, his methods appeared to be sound rather than inspired. But he could handle large masses with a command and a dignity which revealed the nobility of masterpieces.'

Stanford was appointed professor of composition and orchestral playing at the Royal College of Music on its opening in 1883, and professor of music at Cambridge in 1887, holding both appointments until the year of his death. He earned the reputation of being the most successful composition teacher of his time in England. Many of his pupils were destined to become distinguished musicians. Amongst these were Walford Davies, Coleridge Taylor, Vaughan Williams, Gustav Holst, John Ireland, Frank Bridge, Rutland Boughton, Eugène Goossens, Arthur Bliss, and Herbert Howells. This list alone will serve as testimony to the soundness of his training and the catholicity of his sympathies. In 1911 he published his treatise on *Musical Composition*, a little volume which was the fruit of long experience and presented an admirable epitome of his methods, set forth without didactic heaviness or pedantry.

Stanford's other contributions to literature are not numerous, and may be regarded mainly as diversions in the course of a busy life. His chapters in *A History of Music* (1916), written in collaboration with Cecil Forsyth, are terse in style and exhibit sound critical judgements. Mention should also be made of his *Studies and Memories* (1908) and *Interludes* (1922).

Stanford was the recipient of many academic distinctions, including the honorary degrees of Mus.D. of Oxford (1883) and Cambridge (1888), D.C.L. of Durham (1894), and LL.D. of Leeds (1904). He was knighted in 1902.

Stanford married in 1878 Jane Anna Maria, daughter of Henry Champion Wetton, of Joldwynds, Shere, near Guildford. They had one son and one daughter. Stanford died in London 29 March 1924 and his ashes are buried in Westminster Abbey.

Stanford's personality was very striking. He was tall in stature, and his countenance, somewhat grim in repose, assumed, in conversation, immense earnestness and animation. He was easily led by his fiery temperament into indiscretions of utterance. He delighted to triumph over enemies, but seldom bore malice. He could stab with sarcasm and heal the wound with affectionate good-humour. None could question his intense loyalty to his art, to his friends, to those who served him, and to those whom he delighted to honour.

An excellent portrait of Stanford, painted by Sir William Orpen, hangs in the hall of Trinity College, Cambridge. A cartoon of him by 'Spy' appeared in *Vanity Fair* 2 February 1905.

[Sir George Grove, *Dictionary of Music and Musicians*, 3rd ed., 1928; Sir C. V. Stanford, *Pages from an Unwritten Diary*, 1914; *Proceedings* of the Musical Association, 1926–1927; private information; personal knowledge.]

T. F. Dunhill.

STANLEY, EDWARD LYULPH, fourth Baron Sheffield, of Roscommon, in the peerage of Ireland, and fourth Baron Stanley of Alderley, in the peerage of the United Kingdom (1839–1925), was born in London 16 May 1839. He was the third son of Edward John, second Baron Stanley of Alderley [q.v.], by his wife, Henrietta Maria [q.v.], eldest daughter of Henry Augustus Lee-Dillon, thirteenth Viscount Dillon. He succeeded his eldest brother, Henry Edward John, third Baron Stanley of Alderley [q.v.], in 1903, and, by special remainder, succeeded to the barony of Sheffield on the death in 1909 of his kinsman, Henry North Holroyd, third Earl of Sheffield and third Baron Sheffield [q.v.].

Stanley was educated at Eton and at Balliol College, Oxford, where he obtained a second class in classical moderations (1859) and a first class in *literae humaniores* (1861). He was elected a fellow of Balliol in 1862, and held his fellowship until 1869. He was called to the bar by the Inner Temple in 1865, became an assistant commissioner under the Friendly Societies Commission in 1872, and in 1876 a member of the London School Board, on which he served, with one interruption (1885–1888), until its abolition in 1904. After two unsuccessful attempts, Stanley was elected member of parliament for Oldham in the liberal interest in 1880, and retained his seat until 1885. In 1884 he was appointed a member of the royal commission on the housing of the poor, and in 1886 a member of the royal commission (the Cross commission) 'to inquire into the working of the Elementary Education Acts'; when the latter commission reported in 1888 he was the first signatory of a strong minority report, in which his characteristic style is conspicuous.

In 1889 Stanley took a leading part, as chairman of the executive committee and treasurer, in the formation of the National Education Association, which may be regarded as the descendant of the National Education League, an organization very prominent in the controversies connected with the Education Bill of 1870.

In 1897 Stanley became vice-chairman of the London School Board (which then reverted to the practice of appointing an outside chairman—Lord Reay), and he held that office until 1904. On the abolition of the School Board, the London County Council omitted, somewhat ungraciously as it appeared to him, to find an opening for a continuance of his services. His long and valuable work in the development and administration of education in London therefore came to an end. Subsequently, however, he did good service in the same cause in Anglesey, where he was a landowner.

Stanley was always active with his pen. He wrote a small book called *Our National System*, published in 1909, and between 1895 and 1917 expressed his views forcibly in many articles contributed to the *Nineteenth Century*, and the *Fortnightly*, *English*, and *Contemporary* Reviews. He supported the Education Bill of 1918, and in 1923, at the age of eighty-four, he delivered an address to the National Education Association vigorously criticizing two proposals, put forward respectively by the archbishop of Wales and Mr. H. A. L. Fisher, for a 'concordat' solution of the denominational controversy.

In the controversies which the organization and administration of public education have always excited in England, Stanley took an active part. He was a strong advocate of public control, and although he accepted the settlement or compromise of 1870, he held that the development of a public system of education was the business of public authorities (preferably of *ad hoc* authorities), and he offered stout resistance to all proposals which tended to enlarge the influence or strengthen the position of voluntary or denominational bodies in that system. Thus he strongly criticized a circular issued by the London School Board in 1894 relating to religious instruction in Board schools, as giving a new opening to denominational influences in those schools. The controversy was ended by the victory of the Progressive party in 1897, and Stanley for the next seven years exercised a dominant authority on the Board.

The result of another controversy was less happy for Stanley, and indeed it led to the dramatic collapse of the scheme of higher education which he had been instrumental in devising, and to the defeat of his cherished hope that the School Board would become the public authority responsible for all grades and branches of public education. The London School Board had, with the concurrence and aid of the Science and Art Department, developed a large system of 'higher grade schools', 'evening continuation schools', &c., in which free instruction far above the standard of ordinary elementary schools was given to pupils of an age much above the ordinary elementary school age. In discussing with Sir John Eldon Gorst [q.v.] in 1899 the powers of the School Board to provide higher education, Stanley put its claims so high that the Education Department (shortly afterwards merged in the new Board of Education) felt it necessary to obtain a legal decision. Voluntary schools and institutions were also at that time feeling the competition of rate-aided Board schools and institutions, which charged no fees, very severely. Certain items of the London School Board's expenditure on higher education were accordingly challenged before Mr. Cockerton, the auditor, and his disallowance of them was upheld by the Court of Queen's Bench and the Court of Appeal. The courts in effect decided that the power of school boards to provide education out of the rates was limited to elementary instruction, given to children, and not to adults, within the scope of the Elementary School Code as distinguished from the Directory of the Science and Art Department. It was indeed a *cause célèbre*, and in the result led directly to the comprehensive reform of the English system of public education effected by the Act of 1902.

But though Lord Sheffield was an active and determined controversialist, his real achievement lay in the field of detailed and laborious, but nevertheless imaginative and constructive, administration to which he devoted himself for many years. His actual accomplishment, not only in running the machine but in working out big and new ideas, and by a combination of enthusiasm and practical judgement securing their successful application, was great both in volume and quality. He was a pioneer in many branches of education and its organization, and made the London School Board a leading influence in the development of national education. He anticipated many lines of advance which have now become familiar, but he never neglected the humbler conditions on which successful advance depends. He gave constant and personal attention to the provision and improvement of school accommodation in pursuit of his ideal of 'a school place for every child and every child in its place, and that a good place'. But for his previous efforts, the London County Council would have had great difficulty in dealing with the huge problem which it was called on to face in 1904; and in preparing the way for the change from *ad hoc* School Board administration to municipal administration, Sheffield unwittingly contributed to the defeat of one of his own cherished projects.

Lord Sheffield's industry was unflagging; he drove himself and others with extraordinary energy. He was severely critical and caustic in speech, but a genuine kindliness and generosity underlay his antagonisms, and he never bore ill-will. He was not an easy man to deal with, but his disinterested devotion to his chosen task and his capacity for getting things done compelled respect.

Lord Sheffield married in 1873 Mary Katharine, daughter of Sir Isaac Lowthian Bell [q.v.], first baronet, of Washington Hall, co. Durham, and had three sons and five daughters. He was succeeded as fifth Baron Stanley of Alderley and fifth Baron Sheffield by his eldest son, Arthur Lyulph (born 1875). He died at Alderley Park, Cheshire, 18 March 1925.

There is a portrait of Lord Sheffield by P. A. de László at Alderley Park (1904), and others are in the possession of Colonel Oliver Stanley at Plas Llanfawr, Holyhead, and of the Hon. Lyulph Stanley at Penrhos, Holyhead.

[*The Times*, 19 March 1925; *The School Child*, April 1925; *Educational Record*, April 1929; private information.]

L. A. SELBY BIGGE.

STARLING, ERNEST HENRY (1866–1927), physiologist, was born 17 April 1866 in Barnsbury Square, North London, the eldest son of Matthew Henry Starling, clerk of the crown, Bombay, by his wife, Ellen Mathilda, daughter of Henry George Watkins, artist and engraver, of Islington. He was educated at King's College School, London, and at Guy's Hospital, which he entered in 1882. As a student he won numerous distinctions, became demonstrator in physiology at Guy's in 1889, and later on head of the physiology department at that hospital. His tenure of office was marked by a complete reconstruction of the building available for physiology, with the result that, instead of being poorly equipped, Guy's came to have the best physiological laboratory in London. In 1899 Starling was elected to the Jodrell chair of physiology at University College, a position which he filled until 1923. In 1922 he was appointed to the Foulerton research professorship of the Royal Society, of which he was the first holder. He was elected a fellow of the Royal Society in 1899, was awarded the Society's royal medal in 1913, and the Baly medal of the Royal College of Physicians in 1907. He received honorary doctorates from Trinity College, Dublin, and from the universities of Sheffield, Cambridge, Breslau, Strasburg, and Heidelberg. He was created C.M.G. in 1917.

Starling married in 1891 Florence Amelia, daughter of Sir Edward Henry Sieveking [q.v.], the physician, and widow of Leonard Charles Wooldridge, a distinguished physiologist. They had one son and three daughters. His wife assisted him indefatigably in his work. Starling died on board a steamer as it was entering Kingston harbour, Jamaica, 2 May 1927, while he was travelling for his health.

Starling wrote several books, outstanding among which was his *Principles of Human Physiology* (1912, 4th ed. 1925), the classical English physiological textbook of its time; but it is as an original investigator that he has the greatest claim to be remembered. So meagre at that time was the equipment at Guy's Hospital, that for purposes of research Starling was driven in 1890 to University College, which then contained a brilliant group of workers under the leadership of (Sir) E. A. (Sharpey-) Schäfer, the Jodrell professor. This group included (Sir) William Maddock Bayliss [q.v.], who in 1893 married Starling's sister Gertrude. Starling formed with Bayliss a lifelong intellectual alliance of the most fruitful character. Starling's investigations covered an unusually wide field, but three subjects stand out pre-eminently: (1) the secretion of lymph and other body fluids, (2) the discovery of secretin, (3) the laws which govern the activity of the heart.

In 1892 Starling went to Breslau in order to work with R. Heidenhain on the subject of lymph formation. Heidenhain at that time was the protagonist of the 'vital' theory of the secretion of serous fluids, which regarded the cells of the capillary wall as having secretory powers similar to those of the salivary or pancreatic cells. This theory was supported by certain experiments on the ligature of vessels, but principally perhaps by the alleged action of the so-called lymphagogues. It is said, and the saying is approximately correct, that Starling verified all Heidenhain's experiments and disproved all the conclusions; but the advance was made by supplementing the work of the master by other and crucial experiments of his own. Starling showed, in fact, that most of the phenomena which govern the flow of lymph could be explained, if proper account were taken of the factors which govern the hydrostatic pressure of blood in the capillaries together with the osmotic properties of the fluids concerned. In this connexion special stress was laid on the osmotic pressure of the colloid constituents of those fluids. The work, although undertaken with special reference to lymph flow, soon extended to the secretion and absorption of other fluids, such as urine and serous fluids generally. It so completely superseded previous work in this field as to put Starling, in his early thirties, into the first rank of experimental physiologists.

Starling's second achievement, and probably his greatest, was his discovery in 1902 in collaboration with Bayliss of secretin, a performance so noteworthy as to require no comment except that as time has passed that achievement appears to rank more and more as one of the most important discoveries of physiology. The conception of an internal secretion was not new, for Schäfer had established that by his discovery of adrenaline in 1894; moreover, although thyroxine had not then been isolated, its main physiological reactions were known. But the idea of a chemical stimulus from one part of the body producing a specific response elsewhere, such as the secretion of pancreatic juice, was new. The degree of importance to which humoral secretions have now attained is merely evidence of the fundamental nature of the discovery of secretin.

The years immediately preceding the European War of 1914–1918 were devoted by Starling to the study of the heart, which, indeed, was the subject of perhaps his earliest research. The 'heart-lung preparation' had been used by Henry Newell Martin (1848–1896), of Johns Hopkins University, and others, but Starling converted it into a technical method of the first importance by the introduction of a suitable and variable resistance on the arterial side. On the 'heart-lung preparation' he studied, *seriatim*, the effect of varying the numerous factors which influence the beat of that organ, e.g. arterial pressure, venous inflow, temperature, the chemical composition of the blood, and so forth; finally, he expounded the generalization known as 'Starling's law of the heart', namely, that 'the energy of contraction is a function of the length of the muscle-fibres'. Then came the War, and Starling never carried out his full programme, which was to apply all the knowledge acquired on the 'heart-lung preparation' to the innervated organ. Apart from his activities in the War, Starling worked at many other subjects, such as the movement of the gut and renal secretion.

On the outbreak of war Starling at once obtained a commission in the Royal Army Medical Corps, and at first served as a medical officer at the Herbert Hospital at Woolwich; later he performed important work in the gas warfare department at home. In 1917 he was sent on a commission to the Italian army in order to convince the military authorities of the advantages of equipping their soldiers with a more perfect respirator. The sequel was that in the first three months of 1918 Great Britain made about one million respirators for the Italian army of such efficiency as to render quite innocuous an offensive launched against it by the Austrians on a great scale, an offensive which, had it been successful, might have proved decisive.

No account of Starling's work would be complete without some reference to his magnetic personality. Of not more than middle height, and with a penetrating but sympathetic eye, he gave the impression of personified alertness. His energy, mental and physical, appeared inexhaustible, his reactions and judgements were rapid, and if, as was inevitable, they occasionally proved wrong he was not prevented by any misplaced feeling for consistency from revising and correcting them. Yet his searching intellect was coupled with a heart of great generosity; to help younger workers was his supreme pleasure, and no one more fully enjoyed the companionship of his fellows. His outlook on life he once voiced in the words 'An objective life is a happy one'.

[*The Times*, 4 May 1927; *Proceedings* of the Royal Society, vol. cii, B, 1928; private information; personal knowledge.]

J. Barcroft.

STEEL, FLORA ANNIE (1847–1929), novelist, was born at Sudbury Priory, Harrow-on-the-Hill, 2 April 1847, the sixth child and second daughter of George Webster, sheriff-clerk of Forfarshire, by his wife, Isabella, daughter and heiress of Alexander Macallum, sugar planter, of Cousins Cove, Jamaica. Until she was nine years old she lived at Harrow and at her father's London house in Palace Yard, Westminster, where Thackeray and George Cruikshank were among his friends. Her parents moved in 1857 to Burnside, Forfar, and she quickly developed a deep love of the Highlands. News of the Indian Mutiny impressed her childish imagination: she was even then a creature of energetic action, and she burned and hanged the Nana Sahib in effigy many times. She was educated by governesses and at a private school in Brussels where the headmistress described her as 'diligente mais point gracieuse'. During 1866 she lived with her parents in Heriot Row, Edinburgh, and 'dressed on twenty pounds a year'. At the end of 1867 she married Henry William Steel, of the Indian civil service, the son of the Rev. Thomas Henry Steel, vicar of St. Ippollyts with Great Wymondley, Hertfordshire. Although she claimed in her autobiography, *The Garden of Fidelity*, that she was never in love, the marriage was a happy one, and her husband thought her 'the one entirely right thing in this world'.

Mrs. Steel landed in Madras in 1868 and travelled to Delhi. From there she continued the journey by road to Lahore and thence to Ludhiana, where she was the only European woman. Her husband was soon transferred to Dalhousie. There her first child was born dead, but her only other child, a daughter born in 1870, survived. She was a devoted mother, a studious reader, and a keen conversationalist; she also sang, acted in theatricals, and painted with infinite gusto and satisfaction to herself. In 1870 she joined her husband in Kasur, a subdivision of the Lahore district, and made it her business to acquire a special knowledge of India.

Mrs. Steel, alone of the Englishwomen then married to officials in India, flung herself heart and soul into the lives of Indians, and she wrote memorable fiction inspired by the insight which she acquired. Thrown upon her own resources—for there were no other Europeans in Kasur—she interested herself at first in municipal administration and in entertaining local magnates. When riding with her husband through the district, escorted by petty officials and farmers, she became familiar with the life of the country-side and the customs of the people. Later, she penetrated behind the purdah to the secluded women, and thus gained information not available to men. There was that in her Highland blood which was sympathetic to legend, pilgrimage, and religious disputation. She was impatient of the superstitions of others, yet she seems 'with her mind's eye' to have believed in the reality of the Indian railway guard who asserted that his name was Nathaniel James Craddock and who told her the story which she published in 1897 called *In the Permanent Way*.

Over Indian women Mrs. Steel exercised remarkable influence. The need for social reform was clear to her, but at that time there was no revolutionary party in India capable of emancipating women in a nationalist cause. She took a long view of the situation and attacked the deeply rooted social system by strongly advocating the education of Indian women. In this matter she was a pioneer, and her great ability was recognized, although her enthusiasms occasionally brought her into conflict with the constituted authorities. She started a school for little girls at Kasur in 1874, and when she roundly told the government that it ought to appoint inspectresses of girls' schools, it made her the first one (1884). She was a member of the Provincial Educational Board from 1885 to 1888, and served on it with John Lockwood Kipling, the artist, father of Rudyard Kipling. When Mr. Steel retired in 1889, she left India with regret and almost immediately began her literary career in earnest.

Mrs. Steel's first book, *Wide Awake Stories* (1884), had been followed by *The Complete Indian Cook and Housekeeper* (1887), written in collaboration with a friend, Mrs. Grace Gardiner. Neither lady was regarded as an ideal housekeeper, but the book was appreciated by hundreds of Englishwomen in India and is a valuable record of contemporary prices, wages, remedies, conditions, and customs. In 1896 her great novel of the Indian Mutiny, *On the Face of the Waters*, was published and won for its author instant recognition. No future novelist who may write of the Indian Mutiny will possess Mrs. Steel's knowledge of that tragedy. The Northern India which she knew so well had changed but little in custom and sentiment since 1857, and she had listened to many a tale told by an old Moslem servant and other Punjabis. Colonel Reynell George Taylor [q.v.] and Sir George Stuart White [q.v.], who served through the Mutiny, were her friends. The novel was long astir in her mind, and during 1894 she returned to India, going back to live in Kasur, a predominantly Moslem district. From there she went to Delhi and spent much time with the descendants of the old Mogul dynasty. This weaving together of scenes and talks was a method in which she delighted, and her books give a remarkable tapestry of Indian life, sometimes blurred, often confusing, but never false. *On the Face of the Waters* is written with faithful accuracy and complete impartiality. She visited India only once more, during the winter of 1897, and left it finally in May 1898. *The Potter's Thumb* (1894), *In the Permanent Way* (1897), and *Hosts of the Lord* (1900) are convincing in their sincerity and are without rivals as contemporary pictures of life in the cantonments and villages of Northern India. Her series of Indian historical romances is more sentimental, but she never wrote of India without re-creating the Indian scene.

Mrs. Steel lived to be old, energetic to the end. From 1900 until 1913 she lived at Talgarth, near Machynlleth, North Wales, where she enjoyed her garden, and then moved to Court o' Hill, Tenbury. She supported the movement for women's suffrage, but was not a leader nor militant. In 1928 she wrote her autobiography, but died before it was published. It is a self-revealing book. After her husband's death in 1923 she lived with her daughter and son-in-law at Springfield, Minchinhampton, Gloucestershire, where she died 12 April 1929.

[*The Times*, 15 April 1929; *Morning Post*, 15 April 1929; Mrs. Steel's autobiography, *The Garden of Fidelity*, 1929; private information.] E. M. Bell.

STERNDALE, Baron (1848–1923), judge. [See Pickford, William.]

STEVENSON, JAMES, Baron Stevenson, of Holmbury (1873–1926), administrator, was born at Kilmarnock, Ayrshire, 2 April 1873, the elder son of Archibald Stewart Stevenson, of Carriden, Kilmarnock, by his wife, Elizabeth, daughter of James Morrison. He was educated at Kilmarnock Academy, but while still a very young man went into business as a travelling salesman. He became connected with the firm of John Walker and Sons, distillers, of Kilmarnock, and worked his way up to be managing director. With the help of extensive advertising, the sales of the company's whisky were much increased, and the concern prospered under Stevenson's management.

When the European War broke out in 1914 Stevenson offered his services gratuitously to the government in any capacity in which they could be used. On the formation, in the following year, of the Ministry of Munitions under Mr. Lloyd George, he was made director of area organization, an office which he held until 1917. He was then appointed vice-chairman of the Ministry of Munitions advisory committee, and in 1918 a member of the Munitions Council for ordnance. The value of his services in the provision of supplies of war was undoubted. He brought to bear on whatever work he undertook great industry and power of concentration.

After the War Stevenson was appointed chairman of the Munitions Council committee on demobilization and reconstruction, and from 1919 to 1921 he was surveyor-general of supply to the War Office. He was also a member of the Army Council (1919–1921) and of the Air Council (1919–1921), and vice-chairman of the advisory committee on civil aviation (1919–1920). In 1921 he was appointed personal adviser on commercial affairs to the secretary-of-state for the Colonies, a post which he held until 1923. It was while acting in this capacity that he was chosen to be chairman of the Rubber Investigation Committee, which produced the scheme, known as the Stevenson plan, for the restriction of the output of rubber. Those who support this scheme claim that it saved the planters of Malaya and Ceylon from conditions which, when the plan was put into effect (in 1922), were threatening the existence of the rubber industry.

The most striking example of Stevenson's powers of organization was his management of the British Empire Exhibition, held at Wembley in 1924, and reopened the following summer. When it was decided to hold this great display, the biggest effort of the kind hitherto attempted in Great Britain, Stevenson was chosen to be the chairman of the Exhibition board. Exhibits from every part of the British Empire were collected, and there was hardly any industry or art which was not represented. Wide interest was, of course, aroused, and the exhibition proved, as was expected, the event of the summer. The control of this vast enterprise, with all its various sections, was in the hands of Stevenson. Great exertions were required to ensure the opening of the exhibition for its first season on the appointed date. Partly owing to delays caused by unfavourable weather, the work of erecting the buildings and arranging the exhibits in order had been much hindered, and a week before the day fixed for the opening ceremony the scene was one of almost hopeless confusion. Yet thanks to the efforts of the chairman of the board, the opening was made possible at the proper time. Furthermore, Stevenson's initiative and support ensured the successful reopening of the exhibition for a second year, whereby added stimulus was given to the growing sentiment of trading within the Empire.

Stevenson took no share in political controversy, and never declared himself an adherent of any particular party, but worked with and for all governments alike with the same impartial energy. Nor would he have considered himself a public man, yet his record of public service over a period of ten years is notable.

Stevenson was created a baronet in 1917 and G.C.M.G. in 1922. In 1924 he was raised to the peerage as Baron Stevenson, of Holmbury, Surrey. He was twice married: first, in 1897 to Jessie Baird (died 1917), daughter of James Hogarth, of Ardrossan, Ayrshire; and secondly, in 1918 to Stella, fifth daughter of William John Fraser, of Herne, Kent, and widow of Edward Johnstone. Lord Stevenson died at Holmbury St. Mary 10 June 1926, and, as he left no children, the barony became extinct.

[*The Times*, 11 June 1926. Portrait, *Royal Academy Pictures*, 1923.] A. Cochrane.

STEVENSON, WILLIAM HENRY (1858–1924), historian and philologist, was born at Nottingham 7 September 1858, the elder son of William Stevenson, timber merchant and antiquary, by his wife, Mary Ann, daughter of John and Rosina Lennon, of Banbridge, co. Down. The family moved in 1869 to Hull, where Stevenson was educated at the grammar school (now Hymers College). After leaving school he worked for a short time in his father's office on the Queen's dock, and, through the business connexion with Scandinavia, he became interested in Scandinavian languages. He learned Norwegian from a Norwegian sailor. But he never took to the timber trade, and in 1878 he returned to Nottingham, where he was engaged by the town council to edit the records of the borough (4 vols., 1882–1889). At this time Stevenson made the acquaintance of Lord Middleton, whose collection of manuscripts at Wollaton Hall he later calendared for the Historical Manuscripts Commission (1911).

Stevenson's connexion with Oxford was due to Professor E. A. Freeman, with whom he had corresponded and whom he visited at Oxford in 1886. From 1887 he became a regular contributor to the recently founded *English Historical Review*, which contains much of his original work. In 1888, on the recommendation of Freeman, Stevenson was engaged to calendar the muniments of Merton College. He was given rooms in the college and soon became known to many Oxford scholars, including Professor A. S. Napier, with whom he collaborated in editing the important Crawford collection of early charters now in the Bodleian Library (1895). While at Merton he entertained the idea of reading for a degree, but was dissuaded by the warden, G. C. Brodrick, who considered his work on the college muniments incompatible with other studies. He never, in fact, took a degree by the passing of university examinations; but he received the M.A. degree by decree of convocation in 1896, after his election to a research fellowship at Exeter College in the preceding year.

After completing his work at Merton, Stevenson was employed on the records of Gloucester, and edited a *Rental of all the Houses in Gloucester, A.D. 1455* (1890), a *Report on the Records of the Dean and Chapter and of the Corporation* (Historical MSS. Commission, 12th Report, 1891), and a *Calendar of the Records of the Corporation* (1893). In 1890 he was invited by Sir Henry Maxwell-Lyte, then deputy-keeper, to undertake regular work at the Public Record Office. Between 1892 and 1908 he produced eleven volumes of the *Calendars of Close Rolls*, comprising the reigns of Edward I and Edward II, and the first six years of Edward III. He found the work, however, both irksome and a strain on his eyesight; moreover, since his election to a fellowship at Exeter College, he was spending more and more of his time at Oxford. In his later years Stevenson was responsible for but one volume of the Record Office publications, a volume of *Liberate Rolls* of Henry III (1916), which interested him on account of the linguistic difficulties which it presented. In 1904 he published his edition of *Asser's Life of King Alfred* with elaborate introduction and notes, which is perhaps his best work. He was appointed Sandars reader in the university of Cambridge in 1898, and gave a course of lectures on the Anglo-Saxon chancery to a small but distinguished audience which included Professor F. W. Maitland and Mary Bateson. In 1904, shortly after the expiration of his fellowship at Exeter College, he was elected at St. John's, where he spent the remainder of his life, as fellow and librarian, devoting much time to amassing material for the history of the college.

In spite of his interest in, and remarkable knowledge of, topography Stevenson cared little for travel, and, except for a visit which he paid with Maitland to the Canary Islands, he never left England. Both in term and vacation he made his home at Oxford, where the natural simplicity of his character, his kindliness, and sympathy endeared him to a wide circle of friends, and enabled him to enter easily into the lives and interests of undergraduates although he had never been one himself. He died at Oxford 22 October 1924. He was unmarried.

Stevenson's qualifications for historical work were exceptional. He had an exact knowledge of all the languages requisite for the study of early English history, and no professed philologist could compare with him in extent of historical learning and knowledge of diplomatic. It was this remarkable combination that made him the first authority of his time on English place-names. He compiled in the course of his work a vast index of place and personal names, which has since been in part used by the editors of the English Place-Name Society in their publications. His philological work is scattered through his editions, reports, and articles, and he left in the press an edition of *Early Scholastic Colloquies* (published 1929).

[*Oxford Magazine*, 6 November 1924; private information; personal knowledge.]

A. L. Poole.

STOKES, ADRIAN (1887–1927), pathologist, born at Lausanne 9 February 1887, was the youngest son of Henry John Stokes, Indian civil service, of Howth, co. Dublin, by his wife, Mary Anne, daughter of William MacDougall. He was great-grandson of Whitley Stokes [q.v.], sometime regius professor of medicine at Trinity College, Dublin, and grandson of William Stokes [q.v.], the well-known clinician. Sir William Stokes [q.v.], surgeon, and Margaret McNair Stokes [q.v.], Irish archaeologist, were his uncle and aunt. He was educated at St. Stephen's Green School and at Trinity College, Dublin, where he obtained honours in anatomy, and graduated M.B. in 1910 and M.D. in 1911. In 1910–1911 he was working at St. Mary's Hospital, and was house-surgeon at the Royal Sussex County Hospital, Brighton. In the latter year he was awarded the medical travelling prize and the Banks medal by Trinity College. After spending six months with his travelling prize at the Rockefeller Institute for medical research in New York, he was appointed assistant to the professor of pathology in Dublin, a position which he retained until the outbreak of the European War. Stokes went out to France in September 1914 as a lieutenant in the Royal Army Medical Corps, and was appalled by the great number of men who reached the base in the agonies of tetanus. He packed the sidecar of his old motor-bicycle with anti-tetanic serum and set off by himself to visit the field dressing-stations, saving lives at every halting place. In this way the first mobile laboratory of the British Expeditionary Force was established. Stokes invented the method of giving oxygen continuously through a nasal catheter to victims of gassing, a method which has extended since to civilian practice and has saved countless lives. He did invaluable work on typhoid and cerebro-spinal fever, gas-gangrene, trench nephritis, dysentery, and wound infections. In 1916, when an epidemic of jaundice appeared in the Ypres salient, he proved by animal experiment that the disease was spirochaetal in origin and identical with that described by Japanese investigators in 1914. He showed that it was conveyed by rats which infested the trenches, and he helped to locate the infected areas with the result that the epidemic was stamped out. For his war services he received the D.S.O. in 1918 and the O.B.E. in 1919.

In 1919 Stokes returned to Dublin as

professor of bacteriology and preventive medicine at Trinity College. His investigations on epidemic jaundice led to a request in 1920 from the Rockefeller Yellow Fever Commission that he should go to Lagos, but as no cases were available for investigation, the expedition proved fruitless. In 1922 Stokes was appointed Sir William Dunn professor of pathology in London University, working at the pathological department of Guy's Hospital. There he quickly made a unique position for himself. Members of the staff, house-officers, and students constantly sought his help, and they rarely failed to profit from his wide knowledge and great experience. Many important contributions to scientific literature, generally published in the hospital *Reports*, came from his laboratory.

In 1927 the Rockefeller Commission again sought Stokes's assistance. Its investigations had led to no definite results, and it was hoped that his clear judgement and genius for research would help to unravel the problems of yellow fever. Stokes proceeded to Lagos in June of that year, and carried out some decisive experiments. He showed that yellow fever could be transmitted to monkeys, and thus ensured further progress by animal experiment. On 15 September he developed yellow fever and died at Lagos on the 19th at the early age of forty. During the few days of his illness he insisted that mosquitoes should be fed on him, that his blood should be taken for inoculation into monkeys, and that an autopsy should be performed if he died. The mosquitoes were subsequently allowed to bite a monkey which developed yellow fever, the first time that the disease had been thus transmitted; the inoculated monkeys developed the disease, and his own autopsy showed the characteristic changes of yellow fever.

Stokes was a keen sportsman, and especially delighted in fishing, shooting, and cricket. He was extremely popular, and in his short life he exerted an enormous influence for good on all those with whom he came in contact at Trinity College, Dublin, in the Royal Army Medical Corps, and at Guy's Hospital. He was unmarried.

[*Adrian Stokes* by A. F. H. and J. A. R. in Guy's Hospital *Reports*, vol. lxxviii, 1928; personal knowledge.] A. F. Hurst.

STOKES, Sir FREDERICK WILFRID SCOTT (1860–1927), civil engineer and inventor, born 9 April 1860, was the fifth and youngest son of Scott Nasmyth Stokes, barrister, and inspector of schools, a friend of Matthew Arnold, by his wife, Emma Louisa, youngest daughter of Benjamin Walsh, of Worcestershire. An elder brother was the artist Adrian Stokes, R.A. (1854–1935). He was educated at St. Francis Xavier's College, Liverpool, the Kensington Catholic public school, and the Catholic University College in Kensington. At the age of eighteen he was articled to Lancaster Owen, civil engineer, of the Great Western Railway Company. From 1881 to 1885 he was engaged, under Sir William Shelford [q.v.], in designing bridges and other steelwork construction for the old Hull and Barnsley Railway.

On the termination of this employment Stokes began his lifelong connexion with the firm of Messrs. Ransomes & Rapier of Ipswich, by becoming assistant to Richard Christopher Rapier, the managing director. In 1896 when the firm was converted into a limited company, Stokes was appointed engineer and managing director of the London office. On Rapier's death in 1897 he succeeded him as managing director, and in 1907 became chairman of the company, both of which offices he held until his death.

From 1886 to 1888 Stokes took out patents for rotary kilns for cement-making, which were a distinct advance on the Ransome kiln of 1885. His improvements were widely adopted by cement-makers in the United States, and from that country the rotary kiln was later reintroduced into Great Britain in a modified form. He also improved Ransomes & Rapier's break-down crane and invented a shallow traverser for railway carriage and wagon stock. Subsequent to 1880 Ransomes & Rapier acquired the patent rights of the sluices invented by Francis Goold Morony Stoney in 1874 and 1880 [*Proceedings* of the Institution of Civil Engineers, vol. cxxx, pp. 317–18, 1896–1897]. Stokes superintended the erection of these sluices on the Manchester ship canal, and while so engaged he greatly improved their design, notably by arrangements for protecting the rollers from scour when the sluice is open, and by devices for ensuring complete watertightness, and for preventing vibration of the rollers. These sluices were subsequently employed for the Assuan dam on the Nile and for the Sennar dam on the Blue Nile. Stokes visited the Assuan dam in May 1898 and in January 1899, and represented his firm at the opening of the first sluice in December 1901. He was also present at the opening of the Sennar dam in January 1926. For his services in connexion with the Assuan dam he received from the khedive the decorations of the order of the Osmanie (second class) and the Medjidie (second class). These sluices have also been employed in the Argentine, in India, New Zealand, China, and elsewhere.

The original design of the Stokes gun, the invention for which he is most widely known, was rejected by the War Office in December 1914, but the gun was subsequently used in the trenches at the battle of Loos in September 1915, firing smoke shells. It was a trench mortar consisting of a smooth-bored tube of iron or steel, three or four inches in diameter. The projectile carried its own propelling charge and igniter, and when it was dropped down the tube ignition occurred automatically by contact with a striker. Although the gun was not at first very popular in the trenches, it came to be much employed later, when it had been improved. At that time two sizes were used, a smaller for firing high explosive bombs, and a larger for gas, smoke, and incendiary shells. It was employed not only on land, but in naval operations such as the attack on the Zeebrugge mole on 23 April 1918.

Stokes was elected an associate of the Institution of Civil Engineers in 1885, and became a member in 1903. He was president of the British Engineers' Association from 1915 to 1917. He was a member of four committees of the Inventions Department of the Ministry of Munitions, and president of the Industrial Reconstruction Council in 1918. In 1917 he was created K.B.E. He contributed a paper on 'Sluices and Lock-gates of the Nile Reservoir, Assuan', to the *Proceedings* of the Institution of Civil Engineers, vol. clii, p. 108, 1902–1903. He died 7 February 1927 at Ruthin, and was buried at Mortlake.

Stokes married in 1900 Irene, daughter of Luke Ionides, and niece of the donor of the Ionides collection to the South Kensington Museum, Constantine Alexander Ionides [q.v.]. There were no children of the marriage.

[*The Times*, 8 February 1927; *Engineering*, 11 February 1927. See also *Proceedings* of the Institution of Civil Engineers, vol. ccxxii, p. 107, 1925–1926; *Engineering*, vol. cv, p. 719, 1918; vol. cxxi, p. 104, 1926.]

E. I. Carlyle.

STOPFORD, Sir FREDERICK WILLIAM (1854–1929), general, was born in Dublin 22 February 1854, the second son of James Thomas Stopford, fourth Earl of Courtown, by his second wife, Dora, daughter of Edward Pennefather [q.v.], chief-justice of the Queen's Bench, Ireland. He was educated at Eton, and while there became a page of honour to Queen Victoria. In October 1871 he was commissioned as ensign and lieutenant in the Grenadier Guards. From 1877 to 1881 he was adjutant of the regiment, and in August 1882 he was appointed aide-de-camp to General Sir John Miller Adye [q.v.], chief of the staff of the Egyptian Expeditionary Force. Stopford was present at the battle of Tel-el-Kebir (13 September), was mentioned in dispatches, and received the medal and clasp, the bronze star, and the order of the Medjidie (fifth class). In May 1884 he was promoted captain, and in the same year was appointed aide-de-camp to the commander of the British troops in Egypt. In February 1885, on the formation of the Suakin Expeditionary Force, Stopford was appointed aide-de-camp to Major-General Fremantle, commander of the Guards brigade in that expedition, and soon after was made brigade-major of the brigade. He was mentioned in dispatches and received the clasp for Suakin and the brevet of major. From 1886 to 1889 he was brigade-major at Aldershot, and in July 1890 he was promoted substantive-major in the Grenadier Guards.

After serving as deputy-assistant-adjutant-general at the War Office and at Aldershot, Stopford was chosen to command a composite half battalion in the Ashanti expedition of 1895. He was again mentioned in dispatches and received the star for the expedition. In March 1896 he was gazetted as brevet-colonel. In that year he was appointed assistant-adjutant-general at the War Office and was holding that post on the outbreak of the South African War in 1899. Stopford was then appointed military secretary to Sir Redvers Buller. He was present at the battle of Colenso (15 December) and at the actions of Spion Kop (24 January 1900), Vaal Krantz (5 February), Tugela Heights (18 February), Pieter's Hill (27 February), the relief of Ladysmith (28 February), and Laing's Nek (9 June). Later he took part in the operations in the Eastern Transvaal, and was present at the actions of Belfast (26–27 August) and Lydenberg (6 September). He received a number of mentions in dispatches, was awarded the Queen's medal with six clasps, and was created K.C.M.G. in 1900. On his return home Stopford was appointed in 1902 chief of the staff of the I Army Corps, and while holding that position he was, in February 1904, promoted major-general and appointed director of military training at the War Office. He held this position until 1906, when he was appointed to the command of the London district. In that position he took an active part in the organization and development of the Naval and Military Tournament, which had recently been moved from the Agricultural Hall to Olympia, and devoted much of his spare time to service charities, becoming chairman of the Soldiers' and Sailors' Families Association and vice-president of the Royal Patriotic Fund. In 1909 he was created K.C.V.O. and promoted lieutenant-general, and in 1912 he was appointed lieutenant of the Tower of London, which position he was holding on the outbreak of the European War in August 1914.

Soon after that event, Stopford was appointed to the command of the First Home Defence Army, and thus was actively concerned both in the training of troops and in the organization of home defence. When, in June 1915, Sir Ian Hamilton called for reinforcements for the Dardanelles, Stopford was chosen to command the IX Corps of the New or 'Kitchener' Army troops destined for that theatre of war. Although in his sixty-first year, and not in good health, his service in the trying climate of tropical Africa having left its mark on him, Stopford eagerly accepted the offer of an active command, and, preceding his troops, he reached the Eastern Aegean in the middle of July. Here he was for a short time appointed to the command of the VIII Corps on the Krithia front in order to gain local experience. While there he learned from Sir Ian Hamilton that he was to command the IX Corps in a surprise landing at Suvla Bay. He, at first, expressed his entire agreement with Hamilton's plan; but later, on examining it more closely, he informed the commander-in-chief that he had grave doubts whether the amount of artillery support for the landing was sufficient. The landing was begun on the night of 6–7 August, and was at first successful. The Turks were surprised and had but small forces on the spot. The success of the enterprise depended on seizing promptly the Tekke Tehe ridge about five miles from the landing-place; but a landing on a beach is one of the most difficult operations of war, the troops were inexperienced and had been trained mainly for trench warfare in France, while the commanders with their experience of France in their minds, were loth to advance without adequate artillery support, and the naval arrangements for the landing of guns and of water were defective. Owing to the delays thus caused and to the personal and timely intervention of Kemal Pasha on the Turkish front, the opportunity of securing the vital ridge was lost and the landing ended in a dead-lock on the Suvla Plain.

On 16 August Stopford was relieved of his command and came home. A committee of general officers appointed by Lord Kitchener investigated Stopford's conduct of the operations, and this committee, while refusing to blame him, found grounds for criticizing general headquarters. It is possible that a younger man in better health might have been able to inspire his troops by personal example with the necessary enterprise, but it is also possible that more active assistance given to the corps commander by general headquarters on 7 August would have had a like result.

Stopford returned to his post as lieutenant of the Tower, which he held until 1917. He retired from the army in 1920, when he was created K.C.B. He died in London 4 May 1929 at the age of seventy-five. He never married.

[*The Times*, 6 May 1929; Sir J. F. Maurice and M. H. Grant, (Official) *History of the War in South Africa, 1899–1902*, 1906–1910; C. F. Aspinall-Oglander, *History of the Great War. Military Operations. Gallipoli*, vol. ii, 1932.]

F. Maurice.

STOUT, Sir ROBERT (1844–1930), prime minister and chief justice of New Zealand, was born at Lerwick, in the Shetland Islands, 28 September 1844, the son of Thomas Stout, merchant and landed proprietor, of Lerwick. He was educated at the parish school, Lerwick, where he became a pupil teacher at the age of thirteen. In 1863 he went out to New Zealand, and was appointed an assistant master first at Dunedin grammar school and subsequently at North Dunedin district high school. In 1867 Stout began to study law, and in 1871 he gained first place at Otago University in the mental and moral science and political economy examinations. In the same year he was admitted to practise as a solicitor and barrister. In 1872 he was elected to the Otago provincial council and remained a member until the abolition of the provinces in 1876; and from May 1874 to May 1875 he was provincial solicitor. From 1873 to 1875 he was law lecturer at Otago University. In August 1875 he was elected to the house of representatives, at a by-election, for Caversham, as an opponent of the Abolition of Provinces Bill then before the house. At the following general election, in 1876, he became one of the members for Dunedin; and he played a part in the transformation of the provincialist party, whose *raison d'être* had disappeared in 1876, into a new liberal party. Two years later, in 1878, he was appointed attorney-general and minister for lands and immigration in the ministry of Sir George Grey [q.v.].

Finding that politics interfered with his profession, Stout resigned his official posts in 1879, but returned to parliament in 1884 as a member for Dunedin East. In the same year he joined Sir Julius Vogel [q.v.] in the formation of the Stout-Vogel ministry, he himself becoming premier, attorney-general, and minister of education. He was considered chiefly responsible for the important Hospitals and Charitable Institutions Act of 1885. This coalition ministry was defeated in 1887, criticism being chiefly directed against its financial policy, and Stout withdrew from politics for six years. In June 1893 he was returned, at a by-election, for Inangahua. John Ballance [q.v.], who had died in April, is said to have regarded Stout as his natural successor. But Richard John Seddon [q.v.] succeeded to the premiership. For some time afterwards Stout remained somewhat aloof and critical of the Seddon administration. He represented the city of Wellington in parliament from 1893 to 1898, when he resigned, and was appointed in 1899 chief justice of New Zealand, a position which he held until 1926.

Throughout his life Stout kept in close touch with educational matters, though his educational views were regarded as conservative in his later years. He was a member of the senate of the New Zealand University for forty-six years (1884–1930), of the council of Otago University from 1891 to 1898, and of the council of Victoria College for many years. He was chancellor of the New Zealand University from 1903 to 1923. He received honorary degrees from the universities of Oxford, Edinburgh, and Manchester. He was created K.C.M.G. in 1886, was admitted a privy councillor in 1921, and was a member of the Judicial Committee of the Privy Council. When he resigned from the chief justiceship in 1926 he was appointed to the legislative council of New Zealand. This appointment he retained until his death, which occurred at Wellington 19 July 1930 in his eighty-sixth year. Stout married in 1876 Anna Paterson, daughter of John Logan, of Dunedin, clerk to the superintendent of the province of Otago, and had four sons and two daughters.

Stout was one of the greatest advocates the New Zealand bar has ever known; of striking appearance, with a voice of great flexibility and charm, he was a man of outstanding ability, and a formidable antagonist—especially before a jury. He was a courageous upholder of freethinking opinions in religion. He was one of the strongest advocates of prohibition in the country. He was largely responsible for placing the first measure of local option upon the New Zealand statute book, and helped to pass a bill for the introduction of women's suffrage.

As chief justice, Stout, the kindliest of men, endeared himself greatly to the legal profession. He took a leading part in helping to frame the First Offenders' Probation Act (1886), and when as judge he administered the provisions of that Act he was fond of calling attention to its good results. His legal opinions were not always shared by his colleagues on the bench. But his was one of the ablest minds ever devoted to public affairs in New Zealand.

[*The Times*, 21 July 1930; New Zealand Parliamentary Record, 1840–1925; T. M. Hocken, *Contributions to the Early History of New Zealand* (Settlement of Otago), 1898; J. B. Condliffe, *New Zealand in the Making*, 1930.] T. M. Wilford.

STRACHEY, JOHN ST. LOE (1860–1927), journalist, was born at Clifton 9 February 1860, the second son of Sir Edward Strachey, third baronet [q.v.], of Sutton Court, Somerset, by his second wife, Mary Isabella, second daughter of John Addington Symonds, M.D. [q.v.], and sister of the author John Addington Symonds [q.v.]. He was the great-grandson of Sir Henry Strachey, first baronet [q.v.], politician, and nephew of Sir John Strachey [q.v.], Anglo-Indian administrator, and Sir Richard Strachey [q.v.], lieutenant-general. He was educated privately, mainly by his father at home and at Cannes, until he went to live with his uncle by marriage, Thomas Hill Green [q.v.], at Oxford in order to work for responsions. He entered Balliol College in 1878 and read history. He was already widely read, and wrote verse, but he lacked the conventional school education and discipline, and he did not make a favourable impression on the master of Balliol, Jowett, and the dons, nor did he appreciate their merits. However, he obtained a first class in the honour school of modern history in 1882. His quality was proved by the lasting friendships which he made with the best of his Balliol contemporaries, such as (Sir) Herbert Warren, afterwards president of Magdalen College, H. C. Beeching, afterwards dean of Norwich, and (Sir) Bernard Mallet, and with W. T. Arnold, of University College.

In 1884 Strachey settled in London intending to read for the bar, to which he was called by the Inner Temple in 1885, but he plunged eagerly into journalism. He was soon contributing to the *Saturday Review*, the *Pall Mall Gazette*, the *Economist*, the *Manchester Guardian*, and, regularly, to the *Standard*, which accepted him in spite of the whiggism which he had inherited and the liberalism which he professed. For the liberal-unionist party, which he joined in 1886, he edited with C. L. Graves the *Liberal Unionist*, and he then began to write for the *Spectator*, edited by his father's friends Richard Holt Hutton [q.v.] and Meredith White Townsend [q.v.]. In 1896 he was appointed editor of the *Cornhill Magazine*, but in 1898 Townsend handed the *Spectator* over to him, and Strachey became editor and proprietor, a position which he retained until December 1925. The paper lost nothing in vigour as its interests expanded. The circulation increased throughout the English-speaking world, and for years it was the most influential unionist weekly paper. It strengthened Imperial and Anglo-American friendship, and the interest in Indian affairs, which Townsend had made prominent, was not diminished by an editor whose family had sent to India distinguished administrators since the days of Henry Strachey, secretary to Lord Clive.

Strachey married in 1887 Henrietta Mary Amy, daughter of Charles Turner Simpson, and granddaughter of the economist Nassau Senior [q.v.]. This connexion confirmed his individualistic views on social questions. He opposed state-socialism as contrary to the freedom of contract and exchange. Similarly, he opposed the tariff reform movement at the beginning of the twentieth century and became an active and influential unionist free-trader. At the general election of 1906 he unsuccessfully contested the seat for Edinburgh and St. Andrews Universities. He had built a house for himself at Newlands Corner in Surrey, and became enthusiastic over new materials and methods of building. In 1905 he organized the Cheap Cottages Exhibition at Letchworth in order to stimulate progress in cottage-building. In a practical matter like building he had the same naïvely eager love of experiment as he showed in literature, politics, and travel.

Strachey felt it to be his duty to warn Great Britain of the inevitability of the European War, which he foresaw. In his paper and personally in Surrey he took up rifle-shooting as advocated by Lord Roberts, Red Cross Voluntary Aid, and the registration of 'Surrey Veterans', ex-soldiers, and trained men. This led to his greatest contribution to the country's forces, for his scheme was copied beyond Surrey, and in 1914 the War Office had ready a register of 250,000 trained men upon whom there would have been no other means of calling. Strachey was high sheriff of Surrey in 1914 and threw himself into recruiting and other work with a feverish vigour which brought on a serious illness in 1916. A valuable piece of work done in London was the gathering of American and other journalists week by week at his house in Queen Anne's Gate in order to meet Cabinet ministers and others and to discuss the War with them. After the War he recovered his health sufficiently to visit Canada and the United States and to lecture there in 1926, but he died in London 26 August 1927. His elder son predeceased him; his younger son and his only daughter survived him.

Strachey's published works include *The Great Bread Riots* (1885, reissued 1903); *Industrial and Social Life and the Empire* (1895) (*The Citizen and the State*, Part ii); *From Grave to Gay* (essays and studies, 1897); *The Problems and Perils of Socialism* (1908); *The Practical Wisdom of the Bible* (1908); *A New Way of Life* (articles reprinted from the *Spectator*, 1909); *The Adventure of Living, a subjective autobiography* (1922); *The River of Life* (diaries, 1924); *The Madonna of the Barricades* (a novel, 1925); *American Soundings* (1926).

A portrait sketch of Strachey made in 1922 by Sir William Rothenstein is in the possession of Mrs. Strachey.

[Strachey's writings; Amy Strachey, *St. Loe Strachey: his Life and his Paper*, 1930; personal knowledge.] W. V. Cooper.

STRATHCLYDE, Baron (1853–1928), lawyer and politician. [See Ure, Alexander.]

STRUTHERS, Sir JOHN (1857–1925), educationist and civil servant, was born in Adelphi Street, Glasgow, 19 January 1857, the eldest son of Robert Struthers, described as a provision-merchant, by his wife, Agnes Muir. He was one of a numerous family, and was practically adopted and brought up by his father's sister, who was well married in Renfrewshire and was childless. Struthers was educated at the parish school at Mearns, Renfrewshire, where he served for five years as a pupil-teacher. Thence he went to the Church of Scotland Training College, Glasgow, and, combining his course at the college with a university course, he took his degree at Glasgow University with first-class honours in mental philosophy and a second class in classics. In 1881 he won an exhibition at Worcester College, Oxford, where he obtained a second class in classical moderations (1883) and a first class in *literae humaniores* (1885). In 1886 he was appointed an inspector of schools in Scotland; in 1898 he was taken on to the administrative staff of the Scottish Education Department as senior examiner; in 1900 he became assistant secretary, and in 1904 succeeded Sir Henry Craik [q.v.] as secretary; that post he held until his retirement under the age limit in 1922.

In the department Struthers's intimate knowledge of Scottish life and educational questions, his untiring industry, his consistency of purpose, and the sanity of his personal outlook were of the greatest value to Scottish education. Between 1898 and 1904 the framework of Scottish education was reshaped in every part and formed into a complete structure by means of a series of departmental minutes and circulars. The rationalization of the grant system was completed; post-primary education was re-classified and developed in new directions by the institution of 'higher grade schools' and 'supplementary courses'; continuation classes were regulated in a single system and grouped round 'central institutions'; the training of teachers was reorganized. It is not too much to say that the initiation of these reforms was the work of Struthers, and their consolidation was the most characteristic part of what he accomplished as secretary. To some extent they hinged upon the Scottish Education Act of 1901, which raised the school-leaving age effectually to fourteen.

The ensuing Acts of 1908, 1913, and 1918, which, among other reforms, substituted county education authorities for small school boards, settled the voluntary school question, greatly improved the condition of the teaching profession, instituted a general system of medical inspection, with medical treatment and the provision of food and clothing in necessitous cases, and extended the facilities provided by the existing bursary system, were largely due to Struthers's initiative.

While an examiner Struthers had been a member (1898) of the royal commission on manual and practical instruction in Ireland; and (as head of his department) of the committee on local and imperial taxation (1912), and other committees. He was an active trustee of the Carnegie Library Trust and a member of the executive committee of the Central Library for Students.

Struthers married in 1912 Gertrude, daughter of Julian Hill, of Dean's Yard, Westminster, nephew of Sir Rowland Hill; they had no children. He was created C.B. in 1902, K.C.B. in 1910, and given the honorary degree of LL.D. by Aberdeen University in 1905. His portrait by Maurice Greiffenhagen, remarkable both as a likeness and a work of art, was presented to him on his retirement. He died at his house in Chelsea 25 October 1925.

[*The Times*, 26 October 1925; *Glasgow Herald*, 26 and 29 October 1925; private information.] M. F. Headlam.

STRUTT, EDWARD GERALD (1854–1930), agriculturist, the fifth son of John James Strutt, second Baron Rayleigh, by his wife, Clara Elizabeth La Touche, eldest daughter of Captain Richard Vicars, R.E., and sister of Hedley Shafto Johnstone Vicars [q.v.], was born at his father's country seat, Terling Place, Essex, 10 April 1854. He was educated at Winchester and at Trinity College, Cambridge. He then became a pupil of Messrs. Rawlence and Squarey, land agents, of Salisbury. In 1876 he was called upon by his eldest brother, John William Strutt, third Baron Rayleigh [q.v.], to undertake the management of the latter's Essex estates. The farms were then for the most part in the hands of tenants, and he was able to do what was required while completing his training.

In 1877 Strutt went into partnership with Charles Parker, a friend of his boyhood, and the London firm of Strutt & Parker, land agents and surveyors, was founded, primarily in order to undertake the office of receiver (land agent) for the Lincolnshire and Essex estates of Guy's Hospital. A few years of Strutt's administration nearly doubled the income of the hospital from the estates, mainly by means of raising the rents. He ultimately (1919) negotiated the sale of the Lincolnshire estates to the Board of Agriculture, which desired control for the establishment of small holdings. A perpetual rent-charge was accepted in preference to a cash payment, and the hospital gained £5,000 per annum by the transaction.

In the meantime, the tenants on the Rayleigh estates had for the most part left, owing to the bad harvests and disastrous fall of wheat prices from 1878 onwards. They could not be replaced, and it became necessary to take the land in hand. Strutt looked round for some alternative farming policy, and he found it in the development of large-scale arable dairy farming, lucerne and other rotational grasses being used to supplement the limited amount of pasture. His system depended above everything on carefully kept records of milk yield. These were initiated in 1883. By weeding out the cows, the yield per head was progressively increased to more than double what it had been at first. From 1896 the use of the tuberculin test was progressively extended, and the reacting cows, which were at first found to be at least 50 per cent. of the whole number, were got rid of. The old cow houses were replaced by new ones of hygienic construction, and other exacting standards of cleanliness introduced. At the time that these improvements were made, they had a large measure of originality. In 1928, towards the end of Strutt's career, there was on the Rayleigh estate a herd of 850 cows which won the championship for clean milk herds in England.

Concurrently with these developments, a retail selling organization was formed in London, with a number of centres, incorporated as Lord Rayleigh's Dairies, Ltd. The farms on which the dairy herd was developed were and are preponderantly arable, and this aspect was not neglected. Here, too, a system of records was instituted much in advance of current practice. The computed profit or loss on each field was shown, and these figures, when added up, were found to give a good approximation to the actual profit. From these records, which were in full operation from about 1894, the average profit or loss on each crop could be determined. In the published records from 1894 to 1911 profit was always shown on corn crops. On other crops there was usually, but not invariably, a profit. The financial result for cows, cattle, pigs, sheep, and poultry were separately shown. A system of profit-sharing was instituted, and the employees were encouraged to invest their savings in the concern, on special terms.

These facts are taken for the most part from Strutt's presidential address to the Surveyors' Institution, delivered on 11 November 1912. This was the chief occasion on which he gave a public exposition of his views on agricultural policy. He emphasized the national importance of maintaining the agricultural population, and discussed with moderation and restraint what could be done to this end. His suggestions were: (1) an increase of arable land; (2) extension of small holdings; (3) agricultural education and research; (4) light railways; (5) government assistance in building rural cottages; and (6) no adverse legislation against capital invested in the soil. In the concluding part of his address he cited facts and figures to show that if the capital which had been expended on improving agricultural land were deducted, little or nothing remained which could be reckoned as the 'site value' postulated by radical politicians.

During the European War of 1914–1918, Strutt's help was largely relied on by the government in framing its agricultural policy. In 1915 the submarine menace became serious and it was vital to increase to the utmost the home production of food, in order to set overseas transport free for other purposes, and, in the last resort, to avert the threat of starvation. Strutt sat on Lord Milner's food production committee of 1915, and on Lord Selborne's committee of 1916 on post-War agricultural policy. In the meantime Mr. R. E. Prothero (afterwards Lord Ernle) had been appointed minister of agriculture, and Strutt was attached to the ministry as 'agricultural adviser'. He was consulted on most matters of real difficulty, and it was largely in reliance on his advice that compulsion was applied to secure the ploughing up of additional grasslands. He judged that most British farmers would loyally accept such a policy, if prices were guaranteed. The Corn Production Act of 1917 was the result: it proved that Strutt had correctly anticipated the attitude of the British farmers, who from reasons of discretion could not be fully informed of the necessities of the case. For his war services, he was made a Companion of Honour, on the institution of the order in 1917.

Strutt advised his friends not to oppose the minimum wage for agricultural labourers, but as a compensation to the farmer he tried, without ultimate success, to get the guarantee of corn prices continued. After the harvest of 1922–1923 this was abandoned.

Both before and after the War Strutt's agricultural enterprises steadily increased. The firm of Strutt & Parker (Farms) Ltd. was incorporated just before the War. In 1876 he had begun farming 1,000 acres, and at the time of his death this had increased to 25,000 acres. During the post-War period Strutt gave much of his energies to the development of the sugar-beet industry. He served on the royal commission on Oxford and Cambridge Universities (1920–1922), and also on the royal commission on tariffs (1923) under Lord Milner.

Strutt married in 1878 Maria Louisa, daughter of John Jolliffe Tufnell, of Langleys, Essex. They had five sons (two of whom died in infancy) and three daughters. His home was at Whitelands, Hatfield Peverel, on the Rayleigh property, and there he died 8 March 1930.

As an agriculturist, Strutt was essentially practical, and his farming was wholly directed to financial results. He was not by temperament a student, and he sought his information more from men than from books. He had a keen eye to avail himself of the resources of science, but valued it mainly for results. He had, however, the same capacity as his eldest brother for attending to essentials, and for closely adjusting means to ends. There was also some personal resemblance. He was of medium height, with fair complexion and somewhat rugged features. Up to about his fiftieth year he was fond of hunting, but otherwise his work was his chief interest and pleasure. In his personal relationships a strong human sympathy was his most marked quality. Inefficiency or slackness moved him to anger, but his anger left no permanent sting. His death was mourned by a whole country-side, as was very evident at his funeral.

A portrait of Strutt by Fiddes Watt is in possession of the family.

[Lord Ernle in *The Nineteenth Century and After*, April 1931; H. Rider Haggard, *Rural England*, vol. i, pp. 462–470, 1902; *Essex Weekly News*, 14 March 1930; personal knowledge.]

Rayleigh.

STURDEE, Sir FREDERICK CHARLES DOVETON, first baronet (1859–1925), admiral of the fleet, was born at Charlton, Kent, 9 June 1859, the eldest son of Captain Frederick Rannie Sturdee, R.N., by his wife, Anna Frances, daughter of Colonel Charles Hodson, of Oakbank, St. Helena. He was sent to the Royal Naval School at New Cross, and entered the *Britannia* as a naval cadet in July 1871. He passed first out of the training ship and went to sea as a midshipman in July 1873, serving until 1878 in the Channel squadron and on the East Indies station. After promotion to sub-lieutenant in June 1878, Sturdee was for nearly two years at Portsmouth in the gunnery school ship *Excellent* for courses and examinations which he passed with great distinction. He was promoted lieutenant in May 1880. From February 1881 to September 1882 he was in the *Hecla* on the Mediterranean station and took part in the operations at Alexandria in 1882, for his services in which he received the medal and bronze star.

From September 1882 to December 1885 Sturdee was in the *Vernon* torpedo school, and made his mark as a brilliant torpedo officer. For the next three and a half years he served as torpedo lieutenant in the *Bellerophon*, Lord Clanwilliam's flagship on the North American and West Indies station. From 1889 to 1893 he was on the staff of the *Vernon* and was continuously in command of torpedo boats: he gained more experience of these craft than any other lieutenant in the service. He was promoted commander in June 1893, and then served at the Admiralty for four years in the naval ordnance department as a torpedo specialist. He was awarded the gold medal of the Royal United Service Institution in 1894, having won it previously as a lieutenant. In November 1897 he went for two years in command of the *Porpoise* on the Australian station, and took command of the British force in Samoa in the summer of 1899 at the time of the trouble between Germany and the United States. For his services in handling a delicate international situation Sturdee was awarded the C.M.G. and promoted captain. He then returned to the Admiralty as assistant director of naval intelligence until October 1902, when he again went to sea and commanded successive cruisers in home waters until, in May 1905, he became chief of staff to Lord Charles Beresford, commander-in-chief of the Mediterranean fleet. Sturdee continued with Beresford on the latter's transfer to the command of the Channel fleet in 1907; he had received the C.V.O. in 1906. His last year, before promotion to flag rank in September 1908, was spent in command of the *New Zealand* battleship in the Channel fleet. In 1910 he commanded the first battle squadron for a year, and after presiding over the submarine committee at the Admiralty in 1911, was again employed afloat in command of cruiser squadrons, being the senior cruiser admiral in the home fleet, until his promotion to vice-admiral in December 1913. He had been created K.C.B. in the previous June.

In July 1914, immediately before the outbreak of the European War, Sturdee relieved Admiral Sir Henry Jackson as chief of the war staff under Prince Louis of Battenberg, first sea lord. The destruction of the cruiser squadron under Sir Christopher Cradock [q.v.] at Coronel on 1 November 1914 made it urgently necessary to deal with Admiral von Spee's German cruisers; and, on Lord Fisher succeeding Prince Louis as first sea lord, it was decided that Sturdee should be appointed commander-in-chief in the South Atlantic and South Pacific for this purpose. He reached Port Stanley in the Falkland Islands in the evening of 7 December 1914, and von Spee's squadron was sighted the next morning. The decisive victory of the Falkland Islands followed, in which Sturdee with two battle cruisers, five cruisers, and one armed merchant cruiser annihilated the German squadron of two armoured cruisers, three light cruisers, and two colliers, one light cruiser alone escaping. Sturdee's services in this action were rewarded by a baronetcy in January 1916.

Early in 1915 Sturdee hoisted his flag in the *Benbow* in command of the fourth battle squadron, which he commanded at the battle of Jutland on 31 May 1916. In the honours awarded after that battle he was promoted K.C.M.G., and he remained in command of the fourth battle squadron until February 1918, being promoted admiral in May 1917. During his period in the grand fleet he devoted much time and thought to fleet tactics and to tactical and strategical games. He then became commander-in-chief at the Nore until 1921, when he was promoted admiral of the fleet and G.C.B. At the end of the War he received the thanks of parliament and a grant of £10,000. Soon after ceasing active service he succeeded Lord Milford Haven (Prince Louis of Battenberg) as president of the Society for Nautical Research, and applied himself with whole-hearted devotion and energy to the scheme for preserving Nelson's flagship *Victory* and restoring her to her original Trafalgar rig and condition. He had successfully achieved this object before he died at his residence, Wargrave House, Camberley, 7 May 1925.

Sturdee was a really able naval officer, and an indefatigable student of his profession, who made his way to the highest rank entirely by his own merits, hard work, and devotion to the Service.

Sturdee married in 1882 Marion Adela, daughter of William John Andrews, of Fortis Green, Middlesex. They had two children, Lionel Arthur Doveton (born 1884), who succeeded to the baronetcy, and Margaret Adela, who married Vice-Admiral Cecil Minet Staveley.

[Admiralty records; private information.]

V. W. Baddeley.

STURT, GEORGE (1863–1927), author, who wrote under the pseudonym of George Bourne, the younger son of Francis Sturt, by his wife, Ellen, daughter of William Smith, was born at Farnham, Surrey, 18 June 1863. His paternal ancestors had worked at East Street, Farnham, in a firm of wheelwrights which had existed since 1706. His grandfather had bought the business in 1810; his father became head of it in 1865, and died in 1884. Of his early life George Sturt has left a vivid account in *A Small Boy in the Sixties* (1927). He was educated at Farnham grammar school, where he was a teacher from 1878 until 1885, when he entered the family business. He had learned, under the influence of Ruskin, to set handwork above the labour of the desk; and while acting as manager of the shop he took his share in all the branches of the craft. In the early 'nineties he took a partner, William Goatcher, and himself went to live at Vine Cottage in the village of The

Bourne, near Farnham, where he found leisure for writing.

In 1901 Sturt published, under the name 'George Bourne', *The Bettesworth Book*, a study of an old labourer who worked in his garden. It has humour and sympathy, but the stories told by the old labourer, Frederick Bettesworth, are apt to be prolix and somewhat pointless, and the author as interlocutor has rather too large a part in the scene. This book was followed in 1907 by *Memoirs of a Surrey Labourer*, a continuation of Bettesworth's history up to his death. Sturt's subsequent work included *The Ascending Effort* (1910), *Change in the Village* (1912), *Lucy Bettesworth* (1913), *William Smith, Potter and Farmer* (1920), and *A Farmer's Life* (1922). The last two are collected memories of his mother's ancestors in the corner of Surrey round about Frimley and Farnborough. William Smith was Sturt's maternal grandfather; John Smith, of *A Farmer's Life*, his uncle; both were men of the old school, of fine character and strong personality. The background to their histories is the life of the country in days when Aldershot was open heath, and the labours and humours of the people—small tradesmen, farmers, and squatters. Everywhere the author, whose writing is generally lucid and graceful, displays a deep appreciation of the mental vigour and sound sense of the older generation, and of the distinctive character of the landscape.

In 1923 appeared Sturt's best book, *The Wheelwright's Shop*, a chronicle of the family business at Farnham during the author's management of it from 1885 to 1920. This book reveals not only the spirit of the wheelwright's craft before the coming of the machine age, but also the traditional methods and manual skill of the workers. In their hands the English farm-wagon, for instance, is shown to be a thing of beauty in the ordering of its lines and the perfect adaptation of its parts to the work it had to do. Every detail of the craft is explained, the characters of the workers are portrayed, and, unconsciously, a striking self-portrait of the author is furnished.

Sturt's last book, *A Small Boy in the Sixties* (1927), and *The Wheelwright's Shop* appeared under his own name. He died 4 February 1927 at Vine Cottage, The Bourne. He was unmarried.

[*The Times Literary Supplement*, 31 May 1923; J. Conrad, *Notes on Life and Letters*, 1921; Sturt's own works; private information.] G. F. Scott.

SUTHERLAND, Sir THOMAS (1834–1922), chairman of the Peninsular and Oriental Steamship Company from 1881 to 1914, was born at Aberdeen 16 August 1834, the eldest son of Robert Sutherland, a house-painter, of Aberdeen, by his wife, Christian, daughter of Thomas Webster. Thomas Sutherland, while still a child, lost his father, and he and his widowed mother went to live with her parents, the Websters. The earliest influence in his life was the sober and self-respecting atmosphere of his grandparents' house. He was educated at the grammar school and university of Aberdeen, and at the age of nineteen came to London in order to enter as a junior clerk the office of the Peninsular and Oriental Steamship Company, to the service of which he devoted almost the whole of his business life.

In 1854 Sutherland was sent out to Bombay, and had his first experience of Eastern travel. This was six years before the railway from Alexandria to Suez was built, and the overland journey between these two ports occupied three or four days. After a short stay in Bombay, Sutherland was transferred to Hong Kong, where he gave such proof of his ability that by the time he was twenty-six he was appointed superintendent of the company's Japan and China agencies. He was one of the founders of the Hong Kong docks, as well as of the Hong Kong and Shanghai Banking Corporation, of which he became the first vice-chairman. His services to the mercantile community were recognized by his being appointed by the governor, Sir Hercules Robinson, a member of the legislative council of Hong Kong.

After twelve years' work in the East, Sutherland returned in 1867 to London, and was promoted to be inspector, and then assistant manager, of the Peninsular and Oriental Steamship Company. About this time the completion of the Suez canal threatened to rob the company of its monopoly of the Eastern carrying trade, and Sutherland was the moving spirit in the necessary reconstruction of the Peninsular and Oriental fleet. Continuing to show administrative capacity, he was advanced to the position of a managing director in 1873, and eventually in 1881 he was elected chairman of the board.

The most important as well as the most interesting business which Sutherland undertook on behalf of his company was the conduct of the negotiations for an arrangement between British shipowners and the Suez Canal Company. An agreement to obviate delays in working traffic through the canal had been reached in the spring of 1883 by the liberal government of the day, represented by Mr. Gladstone and Lord Granville. But this agreement had been considered so unsuitable that it was never submitted to the House of Commons, and the shipowners, acting on a hint from the government, took the matter in hand themselves. In October of the same year negotiations with M. Ferdinand de Lesseps and his son, M. Charles de Lesseps, were opened by a visit paid by the latter to the London offices of the Peninsular and Oriental Steamship Company. Sutherland explained the requirements of the shipowners, and the result was the agreement of November 1883 known as the 'Programme de Londres'. By this instrument British shipowners were admitted to a share in the management of the canal, with a right to appoint seven directors, and it was also agreed that after the Canal Company had received a fair dividend, the balance of profit should be applied to the reduction of dues. This settlement was of much more advantage to Great Britain than the agreement previously negotiated by the government, under which a substantial loan was to be made to the Canal Company; for under Sutherland's settlement the Canal Company itself was to provide funds for widening the canal. The arrangements at the time gave general satisfaction. The tolls began to be reduced in 1884, and, in addition, a considerable sum was saved annually by the shipowners in pilotage dues. Sutherland himself became one of the directors of the Canal Company, and at the time of his death was senior vice-president. The services rendered by him in this affair were appreciated so highly by his own company that the shareholders presented him with the money necessary to qualify him as a director of the Canal Company.

Sutherland resigned the chairmanship of the Peninsular and Oriental Steamship Company in 1914, after being connected with that undertaking for sixty years, for the last thirty-three of which he had been chairman. His successor in office, paying a tribute to his memory, said that Sutherland had done much to maintain the supremacy of British shipping and the high regard in which British shipowners and their methods are held among foreign competitors.

Sutherland entered the House of Commons as member for Greenock in 1884, and sat for that constituency, first as a liberal, and then as a liberal unionist, until 1900. He was a member of the Load Line commission (1882), and also a member of the royal commission on the financial relations between Great Britain and Ireland (1893). He was one of His Majesty's lieutenants for the City of London and was created K.C.M.G. in 1891 and advanced to G.C.M.G. in 1897.

Sutherland married in 1880 Alice (died 1920), daughter of the Rev. John Macnaught, vicar of St. Chrysostom's, Liverpool, and had two sons and one daughter. His sons were both killed in action, one in the South African War and one in the European War. Sutherland died at his London house in Buckingham Gate 1 January 1922.

[*The Times*, 2 and 9 January 1922; private information.] A. Cochrane.

SWINTON, ALAN ARCHIBALD CAMPBELL (1863–1930), electrical engineer, born at 9 Albyn Place, Edinburgh, 18 October 1863, was the third son of Archibald Campbell Swinton, D.L., of Kimmerghame, Berwickshire, professor of civil law in the university of Edinburgh 1842–1862, by his wife, Georgiana Caroline, daughter of Sir George Sitwell, second baronet, of Renishaw, Derbyshire. As a child, Swinton showed a decided bent towards engineering, and developed considerable skill in photography, which remained a lifelong hobby. In 1878 he was sent to Fettes College, where his hatred of games and dislike of orthodox methods of instruction seem to have made life very difficult for him. At the age of fifteen, two years after the invention of the telephone, he made, at school, an excellently working installation connecting two houses. In 1881 he went to Havre to study French and mathematics, and visited the Paris exhibition, where he was deeply impressed by the electrical inventions which he saw.

In 1882 Swinton began a five years' apprenticeship in the engineering works of Sir W. G. (afterwards Lord) Armstrong at Elswick-on-Tyne. In 1883 his book *The Principles and Practice of Electric Lighting* was published by Messrs. Longman, and thereafter he became chiefly interested in the electrical side of Armstrong's business. He was the first to employ lead-covered wires and cables for electric wiring in ships, in place of the cumbersome methods then employed to prevent the penetration of moisture.

In 1887 Swinton went to London to work up an independent practice as electrical contractor and consulting engineer. He carried out electric lighting installations in many country houses, and was connected with several of the earliest electric supply companies, notably those which were the first to employ steam turbines—for example, the Scarborough Electric Supply Co. and the Cambridge Electric Supply Co., of which latter he became managing director. He was also connected with Messrs. Crompton & Co. and was consultant to Sir William Armstrong. He gave up the contracting side of his business in 1904.

His ability to estimate rapidly the value of new discoveries marked out Swinton as a pioneer in the application of electricity in this country. The first photograph produced by X-rays in England was taken by him and published in *Nature* (23 January 1896) within a month of the announcement of Röntgen's discovery. By 1897 doctors and surgeons were bringing him their patients for examination with the aid of X-rays, so that Swinton must have been one of the first radiographers employed by the medical profession. From this date onwards Swinton read many papers of fundamental importance before the Royal Society and other learned societies, dealing with his observations on X-rays and cathode rays. His writings were, in general, of a descriptive nature, his great skill as an experimenter and his extraordinarily wide scientific knowledge being his greatest assets. His discovery of the high temperatures obtainable by the focusing of cathode rays led to a study of the luminosity of rare earths and was demonstrated by the conversion of a diamond into coke.

In association with Sir Charles Parsons, Swinton was intimately connected with the early development of the steam turbine and with the construction of the turbine ship *Turbinia*, a torpedo-boat destroyer which at the naval review of 1897 attained the then astonishing speed of 33½ knots.

Swinton, who lived in London in Chester Square, met nearly all the eminent men of science of his day, and received much encouragement in his work from Lord Kelvin, Lord Armstrong, and Sir William Crookes. In 1896 he introduced Guglielmo Marconi to (Sir) William Preece, who was then engineer-in-chief to the Post Office; and rapid developments in radio-telegraphy ensued. Swinton was also responsible for investigating the papers left by the inventor, David Edward Hughes [q.v.], and proved that Hughes had made successful experiments in wireless telegraphy over short distances in 1879, some years before Hertz's discovery.

Swinton was a member of the Institutions of Civil, Mechanical, and Electrical Engineers, and was for four years vice-president of the last. In 1911 he was president of the Röntgen Society, and in 1913 of the Radio Society. For several years he was chairman of the Royal Society of Arts, and in 1915 was elected a fellow of the Royal Society. He gave his services freely to many scientific societies, which owe much to his philanthropy. He died at his house, 40 Chester Square, 19 February 1930. He was unmarried.

[*Nature*, 8 March 1930; *Proceedings* of the Royal Society, vol. cxxx, A, 1931; Alan A. Campbell Swinton, *Autobiographical and other writings*, 1930.] S. E. A. Landale.

TAYLOR, HENRY MARTYN (1842–1927), mathematician, was born at Bristol 6 June 1842, the second son of the Rev. James Taylor, who afterwards became headmaster of Wakefield grammar school, by his wife, Eliza Johnson. He was educated at Wakefield and at Trinity College, Cambridge, which he entered as a minor scholar in 1861. He graduated as third wrangler in 1865, and was awarded the second Smith's prize.

Taylor cherished for a time the intention of going to the bar, and was in fact called by Lincoln's Inn, but soon relinquished the design. After holding the post of vice-principal of the School of Naval Architecture and Marine Engineering at Kensington (1865–1869), he returned to Cambridge in 1869 as assistant tutor on the mathematical staff of Trinity College. He had been elected a fellow, under the old competitive system, in 1866. Thenceforward his life was spent in the service of his college and university until his retirement in 1894. He became tutor of the college in 1874, and held the position for the usual period of ten years.

Taylor's mathematical leanings were mainly towards geometry, in its intuitive aspect, as is indicated by the papers which he contributed to the London Mathematical Society (of which he was one of the earliest members), to the *Philosophical Transactions*, and the *Cambridge Transactions*. Special reference may be made to his papers on *Inversion*, on *Plane Curves*, and on *Solid Geometry*. He had a rigid standard of verbal and logical accuracy, and was often consulted by friends, including Lord Rayleigh, on stylistic and other matters, where his judgement was valued.

When released from tutorial duties at the early age of fifty-two, Taylor might reasonably have looked forward to some years of useful mathematical work, but these expectations were defeated by the severe calamity which soon befell him. An attack of influenza was followed by partial, and later by complete, blindness. He met this disaster with admirable courage. He continued for a time to interest himself in mathematical questions, with something like enthusiasm, and indeed his two most original papers, requiring a high degree of constructive imagination, were those which he contributed, after his blindness, to the *Philosophical Transactions* and to the volume commemorating the jubilee of Sir G. Gabriel Stokes (1900).

Taylor's most notable work, however, was yet to come, and lay in a somewhat different direction. His own affliction had led him to consider how, with his own special training and acquirements, he could most usefully help those in like case. He found that although a certain amount of literature was accessible to the blind through the medium of the Braille script, there was no provision of a scientific kind. Taylor made it his duty to try to throw open to them in some degree this province also. He soon made himself expert on the Braille typing machine, and with his own hands transcribed a series of elementary books on mathematics and various branches of natural science. He was here faced with the problem that the Braille system had no provision for mathematical notation, whilst diagrams were, of course, a special difficulty. Taylor accordingly gave much thought to the invention of suitable symbols and contrivances. The question of expense was a further difficulty; the reproduction and multiplication of the bulky volumes was costly. In order to meet this, Taylor, with the assistance of his friends, started an Embossed Scientific Book Fund, which was, to his great satisfaction, accepted as a trust by the Royal Society, and is now administered by a special committee of the fellows. Taylor had himself been elected a fellow in 1898.

In addition to his scientific and educational interests, Taylor had a strong practical sense which found an outlet in the administrative business of his college, and also, later, in municipal affairs. He was one of the university representatives on the Cambridge town council and was in due course elected alderman, and finally mayor in 1904.

Taylor was a singularly modest man, and devoid of personal ambition. He was a loyal and generous friend, and a scrupulously fair opponent. Before his blindness, he had shared in the usual recreations of his time, 'real' tennis, cricket, shooting, fishing, and billiards, in all of which he was competent. He had also been fond of travel, and of mountain excursions. His last few years were clouded by increasing infirmity. He died at Cambridge 16 October 1927. He never married.

[*Proceedings* of the Royal Society, vol. cxvii, A, 1928 (portrait); personal knowledge.]

H. Lamb.

TEALE, THOMAS PRIDGIN (1831–1923), surgeon, the eldest son of Thomas Pridgin Teale, by his wife, Frances Ann, daughter of the Rev. Charles Isherwood, curate-in-charge of Brotherton, Yorkshire, was born at Leeds 28 June 1831. He was the son, grandson, and nephew of Leeds surgeons. His father was a distinguished F.R.S., the inventor of the 'long anterior flap' method of amputation of the leg, and author of the standard work of his day on hernia. The name Pridgin, a corruption of Prujean, is an indication of Teale's Huguenot descent through his paternal grandmother.

Thomas Pridgin Teale the younger was educated first at Leeds grammar school, and from the age of thirteen to eighteen at Winchester College under the headmastership of Dr. George Moberly. Thence he proceeded to Brasenose College, Oxford, where he read mathematics. He received his medical training at King's College, London, of which he was later elected an honorary fellow. After a short period of continental travel and study, he began practice in Leeds in 1856. He was elected surgeon to the Leeds General Infirmary in 1864 and served for twenty years, being afterwards appointed to the consulting staff. In collaboration with his eminent colleague (Sir) Thomas Clifford Allbutt [q.v.] Teale was a pioneer in 'team work' in medicine and in the surgical treatment of scrofulous neck. At the instigation of Allbutt, Teale undertook the experiment of removing enlarged tuberculous glands before supperation had occurred; his example was soon generally followed. Teale, like his father, was expert in the treatment of vesical calculus, and their joint experiences at the Leeds General Infirmary in this branch of surgery covered a period of almost eighty years. He favoured the crushing of stones by the delicate operation of lithotrity, provided the surgeon was trained in the use of an instrument requiring special skill. In the days when the *Lancet* expressed the view that a surgeon who lost a patient after the operation of ovariotomy should be indicted for manslaughter, Teale advocated and employed this method, and his success did much to rescue it from disrepute. His contributions to literature were not numerous; but he wrote important papers on tracheotomy, on ruptured perinaeum, and on dilatation of the anal sphincter. In his ophthalmic practice Teale designed a suction curette for the extraction of soft cataract; he invented an operation for symblepharon; he showed the value of atropine in the treatment of iritis; and he described two cases of cysticercus in the eye, discovered by the ophthalmoscope. He lectured on the abandonment of iridectomy in the extraction of hard cataract. All his writings were expressed with modesty which won for them a most favourable reception.

Perhaps one of the greatest services rendered by Teale to the cause of surgery was his early recognition and enforcement of the truth of the teaching of Lord Lister [q.v.]. At the Leeds General Infirmary, when senior colleagues were hesitant or scoffing, he practised antiseptic surgery, and was one of the most successful apostles in spreading the new gospel. He was an advocate of ether anaesthesia, as opposed to all other methods, and chloroform was vigorously excluded from his practice. As lecturer and teacher by the bedside, Teale, denied the gift of oratory, made a strong and almost unforgettable impression by his earnestness, directness, simplicity, contagious enthusiasm, and sturdy reliance upon personal experience.

Teale's interests extended to sanitation. He invented new fireplaces and new pokers; he taught the virtues of ventilation; he was an eager and exacting authority upon sewers. On domestic hygiene he lectured to the Royal Institution in 1886, and in this important matter no man had so quick and vivid an influence upon his generation. He wrote *Dangers to Health; a pictorial guide to domestic sanitary defects*, which passed through four editions (1879 (two), 1881, and 1883) and was translated into French, Spanish, and Italian, and into German by Princess Helena (Princess Christian of Schleswig-Holstein). In 1888 Teale was elected F.R.S. He was for many years examiner in surgery at the university of Oxford, and from 1876 to 1901 he was a member of the General Medical Council.

Teale added much to the science of surgery, and practised the craft with hands which, for deftness, gentleness, exquisite delicacy of touch, and effective movement, were unsurpassed in his day. Those two great advances, anaesthesia and antiseptic surgery, were advocated and practised by Teale when the minds of other men were unprepared fully to understand their significance. The advocacy of such a man at that time was a great asset, for he was known to be averse from wild adventures. His vision was acute and penetrating; his judgement grave, sane, and cautious; but when convinced of the right way he was joyous and eager in its pursuit and practice.

Teale married twice: first, in 1862 his cousin Alice (died 1891), daughter of the Rev. William Henry Teale, rector of Devizes, and had four sons and four daughters; secondly, in 1899 Mary Jane Elizabeth, second daughter of Daniel Charles Jones, of Tamworth, and had no issue. Teale died at Leeds 13 November 1923.

[*Proceedings* of the Royal Society, vol. xcvi, B, 1924 (portrait).] MOYNIHAN.

TEALL, SIR JETHRO JUSTINIAN HARRIS (1849–1924), geologist, born at Northleach, Gloucestershire, 5 January 1849, was the only and posthumous son of Jethro Teall, landowner, of Sandwich, Kent, by his wife, Mary, daughter of Justinian Hathaway, of Northleach. He received his early education at Northleach grammar school, and later was sent to Berkeley Villa school, Cheltenham, where he developed a taste for natural history and the sciences, especially chemistry, botany, and geology. Having obtained a sound mathematical training, he proceeded to St. John's College, Cambridge, in 1869, with the intention of reading for the mathematical tripos, but falling under the inspiring influence of his college tutor, (Professor) Thomas George Bonney [q.v.], he forsook mathematics and devoted himself wholly to natural science. He was privileged to attend the last course of lectures delivered by Adam Sedgwick [q.v.], the Woodwardian professor of geology, obtained a first class in the natural sciences tripos of 1872, graduated B.A. the following year, and M.A. in 1876.

In 1874 Teall was the first recipient of the Sedgwick prize for geology, endowed in memory of the late Woodwardian professor. The following year (1875) he was elected to a fellowship at his college, and he held it until his marriage, four years later (1879), with Harriet, daughter of George Roberts Cowen, of Nottingham. After taking his degree he devoted himself to lecturing under the university extension scheme and to petrographical research. Teall's earlier contributions to petrology include outstanding papers on the 'Cheviot Lavas' (1883), 'The North of England Dykes' (1884), 'The Whin Sill' (1884), 'The Metamorphosis of Dolerite into Hornblendeschist' (1885), and the 'Origin of Banded Gneisses' (1887); most of these appeared either in the *Quarterly Journal* of the Geological Society or in the *Geological Magazine.* His concurrent mineralogical studies on such subjects as 'Andalusite from the Cheesewring, Cornwall' (1887), 'Rutile-needles in Clays' (1887), 'Minerals from the Lizard' (1888) found ready publication in the *Mineralogical Magazine.* He was one of the first geologists to draw attention to mineralogical changes induced by stress within the earth's crust, and to deal scientifically with the natural history and genesis of many important minerals of metamorphic origin.

Teall's extensive study of British igneous rocks inspired him with the idea of publishing in parts a monograph on *British Petrography,* of which subject his mineralogical and geological knowledge and his intimacy with current petrographical literature made him the best possible exponent. He began the publication of this valuable and beautifully illustrated work in 1886, but owing to the failure of his original publishers its completion was delayed until 1888. This work remains a monument to his scientific ability, his broad outlook, and clear, unbiased interpretation of geological observations.

At the invitation of (Sir) Archibald Geikie [q.v.], Teall joined the Geological Survey of Great Britain in 1888, and at once undertook petrographical work connected with the detailed survey in progress in Scotland and south-west England. This led him to publish in official memoirs the results of many important petrographical investigations, mainly connected with the Lewisian Gneisses, the Torridon Sandstone, and the post-Cambrian igneous rocks. Extra-official publications of exceptional scientific value were those on the *Plutonic Rocks of Garabal Hill* (with J. R. Dakyns, 1892), on *Borolanite* (with J. Horne, 1893), and several papers on the rocks of the Lizard, Cornwall (with Howard Fox, 1891, 1893). Teall succeeded Geikie as director of the Geological Survey of Great Britain in 1901. His able administration, which terminated on his retirement in 1914, left a lasting impression upon that institution: the scope of its activities was enlarged, its scientific status studiously upheld, and its general utility and educational value still further increased.

Teall was elected a fellow of the Geological Society in 1873 and of the Royal Society in 1890; of the former he was secretary (1893–1897) and president (1900–1902). He received from the Geological Society first the Bigsby medal (1889), and later (1905) its highest award, the Wollaston medal; the Académie des Sciences of Paris awarded him the Delesse prize in 1907. He also held doctorates of the universities of Oxford, Cambridge, Dublin, and St. Andrews. He was knighted in 1916. He died at his home at Dulwich 2 July 1924. His wife and two sons survived him.

Teall was a true scientist with the widest scientific sympathies. He was never rash in his conclusions, always free from the tyranny of theories, and always regardful of any piece of evidence however small. Thus his published works hold to-day an important and honoured place in geological literature, and many of them, such as his presidential addresses to the Geological Society and the Geologists' Association, influenced greatly the trend of modern petrographical thought.

['Eminent Living Geologists' in the *Geological Magazine*, vol. vi, 1909 (portrait); *Proceedings* of the Royal Society, vol. xcvii, B, 1925; *Quarterly Journal* of the Geological Society, vol. lxxxi, 1925.] H. H. Thomas.

TERRY, Dame (ALICE) ELLEN (1847–1928), actress, was born in Smithford Street, Coventry, 27 February 1847, the third daughter and third of the eleven children of Benjamin Terry, actor, by his wife, Sarah Ballard, actress, daughter of a Scottish minister at Portsmouth. Benjamin Terry's father was H. B. Terry, an innkeeper at Portsmouth. Three of Ellen Terry's sisters, Kate, Marion, and

Florence, and a brother, Fred, also went on the stage. Ellen's first appearance on the stage was as the boy Mamillius in Charles Kean's production of *The Winter's Tale* at the Princess's Theatre, London, 28 April 1856. With Kean she also acted Puck in *A Midsummer-Night's Dream* (1856), Arthur in *King John* (1858), and Fleance in *Macbeth* (1859), besides a fairy in a pantomime and many other parts.

Ellen Terry's childhood was full of work, and in 1862 she went to the Theatre Royal, Bristol, to the company of J. H. Chute, for whom she appeared as Titania at the opening of the Theatre Royal, Bath, in March 1863. Her dress for that part was designed by the architect Edward William Godwin [q.v.], whose acquaintance she first made at Bristol. In the spring of 1863 she joined the company of John Baldwin Buckstone [q.v.] at the Haymarket Theatre. Her parts there included Hero, Desdemona, Nerissa, Lady Touchwood in *The Belle's Stratagem*, Flora in *The Duke's Motto*, Julia in *The Rivals*, and Mary Meredith in *Our American Cousin* by Tom Taylor [q.v.], in which Edward Askew Sothern [q.v.] was giving his celebrated performance of Lord Dundreary. But Ellen Terry regarded her season at the Haymarket as a lost opportunity. She was restless and not happy, and the theatre had come to seem to her less interesting than the studio. Tom Taylor had introduced her to the painter George Frederic Watts [q.v.], who was enchanted with her beauty; and on 20 February 1864 she was married to him at St. Barnabas church, Kensington. Watts was then nearly forty-seven years old. He and his circle treated his wife like a child—not without some provocation from her playful high spirits. Against her will a separation was arranged in June 1865. She went back to the stage, and in October 1867 joined Alfred Sydney Wigan [q.v.] at the New Queen's Theatre, Long Acre, to play Mrs. Mildmay in Tom Taylor's *Still Waters Run Deep* and other parts, among them Katharine in *Katharine and Petruchio* (Garrick's version of *The Taming of the Shrew*), in which, in December 1867, she acted for the first time with (Sir) Henry Irving [q.v.]. She was still neither happy nor successful on the stage, and in 1868 she left it and set up house in Hertfordshire with her friend Godwin. The theatre saw her no more for six years, during which time she gave birth to her daughter Edith Craig, and her son Edward Gordon Craig.

Anxiety for her children's future induced Ellen Terry to accept an offer from Charles Reade [q.v.]. On 28 February 1874 she took up the part of Philippa in Reade's *The Wandering Heir* at the New Queen's Theatre, and in the summer toured with Reade, from whom she learned much of the art of acting. On 17 April 1875, at the age of twenty-eight, she reached the turning-point of her career, when she appeared as Portia in the production of *The Merchant of Venice* at the old Prince of Wales's Theatre staged by (Sir) Squire Bancroft [q.v.] and his wife. The play ran for only three weeks, but Ellen Terry, in looks and in acting, was the high point of beauty in a beautiful production. Her personal success led to further work with the Bancrofts.

In November 1876 Ellen Terry went for eighteen months to the Court Theatre, where (Sir) John Hare [q.v.] gave her her second great opportunity, namely the part of Olivia in the adaptation by W. G. Wills [q.v.] of Goldsmith's *Vicar of Wakefield* (28 March 1878). In that part, which remained in her repertory until 1900, she proved her power of reducing her audience to tears. Godwin and she had parted company, but not friendship, in 1875; and on 21 November 1877 (Watts having divorced her in that year) she married Charles Clavering Wardell, who acted under the name of Charles Kelly. In 1881 they were judicially separated.

In 1878 Henry Irving, having become sole lessee of the Lyceum Theatre, engaged Ellen Terry to play Ophelia in his forthcoming production of *Hamlet*, and she appeared in that part on the opening night of his management (30 December). Thus began an association which lasted unimpaired until 1896 and unbroken until 1902. Up till 1896 Ellen Terry played the leading female parts in all Irving's productions. The list (excluding revivals and single performances for charity) is as follows: 1878, Ophelia. 1879, Pauline in *The Lady of Lyons*; Ruth in *Eugene Aram*; Henrietta Maria in *Charles I*; Portia. 1880, Iolanthe in a play of that name by Wills. 1881, Camma in *The Cup*; Letitia Hardy in *The Belle's Stratagem*; Desdemona. 1882, Juliet; Beatrice. 1883, Jeannette in *The Lyons Mail*; Clementine in *Robert Macaire*. 1884, Viola. 1885, Olivia in *Olivia*; Marguerite in *Faust*. 1886, Peggy in James Kenney's farce *Raising the Wind*. 1887, Ellaline in *The Amber Heart*. 1888, Lady Macbeth. 1889, Catherine Duval in *The Dead Heart*. 1890,

Lucy Ashton in *Ravenswood* by H. C. Merivale. 1891, Nance Oldfield in the play of that name by Charles Reade. 1892, Queen Katharine in *King Henry VIII*; Cordelia. 1893, Rosamund in *Becket*. 1894, Guinevere in *King Arthur* by Joseph Comyns Carr. 1896, Imogen. 1897, Catharine in *Madame Sans-Gêne*. 1898, Catherine in *Peter the Great* by Laurence Irving; Sylvia Wynford in *The Medicine Man* by Robert Hichens and H. D. Traill. 1899, Clarice in *Robespierre*, an adaptation by Laurence Irving from the French. 1901, Volumnia. She took part in Irving's eight American tours between 1883 and 1901. In the summer of 1902 she was acting at the Lyceum only twice a week, in matinées of *Charles I* and *The Merchant of Venice*. Her last appearance at that theatre was as Portia, 19 July 1902. She decided not to go to America with Irving to act a part in *Dante*; and in the autumn of that year, neither at her suggestion nor by her desire, they finally parted.

Egoist though he was, Irving had too much sense to stint his theatre of the genius of Ellen Terry at her best. Certain plays he chose rather for her sake than for his own. And Ellen Terry made the most of her chances. In face, dress, and movement she was so beautiful, her voice was so thrilling, her personal charm so inextinguishable, and, above all, her vitality so exuberant that these qualities won much of the credit due to histrionic power dependent upon nothing but her intelligence, sympathy, and hard work. As Lucy Ashton she showed that she could conquer her besetting temptation to restlessness. In Madame Sans-Gêne and Volumnia, parts out of line with her personality, she showed her accomplishment and power of impersonation. When her natural attractions (which she had perfectly at command) chimed with her skill, she was a great actress. There was nothing insipid about her. In the young women of Shakespeare, Desdemona or Ophelia, she found character; as Lady Macbeth she was an exquisite woman aflame with ambitious imagination; in Queen Katharine her majesty proved her patience to be no weakness. But she was at her best when her sense of fun and her high spirits could join forces with her strength, her intensity, and her grace. Her Beatrice, surpassing even her Portia, was as near perfection as acting can go. With every sign of complete spontaneity, it was a work of precisely calculated art.

In April 1902, while Irving was acting *Faust* with Cissie Loftus as Marguerite, Ellen Terry went to Stratford-upon-Avon in order to play Queen Katharine with (Sir) Frank Benson's company. In June she appeared with great success at His Majesty's Theatre as Mrs. Page in *The Merry Wives of Windsor* produced by (Sir) Herbert Beerbohm Tree [q.v.]. In 1903 she ventured into management. The theatre was the Imperial, in Westminster; and there in April she produced *The Vikings*, an English version by William Archer of Ibsen's *The Vikings at Helgeland*, herself taking the part of Hiordis. The staging was by Gordon Craig, and was the first example of his art on a large scale. It won golden opinions, but the cost was very heavy and the public rather shy. The play was soon withdrawn. The same ill-success attended her production, also staged by Gordon Craig, of *Much Ado about Nothing*; and in June she closed the theatre. In July 1903 at a charity performance at Drury Lane Theatre Ellen Terry played Portia and acted for the last time in her life with Henry Irving. The next two years saw her well established in modern prose drama. She showed her own faith in it by producing Christopher St. John's (Miss Christabel Marshall's) version of *The Good Hope* by Hermann Heijermans, in which for the first time she played the part of an old woman. On 5 April 1905 she created the part of Alice Grey in (Sir) J. M. Barrie's *Alice Sit-by-the-Fire* at the Duke of York's Theatre; and on 20 March 1906 at the Court Theatre she played Lady Cecily Waynflete in G. Bernard Shaw's *Captain Brassbound's Conversion*.

That month saw the fiftieth anniversary of Ellen Terry's first appearance on the stage; and the occasion was taken to pay public tribute to her. On 12 June a 'jubilee' matinée was held at Drury Lane, in the course of which she played Beatrice in the first act of *Much Ado about Nothing*, with scenery designed by her son and with twenty-two other members of her family in the cast. Foreigners as well as English people joined in the expression of admiration and affection; and nearly £10,000 was subscribed as a gift to her. In September 1906 at His Majesty's Theatre she played Hermione in *The Winter's Tale*. In the early part of 1907 she took *Captain Brassbound's Conversion* and *The Good Hope* on tour in the United States; and on 22 March of that year she was married at Pittsburg, Pennsylvania, to James Usselmann, a young American acting in her company under the name of James Carew, with whom she lived until 1910.

Failure of memory now made it difficult for Ellen Terry to take up new parts; but she appeared not infrequently in special performances. On 19 December 1908 at His Majesty's Theatre she created the part of a sweet old lady, Aunt Imogen, in Walford Graham Robertson's *Pinkie and the Fairies*; in 1917 and 1918 she acted the trial scene from *The Merchant of Venice* and scenes from *The Merry Wives of Windsor* at the Coliseum, and on 12 April 1919 at the Lyric Theatre she took the part of the Nurse in Doris Keane's production of *Romeo and Juliet*. Her last appearance on the stage was at the Lyric Theatre, Hammersmith, in Walter de la Mare's *Crossings* on 19 November 1925. Meanwhile in 1922 and 1923 she had taken part in four productions for the cinematograph. But she had found a wider outlet for her genius.

In 1903 Ellen Terry had composed, with the help of Christopher St. John, and delivered a lecture on 'The Letters in Shakespeare's Plays'. A few years later, with the same assistance, she composed two lectures on Shakespeare's heroines and one on the children in Shakespeare. That she had a talent for verbal expression, and much to say by that means, is proved by her memoirs and by her published letters to Bernard Shaw; and these lectures, with illustrations recited by the lecturer, proved her to be a fine critic and provided a delightful entertainment. In 1910–1911 she delivered the lectures on tour in America; in 1911 and 1912 she gave them in England, and in May 1914 she began a tour of Australia and the United States which lasted until the spring of 1915.

Ellen Terry's eyesight had long been troubling her and sometimes causing her acute pain; and in February 1915 she underwent an operation for cataract in New York. From 1921 onwards her health was failing, and her too lavish generosity had much reduced her means. She seldom went into public, but she was not forgotten. In 1922 the university of St. Andrews conferred upon her the honorary degree of LL.D.; and at the New Year, 1925, she was created G.B.E. She died 21 July 1928 at her house at Small Hythe, Tenterden, Kent. Her ashes were placed in a casket on the wall of St. Paul's church, Covent Garden. Her house at Small Hythe was bought by public subscription and converted into an Ellen Terry museum.

Portraits of Ellen Terry are very many, the most important being as follows. In the Tate Gallery hangs a well-known oil-painting by J. S. Sargent of Ellen Terry as Lady Macbeth. In the National Portrait Gallery are a profile head of her at the age of seventeen by G. F. Watts, and an oil-sketch in black and white of her as Lady Macbeth coming out to meet Duncan, made by J. S. Sargent for reproduction in the *Souvenir* of her jubilee. The Watts Gallery at Compton, Surrey, possesses Watts's portrait of Ellen Terry as Ophelia. Lord Somers owns 'Ellen Terry and her Sister' (Kate) by Watts, and Mr. Kerrison Preston the portrait by Watts entitled 'Choosing'. Mr. W. Graham Robertson retains in his collection his pastel head of Ellen Terry, which Irving used to call 'Ellen in Heaven', his large oil-portrait, and a portrait which he painted in 1923. Miss Edith Craig owns an oil-portrait painted in 1926 by Clare Atwood; and in the Memorial Museum at Small Hythe there is a replica in oils by W. Graham Robertson of his pastel head, besides many other portraits. At His Majesty's Theatre Ellen Terry is seen as Mistress Page, with Madge Kendal as Mrs. Ford and Tree as Falstaff, in a picture by the Hon. John Collier.

[*The Times*, 22 July 1928; *Ellen Terry's Memoirs*, with notes and additional chapters by E. Craig and C. St. John, 1933; Ellen Terry, *Four Lectures on Shakespeare*, edited by C. St. John, 1932; *Ellen Terry and Bernard Shaw, A Correspondence*, edited by C. St. John, 1931; Edward Gordon Craig, *Ellen Terry and her Secret Self*, 1931; Walford Graham Robertson, *Time Was*, 1931; Bram Stoker, *Personal Reminiscences of Henry Irving*, 2 vols., 1906; Austin Brereton, *Life of Henry Irving*, 2 vols., 1908; *Souvenir Programme, Ellen Terry Jubilee Commemoration*, 1906.]

H. H. CHILD.

THISELTON-DYER, SIR WILLIAM TURNER (1843–1928), botanist, was born in Westminster 28 July 1843, the elder son of William George Thiselton Dyer (1812–1868), physician, of Westminster, by his wife, Catherine Jane, daughter of Thomas Firminger, assistant astronomer royal at Greenwich Observatory, and sister of T. A. C. Firminger, author of the standard *Manual of Gardening for Bengal and Upper India* (1864). Thiselton-Dyer's paternal grandparents were William Matthew Thiselton (1783–1842), printer and barrister, who assumed the additional surname of Dyer by royal licence in 1840, and his wife, Louisa

Merzeau, who came of a Huguenot family settled in Spitalfields. He was sent to King's College School, London, where he formed a friendship with Henry Trimen [q.v.], and began with him the botanical rambles which ultimately led to the publication of their *Flora of Middlesex* (1869). In 1861 he entered King's College, London, as a student of medicine, and there met (Sir) Charles James Lyall [q.v.], with whom he was still exchanging notes on Indian botany and on Sanskrit and Arabic plant-names fifty years later. Thiselton-Dyer proceeded to Christ Church, Oxford, in 1863, read mathematics under the tuition of Henry J. S. Smith, Savilian professor of geometry, and obtained a second class in mathematical moderations (1865). He had thought of going out to India with Lyall, but changing his mind, under the influence of his lifelong friends Henry Nottidge Moseley and (Sir) Edwin Ray Lankester, he turned to the study of natural science and obtained a first class in the final school in 1867.

In the following year Thiselton-Dyer was appointed professor of natural history at the Royal Agricultural College, Cirencester, where, with his colleague, A. H. Church, the professor of chemistry, he edited in 1869 S. W. Johnson's *How Crops Grow*, a famous book in its day. He was professor of botany in the Royal College of Science, Dublin, from 1870 to 1872, and at the Royal Horticultural Society at South Kensington and Chiswick from 1872 to 1875; this latter post brought him into touch with the Royal Botanic Gardens at Kew, and introduced him to the scientific world of London. Sir Joseph Dalton Hooker [q.v.] found him work at Kew on the recently begun *Flora of British India*, and for it, in addition to editorial work, Thiselton-Dyer described the Indian species of six families of flowering plants. In 1872 also he became one of T. H. Huxley's demonstrators at the Royal School of Mines, South Kensington, and in 1873 he organized and conducted the botanical side of the famous course of elementary biology. Long afterwards, on the occasion of Huxley's centenary, he wrote an account for *Nature* (1925) of these early days. In 1875 he edited A. W. Bennett's translation of Julius von Sachs's *Text-book of Botany*, which marked an epoch in the teaching of botany in England.

Colonial planters, and the Colonial Office on their behalf, were now turning to Kew for guidance, and Hooker, having persuaded the government to revive the office of assistant-director, appointed Thiselton-Dyer to that post in 1875, to deal chiefly with colonial business. The new assistant-director made a great and immediate success of his office. In his first year he sent out to Ceylon some young Hevea plants from South America, which presently grew into the rubber-plantations of the East. In 1880 he dispatched to Henry Trimen, then director of the botanical gardens at Peradeniya, certain varieties of cacao from Trinidad, which flourished and are still under cultivation in Ceylon. In 1887 Thiselton-Dyer founded the *Kew Bulletin*, for the exchange of information among the many colonial institutions associated with Kew, and very soon this journal became indispensable to planters, agriculturists, and botanists throughout the British Empire. Mr. Joseph Chamberlain and Thiselton-Dyer were close friends, and when Chamberlain was at the Colonial Office (1895–1903) the two worked together for the development of economic botany and colonial agriculture. India, Ceylon, the West Indies, and West Africa were all materially helped and benefited by Kew. The rubber export from the Gold Coast grew from nothing in 1882 to half a million of money in 1898, all owing to the identification of a rubber plant at Kew; and the export of cocoa rose from £4 in 1892 to over £200,000 twelve years later, under the guidance of an officer trained at and sent out by Kew. In 1902 Thiselton-Dyer was formally appointed botanical adviser to the secretary of state for the colonies and held that office until 1906.

On Hooker's retirement in 1885 Thiselton-Dyer was appointed director of Kew Gardens. The Gardens, which had become world-famous under the direction of Hooker and his father Sir William Jackson Hooker [q.v.], more than maintained their reputation under Thiselton-Dyer. From the first his powers of organization showed themselves on every side. He vastly improved and beautified the garden, enlarged the library and the herbarium building, initiated a forestry museum, and made the Jodrell laboratory (the munificent gift of a friend) 'the best botanical laboratory in Europe'. As the herbarium had long been a great centre of systematic botany under Sir William and Sir Joseph Hooker, George Bentham [q.v.], Daniel Oliver, and J. G. Baker, so the laboratory became famous under Thiselton-Dyer and D. H. Scott, and was used by I. Bailey Balfour, F. O. Bower, Marshall Ward,

F. W. Oliver—in short by many who became the botanical teachers of the next generation, and by others, such as Horace T. Brown and F. Escombe in their work on the diffusion of gases and liquids in relation to the assimilation of carbon in plants.

Thiselton-Dyer was president of Section D of the British Association at Bath in 1888, and president at Ipswich in 1895 of the new Botanical Section (K), of which he was virtually the founder. He was a sound and accomplished systematic botanist. He edited with the utmost care the *Flora Capensis* begun by William Henry Harvey [q.v.] in 1859 (1896–1925), the *Flora of Tropical Africa* (1897–1913), the *Icones Plantarum* (1896–1906), and the *Botanical Magazine* (1905–1906). He made a special study of the Cycads, and went far towards compiling a monograph of that extensive order, but other work stood in the way; the account was published, by other hands, as a supplement to Volume v of the *Flora Capensis* (1933), and the preface to this supplementary volume records Thiselton-Dyer's share in the work. A good example of Thiselton-Dyer's style, scientific and literary, may be found in an admirable article on the 'Geographical Distribution of Plants', written from the Darwinian standpoint and published in A. S. Seward's *Darwin and Modern Science* (1909).

As director of Kew Gardens, as a great administrator, as an adviser of botanical students, in touch both with the old learning and with the new, Thiselton-Dyer was the acknowledged leader of English botanists, and his appearance, manner, and conversation marked and justified his unquestioned supremacy. He was, withal, at heart a modest man, constantly at work, doing nothing for publicity, caring only for the work to be done. He was elected F.R.S. in 1880, created C.M.G. in 1882, C.I.E. in 1892, and K.C.M.G. in 1899. In 1905 he retired, and went to live at Witcombe in Gloucestershire. From 1908 to 1916 he represented the university of Oxford on the Gloucestershire education committee, and he was a member of the court of the university of Bristol from 1909. Withdrawing from his old associates, even from the Royal Society, he lived the life of a country gentleman, served as a justice of the peace, and, returning to the favourite lessons of his boyhood, became a student, *facile princeps*, of ancient botany. Classical scholarship was not the least of Thiselton-Dyer's accomplishments. *The Georgicks* of John Martyn [q.v.] had been his favourite school-book, and to identify the plants of Virgil, Pliny, Theophrastus, Galen, and Dioscorides became the occupation of his later years. He revised the whole vocabulary of Greek plant-names for the ninth edition of Liddell and Scott's *Greek-English Lexicon*; helped Sir Arthur Hort in his edition of the *De Historia Plantarum* of Theophrastus (2 vols., 1916); contributed the botanical chapters to *A Companion to Greek Studies* (edited by Leonard Whibley, 1905) and *A Companion to Latin Studies* (edited by Sir J. E. Sandys, 1910); and wrote three articles, dealing with some thirty 'Ancient Plant-Names', all more or less obscure and difficult, for the *Journal of Philology* (edited by Ingram Bywater and Henry Jackson).

Thiselton-Dyer's scholarship was sound, his reading wide, his knowledge of old books prodigious. His notes on Cassia, Colocasia, Amomum, Cardamom, &c. in the *Journal of Philology* are models of care, patience, and erudition. His life-work at Kew dealt with botany on its most practical side, but as part and parcel of the humanities it employed his learning and occupied his old age. He died at Witcombe 23 December 1928.

Thiselton-Dyer married in 1877 Harriet Ann, eldest daughter of Sir Joseph Dalton Hooker. They had one son and one daughter.

[*Nature*, 9 February 1929; *Kew Bulletin*, 1929, pp. 65–75 (with photograph); *Proceedings* of the Royal Society, vol. cvi, B, 1930; private information; personal knowledge.]

D'Arcy W. Thompson.

THOMAS, GEORGE HOLT (1869–1929), pioneer in aircraft manufacture, was born at Brixton Hill, London, 31 March 1869, the seventh son of William Luson Thomas, newspaper proprietor, by his wife, Annie Carmichael. He was educated privately and at Queen's College, Oxford (1888–1890), and entered his father's business, joining in 1899 the staff of the *Graphic* weekly illustrated newspaper, of which, together with the *Daily Graphic*, his father was the founder. In due course Holt Thomas became a director of the business, which he extended by founding the *Bystander* illustrated weekly and the *Empire Illustrated* magazine. After acting for some years as general manager of a group of these papers, he retired from an active share in the business in 1906.

At the time when Holt Thomas gave

up newspaper management, the art of flying was in its infancy, but was being actively developed. On 17 November 1906 the *Daily Mail* had announced its offer of a prize of £10,000 for the first successful flight from London to Manchester, and on 21 November Holt Thomas was prompted, through the medium of his newspapers, to offer £1,000 for a successful flight of one mile. He had social position, money, energy, and imagination, and it was not long before he was devoting his substance and his qualities to stimulating public interest in aviation. What convinced him was a talk which he had in Paris, probably about the end of 1906, with the French aircraft pioneer, Henri Farman, who made it clear that immediately a suitable engine was produced successful flying would be achieved. Holt Thomas followed the subsequent progress of Farman with eager interest; and when, in 1907, Farman succeeded in making short flights in France, Holt Thomas, through his own and other newspapers, pointed out the danger to which Great Britain would become exposed if she neglected to keep abreast of, and develop, the new art of aviation. He urged the War Office to form a military air service.

It cannot be said that Holt Thomas received much encouragement either from officials or from the public; but his convictions were strong, and he continued his propaganda with unabated zeal. In July 1909 he spent his time between Dover and Calais, watching the details of the preparation for the first cross-Channel flight, and after Louis Blériot had made his successful crossing (25 July 1909), Holt Thomas went on to Rheims for a flying-meeting which took place there in August. At Rheims he was much impressed by the skilful piloting of Louis Paulhan, and by the efficiency of the rotary Gnome engine with which Paulhan's Voisin aeroplane was fitted.

When Holt Thomas returned home from Rheims, he organized a flying-meeting for the Blackpool corporation, at which the pilot, Hubert Latham, gave a remarkable display of flying, in a wind of forty miles an hour. Holt Thomas thereupon decided to organize an air display for London, and he persuaded the authorities at Brooklands to clear an area for the purpose. There, in October 1909, Louis Paulhan gave a series of exhibition flights, and as a result of the success of the display a regular aerodrome was laid out at Brooklands, where, later on, many of the earliest pilots in this country were trained. In April 1910, at the instigation of Holt Thomas, Paulhan made a successful flight from London to Manchester, thereby gaining the *Daily Mail* prize. He used as a starting-place a field at Hendon, which later became the well-known Hendon aerodrome.

In September 1910 Holt Thomas attended the military manœuvres in France, where for the first time aeroplanes were employed for reconnaissance. He then went on to Salisbury Plain for the British army manœuvres, and as the result of his experience became an outspoken critic of the backward state of British military aviation. In 1911 the government formed an air battalion of the Royal Engineers, the beginnings of the national air service.

Holt Thomas now turned his attention to the manufacture of aeroplanes. Finding that British engineers and financiers were unwilling to take the initiative, he himself took up the Farman rights and with his own money founded the Aircraft Manufacturing Company. He also acquired the English rights to manufacture Gnome and Le Rhone engines, which were almost exclusively used in British aircraft in the early days of the European War. Farman aircraft were also extensively used by the Royal Flying Corps until British-designed aircraft became available. Just before the outbreak of war in 1914 he acquired the services as chief designer of Geoffrey de Havilland, an engineer who had been designing official types of aeroplane for the Royal Aircraft Factory at Farnborough. Hereafter the Aircraft Manufacturing Company produced at their Hendon works the well-known 'D.H.' series of aeroplanes which proved of great value during the European War. So great did the demand for them become—particularly for the two-seater day-bomber, the D.H. 4—that the factory at Hendon was continuously expanded, subsidiary companies in Gloucester, Wycombe, and other parts of the country were acquired, and these works and others building to D.H. designs, produced thirty per cent. of the aircraft used by the Allied forces. Holt Thomas, without seeking it, made a fortune. During the War one of Holt Thomas's companies manufactured flying-boats, for the production of which works were set up at Hythe, on Southampton Water, and another was engaged in the manufacture of airships, which Lord Fisher demanded for submarine patrol work.

After the War Holt Thomas took up the question of air transport. He founded a new company, Air Travel and Transport, Ltd., in which he was joined by Sir Sefton Brancker [q.v.]. He spent money lavishly in the organization of the first commercial air line to Paris, which opened its services to the public in August 1919, the operating aeroplanes being chiefly converted D.H. 9 bombers. He next formed an alliance with the Birmingham Small Arms group of companies; but when the post-War industrial slump came in 1920, the manufacture of aeroplanes at Hendon ceased. After undergoing reorganization and a change of name, the Air Transport company was eventually merged in Imperial Airways, Ltd., but the Aircraft Manufacturing Company closed down (October 1922) and de Havilland, with a few of his former associates, and with financial backing by Holt Thomas, founded the de Havilland Aircraft Company. Thenceforth Holt Thomas ceased to take active interest in the aircraft industry, and devoted his energies to highly successful dairy-farming.

Holt Thomas received no official recognition of the great services which he rendered his country during a critical period of its history; but if he felt resentment at this neglect he never showed it. Tall and bearded, with strongly marked features, he was a dominant and impressive figure. It was impossible to be long in his company without being aware of his inward fires. There can be little doubt that by his foresight and energy in aircraft manufacture and development, he made possible for England that victory in air-fighting which her airmen gained for her in the European War.

Holt Thomas married in 1894 Gertrude, youngest daughter of Thomas Oliver, F.R.I.B.A., of Newcastle-upon-Tyne, and had no children. He died at Cimiez, France, 1 January 1929.

[Sir W. A. Raleigh, *The War in the Air*, vol. i, 1922; *The Aeroplane*, 9 January 1929; private information; personal knowledge.]

H. A. Jones.

THOMAS, Sir HUGH EVAN- (1862–1928), admiral. [See Evan-Thomas.]

THOMPSON, Sir EDWARD MAUNDE (1840–1929), palaeographer and director of the British Museum, was born at Clarendon, Jamaica, 4 May 1840, the eldest son of Edward Thompson, who held the office of *custos* of Clarendon. His family had been connected with the island for several generations. His mother was Elizabeth Hayhurst, daughter of Samuel Poole, also of Clarendon, and subsequently of Twyford, Buckinghamshire. He was sent to England for education, and proceeded in 1859 from Rugby to University College, Oxford. Owing, however, to a change in his father's financial circumstances, he had to leave the university without taking a degree.

In 1861 Thompson entered the British Museum as an assistant, at first in the principal librarian's office, from which he was soon transferred to the department of manuscripts, then under the direction of Sir Frederic Madden [q.v.]. At first he had doubts as to his wishing to continue in the Museum, and in 1863 he entered at the Middle Temple, and was called to the bar in 1867; but by this time he had settled down to his work, and he never practised at the bar. His industry and ability soon made themselves manifest, and when (Sir) Edward Augustus Bond [q.v.] succeeded Madden as keeper of the department in 1866, Thompson became his principal associate. For several years Thompson's main work was in connexion with the preparation of the 'Class Catalogue' of all the manuscripts in the department, which gave him an acquaintance with a large proportion of the collections, especially in the sections concerned with history and illuminated manuscripts. This laid the foundations for a thorough knowledge of medieval chronicles, of palaeography, and of illumination, with which subjects most of his published work was concerned. In 1871 he was promoted to be assistant-keeper, in succession to William Wright [q.v.].

The next fifteen years were a period of great productiveness for Thompson, in respect both of official and of unofficial work, the latter, although done out of Museum hours, being directly based on his knowledge of manuscripts. On the completion of the 'Class Catalogue', the main departmental duty was the clearing up of arrears in the cataloguing of recent accessions, which was accomplished by two stout volumes (covering the period 1854–1875) published in 1875 and 1877, with an enormous index (1880); in this Thompson had a large part. Meanwhile, he had, in 1873, joined Bond in founding the Palaeographical Society, the successive publications of which for the first time provided students with specimen photographic facsimiles of the most important classical and medieval manuscripts, and thereby laid the foundations of the modern science of palaeography. The society produced two series (comprising 420 plates) during the years 1873–1895, and its work was carried on by the New Palaeographical Society from 1903 to 1930. Both series emanated from the department of manuscripts of the Museum, and Thompson was an editor of both from first to last. Other official publications were the two volumes of the *Catalogue of Ancient Manuscripts in the British Museum* (Greek 1881, Latin 1884), of which his friend and colleague (Sir) George Frederic Warner was joint author with him. Unofficially, he contributed an admirable article on 'English Chronicles' to the *English Encyclopædia* (Arts and Sciences Supplement) in 1873, and an article on 'Palaeography' to the *Encyclopædia Britannica* (9th edition, 1885). The latter of these articles was subsequently enlarged into a *Handbook of Greek and Latin Palaeography* (1893), which is still the best short introduction to the subject. He also supervised and contributed introductions to facsimiles of three important manuscripts, the Utrecht Psalter (1874), the Codex Alexandrinus (1879–1883), and (with Sir Richard Claverhouse Jebb, q.v.) the Laurentian manuscript of Sophocles (1885).

Thompson was also active in editing chronicles and other documents for various societies. These included the *Chronicon Angliae, 1328–1388* (the anonymous chronicle of St. Albans, Rolls Series, 1874), the *Letters of Humphrey Prideaux to John Ellis, 1674–1722* (Camden Society, 1875), the *Chronicon Adae de Usk, 1377–1421* (Royal Society of Literature, 1876; second edition, embodying the recently discovered conclusion 1904), the *Correspondence of the Family of Hatton, 1601–1704* (Camden Society, 1878), the *Diary of Richard Cocks, 1615–1622* (Hakluyt Society, 1883), the *Adae Murimuth Continuatio Chronicorum, 1303–1347*, and *Robertus de Avesbury, De Gestis Mirabilibus regis Edwardi tertii* (Rolls Series, 1889). As a separate work he edited the *Chronicon Galfridi Le Baker de Swynebroke, 1303–1356* (1889); and this was regarded by both himself and others as his most important contribution to medieval history. His catalogue of the manuscripts in Salisbury Cathedral library appeared in 1880. As a palaeographer he had a first-rate eye and a sound judgement, based upon an extensive knowledge of classical and medieval manuscripts over their entire range. As an editor of texts, although he was not a professional historian, he was so accurate in reading and transcribing that his work formed an entirely trustworthy basis for the studies of others.

In 1878 Thompson had become keeper of the department of manuscripts in succession to Bond; and in 1888 he again succeeded Bond as principal librarian (to which the title of director was prefixed in 1898). This practically put an end to his output of published work for the next twenty-one years, during which time almost the whole of his energy was devoted to the duties of administration. The only exceptions were the production of his *Handbook of Greek and Latin Palaeography* (1893), already mentioned; a series of articles on illuminated manuscripts in the periodical *Bibliographica* (1895–1897), the first three of which were reprinted in book form under the title *English Illuminated Manuscripts* (1895); and an edition of the *Customary of the Benedictine Monasteries of St. Augustine, Canterbury, and St. Peter, Westminster* for the Henry Bradshaw Society (1902).

As director of the British Museum Thompson was a masterful administrator, wholly devoted to the interests of the institution, intolerant of anything that he regarded as superficial or prompted by motives of self-seeking, but unflinching in support of those in whom he had confidence. He was urgent in promoting the production of catalogues of the contents of the Museum, which is one of the first duties of a curatorial staff; but perhaps the chief note of his administration was the development of the educational and popular side of the Museum. Objects were better exhibited and better labelled, and he vastly increased, if he did not wholly originate, the production of departmental guidebooks, which were in fact cheap and amply illustrated handbooks to their respective subjects. He also encouraged excavations abroad, in order to add to the collections in the Museum, and was responsible for expeditions to Mesopotamia, Egypt, Cyprus, Ephesus, and Carchemish, and for assistance to Sir Aurel Stein's second expedition to Central Asia in 1906–1908. He carried through reorganizations, with improvements of pay, of the whole Museum staff, and in his latter years was much occupied in planning and supervising the new wing on the north side of the Museum, now known as the King Edward VII galleries.

In the winter of 1908–1909 Thompson's

health, which had hitherto been vigorous, began to give way, and in August 1909 he retired. He lived thenceforward out of London, successively at Mayfield in Sussex, Wells, Worthing, Tunbridge Wells, and finally at Mayfield again, where he built himself a house. His health was never fully re-established, and he was liable to heart trouble, but his mind remained vigorous. He enlarged his *Handbook* into a full-sized, copiously illustrated *Introduction to Greek and Roman Palaeography* (1912); he contributed a chapter to *Shakespeare's England*, which was enlarged into a separate volume entitled *Shakespeare's Handwriting* (1916), and he wrote a chapter on the same subject in his friend A. W. Pollard's *Shakespeare's Hand in the play of Sir Thomas More* (1923).

Thompson took an active part in the foundation of the British Academy, and presided at the meeting at which it was established in June 1901. He was one of the original fellows, and held the office of president from 1907 to 1909. He was made C.B. in 1893, and created K.C.B. in 1895, and G.C.B. on his retirement in 1909. He received honorary degrees from the universities of Oxford, Durham, St. Andrews, and Manchester, and was a corresponding member of the Institut de France and of the Royal Prussian Academy of Sciences, and an honorary fellow of University College, Oxford. He was Sandars reader in bibliography at Cambridge University in 1895–1896 and 1905–1906.

Thompson married in 1864 Georgina (died 1917), daughter of George Mackenzie, of Frankfield, Jamaica, and had three sons and one daughter. He died at Mayfield 14 September 1929 in his ninetieth year, and is buried in Brookwood cemetery.

A good portrait of Thompson by Sir Edward Poynter, painted in 1909, is in the board room of the British Museum, and has been reproduced in photogravure.

[Sir F. G. Kenyon, *Sir Edward Maunde Thompson, 1840–1929*, in *Proceedings* of the British Academy, vol. xv, 1929; private information; personal knowledge.]

F. G. Kenyon.

THOMPSON, HENRY YATES (1838–1928), book-collector, was born at Dingle Cottage, near Liverpool, 15 December 1838, the eldest son of Samuel Henry Thompson, of Thingwall Hall, Lancashire, a partner in the local banking firm of Arthur Heywood, Sons & Co. His mother was the eldest daughter of Joseph Brooks Yates [q.v.], merchant and antiquary, from whom he inherited a number of books and manuscripts. He was educated at Harrow, where he became head of the school, and at Trinity College, Cambridge. Here he won the Porson prize for Greek verse in 1860, and graduated as sixteenth classic in 1862. The university of Cambridge appointed him Sandars reader in bibliography in 1901 and 1904. Thompson was called to the bar by Lincoln's Inn in 1867, but never practised. He unsuccessfully contested three different Lancashire constituencies in the liberal interest in 1865, 1868, and again in 1881. From 1868 to 1873 he was private secretary to the fifth Earl Spencer, viceroy of Ireland. During the years between 1862 and 1875 he travelled widely in Europe, Asia, Egypt, and the United States of America. In 1878 Thompson married Elizabeth, eldest daughter of George Smith, the founder and publisher of this Dictionary [see the memoir now prefixed to the first volume of the Dictionary]. In 1880 Smith made over to him the *Pall Mall Gazette*, which Thompson, after temporarily converting it into a liberal paper, sold in 1892 to Mr. William Waldorf (afterwards Viscount) Astor.

By this time Thompson had begun to form the famous collection of illuminated manuscripts with which his name will always be associated. He ensured its high quality from the first by limiting its number to one hundred, and by gradually discarding manuscripts in order to make room for finer examples. His largest accession was the purchase *en bloc* in 1897 of the portion of Lord Ashburnham's library known as the Appendix, of which he retained the most important manuscripts only. His catalogue, with descriptions by M. R. James, (Sir) S. C. Cockerell, (Sir) G. F. Warner, and others, was privately printed in four volumes in 1898, 1902, 1907, and 1912 respectively, and was supplemented by seven larger volumes of illustrations, issued between 1907 and 1918; these and a few other privately printed volumes remain the chief memorial of an unrivalled collection. The manuscripts were partly dispersed at three sales at Sotheby's in 1919, 1920, and 1921—one manuscript, the 'Hours' of Jeanne de Navarre, fetching at the first sale the record auction price at that date for an illuminated manuscript (£11,800). Thompson had previously given two of his finest manuscripts, the St. Omer Psalter and the Metz Pontifical, to the British Museum and the Fitzwilliam Museum respectively. In 1906 he presented the second volume of the famous 'Anciennetés des Juifs' of Josephus, illuminated by Jean Fouquet, to King Edward VII, in order that it might be presented to the French nation, for preservation with the first volume in the Bibliothèque Nationale, after the insertion of ten of its missing miniatures which had been discovered in the Royal Library at Windsor Castle; for this action he received the legion of honour from the French government.

Thompson's various benefactions included two fine winter gardens in the Liverpool parks, for which he was given the freedom of the city of Liverpool in 1901; hospitals at Crewe and at Horwich railway works of the Lancashire and Yorkshire Railway, of which he was for many years a director; an art school to Harrow; a library to Newnham College, Cambridge; and three additional rooms to the Dulwich Picture Gallery. He died at his London house 8 July 1928, leaving no children.

[*The Times*, 10 July 1928; Seymour de Ricci, 'Les Manuscrits de la Collection Henry Yates Thompson', in *Bulletin de la Société Française de Reproductions de MSS. à Peintures*, 1926; Seymour de Ricci, *English Collectors of Books and Manuscripts*, 1930; private information; personal knowledge.]

E. G. Millar.

THOMSON, CHRISTOPHER BIRDWOOD, Baron Thomson, of Cardington (1875–1930), soldier and politician, was born at Nasik in India 13 April 1875, the third son of David Thomson, major-general, Royal Engineers, by his wife, Emily, daughter of General Christopher Birdwood, and sister of Sir G. C. M. Birdwood [q.v.] and H. M. Birdwood [q.v.]. He was educated at Cheltenham College, where he distinguished himself in modern languages, and at the Royal Military Academy, Woolwich, whence he entered the Royal Engineers in 1894. After spending some time studying submarine mining at Plymouth, Thomson took part in the operations in Mashonaland under Sir Frederick Carrington [q.v.] in 1896 and received the medal. Thence he went to Mauritius, where he spent three years, and from 1899 to 1902 served through the South African War. He took part in the advance on Kimberley and was commended by Lord Kitchener for the manner in which he cleared a block on the railway (February 1900): in the operations in the Transvaal he was present at the actions of Elands River (4–16 August 1900) and Lydenberg (6 September 1900), and in the operations in the Orange River Colony he was present at the actions of Lindley (1 June 1900) and Rhenoster River (29 November 1900). He distinguished himself in command of a field company section and received a brevet majority, the two war medals, and was mentioned in dispatches.

After the War Thomson served first as an instructor at the Engineering School at Chatham and then at Sierra Leone. He became a captain and brevet-major in 1904, and in 1909 joined the Staff College, Camberley, where Sir Henry Hughes Wilson [q.v.] was then commandant. After leaving the Staff College in 1911 he went to the War Office, where he served under Wilson, who had become director of military operations. In 1912 Thomson was appointed military attaché with the Serbian army, serving throughout the Turkish and subsequent Bulgarian campaigns, and returning to the War Office in 1913.

On the outbreak of war in 1914 Thomson served first as *liaison* officer with the Belgian army and then with the British I Corps, proceeding in February 1915 as military attaché to Bucharest, where he spent two years. He regarded the entry of Rumania into the War as ill timed, and protested that her value was greater as a neutral than as one of the Allies, since the Rumanian supplies of corn and oil would thenceforth be at Germany's mercy. After being present at the inter-allied conference at Petrograd in 1917, Thomson joined the 60th division in Palestine as C.R.E. He took part in the advance on Jerusalem and temporarily commanded a brigade at the capture of Jericho, receiving the D.S.O. in 1918. In the same year he was promoted brigadier-general on the staff of the Supreme War Council at Versailles, whence he was sent to Mudros as bearer of the terms of the British armistice with the Turks. He received the C.B.E. at the end of the War in 1919.

After serving on the British delegation to the Peace Conference in Paris, Thomson left the army in 1919 with the rank of honorary brigadier-general in order to enter politics, and stood for parliament as socialist candidate at Bristol. He was defeated in 1919 and in 1922 and again at St. Albans in 1923, so that he never sat in the House of Commons. In 1920 he went to Ireland as a member of the socialist committee of investigation into the rebellion then in progress and the measures taken to combat it. In 1921 he served on an international Red Cross committee which inquired into the condition of refugees in Russia and the Near East, and in 1923 he took part in the socialist deputation to the Ruhr. At this time he also devoted himself to writing, and published *Old Europe's Suicide* (1919), an account of events from 1912 to 1919, and *Victors and Vanquished* (1924).

In 1924 Thomson was appointed secretary of state for air in the first labour government, sworn a privy councillor, and raised to the peerage as Baron Thomson of Cardington, taking his title from the place in Bedfordshire where the government airship works were situated. He set to work to master the technicalities of the air service and visited Egypt and Palestine on an air inspection tour. Thomson was largely responsible for the government's decision on a three years' scheme of airship development, which involved the construction of two airships and experiments with them in flight overseas. These airships were the R.100 and R.101. Thomson also encouraged the study of the problem of the replacement of petrol by heavy oil, for he had a great belief in the future of lighter-than-air craft.

After the fall of the labour government in 1924, Thomson was one of the most indefatigable of the small number of socialist peers in opposition. He was a clear and vigorous speaker, and his cheerfulness and good temper gained him many friends in the House; indeed, he seemed marked out as the future leader of the socialist party in the House of Lords. In opposition he still maintained his interest in the air, and associated himself with the Royal Aero Club, of which he was chairman, and with the Aeronautical Society and the Air League. He undertook a lecturing tour in the United States in 1926, and in 1928 represented the government at an international air conference in New York. He also contributed to the press, and in 1927 published a collection of articles and lectures on aviation entitled *Air Facts and Problems* in which he emphasized his belief in the future of airships.

In 1929, on the formation of the second labour government, Thomson returned to the Air Ministry more than ever convinced that the Royal Air Force had become the first line of home defence. In the House of Lords the defence of the government in important debates was largely entrusted to him, and he spoke on many leading questions of the day, such as the resumption of relations with Russia (4 December 1929), British policy in Egypt (9 December 1929), the Singapore dock question (18 December 1929); and he conducted the Coal Miners Bill through committee in 1930. He was also actively concerned in representing the government at the Naval Conference in London in 1930 and defended the Naval Treaty, which was its outcome, in parliament.

When Thomson came to the Air Ministry for the second time he found that the development of lighter-than-air craft had progressed, and on 28 July 1930 the airship R.100 left Cardington for Canada, reaching Montreal in 79 hours. She returned on 16 August after a flight of 57 hours. The R.100 had petrol burning engines, so that when a flight was contemplated to India the task necessarily fell upon the airship R.101, which used heavy oil, a fuel which could be safely carried and burnt in the tropics. The flight was at first designed to coincide with the Imperial Conference, and there seems no doubt that the later decision to start as early as 4 October was influenced by considerations of public policy and by the strong desire of the secretary of state that a start should be made in time to enable him to take the flight himself and return for the Imperial Conference. But the subsequent commission of inquiry expressly exonerated both Thomson and his advisers from deciding to take an unjustifiable risk. The R.101 left Cardington on 4 October 1930 at 6.36 p.m. Sir William Sefton Brancker [q.v.], director of civil aviation, and ten other passengers and officials accompanied Thomson, and the crew numbered forty-two. The voyage proved uneventful until 2 a.m. on 5 October when the R.101 was over Beauvais, the weather being exceedingly bad with a strong south-west wind blowing in fierce gusts. The ship was rolling badly and failing to keep height, although she was 1,000 feet above the ground. At 2 a.m. the watch changed and a new height coxswain took the helm. Although no blame is attached to officers or crew it is known that in bumpy weather there is difficulty in a new hand getting the 'feel' of a ship and therefore in judging the extent of elevator action needed to counteract a dive. A dive occurred shortly after 2 a.m., but the ship was brought to a level keel after losing some hundreds of feet. A second dive, however, occurred almost immediately which brought the R.101 nose first to the ground, and she immediately burst into flames. There were only eight survivors, two of whom died shortly after at Beauvais. Thomson was killed, and was buried with the other members of the expedition at Cardington. Subsequently, an inquiry into the disaster was held under the chairmanship of Sir John Simon.

Thomson was a man of varied tastes. He was widely, if not deeply, read in several languages, and was accustomed to memorize his favourite passages, so that he had an abundant fund of quotations. He was devoted to music and interested in painting and sculpture. Besides the works mentioned above, he was the author of *Smaranda* (1926), a book of war memories and tales of the Near East, in which he manifested his love of Rumania. He was fond of sport and rode well to hounds. Thomson was unmarried, and the barony became extinct on his death.

[Lord Thomson, *Old Europe's Suicide*, 1919, *Victors and Vanquished*, 1924, *Smaranda* (with an introduction by J. Ramsay MacDonald), 1926, *Air Facts and Problems*, 1927; War Office Records; Hansard, *Parliamentary Debates*; *Journal* of the Royal Engineers, March 1931; *Report* of the R.101 Inquiry, March 1931; private information; personal knowledge.] ONSLOW.

THOMSON, JOHN (1856–1926), physician and writer on diseases of children, was born in Edinburgh 23 November 1856, the second of three children and only son of Thomas Thomson, writer to the signet, by his wife, Elizabeth, daughter of Alexander Cleghorn. Educated at the Edinburgh Academy, he graduated in medicine at Edinburgh University in 1881, and after holding resident posts at the Royal Infirmary, spent seven months in Vienna and Berlin. In Berlin he came under the influence of E. H. Henoch, the famous German paediatrist. On returning to England in 1884 he was appointed resident medical officer at the Hospital for Sick Children, Great Ormond Street, London, where he worked under Walter Butler Cheadle [q.v.] and (Sir) Thomas Barlow. He next became physician to the New Town Dispensary, Edinburgh, and established there a clinic for diseases of children; in this post he accumulated much of that wealth of observation which formed the basis of his writings. In 1888 he published a translation of Henoch's *Vorlesungen über Kinderkrankheiten*.

In 1889 Thomson was appointed extra physician to the Royal Hospital for Sick Children, Edinburgh, and with this hospital he was actively associated for the rest of his life. From this time onwards he contributed to journals and text-books articles upon diseases of childhood, which were characterized by accurate and detailed observation: congenital pyloric stenosis, acute pyelitis in infants, and mongolism were some of the affections which, although previously described, had attracted little notice until his descriptions drew attention to them. In 1898 appeared his *Guide to the Clinical Study and Treatment of Sick Children*, based on his own records and so of particular value. He gave, however, generous recognition to the work of others, and was the better able to do so, since he had extensive knowledge of the literature of paediatrics in other countries.

When, on the expiry of his period of office as physician at the Children's Hospital in 1918, he was appointed consulting physician, Thomson retained a clinic for mentally defective children, in whom he took great interest. For the parents of these he wrote a booklet, *Opening Doors*, in the simplest language, giving valuable hints for training.

Thomson's writings were widely appreciated. In the United States and Canada he was made an honorary member of many paediatric societies; his own university in 1922 conferred on him the honorary degree of LL.D., and the Royal College of Physicians, London, in recognition of his valuable work, elected him a fellow in 1926.

Thomson died in Edinburgh 2 July 1926, and was buried in the Dean cemetery, Edinburgh. He married in 1887 Isobel Finlayson, daughter of the Rev. John S. McPhail, of the United Free Church, Benbecula, and had four sons and two daughters.

[*Edinburgh Medical Journal*, August 1926 (portrait); private information; personal knowledge.] G. F. STILL.

THORNYCROFT, SIR JOHN ISAAC (1843–1928), naval architect, born in Rome 1 February 1843, was the elder son of Thomas Thornycroft [q.v.] by his wife, Mary Thornycroft [q.v.], daughter of John Francis [q.v.]. His father, his mother, and her father were all sculptors, as was his younger brother, Sir William Hamo Thornycroft [q.v.]. His father was also an amateur engineer, and his studio a workshop furnished with model engines and railways. John's career began in this workshop, where after making smaller craft he constructed the *Nautilus*, a steam launch which was the first that was able to keep pace with the crews in the university boat race of 1862. Shortly after this success his father sent him to work as a draughtsman with Palmer's Shipbuilding Company at Jarrow-on-Tyne and thence to Glasgow University, where he studied natural philosophy and engineering under Sir William Thomson (afterwards Lord Kelvin) and Professor MacQuorn Rankine and obtained a certificate in engineering science. He then worked for some time in the drawing office of Messrs. Randolph, Elder & Co. at Fairfield, Govan, near Glasgow (afterwards the well-known Fairfield Shipbuilding Company). At that time the firm was engaged in the construction of the Popofga circular ships for the Russian government, and in 1869 Thornycroft wrote for the Institution of Naval Architects a paper dealing with the work that he had carried out in calculating the resistance of these vessels.

In 1866 his father assisted Thornycroft to establish at Chiswick the shipyard which later became noted for the production of high-speed launches and torpedo craft. Between 1866 and 1870 he also studied at the South Kensington School of Naval Architecture, where he was a contemporary of (Sir) Philip Watts [q.v.]. In 1872 John Donaldson, who had been engineer in the Public Works Department of India and who married Thornycroft's sister, Frances Sarah, in that year, became his partner in the shipyard, Thornycroft devoting most of his attention to design, and his partner to administration. In 1870 the torpedo invented by Robert Whitehead [q.v.] was adopted in the royal navy, and it was realized that to make it effective a fast launch was needed to carry it. In 1871 Thornycroft built the first small high-speed boat of which there is any record, the *Miranda*, a launch with a hull of light steel and an engine of 58 horsepower, which attained a speed of 16·4 knots. In 1873 a somewhat larger boat, the *Gitana*, constructed for the Norwegian government, is said to have reached 20·8 knots with engines of 458 h.p. This boat, being fitted with a spar torpedo, was in fact the first torpedo boat. She had also a closed stokehold system of forced draught, and served as a model for the first torpedo boat of the English navy, the *Lightning*, built by Thornycroft in 1877, which, however, was furnished with a revolving torpedo tube. In the succeeding years he turned out large numbers of torpedo boats, and when in 1892 torpedo-boat destroyers were introduced he was commissioned to build the *Daring* and the *Decoy*, two of the first four vessels of this class [*Transactions* of the Institution of Naval Architects, vol. liii, part ii, pp. 325–330, 1911].

During this period Thornycroft's vessels showed rapid improvement, owing to his continual experiments with hull form and propeller design. He introduced the flat, wide, form of stern at the water-line to prevent 'squatting', with the propeller shaft at downward inclination (a feature of his first juvenile launch), and wing-rudders on each side of the stern. He was the first to carry out experiments with screw propellers, measuring simultaneously the thrust, power transmitted, and speed. He took out patents for improvements in turbine screw propellers and for the tunnel form of stern for high-speed vessels navigating shallow rivers—devices which were successfully employed in 1875 in a twin-screw launch built for Sir John Fowler [q.v.] to navigate the Nile, and in five river gunboats which he was commissioned to build in 1885 for the Gordon relief expedition.

Thornycroft also improved the type of boiler employed in torpedo craft. He soon recognized that the locomotive type would not stand the high rate of forcing to which it was subjected in these vessels, and turned his attention to boilers of the water-tube type. The *Ariete*, a torpedo boat which he built for Spain in 1887, held the record for speed at the time, developing over 26 knots. In 1893, in spite of difficulties, he induced the British Admiralty to fit the *Speedy*, a torpedo gunboat, with water-tube boilers of his own design, and they proved entirely successful. His boats the *Daring* and the *Decoy* (already mentioned) were also fitted with this type of boiler. Ultimately he evolved a light, fast-running reciprocating engine of the triple expansion type, which was adopted in a large number of torpedo craft, but eventually was superseded by the Parsons turbine. Thornycroft was one of the civilian members of the famous Admiralty committee of design, appointed at the instance of Lord Fisher [q.v.] in December 1904, which recommended the adoption of the Parsons turbine for the *Dreadnought* class of battleship and for new destroyers.

The increased size of destroyers and torpedo boats was the principal reason for the removal of the Chiswick shipyard to Woolston, Southampton, in 1906. Even then, however, Thornycroft was bringing to fruition work which led to a partial return to the small torpedo craft of earlier days. Already in 1877 he had patented a special form of hull designed to skim over the water rather than to cut through it, but no light engine then existed powerful enough to generate the speed required for skimming. With the development of the light internal-combustion engine he saw the possibility of success, and after experimenting for several years with aluminium models in a testing tank at Bembridge, Isle of Wight, close to his home, he patented a 'single-step' form of hull which was generally adopted, not only for racing-boats, but also for seaplanes. In the first year of the European War Thornycroft's patent was seen to have great possibilities, and in 1916 the Admiralty placed with his firm an order for a dozen torpedo boats of high speed and of such shallow draught that they could pass safely over mine-fields. These were built with the greatest secrecy on an island in the Thames at Hampton, and subsequently over a hundred more were constructed. These were the coastal motor-boats, known familiarly as 'scooters', which were successfully used in the attacks on Zeebrugge, Ostend, and elsewhere. A vessel of the type, built for the French government after the War, attained a speed of 41·6 knots over the measured mile. Towards the end of the War Thornycroft designed a decoy-ship of shallow draught, 240 feet long by 35 feet beam, which was able to pass over mine-fields and torpedoes. This vessel was given priority over all others under construction, and was completed in three months. In much of his experimenting during the War Thornycroft was assisted by his daughter Blanche, an associate of the Institution of Naval Architects.

Other problems engaged Thornycroft's attention at various times. He was early in the field with the use of oil for raising steam; this he adopted in a life-boat in 1892, and about the same time he fitted a 300-ton yacht with an anti-rolling device. In 1898 he established at Basingstoke works for the manufacture of motor vehicles, chiefly lorries and 'buses; and in later years he invented improvements in sugar-making machinery.

Thornycroft was elected a fellow of the Royal Society in 1893, and received the honorary degree of LL.D. from Glasgow University in 1901. He was knighted in 1902. He served on the council of the Institution of Naval Architects from 1881 and on the council of the Institution of Civil Engineers from 1899 to 1908. He was a pioneer in naval architecture. The advances which he made in the hull design and machinery of small, high-speed craft served to show what could be done in much larger vessels. Of his early boats he designed every detail himself. He was a remarkably neat draughtsman and his line drawings were works of art. To the end of his life he was able to make freehand sketches of complicated details of mechanism which would fit together directly without an assembly drawing.

Thornycroft died at Bembridge 28 June 1928, and was buried there. He married in 1870 Blanche, daughter of Frederick Coules, of Gloucester, and by her he had two sons and five daughters. His elder son, Sir John Edward Thornycroft, succeeded his father as head of the firm.

A cartoon of Thornycroft by 'Spy' appeared in *Vanity Fair* 19 January 1905.

[*The Times*, 29 June 1928; *Transactions* of the Institution of Naval Architects, vol. lxx, 1928 (with portrait); *Proceedings* of the Royal Society, vol. cxxi, A, 1928; *Proceedings* of the Institution of Civil Engineers, vols. cxl, 1899–1900, ccxxvii, 1928–1929; Miss E. Thornycroft, *Bronze and Steel*, 1932; Sir P. Watts in *Encyclopædia Britannica*, 11th edition, vol. xxiv, pp. 915–916. Portrait, *Royal Academy Pictures*, 1919.]

E. I. Carlyle.

THORNYCROFT, Sir (WILLIAM) HAMO (1850–1925), sculptor, was born in London 9 March 1850, the younger son of the sculptor Thomas Thornycroft [q.v.] by his wife, Mary Thornycroft [q.v.], daughter of the sculptor John Francis [q.v.], and herself a sculptor; his elder brother was Sir John Isaac Thornycroft [q.v.], the naval architect. Hamo Thornycroft was educated at Macclesfield grammar school and at University College School, then in Gower Street, London; about 1868 he began to study sculpture, first under his father and subsequently at the Royal Academy Schools. In 1871 he exhibited for the first time at the Academy, his contribution being a portrait-bust of Professor William Sharpey (now at University College, London); soon afterwards he visited Italy, devoting much study to the works of Michelangelo. On his return he assisted his father in the execution of the 'Poets' Fountain' in Park Lane, the figures of Shakespeare, Comedy, and Fame being by the son. The fountain was unveiled in 1875, in which year Thornycroft was awarded the gold medal of the Royal Academy for his group 'A Warrior bearing a Wounded Youth'. Much attention was attracted by his statue 'Lot's Wife', exhibited in 1878; but he achieved his most signal success when in 1880 he exhibited his 'Artemis'. This was commissioned from him in marble by the Duke of Westminster, the marble version being now at Eaton Hall. The following year he exhibited his bronze 'Teucer', which was bought by the Chantrey trustees for £1,000 and is now in the Tate Gallery; in the same year (1881) Thornycroft, now well to the fore among the younger English sculptors of the day, was elected A.R.A.

In his work up to this time, Thornycroft had, as regards subject, kept more or less within the convention of the antique, although in vitality of form and treatment he had advanced well beyond the formula of neo-classicism. Thenceforward he brought within the range of his art the subjects affected by contemporary realism in painting, exhibiting in 1884 'The Mower' (now in the Walker Art Gallery, Liverpool) and in 1886 'A Sower', both probably the result of impulses received from the paintings of Jean François Millet, and displaying a type of subject and treatment which very shortly afterwards was to be exploited quite independently by the Belgian sculptor Constantin Meunier.

Much noticed though these 'realistic' sculptures were, and although he occasionally reverted later on to this type of rendering, these figures nevertheless represent only an episode in Thornycroft's work; his energies were mainly absorbed by the steadily increasing flow of orders for public or semi-public statues, portrait busts, &c., which came to him. Among his best-known public monuments in London are the statues of General Gordon in Trafalgar Square (1888) and Oliver Cromwell in Old Palace Yard (1899), which latter won the *médaille d'honneur* at the Paris world exhibition of 1900; the group of Dean Colet and two kneeling scholars at St. Paul's School, West Kensington (1902); the national memorial to Gladstone in East Aldwych (1905); and the circular bas-relief in stone of Richard Norman Shaw in New Scotland Yard (1914). There is also by Thornycroft a statue of Queen Victoria in the Royal Exchange, and a bronze effigy of Mandell Creighton, bishop of London, in St. Paul's Cathedral. Of his works to be found outside London, mention should be made of the statue of King Alfred at Winchester (1901); the monument of Bishop Harvey Goodwin in Carlisle Cathedral; the Lord Armstrong memorial at Newcastle-upon-Tyne; the memorial of the viceroyalty of Lord Curzon, set up in Calcutta in 1912; the King Edward VII memorial at Karachi (1915); the war memorial at Luton (1923); and the statue of Bishop H. W. Yeatman-Biggs in Coventry Cathedral (1925). A large equestrian statue of Edward I, intended for Blackfriars Bridge, London, was never set up, although several models for it were shown in successive Academy exhibitions between 1885 and 1894. Realism remained to the end the key-note of Thornycroft's style: in one of his later works, the marble group 'The Kiss' (1916, purchased by the Chantrey trustees and now in the Tate Gallery), there is even something like a half-hearted approximation to the manner of Auguste Rodin.

Thornycroft was elected R.A. in 1888, his diploma work being 'The Mirror', a marble relief exhibited in 1890; he was knighted in 1917. In 1923 he received the gold medal of the Royal Society of British Sculptors for his distinguished services to sculpture. He died at Oxford 18 December 1925. He married in 1884 Agatha, second daughter of Homersham Cox, of Tonbridge, and had one son and three daughters. A retrospective selection of his works was shown at the Burlington House Winter Exhibition in 1927.

[*The Times*, 21 December 1925; Algernon Graves, *The Royal Academy of Arts, a complete dictionary of contributors and their works*, vol. vii, 1905; subsequent Royal Academy Exhibition Catalogues including that of the Memorial Exhibition, 1927.] T. Borenius.

THORPE, Sir THOMAS EDWARD (1845–1925), chemist, was born at Barnes Green, Harpurhey, near Manchester, 8 December 1845, the eldest son of George Thorpe, cotton merchant, of Trafford Bank, near Manchester, by his wife, Mary Wilde. From Hulme grammar school, where he received his early education, he passed in 1863 to the chemistry department of Owens College, Manchester, then under the direction of Professor (Sir) Henry Enfield Roscoe [q.v.]. Here Thorpe was initiated into the methods of chemical research, and in association with Roscoe made the first of his many notable contributions to scientific knowledge.

In 1867, fortified with a letter of introduction to the famous R. W. von Bunsen, Thorpe proceeded to the university of Heidelberg, where two years later he graduated Ph.D. Subsequently, he worked for a time in the laboratory of Friedrich August Kekulé at Bonn, and after his return to England in 1870 was appointed to the chair of chemistry in the Andersonian College, Glasgow. An active period of four years in this institution was ended by Thorpe's removal to the Yorkshire College of Science at Leeds, where, besides spending much time and energy in the development of this new enterprise, he maintained a steady output of scientific work.

A further migration brought Thorpe to London, where for two periods, 1885–1894 and 1909–1912, he occupied the chair of chemistry at the Royal College of Science, South Kensington. For the fifteen years between these two periods he occupied the responsible position of government chemist, in which capacity he conducted numerous investigations bearing on industrial and public welfare. The detection of arsenic in beer, the elimination of lead from pottery glazes and of white phosphorus from matches, may be cited as examples of the problems which were tackled successfully in the government laboratories under Thorpe's supervision.

The more academic investigations with which Thorpe was concerned lay mainly in the field of inorganic chemistry. In his early years he shared in Roscoe's pioneer work on vanadium, and this led on to an intensive study of certain phosphorus compounds, notably the fluorides and oxides: his discovery of the pentafluoride provided conclusive evidence for the higher valency of phosphorus. The relation of the molecular weights of substances to their specific gravities in the liquid state was another line of investigation to which Thorpe devoted much attention and the results of which were largely responsible for the award to him of the Longstaff medal of the Chemical Society in 1881. With the assistance of his pupils, Thorpe did valuable work in the accurate determination of the atomic weights of titanium, silicon, gold, strontium, and radium. The results of these and other scientific investigations are recorded in numerous memoirs, published for the most part in the *Journal* of the Chemical Society.

It was not only chemical investigation which claimed Thorpe's active interest. He took part in four eclipse expeditions, and in collaboration with Sir Arthur Rücker he made, in 1884–1888, an extensive magnetic survey of the British Isles, the earlier results of which formed the subject of a joint Bakerian lecture before the Royal Society in 1889.

Besides originality as an investigator Thorpe possessed marked literary talent, as is shown by his *Essays in Historical Chemistry* (first edition, 1894), *Joseph Priestley* (1906), and other biographies, while the well-known *Dictionary of Applied Chemistry* (first edition, 3 vols., 1893, third edition, 7 vols., 1921) is a monument to his energy and ability as an editor. Two books on his favourite recreation of yachting, *A Yachtsman's Guide to the Dutch Waterways* (1905) and *The Seine from Havre to Paris* (1913), bear witness to his exploration of the waterways of Holland and France.

In the activities of British scientific bodies Thorpe took a prominent part. Elected a fellow of the Royal Society in 1876, he was awarded a royal medal in 1889, and acted as foreign secretary of the Society from 1899 to 1903. He was president of the Society of Chemical Industry in 1895, and of the Chemical Society 1899–1901. Finally, in 1921 he was president of the British Association at its Edinburgh meeting.

Thorpe married in 1870 Caroline Emma, daughter of Dr. John Watts, a prominent Manchester citizen and educationist. There were no children of the marriage. He died at his home at Salcombe, South Devon, 23 February 1925.

[*The Times*, 24 February 1925; *Proceedings* of the Royal Society, vol. cix, A, 1925; *Journal* of the Chemical Society, April 1926.]

J. C. Philip.

THURSFIELD, Sir JAMES (1840–1923), naval historian and journalist, was born at Kidderminster 16 November 1840, the younger son of Thomas Thursfield, M.R.C.S., by his wife, Sarah, daughter of Thomas Pardoe. On his father's death in 1855, his mother brought him to London, where he was educated at Merchant Taylors' School. In 1859 he proceeded with a scholarship to Corpus Christi College, Oxford, where he gained first classes in classical moderations (1861) and *literae humaniores* (1863). In 1864 he was elected to a fellowship at Jesus College, of which he eventually became a tutor. He was an examiner in the classical honour schools in 1873, and junior proctor for the year 1875. Among his closest friends at Oxford were Mandell Creighton, Walter

Pater, Mark Pattison, (Sir) Charles Dilke, and Mr. and Mrs. Humphry Ward. Resident fellowships were then held on condition of celibacy, and Thursfield had to relinquish his in 1881 subsequent to his marriage the previous year.

Returning to London, Thursfield joined the staff of *The Times* as leader-writer, and quickly gained recognition by his wide knowledge of public affairs. His political views were radical and not always consonant with the policy of the paper, more especially on the question of Home Rule. This was fully recognized by successive editors. Appreciating his service in other directions, they never asked him to write in support of any policy in which he did not believe. Of this earlier period of his career as a journalist, his *Peel*, contributed in 1891 to the popular series known as 'Twelve English Statesmen', is the landmark.

Perhaps as a result of acting as *The Times* correspondent at the naval manœuvres of 1887, Thursfield began at this time to specialize in a new direction. Himself the most peace-loving of men, he devoted himself to a study of naval policy and, later, of naval history—a study which was thenceforth to be one of the main interests of his life. He attended successive manœuvres and became acquainted with many of the leading naval officers of the day. He did not, however, cease to write on general topics, and from 1891 was for some years in charge of the 'Books of the Week' section of *The Times*. This, in 1902, developed into *The Times Literary Supplement*, of which Thursfield was the first editor, and to which he was a frequent contributor throughout his life.

Thursfield's interest in naval history was strengthened by the publication in 1890 of Captain A. T. Mahan's book, *The Influence of Sea Power upon History*. One of the first to grasp the importance of this work, it was he who directed public attention to it; the views which Mahan expressed being very largely those which Thursfield himself already held. In 1897 *The Navy and the Nation* was published, a collection of essays written by Thursfield and by Sir George Sydenham Clarke, afterwards Lord Sydenham of Combe. Thursfield's established reputation as a writer on naval affairs led to his being invited, in January 1900, to lecture at the Royal United Service Institution. He spoke on the training of seamen, and urged the need for full and impartial inquiry as a preliminary to reform. In 1903, an even more important occasion, he lectured at the Staff College, Camberley, on 'The Higher Policy of Defence'. From 1902 to 1914 he advocated the need of naval development, and enjoyed the confidence of several first lords of the Admiralty, among them being Lord George Hamilton, Lord Selborne, Lord Cawdor, and Lord Tweedmouth. In 1909 his *Nelson and other Naval Studies* appeared, followed in 1913 by a smaller work on *Naval Warfare*.

Thursfield was made an honorary fellow of Jesus College in 1908, and was knighted in 1920 at the age of eighty. He died at his house at Golders Green 22 November 1923.

Thursfield married in 1880 Emily, eldest daughter of the Rev. Samuel Asher Herbert, rector of St. James's, Gateshead, and had one son and one daughter.

[*The Times*, 23 November 1923; private information.] G. A. R. Callender.

TIZARD, THOMAS HENRY (1839–1924), oceanographer, hydrographic surveyor, and navigator, was born at Weymouth 13 March 1839, the third son of Joseph Tizard, shipowner and coal-merchant, by his wife, Sarah Parsons. He was educated at the Royal Hospital School, Greenwich—at that time noted for its sound mathematical training—and entered the royal navy by competitive examination as master's assistant in 1854. At the early age of fifteen he saw active service on H.M.S. *Dragon* with the Baltic fleet during the Russian War (1854–1856). Tizard next served on H.M.S. *Indus* on the West Indies station, and gained his first experience of surveying on the Newfoundland coast. He was promoted second master in 1860, and appointed to H.M. surveying vessel *Rifleman* on the China station. During his seven years' service in that ship he laid the foundation of his subsequent reputation as a surveyor. The survey of the reefs and shoals abounding in the South China sea necessitated the use of the schooner *Saracen* to act as tender to the *Rifleman*. Tizard was in command of the *Saracen* for three years after his promotion to the rank of master in 1864.

From 1868 to 1871 Tizard served as navigating lieutenant and senior assistant surveyor of H.M.S. *Newport* in the Mediterranean and Red Sea, and was present at the official opening of the Suez Canal in 1869, when he led the long procession of ships. During this period he brought out the 'Table of Chords' which has proved an inestimable boon to his brother surveyors. In 1871 the officers and crew of the *Newport* were transferred to the *Sheerwater*, and on the way out from England in the latter ship to continue the survey of the Gulf of Suez, Tizard was largely responsible for an important series of observations on the surface and undercurrents in the Straits of Gibraltar, which set at rest the vexed question of the movements of these waters.

Towards the end of 1872 the appointment of Captain (afterwards Sir) George Strong Nares [q.v.] to the command of the famous *Challenger* expedition led to Tizard's transference to the *Challenger*. He was by this time a man of strong personality and resourcefulness, an experienced navigator, and a master at handling a ship. The appointment opened out to him the great opportunity of his life in bringing him into contact with the leaders of the science of oceanography. The *Challenger* expedition resulted in a vast increase of knowledge of the physical condition of the oceans and of the distribution of marine life, and in the progressive improvement of apparatus and methods of research. As navigating officer Tizard's duties involved close collaboration with the leader of the expedition and the scientific staff. The influence which he exerted was increasingly apparent as time went on, and when Captain Nares left the ship in order to take command of the Arctic expedition of 1875, the prospect of taking Tizard with him could not be entertained. Tizard remained with the *Challenger* until she paid off in 1876, and spent the next three years at the Admiralty writing the narrative of the voyage in association with Sir John Murray [q.v.].

In 1879 Tizard, who had been promoted staff commander in 1874, resumed surveying duties afloat, and in the following year took charge of the Home survey. During the nine years that he held this command he wrote many papers of scientific value and interest. Among these may be mentioned a report on deep-sea exploration in the Faroe Channel (*Proceedings* of the Royal Society, vol. xxxv, 1883, and of the Royal Society of Edinburgh, vol. xi, 1882); lectures on *Marine Surveying* and *Hydrographic Surveying* (Professional Papers of the Corps of Royal Engineers, 1885 and 1890), and an article on the 'Thames Estuary' (*Nature*, April 1890) which is of great permanent value. He was promoted to staff captain in 1889, and in 1891 was appointed assistant hydrographer of the navy, and was elected a fellow of the Royal Society. He was placed on the retired list with the rank of captain in 1896, but continued to serve at the Admiralty until the autumn of 1907. In 1899 he was awarded a civil C.B.

Tizard's last, and not least, public service was to assist the committee appointed by the Admiralty in 1912 'to examine and consider the evidence relating to the tactics employed by Nelson at the Battle of Trafalgar'. An exhaustive examination of ships' logs and journals enabled him to prepare 'the first and only plans representing any phase of the battle of Trafalgar which have been exactly drawn to scale'.

Tizard married in 1881 Mary Elizabeth, daughter of William Henry Churchward, civil engineer, and had one son and four daughters. He died at Kingston-on-Thames 17 February 1924.

[*Proceedings* of the Royal Society, vol. cv, A, 1924; *Geographical Journal*, May 1924; *Nature*, March 1924; private information; personal knowledge.] A. M. Field.

TOUT, THOMAS FREDERICK (1855–1929), historian and teacher, was born at Norwood 28 September 1855, the only child of Thomas Edward Tout, wine merchant—whose father, of a Somersetshire family, had settled in London—by his wife, Anne Charlotte Finch. Educated at St. Olave's grammar school, Southwark, he became head of the school, won the Brackenbury history scholarship at Balliol College, Oxford, in 1874, and went into residence in January 1875. Among his contemporaries at Balliol were (Sir) Charles Harding Firth, Reginald Lane Poole, John Horace Round, (Sir) Sidney Lee, (Sir) Richard Lodge, and Charles Edwyn Vaughan: all these became his lifelong friends. Tout obtained a first class in modern history in 1877 and a second class in *literae humaniores* in 1879. From the first his interests centred in medieval history, and the teacher to whom he owed most was William Stubbs [q.v.], whose place in English medieval studies he was later to fill.

In 1881 Tout was appointed professor of modern history at St. David's College, Lampeter, where he remained until his election, nine years later, to the chair of medieval and modern history at the Victoria University of Manchester. The years at Lampeter were the making of Tout, and most of the ideas with which he was later associated at Manchester received trial there. He studied Welsh history; he took a large part in reconstituting and reviving the college, and to the abounding energy of his Oxford days was now added the self-confidence of the successful professor. In 1883 he was elected to a prize fellowship at Pembroke College, Oxford, and from 1889 to 1891 he was an examiner in the Oxford school of modern history.

Tout went to Manchester in 1890. There he remained until his retirement in 1925, and there his life's work was done in the triple capacity of administrator, teacher, and writer. As an administrator he took a prominent part in securing the severance in 1903 of the university of Manchester from the older federal body which included the universities of Liverpool and Leeds. To the task of building up the new university Tout brought tireless energy, vision, and a strength of will which was almost ruthless. His robust and practical sense made him an extremely useful counsellor, while his criticisms were always of the constructive kind, not sceptical and discouraging. He was a hard fighter, but he had a faith in his ideas which inspired respect, and in all personal relations a warm-hearted, human sympathy which rendered transient the animosities of debate. It was this almost paradoxical contrast which prompted the *bon mot—Tout comprendre c'est Tout pardonner*. Apart from the struggle for the new charter of 1903, Tout is best remembered as an administrator by his work in the building up of the faculty of arts, in the establishment of the undenominational faculty of theology, in the founding of the Manchester University Settlement, in insisting upon the same opportunities in the university for women as for men, and by his creation of the Manchester University Press. He also did invaluable and characteristic work in securing better conditions of pay and service for university lecturers and administrative officers, and as chairman of the Manchester high school for girls in establishing 'sabbatical' terms for the staff on full salary.

These tasks, on which Tout worked unsparingly, at no time overshadowed his main purpose, the development of the history school at Manchester. In this work he had the solid foundation of his predecessor, Sir Adolphus William Ward [q.v.], on which to build, and the whole-hearted co-operation of his colleague James Tait. It was Tout's conviction—and herein he was at variance with established ideas—that the undergraduate training which should produce historians and researchers was also the best for the ordinary educated man. In the last year of the undergraduate course a real effort was made to give the student a grasp of the original sources of history. From the year 1907 this was done by means of a thesis which occupied a large part of the third year and was closely related to a short special period studied intensively with plenty of expert guidance. The essence of Tout's method lay in a nice adjustment between the 'broad outlines of general European History' and early but limited specialization: its success depended on Tout's splendid gifts as a teacher. He was a fine lecturer. He carried his subject in his head, speaking always without notes or even immediate preparation, but with illuminating digressions suggested by his own special studies or his travels. A bicyclist and a walker, he had a lifelong interest in medieval antiquities and archaeology. England and Wales he knew through and through, while there was no department in France, and few countries in Europe, which he had not visited.

Tout's highest gifts, however, lay in his personal relations with his students. Wholly without vanity, he met them on a footing of equality, not less interested in themselves and their future than in their work. Through the teacher the subject became alive to all, while his own energetic example and his faith in learning inspired some to choose the life of scholarship. His success as a teacher was made evident by the character of the graduates whom he produced. They were trained historians in a degree seldom found elsewhere; and many were stimulated to pursue their studies after graduation. From these beginnings there slowly grew up a post-graduate school, the work of which gained increasing recognition through the publications of the Manchester University Press. In 1920 Tout gave up most of his active teaching, and devoted himself to the organization of this post-graduate school.

Tout's writings fall into two well-marked groups, divided from each other by the year 1908. Before this year the easy adaptation to circumstances which marked his whole life was accurately reflected in his work. What his hand found to do he did with all his might. He wrote a number of successful text-books, including a standard *History of England* for schools (in conjunction with Professor

F. York Powell, Part III, 1890, Part II, 1898), and threw himself with enthusiasm into the great new venture of his time, the DICTIONARY OF NATIONAL BIOGRAPHY, of which the first volume appeared in 1885. Tout's contributions—spread out over more than forty volumes and together amounting to a whole volume [see DICTIONARY OF NATIONAL BIOGRAPHY, vol. lxiii, *A Statistical Account*, pp. xv, xviii *et seq.*]—ranged over the whole middle ages, but found a focus in the reign of Edward I and his relations with Wales. It was good work, conceived at first on the old-fashioned, optimistic lines and largely drawn from printed materials, but broadening and deepening with the years as it found a firmer basis in the manuscript sources. Apart from these articles, the research of this period bore fruit in three works of first-rate importance, viz. an article on 'The Welsh Shires' (*Y Cymmrodor*, vol. ix, pp. 201–226, 1888); Volume III (1216–1377) in Longman's *Political History of England* (1905), and *State Trials of the Reign of Edward I, 1289–1293* (in conjunction with his sister-in-law, Miss Hilda Johnstone, Camden series of the Royal Historical Society's publications, 1906). The last of these brought Tout into immediate touch with the unexplored materials in the Public Record Office and foreshadowed the work of his second period.

Tout had always practised, as he had preached, historical research: henceforth he was absorbed by it. In 1912, in evidence before the royal commission on public records, he set forth in considerable detail certain conclusions to which work among archives had led him [First *Report* of Royal Commission on Public Records, vol. i, part iii, pp. 102–108]. The actual stimulus was supplied by Eugène Déprez' *Études de la diplomatique anglaise*, which Tout reviewed in the *English Historical Review* (1908). For the rest of his life he was concerned with administrative history, and his work in this subject is his peculiar contribution to medieval history. It was embodied in two books, *The Place of the Reign of Edward II in English History* (1914) and *Chapters in the Administrative History of Medieval England* (6 vols. 1920–1931). The first of these works grew out of his Ford lectures delivered at Oxford in 1913: of the *Chapters*, the last two volumes, although virtually finished before his death, were published posthumously. Hitherto Tout's originality had lain in his advanced conception of historical teaching. He was now to give a permanent deflection to the study of institutional history such as had earlier been given by Stubbs, and to supply the first constructive criticism of his master's interpretation of the Middle Ages. The basic idea of these books is that, owing to the prevailing absorption in the history of parliament, English medieval history has been seen out of focus, since to contemporaries the administrative side of government bulked immensely larger. Tout's object was to supplement Stubbs's work 'by setting forth in detail the history of the great administrative departments and their offshoots'.

To a great extent Tout was applying to English institutional history ideas which had already been worked out with remarkable results by the historians of France, and one effect of his work was to emphasize the underlying similarity of French and English institutions. The meaning of this 'common heritage' he developed in his *France and England, Their Relations in the Middle Ages and Now* (1922), based mainly upon four lectures given at Rennes, at the invitation of the university of Rennes, in 1921. In this book and in a number of vigorous popular lectures given during the last fifteen years of his life he generalized the results of his special studies, to which they form an excellent introduction. To the end of his life, Tout was also closely connected with the *English Historical Review*, the *Scottish Historical Review*, and *History*. To each of these journals he contributed many valuable articles, notably that on 'Firearms in England in the Fourteenth Century' in the *English Historical Review*, (vol. xxvi, 1911), and for each of them he was an indefatigable reviewer. A careful list of all his writings to the year 1925, compiled by his wife, was included in the *Essays in Medieval History* presented to him by friends and pupils in that year. A note appended to Dr. A. G. Little's memoir in *History* (January 1930) carried the list down to Tout's death. A collection of his miscellaneous writings, historical articles, and public lectures was published posthumously as *The Collected Papers of Thomas Frederick Tout* (3 vols., 1932–1934).

Behind all these activities lay the force and charm of a remarkable personality. Tout was of middle height and thick set; an excellent talker and raconteur, with slow and emphatic utterance, delighting in pungent epithets. Warm-hearted and kindly, he shared naturally the joys and troubles of his friends, and he had the understanding which won the devotion of all who worked with him or for him. The busiest of men, there was no limit to the time he could spare to help and counsel all who sought his advice. Therein he was assisted by the happy circumstances of his domestic life. In 1895 he had married Mary, daughter of Herbert Alison Johnstone, of Stockport. His wife shared his public work as well as his personal interest in his students, and their home became the centre of an ever-widening circle of friends.

Tout resigned his chair at Manchester in 1925. He returned to London, settling at Hampstead, where he had all but completed his *Administrative History* at the time of his death, which took place there 23 October 1929. In these years he maintained his public interests to the full. He was president of the Royal Historical Society from 1926; he directed the medieval publications of the British Academy, of which he had been elected a fellow in 1911 and which, as an active member of the council, he represented at the meetings of the Union Académique Internationale at Brussels in 1920 and 1921; he was elected a member of the Athenaeum Club under Rule II; he was a member of the committee of the Institute of Historical Research and of the advisory committee of the British Broadcasting Company for national lectures. In 1928 he travelled in the United States of America, where he delivered the Messenger lectures at Cornell University, and in Canada. The last ten years of his life were marked by widening recognition of his pre-eminent position in medieval studies. Honorary degrees were conferred on him by the universities of Durham (1921), Liverpool and Edinburgh (1925), Oxford (1926), and Colorado (1928), he was made an honorary fellow of Pembroke College, Oxford, and a corresponding fellow of the Academy of Caen and of the Mediaeval Academy of America. These years were also marked by an ever-increasing interest in the International Congress of Historical Studies. He had much to do with its development from the beginning. At the International Congress held in London in 1913 he was president of the medieval section, and again at Brussels in 1923. He was an active member of its standing committee, president of the British National Committee, and was arranging for the annual meeting in England in 1930 at the time of his death.

Tout was survived by Mrs. Tout and by two sons and a daughter. The eldest son died in infancy.

[A. G. Little in *History*, January 1930; James Tait in *English Historical Review*, January 1930; F. M. Powicke, *Thomas Frederick Tout, 1855–1929* in *Proceedings* of the British Academy, vol. xv, 1929, reprinted in *Collected Papers*, vol. i; Henry Guppy in *Bulletin* of the John Rylands Library, January 1930; personal knowledge.]

V. H. Galbraith.

TOWNSHEND, Sir CHARLES VERE FERRERS (1861–1924), major-general, was born 21 February 1861 in Southwark, the eldest son of Charles Thornton Townshend, by his wife, Louisa, daughter of John Graham, of Melbourne, Australia. His father was the eldest son of the Rev. Lord George Townshend, and a great-grandson of the first Marquess Townshend. Although he was for a time heir presumptive to the marquessate, the father lived in humble circumstances, earning his livelihood as a minor railway official. After his death in 1889 Charles Vere Townshend remained until 1916 heir presumptive to the sixth Marquess Townshend.

Townshend's home life was not happy; he was educated at Cranleigh School, Kent, until his relatives obtained a nomination for him to enter the royal navy. This, however, he did not accept, preferring to work for entrance into the Royal Military College, Sandhurst. Eventually, in February 1881 he was gazetted to the Royal Marine Light Infantry. In 1884 he proceeded to Suakin with a battalion of marines, which, shortly afterwards, was attached to the column with which Sir Herbert Stewart [q.v.] advanced up the Nile valley in an endeavour to relieve General Gordon, then besieged in Khartoum. Townshend was thus present at the fierce actions at Abu Klea and Gubat, and when the fall of Khartoum became known, participated in Stewart's retreat across the Bayuda desert. After being mentioned in dispatches for his work in the Sudan, he was transferred to the Indian army in January 1886.

On arrival in India Townshend was first posted to the seventh Madras Infantry, exchanging very soon into the third Sikh Infantry, and finally into the Central India Horse. The facility with which he changed regiments and sought appointments became a characteristic of Townshend's career. In 1891 he had the good fortune to be selected for service in the Himalayas, and was sent to Gilgit, where he assumed command of the first, or Raga Pertab, battalion of the Imperial Kashmir Contingent. Not long afterwards the Hunza-Nagar expedition was organized at Gilgit, and Townshend thus came to take a prominent part in the capture of the hill forts of Nilt and Hunza. After obtaining another mention in dispatches and acting as military governor of Hunza, he returned to his regiment late in 1892, having been promoted to captain's rank earlier in that year. In 1893 he was once more sent to the Himalayas, being selected for the command of Fort Gupis, which stood midway between Gilgit and Chitral. A series of political murders and the subsequent disaffection of Sher Afzul, the usurping ruler of Chitral, led to the dispatch of the political agent, Sir George Scott Robertson [q.v.], to Chitral, escorted by Townshend and a detachment of troops from Gupis early in 1895. This little force reached Chitral, but was soon driven into the fortified palace of Chitral and there besieged, suffering severe privations during an investment of forty-six days (4 March–20 April). For Townshend, as commander of the garrison, the situation was difficult: the enemy displayed boldness; his own men were apathetic; and the presence of the political agent complicated his position as military commander. In April 1895 Chitral was relieved. For the skill and judgement displayed in its defence, Townshend received the thanks of the government of India, a brevet majority, and the C.B.—a remarkable reward for so young an officer.

On returning to England Townshend found himself a celebrity, and had little difficulty in obtaining a transfer to the Egyptian army. Accordingly in February 1896 he arrived in Cairo to assume command of the twelfth Sudanese battalion. A few weeks later he set out with (Lord) Kitchener's expedition for the reconquest of the Sudan. During that year he took part in the operations for the recovery of Dongola, obtaining another mention and a brevet lieutenant-colonelcy. Throughout 1897 he remained engaged in the Nile valley, and in 1898 commanded his battalion at the battles of the Atbara and of Khartoum, obtaining the D.S.O. for his services. After resigning his appointment in Egypt, Townshend returned to India in 1899, nominally to take up a staff appointment, but, on the outbreak of the war in South Africa, he made every endeavour to be sent to the Cape. This at length he effected, and he arrived at Bloemfontein in March 1900, to act as assistant-adjutant-general on the staff of the military governor of the Orange Free State. The work and surroundings proved uncongenial and Townshend returned home in September 1900, to be reinstated in the British service as a major in the Royal Fusiliers. In spite of his record of service and of his proved military qualities Townshend now antagonized not a few high authorities. Many idiosyncrasies, regarded with amused tolerance in the young officer, proved less becoming in a soldier of standing and distinction. A passion for theatrical society, gifts as an excellent raconteur and entertainer, a constant flow of quips and quotations in French obscured some true merit. A remarkable knowledge of military history was warped by a lack of systematic training and by a self-confidence that often failed to impress. Townshend's abilities were thus, perhaps not unjustly, regarded as unbalanced, and he now went through a period of lean years. Until March 1903 he served at home, growing more dissatisfied with regimental duty. He then exchanged into the battalion of his regiment stationed in India. Promotion to brevet colonel came in January 1904. He returned home in December of that year, and in 1905 acted for a time as military attaché in Paris. But his restlessness was unabated until, in March 1906, he was transferred to the Shropshire Light Infantry and again went to India. There in August 1907 he became assistant-adjutant-general of the ninth division. In February 1908 he was promoted substantive colonel, while a year later he was appointed commander of the Orange River Colony District, a position carrying the rank of brigadier-general. Townshend remained in South Africa until promoted major-general in July 1911, when he returned to England. He had in the meantime become an ardent admirer of the French army and of the future Marshal Foch; so much so that this predilection even coloured the training of his troops. The command of the East Anglian division of the Territorial Force was next given him; but he preferred more active employment, and was gratified when in June 1913 he left for India to assume command of the Jhanzi brigade. A few months later he left this unit for the Rawal Pindi brigade, and he was at Pindi at the time of the outbreak of the European War.

Townshend's persistent efforts to obtain a command at the front were at length satisfied in April 1915 by his appointment to the sixth (Indian) division, that being one of the two divisions operating in Mesopotamia, under the command of Sir John Eccles Nixon [q.v.]. In the ensuing campaign the brunt of the fighting fell upon Townshend's division. His first task was to drive the Turks northwards from Kurna on the Tigris, which was then in full flood. The water was so high that the fortified Turkish position stood out of the marshy flats almost like a string of islands. Townshend accordingly organized a fleet of ancient Tigris barges, known as *bellums*, on which he embarked two brigades, supported by three naval sloops and other odd craft. With this curious armada on 31 May he delivered a frontal attack on the enemy—a seemingly hazardous proceeding, since the Turkish position was guarded by mines and the depth of water was uncertain. Luckily the mines proved ineffective and most of the defenders fled. Emboldened by success Townshend pursued the Turks with a handful of men, embarked on a few naval craft, until he reached Amara (90 miles up the river from Kurna). There the bulk of the Turkish force surrendered before discovering the weakness of the pursuit. Townshend's audacity was thus amply rewarded.

Shortly afterwards Townshend fell ill and was sent to India for treatment. On resuming his command in September, he found his division distributed along the Tigris with the Turks entrenched astride the river in front of Kut el Amara (150 miles above Amara). Difficulties of transport and supply were already hampering the movements of the British troops, who were, moreover, sorely in need of reinforcement; the Turks on the other hand were growing in numbers and boldness. Nevertheless, an advance on Bagdad had been decided upon by higher authority, and Townshend was not unwilling to fall in with the plan. On 27 September he attacked the Turkish position. It was a bold move, involving a night march and a turning movement. Having divided his force Townshend cleverly feinted on the right bank of the river whilst driving home his main attack away from the left bank. The Turks were defeated and Kut was captured (29 September); but the victory could not be effectively followed up owing to the weakness and fatigue of the British forces. Retreating in good order, the Turks took up a fortified position at Ctesiphon, covering Bagdad. The Tigris now grew so shallow that Townshend, depending largely on water transport, found his supply services still further hampered, so that he was compelled to halt at Azizieh (60 miles beyond Kut).

The final move on Bagdad was then ordered. Townshend raised objections to the proposed operations without the assistance of a second division, but deferred to the judgement of his commander-in-chief, Sir John Nixon. Difficulties were minimized by all authorities concerned in the campaign; and a successful preliminary attack on a Turkish advanced post at El Kutuniya encouraged optimism. But the Turks had in the meanwhile been reinforced, before Townshend, on 22 November, could attack their position. Once more he cleverly manœuvred to turn the Turkish left while launching his main attack at a specially selected point in their main line of resistance. This point was taken after fierce fighting, but only at heavy cost. The Turks, now strengthened by some good troops from the Caucasus, counter-attacked the next day. Townshend's resources proved quite inadequate to the task in hand, and the situation, aggravated by the difficulty of navigating the low waters of the Tigris, grew critical.

After a week's fighting and retreating, holding at bay the enemy's greatly superior forces, Townshend led his men back into Kut on 3 December with 1,350 prisoners. It is more than doubtful whether he could have withdrawn farther. After one or two attempts to carry the place by assault the Turks invested it closely. Townshend expected to be relieved, but attempts by Lieutenant-General Aylmer and Major-General Gorringe in January and February proved unavailing. Townshend conducted the defence skilfully, although the fall of Kut had become inevitable when Aylmer failed to break through the Turkish lines in January. The garrison suffered severely, and men were actually dying of starvation when Townshend opened negotiations with the Turks. The surrender of Kut took place on 29 April 1916.

Townshend and his garrison became prisoners of war. The troops fared lamentably in captivity, but Townshend himself was well treated, being interned on Prinkipo Island, near Constantinople. In October 1917 he was created a K.C.B. A year later he was released by the Turks in order that he should plead on their behalf for the best possible terms of surrender. The armistice with Turkey was signed on

30 October 1918, when Townshend returned to England.

After the War Townshend failed to obtain any further military appointment; he therefore retired and took to political life, and was elected to parliament in November 1920, as an independent conservative for the Wrekin division of Shropshire. In the House he occasionally spoke on matters that concerned the East or the ex-service man, but on the whole he proved ineffective, and did not seek re-election. Subsequently, he sought opportunities of acting as negotiator between Great Britain and Turkey in the final settlement of questions arising out of the War; but his services were curtly declined by the government. Undeterred, he proceeded to Angora in June 1922, and was well received by Kemal Pasha, his pro-Turkish sympathies being thereby strengthened. On his return to London he strongly advocated the Turkish case, but failed to find support. He visited Angora again in 1923. His health, however, was failing, and he died in Paris 18 May 1924.

Townshend married in 1898 Alice, daughter of Count Louis Cahen d'Anvers. He left one daughter.

[*The Times*, 19 May 1924; E. Sherson, *Townshend of Chitral and Kut*, 1928; Sir C. V. F. Townshend, *My Campaign in Mesopotamia*, 1920; Army Lists. Portrait, *Royal Academy Pictures*, 1920.]

H. DE WATTEVILLE.

TRELOAR, SIR WILLIAM PURDIE, baronet (1843–1923), carpet manufacturer and philanthropist, the second son of Thomas Treloar, mat manufacturer, of Helston, Cornwall, by his wife, Elizabeth, daughter of John Robertson, of Pitlochry, Perthshire, was born in Southwark 13 January 1843. His family soon moved to Blackheath, and in 1854, at the age of eleven, Treloar was sent to King's College School, then situated in the Strand, travelling thither daily alone in a third-class carriage—the carriages being roofless, windowless, and without seats. He left school at the age of fifteen and entered his father's business. He passed through every department of the factory, beginning at the bottom as a workman, later acting as foreman, and eventually succeeding to the post of manager.

Treloar's civic career began in 1880, when he was elected to the Court of Common Council in the ward of Farringdon Without. Thenceforth he took an active part in the municipal affairs of the City of London. In the annual elections of his ward he was always successful, and generally headed the poll. In 1891 he was elected chairman of the City commission of sewers, which, nominally a separate body, was managed by the City Corporation and afterwards absorbed by it by Act of Parliament. In 1892 he was unanimously elected alderman of the ward of Farringdon Without. In 1899–1900 he served as sheriff, and entered with great spirit into the raising of the City Imperial Volunteers for service in South Africa during the Boer War. He was knighted in 1900.

Amongst Treloar's civic activities certain matters of public interest deserve special mention. In 1886 he moved and carried a resolution that election to the Court of Common Council should be by ballot. In 1894, in the face of much bitter opposition, he moved and finally carried a resolution expressing the desirability of opening the Guildhall Art Gallery on Sunday afternoons. This decision did much to encourage the activities of the National Sunday League, of which Treloar was president.

In 1906 Treloar was elected lord mayor of London, and began a brilliant year of office, during which King Edward VII and Queen Alexandra opened the New Central Criminal Court, Old Bailey. Treloar himself, as lord mayor, paid an official visit to Berlin, on an occasion which called for unusually tactful exchanges. But his most enduring work as lord mayor was the launching of an appeal for the foundation of a home for crippled children. The scheme received royal approval and support. Treloar collected £60,000 and obtained for the home the Princess Louise Military Hospital, built at Alton, Hampshire, during the South African War, with the proceeds of the 'Absent-minded Beggar' appeal by the *Daily Mail*. To the interests of this institution, which was named the Lord Mayor Treloar Cripples' Hospital and College, Treloar devoted the greater part of his remaining life. Such an institution had never previously been conceived. Its objects, from the beginning, were the combined treatment and education of crippled children under the age of twelve years—priority being given to children suffering from surgical tuberculosis—and the training of crippled boys between the ages of fourteen and eighteen in trades suited to their limitations. The hospital met a very real need, and since its opening in September 1908 many thousands of crippled children have been successfully treated, educated, and trained therein. In 1919 Treloar founded a sea-side branch of the hospital at Hayling Island. As a result of this pioneer work, other hospital schools were established in 1911 and are now numerous in the country.

Treloar possessed a most genial personality, and was a member of the Carlton, Junior Carlton, Authors, Savage, Press, and Whitefriars Clubs. He was author of *Ludgate Hill; Past and Present* (1881), *Prince of Palms* (1884), *With the Kaiser in the East, 1898* (1915), *Wilkes and the City* (1917), and *A Lord Mayor's Diary* (1920).

Treloar married in 1865 Annie (died 1909), daughter of George Blake; they had no children. He adopted a nephew and a niece. He was created a baronet in 1907, but the title became extinct on his death, which took place at Grange Mount, Norwood, 6 September 1923.

A portrait of Treloar by P. Tennyson Cole hangs in the Guildhall Art Gallery, and a marble bust by Albert Toft was recently in the Mansion House.

[C. E. Lawrence, *William Purdie Treloar*, 1925; personal knowledge.] H. Gauvain.

TRENCH, FREDERIC HERBERT (1865–1923), poet and playwright, was born at Avoncore, co. Cork, 26 November 1865, the son of W. W. Trench, of Ballater, Bournemouth. In 1880 he went to Haileybury College (Melvill House), and from there in 1884, having won an open exhibition in modern history, to Keble College, Oxford. His university studies were at first hindered by ill-health, but he obtained a first class in modern history in 1888 and was elected a fellow of All Souls College in 1889. He had meanwhile travelled in southern Europe and the Near East. As an undergraduate Trench is described by a contemporary as of engaging manners and striking appearance, with fine eyes, straight black hair, a fresh complexion, and a heavy black moustache. His tutors found him an interesting but somewhat dreamy person, of obvious ability, and of a fine character, steadily developing through discipline. He was appointed a temporary examiner by the Board of Education in 1891, was placed on the permanent staff in 1892, and promoted to be a senior examiner in 1900. He retired in 1909. From then until 1911 he was 'artistic director' at the Haymarket Theatre. Shortly after this he went to live at Settignano, near Florence. He died in hospital at Boulogne-sur-Mer on 11 June 1923, having fallen ill on a journey to England. He had married in 1891 Lilian Isabel, daughter of Robert Fox, of Grove Hall, Falmouth, and Penjerrick, Cornwall. They had two sons and three daughters.

Trench was a man of letters who was temperamentally unsuited to administrative work. When the burden of routine at the Board of Education was much increased after the Education Act of 1902, it was probably with feelings of mutual relief that his retirement was arranged. But before this he had made his mark as a poet; first, in 1900 with *Deirdre Wed and other Poems* and, more definitely, in 1907 with the volume containing 'Apollo and the Seaman'. Later came poems, long and short, inspired by his life in Italy and by the European War, and various lyrics, notably a sequence, 'To Arolilia'. It was probably his short term of responsibility at the Haymarket Theatre (in itself notable for productions of *King Lear* and Maeterlinck's *The Blue Bird*) that turned him to play-writing. He completed a four-act play, *Napoleon*, which was produced by the Stage Society in 1919, and he was at work upon another, *Talleyrand*, when he died. He also published some *Fables in Prose*, which are not remarkable, and a translation (1901) of Merejkowski's *Death of the Gods*.

Trench had a generous share of the attributes of a poet. He was sensitive and imaginative; he had an ear for the music of words and a scholarly taste in their use. His simpler poems are the most likely to survive, and those in which the emotion and the thought meet, as it were, upon equal terms. He is at his best when he is least self-conscious. Such a lyric as 'Come, let us make love deathless, thou and I . . .' is memorable, and there are others as good. Such poems as 'The Shepherd' and 'The Song of the Vine' have authentic beauty, and the swinging melodies of 'Apollo and the Seaman' promise life to a great theme. The vigorous

'Apollo through the woods came down
Furred like a merchant fine,
And sate with a sailor at an inn
Sharing a jug of wine . . .'

is, for the opening of a 'philosophic ballad', hardly to be bettered; so, too, the sailor's

'I heard them calling in the streets
That the ship I serve upon—
The great ship Immortality—
Was gone down, like the sun . . .'

But the promise is only partly fulfilled; the method is incompatible with the portentous weight of matter. The weakness of the more patently ambitious work lies, it is to be feared, in a certain pretentiousness. The poet is possessed, seemingly, by some transcendental idea. But he either cannot or will not forge it as a whole into clear thought and adequate expression. He is apt instead to elaborate its vagueness in fine words and images, which leave us at the poem's end conscious of having read some very noble lines but disposed to wonder what it is all about—and a little suspicious that Trench himself may have been left wondering too.

Napoleon is a play with an idea, a very good idea, and the dramatic medium itself invites clarity. Trench chose, moreover, to cast it in prose, save for one scene, and that not among the best. The stage-craft is efficient, even if the action is, now and then, needlessly crowded with incident. Some of the characters may lack autonomous life, but the result of the whole is often striking, occasionally moving, and never less than interesting. It is distinguished drama, and might well have led him to other and more complete achievement in this kind.

The following is a list of Trench's works: *Deirdre Wed and other Poems* (1900); *The Death of the Gods, translated from Merejkowski* (1901); *New Poems* ('Apollo and the Seaman', 'The Questioners', &c., 1907); *Lyrics and Narrative Poems* (1911); *Ode from Italy in time of War* (1915); *Poems, with Fables in Prose* (1918); *Napoleon, a play* (1919). His *Collected Works* were published in three volumes in 1924.

[*Memoir* by Harold Williams in *Collected Works*, 1924; private information.]

H. Granville-Barker.

TREVELYAN, Sir GEORGE OTTO, second baronet (1838–1928), historian, man of letters, and statesman, was born at Rothley Temple, Leicestershire, 20 July 1838. He was the only son of Sir Charles Edward Trevelyan, first baronet [q.v.], governor of Madras, by his first wife, Hannah More, daughter of Zachary Macaulay [q.v.] and sister of Lord Macaulay [q.v.]. During the first twenty years of Trevelyan's life his father resided in England, occupying, as assistant secretary to the Treasury, a leading position in the English civil service, between two periods of his Indian career. At Clapham and afterwards in London the Trevelyans' house was almost a second home to the bachelor Macaulay. George Trevelyan was from the first a favourite companion of his uncle, and acquired in very early years a picturesque and vivid realization of the past, and 'strong bookmindedness' in relation to classical and English literature, although he never had his uncle's easy familiarity with modern European languages. His elder sister Margaret, who afterwards married the first Viscount Knutsford [q.v.], and his younger sister Alice, afterwards Mrs. Stratford Dugdale, completed this affectionate and like-minded family group.

After a few years at a private school of no special note, Trevelyan went in 1851 to Harrow, then at the height of the scholarly eminence which it reached under Dr. Charles John Vaughan [q.v.]. Trevelyan was at The Grove, Mr. Steel's house: he became head of the school and Gregory prizeman, swept up the school honours, winning the English prize poem three years running, and distinguishing himself by an output of English verse on topical school subjects, some in imitation of Juvenal. In 1857 he went up to Trinity College, Cambridge, where he obtained an undergraduate reputation which long outlasted his residence there. This reputation was not based on Trevelyan's performance in scholarship, although he was placed second in the classical tripos (1861) in a period of very high competition; it rested principally on his intellectual high spirits, above all on his light verse and satires ('The Bear' and 'The Cambridge Dionysia', which made a butt of a pretentious university magazine, *The Lion*). This phase of his literary activity culminated in *Horace at the University of Athens*, first printed by Jonathan Palmer at Cambridge in 1861, a piece of not too recondite fun which long remained a favourite among Cambridge men of the old classical tradition. But, however popular among Trevelyan's contemporaries, it was less highly appreciated by some of the authorities; and William Whewell, as master of Trinity, considered the author lacking in deference.

In any case Trevelyan failed to obtain a fellowship at Trinity in October 1862, and as he had no very high opinion of the scholarship of some of the successful candidates (R. C. Jebb was also passed over that year), he decided not to sit the next year, as he might have done, but to go out to India as private secretary to his father, then financial member of the governor-general's council. His feeling for Trinity remained all his life akin to that of an Athenian for Athens, and one of the honours which he most appreciated in later life was his election in 1885 to an honorary fellowship. His full-length portrait by Frank Holl now hangs in the Old Combination Room of the college, and is by far the best picture of him. His friends among his Trinity contemporaries remained the most intimate friends of his life—Henry and Arthur Sidgwick, Edward Bowen, Henry Jackson, Richard Jebb, Henry Yates Thompson, George Howard (afterwards ninth Earl of Carlisle), Sir George Young, and Henry Montagu Butler, who was a few years his senior.

In December 1859 Lord Macaulay died: in its main outlines Trevelyan's mind never lost the impress made upon it by his uncle's society. But during the following decade his mental equipment for life was completed by two fresh influences—the works of Carlyle, Ruskin, and Browning, which to some extent modernized his literary tastes in a manner which his uncle would not have approved, and in politics the new liberal movement of the 'sixties. Largely intellectual in origin, that movement was closely connected with the desire to reform the older universities and to open them to all, irrespective of religious beliefs. The movement enlisted the enthusiasm of all Trevelyan's Cambridge friends, such as the Sidgwicks and Henry Jackson, and of new Oxford friends in the early days of the 'Ad Eundem' dining club. The memory of his personal connexions with Oxford at this period made him take a particular pleasure as an old man in his election to an honorary fellowship at Oriel College in 1920.

While he was still at Cambridge and still a Palmerstonian whig, rather than a liberal, Trevelyan had been touched by the prevalent enthusiasm for the cause of Italian liberty; in 1862 he had written, in boyish high spirits, a poetic skit on the subject entitled *The Pope and his Patron*; and in 1867 he went out to be present at Garibaldi's attack on Rome, but arrived the day after the battle of Mentana, only in time to witness Garibaldi's arrest by the Italian royal troops. To the end of his life he was devoted to Italian travel and enjoyed it with a full mind.

The work which first brought Trevelyan to the notice of London as distinct from Cambridge society was *The Competition Wallah*, which originally appeared as letters in *Macmillan's Magazine*, and in 1864 in book form; it contained the observations made during his long visit to India in 1863. The work, favourably looked on by those who knew India well, at once became popular in England. It remains the most vivid account of Anglo-Indian life in the decade after the Mutiny. He followed it up with *Cawnpore* (1865), a striking piece of historical narrative.

In the parliament of 1865 to 1868 Trevelyan, although returned for Tynemouth as a Palmerstonian, became an enthusiastic supporter of John Bright. He often sat next to him in the House during the debates and vicissitudes of the struggle which ended in the second Reform Bill (1867). The dramatic events of the Reform Bill session of 1866 inspired him to write *Ladies in Parliament*, the last and not the least happy effort of his poetical and social muse. The Aristophanic chorus 'We much revere our sires' was the best thing of the kind that he wrote.

Trevelyan became at this time a prominent advocate of army reform, particularly of the abolition of the purchase system, in which controversy he was to no small degree inspired and coached by his father. This cause, unpopular with the court and the army chiefs but serviceable to the efficiency of the army, triumphed in 1870 owing to the energetic measures of Mr. Gladstone and (Viscount) Cardwell. In 1868 Gladstone formed his first ministry, and Trevelyan, who had been returned to parliament for the Border (Hawick) Burghs, became civil lord of the Admiralty. In 1870 he resigned office because he differed from the government's decision to increase the grant to the Church schools as part of the arrangements of W. E. Forster's famous Education Bill. This action permanently retarded Trevelyan's rise in the official hierarchy of the party, and throughout life his relations with Gladstone, although correct, were seldom cordial. During the 'seventies he remained in parliament, sitting for the Border Burghs, a centre of Scottish radicalism, until 1886. During the period of liberal opposition (1874–1880) he brought forward year after year a motion for the extension of the working-class franchise to the county divisions, a measure finally passed by Gladstone in 1884–1885, largely as a result of Trevelyan's efforts in bringing the question to the front.

If the 'seventies were a period of comparative obscurity for Trevelyan as a politician, they were the principal period of his literary achievement. In 1876 appeared his *Life and Letters of Lord Macaulay*, a work which has always been regarded as a model of that type of biography, and by which his name is likely to survive longest on this side of the Atlantic. In 1880 he brought out his *Early History of Charles James Fox*, a biography of a totally different kind, giving satisfaction more as a brilliant picture of a state of society than as the portrait of a statesman of whom nothing is there recorded except the years of his irresponsible boyhood and youth. It is a work of historical art which has the effect of giving the reader the *entrée*, as an intimate member, to a bygone aristocratic society.

The death of Trevelyan's mother in 1872 and the marriages of his two sisters had now quite broken up the old family circle, but his own marriage in 1869 to Caroline, daughter of Robert Needham Philips, of Manchester, a leading Lancashire merchant and politician in the heyday of the Manchester School, opened for him fifty-nine years of unbroken domestic happiness. He always spoke of his marriage as the most fortunate event in a very fortunate life. There were three sons of the marriage: Charles Philips, sometime labour minister for education; Robert Calverley, the poet; and George Macaulay, regius professor of modern history in the university of Cambridge, author of this article. He had something of his uncle's power of interesting children in literature and history, especially military history, as much through familiar jokes and allusions as by direct instruction.

In 1880 Gladstone formed his second ministry and Trevelyan was left out of it. In 1881, however, he was appointed parliamentary secretary to the Admiralty, and in 1882 the murder of his friend, Lord Frederick Cavendish, in the Phoenix Park, Dublin, led to Trevelyan's appointment as his successor in the office of chief secretary for Ireland, under the fifth Earl Spencer as lord-lieutenant. The secretary had to face the organized Irish opposition in the Commons, as well as to share with Lord Spencer the difficulties in Ireland, including on one occasion a mutiny of the Dublin police. Trevelyan became warmly attached to Lord Spencer; they endeavoured to carry on the policy of conciliation which Lord Frederick had been sent over to initiate, though their difficulties were greatly increased by his assassination.

In October 1884 Trevelyan entered the Cabinet as chancellor of the duchy of Lancaster. In Gladstone's third ministry, formed after the election of 1885, Trevelyan became secretary for Scotland and in 1886 introduced his Crofters' Bill, the principles of which, when subsequently put into law, did much to solve the crofter question in the highlands on the lines of previous Irish land legislation. But in the spring of 1886 Gladstone introduced Home Rule for Ireland, and Trevelyan resigned, being unable to accept Home Rule, especially in connexion with the accompanying land-purchase scheme. He stood as a liberal-unionist at the general election of 1886, an election which he always thought Gladstone ought to have avoided, as it led inevitably to the break-up of the liberal party. He was defeated by a Gladstonian at the Border Burghs, for which he had sat for twenty-eight years. But alliance with conservatives was not congenial to him; after the abortive Round Table Conference (January–February 1887), in which he took part, had failed to reunite the liberal chiefs, his liberalism overcame his objections to Home Rule. He was returned for the Bridgeton division of Glasgow as a Gladstonian liberal in 1887. This change naturally exposed Trevelyan to a good deal of censure at a time of intense political feeling.

If politics and London society were becoming less entirely congenial to Trevelyan than before, his country home at Wallington in Northumberland, which he inherited when he succeeded his father as second baronet in 1886, gave a happy background to his life. This combined with a love of letters to draw him out of public life in January 1897, after another period in the Cabinet as secretary for Scotland in the Home Rule parliament of 1892–1895. During his later years in politics he had formed friendships—personal and literary even more than political—with colleagues such as Lord Rosebery, (Lord) Bryce, (Lord) Morley, and Sir William Harcourt, and among younger men with Sir Edward (afterwards Viscount) Grey, a neighbour in Northumberland.

From his retirement in 1897 until his death in 1928, Trevelyan seldom spent more than three months a year in London, and in the last dozen years of his life never visited town. He lived during the summer at Wallington and during the winter at his wife's house at Welcombe, Stratford-on-Avon. He was fond of shooting, particularly blackcock and grouse on the moors; in pursuit of game he was an active walker until old age overtook him, when he became devoted to his garden and woods. He was never too old to read the Greek, Latin, and English classics with an avidity rare even among scholars.

Until he became too old for regular work, Trevelyan was employed in writing his history of the American Revolution, which appeared in the following order: *The American Revolution*, Part I, 1766–1776 (1899), Part II (2 vols., 1903–1905), Part III (1907), and *George III and Charles Fox, the concluding part of the American Revolution* (2 vols., 1912 and 1914). This, his last work, completed on the very outbreak of the European War, retains many of the qualities of his earlier work. But, although not ill received, it was not generally popular in England, for the story of the loss of the American colonies can hardly be made an agreeable story to Englishmen, and part of the public regarded his point of view as too favourable to the Americans. On the other hand, the work had a great effect in the United States, where its chief sale has always been. It did much to help the movement over there for reconciliation to England, by emphasizing the strong element of opposition to the policy of George III that had existed in this country, by disposing of many anti-English myths, and by representing English life and people of that day in a pleasanter and more intimate light than any to which American readers were accustomed. The book brought him many American friendships, and put him into close personal and epistolary contact with Theodore Roosevelt, Cabot Lodge, J. H. Choate, the Adamses, the historians J. F. Rhodes and C. H. Van Tyne, and many more. His voluminous correspondence with Roosevelt (some of it published in J. B. Bishop's *Life of Roosevelt*, 1920), Cabot Lodge, and other influential Americans was continued during the European War in the interest of England's quarrel with Germany and the cause of Anglo-Saxon solidarity. He was too old to render his country any more active services between the years 1914 and 1918. He lived until the age of ninety, dying at his home at Wallington 17 August 1928, six months after his wife's death and nine years after their golden wedding. He was succeeded as third baronet by his eldest son (born 1870). In 1911 the Order of Merit had been conferred on him.

[G. M. Trevelyan, *Sir George Otto Trevelyan. A Memoir*, 1932.] G. M. Trevelyan.

TREVES, Sir FREDERICK, baronet (1853–1923), surgeon, was born at Dorchester, Dorset, 15 February 1853, the youngest son of William Treves, upholsterer, of that town, by his wife, Jane, daughter of John Knight, of Honiton. His father's family had been settled in Dorset for many generations, most of its members being yeoman farmers. In 1860, at the age of seven, Treves was sent to the school in Dorchester kept by the Rev. William Barnes [q.v.], the Dorset poet, where he remained until 1864, when he entered Merchant Taylors' School, in the City of London. Here he spent seven years, leaving in 1871, at the age of eighteen, to enter upon the study of medicine. There is no record of his having shown special ability during his school-days. At Merchant Taylors' he became a member of the football XV.

The London Hospital, at which Treves obtained his medical education, although offering its students ample opportunities for clinical observation, did not then enjoy the highest reputation amongst the metropolitan medical schools. Yet on its staff were men of scientific distinction, such as John Hughlings Jackson and (Sir) Jonathan Hutchinson, and others, like (Sir) Andrew Clark, who were eminently practical. It was the practical rather than the scientific aspect of medicine which appealed to Treves. He proved to have excellent manipulative ability, an asset of great value to one destined to become eminent both as anatomist and surgeon.

In 1875, after four years of study, Treves passed the examinations which qualified him as a member of the Royal College of Surgeons of England; in the previous year he had become a licentiate of the Apothecaries Hall. After holding a house-surgeonship at the London Hospital, he became in 1876 resident medical officer at the Royal National Hospital for Scrofula (later it became the Royal Sea-Bathing Hospital) at Margate, to which his brother William (Frederick's senior by ten years) was honorary surgeon. Scrofula and tuberculosis became the subjects of his first research.

Meantime Treves became engaged to Anne Elizabeth, youngest daughter of Alfred Samuel Mason, of Dorchester, and went into practice in Derbyshire in order to provide a home for her. He married in 1877 at the age of twenty-four, but continued to study and passed the examinations for the fellowship of the Royal College of Surgeons of England in 1878.

In the following year he gave up practice in Derbyshire and returned to the London Hospital in order to fill the post of surgical registrar. He had scarcely entered on this office when a vacancy occurred on the surgical staff of the hospital; he was appointed assistant surgeon in September 1879, and became full surgeon in 1884, being then only thirty-one years of age.

Having obtained a place on the surgical staff of his hospital Treves, like other young surgeons in a similar position, had to find a means of livelihood until he had built up a consulting practice. He therefore became a 'demonstrator' of anatomy in the medical school attached to the London Hospital. His reputation as a demonstrator soon spread beyond the walls of the hospital; his clear, incisive style, his power of happy description, his racy humour, and the applicability of his teaching brought crowds of students to his daily demonstrations. His success as a writer, both of medical treatises and of books of travel, can be traced to his experience as a demonstrator of anatomy. He was in charge of the practical teaching of anatomy from 1881 to 1884, when he became lecturer on anatomy, a post which he held until 1893. This he gave up in order to teach operative surgery, which he did for only one year, becoming lecturer on surgery 1894–1897. Meanwhile, Treves was diligent in the wards of the hospital, building up a reputation as a leading surgeon. His consulting-room at No. 6 Wimpole Street became one of the best known in England.

During the period in which he held these teaching posts, Treves also produced a succession of successful text-books. In 1883 appeared *Surgical Applied Anatomy*; he edited *A Manual of Surgery* (3 vols., 1886), *A Manual of Operative Surgery* (1891), *The Student's Handbook of Surgical Operations* (1892), and *A System of Surgery* (2 vols., 1895). All these books are characterized by a lively, clear style and many practical observations.

In quite another category are the books which brought Treves fame as an investigator. His early experience with his brother at Margate led him to join in the search into the nature of the condition then known as scrofula. In 1882, at the age of twenty-nine, he published the results of his research in a book entitled *Scrofula and its Gland Diseases*. In the same year as this book appeared, Robert Koch, the German bacteriologist, demonstrated that the disorder which had so greatly puzzled Treves and all previous investigators was due to the action of a bacillus.

Just at the time when Treves began his surgical career, the abdomen became a field of advance in surgery. The application of the discoveries of Louis Pasteur and of (Lord) Lister [q.v.] made this possible. Treves applied himself to this new field, making a survey of the anatomy of the abdomen, especially in so far as anatomical details could throw light upon the causes of obstruction. In 1883 the Royal College of Surgeons, of which he was one of the Hunterian professors of anatomy in 1885 and Erasmus Wilson lecturer in pathology in 1881, awarded him the Jacksonian prize for a dissertation on *The Pathology, Diagnosis and Treatment of Obstruction of the Intestine* (published 1884). In 1899 a new and revised edition of this work appeared under the title *Intestinal Obstruction, its Varieties, with their Pathology, Diagnosis and Treatment*. A final and much amended edition, almost a new work, appeared in 1902. In 1885 appeared his Hunterian lectures on *The Anatomy of the Intestinal Canal and Peritoneum*, a book which contains his best original work.

When Treves began the study of medicine the condition known as *perityphlitis* was still obscure. By 1886 R. H. Fitz, of Boston, Massachusetts, had examined 290 cases and observed that in 257 of them it was not the caecum but its appendix which was the site of the disease; hence he named the condition *appendicitis*. Treves operated on his first case of perityphlitis (he at first rejected the name appendicitis) in 1887; by 1890 he, too, was convinced that it was the appendix and not the caecum that was the site of the disease. He did great service to surgery in England by his advocacy of the operative treatment of appendicitis. It was he who first advised that in chronic cases operation should be delayed until a quiescent interval was reached.

So extensive did Treves's private practice become that he gave up his surgeonship at the London Hospital in 1898 at the age of forty-five. In 1899, on the outbreak of war in South Africa, he was called to serve as consulting surgeon to the forces then in the field. On his return to England, he was appointed surgeon extraordinary to Queen Victoria in 1900; he was made C.B. and created K.C.V.O. in 1901.

In the summer of 1902 Treves's fame became suddenly world-wide. On 24 June, two days before the date fixed for his coronation, King Edward VII became acutely ill. His condition was diagnosed as perityphlitis. Treves had been called in by the physicians in attendance. After consultation with Lord Lister and (Sir) Thomas Smith [q.v.], he operated. The king made a good recovery and was crowned on 9 August. Treves was created a baronet in the same year.

In 1900 Treves published an account of his experiences of the South African War under the title *Tale of a Field Hospital*. This was the first of a series of books in which he applied to the description of countries and peoples the gifts which had made him famous as a teacher of anatomy and of surgery. *The Other Side of the Lantern* (1905) is based on a tour round the world; *Highways and Byways of Dorset* (1906) is a guide to his native county; a voyage to the West Indies gave him the materials for *The Cradle of the Deep* (1908); *Uganda for a Holiday* (1910) has a self-explanatory title. His impressions of Palestine are vividly reproduced in *The Land that is Desolate* (1912). Treves visited Italy in order to work out the topography of Robert Browning's *The Ring and the Book*. His inquiries provided the basis for *The Country of 'The Ring and the Book'* (1913).

After the European War of 1914–1918, during which he served at the War Office as president of the Head-quarters Medical Board, the state of Treves's health made it advisable for him to live abroad, first in the south of France, afterwards at Vevey on the shores of the Lake of Geneva. His experiences and impressions of these years are published in *The Riviera of the Corniche Road* (1921) and *The Lake of Geneva* (1922). His last book, entitled *The Elephant Man and other Reminiscences* (1923), is devoted to recollections of medical experiences.

Treves died after a few days' illness at his home at Vevey 7 December 1923. His ashes were buried in Dorchester cemetery, his friend Thomas Hardy being present at the ceremony. He had two daughters, the younger of whom predeceased her father, and the baronetcy became extinct on his death without male issue.

Many honours were conferred upon Treves in addition to those already mentioned: C.B. (1901), sergeant-surgeon to King Edward VII (1902) and to King George V (1910), and G.C.V.O. (1905). He received honorary degrees from several universities, and the students of the university of Aberdeen elected him to the rectorship of their university (1905–1908).

Treves loved the sea, holding a master's certificate. He was a strong swimmer and fond of bicycling. He avoided social entertainments, preferring to be in bed by ten o'clock so as to be fresh for work at six in the morning. His early morning hours he devoted to study and correspondence.

There is a portrait of Treves by Sir Luke Fildes at the London Hospital Medical College. A cartoon by 'Spy' appeared in *Vanity Fair* 19 July 1900.

[*The Times*, 10 December 1923; V. G. Plarr, *Lives of the Fellows of the Royal College of Surgeons of England*, 2 vols., revised by Sir D'A. Power and others, 1930; *British Medical Journal*, 1923, vol. ii, p. 1185 (portrait).]

A. Keith.

TROUBRIDGE, Sir ERNEST CHARLES THOMAS (1862–1926), admiral, was born 15 July 1862 at Hampstead. He belonged to a family which for several generations had been connected with the fighting services. Rear-Admiral Sir Thomas Troubridge, the first baronet [q.v.], who gained distinction at the battles of Cape St. Vincent and the Nile, was described by Nelson, his close friend, as 'the most meritorious sea officer of his standing in the service'. His only son, Sir Edward Thomas Troubridge, the second baronet [q.v.], was present at the battle of Copenhagen. Troubridge's father, Colonel Sir Thomas St. Vincent Hope Cochrane Troubridge, the third baronet [q.v.], fought in the Crimean War, losing his right leg and left foot at the battle of Inkermann. He married Louisa Jane, daughter of Daniel Gurney, of North Runcton, Norfolk, and Ernest Troubridge was their third son.

After a short time at Wellington College, Troubridge entered the *Britannia* as a naval cadet in 1875, and was promoted lieutenant out of the royal yacht *Victoria and Albert* in 1884. While serving in the *Sultan* in Suda Bay, Crete, four years later, he saved the life of a young signalman who fell overboard, in the darkness, from a torpedo boat which was going at full speed. He was awarded the silver medal of the Royal Humane Society. In 1895 he was promoted commander, and was appointed in the following year to the *Revenge*, flagship successively of Rear-Admirals Sir Robert Harris and Sir Gerard Noel, and thus came to take part in the international blockade of Crete, in 1897–1898, which was praised by Lord Salisbury in the House of Lords as an example of successful naval diplomacy.

After his promotion to captain in 1901, Troubridge acted successively as naval attaché to the courts of Vienna, Madrid, and Tokio. He was serving in Tokio when the Russo-Japanese War broke out early in 1904, and by special permission of the Japanese government was embarked in one of the Japanese warships. He was the only non-combatant European officer to witness the battle of Chemulpo (9 February 1904) and the actions off Port Arthur, but he subsequently denied that he had taken any part, as had been suggested, in the preparation of Admiral Togo's plans. He furnished the British Admiralty with reports which were of the highest value in the evolution of naval policy. Besides being decorated by the Emperor of Japan, he was created a C.M.G. (1904) and received the M.V.O. (1904) 'as a mark of his Majesty's personal appreciation of his services in the Far East'.

Soon after returning to England, Troubridge was attached to the suite of King Edward VII during the king's visit to Kiel in 1904. In March 1907 he was appointed to the battleship *Queen* as captain of the flagship and chief of the staff to the commander-in-chief, Admiral Sir Charles Drury, and as commodore was subsequently (1908–1910) in command of the Royal Naval Barracks at Chatham. In 1910 he was selected for the position of private secretary to the first lord of the Admiralty. He served both Mr. Reginald McKenna and Mr. Winston Churchill in that capacity, and on the formation of the Naval War Staff in January 1912 was chosen by the latter to organize and direct the new 'brain of the navy', and became chief of the War Staff. Whilst serving at the Admiralty he was promoted to rear-admiral (1911).

In January 1913 Troubridge was appointed, with his flag in the *Defence*, to command the cruiser squadron of the Mediterranean fleet, of which Admiral Sir Archibald Berkeley Milne was commander-in-chief. He was thus destined to play a leading part in one of the decisive incidents of the European War, the fruitless attempt, in the opening days of the War, to intercept the German cruisers *Goeben* and *Breslau* in the Mediterranean. For the failure to bring these two vessels to action, the former one of the fastest and most powerful battle-cruisers afloat, both the commander-in-chief and the rear-admiral of the cruiser squadron were blamed when it became known that the two vessels had eluded the British forces south of Greece and escaped into the Dardanelles, on 10 August 1914, to the great satisfaction of the Turks. It was suggested that this German naval move was the decisive factor in causing the Turkish government to throw in its lot with the Central Powers. Upon his return to England in consequence of the Franco-British agreement under which the French assumed supreme command in the Mediterranean, Milne gave an explanation to the Admiralty of his action and he was exonerated. Subsequently, Troubridge appeared before a court-martial, being charged that 'from negligence or default he did on 7 August forbear to chase H.I.G.M.'s *Goeben*, being an enemy then flying'. The court decided that Troubridge had acted loyally in accordance with his instructions, that he was justified in regarding the enemy's forces as superior to his own, in daylight, and that although, if he had carried on the chase, he might have brought the *Goeben* to action in the Cervi channel, south of Greece, he would not have been justified, without further orders, in quitting the station allotted to him. The charge was held to have been not proved, and Troubridge was 'fully and honourably' acquitted in November 1914. In order that he might attend the court-martial he had been recalled from the blockade of the Dardanelles which he had assumed under the orders of the French commander-in-chief.

In January 1915 Troubridge went out to Serbia as head of the British naval mission, and organized the evacuation of the Serbian army and refugees. During the Serbian retreat Troubridge rendered conspicuous services. His 'influence with the Serbian generals was very great. From the moment when he arrived on the Danube he had won their affection and respect. Throughout the retreat his proud military bearing and the self-control of his officers had been noticed by everybody. The Serbian authorities were very bitter about the Allies; but their affection for the British admiral had never wavered, and when they arrived at the coast one of their first acts had been to give him authority over their own soldiers and fellow countrymen' [*Naval Operations*, vol. iv, p. 118].

Troubridge returned home early in 1916 and was subsequently, in September 1916, appointed on the personal staff of the Crown Prince of Serbia. He was given command of a naval contingent which was successful in preventing Belgrade from being bombarded and the Serbian troops harassed. His association with the Serbian government continued until after peace was signed in June 1919. In June 1920 he was appointed British representative on the International Danube commission, and acted as its president till March 1924. This was his last active service. He had retired from the navy in 1921, having been promoted vice-admiral in June 1916 and admiral in January 1919.

Troubridge died suddenly from heart failure, at Biarritz, 28 January 1926. His attractive personality and genial manners made him one of the most popular naval officers of his day. He was twice married: first, in 1891 to Edith (died 1900), younger daughter of William Duffus, of Halifax, Nova Scotia, by whom he had one son and two daughters; secondly, in 1908 to Una Elena, daughter of Captain Henry Ashworth Taylor, M.V.O., and granddaughter of Sir Henry Taylor [q.v.]; by her he had one daughter.

[*The Times*, 30 January 1926; *Navy Lists*; Sir H. Newbolt, (Official) *History of the Great War. Naval Operations*, vol. iv, 1928; Admiral Sir A. Berkeley Milne, *The Flight of the Goeben and the Breslau*, 1921; personal knowledge.]

A. Hurd.

TUKE, HENRY SCOTT (1858–1929), painter, the younger son of Daniel Hack Tuke [q.v.], physician and governor of Bethlehem Hospital, by his wife, Esther Maria Stickney, of Ridgmont, Holderness, Yorkshire, was born at York 12 June 1858. He was great-great-grandson of William Tuke [q.v.], quaker philanthropist, great-grandson of Henry Tuke [q.v.], quaker writer, grandson of Samuel Tuke [q.v.], and nephew of James Hack Tuke [q.v.], both of whom were also quaker philanthropists. The family, which belonged to the quaker aristocracy, inherited traditions of culture. He showed a precocious talent for drawing, and entered the Slade School of Art in 1875. His first work was hung in the Royal Academy in 1879, and in the following year a portrait group of the Misses Santley attracted attention there. After passing the winter in Florence, he joined Arthur Lemon at Forte dei Marmi in the spring of 1881, and in this friend's company made his first studies of nude figures in the open air, and realized, as he afterwards put it, 'what one's calling in life was'. In the following autumn Tuke entered the studio of Jean Paul Laurens, and remained in Paris until 1883. Besides working in the atelier he was very much alive to the influences of contemporary French art, visiting exhibitions and making useful acquaintances, particularly that of Bastien-Lepage, for whom he felt the profoundest admiration, and whose example, especially in relation to the degree of finish used to accentuate various parts of a picture, can be traced in Tuke's earlier works.

From childhood Tuke had known and loved Cornwall, and on returning to England he settled there, at first in the artistic colony at Newlyn. In June 1885 he discovered quarters in a cottage on the cliffs above Swanpool, a little west of Falmouth, with neighbouring coves and beaches where he could paint from a nude model undisturbed. He gradually added studios to the cottage, which remained his home until his death. The foundries in the town and the maritime population supplied him with a succession of young male models. At first his subjects included scenes on board ship, of which the large 'All Hands to the Pumps' exhibited at the Royal Academy in 1889, bought by the Chantrey trustees, and now in the Tate Gallery, is a typical example. These were gradually superseded by the studies of nude youths in a sunlit atmosphere, against backgrounds of sea or shore—his most characteristic works and his own favourites as well as those of his public. One of the earliest and the finest, 'August Blue', exhibited in the Academy of 1894, created a stir not only by its artistic qualities but by the contrast which it presented to the frigid, studio nudes uneasily tolerated by the prudery of the time. Its purchase by the Chantrey trustees has been generally applauded: it is now in the Tate Gallery.

Throughout his life Tuke was also employed in painting portraits, the best of which rank with all but the most accomplished works of their class and period. He was elected A.R.A. in 1900 and R.A. in 1914. He was also an associate (1904) and member (1911) of the Royal Society of Painters in Water Colours, and his water colours, especially those of harbour scenes and sailing ships, are distinguished by an ethereal, fairy-like charm.

Tuke more than once visited Marseilles, Venice, and the Italian Riviera, and in 1923, at the age of sixty-five, was tempted, unfortunately as it proved, to accompany some scientific friends on a five-months' excursion to the West Indies and Central America. He failed to find the inspiring subjects he had hoped for; the climate made him ill; and the party had experiences which might have tried the strength of a younger man. He returned home unwell in April 1924, and never fully recovered his vigour, although he took up his work and social life with his old zest. By the end of 1927 his health was causing anxiety, and after long periods of illness he died at Swanpool 13 March 1929, and was buried in Falmouth cemetery. He never married.

Tuke was one of those highly individual painters who make the British school the delight of the English public and the despair of philosophic art critics. He had been thoroughly grounded as a draughtsman at the Slade School, but problems of form and design did not greatly interest him. With a single figure, or a pair, his composition was often felicitous, but he rarely combined a larger number without confusion. His technique as a painter, assimilated by an inquiring and receptive temperament in Parisian studios with traditional tendencies, and modified later by study of the French impressionists, was in general experimental, but usually skilful and apposite. As a colourist he was sure of succeeding with certain prescribed schemes. His pictures were never merely illustrations, indeed his few mythological subjects are wholly unconvincing. Allowing for complete dissimilarity of theme, his works may be compared not inaptly with those of George Morland: both appeal to a distinct class of admirers for reasons connected with their subjects apart from their art, and the best works of each claim respect for their art quite apart from their subjects.

Although an extremely industrious painter, Tuke successfully pursued sports and games—yacht-racing, deep-sea fishing, cricket, bicycling, and bridge; and to those not familiar with his habits he seemed almost as eager about them as in his profession. His sympathy with the young kept him youthful in spirit. His considerable reading filled the background of a serious and reflective mind. His views on political, religious, and moral questions were shared with a large circle of close friends, and his social attachments in all ranks of life were numberless.

An excellent self-portrait of Tuke belongs to Mr. Colin W. Kennedy.

[*The Times*, 14 March 1929; Maria Tuke Sainsbury, *Henry Scott Tuke. A Memoir*, 1933 (compiled by his sister with the aid of summary journals kept by him, with illustrations of his works including the self-portrait, and containing three interesting letters from Samuel Butler); personal knowledge.] C. F. Bell.

TURNER, CUTHBERT HAMILTON (1860–1930), ecclesiastical historian and New Testament scholar, was born in Paddington 7 July 1860, the eldest son of Edwin Goldwin Turner, solicitor, by his wife, Catharine, daughter of Cuthbert Finch, M.D. In 1872 he was elected at the same time as (Sir) Charles Oman, his lifelong friend, and (Professor) D. S. Margoliouth, to a scholarship at Winchester. There he laid the foundations of his accurate scholarship, acquired a beautiful handwriting, discussed theology—he was even then an earnest high churchman—and maintained in debate the cause of Gladstonian liberalism.

In 1879 Turner proceeded, as a scholar, to New College, Oxford; and in Oxford the whole of his maturer life was spent. He did brilliantly in classical honour moderations, obtaining in 1881 one of the best first-classes of the year. With every aptitude for historical study, he was not born to be a philosopher, and it must have been a consolation that the second class in *literae humaniores* in 1883 included, besides his own, the names of F. J. Haverfield and T. B. Strong.

After taking his degree, Turner stayed on in Oxford, writing reviews for the *Guardian* and political articles for the *Oxford Review*; he hoped in vain for a fellowship and for the opportunity of teaching at his own college theology, which he was studying with keen interest and in which he obtained a first class in 1884; but no college work came his way until 1885, when he was appointed theological lecturer at St. John's College. In the following year he won the Denyer and Johnson scholarship; by that time he had acquired a deep knowledge of the methods and problems of chronology in their bearing on the history of the Early Church. This knowledge enabled him in 1887 to complete a first-rate piece of research, and to establish conclusively the correct date (Saturday, 22 February 156) of the martyrdom of St. Polycarp [*Studia Biblica*, vol. xi]. Turner had the knack of regarding all historical questions *sub specie temporis*, and it was characteristic of him that his earliest original work should have been a minute inquiry in that field.

In 1888 William Bright [q.v.], the regius professor of ecclesiastical history at Oxford, appointed Turner as his assistant-lecturer, a recognition which Turner never forgot. He continued to work for Bright until the latter's death in 1901, after which he repaid his debt of gratitude by preparing for publication the professor's lectures on *The Age of the Fathers* (1903). In 1889 Turner became a fellow of Magdalen College. The prize fellowship to which he was then elected—after a close contest with F. E. Brightman and R. B. Rackham—was renewed as a research fellowship in 1896, and at regular intervals thereafter; so that for forty-one years he retained his place in the college which had adopted him.

As a fellow of Magdalen, Turner always took some share in the work of lecturing for the theological school, and in such tutorial work as came to him from the colleges (from New College in particular); but he was above all bent on making a substantial contribution to the study of Christian antiquity. It was not easy for him to choose one direct road of research. He wanted to write history; but he was keenly interested in textual criticism and alive to the importance of producing accurate texts. When he chose to concentrate primarily upon the textual material of early Western canon law, he had it in mind to work at the same time upon a book which would have been similar in scale to Duchesne's *Histoire de l'Église*. But he found himself drawn to follow by-roads of learning: his studies in canon law involved complex investigations into the history of manuscripts and manuscript tradition; he became increasingly interested in New Testament studies; and in the end he left behind him no such church history as he had planned to write, but one *magnum opus* carried a long way towards completion, and a large number of *opuscula* which ranged in subject over many fields of research.

Turner's position down to 1920 was that of a research fellow. He was also the first holder of the Speaker's lecturership in biblical studies from 1906 to 1910, and a university lecturer in early Christian history and literature from 1914 to 1920. During this period he was an active member of the board of the faculty of theology. In 1920, when Walter Lock succeeded William Sanday in the Lady Margaret chair of divinity, Turner succeeded Lock in Dean Ireland's professorship of exegesis, a position which he held for the remainder of his life.

Turner's main vocation as a scholar was to edit the successive *fasciculi* of his great work, *Ecclesiae Occidentalis Monumenta Juris Antiquissima*. A general sketch of the development of early canon law, in a chapter contributed by Turner to the *Cambridge Medieval History*, vol. i (1911), on 'The Organization of the Church', and a course of Birkbeck lectures given at Trinity College, Cambridge, in 1921 and 1922 (but never published) were the only elucidations which he ever supplied of the documents published in his *Monumenta*. The nucleus of early Western canon law was formed by what was believed in the West to be Nicene material; but the word 'Nicene' did not cover the whole Nicene code and was allowed to include much that was not Nicene at all; other Eastern councils, such as those of Ancyra, Neo-Caesarea, Gangra, and Antioch, were appended to it, and the canons of Sardica were commonly joined without a break to those of Nicaea. In the early collections of canon law, its three elements—the 'Nicene', the Latin, and the papal decretals—were combined with bewildering diversity. Turner set himself to edit all these collections, beginning with the Latin versions of the Canons of the Apostles, going on to Nicaea and beyond that as far as Ephesus and Chalcedon, and including also the fourth- and fifth-century councils of Africa, Gaul, and Spain. Six sections of this work were published (tom. i, four parts, 1899, 1904, 1913, 1930; tom. ii, two parts, 1907, 1913); they contain the Canons of the Apostles, the Nicene Council, and those of Ancyra, Neo-Caesarea, Gangra, and Antioch; two *fasciculi* also include matter supplementary to Nicaea, a fine piece of work upon the Council of Sardica, and the *Gesta de nomine Apiarii*, the record of a crucial dispute between the Churches of Rome and Carthage. Two more sections, containing the first and second Councils of Arles, with that of Valence, and the Councils of Laodicea and Constantinople respectively, were all but finished at the time of Turner's death. The editing of this material involved the collation of a large number of manuscripts and many visits to foreign libraries. In his yearly journeys abroad for this purpose Turner, who never married, enjoyed, for twenty-two years, the companionship of his mother, whose aid and sympathy are acknowledged in the touching dedication prefixed to a section published in 1930.

Of Turner's minor works the best known is his article on the 'Chronology of the New Testament' in the first volume of

Hastings's *Dictionary of the Bible* (1898). He also contributed an essay on the 'Text of the New Testament' to *Murray's Illustrated Bible Dictionary* (1908), and an elaborate treatise on 'Greek Patristic Commentaries on the Pauline Epistles' to the supplementary volume of the larger work (1904). Each of these is masterly, but the 'Chronology', as Professor Burkitt said, 'took its place from the first as a classic'. Turner did the major part of the work needed to complete an enterprise begun by Sanday—the editing of the New Testament quotations in Irenaeus, a labour begun as early as 1884, and not completed until 1923, when the *Novum Testamentum S. Irenaei* appeared as No. VII in the series *Old Latin Biblical Texts*. For the dean and chapter of Worcester Cathedral he devoted great pains and palaeographical skill to the editing of early manuscript fragments preserved as guard-leaves to books in the chapter library; a stately volume of *Early Worcester MSS.* published by the Clarendon Press in 1916 is the fruit of this research. In 1912 Turner collected some of his earlier work into a volume of essays with the title *Studies in Early Church History*; this included a valuable paper on the 'Letters of St. Cyprian', but an essay on *The History and Use of Creeds and Anathemas in the Early Centuries of the Church*, which had been published for the Church Historical Society in 1906, was too long for inclusion.

From 1910 onwards Turner was greatly interested in the preparation of the volume planned by Henry Barclay Swete [q.v.], *Essays on the Early History of the Church and the Ministry* (1918), and after Swete's death in 1917 he took over the editorial supervision of the volume. His own contribution, an essay on 'Apostolic Succession', was a fully documented study of the word διαδοχή in the earliest centuries and of the problem of non-Catholic orders in the time of St. Augustine. Turner's exposition of 'succession language' in the early Fathers, and of the controversy about Donatist ordinations, attracted a considerable measure of attention; it has also been largely misunderstood, as implying that there was nothing in the early conception of ministerial continuity beyond the numerical following of one bishop by another. It is only just to Turner's memory to say that, as is clear from pp. 107 f. and 195 f. of this essay, he did in fact hold a diametrically opposite view.

Before he was elected professor, Turner undertook for Bishop Gore the revision (1919) of the latter's work on *The Church and the Ministry*, a revision so thorough as to give the book, in its author's opinion, an entirely new value. As professor, he inaugurated his work with a lecture on *The Study of the New Testament, 1883 and 1920*, particularly valuable for its full and just estimate of Sanday's place in the history of scholarship. Another lecture, delivered and published in 1924, on *The Early Printed Editions of the Greek Testament*, had an interesting context, for it was based upon an all but complete collection of sixteenth-century Greek Testaments (including the Complutensian Polyglot) which he had made himself in order to give it to his old school. He was happy to be able to transfer the collection to Winchester in the summer before his death. As professor also, Turner made an intensive study of St. Mark's Gospel, and this study bore fruit both in the luminous exposition which he contributed to the one-volume *New Commentary on Holy Scripture* issued by the Society for Promoting Christian Knowledge in 1928, and in the 'Notes on Marcan Usage' referred to below.

Among the minor interests which absorbed so much of Turner's working time, mention should be made of the *Lexicon of Patristic Greek*, for which he schemed and planned harder than anyone, and above all, of the *Journal of Theological Studies*, of which he was first editor, 1899–1902. His work for the *Journal* ended only with a paper on the *Actus Petri* which appeared after his death. It was a continuous flood of articles, documents, notes, and reviews; there are studies in the textual history of St. Cyprian, and of his own *Monumenta*, texts of Niceta of Remesiana, a re-collation of Codex Bobiensis (*k*), and documents from the chapter library of Verona; and in vols. xxv–xxix there is a notable series of 'Notes on Marcan Usage' which no future editor of St. Mark can afford to neglect.

Part of the material for a second volume of papers was collected by Turner about 1926; this was put into shape in 1931 at the desire of his literary executors under the title of *Catholic and Apostolic*, with a memoir by his friend and former colleague, H. N. Bate (afterwards dean of York). Some of Turner's projects of work were carried so far by him as to justify their being completed after his death. A study of the St. Gall palimpsest fragments (St. Gall 1395) had been in type since 1909: it was finished and published in 1931, with the title *The Oldest Manuscript of the Vulgate Gospels*, by Professor Alexander

Souter, of Aberdeen University. It remains to complete Turner's text of the *Testimonia* and *Ad Fortunatum* of St. Cyprian, and of the Latin version of the *Shepherd of Hermas*.

Turner's journeys in pursuit of learning brought him into contact with many eminent scholars; he was a welcome guest at the great libraries in Rome, Milan, Paris, Verona, and elsewhere: he maintained a constant correspondence with Ehrle, Delisle, Omont, Mercati, Morin, Spagnolo, and interchanged letters with Pope Pius XI when he was prefect of the Ambrosian Library at Milan. He cherished an especial affection for Verona and its librarian, but the Belgian hagiographer, Père Delehaye, was perhaps his most intimate foreign friend.

With all these and many more Turner moved on terms of equality. He was happy everywhere on the Continent; but although his reverence for such German scholars as Ludwig Traube was very deep, he found French and Italian erudition more congenial than that of the Germans, whose language he never fully mastered. His own mind was of the Latin order: it was accurate, clear, logical, and not given to the pursuit of abstractions. It was at this point that he diverged from William Sanday [q.v.]; united with him in all his interests as a palaeographer, as a critic, as a student of documentary history, although more conservative in his adhesion to the verdicts of tradition, he was not able, like Sanday, to absorb and appraise the mass of German work in those fields. But he knew—and perhaps enjoyed—his own limitations. The history of doctrine and the systematizing of theology did not attract him; the study of texts, their origin, their critical history, was his *métier*, and in that area his work was consistently first-rate. Sanday paid him a tribute which Turner would have valued above all others, in comparing his work with that of F. J. A. Hort. 'At the present time,' he wrote in 1910, 'and taking the whole world over, there is no one who occupies so nearly the position that Hort had in the last generation—with an added effectiveness and force to which Hort did not attain.'

Turner was never robust, though his alertness and vivacity made him seem stronger than he was, and led his friends to think him too minutely careful of his health. Some years after his mother's death in 1914 he moved out of college to a house in North Oxford, where he was always accessible to his old friends, to the younger scholars who attended his seminar on St. Mark, and to a group of promising undergraduates from Eton and Winchester whose friendship gave him the keenest pleasure. He held his professorship for ten years, and seemed likely to hold it for many more. But in the autumn of 1930 he had a sudden seizure and died at Oxford 10 October. He was buried, as he had desired, in his mother's grave at Abingdon.

[Memoir by H. N. Bate prefixed to *Catholic and Apostolic*, 1931; personal knowledge.]

H. N. Bate.

TURNER, HERBERT HALL (1861–1930), astronomer, was born at Leeds 13 August 1861, the eldest son of John Turner, artist, of that town, by his wife, Isabella Hall, of Hexham. He was sent first to Leeds modern school and then to Clifton College, whence he proceeded with a scholarship to Trinity College, Cambridge, in 1879. He graduated as second wrangler in 1882, and was second Smith's prizeman in 1883. Turner was elected a fellow of Trinity in 1884, but left Cambridge that year in order to become chief assistant at the Royal Observatory, Greenwich. There he remained until 1893, when he was appointed to succeed Charles Pritchard [q.v.] as Savilian professor of astronomy at Oxford, with a fellowship at New College. He remained at Oxford for the rest of his life. He was elected F.R.S. in 1896, and was president of the Royal Astronomical Society 1903–1904. He received honorary degrees from various British and foreign universities, was a corresponding member of the Institut de France, and was awarded the Bruce gold medal of the Astronomical Society of the Pacific in 1927. Turner married in 1899 Agnes Margaret, eldest daughter of Robert Whyte, of Blackheath, who survived him with their only child, a daughter. He died of cerebral haemorrhage in Stockholm 20 August 1930 while presiding at a meeting of the International Commission on Seismology.

The first general work in which Turner took part, after going to Greenwich, was the co-ordination of the use of photography in astronomy. A congress was summoned in Paris in 1887, which resulted in the formulation of an international scheme for an astrographic chart and catalogue. The scheme was taken up enthusiastically at the time, although its course was diverted before it was fully under way in order to make photographic observations of the minor planet, Eros, from which the dimensions of the solar system may most favourably be derived. The original scheme is still (1934) in large measure uncompleted. Turner devoted all his energies to the work, writing some papers which have become authoritative, and devising means for expediting progress. He continued at Oxford, and the Oxford University Observatory competed closely with Greenwich in being the first to complete and publish its share. From the beginning he realized the magnitude of the undertaking, and used all his energy to secure early and economical publication. In this he followed no more than his natural bent. Just as he was a convinced advocate of the use of photography in astronomy, so he always urged early publication and the full use of material in hand, a counsel which he did not fail to carry out by his own work. The material in question was necessarily statistical, and often rough, but Turner was very skilful in making simple, harmonic analyses of it. He was also a strong believer in the advantages of good personal relations between scientists, and this he constantly illustrated by his relations with other, especially American, astronomers. He was a vigorous personality, who seldom masked his feelings—a trait which in the eyes of those who valued him mattered little.

Astronomy, first of all the sciences, demands a widespread organization, since it is impossible to make all the necessary observations at a single spot. When international co-operation was re-established in 1919 after the end of the European War, the astrographic catalogue was included as one of the commissions of the International Astronomical Union, and Turner became its first president the same year. Here he used his energy and influence in order to spur the laggards into completing their undertakings. At the same time he was elected first president of the commission on seismology in the International Union for Geodesy and Geophysics. His connexion with seismology was in its origin no more than the expression of his friendship with John Milne [q.v.]. When Milne died in 1913, the world-wide organization which he had built up demanded some one to carry it on. It also needed some reasonable reforms. Partly because no one else was forthcoming, Turner took up the task, first partly at Shide in the Isle of Wight, and afterwards wholly at Oxford. Gradually he became more and more interested in the work, gathered more strings into his hands, and developed it, with the help of some zealous co-workers. In much the same way he first became interested in variable stars, by editing a volume for the *Memoirs* of the Royal Astronomical Society in which are the accumulated observations of George Knott. He never lost that interest, and it was subsequently drawn upon when he edited in the same *Memoirs* the records of Sir Cuthbert Edgar Peek, second baronet [q.v.], and those of Peek's observer, Charles Grover.

Turner entered fully into his environment. When he became a fellow of New College he shared whole-heartedly in its life. In the same way, he took a full part in university affairs, including the inevitable quarrels. He was a frequent writer of letters to *The Times*, and a hearty supporter of many causes before they became popular, such as 'daylight saving'. Although a man of strong feelings, who played his various games in earnest, he was a good loser. He was an incessant worker, and, perhaps because of this, he always seemed free to discuss other people's affairs, and, in a remarkable degree, to help to forward them.

[*The Times*, 21 August 1930; personal knowledge.] R. A. SAMPSON.

URE, ALEXANDER, BARON STRATHCLYDE (1853–1928), lawyer and politician, the second son of John Ure, of Cairndhu, Helensburgh, merchant and in his day a distinguished lord provost of Glasgow, by his wife, Isabella, daughter of John Gibb, of Glasgow, was born in that city 24 February 1853. He was educated at Larchfield Academy, Helensburgh, and at the university of Glasgow, where he graduated M.A. in 1872, B.L. in 1874, and LL.B. in 1878, and from which he received the honorary degree of LL.D. in 1907. In 1878 he was admitted a member of the Faculty of Advocates and began his career at the Scottish bar. In the following year he married Margaret McDowall, daughter of Thomas Steven, iron merchant in Glasgow. They had one daughter, who died in 1918.

Success came early to Ure, and for him there was no weary waiting for briefs. His influential connexion with the West of Scotland, the source of most of the lucrative commercial litigations in the Parliament House, and a natural gift of robust and telling advocacy secured for him from the outset a steady flow of business. After only fourteen years of junior practice he 'gave up writing', the step which then marked the transition of a Scottish advocate to senior rank, and on the institution of a roll of Queen's Counsel for Scotland in 1897 he was one of the first new Scottish silks. For ten years after his call to the bar (1878–1888) Ure held the lecturership of constitutional law and history in Glasgow University, but this appointment, which did not require him to reside in Glasgow, in no way interfered with his professional advancement. Like so many other ambitious young advocates he took to politics, and Gladstonian Home Rule found in him an ardent supporter. His first attempt to enter parliament as a candidate for West Perthshire in 1892 was unsuccessful. He also failed in 1893 to secure election for Linlithgowshire, but at the general election in 1895 he was returned in the liberal interest as member for that constituency, which he continued to represent until his elevation to the bench in 1913. From 1905 to 1909 he was solicitor-general for Scotland, and in the latter year he succeeded Lord Shaw (afterwards Lord Craigmyle) as lord advocate and was admitted a privy councillor.

Ure's activities during his tenure of the lord advocateship brought him into conspicuous prominence. It was a period of political high tension, and Mr. Lloyd George's budget for 1909–1910 was the storm-centre. Ure threw himself into the fray with characteristic energy and devoted himself especially to advocating the taxation of land values. His physical vigour, his ubiquity, and his powers of relentless rhetoric rendered him an invaluable party henchman. There were few towns of any importance in England or Scotland which did not resound with his perfervid oratory. Unfortunately, there were occasions when his enthusiasm led him to outstep the generally accepted limits of political controversy, notably in his utterances regarding the unionist party's policy in the matter of old-age pensions. These brought upon him a severe rebuke by Mr. Arthur Balfour, who at a meeting in the Constitutional Club on 26 October 1909 charged him with having been guilty of a 'frigid and calculated lie'. The phrase, singularly inappropriate to Ure's sanguine temperament, passed into currency, and its imputation was not entirely dispelled by Ure's brilliant defence of himself in a speech in the House of Commons on 3 November 1909. It was in that year also that Ure conducted the prosecution in the trial of Oscar Slater for murder and secured from the jury a verdict of guilty by a majority of nine to six. The death sentence was commuted, but the verdict gave rise to a prolonged agitation which a somewhat inconclusive departmental inquiry failed to satisfy, and which was not finally set at rest until, in July 1928, after Slater's liberation, his conviction was reviewed and quashed by the High Court of Justiciary under the Criminal Appeal Act [see DOYLE, Sir Arthur Conan].

In 1913 Ure succeeded Lord Dunedin as lord justice-general for Scotland and lord president of the Court of Session, and in 1914 was raised to the peerage under the title of Baron Strathclyde, of Sandyford, co. Lanark. The transition from party polemics to the dispassionate atmosphere of the judiciary was abrupt, but it was achieved with remarkable success, for the new lord president proved himself from the first an efficient and capable judge, courteous, attentive, and unusually alert. He always had an eye to the practical issue, and his judgments are models of clarity. But the easy certitude which stood him in such good stead in his political career was a less suitable endowment for a judge, and his reported opinions exhibit little of that balanced discussion of legal principles which best contributes to the elucidation and advancement of the law. Undoubtedly Ure was better as an advocate than as a judge, though in neither capacity was he learned in the technical sense. He particularly excelled in cross-examination, where his direct methods and his masterful style found full scope. He had a quite admirable gift, too, of lucid exposition, aided by a retentive memory, which enabled him to handle intricate matters with enviable facility. Sometimes, however, his invincible optimism led him to see both facts and law as he wished them to be rather than as they were.

Ure's mental vigour found its counterpart in his physical constitution, and he was an intrepid yachtsman and an untiring walker. On one occasion he tramped from Edinburgh to London, and on another from London to Land's End. During the European War he rendered valuable service in the promotion of the Scottish War Savings Association, in recognition of which he was created G.B.E. in 1917.

In 1920 Ure was compelled by ill-health to resign from the bench, and he then retired to Cairndhu, the family residence on the Clyde at Helensburgh. It was characteristic of him that he gave up the pension to which he was entitled, but with which his private means enabled him to dispense. In 1921 he published a pleasantly written biographical study of Lord Fullerton, a learned senator of the College of Justice for whom he had a great admiration. He died at Helensburgh 2 October 1928, survived by his wife, and the peerage then became extinct.

[*The Times*, 3 October 1928; *Scotsman*, 3 October 1928; *Glasgow Herald*, 3 October 1928; Hansard, *Parliamentary Debates*; *Annual Register*; personal knowledge.]

MACMILLAN.

VAUGHAN, BERNARD JOHN (1847–1922), Jesuit priest, was born at Courtfield, Herefordshire, 20 September 1847, the sixth son in the family of thirteen children born to Colonel John Francis Vaughan and his first wife, Louisa Elizabeth, third daughter of John Rolls, of The Hendre, Monmouth, grandfather of the first Baron Llangattock. The family inherited an intensely Catholic tradition from pre-Reformation times; and through fines and double land-tax they had lost all but a fraction of the fifty thousand acres they once owned. Of Colonel Vaughan's children, four of the five daughters became nuns, and six sons became priests; the eldest being Herbert Alfred Vaughan [q.v.], cardinal archbishop of Westminster, and the second, Roger William Bede Vaughan [q.v.], archbishop of Sydney.

Bernard Vaughan was sent in 1859 to Stonyhurst College, which had been given to the Jesuits by his great-grandfather, Thomas Weld, father of Cardinal Thomas Weld [q.v.]; and he never faltered in his early desire to become a Jesuit. Undistinguished at school, although he had abundant vitality and enthusiasm, he became a Jesuit novice in 1866. Subsequently he filled minor teaching and other posts at Jesuit colleges, chiefly at Beaumont College, Windsor. In 1880 he was ordained priest, and in 1883 was sent to the church of the Holy Name in Manchester; his eldest brother, Herbert, the future cardinal, was then bishop of Salford. Vaughan developed his church rapidly, and became its superior in 1888. His unconventional methods as a preacher and organizer soon made him a local celebrity, especially when, in order to raise funds for building, he hired the St. James's Hall in October 1890 and converted it into a replica of St. Peter's Piazza, Rome, with all manner of entertainments and scientific exhibits which attracted great crowds from Lancashire and Yorkshire. He revealed unsuspected powers as a popular preacher, with his distinguished bearing, fine voice and delivery, startling use of slang and of homely allusions, and peculiar aptitude for crude epigrams. A series of local controversies enhanced his popularity as a formidable debater, who never failed in good humour and quick repartee. But his wide following in Lancashire arose chiefly from his devoted work among the poorest classes, and his ceaseless agitation to improve the conditions of housing and of factory labour.

As Vaughan's reputation grew, he was invited to preach courses of sermons in Rome and on the Riviera; and in 1898 his preaching at Cannes attracted the notice of the Prince of Wales. A close personal friendship with the prince and other royal personages followed, and these connexions soon led to his being transferred, albeit reluctantly, from Manchester to the Jesuit house at Farm Street, Mayfair, in 1899. His crudely sensational methods seemed unlikely to succeed in London, but he became conspicuous when he brought an action for libel against a protêstant paper, *The Rock*, and was awarded substantial damages (1902). His public reputation increased and culminated in 1906 when, during the London 'season', he preached in Farm Street church a series of sermons on the 'sins of society'—a vigorous denunciation of the selfishness and ostentatious vulgarity of the rich, the growing disregard of marriage ties, and the increase of birth restriction. In subsequent years he preached other courses of sermons with titles such as 'Is England Christian?', 'Is Religion Worth While?', 'The Gospel of Doing Good', and he was in constant demand as a preacher and public speaker.

Vaughan's sermons, when published, had a wide sale, but they were much less sensational than the selected passages which had been eagerly quoted in the press. He took great pains to be accurate in theology and history, and most of his sermons, even on topical questions, were carefully revised for him. His reputation was extended by a visit to Canada in 1910, when he was cathedral preacher at the Eucharistic Congress at Montreal, and subsequent tours in the United States of America (1911–1913), China and Japan (1913), and Africa (1922). During the European War his native patriotism and his enthusiasm for the British Empire found full scope, and he worked ceaselessly to raise funds for war charities.

Vaughan had so deliberately courted publicity in order to obtain the widest audience that his real character was generally misunderstood. Profoundly humble and simple, he was unfailing in obedience to his Jesuit superiors, and for years he went to confession every day. The dominating interest of his life was his personal work among the poor, first in Manchester and later in the East end of London. For them he used all his success and influence, as when he persuaded Madame Adelina Patti to return to London in 1904 and 1908 for Albert Hall concerts which he organized in order to raise funds for a club-house and an orphanage in Whitechapel. He was no socialist, but for years his energies were mainly devoted to campaigns for social reform, and in the many great cities which he visited he always investigated the poorest districts himself, and denounced remorselessly whatever seemed unjust or disgraceful. His published works include several pamphlets issued by the Catholic Truth Society, notably *The Roman Claims* and *Faith and Reason*, *Socialism* (1910), *Socialism from the Christian Standpoint*, (1913), besides several volumes of sermons. A posthumous volume, *Loaves and Fishes*, compiled from his note-books, was issued in 1923. Years of insomnia and nervous strain undermined his strength, and he died at Manresa, the Jesuit novitiate at Roehampton, 31 October 1922.

A cartoon of Vaughan by 'Spy' appeared in *Vanity Fair* 30 January 1907.

[C. C. Martindale, *Father Bernard Vaughan*, 1923; J. G. Snead-Cox, *Life of Cardinal Vaughan*, 1910; private information. Portrait, *Royal Academy Pictures*, 1908.]

D. Gwynn.

VEITCH, Sir HARRY JAMES (1840–1924), horticulturist, was born at Exeter 29 June 1840, the second of the three sons of James Veitch, junior (1815–1869), the foremost horticulturist of his day. He was grandson of James Veitch, the elder (1792–1863), who founded the Veitch nurseries at Exeter and purchased in 1853 the nurseries of Messrs. Knight & Perry at Chelsea, and uncle of James Herbert Veitch [q.v.]. He was educated at Exeter grammar school and continued his training at Altona, near Hamburg, and at Paris with the firm of Vilmorin-Andrieux. He joined his father's business in Chelsea (which was carried on separately from the Exeter business after 1864) when he was eighteen, and was connected with the firm of James Veitch & Son during the long period when the nurseries at Chelsea and at Coombe Wood, Surrey, and Langley, Buckinghamshire, had a world-wide reputation.

Realizing the importance of introducing new plants to cultivation, the firm sent out travellers to various parts of the world, and to its enterprise in this respect are owed many excellent plants grown in English gardens to-day. Harry Veitch was keenly interested in this side of the work. Among the firm's plant-collectors may be mentioned Richard Pearce, who visited Chile, Peru, and Bolivia and introduced *Eucryphia pinnatifolia*, the begonias which are the parents of the large-flowered, tuberous begonias of the hot-house, and many other plants now in cultivation. To John Gould Veitch, Harry Veitch's elder brother, who was sent to Japan, is due the introduction of the well-known *Ampelopsis Veitchii*, and many trees, including the Japanese umbrella pine. Frederick William Burbidge [q.v.], afterwards the curator of the botanic gardens of Trinity College, Dublin, another of the firm's collectors, was sent to Borneo in 1877, and brought back the giant pitcher plant, *Nepenthes Rajah*, from Kina Balu, *N. bicalcarata*, and several orchids. Other collectors were sent to Central and South America, particularly in search of orchids, ferns, and stove plants. But the best-known of the Veitch travellers was Ernest Henry Wilson, afterwards of the Arnold arboretum, Boston, Massachusetts, whose introductions from China are to be found in many English gardens. The firm were pioneers in orchid hybridization and introduced many hybrid orchids and the hybrid *streptocarpus*, begonias, Javan rhododendrons, hippeastrums, and many other plants now commonly grown.

Veitch's active influence in the firm extended over almost the whole of his lifetime, for although he had retired in 1900 he had again to resume control in 1906 owing to the illness of his nephew James Herbert Veitch. He finally retired in 1914. As there was no successor in the family, the nursery at Coombe Wood was sold.

Veitch was closely connected for many years with the Royal Horticultural Society, of which he became treasurer in 1918 at the age of seventy-eight, and later was elected a vice-president. He was awarded the Victoria medal of honour by the Society in 1906 and received several foreign distinctions. In 1912 he was knighted.

Veitch published *The Manual of Coniferae* (1881, second edition 1900) and *The Manual of Orchidaceous Plants* (1887–1894), both works containing much information about plants brought to England by the collectors of the firm. He died at East Burnham Park, Slough, 6 July 1924. Veitch married in 1867 Louisa Mary (died 1921), daughter of Frederick W. Johnston, of Stoke Newington. There were no children of the marriage. His portrait, painted in 1909 by H. G. Riviere, hangs in the council room of the Royal Horticultural Society, Vincent Square.

[J. H. Veitch, *Hortus Veitchii*, 1906; *Gardeners' Chronicle*, 12 July 1924; *Kew Bulletin*, 1924, p. 300; *Nature*, 19 July 1924; personal knowledge.] A. W. Hill.

VENN, JOHN (1834–1923), logician and man of letters, was born at Drypool, Hull, 4 August 1834, the elder son of the Rev. Henry Venn [q.v.], then rector of that parish, by his wife, Martha, daughter of Nicholas Sykes, of Swanland, near Hull. Descended from a Devonshire family of considerable intellectual distinction, his grandfather was the Rev. John Venn [q.v.], the leader of the Clapham Evangelicals, and his great-grandfather was Henry Venn [q.v.], sometime vicar of Huddersfield. Venn was educated first at Sir Roger Cholmley's School, Highgate (now Highgate School), to which place his father had removed upon becoming honorary secretary of the Church Missionary Society, and subsequently at Islington proprietary school. In October 1853 he entered Gonville and Caius College, Cambridge, representing the eighth generation of his family to be admitted to (and to graduate at) Cambridge, or the sister university, and beginning an association with Gonville and Caius College which lasted for seventy years. Elected mathematical scholar in the following year, he took his degree, as sixth wrangler, in January 1857, and was elected fellow of his college a few months later.

Rigidly brought up, as he had been, in the family tradition, it is not surprising that Venn should forthwith have prepared himself for holy orders. Ordained deacon at Ely in 1858, and priest in 1859, he held curacies successively at Cheshunt, Hertfordshire, and at Mortlake, Surrey. After this short experience of parochial work he returned to Cambridge in 1862, and was appointed to the newly created post of college lecturer in moral science, acting for a few months simultaneously as curate at St. Edward's church. Since taking his degree, Venn's attention had been directed more and more to the works of philosophical and metaphysical writers. Augustus De Morgan's treatises, George Boole's *Laws of Thought*, John Austin's *Jurisprudence*, and, most of all, John Stuart Mill's *Logic* so affected him as to cause a revolution in his critical outlook which *Essays and Reviews* (1860) could not counter. Upon resuming academic life, moreover, he found himself in close contact with such men as Henry Sidgwick, J. R. Seeley, Isaac Todhunter, and John Westlake, while outside Cambridge he saw much of his cousins, E. J. S. and A. V. Dicey, and James and Leslie Stephen. It had long ceased to be regarded as an anomaly for a clergyman to preach the then circumscribed evangelical creed and at the same time, without the slightest insincerity, to devote himself actively to philosophical studies; yet, some years later (1883), finding himself still less in sympathy with the orthodox clerical outlook, Venn availed himself of the provisions of the Clerical Disabilities Act. Of a naturally speculative frame of mind, he was wont to say in after-life that, owing to subsequent change in accepted opinion regarding the Thirty-nine Articles, he could consistently have retained his orders; he remained, indeed, throughout his life a man of sincere religious conviction. As Hulsean lecturer in 1869 he published *Some Characteristics of Belief, Scientific and Religious*.

For the next thirty years Venn devoted himself to the study and teaching of logic, at the outset, owing to his mathematical training, paying particular attention to the theory of probability. His first published work was *The Logic of Chance* (1866), which owed its inception to H. T. Buckle's well-known discussion concerning the impossibility of checking the statistical regularity of human actions. Similarly, *Symbolic Logic* (1881) represented a successful attempt, hitherto neglected even by W. S. Jevons, to rationalize and interpret the mechanism of Boole's processes. Many years earlier Venn had adopted the diagrammatic method of illustrating propositions by inclusive and exclusive circles, and he now added the new device of shading the segments of the circles in order to represent the possibilities excluded by the propositions. The moral science tripos was then attracting a growing number of students, among whom were to be found men of such promise and ability as Arthur Balfour, William Cunningham, F. W. Maitland, James Ward, and F. W. H. Myers. As lecturer and examiner Venn played an important part in the development of this tripos, which was characterized by freedom from extraneous control and rested, as is essential with a new subject, upon a friendly intercourse between teachers and taught. In 1889 he completed his trilogy by issuing *The Principles of Empirical Logic*, which, in common with its predecessors, at once became a standard text-book. During this period of his life Venn gradually acquired what was probably the largest private collection of works upon logic ever brought together; this he presented to the University Library in 1888.

Thereafter, apart from lecturing and preparing fresh editions of his books and writing monographs upon statistical and anthropometrical subjects, Venn's activities were devoted to the hitherto neglected subject of university history. In this field his largest single-handed undertaking was represented by the three volumes of the *Biographical History of Gonville and Caius College* (1897), which involved a vast amount of painstaking and methodical search among university, episcopal, and other records. He also edited several volumes of the university archives, e.g., Grace Book Δ (1910) and, with his son, *Matriculations and Degrees, 1544–1659* (1913). *Venn Family Annals* appeared in 1904, and in 1913 he brought together, under the title of *Early Collegiate Life*, many of his own writings and speeches descriptive of Cambridge life and habits in bygone periods. In 1910 he produced *John Caius, a biographical sketch*. Finally, during his latter years, he collaborated with his son in the preparation of the monumental *Alumni Cantabrigienses*, the first two volumes of which (1922) he lived to see in print.

Venn took the Cambridge Sc.D. degree in 1883, and was elected F.R.S. the same year. He married in 1867 Susanna Carnegie, eldest daughter of the Rev. Charles Welland Edmonstone, and had one child, John Archibald, president of Queens' College, Cambridge, since 1932. Of spare build, he was throughout his life a fine walker and mountain climber, a keen botanist, and an excellent talker and linguist. He died at Cambridge 4 April 1923, and was buried at Trumpington. At the time of his death he had been a fellow of his college for sixty-six years, and its president since 1903.

There is a portrait of Venn by C. E. Brock in the combination room of Gonville and Caius College.

[An autobiography (unpublished) written for his family; private information; personal knowledge.] J. A. Venn.

VERNEY, MARGARET MARIA, Lady Verney (1844–1930), historical writer, was born in London 3 December 1844, the elder daughter and co-heiress of Sir John Hay Williams, second baronet, of Bodelwyddan, co. Flint, by his wife, Lady Sarah Elizabeth Pitt, only daughter of William, first Earl Amherst of Arracan [q.v.]. On Sir John Hay Williams's death in 1859, his family retired to Rhianva, a house which he had built for them on the Menai Straits.

Miss Hay Williams married in 1868 Captain Edmund Hope Verney, R.N., liberal member of parliament for North Buckinghamshire, 1885–1886 and 1889–1891, who succeeded his father, Sir Harry Verney, second baronet [q.v.], of Claydon House, Buckinghamshire, in 1894 and died in 1910. They had one son, Sir Harry Calvert Williams Verney (born 1881), fourth baronet, and three daughters. Lady Verney died at Rhianva 7 October 1930, and was buried at Llandegfan.

From 1868 Lady Verney's time and interests were divided between her two homes. Both in Anglesey and in Buckinghamshire she took an active interest in village life, especially in education and nursing. She served on the rural school boards, was co-opted to the Buckinghamshire county education committee, and originated the association for the loan of pictures to schools; later she started a similar scheme for Anglesey. In Wales her activities extended to higher education in connexion with the University College of North Wales at Bangor; she was an original member of the court of governors, and was prominent on the hostels committee. She was a member of the University of Wales court (afterwards the council) from 1894 to 1922, and she continued to represent that body on the court of the National Library of Wales and on the Bangor council. In 1919 she was appointed junior deputy chancellor of the university, and received the honorary degree of LL.D.

As a convinced liberal in politics, Lady Verney worked enthusiastically for her husband and son in election campaigns.

Throughout her life she showed indomitable industry and real breadth of view, well supported by unfailing courage, patience, and humour.

Lady Verney's principal achievement, however, lay in the literary work which she took up as an amateur and completed as an acknowledged authority. Between 1858 and 1890 Frances Parthenope (*née* Nightingale, the sister of Florence Nightingale), second wife of Sir Harry Verney, had discovered the historical value of the seventeenth and eighteenth century letters, diaries, and accounts preserved at Claydon House. Beginning with magazine articles, she gradually worked up a connected history of the Verney family down to 1650, which, finely illustrated by reproductions of portraits, was completed for the press by M. M. Verney as Volumes I and II of *Memoirs of the Verney Family* with a preface by Dr. S. R. Gardiner, in 1892. These were followed by Volume III (1650–1660) in 1894, and by Volume IV (1660–1696) in 1899, which were wholly the work of the younger lady. The Claydon manuscripts, including over 30,000 letters dated before 1700, with drafts and copies of answers, required elaborate arrangement and comparison. The original work attracted so much attention that a thoroughly revised re-issue in two volumes was called for in 1904, and a third edition in 1925.

In addition to contributions about the Verneys to magazines and to this DICTIONARY, Lady Verney published a short *Memoir of Sir Henry Cunningham* (1923), and a text-book of county history, *Bucks. Biographies* (1912), for use in elementary schools. Later on she returned to the family papers, and just before her death (1930) saw through the press two supplementary volumes, the first dealing with the correspondence of John Verney, Viscount Fermanagh (1696–1717), the second with that of the two Earls Verney (1717–1791). The material is of inferior interest, but the workmanship shows no sign of weakness. The prominence given in Lady Verney's works to domestic as well as public matters has done much to encourage similar research; and they form as a whole a serious contribution to English history.

A full-length portrait of Lady Verney as a bride, by Sir William Richmond, hangs at Claydon House. A memorial tablet was placed in Middle Claydon church in 1936.

[*In Memoriam, M. M. Verney 1930*, privately printed, with added bibliography, 1932; private information; personal knowledge.]

H. E. D. BLAKISTON.

VINOGRADOFF, SIR PAUL GAVRILOVITCH (1854–1925), jurist and historian, was born at Kostroma, Russia, 1 December 1854, the eldest son (three sons having been born of a previous marriage) of Gavril (Gabriel) Kiprianovitch Vinogradoff by his second wife, Elena Pavlovna, daughter of General Kobeloff, who had fought in the war of 1812. Kiprianovitch was a schoolmaster of more than average attainments, and a year after Paul's birth he was transferred from Kostroma to a boys' school of high standing at Moscow. Here Vinogradoff was educated at a gymnasium and entered the university in the faculty of history and philosophy at the age of sixteen. On graduating (1875) he obtained a scholarship which enabled him to study at Berlin under Theodor Mommsen and Heinrich Brunner. Instruction under such masters dedicated him decisively to a career of learning. He was accustomed to say that the three greatest minds which he had encountered, and the three most powerful intellectual influences in his life, were the German Mommsen, the Russian Vasili Kluchevsky, and the Englishman Frederic William Maitland [q.v.].

Vinogradoff's first learned paper (1876), written in German, was the fruit of his Berlin training; and in the next few years he immersed himself in the study of a subject which was to prove a special preoccupation throughout his life. His first book, *The Origin of Feudal Relations in Lombard Italy* (Russian, 1881), embodied researches which had been begun by him three years previously in Italy. He was next attracted by the feudal land system in England, and in 1883 came to London to investigate in the Public Record Office material which at that time had been insufficiently explored. During this visit he not only gained a sympathetic insight into English life, but came in contact with some of the most distinguished scholars of the day, such as Sir Henry Maine, Sir Frederick Pollock, and Frederic Seebohm [q.v.]. But the most pregnant friendship which he formed was with Frederic William Maitland, then a young man of brilliant gifts who had not yet devoted himself definitely to a life of scholarship. Vinogradoff's eloquent and enthusiastic discourse decided Maitland upon his vocation; and the influence was not only reciprocal, but led immediately to tangible results of the first importance to English legal history. In a letter to the *Athenaeum* (19 July 1884) Vinogradoff called attention to a manuscript in the British Museum which had been forgotten since Sir Anthony Fitzherbert [q.v.] had used it for his *La Graunde Abridgement* (1514). This was the celebrated 'Note Book' of Henry de Bracton [q.v.], out of which grew the first-fruits of Maitland's genius—one of the richest contributions to modern legal scholarship in England.

The results of Vinogradoff's inquiry into English feudal institutions gained him the doctorate at Moscow in 1884, and were published in Russian in 1887 and in an English translation in 1892 as *Villainage in England*, which many critics still regard as his best and most lucid work. His reputation was now firmly established, and in 1887, after three years' probation as extraordinary professor, he was appointed full professor of history in the university of Moscow. His sympathies had always been liberal, though in no sense revolutionary: and his cosmopolitan training set him in opposition to the narrow and reactionary Slavophilism which at that time stunted education in Russia. He at once became both a teacher of galvanic influence and an indefatigable apostle of educational reform. According to his own account, he 'endeavoured not only to form a school of historians, trained in the methods of western scholarship, but also to influence the progress of general education in Russia'. He was elected councillor of the municipal Duma and became chairman of its educational committee. This gave him an opportunity to promote an extension of the network of elementary schools which made it possible for every child living in Moscow to go through a course of primary education. In 1896 he founded a paedogogic society in which teachers of all grades could meet to discuss problems and conditions of education. Not content with these arduous administrative labours, Vinogradoff wrote several elementary text-books of history, some of which still remain current. In many respects he succeeded in introducing permanent reforms; but a reactionary element in the government steadily gained the ascendant; free speech and free thought among the university students were repressed with increasing severity, until the university itself was closed in 1899. Vinogradoff's moderate and carefully elaborated plan for a *modus vivendi* was rejected. This he felt to be a test case, and, finding his position impossible, he resigned his professorship in 1901.

In 1897, while on a visit to Norway, Vinogradoff had married Louise, daughter of Judge August Stang, of Arendal, Norway, whose wife was an Englishwoman, Isabel Mary Newbold. A daughter was born of this marriage in 1898 and a son in 1901. With his wife and children Vinogradoff came to England after his resignation, and in 1903 was elected to the Corpus Christi chair of jurisprudence at Oxford, in succession to Sir Frederick Pollock. This position he held until his death. He at once introduced into Oxford a hitherto unfamiliar method of seminar teaching, which gathered round him a group of enthusiastic students of history and law. Their versatile and meticulous researches are to be found in an edition of the *Survey of the Honour of Denbigh, 1334* (1914) and in the valuable series of *Oxford Studies in Social and Legal History* (1909–1927). Another direct outcome of the seminar was Vinogradoff's own *English Society in the Eleventh Century* (1908), which had been preceded in 1905 by *The Growth of the Manor*. His output was prolific during the whole period of his professorship; besides innumerable articles and reviews in learned periodicals all over the world, he contributed copiously to encyclopædias and to the *Cambridge Medieval History*; and, before the monumental *Outlines of Historical Jurisprudence* (1920–1922) of his latest years, he produced a luminous short study of *Roman Law in Mediaeval Europe* (1909) and a less successful sketch of English jurisprudence, *Common Sense in Law* (1914). In addition, he served as a director of publications for both the British Academy and the Selden Society. He delivered special courses of lectures in many European countries, in the United States, and in India.

Vinogradoff did not lose touch with Russia, and for many years made annual visits. He was in St. Petersburg during the revolution of 1905, and might have accepted the portfolio of public instruction in the new liberal government but for his disapproval of anti-Semitic restriction in education. In 1908, 1909, and 1911 he lectured in Moscow; but the government was again pursuing an oppressive policy, and Vinogradoff resigned, in common with sixty other instructors, when he found police spies in his lecture-room. The outbreak of the European War found him in high hopes for the moral and social regeneration of Russia. He worked untiringly for the mutual understanding of Russia and England, using to the utmost, by pen and by tongue, his unrivalled knowledge of both countries; and in 1917 he was knighted for these services. The disillusionment which awaited him dealt a mortal blow. In 1914 he had written: 'It is our firm conviction that the sad tale of reaction and oppression is at an end in Russia, and that our country will issue from this momentous crisis with the insight and strength required for the constructive and progressive statesmanship of which it stands in need.' The Russian *débâcle*, the 'Red Terror', and the triumph of Bolshevism shattered, one by one, Vinogradoff's lifelong patriotic aspirations, which were a part of his deepest nature. He never recovered from the wound, and a part of him died when he renounced his Russian nationality in 1918. To his spiritual suffering were added personal distresses: he was obliged to stand by helpless while friends and kindred endured untold miseries in Russia; his own material losses changed his circumstances from comfort to exiguity; and rapidly failing eyesight supplied a crowning affliction. Although in his last years he was extremely active in writing, travelling, and lecturing, nothing of the savour of life remained for him except his intellectual pursuits and his strong family ties. He died suddenly of pneumonia in Paris 19 December 1925, shortly after adding the doctorate of Paris University to his numerous honorary degrees.

In the preface to his earliest English work, *Villainage in England*, Vinogradoff wrote: 'Nobody will deny that historical study is extending more and more in the direction of what is now called anthropology and social science.' The words were prophetic of the future trend of his life-work. Although he remained primarily an historian, and a medieval historian, to the end, his mind moved constantly in the direction of embracing history and, indeed, all the many departments of his learning, in one comprehensive scheme of the structure, the elements, and the cohesive forces of human society. For him, therefore, history and jurisprudence were not only allied, but grew naturally into each other. His range of reading was prodigious, his linguistic equipment extraordinary, his memory apparently without limit; and to these attainments were added a capacity for seeing any portion of knowledge, however minute and detailed, in its relation to a grand perspective of knowledge. His general juristic position which has been described as 'neo-Kantian', was based on a strong individualism, not oblivious, however, of the concessions demanded by the socialistic tendencies of modern states. It is to be regretted that the different elements of his immensely varied studies were never brought together and interrelated in any one published work, except in the Introduction to his *Historical Jurisprudence*, where they suffer not only from the limits of space which he had imposed upon himself, but also from a certain obscurity of expression which grew upon him in his later years. Although he could write eloquently upon a theme which stirred him, and although he had a command of English which few foreigners possess, he was never, in his more technical works, an entirely felicitous stylist.

Vinogradoff's catholicity and constructive power made him an extraordinarily stimulating teacher. His lectures were somewhat beyond the ordinary undergraduate, but for advanced and receptive students he revealed unsuspected worlds both of method and of knowledge. Endowed with a powerful constitution and himself capable of great feats of sustained labour—he would often work twelve hours a day for long periods—he expected and obtained a high standard of industry from his pupils, and would accept no excuse for second-best. Yet, while unrelenting in all matters of scholarship, he was far from being severe or unsympathetic in private relationships, and would not only go to infinite pains to help his pupils in their studies, but would advance their interests by many personal kindnesses.

Vinogradoff was not, like his first master, Mommsen, a man who lived solely in his work, although in his later, darkened years he tended more and more to seek refuge from an uncongenial world in things of the mind. In his prime, he had a lively and spontaneous variety of interests: he was fond of society, and shone in it by the range and adaptability of his conversation; he loved and followed all the arts, especially the theatre, but above all music, in which, as a young man, he had considerable skill as a pianist; and he took a healthy, temperate pleasure in the material amenities of life. His favourite relaxation was chess, which he played with more than average proficiency. Beneath his naturally magisterial manner there lay great amiability, shrewd worldly perception, and a quick, somewhat satirical, humour. The outstanding qualities of his massive personality—besides his intellect—were his sturdy courage, his power of decision, and his inflexible adherence to what he deemed to be right and wise. This last quality made him not only a man of the highest intellectual rectitude, but a somewhat uncompromising controversialist.

Vinogradoff's most enduring works will be his contributions to medieval history. His theories of law and of the social order must be sought in a number of essays, many of which are assembled in his posthumous *Collected Papers* (1928). His *Historical Jurisprudence* was to be the crown and epitome of his many years of untiring research, but unfortunately he did not live to complete more than part of its grand, if somewhat arbitrary, design. Enough remains to show him a master, unequalled in England, of the social and legal institutions both of the ancient and the modern world.

A portrait of Vinogradoff by Henry Lamb was presented to him in June 1925 and hangs in the Maitland Library in the Examination Schools at Oxford.

[*The Times*, 21 December 1925; H. A. L. Fisher, *Memoir* prefixed to *Collected Papers of Paul Vinogradoff* (also printed separately, 1927); F. M. Powicke in *English Historical Review*, April 1926; Sir William Holdsworth, *Professor Sir Paul Vinogradoff, 1854–1925*, in *Proceedings* of the British Academy, vol. xi, 1924–1925; F. de Zulueta in *Law Quarterly Review*, April 1926; Sir Bernard Pares and Baron Alexander Meyendorff in *Slavonic Review*, March 1926; private information. A complete bibliography of Vinogradoff's writings is published as an appendix to the *Collected Papers*.] C. K. Allen.

VON HÜGEL, FRIEDRICH, Baron of the Holy Roman Empire (1852–1925), theologian, was born at Florence 8 May 1852, the elder son of Carl Alexander Anselm, Baron von Hügel (1795–1870), naturalist and traveller, who was Austrian minister successively to Tuscany and to Belgium, by his wife, Elizabeth, daughter of General Francis Farquharson, and niece of Sir James Outram [q.v.]. His mother was a convert from Presbyterianism to the Roman Catholic Church, and von Hügel was brought up as a Roman Catholic, first at Florence, later in Brussels (1860–1867), and, after his father's retirement in 1867, at Torquay. Taught in childhood by an Anglican governess, and for seven years the devoted pupil of a German Lutheran tutor, with the Catholic historian Alfred von Reumont as supervisor of his studies, he was early familiar with various environments, political and religious. In 1870 an attack of typhus permanently impaired his hearing and general health. A religious and moral crisis followed; but he was 'regained to purity and to God' by the Dutch Dominican Raymond Hocking in Vienna. To Hocking and to the Abbé Huvelin in Paris, under whose influence von Hügel came in 1886 (for notes of Huvelin's advice and acute estimate of von Hügel's character see Holland's *Memoir*, pp. 58 ff.), he 'owed infinitely much'; and he acknowledged a similar debt to William George Ward [q.v.], while he once said to a friend 'with emphasis': 'Under God, I owe my salvation to the Jesuits, but don't *you* ever have anything to do with them' [Holland, *Memoir*, p. 6, n. 1].

In 1873 von Hügel married Mary Catherine, daughter of Sidney, first Lord Herbert of Lea [q.v.], and sister of the thirteenth Earl of Pembroke. His wife and two of their three daughters survived him; the eldest (married to Count Salomei), who of all his family most fully shared his interests, died in 1915. After his marriage his home was in England (from 1876 to 1903 at Hampstead, from 1903 to 1925 at 13 Vicarage Gate, Kensington), but until 1903 the winters were frequently spent abroad, most often in Rome. He studied natural science, philosophy, and religious history and literature, learning Hebrew, and adopting 'critical' views of the Old Testament. These views he defended before a Roman Catholic congress at Freiburg in 1897; while in a pamphlet published in 1906, in collaboration with the American Presbyterian scholar Charles Augustus Briggs, he contended that the report of a papal commission, in June of that year, in favour of the Mosaic authorship of the Pentateuch need not be interpreted as a final condemnation of the opposite view. His biblical studies brought him into contact with men like Duchesne, Loisy, Mignot, and Semeria, who were endeavouring, amid much discouragement from the authorities, to domesticate within their own communion the methods which elsewhere had revolutionized the study of scripture and of Christian antiquity. With Loisy, despite a profound dissimilarity in temperament and interests (revealed in Loisy's *Mémoires*), von Hügel maintained from 1893 until his death a constant and intimate correspondence; while George Tyrrell [q.v.], whose acquaintance he made in 1897, became his 'friend of friends'. Von Hügel's social standing and cosmopolitan connexions combined with his impressive and attractive personality to place him at the centre of the 'modernist' group, of which Paul Sabatier described him as 'the lay bishop' and a less sympathetic observer, Salomon Reinach, as 'the pope'. He also cultivated friendly relations with protestant scholars abroad, especially with Rudolf Eucken and Ernst Troeltsch; the latter's death in 1923, on the eve of a visit to England arranged by von Hügel, was a serious blow. In 1896 he became an original member of the Synthetic Society with Arthur (afterwards Earl of) Balfour and others; and he himself founded in 1905 the London Society for the Study of Religion; the obituary notice of him in *The Times* gives a vivid description of him as he appeared at its meetings. In 1908 his *Mystical Element of Religion as studied in St. Catherine of Genoa and her friends* established his reputation as a religious thinker. *Eternal Life, a Study of its Implications and Applications*, followed in 1912, and in 1921 a volume of *Essays and Addresses on the Philosophy of Religion*; of the latter a second series appeared posthumously in 1926. His style, although difficult, and German rather than English in structure, is highly expressive of his individuality.

Although to the last 'impenitent' as regards biblical criticism—his *Encyclopædia Britannica* article on the fourth Gospel (in the 11th edition, 1910) was published three years after the papal condemnation of modernism in 1907—faithful to the principle of free scientific and historical investigation, loyal to friends suffering under ecclesiastical censures, supporting and contributing to the short-lived Italian modernist review *Il Rinnovamento* (1907–1909) and keenly lamenting its enforced decease, von Hügel was yet increasingly repelled by the 'immanentism' of many modernists, as tending towards denial of 'the objective full reality of God' postulated by 'adoration', which he regarded as the essence of religion. Despite his sympathetic study of mysticism, he came to distrust 'all and every monism' as destructive of man's sense of his own 'creatureliness' and God's transcendence, and to value ecclesiastical institutions as the safeguard of a truly religious temper. Himself ever a humble and devout Roman Catholic, careful—for example, by regular use of the rosary—to worship as far as possible in unison with the majority of his fellow churchmen, and convinced that no Church afforded so favourable a soil for the highest type of religion as his own, he yet recognized in every historical religion, although by no means in equal measure, a medium of divine revelation. He therefore 'would not cross the room' to make a convert, although he rejoiced when any one, after fully utilizing the opportunities afforded by his own communion, felt himself compelled to seek in Roman Catholicism a fuller scope for his Godward aspirations. He could conscientiously prepare a child for Anglican confirmation; and it was only after his death that a niece, his spiritual letters to whom were posthumously published, ventured on a step to which he had never encouraged her and became herself a Roman Catholic.

That von Hügel escaped ecclesiastical censure during the campaign against modernism was probably due to a greater extent than he realized to his social position. He never risked refusal by applying for the *imprimatur*; he did not court martyrdom, but there is no reason to suppose that he would have declined the palm, had the Church seen fit to condemn one for whom the deep reverence felt by many outsiders was an advantage to its cause.

In 1914 von Hügel threw in his lot with his country of domicile, and was naturalized as a British subject. To the literature of the European War he contributed an interesting study of *The German Soul in its attitude towards Ethics and Christianity, the State and War* (1916). In 1919 he was given the honorary degree of LL.D. of St. Andrews (to this, his first university, he bequeathed his library), and in 1920, when divinity degrees at Oxford were open to others than Anglican clergymen, he received the honorary D.D. of Oxford. In 1922 he was elected Gifford lecturer at Edinburgh. The lectures, which his health never permitted him to deliver, are represented by *The Reality of God*, edited by E. G. Gardner and posthumously published in 1931 along with part of a projected study of his friend Sir Alfred Lyall [q.v.], entitled *Religion and Agnosticism*.

Von Hügel's influence on recent religious thought, greater outside his own communion than within, is due to the impression conveyed by his writings of a richly endowed and cultured personality, profoundly Christian and catholic, inspired by a passion for communion with God, and sympathetic with all genuine religion wherever found. Of his characteristic ideas the most noteworthy are perhaps his insistence on the necessity of sensory stimulation in every human activity, not excluding the religious; his suggestion that the scientific view of the world may discharge for Christianity the purifying function formerly performed by eschatology, and his defence of the doctrine of two levels in human life, natural and supernatural, each with a value of its own.

Von Hügel died at his house in Kensington 27 January 1925, and was buried near Downside Abbey at Stratton-on-the-Fosse, Somerset.

The personal appearance of von Hügel was singularly impressive. The intensely pale face, lined with marks of physical suffering, the eyes deep set under bushy eyebrows, the dark hair and beard, turning white as he grew older, set off alike the delightful freedom, the eager human interest, the humour and ripe wisdom of his intimate conversation—in general conversation his deafness disabled him from taking part—and the prophetic earnestness of his more public utterances, which were all the more effective for the quaint and striking phrases and illustrations with which they abounded. In both he gave characteristic expression to a religious experience, remarkable for its richness and depth, its intellectual and moral discipline, its balance and sanity, and peculiarly fitted to communicate to others that sense of the reality of God which was the centre of the speaker's own life. Dom Cuthbert Butler has described (*Tablet*, 14 February 1925, quoted by Holland, p. 49) how he would 'watch him sitting' in church, 'the great deep eyes fixed on the Tabernacle, the whole being wrapt in an absorption of prayer, devotion, contemplation', and adds: 'Those who have not seen him so know only half the man.'

[*The Times*, 28 January 1925; *The Times Literary Supplement*, 25 May 1922; *Baron Friedrich von Hügel. Selected Letters 1896–1924*, edited with a memoir by Bernard Holland, 1927; Paul Sabatier, *Les Modernistes*, 1909; M. D. Petre, *Autobiography and Life of George Tyrrell*, 2 vols., 1912; A. Loisy, *Mémoires*, 3 vols., 1930–1931; Maisie Ward, *The Wilfrid Wards and the Transition*, vol. i, 1934; personal knowledge.] C. C. J. WEBB.

WACE, HENRY (1836–1924), dean of Canterbury, was born at Islington 10 December 1836, the eldest son and second child in the family of twelve children of the Rev. Richard Henry Wace, by his wife, Eulielia, daughter of Charles Grey. His father was at one time curate of St. Sepulchre's church, Holborn, but the strain involved by his work during the cholera epidemic of 1848 and 1849 left him with a nervous hesitation of speech, and he was obliged to resign his curacy. He took pupils, first at Goring, and afterwards at Hill House, Wadhurst, a property left to him by an uncle.

Henry Wace, after careful training and tuition at home, was sent to Marlborough College in February 1848. He was physically unequal to the rough disorder of that school, not yet under the capable rule of Dr. George Cotton, and it was thought well to remove him to Rugby, where he was in the School House under Edward Meyrick Goulburn [q.v.]. After staying less than the ordinary time at Rugby, he went to King's College, London, where he lived as a pupil with the Rev. Charles Hole, to whose influence and friendship he owed much. In May 1856 he entered Trinity College, Oxford, but winning a scholarship a few days later at Brasenose College, he migrated thither. He obtained a first class in mathematical moderations in 1858, and graduated in 1860 with second classes in *literae humaniores* and mathematical 'Greats'.

After studying a year for holy orders, Wace was ordained deacon in 1861, and priest in 1862, by Dr. A. C. Tait, bishop of London. His first licence was the curacy of St. Luke's, Berwick Street, a daughter church of St. James's, Piccadilly, and in 1863 the Rev. John Edward Kempe, the rector of St. James's, invited Wace to become his curate, an offer which Wace accepted.

The same year Wace began to write regularly for *The Times*. He had contributed a letter protesting against the treatment of Bishop John William Colenso [q.v.], and this attracted the attention of John Thaddeus Delane [q.v.], the editor. Shortly afterwards Wace was invited to become a writer of leading articles. His terse and vigorous style of writing commended him to Delane, who acknowledged freely the value of his services, and himself gained the admiration of Wace by his masterly notes, which gave his assistants the line to take on any subject. Wace's official association with *The Times* lasted for more than twenty years.

After seven years' work at St. James's, Piccadilly, Wace left in 1870 for the lecturership of Grosvenor chapel. In 1872 he was appointed to the chaplaincy of Lincoln's Inn, and in 1880 he was made preacher of the Inn. When in 1896 he resigned that office, the Society made him an honorary member of its high table, a distinction which he valued greatly. In 1874 and 1875 Wace was chosen to deliver the Boyle lectures in the Chapel Royal, Whitehall. These lectures he collected and published (1876) under the title of *Christianity and Morality*, a work which ran through several editions. He was also Bampton lecturer at Oxford in 1879, choosing as his subject 'The Foundations of Faith'. He resumed his connexion with King's College, London, in 1875 on his appointment to the professorship of ecclesiastical history. About the same time he collaborated with (Sir) William Smith [q.v.] in preparing and editing the *Dictionary of Christian Biography, Literature, Sects, and Doctrines, during the first Eight Centuries*. This work was issued in four volumes between 1877 and 1887. He was also responsible for the section of the *Speaker's Commentary* on the Bible which dealt with the Apocrypha.

In 1883, on the resignation of Dr. Alfred Barry [q.v.], Wace was appointed principal of King's College, a position which he held until 1897. He took a leading part in the struggle for uniting King's College, University College, and Gresham College into one university, a scheme which, owing to the opposition of the Victoria University of Manchester, was defeated in parliament. It was during his term of office as principal that the government grant was withdrawn from King's as being a denominational institution; Wace thereupon raised £15,000 by an appeal for subscriptions to meet the emergency.

In 1896 Wace was nominated by the Drapers' Company to the valuable benefice of St. Michael's, Cornhill. Although this preferment brought with it comparative ease, and enabled him to re-establish a strong constitution overstrained by hard work, his activities continued. Known already as a churchman of wide learning, a controversialist of decided views, and a stout champion of the Reformation settlement, he was able now in various directions to show a remarkable business capacity. The councils and committees on which he served, and over many of which he presided, are too numerous to give in detail. He made an admirable chairman, for, strong partisan as he was, his fairness and ability were generally recognized, and won the confidence of many whose opinions differed from his own.

Up to the age of sixty Wace had not received from the Church authorities any honour except a prebendal stall at St. Paul's Cathedral (1881). But in 1903 promotion came from the Crown, and he succeeded Dr. Frederic William Farrar as dean of Canterbury. The choice of the prime minister, Mr. Balfour, met with general approval, and the work at Canterbury was congenial to Wace himself. He continued the task of repairing the fabric of the cathedral, especially the famous Angel steeple. He did great service at Canterbury in educational and hospital work, and his popularity was shown by the presentation to him in 1921, on the occasion of his eighty-fifth birthday, of the honorary freedom of the city.

As dean, Wace became for the first time a member of the Convocation of Canterbury, where his ability in debate soon gained him the ear of the house. To the end of his long life he took a determined stand upon the ancient ways, and he was the outspoken opponent of innovations which, in the view of other leaders of the Anglican Church, were advisable in order to meet modern conditions. He could not tolerate the methods of the 'higher criticism' of Holy Scripture, and the revision of the Prayer Book found in him a convinced antagonist. Although such an attitude involved the support of many losing causes, he defended his position with a logical keenness and a wealth of learning to which few of his opponents could aspire. In private life he was most attractive, witty, and stimulating in conversation, and considerate to those whose intellectual powers were far less than his own. As a host at the deanery he was ideal, and as a friend loyal and dependable.

Wace made a special study of the Reformation period, and he was deeply read in Lutheran literature. His writings, besides those already mentioned, include an edition of Luther's primary works (in collaboration with Dr. C. A. Buchheim, 1896), lectures on *The Gospel and its Witnesses* (1883), *Sermons on the Sacrifice of Christ* (1898), and *The Bible and Modern Investigations* (1903). His contributions to newspapers and magazines were numerous.

Wace married twice: first, in 1863 his second cousin, Elizabeth (died 1893), eldest daughter of Henry Arnett; secondly, in 1894 Cornelia Gertrude, daughter of Dr. Leonard Schmitz. His second wife, who had been vice-principal of the Ladies' Department of King's College, survived him by nearly a year. By his first wife he had four sons, one of whom died in infancy. He died at Canterbury 9 January 1924.

A portrait of Wace by William Logsdail (1903) hangs in the Deanery, Canterbury.

[*The Times*, 10 January 1924; private information.] A. Cochrane.

WALKER, Sir BYRON EDMUND (1848–1924), Canadian banker, the eldest son of Alfred Edmund Walker, by his wife, Fanny, daughter of William Murton, of East Stour, Kent, was born on a farm in Seneca township, co. Haldimand, Canada West, 14 October 1848. Both his parents were of English origin. He went to the central school in Hamilton, Ontario, at the early age of four, but left when only twelve on account of ill-health. In 1861, while still under thirteen years of age, he was taken into the exchange office of his uncle, J. W. Murton, in Hamilton, where he learnt to understand the various complicated currencies in use, and became a recognized expert in the detection of counterfeit money. In July 1868 he entered the Canadian Bank of Commerce in Hamilton as a discount clerk. In spite of offers from other institutions, Walker remained for the rest of his life in the Bank of Commerce, rapidly acquiring a thorough knowledge of banking by holding a variety of posts. In 1872 he became chief accountant in Toronto; in 1873 accountant in the New York agency; in 1875 manager in Windsor, Ontario; in 1878 manager in London, Ontario; in 1879 inspector at the head office; in 1880 manager in Hamilton; in 1881 joint agent in New York; in 1886 general manager; in 1906 director; and in 1907 president. Not only was the growth of the Bank of Commerce due in great part to Walker's skill and personality, but the Canadian banking system as a whole owes its present form largely to his efforts. Soon after the Bank Act of 1871 had been passed, attempts were made to change it in such a way as to make it possible for the development in Canada of a banking system similar to the American system. In 1880 and again in 1890 when the Act came up for revision, it was Walker who bore the brunt of defending it against such a change. Walker, indeed, was a lifelong advocate of the branch-banking system, and always strenuously opposed the system of local banks which prevails in the United States. This opposition was due not merely to his traditional sentiments, but to reasons of sound finance. The need of co-operation amongst the Canadian banks, thus demonstrated, led him and others to found in 1891 the Canadian Bankers' Association, of which he was successively vice-president and president.

Walker early became recognized as an authority on Canadian finance. In 1899 he was made chairman of a royal commission appointed to report on the financial position of the province of Ontario; in 1909 he was elected vice-president of the American Bankers' Association; and in the last few years of his life he was consulted by the English authorities in reference to the public finance of England. In addition, as director on the boards of many companies, he made valuable contributions to the development of Canadian business and finance. Perhaps, however, the greatest tribute to his financial ability was the stability of Canadian finance during the European War of 1914–1918. Immediately on the outbreak of war, Walker was called to Ottawa in company with two or three other financiers, and within a few hours the plan of war-time finance for Canada was drawn up and approved.

Although Walker's genius lay preeminently in banking and finance, his interests were unusually wide. He himself had never received a university education, but he gave much time and thought to the affairs of the university of Toronto. His first official connexion was as one of the trustees (1892), which office he held until the reorganization of the university following the report of the royal commission of 1905, of which he himself was a prominent member. Thereafter he served as a governor of the university, and as chairman of the board from 1910 until 1923, when he became chancellor.

Walker was connected with a host of organizations, large and small, which had for their object promotion of the arts. Nor was he a mere figure-head in these enterprises; on the contrary, he took an active interest in them all, so far as time allowed. He was honorary president of the Mendelssohn choir of Toronto from 1900, and chairman of the governors of the Toronto conservatoire of music. The opening of the Royal Ontario Museum in 1914 was in no small degree due to his efforts; many of his interests were represented there, and he took an active interest in the acquisition as well as the management of the museum. In palaeontology he was something of an expert, and for years gave much time and money to the collection of specimens. In 1907 Walker was made one of three members of an advisory arts council (later known as the Board of Trustees of the National Gallery) appointed by the Dominion government. To this, as to all the other similar organizations, he was able to lend both his advice on finance and his skilled opinion on artistic questions. He now turned to public purposes that knowledge of pictures which for many years previously had been sought for its own end. In addition he acquired one of the finest and largest collections of Japanese prints in the world.

Walker had a keen sense of public duty, and never shrank from public affairs. But he took little part in politics, and only once was moved to vigorous action in an election. This was at the general election of 1911, when he joined with other liberals of Toronto in opposing the Laurier government's policy of reciprocity with the United States, in which he and they saw serious political and economic harm to Canada.

Amongst Walker's more important writings are 'Canadian Banking' in Palgrave's *Dictionary of Political Economy* (1894–1908), *A History of Banking in Canada* (1896), and 'East and West' (J. O. Miller (ed.), *The New Era in Canada*, Toronto, 1917). He left behind him a remarkable and carefully arranged collection of private papers, which relate to Canadian life and international finance in all their important activities.

Walker married in 1874 Mary (died 1923), daughter of Alexander Alexander, of Hamilton, and had four sons and three daughters. He was knighted in 1910, and received honorary degrees from Trinity University, Toronto, and the university of Toronto (1906). There is a portrait by Sir John Lavery in the National Gallery at Ottawa. He died in Toronto 27 March 1924.

[Victor Ross, *History of the Canadian Bank of Commerce*, 2 vols., Toronto, 1922; letters and papers in possession of the family; personal knowledge.] W. P. M. Kennedy.

WALKLEY, ARTHUR BINGHAM (1855–1926), dramatic and literary critic, was born at Bedminster, Bristol, 17 December 1855, the only child of Arthur Hickman Walkley, bookseller, of Bristol, by his wife, Caroline Charlotte, daughter of Joseph Bingham, bookseller, of Bristol. From Warminster School he gained an exhibition at Balliol College, Oxford, and matriculated there in October 1873. In January 1874 he was admitted a scholar of Corpus Christi College, Oxford. He obtained first classes in mathematical moderations (1875) and in the final school of mathematics (1877).

In June 1877 Walkley was appointed a third class clerk in the secretary's office of the General Post Office. In November 1882 he was promoted second class clerk, in January 1892 first class clerk, in November 1899 principal clerk, and in August 1911 assistant secretary (in charge of the telegraph branch). In 1897 he was secretary to the British delegation to the Washington Postal Congress, in 1898 secretary to the Imperial Penny Postage Conference, and in 1906 a delegate to the Rome Postal Congress. He was superannuated in June 1919.

Side by side with his career as civil servant ran Walkley's more brilliant career as writer. He began by reviewing books in the periodical press. Interested by the dramatic criticisms of his friend William Archer [q.v.] and especially by his book *English Dramatists of To-day* (1882), Walkley turned his attention to the theatre. When the *Star* evening newspaper was founded in January 1888 he was appointed its dramatic critic and held the post until 1900. As 'Spectator' he wrote for the *Star*, besides his notices of plays, a periodical contribution on theatrical affairs and the drama in general; this prepared his way as essayist. In the *Star* he wrote also, under his own name, a series of miscellaneous papers entitled 'Fly Leaves', some of which concerned a certain Pettifer, who was intended for a 'fantasticated, burlesqued, and belittled projection' of the writer. In November 1890 he became dramatic critic of the *Speaker*, a weekly paper, and held the post until the paper changed hands at the end of September 1899.

Dramatic criticisms which he had written for the *Speaker*, the *National Observer*, and other periodicals, Walkley collected into a volume, *Playhouse Impressions* (1892); and a selection from his miscellaneous papers in the *Speaker*, the *Star*, and other journals was published as *Frames of Mind* in 1899. In that year he began to contribute dramatic criticism to *The Times*, his first notice being a review in the issue of 21 September 1899 of (Sir) Herbert Beerbohm Tree's production of *King John*; and on 1 March 1900 he was formally engaged as dramatic critic. He contributed in 1900 and 1901 to *Literature*, a weekly paper published by *The Times*, and to *The Times Literary Supplement* after its foundation in January 1902. Some of these articles composed his volume *Drama and Life* (1907). In February 1903 he delivered three lectures at the Royal Institution, which he published as *Dramatic Criticism* (1903). After his retirement from the Post Office he began the series of miscellaneous articles published in *The Times* on Wednesdays, some of which he collected into his three volumes, *Pastiche and Prejudice* (1921), *More Prejudice* (1923), and *Still More Prejudice* (1925).

Walkley's view of criticism may best be learned from his book, *Dramatic Criticism*. He professed himself an 'impressionist', one whose task was to estimate and analyse his own sensations in the presence of a work of art, not to judge it by rule. 'The primary aim of all art', he wrote, 'is to give pleasure. And this pleasure of art . . . is in the first instance . . . a pleasure of the senses.' In practice he was not entirely consistent, being inclined, as Archer told him, to let aesthetic and philosophical theory intrude between him and the work of art; but his idea of criticism enabled him to come unprejudiced and fresh to each new book or play. This, especially in his earlier years, was of great help to the English drama, which was then beginning a new period and breaking free from certain conventions of dramatic form and content. In particular Walkley's welcome of Ibsen, not as moralist or reformer, but as a great artist in play-making, did much to counteract both the foolish abuse and the genuine misunderstanding with which Ibsen's plays were at first received in London. Later in life Walkley's fastidious love of form, clarity, and finish gave him a distaste for the development, in plays by Bernard Shaw and others, of the very 'drama of ideas' which his admiration for the French drama of the period had led him to desire. He lost his love of Ibsen and came to prefer light comedy of the more conventional type. The theatrical profession found him too much of the essayist and too little of the reporter for its taste; and his fearless gaiety in attack led to his being turned away on 2 March 1903 from the doors of the Garrick Theatre, to which, as critic of *The Times*, he had been invited to see *Whitewashing Julia*, a new play by Henry Arthur Jones produced by Arthur Bourchier. The insult did nothing to prevent Jones and Walkley from later becoming firm friends.

Whatever his opinions, Walkley's criticisms were always in themselves works of art. He was widely read in French drama, fiction, and criticism (he liked to be as French as possible in appearance and in bearing), fairly well read in the classics and in English prose, and with some knowledge of Spanish and Italian. Alike in dramatic and literary criticism and in the short miscellaneous essay (a form in which he was a master), his sensitiveness to impression, his accurate and retentive memory, his ease and grace of manner, and his playfulness and wit produced delightful results.

Next to criticism, Walkley was most interested in fruit-growing and rock-gardening, which he practised at his country home at Pound Hill, near Crawley in Sussex. In 1919 he left it for a house at Brightlingsea in Essex, where he died 8 October 1926. He married in 1881 Frances, daughter of Charles Eldridge, bootmaker's manager, and had one daughter.

[*The Times*, 9 October 1926; H. H. Child, 'Arthur Bingham Walkley' in *The Post-Victorians*, 1933; personal knowledge.]

H. H. Child.

WALSH, STEPHEN (1859–1929), trade union leader and politician, was born in Liverpool of parents in humble circumstances 26 August 1859. Further details of his parentage are not available. In infancy he was admitted as a foundling to the Kirkdale Industrial School and Orphanage, near Liverpool. There he received an elementary education, showing proficiency in mathematics, and acquired in childhood a love of books which enabled him in later years to display to the House of Commons considerable knowledge of English literature and social history. At the age of thirteen Walsh became a working miner at Ashton-in-Makerfield, near Wigan. His native intelligence and trustworthy character attracted the attention of his fellow workers, and in 1901 he was appointed agent of the Lancashire and Cheshire Miners' Federation; subsequently he became president of that federation, and in 1922 vice-president of the Miners' Federation of Great Britain. In 1906 he was invited by the Miners' Federation to contest the Ince division of Lancashire as a labour candidate. He won the seat, and retained it for the remainder of his life. He was also a J.P. and D.L. for the county of Lancaster.

In parliament Walsh spoke with effect on industrial questions, and he made valuable contributions to debates on the Mines Act 1911 and on the Minimum Wage Act 1912. He became expert in wage negotiations, having remarkable facility in dealing with intricate calculations, and from 1914 to 1920 he was chairman of the miners' section of the English Conciliation Board. He was elected a vice-chairman of the parliamentary labour party in 1922. During the European War Walsh devoted himself to recruiting and to the question of man power; he was parliamentary secretary to the Ministry of National Service in 1917, and to the Local Government Board during 1917–1918. He was an advocate of compulsory military service, consistently maintaining during the War, as he had maintained during the coal-mining crisis in 1912, that the claims of citizenship are superior to those of trade unionism. In January 1924, on the formation of the first labour government, Walsh was appointed secretary of state for war and president of the Army Council; when the government resigned in November of the same year he was already recognized as a capable and popular minister. In November 1927 he was appointed a member of the (Simon) statutory commission set up under the provisions of the Government of India Act 1919, but owing to failing health he was unable to serve. He died at his home in Wigan 16 March 1929.

Walsh was a man of exceptionally small stature and homely presence: his personality was acceptable in a marked degree to members of all parties in the House of Commons and to the public. Without any hereditary or educational advantages, he was called to a great position in the public service, and he performed the duties of that position with generally acknowledged efficiency. His career affords an example of success in high administrative office of a man possessed of no obvious qualifications for such responsibilities save integrity, courage, and abundant common sense. Walsh married in 1885 Anne, daughter of John Adamson, a Lancashire miner. She survived him with three sons and five daughters. The eldest son, Arthur, a young man of scholarly attainments, was awarded the military cross and fell in action in 1918.

[*The Times*, 18 March 1929; private information.] A. E. Watkin.

WARD, Sir ADOLPHUS WILLIAM (1837–1924), historian, born at Hampstead 2 December 1837, was the second son of John Ward, diplomatist [q.v.], by his wife, Caroline, daughter of the Rev. John Bullock, rector of Radwinter, Essex. In 1841 John Ward was sent to Germany on the first of a series of missions and appointments which kept him there until his retirement in 1870. This transplantation exerted a profound influence on his son, whose schooling began at Leipzig, where his father was then consul-general, and whose youthful interest in Germany never waned. At the age of sixteen he was removed to King Edward VI School, Bury St. Edmunds, of which John William Donaldson [q.v.] was then headmaster, and in 1855 he entered Peterhouse, Cambridge, as a pensioner. He graduated in 1859 with a first class in the classical tripos, and was elected a fellow of his college in 1862. He entered the Inner Temple in 1860, and was called to the bar in 1866, but never practised. After brief periods as classical lecturer at Peterhouse, examiner at the Education Office, and assistant to George Gilbert Ramsay, professor of humanity in the university of Glasgow, he was appointed professor of history and English language and literature at Owens College, Manchester, in 1866.

For the next thirty-one years Ward laboured with unflagging zeal as a teacher and an administrator. His commanding presence and impressive lectures combined with his enthusiasm for letters and great range of knowledge to render him one of the leading teachers of his time. He was the founder of the history school which placed Manchester next to Oxford and Cambridge in that department of study. The appointment of T. N. Toller as professor of English philology in 1880 relieved him of part of his burden; but until he became principal in 1889 Ward remained responsible both for English literature and for the whole range of history, and he continued to lecture on history until he left Manchester in 1897.

No member of the staff played a more active part than Ward in raising the academic status of Owens College. In 1875, with three of his colleagues, he began to advocate its transformation into an independent university. Instead, the federal Victoria University was created in 1880, with its seat in Manchester, and Owens College as its first constituent member, to which the colleges of Liverpool and Leeds were added later. Ward was vice-chancellor of the new university from 1886 to 1890 and again from 1894 to 1896. In recognition of his services to the community 'Ward of Manchester', as he was often called, received the freedom of the city in 1897, the year in which he left Manchester. He remained in close touch with his old friends, and rejoiced at the establishment of an independent university of Manchester in 1903.

Ward's output during the Manchester years was mainly in the field of English literature, although his translation in five volumes of the *History of Greece* by Ernst Curtius (1868–1873) revealed his interest in ancient history and his admiration for German scholarship. His *History of English Dramatic Literature to the Death of Queen Anne* (2 vols., 1875), the first systematic attempt to cover this immense field, won him a place in the front rank of British scholars. The revised and enlarged edition in three volumes (1899) remains an indispensable work of reference. His editions of works by Marlowe, Robert Greene, and Thomas Heywood, his article on the 'Drama' written for the ninth edition of the *Encyclopædia Britannica*, and his contributions to the *Manchester Guardian*, of which he was for many years dramatic critic, supply additional evidence of his interest in plays new and old. The volumes on *Chaucer* (1879) and *Dickens* (1882) in the 'English Men of Letters' series, his editions of the works of Pope, of John Byrom, the Manchester Jacobite, and, in later years, of Crabbe and of Mrs. Gaskell, proved that he maintained his interest in poetry and fiction. The only substantial historical work of the Manchester period was *The Counter-Reformation* (1889) in Longman's 'Epochs of Church History' series. He contributed some 300 articles, chiefly seventeenth-century lives, to this DICTIONARY, and he was one of the chief supporters of the *English Historical Review* from its foundation in 1886.

On leaving Manchester at the age of sixty, Ward settled in London. A little volume on *Sir Henry Wotton* (1898) was followed by the Ford lectures on *Great Britain and Hanover* (1899, German translation 1906); and he began to work at *The Electress Sophia and the Hanoverian Succession* for Goupil's illustrated monographs (1903, revised and enlarged without illustrations, 1909). In 1900 his old college recalled him as its master. His inspiring influence was quickly felt in Peterhouse, and he took his full share in the life of the university, of which he was vice-chancellor in 1901. He was an admirable chairman of the Press Syndicate from 1905 to 1919, and he was scarcely less active on the Library Syndicate.

The death of Lord Acton [q.v.] in 1902 deprived the editors of the *Cambridge Modern History* of his guiding hand. As editor-in-chief, with the aid of (Sir) George Walter Prothero [q.v.] and (Sir) Stanley Leathes, Ward carried through the immense undertaking in eleven years (1901–1912). Of his own contributions, appearing in seven of the twelve volumes, the most important are the six chapters on the Thirty Years War, which reveal his unsurpassed knowledge of that period. The success of the enterprise encouraged him to suggest and the University Press to undertake the *Cambridge History of English Literature*, edited by Ward and Alfred Rayney Waller, and published 1907–1916, in which Ward's contributions, mainly on the dramatists and historians of the last three centuries, appear in nine of the fourteen volumes. These chapters are on the whole shorter and less impressive than those which he wrote for the *Cambridge Modern History*.

The outbreak of the European War in 1914 was a poignant grief to Ward, who was bound to Germany by numerous ties. His dislike of German militarism in no way disturbed the balance of his chief historical work, *Germany, 1815–1890* (1916–1918), written for the 'Cambridge Historical Series'. The first two volumes, bringing the narrative down to 1871, displayed his power unabated, and in describing the making of the German Empire he was able to draw on the experiences of his early manhood. The third volume, with an epilogue extending to 1907, is shorter and slighter, for the octogenarian was anxious not to leave an unfinished work.

Ward next wrote two little volumes of minor importance on *The Period of Congresses* and *Securities of Peace* (1919) in S.P.C.K. 'Helps for Students of History'. The publication of his *Collected Papers* (1921), at the suggestion of the Cambridge University Press, was a fitting tribute to his services. Two volumes were devoted to history, two to literature, one to travel and miscellanies. His selection was not impeccable; for some important material was omitted, and a few ephemeral reviews were included. Though now over eighty and rather deaf, Ward was still full of energy. The *Cambridge History of British Foreign Policy, 1783–1919*, edited by Ward and Dr. G. P. Gooch, appeared in three volumes in 1922–1923. His chapter on the Schleswig-Holstein question, for which he used the unpublished papers of his father, is more valuable than his lengthy introduction sketching the evolution of diplomacy up to 1783. A briefer survey of British policy in Greece and the Ionian Islands, 1832–1864, derive a personal interest from an early visit of his to Athens, where he had conversed in modern Greek with veterans of the War of Independence. After the completion of this, his last editorial enterprise, Ward contented himself with articles and reviews. He died at Cambridge 19 June 1924.

Ward received many honours at home and abroad. He was knighted in 1913, the year in which he presided over the International Historical Congress in London, and he was created a knight of the Prussian order of the Crown in 1911. He received honorary degrees from the universities of Manchester, Glasgow, St. Andrews, and Leipzig. He was president of the British Academy (of which he was an original member), 1911–1913, of the Royal Historical Society, 1899–1901, of the English Goethe Society, 1912–1922, of the Chetham Society, 1901–1914, and of the Spenser Society, 1883–1894.

Ward's main strength as a historian lay in his unrivalled knowledge of the political evolution of Europe since the Middle Ages, and no British scholar was so intimately acquainted with the results of German scholarship in this field. He owed most to Leopold von Ranke, whose objective treatment he endeavoured to emulate. Like Ranke he was better fitted to describe the policy of states than to portray an individual or to recapture the atmosphere of an epoch. His lack of colour and his lengthy sentences limited his appeal, but on occasion he could rise to passages of restrained eloquence. He belonged to the category of political historians, for he was more interested in events and institutions than in economic factors or political and religious ideas.

Ward was fortunate in his home life. His marriage in 1879 to his cousin, Adelaide Laura, daughter of the Rev. Thomas Burne Lancaster, rector of Grittleton, Wiltshire, like himself a grandchild of the sister of Thomas Arnold of Rugby, brought him enduring happiness; and the marriage in 1916 of their only surviving child to Dr. E. W. Barnes, master of the Temple, afterwards bishop of Birmingham, added to the interest of his later years.

Ward was conspicuous in every gathering he attended, and his hospitality made him an ideal host. He took special pleasure in entertaining foreign scholars. Despite his stately courtesy he was fundamentally simple and human, and his kindness to students was inexhaustible. In national as in academic questions he was a liberal, and he disliked Imperialism both at home and abroad. He remained young in spirit, working to the last with untiring energy.

There is a portrait of Ward by Sir Hubert von Herkomer in the university of Manchester, and another by Hugh Riviere at Peterhouse, Cambridge.

[*The Times*, 20 June 1924; *Manchester Guardian*, 20 June 1924; A. T. Bartholomew, *A Bibliography of Sir A. W. Ward with a Memoir by T. F. Tout*, 1926; *In Memoriam A. W. Ward, Master of Peterhouse*, 1924; *Cambridge Historical Journal*, vol. i, no. 2, 1924; personal knowledge.] G. P. Gooch.

WARD, Sir EDWARD WILLIS DUNCAN, first baronet (1853–1928), soldier and military administrator, the only son of Captain John Ward, R.N., of Oban, by his wife, Mary Hope, daughter of John Bowie, was born there 17 December 1853. Privately educated, he entered in 1874 the commissariat branch of the Control Department, an organization of military officials outside the army, like the French Intendance Militaire. He was promoted assistant commissary-general for active service in the Sudan (1885), and when the Army Service Corps was instituted (1888) as part of the army he was commissioned in it as major and promoted lieutenant-colonel in 1890. Having been noticed by Lord Wolseley in the Sudan, and in Ireland, where he served from 1888 to 1892, Ward held staff appointments in Dublin (1892–1895), on the Ashanti expedition (1895–1896, when he was made C.B.), and in London (1895–1899), where, being given official charge of the (originally unofficial) Military Tournament at Islington, his energy and business ability prepared its later triumphs at Olympia and promoted its substantial contributions to service charities. He published (1897) a good practical *Handbook of Army Service Corps Duties in Peace and War*.

In 1899, war in South Africa being imminent, Ward was among the officers sent out in advance and, as chief supply officer in Natal, collected large stocks at Ladysmith, which was invested on 2 November. Commandeering all traders' supplies, he took responsibility for feeding both troops and inhabitants until relief came on 28 February 1900. He had only two and a half months' rations, eked out with horseflesh; but they were administered so ably that Sir George Stuart White [q.v.] proclaimed Ward 'the best commissariat officer since Moses', forgetting that only miracles saved Israel in the desert from hunger and thirst and that the supreme feat in Egyptian commissariat was Joseph's. Three weeks after the relief Ward, now director of supplies to Lord Roberts, was at Bloemfontein preparing for the advance to Pretoria. That phase of the War ended, he came home with his chief late in 1900, promoted full colonel and created K.C.B.

In April 1901 the secretary of state for war, Mr. Brodrick (afterwards Lord Midleton), who after nine years at the War Office desired to deal with the military heads of departments without a civilian interposed by official rule as permanent under-secretary of state, tried to turn the position by giving that post to Ward. But to those heads Ward's commissariat record, however brilliant, stamped him as more official than soldier; while to Mr. Arnold-Forster, who succeeded Brodrick in 1903, he was more soldier than official, lacking the civil servant's special knowledge and experience. In 1904 the War Office Reconstitution Committee under Viscount Esher [q.v.] established direct dealings between the secretary of state and soldiers as colleagues on the Army Council, while the permanent under-secretary, no longer interposed, shrank to the position of secretary of the Army Council, retaining the (civil) headship of the department. Loyal in disappointment, without troubling overmuch about theories of administration, Ward concentrated on making the new machinery work smoothly, with the devoted help of the civilian staff. Ill-yoked with Mr. (afterwards Viscount) Haldane [q.v.], he yet made a notable contribution to the 'New Model' as chairman of the committee which designed the Officers Training Corps. With his driving-power, knowledge of men, and tact, he was at his best in the chair of a committee with a definite task, other instances of such success being the substitution of ex-military clerks for civilians in the military departments of the War Office, the Brodrick reorganization of the Army Medical Department, and the compilation of the original War Book detailing War Office action on mobilization. By organizing the War Office Sports Club, comprising officers, private soldiers, and civilians, he gave the Office personnel a *camaraderie* formerly lacking. Devoted to the welfare of soldiers past and present, Ward interested himself in schemes for civil employment of discharged men and reservists, and took the lead in founding the Union Jack Club for soldiers and sailors passing through London—an immeasurable boon—of which, after presiding over the originating committee (1902), he was president for twenty-two years.

Ward was created K.C.V.O. in 1907 and a baronet on retiring from the civil service in January 1914, when he became chairman and director of substantial companies. By the autumn he was again immersed in public duties: organizer and commandant-in-chief of the Metropolitan Special Constabulary, Lord Kitchener's deputy in superintending the personal welfare of all overseas troops, organizer of the War Camps Library, director-general of the voluntary organizations of helpers in war hospitals, munition workers' canteens, &c.—there seemed no limit to Ward's powers of leadership, with his genius for wise delegation to the right man. When peace returned he was created G.B.E. in 1919.

A strong but genial personality, welcoming responsibility, imperturbable, somewhat inarticulate, Ward's forte lay in execution rather than in counsel. He married in 1880 Florence Caroline, daughter of Henry Minchin Simons, merchant, of London and Singapore, and had two sons, the elder of whom, Edward Simons (born 1882), succeeded him as second baronet. Ward died 11 September 1928 in Paris, of ptomaine poisoning, and was buried at Brompton.

A cartoon of Ward by 'Spy' appeared in *Vanity Fair* 30 May 1901.

[Official records; private information; personal knowledge.] C. Harris.

WARD, JAMES (1843–1925), philosopher and psychologist, was born at Hull 27 January 1843, the eldest of the nine children of James Ward, by his wife, Hannah Aston. His father was a clever, ambitious, but unsuccessful merchant in Liverpool, whose vicissitudes of fortune made the support of his large family a difficult problem. James Ward was educated for a short time at the Liverpool Institute and then, at the age of eleven, sent to a preparatory school at Parkgate on the Wirral peninsula, expecting thereafter to proceed to Rugby; but his schooldays were cut short, when he was thirteen, by his father's failure in business, and for the remainder of his boyhood he was self-taught. The Wards settled in a small house at Waterloo, then a village, near Liverpool, and James was left free to roam the neighbouring sandhills. In this solitude his senses were quickened, and the town-boy became a lover of nature. As he said long afterwards, 'it was here that the optimism began, in those wild wastes absolutely untouched by the hand of man; . . . all was beautiful, all was good, and I was one with it all'. He had some skill as a draughtsman also, and this led, before he was sixteen, to his apprenticeship to a firm of architects. There he made acquaintances, started a debating society, and began to study Greek and logic. He was also an ardent Sunday-school teacher; and, after four years' office-work, determined to become a minister.

Ward's family were Congregationalists, biblical and Calvinist in their theology, and he shared their creed. In 1863, after many difficulties, financial and scholastic, he entered Spring Hill College, near Birmingham (now absorbed in Mansfield College, Oxford). He remained there till 1869, taking the London B.A. degree, as well as completing his theological course. His time there was on the whole not unhappy, although he was harassed by bad health and insufficient means, and perhaps by the rise of doubts concerning the security of his theological beliefs. Before beginning practical work, Ward determined on further study, and a scholarship made a year in Germany possible for him. Living at the Dom Candidatenstift in Berlin and attending the lectures of Isaac August Dorner, he entered a new theological environment and became immersed in speculations on fundamental problems. In the spring of 1870 he moved to Göttingen in order to study under Rudolf Hermann Lotze, who exerted a permanent influence on his thought; he remained there until the university dispersed on the outbreak of the Franco-Prussian War. Unsettled and unsettling as his speculations were, Ward still looked upon them as a support of Christian belief. He was asked and agreed to preach for a month at Emmanuel Congregational chapel in Cambridge, accepted a call to be its minister in January 1871, and, although never ordained, remained in charge of the congregation until March 1872, when he finally demitted his office. His preaching made a powerful impression on the greater number of his hearers and the congregation tried to dissuade him from resignation; but there were some who resented the liberal tone of his sermons and the absence of familiar doctrines; at the same time a struggle was going on in his own mind which issued in the conviction that his teaching was out of place in the Christian pulpit. It was the most unhappy year of his life; and, in the midst of his own trials, he envied the studious life of the university.

A new period of Ward's career began at the age of twenty-nine. He entered Cambridge University as a non-collegiate student, gained an open scholarship at Trinity College in 1873, was placed alone in the first class in the moral sciences tripos in 1874, and in 1875 was elected to a fellowship at his college which he held for the remainder of his life. The break with his former career was complete; for the future he held himself aloof from all institutional religion: but he did not tend towards secularism or even agnosticism; his early belief in spiritual values and his respect for all sincere religion never left him: 'he buried the past, he burned his boats; but he remained for all that a native of other shores'. His passion for nature also, which had not received much encouragement in a domestic circle whose chief interests were business and sermons, and which seemed to have died away in his years of theological study and struggle, revived; and one day, on a walk, 'the old feeling of the would-be naturalist of ten years ago rose up and confronted the self-excommunicated sceptic'. It is worth noting that the first publications of this new period were two short communications on 'Animal Locomotion' in *Nature* (1874).

At this time Ward was working hard at psychology and philosophy. His fellowship dissertation on 'The Relation of Physiology to Psychology' was printed but not published, although a portion of it, 'An Attempt to Interpret Fechner's Law,' appeared in the first volume of *Mind* (1876). After election to a fellowship, he worked for the greater part of a year in the physiological laboratory at Leipzig, and for some time, on his return to Cambridge, in the physiological laboratory there. The result was two considerable papers: 'Ueber die Auslösung von Reflexbewegungen durch eine Summe schwacher Reize' (*Archiv für Physiologie*, 1880), and 'The Physiology of the Nervous System of the Freshwater Crayfish' (*Journal of Physiology*, 1879; abstract in *Proceedings* of the Royal Society, 1879). But, attracted as he was, and always remained, to research in natural science, Ward was deliberately working up towards the domain of mind. In 1880 he contributed the article on Johann Friedrich Herbart to the ninth edition of the *Encyclopædia Britannica*, in 1880–1881 he printed (without publishing) four papers, on 'General Analysis of Mind' and other fundamental problems in psychology, and in 1883 began a series of articles in *Mind* on 'Psychological Principles'. These writings were obviously prolegomena for a more extended treatise, and circumstances made this treatise take the form of the article 'Psychology' in the ninth edition of the *Encyclopædia Britannica*. It had an immediate and profound effect upon the study and teaching of psychology and, along with two other articles on the same subject in subsequent editions of the *Encyclopædia*, remained the standard expression of Ward's views until the publication of his comprehensive treatise, *Psychological Principles*, in 1918.

Meanwhile Ward's academic career followed a normal course, but rather slowly. He began lecturing for the moral sciences tripos in 1878, became a college lecturer in 1881, and in 1897 was appointed to the newly founded professorship of mental philosophy and logic. In 1880 and for a few years afterwards he also lectured on education, and these lectures form the basis of his *Psychology applied to Education* (1926). He was Gifford lecturer at Aberdeen University, 1895–1898, and again at St. Andrews University, 1907–1910. In each case the twenty lectures required were spread over a longer period than the customary two years, and in each case the result was an important philosophical treatise—*Naturalism and Agnosticism* (1899) and *The Realm of Ends, or Pluralism and Theism* (1911). In 1912 he gave the Henry Sidgwick memorial lecture at Newnham College, Cambridge, on *Heredity and Memory* (published 1913). He received the honorary degree of LL.D. from Edinburgh University in 1889 and from his own university in 1920, was an original fellow of the British Academy, and was elected a *correspondent* of the Institut de France. He spent the summer and early autumn of 1904 in America, lecturing for a term at Berkeley in California, reading a paper at the Congress of Arts and Sciences held in connexion with the St. Louis exhibition, and visiting friends in several universities.

During the earlier part of his literary career, Ward's published work was almost entirely psychological, although he always looked to the philosophical bearings of his views and on occasion wrote philosophical papers; after about 1894 his work was mainly philosophical. The most controversial of his psychological doctrines concerned the standpoint of the science and what he called the 'general analysis' of mind. Neither the physiological approach nor the start with sensations or presentations as ultimate data could withstand his criticism. 'The standpoint of psychology is individualistic; by whatever method, from whatever sources its facts are ascertained, they must—to have a psychological import—be regarded as having place in, or as being part of, *some one's consciousness*.' By 'consciousness', as the term is used here, he means that where and only where there is an object presented to a subject, are we in the domain of mind. The other sciences disregard this fact of presentation as irrelevant for their purposes; but it is fundamental for psychology, and psychology cannot transcend it. The 'subject', however, is not to be identified either with the 'soul' of rational psychology or with a nondescript 'mind-stuff'. It is not a mere passive recipient of presentations; it feels and it acts (or attends). The feeling and the activity characterize the 'subject' only. From this fundamental position a system of psychology was worked out which contained many points of novelty—as in the account of space and time, the clear distinction between the perception and the conception of each, the bold extension of the doctrine of secondary automatism, the emphasis on the importance of subjective as well as natural selection in mental development, and the stress laid on the function of inter-subjective intercourse in leading to knowledge of the external world and of self.

Ward's philosophy is worked out in his two sets of Gifford lectures, in both of which construction is preceded by an elaborate criticism. In the earlier book he begins by making clear the distinction between science and the philosophical theory to which it had been supposed to lead and with which it was often confused, and this opens the way for his refutation of naturalism with its satellite doctrines such as the mechanical theory of reality and psychophysical parallelism. Not all his points were new, but Ward's criticism gave the final blow to the competency of naturalism and to its alliance with agnosticism as promulgated by Herbert Spencer and other leaders of contemporary thought. 'Reality', says Ward, 'consists in the concrete things and events that science sets out from, and not in the network of relations which is its goal'; but science itself starts with the abstraction of things from the experience of them; in philosophy we must proceed from an experience which implies subject-object. In the argument which follows the subjective element is given a position of primacy, and the result is a theory of 'spiritualistic monadism' which interprets the whole of reality from the side of the subject whose objects are themselves always monads or arrangements of monads. This view is elaborated in *The Realm of Ends*, after criticism of other forms of pluralism. Ward held, with Spinoza and Leibniz, that 'all individual things are animated, although in diverse degrees'. According to this form of pluralism reality consists of active subjects of experience interacting with an environment which consists of other spiritual monads; and these active beings have all a nisus towards goodness. It was chiefly this that led Ward to see the unity of the whole from the theistic standpoint. He did not think that theism could be proved, but he held that the idea of God alone enables us to co-ordinate our experience, and the concluding chapters of this book are a series of reflections on the cosmology of theism.

Ward's last book, *A Study of Kant* (1922), was published when he was seventy-nine, and several shorter writings appeared in the three years that followed. They were not marked by the novelty of much of his previous work, but in criticism and exposition they show that his mental powers were unimpaired.

Ward married in 1884 Mary, daughter of the Rev. Henry Martin, Congregationalist minister, herself a lecturer at Newnham College, Cambridge; they had one son and two daughters. He died at Cambridge 4 March 1925.

A portrait of Ward by Ambrose McEvoy was presented by subscribers to the university of Cambridge in 1914 and hangs in the Fitzwilliam Museum.

[Olwen Ward Campbell, *Memoir* prefixed to Ward's *Essays in Philosophy*, 1927; G. F. Stout and others in *The Monist*, Ward Commemoration Number, January 1926; G. Dawes Hicks in *Mind*, July 1925; W. R. Sorley in *Proceedings* of the British Academy, vol. xii, 1926 (including, p. 310 *n.*, some additions to the bibliography contained in *The Monist*); personal knowledge; private information.]

W. R. Sorley.

WARD, Sir JOSEPH GEORGE, first baronet (1856–1930), prime minister of New Zealand, was born at Emerald Hill, Melbourne, Victoria, 26 April 1856, the son of William Thomas Ward, merchant. His parents soon removed to the Awarua district of Southland, where he attended the primary school at the Bluff. At the age of thirteen he entered the New Zealand post and telegraph department as a telegraph messenger. Later he joined the railway department, and in 1877 he set up in business as an export merchant at Invercargill.

Ward took a prominent part in local affairs, and in 1887 was made a J.P. In the same year he was elected liberal member of the house of representatives for Awarua. In 1891, during the premiership of John Ballance [q.v.], he became postmaster-general, and established the San Francisco mail service contract for fortnightly services. He also opened a campaign to secure penny postage. In 1893, in the ministry of Richard John Seddon [q.v.], Ward was appointed colonial treasurer (i.e. minister of finance), and in 1894 had charge of the legislation for the state guarantee to the Bank of New Zealand. He devised and put through parliament the Advances to Settlers Act (1894)—a measure considered daringly experimental—raising £3,000,000 in London at 3 per cent., a record loan for Australasia. In 1894 he became the first minister of industries and commerce; he also had charge of the marine department. He resigned office in 1896 as his firm had been obliged to go into liquidation, but he retained his seat in parliament. In 1899 he rejoined the government as colonial secretary, postmaster-general, and minister of industries and commerce: shortly afterwards he became minister of public health, the first man in the world to hold this office. In 1901 he introduced inland penny postage, and in the same year he was created K.C.M.G. In 1902 he was acting prime minister during Seddon's attendance at the coronation of King Edward VII. The same year he introduced the first superannuation scheme for railway servants, and in 1903 he established state fire insurance for New Zealand. In 1906 he attended the Postal Union Conference held in Rome, and advocated the adoption of universal penny postage.

When Seddon died in June 1906, Ward succeeded him as prime minister after a short interval due to his absence from New Zealand. In 1907 he was sworn of the Privy Council. His first act as premier was to undertake tariff revision; he placed practically all the necessaries of life on the free list. In 1907 he attended the Imperial Conference held in London, and secured the recognition of New Zealand as a Dominion. In 1908 he passed the Workers' Compensation Act, and in 1909 he offered the British government, on behalf of New Zealand, a battle-cruiser, or two if necessary, for the British navy. The offer of one cruiser, H.M.S. *New Zealand*, was accepted. Ward attended the Imperial Defence Conference held in London in 1909, and then returned to New Zealand in order to inaugurate the first hydro-electric scheme for the Dominion. In 1910 he instituted compulsory military training. In 1911 he again went to London in order to attend the Imperial Conference, at which he advocated the creation of an Imperial Parliament of Defence and an Imperial Council, but he received no support and withdrew the motion. The same year he was created a baronet.

The elections of 1911 were inconclusive. Ward met the House, but finding he had not a working majority resigned in March 1912. (Sir) Thomas Mackenzie became prime minister, but he only held office from March to July 1912, when William Ferguson Massey [q.v.] formed a government. In 1915 a national government, composed of a coalition of the reform and liberal parties, was formed, and Ward became minister of finance and post-master-general. He and Massey represented New Zealand at the Imperial War Cabinet and Conferences held in London in 1917 and 1918, and at the Paris Peace Conference in 1919. In 1919 the coalition government was dissolved, owing to the withdrawal of the liberal party. In the ensuing general election the liberal party was defeated, and Ward lost the seat which he had held since 1887. He was out of parliament from 1919 until 1925, when he was returned as member for Invercargill. In 1928, at the invitation of the reorganized national (former liberal) party, he took office as prime minister. He successfully carried out difficult financial operations, but in May 1930 he resigned owing to ill-health, and he died at Wellington 7 July 1930.

Ward married in 1883 Theresa Dorothea (died 1927), daughter of Henry Joseph de Smidt, of New Zealand, and had four sons and one daughter. He was succeeded as second baronet by his eldest son, Cyril Rupert Joseph (born 1884). He received honorary degrees from the universities of Oxford, Cambridge, Edinburgh, Dublin, and Birmingham. He was created G.C.M.G. in 1930.

Ward was an Imperialist, and accomplished much for New Zealand, on the political history of which he left an indelible mark. He was often referred to in the press as a wizard of finance, and his extraordinary memory for figures, which he could quote accurately without notes for lengthy periods, stood him in great stead in parliamentary controversies. A bold administrator, though no great orator, he possessed the gift of inspiring public confidence, and seemed in his last political campaign in 1928 to personify the whole history of the New Zealand liberal movement. He died with his political prestige at its height in his own country, and with many friends, whom his urbanity and generosity had made for him, all over the world.

[*The Times*, 8 July 1930; New Zealand Parliamentary Record, 1840–1925.]

T. M. Wilford.

WARD, Sir LESLIE (1851–1922), cartoonist, was born in Harewood Square, London, 21 November 1851, the eldest son of Edward Matthew Ward [q.v.], historical painter, by his wife, Henrietta Mary Ada Ward. The two families, although they had the same surname, were not related. Mrs. Ward (who died in 1924 at the age of ninety-two) was herself a painter; her father, George Raphael Ward [q.v.], was a mezzotint engraver and miniaturist; her grandfather, James Ward [q.v.], was an engraver and animal painter; and she was niece and great-niece respectively of John Jackson [q.v.], portrait-painter, and of George Morland [q.v.]. After preparatory instruction at Mr. Chase's school at Salt Hill, near Slough, Ward was sent to Eton. His home was visited by many famous artists; and both heredity and environment tended to foster in him precocious artistic development; he exhibited at the Royal Academy while still at school a bust of his brother and a painting (1867). After a brief period of architectural study under Sydney Smirke [q.v.], he joined the Royal Academy Schools in 1871. (Sir) John Everett Millais was much struck by his caricatures, and introduced him to Thomas Gibson Bowles [q.v.], the proprietor of *Vanity Fair*, who chanced to be in need of a new cartoonist.

From the year 1873 onwards Ward contributed regularly to *Vanity Fair*, under the pseudonym of 'Spy'; and for thirty-six years produced cartoons of large numbers of well-known people—politicians, hunting men, judges, jockeys, authors, musicians, bishops, generals—executed in colour and reproduced by lithography. These prints had a wide vogue, and were framed for the walls of innumerable clubs, common-rooms, restaurants, and other places of resort. Ward also did a certain amount of serious portraiture and some architectural drawings. In 1915 he wrote a book of recollections, *Forty Years of 'Spy'*, a pleasant but feeble work. He was knighted in 1918. He died in London 15 May 1922.

Ward married in 1899 Judith Mary Topham-Watney, only daughter of Major Richard Topham, 4th Hussars and 16th Bengal Cavalry, and had one daughter.

Ward was a character-portraitist rather than a caricaturist in the strict sense of the word. He produced good likenesses of his subjects, dressed in their ordinary clothes; and neither presented them in dramatic or mythological guise nor used them to point a political or social moral. He was not a sensitive draughtsman, nor was he a decorator; and the *Vanity Fair* plates may best be described as very good pictorial journalism, largely dependent on topical appositeness for their appeal. His best work, in his own opinion, was done not from formal sittings, but when the model was unaware of his scrutiny.

[*The Times*, 16 May 1922; Sir L. Ward, *Forty Years of 'Spy'*, 1915; *Vanity Fair* albums, *passim*.] H. B. Grimsditch.

WARLOCK, PETER (pseudonym), musical composer and writer on music. [See Heseltine, Philip Arnold.]

WARREN, Sir CHARLES (1840–1927), general and archaeologist, was born at Bangor 7 February 1840, the second son of Major-General Sir Charles Warren [q.v.], by his first wife, Mary, daughter of William Hughes, of Dublin and Carlow. He was educated at Cheltenham College, Sandhurst, and Woolwich, and joined the Royal Engineers in 1857. From 1859 to 1865 he was employed on the Gibraltar survey, and in the latter year became assistant instructor in surveying at the school of military engineering at Chatham. In 1867 he was selected for special service in Palestine, where he made, for the Palestine Exploration Fund, a reconnaissance of Philistia, the Jordan valley, and Gilead, and also excavated extensively in Jerusalem. He published the results in three books—*The Recovery of Jerusalem* (with (Sir) Charles William Wilson, q.v., 1871), *Underground Jerusalem* (1874), and *The Temple or the Tomb* (1880).

Owing to ill-health, Warren was obliged to return to England in 1870. After serving at Dover from 1871 to 1872, he held an appointment at the school of gunnery at Shoeburyness from 1872 to 1876, where he found himself against his will drifting into civil life. He was considering the acceptance of an appointment as engineer to harbour works in Australia when he was asked by the Colonial Office to act as special commissioner to delimit the Griqualand West and Orange Free State boundary. This he completed in 1877, when he received the C.M.G. for his services. He then travelled through the Transvaal to Delagoa Bay, but was sent back to Griqualand in order to investigate and settle the land question, a task which he successfully performed.

During the Kafir War of 1877–1878 Warren received the command of the Diamond Fields Horse. He took part in the actions of Perie Bush (in which he was severely wounded), Debickek, and Tankoon. For his services he was thrice mentioned in dispatches and received the medal and clasp and the brevet of lieutenant-colonel. On the conclusion of the war he was appointed special commissioner to investigate native questions in Bechuanaland, and in 1879 administrator and commander-in-chief of Griqualand West.

From 1880 to 1884 Warren was chief instructor in surveying at the school of military engineering at Chatham, but in the course of his service there he was detached for special duty under the Admiralty in Egypt. He was commissioned to lead a search party to discover the fate of the expedition of Professor Edward Henry Palmer [q.v.], which had left Suez on 8 August 1882. Warren discovered that Palmer and his companions had been robbed and murdered; he recovered their remains, and secured the punishment of the criminals. For this he received the K.C.M.G., medal, bronze star, and third class Medjidie, and in 1883 he was created a knight of justice of the Order of St. John of Jerusalem.

In 1884 difficulties arose in Bechuanaland between the natives and Boer immigrants from the Transvaal, and it became necessary to send a military expedition to Bechuanaland to restore order. Warren was sent out from England to take command. He arrived in December at the Cape, where he mobilized a force of 4,000 men and started for Bechuanaland. Here he met Cecil Rhodes [q.v.], who was acting as deputy-commissioner, and President Kruger. Warren was vested with full civil and military powers, and proceeded to administer the protectorate after forcing the two republics of Stellaland and Goshen, which had been formed by Boer freebooters on territory stolen from the natives, to capitulate. The expedition was a complete success, the more so because it was carried out in the face of very considerable difficulties and entirely without bloodshed. Some friction arose between Warren and the Cape government, but the home government supported Warren. He was, however, recalled in September and his place was taken by Colonel (afterwards Sir) Frederick Carrington [q.v.] in command of a newly created police force. For his services Warren was created G.C.M.G.

After a few weeks spent in command of the troops at Suakin, Warren was appointed to succeed Sir Edmund Y. W. Henderson [q.v.] as chief-commissioner of the London metropolitan police in 1886. The office was one of great difficulty. Much dissatisfaction had been caused by the action of the police in the disturbances in Pall Mall and Oxford Street in the spring of that year, and in consequence Warren was called upon to reorganize the force. On the occasion of Queen Victoria's jubilee in June 1887, Warren was responsible for the police arrangements, which proved completely successful. In that year further disturbances took place in Trafalgar Square, and the police, in quelling them, were popularly accused of 'military high-handedness'. The case of Miss Cass (1887) opened afresh the question of the treatment of women by the police, and the 'Ripper' murders caused much public indignation. Relations between Warren and the home secretary, Henry Matthews (afterwards Viscount Llandaff, q.v.) became strained. Strong difference of opinion arose as to the right of the home secretary to issue orders to the police, and Warren resigned in consequence in 1888, receiving the K.C.B. for his services.

Warren was appointed in 1889 to the command at Singapore, a post which he held until 1894. He proceeded to organize a defence scheme, to frame mobilization regulations, and to reform infantry-training. He conducted experiments in communication and even attempted a wireless communication between two forts. During his time at Singapore he spent his periods of leave in travelling in India, Burma, Japan, and the Dutch East Indies, and on leaving the Straits Settlements he returned home through North America. He was appointed in 1895 to the command of the Thames district. Here he devoted himself to the completion of the Thames defence schemes, but the routine work of the command scarcely gave scope to a man of Warren's restless energy. He was placed on the retired list for a year after completing the period of this command; but after the outbreak of the war in South Africa he was appointed, in November 1899, to the command of the 5th division, and sailed for the Cape.

Warren had been promoted lieutenant-general in 1897, and when he with the fifth division joined Sir Redvers Buller [q.v.] in Natal on 21 December 1899 he was the senior divisional commander. At the beginning of January 1900 Buller planned a further attempt to relieve Ladysmith. It was intended to turn the Boer position in front of Potgieter's Drift by crossing the Tugela near Trichardt's Drift and gaining the open plain north of Spion Kop. The conduct of the operations was placed directly under Warren, whose force consisted of the 2nd division under General (Sir) Francis Clery [q.v.], the mounted brigade under Lord Dundonald [q.v.], and the 5th division less one brigade. The Tugela was crossed on 18 January, and heavy fighting took place from 20 to 23 January. Dundonald advanced along the road to Acton Homes, and Clery made some progress to the north-west. Major-General (Sir) Neville Lyttelton in command of the 4th brigade, who had crossed the Tugela some five miles to the east of Trichardt's Drift, co-operated, although not under Warren's direct command.

On 23 January Warren decided that it was impossible to carry out the flanking movement to the north of Spion Kop for lack of supplies, so it was determined to advance by the more direct road leading north-east. On that day Buller came to Warren's head-quarters, and it was decided to attack Spion Kop that night. Spion Kop was occupied and held during the whole of 24 January, but late in the evening Colonel Alexander Thorneycroft, who was in command, decided on his own responsibility that the position was untenable and evacuated it. On 25 January Buller again visited Warren's head-quarters, and resuming direct command, decided to withdraw his forces and retire south of the Tugela. Spion Kop was a reverse, but although Warren was in direct command of the operations, Buller was often present and exercised occasional control. There was divided responsibility, and Warren's report with the comments of Buller and Lord Roberts led to much subsequent recrimination.

Warren remained in command of the 5th division during the main operations for the relief of Ladysmith, shortly after which a rebellion broke out (April 1900) in North-West Cape Colony, Griqualand West, and British Bechuanaland. On the advice of (Lord) Milner, Warren was placed in command of an expedition to quell this rebellion. He cleared the country between the Orange River and the Vaal, captured Douglas, and defeated a Boer force at Faber's Put (30 May), after which he advanced without further difficulties. In July the rebellion was quelled, the force withdrawn, and peace restored. Warren returned to England in August 1900. He was promoted general in 1904, and colonel commandant of the Royal Engineers in 1905.

Warren was deeply interested in the Boy Scout movement which was founded in 1908; he was an original member, and for many years the oldest member. He gave a very large proportion of his time during the last nineteen years of his life to active work with scouts in the Ramsgate, Canterbury, and Weston-super-Mare districts successively. He maintained his interest in scientific matters—he had been elected F.R.S. in 1884—and in archaeology, and published several books and articles, notably on questions of early weights and measures. He was an enthusiastic freemason, and devoted much time to masonic research. He was also deeply interested in, and a prolific writer upon, religious questions. He also published a volume of reminiscences, *On the Veldt in the Seventies* (1902).

Warren married in 1864 Fanny Margaretta (died 1919), daughter of Samuel Haydon, of Guildford. They had two sons and two daughters. He died at Weston-super-Mare 21 January 1927, and was buried near to his wife's grave at their old country home at Westbere, Kent, after a military funeral in Canterbury Cathedral.

[*The Times*, 24 January 1927; W. Porter, *History of the Corps of Royal Engineers*, vol. ii, 1889; *The Diamond Jubilee of the Palestine Exploration Fund*, 1924; Hansard, *Parliamentary Debates*, House of Commons, November 1888; Sir J. F. Maurice and M. H. Grant, (Official) *History of the War in South Africa 1899–1902*, 1906–1910; *Spion Kop Dispatches*, Cd. 968, 17 April 1902; Blake Knox, *Buller's Campaign in Natal*, 1902; Lord Newton, *Lord Lansdowne*, 1929; War Office Records; private information.]

ONSLOW.

WARREN, SIR THOMAS HERBERT (1853–1930), president of Magdalen College, Oxford, scholar, and man of letters, was born at Cotham, a suburb of Bristol, 21 October 1853, the second son of Algernon William Warren, a business man in Bristol, who held a leading position in the city as town councillor, alderman, and J.P. His mother, Cecil, was the daughter of Thomas Thomas, of Llangadock, Carmarthenshire, and sister of Christopher Thomas, mayor of Bristol in 1878; to her family Warren owed his first christian name. His father had literary and artistic interests, his mother both practical capacity and something of the Welsh imaginative temperament. Herbert—he was always known by his second name—was educated at Manilla Hall school, Clifton, until he was fifteen, when he entered Clifton College, then recently founded with John Percival [q.v.] as its first headmaster. He quickly made his mark both in work and games, and left in 1872 as head of the school and scholar-elect of Balliol College, Oxford, captain of football and fives champion.

When Warren came up to Balliol, Jowett had been two years master and the college was at the height of its reputation. Among the contemporaries whom Warren came to know well were H. H. Asquith and his brother, W. W. Asquith (afterwards a master at Clifton), Charles Lucas, Thomas Raleigh, and Alfred Milner; W. P. Ker and A. D. Godley were his juniors by two years. In this distinguished society Warren more than held his own; he obtained first classes in classical moderations (1873) and in *literae humaniores* (1876), and won the Hertford scholarship (1873), the Craven scholarship (1878), and the Gaisford prize for Greek verse (1875). He was occasionally chosen to represent the university at Rugby football, maintained his supremacy at fives, a game which he continued to play with skill and vigour even after he became president of Magdalen College, and held the office of librarian at the Union in 1875–1876. Francis de Paravicini helped to put the finer edge on his scholarship, and Milner, his closest friend, introduced him to German learning and did much to form his mind and interests. But probably the main influence was that of Jowett himself, whose ideal of a college as not merely a home of learning but a training ground for public life, was destined to guide Warren's policy in his direction of Magdalen.

In October 1877, a year after he had

taken his degree, Warren was elected to a prize fellowship at Magdalen and succeeded in the following term to a classical tutorship. The college in the later years of the presidency of Frederic Bulley had already ceased to be a close corporation and was coming to the front, but Warren himself made the greatest contribution to its remarkable development in the next twenty years. Not only was his brilliant scholarship a stimulus to his pupils' success, but he set himself to know and help them as a personal friend. He also cultivated acquaintance with the public schools, and made every effort to improve the quality of the scholars and commoners who entered the college.

On the death of Dr. Bulley in 1885 Warren, at the unusually early age of thirty-two, was elected president, and held the office until 1928, a period of forty-three years. He threw himself even more vigorously than before into the task of developing the college, gathering round him a distinguished staff of teachers, including H. W. Greene, C. R. L. Fletcher, C. C. J. Webb, and Christopher Cookson—A. D. Godley was already a classical tutor—and welcoming as a new strength to the college the professorial fellows added by the royal commission of 1878. At the same time he increased the numbers of the undergraduates and raised the standard of the college, both intellectually and in other ways. It was sometimes said by outside critics that Warren was over-anxious about the social standing of his undergraduates; if so, this was only a part of his desire to secure for Magdalen the best in every way. It was a marked tribute to the position which the college held in the university and outside it that King George V in 1912 chose it for the Prince of Wales.

Meanwhile Warren was coming to hold a prominent position in university affairs. He was for many years a member of the Hebdomadal Council, a delegate of the University Museum, and a curator of the Taylor Institution. In these capacities he did much to promote the studies of natural science and of modern languages in Oxford, and his courtesy, tact, and good judgement made him a valued member of any body on which he served. He spoke often in Congregation and, if he was sometimes prolix and over-conciliatory, he always gave the impression that he knew his subject thoroughly and carried weight accordingly. From 1906 to 1910 he was vice-chancellor. Lord Curzon [q.v.], as chancellor, was then engaged in drawing up his programme of university reform; Warren supported him whole-heartedly and, if at the time the results appeared meagre, many of the ideas then promoted were adopted by the royal commission of 1919.

Outside the university Warren's services were employed on several government commissions and committees; he was a member, and later chairman, of the governing body of Clifton College, a councillor of the university of Bristol, and for a time a governor of St. Paul's School. Politically he was a liberal of the old school, and preferred gradual reform to hasty change. Brought up as a nonconformist, he was confirmed in the Church of England while a fellow of Magdalen, and proved himself a staunch churchman.

All these practical activities never swamped Warren's devotion to literature. Although his only contribution to classical scholarship was a useful though unpretentious edition of the first five books of Plato's *Republic* (1888, seven times reprinted), his scholarship showed itself in other ways. The two great literary enthusiasms of his life were for Virgil and for Tennyson. In his two published volumes of poems, *By Severn Sea* (1897) and *The Death of Virgil* (1907), he is seen as an eager disciple of both poets, and an attractive, if sometimes rather laboured, writer of verse. His wider literary interests found expression in his lectures as professor of poetry at Oxford (1911–1916), which exhibit his range of reading, his taste, and his mature powers of criticism. The Creweian orations, which it fell to his lot to deliver at the Encaenia, proved also that his fine scholarship and 'Attic wit' remained unimpaired. His ability as a writer was also shown in contributions—particularly in obituary notices—which he made to *The Times*, as its correspondent for the university, and for many years to the *Oxford Magazine*, of which he was one of the founders and a constant supporter. The honorary degree of D.C.L. was conferred upon him at Lord Curzon's first Encaenia in 1907, and he was also an honorary LL.D. of Birmingham University, an honorary D.Litt. of Bristol University, and an honorary fellow of Balliol (1924). He was created K.C.V.O. by the king when the prince left Magdalen on the outbreak of war in 1914.

The long years of Warren's presidency were a time of almost unbroken prosperity for Magdalen College and of personal happiness to himself. As the generations passed, the number of his old Magdalen friends was always increasing, but, with the loyalty and kindness of heart which always characterized him, he kept in touch with them and followed their careers with unfailing interest. He was an ideal host both in the college common room and in his own lodgings. In all this personal side of his life he was greatly helped by his wife, Mary Isabel, youngest daughter of the chemist Sir Benjamin Collins Brodie, second baronet [q.v.], whom he married in 1886. The years of the European War, when he received almost daily the news of the death of some Magdalen man, brought him great distress, but he steered the college through this time of anxiety and through the hardly less difficult period of reconstruction which followed. In 1928 age and increasing infirmity made him decide to resign: he received many tokens of affection and gratitude, and was elected an honorary fellow of the college. He continued to live in Oxford, and died there suddenly 9 June 1930. He had no children.

Warren was naturally a fine athletic figure, tall and broad, with very dark hair, a full beard, and slightly prominent teeth, but in the last twenty years of his life he became more and more crippled by arthritis. A portrait painted by Sir W. B. Richmond in 1899, which hangs in the President's Lodgings, Magdalen College, represents him in middle life; a later portrait by Glyn Philpot, presented to him by Magdalen men on his retirement in 1928, hangs in the college hall and gives an admirable likeness of him in his later years, although the features are perhaps too grim.

A cartoon of Warren by 'Spy' appeared in *Vanity Fair* 8 April 1893.

[*The Times*, 10 and 11 June 1930; Laurie Magnus, *Herbert Warren of Magdalen*, 1932; personal knowledge.] C. Bailey.

WATERHOUSE, PAUL (1861–1924), architect, was the eldest son of the architect, Alfred Waterhouse, R.A. [q.v.], by his wife, Elizabeth, daughter of John Hodgkin, conveyancer, and sister of Thomas Hodgkin [q.v.], the historian. He was born 29 October 1861 at Manchester, and he lived there until his father, having won the competition for the design of the new Natural History Museum in South Kensington (1865), moved with his family to London. Paul Waterhouse was sent to St. Michael's school, Aldin House, Slough, kept by the Rev. J. W. Hawtrey, and from there to Eton. He proceeded to Balliol College, Oxford, and obtained a second class in classical moderations (1882) and in *literae humaniores* (1884). Delicate in health, he did not take any great part in games, but at Balliol he coxed the college eight, was captain of the college boat-club in 1883, and coxed one of the trial eights, though he failed to get his blue. A contemporary in the college boat speaks of his initiative, tact, and insight into character—qualities which marked his professional career.

After leaving Oxford, Waterhouse went into his father's office. He became a partner in 1891, and, after the senior partner's death in 1905, carried on the practice alone, until joined by his own son Michael in 1919. His individual, and especially his more intimate, work has a quality of its own, contrasting in character with the specialized style of the large business and public buildings for which his father had become famous—a tradition which he carried on in the continuation of his father's practice. He inherited a facility for admirable planning, described by a good judge as 'exquisite and workable'. He completed many of his father's works, among them being buildings at Liverpool for the Royal Infirmary and for the University, laboratories at Manchester and Leeds Universities, and St. Mary's Hospital, Manchester.

Among the more important of Waterhouse's own works are the chemical laboratories at Oxford University (1913), and the university Union (1921), the St. Regulus Club (1922), and the Younger commemoration hall (1925) at St. Andrews University. Hospital buildings designed by him include the medical school and the nurses' home, University College, London (1905), the offices of the Royal National Pension Fund for Nurses, Buckingham Street, Strand (1906), extensions to the Lister Institute of Preventive Medicine, Chelsea Bridge Road (1908), and new wards for the Bromley (Kent) and District Hospital (1910), the Yeovil and District Hospital (1921), and St. Leonard's Hospital, Sudbury (1922).

Alfred Waterhouse had been responsible for designing important office buildings for the Prudential Assurance and Refuge Assurance Companies, and his son continued this connexion, designing premises for the former at Stockport, Leicester, Liverpool, Manchester, Ipswich, Middlesbrough, and other towns. The Atlas Assurance Company's office at Birmingham is also from his design. He extended the premises of the National Provincial Bank in Bishopsgate, London, and built branches for Lloyds Bank and for the National Provincial Foreign Bank in Paris, Brussels, and Antwerp.

Among examples of Waterhouse's domestic work, No. 73 South Audley Street, London, and Mount Melville, St. Andrews, with its home-farm and buildings, gardens, cottages, and bailiff's house, may be mentioned. His ecclesiastical work includes All Saints' church, St. Andrews (1918), St. Francis's church, Hammerfield, Hertfordshire, and the convent of the Incarnation at Oxford.

In 1886 Waterhouse was awarded the essay medal of the Royal Institute of British Architects. He was elected an associate of that body in 1889 by examination, with the award of a special prize, and proceeded to the fellowship in 1895. During a lifelong association with the Institute, he devoted himself to the furtherance of its objects and gave unstinted time to its committees, including the Board of Architectural Education. He took particular interest in the education and training of students and in the development of schools of architecture in London and the provinces. In 1921 and 1922 he occupied the president's chair, previously held by his father from 1888 to 1891, and during his years of office did much to promote the unification of the architectural profession. The Institute was passing through a period of difficulty, and Waterhouse's powers of firm but tactful leadership were invaluable. By means of visits and addresses in all parts of the country he succeeded in greatly strengthening the relations between the Institute and its allied societies.

Town Planning was a subject of which Waterhouse made a special study, and he was an authority on London bridges. He excelled as a draughtsman; and his line and wash drawings have much delicacy and charm. Examples of such work are his illustrations to William Sanday's *Sacred Sites of the Gospels* (1903). He was an accomplished speaker and writer. His literary work was confined mainly to professional subjects, which he treated in a style that was scholarly, humorous, and allusive. *Paul Waterhouse. A Collection of certain of his Papers and Addresses* was published by the Oxford University Press in 1930.

Waterhouse married in 1887 Lucy Grace, daughter of Sir Reginald Francis Douce Palgrave [q.v.], clerk of the House of Commons, and had one son, who succeeded him in his practice, and two daughters. Monica Mary, the elder of his two sisters, married Robert Bridges [q.v.], the poet laureate. He died at his home at Yattendon, Berkshire, 19 December 1924.

[*The Times*, 20 December 1924; *Journal* of the Royal Institute of British Architects, 10 January 1925; private information; personal knowledge.] P. S. WORTHINGTON.

WATSON, FOSTER (1860–1929), historian of education, was born at Lincoln 27 June 1860, the third in the family of five sons of Thomas Watson, of Lincoln, engaged in the agricultural machinery business, by his wife, Ann, daughter of Thomas Booth, worsted stuff manufacturer, of Little Horton, Bradford, Yorkshire. He was educated at Lincoln grammar school and at Owens College, Manchester, where he obtained the M.A. (London) degree in 1881. From 1885 to 1891 he was second master at the Cowper Street Middle Class School (afterwards the Central Foundation School, E.C.). In 1894 he was appointed lecturer on education at the University College of Wales, Aberystwyth, and in 1895 was raised to the status of professor. After resigning the professorship in 1913 he was professor emeritus and special lecturer until his death, which took place 13 February 1929, at Green Street Green, near Farnborough, Kent. From 1915 to 1929 he was professor of rhetoric at Gresham College, London.

Foster Watson's work as a writer and as lecturer at Aberystwyth, Gresham College, and elsewhere, covered a great variety of subjects in education, philosophy, and literature, and may be summarized under three heads. In the first group comes the history of education in the period 1500–1660, especially in England. His chief work under this head is *The English Grammar Schools to 1660: their curriculum and practice* (1908), to which he added a companion volume, *The Beginnings of the Teaching of Modern Subjects in England* (1909). He was engaged for many years on the collection of material (much of which he published in journals and magazines between 1892 and 1909) for a projected work on the 'English Educational Renascence', a history of English education in the time of the Commonwealth. Secondly, he made a special study of the life and work of Juan Luis Vives, the friend and counsellor of Erasmus and More. He published *Vives on Educa-*

tion; a translation of the De Tradendis Disciplinis (1912), *Vives and the Renascence Education of Women* (1912), and many articles on the subject in English, Spanish, Catalan, and Italian magazines; he also lectured at Barcelona and Valencia, and presented a tablet to Corpus Christi College, Oxford, in 1925 in memory of Vives's residence there from 1523 to 1525. Thirdly, Foster Watson contributed copiously to dictionaries and encyclopaedias. He wrote the chapter on 'Scholars and Scholarship' in volume vii of the *Cambridge History of English Literature* and a number of educational biographies in this DICTIONARY; he contributed the article on Wales to F. E. Buisson's *Nouveau Dictionnaire de Pédagogie* and, as departmental editor, some 150 articles to Paul Monroe's *Cyclopaedia of Education* (1911–1913). He also edited *The Encyclopaedia and Dictionary of Education* (four vols., 1921, 1922).

Had Watson lived long enough it is probable that he would have endeavoured to construct a theory of education based on the underlying causes of the success of great teachers, as well as on the evidence, positive and negative, furnished by the history of education. No one who heard him lecture will forget the vigour and conviction of his opinions or the dynamic enthusiasm of his delivery.

Watson married twice: first, in 1914 Amy (died 1918), daughter of S. Smith Kimpster, of Masbrough, Yorkshire; secondly, in 1925 Nancy, eldest daughter of L. Wynne Roberts, of Buxton. He had no children. He was a member of several learned societies at home and abroad, and in recognition of his work on the history of education received the honorary D.Litt. degree from the university of Wales (1922). He also obtained the D.Lit. degree of the university of London (1912).

[Private information; personal knowledge. A bibliography of Foster Watson's work in the subject of education was published by the University College of Wales, Aberystwyth, in December 1913.] C. R. CHAPPLE.

WATTS, SIR PHILIP (1846–1926), naval architect, born at Deptford 30 May 1846, was the son of John Watts, of Havelock Park, Southsea, then chief assistant to John Fincham, shipwright at Portsmouth dockyard, a famous builder of warships, and author of *The History of Naval Architecture* (1851), in the preparation of which John Watts assisted. His mother was Mary Ann Featherstone. Watts's father, grandfather, and great-grandfather were all master shipwrights, and his great-grandfather took part in the building of Nelson's flagship *Victory*. Philip Watts was educated at the principal school at Portsmouth, and in 1860 was apprenticed as a shipwright in the royal dockyard, where he was taught mathematics and physical science in the dockyard school. He was selected to receive a 'superior course' in naval construction, and in 1866 was one of the three Admiralty students promoted to the Royal School of Naval Architecture at South Kensington. In April 1870 he left the Royal School with the title of fellow, and was appointed to assist the chief constructor's staff at the Admiralty (which in 1883 became the royal corps of naval constructors) in making calculations with regard to the design of new ships, and to act as Admiralty overseer on several ships then building by contract. In this capacity Watts made a practice of calculating on scientific principles the proper size of various parts of a ship's structure and did much to break down the determination of scantlings by rule of thumb. On completing this work he was engaged for over two years at Torquay in assisting William Froude [q.v.], who was the first to develop an accurate theory of the behaviour of ships in a sea way, in his investigations on that subject undertaken at the request of the Admiralty. This association was the beginning of a lifelong friendship between Watts and Froude and the latter's son and assistant, Robert Edward Froude (1856–1924).

In 1872 Watts became a draughtsman of the third class on the constructor's staff, and on the completion of his service with Froude he was appointed assistant constructor at Pembroke dockyard during the building of the battleship *Shannon*, launched in 1875, and while so engaged became notable as an ingenious designer of mechanical appliances and details of all sorts. On returning to the Admiralty he was entrusted with the organization and supervision of a 'calculating section' rendered necessary by the novelty and growing complexity of naval designs. Among other work the director of naval construction, (Sir) Nathaniel Barnaby [q.v.], placed in Watts's hands the calculations relating to the torpedo-ram *Polyphemus*, laid down in 1878, a vessel of novel construction with a very small reserve of buoyancy, which made extreme accuracy necessary in calculating her metacentric height, range of stability, and increased immersion in case of damage. He was also concerned in the controversy with regard to the battleship *Inflexible*, launched in 1876 [see Barnaby, Sir Nathaniel], and in connexion with it conducted some steering experiments on the battleship *Thunderer* in Portland harbour, the results of which were afterwards issued in a blue book for the instruction of the fleet. In connexion with the *Inflexible* Watts experimented with water chambers for the purpose of moderating the rolling of ships of great metacentric height [cf. Sir Reginald Bacon, *Life of Lord Fisher*, i, 75–6, 1929]. In 1883 he was promoted to the grade of constructor, and in November 1884 appointed to the staff of Chatham dockyard; but in October 1885 he left the Admiralty's service in order to succeed Sir William Henry White [q.v.] as naval designer and general manager to Armstrong & Co. at their warship-yard at Elswick-on-Tyne, White succeeding Barnaby at the Admiralty as director of naval construction.

Watts had now spent fifteen years of very strenuous professional life in the service of the Admiralty. The greater part of his work had consisted in carrying out original investigations and in organizing sections for making and recording many kinds of calculations in the construction department. This experience prepared him for his later career, in which first at Elswick he built cruisers for the navies of the world, and subsequently at the Admiralty, on the eve of a world-wide war, he armed Great Britain with battleships. During his seventeen years at Elswick he was placed in a position of great responsibility, both as a naval designer and as a captain of labour on a large scale; he brought the Elswick shipyard to the foremost position by designing and constructing foreign warships, and also by building several British warships designed by the Admiralty and secured for the Elswick yard in open competition. The ships designed for foreign powers were remarkable for those qualities of gunpower and speed which later were the outstanding features of Watts's additions to the British fighting fleet. He had signal success in obtaining high speed and heavy armament on abnormally small displacements. Cruisers of note designed by him for Japan, the Argentine, Brazil, Chile, Norway, Portugal, Roumania, and Turkey established his reputation as a constructor and gave him experience for his great achievements later. Nearly all the warship fighting done by the Japanese fleet in 1904 and 1905 was carried out by Watts's ships, the battleships *Yashima* and *Hatsuse*, and the cruisers *Idzumo*, *Iwate*, *Asama*, and *Tokiwa*. For his services he was awarded the Japanese order of the Rising Sun. Among Watts's Elswick ships may be mentioned especially the Italian cruiser *Piemonte*, built in 1888, then for her size the most heavily armed war vessel in the world, and the Japanese *Yashima*, launched in 1896, a battleship with the speed of a cruiser, and in many respects the forerunner of his battle-cruisers of later times. From 1894 to 1910 Watts was lieutenant-colonel and honorary colonel of the first brigade of the Royal Garrison Artillery Volunteers, and while at Elswick he equipped and sent out to the South African War the Elswick battery.

In February 1902 Watts succeeded White at the Admiralty as director of naval construction. At that time two of the *King Edward VII* class of eight battleships had been begun, and three more were to be laid down before the end of the year. In this class the main armament was much the same as that of the *Collingwood* class of battleships designed in 1880, though the secondary armament was heavier. Watts considered the class not powerful enough. The immense developments in naval machinery and gun power, the increased possibilities of speed and of the conservation of fuel, all seemed to forecast the evolution of a much more powerful type of warship. But Watts was not able immediately to carry out his ideas to the full. In 1903 he produced designs for battleships of much greater gun power. The Admiralty, however, while approving what afterwards was named the *Lord Nelson* type, resolved to build first the three remaining vessels of the *King Edward* class, which were accordingly laid down in 1903, and were followed by the *Lord Nelson* and *Agamemnon*, of the new and more powerful type, in 1904 and 1905. The appointment on 21 October 1904 of Sir John Arbuthnot Fisher (afterwards Lord Fisher, q.v.) as first sea lord gave Watts the opportunity of realizing more completely his desire for powerful ships. So far back as 1881 he had accompanied the *Inflexible* in the Mediterranean when Fisher was in command, had had the opportunity of discussing with him matters of naval construction, and had brought away an outline design, evolved during the cruise, for a battleship with an 'all big gun' armament of four pairs of 16-inch

80-ton guns mounted in turrets. This design, however, Barnaby had rejected on account of the large displacement involved [*Transactions* of the Institution of Naval Architects, 1919, vol. xli, pp. 3–4]. Fisher, on becoming first lord, introduced a design for an 'all big gun' battleship having six pairs of 12-inch guns all mounted on the middle line, three pairs at each end of the ship in steps. A vessel so armed could fire six guns directly ahead and six directly astern, and all twelve guns on either broadside.

Fisher got a powerful committee of design appointed by Lord Selborne, including Prince Louis of Battenburg [q.v.], naval officers such as John (afterwards Earl) Jellicoe, (Sir) Henry Bradwardine Jackson [q.v.], (Sir) Reginald Bacon, (Sir) Charles Madden, Sir Albert John Durston, and (Sir) Alfred Winsloe, and men of expert knowledge such as Lord Kelvin [q.v.], Sir John Isaac Thornycroft [q.v.], R. E. Froude, (Sir) John Harvard Biles, (Sir) Alexander Gracie, and Watts. Fisher's proposal of a twelve-gun battleship was generally approved, but on consideration it was found too large and costly. The *Dreadnought* was as near an approach as was possible, taking into account dockyard capacity and naval estimates. The final result of the committee's aspirations, as interpreted by Watts, was the recommendation of the remarkable series of ship-types of which the *Dreadnought* battleship and *Indomitable* battle-cruiser were the chief. The principles underlying these new designs were a much more powerful armament on a given displacement, higher speed through the use of steam turbines and the water-tube boiler, unification of gun-calibre to secure gun control, greater manœuvring power, the internal subdivision of the vessel into separate water-tight compartments, each self-contained as regards access, drainage, and ventilation, and greater protection against guns and torpedoes in the arrangement of the armoured decks, and the underwater protection of the sides. In the *Dreadnought* battleship class the main armament was raised from the four 12-inch, and four 9·2-inch guns of the *King Edward VII* class to ten 12-inch guns, mounted in pairs *en barbette*, three pairs on the centre line, and a pair on each broadside opposite each other amidships. The secondary armament disappeared and was replaced by quickfirers to deal with torpedo craft. But in later classes of *Dreadnoughts* the secondary armament was restored, to meet the increased menace from air and torpedo attack.

The first *Dreadnought* was laid down at Plymouth on 2 October 1905 and began her sea trials on 3 October 1906. She had a speed of over 21·6 knots, and owing to her rectangular construction amidships was comparatively free from rolling. During his ten years of office Watts improved and developed the *Dreadnought* type. He was the designer of the *Bellerophon, St. Vincent, Neptune, Orion, King George V, Iron Duke,* and *Queen Elizabeth* classes, each containing several battleships, and each marking an increase in armament, displacement, and speed. He himself considered that the *Orion* class, laid down in 1909–1910, practically realized Fisher's first design. In the *Elizabeth* class, 1912–1913, eight 15-inch guns were substituted for ten 13·5-inch guns. The main armament of the *Dreadnought* type set the fashion to the whole world. 'If Sir Philip's fame rested on no other basis than that of the armament of the *Dreadnought*, his name would be handed down as one of the world's great naval designers' [*Transactions* of the Institution of Naval Architects, 1926, vol. lxviii, p. 289]. Lord Fisher wrote: 'The *Dreadnought* could not have been born but for Sir Philip Watts' [*Memories*, p. 258, 1919].

Hardly less remarkable was the creation of the battle-cruiser. At the outbreak of the European War in 1914 all the effective battle-cruisers in the royal navy were of Watts's design. The battle-cruisers *Indomitable, Inflexible,* and *Invincible* were launched in 1907. They were armed with eight 12-inch guns and had a speed of twenty-four knots. On account of their heavy armament and substantial armour protection they might have been classed as battleships. They were followed by the *Indefatigable* class, launched in 1909, which included besides the *Indefatigable* the Australian cruisers *Australia* and *New Zealand*. In 1910 were launched the *Lion, Princess Royal,* and *Queen Mary*, of greater size and a speed of twenty-eight knots, and in 1912 the *Tiger*, with a speed of thirty knots. It was the speedy arrival and intervention of the *Inflexible* and *Invincible*—wholly unexpected by the enemy—which proved the decisive factor in the action with Admiral von Spee off the Falkland Islands on 8 December 1914. Considerable improvements were also made by Watts in the designs of light cruisers and destroyers.

All these changes in design were fundamental and not merely developments of pre-existing types. As they were made in time of peace it was not easy to explain their desirability to the public and they met with considerable opposition. In parliament in July 1906 Mr. Balfour criticized the designing and building of *Dreadnoughts*, and Sir William White, Watts's predecessor as constructor, suggested in the *Nineteenth Century* in April 1908 that England had started an unnecessary naval armament race. There were strong reasons, however, for thinking that the improvements in naval construction were making the race inevitable. It has been asserted that Germany designed more powerful ships as early as 1904 [*Navy League Annual*, 1910–1911, pp. 188–190]. If an advance was certain, it was important to have the initiative. Subsequent events showed this. Watts's work designed in time of peace stood the vital test of war. The naval developments in Great Britain, when realized, caused the continental powers to change their whole outlook on naval affairs. The Kiel canal had to be widened and harbours reconstructed, and when war broke out in 1914 the German navy with a greatly inferior weight of broadside, in the proportion of about four to seven, was not in a position to meet the demands made on it by the military chiefs in Berlin. The fact that England from the beginning was greatly superior at sea was of primary importance. At the battle of Jutland (31 May 1916) twenty-nine of the thirty-four British battleships and battle-cruisers engaged were of Watts's design.

In August 1912 Watts resigned his post as director of naval construction, but his services were retained in an advisory capacity until January 1916, when he returned to Elswick and became a director of Armstrong, Whitworth & Co. He was created K.C.B. in 1905, and in 1900 was elected a fellow of the Royal Society, of which he was afterwards a member of council and a vice-president. He received the honorary degree of LL.D. from Glasgow University and that of Sc.D. from Trinity College, Dublin. He became a member of the Institution of Naval Architects in 1873, of the Institution of Civil Engineers in 1901, and of the Institution of Mechanical Engineers in 1902. On the formation of the Society of Nautical Research in 1910 he was made a vice-president. In June 1921, at the annual meeting of that society, he called attention to the dangerous state of Nelson's *Victory* in Portsmouth harbour, and as a result of his efforts and those of Sir F. C. Doveton Sturdee [q.v.] the famous ship was re-fitted and preserved. In restoring her to her Trafalgar conditions Watts was assisted by old plans of the ship which had come down to him from his great-grandfather. He contributed an article on this subject in 1923 to the *Transactions* of the Institution of Naval Architects. Like all great organizers, he attached a high value to education. He assisted in the creation of the professorial chairs and the schools of naval architecture in the universities of Glasgow, Durham, and Liverpool.

Watts died of pneumonia at his residence, 4 Hans Crescent, London, 15 March 1926 and was buried in Brompton cemetery. He married in 1875 Elise Isabelle, daughter of Chevalier Gustave Simoneau de St. Omer, of Brussels. His wife and his two daughters survived him. His written work consists of articles, some of which may be regarded as primary sources of information for his own work. He contributed ten papers to the *Transactions* of the Institution of Naval Architects. Two of these are of particular importance, 'Warship Building (1860–1910)', published in 1911, and 'Ships of the British Navy on August 4, 1914', published in 1919. He wrote for the tenth edition of the *Encyclopædia Britannica*, and revised and extended for the eleventh edition, the articles on 'Ships' and 'Shipbuilding', which really are treatises of great value in a concise form and are of particular interest because so largely drawn from his own knowledge and experience. The particulars there given of the composition and distribution of the British navy from 1880 and the detailed information concerning foreign fleets are very useful. He also wrote several articles on naval constructors for this DICTIONARY.

A cartoon of Watts by 'Spy' appeared in *Vanity Fair* 7 April 1910.

[*The Times*, 16 March 1926; Watts's articles mentioned above; *Transactions* of the Institution of Naval Architects, 1926, vol. lxviii, p. 285; *The Engineer*, 19 March 1926; *Engineering*, 19 March 1926; *Nature*, 27 March 1926; Frederic Manning, *Life of Sir William White*, pp. 464–480, 1923; E. L. Woodward, *Great Britain and the German Navy*, pp. 104–116, 1935; Lord Fisher, *Memories*, pp. 257–259, 1919.] E. I. CARLYLE.

WEAVER, SIR LAWRENCE (1876–1930), architectural critic, was born at Clifton 2 July 1876, the only child of Walter Weaver, by his wife, Frances Mary Taylor. He was brought up at Clifton by his mother, and was educated at Clifton College. He left school at the age of seventeen with the intention of becoming a dentist; but he found better scope for his abilities in the occupation of commercial traveller, principally in builders' ironmongery.

Study of old leadwork in his spare time led Weaver to write for *Country Life* a series of articles which were published in 1909 as *English Leadwork: Its Art and History*. As a result, he was taken on to the staff of *Country Life* in 1910 as architectural editor, a position which he held until 1916. Here his zeal for good craftsmanship and good building, as applied, especially, to the small country house, found an outlet. His writings on this subject are collected in *Small Country Houses of To-day* (2 vols., 1910, revised 1922–1925) and *Houses and Gardens of Edwin Lutyens* (1913, revised 1925). The latter book contributed much to the recognition of (Sir) Edwin Lutyens as one of the leading domestic architects of the time.

After the outbreak of war in 1914 Weaver volunteered as an able-bodied seaman in the Royal Naval Volunteer Reserve (anti-aircraft corps). The attention of the director-general of food production, Sir Arthur Lee (afterwards Lord Lee of Fareham), was called to this waste of Weaver's ability, and he was consequently appointed in April 1917 unpaid controller of the supplies division of the newly formed Food Production Department. In this post Weaver was responsible for organizing the supply of fertilizers, feeding-stuffs, seeds, and other requirements of the agricultural industry; and the operations of his department were very effective in extending war-time allotments.

On the reorganization of the Ministry of Agriculture in 1919, Lord Lee, the minister, appointed Weaver commercial secretary, and in 1920 director-general, of the Land Department. He was made responsible for all questions relating to agricultural supplies, and, when director-general, for the development of small holdings, and especially for the settlement of suitable ex-service men on the land. Here he was again in a position to insist on sound building design and the employment of competent architects. There were no architects on the staff of the ministry until Weaver's appointment. The land settlement scheme was undertaken at a time of particular difficulty, owing to the extravagant cost of building materials. Weaver therefore initiated experiments in the revival of traditional materials, such as cob and weather-boarding. Some of the results are published in *The 'Country Life' Book of Cottages* (1913, revised editions 1919 and 1926) and a *Manual for the guidance of County Councils and their Architects in equipment of Small Holdings* (1919, 3rd ed. 1920) dealing with the planning and construction of cottages and farms, issued by the Ministry of Agriculture under Weaver's direction. Further, his war-time experiences suggested to him the need of a single institution to coordinate and direct experiments in crop improvement. To this end he founded in January 1919 the National Institute of Agricultural Botany at Cambridge, with the help of funds contributed by firms interested and supplemented by a government grant, and he was chairman of its council from 1919 to 1924. He and his first wife were also instrumental in founding the Ashtead Potteries for the employment of disabled ex-service men. He was also honorary treasurer of the Housing Association for Officers' Families, and of the Douglas Haig Memorial Homes. After the closing of his department in 1922 as the result of the economy scheme inaugurated by Sir Eric Geddes, Weaver became director-general of the United Kingdom exhibits section of the British Empire Exhibition at Wembley. A visit to the Gothenburg Exhibition in that year had impressed upon him the then unfamiliar ideals of industrial art, and he sought to realize these ideals in his section of the Wembley Exhibition. Subsequently he was an active speaker and writer on the subject of aesthetic ideals in industry.

After the Wembley Exhibition Weaver returned to a business career, accepting various directorships. In 1925–1926 he served under Lord Lee of Fareham on the royal commission on cross-river traffic in London, the expeditious and practical report of which owed much to his collaboration. In 1927 he succeeded (Sir) J. C. Squire, the founder, as president of the Architecture Club; and it was shortly before a meeting of the club at his office that he had a fatal seizure of *angina pectoris* and died at his house in St. John's Wood 10 January 1930.

The improvement in design and taste shown in industrial and commercial art in recent years owes much to Weaver's energetic advocacy. His character was a combination of strong religious, puritanical, and philanthropic convictions—he was a deacon of the 'Irvingite' church—with hard-headed shrewdness and steadfast loyalty to friends and employers. He was an excellent debater and after-dinner speaker—enthusiastic, confident, and witty.

Weaver was created C.B.E. in 1918 and advanced to K.B.E. in 1920. He was a fellow of the Society of Antiquaries and an honorary associate of the Royal Institute of British Architects. He married twice: first, in 1908 Kathleen (died 1927), daughter of Major-General Edward Tobias Willoughby Purcell, R.A., by whom he had two sons and in whom his idealism found strong support; secondly, in 1928 Elizabeth Margaret, younger daughter of William de Caux, of Norwich.

[*The Times*, 11 January 1930; Clough Williams-Ellis, *Lawrence Weaver, A Memoir*, 1933; *Journal* of the Royal Institute of British Architects, 9 April 1921; private information.] C. Hussey.

WEBB, Sir ASTON (1849–1930), architect, was born in London 22 May 1849, the elder son of Edward Webb, engraver and water-colour painter, by his wife, Anna, daughter of John Evans, of Stoke Newington. His mother died the following year and his father in 1854. He was educated at Brighton. In 1867 he entered the office of Messrs. Banks and Barry, architects, of London, and in 1873 was awarded the Pugin studentship of the Royal Institute of British Architects, a travelling studentship which enabled him to study the medieval architecture of Great Britain.

About 1873, having served his articles, Webb set up in practice on his own account and from small beginnings eventually attained the highest position in his profession. In the architecture of London he was responsible for the principal block of the Victoria and Albert Museum (1891), the Royal College of Science (1900–1906), and the Imperial College of Science and Technology (1911)—all at South Kensington; the architectural surroundings of the memorial to Queen Victoria in front of Buckingham Palace, designed by Sir Thomas Brock [q.v.] in 1911; the new eastern façade of Buckingham Palace (1913); and the Admiralty Arch, designed as an entrance to the east end of the Mall (1911). Among many smaller works by Webb particular mention should be made of the French protestant church in Soho Square (1891–1893), a building with the design of which he is said to have felt especial satisfaction.

In partnership with Edward Ingress Bell, also a very able architect, Webb competed unsuccessfully for the designs of the new Admiralty, the new War Office, and the Imperial Institute. But they won the competitions for the Birmingham Law Courts (1886–1891) and for the new Christ's Hospital near Horsham (1894–1904). In the Birmingham competition a plan was suggested to the competitors by the assessor, Alfred Waterhouse [q.v.], and Webb's courage in discarding this plan for a better arrangement was suitably rewarded by Waterhouse's magnanimity in recognizing the improvement. Webb also designed the Royal College of Science, Dublin (1906–1907), in collaboration with (Sir) Thomas Newenham Deane [q.v.]; the Naval College at Dartmouth (1899–1904); and the University of Birmingham (1906–1909). He was responsible for the restoration of Burford church, near Tenbury (1890), and of the church of St. Bartholomew the Great, Smithfield (1886–1893).

As a designer, Webb was distinguished among his contemporaries for clearsightedness and common sense. The planning of his buildings is simple and direct, and their ornamental character is what in their day was considered appropriate. He was exceptionally skilful and conscientious in construction, almost every work of his being a model of fine and solid building. In the early part of his career his designs were not such as the leaders of architectural taste could recognize or approve; but he evolved in time a highly individual style which has had many admirers. In the buildings in which his name is associated with that of Bell, profuse detail of a *François Premier* character usually predominates, and in this class the extreme cleverness of the façade of the Metropolitan Life Assurance Company's offices in Moorgate Street (1890) attracted a great deal of contemporary notice. In his later buildings the style is severer and the scale of detail larger, although in ornament he would always prefer the piquant to the suave. The church of St. George at Worcester (1894) and Michael's court at Gonville and Caius College, Cambridge (1903), show very happily his ingenious invention at work in the Gothic idiom.

Webb received many honours, the most conspicuous of which were the royal gold medal of the Royal Institute of British Architects (1905), the presidency of the

Royal Academy (1919–1924)—the only previous architect to fill that office being James Wyatt [q.v.] in 1805—and the presidency of the Royal Institute of British Architects (1902–1904). In his earlier years he worked zealously for the Architectural Association, being president of that body in 1884; and throughout his life he was consistently a friend and helper to young architects. He was knighted in 1904 and received the C.B. in 1909, C.V.O. in 1911, K.C.V.O. in 1914, and G.C.V.O. in 1925.

Webb married in 1876 Marian, second daughter of David Everett, F.R.C.S., of Worcester, and had two sons and one daughter. His elder son is the architect, Mr. Maurice Webb; his younger son was killed in the European War. He died in London in his eighty-second year 21 August 1930.

A portrait of Webb by Solomon J. Solomon hangs in the head-quarters of the Royal Institute of British Architects in Portland Place, London. A bust executed by Sir Thomas Brock is illustrated in *Royal Academy Pictures*, 1922.

[*Builder*, 29 August 1930; *Architects' Journal*, 27 August 1930; *Journal* of the Royal Institute of British Architects, 20 September 1930.] H. S. Goodhart-Rendel.

WEBB, MARY GLADYS (1881–1927), novelist, essayist, and poet, was born at Leighton-under-the-Wrekin, Shropshire, 25 March 1881. She was the eldest daughter of George Edward Meredith, a schoolmaster of Welsh ancestry, by his wife, Sarah Alice Scott, daughter of an Edinburgh doctor who belonged to the clan of Sir Walter Scott. From her father, the original of the charming and sympathetic character, John Arden, in *The Golden Arrow*, she inherited her passionate love of all country things. He especially loved bees, and his daughter Mary's intimate knowledge of their habits came from having lived near to hives in her childhood. She was brought up in Shropshire and was educated at home, except for two years spent at a private school at Southport. She began to write poetry and stories as a child. In 1912, at the age of thirty-one, she married Henry Bertram Law Webb, a schoolmaster, son of Thomas Law Webb, M.D. There were no children of the marriage. Mary Webb's married life was spent partly at Weston-super-Mare, partly at Lyth Hill, near Shrewsbury, and partly in Hampstead, where she settled in 1921.

The five novels upon which Mary Webb's reputation as a writer rests were published during the course of twelve years. *The Golden Arrow* appeared first, in 1916. *Gone to Earth* followed in 1917. In the same year she also published *The Spring of Joy*, a collection of essays. In 1920 came *The House in Dormer Forest*; in 1922 *Seven for a Secret*, and in 1924 *Precious Bane*. The earlier books were read and admired by a small circle of discriminating readers, but the general public did not awake for a long time to the beauty and interest of her writing, and, although several reviewers praised her work, the sale of her books was small. It was only when the sixth book, *Precious Bane*, was published that novel readers, especially lovers of the country, began to recognize in Mary Webb a writer of exceptional distinction. In 1925 the Femina Vie Heureuse prize for the best English novel published in 1924–1925 was awarded her for this novel. It came into the hands of Mr. Stanley Baldwin, then prime minister, who wrote to her, 17 January 1927, to say how greatly, as a lover of old Shropshire days, he admired her work. A facsimile of his letter is printed at the beginning of *Armour wherein he Trusted*.

Mary Webb died 8 October 1927 at St. Leonards, Sussex, after a short illness. Obituary notices in the press were brief and few, but Mr. Baldwin pronounced an *éloge* on her work at the Royal Literary Fund dinner at which he presided on 25 April 1928. Next day her name was famous. The lending libraries were beset by people demanding copies of her books, which were not easy to find, as they had only been printed in small editions. In order to meet the demand, Mary Webb's five novels were reprinted in 1928 with introductions by Stanley Baldwin, John Buchan, H. R. L. Sheppard, Robert Lynd, and G. K. Chesterton. Her poems, with an introduction by Walter de la Mare, were published along with a reprint of her essays, *The Spring of Joy*, in 1929. The same year an unfinished romance of the Crusades, *Armour wherein he Trusted*, appeared with an introduction by Martin Armstrong, together with some short stories.

Mary Webb's prose in her novels and essays has moments of great beauty, and her cadences derive from seventeenth-century models, especially Sir Thomas Browne. Her narrative style often kindles to a fiery intensity. The plots of her novels are nearly always sombre, although *The*

Golden Arrow and *Seven for a Secret* have happier endings. She was acutely conscious of the cruelties of human life, but curiously insensitive to the cruelty of Nature. In her essays, in which she describes aspects of the country, her knowledge is complete, and her observation minute and unerring. Both in prose and poetry subtlety of observation is combined with a remarkable beauty of thought and phrasing. 'All that she wrote is suffused with poetry,' Walter de la Mare wrote of her [Introduction to *Poems*]. She created in her novels a world of love, hatred, cruelty, beauty, and magic, seen through the medium of an intensely poetic and romantic temperament. Her taste is not always perfect: she is inclined to be didactic, and her style is sometimes a little over-coloured. Her work will always find readers, for she is a true interpreter of the English countryside, especially of that borderland where Celt and Saxon are intermingled.

[Uniform edition of Mary Webb's novels, 1928; private information; personal knowledge.] SUSAN TWEEDSMUIR.

WESTON, FRANK (1871–1924), bishop of Zanzibar, born at Roupell Park, South London, 13 September 1871, was the fourth son and fifth child of Robert Gibbs Weston, a tea-broker in Mincing Lane, by his wife, Amelia, daughter of Dr. Robert Valentine. His father came of a Leicestershire family, but three of his grandparents were Scots, and he was proud of his descent from two seventeenth-century bishops of Brechin—stalwart episcopalians in dark days. He was educated at Dulwich College and Trinity College, Oxford, where he obtained a first class in the honour school of theology in 1893. He was ordained deacon in 1894 and priest in 1895. His first curacy (1894–1896) was at the Trinity College mission in Stratford, East London, his second (1896–1898) at St. Matthew's, Westminster.

In 1898 Weston joined the Universities' Mission to Central Africa, and for nine years was stationed at Zanzibar. His work there was chiefly educational—from 1901 to 1908 he was principal of St. Andrew's Training College, Kiungani—and he lived an ascetic life, almost entirely with Africans, learning, as few have done, what was in their minds. He found time, however, to write *The One Christ* (1907), dealing with the *Kenosis* of Our Lord, a book which won the approval of Professors Sanday and Swete, of Bishop Gore, and of Canon Scott Holland. In 1908 Weston was consecrated bishop of Zanzibar on the resignation of Dr. J. E. Hine. He at once set to work, organizing and reorganizing mission stations throughout his diocese, walking hundreds of miles each year on the mainland, settling vexed questions of morals and administering discipline. In Zanzibar he superintended work among Mohammedans, and did much for the spiritual life of his diocese by founding the Order of the Divine Compassion in 1910.

In June 1913, without consulting Weston, the bishops of Mombasa and Uganda concluded at Kikuyu a concordat with certain protestant denominations, which, in Weston's view, compromised the Church of England, and he denounced the scheme to the archbishop of Canterbury. At the same time he was much concerned about certain modernist teaching in England, and wrote a pamphlet—*Ecclesia Anglicana—For what does she stand?* (1913). Both Weston's action and his pamphlet occasioned a stir; bishops and scholars wrote pamphlets for and against the author, while the newspapers were deluged with correspondence. Archbishop Davidson [q.v.] summoned Weston to come home, referred the one subject to the standing committee of the Lambeth Conference, and the other to Convocation. Finally in 1915 he published a decision on the Kikuyu question which was a very diplomatic document. Weston defended his views on the Church in *The Fulness of Christ* (1916), but the book was too original for most theologians and too abstract for the general public. Against the modernists he wrote *The Christ and His Critics* (1919), which was not persuasive.

Meantime the European War had broken out, and Weston returned to his diocese to find all his staff on the mainland interned by the Germans. He wrote a little book which had a wide circulation, *Conquering and to Conquer* (1918), based on the sufferings of Our Lord, with the object of consoling mourners and sustaining combatants in the Faith. He next made an offer to the embarrassed government of Zanzibar to raise a corps of carriers for the conveyance of supplies up country. Six hundred volunteered at once in Zanzibar, and crossing with them to the mainland, he commanded, with the rank of major, first and last, 2,500 men. He led them up country, and did not lose a single case. There was some sickness, but no one died, although previously the mortality among the carriers had been terrible. For this service he received the O.B.E.

In 1920 Weston came to England for the Lambeth Conference. The bishops who did not know him expected a wild fanatic; they found a great orator, full of sweet reasonableness. The appeal for unity which they issued was partly drafted by Weston and owed much to his inspiration. While at home he was indignant at the circular which was issued by Lord Milner, the secretary of state for the Colonies, on forced and 'encouraged' labour in Africa. His *Serfs of Great Britain* (1920) was fierce, but Mr. J. H. Oldham, of the World Missionary Conference, prevailed on him to moderate his attitude, and the memorandum drawn up by both of them was signed by leading politicians of all parties. The circular was ultimately withdrawn by Lord Milner's successor, Mr. Winston Churchill. In 1923 Weston paid another short visit to England, and presided at the second Anglo-Catholic Congress. For a week his personality dominated great audiences in the Albert Hall; and with his usual impulsiveness he sent greetings from the congress to the archbishop of Canterbury, the ecumenical patriarch, and the pope. He maintained quite correctly that this was in accord with the Lambeth resolution, but it was misunderstood both at Rome and in England. On returning to Africa in August 1923, he started once more on a visitation of his diocese, walking several hundreds of miles. In October 1924 he contracted blood poisoning through having a carbuncle cut by his cook-boy. He managed to reach his palace, a hut which he had built for himself at Hegongo, and died 2 November 1924.

Weston might have been a great theologian if he had stayed on in Oxford after taking his degree, as Professor Sanday wished him to do; but he was a born leader of men with a magnetic influence over individuals. His eloquence could hold 10,000 people in the Albert Hall enthralled; he could also fascinate little African boys in a remote village. He was equally at home in England and in Africa, and his sympathy was such that Africans regarded him as one of themselves. He devoted all his great powers to building up an African Church in native African communities and providing them with a stern discipline which they were to be encouraged to enforce themselves. He thought that only in this way could the race slowly develop on its own lines, and be preserved from the disintegrating force of an alien civilization.

[H. Maynard Smith, *Frank, Bishop of Zanzibar* (containing photographs of Weston), 1926.]

H. MAYNARD SMITH.

WET, CHRISTIAAN RUDOLPH DE (1854–1922), Boer general and politician. [See DE WET.]

WEYMAN, STANLEY JOHN (1855–1928), novelist, the second son of Thomas Weyman, a Ludlow solicitor, by his wife, Mary Maria, daughter of Samuel Black, was born at Ludlow 7 August 1855. He was educated at Ludlow grammar school, at Shrewsbury School, and at Christ Church, Oxford, where he obtained a second class in modern history in 1877. He showed no literary precocity, and wrote nothing save a few trifling sketches of university life and character, more than one of them published in *Chambers's Journal*, until overmuch leisure and scanty income compelled more serious efforts. He had been called to the bar by the Inner Temple in 1881, and had gone on the Oxford circuit, with so little material result that when challenged by the Income Tax authorities he could produce a fee-book showing an annual income of only £130. Some short stories were accepted by the *Cornhill Magazine*, and its editor, James Payn, suggested to him work on a larger scale. The chance of picking up in his club Henry White's *Massacre of St. Bartholomew* led to his writing *The House of the Wolf* (1890). This ran serially in the *English Illustrated Magazine* during 1883, but, as a book, could find no publisher for seven years. *The New Rector* (1891) already revealed what was long afterwards to be amply manifested, Weyman's admiration for Trollope. But for some years he was lured into the writing of highly popular historical romances, in some of which he made admirable use of his knowledge of the by-ways of French history. *A Gentleman of France* (1893) hung fire for three months after publication, and then came into immense demand. Among its successors were: *The Man in Black* (1894), *The Red Cockade* (1895), *Under the Red Robe* (1896, afterwards dramatized at the Haymarket Theatre), *The Castle Inn* (1898), *The Long Night* (1903). *Chippinge* (1906), its author's favourite, well showed his ability to use an English setting and dispense with cloak and sword. *Ovington's Bank* (1922), his second work after a self-imposed silence from 1908 to 1919, is perhaps the most solid proof that Weyman was not dependent on the mere accessories of romance.

The earlier Weyman was regarded by every one as first-rate reading for boys, and by Oscar Wilde, who wished to procure his romances for the inmates of Reading gaol, as first-rate reading for convicts; the later Weyman, although popular, hardly received what was due to his developed power of historical imagination and skill in representing social conditions and broad movements.

Weyman's estimate of himself was modest enough, and he was under no illusions as to his good luck in finding a waiting public. Though fortunate in the moment of his debut, and not least in the misunderstanding which ranked him with R. L. Stevenson, Quiller-Couch, and other masters or popularizers of the 'new' romance—in part as old as Scott or Dumas—Weyman would probably at any time have won recognition for his sense of a situation. The higher gifts which enabled him—in *Chippinge*, for example—to reproduce the atmosphere of a period, not simple nor obviously romantic, were perceptible chiefly by readers who were not much attracted by the picturesque simplicities of his earlier tales.

Weyman made a habit of travelling over any foreign country which was to be the scene of one of his books, often in the company of the novelist, Henry Seton Merriman. At the end of 1885, when his companion was a younger brother, and he was travelling in the south of France, he was arrested on an absurd suspicion of being a spy, an incident which evoked the intervention of the British ambassador, Lord Lyons, a protest in the British press, and some notice in parliament. Switzerland yielded him a pleasanter experience, when the municipal authorities of Geneva made him a presentation as a tribute to the historical accuracy of his romance, *The Long Night*.

For the last thirty years of his life Weyman lived at Ruthin, Denbighshire, where he was chairman of the bench of magistrates and did other useful service in local affairs. He married in 1895 Charlotte, daughter of the Rev. Richard Panting; they had no children. He died at Ruthin 10 April 1928.

[*The Bookman*, August 1908; *Cornhill Magazine*, June 1928; private information.]

T. E. Welby.

WHEATLEY, JOHN (1869–1930), labour politician, was born at Bonmahon, co. Waterford, 24 May 1869, the eldest child of Thomas Wheatley, a labourer, by his wife, Johanna Ryan. When he was nine years old his family migrated to the mining village of Bargeddie, Lanarkshire, where the father found employment in a local coal pit; and from Bargeddie John travelled daily to the Roman Catholic school at Baillieston. The extreme poverty and miserable housing conditions of his childhood—the future minister of health was reared with ten brothers and sisters in a single-apartment house with neither drainage nor water supply—left him with bitter memories and coloured much of his political activity in later years. At the age of eleven he had to leave school and go down the coal-mine to assist his father, but he attended evening classes, read omnivorously, especially the political prints of the United Irish League, and taught himself shorthand. At the age of twenty-four he left the coal-pits and secured employment as a shop assistant, later engaging in a small grocery venture of his own, which, however, did not prosper. In 1896 he married Mary, daughter of Bernard Machan, publisher, of Glasgow.

After his grocery venture Wheatley in 1902 secured employment for a short period as a reporter, and then as an advertisement canvasser for the *Glasgow Observer and Catholic Herald*; but in 1912 he conceived the idea of engaging in partnership with another employee and setting up a publishing business in Glasgow dealing chiefly with shopkeepers' advertisement calendars. This project rapidly developed under Wheatley's guidance into a limited company (Hoxton and Walsh Ltd.), with widespread ramifications and agencies, freeing him from financial anxiety, and enabling him to give his two children a university education.

As a young man Wheatley was a keen adherent of the politics of the United Irish League, at that time an all-powerful organization among the Irish emigrants and their descendants in the West of Scotland; and it was not until 1908, when he was thirty-nine years old, that he joined the independent labour party. Thenceforward he was an active and influential figure in the labour and socialist movement. He made a special study of local government problems, and attracted large audiences by his speeches and addresses on housing, health, and finance. He formed and became first chairman of the Catholic Socialist Society, an organization which did much to win over Irish voters to the labour party; he engaged in spirited disputations with Catholic clergy, and when he was first elected to the Lanarkshire county council in 1909, by the narrow majority of two votes, it was against a sitting Catholic moderate member. When the Shettleston district of Lanarkshire was incorporated in the city of Glasgow in 1910 he held his seat. He became chairman of the Glasgow town council labour party, a magistrate, and a leading exponent of the policy of municipal housing at rents within the competence of the poor. He urged the erection of cottages by government loan, free of interest charge, arguing that such cottages could then be rented at £8 per annum.

In 1918 Wheatley stood for parliament for the Shettleston division of Glasgow, and was defeated by 72 votes. In 1922 he captured the seat, holding it at the next four elections until his death. In parliament he was soon recognized as a powerful force in debate, and so rapidly came to the front that within two years of his appearance at Westminster he was appointed minister for health in the labour ministry. During his nine months of office (his activities occupy 36 columns in the index to the *Official Report* of the House of Commons) Wheatley was responsible for the Housing (Financial Provisions) Act, commonly referred to by housing reformers and administrators as the Wheatley Act. This Act was designed to assist the local authorities in a fifteen-year programme for building two and a half million houses to be let at rents which the average working-class family could afford to pay; a national subsidy was fixed, by agreement with the local authorities, for a trial period, at £9 per house; the building trades were induced to co-operate by permitting more apprentices, and a supplementary measure to prevent profiteering in building materials was promised.

After the general election of October 1924 Wheatley drifted away from his former government colleagues and, declining to sit with them on the front opposition bench, joined the left wing independent labour party group on the back benches. To a considerable extent he lost his influence in the labour party, and when another labour government was formed in 1929 he was not invited to take office. He became more and more identified with revolutionary socialist views and with left wing criticism of the labour government; but his activities were impaired by indifferent health. He died at Shettleston 12 May 1930, and was survived by his wife and a son and daughter.

[*The Times*, 13 May 1930; files of the *Forward* newspaper 1909–1930; *The Book of the Labour Party*, vols. i–iii, 1926; *The Encyclopædia of the Labour Movement*, vol. iii, March 1928.] T. JOHNSTON.

WHIBLEY, CHARLES (1859–1930), scholar, critic, and journalist, born at Sittingbourne, Kent, 9 December 1859, was the eldest son of Ambrose Whibley, merchant, by his second wife, Mary Jenn Davey. Whibley was educated at Bristol grammar school and at Jesus College, Cambridge, where he won a scholarship in 1879, and obtained a first class in the classical tripos of 1883. He was always attached to his college, and kept in touch with it by frequent visits to Cambridge. In 1912 he was elected an honorary fellow of Jesus College, a distinction which he greatly prized.

On taking his degree Whibley at once adopted the profession of letters. For about three years he was in the editorial department of Cassell & Co.; but salaried work was not congenial to one who prized independence as he did. It was his association with literary friends of like tastes with himself which mainly determined the course of his life. In 1889 he published *In Cap and Gown: Three Centuries of Cambridge Wit*, a collection of Cambridge verses for which he wrote an introduction and notes. The most important of his early connexions was with W. E. Henley [q.v.], whom he assisted in the conduct of the *Scots Observer* (afterwards called the *National Observer*), one of the leading critical and political publications of its day. Whibley found in Henley a kindred spirit, a high tory, a poet and scholar of the finest taste, and a fierce denouncer of all that was pretentious and insincere. When Henley projected 'The Tudor Translations', a series of reprints, with critical introductions, of the best-known translations of classical and other authors into English of the Elizabethan and Jacobean periods, Whibley was responsible for many of the introductions, including those to Philemon Holland's Suetonius (1899) and Urquhart and Motteux's Rabelais (1900). At a later date (1924) he himself edited a second series, and wrote the introduction to Thomas Heywood's Sallust.

In 1893 Henley resigned the editorship of the *National Observer*, and Whibley allied himself with H. J. C. Cust [q.v.], then editor of the *Pall Mall Gazette*, which was at that time the most brilliant of the London evening newspapers. He also wrote for the *New Review*. In 1894 Whibley went to Paris as correspondent for the *Pall Mall Gazette*, and there spent some of his happiest days in the society of French poets and *littérateurs*, particularly of Stéphane Mallarmé (of whom in later life he would tell many delightful stories), of Marcel Schwob (the great authority on François Villon), and of Paul Valéry. There also, in 1896, Whibley married his first wife, Ethel, daughter of the sculptor John Birnie Philip [q.v.] and a sister-in-law of J. M. Whistler.

Soon afterwards Whibley returned to England and formed an association with *Blackwood's Magazine* which remained unbroken during most of the rest of his life. Month by month for more than twenty-five years he contributed to that magazine the articles headed 'Musings without Method'. They were anonymous, but Whibley's authorship of them was an open secret; and he was justly proud of the fact that during a quarter of a century he had only failed to contribute to two or three numbers of *Blackwood*. The articles ranged over a great variety of subjects. He dealt with current politics from the standpoint of the highest toryism, and with ethical and literary matters as a critic whose equipment of wit and learning rendered him formidable in the castigation of all which seemed to him to fall short of his own high standard of manners and sincerity.

Between 1897 and 1904 Whibley published *A Book of Scoundrels* (1897), *Studies in Frankness* (1898), *The Pageantry of Life* (1900), and *Literary Portraits* (1904). These were volumes of critical and historical essays, many of which had appeared before, either in magazines or as contributions to such works as the *Cambridge History of English Literature* or as introductions to books which he had edited. He also wrote brief studies of *Thackeray* (1903) and of *William Pitt* (1906), as well as introductions to Edward Hall's *Henry VIII* (1904), Disraeli's *Life of Lord George Bentinck* (1905), Sir Thomas Browne's *Religio Medici* (1906), and selected poems of Byron (1907). During these years Whibley formed a warm friendship with Lord Northcliffe [q.v.], and at his instance contributed for some years to the *Daily Mail* the 'Letters of an Englishman' (collected and published in 1915), full of vigorous and often ironical comments on the affairs or the follies of the day. With Lord Northcliffe he paid a visit in 1907 to the United States, which led to his writing his *American Sketches*, published in 1908. In these he recorded his observations and impressions of a people who, in his judgement, were to be regarded not as a young but as an old nation.

In 1914 Whibley published *A Call to Arms*, and in 1917 an essay on Hazlitt and a volume of *Political Portraits*. In the same year he gave the Leslie Stephen lecture at Cambridge on *Swift*, subsequently published. About this time he built for himself at Great Brickhill, near Bletchley, a pleasant country house, with a large library to house the books which his successful literary labours had enabled him to collect. After the European War Whibley published *Literary Studies* (1919), an edition of George Wyndham's *Essays in Romantic Literature* (1919), a second series of *Political Portraits* (1923), *Lord John Manners and his Friends* (1925), and an introduction to *Robinson Crusoe* (1925), besides editing the *Collected Essays* (1925) of his old friend, Professor William Paton Ker [q.v.]. He also worked for many years as reader for the publishing firm of Macmillan and Co., the head of which, Sir Frederick Macmillan, was another friend to whom he was bound by strong ties and who bore testimony to the great value to his firm of Whibley's keen judgement.

In 1927 Whibley, whose first wife had died in 1920, married Philippa, daughter of Sir Walter Raleigh [q.v.], professor of English literature at Oxford. But his health was now beginning to fail. For some years he suffered from acute neuralgia, the weakening effect of which undoubtedly shortened his life. He died at Hyères 4 March 1930, at the age of seventy. He had no children.

A bare record of his work can give but little idea of Whibley's place in the estimation of his contemporaries, which is attributable at least as much to the effect of his personality on those who came into contact with him as to his literary eminence. The warmth of his human sympathies, his brilliant wit, his love of good cheer, of good talk, and of all that was vital and sincere made him the best of companions. He had his prejudices, to which he would sometimes give alarming expression; but his impeccable intellectual honesty and the courageous vigour of mind and spirit which shone out in his conversation made him an acknowledged leader among his intimates. In this, as in some of his other qualities, including his unbending toryism, he resembled Dr. Johnson; and it may well be that like Johnson he will rather live through the influence which he exerted on those who were privileged to know him than through the written word. Nevertheless, he was a great master of the written word. He maintained throughout his life the loftiest standards of his craft: his literary style was in the highest degree chaste and austere. His most ephemeral work—and much of it was ephemeral—was always that of a scholar; and although as a writer he was critical rather than constructive, he was a power in his time.

[*The Times*, 5 March 1930; private information; personal knowledge.]

D. O. MALCOLM.

WHITEING, RICHARD (1840–1928), journalist and novelist, was born in London 27 July 1840, the only child of William Whiteing, a clerk in the Stamp Office, by his wife, Mary Lander, who died when her son was an infant. Richard Whiteing lived with his father in Norfolk Street, Strand, until he was nearly eight years of age, when he was sent to a school which was conducted in the old palace at Bromley-by-Bow, and then 'as too young to be without a woman's care', he went to live with foster-parents in St. John's Wood, and finished his schooling there under a French refugee. He was then apprenticed for seven years to Benjamin Wyon [q.v.], medallist and engraver of seals. In the evenings he attended art classes, first at the Department of Science and Art at Marlborough House, then at Leigh's Art School in Newman Street, and, for a short time, at the Working Men's College in Great Ormond Street, where he came into contact with F. D. Maurice, John Ruskin, and F. J. Furnivall. Furnivall and his rowing-club for working girls figure in Whiteing's novel, *Ring in the New* (1906).

When he had finished his apprenticeship, Whiteing set up for himself as an engraver, 'with parental aid, and with varied fortunes, mostly bad'. About 1866 he undertook the secretaryship, at a salary of £2 a week, in Paris, of an Anglo-French working-class exhibition. He was 'without a word of French, but with plentiful pigeon-German', learned from a fellow engraver of seals, 'and by good hap they served'. At a later period he came to know Jules Simon officially, Yves Guyot personally, Hilaire Degas by sight, and the brothers Elie Reclus (the ethnologist) and Elisée Reclus (the geographer) intimately. Elie appears as Azrael, a Russian anarchist, in *No. 5 John Street* (1899). Having thus broken with seal-engraving, and made acquaintance with continental life, Whiteing in 1866 made his first essay in journalism with a series of satirical articles on political and social subjects, in the *Evening Star*. These were published in book form in 1867 under the title of *Mr. Sprouts—His Opinions*. Mr. Sprouts is 'a costermonger who gets into parliament and becomes one of the most practical members, rivalling Bernal Osborne in his wit and Roebuck in his satire'. In 1866 Whiteing joined the staff, under the editorship of Justin M'Carthy, of the *Morning Star*, for which he wrote articles on the Paris Exhibition of 1867. He then became the Paris correspondent of both the London *World* and the New York *World*. He lived in Paris, travelling as correspondent to Geneva (for the *Alabama* arbitration, 1871–1872), to Spain (1873), to Vienna, to Berlin, to Russia, and to Rome. In 1876 and 1878 he visited the United States of America.

In 1876 Whiteing published his first novel, *The Democracy*, under the pseudonym of 'Whyte Thorn'. This was 'a book of promise, but not of much positive merit', nor was it followed up until after twelve years—by *The Island* (1888), which in its turn was succeeded after another eleven years by *No. 5 John Street* (1899). From January 1874 to May 1875 Whiteing was serving on the staff of the *Manchester Guardian*, but he soon returned to Paris, where he was contributing to that paper in 1880. He did not leave Paris until about 1886, when he went back to London in order to join the staff of the *Daily News*, from which he resigned in 1899. His long settlement in Paris resulted, in 1886, in the publication of *Living Paris and France* (under the pseudonym of 'Alb') and, in 1900, of *The Life of Paris*. Three other novels and one book of essays followed Whiteing's retirement from journalism at the age of fifty-nine: *The Yellow Van* (1903), *Ring in the New* (1906), *All Moonshine* (1907), and *Little People* (essays on 'the world's nobodies and failures', 1908). In 1915 he published a pleasant volume of autobiography, *My Harvest*, in which he mentions neither his marriage, nor, apart from mere passing allusions to two of them, any of his novels.

Whiteing would not be thought of as a novelist had it not been for the success of *No. 5 John Street*. This was in some degree a sequel to *The Island*, in which Pitcairn Island is imagined as an unsophisticated polity, its inhabitants innocently proud of their membership of a British Empire of which they know nothing. The 'Person of Quality', who depicts their happy state in 1888, dies and leaves it to the narrator of *No. 5 John Street* to send them reports of Queen Victoria's diamond jubilee in 1897. No. 5 John Street is a tenement-house, with a horrible basement and worse cellar. The narrator, himself a 'person of quality', lives there in disguise, for the purposes of his report to the Pitcairn Islanders, and introduces the reader to the other inmates—a flower-girl (a virtuous Amazon, reminiscent of Borrow's Isopel Berners), a consumptive factory-girl, an amiable ruffian, a Russian anarchist, and an old Chartist, who is also a survivor of the charge of the Light Brigade. There is a story, for the consumptive girl is to die, as a protest against conditions in a rubber factory. The flower-girl is to die, too, in an heroic attempt to prevent the anarchist from bombing the house of the factory-owner. The book, as a work of art, suffers from the tendentious character of the story, while the reports of the state of England to the Pitcairn Islanders aim at a humour akin to *Gulliver's Travels* and *Sartor Resartus*. Whiteing's novel, *All Moonshine*, is likewise a fantasy.

Whiteing's autobiography, by its style, suggests that a fine mind had been in part sacrificed during a long life to anonymous journalism. His novels bear witness to a kind heart. He was granted a civil list pension in 1910, and he died at Hampstead 29 June 1928 in his eighty-eighth year. He married in 1869 Helen (who predeceased him by many years), niece of Townsend Harris, the first United States minister to Japan. They had one son.

Among Whiteing's writings not previously mentioned are: *Wonderful Escapes* (revised . . . and original chapters added by R. Whiteing, &c., 1870), *Drawing from Delight* (1912), and *Both Sides of the Curtain* (in collaboration with the Countess Geneviève de Guerbel, née Ward, 1918). In addition to these he wrote introductions to Emerson's *Essays*, first series (1903), Thoreau's *Walden* (1906), F. Loliée's *Women of the Second Empire* (1907), and V. V. Vereshchagin's '*1812*': *Napoleon I in Russia* (1899).

[*The Times*, 30 June 1928; Richard Whiteing, *My Harvest*, 1915 (this gives very few dates).] F. Page.

WILLCOCKS, Sir JAMES (1857–1926), general, was born 1 April 1857 at Baraut in the Delhi district, India, the fourth son of Captain William Willcocks, of the East India Company's service, by his wife, Mary Martin. He was educated privately in England, chiefly at Easton in Somerset. Like not a few famous soldiers he failed more than once in the entrance examination for the army. He was twice unsuccessful for the Royal Military College, Sandhurst, and was nearly twenty-one when he left the College and was gazetted in January 1878 to the 100th Foot, which he joined at Jullundur in the Punjab. Owing to an epidemic of cholera his regiment was not able to take part in the second Afghan War; but when the second stage of it began after the murder of Sir Louis Cavagnari [q.v.] in September 1879, young Willcocks determined to get to the front. He took the audacious step of telegraphing direct to head-quarters at Simla, offering his services. In ninety-nine cases out of a hundred such irregular action would have led to a severe official reprimand. In this case, however, Willcocks received a telegram directing him to proceed to the front at once and to report at Peshawar.

In this second phase of the Afghan War Willcocks served as a transport officer and learned many lessons which were later to stand him in good stead. Early in 1881 he was again on active service as transport officer in the Mahsud Waziri expedition, rejoining the 100th Foot at Umballa in the following year. In 1884 he accepted an appointment in the newly formed Army Transport Department in India, and was soon put in charge of army transport in the Eastern Frontier districts with head-quarters at Assam. India was now called upon to provide a contingent for service in the Sudan, and Captain Willcocks, as he had now become, was selected for transport duties. Returning in due course to Assam, he was once more selected for transport duties in the Burmese Frontier expedition of 1886. At the conclusion of the expedition in December 1887 he was offered a permanent appointment in the amalgamated Commissariat-Transport Department, and at the same time he received a letter from his regimental commanding officer offering him the appointment of adjutant of the 100th Foot, which had now become the 1st battalion Prince of Wales's Leinster Regiment (Royal Canadians).

Although it entailed a pecuniary loss, Willcocks wisely rejoined his battalion. He arrived with five 'ribbons', including the D.S.O., a remarkable number for a comparatively junior officer of those days. Willcocks's tenure of the adjutancy was not of long duration, for in 1889 he was again ordered on active service, this time as intelligence officer in the Chin-Lushai expedition, and this was followed by a further spell of active service in the Manipur expedition of 1891.

For the next five years leave, polo, big-game shooting, and staff appointments in India were Willcocks's lot until, on 18 June 1897, he received a telegram from Simla informing him that he had been selected as assistant adjutant-general of the field force then being formed in the Tochi valley in Baluchistan on the North-West Frontier. On the conclusion of that campaign in November Willcocks was offered by the War Office the post of second-in-command of the new force about to be raised by Major F. J. D. (afterwards Lord) Lugard on the Niger in West Africa. Accepting the appointment, Willcocks proceeded to England and thence to West Africa, arriving at Sierra Leone in March 1898.

In that year Willcocks took part in the Borgu campaign, and became in 1899 colonel-commandant of the West African Frontier force. Then came his first real chance as a commander, when he was appointed to command the Ashanti field force for the relief of Kumassi. In spite of appalling difficulties Willcocks duly relieved the place on 15 July 1900, and for his services he was created K.C.M.G., was mentioned in the king's speech at the opening of the first parliament of King Edward VII, and given the freedom of the City of London.

In 1902 Willcocks joined the field force in South Africa, but he had no opportunity of displaying his genius for organization. Returning to India, he was promoted major-general in 1906 and commanded two expeditions on the North-West Frontier in 1908—such was his rapidity of action that *Punch* began to talk of 'Willcocks's Week-End Wars'. The same year he was promoted lieutenant-general. Two years later (1910) he was appointed to the command of the Northern army in India.

Willcocks reached the zenith of his military career when, in 1914, he was ordered to proceed to France in command of the Indian Army Corps, then on its way to take part in the European War. Everything pointed to his ultimate appointment to the high position of commander-in-chief in India. But it was not to be. Although at the end of the first year's fighting in France Willcocks was awarded the G.C.M.G., friction had developed between him and Sir Douglas (afterwards Earl) Haig [q.v.], who had been promoted general in November 1914 and commander of the newly formed First Army at the beginning of 1915. Hitherto Haig had been junior to Willcocks. Now the situation was reversed, and Willcocks felt compelled to suggest to the general officer commanding the First Army that, as his services apparently no longer met with the army commander's approval, he might be relieved of command of the Indian Corps. Accordingly, having been promoted full general in May, he resigned in September.

Willcocks's military career was now at an end, and a dignified retirement was found for him as governor of Bermuda from 1917 to 1922. He died at Bharatpur 18 December 1926.

Willcocks was the author of three very readable books: *From Kabul to Kumassi* (1904), *With the Indians in France* (1920), and *The Romance of Soldiering and Sport* (1925).

Willcocks married in 1889 Winifred, second daughter of Colonel George Augustus Way, 7th Bengal Infantry, and had one son.

[Official records; Willcocks's own writings; *The Prince of Wales's Leinster Regiment*, 1911; *Frederick Edwin, Earl of Birkenhead, by his son* (the Earl of Birkenhead), vol. i, 1933; private information; personal knowledge.]

F. E. Whitton.

WILLS, Sir GEORGE ALFRED, first baronet, of Blagdon (1854–1928), president of the Imperial Tobacco Company, philanthropist, was born at Bristol 3 June 1854, the eldest son of Henry Overton Wills, of Kelston Knoll, near Bath, by his wife, Alice Hopkinson, of Manchester. He was educated first at Dr. Hudson's private school, Manilla Hall, Clifton, where he was contemporary with T. H. Warren (afterwards Sir Herbert Warren, president of Magdalen College, Oxford), with whom he retained a lifelong friendship. From about 1868 to 1872 he was at Mill Hill School, where he developed an interest in history which was maintained throughout his life. It was not customary at that time to send to the university boys who were intended for a business career. Wills always regretted his lack of a university education, a subject in which in later life he took the keenest interest.

In October 1874, at the age of twenty,

Wills entered the Bristol tobacco firm of W. D. and H. O. Wills. This firm had had a continuous history from the early eighteenth century. Wills's father, Henry Overton Wills, had retired from the business and took no further part in the management. Wills quickly proved his capacity. He was trained in every department of the business, and in 1888 was made manager of the head-quarters and factory at Bedminster, near Bristol. In 1904 the tobacco trade in Great Britain was seriously threatened by American interests. George Wills and his cousin, William Henry Wills (afterwards Baron Winterstoke, q.v.), were together responsible for conducting the intricate and difficult negotiations which resulted in the foundation of the Imperial Tobacco Company of Great Britain and Ireland in 1901. This industrial 'combine', typical of many formed about that time, had, unlike many others, remarkable success from the beginning; and this was largely due to the personality and ability of Wills. On the death of Lord Winterstoke in 1911 he became chairman of the company, and he remained actively in business until 1924, when he retired on account of failing health; he continued, however, to act in an advisory capacity, with the title of president of the company, until his death.

Wills took no part in politics, and never stood for municipal office, although he was sheriff of Bristol from 1899 to 1900; but throughout his life he took a keen interest in Bristol charitable institutions, particularly the General Hospital. After long association with it he became president of the hospital in 1913. He not merely contributed munificently to its development and maintenance, but he was active and constant in administration, and also in visitation of the wards. He was a generous supporter of other hospitals and institutions. In 1909 he purchased the Leigh Woods, on the banks of the Avon, and presented them to the National Trust, in order to preserve them for the public.

Wills's greatest public work was done for the university of Bristol, of which his father was the founder and first chancellor. The University College of Bristol had been opened in 1876. In the early years of the twentieth century a movement was set on foot to erect the college into a university, but little progress was made with the scheme, in spite of the labours of an energetic committee under the chairmanship of Lewis Fry. In 1908 Wills was president, for the year, of the Colston Society, a local body for the encouragement of research; and at the annual dinner of the society in that year he announced the gift of £100,000 from his father, towards the establishing of a university in Bristol. Wills himself purchased the Coombe Dingle estate, and equipped it as playing fields for the University. A charter for the University was granted in 1909. Four years later, in February 1913, Wills wrote to Lewis Fry, chairman of the council, stating simply that he and his brother, Henry Herbert Wills, considered the time to be due for extending the University and ensuring to it a building worthy of the city; accordingly, they offered the sum of £150,000. The European War supervened when the work of building had made only a little progress, and costs rose enormously; but Wills, who always saw through to completion every project which he had initiated, gave continued support, notwithstanding that the total expenditure on the new building—great hall, reception and lecture rooms, tower, and offices—amounted to £600,000. Wills always made it a rule to give funds for maintenance as well as for construction, and thus the University was relieved of very considerable charges in the future. He purchased the Victoria Rooms, Clifton, and equipped them as a University union, with a fund for maintenance. His final gift was to purchase an estate on the downs, at Stoke Bishop, and to build and endow a magnificent hall of residence for men. This was completed in 1929, the year after his death.

Besides his princely generosity to the university of Bristol, Wills devoted much time and energy to its affairs. He was a governor of the old University College, and treasurer of the University from its foundation in 1909 until 1918. He became a pro-chancellor in 1911; and in 1913 he succeeded Lewis Fry in the onerous position of chairman of the council.

Wills was a man of retiring but lovable nature, and he exercised a wide personal influence. Sympathetic, and with a keen sense of humour, he was always approachable. He knew his tobacco business thoroughly, being a great judge of leaf, and an unsurpassed manager of men. He was opposed to all forms of speculation or gambling. He was favourable to his workmen joining a trade union, although he felt that no union could offer them benefits equal to those which they already enjoyed in his works. He was personally well known to very large numbers of the workers in the tobacco factory and was on the best possible terms with them; it was a source of satisfaction to him that there was never a strike in the factory in his time.

Wills lived chiefly at Burwalls, Leigh Woods, outside Clifton, and at Blagdon, Somerset, but he usually went with his family for three or four weeks each year to Scotland, or to a farm which he owned at Aale, in Ramsdelen, Norway. Fishing and walking were his chief recreations. He was also keenly interested in music and pictures.

Wills married in 1878 Susan Britton, daughter of Robert Proctor, of Clifton, and had one son and four daughters. He was created a baronet in 1923, and received the honorary degree of D.C.L. from the university of Oxford in 1926: as he was unable to travel, the vice-chancellor visited Bristol and conferred the degree on him in his own house—a signal honour. He died at Burwalls 11 July 1928, and was succeeded as second baronet by his son, George Vernon Proctor (born 1887).

There is a portrait of Wills by Hugh Riviere in the University buildings, Bristol, and another by Glyn Philpot in the offices of the Imperial Tobacco Company, Bedminster.

[Private information.] R. B. Mowat.

WILMOT, Sir SAINTHILL EARDLEY- (1852–1929), forester, was born at Hobart, Tasmania, 17 July 1852, the third son of Augustus Hillier Eardley-Wilmot, police magistrate in Hobart, and after 1855 resident in London, by his wife, Matilda Jessie, daughter of John Dunn, banker, of Hobart. He was educated at East Budleigh, Devon, and after a forestry training in Germany joined the Indian Forest service in December 1873, and was posted assistant conservator of forests in the old North-West Provinces and Oudh, Dr. (afterwards Sir) Dietrich Brandis [q.v.] being at the time inspector-general of this new service, inaugurated in 1864.

Eardley-Wilmot spent sixteen years as an executive officer in the province. In 1890 he was promoted to administrative rank. The following eight years he passed as conservator in Oudh, and it was there that his organizing ability, driving power, and great professional knowledge attracted the attention of the local government and marked him out for subsequent preferment. After further service in the north of the province, Eardley-Wilmot was transferred in 1900 to Burma, where he spent three years. It was considered at the time that an officer who might be chosen for the head of the service must possess an acquaintance with the very valuable Burmese forests. He was never at home in Burma, and made no secret of his dislike of service in that country. Early in 1903 he was about to ask for the charge of the forest school and circle at Dehra Dun in the Meerut division of the United Provinces; failing this appointment he proposed to retire. At this juncture Mr. H. C. Hill, the inspector-general of Indian forests, suddenly died, and Eardley-Wilmot was appointed to the vacancy in February 1903.

As inspector-general, apart from his activity in administrative matters, notably in effecting improvements in the emoluments of the staff and in the forestry education of the subordinate grades, Eardley-Wilmot's greatest achievement was connected with the inauguration of the Imperial Forest Research Institute at Dehra Dun. The viceroy, Lord Curzon, was keenly interested in the introduction of the scientific expert into India, and had already established an Agricultural Research Institute. The Forest Institute, the officers of which were selected from the Indian Forest department, came into being in 1906. From this small beginning —for buildings and equipment had to be gradually obtained—was built up the magnificent Forest Research Institute, the largest of its kind in the world, which was formally opened by the viceroy, Lord Irwin, in 1929, only six days before Eardley-Wilmot's death—evidence of the great value of the step taken in 1906.

Eardley-Wilmot retired from the service in 1909, and in 1910 was appointed one of the commissioners of the newly formed Development Commission. He served as a commissioner for five years, and was then appointed forestry adviser to the commissioners, a post which he held until 1919 when, on the passing of the Forestry Act, 1911, the Forestry Commission was formed; he then retired into private life. During his service on the Development Commission the improvement of forestry education at the universities and in the agricultural colleges was a chief aim, as was also, where possible, the encouragement of afforestation amongst private proprietors. Grants with these objects in view were made by the commission.

It was during his service as conservator in the North-West Provinces and Oudh that Eardley-Wilmot began writing a series of papers on the silviculture of Indian trees, comprising *Notes on the Regeneration of Sal* (*Shorea robusta*), *Notes on Sal Forests*, *Notes on Improvement Fellings*, *Sal Coppice Forests of Oudh*, *Notes on the Treatment of Shisham* (*Dalbergia Sissoo*) *and Khair* (*Acacia Catechu*) *in the Sub-Himalayan Tracts*. These were published by the Government of India in the *Appendix Series* of the *Indian Forester* and formed an important contribution to the meagre silvicultural knowledge of Indian trees of that day. When inspector-general he published *Notes on the Influence of Forests on the storage and regulation of the Water Supply* (1906). In 1910 appeared his *Forest Life and Sport in India*, a book which has considerable literary merit and, from the point of view of forestry as well as of natural history and sport, is regarded as a classic. Two other works followed, *The Life of a Tiger* (1911) and *The Life of an Elephant* (1912), both of which give evidence of a close study of the lore of the jungle.

Eardley-Wilmot was created C.I.E. in 1908 and K.C.I.E. in 1911. He was twice married: first, in 1884 to Emma Elizabeth (died 1890), daughter of George Casey, of Winterbourne St. Leonards; secondly, in 1891 to Mabel Boisragon, daughter of William Henry Winter, head of the telegraph department, General Post Office. There was one daughter of each marriage. He died at Henley-on-Thames 13 November 1929.

[*The Times*, 14 November 1929; *Nature*, 21 December 1929.] E. P. Stebbing.

WILSON, Sir HENRY HUGHES, baronet (1864–1922), field-marshal, the second son of James Wilson, of Currygrane, Edgeworthstown, co. Longford, by his wife, Constance Grace Martha, eldest daughter of James Freeman Hughes, of The Grove, Stillorgan, co. Dublin, was born at Currygrane 5 May 1864. In 1877 he was sent to Marlborough College, where he worked for entrance into the army. Failing twice to gain admission into Woolwich and three times into Sandhurst, in December 1882 he obtained a commission without examination in the Longford Militia (then 6th battalion, Rifle Brigade); through this channel he gained admission into the 18th Royal Irish Regiment, but was immediately transferred to the Rifle Brigade, being gazetted into it in November 1884. The 1st battalion, which he joined in India, proceeded to Burma soon after in order to take part in the troublesome operations for the suppression of armed brigandage. While engaged on this duty in 1886, Wilson received a severe wound over the right eye and, as a result of the injury, returned home late in 1887. Whilst on sick leave he set to work for entrance to the Staff College, and, after passing the entrance examination in 1891, joined the College at Camberley in January 1892. At the Staff College he made no particular mark as a student but he made many friends. Meanwhile he had married, in 1891, Cecil Mary, youngest daughter of George Cecil Gore Wray, J.P., of Ardnamona, co. Donegal.

On leaving Camberley, after having been promoted captain in December 1893, Wilson remained at home until, early in 1894, he received a temporary appointment in the Intelligence Department at the War Office, at the head of which was his friend, another Irishman, Sir John Ardagh [q.v.]. There he was employed in dealing mainly with South African questions. But he did not complete the normal tenure of his appointment, being transferred in 1897, at the instance of the director of the department, as brigade-major to the 3rd Infantry brigade. On the outbreak of the South African War, Wilson's brigade was sent to the Cape under the command of Major-General (Sir) Neville Lyttelton, as the 4th brigade of the 2nd division. On arrival the troops were ordered to Natal, where the 4th brigade took part in the unfortunate battle of Colenso (15 December 1899). After this failure a deadlock arose until Sir Redvers Buller [q.v.] tried to turn the Boer position by moving westwards and then crossing the Tugela river. The attempt, in which Wilson took a full share, ended in the reverse at Spion Kop (24–25 January 1900). After these operations Lyttelton was promoted to command a division and left the 4th brigade, having formed a high opinion of his brigade-major and conceived a friendship for him which later proved to be greatly to Wilson's advantage.

After the relief of Ladysmith on 1 March the Natal field force, Wilson with it, eventually made its way into the Transvaal. After visiting Pretoria in order to see Lord Roberts, whose only son, killed at Colenso, had been one of Wilson's Irish friends, he was selected for service on the head-quarters staff, first as deputy-assistant-quartermaster-general and then as assistant-military-secretary. In the latter capacity he returned to England with Lord Roberts in January 1901. For his South African service he received the D.S.O. in June and was promoted brevet-lieutenant-colonel on 3 December, the day following his attaining the rank of major in his own regiment. This early promotion, combined with the support of such influential patrons, was certain to lead to further advancement.

Anxious to secure a home appointment, Wilson, in February 1902, obtained command of the 9th provisional battalion at Colchester, and held that position for exactly one year. Having thus qualified for fresh staff appointment, he was made a deputy-assistant-adjutant-general in the military training branch of the War Office in April 1903, being advanced to assistant-adjutant-general in the following June. His work was connected with the training of the auxiliary forces, and in that capacity he often accompanied Lord Roberts on official tours. In 1904 there began the reorganization of the War Office and the formation of the new general staff; during the unsettled period which ensued Wilson was busily engaged on tasks that were after his own heart. Largely as the result of these he was promoted brevet-colonel in December 1904, and finally appointed by Sir Neville Lyttelton, now chief of the general staff, to be commandant of the Staff College, with the rank of brigadier-general, in January 1907.

At Camberley Wilson soon displayed many attributes of the successful teacher, and, thanks to a vivid personality, a remarkable facility for public speaking, a never-failing humorous turn of expression, and a penchant for the dramatic, he achieved great popularity among the students, while his reputation as a lecturer spread throughout the army. In addition, he soon made himself the leading exponent of the policy of close co-operation with France in the event of a continental war. Here he found a virgin field for his talent for lecturing, and he availed himself of the opportunity to the full. More pregnant with fateful consequences was the friendship which at this period he formed with General (afterwards Marshal) Foch, then head of the French École Supérieure de Guerre. As time went on Wilson became more and more possessed by the idea of placing the British army at the disposal of France in the event of war.

In 1910 Wilson was chosen for the post of director of military operations at the War Office, and on leaving Camberley in August of that year he was made the subject of unusual demonstrations of popularity. He had been created a C.B. in 1908. In his new position he rapidly acquired great influence, and concentrated his energies on elaborating schemes for the instant support of France by the entire armed resources of Great Britain in the event of an outbreak of war with Germany. He often visited France, sometimes in company with Sir John French (afterwards Earl of Ypres, q.v.), and thereby still further committed the British government to the policy of armed support of France. But his plans, admirably worked out in detail, were largely based on two faulty premisses: first, they relegated to a merely secondary place any potential intervention of the British fleet; secondly, they entirely subordinated the action of the British army to French plans, with inadequate advantages to, or regard for, British military needs. Moreover, insufficient thought was paid to many practical details of command. The Franco-German crisis of 1911 passed off, and Wilson accelerated his plans for the warlike action which he now advocated in public utterances, while in the meantime his relations with General Foch grew still more intimate. In November 1913 he was promoted major-general. Then, in the spring of 1914, occurred the Curragh incident, the result of the British government's apparent intention of coercing Ulster by armed force to participate in the grant of Irish Home Rule. The cavalry officers at the Curragh declared that they would resign their commissions rather than take action against Ulster, and the episode led to the resignation of Sir John French, then chief of the Imperial General Staff, and of Sir John Spencer Ewart [q.v.], the adjutant-general. Throughout the crisis Wilson, as a protestant Irishman, was active behind the scenes in his support of the Ulster cause. The state of tension, both in Ireland and in the general European situation, continued with little abatement until the sequel to the murders at Serajevo in July 1914 led up to the British declaration of war against Germany in support of France on 4 August. Lord Kitchener [q.v.] thereupon became secretary of state for war. Of his views on matters both of strategy and of raising the 'new armies', Wilson strongly and openly disapproved.

The British Expeditionary Force landed in France under the orders of Sir John French, with Sir Archibald Murray as chief, and Wilson in the entirely new position of sub-chief, of the general staff. The whole scheme of mobilization, which

Wilson had inspired, worked admirably. On 14 August British head-quarters crossed to France; the troops followed, and on 23 August were attacked by the German First Army at Mons. The French plan of campaign already showed signs of collapse, whilst co-operation between French and British armies proved faulty. The retreat began, General Murray's health broke down, and Wilson became largely responsible for the work of general head-quarters. In spite of an assumed air of light-heartedness he could do little to retrieve the situation; indeed, at one moment he seemed to be filled with such forebodings that he sent instructions to the troops to burn their baggage and retreat at full speed; but both corps commanders, Sir Douglas Haig and Sir Horace Smith-Dorrien [q.v.], declined to issue such orders. The tide turned at the River Marne on 6 September; the inconclusive battle of the Aisne followed, until, at the beginning of October, the British army was transferred to Flanders. Throughout this period Wilson performed the work of his office interrupted by frequent visits to French head-quarters. The battle of Ypres was next fought to the bitter end (October–November), but it was scarcely possible for the high command to influence the result, except by a display of remarkable tenacity. In November the question arose whether Wilson should not succeed General Murray as chief of staff. The final decision, however, was not taken until 25 January 1915, when Sir William Robertson became chief of staff, while Wilson was appointed chief liaison officer with French head-quarters, receiving the temporary rank of lieutenant-general, the latter distinction being gazetted on 19 February. He now ceased to exercise any direct influence over the course of events in the field, and busied himself with the political conduct of the War. In June he appears to have become less hostile to the formation of the new armies by Lord Kitchener, a fact which smoothed down the acrimony subsisting between the secretary of state and himself. He was created K.C.B. in the spring.

In August 1915 Wilson received from Sir John French the offer of the command of an army corps; it was also intimated to him privately that his refusal of that offer would not be unacceptable to the secretary of state. In the end the IV Army Corps was entrusted to him in December 1915. During his tenure of command throughout 1916, he was not called upon to participate in any noteworthy action, although on 19 May, after taking over some poorly constructed and sited trenches from the French at the northern end of Vimy Ridge, the Germans developed a heavy surprise attack at that point, which drove the British back a considerable distance with some loss. Wilson thereupon made plans to retake the lost ground, but was ordered to desist, as the attempt promised to be too costly. The IV Corps was gradually denuded of troops for the battle of the Somme, and on 1 December Wilson himself was selected as head of a mission which was to proceed to Russia in order to discuss the supply of war material. After his return in March 1917 he went back to France in order to act as chief liaison officer with French head-quarters, his rank of lieutenant-general being then made permanent. After General Nivelle had been succeeded as commander-in-chief of the French armies by General Pétain on 15 May, the latter informed British head-quarters that he considered Wilson to be a *persona non grata*. Wilson thereupon returned to England.

After a spell of unemployment Wilson, at the instance of Sir William Robertson, was appointed to the Eastern command at home in September 1917, a position which suited him well since it enabled him to reside in London and keep in close touch with military and political authorities alike: it was in these circumstances that Wilson came into close contact with the prime minister, Mr. Lloyd George. Soon afterwards, on 24 October, occurred the serious defeat of the Italian army, initiated by an Austro-German surprise attack at Caporetto. By threatening the complete collapse of Italy, this event produced a grave crisis in the Allied conduct of the War. A conference of the Powers was accordingly summoned at Rapallo, and thither Wilson hastened in an entirely unofficial capacity, in company with the prime minister on 7 November. As prearranged by Mr. Lloyd George and M. Painlevé, the French premier, there was created at this meeting a 'Supreme War Council', designed to co-ordinate the various war policies and military plans of the Allied countries. This council, which was to meet as required, comprised two leading ministers from Great Britain, France, Italy, and the United States respectively, and these statesmen were supported by a group of permanent military representatives who were to work out all military plans on their behalf. One representative was selected by each Power, and, as the chiefs of staff were not eligible, the choice of British representative fell upon Wilson, who might indeed be considered as one of the chief instigators of the creation of the council. He was then given the temporary rank of general. At Versailles, the seat of the new council, Wilson and the other Allied military representatives set up their offices, surrounded by numerous staffs, on 1 December. For the next ten weeks the military representatives compiled a number of joint notes for the benefit of the council, the fourteenth and last of which alone acquired much importance, since it adumbrated the formation of a general reserve of troops for the entire Western front, inclusive of Italy. The use of this reserve was to be controlled by an executive War Board, of which Wilson was to be the British member. But numerous obstacles at once arose, mainly owing to the disinclination of the various national commanders-in-chief to part with their troops, of which they had all too few; still more, perhaps, owing to the difficulties involved in the command of such a body. The consequent discussions dragged on for many weeks, indeed long after Wilson had left Versailles for London.

For some time it had been apparent that Mr. Lloyd George preferred Wilson's facile personality and his pungent modes of expression to the uncompromising attitude and blunt opinions of Sir William Robertson, then chief of the Imperial General Staff. Supported by Lord Milner [q.v.] alone in the Cabinet, Mr. Lloyd George finally decided that Wilson should supersede Robertson, and the change took place on 18 February 1918. As chief of the Imperial General Staff Wilson found full scope in the political sphere for the exercise of his particular abilities; but he had scarcely settled down in his new office when, on 21 March, the Germans launched their great onslaught against the British Fifth Army. The offensive, although long expected, fell at a point which had not been foreseen by the Versailles Council. Heavily outnumbered, the British gave ground until it seemed as though the Allied front might break. The general reserve, as proposed by the Supreme War Council, not having come into existence, it was clear that some drastic remedy was needed to save the situation. Wilson hastened to France, whither Lord Milner had already proceeded, and on 26 March, after a conference of Allied statesmen and commanders at Doullens, north of Amiens, it was decided to confer the control of the combined Allied armies on General Foch. As the direction of the military operations of the Allies now virtually passed into Foch's hands, Wilson's work became merged in the results of the numerous committees and conferences which grew to be synonymous with the higher conduct of the War. In France the next three months continued to be full of anxiety, as the Germans, after being checked before Amiens, renewed their attacks at other points. At length on 18 July the tide turned, the Allied advance began, and the Germans slowly gave way until they were eventually compelled to accept the Allied terms of armistice on 11 November.

The months which elapsed between the Armistice and the signing of the Peace Treaty at Versailles on 28 June 1919, were spent by Wilson mostly in Paris. During that time he began to drift away somewhat from his close association with Mr. Lloyd George. Eventually he made no secret of his dissatisfaction both with the terms of peace and with the whole management of the political situation by the Allied statesmen. He opposed any British participation in the League of Nations, expressed himself against a pro-Greek policy in Asia Minor, and was an advocate of strong British rule in the East generally; whilst he continued to urge the enforcement of rigorous measures in Ireland. In July 1919 he was promoted field-marshal, and in August was created a baronet, receiving the thanks of parliament and a grant of £10,000.

Affairs in Poland, at Constantinople, and in Mesopotamia occupied Wilson in his official capacity very fully during the next two and a half years. He persisted in recommending vigorous measures, not hesitating to advise military action in each minor crisis as it arose; but the main objects of his deepest antipathy remained the Bolshevik governors of Russia and still more the leaders of Sinn Fein in Ireland; against the latter he never ceased to recommend a system of drastic coercion. Throughout 1921 the breach which was growing between Wilson and Mr. Lloyd George widened, and he became ever more preoccupied with Irish affairs and with the intricacies of party politics. Eventually, on 21 February 1922, he was elected unopposed as conservative member of parliament for North Down (Ireland). At the same time he took leave of the War Office on completing his four years as chief of the Imperial General Staff, Mr.

Lloyd George having declined to extend his tenure of that office, and retired from the army.

In the House of Commons Wilson delivered a maiden speech, on 15 March, in the debate concerning the state of the army. The subject had long been a favourite theme with him; his manner and delivery were perfectly suited to the occasion. He was loudly applauded, and although strongly attacked by the labour party in opposition, was welcomed as a great accession to the conservative party and as an opponent of Mr. Lloyd George. In May he visited Northern Ireland, and made public speeches on the Irish problem in a manner which could not fail to arouse violent hostility in the ranks of Sinn Fein. The leaders of that movement thereafter regarded Wilson as an implacable enemy, and fears began to be entertained in London for his personal safety. That these were justified was proved when in the following month he was assassinated by two Sinn Feiners on the doorstep of his London House, No. 36 Eaton Place (22 June). Rumour was prevalent to the effect that his murder was the outcome of an organized conspiracy. But that was never proved, even at the trial of his murderers. He was granted a public funeral and buried in the crypt of St. Paul's Cathedral.

Opinions as to Wilson's talents and as to his place among the great figures of the European War have varied greatly. Even before 1914 some of his own colleagues had looked with growing distrust on his rapid advancement to highly responsible positions. Many saw in him a very great soldier; in that respect his personality and his facility for public speaking served him well; while a whimsical turn of expression and never-failing geniality brought him many friends and admirers. Others were concerned at his perpetual avoidance of responsibility, his lack of any real experience of military command, and his love of intrigue. The publication of his diaries in 1927, full of violently expressed prejudices and mistaken opinions, was followed by the appearance of further literature which went a long way to shatter belief in the superiority of his military talents. It was recognized that he was at heart a politician rather than a soldier.

Wilson left no child, and the baronetcy became extinct on his death. He received honorary degrees from the universities of Oxford and Cambridge and from Trinity College, Dublin; he was colonel of the Royal Irish Rifles (1915) and a colonel commandant of the Rifle Brigade (1919).

There is a portrait of Wilson by Sir William Orpen in the Imperial War Museum, South Kensington; another, by Oswald Birley, appears in *Royal Academy Pictures*, 1922; he also figures in J. S. Sargent's picture 'Some General Officers of the Great War', which hangs in the National Portrait Gallery.

[*The Times*, 23 June 1922; Sir J. E. Edmonds, (Official) *History of the Great War. Military Operations. France and Belgium, 1914–1916* and *1918*, 1922–1935; Sir C. E. Callwell, *Field-Marshal Sir Henry Wilson, his life and diaries*, 2 vols., 1927; Sir Andrew Macphail, *Three Persons*, 1929; John Charteris, *At G.H.Q.*, 1931; Army Lists; personal knowledge.] H. de Watteville.

WILSON, JOSEPH HAVELOCK (1858–1929), founder of the National Union of Seamen, was born at Sunderland 16 August 1858, the third son of John Wilson, foreman draper of that town, by his wife, Hannah, daughter of John Joseph Robson. Both his parents were descended from seafaring families. After intermittent attendance at a local school, Wilson in 1867 was unwillingly apprenticed to a lithographic printer, but hereditary instincts led him in 1870 to run away to sea. His experiences of life before the mast during the succeeding fifteen years decided the course of his future career.

In 1887 Wilson founded the National Amalgamated Sailors' and Firemen's Union, afterwards known as the National Union of Seamen. He determined to obtain recognition of his union by shipowners, and to secure generally improved conditions, especially as regards accommodation, food, and wages, for all seamen. After an inauspicious beginning the Union grew rapidly in strength: the shipowners thereupon formed in 1890 the Shipping Federation. Violent antagonism between the two organizations prevailed until, in 1912, the recognition of Wilson's union by the Federation brought about a mutual desire for the solution in conference of outstanding questions. Wilson meanwhile had frequently been involved in legal proceedings, and he served a short term of imprisonment for unlawful assembly in 1891. In that year he came under the influence of Samuel Plimsoll [q.v.], the 'Sailors' Friend'. Plimsoll deprecated aggressive industrial action and urged Wilson to bring his cause before parliament. Wilson represented Middlesbrough in the liberal interest from 1892 to 1900, and again from 1906 to 1910; he returned to parliament as coalition liberal member for South Shields in 1918. Defeated in 1922, he did not seek re-election: the reforms for which he had laboured, including the amendment of the Merchant Shipping Act in 1907 and the extension of the Workmen's Compensation Act to seafarers, had already been enacted. In 1922 he was made C.H.

Wilson was never a revolutionary socialist, but zeal unqualified by experience caused him as a youthful leader to adopt extreme rather than conciliatory methods. Eventually he became an advocate of peaceful negotiation, and in his uncompleted autobiography entitled *My Stormy Voyage through Life* (1925) he made commendably frank confession of early mistakes. Wilson was at all times a patriot. During the European War British seamen under his leadership boycotted German nationals and cargoes suspected of an ultimate German destination; similarly, passages oversea were refused to certain political leaders then credited with defeatist intentions. For his services in connexion with recruiting Wilson received the C.B.E. in 1918. The General Strike of 1926 was declared by him to be a 'revolutionary plot', and was condemned by his union. He held that the trades union movement, rightly directed, must be industrial and not political, and to trades unionism thus conceived he remained faithful.

Despite ill-health Wilson was persuaded to remain president of the National Union of Seamen until his death, which occurred in London 16 April 1929. He married in 1879 Jane Anne, only child of Thomas Whatham, of South Shields. She survived him with two sons and one daughter.

[*The Times*, 17 April 1929; J. Havelock Wilson, *My Stormy Voyage through Life* (with an introduction by Lord Runciman), 1925; private information.] A. E. Watkin.

WOLLASTON, ALEXANDER FREDERICK RICHMOND (1875–1930), naturalist and explorer, born 22 May 1875 at Clifton, was the second son of George Hyde Wollaston. His parents came of gifted families. His mother, Sarah Constance, daughter of Thomas Richmond and granddaughter of Thomas Richmond [q.v.], miniature painters, and niece of the portrait-painter, George Richmond [q.v.], was a very talented woman. His father, George Hyde Wollaston, was a man of wide culture and one of the most outstanding figures at Clifton College during the headmastership of John Percival. He was a direct descendant of William Wollaston [q.v.] and of Francis Wollaston [q.v.]; Francis John Hyde Wollaston [q.v.] and William Hyde Wollaston [q.v.] were his great-great-uncles, while the entomologist Thomas Vernon Wollaston [q.v.] was more distantly related. No other family name occurs more often in the annals of the Royal Society.

From a private school Wollaston entered Clifton College as a day-boy. He was a born naturalist, caring little for school life and games, but delighting in the study of birds and wild life. In 1893 he went up to King's College, Cambridge. Throughout his life his feelings for his college amounted to devotion. He was one of the select few who attended the zoology lectures of Alfred Newton [q.v.], whose life he wrote in 1921. During a long vacation he began a career of travel by walking from Hammerfest through Lappland to the Baltic. He took only a poll degree in 1896, but stayed up at King's for another two years. Having early made up his mind to be an explorer, he decided to obtain a medical qualification in order to facilitate his chances of travel, and accordingly went to the London Hospital, taking his 'conjoint' in 1903 and his B.Ch. at Cambridge in 1913.

Finding life as a medical student in London very irksome, Wollaston took every opportunity to escape into the country. Mountain country attracted him greatly, and he spent many holidays climbing in Great Britain and in the Alps, but he was stirred rather by a love of exploration and of natural beauty than by the gymnastic side of mountaineering. He was elected to the Alpine Club in 1903 and served on its committee 1922–1924. In 1901 and 1904 he visited the Sudan with N. C. Rothschild in order to collect birds and animals, and later travelled round the world, visiting New Zealand, the Malay States, and Japan.

In 1906 Wollaston took part, as doctor and collector of plants and insects, in the British Museum expedition, led by R. B. Woosnam, to the Ruwenzori mountains in Central Africa. He climbed what was then supposed to be the highest peak (15,286 feet), afterwards named Wollaston Peak by the Duke of Abruzzi, and returned home down the Congo with Douglas Carruthers, publishing a charming account of his travels and observations in *From Ruwenzori to the Congo* (1908). A marked trait in his character was his sympathy with the outlook of primitive native peoples, but his consistent regard for accuracy forced him on this occasion to protest strongly against the calumnies then prevalent in England concerning the Belgian administration on the Congo.

In 1909 Wollaston joined the expedition to Dutch New Guinea organized by the British Ornithologists' Union under the leadership of Walter Goodfellow. The expedition, of which Cecil Godfrey Rawling [q.v.] was surveyor, failed to reach the Nassau range, and there was much sickness; but Wollaston made a valuable collection of natural history specimens, and an extremely interesting study of the very primitive pygmy Tapiro tribe, discovered by the expedition. At the request of the committee of the expedition he wrote an account of it in *Pygmies and Papuans* (1912).

Wollaston was so much disappointed at the failure of this expedition to reach the snows that in 1912–1913 he returned to New Guinea, taking C. B. Kloss as his only white companion. Working up the Utakwa and Setakwa rivers, he succeeded after four months in reaching the glaciers of Mount Carstensz (15,706 feet) and in attaining a height of 14,866 feet. The expedition was very arduous: great physical difficulties of access were accentuated by dense vegetation, bad climate, noxious insects, and complete absence of any local food supplies; but all Wollaston's arrangements were excellent, and by means of suitable diet beri-beri was entirely avoided. His sympathy with the hitherto unknown stone-age natives ensured a friendly reception. He secured a valuable collection of ethnological and natural history specimens, and described the journey in a delightful lecture [*Geographical Journal*, March 1914]. For this expedition, organized by himself, and for his part in former expeditions, he was awarded the Gill memorial by the Royal Geographical Society in 1914. He was planning a third expedition to New Guinea when the European War broke out.

Wollaston volunteered as a surgeon in the royal navy, and was attached to the northern patrol on 4 August 1914 and later to H.M.S. *Agincourt*. In 1915 he joined the East African Expeditionary Force, and served in it for two years. During 1918 he served in a monitor off the Belgian coast, and in 1919 joined the British force sent to Murmansk, the Russian port on the Kola peninsula. He was mentioned in dispatches and awarded the D.S.C. for conspicuous devotion to duty throughout operations in East Africa. He was demobilized in October 1919.

In 1921 Wollaston took part as doctor and naturalist in the first Mount Everest expedition, led by Lieutenant-Colonel C. K. Howard-Bury. His medical services both to members of the expedition and to native Tibetans were highly appreciated; he made excellent collections containing specimens of animals and plants new to science, and also brought back some of the finest photographs in a collection remarkable for its beauty. He wrote a paper in the *Geographical Journal* (July 1922) and two excellent chapters and an appendix in *Mount Everest, the Reconnaisance* (1921).

Wollaston married in 1923 Mary, daughter of Daniel Meinertzhagen, head of the banking house of Frederick Huth. In the same year, with his wife, Wollaston visited the unexplored Sierra Nevada of Santa Marta, in Colombia, a region very difficult of access. He described the venture in a paper read to the Royal Geographical Society [*Geographical Journal*, August 1925]. In 1925 he received the Patron's medal from the Royal Geographical Society, and in 1928 was appointed honorary secretary.

In view of his lack of scholastic achievements, Wollaston's election to a six-years' fellowship at King's College in 1920 was a signal tribute to his character. In 1925 he settled at Uley in Gloucestershire, but in 1928 he was re-elected fellow and appointed tutor to his college and went to live at Cambridge. Despite an extreme personal reticence, he had the gift of inspiring friendship; this, combined with his sense of humour, astonishing insight, and broad outlook, made him remarkably successful with undergraduates. After his death, Mr. J. M. Keynes wrote of him that 'he could unlock hearts with a word and a look, and break down everyone's reserves, except his own', while Mr. Stanley Baldwin as chancellor of the University spoke of Cambridge 'mourning a prince among men'. The affection with which he was regarded intensified the horror and indignation aroused amongst a very wide circle of friends when on 3 June 1930 he was shot dead in his college rooms by a demented undergraduate, who took his own life at the same time. His ashes lie in the chapel of King's College. He left a widow and one son and two daughters.

Wollaston was a distinguished naturalist, ethnologist, and explorer of tropical mountain regions, a geographer in the widest sense, with a marked understanding of primitive races. His writing was distinguished by a notable sensitiveness, and in accuracy of detail and avoidance of error he exhibited the characteristic merit of the scientist William Hyde Wollaston. He was a man of wide knowledge and noble character. He was master of himself in a rare degree: a great adventurer and a wonderful friend.

[*The Times*, 4, 6, and 7 June 1930; *Cambridge Review*, 6 June 1930; J. M. Keynes in *The Nation*, 14 June 1930; *Alpine Journal*, August 1914 and November 1930; *Geographical Journal*, June and November 1906, March 1914, August 1925, and July 1930; *Ibis*, January 1902 and July 1930; Wollaston's writings and diaries (*Letters and Diaries of A. F. R. Wollaston*, selected and edited by Mary Wollaston, 1933); private information; personal knowledge.] T. G. Longstaff.

WOOD, CHARLES (1866–1926), composer, was born at Armagh 14 June 1866, the third son and fifth child of Charles Wood, lay vicar of Armagh Cathedral and diocesan registrar of the diocese of Armagh, by his wife, Jemima Taylor. He was educated at the Cathedral School, Armagh.

In 1883 Wood came to London, having won a scholarship for composition at the Royal College of Music, which in that year began its great and in some ways risky experiment in musical education with fifty scholars and a few students. (Sir) Charles Villiers Stanford [q.v.] and (Sir) Hubert Parry [q.v.] were its two teachers of composition. To Stanford came Wood as a pupil, an unassuming youth not quite seventeen years of age. He at once made his mark. At an epoch of attenuated technique, false sentiment, deliberate showiness, he appeared as one who, by instinct, had kept to the straight, classical line, thorough, sincere, correct; undeveloped, of course, but already, perhaps through his training at Armagh Cathedral, possessing a knowledge of counterpoint and a sense of vocal style beyond his teacher's power to improve. Stanford taught him how to expand his instrumental style; how to make use of the more modern harmonies which Brahms and, in another school, Wagner were developing; how to manage musical forms: but wisely left him alone, for the most part, to achieve his own manner of expression. His other teachers were (Sir) Frederick Bridge [q.v.], harmony and counterpoint, Franklin Taylor, pianoforte, and Thomas Mann, French horn, which instrument Wood played adequately, if not brilliantly, in the College orchestra.

Greater perhaps than the influence of Wood's teachers—though he could have had no more skilful and appreciative guide than Stanford—was that of his environment. He had, even then, an astonishing, self-acquired knowledge of the classical composers; but Brahms, Dvořák, Wagner, and probably most of Schumann were unknown to him. At the College he had access to their works, and could hear them played. Not only that, did he himself write a song, or a violin sonata, or a string quartet he could quite easily get it performed *con amore* by his fellow students. Sir George Grove [q.v.], then director of the College, a passionate if not always discriminating lover of music and literature, quickly recognized the power and promise of Wood, and took an important part in the moulding of his literary tastes. He can be said to have made the poets known to Wood, but in return had Beethoven made known to himself through the medium of Wood's illuminating knowledge.

Wood stayed at the Royal College until 1888. By that time he had written, with much besides, the first of his string quartets and his setting of Shelley's *Ode to the West Wind* for chorus and orchestra. He then went as an undergraduate to Selwyn College, Cambridge, and shortly afterwards as organist scholar to Gonville and Caius College, his Royal College scholarship being made tenable at the University. In 1889 he was appointed to the staff of the Royal College of Music as a teacher of harmony and counterpoint (subjects which were soon understood to include composition), and in 1891 he was made organist of Caius College. Both these appointments he held until his death. He made his home in Cambridge, and settled down to a valuable and influential life of routine. He was made a fellow of Caius College in 1894, took the degree of Mus.D., Cambridge, in 1895 (he had graduated B.A., Mus.Bac. in 1890), and received the honorary degree of LL.D. from the university of Leeds in 1904, and that of D.Mus. from the university of Oxford in 1926. Having been for many years lecturer in harmony and counterpoint to the university of Cambridge, he was made professor of music in that university in 1924, in succession to Sir C. V. Stanford, his former teacher.

Wood's busy and ordered life had two main interests, teaching and composition.

As a teacher he worked in two centres, the Royal College of Music and Cambridge. His most evident characteristic was a sort of natural authority, as of one whose taste and judgement were almost as unquestionable as a law of nature. The most modest of men, he was quite unconscious of his own wisdom; but all who knew him and learned from him felt that he had a curious quality of finality. He knew, and his pupils knew that he knew, right from wrong, good from bad. It was not merely that he could and did teach admirably how music should be shaped and presented; he could make good music live and bad music die in the heart and mind of the student. Something instinctively true and perceptive in his nature enabled him to separate grain from chaff without effort. He hated ostentation, rhetoric, pretentiousness, whether in music, in literature, or in conduct. The wholesomeness and sanity of approach to be found in the music of Handel, Haydn, Beethoven, and Schubert perhaps appealed to him most vitally. It is no exaggeration to say that Wood had a more beneficent and far-reaching effect on contemporary musical production than any other teacher. Most of the present English composers have come under his influence either directly or at one remove, and the result is to be seen in the thoroughness of workmanship and dignity of style which inform the work of the best of them, however far they may have developed or departed from Wood's idiom.

Much of Wood's more ambitious creative work was done in his youth and early manhood: the *Ode to Music* (a setting of a poem specially written by Swinburne for the opening of the new Royal College of Music) in 1890; the music to the *Ion* of Euripides in 1890, and that to *Iphigenia in Tauris* in 1894; his beautiful *Dirge for two Veterans* and his neglected but fine *Ballad of Dundee* for the Leeds festivals of 1901 and 1904 respectively; his *Song of the Tempest* for the Hovingham festival, 1903. He wrote, in addition, eight string quartets at various periods, a set of variations for orchestra on the Irish air *Sir Patrick Sarsfield*, two *Opera Scenes from Dickens*, sixteen preludes for the organ, a very large number of songs, part-songs, services, and anthems, and a setting of the *Passion according to St. Mark*. His music is remarkable for the flawless ease, certainty, and ingenuity of its workmanship, and the purity and nobility of its imaginative quality. At its best it rises very high, by force of its simple dignity and beauty. Wood was no conscious reformer, no shouter of new messages. His aim was to make music as he felt it ought to be, sincere, unextravagant, expressive of the best that was in him. These being the qualities which most endure and grow, his work is steadily advancing in the esteem of musicians and of the discriminating section of the general public. His vocal music and his string quartets in particular are now accepted as models. Of both mediums he had a command which students cannot afford to leave unstudied. His church music can already be regarded as classical. It is performed regularly and frequently in all the cathedrals and in many churches.

As a man Wood was shy and retiring, but he had a great sense of humour and a fundamental common sense which made him quite indifferent to things which seemed to him not to matter. Psychological problems and philosophical speculations left him quite unmoved. Many of his sayings are still repeated. He died at Cambridge 12 July 1926.

Wood married in 1898 Charlotte Georgina, daughter of Captain William Robert Wills Sandford, Scots Greys, of Castlerea House, co. Roscommon, and had two sons, the elder of whom was killed on active service in 1918, and three daughters.

[Private information; personal knowledge.]

S. P. Waddington.

WOOD, FRANCIS DERWENT (1871–1926) sculptor, was born at Keswick 15 October 1871, the son of Alpheus Bayliss Wood, a native of Philadelphia, by his English wife, Anne Mary, daughter of John Hornby Maw. At a very early age he was sent to school at Lausanne, and subsequently for two years studied art at Karlsruhe under Otto Weltring and Hermann Götz. In 1889 he returned to England, and worked as a modeller first in the potteries of Messrs. Maw & Co. at Jackfield, Shropshire, and later for the Coalbrookdale Co., iron-moulders, in the same county. He was meanwhile continuing his artistic education in the local art school, whence he proceeded to the National Art Training Schools at South Kensington (afterwards the Royal College of Art) and there studied sculpture under Professor Edouard Lantéri and gained a national scholarship. In 1890 he became assistant to Professor Alphonse Legros [q.v.] at the Slade School of Art, and held this post until the resignation of Legros at the end of 1892.

At the age of twenty-one Wood could thus look back upon a course of training which had brought him considerable experience: in 1894 he nevertheless entered upon a three years' course at the Royal Academy Schools, continuing to gain many student distinctions: in 1895 he was awarded the gold medal and travelling scholarship for his group 'Daedalus and Icarus'. In the same year he contributed a relief, in plaster, entitled 'Circe', to the Academy exhibition. During his years of study at the Academy Wood acted as assistant to (Sir) Thomas Brock [q.v.], and he continued to do so after a stay in Paris, where he gained the *mention honorable* at the Salon of 1897 for his group 'Maternity'. Shortly afterwards he was appointed modelling master at the Glasgow School of Art, but in 1901 he returned to London and settled in Glebe Place, Chelsea. In 1910 he was elected A.R.A. and in 1920 R.A., his diploma work being a bronze statuette 'The Dancer'. He succeeded his teacher, Lantéri, as professor of sculpture at the Royal College of Art in 1918, resigning the post in 1923; he also taught sculpture in the Royal Academy Schools. During the European War of 1914–1918 he enlisted in the Royal Army Medical Corps in 1915, receiving a commission in the following year.

Wood was gifted with great facility of artistic expression; his work as a sculptor reflects his cultured personality and, as regards style, is perhaps best described as being of a neo-baroque character in its fullness, flexibility, and realism of form. He was an expert at many techniques of craftsmanship and also a draughtsman and water-colour painter of no mean ability. Notable examples of his work in London are the Machine Gun Corps memorial at Hyde Park Corner (1925), one of his best performances, and the pair of groups symbolizing Australia on two of the gate piers of the Queen Victoria memorial in front of Buckingham Palace. The Tate Gallery possesses his life-size bronze statue 'Psyche' (exhibited at the Royal Academy in 1919 and purchased by the Chantrey trustees) and three portrait busts, namely, of Henry James (exhibited at the Royal Academy in 1914 and purchased by the Chantrey trustees), of Colonel T. E. Lawrence, and of Miss Bess Norris (a Chantrey Fund purchase, 1926). Wood was much employed as a sculptor of portrait busts, and in this connexion it should be mentioned that during and after the War he gave devoted service when in charge of the department of masks for facial wounds. Other important examples of his work are the statue of William Pitt, in marble, commissioned by the women of the United States of America living in England in celebration of one hundred years of peace between the two countries, and set up in the National Gallery of Art at Washington in 1920; the war memorial at Ditchingham, Norfolk; statues of General Wolfe at Westerham, of Lord Nunburnholme at Hull, and of Lord Ripon in the spa gardens at Ripon; and a number of public monuments in India, including those of Queen Victoria and King Edward VII at Patiala, of King Edward VII at Rangoon, of Lord Ripon at Madras and at Calcutta, and of the Maharajah Gaekwar of Baroda, this last an equestrian statue. Several works at Glasgow (forming part of the decorations of the Art Galleries, Kelvingrove, the Mercantile Buildings, Bothwell Street, and the Caledonian low level railway station) were the result of Wood's association with the Glasgow School of Art. Among his numerous individual works of statuary reference should also be made to the group 'Dante at Ravenna' (1899) and 'Atalanta' (1909, now in the Manchester Art Gallery).

Wood died in London after an operation 19 February 1926. He married in 1903 the Australian singer, Florence Schmidt, and had one son. A selection of his works was shown at the Burlington House Winter Exhibition in 1927.

[*The Times*, 20 February 1926; Algernon Graves, *The Royal Academy of Arts, a complete dictionary of contributors and their work*, vol. viii, 1906; subsequent Academy exhibition catalogues, including that of the Memorial Exhibition, 1927.] T. Borenius.

WOOD, MATILDA ALICE VICTORIA (1870–1922), music-hall comedian, professionally known as Marie Lloyd, was born at 36 Plumber Street, Hoxton, 12 February 1870, the eldest of the eleven children of John Wood, artificial flower-maker, by his wife, Matilda Mary Caroline Archer. In childhood she formed a troupe of little girls, the Fairy Bell Minstrels, who sang and acted in schoolrooms and mission halls. At the age of fourteen she appeared on the stage of the Grecian music-hall, which was attached to the Eagle public-house in the City Road; her salary was fifteen shillings a week and her stage name Bella Delmare, which she soon changed to Marie Lloyd. Before she was sixteen she was performing in the West end of London, and in 1886 she was earning £100 a week.

In 1891, 1892, and 1893 Marie Lloyd was engaged by Sir Augustus Henry Glossop Harris [q.v.] for his pantomimes at Drury Lane Theatre; she also appeared in a few other pantomimes in suburban and provincial theatres. But her real bent was for the music-halls, which during her career were developing into imposing theatres of variety. Her songs were all written and composed for her by others; but she moulded them as she pleased by means of look, gesture, and tone of voice, making most of them openly and joyfully improper; yet, attractive as she was with her golden hair and blue eyes, she kept her performance free from any personal display or invitation, and appealed to the women as much as to the men. Her power lay in her cheery vitality, her thorough knowledge of vulgar English—and especially Cockney—manners and humour, and her highly cultivated skill in swift and significant expression, which won praise from judges so good as Ellen Terry [q.v.] and Sarah Bernhardt. Tours in Australia, South Africa, and the United States of America showed that her very English humour could be enjoyed outside England.

Marie Lloyd's work fell into three periods. In the first she was girlish, almost childish, as when she made her first great hit with the song 'The boy I love sits up in the gallery'. Next came a long series of songs which she sang as a grown woman dressed in, and beyond, the height of fashion, such as 'Oh, Mr. Porter', 'Everything in the garden's lovely', and 'When you wink the other eye'. Last came certain studies of shabby and broken-down women, in which she mingled sadness and humour, and showed considerable skill in the impersonation of character.

Over the music-hall public Marie Lloyd held undisputed dominion. Some of the affection for her was due to her notorious generosity. She lavished both money and care on the poor and the unhappy; and in 1907 in a music-hall strike on behalf of the minor performers, she came out on strike with the rest and took her turn as picket. Overwork and domestic trouble hastened her end. She was taken ill on the stage of the Alhambra (the audience loudly applauding what they took for a very realistic piece of acting) and died at her home at Golders Green 7 October 1922, aged fifty-two.

Marie Lloyd married three times: first, in 1887 Percy Charles Courtenay, general dealer, by whom she had her only child, a daughter; secondly, in 1906 Alexander (Alec) Hurley, comedian; and thirdly, in 1914 Bernard Dillon, jockey.

[*The Times*, 3 and 6 October 1913, 23 February 1914, 16 July 1920, and 9 October 1922; Naomi Jacob, *Our Marie*, 1936.]

H. H. Child.

WOOD, THOMAS McKINNON (1855–1927), politician, was born 26 January 1855 at 22 Leslie Street, Stepney, London. His father, Hugh Wood, the son of an Orkney farmer, was in business first in Kirkwall, then in Leith, and afterwards moved to London, where he set up as merchant and ship-owner at 141–142 The Minories.

Thomas, the only son of Hugh Wood by his second wife, Jessie, daughter of the Rev. Thomas McKinnon, of Sauchieburn, Kincardineshire, was educated at the Brewers' Company grammar school, Mill Hill School, and University College, London. He won many prizes at school and college, and graduated with honours in English, logic, and moral philosophy. His ambitions were literary, and for a short time he worked on the staff of the *Encyclopædia Britannica* at Edinburgh. In 1878 his father lost his sight, and Thomas returned to London and joined the business as a partner, developing it, and adding a branch in Liverpool and interests in other companies. When he afterwards entered politics he ceased to take an active part in business; but he resumed his interest on leaving the government, and was chairman of three companies at the time of his death.

The Wood family were active members of the King's Weigh House chapel, and through its minister, Alexander Sandison, Thomas Wood met and married in 1883 Isabella (died 1927), sister of the minister and daughter of Alexander Sandison, J.P., of Unst, Shetland. Under these influences, and not primarily as a politician, Wood entered the London County Council as a progressive, representing Central Hackney from 1892 until 1907, when he became an alderman (1907–1909). He soon made his mark, becoming vice-chairman of the parliamentary committee (1893–1895) and chairman (1895–1898 and March to July 1906). He was chairman of the Council (1898–1899), chairman of the water committee (1900–1904), chairman of the general purposes committee (1904–1906), and for a long period leader of the progressive party.

Wood entered parliament in 1906 as liberal member for the St. Rollox division of Glasgow, after unsuccessful attempts at East Islington (1895), St. Rollox (1900), and Orkney and Shetland (1902). He retained the seat without a break until 1918. In April 1908 he was appointed by Mr. Asquith parliamentary secretary to the Board of Education, and in that position found himself chiefly concerned with the progress of Mr. Reginald McKenna's (abortive) Elementary Education Bill. In October 1908 he was appointed under-secretary of state at the Foreign Office. Here, while doing all his work with conscientious ability, his chief interest, natural in his case though by no means usual, was the effect of foreign affairs on trading and commercial conditions.

In 1911 Wood was appointed financial secretary to the Treasury, and in 1912 secretary for Scotland, with a seat in the Cabinet. His first task in the latter capacity was to bring into operation the Small Land-holders (Scotland) Act passed by his predecessor, Lord Pentland [q.v.], in 1911. He himself secured the passing of the Mental Deficiency and Lunacy (Scotland) Act in 1913, skilfully over-coming much opposition to the new system of treating mental defectives. In the same year he passed the Temperance (Scotland) Act, the Highlands and Islands (Medical Service) Act, and the Bankruptcy (Scotland) Act; and, in 1914, the Milk and Dairies (Scotland) Act. In the application to Scotland of the many legislative and administrative measures necessitated by the European War, he showed skill and tact. In July 1916 Wood again became financial secretary to the Treasury, succeeding E. S. Montagu [q.v.] in that post, which was of peculiar importance in war-time, and also in that of chancellor of the duchy of Lancaster. These posts he held until December 1916, when the government was reconstituted and the War Cabinet formed. He was defeated at St. Rollox in the election of 1918, and was also unsuccessful in 1924 at Central Hackney. He died in London 26 March 1927.

Wood was appointed a deputy lieutenant for the county of London in 1899, received the honorary degree of LL.D. from St. Andrews University in the same year, and was admitted a privy councillor in 1911. He had six sons and two daughters, two sons and one daughter dying before him.

A portrait of Wood by Leonard Watts, painted about 1899, hangs in the offices of the London County Council.

[*The Times*, 28 March 1927; official records; private information.] M. F. HEADLAM.

WRIGHT, JOSEPH (1855–1930), philologist, born 31 October 1855 at Thackley, near Bradford, was the second son of Dufton Wright, a weaver and later a quarryman, whom Joseph Wright described as 'a cheerful, good-tempered chap' who 'was fond of poaching . . . but never wanted to work'. Dufton's wife, Sarah Anne Atkinson, had thus to depend largely on her own efforts in bringing up her four children. At the age of six Joseph Wright began work as a donkey-boy, carrying quarrymen's tools to the black-smith's, for which he received eighteen-pence a week from the smith and a penny a week from each quarryman. At seven he became a 'doffer' at the mill belonging to (Sir) Titus Salt [q.v.] at Saltaire, where his duties consisted in removing the full bobbins from the spindles and replacing them with empty ones. His wages here amounted after a time to three and six-pence a week; and it was at the factory school that he received the first elements of education. At thirteen Wright moved to Wildman's mill at Bingley, where his wages rose to nine shillings a week. He then became a wool-sorter, and as his work was now more exacting and paid by the piece, his earnings rose to between twenty and thirty shillings a week. After the death of his father in 1866, Wright was the main support of his mother and his two younger brothers; he became, as he put it, 'father, husband, son, and companion . . . plunged, when a mere child, into the severest battles of life.'

The first incentive to acquire education came to Wright when he heard the men in the mill talking about the Franco-Prussian War. He then taught himself to read and to write. After attending local evening-classes, where he learned some French and German, he studied arithmetic, Euclid, algebra, and shorthand at the Mechanics' Institute at Bradford. He also organized classes of his own, which were held in the evenings in the two bedrooms of his mother's cottage and attended by about a dozen lads, each paying two-pence a week. By this time he had saved £40, and, as in 1876 the mill was temporarily closed, he went to Heidelberg, where he studied for eleven weeks. On his return he obtained a post as teacher at Springfield

School, Bradford, at a salary of £40 a year. He worked there from September 1876 to April 1879, at the same time attending classes at the Yorkshire College of Science at Leeds. In 1878 he passed the London matriculation examination, and in April 1879 received an appointment at Grove School, Wrexham. About two years later he became an under-master at a school at Margate, where he remained for a few months.

In 1882, having passed the London intermediate examination, Wright determined to study in Germany, and matriculated in the spring at Heidelberg. Mathematics had so far been his chief study, but under the stimulus of Professor Hermann Osthoff he transferred his interest to comparative philology. In the examination for the Ph.D. degree, which he obtained *insigni cum laude* in 1885, Wright offered, as principal and subsidiary subjects respectively, comparative philology, with a detailed study of the Germanic languages, and Anglo-Saxon language and literature; and presented a dissertation on 'The Qualitative and Quantitative Changes in the Indo-Germanic Vowel System in Greek'. While at Heidelberg he earned a small income by teaching mathematics at Neuenheim College, kept by the Rev. Frederick Armitage, previously a master at Clifton College, and by revising educational books published by Julius Groos, of Heidelberg. He was also commissioned to prepare, under the supervision of the author, an English translation of Karl Brugmann's *Grundriss der vergleichenden Grammatik der indo-germanischen Sprachen*, which appeared in 1888.

After spending a short time at Leipzig, where he became interested in Lithuanian, Wright went to London in 1887, and in the following year, on the recommendation of Friedrich Max Müller [q.v.], was appointed lecturer to the Association for the Higher Education of Women in Oxford, to teach Gothic, Old English, and Old German. In the same year he was appointed deputy lecturer in German at the Taylor Institution for four terms at £50 a term. When this period expired the curators offered him a special lecturership in Teutonic philology at a salary of £25 a term; this he later described as his first real start in life and the reason for his lifelong devotion to the Taylor Institution. His first task was to prepare a number of grammars necessary for the teaching of medieval languages. In 1888 the Clarendon Press published his *Old High German Primer* and *Middle High German Primer*, and in 1892 his *Gothic Primer*; and in the same year the Dialect Society published his *Grammar of the Dialect of Windhill in the West Riding of Yorkshire.*

Wright's great achievement was the compilation of *The English Dialect Dictionary*; and fortune favoured him in providing him just at this juncture with the necessary leisure for his formidable task, as in February 1891 he was appointed deputy to the professor of comparative philology at Oxford in succession to the Rev. A. H. Sayce. A dialect dictionary had been projected by the English Dialect Society soon after its foundation in 1873; but after some time Professor Walter William Skeat [q.v.], who was 'the father and originator' of the scheme, became convinced that the work could be successfully carried out only by 'an accomplished phonetician', and declared Wright 'the only man capable of undertaking the task'. Accordingly, in 1891 Wright took over the material which had been collected—about a million slips, weighing a ton; and when the Dialect Society came to an end in 1896, Wright became responsible not only for the actual work on the *Dictionary*, but also for the business side of the undertaking. New material was required, and in the first five months he estimated that he had sent out 50,000 prospectuses and had written 3,000 letters, besides addressing meetings wherever there was a likelihood of obtaining subscribers. His entire savings, amounting to £2,000, went into the undertaking; dictionaries and glossaries alone, which were necessary for the preparatory work, cost £600. He found 1,000 contributors in various parts of the country, who furnished information which could only be obtained on the spot; and to these some 6,000 queries were issued annually from the 'workshop' at Oxford. When publication had to be seriously considered, it was found that no publisher was prepared to face the risk; and Wright decided to publish it himself. The first volume appeared in July 1896, and by February 1905, the work, which it was estimated had cost £25,000, was finished. The *English Dialect Grammar*, which serves as an introduction to the whole *Dictionary*, was published in the latter year, and was, in Wright's opinion, 'philologically far more important than the *Dictionary*'. The six volumes of the *Dictionary* contain 5,000 pages and include about 100,000 words, explained by some

500,000 quotations. The work was undertaken none too soon; as early as 1895 Wright wrote: 'Pure dialect is disappearing, even in the country districts, owing to the spread of education and to the modern facilities of intercommunication,' and some thirty years later, in 1926, he complained: 'It is very difficult to find people who can speak a dialect without being seriously mixed up with the so-called standard language.'

In 1901 Wright was elected to succeed Max Müller as Corpus Christi professor of comparative philology at Oxford, and after the completion of the *Dictionary* he was able to take a greater share in the ordinary activities of the university. From 1908 to 1914 he was a member of the Hebdomadal Council; as professor of comparative philology he became *ex officio* a curator of the Taylor Institution; and from 1909 to 1926—he retired from the chair in 1924—he acted as secretary to the Board. These years saw the real growth of modern language studies in Oxford. In 1903 an honour school of modern languages had been founded; soon new chairs, readerships, and lecturerships were instituted, the library of the Taylor Institution was increased, and provision made for the future. In all this development Wright was the moving spirit. He also turned to his first love, the writing of educational books, for Wright was a born teacher. In 1906 he published a revised edition of the *Old High German Primer*, which was followed by a third edition in 1917. His 'Students' Series of Historical and Comparative Grammars' was opened by the *Historical German Grammar* in 1907. In 1908 the *Old English Grammar* appeared, in 1910 the *Grammar of the Gothic Language*, and in 1912 a *Comparative Grammar of the Greek Language*. A Latin Grammar, at which he was working about this time, was almost finished before his death, but was never published. The *Middle High German Primer* was revised and enlarged in 1917, and, after a serious illness in 1920, he set to work on a series of English grammars: the *Elementary Old English Grammar* and *Elementary Middle English Grammar* appeared in 1923, and the *Elementary Historical New English Grammar* in 1924.

In 1896 Wright married Elizabeth Mary, eldest daughter of the Rev. Frederic Simcox Lea, rector of Tedstone Delamere, Herefordshire, formerly perpetual curate of Trinity Church, Stepney. Mrs. Wright was a student at Lady Margaret Hall (1887–1890) and had attended Wright's lectures. Under his supervision she prepared a grammar of the Northumbrian dialect, and, after their marriage, not only undertook much of the secretarial work of the *Dialect Dictionary*, but also shared in the work of the grammars. There were two children of the marriage, a son and a daughter, who both died in childhood. Wright died at his home in Oxford 27 February 1930, of an attack of pneumonia, the strain of which his robust constitution, undermined by years of failing health and incessant labour, was unable to bear.

Wright was a man of sterling qualities. He was gifted with a vast amount of practical common sense, enormous self-reliance, and almost ruthless determination. 'Necessity', he said, 'taught me at a very early age to trust myself.' If the latter qualities of the self-made man sometimes jarred in common-room circles, he could nevertheless be a good and faithful friend. His actions were inspired by a noble, generous simplicity. His humour and good spirits were infectious: 'I have never been depressed in my life,' he used to say. He was a lover and a buyer of books, and had the scholar's love of learning for its own sake; and he used his vast learning for the advancement of others.

Wright's scholarship was recognized by several universities and learned societies. He received honorary degrees from the universities of Durham (1898), Aberdeen (1902), Leeds (1904), Dublin (1906), and Oxford (1926). He was made an honorary member of the Royal Flemish Academy (1919), of the Utrecht Society (1926), of the Modern Language Association of America (1926), and of the Royal Society of Letters of Lund (1928). In 1904 he was elected a fellow of the British Academy, and in 1925 was awarded its first biennial prize for English studies.

In 1927, as the result of a subscription raised among his many friends and admirers, Wright's portrait was painted by Ernest Moore and was presented to the Taylor Institution, where it now hangs.

[Elizabeth Mary Wright, *The Life of Joseph Wright*, 2 vols., 1932; Sir Charles Firth, *Joseph Wright, 1855–1930*, in *Proceedings* of the British Academy, vol. xviii, 1932; personal knowledge.]

J. Boyd.

WYNDHAM-QUIN, WINDHAM THOMAS, fourth Earl of Dunraven (1841–1926), Irish politician. [See Quin.]

WYNN-CARRINGTON, CHARLES ROBERT, third Baron Carrington and Marquess of Lincolnshire (1843–1928), politician, was born in Whitehall, London, 16 May 1843. He was the eldest son of Robert John Carrington (formerly Smith), second Baron Carrington, by his second wife, Charlotte, younger daughter of Peter Robert, twenty-first Baron Willoughby de Eresby. He was educated at Eton, where Mrs. de Rosen was his dame and the Rev. William Wayte his tutor. In 1861 he proceeded to Trinity College, Cambridge, and after taking his degree entered the Royal Horse Guards. He was promoted captain in 1869, and retired in 1878. At the general election of 1865 he was returned unopposed as liberal member of parliament for the borough of High Wycombe. In 1868 he succeeded his father as third Baron Carrington.

When the Prince of Wales (afterwards King Edward VII) visited India in 1875–1876, Lord Carrington was in attendance as aide-de-camp. He was an intimate friend of the royal family, and in 1881, during Gladstone's second ministry, he received the post of captain of the corps of the Gentlemen-at-Arms. From 1885 to 1890 he was governor of New South Wales, where both he and his wife made themselves popular. He held the office of lord chamberlain of the household from 1892 to 1895, and also sat for a time on the London County Council as a progressive member. In 1893 he was appointed chairman of Lord Rosebery's Welsh land tenure commission, and in 1901 he went as special envoy to France, Spain, and Portugal in order to make formal announcement of the accession of King Edward.

On the formation of Sir Henry Campbell-Bannerman's ministry in 1905, Lord Carrington was appointed president of the Board of Agriculture and Fisheries, with a seat in the Cabinet. His term of office was marked by the passing of two important measures, the Agricultural Holdings Amendment Act and the Small Holdings and Allotments Act, both in 1908. Neither measure was popular with landowners, and Carrington had a difficult task in answering those who criticized the displacement of men farming under sound economic conditions by a class without experience and working at a disadvantage as regards capital and equipment. He showed his interest in stock-breeding by appointing, in the later years of his presidency, two committees to inquire into the exportation of stock and into swine-fever respectively.

When the liberal ministry was partially reconstructed in 1911, Lord Carrington became lord privy seal, but he resigned in the following year. On the accession of King George V (1910), he exercised the office of lord great chamberlain. His hereditary right to act for a reign in turn with two other representatives, the Earl of Ancaster and the Marquess of Cholmondeley, the latter of whom he succeeded, had been determined by the Court of Claims which sat before the coronation of King Edward VII. It was derived through his mother as one of the co-heirs to the barony of Willoughby de Eresby.

Lord Carrington was always a sturdy liberal of an extreme type, but his geniality made him popular with many friends who disapproved of his political views. He was created Viscount Wendover and Earl Carrington in 1895, and Marquess of Lincolnshire in 1912. He received the G.C.M.G. in 1885 and the K.G. in 1906. He was sworn of the Privy Council in 1881, and was lord-lieutenant of Buckinghamshire from 1915 to 1923. He died at Daw's Hill House, High Wycombe, 13 June 1928.

Lord Carrington married in 1878 the Hon. Cecilia Margaret Harbord, daughter of Charles, fifth Baron Suffield, and had one son and five daughters. His son, Lord Wendover, died in 1915 of wounds received in action. The marquessate therefore became extinct in 1928, but the barony descended to Lord Lincolnshire's younger brother, Rupert Clement George (born 1852).

[*The Times*, 14 June 1928.]

A. Cochrane.

YOUNG, Sir GEORGE, third baronet, of Formosa Place (1837–1930), administrator and author, born at Formosa Fishery, Cookham, Berkshire, 15 September 1837, the eldest of the five sons of Sir George Young, second baronet, came of naval and literary stock. His great-grandfather, Admiral Sir George Young, F.R.S. [q.v.], was present at the capture of Louisburg and Quebec; his grandfather, Sir Samuel Young, the first baronet, also an F.R.S., began his career in the navy; his father retired from the service as a captain; and the family house, Formosa Place, opposite Cliveden woods on the Thames, was constructed by the admiral to resemble his quarters on the poop of a man-of-war. Young's mother was Susan, daughter of William Mackworth Praed, serjeant-at-law, of Bitton, Teignmouth, and sister and favourite correspondent of Winthrop Mackworth Praed [q.v.], the poet.

Young and his brothers, one of whom was Sir William Mackworth Young [q.v.], governor of the Punjab, were all educated at Eton, where they were conspicuous both for scholarship and games, he himself winning the Newcastle medal in 1855. At Trinity College, Cambridge, he obtained only second classes in classics and mathematics in 1859, but this set-back merely served to strengthen his precocious powers of self-analysis and his determination to make the fullest use of his remarkable capacity for dogged work. 'I sat down after my failures to obtain a first class either in mathematics or classical honours,' he wrote in some autobiographical notes found among his papers, 'to consider what chance I had of a Trinity fellowship, which must cost me two-and-a-half years of renewed labour at learning of no direct use to me in life'; and, after making an elaborate analysis of his own and his possible rivals' chances, he decided to drop mathematics and to concentrate on classics and philosophy during the next three years. He obtained the Le Bas prize for an essay on *The History of Greek Literature in England* (published 1862), and recorded on the eve of his third and final attempt for a fellowship in 1862: 'I had learned the lesson that my powers of study were not, as I had assumed, physically inexhaustible. I read very hard, but resolved not to look at a book for a whole month before the examination.' His judicious industry was rewarded by the first of the Trinity fellowships on the list for that year. Nothing illustrates better the course of his future life, his tenacity and thoroughness, with a certain narrowness of scope, than the reflections which he jotted down on the results of his education: 'The course of my studies was not that of the usual good boy, nor yet of the boy who was not good. I studied hard, preferring what was a little beyond my powers, detesting abridgements, despising too much the established routine of grammar and arithmetic, enjoying the romance of history and the rhythm of good verse, greedy of knowledge, too apt to think I was gaining it by poring over what was in appearance learned, even if dull. . . . The best bit of out-of-the-way knowledge I assimilated was the Theory of Induction, as expounded by Whewell . . . I feel the better able, for it, to retain a balance between acceptance and reservation as to, for instance, the "origin of species", and to refuse even a momentary attraction to the "theory of relativity".'

Young's Trinity fellowship, the baronetcy inherited from his father in 1848, the presidency of the Union (1860)—held previously by his uncle, W. M. Praed, and subsequently by his third son, (Sir) Hilton Young—and the friendships which he had formed at Eton and Cambridge with A. C. Swinburne, G. O. Trevelyan, Henry Jackson, Henry Sidgwick, Richard Jebb, Edward Bowen, and Leslie Stephen, smoothed his path in the larger world of affairs. Although called to the bar by Lincoln's Inn in 1864, he never practised as a barrister, but at first devoted himself to active politics, vainly contesting Plymouth three times (1874, 1880, 1881) in the liberal interest. His political enthusiasm brought him to the notice of Mr. Gladstone, who, in 1870, gave him his first opening in the field of public work as a member of the royal commission on coolie immigration to British Guiana. This appointment was followed by those of assistant-commissioner on the Friendly Societies commission (1871), secretary to the Factory and Workshop Acts commission (1874), and secretary to the Bessborough commission on the Irish Land Acts (1880). Young was entirely responsible for drawing up the report on the Irish Land Acts, characterized by Gladstone as the 'very ablest' he had read. Shortly after the issue of this report he was pressingly invited by Lord Frederick Cavendish, on the latter's appointment as Irish secretary, to join him as his private secretary, with the prospect of succeeding T. H. Burke as permanent under-secretary: Young's telegram gladly accepting the offer was in Lord Frederick's pocket when he and Burke were murdered in Phoenix Park, Dublin, on 6 May 1882.

Three months later Gladstone appointed Young a charity commissioner under the Endowed Schools Acts, a post in which he found work exactly suited to his great legal and historical knowledge and which gave full scope to his genius for taking decisions based on the most exhaustive consideration of evidence. The duty of the charity commissioners was to form schemes for the better employment of ancient endowments which in course of time had become diverted from, or excessive for, their original purposes, and at the same time to diverge as little as possible from the broad intentions of the pious donors. For a long time Young's office was only 'temporary', and his activities were looked at askance by a Treasury unfavourable to 'temporary' appointments, a conservative government tender to ancient endowments, and radicals like Joseph Chamberlain who accused the Commission of being 'robbers of the poor'. Young's difficulties were also, it must be admitted, to some extent of his own making; for his very merits of logical integrity and a just conviction of his exhaustive impartiality made him a difficult colleague and an uncompromising adversary. Nevertheless, his decisions proved so unassailable in principle—'No scheme in my personal charge', he wrote with pride, 'was ever defeated or modified on a point of law'—and so generally acceptable to the persons chiefly concerned that he became indispensable; and in 1903, after being confirmed as third and then as second commissioner on a permanent basis, he was made chief charity commissioner for England and Wales.

In 1906 Young retired, spending the rest of his long life at his beautiful Cookham home, but not ceasing his labours; for to the end he took a prominent part in the public affairs of the country, especially in educational matters. The interests of education, apart from his Charity Commission work, had always been dear to him. He took a large part in the abolition of tests and in promoting the university education of women at Cambridge. From 1881 to 1886 he was president of the senate of University College, London, and he was prominent in helping to establish London as a teaching university.

With all his public work Young always found time to do 'something', as he wrote in his notes, 'to lighten the numerous griefs of life by excursions on the lower slopes of Parnassus'. His original verse was scanty, but he was notable as a translator of poetry. His best-known work of translation is *The Dramas of Sophocles rendered in English Verse, Dramatic and Lyric* (1888); another pleasing volume is *Poems from Victor Hugo in English Verse* (1901). Both are remarkable for their ease and beauty without the sacrifice of accuracy, and for skill in the choice of metre most fitting to the originals. *An English Prosody*, published in his ninety-second year (1928), and *Homer and the Greek Accents* (1930) were a fitting crown to his lifelong devotion to scholarship and literary criticism. An earlier publication, however, *The political and occasional Poems of Winthrop Mackworth Praed* (1888), is the most likely to survive, since by its pithy and lucid explanation of out-of-date allusions it has helped to keep fresh the interest in his uncle's famous verses. Always a man of singular athletic prowess, after leaving Cambridge Young bade fair, like his second son, Geoffrey, to become one of the most intrepid of Alpine climbers; but, after the death by his side in 1866 of his youngest brother on Mont Blanc [see *Alpine Journal*, ii, 382] he never again climbed the Alps. He shared (Sir) Leslie Stephen's delight in long walks at a tremendous pace, was a good oar, and till after his eightieth year retained his love of swimming in the Thames.

Young married in 1871 Alice Eacy, daughter of a noted Irish physician, Evory Kennedy, M.D., of Belgard, co. Dublin, and widow of Sir Alexander Hutchinson Lawrence, first baronet. A beautiful, witty, and most lovable woman, she with her charm and he with his distinguished presence, his mellow knowledge, and his decided opinions made Formosa Place, and later the smaller Formosa Fishery to which they retired, stimulating centres of attraction, not only for the ablest men and women of the time but also for the young, for whom she especially had a warm corner in her heart. She died in 1922, leaving three sons: the only daughter died young. Sir George Young, who in his ninety-third year wrote to *The Times* that he was not dead, as had been announced, but, though slightly deaf, still capable of work, died at Formosa Fishery 4 July 1930. He was succeeded as fourth baronet by his eldest son, George (born 1872).

A portrait of Young by C. N. Kennedy and two pencil drawings by John Brett hang at Formosa Fishery.

[*The Times*, 5 July 1930; autobiographical notes; private information; personal knowledge.] B. Williams.

YOUNG, Sir WILLIAM MACKWORTH (1840–1924), Anglo-Indian administrator, the third son of Captain Sir George Young, second baronet, R.N., of Formosa Place, Cookham, Berkshire, and younger brother of Sir George Young, third baronet [q.v.], was born at Cookham 15 August 1840. Through his mother, Susan, daughter of William Mackworth Praed, serjeant-at-law, of Bitton, Teignmouth, he was nephew to Winthrop Mackworth Praed [q.v.], the poet. He was a scholar of Eton and of King's College, Cambridge, and in 1863 was elected, under the old statutes, a fellow of King's, a position which he held until his marriage in 1869.

Young passed the examination for the Indian civil service in 1862, and was posted to the Punjab, where he took up his first appointment in December 1863. In 1878 he acted as superintendent of the Kapurthala State, and two years later became secretary to the Punjab government, a post which he held for seven years and in which he made his mark. After occupying administrative positions as commissioner and financial commissioner, he was chosen in October 1893 to be president of a commission appointed to inquire into the consumption and control of hemp drugs in India. Two years later (1895) he was made resident at Mysore in Southern India, and in March 1897 was appointed lieutenant-governor of his old province, the Punjab, being created K.C.S.I. in the following June.

Young's official career had been very successful, but the labour, to which his success was largely due, had taken its toll of a constitution naturally delicate, and there were doubts—to be extraordinarily falsified by his subsequent longevity—as to his physical capacity to stand the strain of the lieutenant-governorship. His tenure of that office proved to be in some respects unquiet, but it brought out the tenacity both of his physical and of his mental equipment. The general characteristics of his rule were the steady development of the province, the efficiency of the steps taken to meet occurrences of famine, and the maintenance of good relations with the people; but the official opinion of the day was distracted from these outstanding features by the interest attaching to the emergence of strained relations between his government and that of the viceroy, Lord Curzon [q.v.].

In 1900 Lord Curzon had taken up the question of the administration of the North-West Frontier, which was at that time under the control of the Punjab government, and in December of that year the secretary-of-state approved of his proposal to remove the frontier districts from the Punjab and place them directly under the government of India. Young much resented the proposed dismemberment of the province with which he had so long been associated, the strictures which had been passed on the previous administration of the Frontier under the Punjab government, and certain features of the manner in which Lord Curzon had conducted the correspondence. The disregard of his known opinions in the matter tended to embitter the feelings both of Young and of some of his leading officers during the remainder of his tenure of office.

After holding the lieutenant-governorship for the usual period of five years, Young retired in 1902, and shortly afterwards settled at Silverhill, St. Leonards-on-Sea. Here he employed himself in local affairs, but was able also, in spite of his increasing age and indifferent health, to meet with considerable regularity the calls of his various interests in London during the next twenty years. He had throughout his life been a supporter of missionary work, and before leaving India he had been elected vice-president of the Church Missionary Society. On his return to England he threw himself whole-heartedly into missionary activity in London. The Church Missionary Society made him chairman of its India committee, and he also became chairman of the Church of England Zenana Missionary Society, in which he took special interest, as well as chairman of the Church Education Corporation, and a member of the Central Board of Missions.

Shortly before his death Young had moved from St. Leonards to Weybridge, where he died 10 May 1924. He was twice married: first, in 1869 to Isabel Maria (died 1870), daughter of the Rev. Charles Boileau Elliott, rector of Tattingstone, Suffolk, by whom he had one daughter; secondly, in 1881 to Frances Mary, daughter of Sir Robert Eyles Egerton, who was at that time lieutenant-governor of the Punjab: by her he had four sons and a daughter.

Young was endowed with a remarkably acute and well-ordered mind, and was able to express himself, especially on paper, with a terseness and lucidity which few of his contemporaries in India could rival. Although tenacious of his views and involved at times in official disputes of some consequence, he was not by nature a controversialist and his disposition tended rather towards peace and conciliation. As an administrator, he was sage and business-like in procedure, following, as a rule, prescribed official lines; and he treated his subordinates with unvarying courtesy and patience. In private life he was a man of charming manners and refined tastes, possessing a scholarly mind and a remarkably fine ear for music. His spare, almost ascetic frame, bearded face, and expressive eyes reflected in no small degree the spiritual qualities of his character and life.

[*The Times*, 12 May 1924; official records of service; personal knowledge.]

E. D. Maclagan.

YOUNGER, Sir GEORGE, first Viscount Younger of Leckie (1851–1929), politician, was born 13 October 1851 at the Brewery House, Bank Street, Alloa, Clackmannanshire, the eldest son of James Younger, head of the brewing firm of George Younger & Son, by his wife, Janet, eldest daughter of John McEwan, of Alloa. The youngest son, Robert, was created Baron Blanesburgh in 1923. The firm had been founded by his great-great-grandfather, George Younger (1722–1788), and the management continued in the direct line of the family. Thus when James Younger died in August 1868, George, who had been educated at the Edinburgh Academy and had proceeded to Edinburgh University, took charge of the business when he was not yet seventeen. He entered politics by way of the county council of Clackmannan, to which he was first elected in 1890 and of which he was convener 1895–1906. He was president of the County Councils Association of Scotland 1902–1904, and president of the National Union of Conservative Associations of Scotland in 1904. But it was only in 1906 that he entered the House of Commons, having contested Clackmannan and Kinross unsuccessfully in 1895, 1899, and 1900, and Ayr Burghs in 1904. He was returned by the latter constituency in 1906, and continued to represent it until 1922.

In the House of Commons Younger was prominent in the small conservative opposition as a clear and forcible speaker, and took an active part in the attack on Mr. Lloyd George's budget for 1909–1910. But he was popular with both liberals and conservatives, and received a baronetcy in 1911 from his political opponents. His great talent, however, lay in party management rather than in detailed organization; and in 1917, on the invitation of Mr. Bonar Law [q.v.], he became chairman of the unionist party organization, then not showing much activity owing to the European War and the formation of the Coalition government. He was thereby mainly responsible for the success of the Coalition in the 'coupon' election of December 1918; this device he adopted in order to avoid the sacrifice of seats to labour and independent liberalism. One of Younger's chief aims was the reform of the House of Lords and the establishment of a strong second chamber—a policy to which the Coalition was pledged. Hence, in 1922, he joined (Sir) Leslie Orme Wilson, then chief Coalition whip, in opposing, successfully, two attempts made to hold a fresh general election. But the feeling in the conservative party against the Coalition was growing strong, and, as Younger considered that party to be the best instrument for furthering the country's interests, he supported Mr. Bonar Law at the meeting held at the Carlton Club on 19 October 1922 which brought the Coalition to an end. In Younger's own words, 'this brought the party together with a snap'; and the conservatives were successful in the ensuing general election, without the help of certain of the conservative leaders, notably Lord Birkenhead [q.v.], who had stigmatized Younger's activities in his capacity as chairman of the party as the insubordination of 'the cabin-boy'.

In February 1923 Younger was raised to the peerage as Viscount Younger of Leckie, but he remained treasurer of the unionist party from that year until his death, which occurred suddenly in London 29 April 1929 after a seizure in the Prince of Wales's Theatre. Younger married in 1879 Lucy (died 1921), daughter of Edward Smith, M.D., F.R.S., of Harley Street, and Heanor Fall House, Heanor, Derbyshire, and had three sons. He was succeeded as second viscount by his eldest son, James (born 1880). His two younger sons were both killed in action, the second in the South African War, and the third in the European War.

Lord Younger, who was an excellent man of business, retained the chairmanship of the family brewery until his death. He was also a director of Lloyds Bank, the Southern Railway, the National Bank of Scotland, and the North British & Mercantile Insurance Co. He was a member of the royal commission on the licensing laws (1896); and he was a J.P. and D.L. for the county of Stirling, lord-lieutenant of Stirlingshire (1925), and vice-lieutenant of Clackmannanshire (1922).

There is a portrait of Lord Younger by Sir William Orpen at Leckie, and a replica is at the Carlton Club. A cartoon appeared in *Vanity Fair* 6 January 1910.

[*The Times*, 30 April 1929; Conservative Central Office records; private information.]

M. F. Headlam.

YOXALL, Sir JAMES HENRY (1857–1925), educationist, was born at Redditch,

Worcestershire, 15 July 1857, the eldest son of Henry Houghton Yoxall, manufacturer of fishing-tackle, by his wife, Elizabeth, daughter of James Smallwood. The family were earnest Wesleyans. Before he was fourteen, their circumstances compelled Yoxall to leave the Wesleyan elementary school in Redditch and become a pupil-teacher at Sheffield in the Bridgehouses Wesleyan school. From 1876 to 1878 he was at the Westminster Training College for Teachers, where he was examined by Matthew Arnold and told that he had an ear for the pronunciation of verse. He prosecuted this acquaintance and profited by it.

As a certificated teacher Yoxall served in Sheffield in his old school among others, and in 1887 became headmaster of the Sharrow Lane board school, where he soon became known for his enterprise in encouraging the interest of the pupils in pictures, music, and poetry. He wrote articles on education, was an active member of the local branch of the National Union of Teachers, and in 1889 was elected to its executive council. There followed 'four years of intense labour in school by day, at the writing-desk by night, and on Union duty every week-end'. After being president of the Union for 1891 he was next year appointed its general secretary and gave up teaching.

In the same year (1892) Yoxall stood for parliament as a liberal, in the Bassetlaw division of Nottinghamshire, unsuccessfully; but in 1895 he was returned for Nottingham West, which he represented until he retired in 1918. He did not speak often in the House of Commons except on the education estimates and on education bills, when he made his points clearly and vigorously. During Yoxall's time as general secretary the membership of the National Union rose from 23,000 to 120,000, its organization was improved and developed, its social, political, and educational activities grew in number and variety, and its financial position became very strong. In 1909 Yoxall took over the editorship of *The Schoolmaster*, the weekly magazine and official organ of the Union.

Both before and after the Education Act of 1902, the Union was much concerned about the status of teachers in public elementary schools and the conditions of their service, as regards, for example, the duties of head teachers in church schools, the employment of uncertificated teachers and other less qualified persons, the size of classes, and the state of school-buildings. As the chief permanent official of the Union, Yoxall exercised great influence over its policy and was largely responsible for carrying it into effect. He was thus continually in communication with the Education Department and its successor, the Board of Education, on questions of policy, and with local education authorities and school managers about their practice in administration. Of his handling of such matters it was said that, although formidable in controversy, he never shut his eyes to the arguments on the other side or to the practical difficulties of conceding all that he claimed. This made him invaluable to his Union in establishing good working relations with Whitehall and in conciliating the new local authorities, who at first were suspicious of teachers' organizations. It was his ambition 'to make the teaching profession an honoured one and to lift education out of the ruck of faction'. He held that the interests of teachers and their schools were interdependent. So long as the teacher's financial, and consequently his social, position remained depressed, the school in which he worked would be looked down upon and not be fairly treated. Improvement of conditions of service, especially in pay and pension, would attract better-qualified persons to the profession; difficulties in the supply of candidates gave Yoxall opportunities to press this point.

In 1898 Yoxall had advised his council to agree to the Teachers' Superannuation Bill of that year because it would enable all certificated teachers to get some pension, however small, at the age of sixty-five. The passage of the Superannuation Bill of 1918, which gave great benefits to teachers, was assisted by the Union; the Bill of 1922, which required contributions from teachers, met with less approval. Before the Bill of 1925 Yoxall had retired. In the work upon pensions he was closely associated with another past president of the Union, Charles W. Crook, and on the educational side of his duties with Sir Ernest Gray, past president, and secretary to the educational committee of the Union.

After the European War the question of teachers' pay became acute, and disputes in some areas interrupted the work of the elementary schools. Yoxall was thus engaged in a series of negotiations between the Union, the Local Education Authority, and the Board of Education for the settlement of individual cases. His conduct of such cases and the loyalty which he evoked made him the obvious leader of the teachers upon the standing joint committee on the salaries of teachers in public elementary schools which was set up in 1919 under the chairmanship of Lord Burnham. On the one side were the representatives of the associations of Local Authorities and the London County Council; on the other those of the Union, which had successfully claimed to represent all teachers in the schools in question. Here Yoxall's control of his 'panel' and ability in presenting its case were very remarkable. That the results in 1920 and 1921 were, on the whole, very favourable to the teachers was largely due to his tact, firmness, and good sense.

In 1918 Yoxall retired from parliament, and in 1924 from his secretaryship and editorship, and he died 2 February 1925 at Kew.

Yoxall was a member of the royal commission on secondary education (1894–1895), and of the committee on the teaching of modern languages (1916). He received the honorary degree of M.A. from Cambridge University in 1899 and from Oxford in 1907, when the annual conference of the Union was held in those places. In 1909 he was knighted, being, it was believed, the first certificated teacher to receive that honour. In his professional writings he aimed at making the subject of education more attractive to ordinary people and thus creating more sympathy for teachers. In editing *The Schoolmaster* he tried to combine its primary objects with matters of general interest, and himself wrote in it regularly on travel, books, and art. He spent many holidays in France, and was a collector of old Wedgwood and of the English water-colours of 1810 to 1840. Besides magazine articles, he published a number of novels, including *The Courtier Stoops* (1911), several books about collecting, *The A.B.C. about Collecting* (1910), *Collecting Old Miniatures* (1916), and *Collecting Old Glass* (1916), and two volumes of essays, *The Wander Years* (1909), and *The Villa for Coelebs* (1914).

Short, good-looking, with a small beard, Yoxall was to the end of his life a trim, alert, and interesting figure. He married in 1886 Elizabeth, daughter of Lieutenant-Colonel William Coles, R.E., and had one son and two daughters.

[*The Times*, 3 February, 1925; *The Schoolmaster*, 6 and 13 February 1925; private information; personal knowledge.]

E. B. Phipps.

YPRES, first Earl of (1852–1925), field-marshal. [See French, John Denton Pinkstone.]

ZANGWILL, ISRAEL (1864–1926), author and philanthropist, was born in London 14 February 1864, the eldest son of Moses Zangwill by his wife, Ellen Hannah Marks. His father was a Russian refugee, who had come to England as a lad in 1848, alone and friendless, in order to escape the severe decree of Jewish child-conscription instituted by the Tsar, Nicholas I. Israel Zangwill showed great promise at the school to which he was sent in Bristol, where his parents were then residing; they moved to London in 1872 in order to provide the boy with more advanced education at the Jews' Free School at Spitalfields. There he quickly distinguished himself, winning all the available scholarships. In due course he was articled as a teacher and appointed master of the senior form, having in the meanwhile graduated at London University with triple honours.

Zangwill's father was a very pious man, who throughout a laborious career as a small trader retained his connexion with the synagogue as a scripture-reader. Israel Zangwill soon discarded dogma, although he still clung almost passionately to his race, and to the end of his days exercised a very great influence on his co-religionists. He gave up teaching after a year or two, and took to journalism, a profession in which he quickly made his mark. In 1888 he wrote a fantastic novel, *The Premier and the Painter*, in collaboration with a friend, following this with a couple of witty, light-hearted stories, *The Bachelors' Club* (1891) and *The Old Maids' Club* (1892), which appeared in *Ariel*, a comic journal of which he was for some time the editor. There was much spiritual unrest at this period, and it had extended to Jewry. Zangwill was invited to write a Jewish novel for the newly founded Jewish Publication Society of America. He accepted the invitation, and the result was *The Children of the Ghetto* (1892), a work which at once, and solidly, established his reputation. In this book Zangwill gave the real Jew to the world, revealing him as he had never been revealed before; minimizing nothing, extenuating nothing, exaggerating nothing, handling him with profound knowledge and with affection, but also with justice. *Ghetto Tragedies* followed in 1893, and *Dreamers of the Ghetto* in 1898; both works of high quality, which powerfully influenced cultured Jews in every country of the world.

Zangwill wrote other novels, *The King of Schnorrers* (1894), *The Master* (1895), *The Mantle of Elijah* (1900), *The Grey Wig* (1903), *Jinny the Carrier* (1919), all of which had distinction and achieved a fair measure of success. A small volume of poems, *Blind Children*, appeared in 1903, and in 1910 a collection of essays, *Italian Fantasies*, in which he displayed both erudition and wit. But it is primarily and essentially as a depicter of Jewish life, Jewish ideals and aspirations, that Zangwill has secured his place in literature. He wrote many comedies and tragedies, all, or nearly all, works of merit; but a certain formlessness that was apparent in his novels bulked more largely in his plays and detracted from their value. *The Melting Pot* (1908), which dealt with the life of the Jewish emigrant in America, created almost a sensation in that country and ran for many years; and there were others, notably *The War God* (1911), *The Cockpit* (1921), *The Forcing House* (1922), which, although they possessed no element of popularity, revealed high dramatic gift and penetrating insight.

When Dr. Theodor Herzl came to London in 1896 to plead the Zionist cause, to which he was devoting his life, Zangwill was immediately attracted, and threw himself heart and soul into the movement. It was a time of pogroms in Russia, of persecution in Rumania and Galicia, and the need was urgent. Palestine was the passionately desired haven of refuge; but Herzl and Zangwill were soon compelled to realize that this was then an unattainable dream, and that the salvation of the Jews, their land of liberty, must be sought elsewhere. The great mass of ardent religionists, however, clamoured for Zion; and at the seventh Zionist congress, in 1904, Herzl was shouted down, and his burningly eloquent appeal fell on deaf ears. He died a few months later, brokenhearted, worn out by the struggle against hopeless odds. Zangwill at once took up the leadership, founded the Jewish Territorial Organization, and for the next seven years devoted all his power, energy, and time to the cause. The result was disappointing. Vast labours were undertaken, exploring expeditions sent out, masses of statistics compiled, potentates interviewed all over the world; but the difficulties were overwhelming. Zangwill addressed countless meetings and poured forth tracts and pamphlets, but at last had to acknowledge himself beaten. There was the achievement at least that the stream of Jewish emigration had been diverted from New York to Galveston, and that officials of the International Jewish Territorial Organization accompanied the wanderers on their journey, and reduced the hardships which they had to encounter.

Zangwill was a man of unflinching courage: addressing a great American meeting in 1924 he unsparingly attacked the indolent subservience of the prosperous Jews and the American cult of money. An eloquent speaker and a master of epigram, it was he who said that to the actor the part was greater than the whole. Under a somewhat truculent exterior he was curiously unselfish and tender-hearted. His health had long been undermined by his labours, and he died of pneumonia at Midhurst, Sussex, 1 August 1926. A fiery spirit, a man who all his life followed a great idea, he was fitly apostrophized by Rabbi Wise in his funeral address: 'Flame thou wert, to flame thou hast returned.'

Zangwill married in 1903 Edith Chaplin, daughter of Professor William Edward Ayrton [q.v.], electrical engineer and physicist; they had two sons and one daughter. His wife, although not of his race, whole-heartedly shared his labours and supported his efforts.

A cartoon of Zangwill appeared in *Vanity Fair* 25 February 1897.

[Lucien Wolf, Address delivered before the Jewish Historical Society of England, 26 October 1928; André Spire, *Quelques Juifs*, 1928; personal knowledge. Portrait, *Royal Academy Pictures*, 1894.] A. Sutro.

CUMULATIVE INDEX TO THE TWENTIETH CENTURY DICTIONARY OF NATIONAL BIOGRAPHY 1901-1930

Any Worthy who died in or before 1911 is in the *D. N. B.* **1901–1911** in *three* volumes (now *bound* in one volume).

Any Worthy who died in the years 1912–1921 is in the *D. N. B.* **1912–1921** (one volume).

Any Worthy who died after 1921 is in the *D. N. B.* **1922–1930** (one volume).

The position (within his period) of any Worthy depends on the initial of his *surname* (not of his title or pseudonym, if any).

Anson, Sir William Reynell, third baronet 1843–1914
Arber, Edward 1836–1912
Arbuthnot, Sir Alexander John . 1822–1907
Arbuthnot, Forster Fitzgerald . 1833–1901
Arbuthnot, Sir Robert Keith, fourth baronet 1864–1916
Arch, Joseph 1826–1919
Archer, James 1823–1904
Archer, William 1856–1924
Archer-Hind (formerly **Hodgson**), Richard Dacre 1849–1910
Ardagh, Sir John Charles . . 1840–1907
Ardilaun, first Baron. See Guinness, Sir Arthur Edward.
Arditi, Luigi 1822–1903
Ardwall, Lord. See Jameson, Andrew.
Argyll, ninth Duke of. See Campbell, John Douglas Sutherland.
Armes, Philip 1836–1908
Armour, John Douglas . . . 1830–1903
Armstead, Henry Hugh . . . 1828–1905
Armstrong, Edward 1846–1928
Armstrong, Sir George Carlyon Hughes, first baronet . . . 1836–1907
Armstrong, Thomas. . . . 1832–1911
Arnold, Sir Arthur 1833–1902
Arnold, Sir Edwin 1832–1904
Arnold, George Benjamin . . 1832–1902
Arnold, Sir Thomas Walker . . 1864–1930
Arnold, William Thomas . . 1852–1904
Arnold-Forster, Hugh Oakeley . 1855–1909
Arrol, Sir William 1839–1913
Arthur, William 1819–1901
Ashbourne, first Baron. See Gibson, Edward.
Ashby, Henry 1846–1908
Asher, Alexander 1835–1905
Ashley, Evelyn 1836–1907
Ashley, Sir William James . . 1860–1927
Ashmead Bartlett, Sir Ellis. See Bartlett.
Asquith, Herbert Henry, first Earl of Oxford and Asquith . 1852–1928
Aston, William George . . . 1841–1911
Atkinson, Robert 1839–1908
Atthill, Lombe 1827–1910
Aumonier, James 1832–1911
Austen, Henry Haversham Godwin-. See Godwin-Austen.
Austen, Sir William Chandler Roberts-. See Roberts-Austen.
Austen Leigh, Augustus . . . 1840–1905
Austin, Alfred. 1835–1913
Avebury, first Baron. See Lubbock, Sir John.
Ayerst, William 1830–1904
Ayrton, William Edward . . . 1847–1908

Babington Smith, Sir Henry. See Smith.
Bacon, John Mackenzie . . . 1846–1904
Badcock, Sir Alexander Robert. 1844–1907
Baddeley, Mountford John Byrde 1843–1906
Bailey, Philip James . . . 1816–1902
Bailhache, Sir Clement Meacher 1856–1924
Bain, Alexander 1818–1903
Bain, Robert Nisbet . . . 1854–1909
Bainbridge, Francis Arthur . . 1874–1921
Baines, Frederick Ebenezer . . 1832–1911
Baird, Andrew Wilson . . . 1842–1908
Baker, Sir Benjamin . . . 1840–1907
Baker, Shirley Waldemar . . 1835–1903
Balfour, Arthur James, first Earl of Balfour 1848–1930
Balfour of Burleigh, sixth Baron. See Bruce, Alexander Hugh.
Balfour, George William . . 1823–1903
Balfour, Sir Isaac Bayley . . 1853–1922
Balfour, John Blair, first Baron Kinross 1837–1905
Balfour, Sir Thomas Graham . 1858–1929
Ball, Albert 1896–1917
Ball, Francis Elrington . . . 1863–1928
Ball, Sir Robert Stawell . . 1840–1913
Bancroft, Marie Effie Wilton, Lady. See under Bancroft, Sir Squire Bancroft.
Bancroft, Sir Squire Bancroft . 1841–1926
Banks, Sir John Thomas . . 1815?–1908
Banks, Sir William Mitchell . 1842–1904
Bannerman, Sir Henry Campbell-. See Campbell-Bannerman.
Barbellion, W. N. P., *pseudonym*. See Cummings, Bruce Frederick.
Barbour, Sir David Miller. . 1841–1928
Bardsley, John Wareing . . 1835–1904
Baring, Evelyn, first Earl of Cromer 1841–1917
Baring, Thomas George, first Earl of Northbrook . . 1826–1904
Baring-Gould, Sabine . . . 1834–1924
Barker, Thomas 1838–1907
Barlow, William Hagger . . 1833–1908
Barlow, William Henry . . 1812–1902
Barnaby, Sir Nathaniel . . 1829–1915
Barnardo, Thomas John . . 1845–1905
Barnes, John Gorell, first Baron Gorell 1848–1913
Barnes, Robert 1817–1907
Barnett, Samuel Augustus . . 1844–1913
Baron, Bernhard 1850–1929
Barrett, Wilson 1846–1904
Barrington, Rutland . . . 1853–1922
Barry, Alfred 1826–1910
Barry, Sir John Wolfe Wolfe-. See Wolfe-Barry.
Bartholomew, John George . 1860–1920
Bartlett, Sir Ellis Ashmead . 1849–1902
Bartley, Sir George Christopher Trout 1842–1910
Barton, Sir Edmund . . . 1849–1920
Barton, John 1836–1908
Bashforth, Francis . . . 1819–1912
Bass, Michael Arthur, first Baron Burton 1837–1909
Bates, Cadwallader John . . 1853–1902
Bateson, Mary 1865–1906
Bateson, William 1861–1926
Battenberg, Prince Louis Alexander of. See Mountbatten.
Bauerman, Hilary 1835–1909
Baxter, Lucy, 'Leader Scott' . 1837–1902
Bayley, Sir Steuart Colvin . . 1836–1925
Baylis, Thomas Henry . . . 1817–1908

Botha, Louis 1862–1919
Boucherett, Emilia Jessie 1825–1905
Boucicault, Dion, the younger 1859–1929
Boughton, George Henry 1833–1905
Bourchier, Arthur 1863–1927
Bourchier, James David 1850–1920
Bourinot, Sir John George 1837–1902
Bourke, Robert, Baron Connemara 1827–1902
Bourne, Henry Richard Fox 1837–1909
Bousfield, Henry Brougham 1832–1902
Bowen, Edward Ernest 1836–1901
Bowes, Robert 1835–1919
Bowlby, Sir Anthony Alfred, first baronet 1855–1929
Bowler, Henry Alexander 1824–1903
Bowles, Thomas Gibson 1842–1922
Boyce, Sir Rubert William 1863–1911
Boyd, Henry 1831–1922
Boyd, Sir Thomas Jamieson 1818–1902
Boyd Carpenter, William. See Carpenter.
Boyle, Sir Courtenay Edmund 1845–1901
Boyle, Sir Edward, first baronet 1848–1909
Boyle, George David 1828–1901
Boyle, Richard Vicars 1822–1908
Brabazon, Hercules Brabazon 1821–1906
Brabazon, Reginald, twelfth Earl of Meath 1841–1929
Brackenbury, Sir Henry 1837–1914
Braddon, Sir Edward Nicholas Coventry 1829–1904
Braddon, Mary Elizabeth. See Maxwell.
Bradford, Sir Edward Ridley Colborne, first baronet 1836–1911
Bradley, Francis Herbert 1846–1924
Bradley, George Granville 1821–1903
Bradley, Henry 1845–1923
Brampton, Baron. See Hawkins, Henry.
Bramwell, Sir Frederick Joseph 1818–1903
Brancker, Sir William Sefton 1877–1930
Brand, Henry Robert, second Viscount Hampden 1841–1906
Brand, Herbert Charles Alexander 1839–1901
Brandis, Sir Dietrich 1824–1907
Brassey, Thomas, first Earl Brassey 1836–1918
Bray, Caroline 1814–1905
Bray, Sir Reginald More 1842–1923
Brereton, Joseph Lloyd 1822–1901
Brett, John 1831–1902
Brett, Reginald Baliol, second Viscount Esher 1852–1930
Brewer, Sir Alfred Herbert 1865–1928
Brewtnall, Edward Frederick 1846–1902
Bridge, Sir Cyprian Arthur George 1839–1924
Bridge, Sir John Frederick 1844–1924
Bridge, Thomas William 1848–1909
Bridgeman, Sir Francis Charles Bridgeman 1848–1929
Bridges, John Henry 1832–1906
Bridges, Robert Seymour 1844–1930
Bridges, Sir William Throsby 1861–1915
Briggs, John 1862–1902
Bright, James Franck 1832–1920
Bright, William 1824–1901
Brightwen, Eliza 1830–1906
Broadbent, Sir William Henry, first baronet 1835–1907
Broadhurst, Henry 1840–1911
Brock, Sir Thomas 1847–1922
Brodribb, William Jackson 1829–1905
Brodrick, George Charles 1831–1903
Bromby, Charles Hamilton. See under Bromby, Charles Henry.
Bromby, Charles Henry 1814–1907
Brooke, Sir Charles Anthony Johnson 1829–1917
Brooke, Rupert Chawner 1887–1915
Brooke, Stopford Augustus 1832–1916
Brooking Rowe, Joshua. See Rowe.
Brotherhood, Peter 1838–1902
Brough, Bennett Hooper 1860–1908
Brough, Lionel 1836–1909
Brough, Robert 1872–1905
Broughton, Rhoda 1840–1920
Brown, George Douglas, 'George Douglas' 1869–1902
Brown, Sir George Thomas 1827–1906
Brown, Horatio Robert Forbes 1854–1926
Brown, Joseph 1809–1902
Brown, Peter Hume 1849–1918
Brown, William Haig-. See Haig-Brown.
Browne, Edward Granville 1862–1926
Browne, George Forrest 1833–1930
Browne, Sir James Frankfort Manners 1823–1910
Browne, Sir Samuel James 1824–1901
Browne, Thomas 1870–1910
Browning, Oscar 1837–1923
Bruce, Alexander Hugh, sixth Baron Balfour of Burleigh 1849–1921
Bruce, Sir George Barclay 1821–1908
Bruce, Victor Alexander, ninth Earl of Elgin 1849–1917
Bruce, William Speirs 1867–1921
Brunton, Sir Thomas Lauder, first baronet 1844–1916
Brushfield, Thomas Nadauld 1828–1910
Bryce, James, Viscount Bryce 1838–1922
Brydon, John McKean 1840–1901
Buchan, Alexander 1829–1907
Buchanan, George 1827–1905
Buchanan, Sir George William 1854–1924
Buchanan, Robert Williams 1841–1901
Buckton, George Bowdler 1818–1905
Bullen, Arthur Henry 1857–1920
Buller, Sir Redvers Henry 1839–1908
Buller, Sir Walter Lawry 1838–1906
Bulwer, Sir Edward Earle Gascoyne 1829–1910
Bunsen, Ernest de 1819–1903
Bunting, Sir Percy William 1836–1911
Burbidge, Edward 1839–1903
Burbidge, Frederick William 1847–1905
Burbury, Samuel Hawksley 1831–1911
Burdett-Coutts, Angela Georgina, Baroness Burdett-Coutts 1814–1906
Burdon, John Shaw 1826–1907
Burdon-Sanderson, Sir John Scott, baronet 1828–1905
Burge, Hubert Murray 1862–1925

Channell, Sir Arthur Moseley . 1838–1928
Channer, George Nicholas . 1842–1905
Chaplin, Henry, first Viscount Chaplin . 1840–1923
Chapman, Edward John . 1821–1904
Charles, James . 1851–1906
Charley, Sir William Thomas . 1833–1904
Charteris, Archibald Hamilton . 1835–1908
Chase, Drummond Percy . 1820–1902
Chase, Frederic Henry . 1853–1925
Chase, Marian Emma . 1844–1905
Chase, William St. Lucian . 1856–1908
Chavasse, Francis James . 1846–1928
Cheadle, Walter Butler . 1835–1910
Cheatle, Arthur Henry . 1866–1929
Cheetham, Samuel . 1827–1908
Chelmsford, second Baron. See Thesiger, Frederic Augustus.
Chermside, Sir Herbert Charles . 1850–1929
Chevalier, Albert . 1861–1923
Cheylesmore, third Baron. See Eaton, Herbert Francis.
Cheylesmore, second Baron. See Eaton, William Meriton.
Cheyne, Thomas Kelly . 1841–1915
Child, Thomas . 1839–1906
Child-Villiers, Victor Albert George, seventh Earl of Jersey. See Villiers.
Childers, Robert Erskine . 1870–1922
Chilston, first Viscount. See Akers-Douglas, Aretas.
Chirol, Sir (Ignatius) Valentine . 1852–1929
Chisholm, Hugh . 1866–1924
Christie, Sir William Henry Mahoney . 1845–1922
Chrystal, George . 1851–1911
Church, Sir William Selby, first baronet . 1837–1928
Clanricarde, second Marquess of. See Burgh Canning, Hubert George De.
Clanwilliam, fourth Earl of. See Meade, Richard James.
Clark, John Willis . 1833–1910
Clarke, Sir Andrew . 1824–1902
Clarke, Sir Caspar Purdon . 1846–1911
Clarke, Charles Baron . 1832–1906
Clarke, Henry Butler . 1863–1904
Clarke, Sir Marshal James . 1841–1909
Clasper, John Hawks . 1836–1908
Clayden, Peter William . 1827–1902
Clayton, Sir Gilbert Falkingham 1875–1929
Clerke, Agnes Mary . 1842–1907
Clerke, Ellen Mary. See under Clerke, Agnes Mary.
Clery, Sir Cornelius Francis . 1838–1926
Cleworth, Thomas Ebenezer . 1854–1909
Clifford, Frederick . 1828–1904
Clifford, John . 1836–1923
Clodd, Edward . 1840–1930
Close, Maxwell Henry . 1822–1903
Clowes, Sir William Laird . 1856–1905
Clunies-Ross, George . 1842–1910
Clutton, Henry Hugh . 1850–1909
Clutton-Brock, Arthur . 1868–1924
Cobb, Gerard Francis . 1838–1904
Cobbe, Frances Power . 1822–1904
Cobden-Sanderson, Thomas James 1840–1922

Coghlan, Sir Charles Patrick John 1863–1927
Cohen, Arthur . 1829–1914
Coillard, François . 1834–1904
Cokayne, George Edward . 1825–1911
Coke, Thomas William, second Earl of Leicester . 1822–1909
Coleman, William Stephen 1829–1904
Coleridge, Bernard John Seymour, second Baron Coleridge . 1851–1927
Coleridge, Mary Elizabeth . 1861–1907
Coleridge-Taylor, Samuel . 1875–1912
Coles, Charles Edward [Pasha] . 1853–1926
Coles, Vincent Stuckey Stratton 1845–1929
Collen, Sir Edwin Henry Hayter 1843–1911
Collett, Sir Henry . 1836–1901
Collings, Jesse . 1831–1920
Collingwood, Cuthbert . 1826–1908
Collins, John Churton . 1848–1908
Collins, Michael . 1890–1922
Collins, Richard Henn, Baron Collins . 1842–1911
Collins, William Edward . 1867–1911
Colnaghi, Martin Henry . 1821–1908
Colomb, Sir John Charles Ready 1838–1909
Colton, Sir John . 1823–1902
Colvile, Sir Henry Edward . 1852–1907
Colvin, Sir Auckland . 1838–1908
Colvin, Sir Sidney . 1845–1927
Colvin, Sir Walter Mytton. See under Colvin, Sir Auckland.
Commerell, Sir John Edmund . 1829–1901
Common, Andrew Ainslie . 1841–1903
Compton, Lord Alwyne Frederick 1825–1906
Conder, Charles . 1868–1909
Conder, Claude Reignier . 1848–1910
Congreve, Sir Walter Norris . 1862–1927
Connemara, Baron. See Bourke, Robert.
Conquest, George (Augustus) . 1837–1901
Conrad, Joseph . 1857–1924
Conybeare, Frederick Cornwallis 1856–1924
Cook, Sir Edward Tyas . 1857–1919
Cook, Sir Francis, first baronet . 1817–1901
Coolidge, William Augustus Brevoort . 1850–1926
Cooper, Sir Alfred . 1838–1908
Cooper, Sir Daniel, first baronet 1821–1902
Cooper, Edward Herbert . 1867–1910
Cooper, James . 1846–1922
Cooper, James Davis . 1823–1904
Cooper, Thomas Sidney . 1803–1902
Cooper, Thompson . 1837–1904
Copeland, Ralph . 1837–1905
Copinger, Walter Arthur . 1847–1910
Coppin, George Selth . 1819–1906
Coppinger, Richard William . 1847–1910
Corbet, Matthew Ridley . 1850–1902
Corbett, John . 1817–1901
Corbett, Sir Julian Stafford . 1854–1922
Corbould, Edward Henry . 1815–1905
Corelli, Marie, *pseudonym*. See Mackay, Mary.
Corfield, William Henry . 1843–1903
Cornish, Charles John . 1858–1906
Cornish, Francis Warre Warre-See Warre-Cornish.
Cornwell, James . 1812–1902
Corry, Montagu William Lowry, Baron Rowton . 1838–1903

De Montmorency, Raymond Harvey, third Viscount Frankfort de Montmorency . 1835–1902
De Morgan, William Frend . 1839–1917
Denney, James . . . 1856–1917
Dent, Joseph Malaby . 1849–1926
Derby, sixteenth Earl of. See Stanley, Frederick Arthur.
De Robeck, Sir John Michael, baronet 1862–1928
De Saulles, George William . 1862–1903
Des Vœux, Sir (George) William 1834–1909
Detmold, Charles Maurice . 1883–1908
De Vere, Aubrey Thomas . 1814–1902
De Vere, Sir Stephen Edward, fourth baronet . . . 1812–1904
De Villiers, John Henry, first Baron de Villiers . . . 1842–1914
Devonshire, eighth Duke of. See Cavendish, Spencer Compton.
Dewar, Sir James . . . 1842–1923
De Wet, Christiaan Rudolph . 1854–1922
De Winton, Sir Francis Walter . 1835–1901
De Worms, Henry, Baron Pirbright 1840–1903
Dibbs, Sir George Richard . 1834–1904
Dicey, Albert Venn . . . 1835–1922
Dicey, Edward James Stephen . 1832–1911
Dickinson, Hercules Henry . 1827–1905
Dickinson, Lowes (Cato) . 1819–1908
Dicksee, Sir Francis Bernard (Frank) 1853–1928
Dickson, Sir Collingwood . . 1817–1904
Dickson, William Purdie . . 1823–1901
Digby, William . . . 1849–1904
Dilke, Sir Charles Wentworth, second baronet . . . 1843–1911
Dilke, Emilia Francis Strong, Lady Dilke 1840–1904
Dill, Sir Samuel . . . 1844–1924
Dillon, Frank 1823–1909
Dillon, John 1851–1927
Dimock, Nathaniel . . . 1825–1909
Dines, William Henry . . 1855–1927
Dixie, Lady Florence Caroline . 1857–1905
Dobell, Bertram . . . 1842–1914
Dobson, (Henry) Austin . . 1840–1921
Dods, Marcus 1834–1909
Doherty, Hugh Lawrence . 1875–1919
Dolling, Robert William Radclyffe [Father Dolling] . . 1851–1902
Donaldson, Sir James . . 1831–1915
Donkin, Bryan . . . 1835–1902
Donnelly, Sir John Fretcheville Dykes 1834–1902
Donnet, Sir James John Louis . 1816–1905
Dorrien, Sir Horace Lockwood Smith-. See Smith-Dorrien.
Doughty, Charles Montagu . 1843–1926
Doughty-Wylie, Charles Hotham Montagu 1868–1915
Douglas, Sir Adye . . . 1815–1906
Douglas, Sir Charles Whittingham Horsley . . . 1850–1914
Douglas, George, *pseudonym*. See Brown, George Douglas.
Douglas, George Cunninghame Monteath 1826–1904
Douglas-Pennant, George Sholto Gordon, second Baron Penrhyn 1836–1907
Douglas-Scott-Montagu, John Walter Edward, second Baron Montagu of Beaulieu . . 1866–1929
Dowden, Edward . . . 1843–1913
Dowden, John . . . 1840–1910
Dowie, John Alexander . . 1847–1907
Doyle, Sir Arthur Conan . . 1859–1930
Doyle, John Andrew . . 1844–1907
Dredge, James . . . 1840–1906
Dreschfeld, Julius . . . 1846–1907
Drew, Sir Thomas . . . 1838–1910
Dreyer, John Louis Emil . . 1852–1926
Driver, Samuel Rolles . . 1846–1914
Drummond, Sir George Alexander 1829–1910
Drummond, James . . . 1835–1918
Drummond, William Henry . 1854–1907
Drury-Lowe, Sir Drury Curzon . 1830–1908
Drysdale, Learmont. . . . 1866–1909
Du Cane, Sir Edmund Frederick 1830–1903
Duckett, Sir George Floyd, third baronet 1811–1902
Duckworth, Sir Dyce, first baronet 1840–1928
Dudgeon, Robert Ellis . . 1820–1904
Duff, Sir Beauchamp . . 1855–1918
Duff, Sir Mountstuart Elphinstone Grant. See Grant Duff.
Dufferin, first Marquess of. See Blackwood, Frederick Temple Hamilton-Temple.
Duffy, Sir Charles Gavan . 1816–1903
Duffy, Patrick Vincent . . 1836–1909
Duke, Sir Frederick William 1863–1924
Dunlop, John Boyd . . 1840–1921
Dunmore, seventh Earl of. See Murray, Charles Adolphus.
Dunphie, Charles James . 1820–1908
Dunraven and Mount-Earl, fourth Earl of. See Quin, Windham Thomas Wyndham-.
Dupré, August . . . 1835–1907
Durand, Sir Henry Mortimer . 1850–1924
Durnford, Sir Walter . . 1847–1926
Dutt, Romesh Chunder . . 1848–1909
Dutton, Joseph Everett . . 1874–1905
Duveen, Sir Joseph Joel . . 1843–1908
Dyer, Reginald Edward Harry . 1864–1927
Dyer, Sir William Turner Thiselton-. See Thiselton-Dyer.

Eady, Charles Swinfen, first Baron Swinfen . . . 1851–1919
Eardley-Wilmot, Sir Sainthill. See Wilmot.
Earle, John 1824–1903
East, Sir Alfred . . . 1849–1913
East, Sir Cecil James . . 1837–1908
Eastlake, Charles Locke . . 1836–1906
Eaton, Herbert Francis, third Baron Cheylesmore . . 1848–1925
Eaton, William Meriton, second Baron Cheylesmore . . 1843–1902
Ebsworth, Joseph Woodfall . 1824–1908
Eddis, Eden Upton . . . 1812–1901
Edge, Sir John . . . 1841–1926
Edgeworth, Francis Ysidro [originally Ysidro Francis] . 1845–1926
Edouin, Willie . . . 1846–1908
Edward VII, King . . . 1841–1910

Hall, FitzEdward . . . 1825–1901
Hall, Harry Reginald Holland . 1873–1930
Hall, Sir John 1824–1907
Hallé (formerly Norman-Neruda), Wilma Maria Francisca, Lady 1839–1911
Halliday, Sir Frederick James . 1806–1901
Halsbury, first Earl of. See Giffard, Hardinge Stanley.
Hambleden, second Viscount. See Smith, William Frederick Danvers.
Hamblin Smith, James. See Smith.
Hamilton, David James . 1849–1909
Hamilton, Sir Edward Walter . 1847–1908
Hamilton, Eugene Jacob Lee-. See Lee-Hamilton.
Hamilton, Lord George Francis . 1845–1927
Hamilton, James, second Duke of Abercorn . . . 1838–1913
Hamilton, Sir Richard Vesey . 1829–1912
Hampden, second Viscount. See Brand, Henry Robert.
Hanbury, Charlotte. See under Hanbury, Elizabeth.
Hanbury, Elizabeth . 1793–1901
Hanbury, Sir James Arthur . 1832–1908
Hanbury, Robert William . 1845–1903
Hankin, St. John Emile Clavering 1869–1909
Hanlan (properly Hanlon), Edward 1855–1908
Harben, Sir Henry . . . 1823–1911
Harcourt, Augustus George Vernon 1834–1919
Harcourt, Leveson Francis Vernon-. See Vernon-Harcourt.
Harcourt, Lewis, first Viscount Harcourt 1863–1922
Harcourt, Sir William George Granville Venables Vernon . 1827–1904
Hardie, James Keir . . . 1856–1915
Hardie, William Ross . . 1862–1916
Hardwicke, sixth Earl of. See Yorke, Albert Edward Philip Henry.
Hardy, Frederic Daniel . . 1827–1911
Hardy, Gathorne Gathorne-, first Earl of Cranbrook. See Gathorne-Hardy.
Hardy, Herbert Hardy Cozens-, first Baron Cozens-Hardy. See Cozens-Hardy.
Hardy, Thomas 1840–1928
Hare, Augustus John Cuthbert . 1834–1903
Hare, Sir John 1844–1921
Harland, Henry 1861–1905
Harley, Robert 1828–1910
Harmsworth, Alfred Charles William, Viscount Northcliffe . 1865–1922
Harper, Sir George Montague . 1865–1922
Harrington, Timothy Charles . 1851–1910
Harris, Frederick Leverton . 1864–1926
Harris, Thomas Lake . . . 1823–1906
Harrison, Frederic . . . 1831–1923
Harrison, Jane Ellen . . . 1850–1928
Harrison, Reginald . . . 1837–1908
Hart, Sir Robert, first baronet . 1835–1911
Hartington, Marquess of. See Cavendish, Spencer Compton.
Hartley, Sir Charles Augustus . 1825–1915
Hartshorne, Albert . . . 1839–1910
Hastie, William 1842–1903
Hastings, James 1852–1922
Hatton, Harold Heneage Finch-. See Finch-Hatton.
Hatton, Joseph 1841–1907
Havelock, Sir Arthur Elibank . 1844–1908
Haverfield, Francis John . . 1860–1919
Haweis, Hugh Reginald . . 1838–1901
Haweis, Mary. See under Haweis, Hugh Reginald.
Hawker, Mary Elizabeth, 'Lanoe Falconer' 1848–1908
Hawkins, Henry, Baron Brampton 1817–1907
Hawtrey, Sir Charles Henry . 1858–1923
Hayes, Edwin 1819–1904
Hayman, Henry 1823–1904
Hayne, Charles Hayne Seale-. See Seale-Hayne.
Hayward, Robert Baldwin . 1829–1903
Hazlitt, William Carew . . 1834–1913
Head, Barclay Vincent . . 1844–1914
Headlam, Walter George . . 1866–1908
Headlam-Morley, Sir James Wycliffe 1863–1929
Hearn, Mary Anne, 'Marianne Farningham' 1834–1909
Heath, Christopher . . . 1835–1905
Heath, Sir Leopold George . 1817–1907
Heathcote, John Moyer . . 1834–1912
Heaton, Sir John Henniker, first baronet 1848–1914
Heaviside, Oliver . . . 1850–1925
Hector, Annie French, 'Mrs. Alexander' 1825–1902
Hector, Sir James . . . 1834–1907
Heinemann, William . . 1863–1920
Hellmuth, Isaac 1817–1901
Hemming, George Wirgman . 1821–1905
Hemphill, Charles Hare, first Baron Hemphill . . . 1822–1908
Henderson, Sir David . . 1862–1921
Henderson, George Francis Robert 1854–1903
Henderson, Joseph . . . 1832–1908
Henderson, William George . 1819–1905
Henley, William Ernest . . 1849–1903
Hennell, Sara. See under Bray, Caroline.
Hennessey, John Bobanau Nickerlieu 1829–1910
Hennessy, Henry 1826–1901
Henry, Mitchell 1826–1910
Henty, George Alfred . . . 1832–1902
Herbert, Auberon Edward William Molyneux . . . 1838–1906
Herbert, Auberon Thomas, eighth Baron Lucas . . . 1876–1916
Herbert, George Edward Stanhope Molyneux, fifth Earl of Carnarvon 1866–1923
Herbert, Sir Robert George Wyndham 1831–1905
Herdman, Sir William Abbott . 1858–1924
Herford, Brooke 1830–1903
Herford, William Henry . . 1820–1908
Herkomer, Sir Hubert von . 1849–1914

Hunt, William Holman . . 1827–1910
Hunter, Colin 1841–1904
Hunter, Sir Robert . . . 1844–1913
Hunter, Sir William Guyer . 1827–1902
Huntington, George . . 1825–1905
Hurlstone, William Yeates . 1876–1906
Hutchinson, Sir Jonathan . 1828–1913
Huth, Alfred Henry. . . 1850–1910
Hutton, Alfred . . . 1839–1910
Hutton, Frederick Wollaston . 1836–1905
Hutton, George Clark . . 1825–1908
Hutton, William Holden . . 1860–1930
Hyndman, Henry Mayers . 1842–1921

Ibbetson, Sir Denzil Charles Jelf 1847–1908
Ibbetson, Sir Henry John Selwin-, seventh baronet, and first Baron Rookwood. See Selwin-Ibbetson.
Ignatius, Father. See Lyne, Joseph Leycester.
Ilbert, Sir Courtenay Peregrine . 1841–1924
Image, Selwyn 1849–1930
Ince, William 1825–1910
Inderwick, Frederick Andrew . 1836–1904
Inglis, Elsie Maud . . . 1864–1917
Ingram, John Kells . . . 1823–1907
Ingram, Thomas Dunbar . . 1826–1901
Innes, James John McLeod . 1830–1907
Irby, Leonard Howard Loyd . 1836–1905
Ireland, William Wotherspoon . 1832–1909
Irvine, William 1840–1911
Irving, Sir Henry . . . 1838–1905
Iveagh, first Earl of. See Guinness, Edward Cecil.
Iwan-Müller, Ernest Bruce . 1853–1910

Jacks, William 1841–1907
Jackson, Sir Cyril . . . 1863–1924
Jackson, Sir Frederick John . 1860–1929
Jackson, Henry 1839–1921
Jackson, Sir Henry Bradwardine 1855–1929
Jackson, John. 1833–1901
Jackson, John Hughlings . . 1835–1911
Jackson, Mason 1819–1903
Jackson, Samuel Phillips . . 1830–1904
Jackson, Sir Thomas Graham, first baronet 1835–1924
Jackson, William Lawies, first Baron Allerton . . . 1840–1917
Jacob, Edgar 1844–1920
James, Henry, Lord James of Hereford 1828–1911
James, Henry 1843–1916
James, James 1832–1902
Jameson, Andrew, Lord Ardwall 1845–1911
Jameson, Sir Leander Starr, baronet 1853–1917
Japp, Alexander Hay, 'H. A. Page' 1837–1905
Jardine, Sir Robert, first baronet 1825–1905
Jayne, Francis John . . . 1845–1921
Jeaffreson, John Cordy . . 1831–1901
Jebb, Eglantyne 1876–1928
Jebb, Sir Richard Claverhouse . 1841–1905
Jelf, George Edward . . 1834–1908
Jenkins, Ebenezer Evans . . 1820–1905
Jenkins, John Edward . . 1838–1910
Jenkins, Sir Lawrence Hugh . 1857–1928
Jenkinson, Francis John Henry. 1853–1923
Jenner-Fust, Herbert . . 1806–1904
Jephson, Arthur Jermy Mounteney 1858–1908
Jerome, Jerome Klapka . . 1859–1927
Jersey, seventh Earl of. See Villiers, Victor Albert George Child-.
Jessopp, Augustus . . . 1823–1914
Jeune, Francis Henry, Baron St. Helier 1843–1905
Jex-Blake, Sophia Louisa . 1840–1912
Jex-Blake, Thomas William . 1832–1915
Johns, Claude Hermann Walter 1857–1920
Johnson, Lionel Pigot . . 1867–1902
Johnson, William Percival . 1854–1928
Johnston, Sir Harry Hamilton . 1858–1927
Johnston, William . . 1829–1902
Joly, Charles Jasper . . . 1864–1906
Joly de Lotbinière, Sir Henry Gustave 1829–1908
Jones, Sir Alfred Lewis . . 1845–1909
Jones, Sir Henry . . . 1852–1922
Jones, Henry Arthur . . 1851–1929
Jones, Henry Cadman . . 1818–1902
Jones, Sir John Morris-. See Morris-Jones.
Jones, John Viriamu . . 1856–1901
Jones, Thomas Rupert . . 1819–1911
Jones, William West . . 1838–1908
Jordan, Sir John Newell . . 1852–1925
Joyce, Sir Matthew Ingle . 1839–1930

Kane, Robert Romney . . 1842–1902
Keay, John Seymour . . 1839–1909
Keetley, Charles Robert Bell . 1848–1909
Kekewich, Sir Arthur . . 1832–1907
Kekewich, Robert George. . 1854–1914
Kelly, Frederick Septimus . 1881–1916
Kelly, James Fitzmaurice-. See Fitzmaurice-Kelly.
Kelly, Mary Anne, 'Eva'. See under O'Doherty, Kevin Izod.
Kelly, William 1821–1906
Kelly-Kenny, Sir Thomas. . 1840–1914
Keltie, Sir John Scott . . 1840–1927
Kelvin, Baron. See Thomson, William.
Kemball, Sir Arnold Burrowes . 1820–1908
Kemble, Henry 1848–1907
Kendal, William Hunter . . 1843–1917
Kennedy, Sir Alexander Blackie William 1847–1928
Kennedy, Sir William Rann . 1846–1915
Kenny, Courtney Stanhope . 1847–1930
Kensit, John 1853–1902
Kent, (William) Charles (Mark) . 1823–1902
Kenyon, George Thomas . . 1840–1908
Kenyon-Slaney, William Slaney 1847–1908
Keppel, Sir George Olof Roos-. See Roos-Keppel.
Keppel, Sir Henry . . . 1809–1904
Ker, William Paton . . . 1855–1923
Kerr, John 1824–1907
Kerr, Robert 1823–1904
Kerr, Lord Walter Talbot . 1839–1927
Kidd, Benjamin . . . 1858–1916
Killen, William Dool . . 1806–1902

Lewis, Sir George Henry, first baronet 1833–1911
Lewis, John Travers . . . 1825–1901
Lewis, Richard . . . 1821–1905
Lewis, William Thomas, first Baron Merthyr . . . 1837–1914
Liberty, Sir Arthur Lasenby . 1843–1917
Lidderdale, William . . 1832–1902
Lincolnshire, Marquess of. See Wynn-Carrington, Charles Robert.
Lindley, Nathaniel, Baron Lindley 1828–1921
Lindsay, David 1856–1922
Lindsay, James Gavin . . 1835–1903
Lindsay, James Ludovic, twenty-sixth Earl of Crawford . . 1847–1913
Lindsay (afterwards Loyd-Lindsay), Robert James, Baron Wantage 1832–1901
Lindsay, Thomas Martin . . 1843–1914
Lingen, Ralph Robert Wheeler, Baron Lingen . . . 1819–1905
Linlithgow, first Marquess of. See Hope, John Adrian Louis.
Lister, Arthur . . . 1830–1908
Lister, Joseph, first Baron Lister 1827–1912
Lister, Samuel Cunliffe, first Baron Masham . . . 1815–1906
Little, William John Knox-. See Knox-Little.
Littler, Sir Ralph Daniel Makinson 1835–1908
Liveing, George Downing . 1827–1924
Livesey, Sir George Thomas . 1834–1908
Llandaff, Viscount. See Matthews, Henry.
Lloyd, Marie, *pseudonym.* See Wood, Matilda Alice Victoria.
Loates, Thomas 1867–1910
Loch, Sir Charles Stewart . 1849–1923
Locke, William John . . 1863–1930
Lockey, Charles 1820–1901
Lockwood, Amelius Mark Richard, first Baron Lambourne 1847–1928
Lockyer, Sir (Joseph) Norman . 1836–1920
Loftie, William John . . 1839–1911
Loftus, Lord Augustus William Frederick Spencer . . . 1817–1904
Logue, Michael 1840–1924
Lohmann, George Alfred . . 1865 1901
Londonderry, sixth Marquess of. See Vane-Tempest-Stewart, Charles Stewart.
Long, Walter Hume, first Viscount Long of Wraxall . . 1854–1924
Longhurst, William Henry . 1819–1904
Lopes, Sir Lopes Massey, third baronet 1818–1908
Lord, Thomas 1808–1908
Loreburne, Earl. See Reid, Robert Threshie.
Lorimer, Sir Robert Stodart . 1864–1929
Lotbinière, Sir Henry Gustave Joly de. See Joly de Lotbinière.
Lovelace, second Earl of. See Milbanke, Ralph Gordon Noel King.
Lovett, Richard 1851–1904
Low, Alexander, Lord Low . 1845–1910
Low, Sir Robert Cunliffe . 1838–1911
Lowe, Sir Drury Curzon Drury-. See Drury-Lowe.
Lowry, Henry Dawson . . 1869–1906
Lowther, James . . . 1840–1904
Löwy, Albert or Abraham . 1816–1908
Loyd-Lindsay. See Lindsay, Robert James, Baron Wantage.
Luard, Sir William Garnham . 1820–1910
Lubbock, Sir John, fourth baronet, and first Baron Avebury 1834–1913
Luby, Thomas Clarke . . 1821–1901
Lucas, eighth Baron. See Herbert, Auberon Thomas.
Lucas, Keith 1879–1916
Luckock, Herbert Mortimer . 1833–1909
Lucy, Sir Henry William . . 1843–1924
Ludlow, John Malcolm Forbes 1821–1911
Luke, Jemima 1813–1906
Lukin, Sir Henry Timson . 1860–1925
Lupton, Joseph Hirst . . 1836–1905
Lush, Sir Charles Montague . 1853–1930
Lusk, Sir Andrew, baronet . 1810–1909
Lutz, (Wilhelm) Meyer . . 1829–1903
Lyall, Sir Alfred Comyn . . 1835–1911
Lyall, Sir Charles James . . 1845–1920
Lyall, Edna, *pseudonym.* See Bayly, Ada Ellen.
Lyne, Joseph Leycester [Father Ignatius] 1837–1908
Lyne, Sir William John . . 1844–1913
Lyons, Sir Algernon McLennan . 1833–1908
Lyttelton, Alfred . . . 1857–1913
Lyttelton, Arthur Temple . 1852–1903

Macan, Sir Arthur Vernon . 1843–1908
Macara, Sir Charles Wright, first baronet 1845–1929
McArthur, Charles . . . 1844–1910
Macarthur, Mary Reid. See Anderson.
M'Carthy, Justin 1830–1912
Macartney, Sir Samuel Halliday 1833–1906
Macaulay, James 1817–1902
Macbain, Alexander . . . 1855–1907
Macbeth, Robert Walker . . 1848–1910
MacCallum, Andrew . . . 1821–1902
McCalmont, Harry Leslie Blundell 1861–1902
McClean, Frank 1837–1904
McClintock, Sir Francis Leopold 1819–1907
McClure, Sir John David . . 1860–1922
McCoan, James Carlile . . 1829–1904
MacColl, Malcolm . . . 1831–1907
MacColl, Norman . . . 1843–1904
MacCormac, Sir William, first baronet 1836–1901
McCormick, Sir William Symington 1859–1930
McCudden, James Thomas Byford 1895–1918
Maccunn, Hamish [James] . 1868–1916
MacDermot, Hugh Hyacinth O'Rorke, The MacDermot . 1834–1904
Macdermott, Gilbert Hastings . 1845–1901
MacDermott, Martin . . 1823–1905
Macdonald, Sir Claude Maxwell. 1852–1915

Sharpe, Richard Bowdler . . 1847–1909
Shattock, Samuel George . . 1852–1924
Shaughnessy, Thomas George, first Baron Shaughnessy . 1853–1923
Shaw, Alfred 1842–1907
Shaw, Sir Eyre Massey . . 1830–1908
Shaw, James Johnston . . 1845–1910
Shaw, John Byam Lister . . 1872–1919
Shaw, Richard Norman . . 1831–1912
Shaw-Lefevre, George John, Baron Eversley . . . 1831–1928
Shearman, Sir Montague . . 1857–1930
Sheffield, third Earl of. See Holroyd, Henry North.
Sheffield, fourth Baron. See Stanley, Edward Lyulph.
Shelford, Sir William . . 1834–1905
Shenstone, William Ashwell . 1850–1908
Sherborn, Charles William . 1831–1912
Sherrington, Helen Lemmens-. See Lemmens-Sherrington.
Shields, Frederic James . . 1833–1911
Shipley, Sir Arthur Everett . 1861–1927
Shippard, Sir Sidney Godolphin Alexander 1837–1902
Shirreff. See Grey, Maria Georgina.
Shore, Thomas William . . 1840–1905
Shorter, Clement King . . 1857–1926
Shorthouse, Joseph Henry . 1834–1903
Shrewsbury, Arthur . . 1856–1903
Shuckburgh, Evelyn Shirley . 1843–1906
Sieveking, Sir Edward Henry . 1816–1904
Sifton, Sir Clifford . . . 1861–1929
Simmons, Sir John Lintorn Arabin 1821–1903
Simon, Sir John . . . 1816–1904
Simonds, James Beart . . 1810–1904
Simpson, Maxwell . . 1815–1902
Simpson, Wilfred Hudleston. See Hudleston.
Sims, Charles 1873–1928
Sinclair, John, first Baron Pentland 1860–1925
Singleton, Mary Montgomerie. See Currie, Baroness.
Sinha, Satyendra Prasanno, first Baron Sinha 1864–1928
Skeat, Walter William . . 1835–1912
Skipsey, Joseph 1832–1903
Slaney, William Slaney Kenyon-. See Kenyon-Slaney.
Smartt, Sir Thomas William . 1858–1929
Smeaton, Donald Mackenzie . 1846–1910
Smiles, Samuel 1812–1904
Smith, Sir Archibald Levin . 1836–1901
Smith, Arthur Lionel . . 1850–1924
Smith, Sir Charles Bean Euan-. See Euan-Smith.
Smith, Donald Alexander, first Baron Strathcona . . 1820–1914
Smith, Sir Francis (afterwards Sir Francis Villeneuve) . 1819–1909
Smith, Sir Frederick . . 1857–1929
Smith, Frederick Edwin, first Earl of Birkenhead . . 1872–1930
Smith, George Barnett . . 1841–1909
Smith, George Vance . . 1816?–1902
Smith, Goldwin . . . 1823–1910
Smith, Sir Henry Babington . 1863–1923
Smith, Henry Spencer . . . 1812–1901
Smith, James Hamblin . . 1829–1901
Smith, Lucy Toulmin . . 1838–1911
Smith, Reginald Bosworth . 1839–1908
Smith, Reginald John . . 1857–1916
Smith, Sir Ross Macpherson . 1892–1922
Smith, Samuel . . . 1836–1906
Smith, Sarah, 'Hesba Stretton'. 1832–1911
Smith, Thomas 1817–1906
Smith, Sir Thomas, first baronet 1833–1909
Smith, Thomas Roger . . 1830–1903
Smith, Vincent Arthur . . 1848–1920
Smith, Walter Chalmers . . 1824–1908
Smith, William Frederick Danvers, second Viscount Hambleden 1868–1928
Smith, William Saumarez . 1836–1909
Smith-Dorrien, Sir Horace Lockwood 1858–1930
Smyly, Sir Philip Crampton . 1838–1904
Smyth, Sir Henry Augustus . 1825–1906
Snelus, George James . . 1837–1906
Snow, Herbert. See Kynaston.
Solomon, Sir Richard . . 1850–1913
Solomon, Simeon . . . 1840–1905
Solomon, Solomon Joseph . 1860–1927
Somerset, Lady Isabella Caroline [Lady Henry Somerset] . 1851–1921
Sonnenschein, Edward Adolf . 1851–1929
Sorby, Henry Clifton . . 1826–1908
Sotheby, Sir Edward Southwell. 1813–1902
Soutar, Ellen. See Farren.
Southesk, ninth Earl of. See Carnegie, James.
Southey, Sir Richard . . 1808–1901
Southward, John . . . 1840–1902
Southwell, Thomas . . . 1831–1909
Spencer, Herbert . . . 1820–1903
Spencer, John Poyntz, fifth Earl Spencer 1835–1910
Spencer, Sir Walter Baldwin . 1860–1929
Spiers, Richard Phené . . 1838–1916
Spofforth, Frederick Robert . 1853–1926
Spooner, William Archibald . 1844–1930
Sprengel, Hermann Johann Philipp 1834–1906
Sprigg, Sir John Gordon . . 1830–1913
Spring-Rice, Sir Cecil Arthur . 1859–1918
Sprott, George Washington . 1829–1909
Spy, *pseudonym*. See Ward, Sir Leslie.
Squire, William Barclay . . 1855–1927
Stables, William (Gordon) . 1840–1910
Stack, Sir Lee Oliver Fitzmaurice 1868–1924
Stacpoole, Frederick . . 1813–1907
Stafford, Sir Edward William . 1819–1901
Stainer, Sir John . . . 1840–1901
Stalbridge, first Baron. See Grosvenor, Richard De Aquila.
Stamer, Sir Lovelace Tomlinson, third baronet 1829–1908
Stanford, Sir Charles Villiers . 1852–1924
Stanley, Edward Lyulph, fourth Baron Sheffield, and fourth Baron Stanley of Alderley . 1839–1925
Stanley, Frederick Arthur, sixteenth Earl of Derby . . 1841–1908
Stanley, Henry Edward John, third Baron Stanley of Alderley 1827–1903

Terry, Dame (Alice) Ellen . 1847–1928
Thesiger, Frederic Augustus, second Baron Chelmsford . 1827–1905
Thiselton-Dyer, Sir William Turner 1843–1928
Thomas, David Alfred, Viscount Rhondda . . . 1856–1918
Thomas, George Holt . . 1869–1929
Thomas, Sir Hugh Evan-. See Evan-Thomas.
Thomas, (Philip) Edward . . 1878–1917
Thomas, William Moy . . 1828–1910
Thompson, D'Arcy Wentworth . 1829–1902
Thompson, Edmund Symes-. See Symes-Thompson.
Thompson, Sir Edward Maunde 1840–1929
Thompson, Francis . . . 1859–1907
Thompson, Sir Henry, first baronet 1820–1904
Thompson, Henry Yates . . 1838–1928
Thompson, Lydia . . . 1836–1908
Thompson, Silvanus Phillips . 1851–1916
Thompson, William Marcus . 1857–1907
Thomson, Christopher Birdwood, Baron Thomson . . . 1875–1930
Thomson, Hugh . . . 1860–1920
Thomson, Jocelyn Home . . 1859–1908
Thomson, John . . . 1856–1926
Thomson, William, Baron Kelvin 1824–1907
Thomson, Sir William . . 1843–1909
Thornton, Sir Edward . . 1817–1906
Thornycroft, Sir John Isaac . 1843–1928
Thornycroft, Sir (William) Hamo 1850–1925
Thorpe, Sir Thomas Edward . 1845–1925
Thring, Godfrey . . . 1823–1903
Thring, Henry, Baron Thring . 1818–1907
Thrupp, George Athelstane . 1822–1905
Thuillier, Sir Henry Edward Landor 1813–1906
Thursfield, Sir James . . 1840–1923
Thurston (formerly Madden), Katherine Cecil . . . 1875–1911
Tinsley, William . . . 1831–1902
Tinworth, George . . . 1843–1913
Tizard, Thomas Henry . . 1839–1924
Todd, Sir Charles . . . 1826–1910
Tomson, Arthur . . . 1859–1905
Toole, John Lawrence . . 1830–1906
Torrance, George William. . 1835–1907
Tout, Thomas Frederick . . 1855–1929
Townsend, Meredith White . 1831–1911
Townshend, Sir Charles Vere Ferrers 1861–1924
Tracey, Sir Richard Edward . 1837–1907
Trafford, F. G., *pseudonym*. See Riddell, Charlotte Eliza Lawson.
Traill, Anthony . . . 1838–1914
Traill-Burroughs, Sir Frederick William. See Burroughs.
Tree, Sir Herbert Beerbohm . 1852–1917
Treloar, Sir William Purdie, baronet 1843–1923
Trench, Frederic Herbert . . 1865–1923
Trevelyan, Sir George Otto, second baronet . . . 1838–1928
Treves, Sir Frederick, baronet . 1853–1923
Trevor, William Spottiswoode . 1831–1907
Tristram, Henry Baker . . 1822–1906
Troubridge, Sir Ernest Charles Thomas 1862–1926
Truman, Edwin Thomas . . 1818–1905
Tucker, Alfred Robert . . 1849–1914
Tucker, Henry William . . 1830–1902
Tuke, Henry Scott . . . 1858–1929
Tupper, Sir Charles, first baronet 1821–1915
Tupper, Sir Charles Lewis . 1848–1910
Turner, Charles Edward . . 1831–1903
Turner, Cuthbert Hamilton . 1860–1930
Turner, Herbert Hall . . 1861–1930
Turner, James Smith . . 1832–1904
Turner, Sir William . . 1832–1916
Turpin, Edmund Hart . . 1835–1907
Tweedmouth, second Baron. See Marjoribanks, Edward.
Tyabji, Badruddin . . . 1844–1906
Tyler, Thomas . . . 1826–1902
Tylor, Sir Edward Burnett . 1832–1917
Tylor, Joseph John . . . 1851–1901
Tyrrell, George . . . 1861–1909
Tyrrell, Robert Yelverton . 1844–1914

Underhill, Edward Bean . . 1813–1901
Ure, Alexander, Baron Strathclyde 1853–1928
Urwick, William . . . 1826–1905

Vallance, William Fleming . 1827–1904
Vandam, Albert Dresden . . 1843–1903
Vane-Tempest-Stewart, Charles Stewart, sixth Marquess of Londonderry . . . 1852–1915
Van Horne, Sir William Cornelius 1843–1915
Vansittart, Edward Westby . 1818–1904
Vaughan, Bernard John . . 1847–1922
Vaughan, David James . . 1825–1905
Vaughan, Herbert Alfred . . 1832–1903
Vaughan, Kate . . . 1852?–1903
Veitch, Sir Harry James . . 1840–1924
Veitch, James Herbert . . 1868–1907
Venn, John 1834–1923
Verney, Margaret Maria, Lady Verney 1844–1930
Vernon-Harcourt, Leveson Francis 1839–1907
Verrall, Arthur Woollgar . . 1851–1912
Vezin, Hermann . . . 1829–1910
Vezin (formerly Mrs. Charles Young), Jane Elizabeth . 1827–1902
Victoria Adelaide Mary Louise, Princess Royal of Great Britain and German Empress . . 1840–1901
Villiers, John Henry De, first Baron De Villiers. See De Villiers.
Villiers, Victor Albert George Child-, seventh Earl of Jersey 1845–1915
Vincent, Sir (Charles Edward) Howard 1849–1908
Vincent, James Edmund . . 1857–1909
Vinogradoff, Sir Paul Gavrilovitch 1854–1925
Von Hügel, Friedrich, Baron of the Holy Roman Empire . 1852–1925
Voysey, Charles . . . 1828–1912

Wace, Henry 1836–1924
Wade, Sir Willoughby Francis . 1827–1906
Wakley, Thomas. See under Wakley, Thomas Henry.